THE OFFICIAL® 2009 PRICE GUIDE TO FOOTBALL CARDS

DR. JAMES BECKETT

TWENTY-EIGHTH EDITION

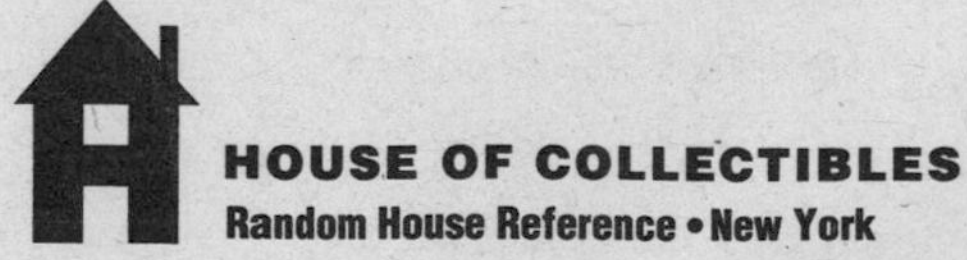

Important Notice: All of the information, including valuations, in this book has been compiled from the most reliable sources, and every effort has been made to eliminate errors and questionable data. Nevertheless, the possibility of error, in a work of such immense scope, always exists. The publisher will not be held responsible for losses that may occur in the purchase, sale, or other transaction of items because of information contained herein. Readers who feel they have discovered errors are invited to *write* and inform us, so they may be corrected in subsequent editions. Those seeking further information on the topics covered in this book are advised to refer to the complete line of *Official Price Guides* published by the House of Collectibles.

House of Collectibles and colophon
are trademarks of Random House, Inc.

www.houseofcollectibles.com

Published by:
House of Collectibles
Random House Reference
New York, New York

Distributed by The Random House Information Group,
a division of Random House, Inc.,
New York, and simultaneously in Canada by
Random House of Canada Limited, Toronto.
Random House is a registered trademark of Random House, Inc.

www.randomhouse.com

Manufactured in the United States of America

ISSN: 0748-1365

ISBN: 978-0-375-72298-1

10 9 8 7 6 5 4 3 2 1

Twenty-Eighth Edition: August 2008

Table of Contents

Table of Contents

Table of Contents

Table of Contents

Table of Contents

Table of Contents

Table of Contents

Table of Contents

About the Author

Jim Beckett, the leading authority on sportscard values in the United States, maintains a wide range of activities in the world of sports. He possesses one of the finest collections of sportscards and autographs in the world, has made numerous appearances on radio and television, and has been frequently cited in many national publications. He was awarded the first "Special Achievement Award for Contributions to the Hobby" by the National Sports Collectors Convention in 1980, the "Jock-Jaspersen Award for Hobby Dedication" in 1983, and the "Buck Barker, Spirit of the Hobby Award" in 1991.

Dr. Beckett is the author of *Beckett Baseball Card Price Guide, The Official Price Guide to Baseball Cards, Beckett Almanac of Baseball Cards and Collectibles, Beckett Football Card Price Guide, The Official Price Guide to Football Cards, Beckett Hockey Card Price Guide and Alphabetical Checklist, Beckett Basketball Card Price Guide, The Official Price Guide to Basketball Cards*, and *Beckett Baseball Card Alphabetical Checklist*. In addition, he is the founder and publisher of sports collectible magazines: *Beckett Baseball, Beckett Basketball, Beckett Football, Beckett Hockey*, and *Beckett Sports Card Monthly*.

Jim Beckett received his Ph.D. in Statistics from Southern Methodist University in 1975. Prior to starting Beckett Publications in 1984, Dr. Beckett served as an Associate Professor of Statistics at Bowling Green State University and as a Vice President of a consulting firm in Dallas, Texas. He currently resides in Dallas.

How to Use This Book

Isn't it great? Every year this book gets better with all the new sets coming out. But even more exciting is that every year there are more attractive choices and, subsequently, more interest in the cards we love so much. This edition has been enhanced and expanded from the previous edition. The cards you collect —who appears on them, what they look like, where they are from, and (most important to most of you) what their current values are—are enumerated within. Many of the features contained in the other *Beckett Price Guides* have been incorporated into this volume since condition-grading, terminology, and many other aspects of collecting are common to the card hobby in general. We hope you find the book both interesting and useful in your collecting pursuits.

The Beckett Guide has been successful where other attempts have failed because it is complete, current, and valid. This price guide contains not just one but two price columns for all the football cards listed. These account for most of the major releases in existence. The prices were added to the card lists just prior to printing and reflect not the author's opinions or desires but the going retail prices for each card, based on the marketplace (sports memorabilia conventions and shows, sportscard shops, hobby papers, current mail-order catalogs, Internet sales, auction results, and other firsthand reporting of actually realized prices).

What is the best price guide available on the market today? Of course card sellers will prefer the price guide with the highest prices, while card buyers will naturally prefer the one with the lowest prices. Accuracy, however, is the true test. Use the price guide used by more collectors and dealers than all the others combined. Look for the Beckett name. I won't put my name on anything I won't stake my reputation on. Not the lowest and not the highest—but the most accurate, with integrity.

To facilitate your use of this book, read the complete introductory section on the following pages before going to the pricing pages. Every collectible field has its own terminology; we've tried to capture most of these terms and definitions in our glossary. Please read carefully the section on grading and the condition of your cards, as you will not be able to determine which price column is appropriate for a given card without first knowing its condition.

Prices in This Guide

Prices found in this guide reflect current retail rates just prior to the printing of this book. They do not reflect the for-sale prices of the author, the publisher, the distributors, the advertisers, or any card dealers associated with this guide. No one is obligated in any way to buy, sell, or trade his or her cards based on these prices. The price listings were compiled by the author from actual buy/sell transactions at sports conventions, sportscard shops, buy/sell advertisements in the hobby papers, for-sale prices from dealer catalogs and price lists, and discussions with leading hobbyists in the U.S. and Canada. All prices are in U.S. dollars.

Introduction

Welcome to the exciting world of sportscard collecting, one of America's most popular avocations. You have made a good choice in buying this book, since it will open up to you the entire panorama of this field in the simplest, most concise way.

The growth of *Beckett Baseball, Beckett Basketball, Beckett Football, Beckett Hockey,* and *Beckett Sports Card Monthly* is an indication of the unprecedented popularity of sportscards. Founded in 1984 by Dr. James Beckett, *Beckett Baseball* contains the most extensive and accepted monthly price guide, collectible glossy superstar covers, colorful feature articles, "Hot List," Convention Calendar, tips for beginners, "Readers Write" letters to and responses from the editor, information on errors and varieties, autograph collecting tips, and profiles of the sport's hottest stars. Published every month, *Beckett Baseball* is the hobby's largest paid circulation periodical. The other five magazines were built on the success of Baseball.

So collecting sportscards—while still pursued as a hobby with youthful exuberance by kids in the neighborhood—has also taken on the trappings of an industry, with thousands of full- and part-time card dealers, as well as vendors of supplies, clubs, and conventions. In fact, each year since 1980 thousands of hobbyists have assembled for a National Sports Collectors Convention, at which hundreds of dealers have displayed their wares, seminars have been conducted, autographs penned by sports notables, and millions of cards changed hands. The Beckett Guide is the best annual guide available to the exciting world of football cards. Read it and use it. May your enjoyment and your card collection increase in the coming months and years.

How to Collect

Each collection is personal and reflects the individuality of its owner. There are no set rules on how to collect cards. Since card collecting is a hobby or leisure pastime, what you collect, how much you collect, and how much time and money you spend collecting are entirely up to you. The funds you have available for collecting and your own personal taste should determine how you collect. The information and ideas presented here are intended to help you get the most enjoyment from this hobby.

It is impossible to collect every card ever produced. Therefore, beginners as well as intermediate and advanced collectors usually specialize in some way. One of the reasons this hobby is popular is that individual collectors can define and tailor their collecting methods to match their own tastes. To give you some ideas of the various approaches to collecting, we will list some of the more popular areas of specialization.

Many collectors select complete sets from particular years. For example, they may concentrate on assembling complete sets from all the years since their birth or since they became avid sports fans. They may try to collect a card for every player during that specified period of time. Many others wish to acquire only certain players. Usually such players are the superstars of the sport, but occasionally collectors will specialize in all the cards of players who attended a particular college or came from a certain town. Some collectors are only interested in the first cards or Rookie Cards of certain players.

Another fun way to collect cards is by team. Most fans have a favorite team, and it is natural for that loyalty to be translated into a desire for cards of the players on that favorite team. For most of the recent years, team sets (all the cards from a given team for that year) are readily available at a reasonable price. See Beckett.com for searchable player checklists.

Preserving Your Cards

Cards are fragile. They must be handled properly in order to retain their value. Careless handling can easily result in creased or bent cards. It is, however, not recommended that tweezers or tongs be used to pick up your cards since such utensils might mar or indent card surfaces and thus reduce those cards' conditions and values. In general, your cards should be handled directly as little as possible. This is sometimes easier to say than to do.

Although there are still many who use custom boxes, storage trays, or even shoe boxes, plastic sheets are the preferred method of many collectors for storing cards. A collection stored in plastic pages in a three-ring album allows you to view your collection at any time without the need to touch the card itself. Cards can also be kept in single holders (of various types and thicknesses) designed for the enjoyment of each card individually. For a large collection, some collectors may use a combination of the above methods. When purchasing plastic sheets for your cards, be sure that you find the pocket size that fits the cards snugly. Don't put your 1951 Bowman in a sheet designed to fit 1981 Topps.

Most hobby and collectibles shops and virtually all collectors' conventions will have these plastic pages available in quantity for the various sizes offered, or you can purchase them directly from the advertisers in this book. Also, remember that pocket size isn't the only factor to consider when looking for plastic sheets. Other factors such as safety, economy, appearance, availability, or personal preference also may indicate which types of sheets a collector may want to buy.

Damp, sunny, and/or hot conditions. No, this is not a weather forecast, but rather three elements to avoid in extremes if you are interested in preserving your collection. Too much (or too little) humidity can cause gradual deterioration of a card. Direct, bright sun (or fluorescent light) over time will bleach out the color of a card. Extreme heat accelerates the decomposition of the card. On the other hand, many cards have lasted more than 50 years without much scientific intervention. So be cautious, even if the above factors typically present a problem only when present in the extreme. It never hurts to be prudent.

Terminology

Each hobby has its own language to describe its area of interest. The following list defines the most important terminology and abbreviations that may appear in this book:

AS - All-Star.

CL - Checklist card. A card that lists in order the cards and players in the set or series. Older checklist cards in mint condition that have not been checked off are very desirable and command large premiums.

COMMON CARD - The typical card of any set; it has no premium value accruing from subject matter, numerical scarcity, popular demand, or anomaly.

COR - Corrected card. A version of an error card that was fixed by the manufacturer.

DIE-CUT - A card with its stock partially cut. In some cases, after removal or appropriate folding, the remaining part of the card can be made to stand up.

DP - Double Print. A card that was printed in approximately double the quantity compared to other cards in the same series, or draft pick card.

ERR - Error card. A card with erroneous information, spelling, or depiction on either side of the card. Most errors are never corrected by the producing card company.

FOIL - A special type of sticker with a metallic-looking surface.

HL - Highlight card, for example from the 1978 Topps subset.

HOF - Hall of Fame, or Hall of Famer (also abbreviated HOFer).

HOR - Horizontal pose on a card as opposed to the standard vertical orientation found on most cards.

IA - In Action card. A special type of card depicting a player in an action photo, such as the 1982 Topps cards.

LL - League leader card. A card depicting the leader or leaders in a specific statistical category from the previous season. Not to be confused with team leader (TL).

LOGO - NFLPA logo on card.

MVP - Most Valuable Player.

NO LOGO - No NFLPA logo on card.

NO TR - No trade reference on card.

NPO - No position.

OFF - Officials cards.

O-ROY - Offensive Rookie of the Year.

PARALLEL - A card that is similar in design to its counterpart from a basic set, but offers a distinguishing quality.

PB - Pro Bowl.

RB - Record Breaker card or running back.

RC - Rookie Card. A player's first appearance on a regular issue card from one of the major card companies. With a few exceptions, each player has only one RC in any given set. A Rookie Card typically cannot be an All-Star, Highlight, In Action, league leader, Super Action, or team leader card. It can, however, be a coach card or draft pick card.

REDEMPTION - A program established by manufacturers that allows collectors to mail in a special card (usually a random insert) in return for special cards, sets, or other prizes not available through conventional channels.

RET - Retired.

REV NEG - Reversed or flopped photo side of the card. This is a major type of error card, but only some are corrected.

ROY - Rookie of the Year.

SB - Super Bowl.

SET - One each of an entire run of cards of the same type, produced by a particular manufacturer during a single season. In other words, if you have a complete set of 1975 Topps football cards, then you have every card from #1 up to and including #528; i.e., all the different cards that were produced.

SP - Single or Short Print. A card which was printed in lesser quantity compared to the other cards in the same series (also see DP). This term can only be used in a relative sense and in reference to one particular set. For instance, the 1989 Pro Set Pete Rozelle SP is less common than the other cards in that set, but it isn't necessarily scarcer than regular cards of any other set.

TC - Team card or team checklist card.

TL - Team leader card or Top Leader.

UER - Uncorrected error card.

XRC - Extended Rookie Card. A player's first appearance on a card, but issued in a set that was not distributed nationally or in packs. In football sets, this term generally refers to the 1984 and 1985 Topps USFL sets.

Understanding Card Values

Determining Value

Why are some cards more valuable than others? Obviously, the economic laws of supply and demand are applicable to card collecting just as they are to any other field where a commodity is bought, sold, or traded in a free, unregulated market.

Supply (the number of cards available on the market) is less than the total number of cards originally produced since attrition diminishes that original quantity. Each year a percentage of cards is typically thrown away, destroyed, or otherwise lost to collectors. This percentage is much, much smaller today than it was in the past because more and more people have become increasingly aware of the value of their cards.

For those who collect only mint condition cards, the supply of older cards can be quite small indeed. Until recently, collectors were not so conscious of the need to preserve the condition of their cards. For this reason, it is difficult to know exactly how many 1962 Topps are currently available, mint or otherwise. It is generally accepted that there are fewer 1962 Topps available than 1972, 1982, or 1992 Topps cards. If demand were equal for each of these sets, the law of supply and demand would increase the price for the least available sets.

Demand, however, is never equal for all sets, so price correlations can be complicated. The demand for a card is influenced by many factors. These include: (1) the age of the card; (2) the number of cards printed; (3) the player(s) portrayed on the card; (4) the attractiveness and popularity of the set; and (5) the physical condition of the card.

In general, (1) the older the card, (2) the fewer the number of the cards printed, (3) the more famous, popular, and talented the player, (4) the more attractive and popular the set, and (5) the better the condition of the card, the higher the value of the card will be. There are exceptions to all but one of these factors: the condition of the card. Given two cards similar in all respects except condition, the one in the better condition will always be valued higher.

While those guidelines help to establish the value of a card, the countless exceptions and peculiarities make any simple, direct mathematical formula to determine card values impossible.

Regional Variation

Since the market varies from region to region, card prices of local players may be higher. This is known as a regional premium. How significant the premium is—and if there is any premium at all—depends on the local popularity of the team and the player.

The largest regional premiums usually do not apply to superstars, who often are so well known nationwide that the prices of their key cards are too high for local dealers to realize a premium.

Lesser stars often command the strongest premiums. Their popularity is concentrated in their home region, creating local demand that greatly exceeds overall demand.

Regional premiums can apply to popular retired players and sometimes can be found in the areas where the players grew up or starred in college.

A regional discount is the converse of a regional premium. Regional discounts occur when a player has been so popular in his region for so long that local collectors and dealers have accumulated quantities of his cards. The abundant supply may make the cards available in that area at the lowest prices anywhere.

Set Prices

A somewhat paradoxical situation exists in the price of a complete set vs. the combined cost of the individual cards in the set. In nearly every case, the sum of the prices for the individual cards is higher than the cost for the complete set. This is prevalent especially in the cards of the past few years. The reasons for this apparent anomaly stem from the habits of collectors and from the carrying costs to dealers. Today, each card in a set normally is produced in the same quantity as all others in its set.

Many collectors pick up only stars, superstars, and particular teams. As a result, the dealer is left with a shortage of certain player cards and an abundance of others. He therefore incurs an expense in simply "carrying" these less desirable cards in stock. On the other hand, if he sells a complete set, he gets rid of large numbers of cards at one time. For this reason, he generally is willing to receive less money for a complete set. By doing this, he recovers all of his costs and also makes a profit.

Set prices do not include rare card varieties, unless specifically stated. Of course, the prices for sets do include one example of each type for the given set, but this is the least expensive variety.

Grading Your Cards

Each hobby has its own grading terminology—stamps, coins, comic books, record collecting, etc. Collectors of sportscards are no exception. The one invariable criterion for determining the value of a card is its condition: the better the condition of the card, the more valuable it is. Condition grading, however, is subjective. Individual card dealers and collectors differ in the strictness of their grading, but the stated condition of a card should be determined without regard to whether it is being bought or sold.

No allowance is made for age. A 1952 card is judged by the same standards as a 1992 card. But there are specific sets and cards that are condition-sensitive because of their border color, consistently poor centering, etc. Such cards and sets sometimes command premiums above the listed percentages in mint condition.

Condition Guide

Grades

Mint (Mt) - A card with no flaws or wear. The card has four perfect corners, 55/45 or better centering from top to bottom and from left to right, original gloss, smooth edges, and original color borders. A mint card does not have print spots, color, or focus imperfections.

Near Mint-Mint (NrMt-Mt) - A card with one minor flaw. Any one of the following would lower a mint card to near mint-mint: one corner with a slight touch of wear, barely noticeable print spots, color or focus imperfections. The card must have 60/40 or better centering in both directions, original gloss, smooth edges, and original color borders.

Near Mint (NrMt) - A card with one minor flaw. Any one of the following would lower a mint card to near mint: one fuzzy corner or two to four corners with slight touches of wear, 70/30 to 60/40 centering, slightly rough edges, minor print spots, color or focus imperfections. The card must have original gloss and original color borders.

Excellent-Mint (ExMt) - A card with two or three fuzzy, but not rounded, corners and centering no worse than 80/20. The card may have no more than two of the following: slightly rough edges, very slightly discolored borders, minor print spots, color or focus imperfections. The card must have original gloss.

Excellent (Ex) - A card with four fuzzy but definitely not rounded corners and centering no worse than 80/20. The card may have a small amount of original gloss lost, rough edges, slightly discolored borders and minor print spots, color or focus imperfections.

Very Good (Vg) - A card that has been handled but not abused: slightly rounded corners with slight layering, slight notching on edges, a significant amount of gloss lost from the surface but no scuffing and moderate discoloration of borders. The card may have a few light creases.

Good (G), Fair (F), Poor (P) - A well-worn, mishandled, or abused card: badly rounded and layered corners, scuffing, most or all original gloss missing, seriously discolored borders, moderate or heavy creases, and one or more serious flaws. The grade of good, fair, or poor depends on the severity of wear and flaws. Good, fair, and poor cards generally are used only as fillers.

Selling Your Cards

Just about every collector sells cards or will sell cards eventually. Someday you may be interested in selling your duplicates or maybe even your whole collection. You may sell to other collectors, friends, or dealers. You may even sell cards you purchased from a certain dealer back to that same dealer. In any event, it helps to know some of the mechanics of the typical transaction between buyer and seller.

Dealers will buy cards in order to resell them to other collectors who are interested in the cards. Dealers will always pay a higher percentage for items that (in their opinion) can be resold quickly, and a much lower percentage for those items that are perceived as having low demand and hence are slow moving. In either case, dealers must buy at a price that allows for the expense of doing business and a margin for profit.

If you have cards for sale, the best advice we can give is that you get several offers for your cards—either from card shops or at a card show—and take the best offer, all things considered. Note, the "best" offer may not be the one for the highest amount. And remember, if a dealer really wants your cards, he won't let you get away without making his best competitive offer. Another alternative is to place your cards in an auction as one or several lots.

Many people think nothing of going into a department store and paying $15 for an item of clothing for which the store paid $5. But if you were selling your $15 card to a dealer and he offered you $5 for it, you might think his markup unreasonable. To complete the analogy, most department stores (and card dealers) that consistently pay $10 for $15 items eventually go out of business. An exception is when the dealer has lined up a willing buyer for the item(s) you are attempting to sell, or if the cards are so hot that it's likely he'll have to hold the cards for only a short period of time.

In those cases, an offer of up to 75% of book value still will allow the dealer to make a reasonable profit considering the short time he will need to hold the merchandise. In general, however, most cards and collections will bring offers in the range of 25% to 50% of retail price. Also consider that most material from the past five to 20 years is plentiful. If that's what you're selling, don't be surprised if your best offer is well below that range.

1995 Absolute

❑ COMPLETE SET (200)	20.00	7.50
❑ 1 John Elway	2.00	.75
❑ 2 Reggie White	.40	.15
❑ 3 Errict Rhett	.20	.07
❑ 4 Deion Sanders	.50	.20
❑ 5 Rocket Ismail	.20	.07
❑ 6 Jerome Bettis	.40	.15
❑ 7 Randall Cunningham	.40	.15
❑ 8 Mario Bates	.20	.07
❑ 9 Dave Brown	.20	.07
❑ 10 Stan Humphries	.20	.07
❑ 11 Drew Bledsoe	.60	.25
❑ 12 Neil O'Donnell	.20	.07
❑ 13 Dan Marino	2.00	.75
❑ 14 Larry Centers	.20	.07
❑ 15 Craig Heyward	.20	.07
❑ 16 Bruce Smith	.40	.15
❑ 17 Erik Kramer	.10	.02
❑ 18 Jeff Blake RC	1.00	.40
❑ 19 Vinny Testaverde	.20	.07
❑ 20 Barry Sanders	1.50	.60
❑ 21 Boomer Esiason	.20	.07
❑ 22 Emmitt Smith	1.50	.60
❑ 23 Warren Moon	.20	.07
❑ 24 Junior Seau	.40	.15
❑ 25 Heath Shuler	.20	.07
❑ 26 Jackie Harris	.10	.02
❑ 27 Terance Mathis	.20	.07
❑ 28 Raymont Harris	.10	.02
❑ 29 Jim Kelly	.40	.15
❑ 30 Dan Wilkinson	.20	.07
❑ 31 Herman Moore	.40	.15
❑ 32 Shannon Sharpe	.20	.07
❑ 33 Antonio Langham	.10	.02
❑ 34 Charles Haley	.20	.07
❑ 35 Brett Favre	2.00	.75
❑ 36 Marshall Faulk	1.25	.50
❑ 37 Neil Smith	.20	.07
❑ 38 Harvey Williams	.10	.02
❑ 39 Johnny Bailey	.10	.02
❑ 40 O.J. McDuffie	.40	.15
❑ 41 David Palmer	.20	.07
❑ 42 Willie McGinest	.20	.07
❑ 43 Quinn Early	.20	.07
❑ 44 Johnny Johnson	.10	.02
❑ 45 Derek Brown TE	.10	.02
❑ 46 Charlie Garner	.40	.15
❑ 47 Byron Bam Morris	.10	.02
❑ 48 Natrone Means	.20	.07
❑ 49 Ken Norton Jr.	.20	.07
❑ 50 Troy Aikman	1.00	.40
❑ 51 Reggie Brooks	.20	.07
❑ 52 Trent Dilfer	.40	.15
❑ 53 Cortez Kennedy	.20	.07
❑ 54 Chuck Levy	.10	.02
❑ 55 Jeff George	.20	.07
❑ 56 Steve Young	.75	.30
❑ 57 Lewis Tillman	.10	.02
❑ 58 Carl Pickens	.20	.07
❑ 59 Jake Reed	.20	.07
❑ 60 Jay Novacek	.20	.07
❑ 61 Greg Hill	.20	.07
❑ 62 James Jett	.20	.07
❑ 63 Terry Kirby	.20	.07
❑ 64 Qadry Ismail	.20	.07
❑ 65 Ben Coates	.20	.07
❑ 66 Kevin Greene	.20	.07
❑ 67 Bryant Young	.20	.07
❑ 68 Brian Mitchell	.10	.02
❑ 69 Steve Walsh	.10	.02
❑ 70 Darnay Scott	.20	.07
❑ 71 Daryl Johnston	.20	.07
❑ 72 Glyn Milburn	.10	.02
❑ 73 Tim Brown	.40	.15
❑ 74 Isaac Bruce	.75	.30
❑ 75 Bernie Parmalee	.20	.07
❑ 76 Terry Allen	.20	.07
❑ 77 Jim Everett	.10	.02
❑ 78 Thomas Lewis	.20	.07
❑ 79 Vaughn Hebron	.10	.02
❑ 80 Rod Woodson	.20	.07
❑ 81 Rick Mirer	.20	.07
❑ 82 Dana Stubblefield	.20	.07
❑ 83 Bert Emanuel	.40	.15
❑ 84 Andre Reed	.20	.07
❑ 85 Jeff Graham	.10	.02
❑ 86 Johnnie Morton	.20	.07
❑ 87 LeShon Johnson	.20	.07
❑ 88 Michael Irvin	.40	.15
❑ 89 Derrick Alexander WR	.40	.15
❑ 90 Lake Dawson	.20	.07
❑ 91 Cody Carlson	.10	.02
❑ 92 Chris Warren	.20	.07
❑ 93 William Floyd	.20	.07
❑ 94 Charles Johnson	.20	.07
❑ 95 Roosevelt Potts	.10	.02
❑ 96 Cris Carter	.40	.15
❑ 97 Aaron Glenn	.10	.02
❑ 98 Curtis Conway	.40	.15
❑ 99 Kevin Williams WR	.20	.07
❑ 100 Jerry Rice	1.00	.40
❑ 101 Frank Reich	.10	.02
❑ 102 Harold Green	.10	.02
❑ 103 Russell Copeland	.10	.02
❑ 104 Rob Moore	.20	.07
❑ 105 Edgar Bennett	.20	.07
❑ 106 Darren Carrington	.10	.02
❑ 107 Tommy Maddox	.40	.15
❑ 108 Dave Meggett	.10	.02
❑ 109 Fred Barnett	.20	.07
❑ 110 Mark Seay	.20	.07
❑ 111 Gus Frerotte	.20	.07
❑ 112 Brent Jones	.10	.02
❑ 113 Chris Miller	.10	.02
❑ 114 Cedric Tillman	.10	.02
❑ 115 Mark Ingram	.10	.02
❑ 116 Eric Turner	.10	.02
❑ 117 Mark Carrier WR	.20	.07
❑ 118 Garrison Hearst	.40	.15
❑ 119 Craig Erickson	.10	.02
❑ 120 Derek Russell	.10	.02
❑ 121 Mike Sherrard	.10	.02
❑ 122 Horace Copeland	.10	.02
❑ 123 Jack Trudeau	.10	.02
❑ 124 Leroy Hoard	.10	.02
❑ 125 Gary Brown	.10	.02
❑ 126 Mel Gray	.10	.02
❑ 127 Steve Beuerlein	.20	.07
❑ 128 Marcus Allen	.40	.15
❑ 129 Irving Fryar	.20	.07
❑ 130 Marion Butts	.10	.02
❑ 131 Ricky Watters	.20	.07
❑ 132 Tony Martin	.20	.07
❑ 133 Lawrence Dawsey	.10	.02
❑ 134 Ronnie Harmon	.10	.02
❑ 135 Herschel Walker	.20	.07
❑ 136 Michael Haynes	.20	.07
❑ 137 Eric Green	.10	.02
❑ 138 Steve Bono	.20	.07
❑ 139 Jamir Miller	.10	.02
❑ 140 Rod Smith DB	.20	.07
❑ 141 Andre Rison	.20	.07
❑ 142 Eric Metcalf	.20	.07
❑ 143 Michael Timpson	.10	.02
❑ 144 Cornelius Bennett	.20	.07
❑ 145 Sean Dawkins	.20	.07
❑ 146 Scott Mitchell	.20	.07
❑ 147 Ray Childress	.10	.02
❑ 148 Jim Harbaugh	.20	.07
❑ 149 Reggie Cobb	.10	.02
❑ 150 Willie Roaf	.10	.02
❑ 151 Stevie Anderson	.10	.02
❑ 152 Barry Foster	.20	.07
❑ 153 Joe Montana	2.00	.75
❑ 154 David Klingler	.20	.07
❑ 155 Chris Chandler	.20	.07
❑ 156 Carnell Lake	.10	.02
❑ 157 Calvin Williams	.20	.07
❑ 158 Kenneth Davis	.10	.02
❑ 159 Tydus Winans	.10	.02
❑ 160 Sam Adams	.10	.02
❑ 161 Ronald Moore	.10	.02
❑ 162 Vincent Brisby	.10	.02
❑ 163 Alvin Harper	.10	.02
❑ 164 Jake Reed	.20	.07
❑ 165 Jeff Hostetler	.20	.07
❑ 166 Mark Brunell	.60	.25
❑ 167 Leonard Russell	.10	.02
❑ 168 Greg Truitt	.10	.02
❑ 169 Pete Metzelaars	.10	.02
❑ 170 Dave Krieg	.10	.02
❑ 171 Lorenzo White	.10	.02
❑ 172 Robert Brooks	.40	.15
❑ 173 Willie Davis	.20	.07
❑ 174 Irving Spikes	.20	.07
❑ 175 Rodney Hampton	.20	.07
❑ 176 Erric Pegram	.20	.07
❑ 177 Brian Blades	.20	.07
❑ 178 Shawn Jefferson	.10	.02
❑ 179 Tyrone Poole RC	.40	.15
❑ 180 Rob Johnson RC	1.50	.60
❑ 181 Ki-Jana Carter RC	.40	.15
❑ 182 Steve McNair RC	5.00	2.00
❑ 183 Michael Westbrook RC	.40	.15
❑ 184 Kerry Collins RC	2.50	1.00
❑ 185 Kevin Carter RC	.40	.15
❑ 186 Tony Boselli RC	.40	.15
❑ 187 Joey Galloway RC	2.50	1.00
❑ 188 Kyle Brady RC	.40	.15
❑ 189 J.J. Stokes RC	.40	.15
❑ 190 Warren Sapp RC	2.50	1.00
❑ 191 Tyrone Wheatley RC	1.50	.60
❑ 192 Napoleon Kaufman RC	2.00	.75
❑ 193 James O. Stewart RC	1.50	.60
❑ 194 Rashaan Salaam RC	.20	.07
❑ 195 Ray Zellars RC	.20	.07
❑ 196 Todd Collins RC	.20	.07
❑ 197 Sherman Williams RC	.10	.02
❑ 198 Frank Sanders RC	.40	.15
❑ 199 Terrell Fletcher RC	.10	.02
❑ 200 Chad May RC	.10	.02
❑ DP1G Tony Boselli Draft Gold	3.00	1.50
❑ DP1S Tony Boselli Draft Silver	2.00	.75
❑ DP2G Kerry Collins Draft Gold	5.00	2.00
❑ DP2S Kerry Collins Draft Silver	5.00	2.00

1996 Absolute

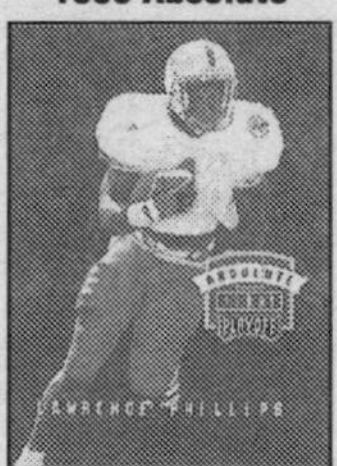

❑ COMPLETE SET (200)	60.00	25.00
❑ COMP.RED SET (100)	15.00	6.00
❑ 1 Jim Kelly	.60	.25
❑ 2 Michael Irvin	.60	.25
❑ 3 Jim Harbaugh	.30	.10
❑ 4 Warren Moon	.30	.10
❑ 5 Rick Mirer	.30	.10
❑ 6 Drew Bledsoe	1.00	.40
❑ 7 Steve Young	1.25	.50
❑ 8 Junior Seau	.60	.25
❑ 9 Sherman Williams	.15	.05
❑ 10 Jay Novacek	.15	.05
❑ 11 Bill Brooks	.15	.05
❑ 12 Steve Bono	.15	.05
❑ 13 Leroy Hoard	.15	.05
❑ 14 Willie Jackson	.30	.10
❑ 15 Irving Fryar	.30	.10
❑ 16 Tony McGee	.15	.05
❑ 17 Neil O'Donnell	.30	.10
❑ 18 Fred Barnett	.15	.05
❑ 19 Erric Pegram	.15	.05
❑ 20 Derrick Moore	.15	.05
❑ 21 Johnnie Morton	.30	.10
❑ 22 James Jett	.30	.10

❑ 23 Tim Brown .60 .25
❑ 24 Kevin Miniefield .15 .05
❑ 25 Jim McMahon .30 .10
❑ 26 Brian Blades .15 .05
❑ 27 Henry Ellard .15 .05
❑ 28 Calvin Williams .15 .05
❑ 29 Chris Chandler .30 .10
❑ 30 Rod Woodson .30 .10
❑ 31 Ronnie Harmon .15 .05
❑ 32 Brent Jones .15 .05
❑ 33 Qadry Ismail .30 .10
❑ 34 Steve Tasker .15 .05
❑ 35 Eric Green .15 .05
❑ 36 Brian Mitchell .15 .05
❑ 37 Herschel Walker .30 .10
❑ 38 Sean Dawkins .15 .05
❑ 39 Bryce Paup .15 .05
❑ 40 Dorsey Levens .60 .25
❑ 41 Andre Rison .30 .10
❑ 42 Lamont Warren .15 .05
❑ 43 Earnest Byner .15 .05
❑ 44 Bobby Engram RC .60 .25
❑ 45 Simeon Rice RC 1.50 .60
❑ 46 Michael Jackson .30 .10
❑ 47 Marvin Harrison RC 4.00 1.50
❑ 48 Thurman Thomas .60 .25
❑ 49 Charles Haley .30 .10
❑ 50 Rob Moore .30 .10
❑ 51 Bryan Cox .15 .05
❑ 52 Horace Copeland .15 .05
❑ 53 Rodney Peete .15 .05
❑ 54 Jeff Graham .15 .05
❑ 55 Charles Johnson .15 .05
❑ 56 Natrone Means .30 .10
❑ 57 Terrell Fletcher .15 .05
❑ 58 Eric Bieniemy .15 .05
❑ 59 Karim Abdul-Jabbar RC .60 .25
❑ 60 Quinn Early .15 .05
❑ 61 Mark Bruener .15 .05
❑ 62 Shawn Jefferson .15 .05
❑ 63 Vinny Testaverde .30 .10
❑ 64 Derrick Mayes RC .60 .25
❑ 65 Mario Bates .30 .10
❑ 66 J.J. Birden .15 .05
❑ 67 Eddie Kennison RC .60 .25
❑ 68 Steve Walsh .15 .05
❑ 69 Mark Chmura .30 .10
❑ 70 Mike Sherrard .15 .05
❑ 71 Boomer Esiason .30 .10
❑ 72 Alex Van Dyke RC .30 .10
❑ 73 Jake Reed .30 .10
❑ 74 Jackie Harris .15 .05
❑ 75 Mark Rypien .15 .05
❑ 76 Chris Calloway .15 .05
❑ 77 Amani Toomer RC 1.50 .60
❑ 78 Terrell Davis 3.00 1.25
❑ 79 Rocket Ismail .15 .05
❑ 80 Derek Loville .15 .05
❑ 81 Ben Coates .30 .10
❑ 82 Kyle Brady .15 .05
❑ 83 Willie Green .15 .05
❑ 84 Randall Cunningham .60 .25
❑ 85 Amp Lee .15 .05
❑ 86 Bert Emanuel .30 .10
❑ 87 Jason Dunn RC .30 .10
❑ 88 Michael Haynes .15 .05
❑ 89 Robert Green .15 .05
❑ 90 Willie Davis .15 .05
❑ 91 O.J. McDuffie .30 .10
❑ 92 Harold Green .15 .05
❑ 93 Ken Dilger .30 .10
❑ 94 Brett Perriman .15 .05
❑ 95 Eric Zeier .15 .05
❑ 96 Jerome Bettis .60 .25
❑ 97 Rickey Dudley RC .60 .25
❑ 98 Darnay Scott .30 .10
❑ 99 Mark Brunell 1.00 .40
❑ 100 Christian Fauria .15 .05
❑ 101 Jeff Blake 1.50 .60
❑ 102 Troy Aikman 4.00 1.50
❑ 103 John Elway 8.00 3.00
❑ 104 Barry Sanders 6.00 2.50
❑ 105 Curtis Conway 1.50 .60
❑ 106 Wayne Chrebet 2.00 .75
❑ 107 Lake Dawson .75 .30
❑ 108 Jerry Rice 4.00 1.50
❑ 109 Kevin Williams .25 .08
❑ 110 Zack Crockett .25 .08
❑ 111 Vincent Brisby .25 .08
❑ 112 Rodney Thomas .25 .08
❑ 113 Rodney Hampton .75 .30
❑ 114 Adrian Murrell .30 .10
❑ 115 Bruce Smith 1.50 .60
❑ 116 Napoleon Kaufman 1.50 .60
❑ 117 Byron Bam Morris .25 .08
❑ 118 Anthony Miller .75 .30
❑ 119 Aaron Hayden RC .75 .30
❑ 120 Joey Galloway .60 .25
❑ 121 Trent Dilfer .75 .30
❑ 122 Stoney Case .25 .08
❑ 123 Tamarick Vanover .30 .10
❑ 124 Eric Metcalf .75 .30
❑ 125 Marcus Allen 1.50 .60
❑ 126 James O. Stewart .75 .30
❑ 127 Charlie Garner .75 .30
❑ 128 Yancey Thigpen .75 .30
❑ 129 William Floyd .75 .30
❑ 130 Terry Allen .75 .30
❑ 131 Robert Smith .75 .30
❑ 132 Todd Kinchen .25 .08
❑ 133 Gus Frerotte .75 .30
❑ 134 Frank Sanders .75 .30
❑ 135 Scott Mitchell .75 .30
❑ 136 Greg Hill .75 .30
❑ 137 Edgar Bennett .75 .30
❑ 138 Alvin Harper .25 .08
❑ 139 Reggie White 1.50 .60
❑ 140 Craig Heyward .25 .08
❑ 141 Todd Collins .75 .30
❑ 142 Ernie Mills .25 .08
❑ 143 Keyshawn Johnson RC 2.50 1.00
❑ 144 Mark Carrier WR .25 .08
❑ 145 Robert Brooks 1.50 .60
❑ 146 Bernie Parmalee .25 .08
❑ 147 Carl Pickens .75 .30
❑ 148 Kevin Hardy RC 1.50 .60
❑ 149 Jonathan Ogden RC 1.50 .60
❑ 150 Lawrence Phillips RC 1.50 .60
❑ 151 Emmitt Smith 10.00 4.00
❑ 152 Brett Favre 12.00 5.00
❑ 153 Dan Marino 12.00 5.00
❑ 154 Jim Everett .60 .25
❑ 155 Dave Brown 1.25 .50
❑ 156 Jeff Hostetler 1.25 .50
❑ 157 Heath Shuler 1.25 .50
❑ 158 Daryl Johnston 1.25 .50
❑ 159 Terance Mathis 1.25 .50
❑ 160 Curtis Martin 5.00 2.00
❑ 161 Ray Zellars .60 .25
❑ 162 Ricky Watters 1.25 .50
❑ 163 Chris Warren 1.25 .50
❑ 164 Larry Centers 1.25 .50
❑ 165 Steve McNair 5.00 2.00
❑ 166 Terry Kirby 1.25 .50
❑ 167 Rob Johnson 2.50 1.00
❑ 168 Dave Meggett .60 .25
❑ 169 Antonio Freeman .60 .25
❑ 170 Marshall Faulk 4.00 1.50
❑ 171 Andre Hastings .15 .05
❑ 172 Stan Humphries 1.25 .50
❑ 173 Errict Rhett 1.25 .50
❑ 174 Michael Westbrook 2.50 1.00
❑ 175 Deion Sanders 4.00 1.50
❑ 176 Jeff George 1.25 .50
❑ 177 Cris Carter 2.50 1.00
❑ 178 Chris Sanders 1.25 .50
❑ 179 Ki-Jana Carter 1.25 .50
❑ 180 Kordell Stewart 2.50 1.00
❑ 181 Isaac Bruce 2.50 1.00
❑ 182 Terry Glenn RC 5.00 2.00
❑ 183 Garrison Hearst 1.25 .50
❑ 184 Erik Kramer .60 .25
❑ 185 Leeland McElroy RC 1.25 .50
❑ 186 Rashaan Salaam 1.25 .50
❑ 187 Kimble Anders .60 .25
❑ 188 Chad May .60 .25
❑ 189 Tony Martin 1.25 .50
❑ 190 J.J. Stokes 2.50 1.00
❑ 191 Darick Holmes .60 .25
❑ 192 Eric Moulds RC 6.00 2.50
❑ 193 Shannon Sharpe 1.25 .50
❑ 194 Tim Biakabutuka RC 2.50 1.00
❑ 195 Eddie George RC 6.00 2.50
❑ 196 Mike Alstott RC 5.00 2.00
❑ 197 Kerry Collins 2.50 1.00
❑ 198 Harvey Williams .60 .25
❑ 199 Herman Moore 1.25 .50
❑ 200 Tyrone Wheatley 1.25 .50

1997 Absolute

❑ COMPLETE SET (200) 80.00 30.00
❑ COMP.GREEN SET (100) 25.00 10.00
❑ 1 Marcus Allen .50 .20
❑ 2 Eric Bieniemy .20 .07
❑ 3 Jason Dunn .20 .07
❑ 4 Jim Harbaugh .30 .10
❑ 5 Michael Westbrook .30 .10
❑ 6 Tiki Barber RC 4.00 1.50
❑ 7 Frank Reich .20 .07
❑ 8 Irving Fryar .30 .10
❑ 9 Courtney Hawkins .20 .07
❑ 10 Eric Zeier .30 .10
❑ 11 Kent Graham .20 .07
❑ 12 Trent Dilfer .50 .20
❑ 13 Neil O'Donnell .30 .10
❑ 14 Reidel Anthony RC .50 .20
❑ 15 Jeff Hostetler .20 .07
❑ 16 Lawrence Phillips .20 .07
❑ 17 Dave Brown .20 .07
❑ 18 Mike Tomczak .20 .07
❑ 19 Jake Reed .30 .10
❑ 20 Anthony Miller .20 .07
❑ 21 Eric Metcalf .30 .10
❑ 22 Sedrick Shaw RC .30 .10
❑ 23 Anthony Johnson .20 .07
❑ 24 Mario Bates .20 .07
❑ 25 Dorsey Levens .50 .20
❑ 26 Stan Humphries .30 .10
❑ 27 Ben Coates .30 .10
❑ 28 Tyrone Wheatley .30 .10
❑ 29 Adrian Murrell .30 .10
❑ 30 William Henderson .30 .10
❑ 31 Warrick Dunn RC 2.00 .75
❑ 32 LeShon Johnson .20 .07
❑ 33 James O.Stewart .30 .10
❑ 34 Edgar Bennett .30 .10
❑ 35 Raymont Harris .20 .07
❑ 36 LeRoy Butler .20 .07
❑ 37 Darren Woodson .20 .07
❑ 38 Darnell Autry RC .30 .10
❑ 39 Johnnie Morton .30 .10
❑ 40 William Floyd .30 .10
❑ 41 Terrell Fletcher .20 .07
❑ 42 Leonard Russell .20 .07
❑ 43 Henry Ellard .20 .07
❑ 44 Terrell Owens .50 .20
❑ 45 John Friesz .20 .07
❑ 46 Antowain Smith RC 1.50 .60
❑ 47 Charles Johnson .30 .10
❑ 48 Rickey Dudley .30 .10
❑ 49 Lake Dawson .20 .07
❑ 50 Bert Emanuel .30 .10
❑ 51 Zach Thomas .50 .20
❑ 52 Earnest Byner .20 .07
❑ 53 Yatil Green RC .30 .10
❑ 54 Chris Spielman .20 .07
❑ 55 Muhsin Muhammad .30 .10
❑ 56 Bobby Engram .30 .10
❑ 57 Eric Bjornson .20 .07
❑ 58 Willie Green .20 .07
❑ 59 Derrick Mayes .30 .10
❑ 60 Chris Sanders .20 .07
❑ 61 Jimmy Smith .30 .10
❑ 62 Tony Gonzalez RC 2.00 .75
❑ 63 Rich Gannon .50 .20
❑ 64 Stanley Pritchett .20 .07
❑ 65 Brad Johnson .50 .20
❑ 66 Rodney Peete .20 .07
❑ 67 Sam Gash .20 .07
❑ 68 Chris Calloway .20 .07

69 Chris T. Jones	.20	.07
70 Will Blackwell RC	.30	.10
71 Mark Bruener	.20	.07
72 Terry Kirby	.30	.10
73 Brian Blades	.20	.07
74 Craig Heyward	.20	.07
75 Jamie Asher	.20	.07
76 Terance Mathis	.30	.10
77 Troy Davis RC	.30	.10
78 Bruce Smith	.30	.10
79 Simeon Rice	.30	.10
80 Fred Barnett	.20	.07
81 Tim Brown	.50	.20
82 James Jett	.30	.10
83 Mark Carrier WR	.20	.07
84 Shawn Jefferson	.20	.07
85 Ken Dilger	.20	.07
86 Rae Carruth RC	.20	.07
87 Keenan McCardell	.30	.10
88 Michael Irvin	.50	.20
89 Mark Chmura	.30	.10
90 Derrick Alexander WR	.30	.10
91 Andre Reed	.30	.10
92 Ed McCaffrey	.30	.10
93 Erik Kramer	.20	.07
94 Albert Connell RC	.50	.20
95 Frank Wycheck	.20	.07
96 Zack Crockett	.20	.07
97 Jim Everett	.20	.07
98 Michael Haynes	.20	.07
99 Jeff Graham	.20	.07
100 Brent Jones	.30	.10
101 Troy Aikman	3.00	1.25
102 Byron Hanspard RC	.30	.10
103 Robert Brooks	1.25	.50
104 Karim Abdul-Jabbar	1.25	.50
105 Drew Bledsoe	1.50	.60
106 Napoleon Kaufman	1.25	.50
107 Steve Young	2.00	.75
108 Leeland McElroy	.20	.07
109 Jamal Anderson	.50	.20
110 David LaFleur RC	.50	.20
111 Vinny Testaverde	.75	.30
112 Eric Moulds	1.25	.50
113 Tim Biakabutuka	1.25	.50
114 Rick Mirer	.50	.20
115 Jeff Blake	1.25	.50
116 Jim Schwantz RC	.50	.20
117 Herman Moore	.75	.30
118 Ike Hilliard RC	2.50	1.00
119 Reggie White	1.25	.50
120 Steve McNair	2.00	.75
121 Marshall Faulk	2.00	.75
122 Natrone Means	.75	.30
123 Greg Hill	.75	.30
124 O.J. McDuffie	.75	.30
125 Robert Smith	.75	.30
126 Bryant Westbrook RC	1.25	.50
127 Ray Zellars	.50	.20
128 Rodney Hampton	.75	.30
129 Wayne Chrebet	.50	.20
130 Desmond Howard	.75	.30
131 Ty Detmer	.75	.30
132 Erric Pegram	.50	.20
133 Yancey Thigpen	.75	.30
134 Danny Wuerffel RC	.50	.20
135 Charlie Jones	.50	.20
136 Chris Warren	.75	.30
137 Isaac Bruce	1.25	.50
138 Errict Rhett	.75	.30
139 Gus Frerotte	1.25	.50
140 Frank Sanders	.75	.30
141 Todd Collins	.75	.30
142 Jake Plummer RC	12.00	5.00
143 Darnay Scott	.75	.30
144 Rashaan Salaam	1.25	.50
145 Terrell Davis	2.00	.75
146 Scott Mitchell	.75	.30
147 Junior Seau	1.25	.50
148 Warren Moon	.75	.30
149 Wesley Walls	.50	.20
150 Daryl Johnston	.75	.30
151 Brett Favre	12.00	5.00
152 Emmitt Smith	10.00	4.00
153 Dan Marino	12.00	5.00
154 Larry Centers	1.25	.50
155 Michael Jackson	1.25	.50
156 Kerry Collins	.50	.20
157 Curtis Conway	1.25	.50
158 Peter Boulware RC	2.00	.75
159 Carl Pickens	1.25	.50
160 Shannon Sharpe	1.25	.50
161 Brett Perriman	.75	.30
162 Eddie George	2.00	.75
163 Mark Brunell	4.00	1.50
164 Tamarick Vanover	1.25	.50
165 Cris Carter	2.00	.75
166 Corey Dillon RC	15.00	6.00
167 Curtis Martin	4.00	1.50
168 Amani Toomer	1.25	.50
169 Jeff George	1.25	.50
170 Kordell Stewart	2.00	.75
171 Garrison Hearst	1.25	.50
172 Tony Banks	1.25	.50
173 Mike Alstott	2.00	.75
174 Jim Druckenmiller RC	.30	.10
175 Chris Chandler	1.25	.50
176 Byron Bam Morris	.75	.30
177 Billy Joe Hobert	1.25	.50
178 Ernie Mills	.75	.30
179 Ki-Jana Carter	.75	.30
180 Deion Sanders	2.00	.75
181 Ricky Watters	1.25	.50
182 Shawn Springs RC	2.00	.75
183 Barry Sanders	10.00	4.00
184 Antonio Freeman	2.00	.75
185 Marvin Harrison	2.00	.75
186 Elvis Grbac	1.25	.50
187 Terry Glenn	2.00	.75
188 Willie Roaf	.75	.30
189 Keyshawn Johnson	2.00	.75
190 Orlando Pace RC	2.00	.75
191 Jerome Bettis	2.00	.75
192 Tony Martin	1.25	.50
193 Jerry Rice	6.00	2.50
194 Joey Galloway	1.25	.50
195 Terry Allen	2.00	.75
196 Eddie Kennison	1.25	.50
197 Thurman Thomas	2.00	.75
198 Darrell Russell RC	.75	.30
199 Rob Moore	1.25	.50
200 John Elway	12.00	5.00

1998 Absolute Hobby

COMPLETE SET (200)	100.00	40.00
1 John Elway	10.00	4.00
2 Marcus Nash RC	1.50	.60
3 Brian Griese RC	6.00	2.50
4 Terrell Davis	2.50	1.00
5 Rod Smith WR	1.50	.60
6 Shannon Sharpe	1.50	.60
7 Ed McCaffrey	1.50	.60
8 Brett Favre	10.00	4.00
9 Dorsey Levens	2.50	1.00
10 Derrick Mayes	1.50	.60
11 Antonio Freeman	2.50	1.00
12 Robert Brooks	1.50	.60
13 Mark Chmura	1.50	.60
14 Reggie White	2.50	1.00
15 Kordell Stewart	2.50	1.00
16 Hines Ward RC	12.00	6.00
17 Jerome Bettis	2.50	1.00
18 Charles Johnson	1.00	.40
19 Courtney Hawkins	1.00	.40
20 Will Blackwell	1.00	.40
21 Mark Bruener	1.00	.40
22 Steve Young	4.00	1.50
23 Jim Druckenmiller	1.00	.40
24 Garrison Hearst	2.50	1.00
25 R.W. McQuarters RC	2.50	1.00
26 Marc Edwards	1.00	.40
27 Irv Smith	1.00	.40
28 Jerry Rice	5.00	2.00
29 Terrell Owens	2.50	1.00
30 J.J. Stokes	1.50	.60
31 Elvis Grbac	1.50	.60
32 Rashaan Shehee RC	2.50	1.00
33 Donnell Bennett	1.00	.40
34 Kimble Anders	1.50	.60
35 Ted Popson	1.00	.40
36 Derrick Alexander WR	1.50	.60
37 Tony Gonzalez	2.50	1.00
38 Andre Rison	1.50	.60
39 Brad Johnson	2.50	1.00
40 Randy Moss RC	25.00	12.50
41 Robert Smith	2.50	1.00
42 Leroy Hoard	1.00	.40
43 Cris Carter	2.50	1.00
44 Jake Reed	1.50	.60
45 Drew Bledsoe	4.00	1.50
46 Tony Simmons RC	2.50	1.00
47 Chris Floyd RC	1.50	.60
48 Robert Edwards RC	2.50	1.00
49 Shawn Jefferson	1.00	.40
50 Ben Coates	1.50	.60
51 Terry Glenn	2.50	1.00
52 Trent Dilfer	2.50	1.00
53 Jacquez Green RC	2.50	1.00
54 Warrick Dunn	2.50	1.00
55 Mike Alstott	2.50	1.00
56 Reidel Anthony	1.50	.60
57 Bert Emanuel	1.50	.60
58 Warren Sapp	1.50	.60
59 Charlie Batch RC	3.00	1.25
60 Germane Crowell RC	2.50	1.00
61 Scott Mitchell	1.50	.60
62 Barry Sanders	8.00	3.00
63 Tommy Vardell	1.00	.40
64 Herman Moore	1.50	.60
65 Johnnie Morton	1.50	.60
66 Mark Brunell	2.50	1.00
67 Jonathan Quinn RC	3.00	1.25
68 Fred Taylor RC	5.00	2.00
69 James Stewart	1.50	.60
70 Jimmy Smith	1.50	.60
71 Damon Jones	1.00	.40
72 Keenan McCardell	1.50	.60
73 Dan Marino	10.00	4.00
74 Larry Shannon RC	1.50	.60
75 John Avery RC	2.50	1.00
76 Troy Drayton	1.00	.40
77 Stanley Pritchett	1.00	.40
78 Karim Abdul-Jabbar	2.50	1.00
79 O.J. McDuffie	1.50	.60
80 Yatil Green	1.00	.40
81 Danny Kanell	1.50	.60
82 Tiki Barber	2.50	1.00
83 Tyrone Wheatley	1.50	.60
84 Charles Way	1.00	.40
85 Gary Brown	1.00	.40
86 Brian Alford RC	1.50	.60
87 Joe Jurevicius RC	3.00	1.25
88 Ike Hilliard	1.50	.60
89 Troy Aikman	5.00	2.00
90 Deion Sanders	2.50	1.00
91 Emmitt Smith	8.00	3.00
92 Chris Warren	1.50	.60
93 Daryl Johnston	1.50	.60
94 Michael Irvin	2.50	1.00
95 David LaFleur	1.00	.40
96 Kevin Dyson RC	3.00	1.25
97 Steve McNair	2.50	1.00
98 Eddie George	2.50	1.00
99 Yancey Thigpen	1.00	.40
100 Frank Wycheck	1.00	.40
101 Glenn Foley	1.50	.60
102 Vinny Testaverde	1.50	.60
103 Keyshawn Johnson	2.50	1.00
104 Curtis Martin	2.50	1.00
105 Keith Byars	1.00	.40
106 Scott Frost RC	1.50	.60
107 Wayne Chrebet	2.50	1.00
108 Warren Moon	2.50	1.00
109 Ahman Green RC	15.00	6.00
110 Steve Broussard	1.00	.40
111 Ricky Watters	1.50	.60
112 Joey Galloway	1.50	.60
113 Mike Pritchard	1.00	.40
114 Brian Blades	1.00	.40
115 Gus Frerotte	1.00	.40

❑ 116 Skip Hicks RC 2.50 1.00
❑ 117 Terry Allen 2.50 1.00
❑ 118 Michael Westbrook 1.50 .60
❑ 119 Jamie Asher 1.00 .40
❑ 120 Leslie Shepherd 1.00 .40
❑ 121 Jeff Blake 1.50 .60
❑ 122 Corey Dillon 2.50 1.00
❑ 123 Carl Pickens 1.50 .60
❑ 124 Tony McGee 1.00 .40
❑ 125 Darnay Scott 1.50 .60
❑ 126 Kerry Collins 1.50 .60
❑ 127 Fred Lane 1.00 .40
❑ 128 William Floyd 1.00 .40
❑ 129 Rae Carruth 1.00 .40
❑ 130 Wesley Walls 1.50 .60
❑ 131 Muhsin Muhammad 1.50 .60
❑ 132 Jake Plummer 2.50 1.00
❑ 133 Adrian Murrell 1.50 .60
❑ 134 Michael Pittman RC 4.00 2.00
❑ 135 Larry Centers 1.00 .40
❑ 136 Frank Sanders 1.50 .60
❑ 137 Rob Moore 1.50 .60
❑ 138 Andre Wadsworth RC 2.50 1.00
❑ 139 Mario Bates 1.50 .60
❑ 140 Chris Chandler 1.50 .60
❑ 141 Byron Hanspard 1.00 .40
❑ 142 Jamal Anderson 2.50 1.00
❑ 143 Terance Mathis 1.50 .60
❑ 144 O.J. Santiago 1.00 .40
❑ 145 Tony Martin 1.50 .60
❑ 146 Jammi German RC 1.50 .60
❑ 147 Jim Harbaugh 1.50 .60
❑ 148 Errict Rhett 1.50 .60
❑ 149 Michael Jackson 1.00 .40
❑ 150 Pat Johnson RC 2.50 1.00
❑ 151 Eric Green 1.00 .40
❑ 152 Doug Flutie 2.50 1.00
❑ 153 Rob Johnson 1.50 .60
❑ 154 Antowain Smith 2.50 1.00
❑ 155 Bruce Smith 1.50 .60
❑ 156 Eric Moulds 2.50 1.00
❑ 157 Andre Reed 1.50 .60
❑ 158 Erik Kramer 1.00 .40
❑ 159 Darnell Autry 1.00 .40
❑ 160 Edgar Bennett 1.00 .40
❑ 161 Curtis Enis RC 1.50 .60
❑ 162 Curtis Conway 1.50 .60
❑ 163 E.G. Green RC 2.50 1.00
❑ 164 Jerome Pathon RC 3.00 1.25
❑ 165 Peyton Manning RC 30.00 12.50
❑ 166 Marshall Faulk 3.00 1.25
❑ 167 Zack Crockett 1.00 .40
❑ 168 Ken Dilger 1.00 .40
❑ 169 Marvin Harrison 2.50 1.00
❑ 170 Danny Wuerffel 1.50 .60
❑ 171 Lamar Smith 1.50 .60
❑ 172 Ray Zellars 1.00 .40
❑ 173 Qadry Ismail 1.50 .60
❑ 174 Sean Dawkins 1.00 .40
❑ 175 Andre Hastings 1.00 .40
❑ 176 Jeff George 1.50 .60
❑ 177 Charles Woodson RC 4.00 1.50
❑ 178 Napoleon Kaufman 2.50 1.00
❑ 179 Jon Ritchie RC 2.50 1.00
❑ 180 Desmond Howard 1.50 .60
❑ 181 Tim Brown 2.50 1.00
❑ 182 James Jett 1.50 .60
❑ 183 Rickey Dudley 1.00 .40
❑ 184 Bobby Hoying 1.50 .60
❑ 185 Rodney Peete 1.00 .40
❑ 186 Charlie Garner 1.50 .60
❑ 187 Irving Fryar 1.50 .60
❑ 188 Chris T. Jones 1.00 .40
❑ 189 Jason Dunn 1.00 .40
❑ 190 Tony Banks 1.50 .60
❑ 191 Robert Holcombe RC 2.50 1.00
❑ 192 Craig Heyward 1.00 .40
❑ 193 Isaac Bruce 2.50 1.00
❑ 194 Az-Zahir Hakim RC 3.00 1.25
❑ 195 Eddie Kennison 1.50 .60
❑ 196 Mikhael Ricks RC 2.50 1.00
❑ 197 Ryan Leaf RC 3.00 1.25
❑ 198 Natrone Means 1.50 .60
❑ 199 Junior Seau 2.50 1.00
❑ 200 Freddie Jones 1.00 .40

1999 Absolute EXP

❑ COMPLETE SET (200) 50.00 25.00
❑ 1 Tim Couch RC 1.25 .50

❑ 2 Donovan McNabb RC 6.00 2.50
❑ 3 Akili Smith RC .75 .30
❑ 4 Edgerrin James RC 5.00 2.00
❑ 5 Ricky Williams RC 2.50 1.00
❑ 6 Torry Holt RC 3.00 1.25
❑ 7 Champ Bailey RC 1.50 .60
❑ 8 David Boston RC 1.25 .50
❑ 9 Chris Claiborne RC .50 .20
❑ 10 Chris McAlister RC .75 .30
❑ 11 Daunte Culpepper RC 5.00 2.00
❑ 12 Cade McNown RC .75 .30
❑ 13 Troy Edwards RC .75 .30
❑ 14 Kevin Johnson RC 1.25 .50
❑ 15 James Johnson RC .75 .30
❑ 16 Rob Konrad RC 1.25 .50
❑ 17 Jim Kleinsasser RC 1.25 .50
❑ 18 Kevin Faulk RC 1.25 .50
❑ 19 Joe Montgomery RC .75 .30
❑ 20 Shaun King RC .75 .30
❑ 21 Peerless Price RC 1.25 .50
❑ 22 Mike Cloud RC .75 .30
❑ 23 Jermaine Fazande RC .75 .30
❑ 24 D'Wayne Bates RC .75 .30
❑ 25 Brock Huard RC 1.25 .50
❑ 26 Marty Booker RC 1.25 .50
❑ 27 Karsten Bailey RC .75 .30
❑ 28 Shawn Bryson RC 1.25 .50
❑ 29 Jeff Paulk RC .50 .20
❑ 30 Sedrick Irvin RC .50 .20
❑ 31 Craig Yeast RC .75 .30
❑ 32 Joe Germaine RC .75 .30
❑ 33 Dameane Douglas RC 1.25 .50
❑ 34 Brandon Stokley RC 1.50 .60
❑ 35 Larry Parker RC 1.25 .50
❑ 36 Wane McGarity RC .50 .20
❑ 37 Na Brown RC .75 .30
❑ 38 Cecil Collins RC .50 .20
❑ 39 Darrin Chiaverini RC .75 .30
❑ 40 Madre Hill RC .50 .20
❑ 41 Adrian Murrell .50 .20
❑ 42 Jake Plummer .50 .20
❑ 43 Frank Sanders .50 .20
❑ 44 Rob Moore .50 .20
❑ 45 Andre Wadsworth .30 .10
❑ 46 Simeon Rice .50 .20
❑ 47 Eric Swann .30 .10
❑ 48 Terance Mathis .50 .20
❑ 49 Tim Dwight .75 .30
❑ 50 Jamal Anderson .75 .30
❑ 51 Chris Chandler .50 .20
❑ 52 Chris Calloway .30 .10
❑ 53 O.J. Santiago .30 .10
❑ 54 Jermaine Lewis .50 .20
❑ 55 Priest Holmes 1.25 .50
❑ 56 Scott Mitchell .30 .10
❑ 57 Tony Banks .50 .20
❑ 58 Rod Woodson .50 .20
❑ 59 Andre Reed .50 .20
❑ 60 Thurman Thomas .50 .20
❑ 61 Bruce Smith .50 .20
❑ 62 Rob Johnson .50 .20
❑ 63 Eric Moulds .75 .30
❑ 64 Doug Flutie .75 .30
❑ 65 Antowain Smith .75 .30
❑ 66 Tim Biakabutuka .50 .20
❑ 67 Muhsin Muhammad .50 .20
❑ 68 Steve Beuerlein .30 .10
❑ 69 Bobby Engram .50 .20
❑ 70 Curtis Conway .50 .20
❑ 71 Curtis Enis .30 .10
❑ 72 Edgar Bennett .30 .10
❑ 73 Jeff Blake .50 .20
❑ 74 Darnay Scott .30 .10
❑ 75 Carl Pickens .50 .20
❑ 76 Corey Dillon .75 .30
❑ 77 Ty Detmer .50 .20
❑ 78 Leslie Shepherd .30 .10
❑ 79 Sedrick Shaw .30 .10
❑ 80 Rocket Ismail .50 .20
❑ 81 Emmitt Smith 1.50 .60
❑ 82 Michael Irvin .50 .20
❑ 83 Troy Aikman 1.50 .60
❑ 84 Deion Sanders .75 .30
❑ 85 Darren Woodson .30 .10
❑ 86 Chris Warren .30 .10
❑ 87 John Elway 2.50 1.00
❑ 88 Brian Griese .75 .30
❑ 89 Shannon Sharpe .50 .20
❑ 90 Terrell Davis .75 .30
❑ 91 Bubby Brister .30 .10
❑ 92 Ed McCaffrey .50 .20
❑ 93 Rod Smith .50 .20
❑ 94 Germane Crowell .30 .10
❑ 95 Johnnie Morton .50 .20
❑ 96 Barry Sanders 2.50 1.00
❑ 97 Herman Moore .50 .20
❑ 98 Charlie Batch .75 .30
❑ 99 Mark Chmura .30 .10
❑ 100 Derrick Mayes .30 .10
❑ 101 Dorsey Levens .75 .30
❑ 102 Brett Favre 2.50 1.00
❑ 103 Antonio Freeman .75 .30
❑ 104 Robert Brooks .50 .20
❑ 105 Desmond Howard .50 .20
❑ 106 Jerome Pathon .30 .10
❑ 107 Marvin Harrison .75 .30
❑ 108 Peyton Manning 2.50 1.00
❑ 109 E.G. Green .30 .10
❑ 110 Tavian Banks .30 .10
❑ 111 Keenan McCardell .50 .20
❑ 112 Jimmy Smith .50 .20
❑ 113 Mark Brunell .75 .30
❑ 114 Fred Taylor .75 .30
❑ 115 Byron Bam Morris .30 .10
❑ 116 Andre Rison .50 .20
❑ 117 Elvis Grbac .50 .20
❑ 118 Warren Moon .75 .30
❑ 119 Tony Gonzalez .75 .30
❑ 120 Derrick Alexander WR .50 .20
❑ 121 Rashaan Shehee .30 .10
❑ 122 Zach Thomas .75 .30
❑ 123 Oronde Gadsden .50 .20
❑ 124 Dan Marino 2.50 1.00
❑ 125 Karim Abdul-Jabbar .50 .20
❑ 126 O.J. McDuffie .50 .20
❑ 127 Jake Reed .50 .20
❑ 128 John Randle .50 .20
❑ 129 Randy Moss 2.00 .75
❑ 130 Cris Carter .75 .30
❑ 131 Randall Cunningham .75 .30
❑ 132 Robert Smith .75 .30
❑ 133 Terry Glenn .75 .30
❑ 134 Ben Coates .50 .20
❑ 135 Drew Bledsoe 1.00 .40
❑ 136 Ty Law .50 .20
❑ 137 Tony Simmons .30 .10
❑ 138 Eddie Kennison .50 .20
❑ 139 Cam Cleeland .30 .10
❑ 140 Ike Hilliard .30 .10
❑ 141 Joe Jurevicius .50 .20
❑ 142 Gary Brown .30 .10
❑ 143 Kerry Collins .50 .20
❑ 144 Tiki Barber .75 .30
❑ 145 Jason Sehorn .30 .10
❑ 146 Dedric Ward .30 .10
❑ 147 Vinny Testaverde .50 .20
❑ 148 Wayne Chrebet .50 .20
❑ 149 Curtis Martin .75 .30
❑ 150 Keyshawn Johnson .75 .30
❑ 151 James Jett .50 .20
❑ 152 Napoleon Kaufman .75 .30
❑ 153 Tim Brown .75 .30
❑ 154 Charles Woodson .75 .30
❑ 155 Rickey Dudley .30 .10
❑ 156 Charles Johnson .30 .10
❑ 157 Duce Staley .75 .30
❑ 158 Chris Fuamatu-Ma'afala .30 .10
❑ 159 Jerome Bettis .75 .30
❑ 160 Kordell Stewart .50 .20
❑ 161 Levon Kirkland .30 .10
❑ 162 Hines Ward .75 .30

❑ 163 Mikhael Ricks .30 .10
❑ 164 Natrone Means .50 .20
❑ 165 Ryan Leaf .75 .30
❑ 166 Jim Harbaugh .50 .20
❑ 167 Junior Seau .75 .30
❑ 168 Steve Young 1.00 .40
❑ 169 J.J. Stokes .50 .20
❑ 170 Terrell Owens .75 .30
❑ 171 Jerry Rice 1.50 .60
❑ 172 Garrison Hearst .50 .20
❑ 173 Ricky Watters .50 .20
❑ 174 Jon Kitna .75 .30
❑ 175 Joey Galloway .50 .20
❑ 176 Ahman Green .75 .30
❑ 177 Isaac Bruce .75 .30
❑ 178 Marshall Faulk 1.00 .40
❑ 179 Trent Green .75 .30
❑ 180 Amp Lee .30 .10
❑ 181 Greg Hill .30 .10
❑ 182 Warren Sapp .30 .10
❑ 183 Hardy Nickerson .30 .10
❑ 184 Trent Dilfer .50 .20
❑ 185 Reidel Anthony .50 .20
❑ 186 Jacquez Green .30 .10
❑ 187 Warrick Dunn .75 .30
❑ 188 Mike Alstott .75 .30
❑ 189 Kevin Dyson .50 .20
❑ 190 Eddie George .75 .30
❑ 191 Yancey Thigpen .30 .10
❑ 192 Steve McNair .75 .30
❑ 193 Chris Sanders .30 .10
❑ 194 Frank Wycheck .30 .10
❑ 195 Darrell Green .30 .10
❑ 196 Stephen Alexander .30 .10
❑ 197 Albert Connell .30 .10
❑ 198 Michael Westbrook .50 .20
❑ 199 Brad Johnson .75 .30
❑ 200 Skip Hicks .30 .10

1999 Absolute SSD

❑ COMPLETE SET (200) 250.00 125.00
❑ 1 Rob Moore 1.25 .50
❑ 2 Frank Sanders 1.25 .50
❑ 3 Jake Plummer 1.25 .50
❑ 4 Adrian Murrell 1.25 .50
❑ 5 Chris Chandler 1.25 .50
❑ 6 Jamal Anderson 2.00 .75
❑ 7 Tim Dwight 2.00 .75
❑ 8 Terance Mathis 1.25 .50
❑ 9 Priest Holmes 3.00 1.25
❑ 10 Jermaine Lewis 1.25 .50
❑ 11 Antowain Smith 2.00 .75
❑ 12 Doug Flutie 2.00 .75
❑ 13 Eric Moulds 2.00 .75
❑ 14 Muhsin Muhammad 1.25 .50
❑ 15 Tim Biakabutuka 1.25 .50
❑ 16 Curtis Enis .75 .30
❑ 17 Curtis Conway 1.25 .50
❑ 18 Bobby Engram 1.25 .50
❑ 19 Corey Dillon 2.00 .75
❑ 20 Carl Pickens 1.25 .50
❑ 21 Darnay Scott .75 .30
❑ 22 Sedrick Shaw .75 .30
❑ 23 Leslie Shepherd .75 .30
❑ 24 Ty Detmer 1.25 .50
❑ 25 Deion Sanders 2.00 .75
❑ 26 Troy Aikman 4.00 1.50
❑ 27 Michael Irvin 1.25 .50
❑ 28 Emmitt Smith 4.00 1.50
❑ 29 Rocket Ismail 1.25 .50
❑ 30 Rod Smith WR 1.25 .50
❑ 31 Ed McCaffrey 1.25 .50
❑ 32 Bubby Brister .75 .30
❑ 33 Terrell Davis 2.00 .75
❑ 34 Shannon Sharpe 1.25 .50
❑ 35 Brian Griese 2.00 .75
❑ 36 John Elway 6.00 2.50
❑ 37 Charlie Batch 2.00 .75
❑ 38 Herman Moore 1.25 .50
❑ 39 Barry Sanders 6.00 2.50
❑ 40 Johnnie Morton 1.25 .50
❑ 41 Antonio Freeman 2.00 .75
❑ 42 Brett Favre 6.00 2.50
❑ 43 Dorsey Levens 2.00 .75
❑ 44 Derrick Mayes 1.25 .50
❑ 45 Mark Chmura .75 .30
❑ 46 Peyton Manning 6.00 2.50
❑ 47 Marvin Harrison 2.00 .75
❑ 48 Jerome Pathon .75 .30
❑ 49 Fred Taylor 2.00 .75
❑ 50 Mark Brunell 2.00 .75
❑ 51 Jimmy Smith 1.25 .50
❑ 52 Keenan McCardell 1.25 .50
❑ 53 Elvis Grbac 1.25 .50
❑ 54 Andre Rison 1.25 .50
❑ 55 Byron Bam Morris .75 .30
❑ 56 O.J. McDuffie 1.25 .50
❑ 57 Karim Abdul-Jabbar 1.25 .50
❑ 58 Dan Marino 6.00 2.50
❑ 59 Oronde Gadsden 1.25 .50
❑ 60 Robert Smith 2.00 .75
❑ 61 Randall Cunningham 2.00 .75
❑ 62 Cris Carter 2.00 .75
❑ 63 Randy Moss 5.00 2.00
❑ 64 Drew Bledsoe 2.50 1.00
❑ 65 Ben Coates 1.25 .50
❑ 66 Terry Glenn 2.00 .75
❑ 67 Cam Cleeland .75 .30
❑ 68 Eddie Kennison 1.25 .50
❑ 69 Kerry Collins 1.25 .50
❑ 70 Gary Brown .75 .30
❑ 71 Joe Jurevicius 1.25 .50
❑ 72 Ike Hilliard .75 .30
❑ 73 Keyshawn Johnson 2.00 .75
❑ 74 Curtis Martin 2.00 .75
❑ 75 Wayne Chrebet 1.25 .50
❑ 76 Tim Brown 2.00 .75
❑ 77 Napoleon Kaufman 2.00 .75
❑ 78 James Jett 1.25 .50
❑ 79 Duce Staley 2.00 .75
❑ 80 Charles Johnson .75 .30
❑ 81 Kordell Stewart 1.25 .50
❑ 82 Jerome Bettis 2.00 .75
❑ 83 Chris Fuamatu-Ma'afala .75 .30
❑ 84 Jim Harbaugh 1.25 .50
❑ 85 Ryan Leaf 2.00 .75
❑ 86 Natrone Means 1.25 .50
❑ 87 Mikhael Ricks .75 .30
❑ 88 Garrison Hearst 1.25 .50
❑ 89 Jerry Rice 4.00 1.50
❑ 90 Terrell Owens 2.00 .75
❑ 91 J.J. Stokes 1.25 .50
❑ 92 Steve Young 2.50 1.00
❑ 93 Joey Galloway 1.25 .50
❑ 94 Jon Kitna 2.00 .75
❑ 95 Ricky Watters 1.25 .50
❑ 96 Trent Green 2.00 .75
❑ 97 Marshall Faulk 2.50 1.00
❑ 98 Isaac Bruce 2.00 .75
❑ 99 Mike Alstott 2.00 .75
❑ 100 Warrick Dunn 2.00 .75
❑ 101 Jacquez Green .75 .30
❑ 102 Reidel Anthony 1.25 .50
❑ 103 Trent Dilfer 1.25 .50
❑ 104 Steve McNair 2.00 .75
❑ 105 Yancey Thigpen .75 .30
❑ 106 Eddie George 2.00 .75
❑ 107 Kevin Dyson 1.25 .50
❑ 108 Skip Hicks .75 .30
❑ 109 Brad Johnson 2.00 .75
❑ 110 Michael Westbrook 1.25 .50
❑ 111 Thurman Thomas CA 4.00 1.50
❑ 112 Andre Reed CA 4.00 1.50
❑ 113 Emmitt Smith CA 10.00 4.00
❑ 114 Troy Aikman CA 10.00 4.00
❑ 115 Deion Sanders CA 5.00 2.00
❑ 116 John Elway CA 15.00 6.00
❑ 117 Terrell Davis CA 5.00 2.00
❑ 118 Barry Sanders CA 15.00 6.00
❑ 119 Brett Favre CA 15.00 6.00
❑ 120 Warren Moon CA 5.00 2.00
❑ 121 Dan Marino CA 15.00 6.00
❑ 122 Cris Carter CA 5.00 2.00
❑ 124 Tim Brown CA 5.00 2.00
❑ 125 Jerome Bettis CA 4.00 1.50
❑ 126 Junior Seau CA 5.00 2.00
❑ 127 Jerry Rice CA 10.00 4.00
❑ 127 Vinny Testaverde CA 4.00 1.50
❑ 128 Steve Young CA 6.00 2.50
❑ 129 Eddie George CA 5.00 2.00
❑ 130 Cardinals CL 3.00 1.25
❑ 131 Falcons CL 3.00 1.25
❑ 132 Ravens CL 8.00 3.00
❑ 133 Bills CL 6.00 2.50
❑ 134 Panthers CL 3.00 1.25
❑ 135 Bears CL 4.00 1.50
❑ 136 Bengals CL 3.00 1.25
❑ 137 Browns CL 8.00 3.00
❑ 138 Cowboys CL 8.00 3.00
❑ 139 Broncos CL 8.00 3.00
❑ 140 Lions CL 8.00 3.00
❑ 141 Packers CL 8.00 3.00
❑ 142 Colts CL 8.00 3.00
❑ 143 Jaguars CL 4.00 1.50
❑ 144 Chiefs CL 3.00 1.25
❑ 145 Dolphins CL 3.00 1.25
❑ 146 Vikings CL 8.00 3.00
❑ 147 Patriots CL 3.00 1.25
❑ 148 Saints CL 8.00 3.00
❑ 149 Giants CL 3.00 1.25
❑ 150 Jets CL 4.00 1.50
❑ 151 Raiders CL 4.00 1.50
❑ 152 Eagles CL 4.00 1.50
❑ 153 Steelers CL 3.00 1.25
❑ 154 Chargers CL 8.00 3.00
❑ 155 49ers CL 8.00 3.00
❑ 156 Seahawks CL 3.00 1.25
❑ 157 Rams CL 4.00 1.50
❑ 158 Buccaneers CL 3.00 1.25
❑ 159 Titans CL 4.00 1.50
❑ 160 Redskins CL 3.00 1.25
❑ 161 Tim Couch RC 2.50 1.00
❑ 162 Donovan McNabb RC 12.00 5.00
❑ 163 Akili Smith RC 4.00 1.50
❑ 164 Edgerrin James RC 10.00 4.00
❑ 165 Ricky Williams RC 5.00 2.00
❑ 166 Torry Holt RC 6.00 2.50
❑ 167 Champ Bailey RC 3.00 1.25
❑ 168 David Boston RC 5.00 2.00
❑ 169 Chris Claiborne RC 1.00 .40
❑ 170 Chris McAlister RC 1.50 .60
❑ 171 Daunte Culpepper RC 10.00 4.00
❑ 172 Cade McNown RC 1.50 .60
❑ 173 Troy Edwards RC 1.50 .60
❑ 174 Kevin Johnson RC 2.50 1.00
❑ 175 James Johnson RC 1.50 .60
❑ 176 Rob Konrad RC 2.50 1.00
❑ 177 Jim Kleinsasser RC 2.50 1.00
❑ 178 Kevin Faulk RC 2.50 1.00
❑ 179 Joe Montgomery RC 1.50 .60
❑ 180 Shaun King RC 1.50 .60
❑ 181 Peerless Price RC 2.50 1.00
❑ 182 Mike Cloud RC 1.50 .60
❑ 183 Jermaine Fazande RC 1.50 .60
❑ 184 D'Wayne Bates RC 1.50 .60
❑ 185 Brock Huard RC 2.50 1.00
❑ 186 Marty Booker RC 2.50 1.00
❑ 187 Karsten Bailey RC 1.50 .60
❑ 188 Shawn Bryson RC 2.50 1.00
❑ 189 Jeff Paulk RC 1.00 .40
❑ 190 Sedrick Irvin RC 1.00 .40
❑ 191 Craig Yeast RC 1.50 .60
❑ 192 Joe Germaine RC 1.50 .60
❑ 193 Dameane Douglas RC 2.50 1.00
❑ 194 Brandon Stokley RC 3.00 1.25
❑ 195 Larry Parker RC 2.50 1.00
❑ 196 Wane McGarity RC 1.00 .40
❑ 197 Na Brown RC 1.50 .60
❑ 198 Cecil Collins RC 1.00 .40
❑ 199 Darrin Chiaverini RC 1.50 .60
❑ 200 Madre Hill RC 1.00 .40

2000 Absolute

❑ COMPLETE SET (250) 250.00 125.00
❑ COMP.SET w/o SP's (150) 20.00 7.50
❑ 1 Frank Sanders .50 .20
❑ 2 Rob Moore .50 .20
❑ 3 Jake Plummer .50 .20
❑ 4 David Boston .75 .30
❑ 5 Chris Chandler .50 .20
❑ 6 Tim Dwight .75 .30

❑ 7 Terance Mathis	.50	.20
❑ 8 Jamal Anderson	.75	.30
❑ 9 Priest Holmes	1.00	.40
❑ 10 Tony Banks	.50	.20
❑ 11 Jermaine Lewis	.30	.10
❑ 12 Qadry Ismail	.50	.20
❑ 13 Brandon Stokley	.50	.20
❑ 14 Shannon Sharpe	.50	.20
❑ 15 Trent Dilfer	.50	.20
❑ 16 Eric Moulds	.75	.30
❑ 17 Doug Flutie	.75	.30
❑ 18 Antowain Smith	.50	.20
❑ 19 Jonathan Linton	.30	.10
❑ 20 Peerless Price	.50	.20
❑ 21 Rob Johnson	.50	.20
❑ 22 Muhsin Muhammad	.50	.20
❑ 23 Wesley Walls	.30	.10
❑ 24 Tim Biakabutuka	.50	.20
❑ 25 Steve Beuerlein	.50	.20
❑ 26 Patrick Jeffers	.75	.30
❑ 27 Natrone Means	.30	.10
❑ 28 Curtis Enis	.30	.10
❑ 29 Bobby Engram	.50	.20
❑ 30 Marcus Robinson	.75	.30
❑ 31 Marty Booker	.50	.20
❑ 32 Cade McNown	.30	.10
❑ 33 Darnay Scott	.50	.20
❑ 34 Carl Pickens	.50	.20
❑ 35 Corey Dillon	.75	.30
❑ 36 Akili Smith	.30	.10
❑ 37 Michael Basnight	.30	.10
❑ 38 Karim Abdul-Jabbar	.50	.20
❑ 39 Tim Couch	.50	.20
❑ 40 Kevin Johnson	.75	.30
❑ 41 Darrin Chiaverini	.30	.10
❑ 42 Errict Rhett	.50	.20
❑ 43 Emmitt Smith	1.50	.60
❑ 44 Michael Irvin	.50	.20
❑ 45 Rocket Ismail	.50	.20
❑ 46 Troy Aikman	1.50	.60
❑ 47 Jason Tucker	.30	.10
❑ 48 Randall Cunningham	.75	.30
❑ 49 Joey Galloway	.50	.20
❑ 50 Ed McCaffrey	.75	.30
❑ 51 Rod Smith	.50	.20
❑ 52 Brian Griese	.75	.30
❑ 53 John Elway	2.50	1.00
❑ 54 Terrell Davis	.75	.30
❑ 55 Olandis Gary	.75	.30
❑ 56 Johnnie Morton	.50	.20
❑ 57 Charlie Batch	.75	.30
❑ 58 Barry Sanders	2.00	.75
❑ 59 Germane Crowell	.30	.10
❑ 60 Herman Moore	.50	.20
❑ 61 James Stewart	.50	.20
❑ 62 Corey Bradford	.30	.10
❑ 63 Dorsey Levens	.50	.20
❑ 64 Antonio Freeman	.75	.30
❑ 65 Brett Favre	2.50	1.00
❑ 66 Bill Schroeder	.50	.20
❑ 67 Marvin Harrison	.75	.30
❑ 68 Peyton Manning	1.50	.60
❑ 69 Terrence Wilkins	.30	.10
❑ 70 Edgerrin James	1.25	.50
❑ 71 Keenan McCardell	.50	.20
❑ 72 Mark Brunell	.75	.30
❑ 73 Fred Taylor	.75	.30
❑ 74 Jimmy Smith	.50	.20
❑ 75 Elvis Grbac	.50	.20
❑ 76 Tony Gonzalez	.50	.20
❑ 77 Donnell Bennett	.30	.10
❑ 78 Warren Moon	.75	.30
❑ 79 Kimble Anders	.30	.10
❑ 80 Dan Marino	2.50	1.00
❑ 81 O.J. McDuffie	.50	.20
❑ 82 Tony Martin	.50	.20
❑ 83 James Johnson	.30	.10
❑ 84 Thurman Thomas	.50	.20
❑ 85 Randy Moss	1.25	.50
❑ 86 Cris Carter	.75	.30
❑ 87 Robert Smith	.75	.30
❑ 88 Daunte Culpepper	1.00	.40
❑ 89 Terry Glenn	.50	.20
❑ 90 Drew Bledsoe	1.00	.40
❑ 91 Kevin Faulk	.50	.20
❑ 92 Ricky Williams	.75	.30
❑ 93 Jeff Blake	.50	.20
❑ 94 Jake Reed	.50	.20
❑ 95 Amani Toomer	.50	.20
❑ 96 Kerry Collins	.50	.20
❑ 97 Tiki Barber	.75	.30
❑ 98 Ike Hilliard	.50	.20
❑ 99 Curtis Martin	.75	.30
❑ 100 Vinny Testaverde	.50	.20
❑ 101 Wayne Chrebet	.50	.20
❑ 102 Ray Lucas	.50	.20
❑ 103 Tyrone Wheatley	.50	.20
❑ 104 Napoleon Kaufman	.50	.20
❑ 105 Tim Brown	.75	.30
❑ 106 Rich Gannon	.75	.30
❑ 107 Duce Staley	.75	.30
❑ 108 Donovan McNabb	1.25	.50
❑ 109 Kordell Stewart	.50	.20
❑ 110 Jerome Bettis	.75	.30
❑ 111 Troy Edwards	.30	.10
❑ 112 Junior Seau	.75	.30
❑ 113 Jim Harbaugh	.50	.20
❑ 114 Ryan Leaf	.50	.20
❑ 115 Jermaine Fazande	.30	.10
❑ 116 Curtis Conway	.50	.20
❑ 117 Terrell Owens	.75	.30
❑ 118 Charlie Garner	.50	.20
❑ 119 Jerry Rice	1.50	.60
❑ 120 Steve Young	1.00	.40
❑ 121 Jeff Garcia	.75	.30
❑ 122 Derrick Mayes	.50	.20
❑ 123 Ricky Watters	.50	.20
❑ 124 Jon Kitna	.75	.30
❑ 125 Sean Dawkins	.30	.10
❑ 126 Az-Zahir Hakim	.50	.20
❑ 127 Isaac Bruce	.75	.30
❑ 128 Marshall Faulk	1.00	.40
❑ 129 Trent Green	.75	.30
❑ 130 Kurt Warner	1.50	.60
❑ 131 Torry Holt	.75	.30
❑ 132 Jacquez Green	.30	.10
❑ 133 Warren Sapp	.50	.20
❑ 134 Mike Alstott	.75	.30
❑ 135 Warrick Dunn	.75	.30
❑ 136 Shaun King	.30	.10
❑ 137 Keyshawn Johnson	.75	.30
❑ 138 Eddie George	.75	.30
❑ 139 Yancey Thigpen	.30	.10
❑ 140 Steve McNair	.75	.30
❑ 141 Kevin Dyson	.50	.20
❑ 142 Frank Wycheck	.30	.10
❑ 143 Jevon Kearse	.75	.30
❑ 144 Stephen Davis	.75	.30
❑ 145 Brad Johnson	.75	.30
❑ 146 Michael Westbrook	.50	.20
❑ 147 Albert Connell	.30	.10
❑ 148 Bruce Smith	.50	.20
❑ 149 Jeff George	.50	.20
❑ 150 Deion Sanders	.75	.30
❑ 151 Peter Warrick RC	4.00	1.50
❑ 152 Courtney Brown RC	4.00	1.50
❑ 153 Plaxico Burress RC	8.00	3.00
❑ 154 Corey Simon RC	4.00	1.50
❑ 155 Thomas Jones RC	6.00	2.50
❑ 156 Travis Taylor RC	4.00	1.50
❑ 157 Shaun Alexander RC	15.00	6.00
❑ 158 Chris Redman RC	3.00	1.25
❑ 159 Chad Pennington RC	10.00	4.00
❑ 160 Jamal Lewis RC	10.00	4.00
❑ 161 Brian Urlacher RC	20.00	7.50
❑ 162 Bubba Franks RC	4.00	1.50
❑ 163 Dez White RC	4.00	1.50
❑ 164 Ahmed Plummer RC	4.00	1.50
❑ 165 Ron Dayne RC	4.00	1.50
❑ 166 Shaun Ellis RC	4.00	1.50
❑ 167 Sylvester Morris RC	.50	.20
❑ 168 Deltha O'Neal RC	4.00	1.50
❑ 169 R.Jay Soward RC	3.00	1.25
❑ 170 Sherrod Gideon RC	2.00	.75
❑ 171 John Abraham RC	4.00	1.50
❑ 172 Travis Prentice RC	3.00	1.25
❑ 173 Darrell Jackson RC	8.00	3.00
❑ 174 Giovanni Carmazzi RC	2.00	.75
❑ 175 Anthony Lucas RC	2.00	.75
❑ 176 Danny Farmer RC	3.00	1.25
❑ 177 Dennis Northcutt RC	4.00	1.50
❑ 178 Troy Walters RC	4.00	1.50
❑ 179 Laveranues Coles RC	5.00	2.00
❑ 180 Kwame Cavil RC	2.00	.75
❑ 181 Tee Martin RC	4.00	1.50
❑ 182 J.R. Redmond RC	3.00	1.25
❑ 183 Tim Rattay RC	4.00	1.50
❑ 184 Jerry Porter RC	3.00	2.00
❑ 185 Sebastian Janikowski RC	4.00	1.50
❑ 186 Michael Wiley RC	3.00	1.25
❑ 187 Reuben Droughns RC	5.00	2.00
❑ 188 Trung Canidate RC	3.00	1.25
❑ 189 Shyrone Stith RC	3.00	1.25
❑ 190 Ian Gold RC	3.00	1.25
❑ 191 Hank Poteat RC	3.00	1.25
❑ 192 Darren Howard RC	3.00	1.25
❑ 193 Rob Morris RC	3.00	1.25
❑ 194 Marc Bulger RC	8.00	3.00
❑ 195 Tom Brady RC	100.00	50.00
❑ 196 Doug Johnson RC	4.00	1.50
❑ 197 Todd Husak RC	4.00	1.50
❑ 198 Gari Scott RC	2.00	.75
❑ 199 Erron Kinney RC	4.00	1.50
❑ 200 Nate Webster RC	2.00	.75
❑ 201 Anthony Becht RC	4.00	1.50
❑ 202 Sammy Morris RC	4.00	1.50
❑ 203 Rondell Mealey RC	2.00	.75
❑ 204 Doug Chapman RC	3.00	1.25
❑ 205 Rogers Beckett RC	3.00	1.25
❑ 206 Ron Dugans RC	2.00	.75
❑ 207 Deon Dyer RC	3.00	1.25
❑ 208 Marcus Knight RC	3.00	1.25
❑ 209 Thomas Hamner RC	2.00	.75
❑ 210 Joe Hamilton RC	3.00	1.25
❑ 211 Todd Pinkston RC	4.00	1.50
❑ 212 Chris Cole RC	3.00	1.25
❑ 213 Ron Dixon RC	3.00	1.25
❑ 214 JaJuan Dawson RC	2.00	.75
❑ 215 Terrelle Smith RC	3.00	1.25
❑ 216 Curtis Keaton RC	3.00	1.25
❑ 217 Keith Bulluck RC	4.00	1.50
❑ 218 John Engelberger RC	3.00	1.25
❑ 219 Raynoch Thompson RC	3.00	1.25
❑ 220 Cornelius Griffin RC	3.00	1.25
❑ 221 William Bartee RC	3.00	1.25
❑ 222 Fred Robbins RC	2.00	.75
❑ 223 Dwayne Goodrich RC	2.00	.75
❑ 224 Deon Grant RC	3.00	1.25
❑ 225 Jacoby Shepherd RC	3.00	1.25
❑ 226 Ben Kelly RC	2.00	.75
❑ 227 Corey Moore RC	2.00	.75
❑ 228 Aaron Shea RC	3.00	1.25
❑ 229 Trevor Gaylor RC	3.00	1.25
❑ 230 Frank Moreau RC	3.00	1.25
❑ 231 Avion Black RC	3.00	1.25
❑ 232 Paul Smith RC	3.00	1.25
❑ 233 Dante Hall RC	8.00	3.00
❑ 234 Muneer Moore RC	2.00	.75
❑ 235 James Whalen RC	2.00	.75
❑ 236 Chad Morton RC	4.00	1.50
❑ 237 Frank Murphy RC	2.00	.75
❑ 238 Mareno Philyaw RC	2.00	.75
❑ 239 James Williams RC	3.00	1.25
❑ 240 Mike Anderson RC	5.00	2.00
❑ 241 Jarious Jackson RC	3.00	1.25
❑ 242 Demario Brown RC	2.00	.75
❑ 243 Chris Coleman RC	4.00	1.50
❑ 244 Rashard Anderson RC	3.00	1.25
❑ 245 John Jones RC	3.00	1.25
❑ 246 Erik Flowers RC	3.00	1.25
❑ 247 JaJuan Seider RC	2.00	.75
❑ 248 Leon Murray RC	2.00	.75
❑ 249 Bashir Yamini RC	2.00	.75
❑ 250 Na'il Diggs RC	3.00	1.25

2001 Absolute Memorabilia

❑ COMP.SET w/o SP's (100)	30.00	12.50
❑ 1 David Boston	1.25	.50
❑ 2 Jake Plummer	.75	.30

❑ 3	Thomas Jones	.75	.30
❑ 4	Jamal Anderson	1.25	.50
❑ 5	Chris Redman	.50	.20
❑ 6	Jamal Lewis	2.00	.75
❑ 7	Qadry Ismail	.75	.30
❑ 8	Ray Lewis	1.25	.50
❑ 9	Shannon Sharpe	.75	.30
❑ 10	Travis Taylor	.75	.30
❑ 11	Trent Dilfer	.75	.30
❑ 12	Elvis Grbac	.75	.30
❑ 13	Eric Moulds	.75	.30
❑ 14	Rob Johnson	.75	.30
❑ 15	Muhsin Muhammad	.75	.30
❑ 16	Brian Urlacher	2.00	.75
❑ 17	Cade McNown	.50	.20
❑ 18	Marcus Robinson	1.25	.50
❑ 19	Akili Smith	.50	.20
❑ 20	Corey Dillon	1.25	.50
❑ 21	Peter Warrick	1.25	.50
❑ 22	Courtney Brown	.75	.30
❑ 23	Tim Couch	.75	.30
❑ 24	Emmitt Smith	2.50	1.00
❑ 25	Troy Aikman	2.00	.75
❑ 26	Brian Griese	1.25	.50
❑ 27	Ed McCaffrey	1.25	.50
❑ 28	John Elway	4.00	1.50
❑ 29	Mike Anderson	1.25	.50
❑ 30	Rod Smith	.75	.30
❑ 31	Terrell Davis	1.25	.50
❑ 32	Barry Sanders	2.50	1.00
❑ 33	James Stewart	.75	.30
❑ 34	Ahman Green	1.25	.50
❑ 35	Antonio Freeman	1.25	.50
❑ 36	Brett Favre	4.00	1.50
❑ 37	Edgerrin James	1.50	.60
❑ 38	Marvin Harrison	1.25	.50
❑ 39	Peyton Manning	3.00	1.25
❑ 40	Fred Taylor	1.25	.50
❑ 41	Jimmy Smith	.75	.30
❑ 42	Keenan McCardell	.50	.20
❑ 43	Mark Brunell	1.25	.50
❑ 44	Sylvester Morris	.50	.20
❑ 45	Tony Gonzalez	.75	.30
❑ 46	Dan Marino	4.00	1.50
❑ 47	Jay Fiedler	1.25	.50
❑ 48	Lamar Smith	.75	.30
❑ 49	Cris Carter	1.25	.50
❑ 50	Daunte Culpepper	1.25	.50
❑ 51	Randy Moss	2.50	1.00
❑ 52	Drew Bledsoe	1.50	.60
❑ 53	Terry Glenn	.75	.30
❑ 54	Aaron Brooks	1.25	.50
❑ 55	Joe Horn	.75	.30
❑ 56	Ricky Williams	1.25	.50
❑ 57	Amani Toomer	.75	.30
❑ 58	Ike Hilliard	.75	.30
❑ 59	Kerry Collins	.75	.30
❑ 60	Ron Dayne	1.25	.50
❑ 61	Tiki Barber	1.25	.50
❑ 62	Chad Pennington	2.00	.75
❑ 63	Curtis Martin	1.25	.50
❑ 64	Laveranues Coles	1.25	.50
❑ 65	Vinny Testaverde	.75	.30
❑ 66	Wayne Chrebet	.75	.30
❑ 67	Charles Woodson	.75	.30
❑ 68	Rich Gannon	1.25	.50
❑ 69	Tim Brown	1.25	.50
❑ 70	Tyrone Wheatley	.75	.30
❑ 71	Corey Simon	.75	.30
❑ 72	Donovan McNabb	1.50	.60
❑ 73	Duce Staley	1.25	.50
❑ 74	Jerome Bettis	1.25	.50
❑ 75	Plaxico Burress	1.25	.50
❑ 76	Doug Flutie	1.25	.50
❑ 77	Junior Seau	1.25	.50
❑ 78	Charlie Garner	.75	.30
❑ 79	Jeff Garcia	1.25	.50
❑ 80	Jerry Rice	2.50	1.00
❑ 81	Steve Young	1.25	.50
❑ 82	Terrell Owens	1.25	.50
❑ 83	Darrell Jackson	1.25	.50
❑ 84	Ricky Watters	.50	.20
❑ 85	Shaun Alexander	1.50	.60
❑ 86	Isaac Bruce	1.25	.50
❑ 87	Kurt Warner	2.50	1.00
❑ 88	Marshall Faulk	1.50	.60
❑ 89	Torry Holt	1.25	.50
❑ 90	Brad Johnson	1.25	.50
❑ 91	Keyshawn Johnson	1.25	.50
❑ 92	Mike Alstott	1.25	.50
❑ 93	Shaun King	.50	.20
❑ 94	Warren Sapp	.75	.30
❑ 95	Warrick Dunn	1.25	.50
❑ 96	Eddie George	1.25	.50
❑ 97	Jevon Kearse	.75	.30
❑ 98	Steve McNair	1.25	.50
❑ 99	Jeff George	.75	.30
❑ 100	Stephen Davis	1.25	.50
❑ 101	Jason McKinley RC	4.00	1.50
❑ 102	Bobby Newcombe RC	4.00	1.50
❑ 103	Cedrick Wilson RC	6.00	2.50
❑ 104	Ken-Yon Rambo RC	4.00	1.50
❑ 105	Kevin Kasper RC	6.00	2.50
❑ 106	Jamal Reynolds RC	6.00	2.50
❑ 107	Scotty Anderson RC	4.00	1.50
❑ 108	T.J. Houshmandzadeh RC	8.00	3.00
❑ 109	Chris Taylor RC	4.00	1.50
❑ 110	Vinny Sutherland RC	4.00	1.50
❑ 111	Jabari Holloway RC	4.00	1.50
❑ 112	Shad Meier RC	4.00	1.50
❑ 113	Correll Buckhalter RC	8.00	3.00
❑ 114	Dan Alexander RC	6.00	2.50
❑ 115	David Allen RC	4.00	1.50
❑ 116	LaMont Jordan RC	12.00	5.00
❑ 117	Nate Clements RC	6.00	2.50
❑ 118	Reggie White RC	4.00	1.50
❑ 119	Javon Green RC	4.00	1.50
❑ 120	Shaun Rogers RC	6.00	2.50
❑ 121	Heath Evans RC	4.00	1.50
❑ 122	Moran Norris RC	2.50	1.00
❑ 123	Ben Leard RC	4.00	1.50
❑ 124	David Rivers RC	4.00	1.50
❑ 125	A.J. Feeley RC	6.00	2.50
❑ 126	Boo Williams RC	4.00	1.50
❑ 127	Ronney Daniels RC	2.50	1.00
❑ 128	Alge Crumpler RC	8.00	4.00
❑ 129	Todd Heap RC	6.00	2.50
❑ 130	Tim Hasselbeck RC	6.00	2.50
❑ 131	Josh Booty RC	6.00	2.50
❑ 132	Jamie Winborn RC	4.00	1.50
❑ 133	Brian Allen RC	2.50	1.00
❑ 134	Sedrick Hodge RC	2.50	1.00
❑ 135	Tommy Polley RC	6.00	2.50
❑ 136	Torrance Marshall RC	6.00	2.50
❑ 137	Damione Lewis RC	4.00	1.50
❑ 138	Marcus Stroud RC	6.00	2.50
❑ 139	Aaron Schobel RC	6.00	2.50
❑ 140	DeLawrence Grant RC	2.50	1.00
❑ 141	Fred Smoot RC	6.00	2.50
❑ 142	Jamar Fletcher RC	4.00	1.50
❑ 143	Ken Lucas RC	4.00	1.50
❑ 144	Will Allen RC	4.00	1.50
❑ 145	Adam Archuleta RC	6.00	2.50
❑ 146	Derrick Gibson RC	4.00	1.50
❑ 147	Jarrod Cooper RC	6.00	2.50
❑ 148	Eddie Berlin RC	4.00	1.50
❑ 149	Steve Smith RC	15.00	7.50
❑ 150	Willie Middlebrooks RC	4.00	1.50
❑ 151	Michael Vick RPM RC	50.00	20.00
❑ 152	Drew Brees RPM RC	50.00	20.00
❑ 153	Chris Weinke RPM RC	15.00	6.00
❑ 154	Mar Tuiasosopo RPM RC	15.00	6.00
❑ 155	Mike McMahon RPM RC	15.00	6.00
❑ 156	Deuce McAllister RPM RC	30.00	12.50
❑ 157	Leonard Davis RPM RC	10.00	4.00
❑ 158	LaD Tomlinson RPM RC	80.00	40.00
❑ 159	Anthony Thomas RPM RC	15.00	6.00
❑ 160	Travis Henry RPM RC	30.00	12.50
❑ 161	James Jackson RPM RC	15.00	6.00
❑ 162	Michael Bennett RPM RC	15.00	6.00
❑ 163	Kevan Barlow RPM RC	15.00	6.00
❑ 164	Travis Minor RPM RC	10.00	4.00
❑ 165	David Terrell RPM RC	15.00	6.00
❑ 166	Santana Moss RPM RC	25.00	10.00
❑ 167	Rod Gardner RPM RC	15.00	6.00
❑ 168	Quincy Morgan RPM RC	15.00	6.00
❑ 169	Freddie Mitchell RPM RC	15.00	6.00
❑ 170	Reggie Wayne RPM RC	30.00	12.50
❑ 171	Koren Robinson RPM RC	15.00	6.00
❑ 172	Chad Johnson RPM RC	40.00	15.00
❑ 173	Chris Chambers RPM RC	25.00	10.00
❑ 174	Josh Heupel RPM RC	15.00	6.00
❑ 175	Andre Carter RPM RC	15.00	6.00
❑ 176	Justin Smith RPM RC	15.00	6.00
❑ 177	Richard Seymour RPM RC	15.00	6.00
❑ 178	Dan Morgan RPM RC	15.00	6.00
❑ 179	Gerard Warren RPM RC	15.00	6.00
❑ 180	Robert Ferguson RPM RC	15.00	6.00
❑ 181	Sage Rosenfels RPM RC	15.00	6.00
❑ 182	Rudi Johnson RPM RC	30.00	12.50
❑ 183	Snoop Minnis RPM RC	10.00	4.00
❑ 184	Jesse Palmer RPM RC	15.00	6.00
❑ 185	Quincy Carter RPM RC	15.00	6.00

2002 Absolute Memorabilia

❑	COMP.SET w/o SP's (150)	30.00	12.50
❑ 1	Aaron Brooks	1.25	.50
❑ 2	Ahman Green	1.25	.50
❑ 3	Alge Crumpler	.75	.30
❑ 4	Amani Toomer	.75	.30
❑ 5	Andre Carter	.50	.20
❑ 6	Anthony Thomas	.75	.30
❑ 7	Antonio Freeman	1.25	.50
❑ 8	Antowain Smith	.75	.30
❑ 9	Az-Zahir Hakim	.50	.20
❑ 10	Bill Schroeder	.75	.30
❑ 11	Brad Johnson	.75	.30
❑ 12	Brett Favre	3.00	1.25
❑ 13	Brian Griese	1.25	.50
❑ 14	Brian Urlacher	2.00	.75
❑ 15	Chad Johnson	1.25	.50
❑ 16	Chad Pennington	1.50	.60
❑ 17	Champ Bailey	.75	.30
❑ 18	Charles Woodson	.75	.30
❑ 19	Charlie Batch	.75	.30
❑ 20	Charlie Garner	.75	.30
❑ 21	Chris Chambers	1.25	.50
❑ 22	Chris Redman	.50	.20
❑ 23	Chris Weinke	.75	.30
❑ 24	Corey Dillon	.75	.30
❑ 25	Correll Buckhalter	.75	.30
❑ 26	Cris Carter	1.25	.50
❑ 27	Curtis Martin	1.25	.50
❑ 28	Darnay Scott	.75	.30
❑ 29	Darrell Jackson	.75	.30
❑ 30	Daunte Culpepper	1.25	.50
❑ 31	David Boston	1.25	.50
❑ 32	David Terrell	1.25	.50
❑ 33	Derrick Alexander	.75	.30
❑ 34	Derrick Mason	.75	.30
❑ 35	Deuce McAllister	1.50	.60
❑ 36	Dominic Rhodes	1.25	.50
❑ 37	Donald Hayes	.50	.20
❑ 38	Donovan McNabb	1.50	.60
❑ 39	Doug Flutie	1.25	.50
❑ 40	Drew Bledsoe	1.50	.60
❑ 41	Drew Brees	1.25	.50
❑ 42	Duce Staley	1.25	.50
❑ 43	Ed McCaffrey	1.25	.50
❑ 44	Eddie George	1.25	.50
❑ 45	Edgerrin James	1.50	.60

❑ 46	Elvis Joseph	.50	.20
❑ 47	Emmitt Smith	3.00	1.25
❑ 48	Eric Moulds	.75	.30
❑ 49	Frank Sanders	.50	.20
❑ 50	Fred Taylor	1.25	.50
❑ 51	Freddie Mitchell	.75	.30
❑ 52	Garrison Hearst	.75	.30
❑ 53	Gerard Warren	.50	.20
❑ 54	Germane Crowell	.50	.20
❑ 55	Isaac Bruce	1.25	.50
❑ 56	Jake Plummer	.75	.30
❑ 57	Jamal Anderson	.75	.30
❑ 58	Jamal Lewis	1.25	.50
❑ 59	James Allen	.75	.30
❑ 60	James Jackson	.50	.20
❑ 61	James Stewart	.75	.30
❑ 62	Jason Brookins	.50	.20
❑ 63	Jay Fiedler	.75	.30
❑ 64	Jeff Garcia	1.25	.50
❑ 65	Jerome Bettis	1.25	.50
❑ 66	Jerry Rice	2.50	1.00
❑ 67	Jevon Kearse	.75	.30
❑ 68	Jim Miller	.50	.20
❑ 69	Jimmy Smith	.75	.30
❑ 70	Joe Horn	.75	.30
❑ 71	Joey Galloway	.75	.30
❑ 72	Jon Kitna	.75	.30
❑ 73	Junior Seau	1.25	.50
❑ 74	Keenan McCardell	.50	.20
❑ 75	Kendrell Bell	1.25	.50
❑ 76	Kerry Collins	.75	.30
❑ 77	Kevan Barlow	.75	.30
❑ 78	Kevin Dyson	.75	.30
❑ 79	Kevin Johnson	.75	.30
❑ 80	Kevin Kasper	.50	.20
❑ 81	Keyshawn Johnson	1.25	.50
❑ 82	Kordell Stewart	.75	.30
❑ 83	Koren Robinson	.75	.30
❑ 84	Kurt Warner	1.25	.50
❑ 85	LaDainian Tomlinson	2.50	1.00
❑ 86	Lamar Smith	.75	.30
❑ 87	Laveranues Coles	.75	.30
❑ 88	MarTay Jenkins	.50	.20
❑ 89	Mark Brunell	1.25	.50
❑ 90	Marshall Faulk	1.25	.50
❑ 91	Marty Booker	.75	.30
❑ 92	Marvin Harrison	1.25	.50
❑ 93	Snoop Minnis	.50	.20
❑ 94	Michael Bennett	.75	.30
❑ 95	Michael Strahan	.75	.30
❑ 96	Michael Vick	2.50	1.00
❑ 97	Mike Alstott	1.25	.50
❑ 98	Mike Anderson	1.25	.50
❑ 99	Mike McMahon	1.25	.50
❑ 100	Muhsin Muhammad	.75	.30
❑ 101	Nate Clements	.50	.20
❑ 102	Orande Gadsden	.75	.30
❑ 103	Peter Warrick	.75	.30
❑ 104	Peyton Manning	2.50	1.00
❑ 105	Plaxico Burress	.75	.30
❑ 106	Priest Holmes	1.50	.60
❑ 107	Quincy Carter	.75	.30
❑ 108	Quincy Morgan	.75	.30
❑ 109	Rocket Ismail	.75	.30
❑ 110	Randy Moss	2.50	1.00
❑ 111	Ray Lewis	1.25	.50
❑ 112	Reggie Wayne	1.25	.50
❑ 113	Rich Gannon	1.25	.50
❑ 114	Rickey Dudley	.50	.20
❑ 115	Ricky Watters	.75	.30
❑ 116	Ricky Williams	1.25	.50
❑ 117	Rod Gardner	.75	.30
❑ 118	Rod Smith	.75	.30
❑ 119	Robert Ferguson	.50	.20
❑ 120	Santana Moss	1.25	.50
❑ 121	Shaun Alexander	1.50	.60
❑ 122	Stephen Davis	.75	.30
❑ 123	Steve McNair	1.25	.50
❑ 124	Steve Smith	1.25	.50
❑ 125	Terrell Davis	1.25	.50
❑ 126	Terrell Owens	1.25	.50
❑ 127	Terry Glenn	.75	.30
❑ 128	Thomas Jones	.75	.30
❑ 129	Tiki Barber	1.25	.50
❑ 130	Tim Brown	1.25	.50
❑ 131	Tim Couch	.75	.30
❑ 132	Todd Heap	.75	.30
❑ 133	Todd Pinkston	.75	.30
❑ 134	Tom Brady	3.00	1.25
❑ 135	Tony Boselli	.50	.20
❑ 136	Tony Gonzalez	.75	.30
❑ 137	Torry Holt	1.25	.50
❑ 138	Travis Henry	1.25	.50
❑ 139	Travis Taylor	.75	.30
❑ 140	Trent Dilfer	.75	.30
❑ 141	Trent Green	.75	.30
❑ 142	Troy Brown	.75	.30
❑ 143	Troy Hambrick	.50	.20
❑ 144	Trung Canidate	.75	.30
❑ 145	Vinny Testaverde	.75	.30
❑ 146	Warren Sapp	.75	.30
❑ 147	Warrick Dunn	1.25	.50
❑ 148	Wayne Chrebet	.75	.30
❑ 149	Wesley Walls	.50	.20
❑ 150	Zach Thomas	1.25	.50
❑ 151	Quentin Jammer RC	6.00	2.50
❑ 152	Randy Fasani RC	5.00	2.00
❑ 153	Kurt Kittner RC	5.00	2.00
❑ 154	Chad Hutchinson RC	5.00	2.00
❑ 155	Major Applewhite RC	6.00	2.50
❑ 156	Wes Pate RC	3.00	1.25
❑ 157	J.T. O'Sullivan RC	5.00	2.00
❑ 158	Ryan Denney RC	5.00	2.00
❑ 159	Ronald Curry RC	6.00	2.50
❑ 160	Lamar Gordon RC	6.00	2.50
❑ 161	Brian Westbrook RC	12.00	5.00
❑ 162	Jonathan Wells RC	6.00	2.50
❑ 163	Ricky Williams RC	5.00	2.00
❑ 164	Verron Haynes RC	6.00	2.50
❑ 165	Josh Scobey RC	6.00	2.50
❑ 166	Larry Ned RC	5.00	2.00
❑ 167	Adrian Peterson RC	8.00	3.00
❑ 168	Chester Taylor RC	12.00	5.00
❑ 169	Luke Staley RC	5.00	2.00
❑ 170	Damien Anderson RC	5.00	2.00
❑ 171	Lee Mays RC	5.00	2.00
❑ 172	Deion Branch RC	10.00	4.00
❑ 173	Terry Charles RC	5.00	2.00
❑ 174	Woody Dantzler RC	5.00	2.00
❑ 175	Jason McAddley RC	5.00	2.00
❑ 176	Kelly Campbell RC	5.00	2.00
❑ 177	Freddie Milons RC	5.00	2.00
❑ 178	Kahlil Hill RC	5.00	2.00
❑ 179	Brian Poli-Dixon RC	5.00	2.00
❑ 180	Mike Echols RC	3.00	1.25
❑ 181	Pete Rebstock RC	3.00	1.25
❑ 182	Dwight Freeney RC	10.00	4.00
❑ 183	Bryan Thomas RC	5.00	2.00
❑ 184	Charles Grant RC	6.00	2.50
❑ 185	Kalimba Edwards RC	6.00	2.50
❑ 186	Ryan Sims RC	6.00	2.50
❑ 187	John Henderson RC	6.00	2.50
❑ 188	Wendell Bryant RC	3.00	1.25
❑ 189	Albert Haynesworth RC	5.00	2.00
❑ 190	Larry Tripplett RC	3.00	1.25
❑ 191	Phillip Buchanon RC	6.00	2.50
❑ 192	Lito Sheppard RC	6.00	2.50
❑ 193	Mike Rumph RC	6.00	2.50
❑ 194	Levar Fisher RC	3.00	1.25
❑ 195	Ed Reed RC	10.00	4.00
❑ 196	Rocky Calmus RC	6.00	2.50
❑ 197	Michael Lewis RC	6.00	2.50
❑ 198	Napoleon Harris RC	6.00	2.50
❑ 199	Robert Thomas RC	6.00	2.50
❑ 200	Anthony Weaver RC	5.00	2.00
❑ 201	Ladell Betts RPM RC	12.00	6.00
❑ 202	Antonio Bryant RPM RC	12.00	6.00
❑ 203	Reche Caldwell RPM RC	12.00	6.00
❑ 204	David Carr RPM RC	15.00	6.00
❑ 205	Tim Carter RPM RC	6.00	3.00
❑ 206	Eric Crouch RPM RC	12.00	6.00
❑ 207	Rohan Davey RPM RC	12.00	5.00
❑ 208	Andre Davis RPM RC	6.00	3.00
❑ 209	T.J. Duckett RPM RC	12.00	5.00
❑ 210	DeShaun Foster RPM RC	12.00	6.00
❑ 211	Jabar Gaffney RPM RC	12.00	6.00
❑ 212	Daniel Graham RPM RC	12.00	6.00
❑ 213	William Green RPM RC	12.00	6.00
❑ 214	Joey Harrington RPM RC	10.00	4.00
❑ 215	David Garrard RPM RC	15.00	6.00
❑ 216	Ron Johnson RPM RC	6.00	3.00
❑ 217	Ashley Lelie RPM RC	25.00	10.00
❑ 218	Josh McCown RPM RC	10.00	4.00
❑ 219	Maurice Morris RPM RC	12.00	6.00
❑ 220	Julius Peppers RPM RC	10.00	4.00
❑ 221	Clinton Portis RPM RC	20.00	8.00
❑ 222	Patrick Ramsey RPM RC	12.00	5.00
❑ 223	Antwaan Randle El RPM RC	10.00	4.00
❑ 224	Josh Reed RPM RC	12.00	6.00
❑ 225	Cliff Russell RPM RC	6.00	3.00
❑ 226	Jeremy Shockey RPM RC	20.00	8.00
❑ 227	Donte Stallworth RPM RC	12.00	5.00
❑ 228	Travis Stephens RPM RC	6.00	3.00
❑ 229	Javon Walker RPM RC	12.00	5.00
❑ 230	Marquise Walker RPM RC	6.00	3.00
❑ 231	Roy Williams RPM RC	15.00	6.00
❑ 232	Mike Williams RPM RC	6.00	3.00

2003 Absolute Memorabilia

❑	COMP.SET w/o SP's (100)	25.00	10.00
❑ 1	Jamal Lewis	1.25	.50
❑ 2	Ray Lewis	1.25	.50
❑ 3	Todd Heap	.75	.30
❑ 4	Drew Bledsoe	1.25	.50
❑ 5	Travis Henry	.75	.30
❑ 6	Peerless Price	.75	.30
❑ 7	Corey Dillon	.75	.30
❑ 8	Chad Johnson	1.25	.50
❑ 9	Tim Couch	.50	.20
❑ 10	William Green	.75	.30
❑ 11	Andre Davis	.50	.20
❑ 12	Brian Griese	1.25	.50
❑ 13	Ashley Lelie	1.25	.50
❑ 14	Clinton Portis	2.00	.75
❑ 15	Rod Smith	.75	.30
❑ 16	David Carr	2.00	.75
❑ 17	Corey Bradford	.50	.20
❑ 18	Jonathan Wells	.50	.20
❑ 19	Peyton Manning	2.00	.75
❑ 20	Edgerrin James	1.25	.50
❑ 21	Marvin Harrison	1.25	.50
❑ 22	Mark Brunell	.75	.30
❑ 23	Fred Taylor	1.25	.50
❑ 24	Jimmy Smith	.75	.30
❑ 25	Trent Green	.75	.30
❑ 26	Priest Holmes	1.50	.60
❑ 27	Tony Gonzalez	.75	.30
❑ 28	Jay Fiedler	.75	.30
❑ 29	Ricky Williams	1.25	.50
❑ 30	Chris Chambers	1.25	.50
❑ 31	Zach Thomas	1.25	.50
❑ 32	Tom Brady	3.00	1.25
❑ 33	Troy Brown	.75	.30
❑ 34	Antowain Smith	.75	.30
❑ 35	Chad Pennington	1.50	.60
❑ 36	Curtis Martin	1.25	.50
❑ 37	Laveranues Coles	.75	.30
❑ 38	Rich Gannon	.75	.30
❑ 39	Charlie Garner	.50	.20
❑ 40	Jerry Rice	2.50	1.00
❑ 41	Tim Brown	1.25	.50
❑ 42	Tommy Maddox	1.25	.50
❑ 43	Jerome Bettis	1.25	.50
❑ 44	Plaxico Burress	.75	.30
❑ 45	Hines Ward	1.25	.50
❑ 46	Drew Brees	1.25	.50
❑ 47	LaDainian Tomlinson	1.25	.50
❑ 48	Junior Seau	1.25	.50
❑ 49	Steve McNair	1.25	.50
❑ 50	Eddie George	.75	.30
❑ 51	Jevon Kearse	.75	.30
❑ 52	Jake Plummer	.75	.30
❑ 53	David Boston	.75	.30
❑ 54	Marcel Shipp	.75	.30
❑ 55	Michael Vick	3.00	1.25
❑ 56	T.J. Duckett	.75	.30
❑ 57	Warrick Dunn	.75	.30
❑ 58	Muhsin Muhammad	.75	.30

❑ 59 Julius Peppers	1.25	.50
❑ 60 Steve Smith	1.25	.50
❑ 61 Anthony Thomas	.75	.30
❑ 62 Brian Urlacher	2.00	.75
❑ 63 Marty Booker	.75	.30
❑ 64 Antonio Bryant	.75	.30
❑ 65 Chad Hutchinson	.50	.20
❑ 66 Roy Williams	1.25	.50
❑ 67 Emmitt Smith	3.00	1.25
❑ 68 Joey Harrington	2.00	.75
❑ 69 James Stewart	.75	.30
❑ 70 Az-Zahir Hakim	.50	.20
❑ 71 Brett Favre	3.00	1.25
❑ 72 Ahman Green	1.25	.50
❑ 73 Donald Driver	.75	.30
❑ 74 Daunte Culpepper	1.25	.50
❑ 75 Randy Moss	2.00	.75
❑ 76 Michael Bennett	.75	.30
❑ 77 Aaron Brooks	1.25	.50
❑ 78 Deuce McAllister	1.25	.50
❑ 79 Donte Stallworth	1.25	.50
❑ 80 Tiki Barber	1.25	.50
❑ 81 Kerry Collins	.75	.30
❑ 82 Jeremy Shockey	2.00	.75
❑ 83 Donovan McNabb	1.50	.60
❑ 84 Duce Staley	.75	.30
❑ 85 Antonio Freeman	.75	.30
❑ 86 Jeff Garcia	1.25	.50
❑ 87 Terrell Owens	1.25	.50
❑ 88 Garrison Hearst	.75	.30
❑ 89 Matt Hasselbeck	.75	.30
❑ 90 Koren Robinson	.75	.30
❑ 91 Shaun Alexander	1.25	.50
❑ 92 Kurt Warner	1.25	.50
❑ 93 Marshall Faulk	1.25	.50
❑ 94 Isaac Bruce	1.25	.50
❑ 95 Brad Johnson	.75	.30
❑ 96 Keyshawn Johnson	1.25	.50
❑ 97 Warren Sapp	.75	.30
❑ 98 Patrick Ramsey	1.25	.50
❑ 99 Rod Gardner	.75	.30
❑ 100 Stephen Davis	.75	.30
❑ 101 Jason Gesser RC	6.00	2.50
❑ 102 Brandon Lloyd RC	6.00	2.50
❑ 103 Ken Dorsey RC	6.00	2.50
❑ 104 Avon Cobourne RC	3.00	1.25
❑ 105 Cecil Sapp RC	5.00	2.00
❑ 106 Derek Watson RC	5.00	2.00
❑ 107 Dwone Hicks RC	3.00	1.25
❑ 108 Earnest Graham RC	6.00	.50
❑ 109 LaBrandon Toefield RC	6.00	2.50
❑ 110 Quentin Griffin RC	6.00	2.50
❑ 111 Sultan McCullough RC	5.00	2.00
❑ 112 Lee Suggs RC	6.00	2.50
❑ 113 Talman Gardner RC	6.00	2.50
❑ 114 Arnaz Battle RC	6.00	2.50
❑ 115 Billy McMullen RC	5.00	2.00
❑ 116 Doug Gabriel RC	6.00	2.50
❑ 117 Justin Gage RC	6.00	2.50
❑ 118 Kareem Kelly RC	5.00	2.00
❑ 119 Paul Arnold RC	5.00	2.00
❑ 120 Sam Aiken RC	5.00	2.00
❑ 121 Shaun McDonald RC	6.00	2.50
❑ 122 Terrence Edwards	5.00	2.00
❑ 123 Walter Young RC	3.00	1.25
❑ 124 Ryan Hoag RC	3.00	1.25
❑ 125 Jason Witten RC	15.00	6.00
❑ 126 Bennie Joppru RC	6.00	2.50
❑ 127 George Wrighster RC	5.00	2.00
❑ 128 L.J. Smith RC	6.00	2.50
❑ 129 Robert Johnson RC	3.00	1.25
❑ 130 Chris Kelsay RC	6.00	2.50
❑ 131 Cory Redding RC	5.00	2.00
❑ 132 DeWayne White RC	5.00	2.00
❑ 133 Kenny Peterson RC	5.00	2.00
❑ 134 Jerome McDougle RC	6.00	2.50
❑ 135 Michael Haynes RC	6.00	2.50
❑ 136 Jimmy Kennedy RC	6.00	2.50
❑ 137 Kevin Williams RC	6.00	2.50
❑ 138 Johnathan Sullivan RC	5.00	2.00
❑ 139 Rien Long RC	3.00	1.25
❑ 140 Ty Warren RC	6.00	2.50
❑ 141 William Joseph RC	6.00	2.50
❑ 142 E.J. Henderson RC	6.00	2.50
❑ 143 Boss Bailey RC	6.00	2.50
❑ 144 Dennis Weathersby RC	3.00	1.25
❑ 145 Chris Simms RC	10.00	4.00
❑ 146 Rashean Mathis RC	5.00	2.00
❑ 147 Charles Rogers RC	6.00	2.50
❑ 148 Andre Woolfolk RC	6.00	2.50
❑ 149 Troy Polamalu RC	25.00	12.50
❑ 150 Mike Doss RC	6.00	2.50
❑ 151 Carson Palmer RPM RC	40.00	20.00
❑ 152 Byron Leftwich RPM RC	30.00	12.50
❑ 153 Kyle Boller RPM RC	12.00	5.00
❑ 154 Rex Grossman RPM RC	30.00	15.00
❑ 155 Dave Ragone RPM RC	12.00	5.00
❑ 156 Kliff Kingsbury RPM RC	10.00	4.00
❑ 157 Seneca Wallace RPM RC	12.00	5.00
❑ 158 Larry Johnson RPM RC	40.00	20.00
❑ 159 Willis McGahee RPM RC	25.00	12.50
❑ 160 Justin Fargas RPM RC	12.00	5.00
❑ 161 Onterrio Smith RPM RC	12.00	5.00
❑ 162 Chris Brown RPM RC	12.00	5.00
❑ 163 Musa Smith RPM RC	12.00	5.00
❑ 164 Artose Pinner RPM RC	12.00	5.00
❑ 165 Andre Johnson RPM RC	20.00	7.50
❑ 166 Kelley Washington RPM RC	12.00	5.00
❑ 167 Taylor Jacobs RPM RC	10.00	4.00
❑ 168 Bryant Johnson RPM RC	12.00	5.00
❑ 169 Tyrone Calico RPM RC	12.00	5.00
❑ 170 Anquan Boldin RPM RC	25.00	10.00
❑ 171 Bethel Johnson RPM RC	12.00	5.00
❑ 172 Nate Burleson RPM RC	12.00	5.00
❑ 173 Kevin Curtis RPM RC	15.00	6.00
❑ 174 Dallas Clark RPM RC	12.00	5.00
❑ 175 Teyo Johnson RPM RC	12.00	5.00
❑ 176 Terrell Suggs RPM RC	20.00	7.50
❑ 177 DeWayne Robertson RPM RC	12.00	5.00
❑ 178 Brian St.Pierre RPM RC	12.00	5.00
❑ 179 Terence Newman RPM RC	20.00	7.50
❑ 180 Marcus Trufant RPM RC	12.00	5.00

2004 Absolute Memorabilia

❑ COMP.SET w/o SP's (150)	80.00	40.00
❑ 151-233 PRINT RUN 750 SER.#'d SETS		
❑ UNPRICED SPECTRUM PLATINUM #'d TO 1		
❑ 1 Anquan Boldin	3.00	1.25
❑ 2 Emmitt Smith	6.00	2.50
❑ 3 Josh McCown	2.00	.75
❑ 4 Marcel Shipp	2.00	.75
❑ 5 Michael Vick	6.00	2.50
❑ 6 Peerless Price	2.00	.75
❑ 7 T.J. Duckett	2.00	.75
❑ 8 Warrick Dunn	2.00	.75
❑ 9 Jamal Lewis	3.00	1.25
❑ 10 Kyle Boller	3.00	1.25
❑ 11 Ray Lewis	3.00	1.25
❑ 12 Terrell Suggs	2.00	.75
❑ 13 Drew Bledsoe	3.00	1.25
❑ 14 Eric Moulds	2.00	.75
❑ 15 Josh Reed	1.25	.50
❑ 16 Travis Henry	2.00	.75
❑ 17 DeShaun Foster	2.00	.75
❑ 18 Jake Delhomme	3.00	1.25
❑ 19 Julius Peppers	3.00	1.25
❑ 20 Muhsin Muhammad	2.00	.75
❑ 21 Stephen Davis	2.00	.75
❑ 22 Steve Smith	3.00	1.25
❑ 23 Anthony Thomas	2.00	.75
❑ 24 Brian Urlacher	4.00	1.50
❑ 25 Marty Booker	2.00	.75
❑ 26 Rex Grossman	3.00	1.25
❑ 27 Carson Palmer	4.00	1.50
❑ 28 Chad Johnson	3.00	1.25
❑ 29 Corey Dillon	2.00	.75
❑ 30 Peter Warrick	2.00	.75
❑ 31 Rudi Johnson	2.00	.75
❑ 32 Andre Davis	1.25	.50
❑ 33 Dennis Northcutt	1.25	.50
❑ 34 Lee Suggs	3.00	1.25
❑ 35 Tim Couch	1.25	.50
❑ 36 Jeff Garcia	3.00	1.25
❑ 37 William Green	2.00	.75
❑ 38 Antonio Bryant	2.00	.75
❑ 39 Quincy Carter	2.00	.75
❑ 40 Roy Williams S	2.00	.75
❑ 41 Terence Newman	2.00	.75
❑ 42 Keyshawn Johnson	2.00	.75
❑ 43 Garrison Hearst	2.00	.75
❑ 44 Champ Bailey	2.00	.75
❑ 45 Ashley Lelie	2.00	.75
❑ 46 Jake Plummer	2.00	.75
❑ 47 Rod Smith	2.00	.75
❑ 48 Shannon Sharpe	2.00	.75
❑ 49 Charles Rogers	2.00	.75
❑ 50 Joey Harrington	3.00	1.25
❑ 51 Ahman Green	3.00	1.25
❑ 52 Brett Favre	8.00	3.00
❑ 53 Donald Driver	2.00	.75
❑ 54 Javon Walker	2.00	.75
❑ 55 Robert Ferguson	1.25	.50
❑ 56 Andre Johnson	3.00	1.25
❑ 57 David Carr	3.00	1.25
❑ 58 Domanick Davis	3.00	1.25
❑ 59 Edgerrin James	3.00	1.25
❑ 60 Marvin Harrison	3.00	1.25
❑ 61 Peyton Manning	5.00	2.00
❑ 62 Reggie Wayne	2.00	.75
❑ 63 Byron Leftwich	4.00	1.50
❑ 64 Fred Taylor	2.00	.75
❑ 65 Jimmy Smith	2.00	.75
❑ 66 Dante Hall	3.00	1.25
❑ 67 Priest Holmes	4.00	1.50
❑ 68 Tony Gonzalez	2.00	.75
❑ 69 Trent Green	2.00	.75
❑ 70 Chris Chambers	2.00	.75
❑ 71 Jay Fiedler	1.25	.50
❑ 72 David Boston	2.00	.75
❑ 73 Ricky Williams	3.00	1.25
❑ 74 Zach Thomas	3.00	1.25
❑ 75 Daunte Culpepper	3.00	1.25
❑ 76 Michael Bennett	2.00	.75
❑ 77 Moe Williams	1.25	.50
❑ 78 Randy Moss	4.00	1.50
❑ 79 David Givens	2.00	.75
❑ 80 Deion Branch	3.00	1.25
❑ 81 Kevin Faulk	1.25	.50
❑ 82 Richard Seymour	1.25	.50
❑ 83 Tom Brady	8.00	3.00
❑ 84 Troy Brown	2.00	.75
❑ 85 Ty Law	2.00	.75
❑ 86 Aaron Brooks	2.00	.75
❑ 87 Deuce McAllister	3.00	1.25
❑ 88 Donte Stallworth	2.00	.75
❑ 89 Joe Horn	2.00	.75
❑ 90 Amani Toomer	2.00	.75
❑ 91 Jeremy Shockey	3.00	1.25
❑ 92 Kerry Collins	2.00	.75
❑ 93 Michael Strahan	2.00	.75
❑ 94 Tiki Barber	3.00	1.25
❑ 95 Chad Pennington	3.00	1.25
❑ 96 Curtis Martin	3.00	1.25
❑ 97 Santana Moss	2.00	.75
❑ 98 Wayne Chrebet	2.00	.75
❑ 99 Justin McCareins	1.25	.50
❑ 100 Charles Woodson	2.00	.75
❑ 101 Jerry Porter	2.00	.75
❑ 102 Jerry Rice	6.00	2.50
❑ 103 Rich Gannon	2.00	.75
❑ 104 Tim Brown	3.00	1.25
❑ 105 Warren Sapp	2.00	.75
❑ 106 A.J. Feeley	3.00	1.25
❑ 107 Brian Westbrook	2.00	.75
❑ 108 Correll Buckhalter	2.00	.75
❑ 109 Donovan McNabb	4.00	1.50
❑ 110 Freddie Mitchell	2.00	.75
❑ 111 Terrell Owens	3.00	1.25
❑ 112 Jevon Kearse	2.00	.75
❑ 113 Todd Pinkston	1.25	.50
❑ 114 Antwaan Randle El	3.00	1.25
❑ 115 Hines Ward	3.00	1.25
❑ 116 Jerome Bettis	3.00	1.25
❑ 117 Kendrell Bell	2.00	.75
❑ 118 Plaxico Burress	2.00	.75
❑ 119 Tommy Maddox	2.00	.75
❑ 120 Duce Staley	2.00	.75
❑ 121 Drew Brees	3.00	1.25

☐ 122 LaDainian Tomlinson 4.00 1.50
☐ 123 Kevan Barlow 2.00 .75
☐ 124 Tai Streets 1.25 .50
☐ 125 Tim Rattay 1.25 .50
☐ 126 Darrell Jackson 2.00 .75
☐ 127 Koren Robinson 2.00 .75
☐ 128 Matt Hasselbeck 2.00 .75
☐ 129 Shaun Alexander 3.00 1.25
☐ 130 Isaac Bruce 2.00 .75
☐ 131 Kurt Warner 3.00 1.25
☐ 132 Marc Bulger 3.00 1.25
☐ 133 Marshall Faulk 3.00 1.25
☐ 134 Torry Holt 3.00 1.25
☐ 135 Derrick Brooks 2.00 .75
☐ 136 Keenan McCardell 1.25 .50
☐ 137 Mike Alstott 2.00 .75
☐ 138 Thomas Jones 2.00 .75
☐ 139 Charlie Garner 2.00 .75
☐ 140 Derrick Mason 2.00 .75
☐ 141 Drew Bennett 2.00 .75
☐ 142 Eddie George 2.00 .75
☐ 143 Keith Bulluck 1.25 .50
☐ 144 Steve McNair 3.00 1.25
☐ 145 LaVar Arrington 6.00 2.50
☐ 146 Laveranues Coles 2.00 .75
☐ 147 Patrick Ramsey 2.00 .75
☐ 148 Rod Gardner 2.00 .75
☐ 149 Clinton Portis 3.00 1.25
☐ 150 Mark Brunell 2.00 .75
☐ 151 Craig Krenzel AU RC 15.00 7.50
☐ 152 Andy Hall AU RC EXCH 12.00 6.00
☐ 153 Josh Harris RC 6.00 2.50
☐ 154 Jim Sorgi AU RC 15.00 7.50
☐ 155 Jeff Smoker AU RC 15.00 7.50
☐ 156 John Navarre AU RC EXCH 15.00 7.50
☐ 157 Jared Lorenzen AU RC 12.00 6.00
☐ 158 Cody Pickett AU RC 15.00 7.50
☐ 159 Casey Bramlet RC 5.00 2.00
☐ 160 Matt Mauck AU RC 15.00 7.50
☐ 161 B.J. Symons AU RC 15.00 7.50
☐ 162 Bradlee Van Pelt RC 10.00 4.00
☐ 163 Ryan Dinwiddie RC 5.00 2.00
☐ 164 Michael Turner RC 8.00 3.00
☐ 165 Drew Henson RC 6.00 2.50
☐ 166 Troy Fleming RC 5.00 2.00
☐ 167 Adimchinobe Echemandu RC 5.00 2.00
☐ 168 Quincy Wilson RC 5.00 2.00
☐ 169 Derrick Ward RC 6.00 2.50
☐ 170 Bruce Perry RC 6.00 2.50
☐ 171 Brandon Miree RC 5.00 2.00
☐ 172 Jarrett Payton AU RC 12.00 5.00
☐ 173 Ran Carthon RC 5.00 2.00
☐ 174 Carlos Francis AU RC EXCH 12.00 6.00
☐ 175 Samie Parker RC 6.00 2.50
☐ 176 Jerricho Cotchery RC 6.00 2.50
☐ 177 Ernest Wilford RC 6.00 2.50
☐ 178 Johnnie Morant RC 6.00 2.50
☐ 179 Maurice Mann AU RC 15.00 7.50
☐ 180 D.J. Hackett RC 5.00 2.00
☐ 181 Drew Carter RC 6.00 2.50
☐ 182 P.K. Sam RC 5.00 2.00
☐ 183 Jamaar Taylor RC 6.00 2.50
☐ 184 Ryan Krause RC 5.00 2.00
☐ 185 Triandos Luke RC 6.00 2.50
☐ 186 Jeris McIntyre RC 5.00 2.00
☐ 187 Clarence Moore AU RC 15.00 7.50
☐ 188 Mark Jones RC 5.00 2.00
☐ 189 Sloan Thomas AU RC 12.00 6.00
☐ 190 Sean Taylor RC 6.00 2.50
☐ 191 Derek Abney RC 6.00 2.50
☐ 192 Jonathan Vilma RC 6.00 2.50
☐ 193 Tommie Harris RC 6.00 2.50
☐ 194 D.J. Williams RC 6.00 2.50
☐ 195 Will Smith RC 6.00 2.50
☐ 196 Kenechi Udeze RC 6.00 2.50
☐ 197 Vince Wilfork RC 6.00 2.50
☐ 198 Ahmad Carroll RC 6.00 2.50
☐ 199 Jason Babin RC 6.00 2.50
☐ 200 Chris Gamble RC 6.00 2.50
☐ 201 Larry Fitzgerald RPM RC 25.00 10.00
☐ 202 DeAngelo Hall RPM RC 10.00 4.00
☐ 203 Matt Schaub RPM RC 25.00 10.00
☐ 204 Michael Jenkins RPM AU RC 25.00 10.00
☐ 205 Devard Darling RPM AU RC 25.00 10.00
☐ 206 J.P. Losman RPM RC 15.00 6.00
☐ 207 Lee Evans RPM RC 10.00 4.00
☐ 208 Keary Colbert RPM AU RC 25.00 10.00
☐ 209 Bernard Berrian RPM AU RC 30.00 12.50
☐ 210 Chris Perry RPM RC 10.00 4.00
☐ 211 Kellen Winslow RPM RC 15.00 6.00
☐ 212 Luke McCown RPM RC 8.00 3.00
☐ 213 Julius Jones RPM RC 25.00 10.00
☐ 214 Darius Watts RPM RC 8.00 3.00
☐ 215 Tatum Bell RPM AU RC 40.00 20.00
☐ 216 Kevin Jones RPM RC 20.00 8.00
☐ 217 Roy Williams RPM RC 20.00 7.50
☐ 218 Dunta Robinson RPM RC 8.00 3.00
☐ 219 Greg Jones RPM AU RC 25.00 12.50
☐ 220 Reggie Williams RPM RC 10.00 4.00
☐ 221 Mewelde Moore RPM RC 10.00 4.00
☐ 222 Ben Watson RPM RC 8.00 3.00
☐ 223 Cedric Cobbs RPM RC 15.00 7.50
☐ 224 Dev Henderson RPM AU RC 25.00 10.00
☐ 225 Eli Manning RPM RC 50.00 25.00
☐ 226 Robert Gallery RPM RC [illegible] [illegible]
☐ 228 Philip Rivers RPM RC 25.00 12.50
☐ 229 Derrick Hamilton RPM RC 6.00 2.50
☐ 230 Rashaun Woods RPM RC 8.00 3.00
☐ 231 Steven Jackson RPM RC 25.00 10.00
☐ 232 Michael Clayton RPM RC 15.00 6.00
☐ 233 Ben Troupe RPM RC 8.00 3.00
☐ 227 Roethlisberger RPM RC 60.00 30.00

2005 Absolute Memorabilia

☐ 151-205 PRINT RUN 999 SER.#'d SETS
☐ 206-234 PRINT RUN 750 SER.#'d SETS
☐ UNPRICED PLATINUM PRINT RUN 1 SET
☐ HOBBY PRINTED ON HOLOFOIL STOCK
☐ 1 Anquan Boldin 2.00 .75
☐ 2 Kurt Warner 2.00 .75
☐ 3 Josh McCown 2.00 .75
☐ 4 Larry Fitzgerald 3.00 1.25
☐ 5 Alge Crumpler 2.00 .75
☐ 6 Michael Vick 5.00 2.00
☐ 7 Peerless Price 1.50 .60
☐ 8 T.J. Duckett 2.00 .75
☐ 9 Warrick Dunn 2.00 .75
☐ 10 Deion Sanders 3.00 1.25
☐ 11 Derrick Mason 2.00 .75
☐ 12 Ed Reed 2.00 .75
☐ 13 Jamal Lewis 3.00 1.25
☐ 14 Kyle Boller 2.00 .75
☐ 15 Ray Lewis 3.00 1.25
☐ 16 Todd Heap 2.00 .75
☐ 17 Eric Moulds 2.00 .75
☐ 18 J.P. Losman 3.00 1.25
☐ 19 Lee Evans 2.00 .75
☐ 20 Travis Henry 2.00 .75
☐ 21 Willis McGahee 3.00 1.25
☐ 22 DeShaun Foster 2.00 .75
☐ 23 Jake Delhomme 3.00 1.25
☐ 24 Julius Peppers 2.00 .75
☐ 25 Keary Colbert 2.00 .75
☐ 26 Stephen Davis 2.00 .75
☐ 27 Steve Smith 2.00 .75
☐ 28 Brian Urlacher 3.00 1.25
☐ 29 Muhsin Muhammad 2.00 .75
☐ 30 Thomas Jones 2.00 .75
☐ 31 Rex Grossman 2.00 .75
☐ 32 Carson Palmer 3.00 1.25
☐ 33 Chad Johnson 3.00 1.25
☐ 34 Peter Warrick 1.50 .60
☐ 35 Rudi Johnson 2.00 .75
☐ 36 T.J. Houshmandzadeh 1.50 .60
☐ 37 Antonio Bryant 1.50 .60
☐ 38 Dennis Northcutt 1.50 .60
☐ 39 Trent Dilfer 2.00 .75
☐ 40 Kellen Winslow 3.00 1.25
☐ 41 Lee Suggs 2.00 .75
☐ 42 Reuben Droughns 2.00 .75
☐ 43 Drew Bledsoe 3.00 1.25
☐ 44 Jason Witten 2.00 .75
☐ 45 Julius Jones 4.00 1.50
☐ 46 Keyshawn Johnson 2.00 .75
☐ 47 Terence Newman 1.50 .60
☐ 48 Roy Williams S 2.00 .75
☐ 49 Jake Plummer 2.00 .75
☐ 50 Rod Smith 2.00 .75
☐ 51 Ashley Lelie 2.00 .75
☐ 52 Tatum Bell 2.00 .75
☐ 53 Charles Rogers 2.00 .75
☐ 54 Joey Harrington 3.00 1.25
☐ 55 Kevin Jones 3.00 1.25
☐ 56 Roy Williams WR 3.00 1.25
☐ 57 [illegible]
☐ 58 Brett Favre 8.00 3.00
☐ 59 Donald Driver 2.00 .75
☐ 60 Javon Walker 2.00 .75
☐ 61 Andre Johnson 2.00 .75
☐ 62 David Carr 3.00 1.25
☐ 63 Domanick Davis 2.00 .75
☐ 64 Brandon Stokley 2.00 .75
☐ 65 Dallas Clark 1.50 .60
☐ 66 Edgerrin James 3.00 1.25
☐ 67 Marvin Harrison 3.00 1.25
☐ 68 Peyton Manning 5.00 2.00
☐ 69 Reggie Wayne 2.00 .75
☐ 70 Reggie Williams 2.00 .75
☐ 71 Byron Leftwich 3.00 1.25
☐ 72 Fred Taylor 2.00 .75
☐ 73 Jimmy Smith 2.00 .75
☐ 74 Priest Holmes 3.00 1.25
☐ 75 Tony Gonzalez 2.00 .75
☐ 76 Dante Hall 2.00 .75
☐ 77 Trent Green 2.00 .75
☐ 78 Eddie Kennison 1.50 .60
☐ 79 A.J. Feeley 2.00 .75
☐ 80 Chris Chambers 2.00 .75
☐ 81 Zach Thomas 3.00 1.25
☐ 82 Junior Seau 2.00 .75
☐ 83 Marty Booker 2.00 .75
☐ 84 Daunte Culpepper 3.00 1.25
☐ 85 Nate Burleson 2.00 .75
☐ 86 Michael Bennett 2.00 .75
☐ 87 Onterrio Smith 2.00 .75
☐ 88 Corey Dillon 2.00 .75
☐ 89 Deion Branch 2.00 .75
☐ 90 Tom Brady 8.00 3.00
☐ 91 Troy Brown 2.00 .75
☐ 92 Tedy Bruschi 2.00 .75
☐ 93 Aaron Brooks 2.00 .75
☐ 94 Donte Stallworth 2.00 .75
☐ 95 Joe Horn 2.00 .75
☐ 96 Deuce McAllister 3.00 1.25
☐ 97 Amani Toomer 2.00 .75
☐ 98 Plaxico Burress [illegible] [illegible]
☐ 99 Jeremy Shockey 3.00 1.25
☐ 100 Eli Manning 6.00 2.50
☐ 101 Tiki Barber 3.00 1.25
☐ 102 Chad Pennington 3.00 1.25
☐ 103 Laveranues Coles 2.00 .75
☐ 104 Curtis Martin 3.00 1.25
☐ 105 Justin McCareins 1.50 .60
☐ 106 Wayne Chrebet 2.00 .75
☐ 107 Jerry Porter 2.00 .75
☐ 108 LaMont Jordan 3.00 1.25
☐ 109 Randy Moss 3.00 1.25
☐ 110 Kerry Collins 2.00 .75
☐ 111 Charles Woodson 2.00 .75
☐ 112 Brian Westbrook 2.00 .75
☐ 113 Donovan McNabb 4.00 1.50
☐ 114 Jevon Kearse 2.00 .75
☐ 115 Terrell Owens 3.00 1.25
☐ 116 Ben Roethlisberger 8.00 3.00
☐ 117 Hines Ward 3.00 1.25
☐ 118 Duce Staley 2.00 .75
☐ 119 Jerome Bettis 3.00 1.25
☐ 120 Antonio Gates 3.00 1.25
☐ 121 Eric Parker 1.50 .60
☐ 122 Keenan McCardell 1.50 .60
☐ 123 Drew Brees 3.00 1.25
☐ 124 LaDainian Tomlinson 4.00 1.50
☐ 125 Brandon Lloyd 1.50 .60
☐ 126 Kevan Barlow 2.00 .75
☐ 127 Tim Rattay 1.50 .60
☐ 128 Koren Robinson 2.00 .75
☐ 129 Darrell Jackson 2.00 .75
☐ 130 Jerry Rice 6.00 2.50

❑ 131 Matt Hasselbeck 2.00 .75
❑ 132 Shaun Alexander 4.00 1.25
❑ 133 Isaac Bruce 2.00 .75
❑ 134 Marc Bulger 3.00 1.25
❑ 135 Marshall Faulk 3.00 1.25
❑ 136 Steven Jackson 4.00 1.50
❑ 137 Torry Holt 3.00 1.25
❑ 138 Brian Griese 2.00 .75
❑ 139 Michael Clayton 3.00 1.25
❑ 140 Michael Pittman 1.50 .60
❑ 141 Mike Alstott 2.00 .75
❑ 142 Chris Brown 2.00 .75
❑ 143 Drew Bennett 2.00 .75
❑ 144 Steve McNair 3.00 1.25
❑ 145 Clinton Portis 3.00 1.25
❑ 146 LaVar Arrington 3.00 1.25
❑ 147 Santana Moss 2.00 .75
❑ 148 Patrick Ramsey 2.00 .75
❑ 149 Rod Gardner 2.00 .75
❑ 150 Sean Taylor 2.00 .75
❑ 151 DeMarcus Ware RC 10.00 4.00
❑ 152 Shawne Merriman RC 10.00 4.00
❑ 153 Thomas Davis RC 6.00 2.50
❑ 154 Derrick Johnson RC 10.00 4.00
❑ 155 Travis Johnson RC 5.00 2.00
❑ 156 David Pollack RC 5.00 2.00
❑ 157 Erasmus James RC 6.00 2.50
❑ 158 Marcus Spears RC 6.00 2.50
❑ 159 Fabian Washington RC 6.00 2.50
❑ 160 Marlin Jackson RC 6.00 2.50
❑ 161 Cedric Benson RC 15.00 6.00
❑ 162 Matt Roth RC 6.00 2.50
❑ 163 Dan Cody RC 6.00 2.50
❑ 164 Bryant McFadden RC 6.00 2.50
❑ 165 Chris Henry RC 6.00 2.50
❑ 166 Brandon Jones RC 6.00 2.50
❑ 167 Marion Barber RC 10.00 4.00
❑ 168 Brandon Jacobs RC 8.00 3.00
❑ 169 Jerome Mathis RC 6.00 2.50
❑ 170 Craphonso Thorpe RC 5.00 2.00
❑ 171 Alvin Pearman RC 6.00 2.50
❑ 172 Darren Sproles RC 6.00 2.50
❑ 173 Fred Gibson RC 5.00 2.00
❑ 174 Roydell Williams RC 6.00 2.50
❑ 175 Airese Currie RC 6.00 2.50
❑ 176 Damien Nash RC 5.00 2.00
❑ 177 Dan Orlovsky RC 5.00 2.00
❑ 178 Adrian McPherson RC 6.00 2.50
❑ 179 Larry Brackins RC 3.00 1.25
❑ 180 Aaron Rodgers RC 20.00 8.00
❑ 181 Cedric Houston RC 6.00 2.50
❑ 182 Mike Williams 6.00 2.50
❑ 183 Heath Miller RC 12.00 5.00
❑ 184 Dante Ridgeway RC 5.00 2.00
❑ 185 Craig Bragg RC 5.00 2.00
❑ 186 Deandra Cobb RC 5.00 2.00
❑ 187 Derek Anderson RC 10.00 4.00
❑ 188 Paris Warren RC 5.00 2.00
❑ 189 David Greene RC 6.00 2.00
❑ 190 Lionel Gates RC 5.00 2.00
❑ 191 Anthony Davis RC 5.00 2.00
❑ 192 Noah Herron RC 6.00 2.50
❑ 193 Ryan Fitzpatrick RC 6.00 2.50
❑ 194 J.R. Russell RC 5.00 2.00
❑ 195 Jason White RC 6.00 2.50
❑ 196 Kay-Jay Harris RC 5.00 2.00
❑ 197 Steve Savoy RC 3.00 1.25
❑ 198 T.A. McLendon RC 3.00 1.25
❑ 199 Taylor Stubblefield RC 3.00 1.25
❑ 200 Josh Davis RC 5.00 2.00
❑ 201 Shaun Cody RC 6.00 2.50
❑ 202 Rasheed Marshall RC 6.00 2.50
❑ 203 Chad Owens RC 6.00 2.50
❑ 204 Tab Perry RC 6.00 2.50
❑ 205 James Kilian RC 6.00 2.50
❑ 206 Adam Jones RPM RC 10.00 4.00
❑ 207 Alex Smith QB RPM RC 30.00 12.50
❑ 208 Antrel Rolle RPM RC 10.00 4.00
❑ 209 Andrew Walter RPM RC 10.00 4.00
❑ 210 Braylon Edwards RPM RC 30.00 12.50
❑ 211 Cadillac Williams RPM RC 30.00 12.50
❑ 212 Carlos Rogers RPM RC 12.00 5.00
❑ 213 Charlie Frye RPM RC 10.00 4.00
❑ 214 Ciatrick Fason RPM RC 10.00 4.00
❑ 215 Courtney Roby RPM RC 10.00 4.00
❑ 216 Eric Shelton RPM RC 10.00 4.00
❑ 217 Frank Gore RPM RC 20.00 10.00
❑ 218 J.J. Arrington RPM RC 10.00 4.00
❑ 219 Kyle Orton RPM RC 10.00 4.00
❑ 220 Jason Campbell RPM RC 15.00 6.00
❑ 221 Mark Bradley RPM RC 10.00 4.00
❑ 222 Mark Clayton RPM RC 10.00 4.00
❑ 223 Matt Jones RPM RC 15.00 6.00
❑ 224 Maurice Clarett RPM 10.00 4.00
❑ 225 Reggie Brown RPM RC 10.00 4.00
❑ 226 Ronnie Brown RPM RC 30.00 12.50
❑ 227 Roddy White RPM RC 10.00 4.00
❑ 228 Ryan Moats RPM RC 10.00 4.00
❑ 229 Roscoe Parrish RPM RC 10.00 4.00
❑ 230 Stefan LeFors RPM RC 10.00 4.00
❑ 231 Terrence Murphy RPM RC 10.00 4.00
❑ 232 Troy Williamson RPM RC 10.00 4.00
❑ 233 Vernand Morency RPM RC 10.00 4.00
❑ 234 Vincent Jackson RPM RC 12.00 5.00

2005 Absolute Memorabilia Retail

❑ COMPLETE SET (150) 30.00 15.00
❑ *VETERANS: .1X TO .25X BASIC CARDS
❑ *ROOKIES 151-205: .2X TO .5X BASIC CARDS
❑ RETAIL PRINTED ON WHITE STOCK

2006 Absolute Memorabilia

❑ 1 Anquan Boldin 2.00 .75
❑ 2 J.J. Arrington 2.00 .75
❑ 3 Kurt Warner 2.00 .75
❑ 4 Larry Fitzgerald 3.00 1.25
❑ 5 Marcel Shipp 1.50 .60
❑ 6 Alge Crumpler 2.00 .75
❑ 7 Michael Jenkins 2.00 .75
❑ 8 Michael Vick 3.00 1.25
❑ 9 T.J. Duckett 2.00 .75
❑ 10 Warrick Dunn 2.00 .75
❑ 11 Derrick Mason 1.50 .60
❑ 12 Jamal Lewis 2.00 .75
❑ 13 Kyle Boller 1.50 .60
❑ 14 Mark Clayton 3.00 1.25
❑ 15 Ray Lewis 3.00 1.25
❑ 16 Todd Heap 2.00 .75
❑ 17 Eric Moulds 2.00 .75
❑ 18 J.P. Losman 2.00 .75
❑ 19 Josh Reed 1.50 .60
❑ 20 Lee Evans 2.00 .75
❑ 21 Willis McGahee 3.00 1.25
❑ 22 DeShaun Foster 2.00 .75
❑ 23 Jake Delhomme 2.00 .75
❑ 24 Julius Peppers 2.00 .75
❑ 25 Keary Colbert 1.50 .60
❑ 26 Stephen Davis 2.00 .75
❑ 27 Steve Smith 3.00 1.25
❑ 28 Brian Urlacher 3.00 1.25
❑ 29 Cedric Benson 3.00 1.25
❑ 30 Rex Grossman 3.00 1.25
❑ 31 Thomas Jones 2.00 .75
❑ 32 Muhsin Muhammad 2.00 .75
❑ 33 Carson Palmer 3.00 1.25
❑ 34 Chad Johnson 2.00 .75
❑ 35 Rudi Johnson 2.00 .75
❑ 36 T.J. Houshmandzadeh 2.00 .75
❑ 37 Charlie Frye 2.00 .75
❑ 38 Dennis Northcutt 1.50 .60
❑ 39 Reuben Droughns 2.00 .75
❑ 40 Braylon Edwards 3.00 1.25
❑ 41 Drew Bledsoe 3.00 1.25
❑ 42 Jason Witten 2.00 .75
❑ 43 Julius Jones 3.00 1.25
❑ 44 Keyshawn Johnson 2.00 .75
❑ 45 Roy Williams S 2.00 .75
❑ 46 Terry Glenn 2.00 .75
❑ 47 Ashley Lelie 2.00 .75
❑ 48 Jake Plummer 2.00 .75
❑ 49 Rod Smith 2.00 .75
❑ 50 Tatum Bell 2.00 .75
❑ 51 Mike Anderson 2.00 .75
❑ 52 Joey Harrington 2.00 .75
❑ 53 Kevin Jones 3.00 1.25
❑ 54 Mike Williams 3.00 1.25
❑ 55 Roy Williams WR 3.00 1.25
❑ 56 Marcus Pollard 1.50 .60
❑ 57 Aaron Rodgers 3.00 1.25
❑ 58 Brett Favre 6.00 2.50
❑ 59 Donald Driver 2.00 .75
❑ 60 Javon Walker 2.00 .75
❑ 61 Samkon Gado 2.00 .75
❑ 62 Bubba Franks 1.50 .60
❑ 63 Andre Johnson 2.00 .75
❑ 64 Corey Bradford 1.50 .60
❑ 65 David Carr 2.00 .75
❑ 66 Domanick Davis 2.00 .75
❑ 67 Jabar Gaffney 1.50 .60
❑ 68 Edgerrin James 3.00 1.25
❑ 69 Dallas Clark 1.50 .60
❑ 70 Marvin Harrison 3.00 1.25
❑ 71 Peyton Manning 5.00 2.00
❑ 72 Reggie Wayne 2.00 .75
❑ 73 Brandon Stokley 2.00 .75
❑ 74 Byron Leftwich 2.00 .75
❑ 75 Fred Taylor 2.00 .75
❑ 76 Jimmy Smith 2.00 .75
❑ 77 Matt Jones 2.00 .75
❑ 78 Ernest Wilford 1.50 .60
❑ 79 Larry Johnson 4.00 1.50
❑ 80 Tony Gonzalez 2.00 .75
❑ 81 Trent Green 2.00 .75
❑ 82 Eddie Kennison 1.50 .60
❑ 83 Dante Hall 2.00 .75
❑ 84 Chris Chambers 2.00 .75
❑ 85 Randy McMichael 1.50 .60
❑ 86 Terrell Owens 3.00 1.25
❑ 87 Ronnie Brown 3.00 1.25
❑ 88 Zach Thomas 3.00 1.25
❑ 89 Marty Booker 1.50 .60
❑ 90 Daunte Culpepper 3.00 1.25
❑ 91 Mewelde Moore 1.50 .60
❑ 92 Nate Burleson 2.00 .75
❑ 93 Troy Williamson 2.00 .75
❑ 94 Corey Dillon 2.00 .75
❑ 95 David Givens 2.00 .75
❑ 96 Deion Branch 2.00 .75
❑ 97 Tedy Bruschi 3.00 1.25
❑ 98 Tom Brady 5.00 2.00
❑ 99 Aaron Brooks 2.00 .75
❑ 100 Deuce McAllister 2.00 .75
❑ 101 Donte Stallworth 2.00 .75
❑ 102 Joe Horn 2.00 .75
❑ 103 Eli Manning 4.00 1.50
❑ 104 Jeremy Shockey 3.00 1.25
❑ 105 Plaxico Burress 2.00 .75
❑ 106 Tiki Barber 3.00 1.25
❑ 107 Chad Pennington 2.00 .75
❑ 108 Curtis Martin 3.00 1.25
❑ 109 Laveranues Coles 2.00 .75
❑ 110 Justin McCareins 1.50 .60
❑ 111 Kerry Collins 2.00 .75
❑ 112 LaMont Jordan 2.00 .75
❑ 113 Randy Moss 3.00 1.25
❑ 114 Jerry Porter 2.00 .75
❑ 115 Brian Westbrook 2.00 .75
❑ 116 Donovan McNabb 3.00 1.25
❑ 117 Reggie Brown 2.50 1.00

❑	118 Ryan Moats	1.50	.60
❑	119 Antwaan Randle El	2.00	.75
❑	120 Ben Roethlisberger	5.00	2.00
❑	121 Willie Parker	4.00	1.50
❑	122 Hines Ward	3.00	1.25
❑	123 Antonio Gates	3.00	1.25
❑	124 Drew Brees	3.00	1.25
❑	125 Keenan McCardell	1.50	.60
❑	126 LaDainian Tomlinson	4.00	1.50
❑	127 Alex Smith QB	3.00	1.25
❑	128 Brandon Lloyd	2.00	.75
❑	129 Frank Gore	3.00	1.25
❑	130 Kevan Barlow	2.00	.75
❑	131 Darrell Jackson	2.00	.75
❑	132 Joe Jurevicius	[illegible]	[illegible]
❑	133 Matt Hasselbeck	2.00	.75
❑	134 Shaun Alexander	3.00	1.25
❑	135 Isaac Bruce	2.00	.75
❑	136 Marc Bulger	2.00	.75
❑	137 Steven Jackson	3.00	1.25
❑	138 Torry Holt	2.00	.75
❑	139 Cadillac Williams	3.00	1.25
❑	140 Chris Simms	2.00	.75
❑	141 Joey Galloway	2.00	.75
❑	142 Michael Clayton	2.00	.75
❑	143 Chris Brown	2.00	.75
❑	144 Drew Bennett	1.50	.60
❑	145 Steve McNair	2.00	.75
❑	146 Tyrone Calico	1.50	.60
❑	147 Clinton Portis	3.00	1.25
❑	148 LaVar Arrington	3.00	1.25
❑	149 Mark Brunell	2.00	.75
❑	150 Santana Moss	2.00	.75
❑	151 Greg Jennings RC	10.00	4.00
❑	152 Joseph Addai RC	20.00	8.00
❑	153 Erik Meyer RC	5.00	2.00
❑	154 Drew Olson RC	5.00	2.00
❑	155 Darrell Hackney RC	5.00	2.00
❑	156 Paul Pinegar RC	5.00	2.00
❑	157 Brandon Kirsch RC	6.00	2.50
❑	158 Andre Hall RC	5.00	2.00
❑	159 Taurean Henderson RC	6.00	2.50
❑	160 Derrick Ross RC	5.00	2.00
❑	161 Mike Bell RC	6.00	2.50
❑	162 Wendell Mathis RC	5.00	2.00
❑	163 Gerald Riggs RC	6.00	2.50
❑	164 John David Washington RC	5.00	2.00
❑	165 Devin Aromashodu RC	5.00	2.00
❑	166 Ben Obomanu RC	5.00	2.00
❑	167 David Anderson RC	5.00	2.00
❑	168 Marques Colston RC	25.00	10.00
❑	169 Kevin McMahan RC	5.00	2.00
❑	170 Miles Austin RC	5.00	2.00
❑	171 Martin Nance RC	5.00	2.00
❑	172 Greg Lee RC	5.00	2.00
❑	173 Hank Baskett RC	[illegible]	[illegible]
❑	174 Anthony Mix RC	5.00	2.00
❑	175 D'Brickashaw Ferguson RC	6.00	2.50
❑	176 Kamerion Wimbley RC	6.00	2.50
❑	177 Tamba Hali RC	6.00	2.50
❑	178 Mathias Kiwanuka RC	8.00	3.00
❑	179 Brodrick Bunkley RC	6.00	2.50
❑	180 John McCargo RC	5.00	2.00
❑	181 Claude Wroten RC	3.00	1.25
❑	182 Gabe Watson RC	5.00	2.00
❑	183 D'Qwell Jackson RC	5.00	2.00
❑	184 Abdul Hodge RC	6.00	2.50
❑	185 Ernie Sims RC	8.00	3.00
❑	186 Chad Greenway RC	6.00	2.50
❑	187 Bobby Carpenter RC	6.00	2.50
❑	188 Manny Lawson RC	6.00	2.50
❑	189 DeMeco Ryans RC	8.00	3.00
❑	190 Rocky McIntosh RC	6.00	2.50
❑	191 Thomas Howard RC	6.00	2.50
❑	192 Jon Alston RC	6.00	2.50
❑	193 A.J. Nicholson RC	3.00	1.25
❑	194 Tye Hill RC	6.00	2.50
❑	195 Antonio Cromartie RC	6.00	2.50
❑	196 Johnathan Joseph RC	5.00	2.00
❑	197 Kelly Jennings RC	6.00	2.50
❑	198 Jimmy Williams RC	6.00	2.50
❑	199 Ashton Youboty RC	6.00	2.50
❑	200 Alan Zemaitis RC	6.00	2.50
❑	201 Anwar Phillips RC	5.00	2.00
❑	202 Jason Allen RC	6.00	2.50
❑	203 Cedric Griffin RC	5.00	2.00
❑	204 Ko Simpson RC	5.00	2.00
❑	205 Pat Watkins RC	6.00	2.50
❑	206 Donte Whitner RC	6.00	2.50
❑	207 Bernard Pollard RC	5.00	2.00
❑	208 Darnell Bing RC	6.00	2.50
❑	209 De'Arrius Howard RC	6.00	2.50
❑	210 Ethan Kilmer RC	6.00	2.50
❑	211 Bennie Brazell RC	5.00	2.00
❑	212 Haloti Ngata RC	6.00	2.50
❑	213 Jeremy Bloom RC	5.00	2.00
❑	214 Jay Cutler RC	20.00	8.00
❑	215 Marcus Vick RC	5.00	2.00
❑	216 Roman Harper RC	5.00	2.00
❑	217 Anthony Smith RC	8.00	3.00
❑	218 Daniel Bullocks RC	6.00	2.50
❑	219 Eric Smith RC	5.00	2.00
❑	220 Dusty Dvoracek RC	6.00	2.50
❑	221 Brodie Croyle AU RC	40.00	20.00
❑	222 [illegible]	15.00	6.00
❑	223 Reggie McNeal AU RC	12.00	5.00
❑	224 Bruce Gradkowski AU RC	40.00	15.00
❑	225 D.J. Shockley AU RC	15.00	6.00
❑	226 P.J. Daniels AU RC	12.00	5.00
❑	227 Marques Hagans AU RC	12.00	5.00
❑	228 Jerome Harrison RC	12.00	5.00
❑	229 Wali Lundy AU RC	15.00	6.00
❑	230 Cedric Humes AU RC	15.00	6.00
❑	231 Quinton Ganther AU RC	12.00	5.00
❑	232 Garrett Mills AU RC	15.00	6.00
❑	233 Anthony Fasano AU RC	15.00	6.00
❑	234 Tony Scheffler AU RC	15.00	6.00
❑	235 Leonard Pope AU RC	15.00	6.00
❑	236 David Thomas AU RC	15.00	6.00
❑	237 Dominique Byrd AU RC	12.00	5.00
❑	238 Jai Lewis AU/299 RC	12.00	5.00
❑	239 Devin Hester AU RC	50.00	30.00
❑	240 Willie Reid AU RC	15.00	6.00
❑	241 Brad Smith AU RC	15.00	6.00
❑	242 Cory Rodgers AU RC	15.00	6.00
❑	243 Skyler Green AU RC	15.00	6.00
❑	244 Domenik Hixon AU RC	12.00	5.00
❑	245 Mike Hass AU RC	15.00	6.00
❑	246 Jonathan Orr AU/299 RC	12.00	5.00
❑	247 Delanie Walker AU/299 RC	12.00	5.00
❑	248 Adam Jennings AU/299 RC	12.00	5.00
❑	249 Jeff Webb AU/299 RC	12.00	5.00
❑	250 Todd Watkins AU RC	12.00	5.00
❑	251 Chad Jackson RPM RC	10.00	4.00
❑	252 Laurence Maroney RPM RC	25.00	10.00
❑	253 Tarvaris Jackson RPM RC	15.00	6.00
❑	254 Michael Huff RPM RC	12.00	5.00
❑	255 Mario Williams RPM RC	15.00	6.00
❑	256 Marcedes Lewis RPM RC	10.00	4.00
❑	257 Maurice Drew RPM RC	25.00	10.00
❑	258 Vince Young RPM RC	40.00	15.00
❑	259 LenDale White RPM RC	20.00	8.00
❑	260 Reggie Bush RPM RC	40.00	15.00
❑	261 Matt Leinart RPM RC	30.00	12.00
❑	262 Michael Robinson RPM RC	10.00	4.00
❑	263 Vernon Davis RPM RC	20.00	8.00
❑	264 Brandon Williams RPM RC	10.00	4.00
❑	265 Derek Hagan RPM RC	10.00	4.00
❑	266 Jason Avant RPM RC	10.00	4.00
❑	267 Brandon Marshall RPM RC	10.00	4.00
❑	268 Omar Jacobs RPM RC	8.00	3.00
❑	269 Santonio Holmes RPM RC	20.00	8.00
❑	270 Jerious Norwood RPM RC	15.00	6.00
❑	271 Demetrius Williams RPM RC	10.00	4.00
❑	272 Sinorice Moss RPM RC	10.00	4.00
❑	273 Leon Washington RPM RC	15.00	6.00
❑	274 Kellen Clemens RPM RC	15.00	6.00
❑	275 A.J. Hawk RPM RC	20.00	8.00
❑	276 Maurice Stovall RPM RC	10.00	4.00
❑	277 DeAngelo Williams RPM RC	25.00	10.00
❑	278 Charlie Whitehurst RPM RC	10.00	4.00
❑	279 Travis Wilson RPM RC	10.00	4.00
❑	280 Joe Klopfenstein RPM RC	8.00	3.00
❑	281 Brian Calhoun RPM RC	10.00	4.00

2007 Absolute Memorabilia

❑	1 Tony Romo	6.00	2.50
❑	2 Julius Jones	2.50	1.00
❑	3 Terry Glenn	2.50	1.00
❑	4 Terrell Owens	3.00	1.25
❑	5 Marion Barber	2.50	1.00
❑	6 Reuben Droughns	2.50	1.00
❑	7 Eli Manning	3.00	1.25
❑	8 Plaxico Burress	2.50	1.00
❑	9 Jeremy Shockey	2.50	1.00
❑	10 Brandon Jacobs	2.50	1.00
❑	11 Donovan McNabb	3.00	1.25
❑	12 Brian Westbrook	2.50	1.00

❑	13 Reggie Brown	2.50	1.00
❑	14 Hank Baskett	2.50	1.00
❑	15 Jason Campbell	2.50	1.00
❑	16 Clinton Portis	2.50	1.00
❑	17 Santana Moss	2.50	1.00
❑	18 Ladell Betts	2.00	.75
❑	19 Brandon Lloyd	2.50	1.00
❑	20 Chris Cooley	2.00	.75
❑	21 Rex Grossman	2.50	1.00
❑	22 Cedric Benson	2.50	1.00
❑	23 Muhsin Muhammad	2.50	1.00
❑	24 Bernard Berrian	2.00	.75
❑	25 Devin Hester	3.00	1.25
❑	26 Brian Urlacher	3.00	1.25
❑	27 Jon Kitna	2.00	.75
❑	28 Kevin Jones	2.00	.75
❑	29 Roy Williams	2.50	1.00
❑	30 Mike Furrey	2.50	1.00
❑	31 Ernie Sims	2.00	.75
❑	32 Tatum Bell	2.50	1.00
❑	33 Brett Favre	6.00	2.50
❑	34 Vernand Morency	2.50	1.00
❑	35 Donald Driver	2.50	1.00
❑	36 Greg Jennings	2.50	1.00
❑	37 AJ Hawk	3.00	1.25
❑	38 Tarvaris Jackson	3.00	1.25
❑	39 Chester Taylor	2.00	.75
❑	40 Troy Williamson	2.00	.75
❑	41 Mewelde Moore	2.00	.75
❑	42 Michael Vick	3.00	1.25
❑	43 Warrick Dunn	2.50	1.00
❑	44 Joe Horn	2.50	1.00
❑	45 Alge Crumpler	2.50	1.00
❑	46 Jerious Norwood	2.50	1.00
❑	47 Jake Delhomme	2.50	1.00
❑	48 DeShaun Foster	2.50	1.00
❑	49 Steve Smith	2.50	1.00
❑	50 DeAngelo Williams	3.00	1.25
❑	51 Drew Brees	2.50	1.00
❑	52 Deuce McAllister	2.50	1.00
❑	53 Marques Colston	3.00	1.25
❑	54 Devery Henderson	2.00	.75
❑	55 Reggie Bush	4.00	1.50
❑	56 Jeff Garcia	2.50	1.00
❑	57 Cadillac Williams	2.50	1.00
❑	58 Joey Galloway	2.50	1.00
❑	59 Michael Clayton	2.50	1.00
❑	60 Matt Leinart	3.00	1.25
❑	61 Edgerrin James	3.00	1.25
❑	62 Anquan Boldin	2.50	1.00
❑	63 Larry Fitzgerald	2.50	1.00
❑	64 Marc Bulger	2.50	1.00
❑	65 Steven Jackson	3.00	1.25
❑	66 Torry Holt	2.50	1.00
❑	67 Isaac Bruce	2.50	1.00
❑	68 Randy McMichael	2.00	.75
❑	69 Drew Bennett	2.00	.75
❑	70 Alex Smith	3.00	1.25
❑	71 Frank Gore	3.00	1.25
❑	72 Darrell Jackson	2.50	1.00
❑	73 Ashley Lelie	2.50	1.00
❑	74 Vernon Davis	2.50	1.00
❑	75 Matt Hasselbeck	2.50	1.00
❑	76 Shaun Alexander	2.50	1.00
❑	77 Deion Branch	2.50	1.00
❑	78 J.P. Losman	2.50	1.00
❑	79 Lee Evans	2.50	1.00
❑	80 Josh Reed	2.00	.75
❑	81 Daunte Culpepper	2.50	1.00
❑	82 Ronnie Brown	2.50	1.00
❑	83 Chris Chambers	2.50	1.00
❑	84 Marty Booker	2.00	.75

Card	Hi	Lo
❑ 85 Zach Thomas	2.50	1.00
❑ 86 Tom Brady	6.00	2.50
❑ 87 Laurence Maroney	3.00	1.25
❑ 88 Randy Moss	3.00	1.25
❑ 89 Chad Jackson	2.00	.75
❑ 90 Ben Watson	2.00	.75
❑ 91 Donte' Stallworth	2.50	1.00
❑ 92 Chad Pennington	2.50	1.00
❑ 93 Thomas Jones	2.50	1.00
❑ 94 Laveranues Coles	2.50	1.00
❑ 95 Jerricho Cotchery	2.00	.75
❑ 96 Leon Washington	2.50	1.00
❑ 97 Steve McNair	2.50	1.00
❑ 98 Willis McGahee	2.50	1.00
❑ 99 Derrick Mason	2.00	.75
❑ 100 Demetrius Williams	2.00	.75
❑ 101 Mark Clayton	2.50	1.00
❑ 102 Carson Palmer	3.00	1.25
❑ 103 Rudi Johnson	2.50	1.00
❑ 104 Chad Johnson	2.50	1.00
❑ 105 T.J. Houshmandzadeh	2.50	1.00
❑ 106 Charlie Frye	2.50	1.00
❑ 107 Braylon Edwards	2.50	1.00
❑ 108 Travis Wilson	2.00	.75
❑ 109 Kellen Winslow	2.50	1.00
❑ 110 Jamal Lewis	2.50	1.00
❑ 111 Ben Roethlisberger	4.00	1.50
❑ 112 Willie Parker	3.00	1.25
❑ 113 Hines Ward	3.00	1.25
❑ 114 Santonio Holmes	2.50	1.00
❑ 115 Ahman Green	2.50	1.00
❑ 116 Andre Johnson	2.50	1.00
❑ 117 Matt Schaub	2.50	1.00
❑ 118 DeMeco Ryans	2.50	1.00
❑ 119 Owen Daniels	2.00	.75
❑ 120 Peyton Manning	5.00	2.00
❑ 121 Joseph Addai	4.00	1.50
❑ 122 Marvin Harrison	3.00	1.25
❑ 123 Reggie Wayne	2.50	1.00
❑ 124 Dallas Clark	2.00	.75
❑ 125 Byron Leftwich	2.50	1.00
❑ 126 Fred Taylor	2.50	1.00
❑ 127 Matt Jones	2.50	1.00
❑ 128 Reggie Williams	2.50	1.00
❑ 129 Marcedes Lewis	2.00	.75
❑ 130 Maurice Jones-Drew	3.00	1.25
❑ 131 Vince Young	4.00	1.50
❑ 132 LenDale White	2.50	1.00
❑ 133 Brandon Jones	2.00	.75
❑ 134 Jay Cutler	3.00	1.25
❑ 135 Travis Henry	2.50	1.00
❑ 136 Javon Walker	2.50	1.00
❑ 137 Rod Smith	2.50	1.00
❑ 138 Mike Bell	2.50	1.00
❑ 139 Brandon Marshall	2.50	1.00
❑ 140 Larry Johnson	3.00	1.25
❑ 141 Eddie Kennison	2.00	.75
❑ 142 Tony Gonzalez	2.50	1.00
❑ 143 Brodie Croyle	3.00	1.25
❑ 144 LaMont Jordan	2.50	1.00
❑ 145 Ronald Curry	2.50	1.00
❑ 146 Philip Rivers	3.00	1.25
❑ 147 LaDainian Tomlinson	4.00	1.50
❑ 148 Vincent Jackson	2.00	.75
❑ 149 Michael Turner	2.50	1.00
❑ 150 Antonio Gates	2.50	1.00
❑ 151 A.J. Davis RC	8.00	3.00
❑ 152 Aaron Rouse RC	12.00	5.00
❑ 153 Ahmad Bradshaw RC	15.00	6.00
❑ 154 Alonzo Coleman RC	10.00	4.00
❑ 155 Anthony Spencer RC	12.00	5.00
❑ 156 Brandon Siler RC	10.00	4.00
❑ 157 Buster Davis RC	10.00	4.00
❑ 158 Chris Houston RC	10.00	4.00
❑ 159 Dallas Baker RC	10.00	4.00
❑ 160 Dan Bazuin RC	10.00	4.00
❑ 161 Danny Ware RC	12.00	5.00
❑ 162 David Ball RC	8.00	3.00
❑ 163 David Irons RC	8.00	3.00
❑ 164 D'Juan Woods RC	10.00	4.00
❑ 165 Earl Everett RC	10.00	4.00
❑ 166 Eric Frampton RC	10.00	4.00
❑ 167 Eric Weddle RC	10.00	4.00
❑ 168 Eric Wright RC	12.00	5.00
❑ 169 Fred Bennett RC	8.00	3.00
❑ 170 Gary Russell RC	12.00	5.00
❑ 171 H.B. Blades RC	10.00	4.00
❑ 172 Jarrett Hicks RC	10.00	4.00
❑ 173 Jarvis Moss RC	12.00	5.00

Card	Hi	Lo
❑ 174 Jason Snelling RC	10.00	4.00
❑ 175 Jerard Rabb RC	10.00	4.00
❑ 176 Jemalle Cornelius RC	10.00	4.00
❑ 177 Tyler Thigpen RC	12.00	5.00
❑ 178 Jon Beason RC	12.00	5.00
❑ 179 Jonathan Wade RC	10.00	4.00
❑ 180 Jordan Kent RC	10.00	4.00
❑ 181 Josh Gattis RC	8.00	3.00
❑ 182 Kenneth Darby RC	12.00	5.00
❑ 183 DeMarcus Tank Tyler RC	10.00	4.00
❑ 184 Levi Brown RC	12.00	5.00
❑ 185 Marcus McCauley RC	10.00	4.00
❑ 186 Tim Shaw RC	10.00	4.00
❑ 187 Michael Okwo RC	10.00	4.00
❑ 188 Mike Walker RC	10.00	4.00
❑ 189 Nate Ilaoa RC	12.00	5.00
❑ 190 Reggie Ball RC	10.00	4.00
❑ 191 Rhema McKnight RC	10.00	4.00
❑ 192 Zak DeOssie RC	10.00	4.00
❑ 193 Rufus Alexander RC	12.00	5.00
❑ 194 Ryan McBean RC	12.00	5.00
❑ 195 Ryne Robinson RC	10.00	4.00
❑ 196 Selvin Young RC	15.00	6.00
❑ 197 Steve Breaston RC	10.00	4.00
❑ 198 Stewart Bradley RC	12.00	5.00
❑ 199 Thomas Clayton RC	10.00	4.00
❑ 200 Tim Crowder RC	12.00	5.00
❑ 201 Aaron Ross AU RC	15.00	6.00
❑ 202 Adam Carriker AU RC	12.00	5.00
❑ 203 Alan Branch AU RC EXCH	12.00	5.00
❑ 204 Amobi Okoye AU RC	15.00	6.00
❑ 205 Aundrae Allison AU RC EXCH	12.00	5.00
❑ 206 Ben Patrick AU RC	12.00	5.00
❑ 207 Brandon Meriweather AU RC	15.00	6.00
❑ 208 Chansi Stuckey AU RC	12.00	5.00
❑ 209 Charles Johnson AU RC EXCH	10.00	4.00
❑ 210 Chris Davis AU RC	12.00	5.00
❑ 211 Chris Leak AU RC	12.00	5.00
❑ 212 Courtney Taylor AU RC	12.00	5.00
❑ 213 Craig Buster Davis AU RC EXCH	15.00	6.00
❑ 214 Darius Walker AU RC	15.00	6.00
❑ 215 Darrelle Revis AU RC	15.00	6.00
❑ 216 David Clowney AU RC	15.00	6.00
❑ 217 David Harris AU RC	12.00	5.00
❑ 218 Daymeion Hughes AU RC	12.00	5.00
❑ 219 DeShawn Wynn AU RC	15.00	6.00
❑ 220 Dwayne Wright AU RC	12.00	5.00
❑ 221 Ikaika Alama-Francis AU RC	15.00	6.00
❑ 222 Isaiah Stanback AU RC	15.00	6.00
❑ 223 Jacoby Jones AU RC	25.00	12.50
❑ 224 Jamaal Anderson AU RC	12.00	5.00
❑ 225 James Jones AU RC	30.00	15.00
❑ 226 Jared Zabransky AU RC	15.00	6.00
❑ 227 Jeff Rowe AU RC	12.00	5.00
❑ 228 Joel Filani AU RC	12.00	5.00
❑ 229 Jordan Palmer AU RC	15.00	6.00
❑ 230 Josh Wilson AU RC	12.00	5.00
❑ 231 Kenny Scott AU RC	10.00	4.00
❑ 232 Kolby Smith AU RC	20.00	8.00
❑ 233 LaMarr Woodley AU RC	15.00	6.00
❑ 234 LaRon Landry AU RC	20.00	8.00
❑ 235 Laurent Robinson AU RC	12.00	5.00
❑ 236 Lawrence Timmons AU RC	15.00	6.00
❑ 237 Leon Hall AU RC	12.00	5.00
❑ 238 Matt Spaeth AU RC	15.00	6.00
❑ 239 Michael Griffin AU RC	15.00	6.00
❑ 240 Paul Posluszny AU RC	20.00	8.00
❑ 241 Quentin Moses AU RC	12.00	5.00
❑ 242 Ray McDonald AU RC	12.00	5.00
❑ 243 Reggie Nelson AU RC	12.00	5.00
❑ 244 Ronnie McGill AU RC	12.00	5.00
❑ 245 Sabby Piscitelli AU RC	15.00	6.00
❑ 246 Scott Chandler AU RC	12.00	5.00
❑ 247 Toby Korrodi AU RC	12.00	5.00
❑ 248 Tyler Palko AU RC	15.00	6.00
❑ 249 Victor Abiamiri AU RC	15.00	6.00
❑ 250 Zach Miller AU RC	15.00	6.00
❑ 251 JaMarcus Russell RPM RC	25.00	10.00
❑ 252 Calvin Johnson RPM RC	30.00	12.00
❑ 253 Joe Thomas RPM RC	10.00	4.00
❑ 254 Gaines Adams RPM RC	10.00	4.00
❑ 255 Greg Olsen RPM RC	12.00	5.00
❑ 256 Adrian Peterson RPM RC	80.00	30.00
❑ 257 Ted Ginn RPM RC	15.00	6.00
❑ 258 Patrick Willis RPM RC	20.00	8.00
❑ 259 Marshawn Lynch RPM RC	20.00	8.00
❑ 260 Brady Quinn RPM RC	30.00	12.00
❑ 261 Dwayne Bowe RPM RC	20.00	8.00
❑ 262 Robert Meachem RPM RC	10.00	4.00

Card	Hi	Lo
❑ 263 Anthony Gonzalez RPM RC	15.00	6.00
❑ 264 Kevin Kolb RPM RC	15.00	6.00
❑ 265 John Beck RPM RC	20.00	8.00
❑ 266 Drew Stanton RPM RC	12.00	5.00
❑ 267 Sidney Rice RPM RC	15.00	6.00
❑ 268 Dwayne Jarrett RPM RC	12.00	5.00
❑ 269 Kenny Irons RPM RC	10.00	4.00
❑ 270 Chris Henry RPM RC	10.00	4.00
❑ 271 Steve Smith RPM RC	12.00	5.00
❑ 272 Brian Leonard RPM RC	12.00	5.00
❑ 273 Brandon Jackson RPM RC	12.00	5.00
❑ 274 Lorenzo Booker RPM RC	10.00	4.00
❑ 275 Yamon Figurs RPM RC	10.00	4.00
❑ 276 Jason Hill RPM RC	10.00	4.00
❑ 277 Paul Williams RPM RC	8.00	3.00
❑ 278 Tony Hunt RPM RC	10.00	4.00
❑ 279 Trent Edwards RPM RC	20.00	8.00
❑ 280 Garrett Wolfe RPM RC	12.00	5.00
❑ 281 Johnnie Lee Higgins RPM RC	8.00	3.00
❑ 282 Michael Bush RPM RC	12.00	5.00
❑ 283 Antonio Pittman RPM RC	8.00	3.00
❑ 284 Troy Smith RPM RC	12.00	5.00

2007 Artifacts

Card	Hi	Lo
❑ 1 Matt Leinart	1.25	.50
❑ 2 Edgerrin James	1.25	.50
❑ 3 Larry Fitzgerald	1.00	.40
❑ 4 Anquan Boldin	1.00	.40
❑ 5 Michael Vick	1.25	.50
❑ 6 Warrick Dunn	1.00	.40
❑ 7 Alge Crumpler	1.00	.40
❑ 8 Steve McNair	1.00	.40
❑ 9 Willis McGahee	1.00	.40
❑ 10 Mark Clayton	1.00	.40
❑ 11 J.P. Losman	1.00	.40
❑ 12 Anthony Thomas	.75	.30
❑ 13 Lee Evans	1.00	.40
❑ 14 Jake Delhomme	1.00	.40
❑ 15 DeShaun Foster	1.00	.40
❑ 16 Steve Smith	1.00	.40
❑ 17 Rex Grossman	1.00	.40
❑ 18 Cedric Benson	1.00	.40
❑ 19 Brian Urlacher	1.25	.50
❑ 20 Carson Palmer	1.25	.50
❑ 21 Rudi Johnson	1.00	.40
❑ 22 Chad Johnson	1.00	.40
❑ 23 T.J. Houshmandzadeh	1.00	.40
❑ 24 Charlie Frye	1.00	.40
❑ 25 Braylon Edwards	1.00	.40
❑ 26 Kellen Winslow	1.00	.40
❑ 27 Tony Romo	2.50	1.00
❑ 28 Julius Jones	1.00	.40
❑ 29 Terrell Owens	1.25	.50
❑ 30 Terry Glenn	1.00	.40
❑ 31 Jay Cutler	1.25	.50
❑ 32 Travis Henry	1.00	.40
❑ 33 Javon Walker	1.00	.40
❑ 34 Jon Kitna	.75	.30
❑ 35 Kevin Jones	.75	.30
❑ 36 Roy Williams WR	1.00	.40
❑ 37 Mike Furrey	1.00	.40
❑ 38 Brett Favre	2.50	1.00
❑ 39 Greg Jennings	1.00	.40
❑ 40 Donald Driver	1.00	.40
❑ 41 David Carr	1.00	.40
❑ 42 Ron Dayne	1.00	.40
❑ 43 Andre Johnson	1.00	.40
❑ 44 Peyton Manning	2.00	.75
❑ 45 Joseph Addai	1.50	.60
❑ 46 Marvin Harrison	1.25	.50
❑ 47 Reggie Wayne	1.00	.40
❑ 48 David Garrard	1.00	.40

❑ 49 Fred Taylor	1.00	.40
❑ 50 Maurice Jones-Drew	1.25	.50
❑ 51 Trent Green	1.00	.40
❑ 52 Larry Johnson	1.25	.50
❑ 53 Tony Gonzalez	1.00	.40
❑ 54 Daunte Culpepper	1.00	.40
❑ 55 Ronnie Brown	1.00	.40
❑ 56 Chris Chambers	1.00	.40
❑ 57 Tarvaris Jackson	1.25	.50
❑ 58 Chester Taylor	.75	.30
❑ 59 Travis Taylor	.75	.30
❑ 60 Tom Brady	2.50	1.00
❑ 61 Laurence Maroney	1.25	.50
❑ 62 Reche Caldwell	.75	.30
❑ 63 Drew Brees	1.00	.40
❑ 64 Deuce McAllister	1.00	.40
❑ 65 Reggie Bush	1.50	.60
❑ 66 Marques Colston	1.25	.50
❑ 67 Eli Manning	1.25	.50
❑ 68 Brandon Jacobs	1.00	.40
❑ 69 Plaxico Burress	1.00	.40
❑ 70 Chad Pennington	1.00	.40
❑ 71 Leon Washington	1.00	.40
❑ 72 Laveranues Coles	1.00	.40
❑ 73 Ronald Curry	1.00	.40
❑ 74 LaMont Jordan	1.00	.40
❑ 75 Randy Moss	1.25	.50
❑ 76 Donovan McNabb	1.25	.50
❑ 77 Brian Westbrook	1.00	.40
❑ 78 Reggie Brown	1.00	.40
❑ 79 Ben Roethlisberger	1.50	.60
❑ 80 Willie Parker	1.25	.50
❑ 81 Hines Ward	1.25	.50
❑ 82 Santonio Holmes	1.00	.40
❑ 83 Philip Rivers	1.25	.50
❑ 84 LaDainian Tomlinson	1.50	.60
❑ 85 Antonio Gates	1.00	.40
❑ 86 Matt Hasselbeck	1.00	.40
❑ 87 Shaun Alexander	1.00	.40
❑ 88 Deion Branch	1.00	.40
❑ 89 Marc Bulger	1.00	.40
❑ 90 Steven Jackson	1.25	.50
❑ 91 Torry Holt	1.00	.40
❑ 92 Chris Simms	.75	.30
❑ 93 Cadillac Williams	1.00	.40
❑ 94 Joey Galloway	1.00	.40
❑ 95 Vince Young	1.50	.60
❑ 96 LenDale White	1.00	.40
❑ 97 Drew Bennett	.75	.30
❑ 98 Jason Campbell	1.00	.40
❑ 99 Clinton Portis	1.00	.40
❑ 100 Santana Moss	1.00	.40
❑ 101 Aaron Ross RC	6.00	2.50
❑ 102 Aaron Rouse RC	6.00	2.50
❑ 103 Alvin Banks RC	5.00	2.00
❑ 104 Anthony Spencer RC	6.00	2.50
❑ 105 Ben Patrick RC	5.00	2.00
❑ 106 Brandon Siler RC	5.00	2.00
❑ 107 Buster Davis RC	5.00	2.00
❑ 108 Clark Harris RC	6.00	2.50
❑ 109 Chris Henry RC	6.00	2.50
❑ 110 Chris Houston RC	5.00	2.00
❑ 111 Courtney Taylor RC	5.00	2.00
❑ 112 Dallas Baker RC	5.00	2.00
❑ 113 Danny Ware RC	6.00	2.50
❑ 114 Darius Walker RC	6.00	2.50
❑ 115 Darrelle Revis RC	6.00	2.50
❑ 116 David Ball RC	4.00	1.50
❑ 117 D'Juan Woods RC	5.00	2.00
❑ 118 Drew Tate RC	5.00	2.00
❑ 119 Dwayne Wright RC	5.00	2.00
❑ 120 Isaiah Stanback RC	6.00	2.50
❑ 121 Garrett Wolfe RC	8.00	3.00
❑ 122 Gary Russell RC	6.00	2.50
❑ 123 Jared Zabransky RC	6.00	2.50
❑ 124 Jarvis Moss RC	6.00	2.50
❑ 125 Jason Hill RC	6.00	2.50
❑ 126 Justin Harrell RC	6.00	2.50
❑ 127 John Beck RC	12.00	5.00
❑ 128 Johnnie Lee Higgins RC	5.00	2.00
❑ 129 Kolby Smith RC	8.00	3.00
❑ 130 LaMarr Woodley RC	6.00	2.50
❑ 131 Le'Ron McClain RC	5.00	2.00
❑ 132 Levi Brown RC	6.00	2.50
❑ 133 Mason Crosby RC	6.00	2.50
❑ 134 Matt Moore RC	10.00	4.00
❑ 135 Matt Trannon RC	5.00	2.00
❑ 136 Ahmad Bradshaw RC	8.00	3.00
❑ 137 Michael Griffin RC	6.00	2.50
❑ 138 Paul Williams RC	5.00	2.00
❑ 139 Rhema McKnight RC	5.00	2.00
❑ 140 Martrez Milner RC	5.00	2.00
❑ 141 Scott Chandler RC	5.00	2.00
❑ 142 Selvin Young RC	8.00	3.00
❑ 143 Steve Breaston RC	5.00	2.00
❑ 144 Matt Spaeth RC	6.00	2.50
❑ 145 DeMarcus Tank Tyler RC	5.00	2.00
❑ 146 Thomas Clayton RC	5.00	2.00
❑ 147 Tim Crowder RC	6.00	2.50
❑ 148 Tony Ugoh RC	5.00	2.00
❑ 149 Trent Edwards RC	12.00	5.00
❑ 150 Tyler Palko RC	6.00	2.50
❑ 151 Adam Carriker SP RC	5.00	2.00
❑ 152 Adrian Peterson SP RC	50.00	20.00
❑ 153 Alan Branch SP RC	5.00	2.00
❑ 154 Amobi Okoye SP RC	6.00	2.50
❑ 155 Anthony Gonzalez SP RC	10.00	4.00
❑ 156 Antonio Pittman SP RC	5.00	2.00
❑ 157 Aundrae Allison SP RC	5.00	2.00
❑ 158 Brady Quinn SP RC	20.00	8.00
❑ 159 Brandon Jackson SP RC	8.00	3.00
❑ 160 Brian Leonard SP RC	6.00	2.50
❑ 161 Calvin Johnson SP RC	20.00	8.00
❑ 162 Chansi Stuckey SP RC	5.00	2.00
❑ 163 Charles Johnson SP RC	4.00	1.50
❑ 164 Chris Leak SP RC	5.00	2.00
❑ 165 Craig Buster Davis SP RC	6.00	2.50
❑ 166 David Clowney SP RC	6.00	2.50
❑ 167 Daymeion Hughes SP RC	5.00	2.00
❑ 168 DeShawn Wynn SP RC	6.00	2.50
❑ 169 Drew Stanton SP RC	8.00	3.00
❑ 170 Dwayne Bowe SP RC	12.00	5.00
❑ 171 Dwayne Jarrett SP RC	8.00	3.00
❑ 172 Gaines Adams SP RC	6.00	2.50
❑ 173 Greg Olsen SP RC	8.00	3.00
❑ 174 Jamaal Anderson SP RC	5.00	2.00
❑ 175 JaMarcus Russell SP RC	15.00	6.00
❑ 176 Joe Thomas SP RC	6.00	2.50
❑ 177 Joel Filani SP RC	5.00	2.00
❑ 178 Jordan Palmer SP RC	6.00	2.50
❑ 179 Kenneth Darby SP RC	6.00	2.50
❑ 180 Kenny Irons SP RC	6.00	2.50
❑ 181 Kevin Kolb SP RC	10.00	4.00
❑ 182 LaRon Landry SP RC	8.00	3.00
❑ 183 Lawrence Timmons SP RC	6.00	2.50
❑ 184 Leon Hall SP RC	5.00	2.00
❑ 185 Lorenzo Booker SP RC	6.00	2.50
❑ 186 Marcus McCauley SP RC	5.00	2.00
❑ 187 Marshawn Lynch SP RC	12.00	5.00
❑ 188 Michael Bush SP RC	8.00	3.00
❑ 189 Patrick Willis SP RC	12.00	5.00
❑ 190 Paul Posluszny SP RC	8.00	3.00
❑ 191 Quentin Moses SP RC	5.00	2.00
❑ 192 Reggie Nelson SP RC	5.00	2.00
❑ 193 Robert Meachem SP RC	6.00	2.50
❑ 194 Sidney Rice SP RC	10.00	4.00
❑ 195 Steve Smith USC SP RC	8.00	3.00
❑ 196 Ted Ginn Jr. SP RC	10.00	4.00
❑ 197 Tony Hunt SP RC	6.00	2.50
❑ 198 Troy Smith SP RC	8.00	3.00
❑ 199 Tyrone Moss SP RC	4.00	1.50
❑ 200 Zach Miller SP RC	6.00	2.50

2004 Bazooka

❑ COMPLETE SET (220)	50.00	20.00
❑ 1 Peyton Manning	1.25	.50
❑ 2 Rod Gardner	.50	.20
❑ 3 Marc Bulger	.75	.30
❑ 4 Champ Bailey	.50	.20
❑ 5 Moe Williams	.40	.15
❑ 6 Andre' Davis	.40	.15
❑ 7 Corey Dillon	.50	.20
❑ 8 Trent Green	.50	.20
❑ 9 Daunte Culpepper	.75	.30
❑ 10 Chad Pennington	.75	.30
❑ 11 Hines Ward	.75	.30
❑ 12 Tim Brown	.75	.30
❑ 13 Jerome Pathon	.40	.15
❑ 14 Drew Brees	.75	.30
❑ 15 Eddie George	.50	.20
❑ 16 Duce Staley	.50	.20
❑ 17 Marques Tuiasosopo	.50	.20
❑ 18 Willis McGahee	.75	.30
❑ 19 T.J. Duckett	.50	.20
❑ 20 Brian Urlacher	1.00	.40
❑ 21 Ashley Lelie	.50	.20
❑ 22 Robert Ferguson	.40	.15
❑ 23 Tai Streets	.40	.15
❑ 24 Junior Seau	.75	.30
❑ 25 Priest Holmes	1.00	.40
❑ 26 Ty Law	.50	.20
❑ 27 Correll Buckhalter	.50	.20
❑ 28 Plaxico Burress	.50	.20
❑ 29 Brad Johnson	.50	.20
❑ 30 Shaun Alexander	.75	.30
❑ 31 Mark Brunell	.50	.20
❑ 32 Julian Peterson	.40	.15
❑ 33 Marcel Shipp	.50	.20
❑ 34 Kyle Boller	.75	.30
❑ 35 Rudi Johnson	.50	.20
❑ 36 Quincy Carter	.50	.20
❑ 37 Jabar Gaffney	.50	.20
❑ 38 Reggie Wayne	.50	.20
❑ 39 Deion Branch	.75	.30
❑ 40 Terrell Owens	.75	.30
❑ 41 Chris Brown	.75	.30
❑ 42 Bobby Engram	.40	.15
❑ 43 Josh Reed	.40	.15
❑ 44 Thomas Jones	.50	.20
❑ 45 Stephen Davis	.50	.20
❑ 46 Mike Anderson	.50	.20
❑ 47 Javon Walker	.50	.20
❑ 48 Edgerrin James	.75	.30
❑ 49 Randy McMichael	.40	.15
❑ 50 Deuce McAllister	.75	.30
❑ 51 Nate Burleson	.75	.30
❑ 52 Jevon Kearse	.50	.20
❑ 53 Jay Fiedler	.40	.15
❑ 54 Patrick Ramsey	.50	.20
❑ 55 Brian Westbrook	.50	.20
❑ 56 Tyrone Calico	.50	.20
❑ 57 Alge Crumpler	.50	.20
❑ 58 Josh McCown	.50	.20
❑ 59 Quincy Morgan	.50	.20
❑ 60 Jeff Garcia	.75	.30
❑ 61 Garrison Hearst	.50	.20
❑ 62 Chad Johnson	.75	.30
❑ 63 Byron Leftwich	1.00	.40
❑ 64 Donald Driver	.50	.20
❑ 65 Ricky Williams	.75	.30
❑ 66 Todd Pinkston	.40	.15
❑ 67 Amani Toomer	.50	.20
❑ 68 David Givens	.50	.20
❑ 69 Jerome Bettis	.75	.30
❑ 70 Derrick Mason	.50	.20
❑ 71 Darrell Jackson	.50	.20
❑ 72 Kassim Osgood	.40	.15
❑ 73 Todd Heap	.50	.20
❑ 74 Warrick Dunn	.50	.20
❑ 75 Brett Favre	2.00	.75
❑ 76 Chris Chambers	.50	.20
❑ 77 Fred Taylor	.50	.20
❑ 78 Charles Rogers	.50	.20
❑ 79 Onterrio Smith	.50	.20
❑ 80 Joe Horn	.50	.20
❑ 81 Justin McCareins	.40	.15
❑ 82 Ike Hilliard	.40	.15
❑ 83 Kevan Barlow	.50	.20
❑ 84 Charlie Garner	.50	.20
❑ 85 Anquan Boldin	.75	.30
❑ 86 Anthony Thomas	.50	.20
❑ 87 Julius Peppers	.75	.30
❑ 88 Dat Nguyen	.40	.15
❑ 89 Peerless Price	.50	.20
❑ 90 Randy Moss	1.00	.40
❑ 91 Jamie Sharper	.40	.15
❑ 92 Travis Henry	.50	.20
❑ 93 Terrell Suggs	.50	.20
❑ 94 Joey Galloway	.50	.20
❑ 95 Torry Holt	.75	.30

❑ 96 Freddie Mitchell .50 .20
❑ 97 Jerry Porter .50 .20
❑ 98 Dwight Freeney .50 .20
❑ 99 Joey Harrington .75 .30
❑ 100 Michael Vick 1.50 .60
❑ 101 Kelley Washington .40 .15
❑ 102 Marty Booker .50 .20
❑ 103 Tim Rattay .40 .15
❑ 104 Derrick Brooks .50 .20
❑ 105 Laveranues Coles .50 .20
❑ 106 Ray Lewis .75 .30
❑ 107 Jon Kitna .50 .20
❑ 108 Terry Glenn .40 .15
❑ 109 Steve Smith .75 .30
❑ 110 Ahman Green .75 .30
❑ 111 Andre Johnson .75 .30
❑ 112 Dallas Clark .50 .20
❑ 113 Kevin Faulk .40 .15
❑ 114 Michael Bennett .50 .20
❑ 115 Tony Gonzalez .50 .20
❑ 116 Michael Strahan .50 .20
❑ 117 Tommy Maddox .50 .20
❑ 118 Isaac Bruce .50 .20
❑ 119 Brandon Lloyd .50 .20
❑ 120 Steve McNair .75 .30
❑ 121 Keith Brooking .40 .15
❑ 122 Drew Bledsoe .75 .30
❑ 123 Peter Warrick .50 .20
❑ 124 Antonio Bryant .50 .20
❑ 125 Clinton Portis .75 .30
❑ 126 Kelly Holcomb .50 .20
❑ 127 Jake Delhomme .75 .30
❑ 128 Rod Smith .50 .20
❑ 129 Lee Suggs .75 .30
❑ 130 Domanick Davis .75 .30
❑ 131 Carson Palmer 1.00 .40
❑ 132 Kerry Collins .50 .20
❑ 133 Teyo Johnson .40 .15
❑ 134 Curtis Martin .75 .30
❑ 135 Matt Hasselbeck .50 .20
❑ 136 Cedrick Wilson .40 .15
❑ 137 Eric Moulds .50 .20
❑ 138 Keyshawn Johnson .50 .20
❑ 139 Dante Hall .75 .30
❑ 140 Jamal Lewis .75 .30
❑ 141 Kelly Campbell .40 .15
❑ 142 Jeremy Shockey .75 .30
❑ 143 Jerry Rice 1.50 .60
❑ 144 Kurt Warner .75 .30
❑ 145 Jake Plummer .50 .20
❑ 146 Keenan McCardell .40 .15
❑ 147 Jimmy Smith .50 .20
❑ 148 Zach Thomas .75 .30
❑ 149 Eddie Kennison .40 .15
❑ 150 Tom Brady 2.00 .75
❑ 151 Donte' Stallworth .50 .20
❑ 152 John Abraham .40 .15
❑ 153 Koren Robinson .50 .20
❑ 154 Rex Grossman .75 .30
❑ 155 Donovan McNabb 1.00 .40
❑ 156 David Carr .75 .30
❑ 157 David Boston .50 .20
❑ 158 Tiki Barber .75 .30
❑ 159 Santana Moss .50 .20
❑ 160 LaDainian Tomlinson 1.25 .50
❑ 161 Justin Fargas .50 .20
❑ 162 Troy Brown .50 .20
❑ 163 Marshall Faulk .75 .30
❑ 164 Aaron Brooks .50 .20
❑ 165 Marvin Harrison .75 .30
❑ 166 Kevin Jones RC 4.00 1.50
❑ 167 Michael Clayton RC 3.00 1.25
❑ 168 Bernard Berrian RC 2.00 .75
❑ 169 Ben Watson RC 1.50 .60
❑ 170 Philip Rivers RC 5.00 2.00
❑ 171 Vince Wilfork RC 1.50 .60
❑ 172 Jason Babin RC 1.50 .60
❑ 173 Marcus Tubbs RC 1.50 .60
❑ 174 Sean Taylor RC 1.50 .60
❑ 175 Larry Fitzgerald RC 5.00 2.00
❑ 176 Craig Krenzel RC 1.50 .60
❑ 177 Cedric Cobbs RC 1.50 .60
❑ 178 Lee Evans RC 2.00 .75
❑ 179 Johnnie Morant RC 1.50 .60
❑ 180 Kellen Winslow RC 3.00 1.25
❑ 181 Mewelde Moore RC 1.50 .60
❑ 182 Carlos Francis RC 1.25 .50
❑ 183 Josh Harris RC 1.50 .60
❑ 184 Julius Jones RC 5.00 2.00
❑ 185 Reggie Williams RC 2.00 .75
❑ 186 DeAngelo Hall RC 2.00 .75
❑ 187 D.J. Williams RC 1.50 .60
❑ 188 Cody Pickett RC 1.50 .60
❑ 189 Dunta Robinson RC 1.50 .60
❑ 190 J.P. Losman RC 3.00 1.25
❑ 191 Jonathan Vilma RC 1.50 .60
❑ 192 Jerricho Cotchery RC 1.50 .60
❑ 193 Keary Colbert RC 1.50 .60
❑ 194 Ben Troupe RC 1.50 .60
❑ 195 Drew Henson RC 1.50 .60
❑ 196 Chris Gamble RC 1.50 .60
❑ 197 Samie Parker RC 1.50 .60
❑ 198 Tatum Bell RC 3.00 1.25
❑ 199 Robert Gallery RC 1.50 .60
❑ 200 Eli Manning RC 12.00 6.00
❑ 201 Ahmad Carroll RC 1.50 .60
❑ 202 Devery Henderson RC 1.50 .60
❑ 203 Matt Schaub RC 5.00 2.00
❑ 204 Greg Jones RC 1.50 .60
❑ 205 Roy Williams RC 4.00 1.50
❑ 206 Tommie Harris RC 1.50 .60
❑ 207 Jeff Smoker RC 1.50 .60
❑ 208 Kenechi Udeze RC 1.50 .60
❑ 209 Derrick Hamilton RC 1.25 .50
❑ 210 Ben Roethlisberger RC 15.00 6.00
❑ 211 Darius Watts RC 1.50 .60
❑ 212 John Navarre RC 1.50 .60
❑ 213 Ernest Wilford RC 1.50 .60
❑ 214 Rashaun Woods RC 1.50 .60
❑ 215 Steven Jackson RC 5.00 2.00
❑ 216 Michael Jenkins RC 1.50 .60
❑ 217 Will Smith RC 1.50 .60
❑ 218 Devard Darling RC 1.50 .60
❑ 219 Chris Perry RC 2.00 .75
❑ 220 Luke McCown RC 1.50 .60

2005 Bazooka

❑ COMPLETE SET (220) 50.00 20.00
❑ COMP.SET w/o RC's (165) 25.00 10.00
❑ 1 Willis McGahee .75 .30
❑ 2 Aaron Brooks .50 .20
❑ 3 Allen Rossum .40 .15
❑ 4 Brett Favre 2.00 .75
❑ 5 Donovan McNabb 1.00 .40
❑ 6 Torry Holt .75 .30
❑ 7 Michael Vick 1.25 .50
❑ 8 David Carr .75 .30
❑ 9 Eric Moulds .50 .20
❑ 10 Chad Pennington .75 .30
❑ 11 Larry Fitzgerald .75 .30
❑ 12 Tom Brady 2.00 .75
❑ 13 Derrick Brooks .50 .20
❑ 14 Brandon Stokley .50 .20
❑ 15 Justin McCareins .40 .15
❑ 16 Champ Bailey .50 .20
❑ 17 Jake Delhomme .75 .30
❑ 18 Peyton Manning 1.25 .50
❑ 19 Keyshawn Johnson .50 .20
❑ 20 Daunte Culpepper .75 .30
❑ 21 Chester Taylor .50 .20
❑ 22 Kurt Warner .50 .20
❑ 23 Cedrick Wilson .40 .15
❑ 24 Brian Westbrook .50 .20
❑ 25 Rodney Harrison .50 .20
❑ 26 Clinton Portis .75 .30
❑ 27 A.J. Feeley .50 .20
❑ 28 Curtis Martin .75 .30
❑ 29 Chris Perry .50 .20
❑ 30 Randy Moss .75 .30
❑ 31 Darrell Jackson .50 .20
❑ 32 Edgerrin James .75 .30
❑ 33 Ben Roethlisberger 2.00 .75
❑ 34 Kevin Jones .75 .30
❑ 35 LaMont Jordan .75 .30
❑ 36 Jerome Bettis .75 .30
❑ 37 Ahman Green .75 .30
❑ 38 Tyrone Calico .50 .20
❑ 39 Anquan Boldin .50 .20
❑ 40 Dante Hall .50 .20
❑ 41 Todd Heap .50 .20
❑ 42 Corey Dillon .50 .20
❑ 43 Julius Peppers .50 .20
❑ 44 Antonio Bryant .40 .15
❑ 45 Dunta Robinson .50 .20
❑ 46 Michael Pittman .40 .15
❑ 47 Billy Volek .50 .20
❑ 48 Jimmy Smith .50 .20
❑ 49 Carson Palmer .75 .30
❑ 50 Derrick Blaylock .40 .15
❑ 51 Deuce McAllister .75 .30
❑ 52 Ray Lewis .75 .30
❑ 53 Chad Johnson .75 .30
❑ 54 Zach Thomas .75 .30
❑ 55 Julius Jones 1.00 .40
❑ 56 D.J. Williams .40 .15
❑ 57 Stephen Davis .50 .20
❑ 58 Greg Jones .40 .15
❑ 59 J.P. Losman .75 .30
❑ 60 Trent Green .50 .20
❑ 61 Drew Bennett .50 .20
❑ 62 Joe Horn .50 .20
❑ 63 Mewelde Moore .50 .20
❑ 64 Alge Crumpler .50 .20
❑ 65 Javon Walker .50 .20
❑ 66 Jake Plummer .50 .20
❑ 67 Aaron Stecker .40 .15
❑ 68 Keary Colbert .50 .20
❑ 69 Joey Harrington .75 .30
❑ 70 Brian Urlacher .75 .30
❑ 71 Jeremy Shockey .75 .30
❑ 72 Duce Staley .50 .20
❑ 73 Tim Rattay .40 .15
❑ 74 Jerry Porter .50 .20
❑ 75 Steven Jackson 1.00 .40
❑ 76 David Givens .50 .20
❑ 77 Byron Leftwich .75 .30
❑ 78 T.J. Duckett .50 .20
❑ 79 Jason Witten .50 .20
❑ 80 Andre Johnson .50 .20
❑ 81 Amani Toomer .50 .20
❑ 82 Kellen Winslow .75 .30
❑ 83 Kyle Boller .50 .20
❑ 84 Santana Moss .50 .20
❑ 85 Antonio Gates .75 .30
❑ 86 Lee Evans .50 .20
❑ 87 Larry Johnson .75 .30
❑ 88 Plaxico Burress .50 .20
❑ 89 Reuben Droughns .50 .20
❑ 90 Eli Manning 1.50 .60
❑ 91 Lito Sheppard .40 .15
❑ 92 DeAngelo Hall .50 .20
❑ 93 Josh McCown .50 .20
❑ 94 Eric Parker .40 .15
❑ 95 Drew Brees .75 .30
❑ 96 Fred Taylor .50 .20
❑ 97 Jonathan Vilma .50 .20
❑ 98 Michael Strahan .50 .20
❑ 99 Dwight Freeney .50 .20
❑ 100 Kerry Collins .50 .20
❑ 101 Hines Ward .75 .30
❑ 102 Lee Suggs .50 .20
❑ 103 Luke McCown .40 .15
❑ 104 Laveranues Coles .50 .20
❑ 105 LaDainian Tomlinson 1.00 .40
❑ 106 Jeff Garcia .50 .20
❑ 107 Michael Clayton .75 .30
❑ 108 DeShaun Foster .50 .20
❑ 109 Rex Grossman .50 .20
❑ 110 Priest Holmes .75 .30
❑ 111 Roy Williams WR .75 .30
❑ 112 Drew Henson .50 .20
❑ 113 Derrick Mason .50 .20
❑ 114 Michael Bennett .50 .20
❑ 115 Chris Simms .50 .20
❑ 116 Isaac Bruce .50 .20
❑ 117 Deion Branch .50 .20
❑ 118 Rudi Johnson .50 .20
❑ 119 Nate Burleson .50 .20
❑ 120 Warrick Dunn .50 .20
❑ 121 Brian Griese .50 .20

❑ 122 T.J. Houshmandzadeh .40 .15
❑ 123 Jamaar Taylor .40 .15
❑ 124 Drew Bledsoe .75 .30
❑ 125 Najeh Davenport .40 .15
❑ 126 Charles Rogers .50 .20
❑ 127 Ronald Curry .50 .20
❑ 128 Chris Brown .50 .20
❑ 129 Doug Gabriel .40 .15
❑ 130 Todd Pinkston .40 .15
❑ 131 Marc Bulger .75 .30
❑ 132 Marshall Faulk .75 .30
❑ 133 Marvin Harrison .75 .30
❑ 134 Matt Hasselbeck .50 .20
❑ 135 Tiki Barber .75 .30
❑ 136 Muhsin Muhammad .50 .20
❑ 137 Kevan Barlow .50 .20
❑ 138 Chris Chambers .50 .20
❑ 139 Donald Driver .50 .20
❑ 140 Jamal Lewis .75 .30
❑ 141 Rashaun Woods .50 .20
❑ 142 Steve McNair .75 .30
❑ 143 Reggie Wayne .50 .20
❑ 144 Jevon Kearse .50 .20
❑ 145 Domanick Davis .50 .20
❑ 146 Donte Stallworth .50 .20
❑ 147 Chris Gamble .50 .20
❑ 148 Philip Rivers .75 .30
❑ 149 Sean Taylor .50 .20
❑ 150 Antwaan Randle El .50 .20
❑ 151 Koren Robinson .50 .20
❑ 152 Tatum Bell .50 .20
❑ 153 Tony Gonzalez .50 .20
❑ 154 Reggie Williams .50 .20
❑ 155 Onterrio Smith .50 .20
❑ 156 Patrick Ramsey .50 .20
❑ 157 Thomas Jones .50 .20
❑ 158 Michael Jenkins .50 .20
❑ 159 Rod Smith .50 .20
❑ 160 Trent Dilfer .50 .20
❑ 161 Randy McMichael .40 .15
❑ 162 Terrell Owens .75 .30
❑ 163 Travis Henry .50 .20
❑ 164 Travis Taylor .40 .15
❑ 165 Shaun Alexander 1.00 .40
❑ 166 J.J. Arrington RC 1.50 .60
❑ 167 Cedric Benson RC 4.00 1.50
❑ 168 Carlos Rogers RC 2.00 .75
❑ 169 Troy Williamson RC 1.50 .60
❑ 170 Ronnie Brown RC 5.00 2.00
❑ 171 Jason Campbell RC 2.50 1.00
❑ 172 Alvin Pearman RC 1.50 .60
❑ 173 Reggie Brown RC 1.50 .60
❑ 174 Lionel Gates RC 1.25 .50
❑ 175 Derek Anderson RC 2.50 1.00
❑ 176 Craphonso Thorpe RC 1.25 .50
❑ 177 Frank Gore RC 3.00 1.25
❑ 178 David Greene RC 1.50 .60
❑ 179 Vincent Jackson RC 1.50 .60
❑ 180 Adam Jones RC 1.50 .60
❑ 181 Derrick Johnson RC 2.50 1.00
❑ 182 Stefan LeFors RC 1.50 .60
❑ 183 Heath Miller RC 3.00 1.25
❑ 184 Ryan Moats RC 1.50 .60
❑ 185 Vernand Morency RC 1.50 .60
❑ 186 Brandon Jacobs RC 2.00 .75
❑ 187 Kyle Orton RC 1.50 .60
❑ 188 Roscoe Parrish RC 1.50 .60
❑ 189 Courtney Roby RC 1.50 .60
❑ 190 Aaron Rodgers RC 6.00 2.50
❑ 191 Marion Barber RC 2.50 1.00
❑ 192 Antrel Rolle RC 1.50 .60
❑ 193 Airese Currie RC 1.50 .60
❑ 194 Alex Smith QB RC 5.00 2.00
❑ 195 Andrew Walter RC 1.50 .60
❑ 196 Roddy White RC 1.50 .60
❑ 197 Cadillac Williams RC 5.00 2.00
❑ 198 Mike Williams 1.50 .60
❑ 199 Rasheed Marshall RC 1.50 .60
❑ 200 Charlie Frye RC 1.50 .60
❑ 201 Justin Miller RC 1.25 .50
❑ 202 Fabian Washington RC 1.50 .60
❑ 203 Mark Bradley RC 1.50 .60
❑ 204 Adrian McPherson RC 1.50 .60
❑ 205 Marcus Spears RC 1.50 .60
❑ 206 Matt Jones RC 5.00 1.00
❑ 207 Darren Sproles RC 1.50 .60
❑ 208 Eric Shelton RC 1.50 .60
❑ 209 Fred Gibson RC 1.25 .50
❑ 210 Anthony Davis RC 1.25 .50
❑ 211 Mark Clayton RC 1.50 .60
❑ 212 Braylon Edwards RC 5.00 2.00
❑ 213 Ciatrick Fason RC 1.50 .60
❑ 214 DeMarcus Ware RC 2.50 1.00
❑ 215 Dan Orlovsky RC 1.50 .60
❑ 216 Maurice Clarett 1.50 .60
❑ 217 Erasmus James RC 1.50 .60
❑ 218 Chris Henry RC 1.50 .60
❑ 219 Jerome Mathis RC 1.50 .60
❑ 220 Terrence Murphy RC 1.50 .60

1948 Bowman

❑ COMPLETE SET (108) 6000.00 4500.00
❑ COMMON 1/4/7/-/-/- 20.00 12.00
❑ COMMON 2/5/8/-/-/- 25.00 15.00
❑ COMMON SP 3/6/9 /-/-/- 100.00 65.00
❑ WRAPPER (1-CENT) 250.00 150.00
❑ 1 Joe Tereshinski RC ! 150.00 80.00
❑ 2 Larry Olsonoski 25.00 15.00
❑ 3 Johnny Lujack RC SP 350.00 250.00
❑ 4 Ray Poole 20.00 12.00
❑ 5 Bill DeCorrevont RC 25.00 15.00
❑ 6 Paul Briggs SP 100.00 65.00
❑ 7 Steve Van Buren RC 200.00 125.00
❑ 8 Kenny Washington RC 60.00 40.00
❑ 9 Nolan Luhn SP 100.00 65.00
❑ 10 Chris Iversen 20.00 12.00
❑ 11 Jack Wiley 25.00 15.00
❑ 12 Charley Conerly RC SP 350.00 250.00
❑ 13 Hugh Taylor RC 25.00 15.00
❑ 14 Frank Seno 25.00 15.00
❑ 15 Gil Bouley SP 100.00 65.00
❑ 16 Tommy Thompson RC 35.00 20.00
❑ 17 Charley Trippi RC 100.00 60.00
❑ 18 Vince Banonis SP 100.00 65.00
❑ 19 Art Faircloth 20.00 12.00
❑ 20 Clyde Goodnight 25.00 15.00
❑ 21 Bill Chipley SP 100.00 65.00
❑ 22 Sammy Baugh RC 500.00 350.00
❑ 23 Don Kindt 25.00 15.00
❑ 24 John Koniszewski SP 100.00 65.00
❑ 25 Pat McHugh 20.00 12.00
❑ 26 Bob Waterfield RC 200.00 125.00
❑ 27 Tony Compagno SP 100.00 65.00
❑ 28 Paul Governali RC 25.00 15.00
❑ 29 Pat Harder RC 60.00 40.00
❑ 30 Vic Lindskog SP 100.00 65.00
❑ 31 Salvatore Rosato 20.00 12.00
❑ 32 John Mastrangelo 25.00 15.00
❑ 33 Fred Gehrke SP 100.00 65.00
❑ 34 Bosh Pritchard 20.00 12.00
❑ 35 Mike Micka 25.00 15.00
❑ 36 Bulldog Turner RC SP 250.00 160.00
❑ 37 Len Younce 20.00 12.00
❑ 38 Pat West 25.00 15.00
❑ 39 Russ Thomas SP 100.00 65.00
❑ 40 James Peebles 20.00 12.00
❑ 41 Bob Skoglund 25.00 15.00
❑ 42 Walt Stickle SP 100.00 65.00
❑ 43 Whitey Wistert RC 25.00 15.00
❑ 44 Paul Christman RC 60.00 40.00
❑ 45 Jay Rhodemyre SP 100.00 65.00
❑ 46 Tony Minisi 20.00 12.00
❑ 47 Bob Mann 25.00 15.00
❑ 48 Mal Kutner RC SP 110.00 70.00
❑ 49 Dick Poillon 20.00 12.00
❑ 50 Charles Cherundolo 25.00 15.00
❑ 51 Gerald Cowhig SP 100.00 65.00
❑ 52 Neill Armstrong RC 25.00 15.00
❑ 53 Frank Maznicki 25.00 15.00
❑ 54 John Sanchez SP 100.00 65.00
❑ 55 Frank Reagan 20.00 12.00
❑ 56 Jim Hardy 25.00 15.00
❑ 57 John Badaczewski SP 100.00 65.00
❑ 58 Robert Nussbaumer 20.00 12.00
❑ 59 Marvin Pregulman 25.00 15.00
❑ 60 Elbie Nickel RC SP 125.00 75.00
❑ 61 Alex Wojciechowicz RC 150.00 90.00
❑ 62 Walt Schlinkman 25.00 15.00
❑ 63 Pete Pihos RC SP 225.00 150.00
❑ 64 Joseph Sulaitis 20.00 12.00
❑ 65 Mike Holovak RC 50.00 30.00
❑ 66 Cy Souders SP RC 100.00 65.00
❑ 67 Paul McKee 20.00 12.00
❑ 68 Bill Moore 25.00 15.00
❑ 69 Frank Minini SP 100.00 65.00
❑ 70 Jack Ferrante 20.00 12.00
❑ 71 Les Horvath RC 50.00 35.00
❑ 72 Ted Fritsch Sr. RC SP 110.00 70.00
❑ 73 Tex Coulter RC 25.00 15.00
❑ 74 Boley Dancewicz 25.00 15.00
❑ 75 Dante Mangani SP 100.00 65.00
❑ 76 James Hefti 20.00 12.00
❑ 77 Paul Sarringhaus 25.00 15.00
❑ 78 Joe Scott SP 100.00 65.00
❑ 79 Bucko Kilroy RC 25.00 15.00
❑ 80 Bill Dudley RC 125.00 75.00
❑ 81 Mal Goldberg RC SP 110.00 70.00
❑ 82 John Cannady 20.00 12.00
❑ 83 Perry Moss 25.00 15.00
❑ 84 Harold Crisler RC SP 110.00 70.00
❑ 85 Bill Gray 20.00 12.00
❑ 86 John Clement 25.00 15.00
❑ 87 Dan Sandifer SP 100.00 65.00
❑ 88 Ben Kish 20.00 12.00
❑ 89 Herbert Banta 25.00 15.00
❑ 90 Bill Garnaas SP 100.00 65.00
❑ 91 Jim White RC 20.00 12.00
❑ 92 Frank Barzilauskas 25.00 15.00
❑ 93 Vic Sears SP 100.00 65.00
❑ 94 John Adams 20.00 12.00
❑ 95 George McAfee RC 150.00 90.00
❑ 96 Ralph Heywood SP 100.00 65.00
❑ 97 Joe Muha 20.00 12.00
❑ 98 Fred Enke 25.00 15.00
❑ 99 Harry Gilmer RC SP 175.00 100.00
❑ 100 Bill Miklich 20.00 12.00
❑ 101 Joe Gottlieb 25.00 15.00
❑ 102 Bud Angsman RC SP 110.00 70.00
❑ 103 Tom Farmer 20.00 12.00
❑ 104 Bruce Smith RC 75.00 40.00
❑ 105 Bob Cifers SP 100.00 65.00
❑ 106 Ernie Steele 20.00 12.00
❑ 107 Sid Luckman RC 300.00 175.00
❑ 108 Buford Ray RC SP ! 400.00 250.00

1950 Bowman

❑ COMPLETE SET (144) 4000.00 3000.00
❑ WRAPPER (5-CENT) 175.00 100.00
❑ 1 Doak Walker ! 250.00 150.00
❑ 2 John Greene 25.00 18.00
❑ 3 Bob Nowasky 25.00 18.00
❑ 4 Jonathan Jenkins 25.00 18.00
❑ 5 Y.A.Tittle RC 250.00 175.00
❑ 6 Lou Groza RC 175.00 100.00
❑ 7 Alex Agase RC 30.00 20.00
❑ 8 Mac Speedie RC 50.00 30.00
❑ 9 Tony Canadeo RC 90.00 50.00
❑ 10 Larry Craig 30.00 20.00
❑ 11 Ted Fritsch Sr. 30.00 20.00
❑ 12 Joe Golding 25.00 18.00
❑ 13 Martin Ruby 25.00 18.00
❑ 14 George Taliaferro 30.00 20.00
❑ 15 Tank Younger RC 50.00 30.00
❑ 16 Glenn Davis RC 125.00 75.00
❑ 17 Bob Waterfield 125.00 75.00
❑ 18 Val Jansante 25.00 18.00
❑ 19 Joe Geri 25.00 18.00
❑ 20 Jerry Nuzum 25.00 18.00

❑ 21 Elmer Bud Angsman 25.00 18.00
❑ 22 Billy Dewell 25.00 18.00
❑ 23 Steve Van Buren 90.00 50.00
❑ 24 Cliff Patton 25.00 18.00
❑ 25 Bosh Pritchard 25.00 18.00
❑ 26 Johnny Lujack 80.00 50.00
❑ 27 Sid Luckman 125.00 75.00
❑ 28 Bulldog Turner 60.00 35.00
❑ 29 Bill Dudley 60.00 35.00
❑ 30 Hugh Taylor 30.00 20.00
❑ 31 George Thomas 25.00 18.00
❑ 32 Ray Poole 25.00 18.00
❑ 33 Travis Tidwell 25.00 18.00
❑ 34 Gail Bruce 25.00 18.00
❑ 35 Joe Perry RC 200.00 125.00
❑ 36 Frankie Albert RC 40.00 25.00
❑ 37 Bobby Layne 200.00 125.00
❑ 38 Leon Hart 40.00 25.00
❑ 39 B.Hoernschemeyer RC 30.00 20.00
❑ 40 Dick Barwegan RC 25.00 18.00
❑ 41 Adrian Burk RC 30.00 20.00
❑ 42 Barry French 25.00 18.00
❑ 43 Marion Motley RC 250.00 150.00
❑ 44 Jim Martin 30.00 20.00
❑ 45 Otto Graham RC 450.00 300.00
❑ 46 Al Baldwin 25.00 18.00
❑ 47 Larry Coutre 30.00 20.00
❑ 48 John Rauch 25.00 18.00
❑ 49 Sam Tamburo 25.00 18.00
❑ 50 Mike Swistowicz 25.00 18.00
❑ 51 Tom Fears RC 150.00 90.00
❑ 52 Elroy Hirsch RC 225.00 125.00
❑ 53 Dick Huffman 25.00 18.00
❑ 54 Bob Gage 25.00 18.00
❑ 55 Buddy Tinsley 25.00 18.00
❑ 56 Bill Blackburn 25.00 18.00
❑ 57 John Cochran 25.00 18.00
❑ 58 Bill Fischer 25.00 18.00
❑ 59 Whitey Wistert 30.00 20.00
❑ 60 Clyde Scott 25.00 18.00
❑ 61 Walter Barnes 25.00 18.00
❑ 62 Bob Perina 25.00 18.00
❑ 63 Bill Wightkin 25.00 18.00
❑ 64 Bob Goode 25.00 18.00
❑ 65 Al Demao 25.00 18.00
❑ 66 Harry Gilmer 30.00 20.00
❑ 67 Bill Austin 25.00 18.00
❑ 68 Joe Scott 25.00 18.00
❑ 69 Tex Coulter 30.00 20.00
❑ 70 Paul Salata 25.00 18.00
❑ 71 Emil Sitko RC 30.00 20.00
❑ 72 Bill Johnson C 25.00 18.00
❑ 73 Don Doll RC 25.00 18.00
❑ 74 Dan Sandifer 25.00 18.00
❑ 75 John Panelli 25.00 18.00
❑ 76 Bill Leonard 25.00 18.00
❑ 77 Bob Kelly 25.00 18.00
❑ 78 Dante Lavelli RC 175.00 100.00
❑ 79 Tony Adamle 30.00 20.00
❑ 80 Dick Wildung 25.00 18.00
❑ 81 Tobin Rote RC 50.00 30.00
❑ 82 Paul Burris 25.00 18.00
❑ 83 Lowell Tew 25.00 18.00
❑ 84 Barney Poole 25.00 18.00
❑ 85 Fred Naumetz 25.00 18.00
❑ 86 Dick Hoerner 25.00 18.00
❑ 87 Bob Reinhard 25.00 18.00
❑ 88 Howard Hartley RC 25.00 18.00
❑ 89 Darrell Hogan RC 25.00 18.00
❑ 90 Jerry Shipkey 25.00 18.00
❑ 91 Frank Tripucka 30.00 20.00
❑ 92 Buster Ramsey RC 25.00 18.00
❑ 93 Pat Harder 30.00 20.00
❑ 94 Vic Sears 25.00 18.00
❑ 95 Tommy Thompson QB 30.00 20.00
❑ 96 Bucko Kilroy 30.00 20.00
❑ 97 George Connor 50.00 30.00
❑ 98 Fred Morrison 25.00 18.00
❑ 99 Rookie 25.00 18.00
❑ 100 Sammy Baugh 250.00 150.00
❑ 101 Harry Ulinski 25.00 18.00
❑ 102 Frank Spaniel 25.00 18.00
❑ 103 Charley Conerly 90.00 50.00
❑ 104 Dick Hensley 25.00 18.00
❑ 105 Eddie Price 25.00 18.00
❑ 106 Ed Carr 25.00 18.00
❑ 107 Leo Nomellini 75.00 45.00
❑ 108 Verl Lillywhite 25.00 18.00
❑ 109 Wallace Triplett 25.00 18.00
❑ 110 Joe Watson 25.00 18.00
❑ 111 Cloyce Box RC 30.00 20.00
❑ 112 Billy Stone 25.00 18.00
❑ 113 Earl Murray 25.00 18.00
❑ 114 Chet Mutryn RC 30.00 20.00
❑ 115 Ken Carpenter 30.00 20.00
❑ 116 Lou Rymkus RC 30.00 20.00
❑ 117 Dub Jones RC 30.00 20.00
❑ 118 Clayton Tonnemaker 25.00 18.00
❑ 119 Walt Schlinkman 25.00 18.00
❑ 120 Billy Grimes 25.00 18.00
❑ 121 George Ratterman RC 30.00 20.00
❑ 122 Bob Mann 25.00 18.00
❑ 123 Buddy Young RC 50.00 30.00
❑ 124 Jack Zilly 25.00 18.00
❑ 125 Tom Kalmanir 25.00 18.00
❑ 126 Frank Sinkovitz 25.00 18.00
❑ 127 Elbert Nickel 30.00 20.00
❑ 128 Jim Finks RC 75.00 40.00
❑ 129 Charley Trippi 60.00 35.00
❑ 130 Tom Wham 25.00 18.00
❑ 131 Ventan Yablonski 25.00 18.00
❑ 132 Chuck Bednarik 125.00 75.00
❑ 133 Joe Muha 25.00 18.00
❑ 134 Pete Pihos 80.00 45.00
❑ 135 Washington Serini 25.00 18.00
❑ 136 George Gulyanics 25.00 18.00
❑ 137 Ken Kavanaugh 30.00 20.00
❑ 138 Howie Livingston 25.00 18.00
❑ 139 Joe Tereshinski 25.00 18.00
❑ 140 Jim White 25.00 18.00
❑ 141 Gene Roberts 25.00 18.00
❑ 142 Bill Swiacki 30.00 20.00
❑ 143 Norm Standlee 25.00 18.00
❑ 144 Knox Ramsey RC ! 100.00 50.00

1951 Bowman

❑ COMPLETE SET (144) 3500.00 2500.00
❑ WRAPPER (1-CENT) 250.00 150.00
❑ WRAPPER (5-CENT) 300.00 175.00
❑ 1 Weldon Humble RC ! 80.00 50.00
❑ 2 Otto Graham 250.00 150.00
❑ 3 Mac Speedie 35.00 20.00
❑ 4 Norm Van Brocklin RC 300.00 200.00
❑ 5 Woodley Lewis RC 25.00 15.00
❑ 6 Tom Fears 50.00 30.00
❑ 7 George Musacco 20.00 12.00
❑ 8 George Taliaferro 25.00 15.00
❑ 9 Barney Poole 20.00 12.00
❑ 10 Steve Van Buren 60.00 35.00
❑ 11 Whitey Wistert 25.00 15.00
❑ 12 Chuck Bednarik 80.00 50.00
❑ 13 Bulldog Turner 50.00 30.00
❑ 14 Bob Williams 20.00 12.00
❑ 15 Johnny Lujack 60.00 35.00
❑ 16 Roy Rebel Steiner 20.00 12.00
❑ 17 Jug Girard 25.00 15.00
❑ 18 Bill Neal 20.00 12.00
❑ 19 Travis Tidwell 20.00 12.00
❑ 20 Tom Landry RC 500.00 350.00
❑ 21 Arnie Weinmeister RC 60.00 35.00
❑ 22 Joe Geri 20.00 12.00
❑ 23 Bill Walsh C RC 30.00 15.00
❑ 24 Fran Rogel 20.00 12.00
❑ 25 Doak Walker 60.00 35.00
❑ 26 Leon Hart 35.00 20.00
❑ 27 Thurman McGraw 20.00 12.00
❑ 28 Buster Ramsey 20.00 12.00
❑ 29 Frank Tripucka 35.00 20.00
❑ 30 Don Paul DB 20.00 12.00
❑ 31 Alex Loyd 20.00 12.00
❑ 32 Y.A.Tittle 135.00 75.00
❑ 33 Verl Lillywhite 20.00 12.00
❑ 34 Sammy Baugh 175.00 110.00
❑ 35 Chuck Drazenovich 20.00 12.00
❑ 36 Bob Goode 20.00 12.00
❑ 37 Horace Gillom RC 25.00 15.00
❑ 38 Lou Rymkus 25.00 15.00
❑ 39 Ken Carpenter 20.00 12.00
❑ 40 Bob Waterfield 75.00 45.00
❑ 41 Vitamin Smith RC 25.00 15.00
❑ 42 Glenn Davis 60.00 35.00
❑ 43 Dan Edwards 20.00 12.00
❑ 44 John Rauch 20.00 12.00
❑ 45 Zollie Toth 20.00 12.00
❑ 46 Pete Pihos 60.00 35.00
❑ 47 Russ Craft 20.00 12.00
❑ 48 Walter Barnes 20.00 12.00
❑ 49 Fred Morrison 20.00 12.00
❑ 50 Ray Bray 20.00 12.00
❑ 51 Ed Sprinkle RC 25.00 15.00
❑ 52 Floyd Reid 20.00 12.00
❑ 53 Billy Grimes 20.00 12.00
❑ 54 Ted Fritsch Sr. 25.00 15.00
❑ 55 Al DeRogatis 25.00 15.00
❑ 56 Charley Conerly 75.00 45.00
❑ 57 Jon Baker 20.00 12.00
❑ 58 Tom McWilliams 20.00 12.00
❑ 59 Jerry Shipkey 20.00 12.00
❑ 60 Lynn Chandnois RC 25.00 15.00
❑ 61 Don Doll 20.00 12.00
❑ 62 Lou Creekmur 50.00 30.00
❑ 63 Bob Hoernschemeyer 25.00 15.00
❑ 64 Tom Wham 20.00 12.00
❑ 65 Bill Fischer 20.00 12.00
❑ 66 Robert Nussbaumer 20.00 12.00
❑ 67 Gordy Soltau RC 20.00 12.00
❑ 68 Visco Grgich 20.00 12.00
❑ 69 John Strzykalski RC 20.00 12.00
❑ 70 Pete Stout 20.00 12.00
❑ 71 Paul Lipscomb 20.00 12.00
❑ 72 Harry Gilmer 35.00 20.00
❑ 73 Dante Lavelli 50.00 30.00
❑ 74 Dub Jones 25.00 15.00
❑ 75 Lou Groza 75.00 45.00
❑ 76 Elroy Hirsch 75.00 45.00
❑ 77 Tom Kalmanir 20.00 12.00
❑ 78 Jack Zilly 20.00 12.00
❑ 79 Bruce Alford 20.00 12.00
❑ 80 Art Weiner 20.00 12.00
❑ 81 Brad Ecklund 20.00 12.00
❑ 82 Bosh Pritchard 20.00 12.00
❑ 83 John Green 20.00 12.00
❑ 84 Ebert Van Buren 20.00 12.00
❑ 85 Julie Rykovich 20.00 12.00
❑ 86 Fred Davis 20.00 12.00
❑ 87 John Hoffman RC 20.00 12.00
❑ 88 Tobin Rote 25.00 15.00
❑ 89 Paul Burris 20.00 12.00
❑ 90 Tony Canadeo 50.00 30.00
❑ 91 Emlen Tunnell RC 100.00 60.00
❑ 92 Otto Schnellbacher RC 20.00 12.00
❑ 93 Ray Poole 20.00 12.00
❑ 94 Darrell Hogan 20.00 12.00
❑ 95 Frank Sinkovitz 20.00 12.00
❑ 96 Ernie Stautner 75.00 45.00
❑ 97 Elmer Bud Angsman 20.00 12.00
❑ 98 Jack Jennings 20.00 12.00
❑ 99 Jerry Groom 20.00 12.00
❑ 100 John Prchlik 20.00 12.00
❑ 101 J. Robert Smith 20.00 12.00
❑ 102 Bobby Layne 135.00 75.00
❑ 103 Frankie Albert 35.00 20.00
❑ 104 Gail Bruce 20.00 12.00
❑ 105 Joe Perry 75.00 45.00
❑ 106 Leon Heath 20.00 12.00
❑ 107 Ed Quirk 20.00 12.00
❑ 108 Hugh Taylor 25.00 15.00
❑ 109 Marion Motley 100.00 60.00
❑ 110 Tony Adamle 20.00 12.00
❑ 111 Alex Agase 25.00 15.00
❑ 112 Tank Younger 35.00 20.00
❑ 113 Bob Boyd 20.00 12.00
❑ 114 Jerry Williams 20.00 12.00
❑ 115 Joe Golding 20.00 12.00
❑ 116 Sherman Howard 20.00 12.00
❑ 117 John Wozniak 20.00 12.00
❑ 118 Frank Reagan 20.00 12.00
❑ 119 Vic Sears 20.00 12.00
❑ 120 Clyde Scott 20.00 12.00
❑ 121 George Gulyanics 20.00 12.00

- ❑ 122 Bill Wightkin 20.00 12.00
- ❑ 123 Chuck Hunsinger 20.00 12.00
- ❑ 124 Jack Cloud 20.00 12.00
- ❑ 125 Abner Wimberly 20.00 12.00
- ❑ 126 Dick Wildung 20.00 12.00
- ❑ 127 Eddie Price 20.00 12.00
- ❑ 128 Joe Scott 20.00 12.00
- ❑ 129 Jerry Nuzum 20.00 12.00
- ❑ 130 Jim Finks 35.00 20.00
- ❑ 131 Bob Gage 20.00 12.00
- ❑ 132 Bill Swiackl 25.00 15.00
- ❑ 133 Joe Watson 20.00 12.00
- ❑ 134 Ollie Cline 20.00 12.00
- ❑ 135 Jack Lininger 20.00 12.00
- ❑ 136 Fran Polsfoot 20.00 12.00
- ❑ 137 Charley Trippi 50.00 30.00
- ❑ 138 Ventan Yablonski 20.00 12.00
- ❑ 139 Emil Sitko 20.00 12.00
- ❑ 140 Leo Nomellini 60.00 30.00
- ❑ 141 Norm Standlee 20.00 12.00
- ❑ 142 Eddie Saenz 20.00 12.00
- ❑ 143 Al Demao 20.00 12.00
- ❑ 144 Bill Dudley ! 150.00 75.00
- ❑ NNO Johnny Lujack Proof 300.00 175.00
- ❑ NNO Bob Gage Proof 125.00 75.00
- ❑ NNO Darrell Hogan Proof 125.00 75.00

1952 Bowman Large

- ❑ COMPLETE SET (144) 12500.00 9500.00
- ❑ COMMON CARD (1-72) 35.00 20.00
- ❑ COMMON CARD (73-144) 40.00 25.00
- ❑ WRAPPER (5-CENT) 60.00 30.00
- ❑ 1 Norm Van Brocklin SP ! 500.00 350.00
- ❑ 2 Otto Graham 300.00 200.00
- ❑ 3 Doak Walker 100.00 60.00
- ❑ 4 Steve Owen RC CO 80.00 50.00
- ❑ 5 Frankie Albert 50.00 30.00
- ❑ 6 Laurie Niemi 35.00 20.00
- ❑ 7 Chuck Hunsinger 35.00 20.00
- ❑ 8 Ed Modzelewski 50.00 30.00
- ❑ 9 Joe Spencer SP 75.00 40.00
- ❑ 10 Chuck Bednarik SP 300.00 200.00
- ❑ 11 Barney Poole 35.00 20.00
- ❑ 12 Charley Trippi 75.00 40.00
- ❑ 13 Tom Fears 75.00 40.00
- ❑ 14 Paul Brown RC CO 250.00 150.00
- ❑ 15 Leon Hart 50.00 30.00
- ❑ 16 Frank Gifford RC 500.00 350.00
- ❑ 17 Y.A.Tittle 300.00 200.00
- ❑ 18 Charlie Justice SP 175.00 100.00
- ❑ 19 George Connor SP 175.00 100.00
- ❑ 20 Lynn Chandnois 35.00 20.00
- ❑ 21 Billy Howton RC 50.00 30.00
- ❑ 22 Kenneth Snyder 35.00 20.00
- ❑ 23 Gino Marchetti RC 250.00 150.00
- ❑ 24 John Karras 35.00 20.00
- ❑ 25 Tank Younger 50.00 30.00
- ❑ 26 Tommy Thompson LB 35.00 20.00
- ❑ 27 Bob Miller SP RC! 300.00 200.00
- ❑ 28 Kyle Rote RC SP 175.00 100.00
- ❑ 29 Hugh McElhenny RC 250.00 150.00
- ❑ 30 Sammy Baugh 350.00 225.00
- ❑ 31 Jim Dooley RC 45.00 25.00
- ❑ 32 Ray Mathews 35.00 20.00
- ❑ 33 Fred Cone 35.00 20.00
- ❑ 34 Al Pollard 35.00 20.00
- ❑ 35 Brad Ecklund 35.00 20.00
- ❑ 36 John Hancock RC SP! 350.00 225.00
- ❑ 37 Elroy Hirsch SP 200.00 125.00
- ❑ 38 Keever Jankovich 35.00 20.00
- ❑ 39 Emlen Tunnell 125.00 75.00
- ❑ 40 Steve Dowden 35.00 20.00
- ❑ 41 Claude Hipps 35.00 20.00
- ❑ 42 Norm Standlee 35.00 20.00
- ❑ 43 Dick Todd CO 35.00 20.00
- ❑ 44 Babe Parilli 50.00 30.00
- ❑ 45 Steve Van Buren SP 300.00 200.00
- ❑ 46 Art Donovan RC SP 350.00 250.00
- ❑ 47 Bill Fischer 35.00 20.00
- ❑ 48 George Halas RC CO 275.00 160.00
- ❑ 49 Jerrell Price 35.00 20.00
- ❑ 50 John Sandusky RC 35.00 20.00
- ❑ 51 Ray Beck 35.00 20.00
- ❑ 52 Jim Martin 45.00 25.00
- ❑ 53 Joe Bach CO UER 35.00 20.00
- ❑ 54 Glen Christian SP 75.00 40.00
- ❑ 55 Andy Davis SP 75.00 40.00
- ❑ 56 Tobin Rote 45.00 25.00
- ❑ 57 Wayne Millner RC CO 90.00 50.00
- ❑ 58 Zollie Toth 35.00 20.00
- ❑ 59 Jack Jennings 35.00 20.00
- ❑ 60 Bill McColl 35.00 20.00
- ❑ 61 Les Richter RC 45.00 25.00
- ❑ 62 Walt Michaels RC 45.00 25.00
- ❑ 63 Charley Conerly SP 700.00 400.00
- ❑ 64 Howard Hartley SP 75.00 40.00
- ❑ 65 Jerome Smith 35.00 20.00
- ❑ 66 James Clark 35.00 20.00
- ❑ 67 Dick Logan 35.00 20.00
- ❑ 68 Wayne Robinson 35.00 20.00
- ❑ 69 James Hammond 35.00 20.00
- ❑ 70 Gene Schroeder 35.00 20.00
- ❑ 71 Tex Coulter 45.00 25.00
- ❑ 72 John Schweder RC SP! 600.00 400.00
- ❑ 73 Vitamin Smith SP 150.00 90.00
- ❑ 74 Joe Campanella RC 40.00 25.00
- ❑ 75 Joe Kuharich RC CO 50.00 30.00
- ❑ 76 Herman Clark 40.00 25.00
- ❑ 77 Dan Edwards 40.00 25.00
- ❑ 78 Bobby Layne 300.00 175.00
- ❑ 79 Bob Hoernschemeyer 50.00 30.00
- ❑ 80 John Carr Blount 40.00 25.00
- ❑ 81 John Kastan RC SP 150.00 90.00
- ❑ 82 Harry Minarik RC SP 150.00 90.00
- ❑ 83 Joe Perry 125.00 75.00
- ❑ 84 Buddy Parker RC CO 50.00 30.00
- ❑ 85 Andy Robustelli RC 200.00 125.00
- ❑ 86 Dub Jones 50.00 30.00
- ❑ 87 Mal Cook 40.00 25.00
- ❑ 88 Billy Stone 40.00 25.00
- ❑ 89 George Taliaferro 50.00 30.00
- ❑ 90 Thomas Johnson RC SP 150.00 90.00
- ❑ 91 Leon Heath SP 100.00 60.00
- ❑ 92 Pete Pihos 100.00 60.00
- ❑ 93 Fred Benners 40.00 25.00
- ❑ 94 George Tarasovic 40.00 25.00
- ❑ 95 Buck Shaw RC CO 40.00 25.00
- ❑ 96 Bill Wightkin 40.00 25.00
- ❑ 97 John Wozniak 40.00 25.00
- ❑ 98 Bobby Dillon RC 50.00 30.00
- ❑ 99 Joe Stydahar RC SP CO! 650.00 450.00
- ❑ 100 Dick Alban RC SP 150.00 90.00
- ❑ 101 Arnie Weinmeister 60.00 35.00
- ❑ 102 Bobby Cross 40.00 25.00
- ❑ 103 Don Paul DB 40.00 25.00
- ❑ 104 Buddy Young 60.00 35.00
- ❑ 105 Lou Groza 125.00 75.00
- ❑ 106 Ray Pelfrey 40.00 25.00
- ❑ 107 Maurice Nipp 40.00 25.00
- ❑ 108 Hubert Johnston RC SP! 650.00 450.00
- ❑ 109 Vol.Quinlan RC SP 100.00 60.00
- ❑ 110 Jack Simmons 40.00 25.00
- ❑ 111 George Ratterman 50.00 30.00
- ❑ 112 John Badaczewski 40.00 25.00
- ❑ 113 Bill Reichardt 40.00 25.00
- ❑ 114 Art Weiner 40.00 25.00
- ❑ 115 Keith Flowers 40.00 25.00
- ❑ 116 Russ Craft 40.00 25.00
- ❑ 117 J.O'Donahue RC SP 150.00 90.00
- ❑ 118 Darrell Hogan SP 100.00 60.00
- ❑ 119 Frank Ziegler 40.00 25.00
- ❑ 120 Dan Towler 60.00 35.00
- ❑ 121 Fred Williams 40.00 25.00
- ❑ 122 Jimmy Phelan CO 40.00 25.00
- ❑ 123 Eddie Price 40.00 25.00
- ❑ 124 Chet Ostrowski 40.00 25.00
- ❑ 125 Leo Nomellini 100.00 60.00
- ❑ 126 S.Romanik RC SP! 300.00 200.00
- ❑ 127 Ollie Matson RC SP 300.00 200.00
- ❑ 128 Dante Lavelli 90.00 50.00
- ❑ 129 Jack Christiansen RC 175.00 100.00
- ❑ 130 Dom Moselle 40.00 25.00
- ❑ 131 John Rapacz 40.00 25.00
- ❑ 132 Chuck Ortmann UER 40.00 25.00
- ❑ 133 Bob Williams 40.00 25.00
- ❑ 134 Chuck Ulrich 40.00 25.00
- ❑ 135 Gene Ronzani CO SP RC! 650.00 450.00
- ❑ 136 Bert Rechichar SP 100.00 60.00
- ❑ 137 Bob Waterfield 125.00 75.00
- ❑ 138 Bobby Walston RC 50.00 30.00
- ❑ 139 Jerry Shipkey 40.00 25.00
- ❑ 140 Yale Lary RC 175.00 100.00
- ❑ 141 Gordy Soltau 40.00 25.00
- ❑ 142 Tom Landry 600.00 450.00
- ❑ 143 John Papit 40.00 25.00
- ❑ 144 [illegible]

1952 Bowman Small

- ❑ COMPLETE SET (144) 5000.00 3500.00
- ❑ COMMON CARD (1-72) 25.00 15.00
- ❑ COMMON CARD (73-144) 30.00 18.00
- ❑ WRAPPER (1-CENT) 60.00 40.00
- ❑ 1 Norm Van Brocklin ! 350.00 200.00
- ❑ 2 Otto Graham 200.00 125.00
- ❑ 3 Doak Walker 60.00 35.00
- ❑ 4 Steve Owen RC CO 60.00 35.00
- ❑ 5 Frankie Albert 35.00 20.00
- ❑ 6 Laurie Niemi 25.00 15.00
- ❑ 7 Chuck Hunsinger 25.00 15.00
- ❑ 8 Ed Modzelewski 35.00 20.00
- ❑ 9 Joe Spencer 25.00 15.00
- ❑ 10 Chuck Bednarik 75.00 45.00
- ❑ 11 Barney Poole 25.00 15.00
- ❑ 12 Charley Trippi 60.00 35.00
- ❑ 13 Tom Fears 60.00 35.00
- ❑ 14 Paul Brown RC CO 150.00 90.00
- ❑ 15 Leon Hart 35.00 20.00
- ❑ 16 Frank Gifford RC 400.00 200.00
- ❑ 17 Y.A.Tittle 125.00 75.00
- ❑ 18 Charlie Justice 45.00 30.00
- ❑ 19 George Connor 35.00 20.00
- ❑ 20 Lynn Chandnois 25.00 15.00
- ❑ 21 Billy Howton RC 40.00 25.00
- ❑ 22 Kenneth Snyder 25.00 15.00
- ❑ 23 Gino Marchetti RC 125.00 75.00
- ❑ 24 John Karras 25.00 15.00
- ❑ 25 Tank Younger 35.00 20.00
- ❑ 26 Tommy Thompson LB 25.00 15.00
- ❑ 27 Bob Miller RC 25.00 15.00
- ❑ 28 Kyle Rote RC 50.00 30.00
- ❑ 29 Hugh McElhenny RC 175.00 100.00
- ❑ 30 Sammy Baugh 250.00 150.00
- ❑ 31 Jim Dooley RC 30.00 18.00
- ❑ 32 Ray Mathews 25.00 15.00
- ❑ 33 Fred Cone 25.00 15.00
- ❑ 34 Al Pollard 25.00 15.00
- ❑ 35 Brad Ecklund 25.00 15.00
- ❑ 36 John Lee Hancock 25.00 15.00
- ❑ 37 Elroy Hirsch 60.00 35.00
- ❑ 38 Keever Jankovich 25.00 15.00
- ❑ 39 Emlen Tunnell 50.00 30.00
- ❑ 40 Steve Dowden 25.00 15.00
- ❑ 41 Claude Hipps 25.00 15.00
- ❑ 42 Norm Standlee 25.00 15.00
- ❑ 43 Dick Todd CO 25.00 15.00
- ❑ 44 Babe Parilli 35.00 20.00
- ❑ 45 Steve Van Buren 75.00 40.00
- ❑ 46 Art Donovan RC 200.00 125.00
- ❑ 47 Bill Fischer 25.00 15.00
- ❑ 48 George Halas RC CO 250.00 150.00
- ❑ 49 Jerrell Price 25.00 15.00
- ❑ 50 John Sandusky RC 25.00 15.00
- ❑ 51 Ray Beck 25.00 15.00

- ❑ 52 Jim Martin 30.00 18.00
- ❑ 53 Joe Bach CO UER 25.00 15.00
- ❑ 54 Glen Christian 25.00 15.00
- ❑ 55 Andy Davis 25.00 15.00
- ❑ 56 Tobin Rote 30.00 18.00
- ❑ 57 Wayne Millner RC CO 50.00 30.00
- ❑ 58 Zollie Toth 25.00 15.00
- ❑ 59 Jack Jennings 25.00 15.00
- ❑ 60 Bill McColl 25.00 15.00
- ❑ 61 Les Richter RC 30.00 18.00
- ❑ 62 Walt Michaels RC 30.00 18.00
- ❑ 63 Charley Conerly 75.00 40.00
- ❑ 64 Howard Hartley 25.00 15.00
- ❑ 65 Jerome Smith 25.00 15.00
- ❑ 66 James Clark 25.00 15.00
- ❑ 67 Dick Logan 25.00 15.00
- ❑ 68 Wayne Robinson 25.00 15.00
- ❑ 69 James Hammond 25.00 15.00
- ❑ 70 Gene Schroeder 25.00 15.00
- ❑ 71 Tex Coulter 30.00 18.00
- ❑ 72 John Schweder 25.00 15.00
- ❑ 73 Vitamin Smith 35.00 20.00
- ❑ 74 Joe Campanella RC 30.00 18.00
- ❑ 75 Joe Kuharich RC CO 35.00 20.00
- ❑ 76 Herman Clark 30.00 18.00
- ❑ 77 Dan Edwards 30.00 18.00
- ❑ 78 Bobby Layne 150.00 90.00
- ❑ 79 Bob Hoernschemeyer 35.00 20.00
- ❑ 80 John Carr Blount 30.00 18.00
- ❑ 81 John Kastan RC 30.00 18.00
- ❑ 82 Harry Minarik 30.00 18.00
- ❑ 83 Joe Perry 75.00 40.00
- ❑ 84 Buddy Parker RC CO 35.00 20.00
- ❑ 85 Andy Robustelli RC 125.00 75.00
- ❑ 86 Dub Jones 35.00 20.00
- ❑ 87 Mal Cook 30.00 18.00
- ❑ 88 Billy Stone 30.00 18.00
- ❑ 89 George Taliaferro 35.00 20.00
- ❑ 90 Thomas Johnson RC 30.00 18.00
- ❑ 91 Leon Heath 30.00 18.00
- ❑ 92 Pete Pihos 50.00 35.00
- ❑ 93 Fred Benners 30.00 18.00
- ❑ 94 George Tarasovic 30.00 18.00
- ❑ 95 Buck Shaw RC CO 30.00 18.00
- ❑ 96 Bill Wightkin 30.00 18.00
- ❑ 97 John Wozniak 30.00 18.00
- ❑ 98 Bobby Dillon RC 35.00 20.00
- ❑ 99 Joe Stydahar RC CO 45.00 30.00
- ❑ 100 Dick Alban RC 30.00 18.00
- ❑ 101 Arnie Weinmeister 40.00 25.00
- ❑ 102 Bobby Cross 30.00 18.00
- ❑ 103 Don Paul DB 30.00 18.00
- ❑ 104 Buddy Young 40.00 25.00
- ❑ 105 Lou Groza 75.00 45.00
- ❑ 106 Ray Pelfrey 30.00 18.00
- ❑ 107 Maurice Nipp 30.00 18.00
- ❑ 108 Hubert Johnston 30.00 18.00
- ❑ 109 Volney Quinlan RC 30.00 18.00
- ❑ 110 Jack Simmons 30.00 18.00
- ❑ 111 George Ratterman 35.00 20.00
- ❑ 112 John Badaczewski 30.00 18.00
- ❑ 113 Bill Reichardt 30.00 18.00
- ❑ 114 Art Weiner 30.00 18.00
- ❑ 115 Keith Flowers 30.00 18.00
- ❑ 116 Russ Craft 30.00 18.00
- ❑ 117 Jim O'Donahue RC 30.00 18.00
- ❑ 118 Darrell Hogan 30.00 18.00
- ❑ 119 Frank Ziegler 30.00 18.00
- ❑ 120 Dan Towler 40.00 25.00
- ❑ 121 Fred Williams 30.00 18.00
- ❑ 122 Jimmy Phelan CO 30.00 18.00
- ❑ 123 Eddie Price 30.00 18.00
- ❑ 124 Chet Ostrowski 30.00 18.00
- ❑ 125 Leo Nomellini 75.00 40.00
- ❑ 126 Steve Romanik 30.00 18.00
- ❑ 127 Ollie Matson RC 125.00 75.00
- ❑ 128 Dante Lavelli 60.00 35.00
- ❑ 129 Jack Christiansen RC 80.00 50.00
- ❑ 130 Dom Moselle 30.00 18.00
- ❑ 131 John Rapacz 30.00 18.00
- ❑ 132 Chuck Ortmann UER 30.00 18.00
- ❑ 133 Bob Williams 30.00 18.00
- ❑ 134 Chuck Ulrich 30.00 18.00
- ❑ 135 Gene Ronzani RC CO 30.00 18.00
- ❑ 136 Bert Rechichar 35.00 20.00
- ❑ 137 Bob Waterfield 75.00 45.00
- ❑ 138 Bobby Walston RC 35.00 20.00
- ❑ 139 Jerry Shipkey 30.00 18.00
- ❑ 140 Yale Lary RC 80.00 50.00
- ❑ 141 Gordy Soltau 30.00 18.00
- ❑ 142 Tom Landry 400.00 250.00
- ❑ 143 John Papit 30.00 18.00
- ❑ 144 Jim Lansford RC ! 175.00 100.00

1953 Bowman

- ❑ COMPLETE SET (96) 3400.00 2200.00
- ❑ WRAPPER (5-CENT) 150.00 90.00
- ❑ 1 Eddie LeBaron RC ! 125.00 75.00
- ❑ 2 John Dottley 30.00 18.00
- ❑ 3 Babe Parilli 35.00 20.00
- ❑ 4 Bucko Kilroy 35.00 20.00
- ❑ 5 Joe Tereshinski 30.00 18.00
- ❑ 6 Doak Walker 75.00 45.00
- ❑ 7 Fran Polsfoot 30.00 18.00
- ❑ 8 Sisto Averno 30.00 18.00
- ❑ 9 Marion Motley 75.00 45.00
- ❑ 10 Pat Brady 30.00 18.00
- ❑ 11 Norm Van Brocklin 125.00 75.00
- ❑ 12 Bill McColl 30.00 18.00
- ❑ 13 Jerry Groom 30.00 18.00
- ❑ 14 Al Pollard 30.00 18.00
- ❑ 15 Dante Lavelli 50.00 30.00
- ❑ 16 Eddie Price 30.00 18.00
- ❑ 17 Charley Trippi 50.00 30.00
- ❑ 18 Elbert Nickel 35.00 20.00
- ❑ 19 George Taliaferro 35.00 20.00
- ❑ 20 Charley Conerly 80.00 50.00
- ❑ 21 Bobby Layne 125.00 75.00
- ❑ 22 Elroy Hirsch 100.00 60.00
- ❑ 23 Jim Finks 40.00 25.00
- ❑ 24 Chuck Bednarik 75.00 45.00
- ❑ 25 Kyle Rote 40.00 25.00
- ❑ 26 Otto Graham 175.00 100.00
- ❑ 27 Harry Gilmer 35.00 20.00
- ❑ 28 Tobin Rote 35.00 20.00
- ❑ 29 Billy Stone 30.00 18.00
- ❑ 30 Buddy Young 40.00 25.00
- ❑ 31 Leon Hart 40.00 25.00
- ❑ 32 Hugh McElhenny 75.00 45.00
- ❑ 33 Dale Samuels 30.00 18.00
- ❑ 34 Lou Creekmur 50.00 30.00
- ❑ 35 Tom Catlin 30.00 18.00
- ❑ 36 Tom Fears 60.00 35.00
- ❑ 37 George Connor 40.00 25.00
- ❑ 38 Bill Walsh C 30.00 18.00
- ❑ 39 Leo Sanford SP 45.00 30.00
- ❑ 40 Horace Gillom 35.00 20.00
- ❑ 41 John Schweder SP 45.00 30.00
- ❑ 42 Tom O'Connell 30.00 18.00
- ❑ 43 Frank Gifford SP 300.00 175.00
- ❑ 44 Frank Continetti SP 45.00 30.00
- ❑ 45 John Olszewski SP 45.00 30.00
- ❑ 46 Dub Jones 35.00 20.00
- ❑ 47 Don Paul LB SP 45.00 30.00
- ❑ 48 Gerald Weatherly 30.00 18.00
- ❑ 49 Fred Bruney SP 45.00 30.00
- ❑ 50 Jack Scarbath 30.00 18.00
- ❑ 51 John Karras 30.00 18.00
- ❑ 52 Al Conway 30.00 18.00
- ❑ 53 Emlen Tunnell SP 125.00 75.00
- ❑ 54 Gern Nagler SP 45.00 30.00
- ❑ 55 Kenneth Snyder SP 45.00 30.00
- ❑ 56 Y.A.Tittle 150.00 90.00
- ❑ 57 John Rapacz SP 45.00 30.00
- ❑ 58 Harley Sewell SP 45.00 30.00
- ❑ 59 Don Bingham 30.00 18.00
- ❑ 60 Darrell Hogan 30.00 18.00
- ❑ 61 Tony Curcillo 30.00 18.00
- ❑ 62 Ray Renfro RC SP 50.00 30.00
- ❑ 63 Leon Heath 30.00 18.00
- ❑ 64 Tex Coulter SP 45.00 30.00
- ❑ 65 Dewayne Douglas 30.00 18.00
- ❑ 66 J. Robert Smith SP 45.00 30.00
- ❑ 67 Bob McChesney SP 45.00 30.00
- ❑ 68 Dick Alban SP 45.00 30.00
- ❑ 69 Andy Kozar 30.00 18.00
- ❑ 70 Merwin Hodel SP 45.00 30.00
- ❑ 71 Thurman McGraw 30.00 18.00
- ❑ 72 Cliff Anderson 30.00 18.00
- ❑ 73 Pete Pihos 60.00 35.00
- ❑ 74 Julie Rykovich 30.00 18.00
- ❑ 75 John Kreamcheck SP 45.00 30.00
- ❑ 76 Lynn Chandnois 30.00 18.00
- ❑ 77 Cloyce Box SP 45.00 30.00
- ❑ 78 Ray Mathews 30.00 18.00
- ❑ 79 Bobby Walston 35.00 20.00
- ❑ 80 Jim Dooley 30.00 18.00
- ❑ 81 Pat Harder SP 45.00 30.00
- ❑ 82 Jerry Shipkey 30.00 18.00
- ❑ 83 Bobby Thomason RC 30.00 18.00
- ❑ 84 Hugh Taylor 35.00 20.00
- ❑ 85 George Ratterman 35.00 20.00
- ❑ 86 Don Stonesifer 30.00 18.00
- ❑ 87 John Williams SP RC 45.00 30.00
- ❑ 88 Leo Nomellini 50.00 30.00
- ❑ 89 Frank Ziegler 30.00 18.00
- ❑ 90 Don Paul DB UER 30.00 18.00
- ❑ 91 Tom Dublinski 30.00 18.00
- ❑ 92 Ken Carpenter 30.00 18.00
- ❑ 93 Ted Marchibroda RC 40.00 25.00
- ❑ 94 Chuck Drazenovich 30.00 18.00
- ❑ 95 Lou Groza SP 125.00 75.00
- ❑ 96 William Cross RC SP ! 100.00 50.00

1954 Bowman

- ❑ COMPLETE SET (128) 1800.00 1200.00
- ❑ COMMON CARD (1-64) 5.00 3.00
- ❑ COMMON SP (65-96) 25.00 15.00
- ❑ COMMON CARD (97-128) 5.00 3.00
- ❑ WRAPPER (1-CENT) 15.00 10.00
- ❑ WRAPPER (5-CENT) 30.00 25.00
- ❑ 1 Ray Mathews ! 30.00 15.00
- ❑ 2 John Huzvar 5.00 3.00
- ❑ 3 Jack Scarbath 5.00 3.00
- ❑ 4 Doug Atkins RC 50.00 30.00
- ❑ 5 Bill Stits 5.00 3.00
- ❑ 6 Joe Perry 30.00 18.00
- ❑ 7 Kyle Rote 15.00 7.50
- ❑ 8 Norm Van Brocklin 50.00 25.00
- ❑ 9 Pete Pihos 20.00 12.00
- ❑ 10 Babe Parilli 8.00 4.00
- ❑ 11 Zeke Bratkowski RC 25.00 15.00
- ❑ 12 Ollie Matson 25.00 15.00
- ❑ 13 Pat Brady 5.00 3.00
- ❑ 14 Fred Enke 5.00 3.00
- ❑ 15 Harry Ulinski 5.00 3.00
- ❑ 16 Bob Garrett 5.00 3.00
- ❑ 17 Bill Bowman 5.00 3.00
- ❑ 18 Leo Rucka 5.00 3.00
- ❑ 19 John Cannady 5.00 3.00
- ❑ 20 Tom Fears 25.00 15.00
- ❑ 21 Norm Willey 5.00 3.00
- ❑ 22 Floyd Reid 5.00 3.00
- ❑ 23 George Blanda RC 175.00 100.00
- ❑ 24 Don Doheney 5.00 3.00
- ❑ 25 John Schweder 5.00 3.00
- ❑ 26 Bert Rechichar 5.00 3.00
- ❑ 27 Harry Dowda 5.00 3.00
- ❑ 28 John Sandusky 5.00 3.00
- ❑ 29 Les Bingaman RC 15.00 7.50
- ❑ 30 Joe Arenas 5.00 3.00
- ❑ 31 Ray Wietecha RC 5.00 3.00
- ❑ 32 Elroy Hirsch 30.00 18.00

❑	33 Harold Giancanelli	5.00	3.00
❑	34 Billy Howton	8.00	4.00
❑	35 Fred Morrison	5.00	3.00
❑	36 Bobby Cavazos	5.00	3.00
❑	37 Darrell Hogan	5.00	3.00
❑	38 Buddy Young	8.00	4.00
❑	39 Charlie Justice	20.00	12.00
❑	40 Otto Graham	80.00	50.00
❑	41 Doak Walker	35.00	20.00
❑	42 Y.A.Tittle	60.00	35.00
❑	43 Buford Long	5.00	3.00
❑	44 Volney Quinlan	5.00	3.00
❑	45 Bobby Thomason	5.00	3.00
❑	46 Fred Cone	5.00	3.00
❑	47 Gerald Weatherly	5.00	3.00
❑	[illegible]	[illegible]	[illegible]
❑	49A Lynn Chandnois ERR	5.00	3.00
❑	49B Lynn Chandnois COR	5.00	3.00
❑	50 George Taliaferro	5.00	3.00
❑	51 Dick Alban	5.00	3.00
❑	52 Lou Groza	35.00	20.00
❑	53 Bobby Layne	60.00	35.00
❑	54 Hugh McElhenny	40.00	20.00
❑	55 Frank Gifford	100.00	60.00
❑	56 Leon McLaughlin	5.00	3.00
❑	57 Chuck Bednarik	40.00	20.00
❑	58 Art Hunter	5.00	3.00
❑	59 Bill McColl	5.00	3.00
❑	60 Charley Trippi	25.00	15.00
❑	61 Jim Finks	15.00	7.50
❑	62 Bill Lange G	5.00	3.00
❑	63 Laurie Niemi	5.00	3.00
❑	64 Ray Renfro	8.00	4.00
❑	65 Dick Chapman	25.00	15.00
❑	66 Bob Hantla	25.00	15.00
❑	67 Ralph Starkey	25.00	15.00
❑	68 Don Paul LB	25.00	15.00
❑	69 Kenneth Snyder	25.00	15.00
❑	70 Tobin Rote SP	30.00	18.00
❑	71 Art DeCarlo	25.00	15.00
❑	72 Tom Keane SP	25.00	15.00
❑	73 Hugh Taylor SP	30.00	18.00
❑	74 Warren Lahr RC SP	25.00	15.00
❑	75 Jim Neal	25.00	15.00
❑	76 Leo Nomellini SP	60.00	35.00
❑	77 Dick Yelvington	25.00	15.00
❑	78 Les Richter SP	30.00	18.00
❑	79 Bucko Kilroy SP	30.00	18.00
❑	80 John Martinkovic	25.00	15.00
❑	81 Dale Dodrill RC SP	25.00	15.00
❑	82 Ken Jackson	25.00	15.00
❑	83 Paul Lipscomb	25.00	15.00
❑	84 John Bauer	25.00	15.00
❑	85 Lou Creekmur SP	50.00	30.00
❑	86 Eddie Price	25.00	15.00
❑	87 Kenneth Farragut	25.00	15.00
❑	88 [illegible]	[illegible]	18.00
❑	89 Don Boll	25.00	15.00
❑	90 Chet Hanulak	25.00	15.00
❑	91 Thurman McGraw	25.00	15.00
❑	92 Don Heinrich RC SP	30.00	18.00
❑	93 Dan McKown	25.00	15.00
❑	94 Bob Fleck	25.00	15.00
❑	95 Jerry Hilgenberg	25.00	15.00
❑	96 Bill Walsh C	25.00	15.00
❑	97A Tom Finnin ERR	60.00	35.00
❑	97B Tom Finnan COR	8.00	4.00
❑	98 Paul Barry	5.00	3.00
❑	99 Chick Jagade	5.00	3.00
❑	100 Jack Christiansen	20.00	12.00
❑	101 Gordy Soltau	5.00	3.00
❑	102A Emlen Tunnel ERR	20.00	12.00
❑	102B Emlen Tunnell COR	20.00	12.00
❑	102C Emlen Tunnell COR	20.00	12.00
❑	103 Stan West	5.00	3.00
❑	104 Jerry Williams	5.00	3.00
❑	105 Veryl Switzer	5.00	3.00
❑	106 Billy Stone	5.00	3.00
❑	107 Jerry Watford	5.00	3.00
❑	108 Elbert Nickel	8.00	4.00
❑	109 Ed Sharkey	5.00	3.00
❑	110 Steve Meilinger	5.00	3.00
❑	111 Dante Lavelli	20.00	12.00
❑	112 Leon Hart	15.00	7.50
❑	113 Charley Conerly	30.00	18.00
❑	114 Richard Lemmon	5.00	3.00
❑	115 Al Carmichael	5.00	3.00
❑	116 George Connor	20.00	12.00
❑	117 John Olszewski	5.00	3.00
❑	118 Ernie Stautner	25.00	15.00
❑	119 Ray Smith	5.00	3.00
❑	120 Neil Worden	5.00	3.00
❑	121 Jim Dooley	5.00	3.00
❑	122 Arnold Galiffa	5.00	3.00
❑	123 Kline Gilbert	5.00	3.00
❑	124 Bob Hoernschemeyer	8.00	4.00
❑	125 Wilford White RC	15.00	7.50
❑	126 Art Spinney	5.00	3.00
❑	127 Joe Koch	5.00	3.00
❑	128 John Lattner RC !	80.00	40.00

1955 Bowman

❑	COMPLETE SET (160)	1600.00	1000.00
❑	COMMON CARD (1-64)	5.00	3.00
❑	COMMON CARD (65-160)	8.00	5.00
❑	WRAPPER (1 CENT)	225.00	150.00
❑	WRAPPER (5-CENT)	120.00	60.00
❑	1 Doak Walker !	75.00	40.00
❑	2 Mike McCormack RC	30.00	18.00
❑	3 John Olszewski	5.00	3.00
❑	4 Dorne Dibble	5.00	3.00
❑	5 Lindon Crow	5.00	3.00
❑	6 Hugh Taylor UER	8.00	4.00
❑	7 Frank Gifford	75.00	45.00
❑	8 Alan Ameche RC	40.00	25.00
❑	9 Don Stonesifer	5.00	3.00
❑	10 Pete Pihos	15.00	7.50
❑	11 Bill Austin	5.00	3.00
❑	12 Dick Alban	5.00	3.00
❑	13 Bobby Walston	8.00	4.00
❑	14 Len Ford RC	40.00	25.00
❑	15 Jug Girard	5.00	3.00
❑	16 Charley Conerly	25.00	15.00
❑	17 Volney Peters	5.00	3.00
❑	18 Max Boydston	5.00	3.00
❑	19 Leon Hart	12.00	6.00
❑	20 Bert Rechichar	5.00	3.00
❑	21 Lee Riley	5.00	[illegible]
❑	22 Johnny Carson	5.00	3.00
❑	23 Harry Thompson	5.00	3.00
❑	24 Ray Wietecha	5.00	3.00
❑	25 Ollie Matson	25.00	15.00
❑	26 Eddie LeBaron	15.00	7.50
❑	27 Jack Simmons	5.00	3.00
❑	28 Jack Christiansen	15.00	7.50
❑	29 Bucko Kilroy	8.00	4.00
❑	30 Tom Keane	5.00	3.00
❑	31 Dave Leggett	5.00	3.00
❑	32 Norm Van Brocklin	40.00	25.00
❑	33 Harlon Hill RC	8.00	4.00
❑	34 Robert Haner	5.00	3.00
❑	35 Veryl Switzer	5.00	3.00
❑	36 Dick Stanfel RC	12.00	6.00
❑	37 Lou Groza	25.00	15.00
❑	38 Tank Younger	12.00	6.00
❑	39 Dick Flanagan	5.00	3.00
❑	40 Jim Dooley	5.00	3.00
❑	41 Ray Collins	5.00	3.00
❑	42 John Henry Johnson RC	40.00	25.00
❑	43 Tom Fears	15.00	7.50
❑	44 Joe Perry	30.00	18.00
❑	45 Gene Brito RC	5.00	3.00
❑	46 Bill Johnson C	5.00	3.00
❑	47 Dan Towler	12.00	6.00
❑	48 Dick Moegle	8.00	4.00
❑	49 Kline Gilbert	5.00	3.00
❑	50 Les Gobel	5.00	3.00
❑	51 Ray Krouse RC	5.00	3.00
❑	52 Pat Summerall RC	70.00	35.00
❑	53 Ed Brown RC	12.00	6.00
❑	54 Lynn Chandnois	5.00	3.00
❑	55 Joe Heap	5.00	3.00
❑	56 John Hoffman	5.00	3.00
❑	57 Howard Ferguson	5.00	3.00
❑	58 Bobby Watkins	5.00	3.00
❑	59 Charlie Ane RC	5.00	3.00
❑	60 Ken MacAfee E RC	8.00	4.00
❑	61 Ralph Guglielmi RC	8.00	4.00
❑	62 George Blanda	60.00	35.00
❑	63 Kenneth Snyder	5.00	3.00
❑	64 Chet Ostrowski	5.00	3.00
❑	65 Buddy Young	15.00	7.50
❑	66 Gordy Soltau	8.00	5.00
❑	67 Eddie Bell	8.00	5.00
❑	68 Ben Agajanian RC	12.00	6.00
❑	69 Tom Dahms	8.00	5.00
❑	70 Jim Ringo RC	50.00	30.00
❑	71 Bobby Layne	75.00	45.00
❑	72 Y.A.Tittle	75.00	45.00
❑	73 Bob Gaona	8.00	5.00
❑	74 Tobin Rote	12.00	6.00
❑	75 Hugh McElhenny	30.00	18.00
❑	76 John Kreamcheck	8.00	5.00
❑	77 Al Dorow	12.00	6.00
❑	78 Bill Wade	15.00	7.50
❑	79 Dale Dodrill	8.00	5.00
❑	80 Chuck Drazenovich	8.00	5.00
❑	81 Billy Wilson RC	12.00	6.00
❑	82 Les Richter	12.00	6.00
❑	83 Pat Brady	8.00	5.00
❑	84 Bob Hoernschemeyer	12.00	6.00
❑	85 Joe Arenas	8.00	5.00
❑	86 Len Szafaryn UER	8.00	5.00
❑	87 Rick Casares RC	20.00	12.00
❑	88 Leon McLaughlin	8.00	5.00
❑	89 Charley Toogood	8.00	5.00
❑	90 Tom Bettis	8.00	5.00
❑	91 John Sandusky	8.00	5.00
❑	92 Bill Wightkin	8.00	5.00
❑	93 Darrel Brewster	8.00	5.00
❑	94 Marion Campbell	15.00	7.50
❑	95 Floyd Reid	8.00	5.00
❑	96 Chick Jagade	8.00	5.00
❑	97 George Taliaferro	8.00	5.00
❑	98 Carlton Massey	8.00	5.00
❑	99 Fran Rogel	8.00	5.00
❑	100 Alex Sandusky	8.00	5.00
❑	101 Bob St.Clair RC	35.00	20.00
❑	102 Al Carmichael	8.00	5.00
❑	103 Carl Taseff RC	8.00	5.00
❑	104 Leo Nomellini	25.00	15.00
❑	105 Tom Scott	8.00	5.00
❑	106 Ted Marchibroda	15.00	7.50
❑	107 Art Spinney	8.00	5.00
❑	108 Wayne Robinson	8.00	5.00
❑	109 Jim Ricca	8.00	5.00
❑	110 Lou Ferry	8.00	5.00
❑	111 [illegible]	8.00	5.00
❑	112 Lou Creekmur	15.00	7.50
❑	113 Kenny Konz	8.00	5.00
❑	114 Doug Eggers	8.00	5.00
❑	115 Bobby Thomason	8.00	5.00
❑	116 Bill McPeak	8.00	5.00
❑	117 William Brown	8.00	5.00
❑	118 Royce Womble	8.00	5.00
❑	119 Frank Gatski RC	35.00	20.00
❑	120 Jim Finks	15.00	7.50
❑	121 Andy Robustelli	25.00	15.00
❑	122 Bobby Dillon	8.00	5.00
❑	123 Leo Sanford	8.00	5.00
❑	124 Elbert Nickel	12.00	6.00
❑	125 Wayne Hansen	8.00	5.00
❑	126 Buck Lansford RC	8.00	5.00
❑	127 Gern Nagler	8.00	5.00
❑	128 Jim Salsbury	8.00	5.00
❑	129 Dale Atkeson RC	8.00	5.00
❑	130 John Schweder	8.00	5.00
❑	131 Dave Hanner	12.00	6.00
❑	132 Eddie Price	8.00	5.00
❑	133 Vic Janowicz	30.00	15.00
❑	134 Ernie Stautner	25.00	15.00
❑	135 James Parmer	8.00	5.00
❑	136 Emlen Tunnell UER	20.00	12.00
❑	137 Kyle Rote	15.00	7.50
❑	138 Norm Willey	8.00	5.00
❑	139 Charley Trippi	20.00	12.00
❑	140 Billy Howton	12.00	6.00
❑	141 Bobby Clatterbuck	8.00	5.00
❑	142 Bob Boyd	8.00	5.00
❑	143 Bob Toneff RC	12.00	6.00

❑ 144 Jerry Helluin	8.00	5.00
❑ 145 Adrian Burk	8.00	5.00
❑ 146 Walt Michaels	12.00	6.00
❑ 147 Zollie Toth	8.00	5.00
❑ 148 Frank Varrichione RC	8.00	5.00
❑ 149 Dick Bielski RC	8.00	5.00
❑ 150 George Ratterman	12.00	6.00
❑ 151 Mike Jarmoluk	8.00	5.00
❑ 152 Tom Landry	200.00	125.00
❑ 153 Ray Renfro	12.00	6.00
❑ 154 Zeke Bratkowski	12.00	6.00
❑ 155 Jerry Norton	8.00	5.00
❑ 156 Maurice Bassett	8.00	5.00
❑ 157 Volney Quinlan	8.00	5.00
❑ 158 Chuck Bednarik	30.00	18.00
❑ 159 Don Colo	8.00	5.00
❑ 160 L.G. Dupre RC !	40.00	20.00

1991 Bowman

❑ COMPLETE SET (561)	12.00	5.00
❑ COMP.FACT.SET (561)	12.00	5.00
❑ 1 Jeff George RS	.25	.08
❑ 2 Richmond Webb RS	.05	.01
❑ 3 Emmitt Smith RS	1.25	.50
❑ 4 Mark Carrier DB RS UER	.05	.01
❑ 5 Steve Christie RS	.05	.01
❑ 6 Keith Sims RS	.05	.01
❑ 7 Rob Moore RS UER	.25	.08
❑ 8 Johnny Johnson RS	.05	.01
❑ 9 Eric Green RS	.05	.01
❑ 10 Ben Smith RS	.05	.01
❑ 11 Tory Epps RS	.05	.01
❑ 12 Andre Rison	.10	.02
❑ 13 Shawn Collins	.05	.01
❑ 14 Chris Hinton	.05	.01
❑ 15 Deion Sanders	.40	.15
❑ 16 Darion Conner	.05	.01
❑ 17 Michael Haynes	.25	.08
❑ 18 Chris Miller	.10	.02
❑ 19 Jessie Tuggle	.05	.01
❑ 20 Scott Fulhage	.05	.01
❑ 21 Bill Fralic	.05	.01
❑ 22 Floyd Dixon	.05	.01
❑ 23 Oliver Barnett	.05	.01
❑ 24 Mike Rozier	.05	.01
❑ 25 Tory Epps	.05	.01
❑ 26 Tim Green	.05	.01
❑ 27 Steve Broussard	.05	.01
❑ 28 Bruce Pickens RC	.05	.01
❑ 29 Mike Pritchard RC	.25	.08
❑ 30 Andre Reed	.10	.02
❑ 31 Darryl Talley	.05	.01
❑ 32 Nate Odomes	.05	.01
❑ 33 Jamie Mueller	.05	.01
❑ 34 Leon Seals	.05	.01
❑ 35 Keith McKeller	.05	.01
❑ 36 Al Edwards	.05	.01
❑ 37 Butch Rolle	.05	.01
❑ 38 Jeff Wright RC	.05	.01
❑ 39 Will Wolford	.05	.01
❑ 40 James Williams	.05	.01
❑ 41 Kent Hull	.05	.01
❑ 42 James Lofton	.10	.02
❑ 43 Frank Reich	.10	.02
❑ 44 Bruce Smith	.25	.08
❑ 45 Thurman Thomas	.25	.08
❑ 46 Leonard Smith	.05	.01
❑ 47 Shane Conlan	.05	.01
❑ 48 Steve Tasker	.10	.02
❑ 49 Ray Bentley	.05	.01
❑ 50 Cornelius Bennett	.10	.02
❑ 51 Stan Thomas	.05	.01

❑ 52 Shaun Gayle	.05	.01
❑ 53 Wendell Davis	.05	.01
❑ 54 James Thornton	.05	.01
❑ 55 Mark Carrier DB	.10	.02
❑ 56 Richard Dent	.10	.02
❑ 57 Ron Morris	.05	.01
❑ 58 Mike Singletary	.10	.02
❑ 59 Jay Hilgenberg	.05	.01
❑ 60 Donnell Woolford	.05	.01
❑ 61 Jim Covert	.05	.01
❑ 62 Jim Harbaugh	.25	.08
❑ 63 Neal Anderson	.10	.02
❑ 64 Brad Muster	.05	.01
❑ 65 Kevin Butler	.05	.01
❑ 66 Trace Armstrong UER	.05	.01
❑ 67 Ron Cox	.05	.01
❑ 68 Peter Tom Willis	.05	.01
❑ 69 Johnny Bailey	.05	.01
❑ 70 Mark Bortz UER	.05	.01
❑ 71 Chris Zorich RC	.25	.08
❑ 72 Lamar Rogers RC	.05	.01
❑ 73 David Grant UER	.05	.01
❑ 74 Lewis Billups	.05	.01
❑ 75 Harold Green	.10	.02
❑ 76 Ickey Woods	.05	.01
❑ 77 Eddie Brown	.05	.01
❑ 78 David Fulcher	.05	.01
❑ 79 Anthony Munoz	.10	.02
❑ 80 Carl Zander	.05	.01
❑ 81 Rodney Holman	.05	.01
❑ 82 James Brooks	.10	.02
❑ 83 Tim McGee	.05	.01
❑ 84 Boomer Esiason	.10	.02
❑ 85 Leon White	.05	.01
❑ 86 James Francis UER	.05	.01
❑ 87 Mitchell Price RC	.05	.01
❑ 88 Ed King RC	.05	.01
❑ 89 Eric Turner RC	.10	.02
❑ 90 Rob Burnett RC	.10	.02
❑ 91 Leroy Hoard	.10	.02
❑ 92 Kevin Mack UER	.05	.01
❑ 93 Thane Gash UER	.05	.01
❑ 94 Gregg Rakoczy	.05	.01
❑ 95 Clay Matthews	.10	.02
❑ 96 Eric Metcalf	.10	.02
❑ 97 Stephen Braggs	.05	.01
❑ 98 Frank Minnifield	.05	.01
❑ 99 Reggie Langhorne	.05	.01
❑ 100 Mike Johnson	.05	.01
❑ 101 Brian Brennan	.05	.01
❑ 102 Anthony Pleasant	.05	.01
❑ 103 Godfrey Myles RC UER	.05	.01
❑ 104 Russell Maryland RC	.25	.08
❑ 105 James Washington RC	.05	.01
❑ 106 Nate Newton	.10	.02
❑ 107 Jimmie Jones	.05	.01
❑ 108 Jay Novacek	.25	.08
❑ 109 Alexander Wright	.05	.01
❑ 110 Jack Del Rio	.10	.02
❑ 111 Jim Jeffcoat	.05	.01
❑ 112 Mike Saxon	.05	.01
❑ 113 Troy Aikman	.75	.30
❑ 114 Issiac Holt	.05	.01
❑ 115 Ken Norton	.10	.02
❑ 116 Kelvin Martin	.05	.01
❑ 117 Emmitt Smith	2.50	1.00
❑ 118 Ken Willis	.05	.01
❑ 119 Daniel Stubbs	.05	.01
❑ 120 Michael Irvin	.25	.08
❑ 121 Danny Noonan	.05	.01
❑ 122 Alvin Harper RC	.25	.08
❑ 123 Reggie Johnson RC	.05	.01
❑ 124 Vance Johnson	.05	.01
❑ 125 Steve Atwater	.05	.01
❑ 126 Greg Kragen	.05	.01
❑ 127 John Elway	1.25	.50
❑ 128 Simon Fletcher	.05	.01
❑ 129 Wymon Henderson	.05	.01
❑ 130 Ricky Nattiel	.05	.01
❑ 131 Shannon Sharpe	.50	.20
❑ 132 Ron Holmes	.05	.01
❑ 133 Karl Mecklenburg	.05	.01
❑ 134 Bobby Humphrey	.05	.01
❑ 135 Clarence Kay	.05	.01
❑ 136 Dennis Smith	.05	.01
❑ 137 Jim Juriga	.05	.01
❑ 138 Melvin Bratton	.05	.01
❑ 139 Mark Jackson UER	.05	.01
❑ 140 Michael Brooks	.05	.01

❑ 141 Alton Montgomery	.05	.01
❑ 142 Mike Croel RC	.05	.01
❑ 143 Mel Gray	.10	.02
❑ 144 Michael Cofer	.05	.01
❑ 145 Jeff Campbell	.05	.01
❑ 146 Dan Owens	.05	.01
❑ 147 Robert Clark UER	.05	.01
❑ 148 Jim Arnold	.05	.01
❑ 149 William White	.05	.01
❑ 150 Rodney Peete	.10	.02
❑ 151 Jerry Ball	.05	.01
❑ 152 Bennie Blades	.05	.01
❑ 153 Barry Sanders UER	1.25	.50
❑ 154 Andre Ware	.10	.02
❑ 155 Lomas Brown	.05	.01
❑ 156 Chris Spielman	.10	.02
❑ 157 Kelvin Pritchett RC	.10	.02
❑ 158 Herman Moore RC	.25	.08
❑ 159 Chris Jacke	.05	.01
❑ 160 Tony Mandarich	.05	.01
❑ 161 Perry Kemp	.05	.01
❑ 162 Johnny Holland	.05	.01
❑ 163 Mark Lee	.05	.01
❑ 164 Anthony Dilweg	.05	.01
❑ 165 Scott Stephen RC	.05	.01
❑ 166 Ed West	.05	.01
❑ 167 Mark Murphy	.05	.01
❑ 168 Darrell Thompson	.05	.01
❑ 169 James Campen RC	.05	.01
❑ 170 Jeff Query	.05	.01
❑ 171 Brian Noble	.05	.01
❑ 172 Sterling Sharpe UER	.25	.08
❑ 173 Robert Brown	.05	.01
❑ 174 Tim Harris	.05	.01
❑ 175 LeRoy Butler	.10	.02
❑ 176 Don Majkowski	.05	.01
❑ 177 Vinnie Clark RC	.05	.01
❑ 178 Esera Tuaolo RC	.05	.01
❑ 179 Lorenzo White UER	.05	.01
❑ 180 Warren Moon	.25	.08
❑ 181 Sean Jones	.10	.02
❑ 182 Curtis Duncan	.05	.01
❑ 183 Al Smith	.05	.01
❑ 184 Richard Johnson CB RC	.05	.01
❑ 185 Tony Jones WR	.05	.01
❑ 186 Bubba McDowell	.05	.01
❑ 187 Bruce Matthews	.10	.02
❑ 188 Ray Childress	.05	.01
❑ 189 Haywood Jeffires	.10	.02
❑ 190 Ernest Givins	.10	.02
❑ 191 Mike Munchak	.10	.02
❑ 192 Greg Montgomery	.05	.01
❑ 193 Cody Carlson RC	.05	.01
❑ 194 Johnny Meads	.05	.01
❑ 195 Drew Hill UER	.05	.01
❑ 196 Mike Dumas RC	.05	.01
❑ 197 Darryll Lewis RC	.10	.02
❑ 198 Rohn Stark	.05	.01
❑ 199 Clarence Verdin UER	.05	.01
❑ 200 Mike Prior	.05	.01
❑ 201 Eugene Daniel	.05	.01
❑ 202 Dean Biasucci	.05	.01
❑ 203 Jeff Herrod	.05	.01
❑ 204 Keith Taylor	.05	.01
❑ 205 Jon Hand	.05	.01
❑ 206 Pat Beach	.05	.01
❑ 207 Duane Bickett	.05	.01
❑ 208 Jessie Hester UER	.05	.01
❑ 209 Chip Banks	.05	.01
❑ 210 Ray Donaldson	.05	.01
❑ 211 Bill Brooks	.05	.01
❑ 212 Jeff George	.25	.08
❑ 213 Tony Siragusa RC	.10	.02
❑ 214 Albert Bentley	.05	.01
❑ 215 Joe Valerio	.05	.01
❑ 216 Chris Martin	.05	.01
❑ 217 Christian Okoye	.05	.01
❑ 218 Stephone Paige	.05	.01
❑ 219 Percy Snow	.05	.01
❑ 220 David Szott	.05	.01
❑ 221 Derrick Thomas	.25	.08
❑ 222 Todd McNair	.05	.01
❑ 223 Albert Lewis	.05	.01
❑ 224 Neil Smith	.25	.08
❑ 225 Barry Word	.05	.01
❑ 226 Robb Thomas	.05	.01
❑ 227 John Alt	.05	.01
❑ 228 Jonathan Hayes	.05	.01
❑ 229 Kevin Ross	.05	.01

❑ 230 Nick Lowery .05 .01
❑ 231 Tim Grunhard .05 .01
❑ 232 Dan Saleaumua .05 .01
❑ 233 Steve DeBerg .05 .01
❑ 234 Harvey Williams RC .25 .08
❑ 235 Nick Bell RC UER .05 .01
❑ 236 Mervyn Fernandez UER .05 .01
❑ 237 Howie Long .25 .08
❑ 238 Marcus Allen .25 .08
❑ 239 Eddie Anderson .05 .01
❑ 240 Ethan Horton .05 .01
❑ 241 Lionel Washington .05 .01
❑ 242 Steve Wisniewski UER .05 .01
❑ 243 Bo Jackson UER .30 .10
❑ 244 Greg Townsend .05 .01
❑ 245 Jeff Jaeger .05 .01
❑ [illegible] [illegible] [illegible] .01
❑ 247 Garry Lewis .05 .01
❑ 248 Steve Smith .05 .01
❑ 249 Willie Gault UER .05 .01
❑ 250 Scott Davis .05 .01
❑ 251 Jay Schroeder .05 .01
❑ 252 Don Mosebar .05 .01
❑ 253 Todd Marinovich RC .05 .01
❑ 254 Irv Pankey .05 .01
❑ 255 Flipper Anderson .05 .01
❑ 256 Tom Newberry .05 .01
❑ 257 Kevin Greene .10 .02
❑ 258 Mike Wilcher .05 .01
❑ 259 Bern Brostek .05 .01
❑ 260 Buford McGee .05 .01
❑ 261 Cleveland Gary .05 .01
❑ 262 Jackie Slater .05 .01
❑ 263 Henry Ellard .10 .02
❑ 264 Alvin Wright .05 .01
❑ 265 Darryl Henley RC .05 .01
❑ 266 Damone Johnson RC .05 .01
❑ 267 Frank Stams .05 .01
❑ 268 Jerry Gray .05 .01
❑ 269 Jim Everett .10 .02
❑ 270 Pat Terrell .05 .01
❑ 271 Todd Lyght RC .05 .01
❑ 272 Aaron Cox .05 .01
❑ 273 Barry Sanders LL .50 .20
❑ 274 Jerry Rice LL .40 .15
❑ 275 Derrick Thomas LL .25 .08
❑ 276 Mark Carrier DB LL .10 .02
❑ 277 Warren Moon LL .25 .08
❑ 278 Randall Cunningham LL .10 .02
❑ 279 Nick Lowery LL .05 .01
❑ 280 Clarence Verdin LL .05 .01
❑ 281 Thurman Thomas LL .25 .08
❑ 282 Mike Horan LL .05 .01
❑ 283 Flipper Anderson LL .05 .01
❑ 284 John Offerdahl .05 .01
❑ 285 Dan Marino UER 1.25 .50
❑ 286 Mark Clayton .10 .02
❑ 287 Tony Paige .05 .01
❑ 288 Keith Sims .05 .01
❑ 289 Jeff Cross .05 .01
❑ 290 Pete Stoyanovich .05 .01
❑ 291 Ferrell Edmunds .05 .01
❑ 292 Reggie Roby .05 .01
❑ 293 Louis Oliver .05 .01
❑ 294 Jarvis Williams .05 .01
❑ 295 Sammie Smith .05 .01
❑ 296 Richmond Webb .05 .01
❑ 297 J.B. Brown .05 .01
❑ 298 Jim C.Jensen .05 .01
❑ 299 Mark Duper .10 .02
❑ 300 David Griggs .05 .01
❑ 301 Randal Hill RC .10 .02
❑ 302 Aaron Craver RC .05 .01
❑ 303 Keith Millard .05 .01
❑ 304 Steve Jordan .05 .01
❑ 305 Anthony Carter .10 .02
❑ 306 Mike Merriweather .05 .01
❑ 307 Audray McMillian RC UER .05 .01
❑ 308 Randall McDaniel .05 .01
❑ 309 Gary Zimmerman .05 .01
❑ 310 Carl Lee .05 .01
❑ 311 Reggie Rutland .05 .01
❑ 312 Hassan Jones .05 .01
❑ 313 Kirk Lowdermilk UER .05 .01
❑ 314 Herschel Walker .10 .02
❑ 315 Chris Doleman .05 .01
❑ 316 Joey Browner .05 .01
❑ 317 Wade Wilson .10 .02
❑ 318 Henry Thomas .05 .01
❑ 319 Rich Gannon .25 .08
❑ 320 Al Noga UER .05 .01
❑ 321 Pat Harlow RC .05 .01
❑ 322 Bruce Armstrong .05 .01
❑ 323 Maurice Hurst .05 .01
❑ 324 Brent Williams .05 .01
❑ 325 Chris Singleton .05 .01
❑ 326 Jason Staurovsky .05 .01
❑ 327 Marvin Allen .05 .01
❑ 328 Hart Lee Dykes .05 .01
❑ 329 Johnny Rembert .05 .01
❑ 330 Andre Tippett .05 .01
❑ 331 Greg McMurtry .05 .01
❑ 332 John Stephens .05 .01
❑ 333 Ray Agnew .05 .01
❑ 334 Tommy Hodson .05 .01
❑ 335 Ronnie Lippett .05 .01
❑ 336 Marv Cook .05 .01
❑ 337 Tommy Barnhardt RC .05 .01
❑ 338 Dalton Hilliard .05 .01
❑ 339 Sam Mills .05 .01
❑ 340 Morten Andersen .05 .01
❑ 341 Stan Brock .05 .01
❑ 342 Brett Maxie .05 .01
❑ 343 Steve Walsh .05 .01
❑ 344 Vaughan Johnson .05 .01
❑ 345 Rickey Jackson .05 .01
❑ 346 Renaldo Turnbull .05 .01
❑ 347 Joel Hilgenberg .05 .01
❑ 348 Toi Cook RC .05 .01
❑ 349 Robert Massey .05 .01
❑ 350 Pat Swilling .10 .02
❑ 351 Eric Martin .05 .01
❑ 352 Rueben Mayes UER .05 .01
❑ 353 Vince Buck .05 .01
❑ 354 Brett Perriman .25 .08
❑ 355 Wesley Carroll RC .05 .01
❑ 356 Jarrod Bunch RC .05 .01
❑ 357 Pepper Johnson .05 .01
❑ 358 Dave Meggett .10 .02
❑ 359 Mark Collins .05 .01
❑ 360 Sean Landeta .05 .01
❑ 361 Maurice Carthon .05 .01
❑ 362 Mike Fox UER .05 .01
❑ 363 Jeff Hostetler .10 .02
❑ 364 Phil Simms .10 .02
❑ 365 Leonard Marshall .05 .01
❑ 366 Gary Reasons .05 .01
❑ 367 Rodney Hampton .25 .08
❑ 368 Greg Jackson RC .05 .01
❑ 369 Jumbo Elliott .05 .01
❑ 370 Bob Kratch RC .05 .01
❑ 371 Lawrence Taylor .25 .08
❑ 372 Erik Howard .05 .01
❑ 373 Carl Banks .05 .01
❑ 374 Stephen Baker .05 .01
❑ 375 Mark Ingram .10 .02
❑ 376 Browning Nagle RC .05 .01
❑ 377 Jeff Lageman .05 .01
❑ 378 Ken O'Brien .05 .01
❑ 379 Al Toon .10 .02
❑ 380 Joe Prokop .05 .01
❑ 381 Tony Stargell .05 .01
❑ 382 Blair Thomas .05 .01
❑ 383 Erik McMillan .05 .01
❑ 384 Dennis Byrd .05 .01
❑ 385 Freeman McNeil .05 .01
❑ 386 Brad Baxter .05 .01
❑ 387 Mark Boyer .05 .01
❑ 388 Terance Mathis .10 .02
❑ 389 Jim Sweeney .05 .01
❑ 390 Kyle Clifton .05 .01
❑ 391 Pat Leahy .05 .01
❑ 392 Rob Moore .25 .08
❑ 393 James Hasty .05 .01
❑ 394 Blaise Bryant .05 .01
❑ 395A Jesse Campbell RC ERR 1.00 .40
❑ 395B Jesse Campbell RC COR .05 .01
❑ 396 Keith Jackson .10 .02
❑ 397 Jerome Brown .05 .01
❑ 398 Keith Byars .05 .01
❑ 399 Seth Joyner .10 .02
❑ 400 Mike Bellamy .05 .01
❑ 401 Fred Barnett .25 .08
❑ 402 Reggie Singletary RC .05 .01
❑ 403 Reggie White .25 .08
❑ 404 Randall Cunningham .25 .08
❑ 405 Byron Evans .05 .01
❑ 406 Wes Hopkins .05 .01
❑ 407 Ben Smith .05 .01
❑ 408 Roger Ruzek .05 .01
❑ 409 Eric Allen UER .05 .01
❑ 410 Anthony Toney UER .05 .01
❑ 411 Clyde Simmons .05 .01
❑ 412 Andre Waters .05 .01
❑ 413 Calvin Williams .10 .02
❑ 414 Eric Swann RC .25 .08
❑ 415 Eric Hill .05 .01
❑ 416 Tim McDonald .05 .01
❑ 417 Luis Sharpe .05 .01
❑ 418 Ernie Jones UER .05 .01
❑ 419 Ken Harvey .10 .02
❑ 420 Ricky Proehl .05 .01
❑ 421 Johnny Johnson .05 .01
❑ 422 Anthony Bell .05 .01
❑ 423 Timm Rosenbach .05 .01
❑ 424 Rich Camarillo .05 .01
❑ 425 Walter Reeves .05 .01
❑ 426 Freddie Joe Nunn .05 .01
❑ 427 Anthony Thompson UER .05 .01
❑ 428 Bill Lewis .05 .01
❑ 429 Jim Wahler RC .05 .01
❑ 430 Cedric Mack .05 .01
❑ 431 Mike Jones DE RC .05 .01
❑ 432 Ernie Mills RC .10 .02
❑ 433 Tim Worley .05 .01
❑ 434 Greg Lloyd .25 .08
❑ 435 Dermontti Dawson .05 .01
❑ 436 Louis Lipps .05 .01
❑ 437 Eric Green .05 .01
❑ 438 Donald Evans .05 .01
❑ 439 D.J. Johnson .05 .01
❑ 440 Tunch Ilkin .05 .01
❑ 441 Bubby Brister .05 .01
❑ 442 Chris Calloway .05 .01
❑ 443 David Little .05 .01
❑ 444 Thomas Everett .05 .01
❑ 445 Carnell Lake .05 .01
❑ 446 Rod Woodson .25 .08
❑ 447 Gary Anderson K .05 .01
❑ 448 Merril Hoge .05 .01
❑ 449 Gerald Williams .05 .01
❑ 450 Eric Moten RC .05 .01
❑ 451 Marion Butts .10 .02
❑ 452 Leslie O'Neal .10 .02
❑ 453 Ronnie Harmon .05 .01
❑ 454 Gill Byrd .05 .01
❑ 455 Junior Seau .25 .08
❑ 456 Nate Lewis RC .05 .01
❑ 457 Leo Goeas .05 .01
❑ 458 Burt Grossman .05 .01
❑ 459 Courtney Hall .05 .01
❑ 460 Anthony Miller .10 .02
❑ 461 Gary Plummer .05 .01
❑ 462 Billy Joe Tolliver .05 .01
❑ 463 Lee Williams .05 .01
❑ 464 Arthur Cox .05 .01
❑ 465 John Kidd UER .05 .01
❑ 466 Frank Cornish .05 .01
❑ 467 John Carney .05 .01
❑ 468 Eric Bieniemy RC .05 .01
❑ 469 Don Griffin .05 .01
❑ 470 Jerry Rice .75 .30
❑ 471 Keith DeLong .05 .01
❑ 472 John Taylor .10 .02
❑ 473 Brent Jones .25 .08
❑ 474 Pierce Holt .05 .01
❑ 475 Kevin Fagan .05 .01
❑ 476 Bill Romanowski .05 .01
❑ 477 Dexter Carter .05 .01
❑ 478 Guy McIntyre .05 .01
❑ 479 Joe Montana 1.25 .50
❑ 480 Charles Haley .10 .02
❑ 481 Mike Cofer .05 .01
❑ 482 Jesse Sapolu .05 .01
❑ 483 Eric Davis .05 .01
❑ 484 Mike Sherrard .05 .01
❑ 485 Steve Young .75 .30
❑ 486 Darryl Pollard .05 .01
❑ 487 Tom Rathman .05 .01
❑ 488 Michael Carter .05 .01
❑ 489 Ricky Watters RC 1.50 .60
❑ 490 John Johnson RC .05 .01
❑ 491 Eugene Robinson .05 .01
❑ 492 Andy Heck .05 .01
❑ 493 John L. Williams .05 .01
❑ 494 Norm Johnson .05 .01
❑ 495 David Wyman .05 .01

❑ 496 Derrick Fenner UER .05 .01
❑ 497 Rick Donnelly .05 .01
❑ 498 Tony Woods .05 .01
❑ 499 Derrick Loville RC .05 .01
❑ 500 Dave Krieg .10 .02
❑ 501 Joe Nash .05 .01
❑ 502 Brian Blades .10 .02
❑ 503 Cortez Kennedy .25 .08
❑ 504 Jeff Bryant .05 .01
❑ 505 Tommy Kane .05 .01
❑ 506 Travis McNeal .05 .01
❑ 507 Terry Wooden .05 .01
❑ 508 Chris Warren .25 .08
❑ 509A Dan McGwire RC ERR .05 .01
❑ 509B Dan McGwire RC COR .05 .01
❑ 510 Mark Robinson .05 .01
❑ 511 Ron Hall .05 .01
❑ 512 Paul Gruber .05 .01
❑ 513 Harry Hamilton .05 .01
❑ 514 Keith McCants .05 .01
❑ 515 Reggie Cobb .05 .01
❑ 516 Steve Christie UER .05 .01
❑ 517 Broderick Thomas .05 .01
❑ 518 Mark Carrier WR .25 .08
❑ 519 Vinny Testaverde .10 .02
❑ 520 Ricky Reynolds .05 .01
❑ 521 Jesse Anderson .05 .01
❑ 522 Reuben Davis .05 .01
❑ 523 Wayne Haddix .05 .01
❑ 524 Gary Anderson RB UER .05 .01
❑ 525 Bruce Hill .05 .01
❑ 526 Kevin Murphy .05 .01
❑ 527 Lawrence Dawsey RC .10 .02
❑ 528 Ricky Ervins RC .10 .02
❑ 529 Charles Mann .05 .01
❑ 530 Jim Lachey .05 .01
❑ 531 Mark Rypien UER .10 .02
❑ 532 Darrell Green .05 .01
❑ 533 Stan Humphries .25 .08
❑ 534 Jeff Bostic UER .05 .01
❑ 535 Earnest Byner .05 .01
❑ 536 Art Monk UER .10 .02
❑ 537 Don Warren .05 .01
❑ 538 Darryl Grant .05 .01
❑ 539 Wilber Marshall .05 .01
❑ 540 Kurt Gouveia RC .05 .01
❑ 541 Markus Koch .05 .01
❑ 542 Andre Collins .05 .01
❑ 543 Chip Lohmiller .05 .01
❑ 544 Alvin Walton .05 .01
❑ 545 Gary Clark .25 .08
❑ 546 Ricky Sanders .05 .01
❑ 547 Redskins vs. Eagles .05 .01
❑ 548 Bengals vs. Oilers .05 .01
❑ 549 Dolphins vs. Chiefs .05 .01
❑ 550 Bears vs. Saints UER .05 .01
❑ 551 Playoffs/Thurman Thomas .10 .02
❑ 552 49ers vs. Redskins .05 .01
❑ 553 Giants vs. Bears .05 .01
❑ 554 Playoffs/Bo Jackson .10 .02
❑ 555 AFC Championship .05 .01
❑ 556 NFC Championship .05 .01
❑ 557 Super Bowl XXV .05 .01
❑ 558 Checklist 1-140 .05 .01
❑ 559 Checklist 141-280 .05 .01
❑ 560 Checklist 281-420 UER .05 .01
❑ 561 Checklist 421-561 UER .05 .01

1992 Bowman

❑ COMPLETE SET (573) 50.00 25.00
❑ 1 Reggie White 1.00 .40
❑ 2 Johnny Meads .25 .08
❑ 3 Chip Lohmiller .25 .08
❑ 4 James Lofton .50 .20
❑ 5 Ray Horton .25 .08
❑ 6 Rich Moran .25 .08
❑ 7 Howard Cross .25 .08
❑ 8 Mike Horan .25 .08
❑ 9 Erik Kramer .50 .20
❑ 10 Steve Wisniewski .25 .08
❑ 11 Michael Haynes .50 .20
❑ 12 Donald Evans .25 .08
❑ 13 Michael Irvin FOIL 1.00 .40
❑ 14 Gary Zimmerman .25 .08
❑ 15 John Friesz .50 .20
❑ 16 Mark Carrier WR 1.00 .40
❑ 17 Mark Duper .25 .08
❑ 18 James Thornton .25 .08
❑ 19 Jon Hand .25 .08
❑ 20 Sterling Sharpe 1.00 .40
❑ 21 Jacob Green .25 .08
❑ 22 Wesley Carroll .25 .08
❑ 23 Clay Matthews .50 .20
❑ 24 Kevin Greene .50 .20
❑ 25 Brad Baxter .25 .08
❑ 26 Don Griffin .25 .08
❑ 27 Robert Delpino 1.50 .60
❑ 28 Lee Johnson .25 .08
❑ 29 Jim Wahler .25 .08
❑ 30 Leonard Russell .50 .20
❑ 31 Eric Moore .25 .08
❑ 32 Dino Hackett .25 .08
❑ 33 Simon Fletcher .25 .08
❑ 34 Al Edwards .25 .08
❑ 35 Brad Edwards .25 .08
❑ 36 James Joseph .25 .08
❑ 37 Rodney Peete .50 .20
❑ 38 Ricky Reynolds .25 .08
❑ 39 Eddie Anderson .25 .08
❑ 40 Ken Clarke .25 .08
❑ 41 Tony Bennett .50 .20
❑ 42 Larry Brown DB .25 .08
❑ 43 Ray Childress .25 .08
❑ 44 Mike Kenn .25 .08
❑ 45 Vestee Jackson .25 .08
❑ 46 Neil O'Donnell .50 .20
❑ 47 Bill Brooks .25 .08
❑ 48 Kevin Butler .25 .08
❑ 49 Joe Phillips .25 .08
❑ 50 Cortez Kennedy .50 .20
❑ 51 Rickey Jackson .25 .08
❑ 52 Vinnie Clark .25 .08
❑ 53 Michael Jackson .50 .20
❑ 54 Ernie Jones .25 .08
❑ 55 Tom Newberry .25 .08
❑ 56 Pat Harlow .25 .08
❑ 57 Craig Taylor .25 .08
❑ 58 Joe Prokop .25 .08
❑ 59 Warren Moon FOIL SP 2.00 .75
❑ 60 Jeff Lageman .25 .08
❑ 61 Neil Smith 1.00 .40
❑ 62 Jim Jeffcoat .25 .08
❑ 63 Bill Fralic .25 .08
❑ 64 Mark Schlereth RC .25 .08
❑ 65 Keith Byars .25 .08
❑ 66 Jeff Hostetler .50 .20
❑ 67 Joey Browner .25 .08
❑ 68 Bobby Hebert FOIL SP 1.50 .60
❑ 69 Keith Sims .25 .08
❑ 70 Warren Moon 1.00 .40
❑ 71 Pio Sagapolutele RC .25 .08
❑ 72 Cornelius Bennett .50 .20
❑ 73 Greg Davis .25 .08
❑ 74 Ronnie Harmon .25 .08
❑ 75 Ron Hall .25 .08
❑ 76 Howie Long 1.00 .40
❑ 77 Greg Lewis .25 .08
❑ 78 Carnell Lake .25 .08
❑ 79 Ray Crockett .25 .08
❑ 80 Tom Waddle .25 .08
❑ 81 Vincent Brown .25 .08
❑ 82 Bill Brooks .50 .20
❑ 83 John L. Williams .25 .08
❑ 84 Floyd Turner .25 .08
❑ 85 Scott Radecic .25 .08
❑ 86 Anthony Munoz .50 .20
❑ 87 Lonnie Young .25 .08
❑ 88 Dexter Carter .25 .08
❑ 89 Tony Zendejas .25 .08
❑ 90 Tim Jorden .25 .08
❑ 91 LeRoy Butler .25 .08
❑ 92 Richard Brown RC .25 .08
❑ 93 Erric Pegram .50 .20
❑ 94 Sean Landeta .25 .08
❑ 95 Clyde Simmons .25 .08
❑ 96 Martin Mayhew .25 .08
❑ 97 Jarvis Williams .25 .08
❑ 98 Barry Word .25 .08
❑ 99 John Taylor FOIL .50 .20
❑ 100 Emmitt Smith 8.00 3.00
❑ 101 Leon Seals .25 .08
❑ 102 Marion Butts .25 .08
❑ 103 Mike Merriweather .25 .08
❑ 104 Ernest Givins .50 .20
❑ 105 Wymon Henderson .25 .08
❑ 106 Robert Wilson .25 .08
❑ 107 Bobby Hebert .25 .08
❑ 108 Terry McDaniel .25 .08
❑ 109 Jerry Ball .25 .08
❑ 110 John Taylor .50 .20
❑ 111 Rob Moore .50 .20
❑ 112 Thurman Thomas FOIL 1.00 .40
❑ 113 Checklist 1-115 .25 .08
❑ 114 Brian Blades .50 .20
❑ 115 Larry Kelm .25 .08
❑ 116 James Francis .25 .08
❑ 117 Rod Woodson 1.00 .40
❑ 118 Trace Armstrong .25 .08
❑ 119 Eugene Daniel .25 .08
❑ 120 Andre Tippett .25 .08
❑ 121 Chris Jacke .25 .08
❑ 122 Jessie Tuggle .25 .08
❑ 123 Chris Chandler 1.00 .40
❑ 124 Tim Johnson .25 .08
❑ 125 Mark Collins .25 .08
❑ 126 Aeneas Williams SP 1.50 .60
❑ 127 James Jones DT .25 .08
❑ 128 George Jamison .25 .08
❑ 129 Deron Cherry .25 .08
❑ 130 Mark Clayton .50 .20
❑ 131 Keith DeLong .25 .08
❑ 132 Marcus Allen 1.00 .40
❑ 133 Joe Walter RC .25 .08
❑ 134 Reggie Rutland .25 .08
❑ 135 Kent Hull .25 .08
❑ 136 Jeff Feagles .25 .08
❑ 137 Ronnie Lott FOIL SP 2.00 .75
❑ 138 Henry Rolling .25 .08
❑ 139 Gary Anderson RB .25 .08
❑ 140 Morten Andersen .25 .08
❑ 141 Cris Dishman .25 .08
❑ 142 David Treadwell .25 .08
❑ 143 Kevin Gogan .25 .08
❑ 144 James Hasty .25 .08
❑ 145 Robert Delpino .25 .08
❑ 146 Patrick Hunter .25 .08
❑ 147 Gary Anderson K .25 .08
❑ 148 Chip Banks .25 .08
❑ 149 Dan Fike .25 .08
❑ 150 Chris Miller .50 .20
❑ 151 Hugh Millen .25 .08
❑ 152 Courtney Hall .25 .08
❑ 153 Gary Clark .50 .20
❑ 154 Michael Brooks .25 .08
❑ 155 Jay Hilgenberg .25 .08
❑ 156 Tim McDonald .25 .08
❑ 157 Andre Tippett .50 .20
❑ 158 Doug Riesenberg .25 .08
❑ 159 Bill Maas .25 .08
❑ 160 Fred Barnett .50 .20
❑ 161 Pierce Holt .25 .08
❑ 162 Brian Noble .25 .08
❑ 163 Harold Green .25 .08
❑ 164 Joel Hilgenberg .25 .08
❑ 165 Mervyn Fernandez .25 .08
❑ 166 John Offerdahl .25 .08
❑ 167 Shane Conlan .25 .08
❑ 168 Mark Higgs FOIL SP 1.50 .60
❑ 169 Bubba McDowell .25 .08
❑ 170 Barry Sanders 6.00 2.50
❑ 171 Larry Roberts .25 .08
❑ 172 Herschel Walker .50 .20
❑ 173 Steve McMichael .50 .20
❑ 174 Kelly Stouffer .25 .08
❑ 175 Louis Lipps .25 .08
❑ 176 Jim Everett .50 .20
❑ 177 Tony Tolbert .25 .08
❑ 178 Mike Baab .25 .08
❑ 179 Eric Swann .50 .20
❑ 180 Emmitt Smith FOIL SP 12.00 5.00

❑ 181 Tim Brown 1.00 .40
❑ 182 Dennis Smith .25 .08
❑ 183 Moe Gardner .25 .08
❑ 184 Derrick Walker .25 .08
❑ 185 Reyna Thompson .25 .08
❑ 186 Esera Tuaolo .25 .08
❑ 187 Jeff Wright .25 .08
❑ 188 Mark Rypien .25 .08
❑ 189 Quinn Early .50 .20
❑ 190 Christian Okoye .25 .08
❑ 191 Keith Jackson .50 .20
❑ 192 Doug Smith .25 .08
❑ 193 John Elway FOIL 10.00 4.00
❑ 194 Reggie Cobb .25 .08
❑ 195 Reggie Roby .25 .08
❑ 196 Clarence Verdin .25 .08
❑ 197 [illegible] .25 .08
❑ 198 Jim Sweeney .25 .08
❑ 199 Marv Cook .25 .08
❑ 200 Ronnie Lott .50 .20
❑ 201 Mel Gray .50 .20
❑ 202 Maury Buford .25 .08
❑ 203 Lorenzo Lynch .25 .08
❑ 204 Jesse Sapolu .25 .08
❑ 205 Steve Jordan .25 .08
❑ 206 Don Majkowski .25 .08
❑ 207 Flipper Anderson .25 .08
❑ 208 Ed King .25 .08
❑ 209 Tony Woods .25 .08
❑ 210 Ron Heller .25 .08
❑ 211 Greg Kragen .25 .08
❑ 212 Scott Case .25 .08
❑ 213 Tommy Barnhardt .25 .08
❑ 214 Charles Mann .25 .08
❑ 215 David Griggs .25 .08
❑ 216 Kenneth Davis FOIL SP 1.50 .60
❑ 217 Lamar Lathon .25 .08
❑ 218 Nate Odomes .25 .08
❑ 219 Vinny Testaverde .50 .20
❑ 220 Rod Bernstine .25 .08
❑ 221 Barry Sanders FOIL 10.00 4.00
❑ 222 Carlton Haselrig RC .25 .08
❑ 223 Steve Beuerlein .50 .20
❑ 224 John Alt .25 .08
❑ 225 Pepper Johnson .25 .08
❑ 226 Checklist 116-230 .25 .08
❑ 227 Irv Eatman .25 .08
❑ 228 Greg Townsend .25 .08
❑ 229 Mark Jackson .25 .08
❑ 230 Robert Blackmon .25 .08
❑ 231 Terry Allen 1.00 .40
❑ 232 Bennie Blades .25 .08
❑ 233 Sam Mills 1.00 .40
❑ 234 Richmond Webb .25 .08
❑ 235 Richard Dent .50 .20
❑ 236 Alonzo Mitz RC .25 .08
❑ 237 Steve Young 5.00 2.00
❑ 238 Pat Swilling .25 .08
❑ 239 James Campen .25 .08
❑ 240 Earnest Byner .25 .08
❑ 241 Pat Terrell .25 .08
❑ 242 Carwell Gardner .25 .08
❑ 243 Charles McRae .25 .08
❑ 244 Vince Newsome .25 .08
❑ 245 Eric Hill .25 .08
❑ 246 Steve Young FOIL 5.00 2.00
❑ 247 Nate Lewis .25 .08
❑ 248 William Fuller .25 .08
❑ 249 Andre Waters .25 .08
❑ 250 Dean Biasucci .25 .08
❑ 251 Andre Rison .50 .20
❑ 252 Brent Williams .25 .08
❑ 253 Todd McNair .25 .08
❑ 254 Jeff Davidson RC .25 .08
❑ 255 Art Monk .50 .20
❑ 256 Kirk Lowdermilk .25 .08
❑ 257 Bob Golic .25 .08
❑ 258 Michael Irvin 1.00 .40
❑ 259 Eric Green .25 .08
❑ 260 David Fulcher .50 .20
❑ 261 Damone Johnson .25 .08
❑ 262 Marc Spindler .25 .08
❑ 263 Alfred Williams .25 .08
❑ 264 Donnie Elder .25 .08
❑ 265 Keith McKeller .25 .08
❑ 266 Steve Bono RC 1.00 .40
❑ 267 Jumbo Elliott .25 .08
❑ 268 Randy Hilliard RC .25 .08
❑ 269 Rufus Porter .25 .08
❑ 270 Neal Anderson .25 .08
❑ 271 Dalton Hilliard .25 .08
❑ 272 Michael Zordich RC .25 .08
❑ 273 Cornelius Bennett FOIL .50 .20
❑ 274 Louie Aguiar RC .25 .08
❑ 275 Aaron Craver .25 .08
❑ 276 Tony Bennett .25 .08
❑ 277 Terry Wooden .25 .08
❑ 278 Mike Munchak .50 .20
❑ 279 Chris Hinton .25 .08
❑ 280 John Elway 6.00 2.50
❑ 281 Randall McDaniel .25 .08
❑ 282 Brad Baxter .50 .20
❑ 283 Wes Hopkins .25 .08
❑ 284 Scott Davis .25 .08
❑ 285 Mark Tuinei [illegible] [illegible]
❑ 286 Broderick Thompson .25 .08
❑ 287 Henry Ellard .50 .20
❑ 288 Adrian Cooper .25 .08
❑ 289 Don Warren .25 .08
❑ 290 Rodney Hampton .50 .20
❑ 291 Kevin Ross .25 .08
❑ 292 Mark Carrier DB .25 .08
❑ 293 Ian Beckles .25 .08
❑ 294 Gene Atkins .25 .08
❑ 295 Mark Rypien FOIL .50 .20
❑ 296 Eric Metcalf .50 .20
❑ 297 Howard Ballard .25 .08
❑ 298 Nate Newton .25 .08
❑ 299 Dan Owens .25 .08
❑ 300 Tim McGee .25 .08
❑ 301 Greg McMurtry .25 .08
❑ 302 Walter Reeves .25 .08
❑ 303 Jeff Herrod .25 .08
❑ 304 Darren Comeaux .25 .08
❑ 305 Pete Stoyanovich .25 .08
❑ 306 Johnny Holland .25 .08
❑ 307 Jay Novacek .50 .20
❑ 308 Steve Broussard .25 .08
❑ 309 Darrell Green .25 .08
❑ 310 Sam Mills .25 .08
❑ 311 Tim Barnett .25 .08
❑ 312 Steve Atwater .25 .08
❑ 313 Tom Waddle FOIL .50 .20
❑ 314 Felix Wright .25 .08
❑ 315 Sean Jones .25 .08
❑ 316 Jim Harbaugh 1.00 .40
❑ 317 Eric Allen .25 .08
❑ 318 Don Mosebar .25 .08
❑ 319 Rob Taylor .25 .08
❑ 320 Terance Mathis .50 .20
❑ 321 Leroy Hoard .50 .20
❑ 322 Kenneth Davis .25 .08
❑ 323 Guy McIntyre .25 .08
❑ 324 Deron Cherry .50 .20
❑ 325 Tunch Ilkin .25 .08
❑ 326 Willie Green .25 .08
❑ 327 Darryl Henley .25 .08
❑ 328 Shawn Jefferson .25 .08
❑ 329 Greg Jackson .25 .08
❑ 330 John Roper .25 .08
❑ 331 Bill Lewis .25 .08
❑ 332 Rodney Holman .25 .08
❑ 333 Bruce Armstrong .25 .08
❑ 334 Robb Thomas .25 .08
❑ 335 Alvin Harper .50 .20
❑ 336 Brian Jordan .50 .20
❑ 337 Morten Andersen .50 .20
❑ 338 Dermontti Dawson .25 .08
❑ 339 Checklist 231-345 .25 .08
❑ 340 Louis Oliver .25 .08
❑ 341 Paul McJulien RC .25 .08
❑ 342 Karl Mecklenburg .25 .08
❑ 343 Lawrence Dawsey .50 .20
❑ 344 Kyle Clifton .25 .08
❑ 345 Jeff Bostic .25 .08
❑ 346 Cris Carter 1.50 .60
❑ 347 Al Smith .25 .08
❑ 348 Mark Kelso .25 .08
❑ 349 Art Monk FOIL 1.00 .40
❑ 350 Michael Carter .25 .08
❑ 351 Ethan Horton .25 .08
❑ 352 Andy Heck .25 .08
❑ 353 Gill Fenerty .25 .08
❑ 354 David Brandon RC .25 .08
❑ 355 Anthony Johnson 1.00 .40
❑ 356 Mike Golic .25 .08
❑ 357 Ferrell Edmunds .25 .08
❑ 358 Dennis Gibson .25 .08
❑ 359 Gill Byrd .25 .08
❑ 360 Todd Lyght .25 .08
❑ 361 Jayice Pearson RC .25 .08
❑ 362 John Rade .25 .08
❑ 363 Keith Van Horne .25 .08
❑ 364 John Kasay .25 .08
❑ 365 Broderick Thomas 1.50 .60
❑ 366 Ken Harvey .25 .08
❑ 367 Rich Gannon 1.00 .40
❑ 368 Darrell Thompson .25 .08
❑ 369 Jon Vaughn .25 .08
❑ 370 Jesse Solomon .25 .08
❑ 371 Erik McMillan .25 .08
❑ 372 Bruce Matthews .25 .08
❑ 373 Wilber Marshall .25 .08
❑ 374 [illegible] 1.50 .60
❑ 375 Vance Johnson .25 .08
❑ 376 Eddie Brown .25 .08
❑ 377 Don Beebe .25 .08
❑ 378 Brent Jones .50 .20
❑ 379 Matt Bahr .25 .08
❑ 380 Dwight Stone .25 .08
❑ 381 Tony Casillas .25 .08
❑ 382 Jay Schroeder .25 .08
❑ 383 Byron Evans .25 .08
❑ 384 Dan Saleaumua .25 .08
❑ 385 Wendell Davis .25 .08
❑ 386 Ron Holmes .25 .08
❑ 387 George Thomas RC .25 .08
❑ 388 Ray Berry .25 .08
❑ 389 Eric Martin .25 .08
❑ 390 Kevin Mack .25 .08
❑ 391 Natu Tuatagaloa RC .25 .08
❑ 392 Bill Romanowski .25 .08
❑ 393 Nick Bell FOIL SP 1.50 .60
❑ 394 Grant Feasel .25 .08
❑ 395 Eugene Lockhart .25 .08
❑ 396 Lorenzo White .25 .08
❑ 397 Mike Farr .25 .08
❑ 398 Eric Bieniemy .25 .08
❑ 399 Kevin Murphy .25 .08
❑ 400 Luis Sharpe .25 .08
❑ 401 Jessie Tuggle 1.50 .60
❑ 402 Cleveland Gary .25 .08
❑ 403 Tony Mandarich .25 .08
❑ 404 Bryan Cox .50 .20
❑ 405 Marvin Washington .25 .08
❑ 406 Fred Stokes .25 .08
❑ 407 Duane Bickett .25 .08
❑ 408 Leonard Marshall .25 .08
❑ 409 Barry Foster .50 .20
❑ 410 Thurman Thomas 1.00 .40
❑ 411 Willie Gault .50 .20
❑ 412 Vinson Smith RC .25 .08
❑ 413 Mark Bortz .25 .08
❑ 414 Johnny Johnson .25 .08
❑ 415 Rodney Hampton FOIL 1.00 .40
❑ 416 Steve Wallace .25 .08
❑ 417 Fuad Reveiz .25 .08
❑ 418 Derrick Thomas .50 .20
❑ 419 Jackie Harris RC 1.00 .40
❑ 420 Derek Russell .25 .08
❑ 421 David Grant .25 .08
❑ 422 Tommy Kane .25 .08
❑ 423 Stan Brock .25 .08
❑ 424 Haywood Jeffires .50 .20
❑ 425 Broderick Thomas .25 .08
❑ 426 John Kidd .25 .08
❑ 427 Shawn McCarthy RC FOIL .50 .20
❑ 428 Jim Arnold .25 .08
❑ 429 Scott Fulhage .25 .08
❑ 430 Jackie Slater .25 .08
❑ 431 Scott Galbraith RC .25 .08
❑ 432 Roger Ruzek .25 .08
❑ 433 Irving Fryar .50 .20
❑ 434A D.Thomas FOIL ERR 494 1.00 .40
❑ 434B D.Thomas FOIL COR 1.00 .40
❑ 435 D.J. Johnson .25 .08
❑ 436 Jim C.Jensen .25 .08
❑ 437 James Washington .25 .08
❑ 438 Phil Hansen .25 .08
❑ 439 Rohn Stark .25 .08
❑ 440 Jarrod Bunch .25 .08
❑ 441 Todd Marinovich .25 .08
❑ 442 Brett Perriman 1.00 .40
❑ 443 Eugene Robinson .25 .08
❑ 444 Robert Massey .25 .08
❑ 445 Nick Lowery .25 .08
❑ 446 Rickey Dixon .25 .08

❑ 447 Jim Lachey .25 .08
❑ 448 Johnny Hector .50 .20
❑ 449 Gary Plummer .25 .08
❑ 450 Robert Brown .25 .08
❑ 451 Gaston Green .25 .08
❑ 452 Checklist 346-459 .25 .08
❑ 453 Darion Conner .25 .08
❑ 454 Mike Cofer .25 .08
❑ 455 Craig Heyward .50 .20
❑ 456 Anthony Carter .50 .20
❑ 457 Pat Coleman RC .25 .08
❑ 458 Jeff Bryant .25 .08
❑ 459 Mark Gunn RC .25 .08
❑ 460 Stan Thomas .25 .08
❑ 461 Simon Fletcher 1.50 .60
❑ 462 Ray Agnew .25 .08
❑ 463 Jessie Hester .25 .08
❑ 464 Rob Burnett .25 .08
❑ 465 Mike Croel .25 .08
❑ 466 Mike Pitts .25 .08
❑ 467 Darryl Talley .25 .08
❑ 468 Rich Camarillo .25 .08
❑ 469 Reggie White FOIL 1.00 .40
❑ 470 Nick Bell .25 .08
❑ 471 Tracy Hayworth RC .25 .08
❑ 472 Eric Thomas .25 .08
❑ 473 Paul Gruber .25 .08
❑ 474 David Richards .25 .08
❑ 475 T.J. Turner .25 .08
❑ 476 Mark Ingram .25 .08
❑ 477 Tim Grunhard .25 .08
❑ 478 Marion Butts FOIL .50 .20
❑ 479 Tom Rathman .25 .08
❑ 480 Brian Mitchell .50 .20
❑ 481 Bryce Paup 1.00 .40
❑ 482 Mike Pritchard .50 .20
❑ 483 Ken Norton Jr. .50 .20
❑ 484 Roman Phifer .25 .08
❑ 485 Greg Lloyd .50 .20
❑ 486 Brett Maxie .25 .08
❑ 487 Richard Dent FOIL SP 1.50 .60
❑ 488 Curtis Duncan .25 .08
❑ 489 Chris Burkett .25 .08
❑ 490 Travis McNeal .25 .08
❑ 491 Carl Lee .25 .08
❑ 492 Clarence Kay .25 .08
❑ 493 Tom Thayer .25 .08
❑ 494 Erik Kramer FOIL SP 2.00 .75
❑ 495 Perry Kemp .25 .08
❑ 496 Jeff Jaeger .25 .08
❑ 497 Eric Sanders .25 .08
❑ 498 Burt Grossman .25 .08
❑ 499 Ben Smith .25 .08
❑ 500 Keith McCants .25 .08
❑ 501 John Stephens .25 .08
❑ 502 John Rienstra .25 .08
❑ 503 Jim Ritcher .25 .08
❑ 504 Harris Barton .25 .08
❑ 505 Andre Rison FOIL SP 2.00 .75
❑ 506 Chris Martin .25 .08
❑ 507 Freddie Joe Nunn .25 .08
❑ 508 Mark Higgs .25 .08
❑ 509 Norm Johnson .25 .08
❑ 510 Stephen Baker .25 .08
❑ 511 Ricky Sanders .25 .08
❑ 512 Ray Donaldson .25 .08
❑ 513 David Fulcher .25 .08
❑ 514 Gerald Williams .25 .08
❑ 515 Toi Cook .25 .08
❑ 516 Chris Warren 1.00 .40
❑ 517 Jeff Gossett .25 .08
❑ 518 Ken Lanier .25 .08
❑ 519 Haywood Jeffires FOIL SP 2.00 .75
❑ 520 Kevin Glover .25 .08
❑ 521 Mo Lewis .25 .08
❑ 522 Bern Brostek .25 .08
❑ 523 Bo Orlando RC .25 .08
❑ 524 Mike Saxon .25 .08
❑ 525 Seth Joyner .25 .08
❑ 526 John Carney .25 .08
❑ 527 Jeff Cross .25 .08
❑ 528 Gary Anderson K FOIL SP 1.50 .60
❑ 529 Chuck Cecil .25 .08
❑ 530 Tim Green .25 .08
❑ 531 Kevin Porter .25 .08
❑ 532 Chris Spielman .50 .20
❑ 533 Willie Drewrey .25 .08
❑ 534 Chris Singleton UER .25 .08
❑ 535 Matt Stover .25 .08
❑ 536 Andre Collins .25 .08
❑ 537 Erik Howard .25 .08
❑ 538 Steve Tasker .50 .20
❑ 539 Anthony Thompson .25 .08
❑ 540 Charles Haley .50 .20
❑ 541 Mike Merriweather .50 .20
❑ 542 Henry Thomas .25 .08
❑ 543 Scott Stephen .25 .08
❑ 544 Bruce Kozerski .25 .08
❑ 545 Tim McKyer .25 .08
❑ 546 Chris Doleman .25 .08
❑ 547 Riki Ellison .25 .08
❑ 548 Mike Prior .25 .08
❑ 549 Dwayne Harper .25 .08
❑ 550 Bubby Brister .25 .08
❑ 551 Dave Meggett .50 .20
❑ 552 Greg Montgomery .25 .08
❑ 553 Kevin Mack .50 .20
❑ 554 Mark Stepnoski .50 .20
❑ 555 Kenny Walker .25 .08
❑ 556 Eric Moten .25 .08
❑ 557 Michael Stewart .25 .08
❑ 558 Calvin Williams .50 .20
❑ 559 Johnny Hector .25 .08
❑ 560 Tony Paige .25 .08
❑ 561 Tim Newton .25 .08
❑ 562 Brad Muster .25 .08
❑ 563 Aeneas Williams .50 .20
❑ 564 Herman Moore 1.00 .40
❑ 565 Checklist 460-573 .25 .08
❑ 566 Jerome Henderson .25 .08
❑ 567 Danny Copeland .25 .08
❑ 568 Alexander Wright .50 .20
❑ 569 Tim Harris .25 .08
❑ 570 Jonathan Hayes .25 .08
❑ 571 Tony Jones T .25 .08
❑ 572 Carlton Bailey RC .25 .08
❑ 573 Vaughan Johnson .25 .08

1993 Bowman

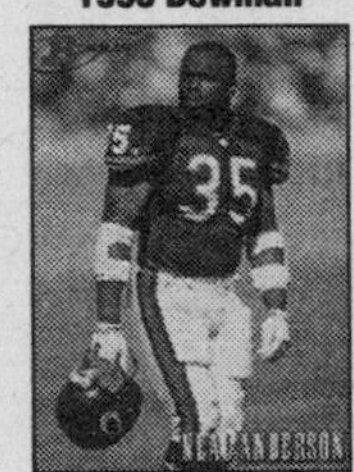

❑ COMPLETE SET (423) 25.00 10.00
❑ 1 Troy Aikman FOIL 3.00 1.50
❑ 2 John Parrella RC .20 .07
❑ 3 Dana Stubblefield RC .75 .30
❑ 4 Mark Higgs .20 .07
❑ 5 Tom Carter RC .40 .15
❑ 6 Nate Lewis .20 .07
❑ 7 Vaughn Hebron RC .20 .07
❑ 8 Ernest Givins .40 .15
❑ 9 Vince Buck .20 .07
❑ 10 Levon Kirkland .20 .07
❑ 11 J.J. Birden .20 .07
❑ 12 Steve Jordan .20 .07
❑ 13 Simon Fletcher .20 .07
❑ 14 Willie Green .20 .07
❑ 15 Pepper Johnson .20 .07
❑ 16 Roger Harper RC .20 .07
❑ 17 Rob Moore .40 .15
❑ 18 David Lang .20 .07
❑ 19 David Klingler .20 .07
❑ 20 Garrison Hearst RC FOIL 2.00 .75
❑ 21 Anthony Johnson .40 .15
❑ 22 Eric Curry RC FOIL .40 .15
❑ 23 Nolan Harrison .20 .07
❑ 24 Earl Dotson RC .20 .07
❑ 25 Leonard Russell .40 .15
❑ 26 Doug Riesenberg .20 .07
❑ 27 Dwayne Harper .20 .07
❑ 28 Richard Dent .40 .15
❑ 29 Victor Bailey RC .20 .07
❑ 30 Junior Seau .75 .30
❑ 31 Steve Tasker .40 .15
❑ 32 Kurt Gouveia .20 .07
❑ 33 Renaldo Turnbull UER .20 .07
❑ 34 Dale Carter .20 .07
❑ 35 Russell Maryland .20 .07
❑ 36 Dana Hall .20 .07
❑ 37 Marco Coleman .20 .07
❑ 38 Greg Montgomery .20 .07
❑ 39 Deon Figures RC .20 .07
❑ 40 Troy Drayton RC .40 .15
❑ 41 Eric Metcalf .40 .15
❑ 42 Michael Husted RC .20 .07
❑ 43 Harry Newsome .20 .07
❑ 44 Kelvin Pritchett .20 .07
❑ 45 Andre Rison FOIL .75 .40
❑ 46 John Copeland RC .40 .15
❑ 47 Greg Biekert RC .20 .07
❑ 48 Johnny Johnson .20 .07
❑ 49 Chuck Cecil .20 .07
❑ 50 Rick Mirer RC FOIL 1.50 .60
❑ 51 Rod Bernstine .20 .07
❑ 52 Steve McMichael .40 .15
❑ 53 Roosevelt Potts RC .20 .07
❑ 54 Mike Sherrard .20 .07
❑ 55 Terrell Buckley .20 .07
❑ 56 Eugene Chung .20 .07
❑ 57 Kimble Anders RC .75 .30
❑ 58 Daryl Johnston .75 .30
❑ 59 Harris Barton .20 .07
❑ 60 Thurman Thomas FOIL 1.50 .60
❑ 61 Eric Martin .20 .07
❑ 62 Reggie Brooks RC FOIL .40 .15
❑ 63 Eric Bieniemy .20 .07
❑ 64 John Offerdahl .20 .07
❑ 65 Wilber Marshall .20 .07
❑ 66 Mark Carrier WR .40 .15
❑ 67 Merril Hoge .20 .07
❑ 68 Cris Carter .75 .30
❑ 69 Marty Thompson RC .20 .07
❑ 70 Randall Cunningham FOIL 1.50 .60
❑ 71 Winston Moss .20 .07
❑ 72 Doug Pelfrey RC .20 .07
❑ 73 Jackie Slater .20 .07
❑ 74 Pierce Holt .20 .07
❑ 75 Hardy Nickerson .40 .15
❑ 76 Chris Burkett .20 .07
❑ 77 Michael Brandon .20 .07
❑ 78 Tom Waddle .20 .07
❑ 79 Walter Reeves .20 .07
❑ 80 Lawrence Taylor FOIL .75 .40
❑ 81 Wayne Simmons RC .20 .07
❑ 82 Brent Williams .20 .07
❑ 83 Shannon Sharpe .75 .30
❑ 84 Robert Blackmon .20 .07
❑ 85 Keith Jackson .40 .15
❑ 86 A.J. Johnson .20 .07
❑ 87 Ryan McNeil RC .75 .30
❑ 88 Michael Dean Perry .40 .15
❑ 89 Russell Copeland RC .40 .15
❑ 90 Sam Mills .20 .07
❑ 91 Courtney Hall .20 .07
❑ 92 Gino Torretta RC .40 .15
❑ 93 Artie Smith RC .20 .07
❑ 94 David Whitmore .20 .07
❑ 95 Charles Haley .40 .15
❑ 96 Rod Woodson .75 .30
❑ 97 Lorenzo White .20 .07
❑ 98 Tom Scott OL RC .20 .07
❑ 99 Tyji Armstrong .20 .07
❑ 100 Boomer Esiason .40 .15
❑ 101 Rocket Ismail FOIL .75 .40
❑ 102 Mark Carrier DB .20 .07
❑ 103 Broderick Thompson .20 .07
❑ 104 Bob Whitfield .20 .07
❑ 105 Ben Coleman RC .20 .07
❑ 106 Jon Vaughn .20 .07
❑ 107 Marcus Buckley RC .20 .07
❑ 108 Cleveland Gary .20 .07
❑ 109 Ashley Ambrose .20 .07
❑ 110 Reggie White FOIL 1.50 .60
❑ 111 Arthur Marshall RC .20 .07
❑ 112 Greg McMurtry .20 .07
❑ 113 Mike Johnson .20 .07
❑ 114 Tim McGee .20 .07
❑ 115 John Carney .20 .07
❑ 116 Neil Smith .75 .30
❑ 117 Mark Stepnoski .20 .07
❑ 118 Don Beebe .20 .07
❑ 119 Scott Mitchell .75 .30
❑ 120 Randall McDaniel .20 .07
❑ 121 Chidi Ahanotu RC .20 .07

❑ 122	Ray Childress	.20	.07
❑ 123	Tony McGee RC	.40	.15
❑ 124	Marc Boutte	.20	.07
❑ 125	Ronnie Lott	.40	.15
❑ 126	Jason Elam RC	.75	.30
❑ 127	Martin Harrison RC	.20	.07
❑ 128	Leonard Renfro RC	.20	.07
❑ 129	Jessie Armstead RC	.40	.15
❑ 130	Quentin Coryatt	.40	.15
❑ 131	Luis Sharpe	.20	.07
❑ 132	Bill Maas	.20	.07
❑ 133	Jesse Solomon	.20	.07
❑ 134	Kevin Greene	.40	.15
❑ 135	Derek Brown RC RBK	.40	.15
❑ 136	Greg Townsend	.30	.07
❑ 137	Neal Anderson	.20	.07
❑ 138	John L. Williams	.20	.07
❑ 139	Vincent Brisby RC	.75	.30
❑ 140	Barry Sanders FOIL	5.00	2.00
❑ 141	Charles Mann	.20	.07
❑ 142	Ken Norton	.40	.15
❑ 143	Eric Moten	.20	.07
❑ 144	John Alt	.20	.07
❑ 145	Dan Footman RC	.20	.07
❑ 146	Bill Brooks	.20	.07
❑ 147	James Thornton	.20	.07
❑ 148	Martin Mayhew	.20	.07
❑ 149	Andy Harmon	.40	.15
❑ 150	Dan Marino FOIL	6.00	2.50
❑ 151	Micheal Barrow RC	.75	.30
❑ 152	Flipper Anderson	.20	.07
❑ 153	Jackie Harris	.20	.07
❑ 154	Todd Kelly RC	.20	.07
❑ 155	Dan Williams RC	.20	.07
❑ 156	Harold Green	.20	.07
❑ 157	David Treadwell	.20	.07
❑ 158	Chris Doleman	.20	.07
❑ 159	Eric Hill	.20	.07
❑ 160	Lincoln Kennedy RC	.20	.07
❑ 161	Devon McDonald RC	.20	.07
❑ 162	Natrone Means RC	.75	.30
❑ 163	Rick Hamilton RC	.20	.07
❑ 164	Kelvin Martin	.20	.07
❑ 165	Jeff Hostetler	.40	.15
❑ 166	Mark Brunell RC	4.00	1.50
❑ 167	Tim Barnett	.20	.07
❑ 168	Ray Crockett	.20	.07
❑ 169	William Perry	.40	.15
❑ 170	Michael Irvin	.75	.30
❑ 171	Marvin Washington	.20	.07
❑ 172	Irving Fryar	.40	.15
❑ 173	Scott Sisson RC	.20	.07
❑ 174	Gary Anderson K	.20	.07
❑ 175	Bruce Smith	.75	.30
❑ 176	Clyde Simmons	.20	.07
❑ 177	Russell White RC	.40	.15
❑ 178	Irv Smith RC	.20	.07
❑ 179	Mark Wheeler	.20	.07
❑ 180	Warren Moon	.75	.30
❑ 181	Del Speer RC	.20	.07
❑ 182	Henry Thomas	.20	.07
❑ 183	Keith Kartz	.20	.07
❑ 184	Ricky Ervins	.20	.07
❑ 185	Phil Simms	.40	.15
❑ 186	Tim Brown	.75	.30
❑ 187	Willis Peguese	.20	.07
❑ 188	Rich Moran	.20	.07
❑ 189	Robert Jones	.20	.07
❑ 190	Craig Heyward	.40	.15
❑ 191	Ricky Watters	.75	.30
❑ 192	Stan Humphries	.40	.15
❑ 193	Larry Webster	.20	.07
❑ 194	Brad Baxter	.20	.07
❑ 195	Randal Hill	.20	.07
❑ 196	Robert Porcher	.20	.07
❑ 197	Patrick Robinson RC	.20	.07
❑ 198	Ferrell Edmunds	.20	.07
❑ 199	Melvin Jenkins	.20	.07
❑ 200	Joe Montana FOIL	6.00	2.50
❑ 201	Marv Cook	.20	.07
❑ 202	Henry Ellard	.40	.15
❑ 203	Calvin Williams	.40	.15
❑ 204	Craig Erickson	.40	.15
❑ 205	Steve Atwater	.20	.07
❑ 206	Najee Mustafaa	.20	.07
❑ 207	Darryl Talley	.20	.07
❑ 208	Jarrod Bunch	.20	.07
❑ 209	Tim McDonald	.20	.07
❑ 210	Patrick Bates RC	.20	.07
❑ 211	Sean Jones	.20	.07
❑ 212	Leslie O'Neal	.40	.15
❑ 213	Mike Golic	.20	.07
❑ 214	Mark Clayton	.20	.07
❑ 215	Leonard Marshall	.20	.07
❑ 216	Curtis Conway RC	1.50	.60
❑ 217	Andre Hastings RC	.40	.15
❑ 218	Barry Word	.20	.07
❑ 219	Will Wolford	.20	.07
❑ 220	Desmond Howard	.40	.15
❑ 221	Rickey Jackson	.20	.07
❑ 222	Alvin Harper	.40	.15
❑ 223	William White	.20	.07
❑ 224	Steve Broussard	.20	.07
❑ 225	Aeneas Williams	.20	.07
❑ 226	Michael Brooks	.20	.07
❑ 227	Reggie Cobb	.20	.07
❑ 228	Derrick Walker	.20	.07
❑ 229	Marcus Allen	.75	.30
❑ 230	Jerry Ball	.20	.07
❑ 231	J.B. Brown	.20	.07
❑ 232	Terry McDaniel	.20	.07
❑ 233	LeRoy Butler	.20	.07
❑ 234	Kyle Clifton	.20	.07
❑ 235	Henry Jones	.20	.07
❑ 236	Shane Conlan	.20	.07
❑ 237	Michael Bates RC	.20	.07
❑ 238	Vincent Brown	.20	.07
❑ 239	William Fuller	.20	.07
❑ 240	Ricardo McDonald	.20	.07
❑ 241	Gary Zimmerman	.20	.07
❑ 242	Fred Barnett	.40	.15
❑ 243	Elvis Grbac RC	4.00	1.50
❑ 244	Myron Baker RC	.20	.07
❑ 245	Steve Emtman	.20	.07
❑ 246	Mike Compton RC	.75	.30
❑ 247	Mark Jackson	.20	.07
❑ 248	Santo Stephens RC	.20	.07
❑ 249	Tommie Agee	.20	.07
❑ 250	Broderick Thomas	.20	.07
❑ 251	Fred Baxter RC	.20	.07
❑ 252	Andre Collins	.20	.07
❑ 253	Ernest Dye RC	.20	.07
❑ 254	Raylee Johnson RC	.40	.15
❑ 255	Rickey Dixon	.20	.07
❑ 256	Ron Heller	.20	.07
❑ 257	Joel Steed	.20	.07
❑ 258	Everett Lindsay RC	.20	.07
❑ 259	Tony Smith RB	.20	.07
❑ 260	Sterling Sharpe UER	.75	.30
❑ 261	Tommy Vardell	.20	.07
❑ 262	Morten Andersen	.20	.07
❑ 263	Eddie Robinson	.20	.07
❑ 264	Jerome Bettis RC	8.00	4.00
❑ 265	Alonzo Spellman	.20	.07
❑ 266	Harvey Williams	.40	.15
❑ 267	Jason Belser RC	.20	.07
❑ 268	Derek Russell	.20	.07
❑ 269	Derrick Lassic RC	.20	.07
❑ 270	Steve Young FOIL	3.00	1.50
❑ 271	Adrian Murrell RC	.75	.30
❑ 272	Lewis Tillman	.20	.07
❑ 273	O.J.McDuffie RC	.75	.30
❑ 274	Marty Carter	.20	.07
❑ 275	Ray Seals	.20	.07
❑ 276	Earnest Byner	.20	.07
❑ 277	Marion Butts	.20	.07
❑ 278	Chris Spielman	.40	.15
❑ 279	Carl Pickens	.40	.15
❑ 280	Drew Bledsoe RC FOIL	6.00	2.50
❑ 281	Mark Kelso	.20	.07
❑ 282	Eugene Robinson	.20	.07
❑ 283	Eric Allen	.20	.07
❑ 284	Ethan Horton	.20	.07
❑ 285	Greg Lloyd	.40	.15
❑ 286	Anthony Carter	.40	.15
❑ 287	Edgar Bennett	.75	.30
❑ 288	Bobby Hebert	.20	.07
❑ 289	Haywood Jeffires	.40	.15
❑ 290	Glyn Milburn RC	.75	.30
❑ 291	Bernie Kosar	.40	.15
❑ 292	Jumbo Elliott	.20	.07
❑ 293	Jessie Hester	.20	.07
❑ 294	Brent Jones	.40	.15
❑ 295	Carl Banks	.20	.07
❑ 296	Brian Washington	.20	.07
❑ 297	Steve Beuerlein	.40	.15
❑ 298	John Lynch RC	2.00	.75
❑ 299	Troy Vincent	.20	.07
❑ 300	Emmitt Smith FOIL	5.00	2.50
❑ 301	Chris Zorich	.20	.07
❑ 302	Wade Wilson	.20	.07
❑ 303	Darrien Gordon RC	.20	.07
❑ 304	Fred Stokes	.20	.07
❑ 305	Nick Lowery	.20	.07
❑ 306	Rodney Peete	.20	.07
❑ 307	Chris Warren	.40	.15
❑ 308	Herschel Walker	.40	.15
❑ 309	Aundray Bruce	.20	.07
❑ 310	Barry Foster FOIL	.40	.15
❑ 311	George Teague RC	.40	.15
❑ 312	Darryl Williams	.20	.07
❑ 313	Thomas Smith RC	.40	.15
❑ 314	Dennis Brown	.20	.07
❑ 315	Marvin Jones RC FOIL	.40	.15
❑ 316	Andre Tippett	.20	.07
❑ 317	Demetrius DuBose RC	.20	.07
❑ 318	Kirk Lowdermilk	.20	.07
❑ 319	Shane Dronett	.20	.07
❑ 320	Terry Kirby RC	.75	.30
❑ 321	Qadry Ismail RC	.75	.30
❑ 322	Lorenzo Lynch	.20	.07
❑ 323	Willie Drewrey	.20	.07
❑ 324	Jessie Tuggle	.20	.07
❑ 325	Leroy Hoard	.40	.15
❑ 326	Mark Collins	.20	.07
❑ 327	Darrell Green	.20	.07
❑ 328	Anthony Miller	.40	.15
❑ 329	Brad Muster	.20	.07
❑ 330	Jim Kelly FOIL	1.50	.60
❑ 331	Sean Gilbert	.40	.15
❑ 332	Tim McKyer	.20	.07
❑ 333	Scott Mersereau	.20	.07
❑ 334	Willie Davis	.75	.30
❑ 335	Brett Favre FOIL	6.00	3.00
❑ 336	Kevin Gogan	.20	.07
❑ 337	Jim Harbaugh	.75	.30
❑ 338	James Trapp RC	.20	.07
❑ 339	Pete Stoyanovich	.20	.07
❑ 340	Jerry Rice FOIL	3.00	1.50
❑ 341	Gary Anderson RB	.20	.07
❑ 342	Carlton Gray RC	.20	.07
❑ 343	Dermontti Dawson	.20	.07
❑ 344	Ray Buchanan RC	.75	.30
❑ 345	Derrick Fenner	.20	.07
❑ 346	Dennis Smith	.20	.07
❑ 347	Todd Rucci RC	.20	.07
❑ 348	Seth Joyner	.20	.07
❑ 349	Jim McMahon	.40	.15
❑ 350	Rodney Hampton	.40	.15
❑ 351	Al Smith	.20	.07
❑ 352	Steve Everitt RC	.20	.07
❑ 353	Vinnie Clark	.20	.07
❑ 354	Eric Swann	.40	.15
❑ 355	Brian Mitchell	.40	.15
❑ 356	Will Shields RC	.75	.30
❑ 357	Cornelius Bennett	.40	.15
❑ 358	Darrin Smith RC	.40	.15
❑ 359	Chris Mims	.20	.07
❑ 360	Blair Thomas	.20	.07
❑ 361	Dennis Gibson	.20	.07
❑ 362	Santana Dotson	.40	.15
❑ 363	Mark Ingram	.20	.07
❑ 364	Don Mosebar	.20	.07
❑ 365	Ty Detmer	.75	.30
❑ 366	Bob Christian RC	.20	.07
❑ 367	Adrian Hardy	.20	.07
❑ 368	Vaughan Johnson	.20	.07
❑ 369	Jim Everett	.40	.15
❑ 370	Ricky Sanders	.20	.07
❑ 371	Jonathan Hayes	.20	.07
❑ 372	Bruce Matthews	.20	.07
❑ 373	Darren Drozdov RC	.75	.30
❑ 374	Scott Brumfield RC	.20	.07
❑ 375	Cortez Kennedy	.40	.15
❑ 376	Tim Harris	.20	.07
❑ 377	Neil O'Donnell	.75	.30
❑ 378	Robert Smith RC	3.00	1.25
❑ 379	Mike Caldwell RC	.20	.07
❑ 380	Burt Grossman	.20	.07
❑ 381	Corey Miller	.20	.07
❑ 382	Kev.Williams WR FOIL RC	.40	.15
❑ 383	Ken Harvey	.20	.07
❑ 384	Greg Robinson RC	.20	.07
❑ 385	Harold Alexander RC	.20	.07
❑ 386	Andre Reed	.40	.15
❑ 387	Reggie Langhorne	.20	.07
❑ 388	Courtney Hawkins	.20	.07

❑ 389 James Hasty .20 .07
❑ 390 Pat Swilling .20 .07
❑ 391 Chris Slade RC .40 .15
❑ 392 Keith Byars .20 .07
❑ 393 Dalton Hilliard .20 .07
❑ 394 David Williams .20 .07
❑ 395 Terry Obee RC .20 .07
❑ 396 Heath Sherman .20 .07
❑ 397 John Taylor .40 .15
❑ 398 Irv Eatman .20 .07
❑ 399 Johnny Holland .20 .07
❑ 400 John Elway FOIL 6.00 2.50
❑ 401 Clay Matthews .40 .15
❑ 402 Dave Meggett .20 .07
❑ 403 Eric Green .20 .07
❑ 404 Bryan Cox .20 .07
❑ 405 Jay Novacek .40 .15
❑ 406 Kenneth Davis .20 .07
❑ 407 Lamar Thomas RC .20 .07
❑ 408 Lance Gunn RC .20 .07
❑ 409 Audray McMillian .20 .07
❑ 410 Derrick Thomas FOIL 1.50 .60
❑ 411 Rufus Porter .20 .07
❑ 412 Coleman Rudolph RC .20 .07
❑ 413 Mark Rypien .20 .07
❑ 414 Duane Bickett .20 .07
❑ 415 Chris Singleton .20 .07
❑ 416 Mitch Lyons RC .20 .07
❑ 417 Bill Fralic .20 .07
❑ 418 Gary Plummer .20 .07
❑ 419 Ricky Proehl .20 .07
❑ 420 Howie Long .75 .30
❑ 421 Willie Roaf RC FOIL .75 .40
❑ 422 Checklist 1-212 .20 .07
❑ 423 Checklist 213-423 .20 .07

1994 Bowman

❑ COMPLETE SET (390) 50.00 20.00
❑ 1 Dan Wilkinson RC .40 .15
❑ 2 Marshall Faulk RC 15.00 6.00
❑ 3 Heath Shuler RC .75 .30
❑ 4 Willie McGinest RC .75 .30
❑ 5 Trent Dilfer RC 3.00 1.25
❑ 6 Brent Jones .40 .15
❑ 7 Sam Adams RC .40 .15
❑ 8 Randy Baldwin .20 .07
❑ 9 Jamir Miller RC .40 .15
❑ 10 John Thierry RC .20 .07
❑ 11 Aaron Glenn RC .75 .30
❑ 12 Joe Johnson RC .20 .07
❑ 13 Bernard Williams RC .20 .07
❑ 14 Wayne Gandy RC .20 .07
❑ 15 Aaron Taylor RC .20 .07
❑ 16 Charles Johnson RC .75 .30
❑ 17 Dew.Washington RC UER 309 .40 .15
❑ 18 Bernie Kosar .40 .15
❑ 19 Johnnie Morton RC 2.50 1.00
❑ 20 Rob Fredrickson RC .40 .15
❑ 21 Shante Carver RC .20 .07
❑ 22 Thomas Lewis RC .40 .15
❑ 23 Greg Hill RC .75 .30
❑ 24 Cris Dishman .20 .07
❑ 25 Jeff Burris RC .40 .15
❑ 26 Isaac Davis RC .20 .07
❑ 27 Bert Emanuel RC .75 .30
❑ 28 Allen Aldridge RC .20 .07
❑ 29 Kevin Lee RC .20 .07
❑ 30 Chris Brantley RC .20 .07
❑ 31 Rich Braham RC .20 .07
❑ 32 Ricky Watters .40 .15
❑ 33 Quentin Coryatt .20 .07
❑ 34 Hardy Nickerson .40 .15
❑ 35 Johnny Johnson .20 .07
❑ 36 Ken Harvey .20 .07
❑ 37 Chris Zorich .20 .07
❑ 38 Chris Warren .40 .15
❑ 39 David Palmer RC .75 .30
❑ 40 Chris Miller .20 .07
❑ 41 Ken Ruettgers .20 .07
❑ 42 Joe Panos RC .20 .07
❑ 43 Mario Bates RC .75 .30
❑ 44 Harry Colon .20 .07
❑ 45 Barry Foster .20 .07
❑ 46 Steve Tasker .40 .15
❑ 47 Richmond Webb .20 .07
❑ 48 James Folston RC .20 .07
❑ 49 Erik Williams .20 .07
❑ 50 Rodney Hampton .40 .15
❑ 51 Derek Russell .20 .07
❑ 52 Greg Montgomery .20 .07
❑ 53 Anthony Phillips .20 .07
❑ 54 Andre Coleman RC .20 .07
❑ 55 Gary Brown .20 .07
❑ 56 Neil Smith .40 .15
❑ 57 Myron Baker .20 .07
❑ 58 Sean Dawkins RC .75 .30
❑ 59 Marvin Washington .20 .07
❑ 60 Steve Beuerlein .40 .15
❑ 61 Brentson Buckner RC .20 .07
❑ 62 William Gaines RC .20 .07
❑ 63 LeShon Johnson RC .40 .15
❑ 64 Errict Rhett RC .75 .30
❑ 65 Jim Everett .40 .15
❑ 66 Desmond Howard .40 .15
❑ 67 Jack Del Rio .20 .07
❑ 68 Isaac Bruce RC 12.00 6.00
❑ 69 Van Malone RC .20 .07
❑ 70 Jim Kelly .75 .30
❑ 71 Leon Lett .20 .07
❑ 72 Greg Robinson .20 .07
❑ 73 Ryan Yarborough RC .20 .07
❑ 74 Terry Wooden .20 .07
❑ 75 Eric Allen .20 .07
❑ 76 Ernest Givins .40 .15
❑ 77 Marcus Spears RC .20 .07
❑ 78 Thomas Randolph RC .20 .07
❑ 79 Willie Clark RC .20 .07
❑ 80 John Elway 4.00 1.50
❑ 81 Aubrey Beavers RC .20 .07
❑ 82 Jeff Cothran RC .20 .07
❑ 83 Norm Johnson .20 .07
❑ 84 Donnell Bennett RC .75 .30
❑ 85 Phillippi Sparks .20 .07
❑ 86 Scott Mitchell .40 .15
❑ 87 Bucky Brooks RC .20 .07
❑ 88 Courtney Hawkins .20 .07
❑ 89 Kevin Greene .40 .15
❑ 90 Doug Nussmeier RC .20 .07
❑ 91 Floyd Turner .20 .07
❑ 92 Anthony Newman .20 .07
❑ 93 Vinny Testaverde .40 .15
❑ 94 Ronnie Lott .40 .15
❑ 95 Troy Aikman 2.00 .75
❑ 96 John Taylor .40 .15
❑ 97 Henry Ellard .40 .15
❑ 98 Carl Lee .20 .07
❑ 99 Terry McDaniel .20 .07
❑ 100 Joe Montana 4.00 1.50
❑ 101 David Klingler .20 .07
❑ 102 Bruce Walker RC .20 .07
❑ 103 Rick Cunningham RC .20 .07
❑ 104 Robert Delpino .20 .07
❑ 105 Mark Ingram .20 .07
❑ 106 Leslie O'Neal .20 .07
❑ 107 Darrell Thompson .20 .07
❑ 108 Dave Meggett .20 .07
❑ 109 Chris Gardocki .20 .07
❑ 110 Andre Rison .40 .15
❑ 111 Kelvin Martin .20 .07
❑ 112 Marcus Robertson .20 .07
❑ 113 Jason Gildon RC 3.00 1.25
❑ 114 Mel Gray .20 .07
❑ 115 Tommy Vardell .20 .07
❑ 116 Dexter Carter .20 .07
❑ 117 Scottie Graham RC .40 .15
❑ 118 Horace Copeland .20 .07
❑ 119 Cornelius Bennett .40 .15
❑ 120 Chris Maumalanga RC .20 .07
❑ 121 Mo Lewis .20 .07
❑ 122 Toby Wright RC .20 .07
❑ 123 George Hegamin RC .20 .07
❑ 124 Chip Lohmiller .20 .07
❑ 125 Calvin Jones RC .20 .07
❑ 126 Steve Shine .20 .07
❑ 127 Chuck Levy RC .20 .07
❑ 128 Sam Mills .20 .07
❑ 129 Terance Mathis .40 .15
❑ 130 Randall Cunningham .75 .30
❑ 131 John Fina .20 .07
❑ 132 Reggie White .75 .30
❑ 133 Tom Waddle .20 .07
❑ 134 Chris Calloway .20 .07
❑ 135 Kevin Mawae RC .75 .30
❑ 136 Lake Dawson RC .40 .15
❑ 137 Alai Kalaniubalu .20 .07
❑ 138 Tom Nalen RC .75 .30
❑ 139 Cody Carlson .20 .07
❑ 140 Dan Marino 4.00 1.50
❑ 141 Harris Barton .20 .07
❑ 142 Don Mosebar .20 .07
❑ 143 Romeo Bandison .20 .07
❑ 144 Bruce Smith .75 .30
❑ 145 Warren Moon .75 .30
❑ 146 David Lutz .20 .07
❑ 147 Dermontti Dawson .20 .07
❑ 148 Ricky Proehl .20 .07
❑ 149 Lou Benfatti RC .20 .07
❑ 150 Craig Erickson .20 .07
❑ 151 Sean Gilbert .20 .07
❑ 152 Zefross Moss .20 .07
❑ 153 Darnay Scott RC 1.25 .50
❑ 154 Courtney Hall .20 .07
❑ 155 Brian Mitchell .20 .07
❑ 156 Joe Burch RC UER 333 .20 .07
❑ 157 Terry Mickens .20 .07
❑ 158 Jay Novacek .40 .15
❑ 159 Chris Gedney .20 .07
❑ 160 Bruce Matthews .20 .07
❑ 161 Marlo Perry RC .20 .07
❑ 162 Vince Buck .20 .07
❑ 163 Michael Bates .20 .07
❑ 164 Willie Davis .40 .15
❑ 165 Mike Pritchard .20 .07
❑ 166 Doug Riesenberg .20 .07
❑ 167 Herschel Walker .40 .15
❑ 168 Tim Ruddy RC .20 .07
❑ 169 William Floyd RC .75 .30
❑ 170 John Randle .40 .15
❑ 171 Winston Moss .20 .07
❑ 172 Thurman Thomas .75 .30
❑ 173 Eric England RC .20 .07
❑ 174 Vincent Brisby .40 .15
❑ 175 Greg Lloyd .40 .15
❑ 176 Paul Gruber .20 .07
❑ 177 Brad Ottis RC .20 .07
❑ 178 George Teague .20 .07
❑ 179 Willie Jackson RC .75 .30
❑ 180 Barry Sanders 3.00 1.25
❑ 181 Brian Washington .20 .07
❑ 182 Michael Jackson .40 .15
❑ 183 Jason Mathews RC .20 .07
❑ 184 Chester McGlockton .20 .07
❑ 185 Tydus Winans RC .20 .07
❑ 186 Michael Haynes .40 .15
❑ 187 Erik Kramer .40 .15
❑ 188 Chris Doleman .20 .07
❑ 189 Haywood Jeffires .40 .15
❑ 190 Larry Whigham RC .20 .07
❑ 191 Shawn Jefferson .20 .07
❑ 192 Pete Stoyanovich .20 .07
❑ 193 Rod Bernstine .20 .07
❑ 194 William Thomas .20 .07
❑ 195 Marcus Allen .75 .30
❑ 196 Dave Brown .40 .15
❑ 197 Harold Bishop RC .20 .07
❑ 198 Lorenzo Lynch .20 .07
❑ 199 Dwight Stone .20 .07
❑ 200 Jerry Rice 2.00 .75
❑ 201 Rocket Ismail .40 .15
❑ 202 LeRoy Butler .20 .07
❑ 203 Glenn Parker .20 .07
❑ 204 Bruce Armstrong .20 .07
❑ 205 Shane Conlan .20 .07
❑ 206 Russell Maryland .20 .07
❑ 207 Herman Moore .75 .30
❑ 208 Eric Martin .20 .07
❑ 209 John Friesz .40 .15
❑ 210 Boomer Esiason .40 .15
❑ 211 Jim Harbaugh .75 .30
❑ 212 Harold Green .20 .07

❑ 213 Perry Klein RC .20 .07
❑ 214 Eric Metcalf .40 .15
❑ 215 Steve Everitt .20 .07
❑ 216 Victor Bailey .20 .07
❑ 217 Lincoln Kennedy .20 .07
❑ 218 Glyn Milburn .40 .15
❑ 219 John Copeland .20 .07
❑ 220 Drew Bledsoe 2.00 .75
❑ 221 Kevin Williams WR .40 .15
❑ 222 Roosevelt Potts .20 .07
❑ 223 Troy Drayton .20 .07
❑ 224 Terry Kirby .75 .30
❑ 225 Ronald Moore .20 .07
❑ 226 Tyrone Hughes .40 .15
❑ 227 Wayne Simmons .20 .07
❑ 228 Tony McGee .20 .07
❑ 229 Derek Brown RBK .20 .07
❑ 230 Jason Elam .40 .15
❑ 231 Qadry Ismail .75 .30
❑ 232 O.J.McDuffie .75 .30
❑ 233 Mike Caldwell .20 .07
❑ 234 Reggie Brooks .40 .15
❑ 235 Rick Mirer .75 .30
❑ 236 Steve Tovar .20 .07
❑ 237 Patrick Robinson .20 .07
❑ 238 Tom Carter .20 .07
❑ 239 Ben Coates .40 .15
❑ 240 Jerome Bettis 1.25 .50
❑ 241 Garrison Hearst .75 .30
❑ 242 Natrone Means .75 .30
❑ 243 Dana Stubblefield .40 .15
❑ 244 Willie Roaf .20 .07
❑ 245 Cortez Kennedy .40 .15
❑ 246 Todd Steussie RC .40 .15
❑ 247 Pat Coleman .20 .07
❑ 248 David Wyman .20 .07
❑ 249 Jeremy Lincoln .20 .07
❑ 250 Carlester Crumpler .20 .07
❑ 251 Dale Carter .20 .07
❑ 252 Corey Raymond RC .20 .07
❑ 253 Bryan Cox .20 .07
❑ 254 Charlie Garner RC 3.00 1.25
❑ 255 Jeff Hostetler .40 .15
❑ 256 Shane Bonham RC .20 .07
❑ 257 Thomas Everett .20 .07
❑ 258 John Jackson T .20 .07
❑ 259 Terry Irving RC .20 .07
❑ 260 Corey Sawyer .40 .15
❑ 261 Rob Waldrop .20 .07
❑ 262 Curtis Conway .75 .30
❑ 263 Winfred Tubbs RC .40 .15
❑ 264 Sean Jones .20 .07
❑ 265 James Washington .20 .07
❑ 266 Lonnie Johnson RC .20 .07
❑ 267 Rob Moore .40 .15
❑ 268 Flipper Anderson .20 .07
❑ 269 Jon Hand .20 .07
❑ 270 Joe Patton RC .20 .07
❑ 271 Howard Ballard .20 .07
❑ 272 Fernando Smith RC .20 .07
❑ 273 Jessie Tuggle .20 .07
❑ 274 John Alt .20 .07
❑ 275 Corey Miller .20 .07
❑ 276 Gus Frerotte RC .75 .30
❑ 277 Jeff Cross .20 .07
❑ 278 Kevin Smith .20 .07
❑ 279 Corey Louchiey RC .20 .07
❑ 280 Micheal Barrow .20 .07
❑ 281 Jim Flanigan RC .40 .15
❑ 282 Calvin Williams .40 .15
❑ 283 Jeff Jaeger .20 .07
❑ 284 John Reece RC .20 .07
❑ 285 Jason Hanson .20 .07
❑ 286 Kurt Haws RC .20 .07
❑ 287 Eric Davis .20 .07
❑ 288 Maurice Hurst .20 .07
❑ 289 Kirk Lowdermilk .20 .07
❑ 290 Rod Woodson .40 .15
❑ 291 Andre Reed .40 .15
❑ 292 Vince Workman .20 .07
❑ 293 Wayne Martin .20 .07
❑ 294 Keith Lyle RC .20 .07
❑ 295 Brett Favre 4.00 1.50
❑ 296 Doug Brien RC .20 .07
❑ 297 Junior Seau .75 .30
❑ 298 Randall McDaniel .20 .07
❑ 299 Johnny Mitchell .20 .07
❑ 300 Emmitt Smith 3.00 1.25
❑ 301 Michael Brooks .20 .07
❑ 302 Steve Jackson .20 .07
❑ 303 Jeff George .75 .30
❑ 304 Irving Fryar .40 .15
❑ 305 Derrick Thomas .75 .30
❑ 306 Dante Jones .20 .07
❑ 307 Darrell Green .20 .07
❑ 308 Mark Bavaro .20 .07
❑ 309 Eugene Robinson .20 .07
❑ 310 Shannon Sharpe .40 .15
❑ 311 Michael Timpson .20 .07
❑ 312 Kevin Mitchell RC .20 .07
❑ 313 Stevon Moore .20 .07
❑ 314 Eric Swann .40 .15
❑ 315 James Bostic RC .75 .30
❑ 316 Robert Brooks .75 .30
❑ 317 Pete Pierson RC .20 .07
❑ 318 Jim Sweeney .20 .07
❑ 319 Anthony Smith .20 .07
❑ 320 Rohn Stark .20 .07
❑ 321 Gary Anderson K .20 .07
❑ 322 Robert Porcher .20 .07
❑ 323 Darryl Talley .20 .07
❑ 324 Stan Humphries .40 .15
❑ 325 Shelly Hammonds RC .20 .07
❑ 326 Jim McMahon .40 .15
❑ 327 Lamont Warren RC .20 .07
❑ 328 Chris Penn RC .20 .07
❑ 329 Tony Woods .20 .07
❑ 330 Raymont Harris RC .75 .30
❑ 331 Mitch Davis RC .20 .07
❑ 332 Michael Irvin .75 .30
❑ 333 Kent Graham .40 .15
❑ 334 Brian Blades .40 .15
❑ 335 Lomas Brown .20 .07
❑ 336 Willie Drewrey .20 .07
❑ 337 Russell Freeman .20 .07
❑ 338 Eric Zomalt RC .20 .07
❑ 339 Santana Dotson .40 .15
❑ 340 Sterling Sharpe .40 .15
❑ 341 Ray Crittenden RC .20 .07
❑ 342 Perry Carter RC .20 .07
❑ 343 Austin Robbins .20 .07
❑ 344 Mike Wells DT RC .20 .07
❑ 345 Toddrick McIntosh RC .20 .07
❑ 346 Mark Carrier WR .40 .15
❑ 347 Eugene Daniel .20 .07
❑ 348 Tre Johnson RC .20 .07
❑ 349 D.J. Johnson .20 .07
❑ 350 Steve Young 1.50 .60
❑ 351 Jim Pyne RC .20 .07
❑ 352 Joselyn Borgella RC .20 .07
❑ 353 Pat Carter .20 .07
❑ 354 Sam Rogers RC .20 .07
❑ 355 Jason Sehorn RC 1.25 .50
❑ 356 Darren Carrington .20 .07
❑ 357 Lamar Smith RC 4.00 1.50
❑ 358 James Burton RC .20 .07
❑ 359 Darrin Smith .20 .07
❑ 360 Marco Coleman .20 .07
❑ 361 Webster Slaughter .20 .07
❑ 362 Lewis Tillman .20 .07
❑ 363 David Alexander .20 .07
❑ 364 Bradford Banta RC .20 .07
❑ 365 Erric Pegram .20 .07
❑ 366 Mike Fox .20 .07
❑ 367 Jeff Lageman .20 .07
❑ 368 Kurt Gouveia .20 .07
❑ 369 Tim Brown .75 .30
❑ 370 Seth Joyner .20 .07
❑ 371 Irv Eatman .20 .07
❑ 372 Dorsey Levens RC 4.00 1.50
❑ 373 Anthony Pleasant .20 .07
❑ 374 Henry Jones .20 .07
❑ 375 Cris Carter 1.00 .40
❑ 376 Morten Andersen .20 .07
❑ 377 Neil O'Donnell .75 .30
❑ 378 Tyronne Drakeford RC .20 .07
❑ 379 John Carney .20 .07
❑ 380 Vincent Brown .20 .07
❑ 381 J.J. Birden .20 .07
❑ 382 Chris Spielman .40 .15
❑ 383 Mark Bortz .20 .07
❑ 384 Ray Childress .20 .07
❑ 385 Carlton Bailey .20 .07
❑ 386 Charles Haley .40 .15
❑ 387 Shane Dronett .20 .07
❑ 388 Jon Vaughn .20 .07
❑ 389 Checklist 1-195 .20 .07
❑ 390 Checklist 196-390 .20 .07

1995 Bowman

❑ COMPLETE SET (357) 60.00 25.00
❑ 1 Ki-Jana Carter RC .75 .30
❑ 2 Tony Boselli RC .75 .30
❑ 3 Steve McNair RC 8.00 3.00
❑ 4 Michael Westbrook RC .60 .25
❑ 5 Kerry Collins RC 4.00 1.50
❑ 6 Kevin Carter RC .75 .30
❑ 7 Mike Mamula RC .20 .05
❑ 8 Joey Galloway RC 4.00 1.50
❑ 9 Kyle Brady RC .75 .30
❑ 10 J.J. Stokes RC .75 .30
❑ 11 Derrick Alexander DE RC .20 .05
❑ 12 Warren Sapp RC 4.00 1.50
❑ 13 Mark Fields RC .75 .30
❑ 14 Ruben Brown RC .75 .30
❑ 15 Ellis Johnson RC .20 .05
❑ 16 Hugh Douglas RC .75 .30
❑ 17 Mike Pelton RC .20 .05
❑ 18 Napoleon Kaufman RC 3.00 1.25
❑ 19 James O. Stewart RC 2.50 1.00
❑ 20 Luther Elliss RC .20 .05
❑ 21 Rashaan Salaam RC .40 .15
❑ 22 Tyrone Poole RC .75 .30
❑ 23 Ty Law RC 3.00 1.25
❑ 24 Korey Stringer RC .40 .15
❑ 25 Billy Milner RC .20 .05
❑ 26 Devin Bush RC .20 .05
❑ 27 Mark Bruener RC .40 .15
❑ 28 Derrick Brooks RC 4.00 1.50
❑ 29 Blake Brockermeyer RC .20 .05
❑ 30 Alundis Brice RC .20 .05
❑ 31 Trezelle Jenkins RC .20 .05
❑ 32 Craig Newsome RC .20 .05
❑ 33 Fred Barnett .30 .10
❑ 34 Ray Childress .15 .05
❑ 35 Chris Miller .15 .05
❑ 36 Charles Haley .30 .10
❑ 37 Ray Crittenden .15 .05
❑ 38 Gus Frerotte .30 .10
❑ 39 Jeff George .30 .10
❑ 40 Dan Marino 3.00 1.25
❑ 41 Shawn Lee .15 .05
❑ 42 Herman Moore .60 .25
❑ 43 Chris Calloway .15 .05
❑ 44 Jeff Graham .15 .05
❑ 45 Ray Buchanan .15 .05
❑ 46 Doug Pelfrey .15 .05
❑ 47 Lake Dawson .30 .10
❑ 48 Glenn Parker .15 .05
❑ 49 Terry McDaniel .15 .05
❑ 50 Rod Woodson .30 .10
❑ 51 Santana Dotson .15 .05
❑ 52 Anthony Miller .30 .10
❑ 53 Bo Orlando .15 .05
❑ 54 David Palmer .30 .10
❑ 55 William Floyd .30 .10
❑ 56 Edgar Bennett .30 .10
❑ 57 Jeff Blake RC 2.50 1.00
❑ 58 Anthony Pleasant .15 .05
❑ 59 Quinn Early .30 .10
❑ 60 Bobby Houston .15 .05
❑ 61 Terrell Fletcher RC .20 .05
❑ 62 Gary Brown .15 .05
❑ 63 Dwayne Sabb .15 .05
❑ 64 Roman Phifer .15 .05
❑ 65 Sherman Williams RC .20 .05
❑ 66 Roosevelt Potts .15 .05
❑ 67 Darnay Scott .30 .10
❑ 68 Charlie Garner .60 .25
❑ 69 Bert Emanuel .60 .25

❑ 70 Herschel Walker .30 .10
❑ 71 Lorenzo Styles RC .20 .05
❑ 72 Andre Coleman .15 .05
❑ 73 Tyronne Drakeford .15 .05
❑ 74 Jay Novacek .30 .10
❑ 75 Raymont Harris .15 .05
❑ 76 Tamarick Vanover RC .75 .30
❑ 77 Tom Carter .15 .05
❑ 78 Eric Green .15 .05
❑ 79 Patrick Hunter .15 .05
❑ 80 Jeff Hostetler .30 .10
❑ 81 Robert Blackmon .15 .05
❑ 82 Anthony Cook RC .20 .05
❑ 83 Craig Erickson .15 .05
❑ 84 Glyn Milburn .15 .05
❑ 85 Greg Lloyd .30 .10
❑ 86 Brent Jones .15 .05
❑ 87 Barrett Brooks RC .20 .05
❑ 88 Alvin Harper .15 .05
❑ 89 Sean Jones .15 .05
❑ 90 Cris Carter .60 .25
❑ 91 Russell Copeland .15 .05
❑ 92 Frank Sanders RC .75 .30
❑ 93 Mo Lewis .15 .05
❑ 94 Michael Haynes .30 .10
❑ 95 Andre Rison .30 .10
❑ 96 Jesse James RC .20 .05
❑ 97 Stan Humphries .30 .10
❑ 98 James Hasty .15 .05
❑ 99 Ricardo McDonald .15 .05
❑ 100 Jerry Rice 1.50 .60
❑ 101 Chris Hudson RC .20 .05
❑ 102 Dave Meggett .15 .05
❑ 103 Brian Mitchell .15 .05
❑ 104 Mike Johnson .15 .05
❑ 105 Kordell Stewart RC 4.00 1.50
❑ 106 Michael Brooks .15 .05
❑ 107 Steve Walsh .15 .05
❑ 108 Eric Metcalf .30 .10
❑ 109 Ricky Watters .30 .10
❑ 110 Brett Favre 3.00 1.25
❑ 111 Aubrey Beavers .15 .05
❑ 112 Brian Williams LB RC .20 .05
❑ 113 Eugene Robinson .15 .05
❑ 114 Matt O'Dwyer RC .20 .05
❑ 115 Micheal Barrow .15 .05
❑ 116 Rocket Ismail .30 .10
❑ 117 Scott Gragg RC .20 .05
❑ 118 Leon Lett .15 .05
❑ 119 Reggie Roby .15 .05
❑ 120 Marshall Faulk 2.00 .75
❑ 121 Jack Jackson RC .20 .05
❑ 122 Keith Byars .15 .05
❑ 123 Eric Hill .15 .05
❑ 124 Todd Sauerbrun RC .20 .05
❑ 125 Dexter Carter .15 .05
❑ 126 Vinny Testaverde .30 .10
❑ 127 Shane Conlan .15 .05
❑ 128 Terrance Shaw RC .20 .05
❑ 129 Willie Roaf .15 .05
❑ 130 Jim Kelly .60 .25
❑ 131 Neil O'Donnell .30 .10
❑ 132 Ray McElroy RC .20 .05
❑ 133 Ed McDaniel .15 .05
❑ 134 Brian Gelzheiser RC .20 .05
❑ 135 Marcus Allen .60 .25
❑ 136 Carl Pickens .30 .10
❑ 137 Mike Verstegan RC .20 .05
❑ 138 Chris Mims .15 .05
❑ 139 Darryl Pounds RC .20 .05
❑ 140 Emmitt Smith 2.50 1.25
❑ 141 Mike Frederick RC .20 .05
❑ 142 Henry Ellard .30 .10
❑ 143 Willie McGinest .30 .10
❑ 144 Michael Roan RC .20 .05
❑ 145 Chris Spielman .30 .10
❑ 146 Darryl Talley .15 .05
❑ 147 Randall Cunningham .60 .25
❑ 148 Andrew Greene RC .20 .05
❑ 149 George Teague .15 .05
❑ 150 Tyrone Hughes .30 .10
❑ 151 Ron Davis RC .20 .05
❑ 152 Stevon Moore .15 .05
❑ 153 Merton Hanks .15 .05
❑ 154 Darren Perry .15 .05
❑ 155 Dave Brown .30 .10
❑ 156 Mike Morton RC .20 .05
❑ 157 Seth Joyner .15 .05
❑ 158 Bryan Cox .15 .05
❑ 159 Corey Fuller RC .20 .05
❑ 160 John Elway 3.00 1.25
❑ 161 Dewayne Washington .30 .10
❑ 162 Chris Warren .30 .10
❑ 163 Jeff Kopp RC .20 .05
❑ 164 Sean Dawkins .30 .10
❑ 165 Mark Carrier DB .15 .05
❑ 166 Andre Hastings .30 .10
❑ 167 Derek West RC .20 .05
❑ 168 Glenn Montgomery .15 .05
❑ 169 Trent Dilfer .60 .25
❑ 170 Rob Johnson RC 2.50 1.00
❑ 171 Todd Scott .15 .05
❑ 172 Charles Johnson .30 .10
❑ 173 Kez McCorvey RC .20 .05
❑ 174 Rob Fredrickson .15 .05
❑ 175 Corey Sawyer .15 .05
❑ 176 Brett Perriman .30 .10
❑ 177 Ken Dilger RC .75 .30
❑ 178 Dana Stubblefield .30 .10
❑ 179 Eric Allen .15 .05
❑ 180 Drew Bledsoe 1.00 .40
❑ 181 Tyrone Davis RC .20 .05
❑ 182 Reggie Brooks .30 .10
❑ 183 Dale Carter .30 .10
❑ 184 William Henderson RC 3.00 1.25
❑ 185 Reggie White .60 .25
❑ 186 Lorenzo White .15 .05
❑ 187 Leslie O'Neal .30 .10
❑ 188 Stoney Case RC .20 .05
❑ 189 Jeff Burris .15 .05
❑ 190 Leroy Hoard .15 .05
❑ 191 Thomas Randolph .15 .05
❑ 192 Rodney Thomas RC .40 .15
❑ 193 Quentin Coryatt .30 .10
❑ 194 Terry Wooden .15 .05
❑ 195 David Sloan RC .20 .05
❑ 196 Bernie Parmalee .30 .10
❑ 197 Zack Crockett RC .40 .15
❑ 198 Troy Aikman 1.50 .60
❑ 199 Bruce Smith .60 .25
❑ 200 Eric Zeier RC .75 .30
❑ 201 Anthony Smith .15 .05
❑ 202 Jake Reed .30 .10
❑ 203 Hardy Nickerson .15 .05
❑ 204 Patrick Riley RC .20 .05
❑ 205 Bruce Matthews .15 .05
❑ 206 Larry Centers .30 .10
❑ 207 Troy Drayton .15 .05
❑ 208 John Burrough RC .20 .05
❑ 209 Jason Elam .30 .10
❑ 210 Donnell Woolford .15 .05
❑ 211 Sam Shade RC .20 .05
❑ 212 Kevin Greene .30 .10
❑ 213 Ronald Moore .15 .05
❑ 214 Shane Hannah RC .20 .05
❑ 215 Jim Everett .15 .05
❑ 216 Scott Mitchell .30 .10
❑ 217 Antonio Freeman RC 3.00 1.25
❑ 218 Tony McGee .15 .05
❑ 219 Clay Matthews .30 .10
❑ 220 Neil Smith .30 .10
❑ 221 Mark Williams FOIL .40 .15
❑ 222 Derrick Graham FOIL .40 .15
❑ 223 Mike Hollis FOIL .40 .15
❑ 224 Darion Conner FOIL .40 .15
❑ 225 Steve Beuerlein FOIL .40 .15
❑ 226 Rod Smith DB FOIL .40 .15
❑ 227 James Williams LB FOIL .40 .15
❑ 228 Bob Christian FOIL .40 .15
❑ 229 Jeff Lageman FOIL .40 .15
❑ 230 Frank Reich FOIL .40 .15
❑ 231 Harry Colon FOIL .40 .15
❑ 232 Carlton Bailey FOIL .40 .15
❑ 233 Mickey Washington FOIL .40 .15
❑ 234 Shawn Bouwens FOIL .40 .15
❑ 235 Don Beebe FOIL .40 .15
❑ 236 Kelvin Pritchett FOIL .40 .15
❑ 237 Tommy Barnhardt FOIL .40 .15
❑ 238 Mike Dumas FOIL .40 .15
❑ 239 Brett Maxie FOIL .40 .15
❑ 240 Desmond Howard FOIL .40 .15
❑ 241 Sam Mills FOIL .40 .15
❑ 242 Keith Goganious FOIL .40 .15
❑ 243 Bubba McDowell FOIL .40 .15
❑ 244 Vinnie Clark FOIL .40 .15
❑ 245 Lamar Lathon FOIL .40 .15
❑ 246 Bryan Barker FOIL .40 .15
❑ 247 Darren Carrington FOIL .40 .15
❑ 248 Jay Barker RC .20 .05
❑ 249 Eric Davis .15 .05
❑ 250 Heath Shuler .30 .10
❑ 251 Donta Jones RC .20 .05
❑ 252 LeRoy Butler .15 .05
❑ 253 Michael Zordich .15 .05
❑ 254 Cortez Kennedy .30 .10
❑ 255 Brian DeMarco RC .20 .05
❑ 256 Randal Hill .15 .05
❑ 257 Michael Irvin .60 .25
❑ 258 Natrone Means .30 .10
❑ 259 Linc Harden RC .20 .05
❑ 260 Jerome Bettis .60 .25
❑ 261 Tony Bennett .15 .05
❑ 262 Dameian Jeffries RC .20 .05
❑ 263 Cornelius Bennett .30 .10
❑ 264 Chris Zorich .15 .05
❑ 265 Bobby Taylor RC .75 .30
❑ 266 Terrell Buckley .15 .05
❑ 267 Troy Dumas RC .20 .05
❑ 268 Rodney Hampton .30 .10
❑ 269 Steve Everitt .15 .05
❑ 270 Mel Gray .15 .05
❑ 271 Antonio Armstrong RC .20 .05
❑ 272 Jim Harbaugh .30 .10
❑ 273 Gary Clark .15 .05
❑ 274 Tau Pupua RC .20 .05
❑ 275 Warren Moon .30 .10
❑ 276 Corey Croom .15 .05
❑ 277 Tony Berti RC .20 .05
❑ 278 Shannon Sharpe .30 .10
❑ 279 Boomer Esiason .30 .10
❑ 280 Aeneas Williams .15 .05
❑ 281 Lethon Flowers RC .20 .05
❑ 282 Derek Brown TE .15 .05
❑ 283 Charlie Williams RC .20 .05
❑ 284 Dan Wilkinson .30 .10
❑ 285 Mike Sherrard .15 .05
❑ 286 Evan Pilgrim RC .20 .05
❑ 287 Kimble Anders .30 .10
❑ 288 Greg Jefferson RC .20 .05
❑ 289 Ken Norton .30 .10
❑ 290 Terance Mathis .30 .10
❑ 291 Torey Hunter RC .20 .05
❑ 292 Ken Harvey .15 .05
❑ 293 Irving Fryar .30 .10
❑ 294 Michael Reed RC .20 .05
❑ 295 Andre Reed .30 .10
❑ 296 Vencie Glenn .15 .05
❑ 297 Corey Swinson .15 .05
❑ 298 Harvey Williams .15 .05
❑ 299 Willie Davis .30 .10
❑ 300 Barry Sanders 2.50 1.00
❑ 301 Curtis Martin RC 8.00 3.00
❑ 302 Johnny Mitchell .15 .05
❑ 303 Daryl Johnston .30 .10
❑ 304 Lorenzo Lynch .15 .05
❑ 305 Christian Fauria RC .40 .15
❑ 306 Sean Gilbert .30 .10
❑ 307 Ray Zellars RC .40 .15
❑ 308 William Strong RC .20 .05
❑ 309 Jack Del Rio .15 .05
❑ 310 Junior Seau .60 .25
❑ 311 Justin Armour RC .20 .05
❑ 312 Eric Bjornson RC .20 .05
❑ 313 Vincent Brown .15 .05
❑ 314 Darius Holland RC .20 .05
❑ 315 Chad May RC .20 .05
❑ 316 Simon Fletcher .15 .05
❑ 317 Roell Preston RC .30 .10
❑ 318 John Thierry .15 .05
❑ 319 Orlando Thomas RC .20 .05
❑ 320 Zach Wiegert RC .20 .05
❑ 321 Derrick Alexander WR .60 .25
❑ 322 Chris Cowart RC .20 .05
❑ 323 Chris Sanders RC .40 .15
❑ 324 Robert Brooks .60 .25
❑ 325 Todd Collins RC 2.50 1.00
❑ 326 Ken Irvin RC .20 .05
❑ 327 Erric Pegram .30 .10
❑ 328 Damien Covington RC .20 .05
❑ 329 Brendan Stai RC .20 .05
❑ 330 James A.Stewart RC .20 .05
❑ 331 Jessie Tuggle .15 .05
❑ 332 Marco Coleman .15 .05
❑ 333 Steve Young 1.25 .50
❑ 334 Greg Hill .30 .10
❑ 335 Darryl Williams .15 .05
❑ 336 Calvin Williams .30 .10

❑ 337 Cris Dishman .15 .05
❑ 338 Anthony Morgan .15 .05
❑ 339 Renaldo Turnbull .15 .05
❑ 340 Rick Mirer .30 .10
❑ 341 Tim Brown .60 .25
❑ 342 Dennis Gibson .15 .05
❑ 343 Brad Baxter .15 .05
❑ 344 Henry Jones .15 .05
❑ 345 Johnny Bailey .15 .05
❑ 346 Rocket Ismail .30 .10
❑ 347 Richmond Webb .15 .05
❑ 348 Robert Jones .15 .05
❑ 349 Garrison Hearst .60 .25
❑ 350 Errict Rhett .30 .10
❑ 351 Steve Atwater .15 .05
❑ 352 Joe Cain .15 .05
❑ 353 Ben Coates .30 .10
❑ 354 Aaron Glenn .15 .05
❑ 355 Antonio Langham .15 .05
❑ 356 Eugene Daniel .15 .05
❑ 357 Tim Bowens .15 .05

1998 Bowman

❑ COMPLETE SET (220) 50.00 20.00
❑ 1 Peyton Manning RC 25.00 12.50
❑ 2 Keith Brooking RC 1.50 .60
❑ 3 Duane Starks RC .75 .30
❑ 4 Takeo Spikes RC 1.50 .60
❑ 5 Andre Wadsworth RC 1.25 .50
❑ 6 Greg Ellis RC .75 .30
❑ 7 Brian Griese RC 3.00 1.25
❑ 8 Germane Crowell RC 1.25 .50
❑ 9 Jerome Pathon RC 1.50 .60
❑ 10 Ryan Leaf RC 1.50 .60
❑ 11 Fred Taylor RC 2.50 1.00
❑ 12 Robert Edwards RC 1.25 .50
❑ 13 Grant Wistrom RC 1.25 .50
❑ 14 Robert Holcombe RC 1.25 .50
❑ 15 Tim Dwight RC 1.50 .60
❑ 16 Jacquez Green RC 1.25 .50
❑ 17 Marcus Nash RC .75 .30
❑ 18 Jason Peter RC .75 .30
❑ 19 Anthony Simmons RC 1.25 .50
❑ 20 Curtis Enis RC .75 .30
❑ 21 John Avery RC 1.25 .50
❑ 22 Pat Johnson RC 1.25 .50
❑ 23 Joe Jurevicius RC 1.50 .60
❑ 24 Brian Simmons RC 1.25 .50
❑ 25 Kevin Dyson RC 1.50 .60
❑ 26 Skip Hicks RC 1.25 .50
❑ 27 Hines Ward RC 8.00 3.00
❑ 28 Tavian Banks RC 1.25 .50
❑ 29 Ahman Green RC 8.00 3.00
❑ 30 Tony Simmons RC 1.25 .50
❑ 31 Charles Johnson .30 .10
❑ 32 Freddie Jones .30 .10
❑ 33 Joey Galloway .50 .20
❑ 34 Tony Banks .50 .20
❑ 35 Jake Plummer .75 .30
❑ 36 Reidel Anthony .50 .20
❑ 37 Steve McNair .75 .30
❑ 38 Michael Westbrook .50 .20
❑ 39 Chris Sanders .30 .10
❑ 40 Isaac Bruce .75 .30
❑ 41 Charlie Garner .50 .20
❑ 42 Wayne Chrebet .75 .30
❑ 43 Michael Strahan .50 .20
❑ 44 Brad Johnson .75 .30
❑ 45 Mike Alstott .75 .30
❑ 46 Tony Gonzalez .75 .30
❑ 47 Johnnie Morton .50 .20
❑ 48 Darnay Scott .50 .20
❑ 49 Rae Carruth .30 .10
❑ 50 Terrell Davis .75 .30
❑ 51 Jermaine Lewis .50 .20
❑ 52 Frank Sanders .50 .20
❑ 53 Byron Hanspard .30 .10
❑ 54 Gus Frerotte .30 .10
❑ 55 Terry Glenn .75 .30
❑ 56 J.J. Stokes .50 .20
❑ 57 Will Blackwell .30 .10
❑ 58 Keyshawn Johnson .75 .30
❑ 59 Tiki Barber .75 .30
❑ 60 Dorsey Levens .75 .30
❑ 61 Zach Thomas .75 .30
❑ 62 Corey Dillon .75 .30
❑ 63 Antowain Smith .75 .30
❑ 64 Michael Sinclair .30 .10
❑ 65 Rod Smith .50 .20
❑ 66 Trent Dilfer .75 .30
❑ 67 Warren Sapp .50 .20
❑ 68 Charles Way .30 .10
❑ 69 Tamarick Vanover .30 .10
❑ 70 Drew Bledsoe 1.25 .50
❑ 71 John Mobley .30 .10
❑ 72 Kerry Collins .50 .20
❑ 73 Peter Boulware .30 .10
❑ 74 Simeon Rice .50 .20
❑ 75 Eddie George .75 .30
❑ 76 Fred Lane .30 .10
❑ 77 Jamal Anderson .75 .30
❑ 78 Antonio Freeman .75 .30
❑ 79 Jason Sehorn .50 .20
❑ 80 Curtis Martin .75 .30
❑ 81 Bobby Hoying .50 .20
❑ 82 Garrison Hearst .75 .30
❑ 83 Glenn Foley .50 .20
❑ 84 Danny Kanell .50 .20
❑ 85 Kordell Stewart .75 .30
❑ 86 O.J. McDuffie .50 .20
❑ 87 Marvin Harrison .75 .30
❑ 88 Bobby Engram .50 .20
❑ 89 Chris Slade .30 .10
❑ 90 Warrick Dunn .75 .30
❑ 91 Ricky Watters .50 .20
❑ 92 Rickey Dudley .30 .10
❑ 93 Terrell Owens .75 .30
❑ 94 Karim Abdul-Jabbar .75 .30
❑ 95 Napoleon Kaufman .75 .30
❑ 96 Darrell Green .50 .20
❑ 97 Levon Kirkland .30 .10
❑ 98 Jeff George .50 .20
❑ 99 Andre Hastings .30 .10
❑ 100 John Elway 3.00 1.25
❑ 101 John Randle .50 .20
❑ 102 Andre Rison .50 .20
❑ 103 Keenan McCardell .50 .20
❑ 104 Marshall Faulk 1.00 .40
❑ 105 Emmitt Smith 2.50 1.00
❑ 106 Robert Brooks .50 .20
❑ 107 Scott Mitchell .50 .20
❑ 108 Shannon Sharpe .50 .20
❑ 109 Deion Sanders .75 .30
❑ 110 Jerry Rice 1.50 .60
❑ 111 Erik Kramer .30 .10
❑ 112 Michael Jackson .30 .10
❑ 113 Aeneas Williams .30 .10
❑ 114 Terry Allen .75 .30
❑ 115 Steve Young 1.00 .40
❑ 116 Warren Moon .75 .30
❑ 117 Junior Seau .75 .30
❑ 118 Jerome Bettis .75 .30
❑ 119 Irving Fryar .50 .20
❑ 120 Barry Sanders 2.50 1.00
❑ 121 Tim Brown .75 .30
❑ 122 Chad Brown .30 .10
❑ 123 Ben Coates .50 .20
❑ 124 Robert Smith .75 .30
❑ 125 Brett Favre 3.00 1.25
❑ 126 Derrick Thomas .75 .30
❑ 127 Reggie White .75 .30
❑ 128 Troy Aikman 1.50 .60
❑ 129 Jeff Blake .50 .20
❑ 130 Mark Brunell .75 .30
❑ 131 Curtis Conway .50 .20
❑ 132 Wesley Walls .50 .20
❑ 133 Thurman Thomas .75 .30
❑ 134 Chris Chandler .50 .20
❑ 135 Dan Marino 3.00 1.25
❑ 136 Larry Centers .30 .10
❑ 137 Shawn Jefferson .30 .10
❑ 138 Andre Reed .50 .20
❑ 139 Jake Reed .50 .20
❑ 140 Cris Carter .75 .30
❑ 141 Elvis Grbac .50 .20
❑ 142 Mark Chmura .50 .20
❑ 143 Michael Irvin .75 .30
❑ 144 Carl Pickens .50 .20
❑ 145 Herman Moore .50 .20
❑ 146 Marvin Jones .30 .10
❑ 147 Terance Mathis .50 .20
❑ 148 Rob Moore .50 .20
❑ 149 Bruce Smith .50 .20
❑ 150 Rob Johnson CL .30 .10
❑ 151 Leslie Shepherd .30 .10
❑ 152 Chris Spielman .30 .10
❑ 153 Tony McGee .30 .10
❑ 154 Kevin Smith .30 .10
❑ 155 Bill Romanowski .30 .10
❑ 156 Stephen Boyd .30 .10
❑ 157 James Stewart .50 .20
❑ 158 Jason Taylor .50 .20
❑ 159 Troy Drayton .30 .10
❑ 160 Mark Fields .30 .10
❑ 161 Jessie Armstead .30 .10
❑ 162 James Jett .50 .20
❑ 163 Bobby Taylor .30 .10
❑ 164 Kimble Anders .50 .20
❑ 165 Jimmy Smith .50 .20
❑ 166 Quentin Coryatt .30 .10
❑ 167 Bryant Westbrook .30 .10
❑ 168 Neil Smith .50 .20
❑ 169 Darren Woodson .30 .10
❑ 170 Ray Buchanan .30 .10
❑ 171 Earl Holmes .30 .10
❑ 172 Ray Lewis .75 .30
❑ 173 Steve Broussard .30 .10
❑ 174 Derrick Brooks .75 .30
❑ 175 Ken Harvey .30 .10
❑ 176 Darryll Lewis .30 .10
❑ 177 Derrick Rodgers .30 .10
❑ 178 James McKnight .75 .30
❑ 179 Cris Dishman .30 .10
❑ 180 Hardy Nickerson .30 .10
❑ 181 Charles Woodson RC 2.00 .75
❑ 182 Randy Moss RC 15.00 7.50
❑ 183 Stephen Alexander RC 1.25 .50
❑ 184 Samari Rolle RC .75 .30
❑ 185 Jamie Duncan RC .75 .30
❑ 186 Lance Schulters RC .75 .30
❑ 187 Tony Parrish RC 1.50 .60
❑ 188 Corey Chavous RC 1.50 .60
❑ 189 Jammi German RC .75 .30
❑ 190 Sam Cowart RC 1.25 .50
❑ 191 Donald Hayes RC 1.25 .50
❑ 192 R.W. McQuarters RC 1.25 .50
❑ 193 Az-Zahir Hakim RC 1.50 .60
❑ 194 Chris Fuamatu-Ma'afala RC 1.25 .50
❑ 195 Allen Rossum RC 1.25 .50
❑ 196 Jon Ritchie RC 1.25 .50
❑ 197 Blake Spence RC .75 .30
❑ 198 Brian Alford RC .75 .30
❑ 199 Fred Weary RC .75 .30
❑ 200 Rod Rutledge RC .75 .30
❑ 201 Michael Myers RC .75 .30
❑ 202 Rashaan Shehee RC 1.25 .50
❑ 203 Donovin Darius RC 1.25 .50
❑ 204 E.G. Green RC 1.25 .50
❑ 205 Vonnie Holliday RC 1.25 .50
❑ 206 Charlie Batch RC 1.50 .60
❑ 207 Michael Pittman RC 2.00 .75
❑ 208 Artrell Hawkins RC .75 .30
❑ 209 Jonathan Quinn RC 1.50 .60
❑ 210 Kailee Wong RC .75 .30
❑ 211 DeShea Townsend RC .75 .30
❑ 212 Patrick Surtain RC 1.50 .60
❑ 213 Brian Kelly RC 1.25 .50
❑ 214 Tebucky Jones RC .75 .30
❑ 215 Pete Gonzalez RC .75 .30
❑ 216 Shaun Williams RC 1.25 .50
❑ 217 Scott Frost RC .75 .30
❑ 218 Leonard Little RC 1.50 .60
❑ 219 Alonzo Mayes RC .75 .30
❑ 220 Cordell Taylor RC .75 .30

1999 Bowman

❑ COMPLETE SET (220) 40.00 15.00
❑ 1 Dan Marino 2.50 1.00
❑ 2 Michael Westbrook .50 .20
❑ 3 Yancey Thigpen .30 .10

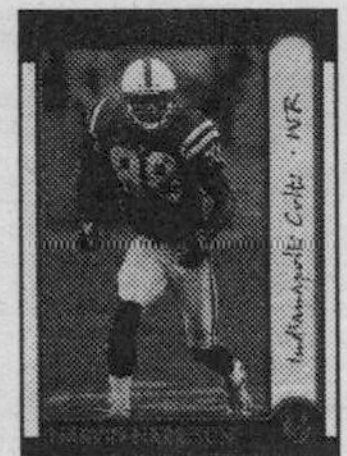

❑ 4 Tony Martin	.50	.20
❑ 5 Michael Strahan	.50	.20
❑ 6 Dedric Ward	.30	.10
❑ 7 Joey Galloway	.50	.20
❑ 8 Bobby Engram	.50	.20
❑ 9 Frank Sanders	.50	.20
❑ 10 Jake Plummer	.50	.20
❑ 11 Eddie Kennison	.50	.20
❑ 12 Curtis Martin	.75	.30
❑ 13 Chris Spielman	.30	.10
❑ 14 Trent Dilfer	.50	.20
❑ 15 Tim Biakabutuka	.50	.20
❑ 16 Elvis Grbac	.50	.20
❑ 17 Charlie Batch	.75	.30
❑ 18 Takeo Spikes	.30	.10
❑ 19 Tony Banks	.50	.20
❑ 20 Doug Flutie	.75	.30
❑ 21 Ty Law	.50	.20
❑ 22 Isaac Bruce	.75	.30
❑ 23 James Jett	.50	.20
❑ 24 Kent Graham	.30	.10
❑ 25 Derrick Mayes	.30	.10
❑ 26 Amani Toomer	.30	.10
❑ 27 Ray Lewis	.75	.30
❑ 28 Shawn Springs	.30	.10
❑ 29 Warren Sapp	.30	.10
❑ 30 Jamal Anderson	.75	.30
❑ 31 Byron Bam Morris	.30	.10
❑ 32 Johnnie Morton	.30	.10
❑ 33 Terance Mathis	.30	.10
❑ 34 Terrell Davis	.75	.30
❑ 35 John Randle	.50	.20
❑ 36 Vinny Testaverde	.30	.10
❑ 37 Junior Seau	.75	.30
❑ 38 Reidel Anthony	.50	.20
❑ 39 Brad Johnson	.30	.10
❑ 40 Emmitt Smith	1.50	.60
❑ 41 Mo Lewis	.30	.10
❑ 42 Terry Glenn	.75	.30
❑ 43 Dorsey Levens	.75	.30
❑ 44 Thurman Thomas	.50	.20
❑ 45 Rob Moore	.50	.20
❑ 46 Corey Dillon	.75	.30
❑ 47 Jessie Armstead	.30	.10
❑ 48 Marshall Faulk	1.00	.40
❑ 49 Charles Woodson	.30	.10
❑ 50 John Elway	2.50	1.00
❑ 51 Kevin Dyson	.50	.20
❑ 52 Tony Simmons	.30	.10
❑ 53 Keenan McCardell	.50	.20
❑ 54 O.J. Santiago	.30	.10
❑ 55 Jermaine Lewis	.50	.20
❑ 56 Herman Moore	.50	.20
❑ 57 Gary Brown	.30	.10
❑ 58 Jim Harbaugh	.50	.20
❑ 59 Mike Alstott	.75	.30
❑ 60 Brett Favre	2.50	1.00
❑ 61 Tim Brown	.75	.30
❑ 62 Steve McNair	.75	.30
❑ 63 Ben Coates	.50	.20
❑ 64 Jerome Pathon	.30	.10
❑ 65 Ray Buchanan	.30	.10
❑ 66 Troy Aikman	1.50	.60
❑ 67 Andre Reed	.50	.20
❑ 68 Bubby Brister	.30	.10
❑ 69 Karim Abdul-Jabbar	.50	.20
❑ 70 Peyton Manning	2.50	1.00
❑ 71 Charles Johnson	.30	.10
❑ 72 Natrone Means	.50	.20
❑ 73 Michael Sinclair	.30	.10
❑ 74 Skip Hicks	.30	.10
❑ 75 Derrick Alexander	.50	.20
❑ 76 Wayne Chrebet	.50	.20
❑ 77 Rod Smith	.50	.20
❑ 78 Carl Pickens	.50	.20
❑ 79 Adrian Murrell	.50	.20
❑ 80 Fred Taylor	.75	.30
❑ 81 Eric Moulds	.75	.30
❑ 82 Lawrence Phillips	.50	.20
❑ 83 Marvin Harrison	.75	.30
❑ 84 Cris Carter	.75	.30
❑ 85 Ike Hilliard	.30	.10
❑ 86 Hines Ward	.75	.30
❑ 87 Terrell Owens	.75	.30
❑ 88 Ricky Proehl	.30	.10
❑ 89 Bert Emanuel	.50	.20
❑ 90 Randy Moss	2.00	.75
❑ 91 Aaron Glenn	.30	.10
❑ 92 Robert Smith	.75	.30
❑ 93 Andre Hastings	.30	.10
❑ 94 Jake Reed	.50	.20
❑ 95 Curtis Enis	.30	.10
❑ 96 Andre Wadsworth	.30	.10
❑ 97 Ed McCaffrey	.50	.20
❑ 98 Zach Thomas	.75	.30
❑ 99 Kerry Collins	.50	.20
❑ 100 Drew Bledsoe	1.00	.40
❑ 101 Germane Crowell	.30	.10
❑ 102 Bryan Still	.30	.10
❑ 103 Chad Brown	.30	.10
❑ 104 Jacquez Green	.30	.10
❑ 105 Garrison Hearst	.50	.20
❑ 106 Napoleon Kaufman	.75	.30
❑ 107 Ricky Watters	.50	.20
❑ 108 O.J. McDuffie	.50	.20
❑ 109 Keyshawn Johnson	.75	.30
❑ 110 Jerome Bettis	.75	.30
❑ 111 Duce Staley	.75	.30
❑ 112 Curtis Conway	.50	.20
❑ 113 Chris Chandler	.50	.20
❑ 114 Marcus Nash	.30	.10
❑ 115 Stephen Alexander	.30	.10
❑ 116 Darnay Scott	.30	.10
❑ 117 Bruce Smith	.50	.20
❑ 118 Priest Holmes	1.25	.50
❑ 119 Mark Brunell	.75	.30
❑ 120 Jerry Rice	1.50	.60
❑ 121 Randall Cunningham	.75	.30
❑ 122 Scott Mitchell	.30	.10
❑ 123 Antonio Freeman	.75	.30
❑ 124 Kordell Stewart	.50	.20
❑ 125 Jon Kitna	.75	.30
❑ 126 Ahman Green	.75	.30
❑ 127 Warrick Dunn	.75	.30
❑ 128 Robert Brooks	.50	.20
❑ 129 Derrick Thomas	.75	.30
❑ 130 Steve Young	1.00	.40
❑ 131 Peter Boulware	.30	.10
❑ 132 Michael Irvin	.50	.20
❑ 133 Shannon Sharpe	.30	.10
❑ 134 Jimmy Smith	.50	.20
❑ 135 John Avery	.30	.10
❑ 136 Fred Lane	.30	.10
❑ 137 Trent Green	.75	.30
❑ 138 Andre Rison	.50	.20
❑ 139 Antowain Smith	.30	.10
❑ 140 Eddie George	.75	.30
❑ 141 Jeff Blake	.50	.20
❑ 142 Rocket Ismail	.50	.20
❑ 143 Rickey Dudley	.30	.10
❑ 144 Courtney Hawkins	.30	.10
❑ 145 Mikhael Ricks	.30	.10
❑ 146 J.J. Stokes	.50	.20
❑ 147 Levon Kirkland	.30	.10
❑ 148 Deion Sanders	.75	.30
❑ 149 Barry Sanders	2.50	1.00
❑ 150 Tiki Barber	.75	.30
❑ 151 David Boston RC	2.00	.75
❑ 152 Chris McAlister RC	1.50	.60
❑ 153 Peerless Price RC	2.00	.75
❑ 154 D'Wayne Bates RC	1.50	.60
❑ 155 Cade McNown RC	1.50	.60
❑ 156 Akili Smith RC	1.50	.60
❑ 157 Kevin Johnson RC	2.00	.75
❑ 158 Tim Couch RC	2.00	.75
❑ 159 Sedrick Irvin RC	.75	.30
❑ 160 Chris Claiborne RC	.75	.30
❑ 161 Edgerrin James RC	8.00	3.00
❑ 162 Mike Cloud RC	1.50	.60
❑ 163 Cecil Collins RC	.75	.30
❑ 164 James Johnson RC	1.50	.60
❑ 165 Rob Konrad RC	2.00	.75
❑ 166 Daunte Culpepper RC	8.00	3.00
❑ 167 Kevin Faulk RC	2.00	.75
❑ 168 Donovan McNabb RC	10.00	4.00
❑ 169 Troy Edwards RC	1.50	.60
❑ 170 Amos Zereoue RC	2.00	.75
❑ 171 Karsten Bailey RC	1.50	.60
❑ 172 Brock Huard RC	2.00	.75
❑ 173 Joe Germaine RC	1.50	.60
❑ 174 Torry Holt RC	5.00	2.00
❑ 175 Shaun King RC	1.50	.60
❑ 176 Jevon Kearse RC	3.00	1.25
❑ 177 Champ Bailey RC	2.50	1.00
❑ 178 Ebenezer Ekuban RC	1.50	.60
❑ 179 Andy Katzenmoyer	1.50	.60
❑ 180 Antoine Winfield RC	1.50	.60
❑ 181 Jermaine Fazande RC	1.50	.60
❑ 182 Ricky Williams RC	4.00	1.50
❑ 183 Joel Makovicka RC	2.00	.75
❑ 184 Reginald Kelly RC	.75	.30
❑ 185 Brandon Stokley RC	2.50	1.00
❑ 186 L.C. Stevens RC	.75	.30
❑ 187 Marty Booker RC	2.00	.75
❑ 188 Jerry Azumah	2.00	.75
❑ 189 Ted White RC	.75	.30
❑ 190 Scott Covington RC	2.00	.75
❑ 191 Tim Alexander RC	.75	.30
❑ 192 Darrin Chiaverini RC	1.50	.60
❑ 193 Dat Nguyen RC	2.00	.75
❑ 194 Wane McGarity RC	.75	.30
❑ 195 Al Wilson RC	2.00	.75
❑ 196 Travis McGriff RC	.75	.30
❑ 197 Stacey Mack RC	2.00	.75
❑ 198 Antuan Edwards RC	.75	.30
❑ 199 Aaron Brooks RC	4.00	1.50
❑ 200 De'Mond Parker RC	.75	.30
❑ 201 Jed Weaver RC	.75	.30
❑ 202 Madre Hill RC	.75	.30
❑ 203 Jim Kleinsasser RC	2.00	.75
❑ 204 Michael Bishop RC	2.00	.75
❑ 205 Michael Basnight RC	.75	.30
❑ 206 Sean Bennett RC	.75	.30
❑ 207 Dameane Douglas RC	1.50	.60
❑ 208 Na Brown RC	1.50	.60
❑ 209 Patrick Kerney RC	2.00	.75
❑ 210 Malcolm Johnson RC	.75	.30
❑ 211 Dre Bly RC	2.00	.75
❑ 212 Terry Jackson RC	1.50	.60
❑ 213 Eugene Baker RC	.75	.30
❑ 214 Autry Denson RC	1.50	.60
❑ 215 Darnell McDonald RC	1.50	.60
❑ 216 Charlie Rogers RC	1.50	.60
❑ 217 Joe Montgomery RC	1.50	.60
❑ 218 Cecil Martin RC	1.50	.60
❑ 219 Larry Parker RC	2.00	.75
❑ 220 Mike Peterson RC	2.00	.75

2000 Bowman

❑ COMPLETE SET (240)	80.00	30.00
❑ 1 Eddie George	.60	.25
❑ 2 Ike Hilliard	.40	.15
❑ 3 Terrell Owens	.60	.25
❑ 4 James Stewart	.40	.15
❑ 5 Joey Galloway	.40	.15
❑ 6 Jake Reed	.40	.15
❑ 7 Derrick Alexander	.40	.15
❑ 8 Jeff George	.40	.15
❑ 9 Kerry Collins	.40	.15
❑ 10 Tony Gonzalez	.40	.15
❑ 11 Marcus Robinson	.60	.25
❑ 12 Charles Woodson	.40	.15
❑ 13 Germane Crowell	.25	.08

❑ 14 Yancey Thigpen	.25	.08
❑ 15 Tony Martin	.40	.15
❑ 16 Frank Sanders	.40	.15
❑ 17 Napoleon Kaufman	.40	.15
❑ 18 Jay Fiedler	.60	.25
❑ 19 Patrick Jeffers	.60	.25
❑ 20 Steve McNair	.60	.25
❑ 21 Herman Moore	.40	.15
❑ 22 Tim Brown	.60	.25
❑ 23 Olandis Gary	.60	.25
❑ 24 Corey Dillon	.60	.25
❑ 25 Warren Sapp	.40	.15
❑ 26 Curtis Enis	.25	.08
❑ 27 Vinny Testaverde	.40	.15
❑ 28 Tim Biakabutuka	.40	.15
❑ 29 Kevin Johnson	.60	.25
❑ 30 Charlie Batch	.60	.25
❑ 31 Jermaine Fazande	.25	.08
❑ 32 Shaun King	.25	.08
❑ 33 Errict Rhett	.40	.15
❑ 34 O.J. McDuffie	.40	.15
❑ 35 Bruce Smith	.40	.15
❑ 36 Antonio Freeman	.60	.25
❑ 37 Tim Couch	.40	.15
❑ 38 Duce Staley	.60	.25
❑ 39 Jeff Blake	.40	.15
❑ 40 Jim Harbaugh	.40	.15
❑ 41 Jeff Graham	.25	.08
❑ 42 Drew Bledsoe	.75	.30
❑ 43 Mike Alstott	.60	.25
❑ 44 Terance Mathis	.40	.15
❑ 45 Antowain Smith	.40	.15
❑ 46 Johnnie Morton	.40	.15
❑ 47 Chris Chandler	.40	.15
❑ 48 Keith Poole	.40	.15
❑ 49 Ricky Watters	.40	.15
❑ 50 Darnay Scott	.40	.15
❑ 51 Damon Huard	.60	.25
❑ 52 Peerless Price	.40	.15
❑ 53 Brian Griese	.60	.25
❑ 54 Frank Wycheck	.25	.08
❑ 55 Kevin Dyson	.40	.15
❑ 56 Junior Seau	.60	.25
❑ 57 Curtis Conway	.40	.15
❑ 58 Jamal Anderson	.60	.25
❑ 59 Jim Miller	.25	.08
❑ 60 Rob Johnson	.25	.08
❑ 61 Mark Brunell	.60	.25
❑ 62 Wayne Chrebet	.40	.15
❑ 63 James Johnson	.25	.08
❑ 64 Sean Dawkins	.25	.08
❑ 65 Stephen Davis	.60	.25
❑ 66 Daunte Culpepper	.75	.30
❑ 67 Doug Flutie	.60	.25
❑ 68 Pete Mitchell	.25	.08
❑ 69 Bill Schroeder	.40	.15
❑ 70 Terrence Wilkins	.25	.08
❑ 71 Cade McNown	.25	.08
❑ 72 Muhsin Muhammad	.40	.15
❑ 73 E.G. Green	.25	.08
❑ 74 Edgerrin James	1.00	.40
❑ 75 Troy Edwards	.25	.08
❑ 76 Terry Glenn	.40	.15
❑ 77 Tony Banks	.40	.15
❑ 78 Derrick Mayes	.40	.15
❑ 79 Curtis Martin	.60	.25
❑ 80 Kordell Stewart	.40	.15
❑ 81 Amani Toomer	.40	.15
❑ 82 Dorsey Levens	.40	.15
❑ 83 Brad Johnson	.60	.25
❑ 84 Ed McCaffrey	.60	.25
❑ 85 Charlie Garner	.40	.15
❑ 86 Brett Favre	2.00	.75
❑ 87 J.J. Stokes	.40	.15
❑ 88 Steve Young	.75	.30
❑ 89 Jonathan Linton	.25	.08
❑ 90 Isaac Bruce	.60	.25
❑ 91 Shawn Jefferson	.25	.08
❑ 92 Rod Smith	.40	.15
❑ 93 Champ Bailey	.40	.15
❑ 94 Ricky Williams	.60	.25
❑ 95 Priest Holmes	.75	.30
❑ 96 Corey Bradford	.40	.15
❑ 97 Eric Moulds	.60	.25
❑ 98 Warrick Dunn	.60	.25
❑ 99 Jevon Kearse	.60	.25
❑ 100 Albert Connell	.25	.08
❑ 101 Az-Zahir Hakim	.25	.08
❑ 102 Marvin Harrison	.60	.25
❑ 103 Qadry Ismail	.40	.15
❑ 104 Oronde Gadsden	.40	.15
❑ 105 Rob Moore	.40	.15
❑ 106 Marshall Faulk	.75	.30
❑ 107 Steve Beuerlein	.25	.08
❑ 108 Torry Holt	.60	.25
❑ 109 Donovan McNabb	1.00	.40
❑ 110 Rich Gannon	.60	.25
❑ 111 Jerome Bettis	.60	.25
❑ 112 Peyton Manning	1.50	.60
❑ 113 Cris Carter	.60	.25
❑ 114 Jake Plummer	.40	.15
❑ 115 Kent Graham	.25	.08
❑ 116 Keenan McCardell	.40	.15
❑ 117 Tim Dwight	.60	.25
❑ 118 Fred Taylor	.60	.25
❑ 119 Jerry Rice	1.25	.50
❑ 120 Michael Westbrook	.40	.15
❑ 121 Kurt Warner	1.25	.50
❑ 122 Jimmy Smith	.40	.15
❑ 123 Emmitt Smith	1.25	.50
❑ 124 Terrell Davis	.60	.25
❑ 125 Randy Moss	1.25	.50
❑ 126 Akili Smith	.25	.08
❑ 127 Rocket Ismail	.40	.15
❑ 128 Jon Kitna	.60	.25
❑ 129 Elvis Grbac	.40	.15
❑ 130 Wesley Walls	.25	.08
❑ 131 Torrance Small	.25	.08
❑ 132 Tyrone Wheatley	.40	.15
❑ 133 Carl Pickens	.40	.15
❑ 134 Zach Thomas	.60	.25
❑ 135 Jacquez Green	.25	.08
❑ 136 Robert Smith	.60	.25
❑ 137 Keyshawn Johnson	.60	.25
❑ 138 Matthew Hatchette	.25	.08
❑ 139 Troy Aikman	1.25	.50
❑ 140 Charles Johnson	.40	.15
❑ 141 Terry Battle EP	.30	.12
❑ 142 Pepe Pearson EP RC	.75	.30
❑ 143 Cory Sauter EP	.30	.12
❑ 144 Brian Shay EP	.30	.12
❑ 145 Marcus Crandell EP RC	.50	.20
❑ 146 Danny Wuerffel EP	.50	.20
❑ 147 L.C. Stevens EP	.30	.12
❑ 148 Ted White EP	.30	.12
❑ 149 Matt Lytle EP RC	.50	.20
❑ 150 Vershan Jackson EP RC	.30	.12
❑ 151 Mario Bailey EP	.30	.12
❑ 152 Darryl Daniel EP RC	.50	.20
❑ 153 Sean Morey EP RC	.50	.20
❑ 154 Jim Kubiak EP RC	.60	.20
❑ 155 Aaron Stecker EP RC	.75	.30
❑ 156 Damon Dunn EP RC	.50	.20
❑ 157 Kevin Daft EP	.30	.12
❑ 158 Corey Thomas EP	.30	.12
❑ 159 Deon Mitchell EP RC	.50	.20
❑ 160 Todd Floyd EP RC	.30	.12
❑ 161 Norman Miller EP RC	.30	.12
❑ 162 Jeremaine Copeland EP	.30	.12
❑ 163 Michael Blair EP	.30	.12
❑ 164 Ron Powlus EP RC	.75	.30
❑ 165 Pat Barnes EP	.50	.20
❑ 166 Dez White RC	1.00	.40
❑ 167 Trung Canidate RC	.75	.30
❑ 168 Thomas Jones RC	1.50	.60
❑ 169 Courtney Brown RC	1.00	.40
❑ 170 Jamal Lewis RC	2.50	1.00
❑ 171 Chris Redman RC	.75	.30
❑ 172 Ron Dayne RC	1.00	.40
❑ 173 Chad Pennington RC	2.50	1.00
❑ 174 Plaxico Burress RC	2.00	.75
❑ 175 R.Jay Soward RC	.75	.30
❑ 176 Travis Taylor RC	1.00	.40
❑ 177 Shaun Alexander RC	5.00	2.00
❑ 178 Brian Urlacher RC	4.00	1.50
❑ 179 Danny Farmer RC	.75	.30
❑ 180 Tee Martin RC	1.00	.40
❑ 181 Sylvester Morris RC	.75	.30
❑ 182 Curtis Keaton RC	.75	.30
❑ 183 Peter Warrick RC	1.00	.40
❑ 184 Anthony Becht RC	1.00	.40
❑ 185 Travis Prentice RC	1.00	.40
❑ 186 J.R. Redmond RC	.75	.30
❑ 187 Bubba Franks RC	1.00	.40
❑ 188 Ron Dugans RC	.50	.20
❑ 189 Reuben Droughns RC	1.25	.50
❑ 190 Corey Simon RC	1.00	.40
❑ 191 Joe Hamilton RC	.75	.30
❑ 192 Laveranues Coles RC	1.25	.50
❑ 193 Todd Pinkston RC	1.00	.40
❑ 194 Jerry Porter RC	1.25	.50
❑ 195 Dennis Northcutt RC	1.00	.40
❑ 196 Tim Rattay RC	1.00	.40
❑ 197 Giovanni Carmazzi RC	.50	.20
❑ 198 Mareno Philyaw RC	.50	.20
❑ 199 Avion Black RC	.75	.30
❑ 200 Chafie Fields RC	.50	.20
❑ 201 Rondell Mealey RC	.50	.20
❑ 202 Troy Walters RC	1.00	.40
❑ 203 Frank Moreau RC	.75	.30
❑ 204 Vaughn Sanders RC	.50	.20
❑ 205 Sherrod Gideon RC	.50	.20
❑ 206 Doug Chapman RC	[illegible]	[illegible]
❑ 207 Marcus Knight RC	.75	.30
❑ 208 Jamel White RC	.75	.30
❑ 209 Windrell Hayes RC	.75	.30
❑ 210 Reggie Jones RC	1.00	.40
❑ 211 Jarious Jackson RC	.75	.30
❑ 212 Ronney Jenkins RC	.75	.30
❑ 213 Quinton Spotwood RC	.50	.20
❑ 214 Rob Morris RC	.75	.30
❑ 215 Gari Scott RC	.50	.20
❑ 216 Kevin Thompson RC	.50	.20
❑ 217 Trevor Insley RC	.50	.20
❑ 218 Frank Murphy RC	.50	.20
❑ 219 Patrick Pass RC	.75	.30
❑ 220 Mike Anderson RC	1.25	.50
❑ 221 Deltha Thompson RC	1.00	.40
❑ 222 John Abraham RC	1.00	.40
❑ 223 Dante Hall RC	2.00	.75
❑ 224 Chad Morton RC	1.00	.40
❑ 225 Ahmed Plummer RC	1.00	.40
❑ 226 Julian Peterson RC	1.00	.40
❑ 227 Mike Green RC	.75	.30
❑ 228 Michael Wiley RC	.75	.30
❑ 229 Spergon Wynn RC	.75	.30
❑ 230 Trevor Gaylor RC	.75	.30
❑ 231 Doug Johnson RC	1.00	.40
❑ 232 Marc Bulger RC	2.00	.75
❑ 233 Ron Dixon RC	.75	.30
❑ 234 Aaron Shea RC	.75	.30
❑ 235 Thomas Hamner RC	.50	.20
❑ 236 Tom Brady RC	50.00	30.00
❑ 237 Deltha O'Neal RC	1.00	.40
❑ 238 Todd Husak RC	1.00	.40
❑ 239 Erron Kinney RC	1.00	.40
❑ 240 JaJuan Dawson RC	.50	.20

2001 Bowman

❑ COMPLETE SET (275)	70.00	35.00
❑ 1 Emmitt Smith	1.25	.50
❑ 2 James Stewart	.40	.15
❑ 3 Jeff Graham	.25	.08
❑ 4 Keyshawn Johnson	.60	.25
❑ 5 Stephen Davis	.60	.25
❑ 6 Chad Lewis	.25	.08
❑ 7 Drew Bledsoe	.75	.30
❑ 8 Fred Taylor	.60	.25
❑ 9 Mike Anderson	.60	.25
❑ 10 Tony Gonzalez	.40	.15
❑ 11 Aaron Brooks	.60	.25
❑ 12 Vinny Testaverde	.40	.15
❑ 13 Jerome Bettis	.60	.25
❑ 14 Marshall Faulk	.75	.30
❑ 15 Jeff Garcia	.60	.25
❑ 16 Terry Glenn	.40	.15
❑ 17 Jay Fiedler	.60	.25
❑ 18 Ahman Green	.60	.25
❑ 19 Cade McNown	.25	.08
❑ 20 Rob Johnson	.40	.15

❑ 21 Jamal Anderson	.60	.25
❑ 22 Corey Dillon	.60	.25
❑ 23 Jake Plummer	.40	.15
❑ 24 Rod Smith	.40	.15
❑ 25 Trent Green	.60	.25
❑ 26 Ricky Williams	.60	.25
❑ 27 Charlie Garner	.40	.15
❑ 28 Shaun Alexander	.75	.30
❑ 29 Jeff George	.40	.15
❑ 30 Torry Holt	.60	.25
❑ 31 James Thrash	.40	.15
❑ 32 Rich Gannon	.60	.25
❑ 33 Ron Dayne	.60	.25
❑ 34 Dedric Ward	.25	.08
❑ 35 Edgerrin James	.75	.30
❑ 36 Cris Carter	.60	.25
❑ 37 Derrick Mason	.40	.15
❑ 38 Brad Johnson	.60	.25
❑ 39 Charlie Batch	.60	.25
❑ 40 Joey Galloway	.40	.15
❑ 41 James Allen	.40	.15
❑ 42 Tim Biakabutuka	.40	.15
❑ 43 Ray Lewis	.60	.25
❑ 44 David Boston	.60	.25
❑ 45 Kevin Johnson	.40	.15
❑ 46 Jimmy Smith	.40	.15
❑ 47 Joe Horn	.40	.15
❑ 48 Terrell Owens	.60	.25
❑ 49 Eddie George	.60	.25
❑ 50 Brett Favre	2.00	.75
❑ 51 Wayne Chrebet	.40	.15
❑ 52 Hines Ward	.60	.25
❑ 53 Warrick Dunn	.60	.25
❑ 54 Matt Hasselbeck	.40	.15
❑ 55 Tiki Barber	.60	.25
❑ 56 Lamar Smith	.40	.15
❑ 57 Tim Couch	.40	.15
❑ 58 Eric Moulds	.40	.15
❑ 59 Shawn Jefferson	.25	.08
❑ 60 Donald Hayes	.25	.08
❑ 61 Brian Urlacher	1.00	.40
❑ 62 Steve McNair	.60	.25
❑ 63 Kurt Warner	1.25	.50
❑ 64 Tim Brown	.60	.25
❑ 65 Troy Brown	.40	.15
❑ 66 Albert Connell	.25	.08
❑ 67 Peyton Manning	1.50	.60
❑ 68 Peter Warrick	.60	.25
❑ 69 Elvis Grbac	.40	.15
❑ 70 Chris Chandler	.40	.15
❑ 71 Akili Smith	.25	.08
❑ 72 Keenan McCardell	.25	.08
❑ 73 Kerry Collins	.40	.15
❑ 74 Junior Seau	.60	.25
❑ 75 Donovan McNabb	.75	.30
❑ 76 Tony Banks	.40	.15
❑ 77 Steve Beuerlein	.25	.08
❑ 78 Daunte Culpepper	.60	.25
❑ 79 Darrell Jackson	.60	.25
❑ 80 Isaac Bruce	.60	.25
❑ 81 Tyrone Wheatley	.40	.15
❑ 82 Derrick Alexander	.40	.15
❑ 83 Germane Crowell	.25	.08
❑ 84 Jon Kitna	.40	.15
❑ 85 Jamal Lewis	1.00	.40
❑ 86 Ed McCaffrey	.60	.25
❑ 87 Mark Brunell	.60	.25
❑ 88 Jeff Blake	.40	.15
❑ 89 Duce Staley	.60	.25
❑ 90 Doug Flutie	.60	.25
❑ 91 Kordell Stewart	.40	.15
❑ 92 Randy Moss	1.25	.50
❑ 93 Marvin Harrison	.60	.25
❑ 94 Muhsin Muhammad	.40	.15
❑ 95 Brian Griese	.60	.25
❑ 96 Antonio Freeman	.60	.25
❑ 97 Amani Toomer	.40	.15
❑ 98 Oronde Gadsden	.40	.15
❑ 99 Curtis Martin	.60	.25
❑ 100 Jerry Rice	1.25	.50
❑ 101 Michael Pittman	.25	.08
❑ 102 Shannon Sharpe	.40	.15
❑ 103 Peerless Price	.40	.15
❑ 104 Bill Schroeder	.40	.15
❑ 105 Ike Hilliard	.40	.15
❑ 106 Freddie Jones	.25	.08
❑ 107 Tai Streets	.25	.08
❑ 108 Ricky Watters	.40	.15
❑ 109 Az-Zahir Hakim	.25	.08
❑ 110 Jacquez Green	.25	.08
❑ 111 Bobby Shaw	.25	.08
❑ 112 Johnnie Morton	.40	.15
❑ 113 Laveranues Coles	.60	.25
❑ 114 Chad Pennington	1.00	.40
❑ 115 Champ Bailey	.40	.15
❑ 116 Charles Woodson	.40	.15
❑ 117 Curtis Conway	.40	.15
❑ 118 Marcus Robinson	.60	.25
❑ 119 Michael Westbrook	.40	.15
❑ 120 Mike Alstott	.60	.25
❑ 121 Priest Holmes	.75	.30
❑ 122 Qadry Ismail	.40	.15
❑ 123 Rocket Ismail	.40	.15
❑ 124 Shawn Bryson	.25	.08
❑ 125 Jeff Lewis	.25	.08
❑ 126 Jeremy Mcdaniel	.25	.08
❑ 127 Terance Mathis	.25	.08
❑ 128 Travis Prentice	.25	.08
❑ 129 Warren Sapp	.40	.15
❑ 130 Jevon Kearse	.40	.15
❑ 131 George Layne RC	.75	.30
❑ 132 Correll Buckhalter RC	1.50	.60
❑ 133 Tony Stewart RC	1.25	.50
❑ 134 Chris Barnes RC	.75	.30
❑ 135 A.J. Feeley RC	1.25	.50
❑ 136 Margin Hooks RC	.50	.20
❑ 137 Anthony Henry RC	1.25	.50
❑ 138 Dwight Smith RC	.50	.20
❑ 139 Torrance Marshall RC	1.25	.50
❑ 140 Gary Baxter RC	.75	.30
❑ 141 Derek Combs RC	.75	.30
❑ 142 Marcus Bell DT RC	.75	.30
❑ 143 Delawrence Grant RC	.50	.20
❑ 144 Jameel Cook RC	.75	.30
❑ 145 Eric Downing RC	.50	.20
❑ 146 Marlon McCree RC	.75	.30
❑ 147 Tay Cody RC	.50	.20
❑ 148 Mario Monds RC	.50	.20
❑ 149 Kenny Smith RC	.75	.30
❑ 150 Sedrick Hodge RC	.50	.20
❑ 151 Marcus Stroud RC	1.25	.50
❑ 152 Steve Smith RC	3.00	1.25
❑ 153 Tyrone Robertson RC	.50	.20
❑ 154 James Reed RC	.50	.20
❑ 155 Kris Kocurek RC	.50	.20
❑ 156 Dan O'Leary RC	.75	.30
❑ 157 Harold Blackmon RC	.50	.20
❑ 158 Fred Smoot RC	1.25	.50
❑ 159 Billy Baber RC	.50	.20
❑ 160 Jarrod Cooper RC	1.25	.50
❑ 161 Travis Henry RC	2.50	1.00
❑ 162 David Terrell RC	1.25	.50
❑ 163 Josh Heupel RC	1.25	.50
❑ 164 Drew Brees RC	4.00	1.50
❑ 165 T.J. Houshmandzadeh RC	1.50	.60
❑ 166 Rod Gardner RC	1.25	.50
❑ 167 Richard Seymour RC	1.25	.50
❑ 168 Koren Robinson RC	1.25	.50
❑ 169 Scotty Anderson RC	.75	.30
❑ 170 Marques Tuiasosopo RC	1.25	.50
❑ 171 John Capel RC	.75	.30
❑ 172 LaMont Jordan RC	2.50	1.00
❑ 173 James Jackson RC	1.25	.50
❑ 174 Bobby Newcombe RC	1.25	.50
❑ 175 Anthony Thomas RC	1.25	.50
❑ 176 Dan Alexander RC	1.25	.50
❑ 177 Quincy Carter RC	1.25	.50
❑ 178 Morlon Greenwood RC	.75	.30
❑ 179 Robert Ferguson RC	1.25	.50
❑ 180 Sage Rosenfels RC	1.25	.50
❑ 181 Michael Stone RC	.50	.20
❑ 182 Chris Weinke RC	1.25	.50
❑ 183 Travis Minor RC	.75	.30
❑ 184 Gerard Warren RC	1.25	.50
❑ 185 Jamar Fletcher RC	.75	.30
❑ 186 Andre Carter RC	1.25	.50
❑ 187 Deuce McAllister RC	2.50	1.00
❑ 188 Dan Morgan RC	1.25	.50
❑ 189 Todd Heap RC	1.25	.50
❑ 190 Snoop Minnis RC	.75	.30
❑ 191 Will Allen RC	.75	.30
❑ 192 Freddie Mitchell RC	1.25	.50
❑ 193 Rudi Johnson RC	2.50	1.00
❑ 194 Kevan Barlow RC	1.25	.50
❑ 195 Jamie Winborn RC	.75	.30
❑ 196 Onomo Ojo RC	.75	.30
❑ 197 Leonard Davis RC	.75	.30
❑ 198 Santana Moss RC	2.00	.75
❑ 199 Chris Chambers RC	2.00	.75
❑ 200 Michael Vick RC	4.00	1.50
❑ 201 Michael Bennett RC	1.25	.50
❑ 202 Mike McMahon RC	1.25	.50
❑ 203 Jonathan Carter RC	.75	.30
❑ 204 Jamal Reynolds RC	1.25	.50
❑ 205 Justin Smith RC	1.25	.50
❑ 206 Quincy Morgan RC	1.25	.50
❑ 207 Chad Johnson RC	3.00	1.25
❑ 208 Jesse Palmer RC	1.25	.50
❑ 209 Reggie Wayne RC	2.50	1.00
❑ 210 LaDainian Tomlinson RC	25.00	10.00
❑ 211 Andre King RC	.75	.30
❑ 212 Richmond Flowers RC	.75	.30
❑ 213 Derrick Blaylock RC	1.25	.50
❑ 214 Cedrick Wilson RC	1.25	.50
❑ 215 Zeke Moreno RC	1.25	.50
❑ 216 Tommy Polley RC	1.25	.50
❑ 217 Damione Lewis RC	.75	.30
❑ 218 Aaron Schobel RC	1.25	.50
❑ 219 Alge Crumpler RC	1.50	.60
❑ 220 Nate Clements RC	1.25	.50
❑ 221 Quentin McCord RC	.75	.30
❑ 222 Ken-Yon Rambo RC	.75	.30
❑ 223 Milton Wynn RC	.75	.30
❑ 224 Derrick Gibson RC	.75	.30
❑ 225 Chris Taylor RC	.75	.30
❑ 226 Corey Hall RC	.50	.20
❑ 227 Vinny Sutherland RC	.75	.30
❑ 228 Kendrell Bell RC	2.00	.75
❑ 229 Casey Hampton RC	1.25	.50
❑ 230 Demetric Evans RC	.50	.20
❑ 231 Brian Allen RC	.50	.20
❑ 232 Rodney Bailey RC	.50	.20
❑ 233 Otis Leverette RC	.50	.20
❑ 234 Ron Edwards RC	.50	.20
❑ 235 Michael Jameson RC	.50	.20
❑ 236 Markus Steele RC	.75	.30
❑ 237 Jimmy Williams RC	.50	.20
❑ 238 Roger Knight RC	.50	.20
❑ 239 Randy Garner RC	.50	.20
❑ 240 Raymond Perryman RC	.50	.20
❑ 241 Karon Riley RC	.50	.20
❑ 242 Adam Archuleta RC	1.25	.50
❑ 243 Arnold Jackson RC	.75	.30
❑ 244 Ryan Pickett RC	.50	.20
❑ 245 Shad Meier RC	.75	.30
❑ 246 Reggie Germany RC	.75	.30
❑ 247 Justin McCareins RC	1.25	.50
❑ 248 Idrees Bashir RC	.50	.20
❑ 249 Josh Booty RC	1.25	.50
❑ 250 Eddie Berlin RC	.75	.30
❑ 251 Heath Evans RC	.75	.30
❑ 252 Alex Bannister RC	.75	.30
❑ 253 Corey Alston RC	.50	.20
❑ 254 Reggie White RC	.75	.30
❑ 255 Orlando Huff RC	.50	.20
❑ 256 Ken Lucas RC	.75	.30
❑ 257 Matt Stewart RC	.50	.20
❑ 258 Cedric Scott RC	.75	.30
❑ 259 Ronney Daniels RC	.50	.20
❑ 260 Kevin Kasper RC	1.25	.50
❑ 261 Tony Driver RC	.75	.30
❑ 262 Kyle Vanden Bosch RC	1.25	.50
❑ 263 T.J. Turner RC	.50	.20
❑ 264 Eric Westmoreland RC	.75	.30
❑ 265 Ronald Flemons RC	.50	.20
❑ 266 Eric Kelly RC	.50	.20
❑ 267 Moran Norris RC	.50	.20
❑ 268 Damerien McCants RC	.75	.30
❑ 269 James Boyd RC	.50	.20
❑ 270 Keith Adams RC	.50	.20
❑ 271 Brandon Manumaleuna RC	.75	.30
❑ 272 Dee Brown RC	1.25	.50
❑ 273 Ross Kolodziej RC	.50	.20
❑ 274 Boo Williams RC	.75	.30
❑ 275 Patrick Chukwurah RC	.50	.20

2002 Bowman

❑ COMPLETE SET (275)	50.00	20.00
❑ 1 Emmitt Smith	1.50	.60
❑ 2 Drew Brees	.60	.25
❑ 3 Duce Staley	.60	.25
❑ 4 Curtis Martin	.60	.25
❑ 5 Isaac Bruce	.60	.25
❑ 6 Stephen Davis	.40	.15
❑ 7 Darrell Jackson	.40	.15
❑ 8 James Stewart	.40	.15
❑ 9 Tim Couch	.40	.15
❑ 10 Travis Henry	.60	.25

❑ 11 Thomas Jones .40 .15
❑ 12 Jamal Lewis .60 .25
❑ 13 Chris Chambers .60 .25
❑ 14 Jeff Blake .40 .15
❑ 15 Plaxico Burress .60 .25
❑ 16 Michael Pittman .25 .08
❑ 17 Jeff Garcia .60 .25
❑ 18 Tim Brown .60 .25
❑ 19 Kent Graham .25 .08
❑ 20 Shannon Sharpe .40 .15
❑ 21 Corey Dillon .40 .15
❑ 22 Muhsin Muhammad .40 .15
❑ 23 Tony Gonzalez .40 .15
❑ 24 Qadry Ismail .40 .15
❑ 25 Mike McMahon .60 .25
❑ 26 Edgerrin James .75 .30
❑ 27 Daunte Culpepper .60 .25
❑ 28 Deuce McAllister .75 .30
❑ 29 Kerry Collins .40 .15
❑ 30 Eddie George .60 .25
❑ 31 Torry Holt .60 .25
❑ 32 Todd Pinkston .40 .15
❑ 33 Quincy Carter .40 .15
❑ 34 Rod Smith .40 .15
❑ 35 Michael Vick 1.25 .50
❑ 36 Jim Miller .25 .08
❑ 37 Troy Brown .40 .15
❑ 38 Wayne Chrebet .40 .15
❑ 39 Curtis Conway .25 .08
❑ 40 Reidel Anthony .25 .08
❑ 41 Mark Brunell .60 .25
❑ 42 Chris Weinke .40 .15
❑ 43 Eric Moulds .40 .15
❑ 44 Ike Hilliard .25 .08
❑ 45 Jay Fiedler .40 .15
❑ 46 Keyshawn Johnson .60 .25
❑ 47 Rod Gardner .40 .15
❑ 48 Chris Redman .25 .08
❑ 49 James Allen .40 .15
❑ 50 Kordell Stewart .40 .15
❑ 51 Priest Holmes .75 .30
❑ 52 Anthony Thomas .40 .15
❑ 53 Peter Warrick .40 .15
❑ 54 Jake Plummer .40 .15
❑ 55 Jerry Rice 1.25 .50
❑ 56 Joe Horn .40 .15
❑ 57 Derrick Mason .40 .15
❑ 58 Kurt Warner .60 .25
❑ 59 Antowain Smith .40 .15
❑ 60 Randy Moss 1.25 .50
❑ 61 Warrick Dunn .60 .25
❑ 62 Laveranues Coles .40 .15
❑ 63 LaDainian Tomlinson 1.00 .40
❑ 64 Michael Westbrook .25 .08
❑ 65 Travis Taylor .25 .08
❑ 66 Brian Griese .60 .25
❑ 67 Bill Schroeder .40 .15
❑ 68 Ahman Green .60 .25
❑ 69 Jimmy Smith .40 .15
❑ 70 Charlie Garner .40 .15
❑ 71 Terrell Owens .60 .25
❑ 72 Brad Johnson .40 .15
❑ 73 James Thrash .40 .15
❑ 74 Marvin Harrison .60 .25
❑ 75 Brett Favre 1.50 .60
❑ 76 Rocket Ismail .40 .15
❑ 77 David Boston .60 .25
❑ 78 Jermaine Lewis .25 .08
❑ 79 Aaron Brooks .60 .25
❑ 80 Shaun Alexander .75 .30
❑ 81 Steve McNair .60 .25
❑ 82 Marshall Faulk .60 .25
❑ 83 Terrell Davis .60 .25
❑ 84 Corey Bradford .25 .08
❑ 85 David Terrell .60 .25
❑ 86 Kevin Johnson .40 .15
❑ 87 Jon Kitna .40 .15
❑ 88 Az-Zahir Hakim .25 .08
❑ 89 Drew Bledsoe .75 .30
❑ 90 Garrison Hearst .40 .15
❑ 91 Doug Flutie .60 .25
❑ 92 Jerome Bettis .60 .25
❑ 93 Vinny Testaverde .40 .15
❑ 94 Tiki Barber .60 .25
❑ 95 Johnnie Morton .40 .15
❑ 96 Lamar Smith .40 .15
❑ 97 Marcus Robinson .40 .15
❑ 98 Fred Taylor .60 .25
❑ 99 Tom Brady 1.50 .60
❑ 100 Peyton Manning 1.25 .50
❑ 101 Donovan McNabb .75 .30
❑ 102 Rich Gannon .60 .25
❑ 103 Hines Ward .60 .25
❑ 104 Michael Bennett .60 .25
❑ 105 Ricky Williams .60 .25
❑ 106 Germane Crowell .25 .08
❑ 107 Joey Galloway .40 .15
❑ 108 Amani Toomer .40 .15
❑ 109 Trent Green .40 .15
❑ 110 Terry Glenn .40 .15
❑ 111 Donte Stallworth RC 2.50 1.00
❑ 112 Mike Williams RC 1.25 .50
❑ 113 Kurt Kittner RC 1.25 .50
❑ 114 Josh Reed RC 1.50 .60
❑ 115 Raonall Smith RC 1.25 .50
❑ 116 David Garrard RC 3.00 1.25
❑ 117 Eric Crouch RC 1.50 .60
❑ 118 Bryan Thomas RC 1.25 .50
❑ 119 Levi Jones RC 1.25 .50
❑ 120 Andre Davis RC 1.25 .50
❑ 121 Herb Haygood RC .75 .30
❑ 122 Josh McCown RC 2.00 .75
❑ 123 Quentin Jammer RC 1.50 .60
❑ 124 Cliff Russell RC 1.25 .50
❑ 125 Jeremy Shockey RC 5.00 2.00
❑ 126 Jamin Elliott RC .75 .30
❑ 127 Roy Williams RC 3.00 1.25
❑ 128 Marquise Walker RC 1.25 .50
❑ 129 Kalimba Edwards RC 1.50 .60
❑ 130 Daniel Graham RC 1.50 .60
❑ 131 Freddie Milons RC 1.25 .50
❑ 132 Anthony Weaver RC 1.25 .50
❑ 133 Jake Schifino RC 1.25 .50
❑ 134 Antonio Bryant RC 1.50 .60
❑ 135 DeShaun Foster RC 1.50 .60
❑ 136 Antwaan Randle El RC 2.00 .75
❑ 137 William Green RC 1.50 .60
❑ 138 Ed Reed RC 2.50 1.00
❑ 139 Maurice Morris RC 1.50 .60
❑ 140 Joey Harrington RC 2.00 .75
❑ 141 T.J. Duckett RC 1.50 .60
❑ 142 Javon Walker RC 2.50 1.00
❑ 143 Albert Haynesworth RC 1.25 .50
❑ 144 Julius Peppers RC 3.00 1.25
❑ 145 Clinton Portis RC 5.00 2.00
❑ 146 Craig Nall RC 1.50 .60
❑ 147 Ashley Lelie RC 3.00 1.25
❑ 148 Reche Caldwell RC 1.50 .60
❑ 149 Rohan Davey RC 1.50 .60
❑ 150 Patrick Ramsey RC 1.50 .60
❑ 151 Jabar Gaffney RC 1.50 .60
❑ 152 Tank Williams RC 1.25 .50
❑ 153 Ron Johnson RC 1.25 .50
❑ 154 Ladell Betts RC 1.50 .60
❑ 155 Brian Westbrook RC 3.00 1.25
❑ 156 Jamar Martin RC 1.25 .50
❑ 157 Travis Stephens RC 1.25 .50
❑ 158 Tim Carter RC 1.25 .50
❑ 159 Darrell Hill RC 1.50 .60
❑ 160 Luke Staley RC 1.25 .50
❑ 161 Randy Fasani RC 1.25 .50
❑ 162 Matt Schobel RC 1.25 .50
❑ 163 Jon McGraw RC .75 .30
❑ 164 Dwight Freeney RC 2.50 1.00
❑ 165 Chad Hutchinson RC 1.25 .50
❑ 166 Adrian Peterson RC 2.00 .75
❑ 167 Josh Scobey RC 1.50 .60
❑ 168 Jonathan Wells RC 1.50 .60
❑ 169 Sam Simmons RC .75 .30
❑ 170 Jerramy Stevens RC 1.50 .60
❑ 171 Jason McAddley RC 1.25 .50
❑ 172 Ken Simonton RC .75 .30
❑ 173 Chester Taylor RC 3.00 1.25
❑ 174 Brandon Doman RC 1.25 .50
❑ 175 Javin Hunter RC .75 .30
❑ 176 Eddie Drummond RC 1.25 .50
❑ 177 Andre Lott RC 1.50 .60
❑ 178 Travis Fisher RC 1.50 .60
❑ 179 Jarvis Green RC 1.25 .50
❑ 180 Ross Tucker RC .75 .30
❑ 181 Lamont Brightful RC .75 .30
❑ 182 Rocky Calmus RC 1.50 .60
❑ 183 Wes Pate RC .75 .30
❑ 184 Lamar Gordon RC 1.50 .60
❑ 185 Terry Jones RC 1.25 .50
❑ 186 [illegible]
❑ 187 Daryl Jones RC 1.25 .50
❑ 188 Tellis Redmon RC 1.25 .50
❑ 189 Howard Green RC .75 .30
❑ 190 Jarrod Baxter RC 1.25 .50
❑ 191 Delvon Flowers RC 1.25 .50
❑ 192 Kevin Curtis RC .75 .30
❑ 193 Kelly Campbell RC 1.25 .50
❑ 194 Eddie Freeman RC .75 .30
❑ 195 Atrews Bell RC .75 .30
❑ 196 Omar Easy RC 1.50 .60
❑ 197 Jeremy Allen RC .75 .30
❑ 198 Andra Davis RC 1.25 .50
❑ 199 Jack Brewer RC 1.25 .50
❑ 200 Mike Rumph RC 1.50 .60
❑ 201 Seth Burford RC 1.25 .50
❑ 202 Marquand Manuel RC .75 .30
❑ 203 Marques Anderson RC 1.50 .60
❑ 204 Ben Leber RC 1.50 .60
❑ 205 Ryan Denney RC 1.25 .50
❑ 206 Justin Peelle RC .75 .30
❑ 207 Lito Sheppard RC 1.50 .60
❑ 208 Damien Anderson RC 1.25 .50
❑ 209 Lamont Thompson RC 1.25 .50
❑ 210 David Priestley RC 1.25 .50
❑ 211 Michael Lewis RC 1.50 .60
❑ 212 Lee Mays RC 1.25 .50
❑ 213 Alan Harper RC .75 .30
❑ 214 Verron Haynes RC 1.50 .60
❑ 215 Chris Hope RC 1.50 .60
❑ 216 David Thornton RC .75 .30
❑ 217 Derek Ross RC 1.25 .50
❑ 218 Brett Keisel RC 4.00 1.50
❑ 219 Joseph Jefferson RC 1.25 .50
❑ 220 Andre Goodman RC 1.50 .60
❑ 221 Robert Royal RC 1.50 .60
❑ 222 Sheldon Brown RC 1.50 .60
❑ 223 DeVeren Johnson RC 1.25 .50
❑ 224 Rock Cartwright RC 2.00 .75
❑ 225 Quincy Monk RC .75 .30
❑ 226 Nick Rogers RC 1.25 .50
❑ 227 Kendall Simmons RC 1.50 .60
❑ 228 Joe Burns RC 1.25 .50
❑ 229 Wesly Mallard RC 1.25 .50
❑ 230 Chris Cash RC 1.25 .50
❑ 231 David Givens RC 5.00 2.00
❑ 232 John Owens RC 1.25 .50
❑ 233 Jarrett Ferguson RC 1.25 .50
❑ 234 Randy McMichael RC 2.50 1.00
❑ 235 Chris Baker RC 1.25 .50
❑ 236 Rashad Bauman RC 1.25 .50
❑ 237 Matt Murphy RC 1.25 .50
❑ 238 LaVar Glover RC .75 .30
❑ 239 Steve Bellisari RC 1.25 .50
❑ 240 Chad Williams RC 1.25 .50
❑ 241 Kevin Thomas RC 1.25 .50
❑ 242 Carlos Hall RC 1.50 .60
❑ 243 Nick Greisen RC .75 .30
❑ 244 Justin Bannan RC 1.25 .50
❑ 245 Charles Hill RC .75 .30
❑ 246 Mark Anelli RC .75 .30
❑ 247 Coy Wire RC 1.50 .60
❑ 248 Darnell Sanders RC 1.25 .50
❑ 249 Larry Foote RC 4.00 1.50
❑ 250 David Carr RC 3.00 1.25
❑ 251 Ricky Williams RC 1.25 .50
❑ 252 Napoleon Harris RC 1.50 .60
❑ 253 Ennis Haywood RC 1.25 .50
❑ 254 Keyuo Craver RC 1.25 .50
❑ 255 Kahlil Hill RC 1.25 .50
❑ 256 J.T. O'Sullivan RC 1.25 .50
❑ 257 Woody Dantzler RC 1.25 .50
❑ 258 Phillip Buchanon RC 1.50 .60
❑ 259 Charles Grant RC 1.50 .60
❑ 260 Dusty Bonner RC .75 .30

❑ 261 James Allen RC	.75	.30
❑ 262 Ronald Curry RC	1.50	.60
❑ 263 Deion Branch RC	2.50	1.00
❑ 264 Larry Ned RC	1.25	.50
❑ 265 Mel Mitchell RC	1.25	.50
❑ 266 Kendall Newson RC	.75	.30
❑ 267 Shaun Hill RC	1.50	.60
❑ 268 David Pugh RC	.75	.30
❑ 269 Dante Wesley RC	.75	.30
❑ 270 Josh Mallard RC	.75	.30
❑ 271 Akin Ayodele RC	.75	.30
❑ 272 Pete Hunter RC	1.25	.50
❑ 273 Kevin McCadam RC	1.25	.50
❑ 274 Jeff Kelly RC	1.25	.50
❑ 275 John Henderson RC	1.50	.60

2003 Bowman

❑ COMPLETE SET (273)	80.00	40.00
❑ 1 Brett Favre	2.00	.75
❑ 2 Jeremy Shockey	1.25	.50
❑ 3 Fred Taylor	.75	.30
❑ 4 Rich Gannon	.50	.20
❑ 5 Joey Galloway	.50	.20
❑ 6 Ray Lewis	.75	.30
❑ 7 Jeff Blake	.30	.10
❑ 8 Stacey Mack	.30	.10
❑ 9 Matt Hasselbeck	.50	.20
❑ 10 Laveranues Coles	.50	.20
❑ 11 Brad Johnson	.50	.20
❑ 12 Tommy Maddox	.75	.30
❑ 13 Curtis Martin	.75	.30
❑ 14 Tom Brady	2.00	.75
❑ 15 Ricky Williams	.75	.30
❑ 16 Stephen Davis	.50	.20
❑ 17 Chad Johnson	.75	.30
❑ 18 Joey Harrington	1.25	.50
❑ 19 Tony Gonzalez	.50	.20
❑ 20 Peerless Price	.50	.20
❑ 21 LaDainian Tomlinson	.75	.30
❑ 22 James Thrash	.30	.10
❑ 23 Charlie Garner	.50	.20
❑ 24 Eddie George	.50	.20
❑ 25 Terrell Owens	.75	.30
❑ 26 Brian Urlacher	1.25	.50
❑ 27 Eric Moulds	.50	.20
❑ 28 Emmitt Smith	2.00	.75
❑ 29 Tim Couch	.30	.10
❑ 30 Jake Plummer	.50	.20
❑ 31 Marvin Harrison	.75	.30
❑ 32 Chris Chambers	.75	.30
❑ 33 Tiki Barber	.75	.30
❑ 34 Kurt Warner	.75	.30
❑ 35 Michael Pittman	.30	.10
❑ 36 Kevin Dyson	.50	.20
❑ 37 Clinton Portis	1.25	.50
❑ 38 Peyton Manning	1.25	.50
❑ 39 Travis Taylor	.50	.20
❑ 40 Jeff Garcia	.75	.30
❑ 41 Patrick Ramsey	.75	.30
❑ 42 Shaun Alexander	.75	.30
❑ 43 Joe Horn	.50	.20
❑ 44 Daunte Culpepper	.75	.30
❑ 45 Travis Henry	.50	.20
❑ 46 Brian Finneran	.30	.10
❑ 47 William Green	.50	.20
❑ 48 Kordell Stewart	.50	.20
❑ 49 Reggie Wayne	.50	.20
❑ 50 Priest Holmes	1.00	.40
❑ 51 Jay Fiedler	.50	.20
❑ 52 Corey Dillon	.50	.20
❑ 53 Jamal Lewis	.75	.30
❑ 54 Mark Brunell	.50	.20
❑ 55 Santana Moss	.50	.20
❑ 56 Duce Staley	.50	.20
❑ 57 Torry Holt	.75	.30
❑ 58 Rod Gardner	.50	.20
❑ 59 Kerry Collins	.50	.20
❑ 60 Randy Moss	1.25	.50
❑ 61 Jerry Porter	.50	.20
❑ 62 Plaxico Burress	.50	.20
❑ 63 Steve McNair	.75	.30
❑ 64 Muhsin Muhammad	.50	.20
❑ 65 Drew Bledsoe	.75	.30
❑ 66 T.J. Duckett	.50	.20
❑ 67 Ahman Green	.75	.30
❑ 68 Rod Smith	.50	.20
❑ 69 Jimmy Smith	.50	.20
❑ 70 Trent Green	.50	.20
❑ 71 Tim Brown	.75	.30
❑ 72 Jerome Bettis	.75	.30
❑ 73 Isaac Bruce	.75	.30
❑ 74 Derrick Mason	.50	.20
❑ 75 Donovan McNabb	1.00	.40
❑ 76 Deuce McAllister	.75	.30
❑ 77 Zach Thomas	.75	.30
❑ 78 Garrison Hearst	.50	.20
❑ 79 Koren Robinson	.50	.20
❑ 80 Marshall Faulk	.75	.30
❑ 81 Keyshawn Johnson	.75	.30
❑ 82 Jake Delhomme	.75	.30
❑ 83 Marty Booker	.50	.20
❑ 84 James Stewart	.50	.20
❑ 85 Corey Bradford	.30	.10
❑ 86 Derrius Thompson	.30	.10
❑ 87 Edgerrin James	.75	.30
❑ 88 Darrell Jackson	.50	.20
❑ 89 Hines Ward	.75	.30
❑ 90 David Boston	.50	.20
❑ 91 Curtis Conway	.50	.20
❑ 92 David Patten	.30	.10
❑ 93 Michael Bennett	.50	.20
❑ 94 Todd Pinkston	.50	.20
❑ 95 Jerry Rice	1.50	.60
❑ 96 Jon Kitna	.50	.20
❑ 97 Ed McCaffrey	.75	.30
❑ 98 Donald Driver	.50	.20
❑ 99 Anthony Thomas	.50	.20
❑ 100 Michael Vick	2.00	.75
❑ 101 Terry Glenn	.30	.10
❑ 102 Quincy Morgan	.50	.20
❑ 103 David Carr	1.25	.50
❑ 104 Troy Brown	.50	.20
❑ 105 Aaron Brooks	.75	.30
❑ 106 Amani Toomer	.50	.20
❑ 107 Drew Brees	.75	.30
❑ 108 Chad Hutchinson	.30	.10
❑ 109 Warrick Dunn	.50	.20
❑ 110 Chad Pennington	1.00	.40
❑ 111 Carson Palmer RC	6.00	2.50
❑ 112 Brian St.Pierre RC	1.50	.60
❑ 113 Keenan Howry RC	1.50	.60
❑ 114 Sultan McCullough RC	1.25	.50
❑ 115 Terence Newman RC	3.00	1.25
❑ 116 Kelley Washington RC	1.50	.60
❑ 117 Musa Smith RC	1.50	.60
❑ 118 Kevin Williams RC	1.50	.60
❑ 119 Jordan Gross RC	1.25	.50
❑ 120 Lance Briggs RC	5.00	2.00
❑ 121 Victor Hobson RC	1.50	.60
❑ 122 Bryant Johnson RC	1.50	.60
❑ 123 Travis Anglin RC	.75	.30
❑ 124 Artose Pinner RC	1.50	.60
❑ 125 Willis McGahee RC	4.00	1.50
❑ 126 Rashean Mathis RC	1.25	.50
❑ 127 B.J. Askew RC	1.50	.60
❑ 128 DeWayne White RC	1.25	.50
❑ 129 Kevin Curtis RC	2.00	.75
❑ 130 Tyrone Calico RC	2.00	.75
❑ 131 Julian Battle RC	1.25	.50
❑ 132 Ricky Manning RC	1.50	.60
❑ 133 Cory Redding RC	1.25	.50
❑ 134 Michael Haynes RC	1.50	.60
❑ 135 Dallas Clark RC	1.50	.60
❑ 136 Shaun McDonald RC	1.50	.60
❑ 137 Marcus Trufant RC	1.50	.60
❑ 138 Kareem Kelly RC	1.25	.50
❑ 139 Sam Aiken RC	1.25	.50
❑ 140 Terrell Suggs RC	2.50	1.00
❑ 141 Gibran Hamdan RC	.75	.30
❑ 142 Bobby Wade RC	1.50	.60
❑ 143 Aaron Walker RC	1.25	.50
❑ 144 Calvin Pace RC	1.25	.50
❑ 145 Quentin Griffin RC	1.50	.60
❑ 146 Ken Dorsey RC	1.50	.60
❑ 147 Jerome McDougle RC	1.50	.60
❑ 148 Earnest Graham RC	1.50	.60
❑ 149 Rashad Moore RC	1.25	.50
❑ 150 Charles Rogers RC	1.50	.60
❑ 151 Cecil Sapp RC	1.25	.50
❑ 152 Cato June RC	2.00	.75
❑ 153 Ahmaad Galloway RC	1.25	.50
❑ 154 William Joseph RC	1.50	.60
❑ 155 Anquan Boldin RC	4.00	1.50
❑ 156 L.J. Smith RC	1.50	.60
❑ 157 Antwoine Sanders RC	.75	.30
❑ 158 Justin Griffith RC	1.25	.50
❑ 159 Kevin Garrett RC	.75	.30
❑ 160 Teyo Johnson RC	1.50	.60
❑ 161 Chris Crocker RC	1.50	.60
❑ 162 Brad Banks RC	1.25	.50
❑ 163 Justin Gage RC	1.50	.60
❑ 164 Doug Gabriel RC	1.50	.60
❑ 165 Terry Pierce RC	1.25	.50
❑ 166 Bradie James RC	1.50	.60
❑ 167 Bennie Joppru RC	1.50	.60
❑ 168 Malaefou Mackenzie RC	.75	.30
❑ 169 Terrence Edwards RC	1.25	.50
❑ 170 E.J. Henderson RC	1.50	.60
❑ 171 Tony Romo RC	30.00	15.00
❑ 172 DeWayne Robertson RC	1.50	.60
❑ 173 Dwone Hicks RC	.75	.30
❑ 174 Carl Ford RC	.75	.30
❑ 175 Byron Leftwich RC	5.00	2.00
❑ 176 Ken Hamlin RC	1.50	.60
❑ 177 Domanick Davis RC	1.50	.60
❑ 178 Adrian Madise RC	1.25	.50
❑ 179 Siddeeq Shabazz RC	.75	.30
❑ 180 Dave Ragone RC	1.50	.60
❑ 181 Mike Seidman RC	.75	.30
❑ 182 Brooks Bollinger RC	1.50	.60
❑ 183 DeAndrew Rubin RC	.75	.30
❑ 184 Mike Pinkard RC	.75	.30
❑ 185 Nate Burleson RC	1.50	.60
❑ 186 LaBrandon Toefield RC	1.50	.60
❑ 187 Angelo Crowell RC	1.25	.50
❑ 188 J.R. Tolver RC	1.25	.50
❑ 189 Osi Umenyiora RC	2.50	1.00
❑ 190 Larry Johnson RC	6.00	3.00
❑ 191 Nick Barnett RC	1.50	.60
❑ 192 Brandon Drumm RC	.75	.30
❑ 193 Rien Long RC	.75	.30
❑ 194 Zuriel Smith RC	.75	.30
❑ 195 Onterrio Smith RC	1.50	.60
❑ 196 Ronald Bellamy RC	1.25	.50
❑ 197 Kenny Peterson RC	1.25	.50
❑ 198 Charles Tillman RC	2.00	.75
❑ 199 Chaun Thompson RC	.75	.30
❑ 200 Andre Johnson RC	3.00	1.25
❑ 201 Gerald Hayes RC	.75	.30
❑ 202 Terrence Holt RC	1.25	.50
❑ 203 Ovie Mughelli RC	.75	.30
❑ 204 Talman Gardner RC	1.50	.60
❑ 205 Bethel Johnson RC	1.50	.60
❑ 206 Avon Cobourne RC	.75	.30
❑ 207 Brandon Lloyd RC	1.50	.60
❑ 208 Andre Woolfolk RC	1.50	.60
❑ 209 George Wrighster RC	1.25	.50
❑ 210 Justin Fargas RC	1.50	.60
❑ 211 Jimmy Kennedy RC	1.50	.60
❑ 212 Arnaz Battle RC	1.50	.60
❑ 213 Marquel Blackwell RC	.75	.30
❑ 214 Walter Young RC	.75	.30
❑ 215 Kliff Kingsbury RC	1.25	.50
❑ 216 Kawika Mitchell RC	1.50	.60
❑ 217 Drayton Florence RC	.75	.30
❑ 218 Jeremi Johnson RC	1.25	.50
❑ 219 Billy McMullen RC	1.25	.50
❑ 220 Lee Suggs RC	1.50	.60
❑ 221 David Kircus RC	1.50	.60
❑ 222 Rod Babers RC	1.25	.50
❑ 223 Jon Olinger RC	.75	.30
❑ 224 Ty Warren RC	1.50	.60
❑ 225 Kyle Boller RC	1.50	.60
❑ 226 Danny Curley RC	.75	.30
❑ 227 Andrew Pinnock RC	1.25	.50
❑ 228 Kirk Farmer RC	.75	.30
❑ 229 Tully Banta-Cain RC	1.25	.50
❑ 230 Alonzo Jackson RC	1.25	.50
❑ 231 Anthony Adams RC	1.25	.50
❑ 232 Trent Smith RC	1.50	.60

❑ 233 Seneca Wallace RC	1.50	.60
❑ 234 Shane Walton RC	.75	.30
❑ 235 Chris Brown RC	1.50	.60
❑ 236 Dahrran Diedrick RC	1.50	.60
❑ 237 Juston Wood RC	.75	.30
❑ 238 Mike Doss RC	1.50	.60
❑ 239 Visanthe Shiancoe RC	1.25	.50
❑ 240 Rex Grossman RC	4.00	1.50
❑ 241 David Young RC	.75	.30
❑ 242 Jimmy Wilkerson RC	1.25	.50
❑ 243 Jason Witten RC	3.00	1.25
❑ 244 Dennis Weathersby RC	.75	.30
❑ 245 Taylor Jacobs RC	1.25	.50
❑ 246 Chris Davis RC	1.25	.50
❑ 247 LaTarence Dunbar RC	1.25	.50
❑ 248 Eugene Wilson RC	1.50	.60
❑ 249 Ryan Hoag RC	.75	.30
❑ 250 Chris Simms RC	2.50	1.00
❑ 251 Ike Taylor RC	2.50	1.00
❑ 252 Brock Forsey RC	1.50	.60
❑ 253 Curt Anes RC	.75	.30
❑ 254 Taco Wallace RC	1.25	.50
❑ 255 Johnathan Sullivan RC	1.25	.50
❑ 256 David Tyree RC	1.25	.50
❑ 257 Troy Polamalu RC	12.00	6.00
❑ 258 Nate Hybl RC	1.50	.60
❑ 259 Spencer Nead RC	1.25	.50
❑ 260 Boss Bailey RC	1.50	.60
❑ 261 LaMarcus McDonald RC	.75	.30
❑ 262 Casey Moore RC	1.25	.50
❑ 263 Pisa Tinoisamoa RC	1.50	.60
❑ 264 Willie Ponder RC	.75	.30
❑ 265 Donald Lee RC	1.25	.50
❑ 266 Nnamdi Asomugha RC	1.25	.50
❑ 267 Sammy Davis RC	1.50	.60
❑ 268 Joffrey Reynolds RC	.75	.30
❑ 269 Eddie Moore RC	1.25	.50
❑ 270 Tony Hollings RC	1.50	.60
❑ 271 Nick Maddox RC	.75	.30
❑ 272 Kevin Walter RC	1.25	.50
❑ 273 Dan Klecko RC	1.50	.60
❑ 274 Antwan Peek RC	1.25	.50
❑ 275 Tyler Brayton RC	1.50	.60

2004 Bowman

❑ COMPLETE SET (275)	60.00	30.00
❑ 1 Brett Favre	2.00	.75
❑ 2 Jay Fiedler	.30	.10
❑ 3 Andre Davis	.30	.10
❑ 4 Travis Henry	.50	.20
❑ 5 Jimmy Smith	.50	.20
❑ 6 Santana Moss	.50	.20
❑ 7 Correll Buckhalter	.50	.20
❑ 8 Randy Moss	1.00	.40
❑ 9 Edgerrin James	.75	.30
❑ 10 Marc Bulger	.75	.30
❑ 11 Derrick Mason	.50	.20
❑ 12 Mark Brunell	.50	.20
❑ 13 Donte' Stallworth	.50	.20
❑ 14 Deion Branch	.75	.30
❑ 15 Jake Plummer	.50	.20
❑ 16 Steve Smith	.75	.30
❑ 17 Jon Kitna	.50	.20
❑ 18 Andre Johnson	.75	.30
❑ 19 A.J. Feeley	.75	.30
❑ 20 Drew Bledsoe	.75	.30
❑ 21 Antonio Bryant	.50	.20
❑ 22 Reggie Wayne	.50	.20
❑ 23 Thomas Jones	.50	.20
❑ 24 Alge Crumpler	.50	.20
❑ 25 Anquan Boldin	.75	.30
❑ 26 Tim Rattay	.30	.10
❑ 27 Charlie Garner	.50	.20
❑ 28 James Thrash	.30	.10
❑ 29 Koren Robinson	.50	.20
❑ 30 Terrell Owens	.75	.30
❑ 31 Amani Toomer	.50	.20
❑ 32 Kelly Campbell	.30	.10
❑ 33 Patrick Ramsey	.50	.20
❑ 34 Plaxico Burress	.50	.20
❑ 35 Chad Pennington	.75	.30
❑ 36 Fred Taylor	.50	.20
❑ 37 Domanick Davis	.75	.30
❑ 38 DeShaun Foster	.50	.20
❑ 39 T.J. Duckett	.50	.20
❑ 40 Ahman Green	.75	.30
❑ 41 Lee Suggs	.75	.30
❑ 42 Tony Gonzalez	.50	.20
❑ 43 Rich Gannon	.50	.20
❑ 44 Kevan Barlow	.50	.20
❑ 45 Torry Holt	.75	.30
❑ 46 Aaron Brooks	.50	.20
❑ 47 Tyrone Calico	.50	.20
❑ 48 Keenan McCardell	.30	.10
❑ 49 Hines Ward	.75	.30
❑ 50 LaDainian Tomlinson	1.00	.40
❑ 51 Dante Hall	.75	.30
❑ 52 Marcus Pollard	.30	.10
❑ 53 Corey Dillon	.50	.20
❑ 54 Justin McCareins	.30	.10
❑ 55 Stephen Davis	.50	.20
❑ 56 Jeff Garcia	.75	.30
❑ 57 Ashley Lelie	.50	.20
❑ 58 Javon Walker	.50	.20
❑ 59 Kyle Boller	.75	.30
❑ 60 Chad Johnson	.75	.30
❑ 61 Anthony Thomas	.50	.20
❑ 62 Byron Leftwich	1.00	.40
❑ 63 David Boston	.50	.20
❑ 64 Onterrio Smith	.50	.20
❑ 65 Deuce McAllister	.75	.30
❑ 66 Antwaan Randle El	.75	.30
❑ 67 Justin Fargas	.50	.20
❑ 68 Laveranues Coles	.50	.20
❑ 69 Quincy Morgan	.50	.20
❑ 70 Priest Holmes	1.00	.40
❑ 71 Robert Ferguson	.30	.10
❑ 72 Charles Rogers	.50	.20
❑ 73 Drew Brees	.75	.30
❑ 74 Matt Hasselbeck	.50	.20
❑ 75 Peyton Manning	1.25	.50
❑ 76 Rudi Johnson	.50	.20
❑ 77 Jake Delhomme	.75	.30
❑ 78 Tiki Barber	.75	.30
❑ 79 Brad Johnson	.50	.20
❑ 80 Steve McNair	.75	.30
❑ 81 Willis McGahee	.75	.30
❑ 82 Josh McCown	.50	.20
❑ 83 Garrison Hearst	.50	.20
❑ 84 Quincy Carter	.50	.20
❑ 85 Ricky Williams	.75	.30
❑ 86 Trent Green	.50	.20
❑ 87 Curtis Martin	.75	.30
❑ 88 Jerry Porter	.50	.20
❑ 89 Brian Westbrook	.50	.20
❑ 90 Clinton Portis	.75	.30
❑ 91 Eric Moulds	.50	.20
❑ 92 Marcel Shipp	.50	.20
❑ 93 Joey Harrington	.75	.30
❑ 94 David Carr	.75	.30
❑ 95 Marvin Harrison	.75	.30
❑ 96 Joe Horn	.50	.20
❑ 97 Chris Chambers	.50	.20
❑ 98 Darrell Jackson	.50	.20
❑ 99 Eddie George	.50	.20
❑ 100 Donovan McNabb	1.00	.40
❑ 101 Marshall Faulk	.75	.30
❑ 102 Rex Grossman	.75	.30
❑ 103 Tai Streets	.30	.10
❑ 104 Jeremy Shockey	.75	.30
❑ 105 Jamal Lewis	.75	.30
❑ 106 Tom Brady	2.00	.75
❑ 107 Shaun Alexander	.75	.30
❑ 108 Carson Palmer	1.00	.40
❑ 109 Daunte Culpepper	.75	.30
❑ 110 Michael Vick	1.50	.60
❑ 111 Eli Manning RC	15.00	6.00
❑ 112 Kevin Jones RC	2.50	1.00
❑ 113 Philip Rivers RC	5.00	2.00
❑ 114 Ben Roethlisberger RC	20.00	8.00
❑ 115 Roy Williams RC	4.00	1.50
❑ 116 Tommie Harris RC	1.50	.60
❑ 117 Vontez Duff RC	1.25	.50
❑ 118 Karlos Dansby RC	1.50	.60
❑ 119 Thomas Tapeh RC	1.25	.50
❑ 120 Matt Schaub RC	5.00	2.00
❑ 121 Dexter Reid RC	.75	.30
❑ 122 Jonathan Smith RC	1.25	.50
❑ 123 Ricardo Colclough RC	1.50	.60
❑ 124 Jeff Dugan RC	.75	.30
❑ 125 Larry Fitzgerald RC	5.00	2.00
❑ 126 Gibril Wilson RC	1.50	.60
❑ 127 Sean Taylor RC	1.50	.60
❑ 128 Marquise Hill RC	1.25	.50
❑ 129 Ernest Wilford RC	1.50	.60
❑ 130 Cedric Cobbs RC	1.50	.60
❑ 131 Rich Gardner RC	1.25	.50
❑ 132 Chris Cooley RC	1.50	.60
❑ 133 Kenechi Udeze RC	1.50	.60
❑ 134 John Navarre RC	1.50	.60
❑ 135 Ben Troupe RC	1.50	.60
❑ 136 Dave Ball RC	.75	.30
❑ 137 Antwan Odom RC	1.50	.60
❑ 138 Stuart Schweigert RC	1.50	.60
❑ 139 Derek Abney RC	1.50	.60
❑ 140 Keary Colbert RC	1.50	.60
❑ 141 Jeris McIntyre RC	1.25	.50
❑ 142 Matt Kranchick RC	1.50	.60
❑ 143 Rodney Leisle RC	.75	.30
❑ 144 Vince Wilfork RC	1.50	.60
❑ 145 Lee Evans RC	2.00	.75
❑ 146 Darnell Dockett RC	1.25	.50
❑ 147 Jeremy LeSueur RC	1.25	.50
❑ 148 Gilbert Gardner RC	1.25	.50
❑ 149 Amon Gordon RC	.75	.30
❑ 150 Darius Watts RC	1.50	.60
❑ 151 Junior Siavii RC	1.50	.60
❑ 152 Igor Olshansky RC	1.50	.60
❑ 153 Courtney Watson RC	1.50	.60
❑ 154 D.J. Williams RC	1.50	.60
❑ 155 Mewelde Moore RC	1.50	.60
❑ 156 Teddy Lehman RC	1.50	.60
❑ 157 Nathan Vasher RC	2.00	.75
❑ 158 Randy Starks RC	1.25	.50
❑ 159 Isaac Sopoaga RC	.75	.30
❑ 160 Drew Henson RC	1.50	.60
❑ 161 Erik Coleman RC	1.50	.60
❑ 162 Robert Kent RC	.75	.30
❑ 163 Jammal Lord RC	1.50	.60
❑ 164 Richard Seigler RC	1.25	.50
❑ 165 Jeff Smoker RC	1.50	.60
❑ 166 Niko Koutouvides RC	1.25	.50
❑ 167 Adimchinobe Echemandu RC	1.25	.50
❑ 168 Matt Mauck RC	1.50	.60
❑ 169 Brandon Miree RC	1.25	.50
❑ 170 Dunta Robinson RC	1.50	.60
❑ 171 B.J. Symons RC	1.50	.60
❑ 172 Courtney Anderson RC	1.25	.50
❑ 173 Bruce Perry RC	1.50	.60
❑ 174 Shaun Phillips RC	1.25	.50
❑ 175 Greg Jones RC	1.50	.60
❑ 176 Ryan Krause RC	1.25	.50
❑ 177 Charlie Anderson RC	.75	.30
❑ 178 Tank Johnson RC	1.25	.50
❑ 179 Dwan Edwards RC	.75	.30
❑ 180 Julius Jones RC	5.00	2.00
❑ 181 Chad Lavalais RC	1.25	.50
❑ 182 Tim Anderson RC	1.50	.60
❑ 183 Jarrett Payton RC	1.50	.60
❑ 184 Matt Ware RC	1.50	.60
❑ 185 DeAngelo Hall RC	2.00	.75
❑ 186 Ben Hartsock RC	1.50	.60
❑ 187 Bradlee Van Pelt RC	1.50	.60
❑ 188 Michael Boulware RC	1.50	.60
❑ 189 Keith Smith RC	1.25	.50
❑ 190 Michael Jenkins RC	1.50	.60
❑ 191 Quincy Wilson RC	1.25	.50
❑ 192 Dontarrious Thomas RC	1.50	.60
❑ 193 Sloan Thomas RC	1.25	.50
❑ 194 Tony Hargrove RC	1.25	.50
❑ 195 Ben Watson RC	1.50	.60
❑ 196 Craig Krenzel RC	1.50	.60
❑ 197 Jason Babin RC	1.50	.60
❑ 198 Jim Sorgi RC	1.50	.60
❑ 199 Triandos Luke RC	1.50	.60
❑ 200 Kellen Winslow RC	3.00	1.25
❑ 201 Patrick Crayton RC	1.50	.60
❑ 202 Michael Waddell RC	.75	.30
❑ 203 Chris Gamble RC	1.50	.60
❑ 204 Josh Harris RC	1.50	.60

❑ 205 Devard Darling RC	1.50	.60
❑ 206 Shawntae Spencer RC	1.50	.60
❑ 207 Will Smith RC	1.50	.60
❑ 208 Samie Parker RC	1.50	.60
❑ 209 Darrion Scott RC	1.50	.60
❑ 210 Chris Perry RC	2.00	.75
❑ 211 P.K. Sam RC	1.25	.50
❑ 212 Wes Welker RC	4.00	1.50
❑ 213 Ryan Dinwiddie RC	1.25	.50
❑ 214 Rod Davis RC	.75	.30
❑ 215 Casey Clausen RC	1.50	.60
❑ 216 Clarence Moore RC	1.50	.60
❑ 217 D.J. Hackett RC	1.25	.50
❑ 218 Casey Bramlet RC	1.25	.50
❑ 219 Jared Lorenzen RC	1.25	.50
❑ 220 Devery Henderson RC	1.50	.60
❑ 221 Sean Jones RC	1.25	.50
❑ 222 Maurice Mann RC	1.25	.50
❑ 223 Jared Allen RC	1.50	.60
❑ 224 Bruce Thornton RC	.75	.30
❑ 225 Tatum Bell RC	3.00	1.25
❑ 226 Leon Joe RC	.75	.30
❑ 227 Tim Euhus RC	1.50	.60
❑ 228 John Standeford RC	1.25	.50
❑ 229 Reggie Torbor RC	1.25	.50
❑ 230 Rashaun Woods RC	1.50	.60
❑ 231 Jason Shivers RC	.75	.30
❑ 232 Jason Peters RC	1.50	.60
❑ 233 Ahmad Carroll RC	1.50	.60
❑ 234 Jason David RC	1.50	.60
❑ 235 Keyaron Fox RC	1.25	.50
❑ 236 Corey Williams RC	.75	.30
❑ 237 Raheem Orr RC	.75	.30
❑ 238 Carlos Francis RC	1.25	.50
❑ 239 Von Hutchins RC	1.25	.50
❑ 240 Marcus Tubbs RC	1.50	.60
❑ 241 Daryl Smith RC	1.50	.60
❑ 242 Robert Gallery RC	1.50	.60
❑ 243 Sean Tufts RC	1.25	.50
❑ 244 Marquis Cooper RC	1.25	.50
❑ 245 Bernard Berrian RC	2.00	.75
❑ 246 Derrick Strait RC	1.50	.60
❑ 247 Travis LaBoy RC	1.50	.60
❑ 248 Johnnie Morant RC	1.50	.60
❑ 249 Caleb Miller RC	1.25	.50
❑ 250 Michael Clayton RC	3.00	1.25
❑ 251 Will Poole RC	1.50	.60
❑ 252 Andy Hall RC	1.25	.50
❑ 253 Demorrio Williams RC	1.50	.60
❑ 254 Chris Thompson RC	.75	.30
❑ 255 Derrick Hamilton RC	1.25	.50
❑ 256 Glenn Earl RC	1.25	.50
❑ 257 Jonathan Vilma RC	1.50	.60
❑ 258 Donnell Washington RC	1.50	.60
❑ 259 Drew Carter RC	1.50	.60
❑ 260 Steven Jackson RC	5.00	2.00
❑ 261 Jamaar Taylor RC	1.50	.60
❑ 262 Nate Lawrie RC	1.25	.50
❑ 263 Cody Pickett RC	1.50	.60
❑ 264 Keiwan Ratliff RC	1.25	.50
❑ 265 Luke McCown RC	1.50	.60
❑ 266 Jerricho Cotchery RC	1.50	.60
❑ 267 Joey Thomas RC	1.50	.60
❑ 268 Shawn Andrews RC	1.50	.60
❑ 269 Derrick Ward RC	1.50	.60
❑ 270 Reggie Williams RC	2.00	.75
❑ 271 Rod Rutherford RC	1.25	.50
❑ 272 Michael Turner RC	2.00	.75
❑ 273 Michael Gaines RC	1.25	.50
❑ 274 Will Allen RC	1.50	.60
❑ 275 J.P. Losman RC	3.00	1.25

2005 Bowman

❑ COMP.SET w/o AU's (270)	60.00	25.00
❑ 1 Peyton Manning	1.25	.50
❑ 2 Antonio Gates	.75	.30
❑ 3 Priest Holmes	.75	.30
❑ 4 Anquan Boldin	.50	.20
❑ 5 Donovan McNabb	1.00	.40
❑ 6 Drew Bennett	.50	.20
❑ 7 Michael Vick	1.25	.50
❑ 8 David Carr	.75	.30
❑ 9 Drew Brees	.75	.30
❑ 10 Trent Green	.50	.20
❑ 11 Drew Bledsoe	.75	.30
❑ 12 Randy Moss	.75	.30
❑ 13 Terrell Owens	.75	.30
❑ 14 Donte Stallworth	.50	.20
❑ 15 Alge Crumpler	.50	.20

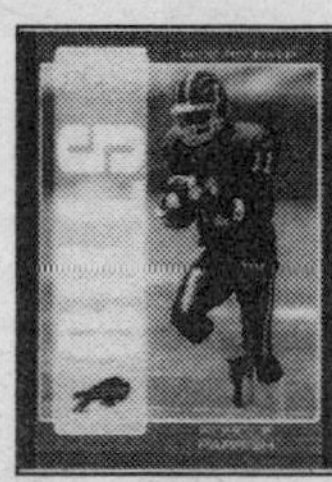

❑ 16 Jake Plummer	.50	.20
❑ 17 Curtis Martin	.75	.30
❑ 18 Jason Witten	.50	.20
❑ 19 Tom Brady	2.00	.75
❑ 20 Thomas Jones	.50	.20
❑ 21 Tiki Barber	.75	.30
❑ 22 Maurice Carthon CO	.50	.20
❑ 23 Rex Grossman	.50	.20
❑ 24 Brett Favre	2.00	.75
❑ 25 Marshall Faulk	.75	.30
❑ 26 LaMont Jordan	.75	.30
❑ 27 Kurt Warner	.50	.20
❑ 28 Corey Dillon	.50	.20
❑ 29 Julius Jones	1.00	.40
❑ 30 Ahman Green	.75	.30
❑ 31 Jamal Lewis	.75	.30
❑ 32 Ben Roethlisberger	2.00	.75
❑ 33 Keary Colbert	.50	.20
❑ 34 Mike Nolan CO RC	.75	.30
❑ 35 Joey Harrington	.75	.30
❑ 36 Brian Westbrook	.50	.20
❑ 37 Domanick Davis	.50	.20
❑ 38 Carson Palmer	.75	.30
❑ 39 Stephen Davis	.50	.20
❑ 40 Eli Manning	1.50	.60
❑ 41 Edgerrin James	.75	.30
❑ 42 Jonathan Vilma	.50	.20
❑ 43 Brad Childress CO RC	.50	.20
❑ 44 Willis McGahee	.75	.30
❑ 45 Steve McNair	.75	.30
❑ 46 Plaxico Burress	.50	.20
❑ 47 Rudi Johnson	.50	.20
❑ 48 Jerry Porter	.50	.20
❑ 49 Chad Pennington	.75	.30
❑ 50 Charles Rogers	.50	.20
❑ 51 Patrick Ramsey	.50	.20
❑ 52 Dwight Freeney	.50	.20
❑ 53 Brian Griese	.50	.20
❑ 54 Jerome Bettis	.75	.30
❑ 55 Tim Lewis CO	.40	.15
❑ 56 Aaron Brooks	.50	.20
❑ 57 Matt Hasselbeck	.50	.20
❑ 58 Chris Chambers	.50	.20
❑ 59 Kyle Boller	.50	.20
❑ 60 Brandon Lloyd	.40	.15
❑ 61 Marc Bulger	.75	.30
❑ 62 Isaac Bruce	.50	.20
❑ 63 Jake Delhomme	.75	.30
❑ 64 Chad Johnson	.75	.30
❑ 65 Shaun Alexander	1.00	.40
❑ 66 Kevin Jones	.75	.30
❑ 67 Eric Moulds	.50	.20
❑ 68 Laveranues Coles	.50	.20
❑ 69 A.J. Feeley	.50	.20
❑ 70 Sean Taylor	.50	.20
❑ 71 Romeo Crennel CO RC	.75	.30
❑ 72 Ashley Lelie	.50	.20
❑ 73 Nick Saban CO RC	.75	.30
❑ 74 Deuce McAllister	.75	.30
❑ 75 Kerry Collins	.50	.20
❑ 76 Chris Brown	.50	.20
❑ 77 Steven Jackson	1.00	.40
❑ 78 Nate Burleson	.50	.20
❑ 79 LaDainian Tomlinson	1.00	.40
❑ 80 Darrell Jackson	.50	.20
❑ 81 Torry Holt	.75	.30
❑ 82 Lee Suggs	.50	.20
❑ 83 Lee Evans	.50	.20
❑ 84 Santana Moss	.50	.20
❑ 85 Jeremy Shockey	.75	.30
❑ 86 Hines Ward	.75	.30
❑ 87 Muhsin Muhammad	.50	.20
❑ 88 Daunte Culpepper	.75	.30
❑ 89 Deion Branch	.50	.20
❑ 90 DeShaun Foster	.50	.20
❑ 91 Travis Henry	.50	.20
❑ 92 Jerry Rice	1.50	.60
❑ 93 Reggie Wayne	.50	.20
❑ 94 Roy Williams WR	.75	.30
❑ 95 Michael Jenkins	.50	.20
❑ 96 Tatum Bell	.50	.20
❑ 97 Andre Johnson	.50	.20
❑ 98 Dante Hall	.50	.20
❑ 99 Javon Walker	.50	.20
❑ 100 Larry Fitzgerald	.75	.30
❑ 101 Joe Horn	.50	.20
❑ 102 Marvin Harrison	.75	.30
❑ 103 Fred Taylor	.50	.20
❑ 104 Byron Leftwich	.75	.30
❑ 105 Tony Gonzalez	.50	.20
❑ 106 T.J. Houshmandzadeh	.40	.15
❑ 107 J.P. Losman	.75	.30
❑ 108 Michael Clayton	.75	.30
❑ 109 Clinton Portis	.75	.30
❑ 110 Ted Cottrell CO RC	.40	.15
❑ 111 Braylon Edwards RC	5.00	2.00
❑ 112 Aaron Rodgers RC	5.00	2.00
❑ 113 Ronnie Brown RC	6.00	2.50
❑ 114 Alex Smith QB RC	6.00	2.50
❑ 115 Cadillac Williams RC	6.00	2.50
❑ 116 Ciatrick Fason RC	1.50	.60
❑ 117 Derrick Johnson RC	2.50	1.00
❑ 118 Carlos Rogers RC	2.00	.75
❑ 119 Ryan Moats RC	1.50	.60
❑ 120 Alvin Pearman RC	1.50	.60
❑ 121 Stefan LeFors RC	1.50	.60
❑ 122 Brandon Jacobs RC	2.00	.75
❑ 123 Kyle Orton RC	1.50	.60
❑ 124 Marion Barber RC	2.50	1.00
❑ 125 Mark Bradley RC	1.50	.60
❑ 126 Travis Johnson RC	1.25	.50
❑ 127 Antrel Rolle RC	1.50	.60
❑ 128 Jason Campbell RC	2.50	1.00
❑ 129 DeMarcus Ware RC	2.50	1.00
❑ 130 Frank Gore RC	3.00	1.25
❑ 131 Justin Miller RC	1.25	.50
❑ 132 J.J. Arrington RC	1.50	.60
❑ 133 Marcus Spears RC	1.50	.60
❑ 134 Roddy White RC	1.50	.60
❑ 135 Fabian Washington RC	1.50	.60
❑ 136 Vincent Jackson RC	1.50	.60
❑ 137 Erasmus James RC	1.50	.60
❑ 138 Roscoe Parrish RC	1.50	.60
❑ 139 Airese Currie RC	1.50	.60
❑ 140 Heath Miller RC	3.00	1.25
❑ 141 Mike Patterson RC	1.50	.60
❑ 142 Troy Williamson RC	1.50	.60
❑ 143 Terrence Murphy RC	1.50	.60
❑ 144 Dan Orlovsky RC	1.50	.60
❑ 145 Eric Shelton RC	1.50	.60
❑ 146 Thomas Davis RC	1.50	.60
❑ 147 Cedric Benson RC	4.00	1.50
❑ 148 Noah Herron RC	1.50	.60
❑ 149 Vernand Morency RC	1.50	.60
❑ 150 Darren Sproles RC	1.50	.60
❑ 151 Alex Smith TE RC	1.50	.60
❑ 152 Mark Clayton RC	1.50	.60
❑ 153 Craphonso Thorpe RC	1.25	.50
❑ 154 Mike Williams	1.50	.60
❑ 155 Anthony Davis RC	1.25	.50
❑ 156 Charlie Frye RC	1.50	.60
❑ 157 Fred Gibson RC	1.25	.50
❑ 158 Reggie Brown RC	1.50	.60
❑ 159 Andrew Walter RC	1.50	.60
❑ 160 Adam Jones RC	1.50	.60
❑ 161 David Greene RC	1.50	.60
❑ 162 Maurice Clarett	1.50	.60
❑ 163 Courtney Roby RC	1.50	.60
❑ 164 Derek Anderson RC	2.50	1.00
❑ 165 Matt Jones RC	2.50	1.00
❑ 166 Chris Henry RC	1.50	.60
❑ 167 Shaun Cody RC	1.50	.60
❑ 168 Khalif Barnes RC	1.25	.50
❑ 169 Matt Roth RC	1.50	.60
❑ 170 Lionel Gates RC	1.25	.50
❑ 171 Kevin Burnett RC	1.50	.60
❑ 172 Taylor Stubblefield RC	.75	.30
❑ 173 Zach Tuiasosopo RC	.75	.30
❑ 174 Alex Barron RC	.75	.30
❑ 175 Mike Nugent RC	1.50	.60
❑ 176 Barrett Ruud RC	1.50	.60

- ❑ 177 Brock Berlin RC 1.25 .50
- ❑ 178 Kirk Morrison RC 1.50 .60
- ❑ 179 David Pollack RC 1.50 .60
- ❑ 180 Ryan Fitzpatrick RC 1.50 .60
- ❑ 181 Kay-Jay Harris RC 1.25 .50
- ❑ 182 Dan Cody RC 1.50 .60
- ❑ 183 Chad Owens RC 1.50 .60
- ❑ 184 Stanley Wilson RC 1.25 .50
- ❑ 185 Rasheed Marshall RC 1.50 .60
- ❑ 186 Bryant McFadden RC 1.50 .60
- ❑ 187 Joel Dreessen RC 1.25 .50
- ❑ 188 Donte Nicholson RC 1.50 .60
- ❑ 189 Scott Starks RC 1.25 .50
- ❑ 190 Walter Reyes RC 1.25 .50
- ❑ 191 Stanford Routt RC 1.25 .50
- ❑ 192 Lance Mitchell RC 1.25 .50
- ❑ 193 Rian Wallace RC 1.25 .50
- ❑ 194 Timmy Chang RC 1.25 .50
- ❑ 195 Oshiomogho Atogwe RC 1.25 .50
- ❑ 196 Larry Brackins RC 1.25 .50
- ❑ 197 Jovan Witherspoon RC .75 .30
- ❑ 198 Boomer Grigsby RC 1.50 .60
- ❑ 199 Darryl Blackstock RC 1.25 .50
- ❑ 200 Jerome Mathis RC 1.50 .60
- ❑ 201 Ellis Hobbs RC 1.50 .60
- ❑ 202 Dante Ridgeway RC 1.25 .50
- ❑ 203 James Kilian RC 1.50 .60
- ❑ 204 Patrick Estes RC 1.25 .50
- ❑ 205 Justin Tuck RC 1.50 .60
- ❑ 206 Channing Crowder RC 1.50 .60
- ❑ 207 Dustin Fox RC 1.50 .60
- ❑ 208 Marlin Jackson RC 1.50 .60
- ❑ 209 Luis Castillo RC 1.50 .60
- ❑ 210 Paris Warren RC 1.25 .50
- ❑ 211 J.R. Russell RC 1.25 .50
- ❑ 212 Cedric Houston RC 1.50 .60
- ❑ 213 Corey Webster RC 1.50 .60
- ❑ 214 Craig Bragg RC 1.25 .50
- ❑ 215 Tab Perry RC 1.50 .60
- ❑ 216 Ryan Riddle RC .75 .30
- ❑ 217 Gino Guidugli RC .75 .30
- ❑ 218 Deandra Cobb RC 1.25 .50
- ❑ 219 Travis Daniels RC 1.25 .50
- ❑ 220 Marcus Maxwell RC 1.25 .50
- ❑ 221 Eric King RC 1.25 .50
- ❑ 222 Matt Cassel RC 2.50 1.00
- ❑ 223 Justin Green RC 1.50 .60
- ❑ 224 Steve Savoy RC .75 .30
- ❑ 225 Shawne Merriman RC 2.50 1.00
- ❑ 226 Damien Nash RC 1.25 .50
- ❑ 227 T.A. McLendon RC .75 .30
- ❑ 228 Vincent Fuller RC 1.25 .50
- ❑ 229 Jordan Beck RC 1.25 .50
- ❑ 230 Lofa Tatupu RC 2.00 .75
- ❑ 231 Will Peoples RC 1.25 .50
- ❑ 232 Chad Friehauf RC 1.25 .50
- ❑ 233 Brady Poppinga RC 1.50 .60
- ❑ 234 Anttaj Hawthorne RC 1.25 .50
- ❑ 235 Adrian McPherson RC 1.50 .60
- ❑ 236 Nick Collins RC 1.50 .60
- ❑ 237 Roydell Williams RC 1.50 .60
- ❑ 238 Craig Ochs RC 1.25 .50
- ❑ 239 Billy Bajema RC 1.25 .50
- ❑ 240 Jon Goldsberry RC 1.50 .60
- ❑ 241 Jared Newberry RC 1.25 .50
- ❑ 242 Odell Thurman RC 1.50 .60
- ❑ 243 Kelvin Hayden RC 1.25 .50
- ❑ 244 Jamaal Brimmer RC .75 .30
- ❑ 245 Jonathan Babineaux RC 1.25 .50
- ❑ 246 Bo Scaife RC 1.25 .50
- ❑ 247 Chris Spencer RC 1.50 .60
- ❑ 248 Manuel White RC 1.25 .50
- ❑ 249 Josh Davis RC 1.25 .50
- ❑ 250 Bryan Randall RC 1.25 .50
- ❑ 251 James Butler RC 1.25 .50
- ❑ 252 Harry Williams RC 1.25 .50
- ❑ 253 Leroy Hill RC 1.50 .60
- ❑ 254 Josh Bullocks RC 1.50 .60
- ❑ 255 Alfred Fincher RC 1.25 .50
- ❑ 256 Antonio Perkins RC 1.25 .50
- ❑ 257 Bobby Purify RC 1.25 .50
- ❑ 258 Rick Razzano RC 1.50 .60
- ❑ 259 Darrent Williams RC 1.50 .60
- ❑ 260 Darian Durant RC 1.50 .60
- ❑ 261 Fred Amey RC 1.25 .50
- ❑ 262 Ronald Bartell RC 1.25 .50
- ❑ 263 Kerry Rhodes RC 1.50 .60
- ❑ 264 Jerome Carter RC 1.25 .50
- ❑ 265 Marcus Randall RC 1.25 .50
- ❑ 266 Nehemiah Broughton RC 1.25 .50
- ❑ 267 Keron Henry RC .75 .30
- ❑ 268 Jerome Collins RC 1.25 .50
- ❑ 269 Trent Cole RC 1.50 .60
- ❑ 270 Alphonso Hodge RC .75 .30
- ❑ 271 Brandon Jones RC 1.50 .60
- ❑ 272 Chase Lyman RC 1.25 .50
- ❑ 273 Marviel Underwood RC 1.25 .50
- ❑ 274 Maurice Washington RC 1.25 .50
- ❑ 275 Madison Hedgecock RC 1.50 .60

2006 Bowman

- ❑ 1 Plaxico Burress .50 .20
- ❑ 2 Lee Evans .50 .20
- ❑ 3 Shaun Alexander .75 .30
- ❑ 4 Muhsin Muhammad .50 .20
- ❑ 5 Jamal Lewis .50 .20
- ❑ 6 Brett Favre 1.50 .60
- ❑ 7 Jake Plummer .50 .20
- ❑ 8 Clinton Portis .75 .30
- ❑ 9 Deuce McAllister .50 .20
- ❑ 10 Rod Marinelli CO RC .50 .20
- ❑ 11 Tom Brady 1.25 .50
- ❑ 12 Torry Holt .50 .20
- ❑ 13 T.J. Houshmandzadeh .50 .20
- ❑ 14 Rudi Johnson .50 .20
- ❑ 15 Priest Holmes .50 .20
- ❑ 16 Tatum Bell .50 .20
- ❑ 17 Carson Palmer .75 .30
- ❑ 18 Jeremy Shockey .75 .30
- ❑ 19 Willis McGahee .75 .30
- ❑ 20 Shawne Merriman .50 .20
- ❑ 21 Alge Crumpler .50 .20
- ❑ 22 Terrell Owens .75 .30
- ❑ 23 Marion Barber .50 .20
- ❑ 24 Fred Taylor .50 .20
- ❑ 25 Dante Hall .50 .20
- ❑ 26 Steve Smith .75 .30
- ❑ 27 Mike McCarthy CO RC .50 .20
- ❑ 28 Brad Johnson .50 .20
- ❑ 29 Reggie Wayne .50 .20
- ❑ 30 David Carr .50 .20
- ❑ 31 DeShaun Foster .50 .20
- ❑ 32 Julius Jones .75 .30
- ❑ 33 Tony Gonzalez .50 .20
- ❑ 34 Chad Johnson .50 .20
- ❑ 35 Javon Walker .50 .20
- ❑ 36 Curtis Martin .75 .30
- ❑ 37 Marc Bulger .50 .20
- ❑ 38 Peyton Manning 1.25 .50
- ❑ 39 LaMont Jordan .50 .20
- ❑ 40 LaDainian Tomlinson 1.00 .40
- ❑ 41 Tiki Barber .75 .30
- ❑ 42 Darrell Jackson .50 .20
- ❑ 43 Byron Leftwich .50 .20
- ❑ 44 J.P. Losman .50 .20
- ❑ 45 Dwight Freeney .50 .20
- ❑ 46 Kevin Jones .75 .30
- ❑ 47 Drew Brees .75 .30
- ❑ 48 Isaac Bruce .50 .20
- ❑ 49 Hines Ward .75 .30
- ❑ 50 Drew Bledsoe .75 .30
- ❑ 51 Randy Moss .75 .30
- ❑ 52 Roy Williams WR .75 .30
- ❑ 53 Edgerrin James .75 .30
- ❑ 54 Donte Stallworth .50 .20
- ❑ 55 Odell Thurman .40 .15
- ❑ 56 Chester Taylor .50 .20
- ❑ 57 Ahman Green .50 .20
- ❑ 58 Steven Jackson .75 .30
- ❑ 59 Randy McMichael .40 .15
- ❑ 60 Larry Fitzgerald .75 .30
- ❑ 61 Ben Roethlisberger 1.25 .50
- ❑ 62 Charlie Frye .50 .20
- ❑ 63 Daunte Culpepper .75 .30
- ❑ 64 Keary Colbert .40 .15
- ❑ 65 Santana Moss .50 .20
- ❑ 66 Patrick Ramsey .50 .20
- ❑ 67 Mark Clayton .75 .30
- ❑ 68 Jonathan Vilma .50 .20
- ❑ 69 Gary Kubiak CO .50 .20
- ❑ 70 Michael Jenkins .50 .20
- ❑ 71 Jake Delhomme .50 .20
- ❑ 72 Marvin Harrison .75 .30
- ❑ 73 Aaron Rodgers .75 .30
- ❑ 74 Trent Green .50 .20
- ❑ 75 Andre Johnson .50 .20
- ❑ 76 Chris Chambers .50 .20
- ❑ 77 Matt Hasselbeck .50 .20
- ❑ 78 Chris Brown .50 .20
- ❑ 79 Reggie Brown .60 .25
- ❑ 80 Eli Manning 1.00 .40
- ❑ 81 Warrick Dunn .50 .20
- ❑ 82 Kurt Warner .50 .20
- ❑ 83 Corey Dillon .50 .20
- ❑ 84 Antonio Gates .75 .30
- ❑ 85 Anquan Boldin .50 .20
- ❑ 86 Terry Glenn .50 .20
- ❑ 87 Donovan McNabb .75 .30
- ❑ 88 Steve McNair .50 .20
- ❑ 89 Drew Bennett .40 .15
- ❑ 90 Jason Witten .50 .20
- ❑ 91 Alex Smith QB .75 .30
- ❑ 92 Joe Horn .50 .20
- ❑ 93 Eric Moulds .50 .20
- ❑ 94 Domanick Davis .50 .20
- ❑ 95 Billy Volek .50 .20
- ❑ 96 Deion Branch .50 .20
- ❑ 97 Chris Cooley .40 .15
- ❑ 98 Todd Heap UER .50 .20
- ❑ 99 Larry Johnson 1.00 .40
- ❑ 100 Chad Pennington .50 .20
- ❑ 101 Willie Parker 1.00 .40
- ❑ 102 Brandon Lloyd .50 .20
- ❑ 103 Cadillac Williams .75 .30
- ❑ 104 Rod Smith .50 .20
- ❑ 105 Philip Rivers .75 .30
- ❑ 106 Ronnie Brown .75 .30
- ❑ 107 Reuben Droughns .50 .20
- ❑ 108 Braylon Edwards .75 .30
- ❑ 109 Joey Galloway .50 .20
- ❑ 110 Michael Vick .75 .30
- ❑ 111 Reggie Bush RC 6.00 2.50
- ❑ 112 Matt Leinart RC 5.00 2.00
- ❑ 113 Vince Young RC 6.00 2.50
- ❑ 114 Jay Cutler RC 5.00 2.00
- ❑ 115 Santonio Holmes RC 3.00 1.25
- ❑ 116 LenDale White RC 3.00 1.25
- ❑ 117 DeAngelo Williams RC 4.00 1.50
- ❑ 118 Mario Williams RC 2.50 1.00
- ❑ 119 A.J. Hawk RC 3.00 1.25
- ❑ 120 Joseph Addai RC 5.00 2.00
- ❑ 121 Leonard Pope RC 1.50 .60
- ❑ 122 Tamba Hali RC 1.50 .60
- ❑ 123 Bruce Gradkowski RC 2.50 1.00
- ❑ 124 Jerome Harrison RC 1.50 .60
- ❑ 125 Jason Allen RC 1.50 .60
- ❑ 126 Laurence Maroney RC 4.00 1.50
- ❑ 127 Mathias Kiwanuka RC 2.00 .75
- ❑ 128 Brodrick Bunkley RC 1.50 .60
- ❑ 129 Brian Calhoun RC 1.50 .60
- ❑ 130 Bobby Carpenter RC 1.50 .60
- ❑ 131 Johnathan Joseph RC 1.25 .50
- ❑ 132 Maurice Stovall RC 1.50 .60
- ❑ 133 Anthony Fasano RC 1.50 .60
- ❑ 134 Travis Wilson RC 1.50 .60
- ❑ 135 Chad Jackson RC 1.50 .60
- ❑ 136 D'Brickashaw Ferguson RC 1.50 .60
- ❑ 137 Tarvaris Jackson RC 2.50 1.00
- ❑ 138 Omar Jacobs RC 1.25 .50
- ❑ 139 Reggie McNeal RC 1.25 .50
- ❑ 140 Jerious Norwood RC 2.50 1.00
- ❑ 141 Haloti Ngata RC 1.50 .60
- ❑ 142 Jason Avant RC 1.50 .60
- ❑ 143 Brandon Marshall RC 1.50 .60
- ❑ 144 Tye Hill RC 1.50 .60
- ❑ 145 Manny Lawson RC 1.50 .60
- ❑ 146 Brandon Williams RC 1.50 .60
- ❑ 147 Demetrius Williams RC 1.50 .60
- ❑ 148 Michael Huff RC 2.00 .75
- ❑ 149 Mike Hass RC 1.50 .60

❑ 150 Vernon Davis RC 3.00 1.25
❑ 151 Donte Whitner RC 1.50 .60
❑ 152 Marcedes Lewis RC 1.50 .60
❑ 153 Michael Robinson RC 1.50 .60
❑ 154 Maurice Drew RC 4.00 1.50
❑ 155 Sinorice Moss RC 1.50 .60
❑ 156 Brodie Croyle RC 4.00 1.50
❑ 157 Derek Hagan RC 1.50 .60
❑ 158 Chad Greenway RC 1.50 .60
❑ 159 Kellen Clemens RC 2.50 1.00
❑ 160 Skyler Green RC 1.50 .60
❑ 161 Devin Hester RC 3.00 1.25
❑ 162 Jeremy Bloom RC 1.25 .50
❑ 163 Ashton Youboty RC 1.50 .60
❑ 164 Kamerion Wimbley RC 1.50 .60
❑ 165 Charlie Whitehurst RC 1.50 .60
❑ 166 Devin Aromashodu RC 1.25 .50
❑ 167 Darnell Bing RC 1.50 .60
❑ 168 Adam Jennings RC 1.25 .50
❑ 169 Joe Klopfenstein RC 1.25 .50
❑ 170 Jeff Webb RC 1.25 .50
❑ 171 D.J. Shockley RC 1.50 .60
❑ 172 Daniel Bullocks RC 1.50 .60
❑ 173 Marcus Vick RC 1.25 .50
❑ 174 Greg Jennings RC 2.50 1.00
❑ 175 David Thomas RC 1.50 .60
❑ 176 Thomas Howard RC 1.50 .60
❑ 177 Todd Watkins RC 1.25 .50
❑ 178 Leon Washington RC 2.50 1.00
❑ 179 Winston Justice RC 1.50 .60
❑ 180 Lawrence Vickers RC 1.25 .50
❑ 181 Bernard Pollard RC 1.25 .50
❑ 182 Davin Joseph RC 1.25 .50
❑ 183 Abdul Hodge RC 1.50 .60
❑ 184 Pat Watkins RC 1.50 .60
❑ 185 Jon Alston RC 1.50 .60
❑ 186 Ernie Sims RC 2.00 .75
❑ 187 Jovon Bouknight RC 1.25 .50
❑ 188 D'Qwell Jackson RC 1.25 .50
❑ 189 Wali Lundy RC 1.50 .60
❑ 190 Corey Bramlet RC 1.25 .50
❑ 191 Jonathan Orr RC 1.25 .50
❑ 192 Gerald Riggs RC 1.50 .60
❑ 193 Antonio Cromartie RC 1.50 .60
❑ 194 Will Blackmon RC 1.25 .50
❑ 195 Chris Gocong RC 1.25 .50
❑ 196 David Pittman RC 1.25 .50
❑ 197 Quinn Sypniewski RC 1.25 .50
❑ 198 A.J. Nicholson RC .75 .30
❑ 199 Richard Marshall RC 1.25 .50
❑ 200 Kevin McMahan RC 1.25 .50
❑ 201 Cedric Humes RC 1.50 .60
❑ 202 J.D. Runnels RC 1.25 .50
❑ 203 Darryl Tapp RC 1.25 .50
❑ 204 Charles Davis RC 1.25 .50
❑ 205 Brad Smith RC 1.50 .60
❑ 206 Tim Massaquoi RC 1.25 .50
❑ 207 Nate Salley RC 1.25 .50
❑ 208 Matt Shelton RC 1.50 .60
❑ 209 Brett Basanez RC 1.50 .60
❑ 210 Demario Minter RC 1.25 .50
❑ 211 Marques Hagans RC 1.25 .50
❑ 212 Rocky Mcintosh RC 1.50 .60
❑ 213 Anthony Mix RC 1.25 .50
❑ 214 Hank Baskett RC 1.50 .60
❑ 215 Jimmy Williams RC 1.50 .60
❑ 216 Andre Hall RC 1.25 .50
❑ 217 Cody Hodges RC 1.25 .50
❑ 218 Greg Lee RC 1.25 .50
❑ 219 Danieal Manning RC 1.50 .60
❑ 220 Jason Hatcher RC 1.25 .50
❑ 221 Ben Obomanu RC 1.25 .50
❑ 222 Dusty Dvoracek RC 1.50 .60
❑ 223 Ingle Martin RC 1.50 .60
❑ 224 Marcus McNeill RC 1.25 .50
❑ 225 DeMeco Ryans RC 2.00 .75
❑ 226 Dwayne Slay RC 1.25 .50
❑ 227 Domenik Hixon RC 1.25 .50
❑ 228 John David Washington RC 1.25 .50
❑ 229 P.J. Daniels RC 1.25 .50
❑ 230 Kelly Jennings RC 1.50 .60
❑ 231 Josh Betts RC 1.25 .50
❑ 232 Marques Colston RC 6.00 2.50
❑ 233 John McCargo RC 1.25 .50
❑ 234 P.J. Pope RC 1.25 .50
❑ 235 Gabe Watson RC 1.25 .50
❑ 236 Paul Pinegar RC 1.25 .50
❑ 237 Ray Edwards RC 1.25 .50
❑ 238 Elvis Dumervil RC .75 .30
❑ 239 Travis Lulay RC 1.25 .50
❑ 240 Alan Zemaitis RC 1.50 .60
❑ 241 Bennie Brazell RC 1.25 .50
❑ 242 Jeff King RC 1.25 .50
❑ 243 Damien Rhodes RC 1.25 .50
❑ 244 Orien Harris RC 1.25 .50
❑ 245 David Anderson RC 1.25 .50
❑ 246 Roman Harper RC 1.25 .50
❑ 247 Garrett Mills RC 1.50 .60
❑ 248 Anthony Schlegel RC 1.25 .50
❑ 249 David Kirtman RC 1.25 .50
❑ 250 Omar Gaither RC 1.25 .50
❑ 251 Freddie Keiaho RC 1.25 .50
❑ 252 J.J. Outlaw RC 1.25 .50
❑ 253 Willie Reid RC 1.50 .60
❑ 254 Tony Scheffler RC 1.50 .60
❑ 255 Dee Webb RC 1.25 .50
❑ 256 Drew Olson RC 1.25 .50
❑ 257 Tim Day RC 1.25 .50
❑ 258 Martin Nance RC 1.25 .50
❑ 259 Spencer Havner RC 1.25 .50
❑ 260 Ko Simpson RC 1.25 .50
❑ 261 Jesse Mahelona RC 1.25 .50
❑ 262 Owen Daniels RC 1.50 .60
❑ 263 Mike Bell RC 1.50 .60
❑ 264 Anwar Phillips RC 1.25 .50
❑ 265 Erik Meyer RC 1.25 .50
❑ 266 Delanie Walker RC 1.25 .50
❑ 267 Dominique Byrd RC 1.25 .50
❑ 268 Eric Smith RC 1.25 .50
❑ 269 Darrell Hackney RC 1.25 .50
❑ 270 Freddie Roach RC 1.25 .50
❑ 271 James Anderson RC .75 .30
❑ 272 Anthony Smith RC 2.00 .75
❑ 273 Quinton Ganther RC 1.25 .50
❑ 274 Nick Mangold RC 1.25 .50
❑ 275 Gerris Wilkinson RC .75 .30

2007 Bowman

❑ 1 Matt Leinart .75 .30
❑ 2 Matt Schaub .60 .25
❑ 3 Jason Campbell .60 .25
❑ 4 Steve McNair .60 .25
❑ 5 J.P. Losman .60 .25
❑ 6 Jake Delhomme .60 .25
❑ 7 Rex Grossman .60 .25
❑ 8 Carson Palmer .75 .30
❑ 9 Tony Romo 1.50 .60
❑ 10 Jay Cutler .75 .30
❑ 11 Brett Favre 1.50 .60
❑ 12 Peyton Manning 1.25 .50
❑ 13 Trent Green .60 .25
❑ 14 Tom Brady 1.50 .60
❑ 15 Drew Brees .60 .25
❑ 16 Eli Manning .75 .30
❑ 17 Chad Pennington .60 .25
❑ 18 Donovan McNabb .75 .30
❑ 19 Ben Roethlisberger 1.00 .40
❑ 20 Philip Rivers .75 .30
❑ 21 Alex Smith QB .75 .30
❑ 22 Matt Hasselbeck .60 .25
❑ 23 Marc Bulger .60 .25
❑ 24 Vince Young 1.00 .40
❑ 25 Edgerrin James .75 .30
❑ 26 Warrick Dunn .60 .25
❑ 27 Jamal Lewis .60 .25
❑ 28 Willis McGahee .60 .25
❑ 29 DeShaun Foster .60 .25
❑ 30 DeAngelo Williams .75 .30
❑ 31 Cedric Benson .60 .25
❑ 32 Thomas Jones .60 .25
❑ 33 Rudi Johnson .60 .25
❑ 34 Julius Jones .60 .25
❑ 35 Dominic Rhodes .60 .25
❑ 36 Joseph Addai 1.00 .40
❑ 37 Fred Taylor .60 .25
❑ 38 Maurice Jones-Drew .75 .30
❑ 39 Larry Johnson .75 .30
❑ 40 Ronnie Brown .60 .25
❑ 41 Chester Taylor .50 .20
❑ 42 Laurence Maroney .75 .30
❑ 43 Deuce McAllister .60 .25
❑ 44 Reggie Bush 1.00 .40
❑ 45 Brandon Jacobs .60 .25
❑ 46 Brian Westbrook .60 .25
❑ 47 Willie Parker .75 .30
❑ 48 LaDainian Tomlinson 1.00 .40
❑ 49 Frank Gore .75 .30
❑ 50 Shaun Alexander .60 .25
❑ 51 Steven Jackson .75 .30
❑ 52 Cadillac Williams .60 .25
❑ 53 Clinton Portis .60 .25
❑ 54 Michael Turner .60 .25
❑ 55 Anquan Boldin .60 .25
❑ 56 Larry Fitzgerald .60 .25
❑ 57 Derrick Mason .50 .20
❑ 58 Lee Evans .60 .25
❑ 59 Steve Smith .60 .25
❑ 60 Muhsin Muhammad .60 .25
❑ 61 Chad Johnson .60 .25
❑ 62 T.J. Houshmandzadeh .60 .25
❑ 63 Braylon Edwards .60 .25
❑ 64 Terrell Owens .75 .30
❑ 65 Terry Glenn .60 .25
❑ 66 Javon Walker .60 .25
❑ 67 Mike Furrey .60 .25
❑ 68 Roy Williams WR .60 .25
❑ 69 Donald Driver .60 .25
❑ 70 Greg Jennings .60 .25
❑ 71 Andre Johnson .60 .25
❑ 72 Reggie Wayne .60 .25
❑ 73 Marvin Harrison .75 .30
❑ 74 Matt Jones .60 .25
❑ 75 Chris Chambers .60 .25
❑ 76 Troy Williamson .50 .20
❑ 77 Devery Henderson .50 .20
❑ 78 Joe Horn .60 .25
❑ 79 Marques Colston .75 .30
❑ 80 Plaxico Burress .60 .25
❑ 81 Amani Toomer .60 .25
❑ 82 Jerricho Cotchery .50 .20
❑ 83 Laveranues Coles .60 .25
❑ 84 Randy Moss .75 .30
❑ 85 Donte Stallworth .60 .25
❑ 86 Reggie Brown .60 .25
❑ 87 Hines Ward .75 .30
❑ 88 Santonio Holmes .60 .25
❑ 89 Keenan McCardell .50 .20
❑ 90 Eric Parker .50 .20
❑ 91 Arnaz Battle .50 .20
❑ 92 Antonio Bryant .60 .25
❑ 93 Deion Branch .60 .25
❑ 94 Darrell Jackson .60 .25
❑ 95 Kevin Curtis .50 .20
❑ 96 Torry Holt .60 .25
❑ 97 Isaac Bruce .60 .25
❑ 98 Antwaan Randle El .50 .20
❑ 99 Santana Moss .60 .25
❑ 100 Alge Crumpler .60 .25
❑ 101 Kellen Winslow .60 .25
❑ 102 Tony Gonzalez .60 .25
❑ 103 Jeremy Shockey .60 .25
❑ 104 Antonio Gates .60 .25
❑ 105 Vernon Davis .60 .25
❑ 106 Tarvaris Jackson .75 .30
❑ 107 Travis Henry .60 .25
❑ 108 Drew Bennett .50 .20
❑ 109 Todd Heap .50 .20
❑ 110 Byron Leftwich .60 .25
❑ 111 JaMarcus Russell RC 4.00 1.50
❑ 112 Brady Quinn RC 5.00 2.00
❑ 113 Drew Stanton RC 2.00 .75
❑ 114 Troy Smith RC 2.00 .75
❑ 115 Kevin Kolb RC 2.50 1.00
❑ 116 Trent Edwards RC 3.00 1.25
❑ 117 John Beck RC 3.00 1.25
❑ 118 Jordan Palmer RC 1.50 .60
❑ 119 Chris Leak RC 1.25 .50
❑ 120 Isaiah Stanback RC 1.50 .60
❑ 121 Tyler Palko RC 1.50 .60
❑ 122 Jared Zabransky RC 1.50 .60

❏ 123 Jeff Rowe RC	1.25	.50
❏ 124 Zac Taylor RC	1.50	.60
❏ 125 Lester Ricard RC	1.25	.50
❏ 126 Adrian Peterson RC	15.00	6.00
❏ 127 Marshawn Lynch RC	3.00	1.25
❏ 128 Brandon Jackson RC	2.00	.75
❏ 129 Michael Bush RC	2.00	.75
❏ 130 Kenny Irons RC	1.50	.60
❏ 131 Antonio Pittman RC	1.25	.50
❏ 132 Tony Hunt RC	1.50	.60
❏ 133 Darius Walker RC	1.50	.60
❏ 134 Dwayne Wright RC	1.25	.50
❏ 135 Lorenzo Booker RC	1.50	.60
❏ 136 Kenneth Darby RC	1.50	.60
❏ 137 Chris Henry RB RC	1.50	.60
❏ 138 Selvin Young RC	2.00	.75
❏ 139 Brian Leonard RC	2.00	.75
❏ 140 Ahmad Bradshaw RC	2.00	.75
❏ 141 Gary Russell RC	1.50	.60
❏ 142 Kolby Smith RC	2.00	.75
❏ 143 Thomas Clayton RC	1.25	.50
❏ 144 Garrett Wolfe RC	2.00	.75
❏ 145 Calvin Johnson RC	5.00	2.00
❏ 146 Ted Ginn Jr. RC	2.50	1.00
❏ 147 Dwayne Jarrett RC	2.00	.75
❏ 148 Dwayne Bowe RC	3.00	1.25
❏ 149 Sidney Rice RC	2.50	1.00
❏ 150 Robert Meachem RC	1.50	.60
❏ 151 Anthony Gonzalez RC	2.50	1.00
❏ 152 Craig Buster Davis RC	1.50	.60
❏ 153 Aundrae Allison RC	1.25	.50
❏ 154 Chansi Stuckey RC	1.25	.50
❏ 155 David Clowney RC	1.50	.60
❏ 156 Steve Smith USC RC	2.00	.75
❏ 157 Courtney Taylor RC	1.25	.50
❏ 158 Paul Williams RC	1.25	.50
❏ 159 Johnnie Lee Higgins RC	1.25	.50
❏ 160 Rhema McKnight RC	1.25	.50
❏ 161 Jason Hill RC	1.50	.60
❏ 162 Dallas Baker RC	1.25	.50
❏ 163 Greg Olsen RC	2.00	.75
❏ 164 Yamon Figurs RC	1.50	.60
❏ 165 Scott Chandler RC	1.25	.50
❏ 166 Matt Spaeth RC	1.50	.60
❏ 167 Ben Patrick RC	1.25	.50
❏ 168 Clark Harris RC	1.50	.60
❏ 169 Martrez Milner RC	1.25	.50
❏ 170 Joe Newton RC	1.25	.50
❏ 171 Alan Branch RC	1.25	.50
❏ 172 Amobi Okoye RC	1.50	.60
❏ 173 DeMarcus Tank Tyler RC	1.25	.50
❏ 174 Justin Harrell RC	1.50	.60
❏ 175 Brandon Mebane RC	1.25	.50
❏ 176 Gaines Adams RC	1.50	.60
❏ 177 Jamaal Anderson RC	1.25	.50
❏ 178 Adam Carriker RC	1.25	.50
❏ 179 Jarvis Moss RC	1.50	.60
❏ 180 Charles Johnson RC	1.00	.40
❏ 181 Anthony Spencer RC	1.50	.60
❏ 182 Quentin Moses RC	1.25	.50
❏ 183 LaMarr Woodley RC	1.50	.60
❏ 184 Victor Abiamiri RC	1.50	.60
❏ 185 Ray McDonald RC	1.25	.50
❏ 186 Tim Crowder RC	1.50	.60
❏ 187 Patrick Willis RC	3.00	1.25
❏ 188 Brandon Siler RC	1.25	.50
❏ 189 David Harris RC	1.25	.50
❏ 190 Buster Davis RC	1.25	.50
❏ 191 Lawrence Timmons RC	1.50	.60
❏ 192 Paul Posluszny RC	2.00	.75
❏ 193 Jon Beason RC	1.50	.60
❏ 194 Rufus Alexander RC	1.50	.60
❏ 195 Earl Everett RC	1.25	.50
❏ 196 Stewart Bradley RC	1.50	.60
❏ 197 Prescott Burgess RC	1.25	.50
❏ 198 Leon Hall RC	1.25	.50
❏ 199 Darrelle Revis RC	1.50	.60
❏ 200 Aaron Ross RC	1.50	.60
❏ 201 Daymeion Hughes RC	1.25	.50
❏ 202 Marcus McCauley RC	1.25	.50
❏ 203 Chris Houston RC	1.25	.50
❏ 204 Tanard Jackson RC	1.00	.40
❏ 205 Jonathan Wade RC	1.25	.50
❏ 206 Josh Wilson RC	1.25	.50
❏ 207 Eric Wright RC	1.50	.60
❏ 208 A.J. Davis RC	1.00	.40
❏ 209 David Irons RC	1.00	.40
❏ 210 LaRon Landry RC	2.00	.75
❏ 211 Reggie Nelson RC	1.25	.50
❏ 212 Michael Griffin RC	1.50	.60
❏ 213 Brandon Meriweather RC	1.50	.60
❏ 214 Eric Weddle RC	1.25	.50
❏ 215 Aaron Rouse RC	1.50	.60
❏ 216 Josh Gattis RC	1.00	.40
❏ 217 Joe Thomas RC	1.50	.60
❏ 218 Levi Brown RC	1.50	.60
❏ 219 Tony Ugoh RC	1.25	.50
❏ 220 Ryan Kalil RC	1.25	.50
❏ 221 Joe Staley RC	1.25	.50
❏ 222 Steve Breaston RC	1.25	.50
❏ 223 Jacoby Jones RC	1.50	.60
❏ 224 Ryne Robinson RC	1.25	.50
❏ 225 Chris Davis RC	1.25	.50
❏ 226 Le'Ron McClain RC	1.25	.50
❏ 227 Joel Filani RC	1.25	.50
❏ 228 Gerald Alexander RC	1.00	.40
❏ 229 Justise Hairston RC	1.25	.50
❏ 230 Nate Ilaoa RC	1.50	.60
❏ 231 Brett Ratliff RC	1.25	.50
❏ 232 Kyle Steffes RC	1.00	.40
❏ 233 Jesse Pellot-Rosa RC	1.00	.40
❏ 234 Roy Hall RC	1.50	.60
❏ 235 Brannon Condren RC	1.00	.40
❏ 236 Clint Session RC	1.25	.50
❏ 237 Dan Bazuin RC	1.25	.50
❏ 238 Michael Okwo RC	1.25	.50
❏ 239 Kevin Payne RC	1.00	.40
❏ 240 Legedu Naanee RC	1.25	.50
❏ 241 Jarrett Hicks RC	1.25	.50
❏ 242 Sonny Shackelford RC	1.25	.50
❏ 243 Arron Sears RC	1.25	.50
❏ 244 Justin Durant RC	1.25	.50
❏ 245 Ikaika Alma-Francis RC	1.50	.60
❏ 246 Sabby Piscitelli RC	1.50	.60
❏ 247 Quincy Black RC	1.25	.50
❏ 248 Jay Alford RC	2.50	1.00
❏ 249 Anthony Waters RC	1.25	.50
❏ 250 Laurent Robinson RC	1.25	.50
❏ 251 Brian Robison RC	1.50	.60
❏ 252 Jay Moore RC	1.25	.50
❏ 253 Stephen Nicholas RC	1.25	.50
❏ 254 John Bowie RC	1.00	.40
❏ 255 Brian Smith RC	1.00	.40
❏ 256 Marvin White RC	1.00	.40
❏ 257 Fred Bennett RC	1.00	.40
❏ 258 Kevin Boss RC	6.00	2.50
❏ 259 Dante Rosario RC	1.25	.50
❏ 260 Brent Celek RC	1.25	.50
❏ 261 Orenthal O'Neal RC	1.00	.40
❏ 262 Reagan Mauia RC	1.00	.40
❏ 263 Deon Anderson RC	1.25	.50
❏ 264 Tyler Ecker RC	1.25	.50
❏ 265 Michael Allan RC	1.00	.40
❏ 266 Jordan Kent RC	1.25	.50
❏ 267 John Broussard RC	1.25	.50
❏ 268 Chandler Williams RC	1.25	.50
❏ 269 Jason Snelling RC	1.25	.50
❏ 270 Derek Stanley RC	1.25	.50
❏ 271 Zach Miller RC	1.50	.60
❏ 272 Ramzee Robinson RC	1.00	.40
❏ 273 Michael Johnson RC	1.25	.50
❏ 274 Syndric Steptoe RC	1.25	.50
❏ 275 Tarell Brown RC	1.00	.40

1998 Bowman Chrome

❏ COMPLETE SET (220)	100.00	50.00
❏ 1 Peyton Manning RC	40.00	20.00
❏ 2 Keith Brooking RC	4.00	1.50
❏ 3 Duane Starks RC	2.00	.75
❏ 4 Takeo Spikes RC	4.00	1.50
❏ 5 Andre Wadsworth RC	3.00	1.25
❏ 6 Greg Ellis RC	2.00	.75
❏ 7 Brian Griese RC	8.00	3.00
❏ 8 Germane Crowell RC	3.00	1.25
❏ 9 Jerome Pathon RC	4.00	1.50
❏ 10 Ryan Leaf RC	4.00	1.50
❏ 11 Fred Taylor RC	6.00	2.50
❏ 12 Robert Edwards RC	3.00	1.25
❏ 13 Grant Wistrom RC	3.00	1.25
❏ 14 Robert Holcombe RC	3.00	1.25
❏ 15 Tim Dwight RC	4.00	1.50
❏ 16 Jacquez Green RC	3.00	1.25
❏ 17 Marcus Nash RC	2.00	.75
❏ 18 Jason Peter RC	2.00	.75
❏ 19 Anthony Simmons RC	3.00	1.25
❏ 20 Curtis Enis RC	2.00	.75
❏ 21 John Avery RC	3.00	1.25
❏ 22 Pat Johnson RC	3.00	1.25
❏ 23 Joe Jurevicius RC	4.00	1.50
❏ 24 Brian Simmons RC	3.00	1.25
❏ 25 Kevin Dyson RC	4.00	1.50
❏ 26 Skip Hicks RC	3.00	1.25
❏ 27 Hines Ward RC	15.00	7.50
❏ 28 Tavian Banks RC	3.00	1.25
❏ 29 Ahman Green RC	20.00	10.00
❏ 30 Tony Simmons RC	3.00	1.25
❏ 31 Charles Johnson	.50	.20
❏ 32 Freddie Jones	.50	.20
❏ 33 Joey Galloway	.75	.30
❏ 34 Tony Banks	.75	.30
❏ 35 Jake Plummer	1.25	.50
❏ 36 Reidel Anthony	.75	.30
❏ 37 Steve McNair	1.25	.50
❏ 38 Michael Westbrook	.75	.30
❏ 39 Chris Sanders	.50	.20
❏ 40 Isaac Bruce	.50	.20
❏ 41 Charlie Garner	.75	.30
❏ 42 Wayne Chrebet	1.25	.50
❏ 43 Michael Strahan	.75	.30
❏ 44 Brad Johnson	1.25	.50
❏ 45 Mike Alstott	.50	.20
❏ 46 Tony Gonzalez	1.25	.50
❏ 47 Johnnie Morton	.75	.30
❏ 48 Darnay Scott	.75	.30
❏ 49 Rae Carruth	.50	.20
❏ 50 Terrell Davis	1.25	.50
❏ 51 Jermaine Lewis	.75	.30
❏ 52 Frank Sanders	.75	.30
❏ 53 Byron Hanspard	.50	.20
❏ 54 Gus Frerotte	.50	.20
❏ 55 Terry Glenn	1.25	.50
❏ 56 J.J. Stokes	.75	.30
❏ 57 Will Blackwell	.50	.20
❏ 58 Keyshawn Johnson	1.25	.50
❏ 59 Tiki Barber	1.25	.50
❏ 60 Dorsey Levens	1.25	.50
❏ 61 Zach Thomas	1.25	.50
❏ 62 Corey Dillon	1.25	.50
❏ 63 Antowain Smith	1.25	.50
❏ 64 Michael Sinclair	.50	.20
❏ 65 Rod Smith	.75	.30
❏ 66 Trent Dilfer	1.25	.50
❏ 67 Warren Sapp	.75	.30
❏ 68 Charles Way	.50	.20
❏ 69 Tamarick Vanover	.50	.20
❏ 70 Drew Bledsoe	2.00	.75
❏ 71 John Mobley	.50	.20
❏ 72 Kerry Collins	.75	.30
❏ 73 Peter Boulware	.50	.20
❏ 74 Simeon Rice	.75	.30
❏ 75 Eddie George	1.25	.50
❏ 76 Fred Lane	.50	.20
❏ 77 Jamal Anderson	1.25	.50
❏ 78 Antonio Freeman	1.25	.50
❏ 79 Jason Sehorn	.75	.30
❏ 80 Curtis Martin	1.25	.50
❏ 81 Bobby Hoying	.75	.30
❏ 82 Garrison Hearst	1.25	.50
❏ 83 Glenn Foley	.75	.30
❏ 84 Danny Kanell	.75	.30
❏ 85 Kordell Stewart	1.25	.50
❏ 86 O.J. McDuffie	.75	.30
❏ 87 Marvin Harrison	1.25	.50
❏ 88 Bobby Engram	.75	.30
❏ 89 Chris Slade	.50	.20
❏ 90 Warrick Dunn	1.25	.50
❏ 91 Ricky Watters	.75	.30
❏ 92 Rickey Dudley	.50	.20
❏ 93 Terrell Owens	1.25	.50
❏ 94 Karim Abdul-Jabbar	1.25	.50

❑ 95 Napoleon Kaufman 1.25 .50
❑ 96 Darrell Green .75 .30
❑ 97 Levon Kirkland .50 .20
❑ 98 Jeff George .75 .30
❑ 99 Andre Hastings .50 .20
❑ 100 John Elway 5.00 2.00
❑ 101 John Randle .75 .30
❑ 102 Andre Rison .75 .30
❑ 103 Keenan McCardell .75 .30
❑ 104 Marshall Faulk 1.50 .60
❑ 105 Emmitt Smith 4.00 1.50
❑ 106 Robert Brooks .75 .30
❑ 107 Scott Mitchell .75 .30
❑ 108 Shannon Sharpe .75 .30
❑ 109 Deion Sanders 1.25 .50
❑ 110 Jerry Rice 2.50 1.00
❑ 111 Erik Kramer .50 .20
❑ 112 Michael Jackson .50 .20
❑ 113 Aeneas Williams .50 .20
❑ 114 Terry Allen 1.25 .50
❑ 115 Steve Young 1.50 .60
❑ 116 Warren Moon 1.25 .50
❑ 117 Junior Seau 1.25 .50
❑ 118 Jerome Bettis 1.25 .50
❑ 119 Irving Fryar .75 .30
❑ 120 Barry Sanders 4.00 1.50
❑ 121 Tim Brown .50 .20
❑ 122 Chad Brown .50 .20
❑ 123 Ben Coates .75 .30
❑ 124 Robert Smith 1.25 .50
❑ 125 Brett Favre 5.00 2.00
❑ 126 Derrick Thomas 1.25 .50
❑ 127 Reggie White 1.25 .50
❑ 128 Troy Aikman 2.50 1.00
❑ 129 Jeff Blake .75 .30
❑ 130 Mark Brunell 1.25 .50
❑ 131 Curtis Conway .75 .30
❑ 132 Wesley Walls .75 .30
❑ 133 Thurman Thomas 1.25 .50
❑ 134 Chris Chandler .75 .30
❑ 135 Dan Marino 5.00 2.00
❑ 136 Larry Centers .50 .20
❑ 137 Shawn Jefferson .50 .20
❑ 138 Andre Reed .75 .30
❑ 139 Jake Reed .75 .30
❑ 140 Cris Carter 1.25 .50
❑ 141 Elvis Grbac .75 .30
❑ 142 Mark Chmura .75 .30
❑ 143 Michael Irvin 1.25 .50
❑ 144 Carl Pickens .75 .30
❑ 145 Herman Moore .75 .30
❑ 146 Marvin Jones .50 .20
❑ 147 Terance Mathis .75 .30
❑ 148 Rob Moore .75 .30
❑ 149 Bruce Smith .75 .30
❑ 150 Rob Johnson CL .50 .20
❑ 151 Leslie Shepherd .50 .20
❑ 152 Chris Spielman .50 .20
❑ 153 Tony McGee .50 .20
❑ 154 Kevin Smith .50 .20
❑ 155 Bill Romanowski .50 .20
❑ 156 Stephen Boyd .50 .20
❑ 157 James Stewart .75 .30
❑ 158 Jason Taylor .75 .30
❑ 159 Troy Drayton .50 .20
❑ 160 Mark Fields .50 .20
❑ 161 Jessie Armstead .50 .20
❑ 162 James Jett .75 .30
❑ 163 Bobby Taylor .50 .20
❑ 164 Kimble Anders .75 .30
❑ 165 Jimmy Smith .75 .30
❑ 166 Quentin Coryatt .50 .20
❑ 167 Bryant Westbrook .50 .20
❑ 168 Neil Smith .75 .30
❑ 169 Darren Woodson .50 .20
❑ 170 Ray Buchanan .50 .20
❑ 171 Earl Holmes .50 .20
❑ 172 Ray Lewis 1.25 .50
❑ 173 Steve Broussard .50 .20
❑ 174 Derrick Brooks 1.25 .50
❑ 175 Ken Harvey .50 .20
❑ 176 Darryll Lewis .50 .20
❑ 177 Derrick Rodgers .50 .20
❑ 178 James McKnight 1.25 .50
❑ 179 Cris Dishman .50 .20
❑ 180 Hardy Nickerson .50 .20
❑ 181 Charles Woodson RC 5.00 2.00
❑ 182 Randy Moss RC 30.00 15.00
❑ 183 Stephen Alexander RC 3.00 1.25
❑ 184 Samari Rolle RC 2.00 .75
❑ 185 Jamie Duncan RC 2.00 .75
❑ 186 Lance Schulters RC 2.00 .75
❑ 187 Tony Parrish RC 4.00 1.50
❑ 188 Corey Chavous RC 4.00 1.50
❑ 189 Jammi German RC 2.00 .75
❑ 190 Sam Cowart RC 3.00 1.25
❑ 191 Donald Hayes RC 3.00 1.25
❑ 192 R.W. McQuarters RC 3.00 1.25
❑ 193 Az-Zahir Hakim RC 4.00 1.50
❑ 194 Chris Fuamatu-Ma'afala RC 3.00 1.25
❑ 195 Allen Rossum RC 2.00 .75
❑ 196 Jon Ritchie RC 3.00 1.25
❑ 197 Blake Spence RC 2.00 .75
❑ 198 Brian Alford RC 2.00 .75
❑ 199 Fred Weary RC 2.00 .75
❑ 200 Rod Rutledge RC 2.00 .75
❑ 201 Michael Myers RC 2.00 .75
❑ 202 Rashaan Shehee RC 3.00 1.25
❑ 203 Donovin Darius RC 3.00 1.25
❑ 204 E.G. Green RC 3.00 1.25
❑ 205 Vonnie Holliday RC 3.00 1.25
❑ 206 Charlie Batch RC 4.00 1.50
❑ 207 Michael Pittman RC 4.00 1.50
❑ 208 Artrell Hawkins RC 2.00 .75
❑ 209 Jonathan Quinn RC 4.00 1.50
❑ 210 Kailee Wong RC 2.00 .75
❑ 211 Deshea Townsend RC 2.00 .75
❑ 212 Patrick Surtain RC 4.00 1.50
❑ 213 Brian Kelly RC 3.00 1.25
❑ 214 Tebucky Jones RC 2.00 .75
❑ 215 Pete Gonzalez RC 2.00 .75
❑ 216 Shaun Williams RC 3.00 1.25
❑ 217 Scott Frost RC 2.00 .75
❑ 218 Leonard Little RC 4.00 1.50
❑ 219 Alonzo Mayes RC 2.00 .75
❑ 220 Cordell Taylor RC 2.00 .75

1999 Bowman Chrome

❑ COMPLETE SET (220) 80.00 40.00
❑ 1 Dan Marino 4.00 1.50
❑ 2 Michael Westbrook .75 .30
❑ 3 Yancey Thigpen .50 .20
❑ 4 Tony Martin .75 .30
❑ 5 Michael Strahan .75 .30
❑ 6 Dedric Ward .50 .20
❑ 7 Joey Galloway .75 .30
❑ 8 Bobby Engram .75 .30
❑ 9 Frank Sanders .75 .30
❑ 10 Jake Plummer .75 .30
❑ 11 Eddie Kennison .75 .30
❑ 12 Curtis Martin 1.25 .50
❑ 13 Chris Spielman .50 .20
❑ 14 Trent Dilfer .75 .30
❑ 15 Tim Biakabutuka .75 .30
❑ 16 Elvis Grbac .75 .30
❑ 17 Charlie Batch 1.25 .50
❑ 18 Takeo Spikes .50 .20
❑ 19 Tony Banks .75 .30
❑ 20 Doug Flutie 1.25 .50
❑ 21 Ty Law .75 .30
❑ 22 Isaac Bruce 1.25 .50
❑ 23 James Jett .75 .30
❑ 24 Kent Graham .50 .20
❑ 25 Derrick Mayes .50 .20
❑ 26 Amani Toomer .50 .20
❑ 27 Ray Lewis 1.25 .50
❑ 28 Shawn Springs .50 .20
❑ 29 Warren Sapp .50 .20
❑ 30 Jamal Anderson 1.25 .50
❑ 31 Byron Bam Morris .50 .20
❑ 32 Johnnie Morton .50 .20
❑ 33 Terance Mathis .50 .20
❑ 34 Terrell Davis 1.25 .50
❑ 35 John Randle .75 .30
❑ 36 Vinny Testaverde .50 .20
❑ 37 Junior Seau 1.25 .50
❑ 38 Reidel Anthony .75 .30
❑ 39 Brad Johnson .50 .20
❑ 40 Emmitt Smith 2.50 1.00
❑ 41 Mo Lewis .50 .20
❑ 42 Terry Glenn 1.25 .50
❑ 43 Dorsey Levens 1.25 .50
❑ 44 Thurman Thomas .75 .30
❑ 45 Rob Moore .75 .30
❑ 46 Corey Dillon 1.25 .50
❑ 47 Jessie Armstead .50 .20
❑ 48 Marshall Faulk 1.50 .60
❑ 49 Charles Woodson .50 .20
❑ 50 John Elway 4.00 1.50
❑ 51 Kevin Dyson .75 .30
❑ 52 Tony Simmons .50 .20
❑ 53 Keenan McCardell .75 .30
❑ 54 O.J. Santiago .50 .20
❑ 55 Jermaine Lewis .75 .30
❑ 56 Herman Moore .75 .30
❑ 57 Gary Brown .50 .20
❑ 58 Jim Harbaugh .75 .30
❑ 59 Mike Alstott 1.25 .50
❑ 60 Brett Favre 4.00 1.50
❑ 61 Tim Brown 1.25 .50
❑ 62 Steve McNair .50 .20
❑ 63 Ben Coates .75 .30
❑ 64 Jerome Pathon .50 .20
❑ 65 Ray Buchanan .50 .20
❑ 66 Troy Aikman 2.50 1.00
❑ 67 Andre Reed .75 .30
❑ 68 Bubby Brister .50 .20
❑ 69 Karim Abdul-Jabbar .75 .30
❑ 70 Peyton Manning 4.00 1.50
❑ 71 Charles Johnson .50 .20
❑ 72 Natrone Means .75 .30
❑ 73 Michael Sinclair .50 .20
❑ 74 Skip Hicks .50 .20
❑ 75 Derrick Alexander .50 .20
❑ 76 Wayne Chrebet .75 .30
❑ 77 Rod Smith .75 .30
❑ 78 Carl Pickens .75 .30
❑ 79 Adrian Murrell .75 .30
❑ 80 Fred Taylor 1.25 .50
❑ 81 Eric Moulds 1.25 .50
❑ 82 Lawrence Phillips .75 .30
❑ 83 Marvin Harrison 1.25 .50
❑ 84 Cris Carter 1.25 .50
❑ 85 Ike Hilliard .50 .20
❑ 86 Hines Ward 1.25 .50
❑ 87 Terrell Owens 1.25 .50
❑ 88 Ricky Proehl .50 .20
❑ 89 Bert Emanuel .75 .30
❑ 90 Randy Moss 3.00 1.25
❑ 91 Aaron Glenn .50 .20
❑ 92 Robert Smith 1.25 .50
❑ 93 Andre Hastings .50 .20
❑ 94 Jake Reed .75 .30
❑ 95 Curtis Enis .50 .20
❑ 96 Andre Wadsworth .50 .20
❑ 97 Ed McCaffrey .75 .30
❑ 98 Zach Thomas 1.25 .50
❑ 99 Kerry Collins .75 .30
❑ 100 Drew Bledsoe 1.50 .60
❑ 101 Germane Crowell .50 .20
❑ 102 Bryan Still .50 .20
❑ 103 Chad Brown .50 .20
❑ 104 Jacquez Green .50 .20
❑ 105 Garrison Hearst .75 .30
❑ 106 Napoleon Kaufman 1.25 .50
❑ 107 Ricky Watters .75 .30
❑ 108 O.J. McDuffie .75 .30
❑ 109 Keyshawn Johnson 1.25 .50
❑ 110 Jerome Bettis 1.25 .50
❑ 111 Duce Staley 1.25 .50
❑ 112 Curtis Conway .75 .30
❑ 113 Chris Chandler .75 .30
❑ 114 Marcus Nash .50 .20
❑ 115 Stephen Alexander .50 .20
❑ 116 Darnay Scott .75 .30
❑ 117 Bruce Smith .75 .30
❑ 118 Priest Holmes 2.00 .75
❑ 119 Mark Brunell 1.25 .50
❑ 120 Jerry Rice 2.50 1.00
❑ 121 Randall Cunningham 1.25 .50

❑ 122 Scott Mitchell .50 .20
❑ 123 Antonio Freeman 1.25 .50
❑ 124 Kordell Stewart .75 .30
❑ 125 Jon Kitna 1.25 .50
❑ 126 Ahman Green 1.25 .50
❑ 127 Warrick Dunn 1.25 .50
❑ 128 Robert Brooks .75 .30
❑ 129 Derrick Thomas 1.25 .50
❑ 130 Steve Young 1.50 .60
❑ 131 Peter Boulware .50 .20
❑ 132 Michael Irvin .75 .30
❑ 133 Shannon Sharpe .75 .30
❑ 134 Jimmy Smith .75 .30
❑ 135 John Avery .50 .20
❑ 136 Fred Lane .50 .20
❑ 137 Trent Green 1.25 .50
❑ 138 Andre Rison .75 .30
❑ 139 Antowain Smith 1.25 .50
❑ 140 Eddie George 1.25 .50
❑ 141 Jeff Blake .75 .30
❑ 142 Rocket Ismail .75 .30
❑ 143 Rickey Dudley .50 .20
❑ 144 Courtney Hawkins .50 .20
❑ 145 Mikhael Ricks .50 .20
❑ 146 J.J. Stokes .75 .30
❑ 147 Levon Kirkland .50 .20
❑ 148 Deion Sanders 1.25 .50
❑ 149 Barry Sanders 4.00 1.50
❑ 150 Tiki Barber 1.25 .50
❑ 151 David Boston RC 2.00 .75
❑ 152 Chris McAlister RC 1.25 .50
❑ 153 Peerless Price RC 2.00 .75
❑ 154 D'Wayne Bates RC 1.25 .50
❑ 155 Cade McNown RC 1.25 .50
❑ 156 Akili Smith RC 1.25 .50
❑ 157 Kevin Johnson RC 2.00 .75
❑ 158 Tim Couch RC 2.00 .75
❑ 159 Sedrick Irvin RC 1.00 .40
❑ 160 Chris Claiborne RC 1.00 .40
❑ 161 Edgerrin James RC 10.00 4.00
❑ 162 Mike Cloud RC 1.25 .50
❑ 163 Cecil Collins RC 1.00 .40
❑ 164 James Johnson RC 1.25 .50
❑ 165 Rob Konrad RC 2.00 .75
❑ 166 Daunte Culpepper RC 10.00 4.00
❑ 167 Kevin Faulk RC 2.00 .75
❑ 168 Donovan McNabb RC 12.00 5.00
❑ 169 Troy Edwards RC 1.25 .50
❑ 170 Amos Zereoue RC 2.00 .75
❑ 171 Karsten Bailey RC 1.25 .50
❑ 172 Brock Huard RC 2.00 .75
❑ 173 Joe Germaine RC 1.25 .50
❑ 174 Torry Holt RC 6.00 2.50
❑ 175 Shaun King RC 1.25 .50
❑ 176 Jevon Kearse RC 4.00 1.50
❑ 177 Champ Bailey RC 3.00 1.25
❑ 178 Ebenezer Ekuban RC 1.25 .50
❑ 179 Andy Katzenmoyer RC 1.25 .50
❑ 180 Antoine Winfield RC 1.25 .50
❑ 181 Jermaine Fazande RC 1.25 .50
❑ 182 Ricky Williams RC 5.00 2.00
❑ 183 Joel Makovicka RC 2.00 .75
❑ 184 Reginald Kelly RC 1.25 .50
❑ 185 Brandon Stokley RC 2.50 1.00
❑ 186 L.C. Stevens RC 1.00 .40
❑ 187 Marty Booker RC 2.00 .75
❑ 188 Jerry Azumah RC 1.25 .50
❑ 189 Ted White RC 1.00 .40
❑ 190 Scott Covington RC 2.00 .75
❑ 191 Tim Alexander RC 1.00 .40
❑ 192 Darrin Chiaverini RC 1.25 .50
❑ 193 Dat Nguyen RC 2.00 .75
❑ 194 Wane McGarity RC 1.00 .40
❑ 195 Al Wilson RC 2.00 .75
❑ 196 Travis McGriff RC 1.00 .40
❑ 197 Stacey Mack RC 2.00 .75
❑ 198 Antuan Edwards RC 1.00 .40
❑ 199 Aaron Brooks RC 5.00 2.00
❑ 200 De'Mond Parker RC 1.00 .40
❑ 201 Jed Weaver RC 1.00 .40
❑ 202 Madre Hill RC 1.00 .40
❑ 203 Jim Kleinsasser RC 2.00 .75
❑ 204 Michael Bishop RC 2.00 .75
❑ 205 Michael Basnight RC 1.00 .40
❑ 206 Sean Bennett RC 1.00 .40
❑ 207 Dameane Douglas RC 1.25 .50
❑ 208 Na Brown RC 1.25 .50
❑ 209 Patrick Kerney RC 2.00 .75
❑ 210 Malcolm Johnson RC 1.00 .40
❑ 211 Dre Bly RC 2.00 .75
❑ 212 Terry Jackson RC 1.25 .50
❑ 213 Eugene Baker RC 1.00 .40
❑ 214 Autry Denson RC 1.25 .50
❑ 215 Darnell McDonald RC 1.25 .50
❑ 216 Charlie Rogers RC 1.25 .50
❑ 217 Joe Montgomery RC 1.25 .50
❑ 218 Cecil Martin RC 1.25 .50
❑ 219 Larry Parker RC 2.00 .75
❑ 220 Mike Peterson RC 1.25 .50

2000 Bowman Chrome

❑ 1 Eddie George 1.00 .40
❑ 2 Ike Hilliard .60 .25
❑ 3 Terrell Owens 1.00 .40
❑ 4 James Stewart .60 .25
❑ 5 Joey Galloway .60 .25
❑ 6 Jake Reed .40 .15
❑ 7 Derrick Alexander .60 .25
❑ 8 Jeff George .60 .25
❑ 9 Kerry Collins .60 .25
❑ 10 Tony Gonzalez .60 .25
❑ 11 Marcus Robinson 1.00 .40
❑ 12 Charles Woodson .60 .25
❑ 13 Germane Crowell .40 .15
❑ 14 Yancey Thigpen .40 .15
❑ 15 Tony Martin .40 .15
❑ 16 Frank Sanders .60 .25
❑ 17 Napoleon Kaufman .60 .25
❑ 18 Jay Fiedler 1.00 .40
❑ 19 Patrick Jeffers 1.00 .40
❑ 20 Steve McNair 1.00 .40
❑ 21 Herman Moore .60 .25
❑ 22 Tim Brown 1.00 .40
❑ 23 Olandis Gary 1.00 .40
❑ 24 Corey Dillon 1.00 .40
❑ 25 Warren Sapp .60 .25
❑ 26 Curtis Enis .40 .15
❑ 27 Vinny Testaverde .60 .25
❑ 28 Tim Biakabutuka .60 .25
❑ 29 Kevin Johnson 1.00 .40
❑ 30 Charlie Batch 1.00 .40
❑ 31 Jermaine Fazande .60 .25
❑ 32 Shaun King .40 .15
❑ 33 Errict Rhett .60 .25
❑ 34 O.J. McDuffie .60 .25
❑ 35 Bruce Smith .60 .25
❑ 36 Antonio Freeman 1.00 .40
❑ 37 Tim Couch .60 .25
❑ 38 Duce Staley 1.00 .40
❑ 39 Jeff Blake .60 .25
❑ 40 Jim Harbaugh .60 .25
❑ 41 Jeff Graham .40 .15
❑ 42 Drew Bledsoe 1.25 .50
❑ 43 Mike Alstott 1.00 .40
❑ 44 Terance Mathis .60 .25
❑ 45 Antowain Smith .60 .25
❑ 46 Johnnie Morton .60 .25
❑ 47 Chris Chandler .60 .25
❑ 48 Keith Poole .40 .15
❑ 49 Ricky Watters .60 .25
❑ 50 Darnay Scott .40 .15
❑ 51 Damon Huard .60 .25
❑ 52 Peerless Price .60 .25
❑ 53 Brian Griese 1.00 .40
❑ 54 Frank Wycheck .60 .25
❑ 55 Kevin Dyson .60 .25
❑ 56 Junior Seau 1.00 .40
❑ 57 Curtis Conway .60 .25
❑ 58 Jamal Anderson 1.00 .40
❑ 59 Jim Miller .40 .15
❑ 60 Rob Johnson .60 .25
❑ 61 Mark Brunell 1.00 .40
❑ 62 Wayne Chrebet .60 .25
❑ 63 James Johnson .40 .15
❑ 64 Sean Dawkins .40 .15
❑ 65 Stephen Davis 1.00 .40
❑ 66 Daunte Culpepper 1.25 .50
❑ 67 Doug Flutie 1.00 .40
❑ 68 Pete Mitchell .40 .15
❑ 69 Bill Schroeder .40 .15
❑ 70 Terrence Wilkins .40 .15
❑ 71 Cade McNown .40 .15
❑ 72 Muhsin Muhammad .60 .25
❑ 73 E.G. Green .40 .15
❑ 74 Edgerrin James 1.50 .60
❑ 75 Troy Edwards .40 .15
❑ 76 Terry Glenn .60 .25
❑ 77 Tony Banks .60 .25
❑ 78 Derrick Mayes .60 .25
❑ 79 Curtis Martin 1.00 .40
❑ 80 Kordell Stewart .60 .25
❑ 81 Amani Toomer .60 .25
❑ 82 Dorsey Levens .60 .25
❑ 83 Brad Johnson 1.00 .40
❑ 84 Ed McCaffrey 1.00 .40
❑ 85 Charlie Garner .60 .25
❑ 86 Brett Favre 3.00 1.25
❑ 87 J.J. Stokes .60 .25
❑ 88 Steve Young 1.25 .50
❑ 89 Jonathan Linton .40 .15
❑ 90 Isaac Bruce 1.00 .40
❑ 91 Shawn Jefferson .40 .15
❑ 92 Rod Smith .60 .25
❑ 93 Champ Bailey .60 .25
❑ 94 Ricky Williams 1.00 .40
❑ 95 Priest Holmes 1.25 .50
❑ 96 Corey Bradford .60 .25
❑ 97 Eric Moulds 1.00 .40
❑ 98 Warrick Dunn 1.00 .40
❑ 99 Jevon Kearse 1.00 .40
❑ 100 Albert Connell .40 .15
❑ 101 Az-Zahir Hakim .40 .15
❑ 102 Marvin Harrison 1.00 .40
❑ 103 Qadry Ismail .60 .25
❑ 104 Oronde Gadsden .60 .25
❑ 105 Rob Moore .60 .25
❑ 106 Marshall Faulk 1.50 .60
❑ 107 Steve Beuerlein .60 .25
❑ 108 Torry Holt 1.00 .40
❑ 109 Donovan McNabb 1.50 .60
❑ 110 Rich Gannon 1.00 .40
❑ 111 Jerome Bettis 1.00 .40
❑ 112 Peyton Manning 2.50 1.00
❑ 113 Cris Carter 1.00 .40
❑ 114 Jake Plummer .60 .25
❑ 115 Kent Graham .40 .15
❑ 116 Keenan McCardell .60 .25
❑ 117 Tim Dwight 1.00 .40
❑ 118 Fred Taylor 1.00 .40
❑ 119 Jerry Rice 2.00 .75
❑ 120 Michael Westbrook .60 .25
❑ 121 Kurt Warner 2.00 .75
❑ 122 Jimmy Smith .60 .25
❑ 123 Emmitt Smith 2.00 .75
❑ 124 Terrell Davis 1.00 .40
❑ 125 Randy Moss 2.00 .75
❑ 126 Akili Smith .40 .15
❑ 127 Rocket Ismail .60 .25
❑ 128 Jon Kitna 1.00 .40
❑ 129 Elvis Grbac .60 .25
❑ 130 Wesley Walls .40 .15
❑ 131 Torrance Small .40 .15
❑ 132 Tyrone Wheatley .60 .25
❑ 133 Carl Pickens .40 .15
❑ 134 Zach Thomas 1.00 .40
❑ 135 Jacquez Green .40 .15
❑ 136 Robert Smith 1.00 .40
❑ 137 Keyshawn Johnson 1.00 .40
❑ 138 Matthew Hatchette .40 .15
❑ 139 Troy Aikman 2.00 .75
❑ 140 Charles Johnson .60 .25
❑ 141 Terry Battle EP 1.00 .40
❑ 142 Pepe Pearson EP RC 2.00 .75
❑ 143 Cory Sauter EP 1.00 .40
❑ 144 Brian Shay EP 1.00 .40
❑ 145 Marcus Crandell EP RC 1.50 .60
❑ 146 Danny Wuerffel EP 1.50 .60
❑ 147 L.C. Stevens EP 1.00 .40
❑ 148 Ted White EP 1.00 .40
❑ 149 Matt Lytle EP RC 1.50 .60

❑ 150 Vershan Jackson EP RC 1.00 .40
❑ 151 Mario Bailey EP 1.00 .40
❑ 152 Darryl Daniel EP RC 1.50 .60
❑ 153 Sean Morey EP RC 1.50 .60
❑ 154 Jim Kubiak EP RC 1.50 .60
❑ 155 Aaron Stecker EP RC 2.00 .75
❑ 156 Damon Dunn EP RC 1.50 .60
❑ 157 Kevin Daft EP 1.00 .40
❑ 158 Corey Thomas EP 1.00 .40
❑ 159 Deon Mitchell EP RC 1.50 .60
❑ 160 Todd Floyd EP RC 1.00 .40
❑ 161 Norman Miller EP RC 1.00 .40
❑ 162 Jeremaine Copeland EP 1.00 .40
❑ 163 Michael Blair EP 1.00 .40
❑ 164 Ron Powlus EP RC 2.00 .75
❑ 165 Pat Barnes EP 1.50 .60
❑ 166 Dez White RC 4.00 1.50
❑ 167 Trung Canidate SP RC 25.00 10.00
❑ 168 Thomas Jones SP RC 40.00 20.00
❑ 169 Courtney Brown SP RC 30.00 12.50
❑ 170 Jamal Lewis SP RC 50.00 20.00
❑ 171 Chris Redman SP RC 25.00 10.00
❑ 172 Ron Dayne SP RC 30.00 12.50
❑ 173 Chad Pennington SP RC 50.00 25.00
❑ 174 Plaxico Burress SP RC 50.00 20.00
❑ 175 R.Jay Soward SP RC 25.00 10.00
❑ 176 Travis Taylor SP RC 30.00 12.50
❑ 177 Shaun Alexander SP RC 60.00 30.00
❑ 178 Brian Urlacher RC 20.00 10.00
❑ 179 Danny Farmer RC 3.00 1.25
❑ 180 Tee Martin SP RC 30.00 12.50
❑ 181 Sylvester Morris SP RC 25.00 10.00
❑ 182 Curtis Keaton RC 3.00 1.25
❑ 183 Peter Warrick SP RC 30.00 12.50
❑ 184 Anthony Becht RC 4.00 1.50
❑ 185 Travis Prentice SP RC 30.00 12.50
❑ 186 J.R. Redmond SP RC 25.00 10.00
❑ 187 Bubba Franks SP RC 30.00 12.50
❑ 188 Ron Dugans SP RC 20.00 7.50
❑ 189 Reuben Droughns RC 5.00 2.00
❑ 190 Corey Simon RC 2.00 .75
❑ 191 Joe Hamilton RC 3.00 1.25
❑ 192 Laveranues Coles RC 5.00 2.00
❑ 193 Todd Pinkston SP RC 30.00 12.50
❑ 194 Jerry Porter SP RC 50.00 20.00
❑ 195 Dennis Northcutt RC 4.00 1.50
❑ 196 Tim Rattay RC 4.00 1.50
❑ 197 Giovanni Carmazzi RC 2.00 .75
❑ 198 Mareno Philyaw RC 2.00 .75
❑ 199 Avion Black RC 3.00 1.25
❑ 200 Chafie Fields RC 2.00 .75
❑ 201 Rondell Mealey RC 2.00 .75
❑ 202 Troy Walters RC 4.00 1.50
❑ 203 Frank Moreau RC 3.00 1.25
❑ 204 Vaughn Sanders RC 2.00 .75
❑ 205 Sherrod Gideon RC 2.00 .75
❑ 206 Doug Chapman RC 3.00 1.25
❑ 207 Marcus Knight RC 3.00 1.25
❑ 208 Jamel White RC 3.00 1.25
❑ 209 Windrell Hayes RC 3.00 1.25
❑ 210 Reggie Jones RC 2.00 .75
❑ 211 Jarious Jackson RC 3.00 1.25
❑ 212 Ronney Jenkins RC 3.00 1.25
❑ 213 Quinton Spotwood RC 2.00 .75
❑ 214 Rob Morris RC 3.00 1.25
❑ 215 Gari Scott RC 2.00 .75
❑ 216 Kevin Thompson RC 2.00 .75
❑ 217 Trevor Insley RC 2.00 .75
❑ 218 Frank Murphy RC 2.00 .75
❑ 219 Patrick Pass RC 3.00 1.25
❑ 220 Mike Anderson RC 2.50 1.00
❑ 221 Derrius Thompson RC 4.00 1.50
❑ 222 John Abraham RC 6.00 2.50
❑ 223 Dante Hall RC 8.00 3.00
❑ 224 Chad Morton RC 4.00 1.50
❑ 225 Ahmed Plummer RC 4.00 1.50
❑ 226 Julian Peterson RC 4.00 1.50
❑ 227 Mike Green RC 3.00 1.25
❑ 228 Michael Wiley RC 3.00 1.25
❑ 229 Spergon Wynn RC 3.00 1.25
❑ 230 Trevor Gaylor RC 3.00 1.25
❑ 231 Doug Johnson RC 4.00 1.50
❑ 232 Marc Bulger RC 8.00 3.00
❑ 233 Ron Dixon RC 3.00 1.25
❑ 234 Aaron Shea RC 1.50 .60
❑ 235 Thomas Hamner RC 2.00 .75
❑ 236 Tom Brady RC 150.00 90.00
❑ 237 Deltha O'Neal RC 4.00 1.50
❑ 238 Todd Husak RC 4.00 1.50
❑ 239 Erron Kinney RC 4.00 1.50
❑ 240 JaJuan Dawson RC 2.00 .75
❑ 241 Nick Williams 1.00 .40
❑ 242 Deon Grant RC 3.00 1.25
❑ 243 Brad Hoover RC 3.00 1.25
❑ 244 Kamil Loud .40 .15
❑ 245 Rashard Anderson RC 3.00 1.25
❑ 246 Clint Stoerner RC 1.50 .60
❑ 247 Antwan Harris RC 2.00 .75
❑ 248 Jason Webster RC 2.00 .75
❑ 249 Kevin McDougal RC 3.00 1.25
❑ 250 Tony Scott RC 2.00 .75
❑ 251 Thabiti Davis RC 2.00 .75
❑ 252 Ian Gold RC 3.00 1.25
❑ 253 Sammy Morris RC 4.00 1.50
❑ 254 Raynoch Thompson RC 3.00 1.25
❑ 255 Jeremy McDaniel 1.00 .40
❑ 256 Terrelle Smith RC 3.00 1.25
❑ 257 Deon Dyer RC 3.00 1.25
❑ 258 Na'il Diggs RC 3.00 1.25
❑ 259 Brandon Short RC 3.00 1.25
❑ 260 Mike Brown RC 8.00 3.00
❑ 261 John Engelberger RC 3.00 1.25
❑ 262 Rogers Beckett RC 3.00 1.25
❑ 263 JaJuan Seider RC 2.00 .75
❑ 264 Desmond Kitchings RC 3.00 1.25
❑ 265 Reggie Davis RC 3.00 1.25
❑ 266 Corey Moore RC 2.00 .75
❑ 267 Cornelius Griffin RC 3.00 1.25
❑ 268 Stockar McDougle RC 2.00 .75
❑ 269 James Williams RC 3.00 1.25
❑ 270 Darrell Jackson RC 6.00 2.50

2001 Bowman Chrome

❑ COMP.SET w/o SP's (110) 25.00 10.00
❑ 1 Emmitt Smith 2.00 .75
❑ 2 James Stewart .60 .25
❑ 3 Jeff Graham .40 .15
❑ 4 Keyshawn Johnson 1.00 .40
❑ 5 Stephen Davis 1.00 .40
❑ 6 Chad Lewis .40 .15
❑ 7 Drew Bledsoe 1.25 .50
❑ 8 Fred Taylor 1.00 .40
❑ 9 Mike Anderson 1.00 .40
❑ 10 Tony Gonzalez .60 .25
❑ 11 Aaron Brooks 1.00 .40
❑ 12 Vinny Testaverde .60 .25
❑ 13 Jerome Bettis 1.00 .40
❑ 14 Marshall Faulk 1.25 .50
❑ 15 Jeff Garcia 1.00 .40
❑ 16 Terry Glenn .60 .25
❑ 17 Jay Fiedler 1.00 .40
❑ 18 Ahman Green 1.00 .40
❑ 19 Cade McNown .40 .15
❑ 20 Rob Johnson .60 .25
❑ 21 Jamal Anderson 1.00 .40
❑ 22 Corey Dillon 1.00 .40
❑ 23 Jake Plummer .60 .25
❑ 24 Rod Smith .60 .25
❑ 25 Trent Green 1.00 .40
❑ 26 Ricky Williams 1.00 .40
❑ 27 Charlie Garner .60 .25
❑ 28 Shaun Alexander 1.25 .50
❑ 29 Jeff George .60 .25
❑ 30 Torry Holt 1.00 .40
❑ 31 James Thrash .60 .25
❑ 32 Rich Gannon 1.00 .40
❑ 33 Ron Dayne 1.00 .40
❑ 34 Dedric Ward .40 .15
❑ 35 Edgerrin James 1.25 .50
❑ 36 Cris Carter 1.00 .40
❑ 37 Derrick Mason .60 .25
❑ 38 Brad Johnson 1.00 .40
❑ 39 Charlie Batch 1.00 .40
❑ 40 Joey Galloway .60 .25
❑ 41 James Allen .60 .25
❑ 42 Tim Biakabutuka .60 .25
❑ 43 Ray Lewis 1.00 .40
❑ 44 David Boston 1.00 .40
❑ 45 Kevin Johnson .60 .25
❑ 46 Jimmy Smith .60 .25
❑ 47 Joe Horn .60 .25
❑ 48 Terrell Owens 1.00 .40
❑ 49 Eddie George 1.00 .40
❑ 50 Brett Favre 3.00 1.25
❑ 51 Wayne Chrebet .60 .25
❑ 52 Hines Ward 1.00 .40
❑ 53 Warrick Dunn 1.00 .40
❑ 54 Matt Hasselbeck .60 .25
❑ 55 Tiki Barber 1.00 .40
❑ 56 Lamar Smith .60 .25
❑ 57 Tim Couch .60 .25
❑ 58 Eric Moulds .60 .25
❑ 59 Shawn Jefferson .40 .15
❑ 60 Donald Hayes .40 .15
❑ 61 Brian Urlacher 1.50 .60
❑ 62 Steve McNair 1.00 .40
❑ 63 Kurt Warner 2.00 .75
❑ 64 Tim Brown 1.00 .40
❑ 65 Troy Brown .60 .25
❑ 66 Albert Connell .40 .15
❑ 67 Peyton Manning 2.50 1.00
❑ 68 Peter Warrick 1.00 .40
❑ 69 Elvis Grbac .60 .25
❑ 70 Chris Chandler .60 .25
❑ 71 Akili Smith .40 .15
❑ 72 Keenan McCardell .40 .15
❑ 73 Kerry Collins .60 .25
❑ 74 Junior Seau 1.00 .40
❑ 75 Donovan McNabb 1.25 .50
❑ 76 Tony Banks .60 .25
❑ 77 Steve Beuerlein .60 .25
❑ 78 Daunte Culpepper 1.00 .40
❑ 79 Darrell Jackson 1.00 .40
❑ 80 Isaac Bruce 1.00 .40
❑ 81 Tyrone Wheatley .60 .25
❑ 82 Derrick Alexander .60 .25
❑ 83 Germane Crowell .40 .15
❑ 84 Jon Kitna .60 .25
❑ 85 Jamal Lewis 1.50 .60
❑ 86 Ed McCaffrey 1.00 .40
❑ 87 Mark Brunell 1.00 .40
❑ 88 Jeff Blake .60 .25
❑ 89 Duce Staley 1.00 .40
❑ 90 Doug Flutie 1.00 .40
❑ 91 Kordell Stewart .60 .25
❑ 92 Randy Moss 2.00 .75
❑ 93 Marvin Harrison 1.00 .40
❑ 94 Muhsin Muhammad .60 .25
❑ 95 Brian Griese 1.00 .40
❑ 96 Antonio Freeman 1.00 .40
❑ 97 Amani Toomer .60 .25
❑ 98 Oronde Gadsden .60 .25
❑ 99 Curtis Martin 1.00 .40
❑ 100 Jerry Rice 2.00 .75
❑ 101 Michael Pittman .40 .15
❑ 102 Shannon Sharpe .60 .25
❑ 103 Peerless Price .60 .25
❑ 104 Bill Schroeder .60 .25
❑ 105 Ike Hilliard .60 .25
❑ 106 Freddie Jones .40 .15
❑ 107 Tai Streets .40 .15
❑ 108 Ricky Watters .60 .25
❑ 109 Az-Zahir Hakim .40 .15
❑ 110 Jacquez Green .40 .15
❑ 111 George Layne RC 5.00 2.00
❑ 112 Correll Buckhalter RC 10.00 4.00
❑ 113 Tony Stewart RC 8.00 3.00
❑ 114 Chris Barnes RC 5.00 2.00
❑ 115 A.J. Feeley RC 8.00 3.00
❑ 116 Margin Hooks RC 3.00 1.25
❑ 117 Anthony Henry RC 8.00 3.00
❑ 118 Dwight Smith RC 3.00 1.25
❑ 119 Torrance Marshall RC 8.00 3.00
❑ 120 Gary Baxter RC 5.00 2.00
❑ 121 Derek Combs RC 5.00 2.00
❑ 122 Marcus Bell RC 5.00 2.00
❑ 123 DeLawrence Grant RC 3.00 1.25
❑ 124 Jameel Cook RC 5.00 2.00
❑ 125 Eric Downing RC 3.00 1.25
❑ 126 Marlon McCree RC 5.00 2.00

❑ 127 Tay Cody RC	3.00	1.25
❑ 128 Mario Monds RC	3.00	1.25
❑ 129 Kenny Smith RC	5.00	2.00
❑ 130 Sedrick Hodge RC	3.00	1.25
❑ 131 Marcus Stroud RC	8.00	3.00
❑ 132 Steve Smith RC	30.00	15.00
❑ 133 Tyrone Robertson RC	3.00	1.25
❑ 134 James Reed RC	3.00	1.25
❑ 135 Kris Kocurek RC	3.00	1.25
❑ 136 Dan O'Leary RC	5.00	2.00
❑ 137 Harold Blackmon RC	3.00	1.25
❑ 138 Fred Smoot RC	8.00	3.00
❑ 139 Billy Baber RC	3.00	1.25
❑ 140 Jarrod Cooper RC	8.00	3.00
❑ 141 Travis Henry RC	15.00	7.50
❑ 142 David Terrell RC	8.00	3.00
❑ 143 Josh Heupel RC	8.00	3.00
❑ 144 Drew Brees RC	40.00	20.00
❑ 145 T.J. Houshmandzadeh RC	10.00	4.00
❑ 146 Rod Gardner RC	8.00	3.00
❑ 147 Richard Seymour RC	8.00	3.00
❑ 148 Koren Robinson RC	8.00	3.00
❑ 149 Scotty Anderson RC	5.00	2.00
❑ 150 Marques Tuiasosopo RC	8.00	3.00
❑ 151 John Capel RC	[illegible]	[illegible]
❑ 152 LaMont Jordan RC	15.00	6.00
❑ 153 James Jackson RC	8.00	3.00
❑ 154 Bobby Newcombe RC	5.00	2.00
❑ 155 Anthony Thomas RC	8.00	3.00
❑ 156 Dan Alexander RC	8.00	3.00
❑ 157 Quincy Carter RC	8.00	3.00
❑ 158 Morlon Greenwood RC	5.00	2.00
❑ 159 Robert Ferguson RC	8.00	3.00
❑ 160 Sage Rosenfels RC	8.00	3.00
❑ 161 Michael Stone RC	3.00	1.25
❑ 162 Chris Weinke RC	8.00	3.00
❑ 163 Travis Minor RC	5.00	2.00
❑ 164 Gerard Warren RC	8.00	3.00
❑ 165 Jamar Fletcher RC	5.00	2.00
❑ 166 Andre Carter RC	8.00	3.00
❑ 167 Deuce McAllister RC	15.00	7.50
❑ 168 Dan Morgan RC	8.00	3.00
❑ 169 Todd Heap RC	8.00	3.00
❑ 170 Snoop Minnis RC	5.00	2.00
❑ 171 Will Allen RC	5.00	2.00
❑ 172 Freddie Mitchell RC	8.00	3.00
❑ 173 Rudi Johnson RC	15.00	6.00
❑ 174 Kevan Barlow RC	8.00	3.00
❑ 175 Jamie Winborn RC	5.00	2.00
❑ 176 Onome Ojo RC	5.00	2.00
❑ 177 Leonard Davis RC	5.00	2.00
❑ 178 Santana Moss RC	12.00	5.00
❑ 179 Chris Chambers RC	12.00	5.00
❑ 180 Michael Vick RC	40.00	15.00
❑ 181 Michael Bennett RC	8.00	3.00
❑ 182 Mike McMahon RC	8.00	3.00
❑ 183 Jonathan Carter RC	5.00	2.00
❑ 184 Jamal Reynolds RC	8.00	3.00
❑ 185 Justin Smith RC	8.00	3.00
❑ 186 Quincy Morgan RC	8.00	3.00
❑ 187 Chad Johnson RC	30.00	12.00
❑ 188 Jesse Palmer RC	8.00	3.00
❑ 189 Reggie Wayne RC	20.00	10.00
❑ 190 LaDainian Tomlinson RC	120.00	60.00
❑ 191 Andre King RC	5.00	2.00
❑ 192 Richmond Flowers RC	5.00	2.00
❑ 193 Derrick Blaylock RC	8.00	3.00
❑ 194 Cedrick Wilson RC	8.00	3.00
❑ 195 Zeke Moreno RC	8.00	3.00
❑ 196 Tommy Polley RC	8.00	3.00
❑ 197 Damione Lewis RC	5.00	2.00
❑ 198 Aaron Schobel RC	8.00	3.00
❑ 199 Alge Crumpler RC	12.00	5.00
❑ 200 Nate Clements RC	8.00	3.00
❑ 201 Quentin McCord RC	5.00	2.00
❑ 202 Ken-Yon Rambo RC	5.00	2.00
❑ 203 Milton Wynn RC	5.00	2.00
❑ 204 Derrick Gibson RC	5.00	2.00
❑ 205 Chris Taylor RC	5.00	2.00
❑ 206 Corey Hall RC	3.00	1.25
❑ 207 Vinny Sutherland RC	5.00	2.00
❑ 208 Kendrell Bell RC	12.00	5.00
❑ 209 Casey Hampton RC	8.00	3.00
❑ 210 Demetric Evans RC	3.00	1.25
❑ 211 Brian Allen RC	3.00	1.25
❑ 212 Rodney Bailey RC	3.00	1.25
❑ 213 Otis Leverette RC	3.00	1.25
❑ 214 Ron Edwards RC	3.00	1.25
❑ 215 Michael Jameson RC	3.00	1.25
❑ 216 Markus Steele RC	5.00	2.00
❑ 217 Jimmy Williams RC	3.00	1.25
❑ 218 Roger Knight RC	3.00	1.25
❑ 219 Randy Garner RC	3.00	1.25
❑ 220 Raymond Perryman RC	3.00	1.25
❑ 221 Karon Riley RC	3.00	1.25
❑ 222 Adam Archuleta RC	8.00	3.00
❑ 223 Arnold Jackson RC	5.00	2.00
❑ 224 Ryan Pickett RC	3.00	1.25
❑ 225 Shad Meier RC	5.00	2.00
❑ 226 Reggie Germany RC	5.00	2.00
❑ 227 Justin McCareins RC	8.00	3.00
❑ 228 Idrees Bashir RC	3.00	1.25
❑ 229 Josh Booty RC	8.00	3.00
❑ 230 Eddie Berlin RC	5.00	2.00
❑ 231 Heath Evans RC	5.00	2.00
❑ 232 Alex Bannister RC	5.00	2.00
❑ 233 Corey Alston RC	3.00	1.25
❑ 234 Reggie White RC	5.00	2.00
❑ 235 Orlando Huff RC	3.00	1.25
❑ 236 Ken Lucas RC	5.00	2.00
❑ 237 Matt Stewart RC	3.00	1.25
❑ 238 Cedric Scott RC	5.00	2.00
❑ 239 Ronney Daniels RC	3.00	1.25
❑ 240 Kevin Kasper RC	8.00	3.00
❑ 241 Tony Driver RC	5.00	2.00
❑ 242 Kyle Vanden Bosch RC	8.00	3.00
❑ 243 T.J. Turner RC	3.00	1.25
❑ 244 Eric Westmoreland RC	5.00	2.00
❑ 245 Ronald Flemons RC	3.00	1.25
❑ 246 Eric Kelly RC	3.00	1.25
❑ 247 Moran Norris RC	3.00	1.25
❑ 248 Damerien McCants RC	5.00	2.00
❑ 249 James Boyd RC	3.00	1.25
❑ 250 Keith Adams RC	3.00	1.25
❑ 251 Brandon Manumaleuna RC	5.00	2.00
❑ 252 Dee Brown RC	8.00	3.00
❑ 253 Ross Kolodziej RC	3.00	1.25
❑ 254 Boo Williams RC	5.00	2.00
❑ 255 Patrick Chukwurah RC	3.00	1.25

2002 Bowman Chrome

❑ COMP.SET w/o SP's (110)	25.00	10.00
❑ 1 Emmitt Smith	2.50	1.00
❑ 2 Drew Brees	1.00	.40
❑ 3 Duce Staley	1.00	.40
❑ 4 Curtis Martin	1.00	.40
❑ 5 Isaac Bruce	1.00	.40
❑ 6 Stephen Davis	.60	.25
❑ 7 Darrell Jackson	.60	.25
❑ 8 James Stewart	.60	.25
❑ 9 Tim Couch	.60	.25
❑ 10 Travis Henry	1.00	.40
❑ 11 Thomas Jones	.60	.25
❑ 12 Jamal Lewis	1.00	.40
❑ 13 Chris Chambers	1.00	.40
❑ 14 Jeff Blake	.60	.25
❑ 15 Plaxico Burress	.60	.25
❑ 16 Michael Pittman	.40	.15
❑ 17 Jeff Garcia	1.00	.40
❑ 18 Tim Brown	1.00	.40
❑ 19 Kent Graham	.40	.15
❑ 20 Shannon Sharpe	.60	.25
❑ 21 Corey Dillon	.60	.25
❑ 22 Muhsin Muhammad	.60	.25
❑ 23 Tony Gonzalez	.60	.25
❑ 24 Qadry Ismail	.60	.25
❑ 25 Mike McMahon	1.00	.40
❑ 26 Edgerrin James	1.25	.50
❑ 27 Daunte Culpepper	1.00	.40
❑ 28 Deuce McAllister	1.25	.50
❑ 29 Kerry Collins	.60	.25
❑ 30 Eddie George	1.00	.40
❑ 31 Torry Holt	1.00	.40
❑ 32 Todd Pinkston	.60	.25
❑ 33 Quincy Carter	.60	.25
❑ 34 Rod Smith	.60	.25
❑ 35 Michael Vick	2.00	.75
❑ 36 Jim Miller	.60	.25
❑ 37 Troy Brown	.60	.25
❑ 38 Wayne Chrebet	.60	.25
❑ 39 Curtis Conway	.40	.15
❑ 40 Reidel Anthony	.40	.15
❑ 41 Mark Brunell	1.00	.40
❑ 42 Chris Weinke	.60	.25
❑ 43 Eric Moulds	.60	.25
❑ 44 Ike Hilliard	.60	.25
❑ 45 Jay Fiedler	.60	.25
❑ 46 Keyshawn Johnson	1.00	.40
❑ 47 Rod Gardner	.60	.25
❑ 48 Chris Redman	.40	.15
❑ 49 James Allen	.60	.25
❑ 50 Kordell Stewart	.60	.25
❑ 51 Priest Holmes	1.25	.50
❑ 52 Anthony Thomas	.60	.25
❑ 53 Peter Warrick	.60	.25
❑ 54 Jake Plummer	.60	.25
❑ 55 Jerry Rice	2.00	.75
❑ 56 Joe Horn	.60	.25
❑ 57 Derrick Mason	.60	.25
❑ 58 Kurt Warner	1.00	.40
❑ 59 Antowain Smith	.60	.25
❑ 60 Randy Moss	2.00	.75
❑ 61 Warrick Dunn	1.00	.40
❑ 62 Laveranues Coles	.60	.25
❑ 63 LaDainian Tomlinson	1.50	.60
❑ 64 Michael Westbrook	.60	.25
❑ 65 Travis Taylor	.60	.25
❑ 66 Brian Griese	1.00	.40
❑ 67 Bill Schroeder	.60	.25
❑ 68 Ahman Green	1.00	.40
❑ 69 Jimmy Smith	.60	.25
❑ 70 Charlie Garner	.60	.25
❑ 71 Terrell Owens	1.00	.40
❑ 72 Brad Johnson	.60	.25
❑ 73 James Thrash	.60	.25
❑ 74 Marvin Harrison	1.00	.40
❑ 75 Brett Favre	2.50	1.00
❑ 76 Rocket Ismail	.60	.25
❑ 77 David Boston	1.00	.40
❑ 78 Jermaine Lewis	.40	.15
❑ 79 Aaron Brooks	1.00	.40
❑ 80 Shaun Alexander	1.25	.50
❑ 81 Steve McNair	1.00	.40
❑ 82 Marshall Faulk	1.00	.40
❑ 83 Terrell Davis	1.00	.40
❑ 84 Corey Bradford	.40	.15
❑ 85 David Terrell	1.00	.40
❑ 86 Kevin Johnson	.60	.25
❑ 87 Jon Kitna	.60	.25
❑ 88 Az-Zahir Hakim	.40	.15
❑ 89 Drew Bledsoe	1.25	.50
❑ 90 Garrison Hearst	.60	.25
❑ 91 Doug Flutie	1.00	.40
❑ 92 Jerome Bettis	1.00	.40
❑ 93 Vinny Testaverde	.60	.25
❑ 94 Tiki Barber	1.00	.40
❑ 95 Johnnie Morton	.60	.25
❑ 96 Lamar Smith	.60	.25
❑ 97 Marcus Robinson	.60	.25
❑ 98 Fred Taylor	1.00	.40
❑ 99 Tom Brady	2.50	1.00
❑ 100 Peyton Manning	2.00	.75
❑ 101 Donovan McNabb	1.25	.50
❑ 102 Rich Gannon	1.00	.40
❑ 103 Hines Ward	1.00	.40
❑ 104 Michael Bennett	.60	.25
❑ 105 Ricky Williams	1.00	.40
❑ 106 Germane Crowell	.40	.15
❑ 107 Joey Galloway	.60	.25
❑ 108 Amani Toomer	.60	.25
❑ 109 Trent Green	.60	.25
❑ 110 Terry Glenn	.60	.25
❑ 111 Donte Stallworth RC	8.00	3.00
❑ 112 Mike Williams RC	4.00	1.50
❑ 113 Kurt Kittner RC	4.00	1.50
❑ 114 Josh Reed RC	5.00	2.00
❑ 115 Raonall Smith RC	4.00	1.50
❑ 116 David Garrard RC	10.00	4.00
❑ 117 Eric Crouch RC	5.00	2.00
❑ 118 Levi Jones RC	4.00	1.50

❑ 119 Quentin Jammer RC	5.00	2.00
❑ 120 Cliff Russell RC	4.00	1.50
❑ 121 Jamin Elliott RC	2.50	1.00
❑ 122 Roy Williams RC	10.00	4.00
❑ 123 Marquise Walker RC	4.00	1.50
❑ 124 Kalimba Edwards RC	5.00	2.00
❑ 125 Daniel Graham RC	5.00	2.00
❑ 126 Anthony Weaver RC	4.00	1.50
❑ 127 Antonio Bryant RC	5.00	2.00
❑ 128 DeShaun Foster RC	5.00	2.00
❑ 129 Antwaan Randle El RC	6.00	2.50
❑ 130 William Green RC	5.00	2.00
❑ 131 Joey Harrington RC	6.00	2.50
❑ 132 T.J. Duckett RC	5.00	2.00
❑ 133 Javon Walker RC	8.00	3.00
❑ 134 Albert Haynesworth RC	4.00	1.50
❑ 135 Julius Peppers RC	10.00	4.00
❑ 136 Clinton Portis RC	15.00	6.00
❑ 137 Ashley Lelie RC	10.00	4.00
❑ 138 Reche Caldwell RC	5.00	2.00
❑ 139 Rohan Davey RC	5.00	2.00
❑ 140 Patrick Ramsey RC	5.00	2.00
❑ 141 Ron Johnson RC	4.00	1.50
❑ 142 Jamar Martin RC	4.00	1.50
❑ 143 Travis Stephens RC	4.00	1.50
❑ 143AU Travis Stephens AU	12.00	5.00
❑ 144 Darrell Hill RC	4.00	1.50
❑ 145 Jon McGraw RC	2.50	1.00
❑ 146 Javin Hunter RC	2.50	1.00
❑ 146AU Javin Hunter AU	10.00	4.00
❑ 147 Eddie Drummond RC	4.00	1.50
❑ 148 Andre Lott RC	5.00	2.00
❑ 149 Travis Fisher RC	5.00	2.00
❑ 150 Lamont Brightful RC	2.50	1.00
❑ 151 Rocky Calmus RC	5.00	2.00
❑ 152 Wes Pate RC	2.50	1.00
❑ 152AU Wes Pate AU	10.00	4.00
❑ 153 Lamar Gordon RC	5.00	2.00
❑ 154 Terry Jones RC	4.00	1.50
❑ 155 Kyle Johnson RC	2.50	1.00
❑ 155AU Kyle Johnson AU	10.00	4.00
❑ 156 Daryl Jones RC	4.00	1.50
❑ 157 Tellis Redmon RC	4.00	1.50
❑ 158 Jarrod Baxter RC	4.00	1.50
❑ 159 Delvon Flowers RC	4.00	1.50
❑ 160 Kelly Campbell RC	4.00	1.50
❑ 161 Eddie Freeman RC	2.50	1.00
❑ 162 Atrews Bell RC	2.50	1.00
❑ 163 Omar Easy RC	5.00	2.00
❑ 164 Jeremy Allen RC	2.50	1.00
❑ 165 Andra Davis RC	4.00	1.50
❑ 166 Mike Rumph RC	5.00	2.00
❑ 167 Seth Burford RC	4.00	1.50
❑ 168 Marquand Manuel RC	2.50	1.00
❑ 169 Marques Anderson RC	5.00	2.00
❑ 170 Ben Leber RC	5.00	2.00
❑ 171 Ryan Denney RC	4.00	1.50
❑ 172 Justin Peelle RC	2.50	1.00
❑ 173 Lito Sheppard RC	5.00	2.00
❑ 174 Damien Anderson RC	4.00	1.50
❑ 175 Lamont Thompson RC	4.00	1.50
❑ 176 David Priestley RC	4.00	1.50
❑ 177 Michael Lewis RC	5.00	2.00
❑ 178 Lee Mays RC	4.00	1.50
❑ 179 Alan Harper RC	2.50	1.00
❑ 180 Verron Haynes RC	5.00	2.00
❑ 181 Chris Hope RC	5.00	2.00
❑ 182 Derek Ross RC	4.00	1.50
❑ 183 Joseph Jefferson RC	4.00	1.50
❑ 184 Carlos Hall RC	5.00	2.00
❑ 185 Robert Royal RC	5.00	2.00
❑ 186 Sheldon Brown RC	5.00	2.00
❑ 187 DeVeren Johnson RC	4.00	1.50
❑ 188 Rock Cartwright RC	6.00	2.50
❑ 189 Kendall Simmons RC	4.00	1.50
❑ 190 Joe Burns RC	4.00	1.50
❑ 191 David Givens RC	12.00	5.00
❑ 192 John Owens RC	4.00	1.50
❑ 193 Jarrett Ferguson RC	4.00	1.50
❑ 194 Randy McMichael RC	8.00	3.00
❑ 195 Chris Baker RC	4.00	1.50
❑ 196 Rashad Bauman RC	4.00	1.50
❑ 197 Matt Murphy RC	4.00	1.50
❑ 198 Steve Bellisari RC	4.00	1.50
❑ 199 Jeff Kelly RC	4.00	1.50
❑ 200 Mark Anelli RC	2.50	1.00
❑ 201 Darnell Sanders RC	4.00	1.50
❑ 202 Coy Wire RC	5.00	2.00
❑ 203 Ricky Williams RC	4.00	1.50
❑ 204 Napoleon Harris RC	5.00	2.00
❑ 205 Ennis Haywood RC	4.00	1.50
❑ 206 Keyuo Craver RC	4.00	1.50
❑ 207 Kahlil Hill RC	4.00	1.50
❑ 208 J.T. O'Sullivan RC	4.00	1.50
❑ 209 Woody Dantzler RC	4.00	1.50
❑ 210 Phillip Buchanon RC	5.00	2.00
❑ 211 Charles Grant RC	5.00	2.00
❑ 212 Dusty Bonner RC	2.50	1.00
❑ 213 James Allen RC	2.50	1.00
❑ 214 Ronald Curry RC	5.00	2.00
❑ 215 Deion Branch RC	8.00	3.00
❑ 216 Larry Ned RC	4.00	1.50
❑ 217 Kendall Newson RC	2.50	1.00
❑ 218 Shaun Hill RC	5.00	2.00
❑ 219 Akin Ayodele RC	2.50	1.00
❑ 220 John Henderson RC	5.00	2.00
❑ 221 Andre Davis AU A RC	12.00	5.00
❑ 222 Bryan Thomas AU A RC	20.00	7.50
❑ 223 Brian Westbrook AU C RC	60.00	35.00
❑ 224 Chad Hutchinson AU C RC	12.00	5.00
❑ 225 Craig Nall AU D RC	20.00	7.50
❑ 226 David Carr AU A RC	50.00	20.00
❑ 227 Dwight Freeney AU D RC	40.00	20.00
❑ 228 Adrian Peterson AU A RC	30.00	12.00
❑ 229 Randy Fasani AU E RC	12.00	5.00
❑ 230 Ed Reed AU A RC	30.00	12.00
❑ 231 Freddie Milons AU B RC	12.00	5.00
❑ 232 Herb Haygood AU E RC	10.00	4.00
❑ 233 Jabar Gaffney AU A RC	15.00	6.00
❑ 234 Josh McCown AU A RC	30.00	12.00
❑ 235 Jeremy Shockey AU A RC	100.00	50.00
❑ 236 Jake Schifino AU F RC	12.00	5.00
❑ 237 Josh Scobey AU E RC	20.00	7.50
❑ 238 Jonathan Wells AU D RC	20.00	7.50
❑ 239 Ladell Betts AU A RC	25.00	12.50
❑ 240 Luke Staley AU E RC	12.00	5.00
❑ 241 Maurice Morris AU B RC	20.00	7.50
❑ 242 Matt Schobel AU D RC	12.00	5.00
❑ 243 Sam Simmons AU C RC	10.00	4.00
❑ 244 Tim Carter AU A RC	12.00	5.00
❑ 245 Tank Williams AU E RC	12.00	5.00
❑ 246 Jerramy Stevens AU A RC	20.00	7.50
❑ 247 Jason McAddley AU C RC	12.00	5.00
❑ 248 Ken Simonton AU D RC	10.00	4.00
❑ 249 Chester Taylor AU F RC	30.00	15.00
❑ 250 Brandon Doman AU C RC	12.00	5.00

2003 Bowman Chrome

❑ COMP.SET w/o SP's (110)	25.00	10.00
❑ 1 Brett Favre	2.50	1.00
❑ 2 Jeremy Shockey	1.50	.60
❑ 3 Fred Taylor	1.00	.40
❑ 4 Rich Gannon	.60	.25
❑ 5 Joey Galloway	.60	.25
❑ 6 Ray Lewis	1.00	.40
❑ 7 Jeff Blake	.40	.15
❑ 8 Stacey Mack	.40	.15
❑ 9 Matt Hasselbeck	.60	.25
❑ 10 Laveranues Coles	.60	.25
❑ 11 Brad Johnson	.60	.25
❑ 12 Tommy Maddox	1.00	.40
❑ 13 Curtis Martin	1.00	.40
❑ 14 Tom Brady	2.50	1.00
❑ 15 Ricky Williams	1.00	.40
❑ 16 Stephen Davis	.60	.25
❑ 17 Chad Johnson	1.00	.40
❑ 18 Joey Harrington	1.50	.60
❑ 19 Tony Gonzalez	.60	.25
❑ 20 Peerless Price	.60	.25
❑ 21 LaDainian Tomlinson	1.00	.40
❑ 22 James Thrash	.60	.25
❑ 23 Charlie Garner	.60	.25
❑ 24 Eddie George	.60	.25
❑ 25 Terrell Owens	1.00	.40
❑ 26 Brian Urlacher	1.50	.60
❑ 27 Eric Moulds	.60	.25
❑ 28 Emmitt Smith	2.50	1.00
❑ 29 Tim Couch	.40	.15
❑ 30 Jake Plummer	.60	.25
❑ 31 Marvin Harrison	1.00	.40
❑ 32 Chris Chambers	1.00	.40
❑ 33 Tiki Barber	1.00	.40
❑ 34 Kurt Warner	1.00	.40
❑ 35 Michael Pittman	.40	.15
❑ 36 Kevin Dyson	.60	.25
❑ 37 Clinton Portis	1.50	.60
❑ 38 Peyton Manning	1.50	.60
❑ 39 Travis Taylor	.60	.25
❑ 40 Jeff Garcia	1.00	.40
❑ 41 Patrick Ramsey	1.00	.40
❑ 42 Shaun Alexander	1.00	.40
❑ 43 Joe Horn	.60	.25
❑ 44 Daunte Culpepper	1.00	.40
❑ 45 Travis Henry	.60	.25
❑ 46 Brian Finneran	.40	.15
❑ 47 William Green	.60	.25
❑ 48 Kordell Stewart	.60	.25
❑ 49 Reggie Wayne	.60	.25
❑ 50 Priest Holmes	1.25	.50
❑ 51 Jay Fiedler	.60	.25
❑ 52 Corey Dillon	.60	.25
❑ 53 Jamal Lewis	1.00	.40
❑ 54 Mark Brunell	.60	.25
❑ 55 Santana Moss	.60	.25
❑ 56 Duce Staley	.60	.25
❑ 57 Torry Holt	1.00	.40
❑ 58 Rod Gardner	.60	.25
❑ 59 Kerry Collins	.60	.25
❑ 60 Randy Moss	1.50	.60
❑ 61 Jerry Porter	.60	.25
❑ 62 Plaxico Burress	.60	.25
❑ 63 Steve McNair	1.00	.40
❑ 64 Muhsin Muhammad	.60	.25
❑ 65 Drew Bledsoe	1.00	.40
❑ 66 T.J. Duckett	.60	.25
❑ 67 Ahman Green	1.00	.40
❑ 68 Rod Smith	.60	.25
❑ 69 Jimmy Smith	.60	.25
❑ 70 Trent Green	.60	.25
❑ 71 Tim Brown	1.00	.40
❑ 72 Jerome Bettis	1.00	.40
❑ 73 Isaac Bruce	1.00	.40
❑ 74 Derrick Mason	.60	.25
❑ 75 Donovan McNabb	1.25	.50
❑ 76 Deuce McAllister	1.00	.40
❑ 77 Zach Thomas	1.00	.40
❑ 78 Garrison Hearst	.60	.25
❑ 79 Koren Robinson	.60	.25
❑ 80 Marshall Faulk	1.00	.40
❑ 81 Keyshawn Johnson	1.00	.40
❑ 82 Jake Delhomme	1.00	.40
❑ 83 Marty Booker	.60	.25
❑ 84 James Stewart	.60	.25
❑ 85 Corey Bradford	.40	.15
❑ 86 Derrius Thompson	.40	.15
❑ 87 Edgerrin James	1.00	.40
❑ 88 Darrell Jackson	.60	.25
❑ 89 Hines Ward	1.00	.40
❑ 90 David Boston	.60	.25
❑ 91 Curtis Conway	.40	.15
❑ 92 David Patten	.40	.15
❑ 93 Michael Bennett	.60	.25
❑ 94 Todd Pinkston	.60	.25
❑ 95 Jerry Rice	2.00	.75
❑ 96 Jon Kitna	.60	.25
❑ 97 Ed McCaffrey	1.00	.40
❑ 98 Donald Driver	.60	.25
❑ 99 Anthony Thomas	.60	.25
❑ 100 Michael Vick	2.50	1.00
❑ 101 Terry Glenn	.40	.15
❑ 102 Quincy Morgan	.60	.25
❑ 103 David Carr	1.50	.60
❑ 104 Troy Brown	.60	.25
❑ 105 Aaron Brooks	1.00	.40
❑ 106 Amani Toomer	.60	.25
❑ 107 Drew Brees	1.00	.40
❑ 108 Chad Hutchinson	.40	.15
❑ 109 Warrick Dunn	.60	.25
❑ 110 Chad Pennington	1.25	.50
❑ 111 Brian St.Pierre RC	5.00	2.00

❑ 112 Keenan Howry RC 5.00 2.00
❑ 113 Sultan McCullough RC 4.00 1.50
❑ 114 Terence Newman RC 10.00 4.00
❑ 115 Kelley Washington RC 5.00 2.00
❑ 116 Musa Smith RC 5.00 2.00
❑ 117 Victor Hobson RC 5.00 2.00
❑ 118 Travis Anglin RC 2.50 1.00
❑ 119 Artose Pinner RC 5.00 2.00
❑ 120 Rashean Mathis RC 4.00 1.50
❑ 121 DeWayne White RC 4.00 1.50
❑ 122 Kevin Curtis RC 6.00 2.50
❑ 123 Tyrone Calico RC 6.00 2.50
❑ 124 Ricky Manning RC 5.00 2.00
❑ 125 Cory Redding RC 4.00 1.50
❑ 126 Dallas Clark RC 5.00 2.00
❑ 127 Marcus Trufant RC 5.00 2.00
❑ 128 Terrell Suggs RC 8.00 3.00
❑ 129 Aaron Walker RC 4.00 1.50
❑ 130 Calvin Pace RC 4.00 1.50
❑ 131 Ken Dorsey RC 5.00 2.00
❑ 132 Earnest Graham RC 5.00 2.00
❑ 133 Cecil Sapp RC 4.00 1.50
❑ 134 William Joseph RC 5.00 2.00
❑ 135 Anquan Boldin RC 15.00 6.00
❑ 136 Justin Griffith RC 4.00 1.50
❑ 137 Teyo Johnson RC 5.00 2.00
❑ 138 Chris Crocker RC 2.50 1.00
❑ 139 Doug Gabriel RC 6.00 2.50
❑ 140 Terry Pierce RC 4.00 1.50
❑ 141 Bradie James RC 5.00 2.00
❑ 142 Terrence Edwards RC 4.00 1.50
❑ 143 E.J. Henderson RC 5.00 2.00
❑ 144 Tony Romo RC 60.00 30.00
❑ 145 DeWayne Robertson RC 5.00 2.00
❑ 146 Dwone Hicks RC 2.50 1.00
❑ 147 Carl Ford RC 2.50 1.00
❑ 148 Ken Hamlin RC 5.00 2.00
❑ 149 Adrian Madise RC 4.00 1.50
❑ 150 Siddeeq Shabazz RC 2.50 1.00
❑ 151 Dave Ragone RC 5.00 2.00
❑ 152 Mike Seidman RC 2.50 1.00
❑ 153 DeAndrew Rubin RC 2.50 1.00
❑ 154 Mike Pinkard RC 2.50 1.00
❑ 155 Nate Burleson RC 5.00 2.00
❑ 156 Angelo Crowell RC 4.00 1.50
❑ 157 J.R. Tolver RC 4.00 1.50
❑ 158 Osi Umenyiora RC 8.00 3.00
❑ 159 Nick Barnett RC 5.00 2.00
❑ 160 Brandon Drumm RC 2.50 1.00
❑ 161 Rien Long RC 2.50 1.00
❑ 162 Zuriel Smith RC 2.50 1.00
❑ 163 Ontorrio Smith RC 5.00 2.00
❑ 164 Kenny Peterson RC 4.00 1.50
❑ 165 Chaun Thompson RC 2.50 1.00
❑ 166 Terrence Holt RC 4.00 1.50
❑ 167 Ovie Mughelli RC 2.50 1.00
❑ 168 Bethel Johnson RC 5.00 2.00
❑ 169 Avon Cobourne RC 2.50 1.00
❑ 170 Andre Woolfolk RC 5.00 2.00
❑ 171 George Wrighster RC 4.00 1.50
❑ 172 Justin Fargas RC 5.00 2.00
❑ 173 Marquel Blackwell RC 2.50 1.00
❑ 174 Walter Young RC 2.50 1.00
❑ 175 Kawika Mitchell RC 5.00 2.00
❑ 176 Drayton Florence RC 2.50 1.00
❑ 177 Jeremi Johnson RC 4.00 1.50
❑ 178 Lee Suggs RC 5.00 2.00
❑ 179 David Kircus RC 5.00 2.00
❑ 180 Rex Grossman RC 15.00 6.00
❑ 180AU Rex Grossman AU B 60.00 25.00
❑ 181 Jon Olinger RC 2.50 1.00
❑ 182 Dan Curley RC 2.50 1.00
❑ 183 Andrew Pinnock RC 4.00 1.50
❑ 184 Kirk Farmer RC 2.50 1.00
❑ 185 Charles Rogers RC 5.00 2.00
❑ 186 Alonzo Jackson RC 4.00 1.50
❑ 187 Trent Smith RC 4.00 1.50
❑ 188 Seneca Wallace RC 5.00 2.00
❑ 189 Shane Walton RC 2.50 1.00
❑ 190 Chris Brown RC 5.00 2.00
❑ 191 Dahrran Diedrick RC 5.00 2.00
❑ 192 Juston Wood RC 2.50 1.00
❑ 193 Mike Doss RC 5.00 2.00
❑ 194 Visanthe Shiancoe RC 4.00 1.50
❑ 195 Andre Johnson RC 10.00 4.00
❑ 196 Dennis Weathersby RC 2.50 1.00
❑ 197 Chris Davis RC 4.00 1.50
❑ 198 LaTarence Dunbar RC 4.00 1.50
❑ 199 Eugene Wilson RC 5.00 2.00
❑ 200 Ryan Hoag RC 2.50 1.00
❑ 201 Chris Simms RC 8.00 3.00
❑ 202 Curt Anes RC 2.50 1.00
❑ 203 Taco Wallace RC 4.00 1.50
❑ 204 David Tyree RC 4.00 1.50
❑ 205 Nate Hybl RC 5.00 2.00
❑ 206 Willis McGahee RC 15.00 6.00
❑ 207 Casey Moore RC 4.00 1.50
❑ 208 Pisa Tinoisamoa RC 5.00 2.00
❑ 209 Willie Ponder RC 2.50 1.00
❑ 210 Donald Lee RC 4.00 1.50
❑ 211 Nnamdi Asomugha RC 4.00 1.50
❑ 212 Sammy Davis RC 5.00 2.00
❑ 213 Joffrey Reynolds RC 2.50 1.00
❑ 214 Eddie Moore RC 4.00 1.50
❑ 215 Tony Hollings RC 5.00 2.00
❑ 216 Nick Maddox RC 2.50 1.00
❑ 217 Kevin Walter RC 4.00 1.50
❑ 218 Dan Klecko RC 5.00 2.00
❑ 219 Antwan Peek RC 4.00 1.50
❑ 220 Tyler Brayton RC 5.00 2.00
❑ 221 Byron Leftwich AU B RC 40.00 15.00
❑ 222 Bobby Wade AU D RC 15.00 6.00
❑ 223 Jerome McDougle AU C RC 12.00 5.00
❑ 224 Michael Haynes AU D RC 12.00 5.00
❑ 225 Taylor Jacobs AU C RC 15.00 6.00
❑ 226 Shaun McDonald AU D RC 12.00 5.00
❑ 227 Bry.Johnson AU B RC EXCH
❑ 228 Talman Gardner AU D RC 12.00 5.00
❑ 229 Domanick Davis AU D RC 25.00 10.00
❑ 230 Jason Witten AU D RC 40.00 20.00
❑ 231 Kyle Boller AU B RC 20.00 8.00
❑ 232 L.J. Smith AU C RC 20.00 8.00
❑ 233 Boss Bailey AU C RC 15.00 6.00
❑ 234 Billy McMullen AU D RC 10.00 4.00
❑ 235 Larry Johnson AU B RC 150.00 75.00
❑ 236 Kareem Kelly AU E RC 10.00 4.00
❑ 237 Carson Palmer AU A RC 300.00 150.00
❑ 238 Quentin Griffin AU D RC 15.00 6.00
❑ 239 Kevin Garrett AU E RC 10.00 4.00
❑ 240 Charles Tillman AU E RC 15.00 6.00
❑ 241 Arnaz Battle AU D RC 20.00 8.00
❑ 242 Brooks Bollinger AU E RC 12.00 5.00
❑ 243 LaBrandon Toefield AU D RC 12.00 5.00
❑ 244 Sam Aiken AU D RC 10.00 4.00
❑ 245 Justin Gage AU D RC 12.00 5.00
❑ 246 Gibran Hamdan AU D RC 10.00 4.00

2004 Bowman Chrome

❑ COMP.SET w/o SP's (220) 175.00 100.00
❑ COMP.SET w/o RC's (110) 30.00 12.50
❑ ROOKIE AU/199 GROUP A ODDS 1:603
❑ ROOKIE AU GROUP B ODDS 1:1293
❑ ROOKIE AU GROUP C ODDS 1:359
❑ ROOKIE AU GROUP D ODDS 1:21
❑ 1 Brett Favre 2.50 1.00
❑ 2 Jay Fiedler .40 .15
❑ 3 Andre Davis .40 .15
❑ 4 Travis Henry .60 .25
❑ 5 Jimmy Smith .60 .25
❑ 6 Santana Moss .60 .25
❑ 7 Correll Buckhalter .60 .25
❑ 8 Randy Moss 1.25 .50
❑ 9 Edgerrin James 1.00 .40
❑ 10 Marc Bulger 1.00 .40
❑ 11 Derrick Mason .60 .25
❑ 12 Mark Brunell .60 .25
❑ 13 Donte Stallworth .60 .25
❑ 14 Deion Branch 1.00 .40
❑ 15 Jake Plummer .60 .25
❑ 16 Steve Smith 1.00 .40
❑ 17 Jon Kitna .60 .25
❑ 18 Andre Johnson 1.00 .40
❑ 19 A.J. Feeley 1.00 .40
❑ 20 Drew Bledsoe 1.00 .40
❑ 21 Antonio Bryant .60 .25
❑ 22 Reggie Wayne .60 .25
❑ 23 Thomas Jones .60 .25
❑ 24 Alge Crumpler .60 .25
❑ 25 Anquan Boldin 1.00 .40
❑ 26 Tim Rattay .40 .15
❑ 27 Charlie Garner .60 .25
❑ 28 James Thrash .40 .15
❑ 29 Koren Robinson .60 .25
❑ 30 Terrell Owens 1.00 .40
❑ 31 Amani Toomer .60 .25
❑ 32 Kelly Campbell .40 .15
❑ 33 Patrick Ramsey .60 .25
❑ 34 Plaxico Burress .60 .25
❑ 35 Chad Pennington 1.00 .40
❑ 36 Fred Taylor .60 .25
❑ 37 Domanick Davis 1.00 .40
❑ 38 DeShaun Foster .60 .25
❑ 39 T.J. Duckett .60 .25
❑ 40 Ahman Green 1.00 .40
❑ 41 Lee Suggs 1.00 .40
❑ 42 Tony Gonzalez .60 .25
❑ 43 Rich Gannon .60 .25
❑ 44 Kevan Barlow .60 .25
❑ 45 Torry Holt 1.00 .40
❑ 46 Aaron Brooks .60 .25
❑ 47 Tyrone Calico .60 .25
❑ 48 Keenan McCardell .40 .15
❑ 49 Hines Ward 1.00 .40
❑ 50 LaDainian Tomlinson 1.25 .50
❑ 51 Dante Hall 1.00 .40
❑ 52 Marcus Pollard .40 .15
❑ 53 Corey Dillon .60 .25
❑ 54 Justin McCareins .40 .15
❑ 55 Stephen Davis .60 .25
❑ 56 Jeff Garcia 1.00 .40
❑ 57 Ashley Lelie .60 .25
❑ 58 Javon Walker .60 .25
❑ 59 Kyle Boller 1.00 .40
❑ 60 Chad Johnson 1.00 .40
❑ 61 Anthony Thomas .60 .25
❑ 62 Byron Leftwich 1.25 .50
❑ 63 David Boston .60 .25
❑ 64 Onterrio Smith .60 .25
❑ 65 Deuce McAllister 1.00 .40
❑ 66 Antwaan Randle El 1.00 .40
❑ 67 Justin Fargas .60 .25
❑ 68 Laveranues Coles .60 .25
❑ 69 Quincy Morgan .60 .25
❑ 70 Priest Holmes 1.25 .50
❑ 71 Robert Ferguson .40 .15
❑ 72 Charles Rogers .60 .25
❑ 73 Drew Brees 1.00 .40
❑ 74 Matt Hasselbeck .60 .25
❑ 75 Peyton Manning 1.50 .60
❑ 76 Rudi Johnson .60 .25
❑ 77 Jake Delhomme 1.00 .40
❑ 78 Tiki Barber 1.00 .40
❑ 79 Brad Johnson .60 .25
❑ 80 Steve McNair 1.00 .40
❑ 81 Willis McGahee 1.00 .40
❑ 82 Josh McCown .60 .25
❑ 83 Garrison Hearst .60 .25
❑ 84 Quincy Carter .60 .25
❑ 85 Ricky Williams 1.00 .40
❑ 86 Trent Green .60 .25
❑ 87 Curtis Martin 1.00 .40
❑ 88 Jerry Porter .60 .25
❑ 89 Brian Westbrook .60 .25
❑ 90 Clinton Portis 1.00 .40
❑ 91 Eric Moulds .60 .25
❑ 92 Marcel Shipp .60 .25
❑ 93 Joey Harrington 1.00 .40
❑ 94 David Carr 1.00 .40
❑ 95 Marvin Harrison 1.00 .40
❑ 96 Joe Horn .60 .25
❑ 97 Chris Chambers .60 .25
❑ 98 Darrell Jackson .60 .25
❑ 99 Eddie George .60 .25
❑ 100 Donovan McNabb 1.25 .50
❑ 101 Marshall Faulk 1.00 .40
❑ 102 Rex Grossman 1.00 .40
❑ 103 Tai Streets .40 .15
❑ 104 Jeremy Shockey 1.00 .40
❑ 105 Jamal Lewis 1.00 .40
❑ 106 Tom Brady 2.50 1.00

❑ 107 Shaun Alexander 1.00 .40
❑ 108 Carson Palmer 1.25 .50
❑ 109 Daunte Culpepper 1.00 .40
❑ 110 Michael Vick 2.00 .75
❑ 111 Roethlis AU/199 RC 350.00 200.00
❑ 112 Tommie Harris RC 4.00 1.50
❑ 113 Thomas Tapeh RC 3.00 1.25
❑ 114 Matt Schaub RC 12.00 5.00
❑ 115 Jonathan Smith RC 3.00 1.25
❑ 116 Ricardo Colclough RC 4.00 1.50
❑ 117 Jeff Dugan RC 2.00 .75
❑ 118 Larry Fitzgerald RC 12.00 5.00
❑ 119 Gibril Wilson RC 4.00 1.50
❑ 120 Sean Taylor RC 4.00 1.50
❑ 121 Marquise Hill RC 3.00 1.25
❑ 122 Cedric Cobbs RC 4.00 1.50
❑ 123 Rich Gardner RC 3.00 1.25
❑ 124 Chris Cooley RC 4.00 1.50
❑ 125 Ben Troupe RC 4.00 1.50
❑ 126 Antwan Odom RC 4.00 1.50
❑ 127 Stuart Schweigert RC 4.00 1.50
❑ 128 Derek Abney RC 4.00 1.50
❑ 129 Keary Colbert RC 4.00 1.50
❑ 130 Jeris McIntyre RC 3.00 1.25
❑ 131 Matt Kranchick RC 4.00 1.50
❑ 132 Rodney Leisle RC 2.00 .75
❑ 133 Vince Wilfork RC 4.00 1.50
❑ 134 Darnell Dockett RC 3.00 1.25
❑ 135 Jeremy LeSueur RC 3.00 1.25
❑ 136 Gilbert Gardner RC 3.00 1.25
❑ 137 Amon Gordon RC 2.00 .75
❑ 138 Darius Watts RC 4.00 1.50
❑ 139 Junior Siavii RC 4.00 1.50
❑ 140 Igor Olshansky RC 4.00 1.50
❑ 141 Mewelde Moore RC 4.00 1.50
❑ 142 Nathan Vasher RC 5.00 2.00
❑ 143 Randy Starks RC 3.00 1.25
❑ 144 Isaac Sopoaga RC 2.00 .75
❑ 145 Drew Henson RC 4.00 1.50
❑ 146 Erik Coleman RC 4.00 1.50
❑ 147 Robert Kent RC 2.00 .75
❑ 148 Jammal Lord RC 4.00 1.50
❑ 149 Richard Seigler RC 3.00 1.25
❑ 150 Niko Koutouvides RC 3.00 1.25
❑ 151 Brandon Miree RC 3.00 1.25
❑ 152 Dunta Robinson RC 4.00 1.50
❑ 153 Courtney Anderson RC 3.00 1.25
❑ 154 Bruce Perry RC 4.00 1.50
❑ 155 Shaun Phillips RC 3.00 1.25
❑ 156 Greg Jones RC 4.00 1.50
❑ 157 Tank Johnson RC 3.00 1.25
❑ 158 Dwan Edwards RC 2.00 .75
❑ 159 Julius Jones RC 12.00 5.00
❑ 160 Chad Lavalais RC 3.00 1.25
❑ 161 Tim Anderson RC 4.00 1.50
❑ 162 Jarrett Payton RC 4.00 1.50
❑ 163 Matt Ware RC 4.00 1.50
❑ 164 DeAngelo Hall RC 5.00 2.00
❑ 165 Ben Hartsock RC 4.00 1.50
❑ 166 Keith Smith RC 3.00 1.25
❑ 167 Michael Jenkins RC 4.00 1.50
❑ 168 Quincy Wilson RC 3.00 1.25
❑ 169 Dontarrious Thomas RC 4.00 1.50
❑ 170 Tony Hargrove RC 3.00 1.25
❑ 171 Ben Watson RC 4.00 1.50
❑ 172 Triandos Luke RC 4.00 1.50
❑ 173 Kellen Winslow RC 8.00 3.00
❑ 174 Patrick Crayton RC 4.00 1.50
❑ 175 Devard Darling RC 4.00 1.50
❑ 176 Shawntae Spencer RC 4.00 1.50
❑ 177 Will Smith RC 4.00 1.50
❑ 178 Darrion Scott RC 4.00 1.50
❑ 179 Wes Welker RC 12.00 5.00
❑ 180 Ryan Dinwiddie RC 3.00 1.25
❑ 181 Rod Davis RC 2.00 .75
❑ 182 Casey Clausen RC 4.00 1.50
❑ 183 Clarence Moore RC 4.00 1.50
❑ 184 D.J. Hackett RC 3.00 1.25
❑ 185 Devery Henderson RC 4.00 1.50
❑ 186 Sean Jones RC 3.00 1.25
❑ 187 Bruce Thornton RC 2.00 .75
❑ 188 Tatum Bell RC 8.00 3.00
❑ 189 Tim Euhus RC 4.00 1.50
❑ 190 John Standeford RC 3.00 1.25
❑ 191 Reggie Torbor RC 3.00 1.25
❑ 192 Rashaun Woods RC 4.00 1.50
❑ 193 Jason Shivers RC 2.00 .75
❑ 194 Ahmad Carroll RC 4.00 1.50
❑ 195 Keyaron Fox RC 3.00 1.25
❑ 196 Von Hutchins RC 3.00 1.25
❑ 197 Marcus Tubbs RC 4.00 1.50
❑ 198 Daryl Smith RC 4.00 1.50
❑ 199 Robert Gallery RC 4.00 1.50
❑ 200 Marquis Cooper RC 3.00 1.25
❑ 201 Bernard Berrian RC 5.00 2.00
❑ 202 Derrick Strait RC 4.00 1.50
❑ 203 Travis LaBoy RC 4.00 1.50
❑ 204 Caleb Miller RC 3.00 1.25
❑ 205 Michael Clayton RC 8.00 3.00
❑ 206 Will Poole RC 4.00 1.50
❑ 207 Derrick Hamilton RC 3.00 1.25
❑ 208 Glenn Earl RC 3.00 1.25
❑ 209 Donnell Washington RC 4.00 1.50
❑ 210 Nate Lawrie RC 3.00 1.25
❑ 211 Keiwan Ratliff RC 3.00 1.25
❑ 212 Luke McCown RC 4.00 1.50
❑ 213 Joey Thomas RC 4.00 1.50
❑ 214 Shawn Andrews RC 4.00 1.50
❑ 215 Derrick Ward RC 4.00 1.50
❑ 216 Reggie Williams RC 5.00 2.00
❑ 217 Rod Rutherford RC 3.00 1.25
❑ 218 Michael Gaines RC 3.00 1.25
❑ 219 Will Allen RC 4.00 1.50
❑ 220 J.P. Losman RC 8.00 3.00
❑ 221 Roy Williams AU/199 RC 120.00 60.00
❑ 222 Kevin Jones AU/199 RC 100.00 40.00
❑ 223 Philip Rivers AU/199 RC 250.00125.00
❑ 224 Steven Jackson AU/199 RC 250.00 150.00
❑ 225 Eli Manning AU/199 RC 350.00 200.00
❑ 226 Cody Pickett AU D RC 20.00 7.50
❑ 227 P.K. Sam AU D RC 15.00 6.00
❑ 228 Maurice Mann AU D RC 15.00 6.00
❑ 229 Andy Hall AU D RC 15.00 6.00
❑ 230 Chris Perry AU D RC 20.00 7.50
❑ 231 Ernest Wilford AU C RC 20.00 7.50
❑ 232 Kenechi Udeze AU D RC 20.00 7.50
❑ 233 Michael Boulware AU D RC 20.00 7.50
❑ 234 B.J. Symons AU D RC 20.00 7.50
❑ 235 Jared Lorenzen AU D RC 15.00 6.00
❑ 236 Matt Mauck AU D RC 20.00 7.50
❑ 237 Carlos Francis AU D RC 15.00 6.00
❑ 238 Michael Turner AU D RC 50.00 25.00
❑ 239 Lee Evans AU B RC 40.00 20.00
❑ 240 Jerricho Cotchery AU D RC 20.00 7.50
❑ 241 John Navarre AU D RC 20.00 7.50
❑ 242 Jonathan Vilma AU D RC 25.00 10.00
❑ 243 Josh Harris AU D RC 20.00 7.50
❑ 244 Jeff Smoker AU C RC 20.00 7.50
❑ 245 Jamaar Taylor AU D RC 20.00 7.50

2005 Bowman Chrome

❑ COMP.SET w/o AU's (220) 100.00 40.00
❑ COMP.SET w/o RC's (110) 30.00 12.50
❑ ROOK.AU GROUP A ODDS 1:381 H, 1:1011 R
❑ ROOK.AU GROUP B ODDS 1:156 H, 1:449 R
❑ ROOK.AU GROUP C ODDS 1:318 H, 1:899 R
❑ ROOK.AU GROUP D ODDS 1:296 H, 1:899 R
❑ ROOK.AU GROUP E ODDS 1:281 H, 1:809 R
❑ ROOK.AU GROUP F ODDS 1:132 H, 404 R
❑ ROOK.AU GROUP G ODDS 1:39 H, 1:108 R
❑ ROOKIE AU/199 ODDS 1:685 H, 1:1348 R
❑ UNPRICED PRINT.PLATE 1/1 ODDS 1:975 H
❑ 1 Peyton Manning 1.50 .60
❑ 2 Priest Holmes 1.00 .40
❑ 3 Anquan Boldin .60 .25
❑ 4 Michael Vick 1.50 .60
❑ 5 Drew Brees 1.00 .40
❑ 6 Terrell Owens 1.00 .40
❑ 7 Curtis Martin 1.00 .40
❑ 8 Tom Brady 2.50 1.00
❑ 9 Maurice Carthon CO .60 .25
❑ 10 Brett Favre 2.50 1.00
❑ 11 Marshall Faulk 1.00 .40
❑ 12 Corey Dillon .60 .25
❑ 13 Julius Jones 1.25 .50
❑ 14 Jamal Lewis 1.00 .40
❑ 15 Keary Colbert .60 .25
❑ 16 Joey Harrington 1.00 .40
❑ 17 Domanick Davis .60 .25
❑ 18 Eli Manning 2.00 .75
❑ 19 Brad Childress CO .60 .25
❑ 20 Steve McNair 1.00 .40
❑ 21 Plaxico Burress .60 .25
❑ 22 Chad Pennington 1.00 .40
❑ 23 Patrick Ramsey .60 .25
❑ 24 Brian Griese .60 .25
❑ 25 Matt Hasselbeck .60 .25
❑ 26 Chris Chambers .60 .25
❑ 27 Marc Bulger 1.00 .40
❑ 28 Jake Delhomme 1.00 .40
❑ 29 Shaun Alexander 1.25 .50
❑ 30 Laveranues Coles .60 .25
❑ 31 A.J. Feeley .60 .25
❑ 32 Ashley Lelie .60 .25
❑ 33 Deuce McAllister 1.00 .40
❑ 34 Chris Brown .60 .25
❑ 35 Nate Burleson .60 .25
❑ 36 Darrell Jackson .60 .25
❑ 37 Lee Evans .60 .25
❑ 38 Jeremy Shockey 1.00 .40
❑ 39 Muhsin Muhammad .60 .25
❑ 40 Deion Branch .60 .25
❑ 41 DeShaun Foster .60 .25
❑ 42 Reggie Wayne .60 .25
❑ 43 Michael Jenkins .60 .25
❑ 44 Andre Johnson .60 .25
❑ 45 Javon Walker .60 .25
❑ 46 Joe Horn .60 .25
❑ 47 Fred Taylor .60 .25
❑ 48 Tony Gonzalez .60 .25
❑ 49 J.P. Losman 1.00 .40
❑ 50 Clinton Portis 1.00 .40
❑ 51 Randy Moss 1.00 .40
❑ 52 Jake Plummer .60 .25
❑ 53 Tiki Barber 1.00 .40
❑ 54 Edgerrin James 1.00 .40
❑ 55 Jerome Bettis 1.00 .40
❑ 56 Brandon Lloyd .50 .20
❑ 57 Romeo Crennel CO 1.00 .40
❑ 58 Antonio Gates 1.00 .40
❑ 59 Donovan McNabb 1.25 .50
❑ 60 Drew Bennett .60 .25
❑ 61 David Carr 1.00 .40
❑ 62 Trent Green .60 .25
❑ 63 Drew Bledsoe 1.00 .40
❑ 64 Donte Stallworth .60 .25
❑ 65 Alge Crumpler .60 .25
❑ 66 Jason Witten .60 .25
❑ 67 Thomas Jones .60 .25
❑ 68 Rex Grossman .60 .25
❑ 69 LaMont Jordan 1.00 .40
❑ 70 Kurt Warner .60 .25
❑ 71 Ahman Green 1.00 .40
❑ 72 Ben Roethlisberger 2.50 1.00
❑ 73 Mike Nolan CO 1.00 .40
❑ 74 Brian Westbrook .60 .25
❑ 75 Carson Palmer 1.00 .40
❑ 76 Stephen Davis .60 .25
❑ 77 Jonathan Vilma .60 .25
❑ 78 Willis McGahee 1.00 .40
❑ 79 Rudi Johnson .60 .25
❑ 80 Jerry Porter .60 .25
❑ 81 Charles Rogers .60 .25
❑ 82 Dwight Freeney .60 .25
❑ 83 Tim Lewis CO .50 .20
❑ 84 Aaron Brooks .60 .25
❑ 85 Kyle Boller .60 .25
❑ 86 Isaac Bruce .60 .25
❑ 87 Chad Johnson 1.00 .40
❑ 88 Kevin Jones 1.00 .40
❑ 89 Eric Moulds .60 .25
❑ 90 Sean Taylor .60 .25
❑ 91 Chris Perry .60 .25
❑ 92 Kerry Collins .60 .25
❑ 93 Steven Jackson 1.25 .50
❑ 94 LaDainian Tomlinson 1.25 .50
❑ 95 Torry Holt 1.00 .40
❑ 96 Lee Suggs .60 .25
❑ 97 Santana Moss .60 .25
❑ 98 Hines Ward 1.00 .40

❑ 99 Daunte Culpepper 1.00 .40
❑ 100 Travis Henry .60 .25
❑ 101 Ricky Williams .60 .25
❑ 102 Roy Williams WR 1.00 .40
❑ 103 Tatum Bell .60 .25
❑ 104 Dante Hall .60 .25
❑ 105 Larry Fitzgerald 1.00 .40
❑ 106 Marvin Harrison 1.00 .40
❑ 107 Byron Leftwich 1.00 .40
❑ 108 T.J. Houshmandzadeh .50 .20
❑ 109 Michael Clayton 1.00 .40
❑ 110 Ted Cottrell CO .50 .20
❑ 111 Carlos Rogers RC 5.00 2.00
❑ 112 Kyle Orton RC 4.00 1.50
❑ 113 Marion Barber RC 6.00 2.50
❑ 114 Mark Bradley RC 4.00 1.50
❑ 115 Travis Johnson RC 3.00 1.25
❑ 116 Antrel Rolle RC 4.00 1.50
❑ 117 Jason Campbell RC 6.00 2.50
❑ 118 Justin Miller RC 3.00 1.25
❑ 119 J.J. Arrington RC 4.00 1.50
❑ 120 Marcus Spears RC 4.00 1.50
❑ 121 Vincent Jackson RC 4.00 1.50
❑ 122 Erasmus James RC 4.00 1.50
❑ 123 Heath Miller RC 8.00 3.00
❑ 124 Eric Shelton RC 4.00 1.50
❑ 125 Cedric Benson RC 10.00 4.00
❑ 126 Mark Clayton RC 4.00 1.50
❑ 127 Anthony Davis RC 3.00 1.25
❑ 128 Charlie Frye RC 4.00 1.50
❑ 129 Fred Gibson RC 3.00 1.25
❑ 130 Reggie Brown RC 4.00 1.50
❑ 131 Andrew Walter RC 4.00 1.50
❑ 132 Adam Jones RC 4.00 1.50
❑ 133 David Greene RC 4.00 1.50
❑ 134 Maurice Clarett 4.00 1.50
❑ 135 Roscoe Parrish RC 4.00 1.50
❑ 136 Chris Henry RC 4.00 1.50
❑ 137 Mike Nugent RC 4.00 1.50
❑ 138 Kevin Burnett RC 4.00 1.50
❑ 139 Matt Roth RC 4.00 1.50
❑ 140 Barrett Ruud RC 4.00 1.50
❑ 141 Kirk Morrison RC 4.00 1.50
❑ 142 Brock Berlin RC 3.00 1.25
❑ 143 Bryant McFadden RC 4.00 1.50
❑ 144 Scott Starks RC 3.00 1.25
❑ 145 Stanford Routt RC 3.00 1.25
❑ 146 Oshiomogho Atogwe RC 3.00 1.25
❑ 147 Jovan Witherspoon RC 2.00 .75
❑ 148 Boomer Grigsby RC 4.00 1.50
❑ 149 Lance Mitchell RC 3.00 1.25
❑ 150 Darryl Blackstock RC 3.00 1.25
❑ 151 Ellis Hobbs RC 4.00 1.50
❑ 152 James Kilian RC 4.00 1.50
❑ 153 Willie Parker 10.00 4.00
❑ 154 Justin Tuck RC 4.00 1.50
❑ 155 Luis Castillo RC 4.00 1.50
❑ 156 Paris Warren RC 3.00 1.25
❑ 157 Corey Webster RC 4.00 1.50
❑ 158 Tab Perry RC 4.00 1.50
❑ 159 Rian Wallace RC 3.00 1.25
❑ 160 Joel Dreessen RC 3.00 1.25
❑ 161 Khalif Barnes RC 3.00 1.25
❑ 162 David Pollack RC 4.00 1.50
❑ 163 Zach Tuiasosopo RC 2.00 .75
❑ 164 Ryan Riddle RC 2.00 .75
❑ 165 Travis Daniels RC 3.00 1.25
❑ 166 Eric King RC 3.00 1.25
❑ 167 Justin Green RC 4.00 1.50
❑ 168 Manuel White RC 3.00 1.25
❑ 169 Jordan Beck RC 3.00 1.25
❑ 170 Lofa Tatupu RC 5.00 2.00
❑ 171 Will Peoples RC 3.00 1.25
❑ 172 Chad Friehauf RC 3.00 1.25
❑ 173 Brady Poppinga RC 4.00 1.50
❑ 174 Anttaj Hawthorne RC 3.00 1.25
❑ 175 Nick Collins RC 4.00 1.50
❑ 176 Craig Ochs RC 3.00 1.25
❑ 177 Billy Bajema RC 3.00 1.25
❑ 178 Jon Goldsberry RC 4.00 1.50
❑ 179 Jared Newberry RC 3.00 1.25
❑ 180 Odell Thurman RC 4.00 1.50
❑ 181 Kelvin Hayden RC 3.00 1.25
❑ 182 Jamaal Brimmer RC 2.00 .75
❑ 183 Jonathan Babineaux RC 3.00 1.25
❑ 184 Bo Scaife RC 3.00 1.25
❑ 185 Bryan Randall RC 3.00 1.25
❑ 186 James Butler RC 3.00 1.25
❑ 187 Harry Williams RC 3.00 1.25
❑ 188 Leroy Hill RC 4.00 1.50
❑ 189 Josh Bullocks RC 4.00 1.50
❑ 190 Alfred Fincher RC 3.00 1.25
❑ 191 Antonio Perkins RC 3.00 1.25
❑ 192 Bobby Purify RC 3.00 1.25
❑ 193 Darrent Williams RC 4.00 1.50
❑ 194 Darian Durant RC 4.00 1.60
❑ 195 Fred Amey RC 3.00 1.25
❑ 196 Ronald Bartell RC 3.00 1.25
❑ 197 Kerry Rhodes RC 4.00 1.50
❑ 198 Jerome Carter RC 3.00 1.25
❑ 199 Roddy White RC 4.00 1.50
❑ 200 Nehemiah Broughton RC 3.00 1.25
❑ 201 Keron Henry RC 2.00 .75
❑ 202 Jerome Collins RC 3.00 1.25
❑ 203 Trent Cole RC 4.00 1.50
❑ 204 Alphonso Hodge RC 2.00 .75
❑ 205 Marviel Underwood RC 3.00 1.25
❑ 206 Marlin Jackson RC 4.00 1.50
❑ 207 Madison Hedgecock RC 4.00 1.50
❑ 208 Chris Spencer RC 4.00 1.50
❑ 209 Vincent Fuller RC 3.00 1.25
❑ 210 Marcus Maxwell RC 3.00 1.25
❑ 211 Dustin Fox RC 4.00 1.50
❑ 212 Timmy Chang RC 3.00 1.25
❑ 213 Walter Reyes RC 3.00 1.25
❑ 214 Donte Nicholson RC 4.00 1.50
❑ 215 Stanley Wilson RC 3.00 1.25
❑ 216 Dan Cody RC 4.00 1.50
❑ 217 Alex Barron RC 2.00 .75
❑ 218 Taylor Stubblefield RC 2.00 .75
❑ 219 Shaun Cody RC 4.00 1.50
❑ 220 Steve Savoy RC 2.00 .75
❑ 221 Aaron Rodgers AU/199 RC 125.00 75.00
❑ 222 Alex Smith QB AU/199 RC 120.00 60.00
❑ 223 Bray.Edwards AU/199 RC 150.00 75.00
❑ 224 Cadill.Williams AU/199 RC 100.00 40.00
❑ 225 Mike Williams AU/199 50.00 20.00
❑ 226 Ronnie Brown AU/199 RC 120.00 50.00
❑ 227 T.Williamson AU/199 RC 50.00 20.00
❑ 228 Dante Ridgeway AU B RC 12.00 5.00
❑ 229 Channing Crowder AU G RC 15.00 6.00
❑ 230 Chase Lyman AU E RC 12.00 5.00
❑ 231 Courtney Roby AU F RC 15.00 6.00
❑ 232 Damien Nash AU G RC 15.00 6.00
❑ 233 Dan Orlovsky AU C RC 20.00 8.00
❑ 234 Fabian Washington AU B RC 20.00 7.50
❑ 235 Shawne Merriman AU B RC 40.00 20.00
❑ 236 Cedric Houston AU G RC 15.00 7.50
❑ 237 Alex Smith TE AU D RC 15.00 6.00
❑ 238 Brandon Jones AU B RC 15.00 6.00
❑ 239 Alvin Pearman AU G RC 15.00 6.00
❑ 240 Derek Anderson AU C RC 40.00 20.00
❑ 241 J.R. Russell AU G RC 12.00 5.00
❑ 242 Jerome Mathis AU F RC 12.00 5.00
❑ 243 Josh Davis AU A RC 15.00 6.00
❑ 244 Kay-Jay Harris AU G RC 12.00 5.00
❑ 245 Rasheed Marshall AU F RC 12.00 5.00
❑ 246 Matt Jones AU/199 RC 60.00 25.00
❑ 247 Chad Owens AU G RC 15.00 6.00
❑ 248 Larry Brackins AU A RC 15.00 6.00
❑ 249 Matt Cassel AU G RC 25.00 12.50
❑ 250 Noah Herron AU G RC 15.00 6.00
❑ 251 Roydell Williams AU G RC 15.00 6.00
❑ 252 Ryan Fitzpatrick AU F RC 15.00 6.00
❑ 253 Derrick Johnson AU E RC 25.00 10.00
❑ 254 DeMarcus Ware AU D RC 30.00 15.00
❑ 255 Brandon Jacobs AU A RC 50.00 30.00
❑ 256 Craig Bragg AU G RC 12.00 5.00
❑ 257 Ryan Moats AU G RC 25.00 12.50
❑ 258 Stefan LeFors AU G RC 15.00 6.00
❑ 259 Frank Gore AU B RC 80.00 50.00
❑ DSB Bogut/A.Smith QB AU/100 200.00 100.00

2006 Bowman Chrome

❑ 1 Devin Aromashodu RC 1.50 .60
❑ 2 Daniel Bullocks RC 2.00 .75
❑ 3 Winston Justice RC 2.00 .75
❑ 4 Lawrence Vickers RC 1.50 .60
❑ 5 Bernard Pollard RC 1.50 .60
❑ 6 Abdul Hodge RC 2.00 .75
❑ 7 Jovon Bouknight RC 1.50 .60
❑ 8 Wali Lundy RC 2.00 .75
❑ 9 Jonathan Orr RC 1.50 .60
❑ 10 Gerald Riggs RC 2.00 .75
❑ 11 Chris Gocong RC 1.50 .60
❑ 12 David Kirtman RC 1.50 .60
❑ 13 Quinn Sypniewski RC 1.50 .60
❑ 14 Richard Marshall RC 1.50 .60
❑ 15 Darryl Tapp RC 1.50 .60
❑ 16 Charles Davis RC 1.50 .60
❑ 17 Tim Massaquoi RC 1.50 .60
❑ 18 DeMario Minter RC 1.50 .60
❑ 19 Hank Baskett RC 2.00 .75
❑ 20 Andre Hall RC 1.50 .60
❑ 21 Cody Hodges RC 1.50 .60
❑ 22 Greg Lee RC 1.50 .60
❑ 23 Danieal Manning RC 2.00 .75
❑ 24 Jason Hatcher RC 1.50 .60
❑ 25 Ben Obomanu RC 1.50 .60
❑ 26 Dusty Dvoracek RC 2.00 .75
❑ 27 Domenik Hixon RC 1.50 .60
❑ 28 Josh Betts RC 1.50 .60
❑ 29 Marques Colston RC 8.00 3.00
❑ 30 P.J. Pope RC 1.50 .60
❑ 31 Gabe Watson RC 1.50 .60
❑ 32 Alan Zemaitis RC 2.00 .75
❑ 33 Jeff King RC 1.50 .60
❑ 34 Damien Rhodes RC 1.50 .60
❑ 35 Orien Harris RC 1.50 .60
❑ 36 David Anderson RC 1.50 .60
❑ 37 Garrett Mills RC 2.00 .75
❑ 38 Anthony Schlegel RC 1.50 .60
❑ 39 Omar Gaither RC 1.50 .60
❑ 40 Freddie Keiaho RC 1.50 .60
❑ 41 J.J. Outlaw RC 1.50 .60
❑ 42 Tony Scheffler RC 2.00 .75
❑ 43 Dee Webb RC 1.50 .60
❑ 44 Drew Olson RC 1.50 .60
❑ 45 Martin Nance RC 1.50 .60
❑ 46 Ko Simpson RC 1.50 .60
❑ 47 Jesse Mahelona RC 1.50 .60
❑ 48 Owen Daniels RC 2.00 .75
❑ 49 Delanie Walker RC 1.50 .60
❑ 50 Eric Smith RC 1.50 .60
❑ 51 Darrell Hackney RC 1.50 .60
❑ 52 Freddie Roach RC 1.50 .60
❑ 53 James Anderson RC 1.00 .40
❑ 54 Anthony Smith RC 2.50 1.00
❑ 55 Gerris Wilkinson RC 1.00 .40
❑ 56 Tamba Hali RC 4.00 1.50
❑ 57 Jerome Harrison RC 4.00 1.50
❑ 58 Jason Allen RC 4.00 1.50
❑ 59 Brodrick Bunkley RC 4.00 1.50
❑ 60 Bobby Carpenter RC 4.00 1.50
❑ 61 Johnathan Joseph RC 3.00 1.25
❑ 62 Travis Wilson RC 4.00 1.50
❑ 63 Reggie McNeal RC 3.00 1.25
❑ 64 Haloti Ngata RC 4.00 1.50
❑ 65 Manny Lawson RC 4.00 1.50
❑ 66 Donte Whitner RC 4.00 1.50
❑ 67 Derek Hagan RC 4.00 1.50
❑ 68 Devin Hester RC 8.00 3.00
❑ 69 Jeremy Bloom RC 3.00 1.25
❑ 70 Ashton Youboty RC 4.00 1.50
❑ 71 Kamerion Wimbley RC 4.00 1.50
❑ 72 Charlie Whitehurst RC 4.00 1.50
❑ 73 Darnell Bing RC 4.00 1.50
❑ 74 Adam Jennings RC 3.00 1.25
❑ 75 Tim Day RC 3.00 1.25
❑ 76 Jeff Webb RC 3.00 1.25
❑ 77 D.J. Shockley RC 4.00 1.50
❑ 78 Marcus Vick RC 3.00 1.25
❑ 79 Thomas Howard RC 4.00 1.50
❑ 80 Todd Watkins RC 3.00 1.25
❑ 81 Davin Joseph RC 3.00 1.25
❑ 82 Pat Watkins RC 4.00 1.50
❑ 83 Jon Alston RC 4.00 1.50
❑ 84 Ernie Sims RC 5.00 2.00
❑ 85 D'Qwell Jackson RC 3.00 1.25
❑ 86 Corey Bramlet RC 3.00 1.25
❑ 87 Antonio Cromartie RC 4.00 1.50

❑ 88 A.J. Nicholson RC	2.00	.75
❑ 89 Kevin McMahan RC	3.00	1.25
❑ 90 J.D. Runnels RC	3.00	1.25
❑ 91 Nate Salley RC	3.00	1.25
❑ 92 Matt Shelton RC	4.00	1.50
❑ 93 Brett Basanez RC	4.00	1.50
❑ 94 Rocky McIntosh RC	4.00	1.50
❑ 95 Anthony Mix RC	3.00	1.25
❑ 96 Jimmy Williams RC	4.00	1.50
❑ 97 Marcus McNeill RC	3.00	1.25
❑ 98 DeMeco Ryans RC	5.00	2.00
❑ 99 Dwayne Slay RC	3.00	1.25
❑ 100 John David Washington RC	3.00	1.25
❑ 101 P.J. Daniels RC	3.00	1.25
❑ 102 Kelly Jennings RC	4.00	1.50
❑ 103 John McCargo RC	3.00	1.25
❑ 104 Paul Pinegar RC	3.00	1.25
❑ 105 Ray Edwards RC	3.00	1.25
❑ 106 Elvis Dumervil RC	2.00	.75
❑ 107 Travis Lulay RC	3.00	1.25
❑ 108 Bennie Brazell RC	3.00	1.25
❑ 109 Dominique Byrd RC	3.00	1.25
❑ 110 Nick Mangold RC	3.00	1.25
❑ 111 Plaxico Burress	.60	.25
❑ 112 Shaun Alexander	1.00	.40
❑ 113 Muhsin Muhammad	.60	.25
❑ 114 Jake Plummer	.60	.25
❑ 115 Deuce McAllister	.60	.25
❑ 116 T.J. Houshmandzadeh	.60	.25
❑ 117 Carson Palmer	1.00	.40
❑ 118 Willis McGahee	1.00	.40
❑ 119 Terrell Owens	1.00	.40
❑ 120 Fred Taylor	.60	.25
❑ 121 Dante Hall	.60	.25
❑ 122 Brad Johnson	.60	.25
❑ 123 Reggie Wayne	.60	.25
❑ 124 DeShaun Foster	.60	.25
❑ 125 Tony Gonzalez	.60	.25
❑ 126 Javon Walker	.60	.25
❑ 127 Marc Bulger	.60	.25
❑ 128 LaDainian Tomlinson	1.25	.50
❑ 129 Byron Leftwich	.60	.25
❑ 130 Dwight Freeney	.60	.25
❑ 131 Kevin Jones	1.00	.40
❑ 132 Hines Ward	1.00	.40
❑ 133 Randy Moss	1.00	.40
❑ 134 Edgerrin James	1.00	.40
❑ 135 Ahman Green	.60	.25
❑ 136 Steven Jackson	1.00	.40
❑ 137 Ben Roethlisberger	1.50	.60
❑ 138 Daunte Culpepper	1.00	.40
❑ 139 Santana Moss	.60	.25
❑ 140 Jonathan Vilma	.60	.25
❑ 141 Gary Kubiak CO	.60	.25
❑ 142 Marvin Harrison	1.00	.40
❑ 143 Trent Green	.60	.25
❑ 144 Chris Chambers	.60	.25
❑ 145 Chris Brown	.60	.25
❑ 146 Eli Manning	1.25	.50
❑ 147 Corey Dillon	.60	.25
❑ 148 Anquan Boldin	.60	.25
❑ 149 Donovan McNabb	1.00	.40
❑ 150 Drew Bennett	.50	.20
❑ 151 Jason Witten	.60	.25
❑ 152 Eric Moulds	.60	.25
❑ 153 Billy Volek	.60	.25
❑ 154 Chris Cooley	.50	.20
❑ 155 Larry Johnson	1.25	.50
❑ 156 Willie Parker	1.25	.50
❑ 157 Cadillac Williams	1.00	.40
❑ 158 Philip Rivers	1.00	.40
❑ 159 Reuben Droughns	.60	.25
❑ 160 Joey Galloway	.60	.25
❑ 161 Lee Evans	.60	.25
❑ 162 Jamal Lewis	.60	.25
❑ 163 Brett Favre	2.00	.75
❑ 164 Clinton Portis	1.00	.40
❑ 165 Rod Marinelli CO	.60	.25
❑ 166 Tom Brady	1.50	.60
❑ 167 Torry Holt	.60	.25
❑ 168 Rudi Johnson	.60	.25
❑ 169 Priest Holmes	.60	.25
❑ 170 Tatum Bell	.60	.25
❑ 171 Jeremy Shockey	1.00	.40
❑ 172 Shawne Merriman	.60	.25
❑ 173 Alge Crumpler	.60	.25
❑ 174 Marion Barber	.60	.25
❑ 175 Steve Smith	1.00	.40
❑ 176 Mike McCarthy CO	.60	.25
❑ 177 David Carr	.60	.25
❑ 178 Julius Jones	1.00	.40
❑ 179 Chad Johnson	.60	.25
❑ 180 Curtis Martin	1.00	.40
❑ 181 Peyton Manning	1.50	.60
❑ 182 LaMont Jordan	.60	.25
❑ 183 Tiki Barber	1.00	.40
❑ 184 Darrell Jackson	.60	.25
❑ 185 J.P. Losman	.60	.25
❑ 186 Drew Brees	1.00	.40
❑ 187 Isaac Bruce	.60	.25
❑ 188 Drew Bledsoe	1.00	.40
❑ 189 Roy Williams WR	1.00	.40
❑ 190 Donte Stallworth	.60	.25
❑ 191 Odell Thurman	.50	.20
❑ 192 Chester Taylor	.60	.25
❑ 193 Randy McMichael	.50	.20
❑ 194 Larry Fitzgerald	1.00	.40
❑ 195 Charlie Frye	.60	.25
❑ 196 Keary Colbert	.50	.20
❑ 197 Patrick Ramsey	.60	.25
❑ 198 Mark Clayton	1.00	.40
❑ 199 Michael Jenkins	.60	.25
❑ 200 Jake Delhomme	.60	.25
❑ 201 Aaron Rodgers	1.00	.40
❑ 202 Andre Johnson	.60	.25
❑ 203 Matt Hasselbeck	.60	.25
❑ 204 Reggie Brown	.75	.30
❑ 205 Warrick Dunn	.60	.25
❑ 206 Kurt Warner	.60	.25
❑ 207 Antonio Gates	1.00	.40
❑ 208 Terry Glenn	.60	.25
❑ 209 Steve McNair	.60	.25
❑ 210 Alex Smith QB	1.00	.40
❑ 211 Joe Horn	.60	.25
❑ 212 Domanick Davis	.60	.25
❑ 213 Deion Branch	.60	.25
❑ 214 Todd Heap	.60	.25
❑ 215 Chad Pennington	.60	.25
❑ 216 Brandon Lloyd	.60	.25
❑ 217 Rod Smith	.60	.25
❑ 218 Ronnie Brown	1.00	.40
❑ 219 Braylon Edwards	1.00	.40
❑ 220 Michael Vick	1.00	.40
❑ 221 Vince Young RC	20.00	8.00
❑ 222 Jay Cutler RC	12.00	5.00
❑ 223 Reggie Bush RC	25.00	10.00
❑ 224 Matt Leinart RC	12.00	5.00
❑ 225 Vernon Davis RC	8.00	3.00
❑ 226 A.J. Hawk RC	8.00	3.00
❑ 227 Santonio Holmes RC	8.00	3.00
❑ 228 DeAngelo Williams RC	10.00	4.00
❑ 229 LenDale White RC	8.00	3.00
❑ 230 Sinorice Moss RC	4.00	1.50
❑ 231 Joseph Addai RC	12.00	5.00
❑ 232 Mike Bell RC	4.00	1.50
❑ 233 Will Blackmon RC	3.00	1.25
❑ 234 Brian Calhoun RC	4.00	1.50
❑ 235 Kellen Clemens RC	6.00	2.50
❑ 236 Brodie Croyle RC	10.00	4.00
❑ 237 Maurice Drew RC	10.00	4.00
❑ 238 Anthony Fasano RC	4.00	1.50
❑ 239 D'Brickashaw Ferguson RC	4.00	1.50
❑ 240 Quinton Ganther RC	3.00	1.25
❑ 241 Bruce Gradkowski RC	6.00	2.50
❑ 242 Skyler Green RC	4.00	1.50
❑ 243 Chad Greenway RC	4.00	1.50
❑ 244 Marques Hagans RC	3.00	1.25
❑ 245 Michael Huff RC	5.00	2.00
❑ 246 Cedric Humes RC	4.00	1.50
❑ 247 Tarvaris Jackson RC	6.00	2.50
❑ 248 Omar Jacobs RC	3.00	1.25
❑ 249 Greg Jennings RC	6.00	2.50
❑ 250 Mathias Kiwanuka RC	5.00	2.00
❑ 251 Joe Klopfenstein RC	3.00	1.25
❑ 252 Marcedes Lewis RC	4.00	1.50
❑ 253 Brandon Marshall RC	4.00	1.50
❑ 254 Ingle Martin RC	4.00	1.50
❑ 255 Dontrell Moore RC	3.00	1.25
❑ 256 Jerious Norwood RC	6.00	2.50
❑ 257 Leonard Pope RC	4.00	1.50
❑ 258 Willie Reid RC	4.00	1.50
❑ 259 Michael Robinson RC	4.00	1.50
❑ 260 Brad Smith RC	4.00	1.50
❑ 261 Maurice Stovall RC	4.00	1.50
❑ 262 David Thomas RC	4.00	1.50
❑ 263 Leon Washington RC	6.00	2.50
❑ 264 Brandon Williams RC	4.00	1.50
❑ 265 Demetrius Williams RC	4.00	1.50
❑ 266 Tye Hill RC	4.00	1.50
❑ 267 Mike Hass RC	4.00	1.50
❑ 268 Jason Avant RC	4.00	1.50
❑ 269 Chad Jackson RC	4.00	1.50
❑ 270 Laurence Maroney RC	10.00	4.00
❑ 271 Anwar Phillips RC	3.00	1.25
❑ 272 David Kirtman RC	3.00	1.25
❑ 273 Roman Harper RC	3.00	1.25
❑ 274 Spencer Havner RC	3.00	1.25
❑ 275 Erik Meyer RC	3.00	1.25

2007 Bowman Chrome

❑ COMPLETE SET (220)	100.00	40.00
❑ COMP.SHORT SET (55)	20.00	8.00
❑ COMP.VET SET (110)	15.00	6.00
❑ 1-55 INSERTED IN BOWMAN PACKS		
❑ BC1 Kenny Irons RC	1.50	.60
❑ BC2 David Clowney RC	1.50	.60
❑ BC3 Courtney Taylor RC	1.25	.50
❑ BC4 Amobi Okoye RC	1.50	.60
❑ BC5 Jamaal Anderson RC	1.25	.50
❑ BC6 Adam Carriker RC	1.25	.50
❑ BC7 Jarvis Moss RC	1.50	.60
❑ BC8 Anthony Spencer RC	1.50	.60
❑ BC9 Jon Beason RC	1.50	.60
❑ BC10 Darrelle Revis RC	1.50	.60
❑ BC11 Aaron Ross RC	1.50	.60
❑ BC12 Reggie Nelson RC	1.25	.50
❑ BC13 Michael Griffin RC	1.50	.60
❑ BC14 Brandon Meriweather RC	1.50	.60
❑ BC15 Tyler Palko RC	1.50	.60
❑ BC16 Jared Zabransky RC	1.50	.60
❑ BC17 Lester Ricard RC	1.25	.50
❑ BC18 Darius Walker RC	1.50	.60
❑ BC19 Ahmad Bradshaw RC	2.00	.75
❑ BC20 Thomas Clayton RC	1.25	.50
❑ BC21 Rhema McKnight RC	1.25	.50
❑ BC22 Scott Chandler RC	1.25	.50
❑ BC23 Matt Spaeth RC	1.50	.60
❑ BC24 Ben Patrick RC	1.25	.50
❑ BC25 Clark Harris RC	1.50	.60
❑ BC26 Martrez Milner RC	1.25	.50
❑ BC27 Joe Newton RC	1.25	.50
❑ BC28 DeMarcus Tank Tyler RC	1.25	.50
❑ BC29 Justin Harrell RC	1.50	.60
❑ BC30 LaMarr Woodley RC	1.50	.60
❑ BC31 David Harris RC	1.25	.50
❑ BC32 Buster Davis RC	1.25	.50
❑ BC33 Rufus Alexander RC	1.50	.60
❑ BC34 Earl Everett RC	1.25	.50
❑ BC35 Stewart Bradley RC	1.50	.60
❑ BC36 Prescott Burgess RC	1.25	.50
❑ BC37 Daymeion Hughes RC	1.25	.50
❑ BC38 Marcus McCauley RC	1.25	.50
❑ BC39 Chris Houston RC	1.25	.50
❑ BC40 David Irons RC	1.00	.40
❑ BC41 Levi Brown RC	1.50	.60
❑ BC42 Joe Staley RC	1.25	.50
❑ BC43 Steve Breaston RC	1.25	.50
❑ BC44 Le'Ron McClain RC	1.25	.50
❑ BC45 Joel Filani RC	1.25	.50
❑ BC46 Justise Hairston RC	1.25	.50
❑ BC47 Nate Ilaoa RC	1.50	.60
❑ BC48 Brett Ratliff RC	1.25	.50
❑ BC49 Roy Hall RC	1.50	.60
❑ BC50 Legedu Naanee RC	1.25	.50
❑ BC51 Jarrett Hicks RC	1.25	.50
❑ BC52 Sonny Shackelford RC	1.25	.50
❑ BC53 Jordan Kent RC	1.25	.50
❑ BC54 John Broussard RC	1.25	.50
❑ BC55 Chandler Williams RC	1.25	.50
❑ BC56 JaMarcus Russell RC	10.00	4.00

❑ BC57 Brady Quinn RC 12.00 5.00
❑ BC58 Drew Stanton RC 5.00 2.00
❑ BC59 Troy Smith RC 5.00 2.00
❑ BC60 Kevin Kolb RC 6.00 2.50
❑ BC61 Trent Edwards RC 8.00 3.00
❑ BC62 John Beck RC 8.00 3.00
❑ BC63 Jordan Palmer RC 4.00 1.50
❑ BC64 Chris Leak RC 3.00 1.25
❑ BC65 Adrian Peterson RC 30.00 12.00
❑ BC66 Marshawn Lynch RC 8.00 3.00
❑ BC67 Brandon Jackson RC 5.00 2.00
❑ BC68 Michael Bush RC 5.00 2.00
❑ BC69 Antonio Pittman RC 3.00 1.25
❑ BC70 Tony Hunt RC 4.00 1.50
❑ BC71 [illegible] RC 4.00 1.50
❑ BC72 Chris Henry RC 4.00 1.50
❑ BC73 Brian Leonard RC 4.00 1.50
❑ BC74 Garrett Wolfe RC 5.00 2.00
❑ BC75 Calvin Johnson RC 12.00 5.00
❑ BC76 Ted Ginn RC 6.00 2.50
❑ BC77 Dwayne Jarrett RC 5.00 2.00
❑ BC78 Dwayne Bowe RC 8.00 3.00
❑ BC79 Sidney Rice RC 6.00 2.50
❑ BC80 Robert Meachem RC 4.00 1.50
❑ BC81 Anthony Gonzalez RC 6.00 2.50
❑ BC82 Craig Buster Davis RC 4.00 1.50
❑ BC83 Aundrae Allison RC 3.00 1.25
❑ BC84 Chansi Stuckey RC 3.00 1.25
❑ BC85 Alan Branch RC 3.00 1.25
❑ BC86 Steve Smith USC RC 5.00 2.00
❑ BC87 Paul Williams RC 3.00 1.25
❑ BC88 Johnnie Lee Higgins RC 3.00 1.25
❑ BC89 Jason Hill RC 4.00 1.50
❑ BC90 Greg Olsen RC 5.00 2.00
❑ BC91 Yamon Figurs RC 4.00 1.50
❑ BC92 Gaines Adams RC 4.00 1.50
❑ BC93 Patrick Willis RC 8.00 3.00
❑ BC94 Joe Thomas RC 4.00 1.50
❑ BC95 Isaiah Stanback RC 4.00 1.50
❑ BC96 Paul Posluszny RC 5.00 2.00
❑ BC97 Jeff Rowe RC 3.00 1.25
❑ BC98 Zac Taylor RC 4.00 1.50
❑ BC99 Dwayne Wright RC 3.00 1.25
❑ BC100 Kenneth Darby RC 4.00 1.50
❑ BC101 Selvin Young RC 5.00 2.00
❑ BC102 Gary Russell RC 4.00 1.50
❑ BC103 Kolby Smith RC 5.00 2.00
❑ BC104 Dallas Baker RC 3.00 1.25
❑ BC105 Jacoby Jones RC 4.00 1.50
❑ BC106 Ryne Robinson RC 3.00 1.25
❑ BC107 Chris Davis RC 3.00 1.25
❑ BC108 Laron Landry RC 5.00 2.00
❑ BC109 Leon Hall RC 3.00 1.25
❑ BC110 Lawrence Timmons RC 4.00 1.50
❑ BC111 Matt Leinart 1.00 .40
❑ BC112 Jason Campbell .75 .30
❑ BC113 J.P. Losman .75 .30
❑ BC114 Rex Grossman .75 .30
❑ BC115 Tony Romo 2.00 .75
❑ BC116 Brett Favre 2.00 .75
❑ BC117 Trent Green .75 .30
❑ BC118 Drew Brees .75 .30
❑ BC119 Chad Pennington .75 .30
❑ BC120 Ben Roethlisberger 1.25 .50
❑ BC121 Alex Smith QB 1.00 .40
❑ BC122 Marc Bulger .75 .30
❑ BC123 Edgerrin James 1.00 .40
❑ BC124 Jamal Lewis .75 .30
❑ BC125 DeShaun Foster .75 .30
❑ BC126 Cedric Benson .75 .30
❑ BC127 Rudi Johnson .75 .30
❑ BC128 Dominic Rhodes .75 .30
❑ BC129 Fred Taylor .75 .30
❑ BC130 Larry Johnson 1.00 .40
❑ BC131 Chester Taylor .60 .25
❑ BC132 Deuce McAllister .75 .30
❑ BC133 Brandon Jacobs .75 .30
❑ BC134 Willie Parker 1.00 .40
❑ BC135 Frank Gore 1.00 .40
❑ BC136 Steven Jackson 1.00 .40
❑ BC137 Clinton Portis .75 .30
❑ BC138 Anquan Boldin .75 .30
❑ BC139 Derrick Mason .60 .25
❑ BC140 Steve Smith .75 .30
❑ BC141 Chad Johnson .75 .30
❑ BC142 Braylon Edwards .75 .30
❑ BC143 Terry Glenn .75 .30
❑ BC144 Mike Furrey .75 .30
❑ BC145 Donald Driver .75 .30
❑ BC146 Andre Johnson .75 .30
❑ BC147 Marvin Harrison 1.00 .40
❑ BC148 Chris Chambers .75 .30
❑ BC149 Devery Henderson .60 .25
❑ BC150 Marques Colston 1.00 .40
❑ BC151 Amani Toomer .75 .30
❑ BC152 Laveranues Coles .75 .30
❑ BC153 Donte Stallworth .75 .30
❑ BC154 Hines Ward 1.00 .40
❑ BC155 Keenan McCardell .60 .25
❑ BC156 Arnaz Battle .60 .25
❑ BC157 Deion Branch .75 .30
❑ BC158 Kevin Curtis .60 .25
❑ BC159 Isaac Bruce .75 .30
❑ BC160 Santana Moss .75 .30
❑ BC161 Kellen Winslow .75 .30
❑ BC162 Jeremy Shockey .75 .30
❑ BC163 Vernon Davis .75 .30
❑ BC164 Travis Henry .75 .30
❑ BC165 Todd Heap .60 .25
❑ BC166 Matt Schaub .75 .30
❑ BC167 Steve McNair .75 .30
❑ BC168 Jake Delhomme .75 .30
❑ BC169 Carson Palmer 1.00 .40
❑ BC170 Jay Cutler 1.00 .40
❑ BC171 Peyton Manning 1.50 .60
❑ BC172 Tom Brady 2.00 .75
❑ BC173 Eli Manning 1.00 .40
❑ BC174 Donovan Mcnabb 1.00 .40
❑ BC175 Philip Rivers 1.00 .40
❑ BC176 Matt Hasselbeck .75 .30
❑ BC177 Vince Young 1.25 .50
❑ BC178 Warrick Dunn .75 .30
❑ BC179 Willis McGahee .75 .30
❑ BC180 DeAngelo Williams 1.00 .40
❑ BC181 Thomas Jones .75 .30
❑ BC182 Julius Jones .75 .30
❑ BC183 Joseph Addai 1.25 .50
❑ BC184 Maurice Jones-Drew 1.00 .40
❑ BC185 Ronnie Brown .75 .30
❑ BC186 Laurence Maroney 1.00 .40
❑ BC187 Reggie Bush 1.25 .50
❑ BC188 Brian Westbrook .75 .30
❑ BC189 LaDainian Tomlinson 1.25 .50
❑ BC190 Shaun Alexander .75 .30
❑ BC191 Cadillac Williams .75 .30
❑ BC192 Michael Turner .75 .30
❑ BC193 Larry Fitzgerald .75 .30
❑ BC194 Lee Evans .75 .30
❑ BC195 Muhsin Muhammad .75 .30
❑ BC196 T.J. Houshmandzadeh .75 .30
❑ BC197 Terrell Owens 1.00 .40
❑ BC198 Javon Walker .75 .30
❑ BC199 Roy Williams WR .75 .30
❑ BC200 Greg Jennings .75 .30
❑ BC201 Reggie Wayne .75 .30
❑ BC202 Matt Jones .75 .30
❑ BC203 Troy Williamson .60 .25
❑ BC204 Joe Horn .75 .30
❑ BC205 Plaxico Burress .75 .30
❑ BC206 Jerricho Cotchery .60 .25
❑ BC207 Randy Moss 1.00 .40
❑ BC208 Reggie Brown .75 .30
❑ BC209 Santonio Holmes .75 .30
❑ BC210 Eric Parker .60 .25
❑ BC211 Antonio Bryant .75 .30
❑ BC212 Darrell Jackson .75 .30
❑ BC213 Torry Holt .75 .30
❑ BC214 Antwaan Randle El .60 .25
❑ BC215 Alge Crumpler .75 .30
❑ BC216 Tony Gonzalez .75 .30
❑ BC217 Antonio Gates .75 .30
❑ BC218 Tarvaris Jackson 1.00 .40
❑ BC219 Drew Bennett .60 .25
❑ BC220 Byron Leftwich .75 .30

2006 Bowman Sterling

❑ COMP.RC SET (50) 50.00 20.00
❑ 1 Jon Alston RC 3.00 1.25
❑ 2 Daniel Bullocks RC 3.00 1.25
❑ 3 Damien Rhodes RC 2.50 1.00
❑ 4 Josh Betts RC 2.50 1.00
❑ 5 Garrett Mills RC 3.00 1.25
❑ 6 Anthony Schlegel RC 2.50 1.00
❑ 7 Lawrence Vickers RC 2.50 1.00
❑ 8 Abdul Hodge RC 3.00 1.25
❑ 9 Kevin McMahan RC 2.50 1.00
❑ 10 Orien Harris RC 2.50 1.00
❑ 11 Charles Davis RC 2.50 1.00

❑ 12 Haloti Ngata RC 3.00 1.25
❑ 13 Kelly Jennings RC 3.00 1.25
❑ 14 Corey Bramlet RC 2.50 1.00
❑ 15 Manny Lawson RC 3.00 1.25
❑ 16 David Kirtman RC 2.50 1.00
❑ 17 Jeremy Bloom RC 2.50 1.00
❑ 18 Jason Allen RC 3.00 1.25
❑ 19 Owen Daniels RC 3.00 1.25
❑ 20 Ray Edwards RC 2.50 1.00
❑ 21 DeMario Minter RC 2.50 1.00
❑ 22 Ernie Sims RC 4.00 1.50
❑ 23 Jovon Bouknight RC 2.50 1.00
❑ 24 Sinorice Moss RC 3.00 1.25
❑ 25 Travis Lulay RC 2.50 1.00
❑ 26 Quinn Sypniewski RC 2.50 1.00
❑ 27 T.J. Rushing RC 1.50 .60
❑ 28 J.J. Outlaw RC 2.50 1.00
❑ 29 Donte Whitner RC 3.00 1.25
❑ 30 Freddie Keiaho RC 2.50 1.00
❑ 31 Rocky McIntosh RC 3.00 1.25
❑ 32 Tamba Hali RC 3.00 1.25
❑ 33 Johnathan Joseph RC 2.50 1.00
❑ 34 Omar Gaither RC 2.50 1.00
❑ 35 Elvis Dumervil RC 1.50 .60
❑ 36 Thomas Howard RC 3.00 1.25
❑ 37 Gabe Watson RC 2.50 1.00
❑ 38 Tony Scheffler RC 3.00 1.25
❑ 39 Tim Massaquoi RC 2.50 1.00
❑ 40 Chris Gocong RC 2.50 1.00
❑ 41 Ko Simpson RC 2.50 1.00
❑ 42 D'Qwell Jackson RC 2.50 1.00
❑ 43 James Anderson RC 1.50 .60
❑ 44 P.J. Pope RC 2.50 1.00
❑ 45 Bennie Brazell RC 2.50 1.00
❑ 46 Jeff King RC 2.50 1.00
❑ 47 Dusty Dvoracek RC 3.00 1.25
❑ 48 Doo Webb RC 2.50 1.00
❑ 49 Jimmy Williams RC 3.00 1.25
❑ 50 [illegible] RC [illegible] [illegible]
❑ AC1 Antonio Cromartie AU RC 12.00 5.00
❑ AC2 Alge Crumpler JSY 10.00 4.00
❑ AF Anthony Fasano AU RC 12.00 5.00
❑ AH1 A.J. Hawk JSY RC 15.00 6.00
❑ AH2 A.J. Hawk JSY AU 80.00 40.00
❑ AHA Andre Hall AU RC 10.00 4.00
❑ AJ Adam Jennings AU RC 10.00 4.00
❑ AW Al Wilson JSY 8.00 3.00
❑ AY Ashton Youboty AU RC 12.00 5.00
❑ AZ Alan Zemaitis AU RC 12.00 5.00
❑ BB Brett Basanez AU RC 12.00 5.00
❑ BC1 Brian Calhoun JSY RC 8.00 3.00
❑ BC2 Brian Calhoun JSY AU 15.00 6.00
❑ BCR Brodie Croyle AU RC SP 60.00 25.00
❑ BF Brett Favre JSY 25.00 10.00
❑ BG Bruce Gradkowski AU RC 30.00 12.00
❑ BM Brandon Marshall JSY RC 8.00 3.00
❑ BO Ben Obomanu AU RC 10.00 4.00
❑ BS1 Bob Sanders JSY 10.00 4.00
❑ BS2 Brad Smith AU RC SP 12.00 5.00
❑ BW1 Brandon Williams JSY RC 8.00 3.00
❑ BW2 Brandon Williams JSY AU 15.00 6.00
❑ CB1 Chris Brown JSY 8.00 3.00
❑ CB2 Chris Brown JSY AU 10.00 4.00
❑ CG Chad Greenway AU RC 12.00 5.00
❑ CH Cedric Humes AU RC 12.00 5.00
❑ CHO Cody Hodges AU RC 10.00 4.00
❑ CJ Chad Jackson JSY RC 8.00 3.00
❑ CM Curtis Martin JSY 12.00 5.00
❑ CP Carson Palmer JSY 12.00 5.00
❑ CW Charlie Whitehurst JSY RC 8.00 3.00
❑ DAN David Anderson AU RC 10.00 4.00
❑ DB1 Derrick Burgess JSY 8.00 3.00

❑ DB2 Dominique Byrd AU RC 12.00 5.00
❑ DEH Derek Hagan JSY RC 8.00 3.00
❑ DEW Demetrius Williams JSY RC 8.003.00
❑ DF Dwight Freeney JSY 10.00 4.00
❑ DFE D.Ferguson AU RC SP 12.00 5.00
❑ DHA Darrell Hackney AU RC SP 10.004.00
❑ DHE Devin Hester AU RC 50.00 30.00
❑ DHI Domenik Hixon AU RC 10.00 4.00
❑ DM Donovan McNabb JSY 12.00 5.00
❑ DOL Drew Olson AU RC 10.00 4.00
❑ DON Deltha O'Neal JSY SP 12.00 5.00
❑ DRY DeMeco Ryans AU RC 20.00 8.00
❑ DS1 Darren Sharper JSY 8.00 3.00
❑ DS2 D.J. Shockley AU RC 12.00 5.00
❑ DT David Thomas AU RC 12.00 5.00
❑ DW DeAngelo Williams JSY RC 20.00 8.00
❑ DWA Delanie Walker AU RC 10.00 4.00
❑ GJ Greg Jennings AU RC 30.00 15.00
❑ HB Hank Baskett AU RC 15.00 6.00
❑ IM Ingle Martin AU RC 10.00 4.00
❑ JA1 Joseph Addai AU RC 125.00 75.00
❑ JA2 Jason Avant JSY RC 8.00 3.00
❑ JD Jake Delhomme JSY 10.00 4.00
❑ JH Jerome Harrison AU RC 12.00 5.00
❑ JJ Julius Jones JSY 12.00 5.00
❑ JK1 Joe Klopfenstein JSY RC 8.00 3.00
❑ JK2 Joe Klopfenstein JSY AU 12.00 5.00
❑ JL Jamal Lewis JSY 10.00 4.00
❑ JM Jerome Mathis JSY 8.00 3.00
❑ JN1 Jerious Norwood JSY RC 10.00 4.00
❑ JN2 Jerious Norwood AU 30.00 12.00
❑ JN3 Jerious Norwood JSY AU 40.00 15.00
❑ JO Jonathan Orr AU RC 10.00 4.00
❑ JP Julius Peppers JSY 10.00 4.00
❑ JS Jeremy Shockey JSY 12.00 5.00
❑ JSM Jimmy Smith JSY 10.00 4.00
❑ JT Jeremiah Trotter JSY 8.00 3.00
❑ JW Javon Walker JSY 10.00 4.00
❑ JWE Jeff Webb AU RC 10.00 4.00
❑ KC1 Kellen Clemens JSY RC 10.00 4.00
❑ KC2 Kellen Clemens JSY AU 30.00 15.00
❑ KR Koren Robinson JSY 10.00 4.00
❑ KW Kamerion Wimbley AU RC 12.00 5.00
❑ LB Lance Briggs JSY 8.00 3.00
❑ LE Lee Evans JSY 10.00 4.00
❑ LF Larry Fitzgerald JSY 12.00 5.00
❑ LJ Larry Johnson JSY 15.00 6.00
❑ LM Laurence Maroney JSY RC 20.00 8.00
❑ LN Lorenzo Neal JSY 8.00 3.00
❑ LP Leonard Pope AU RC SP 12.00 5.00
❑ LW LenDale White JSY RC 12.00 5.00
❑ LWA1 Leon Washington JSY RC 12.00 5.00
❑ LWA2 Leon Washington JSY AU 25.00 10.00
❑ MB Marion Barber JSY 10.00 4.00
❑ MBE Mike Bell AU RC 12.00 5.00
❑ MD Maurice Drew JSY RC 12.00 5.00
❑ MH Marvin Harrison JSY 12.00 5.00
❑ MHA Marques Hagans AU RC 10.00 4.00
❑ MHU Michael Huff JSY RC 10.00 4.00
❑ MIH Mike Hass AU RC SP 12.00 5.00
❑ MK Mathias Kiwanuka AU RC 15.00 6.00
❑ ML Matt Leinart JSY RC 25.00 10.00
❑ MLE Marcedes Lewis JSY RC 8.00 3.00
❑ MN Martin Nance AU RC 10.00 4.00
❑ MR1 Michael Robinson JSY RC 8.00 3.00
❑ MR2 Michael Robinson JSY AU 12.00 5.00
❑ MS Michael Strahan JSY 10.00 4.00
❑ MST Marcus Stroud JSY 8.00 3.00
❑ MST1 Maurice Stovall JSY RC 8.00 3.00
❑ MST2 Maurice Stovall AU 12.00 5.00
❑ MV Michael Vick JSY 12.00 5.00
❑ MW1 Mario Williams JSY RC 10.00 4.00
❑ MW2 Mario Williams JSY AU 20.00 8.00
❑ OJ Omar Jacobs JSY RC 8.00 3.00
❑ OU Osi Umenyiora JSY 8.00 3.00
❑ PB Plaxico Burress JSY 10.00 4.00
❑ PM Peyton Manning JSY 20.00 8.00
❑ PP Paul Pinegar AU RC SP 10.00 4.00
❑ QG Quinton Ganther AU RC 10.00 4.00
❑ RB1 Reggie Bush JSY RC 30.00 12.00
❑ RB2 Reggie Bush JSY AU SP 300.00 150.00
❑ RB3 Ronnie Brown JSY 12.00 5.00
❑ RBA Ronde Barber JSY 8.00 3.00
❑ RJ Rudi Johnson JSY AU 20.00 8.00
❑ RM Reggie McNeal AU RC 10.00 4.00
❑ RS Rod Smith JSY 10.00 4.00
❑ RW Reggie Wayne JSY 10.00 4.00
❑ RWI Roy Williams S JSY 10.00 4.00
❑ SG Skyler Green AU RC SP 12.00 5.00

❑ SH1 Santonio Holmes JSY RC 12.00 5.00
❑ SH2 S.Holmes JSY AU SP 60.00 30.00
❑ SMO Santana Moss JSY 10.00 4.00
❑ SR Shaun Rogers JSY 8.00 3.00
❑ SS Steve Smith JSY AU SP 50.00 25.00
❑ TB Tatum Bell JSY AU 15.00 6.00
❑ TBA Tiki Barber JSY 12.00 5.00
❑ TG Tony Gonzalez JSY 10.00 4.00
❑ TH Tommie Harris JSY 8.00 3.00
❑ THO Torry Holt JSY 10.00 4.00
❑ TJ1 Tarvaris Jackson JSY RC 10.00 4.00
❑ TJ2 Tarvaris Jackson JSY AU 40.00 15.00
❑ TW Travis Wilson JSY RC 8.00 3.00
❑ TYH Tye Hill AU RC 12.00 5.00
❑ VD1 Vernon Davis JSY RC 15.00 6.00
❑ VD2 Vernon Davis JSY AU SP 50.00 25.00
❑ VY1 Vince Young JSY RC 30.00 12.50
❑ VY2 Vince Young JSY AU SP 250.00125.00
❑ WB Will Blackmon AU RC 10.00 4.00
❑ WD Warrick Dunn JSY 10.00 4.00
❑ WJ Winston Justice AU RC 12.00 5.00
❑ WR Willie Reid AU RC 12.00 5.00
❑ ZT Zach Thomas JSY 12.00 5.00

2007 Bowman Sterling

❑ 1 Levi Brown RC 6.00 2.50
❑ 2 Darrelle Revis RC 6.00 2.50
❑ 3 Lawrence Timmons RC 6.00 2.50
❑ 4 Justin Harrell RC 6.00 2.50
❑ 5 Jarvis Moss RC 6.00 2.50
❑ 6 Michael Griffin RC 6.00 2.50
❑ 7 Aaron Ross RC 6.00 2.50
❑ 8 Reggie Nelson RC 5.00 2.00
❑ 9 Brandon Meriweather RC 6.00 2.50
❑ 10 Jon Beason RC 6.00 2.50
❑ 11 Anthony Spencer RC 6.00 2.50
❑ 12 David Irons RC 4.00 1.50
❑ 13 Matt Spaeth RC 6.00 2.50
❑ 14 Zak DeOssie RC 5.00 2.00
❑ 15 Matt Moore RC 10.00 4.00
❑ 16 Brett Ratliff RC 5.00 2.00
❑ 17 John Broussard RC 5.00 2.00
❑ 18 Chandler Williams RC 5.00 2.00
❑ 19 Chansi Stuckey RC 5.00 2.00
❑ 20 Derek Stanley RC 5.00 2.00
❑ 21 Ahmad Bradshaw RC 8.00 3.00
❑ 22 Jason Snelling RC 5.00 2.00
❑ 23 Tyler Palko RC 6.00 2.50
❑ 24 Tyrone Moss RC 4.00 1.50
❑ 25 Drew Tate RC 5.00 2.00
❑ 26 Joe Staley RC 5.00 2.00
❑ 27 Ben Grubbs RC 5.00 2.00
❑ 28 Eric Weddle RC 5.00 2.00
❑ 29 Chris Houston RC 5.00 2.00
❑ 30 Justin Durant RC 5.00 2.00
❑ 31 Eric Wright RC 6.00 2.50
❑ 32 Josh Wilson RC 5.00 2.00
❑ 33 Tim Crowder RC 6.00 2.50
❑ 34 Victor Abiamiri RC 6.00 2.50
❑ 35 Ramzee Robinson RC 4.00 1.50
❑ 36 Jonathan Wade RC 5.00 2.00
❑ 37 Aaron Rouse RC 6.00 2.50
❑ 38 Daymeion Hughes RC 5.00 2.00
❑ 39 Ray McDonald RC 5.00 2.00
❑ 40 Tanard Jackson RC 4.00 1.50
❑ 41 Martrez Milner RC 5.00 2.00
❑ 42 Le'Ron McClain RC 5.00 2.00
❑ 43 Kevin Boss RC 15.00 6.00
❑ 44 C.J. Gaddis RC 4.00 1.50
❑ 45 Rufus Alexander RC 6.00 2.50
❑ 46 Courtney Taylor RC 5.00 2.00
❑ 47 Prescott Burgess RC 5.00 2.00

❑ 48 Jordan Kent RC 5.00 2.00
❑ 49 Ben Patrick RC 5.00 2.00
❑ 50 Tyler Thigpen RC 6.00 2.50
❑ AA Aundrae Allison AU RC 8.00 3.00
❑ AB Anquan Boldin JSY 10.00 4.00
❑ ABR Alan Branch AU RC 8.00 3.00
❑ AC Adam Carriker AU RC 8.00 3.00
❑ ACR Alge Crumpler JSY 10.00 4.00
❑ AG1 Anthony Gonzalez JSY RC 12.00 5.00
❑ AG2 Anthony Gonzalez JSY AU 40.00 15.00
❑ AGA Antonio Gates JSY 10.00 4.00
❑ AJ Andre Johnson JSY 10.00 4.00
❑ AO Amobi Okoye AU RC 10.00 4.00
❑ AP1 Antonio Pittman JSY RC 6.00 2.50
❑ AP2 Antonio Pittman JSY AU 12.00 5.00
❑ APE1 Adrian Peterson JSY RC 60.00 25.00
❑ APE2 Adrian Peterson JSY AU 300.00 175.00
❑ AS Aaron Schobel JSY 8.00 3.00
❑ AT Adalius Thomas JSY 8.00 3.00
❑ AW Adrian Wilson JSY 8.00 3.00
❑ BE Braylon Edwards JSY 10.00 4.00
❑ BF Brett Favre JSY 25.00 10.00
❑ BJ1 Brandon Jackson JSY RC 10.00 4.00
❑ BJ2 Brandon Jackson JSY AU 20.00 8.00
❑ BL1 Brian Leonard JSY RC 10.00 4.00
❑ BL2 Brian Leonard JSY AU 15.00 6.00
❑ BQ1 Brady Quinn JSY RC 25.00 10.00
❑ BQ2 Brady Quinn JSY AU 150.00 90.00
❑ BW Brian Westbrook JSY 10.00 4.00
❑ CD Craig Buster Davis AU RC 10.00 4.00
❑ CDA Chris Davis AU RC 8.00 3.00
❑ CH1 Chris Henry JSY RC 8.00 3.00
❑ CH2 Chris Henry JSY AU 15.00 6.00
❑ CJ Chad Johnson JSY 10.00 4.00
❑ CJO1 Calvin Johnson JSY RC 25.00 10.00
❑ CJO2 Calvin Johnson JSY AU 125.0075.00
❑ CL Chris Leak AU RC 8.00 3.00
❑ CM Chris McAlister JSY 8.00 3.00
❑ CP Chad Pennington JSY 10.00 4.00
❑ CPO Clinton Portis JSY 10.00 4.00
❑ DB1 Dwayne Bowe JSY RC 15.00 6.00
❑ DB2 Dwayne Bowe JSY AU 40.00 15.00
❑ DBA Dallas Baker AU RC 8.00 3.00
❑ DC David Clowney AU RC 10.00 4.00
❑ DD Donald Driver JSY 10.00 4.00
❑ DH DeAngelo Hall JSY 10.00 4.00
❑ DHA David Harris AU RC 8.00 3.00
❑ DJ1 Dwayne Jarrett JSY RC 10.00 4.00
❑ DJ2 Dwayne Jarrett JSY AU 20.00 8.00
❑ DM Deuce McAllister JSY 10.00 4.00
❑ DS1 Drew Stanton JSY RC 10.00 4.00
❑ DS2 Drew Stanton JSY AU 30.00 15.00
❑ DW Darius Walker AU RC 10.00 4.00
❑ DWA DeMarcus Ware JSY 10.00 4.00
❑ DWR Dwayne Wright AU RC 8.00 3.00
❑ EJ Edgerrin James JSY 12.00 5.00
❑ ER Ed Reed JSY 10.00 4.00
❑ FG Frank Gore JSY 12.00 5.00
❑ GA1 Gaines Adams JSY RC 8.00 3.00
❑ GA2 Gaines Adams JSY AU 15.00 6.00
❑ GO1 Greg Olsen JSY RC 10.00 4.00
❑ GO2 Greg Olsen JSY AU 20.00 8.00
❑ GR Gary Russell AU RC 10.00 4.00
❑ GW1 Garrett Wolfe JSY RC 10.00 4.00
❑ GW2 Garrett Wolfe JSY AU 20.00 8.00
❑ IS Isaiah Stanback AU RC 10.00 4.00
❑ JA Jamaal Anderson AU RC 8.00 3.00
❑ JAD Joseph Addai JSY 15.00 6.00
❑ JB1 John Beck JSY RC 15.00 6.00
❑ JB2 John Beck JSY AU 40.00 15.00
❑ JC Jerricho Cotchery JSY 8.00 3.00
❑ JF Joel Filani AU RC 8.00 3.00
❑ JH1 Jason Hill JSY RC 8.00 3.00
❑ JH2 Jason Hill JSY AU 15.00 6.00
❑ JHA Justise Hairston AU RC 8.00 3.00
❑ JJ Jacoby Jones AU RC 10.00 4.00
❑ JJO James Jones AU RC 25.00 10.00
❑ JL J.P. Losman JSY 10.00 4.00
❑ JLH1 Johnnie Lee Higgins JSY RC 6.00 2.50
❑ JLH2 Johnnie Lee Higgins JSY AU 12.00 5.00
❑ JLY John Lynch JSY 10.00 4.00
❑ JM Justin Miller JSY 8.00 3.00
❑ JP Jordan Palmer AU RC 10.00 4.00
❑ JPE Julian Peterson JSY 8.00 3.00
❑ JR1 JaMarcus Russell JSY RC 20.00 8.00
❑ JR2 JaMarcus Russell JSY AU 125.00 75.00
❑ JRO Jeff Rowe AU RC 8.00 3.00
❑ JT Jason Taylor JSY 8.00 3.00
❑ JTH1 Joe Thomas JSY RC 8.00 3.00

❑ JTH2 Joe Thomas JSY AU	15.00	6.00
❑ JW Javon Walker JSY	10.00	4.00
❑ JZ Jared Zabransky AU RC	10.00	4.00
❑ KD Ken Darby AU RC	10.00	4.00
❑ KI1 Kenny Irons JSY RC	8.00	3.00
❑ KI2 Kenny Irons JSY AU	15.00	6.00
❑ KK1 Kevin Kolb JSY RC	12.00	5.00
❑ KK2 Kevin Kolb JSY AU	30.00	15.00
❑ KS Kolby Smith AU RC	20.00	10.00
❑ LB1 Lorenzo Booker JSY RC	8.00	3.00
❑ LB2 Lorenzo Booker JSY AU	15.00	6.00
❑ LC Laveranues Coles JSY	10.00	4.00
❑ LG Luke Getsy AU RC	10.00	4.00
❑ LH Leon Hall AU RC	8.00	3.00
❑ LN Legedu Naane AU RC	8.00	3.00
❑ LR Laurent Robinson AU RC	8.00	3.00
❑ LW LaMarr Woodley AU RC	10.00	4.00
❑ MB Marc Bulger JSY	10.00	4.00
❑ MBU1 Michael Bush JSY RC	10.00	4.00
❑ MBU2 Michael Bush JSY AU	20.00	8.00
❑ MH Matt Hasselbeck JSY	10.00	4.00
❑ ML1 Marshawn Lynch JSY RC	15.00	6.00
❑ ML2 Marshawn Lynch JSY AU	80.00	30.00
❑ MS Michael Strahan JSY	10.00	4.00
❑ MST Mack Strong JSY	8.00	3.00
❑ MW Mike Walker AU RC	8.00	3.00
❑ PB Plaxico Burress JSY	10.00	4.00
❑ PP Paul Posluszny AU RC	12.00	5.00
❑ PW1 Patrick Willis JSY RC	15.00	6.00
❑ PW2 Patrick Willis JSY AU	30.00	12.00
❑ PWI1 Paul Williams JSY RC	6.00	2.50
❑ PWI2 Paul Williams JSY AU	12.00	5.00
❑ RB Reggie Brown JSY	10.00	4.00
❑ RBR Ronnie Brown JSY	10.00	4.00
❑ RH Roy Hall AU RC	10.00	4.00
❑ RM Rhema McKnight AU RC	8.00	3.00
❑ RMA Rashean Mathis JSY	8.00	3.00
❑ RME1 Robert Meachem JSY RC	8.00	3.00
❑ RME2 Robert Meachem JSY AU	15.00	6.00
❑ RR Ryne Robinson AU RC	8.00	3.00
❑ RW Reggie Wayne JSY	10.00	4.00
❑ RWI Roy Williams S JSY	10.00	4.00
❑ RWL Roy Williams WR JSY	10.00	4.00
❑ SB Steve Breaston AU RC	8.00	3.00
❑ SC Scott Chandler AU RC	8.00	3.00
❑ SH Steve Hutchinson JSY	8.00	3.00
❑ SJ Steven Jackson JSY	12.00	5.00
❑ SR1 Sidney Rice JSY RC	12.00	5.00
❑ SR2 Sidney Rice JSY AU	25.00	10.00
❑ SS1 Steve Smith USC JSY RC	10.00	4.00
❑ SS2 Steve Smith USC JSY AU	30.00	15.00
❑ SSM Steve Smith JSY	10.00	4.00
❑ SY Selvin Young AU RC	20.00	8.00
❑ TC Thomas Clayton AU RC	8.00	3.00
❑ TE1 Trent Edwards JSY RC	15.00	6.00
❑ TE2 Trent Edwards JSY AU	40.00	15.00
❑ TG1 Ted Ginn JSY RC	12.00	5.00
❑ TG2 Ted Ginn JSY AU	25.00	10.00
❑ TH1 Tony Hunt JSY RC	8.00	3.00
❑ TH2 Tony Hunt JSY AU	15.00	6.00
❑ THO T.J. Houshmandzadeh JSY	10.00	4.00
❑ TS1 Troy Smith JSY RC	10.00	4.00
❑ TS2 Troy Smith JSY AU	30.00	15.00
❑ WD Warrick Dunn JSY	10.00	4.00
❑ WP Willie Parker JSY	12.00	5.00
❑ WPI Willie Parker PB JSY	12.00	5.00
❑ WS Will Smith JSY	8.00	3.00
❑ YF1 Yamon Figurs JSY RC	8.00	3.00
❑ YF2 Yamon Figurs JSY AU	15.00	6.00
❑ ZM Zach Miller AU RC	10.00	4.00
❑ ZT Zac Taylor AU RC	10.00	4.00
❑ ZTH Zach Thomas JSY	10.00	4.00

1995 Bowman's Best

❑ COMPLETE SET (180)	100.00	40.00
❑ R1 Ki-Jana Carter RC	1.50	.60
❑ R2 Tony Boselli RC	1.50	.60
❑ R3 Steve McNair RC	15.00	6.00
❑ R4 Michael Westbrook RC	1.50	.60
❑ R5 Kerry Collins RC	6.00	2.50
❑ R6 Kevin Carter RC	1.50	.60
❑ R7 Mike Mamula RC	.40	.15
❑ R8 Joey Galloway RC	6.00	2.50
❑ R9 Kyle Brady RC	1.50	.60
❑ R10 Ray McElroy RC	.40	.15
❑ R11 Derrick Alexander DE RC	.40	.15
❑ R12 Warren Sapp RC	6.00	2.50
❑ R13 Mark Fields RC	1.50	.60
❑ R14 Ruben Brown RC	1.50	.60

❑ R15 Ellis Johnson RC	.40	.15
❑ R16 Hugh Douglas RC	1.50	.60
❑ R17 Alundis Brice RC	.40	.15
❑ R18 Napoleon Kaufman RC	5.00	2.00
❑ R19 James O. Stewart RC	3.00	1.25
❑ R20 Luther Elliss RC	.40	.15
❑ R21 Rashaan Salaam RC	.75	.30
❑ R22 Tyrone Poole RC	1.50	.60
❑ R23 Ty Law RC	4.00	1.50
❑ R24 Korey Stringer RC	.75	.30
❑ R25 Billy Milner RC	.40	.15
❑ R26 Roell Preston RC	.75	.30
❑ R27 Mark Bruener RC	.75	.30
❑ R28 Derrick Brooks RC	6.00	2.50
❑ R29 Blake Brockermeyer RC	.40	.15
❑ R30 Mike Frederick RC	.40	.15
❑ R31 Trezelle Jenkins RC	.40	.15
❑ R32 Craig Newsome RC	.40	.15
❑ R33 Matt O'Dwyer RC	.40	.15
❑ R34 Terrance Shaw RC	.40	.15
❑ R35 Anthony Cook RC	.40	.15
❑ R36 Darick Holmes RC	.75	.30
❑ R37 Cory Raymer RC	.40	.15
❑ R38 Zach Wiegert RC	.40	.15
❑ R39 Sam Shade RC	.40	.15
❑ R40 Brian DeMarco RC	.40	.15
❑ R41 Ron Davis RC	.40	.15
❑ R42 Orlando Thomas RC	.40	.15
❑ R43 Derek West RC	.40	.15
❑ R44 Ray Zellars RC	.75	.30
❑ R45 Todd Collins RC	5.00	2.00
❑ R46 Linc Harden RC	.40	.15
❑ R47 Frank Sanders RC	1.50	.60
❑ R48 Ken Dilger RC	1.50	.60
❑ R49 Barrett Robbins RC	.40	.15
❑ R50 Bobby Taylor RC	2.50	1.00
❑ R51 Terrell Fletcher RC	.40	.15
❑ R52 Jack Jackson RC	.40	.15
❑ R53 Jeff Kopp RC	.40	.15
❑ R54 Brendan Stai RC	.40	.15
❑ R55 Corey Fuller RC	.40	.15
❑ R56 Todd Sauerbrun RC	.40	.15
❑ R57 Dameian Jeffries RC	.40	.15
❑ R58 Troy Dumas RC	.40	.15
❑ R59 Charlie Williams RC	.40	.15
❑ R60 Kordell Stewart RC	6.00	2.50
❑ R61 Jay Barker RC	.40	.15
❑ R62 Jesse James RC	.40	.15
❑ R63 Shane Hannah RC	.40	.15
❑ R64 Rob Johnson RC	4.00	1.50
❑ R65 Darius Holland RC	.40	.15
❑ R66 William Henderson RC	5.00	2.00
❑ R67 Chris Sanders RC	.75	.30
❑ R68 Darryl Pounds RC	.40	.15
❑ R69 Melvin Tuten RC	.40	.15
❑ R70 David Sloan RC	.40	.15
❑ R71 Chris Hudson RC	.40	.15
❑ R72 William Strong RC	.40	.15
❑ R73 Brian Williams LB RC	.40	.15
❑ R74 Curtis Martin RC	15.00	6.00
❑ R75 Mike Verstegen RC	.40	.15
❑ R76 Justin Armour RC	.40	.15
❑ R77 Lorenzo Styles RC	.40	.15
❑ R78 Oliver Gibson RC	.40	.15
❑ R79 Zack Crockett RC	.75	.30
❑ R80 Tau Pupua RC	.40	.15
❑ R81 Tamarick Vanover RC	1.50	.60
❑ R82 Steve McLaughlin RC	.40	.15
❑ R83 Sean Harris RC	.40	.15
❑ R84 Eric Zeier RC	1.50	.60
❑ R85 Rodney Young RC	.40	.15
❑ R86 Chad May RC	.40	.15
❑ R87 Evan Pilgrim RC	.40	.15
❑ R88 James A.Stewart RC	.40	.15
❑ R89 Torey Hunter RC	.40	.15
❑ R90 Antonio Freeman RC	4.00	1.50
❑ V1 Rob Moore	.60	.25
❑ V2 Craig Heyward	.60	.25
❑ V3 Jim Kelly	1.25	.50
❑ V4 John Kasay	.30	.10
❑ V5 Jeff Graham	.30	.10
❑ V6 Jeff Blake RC	2.50	1.00
❑ V7 Antonio Langham	.30	.10
❑ V8 Troy Aikman	3.00	1.25
❑ V9 Simon Fletcher	.30	.10
❑ V10 Barry Sanders	5.00	2.00
❑ V11 Edgar Bennett	.60	.25
❑ V12 Ray Childress	.30	.10
❑ V13 Ray Buchanan	.30	.10
❑ V14 Desmond Howard	.60	.25
❑ V15 Dale Carter	.60	.25
❑ V16 Troy Vincent	.30	.10
❑ V17 David Palmer	.60	.25
❑ V18 Ben Coates	.60	.25
❑ V19 Derek Brown TE	.30	.10
❑ V20 Dave Brown	.60	.25
❑ V21 Mo Lewis	.30	.10
❑ V22 Harvey Williams	.30	.10
❑ V23 Randall Cunningham	1.25	.50
❑ V24 Kevin Greene	.60	.25
❑ V25 Junior Seau	1.25	.50
❑ V26 Merton Hanks	.30	.10
❑ V27 Cortez Kennedy	.60	.25
❑ V28 Troy Drayton	.30	.10
❑ V29 Hardy Nickerson	.30	.10
❑ V30 Brian Mitchell	.30	.10
❑ V31 Raymont Harris	.30	.10
❑ V32 Keith Goganious	.30	.10
❑ V33 Andre Reed	.60	.25
❑ V34 Terance Mathis	.60	.25
❑ V35 Garrison Hearst	1.25	.50
❑ V36 Glyn Milburn	.30	.10
❑ V37 Emmitt Smith	5.00	2.00
❑ V38 Vinny Testaverde	.60	.25
❑ V39 Darnay Scott	.60	.25
❑ V40 Mickey Washington	.30	.10
❑ V41 Craig Erickson	.30	.10
❑ V42 Chris Chandler	1.25	.50
❑ V43 Brett Favre	6.00	2.50
❑ V44 Scott Mitchell	.60	.25
❑ V45 Chris Slade	.30	.10
❑ V46 Warren Moon	.60	.25
❑ V47 Dan Marino	6.00	2.50
❑ V48 Greg Hill	.60	.25
❑ V49 Rocket Ismail	.60	.25
❑ V50 Bobby Houston	.30	.10
❑ V51 Rodney Hampton	.60	.25
❑ V52 Jim Everett	.30	.10
❑ V53 Rick Mirer	.60	.25
❑ V54 Steve Young	2.50	1.00
❑ V55 Dennis Gibson	.30	.10
❑ V56 Rod Woodson	.60	.25
❑ V57 Calvin Williams	.60	.25
❑ V58 Tom Carter	.30	.10
❑ V59 Trent Dilfer	1.25	.50
❑ V60 Shane Conlan	.30	.10
❑ V61 Cornelius Bennett	.60	.25
❑ V62 Eric Metcalf	.60	.25
❑ V63 Frank Reich	.30	.10
❑ V64 Eric Hill	.30	.10
❑ V65 Erik Kramer	.30	.10
❑ V66 Michael Irvin	1.25	.50
❑ V67 Tony McGee	.30	.10
❑ V68 Andre Rison	.60	.25
❑ V69 Shannon Sharpe	.60	.25
❑ V70 Quentin Coryatt	.60	.25
❑ V71 Robert Brooks	1.25	.50
❑ V72 Steve Beuerlein	.60	.25
❑ V73 Herman Moore	1.25	.50
❑ V74 Jack Del Rio	.30	.10
❑ V75 Dave Meggett	.30	.10
❑ V76 Pete Stoyanovich	.30	.10
❑ V77 Neil Smith	.60	.25
❑ V78 Corey Miller	.30	.10
❑ V79 Tim Brown	1.25	.50
❑ V80 Tyrone Hughes	.60	.25
❑ V81 Boomer Esiason	.60	.25
❑ V82 Natrone Means	.60	.25
❑ V83 Chris Warren	.60	.25
❑ V84 Byron Bam Morris	.30	.10
❑ V85 Jerry Rice	3.00	1.25

❑ V86	Michael Zordich	.30	.10
❑ V87	Errict Rhett	.60	.25
❑ V88	Henry Ellard	.60	.25
❑ V89	Chris Miller	.30	.10
❑ V90	John Elway	6.00	2.50

1996 Bowman's Best

❑	COMPLETE SET (180)	80.00	40.00
❑ 1	Emmitt Smith	3.00	1.25
❑ 2	Kordell Stewart	.75	.30
❑ 3	Mark Chmura	.40	.15
❑ 4	Sean Dawkins	.20	.07
❑ 5	Steve Young	1.50	.60
❑ 6	Tamarick Vanover	.40	.15
❑ 7	Scott Mitchell	.40	.15
❑ 8	Aaron Hayden	.20	.07
❑ 9	William Thomas	.20	.07
❑ 10	Dan Marino	4.00	1.50
❑ 11	Curtis Conway	.75	.30
❑ 12	Steve Atwater	.20	.07
❑ 13	Derrick Brooks	.75	.30
❑ 14	Rick Mirer	.40	.15
❑ 15	Mark Brunell	1.00	.40
❑ 16	Garrison Hearst	.40	.15
❑ 17	Eric Turner	.20	.07
❑ 18	Mark Carrier WR	.20	.07
❑ 19	Darnay Scott	.40	.15
❑ 20	Steve McNair	1.50	.60
❑ 21	Jim Everett	.20	.07
❑ 22	Wayne Chrebet	1.00	.40
❑ 23	Ben Coates	.40	.15
❑ 24	Harvey Williams	.20	.07
❑ 25	Michael Westbrook	.75	.30
❑ 26	Kevin Carter	.20	.07
❑ 27	Dave Brown	.20	.07
❑ 28	Jake Reed	.40	.15
❑ 29	Thurman Thomas	.75	.30
❑ 30	Jeff George	.40	.15
❑ 31	Carnell Lake	.20	.07
❑ 32	J.J. Stokes	.75	.30
❑ 33	Jay Novacek	.20	.07
❑ 34	Brett Perriman	.20	.07
❑ 35	Robert Brooks	.75	.30
❑ 36	Neil Smith	.40	.15
❑ 37	Chris Zorich	.20	.07
❑ 38	Micheal Barrow	.20	.07
❑ 39	Quentin Coryatt	.20	.07
❑ 40	Kerry Collins	.75	.30
❑ 41	Aeneas Williams	.20	.07
❑ 42	James O.Stewart	.40	.15
❑ 43	Warren Moon	.40	.15
❑ 44	Willie McGinest	.20	.07
❑ 45	Rodney Hampton	.40	.15
❑ 46	Jeff Hostetler	.20	.07
❑ 47	Darrell Green	.20	.07
❑ 48	Warren Sapp	.20	.07
❑ 49	Troy Drayton	.20	.07
❑ 50	Junior Seau	.75	.30
❑ 51	Mike Mamula	.20	.07
❑ 52	Antonio Langham	.20	.07
❑ 53	Eric Metcalf	.20	.07
❑ 54	Adrian Murrell	.40	.15
❑ 55	Joey Galloway	.75	.30
❑ 56	Anthony Miller	.40	.15
❑ 57	Carl Pickens	.40	.15
❑ 58	Bruce Smith	.40	.15
❑ 59	Merton Hanks	.20	.07
❑ 60	Troy Aikman	2.00	.75
❑ 61	Erik Kramer	.20	.07
❑ 62	Tyrone Poole	.20	.07
❑ 63	Michael Jackson	.40	.15
❑ 64	Rob Moore	.40	.15
❑ 65	Marcus Allen	.75	.30
❑ 66	Orlando Thomas	.20	.07
❑ 67	Dave Meggett	.20	.07
❑ 68	Trent Dilfer	.75	.30
❑ 69	Herman Moore	.40	.15
❑ 70	Brett Favre	4.00	1.50
❑ 71	Blaine Bishop	.20	.07
❑ 72	Eric Allen	.20	.07
❑ 73	Bernie Parmalee	.20	.07
❑ 74	Kyle Brady	.20	.07
❑ 75	Terry McDaniel	.20	.07
❑ 76	Rodney Peete	.20	.07
❑ 77	Yancey Thigpen	.40	.15
❑ 78	Stan Humphries	.40	.15
❑ 79	Craig Heyward	.20	.07
❑ 80	Rashaan Salaam	.40	.15
❑ 81	Shannon Sharpe	.40	.15
❑ 82	Jim Harbaugh	.40	.15
❑ 83	Vinnie Clark	.20	.07
❑ 84	Steve Bono	.20	.07
❑ 85	Drew Bledsoe	1.00	.40
❑ 86	Ken Norton	.20	.07
❑ 87	Brian Mitchell	.20	.07
❑ 88	Hardy Nickerson	.20	.07
❑ 89	Todd Lyght	.20	.07
❑ 90	Barry Sanders	3.00	1.25
❑ 91	Robert Blackmon	.20	.07
❑ 92	Larry Centers	.40	.15
❑ 93	Jim Kelly	.75	.30
❑ 94	Lamar Lathon	.20	.07
❑ 95	Cris Carter	.75	.30
❑ 96	Hugh Douglas	.40	.15
❑ 97	Michael Strahan	.40	.15
❑ 98	Lee Woodall	.20	.07
❑ 99	Michael Irvin	.75	.30
❑ 100	Marshall Faulk	1.00	.40
❑ 101	Terance Mathis	.20	.07
❑ 102	Eric Zeier	.20	.07
❑ 103	Marty Carter	.20	.07
❑ 104	Steve Tovar	.20	.07
❑ 105	Isaac Bruce	.75	.30
❑ 106	Tony Martin	.40	.15
❑ 107	Dale Carter	.20	.07
❑ 108	Terry Kirby	.40	.15
❑ 109	Tyrone Hughes	.20	.07
❑ 110	Bryce Paup	.20	.07
❑ 111	Errict Rhett	.40	.15
❑ 112	Ricky Watters	.40	.15
❑ 113	Chris Chandler	.40	.15
❑ 114	Edgar Bennett	.40	.15
❑ 115	John Elway	4.00	1.50
❑ 116	Sam Mills	.20	.07
❑ 117	Seth Joyner	.20	.07
❑ 118	Jeff Lageman	.20	.07
❑ 119	Chris Calloway	.20	.07
❑ 120	Curtis Martin	1.50	.60
❑ 121	Ken Harvey	.20	.07
❑ 122	Eugene Daniel	.20	.07
❑ 123	Tim Brown	.75	.30
❑ 124	Mo Lewis	.20	.07
❑ 125	Jeff Blake	.75	.30
❑ 126	Jessie Tuggle	.20	.07
❑ 127	Vinny Testaverde	.40	.15
❑ 128	Chris Warren	.40	.15
❑ 129	Terrell Davis	1.50	.60
❑ 130	Greg Lloyd	.40	.15
❑ 131	Deion Sanders	1.00	.40
❑ 132	Derrick Thomas	.75	.30
❑ 133	Darryll Lewis	.20	.07
❑ 134	Reggie White	.75	.30
❑ 135	Jerry Rice	2.00	.75
❑ 136	Tony Banks RC	1.00	.40
❑ 137	Derrick Mayes RC	1.00	.40
❑ 138	Leeland McElroy RC	.50	.20
❑ 139	Bryan Still RC	.50	.20
❑ 140	Tim Biakabutuka RC	1.00	.40
❑ 141	Rickey Dudley RC	1.00	.40
❑ 142	Tory James RC	.50	.20
❑ 143	Lawyer Milloy RC	1.25	.50
❑ 144	Mike Ulufale RC	.25	.08
❑ 145	Bobby Engram RC	1.00	.40
❑ 146	Willie Anderson RC	.25	.08
❑ 147	Terrell Owens RC	15.00	7.50
❑ 148	Jonathan Ogden RC	1.00	.40
❑ 149	Darrius Johnson RC	.25	.08
❑ 150	Kevin Hardy RC	1.00	.40
❑ 151	Simeon Rice RC	2.50	1.00
❑ 152	Alex Molden RC	.25	.08
❑ 153	Cedric Jones RC	.25	.08
❑ 154	Duane Clemons RC	.25	.08
❑ 155	Karim Abdul-Jabbar RC	1.00	.40
❑ 156	Dedric Mathis RC	.25	.08
❑ 157	John Michels RC	.25	.08
❑ 158	Winslow Oliver RC	.25	.08
❑ 159	Stepfret Williams RC	.25	.08
❑ 160	Eddie Kennison RC	1.00	.40
❑ 161	Marcus Coleman RC	.25	.08
❑ 162	Tedy Bruschi RC	20.00	10.00
❑ 163	Detron Smith RC	.25	.08
❑ 164	Ray Lewis RC	25.00	12.50
❑ 165	Marvin Harrison RC	15.00	7.50
❑ 166	Je'rod Cherry RC	.25	.08
❑ 167	Jerris McPhail RC	.25	.08
❑ 168	Eric Moulds RC	8.00	3.00
❑ 169	Walt Harris RC	.25	.08
❑ 170	Eddie George RC	8.00	3.00
❑ 171	Jermaine Lewis RC	1.00	.40
❑ 172	Jeff Lewis RC	.50	.20
❑ 173	Ray Mickens RC	.25	.08
❑ 174	Amani Toomer RC	5.00	2.00
❑ 175	Zach Thomas RC	3.00	1.25
❑ 176	Lawrence Phillips RC	.50	.20
❑ 177	John Mobley RC	.25	.08
❑ 178	Anthony Dorsett RC	.25	.08
❑ 179	DeRon Jenkins	.20	.07
❑ 180	Keyshawn Johnson RC	6.00	2.50

1997 Bowman's Best

❑	COMPLETE SET (125)	30.00	12.50
❑ 1	Brett Favre	4.00	1.50
❑ 2	Larry Centers	.60	.25
❑ 3	Trent Dilfer	1.00	.40
❑ 4	Rodney Hampton	.60	.25
❑ 5	Wesley Walls	.60	.25
❑ 6	Jerome Bettis	1.00	.40
❑ 7	Keyshawn Johnson	1.00	.40
❑ 8	Keenan McCardell	.60	.25
❑ 9	Terry Allen	1.00	.40
❑ 10	Troy Aikman	2.00	.75
❑ 11	Tony Banks	.60	.25
❑ 12	Ty Detmer	.60	.25
❑ 13	Chris Chandler	.60	.25
❑ 14	Marshall Faulk	1.25	.50
❑ 15	Heath Shuler	.40	.15
❑ 16	Stan Humphries	.60	.25
❑ 17	Bryan Cox	.40	.15
❑ 18	Chris Spielman	.40	.15
❑ 19	Derrick Thomas	1.00	.40
❑ 20	Steve Young	1.25	.50
❑ 21	Desmond Howard	.60	.25
❑ 22	Jeff Blake	.60	.25
❑ 23	Michael Jackson	.60	.25
❑ 24	Cris Carter	1.00	.40
❑ 25	Joey Galloway	.60	.25
❑ 26	Simeon Rice	.60	.25
❑ 27	Reggie White	1.00	.40
❑ 28	Dave Brown	.40	.15
❑ 29	Mike Alstott	1.00	.40
❑ 30	Emmitt Smith	3.00	1.25
❑ 31	Anthony Johnson	.40	.15
❑ 32	Mark Brunell	1.25	.50
❑ 33	Ricky Watters	.60	.25
❑ 34	Terrell Davis	1.25	.50
❑ 35	Ben Coates	.60	.25
❑ 36	Gus Frerotte	.40	.15
❑ 37	Andre Reed	.60	.25
❑ 38	Isaac Bruce	1.00	.40
❑ 39	Junior Seau	1.00	.40
❑ 40	Eddie George	1.00	.40
❑ 41	Adrian Murrell	.60	.25
❑ 42	Jake Reed	.60	.25

❑ 43 Karim Abdul-Jabbar	.60	.25
❑ 44 Scott Mitchell	.60	.25
❑ 45 Ki-Jana Carter	.40	.15
❑ 46 Curtis Conway	.60	.25
❑ 47 Jim Harbaugh	.60	.25
❑ 48 Tim Brown	1.00	.40
❑ 49 Mario Bates	.40	.15
❑ 50 Jerry Rice	2.00	.75
❑ 51 Byron Bam Morris	.40	.15
❑ 52 Marcus Allen	1.00	.40
❑ 53 Errict Rhett	.40	.15
❑ 54 Steve McNair	1.25	.50
❑ 55 Kerry Collins	1.00	.40
❑ 56 Bert Emanuel	.60	.25
❑ 57 Curtis Martin	1.25	.50
❑ 58 [illegible]	.40	.15
❑ 59 Brad Johnson	1.00	.40
❑ 60 John Elway	4.00	1.50
❑ 61 Natrone Means	.60	.25
❑ 62 Deion Sanders	1.00	.40
❑ 63 Tony Martin	.60	.25
❑ 64 Michael Westbrook	.60	.25
❑ 65 Chris Calloway	.40	.15
❑ 66 Antonio Freeman	1.00	.40
❑ 67 Rob Johnson	1.00	.40
❑ 68 Kent Graham	.40	.15
❑ 69 O.J. McDuffie	.60	.25
❑ 70 Barry Sanders	3.00	1.25
❑ 71 Chris Warren	.60	.25
❑ 72 Kordell Stewart	1.00	.40
❑ 73 Thurman Thomas	1.00	.40
❑ 74 Marvin Harrison	1.00	.40
❑ 75 Carl Pickens	.60	.25
❑ 76 Brent Jones	.40	.15
❑ 77 Irving Fryar	.60	.25
❑ 78 Neil O'Donnell	.60	.25
❑ 79 Elvis Grbac	.60	.25
❑ 80 Drew Bledsoe	1.25	.50
❑ 81 Shannon Sharpe	.60	.25
❑ 82 Vinny Testaverde	.60	.25
❑ 83 Chris Sanders	.40	.15
❑ 84 Herman Moore	.60	.25
❑ 85 Jeff George	.60	.25
❑ 86 Bruce Smith	.60	.25
❑ 87 Robert Smith	.60	.25
❑ 88 Kevin Hardy	.40	.15
❑ 89 Kevin Greene	.60	.25
❑ 90 Dan Marino	4.00	1.50
❑ 91 Michael Irvin	1.00	.40
❑ 92 Garrison Hearst	.60	.25
❑ 93 Lake Dawson	.40	.15
❑ 94 Lawrence Phillips	.40	.15
❑ 95 Terry Glenn	1.00	.40
❑ 96 Jake Plummer RC	6.00	2.50
❑ 97 Byron Hanspard RC	.60	.25
❑ 98 Bryant Westbrook RC	.40	.15
❑ 99 Troy Davis RC	.60	.25
❑ 100 Danny Wuerffel RC	1.00	.40
❑ 101 Tony Gonzalez RC	4.00	1.50
❑ 102 Jim Druckenmiller RC	.60	.25
❑ 103 Kevin Lockett RC	.60	.25
❑ 104 Renaldo Wynn RC	.40	.15
❑ 105 James Farrior RC	1.00	.40
❑ 106 Rae Carruth RC	.40	.15
❑ 107 Tom Knight RC	.40	.15
❑ 108 Corey Dillon RC	8.00	3.00
❑ 109 Kenny Holmes RC	1.00	.40
❑ 110 Orlando Pace RC	1.00	.40
❑ 111 Reidel Anthony RC	1.00	.40
❑ 112 Chad Scott RC	.60	.25
❑ 113 Antowain Smith RC	3.00	1.25
❑ 114 David LaFleur RC	.40	.15
❑ 115 Yatil Green RC	.60	.25
❑ 116 Darrell Russell RC	.40	.15
❑ 117 Joey Kent RC	1.00	.40
❑ 118 Darnell Autry RC	.60	.25
❑ 119 Peter Boulware RC	1.00	.40
❑ 120 Shawn Springs RC	.60	.25
❑ 121 Ike Hilliard RC	1.50	.60
❑ 122 Dwayne Rudd RC	1.00	.40
❑ 123 Reinard Wilson RC	.60	.25
❑ 124 Michael Booker RC	.40	.15
❑ 125 Warrick Dunn RC	4.00	1.50

1998 Bowman's Best

❑ COMPLETE SET (125)	80.00	30.00
❑ 1 Emmitt Smith	3.00	1.25
❑ 2 Reggie White	1.00	.40
❑ 3 Jake Plummer	1.00	.40
❑ 4 Ike Hilliard	.40	.15
❑ 5 Isaac Bruce	.40	.15
❑ 6 Trent Dilfer	1.00	.40
❑ 7 Ricky Watters	.60	.25
❑ 8 Jeff George	.60	.25
❑ 9 Wayne Chrebet	1.00	.40
❑ 10 Brett Favre	4.00	1.50
❑ 11 Terry Allen	1.00	.40
❑ 12 Bert Emanuel	.40	.15
❑ 13 Andre Reed	.60	.25
❑ 14 Andre Rison	.60	.25
❑ 15 Jeff Blake	.60	.25
❑ 16 Steve McNair	1.00	.40
❑ 17 Joey Galloway	.60	.25
❑ 18 Irving Fryar	.60	.25
❑ 19 Dorsey Levens	1.00	.40
❑ 20 Jerry Rice	2.00	.75
❑ 21 Kerry Collins	.60	.25
❑ 22 Michael Jackson	.40	.15
❑ 23 Kordell Stewart	1.00	.40
❑ 24 Junior Seau	1.00	.40
❑ 25 Jimmy Smith	.60	.25
❑ 26 Michael Westbrook	.60	.25
❑ 27 Eddie George	1.00	.40
❑ 28 Cris Carter	1.00	.40
❑ 29 Jason Sehorn	.60	.25
❑ 30 Warrick Dunn	1.00	.40
❑ 31 Garrison Hearst	1.00	.40
❑ 32 Erik Kramer	.40	.15
❑ 33 Chris Chandler	.60	.25
❑ 34 Michael Irvin	1.00	.40
❑ 35 Marshall Faulk	1.25	.50
❑ 36 Warren Moon	1.00	.40
❑ 37 Rickey Dudley	.40	.15
❑ 38 Drew Bledsoe	1.50	.60
❑ 39 Antowain Smith	1.00	.40
❑ 40 Terrell Davis	1.00	.40
❑ 41 Gus Frerotte	.40	.15
❑ 42 Robert Brooks	.60	.25
❑ 43 Tony Banks	.60	.25
❑ 44 Terrell Owens	1.00	.40
❑ 45 Edgar Bennett	.40	.15
❑ 46 Rob Moore	.60	.25
❑ 47 J.J. Stokes	.60	.25
❑ 48 Yancey Thigpen	.40	.15
❑ 49 Elvis Grbac	.60	.25
❑ 50 John Elway	4.00	1.50
❑ 51 Charles Johnson	.40	.15
❑ 52 Karim Abdul-Jabbar	1.00	.40
❑ 53 Carl Pickens	.60	.25
❑ 54 Peter Boulware	.40	.15
❑ 55 Chris Warren	.40	.15
❑ 56 Terance Mathis	.60	.25
❑ 57 Andre Hastings	.40	.15
❑ 58 Jake Reed	.60	.25
❑ 59 Mike Alstott	.40	.15
❑ 60 Mark Brunell	1.00	.40
❑ 61 Herman Moore	.60	.25
❑ 62 Troy Aikman	2.00	.75
❑ 63 Fred Lane	.40	.15
❑ 64 Rod Smith	.60	.25
❑ 65 Terry Glenn	1.00	.40
❑ 66 Jerome Bettis	1.00	.40
❑ 67 Derrick Thomas	1.00	.40
❑ 68 Marvin Harrison	1.00	.40
❑ 69 Adrian Murrell	.40	.15
❑ 70 Curtis Martin	1.00	.40
❑ 71 Bobby Hoying	.60	.25
❑ 72 Darrell Green	.60	.25
❑ 73 Sean Dawkins	.40	.15
❑ 74 Robert Smith	1.00	.40
❑ 75 Antonio Freeman	1.00	.40
❑ 76 Scott Mitchell	.60	.25
❑ 77 Curtis Conway	.60	.25
❑ 78 Rae Carruth	.40	.15
❑ 79 Jamal Anderson	1.00	.40
❑ 80 Dan Marino	4.00	1.50
❑ 81 Brad Johnson	1.00	.40
❑ 82 Danny Kanell	.60	.25
❑ 83 Charlie Garner	.60	.25
❑ 84 Rob Johnson	.60	.25
❑ 85 Natrone Means	.60	.25
❑ 86 Tim Brown	1.00	.40
❑ 87 Keyshawn Johnson	1.00	.40
❑ 88 Ben Coates	.60	.25
❑ 89 Derrick Alexander	.60	.25
❑ 90 Steve Young	1.25	.50
❑ 91 Shannon Sharpe	.60	.25
❑ 92 Corey Dillon	1.00	.40
❑ 93 Bruce Smith	.60	.25
❑ 94 Errict Rhett	.60	.25
❑ 95 Jim Harbaugh	.40	.15
❑ 96 Napoleon Kaufman	1.00	.40
❑ 97 Glenn Foley	.60	.25
❑ 98 Tony Gonzalez	1.00	.40
❑ 99 Keenan McCardell	.60	.25
❑ 100 Barry Sanders	3.00	1.25
❑ 101 Charles Woodson RC	3.00	1.25
❑ 102 Tim Dwight RC	2.50	1.00
❑ 103 Marcus Nash RC	1.25	.50
❑ 104 Joe Jurevicius RC	2.50	1.00
❑ 105 Jacquez Green RC	2.00	.75
❑ 106 Kevin Dyson RC	2.50	1.00
❑ 107 Keith Brooking RC	2.50	1.00
❑ 108 Andre Wadsworth RC	2.00	.75
❑ 109 Randy Moss RC	15.00	7.50
❑ 110 Robert Edwards RC	2.00	.75
❑ 111 Pat Johnson RC	2.00	.75
❑ 112 Peyton Manning RC	25.00	12.50
❑ 113 Duane Starks RC	1.25	.50
❑ 114 Grant Wistrom RC	2.00	.75
❑ 115 Anthony Simmons RC	2.00	.75
❑ 116 Takeo Spikes RC	2.50	1.00
❑ 117 Tony Simmons RC	2.00	.75
❑ 118 Jerome Pathon RC	2.50	1.00
❑ 119 Ryan Leaf RC	2.50	1.00
❑ 120 Skip Hicks RC	2.00	.75
❑ 121 Curtis Enis RC	1.25	.50
❑ 122 Germane Crowell RC	2.00	.75
❑ 123 John Avery RC	2.00	.75
❑ 124 Hines Ward RC	10.00	5.00
❑ 125 Fred Taylor RC	4.00	1.50

1999 Bowman's Best

❑ COMPLETE SET (133)	80.00	30.00
❑ 1 Randy Moss	2.50	1.00
❑ 2 Skip Hicks	.40	.15
❑ 3 Robert Smith	1.00	.40
❑ 4 Drew Bledsoe	1.25	.50
❑ 5 Tim Brown	1.00	.40
❑ 6 Marshall Faulk	1.25	.50
❑ 7 Terance Mathis	.60	.25
❑ 8 Sean Dawkins	.40	.15
❑ 9 Ed McCaffrey	.60	.25
❑ 10 Jamal Anderson	1.00	.40
❑ 11 Antonio Freeman	1.00	.40
❑ 12 Terry Kirby	.60	.25
❑ 13 Vinny Testaverde	.60	.25
❑ 14 Eddie George	1.00	.40
❑ 15 Ricky Watters	.60	.25
❑ 16 Johnnie Morton	.60	.25
❑ 17 Natrone Means	.60	.25
❑ 18 Terry Glenn	1.00	.40
❑ 19 Michael Westbrook	.60	.25

❑	20 Doug Flutie	1.00	.40
❑	21 Jake Plummer	.60	.25
❑	22 Darnay Scott	.60	.25
❑	23 Andre Rison	.60	.25
❑	24 Jon Kitna	1.00	.40
❑	25 Dan Marino	3.00	1.25
❑	26 Ike Hilliard	.60	.25
❑	27 Warrick Dunn	1.00	.40
❑	28 Jerome Bettis	1.00	.40
❑	29 Curtis Conway	.60	.25
❑	30 Emmitt Smith	2.00	.75
❑	31 Jimmy Smith	.60	.25
❑	32 Isaac Bruce	1.00	.40
❑	33 Jerry Rice	2.00	.75
❑	34 Curtis Martin	1.00	.40
❑	35 Steve McNair	1.00	.40
❑	36 Jeff Blake	.60	.25
❑	37 Rob Moore	.60	.25
❑	38 Dorsey Levens	1.00	.40
❑	39 Terrell Davis	1.00	.40
❑	40 John Elway	3.00	1.25
❑	41 Trent Dilfer	.60	.25
❑	42 Joey Galloway	.60	.25
❑	43 Keyshawn Johnson	1.00	.40
❑	44 O.J. McDuffie	.60	.25
❑	45 Fred Taylor	1.00	.40
❑	46 Andre Reed	.60	.25
❑	47 Frank Sanders	.60	.25
❑	48 Keenan McCardell	.60	.25
❑	49 Elvis Grbac	.60	.25
❑	50 Barry Sanders	3.00	1.25
❑	51 Terrell Owens	1.00	.40
❑	52 Trent Green	1.00	.40
❑	53 Brad Johnson	1.00	.40
❑	54 Rich Gannon	1.00	.40
❑	55 Randall Cunningham	1.00	.40
❑	56 Tony Martin	.60	.25
❑	57 Rod Smith	.60	.25
❑	58 Eric Moulds	1.00	.40
❑	59 Yancey Thigpen	.40	.15
❑	60 Brett Favre	3.00	1.25
❑	61 Cris Carter	1.00	.40
❑	62 Marvin Harrison	1.00	.40
❑	63 Chris Chandler	.60	.25
❑	64 Antowain Smith	1.00	.40
❑	65 Carl Pickens	.60	.25
❑	66 Shannon Sharpe	.60	.25
❑	67 Mike Alstott	1.00	.40
❑	68 J.J. Stokes	.60	.25
❑	69 Ben Coates	.60	.25
❑	70 Peyton Manning	3.00	1.25
❑	71 Duce Staley	1.00	.40
❑	72 Michael Irvin	.60	.25
❑	73 Tim Biakabutuka	.60	.25
❑	74 Priest Holmes	1.50	.60
❑	75 Steve Young	1.25	.50
❑	76 Jerome Pathon	.60	.25
❑	77 Wayne Chrebet	1.00	.40
❑	78 Bert Emanuel	.40	.15
❑	79 Curtis Enis	.40	.15
❑	80 Mark Brunell	1.00	.40
❑	81 Herman Moore	.60	.25
❑	82 Corey Dillon	1.00	.40
❑	83 Jim Harbaugh	.60	.25
❑	84 Gary Brown	.40	.15
❑	85 Kordell Stewart	.60	.25
❑	86 Garrison Hearst	.60	.25
❑	87 Rocket Ismail	.60	.25
❑	88 Charlie Batch	1.00	.40
❑	89 Napoleon Kaufman	1.00	.40
❑	90 Troy Aikman	2.00	.75
❑	91 Brett Favre BP	1.50	.60
❑	92 Randy Moss BP	1.25	.50
❑	93 Terrell Davis BP	1.00	.40
❑	94 Barry Sanders BP	1.50	.60
❑	95 Peyton Manning BP	1.50	.60
❑	96 Troy Edwards BP	.60	.25
❑	97 Cade McNown BP	.60	.25
❑	98 Edgerrin James BP	2.50	1.00
❑	99 Torry Holt BP	1.00	.40
❑	100 Tim Couch BP	1.00	.40
❑	101 Chris Claiborne RC	1.00	.40
❑	102 Brock Huard RC	2.00	.75
❑	103 Amos Zereoue RC	2.00	.75
❑	104 Sedrick Irvin RC	1.00	.40
❑	105 Kevin Faulk RC	2.00	.75
❑	106 Ebenezer Ekuban RC	1.00	.40
❑	107 Daunte Culpepper RC	8.00	3.00
❑	108 Rob Konrad RC	1.50	.60
❑	109 James Johnson RC	1.50	.60
❑	110 Kurt Warner RC	10.00	4.00
❑	111 Mike Cloud RC	1.50	.60
❑	112 Andy Katzenmoyer RC	1.50	.60
❑	113 Jevon Kearse RC	3.00	1.25
❑	114 Akili Smith RC	1.50	.60
❑	115 Edgerrin James RC	8.00	3.00
❑	116 Cecil Collins RC	1.00	.40
❑	117 Chris McAlister RC	1.50	.60
❑	118 Donovan McNabb RC	10.00	4.00
❑	119 Kevin Johnson RC	2.00	.75
❑	120 Torry Holt RC	5.00	2.00
❑	121 Antoine Winfield RC	1.50	.60
❑	122 Michael Bishop RC	2.00	.75
❑	123 Joe Germaine RC	1.50	.60
❑	124 David Boston RC	2.00	.75
❑	125 D'Wayne Bates RC	1.50	.60
❑	126 Champ Bailey RC	2.50	1.00
❑	127 Cade McNown RC	1.50	.60
❑	128 Shaun King RC	1.50	.60
❑	129 Peerless Price RC	2.00	.75
❑	130 Troy Edwards RC	1.50	.60
❑	131 Karsten Bailey RC	1.50	.60
❑	132 Tim Couch RC	2.00	.75
❑	133 Ricky Williams RC	4.00	1.50
❑	C1 Rookie Class Photo	8.00	3.00

2000 Bowman's Best

❑	COMPLETE SET (150)	500.00	250.00
❑	1 Troy Edwards	.30	.10
❑	2 Kurt Warner	1.50	.60
❑	3 Steve McNair	.75	.30
❑	4 Terry Glenn	.50	.20
❑	5 Charlie Batch	.75	.30
❑	6 Patrick Jeffers	.75	.30
❑	7 Jake Plummer	.50	.20
❑	8 Derrick Alexander	.50	.20
❑	9 Joey Galloway	.50	.20
❑	10 Tony Banks	.50	.20
❑	11 Robert Smith	.75	.30
❑	12 Jerry Rice	1.50	.60
❑	13 Jeff Garcia	.75	.30
❑	14 Michael Westbrook	.50	.20
❑	15 Curtis Conway	.50	.20
❑	16 Brian Griese	.75	.30
❑	17 Peyton Manning	2.00	.75
❑	18 Daunte Culpepper	1.00	.40
❑	19 Frank Sanders	.50	.20
❑	20 Muhsin Muhammad	.50	.20
❑	21 Corey Dillon	.75	.30
❑	22 Brett Favre	2.50	1.00
❑	23 Warrick Dunn	.75	.30
❑	24 Tim Brown	.75	.30
❑	25 Kerry Collins	.50	.20
❑	26 Brad Johnson	.75	.30
❑	27 Rocket Ismail	.50	.20
❑	28 Jamal Anderson	.75	.30
❑	29 Jimmy Smith	.50	.20
❑	30 Torry Holt	.75	.30
❑	31 Duce Staley	.75	.30
❑	32 Drew Bledsoe	1.00	.40
❑	33 Jerome Bettis	.75	.30
❑	34 Keyshawn Johnson	.75	.30
❑	35 Fred Taylor	.75	.30
❑	36 Akili Smith	.30	.10
❑	37 Rob Johnson	.50	.20
❑	38 Elvis Grbac	.50	.20
❑	39 Antonio Freeman	.75	.30
❑	40 Curtis Enis	.30	.10
❑	41 Terance Mathis	.50	.20
❑	42 Terrell Davis	.75	.30
❑	43 Randy Moss	1.50	.60
❑	44 Jon Kitna	.75	.30
❑	45 Curtis Martin	.75	.30
❑	46 Terrell Owens	.75	.30
❑	47 Robert Smith	.75	.30
❑	48 Albert Connell	.30	.10
❑	49 Edgerrin James	1.25	.50
❑	50 Tony Gonzalez	.50	.20
❑	51 Eric Moulds	.75	.30
❑	52 Natrone Means	.50	.20
❑	53 Carl Pickens	.50	.20
❑	54 Mark Brunell	.75	.30
❑	55 Rob Moore	.50	.20
❑	56 Marshall Faulk	1.00	.40
❑	57 Stephen Davis	.75	.30
❑	58 Rich Gannon	.75	.30
❑	59 Ricky Williams	.75	.30
❑	60 Emmitt Smith	1.50	.60
❑	61 Germane Crowell	.30	.10
❑	62 Doug Flutie	.75	.30
❑	63 O.J. McDuffie	.50	.20
❑	64 Chris Chandler	.50	.20
❑	65 Qadry Ismail	.50	.20
❑	66 Tim Couch	.50	.20
❑	67 James Stewart	.50	.20
❑	68 Marvin Harrison	.75	.30
❑	69 Cris Carter	.75	.30
❑	70 Cade McNown	.30	.10
❑	71 Marcus Robinson	.75	.30
❑	72 Steve Beuerlein	.50	.20
❑	73 Jevon Kearse	.75	.30
❑	74 Eddie George	.75	.30
❑	75 Donovan McNabb	1.25	.50
❑	76 Jeff Blake	.50	.20
❑	77 Wayne Chrebet	.50	.20
❑	78 Kordell Stewart	.50	.20
❑	79 Steve Young	1.00	.40
❑	80 Mike Alstott	.75	.30
❑	81 Ricky Watters	.50	.20
❑	82 Charlie Garner	.50	.20
❑	83 Troy Aikman	1.50	.60
❑	84 Dorsey Levens	.50	.20
❑	85 Ike Hilliard	.50	.20
❑	86 Shaun King	.30	.10
❑	87 Isaac Bruce	.75	.30
❑	88 Tyrone Wheatley	.50	.20
❑	89 Amani Toomer	.50	.20
❑	90 Ed McCaffrey	.75	.30
❑	91 E.James/M.Faulk BP	.75	.30
❑	92 D.Bledsoe/B.Johnson BP	.75	.30
❑	93 J.Smith/R.Moss BP	1.00	.40
❑	94 E.George/S.Davis BP	.50	.20
❑	95 M.Brunell/T.Aikman BP	1.00	.40
❑	96 M.Harrison/C.Carter BP	.75	.30
❑	97 C.Martin/E.Smith BP	1.00	.40
❑	98 T.Brown/I.Bruce BP	.50	.20
❑	99 F.Taylor/R.Williams BP	.75	.30
❑	100 K.Warner/P.Manning BP	1.00	.40
❑	101 Shaun Alexander RC	30.00	15.00
❑	102 Thomas Jones RC	12.00	5.00
❑	103 Courtney Brown RC	8.00	3.00
❑	104 Curtis Keaton RC	6.00	2.50
❑	105 Jerry Porter RC	10.00	4.00
❑	106 Corey Simon RC	8.00	3.00
❑	107 Dez White RC	8.00	3.00
❑	108 Jamal Lewis RC	15.00	6.00
❑	109 Ron Dayne RC	8.00	3.00
❑	110 R.Jay Soward RC	6.00	2.50
❑	111 Tee Martin RC	8.00	3.00
❑	112 Brian Urlacher RC	25.00	10.00
❑	113 Reuben Droughns RC	10.00	4.00
❑	114 Travis Taylor RC	8.00	3.00
❑	115 Plaxico Burress RC	15.00	6.00
❑	116 Chad Pennington RC	15.00	6.00
❑	117 Sylvester Morris RC	6.00	2.50
❑	118 Ron Dugans RC	4.00	1.50
❑	119 Joe Hamilton RC	6.00	2.50
❑	120 Chris Redman RC	6.00	2.50
❑	121 Trung Canidate RC	6.00	2.50
❑	122 J.R. Redmond RC	6.00	2.50
❑	123 Danny Farmer RC	6.00	2.50
❑	124 Todd Pinkston RC	8.00	3.00
❑	125 Dennis Northcutt RC	8.00	3.00
❑	126 Laveranues Coles RC	10.00	4.00
❑	127 Bubba Franks RC	8.00	3.00
❑	128 Travis Prentice RC	6.00	2.50
❑	129 Peter Warrick RC	8.00	3.00
❑	130 Anthony Becht RC	8.00	3.00
❑	131 Ike Charlton RC	4.00	1.50
❑	132 Shaun Ellis RC	8.00	3.00

❑ 133 Sean Morey RC 6.00 2.50
❑ 134 Sebastian Janikowski RC 8.00 3.00
❑ 135 Aaron Stecker RC 8.00 3.00
❑ 136 Ronney Jenkins RC 6.00 2.50
❑ 137 Jamel White RC 6.00 2.50
❑ 138 Nick Williams 4.00 1.50
❑ 139 Andy McCullough 4.00 1.50
❑ 140 Kevin Daft 4.00 1.50
❑ 141 Thomas Hamner RC 4.00 1.50
❑ 142 Tim Rattay RC 8.00 3.00
❑ 143 Spergon Wynn RC 6.00 2.50
❑ 144 Brandon Short RC 6.00 2.50
❑ 145 Chad Morton RC 8.00 3.00
❑ 146 Gari Scott RC 4.00 1.50
❑ 147 Frank Murphy RC 4.00 1.50
[illegible]
❑ 149 Windrell Hayes RC 6.00 2.50
❑ 150 Doug Johnson RC 8.00 3.00

2001 Bowman's Best

❑ COMP.SET w/o SP's (100) 20.00 7.50
❑ 1 Jerry Rice 1.50 .60
❑ 2 Doug Flutie .75 .30
❑ 3 Drew Bledsoe 1.00 .40
❑ 4 Edgerrin James 1.00 .40
❑ 5 Muhsin Muhammad .50 .20
❑ 6 Charlie Batch .75 .30
❑ 7 Marshall Faulk 1.00 .40
❑ 8 Trent Green .75 .30
❑ 9 Rich Gannon .75 .30
❑ 10 Emmitt Smith 1.50 .60
❑ 11 Steve McNair .75 .30
❑ 12 Darrell Jackson .75 .30
❑ 13 Amani Toomer .50 .20
❑ 14 Jimmy Smith .50 .20
❑ 15 Kevin Johnson .50 .20
❑ 16 Ray Lewis .75 .30
❑ 17 Peter Warrick .75 .30
❑ 18 Cris Carter .75 .30
❑ 19 Jerome Bettis .75 .30
❑ 20 Keyshawn Johnson .75 .30
❑ 21 Joey Galloway .50 .20
❑ 22 Chris Chandler .50 .20
❑ 23 Brett Favre 2.50 1.00
❑ 24 Aaron Brooks .75 .30
❑ 25 Kurt Warner 1.50 .60
❑ 26 Jeff Graham .30 .10
❑ 27 Curtis Martin .75 .30
❑ 28 Mike Anderson .75 .30
❑ 29 Eric Moulds .50 .20
❑ 30 David Boston .75 .30
❑ 31 Elvis Grbac .50 .20
❑ 32 James Stewart .50 .20
❑ 33 Randy Moss 1.50 .60
❑ 34 Donovan McNabb 1.00 .40
❑ 35 Matt Hasselbeck .50 .20
❑ 36 Stephen Davis .75 .30
❑ 37 Brad Johnson .75 .30
❑ 38 Jamal Anderson .75 .30
❑ 39 Tim Biakabutuka .50 .20
❑ 40 Antonio Freeman .75 .30
❑ 41 Mark Brunell .75 .30
❑ 42 Tiki Barber .75 .30
❑ 43 Charlie Garner .50 .20
❑ 44 Eddie George .75 .30
❑ 45 Ricky Williams .75 .30
❑ 46 Rob Johnson .50 .20
❑ 47 Jake Plummer .50 .20
❑ 48 Peyton Manning 2.00 .75
❑ 49 Lamar Smith .50 .20
❑ 50 Corey Dillon .75 .30
❑ 51 Derrick Alexander .50 .20
❑ 52 Troy Brown .50 .20
❑ 53 Wayne Chrebet .50 .20
❑ 54 Shaun Alexander 1.00 .40
❑ 55 Jeff George .50 .20
❑ 56 Tim Brown .75 .30
❑ 57 Brian Griese .75 .30
❑ 58 Cade McNown .30 .10
❑ 59 Jamal Lewis 1.25 .50
❑ 60 Germane Crowell .30 .10
❑ 61 Junior Seau .75 .30
❑ 62 Warrick Dunn .75 .30
❑ 63 Isaac Bruce .75 .30
❑ 64 Terry Glenn .50 .20
❑ 65 Fred Taylor .75 .30
❑ 66 Tim Couch .50 .20
[illegible]
❑ 68 Tony Gonzalez .50 .20
❑ 69 Kerry Collins .50 .20
❑ 70 James Thrash .50 .20
❑ 71 Terrell Owens .75 .30
❑ 72 Derrick Mason .50 .20
❑ 73 Tyrone Wheatley .50 .20
❑ 74 Oronde Gadsden .50 .20
❑ 75 Ahman Green .75 .30
❑ 76 Jon Kitna .50 .20
❑ 77 Tony Banks .50 .20
❑ 78 Marvin Harrison .75 .30
❑ 79 Daunte Culpepper .75 .30
❑ 80 Vinny Testaverde .50 .20
❑ 81 Chad Lewis .30 .10
❑ 82 Torry Holt .75 .30
❑ 83 Jeff Garcia .75 .30
❑ 84 Rod Smith .50 .20
❑ 85 Marcus Robinson .75 .30
❑ 86 Keenan McCardell .30 .10
❑ 87 Joe Horn .50 .20
❑ 88 Kordell Stewart .50 .20
❑ 89 Jay Fiedler .75 .30
❑ 90 Ed McCaffrey .75 .30
❑ 91 E.George/S.Davis .50 .20
❑ 92 P.Manning/J.Garcia 1.50 .60
❑ 93 R.Smith/T.Holt .75 .30
❑ 94 E.James/M.Faulk 1.50 .60
❑ 95 E.Grbac/D.Culpepper .75 .30
❑ 96 M.Harrison/R.Moss 1.25 .50
❑ 97 M.Anderson/E.Smith .75 .30
❑ 98 B.Griese/K.Warner 1.00 .40
❑ 99 M.Muhammad/E.McCaffrey .75 .30
❑ 100 E.Moulds/T.Owens .75 .30
❑ 101 David Terrell JSY RC 8.00 3.00
❑ 102 Kevan Barlow JSY RC 8.00 3.00
❑ 103 Quincy Morgan JSY RC 8.00 3.00
❑ 104 Chris Weinke JSY RC 8.00 3.00
❑ 105 Josh Heupel JSY RC 8.00 3.00
❑ 106 Chris Chambers JSY RC 15.00 6.00
❑ 107 Reggie Wayne JSY RC 20.00 7.50
❑ 108 Gerard Warren JSY RC [illegible] [illegible]
❑ 109 Freddie Mitchell JSY RC 8.00 3.00
❑ 110 Anthony Thomas JSY RC 8.00 3.00
❑ 111 Robert Ferguson JSY RC 8.00 3.00
❑ 112 Deuce McAllister JSY RC 20.00 7.50
❑ 113 Travis Henry JSY RC 20.00 7.50
❑ 114 Rod Gardner JSY RC 8.00 3.00
❑ 115 Michael Bennett JSY RC 8.00 3.00
❑ 116 Santana Moss JSY RC 15.00 6.00
❑ 117 Chad Johnson JSY RC 25.00 10.00
❑ 118 Jesse Palmer JSY RC 8.00 3.00
❑ 119 James Jackson JSY RC 8.00 3.00
❑ 120 Dan Morgan JSY RC 8.00 3.00
❑ 121 Drew Brees RC 20.00 10.00
❑ 122 Travis Minor RC 4.00 1.50
❑ 123 Quincy Carter RC 6.00 2.50
❑ 124 LaDainian Tomlinson RC 80.00 40.00
❑ 125 Michael Vick RC 25.00 10.00
❑ 126 Ryan Pickett RC 2.50 1.00
❑ 127 Mike McMahon RC 6.00 2.50
❑ 128 Alex Bannister RC 4.00 1.50
❑ 129 A.J. Feeley RC 6.00 2.50
❑ 130 Shad Meier RC 4.00 1.50
❑ 131 Jamie Winborn RC 4.00 1.50
❑ 132 Fred Smoot RC 6.00 2.50
❑ 133 Milton Wynn RC 4.00 1.50
❑ 134 Onome Ojo RC 4.00 1.50
❑ 135 Jonathan Carter RC 4.00 1.50
❑ 136 Todd Heap RC 6.00 2.50
❑ 137 Bobby Newcombe RC 4.00 1.50
❑ 138 Tony Stewart RC 6.00 2.50
❑ 139 Torrance Marshall RC 6.00 2.50
❑ 140 Jamal Reynolds RC 6.00 2.50
❑ 141 Jamar Fletcher RC 4.00 1.50
❑ 142 Richard Seymour RC 6.00 2.50
❑ 143 Tay Cody RC 2.50 1.00
❑ 144 Koren Robinson RC 6.00 2.50
❑ 145 Eddie Berlin RC 4.00 1.50
❑ 146 Damione Lewis RC 4.00 1.50
❑ 147 Marques Tuiasosopo RC 8.00 3.00
❑ 148 Snoop Minnis RC 4.00 1.50
❑ 149 Chris Barnes RC 4.00 1.50
❑ 150 Leonard Davis RC 4.00 1.50
❑ 151 Vinny Sutherland RC 4.00 1.50
❑ 152 Rudi Johnson RC 12.00 5.00
❑ 153 Derrick Gibson RC 4.00 1.50
❑ 154 Dan Alexander RC 6.00 2.50
❑ 155 Damerien McCants RC 4.00 1.50
[illegible]
❑ 157 Correll Buckhalter RC 8.00 3.00
❑ 158 LaMont Jordan RC 12.00 5.00
❑ 159 Quentin McCord RC 4.00 1.50
❑ 160 Justin Smith RC 6.00 2.50
❑ 161 Nate Clements RC 6.00 2.50
❑ 162 Alge Crumpler RC 8.00 4.00
❑ 163 Dan O'Leary RC 4.00 1.50
❑ 164 Sage Rosenfels RC 8.00 3.00
❑ 165 Andre Carter RC 6.00 2.50
❑ 166 Marcus Stroud RC 6.00 2.50
❑ 167 Will Allen RC 4.00 1.50
❑ 168 Tommy Polley RC 6.00 2.50
❑ 169 Justin McCareins RC 6.00 2.50
❑ 170 Josh Booty RC 6.00 2.50

2002 Bowman's Best

❑ COMP.SET w/o SP's (90) 40.00 15.00
❑ 1 Peyton Manning 3.00 1.25
❑ 2 Chris Weinke 1.00 .40
❑ 3 Daunte Culpepper 1.50 .60
❑ 4 Deuce McAllister 2.00 .75
❑ 5 Duce Staley 1.50 .60
❑ 6 Koren Robinson 1.00 .40
❑ 7 Emmitt Smith 4.00 1.50
❑ 8 Jamal Lewis 1.50 .60
❑ 9 Jake Plummer 1.00 .40
❑ 10 Tim Brown 1.50 .60
❑ 11 LaDainian Tomlinson 2.50 1.00
❑ 12 Derrick Mason 1.00 .40
❑ 13 Keyshawn Johnson 1.50 .60
❑ 14 Priest Holmes 2.00 .75
❑ 15 Marcus Robinson 1.00 .40
❑ 16 Drew Bledsoe 2.00 .75
❑ 17 Troy Brown 1.00 .40
❑ 18 Ahman Green 1.50 .60
❑ 19 Edgerrin James 2.00 .75
❑ 20 Hines Ward 1.50 .60
❑ 21 Marshall Faulk 1.50 .60
❑ 22 Rod Gardner 1.00 .40
❑ 23 Amani Toomer 1.00 .40
❑ 24 Ricky Williams 1.50 .60
❑ 25 Peter Warrick 1.00 .40
❑ 26 Ray Lewis 1.50 .60
❑ 27 Warrick Dunn 1.50 .60
❑ 28 Jermaine Lewis 1.00 .40
❑ 29 Mark Brunell 1.50 .60
❑ 30 Randy Moss 3.00 1.25
❑ 31 Laveranues Coles 1.00 .40
❑ 32 Kordell Stewart 1.00 .40
❑ 33 Darrell Jackson 1.00 .40
❑ 34 Jeff Garcia 1.50 .60
❑ 35 Eddie George 1.50 .60
❑ 36 Tim Dwight 1.00 .40
❑ 37 Trent Green 1.00 .40
❑ 38 Quincy Carter 1.00 .40
❑ 39 Mike McMahon 1.50 .60

❑ 40 Corey Dillon 1.00 .40
❑ 41 Corey Bradford .60 .25
❑ 42 Aaron Brooks 1.50 .60
❑ 43 Todd Pinkston 1.00 .40
❑ 44 Isaac Bruce 1.50 .60
❑ 45 Shane Matthews 1.00 .40
❑ 46 Eric Moulds 1.00 .40
❑ 47 Anthony Thomas 1.00 .40
❑ 48 David Boston 1.50 .60
❑ 49 Kevin Johnson 1.00 .40
❑ 50 Brett Favre 4.00 1.50
❑ 51 Ron Dayne 1.00 .40
❑ 52 Donovan McNabb 2.00 .75
❑ 53 Brad Johnson 1.00 .40
❑ 54 Garrison Hearst 1.00 .40
❑ 55 Jimmy Smith 1.00 .40
❑ 56 Muhsin Muhammad 1.00 .40
❑ 57 Michael Vick 3.00 1.25
❑ 58 Kerry Collins 1.00 .40
❑ 59 Jerome Bettis 1.50 .60
❑ 60 Trent Dilfer 1.00 .40
❑ 61 Torry Holt 1.50 .60
❑ 62 Stephen Davis 1.00 .40
❑ 63 Steve McNair 1.50 .60
❑ 64 Marvin Harrison 1.50 .60
❑ 65 Zach Thomas 1.50 .60
❑ 66 Antowain Smith 1.00 .40
❑ 67 Joe Horn 1.00 .40
❑ 68 Jim Miller 1.00 .40
❑ 69 Travis Taylor 1.00 .40
❑ 70 James Allen 1.00 .40
❑ 71 Tom Brady 4.00 1.50
❑ 72 Tiki Barber 1.50 .60
❑ 73 Doug Flutie 1.50 .60
❑ 74 Rich Gannon 1.50 .60
❑ 75 Kurt Warner 1.50 .60
❑ 76 Michael Pittman .60 .25
❑ 77 Curtis Martin 1.50 .60
❑ 78 Plaxico Burress 1.50 .60
❑ 79 Terrell Owens 1.50 .60
❑ 80 Tony Gonzalez 1.00 .40
❑ 81 Michael Bennett 1.50 .60
❑ 82 Brian Griese 1.50 .60
❑ 83 Tim Couch 1.00 .40
❑ 84 Shaun Alexander 2.00 .75
❑ 85 Drew Brees 1.50 .60
❑ 86 Vinny Testaverde 1.00 .40
❑ 87 Chris Chambers 1.50 .60
❑ 88 David Terrell 1.50 .60
❑ 89 Rod Smith 1.00 .40
❑ 90 Jerry Rice 3.00 1.25
❑ 91 David Carr JSY RC 15.00 6.00
❑ 92 Joey Harrington JSY RC 10.00 4.00
❑ 93 Marquise Walker JSY RC 6.00 2.50
❑ 94 Ladell Betts JSY RC 8.00 3.00
❑ 95 David Garrard JSY RC 15.00 6.00
❑ 96 Antwaan Randle El JSY RC 10.00 4.00
❑ 97 Antonio Bryant JSY RC 8.00 3.00
❑ 98 Eric Crouch JSY RC 8.00 3.00
❑ 99 Tim Carter JSY RC 6.00 2.50
❑ 100 William Green JSY RC 8.00 3.00
❑ 101 Rohan Davey JSY RC 8.00 3.00
❑ 102 Julius Peppers JSY RC 15.00 6.00
❑ 103 Donte Stallworth JSY RC 12.00 5.00
❑ 104 Ashley Lelie JSY RC 8.00 3.00
❑ 105 Jeremy Shockey JSY RC 25.00 10.00
❑ 106 Javon Walker JSY RC 12.00 5.00
❑ 107 Patrick Ramsey JSY RC 10.00 4.00
❑ 108 Roy Williams JSY RC 15.00 6.00
❑ 109 T.J. Duckett JSY RC 10.00 4.00
❑ 110 Jabar Gaffney JSY RC 8.00 3.00
❑ 111 Andre Davis JSY RC 6.00 2.50
❑ 112 Reche Caldwell JSY RC 8.00 3.00
❑ 113 Josh McCown JSY RC 10.00 4.00
❑ 114 Maurice Morris JSY RC 8.00 3.00
❑ 115 Ron Johnson JSY RC 6.00 2.50
❑ 116 DeShaun Foster JSY RC 8.00 3.00
❑ 117 Clinton Portis JSY RC 25.00 10.00
❑ 118 Aaron Lockett AU RC 6.00 2.50
❑ 119 Robert Thomas AU RC 12.00 5.00
❑ 121 Atrews Bell AU RC 6.00 2.50
❑ 122 Brandon Doman AU RC 10.00 4.00
❑ 124 Bryan Thomas AU RC 10.00 4.00
❑ 125 Bryant McKinnie AU RC 10.00 4.00
❑ 126 Chad Hutchinson AU RC 10.00 4.00
❑ 127 Charles Grant AU RC 12.00 5.00
❑ 128 Chester Taylor AU RC 30.00 15.00
❑ 129 Craig Nall AU RC 15.00 6.00
❑ 130 Deion Branch AU RC 30.00 15.00
❑ 131 Doug Jolley AU RC 12.00 5.00
❑ 132 Dwight Freeney AU RC 40.00 20.00
❑ 133 Ed Reed AU RC 40.00 15.00
❑ 134 Freddie Milons AU RC 10.00 4.00
❑ 135 Herb Haygood AU RC 6.00 2.50
❑ 136 J.T. O'Sullivan AU RC 10.00 4.00
❑ 137 Jake Schifino AU RC 10.00 4.00
❑ 138 Jason McAddley AU RC 10.00 4.00
❑ 139 Jeff Kelly AU RC 10.00 4.00
❑ 140 Jerramy Stevens AU RC 12.00 5.00
❑ 141 John Henderson AU RC 12.00 5.00
❑ 142 Jonathan Wells AU RC 12.00 5.00
❑ 143 Josh Scobey AU RC 12.00 5.00
❑ 144 Kelly Campbell AU RC 10.00 4.00
❑ 145 Kahlil Hill AU RC 10.00 4.00
❑ 146 Kalimba Edwards AU RC 12.00 5.00
❑ 147 Ken Simonton AU RC 6.00 2.50
❑ 148 Kurt Kittner AU RC 10.00 4.00
❑ 149 Lamar Gordon AU RC 12.00 5.00
❑ 150 Leonard Henry AU RC 10.00 4.00
❑ 151 Lito Sheppard AU RC 12.00 5.00
❑ 152 Luke Staley AU RC 10.00 4.00
❑ 153 Matt Schobel AU RC 10.00 4.00
❑ 154 Mike Rumph AU RC 12.00 5.00
❑ 155 Najeh Davenport AU RC 12.00 5.00
❑ 156 Napoleon Harris AU RC 12.00 5.00
❑ 158 Quentin Jammer AU RC 12.00 5.00
❑ 159 Randy Fasani AU RC 10.00 4.00
❑ 160 Ronald Curry AU RC 20.00 8.00
❑ 161 Ryan Sims AU RC 12.00 5.00
❑ 162 Sam Simmons AU RC 6.00 2.50
❑ 163 Seth Burford AU RC 10.00 4.00
❑ 164 Tellis Redmon AU RC 10.00 4.00
❑ 165 Terry Charles AU RC 10.00 4.00
❑ 166 Tracey Wistrom AU RC 10.00 4.00
❑ 167 Verron Haynes AU RC 20.00 7.50
❑ 168 Wes Pate AU RC 6.00 2.50
❑ 169 Wendell Bryant AU RC 6.00 2.50
❑ 170 Damien Anderson AU RC 10.00 4.00

2003 Bowman's Best

❑ COMP.SET w/o SP's (80) 30.00 12.50
❑ ROOKIE AU STATED ODDS 1:136
❑ CARDS 170, 175 NOT RELEASED
❑ 1 Terrell Owens 1.50 .60
❑ 2 Peerless Price 1.00 .40
❑ 3 Joey Harrington 2.50 1.00
❑ 4 Ricky Williams 1.50 .60
❑ 5 David Boston 1.00 .40
❑ 6 Troy Brown 1.00 .40
❑ 7 Deuce McAllister 1.50 .60
❑ 8 Marvin Harrison 1.50 .60
❑ 9 Ahman Green 1.50 .60
❑ 10 Emmitt Smith 4.00 1.50
❑ 11 Brian Urlacher 2.50 1.00
❑ 12 Jamal Lewis 1.50 .60
❑ 13 Keyshawn Johnson 1.50 .60
❑ 14 Kurt Warner 1.50 .60
❑ 15 Rod Gardner 1.00 .40
❑ 16 Plaxico Burress 1.00 .40
❑ 17 Chad Pennington 2.00 .75
❑ 18 Jeremy Shockey 2.50 1.00
❑ 19 Donovan McNabb 2.00 .75
❑ 20 T.J. Duckett 1.00 .40
❑ 21 Fred Taylor 1.50 .60
❑ 22 Daunte Culpepper 1.50 .60
❑ 23 Tiki Barber 1.50 .60
❑ 24 Brian Griese 1.50 .60
❑ 25 Chad Johnson 1.50 .60
❑ 26 Julius Peppers 1.50 .60
❑ 27 Chad Hutchinson .60 .25
❑ 28 Eddie George 1.00 .40
❑ 29 Torry Holt 1.50 .60
❑ 30 Drew Brees 1.50 .60
❑ 31 Rich Gannon 1.00 .40
❑ 32 Trent Green 1.00 .40
❑ 33 Clinton Portis 2.50 1.00
❑ 34 Tom Brady 4.00 1.50
❑ 35 Aaron Brooks 1.50 .60
❑ 36 Ray Lewis 1.50 .60
❑ 37 David Carr 2.50 1.00
❑ 38 Chris Chambers 1.50 .60
❑ 39 Brad Johnson 1.00 .40
❑ 40 Tommy Maddox 1.50 .60
❑ 41 Curtis Martin 1.50 .60
❑ 42 Travis Henry 1.00 .40
❑ 43 Brett Favre 4.00 1.50
❑ 44 Randy Moss 2.50 1.00
❑ 45 Jimmy Smith 1.00 .40
❑ 46 Joey Galloway 1.00 .40
❑ 47 Derrick Mason 1.00 .40
❑ 48 Darrell Jackson 1.00 .40
❑ 49 Curtis Conway .60 .25
❑ 50 Michael Vick 4.00 1.50
❑ 51 Rod Smith 1.00 .40
❑ 52 Muhsin Muhammad 1.00 .40
❑ 53 Drew Bledsoe 1.50 .60
❑ 54 Michael Bennett 1.00 .40
❑ 55 Joe Horn 1.00 .40
❑ 56 Stephen Davis 1.00 .40
❑ 57 Isaac Bruce 1.50 .60
❑ 58 Shaun Alexander 1.50 .60
❑ 59 Jerry Rice 3.00 1.25
❑ 60 Peyton Manning 2.50 1.00
❑ 61 Tony Gonzalez 1.00 .40
❑ 62 Jake Plummer 1.00 .40
❑ 63 Tim Couch .60 .25
❑ 64 Marty Booker 1.00 .40
❑ 65 Corey Dillon 1.00 .40
❑ 66 Steve McNair 1.50 .60
❑ 67 Jeff Garcia 1.50 .60
❑ 68 Hines Ward 1.50 .60
❑ 69 Laveranues Coles 1.00 .40
❑ 70 Amani Toomer 1.00 .40
❑ 71 Eric Moulds 1.00 .40
❑ 72 Donald Driver 1.00 .40
❑ 73 Jay Fiedler 1.00 .40
❑ 74 Charlie Garner 1.00 .40
❑ 75 Priest Holmes 2.00 .75
❑ 76 Edgerrin James 1.50 .60
❑ 77 Kerry Collins 1.00 .40
❑ 78 LaDainian Tomlinson 1.50 .60
❑ 79 Mark Brunell 1.00 .40
❑ 80 Marshall Faulk 1.50 .60
❑ 81 Lee Suggs RC 5.00 2.00
❑ 82 William Joseph RC 4.00 1.50
❑ 83 Brandon Lloyd RC 5.00 2.00
❑ 84 Nick Barnett RC 5.00 2.00
❑ 85 Andre Woolfolk RC 4.00 1.50
❑ 86 Jimmy Kennedy RC 4.00 1.50
❑ 87 Kliff Kingsbury RC 4.00 1.50
❑ 88 Andrew Williams RC 4.00 1.50
❑ 89 Mike Doss RC 4.00 1.50
❑ 90 Troy Polamalu RC 20.00 10.00
❑ 91 Bryant Johnson JSY RC 6.00 2.50
❑ 92 Justin Fargas JSY RC 6.00 2.50
❑ 93 Terence Newman JSY RC 12.00 6.00
❑ 94 Brian St.Pierre JSY RC 6.00 2.50
❑ 95 DeWayne Robertson JSY RC 6.00 2.50
❑ 96 Dave Ragone JSY RC 6.00 2.50
❑ 97 Teyo Johnson JSY RC 6.00 2.50
❑ 98 Bethel Johnson JSY RC 6.00 2.50
❑ 99 Tyrone Calico JSY RC 6.00 2.50
❑ 100 Carson Palmer JSY RC 25.00 12.50
❑ 101 Marcus Trufant JSY RC 6.00 2.50
❑ 102 Nate Burleson JSY RC 6.00 2.50
❑ 103 Musa Smith JSY RC 6.00 2.50
❑ 104 Anquan Boldin JSY RC 15.00 6.00
❑ 105 Chris Simms JSY RC 10.00 4.00
❑ 106 Taylor Jacobs JSY RC 6.00 2.50
❑ 107 Dallas Clark JSY RC 6.00 2.50
❑ 108 Seneca Wallace JSY RC 6.00 2.50
❑ 109 Ken Dorsey JSY RC 6.00 2.50
❑ 110 Willis McGahee JSY RC 15.00 6.00
❑ 111 Chris Brown JSY RC 6.00 2.50
❑ 112 Terrell Suggs JSY RC 10.00 4.00
❑ 113 Kelley Washington JSY RC 6.00 2.50
❑ 114 Onterrio Smith JSY RC 6.00 2.50
❑ 115 Rex Grossman JSY RC 25.00 10.00
❑ 116 LaBrandon Toefield AU RC 12.00 5.00
❑ 117 Sam Aiken AU RC 10.00 4.00

- ❑ 118 Malaefou Mackenzie AU RC 8.00 3.00
- ❑ 119 David Tyree AU RC 30.00 15.00
- ❑ 120 Jerome McDougle AU RC 12.00 5.00
- ❑ 121 DeWayne White AU RC 10.00 4.00
- ❑ 122 Zuriel Smith AU RC 8.00 3.00
- ❑ 123 Shaun McDonald AU RC 12.00 5.00
- ❑ 124 Andre Johnson AU/199 RC 60.00 30.00
- ❑ 125 Ahmaad Galloway AU RC 10.00 4.00
- ❑ 126 Keenan Howry AU RC 12.00 5.00
- ❑ 127 Kareem Kelly AU RC 10.00 4.00
- ❑ 128 Brooks Bollinger AU RC 12.00 5.00
- ❑ 129 Arnaz Battle AU RC 15.00 6.00
- ❑ 130 Adrian Madise AU RC 10.00 4.00
- ❑ 131 LaTarence Dunbar AU RC 10.00 4.00
- ❑ [illegible]
- ❑ 133 B.J. Askew AU RC 12.00 5.00
- ❑ 134 Michael Haynes AU RC 12.00 5.00
- ❑ 135 David Kircus AU RC 15.00 6.00
- ❑ 136 Kyle Boller AU/199 RC 40.00 15.00
- ❑ 137 Domanick Davis AU RC 20.00 8.00
- ❑ 138 Osi Umenyiora AU RC 35.00 20.00
- ❑ 139 Bobby Wade AU RC 12.00 5.00
- ❑ 140 Boss Bailey AU RC 12.00 5.00
- ❑ 141 Billy McMullen AU RC 10.00 4.00
- ❑ 142 Doug Gabriel AU RC 12.00 5.00
- ❑ 143 J.R. Tolver AU RC 10.00 4.00
- ❑ 144 Gibran Hamdan AU RC 8.00 3.00
- ❑ 145 Walter Young AU RC 8.00 3.00
- ❑ 146 Carl Ford AU RC 8.00 3.00
- ❑ 147 Andrew Pinnock AU RC 10.00 4.00
- ❑ 148 Byron Leftwich AU/199 RC 50.00 20.00
- ❑ 149 Ty Warren AU RC 12.00 5.00
- ❑ 150 Visanthe Shiancoe AU RC 10.00 4.00
- ❑ 151 Justin Gage AU RC 12.00 5.00
- ❑ 152 Brock Forsey AU RC 12.00 5.00
- ❑ 153 Casey Moore AU RC 10.00 4.00
- ❑ 154 Juston Wood AU RC 8.00 3.00
- ❑ 155 Aaron Walker AU RC 10.00 4.00
- ❑ 156 Trent Smith AU RC 12.00 5.00
- ❑ 157 Travis Anglin AU RC 8.00 3.00
- ❑ 158 Jeremi Johnson AU RC 10.00 4.00
- ❑ 159 Justin Griffith AU RC 10.00 4.00
- ❑ 160 Chris Davis AU RC 10.00 4.00
- ❑ 161 J.T. Wall AU RC 8.00 3.00
- ❑ 162 Larry Johnson AU/199 RC 150.00 75.00
- ❑ 163 Jon Olinger AU RC 10.00 4.00
- ❑ 164 Donald Lee AU RC 10.00 4.00
- ❑ 165 Taco Wallace AU RC 10.00 4.00
- ❑ 166 DeAndrew Rubin AU RC 8.00 3.00
- ❑ 167 Ryan Hoag AU RC 8.00 3.00
- ❑ 168 Kevin Williams AU RC 20.00 8.00
- ❑ 169 Ovie Mughelli AU RC 8.00 3.00
- ❑ 171 Brandon Drumm AU RC 10.00 4.00
- ❑ 172 Brad Banks AU RC 10.00 4.00
- ❑ 173 Talman Gardner AU RC 12.00 5.00
- ❑ [illegible]

2004 Bowman's Best

- ❑ COMP.SET w/o SP's (100) 50.00 25.00
- ❑ RC JSY GROUP A ODDS 1:130
- ❑ RC JSY GROUP B ODDS 1:236
- ❑ RC JSY GROUP C ODDS 1:86
- ❑ RC JSY GROUP D ODDS 1:38
- ❑ RC JSY GROUP E ODDS 1:31
- ❑ RC JSY GROUP F ODDS 1:27
- ❑ RC JSY GROUP G ODDS 1:50
- ❑ RC JSY GROUP H ODDS 1:89
- ❑ RC JSY GROUP I ODDS 1:29
- ❑ RC AU/199 STATED ODDS 1:311
- ❑ RC AU STATED ODDS 1:3
- ❑ 1 Brett Favre 4.00 1.50
- ❑ 2 Chris Chambers 1.00 .40
- ❑ 3 Kyle Boller 1.50 .60
- ❑ 4 Brian Urlacher 2.00 .75
- ❑ 5 Marvin Harrison 1.50 .60
- ❑ 6 Matt Hasselbeck 1.00 .40
- ❑ 7 Aaron Brooks 1.00 .40
- ❑ 8 Curtis Martin 1.50 .60
- ❑ 9 Keenan McCardell .60 .25
- ❑ 10 Terrell Owens 1.50 .60
- ❑ 11 Jimmy Smith 1.00 .40
- ❑ 12 Garrison Hearst 1.00 .40
- ❑ 13 Joe Horn 1.00 .40
- ❑ 14 David Carr 1.50 .60
- ❑ 15 Tom Brady 4.00 1.50
- ❑ 16 Shaun Alexander 1.50 .60
- ❑ [illegible]
- ❑ 18 Tiki Barber 1.50 .60
- ❑ 19 Trent Green 1.00 .40
- ❑ 20 Anquan Boldin 1.50 .60
- ❑ 21 Peerless Price 1.00 .40
- ❑ 22 Jake Delhomme 1.50 .60
- ❑ 23 Eric Moulds 1.00 .40
- ❑ 24 Quincy Carter 1.00 .40
- ❑ 25 Steve McNair 1.50 .60
- ❑ 26 Tim Hattay .60 .25
- ❑ 27 Laveranues Coles 1.00 .40
- ❑ 28 Corey Dillon 1.00 .40
- ❑ 29 Byron Leftwich 2.00 .75
- ❑ 30 Chad Pennington 1.50 .60
- ❑ 31 Koren Robinson 1.00 .40
- ❑ 32 Plaxico Burress 1.00 .40
- ❑ 33 Steve Smith 1.50 .60
- ❑ 34 Warrick Dunn 1.00 .40
- ❑ 35 Jamal Lewis 1.50 .60
- ❑ 36 Charles Rogers 1.00 .40
- ❑ 37 Tony Gonzalez 1.00 .40
- ❑ 38 Jake Plummer 1.00 .40
- ❑ 39 Chad Johnson 1.50 .60
- ❑ 40 Peyton Manning 2.50 1.00
- ❑ 41 Daunte Culpepper 1.50 .60
- ❑ 42 Fred Taylor 1.00 .40
- ❑ 43 Amani Toomer 1.00 .40
- ❑ 44 Santana Moss 1.00 .40
- ❑ 45 Deuce McAllister 1.50 .60
- ❑ 46 Rex Grossman 1.50 .60
- ❑ 47 Ray Lewis 1.50 .60
- ❑ 48 Hines Ward 1.50 .60
- ❑ 49 Darrell Jackson 1.00 .40
- ❑ 50 Randy Moss 2.00 .75
- ❑ 51 Carson Palmer 2.00 .75
- ❑ 52 Rod Smith 1.00 .40
- ❑ 53 Drew Bledsoe 1.50 .60
- ❑ 54 Brad Johnson 1.00 .40
- ❑ 55 Travis Henry 1.00 .40
- ❑ 56 Joey Harrington 1.50 .60
- ❑ 57 Edgerrin James 1.50 .60
- ❑ [illegible]
- ❑ 59 Josh McCown 1.00 .40
- ❑ 60 Clinton Portis 1.50 .60
- ❑ 61 Brian Westbrook 1.00 .40
- ❑ 62 Marc Bulger 1.50 .60
- ❑ 63 Charlie Garner 1.00 .40
- ❑ 64 Torry Holt 1.50 .60
- ❑ 65 LaDainian Tomlinson 2.00 .75
- ❑ 66 Mark Brunell 1.00 .40
- ❑ 67 Derrick Mason 1.00 .40
- ❑ 68 Andre Johnson 1.50 .60
- ❑ 69 Keyshawn Johnson 1.00 .40
- ❑ 70 Ahman Green 1.50 .60
- ❑ 71 Rudi Johnson 1.00 .40
- ❑ 72 Stephen Davis 1.00 .40
- ❑ 73 Jeff Garcia 1.50 .60
- ❑ 74 Michael Strahan 1.00 .40
- ❑ 75 Michael Vick 3.00 1.25
- ❑ 76 Ricky Williams 1.50 .60
- ❑ 77 Domanick Davis 1.50 .60
- ❑ 78 Priest Holmes 2.00 .75
- ❑ 79 Marshall Faulk 1.50 .60
- ❑ 80 Donovan McNabb 2.00 .75
- ❑ 81 Dunta Robinson RC 4.00 1.50
- ❑ 82 Robert Gallery RC 4.00 1.50
- ❑ 83 Ben Troupe RC 4.00 1.50
- ❑ 84 Antwan Odom RC 4.00 1.50
- ❑ 85 Brandon Miree RC 3.00 1.25
- ❑ 86 Darnell Dockett RC 3.00 1.25
- ❑ 87 Vince Wilfork RC 4.00 1.50
- ❑ 88 Randy Starks RC 3.00 1.25
- ❑ 89 Chris Cooley RC 4.00 1.50
- ❑ 90 Dwan Edwards RC 2.00 .75
- ❑ 91 Patrick Crayton RC 4.00 1.50
- ❑ 92 Sean Jones RC 3.00 1.25
- ❑ 93 Sean Ryan RC 3.00 1.25
- ❑ 94 Chris Gamble RC 4.00 1.50
- ❑ 95 Will Smith RC 4.00 1.50
- ❑ 96 Sloan Thomas RC 3.00 1.25
- ❑ 97 Tim Euhus RC 4.00 1.50
- ❑ 98 Tommie Harris RC 4.00 1.50
- ❑ 99 Will Poole RC 4.00 1.50
- ❑ 100 Karlos Dansby RC 4.00 1.50
- ❑ 101 Bernard Berrian JSY RC D 8.00 3.00
- ❑ 102 DeAngelo Hall JSY RC A 8.00 3.00
- ❑ 103 Mewelde Moore JSY RC G 6.00 2.50
- ❑ 104 Rashaun Woods JSY RC G 6.00 2.50
- ❑ 105 Reggie Williams JSY RC 8.00 3.00
- ❑ [illegible]
- ❑ 107 Kellen Winslow JSY RC C 12.00 5.00
- ❑ 108 Devard Darling JSY RC D 6.00 2.50
- ❑ 109 Michael Clayton JSY RC B 12.00 5.00
- ❑ 110 Larry Fitzgerald JSY RC E 20.00 7.50
- ❑ 111 Greg Jones JSY RC E 6.00 2.50
- ❑ 112 Chris Perry JSY RC H 10.00 4.00
- ❑ 113 Lee Evans JSY RC F 8.00 3.00
- ❑ 114 Tatum Bell JSY RC E 12.00 5.00
- ❑ 115 Steven Jackson JSY RC I 20.00 7.50
- ❑ 116 Matt Schaub JSY RC A 12.00 5.00
- ❑ 117 Ben Troupe JSY 6.00 2.50
- ❑ 118 Devery Henderson JSY RC F 6.00 2.50
- ❑ 119 Ben Watson JSY RC E 6.00 2.50
- ❑ 120 J.P. Losman JSY RC I 12.00 5.00
- ❑ 121 Keary Colbert JSY RC F 6.00 2.50
- ❑ 122 Darius Watts JSY RC C 6.00 2.50
- ❑ 123 Cedric Cobbs JSY RC D 6.00 2.50
- ❑ 124 Luke McCown JSY RC A 6.00 2.50
- ❑ 125 Michael Jenkins JSY RC A 6.00 2.50
- ❑ 126 Eli Manning AU/199 RC 200.00 125.00
- ❑ 127 Roy Williams AU/199 RC 100.00 50.00
- ❑ 128 Kevin Jones AU/199 RC 80.00 40.00
- ❑ 129 Philip Rivers AU/199 RC 120.00 50.00
- ❑ 130 Roethlis AU/199 RC 250.00 125.00
- ❑ 131 Carlos Francis AU RC 12.00 5.00
- ❑ 132 Bradlee Van Pelt AU RC 15.00 6.00
- ❑ 133 Michael Turner AU RC 40.00 20.00
- ❑ 134 Kenechi Udeze AU RC 15.00 6.00
- ❑ 135 Jeff Smoker AU RC 15.00 6.00
- ❑ 136 Josh Harris AU RC 12.00 5.00
- ❑ 137 Derrick Strait AU RC 12.00 5.00
- ❑ 138 Jonathan Vilma AU RC 20.00 7.50
- ❑ 139 Triandos Luke AU RC 12.00 5.00
- ❑ 140 Jim Sorgi AU RC 15.00 6.00
- ❑ 141 Ryan Krause AU RC 12.00 5.00
- ❑ 142 Julius Jones AU RC 60.00 30.00
- ❑ 143 Mark Jones AU RC 12.00 5.00
- ❑ 144 P.K. Sam AU RC 12.00 5.00
- ❑ 145 B.J. Symons AU RC 15.00 6.00
- ❑ 146 Adimchinobe Echemandu AU RC 12.00 5.00
- ❑ 147 Casey Bramlet AU RC 12.00 5.00
- ❑ 148 Clarence Moore AU RC 15.00 6.00
- ❑ 149 D.J. Williams AU RC 12.00 5.00
- ❑ 150 Jeris McIntyre AU RC 12.00 5.00
- ❑ 151 Jerricho Cotchery AU RC 15.00 6.00
- ❑ 152 Andy Hall AU RC 12.00 5.00
- ❑ 153 Samie Parker AU RC 15.00 6.00
- ❑ 154 Maurice Mann AU RC 12.00 5.00
- ❑ 155 Jonathan Smith AU RC 12.00 5.00
- ❑ 156 Derrick Ward AU RC 20.00 8.00
- ❑ 157 D.J. Hackett AU RC 15.00 6.00
- ❑ 158 Craig Krenzel AU RC 15.00 6.00
- ❑ 159 Jared Lorenzen AU RC 12.00 5.00
- ❑ 160 Cody Pickett AU RC 15.00 6.00
- ❑ 161 Jamaar Taylor AU RC 15.00 6.00
- ❑ 162 Michael Boulware AU RC 15.00 6.00
- ❑ 163 Matt Mauck AU RC 12.00 5.00
- ❑ 164 John Navarre AU RC 15.00 6.00
- ❑ 165 Ahmad Carroll AU RC 12.00 5.00
- ❑ 166 Bruce Perry AU RC 15.00 6.00
- ❑ 167 Erik Jensen AU RC 12.00 5.00
- ❑ 168 Matt Kranchick AU RC 15.00 6.00
- ❑ 169 Courtney Anderson AU RC 12.00 5.00
- ❑ 170 Nate Lawrie AU RC 12.00 5.00
- ❑ 171 Thomas Tapeh AU RC 12.00 5.00
- ❑ 172 Courtney Watson AU RC 15.00 6.00
- ❑ 173 Drew Carter AU RC 15.00 6.00
- ❑ 174 Ricardo Colclough AU RC 15.00 6.00
- ❑ 175 Dontarrious Thomas AU RC 15.00 6.00
- ❑ 176 Ernest Wilford AU RC 15.00 6.00
- ❑ 177 Quincy Wilson AU RC 12.00 5.00
- ❑ 178 Derek Abney AU RC 15.00 6.00
- ❑ 179 Jeff Dugan AU RC 10.00 4.00
- ❑ 180 Ben Hartsock AU RC 15.00 6.00

❑ 181 Matt Kegel AU RC 15.00 6.00
❑ 182 Derrick Knight AU RC 12.00 5.00
❑ 183 Teddy Lehman AU RC 15.00 6.00
❑ 184 Johnnie Morant AU RC 15.00 6.00
❑ 185A B.Sanders AU RC Long AU 150.00 100.00
❑ 185B B.Sanders AU RC Short AU 100.00 50.00
❑ 186 Michael Gaines AU RC 12.00 5.00
❑ 187 Daryl Smith AU RC 15.00 6.00
❑ 188 Jason Babin AU RC 15.00 6.00

2005 Bowman's Best

❑ COMP.SET w/o SPs (100) 40.00 15.00
❑ ROOKIE JSY STATED ODDS 1:14
❑ ROOKIE JSY PRINT RUN 799 SER.#'d SETS
❑ ROOKIE AU/999 STATED ODDS 1:8
❑ ROOKIE AU/199 STATED ODDS 1:296
❑ ROOKIE AU PRINT RUN 999 SER.#'d SETS
❑ AU EXCH EXPIRATION: 10/31/2007
❑ UNPRICED GOLD PRINT RUN 1 SET
❑ UNPRICED PRINT.PLATE PRINT RUN 1 SET
❑ 1 Tiki Barber 1.00 .40
❑ 2 Peyton Manning 2.50 1.00
❑ 3 Tony Gonzalez .60 .25
❑ 4 Terrell Owens 1.00 .40
❑ 5 Brett Favre 2.50 1.00
❑ 6 Rudi Johnson .60 .25
❑ 7 Hines Ward 1.00 .40
❑ 8 Andre Johnson .60 .25
❑ 9 Tom Brady 2.50 1.00
❑ 10 LaDainian Tomlinson 1.25 .50
❑ 11 Daunte Culpepper 1.00 .40
❑ 12 Muhsin Muhammad .60 .25
❑ 13 Dwight Freeney .60 .25
❑ 14 Curtis Martin 1.00 .40
❑ 15 Eli Manning 1.50 .60
❑ 16 Willis McGahee 1.00 .40
❑ 17 Steve McNair 1.00 .40
❑ 18 Jamal Lewis 1.00 .40
❑ 19 Reggie Wayne .60 .25
❑ 20 Trent Green .60 .25
❑ 21 Isaac Bruce .60 .25
❑ 22 Edgerrin James 1.00 .40
❑ 23 Marc Bulger 1.00 .40
❑ 24 Torry Holt 1.00 .40
❑ 25 Deuce McAllister 1.00 .40
❑ 26 Jake Plummer .60 .25
❑ 27 Randy Moss 1.00 .40
❑ 28 Drew Brees 1.00 .40
❑ 29 Ahman Green 1.00 .40
❑ 30 Marvin Harrison 1.00 .40
❑ 31 Michael Vick 1.50 .60
❑ 32 Julius Jones 1.25 .50
❑ 33 Matt Hasselbeck .60 .25
❑ 34 Priest Holmes 1.00 .40
❑ 35 Drew Bennett .60 .25
❑ 36 Donovan McNabb 1.25 .50
❑ 37 Chad Johnson 1.00 .40
❑ 38 Fred Taylor .60 .25
❑ 39 Chris Brown .60 .25
❑ 40 Jake Delhomme 1.00 .40
❑ 41 Joe Horn .60 .25
❑ 42 Chad Pennington 1.00 .40
❑ 43 Corey Dillon .60 .25
❑ 44 Byron Leftwich 1.00 .40
❑ 45 Javon Walker .60 .25
❑ 46 Ben Roethlisberger 2.50 1.00
❑ 47 Eric Moulds .60 .25
❑ 48 Domanick Davis .60 .25
❑ 49 Steven Jackson 1.25 .50
❑ 50 Shaun Alexander 1.25 .50
❑ 51 Stanford Routt RC 4.00 1.50
❑ 52 Marion Barber RC 8.00 3.00
❑ 53 Matt Roth RC 5.00 2.00
❑ 54 James Kilian RC 5.00 2.00
❑ 55 Alex Barron RC 2.50 1.00
❑ 56 Madison Hedgecock RC 5.00 2.00
❑ 57 Patrick Estes RC 4.00 1.50
❑ 58 Bryant McFadden RC 5.00 2.00
❑ 59 Dan Cody RC 5.00 2.00
❑ 60 Justin Miller RC 4.00 1.50
❑ 61 Paris Warren RC 4.00 1.50
❑ 62 Marcus Spears RC 5.00 2.00
❑ 63 Odell Thurman RC 5.00 2.00
❑ 64 Craphonso Thorpe RC 4.00 1.50
❑ 65 Dustin Fox RC 5.00 2.00
❑ 66 David Pollack RC 5.00 2.00
❑ 67 Anthony Davis RC 4.00 1.50
❑ 68 Mike Nugent RC 5.00 2.00
❑ 69 David Greene RC 5.00 2.00
❑ 70 Rick Razzano RC 5.00 2.00
❑ 70AU Rick Razzano AU 12.00 5.00
❑ 71 Mike Patterson RC 5.00 2.00
❑ 72 Derek Anderson RC 8.00 3.00
❑ 72AU Derek Anderson AU 30.00 15.00
❑ 73 Marlin Jackson RC 5.00 2.00
❑ 73AU Marlin Jackson AU 12.00 5.00
❑ 74 Boomer Grigsby RC 5.00 2.00
❑ 75 Kevin Burnett RC 5.00 2.00
❑ 76 Ryan Riddle RC 2.50 1.00
❑ 77 Brock Berlin RC 4.00 1.50
❑ 78 Khalif Barnes RC 4.00 1.50
❑ 79 Marcus Maxwell RC 4.00 1.50
❑ 80 Fred Gibson RC 4.00 1.50
❑ 81 T.A. McLendon RC 2.50 1.00
❑ 82 Kirk Morrison RC 5.00 2.00
❑ 83 Sean Considine RC 5.00 2.00
❑ 84 Luis Castillo RC 5.00 2.00
❑ 85 Darryl Blackstock RC 4.00 1.50
❑ 86 Airese Currie RC 5.00 2.00
❑ 87 Corey Webster RC 5.00 2.00
❑ 88 Kurt Campbell RC 4.00 1.50
❑ 89 Ellis Hobbs RC 5.00 2.00
❑ 90 Timmy Chang RC 4.00 1.50
❑ 91 Travis Johnson RC 4.00 1.50
❑ 92 Eric Moore RC 4.00 1.50
❑ 93 Barrett Ruud RC 5.00 2.00
❑ 94 Erasmus James RC 5.00 2.00
❑ 95 Anttaj Hawthorne RC 4.00 1.50
❑ 96 Manuel White RC 4.00 1.50
❑ 97 Rian Wallace RC 4.00 1.50
❑ 98 Justin Tuck RC 5.00 2.00
❑ 99 Travis Daniels RC 4.00 1.50
❑ 100 Donte Nicholson RC 5.00 2.00
❑ 101 Matt Jones JSY RC 10.00 4.00
❑ 102 J.J. Arrington JSY RC 8.00 3.00
❑ 103 Mark Bradley JSY RC 10.00 4.00
❑ 104 Reggie Brown JSY RC 8.00 3.00
❑ 105 Jason Campbell JSY RC 10.00 4.00
❑ 106 Maurice Clarett JSY 8.00 3.00
❑ 107 Mark Clayton JSY RC 8.00 3.00
❑ 108 Braylon Edwards JSY RC 15.00 6.00
❑ 109 Ciatrick Fason JSY RC 8.00 3.00
❑ 110 Charlie Frye JSY RC 8.00 3.00
❑ 111 Frank Gore JSY RC 12.00 5.00
❑ 112 Vincent Jackson JSY RC 10.00 4.00
❑ 113 Adam Jones JSY RC 8.00 3.00
❑ 114 Stefan LeFors JSY 8.00 3.00
❑ 114AU Stefan LeFors AU RC 12.00 5.00
❑ 115 Ryan Moats JSY 8.00 3.00
❑ 115AU Ryan Moats AU RC 20.00 7.50
❑ 116 Vernand Morency JSY RC 8.00 3.00
❑ 117 Terrence Murphy JSY RC 8.00 3.00
❑ 118 Kyle Orton JSY RC 8.00 3.00
❑ 119 Roscoe Parrish JSY RC 8.00 3.00
❑ 120 Courtney Roby JSY RC 8.00 3.00
❑ 121 Carlos Rogers JSY RC 10.00 4.00
❑ 122 Antrel Rolle JSY RC 8.00 3.00
❑ 123 Eric Shelton JSY RC 8.00 3.00
❑ 124 Andrew Walter JSY RC 8.00 3.00
❑ 125 Roddy White JSY RC 8.00 3.00
❑ 126 Cadillac Williams JSY RC 25.00 10.00
❑ 127 Troy Williamson JSY RC 8.00 3.00
❑ 128 Cedric Benson AU/199 RC 80.00 40.00
❑ 129 Aaron Rodgers AU/199 RC 120.00 60.00
❑ 130 Alex Smith QB AU/199 RC 120.00 60.00
❑ 131 Mike Williams AU/199 20.00 8.00
❑ 132 Ronnie Brown AU/199 RC 120.00 50.00
❑ 133 Adrian McPherson AU RC 15.00 6.00
❑ 134 Brandon Jacobs AU RC 30.00 12.50
❑ 135 Chad Owens AU RC 12.00 5.00
❑ 136 Chase Lyman AU RC 10.00 4.00
❑ 137 Chris Henry AU RC EXCH 12.00 5.00
❑ 138 Craig Bragg AU RC 10.00 4.00
❑ 139 Damien Nash AU RC 10.00 4.00
❑ 140 Dante Ridgeway AU RC 10.00 4.00
❑ 141 Darren Sproles AU RC 12.00 5.00
❑ 142 Deandra Cobb AU RC 10.00 4.00
❑ 143 Gino Guidugli AU RC 8.00 3.00
❑ 144 J.R. Russell AU RC 10.00 4.00
❑ 145 Jerome Mathis AU RC EXCH 12.00 5.00
❑ 146 Josh Davis AU RC 10.00 4.00
❑ 147 Kay-Jay Harris AU RC 10.00 4.00
❑ 148 Larry Brackins AU RC 10.00 4.00
❑ 149 Matt Cassel AU RC 20.00 10.00
❑ 150 Noah Herron AU RC 12.00 5.00
❑ 151 Rasheed Marshall AU RC 12.00 5.00
❑ 152 Roydell Williams AU RC 12.00 5.00
❑ 153 Ryan Fitzpatrick AU RC 12.00 5.00
❑ 154 Steve Savoy AU RC 8.00 3.00
❑ 155 Tab Perry AU RC 12.00 5.00
❑ 156 Shawne Merriman AU RC 30.00 12.50
❑ 157 Charles Frederick AU RC 10.00 4.00
❑ 158 Alvin Pearman AU RC 12.00 5.00
❑ 159 Channing Crowder AU RC 12.00 5.00
❑ 160 Fabian Washington AU RC 12.00 5.00
❑ 161 Dan Orlovsky AU RC 15.00 6.00
❑ 162 Derrick Johnson AU RC 20.00 7.50
❑ 163 Alex Smith TE AU RC 12.00 5.00
❑ 164 Cedric Houston AU RC 12.00 5.00
❑ 165 Brandon Jones AU RC 12.00 5.00
❑ 166 DeMarcus Ware AU RC 25.00 12.50
❑ 167 Lionel Gates AU RC 10.00 4.00

1996 Donruss

❑ COMPLETE SET (240) 20.00 7.50
❑ 1 Barry Sanders 1.50 .60
❑ 2 Flipper Anderson .10 .02
❑ 3 Ben Coates .20 .07
❑ 4 Rob Johnson .40 .15
❑ 5 Rodney Hampton .20 .07
❑ 6 Desmond Howard .20 .07
❑ 7 Craig Heyward .10 .02
❑ 8 Alvin Harper .10 .02
❑ 9 Todd Collins .20 .07
❑ 10 Ken Norton Jr. .10 .02
❑ 11 Stan Humphries .20 .07
❑ 12 Aeneas Williams .10 .02
❑ 13 Jeff Hostetler .10 .02
❑ 14 Frank Sanders .20 .07
❑ 15 J.J. Birden .10 .02
❑ 16 Bryce Paup .10 .02
❑ 17 Bill Brooks .10 .02
❑ 18 Kevin Williams .10 .02
❑ 19 Boomer Esiason .20 .07
❑ 20 O.J. McDuffie .20 .07
❑ 21 Eric Swann .10 .02
❑ 22 Neil Smith .20 .07
❑ 23 Charlie Garner .20 .07
❑ 24 Greg Lloyd .20 .07
❑ 25 Willie Jackson .20 .07
❑ 26 Shawn Jefferson .10 .02
❑ 27 Rodney Peete .10 .02
❑ 28 Michael Westbrook .40 .15
❑ 29 J.J. Stokes .40 .15
❑ 30 Troy Aikman 1.00 .40
❑ 31 Sean Dawkins .10 .02
❑ 32 Larry Centers .20 .07
❑ 33 Herschel Walker .20 .07
❑ 34 Stoney Case .10 .02
❑ 35 Kevin Greene .20 .07
❑ 36 Quinn Early .10 .02
❑ 37 Fred Barnett .10 .02
❑ 38 Andre Coleman .10 .02

❑ 39 Mark Chmura .20 .07
❑ 40 Adrian Murrell .20 .07
❑ 41 Roosevelt Potts .10 .02
❑ 42 Jay Novacek .10 .02
❑ 43 Derrick Alexander .20 .07
❑ 44 Ken Dilger .20 .07
❑ 45 Rob Moore .20 .07
❑ 46 Cris Carter .40 .15
❑ 47 Jeff Blake .40 .15
❑ 48 Derek Loville .10 .02
❑ 49 Tyrone Wheatley .20 .07
❑ 50 Terrell Fletcher .10 .02
❑ 51 Sherman Williams .10 .02
❑ 52 Justin Armour .10 .02
❑ 53 Kordell Stewart [illegible] [illegible]
❑ 54 Tim Brown .40 .15
❑ 55 Kevin Carter .10 .02
❑ 56 Andre Rison .20 .07
❑ 57 James O.Stewart .20 .07
❑ 58 Brent Jones .10 .02
❑ 59 Erik Kramer .10 .02
❑ 60 Floyd Turner .10 .02
❑ 61 Ricky Watters .20 .07
❑ 62 Hardy Nickerson .10 .02
❑ 63 Aaron Craver .10 .02
❑ 64 Dave Krieg .10 .02
❑ 65 Warren Moon .20 .07
❑ 66 Wayne Chrebet .50 .20
❑ 67 Napoleon Kaufman .40 .15
❑ 68 Terance Mathis .10 .02
❑ 69 Chad May .10 .02
❑ 70 Andre Reed .20 .07
❑ 71 Reggie White .40 .15
❑ 72 Brett Favre 2.00 .75
❑ 73 Chris Zorich .10 .02
❑ 74 Kerry Collins .40 .15
❑ 75 Herman Moore .20 .07
❑ 76 Yancey Thigpen .20 .07
❑ 77 Glenn Foley .20 .07
❑ 78 Quentin Coryatt .10 .02
❑ 79 Terry Kirby .20 .07
❑ 80 Edgar Bennett .20 .07
❑ 81 Mark Brunell .60 .25
❑ 82 Heath Shuler .20 .07
❑ 83 Gus Frerotte .20 .07
❑ 84 Deion Sanders .60 .25
❑ 85 Calvin Williams .10 .02
❑ 86 Junior Seau .40 .15
❑ 87 Jim Kelly .40 .15
❑ 88 Daryl Johnston .20 .07
❑ 89 Irving Fryar .20 .07
❑ 90 Brian Blades .10 .02
❑ 91 Willie Davis .10 .02
❑ 92 Jerome Bettis .40 .15
❑ 93 Marcus Allen .40 .15
❑ 94 Jeff Graham .10 .02
❑ 95 Rick Mirer .20 .07
❑ 96 Harvey Williams .10 .02
❑ 97 Steve Atwater .10 .02
❑ 98 Carl Pickens .20 .07
❑ 99 Darick Holmes .10 .02
❑ 100 Bruce Smith .20 .07
❑ 101 Vinny Testaverde .20 .07
❑ 102 Thurman Thomas .40 .15
❑ 103 Drew Bledsoe .60 .25
❑ 104 Bernie Parmalee .10 .02
❑ 105 Greg Hill .20 .07
❑ 106 Steve McNair .75 .30
❑ 107 Andre Hastings .10 .02
❑ 108 Eric Metcalf .10 .02
❑ 109 Kimble Anders .20 .07
❑ 110 Steve Tasker .10 .02
❑ 111 Mark Carrier WR .10 .02
❑ 112 Jerry Rice 1.00 .40
❑ 113 Joey Galloway .40 .15
❑ 114 Robert Smith .20 .07
❑ 115 Hugh Douglas .20 .07
❑ 116 Willie McGinest .10 .02
❑ 117 Terrell Davis .75 .30
❑ 118 Cortez Kennedy .10 .02
❑ 119 Marshall Faulk .50 .20
❑ 120 Michael Haynes .10 .02
❑ 121 Isaac Bruce .40 .15
❑ 122 Brian Mitchell .10 .02
❑ 123 Bryan Cox .10 .02
❑ 124 Tamarick Vanover .20 .07
❑ 125 William Floyd .20 .07
❑ 126 Chris Chandler .20 .07
❑ 127 Carnell Lake .10 .02
❑ 128 Aaron Bailey .10 .02
❑ 129 Darnay Scott .20 .07
❑ 130 Darren Woodson .20 .07
❑ 131 Ernie Mills .10 .02
❑ 132 Charles Haley .20 .07
❑ 133 Rocket Ismail .10 .02
❑ 134 Bert Emanuel .20 .07
❑ 135 Lake Dawson .10 .02
❑ 136 Jake Reed .20 .07
❑ 137 Dave Brown .10 .02
❑ 138 Steve Bono .10 .02
❑ 139 Terry Allen .20 .07
❑ 140 Errict Rhett .20 .07
❑ 141 Rod Woodson .20 .07
❑ 142 Charles Johnson .10 .02
❑ 143 Emmitt Smith 1.50 .60
❑ 144 Ki-Jana Carter .20 .07
❑ 145 Garrison Hearst .20 .07
❑ 146 Rashaan Salaam .20 .07
❑ 147 Tony Boselli .10 .02
❑ 148 Derrick Thomas .40 .15
❑ 149 Mark Seay .10 .02
❑ 150 Derrick Alexander .10 .02
❑ 151 Christian Fauria .10 .02
❑ 152 Aaron Hayden .10 .02
❑ 153 Chris Warren .20 .07
❑ 154 Dave Meggett .10 .02
❑ 155 Jeff George .20 .07
❑ 156 Jackie Harris .10 .02
❑ 157 Michael Irvin .40 .15
❑ 158 Scott Mitchell .20 .07
❑ 159 Trent Dilfer .40 .15
❑ 160 Kyle Brady .10 .02
❑ 161 Dan Marino 2.00 .75
❑ 162 Curtis Martin .75 .30
❑ 163 Mario Bates .20 .07
❑ 164 Erric Pegram .10 .02
❑ 165 Eric Zeier .10 .02
❑ 166 Rodney Thomas .10 .02
❑ 167 Neil O'Donnell .20 .07
❑ 168 Warren Sapp .10 .02
❑ 169 Jim Harbaugh .20 .07
❑ 170 Henry Ellard .10 .02
❑ 171 Anthony Miller .20 .07
❑ 172 Derrick Moore .10 .02
❑ 173 John Elway 2.00 .75
❑ 174 Vincent Brisby .10 .02
❑ 175 Antonio Freeman .40 .15
❑ 176 Chris Sanders .20 .07
❑ 177 Steve Young .75 .30
❑ 178 Shannon Sharpe .20 .07
❑ 179 Brett Perriman .10 .02
❑ 180 Orlando Thomas .10 .02
❑ 181 Eric Bjornson .10 .02
❑ 182 Natrone Means .20 .07
❑ 183 Jim Everett .10 .02
❑ 184 Curtis Conway .40 .15
❑ 185 Robert Brooks .40 .15
❑ 186 Tony Martin .20 .07
❑ 187 Mark Carrier DB .10 .02
❑ 188 LeShon Johnson .10 .02
❑ 189 Bernie Kosar .10 .02
❑ 190 Ray Zellars .10 .02
❑ 191 Steve Walsh .10 .02
❑ 192 Craig Erickson .10 .02
❑ 193 Tommy Maddox .40 .15
❑ 194 Leslie O'Neal .10 .02
❑ 195 Harold Green .10 .02
❑ 196 Steve Beuerlein .20 .07
❑ 197 Ronald Moore .10 .02
❑ 198 Leslie Shepherd .10 .02
❑ 199 Leroy Hoard .10 .02
❑ 200 Michael Jackson .20 .07
❑ 201 Will Moore .10 .02
❑ 202 Ricky Ervins .10 .02
❑ 203 Keith Jennings .10 .02
❑ 204 Eric Green .10 .02
❑ 205 Mark Rypien .10 .02
❑ 206 Torrance Small .10 .02
❑ 207 Sean Gilbert .10 .02
❑ 208 Mike Alstott RC 1.00 .40
❑ 209 Willie Anderson RC .10 .02
❑ 210 Alex Molden RC .10 .02
❑ 211 Jonathan Ogden RC .40 .15
❑ 212 Stepfret Williams RC .20 .07
❑ 213 Jeff Lewis RC .20 .07
❑ 214 Regan Upshaw RC .10 .02
❑ 215 Daryl Gardener RC .10 .02
❑ 216 Danny Kanell RC .40 .15
❑ 217 John Mobley RC .10 .02
❑ 218 Reggie Brown LB RC .10 .02
❑ 219 Muhsin Muhammad RC 1.00 .40
❑ 220 Kevin Hardy RC .40 .15
❑ 221 Stanley Pritchett RC .20 .07
❑ 222 Cedric Jones RC .10 .02
❑ 223 Marco Battaglia RC .10 .02
❑ 224 Duane Clemons RC .10 .02
❑ 225 Jerald Moore RC .20 .07
❑ 226 Simeon Rice RC 1.00 .40
❑ 227 Chris Darkins RC .10 .02
❑ 228 Bobby Hoying RC .40 .15
❑ 229 Stephen Davis RC 1.50 .60
❑ 230 Walt Harris RC .10 .02
❑ 231 Jermane Mayberry RC .10 .02
❑ 232 Tony Brackens RC .40 .15
❑ 233 Eric Moulds RC 1.25 .50
❑ 234 Alex Van Dyke RC .20 .07
❑ 235 Marvin Harrison RC 2.50 1.00
❑ 236 Rickey Dudley RC .40 .15
❑ 237 Terrell Owens RC 2.50 1.00
❑ 238 Jerry Rice CL .40 .15
❑ 239 Dan Marino CL .40 .15
❑ 240 Emmitt Smith CL .40 .15

1997 Donruss

❑ COMPLETE SET (230) 20.00 7.50
❑ 1 Dan Marino 2.00 .75
❑ 2 Brett Favre 2.00 .75
❑ 3 Emmitt Smith 1.50 .60
❑ 4 Eddie George .50 .20
❑ 5 Karim Abdul-Jabbar .30 .10
❑ 6 Terrell Davis .60 .25
❑ 7 Curtis Martin .60 .25
❑ 8 Drew Bledsoe .60 .25
❑ 9 Jerry Rice 1.00 .40
❑ 10 Troy Aikman 1.00 .40
❑ 11 Barry Sanders 1.50 .60
❑ 12 Mark Brunell .60 .25
❑ 13 Kerry Collins .50 .20
❑ 14 Steve Young .60 .25
❑ 15 Kordell Stewart .50 .20
❑ 16 Eddie Kennison .30 .10
❑ 17 Terry Glenn .50 .20
❑ 18 John Elway 2.00 .75
❑ 19 Joey Galloway .30 .10
❑ 20 Deion Sanders .50 .20
❑ 21 Keyshawn Johnson .50 .20
❑ 22 Lawrence Phillips .20 .07
❑ 23 Ricky Watters .30 .10
❑ 24 Marvin Harrison .50 .20
❑ 25 Bobby Engram .30 .10
❑ 26 Marshall Faulk .60 .25
❑ 27 Carl Pickens .30 .10
❑ 28 Isaac Bruce .50 .20
❑ 29 Herman Moore .30 .10
❑ 30 Jerome Bettis .50 .20
❑ 31 Rashaan Salaam .20 .07
❑ 32 Errict Rhett .20 .07
❑ 33 Tim Biakabutuka .30 .10
❑ 34 Robert Brooks .30 .10
❑ 35 Antonio Freeman .50 .20
❑ 36 Steve McNair .60 .25
❑ 37 Jeff Blake .30 .10
❑ 38 Tony Banks .30 .10
❑ 39 Terrell Owens .60 .25
❑ 40 Eric Moulds .50 .20
❑ 41 Leeland McElroy .20 .07
❑ 42 Chris Sanders .20 .07
❑ 43 Thurman Thomas .50 .20
❑ 44 Bruce Smith .30 .10
❑ 45 Reggie White .50 .20

46 Chris Warren	.30	.10
47 J.J. Stokes	.30	.10
48 Ben Coates	.30	.10
49 Tim Brown	.50	.20
50 Marcus Allen	.50	.20
51 Michael Irvin	.50	.20
52 William Floyd	.30	.10
53 Ken Dilger	.20	.07
54 Bobby Taylor	.20	.07
55 Keenan McCardell	.30	.10
56 Raymont Harris	.20	.07
57 Keith Byars	.20	.07
58 O.J. McDuffie	.30	.10
59 Robert Smith	.30	.10
60 Bert Emanuel	.30	.10
61 Rick Mirer	.20	.07
62 Vinny Testaverde	.30	.10
63 Kyle Brady	.20	.07
64 Mark Bruener	.20	.07
65 Neil O'Donnell	.30	.10
66 Anthony Johnson	.20	.07
67 Ken Norton	.20	.07
68 Warren Sapp	.30	.10
69 Amani Toomer	.30	.10
70 Simeon Rice	.30	.10
71 Kevin Hardy	.20	.07
72 Junior Seau	.50	.20
73 Neil Smith	.30	.10
74 LeShon Johnson	.20	.07
75 Quinn Early	.20	.07
76 Andre Reed	.30	.10
77 Jake Reed	.30	.10
78 Elvis Grbac	.30	.10
79 Tyrone Wheatley	.30	.10
80 Adrian Murrell	.30	.10
81 Fred Barnett	.20	.07
82 Darrell Green	.30	.10
83 Stan Humphries	.30	.10
84 Troy Drayton	.20	.07
85 Steve Atwater	.20	.07
86 Quentin Coryatt	.20	.07
87 Dan Wilkinson	.20	.07
88 Scott Mitchell	.30	.10
89 Willie McGinest	.20	.07
90 Kevin Smith	.20	.07
91 Gus Frerotte	.20	.07
92 Byron Bam Morris	.20	.07
93 Darick Holmes	.20	.07
94 Zach Thomas	.50	.20
95 Tom Carter	.20	.07
96 Cortez Kennedy	.20	.07
97 Kevin Williams	.20	.07
98 Michael Haynes	.20	.07
99 Lamont Warren	.20	.07
100 Jeff Graham	.20	.07
101 Alex Van Dyke	.20	.07
102 Jim Everett	.20	.07
103 Chris Chandler	.30	.10
104 Qadry Ismail	.30	.10
105 Ray Zellars	.20	.07
106 Chris T. Jones	.20	.07
107 Charlie Garner	.30	.10
108 Bobby Hoying	.30	.10
109 Mark Chmura	.30	.10
110 Cris Carter	.50	.20
111 Darnay Scott	.30	.10
112 Anthony Miller	.20	.07
113 Desmond Howard	.30	.10
114 Terance Mathis	.30	.10
115 Rodney Hampton	.30	.10
116 Napoleon Kaufman	.50	.20
117 Jim Harbaugh	.30	.10
118 Shannon Sharpe	.30	.10
119 Irving Fryar	.30	.10
120 Garrison Hearst	.30	.10
121 Terry Allen	.50	.20
122 Larry Centers	.30	.10
123 Sean Dawkins	.20	.07
124 Jeff George	.30	.10
125 Tony Martin	.30	.10
126 Mike Alstott	.50	.20
127 Rickey Dudley	.30	.10
128 Kevin Carter	.20	.07
129 Derrick Alexander WR	.30	.10
130 Greg Lloyd	.20	.07
131 Bryce Paup	.20	.07
132 Derrick Thomas	.50	.20
133 Greg Hill	.20	.07
134 Jamal Anderson	.50	.20
135 Curtis Conway	.30	.10
136 Frank Sanders	.30	.10
137 Brett Perriman	.20	.07
138 Edgar Bennett	.30	.10
139 Wayne Chrebet	.50	.20
140 Natrone Means	.30	.10
141 Eric Metcalf	.30	.10
142 Trent Dilfer	.50	.20
143 Terry Kirby	.30	.10
144 Johnnie Morton	.30	.10
145 Dale Carter	.20	.07
146 Michael Westbrook	.30	.10
147 Stanley Pritchett	.20	.07
148 Todd Collins	.20	.07
149 Tamarick Vanover	.30	.10
150 Kevin Greene	.30	.10
151 Lamar Lathon	.20	.07
152 Muhsin Muhammad	.30	.10
153 Dorsey Levens	.50	.20
154 Rod Woodson	.30	.10
155 Brent Jones	.20	.07
156 Michael Jackson	.30	.10
157 Shawn Jefferson	.20	.07
158 Kimble Anders	.30	.10
159 Sean Gilbert	.20	.07
160 Carnell Lake	.20	.07
161 Darren Woodson	.20	.07
162 Dave Meggett	.20	.07
163 Henry Ellard	.20	.07
164 Eric Swann	.20	.07
165 Tony Boselli	.20	.07
166 Daryl Johnston	.30	.10
167 Willie Jackson	.20	.07
168 Wesley Walls	.30	.10
169 Mario Bates	.20	.07
170 Lake Dawson	.20	.07
171 Mike Mamula	.20	.07
172 Ed McCaffrey	.30	.10
173 Tony Brackens	.20	.07
174 Craig Heyward	.20	.07
175 Harvey Williams	.20	.07
176 Dave Brown	.20	.07
177 Aaron Glenn	.20	.07
178 Jeff Hostetler	.20	.07
179 Alvin Harper	.20	.07
180 Ty Detmer	.30	.10
181 James Jett	.30	.10
182 James O.Stewart	.30	.10
183 Warren Moon	.50	.20
184 Herschel Walker	.30	.10
185 Ki-Jana Carter	.20	.07
186 Leslie O'Neal	.20	.07
187 Danny Kanell	.20	.07
188 Eric Bjornson	.20	.07
189 Alex Molden	.20	.07
190 Bryant Young	.20	.07
191 Merton Hanks	.20	.07
192 Heath Shuler	.20	.07
193 Brian Blades	.20	.07
194 Steve Bono	.30	.10
195 Wayne Simmons	.20	.07
196 Warrick Dunn RC	1.50	.60
197 Peter Boulware RC	.50	.20
198 David LaFleur RC	.20	.07
199 Shawn Springs RC	.30	.10
200 Reidel Anthony RC	.50	.20
201 Jim Druckenmiller RC	.30	.10
202 Orlando Pace RC	.50	.20
203 Yatil Green RC	.30	.10
204 Bryant Westbrook RC	.20	.07
205 Tiki Barber RC	3.00	1.25
206 James Farrior RC	.50	.20
207 Rae Carruth RC	.20	.07
208 Danny Wuerffel RC	.50	.20
209 Corey Dillon RC	3.00	1.25
210 Ike Hilliard RC	.75	.30
211 Tony Gonzalez RC	1.50	.60
212 Antowain Smith RC	1.25	.50
213 Pat Barnes RC	.50	.20
214 Troy Davis RC	.30	.10
215 Byron Hanspard RC	.30	.10
216 Joey Kent RC	.50	.20
217 Jake Plummer RC	2.50	1.00
218 Kenny Holmes RC	.50	.20
219 Darnell Autry RC	.30	.10
220 Darrell Russell RC	.20	.07
221 Walter Jones RC	.50	.20
222 Dwayne Rudd RC	.50	.20
223 Tom Knight RC	.20	.07
224 Kevin Lockett RC	.30	.10
225 Will Blackwell RC	.30	.10
226 Dan Marino CL	.40	.15
227 Brett Favre CL	.40	.15
228 Emmitt Smith CL	.50	.20
229 Barry Sanders CL	.50	.20
230 Jerry Rice CL	.25	.08
P1 Drew Bledsoe Promo	1.00	.40
P2 Mark Brunell Promo	1.00	.40
P3 Barry Sanders Promo	1.50	.60

1999 Donruss

COMPLETE SET (200)	100.00	40.00
COMP.SET w/o SP's (150)	20.00	10.00
1 Jake Plummer	.40	.15
2 Rob Moore	.40	.15
3 Adrian Murrell	.40	.15
4 Frank Sanders	.40	.15
5 Jamal Anderson	.60	.25
6 Tim Dwight	.40	.15
7 Terance Mathis	.40	.15
8 Chris Chandler	.40	.15
9 Byron Hanspard	.25	.08
10 Priest Holmes	1.00	.40
11 Jermaine Lewis	.40	.15
12 Errict Rhett	.40	.15
13 Doug Flutie	.60	.25
14 Eric Moulds	.60	.25
15 Antowain Smith	.60	.25
16 Thurman Thomas	.40	.15
17 Andre Reed	.40	.15
18 Bruce Smith	.40	.15
19 Tim Biakabutuka	.40	.15
20 Rae Carruth	.25	.08
21 Muhsin Muhammad	.40	.15
22 Curtis Enis	.25	.08
23 Curtis Conway	.40	.15
24 Bobby Engram	.40	.15
25 Corey Dillon	.60	.25
26 Carl Pickens	.40	.15
27 Jeff Blake	.40	.15
28 Darnay Scott	.40	.15
29 Ty Detmer	.40	.15
30 Leslie Shepherd	.25	.08
31 Emmitt Smith	1.25	.50
32 Troy Aikman	1.25	.50
33 Michael Irvin	.40	.15
34 Deion Sanders	.60	.25
35 Rocket Ismail	.40	.15
36 John Elway	2.00	.75
37 Terrell Davis	.60	.25
38 Ed McCaffrey	.40	.15
39 Shannon Sharpe	.40	.15
40 Rod Smith	.40	.15
41 Bubby Brister	.25	.08
42 Brian Griese	.60	.25
43 Barry Sanders	2.00	.75
44 Charlie Batch	.60	.25
45 Herman Moore	.40	.15
46 Germane Crowell	.25	.08
47 Johnnie Morton	.40	.15
48 Ron Rivers	.25	.08
49 Brett Favre	2.00	.75
50 Antonio Freeman	.60	.25
51 Dorsey Levens	.60	.25
52 Mark Chmura	.25	.08
53 Corey Bradford	.60	.25
54 Bill Schroeder	.60	.25
55 Peyton Manning ERR	2.00	.75
56 Marvin Harrison	.60	.25
57 E.G. Green	.25	.08
58 Fred Taylor	.60	.25

❑ 59 Mark Brunell .60 .25
❑ 60 Tavian Banks .25 .08
❑ 61 Jimmy Smith .40 .15
❑ 62 Keenan McCardell .40 .15
❑ 63 Warren Moon .60 .25
❑ 64 Derrick Alexander WR .40 .15
❑ 65 Byron Bam Morris .25 .08
❑ 66 Elvis Grbac .40 .15
❑ 67 Andre Rison .40 .15
❑ 68 Dan Marino 2.00 .75
❑ 69 Karim Abdul-Jabbar .40 .15
❑ 70 O.J. McDuffie .40 .15
❑ 71 Tony Martin .25 .08
❑ 72 Randy Moss 1.50 .60
❑ 73 Cris Carter .60 .25
❑ 74 Randall Cunningham .60 .25
❑ 75 Robert Smith .60 .25
❑ 76 Jeff George .40 .15
❑ 77 Jake Reed .40 .15
❑ 78 Terry Allen .40 .15
❑ 79 Drew Bledsoe .75 .30
❑ 80 Terry Glenn .60 .25
❑ 81 Ben Coates .40 .15
❑ 82 Tony Simmons .25 .08
❑ 83 Cam Cleeland .25 .08
❑ 84 Eddie Kennison .40 .15
❑ 85 Kerry Collins .25 .08
❑ 86 Ike Hilliard .25 .08
❑ 87 Gary Brown .25 .08
❑ 88 Joe Jurevicius .40 .15
❑ 89 Kent Graham .25 .08
❑ 90 Wayne Chrebet .40 .15
❑ 91 Keyshawn Johnson .60 .25
❑ 92 Curtis Martin .60 .25
❑ 93 Vinny Testaverde .40 .15
❑ 94 Tim Brown .60 .25
❑ 95 Napoleon Kaufman .60 .25
❑ 96 Charles Woodson .60 .25
❑ 97 Tyrone Wheatley .40 .15
❑ 98 Rich Gannon .60 .25
❑ 99 Charles Johnson .25 .08
❑ 100 Duce Staley .60 .25
❑ 101 Kordell Stewart .40 .15
❑ 102 Jerome Bettis .60 .25
❑ 103 Hines Ward .60 .25
❑ 104 Ryan Leaf .60 .25
❑ 105 Natrone Means .40 .15
❑ 106 Jim Harbaugh .40 .15
❑ 107 Junior Seau .60 .25
❑ 108 Mikhael Ricks .25 .08
❑ 109 Jerry Rice 1.25 .50
❑ 110 Steve Young .75 .30
❑ 111 Garrison Hearst .40 .15
❑ 112 Terrell Owens .60 .25
❑ 113 Lawrence Phillips .40 .15
❑ 114 J.J. Stokes .40 .15
❑ 115 Sean Dawkins .25 .08
❑ 116 Derrick Mayes .25 .08
❑ 117 Joey Galloway .40 .15
❑ 118 Jon Kitna .60 .25
❑ 119 Ahman Green .60 .25
❑ 120 Ricky Watters .40 .15
❑ 121 Isaac Bruce .60 .25
❑ 122 Marshall Faulk .75 .30
❑ 123 Az-Zahir Hakim .25 .08
❑ 124 Warrick Dunn .60 .25
❑ 125 Mike Alstott .60 .25
❑ 126 Trent Dilfer .40 .15
❑ 127 Reidel Anthony .40 .15
❑ 128 Jacquez Green .25 .08
❑ 129 Warren Sapp .40 .15
❑ 130 Eddie George .60 .25
❑ 131 Steve McNair .60 .25
❑ 132 Kevin Dyson .40 .15
❑ 133 Yancey Thigpen .25 .08
❑ 134 Frank Wycheck .25 .08
❑ 135 Stephen Davis .60 .25
❑ 136 Brad Johnson .60 .25
❑ 137 Skip Hicks .25 .08
❑ 138 Michael Westbrook .40 .15
❑ 139 Darrell Green .25 .08
❑ 140 Albert Connell .25 .08
❑ 141 Tim Couch RC 2.00 .75
❑ 142 Donovan McNabb RC 8.00 3.00
❑ 143 Akili Smith RC 1.50 .60
❑ 144 Edgerrin James RC 6.00 2.50
❑ 145 Ricky Williams RC 3.00 1.25
❑ 146 Torry Holt RC 4.00 1.50
❑ 147 Champ Bailey RC 2.50 1.00
❑ 148 David Boston RC 2.00 .75
❑ 149 Andy Katzenmoyer RC 1.50 .60
❑ 150 Chris McAlister RC 1.50 .60
❑ 151 Daunte Culpepper RC 6.00 2.50
❑ 152 Cade McNown RC 1.50 .60
❑ 153 Troy Edwards RC 1.50 .60
❑ 154 Kevin Johnson RC 2.00 .75
❑ 155 James Johnson RC 1.50 .60
❑ 156 Rob Konrad RC 1.50 .60
❑ 157 Jim Kleinsasser RC 2.00 .75
❑ 158 Kevin Faulk RC 2.00 .75
❑ 159 Joe Montgomery RC 1.50 .60
❑ 160 Shaun King RC 1.50 .60
❑ 161 Peerless Price RC 2.00 .75
❑ 162 Mike Cloud RC 1.50 .60
❑ 163 Jermaine Fazande RC 1.50 .60
❑ 164 D'Wayne Bates RC 1.50 .60
❑ 165 Brock Huard RC 2.00 .75
❑ 166 Marty Booker RC 2.00 .75
❑ 167 Karsten Bailey RC 1.50 .60
❑ 168 Shawn Bryson RC 2.00 .75
❑ 169 Jeff Paulk RC 1.00 .40
❑ 170 Travis McGriff RC 1.00 .40
❑ 171 Amos Zereoue RC 2.00 .75
❑ 172 Craig Yeast RC 1.50 .60
❑ 173 Joe Germaine RC 1.50 .60
❑ 174 Dameane Douglas RC 1.50 .60
❑ 175 Brandon Stokley RC 2.50 1.00
❑ 176 Larry Parker RC 2.00 .75
❑ 177 Joel Makovicka RC 2.00 .75
❑ 178 Wane McGarity RC 1.00 .40
❑ 179 Na Brown RC 1.50 .60
❑ 180 Cecil Collins RC 1.00 .40
❑ 181 Nick Williams RC 1.50 .60
❑ 182 Charlie Rogers RC 1.50 .60
❑ 183 Darrin Chiaverini RC 1.50 .60
❑ 184 Terry Jackson RC 1.50 .60
❑ 185 De'Mond Parker RC 1.00 .40
❑ 186 Sedrick Irvin RC 1.00 .40
❑ 187 MarTay Jenkins RC 2.00 .75
❑ 188 Kurt Warner RC 12.00 5.00
❑ 189 Michael Bishop RC 2.00 .75
❑ 190 Sean Bennett RC 1.00 .40
❑ 191 Jamal Anderson CL .25 .08
❑ 192 Eric Moulds CL .25 .08
❑ 193 Terrell Davis CL .60 .25
❑ 194 John Elway CL .75 .30
❑ 195 Barry Sanders CL .75 .30
❑ 196 Peyton Manning CL .75 .30
❑ 197 Fred Taylor CL .60 .25
❑ 198 Dan Marino CL .75 .30
❑ 199 Randy Moss CL .60 .25
❑ 200 Terrell Owens CL .40 .15

2000 Donruss

❑ COMPLETE SET (250) 400.00 150.00
❑ 1 Jake Plummer .30 .10
❑ 2 Frank Sanders .30 .10
❑ 3 Rob Moore .30 .10
❑ 4 David Boston .50 .20
❑ 5 Tim Dwight .50 .20
❑ 6 Jamal Anderson .50 .20
❑ 7 Chris Chandler .30 .10
❑ 8 Terance Mathis .30 .10
❑ 9 Tony Banks .30 .10
❑ 10 Jermaine Lewis .30 .10
❑ 11 Shannon Sharpe .30 .10
❑ 12 Trent Dilfer .30 .10
❑ 13 Qadry Ismail .30 .10
❑ 14 Eric Moulds .50 .20
❑ 15 Doug Flutie .50 .20
❑ 16 Antowain Smith .30 .10
❑ 17 Jonathan Linton .20 .07
❑ 18 Peerless Price .30 .10
❑ 19 Rob Johnson .30 .10
❑ 20 Natrone Means .30 .10
❑ 21 Muhsin Muhammad .30 .10
❑ 22 Wesley Walls .30 .10
❑ 23 Tim Biakabutuka .30 .10
❑ 24 Steve Beuerlein .30 .10
❑ 25 Patrick Jeffers .50 .20
❑ 26 Curtis Enis .20 .07
❑ 27 Cade McNown .20 .07
❑ 28 Bobby Engram .30 .10
❑ 29 Marcus Robinson .50 .20
❑ 30 Marty Booker .30 .10
❑ 31 Corey Dillon .50 .20
❑ 32 Darnay Scott .30 .10
❑ 33 Carl Pickens .30 .10
❑ 34 Akili Smith .20 .07
❑ 35 Michael Basnight .20 .07
❑ 36 Tim Couch .30 .10
❑ 37 Kevin Johnson .50 .20
❑ 38 Karim Abdul-Jabbar .30 .10
❑ 39 Errict Rhett .30 .10
❑ 40 Darrin Chiaverini .20 .07
❑ 41 Emmitt Smith 1.00 .40
❑ 42 Troy Aikman 1.00 .40
❑ 43 Joey Galloway .30 .10
❑ 44 Randall Cunningham .50 .20
❑ 45 Michael Irvin .30 .10
❑ 46 Rocket Ismail .30 .10
❑ 47 Jason Tucker .20 .07
❑ 48 Terrell Davis .50 .20
❑ 49 John Elway 1.50 .60
❑ 50 Olandis Gary .30 .10
❑ 51 Ed McCaffrey .50 .20
❑ 52 Rod Smith .30 .10
❑ 53 Brian Griese .50 .20
❑ 54 Charlie Batch .50 .20
❑ 55 Barry Sanders 1.25 .50
❑ 56 Herman Moore .30 .10
❑ 57 Johnnie Morton .30 .10
❑ 58 Germane Crowell .20 .07
❑ 59 James Stewart .30 .10
❑ 60 Brett Favre 1.50 .60
❑ 61 Dorsey Levens .30 .10
❑ 62 Antonio Freeman .50 .20
❑ 63 Corey Bradford .30 .10
❑ 64 Bill Schroeder .30 .10
❑ 65 E.G. Green .20 .07
❑ 66 Peyton Manning 1.25 .50
❑ 67 Edgerrin James .75 .30
❑ 68 Marvin Harrison .50 .20
❑ 69 Terrence Wilkins .20 .07
❑ 70 Mark Brunell .50 .20
❑ 71 Fred Taylor .50 .20
❑ 72 Keenan McCardell .30 .10
❑ 73 Jimmy Smith .30 .10
❑ 74 Warren Moon .50 .20
❑ 75 Elvis Grbac .30 .10
❑ 76 Tony Gonzalez .30 .10
❑ 77 Dan Marino 1.50 .60
❑ 78 O.J. McDuffie .30 .10
❑ 79 Tony Martin .30 .10
❑ 80 James Johnson .20 .07
❑ 81 Thurman Thomas .30 .10
❑ 82 Randy Moss 1.00 .40
❑ 83 Daunte Culpepper .60 .25
❑ 84 Cris Carter .50 .20
❑ 85 Robert Smith .50 .20
❑ 86 John Randle .30 .10
❑ 87 Drew Bledsoe .60 .25
❑ 88 Terry Glenn .30 .10
❑ 89 Kevin Faulk .30 .10
❑ 90 Ricky Williams .50 .20
❑ 91 Jeff Blake .30 .10
❑ 92 Jake Reed .30 .10
❑ 93 Amani Toomer .30 .10
❑ 94 Kerry Collins .30 .10
❑ 95 Tiki Barber .50 .20
❑ 96 Ike Hilliard .30 .10
❑ 97 Curtis Martin .50 .20
❑ 98 Vinny Testaverde .30 .10
❑ 99 Wayne Chrebet .30 .10
❑ 100 Ray Lucas .30 .10
❑ 101 Charles Woodson .30 .10
❑ 102 Napoleon Kaufman .30 .10
❑ 103 Tim Brown .50 .20
❑ 104 Tyrone Wheatley .30 .10
❑ 105 Rich Gannon .50 .20

❑	106	Duce Staley	.50	.20
❑	107	Donovan McNabb	.75	.30
❑	108	Amos Zereoue	.50	.20
❑	109	Kordell Stewart	.30	.10
❑	110	Jerome Bettis	.50	.20
❑	111	Troy Edwards	.20	.07
❑	112	Ryan Leaf	.30	.10
❑	113	Junior Seau	.50	.20
❑	114	Jim Harbaugh	.30	.10
❑	115	Jermaine Fazande	.20	.07
❑	116	Curtis Conway	.30	.10
❑	117	Steve Young	.60	.25
❑	118	Jerry Rice	1.00	.40
❑	119	Terrell Owens	.50	.20
❑	120	Charlie Garner	.30	.10
❑	121	Jeff Garcia	.50	.20
❑	122	Jon Kitna	.50	.20
❑	123	Derrick Mayes	.30	.10
❑	124	Ricky Watters	.30	.10
❑	125	Kurt Warner	1.00	.40
❑	126	Marshall Faulk	.60	.25
❑	127	Torry Holt	.50	.20
❑	128	Az-Zahir Hakim	.30	.10
❑	129	Isaac Bruce	.50	.20
❑	130	Mike Alstott	.50	.20
❑	131	Warrick Dunn	.50	.20
❑	132	Shaun King	.20	.07
❑	133	Keyshawn Johnson	.50	.20
❑	134	Jacquez Green	.20	.07
❑	135	Reidel Anthony	.30	.10
❑	136	Warren Sapp	.30	.10
❑	137	Eddie George	.50	.20
❑	138	Steve McNair	.50	.20
❑	139	Yancey Thigpen	.20	.07
❑	140	Kevin Dyson	.30	.10
❑	141	Frank Wycheck	.30	.10
❑	142	Jevon Kearse	.50	.20
❑	143	Stephen Davis	.50	.20
❑	144	Skip Hicks	.20	.07
❑	145	Brad Johnson	.50	.20
❑	146	Bruce Smith	.30	.10
❑	147	Michael Westbrook	.30	.10
❑	148	Albert Connell	.20	.07
❑	149	Jeff George	.30	.10
❑	150	Deion Sanders	.50	.20
❑	151	Courtney Brown RC	6.00	2.50
❑	152	Corey Simon RC	6.00	2.50
❑	153	Brian Urlacher RC	25.00	10.00
❑	154	Shaun Ellis RC	6.00	2.50
❑	155	John Abraham RC	6.00	2.50
❑	156	Deltha O'Neal RC	6.00	2.50
❑	157	Ahmed Plummer RC	6.00	2.50
❑	158	Chris Hovan RC	5.00	2.00
❑	159	Rob Morris RC	5.00	2.00
❑	160	Keith Bulluck RC	6.00	2.50
❑	161	Darren Howard RC	5.00	2.00
❑	162	John Engelberger RC	5.00	2.00
❑	163	Raynoch Thompson RC	5.00	2.00
❑	164	Cornelius Griffin RC	5.00	2.00
❑	165	William Bartee RC	5.00	2.00
❑	166	Fred Robbins RC	3.00	1.25
❑	167	Micheal Boireau RC	3.00	1.25
❑	168	Brandon Short RC	5.00	2.00
❑	169	Jacoby Shepherd RC	3.00	1.25
❑	170	Peter Warrick RC	6.00	2.50
❑	171	Jamal Lewis RC	15.00	6.00
❑	172	Thomas Jones RC	10.00	4.00
❑	173	Plaxico Burress RC	12.00	5.00
❑	174	Travis Taylor RC	6.00	2.50
❑	175	Ron Dayne RC	6.00	2.50
❑	176	Bubba Franks RC	6.00	2.50
❑	177	Sebastian Janikowski RC	6.00	2.50
❑	178	Chad Pennington RC	15.00	6.00
❑	179	Shaun Alexander RC	30.00	15.00
❑	180	Sylvester Morris RC	5.00	2.00
❑	181	Anthony Becht RC	6.00	2.50
❑	182	R.Jay Soward RC	5.00	2.00
❑	183	Trung Canidate RC	5.00	2.00
❑	184	Dennis Northcutt RC	6.00	2.50
❑	185	Todd Pinkston RC	6.00	2.50
❑	186	Jerry Porter RC	8.00	3.00
❑	187	Travis Prentice RC	5.00	2.00
❑	188	Giovanni Carmazzi RC	3.00	1.25
❑	189	Ron Dugans RC	3.00	1.25
❑	190	Erron Kinney RC	6.00	2.50
❑	191	Dez White RC	6.00	2.50
❑	192	Chris Cole RC	5.00	2.00
❑	193	Ron Dixon RC	5.00	2.00
❑	194	Chris Redman RC	5.00	2.00
❑	195	J.R. Redmond RC	5.00	2.00
❑	196	Laveranues Coles RC	8.00	3.00
❑	197	JaJuan Dawson RC	3.00	1.25
❑	198	Darrell Jackson RC	12.00	5.00
❑	199	Reuben Droughns RC	8.00	3.00
❑	200	Doug Chapman RC	5.00	2.00
❑	201	Terrelle Smith RC	5.00	2.00
❑	202	Curtis Keaton RC	5.00	2.00
❑	203	Gari Scott RC	3.00	1.25
❑	204	Danny Farmer RC	5.00	2.00
❑	205	Hank Poteat RC	5.00	2.00
❑	206	Ben Kelly RC	3.00	1.25
❑	207	Corey Moore RC	3.00	1.25
❑	208	Na'il Diggs RC	5.00	2.00
❑	209	Aaron Shea RC	5.00	2.00
❑	210	Trevor Gaylor RC	5.00	2.00
❑	211	Julian Peterson RC	6.00	2.50
❑	212	Frank Moreau RC	5.00	2.00
❑	213	Deon Dyer RC	5.00	2.00
❑	214	Avion Black RC	5.00	2.00
❑	215	Paul Smith RC	5.00	2.00
❑	216	Michael Wiley RC	5.00	2.00
❑	217	Dante Hall RC	12.00	5.00
❑	218	Mike Brown RC	10.00	4.00
❑	219	Sammy Morris RC	6.00	2.50
❑	220	Billy Volek RC	10.00	4.00
❑	221	Tee Martin RC	6.00	2.50
❑	222	Troy Walters RC	6.00	2.50
❑	223	Chad Morton RC	6.00	2.50
❑	224	Erik Flowers RC	5.00	2.00
❑	225	Ronney Jenkins RC	5.00	2.00
❑	226	Thomas Hamner RC	3.00	1.25
❑	227	Mareno Philyaw RC	3.00	1.25
❑	228	James Williams RC	5.00	2.00
❑	229	Mike Anderson RC	8.00	3.00
❑	230	Tom Brady RC	200.00	125.00
❑	231	Mike Green RC	5.00	2.00
❑	232	Todd Husak RC	6.00	2.50
❑	233	Tim Rattay RC	6.00	2.50
❑	234	Jarious Jackson RC	5.00	2.00
❑	235	Joe Hamilton RC	5.00	2.00
❑	236	Shyrone Stith RC	5.00	2.00
❑	237	Rondell Mealey RC	3.00	1.25
❑	238	Demario Brown RC	3.00	1.25
❑	239	Chris Coleman RC	6.00	2.50
❑	240	Dwayne Goodrich RC	3.00	1.25
❑	241	Drew Haddad RC	3.00	1.25
❑	242	Doug Johnson RC	6.00	2.50
❑	243	Windrell Hayes RC	5.00	2.00
❑	244	Charles Lee RC	3.00	1.25
❑	245	Kevin McDougal RC	5.00	2.00
❑	246	Spergon Wynn RC	5.00	2.00
❑	247	Shockmain Davis RC	3.00	1.25
❑	248	Jamel White RC	5.00	2.00
❑	249	Bashir Yamini RC	3.00	1.25
❑	250	Kwame Cavil RC	3.00	1.25

2002 Donruss

❑		COMPLETE SET (300)	150.00	75.00
❑		COMP.SET w/o SP's (100)	20.00	7.50
❑	1	Jake Plummer	.30	.10
❑	2	David Boston	.50	.20
❑	3	MarTay Jenkins	.20	.07
❑	4	Thomas Jones	.30	.10
❑	5	Frank Sanders	.20	.07
❑	6	Shawn Jefferson	.20	.07
❑	7	Alge Crumpler	.30	.10
❑	8	Michael Vick	1.00	.40
❑	9	Jamal Anderson	.30	.10
❑	10	Warrick Dunn	.50	.20
❑	11	Peter Boulware	.20	.07
❑	12	Jamal Lewis	.50	.20
❑	13	Jeff Blake	.20	.07
❑	14	Travis Taylor	.30	.10
❑	15	Ray Lewis	.50	.20
❑	16	Todd Heap	.20	.07
❑	17	Nate Clements	.20	.07
❑	18	Alex Van Pelt	.20	.07
❑	19	Reggie Germany	.20	.07
❑	20	Larry Centers	.20	.07
❑	21	Eric Moulds	.30	.10
❑	22	Travis Henry	.50	.20
❑	23	Wesley Walls	.20	.07
❑	24	Steve Smith	.50	.20
❑	25	Lamar Smith	.30	.10
❑	26	Patrick Jeffers	.20	.07
❑	27	Chris Weinke	.30	.10
❑	28	Muhsin Muhammad	.30	.10
❑	29	Marcus Robinson	.30	.10
❑	30	Jim Miller	.20	.07
❑	31	Anthony Thomas	.30	.10
❑	32	David Terrell	.50	.20
❑	33	Brian Urlacher	.75	.30
❑	34	Marty Booker	.20	.07
❑	35	Darnay Scott	.20	.07
❑	36	Jon Kitna	.30	.10
❑	37	Chad Johnson	.50	.20
❑	38	T.J. Houshmandzadeh	.30	.10
❑	39	Corey Dillon	.30	.10
❑	40	Peter Warrick	.30	.10
❑	41	Gerard Warren	.20	.07
❑	42	Anthony Henry	.20	.07
❑	43	Quincy Morgan	.20	.07
❑	44	JaJuan Dawson	.20	.07
❑	45	Tim Couch	.30	.10
❑	46	Kevin Johnson	.30	.10
❑	47	James Jackson	.20	.07
❑	48	La'Roi Glover	.20	.07
❑	49	Anthony Wright	.20	.07
❑	50	Rocket Ismail	.30	.10
❑	51	Troy Hambrick	.20	.07
❑	52	Emmitt Smith	1.25	.50
❑	53	Quincy Carter	.30	.10
❑	54	Joey Galloway	.30	.10
❑	55	Shannon Sharpe	.30	.10
❑	56	Kevin Kasper	.20	.07
❑	57	Olandis Gary	.30	.10
❑	58	Brian Griese	.50	.20
❑	59	Rod Smith	.30	.10
❑	60	Terrell Davis	.50	.20
❑	61	Ed McCaffrey	.50	.20
❑	62	Mike Anderson	.50	.20
❑	63	Bill Schroeder	.30	.10
❑	64	Scotty Anderson	.20	.07
❑	65	Mike McMahon	.50	.20
❑	66	James Stewart	.30	.10
❑	67	Az-Zahir Hakim	.20	.07
❑	68	Germane Crowell	.20	.07
❑	69	Kabeer Gbaja-Biamila	.30	.10
❑	70	LeRoy Butler	.20	.07
❑	71	Antonio Freeman	.50	.20
❑	72	Bubba Franks	.30	.10
❑	73	Brett Favre	1.25	.50
❑	74	Ahman Green	.50	.20
❑	75	Terry Glenn	.30	.10
❑	76	Jamie Sharper	.20	.07
❑	77	Tony Simmons	.20	.07
❑	78	James Allen	.30	.10
❑	79	Terrence Wilkins	.20	.07
❑	80	Dominic Rhodes	.50	.20
❑	81	Qadry Ismail	.30	.10
❑	82	Peyton Manning	1.00	.40
❑	83	Edgerrin James	.60	.25
❑	84	Marvin Harrison	.50	.20
❑	85	Reggie Wayne	.50	.20
❑	86	Fred Taylor	.50	.20
❑	87	Elvis Joseph	.20	.07
❑	88	Mark Brunell	.50	.20
❑	89	Keenan McCardell	.20	.07
❑	90	Jimmy Smith	.30	.10
❑	91	Kyle Brady	.20	.07
❑	92	Derrick Alexander	.30	.10
❑	93	Johnnie Morton	.30	.10
❑	94	Trent Green	.30	.10
❑	95	Priest Holmes	.60	.25
❑	96	Tony Gonzalez	.30	.10
❑	97	Snoop Minnis	.20	.07
❑	98	Travis Minor	.20	.07
❑	99	Oronde Gadsden	.30	.10
❑	100	Jay Fiedler	.30	.10
❑	101	Chris Chambers	.50	.20

102	Ricky Williams	.50	.20
103	Zach Thomas	.50	.20
104	Byron Chamberlain	.20	.07
105	Todd Bouman	.20	.07
106	Daunte Culpepper	.50	.20
107	Michael Bennett	.30	.10
108	Randy Moss	1.00	.40
109	Cris Carter	.50	.20
110	David Patten	.20	.07
111	Donald Hayes	.20	.07
112	Tom Brady	1.25	.50
113	Antowain Smith	.30	.10
114	Troy Brown	.30	.10
115	Drew Bledsoe	.60	.25
116	Bryan Cox	.20	.07
117	Moe Williams	.20	.07
118	Aaron Brooks	.50	.20
119	Deuce McAllister	.60	.25
120	Joe Horn	.30	.10
121	Amani Toomer	.30	.10
122	Ron Dayne	.30	.10
123	Kerry Collins	.30	.10
124	Ike Hilliard	.30	.10
125	Tiki Barber	.50	.20
126	Michael Strahan	.30	.10
127	Chad Pennington	.60	.25
128	Santana Moss	.50	.20
129	LaMont Jordan	.50	.20
130	Curtis Martin	.50	.20
131	Wayne Chrebet	.30	.10
132	Laveranues Coles	.30	.10
133	Vinny Testaverde	.30	.10
134	Charles Woodson	.30	.10
135	Tyrone Wheatley	.30	.10
136	Jerry Porter	.20	.07
137	Rich Gannon	.50	.20
138	Charlie Garner	.30	.10
139	Tim Brown	.50	.20
140	Jerry Rice	1.00	.40
141	James Thrash	.30	.10
142	Todd Pinkston	.30	.10
143	A.J. Feeley	.50	.20
144	Donovan McNabb	.60	.25
145	Duce Staley	.50	.20
146	Freddie Mitchell	.30	.10
147	Correll Buckhalter	.30	.10
148	Casey Hampton	.20	.07
149	Hines Ward	.50	.20
150	Chris Fuamatu-Ma'afala	.20	.07
151	Jerome Bettis	.50	.20
152	Kordell Stewart	.30	.10
153	Plaxico Burress	.30	.10
154	Kendrell Bell	.50	.20
155	Trevor Gaylor	.20	.07
156	Curtis Conway	.20	.07
157	Doug Flutie	.50	.20
158	Drew Brees	.50	.20
159	LaDainian Tomlinson	.75	.30
160	Junior Seau	.50	.20
161	Bryant Young	.20	.07
162	Andre Carter	.20	.07
163	Eric Johnson	.20	.07
164	Jeff Garcia	.50	.20
165	Garrison Hearst	.30	.10
166	Terrell Owens	.50	.20
167	Kevan Barlow	.30	.10
168	Levon Kirkland	.20	.07
169	Ricky Watters	.20	.07
170	Trent Dilfer	.30	.10
171	Shaun Alexander	.60	.25
172	Koren Robinson	.30	.10
173	Darrell Jackson	.30	.10
174	Adam Archuleta	.20	.07
175	Aeneas Williams	.20	.07
176	Trung Canidate	.30	.10
177	Kurt Warner	.50	.20
178	Marshall Faulk	.50	.20
179	Torry Holt	.50	.20
180	Isaac Bruce	.50	.20
181	John Lynch	.30	.10
182	Joe Jurevicius	.20	.07
183	Brad Johnson	.30	.10
184	Rob Johnson	.30	.10
185	Keyshawn Johnson	.50	.20
186	Mike Alstott	.50	.20
187	Warren Sapp	.30	.10
188	Drew Bennett	.50	.20
189	Frank Wycheck	.20	.07
190	Kevin Dyson	.30	.10
191	Steve McNair	.50	.20
192	Eddie George	.50	.20
193	Jevon Kearse	.30	.10
194	Derrick Mason	.30	.10
195	Champ Bailey	.30	.10
196	Darrell Green	.20	.07
197	Bruce Smith	.20	.07
198	Jacquez Green	.20	.07
199	Stephen Davis	.30	.10
200	Rod Gardner	.30	.10
201	David Carr RC	6.00	2.50
202	Joey Harrington RC	4.00	1.50
203	Patrick Ramsey RC	3.00	1.25
204	Kurt Kittner RC	2.50	1.00
205	Rohan Davey RC	3.00	1.25
206	Josh McCown RC	4.00	1.50
207	David Garrard RC	6.00	2.50
208	Randy Fasani RC	2.50	1.00
209	Alrews Bell RC	1.50	.60
210	Brandon Doman RC	2.50	1.00
211	Eric Crouch RC	3.00	1.25
212	Woody Dantzler RC	2.50	1.00
213	Chad Hutchinson RC	2.50	1.00
214	Zak Kustok RC	3.00	1.25
215	Ronald Curry RC	3.00	1.25
216	William Green RC	3.00	1.25
217	T.J. Duckett RC	3.00	1.25
218	Clinton Portis RC	10.00	4.00
219	DeShaun Foster RC	3.00	1.25
220	Lamar Gordon RC	3.00	1.25
221	Jonathan Wells RC	3.00	1.25
222	Adrian Peterson RC	4.00	1.50
223	Ladell Betts RC	3.00	1.25
224	Maurice Morris RC	3.00	1.25
225	Brian Westbrook RC	6.00	2.50
226	Luke Staley RC	2.50	1.00
227	Travis Stephens RC	2.50	1.00
228	Craig Nall RC	3.00	1.25
229	Chester Taylor RC	6.00	2.50
230	Ken Simonton RC	1.50	.60
231	Verron Haynes RC	3.00	1.25
232	Tellis Redmon RC	2.50	1.00
233	J.T. O'Sullivan RC	2.50	1.00
234	Major Applewhite RC	3.00	1.25
235	Ricky Williams RC	2.50	1.00
236	James Mungro RC	3.00	1.25
237	Josh Scobey RC	3.00	1.25
238	Najeh Davenport RC	3.00	1.25
239	Dicenzo Miller RC	1.50	.60
240	Ennis Haywood RC	2.50	1.00
241	Jabar Gaffney RC	3.00	1.25
242	Antonio Bryant RC	3.00	1.25
243	Donte Stallworth RC	5.00	2.00
244	Josh Reed RC	3.00	1.25
245	Ashley Lelie RC	6.00	2.50
246	Reche Caldwell RC	3.00	1.25
247	Marquise Walker RC	2.50	1.00
248	Javon Walker RC	5.00	2.00
249	Andre Davis RC	2.50	1.00
250	Antwaan Randle El RC	4.00	1.50
251	Kelly Campbell RC	2.50	1.00
252	Cliff Russell RC	2.50	1.00
253	Kahlil Hill RC	2.50	1.00
254	Ron Johnson RC	2.50	1.00
255	Deion Branch RC	5.00	2.00
256	Brian Poli-Dixon RC	2.50	1.00
257	Freddie Milons RC	2.50	1.00
258	Lee Mays RC	2.50	1.00
259	Tim Carter RC	2.50	1.00
260	Terry Charles RC	2.50	1.00
261	Jamar Martin RC	2.50	1.00
262	Jason McAddley RC	2.50	1.00
263	Chris Hope RC	3.00	1.25
264	Howard Green RC	1.50	.60
265	Jeremy Shockey RC	10.00	4.00
266	Daniel Graham RC	3.00	1.25
267	Eddie Freeman RC	1.50	.60
268	Julius Peppers RC	6.00	2.50
269	Kalimba Edwards RC	3.00	1.25
270	Dwight Freeney RC	5.00	2.00
271	Dennis Johnson RC	1.50	.60
272	Alex Brown RC	3.00	1.25
273	Bryan Thomas RC	2.50	1.00
274	Bryan Fletcher RC	1.50	.60
275	Will Overstreet RC	1.50	.60
276	Ryan Denney RC	2.50	1.00
277	Charles Grant RC	3.00	1.25
278	John Henderson RC	3.00	1.25
279	Albert Haynesworth RC	2.50	1.00
280	Wendell Bryant RC	1.50	.60
281	Ryan Sims RC	3.00	1.25
282	Anthony Weaver RC	2.50	1.00
283	Larry Tripplett RC	1.50	.60
284	Alan Harper RC	1.50	.60
285	Napoleon Harris RC	3.00	1.25
286	Robert Thomas RC	3.00	1.25
287	Levar Fisher RC	1.50	.60
288	Andra Davis RC	2.50	1.00
289	Quentin Jammer RC	3.00	1.25
290	Phillip Buchanon RC	3.00	1.25
291	Keyuo Craver RC	2.50	1.00
292	Lito Sheppard RC	3.00	1.25
293	Rocky Calmus RC	3.00	1.25
294	Mike Rumph RC	3.00	1.25
295	Mike Echols RC	1.50	.60
296	Joseph Jefferson RC	2.50	1.00
297	Roy Williams RC	6.00	2.50
298	Ed Reed RC	5.00	2.00
299	Michael Lewis RC	3.00	1.25
300	Eddie Drummond RC	2.50	1.00

1999 Donruss Elite

	COMPLETE SET (200)	100.00	40.00
	COMP.SET w/o SP's (160)	30.00	15.00
1	Warren Moon	1.25	.50
2	Terry Allen	.75	.30
3	Jeff George	.75	.30
4	Brett Favre	4.00	1.50
5	Rob Moore	.75	.30
6	Bubby Brister	.50	.20
7	John Elway	4.00	1.50
8	Troy Aikman	2.50	1.00
9	Steve McNair	1.25	.50
10	Charlie Batch	1.25	.50
11	Elvis Grbac	.75	.30
12	Trent Dilfer	.75	.30
13	Kerry Collins	.75	.30
14	Neil O'Donnell	.50	.20
15	Tony Simmons	.50	.20
16	Ryan Leaf	1.25	.50
17	Bobby Hoying	.75	.30
18	Marvin Harrison	1.25	.50
19	Keyshawn Johnson	1.25	.50
20	Cris Carter	1.25	.50
21	Deion Sanders	1.25	.50
22	Emmitt Smith	2.50	1.00
23	Antowain Smith	1.25	.50
24	Terry Fair	.50	.20
25	Robert Holcombe	.50	.20
26	Napoleon Kaufman	1.25	.50
27	Eddie George	1.25	.50
28	Corey Dillon	1.25	.50
29	Adrian Murrell	.75	.30
30	Charles Way	.50	.20
31	Amp Lee	.50	.20
32	Ricky Watters	.75	.30
33	Gary Brown	.50	.20
34	Thurman Thomas	.75	.30
35	Pat Johnson	.50	.20
36	Jerome Bettis	1.25	.50
37	Muhsin Muhammad	.75	.30
38	Kimble Anders	.75	.30
39	Curtis Enis	.50	.20
40	Mike Alstott	1.25	.50
41	Charles Johnson	.50	.20
42	Chris Warren	.50	.20
43	Tony Banks	.75	.30
44	Leroy Hoard	.50	.20
45	Chris Fuamatu-Ma'afala	.50	.20
46	Michael Irvin	1.25	.50
47	Robert Edwards	.50	.20

❑ 48 Hines Ward 1.25 .50
❑ 49 Trent Green 1.25 .50
❑ 50 Eric Zeier .50 .20
❑ 51 Sean Dawkins .50 .20
❑ 52 Yancey Thigpen .50 .20
❑ 53 Jacquez Green .50 .20
❑ 54 Zach Thomas 1.25 .50
❑ 55 Junior Seau 1.25 .50
❑ 56 Darnay Scott .50 .20
❑ 57 Kent Graham .50 .20
❑ 58 O.J. Santiago .50 .20
❑ 59 Tony Gonzalez 1.25 .50
❑ 60 Ty Detmer .50 .20
❑ 61 Albert Connell .50 .20
❑ 62 James Jett .75 .30
❑ 63 Bert Emanuel .75 .30
❑ 64 Derrick Alexander WR .75 .30
❑ 65 Wesley Walls .75 .30
❑ 66 Jake Reed .75 .30
❑ 67 Randall Cunningham 1.25 .50
❑ 68 Leslie Shepherd .50 .20
❑ 69 Mark Chmura .50 .20
❑ 70 Bobby Engram .75 .30
❑ 71 Rickey Dudley .50 .20
❑ 72 Darick Holmes .50 .20
❑ 73 Andre Reed .75 .30
❑ 74 Az-Zahir Hakim .50 .20
❑ 75 Cameron Cleeland .50 .20
❑ 76 Lamar Thomas .50 .20
❑ 77 Oronde Gadsden .75 .30
❑ 78 Ben Coates .75 .30
❑ 79 Bruce Smith .75 .30
❑ 80 Jerry Rice 2.50 1.00
❑ 81 Tim Brown 1.25 .50
❑ 82 Michael Westbrook .75 .30
❑ 83 J.J. Stokes .75 .30
❑ 84 Shannon Sharpe .75 .30
❑ 85 Reidel Anthony .75 .30
❑ 86 Antonio Freeman 1.25 .50
❑ 87 Keenan McCardell .75 .30
❑ 88 Terry Glenn 1.25 .50
❑ 89 Andre Rison .75 .30
❑ 90 Neil Smith .75 .30
❑ 91 Terrance Mathis .75 .30
❑ 92 Rocket Ismail .75 .30
❑ 93 Byron Bam Morris .50 .20
❑ 94 Ike Hilliard .50 .20
❑ 95 Eddie Kennison .75 .30
❑ 96 Tavian Banks .50 .20
❑ 97 Yatil Green .50 .20
❑ 98 Frank Wycheck .50 .20
❑ 99 Warren Sapp .50 .20
❑ 100 Germane Crowell .50 .20
❑ 101 Curtis Martin 2.50 1.00
❑ 102 John Avery 1.00 .40
❑ 103 Eric Moulds 2.50 1.00
❑ 104 Randy Moss 8.00 3.00
❑ 105 Terrell Owens 2.50 1.00
❑ 106 Vinny Testaverde 1.50 .60
❑ 107 Doug Flutie 1.25 .50
❑ 108 Mark Brunell 1.25 .50
❑ 109 Isaac Bruce 2.50 1.00
❑ 110 Kordell Stewart 1.50 .60
❑ 111 Drew Bledsoe 3.00 1.25
❑ 112 Chris Chandler 1.50 .60
❑ 113 Dan Marino 8.00 3.00
❑ 114 Brian Griese 2.50 1.00
❑ 115 Carl Pickens 1.50 .60
❑ 116 Jake Plummer 1.50 .60
❑ 117 Natrone Means 1.50 .60
❑ 118 Peyton Manning 10.00 4.00
❑ 119 Garrison Hearst 2.50 1.00
❑ 120 Barry Sanders 8.00 3.00
❑ 121 Steve Young 3.00 1.25
❑ 122 Rashaan Shehee 1.00 .40
❑ 123 Ed McCaffrey 1.50 .60
❑ 124 Charles Woodson 2.50 1.00
❑ 125 Dorsey Levens 2.50 1.00
❑ 126 Robert Smith 2.50 1.00
❑ 127 Greg Hill 1.00 .40
❑ 128 Fred Taylor 2.50 1.00
❑ 129 Marcus Nash 1.00 .40
❑ 130 Terrell Davis 2.50 1.00
❑ 131 Ahman Green 2.50 1.00
❑ 132 Jamal Anderson 2.50 1.00
❑ 133 Karim Abdul-Jabbar 1.50 .60
❑ 134 Jermaine Lewis 1.50 .60
❑ 135 Jerome Pathon 1.50 .60
❑ 136 Brad Johnson 2.50 1.00
❑ 137 Herman Moore 1.50 .60
❑ 138 Tim Dwight 2.50 1.00
❑ 139 Johnnie Morton 1.00 .40
❑ 140 Marshall Faulk 3.00 1.25
❑ 141 Frank Sanders 1.50 .60
❑ 142 Kevin Dyson 1.50 .60
❑ 143 Curtis Conway 1.50 .60
❑ 144 Derrick Mayes 1.00 .40
❑ 145 O.J. McDuffie 1.50 .60
❑ 146 Joe Jurevicius 1.50 .60
❑ 147 Jon Kitna 2.50 1.00
❑ 148 Joey Galloway 1.50 .60
❑ 149 Jimmy Smith 1.50 .60
❑ 150 Skip Hicks 1.00 .40
❑ 151 Rod Smith 1.50 .60
❑ 152 Duce Staley 2.50 1.00
❑ 153 James Stewart 1.00 .40
❑ 154 Rob Johnson 1.50 .60
❑ 155 Mikhael Ricks 1.00 .40
❑ 156 Wayne Chrebet 1.50 .60
❑ 157 Robert Brooks 1.50 .60
❑ 158 Tim Biakabutuka 1.50 .60
❑ 159 Priest Holmes 4.00 1.25
❑ 160 Warrick Dunn 2.50 1.00
❑ 161 Champ Bailey RC 5.00 2.00
❑ 162 D'Wayne Bates RC 2.50 1.00
❑ 163 Michael Bishop RC 3.00 1.25
❑ 164 David Boston RC 3.00 1.25
❑ 165 Na Brown RC 2.50 1.00
❑ 166 Chris Claiborne RC 1.50 .60
❑ 167 Joe Montgomery RC 2.50 1.00
❑ 168 Mike Cloud RC 2.50 1.00
❑ 169 Travis McGriff RC 1.50 .60
❑ 170 Tim Couch RC 3.00 1.25
❑ 171 Daunte Culpepper RC 12.00 5.00
❑ 172 Autry Denson RC 2.50 1.00
❑ 173 Jermaine Fazande RC 2.50 1.00
❑ 174 Troy Edwards RC 2.50 1.00
❑ 175 Kevin Faulk RC 3.00 1.25
❑ 176 Dee Miller RC 1.50 .60
❑ 177 Brock Huard RC 3.00 1.25
❑ 178 Torry Holt RC 8.00 3.00
❑ 179 Sedrick Irvin RC 1.50 .60
❑ 180 Edgerrin James RC 12.00 5.00
❑ 181 Joe Germaine RC 2.50 1.00
❑ 182 James Johnson RC 2.50 1.00
❑ 183 Kevin Johnson RC 2.50 1.00
❑ 184 Andy Katzenmoyer RC 2.50 1.00
❑ 185 Jevon Kearse RC 6.00 2.50
❑ 186 Shaun King RC 2.50 1.00
❑ 187 Rob Konrad RC 3.00 1.25
❑ 188 Jim Kleinsasser RC 3.00 1.25
❑ 189 Chris McAlister RC 2.50 1.00
❑ 190 Donovan McNabb RC 15.00 6.00
❑ 191 Cade McNown RC 2.50 1.00
❑ 192 De'Mond Parker RC 1.00 .40
❑ 193 Craig Yeast RC 2.50 1.00
❑ 194 Shawn Bryson RC 3.00 1.25
❑ 195 Peerless Price RC 3.00 1.25
❑ 196 Darnell McDonald RC 2.50 1.00
❑ 197 Akili Smith RC 1.50 .60
❑ 198 Tai Streets RC 3.00 1.25
❑ 199 Ricky Williams RC 6.00 2.50
❑ 200 Amos Zereoue RC 2.50 1.00

2000 Donruss Elite

❑ COMPLETE SET (200) 500.00 300.00
❑ 1 Jake Plummer .50 .20
❑ 2 David Boston .75 .30
❑ 3 Rob Moore .50 .20
❑ 4 Chris Chandler .50 .20
❑ 5 Tim Dwight .75 .30
❑ 6 Terance Mathis .50 .20
❑ 7 Jamal Anderson .75 .30
❑ 8 Priest Holmes 1.00 .40
❑ 9 Tony Banks .50 .20
❑ 10 Shannon Sharpe .50 .20
❑ 11 Qadry Ismail .50 .20
❑ 12 Eric Moulds .75 .30
❑ 13 Doug Flutie .75 .30
❑ 14 Antowain Smith .50 .20
❑ 15 Peerless Price .50 .20
❑ 16 Muhsin Muhammad .50 .20
❑ 17 Tim Biakabutuka .50 .20
❑ 18 Patrick Jeffers .75 .30
❑ 19 Steve Beuerlein .50 .20
❑ 20 Wesley Walls .30 .10
❑ 21 Curtis Enis .30 .10
❑ 22 Marcus Robinson .75 .30
❑ 23 Carl Pickens .50 .20
❑ 24 Corey Dillon .75 .30
❑ 25 Akili Smith .30 .10
❑ 26 Darnay Scott .50 .20
❑ 27 Kevin Johnson .75 .30
❑ 28 Errict Rhett .50 .20
❑ 29 Emmitt Smith 1.50 .60
❑ 30 Deion Sanders .75 .30
❑ 31 Troy Aikman 1.50 .60
❑ 32 Joey Galloway .50 .20
❑ 33 Michael Irvin .50 .20
❑ 34 Rocket Ismail .50 .20
❑ 35 Jason Tucker .30 .10
❑ 36 Ed McCaffrey .75 .30
❑ 37 Rod Smith .50 .20
❑ 38 Brian Griese .75 .30
❑ 39 Terrell Davis .75 .30
❑ 40 Olandis Gary .75 .30
❑ 41 Charlie Batch .75 .30
❑ 42 Johnnie Morton .50 .20
❑ 43 Herman Moore .50 .20
❑ 44 James Stewart .50 .20
❑ 45 Dorsey Levens .50 .20
❑ 46 Antonio Freeman .75 .30
❑ 47 Brett Favre 2.50 1.00
❑ 48 Bill Schroeder .50 .20
❑ 49 Peyton Manning 2.00 .75
❑ 50 Keenan McCardell .50 .20
❑ 51 Fred Taylor .75 .30
❑ 52 Jimmy Smith .50 .20
❑ 53 Elvis Grbac .50 .20
❑ 54 Tony Gonzalez .50 .20
❑ 55 Derrick Alexander .50 .20
❑ 56 Dan Marino 2.50 1.00
❑ 57 Tony Martin .50 .20
❑ 58 James Johnson .30 .10
❑ 59 Damon Huard .75 .30
❑ 60 Thurman Thomas .50 .20
❑ 61 Robert Smith .75 .30
❑ 62 Randall Cunningham .75 .30
❑ 63 Jeff George .50 .20
❑ 64 Terry Glenn .50 .20
❑ 65 Drew Bledsoe 1.00 .40
❑ 66 Jeff Blake .50 .20
❑ 67 Amani Toomer .50 .20
❑ 68 Kerry Collins .50 .20
❑ 69 Joe Montgomery .30 .10
❑ 70 Vinny Testaverde .50 .20
❑ 71 Ray Lucas .50 .20
❑ 72 Keyshawn Johnson .75 .30
❑ 73 Wayne Chrebet .50 .20
❑ 74 Napoleon Kaufman .50 .20
❑ 75 Tim Brown .75 .30
❑ 76 Rich Gannon .75 .30
❑ 77 Duce Staley .75 .30
❑ 78 Kordell Stewart .50 .20
❑ 79 Jerome Bettis .75 .30
❑ 80 Troy Edwards .30 .10
❑ 81 Natrone Means .30 .10
❑ 82 Curtis Conway .50 .20
❑ 83 Jim Harbaugh .50 .20
❑ 84 Junior Seau .75 .30
❑ 85 Jermaine Fazande .30 .10
❑ 86 Terrell Owens .75 .30
❑ 87 Charlie Garner .50 .20
❑ 88 Steve Young 1.00 .40
❑ 89 Jeff Garcia .75 .30
❑ 90 Derrick Mayes .50 .20
❑ 91 Ricky Watters .50 .20
❑ 92 Az-Zahir Hakim .50 .20
❑ 93 Torry Holt .75 .30
❑ 94 Warren Sapp .50 .20

❑ 95 Mike Alstott .75 .30
❑ 96 Warrick Dunn .75 .30
❑ 97 Kevin Dyson .50 .20
❑ 98 Bruce Smith .50 .20
❑ 99 Albert Connell .30 .10
❑ 100 Michael Westbrook .50 .20
❑ 101 Cade McNown .30 .10
❑ 102 Tim Couch 2.00 .75
❑ 103 John Elway 6.00 2.50
❑ 104 Barry Sanders 5.00 2.00
❑ 105 Germane Crowell 1.25 .50
❑ 106 Marvin Harrison 2.00 .75
❑ 107 Edgerrin James 3.00 1.25
❑ 108 Mark Brunell 2.00 .75
❑ 109 Randy Moss 4.00 1.50
❑ 110 Cris Carter 2.00 .75
❑ 111 Daunte Culpepper 2.50 1.00
❑ 112 Ricky Williams .75 .30
❑ 113 Curtis Martin 2.00 .75
❑ 114 Donovan McNabb 3.00 1.25
❑ 115 Jerry Rice 4.00 1.50
❑ 116 Jon Kitna 2.00 .75
❑ 117 Isaac Bruce 2.00 .75
❑ 118 Marshall Faulk 2.50 1.00
❑ 119 Kurt Warner 4.00 1.50
❑ 120 Shaun King .30 .10
❑ 121 Eddie George 2.00 .75
❑ 122 Steve McNair 2.00 .75
❑ 123 Jevon Kearse 2.00 .75
❑ 124 Stephen Davis 2.00 .75
❑ 125 Brad Johnson 2.00 .75
❑ 126 Mike Anderson RC 2.50 1.00
❑ 127 Peter Warrick RC 5.00 2.00
❑ 128 Courtney Brown RC 2.00 .75
❑ 129 Plaxico Burress RC 10.00 4.00
❑ 130 Corey Simon RC 5.00 2.00
❑ 131 Thomas Jones RC 8.00 3.00
❑ 132 Travis Taylor RC 2.00 .75
❑ 133 Shaun Alexander RC 30.00 12.50
❑ 134 Deon Grant RC 4.00 1.50
❑ 135 Chris Redman RC 4.00 1.50
❑ 136 Chad Pennington RC 12.00 5.00
❑ 137 Jamal Lewis RC 12.00 5.00
❑ 138 Brian Urlacher RC 25.00 10.00
❑ 139 Keith Bulluck RC 5.00 2.00
❑ 140 Bubba Franks RC 5.00 2.00
❑ 141 Dez White RC 5.00 2.00
❑ 142 Na'il Diggs RC 4.00 1.50
❑ 143 Ahmed Plummer RC 5.00 2.00
❑ 144 Ron Dayne RC 5.00 2.00
❑ 145 Shaun Ellis RC 5.00 2.00
❑ 146 Sylvester Morris RC 4.00 1.50
❑ 147 Deltha O'Neal RC 5.00 2.00
❑ 148 Raynoch Thompson RC 4.00 1.50
❑ 149 R.Jay Soward RC 4.00 1.50
❑ 150 Mario Edwards RC 4.00 1.50
❑ 151 John Engelberger RC 4.00 1.50
❑ 152 Dwayne Goodrich RC 5.00 2.00
❑ 153 Sherrod Gideon RC 2.50 1.00
❑ 154 John Abraham RC 5.00 2.00
❑ 155 Ben Kelly RC 5.00 2.00
❑ 156 Travis Prentice RC 4.00 1.50
❑ 157 Darrell Jackson RC 10.00 4.00
❑ 158 Giovanni Carmazzi RC 2.50 1.00
❑ 159 Anthony Lucas RC 2.50 1.00
❑ 160 Danny Farmer RC 4.00 1.50
❑ 161 Dennis Northcutt RC 5.00 2.00
❑ 162 Troy Walters RC 5.00 2.00
❑ 163 Laveranues Coles RC 6.00 2.50
❑ 164 Tee Martin RC 5.00 2.00
❑ 165 J.R. Redmond RC 4.00 1.50
❑ 166 Tim Rattay RC 5.00 2.00
❑ 167 Jerry Porter RC 6.00 2.50
❑ 168 Sebastian Janikowski RC 5.00 2.00
❑ 169 Michael Wiley RC 4.00 1.50
❑ 170 Reuben Droughns RC 6.00 2.50
❑ 171 Trung Canidate RC 4.00 1.50
❑ 172 Shyrone Stith RC 5.00 2.00
❑ 173 Chris Hovan RC 4.00 1.50
❑ 174 Brandon Short RC 5.00 2.00
❑ 175 Mark Roman RC 4.00 1.50
❑ 176 Trevor Gaylor RC 4.00 1.50
❑ 177 Chris Cole RC 4.00 1.50
❑ 178 Hank Poteat RC 4.00 1.50
❑ 179 Darren Howard RC 4.00 1.50
❑ 180 Rob Morris RC 5.00 2.00
❑ 181 Spergon Wynn RC 4.00 1.50
❑ 182 Marc Bulger RC 10.00 5.00
❑ 183 Tom Brady RC 175.00 100.00
❑ 184 Todd Husak RC 5.00 2.00
❑ 185 Gari Scott RC 2.50 1.00
❑ 186 Erron Kinney RC 4.00 1.50
❑ 187 Julian Peterson RC 5.00 2.00
❑ 188 Sammy Morris RC 5.00 2.00
❑ 189 Rondell Mealey RC 2.50 1.00
❑ 190 Doug Chapman RC 4.00 1.50
❑ 191 Ron Dugans RC 2.50 1.00
❑ 192 Deon Dyer RC 4.00 1.50
❑ 193 Fred Robbins RC 2.50 1.00
❑ 194 Ike Charlton RC 5.00 2.00
❑ 195 Mareno Philyaw RC 2.50 1.00
❑ 196 Thomas Hamner RC 2.50 1.00
❑ 197 Jarious Jackson RC 4.00 1.50
❑ 198 Anthony Becht RC 5.00 2.00
❑ 199 Joe Hamilton RC 4.00 1.50
❑ 200 Todd Pinkston RC 5.00 2.00

2001 Donruss Elite

❑ COMP.SET w/o SP's (100) 20.00 7.50
❑ 1 David Boston .60 .25
❑ 2 Jake Plummer .40 .15
❑ 3 Thomas Jones .40 .15
❑ 4 Jamal Anderson .60 .25
❑ 5 Chris Redman .25 .08
❑ 6 Jamal Lewis 1.00 .40
❑ 7 Shannon Sharpe .40 .15
❑ 8 Travis Taylor .40 .15
❑ 9 Trent Dilfer .40 .15
❑ 10 Doug Flutie .60 .25
❑ 11 Eric Moulds .40 .15
❑ 12 Rob Johnson .40 .15
❑ 13 Muhsin Muhammad .40 .15
❑ 14 Steve Beuerlein .25 .08
❑ 15 Brian Urlacher 1.00 .40
❑ 16 Cade McNown .25 .08
❑ 17 Marcus Robinson .60 .25
❑ 18 Akili Smith .25 .08
❑ 19 Corey Dillon .60 .25
❑ 20 Peter Warrick .60 .25
❑ 21 Kevin Johnson .40 .15
❑ 22 Tim Couch .40 .15
❑ 23 Emmitt Smith 1.25 .50
❑ 24 Troy Aikman 1.00 .40
❑ 25 Brian Griese .60 .25
❑ 26 John Elway 2.00 .75
❑ 27 Mike Anderson .60 .25
❑ 28 Rod Smith .40 .15
❑ 29 Terrell Davis .60 .25
❑ 30 Barry Sanders 1.25 .50
❑ 31 Charlie Batch .60 .25
❑ 32 James Stewart .40 .15
❑ 33 Ahman Green .60 .25
❑ 34 Antonio Freeman .60 .25
❑ 35 Brett Favre 2.00 .75
❑ 36 Edgerrin James .75 .30
❑ 37 Marvin Harrison .60 .25
❑ 38 Peyton Manning 1.50 .60
❑ 39 Fred Taylor .60 .25
❑ 40 Jimmy Smith .40 .15
❑ 41 Keenan McCardell .25 .08
❑ 42 Mark Brunell .60 .25
❑ 43 Derrick Alexander .40 .15
❑ 44 Elvis Grbac .40 .15
❑ 45 Sylvester Morris .25 .08
❑ 46 Tony Gonzalez .40 .15
❑ 47 Dan Marino 2.00 .75
❑ 48 Jay Fiedler .60 .25
❑ 49 Lamar Smith .40 .15
❑ 50 Oronde Gadsden .40 .15
❑ 51 Cris Carter .60 .25
❑ 52 Daunte Culpepper .60 .25
❑ 53 Randy Moss 1.25 .50
❑ 54 Robert Smith .40 .15
❑ 55 Drew Bledsoe .75 .30
❑ 56 Terry Glenn .25 .08
❑ 57 Aaron Brooks .60 .25
❑ 58 Joe Horn .40 .15
❑ 59 Ricky Williams .60 .25
❑ 60 Amani Toomer .25 .08
❑ 61 Ike Hilliard .40 .15
❑ 62 Kerry Collins .40 .15
❑ 63 Ron Dayne .60 .25
❑ 64 Tiki Barber .60 .25
❑ 65 Chad Pennington 1.00 .40
❑ 66 Curtis Martin .60 .25
❑ 67 Vinny Testaverde .40 .15
❑ 68 Wayne Chrebet .40 .15
❑ 69 Rich Gannon .60 .25
❑ 70 Tim Brown .60 .25
❑ 71 Tyrone Wheatley .40 .15
❑ 72 Donovan McNabb .75 .30
❑ 73 Jerome Bettis .60 .25
❑ 74 Plaxico Burress .60 .25
❑ 75 Junior Seau .60 .25
❑ 76 Charlie Garner .40 .15
❑ 77 Jeff Garcia .60 .25
❑ 78 Jerry Rice 1.25 .50
❑ 79 Terrell Owens .60 .25
❑ 80 Darrell Jackson .60 .25
❑ 81 Ricky Watters .40 .15
❑ 82 Shaun Alexander .75 .30
❑ 83 Isaac Bruce .60 .25
❑ 84 Kurt Warner 1.25 .50
❑ 85 Marshall Faulk .75 .30
❑ 86 Torry Holt .60 .25
❑ 87 Trent Green .60 .25
❑ 88 Keyshawn Johnson .60 .25
❑ 89 Shaun King .25 .08
❑ 90 Warren Sapp .40 .15
❑ 91 Warrick Dunn .60 .25
❑ 92 Eddie George .60 .25
❑ 93 Jevon Kearse .40 .15
❑ 94 Steve McNair .60 .25
❑ 95 Albert Connell .25 .08
❑ 96 Jeff George .40 .15
❑ 97 Brad Johnson .60 .25
❑ 98 Bruce Smith .25 .08
❑ 99 Michael Westbrook .40 .15
❑ 100 Stephen Davis .60 .25
❑ 101 Michael Vick RC 40.00 15.00
❑ 102 Drew Brees RC 40.00 20.00
❑ 103 Chris Weinke RC 10.00 4.00
❑ 104 Quincy Carter RC 10.00 4.00
❑ 105 Sage Rosenfels RC 10.00 4.00
❑ 106 Josh Heupel RC 10.00 4.00
❑ 107 Tony Driver RC 6.00 2.50
❑ 108 Ben Leard RC 6.00 2.50
❑ 109 Marques Tuiasosopo RC 10.00 4.00
❑ 110 Tim Hasselbeck RC 10.00 4.00
❑ 111 Mike McMahon RC 10.00 4.00
❑ 112 Deuce McAllister RC 25.00 10.00
❑ 113 LaMont Jordan RC 25.00 10.00
❑ 114 LaDainian Tomlinson RC 100.00 50.00
❑ 115 James Jackson RC 10.00 4.00
❑ 116 Anthony Thomas RC 10.00 4.00
❑ 117 Travis Henry RC 25.00 10.00
❑ 118 DeAngelo Evans RC 6.00 2.50
❑ 119 Travis Minor RC 6.00 2.50
❑ 120 Rudi Johnson RC 25.00 12.50
❑ 121 Michael Bennett RC 10.00 4.00
❑ 122 Kevan Barlow RC 10.00 4.00
❑ 123 Dan Alexander RC 10.00 4.00
❑ 124 David Allen RC 6.00 2.50
❑ 125 Correll Buckhalter RC 12.00 5.00
❑ 126 David Rivers RC 6.00 2.50
❑ 127 Reggie White RC 6.00 2.50
❑ 128 Moran Norris RC 4.00 1.50
❑ 129 Ja'Mar Toombs RC 6.00 2.50
❑ 130 Jason McKinley RC 6.00 2.50
❑ 131 Scotty Anderson RC 6.00 2.50
❑ 132 Dustin McClintock RC 10.00 4.00
❑ 133 Heath Evans RC 6.00 2.50
❑ 134 David Terrell RC 10.00 4.00
❑ 135 Santana Moss RC 15.00 6.00
❑ 136 Rod Gardner RC 10.00 4.00
❑ 137 Quincy Morgan RC 10.00 4.00
❑ 138 Freddie Mitchell RC 10.00 4.00
❑ 139 Boo Williams RC 6.00 2.50
❑ 140 Reggie Wayne RC 25.00 10.00
❑ 141 Ronney Daniels RC 4.00 1.50

❑ 142 Bobby Newcombe RC 6.00 2.50
❑ 143 Reggie Germany/250 RC 12.00 5.00
❑ 144 Jesse Palmer RC 10.00 4.00
❑ 145 Robert Ferguson RC 10.00 4.00
❑ 146 Ken-Yon Rambo RC 6.00 2.50
❑ 147 Alex Bannister RC 6.00 2.50
❑ 148 Koren Robinson RC 10.00 4.00
❑ 149 Chad Johnson RC 30.00 12.50
❑ 150 Chris Chambers RC 15.00 6.00
❑ 151 Javon Green RC 6.00 2.50
❑ 152 Snoop Minnis RC 6.00 2.50
❑ 153 Vinny Sutherland RC 6.00 2.50
❑ 154 Cedrick Wilson RC 10.00 4.00
❑ 155 John Capel/250 RC 12.00 5.00
❑ 156 T.J. Houshmandzadeh RC 12.00 5.00
❑ 157 Todd Heap RC 10.00 4.00
❑ 158 Alge Crumpler RC 15.00 6.00
❑ 159 Jabari Holloway RC 6.00 2.50
❑ 160 Marcellus Rivers RC 6.00 2.50
❑ 161 Rashon Burns RC 4.00 1.50
❑ 162 Tony Stewart RC 10.00 4.00
❑ 163 Jevaris Johnson RC 4.00 1.50
❑ 164 Jamal Reynolds RC 10.00 4.00
❑ 165 Andre Carter RC 10.00 4.00
❑ 166 David Warren RC 4.00 1.50
❑ 167 Justin Smith RC 10.00 4.00
❑ 168 Josh Booty RC 10.00 4.00
❑ 169 Karon Riley RC 4.00 1.50
❑ 170 Cedric Scott RC 4.00 1.50
❑ 171 Kenny Smith RC 6.00 2.50
❑ 172 Richard Seymour RC 10.00 4.00
❑ 173 Willie Howard RC 6.00 2.50
❑ 174 Markus Steele RC 6.00 2.50
❑ 175 Marcus Stroud RC 10.00 4.00
❑ 176 Damione Lewis RC 6.00 2.50
❑ 177 Casey Hampton RC 10.00 4.00
❑ 178 Ennis Davis RC 4.00 1.50
❑ 179 Gerard Warren RC .60 .25
❑ 180 Tommy Polley RC 10.00 4.00
❑ 181 Kendrell Bell/250 RC 40.00 15.00
❑ 182 Dan Morgan RC 10.00 4.00
❑ 183 Morlon Greenwood RC 6.00 2.50
❑ 184 Quinton Caver/250 10.00 4.00
❑ 185 Keith Adams RC 4.00 1.50
❑ 186 Brian Allen RC 4.00 1.50
❑ 187 Carlos Polk RC 4.00 1.50
❑ 188 Torrance Marshall RC 10.00 4.00
❑ 189 Jamie Winborn RC 6.00 2.50
❑ 190 Jamar Fletcher RC 6.00 2.50
❑ 191 Ken Lucas RC 6.00 2.50
❑ 192 Fred Smoot RC 10.00 4.00
❑ 193 Nate Clements RC 10.00 4.00
❑ 194 Will Allen RC 6.00 2.50
❑ 195 Willie Middlebrooks/250 RC 10.00 4.00
❑ 196 Gary Baxter RC 6.00 2.50
❑ 197 Derrick Gibson RC 6.00 2.50
❑ 198 Robert Carswell/250 RC 10.00 4.00
❑ 199 Hakim Akbar RC 4.00 1.50
❑ 200 Adam Archuleta RC 10.00 4.00

2002 Donruss Elite

❑ COMP.SET w/o SP's (100) 20.00 7.50
❑ 1 Elvis Grbac .30 .10
❑ 2 Jamal Lewis .50 .20
❑ 3 Ray Lewis .50 .20
❑ 4 Travis Henry .50 .20
❑ 5 Eric Moulds .30 .10
❑ 6 Corey Dillon .30 .10
❑ 7 Peter Warrick .30 .10
❑ 8 Tim Couch .30 .10
❑ 9 James Jackson .20 .07
❑ 10 Kevin Johnson .30 .10
❑ 11 Mike Anderson .50 .20
❑ 12 Terrell Davis .50 .20
❑ 13 Brian Griese .50 .20
❑ 14 Rod Smith .30 .10
❑ 15 Marvin Harrison .50 .20
❑ 16 Reggie Wayne .50 .20
❑ 17 Dominic Rhodes .50 .20
❑ 18 Edgerrin James .60 .25
❑ 19 Mark Brunell .50 .20
❑ 20 Keenan McCardell .20 .07
❑ 21 Jimmy Smith .30 .10
❑ 22 Tony Gonzalez .30 .10
❑ 23 Trent Green .30 .10
❑ 24 Priest Holmes .60 .25
❑ 25 Snoop Minnis .20 .07
❑ 26 Chris Chambers .50 .20
❑ 27 Jay Fiedler .30 .10
❑ 28 Travis Minor .20 .07
❑ 29 Lamar Smith .30 .10
❑ 30 Tom Brady 1.25 .50
❑ 31 Troy Brown .30 .10
❑ 32 Antowain Smith .30 .10
❑ 33 Laveranues Coles .30 .10
❑ 34 Curtis Martin .50 .20
❑ 35 Vinny Testaverde .30 .10
❑ 36 Wayne Chrebet .30 .10
❑ 37 Tim Brown .50 .20
❑ 38 Rich Gannon .50 .20
❑ 39 Jerry Rice 1.00 .40
❑ 40 Charlie Garner .30 .10
❑ 41 Jerome Bettis .50 .20
❑ 42 Plaxico Burress .30 .10
❑ 43 Kordell Stewart .30 .10
❑ 44 Kendrell Bell .50 .20
❑ 45 Doug Flutie .50 .20
❑ 46 LaDainian Tomlinson .75 .30
❑ 47 Junior Seau .50 .20
❑ 48 Drew Brees .50 .20
❑ 49 Shaun Alexander .60 .25
❑ 50 Koren Robinson .30 .10
❑ 51 Ricky Watters .30 .10
❑ 52 Eddie George .50 .20
❑ 53 Derrick Mason .30 .10
❑ 54 Steve McNair .50 .20
❑ 55 David Boston .50 .20
❑ 56 Jake Plummer .30 .10
❑ 57 Chris Chandler .30 .10
❑ 58 Jamal Anderson .30 .10
❑ 59 Michael Vick 1.00 .40
❑ 60 Wesley Walls .20 .07
❑ 61 Chris Weinke .30 .10
❑ 62 David Terrell .50 .20
❑ 63 Anthony Thomas .30 .10
❑ 64 Brian Urlacher .75 .30
❑ 65 Quincy Carter .30 .10
❑ 66 Rocket Ismail .30 .10
❑ 67 Emmitt Smith 1.25 .50
❑ 68 James Stewart .30 .10
❑ 69 Germane Crowell .20 .07
❑ 70 Mike McMahon .50 .20
❑ 71 Brett Favre 1.25 .50
❑ 72 Ahman Green .50 .20
❑ 73 Antonio Freeman .50 .20
❑ 74 Michael Bennett .30 .10
❑ 75 Cris Carter .50 .20
❑ 76 Daunte Culpepper .50 .20
❑ 77 Randy Moss 1.00 .40
❑ 78 Aaron Brooks .50 .20
❑ 79 Deuce McAllister .60 .25
❑ 80 Ricky Williams .50 .20
❑ 81 Kerry Collins .30 .10
❑ 82 Ron Dayne .30 .10
❑ 83 Amani Toomer .30 .10
❑ 84 Correll Buckhalter .30 .10
❑ 85 James Thrash .30 .10
❑ 86 Freddie Mitchell .30 .10
❑ 87 Duce Staley .50 .20
❑ 88 Jeff Garcia .50 .20
❑ 89 Garrison Hearst .30 .10
❑ 90 Terrell Owens .50 .20
❑ 91 Isaac Bruce .50 .20
❑ 92 Marshall Faulk .50 .20
❑ 93 Torry Holt .50 .20
❑ 94 Kurt Warner .50 .20
❑ 95 Mike Alstott .50 .20
❑ 96 Brad Johnson .30 .10
❑ 97 Keyshawn Johnson .50 .20
❑ 98 Stephen Davis .30 .10
❑ 99 Rod Gardner .30 .10
❑ 100 Tony Banks .20 .07
❑ 101 David Carr RC 30.00 12.50
❑ 102 Joey Harrington RC 20.00 7.50
❑ 103 Rohan Davey RC 15.00 6.00
❑ 104 Chad Hutchinson RC 12.00 5.00
❑ 105 Patrick Ramsey RC 15.00 6.00
❑ 106 Kurt Kittner RC 12.00 5.00
❑ 107 Eric Crouch RC 15.00 6.00
❑ 108 David Garrard RC 30.00 15.00
❑ 109 Ronald Curry RC 15.00 6.00
❑ 110 Zak Kustok RC 15.00 6.00
❑ 111 Woody Dantzler RC 12.00 5.00
❑ 112 Wes Pate RC 6.00 2.50
❑ 113 Brian Westbrook RC 30.00 12.50
❑ 114 Josh McCown RC 20.00 7.50
❑ 115 Travis Stephens RC 12.00 5.00
❑ 116 Luke Staley RC 12.00 5.00
❑ 117 William Green RC 15.00 6.00
❑ 118 Clinton Portis RC 50.00 20.00
❑ 119 DeShaun Foster RC 15.00 6.00
❑ 120 Verron Haynes RC 15.00 6.00
❑ 121 T.J. Duckett RC 15.00 6.00
❑ 122 Antwoine Womack RC 12.00 5.00
❑ 123 Leonard Henry RC 12.00 5.00
❑ 124 Lamar Gordon RC 15.00 6.00
❑ 125 Adrian Peterson RC 20.00 7.50
❑ 126 Chester Taylor RC 30.00 12.50
❑ 127 Damien Anderson RC 12.00 5.00
❑ 128 Maurice Morris RC 15.00 6.00
❑ 129 Ricky Williams RC 12.00 5.00
❑ 130 Terry Charles RC 12.00 5.00
❑ 131 Demontray Carter RC 6.00 2.50
❑ 132 Jason McAddley RC 12.00 5.00
❑ 133 Ladell Betts RC 15.00 6.00
❑ 134 Cortlen Johnson RC 6.00 2.50
❑ 135 James Mungro RC 15.00 6.00
❑ 136 Atrews Bell RC 6.00 2.50
❑ 137 Josh Scobey RC 15.00 6.00
❑ 138 Justin Peelle RC 6.00 2.50
❑ 139 Najeh Davenport RC 15.00 6.00
❑ 140 Josh Reed RC 15.00 6.00
❑ 141 Marquise Walker RC 12.00 5.00
❑ 142 Jabar Gaffney RC 15.00 6.00
❑ 143 Antwaan Randle El RC 20.00 7.50
❑ 144 Ashley Lelie RC 30.00 12.50
❑ 145 Tavon Mason RC 6.00 2.50
❑ 146 Antonio Bryant RC 15.00 6.00
❑ 147 Javon Walker RC 25.00 10.00
❑ 148 Kelly Campbell RC 12.00 5.00
❑ 149 Ron Johnson RC 12.00 5.00
❑ 150 Andre Davis RC 12.00 5.00
❑ 151 Cliff Russell RC 12.00 5.00
❑ 152 Reche Caldwell RC 15.00 6.00
❑ 153 Kyle Johnson RC 6.00 2.50
❑ 154 Freddie Milons RC 12.00 5.00
❑ 155 Brian Poli-Dixon RC 12.00 5.00
❑ 156 David Thornton RC 6.00 2.50
❑ 157 Bryan Thomas RC 12.00 5.00
❑ 158 Kahlil Hill RC 12.00 5.00
❑ 159 Deion Branch RC 25.00 10.00
❑ 160 Akin Ayodele RC 6.00 2.50
❑ 161 Donte Stallworth RC 25.00 10.00
❑ 162 Tim Carter RC 12.00 5.00
❑ 163 Kenyon Coleman RC 6.00 2.50
❑ 164 Jeremy Shockey RC 40.00 15.00
❑ 165 Eddie Freeman RC 6.00 2.50
❑ 166 Tracey Wistrom RC 12.00 5.00
❑ 167 Daniel Graham RC 15.00 6.00
❑ 168 Julius Peppers RC 30.00 12.50
❑ 169 Alex Brown RC 15.00 6.00
❑ 170 Dwight Freeney RC 25.00 10.00
❑ 171 Kalimba Edwards RC 15.00 6.00
❑ 172 Dennis Johnson RC 6.00 2.50
❑ 173 Travis Fisher RC 15.00 6.00
❑ 174 John Henderson RC 15.00 6.00
❑ 175 Anthony Weaver RC 12.00 5.00
❑ 176 Ryan Sims RC 15.00 6.00
❑ 177 Alan Harper RC 6.00 2.50
❑ 178 Larry Tripplett RC 6.00 2.50
❑ 179 Wendell Bryant RC 6.00 2.50
❑ 180 Albert Haynesworth RC 12.00 5.00
❑ 181 Levar Fisher RC 6.00 2.50
❑ 182 Andra Davis RC 12.00 5.00
❑ 183 Joseph Jefferson RC 12.00 5.00
❑ 184 Lamont Thompson RC 12.00 5.00
❑ 185 Robert Thomas RC 15.00 6.00
❑ 186 Michael Lewis RC 15.00 6.00
❑ 187 Rocky Calmus RC 15.00 6.00
❑ 188 Napoleon Harris RC 15.00 6.00

❑ 189 Lito Sheppard RC	15.00	6.00
❑ 190 Quentin Jammer RC	15.00	6.00
❑ 191 Roy Williams RC	30.00	12.50
❑ 192 Marques Anderson RC	15.00	6.00
❑ 193 Chris Hope RC	15.00	6.00
❑ 194 Raonall Smith RC	12.00	5.00
❑ 195 Mike Rumph RC	15.00	6.00
❑ 196 James Allen RC	6.00	2.50
❑ 197 Ed Reed RC	25.00	12.50
❑ 198 Mike Williams RC	12.00	5.00
❑ 199 Phillip Buchanon RC	15.00	6.00
❑ 200 Bryant McKinnie RC	12.00	5.00

2003 Donruss Elite

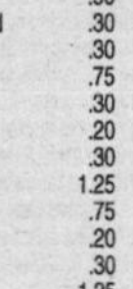
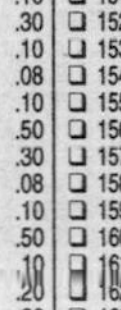

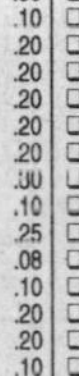

❑ COMP.SET w/o SP's (100)	20.00	7.50
❑ 1 Jamal Lewis	.50	.20
❑ 2 Ray Lewis	.50	.20
❑ 3 Todd Heap	.30	.10
❑ 4 Drew Bledsoe	.50	.20
❑ 5 Travis Henry	.30	.10
❑ 6 Eric Moulds	.30	.10
❑ 7 Peerless Price	.30	.10
❑ 8 Jon Kitna	.30	.10
❑ 9 Corey Dillon	.30	.10
❑ 10 Chad Johnson	.50	.20
❑ 11 Tim Couch	.20	.08
❑ 12 William Green	.30	.10
❑ 13 Andre Davis	.20	.08
❑ 14 Brian Griese	.50	.20
❑ 15 Ashley Lelie	.50	.20
❑ 16 Clinton Portis	.75	.30
❑ 17 Rod Smith	.30	.10
❑ 18 David Carr	.75	.30
❑ 19 Jonathan Wells	.20	.08
❑ 20 Jabar Gaffney	.30	.10
❑ 21 Peyton Manning	.75	.30
❑ 22 Edgerrin James	.50	.20
❑ 23 Marvin Harrison	.50	.20
❑ 24 Mark Brunell	.30	.10
❑ 25 Jimmy Smith	.30	.10
❑ 26 Fred Taylor	.50	.20
❑ 27 Priest Holmes	.60	.25
❑ 28 Trent Green	.30	.10
❑ 29 Tony Gonzalez	.30	.10
❑ 30 Chris Chambers	.50	.20
❑ 31 Zach Thomas	.30	.10
❑ 32 Ricky Williams	.50	.20
❑ 33 Tom Brady	1.25	.50
❑ 34 Antowain Smith	.30	.10
❑ 35 Troy Brown	.30	.10
❑ 36 Chad Pennington	.60	.25
❑ 37 Curtis Martin	.50	.20
❑ 38 Laveranues Coles	.30	.10
❑ 39 Tim Brown	.50	.20
❑ 40 Rich Gannon	.30	.10
❑ 41 Jerry Rice	1.00	.40
❑ 42 Charlie Garner	.30	.10
❑ 43 Antwaan Randle El	.50	.20
❑ 44 Plaxico Burress	.30	.10
❑ 45 Tommy Maddox	.50	.20
❑ 46 Jerome Bettis	.50	.20
❑ 47 Drew Brees	.50	.20
❑ 48 LaDainian Tomlinson	.50	.20
❑ 49 Junior Seau	.50	.20
❑ 50 Eddie George	.30	.10
❑ 51 Steve McNair	.50	.20
❑ 52 Derrick Mason	.30	.10
❑ 53 David Boston	.30	.10
❑ 54 Jake Plummer	.30	.10
❑ 55 Marcel Shipp	.30	.10
❑ 56 Michael Vick	1.25	.50
❑ 57 T.J. Duckett	.30	.10
❑ 58 Warrick Dunn	.30	.10
❑ 59 Julius Peppers	.50	.20
❑ 60 Steve Smith	.50	.20
❑ 61 Muhsin Muhammad	.30	.10
❑ 62 Anthony Thomas	.30	.10
❑ 63 Brian Urlacher	.75	.30
❑ 64 Marty Booker	.30	.10
❑ 65 Chad Hutchinson	.20	.08
❑ 66 Antonio Bryant	.30	.10
❑ 67 Emmitt Smith	1.25	.50
❑ 68 Joey Harrington	.75	.30
❑ 69 Germane Crowell	.20	.08
❑ 70 James Stewart	.30	.10
❑ 71 Brett Favre	1.25	.50
❑ 72 Donald Driver	.30	.10
❑ 73 Ahman Green	.50	.20
❑ 74 Randy Moss	.75	.30
❑ 75 Michael Bennett	.30	.10
❑ 76 Daunte Culpepper	.50	.20
❑ 77 Aaron Brooks	.50	.20
❑ 78 Deuce McAllister	.50	.20
❑ 79 Donte Stallworth	.50	.20
❑ 80 Tiki Barber	.50	.20
❑ 81 Jeremy Shockey	.75	.30
❑ 82 Kerry Collins	.30	.10
❑ 83 Donovan McNabb	.60	.25
❑ 84 James Thrash	.20	.08
❑ 85 Duce Staley	.30	.10
❑ 86 Jeff Garcia	.50	.20
❑ 87 Terrell Owens	.50	.20
❑ 88 Garrison Hearst	.30	.10
❑ 89 Shaun Alexander	.50	.20
❑ 90 Darrell Jackson	.30	.10
❑ 91 Koren Robinson	.20	.08
❑ 92 Marshall Faulk	.50	.20
❑ 93 Kurt Warner	.50	.20
❑ 94 Isaac Bruce	.50	.20
❑ 95 Keyshawn Johnson	.50	.20
❑ 96 Brad Johnson	.30	.10
❑ 97 Warren Sapp	.30	.10
❑ 98 Patrick Ramsey	.50	.20
❑ 99 Rod Gardner	.30	.10
❑ 100 Stephen Davis	.30	.10
❑ 101 Brian St.Pierre RC	12.00	5.00
❑ 102 Byron Leftwich RC	40.00	15.00
❑ 103 Carson Palmer RC	50.00	20.00
❑ 104 Chris Simms RC	20.00	7.50
❑ 105 Dave Ragone RC	12.00	5.00
❑ 106 Ken Dorsey RC	12.00	5.00
❑ 107 Kliff Kingsbury RC	10.00	4.00
❑ 108 Kyle Boller RC	12.00	5.00
❑ 109 Rex Grossman RC	40.00	15.00
❑ 110 Seneca Wallace RC	12.00	5.00
❑ 111 Jason Gesser RC	12.00	5.00
❑ 112 Artose Pinner RC	12.00	5.00
❑ 113 Avon Cobourne RC	6.00	2.50
❑ 114 Cecil Sapp RC	10.00	4.00
❑ 115 Chris Brown RC	12.00	5.00
❑ 116 Derek Watson RC	10.00	4.00
❑ 117 Domanick Davis RC	12.00	5.00
❑ 118 Dwone Hicks/100 RC	30.00	15.00
❑ 119 Earnest Graham RC	12.00	5.00
❑ 120 Justin Fargas RC	12.00	5.00
❑ 121 Larry Johnson RC	50.00	25.00
❑ 122 Lee Suggs RC	12.00	5.00
❑ 123 Musa Smith RC	12.00	5.00
❑ 124 Onterrio Smith RC	12.00	5.00
❑ 125 Quentin Griffin RC	12.00	5.00
❑ 126 Willis McGahee RC	30.00	15.00
❑ 127 Sultan McCullough RC	10.00	4.00
❑ 128 LaBrandon Toefield RC	12.00	5.00
❑ 129 B.J. Askew RC	12.00	5.00
❑ 130 Andre Johnson RC	25.00	10.00
❑ 131 Anquan Boldin RC	30.00	12.50
❑ 132 Arnaz Battle RC	12.00	5.00
❑ 133 Bethel Johnson RC	12.00	5.00
❑ 134 Billy McMullen RC	10.00	4.00
❑ 135 Bobby Wade RC	12.00	5.00
❑ 136 Brandon Lloyd RC	12.00	5.00
❑ 137 Bryant Johnson RC	12.00	5.00
❑ 138 Charles Rogers RC	12.00	5.00
❑ 139 Doug Gabriel RC	12.00	5.00
❑ 140 Justin Gage RC	12.00	5.00
❑ 141 Kareem Kelly RC	10.00	4.00
❑ 142 Kelley Washington RC	12.00	5.00
❑ 143 Kevin Curtis RC	15.00	6.00
❑ 144 Nate Burleson RC	12.00	5.00
❑ 145 Sam Aiken RC	10.00	4.00
❑ 146 Shaun McDonald RC	12.00	5.00
❑ 147 Talman Gardner RC	12.00	5.00
❑ 148 Taylor Jacobs RC	10.00	4.00
❑ 149 Terrence Edwards RC	10.00	4.00
❑ 150 Tyrone Calico RC	12.00	5.00
❑ 151 Walter Young RC	6.00	2.50
❑ 152 Ryan Hoag/100 RC	30.00	15.00
❑ 153 Paul Arnold/100 RC	30.00	15.00
❑ 154 Bennie Joppru RC	12.00	5.00
❑ 155 Dallas Clark RC	12.00	5.00
❑ 156 George Wrighster RC	10.00	4.00
❑ 157 Jason Witten RC	20.00	10.00
❑ 158 Mike Pinkard RC	6.00	2.50
❑ 159 Robert Johnson/100 RC	30.00	15.00
❑ 160 Teyo Johnson RC	12.00	5.00
❑ 161 Andrew Williams RC	10.00	4.00
❑ 162 Chris Kelsay RC	12.00	5.00
❑ 163 Cory Redding RC	10.00	4.00
❑ 164 DeWayne Robertson RC	12.00	5.00
❑ 165 DeWayne White RC	10.00	4.00
❑ 166 Jerome McDougle RC	12.00	5.00
❑ 167 Kenny Peterson RC	10.00	4.00
❑ 168 Kindal Moorehead RC	10.00	4.00
❑ 169 Michael Haynes RC	12.00	5.00
❑ 170 Terrell Suggs RC	20.00	7.50
❑ 171 Tully Banta-Cain RC	10.00	4.00
❑ 172 Jimmy Kennedy RC	12.00	5.00
❑ 173 Johnathan Sullivan RC	6.00	2.50
❑ 174 Kevin Williams RC	12.00	5.00
❑ 175 Nick Eason/100 RC	30.00	15.00
❑ 176 Rien Long RC	6.00	2.50
❑ 177 Ty Warren RC	12.00	5.00
❑ 178 William Joseph RC	12.00	5.00
❑ 179 Boss Bailey RC	12.00	5.00
❑ 180 Bradie James RC	12.00	5.00
❑ 181 Victor Hobson RC	12.00	5.00
❑ 182 Clifton Smith/100 RC	30.00	15.00
❑ 183 E.J. Henderson/100 RC	30.00	15.00
❑ 184 Gerald Hayes/100 RC	30.00	15.00
❑ 185 LaM McDonald/100 RC	30.00	15.00
❑ 186 Nick Barnett RC	12.00	5.00
❑ 187 Terry Pierce RC	10.00	4.00
❑ 188 Andre Woolfolk RC	12.00	5.00
❑ 189 Dennis Weathersby RC	6.00	2.50
❑ 190 Drayton Florence/100 RC	30.00	15.00
❑ 191 Eugene Wilson RC	12.00	5.00
❑ 192 Marcus Trufant RC	12.00	5.00
❑ 193 Rashean Mathis RC	10.00	4.00
❑ 194 Ricky Manning RC	12.00	5.00
❑ 195 Sammy Davis/100 RC	30.00	15.00
❑ 196 Terence Newman RC	25.00	10.00
❑ 197 Julian Battle RC	10.00	4.00
❑ 198 Ken Hamlin RC	12.00	5.00
❑ 199 Mike Doss RC	12.00	5.00
❑ 200 Troy Polamalu/100 RC	100.00	60.00

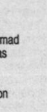

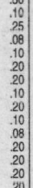

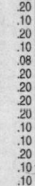

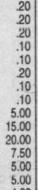

2004 Donruss Elite

❑ COMP.SET w/o SP's (100)	20.00	7.50
❑ ROOKIE PRINT RUN 500 SER.#'d SETS		
❑ 1 Emmitt Smith	2.00	.75
❑ 2 Anquan Boldin	1.00	.40
❑ 3 Michael Vick	2.00	.75
❑ 4 Peerless Price	.60	.25
❑ 5 T.J. Duckett	.60	.25
❑ 6 Warrick Dunn	.60	.25
❑ 7 Jamal Lewis	1.00	.40
❑ 8 Kyle Boller	1.00	.40
❑ 9 Todd Heap	.60	.25
❑ 10 Ray Lewis	1.00	.40
❑ 11 Drew Bledsoe	1.00	.40
❑ 12 Eric Moulds	.60	.25
❑ 13 Travis Henry	.60	.25
❑ 14 Jake Delhomme	1.00	.40

❑ 15	Stephen Davis	.60	.25
❑ 16	Steve Smith	1.00	.40
❑ 17	Anthony Thomas	.60	.25
❑ 18	Brian Urlacher	1.25	.50
❑ 19	Rex Grossman	1.00	.40
❑ 20	Chad Johnson	1.00	.40
❑ 21	Carson Palmer	1.25	.50
❑ 22	Rudi Johnson	.60	.25
❑ 23	Peter Warrick	.60	.25
❑ 24	Andre Davis	.40	.15
❑ 25	Tim Couch	.40	.15
❑ 26	Quincy Carter	.60	.25
❑ 27	Roy Williams S	.60	.25
❑ 28	Terence Newman	.60	.25
❑ 29	Clinton Portis	1.00	.40
❑ 30	Jake Plummer	.60	.25
❑ 31	Rod Smith	.60	.25
❑ 32	Charles Rogers	.60	.25
❑ 33	Joey Harrington	1.00	.40
❑ 34	Ahman Green	1.00	.40
❑ 35	Brett Favre	2.50	1.00
❑ 36	Javon Walker	.60	.25
❑ 37	Andre Johnson	1.00	.40
❑ 38	David Carr	1.00	.40
❑ 39	Domanick Davis	1.00	.40
❑ 40	Edgerrin James	1.00	.40
❑ 41	Marvin Harrison	1.00	.40
❑ 42	Peyton Manning	1.50	.60
❑ 43	Reggie Wayne	.60	.25
❑ 44	Byron Leftwich	1.25	.50
❑ 45	Fred Taylor	.60	.25
❑ 46	Jimmy Smith	.60	.25
❑ 47	Priest Holmes	1.25	.50
❑ 48	Tony Gonzalez	.60	.25
❑ 49	Trent Green	.60	.25
❑ 50	Chris Chambers	.60	.25
❑ 51	Ricky Williams	1.00	.40
❑ 52	Zach Thomas	1.00	.40
❑ 53	Daunte Culpepper	1.00	.40
❑ 54	Michael Bennett	.60	.25
❑ 55	Moe Williams	.40	.15
❑ 56	Randy Moss	1.25	.50
❑ 57	Deion Branch	1.00	.40
❑ 58	Tom Brady	2.50	1.00
❑ 59	Tedy Bruschi	.60	.25
❑ 60	Aaron Brooks	.60	.25
❑ 61	Deuce McAllister	1.00	.40
❑ 62	Joe Horn	.60	.25
❑ 63	Jeremy Shockey	1.00	.40
❑ 64	Kerry Collins	.60	.25
❑ 65	Michael Strahan	.60	.25
❑ 66	Tiki Barber	1.00	.40
❑ 67	Chad Pennington	1.00	.40
❑ 68	Curtis Martin	1.00	.40
❑ 69	Santana Moss	.60	.25
❑ 70	Jerry Porter	.60	.25
❑ 71	Jerry Rice	2.00	.75
❑ 72	Tim Brown	1.00	.40
❑ 73	Brian Westbrook	.60	.25
❑ 74	Correll Buckhalter	.60	.25
❑ 75	Donovan McNabb	1.25	.50
❑ 76	Hines Ward	1.00	.40
❑ 77	Kendrell Bell	.60	.25
❑ 78	Plaxico Burress	.60	.25
❑ 79	David Boston	.60	.25
❑ 80	Drew Brees	1.00	.40
❑ 81	LaDainian Tomlinson	1.25	.50
❑ 82	Jeff Garcia	1.00	.40
❑ 83	Kevan Barlow	.60	.25
❑ 84	Terrell Owens	1.00	.40
❑ 85	Koren Robinson	.60	.25
❑ 86	Matt Hasselbeck	.60	.25
❑ 87	Shaun Alexander	1.00	.40
❑ 88	Isaac Bruce	.60	.25
❑ 89	Marc Bulger	1.00	.40
❑ 90	Marshall Faulk	1.00	.40
❑ 91	Torry Holt	1.00	.40
❑ 92	Brad Johnson	.60	.25
❑ 93	Derrick Brooks	.60	.25
❑ 94	Keenan McCardell	.40	.15
❑ 95	Derrick Mason	.60	.25
❑ 96	Eddie George	.60	.25
❑ 97	Steve McNair	1.00	.40
❑ 98	Jevon Kearse	.60	.25
❑ 99	Laveranues Coles	.60	.25
❑ 100	Patrick Ramsey	.60	.25
❑ 101	Adimchinobe Echemandu RC	6.00	2.50
❑ 102	Ahmad Carroll RC	8.00	3.00
❑ 103	Antwan Odom RC	8.00	3.00
❑ 104	B.J. Johnson RC	6.00	2.50
❑ 105	Ben Roethlisberger RC	60.00	30.00
❑ 106	Ben Troupe RC	8.00	3.00
❑ 107	Ben Watson RC	8.00	3.00
❑ 108	Bernard Berrian RC	10.00	4.00
❑ 109	Bob Sanders RC	20.00	8.00
❑ 110	Brandon Everage RC	6.00	2.50
❑ 111	Brandon Miree RC	6.00	2.50
❑ 112	Carlos Francis RC	6.00	2.50
❑ 113	Cedric Cobbs RC	10.00	4.00
❑ 114	Chad Lavalais RC	6.00	2.50
❑ 115	Chris Collins RC	6.00	2.50
❑ 116	Chris Gamble RC	8.00	3.00
❑ 117	Chris Perry RC	10.00	4.00
❑ 118	Cody Pickett RC	8.00	3.00
❑ 119	Craig Krenzel RC	8.00	3.00
❑ 120	D.J. Hackett RC	6.00	2.50
❑ 121	D.J. Williams RC	8.00	3.00
❑ 122	Darius Watts RC	8.00	3.00
❑ 123	Darnell Dockett RC	6.00	2.50
❑ 124	DeAngelo Hall RC	10.00	4.00
❑ 125	Derek Abney RC	8.00	3.00
❑ 126	Derrick Hamilton RC	6.00	2.50
❑ 127	Derrick Strait RC	8.00	3.00
❑ 128	Devard Darling RC	8.00	3.00
❑ 129	Devery Henderson RC	8.00	3.00
❑ 130	Dontarrious Thomas RC	8.00	3.00
❑ 131	Drew Henson RC	8.00	3.00
❑ 132	Dunta Robinson RC	8.00	3.00
❑ 133	Dwan Edwards RC	4.00	1.50
❑ 134	Eli Manning RC	50.00	25.00
❑ 135	Ernest Wilford RC	8.00	3.00
❑ 136	Fred Russell RC	8.00	3.00
❑ 137	Greg Jones RC	8.00	3.00
❑ 138	Igor Olshansky RC	8.00	3.00
❑ 139	J.P. Losman RC	15.00	6.00
❑ 140	Jared Lorenzen RC	6.00	2.50
❑ 141	Jarrett Payton RC	8.00	3.00
❑ 142	Jason Babin RC	8.00	3.00
❑ 143	Jason Fife RC	6.00	2.50
❑ 144	Jeff Smoker RC	8.00	3.00
❑ 145	Jeremy LeSueur RC	6.00	2.50
❑ 146	Jerricho Cotchery RC	8.00	3.00
❑ 147	John Navarre RC	8.00	3.00
❑ 148	John Standeford RC	6.00	2.50
❑ 149	Johnnie Morant RC	8.00	3.00
❑ 150	Jonathan Vilma RC	8.00	3.00
❑ 151	Josh Davis RC	6.00	2.50
❑ 152	Josh Harris RC	8.00	3.00
❑ 153	Julius Jones RC	25.00	10.00
❑ 154	Justin Jenkins RC	6.00	2.50
❑ 155	Karlos Dansby RC	8.00	3.00
❑ 156	Keary Colbert RC	8.00	3.00
❑ 157	Keith Smith RC	6.00	2.50
❑ 158	Keiwan Ratliff RC	6.00	2.50
❑ 159	Kellen Winslow RC	15.00	6.00
❑ 160	Kendrick Starling RC	4.00	1.50
❑ 161	Kenechi Udeze RC	8.00	3.00
❑ 162	Kevin Jones RC	20.00	8.00
❑ 163	Larry Fitzgerald RC	30.00	12.50
❑ 164	Lee Evans RC	10.00	4.00
❑ 165	Luke McCown RC	8.00	3.00
❑ 166	Marquise Hill RC	6.00	2.50
❑ 167	Matt Schaub RC	25.00	10.00
❑ 168	Matt Ware RC	8.00	3.00
❑ 169	Matt Mauck RC	8.00	3.00
❑ 170	Maurice Mann RC	6.00	2.50
❑ 171	Mewelde Moore RC	8.00	3.00
❑ 172	Michael Boulware RC	8.00	3.00
❑ 173	Michael Clayton RC	15.00	6.00
❑ 174	Michael Jenkins RC	8.00	3.00
❑ 175	Michael Turner RC	10.00	4.00
❑ 176	B.J. Symons RC	8.00	3.00
❑ 177	Nathan Vasher RC	10.00	4.00
❑ 178	P.K. Sam RC	6.00	2.50
❑ 179	Philip Rivers RC	25.00	12.50
❑ 180	Quincy Wilson RC	6.00	2.50
❑ 181	Ran Carthon RC	6.00	2.50
❑ 182	Randy Starks RC	6.00	2.50
❑ 183	Rashaun Woods RC	8.00	3.00
❑ 184	Reggie Williams RC	10.00	4.00
❑ 185	Ricardo Colclough RC	8.00	3.00
❑ 186	Robert Kent RC	4.00	1.50
❑ 187	Roy Williams RC	25.00	10.00
❑ 188	Samie Parker RC	8.00	3.00
❑ 189	Scott Rislov RC	8.00	3.00
❑ 190	Sean Jones RC	6.00	2.50
❑ 191	Sean Taylor RC	8.00	3.00
❑ 192	Steven Jackson RC	25.00	10.00
❑ 193	Stuart Schweigert RC	8.00	3.00
❑ 194	Tatum Bell RC	15.00	6.00
❑ 195	Teddy Lehman RC	8.00	3.00
❑ 196	Tommie Harris RC	8.00	3.00
❑ 197	Troy Fleming RC	6.00	2.50
❑ 198	Vince Wilfork RC	8.00	3.00
❑ 199	Will Poole RC	8.00	3.00
❑ 200	Will Smith RC	8.00	3.00

2005 Donruss Elite

❑	COMP.SET w/o SP's (100)	20.00	7.50
❑	101-200 PRINT RUN 499 SER.#'d SETS		
❑ 1	Kurt Warner	.60	.25
❑ 2	Larry Fitzgerald	1.00	.40
❑ 3	Anquan Boldin	.60	.25
❑ 4	Emmitt Smith	2.00	.75
❑ 5	Michael Vick	1.50	.60
❑ 6	Warrick Dunn	.60	.25
❑ 7	Alge Crumpler	.60	.25
❑ 8	Jamal Lewis	1.00	.40
❑ 9	Kyle Boller	.60	.25
❑ 10	Ray Lewis	1.00	.40
❑ 11	Drew Bledsoe	1.00	.40
❑ 12	Willis McGahee	1.00	.40
❑ 13	Travis Henry	.60	.25
❑ 14	Eric Moulds	.60	.25
❑ 15	Rex Grossman	.60	.25
❑ 16	Brian Urlacher	1.00	.40
❑ 17	Thomas Jones	.60	.25
❑ 18	Carson Palmer	1.00	.40
❑ 19	Rudi Johnson	.60	.25
❑ 20	Chad Johnson	1.00	.40
❑ 21	J.P. Losman	1.00	.40
❑ 22	Lee Suggs	.60	.25
❑ 23	Antonio Bryant	.50	.20
❑ 24	Julius Jones	1.25	.50
❑ 25	Roy Williams S	.60	.25
❑ 26	Keyshawn Johnson	.60	.25
❑ 27	Jake Plummer	.60	.25
❑ 28	Tatum Bell	.60	.25
❑ 29	Rod Smith	.60	.25
❑ 30	Joey Harrington	1.00	.40
❑ 31	Kevin Jones	1.00	.40
❑ 32	Roy Williams WR	1.00	.40
❑ 33	Brett Favre	2.50	1.00
❑ 34	Ahman Green	1.00	.40
❑ 35	Javon Walker	.60	.25
❑ 36	David Carr	1.00	.40
❑ 37	Andre Johnson	.60	.25
❑ 38	Domanick Davis	.60	.25
❑ 39	Peyton Manning	1.50	.60
❑ 40	Edgerrin James	1.00	.40
❑ 41	Brandon Stokley	.60	.25
❑ 42	Reggie Wayne	.60	.25
❑ 43	Marvin Harrison	1.00	.40
❑ 44	Byron Leftwich	1.00	.40
❑ 45	Jimmy Smith	.60	.25
❑ 46	Fred Taylor	.60	.25
❑ 47	Trent Green	.60	.25
❑ 48	Priest Holmes	1.00	.40
❑ 49	Tony Gonzalez	.60	.25
❑ 50	A.J. Feeley	.60	.25
❑ 51	Chris Chambers	.60	.25
❑ 52	Daunte Culpepper	1.00	.40
❑ 53	Randy Moss	1.00	.40
❑ 54	Onterrio Smith	.60	.25
❑ 55	Corey Dillon	.60	.25
❑ 56	Tom Brady	2.50	1.00
❑ 57	David Givens	.60	.25
❑ 58	Aaron Brooks	.60	.25
❑ 59	Deuce McAllister	1.00	.40
❑ 60	Joe Horn	.60	.25
❑ 61	Eli Manning	2.00	.75

❑ 62 Tiki Barber 1.00 .40
❑ 63 Jeremy Shockey 1.00 .40
❑ 64 Chad Pennington 1.00 .40
❑ 65 Curtis Martin 1.00 .40
❑ 66 Santana Moss .60 .25
❑ 67 Kerry Collins .60 .25
❑ 68 Jerry Porter .60 .25
❑ 69 Donovan McNabb 1.25 .50
❑ 70 Terrell Owens 1.00 .40
❑ 71 Brian Westbrook .60 .25
❑ 72 Ben Roethlisberger 2.50 1.00
❑ 73 Plaxico Burress .60 .25
❑ 74 Hines Ward 1.00 .40
❑ 75 Jerome Bettis 1.00 .40
❑ 76 Duce Staley .60 .25
❑ 77 Antonio Gates 1.00 .40
❑ 78 Drew Brees 1.00 .40
❑ 79 LaDainian Tomlinson 1.25 .50
❑ 80 Brandon Lloyd .50 .20
❑ 81 Kevan Barlow .60 .25
❑ 82 Matt Hasselbeck .60 .25
❑ 83 Shaun Alexander 1.25 .50
❑ 84 Darrell Jackson .60 .25
❑ 85 Jerry Rice 2.00 .75
❑ 86 Marc Bulger 1.00 .40
❑ 87 Marshall Faulk 1.00 .40
❑ 88 Steven Jackson 1.25 .50
❑ 89 Isaac Bruce .60 .25
❑ 90 Torry Holt 1.00 .40
❑ 91 Michael Clayton 1.00 .40
❑ 92 Brian Griese .60 .25
❑ 93 Mike Alstott .60 .25
❑ 94 Steve McNair 1.00 .40
❑ 95 Derrick Mason .60 .25
❑ 96 Chris Brown .60 .25
❑ 97 Drew Bennett .60 .25
❑ 98 Patrick Ramsey .60 .25
❑ 99 Clinton Portis 1.00 .40
❑ 100 LaVar Arrington 1.00 .40
❑ 101 Aaron Rodgers RC 40.00 15.00
❑ 102 Adam Jones RC 10.00 4.00
❑ 103 Adrian McPherson RC 10.00 4.00
❑ 104A Alex Smith TE ERR RC 12.00 5.00
❑ 104B Alex Smith TE COR RC 12.00 5.00
❑ 105A Alex Smith QB ERR RC 50.00 20.00
❑ 105B Alex Smith QB COR RC 50.00 20.00
❑ 106 Alvin Pearman RC 10.00 4.00
❑ 107 Andrew Walter RC 10.00 4.00
❑ 108 Anthony Davis RC 8.00 3.00
❑ 109 Antrel Rolle RC 10.00 4.00
❑ 110 Anttaj Hawthorne RC 8.00 3.00
❑ 111 Brandon Browner RC 8.00 3.00
❑ 112 Brandon Jacobs RC 12.00 5.00
❑ 113 Braylon Edwards RC 40.00 15.00
❑ 114 Brock Berlin RC 8.00 3.00
❑ 115 Brandon Jones RC 10.00 4.00
❑ 116 Bryant McFadden RC 10.00 4.00
❑ 117 Carlos Rogers RC 12.00 5.00
❑ 118 Cadillac Williams RC 50.00 20.00
❑ 119 Cedric Benson RC 30.00 12.00
❑ 120 Cedric Houston RC 10.00 4.00
❑ 121 Channing Crowder RC 10.00 4.00
❑ 122 Charles Frederick RC 8.00 3.00
❑ 123 Charlie Frye RC 10.00 4.00
❑ 124 Chase Lyman RC 8.00 3.00
❑ 125 Chris Henry RC 10.00 4.00
❑ 126 Chris Rix RC 8.00 3.00
❑ 127 Ciatrick Fason RC 10.00 4.00
❑ 128 Corey Webster RC 10.00 4.00
❑ 129 Courtney Roby RC 10.00 4.00
❑ 130 Craig Bragg RC 8.00 3.00
❑ 131 Craphonso Thorpe RC 8.00 3.00
❑ 132 Damien Nash RC 8.00 3.00
❑ 133 Dan Cody RC 10.00 4.00
❑ 134 Dan Orlovsky RC 10.00 4.00
❑ 135 Dante Ridgeway RC 8.00 3.00
❑ 136 Darian Durant RC 10.00 4.00
❑ 137 Darren Sproles RC 10.00 4.00
❑ 138 Darryl Blackstock RC 8.00 3.00
❑ 139 David Greene RC 10.00 4.00
❑ 140 David Pollack RC 10.00 4.00
❑ 141 DeMarcus Ware RC 15.00 6.00
❑ 142 Derek Anderson RC 15.00 6.00
❑ 143 Derrick Johnson RC 15.00 6.00
❑ 144 Erasmus James RC 10.00 4.00
❑ 145 Eric Shelton RC 10.00 4.00
❑ 146 Ernest Shazor RC 10.00 4.00
❑ 147 Fabian Washington RC 10.00 4.00
❑ 148 Frank Gore UER RC 25.00 10.00
❑ 149 Fred Amey RC 8.00 3.00
❑ 150 Fred Gibson RC 8.00 3.00
❑ 151 Maurice Clarett 10.00 4.00
❑ 152 Gino Guidugli RC 5.00 2.00
❑ 153 Heath Miller RC 25.00 10.00
❑ 154 J.J. Arrington RC 10.00 4.00
❑ 155 J.R. Russell RC 8.00 3.00
❑ 156 Jason Campbell RC 15.00 6.00
❑ 157 Jason White RC 10.00 4.00
❑ 158 Jerome Mathis RC 10.00 4.00
❑ 159 Josh Bullocks RC 10.00 4.00
❑ 160 Josh Davis RC 8.00 3.00
❑ 161 Justin Miller RC 8.00 3.00
❑ 162 Justin Tuck RC 10.00 4.00
❑ 163 Kay-Jay Harris RC 8.00 3.00
❑ 164 Kevin Burnett RC 10.00 4.00
❑ 165 Kyle Orton RC 10.00 4.00
❑ 166 Larry Brackins RC 5.00 2.00
❑ 167 Marcus Spears RC 10.00 4.00
❑ 168 Marion Barber RC 15.00 6.00
❑ 169 Mark Bradley RC 10.00 4.00
❑ 170 Mark Clayton RC 10.00 4.00
❑ 171 Marlin Jackson RC 10.00 4.00
❑ 172 Matt Jones RC 15.00 6.00
❑ 173 Matt Roth RC 10.00 4.00
❑ 174 Mike Patterson RC 10.00 4.00
❑ 175 Mike Williams 10.00 4.00
❑ 176 Airese Currie RC 10.00 4.00
❑ 177 Reggie Brown RC 10.00 4.00
❑ 178 Roddy White RC 10.00 4.00
❑ 179 Ronnie Brown RC 50.00 20.00
❑ 180 Roscoe Parrish RC 10.00 4.00
❑ 181 Roydell Williams RC 10.00 4.00
❑ 182 Ryan Fitzpatrick RC 10.00 4.00
❑ 183 Rasheed Marshall RC 10.00 4.00
❑ 184 Ryan Moats RC 10.00 4.00
❑ 185 Shaun Cody RC 10.00 4.00
❑ 186 Shawne Merriman RC 15.00 6.00
❑ 187 Chad Owens RC 10.00 4.00
❑ 188 Stefan LeFors RC 10.00 4.00
❑ 189 Steve Savoy RC 5.00 2.00
❑ 190 T.A. McLendon RC 5.00 2.00
❑ 191 Tab Perry RC 10.00 4.00
❑ 192 Taylor Stubblefield RC 5.00 2.00
❑ 193 Terrence Murphy RC 10.00 4.00
❑ 194 Thomas Davis RC 10.00 4.00
❑ 195 Timmy Chang RC 8.00 3.00
❑ 196 Travis Johnson RC 8.00 3.00
❑ 197 Troy Williamson RC 10.00 4.00
❑ 198 Vernand Morency RC 10.00 4.00
❑ 199 Vincent Jackson RC 10.00 4.00
❑ 200 Walter Reyes RC 8.00 3.00

2006 Donruss Elite

❑ COMP.SET w/o RC's (100) 20.00 7.50
❑ ROOKIE PRINT RUN 599 SER.#'d SETS
❑ 1 Anquan Boldin .60 .25
❑ 2 Kurt Warner .60 .25
❑ 3 Larry Fitzgerald 1.00 .40
❑ 4 Marcel Shipp .50 .20
❑ 5 Alge Crumpler .60 .25
❑ 6 Michael Vick 1.00 .40
❑ 7 Warrick Dunn .60 .25
❑ 8 Derrick Mason .50 .20
❑ 9 Jamal Lewis .60 .25
❑ 10 Kyle Boller .50 .20
❑ 11 J.P. Losman .60 .25
❑ 12 Lee Evans .60 .25
❑ 13 Willis McGahee 1.00 .40
❑ 14 Jake Delhomme .60 .25
❑ 15 Stephen Davis .60 .25
❑ 16 Steve Smith 1.00 .40
❑ 17 Cedric Benson 1.00 .40
❑ 18 Kyle Orton .60 .25
❑ 19 Thomas Jones .60 .25
❑ 20 Carson Palmer 1.00 .40
❑ 21 Chad Johnson .60 .25
❑ 22 Rudi Johnson .60 .25
❑ 23 Braylon Edwards 1.00 .40
❑ 24 Reuben Droughns .60 .25
❑ 25 Trent Dilfer .60 .25
❑ 26 Drew Bledsoe 1.00 .40
❑ 27 Julius Jones 1.00 .40
❑ 28 Keyshawn Johnson .60 .25
❑ 29 Jake Plummer .60 .25
❑ 30 Rod Smith .60 .25
❑ 31 Tatum Bell .60 .25
❑ 32 Joey Harrington .60 .25
❑ 33 Kevin Jones 1.00 .40
❑ 34 Roy Williams WR 1.00 .40
❑ 35 Aaron Rodgers 1.00 .40
❑ 36 Brett Favre 2.00 .75
❑ 37 Ahman Green .60 .25
❑ 38 Andre Johnson .60 .25
❑ 39 David Carr .60 .25
❑ 40 Domanick Davis .60 .25
❑ 41 Edgerrin James 1.00 .40
❑ 42 Marvin Harrison 1.00 .40
❑ 43 Peyton Manning 1.50 .60
❑ 44 Byron Leftwich .60 .25
❑ 45 Fred Taylor .60 .25
❑ 46 Jimmy Smith .60 .25
❑ 47 Matt Jones .60 .25
❑ 48 Larry Johnson 1.25 .50
❑ 49 Tony Gonzalez .60 .25
❑ 50 Trent Green .60 .25
❑ 51 Chris Chambers .60 .25
❑ 52 Ricky Williams .60 .25
❑ 53 Ronnie Brown 1.00 .40
❑ 54 Randy McMichael .50 .20
❑ 55 Daunte Culpepper 1.00 .40
❑ 56 Mewelde Moore .50 .20
❑ 57 Nate Burleson .60 .25
❑ 58 Corey Dillon .60 .25
❑ 59 Deion Branch .60 .25
❑ 60 Tom Brady 1.50 .60
❑ 61 Aaron Brooks .60 .25
❑ 62 Deuce McAllister .60 .25
❑ 63 Donte Stallworth .60 .25
❑ 64 Eli Manning 1.25 .50
❑ 65 Jeremy Shockey 1.00 .40
❑ 66 Plaxico Burress .60 .25
❑ 67 Tiki Barber 1.00 .40
❑ 68 Chad Pennington .60 .25
❑ 69 Curtis Martin 1.00 .40
❑ 70 Laveranues Coles .60 .25
❑ 71 Kerry Collins .60 .25
❑ 72 LaMont Jordan .60 .25
❑ 73 Randy Moss 1.00 .40
❑ 74 Donovan McNabb 1.00 .40
❑ 75 Reggie Brown .75 .30
❑ 76 Brian Westbrook .60 .25
❑ 77 Ben Roethlisberger 1.50 .60
❑ 78 Duce Staley .60 .25
❑ 79 Hines Ward 1.00 .40
❑ 80 Antonio Gates 1.00 .40
❑ 81 Drew Brees 1.00 .40
❑ 82 LaDainian Tomlinson 1.25 .50
❑ 83 Alex Smith QB 1.00 .40
❑ 84 Kevan Barlow .60 .25
❑ 85 Brandon Lloyd .60 .25
❑ 86 Darrell Jackson .60 .25
❑ 87 Matt Hasselbeck .60 .25
❑ 88 Shaun Alexander 1.00 .40
❑ 89 Marc Bulger .60 .25
❑ 90 Steven Jackson 1.00 .40
❑ 91 Torry Holt .60 .25
❑ 92 Cadillac Williams 1.00 .40
❑ 93 Joey Galloway .60 .25
❑ 94 Michael Clayton .60 .25
❑ 95 Chris Brown .60 .25
❑ 96 Drew Bennett .50 .20
❑ 97 Steve McNair .60 .25
❑ 98 Clinton Portis 1.00 .40
❑ 99 Mark Brunell .60 .25
❑ 100 Santana Moss .60 .25
❑ 101 A.J. Hawk RC 25.00 10.00
❑ 102 Abdul Hodge RC 12.00 5.00
❑ 103 Adam Jennings RC 10.00 4.00
❑ 104 Alan Zemaitis RC 12.00 5.00
❑ 105 Andre Hall RC 10.00 4.00

106	Anthony Fasano RC	12.00	5.00
107	Anthony Mix RC	10.00	4.00
108	Ashton Youboty RC	12.00	5.00
109	Miles Austin RC	10.00	4.00
110	Barrick Nealy RC	10.00	4.00
111	Ben Obomanu RC	10.00	4.00
112	Bobby Carpenter RC	12.00	5.00
113	Brad Smith RC	12.00	5.00
114	Brandon Kirsch RC	12.00	5.00
115	Brandon Marshall RC	12.00	5.00
116	Brandon Williams RC	12.00	5.00
117	Brett Elliott RC	12.00	5.00
118	Brian Calhoun RC	12.00	5.00
119	Brodie Croyle RC	30.00	12.00
120	Brodrick Bunkley RC	12.00	5.00
121	Bruce Gradkowski RC	20.00	8.00
122	Cedric Griffin RC	10.00	4.00
123	Cedric Humes RC	12.00	5.00
124	Chad Greenway RC	12.00	5.00
125	Chad Jackson RC	12.00	5.00
126	Charlie Whitehurst RC	12.00	5.00
127	Cory Rodgers RC	12.00	5.00
128	D.J. Shockley RC	12.00	5.00
129	Darnell Bing RC	12.00	5.00
130	Darrell Hackney RC	10.00	4.00
131	David Thomas RC	12.00	5.00
132	D'Brickashaw Ferguson RC	12.00	5.00
133	DeAngelo Williams RC	30.00	12.00
134	De'Arrius Howard RC	12.00	5.00
135	Dee Webb RC	10.00	4.00
136	Delanie Walker RC	10.00	4.00
137	DeMeco Ryans RC	15.00	6.00
138	Demetrius Williams RC	12.00	5.00
139	Derek Hagan RC	12.00	5.00
140	Derrick Ross RC	10.00	4.00
141	Devin Aromashodu RC	10.00	4.00
142	Devin Hester RC	25.00	10.00
143	Dominique Byrd RC	10.00	4.00
144	Donte Whitner RC	12.00	5.00
145	DonTrell Moore RC	10.00	4.00
146	D'Qwell Jackson RC	10.00	4.00
147	Drew Olson RC	10.00	4.00
148	Eric Winston RC	6.00	2.50
149	Erik Meyer RC	10.00	4.00
150	Ernie Sims RC	15.00	6.00
151	Gabe Watson RC	10.00	4.00
152	Gerald Riggs RC	12.00	5.00
153	Ryan Gilbert RC	10.00	4.00
154	Greg Jennings RC	20.00	8.00
155	Greg Lee RC	10.00	4.00
156	Haloti Ngata RC	12.00	5.00
157	Hank Baskett RC	12.00	5.00
158	Ingle Martin RC	12.00	5.00
159	Jason Allen RC	12.00	5.00
160	Jason Avant RC	12.00	5.00
161	Jason Carter RC	10.00	4.00
162	Jay Cutler RC	40.00	15.00
163	Jeff King RC	10.00	4.00
164	Jeff Webb RC	10.00	4.00
165	Jeremy Bloom RC	10.00	4.00
166	Jerious Norwood RC	20.00	8.00
167	Jerome Harrison RC	12.00	5.00
168	Jimmy Williams RC	12.00	5.00
169	Joe Klopfenstein RC	10.00	4.00
170	Jon Alston RC	12.00	5.00
171	Johnathan Joseph RC	10.00	4.00
172	Jonathan Orr RC	10.00	4.00
173	Joseph Addai RC	40.00	15.00
174	Kai Parham RC	12.00	5.00
175	Kamerion Wimbley RC	12.00	5.00
176	Kellen Clemens RC	20.00	8.00
177	Kelly Jennings RC	12.00	5.00
178	Kent Smith RC	12.00	5.00
179	Ko Simpson RC	10.00	4.00
180	Laurence Maroney RC	30.00	12.00
181	Lawrence Vickers RC	10.00	4.00
182	LenDale White RC	25.00	10.00
183	Leon Washington RC	20.00	8.00
184	Leonard Pope RC	12.00	5.00
185	Manny Lawson RC	12.00	5.00
186	Marcedes Lewis RC	12.00	5.00
187	Marcus Vick RC	10.00	4.00
188	Mario Williams RC	20.00	8.00
189	Marques Colston RC	50.00	20.00
190	Martin Nance RC	10.00	4.00
191	Mathias Kiwanuka RC	15.00	6.00
192	Matt Leinart RC	40.00	15.00
193	Maurice Drew RC	30.00	12.00
194	Maurice Stovall RC	12.00	5.00
195	Michael Huff RC	15.00	6.00
196	Michael Robinson RC	12.00	5.00
197	Mike Bell RC	12.00	5.00
198	Mike Hass RC	12.00	5.00
199	Omar Jacobs RC	10.00	4.00
200	Owen Daniels RC	12.00	5.00
201	P.J. Daniels RC	10.00	4.00
202	Paul Pinegar RC	10.00	4.00
203	Quinton Ganther RC	10.00	4.00
204	Reggie Bush RC	50.00	20.00
205	Reggie McNeal RC	10.00	4.00
206	Rodrique Wright RC	6.00	2.50
207	Santonio Holmes RC	25.00	10.00
208	Sinorice Moss RC	12.00	5.00
209	Skyler Green RC	12.00	5.00
210	Tamba Hali RC	12.00	5.00
211	Tarvaris Jackson RC	20.00	8.00
212	Taurean Henderson RC	12.00	5.00
213	Terrence Whitehead RC	10.00	4.00
214	Tim Day RC	10.00	4.00
215	Todd Watkins RC	10.00	4.00
216	Tony Scheffler RC	12.00	5.00
217	Travis Lulay RC	10.00	4.00
218	Travis Wilson RC	12.00	5.00
219	Tye Hill RC	12.00	5.00
220	Vernon Davis RC	25.00	10.00
221	Vince Young RC	50.00	20.00
222	Wali Lundy RC	12.00	5.00
223	Wendell Mathis RC	10.00	4.00
224	Willie Reid RC	12.00	5.00
225	Winston Justice RC	12.00	5.00

1992 Finest

	COMPLETE SET (45)	20.00	7.50
1	Neal Anderson	.50	.20
2	Cornelius Bennett	.50	.20
3	Marion Butts	.30	.10
4	Anthony Carter	.50	.20
5	Mike Croel	.30	.10
6	John Elway	5.00	2.00
7	Jim Everett	.50	.20
8	Ernest Givins	.30	.10
9	Rodney Hampton	.50	.20
10	Alvin Harper	.30	.10
11	Michael Irvin	1.00	.40
12	Rickey Jackson	.30	.10
13	Seth Joyner	.30	.10
14	James Lofton	.50	.20
15	Ronnie Lott	.50	.20
16	Eric Metcalf	.50	.20
17	Chris Miller	.50	.20
18	Art Monk	.50	.20
19	Warren Moon	1.00	.40
20	Rob Moore	.50	.20
21	Anthony Munoz	.50	.20
22	Christian Okoye	.30	.10
23	Andre Rison	.50	.20
24	Leonard Russell	.30	.10
25	Mark Rypien	.50	.20
26	Barry Sanders	5.00	2.00
27	Emmitt Smith	6.00	2.50
28	Pat Swilling	.30	.10
29	John Taylor	.50	.20
30	Derrick Thomas	1.00	.40
31	Thurman Thomas	1.00	.40
32	Reggie White	1.00	.40
33	Rod Woodson	1.00	.40
34	Edgar Bennett	.50	.20
35	Terrell Buckley	.30	.10
36	Keith Hamilton	.50	.20
37	Amp Lee	.30	.10
38	Ricardo McDonald	.30	.10
39	Chris Mims	.30	.10
40	Robert Porcher	1.00	.40
41	Leon Searcy	.30	.10
42	Siran Stacy	.30	.10
43	Tommy Vardell	.30	.10
44	Bob Whitfield	.30	.10
NNO	Checklist	.30	.10

1994 Finest

	COMPLETE SET (220)	40.00	15.00
1	Emmitt Smith	6.00	2.50
2	Calvin Williams	.60	.25
3	Mark Collins	.30	.10
4	Steve McMichael	.60	.25
5	Jim Kelly	1.25	.50
6	Michael Dean Perry	.60	.25
7	Wayne Simmons	.30	.10
8	Rocket Ismail	.60	.25
9	Mark Rypien	.30	.10
10	Brian Blades	.60	.25
11	Barry Word	.30	.10
12	Jerry Rice	4.00	1.50
13	Derrick Fenner	.30	.10
14	Karl Mecklenburg	.30	.10
15	Reggie Cobb	.30	.10
16	Eric Swann	.60	.25
17	Neil Smith	.60	.25
18	Barry Foster	.30	.10
19	Willie Roaf	.30	.10
20	Troy Drayton	.30	.10
21	Warren Moon	1.25	.50
22	Richmond Webb	.30	.10
23	Anthony Miller	.60	.25
24	Chris Slade	.30	.10
25	Mel Gray	.30	.10
26	Ronnie Lott	.60	.25
27	Andre Rison	.60	.25
28	Jeff George	1.25	.50
29	John Copeland	.30	.10
30	Derrick Thomas	1.25	.50
31	Sterling Sharpe	.60	.25
32	Chris Doleman	.30	.10
33	Monte Coleman	.30	.10
34	Mark Bavaro	.30	.10
35	Kevin Williams WR	.60	.25
36	Eric Metcalf	.60	.25
37	Brent Jones	.60	.25
38	Steve Tasker	.60	.25
39	Dave Meggett	.30	.10
40	Howie Long	1.25	.50
41	Rick Mirer	1.25	.50
42	Jerome Bettis	4.00	1.50
43	Marion Butts	.30	.10
44	Barry Sanders	6.00	2.50
45	Jason Elam	.60	.25
46	Broderick Thomas	.30	.10
47	Derek Brown RBK	.30	.10
48	Lorenzo White	.30	.10
49	Neil O'Donnell	1.25	.50
50	Chris Burkett	.30	.10
51	John Offerdahl	.30	.10
52	Rohn Stark	.30	.10
53	Neal Anderson	.30	.10
54	Steve Beuerlein	.60	.25
55	Bruce Armstrong	.30	.10
56	Lincoln Kennedy	.30	.10
57	Darrell Green	.30	.10
58	Ricardo McDonald	.30	.10
59	Chris Warren	.60	.25
60	Mark Jackson	.30	.10
61	Pepper Johnson	.30	.10
62	Chris Spielman	.60	.25

63	Marcus Allen	1.25	.50
64	Jim Everett	.60	.25
65	Greg Townsend	.30	.10
66	Cris Carter	1.50	.60
67	Don Beebe	.30	.10
68	Reggie Langhorne	.30	.10
69	Randall Cunningham	1.25	.50
70	Johnny Holland	.30	.10
71	Morten Andersen	.30	.10
72	Leonard Marshall	.30	.10
73	Keith Jackson	.30	.10
74	Leslie O'Neal	.30	.10
75	Hardy Nickerson	.60	.25
76	Dan Williams	.30	.10
77	Steve Young	3.00	1.25
78	Deon Figures	.30	.10
79	Michael Irvin	1.00	.40
80	Luis Sharpe	.30	.10
81	Andre Tippett	.30	.10
82	Ricky Sanders	.30	.10
83	Erric Pegram	.30	.10
84	Albert Lewis	.30	.10
85	Anthony Blaylock	.30	.10
86	Pat Swilling	.30	.10
87	Duane Bickett	.30	.10
88	Myron Guyton	.30	.10
89	Clay Matthews	.30	.10
90	Jim McMahon	.60	.25
91	Bruce Smith	1.25	.50
92	Reggie White	1.25	.50
93	Shannon Sharpe	.60	.25
94	Rickey Jackson	.30	.10
95	Ronnie Harmon	.30	.10
96	Terry McDaniel	.30	.10
97	Bryan Cox	.30	.10
98	Webster Slaughter	.30	.10
99	Boomer Esiason	.60	.25
100	Tim Krumrie	.30	.10
101	Cortez Kennedy	.60	.25
102	Henry Ellard	.60	.25
103	Clyde Simmons	.30	.10
104	Craig Erickson	.30	.10
105	Eric Green	.30	.10
106	Gary Clark	.60	.25
107	Jay Novacek	.60	.25
108	Dana Stubblefield	.60	.25
109	Mike Johnson	.30	.10
110	Ray Crockett	.30	.10
111	Leonard Russell	.30	.10
112	Robert Smith	1.25	.50
113	Art Monk	.60	.25
114	Ray Childress	.30	.10
115	O.J.McDuffie	1.25	.50
116	Tim Brown	1.25	.50
117	Kevin Ross	.30	.10
118	Richard Dent	.60	.25
119	John Elway	8.00	3.00
120	James Hasty	.30	.10
121	Gary Plummer	.30	.10
122	Pierce Holt	.30	.10
123	Eric Martin	.30	.10
124	Brett Favre	8.00	3.00
125	Cornelius Bennett	.60	.25
126	Jessie Hester	.30	.10
127	Lewis Tillman	.30	.10
128	Qadry Ismail	1.25	.50
129	Jay Schroeder	.30	.10
130	Curtis Conway	1.25	.50
131	Santana Dotson	.60	.25
132	Nick Lowery	.30	.10
133	Lomas Brown	.30	.10
134	Reggie Roby	.30	.10
135	John L. Williams	.30	.10
136	Vinny Testaverde	.60	.25
137	Seth Joyner	.30	.10
138	Ethan Horton	.30	.10
139	Jackie Slater	.30	.10
140	Rod Bernstine	.30	.10
141	Rob Moore	.60	.25
142	Dan Marino	8.00	3.00
143	Ken Harvey	.30	.10
144	Ernest Givins	.60	.25
145	Russell Maryland	.30	.10
146	Drew Bledsoe	3.00	1.25
147	Kevin Greene	.60	.25
148	Bobby Hebert	.30	.10
149	Junior Seau	1.25	.50
150	Tim McDonald	.30	.10
151	Thurman Thomas	1.25	.50
152	Phil Simms	.60	.25
153	Terrell Buckley	.30	.10
154	Sam Mills	.30	.10
155	Anthony Carter	.60	.25
156	Kelvin Martin	.30	.10
157	Shane Conlan	.30	.10
158	Irving Fryar	.60	.25
159	Demetrius DuBose	.30	.10
160	David Klingler	.30	.10
161	Herman Moore	1.25	.50
162	Jeff Hostetler	.60	.25
163	Tommy Vardell	.30	.10
164	Craig Heyward	.60	.25
165	Wilber Marshall	.30	.10
166	Quentin Coryatt	.30	.10
167	Glyn Milburn	.60	.25
168	Fred Barnett	.60	.25
169	Charles Haley	.60	.25
170	Carl Banks	.30	.10
171	Ricky Proehl	.30	.10
172	Joe Montana	8.00	3.00
173	Johnny Mitchell	.30	.10
174	Andre Reed	.60	.25
175	Marco Coleman	.30	.10
176	Vaughan Johnson	.30	.10
177	Carl Pickens	.60	.25
178	Dwight Stone	.30	.10
179	Ricky Watters	.60	.25
180	Michael Haynes	.60	.25
181	Roger Craig	.60	.25
182	Cleveland Gary	.30	.10
183	Steve Emtman	.30	.10
184	Patrick Bates	.30	.10
185	Mark Carrier WR	.60	.25
186	Brad Hopkins	.30	.10
187	Dennis Smith	.30	.10
188	Natrone Means	1.25	.50
189	Michael Jackson	.60	.25
190	Ken Norton Jr.	.60	.25
191	Carlton Gray	.30	.10
192	Edgar Bennett	1.25	.50
193	Lawrence Taylor	1.25	.50
194	Marv Cook	.30	.10
195	Eric Curry	.30	.10
196	Victor Bailey	.30	.10
197	Ryan McNeil	.30	.10
198	Rod Woodson	.60	.25
199	Earnest Byner	.30	.10
200	Marvin Jones	.30	.10
201	Thomas Smith	.30	.10
202	Troy Aikman	4.00	1.50
203	Audray McMillian	.30	.10
204	Wade Wilson	.30	.10
205	George Teague	.30	.10
206	Delon Sanders	2.00	.75
207	Will Shields	.60	.25
208	John Taylor	.60	.25
209	Jim Harbaugh	1.25	.50
210	Micheal Barrow	.30	.10
211	Harold Green	.30	.10
212	Steve Everitt	.30	.10
213	Flipper Anderson	.30	.10
214	Rodney Hampton	.60	.25
215	Steve Atwater	.30	.10
216	James Trapp	.30	.10
217	Terry Kirby	1.25	.50
218	Garrison Hearst	1.25	.50
219	Jeff Bryant	.30	.10
220	Roosevelt Potts	.30	.10

1995 Finest

	COMPLETE SET (275)	80.00	30.00
	COMP.SERIES 1 (165)	20.00	10.00
	COMP.SERIES 2 (110)	60.00	25.00
1	Natrone Means	.60	.25
2	Dave Meggett	.25	.08
3	Tim Bowens	.25	.08
4	Jay Novacek	.60	.25
5	Michael Jackson	.60	.25
6	Calvin Williams	.60	.25
7	Neil Smith	.60	.25
8	Chris Gardocki	.25	.08
9	Jeff Burris	.25	.08
10	Warren Moon	.60	.25
11	Gary Anderson K	.25	.08
12	Bert Emanuel	1.25	.50
13	Rick Tuten	.25	.08
14	Steve Wallace	.25	.08
15	Marion Butts	.25	.08
16	Johnnie Morton	.60	.25
17	Rob Moore	.60	.25
18	Wayne Gandy	.25	.08
19	Quentin Coryatt	.60	.25
20	Richmond Webb	.25	.08
21	Errict Rhett	.60	.25
22	Joe Johnson	.25	.08
23	Gary Brown	.25	.08
24	Jeff Hostetler	.60	.25
25	Larry Centers	.60	.25
26	Tom Carter	.25	.08
27	Steve Atwater	.25	.08
28	Doug Pelfrey	.25	.08
29	Bryce Paup	.60	.25
30	Erik Williams	.25	.08
31	Henry Jones	.25	.08
32	Stanley Richard	.25	.08
33	Marcus Allen	1.25	.50
34	Antonio Langham	.25	.08
35	Lewis Tillman	.25	.08
36	Thomas Randolph	.25	.08
37	Byron Bam Morris	.25	.08
38	David Palmer	.60	.25
39	Ricky Watters	.60	.25
40	Brett Perriman	.60	.25
41	Will Wolford	.25	.08
42	Burt Grossman	.25	.08
43	Vincent Brisby	.25	.08
44	Ronnie Lott	.60	.25
45	Brian Blades	.60	.25
46	Brent Jones	.25	.08
47	Anthony Newman	.25	.08
48	Willie Roaf	.25	.08
49	Paul Gruber	.25	.08
50	Jeff George	.60	.25
51	Jamir Miller	.25	.08
52	Anthony Miller	.60	.25
53	Darrell Green	.25	.08
54	Steve Wisniewski	.25	.08
55	Dan Wilkinson	.60	.25
56	Brett Favre	5.00	2.00
57	Leslie O'Neal	.60	.25
58	Keith Byars	.25	.08
59	James Washington	.25	.08
60	Andre Reed	.60	.25
61	Ken Norton Jr.	.60	.25
62	John Randle	.60	.25
63	Lake Dawson	.60	.25
64	Greg Montgomery	.25	.08
65	Erric Pegram	.60	.25
66	Steve Everitt	.25	.08
67	Chris Brantley	.25	.08
68	Rod Woodson	.60	.25
69	Eugene Robinson	.25	.08
70	Dave Brown	.60	.25
71	Ricky Reynolds	.25	.08
72	Rohn Stark	.25	.08
73	Randal Hill	.25	.08
74	Brian Washington	.25	.08
75	Heath Shuler	.60	.25
76	Darion Conner	.25	.08
77	Terry McDaniel	.25	.08
78	Al Del Greco	.25	.08
79	Allen Aldridge	.25	.08
80	Trace Armstrong	.25	.08
81	Darnay Scott	.60	.25
82	Charlie Garner	1.25	.50
83	Harold Bishop	.25	.08
84	Reggie White	1.25	.50
85	Shawn Jefferson	.25	.08
86	Irving Spikes	.60	.25

❑ 87 Mel Gray .25 .08
❑ 88 D.J. Johnson .25 .08
❑ 89 Daryl Johnston .60 .25
❑ 90 Joe Montana 5.00 2.00
❑ 91 Michael Strahan 1.25 .50
❑ 92 Robert Blackmon .25 .08
❑ 93 Ryan Yarborough .60 .25
❑ 94 Terry Allen .60 .25
❑ 95 Michael Haynes .60 .25
❑ 96 Jim Harbaugh .60 .25
❑ 97 Micheal Barrow .25 .08
❑ 98 John Thierry .25 .08
❑ 99 Seth Joyner .25 .08
❑ 100 Deion Sanders 2.00 .75
❑ 101 Eric Turner .25 .08
❑ 102 LeShon Johnson .60 .25
❑ 103 John Copeland .25 .08
❑ 104 Cornelius Bennett .60 .25
❑ 105 Sean Gilbert .60 .25
❑ 106 Herschel Walker .60 .25
❑ 107 Henry Ellard .60 .25
❑ 108 Neil O'Donnell .60 .25
❑ 109 Charles Wilson .25 .08
❑ 110 Willie McGinest .60 .25
❑ 111 Tim Brown 1.25 .50
❑ 112 Simon Fletcher .25 .08
❑ 113 Broderick Thomas .25 .08
❑ 114 Tom Waddle .25 .08
❑ 115 Jessie Tuggle .25 .08
❑ 116 Maurice Hurst .25 .08
❑ 117 Aubrey Beavers .25 .08
❑ 118 Donnell Bennett .60 .25
❑ 119 Shante Carver .25 .08
❑ 120 Eric Metcalf .60 .25
❑ 121 John Carney .25 .08
❑ 122 Thomas Lewis .60 .25
❑ 123 Johnny Mitchell .25 .08
❑ 124 Trent Dilfer 1.25 .50
❑ 125 Marshall Faulk 3.00 1.25
❑ 126 Ernest Givins .25 .08
❑ 127 Aeneas Williams .25 .08
❑ 128 Bucky Brooks .25 .08
❑ 129 Todd Steussie .25 .08
❑ 130 Randall Cunningham 1.25 .50
❑ 131 Reggie Brooks .60 .25
❑ 132 Morten Andersen .25 .08
❑ 133 James Jett .60 .25
❑ 134 George Teague .25 .08
❑ 135 John Taylor .25 .08
❑ 136 Charles Johnson .60 .25
❑ 137 Isaac Bruce 2.50 1.00
❑ 138 Jason Elam .60 .25
❑ 139 Carl Pickens .60 .25
❑ 140 Chris Warren .60 .25
❑ 141 Bruce Armstrong .25 .08
❑ 142 Mark Carrier DB .25 .08
❑ 143 Irving Fryar .60 .25
❑ 144 Van Malone .25 .08
❑ 145 Charles Haley .60 .25
❑ 146 Chris Calloway .25 .08
❑ 147 J.J. Birden .25 .08
❑ 148 Tony Bennett .25 .08
❑ 149 Lincoln Kennedy .25 .08
❑ 150 Stan Humphries .60 .25
❑ 151 Hardy Nickerson .25 .08
❑ 152 Randall McDaniel .25 .08
❑ 153 Marcus Robertson .25 .08
❑ 154 Ronald Moore .25 .08
❑ 155 Thurman Thomas 1.25 .50
❑ 156 Tommy Vardell .25 .08
❑ 157 Ken Ruettgers .25 .08
❑ 158 Rob Fredrickson .25 .08
❑ 159 Johnny Bailey .25 .08
❑ 160 Greg Lloyd .60 .25
❑ 161 David Alexander .25 .08
❑ 162 Kevin Mawae .25 .08
❑ 163 Derek Brown RBK .25 .08
❑ 164 William Floyd .60 .25
❑ 165 Aaron Glenn .25 .08
❑ 166 Joey Galloway RC 8.00 3.00
❑ 167 Troy Drayton .25 .08
❑ 168 Dermontti Dawson .60 .25
❑ 169 Ronald Moore .25 .08
❑ 170 Dan Marino 5.00 2.00
❑ 171 Dennis Gibson .25 .08
❑ 172 Raymont Harris .25 .08
❑ 173 Shannon Sharpe .60 .25
❑ 174 Kevin Williams .60 .25
❑ 175 Jim Everett .25 .08
❑ 176 Rocket Ismail .60 .25
❑ 177 Mark Fields RC 1.25 .50
❑ 178 George Koonce .25 .08
❑ 179 Chris Hudson .25 .08
❑ 180 Jerry Rice 2.50 1.00
❑ 181 Dewayne Washington .60 .25
❑ 182 Dale Carter .60 .25
❑ 183 Pete Stoyanovich .25 .08
❑ 184 Blake Brockermeyer .25 .08
❑ 185 Troy Aikman 2.50 1.00
❑ 186 Jeff Blake RC 2.50 1.00
❑ 187 Troy Vincent .25 .08
❑ 188 Lamar Lathon .25 .08
❑ 189 Tony Boselli 1.25 .50
❑ 190 Emmitt Smith 4.00 1.50
❑ 191 Bobby Houston .25 .08
❑ 192 Edgar Bennett .60 .25
❑ 193 Derrick Brooks RC 8.00 3.00
❑ 194 Ricky Proehl .25 .08
❑ 195 Rodney Hampton .60 .25
❑ 196 Dave Krieg .25 .08
❑ 197 Vinny Testaverde .60 .25
❑ 198 Erik Kramer .25 .08
❑ 199 Ben Coates .60 .25
❑ 200 Steve Young 2.00 .75
❑ 201 Glyn Milburn .25 .08
❑ 202 Bryan Cox .25 .08
❑ 203 Luther Elliss .25 .08
❑ 204 Mark McMillian .25 .08
❑ 205 Jerome Bettis 1.25 .50
❑ 206 Craig Heyward .60 .25
❑ 207 Ray Buchanan .25 .08
❑ 208 Kimble Anders .60 .25
❑ 209 Kevin Greene .60 .25
❑ 210 Eric Allen .25 .08
❑ 211 Ricardo McDonald .25 .08
❑ 212 Ruben Brown RC 1.50 .60
❑ 213 Harvey Williams .25 .08
❑ 214 Broderick Thomas .25 .08
❑ 215 Frank Reich .25 .08
❑ 216 Frank Sanders RC 1.50 .60
❑ 217 Craig Newsome .25 .08
❑ 218 Merton Hanks .25 .08
❑ 219 Chris Miller .25 .08
❑ 220 John Elway 5.00 2.00
❑ 221 Ernest Givins .25 .08
❑ 222 Boomer Esiason .60 .25
❑ 223 Reggie Roby .25 .08
❑ 224 Qadry Ismail .60 .25
❑ 225 Ki-Jana Carter RC 1.50 .60
❑ 226 Leon Lett .25 .08
❑ 227 Eric Hill .25 .08
❑ 228 Scott Mitchell .60 .25
❑ 229 Craig Erickson .25 .08
❑ 230 Drew Bledsoe 2.00 .75
❑ 231 Sean Landeta .25 .08
❑ 232 Barrett Brooks .25 .08
❑ 233 Brian Mitchell .25 .08
❑ 234 Tyrone Poole 1.25 .50
❑ 235 Desmond Howard .60 .25
❑ 236 Wayne Simmons .25 .08
❑ 237 Michael Westbrook RC 1.50 .60
❑ 238 Quinn Early .60 .25
❑ 239 Willie Davis .60 .25
❑ 240 Rashaan Salaam RC .75 .30
❑ 241 Devin Bush .25 .08
❑ 242 Dana Stubblefield .60 .25
❑ 243 Dexter Carter .25 .08
❑ 244 Shane Conlan .25 .08
❑ 245 Keith Elias RC .25 .08
❑ 246 Robert Brooks 1.25 .50
❑ 247 Garrison Hearst 1.25 .50
❑ 248 Eric Zeier RC 1.50 .60
❑ 249 Nate Newton .60 .25
❑ 250 Barry Sanders 4.00 1.50
❑ 251 Dave Meggett .25 .08
❑ 252 Courtney Hawkins .25 .08
❑ 253 Cortez Kennedy .60 .25
❑ 254 Mario Bates .60 .25
❑ 255 Junior Seau 1.25 .50
❑ 256 Brian Washington .25 .08
❑ 257 Darius Holland .25 .08
❑ 258 Jeff Graham .25 .08
❑ 259 Rob Moore .60 .25
❑ 260 Andre Rison .60 .25
❑ 261 Kerry Collins RC 8.00 3.00
❑ 262 Roosevelt Potts .25 .08
❑ 263 Cris Carter 1.25 .50
❑ 264 Curtis Martin RC 15.00 6.00
❑ 265 Rick Mirer .60 .25
❑ 266 Mo Lewis .25 .08
❑ 267 Mike Sherrard .25 .08
❑ 268 Herman Moore 1.25 .50
❑ 269 Eric Metcalf .60 .25
❑ 270 Ray Childress .25 .08
❑ 271 Chris Slade .25 .08
❑ 272 Michael Irvin 1.25 .50
❑ 273 Jim Kelly 1.25 .50
❑ 274 Terance Mathis .60 .25
❑ 275 LeRoy Butler .25 .08

1996 Finest

❑ COMPLETE SET (359) 300.00 150.00
❑ COMP.SERIES 1 (191) 200.00 100.00
❑ COMP.SERIES 2 (168) 100.00 50.00
❑ COMP.BRONZE SER.1 (110) 40.00 15.00
❑ COMP.BRONZE SER.2 (110) 40.00 15.00
❑ B2 Jay Novacek B .60 .25
❑ B3 Ray Buchanan B .30 .10
❑ B5 Phil Hansen B .30 .10
❑ B6 Mike Mamula B .30 .10
❑ B9 Bernie Parmalee B .30 .10
❑ B10 Herman Moore B .60 .25
❑ B11 Shawn Jefferson B .30 .10
❑ B12 Chris Doleman B .30 .10
❑ B13 Erik Kramer B .60 .25
❑ B15 Orlando Thomas B .30 .10
❑ B16 Terrell Davis B 4.00 1.50
❑ B18 Roman Phifer B .30 .10
❑ B19 Trent Dilfer B .60 .25
❑ B21 Darnay Scott B .60 .25
❑ B22 Steve McNair B 4.00 1.50
❑ B23 Lamar Lathon B .30 .10
❑ B26 Thomas Randolph B .30 .10
❑ B27 Michael Jackson B .60 .25
❑ B28 Seth Joyner B .30 .10
❑ B29 Jeff Lageman B .30 .10
❑ B30 Darryl Williams B .30 .10
❑ B32 Erric Pegram B .60 .25
❑ B34 Sean Dawkins B .60 .25
❑ B38 Dan Saleaumua B UER 28 .30 .10
❑ B39 Henry Thomas B .30 .10
❑ B43 Pat Swilling B .30 .10
❑ B44 Marty Carter B .30 .10
❑ B45 Anthony Miller B .60 .25
❑ B48 Chris Warren B .60 .25
❑ B49 Derek Brown RBK B .30 .10
❑ B51 Blaine Bishop B .30 .10
❑ B52 Jake Reed B .60 .25
❑ B55 Vencie Glenn B .30 .10
❑ B58 Derrick Alexander WR B .60 .25
❑ B64 Jessie Tuggle B .30 .10
❑ B65 Terrance Shaw B .30 .10
❑ B66 David Sloan B .60 .25
❑ B68 Brent Jones B .30 .10
❑ B70 William Thomas B .30 .10
❑ B71 Robert Smith B .60 .25
❑ B72 Wayne Simmons B .30 .10
❑ B73 Jim Harbaugh B .60 .25
❑ B76 Wayne Chrebet B 2.00 .75
❑ B77 Chris Hudson B .30 .10
❑ B79 Stevon Moore B .30 .10
❑ B80 Chris Calloway B .30 .10
❑ B81 Tom Carter B .30 .10
❑ B82 Dave Meggett B .30 .10
❑ B83 Sam Mills B .60 .25
❑ B86 Renaldo Turnbull B .30 .10
❑ B87 Derrick Brooks B 1.00 .40
❑ B89 Eugene Robinson B .30 .10
❑ B91 Rodney Thomas B .30 .10
❑ B92 Dan Wilkinson B .30 .10

Card	Player	Mint	Nrmt
B93	Mark Fields B	.30	.10
B94	Warren Sapp B	.30	.10
B95	Curtis Martin B	4.00	1.50
B97	Ray Crockett B	.30	.10
B98	Ed McDaniel B	.30	.10
B101	Craig Heyward B	.30	.10
B102	Ellis Johnson B	.30	.10
B104	O.J. McDuffie B	.60	.25
B105	J.J. Stokes B	1.00	.40
B106	Mo Lewis B	.30	.10
B108	Rob Moore B	.60	.25
B110	Tyrone Wheatley B	.60	.25
B111	Ken Harvey B	.30	.10
B113	Willie Green B	.30	.10
B114	Willie Davis B	.60	.25
B115	Andy Harmon B	.30	.10
B117	Bryan Cox B	.30	.10
B119	Bert Emanuel B	.60	.25
B120	Greg Lloyd B	.60	.25
B122	Willie Jackson B	.60	.25
B123	Lorenzo Lynch B	.30	.10
B124	Pepper Johnson B	.30	.10
B128	Tyrone Poole B	.30	.10
B129	Neil Smith B	.60	.25
B130	Eddie Robinson B	.30	.10
B131	Bryce Paup B	.60	.25
B134	Troy Aikman B	5.00	2.00
B136	Chris Sanders B	.60	.25
B138	Jim Everett B	.30	.10
B139	Frank Sanders B	.60	.25
B141	Cortez Kennedy B	.60	.25
B143	Derrick Alexander DE B	.30	.10
B144	Rob Fredrickson B	.30	.10
B145	Chris Zorich B	.30	.10
B146	Devin Bush B	.30	.10
B149	Troy Vincent B	.30	.10
B151	Deion Sanders B	2.50	1.00
B152	James O. Stewart B	.60	.25
B156	Lawrence Dawsey B	.30	.10
B157	Robert Brooks B	1.00	.40
B158	Rashaan Salaam B	.60	.25
B161	Tim Brown B	.60	.25
B162	Brendan Stai B	.30	.10
B163	Sean Gilbert B	.30	.10
B169	Calvin Williams B	.60	.25
B171	Ruben Brown B	.30	.10
B172	Eric Green B	.30	.10
B175	Jerry Rice B	5.00	2.00
B176	Bruce Smith B	1.00	.40
B177	Mark Bruener B	.30	.10
B179	Lamont Warren B	.30	.10
B180	Tamarick Vanover B	1.00	.40
B182	Scott Mitchell B	.60	.25
B186	Terry Wooden B	.30	.10
B187	Ken Norton B	.60	.25
B188	Jeff Herrod B	.30	.10
B192	Gus Frerotte B	.60	.25
B194	Brett Maxie B	.30	.10
B198	Eddie Kennison B RC	1.25	.50
B201	Marcus Jones B RC	.30	.10
B202	Terry Allen B	.60	.25
B203	Leroy Hoard B	.30	.10
B205	Reggie White B	1.00	.40
B206	Larry Centers B	.60	.25
B208	Vincent Brisby B	.30	.10
B209	Michael Timpson B	.30	.10
B211	John Mobley B RC	.30	.10
B212	Clay Matthews B	.60	.25
B213	Shannon Sharpe B	.60	.25
B214	Tony Bennett B	.30	.10
B216	Mickey Washington B	.30	.10
B217	Fred Barnett B	.60	.25
B218	Michael Haynes B	.60	.25
B219	Stan Humphries B	.60	.25
B221	Winston Moss B	.30	.10
B222	Tim Biakabutuka B RC	1.25	.50
B223	Leeland McElroy B RC	.60	.25
B224	Vinnie Clark B	.30	.10
B225	Keyshawn Johnson B RC	5.00	2.00
B228	Tony Woods B	.30	.10
B231	Anthony Pleasant B	.30	.10
B232	Jeff George B	.60	.25
B233	Curtis Conway B	1.00	.40
B235	Jeff Lewis B RC	.60	.25
B236	Edgar Bennett B	.60	.25
B237	Regan Upshaw B RC	.30	.10
B238	William Fuller B	.30	.10
B241	Willie Anderson B RC	.30	.10
B242	Derrick Thomas B	1.00	.40
B243	Marvin Harrison B RC	15.00	6.00
B244	Darion Conner B	.30	.10
B245	Antonio Langham B	.30	.10
B246	Rodney Peete B	.30	.10
B247	Tim McDonald B	.30	.10
B248	Robert Jones B	.30	.10
B251	Mark Carrier DB B	.30	.10
B252	Stephen Grant B	.30	.10
B254	Jeff Hostetler B	.60	.25
B255	Darrell Green B	.30	.10
B261	Eric Swann B	.60	.25
B263	Irv Smith B	.30	.10
B264	Tim McKyer B	.30	.10
B266	Sean Jones B	.30	.10
B271	Yancey Thigpen B	.60	.25
B273	Quentin Coryatt B	.30	.10
B274	Hardy Nickerson B	.30	.10
B275	Ricardo McDonald B	.30	.10
B277	Robert Blackmon B	.30	.10
B279	Alonzo Spellman B	.30	.10
B281	Rickey Dudley B RC	1.25	.50
B282	Joe Cain B	.30	.10
B284	John Randle B	.60	.25
B286	Vinny Testaverde B	.60	.25
B289	Henry Jones B	.30	.10
B290	Simeon Rice B RC	3.00	1.25
B295	Leslie O'Neal B	.30	.10
B297	Greg Hill B	.60	.25
B301	Eric Metcalf B	.60	.25
B303	Jerome Woods B RC	.30	.10
B306	Anthony Smith B	.30	.10
B307	Darren Perry B	.30	.10
B311	James Hasty B	.30	.10
B312	Cris Carter B	1.00	.40
B314	Lawrence Phillips B RC	.60	.25
B317	Aeneas Williams B	.30	.10
B318	Eric Hill B	.30	.10
B319	Kevin Hardy B RC	1.25	.50
B321	Chris Chandler B	.60	.25
B322	Rocket Ismail B	.60	.25
B323	Anthony Parker B	.30	.10
B324	John Thierry B	.30	.10
B325	Micheal Barrow B	.30	.10
B326	Henry Ford B	.30	.10
B327	Aaron Hayden B RC	.30	.10
B328	Terance Mathis B	.30	.10
B329	Kirk Pointer B RC	.30	.10
B330	Ray Mickens B RC	.30	.10
B331	Jermane Mayberry B RC	.30	.10
B332	Mario Bates B	.60	.25
B333	Carlton Gray B	.30	.10
B334	Derek Loville B	.30	.10
B335	Mike Alstott B RC	5.00	2.00
B336	Eric Guliford B	.30	.10
B337	Marvcus Patton B	.30	.10
B338	Terrell Owens B RC	15.00	6.00
B339	Lance Johnstone B RC	.60	.25
B340	Lake Dawson B	.60	.25
B341	Winslow Oliver B RC	.30	.10
B342	Adrian Murrell B	.60	.25
B343	Jason Belser B	.30	.10
B344	Brian Dawkins B RC	6.00	2.50
B345	Reggie Brown B RC	.30	.10
B346	Shaun Gayle B	.30	.10
B347	Tony Brackens B RC	1.25	.50
B348	Thomas Lewis B	.30	.10
B349	Kelvin Pritchett B	.30	.10
B350	Bobby Engram B RC	1.25	.50
B351	Moe Williams B RC	3.00	1.25
B352	Thomas Smith B	.30	.10
B353	Dexter Carter B	.30	.10
B354	Qadry Ismail B	.60	.25
B355	Marco Battaglia B RC	.30	.10
B356	Levon Kirkland B	.30	.10
B357	Eric Allen B	.30	.10
B358	Bobby Hoying B RC	1.25	.50
B359	Checklist B	.30	.10
G1	Kordell Stewart G	5.00	2.00
G7	Kimble Anders G	1.50	.60
G8	Merton Hanks G	1.50	.60
G17	Rick Mirer G	3.00	1.25
G33	Craig Newsome G	1.50	.60
G36	Bryce Paup G	3.00	1.25
G40	Dan Marino G	20.00	7.50
G42	Andre Coleman G	1.50	.60
G47	Kevin Carter G	1.50	.60
G60	Mark Brunell G	8.00	3.00
G61	David Palmer G	3.00	1.25
G75	Carnell Lake G	1.50	.60
G96	Joey Galloway G	5.00	2.00
G112	Melvin Tuten G	1.50	.60
G121	Aaron Glenn G	1.50	.60
G132	Brett Favre G	20.00	7.50
G133	Ken Dilger G	3.00	1.25
G140	Barry Sanders G	20.00	7.50
G142	Glyn Milburn G	1.50	.60
G148	Brett Perriman G	3.00	1.25
G160	Kerry Collins G	5.00	2.00
G164	Lee Woodall G	1.50	.60
G173	Marshall Faulk G	6.00	2.50
G178	Troy Aikman G	12.00	5.00
G190	Drew Bledsoe G	8.00	3.00
G191	Checklist G	1.50	.60
G193	Michael Irvin G	5.00	2.00
G195	Warren Moon G	3.00	1.25
G200	Steve Young G	10.00	4.00
G207	Alex Van Dyke G RC	3.00	1.25
G220	Cris Carter G	5.00	2.00
G230	John Elway G	20.00	7.50
G234	Charles Haley G	3.00	1.25
G240	Jim Kelly G	5.00	2.00
G250	Rodney Hampton G	3.00	1.25
G256	Errict Rhett G	3.00	1.25
G257	Alex Molden G	1.50	.60
G260	Kevin Hardy G	3.00	1.25
G267	Bryant Young G	3.00	1.25
G268	Jeff Blake G	5.00	2.00
G270	Keyshawn Johnson G	5.00	2.00
G278	Junior Seau G	5.00	2.00
G285	Terry Kirby G	3.00	1.25
G293	Hugh Douglas G	3.00	1.25
G296	Reggie White G	5.00	2.00
G298	Elvis Grbac G	5.00	2.00
G300	Emmitt Smith G	15.00	6.00
G309	Ricky Watters G	3.00	1.25
S4	Brett Favre S	15.00	6.00
S14	Chester McGlockton S	.75	.30
S20	Tyrone Hughes S	.75	.30
S24	Ty Law S	3.00	1.25
S25	Brian Mitchell S	.75	.30
S31	Darren Woodson S	1.50	.60
S35	Brian Mitchell S	.75	.30
S37	Dana Stubblefield S	1.50	.60
S41	Kerry Collins S	3.00	1.25
S46	Orlando Thomas S	.75	.30
S50	Jerry Rice S	8.00	3.00
S53	Willie McGinest S	.75	.30
S54	Blake Brockermeyer S	.75	.30
S56	Michael Westbrook S	3.00	1.25
S57	Garrison Hearst S	3.00	1.25
S59	Kyle Brady S	1.50	.60
S62	Tim Brown S	1.50	.60
S63	Jeff Graham S	.75	.30
S67	Dan Marino S	15.00	6.00
S69	Tamarick Vanover S	3.00	1.25
S74	Daryl Johnston S	1.50	.60
S78	Frank Sanders S	1.50	.60
S84	Darryll Lewis S	.75	.30
S85	Carl Pickens S	1.50	.60
S88	Jerome Bettis S	3.00	1.25
S90	Terrell Davis S	6.00	2.50
S99	Napoleon Kaufman S	3.00	1.25
S100	Rashaan Salaam S	1.50	.60
S103	Barry Sanders S	15.00	6.00
S107	Tony Boselli S	1.50	.60
S109	Eric Zeier S	1.50	.60
S116	Bruce Smith S	3.00	1.25
S118	Zack Crockett S	.75	.30
S125	Joey Galloway S	3.00	1.25
S126	Heath Shuler S	1.50	.60
S127	Curtis Martin S	6.00	2.50
S135	Greg Lloyd S	1.50	.60
S137	Marshall Faulk S	4.00	1.50
S147	Tyrone Poole S	.75	.30
S150	J.J. Stokes S	3.00	1.25
S153	Drew Bledsoe S	5.00	2.00
S154	Terry McDaniel S	.75	.30
S155	Terrell Fletcher S	.75	.30
S159	Dave Brown S	.75	.30
S165	Jim Harbaugh S	1.50	.60
S166	Larry Brown S	.75	.30
S167	Neil Smith S	1.50	.60
S168	Herman Moore S	1.50	.60
S170	Deion Sanders S	5.00	2.00
S174	Mark Chmura S	1.50	.60
S181	Chris Warren S	1.50	.60
S183	Robert Brooks S	3.00	1.25
S184	Steve McNair S	6.00	2.50

❑ S185 Kordell Stewart S 3.00 1.25
❑ S189 Charlie Garner S 1.50 .60
❑ S195 Harvey Williams S .75 .30
❑ S197 Jeff George S 1.50 .60
❑ S199 Ricky Watters S 1.50 .60
❑ S204 Steve Bono S 1.50 .60
❑ S210 Jeff Blake S 3.00 1.25
❑ S215 Phillippi Sparks S .75 .30
❑ S226 William Floyd S 1.50 .60
❑ S227 Troy Drayton S .75 .30
❑ S229 Rodney Hampton S 1.50 .60
❑ S239 Duane Clemons S RC .75 .30
❑ S249 Curtis Conway S 3.00 1.25
❑ S253 John Mobley S .75 .30
❑ S258 Chris Slade S .75 .30
❑ S259 Derrick Thomas S 3.00 1.25
❑ S262 Eric Metcalf S 1.50 .60
❑ S265 Emmitt Smith S 12.00 5.00
❑ S269 Jeff Hostetler S 1.50 .60
❑ S272 Thurman Thomas S 3.00 1.25
❑ S276 Steve Atwater S .75 .30
❑ S280 Isaac Bruce S 3.00 1.25
❑ S283 Neil O'Donnell S 1.50 .60
❑ S287 Jim Kelly S 3.00 1.25
❑ S288 Lawrence Phillips S 3.00 1.25
❑ S291 Terance Mathis S .75 .30
❑ S292 Errict Rhett S 1.50 .60
❑ S294 Santo Stephens S .75 .30
❑ S299 Walt Harris S RC .75 .30
❑ S302 Jamir Miller S .75 .30
❑ S304 Ben Coates S 1.50 .60
❑ S305 Marcus Allen S 3.00 1.25
❑ S308 Jonathan Ogden S RC 3.00 1.25
❑ S310 John Elway S 15.00 6.00
❑ S313 Irving Fryar S 1.50 .60
❑ S315 Junior Seau S 3.00 1.25
❑ S316 Alex Molden S RC .75 .30
❑ S320 Steve Young S 6.00 2.50

1997 Finest

❑ COMPLETE SET (350) 500.00 250.00
❑ COMP.SERIES 1 SET (175) 250.00 125.00
❑ COMP.SERIES 2 SET (175) 250.00 125.00
❑ COMP.BRONZE SER.1 (100) 25.00 10.00
❑ COMP.BRONZE SER.2 (100) 40.00 15.00
❑ 1 Mark Brunell B 2.00 .75
❑ 2 Chris Slade B .60 .25
❑ 3 Chris Doleman B .60 .25
❑ 4 Chris Hudson B .60 .25
❑ 5 Karim Abdul-Jabbar B 1.00 .40
❑ 6 Darren Perry B .60 .25
❑ 7 Daryl Johnston B 1.00 .40
❑ 8 Rob Moore B UER 1.00 .40
❑ 9 Robert Smith B 1.00 .40
❑ 10 Terry Allen B 1.50 .60
❑ 11 Jason Dunn B .60 .25
❑ 12 Henry Thomas B .60 .25
❑ 13 Rod Stephens B .60 .25
❑ 14 Ray Mickens B .60 .25
❑ 15 Ty Detmer B 1.00 .40
❑ 16 Fred Barnett B .60 .25
❑ 17 Derrick Alexander WR B 1.00 .40
❑ 18 Marcus Robertson B .60 .25
❑ 19 Robert Blackmon B .60 .25
❑ 20 Isaac Bruce B 1.50 .60
❑ 21 Chester McGlockton B .60 .25
❑ 22 Stan Humphries B 1.00 .40
❑ 23 Lonnie Marts B .60 .25
❑ 24 Jason Sehorn B 1.00 .40
❑ 25 Bobby Engram B UER 1.00 .40
❑ 26 Brett Perriman B UER .60 .25
❑ 27 Stevon Moore B .60 .25
❑ 28 Jamal Anderson B 1.50 .60
❑ 29 Wayne Martin B .60 .25
❑ 30 Michael Irvin B UER 1.50 .60
❑ 31 Thomas Smith B .60 .25
❑ 32 Tony Brackens B .60 .25
❑ 33 Eric Davis B .60 .25
❑ 34 James O.Stewart B 1.00 .40
❑ 35 Ki-Jana Carter B .60 .25
❑ 36 Ken Norton B .60 .25
❑ 37 William Thomas B .60 .25
❑ 38 Tim Brown B 1.50 .60
❑ 39 Lawrence Phillips B .60 .25
❑ 40 Ricky Watters B 1.00 .40
❑ 41 Tony Bennett B .60 .25
❑ 42 Jessie Armstead B .60 .25
❑ 43 Trent Dilfer B 1.50 .60
❑ 44 Rodney Hampton B 1.00 .40
❑ 45 Sam Mills B .60 .25
❑ 46 Rodney Harrison B RC 3.00 1.25
❑ 47 Rob Fredrickson B .60 .25
❑ 48 Eric Hill B .60 .25
❑ 49 Bennie Blades B .60 .25
❑ 50 Eddie George B 1.50 .60
❑ 51 Dave Brown B .60 .25
❑ 52 Raymont Harris B .60 .25
❑ 53 Steve Tovar B .60 .25
❑ 54 Thurman Thomas B 1.50 .60
❑ 55 Leeland McElroy B .60 .25
❑ 56 Brian Mitchell B UER .60 .25
❑ 57 Eric Allen B .60 .25
❑ 58 Vinny Testaverde B 1.00 .40
❑ 59 Marvin Washington B .60 .25
❑ 60 Junior Seau B 1.50 .60
❑ 61 Bert Emanuel B 1.00 .40
❑ 62 Kevin Carter B .60 .25
❑ 63 Mark Carrier DB B .60 .25
❑ 64 Andre Coleman B .60 .25
❑ 65 Chris Warren B 1.00 .40
❑ 66 Aeneas Williams B .60 .25
❑ 67 Eugene Robinson B .60 .25
❑ 68 Darren Woodson B .60 .25
❑ 69 Anthony Johnson B .60 .25
❑ 70 Terry Glenn B 1.50 .60
❑ 71 Troy Vincent B .60 .25
❑ 72 John Copeland B .60 .25
❑ 73 Warren Sapp B 1.00 .40
❑ 74 Bobby Hebert B .60 .25
❑ 75 Jeff Hostetler B .60 .25
❑ 76 Willie Davis B .60 .25
❑ 77 Mickey Washington B .60 .25
❑ 78 Cortez Kennedy B .60 .25
❑ 79 Michael Strahan B 1.00 .40
❑ 80 Jerome Bettis B 1.50 .60
❑ 81 Andre Hastings B UER .60 .25
❑ 82 Simeon Rice B 1.00 .40
❑ 83 Cornelius Bennett B .60 .25
❑ 84 Napoleon Kaufman B 1.50 .60
❑ 85 Jim Harbaugh B 1.00 .40
❑ 86 Aaron Hayden B .60 .25
❑ 87 Gus Frerotte B .60 .25
❑ 88 Jeff Blake B 1.00 .40
❑ 89 Anthony Miller B UER .60 .25
❑ 90 Deion Sanders B 1.50 .60
❑ 91 Curtis Conway B 1.00 .40
❑ 92 William Floyd B 1.00 .40
❑ 93 Eric Moulds B UER 1.50 .60
❑ 94 Mel Gray B .60 .25
❑ 95 Andre Rison B UER 1.00 .40
❑ 96 Eugene Daniel B .60 .25
❑ 97 Jason Belser B .60 .25
❑ 98 Mike Mamula B .60 .25
❑ 99 Jim Everett B .60 .25
❑ 100 Checklist B .60 .25
❑ 101 Drew Bledsoe S 4.00 1.50
❑ 102 Shannon Sharpe S 2.00 .75
❑ 103 Ken Harvey S 1.25 .50
❑ 104 Isaac Bruce S 3.00 1.25
❑ 105 Terry Allen S 3.00 1.25
❑ 106 Lawyer Milloy S 2.00 .75
❑ 107 Ashley Ambrose S 1.25 .50
❑ 108 Alfred Williams S 1.25 .50
❑ 109 Hugh Douglas S 1.25 .50
❑ 110 Junior Seau S 3.00 1.25
❑ 111 Kordell Stewart S 3.00 1.25
❑ 112 Adrian Murrell S 2.00 .75
❑ 113 Byron Bam Morris S 1.25 .50
❑ 114 Terrell Buckley S 1.25 .50
❑ 115 Dan Marino S 12.00 5.00
❑ 116 Willie Clay S 1.25 .50
❑ 117 Neil Smith S 2.00 .75
❑ 118 Blaine Bishop S 1.25 .50
❑ 119 John Mobley S 1.25 .50
❑ 120 Herman Moore S 2.00 .75
❑ 121 Keyshawn Johnson S 3.00 1.25
❑ 122 Boomer Esiason S 2.00 .75
❑ 123 Marshall Faulk S 4.00 1.50
❑ 124 Keith Jackson S 1.25 .50
❑ 125 Ricky Watters S 2.00 .75
❑ 126 Carl Pickens S 2.00 .75
❑ 127 Cris Carter S 3.00 1.25
❑ 128 Mike Alstott S 3.00 1.25
❑ 129 Simeon Rice S 2.00 .75
❑ 130 Troy Aikman S 6.00 2.50
❑ 131 Tamarick Vanover S 2.00 .75
❑ 132 Marquez Pope S 1.25 .50
❑ 133 Winslow Oliver S 1.25 .50
❑ 134 Edgar Bennett S 2.00 .75
❑ 135 Dave Meggett S 1.25 .50
❑ 136 Marcus Allen S 3.00 1.25
❑ 137 Jerry Rice S 6.00 2.50
❑ 138 Steve Atwater S 1.25 .50
❑ 139 Tim McDonald S 1.25 .50
❑ 140 Barry Sanders S 10.00 4.00
❑ 141 Eddie George S 3.00 1.25
❑ 142 Wesley Walls S 1.25 .50
❑ 143 Jerome Bettis S 3.00 1.25
❑ 144 Kevin Greene S 2.00 .75
❑ 145 Terrell Davis S 4.00 1.50
❑ 146 Gus Frerotte S 2.00 .75
❑ 147 Joey Galloway S 2.00 .75
❑ 148 Vinny Testaverde S 2.00 .75
❑ 149 Hardy Nickerson S 1.25 .50
❑ 150 Brett Favre S 12.00 5.00
❑ 151 Desmond Howard G 1.50 .60
❑ 152 Keyshawn Johnson G 5.00 2.00
❑ 153 Tony Banks G 5.00 2.00
❑ 154 Chris Spielman G 1.50 .60
❑ 155 Reggie White G 5.00 2.00
❑ 156 Zach Thomas G 5.00 2.00
❑ 157 Carl Pickens G 3.00 1.25
❑ 158 Karim Abdul-Jabbar G 5.00 2.00
❑ 159 Chad Brown G 1.50 .60
❑ 160 Kerry Collins G 5.00 2.00
❑ 161 Marvin Harrison G 5.00 2.00
❑ 162 Steve Young G 6.00 2.50
❑ 163 Deion Sanders G 5.00 2.00
❑ 164 Trent Dilfer G 5.00 2.00
❑ 165 Barry Sanders G 15.00 6.00
❑ 166 Cris Carter G 5.00 2.00
❑ 167 Keenan McCardell G 3.00 1.25
❑ 168 Terry Glenn G 5.00 2.00
❑ 169 Emmitt Smith G 15.00 6.00
❑ 170 John Elway G 20.00 7.50
❑ 171 Jerry Rice G 10.00 4.00
❑ 172 Troy Aikman G 10.00 4.00
❑ 173 Curtis Martin G 6.00 2.50
❑ 174 Darrell Green G 1.50 .60
❑ 175 Mark Brunell G 6.00 2.50
❑ 176 Corey Dillon B RC 12.00 5.00
❑ 177 Tyrone Poole B .60 .25
❑ 178 Anthony Pleasant B .60 .25
❑ 179 Frank Sanders B 1.00 .40
❑ 180 Troy Aikman B 3.00 1.50
❑ 181 Bill Romanowski B .60 .25
❑ 182 Ty Law B 1.00 .40
❑ 183 Orlando Thomas B .60 .25
❑ 184 Quentin Coryatt B .60 .25
❑ 185 Kenny Holmes RC B 1.25 .50
❑ 186 Bryant Young B .60 .25
❑ 187 Michael Sinclair B .60 .25
❑ 188 Mike Tomczak B .60 .25
❑ 189 Bobby Taylor B .60 .25
❑ 190 Brett Favre B 6.00 3.00
❑ 191 Kent Graham B .60 .25
❑ 192 Jessie Tuggle B .60 .25
❑ 193 Jimmy Smith B 1.00 .40
❑ 194 Greg Hill B .60 .25
❑ 195 Yatil Green B RC .75 .30
❑ 196 Mark Fields B .60 .25
❑ 197 Phillippi Sparks B .60 .25
❑ 198 Aaron Glenn B .60 .25
❑ 199 Pat Swilling B .60 .25
❑ 200 Barry Sanders B 5.00 2.00
❑ 201 Mark Chmura B 1.00 .40
❑ 202 Marco Coleman B .60 .25
❑ 203 Merton Hanks B .60 .25
❑ 204 Brian Blades B .60 .25
❑ 205 Errict Rhett B .60 .25

❑ 206 Henry Ellard B	.60	.25
❑ 207 Andre Reed B	1.00	.40
❑ 208 Bryan Cox B	.60	.25
❑ 209 Darnay Scott B	1.00	.40
❑ 210 John Elway B	6.00	3.00
❑ 211 Glyn Milburn B	.60	.25
❑ 212 Don Beebe B	.60	.25
❑ 213 Kevin Lockett B RC	.75	.30
❑ 214 Dorsey Levens B	1.50	.60
❑ 215 Kordell Stewart B	1.50	.60
❑ 216 Larry Centers B	1.00	.40
❑ 217 Cris Carter B	1.50	.60
❑ 218 Willie McGinest B	.60	.25
❑ 219 Renaldo Wynn RC B	.30	.10
❑ 220 Jerry Rice B	3.00	1.50
❑ 221 Reidel Anthony B RC	[illegible]	[illegible]
❑ 222 Mark Carrier WR B	.60	.25
❑ 223 Quinn Early B	.60	.25
❑ 224 Chris Sanders B	.60	.25
❑ 225 Shawn Springs B RC	.75	.30
❑ 226 Kevin Smith B	.60	.25
❑ 227 Ben Coates B	1.00	.40
❑ 228 Tyrone Wheatley B	1.00	.40
❑ 229 Antonio Freeman B	1.50	.60
❑ 230 Dan Marino B	6.00	3.00
❑ 231 Dwayne Rudd RC B	1.25	.50
❑ 232 Leslie O'Neal B	.60	.25
❑ 233 Brent Jones B	.60	.25
❑ 234 Jake Plummer B RC	10.00	4.00
❑ 235 Kerry Collins B	1.50	.60
❑ 236 Rashaan Salaam B	.60	.25
❑ 237 Tyrone Braxton B	.60	.25
❑ 238 Herman Moore B	1.00	.40
❑ 239 Keyshawn Johnson B	1.50	.60
❑ 240 Drew Bledsoe B	2.00	.75
❑ 241 Rickey Dudley B	1.00	.40
❑ 242 Antowain Smith B RC	5.00	2.00
❑ 243 Jeff Lageman B	.60	.25
❑ 244 Chris T. Jones B	.60	.25
❑ 245 Steve Young B	2.00	.75
❑ 246 Eddie Robinson B	.60	.25
❑ 247 Chad Cota B	.60	.25
❑ 248 Michael Jackson B	1.00	.40
❑ 249 Robert Porcher B	.60	.25
❑ 250 Reggie White B	1.50	.60
❑ 251 Carnell Lake B	.60	.25
❑ 252 Chris Calloway B	.60	.25
❑ 253 Terance Mathis B	1.00	.40
❑ 254 Carl Pickens B	1.00	.40
❑ 255 Curtis Martin B	2.00	.75
❑ 256 Jeff Graham B	.60	.25
❑ 257 Regan Upshaw RC B	.30	.10
❑ 258 Sean Gilbert B	.60	.25
❑ 259 Will Blackwell B RC	.75	.30
❑ 260 Emmitt Smith B	5.00	2.50
❑ 261 Reinard Wilson RC B	.75	.30
❑ 262 Darrell Russell RC B	.30	.10
❑ 263 Wayne Chrebet B	1.00	.40
❑ 264 Kevin Hardy B	.60	.25
❑ 265 Shannon Sharpe B	1.00	.40
❑ 266 Harvey Williams B	.60	.25
❑ 267 John Randle B	1.00	.40
❑ 268 Tim Bowens B	.60	.25
❑ 269 Tony Gonzalez B RC	6.00	2.50
❑ 270 Warrick Dunn B RC	6.00	2.50
❑ 271 Sean Dawkins B	.60	.25
❑ 272 Darryll Lewis B	.60	.25
❑ 273 Alonzo Spellman B	.60	.25
❑ 274 Mark Collins B	.60	.25
❑ 275 Checklist Card B	.60	.25
❑ 276 Pat Barnes S RC	2.00	.75
❑ 277 Dana Stubblefield S	2.00	.75
❑ 278 Dan Wilkinson S	1.25	.50
❑ 279 Bryce Paup S	1.25	.50
❑ 280 Kerry Collins S	3.00	1.25
❑ 281 Derrick Brooks S	3.00	1.25
❑ 282 Walter Jones S RC	3.00	1.25
❑ 283 Terry McDaniel S	1.25	.50
❑ 284 James Farrior RC S	3.00	1.25
❑ 285 Curtis Martin S	4.00	1.50
❑ 286 O.J. McDuffie S	2.00	.75
❑ 287 Natrone Means S	2.00	.75
❑ 288 Bryant Westbrook RC S	2.00	.75
❑ 289 Peter Boulware RC S	3.00	1.25
❑ 290 Emmitt Smith S	10.00	4.00
❑ 291 Joey Kent S RC	3.00	1.25
❑ 292 Eddie Kennison S	2.00	.75
❑ 293 LeRoy Butler S	1.25	.50
❑ 294 Dale Carter S	1.25	.50
❑ 295 Jim Druckenmiller S RC	2.00	.75
❑ 296 Byron Hanspard S RC	2.00	.75
❑ 297 Jeff Blake S	2.00	.75
❑ 298 Levon Kirkland S	1.25	.50
❑ 299 Michael Westbrook S	2.00	.75
❑ 300 John Elway S	12.00	5.00
❑ 301 Lamar Lathon S	1.25	.50
❑ 302 Ray Lewis S	5.00	2.00
❑ 303 Steve McNair S	4.00	1.50
❑ 304 Shawn Springs S	2.00	.75
❑ 305 Karim Abdul-Jabbar S	2.00	.75
❑ 306 Orlando Pace S RC	3.00	1.25
❑ 307 Scott Mitchell S	1.25	.50
❑ 308 Walt Harris S	1.25	.50
❑ 309 Bruce Smith S	2.00	.75
❑ 310 Reggie White S	[illegible]	1.25
❑ 311 Eric Swann S	1.25	.50
❑ 312 Derrick Thomas S	3.00	1.25
❑ 313 Tony Martin S	2.00	.75
❑ 314 Darrell Russell RC S	2.00	.75
❑ 315 Mark Brunell S	4.00	1.50
❑ 316 Trent Dilfer S	3.00	1.25
❑ 317 Irving Fryar S	1.25	.50
❑ 318 Amani Toomer S	2.00	.75
❑ 319 Jake Reed S	2.00	.75
❑ 320 Steve Young S	4.00	1.50
❑ 321 Troy Davis S RC	2.00	.75
❑ 322 Jim Harbaugh S	2.00	.75
❑ 323 Neil O'Donnell S	1.25	.50
❑ 324 Terry Glenn S	3.00	1.25
❑ 325 Deion Sanders S	3.00	1.25
❑ 326 Gus Frerotte G	3.00	1.25
❑ 327 Tom Knight RC G	3.00	1.25
❑ 328 Peter Boulware G	3.00	1.25
❑ 329 Jerome Bettis G	5.00	2.00
❑ 330 Orlando Pace G	5.00	2.00
❑ 331 Darnell Autry G RC	3.00	1.25
❑ 332 Ike Hilliard G RC	12.00	5.00
❑ 333 David LaFleur G RC	1.50	.60
❑ 334 Jim Harbaugh G	3.00	1.25
❑ 335 Eddie George G	5.00	2.00
❑ 336 Vinny Testaverde G	3.00	1.25
❑ 337 Terry Allen G	3.00	1.25
❑ 338 Jim Druckenmiller G	3.00	1.25
❑ 339 Ricky Watters G	3.00	1.25
❑ 340 Brett Favre G	20.00	7.50
❑ 341 Simeon Rice G	3.00	1.25
❑ 342 Shannon Sharpe G	3.00	1.25
❑ 343 Kordell Stewart G	5.00	2.00
❑ 344 Isaac Bruce G	5.00	2.00
❑ 345 Drew Bledsoe G	6.00	2.50
❑ 346 Jeff Blake G	3.00	1.25
❑ 347 Herman Moore G	3.00	1.25
❑ 348 Junior Seau G	5.00	2.00
❑ 349 Rae Carruth G RC	1.50	.60
❑ 350 Dan Marino G	20.00	7.50
❑ P5 K.Abdul-Jabbar Promo	1.50	.60
❑ P32 Tony Brackens Promo	1.50	.60
❑ P45 Sam Mills Promo	1.50	.60
❑ P70 Terry Glenn Promo	1.50	.60
❑ P87 Gus Frerotte Promo	1.50	.60

1998 Finest

❑ COMPLETE SET (270)	80.00	30.00
❑ COMP.SERIES 1 (150)	50.00	20.00
❑ COMP.SERIES 2 (120)	30.00	12.50
❑ 1 John Elway	4.00	1.50
❑ 2 Terance Mathis	.60	.25
❑ 3 Jermaine Lewis	.60	.25
❑ 4 Fred Lane	.40	.15
❑ 5 Simeon Rice	.60	.25
❑ 6 David Dunn	.40	.15
❑ 7 Dexter Coakley	.40	.15
❑ 8 Carl Pickens	.60	.25
❑ 9 Antonio Freeman	1.00	.40
❑ 10 Herman Moore	.60	.25
❑ 11 Kevin Hardy	.40	.15
❑ 12 Tony Gonzalez	1.00	.40
❑ 13 O.J. McDuffie	.60	.25
❑ 14 David Palmer	.40	.15
❑ 15 Lawyer Milloy	.60	.25
❑ 16 Danny Kanell	.60	.25
❑ 17 Randal Hill	.40	.15
❑ 18 Chris Slade	.40	.15
❑ 19 Charlie Garner	.60	.25
❑ 20 Mark Brunell	1.00	.40
❑ 21 Donnell Woolford	.40	.15
❑ 22 Freddie Jones	.40	.15
❑ 23 Ken Norton	.40	.15
❑ 24 Tony Banks	.60	.25
❑ 25 Isaac Bruce	1.00	.40
❑ 26 Willie Davis	.40	.15
❑ 27 Cris Dishman	.40	.15
❑ 28 Aeneas Williams	.40	.15
❑ 29 Michael Booker	.40	.15
❑ 30 Cris Carter	1.00	.40
❑ 31 Michael McCrary	.40	.15
❑ 32 Eric Moulds	1.00	.40
❑ 33 Rae Carruth	.40	.15
❑ 34 Bobby Engram	.60	.25
❑ 35 Jeff Blake	.60	.25
❑ 36 Deion Sanders	1.00	.40
❑ 37 Rod Smith	.60	.25
❑ 38 Bryant Westbrook	.40	.15
❑ 39 Mark Chmura	.60	.25
❑ 40 Tim Brown	1.00	.40
❑ 41 Bobby Taylor	.40	.15
❑ 42 James Stewart	.60	.25
❑ 43 Kimble Anders	.60	.25
❑ 44 Karim Abdul-Jabbar	1.00	.40
❑ 45 Willie McGinest	.40	.15
❑ 46 Jessie Armstead	.40	.15
❑ 47 Brad Johnson	1.00	.40
❑ 48 Greg Lloyd	.40	.15
❑ 49 Stephen Davis	.40	.15
❑ 50 Jerome Bettis	1.00	.40
❑ 51 Warren Sapp	.60	.25
❑ 52 Horace Copeland	.40	.15
❑ 53 Chad Brown	.40	.15
❑ 54 Chris Canty	.40	.15
❑ 55 Robert Smith	1.00	.40
❑ 56 Pete Mitchell	.40	.15
❑ 57 Aaron Bailey	.40	.15
❑ 58 Robert Porcher	.40	.15
❑ 59 John Mobley	.40	.15
❑ 60 Tony Martin	.60	.25
❑ 61 Michael Irvin	1.00	.40
❑ 62 Charles Way	.40	.15
❑ 63 Raymont Harris	.40	.15
❑ 64 Chuck Smith	.40	.15
❑ 65 Larry Centers	.40	.15
❑ 66 Greg Hill	.40	.15
❑ 67 Kenny Holmes	.40	.15
❑ 68 John Lynch	.60	.25
❑ 69 Michael Sinclair	.40	.15
❑ 70 Steve Young	1.25	.50
❑ 71 Michael Strahan	.60	.25
❑ 72 Levon Kirkland	.40	.15
❑ 73 Rickey Dudley	.40	.15
❑ 74 Marcus Allen	1.00	.40
❑ 75 John Randle	.60	.25
❑ 76 Erik Kramer	.40	.15
❑ 77 Neil Smith	.60	.25
❑ 78 Byron Hanspard	.40	.15
❑ 79 Quinn Early	.40	.15
❑ 80 Warren Moon	1.00	.40
❑ 81 William Thomas	.40	.15
❑ 82 Ben Coates	.60	.25
❑ 83 Lake Dawson	.40	.15
❑ 84 Steve McNair	1.00	.40
❑ 85 Gus Frerotte	.40	.15
❑ 86 Rodney Harrison	.60	.25
❑ 87 Reggie White	1.00	.40
❑ 88 Derrick Thomas	1.00	.40
❑ 89 Dale Carter	.40	.15
❑ 90 Warrick Dunn	1.00	.40
❑ 91 Will Blackwell	.40	.15
❑ 92 Troy Vincent	.40	.15
❑ 93 Johnnie Morton	.60	.25
❑ 94 David LaFleur	.40	.15
❑ 95 Tony McGee	.40	.15

❑ 96	Lonnie Johnson	.40	.15
❑ 97	Thurman Thomas	1.00	.40
❑ 98	Chris Chandler	.60	.25
❑ 99	Jamal Anderson	1.00	.40
❑ 100	Checklist	.40	.15
❑ 101	Marshall Faulk	1.50	.60
❑ 102	Chris Calloway	.40	.15
❑ 103	Chris Spielman	.40	.15
❑ 104	Zach Thomas	1.00	.40
❑ 105	Jeff George	.60	.25
❑ 106	Darrell Russell	.40	.15
❑ 107	Darryll Lewis	.40	.15
❑ 108	Reidel Anthony	.60	.25
❑ 109	Terrell Owens	1.00	.40
❑ 110	Rob Moore	.60	.25
❑ 111	Darrell Green	.60	.25
❑ 112	Merton Hanks	.40	.15
❑ 113	Shawn Jefferson	.40	.15
❑ 114	Chris Sanders	.40	.15
❑ 115	Scott Mitchell	.60	.25
❑ 116	Vaughn Hebron	.40	.15
❑ 117	Ed McCaffrey	.60	.25
❑ 118	Bruce Smith	.60	.25
❑ 119	Peter Boulware	.40	.15
❑ 120	Brett Favre	4.00	1.50
❑ 121	Peyton Manning RC	30.00	15.00
❑ 122	Brian Griese RC	5.00	2.00
❑ 123	Tavian Banks RC	1.50	.60
❑ 124	Duane Starks RC	1.00	.40
❑ 125	Robert Holcombe RC	1.50	.60
❑ 126	Brian Simmons RC	1.50	.60
❑ 127	Skip Hicks RC	1.50	.60
❑ 128	Keith Brooking RC	2.50	1.00
❑ 129	Ahman Green RC	12.00	5.00
❑ 130	Jerome Pathon RC	2.50	1.00
❑ 131	Curtis Enis RC	1.00	.40
❑ 132	Grant Wistrom RC	1.50	.60
❑ 133	Germane Crowell RC	1.50	.60
❑ 134	Jacquez Green RC	1.50	.60
❑ 135	Randy Moss RC	20.00	10.00
❑ 136	Jason Peter RC	1.00	.40
❑ 137	John Avery RC	1.50	.60
❑ 138	Takeo Spikes RC	2.50	1.00
❑ 139	Pat Johnson RC	1.50	.60
❑ 140	Andre Wadsworth RC	1.50	.60
❑ 141	Fred Taylor RC	4.00	1.50
❑ 142	Charles Woodson RC	3.00	1.25
❑ 143	Marcus Nash RC	1.00	.40
❑ 144	Robert Edwards RC	1.50	.60
❑ 145	Kevin Dyson RC	2.50	1.00
❑ 146	Joe Jurevicius RC	2.50	1.00
❑ 147	Anthony Simmons RC	1.50	.60
❑ 148	Hines Ward RC	10.00	5.00
❑ 149	Greg Ellis RC	1.00	.40
❑ 150	Ryan Leaf RC	2.50	1.00
❑ 151	Jerry Rice	2.00	.75
❑ 152	Tony Martin	.60	.25
❑ 153	Checklist	.40	.15
❑ 154	Rob Johnson	.60	.25
❑ 155	Shannon Sharpe	.60	.25
❑ 156	Bert Emanuel	.60	.25
❑ 157	Eric Metcalf	.40	.15
❑ 158	Natrone Means	.60	.25
❑ 159	Derrick Alexander	.60	.25
❑ 160	Emmitt Smith	3.00	1.25
❑ 161	Jeff Burris	.40	.15
❑ 162	Chris Warren	.60	.25
❑ 163	Corey Fuller	.40	.15
❑ 164	Courtney Hawkins	.40	.15
❑ 165	James McKnight	1.00	.40
❑ 166	Shawn Springs	.40	.15
❑ 167	Wayne Martin	.40	.15
❑ 168	Michael Westbrook	.60	.25
❑ 169	Michael Jackson	.40	.15
❑ 170	Dan Marino	4.00	1.50
❑ 171	Amp Lee	.40	.15
❑ 172	James Jett	.60	.25
❑ 173	Ty Law	.60	.25
❑ 174	Kerry Collins	.60	.25
❑ 175	Robert Brooks	.60	.25
❑ 176	Blaine Bishop	.40	.15
❑ 177	Stephen Boyd	.40	.15
❑ 178	Keyshawn Johnson	1.00	.40
❑ 179	Deon Figures	.40	.15
❑ 180	Allen Aldridge	.40	.15
❑ 181	Corey Miller	.40	.15
❑ 182	Chad Lewis	.60	.25
❑ 183	Derrick Rodgers	.40	.15
❑ 184	Troy Drayton	.40	.15
❑ 185	Darren Woodson	.40	.15
❑ 186	Ken Dilger	.40	.15
❑ 187	Elvis Grbac	.60	.25
❑ 188	Terrell Fletcher	.40	.15
❑ 189	Frank Sanders	.60	.25
❑ 190	Curtis Martin	1.00	.40
❑ 191	Derrick Brooks	1.00	.40
❑ 192	Darrien Gordon	.40	.15
❑ 193	Andre Reed	.60	.25
❑ 194	Darnay Scott	.60	.25
❑ 195	Curtis Conway	.60	.25
❑ 196	Tim McDonald	.40	.15
❑ 197	Sean Dawkins	.40	.15
❑ 198	Napoleon Kaufman	1.00	.40
❑ 199	Willie Clay	.40	.15
❑ 200	Terrell Davis	1.00	.40
❑ 201	Wesley Walls	.60	.25
❑ 202	Santana Dotson	.40	.15
❑ 203	Frank Wycheck	.40	.15
❑ 204	Wayne Chrebet	1.00	.40
❑ 205	Andre Rison	.60	.25
❑ 206	Jason Sehorn	.60	.25
❑ 207	Jessie Tuggle	.40	.15
❑ 208	Kevin Turner	.40	.15
❑ 209	Jason Taylor	.60	.25
❑ 210	Yancey Thigpen	.40	.15
❑ 211	Jake Reed	.60	.25
❑ 212	Carnell Lake	.40	.15
❑ 213	Joey Galloway	.60	.25
❑ 214	Andre Hastings	.40	.15
❑ 215	Terry Allen	1.00	.40
❑ 216	Jim Harbaugh	.60	.25
❑ 217	Tony Banks	.60	.25
❑ 218	Greg Clark	.40	.15
❑ 219	Corey Dillon	1.00	.40
❑ 220	Troy Aikman	2.00	.75
❑ 221	Antowain Smith	1.00	.40
❑ 222	Steve Atwater	.40	.15
❑ 223	Trent Dilfer	1.00	.40
❑ 224	Junior Seau	1.00	.40
❑ 225	Garrison Hearst	1.00	.40
❑ 226	Eric Allen	.40	.15
❑ 227	Chad Cota	.40	.15
❑ 228	Vinny Testaverde	.60	.25
❑ 229	Duce Staley	1.25	.50
❑ 230	Drew Bledsoe	1.50	.60
❑ 231	Charles Johnson	.40	.15
❑ 232	Jake Plummer	1.00	.40
❑ 233	Errict Rhett	.60	.25
❑ 234	Doug Evans	.40	.15
❑ 235	Phillippi Sparks	.40	.15
❑ 236	Ashley Ambrose	.40	.15
❑ 237	Bryan Cox	.40	.15
❑ 238	Kevin Smith	.40	.15
❑ 239	Hardy Nickerson	.40	.15
❑ 240	Terry Glenn	1.00	.40
❑ 241	Lee Woodall	.40	.15
❑ 242	Andre Coleman	.40	.15
❑ 243	Michael Bates	.40	.15
❑ 244	Mark Fields	.40	.15
❑ 245	Eddie Kennison	.60	.25
❑ 246	Dana Stubblefield	.40	.15
❑ 247	Bobby Hoying	.60	.25
❑ 248	Mo Lewis	.40	.15
❑ 249	Derrick Mayes	.60	.25
❑ 250	Eddie George	1.00	.40
❑ 251	Mike Alstott	1.00	.40
❑ 252	J.J. Stokes	.60	.25
❑ 253	Adrian Murrell	.60	.25
❑ 254	Kevin Greene	.60	.25
❑ 255	LeRoy Butler	.40	.15
❑ 256	Glenn Foley	.60	.25
❑ 257	Jimmy Smith	.60	.25
❑ 258	Tiki Barber	1.00	.40
❑ 259	Irving Fryar	.60	.25
❑ 260	Ricky Watters	.60	.25
❑ 261	Jeff Graham	.40	.15
❑ 262	Kordell Stewart	1.00	.40
❑ 263	Rod Woodson	.60	.25
❑ 264	Leslie Shepherd	.40	.15
❑ 265	Ryan McNeil	.40	.15
❑ 266	Ike Hilliard	.60	.25
❑ 267	Keenan McCardell	.60	.25
❑ 268	Marvin Harrison	1.00	.40
❑ 269	Dorsey Levens	1.00	.40
❑ 270	Barry Sanders	3.00	1.25

1999 Finest

❑	COMPLETE SET (175)	80.00	30.00
❑	COMP.SET w/o SPs (124)	30.00	15.00
❑ 1	Peyton Manning	3.00	1.25
❑ 2	Priest Holmes	1.50	.60
❑ 3	Kordell Stewart	.60	.25
❑ 4	Shannon Sharpe	.60	.25
❑ 5	Andre Rison	.60	.25
❑ 6	Rickey Dudley	.40	.15
❑ 7	Duce Staley	1.00	.40
❑ 8	Randall Cunningham	1.00	.40
❑ 9	Warrick Dunn	1.00	.40
❑ 10	Dan Marino	3.00	1.25
❑ 11	Kevin Greene	.40	.15
❑ 12	Garrison Hearst	.60	.25
❑ 13	Eric Moulds	1.00	.40
❑ 14	Marvin Harrison	1.00	.40
❑ 15	Eddie George	1.00	.40
❑ 16	Vinny Testaverde	.60	.25
❑ 17	Brad Johnson	1.00	.40
❑ 18	Derrick Thomas	1.00	.40
❑ 19	Chris Chandler	.60	.25
❑ 20	Troy Aikman	2.00	.75
❑ 21	Terance Mathis	.60	.25
❑ 22	Terrell Owens	1.00	.40
❑ 23	Junior Seau	1.00	.40
❑ 24	Cris Carter	1.00	.40
❑ 25	Fred Taylor	1.00	.40
❑ 26	Adrian Murrell	.60	.25
❑ 27	Terry Glenn	1.00	.40
❑ 28	Rod Smith	.60	.25
❑ 29	Darnay Scott	.60	.25
❑ 30	Brett Favre	3.00	1.25
❑ 31	Cam Cleeland	.40	.15
❑ 32	Ricky Watters	.60	.25
❑ 33	Derrick Alexander	.60	.25
❑ 34	Bruce Smith	.60	.25
❑ 35	Steve McNair	1.00	.40
❑ 36	Wayne Chrebet	.60	.25
❑ 37	Herman Moore	.60	.25
❑ 38	Bert Emanuel	.60	.25
❑ 39	Michael Irvin	.60	.25
❑ 40	Steve Young	1.25	.50
❑ 41	Napoleon Kaufman	1.00	.40
❑ 42	Tim Biakabutuka	.60	.25
❑ 43	Isaac Bruce	1.00	.40
❑ 44	J.J. Stokes	.60	.25
❑ 45	Antonio Freeman	1.00	.40
❑ 46	John Randle	.60	.25
❑ 47	Frank Sanders	.60	.25
❑ 48	O.J. McDuffie	.60	.25
❑ 49	Keenan McCardell	.60	.25
❑ 50	Randy Moss	2.50	1.00
❑ 51	Ed McCaffrey	.60	.25
❑ 52	Yancey Thigpen	.40	.15
❑ 53	Curtis Conway	.60	.25
❑ 54	Mike Alstott	1.00	.40
❑ 55	Deion Sanders	1.00	.40
❑ 56	Dorsey Levens	1.00	.40
❑ 57	Joey Galloway	.60	.25
❑ 58	Natrone Means	.60	.25
❑ 59	Tim Brown	1.00	.40
❑ 60	Jerry Rice	2.00	.75
❑ 61	Robert Smith	1.00	.40
❑ 62	Carl Pickens	.60	.25
❑ 63	Ben Coates	.60	.25
❑ 64	Jerome Bettis	1.00	.40
❑ 65	Corey Dillon	1.00	.40
❑ 66	Curtis Martin	1.00	.40
❑ 67	Jimmy Smith	.60	.25
❑ 68	Keyshawn Johnson	1.00	.40
❑ 69	Charlie Batch	1.00	.40
❑ 70	Jamal Anderson	1.00	.40
❑ 71	Mark Brunell	1.00	.40
❑ 72	Antowain Smith	1.00	.40

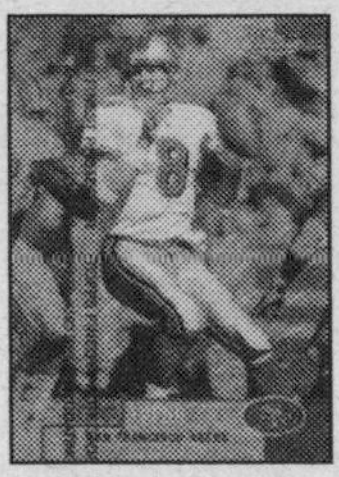

73 Aeneas Williams	.40	.15
74 Wesley Walls	.60	.25
75 Jake Plummer	.60	.25
76 Oronde Gadsden	.60	.25
77 Gary Brown	.40	.15
78 Peter Boulware	.40	.15
79 Stephen Alexander	.40	.15
80 Barry Sanders	3.00	1.25
81 Warren Sapp	.60	.25
82 Michael Sinclair	.40	.15
83 Freddie Jones	.40	.15
84 Ike Hilliard	.40	.15
85 Jake Reed	.60	.25
86 Tim Dwight	1.00	.40
87 Johnnie Morton	.60	.25
[illegible]	[illegible]	[illegible]
89 Rocket Ismail	.60	.25
90 Emmitt Smith	2.00	.75
91 Ricky Proehl	.40	.15
92 James Jett	.60	.25
93 Karim Abdul-Jabbar	.60	.25
94 Mark Chmura	.40	.15
95 Andre Reed	.60	.25
96 Michael Westbrook	.60	.25
97 Michael Strahan	.60	.25
98 Chad Brown	.40	.15
99 Trent Dilfer	.60	.25
100 Terrell Davis	1.00	.40
101 Aaron Glenn	.40	.15
102 Skip Hicks	.40	.15
103 Tony Gonzalez	1.00	.40
104 Ty Law	.60	.25
105 Jermaine Lewis	.60	.25
106 Ray Lewis	1.00	.40
107 Zach Thomas	1.00	.40
108 Reidel Anthony	.60	.25
109 Levon Kirkland	.40	.15
110 Drew Bledsoe	1.25	.50
111 Bobby Engram	.60	.25
112 Jerome Pathon	.40	.15
113 Muhsin Muhammad	.60	.25
114 Vonnie Holliday	.40	.15
115 Bill Romanowski	.40	.15
116 Marshall Faulk	1.25	.50
117 Ty Detmer	.60	.25
118 Mo Lewis	.40	.15
119 Charles Woodson	1.00	.40
120 Doug Flutie	1.00	.40
121 Jon Kitna	1.00	.40
122 Courtney Hawkins	.40	.15
123 Trent Green	1.00	.40
124 John Elway	3.00	1.25
125 Barry Sanders GM	5.00	2.00
126 Brett Favre GM	5.00	2.00
127 Curtis Martin GM	1.50	.60
128 Dan Marino GM	5.00	2.00
129 Eddie George GM	1.00	[illegible]
130 Emmitt Smith GM	5.00	2.00
131 Jamal Anderson GM	1.50	.60
132 Jerry Rice GM	3.00	1.25
133 John Elway GM	5.00	2.00
134 Terrell Davis GM	2.50	1.00
135 Troy Aikman GM	3.00	1.25
136 Skip Hicks SN	.40	.15
137 Charles Woodson SN	1.00	.40
138 Charlie Batch SN	2.50	1.00
139 Curtis Enis SN	1.50	.60
140 Fred Taylor SN	2.50	1.00
141 Jake Plummer SN	1.50	.60
142 Peyton Manning SN	5.00	2.00
143 Randy Moss SN	4.00	1.50
144 Corey Dillon SN	1.50	.60
145 Priest Holmes SN	1.50	.60
146 Warrick Dunn SN	1.50	.60
147 Jevon Kearse RC	4.00	1.50
148 Chris Claiborne RC	1.50	.60
149 Akili Smith RC	1.50	.60
150 Brock Huard RC	3.00	1.25
151 Daunte Culpepper RC	10.00	4.00
152 Edgerrin James RC	10.00	4.00
153 Cecil Collins RC	1.50	.60
154 Kevin Faulk RC	3.00	1.25
155 Amos Zereoue RC	3.00	1.25
156 James Johnson RC	2.50	1.00
157 Sedrick Irvin RC	1.50	.60
158 Ricky Williams RC	5.00	2.00
159 Mike Cloud RC	2.50	1.00
160 Chris McAlister	1.50	.60
161 Rob Konrad RC	2.50	1.00
162 Champ Bailey RC	3.00	1.25
163 Ebenezer Ekuban RC	2.50	1.00
164 Tim Couch RC	3.00	1.25
165 Cade McNown RC	2.50	1.00
166 Donovan McNabb RC	12.00	5.00
167 Joe Germaine RC	2.50	1.00
168 Shaun King RC	2.50	1.00
169 Peerless Price RC	3.00	1.25
170 Kevin Johnson RC	2.50	1.00
171 Troy Edwards RC	2.50	1.00
172 Karsten Bailey RC	2.50	1.00
173 David Boston RC	3.00	1.25
174 D'Wayne Bates RC	2.50	1.00
175 Torry Holt RC	6.00	2.50

2000 Finest

COMPLETE SET (205)	400.00	150.00
1 Tim Dwight	.75	.30
2 Cade McNown	.30	.10
3 Drew Bledsoe	1.00	.40
4 Torry Holt	.75	.30
5 Derrick Mayes	.50	.20
6 Vinny Testaverde	.50	.20
7 Patrick Jeffers	.75	.30
8 Dorsey Levens	.50	.20
9 James Johnson	.30	.10
10 Champ Bailey	.50	.20
11 Jeff George	.50	.20
12 Shawn Jefferson	.30	.10
13 Terrence Wilkins	.30	.10
14 J.J. Stokes	.50	.20
15 Doug Flutie	.75	.30
16 Corey Dillon	.75	.30
17 Rod Smith	.50	.20
18 Jimmy Smith	.50	.20
19 Amani Toomer	.50	.20
20 Curtis Conway	.50	.20
21 Brad Johnson	.75	.30
22 Edgerrin James	1.25	.50
23 Derrick Alexander	.50	.20
24 Terrell Owens	.75	.30
25 Kurt Warner	1.50	.60
26 Frank Sanders	.50	.20
27 Tony Banks	.50	.20
28 Troy Aikman	1.50	.60
29 Curtis Enis	.30	.10
30 Eddie George	.75	.30
31 Bill Schroeder	.50	.20
32 Kent Graham	.30	.10
33 Mike Alstott	.75	.30
34 Steve Young	1.00	.40
35 Jacquez Green	.30	.10
36 Frank Wycheck	.30	.10
37 Kerry Collins	.50	.20
38 Stephen Davis	.75	.30
39 Tony Gonzalez	.50	.20
40 Tyrone Wheatley	.50	.20
41 Brett Favre	2.50	1.00
42 Joey Galloway	.50	.20
43 Terrell Davis	.75	.30
44 Marvin Harrison	.75	.30
45 Zach Thomas	.75	.30
46 Jerry Rice	1.50	.60
47 Keyshawn Johnson	.75	.30
48 Rob Johnson	.50	.20
49 Rocket Ismail	.50	.20
50 Elvis Grbac	.50	.20
51 Warrick Dunn	.75	.30
52 Jevon Kearse	.75	.30
53 Albert Connell	.30	.10
54 Muhsin Muhammad	.50	.20
55 Carl Pickens	.50	.20
56 Peyton Manning	2.00	.75
57 Daunte Culpepper	1.00	.40
58 Ike Hilliard	.50	.20
59 Steve McNair	.75	.30
60 Sean Dawkins	.30	.10
61 Steve Beuerlein	.50	.20
62 Priest Holmes	1.00	.40
63 Jim Harbaugh	.50	.20
64 Germane Crowell	.30	.10
65 Cris Carter	.75	.30
66 Jamal Anderson	.75	.30
67 Kevin Johnson	.75	.30
68 Herman Moore	.50	.20
69 Ricky Williams	.75	.30
70 Rich Gannon	.75	.30
[illegible]	[illegible]	[illegible]
72 Peerless Price	.50	.20
73 Az-Zahir Hakim	.50	.20
74 Mark Brunell	.75	.30
75 Rob Moore	.50	.20
76 Antowain Smith	.50	.20
77 Tim Biakabutuka	.50	.20
78 Ed McCaffrey	.75	.30
79 Tony Martin	.50	.20
80 Marcus Robinson	.75	.30
81 Kevin Dyson	.50	.20
82 Wesley Walls	.30	.10
83 Chris Chandler	.50	.20
84 Keenan McCardell	.50	.20
85 Napoleon Kaufman	.50	.20
86 Emmitt Smith	1.50	.60
87 James Stewart	.50	.20
88 Tim Brown	.75	.30
89 Ricky Watters	.50	.20
90 Johnnie Morton	.50	.20
91 Jake Plummer	.50	.20
92 Olandis Gary	.75	.30
93 Jerome Bettis	.75	.30
94 Terry Glenn	.50	.20
95 Kordell Stewart	.50	.20
96 Charlie Garner	.50	.20
97 Yancey Thigpen	.30	.10
98 Michael Westbrook	.50	.20
99 Bobby Engram	.50	.20
100 Eric Moulds	.75	.30
101 Darnay Scott	.50	.20
102 Antonio Freeman	.75	.30
103 Wayne Chrebet	.50	.20
104 Akili Smith	.30	.10
105 Jeff Blake	.50	.20
106 Curtis Martin	.75	.30
107 Errict Rhett	.50	.20
108 Damon Huard	.75	.30
109 Jeff Graham	.30	.10
110 Terance Mathis	.50	.20
111 Jon Kitna	.75	.30
112 Tim Couch	.50	.20
113 Fred Taylor	.75	.30
114 Qadry Ismail	.50	.20
115 Donovan McNabb	1.25	.50
116 Charles Johnson	.50	.20
117 Troy Edwards	.30	.10
118 Shaun King	.30	.10
119 Charlie Batch	.75	.30
120 Robert Smith	.75	.30
121 Marshall Faulk	1.00	.40
122 Brian Griese	.75	.30
123 O.J. McDuffie	.50	.20
124 Randy Moss	1.50	.60
125 Duce Staley	.75	.30
126 Peter Warrick RC	8.00	3.00
127 Dez White RC	8.00	3.00
128 Ron Dayne RC	8.00	3.00
129 J.R. Redmond RC	6.00	2.50
130 Thomas Jones RC	12.00	5.00
131 Plaxico Burress RC	15.00	6.00
132 Reuben Droughns RC	10.00	4.00
133 Shaun Alexander RC	40.00	20.00
134 Ron Dugans RC	6.00	2.50
135 Travis Prentice RC	6.00	2.50
136 Joe Hamilton RC	6.00	2.50
137 Curtis Keaton RC	6.00	2.50
138 Chris Redman RC	6.00	2.50
139 Chad Pennington RC	20.00	7.50
140 Travis Taylor RC	8.00	3.00
141 Bubba Franks RC	8.00	3.00
142 Dennis Northcutt RC	8.00	3.00
143 Jerry Porter RC	10.00	4.00
144 Sylvester Morris RC	6.00	2.50

❑ 145 Anthony Becht RC	8.00	3.00
❑ 146 Trung Canidate RC	6.00	2.50
❑ 147 Jamal Lewis RC	20.00	7.50
❑ 148 R.Jay Soward RC	6.00	2.50
❑ 149 Tee Martin RC	8.00	3.00
❑ 150 Courtney Brown RC	8.00	3.00
❑ 151 Brian Urlacher RC	30.00	12.50
❑ 152 Danny Farmer RC	6.00	2.50
❑ 153 Laveranues Coles RC	10.00	4.00
❑ 154 Todd Pinkston RC	8.00	3.00
❑ 155 Corey Simon RC	8.00	3.00
❑ 156 Spergon Wynn RC	6.00	2.50
❑ 157 Tim Rattay RC	8.00	3.00
❑ 158 Todd Husak RC	8.00	3.00
❑ 159 Aaron Shea RC	6.00	2.50
❑ 160 Giovanni Carmazzi RC	6.00	2.50
❑ 161 Trevor Gaylor RC	6.00	2.50
❑ 162 JaJuan Dawson RC	6.00	2.50
❑ 163 Jarious Jackson RC	6.00	2.50
❑ 164 Chris Samuels RC	6.00	2.50
❑ 165 Rob Morris RC	6.00	2.50
❑ 166 P.Warrick/R.Moss IF	2.00	.75
❑ 167 R.Moss/P.Warrick IF	2.00	.75
❑ 168 T.Prentice/S.Davis IF	1.50	.60
❑ 169 S.Davis/T.Prentice IF	1.50	.60
❑ 170 C.Redman/K.Warner IF	1.50	.60
❑ 171 K.Warner/C.Redman IF	1.50	.60
❑ 172 Syl.Morris/J.Smith IF	1.50	.60
❑ 173 J.Smith/Syl.Morris IF	1.50	.60
❑ 174 C.Pennington/P.Manning IF	4.00	1.50
❑ 175 P.Manning/C.Pennington IF	4.00	1.50
❑ 176 R.Soward/M.Harrison IF	1.50	.60
❑ 177 M.Harrison/R.Soward IF	1.50	.60
❑ 178 R.Dayne/J.Anderson IF	1.50	.60
❑ 179 J.Anderson/R.Dayne IF	1.50	.60
❑ 180 S.Alexander/E.George IF	4.00	1.50
❑ 181 E.George/S.Alexander IF	3.00	1.25
❑ 182 C.Brown/B.Smith IF	1.50	.60
❑ 183 B.Smith/C.Brown IF	1.50	.60
❑ 184 J.Lewis/E.James IF	3.00	1.25
❑ 185 E.James/J.Lewis IF	3.00	1.25
❑ 186 T.Canidate/E.Smith IF	3.00	1.25
❑ 187 E.Smith/T.Canidate IF	3.00	1.25
❑ 188 T.Taylor/C.Carter IF	2.00	.75
❑ 189 C.Carter/T.Taylor IF	2.00	.75
❑ 190 C.Keaton/M.Faulk IF	2.00	.75
❑ 191 M.Faulk/C.Keaton IF	2.00	.75
❑ 192 P.Burress/J.Rice IF	3.00	1.25
❑ 193 J.Rice/P.Burress IF	3.00	1.25
❑ 194 T.Jones/T.Davis IF	2.00	.75
❑ 195 T.Davis/T.Jones IF	2.00	.75
❑ 196 Peyton Manning GM	5.00	2.00
❑ 197 Randy Moss GM	4.00	1.50
❑ 198 Terrell Davis GM	1.50	.60
❑ 199 Marshall Faulk GM	2.50	1.00
❑ 200 Edgerrin James GM	4.00	1.50
❑ 201 Emmitt Smith GM	4.00	1.50
❑ 202 Ricky Williams GM	1.50	.60
❑ 203 Kurt Warner GM	3.00	1.25
❑ 204 Eddie George GM	1.50	.60
❑ 205 Brett Favre GM	6.00	2.50

2001 Finest

❑ COMP.SET w/o SP's (100)	40.00	20.00
❑ 1 Eddie George	1.25	.50
❑ 2 Jay Fiedler	1.25	.50
❑ 3 Peter Warrick	1.25	.50
❑ 4 Vinny Testaverde	.75	.30
❑ 5 Charles Johnson	.50	.20
❑ 6 Ahman Green	1.25	.50
❑ 7 Isaac Bruce	1.25	.50
❑ 8 Junior Seau	1.25	.50
❑ 9 Daunte Culpepper	1.25	.50
❑ 10 Ike Hilliard	.75	.30
❑ 11 Tony Banks	.75	.30
❑ 12 Steve Beuerlein	.75	.30
❑ 13 Jamal Anderson	1.25	.50
❑ 14 Tyrone Wheatley	.75	.30
❑ 15 Sylvester Morris	.50	.20
❑ 16 Edgerrin James	1.50	.60
❑ 17 Shaun King	.50	.20
❑ 18 Terrell Owens	1.25	.50
❑ 19 Donovan Mcnabb	1.50	.60
❑ 20 Cade Mcnown	.50	.20
❑ 21 Elvis Grbac	.75	.30
❑ 22 James Stewart	.75	.30
❑ 23 Joe Horn	.75	.30
❑ 24 Randy Moss	2.50	1.00
❑ 25 Matt Hasselbeck	.75	.30
❑ 26 Jerome Bettis	1.25	.50
❑ 27 Bill Schroeder	.75	.30
❑ 28 Jake Plummer	.75	.30
❑ 29 Rod Smith	.75	.30
❑ 30 Akili Smith	.50	.20
❑ 31 Jimmy Smith	.75	.30
❑ 32 Oronde Gadsden	.75	.30
❑ 33 Kerry Collins	.75	.30
❑ 34 Warrick Dunn	1.25	.50
❑ 35 Jeff Graham	.50	.20
❑ 36 Ray Lewis	1.25	.50
❑ 37 Joey Galloway	.75	.30
❑ 38 Tim Brown	1.25	.50
❑ 39 Derrick Alexander	.75	.30
❑ 40 Jerry Rice	2.50	1.00
❑ 41 Muhsin Muhammad	.75	.30
❑ 42 Shawn Jefferson	.50	.20
❑ 43 Curtis Martin	1.25	.50
❑ 44 Terry Glenn	.75	.30
❑ 45 Marvin Harrison	1.25	.50
❑ 46 Mike Anderson	1.25	.50
❑ 47 Stephen Davis	1.25	.50
❑ 48 Chad Lewis	.50	.20
❑ 49 Fred Taylor	1.25	.50
❑ 50 Corey Dillon	1.25	.50
❑ 51 Charlie Batch	1.25	.50
❑ 52 Kevin Johnson	.75	.30
❑ 53 Brett Favre	4.00	1.50
❑ 54 Marshall Faulk	1.50	.60
❑ 55 Kordell Stewart	.75	.30
❑ 56 Steve McNair	1.25	.50
❑ 57 Jeff Blake	.75	.30
❑ 58 Eric Moulds	.75	.30
❑ 59 Emmitt Smith	2.50	1.00
❑ 60 David Boston	1.25	.50
❑ 61 Cris Carter	1.25	.50
❑ 62 Peyton Manning	3.00	1.25
❑ 63 Keyshawn Johnson	1.25	.50
❑ 64 Doug Flutie	1.25	.50
❑ 65 Drew Bledsoe	1.50	.60
❑ 66 Ricky Williams	1.25	.50
❑ 67 Keenan Mccardell	.50	.20
❑ 68 Brian Urlacher	2.00	.75
❑ 69 Jamal Lewis	2.00	.75
❑ 70 Ed McCaffrey	1.25	.50
❑ 71 Antonio Freeman	1.25	.50
❑ 72 Darrell Jackson	1.25	.50
❑ 73 Jeff George	.75	.30
❑ 74 Chris Chandler	.75	.30
❑ 75 Germane Crowell	.50	.20
❑ 76 Tim Biakabutuka	.75	.30
❑ 77 Jon Kitna	.75	.30
❑ 78 Troy Brown	.75	.30
❑ 79 Lamar Smith	.75	.30
❑ 80 Derrick Mason	.75	.30
❑ 81 Hines Ward	1.25	.50
❑ 82 Mark Brunell	1.25	.50
❑ 83 Trent Dilfer	.75	.30
❑ 84 Tim Couch	.75	.30
❑ 85 Donald Hayes	.50	.20
❑ 86 Amani Toomer	.75	.30
❑ 87 Tony Gonzalez	.75	.30
❑ 88 Rich Gannon	1.25	.50
❑ 89 Rob Johnson	.75	.30
❑ 90 Torry Holt	1.25	.50
❑ 91 Jeff Garcia	1.25	.50
❑ 92 Kurt Warner	2.50	1.00
❑ 93 Aaron Brooks	1.25	.50
❑ 94 Brian Griese	1.25	.50
❑ 95 James Allen	.75	.30
❑ 96 Wayne Chrebet	.75	.30
❑ 97 Tiki Barber	1.25	.50
❑ 98 Brad Johnson	1.25	.50
❑ 99 Ricky Watters	.75	.30
❑ 100 Charlie Garner	.75	.30
❑ 101 Andre Carter RC	10.00	4.00
❑ 102 Dan Morgan RC	10.00	4.00
❑ 103 Gerard Warren RC	10.00	4.00
❑ 104 Jesse Palmer RC	10.00	4.00
❑ 105 Josh Heupel RC	10.00	4.00
❑ 106 Justin Smith RC	10.00	4.00
❑ 107 LaMont Jordan RC	20.00	10.00
❑ 108 Leonard Davis RC	6.00	2.50
❑ 109 Marques Tuiasosopo RC	10.00	4.00
❑ 110 Snoop Minnis RC	6.00	2.50
❑ 111 Quincy Carter RC	10.00	4.00
❑ 112 Quincy Morgan RC	10.00	4.00
❑ 113 Richard Seymour RC	10.00	4.00
❑ 114 Rudi Johnson RC	20.00	7.50
❑ 115 Sage Rosenfels RC	10.00	4.00
❑ 116 Todd Heap RC	10.00	4.00
❑ 117 Travis Minor RC	6.00	2.50
❑ 118 Will Allen RC	6.00	2.50
❑ 119 Jamal Reynolds RC	10.00	4.00
❑ 120 Scotty Anderson RC	6.00	2.50
❑ 121 Anthony Thomas RC	10.00	4.00
❑ 122 Chad Johnson RC	25.00	10.00
❑ 123 Chris Chambers RC	15.00	6.00
❑ 124 Chris Weinke RC	10.00	4.00
❑ 125 David Terrell RC	10.00	4.00
❑ 126 Deuce McAllister RC	20.00	7.50
❑ 127 Drew Brees RC	40.00	15.00
❑ 128 Freddie Mitchell RC	10.00	4.00
❑ 129 James Jackson RC	10.00	4.00
❑ 130 Kevan Barlow RC	10.00	4.00
❑ 131 Koren Robinson RC	10.00	4.00
❑ 132 LaDainian Tomlinson RC	120.00	60.00
❑ 133 Michael Bennett RC	10.00	4.00
❑ 134 Michael Vick RC	30.00	12.50
❑ 135 Mike McMahon RC	10.00	4.00
❑ 136 Reggie Wayne RC	20.00	7.50
❑ 137 Robert Ferguson RC	10.00	4.00
❑ 138 Rod Gardner RC	10.00	4.00
❑ 139 Santana Moss RC	15.00	6.00
❑ 140 Travis Henry RC	25.00	10.00

2002 Finest

❑ COMP.SET w/o SP's (62)	40.00	15.00
❑ 1 Peyton Manning	2.50	1.00
❑ 2 Troy Brown	.75	.30
❑ 3 Curtis Martin	1.25	.50
❑ 4 Kordell Stewart	.75	.30
❑ 5 Michael Pittman	.50	.20
❑ 6 Rod Gardner	.75	.30
❑ 7 Germane Crowell	.50	.20
❑ 8 Terrell Davis	1.25	.50
❑ 9 Eric Moulds	.75	.30
❑ 10 Jake Plummer	.75	.30
❑ 11 Tony Gonzalez	.75	.30
❑ 12 Ricky Williams	1.25	.50
❑ 13 Deuce McAllister	1.50	.60
❑ 14 Jerry Rice	2.50	1.00
❑ 15 Torry Holt	1.25	.50
❑ 16 Michael Vick	2.50	1.00
❑ 17 David Terrell	1.25	.50
❑ 18 Terry Glenn	.75	.30
❑ 19 Mark Brunell	1.25	.50
❑ 20 Vinny Testaverde	.75	.30
❑ 21 Jerome Bettis	1.25	.50
❑ 22 Randy Moss	2.50	1.00
❑ 23 Marvin Harrison	1.25	.50
❑ 24 Chris Weinke	.75	.30
❑ 25 Tiki Barber	1.25	.50
❑ 26 Corey Bradford	.50	.20

- ❑ 27 David Boston 1.25 .50
- ❑ 28 Emmitt Smith 3.00 1.25
- ❑ 29 Santana Moss 1.25 .50
- ❑ 30 Brian Griese 1.25 .50
- ❑ 31 Priest Holmes 1.50 .60
- ❑ 32 Rich Gannon 1.25 .50
- ❑ 33 Antowain Smith .75 .30
- ❑ 34 Marcus Robinson .75 .30
- ❑ 35 Warrick Dunn 1.25 .50
- ❑ 36 Daunte Culpepper 1.25 .50
- ❑ 37 Shaun Alexander 1.50 .60
- ❑ 38 Kurt Warner 1.25 .50
- ❑ 39 Quincy Carter .75 .30
- ❑ 40 Ray Lewis 1.25 .50
- ❑ 41 Aaron Brooks 1.25 .50
- ❑ 42 Plaxico Burress .75 .30
- ❑ 43 Jamal Lewis 1.25 .50
- ❑ 44 Ahman Green 1.25 .50
- ❑ 45 Rod Smith .75 .30
- ❑ 46 Tim Couch .75 .30
- ❑ 47 Muhsin Muhammad .75 .30
- ❑ 48 Drew Bledsoe 1.50 .60
- ❑ 49 Anthony Thomas .75 .30
- ❑ 50 Tom Brady 3.00 1.25
- ❑ 51 Trent Green .75 .30
- ❑ 52 Charlie Garner .75 .30
- ❑ 53 Darrell Jackson .75 .30
- ❑ 54 Mike McMahon 1.25 .50
- ❑ 55 Donovan McNabb 1.50 .60
- ❑ 56 Fred Taylor 1.25 .50
- ❑ 57 Corey Dillon .75 .30
- ❑ 58 Keyshawn Johnson 1.25 .50
- ❑ 59 Drew Brees 1.25 .50
- ❑ 60 Steve McNair 1.25 .50
- ❑ 61 Jimmy Smith .75 .30
- ❑ 62 Terrell Owens 1.25 .50
- ❑ 63 Eddie George JSY/499 20.00 7.50
- ❑ 64 Jeff Garcia JSY/999 15.00 6.00
- ❑ 65 LaDain Tomlinson JSY/999 25.00 10.00
- ❑ 66 Cris Carter JSY/499 20.00 7.50
- ❑ 67 Chris Chambers JSY/499 20.00 7.50
- ❑ 68 Brian Urlacher JSY/999 25.00 10.00
- ❑ 69 Tim Brown JSY/999 15.00 6.00
- ❑ 70 Marshall Faulk JSY/999 20.00 7.50
- ❑ 71 Stephen Davis JSY/999 12.00 5.00
- ❑ 72 Jevon Kearse JSY/999 12.00 5.00
- ❑ 73 Edgerrin James JSY/999 15.00 6.00
- ❑ 74 Mike Anderson JSY/999 15.00 6.00
- ❑ 75 Warren Sapp JSY/499 20.00 7.50
- ❑ 76 Brett Favre JSY/499 30.00 15.00
- ❑ 77 Julius Peppers RC 6.00 2.50
- ❑ 78 Tim Carter RC 3.00 1.25
- ❑ 79 Travis Stephens RC 3.00 1.25
- ❑ 80 Jabar Gaffney RC 4.00 1.50
- ❑ 81 Cliff Russell RC 3.00 1.25
- ❑ 82 Reche Caldwell RC 4.00 1.50
- ❑ 83 Maurice Morris RC 4.00 1.50
- ❑ 84 Antwaan Randle El RC 5.00 2.00
- ❑ 85 Ladell Betts RC 4.00 1.50
- ❑ 86 Daniel Graham RC 4.00 1.50
- ❑ 87 Jeremy Shockey RC 12.00 5.00
- ❑ 88 Mike Williams RC 3.00 1.25
- ❑ 89 Josh McCown RC 5.00 2.00
- ❑ 90 Rohan Davey RC 4.00 1.50
- ❑ 91 David Garrard RC 8.00 3.00
- ❑ 92 Dwight Freeney RC 6.00 2.50
- ❑ 93 Leonard Henry RC 3.00 1.25
- ❑ 94 Albert Haynesworth RC 3.00 1.25
- ❑ 95 Herb Haygood RC 2.00 .75
- ❑ 96 Kurt Kittner RC 3.00 1.25
- ❑ 97 Jason McAddley RC 3.00 1.25
- ❑ 98 Bryan Thomas RC 3.00 1.25
- ❑ 99 Wendell Bryant RC 2.00 .75
- ❑ 100 Mike Rumph RC 4.00 1.50
- ❑ 101 Chad Hutchinson RC 3.00 1.25
- ❑ 102 Brian Westbrook RC 8.00 3.00
- ❑ 103 Deion Branch RC 6.00 2.50
- ❑ 104 John Henderson RC 4.00 1.50
- ❑ 105 Jerramy Stevens RC 4.00 1.50
- ❑ 106 Tracey Wistrom RC 3.00 1.25
- ❑ 107 Phillip Buchanon RC 4.00 1.50
- ❑ 108 Matt Schobel RC 3.00 1.25
- ❑ 109 Ed Reed RC 6.00 2.50
- ❑ 110 Randy Fasani RC 3.00 1.25
- ❑ 111 Josh Scobey RC 4.00 1.50
- ❑ 112 Luke Staley RC 3.00 1.25
- ❑ 113 Anthony Weaver RC 3.00 1.25
- ❑ 114 Kyle Johnson RC 2.00 .75
- ❑ 115 David Carr AU RC 40.00 20.00
- ❑ 116 Joey Harrington AU RC 25.00 12.50
- ❑ 117 Donte Stallworth AU RC 40.00 15.00
- ❑ 118 Ashley Lelie AU RC 15.00 6.00
- ❑ 119 Patrick Ramsey AU RC 25.00 10.00
- ❑ 120 William Green AU RC 20.00 7.50
- ❑ 121 Josh Reed AU RC 20.00 7.50
- ❑ 122 Clinton Portis AU RC 60.00 30.00
- ❑ 123 Antonio Bryant AU RC 15.00 6.00
- ❑ 124 Javon Walker AU RC 30.00 12.00
- ❑ 125 Roy Williams AU RC 40.00 15.00
- ❑ 126 Marquise Walker AU RC 20.00 7.50
- ❑ 127 Quentin Jammer AU RC 20.00 7.50
- ❑ 128 DeShaun Foster AU RC 25.00 12.50
- ❑ 129 Andre Davis AU RC 20.00 7.50
- ❑ 130 Ron Johnson AU RC 20.00 7.50
- ❑ 131 Lamar Gordon AU RC 20.00 7.50
- ❑ 132 T.J. Duckett AU/300 RC 25.00 10.00
- ❑ 133 Freddie Milons AU RC 20.00 7.50
- ❑ 134 Eric Crouch AU RC 20.00 7.50
- ❑ 135 Adrian Peterson AU RC 25.00 10.00
- ❑ 136 Damien Anderson AU RC 20.00 7.50

2003 Finest

- ❑ COMP.SET w/o SP's (100) 50.00 20.00
- ❑ 101-118 GROUP A ODDS 1:171 MINI-BOXES
- ❑ 101-118 GROUP B ODDS 1:38 MINI-BOXES
- ❑ 101-118 GROUP C ODDS 1:4 MINI-BOXES
- ❑ ROOKIE AU/399 ODDS 1:30 MINI-BOXES
- ❑ ROOKIE AU/999 ODDS 1:3 MINI-BOXES
- ❑ 1 Chad Pennington 1.50 .60
- ❑ 2 Tommy Maddox 1.25 .50
- ❑ 3 Brett Favre 3.00 1.25
- ❑ 4 Eric Moulds .75 .30
- ❑ 5 Randy Moss 2.00 .75
- ❑ 6 Duce Staley .75 .30
- ❑ 7 Derrick Mason .75 .30
- ❑ 8 Shaun Alexander 1.25 .50
- ❑ 9 Peyton Manning 2.00 .75
- ❑ 10 Kerry Collins .75 .30
- ❑ 11 Joe Horn .75 .30
- ❑ 12 Laveranues Coles .75 .30
- ❑ 13 Marty Booker .75 .30
- ❑ 14 Emmitt Smith 3.00 1.25
- ❑ 15 Edgerrin James 1.25 .50
- ❑ 16 Aaron Brooks 1.25 .50
- ❑ 17 Curtis Martin 1.25 .50
- ❑ 18 Hines Ward 1.25 .50
- ❑ 19 Rod Smith .75 .30
- ❑ 20 Priest Holmes 1.50 .60
- ❑ 21 Jerry Rice 2.50 1.00
- ❑ 22 Peerless Price .75 .30
- ❑ 23 Mark Brunell .75 .30
- ❑ 24 Trent Green .75 .30
- ❑ 25 David Boston .75 .30
- ❑ 26 Chris Chambers 1.25 .50
- ❑ 27 Marshall Faulk 1.25 .50
- ❑ 28 Fred Taylor 1.25 .50
- ❑ 29 Tim Couch .50 .20
- ❑ 30 Amani Toomer .75 .30
- ❑ 31 Travis Henry .75 .30
- ❑ 32 Jeff Blake .50 .20
- ❑ 33 Troy Brown .75 .30
- ❑ 34 Charlie Garner .75 .30
- ❑ 35 Tom Brady 3.00 1.25
- ❑ 36 Warrick Dunn .75 .30
- ❑ 37 Plaxico Burress .75 .30
- ❑ 38 Marvin Harrison 1.25 .50
- ❑ 39 Clinton Portis 2.00 .75
- ❑ 40 Deuce McAllister 1.25 .50
- ❑ 41 Matt Hasselbeck .75 .30
- ❑ 42 Jeff Garcia 1.25 .50
- ❑ 43 David Carr 2.00 .75
- ❑ 44 Ahman Green 1.25 .50
- ❑ 45 Eddie George .75 .30
- ❑ 46 Drew Brees 1.25 .50
- ❑ 47 Tiki Barber 1.25 .50
- ❑ 48 Jay Fiedler .75 .30
- ❑ 49 Curtis Conway .75 .30
- ❑ 50 Steve McNair 1.25 .50
- ❑ 51 Donald Driver .75 .30
- ❑ 52 Jake Plummer .75 .30
- ❑ 53 Jamal Lewis 1.25 .50
- ❑ 54 Corey Dillon .75 .30
- ❑ 55 Stephen Davis .75 .30
- ❑ 56 Terrell Owens 1.25 .50
- ❑ 57 Torry Holt 1.25 .50
- ❑ 58 Chad Johnson 1.25 .50
- ❑ 59 Chad Hutchinson .50 .20
- ❑ 60 Kurt Warner 1.25 .50
- ❑ 61 Troy Polamalu RC 20.00 8.00
- ❑ 62 Eugene Wilson RC 3.00 1.25
- ❑ 63 Juston Wood RC 1.50 .60
- ❑ 64 Anquan Boldin RC 8.00 3.00
- ❑ 65 Doug Gabriel RC 3.00 1.25
- ❑ 66 Domanick Davis RC 3.00 1.25
- ❑ 67 J.R. Tolver RC 2.50 1.00
- ❑ 68 Jerome McDougle RC 3.00 1.25
- ❑ 69 Keenan Howry RC 3.00 1.25
- ❑ 70 Teyo Johnson RC 3.00 1.25
- ❑ 71 Bethel Johnson RC 3.00 1.25
- ❑ 72 Ken Hamlin RC 3.00 1.25
- ❑ 73 L.J. Smith RC 3.00 1.25
- ❑ 74 Rashean Mathis RC 1.50 .60
- ❑ 75 Arnaz Battle RC 3.00 1.25
- ❑ 76 B.J. Askew RC 3.00 1.25
- ❑ 77 Mike Doss RC 3.00 1.25
- ❑ 78 Kevin Curtis RC 4.00 1.50
- ❑ 79 Terence Newman RC 6.00 2.50
- ❑ 80 Shaun McDonald RC 3.00 1.25
- ❑ 81 Kevin Williams RC 3.00 1.25
- ❑ 82 Nate Burleson RC 3.00 1.25
- ❑ 83 Tyrone Calico RC 3.00 1.25
- ❑ 84 DeWayne White RC 2.50 1.00
- ❑ 85 Marcus Trufant RC 3.00 1.25
- ❑ 86 Nick Barnett RC 3.00 1.25
- ❑ 87 Bennie Joppru RC 3.00 1.25
- ❑ 88 Andre Woolfolk RC 3.00 1.25
- ❑ 89 Billy McMullen RC 2.50 1.00
- ❑ 90 Boss Bailey RC 3.00 1.25
- ❑ 91 William Joseph RC 3.00 1.25
- ❑ 92 Michael Haynes RC 3.00 1.25
- ❑ 93 DeWayne Robertson RC 3.00 1.25
- ❑ 94 LaTarence Dunbar RC 2.50 1.00
- ❑ 95 David Tyree RC 2.50 1.00
- ❑ 96 Walter Young RC 1.50 .60
- ❑ 97 E.J. Henderson RC 3.00 1.25
- ❑ 98 Ty Warren RC 3.00 1.25
- ❑ 99 Zuriel Smith RC 1.50 .60
- ❑ 100 Brock Forsey RC 3.00 1.25
- ❑ 101 Ricky Williams JSY C 12.00 5.00
- ❑ 102 Drew Bledsoe JSY C 12.00 5.00
- ❑ 103 Joey Harrington JSY C 15.00 6.00
- ❑ 104 Tim Brown JSY C 15.00 6.00
- ❑ 105 Brian Urlacher JSY C 20.00 7.50
- ❑ 106 Zach Thomas JSY C 12.00 5.00
- ❑ 107 Jeremy Shockey JSY C 15.00 6.00
- ❑ 108 Michael Strahan JSY A 12.00 5.00
- ❑ 109 Jason Taylor JSY C 12.00 5.00
- ❑ 110 Donovan McNabb JSY C 20.00 7.50
- ❑ 111 LaDainian Tomlinson JSY B 15.00 6.00
- ❑ 112 Rich Gannon JSY C 12.00 5.00
- ❑ 113 Brad Johnson JSY C 12.00 5.00
- ❑ 114 Daunte Culpepper JSY C 12.00 5.00
- ❑ 115 Michael Vick JSY C 25.00 10.00
- ❑ 116 Jimmy Smith JSY B 10.00 4.00
- ❑ 117 Keyshawn Johnson JSY C 12.00 5.00
- ❑ 118 Keith Brooking JSY C 10.00 4.00
- ❑ 119 Carson Palmer AU/399 RC 150.00 75.00
- ❑ 120 Byron Leftwich AU/399 RC 40.00 15.00
- ❑ 121 Chris Simms AU/399 RC 40.00 15.00
- ❑ 122 Kyle Boller AU/399 RC 25.00 10.00
- ❑ 123 Justin Fargas AU RC 20.00 10.00
- ❑ 124 Seneca Wallace AU RC 15.00 6.00
- ❑ 125 Larry Johnson AU RC 120.00 50.00
- ❑ 126 Kareem Kelly AU RC 15.00 6.00
- ❑ 127 Willis McGahee AU/399 RC 50.00 20.00
- ❑ 128 Kelley Washington AU RC 20.00 10.00
- ❑ 129 Brian St.Pierre AU RC 15.00 6.00
- ❑ 130 Kliff Kingsbury AU RC 15.00 6.00
- ❑ 131 Ken Dorsey AU RC 15.00 6.00
- ❑ 132 Bryant Johnson AU RC 15.00 6.00
- ❑ 133 Dallas Clark AU RC 25.00 10.00

❑ 134 Chris Brown AU RC 20.00 8.00
❑ 135 Taylor Jacobs AU RC 15.00 6.00
❑ 136 Artose Pinner AU RC 15.00 6.00
❑ 137 Lee Suggs AU RC 20.00 7.50
❑ 138 LaBrandon Toefield AU RC 15.00 6.00
❑ 139 Jason Witten AU RC 40.00 20.00
❑ 140 Brad Banks AU RC 15.00 6.00
❑ 141 Earnest Graham AU RC 20.00 8.00
❑ 142 Bobby Wade AU RC 15.00 6.00
❑ 143 Talman Gardner AU RC 15.00 6.00
❑ 144 Justin Gage AU RC 15.00 6.00
❑ 145 Sam Aiken AU RC 15.00 6.00
❑ 146 Musa Smith AU RC 15.00 6.00
❑ 147 Terrell Suggs AU RC 20.00 7.50
❑ 148 Brandon Lloyd AU RC 20.00 7.50
❑ 150 Rex Grossman AU RC 40.00 15.00

2004 Finest

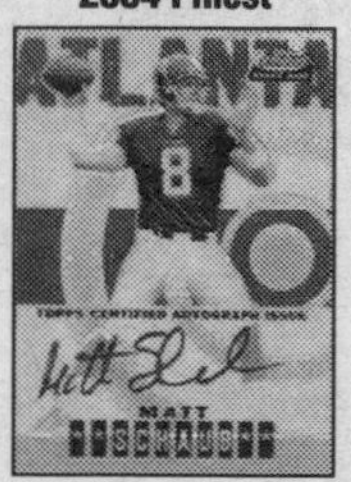

❑ COMP.SET w/o SP's (100) 40.00 15.00
❑ COMP.SET w/o RC's (60) 12.00 5.00
❑ 108-134 AU/399 RC STATED ODDS 1:120
❑ 108-134 AU/999 RC STATED ODDS 1:12
❑ 1 Steve McNair .75 .30
❑ 2 Corey Dillon .50 .20
❑ 3 Joey Harrington .75 .30
❑ 4 Travis Henry .50 .20
❑ 5 Donovan McNabb 1.00 .40
❑ 6 Jamal Lewis .75 .30
❑ 7 Jeff Garcia .75 .30
❑ 8 Fred Taylor .50 .20
❑ 9 Aaron Brooks .50 .20
❑ 10 Marc Bulger .75 .30
❑ 11 Keenan McCardell .30 .10
❑ 12 David Carr .75 .30
❑ 13 Charles Rogers .50 .20
❑ 14 Ray Lewis .75 .30
❑ 15 Priest Holmes 1.00 .40
❑ 16 Curtis Martin .75 .30
❑ 17 Plaxico Burress .50 .20
❑ 18 Shaun Alexander .75 .30
❑ 19 Brad Johnson .50 .20
❑ 20 Marvin Harrison .75 .30
❑ 21 Rod Smith .50 .20
❑ 22 Jake Delhomme .75 .30
❑ 23 Santana Moss .50 .20
❑ 24 Trent Green .50 .20
❑ 25 Michael Vick 1.50 .60
❑ 26 Tim Rattay .30 .10
❑ 27 Chris Chambers .50 .20
❑ 28 Robert Ferguson .30 .10
❑ 29 Tiki Barber .75 .30
❑ 30 Terrell Owens .75 .30
❑ 31 Marshall Faulk .75 .30
❑ 32 Quincy Carter .50 .20
❑ 33 Stephen Davis .50 .20
❑ 34 Josh McCown .50 .20
❑ 35 Jeremy Shockey .75 .30
❑ 36 Tommy Maddox .50 .20
❑ 37 Derrick Mason .50 .20
❑ 38 Kerry Collins .50 .20
❑ 39 Jimmy Smith .50 .20
❑ 40 Chad Pennington .75 .30
❑ 41 Domanick Davis .75 .30
❑ 42 Darrell Jackson .50 .20
❑ 43 Steve Smith .75 .30
❑ 44 Drew Bledsoe .75 .30
❑ 45 Deuce McAllister .75 .30
❑ 46 Jerry Porter .50 .20
❑ 47 Peerless Price .50 .20
❑ 48 Eric Moulds .50 .20
❑ 49 Garrison Hearst .50 .20
❑ 50 Brett Favre 3.00 1.25
❑ 51 Amani Toomer .50 .20
❑ 52 Andre Johnson .75 .30
❑ 53 Edgerrin James .75 .30
❑ 54 Rex Grossman .75 .30
❑ 55 Daunte Culpepper .75 .30
❑ 56 Tony Gonzalez .50 .20
❑ 57 Byron Leftwich 1.00 .40
❑ 58 Mark Brunell .50 .20
❑ 59 Laveranues Coles .50 .20
❑ 60 Matt Hasselbeck .50 .20
❑ 61 Chris Gamble RC 2.00 .75
❑ 62 Michael Turner RC 2.50 1.00
❑ 63 Julius Jones RC 8.00 3.00
❑ 64 Dunta Robinson RC 2.00 .75
❑ 65 Sean Taylor RC 2.00 .75
❑ 66 Ahmad Carroll RC 2.00 .75
❑ 67 Derrick Strait RC 2.00 .75
❑ 68 Dontarrious Thomas RC 2.00 .75
❑ 69 Jason Babin RC 2.00 .75
❑ 70 Reggie Williams RC 2.50 1.00
❑ 71 Dwan Edwards RC 1.00 .40
❑ 72 Rashaun Woods RC 2.00 .75
❑ 73 Ricardo Colclough RC 2.00 .75
❑ 74 Will Smith RC 2.00 .75
❑ 75 Kellen Winslow RC 4.00 1.50
❑ 76 Roy Williams RC 5.00 2.00
❑ 77 B.J. Symons RC 2.00 .75
❑ 78 Carlos Francis RC 1.50 .60
❑ 79 Triandos Luke RC 2.00 .75
❑ 80 Drew Henson RC 2.00 .75
❑ 81 Keiwan Ratliff RC 1.50 .60
❑ 82 Will Poole RC 2.00 .75
❑ 83 Tommie Harris RC 2.00 .75
❑ 84 Steven Jackson RC 6.00 2.50
❑ 85 Greg Jones RC 2.00 .75
❑ 86 Vince Wilfork RC 2.00 .75
❑ 87 DeAngelo Hall RC 2.50 1.00
❑ 88 Daryl Smith RC 2.00 .75
❑ 89 Teddy Lehman RC 2.00 .75
❑ 90 Casey Bramlet RC 1.50 .60
❑ 91 Marcus Tubbs RC 2.00 .75
❑ 92 Andy Hall RC 1.50 .60
❑ 93 Jim Sorgi RC 2.00 .75
❑ 94 Kenechi Udeze RC 2.00 .75
❑ 95 Darius Watts RC 2.00 .75
❑ 96 Tank Johnson RC 1.50 .60
❑ 97 Matt Mauck RC 2.00 .75
❑ 98 Bradlee Van Pelt RC 2.50 1.00
❑ 99 D.J. Williams RC 2.00 .75
❑ 100 Larry Fitzgerald RC 6.00 2.50
❑ 101 Peyton Manning JSY 15.00 6.00
❑ 102 Clinton Portis JSY 8.00 3.00
❑ 103 Chad Johnson JSY 8.00 3.00
❑ 104 Randy Moss JSY 10.00 4.00
❑ 105 Tom Brady JSY 20.00 7.50
❑ 106 LaDainian Tomlinson JSY 10.00 4.00
❑ 107 Ahman Green JSY 8.00 3.00
❑ 108 Roethlisberger AU/399 RC 250.00 125.00
❑ 109 Philip Rivers AU/399 RC 100.00 50.00
❑ 110 Eli Manning AU/399 RC 200.00 125.00
❑ 111 Kevin Jones AU/399 RC 60.00 25.00
❑ 112 Bernard Berrian AU RC 25.00 12.50
❑ 113 Jeff Smoker AU RC 15.00 6.00
❑ 114 Mewelde Moore AU RC 15.00 6.00
❑ 115 Michael Clayton AU RC 30.00 12.50
❑ 116 Jonathan Vilma AU RC 20.00 7.50
❑ 117 Johnnie Morant AU RC 15.00 6.00
❑ 118 Devard Darling AU RC 15.00 6.00
❑ 119 Cedric Cobbs AU RC 15.00 6.00
❑ 120 Chris Perry AU/399 RC 30.00 12.50
❑ 121 Ernest Wilford AU RC 15.00 6.00
❑ 122 Michael Jenkins AU RC 15.00 6.00
❑ 123 Jerricho Cotchery AU RC 15.00 6.00
❑ 124 P.K. Sam AU RC 12.00 5.00
❑ 125 Tatum Bell AU RC 30.00 12.50
❑ 126 Derrick Hamilton AU RC 12.00 5.00
❑ 127 Luke McCown AU RC 15.00 6.00
❑ 128 Devery Henderson AU RC 15.00 6.00
❑ 129 Craig Krenzel AU RC 15.00 6.00
❑ 130 J.P. Losman AU RC 30.00 12.50
❑ 131 Lee Evans AU RC 20.00 10.00
❑ 132 Matt Schaub AU RC 50.00 20.00
❑ 133 Robert Gallery AU RC 15.00 6.00
❑ 134 Keary Colbert AU RC 15.00 6.00

2005 Finest

❑ COMPLETE SET (183)
❑ UNPRICED FRAMED REF. PRINT RUN 1 SET
❑ UNPRICED FRAM.XFRAC. PRINT RUN 1 SET

❑ UNPRICED GOLD XFRAC.PRINT RUN 10 SETS
❑ UNPRICED PRINT.PLATE PRINT RUN 1 SET
❑ UNPRICED SUPERFRACTORS #'d TO 1
❑ 1 Muhsin Muhammad .50 .20
❑ 2 Kevin Jones .75 .30
❑ 3 Eli Manning 1.50 .60
❑ 4 Kevan Barlow .50 .20
❑ 5 Randy Moss .75 .30
❑ 6 Brian Griese .50 .20
❑ 7 Dante Hall .50 .20
❑ 8 Chris Brown .50 .20
❑ 9 Antonio Gates .75 .30
❑ 10 Champ Bailey .50 .20
❑ 11 Eric Moulds .50 .20
❑ 12 Ray Lewis .75 .30
❑ 13 Larry Fitzgerald .75 .30
❑ 14 Byron Leftwich .75 .30
❑ 15 Marvin Harrison .75 .30
❑ 16 Stephen Davis .50 .20
❑ 17 Laveranues Coles .50 .20
❑ 18 Shaun Alexander 1.00 .40
❑ 19 Drew Bledsoe .75 .30
❑ 20 Sean Taylor .50 .20
❑ 21 Deuce McAllister .75 .30
❑ 22 Nate Burleson .50 .20
❑ 23 A.J. Feeley .50 .20
❑ 24 Jerome Bettis .75 .30
❑ 25 Torry Holt .75 .30
❑ 26 LaDainian Tomlinson 1.00 .40
❑ 27 Travis Henry .50 .20
❑ 28 T.J. Houshmandzadeh .40 .15
❑ 29 Fred Taylor .50 .20
❑ 30 Michael Jenkins .50 .20
❑ 31 Edgerrin James .75 .30
❑ 32 Terrell Owens .75 .30
❑ 33 Jason Witten .50 .20
❑ 34 Clinton Portis .75 .30
❑ 35 Deion Branch .50 .20
❑ 36 Priest Holmes .75 .30
❑ 37 Javon Walker .50 .20
❑ 38 Rex Grossman .50 .20
❑ 39 Domanick Davis .50 .20
❑ 40 Allen Rossum .40 .15
❑ 41 Dwight Freeney .50 .20
❑ 42 Jimmy Smith .50 .20
❑ 43 Tiki Barber .75 .30
❑ 44 Steve McNair .75 .30
❑ 45 Steven Jackson 1.00 .40
❑ 46 Joe Horn .50 .20
❑ 47 Randy McMichael .40 .15
❑ 48 J.P. Losman .75 .30
❑ 49 Warrick Dunn .50 .20
❑ 50 Tatum Bell .50 .20
❑ 51 Roy Williams WR .75 .30
❑ 52 Curtis Martin .75 .30
❑ 53 Donovan McNabb 1.00 .40
❑ 54 LaMont Jordan .75 .30
❑ 55 Marc Bulger .75 .30
❑ 56 Drew Bennett .50 .20
❑ 57 Julius Jones 1.00 .40
❑ 58 Santana Moss .50 .20
❑ 59 Michael Bennett .50 .20
❑ 60 Tony Gonzalez .50 .20
❑ 61 Jamal Lewis .75 .30
❑ 62 Keary Colbert .50 .20
❑ 63 Carson Palmer .75 .30
❑ 64 Dunta Robinson .50 .20
❑ 65 Brandon Stokley .50 .20
❑ 66 Brett Favre 2.00 .75
❑ 67 Jonathan Vilma .50 .20
❑ 68 Darrell Jackson .50 .20
❑ 69 Michael Pittman .40 .15

❑ 70 Drew Brees	.75	.30
❑ 71 Amani Toomer	.50	.20
❑ 72 Corey Dillon	.50	.20
❑ 73 Willis McGahee	.75	.30
❑ 74 Michael Vick	1.25	.50
❑ 75 Chad Johnson	.75	.30
❑ 76 Anquan Boldin	.50	.20
❑ 77 Kerry Collins	.50	.20
❑ 78 Marshall Faulk	.75	.30
❑ 79 Roy Williams S	.50	.20
❑ 80 Trent Green	.50	.20
❑ 81 Chris Gamble	.50	.20
❑ 82 Ahman Green	.75	.30
❑ 83 Todd Heap	.50	.20
❑ 84 Brandon Lloyd	.40	.15
❑ 85 Andre Johnson	.50	.20
❑ 86 Lee Suggs	.50	.20
❑ 87 Plaxico Burress	.50	.20
❑ 88 Hines Ward	.75	.30
❑ 89 Rod Smith	.50	.20
❑ 90 Joey Harrington	.75	.30
❑ 91 Derrick Mason	.50	.20
❑ 92 Rudi Johnson	.50	.20
❑ 93 Isaac Bruce	.50	.20
❑ 94 Chris Chambers	.50	.20
❑ 95 Matt Hasselbeck	.50	.20
❑ 96 Donte Stallworth	.50	.20
❑ 97 Philip Rivers	.75	.30
❑ 98 Michael Clayton	.75	.30
❑ 99 Alge Crumpler	.50	.20
❑ 100 Chad Pennington	.75	.30
❑ 101 Brian Westbrook	.50	.20
❑ 102 Daunte Culpepper	.75	.30
❑ 103 Jeremy Shockey	.75	.30
❑ 104 Jerry Porter	.50	.20
❑ 105 Tom Brady	2.00	.75
❑ 106 Lee Evans	.50	.20
❑ 107 Jake Delhomme	.75	.30
❑ 108 Ben Roethlisberger	2.00	.75
❑ 109 Jake Plummer	.50	.20
❑ 110 Charles Rogers	.50	.20
❑ 111 Patrick Ramsey	.50	.20
❑ 112 Reggie Wayne	.50	.20
❑ 113 Reuben Droughns	.50	.20
❑ 114 Aaron Brooks	.50	.20
❑ 115 David Carr	.75	.30
❑ 116 Thomas Jones	.50	.20
❑ 117 Ashley Lelie	.50	.20
❑ 118 Donald Driver	.50	.20
❑ 119 Billy Volek	.50	.20
❑ 120 Peyton Manning	1.25	.50
❑ 121 Frank Gore RC	5.00	2.00
❑ 122 Adam Jones RC	2.50	1.00
❑ 123 Antrel Rolle RC	2.50	1.00
❑ 124 Roddy White RC	2.50	1.00
❑ 125 Derrick Johnson RC	4.00	1.50
❑ 126 Troy Williamson RC	2.50	1.00
❑ 127 Maurice Clarett	2.50	1.00
❑ 128 Dan Orlovsky RC	2.50	1.00
❑ 129 Andrew Walter RC	2.50	1.00
❑ 130 Reggie Brown RC	2.50	1.00
❑ 131 Matt Jones RC	4.00	1.50
❑ 132 David Greene RC	2.50	1.00
❑ 133 Jerome Mathis RC	2.50	1.00
❑ 134 Thomas Davis RC	2.50	1.00
❑ 135 Roscoe Parrish RC	2.50	1.00
❑ 136 Ciatrick Fason RC	2.50	1.00
❑ 137 David Pollack RC	2.50	1.00
❑ 138 Kyle Orton RC	2.50	1.00
❑ 139 Heath Miller RC	5.00	2.00
❑ 140 Courtney Roby RC	2.50	1.00
❑ 141 Terrence Murphy RC	2.50	1.00
❑ 142 DeMarcus Ware RC	4.00	1.50
❑ 143 Fabian Washington RC	2.50	1.00
❑ 144 J.J. Arrington RC	2.50	1.00
❑ 145 Fred Gibson RC	2.00	.75
❑ 146 Carlos Rogers RC	3.00	1.25
❑ 147 Eric Shelton RC	2.50	1.00
❑ 148 Craphonso Thorpe RC	2.00	.75
❑ 149 Anthony Davis RC	2.00	.75
❑ 150 Marion Barber RC	4.00	1.50
❑ 151 Aaron Rodgers AU/299 RC	100.00	50.00
❑ 152 Alex Smith QB AU/299 RC	100.00	40.00
❑ 153 Braylon Edwards AU/299 RC	60.00	30.00
❑ 154 Cadillac Williams AU/299 RC	100.00	40.00
❑ 155 Cedric Benson AU/299 RC	60.00	30.00
❑ 156 Charlie Frye AU/299 RC	40.00	15.00
❑ 157 Jason Campbell AU/299 RC	60.00	35.00
❑ 158 Mark Clayton AU/299 RC	40.00	15.00
❑ 159 Mike Williams AU/299	40.00	15.00
❑ 160 Ronnie Brown AU/299 RC	100.00	40.00
❑ 161 Alex Smith TE AU RC	12.00	5.00
❑ 162 Alvin Pearman AU RC	12.00	5.00
❑ 163 Brandon Jacobs AU RC	30.00	15.00
❑ 164 Channing Crowder AU RC	12.00	5.00
❑ 165 Chris Henry AU RC	15.00	6.00
❑ 166 Courtney Roby AU RC	12.00	5.00
❑ 167 Derek Anderson AU RC	30.00	15.00
❑ 168 Mark Bradley AU RC	15.00	6.00
❑ 169 Ryan Fitzpatrick AU RC	12.00	5.00
❑ 170 Ryan Moats AU RC	20.00	7.50
❑ 171 Stefan LeFors AU RC	12.00	5.00
❑ 172 Steve Savoy AU RC	10.00	4.00
❑ 173 Tab Perry AU RC	12.00	5.00
❑ 174 Timmy Chang AU RC	15.00	6.00
❑ 175 Vincent Jackson AU RC	20.00	8.00
❑ 176 Charles Frederick AU RC	12.00	5.00
❑ 177 Kay-Jay Harris AU RC	10.00	4.00
❑ 178 Darren Sproles AU RC	12.00	5.00
❑ 179 Adrian McPherson AU RC	15.00	6.00
❑ 180 Craig Bragg AU RC	10.00	4.00
❑ 181 J.R. Russell AU RC	10.00	4.00
❑ 182 Gino Guidugli AU RC	10.00	4.00
❑ 183 Vernand Morency AU RC	12.00	5.00

2006 Finest

❑ COMP.SET w/o AU's (150)	30.00	12.50
❑ 1 Muhsin Muhammad	.50	.20
❑ 2 Kevin Jones	.75	.30
❑ 3 Eli Manning	1.00	.40
❑ 4 Marion Barber	.50	.20
❑ 5 Randy Moss	.75	.30
❑ 6 Odell Thurman	.40	.15
❑ 7 Dante Hall	.50	.20
❑ 8 Chris Brown	.50	.20
❑ 9 Antonio Gates	.75	.30
❑ 10 Champ Bailey	.50	.20
❑ 11 Eric Moulds	.50	.20
❑ 12 Ray Lewis	.75	.30
❑ 13 Larry Fitzgerald	.75	.30
❑ 14 Byron Leftwich	.50	.20
❑ 15 Marvin Harrison	.75	.30
❑ 16 Larry Johnson	1.00	.40
❑ 17 Steve Smith	.75	.30
❑ 18 Shaun Alexander	.75	.30
❑ 19 Drew Bledsoe	.75	.30
❑ 20 Joey Galloway	.50	.20
❑ 21 Deuce McAllister	.50	.20
❑ 22 Ben Obomanu RC	3.00	1.25
❑ 23 Chester Taylor	.50	.20
❑ 24 Delanie Walker RC	3.00	1.25
❑ 25 Torry Holt	.50	.20
❑ 26 LaDainian Tomlinson	1.00	.40
❑ 27 Derrick Mason	.40	.15
❑ 28 T.J. Houshmandzadeh	.50	.20
❑ 29 Fred Taylor	.50	.20
❑ 30 Michael Jenkins	.50	.20
❑ 31 Edgerrin James	.75	.30
❑ 32 Terrell Owens	.75	.30
❑ 33 Jason Witten	.50	.20
❑ 34 Clinton Portis	.75	.30
❑ 35 Deion Branch	.50	.20
❑ 36 Priest Holmes	.50	.20
❑ 37 Quinton Ganther RC	3.00	1.25
❑ 38 Kurt Warner	.50	.20
❑ 39 Domanick Davis	.50	.20
❑ 40 Chris Simms	.50	.20
❑ 41 Dwight Freeney	.50	.20
❑ 42 Daniel Bullocks RC	4.00	1.50
❑ 43 Tiki Barber	.75	.30
❑ 44 Steve McNair	.50	.20
❑ 45 Steven Jackson	.75	.30
❑ 46 Joe Horn	.50	.20
❑ 47 Randy McMichael	.40	.15
❑ 48 Cedric Humes RC	4.00	1.50
❑ 49 Warrick Dunn	.50	.20
❑ 50 Tatum Bell	.50	.20
❑ 51 P.J. Pope RC	3.00	1.25
❑ 52 Curtis Martin	.75	.30
❑ 53 Donovan McNabb	.75	.30
❑ 54 LaMont Jordan	.50	.20
❑ 55 Marc Bulger	.50	.20
❑ 56 Drew Bennett	.40	.15
❑ 57 Julius Jones	.75	.30
❑ 58 Santana Moss	.50	.20
❑ 59 Ronnie Brown	.75	.30
❑ 60 Tony Gonzalez	.50	.20
❑ 61 Jamal Lewis	.50	.20
❑ 62 D.J. Shockley RC	4.00	1.50
❑ 63 Carson Palmer	.75	.30
❑ 64 Jonathan Orr RC	3.00	1.25
❑ 65 Brandon Stokley	.50	.20
❑ 66 Brett Favre	1.50	.60
❑ 67 Jonathan Vilma	.50	.20
❑ 68 Darrell Jackson	.50	.20
❑ 69 Brian Urlacher	.75	.30
❑ 70 Drew Brees	.75	.30
❑ 71 Mike Williams	.75	.30
❑ 72 Corey Dillon	.50	.20
❑ 73 Willis McGahee	.75	.30
❑ 74 Michael Vick	.75	.30
❑ 75 Chad Johnson	.50	.20
❑ 76 Anquan Boldin	.50	.20
❑ 77 Shawne Merriman	.50	.20
❑ 78 Willie Parker	1.00	.40
❑ 79 Roy Williams S	.50	.20
❑ 80 Trent Green	.50	.20
❑ 81 Chris Gamble	.40	.15
❑ 82 Ahman Green	.50	.20
❑ 83 Todd Heap	.50	.20
❑ 84 Brett Basanez RC	4.00	1.50
❑ 85 Andre Johnson	.50	.20
❑ 86 Abdul Hodge RC	4.00	1.50
❑ 87 Plaxico Burress	.50	.20
❑ 88 Hines Ward	.75	.30
❑ 89 Rod Smith	.50	.20
❑ 90 Cadillac Williams	.75	.30
❑ 91 Braylon Edwards	.75	.30
❑ 92 Rudi Johnson	.50	.20
❑ 93 Isaac Bruce	.50	.20
❑ 94 Chris Chambers	.50	.20
❑ 95 Matt Hasselbeck	.50	.20
❑ 96 Donte Stallworth	.50	.20
❑ 97 Philip Rivers	.75	.30
❑ 98 Will Blackmon RC	3.00	1.25
❑ 99 Alge Crumpler	.50	.20
❑ 100 Chad Pennington	.50	.20
❑ 101 Darnell Bing RC	4.00	1.50
❑ 102 Daunte Culpepper	.75	.30
❑ 103 Jeremy Shockey	.75	.30
❑ 104 Jerry Porter	.50	.20
❑ 105 Tom Brady	1.25	.50
❑ 106 Jeff Webb RC	3.00	1.25
❑ 107 Jake Delhomme	.50	.20
❑ 108 Ben Roethlisberger	1.25	.50
❑ 109 Jake Plummer	.50	.20
❑ 110 Paul Pinegar RC	3.00	1.25
❑ 111 Kevin McMahan RC	3.00	1.25
❑ 112 Reggie Wayne	.50	.20
❑ 113 Bennie Brazell RC	3.00	1.25
❑ 114 Todd Watkins RC	3.00	1.25
❑ 115 David Carr	.50	.20
❑ 116 Cory Rodgers RC	4.00	1.50
❑ 117 Leon Washington RC	6.00	2.50
❑ 118 Michael Strahan	.50	.20
❑ 119 P.J. Daniels RC	3.00	1.25
❑ 120 Peyton Manning	1.25	.50
❑ 121 Brandon Marshall RC	4.00	1.50
❑ 122 Jerome Harrison RC	4.00	1.50
❑ 123 Mario Williams RC	6.00	2.50
❑ 124 Ernie Sims RC	5.00	2.00
❑ 125 Devin Hester RC	8.00	3.00
❑ 126 Jimmy Williams RC	4.00	1.50
❑ 127 Charlie Whitehurst RC	4.00	1.50
❑ 128 Jason Avant RC	4.00	1.50
❑ 129 Marcus Vick RC	3.00	1.25
❑ 130 Mathias Kiwanuka RC	5.00	2.00
❑ 131 Brodrick Bunkley RC	4.00	1.50
❑ 132 Reggie McNeal RC	3.00	1.25
❑ 133 Dominique Byrd RC	3.00	1.25

❑ 134 Jason Allen RC	4.00	1.50
❑ 135 D'Qwell Jackson RC	3.00	1.25
❑ 136 Donte Whitner RC	4.00	1.50
❑ 137 Willie Reid RC	4.00	1.50
❑ 138 Kamerion Wimbley RC	4.00	1.50
❑ 139 Martin Nance RC	3.00	1.25
❑ 140 Haloti Ngata RC	4.00	1.50
❑ 141 Devin Aromashodu RC	3.00	1.25
❑ 142 Jeremy Bloom RC	3.00	1.25
❑ 143 Manny Lawson RC	4.00	1.50
❑ 144 Johnathan Joseph RC	3.00	1.25
❑ 145 Brad Smith RC	4.00	1.50
❑ 146 Thomas Howard RC	4.00	1.50
❑ 147 Demetrius Williams RC	4.00	1.50
❑ 148 Antonio Cromartie RC	4.00	1.50
❑ 149 Bobby Carpenter RC	4.00	1.50
❑ 150 Tamba Hali RC	4.00	1.50
❑ 151 Reggie Bush AU/199 RC	200.00	100.00
❑ 152 Matt Leinart AU/199 RC	150.00	75.00
❑ 153 Vince Young AU/199 RC	200.00	100.00
❑ 154 Jay Cutler AU/199 RC	150.00	75.00
❑ 155 S.Holmes AU/199 RC	40.00	15.00
❑ 156 LenDale White AU/199 RC	50.00	20.00
❑ 157 DeA.Williams AU/199 RC	80.00	40.00
❑ 158 Sinorice Moss AU/199 RC	20.00	8.00
❑ 159 Vernon Davis AU/199 RC	40.00	15.00
❑ 160 Joseph Addai AU/199 RC	100.00	50.00
❑ 161 Omar Jacobs AU/199 RC	20.00	8.00
❑ 162 Chad Jackson AU/199 RC	20.00	8.00
❑ 163 Chad Greenway AU RC	12.00	5.00
❑ 164 Maurice Drew AU RC	50.00	25.00
❑ 165 D.Ferguson AU RC	12.00	5.00
❑ 166 Anthony Fasano AU RC	12.00	5.00
❑ 167 Derek Hagan AU/199 RC	20.00	8.00
❑ 168 A.J. Hawk AU/199 RC	100.00	50.00
❑ 169 David Thomas AU RC	12.00	5.00
❑ 170 Brian Calhoun AU RC	12.00	5.00
❑ 171 Kellen Clemens AU RC	20.00	10.00
❑ 172 Tarvaris Jackson AU RC	25.00	12.50
❑ 173 M.Stovall AU RC EXCH	12.00	5.00
❑ 174 Michael Huff AU/199 RC	30.00	12.50
❑ 175 Greg Jennings AU RC	30.00	15.00
❑ 176 Joe Klopfenstein AU RC	10.00	4.00
❑ 177 Leonard Pope AU RC	12.00	5.00
❑ 178 Michael Robinson AU RC	12.00	5.00
❑ 179 Ingle Martin AU RC	10.00	4.00
❑ 180 Wali Lundy AU RC	12.00	5.00
❑ 181 Drew Olson AU RC	10.00	4.00
❑ 182 Jerious Norwood AU RC	30.00	12.00
❑ 183 Travis Wilson AU RC	12.00	5.00
❑ 184 Tye Hill AU RC	12.00	5.00
❑ 185 Brandon Williams AU RC	12.00	5.00
❑ 186 Marques Hagans AU RC	10.00	4.00

2007 Finest

❑ COMPLETE SET (150)	60.00	30.00
❑ 1 Peyton Manning	1.25	.50
❑ 2 Drew Brees	.60	.25
❑ 3 Donovan McNabb	.75	.30
❑ 4 Tony Romo	1.50	.60
❑ 5 Carson Palmer	.75	.30
❑ 6 Mark Bulger	.60	.25
❑ 7 Philip Rivers	.75	.30
❑ 8 Tom Brady	1.50	.60
❑ 9 J.P. Losman	.60	.25
❑ 10 Steve McNair	.60	.25
❑ 11 Eli Manning	.75	.30
❑ 12 Matt Hasselbeck	.60	.25
❑ 13 Alex Smith QB	.75	.30
❑ 14 Ben Roethlisberger	1.00	.40
❑ 15 Matt Leinart	.75	.30
❑ 16 Rex Grossman	.60	.25
❑ 17 Brett Favre	1.50	.60
❑ 18 Vince Young	1.00	.40
❑ 19 Jay Cutler	.75	.30
❑ 20 Chad Pennington	.60	.25
❑ 21 LaDainian Tomlinson	1.00	.40
❑ 22 Larry Johnson	.75	.30
❑ 23 Frank Gore	.75	.30
❑ 24 Steven Jackson	.75	.30
❑ 25 Willie Parker	.75	.30
❑ 26 Rudi Johnson	.60	.25
❑ 27 Brian Westbrook	.60	.25
❑ 28 Chester Taylor	.50	.20
❑ 29 Travis Henry	.60	.25
❑ 30 Thomas Jones	.60	.25
❑ 31 Edgerrin James	.75	.30
❑ 32 Fred Taylor	.60	.25
❑ 33 Warrick Dunn	.60	.25
❑ 34 Jamal Lewis	.60	.25
❑ 35 Julius Jones	.60	.25
❑ 36 Joseph Addai	1.00	.40
❑ 37 Ahman Green	.60	.25
❑ 38 Deuce McAllister	.60	.25
❑ 39 Ronnie Brown	.60	.25
❑ 40 Maurice Jones-Drew	.75	.30
❑ 41 DeShaun Foster	.60	.25
❑ 42 Shaun Alexander	.60	.25
❑ 43 Cadillac Williams	.60	.25
❑ 44 Laurence Maroney	.75	.30
❑ 45 Cedric Benson	.60	.25
❑ 46 Dominic Rhodes	.60	.25
❑ 47 Jerious Norwood	.60	.25
❑ 48 Brandon Jacobs	.60	.25
❑ 49 DeAngelo Williams	.75	.30
❑ 50 Willis McGahee	.60	.25
❑ 51 Clinton Portis	.60	.25
❑ 52 Chad Johnson	.60	.25
❑ 53 Marvin Harrison	.75	.30
❑ 54 Roy Williams WR	.60	.25
❑ 55 Reggie Wayne	.60	.25
❑ 56 Donald Driver	.60	.25
❑ 57 Lee Evans	.60	.25
❑ 58 Anquan Boldin	.60	.25
❑ 59 Torry Holt	.60	.25
❑ 60 Terrell Owens	.75	.30
❑ 61 Steve Smith	.60	.25
❑ 62 Andre Johnson	.60	.25
❑ 63 Laveraneus Coles	.60	.25
❑ 64 Javon Walker	.60	.25
❑ 65 T.J. Houshmandzadeh	.60	.25
❑ 66 Marques Colston	.75	.30
❑ 67 Terry Glenn	.60	.25
❑ 68 Plaxico Burress	.60	.25
❑ 69 Hines Ward	.75	.30
❑ 70 Jerricho Cotchery	.50	.20
❑ 71 Larry Fitzgerald	.60	.25
❑ 72 Braylon Edwards	.60	.25
❑ 73 Santana Moss	.60	.25
❑ 74 Santonio Holmes	.60	.25
❑ 75 Mike Furrey	.60	.25
❑ 76 Isaac Bruce	.60	.25
❑ 77 Derrick Mason	.50	.20
❑ 78 Randy Moss	.75	.30
❑ 79 Greg Jennings	.60	.25
❑ 80 Devin Hester	.75	.30
❑ 81 Muhsin Muhammad	.60	.25
❑ 82 Kellen Winslow	.60	.25
❑ 83 Todd Heap	.50	.20
❑ 84 Tony Gonzalez	.60	.25
❑ 85 Antonio Gates	.60	.25
❑ 86 Jeremy Shockey	.60	.25
❑ 87 Jason Witten	.60	.25
❑ 88 Randy McMichael	.50	.20
❑ 89 Alge Crumpler	.60	.25
❑ 90 L.J. Smith	.50	.20
❑ 91 Champ Bailey	.60	.25
❑ 92 DeAngelo Hall	.60	.25
❑ 93 Asante Samuel	.50	.20
❑ 94 Julius Peppers	.60	.25
❑ 95 Jason Taylor	.50	.20
❑ 96 Michael Strahan	.60	.25
❑ 97 Shawne Merriman	.60	.25
❑ 98 Brian Urlacher	.75	.30
❑ 99 Troy Polamalu	.75	.30
❑ 100 Ed Reed	.60	.25
❑ 101 JaMarcus Russell RC	10.00	4.00
❑ 102 Brady Quinn RC	12.00	5.00
❑ 103 John Beck RC	8.00	3.00
❑ 104 Kevin Kolb RC	6.00	2.50
❑ 105 Trent Edwards RC	8.00	3.00
❑ 106 Troy Smith RC	5.00	2.00
❑ 107 Drew Stanton RC	5.00	2.00
❑ 108 Chris Leak RC	3.00	1.25
❑ 109 Jordan Palmer RC	4.00	1.50
❑ 110 Drew Tate RC	3.00	1.25
❑ 111 Isaiah Stanback RC	4.00	1.50
❑ 112 Adrian Peterson RC	30.00	12.00
❑ 113 Marshawn Lynch RC	8.00	3.00
❑ 114 Brandon Jackson RC	5.00	2.00
❑ 115 Kenny Irons RC	4.00	1.50
❑ 116 Michael Bush RC	5.00	2.00
❑ 117 Lorenzo Booker RC	4.00	1.50
❑ 118 Brian Leonard RC	5.00	2.00
❑ 119 Garrett Wolfe RC	5.00	2.00
❑ 120 Antonio Pittman RC	3.00	1.25
❑ 121 Selvin Young RC	5.00	2.00
❑ 122 Chris Henry RB RC	4.00	1.50
❑ 123 Tony Hunt RC	4.00	1.50
❑ 124 Kenneth Darby RC	4.00	1.50
❑ 125 Kolby Smith RC	5.00	2.00
❑ 126 Darius Walker RC	4.00	1.50
❑ 127 Greg Olsen RC	5.00	2.00
❑ 128 Dwayne Bowe RC	8.00	3.00
❑ 129 Craig Buster Davis RC	4.00	1.50
❑ 130 Ted Ginn Jr. RC	6.00	2.50
❑ 131 Anthony Gonzalez RC	6.00	2.50
❑ 132 Yamon Figurs RC	4.00	1.50
❑ 133 Jason Hill RC	4.00	1.50
❑ 134 Dwayne Jarrett RC	5.00	2.00
❑ 135 Calvin Johnson RC	12.00	5.00
❑ 136 Robert Meachem RC	4.00	1.50
❑ 137 Sidney Rice RC	6.00	2.50
❑ 138 Steve Smith USC RC	5.00	2.00
❑ 139 Paul Williams RC	3.00	1.25
❑ 140 Steve Breaston RC	3.00	1.25
❑ 141 David Clowney RC	4.00	1.50
❑ 142 Aundrea Allison RC	3.00	1.25
❑ 143 Ryne Robinson RC	3.00	1.25
❑ 144 Joe Thomas RC	4.00	1.50
❑ 145 Leon Hall RC	3.00	1.25
❑ 146 Gaines Adams RC	4.00	1.50
❑ 147 LaRon Landry RC	5.00	2.00
❑ 148 Amobi Okoye RC	4.00	1.50
❑ 149 Patrick Willis RC	8.00	3.00
❑ 150 Lawrence Timmons RC	4.00	1.50

1960 Fleer

❑ COMPLETE SET (132)	750.00	500.00
❑ WRAPPER (5-CENT)	25.00	20.00
❑ 1 Harvey White RC !	20.00	12.00
❑ 2 Tom Corky Tharp	3.50	2.00
❑ 3 Dan McGrew	3.50	2.00
❑ 4 Bob White	3.50	2.00
❑ 5 Dick Jamieson	3.50	2.00
❑ 6 Sam Salerno	3.50	2.00
❑ 7 Sid Gillman RC CO !	20.00	12.00
❑ 8 Ben Preston	3.50	2.00
❑ 9 George Blanch	3.50	2.00
❑ 10 Bob Stransky	3.50	2.00
❑ 11 Fran Curci	3.50	2.00
❑ 12 George Shirkey	3.50	2.00
❑ 13 Paul Larson	3.50	2.00
❑ 14 John Stolte	3.50	2.00
❑ 15 Serafino Fazio RC	5.00	2.50
❑ 16 Tom Dimitroff	3.50	2.00
❑ 17 Elbert Dubenion RC	12.00	6.00
❑ 18 Hogan Wharton	3.50	2.00
❑ 19 Tom O'Connell	3.50	2.00
❑ 20 Sammy Baugh CO	50.00	30.00
❑ 21 Tony Sardisco	3.50	2.00
❑ 22 Alan Cann	3.50	2.00
❑ 23 Mike Hudock	3.50	2.00

Card	NRMT	VG-E
❑ 24 Bill Atkins	3.50	2.00
❑ 25 Charlie Jackson	3.50	2.00
❑ 26 Frank Tripucka	6.00	3.00
❑ 27 Tony Teresa	3.50	2.00
❑ 28 Joe Amstutz	3.50	2.00
❑ 29 Bob Fee RC	3.50	2.00
❑ 30 Jim Baldwin	3.50	2.00
❑ 31 Jim Yates	3.50	2.00
❑ 32 Don Flynn	3.50	2.00
❑ 33 Ken Adamson	3.50	2.00
❑ 34 Ron Drzewiecki	3.50	2.00
❑ 35 J.W. Slack	3.50	2.00
❑ 36 Bob Yates	3.50	2.00
❑ 37 Gary Cobb	3.50	2.00
❑ 38 Jacky Lee RC	5.00	2.50
❑ 39 [illegible]	3.00	1.50
❑ 40 Jim Padgett	3.50	2.00
❑ 41 Jack Larscheid UER RC	3.50	2.00
❑ 42 Bob Reifsnyder RC	3.50	2.00
❑ 43 Fran Rogel	3.50	2.00
❑ 44 Ray Moss	3.50	2.00
❑ 45 Tony Banfield RC	5.00	2.50
❑ 46 George Herring	3.50	2.00
❑ 47 Willie Smith RC	3.50	2.00
❑ 48 Buddy Allen	3.50	2.00
❑ 49 Bill Brown LB	3.50	2.00
❑ 50 Ken Ford RC	3.50	2.00
❑ 51 Billy Kinard	3.50	2.00
❑ 52 Buddy Mayfield	3.50	2.00
❑ 53 Bill Krisher	3.50	2.00
❑ 54 Frank Bernardi	3.50	2.00
❑ 55 Lou Saban RC CO	5.00	2.50
❑ 56 Gene Cockrell	3.50	2.00
❑ 57 Sam Sanders	3.50	2.00
❑ 58 George Blanda	50.00	30.00
❑ 59 Sherrill Headrick RC	5.00	2.50
❑ 60 Carl Larpenter	3.50	2.00
❑ 61 Gene Prebola	3.50	2.00
❑ 62 Dick Chorovich	3.50	2.00
❑ 63 Bob McNamara	3.50	2.00
❑ 64 Tom Saidock	3.50	2.00
❑ 65 Willie Evans	3.50	2.00
❑ 66 Billy Cannon RC UER	18.00	10.00
❑ 67 Sam McCord	3.50	2.00
❑ 68 Mike Simmons	3.50	2.00
❑ 69 Jim Swink RC	5.00	2.50
❑ 70 Don Hitt	3.50	2.00
❑ 71 Gerhard Schwedes	3.50	2.00
❑ 72 Thurlow Cooper	3.50	2.00
❑ 73 Abner Haynes RC	18.00	10.00
❑ 74 Billy Shoemake	3.50	2.00
❑ 75 Marv Lasater	3.50	2.00
❑ 76 Paul Lowe RC	15.00	7.50
❑ 77 Bruce Hartman	3.50	2.00
❑ 78 Blanche Martin	3.50	2.00
❑ 79 Gene Grabosky	3.50	2.00
❑ 80 Lou Rymkus CO	5.00	2.50
❑ 81 Chris Burford RC	8.00	4.00
❑ 82 Don Allen	3.50	2.00
❑ 83 Bob Nelson C	3.50	2.00
❑ 84 Jim Woodard	3.50	2.00
❑ 85 Tom Rychlec	3.50	2.00
❑ 86 Bob Cox	3.50	2.00
❑ 87 Jerry Cornelison	3.50	2.00
❑ 88 Jack Work	3.50	2.00
❑ 89 Sam DeLuca	3.50	2.00
❑ 90 Rommie Loudd	3.50	2.00
❑ 91 Teddy Edmondson	3.50	2.00
❑ 92 Buster Ramsey CO	3.50	2.00
❑ 93 Doug Asad	3.50	2.00
❑ 94 Jimmy Harris	3.50	2.00
❑ 95 Larry Cundiff	3.50	2.00
❑ 96 Richie Lucas RC	6.00	3.00
❑ 97 Don Norwood	3.50	2.00
❑ 98 Larry Grantham RC	5.00	2.50
❑ 99 Bill Mathis RC	6.00	3.00
❑ 100 Mel Branch RC	5.00	2.50
❑ 101 Marvin Terrell	3.50	2.00
❑ 102 Charlie Flowers	3.50	2.00
❑ 103 John McMullan	3.50	2.00
❑ 104 Charlie Kaaihue	3.50	2.00
❑ 105 Joe Schaffer	3.50	2.00
❑ 106 Al Day	3.50	2.00
❑ 107 Johnny Carson	3.50	2.00
❑ 108 Alan Goldstein	3.50	2.00
❑ 109 Doug Cline	3.50	2.00
❑ 110 Al Carmichael	3.50	2.00
❑ 111 Bob Dee	3.50	2.00
❑ 112 John Bredice	3.50	2.00
❑ 113 Don Floyd	3.50	2.00
❑ 114 Ronnie Cain	3.50	2.00
❑ 115 Stan Flowers	3.50	2.00
❑ 116 Hank Stram RC CO	40.00	25.00
❑ 117 Bob Dougherty	3.50	2.00
❑ 118 Ron Mix RC	40.00	25.00
❑ 119 Roger Ellis	3.50	2.00
❑ 120 Elvin Caldwell	3.50	2.00
❑ 121 Bill Kimber	3.50	2.00
❑ 122 Jim Matheny	3.50	2.00
❑ 123 Curley Johnson RC	3.50	2.00
❑ 124 Jack Kemp RC	175.00	90.00
❑ 125 Ed Denk	3.50	2.00
❑ 126 Jerry McFarland	3.50	2.00
❑ 127 Dan Lanphear	3.50	2.00
❑ 128 Paul Maguire RC	18.00	10.00
❑ 129 Ray Collins	3.50	2.00
❑ 130 Ron Burton RC	6.00	3.00
❑ 131 Eddie Erdelatz CO	3.50	2.00
❑ 132 Ron Beagle RC !	15.00	7.50

1961 Fleer

DON MAYNARD

Card	NRMT	VG-E
❑ COMPLETE SET (220)	1600.00	1000.00
❑ COMMON CARD (1-132)	4.00	2.50
❑ COMMON CARD (133-220)	6.00	3.50
❑ WRAPPER (5-CENT, SER.1)	25.00	20.00
❑ WRAPPER (5-CENT, SER.2)	30.00	25.00
❑ 1 Ed Brown !	15.00	7.50
❑ 2 Rick Casares	6.00	3.00
❑ 3 Willie Galimore	6.00	3.00
❑ 4 Jim Dooley	4.00	2.50
❑ 5 Harlon Hill	4.00	2.50
❑ 6 Stan Jones	7.00	3.50
❑ 7 J.C. Caroline	4.00	2.50
❑ 8 Joe Fortunato	4.00	2.50
❑ 9 Doug Atkins	8.00	4.00
❑ 10 Milt Plum	6.00	3.00
❑ 11 Jim Brown	150.00	90.00
❑ 12 Bobby Mitchell	10.00	5.00
❑ 13 Ray Renfro	6.00	3.00
❑ 14 Gern Nagler	4.00	2.50
❑ 15 Jim Shofner	4.00	2.50
❑ 16 Vince Costello	4.00	2.50
❑ 17 Galen Fiss	4.00	2.50
❑ 18 Walt Michaels	6.00	3.00
❑ 19 Bob Gain	4.00	2.50
❑ 20 Mal Hammack	4.00	2.50
❑ 21 Frank Mestnik RC	4.00	2.50
❑ 22 Bobby Joe Conrad	6.00	3.00
❑ 23 John David Crow	6.00	3.00
❑ 24 Sonny Randle RC	6.00	3.00
❑ 25 Don Gillis	4.00	2.50
❑ 26 Jerry Norton	4.00	2.50
❑ 27 Bill Stacy	4.00	2.50
❑ 28 Leo Sugar	4.00	2.50
❑ 29 Frank Fuller	4.00	2.50
❑ 30 Johnny Unitas	60.00	35.00
❑ 31 Alan Ameche	7.00	3.50
❑ 32 Lenny Moore	15.00	7.50
❑ 33 Raymond Berry	15.00	7.50
❑ 34 Jim Mutscheller	4.00	2.50
❑ 35 Jim Parker	7.00	3.50
❑ 36 Bill Pellington	4.00	2.50
❑ 37 Gino Marchetti	10.00	5.00
❑ 38 Gene Lipscomb	7.00	3.50
❑ 39 Art Donovan	15.00	7.50
❑ 40 Eddie LeBaron	6.00	3.00
❑ 41 Don Meredith RC	150.00	90.00
❑ 42 Don McIlhenny	4.00	2.50
❑ 43 L.G. Dupre	4.00	2.50
❑ 44 Fred Dugan	4.00	2.50
❑ 45 Billy Howton	6.00	3.00
❑ 46 Duane Putnam	4.00	2.50
❑ 47 Gene Cronin	4.00	2.50
❑ 48 Jerry Tubbs	4.00	2.50
❑ 49 Clarence Peaks	4.00	2.50
❑ 50 Ted Dean RC	4.00	2.50
❑ 51 Tommy McDonald	8.00	4.00
❑ 52 Bill Barnes	4.00	2.50
❑ 53 Pete Retzlaff	6.00	3.00
❑ 54 Bobby Walston	4.00	2.50
❑ 55 Chuck Bednarik	12.00	6.00
❑ 56 Maxie Baughan RC	6.00	3.00
❑ 57 Bob Pellegrini	4.00	2.50
❑ 58 Jesse Richardson	4.00	2.50
❑ 59 John Brodie RC	50.00	30.00
❑ 60 J.D. Smith RB	6.00	3.00
❑ 61 Ray Norton RC	4.00	2.50
❑ 62 Monty Stickles RC	4.00	2.50
❑ 63 Bob St.Clair	7.00	3.50
❑ 64 Dave Baker	4.00	2.50
❑ 65 Abe Woodson	4.00	2.50
❑ 66 Matt Hazeltine	4.00	2.50
❑ 67 Leo Nomellini	10.00	5.00
❑ 68 Charley Conerly	10.00	5.00
❑ 69 Kyle Rote	7.00	3.50
❑ 70 Jack Stroud	4.00	2.50
❑ 71 Roosevelt Brown	7.00	3.50
❑ 72 Jim Patton	4.00	2.50
❑ 73 Erich Barnes	4.00	2.50
❑ 74 Sam Huff	15.00	7.50
❑ 75 Andy Robustelli	10.00	5.00
❑ 76 Dick Modzelewski	4.00	2.50
❑ 77 Roosevelt Grier	7.00	3.50
❑ 78 Earl Morrall	7.00	3.50
❑ 79 Jim Ninowski	4.00	2.50
❑ 80 Nick Pietrosante RC	6.00	3.00
❑ 81 Howard Cassady	6.00	3.00
❑ 82 Jim Gibbons	4.00	2.50
❑ 83 Gail Cogdill RC	6.00	3.00
❑ 84 Dick Lane	7.00	3.50
❑ 85 Yale Lary	7.00	3.50
❑ 86 Joe Schmidt	8.00	4.00
❑ 87 Darris McCord	4.00	2.50
❑ 88 Bart Starr	60.00	35.00
❑ 89 Jim Taylor	50.00	30.00
❑ 90 Paul Hornung	55.00	30.00
❑ 91 Tom Moore RC	8.00	4.00
❑ 92 Boyd Dowler RC	15.00	7.50
❑ 93 Max McGee	7.00	3.50
❑ 94 Forrest Gregg	8.00	4.00
❑ 95 Jerry Kramer	10.00	5.00
❑ 96 Jim Ringo	8.00	4.00
❑ 97 Bill Forester	6.00	3.00
❑ 98 Frank Ryan	6.00	3.00
❑ 99 Ollie Matson	12.00	6.00
❑ 100 Jon Arnett	6.00	3.00
❑ 101 Dick Bass RC	6.00	3.00
❑ 102 Jim Phillips	4.00	2.50
❑ 103 Del Shofner	6.00	3.00
❑ 104 Art Hunter	4.00	2.50
❑ 105 Lindon Crow	4.00	2.50
❑ 106 Les Richter	6.00	3.00
❑ 107 Lou Michaels	4.00	2.50
❑ 108 Ralph Guglielmi	4.00	2.50
❑ 109 Don Bosseler	4.00	2.50
❑ 110 John Olszewski	4.00	2.50
❑ 111 Bill Anderson	4.00	2.50
❑ 112 Joe Walton	4.00	2.50
❑ 113 Jim Schrader	4.00	2.50
❑ 114 Gary Glick	4.00	2.50
❑ 115 Ralph Felton	4.00	2.50
❑ 116 Bob Toneff	4.00	2.50
❑ 117 Bobby Layne	40.00	25.00
❑ 118 John Henry Johnson	7.00	3.50
❑ 119 Tom Tracy	6.00	3.00
❑ 120 Jimmy Orr RC	7.00	3.50
❑ 121 John Nisby	4.00	2.50
❑ 122 Dean Derby	4.00	2.50
❑ 123 John Reger	4.00	2.50
❑ 124 George Tarasovic	4.00	2.50
❑ 125 Ernie Stautner	10.00	5.00
❑ 126 George Shaw	4.00	2.50
❑ 127 Hugh McElhenny	12.00	6.00
❑ 128 Dick Haley	4.00	2.50
❑ 129 Dave Middleton	4.00	2.50
❑ 130 Perry Richards	4.00	2.50
❑ 131 Gene Johnson DB	4.00	2.50
❑ 132 Don Joyce !	4.00	2.50
❑ 133 Johnny Green !	8.00	4.00
❑ 134 Wray Carlton RC	8.00	4.00

❑ 135 Richie Lucas 8.00 4.00
❑ 136 Elbert Dubenion ! 8.00 4.00
❑ 137 Tom Rychlec 6.00 3.50
❑ 138 Mack Yoho 6.00 3.50
❑ 139 Phil Blazer 6.00 3.50
❑ 140 Dan McGrew 6.00 3.50
❑ 141 Bill Atkins 6.00 3.50
❑ 142 Archie Matsos RC 6.00 3.50
❑ 143 Gene Grabosky 6.00 3.50
❑ 144 Frank Tripucka 10.00 5.00
❑ 145 Al Carmichael 6.00 3.50
❑ 146 Bob McNamara 6.00 3.50
❑ 147 Lionel Taylor RC 15.00 7.50
❑ 148 Eldon Danenhauer 6.00 3.50
❑ 149 Willie Smith 6.00 3.50
❑ 150 Carl Larpenter 6.00 3.50
❑ 151 Ken Adamson 6.00 3.50
❑ 152 Goose Gonsoulin RC UER 10.00 5.00
❑ 153 Joe Young 6.00 3.50
❑ 154 Gordy Holz RC 6.00 3.50
❑ 155 Jack Kemp 120.00 60.00
❑ 156 Charlie Flowers 6.00 3.50
❑ 157 Paul Lowe 10.00 5.00
❑ 158 Don Norton 6.00 3.50
❑ 159 Howard Clark 6.00 3.50
❑ 160 Paul Maguire 15.00 7.50
❑ 161 Ernie Wright RC 8.00 4.00
❑ 162 Ron Mix 15.00 7.50
❑ 163 Fred Cole 6.00 3.50
❑ 164 Jim Sears 6.00 3.50
❑ 165 Volney Peters 6.00 3.50
❑ 166 George Blanda 45.00 25.00
❑ 167 Jacky Lee 8.00 4.00
❑ 168 Bob White 6.00 3.50
❑ 169 Doug Cline 6.00 3.50
❑ 170 Dave Smith RB 6.00 3.50
❑ 171 Billy Cannon 15.00 7.50
❑ 172 Bill Groman 6.00 3.50
❑ 173 Al Jamison 6.00 3.50
❑ 174 Jim Norton 6.00 3.50
❑ 175 Dennit Morris 6.00 3.50
❑ 176 Don Floyd 6.00 3.50
❑ 177 Butch Songin 6.00 3.50
❑ 178 Billy Lott 6.00 3.50
❑ 179 Ron Burton 10.00 5.00
❑ 180 Jim Colclough 6.00 3.50
❑ 181 Charley Leo 6.00 3.50
❑ 182 Walt Cudzik 6.00 3.50
❑ 183 Fred Bruney 6.00 3.50
❑ 184 Ross O'Hanley 6.00 3.50
❑ 185 Tony Sardisco 6.00 3.50
❑ 186 Harry Jacobs 6.00 3.50
❑ 187 Bob Dee 6.00 3.50
❑ 188 Tom Flores RC 30.00 15.00
❑ 189 Jack Larscheid 6.00 3.50
❑ 190 Dick Christy 6.00 3.50
❑ 191 Alan Miller RC 6.00 3.50
❑ 192 James Smith 6.00 3.50
❑ 193 Gerald Burch 6.00 3.50
❑ 194 Gene Prebola 6.00 3.50
❑ 195 Alan Goldstein 6.00 3.50
❑ 196 Don Manoukian 6.00 3.50
❑ 197 Jim Otto RC 75.00 40.00
❑ 198 Wayne Crow 6.00 3.50
❑ 199 Cotton Davidson RC 8.00 4.00
❑ 200 Randy Duncan RC 8.00 4.00
❑ 201 Jack Spikes 8.00 4.00
❑ 202 Johnny Robinson RC 15.00 7.50
❑ 203 Abner Haynes 15.00 7.50
❑ 204 Chris Burford 8.00 4.00
❑ 205 Bill Krisher 6.00 3.50
❑ 206 Marvin Terrell 6.00 3.50
❑ 207 Jimmy Harris 6.00 3.50
❑ 208 Mel Branch 8.00 4.00
❑ 209 Paul Miller 6.00 3.50
❑ 210 Al Dorow 6.00 3.50
❑ 211 Dick Jamieson 6.00 3.50
❑ 212 Pete Hart 6.00 3.50
❑ 213 Bill Shockley 6.00 3.50
❑ 214 Dewey Bohling 6.00 3.50
❑ 215 Don Maynard RC 80.00 40.00
❑ 216 Bob Mischak 6.00 3.50
❑ 217 Mike Hudock 6.00 3.50
❑ 218 Bob Reifsnyder 6.00 3.50
❑ 219 Tom Saidock 6.00 3.50
❑ 220 Sid Youngelman ! 20.00 12.00

1962 Fleer

❑ COMPLETE SET (88) 900.00 500.00
❑ WRAPPER (5-CENT) 200.00 100.00

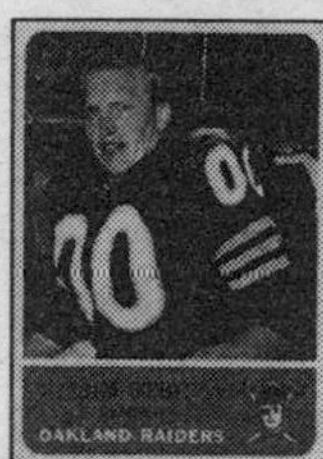

❑ 1 Billy Lott ! 16.00 8.00
❑ 2 Ron Burton 10.00 5.00
❑ 3 Gino Cappelletti RC 15.00 7.50
❑ 4 Babe Parilli 10.00 5.00
❑ 5 Jim Colclough 7.00 3.50
❑ 6 Tony Sardisco 7.00 3.50
❑ 7 Walt Cudzik 7.00 3.50
❑ 8 Bob Dee 7.00 3.50
❑ 9 Tommy Addison RC 8.00 4.00
❑ 10 Harry Jacobs 7.00 3.50
❑ 11 Ross O'Hanley 7.00 3.50
❑ 12 Art Baker 7.00 3.50
❑ 13 Johnny Green 7.00 3.50
❑ 14 Elbert Dubenion 10.00 5.00
❑ 15 Tom Rychlec 7.00 3.50
❑ 16 Billy Shaw RC 40.00 20.00
❑ 17 Ken Rice 7.00 3.50
❑ 18 Bill Atkins 7.00 3.50
❑ 19 Richie Lucas 8.00 4.00
❑ 20 Archie Matsos 7.00 3.50
❑ 21 Laverne Torczon 7.00 3.50
❑ 22 Warren Rabb 7.00 3.50
❑ 23 Jack Spikes 8.00 4.00
❑ 24 Cotton Davidson 8.00 4.00
❑ 25 Abner Haynes 15.00 7.50
❑ 26 Jimmy Saxton 7.00 3.50
❑ 27 Chris Burford 8.00 4.00
❑ 28 Bill Miller 7.00 3.50
❑ 29 Sherrill Headrick 8.00 4.00
❑ 30 E.J.Holub RC 8.00 4.00
❑ 31 Jerry Mays RC 10.00 5.00
❑ 32 Mel Branch 8.00 4.00
❑ 33 Paul Rochester RC 7.00 3.50
❑ 34 Frank Tripucka 10.00 5.00
❑ 35 Gene Mingo 7.00 3.50
❑ 36 Lionel Taylor 12.00 6.00
❑ 37 Ken Adamson 7.00 3.50
❑ 38 Eldon Danenhauer 7.00 3.50
❑ 39 Goose Gonsoulin 10.00 5.00
❑ 40 Gordy Holz 7.00 3.50
❑ 41 Bud McFadin 8.00 4.00
❑ 42 Jim Stinnette 7.00 3.50
❑ 43 Bob Hudson RC 7.00 3.50
❑ 44 George Herring 7.00 3.50
❑ 45 Charley Tolar RC 7.00 3.50
❑ 46 George Blanda 50.00 30.00
❑ 47 Billy Cannon 15.00 7.50
❑ 48 Charlie Hennigan RC 15.00 7.50
❑ 49 Bill Groman 7.00 3.50
❑ 50 Al Jamison 7.00 3.50
❑ 51 Tony Banfield 7.00 3.50
❑ 52 Jim Norton 7.00 3.50
❑ 53 Dennit Morris 7.00 3.50
❑ 54 Don Floyd 7.00 3.50
❑ 55 Ed Husmann UER 7.00 3.50
❑ 56 Robert Brooks 7.00 3.50
❑ 57 Al Dorow 7.00 3.50
❑ 58 Dick Christy 7.00 3.50
❑ 59 Don Maynard 50.00 30.00
❑ 60 Art Powell 10.00 5.00
❑ 61 Mike Hudock 7.00 3.50
❑ 62 Bill Mathis 8.00 4.00
❑ 63 Butch Songin 7.00 3.50
❑ 64 Larry Grantham 7.00 3.50
❑ 65 Nick Mumley 7.00 3.50
❑ 66 Tom Saidock 7.00 3.50
❑ 67 Alan Miller 7.00 3.50
❑ 68 Tom Flores 15.00 7.50
❑ 69 Bob Coolbaugh 7.00 3.50
❑ 70 George Fleming 7.00 3.50
❑ 71 Wayne Hawkins RC 8.00 4.00
❑ 72 Jim Otto 40.00 25.00
❑ 73 Wayne Crow 7.00 3.50
❑ 74 Fred Williamson RC 30.00 18.00
❑ 75 Tom Louderback 7.00 3.50
❑ 76 Volney Peters 7.00 3.50
❑ 77 Charley Powell 7.00 3.50
❑ 78 Don Norton 7.00 3.50
❑ 79 Jack Kemp 125.00 75.00
❑ 80 Paul Lowe 10.00 5.00
❑ 81 Dave Kocourek 7.00 3.50
❑ 82 Ron Mix 15.00 7.50
❑ 83 Ernie Wright 10.00 5.00
❑ 84 Dick Harris 7.00 3.50
❑ 85 Bill Hudson 7.00 3.50
❑ 86 Ernie Ladd RC 25.00 15.00
❑ 87 Earl Faison RC 8.00 4.00
❑ 88 Ron Nery ! 18.00 9.00

1963 Fleer

❑ COMPLETE SET (88) 1800.00 1200.00
❑ WRAPPER (5-CENT) 120.00 60.00
❑ 1 Larry Garron RC 20.00 10.00
❑ 2 Babe Parilli 10.00 5.00
❑ 3 Ron Burton 12.00 6.00
❑ 4 Jim Colclough 8.00 4.00
❑ 5 Gino Cappelletti 12.00 6.00
❑ 6 Charles Long RC SP 150.00 75.00
❑ 7 Billy Neighbors RC 8.00 4.00
❑ 8 Dick Felt 8.00 4.00
❑ 9 Tommy Addison 8.00 4.00
❑ 10 Nick Buoniconti RC 80.00 45.00
❑ 11 Larry Eisenhauer RC 8.00 4.00
❑ 12 Bill Mathis 8.00 4.00
❑ 13 Lee Grosscup RC 10.00 5.00
❑ 14 Dick Christy 8.00 4.00
❑ 15 Don Maynard 50.00 30.00
❑ 16 Alex Kroll RC 8.00 4.00
❑ 17 Bob Mischak 8.00 4.00
❑ 18 Dainard Paulson 8.00 4.00
❑ 19 Lee Riley 8.00 4.00
❑ 20 Larry Grantham 10.00 5.00
❑ 21 Hubert Bobo 8.00 4.00
❑ 22 Nick Mumley 8.00 4.00
❑ 23 Cookie Gilchrist RC 50.00 30.00
❑ 24 Jack Kemp 150.00 75.00
❑ 25 Wray Carlton 8.00 4.00
❑ 26 Elbert Dubenion 10.00 5.00
❑ 27 Ernie Warlick RC 10.00 5.00
❑ 28 Billy Shaw 15.00 7.50
❑ 29 Ken Rice 8.00 4.00
❑ 30 Booker Edgerson 8.00 4.00
❑ 31 Ray Abruzzese 8.00 4.00
❑ 32 Mike Stratton RC 15.00 7.50
❑ 33 Tom Sestak RC 10.00 5.00
❑ 34 Charley Tolar 8.00 4.00
❑ 35 Dave Smith RB 8.00 4.00
❑ 36 George Blanda 55.00 30.00
❑ 37 Billy Cannon 15.00 7.50
❑ 38 Charlie Hennigan 10.00 5.00
❑ 39 Bob Talamini RC 8.00 4.00
❑ 40 Jim Norton 8.00 4.00
❑ 41 Tony Banfield 8.00 4.00
❑ 42 Doug Cline 8.00 4.00
❑ 43 Don Floyd 8.00 4.00
❑ 44 Ed Husmann 8.00 4.00
❑ 45 Curtis McClinton RC 15.00 7.50
❑ 46 Jack Spikes 10.00 5.00
❑ 47 Len Dawson RC 200.00 125.00
❑ 48 Abner Haynes 15.00 7.50
❑ 49 Chris Burford 10.00 5.00
❑ 50 Fred Arbanas RC 12.00 6.00
❑ 51 Johnny Robinson 10.00 5.00
❑ 52 E.J. Holub 10.00 5.00

❑	53 Sherrill Headrick	10.00	5.00
❑	54 Mel Branch	10.00	5.00
❑	55 Jerry Mays	10.00	5.00
❑	56 Cotton Davidson	10.00	5.00
❑	57 Clem Daniels RC	15.00	7.50
❑	58 Bo Roberson RC	10.00	5.00
❑	59 Art Powell	12.00	6.00
❑	60 Bob Coolbaugh	8.00	4.00
❑	61 Wayne Hawkins	8.00	4.00
❑	62 Jim Otto	30.00	18.00
❑	63 Fred Williamson	20.00	10.00
❑	64 Bob Dougherty SP	120.00	60.00
❑	65 Dalva Allen	8.00	4.00
❑	66 Chuck McMurtry	8.00	4.00
❑	67 Gerry McDougall RC	8.00	4.00
❑	68 Tobin Rote	10.00	5.00
❑	69 Paul Lowe	12.00	6.00
❑	70 Keith Lincoln RC	40.00	25.00
❑	71 Dave Kocourek	8.00	4.00
❑	72 Lance Alworth RC	250.00	125.00
❑	73 Ron Mix	25.00	15.00
❑	74 Charley McNeil RC	8.00	4.00
❑	75 Emil Karas	8.00	4.00
❑	76 Ernie Ladd	20.00	10.00
❑	77 Earl Faison	8.00	4.00
❑	78 Jim Stinnette	8.00	4.00
❑	79 Frank Tripucka	12.00	6.00
❑	80 Don Stone	8.00	4.00
❑	81 Bob Scarpitto	8.00	4.00
❑	82 Lionel Taylor	12.00	6.00
❑	83 Jerry Tarr	8.00	4.00
❑	84 Eldon Danenhauer	8.00	4.00
❑	85 Goose Gonsoulin	10.00	5.00
❑	86 Jim Fraser	8.00	4.00
❑	87 Chuck Gavin	8.00	4.00
❑	88 Bud McFadin !	20.00	10.00
❑	NNO Checklist SP !	350.00	250.00

1990 Fleer

❑	COMPLETE SET (400)	10.00	4.00
❑	1 Harris Barton	.04	.01
❑	2 Chet Brooks	.04	.01
❑	3 Michael Carter	.04	.01
❑	4 Mike Cofer UER	.04	.01
❑	5 Roger Craig	.10	.02
❑	6 Kevin Fagan RC	.04	.01
❑	7 Charles Haley UER	.10	.02
❑	8 Pierce Holt RC	.04	.01
❑	9 Ronnie Lott	.10	.02
❑	10A Joe Montana ERR	1.25	.50
❑	10B Joe Montana COR	1.25	.50
❑	11 Bubba Paris	.04	.01
❑	12 Tom Rathman	.04	.01
❑	13 Jerry Rice	.75	.30
❑	14 John Taylor	.25	.08
❑	15 Keena Turner	.04	.01
❑	16 Michael Walter	.04	.01
❑	17 Steve Young	.50	.20
❑	18 Steve Atwater	.04	.01
❑	19 Tyrone Braxton	.04	.01
❑	20 Michael Brooks RC	.04	.01
❑	21 John Elway	1.25	.50
❑	22 Simon Fletcher	.04	.01
❑	23 Bobby Humphrey	.04	.01
❑	24 Mark Jackson	.04	.01
❑	25 Vance Johnson	.04	.01
❑	26 Greg Kragen	.04	.01
❑	27 Ken Lanier RC	.04	.01
❑	28 Karl Mecklenburg	.04	.01
❑	29 Orson Mobley RC	.04	.01
❑	30 Steve Sewell	.04	.01
❑	31 Dennis Smith	.04	.01
❑	32 David Treadwell	.04	.01
❑	33 Flipper Anderson	.04	.01
❑	34 Greg Bell	.04	.01
❑	35 Henry Ellard	.10	.02
❑	36 Jim Everett	.10	.02
❑	37 Jerry Gray	.04	.01
❑	38 Kevin Greene	.10	.02
❑	39 Pete Holohan	.04	.01
❑	40 LeRoy Irvin	.04	.01
❑	41 Mike Lansford	.04	.01
❑	42 Buford McGee RC	.04	.01
❑	43 Tom Newberry	.04	.01
❑	44 Vince Newsome RC	.04	.01
❑	45 Jackie Slater	.04	.01
❑	46 Mike Wilcher	.04	.01
❑	47 Matt Bahr	.04	.01
❑	48 Brian Brennan	.04	.01
❑	49 Thane Gash RC	.04	.01
❑	50 Mike Johnson	.04	.01
❑	51 Bernie Kosar	.10	.02
❑	52 Reggie Langhorne	.04	.01
❑	53 Tim Manoa	.04	.01
❑	54 Clay Matthews	.10	.02
❑	55 Eric Metcalf	.25	.08
❑	56 Frank Minnifield	.04	.01
❑	57 Gregg Rakoczy RC UER	.04	.01
❑	58 Webster Slaughter	.10	.02
❑	59 Bryan Wagner	.04	.01
❑	60 Felix Wright	.04	.01
❑	61 Raul Allegre	.04	.01
❑	62 Ottis Anderson UER	.10	.02
❑	63 Carl Banks	.04	.01
❑	64 Mark Bavaro	.04	.01
❑	65 Maurice Carthon	.04	.01
❑	66 Mark Collins UER	.04	.01
❑	67 Jeff Hostetler RC	.25	.08
❑	68 Erik Howard	.04	.01
❑	69 Pepper Johnson	.04	.01
❑	70 Sean Landeta	.04	.01
❑	71 Lionel Manuel	.04	.01
❑	72 Leonard Marshall	.04	.01
❑	73 Dave Meggett	.10	.02
❑	74 Bart Oates	.04	.01
❑	75 Doug Riesenberg RC	.04	.01
❑	76 Phil Simms	.10	.02
❑	77 Lawrence Taylor	.25	.08
❑	78 Eric Allen	.04	.01
❑	79 Jerome Brown	.04	.01
❑	80 Keith Byars	.04	.01
❑	81 Cris Carter	.50	.20
❑	82A Byron Evans RC ERR	.15	.05
❑	82B Randall Cunningham	.15	.05
❑	83A Ron Heller RC OT ERR	.15	.05
❑	83B Byron Evans RC COR	.15	.05
❑	84 Ron Heller RC OT COR	.04	.01
❑	85 Terry Hoage RC	.04	.01
❑	86 Keith Jackson	.10	.02
❑	87 Seth Joyner	.10	.02
❑	88 Mike Quick	.04	.01
❑	89 Mike Schad	.04	.01
❑	90 Clyde Simmons	.04	.01
❑	91 John Teltschik	.04	.01
❑	92 Anthony Toney	.04	.01
❑	93 Reggie White	.25	.08
❑	94 Ray Berry	.04	.01
❑	95 Joey Browner	.04	.01
❑	96 Anthony Carter	.10	.02
❑	97 Chris Doleman	.04	.01
❑	98 Rick Fenney	.04	.01
❑	99 Rich Gannon RC	1.50	.60
❑	100 Hassan Jones	.04	.01
❑	101 Steve Jordan	.04	.01
❑	102 Rich Karlis	.04	.01
❑	103 Andre Ware RC	.25	.08
❑	104 Kirk Lowdermilk	.04	.01
❑	105 Keith Millard	.04	.01
❑	106 Scott Studwell	.04	.01
❑	107 Herschel Walker	.10	.02
❑	108 Wade Wilson	.10	.02
❑	109 Gary Zimmerman	.04	.01
❑	110 Don Beebe	.10	.02
❑	111 Cornelius Bennett	.10	.02
❑	112 Shane Conlan	.04	.01
❑	113 Jim Kelly	.25	.08
❑	114 Scott Norwood UER	.04	.01
❑	115 Mark Kelso UER	.04	.01
❑	116 Larry Kinnebrew	.04	.01
❑	117 Pete Metzelaars	.04	.01
❑	118 Scott Radecic	.04	.01
❑	119 Andre Reed	.25	.08
❑	120 Jim Ritcher RC	.04	.01
❑	121 Bruce Smith	.25	.08
❑	122 Leonard Smith	.04	.01
❑	123 Art Still	.04	.01
❑	124 Thurman Thomas	.25	.08
❑	125 Steve Brown	.04	.01
❑	126 Ray Childress	.04	.01
❑	127 Ernest Givins	.10	.02
❑	128 John Grimsley	.04	.01
❑	129 Alonzo Highsmith	.04	.01
❑	130 Drew Hill	.04	.01
❑	131 Bruce Matthews	.10	.02
❑	132 Johnny Meads	.04	.01
❑	133 Warren Moon UER	.25	.08
❑	134 Mike Munchak	.10	.02
❑	135 Mike Rozier	.04	.01
❑	136 Dean Steinkuhler	.04	.01
❑	137 Lorenzo White	.04	.01
❑	138 Tony Zendejas	.04	.01
❑	139 Gary Anderson K	.04	.01
❑	140 Bubby Brister	.04	.01
❑	141 Thomas Everett	.04	.01
❑	142 Derek Hill	.04	.01
❑	143 Merril Hoge	.04	.01
❑	144 Tim Johnson	.04	.01
❑	145 Louis Lipps	.10	.02
❑	146 David Little	.04	.01
❑	147 Greg Lloyd	.25	.08
❑	148 Mike Mularkey	.04	.01
❑	149 John Rienstra RC	.04	.01
❑	150 Gerald Williams RC UER	.04	.01
❑	151 Keith Willis UER	.04	.01
❑	152 Rod Woodson	.25	.08
❑	153 Tim Worley	.04	.01
❑	154 Gary Clark	.25	.08
❑	155 Darryl Grant	.04	.01
❑	156 Darrell Green	.10	.02
❑	157 Joe Jacoby	.04	.01
❑	158 Jim Lachey	.04	.01
❑	159 Chip Lohmiller	.04	.01
❑	160 Charles Mann	.04	.01
❑	161 Wilber Marshall	.04	.01
❑	162 Mark May	.04	.01
❑	163 Ralf Mojsiejenko	.04	.01
❑	164 Art Monk UER	.10	.02
❑	165 Gerald Riggs	.10	.02
❑	166 Mark Rypien	.10	.02
❑	167 Ricky Sanders	.04	.01
❑	168 Don Warren	.04	.01
❑	169 Robert Brown RC	.04	.01
❑	170 Blair Bush	.04	.01
❑	171 Brent Fullwood	.04	.01
❑	172 Tim Harris	.04	.01
❑	173 Chris Jacke	.04	.01
❑	174 Perry Kemp	.04	.01
❑	175 Don Majkowski	.04	.01
❑	176 Tony Mandarich	.04	.01
❑	177 Mark Murphy	.04	.01
❑	178 Brian Noble	.04	.01
❑	179 Ken Ruettgers	.04	.01
❑	180 Sterling Sharpe	.25	.08
❑	181 Ed West RC	.04	.01
❑	182 Keith Woodside	.04	.01
❑	183 Morten Andersen	.04	.01
❑	184 Stan Brock	.04	.01
❑	185 Jim Dombrowski RC	.04	.01
❑	186 John Fourcade	.04	.01
❑	187 Bobby Hebert	.04	.01
❑	188 Craig Heyward	.10	.02
❑	189 Dalton Hilliard	.04	.01
❑	190 Rickey Jackson	.10	.02
❑	191 Buford Jordan	.04	.01
❑	192 Eric Martin	.04	.01
❑	193 Robert Massey	.04	.01
❑	194 Sam Mills	.10	.02
❑	195 Pat Swilling	.10	.02
❑	196 Jim Wilks	.04	.01
❑	197 John Alt RC	.04	.01
❑	198 Walker Lee Ashley	.04	.01
❑	199 Steve DeBerg	.04	.01
❑	200 Leonard Griffin	.04	.01
❑	201 Albert Lewis	.04	.01
❑	202 Nick Lowery	.04	.01
❑	203 Bill Maas	.04	.01
❑	204 Pete Mandley	.04	.01
❑	205 Chris Martin RC	.04	.01
❑	206 Christian Okoye	.04	.01
❑	207 Stephone Paige	.04	.01

❑ 208 Kevin Porter RC	.04	.01
❑ 209 Derrick Thomas	.25	.08
❑ 210 Lewis Billups	.04	.01
❑ 211 James Brooks	.10	.02
❑ 212 Jason Buck	.04	.01
❑ 213 Rickey Dixon RC	.04	.01
❑ 214 Boomer Esiason	.10	.02
❑ 215 David Fulcher	.04	.01
❑ 216 Rodney Holman	.04	.01
❑ 217 Lee Johnson	.04	.01
❑ 218 Tim Krumrie	.04	.01
❑ 219 Tim McGee	.04	.01
❑ 220 Anthony Munoz	.10	.02
❑ 221 Bruce Reimers RC	.04	.01
❑ 222 Leon White	.04	.01
❑ 223 Ickey Woods	.04	.01
❑ 224 Harvey Armstrong RC	.04	.01
❑ 225 Michael Ball RC	.04	.01
❑ 226 Chip Banks	.04	.01
❑ 227 Pat Beach	.04	.01
❑ 228 Duane Bickett	.04	.01
❑ 229 Bill Brooks	.04	.01
❑ 230 Jon Hand	.04	.01
❑ 231 Andre Rison	.25	.08
❑ 232 Rohn Stark	.04	.01
❑ 233 Donnell Thompson	.04	.01
❑ 234 Jack Trudeau	.04	.01
❑ 235 Clarence Verdin	.04	.01
❑ 236 Mark Clayton	.10	.02
❑ 237 Jeff Cross	.04	.01
❑ 238 Jeff Dellenbach RC	.04	.01
❑ 239 Mark Duper	.10	.02
❑ 240 Ferrell Edmunds	.04	.01
❑ 241 Hugh Green UER	.04	.01
❑ 242 E.J. Junior	.04	.01
❑ 243 Marc Logan	.04	.01
❑ 244 Dan Marino	1.25	.50
❑ 245 John Offerdahl	.04	.01
❑ 246 Reggie Roby	.04	.01
❑ 247 Sammie Smith	.04	.01
❑ 248 Pete Stoyanovich	.04	.01
❑ 249 Marcus Allen	.25	.08
❑ 250 Eddie Anderson RC	.04	.01
❑ 251 Steve Beuerlein	.10	.02
❑ 252 Mike Dyal	.04	.01
❑ 253 Mervyn Fernandez	.04	.01
❑ 254 Bob Golic	.04	.01
❑ 255 Mike Harden	.04	.01
❑ 256 Bo Jackson	.30	.10
❑ 257 Howie Long UER	.25	.08
❑ 258 Don Mosebar	.04	.01
❑ 259 Jay Schroeder	.04	.01
❑ 260 Steve Smith	.04	.01
❑ 261 Greg Townsend	.04	.01
❑ 262 Lionel Washington	.04	.01
❑ 263 Brian Blades	.10	.02
❑ 264 Jeff Bryant	.04	.01
❑ 265 Grant Feasel RC	.04	.01
❑ 266 Jacob Green	.04	.01
❑ 267 James Jefferson	.04	.01
❑ 268 Norm Johnson	.04	.01
❑ 269 Dave Krieg UER	.10	.02
❑ 270 Travis McNeal	.04	.01
❑ 271 Joe Nash	.04	.01
❑ 272 Rufus Porter	.04	.01
❑ 273 Kelly Stouffer	.04	.01
❑ 274 John L. Williams	.04	.01
❑ 275 Jim Arnold	.04	.01
❑ 276 Jerry Ball	.04	.01
❑ 277 Bennie Blades	.04	.01
❑ 278 Lomas Brown	.04	.01
❑ 279 Michael Cofer	.04	.01
❑ 280 Bob Gagliano	.04	.01
❑ 281 Richard Johnson	.04	.01
❑ 282 Eddie Murray	.04	.01
❑ 283 Rodney Peete	.10	.02
❑ 284 Barry Sanders	1.25	.50
❑ 285 Eric Sanders	.04	.01
❑ 286 Chris Spielman	.25	.08
❑ 287 Eric Williams RC	.04	.01
❑ 288 Neal Anderson	.10	.02
❑ 289A Kevin Butler P/P	.25	.08
❑ 289B Kevin Butler K/P	.25	.08
❑ 289C Kevin Butler P/K	.25	.08
❑ 289D Kevin Butler K/K	.04	.01
❑ 290 Jim Covert	.04	.01
❑ 291 Richard Dent	.10	.02
❑ 292 Dennis Gentry	.04	.01
❑ 293 Jim Harbaugh	.25	.08
❑ 294 Jay Hilgenberg	.04	.01
❑ 295 Vestee Jackson	.04	.01
❑ 296 Steve McMichael	.10	.02
❑ 297 Ron Morris	.04	.01
❑ 298 Brad Muster	.04	.01
❑ 299 Mike Singletary	.10	.02
❑ 300 James Thornton UER	.04	.01
❑ 301 Mike Tomczak	.10	.02
❑ 302 Keith Van Horne	.04	.01
❑ 303 Chris Bahr UER	.04	.01
❑ 304 Martin Bayless RC	.04	.01
❑ 305 Marion Butts	.10	.02
❑ 306 Gill Byrd	.04	.01
❑ 307 Arthur Cox	.04	.01
❑ 308 Burt Grossman	.04	.01
❑ 309 Jamie Holland	.04	.01
❑ 310 Jim McMahon	.10	.02
❑ 311 Anthony Miller	.25	.08
❑ 312 Leslie O'Neal	.10	.02
❑ 313 Billy Ray Smith	.04	.01
❑ 314 Tim Spencer	.04	.01
❑ 315 Broderick Thompson RC	.04	.01
❑ 316 Lee Williams	.04	.01
❑ 317 Bruce Armstrong	.04	.01
❑ 318 Tim Goad RC	.04	.01
❑ 319 Steve Grogan	.10	.02
❑ 320 Roland James	.04	.01
❑ 321 Cedric Jones	.04	.01
❑ 322 Fred Marion	.04	.01
❑ 323 Stanley Morgan	.04	.01
❑ 324 Robert Perryman	.04	.01
❑ 325 Johnny Rembert	.04	.01
❑ 326 Ed Reynolds	.04	.01
❑ 327 Kenneth Sims	.04	.01
❑ 328 John Stephens	.04	.01
❑ 329 Danny Villa RC	.04	.01
❑ 330 Robert Awalt	.04	.01
❑ 331 Anthony Bell	.04	.01
❑ 332 Rich Camarillo	.04	.01
❑ 333 Earl Ferrell	.04	.01
❑ 334 Roy Green	.10	.02
❑ 335 Gary Hogeboom	.04	.01
❑ 336 Cedric Mack	.04	.01
❑ 337 Freddie Joe Nunn	.04	.01
❑ 338 Luis Sharpe	.04	.01
❑ 339 Vai Sikahema	.04	.01
❑ 340 J.T. Smith	.04	.01
❑ 341 Tom Tupa RC	.04	.01
❑ 342 Percy Snow RC	.04	.01
❑ 343 Mark Carrier WR	.25	.08
❑ 344 Randy Grimes	.04	.01
❑ 345 Paul Gruber	.04	.01
❑ 346 Ron Hall	.04	.01
❑ 347 Jeff George RC	.50	.20
❑ 348 Bruce Hill UER	.04	.01
❑ 349 William Howard UER	.04	.01
❑ 350 Donald Igwebuike	.04	.01
❑ 351 Chris Mohr RC	.04	.01
❑ 352 Winston Moss RC	.04	.01
❑ 353 Ricky Reynolds	.04	.01
❑ 354 Mark Robinson	.04	.01
❑ 355 Lars Tate	.04	.01
❑ 356 Vinny Testaverde	.10	.02
❑ 357 Broderick Thomas	.04	.01
❑ 358 Troy Benson	.04	.01
❑ 359 Jeff Criswell RC	.04	.01
❑ 360 Tony Eason	.04	.01
❑ 361 James Hasty	.04	.01
❑ 362 Johnny Hector	.04	.01
❑ 363 Bobby Humphery UER	.04	.01
❑ 364 Pat Leahy	.04	.01
❑ 365 Erik McMillan	.04	.01
❑ 366 Freeman McNeil	.04	.01
❑ 367 Ken O'Brien	.04	.01
❑ 368 Ron Stallworth	.04	.01
❑ 369 Al Toon	.10	.02
❑ 370 Blair Thomas RC	.04	.01
❑ 371 Aundray Bruce	.04	.01
❑ 372 Tony Casillas	.04	.01
❑ 373 Shawn Collins	.04	.01
❑ 374 Evan Cooper	.04	.01
❑ 375 Bill Fralic	.04	.01
❑ 376 Scott Funhage	.04	.01
❑ 377 Mike Gann	.04	.01
❑ 378 Ron Heller TE	.04	.01
❑ 379 Keith Jones	.04	.01
❑ 380 Mike Kenn	.04	.01
❑ 381 Chris Miller	.25	.08
❑ 382 Deion Sanders UER	.50	.20
❑ 383 John Settle	.04	.01
❑ 384 Troy Aikman	.75	.30
❑ 385 Bill Bates	.10	.02
❑ 386 Willie Broughton	.04	.01
❑ 387 Steve Folsom	.04	.01
❑ 388 Ray Horton UER	.04	.01
❑ 389 Michael Irvin	.25	.08
❑ 390 Jim Jeffcoat	.04	.01
❑ 391 Eugene Lockhart	.04	.01
❑ 392 Kelvin Martin RC	.04	.01
❑ 393 Nate Newton	.10	.02
❑ 394 Mike Saxon UER	.04	.01
❑ 395 Derrick Shepard	.04	.01
❑ 396 Steve Walsh	.10	.02
❑ 397 Joe Montana/Rice MVP's	.75	.30
❑ 398 Checklist Card UER	.04	.01
❑ 399 Checklist Card UER	.04	.01
❑ 400 Checklist Card	.04	.01

1990 Fleer Update

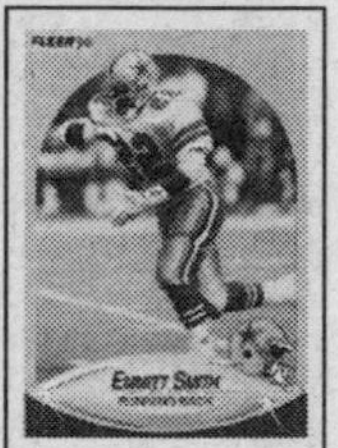

❑ COMP.FACT.SET (120)	25.00	12.50
❑ U1 Albert Bentley	.08	.02
❑ U2 Dean Biasucci	.08	.02
❑ U3 Ray Donaldson	.08	.02
❑ U4 Jeff George	1.25	.50
❑ U5 Ray Agnew RC	.08	.02
❑ U6 Greg McMurtry RC	.08	.02
❑ U7 Chris Singleton RC	.08	.02
❑ U8 James Francis RC	.08	.02
❑ U9 Harold Green RC	.30	.10
❑ U10 John Elliott	.08	.02
❑ U11 Rodney Hampton RC	.30	.10
❑ U12 Gary Reasons	.08	.02
❑ U13 Lewis Tillman	.08	.02
❑ U14 Everson Walls	.08	.02
❑ U15 David Alexander RC	.08	.02
❑ U16 Jim McMahon	.15	.05
❑ U17 Ben Smith RC	.08	.02
❑ U18 Andre Waters	.08	.02
❑ U19 Calvin Williams RC	.15	.05
❑ U20 Earnest Byner	.08	.02
❑ U21 Andre Collins RC	.08	.02
❑ U22 Russ Grimm	.08	.02
❑ U23 Stan Humphries RC	.30	.10
❑ U24 Martin Mayhew RC	.08	.02
❑ U25 Barry Foster RC	.30	.10
❑ U26 Eric Green RC	.15	.05
❑ U27 Tunch Ilkin	.08	.02
❑ U28 Hardy Nickerson	.15	.05
❑ U29 Jerrol Williams	.08	.02
❑ U30 Mike Baab	.08	.02
❑ U31 Leroy Hoard RC	.50	.20
❑ U32 Eddie Johnson RC	.08	.02
❑ U33 William Fuller	.15	.05
❑ U34 Haywood Jeffires RC	.30	.10
❑ U35 Don Maggs RC	.08	.02
❑ U36 Allen Pinkett	.08	.02
❑ U37 Robert Awalt	.08	.02
❑ U38 Dennis McKinnon	.08	.02
❑ U39 Ken Norton Jr. RC	.30	.10
❑ U40 Emmitt Smith RC	20.00	7.50
❑ U41 Alexander Wright RC	.08	.02
❑ U42 Eric Hill	.08	.02
❑ U43 Johnny Johnson RC	.15	.05
❑ U44 Timm Rosenbach	.08	.02
❑ U45 Anthony Thompson RC	.08	.02
❑ U46 Dexter Carter RC	.08	.02
❑ U47 Eric Davis RC UER	.15	.05
❑ U48 Keith DeLong	.08	.02
❑ U49 Brent Jones RC	.30	.10
❑ U50 Darryl Pollard RC	.08	.02
❑ U51 Steve Wallace RC	.30	.10

Card	Player	Price	Price
❑ U52	Bern Brostek RC	.08	.02
❑ U53	Aaron Cox	.08	.02
❑ U54	Cleveland Gary	.08	.02
❑ U55	Fred Strickland RC	.08	.02
❑ U56	Pat Terrell RC	.08	.02
❑ U57	Steve Broussard RC	.08	.02
❑ U58	Scott Case	.08	.02
❑ U59	Brian Jordan RC	.15	.05
❑ U60	Andre Rison	.30	.10
❑ U61	Kevin Haverdink	.08	.02
❑ U62	Rueben Mayes	.08	.02
❑ U63	Steve Walsh	.15	.05
❑ U64	Greg Bell	.08	.02
❑ U65	Tim Brown	.30	.10
❑ U66	Willie Gault	.15	.05
❑ U67	Vance Mueller RC	.08	.02
❑ U68	Bill Pickel	.08	.02
❑ U69	Aaron Wallace RC	.08	.02
❑ U70	Glenn Parker RC	.08	.02
❑ U71	Frank Reich	.30	.10
❑ U72	Leon Seals RC	.08	.02
❑ U73	Darryl Talley	.08	.02
❑ U74	Brad Baxter RC	.08	.02
❑ U75	Jeff Criswell	.08	.02
❑ U76	Jeff Lageman	.08	.02
❑ U77	Rob Moore RC	1.50	.60
❑ U78	Blair Thomas	.15	.05
❑ U79	Louis Oliver	.08	.02
❑ U80	Tony Paige	.08	.02
❑ U81	Richmond Webb RC	.08	.02
❑ U82	Robert Blackmon RC	.08	.02
❑ U83	Derrick Fenner RC	.08	.02
❑ U84	Andy Heck	.08	.02
❑ U85	Cortez Kennedy RC	.30	.10
❑ U86	Terry Wooden RC	.08	.02
❑ U87	Jeff Donaldson	.08	.02
❑ U88	Tim Grunhard RC	.08	.02
❑ U89	Emile Harry RC	.08	.02
❑ U90	Dan Saleaumua	.08	.02
❑ U91	Percy Snow	.08	.02
❑ U92	Andre Ware	.30	.10
❑ U93	Darrell Fullington RC	.08	.02
❑ U94	Mike Merriweather	.08	.02
❑ U95	Henry Thomas	.08	.02
❑ U96	Robert Brown	.08	.02
❑ U97	LeRoy Butler RC	.30	.10
❑ U98	Anthony Dilweg	.08	.02
❑ U99	Darrell Thompson RC	.08	.02
❑ U100	Keith Woodside	.08	.02
❑ U101	Gary Plummer	.08	.02
❑ U102	Junior Seau RC	5.00	2.00
❑ U103	Billy Joe Tolliver	.08	.02
❑ U104	Mark Vlasic	.08	.02
❑ U105	Gary Anderson RB	.08	.02
❑ U106	Ian Beckles RC	.08	.02
❑ U107	Reggie Cobb RC	.08	.02
❑ U108	Keith McCants RC	.08	.02
❑ U109	Mark Bortz RC	.08	.02
❑ U110	Maury Buford	.08	.02
❑ U111	Mark Carrier RC DB	.30	.10
❑ U112	Dan Hampton	.15	.05
❑ U113	William Perry	.15	.05
❑ U114	Ron Rivera	.08	.02
❑ U115	Lemuel Stinson	.08	.02
❑ U116	Melvin Bratton RC	.08	.02
❑ U117	Gary Kubiak RC	.30	.10
❑ U118	Alton Montgomery RC	.08	.02
❑ U119	Ricky Nattiel	.08	.02
❑ U120	Checklist 1-132	.08	.02

1991 Fleer

Card	Player	Price	Price
❑	COMPLETE SET (432)	8.00	4.00
❑ 1	Shane Conlan	.05	.01
❑ 2	John Davis RC	.05	.01
❑ 3	Kent Hull	.05	.01
❑ 4	James Lofton	.10	.02
❑ 5	Keith McKeller	.05	.01
❑ 6	Scott Norwood	.05	.01
❑ 7	Nate Odomes	.05	.01
❑ 8	Andre Reed	.10	.02
❑ 9	Jim Ritcher	.05	.01
❑ 10	Leon Seals	.05	.01
❑ 11	Bruce Smith	.25	.08
❑ 12	Leonard Smith	.05	.01
❑ 13	Steve Tasker	.10	.02
❑ 14	Thurman Thomas	.25	.08
❑ 15	Lewis Billups	.05	.01
❑ 16	James Brooks	.10	.02
❑ 17	Eddie Brown	.05	.01
❑ 18	Carl Carter	.05	.01
❑ 19	Boomer Esiason	.10	.02
❑ 20	James Francis	.05	.01
❑ 21	David Fulcher	.05	.01
❑ 22	Harold Green	.10	.02
❑ 23	Rodney Holman	.05	.01
❑ 24	Bruce Kozerski	.05	.01
❑ 25	Tim McGee	.05	.01
❑ 26	Anthony Munoz	.10	.02
❑ 27	Bruce Reimers	.05	.01
❑ 28	Ickey Woods	.05	.01
❑ 29	Carl Zander	.05	.01
❑ 30	Mike Baab	.05	.01
❑ 31	Brian Brennan	.05	.01
❑ 32	Rob Burnett RC	.10	.02
❑ 33	Paul Farren	.05	.01
❑ 34	Thane Gash	.05	.01
❑ 35	David Grayson	.05	.01
❑ 36	Mike Johnson	.05	.01
❑ 37	Reggie Langhorne	.05	.01
❑ 38	Kevin Mack	.05	.01
❑ 39	Eric Metcalf	.10	.02
❑ 40	Frank Minnifield	.05	.01
❑ 41	Gregg Rakoczy	.05	.01
❑ 42	Felix Wright	.05	.01
❑ 43	Steve Atwater	.05	.01
❑ 44	Michael Brooks	.05	.01
❑ 45	John Elway	1.25	.50
❑ 46	Simon Fletcher	.05	.01
❑ 47	Bobby Humphrey	.05	.01
❑ 48	Mark Jackson	.05	.01
❑ 49	Keith Kartz	.05	.01
❑ 50	Clarence Kay	.05	.01
❑ 51	Greg Kragen	.05	.01
❑ 52	Karl Mecklenburg	.05	.01
❑ 53	Warren Powers	.05	.01
❑ 54	Dennis Smith	.05	.01
❑ 55	Jim Szymanski	.05	.01
❑ 56	David Treadwell	.05	.01
❑ 57	Michael Young	.05	.01
❑ 58	Ray Childress	.05	.01
❑ 59	Curtis Duncan	.05	.01
❑ 60	William Fuller	.10	.02
❑ 61	Ernest Givins	.10	.02
❑ 62	Drew Hill	.05	.01
❑ 63	Haywood Jeffires	.10	.02
❑ 64	Richard Johnson DB	.05	.01
❑ 65	Sean Jones	.10	.02
❑ 66	Don Maggs	.05	.01
❑ 67	Bruce Matthews	.10	.02
❑ 68	Johnny Meads	.05	.01
❑ 69	Greg Montgomery	.05	.01
❑ 70	Warren Moon	.25	.08
❑ 71	Mike Munchak	.10	.02
❑ 72	Allen Pinkett	.05	.01
❑ 73	Lorenzo White	.05	.01
❑ 74	Pat Beach	.05	.01
❑ 75	Albert Bentley	.05	.01
❑ 76	Dean Biasucci	.05	.01
❑ 77	Duane Bickett	.05	.01
❑ 78	Bill Brooks	.05	.01
❑ 79	Sam Clancy	.05	.01
❑ 80	Ray Donaldson	.05	.01
❑ 81	Jeff George	.25	.08
❑ 82	Alan Grant	.05	.01
❑ 83	Jessie Hester	.05	.01
❑ 84	Jeff Herrod	.05	.01
❑ 85	Rohn Stark	.05	.01
❑ 86	Jack Trudeau	.05	.01
❑ 87	Clarence Verdin	.05	.01
❑ 88	John Alt	.05	.01
❑ 89	Steve DeBerg	.05	.01
❑ 90	Tim Grunhard	.05	.01
❑ 91	Dino Hackett	.05	.01
❑ 92	Jonathan Hayes	.05	.01
❑ 93	Albert Lewis	.05	.01
❑ 94	Nick Lowery	.05	.01
❑ 95	Bill Maas UER	.05	.01
❑ 96	Christian Okoye	.05	.01
❑ 97	Stephone Paige	.05	.01
❑ 98	Kevin Porter	.05	.01
❑ 99	David Szott	.05	.01
❑ 100	Derrick Thomas	.25	.08
❑ 101	Barry Word FFC	.05	.01
❑ 102	Marcus Allen	.25	.08
❑ 103	Thomas Benson	.05	.01
❑ 104	Tim Brown	.25	.08
❑ 105	Riki Ellison	.05	.01
❑ 106	Mervyn Fernandez	.05	.01
❑ 107	Willie Gault	.10	.02
❑ 108	Bob Golic	.05	.01
❑ 109	Ethan Horton FFC	.05	.01
❑ 110	Bo Jackson	.30	.10
❑ 111	Howie Long	.25	.08
❑ 112	Don Mosebar	.05	.01
❑ 113	Jerry Robinson	.05	.01
❑ 114	Jay Schroeder	.05	.01
❑ 115	Steve Smith	.05	.01
❑ 116	Greg Townsend	.05	.01
❑ 117	Steve Wisniewski	.05	.01
❑ 118	Mark Clayton	.10	.02
❑ 119	Mark Duper	.10	.02
❑ 120	Ferrell Edmunds	.05	.01
❑ 121	Hugh Green	.05	.01
❑ 122	David Griggs	.05	.01
❑ 123	Jim C. Jensen	.05	.01
❑ 124	Dan Marino	1.25	.50
❑ 125	Tim McKyer	.05	.01
❑ 126	John Offerdahl	.05	.01
❑ 127	Louis Oliver	.05	.01
❑ 128	Tony Paige	.05	.01
❑ 129	Reggie Roby	.05	.01
❑ 130	Keith Sims	.05	.01
❑ 131	Sammie Smith	.05	.01
❑ 132	Pete Stoyanovich	.05	.01
❑ 133	Richmond Webb	.05	.01
❑ 134	Bruce Armstrong	.05	.01
❑ 135	Vincent Brown	.05	.01
❑ 136	Hart Lee Dykes	.05	.01
❑ 137	Irving Fryar	.10	.02
❑ 138	Tim Goad	.05	.01
❑ 139	Tommy Hodson	.05	.01
❑ 140	Maurice Hurst	.05	.01
❑ 141	Ronnie Lippett	.05	.01
❑ 142	Greg McMurtry	.05	.01
❑ 143	Ed Reynolds	.05	.01
❑ 144	John Stephens	.05	.01
❑ 145	Andre Tippett	.05	.01
❑ 146	Danny Villa	.05	.01
❑ 147	Brad Baxter	.05	.01
❑ 148	Kyle Clifton	.05	.01
❑ 149	Jeff Criswell	.05	.01
❑ 150	James Hasty	.05	.01
❑ 151	Jeff Lageman	.05	.01
❑ 152	Pat Leahy	.05	.01
❑ 153	Rob Moore	.25	.08
❑ 154	Al Toon	.10	.02
❑ 155	Gary Anderson K	.05	.01
❑ 156	Bubby Brister	.05	.01
❑ 157	Chris Calloway	.05	.01
❑ 158	Donald Evans	.05	.01
❑ 159	Eric Green	.05	.01
❑ 160	Bryan Hinkle	.05	.01
❑ 161	Merril Hoge	.05	.01
❑ 162	Tunch Ilkin	.05	.01
❑ 163	Louis Lipps	.05	.01
❑ 164	David Little	.05	.01
❑ 165	Mike Mularkey	.05	.01
❑ 166	Gerald Williams	.05	.01
❑ 167	Warren Williams	.05	.01
❑ 168	Rod Woodson	.25	.08
❑ 169	Tim Worley	.05	.01
❑ 170	Martin Bayless	.05	.01
❑ 171	Marion Butts	.10	.02
❑ 172	Gill Byrd	.05	.01
❑ 173	Frank Cornish	.05	.01
❑ 174	Arthur Cox	.05	.01
❑ 175	Burt Grossman	.05	.01
❑ 176	Anthony Miller	.10	.02
❑ 177	Leslie O'Neal	.10	.02

❑ 178 Gary Plummer .05 .01
❑ 179 Junior Seau .25 .08
❑ 180 Billy Joe Tolliver .05 .01
❑ 181 Derrick Walker RC .05 .01
❑ 182 Lee Williams .05 .01
❑ 183 Robert Blackmon .05 .01
❑ 184 Brian Blades .10 .02
❑ 185 Grant Feasel .05 .01
❑ 186 Derrick Fenner .05 .01
❑ 187 Andy Heck .05 .01
❑ 188 Norm Johnson .05 .01
❑ 189 Tommy Kane .05 .01
❑ 190 Cortez Kennedy .25 .08
❑ 191 Dave Krieg .10 .02
❑ 192 Travis McNeal .05 .01
❑ 193 Eugene Robinson .05 .01
❑ 194 Chris Warren FFC .25 .08
❑ 195 John L. Williams .05 .01
❑ 196 Steve Broussard .05 .01
❑ 197 Scott Case .05 .01
❑ 198 Shawn Collins .05 .01
❑ 199 Darion Conner UER .05 .01
❑ 200 Tory Epps .05 .01
❑ 201 Bill Fralic .05 .01
❑ 202 Michael Haynes FFC .25 .08
❑ 203 Chris Hinton .05 .01
❑ 204 Keith Jones .05 .01
❑ 205 Brian Jordan .10 .02
❑ 206 Mike Kenn .05 .01
❑ 207 Chris Miller .10 .02
❑ 208 Andre Rison .10 .02
❑ 209 Mike Rozier .05 .01
❑ 210 Deion Sanders .40 .15
❑ 211 Gary Wilkins .05 .01
❑ 212 Neal Anderson .10 .02
❑ 213 Trace Armstrong .05 .01
❑ 214 Mark Bortz .05 .01
❑ 215 Kevin Butler .05 .01
❑ 216 Mark Carrier DB .10 .02
❑ 217 Wendell Davis FFC .05 .01
❑ 218 Richard Dent .10 .02
❑ 219 Dennis Gentry .05 .01
❑ 220 Jim Harbaugh .25 .08
❑ 221 Jay Hilgenberg .05 .01
❑ 222 Steve McMichael .10 .02
❑ 223 Ron Morris .05 .01
❑ 224 Brad Muster .05 .01
❑ 225 Mike Singletary .10 .02
❑ 226 James Thornton .05 .01
❑ 227 Tommie Agee .05 .01
❑ 228 Troy Aikman .75 .30
❑ 229 Jack Del Rio .10 .02
❑ 230 Issiac Holt .05 .01
❑ 231 Ray Horton .05 .01
❑ 232 Jim Jeffcoat .05 .01
❑ 233 Eugene Lockhart .05 .01
❑ 234 Kelvin Martin .05 .01
❑ 235 Nate Newton .10 .02
❑ 236 Mike Saxon .05 .01
❑ 237 Emmitt Smith 2.50 1.00
❑ 238A Daniel Stubbs .10 .02
❑ 238B Daniel Stubbs .10 .02
❑ 239 Jim Arnold .05 .01
❑ 240 Jerry Ball .05 .01
❑ 241 Bennie Blades .05 .01
❑ 242 Lomas Brown .05 .01
❑ 243 Robert Clark .05 .01
❑ 244 Mike Cofer .05 .01
❑ 245 Mel Gray .10 .02
❑ 246 Rodney Peete .10 .02
❑ 247 Barry Sanders 1.25 .50
❑ 248 Andre Ware .10 .02
❑ 249 Matt Brock RC .05 .01
❑ 250 Robert Brown .05 .01
❑ 251 Anthony Dilweg .05 .01
❑ 252 Johnny Holland .05 .01
❑ 253 Tim Harris .05 .01
❑ 254 Chris Jacke .05 .01
❑ 255 Perry Kemp .05 .01
❑ 256 Don Majkowski UER .05 .01
❑ 257 Tony Mandarich .05 .01
❑ 258 Mark Murphy .05 .01
❑ 259 Brian Noble .05 .01
❑ 260 Jeff Query .05 .01
❑ 261 Sterling Sharpe .25 .08
❑ 262 Ed West .05 .01
❑ 263 Keith Woodside .05 .01
❑ 264 Flipper Anderson .05 .01
❑ 265 Aaron Cox .05 .01
❑ 266 Henry Ellard .10 .02
❑ 267 Jim Everett .10 .02
❑ 268 Cleveland Gary .05 .01
❑ 269 Kevin Greene .10 .02
❑ 270 Pete Holohan .05 .01
❑ 271 Mike Lansford .05 .01
❑ 272 Duval Love RC .05 .01
❑ 273 Buford McGee .05 .01
❑ 274 Tom Newberry .05 .01
❑ 275 Jackie Slater .05 .01
❑ 276 Frank Stams .05 .01
❑ 277 Alfred Anderson .05 .01
❑ 278 Joey Browner .05 .01
❑ 279 Anthony Carter .10 .02
❑ 280 Chris Doleman .05 .01
❑ 281 Rick Fenney .05 .01
❑ 282 Rich Gannon .25 .08
❑ 283 Hassan Jones .05 .01
❑ 284 Steve Jordan .05 .01
❑ 285 Carl Lee .05 .01
❑ 286 Randall McDaniel .05 .01
❑ 287 Keith Millard .05 .01
❑ 288 Herschel Walker .10 .02
❑ 289 Wade Wilson .10 .02
❑ 290 Gary Zimmerman .05 .01
❑ 291 Morten Andersen .05 .01
❑ 292 Jim Dombrowski .05 .01
❑ 293 Gill Fenerty .05 .01
❑ 294 Craig Heyward .10 .02
❑ 295 Dalton Hilliard .05 .01
❑ 296 Rickey Jackson .05 .01
❑ 297 Vaughan Johnson .05 .01
❑ 298 Eric Martin .05 .01
❑ 299 Robert Massey .05 .01
❑ 300 Rueben Mayes .05 .01
❑ 301 Sam Mills .05 .01
❑ 302 Brett Perriman .25 .08
❑ 303 Pat Swilling .10 .02
❑ 304 Steve Walsh .05 .01
❑ 305 Ottis Anderson .10 .02
❑ 306 Matt Bahr .05 .01
❑ 307 Mark Bavaro .05 .01
❑ 308 Maurice Carthon .05 .01
❑ 309 Mark Collins .05 .01
❑ 310 John Elliott .05 .01
❑ 311 Rodney Hampton .25 .08
❑ 312 Jeff Hostetler .10 .02
❑ 313 Erik Howard .05 .01
❑ 314 Pepper Johnson .05 .01
❑ 315 Sean Landeta .05 .01
❑ 316 Dave Meggett .10 .02
❑ 317 Bart Oates .05 .01
❑ 318 Phil Simms .10 .02
❑ 319 Lawrence Taylor .25 .08
❑ 320 Reyna Thompson .05 .01
❑ 321 Everson Walls .05 .01
❑ 322 Eric Allen .05 .01
❑ 323 Fred Barnett FFC .25 .08
❑ 324 Jerome Brown .05 .01
❑ 325 Keith Byars .05 .01
❑ 326 Randall Cunningham .25 .08
❑ 327 Byron Evans .05 .01
❑ 328 Ron Heller .05 .01
❑ 329 Keith Jackson .10 .02
❑ 330 Seth Joyner .10 .02
❑ 331 Heath Sherman .05 .01
❑ 332 Clyde Simmons .05 .01
❑ 333 Ben Smith .05 .01
❑ 334 Anthony Toney .05 .01
❑ 335 Andre Waters .05 .01
❑ 336 Reggie White .25 .08
❑ 337 Calvin Williams .10 .02
❑ 338 Anthony Bell .05 .01
❑ 339 Rich Camarillo .05 .01
❑ 340 Roy Green .05 .01
❑ 341 Tim Jorden RC .05 .01
❑ 342 Cedric Mack .05 .01
❑ 343 Dexter Manley .05 .01
❑ 344 Freddie Joe Nunn .05 .01
❑ 345 Ricky Proehl .05 .01
❑ 346 Tootie Robbins .05 .01
❑ 347 Timm Rosenbach .05 .01
❑ 348 Luis Sharpe .05 .01
❑ 349 Vai Sikahema .05 .01
❑ 350 Anthony Thompson .05 .01
❑ 351 Lonnie Young .05 .01
❑ 352 Dexter Carter .05 .01
❑ 353 Mike Cofer .05 .01
❑ 354 Kevin Fagan .05 .01
❑ 355 Don Griffin .05 .01
❑ 356 Charles Haley UER .10 .02
❑ 357 Pierce Holt .05 .01
❑ 358 Brent Jones .25 .08
❑ 359 Guy McIntyre .05 .01
❑ 360 Joe Montana 1.25 .50
❑ 361 Darryl Pollard .05 .01
❑ 362 Tom Rathman .05 .01
❑ 363 Jerry Rice .75 .30
❑ 364 Bill Romanowski .05 .01
❑ 365 John Taylor .10 .02
❑ 366 Steve Wallace .10 .02
❑ 367 Steve Young .75 .30
❑ 368 Gary Anderson RB .05 .01
❑ 369 Ian Beckles .05 .01
❑ 370 Mark Carrier WR .25 .08
❑ 371 Reggie Cobb .05 .01
❑ 372 Reuben Davis .05 .01
❑ 373 Randy Grimes .05 .01
❑ 374 Wayne Haddix .05 .01
❑ 375 Ron Hall .05 .01
❑ 376 Harry Hamilton .05 .01
❑ 377 Bruce Hill .05 .01
❑ 378 Keith McCants .05 .01
❑ 379 Bruce Perkins .05 .01
❑ 380 Vinny Testaverde UER .10 .02
❑ 381 Broderick Thomas .05 .01
❑ 382 Jeff Bostic .05 .01
❑ 383 Earnest Byner .05 .01
❑ 384 Gary Clark .25 .08
❑ 385 Darryl Grant .05 .01
❑ 386 Darrell Green .05 .01
❑ 387 Stan Humphries .25 .08
❑ 388 Jim Lachey .05 .01
❑ 389 Charles Mann .05 .01
❑ 390 Wilber Marshall .05 .01
❑ 391 Art Monk .10 .02
❑ 392 Gerald Riggs .05 .01
❑ 393 Mark Rypien .10 .02
❑ 394 Ricky Sanders .05 .01
❑ 395 Don Warren .05 .01
❑ 396 Bruce Smith HIT .10 .02
❑ 397 Reggie White HIT .10 .02
❑ 398 Lawrence Taylor HIT .10 .02
❑ 399 David Fulcher HIT .05 .01
❑ 400 Derrick Thomas HIT .10 .02
❑ 401 Mark Carrier DB HIT .05 .01
❑ 402 Mike Singletary HIT .10 .02
❑ 403 Charles Haley HIT .05 .01
❑ 404 Jeff Cross HIT .05 .01
❑ 405 Leslie O'Neal HIT .10 .02
❑ 406 Tim Harris HIT .05 .01
❑ 407 Steve Atwater HIT .05 .01
❑ 408 Joe Montana LL UER .50 .20
❑ 409 Randall Cunningham LL .10 .02
❑ 410 Warren Moon LL .10 .02
❑ 411 Andre Rison LL UER 412 .10 .02
❑ 412 Haywood Jeffires LL .10 .02
❑ 413 Stephone Paige LL .05 .01
❑ 414 Phil Simms LL .10 .02
❑ 415 Barry Sanders LL .50 .20
❑ 416 Bo Jackson LL .10 .02
❑ 417 Thurman Thomas LL .10 .02
❑ 418 Emmitt Smith LL 1.25 .50
❑ 419 John L. Williams LL .05 .01
❑ 420 Nick Bell RC .05 .01
❑ 421 Eric Bieniemy RC .05 .01
❑ 422 Mike Dumas RC UER .05 .01
❑ 423 Russell Maryland RC .25 .08
❑ 424 Derek Russell RC .05 .01
❑ 425 Chris Smith RC .05 .01
❑ 426 Mike Stonebreaker RP .05 .01
❑ 427 Pat Tyrance RP .05 .01
❑ 428 Kenny Walker RC .05 .01
❑ 429 Checklist 1-108 UER .05 .01
❑ 430 Checklist 109-216 .05 .01
❑ 431 Checklist 217-324 .05 .01
❑ 432 Checklist 325-432 .05 .01

1992 Fleer

❑ COMPLETE SET (480) 10.00 5.00
❑ 1 Steve Broussard .05 .01
❑ 2 Rick Bryan .05 .01
❑ 3 Scott Case .05 .01
❑ 4 Tory Epps .05 .01
❑ 5 Bill Fralic .05 .01
❑ 6 Moe Gardner .05 .01
❑ 7 Michael Haynes .10 .02
❑ 8 Chris Hinton .05 .01

❑ 9 Brian Jordan .10 .02
❑ 10 Mike Kenn .05 .01
❑ 11 Tim McKyer .05 .01
❑ 12 Chris Miller .10 .02
❑ 13 Erric Pegram .10 .02
❑ 14 Mike Pritchard .10 .02
❑ 15 Andre Rison .10 .02
❑ 16 Jessie Tuggle .05 .01
❑ 17 Carlton Bailey RC .10 .02
❑ 18 Howard Ballard .05 .01
❑ 19 Don Beebe .05 .01
❑ 20 Cornelius Bennett .10 .02
❑ 21 Shane Conlan .05 .01
❑ 22 Kent Hull .05 .01
❑ 23 Mark Kelso .05 .01
❑ 24 James Lofton .10 .02
❑ 25 Keith McKeller .05 .01
❑ 26 Scott Norwood .05 .01
❑ 27 Nate Odomes .05 .01
❑ 28 Frank Reich .10 .02
❑ 29 Jim Ritcher .05 .01
❑ 30 Leon Seals .05 .01
❑ 31 Darryl Talley .05 .01
❑ 32 Steve Tasker .10 .02
❑ 33 Thurman Thomas .25 .08
❑ 34 Will Wolford .05 .01
❑ 35 Neal Anderson .05 .01
❑ 36 Trace Armstrong .05 .01
❑ 37 Mark Carrier DB .05 .01
❑ 38 Richard Dent .10 .02
❑ 39 Shaun Gayle .05 .01
❑ 40 Jim Harbaugh .25 .08
❑ 41 Jay Hilgenberg .05 .01
❑ 42 Darren Lewis .05 .01
❑ 43 Steve McMichael .10 .02
❑ 44 Brad Muster .05 .01
❑ 45 William Perry .10 .02
❑ 46 John Roper .05 .01
❑ 47 Lemuel Stinson .05 .01
❑ 48 Stan Thomas .05 .01
❑ 49 Keith Van Horne .05 .01
❑ 50 Tom Waddle .05 .01
❑ 51 Donnell Woolford .05 .01
❑ 52 Chris Zorich .10 .02
❑ 53 Eddie Brown .05 .01
❑ 54 James Francis .05 .01
❑ 55 David Fulcher .05 .01
❑ 56 David Grant .05 .01
❑ 57 Harold Green .05 .01
❑ 58 Rodney Holman .05 .01
❑ 59 Lee Johnson .05 .01
❑ 60 Tim Krumrie .05 .01
❑ 61 Anthony Munoz .10 .02
❑ 62 Joe Walter RC .05 .01
❑ 63 Mike Baab .05 .01
❑ 64 Stephen Braggs .05 .01
❑ 65 Richard Brown RC .05 .01
❑ 66 Dan Fike .05 .01
❑ 67 Scott Galbraith RC .05 .01
❑ 68 Randy Hilliard RC .05 .01
❑ 69 Michael Jackson .10 .02
❑ 70 Tony Jones T .05 .01
❑ 71 Ed King .05 .01
❑ 72 Kevin Mack .05 .01
❑ 73 Clay Matthews .10 .02
❑ 74 Eric Metcalf .10 .02
❑ 75 Vince Newsome .05 .01
❑ 76 John Rienstra .05 .01
❑ 77 Steve Beuerlein .10 .02
❑ 78 Larry Brown DB .05 .01
❑ 79 Tony Casillas .05 .01
❑ 80 Alvin Harper .10 .02
❑ 81 Issiac Holt .05 .01
❑ 82 Ray Horton .05 .01
❑ 83 Michael Irvin .25 .08
❑ 84 Daryl Johnston .25 .08
❑ 85 Kelvin Martin .05 .01
❑ 86 Nate Newton .10 .02
❑ 87 Ken Norton .10 .02
❑ 88 Jay Novacek .10 .02
❑ 89 Emmitt Smith 1.50 .60
❑ 90 Vinson Smith RC .05 .01
❑ 91 Mark Stepnoski .10 .02
❑ 92 Steve Atwater .05 .01
❑ 93 Mike Croel .05 .01
❑ 94 John Elway 1.25 .50
❑ 95 Simon Fletcher .05 .01
❑ 96 Gaston Green .05 .01
❑ 97 Mark Jackson .05 .01
❑ 98 Keith Kartz .05 .01
❑ 99 Greg Kragen .05 .01
❑ 100 Greg Lewis .05 .01
❑ 101 Karl Mecklenburg .05 .01
❑ 102 Derek Russell .05 .01
❑ 103 Steve Sewell .05 .01
❑ 104 Dennis Smith .05 .01
❑ 105 David Treadwell .05 .01
❑ 106 Kenny Walker .05 .01
❑ 107 Doug Widell .05 .01
❑ 108 Michael Young .05 .01
❑ 109 Jerry Ball .05 .01
❑ 110 Bennie Blades .05 .01
❑ 111 Lomas Brown .05 .01
❑ 112 Scott Conover RC .05 .01
❑ 113 Ray Crockett .05 .01
❑ 114 Mike Farr .05 .01
❑ 115 Mel Gray .10 .02
❑ 116 Willie Green .05 .01
❑ 117 Tracy Hayworth RC .05 .01
❑ 118 Erik Kramer .10 .02
❑ 119 Herman Moore .25 .08
❑ 120 Dan Owens .05 .01
❑ 121 Rodney Peete .10 .02
❑ 122 Brett Perriman .25 .08
❑ 123 Barry Sanders 1.25 .50
❑ 124 Chris Spielman .10 .02
❑ 125 Marc Spindler .05 .01
❑ 126 Tony Bennett .05 .01
❑ 127 Matt Brock .05 .01
❑ 128 LeRoy Butler .05 .01
❑ 129 Johnny Holland .05 .01
❑ 130 Perry Kemp .05 .01
❑ 131 Don Majkowski .05 .01
❑ 132 Mark Murphy .05 .01
❑ 133 Brian Noble .05 .01
❑ 134 Bryce Paup .25 .08
❑ 135 Sterling Sharpe .25 .08
❑ 136 Scott Stephen .05 .01
❑ 137 Darrell Thompson .05 .01
❑ 138 Mike Tomczak .05 .01
❑ 139 Esera Tuaolo .05 .01
❑ 140 Keith Woodside .05 .01
❑ 141 Ray Childress .05 .01
❑ 142 Cris Dishman .05 .01
❑ 143 Curtis Duncan .05 .01
❑ 144 John Flannery .05 .01
❑ 145 William Fuller .10 .02
❑ 146 Ernest Givins .10 .02
❑ 147 Haywood Jeffires .10 .02
❑ 148 Sean Jones .10 .02
❑ 149 Lamar Lathon .05 .01
❑ 150 Bruce Matthews .05 .01
❑ 151 Bubba McDowell .05 .01
❑ 152 Johnny Meads .05 .01
❑ 153 Warren Moon .25 .08
❑ 154 Mike Munchak .10 .02
❑ 155 Al Smith .05 .01
❑ 156 Doug Smith .05 .01
❑ 157 Lorenzo White .05 .01
❑ 158 Michael Ball .05 .01
❑ 159 Chip Banks .05 .01
❑ 160 Duane Bickett .05 .01
❑ 161 Bill Brooks .05 .01
❑ 162 Ken Clark .05 .01
❑ 163 Jon Hand .05 .01
❑ 164 Jeff Herrod .05 .01
❑ 165 Jessie Hester .05 .01
❑ 166 Scott Radecic .05 .01
❑ 167 Rohn Stark .05 .01
❑ 168 Clarence Verdin .05 .01
❑ 169 John Alt .05 .01
❑ 170 Tim Barnett .05 .01
❑ 171 Tim Grunhard .05 .01
❑ 172 Dino Hackett .05 .01
❑ 173 Jonathan Hayes .05 .01
❑ 174 Bill Maas .05 .01
❑ 175 Chris Martin .05 .01
❑ 176 Christian Okoye .05 .01
❑ 177 Stephone Paige .05 .01
❑ 178 Jayice Pearson RC .05 .01
❑ 179 Kevin Porter .05 .01
❑ 180 Kevin Ross .05 .01
❑ 181 Dan Saleaumua .05 .01
❑ 182 Tracy Simien RC .05 .01
❑ 183 Neil Smith .25 .08
❑ 184 [illegible]
❑ 185 Robb Thomas .05 .01
❑ 186 Mark Vlasic .05 .01
❑ 187 Barry Word .05 .01
❑ 188 Marcus Allen .25 .08
❑ 189 Eddie Anderson .05 .01
❑ 190 Nick Bell .05 .01
❑ 191 Tim Brown .25 .08
❑ 192 Scott Davis .05 .01
❑ 193 Riki Ellison .05 .01
❑ 194 Mervyn Fernandez .05 .01
❑ 195 Willie Gault .10 .02
❑ 196 Jeff Gossett .05 .01
❑ 197 Ethan Horton .05 .01
❑ 198 Jeff Jaeger .05 .01
❑ 199 Howie Long .25 .08
❑ 200 Ronnie Lott .10 .02
❑ 201 Todd Marinovich .05 .01
❑ 202 Don Mosebar .05 .01
❑ 203 Jay Schroeder .05 .01
❑ 204 Greg Townsend .05 .01
❑ 205 Lionel Washington .05 .01
❑ 206 Steve Wisniewski .05 .01
❑ 207 Flipper Anderson .05 .01
❑ 208 Bern Brostek .05 .01
❑ 209 Robert Delpino .05 .01
❑ 210 Henry Ellard .10 .02
❑ 211 Jim Everett .10 .02
❑ 212 Cleveland Gary .05 .01
❑ 213 Kevin Greene .10 .02
❑ 214 Darryl Henley .05 .01
❑ 215 Damone Johnson .05 .01
❑ 216 Larry Kelm .05 .01
❑ 217 Todd Lyght .05 .01
❑ 218 Jackie Slater .05 .01
❑ 219 Michael Stewart .05 .01
❑ 220 Pat Terrell UER .05 .01
❑ 221 Robert Young .05 .01
❑ 222 Mark Clayton .10 .02
❑ 223 Bryan Cox .10 .02
❑ 224 Aaron Craver .05 .01
❑ 225 Jeff Cross .05 .01
❑ 226 Mark Duper .05 .01
❑ 227 Harry Galbreath .05 .01
❑ 228 David Griggs .05 .01
❑ 229 Mark Higgs .05 .01
❑ 230 Vestee Jackson .05 .01
❑ 231 John Offerdahl .05 .01
❑ 232 Louis Oliver .05 .01
❑ 233 Tony Paige .05 .01
❑ 234 Reggie Roby .05 .01
❑ 235 Sammie Smith .05 .01
❑ 236 Pete Stoyanovich .05 .01
❑ 237 Richmond Webb .05 .01
❑ 238 Terry Allen .25 .08
❑ 239 Ray Berry .05 .01
❑ 240 Joey Browner .05 .01
❑ 241 Anthony Carter .10 .02
❑ 242 Cris Carter .50 .20
❑ 243 Chris Doleman .05 .01
❑ 244 Rich Gannon .25 .08
❑ 245 Tim Irwin .05 .01
❑ 246 Steve Jordan .05 .01
❑ 247 Carl Lee .05 .01
❑ 248 Randall McDaniel .05 .01
❑ 249 Mike Merriweather .05 .01
❑ 250 Harry Newsome .05 .01
❑ 251 John Randle .10 .02
❑ 252 Henry Thomas .05 .01
❑ 253 Herschel Walker .10 .02
❑ 254 Ray Agnew .05 .01
❑ 255 Bruce Armstrong .05 .01
❑ 256 Vincent Brown .05 .01
❑ 257 Marv Cook .05 .01
❑ 258 Irving Fryar .10 .02

259	Pat Harlow	.05	.01
260	Tommy Hodson	.05	.01
261	Maurice Hurst	.05	.01
262	Ronnie Lippett	.05	.01
263	Eugene Lockhart	.05	.01
264	Greg McMurtry	.05	.01
265	Hugh Millen	.05	.01
266	Leonard Russell	.10	.02
267	Andre Tippett	.05	.01
268	Brent Williams	.05	.01
269	Morten Andersen	.05	.01
270	Gene Atkins	.05	.01
271	Wesley Carroll	.05	.01
272	Jim Dombrowski	.05	.01
273	Quinn Early	.10	.02
274	Gill Fenerty	.05	.01
275	Bobby Hebert	.05	.01
276	Joel Hilgenberg	.05	.01
277	Rickey Jackson	.05	.01
278	Vaughan Johnson	.05	.01
279	Eric Martin	.05	.01
280	Brett Maxie	.05	.01
281	Fred McAfee RC	.05	.01
282	Sam Mills	.05	.01
283	Pat Swilling	.10	.02
284	Floyd Turner	.05	.01
285	Steve Walsh	.05	.01
286	Frank Warren	.05	.01
287	Stephen Baker	.05	.01
288	Maurice Carthon	.05	.01
289	Mark Collins	.05	.01
290	John Elliott	.05	.01
291	Myron Guyton	.05	.01
292	Rodney Hampton	.10	.02
293	Jeff Hostetler	.10	.02
294	Mark Ingram	.05	.01
295	Pepper Johnson	.05	.01
296	Sean Landeta	.05	.01
297	Leonard Marshall	.05	.01
298	Dave Meggett	.10	.02
299	Bart Oates	.05	.01
300	Phil Simms	.10	.02
301	Reyna Thompson	.05	.01
302	Lewis Tillman	.05	.01
303	Brad Baxter	.05	.01
304	Kyle Clifton	.05	.01
305	James Hasty	.05	.01
306	Joe Kelly	.05	.01
307	Jeff Lageman	.05	.01
308	Mo Lewis	.05	.01
309	Erik McMillan	.05	.01
310	Rob Moore	.10	.02
311	Tony Stargell	.05	.01
312	Jim Sweeney	.05	.01
313	Marvin Washington	.05	.01
314	Lonnie Young	.05	.01
315	Eric Allen	.05	.01
316	Fred Barnett	.25	.08
317	Jerome Brown	.05	.01
318	Keith Byars	.05	.01
319	Wes Hopkins	.05	.01
320	Keith Jackson	.10	.02
321	James Joseph	.05	.01
322	Seth Joyner	.10	.02
323	Jeff Kemp	.05	.01
324	Roger Ruzek	.05	.01
325	Clyde Simmons	.05	.01
326	William Thomas	.05	.01
327	Reggie White	.25	.08
328	Calvin Williams	.10	.02
329	Rich Camarillo	.05	.01
330	Ken Harvey	.05	.01
331	Eric Hill	.05	.01
332	Johnny Johnson	.05	.01
333	Ernie Jones	.05	.01
334	Tim Jorden	.05	.01
335	Tim McDonald	.05	.01
336	Freddie Joe Nunn	.05	.01
337	Luis Sharpe	.05	.01
338	Eric Swann	.10	.02
339	Aeneas Williams	.10	.02
340	Gary Anderson K	.05	.01
341	Bubby Brister	.05	.01
342	Adrian Cooper	.05	.01
343	Barry Foster	.10	.02
344	Eric Green	.05	.01
345	Bryan Hinkle	.05	.01
346	Tunch Ilkin	.05	.01
347	Carnell Lake	.05	.01
348	Louis Lipps	.05	.01
349	David Little	.05	.01
350	Greg Lloyd	.10	.02
351	Neil O'Donnell	.25	.08
352	Dwight Stone	.05	.01
353	Rod Woodson	.25	.08
354	Rod Bernstine	.05	.01
355	Eric Bieniemy	.05	.01
356	Marion Butts	.05	.01
357	Gill Byrd	.05	.01
358	John Friesz	.10	.02
359	Burt Grossman	.05	.01
360	Courtney Hall	.05	.01
361	Ronnie Harmon	.05	.01
362	Shawn Jefferson	.05	.01
363	Nate Lewis	.05	.01
364	Craig McEwen RC	.05	.01
365	Eric Moten	.05	.01
366	Joe Phillips	.05	.01
367	Gary Plummer	.05	.01
368	Henry Rolling	.05	.01
369	Broderick Thompson	.05	.01
370	Harris Barton	.05	.01
371	Steve Bono RC	.25	.08
372	Todd Bowles	.05	.01
373	Dexter Carter	.05	.01
374	Michael Carter	.05	.01
375	Mike Cofer	.05	.01
376	Keith DeLong	.05	.01
377	Charles Haley	.10	.02
378	Merton Hanks	.10	.02
379	Tim Harris	.05	.01
380	Brent Jones	.10	.02
381	Guy McIntyre	.05	.01
382	Tom Rathman	.05	.01
383	Bill Romanowski	.05	.01
384	Jesse Sapolu	.05	.01
385	John Taylor	.10	.02
386	Steve Young	.60	.25
387	Robert Blackmon	.05	.01
388	Brian Blades	.10	.02
389	Jacob Green	.05	.01
390	Dwayne Harper	.05	.01
391	Andy Heck	.05	.01
392	Tommy Kane	.05	.01
393	John Kasay	.05	.01
394	Cortez Kennedy	.10	.02
395	Bryan Millard	.05	.01
396	Rufus Porter	.05	.01
397	Eugene Robinson	.05	.01
398	John L. Williams	.05	.01
399	Terry Wooden	.05	.01
400	Gary Anderson RB	.05	.01
401	Ian Beckles	.05	.01
402	Mark Carrier WR	.10	.02
403	Reggie Cobb	.05	.01
404	Lawrence Dawsey	.10	.02
405	Ron Hall	.05	.01
406	Keith McCants	.05	.01
407	Charles McRae	.05	.01
408	Tim Newton	.05	.01
409	Jesse Solomon	.05	.01
410	Vinny Testaverde	.10	.02
411	Broderick Thomas	.05	.01
412	Robert Wilson	.05	.01
413	Jeff Bostic	.05	.01
414	Earnest Byner	.05	.01
415	Gary Clark	.25	.08
416	Andre Collins	.05	.01
417	Brad Edwards	.05	.01
418	Kurt Gouveia	.05	.01
419	Darrell Green	.05	.01
420	Joe Jacoby	.05	.01
421	Jim Lachey	.05	.01
422	Chip Lohmiller	.05	.01
423	Charles Mann	.05	.01
424	Wilber Marshall	.05	.01
425	Ron Middleton RC	.05	.01
426	Brian Mitchell	.10	.02
427	Art Monk	.10	.02
428	Mark Rypien	.05	.01
429	Ricky Sanders	.05	.01
430	Mark Schlereth RC	.05	.01
431	Fred Stokes	.05	.01
432	Edgar Bennett RC	.25	.08
433	Brian Bollinger RC	.05	.01
434	Joe Bowden RC	.05	.01
435	Terrell Buckley RC	.05	.01
436	Willie Clay RC	.05	.01
437	Steve Gordon RC	.05	.01
438	Keith Hamilton RC	.10	.02
439	Carlos Huerta	.05	.01
440	Matt LaBounty RC	.05	.01
441	Amp Lee RC	.05	.01
442	Ricardo McDonald RC	.05	.01
443	Chris Mims RC	.10	.02
444	Michael Moody RC	.05	.01
445	Patrick Rowe RC	.05	.01
446	Leon Searcy RC	.10	.02
447	Siran Stacy RC	.05	.01
448	Kevin Turner RC	.05	.01
449	Tommy Vardell RC	.10	.02
450	Bob Whitfield RC	.05	.01
451	Darryl Williams RC	.05	.01
452	Thurman Thomas LL	.10	.02
453	Emmitt Smith LL	.75	.30
454	Haywood Jeffires LL	.05	.01
455	Michael Irvin LL	.10	.02
456	Mark Clayton LL	.05	.01
457	Barry Sanders LL	.60	.25
458	Pete Stoyanovich LL	.05	.01
459	Chip Lohmiller LL	.05	.01
460	William Fuller LL	.05	.01
461	Pat Swilling LL	.05	.01
462	Ronnie Lott LL	.05	.01
463	Ray Crockett LL	.05	.01
464	Tim McKyer LL	.05	.01
465	Aeneas Williams LL	.05	.01
466	Rod Woodson LL	.10	.02
467	Mel Gray LL	.05	.01
468	Nate Lewis LL	.05	.01
469	Steve Young LL	.30	.10
470	Reggie Roby LL	.05	.01
471	John Elway PV	.60	.25
472	Ronnie Lott PV	.05	.01
473	Art Monk PV UER	.05	.01
474	Warren Moon PV	.10	.02
475	Emmitt Smith PV	.75	.30
476	Thurman Thomas PV	.10	.02
477	Checklist 1-120	.05	.01
478	Checklist 121-240	.05	.01
479	Checklist 241-360	.05	.01
480	Checklist 361-480	.05	.01

1993 Fleer

	COMPLETE SET (500)	20.00	10.00
1	Dan Saleaumua	.05	.01
2	Bryan Cox	.05	.01
3	Dermontti Dawson	.05	.01
4	Michael Jackson	.10	.02
5	Calvin Williams	.10	.02
6	Terry McDaniel	.05	.01
7	Jack Del Rio	.05	.01
8	Steve Atwater	.05	.01
9	Ernie Jones	.05	.01
10	Brad Muster	.05	.01
11	Harold Green	.05	.01
12	Eric Bieniemy	.05	.01
13	Eric Dorsey	.05	.01
14	Fred Barnett	.10	.02
15	Cleveland Gary	.05	.01
16	Darion Conner	.05	.01
17	Jerry Ball	.05	.01
18	Tony Casillas	.05	.01
19	Brian Blades	.10	.02
20	Tony Bennett	.05	.01
21	Reggie Cobb	.05	.01
22	Kurt Gouveia	.05	.01
23	Greg McMurtry	.05	.01
24	Kyle Clifton	.05	.01

❑ 25	Trace Armstrong	.05	.01
❑ 26	Terry Allen	.25	.08
❑ 27	Steve Bono	.10	.02
❑ 28	Barry Word	.05	.01
❑ 29	Mark Duper	.05	.01
❑ 30	Nate Newton	.10	.02
❑ 31	Will Wolford	.05	.01
❑ 32	Curtis Duncan	.05	.01
❑ 33	Nick Bell	.05	.01
❑ 34	Don Beebe	.05	.01
❑ 35	Mike Croel	.05	.01
❑ 36	Rich Camarillo	.05	.01
❑ 37	Wade Wilson	.05	.01
❑ 38	John Taylor	.10	.02
❑ 39	Marion Butts	.05	.01
❑ 40	Rodney Hampton	.10	.02
❑ 41	Seth Joyner	.05	.01
❑ 42	Wilber Marshall	.05	.01
❑ 43	Bobby Hebert	.05	.01
❑ 44	Bennie Blades	.05	.01
❑ 45	Thomas Everett	.05	.01
❑ 46	Ricky Sanders	.05	.01
❑ 47	Matt Brock	.05	.01
❑ 48	Lawrence Dawsey	.05	.01
❑ 49	Brad Edwards	.05	.01
❑ 50	Vincent Brown	.05	.01
❑ 51	Jeff Lageman	.05	.01
❑ 52	Mark Carrier DB	.05	.01
❑ 53	Cris Carter	.25	.08
❑ 54	Brent Jones	.10	.02
❑ 55	Barry Foster	.10	.02
❑ 56	Derrick Thomas	.25	.08
❑ 57	Scott Zolak	.05	.01
❑ 58	Mark Stepnoski	.05	.01
❑ 59	Eric Metcalf	.10	.02
❑ 60	Al Smith	.05	.01
❑ 61	Ronnie Harmon	.05	.01
❑ 62	Cornelius Bennett	.10	.02
❑ 63	Karl Mecklenburg	.05	.01
❑ 64	Chris Chandler	.10	.02
❑ 65	Toi Cook	.05	.01
❑ 66	Tim Krumrie	.05	.01
❑ 67	Gill Byrd	.05	.01
❑ 68	Mark Jackson	.05	.01
❑ 69	Tim Harris	.05	.01
❑ 70	Shane Conlan	.05	.01
❑ 71	Moe Gardner	.05	.01
❑ 72	Lomas Brown	.05	.01
❑ 73	Charles Haley	.10	.02
❑ 74	Mark Rypien	.05	.01
❑ 75	LeRoy Butler	.05	.01
❑ 76	Steve DeBerg	.05	.01
❑ 77	Darrell Green	.05	.01
❑ 78	Marv Cook	.05	.01
❑ 79	Chris Burkett	.05	.01
❑ 80	Richard Dent	.10	.02
❑ 81	Roger Craig	.10	.02
❑ 82	Amp Lee	.05	.01
❑ 83	Eric Green	.05	.01
❑ 84	Willie Davis	.25	.08
❑ 85	Mark Higgs	.05	.01
❑ 86	Carlton Haselrig	.05	.01
❑ 87	Tommy Vardell	.05	.01
❑ 88	Haywood Jeffires	.10	.02
❑ 89	Tim Brown	.25	.08
❑ 90	Randall McDaniel	.05	.01
❑ 91	John Elway	1.50	.60
❑ 92	Ken Harvey	.05	.01
❑ 93	Joel Hilgenberg	.05	.01
❑ 94	Steve Wallace	.05	.01
❑ 95	Stan Humphries	.10	.02
❑ 96	Greg Jackson	.05	.01
❑ 97	Clyde Simmons	.05	.01
❑ 98	Jim Everett	.10	.02
❑ 99	Michael Haynes	.10	.02
❑ 100	Mel Gray	.10	.02
❑ 101	Alvin Harper	.10	.02
❑ 102	Art Monk	.10	.02
❑ 103	Brett Favre	2.00	.75
❑ 104	Keith McCants	.05	.01
❑ 105	Charles Mann	.05	.01
❑ 106	Leonard Russell	.10	.02
❑ 107	Mo Lewis	.05	.01
❑ 108	Shaun Gayle	.05	.01
❑ 109	Chris Doleman	.05	.01
❑ 110	Tim McDonald	.05	.01
❑ 111	Louis Oliver	.05	.01
❑ 112	Greg Lloyd	.10	.02
❑ 113	Chip Banks	.05	.01
❑ 114	Sean Jones	.05	.01
❑ 115	Ethan Horton	.05	.01
❑ 116	Kenneth Davis	.05	.01
❑ 117	Simon Fletcher	.05	.01
❑ 118	Johnny Johnson	.05	.01
❑ 119	Vaughan Johnson	.05	.01
❑ 120	Derrick Fenner	.05	.01
❑ 121	Nate Lewis	.05	.01
❑ 122	Pepper Johnson	.05	.01
❑ 123	Heath Sherman	.05	.01
❑ 124	Darryl Henley	.05	.01
❑ 125	Pierce Holt	.05	.01
❑ 126	Herman Moore	.25	.08
❑ 127	Michael Irvin	.25	.08
❑ 128	Tommy Kane	.05	.01
❑ 129	Jackie Harris	.05	.01
❑ 130	Hardy Nickerson	.10	.02
❑ 131	Chip Lohmiller	.05	.01
❑ 132	Andre Tippett	.05	.01
❑ 133	Leonard Marshall	.05	.01
❑ 134	Craig Heyward	.10	.02
❑ 135	Anthony Carter	.10	.02
❑ 136	Tom Rathman	.05	.01
❑ 137	Lorenzo White	.05	.01
❑ 138	Nick Lowery	.05	.01
❑ 139	John Offerdahl	.05	.01
❑ 140	Neil O'Donnell	.25	.08
❑ 141	Clarence Verdin	.05	.01
❑ 142	Ernest Givins	.10	.02
❑ 143	Todd Marinovich	.05	.01
❑ 144	Jeff Wright	.05	.01
❑ 145	Michael Brooks	.05	.01
❑ 146	Freddie Joe Nunn	.05	.01
❑ 147	William Perry	.10	.02
❑ 148	Daniel Stubbs	.05	.01
❑ 149	Morten Andersen	.05	.01
❑ 150	Dave Meggett	.05	.01
❑ 151	Andre Waters	.05	.01
❑ 152	Todd Lyght	.05	.01
❑ 153	Chris Miller	.10	.02
❑ 154	Rodney Peete	.05	.01
❑ 155	Jim Jeffcoat	.05	.01
❑ 156	Cortez Kennedy	.10	.02
❑ 157	Johnny Holland	.05	.01
❑ 158	Ricky Reynolds	.05	.01
❑ 159	Kevin Greene	.10	.02
❑ 160	Jeff Herrod	.05	.01
❑ 161	Bruce Matthews	.05	.01
❑ 162	Anthony Smith	.05	.01
❑ 163	Henry Jones	.05	.01
❑ 164	Rob Burnett	.05	.01
❑ 165	Eric Swann	.10	.02
❑ 166	Tom Waddle	.05	.01
❑ 167	Alfred Williams	.05	.01
❑ 168	Darren Carrington RC	.05	.01
❑ 169	Mike Sherrard	.05	.01
❑ 170	Frank Reich	.10	.02
❑ 171	Anthony Newman RC	.05	.01
❑ 172	Mike Pritchard	.10	.02
❑ 173	Andre Ware	.05	.01
❑ 174	Daryl Johnston	.25	.08
❑ 175	Rufus Porter	.05	.01
❑ 176	Reggie White	.25	.08
❑ 177	Charles Mincy RC	.05	.01
❑ 178	Pete Stoyanovich	.05	.01
❑ 179	Rod Woodson	.25	.08
❑ 180	Anthony Johnson	.10	.02
❑ 181	Cody Carlson	.05	.01
❑ 182	Gaston Green	.05	.01
❑ 183	Audray McMillian	.05	.01
❑ 184	Mike Johnson	.05	.01
❑ 185	Aeneas Williams	.05	.01
❑ 186	Jarrod Bunch	.05	.01
❑ 187	Dennis Smith	.05	.01
❑ 188	Quinn Early	.10	.02
❑ 189	James Hasty	.05	.01
❑ 190	Darryl Talley	.05	.01
❑ 191	Jon Vaughn	.05	.01
❑ 192	Andre Rison	.10	.02
❑ 193	Kelvin Pritchett	.05	.01
❑ 194	Ken Norton Jr.	.10	.02
❑ 195	Chris Warren	.10	.02
❑ 196	Sterling Sharpe	.25	.08
❑ 197	Christian Okoye	.05	.01
❑ 198	Richmond Webb	.05	.01
❑ 199	James Francis	.05	.01
❑ 200	Reggie Langhorne	.05	.01
❑ 201	J.J. Birden	.05	.01
❑ 202	Aaron Wallace	.05	.01
❑ 203	Henry Thomas	.05	.01
❑ 204	Clay Matthews	.10	.02
❑ 205	Robert Massey	.05	.01
❑ 206	Donnell Woolford	.05	.01
❑ 207	Ricky Watters	.25	.08
❑ 208	Wayne Martin	.05	.01
❑ 209	Rob Moore	.10	.02
❑ 210	Steve Tasker	.10	.02
❑ 211	Jackie Slater	.05	.01
❑ 212	Steve Young	.75	.30
❑ 213	Barry Sanders	1.25	.50
❑ 214	Jay Novacek	.10	.02
❑ 215	Eugene Robinson	.05	.01
❑ 216	Duane Bickett	.05	.01
❑ 217	Broderick Thomas	.05	.01
❑ 218	David Fulcher	.05	.01
❑ 219	Rohn Stark	.05	.01
❑ 220	Warren Moon	.25	.08
❑ 221	Steve Wisniewski	.05	.01
❑ 222	Nate Odomes	.05	.01
❑ 223	Shannon Sharpe	.25	.08
❑ 224	Byron Evans	.05	.01
❑ 225	Mark Collins	.05	.01
❑ 226	Rod Bernstine	.05	.01
❑ 227	Sam Mills	.05	.01
❑ 228	Marvin Washington	.05	.01
❑ 229	Thurman Thomas	.25	.08
❑ 230	Brent Williams	.05	.01
❑ 231	Jessie Tuggle	.05	.01
❑ 232	Chris Spielman	.10	.02
❑ 233	Emmitt Smith	1.50	.60
❑ 234	John L. Williams	.05	.01
❑ 235	Jeff Cross	.05	.01
❑ 236	Chris Doleman AW	.05	.01
❑ 237	John Elway AW	.75	.30
❑ 238	Barry Foster AW	.05	.01
❑ 239	Cortez Kennedy AW	.05	.01
❑ 240	Steve Young AW	.40	.15
❑ 241	Barry Foster LL	.05	.01
❑ 242	Warren Moon LL	.05	.01
❑ 243	Sterling Sharpe LL	.05	.01
❑ 244	Emmitt Smith LL	.75	.30
❑ 245	Thurman Thomas LL	.10	.02
❑ 246	Michael Irvin PV	.10	.02
❑ 247	Steve Young PV	.40	.15
❑ 248	Barry Foster PV	.05	.01
❑ 249	Checklist	.05	.01
❑ 250	Checklist	.05	.01
❑ 251	Checklist	.05	.01
❑ 252	Checklist	.05	.01
❑ 253	Troy Aikman AW	.40	.15
❑ 254	Jason Hanson AW	.05	.01
❑ 255	Carl Pickens AW	.10	.02
❑ 256	Santana Dotson AW	.05	.01
❑ 257	Dale Carter AW	.05	.01
❑ 258	Clyde Simmons LL	.05	.01
❑ 259	Audray McMillian LL	.05	.01
❑ 260	Henry Jones LL	.05	.01
❑ 261	Deion Sanders LL	.25	.08
❑ 262	Haywood Jeffires LL	.05	.01
❑ 263	Deion Sanders PV	.25	.08
❑ 264	Andre Reed PV	.10	.02
❑ 265	Vince Workman	.05	.01
❑ 266	Robert Brown	.05	.01
❑ 267	Ray Agnew	.05	.01
❑ 268	Ronnie Lott	.10	.02
❑ 269	Wesley Carroll	.05	.01
❑ 270	John Randle	.10	.02
❑ 271	Rodney Culver	.05	.01
❑ 272	David Alexander	.05	.01
❑ 273	Troy Aikman	.75	.30
❑ 274	Bernie Kosar	.10	.02
❑ 275	Scott Case	.05	.01
❑ 276	Dan McGwire	.05	.01
❑ 277	John Alt	.05	.01
❑ 278	Dan Marino	1.50	.60
❑ 279	Santana Dotson	.10	.02
❑ 280	Johnny Mitchell	.05	.01
❑ 281	Alonzo Spellman	.05	.01
❑ 282	Adrian Cooper	.05	.01
❑ 283	Gary Clark	.10	.02
❑ 284	Vance Johnson	.05	.01
❑ 285	Eric Martin	.05	.01
❑ 286	Jesse Solomon	.05	.01
❑ 287	Carl Banks	.05	.01
❑ 288	Harris Barton	.05	.01
❑ 289	Jim Harbaugh	.25	.08
❑ 290	Bubba McDowell	.05	.01
❑ 291	Anthony McDowell RC	.05	.01

❑ 292 Terrell Buckley .05 .01
❑ 293 Bruce Armstrong .05 .01
❑ 294 Kurt Barber .05 .01
❑ 295 Reginald Jones .05 .01
❑ 296 Steve Jordan .05 .01
❑ 297 Kerry Cash .05 .01
❑ 298 Ray Crockett .05 .01
❑ 299 Keith Byars .05 .01
❑ 300 Russell Maryland .05 .01
❑ 301 Johnny Bailey .05 .01
❑ 302 Vinnie Clark .05 .01
❑ 303 Terry Wooden .05 .01
❑ 304 Harvey Williams .10 .02
❑ 305 Marco Coleman .05 .01
❑ 306 Mark Wheeler .05 .01
❑ 307 Greg Townsend .05 .01
❑ 308 Tim McGee .05 .01
❑ 309 Donald Evans .05 .01
❑ 310 Randal Hill .05 .01
❑ 311 Kenny Walker .05 .01
❑ 312 Dalton Hilliard .05 .01
❑ 313 Howard Ballard .05 .01
❑ 314 Phil Simms .10 .02
❑ 315 Jerry Rice 1.00 .40
❑ 316 Courtney Hall .05 .01
❑ 317 Darren Lewis .05 .01
❑ 318 Greg Montgomery .05 .01
❑ 319 Paul Gruber .05 .01
❑ 320 George Koonce RC .05 .01
❑ 321 Eugene Chung .05 .01
❑ 322 Mike Brim .05 .01
❑ 323 Patrick Hunter .05 .01
❑ 324 Todd Scott .05 .01
❑ 325 Steve Emtman .05 .01
❑ 326 Andy Harmon RC .10 .02
❑ 327 Larry Brown DB .05 .01
❑ 328 Chuck Cecil .05 .01
❑ 329 Tim McKyer .05 .01
❑ 330 Jeff Bryant .05 .01
❑ 331 Tim Barnett .05 .01
❑ 332 Irving Fryar .10 .02
❑ 333 Tyji Armstrong .05 .01
❑ 334 Brad Baxter .05 .01
❑ 335 Shane Collins .05 .01
❑ 336 Jeff Graham .10 .02
❑ 337 Ricky Proehl .05 .01
❑ 338 Tommy Maddox .25 .08
❑ 339 Jim Dombrowski .05 .01
❑ 340 Bill Brooks .05 .01
❑ 341 Dave Brown RC .25 .08
❑ 342 Eric Davis .05 .01
❑ 343 Leslie O'Neal .10 .02
❑ 344 Jim Morrissey .05 .01
❑ 345 Mike Munchak .10 .02
❑ 346 Ron Hall .05 .01
❑ 347 Brian Noble .05 .01
❑ 348 Chris Singleton .05 .01
❑ 349 Boomer Esiason .10 .02
❑ 350 Ray Roberts .05 .01
❑ 351 Gary Zimmerman .05 .01
❑ 352 Quentin Coryatt .10 .02
❑ 353 Willie Green .05 .01
❑ 354 Randall Cunningham .25 .08
❑ 355 Kevin Smith .10 .02
❑ 356 Michael Dean Perry .10 .02
❑ 357 Tim Green .05 .01
❑ 358 Dwayne Harper .05 .01
❑ 359 Dale Carter .05 .01
❑ 360 Keith Jackson .10 .02
❑ 361 Martin Mayhew .05 .01
❑ 362 Brian Washington .05 .01
❑ 363 Earnest Byner .05 .01
❑ 364 D.J. Johnson .05 .01
❑ 365 Timm Rosenbach .05 .01
❑ 366 Doug Widell .05 .01
❑ 367 Vaughn Dunbar .05 .01
❑ 368 Phil Hansen .05 .01
❑ 369 Mike Fox .05 .01
❑ 370 Dana Hall .05 .01
❑ 371 Junior Seau .25 .08
❑ 372 Steve McMichael .10 .02
❑ 373 Eddie Robinson .05 .01
❑ 374 Milton Mack RC .05 .01
❑ 375 Mike Prior .05 .01
❑ 376 Jerome Henderson .05 .01
❑ 377 Scott Mersereau .05 .01
❑ 378 Neal Anderson .05 .01
❑ 379 Harry Newsome .05 .01
❑ 380 John Baylor .05 .01
❑ 381 Bill Fralic .05 .01
❑ 382 Mark Bavaro .05 .01
❑ 383 Robert Jones .05 .01
❑ 384 Tyronne Stowe .05 .01
❑ 385 Deion Sanders .50 .20
❑ 386 Robert Blackmon .05 .01
❑ 387 Neil Smith .25 .08
❑ 388 Mark Ingram .05 .01
❑ 389 Mark Carrier WR .10 .02
❑ 390 Browning Nagle .05 .01
❑ 391 Ricky Ervins .05 .01
❑ 392 Carnell Lake .05 .01
❑ 393 Luis Sharpe .05 .01
❑ 394 Greg Kragen .05 .01
❑ 395 Tommy Barnhardt .05 .01
❑ 396 Mark Kelso .05 .01
❑ 397 Kent Graham RC .25 .08
❑ 398 Bill Romanowski .05 .01
❑ 399 Anthony Miller .10 .02
❑ 400 John Roper .05 .01
❑ 401 Lamar Rogers .05 .01
❑ 402 Troy Auzenne .05 .01
❑ 403 Webster Slaughter .05 .01
❑ 404 David Brandon .05 .01
❑ 405 Chris Hinton .05 .01
❑ 406 Andy Heck .05 .01
❑ 407 Tracy Simien .05 .01
❑ 408 Troy Vincent .05 .01
❑ 409 Jason Hanson .05 .01
❑ 410 Rod Jones CB RC .05 .01
❑ 411 Al Noga .05 .01
❑ 412 Ernie Mills .05 .01
❑ 413 Willie Gault .05 .01
❑ 414 Henry Ellard .10 .02
❑ 415 Rickey Jackson .05 .01
❑ 416 Bruce Smith .25 .08
❑ 417 Derek Brown TE .05 .01
❑ 418 Kevin Fagan .05 .01
❑ 419 Gary Plummer .05 .01
❑ 420 Wendell Davis .05 .01
❑ 421 Craig Thompson .05 .01
❑ 422 Wes Hopkins .05 .01
❑ 423 Ray Childress .05 .01
❑ 424 Pat Harlow .05 .01
❑ 425 Howie Long .25 .08
❑ 426 Shane Dronett .05 .01
❑ 427 Sean Salisbury .05 .01
❑ 428 Dwight Hollier RC .05 .01
❑ 429 Brett Perriman .25 .08
❑ 430 Donald Hollas RC .05 .01
❑ 431 Jim Lachey .05 .01
❑ 432 Darren Perry .05 .01
❑ 433 Lionel Washington .05 .01
❑ 434 Sean Gilbert .10 .02
❑ 435 Gene Atkins .05 .01
❑ 436 Jim Kelly .25 .08
❑ 437 Ed McCaffrey .25 .08
❑ 438 Don Griffin .05 .01
❑ 439 Jerrol Williams .05 .01
❑ 440 Bryce Paup .10 .02
❑ 441 Darryl Williams .05 .01
❑ 442 Vai Sikahema .05 .01
❑ 443 Cris Dishman .05 .01
❑ 444 Kevin Mack .05 .01
❑ 445 Winston Moss .05 .01
❑ 446 Tyrone Braxton .05 .01
❑ 447 Mike Merriweather .05 .01
❑ 448 Tony Paige .05 .01
❑ 449 Robert Porcher .05 .01
❑ 450 Ricardo McDonald .05 .01
❑ 451 Danny Copeland .05 .01
❑ 452 Tony Tolbert .05 .01
❑ 453 Eric Dickerson .10 .02
❑ 454 Flipper Anderson .05 .01
❑ 455 Dave Krieg .10 .02
❑ 456 Brad Lamb RC .05 .01
❑ 457 Bart Oates .05 .01
❑ 458 Guy McIntyre .05 .01
❑ 459 Stanley Richard .05 .01
❑ 460 Edgar Bennett .25 .08
❑ 461 Pat Carter .05 .01
❑ 462 Eric Allen .05 .01
❑ 463 William Fuller .05 .01
❑ 464 James Jones DT .05 .01
❑ 465 Chester McGlockton .10 .02
❑ 466 Charles Dimry .05 .01
❑ 467 Tim Grunhard .05 .01
❑ 468 Jarvis Williams .05 .01
❑ 469 Tracy Scroggins .05 .01
❑ 470 David Klingler .05 .01
❑ 471 Andre Collins .05 .01
❑ 472 Erik Williams .05 .01
❑ 473 Eddie Anderson .05 .01
❑ 474 Marc Boutte .05 .01
❑ 475 Joe Montana 1.50 .60
❑ 476 Andre Reed .10 .02
❑ 477 Lawrence Taylor .25 .08
❑ 478 Jeff George .25 .08
❑ 479 Chris Mims .05 .01
❑ 480 Ken Ruettgers .05 .01
❑ 481 Roman Phifer .05 .01
❑ 482 William Thomas .05 .01
❑ 483 Lamar Lathon .05 .01
❑ 484 Vinny Testaverde .10 .02
❑ 485 Mike Kenn .05 .01
❑ 486 Greg Lewis .05 .01
❑ 487 Chris Martin .05 .01
❑ 488 Maurice Hurst .05 .01
❑ 489 Pat Swilling .05 .01
❑ 490 Carl Pickens .10 .02
❑ 491 Tony Smith RB .05 .01
❑ 492 James Washington .05 .01
❑ 493 Jeff Hostetler .10 .02
❑ 494 Jeff Chadwick .05 .01
❑ 495 Kevin Ross .05 .01
❑ 496 Jim Ritcher .05 .01
❑ 497 Jessie Hester .05 .01
❑ 498 Burt Grossman .05 .01
❑ 499 Keith Van Horne .05 .01
❑ 500 Gerald Robinson .05 .01
❑ P1 Promo Panel 5.00 2.00

1994 Fleer

❑ COMPLETE SET (480) 20.00 10.00
❑ 1 Michael Bankston .05 .01
❑ 2 Steve Beuerlein .10 .02
❑ 3 John Booty .05 .01
❑ 4 Rich Camarillo .05 .01
❑ 5 Chuck Cecil .05 .01
❑ 6 Larry Centers .25 .08
❑ 7 Gary Clark .10 .02
❑ 8 Garrison Hearst .25 .08
❑ 9 Eric Hill .05 .01
❑ 10 Randal Hill .05 .01
❑ 11 Ronald Moore .05 .01
❑ 12 Ricky Proehl .05 .01
❑ 13 Luis Sharpe .05 .01
❑ 14 Clyde Simmons .05 .01
❑ 15 Tyronne Stowe .05 .01
❑ 16 Eric Swann .10 .02
❑ 17 Aeneas Williams .05 .01
❑ 18 Darion Conner .05 .01
❑ 19 Moe Gardner .05 .01
❑ 20 Jumpy Geathers .05 .01
❑ 21 Jeff George .25 .08
❑ 22 Roger Harper .05 .01
❑ 23 Bobby Hebert .05 .01
❑ 24 Pierce Holt .05 .01
❑ 25 D.J. Johnson .05 .01
❑ 26 Mike Kenn .05 .01
❑ 27 Lincoln Kennedy .05 .01
❑ 28 Erric Pegram .05 .01
❑ 29 Mike Pritchard .05 .01
❑ 30 Andre Rison .10 .02
❑ 31 Deion Sanders .50 .20
❑ 32 Tony Smith RB .05 .01
❑ 33 Jesse Solomon .05 .01
❑ 34 Jessie Tuggle .05 .01
❑ 35 Don Beebe .05 .01
❑ 36 Cornelius Bennett .10 .02
❑ 37 Bill Brooks .05 .01

❑	38 Kenneth Davis	.05	.01
❑	39 John Fina	.05	.01
❑	40 Phil Hansen	.05	.01
❑	41 Kent Hull	.05	.01
❑	42 Henry Jones	.05	.01
❑	43 Jim Kelly	.25	.08
❑	44 Pete Metzelaars	.05	.01
❑	45 Marvcus Patton	.05	.01
❑	46 Andre Reed	.10	.02
❑	47 Frank Reich	.10	.02
❑	48 Bruce Smith	.25	.08
❑	49 Thomas Smith	.05	.01
❑	50 Darryl Talley	.05	.01
❑	51 Steve Tasker	.10	.02
❑	[illegible]	[illegible]	[illegible]
❑	53 Jeff Wright	.05	.01
❑	54 Neal Anderson	.05	.01
❑	55 Trace Armstrong	.05	.01
❑	56 Troy Auzenne	.05	.01
❑	57 Joe Cain RC	.05	.01
❑	58 Mark Carrier DB	.05	.01
❑	59 Curtis Conway	.25	.08
❑	60 Richard Dent	.10	.02
❑	61 Shaun Gayle	.05	.01
❑	62 Andy Heck	.05	.01
❑	63 Dante Jones	.05	.01
❑	64 Erik Kramer	.10	.02
❑	65 Steve McMichael	.10	.02
❑	66 Terry Obee	.05	.01
❑	67 Vinson Smith	.05	.01
❑	68 Alonzo Spellman	.05	.01
❑	69 Tom Waddle	.05	.01
❑	70 Donnell Woolford	.05	.01
❑	71 Tim Worley	.05	.01
❑	72 Chris Zorich	.05	.01
❑	73 Mike Brim	.05	.01
❑	74 John Copeland	.05	.01
❑	75 Derrick Fenner	.05	.01
❑	76 James Francis	.05	.01
❑	77 Harold Green	.05	.01
❑	78 Rod Jones CB	.05	.01
❑	79 David Klingler	.05	.01
❑	80 Bruce Kozerski	.05	.01
❑	81 Tim Krumrie	.05	.01
❑	82 Ricardo McDonald	.05	.01
❑	83 Tim McGee	.05	.01
❑	84 Tony McGee	.05	.01
❑	85 Louis Oliver	.05	.01
❑	86 Carl Pickens	.10	.02
❑	87 Jeff Query	.05	.01
❑	88 Daniel Stubbs	.05	.01
❑	89 Steve Tovar	.05	.01
❑	90 Alfred Williams	.05	.01
❑	91 Darryl Williams	.05	.01
❑	92 Rob Burnett	.05	.01
❑	93 Mark Carrier WR	.10	.02
❑	94 Leroy Hoard	.05	.01
❑	95 Michael Jackson	.10	.02
❑	96 Mike Johnson	.05	.01
❑	97 Pepper Johnson	.05	.01
❑	98 Tony Jones T	.05	.01
❑	99 Clay Matthews	.05	.01
❑	100 Eric Metcalf	.10	.02
❑	101 Stevon Moore	.05	.01
❑	102 Michael Dean Perry	.10	.02
❑	103 Anthony Pleasant	.05	.01
❑	104 Vinny Testaverde	.10	.02
❑	105 Eric Turner	.05	.01
❑	106 Tommy Vardell	.05	.01
❑	107 Troy Aikman	1.00	.40
❑	108 Larry Brown DB	.05	.01
❑	109 Dixon Edwards	.05	.01
❑	110 Charles Haley	.10	.02
❑	111 Alvin Harper	.10	.02
❑	112 Michael Irvin	.25	.08
❑	113 Jim Jeffcoat	.05	.01
❑	114 Daryl Johnston	.10	.02
❑	115 Leon Lett	.05	.01
❑	116 Russell Maryland	.05	.01
❑	117 Nate Newton	.05	.01
❑	118 Ken Norton Jr.	.10	.02
❑	119 Jay Novacek	.10	.02
❑	120 Darrin Smith	.05	.01
❑	121 Emmitt Smith	1.50	.60
❑	122 Kevin Smith	.05	.01
❑	123 Mark Stepnoski	.05	.01
❑	124 Tony Tolbert	.05	.01
❑	125 Erik Williams	.05	.01
❑	126 Kevin Williams WR	.10	.02
❑	127 Darren Woodson	.10	.02
❑	128 Steve Atwater	.05	.01
❑	129 Rod Bernstine	.05	.01
❑	130 Ray Crockett	.05	.01
❑	131 Mike Croel	.05	.01
❑	132 Robert Delpino	.05	.01
❑	133 Shane Dronett	.05	.01
❑	134 Jason Elam	.10	.02
❑	135 John Elway	2.00	.75
❑	136 Simon Fletcher	.05	.01
❑	137 Greg Kragen	.05	.01
❑	138 Karl Mecklenburg	.05	.01
❑	139 Glyn Milburn	.10	.02
❑	140 Anthony Miller	.10	.02
❑	141 Derek Russell	.05	.01
❑	142 Shannon Sharpe	.10	.02
❑	143 Dennis Smith	.05	.01
❑	144 Dan Williams	.05	.01
❑	145 Gary Zimmerman	.05	.01
❑	146 Bennie Blades	.05	.01
❑	147 Lomas Brown	.05	.01
❑	148 Bill Fralic	.05	.01
❑	149 Mel Gray	.05	.01
❑	150 Willie Green	.05	.01
❑	151 Jason Hanson	.05	.01
❑	152 Robert Massey	.05	.01
❑	153 Ryan McNeil	.05	.01
❑	154 Scott Mitchell	.10	.02
❑	155 Derrick Moore	.05	.01
❑	156 Herman Moore	.25	.08
❑	157 Brett Perriman	.10	.02
❑	158 Robert Porcher	.05	.01
❑	159 Kelvin Pritchett	.05	.01
❑	160 Barry Sanders	1.50	.60
❑	161 Tracy Scroggins	.05	.01
❑	162 Chris Spielman	.10	.02
❑	163 Pat Swilling	.05	.01
❑	164 Edgar Bennett	.25	.08
❑	165 Robert Brooks	.25	.08
❑	166 Terrell Buckley	.05	.01
❑	167 LeRoy Butler	.05	.01
❑	168 Brett Favre	2.00	.75
❑	169 Harry Galbreath	.05	.01
❑	170 Jackie Harris	.05	.01
❑	171 Johnny Holland	.05	.01
❑	172 Chris Jacke	.05	.01
❑	173 George Koonce	.05	.01
❑	174 Bryce Paup	.10	.02
❑	175 Ken Ruettgers	.05	.01
❑	176 Sterling Sharpe	.10	.02
❑	177 Wayne Simmons	.05	.01
❑	178 George Teague	.05	.01
❑	179 Darrell Thompson	.05	.01
❑	180 Reggie White	.25	.08
❑	181 Gary Brown	.05	.01
❑	182 Cody Carlson	.05	.01
❑	183 Ray Childress	.05	.01
❑	184 Cris Dishman	.05	.01
❑	185 Ernest Givins	.10	.02
❑	186 Haywood Jeffires	.10	.02
❑	187 Sean Jones	.05	.01
❑	188 Lamar Lathon	.05	.01
❑	189 Bruce Matthews	.05	.01
❑	190 Bubba McDowell	.05	.01
❑	191 Glenn Montgomery	.05	.01
❑	192 Greg Montgomery	.05	.01
❑	193 Warren Moon	.25	.08
❑	194 Bo Orlando	.05	.01
❑	195 Marcus Robertson	.05	.01
❑	196 Eddie Robinson	.05	.01
❑	197 Webster Slaughter	.05	.01
❑	198 Lorenzo White	.05	.01
❑	199 John Baylor	.05	.01
❑	200 Jason Belser	.05	.01
❑	201 Tony Bennett	.05	.01
❑	202 Dean Biasucci	.05	.01
❑	203 Ray Buchanan	.05	.01
❑	204 Kerry Cash	.05	.01
❑	205 Quentin Coryatt	.05	.01
❑	206 Eugene Daniel	.05	.01
❑	207 Steve Emtman	.05	.01
❑	208 Jon Hand	.05	.01
❑	209 Jim Harbaugh	.25	.08
❑	210 Jeff Herrod	.05	.01
❑	211 Anthony Johnson	.10	.02
❑	212 Roosevelt Potts	.05	.01
❑	213 Rohn Stark	.05	.01
❑	214 Will Wolford	.05	.01
❑	215 Marcus Allen	.25	.08
❑	216 John Alt	.05	.01
❑	217 Kimble Anders	.10	.02
❑	218 J.J. Birden	.05	.01
❑	219 Dale Carter	.05	.01
❑	220 Keith Cash	.05	.01
❑	221 Tony Casillas	.05	.01
❑	222 Willie Davis	.10	.02
❑	223 Tim Grunhard	.05	.01
❑	224 Nick Lowery	.05	.01
❑	225 Charles Mincy	.05	.01
❑	226 Joe Montana	2.00	.75
❑	227 Dan Saleaumua	.05	.01
❑	228 Tracy Simien	.05	.01
❑	229 Neil Smith	.10	.02
❑	230 Derrick Thomas	.25	.08
❑	231 Eddie Anderson	.05	.01
❑	232 Tim Brown	.25	.08
❑	233 Nolan Harrison	.05	.01
❑	234 Jeff Hostetler	.10	.02
❑	235 Rocket Ismail	.10	.02
❑	236 Jeff Jaeger	.05	.01
❑	237 James Jett	.05	.01
❑	238 Joe Kelly	.05	.01
❑	239 Albert Lewis	.05	.01
❑	240 Terry McDaniel	.05	.01
❑	241 Chester McGlockton	.05	.01
❑	242 Winston Moss	.05	.01
❑	243 Gerald Perry	.05	.01
❑	244 Greg Robinson	.05	.01
❑	245 Anthony Smith	.05	.01
❑	246 Steve Smith	.05	.01
❑	247 Greg Townsend	.05	.01
❑	248 Lionel Washington	.05	.01
❑	249 Steve Wisniewski	.05	.01
❑	250 Alexander Wright	.05	.01
❑	251 Flipper Anderson	.05	.01
❑	252 Jerome Bettis	.50	.20
❑	253 Marc Boutte	.05	.01
❑	254 Shane Conlan	.05	.01
❑	255 Troy Drayton	.05	.01
❑	256 Henry Ellard	.10	.02
❑	257 Sean Gilbert	.05	.01
❑	258 Nate Lewis	.05	.01
❑	259 Todd Lyght	.05	.01
❑	260 Chris Miller	.05	.01
❑	261 Anthony Newman	.05	.01
❑	262 Roman Phifer	.05	.01
❑	263 Henry Rolling	.05	.01
❑	264 T.J.Rubley RC	.05	.01
❑	265 Jackie Slater	.05	.01
❑	266 Fred Stokes	.05	.01
❑	267 Robert Young	.05	.01
❑	268 Gene Atkins	.05	.01
❑	269 J.B. Brown	.05	.01
❑	270 Keith Byars	.05	.01
❑	271 Marco Coleman	.05	.01
❑	272 Bryan Cox	.05	.01
❑	273 Jeff Cross	.05	.01
❑	274 Irving Fryar	.10	.02
❑	275 Mark Higgs	.05	.01
❑	276 Dwight Hollier	.05	.01
❑	277 Mark Ingram	.05	.01
❑	278 Keith Jackson	.05	.01
❑	279 Terry Kirby	.25	.08
❑	280 Bernie Kosar	.10	.02
❑	281 Dan Marino	2.00	.75
❑	282 O.J.McDuffie	.25	.08
❑	283 Keith Sims	.05	.01
❑	284 Pete Stoyanovich	.05	.01
❑	285 Troy Vincent	.05	.01
❑	286 Richmond Webb	.05	.01
❑	287 Terry Allen	.10	.02
❑	288 Anthony Carter	.10	.02
❑	289 Cris Carter	.50	.20
❑	290 Jack Del Rio	.05	.01
❑	291 Chris Doleman	.05	.01
❑	292 Vencie Glenn	.05	.01
❑	293 Scottie Graham RC	.10	.02
❑	294 Chris Hinton	.05	.01
❑	295 Qadry Ismail	.25	.08
❑	296 Carlos Jenkins	.05	.01
❑	297 Steve Jordan	.05	.01
❑	298 Carl Lee	.05	.01
❑	299 Randall McDaniel	.05	.01
❑	300 John Randle	.10	.02
❑	301 Todd Scott	.05	.01
❑	302 Robert Smith	.25	.08
❑	303 Fred Strickland	.05	.01
❑	304 Henry Thomas	.05	.01

❑ 305 Bruce Armstrong .05 .01
❑ 306 Harlon Barnett .05 .01
❑ 307 Drew Bledsoe .75 .30
❑ 308 Vincent Brown .05 .01
❑ 309 Ben Coates .10 .02
❑ 310 Todd Collins .05 .01
❑ 311 Myron Guyton .05 .01
❑ 312 Pat Harlow .05 .01
❑ 313 Maurice Hurst .05 .01
❑ 314 Leonard Russell .05 .01
❑ 315 Chris Slade .05 .01
❑ 316 Michael Timpson .05 .01
❑ 317 Andre Tippett .05 .01
❑ 318 Morten Andersen .05 .01
❑ 319 Derek Brown RBK .05 .01
❑ 320 Vince Buck .05 .01
❑ 321 Toi Cook .05 .01
❑ 322 Quinn Early .10 .02
❑ 323 Jim Everett .10 .02
❑ 324 Michael Haynes .10 .02
❑ 325 Tyrone Hughes .10 .02
❑ 326 Rickey Jackson .05 .01
❑ 327 Vaughan Johnson .05 .01
❑ 328 Eric Martin .05 .01
❑ 329 Wayne Martin .05 .01
❑ 330 Sam Mills .05 .01
❑ 331 Willie Roaf .05 .01
❑ 332 Irv Smith .05 .01
❑ 333 Keith Taylor .05 .01
❑ 334 Renaldo Turnbull .05 .01
❑ 335 Carlton Bailey .05 .01
❑ 336 Michael Brooks .05 .01
❑ 337 Jarrod Bunch .05 .01
❑ 338 Chris Calloway .05 .01
❑ 339 Mark Collins .05 .01
❑ 340 Howard Cross .05 .01
❑ 341 Stacey Dillard RC .05 .01
❑ 342 John Elliott .05 .01
❑ 343 Rodney Hampton .10 .02
❑ 344 Greg Jackson .05 .01
❑ 345 Mark Jackson .05 .01
❑ 346 Dave Meggett .05 .01
❑ 347 Corey Miller .05 .01
❑ 348 Mike Sherrard .05 .01
❑ 349 Phil Simms .10 .02
❑ 350 Lewis Tillman .05 .01
❑ 351 Brad Baxter .05 .01
❑ 352 Kyle Clifton .05 .01
❑ 353 Boomer Esiason .10 .02
❑ 354 James Hasty .05 .01
❑ 355 Bobby Houston .05 .01
❑ 356 Johnny Johnson .05 .01
❑ 357 Jeff Lageman .05 .01
❑ 358 Mo Lewis .05 .01
❑ 359 Ronnie Lott .10 .02
❑ 360 Leonard Marshall .05 .01
❑ 361 Johnny Mitchell .05 .01
❑ 362 Rob Moore .10 .02
❑ 363 Eric Thomas .05 .01
❑ 364 Brian Washington .05 .01
❑ 365 Marvin Washington .05 .01
❑ 366 Eric Allen .05 .01
❑ 367 Fred Barnett .10 .02
❑ 368 Bubby Brister .05 .01
❑ 369 Randall Cunningham .25 .08
❑ 370 Byron Evans .05 .01
❑ 371 William Fuller .05 .01
❑ 372 Andy Harmon .05 .01
❑ 373 Seth Joyner .05 .01
❑ 374 William Perry .10 .02
❑ 375 Leonard Renfro .05 .01
❑ 376 Heath Sherman .05 .01
❑ 377 Ben Smith .05 .01
❑ 378 William Thomas .05 .01
❑ 379 Herschel Walker .10 .02
❑ 380 Calvin Williams .10 .02
❑ 381 Chad Brown .05 .01
❑ 382 Dermontti Dawson .05 .01
❑ 383 Deon Figures .05 .01
❑ 384 Barry Foster .05 .01
❑ 385 Jeff Graham .05 .01
❑ 386 Eric Green .05 .01
❑ 387 Kevin Greene .10 .02
❑ 388 Carlton Haselrig .05 .01
❑ 389 Levon Kirkland .05 .01
❑ 390 Carnell Lake .05 .01
❑ 391 Greg Lloyd .10 .02
❑ 392 Neil O'Donnell .25 .08
❑ 393 Darren Perry .05 .01
❑ 394 Dwight Stone .05 .01
❑ 395 Leroy Thompson .05 .01
❑ 396 Rod Woodson .10 .02
❑ 397 Marion Butts .05 .01
❑ 398 John Carney .05 .01
❑ 399 Darren Carrington .05 .01
❑ 400 Burt Grossman .05 .01
❑ 401 Courtney Hall .05 .01
❑ 402 Ronnie Harmon .05 .01
❑ 403 Stan Humphries .10 .02
❑ 404 Shawn Jefferson .05 .01
❑ 405 Vance Johnson .05 .01
❑ 406 Chris Mims .05 .01
❑ 407 Leslie O'Neal .05 .01
❑ 408 Stanley Richard .05 .01
❑ 409 Junior Seau .25 .08
❑ 410 Harris Barton .05 .01
❑ 411 Dennis Brown .05 .01
❑ 412 Eric Davis .05 .01
❑ 413 Merton Hanks .10 .02
❑ 414 John Johnson .05 .01
❑ 415 Brent Jones .10 .02
❑ 416 Marc Logan .05 .01
❑ 417 Tim McDonald .05 .01
❑ 418 Gary Plummer .05 .01
❑ 419 Tom Rathman .05 .01
❑ 420 Jerry Rice 1.00 .40
❑ 421 Bill Romanowski .05 .01
❑ 422 Jesse Sapolu .05 .01
❑ 423 Dana Stubblefield .10 .02
❑ 424 John Taylor .10 .02
❑ 425 Steve Wallace .05 .01
❑ 426 Ted Washington .05 .01
❑ 427 Ricky Watters .10 .02
❑ 428 Troy Wilson RC .05 .01
❑ 429 Steve Young .75 .30
❑ 430 Howard Ballard .05 .01
❑ 431 Michael Bates .05 .01
❑ 432 Robert Blackmon .05 .01
❑ 433 Brian Blades .10 .02
❑ 434 Ferrell Edmunds .05 .01
❑ 435 Carlton Gray .05 .01
❑ 436 Patrick Hunter .05 .01
❑ 437 Cortez Kennedy .10 .02
❑ 438 Kelvin Martin .05 .01
❑ 439 Rick Mirer .25 .08
❑ 440 Nate Odomes .05 .01
❑ 441 Ray Roberts .05 .01
❑ 442 Eugene Robinson .05 .01
❑ 443 Rod Stephens .05 .01
❑ 444 Chris Warren .10 .02
❑ 445 John L. Williams .05 .01
❑ 446 Terry Wooden .05 .01
❑ 447 Marty Carter .05 .01
❑ 448 Reggie Cobb .05 .01
❑ 449 Lawrence Dawsey .05 .01
❑ 450 Santana Dotson .10 .02
❑ 451 Craig Erickson .05 .01
❑ 452 Thomas Everett .05 .01
❑ 453 Paul Gruber .05 .01
❑ 454 Courtney Hawkins .05 .01
❑ 455 Martin Mayhew .05 .01
❑ 456 Hardy Nickerson .10 .02
❑ 457 Ricky Reynolds .05 .01
❑ 458 Vince Workman .05 .01
❑ 459 Reggie Brooks .10 .02
❑ 460 Earnest Byner .05 .01
❑ 461 Andre Collins .05 .01
❑ 462 Brad Edwards .05 .01
❑ 463 Kurt Gouveia .05 .01
❑ 464 Darrell Green .05 .01
❑ 465 Ken Harvey .05 .01
❑ 466 Ethan Horton .05 .01
❑ 467 A.J. Johnson .05 .01
❑ 468 Tim Johnson .05 .01
❑ 469 Jim Lachey .05 .01
❑ 470 Chip Lohmiller .05 .01
❑ 471 Art Monk .10 .02
❑ 472 Sterling Palmer RC .05 .01
❑ 473 Mark Rypien .05 .01
❑ 474 Ricky Sanders .05 .01
❑ 475 Checklist 1-106 .05 .01
❑ 476 Checklist 107-214 .05 .01
❑ 477 Checklist 215-317 .05 .01
❑ 478 Checklist 318-409 .05 .01
❑ 479 Checklist 410-480/Inserts .05 .01
❑ 480 Inserts Checklist .05 .01
❑ P244 Jerome Bettis Promo 1.00 .40

1995 Fleer

❑ COMPLETE SET (400) 25.00 10.00
❑ 1 Michael Bankston .10 .02
❑ 2 Larry Centers .20 .07
❑ 3 Gary Clark .10 .02
❑ 4 Eric Hill .10 .02
❑ 5 Seth Joyner .10 .02
❑ 6 Dave Krieg .10 .02
❑ 7 Lorenzo Lynch .10 .02
❑ 8 Jamir Miller .10 .02
❑ 9 Ronald Moore .10 .02
❑ 10 Ricky Proehl .10 .02
❑ 11 Clyde Simmons .10 .02
❑ 12 Eric Swann .20 .07
❑ 13 Aeneas Williams .10 .02
❑ 14 J.J. Birden .10 .02
❑ 15 Chris Doleman .10 .02
❑ 16 Bert Emanuel .30 .10
❑ 17 Jumpy Geathers .10 .02
❑ 18 Jeff George .20 .07
❑ 19 Roger Harper .10 .02
❑ 20 Craig Heyward .20 .07
❑ 21 Pierce Holt .10 .02
❑ 22 D.J. Johnson .10 .02
❑ 23 Terance Mathis .20 .07
❑ 24 Clay Matthews .20 .07
❑ 25 Andre Rison .20 .07
❑ 26 Chuck Smith .10 .02
❑ 27 Jessie Tuggle .10 .02
❑ 28 Cornelius Bennett .20 .07
❑ 29 Bucky Brooks .10 .02
❑ 30 Jeff Burris .10 .02
❑ 31 Russell Copeland .10 .02
❑ 32 Matt Darby .10 .02
❑ 33 Phil Hansen .10 .02
❑ 34 Henry Jones .10 .02
❑ 35 Jim Kelly .30 .10
❑ 36 Mark Maddox RC .10 .02
❑ 37 Bryce Paup .20 .07
❑ 38 Andre Reed .20 .07
❑ 39 Bruce Smith .30 .10
❑ 40 Darryl Talley .10 .02
❑ 41 Dewell Brewer RC .10 .02
❑ 42 Mike Fox .10 .02
❑ 43 Eric Guliford .10 .02
❑ 44 Lamar Lathon .10 .02
❑ 45 Pete Metzelaars .10 .02
❑ 46 Sam Mills .20 .07
❑ 47 Frank Reich .10 .02
❑ 48 Rod Smith DB .20 .07
❑ 49 Jack Trudeau .10 .02
❑ 50 Trace Armstrong .10 .02
❑ 51 Joe Cain .10 .02
❑ 52 Mark Carrier DB .10 .02
❑ 53 Curtis Conway .30 .10
❑ 54 Shaun Gayle .10 .02
❑ 55 Jeff Graham .10 .02
❑ 56 Raymont Harris .10 .02
❑ 57 Erik Kramer .10 .02
❑ 58 Lewis Tillman .10 .02
❑ 59 Tom Waddle .10 .02
❑ 60 Steve Walsh .10 .02
❑ 61 Donnell Woolford .10 .02
❑ 62 Chris Zorich .10 .02
❑ 63 Jeff Blake RC .60 .25
❑ 64 Mike Brim .10 .02
❑ 65 Steve Broussard .10 .02
❑ 66 James Francis .10 .02
❑ 67 Ricardo McDonald .10 .02
❑ 68 Tony McGee .10 .02
❑ 70 Darnay Scott .20 .07

❑ 71 Steve Tovar .10 .02
❑ 72 Dan Wilkinson .20 .07
❑ 73 Alfred Williams .10 .02
❑ 74 Darryl Williams .10 .02
❑ 75 Derrick Alexander WR .30 .10
❑ 76 Randy Baldwin .10 .02
❑ 77 Carl Banks .10 .02
❑ 78 Rob Burnett .10 .02
❑ 79 Steve Everitt .10 .02
❑ 80 Leroy Hoard .10 .02
❑ 81 Michael Jackson .20 .07
❑ 82 Pepper Johnson .10 .02
❑ 83 Tony Jones T .10 .02
❑ 84 Antonio Langham .10 .02
❑ 85 Eric Metcalf .20 .07
❑ 86 Stevon Moore .10 .02
❑ 87 Anthony Pleasant .10 .02
❑ 88 Vinny Testaverde .20 .07
❑ 89 Eric Turner .10 .02
❑ 90 Troy Aikman 1.00 .40
❑ 91 Charles Haley .20 .07
❑ 92 Michael Irvin .30 .10
❑ 93 Daryl Johnston .20 .07
❑ 94 Robert Jones .10 .02
❑ 95 Leon Lett .10 .02
❑ 96 Russell Maryland .10 .02
❑ 97 Nate Newton .20 .07
❑ 98 Jay Novacek .20 .07
❑ 99 Darrin Smith .10 .02
❑ 100 Emmitt Smith 1.50 .60
❑ 101 Kevin Smith .10 .02
❑ 102 Erik Williams .10 .02
❑ 103 Kevin Williams WR .20 .07
❑ 104 Darren Woodson .20 .07
❑ 105 Elijah Alexander .10 .02
❑ 106 Steve Atwater .10 .02
❑ 107 Ray Crockett .10 .02
❑ 108 Shane Dronett .10 .02
❑ 109 Jason Elam .20 .07
❑ 110 John Elway 2.00 .75
❑ 111 Simon Fletcher .10 .02
❑ 112 Glyn Milburn .10 .02
❑ 113 Anthony Miller .20 .07
❑ 114 Michael Dean Perry .10 .02
❑ 115 Mike Pritchard .10 .02
❑ 116 Derek Russell .10 .02
❑ 117 Leonard Russell .10 .02
❑ 118 Shannon Sharpe .20 .07
❑ 119 Gary Zimmerman .10 .02
❑ 120 Bennie Blades .10 .02
❑ 121 Lomas Brown .10 .02
❑ 122 Willie Clay .10 .02
❑ 123 Mike Johnson .10 .02
❑ 124 Robert Massey .10 .02
❑ 125 Scott Mitchell .20 .07
❑ 126 Herman Moore .30 .10
❑ 127 Brett Perriman .20 .07
❑ 128 Robert Porcher .10 .02
❑ 129 Barry Sanders 1.50 .60
❑ 130 Chris Spielman .20 .07
❑ 131 Henry Thomas .10 .02
❑ 132 Edgar Bennett .20 .07
❑ 134 LeRoy Butler .10 .02
❑ 135 Brett Favre 2.00 .75
❑ 136 Sean Jones .10 .02
❑ 137 John Jurkovic .10 .02
❑ 138 George Koonce .10 .02
❑ 139 Wayne Simmons .10 .02
❑ 140 George Teague .10 .02
❑ 141 Reggie White .30 .10
❑ 142 Micheal Barrow .10 .02
❑ 143 Gary Brown .10 .02
❑ 144 Cody Carlson .10 .02
❑ 145 Ray Childress .10 .02
❑ 146 Cris Dishman .10 .02
❑ 147 Ernest Givins .10 .02
❑ 148 Mel Gray .10 .02
❑ 149 Darryll Lewis .10 .02
❑ 150 Bruce Matthews .10 .02
❑ 151 Marcus Robertson .10 .02
❑ 152 Webster Slaughter .10 .02
❑ 153 Al Smith .10 .02
❑ 154 Mark Stepnoski .10 .02
❑ 155 Trev Alberts .10 .02
❑ 156 Flipper Anderson .10 .02
❑ 157 Jason Belser .10 .02
❑ 158 Tony Bennett .10 .02
❑ 159 Ray Buchanan .10 .02
❑ 160 Quentin Coryatt .20 .07
❑ 161 Sean Dawkins .20 .07
❑ 162 Steve Emtman .10 .02
❑ 163 Marshall Faulk 1.25 .50
❑ 164 Stephen Grant RC .10 .02
❑ 165 Jim Harbaugh .20 .07
❑ 166 Jeff Herrod .10 .02
❑ 167 Tony Siragusa .10 .02
❑ 168 Steve Beuerlein .20 .07
❑ 169 Darren Carrington .10 .02
❑ 170 Reggie Cobb .10 .02
❑ 171 Kelvin Martin .10 .02
❑ 172 Kelvin Pritchett .10 .02
❑ 173 Joel Smeenge .10 .02
❑ 174 James Williams LB .10 .02
❑ 175 Marcus Allen .30 .10
❑ 176 Kimble Anders .20 .07
❑ 177 Dale Carter .20 .07
❑ 178 Mark Collins .10 .02
❑ 179 Willie Davis .20 .07
❑ 180 Lake Dawson .20 .07
❑ 181 Greg Hill .20 .07
❑ 182 Darren Mickell .10 .02
❑ 183 Joe Montana 2.00 .75
❑ 184 Tracy Simien .10 .02
❑ 185 Neil Smith .20 .07
❑ 186 William White .10 .02
❑ 187 Greg Biekert .10 .02
❑ 188 Tim Brown .30 .10
❑ 189 Rob Fredrickson .10 .02
❑ 190 Andrew Glover RC .10 .02
❑ 191 Nolan Harrison .10 .02
❑ 192 Jeff Hostetler .20 .07
❑ 193 Rocket Ismail .20 .07
❑ 194 Terry McDaniel .10 .02
❑ 195 Chester McGlockton .20 .07
❑ 196 Winston Moss .10 .02
❑ 197 Anthony Smith .10 .02
❑ 198 Harvey Williams .10 .02
❑ 199 Steve Wisniewski .10 .02
❑ 200 Johnny Bailey .10 .02
❑ 201 Jerome Bettis .30 .10
❑ 202 Isaac Bruce .50 .20
❑ 203 Shane Conlan .10 .02
❑ 204 Troy Drayton .10 .02
❑ 205 Sean Gilbert .20 .07
❑ 206 Jessie Hester .10 .02
❑ 207 Jimmie Jones .10 .02
❑ 208 Todd Lyght .10 .02
❑ 209 Chris Miller .10 .02
❑ 210 Roman Phifer .10 .02
❑ 211 Marquez Pope .10 .02
❑ 212 Robert Young .10 .02
❑ 213 Gene Atkins .10 .02
❑ 214 Aubrey Beavers .10 .02
❑ 215 Tim Bowens .10 .02
❑ 216 Bryan Cox .10 .02
❑ 217 Jeff Cross .10 .02
❑ 218 Irving Fryar .20 .07
❑ 219 Eric Green .10 .02
❑ 220 Mark Ingram .10 .02
❑ 221 Terry Kirby .20 .07
❑ 222 Dan Marino 2.00 .75
❑ 223 O.J. McDuffie .30 .10
❑ 224 Bernie Parmalee .20 .07
❑ 225 Keith Sims .10 .02
❑ 226 Irving Spikes .20 .07
❑ 227 Michael Stewart .10 .02
❑ 228 Troy Vincent .10 .02
❑ 229 Richmond Webb .10 .02
❑ 230 Terry Allen .20 .07
❑ 231 Cris Carter .30 .10
❑ 232 Jack Del Rio .10 .02
❑ 233 Vencie Glenn .10 .02
❑ 234 Qadry Ismail .20 .07
❑ 235 Carlos Jenkins .10 .02
❑ 236 Ed McDaniel .10 .02
❑ 237 Randall McDaniel .10 .02
❑ 238 Warren Moon .20 .07
❑ 239 Anthony Parker .10 .02
❑ 240 John Randle .20 .07
❑ 241 Jake Reed .20 .07
❑ 242 Fuad Reveiz .10 .02
❑ 243 Broderick Thomas .10 .02
❑ 244 Dewayne Washington .20 .07
❑ 245 Bruce Armstrong .10 .02
❑ 246 Drew Bledsoe .60 .25
❑ 247 Vincent Brisby .10 .02
❑ 248 Vincent Brown .10 .02
❑ 249 Marion Butts .10 .02
❑ 250 Ben Coates .20 .07
❑ 251 Tim Goad .10 .02
❑ 252 Myron Guyton .10 .02
❑ 253 Maurice Hurst .10 .02
❑ 254 Mike Jones .10 .02
❑ 255 Willie McGinest .20 .07
❑ 256 Dave Meggett .10 .02
❑ 257 Ricky Reynolds .10 .02
❑ 258 Chris Slade .20 .07
❑ 259 Michael Timpson .10 .02
❑ 260 Mario Bates .20 .07
❑ 261 Derek Brown RBK .10 .02
❑ 262 Darion Conner .10 .02
❑ 263 Quinn Early .20 .07
❑ 264 Jim Everett .10 .02
❑ 265 Michael Haynes .20 .07
❑ 266 Tyrone Hughes .20 .07
❑ 267 Joe Johnson .10 .02
❑ 268 Wayne Martin .10 .02
❑ 269 Willie Roaf .10 .02
❑ 270 Irv Smith .10 .02
❑ 271 Jimmy Spencer .10 .02
❑ 272 Winfred Tubbs .10 .02
❑ 273 Renaldo Turnbull .10 .02
❑ 274 Michael Brooks .10 .02
❑ 275 Dave Brown .20 .07
❑ 276 Chris Calloway .10 .02
❑ 277 Jesse Campbell .10 .02
❑ 278 Howard Cross .10 .02
❑ 279 John Elliott .10 .02
❑ 280 Keith Hamilton .10 .02
❑ 281 Rodney Hampton .20 .07
❑ 282 Thomas Lewis .20 .07
❑ 283 Thomas Randolph .10 .02
❑ 284 Mike Sherrard .10 .02
❑ 285 Michael Strahan .30 .10
❑ 286 Brad Baxter .10 .02
❑ 287 Tony Casillas .10 .02
❑ 288 Kyle Clifton .10 .02
❑ 289 Boomer Esiason .20 .07
❑ 290 Aaron Glenn .10 .02
❑ 291 Bobby Houston .10 .02
❑ 292 Johnny Johnson .10 .02
❑ 293 Jeff Lageman .10 .02
❑ 294 Mo Lewis .10 .02
❑ 295 Johnny Mitchell .10 .02
❑ 296 Rob Moore .20 .07
❑ 297 Marcus Turner .10 .02
❑ 298 Marvin Washington .10 .02
❑ 299 Eric Allen .10 .02
❑ 300 Fred Barnett .20 .07
❑ 301 Randall Cunningham .30 .10
❑ 302 Byron Evans .10 .02
❑ 303 William Fuller .10 .02
❑ 304 Charlie Garner .30 .10
❑ 305 Andy Harmon .10 .02
❑ 306 Greg Jackson .10 .02
❑ 307 Bill Romanowski .10 .02
❑ 308 William Thomas .10 .02
❑ 309 Herschel Walker .20 .07
❑ 310 Calvin Williams .20 .07
❑ 311 Michael Zordich .10 .02
❑ 312 Chad Brown .20 .07
❑ 313 Dermontti Dawson .20 .07
❑ 314 Barry Foster .20 .07
❑ 315 Kevin Greene .20 .07
❑ 316 Charles Johnson .20 .07
❑ 317 Levon Kirkland .10 .02
❑ 318 Carnell Lake .10 .02
❑ 319 Greg Lloyd .20 .07
❑ 320 Byron Bam Morris .10 .02
❑ 321 Neil O'Donnell .20 .07
❑ 322 Darren Perry .10 .02
❑ 323 Ray Seals .10 .02
❑ 324 John L. Williams .10 .02
❑ 325 Rod Woodson .20 .07
❑ 326 John Carney .10 .02
❑ 327 Andre Coleman .10 .02
❑ 328 Courtney Hall .10 .02
❑ 329 Ronnie Harmon .10 .02
❑ 330 Dwayne Harper .10 .02
❑ 331 Stan Humphries .20 .07
❑ 332 Shawn Jefferson .10 .02
❑ 333 Tony Martin .20 .07
❑ 334 Natrone Means .20 .07
❑ 335 Chris Mims .10 .02
❑ 336 Leslie O'Neal .20 .07
❑ 337 Alfred Pupunu RC .10 .02
❑ 338 Junior Seau .30 .10

❑ 339 Mark Seay .20 .07
❑ 340 Eric Davis .10 .02
❑ 341 William Floyd .20 .07
❑ 342 Merton Hanks .10 .02
❑ 343 Rickey Jackson .10 .02
❑ 344 Brent Jones .10 .02
❑ 345 Tim McDonald .10 .02
❑ 346 Ken Norton Jr. .20 .07
❑ 347 Gary Plummer .10 .02
❑ 348 Jerry Rice 1.00 .40
❑ 349 Deion Sanders .40 .15
❑ 350 Jesse Sapolu .10 .02
❑ 351 Dana Stubblefield .20 .07
❑ 352 John Taylor .10 .02
❑ 353 Steve Wallace .10 .02
❑ 354 Ricky Watters .20 .07
❑ 355 Lee Woodall .10 .02
❑ 356 Bryant Young .20 .07
❑ 357 Steve Young .75 .30
❑ 358 Sam Adams .10 .02
❑ 359 Howard Ballard .10 .02
❑ 360 Robert Blackmon .10 .02
❑ 361 Brian Blades .20 .07
❑ 362 Carlton Gray .10 .02
❑ 363 Cortez Kennedy .20 .07
❑ 364 Rick Mirer .20 .07
❑ 365 Eugene Robinson .10 .02
❑ 366 Chris Warren .20 .07
❑ 367 Terry Wooden .10 .02
❑ 368 Brad Culpepper .10 .02
❑ 369 Lawrence Dawsey .10 .02
❑ 370 Trent Dilfer .30 .10
❑ 371 Santana Dotson .10 .02
❑ 372 Craig Erickson .10 .02
❑ 373 Thomas Everett .10 .02
❑ 374 Paul Gruber .10 .02
❑ 375 Alvin Harper .10 .02
❑ 376 Jackie Harris .10 .02
❑ 377 Courtney Hawkins .10 .02
❑ 378 Martin Mayhew .10 .02
❑ 379 Hardy Nickerson .10 .02
❑ 380 Errict Rhett .20 .07
❑ 381 Charles Wilson .10 .02
❑ 382 Reggie Brooks .20 .07
❑ 383 Tom Carter .10 .02
❑ 384 Andre Collins .10 .02
❑ 385 Henry Ellard .20 .07
❑ 386 Ricky Ervins .10 .02
❑ 387 Darrell Green .10 .02
❑ 388 Ken Harvey .10 .02
❑ 389 Brian Mitchell .10 .02
❑ 390 Stanley Richard .10 .02
❑ 391 Heath Shuler .20 .07
❑ 392 Rod Stephens .10 .02
❑ 393 Tyronne Stowe .10 .02
❑ 394 Tydus Winans .10 .02
❑ 395 Tony Woods .10 .02
❑ 396 Checklist .10 .02
❑ 397 Checklist .10 .02
❑ 398 Checklist .10 .02
❑ 399 Checklist .10 .02
❑ 400 Checklist .10 .02

1996 Fleer

❑ COMPLETE SET (200) 20.00 7.50
❑ 1 Garrison Hearst .20 .07
❑ 2 Rob Moore .20 .07
❑ 3 Frank Sanders .20 .07
❑ 4 Eric Swann .10 .02
❑ 5 Aeneas Williams .10 .02
❑ 6 Jeff George .20 .07
❑ 7 Craig Heyward .10 .02
❑ 8 Terance Mathis .10 .02
❑ 9 Eric Metcalf .10 .02
❑ 10 Michael Jackson .20 .07
❑ 11 Andre Rison .20 .07
❑ 12 Vinny Testaverde .20 .07
❑ 13 Eric Turner .10 .02
❑ 14 Darick Holmes .10 .02
❑ 15 Jim Kelly .30 .10
❑ 16 Bryce Paup .10 .02
❑ 17 Bruce Smith .20 .07
❑ 18 Thurman Thomas .30 .10
❑ 19 Kerry Collins .30 .10
❑ 20 Lamar Lathon .10 .02
❑ 21 Derrick Moore .10 .02
❑ 22 Tyrone Poole .10 .02
❑ 23 Curtis Conway .30 .10
❑ 24 Bryan Cox .10 .02
❑ 25 Erik Kramer .10 .02
❑ 26 Rashaan Salaam .20 .07
❑ 27 Jeff Blake .30 .10
❑ 28 Ki-Jana Carter .20 .07
❑ 29 Carl Pickens .20 .07
❑ 30 Darnay Scott .20 .07
❑ 31 Troy Aikman .75 .30
❑ 32 Charles Haley .20 .07
❑ 33 Michael Irvin .30 .10
❑ 34 Daryl Johnston .20 .07
❑ 35 Jay Novacek .10 .02
❑ 36 Deion Sanders .40 .15
❑ 37 Emmitt Smith 1.25 .50
❑ 38 Steve Atwater .10 .02
❑ 39 Terrell Davis .60 .25
❑ 40 John Elway 1.50 .60
❑ 41 Anthony Miller .20 .07
❑ 42 Shannon Sharpe .20 .07
❑ 43 Scott Mitchell .20 .07
❑ 44 Herman Moore .20 .07
❑ 45 Johnnie Morton .20 .07
❑ 46 Brett Perriman .10 .02
❑ 47 Barry Sanders 1.25 .50
❑ 48 Edgar Bennett .20 .07
❑ 49 Robert Brooks .30 .10
❑ 50 Mark Chmura .20 .07
❑ 51 Brett Favre 1.50 .60
❑ 52 Reggie White .30 .10
❑ 53 Mel Gray .10 .02
❑ 54 Steve McNair .60 .25
❑ 55 Chris Sanders .20 .07
❑ 56 Rodney Thomas .10 .02
❑ 57 Quentin Coryatt .10 .02
❑ 58 Sean Dawkins .10 .02
❑ 59 Ken Dilger .20 .07
❑ 60 Marshall Faulk .40 .15
❑ 61 Jim Harbaugh .20 .07
❑ 62 Tony Boselli .10 .02
❑ 63 Mark Brunell .50 .20
❑ 64 Natrone Means .20 .07
❑ 65 James O.Stewart .20 .07
❑ 66 Marcus Allen .30 .10
❑ 67 Steve Bono .10 .02
❑ 68 Neil Smith .20 .07
❑ 69 Derrick Thomas .30 .10
❑ 70 Tamarick Vanover .20 .07
❑ 71 Fred Barnett .10 .02
❑ 72 Eric Green .10 .02
❑ 73 Dan Marino 1.50 .60
❑ 74 O.J. McDuffie .20 .07
❑ 75 Bernie Parmalee .10 .02
❑ 76 Cris Carter .30 .10
❑ 77 Qadry Ismail .20 .07
❑ 78 Warren Moon .20 .07
❑ 79 Jake Reed .20 .07
❑ 80 Robert Smith .20 .07
❑ 81 Drew Bledsoe .50 .20
❑ 82 Vincent Brisby .10 .02
❑ 83 Ben Coates .20 .07
❑ 84 Curtis Martin .60 .25
❑ 85 Dave Meggett .10 .02
❑ 86 Mario Bates .20 .07
❑ 87 Jim Everett .10 .02
❑ 88 Michael Haynes .10 .02
❑ 89 Renaldo Turnbull .10 .02
❑ 90 Dave Brown .10 .02
❑ 91 Rodney Hampton .20 .07
❑ 92 Thomas Lewis .10 .02
❑ 93 Tyrone Wheatley .20 .07
❑ 94 Kyle Brady .10 .02
❑ 95 Hugh Douglas .20 .07
❑ 96 Aaron Glenn .10 .02
❑ 97 Jeff Graham .10 .02
❑ 98 Adrian Murrell .20 .07
❑ 99 Neil O'Donnell .20 .07
❑ 100 Tim Brown .30 .10
❑ 101 Jeff Hostetler .10 .02
❑ 102 Napoleon Kaufman .30 .10
❑ 103 Chester McGlockton .10 .02
❑ 104 Harvey Williams .10 .02
❑ 105 William Fuller .10 .02
❑ 106 Charlie Garner .20 .07
❑ 107 Ricky Watters .20 .07
❑ 108 Calvin Williams .10 .02
❑ 109 Jerome Bettis .30 .10
❑ 110 Greg Lloyd .20 .07
❑ 111 Byron Bam Morris .10 .02
❑ 112 Kordell Stewart .30 .10
❑ 113 Yancey Thigpen .20 .07
❑ 114 Rod Woodson .20 .07
❑ 115 Isaac Bruce .30 .10
❑ 116 Troy Drayton .10 .02
❑ 117 Leslie O'Neal .10 .02
❑ 118 Steve Walsh .10 .02
❑ 119 Marco Coleman .10 .02
❑ 120 Aaron Hayden .10 .02
❑ 121 Stan Humphries .20 .07
❑ 122 Junior Seau .30 .10
❑ 123 William Floyd .20 .07
❑ 124 Brent Jones .10 .02
❑ 125 Ken Norton .10 .02
❑ 126 Jerry Rice .75 .30
❑ 127 J.J. Stokes .30 .10
❑ 128 Steve Young .60 .25
❑ 129 Brian Blades .10 .02
❑ 130 Joey Galloway .30 .10
❑ 131 Rick Mirer .20 .07
❑ 132 Chris Warren .20 .07
❑ 133 Trent Dilfer .30 .10
❑ 134 Alvin Harper .10 .02
❑ 135 Hardy Nickerson .10 .02
❑ 136 Errict Rhett .20 .07
❑ 137 Terry Allen .20 .07
❑ 138 Henry Ellard .10 .02
❑ 139 Heath Shuler .20 .07
❑ 140 Michael Westbrook .30 .10
❑ 141 Karim Abdul-Jabbar RC .30 .10
❑ 142 Mike Alstott RC 1.00 .40
❑ 143 Marco Battaglia RC .10 .02
❑ 144 Tim Biakabutuka RC .30 .10
❑ 145 Tony Brackens RC .30 .10
❑ 146 Duane Clemons RC .10 .02
❑ 147 Ernie Conwell RC .10 .02
❑ 148 Chris Darkins RC .10 .02
❑ 149 Stephen Davis RC 1.50 .60
❑ 150 Brian Dawkins RC 1.25 .50
❑ 151 Rickey Dudley RC .30 .10
❑ 152 Jason Dunn RC .20 .07
❑ 153 Bobby Engram RC .30 .10
❑ 154 Daryl Gardener RC .10 .02
❑ 155 Eddie George RC 1.25 .50
❑ 156 Terry Glenn RC 1.00 .40
❑ 157 Kevin Hardy RC .30 .10
❑ 158 Walt Harris RC .10 .02
❑ 159 Marvin Harrison RC 2.50 1.00
❑ 160 Bobby Hoying RC .30 .10
❑ 161 Keyshawn Johnson RC 1.00 .40
❑ 162 Cedric Jones RC .10 .02
❑ 163 Marcus Jones RC .10 .02
❑ 164 Eddie Kennison RC .30 .10
❑ 165 Ray Lewis RC 2.50 1.00
❑ 166 Derrick Mayes RC .30 .10
❑ 167 Leeland McElroy RC .20 .07
❑ 168 Johnny McWilliams RC .20 .07
❑ 169 John Mobley RC .10 .02
❑ 170 Alex Molden RC .10 .02
❑ 171 Eric Moulds RC 1.25 .50
❑ 172 Muhsin Muhammad RC 1.00 .40
❑ 173 Jonathan Ogden RC .30 .10
❑ 174 Lawrence Phillips RC .30 .10
❑ 175 Stanley Pritchett RC .20 .07
❑ 176 Simeon Rice RC .75 .30
❑ 177 Bryan Still RC .20 .07
❑ 178 Amani Toomer RC 1.00 .40
❑ 179 Regan Upshaw RC .10 .02
❑ 180 Alex Van Dyke RC .20 .07
❑ 181 Barry Sanders PFW .60 .25
❑ 182 Marcus Allen PFW .30 .10
❑ 183 Bryce Paup PFW .10 .02
❑ 184 Jerry Rice PFW .40 .15
❑ 185 D.Howard/B.Christian PFW .20 .07

❑	186	Leon Lett PFW	.10	.02
❑	187	Brett Favre PFW	.75	.30
❑	188	G.Lloyd/D.Thomas PFW	.10	.02
❑	189	Jeff Blake PFW	.20	.07
❑	190	Emmitt Smith PFW	.60	.25
❑	191	J.Elway/J.Hostetler PFW	.40	.15
❑	192	Chiefs PFW	.10	.02
❑	193	Marshall Faulk PFW	.30	.10
❑	194	T.Aikman/S.Young PFW	.40	.15
❑	195	Dan Marino PFW	.75	.30
❑	196	Donta Jones PFW	.10	.02
❑	197	Jim Kelly PFW	.30	.10
❑	198	Checklist	.10	.02
❑	199	Checklist	.10	.02
❑	200	Checklist	.10	.02
❑	P1	Promo Sheet/WFloyd/TDil/Favre	4.00	1.50

1997 Fleer

❑		COMPLETE SET (450)	40.00	15.00
❑	1	Mark Brunell	1.00	.40
❑	2	Andre Reed	.50	.20
❑	3	Darrell Green	.50	.20
❑	4	Mario Bates	.30	.10
❑	5	Eddie George	.75	.30
❑	6	Cris Carter	.75	.30
❑	7	Terrell Owens	1.00	.40
❑	8	Bill Romanowski	.30	.10
❑	9	Isaac Bruce	.75	.30
❑	10	Eric Curry	.30	.10
❑	11	Danny Kanell	.30	.10
❑	12	Ki-Jana Carter	.30	.10
❑	13	Antonio Freeman	.75	.30
❑	14	Ricky Watters	.50	.20
❑	15	Ty Law	.50	.20
❑	16	Alonzo Spellman	.30	.10
❑	17	Kordell Stewart	.75	.30
❑	18	Jerry Rice	1.50	.60
❑	19	Derrick Alexander WR	.50	.20
❑	20	Barry Sanders	2.50	1.00
❑	21	Keyshawn Johnson	.75	.30
❑	22	Emmitt Smith	2.50	1.00
❑	23	Ricky Proehl	.30	.10
❑	24	Daryl Gardener	.30	.10
❑	25	Dan Saleaumua	.30	.10
❑	26	Kevin Greene	.50	.20
❑	27	Junior Seau	.75	.30
❑	28	Randall McDaniel	.30	.10
❑	29	Marshall Faulk	1.00	.40
❑	30	Lorenzo Lynch	.30	.10
❑	31	Terance Mathis	.50	.20
❑	32	Warren Sapp	.50	.20
❑	33	Chris Sanders	.30	.10
❑	34	Tom Carter	.30	.10
❑	35	Aeneas Williams	.30	.10
❑	36	Lawrence Phillips	.30	.10
❑	37	John Elway	3.00	1.25
❑	38	Stanley Richard	.30	.10
❑	39	Darryl Williams	.30	.10
❑	40	Phillippi Sparks	.30	.10
❑	41	Tedy Bruschi	1.50	.60
❑	42	Merton Hanks	.30	.10
❑	43	Ray Lewis	1.25	.50
❑	44	Erik Williams	.30	.10
❑	45	Jason Gildon	.30	.10
❑	46	George Koonce	.30	.10
❑	47	Louis Oliver	.30	.10
❑	48	Muhsin Muhammad	.50	.20
❑	49	Daryl Hobbs	.30	.10
❑	50	Terry Glenn	.75	.30
❑	51	Marvin Harrison	.75	.30
❑	52	Brian Dawkins	.75	.30
❑	53	Dale Carter	.30	.10
❑	54	Alex Molden	.30	.10
❑	55	Raymont Harris	.30	.10
❑	56	Jeff Burris	.30	.10
❑	57	Don Beebe	.30	.10
❑	58	Jamir Miller	.30	.10
❑	59	Carl Pickens	.50	.20
❑	60	Antonio London	.30	.10
❑	61	Courtney Hall	.30	.10
❑	62	Derrick Brooks	.75	.30
❑	63	Chris Boniol	.30	.10
❑	64	Jeff Lageman	.30	.10
❑	65	Roy Barker	.30	.10
❑	66	Devin Bush	.30	.10
❑	67	Aaron Glenn	.30	.10
❑	68	Wayne Simmons	.30	.10
❑	69	Steve Atwater	.30	.10
❑	70	Jimmie Jones	.30	.10
❑	71	Mark Carrier WR	.30	.10
❑	72	Chris Chandler	.50	.20
❑	73	Andy Harmon	.30	.10
❑	74	John Friesz	.30	.10
❑	75	Karim Abdul-Jabbar	.50	.20
❑	76	Levon Kirkland	.30	.10
❑	77	Torrance Small	.30	.10
❑	78	Harvey Williams	.30	.10
❑	79	Chris Calloway	.30	.10
❑	80	Vinny Testaverde	.50	.20
❑	81	Bryant Young	.30	.10
❑	82	Ray Buchanan	.30	.10
❑	83	Robert Smith	.50	.20
❑	84	Robert Brooks	.50	.20
❑	85	Ray Crockett	.30	.10
❑	86	Bennie Blades	.30	.10
❑	87	Mark Carrier DB	.30	.10
❑	88	Mike Tomczak	.30	.10
❑	89	Darick Holmes	.30	.10
❑	90	Drew Bledsoe	1.00	.40
❑	91	Darren Woodson	.30	.10
❑	92	Dan Wilkinson	.30	.10
❑	93	Charles Way	.30	.10
❑	94	Ray Farmer	.30	.10
❑	95	Marcus Allen	.75	.30
❑	96	Marco Coleman	.30	.10
❑	97	Zach Thomas	.75	.30
❑	98	Wesley Walls	.50	.20
❑	99	Frank Wycheck	.30	.10
❑	100	Troy Aikman	1.50	.60
❑	101	Clyde Simmons	.30	.10
❑	102	Courtney Hawkins	.30	.10
❑	103	Chuck Smith	.30	.10
❑	104	Neil O'Donnell	.50	.20
❑	105	Kevin Carter	.30	.10
❑	106	Chris Slade	.30	.10
❑	107	Jessie Armstead	.30	.10
❑	108	Sean Dawkins	.30	.10
❑	109	Robert Blackmon	.30	.10
❑	110	Kevin Smith	.30	.10
❑	111	Lonnie Johnson	.30	.10
❑	112	Craig Newsome	.30	.10
❑	113	Jonathan Ogden	.30	.10
❑	114	Chris Zorich	.30	.10
❑	115	Tim Brown	.75	.30
❑	116	Fred Barnett	.30	.10
❑	117	Michael Haynes	.30	.10
❑	118	Eric Hill	.30	.10
❑	119	Ronnie Harmon	.30	.10
❑	120	Sean Gilbert	.30	.10
❑	121	Derrick Alexander DE	.30	.10
❑	122	Derrick Thomas	.75	.30
❑	123	Tyrone Wheatley	.50	.20
❑	124	Cortez Kennedy	.30	.10
❑	125	Jeff George	.50	.20
❑	126	Chad Cota	.30	.10
❑	127	Gary Zimmerman	.30	.10
❑	128	Johnnie Morton	.50	.20
❑	129	Chad Brown	.30	.10
❑	130	Marvcus Patton	.30	.10
❑	131	James O.Stewart	.50	.20
❑	132	Terry Kirby	.50	.20
❑	133	Chris Mims	.30	.10
❑	134	William Thomas	.30	.10
❑	135	Steve Tasker	.30	.10
❑	136	Jason Belser	.30	.10
❑	137	Bryan Cox	.30	.10
❑	138	Jessie Tuggle	.30	.10
❑	139	Ashley Ambrose	.30	.10
❑	140	Mark Chmura	.50	.20
❑	141	Jeff Hostetler	.30	.10
❑	142	Rich Owens	.30	.10
❑	143	Willie Davis	.30	.10
❑	144	Hardy Nickerson	.30	.10
❑	145	Curtis Martin	1.00	.40
❑	146	Ken Norton	.30	.10
❑	147	Victor Green	.30	.10
❑	148	Anthony Miller	.30	.10
❑	149	John Kasay	.30	.10
❑	150	O.J. McDuffie	.50	.20
❑	151	Darren Perry	.30	.10
❑	152	Luther Elliss	.30	.10
❑	153	Greg Hill	.30	.10
❑	154	John Randle	.50	.20
❑	155	Stephen Grant	.30	.10
❑	156	Leon Lett	.30	.10
❑	157	Darrien Gordon	.30	.10
❑	158	Ray Zellars	.30	.10
❑	159	Michael Jackson	.50	.20
❑	160	Leslie O'Neal	.30	.10
❑	161	Bruce Smith	.50	.20
❑	162	Santana Dotson	.30	.10
❑	163	Bobby Hebert	.30	.10
❑	164	Keith Hamilton	.30	.10
❑	165	Tony Boselli	.30	.10
❑	166	Alfred Williams	.30	.10
❑	167	Ty Detmer	.50	.20
❑	168	Chester McGlockton	.30	.10
❑	169	William Floyd	.50	.20
❑	170	Bruce Matthews	.30	.10
❑	171	Simeon Rice	.50	.20
❑	172	Scott Mitchell	.50	.20
❑	173	Ricardo McDonald	.30	.10
❑	174	Tyrone Poole	.30	.10
❑	175	Greg Lloyd	.30	.10
❑	176	Bruce Armstrong	.30	.10
❑	177	Erik Kramer	.30	.10
❑	178	Kimble Anders	.50	.20
❑	179	Lamar Smith	.75	.30
❑	180	Tony Tolbert	.30	.10
❑	181	Joe Aska	.30	.10
❑	182	Eric Allen	.30	.10
❑	183	Eric Turner	.30	.10
❑	184	Brad Johnson	.75	.30
❑	185	Tony Martin	.50	.20
❑	186	Mike Mamula	.30	.10
❑	187	Irving Spikes	.30	.10
❑	188	Keith Jackson	.30	.10
❑	189	Carlton Bailey	.30	.10
❑	190	Tyrone Braxton	.30	.10
❑	191	Chad Bratzke	.30	.10
❑	192	Adrian Murrell	.50	.20
❑	193	Roman Phifer	.30	.10
❑	194	Todd Collins	.30	.10
❑	195	Chris Warren	.50	.20
❑	196	Kevin Hardy	.30	.10
❑	197	Rick Mirer	.30	.10
❑	198	Cornelius Bennett	.30	.10
❑	199	Jimmy Hitchcock	.30	.10
❑	200	Michael Irvin	.75	.30
❑	201	Quentin Coryatt	.30	.10
❑	202	Reggie White	.75	.30
❑	203	Larry Centers	.50	.20
❑	204	Rodney Thomas	.30	.10
❑	205	Dana Stubblefield	.30	.10
❑	206	Rod Woodson	.50	.20
❑	207	Rhett Hall	.30	.10
❑	208	Steve Tovar	.30	.10
❑	209	Michael Westbrook	.50	.20
❑	210	Steve Wisniewski	.30	.10
❑	211	Carlester Crumpler	.30	.10
❑	212	Elvis Grbac	.50	.20
❑	213	Tim Bowens	.30	.10
❑	214	Robert Porcher	.30	.10
❑	215	John Carney	.30	.10
❑	216	Anthony Newman	.30	.10
❑	217	Earnest Byner	.30	.10
❑	218	Dewayne Washington	.30	.10
❑	219	Willie Green	.30	.10
❑	220	Terry Allen	.75	.30
❑	221	William Fuller	.30	.10
❑	222	Al Del Greco	.30	.10
❑	223	Trent Dilfer	.75	.30
❑	224	Michael Dean Perry	.30	.10
❑	225	Larry Allen	.30	.10
❑	226	Mark Bruener	.30	.10
❑	227	Clay Matthews	.30	.10
❑	228	Reuben Brown	.30	.10
❑	229	Edgar Bennett	.50	.20
❑	230	Neil Smith	.50	.20
❑	231	Ken Harvey	.30	.10

232	Kyle Brady	.30	.10
233	Corey Miller	.30	.10
234	Tony Siragusa	.30	.10
235	Todd Sauerbrun	.30	.10
236	Daniel Stubbs	.30	.10
237	Robb Thomas	.30	.10
238	Jimmy Smith	.50	.20
239	Marquez Pope	.30	.10
240	Tim Biakabutuka	.50	.20
241	Jamie Asher	.30	.10
242	Steve McNair	1.00	.40
243	Harold Green	.30	.10
244	Frank Sanders	.50	.20
245	Joe Johnson	.30	.10
246	Eric Bieniemy	.30	.10
247	Kevin Turner	.30	.10
248	Rickey Dudley	.50	.20
249	Orlando Thomas	.30	.10
250	Dan Marino	3.00	1.25
251	Deion Sanders	.75	.30
252	Dan Williams	.30	.10
253	Sam Gash	.30	.10
254	Lonnie Marts	.30	.10
255	Mo Lewis	.30	.10
256	Charles Johnson	.50	.20
257	Chris Jacke	.30	.10
258	Keenan McCardell	.50	.20
259	Donnell Woolford	.30	.10
260	Terrance Shaw	.30	.10
261	Jason Dunn	.30	.10
262	Willie McGinest	.30	.10
263	Ken Dilger	.30	.10
264	Keith Lyle	.30	.10
265	Antonio Langham	.30	.10
266	Carlton Gray	.30	.10
267	LeShon Johnson	.30	.10
268	Thurman Thomas	.75	.30
269	Jesse Campbell	.30	.10
270	Carnell Lake	.30	.10
271	Cris Dishman	.30	.10
272	Kevin Williams	.30	.10
273	Troy Brown	.50	.20
274	William Roaf	.30	.10
275	Terrell Davis	1.00	.40
276	Herman Moore	.50	.20
277	Walt Harris	.30	.10
278	Mark Collins	.30	.10
279	Bert Emanuel	.50	.20
280	Qadry Ismail	.50	.20
281	Phil Hansen	.30	.10
282	Steve Young	1.00	.40
283	Michael Sinclair	.30	.10
284	Jeff Graham	.30	.10
285	Sam Mills	.30	.10
286	Terry McDaniel	.30	.10
287	Eugene Robinson	.30	.10
288	Tony Bennett	.30	.10
289	Daryl Johnston	.50	.20
290	Eric Swann	.30	.10
291	Byron Bam Morris	.30	.10
292	Thomas Lewis	.30	.10
293	Terrell Fletcher	.30	.10
294	Gus Frerotte	.30	.10
295	Stanley Pritchett	.30	.10
296	Mike Alstott	.75	.30
297	Will Shields	.30	.10
298	Errict Rhett	.30	.10
299	Garrison Hearst	.50	.20
300	Kerry Collins	.75	.30
301	Darryll Lewis	.30	.10
302	Chris T. Jones	.30	.10
303	Yancey Thigpen	.50	.20
304	Jackie Harris	.30	.10
305	Steve Christie	.30	.10
306	Gilbert Brown	.50	.20
307	Terry Wooden	.30	.10
308	Pete Mitchell	.30	.10
309	Tim McDonald	.30	.10
310	Jake Reed	.50	.20
311	Ed McCaffrey	.50	.20
312	Chris Doleman	.30	.10
313	Eric Metcalf	.50	.20
314	Ricky Reynolds	.30	.10
315	David Sloan	.30	.10
316	Marvin Washington	.30	.10
317	Herschel Walker	.50	.20
318	Michael Timpson	.30	.10
319	Blaine Bishop	.30	.10
320	Irv Smith	.30	.10
321	Seth Joyner	.30	.10
322	Terrell Buckley	.30	.10
323	Michael Strahan	.50	.20
324	Sam Adams	.30	.10
325	Leslie Shepherd	.30	.10
326	James Jett	.50	.20
327	Anthony Pleasant	.30	.10
328	Lee Woodall	.30	.10
329	Shannon Sharpe	.50	.20
330	Jamal Anderson	.75	.30
331	Andre Hastings	.30	.10
332	Troy Vincent	.30	.10
333	Sean LaChapelle	.30	.10
334	Winslow Oliver	.30	.10
335	Sean Jones	.30	.10
336	Darnay Scott	.50	.20
337	Todd Lyght	.30	.10
338	Leonard Russell	.30	.10
339	Nate Newton	.30	.10
340	Zack Crockett	.30	.10
341	Amp Lee	.30	.10
342	Bobby Engram	.50	.20
343	Mike Hollis	.30	.10
344	Rodney Hampton	.50	.20
345	Mel Gray	.30	.10
346	Van Malone	.30	.10
347	Aaron Craver	.30	.10
348	Jim Everett	.30	.10
349	Trace Armstrong	.30	.10
350	Pat Swilling	.30	.10
351	Brent Jones	.30	.10
352	Chris Spielman	.30	.10
353	Brett Perriman	.30	.10
354	Brian Kinchen	.30	.10
355	Joey Galloway	.50	.20
356	Henry Ellard	.30	.10
357	Ben Coates	.50	.20
358	Dorsey Levens	.75	.30
359	Charlie Garner	.50	.20
360	Erric Pegram	.30	.10
361	Anthony Johnson	.30	.10
362	Rashaan Salaam	.30	.10
363	Jeff Blake	.50	.20
364	Kent Graham	.30	.10
365	Broderick Thomas	.30	.10
366	Richmond Webb	.30	.10
367	Alfred Pupunu	.30	.10
368	Mark Stepnoski	.30	.10
369	David Dunn	.30	.10
370	Bobby Houston	.30	.10
371	Anthony Parker	.30	.10
372	Quinn Early	.30	.10
373	LeRoy Butler	.30	.10
374	Kurt Gouveia	.30	.10
375	Greg Biekert	.30	.10
376	Jim Harbaugh	.50	.20
377	Eric Bjornson	.30	.10
378	Craig Heyward	.30	.10
379	Steve Bono	.50	.20
380	Tony Banks	.50	.20
381	John Mobley	.30	.10
382	Irving Fryar	.50	.20
383	Dermontti Dawson	.30	.10
384	Eric Davis	.30	.10
385	Natrone Means	.50	.20
386	Jason Sehorn	.50	.20
387	Michael McCrary	.30	.10
388	Corwin Brown	.30	.10
389	Kevin Glover	.30	.10
390	Jerris McPhail	.30	.10
391	Bobby Taylor	.30	.10
392	Tony McGee	.30	.10
393	Curtis Conway	.50	.20
394	Napoleon Kaufman	.75	.30
395	Brian Blades	.30	.10
396	Richard Dent	.30	.10
397	Dave Brown	.30	.10
398	Stan Humphries	.50	.20
399	Stevon Moore	.30	.10
400	Brett Favre	3.00	1.50
401	Jerome Bettis	.75	.30
402	Darrin Smith	.30	.10
403	Chris Penn	.30	.10
404	Rob Moore	.50	.20
405	Micheal Barrow	.30	.10
406	Tony Brackens	.30	.10
407	Wayne Martin	.30	.10
408	Warren Moon	.75	.30
409	Jason Elam	.50	.20
410	J.J. Birden	.30	.10
411	Hugh Douglas	.30	.10
412	Lamar Lathon	.30	.10
413	John Kidd	.30	.10
414	Bryce Paup	.30	.10
415	Shawn Jefferson	.30	.10
416	Leeland McElroy SS	.30	.10
417	Elbert Shelley SS	.30	.10
418	Jermaine Lewis SS	.50	.20
419	Eric Moulds SS	.75	.30
420	Michael Bates SS	.30	.10
421	John Mangum SS	.30	.10
422	Corey Sawyer SS	.30	.10
423	Jim Schwantz SS RC	.30	.10
424	Rod Smith WR SS	.75	.30
425	Glyn Milburn SS	.30	.10
426	Desmond Howard SS	.50	.20
427	John Henry Mills SS RC	.30	.10
428	Cary Blanchard SS RC	.30	.10
429	Chris Hudson SS	.30	.10
430	Tamarick Vanover SS	.50	.20
431	Kirby Dar Dar SS RC	.50	.20
432	David Palmer SS	.30	.10
433	Dave Meggett SS	.30	.10
434	Tyrone Hughes SS	.30	.10
435	Amani Toomer SS	.50	.20
436	Wayne Chrebet SS	.50	.20
437	Carl Kidd RC SS	.30	.10
438	Derrick Witherspoon SS	.30	.10
439	Jahine Arnold SS	.30	.10
440	Andre Coleman SS	.30	.10
441	Jeff Wilkins SS	.30	.10
442	Jay Bellamy SS RC	.30	.10
443	Eddie Kennison SS	.50	.20
444	Nilo Silvan SS	.30	.10
445	Brian Mitchell SS	.30	.10
446	Garrison Hearst CL	.50	.20
447	Napoleon Kaufman CL	.75	.30
448	Brian Mitchell CL	.30	.10
449	Rodney Hampton CL	.30	.10
450	Edgar Bennett CL	.30	.10
S1	Mark Chmura Sample	1.00	.40
AU1	Reggie White AUTO	125.00	75.00

2006 Fleer

1	Anquan Boldin	.30	.10
2	Larry Fitzgerald	.50	.20
3	J.J. Arrington	.30	.10
4	Michael Vick	.50	.20
5	Warrick Dunn	.30	.10
6	Roddy White	.30	.10
7	Jamal Lewis	.30	.10
8	Kyle Boller	.25	.10
9	Derrick Mason	.25	.10
10	Willis McGahee	.50	.20
11	J.P. Losman	.30	.10
12	Lee Evans	.30	.10
13	Steve Smith	.50	.20
14	Jake Delhomme	.30	.10
15	DeShaun Foster	.30	.10
16	Rex Grossman	.50	.20
17	Brian Urlacher	.50	.20
18	Thomas Jones	.30	.10
19	Carson Palmer	.50	.20
20	Chad Johnson	.30	.10
21	Rudi Johnson	.30	.10
22	Charlie Frye	.30	.12
23	Braylon Edwards	.50	.20
24	Reuben Droughns	.30	.10
25	Julius Jones	.50	.20
26	Drew Bledsoe	.50	.20
27	Terry Glenn	.30	.10

❑ 28 Jake Plummer	.30	.10
❑ 29 Tatum Bell	.30	.10
❑ 30 Champ Bailey	.30	.10
❑ 31 Rod Smith	.30	.10
❑ 32 Roy Williams WR	.50	.20
❑ 33 Kevin Jones	.50	.20
❑ 34 Mike Williams	.50	.20
❑ 35 Brett Favre	1.00	.40
❑ 36 Ahman Green	.30	.10
❑ 37 Javon Walker	.30	.10
❑ 38 David Carr	.30	.10
❑ 39 Andre Johnson	.30	.10
❑ 40 Domanick Davis	.30	.10
❑ 41 Peyton Manning	.75	.30
❑ 42 Edgerrin James	.50	.20
❑ 43 Marvin Harrison	.50	.20
❑ 44 Reggie Wayne	.30	.10
❑ 45 Byron Leftwich	.30	.10
❑ 46 Fred Taylor	.30	.10
❑ 47 Ernest Wilford	.25	.10
❑ 48 Larry Johnson	.60	.25
❑ 49 Trent Green	.30	.10
❑ 50 Tony Gonzalez	.30	.10
❑ 51 Ronnie Brown	.50	.20
❑ 52 Ricky Williams	.30	.10
❑ 53 Chris Chambers	.30	.10
❑ 54 Daunte Culpepper	.50	.20
❑ 55 Troy Williamson	.30	.10
❑ 56 Brad Johnson	.30	.10
❑ 57 Tom Brady	.75	.30
❑ 58 Deion Branch	.30	.10
❑ 59 Corey Dillon	.30	.10
❑ 60 Deuce McAllister	.30	.10
❑ 61 Donte Stallworth	.30	.10
❑ 62 Joe Horn	.30	.10
❑ 63 Eli Manning	.60	.25
❑ 64 Tiki Barber	.50	.20
❑ 65 Plaxico Burress	.30	.10
❑ 66 Jeremy Shockey	.50	.20
❑ 67 Chad Pennington	.30	.10
❑ 68 Curtis Martin	.50	.20
❑ 69 Laveranues Coles	.30	.10
❑ 70 Randy Moss	.50	.20
❑ 71 Aaron Brooks	.30	.10
❑ 72 LaMont Jordan	.30	.10
❑ 73 Donovan McNabb	.50	.20
❑ 74 Brian Westbrook	.30	.10
❑ 75 Terrell Owens	.50	.20
❑ 76 Ben Roethlisberger	.75	.30
❑ 77 Hines Ward	.50	.20
❑ 78 Willie Parker	.60	.25
❑ 79 Heath Miller	.30	.12
❑ 80 LaDainian Tomlinson	.60	.25
❑ 81 Drew Brees	.50	.20
❑ 82 Antonio Gates	.50	.20
❑ 83 Alex Smith QB	.50	.20
❑ 84 Antonio Bryant	.30	.10
❑ 85 Frank Gore	.50	.20
❑ 86 Shaun Alexander	.50	.20
❑ 87 Matt Hasselbeck	.30	.10
❑ 88 Darrell Jackson	.30	.10
❑ 89 Marc Bulger	.30	.10
❑ 90 Steven Jackson	.50	.20
❑ 91 Torry Holt	.30	.10
❑ 92 Cadillac Williams	.50	.20
❑ 93 Chris Simms	.30	.10
❑ 94 Joey Galloway	.30	.10
❑ 95 Steve McNair	.30	.12
❑ 96 Chris Brown	.30	.10
❑ 97 Drew Bennett	.25	.10
❑ 98 Clinton Portis	.50	.20
❑ 99 Santana Moss	.30	.10
❑ 100 Mark Brunell	.30	.10
❑ 101 A.J. Hawk RC	4.00	1.50
❑ 102 A.J. Nicholson RC	1.00	.40
❑ 103 Abdul Hodge RC	2.00	.75
❑ 104 Andre Hall RC	1.50	.60
❑ 105 Anthony Fasano RC	2.00	.75
❑ 106 Antonio Cromartie RC	2.00	.75
❑ 107 Ashton Youboty RC	2.00	.75
❑ 108 Bobby Carpenter RC	2.00	.75
❑ 109 Brad Smith RC	2.00	.75
❑ 110 Greg Jennings RC	3.00	1.25
❑ 111 Brandon Williams RC	2.00	.75
❑ 112 Brian Calhoun RC	2.00	.75
❑ 113 Brodie Croyle RC	5.00	2.00
❑ 114 Brodrick Bunkley RC	2.00	.75
❑ 115 Bruce Gradkowski RC	3.00	1.25
❑ 116 Chad Greenway RC	2.00	.75
❑ 117 Chad Jackson RC	2.00	.75
❑ 118 Charles Davis RC	1.50	.60
❑ 119 Charles Gordon RC	1.50	.60
❑ 120 Charlie Whitehurst RC	2.00	.75
❑ 121 Claude Wroten RC	1.00	.40
❑ 122 Cory Rodgers RC	2.00	.75
❑ 123 D.J. Shockley RC	2.00	.75
❑ 124 Darnell Bing RC	2.00	.75
❑ 125 Darrell Hackney RC	1.50	.60
❑ 126 David Thomas RC	2.00	.75
❑ 127 D'Brickashaw Ferguson RC	2.00	.75
❑ 128 DeAngelo Williams RC	5.00	2.00
❑ 129 DeMeco Ryans RC	2.50	1.00
❑ 130 Demetrius Williams RC	2.00	.75
❑ 131 Derek Hagan RC	2.00	.75
❑ 132 Devin Hester RC	4.00	1.50
❑ 133 Dominique Byrd RC	1.50	.60
❑ 134 DonTrell Moore RC	1.50	.60
❑ 135 D'Qwell Jackson RC	1.50	.60
❑ 136 Drew Olson RC	1.50	.60
❑ 137 Elvis Dumervil RC	1.00	.40
❑ 138 Ernie Sims RC	2.50	1.00
❑ 139 Garrett Mills RC	2.00	.75
❑ 140 Gerald Riggs RC	2.00	.75
❑ 141 Greg Lee RC	1.50	.60
❑ 142 Haloti Ngata RC	2.00	.75
❑ 143 Hank Baskett RC	2.00	.75
❑ 144 Jason Allen RC	2.00	.75
❑ 145 Jason Avant RC	2.00	.75
❑ 146 Jay Cutler RC	6.00	2.50
❑ 147 Jeff Webb RC	1.50	.60
❑ 148 Jeremy Bloom RC	1.50	.60
❑ 149 Jerome Harrison RC	2.00	.75
❑ 150 Jimmy Williams RC	2.00	.75
❑ 151 Joe Klopfenstein RC	1.50	.60
❑ 152 Johnathan Joseph RC	1.50	.60
❑ 153 Joseph Addai RC	6.00	2.50
❑ 154 Jovon Bouknight RC	1.50	.60
❑ 155 Kai Parham RC	2.00	.75
❑ 156 Kamerion Wimbley RC	2.00	.75
❑ 157 Kellen Clemens RC	3.00	1.25
❑ 158 Kelly Jennings RC	2.00	.75
❑ 159 Ko Simpson RC	1.50	.60
❑ 160 Laurence Maroney RC	5.00	2.00
❑ 161 Lawrence Vickers RC	1.50	.60
❑ 162 LenDale White RC	4.00	1.50
❑ 163 Leon Washington RC	3.00	1.25
❑ 164 Leonard Pope RC	2.00	.75
❑ 165 Manny Lawson RC	2.00	.75
❑ 166 Marcedes Lewis RC	2.00	.75
❑ 167 Marcus McNeill RC	1.50	.60
❑ 168 Donte Whitner RC	2.00	.75
❑ 169 Mario Williams RC	3.00	1.25
❑ 170 Martin Nance RC	1.50	.60
❑ 171 Mathias Kiwanuka RC	2.50	1.00
❑ 172 Matt Bernstein RC	1.00	.40
❑ 173 Matt Leinart RC	6.00	2.50
❑ 174 Maurice Drew RC	5.00	2.00
❑ 175 Maurice Stovall RC	2.00	.75
❑ 176 Michael Huff RC	2.50	1.00
❑ 177 Michael Robinson RC	2.00	.75
❑ 178 Mike Hass RC	2.00	.75
❑ 179 Omar Jacobs RC	1.50	.60
❑ 180 Orien Harris RC	1.50	.60
❑ 181 Owen Daniels RC	2.00	.75
❑ 182 Miles Austin RC	1.50	.60
❑ 183 Reggie Bush RC	8.00	3.00
❑ 184 Reggie McNeal RC	1.50	.60
❑ 185 Santonio Holmes RC	4.00	1.50
❑ 186 Sinorice Moss RC	2.00	.75
❑ 187 Skyler Green RC	2.00	.75
❑ 188 Tony Scheffler RC	2.00	.75
❑ 189 Tamba Hali RC	2.00	.75
❑ 190 Tarvaris Jackson RC	3.00	1.25
❑ 191 Thomas Howard RC	2.00	.75
❑ 192 Tim Day RC	1.50	.60
❑ 193 Todd Watkins RC	1.50	.60
❑ 194 Travis Wilson RC	2.00	.75
❑ 195 Tye Hill RC	2.00	.75
❑ 196 Vernon Davis RC	4.00	1.50
❑ 197 Vince Young RC	8.00	3.00
❑ 198 Wali Lundy RC	2.00	.75
❑ 199 Will Blackmon RC	1.50	.60
❑ 200 Winston Justice RC	2.00	.75

1998 Fleer Tradition

❑ COMPLETE SET (250)	40.00	20.00
❑ 1 Brett Favre	2.00	.75
❑ 2 Barry Sanders	1.50	.60
❑ 3 John Elway	2.00	.75
❑ 4 Emmitt Smith	1.50	.60
❑ 5 Dan Marino	2.00	.75
❑ 6 Eddie George	.50	.20
❑ 7 Jerry Rice	1.00	.40
❑ 8 Jake Plummer	.50	.20
❑ 9 Joey Galloway	.30	.10
❑ 10 Mike Alstott	.50	.20
❑ 11 Brian Mitchell	.20	.07
❑ 12 Keyshawn Johnson	.50	.20
❑ 13 Jerald Moore	.20	.07
❑ 14 Randal Hill	.20	.07
❑ 15 Byron Hanspard	.20	.07
❑ 16 Jeff George	.30	.10
❑ 17 Terry Glenn	.50	.20
❑ 18 Jerome Bettis	.50	.20
❑ 19 Curtis Conway	.30	.10
❑ 20 Fred Lane	.20	.07
❑ 21 Isaac Bruce	.50	.20
❑ 22 Tiki Barber	.50	.20
❑ 23 Bobby Hoying	.30	.10
❑ 24 Marcus Allen	.50	.20
❑ 25 Dana Stubblefield	.20	.07
❑ 26 Peter Boulware	.20	.07
❑ 27 John Randle	.30	.10
❑ 28 Jason Sehorn	.30	.10
❑ 29 Rod Smith	.30	.10
❑ 30 Michael Sinclair	.20	.07
❑ 31 Marshall Faulk	.60	.25
❑ 32 Karl Williams	.20	.07
❑ 33 Kordell Stewart	.50	.20
❑ 34 Corey Dillon	.50	.20
❑ 35 Bryant Young	.20	.07
❑ 36 Charlie Garner	.30	.10
❑ 37 Andre Reed	.30	.10
❑ 38 Ray Buchanan	.20	.07
❑ 39 Brett Perriman	.20	.07
❑ 40 Leon Lett	.20	.07
❑ 41 Keenan McCardell	.30	.10
❑ 42 Eric Swann	.20	.07
❑ 43 Leslie Shepherd	.20	.07
❑ 44 Curtis Martin	.50	.20
❑ 45 Andre Rison	.30	.10
❑ 46 Keith Lyle	.20	.07
❑ 47 Rae Carruth	.20	.07
❑ 48 William Henderson	.30	.10
❑ 49 Sean Dawkins	.20	.07
❑ 50 Terrell Davis	.50	.20
❑ 51 Tim Brown	.50	.20
❑ 52 Willie McGinest	.20	.07
❑ 53 Jermaine Lewis	.30	.10
❑ 54 Ricky Watters	.30	.10
❑ 55 Freddie Jones	.20	.07
❑ 56 Robert Smith	.50	.20
❑ 57 Reidel Anthony	.30	.10
❑ 58 James Stewart	.30	.10
❑ 59 Earl Holmes RC	.50	.20
❑ 60 Dale Carter	.20	.07
❑ 61 Michael Irvin	.50	.20
❑ 62 Jason Taylor	.30	.10
❑ 63 Eric Metcalf	.20	.07
❑ 64 LeRoy Butler	.20	.07
❑ 65 Jamal Anderson	.50	.20
❑ 66 Jamie Asher	.20	.07
❑ 67 Chris Sanders	.20	.07
❑ 68 Warren Sapp	.30	.10
❑ 69 Ray Zellars	.20	.07
❑ 70 Carl Pickens	.30	.10
❑ 71 Garrison Hearst	.50	.20
❑ 72 Eddie Kennison	.30	.10
❑ 73 John Mobley	.20	.07
❑ 74 Rob Johnson	.30	.10

❑ 75 William Thomas	.20	.07
❑ 76 Drew Bledsoe	.75	.30
❑ 77 Micheal Barrow	.20	.07
❑ 78 Jim Harbaugh	.30	.10
❑ 79 Terry McDaniel	.20	.07
❑ 80 Johnnie Morton	.30	.10
❑ 81 Danny Kanell	.30	.10
❑ 82 Larry Centers	.20	.07
❑ 83 Courtney Hawkins	.20	.07
❑ 84 Tony Brackens	.20	.07
❑ 85 Tony Gonzalez	.50	.20
❑ 86 Aaron Glenn	.20	.07
❑ 87 Cris Carter	.50	.20
❑ 88 Chuck Smith	.20	.07
❑ 89 Tamarick Vanover	.20	.07
❑ 90 Karim Abdul-Jabbar	.50	.20
❑ 91 Bryant Westbrook	.20	.07
❑ 92 Mike Pritchard	.20	.07
❑ 93 Darren Woodson	.20	.07
❑ 94 Wesley Walls	.30	.10
❑ 95 Tony Banks	.30	.10
❑ 96 Michael Westbrook	.30	.10
❑ 97 Shannon Sharpe	.30	.10
❑ 98 Jeff Blake	.30	.10
❑ 99 Terrell Owens	.50	.20
❑ 100 Warrick Dunn	.50	.20
❑ 101 Levon Kirkland	.20	.07
❑ 102 Frank Wycheck	.20	.07
❑ 103 Gus Frerotte	.20	.07
❑ 104 Simeon Rice	.30	.10
❑ 105 Shawn Jefferson	.20	.07
❑ 106 Irving Fryar	.30	.10
❑ 107 Michael McCrary	.20	.07
❑ 108 Robert Brooks	.30	.10
❑ 109 Chris Chandler	.30	.10
❑ 110 Junior Seau	.50	.20
❑ 111 O.J. McDuffie	.30	.10
❑ 112 Glenn Foley	.30	.10
❑ 113 Darryl Williams	.20	.07
❑ 114 Elvis Grbac	.30	.10
❑ 115 Napoleon Kaufman	.50	.20
❑ 116 Anthony Miller	.20	.07
❑ 117 Troy Davis	.20	.07
❑ 118 Charles Way	.20	.07
❑ 119 Scott Mitchell	.30	.10
❑ 120 Ken Harvey	.20	.07
❑ 121 Tyrone Hughes	.20	.07
❑ 122 Mark Brunell	.50	.20
❑ 123 David Palmer	.20	.07
❑ 124 Rob Moore	.30	.10
❑ 125 Kerry Collins	.30	.10
❑ 126 Will Blackwell	.20	.07
❑ 127 Ray Crockett	.20	.07
❑ 128 Leslie O'Neal	.20	.07
❑ 129 Antowain Smith	.50	.20
❑ 130 Carlester Crumpler	.20	.07
❑ 131 Michael Jackson	.20	.07
❑ 132 Trent Dilfer	.50	.20
❑ 133 Dan Williams	.20	.07
❑ 134 Dorsey Levens	.50	.20
❑ 135 Ty Law	.30	.10
❑ 136 Rickey Dudley	.20	.07
❑ 137 Jessie Tuggle	.20	.07
❑ 138 Darrien Gordon	.20	.07
❑ 139 Kevin Turner	.20	.07
❑ 140 Willie Davis	.20	.07
❑ 141 Zach Thomas	.50	.20
❑ 142 Tony McGee	.20	.07
❑ 143 Dexter Coakley	.20	.07
❑ 144 Troy Brown	.30	.10
❑ 145 Leeland McElroy	.20	.07
❑ 146 Michael Strahan	.30	.10
❑ 147 Ken Dilger	.20	.07
❑ 148 Bryce Paup	.20	.07
❑ 149 Herman Moore	.30	.10
❑ 150 Reggie White	.50	.20
❑ 151 Dewayne Washington	.20	.07
❑ 152 Natrone Means	.30	.10
❑ 153 Ben Coates	.30	.10
❑ 154 Bert Emanuel	.30	.10
❑ 155 Steve Young	.60	.25
❑ 156 Jimmy Smith	.30	.10
❑ 157 Darrell Green	.30	.10
❑ 158 Troy Aikman	1.00	.40
❑ 159 Greg Hill	.20	.07
❑ 160 Raymont Harris	.20	.07
❑ 161 Troy Drayton	.20	.07
❑ 162 Stevon Moore	.20	.07
❑ 163 Warren Moon	.50	.20
❑ 164 Wayne Martin	.20	.07
❑ 165 Jason Gildon	.20	.07
❑ 166 Chris Calloway	.20	.07
❑ 167 Aeneas Williams	.20	.07
❑ 168 Michael Bates	.20	.07
❑ 169 Hugh Douglas	.20	.07
❑ 170 Brad Johnson	.50	.20
❑ 171 Bruce Smith	.30	.10
❑ 172 Neil Smith	.30	.10
❑ 173 James McKnight	.50	.20
❑ 174 Robert Porcher	.20	.07
❑ 175 Merton Hanks	.20	.07
❑ 176 Ki-Jana Carter	.20	.07
❑ 177 Mo Lewis	.20	.07
❑ 178 Chester McGlockton	.20	.07
❑ 179 Zack Crockett	.20	.07
❑ 180 Derrick Thomas	.50	.20
❑ 181 J.J. Stokes	.30	.10
❑ 182 Derrick Rodgers	.20	.07
❑ 183 Daryl Johnston	.30	.10
❑ 184 Chris Penn	.20	.07
❑ 185 Steve Atwater	.20	.07
❑ 186 Amp Lee	.20	.07
❑ 187 Frank Sanders	.30	.10
❑ 188 Chris Slade	.20	.07
❑ 189 Mark Chmura	.30	.10
❑ 190 Kimble Anders	.30	.10
❑ 191 Charles Johnson	.20	.07
❑ 192 William Floyd	.20	.07
❑ 193 Jay Graham	.20	.07
❑ 194 Hardy Nickerson	.20	.07
❑ 195 Terry Allen	.50	.20
❑ 196 James Jett	.30	.10
❑ 197 Jessie Armstead	.20	.07
❑ 198 Yancey Thigpen	.30	.10
❑ 199 Terance Mathis	.30	.10
❑ 200 Steve McNair	.50	.20
❑ 201 Wayne Chrebet	.50	.20
❑ 202 Jamir Miller	.20	.07
❑ 203 Duce Staley	.60	.25
❑ 204 Deion Sanders	.50	.20
❑ 205 Carnell Lake	.20	.07
❑ 206 Ed McCaffrey	.30	.10
❑ 207 Shawn Springs	.20	.07
❑ 208 Tony Martin	.30	.10
❑ 209 Jerris McPhail	.20	.07
❑ 210 Darnay Scott	.30	.10
❑ 211 Jake Reed	.30	.10
❑ 212 Adrian Murrell	.30	.10
❑ 213 Quinn Early	.20	.07
❑ 214 Marvin Harrison	.50	.20
❑ 215 Ryan McNeil	.20	.07
❑ 216 Derrick Alexander	.30	.10
❑ 217 Ray Lewis	.50	.20
❑ 218 Antonio Freeman	.50	.20
❑ 219 Dwayne Rudd	.20	.07
❑ 220 Muhsin Muhammad	.30	.10
❑ 221 Kevin Hardy	.20	.07
❑ 222 Andre Hastings	.20	.07
❑ 223 John Avery RC	.75	.30
❑ 224 Keith Brooking RC	1.25	.50
❑ 225 Kevin Dyson RC	1.25	.50
❑ 226 Robert Edwards RC	.75	.30
❑ 227 Greg Ellis RC	.50	.20
❑ 228 Curtis Enis RC	.50	.20
❑ 229 Terry Fair RC	.75	.30
❑ 230 Ahman Green RC	6.00	2.50
❑ 231 Jacquez Green RC	.75	.30
❑ 232 Brian Griese RC	3.00	1.25
❑ 233 Skip Hicks RC	.75	.30
❑ 234 Ryan Leaf RC	1.25	.50
❑ 235 Peyton Manning RC	15.00	6.00
❑ 236 R.W. McQuarters RC	.75	.30
❑ 237 Randy Moss RC	10.00	5.00
❑ 238 Marcus Nash RC	.50	.20
❑ 239 Anthony Simmons RC	.75	.30
❑ 240 Brian Simmons RC	.75	.30
❑ 241 Takeo Spikes RC	1.25	.50
❑ 242 Duane Starks RC	.50	.20
❑ 243 Fred Taylor RC	2.00	.75
❑ 244 Andre Wadsworth RC	.75	.30
❑ 245 Shaun Williams RC	.75	.30
❑ 246 Grant Wistrom RC	.75	.30
❑ 247 Charles Woodson RC	1.50	.60
❑ 248 Checklist	.20	.07
❑ 249 Checklist	.20	.07
❑ 250 Checklist	.20	.07

1999 Fleer Tradition

❑ COMPLETE SET (300)	40.00	20.00
❑ 1 Randy Moss	1.25	.50
❑ 2 Peyton Manning	1.50	.60
❑ 3 Barry Sanders	1.50	.60
❑ 4 Terrell Davis	.50	.20
❑ 5 Brett Favre	1.50	.60
❑ 6 Fred Taylor	.50	.20
❑ 7 Jake Plummer	.30	.10
❑ 8 John Elway	1.50	.60
❑ 9 Emmitt Smith	1.00	.40
❑ 10 Kerry Collins	.30	.10
❑ 11 Peter Boulware	.20	.07
❑ 12 Jamal Anderson	.50	.20
❑ 13 Doug Flutie	.50	.20
❑ 14 Michael Bates	.20	.07
❑ 15 Corey Dillon	.50	.20
❑ 16 Curtis Conway	.30	.10
❑ 17 Ty Detmer	.30	.10
❑ 18 Robert Brooks	.30	.10
❑ 19 Dale Carter	.20	.07
❑ 20 Charlie Batch	.50	.20
❑ 21 Ken Dilger	.20	.07
❑ 22 Troy Aikman	1.00	.40
❑ 23 Tavian Banks	.20	.07
❑ 24 Cris Carter	.50	.20
❑ 25 Derrick Alexander WR	.30	.10
❑ 26 Chris Bordano RC	.20	.07
❑ 27 Karim Abdul-Jabbar	.30	.10
❑ 28 Jessie Armstead	.20	.07
❑ 29 Drew Bledsoe	.60	.25
❑ 30 Brian Dawkins	.50	.20
❑ 31 Wayne Chrebet	.30	.10
❑ 32 Garrison Hearst	.30	.10
❑ 33 Eric Allen	.20	.07
❑ 34 Tony Banks	.30	.10
❑ 35 Jerome Bettis	.50	.20
❑ 36 Stephen Alexander	.20	.07
❑ 37 Rodney Harrison	.20	.07
❑ 38 Mike Alstott	.50	.20
❑ 39 Chad Brown	.20	.07
❑ 40 Johnny McWilliams	.20	.07
❑ 41 Kevin Dyson	.30	.10
❑ 42 Keith Brooking	.20	.07
❑ 43 Jim Harbaugh	.30	.10
❑ 44 Bobby Engram	.30	.10
❑ 45 John Holecek	.20	.07
❑ 46 Steve Beuerlein	.20	.07
❑ 47 Tony McGee	.20	.07
❑ 48 Greg Ellis	.20	.07
❑ 49 Corey Fuller	.20	.07
❑ 50 Stephen Boyd	.20	.07
❑ 51 Marshall Faulk	.60	.25
❑ 52 LeRoy Butler	.20	.07
❑ 53 Reggie Barlow	.20	.07
❑ 54 Randall Cunningham	.50	.20
❑ 55 Aeneas Williams	.20	.07
❑ 56 Kimble Anders	.30	.10
❑ 57 Cam Cleeland	.20	.07
❑ 58 John Avery	.20	.07
❑ 59 Gary Brown	.20	.07
❑ 60 Ben Coates	.30	.10
❑ 61 Koy Detmer	.20	.07
❑ 62 Bryan Cox	.20	.07
❑ 63 Edgar Bennett	.20	.07
❑ 64 Tim Brown	.50	.20
❑ 65 Isaac Bruce	.50	.20
❑ 66 Eddie George	.50	.20
❑ 67 Reidel Anthony	.30	.10
❑ 68 Charlie Jones	.20	.07
❑ 69 Terry Allen	.30	.10

❑ 70 Joey Galloway	.30	.10
❑ 71 Jamir Miller	.20	.07
❑ 72 Will Blackwell	.20	.07
❑ 73 Ray Buchanan	.20	.07
❑ 74 Priest Holmes	.75	.30
❑ 75 Michael Irvin	.30	.10
❑ 76 Jonathan Linton	.20	.07
❑ 77 Curtis Enis	.20	.07
❑ 78 Neil O'Donnell	.30	.10
❑ 79 Tim Biakabutuka	.30	.10
❑ 80 Terry Kirby	.20	.07
❑ 81 Germane Crowell	.20	.07
❑ 82 Jason Elam	.20	.07
❑ 83 Mark Chmura	.20	.07
❑ 84 Marvin Harrison	.50	.20
❑ 85 Jimmy Hitchcock	.20	.07
❑ 86 Tony Brackens	.20	.07
❑ 87 Sean Dawkins	.20	.07
❑ 88 Tony Gonzalez	.50	.20
❑ 89 Kent Graham	.20	.07
❑ 90 Oronde Gadsden	.30	.10
❑ 91 Hugh Douglas	.20	.07
❑ 92 Robert Edwards	.20	.07
❑ 93 R.W. McQuarters	.20	.07
❑ 94 Aaron Glenn	.20	.07
❑ 95 Kevin Carter	.20	.07
❑ 96 Rickey Dudley	.20	.07
❑ 97 Derrick Brooks	.50	.20
❑ 98 Mark Bruener	.20	.07
❑ 99 Darrell Green	.20	.07
❑ 100 Jessie Tuggle	.20	.07
❑ 101 Freddie Jones	.20	.07
❑ 102 Rob Moore	.30	.10
❑ 103 Ahman Green	.50	.20
❑ 104 Chris Chandler	.30	.10
❑ 105 Steve McNair	.50	.20
❑ 106 Kevin Greene	.20	.07
❑ 107 Jermaine Lewis	.30	.10
❑ 108 Erik Kramer	.20	.07
❑ 109 Eric Moulds	.50	.20
❑ 110 Terry Fair	.20	.07
❑ 111 Carl Pickens	.30	.10
❑ 112 La'Roi Glover RC	1.25	.50
❑ 113 Chris Spielman	.20	.07
❑ 114 Leroy Hoard	.20	.07
❑ 115 Mark Brunell	.50	.20
❑ 116 Patrick Jeffers RC	3.00	1.50
❑ 117 Elvis Grbac	.30	.10
❑ 118 Ike Hilliard	.20	.07
❑ 119 Sam Madison	.20	.07
❑ 120 Terrell Owens	.50	.20
❑ 121 Rich Gannon	.50	.20
❑ 122 Skip Hicks	.20	.07
❑ 123 Eric Green	.20	.07
❑ 124 Trent Dilfer	.30	.10
❑ 125 Terry Glenn	.50	.20
❑ 126 Trent Green	.50	.20
❑ 127 Charles Johnson	.20	.07
❑ 128 Adrian Murrell	.30	.10
❑ 129 Jason Gildon	.20	.07
❑ 130 Tim Dwight	.50	.20
❑ 131 Ryan Leaf	.50	.20
❑ 132 Rocket Ismail	.30	.10
❑ 133 Jon Kitna	.50	.20
❑ 134 Alonzo Mayes	.20	.07
❑ 135 Yancey Thigpen	.20	.07
❑ 136 David LaFleur	.20	.07
❑ 137 Ray Lewis	.50	.20
❑ 138 Herman Moore	.30	.10
❑ 139 Brian Griese	.50	.20
❑ 140 Antonio Freeman	.50	.20
❑ 141 Darnay Scott	.20	.07
❑ 142 Ed McDaniel	.20	.07
❑ 143 Andre Reed	.30	.10
❑ 144 Andre Hastings	.20	.07
❑ 145 Chris Warren	.20	.07
❑ 146 Kevin Hardy	.20	.07
❑ 147 Joe Jurevicius	.30	.10
❑ 148 Jerome Pathon	.20	.07
❑ 149 Duce Staley	.50	.20
❑ 150 Dan Marino	1.50	.60
❑ 151 Jerry Rice	1.00	.40
❑ 152 Byron Bam Morris	.20	.07
❑ 153 Az-Zahir Hakim	.20	.07
❑ 154 Ty Law	.30	.10
❑ 155 Warrick Dunn	.50	.20
❑ 156 Keyshawn Johnson	.50	.20
❑ 157 Brian Mitchell	.20	.07
❑ 158 James Jett	.30	.10

❑ 159 Fred Lane	.20	.07
❑ 160 Courtney Hawkins	.20	.07
❑ 161 Andre Wadsworth	.20	.07
❑ 162 Natrone Means	.30	.10
❑ 163 Andrew Glover	.20	.07
❑ 164 Anthony Simmons	.20	.07
❑ 165 Leon Lett	.20	.07
❑ 166 Frank Wycheck	.20	.07
❑ 167 Barry Minter	.20	.07
❑ 168 Michael McCrary	.20	.07
❑ 169 Johnnie Morton	.30	.10
❑ 170 Jay Riemersma	.20	.07
❑ 171 Vonnie Holliday	.20	.07
❑ 172 Brian Simmons	.20	.07
❑ 173 Joe Johnson	.20	.07
❑ 174 Ed McCaffrey	.30	.10
❑ 175 Jason Sehorn	.20	.07
❑ 176 Keenan McCardell	.30	.10
❑ 177 Bobby Taylor	.20	.07
❑ 178 Andre Rison	.30	.10
❑ 179 Greg Hill	.20	.07
❑ 180 O.J. McDuffie	.30	.10
❑ 181 Darren Woodson	.20	.07
❑ 182 Willie McGinest	.20	.07
❑ 183 J.J. Stokes	.30	.10
❑ 184 Leon Johnson	.20	.07
❑ 185 Bert Emanuel	.30	.10
❑ 186 Napoleon Kaufman	.50	.20
❑ 187 Leslie Shepherd	.20	.07
❑ 188 Levon Kirkland	.20	.07
❑ 189 Simeon Rice	.30	.10
❑ 190 Mikhael Ricks	.20	.07
❑ 191 Robert Smith	.50	.20
❑ 192 Michael Sinclair	.20	.07
❑ 193 Muhsin Muhammad	.30	.10
❑ 194 Duane Starks	.20	.07
❑ 195 Terance Mathis	.30	.10
❑ 196 Antowain Smith	.50	.20
❑ 197 Tony Parrish	.20	.07
❑ 198 Takeo Spikes	.20	.07
❑ 199 Ernie Mills	.20	.07
❑ 200 John Mobley	.20	.07
❑ 202 Pete Mitchell	.20	.07
❑ 203 Darick Holmes	.20	.07
❑ 204 Derrick Thomas	.50	.20
❑ 205 David Palmer	.20	.07
❑ 206 Jason Taylor	.20	.07
❑ 207 Sammy Knight	.20	.07
❑ 208 Dwayne Rudd	.20	.07
❑ 209 Lawyer Milloy	.30	.10
❑ 210 Michael Strahan	.30	.10
❑ 211 Mo Lewis	.20	.07
❑ 212 William Thomas	.20	.07
❑ 213 Darrell Russell	.20	.07
❑ 214 Brad Johnson	.50	.20
❑ 215 Kordell Stewart	.30	.10
❑ 216 Robert Holcombe	.20	.07
❑ 217 Junior Seau	.50	.20
❑ 218 Jacquez Green	.20	.07
❑ 219 Shawn Springs	.20	.07
❑ 220 Michael Westbrook	.30	.10
❑ 221 Rod Woodson	.30	.10
❑ 222 Frank Sanders	.30	.10
❑ 223 Bruce Smith	.30	.10
❑ 224 Eugene Robinson	.20	.07
❑ 225 Bill Romanowski	.20	.07
❑ 226 Wesley Walls	.30	.10
❑ 227 Jimmy Smith	.30	.10
❑ 228 Deion Sanders	.50	.20
❑ 229 Lamar Thomas	.20	.07
❑ 230 Dorsey Levens	.50	.20
❑ 231 Tony Simmons	.20	.07
❑ 232 John Randle	.30	.10
❑ 233 Curtis Martin	.50	.20
❑ 234 Bryant Young	.20	.07
❑ 235 Charles Woodson	.50	.20
❑ 236 Charles Way	.20	.07
❑ 237 Zach Thomas	.50	.20
❑ 238 Ricky Proehl	.20	.07
❑ 239 Ricky Watters	.30	.10
❑ 240 Hardy Nickerson	.20	.07
❑ 241 Shannon Sharpe	.30	.10
❑ 242 O.J. Santiago	.20	.07
❑ 243 Vinny Testaverde	.30	.10
❑ 244 Roell Preston	.20	.07
❑ 245 James Stewart	.30	.10
❑ 246 Jake Reed	.30	.10
❑ 247 Steve Young	.60	.25
❑ 248 Shaun Williams	.20	.07

❑ 249 Rod Smith	.30	.10
❑ 250 Warren Sapp	.30	.10
❑ 251 Champ Bailey RC	1.50	.60
❑ 252 Karsten Bailey RC	.75	.30
❑ 253 D'Wayne Bates RC	.75	.30
❑ 254 Michael Bishop RC	1.25	.50
❑ 255 David Boston RC	1.25	.50
❑ 256 Na Brown RC	.75	.30
❑ 257 Fernando Bryant RC	.75	.30
❑ 258 Shawn Bryson RC	1.25	.50
❑ 259 Darrin Chiaverini RC	.75	.30
❑ 260 Chris Claiborne RC	.40	.15
❑ 261 Mike Cloud RC	.75	.30
❑ 262 Cecil Collins RC	.40	.15
❑ 263 Tim Couch RC	1.25	.50
❑ 264 Scott Covington RC	1.25	.50
❑ 265 Daunte Culpepper RC	5.00	2.00
❑ 266 Antuan Edwards RC	.40	.15
❑ 267 Troy Edwards RC	.75	.30
❑ 268 Ebenezer Ekuban RC	.75	.30
❑ 269 Kevin Faulk RC	1.25	.50
❑ 270 Jermaine Fazande RC	.75	.30
❑ 271 Joe Germaine RC	.75	.30
❑ 272 Martin Gramatica RC	.40	.15
❑ 273 Torry Holt RC	3.00	1.25
❑ 274 Brock Huard RC	1.25	.50
❑ 275 Sedrick Irvin RC	.40	.15
❑ 276 Sheldon Jackson RC	.75	.30
❑ 277 Edgerrin James RC	5.00	2.00
❑ 278 James Johnson RC	.75	.30
❑ 279 Kevin Johnson RC	1.25	.50
❑ 280 Malcolm Johnson RC	.40	.15
❑ 281 Andy Katzenmoyer RC	.75	.30
❑ 282 Jevon Kearse RC	2.00	.75
❑ 283 Patrick Kerney RC	1.25	.50
❑ 284 Shaun King RC	.75	.30
❑ 285 Jim Kleinsasser RC	1.25	.50
❑ 286 Rob Konrad RC	1.25	.50
❑ 287 Chris McAlister RC	.75	.30
❑ 288 Donovan McNabb RC	6.00	2.50
❑ 289 Cade McNown RC	.75	.30
❑ 290 Dee Miller RC	.40	.15
❑ 291 Joe Montgomery RC	.75	.30
❑ 292 De'Mond Parker RC	.40	.15
❑ 293 Peerless Price RC	1.25	.50
❑ 294 Akili Smith RC	.75	.30
❑ 295 Justin Swift RC	.40	.15
❑ 296 Jerame Tuman RC	1.25	.50
❑ 297 Ricky Williams RC	2.50	1.00
❑ 298 Antoine Winfield	.75	.30
❑ 299 Craig Yeast RC	.75	.30
❑ 300 Amos Zereoue RC	1.25	.50
❑ P6 Fred Taylor Promo	1.00	.40

2000 Fleer Tradition

❑ COMPLETE SET (400)	60.00	25.00
❑ 1 Kevin Johnson	.50	.20
❑ 2 Chris Chandler	.30	.10
❑ 3 Peerless Price	.30	.10
❑ 4 Andre Rison	.30	.10
❑ 5 Curtis Enis	.20	.07
❑ 6 Tim Couch	.30	.10
❑ 7 Brian Dawkins	.50	.20
❑ 8 Akili Smith	.20	.07
❑ 9 Kevin Faulk	.30	.10
❑ 10 Joey Galloway	.30	.10
❑ 11 Bill Romanowski	.20	.07
❑ 12 Charlie Batch	.50	.20
❑ 13 Terrence Wilkins	.20	.07
❑ 14 Kevin Hardy	.20	.07
❑ 15 Cade McNown	.20	.07
❑ 16 Elvis Grbac	.30	.10

❑ 17 Cris Carter .50 .20
❑ 18 Willie McGinest .20 .07
❑ 19 Michael Bishop .20 .07
❑ 20 Lee Woodall .20 .07
❑ 21 Jake Reed .30 .10
❑ 22 Bryan Cox .20 .07
❑ 23 Chris Sanders .20 .07
❑ 24 Tavian Banks .20 .07
❑ 25 Levon Kirkland .20 .07
❑ 26 James Hundon .20 .07
❑ 27 Junior Seau .50 .20
❑ 28 Darren Woodson .20 .07
❑ 29 Kevin Carter .20 .07
❑ 30 Joe Jurevicius .20 .07
❑ 31 John Lynch .30 .10
❑ 32 Steve McNair .50 .20
❑ 33 Jake Plummer .30 .10
❑ 34 Antonio Freeman .50 .20
❑ 35 Peter Boulware .20 .07
❑ 36 Brad Johnson .50 .20
❑ 37 Bobby Engram .30 .10
❑ 38 David Boston .50 .20
❑ 39 Jason Tucker .20 .07
❑ 40 Troy Brown .30 .10
❑ 41 Brian Griese .50 .20
❑ 42 Dorsey Levens .30 .10
❑ 43 Cornelius Bennett .20 .07
❑ 44 Donovan McNabb .75 .30
❑ 45 Rob Johnson .30 .10
❑ 46 Robert Smith .50 .20
❑ 47 Stanley Pritchett .20 .07
❑ 48 Tedy Bruschi .50 .20
❑ 49 Dan Marino 1.50 .60
❑ 50 Amani Toomer .30 .10
❑ 51 Aaron Glenn .20 .07
❑ 52 Rickey Dudley .20 .07
❑ 53 Tim Brown .50 .20
❑ 54 Jim Harbaugh .30 .10
❑ 55 Terrell Owens .50 .20
❑ 56 Jason Sehorn .20 .07
❑ 57 Cortez Kennedy .20 .07
❑ 58 London Fletcher RC .30 .10
❑ 59 Simeon Rice .30 .10
❑ 60 Shaun King .20 .07
❑ 61 Stephen Davis .50 .20
❑ 62 Andre Wadsworth .20 .07
❑ 63 Kyle Brady .20 .07
❑ 64 Priest Holmes .60 .25
❑ 65 Patrick Jeffers .50 .20
❑ 66 Barry Minter .20 .07
❑ 67 Curtis Martin .50 .20
❑ 68 Darrin Chiaverini .20 .07
❑ 69 Robert Thomas .20 .07
❑ 70 Samari Rolle .20 .07
❑ 71 Robert Porcher .20 .07
❑ 72 Jerry Rice 1.00 .40
❑ 73 Bill Schroeder .30 .10
❑ 74 Chad Bratzke .20 .07
❑ 75 Tony Brackens .20 .07
❑ 76 O.J. McDuffie .30 .10
❑ 77 John Randle .30 .10
❑ 78 Michael Pittman .20 .07
❑ 79 Drew Bledsoe .60 .25
❑ 80 Ike Hilliard .30 .10
❑ 81 Victor Green .20 .07
❑ 82 Duce Staley .50 .20
❑ 83 Bruce Smith .30 .10
❑ 84 Amos Zereoue .50 .20
❑ 85 Charlie Garner .30 .10
❑ 86 Shawn Springs .20 .07
❑ 87 Kurt Warner 1.00 .40
❑ 88 Eddie George .50 .20
❑ 89 Michael Westbrook .30 .10
❑ 90 Dexter Coakley .20 .07
❑ 91 Rob Moore .30 .10
❑ 92 Duane Starks .20 .07
❑ 93 Steve Beuerlein .30 .10
❑ 94 Marty Booker .30 .10
❑ 95 Karim Abdul-Jabbar .30 .10
❑ 96 Troy Aikman 1.00 .40
❑ 97 Germane Crowell .20 .07
❑ 98 Matt Hasselbeck .30 .10
❑ 99 E.G. Green .20 .07
❑ 100 Mark Brunell .50 .20
❑ 101 Tony Martin .30 .10
❑ 102 Darrell Green .20 .07
❑ 103 Ricky Williams .50 .20
❑ 104 Michael Strahan .30 .10
❑ 105 Vinny Testaverde .30 .10
❑ 106 Charles Johnson .30 .10
❑ 107 Hines Ward .50 .20
❑ 108 Bryant Young .20 .07
❑ 109 Mo Lewis .20 .07
❑ 110 Greg Clark .20 .07
❑ 111 Jon Kitna .50 .20
❑ 112 Jacquez Green .20 .07
❑ 113 Kevin Dyson .30 .10
❑ 114 Stephen Alexander .20 .07
❑ 115 Cam Cleeland .20 .07
❑ 116 Keith Poole .20 .07
❑ 117 Az-Zahir Hakim .30 .10
❑ 118 Tim Dwight .50 .20
❑ 119 Corey Bradford .20 .07
❑ 120 Carlos Emmons .20 .07
❑ 121 Trent Dilfer .30 .10
❑ 122 Lance Schulters .20 .07
❑ 123 Byron Hanspard .20 .07
❑ 124 Tim Biakabutuka .30 .10
❑ 125 Eddie Kennison .30 .10
❑ 126 Terry Kirby .20 .07
❑ 127 Mike McKenzie .20 .07
❑ 128 Fred Beasley .20 .07
❑ 129 Chad Brown .20 .07
❑ 130 Terrell Davis .50 .20
❑ 131 Herman Moore .30 .10
❑ 132 Vonnie Holliday .20 .07
❑ 133 Jim Miller .20 .07
❑ 134 Peyton Manning 1.25 .50
❑ 135 Derrick Alexander .30 .10
❑ 136 Oronde Gadsden .30 .10
❑ 137 Robert Griffith .20 .07
❑ 138 Troy Edwards .20 .07
❑ 139 Damon Huard .50 .20
❑ 140 Jessie Armstead .20 .07
❑ 141 Charles Woodson .30 .10
❑ 142 Troy Vincent .20 .07
❑ 143 Natrone Means .20 .07
❑ 144 Jeff Garcia .50 .20
❑ 145 Terry Glenn .30 .10
❑ 146 Marshall Faulk .60 .25
❑ 147 Pat Johnson .20 .07
❑ 148 Frank Wycheck .20 .07
❑ 149 Champ Bailey .30 .10
❑ 150 Jamal Anderson .50 .20
❑ 151 Doug Flutie .50 .20
❑ 152 Michael Bates .20 .07
❑ 153 Corey Dillon .50 .20
❑ 154 Keith McKenzie .20 .07
❑ 155 Orpheus Roye .20 .07
❑ 156 Olandis Gary .50 .20
❑ 157 Johnnie Morton .30 .10
❑ 158 Brett Favre 1.50 .60
❑ 159 Adrian Murrell .20 .07
❑ 160 Fred Taylor .50 .20
❑ 161 Tony Gonzalez .30 .10
❑ 162 Zach Thomas .50 .20
❑ 163 Randy Moss 1.00 .40
❑ 164 Marcus Robinson .50 .20
❑ 165 Tiki Barber .50 .20
❑ 166 Rich Gannon .50 .20
❑ 167 Jeremiah Trotter RC 1.50 .60
❑ 168 Jermaine Fazande .20 .07
❑ 169 Steve Young .60 .25
❑ 170 Isaac Bruce .50 .20
❑ 171 Warrick Dunn .50 .20
❑ 172 Yancey Thigpen .20 .07
❑ 173 Rod Smith .30 .10
❑ 174 Albert Connell .20 .07
❑ 175 Freddie Jones .20 .07
❑ 176 Terance Mathis .30 .10
❑ 177 Eric Moulds .50 .20
❑ 178 Brian Mitchell .20 .07
❑ 179 Wesley Walls .20 .07
❑ 180 Carl Pickens .30 .10
❑ 181 Errict Rhett .30 .10
❑ 182 Madre Hill .20 .07
❑ 183 Jason Elam .20 .07
❑ 184 Greg Ellis .20 .07
❑ 185 David Sloan .20 .07
❑ 186 Edgerrin James .75 .30
❑ 187 Jimmy Smith .30 .10
❑ 188 Tony Richardson RC .30 .10
❑ 189 James Hasty .20 .07
❑ 190 Sam Madison .20 .07
❑ 191 Tony Simmons .20 .07
❑ 192 Andre Hastings .20 .07
❑ 193 Keyshawn Johnson .50 .20
❑ 194 Na Brown .20 .07
❑ 195 Napoleon Kaufman .30 .10
❑ 196 Torrance Small .20 .07
❑ 197 Curtis Conway .30 .10
❑ 198 Jeff Graham .20 .07
❑ 199 Jason Hanson .20 .07
❑ 200 Derrick Mayes .30 .10
❑ 201 Torry Holt .50 .20
❑ 202 Warren Sapp .30 .10
❑ 203 Kimble Anders .20 .07
❑ 204 Blaine Bishop .20 .07
❑ 205 Leroy Hoard .20 .07
❑ 206 Larry Centers .20 .07
❑ 207 O.J. Santiago .20 .07
❑ 208 Antowain Smith .30 .10
❑ 209 Chuck Smith .20 .07
❑ 210 Takeo Spikes .20 .07
❑ 211 Rocket Ismail .30 .10
❑ 212 Ed McCaffrey .50 .20
❑ 213 Karsten Bailey .20 .07
❑ 214 Terry Fair .20 .07
❑ 215 Ken Dilger .20 .07
❑ 216 Jamie Martin .30 .10
❑ 217 Cris Dishman .20 .07
❑ 218 Jay Fiedler .30 .10
❑ 219 Lawyer Milloy .30 .10
❑ 220 Jake Delhomme RC 3.00 1.25
❑ 221 Wayne Chrebet .30 .10
❑ 222 Darrell Russell .20 .07
❑ 223 Christian Fauria .20 .07
❑ 224 Jerome Bettis .50 .20
❑ 225 Ryan Leaf .30 .10
❑ 226 Ricky Watters .30 .10
❑ 227 Keenan McCardell .30 .10
❑ 228 Grant Wistrom .20 .07
❑ 229 Jevon Kearse .50 .20
❑ 230 Frank Sanders .30 .10
❑ 231 Shannon Sharpe .30 .10
❑ 232 Jonathan Linton .20 .07
❑ 233 Alonzo Mayes .20 .07
❑ 234 Jason Garrett .20 .07
❑ 235 Kordell Stewart .30 .10
❑ 236 David LaFleur .20 .07
❑ 237 Kenny Bynum .20 .07
❑ 238 Byron Chamberlain .20 .07
❑ 239 Tyrone Davis .20 .07
❑ 240 Jerome Pathon .30 .10
❑ 241 Alvis Whitted .20 .07
❑ 242 Kevin Lockett .20 .07
❑ 243 Matthew Hatchette .20 .07
❑ 244 Rod Woodson .30 .10
❑ 245 Joe Horn .30 .10
❑ 246 Ronnie Powell .20 .07
❑ 247 Dedric Ward .20 .07
❑ 248 James Johnson .20 .07
❑ 249 James Jett .20 .07
❑ 250 Bobby Shaw RC .50 .20
❑ 251 J.J. Stokes .30 .10
❑ 252 Paul Shields RC .20 .07
❑ 253 Sean Dawkins .20 .07
❑ 254 Hardy Nickerson .20 .07
❑ 255 Stephen Boyd .20 .07
❑ 256 Chris Warren .20 .07
❑ 257 Kerry Collins .30 .10
❑ 258 Isaac Byrd .20 .07
❑ 259 Bobby Hoying .20 .07
❑ 260 Daunte Culpepper .60 .25
❑ 261 Moe Williams .30 .10
❑ 262 Kamil Loud .20 .07
❑ 263 Derrick Brooks .50 .20
❑ 264 Jay Riemersma .20 .07
❑ 265 Ray Lucas .30 .10
❑ 266 Jason Gildon .20 .07
❑ 267 James Stewart .30 .10
❑ 268 Marcellus Wiley .20 .07
❑ 269 Craig Yeast .20 .07
❑ 270 Michael Basnight .20 .07
❑ 271 Tyrone Wheatley .30 .10
❑ 272 Martin Gramatica .20 .07
❑ 273 Phillip Daniels RC .30 .10
❑ 274 Richard Huntley .20 .07
❑ 275 Muhsin Muhammad .30 .10
❑ 276 Todd Lyght .20 .07
❑ 277 Carlester Crumpler .20 .07
❑ 278 Jeff Lewis .20 .07
❑ 279 Jeff George .30 .10
❑ 280 Jeff Blake .30 .10
❑ 281 Michael McCrary .20 .07
❑ 282 Shawn Jefferson .20 .07
❑ 283 Mark Bruener .20 .07

❑ 284 Donnie Abraham	.20	.07
❑ 285 Yatil Green	.20	.07
❑ 286 Jermaine Lewis	.20	.07
❑ 287 Rob Fredrickson	.20	.07
❑ 288 Thurman Thomas	.30	.10
❑ 289 Kent Graham	.20	.07
❑ 290 Darnay Scott	.30	.10
❑ 291 Tony Graziani	.20	.07
❑ 292 Qadry Ismail	.30	.10
❑ 293 Aeneas Williams	.20	.07
❑ 294 Marvin Harrison	.50	.20
❑ 295 Jimmy Hitchcock	.20	.07
❑ 296 Bob Christian	.20	.07
❑ 297 Pete Mitchell	.20	.07
❑ 298 Mike Alstott	.50	.20
❑ 299 Emmitt Smith	1.00	.40
❑ [illegible]	.20	.07
❑ 301 Tony Banks	.30	.10
❑ 302 Mikhael Ricks	.20	.07
❑ 303 Randall Cunningham	.50	.20
❑ 304 Thomas Jones RC	1.25	.50
❑ 305 Mark Simoneau RC	.60	.25
❑ 306 Jamal Lewis RC	2.00	.75
❑ 307 Kwame Cavil RC	.40	.15
❑ 308 Rashard Anderson RC	.60	.25
❑ 309 Brian Urlacher RC	3.00	1.25
❑ 310 Peter Warrick RC	.75	.30
❑ 311 Courtney Brown RC	.75	.30
❑ 312 Michael Wiley RC	.60	.25
❑ 313 Chris Cole RC	.60	.25
❑ 314 Reuben Droughns RC	1.00	.40
❑ 315 Bubba Franks RC	.75	.30
❑ 316 Rob Morris RC	.60	.25
❑ 317 R.Jay Soward RC	.60	.25
❑ 318 Sylvester Morris RC	.60	.25
❑ 319 Ben Kelly RC	.40	.15
❑ 320 Doug Chapman RC	.60	.25
❑ 321 J.R. Redmond RC	.60	.25
❑ 322 Darren Howard RC	.60	.25
❑ 323 Ron Dayne RC	.75	.30
❑ 324 Chad Pennington RC	2.00	.75
❑ 325 Jerry Porter RC	1.00	.40
❑ 326 Corey Simon RC	.75	.30
❑ 327 Plaxico Burress RC	1.50	.60
❑ 328 Trung Canidate RC	.60	.25
❑ 329 Rogers Beckett RC	.60	.25
❑ 330 Giovanni Carmazzi RC	.40	.15
❑ 331 Shaun Alexander RC	4.00	1.50
❑ 332 Joe Hamilton RC	.60	.25
❑ 333 Keith Bulluck RC	.75	.30
❑ 334 Todd Husak RC	.75	.30
❑ 335 D.Walker RC/R.Thompson RC	.60	.25
❑ 336 M.Philyaw RC/A.Midget RC	.40	.15
❑ 337 C.Redman RC/T.Taylor RC	.75	.30
❑ 338 Sam.Morris RC/A.Black RC	.75	.30
❑ 339 D.Grant RC/A.McKinley RC	.60	.25
❑ 340 D.White RC/F.Murphy RC	.75	.30
❑ 341 [illegible] RC/R.Dugans RC	1.00	.40
❑ 342 Prentice RC/Northcutt RC	.60	.25
❑ 343 O.Grant RC/D.Goodrich RC	.40	.15
❑ 344 D.O'Neal RC/I.Gold RC	.75	.30
❑ 345 S.McDougle RC/B.Green RC	.40	.15
❑ 346 A.Lucas RC/N.Diggs RC	.60	.25
❑ 347 M.Washington RC/D.Kendra RC	.60	.25
❑ 348 T.Slaughter RC/S.Stith RC	.60	.25
❑ 349 W.Bartee RC/F.Moreau RC	.60	.25
❑ 350 D.Dyer RC/T.Wade RC	.60	.25
❑ 351 C.Hovan RC/T.Walters	.75	.30
❑ 352 T.Brady RC/Stachelski RC	30.00	15.00
❑ 353 M.Bulger RC/T.Smith RC	1.50	.60
❑ 354 C.Griffin RC/R.Dixon RC	.60	.25
❑ 355 L.Coles RC/A.Becht RC	.75	.30
❑ 356 Janikowski RC/Lechler RC	.75	.30
❑ 357 T.Pinkston RC/G.Scott RC	.75	.30
❑ 358 D.Farmer RC/T.Martin RC	.60	.25
❑ 359 B.Young RC/J.Shepherd RC	.60	.25
❑ 360 J.Seider RC/T.Gaylor RC	.60	.25
❑ 361 T.Rattay RC/C.Fields RC	.75	.30
❑ 362 D.Jackson RC/J.Williams RC	1.25	.50
❑ 363 N.Webster RC/J.Whalen RC	.40	.15
❑ 364 E.Kinney RC/C.Coleman RC	.75	.30
❑ 365 C.Samuels RC/L.Murray RC	.60	.25
❑ 366 Cardinals IA/Plummer	.30	.10
❑ 367 Falcons IA/Chandlr/Andrson	.30	.10
❑ 368 Ravens IA/Boulware	.20	.07
❑ 369 Bills IA/Flutie	.30	.10
❑ 370 Panthers IA/Beuerlein	.30	.10
❑ 371 Bears IA/McNown	.20	.07
❑ 372 Bengals IA/Dillon	.30	.10
❑ 373 Browns IA/Couch	.30	.10
❑ 374 Cowboys IA/Smith	.50	.20
❑ 375 Broncos IA/Gary	.30	.10
❑ 376 Lions IA/Batch	.30	.10
❑ 377 Packers IA/Levens	.30	.10
❑ 378 Colts IA/James	.60	.25
❑ 379 Jaguars IA/Brackens	.20	.07
❑ 380 Chiefs IA/Grbac	.20	.07
❑ 381 Dolphins IA/Marino	.75	.30
❑ 382 Vikings IA/Rob.Smith	.30	.10
❑ 383 Patriots IA/Bledsoe	.30	.10
❑ 384 Saints IA/Williams	.50	.20
❑ 385 Giants IA/Armstead	.20	.07
❑ 386 Jets IA/Martin	.30	.10
❑ 387 Raiders IA/Kaufman	.30	.10
❑ 388 Eagles IA/McNabb	.30	.10
❑ 389 Steelers IA/Bettis	.30	.10
❑ 390 Rams IA/Faulk	.50	.20
❑ 391 Chargers IA/Fazande	.20	.07
❑ 392 49ers IA/Garner	.30	.10
❑ 393 Seahawks IA/Kennedy	.20	.07
❑ 394 Buccaneers IA/Alstott	.30	.10
❑ 395 Titans IA/McNair	.30	.10
❑ 396 Redskins IA/S.Davis	.30	.10
❑ 397 Tim Couch CL	.30	.10
❑ 398 Peyton Manning CL	.60	.25
❑ 399 Kurt Warner CL	.50	.20
❑ 400 Randy Moss CL	.50	.20

2001 Fleer Tradition

❑ COMPLETE SET (450)	40.00	20.00
❑ 1 Thomas Jones	.40	.15
❑ 2 Bruce Smith	.25	.08
❑ 3 Marvin Harrison	.60	.25
❑ 4 Darrell Jackson	.60	.25
❑ 5 Trent Green	.60	.25
❑ 6 Wesley Walls	.25	.08
❑ 7 Jimmy Smith	.40	.15
❑ 8 Isaac Bruce	.60	.25
❑ 9 Jamal Anderson	.60	.25
❑ 10 Marty Booker	.25	.08
❑ 11 Elvis Grbac	.40	.15
❑ 12 Joe Jurevicius	.25	.08
❑ 13 Reidel Anthony	.25	.08
❑ 14 Darnay Scott	.25	.08
❑ 15 Oronde Gadsden	.40	.15
❑ 16 Shawn Bryson	.25	.08
❑ 17 Jonathan Ogden	.25	.08
❑ 18 Aaron Shea	.25	.08
❑ 19 Randy Moss	1.25	.50
❑ 20 Eddie George	.60	.25
❑ 21 Stephen Davis	.60	.25
❑ 22 Emmitt Smith	1.25	.50
❑ 23 Willie McGinest	.25	.08
❑ 24 Trent Dilfer	.40	.15
❑ 25 Peter Boulware	.25	.08
❑ 26 Rod Smith	.40	.15
❑ 27 Ricky Williams	.60	.25
❑ 28 Albert Connell	.25	.08
❑ 29 Robert Porcher	.25	.08
❑ 30 Jessie Armstead	.25	.08
❑ 31 Shane Matthews	.25	.08
❑ 32 Eric Moulds	.40	.15
❑ 33 Kurt Schulz	.25	.08
❑ 34 Richie Anderson	.25	.08
❑ 35 Ron Dugans	.25	.08
❑ 36 Steve Beuerlein	.40	.15
❑ 37 Darren Sharper	.25	.08
❑ 38 Andre Rison	.40	.15
❑ 39 Courtney Brown	.40	.15
❑ 40 Eddie Kennison	.40	.15
❑ 41 Ken Dilger	.25	.08
❑ 42 Charles Johnson	.25	.08
❑ 43 Dexter Coakley	.25	.08
❑ 44 Akili Smith	.25	.08
❑ 45 R.Jay Soward	.25	.08
❑ 46 Danny Farmer	.25	.08
❑ 47 Dez White	.25	.08
❑ 48 Olandis Gary	.40	.15
❑ 49 Wall Rainer	.25	.08
❑ 50 Derrick Alexander	.40	.15
❑ 51 Donnie Abraham	.25	.08
❑ 52 David Sloan	.25	.08
❑ 53 Larry Allen	.25	.08
❑ 54 Sam Madison	.25	.08
❑ 55 Troy Edwards	.25	.08
❑ 56 Ryan Longwell	.25	.08
❑ 57 Brian Griese	.60	.25
❑ 58 John Randle	.40	.15
❑ 59 Reggie Jones	.25	.08
❑ 60 Mike Peterson	.25	.08
❑ 61 Bill Romanowski	.25	.08
❑ 62 Kevin Faulk	.40	.15
❑ 63 Tai Streets	.25	.08
❑ 64 Tony Brackens	.25	.08
❑ 65 James Stewart	.40	.15
❑ 66 Joe Horn	.40	.15
❑ 67 Kurt Warner	1.25	.50
❑ 68 Eric Hicks RC	.25	.08
❑ 69 Bryan Westbrook	.25	.08
❑ 70 Tiki Barber	.60	.25
❑ 71 Frank Sanders	.25	.08
❑ 72 Olindo Mare	.25	.08
❑ 73 Bill Schroeder	.40	.15
❑ 74 Anthony Becht	.25	.08
❑ 75 Rob Johnson	.40	.15
❑ 76 Troy Brown	.40	.15
❑ 77 Chad Bratzke	.25	.08
❑ 78 Rickey Dudley	.25	.08
❑ 79 Doug Johnson	.25	.08
❑ 80 Joe Johnson	.25	.08
❑ 81 Keenan McCardell	.25	.08
❑ 82 Tim Brown	.60	.25
❑ 83 Blaine Bishop	.25	.08
❑ 84 Ron Dixon	.25	.08
❑ 85 Michael Cloud	.25	.08
❑ 86 Todd Pinkston	.25	.08
❑ 87 Shannon Sharpe	.40	.15
❑ 88 Marvin Jones	.25	.08
❑ 89 Zach Thomas	.60	.25
❑ 90 Kordell Stewart	.40	.15
❑ 91 Champ Bailey	.40	.15
❑ 92 Jacquez Green	.25	.08
❑ 93 Daunte Culpepper	.60	.25
❑ 94 Freddie Jones	.25	.08
❑ 95 Donald Hayes	.25	.08
❑ 96 Rich Gannon	.60	.25
❑ 97 Ty Law	.40	.15
❑ 98 Grant Wistrom	.25	.08
❑ 99 James Allen	.40	.15
❑ 100 Corey Simon	.40	.15
❑ 101 Jeff Blake	.40	.15
❑ 102 Bryant Young	.25	.08
❑ 103 Craig Yeast	.25	.08
❑ 104 Bobby Shaw	.25	.08
❑ 105 Kerry Collins	.40	.15
❑ 106 Brock Huard	.25	.08
❑ 107 JaJuan Dawson	.25	.08
❑ 108 Jeff Graham	.25	.08
❑ 109 Chad Pennington	1.00	.40
❑ 110 Jake Plummer	.40	.15
❑ 111 James McKnight	.40	.15
❑ 112 Terrell Owens	.60	.25
❑ 113 Mo Lewis	.25	.08
❑ 114 Jeremy McDaniel	.25	.08
❑ 115 Ed McCaffrey	.60	.25
❑ 116 Ricky Watters	.25	.08
❑ 117 Jerry Porter	.40	.15
❑ 118 Shawn Jefferson	.25	.08
❑ 119 Charlie Batch	.60	.25
❑ 120 Justin Watson	.25	.08
❑ 121 Donovan McNabb	.75	.30
❑ 122 Shaun King	.25	.08
❑ 123 Brett Favre	2.00	.75
❑ 124 Ronald McKinnon	.25	.08
❑ 125 Richard Huntley	.25	.08
❑ 126 Ray Lewis	.60	.25
❑ 127 Jerome Pathon	.40	.15
❑ 128 Sam Cowart	.25	.08
❑ 129 Ryan Leaf	.40	.15
❑ 130 Greg Clark	.25	.08

❑ 131 Tony Boselli .25 .08
❑ 132 Frank Wycheck .25 .08
❑ 133 Charlie Garner .40 .15
❑ 134 Tony Siragusa .25 .08
❑ 135 Sylvester Morris .25 .08
❑ 136 Qadry Ismail .40 .15
❑ 137 Jon Kitna .40 .15
❑ 138 James Thrash .40 .15
❑ 139 Lamar Smith .40 .15
❑ 140 Brad Johnson .60 .25
❑ 141 London Fletcher .25 .08
❑ 142 Tim Biakabutuka .40 .15
❑ 143 Ed McDaniel .25 .08
❑ 144 Tony Parrish .25 .08
❑ 145 David Boston .60 .25
❑ 146 Brian Urlacher 1.00 .40
❑ 147 Drew Bledsoe .75 .30
❑ 148 David Patten .25 .08
❑ 149 Marcellus Wiley .25 .08
❑ 150 Peter Warrick .60 .25
❑ 151 La'Roi Glover .25 .08
❑ 152 Troy Aikman 1.00 .40
❑ 153 Chris Chandler .40 .15
❑ 154 Travis Prentice .25 .08
❑ 155 Ike Hilliard .40 .15
❑ 156 John Mobley .25 .08
❑ 157 Warren Sapp .40 .15
❑ 158 Joey Galloway .40 .15
❑ 159 Laveranues Coles .60 .25
❑ 160 Germane Crowell .25 .08
❑ 161 Jamal Lewis 1.00 .40
❑ 162 Mike Anderson .60 .25
❑ 163 Charles Woodson .40 .15
❑ 164 Antonio Freeman .60 .25
❑ 165 Derrick Mason .40 .15
❑ 166 Chris Claiborne .25 .08
❑ 167 Brian Mitchell .25 .08
❑ 168 Mike Vanderjagt .25 .08
❑ 169 Rod Woodson .40 .15
❑ 170 Doug Chapman .25 .08
❑ 171 John Lynch .40 .15
❑ 172 Kevin Hardy .25 .08
❑ 173 Sam Shade .25 .08
❑ 174 Edgerrin James .75 .30
❑ 175 Brian Dawkins .40 .15
❑ 176 Donnie Edwards .25 .08
❑ 177 Patrick Jeffers .40 .15
❑ 178 Mark Brunell .60 .25
❑ 179 Junior Seau .60 .25
❑ 180 Trace Armstrong .25 .08
❑ 181 Marcus Robinson .60 .25
❑ 182 Tony Gonzalez .40 .15
❑ 183 J.J. Stokes .40 .15
❑ 184 Jake Reed .40 .15
❑ 185 Corey Dillon .60 .25
❑ 186 Jay Fiedler .60 .25
❑ 187 Christian Fauria .25 .08
❑ 188 Sammy Knight .25 .08
❑ 189 Kevin Johnson .40 .15
❑ 190 Matthew Hatchette .25 .08
❑ 191 Az-Zahir Hakim .40 .15
❑ 192 Keith Hamilton .25 .08
❑ 193 Darren Woodson .25 .08
❑ 194 Terry Glenn .40 .15
❑ 195 Simeon Rice .40 .15
❑ 196 Keyshawn Johnson .60 .25
❑ 197 Terrell Davis .60 .25
❑ 198 William Roaf .25 .08
❑ 199 Doug Flutie .60 .25
❑ 200 Kevin Carter .25 .08
❑ 201 Stephen Boyd .25 .08
❑ 202 Michael Strahan .40 .15
❑ 203 Ray Buchanan .25 .08
❑ 204 Tyrone Wheatley .40 .15
❑ 205 Jason Hanson .25 .08
❑ 206 Wayne Chrebet .40 .15
❑ 207 Samari Rolle .25 .08
❑ 208 Duce Staley .60 .25
❑ 209 Dorsey Levens .40 .15
❑ 210 Sebastian Janikowski .25 .08
❑ 211 Duane Starks .25 .08
❑ 212 Jason Gildon .25 .08
❑ 213 Terrence Wilkins .25 .08
❑ 214 Eric Allen .25 .08
❑ 215 Deion Sanders .60 .25
❑ 216 Curtis Conway .40 .15
❑ 217 Fred Taylor .60 .25
❑ 218 Troy Vincent .25 .08
❑ 219 Mike Minter RC .40 .15
❑ 220 Jeff Garcia .60 .25
❑ 221 Tony Richardson .25 .08
❑ 222 Jerome Bettis .60 .25
❑ 223 Chad Morton .25 .08
❑ 224 Tony Horne .25 .08
❑ 225 Dave Moore .25 .08
❑ 226 Victor Green .25 .08
❑ 227 Chris Sanders .25 .08
❑ 228 Marshall Faulk .75 .30
❑ 229 Cris Carter .60 .25
❑ 230 Rodney Harrison .25 .08
❑ 231 Tim Couch .40 .15
❑ 232 Antowain Smith .40 .15
❑ 233 Lawyer Milloy .40 .15
❑ 234 Lance Schulters .25 .08
❑ 235 Michael Wiley .25 .08
❑ 236 Steve McNair .60 .25
❑ 237 Aaron Brooks .60 .25
❑ 238 Anthony Simmons .25 .08
❑ 239 Dwayne Carswell .25 .08
❑ 240 Priest Holmes .75 .30
❑ 241 Amani Toomer .40 .15
❑ 242 Aeneas Williams .25 .08
❑ 243 MarTay Jenkins .25 .08
❑ 244 Jeff George .40 .15
❑ 245 Vinny Testaverde .40 .15
❑ 246 Peerless Price .40 .15
❑ 247 Bubba Franks .40 .15
❑ 248 Randall Cunningham .60 .25
❑ 249 Aaron Glenn .25 .08
❑ 250 Terance Mathis .40 .15
❑ 251 Peyton Manning 1.50 .60
❑ 252 Terrell Buckley .25 .08
❑ 253 Greg Biekert .25 .08
❑ 254 Martin Gramatica .25 .08
❑ 255 Kyle Brady .25 .08
❑ 256 Johnnie Morton .40 .15
❑ 257 Jeremiah Trotter .40 .15
❑ 258 Travis Taylor .40 .15
❑ 259 Frank Moreau .25 .08
❑ 260 LeRoy Butler .25 .08
❑ 261 Plaxico Burress .60 .25
❑ 262 Randall Godfrey .25 .08
❑ 263 Jason Taylor .25 .08
❑ 264 Jeff Burris .25 .08
❑ 265 Jim Harbaugh .40 .15
❑ 266 Marco Coleman .25 .08
❑ 267 Robert Smith .40 .15
❑ 268 Mike Hollis .25 .08
❑ 269 Jerry Rice 1.25 .50
❑ 270 Muhsin Muhammad .40 .15
❑ 271 J.R. Redmond .25 .08
❑ 272 Brian Walker .25 .08
❑ 273 Orlando Pace .25 .08
❑ 274 Cade McNown .25 .08
❑ 275 Darren Howard .25 .08
❑ 276 Ron Dayne .60 .25
❑ 277 Shaun Alexander .75 .30
❑ 278 Brandon Bennett .25 .08
❑ 279 Jason Sehorn .25 .08
❑ 280 Matt Hasselbeck .40 .15
❑ 281 Michael Pittman .25 .08
❑ 282 Dennis Northcutt .40 .15
❑ 283 Dedric Ward .25 .08
❑ 284 Curtis Martin .60 .25
❑ 285 Sammy Morris .25 .08
❑ 286 Rocket Ismail .40 .15
❑ 287 Jon Ritchie .25 .08
❑ 288 Shaun Ellis .25 .08
❑ 289 Tim Dwight .60 .25
❑ 290 Trevor Pryce .25 .08
❑ 291 Warrick Dunn .60 .25
❑ 292 Napoleon Kaufman .40 .15
❑ 293 Mike Alstott .60 .25
❑ 294 Herman Moore .40 .15
❑ 295 Chad Lewis .25 .08
❑ 296 Hugh Douglas .25 .08
❑ 297 Chris Redman .25 .08
❑ 298 Ahman Green .60 .25
❑ 299 Hines Ward .60 .25
❑ 300 Mark Bruener .25 .08
❑ 301 Jevon Kearse .40 .15
❑ 302 Jermaine Fazande .25 .08
❑ 303 Terrell Fletcher .25 .08
❑ 304 Torry Holt .60 .25
❑ 305 Chris McAlister .25 .08
❑ 306 Jason Elam .25 .08
❑ 307 Fred Beasley .25 .08
❑ 308 Frank Wycheck UH .25 .08
❑ 309 Michael McCrary UH .25 .08
❑ 310 Mark Brunell UH .60 .25
❑ 311 Tim Couch UH .40 .15
❑ 312 Takeo Spikes UH .25 .08
❑ 313 Jerome Bettis UH .40 .15
❑ 314 Zach Thomas UH .60 .25
❑ 315 Drew Bledsoe UH .60 .25
❑ 316 Wayne Chrebet UH .25 .08
❑ 317 Jay Riemersma UH .25 .08
❑ 318 Marvin Harrison UH .40 .15
❑ 319 Ed McCaffrey UH .40 .15
❑ 320 Tony Gonzalez UH .25 .08
❑ 321 Tim Brown UH .40 .15
❑ 322 Junior Seau UH .40 .15
❑ 323 Shawn Springs UH .25 .08
❑ 324 Troy Aikman UH .40 .15
❑ 325 Pat Tillman UH RC 20.00 8.00
❑ 326 David Akers UH RC .40 .15
❑ 327 Michael Strahan UH .40 .15
❑ 328 Darrell Green UH .25 .08
❑ 329 Kurt Warner UH .60 .25
❑ 330 Jeff Garcia UH .40 .15
❑ 331 Aaron Brooks UH .40 .15
❑ 332 Jamal Anderson UH .40 .15
❑ 333 Brad Hoover UH .25 .08
❑ 334 Cris Carter UH .40 .15
❑ 335 Derrick Brooks UH .60 .25
❑ 336 Antonio Freeman UH .40 .15
❑ 337 Luther Elliss UH .25 .08
❑ 338 James Allen UH .25 .08
❑ 339 Arizona Cardinals TC .40 .15
❑ 340 Atlanta Falcons TC .40 .15
❑ 341 Baltimore Ravens TC .25 .08
❑ 342 Buffalo Bills TC .25 .08
❑ 343 Carolina Panthers TC .25 .08
❑ 344 Chicago Bears TC .60 .25
❑ 345 Cincinnati Bengals TC .40 .15
❑ 346 Cleveland Browns TC .25 .08
❑ 347 Cowboys TC/Emmitt .60 .25
❑ 348 Denver Broncos TC .40 .15
❑ 349 Detroit Lions TC .25 .08
❑ 350 Packers TC/Favre 1.00 .40
❑ 351 Colts TC/James .60 .25
❑ 352 Jacksonville Jaguars TC .60 .25
❑ 353 Kansas City Chiefs TC .25 .08
❑ 354 Miami Dolphins TC .40 .15
❑ 355 Minnesota Vikings TC .60 .25
❑ 356 New England Patriots TC .60 .25
❑ 357 New Orleans Saints TC .40 .15
❑ 358 New York Giants TC .40 .15
❑ 359 New York Jets TC .40 .15
❑ 360 Oakland Raiders TC .40 .15
❑ 361 Philadelphia Eagles TC .60 .25
❑ 362 Pittsburgh Steelers TC .40 .15
❑ 363 San Diego Chargers TC .25 .08
❑ 364 San Francisco 49ers TC .25 .08
❑ 365 Seattle Seahawks TC .25 .08
❑ 366 Rams TC/Warner .60 .25
❑ 367 Tampa Bay Buccaneers TC .40 .15
❑ 368 Tennessee Titans TC .40 .15
❑ 369 Washington Redskins TC .40 .15
❑ 370 Buffalo Bills TL .25 .08
❑ 371 Indianapolis Colts TL .60 .25
❑ 372 Miami Dolphins TL .25 .08
❑ 373 New England Patriots TL .40 .15
❑ 374 New York Jets TL .40 .15
❑ 375 Baltimore Ravens TL .40 .15
❑ 376 Cincinnati Bengals TL .25 .08
❑ 377 Cleveland Browns TL .25 .08
❑ 378 Jacksonville Jaguars TL .40 .15
❑ 379 Pittsburgh Steelers TL .40 .15
❑ 380 Tennessee Titans TL .40 .15
❑ 381 Denver Broncos TL .40 .15
❑ 382 Kansas City Chiefs TL .40 .15
❑ 383 Oakland Raiders TL .40 .15
❑ 384 San Diego Chargers TL .40 .15
❑ 385 Seattle Seahawks TL .25 .08
❑ 386 Arizona Cardinals TL .25 .08
❑ 387 Dallas Cowboys TL .60 .25
❑ 388 New York Giants TL .40 .15
❑ 389 Philadelphia Eagles TL .40 .15
❑ 390 Washington Redskins TL .40 .15
❑ 391 Chicago Bears TL .25 .08
❑ 392 Detroit Lions TL .25 .08
❑ 393 Green Bay Packers TL .60 .25
❑ 394 Minnesota Vikings TL .60 .25
❑ 395 Tampa Bay Buccaneers TL .40 .15
❑ 396 Atlanta Falcons TL .25 .08
❑ 397 Carolina Panthers TL .25 .08

❑ 398 New Orleans Saints TL .40 .15
❑ 399 San Francisco 49ersTL .40 .15
❑ 400 St. Louis Rams TL .60 .25
❑ 401 Michael Vick RC 4.00 1.50
❑ 402 Drew Brees RC 4.00 1.50
❑ 403 Michael Bennett RC 1.25 .50
❑ 404 David Terrell RC 1.25 .50
❑ 405 Deuce McAllister RC 2.50 1.00
❑ 406 Santana Moss RC 2.00 .75
❑ 407 Koren Robinson RC 1.25 .50
❑ 408 Chris Weinke RC 1.25 .50
❑ 409 Reggie Wayne RC 2.50 1.00
❑ 410 Rod Gardner RC 1.25 .50
❑ 411 James Jackson RC 1.25 .50
❑ 412 Travis Henry RC 2.50 1.00
[illegible]
❑ 414 LaDainian Tomlinson RC 15.00 7.50
❑ 415 Chad Johnson RC 3.00 1.25
❑ 416 Sage Rosenfels RC 1.25 .50
❑ 417 Quincy Morgan RC 1.25 .50
❑ 418 Ken-Yon Rambo RC .75 .30
❑ 419 LaMont Jordan RC 2.50 1.00
❑ 420 Anthony Thomas RC 1.25 .50
❑ 421 Dave Dickenson RC .75 .30
❑ 422 Travis Minor RC .75 .30
❑ 423 Kevan Barlow RC 1.25 .50
❑ 424 Chris Chambers RC 2.00 .75
❑ 425 Richard Seymour RC 1.25 .50
❑ 426 Gerard Warren RC 1.25 .50
❑ 427 Jamar Fletcher RC .75 .30
❑ 428 Freddie Mitchell RC 1.25 .50
❑ 429 Jamal Reynolds RC 1.25 .50
❑ 430 Marques Tuiasosopo RC 1.25 .50
❑ 431 Snoop Minnis RC .75 .30
❑ 432 Mike McMahon RC 1.25 .50
❑ 433 Robert Ferguson RC 1.25 .50
❑ 434 Ronney Daniels RC .50 .20
❑ 435 Rudi Johnson RC 2.50 1.00
❑ 436 Vinny Sutherland RC .75 .30
❑ 437 Josh Booty RC 1.25 .50
❑ 438 Reggie White RC .75 .30
❑ 439 Todd Heap RC 1.25 .50
❑ 440 Justin Smith RC 1.25 .50
❑ 441 Andre Carter RC 1.25 .50
❑ 442 Bobby Newcombe RC .75 .30
❑ 443 Alex Bannister RC .75 .30
❑ 444 Correll Buckhalter RC 1.50 .60
❑ 445 Quincy Carter RC 1.25 .50
❑ 446 Jesse Palmer RC 1.25 .50
❑ 447 Heath Evans RC .75 .30
❑ 448 Dan Morgan RC 1.25 .50
❑ 449 Justin McCareins RC 1.25 .50
❑ 450 Alge Crumpler RC 1.50 .60

2001 Fleer Tradition Glossy

❑ COMP.SET w/o SP's (400) 40.00 20.00
❑ 1 Thomas Jones .50 .20
❑ 2 Bruce Smith .30 .10
❑ 3 Marvin Harrison .75 .30
❑ 4 Darrell Jackson .75 .30
❑ 5 Trent Green .75 .30
❑ 6 Wesley Walls .30 .10
❑ 7 Jimmy Smith .50 .20
❑ 8 Isaac Bruce .75 .30
❑ 9 Jamal Anderson .75 .30
❑ 10 Marty Booker .30 .10
❑ 11 Elvis Grbac .50 .20
❑ 12 Joe Jurevicius .30 .10
❑ 13 Reidel Anthony .30 .10
❑ 14 Damay Scott .30 .10
❑ 15 Oronde Gadsden .50 .20
❑ 16 Shawn Bryson .30 .10
❑ 17 Jonathan Ogden .30 .10
❑ 18 Aaron Shea .30 .10
❑ 19 Randy Moss 1.50 .60
❑ 20 Eddie George .75 .30
❑ 21 Stephen Davis .75 .30
❑ 22 Emmitt Smith 1.50 .60
❑ 23 Willie McGinest .30 .10
❑ 24 Trent Dilfer .50 .20
❑ 25 Peter Boulware .30 .10
❑ 26 Rod Smith .50 .20
❑ 27 Ricky Williams .75 .30
❑ 28 Albert Connell .30 .10
❑ 29 Robert Porcher .30 .10
[illegible]
❑ 31 Shane Matthews .30 .10
❑ 32 Eric Moulds .50 .20
❑ 33 Kurt Schulz .30 .10
❑ 34 Richie Anderson .30 .10
❑ 35 Ron Dugans .30 .10
❑ 36 Steve Beuerlein .50 .20
❑ 37 Darren Sharper .30 .10
❑ 38 Andre Rison .50 .20
❑ 39 Courtney Brown .50 .20
❑ 40 Eddie Kennison .50 .20
❑ 41 Ken Dilger .30 .10
❑ 42 Charles Johnson .30 .10
❑ 43 Dexter Coakley .30 .10
❑ 44 Akili Smith .30 .10
❑ 45 R.Jay Soward .30 .10
❑ 46 Danny Farmer .30 .10
❑ 47 Dez White .30 .10
❑ 48 Olandis Gary .50 .20
❑ 49 Wali Rainer .30 .10
❑ 50 Derrick Alexander .50 .20
❑ 51 Donnie Abraham .30 .10
❑ 52 David Sloan .30 .10
❑ 53 Larry Allen .30 .10
❑ 54 Sam Madison .30 .10
❑ 55 Troy Edwards .30 .10
❑ 56 Ryan Longwell .30 .10
❑ 57 Brian Griese .75 .30
❑ 58 John Randle .50 .20
❑ 59 Reggie Jones .30 .10
❑ 60 Mike Peterson .30 .10
❑ 61 Bill Romanowski .30 .10
❑ 62 Kevin Faulk .50 .20
❑ 63 Tai Streets .30 .10
❑ 64 Tony Brackens .30 .10
❑ 65 James Stewart .50 .20
❑ 66 Joe Horn .50 .20
❑ 67 Kurt Warner 1.50 .60
❑ 68 Eric Hicks RC .30 .10
❑ 60 Bryan Westbrook .30 .10
❑ 70 Tiki Barber .75 .30
❑ 71 Frank Sanders .30 .10
❑ 72 Olindo Mare .30 .10
❑ 73 Bill Schroeder .50 .20
❑ 74 Anthony Becht .30 .10
❑ 75 Rob Johnson .50 .20
❑ 76 Troy Brown .50 .20
❑ 77 Chad Bratzke .30 .10
❑ 78 Rickey Dudley .30 .10
❑ 79 Doug Johnson .30 .10
❑ 80 Joe Johnson .30 .10
❑ 81 Keenan McCardell .30 .10
❑ 82 Tim Brown .75 .30
❑ 83 Blaine Bishop .30 .10
❑ 84 Ron Dixon .30 .10
❑ 85 Michael Cloud .30 .10
❑ 86 Todd Pinkston .30 .10
❑ 87 Shannon Sharpe .50 .20
❑ 88 Marvin Jones .30 .10
❑ 89 Zach Thomas .75 .30
❑ 90 Kordell Stewart .50 .20
❑ 91 Champ Bailey .50 .20
❑ 92 Jacquez Green .30 .10
❑ 93 Daunte Culpepper .75 .30
❑ 94 Freddie Jones .30 .10
❑ 95 Donald Hayes .30 .10
❑ 96 Rich Gannon .75 .30
❑ 97 Ty Law .50 .20
❑ 98 Grant Wistrom .30 .10
❑ 99 James Allen .50 .20
❑ 100 Corey Simon .50 .20
❑ 101 Jeff Blake .50 .20
❑ 102 Bryant Young .30 .10
❑ 103 Craig Yeast .30 .10
❑ 104 Bobby Shaw .30 .10
❑ 105 Kerry Collins .50 .20
❑ 106 Brock Huard .30 .10
❑ 107 JaJuan Dawson .30 .10
❑ 108 Jeff Graham .30 .10
❑ 109 Chad Pennington 1.25 .50
❑ 110 Jake Plummer .50 .20
❑ 111 James McKnight .50 .20
❑ 112 Terrell Owens .75 .30
❑ 113 Mo Lewis .30 .10
❑ 114 Jeremy McDaniel .30 .10
❑ 115 Ed McCaffrey .75 .30
❑ 116 Ricky Watters .30 .10
❑ 117 Jerry Porter .50 .20
❑ 118 Shawn Jefferson .30 .10
[illegible]
❑ 120 Justin Watson .30 .10
❑ 121 Donovan McNabb 1.00 .40
❑ 122 Shaun King .30 .10
❑ 123 Brett Favre 2.50 1.00
❑ 124 Ronald McKinnon .30 .10
❑ 125 Richard Huntley .30 .10
❑ 126 Ray Lewis .75 .30
❑ 127 Jerome Pathon .50 .20
❑ 128 Sam Cowart .30 .10
❑ 129 Ryan Leaf .50 .20
❑ 130 Greg Clark .30 .10
❑ 131 Tony Boselli .30 .10
❑ 132 Frank Wycheck .30 .10
❑ 133 Charlie Garner .50 .20
❑ 134 Tony Siragusa .30 .10
❑ 135 Sylvester Morris .30 .10
❑ 136 Qadry Ismail .50 .20
❑ 137 Jon Kitna .50 .20
❑ 138 James Thrash .50 .20
❑ 139 Lamar Smith .50 .20
❑ 140 Brad Johnson .75 .30
❑ 141 London Fletcher .30 .10
❑ 142 Tim Biakabutuka .50 .20
❑ 143 Ed McDaniel .30 .10
❑ 144 Tony Parrish .30 .10
❑ 145 David Boston .75 .30
❑ 146 Brian Urlacher 1.25 .50
❑ 147 Drew Bledsoe 1.00 .40
❑ 148 David Patten .30 .10
❑ 149 Marcellus Wiley .30 .10
❑ 150 Peter Warrick .75 .30
❑ 151 La'Roi Glover .30 .10
❑ 152 Troy Aikman 1.25 .50
❑ 153 Chris Chandler .50 .20
❑ 154 Travis Prentice .30 .10
❑ 155 Ike Hilliard .50 .20
❑ 156 John Mobley .30 .10
❑ 157 Warren Sapp .50 .20
❑ 158 Joey Galloway .50 .20
❑ 159 Laveranues Coles .75 .30
❑ 160 Germane Crowell .30 .10
❑ 161 Jamal Lewis 1.25 .50
❑ 162 Mike Anderson .75 .30
❑ 163 Charles Woodson .50 .20
❑ 164 Antonio Freeman .75 .30
❑ 165 Derrick Mason .50 .20
❑ 166 Chris Claiborne .30 .10
❑ 167 Brian Mitchell .30 .10
❑ 168 Mike Vanderjagt .30 .10
❑ 169 Rod Woodson .50 .20
❑ 170 Doug Chapman .30 .10
❑ 171 John Lynch .50 .20
❑ 172 Kevin Hardy .30 .10
❑ 173 Sam Shade .30 .10
❑ 174 Edgerrin James 1.00 .40
❑ 175 Brian Dawkins .50 .20
❑ 176 Donnie Edwards .30 .10
❑ 177 Patrick Jeffers .50 .20
❑ 178 Mark Brunell .75 .30
❑ 179 Junior Seau .75 .30
❑ 180 Trace Armstrong .30 .10
❑ 181 Marcus Robinson .75 .30
❑ 182 Tony Gonzalez .50 .20
❑ 183 J.J. Stokes .50 .20
❑ 184 Jake Reed .50 .20
❑ 185 Corey Dillon .75 .30
❑ 186 Jay Fiedler .75 .30
❑ 187 Christian Fauria .30 .10
❑ 188 Sammy Knight .30 .10
❑ 189 Kevin Johnson .50 .20
❑ 190 Matthew Hatchette .30 .10
❑ 191 Az-Zahir Hakim .50 .20
❑ 192 Keith Hamilton .30 .10

❑ 193 Darren Woodson .30 .10
❑ 194 Terry Glenn .50 .20
❑ 195 Simeon Rice .50 .20
❑ 196 Keyshawn Johnson .75 .30
❑ 197 Terrell Davis .75 .30
❑ 198 William Roaf .30 .10
❑ 199 Doug Flutie .75 .30
❑ 200 Kevin Carter .30 .10
❑ 201 Stephen Boyd .30 .10
❑ 202 Michael Strahan .50 .20
❑ 203 Ray Buchanan .30 .10
❑ 204 Tyrone Wheatley .50 .20
❑ 205 Jason Hanson .30 .10
❑ 206 Wayne Chrebet .50 .20
❑ 207 Samari Rolle .30 .10
❑ 208 Duce Staley .75 .30
❑ 209 Dorsey Levens .50 .20
❑ 210 Sebastian Janikowski .30 .10
❑ 211 Duane Starks .30 .10
❑ 212 Jason Gildon .30 .10
❑ 213 Terrence Wilkins .30 .10
❑ 214 Eric Allen .30 .10
❑ 215 Deion Sanders .75 .30
❑ 216 Curtis Conway .50 .20
❑ 217 Fred Taylor .75 .30
❑ 218 Troy Vincent .30 .10
❑ 219 Mike Minter .50 .20
❑ 220 Jeff Garcia .75 .30
❑ 221 Tony Richardson .30 .10
❑ 222 Jerome Bettis .75 .30
❑ 223 Chad Morton .30 .10
❑ 224 Tony Horne .30 .10
❑ 225 Dave Moore .30 .10
❑ 226 Victor Green .30 .10
❑ 227 Chris Sanders .30 .10
❑ 228 Marshall Faulk 1.00 .40
❑ 229 Cris Carter .75 .30
❑ 230 Rodney Harrison .30 .10
❑ 231 Tim Couch .50 .20
❑ 232 Antowain Smith .50 .20
❑ 233 Lawyer Milloy .50 .20
❑ 234 Lance Schulters .30 .10
❑ 235 Michael Wiley .30 .10
❑ 236 Steve McNair .75 .30
❑ 237 Aaron Brooks .75 .30
❑ 238 Anthony Simmons .30 .10
❑ 239 Dwayne Carswell .30 .10
❑ 240 Priest Holmes 1.00 .40
❑ 241 Amani Toomer .50 .20
❑ 242 Aeneas Williams .30 .10
❑ 243 MarTay Jenkins .30 .10
❑ 244 Jeff George .50 .20
❑ 245 Vinny Testaverde .50 .20
❑ 246 Peerless Price .50 .20
❑ 247 Bubba Franks .50 .20
❑ 248 Randall Cunningham .75 .30
❑ 249 Aaron Glenn .30 .10
❑ 250 Terance Mathis .50 .20
❑ 251 Peyton Manning 2.00 .75
❑ 252 Terrell Buckley .30 .10
❑ 253 Greg Biekert .30 .10
❑ 254 Martin Gramatica .30 .10
❑ 255 Kyle Brady .30 .10
❑ 256 Johnnie Morton .50 .20
❑ 257 Jeremiah Trotter .50 .20
❑ 258 Travis Taylor .50 .20
❑ 259 Frank Moreau .30 .10
❑ 260 LeRoy Butler .30 .10
❑ 261 Plaxico Burress .75 .30
❑ 262 Randall Godfrey .30 .10
❑ 263 Jason Taylor .30 .10
❑ 264 Jeff Burris .30 .10
❑ 265 Jim Harbaugh .50 .20
❑ 266 Marco Coleman .30 .10
❑ 267 Robert Smith .50 .20
❑ 268 Mike Hollis .30 .10
❑ 269 Jerry Rice 1.50 .60
❑ 270 Muhsin Muhammad .50 .20
❑ 271 J.R. Redmond .30 .10
❑ 272 Brian Walker .30 .10
❑ 273 Orlando Pace .30 .10
❑ 274 Cade McNown .30 .10
❑ 275 Darren Howard .30 .10
❑ 276 Ron Dayne .75 .30
❑ 277 Shaun Alexander 1.00 .40
❑ 278 Brandon Bennett .30 .10
❑ 279 Jason Sehorn .30 .10
❑ 280 Matt Hasselbeck .50 .20
❑ 281 Michael Pittman .30 .10
❑ 282 Dennis Northcutt .50 .20
❑ 283 Dedric Ward .30 .10
❑ 284 Curtis Martin .75 .30
❑ 285 Sammy Morris .30 .10
❑ 286 Rocket Ismail .50 .20
❑ 287 Jon Ritchie .30 .10
❑ 288 Shaun Ellis .30 .10
❑ 289 Tim Dwight .75 .30
❑ 290 Trevor Pryce .30 .10
❑ 291 Warrick Dunn .75 .30
❑ 292 Napoleon Kaufman .50 .20
❑ 293 Mike Alstott .75 .30
❑ 294 Herman Moore .50 .20
❑ 295 Chad Lewis .30 .10
❑ 296 Hugh Douglas .30 .10
❑ 297 Chris Redman .30 .10
❑ 298 Ahman Green .75 .30
❑ 299 Hines Ward .75 .30
❑ 300 Mark Bruener .30 .10
❑ 301 Jevon Kearse .50 .20
❑ 302 Jermaine Fazande .30 .10
❑ 303 Terrell Fletcher .30 .10
❑ 304 Torry Holt .75 .30
❑ 305 Chris McAlister .30 .10
❑ 306 Jason Elam .30 .10
❑ 307 Fred Beasley .30 .10
❑ 308 Frank Wycheck UH .30 .10
❑ 309 Michael McCrary UH .30 .10
❑ 310 Mark Brunell UH .75 .30
❑ 311 Tim Couch UH .50 .20
❑ 312 Takeo Spikes UH .30 .10
❑ 313 Jerome Bettis UH .50 .20
❑ 314 Zach Thomas UH .75 .30
❑ 315 Drew Bledsoe UH .75 .30
❑ 316 Wayne Chrebet UH .30 .10
❑ 317 Jay Riemersma UH .30 .10
❑ 318 Marvin Harrison UH .50 .20
❑ 319 Ed McCaffrey UH .50 .20
❑ 320 Tony Gonzalez UH .30 .10
❑ 321 Tim Brown UH .50 .20
❑ 322 Junior Seau UH .50 .20
❑ 323 Shawn Springs UH .30 .10
❑ 324 Troy Aikman UH .75 .30
❑ 325 Pat Tillman UH RC 20.00 8.00
❑ 326 David Akers UH RC .50 .20
❑ 327 Michael Strahan UH .50 .20
❑ 328 Darrell Green UH .30 .10
❑ 329 Kurt Warner UH 1.00 .40
❑ 330 Jeff Garcia UH .50 .20
❑ 331 Aaron Brooks UH .50 .20
❑ 332 Jamal Anderson UH .50 .20
❑ 333 Brad Hoover UH .30 .10
❑ 334 Cris Carter UH .50 .20
❑ 335 Derrick Brooks UH .75 .30
❑ 336 Antonio Freeman UH .50 .20
❑ 337 Luther Elliss UH .30 .10
❑ 338 James Allen UH .30 .10
❑ 339 Arizona Cardinals TC .50 .20
❑ 340 Atlanta Falcons TC .50 .20
❑ 341 Baltimore Ravens TC .30 .10
❑ 342 Buffalo Bills TC .30 .10
❑ 343 Carolina Panthers TC .30 .10
❑ 344 Chicago Bears TC .75 .30
❑ 345 Cincinnati Bengals TC .50 .20
❑ 346 Cleveland Browns TC .30 .10
❑ 347 Cowboys TC/Emmitt .75 .30
❑ 348 Denver Broncos TC .50 .20
❑ 349 Detroit Lions TC .30 .10
❑ 350 Packers TC/Favre 1.25 .50
❑ 351 Colts TC/James .75 .30
❑ 352 Jacksonville Jaguars TC .75 .30
❑ 353 Kansas City Chiefs TC .30 .10
❑ 354 Miami Dolphins TC .50 .20
❑ 355 Minnesota Vikings TC .75 .30
❑ 356 New England Patriots TC .75 .30
❑ 357 New Orleans Saints TC .50 .20
❑ 358 New York Giants TC .50 .20
❑ 359 New York Jets TC .50 .20
❑ 360 Oakland Raiders TC .50 .20
❑ 361 Philadelphia Eagles TC .75 .30
❑ 362 Pittsburgh Steelers TC .50 .20
❑ 363 San Diego Chargers TC .30 .10
❑ 364 San Francisco 49ers TC .30 .10
❑ 365 Seattle Seahawks TC .30 .10
❑ 366 Rams TC/Warner .75 .30
❑ 367 Tampa Bay Buccaneers TC .50 .20
❑ 368 Tennessee Titans TC .50 .20
❑ 369 Washington Redskins TC .50 .20
❑ 370 Buffalo Bills TL .50 .20
❑ 371 Indianapolis Colts TL .75 .30
❑ 372 Miami Dolphins TL .30 .10
❑ 373 New England Patriots TL .50 .20
❑ 374 New York Jets TL .50 .20
❑ 375 Baltimore Ravens TL .50 .20
❑ 376 Cincinnati Bengals TL .30 .10
❑ 377 Cleveland Browns TL .30 .10
❑ 378 Jacksonville Jaguars TL .50 .20
❑ 379 Pittsburgh Steelers TL .50 .20
❑ 300 Tennessee Titans TL .50 .20
❑ 381 Denver Broncos TL .50 .20
❑ 382 Kansas City Chiefs TL .50 .20
❑ 383 Oakland Raiders TL .50 .20
❑ 384 San Diego Chargers TL .50 .20
❑ 385 Seattle Seahawks TL .30 .10
❑ 386 Arizona Cardinals TL .30 .10
❑ 387 Dallas Cowboys TL .75 .30
❑ 388 New York Giants TL .50 .20
❑ 389 Philadelphia Eagles TL .50 .20
❑ 390 Washington Redskins TL .50 .20
❑ 391 Chicago Bears TL .30 .10
❑ 392 Detroit Lions TL .30 .10
❑ 393 Green Bay Packers TL .75 .30
❑ 394 Minnesota Vikings TL .75 .30
❑ 395 Tampa Bay Buccaneers TL .50 .20
❑ 396 Atlanta Falcons TL .30 .10
❑ 397 Carolina Panthers TL .30 .10
❑ 398 New Orleans Saints TL .50 .20
❑ 399 San Francisco 49ersTL .50 .20
❑ 400 St. Louis Rams TL .75 .30
❑ 401 Michael Vick RC 15.00 6.00
❑ 402 Drew Brees RC 15.00 6.00
❑ 403 Michael Bennett RC 4.00 1.50
❑ 404 David Terrell RC 4.00 1.50
❑ 405 Deuce McAllister RC 10.00 4.00
❑ 406 Santana Moss RC 8.00 3.00
❑ 407 Koren Robinson RC 4.00 1.50
❑ 408 Chris Weinke RC 4.00 1.50
❑ 409 Reggie Wayne RC 10.00 4.00
❑ 410 Rod Gardner RC 4.00 1.50
❑ 411 James Jackson RC 4.00 1.50
❑ 412 Travis Henry RC 10.00 4.00
❑ 413 Josh Heupel RC 4.00 1.50
❑ 415 Chad Johnson RC 12.00 5.00
❑ 416 Sage Rosenfels RC 4.00 1.50
❑ 417 Quincy Morgan RC 4.00 1.50
❑ 418 Ken-Yon Rambo RC 3.00 1.25
❑ 419 LaMont Jordan RC 10.00 4.00
❑ 420 Anthony Thomas RC 4.00 1.50
❑ 421 Dave Dickenson RC 3.00 1.25
❑ 422 Travis Minor RC 3.00 1.25
❑ 423 Kevan Barlow RC 4.00 1.50
❑ 424 Chris Chambers RC 8.00 3.00
❑ 425 Richard Seymour RC 4.00 1.50
❑ 426 Gerard Warren RC 4.00 1.50
❑ 427 Jamar Fletcher RC 3.00 1.25
❑ 428 Freddie Mitchell RC 4.00 1.50
❑ 429 Jamal Reynolds RC 4.00 1.50
❑ 430 Marques Tuiasosopo RC 4.00 1.50
❑ 431 Snoop Minnis RC 3.00 1.25
❑ 432 Mike McMahon RC 4.00 1.50
❑ 433 Robert Ferguson RC 4.00 1.50
❑ 434 Ronney Daniels RC 3.00 1.25
❑ 435 Rudi Johnson RC 10.00 4.00
❑ 436 Vinny Sutherland RC 3.00 1.25
❑ 437 Josh Booty RC 4.00 1.50
❑ 438 Reggie White RC 3.00 1.25
❑ 439 Todd Heap RC 4.00 1.50
❑ 440 Justin Smith RC 4.00 1.50
❑ 441 Andre Carter RC 4.00 1.50
❑ 442 Bobby Newcombe RC 3.00 1.25
❑ 443 Alex Bannister RC 3.00 1.25
❑ 444 Correll Buckhalter RC 6.00 2.50
❑ 445 Quincy Carter RC 4.00 1.50
❑ 446 Jesse Palmer RC 4.00 1.50
❑ 447 Heath Evans RC 3.00 1.25
❑ 448 Dan Morgan RC 4.00 1.50
❑ 449 Justin McCareins RC 4.00 1.50
❑ 450 Alge Crumpler RC 5.00 2.00
❑ 414 LaDainian Tomlinson RC 50.00 20.00

2002 Fleer Tradition

❑ COMPLETE SET (300) 80.00 30.00
❑ 1 Jeff Garcia .60 .25
❑ 2 Brian Simmons .25 .08
❑ 3 Kordell Stewart .40 .15
❑ 4 Chris Weinke .40 .15
❑ 5 Donovan McNabb .75 .30
❑ 6 Antoine Winfield .25 .08

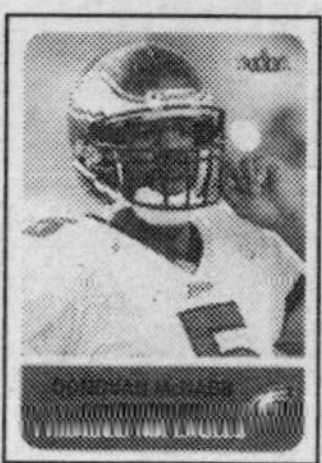

❑	7	Ray Lewis	.60	.25
❑	8	Drew Brees	.60	.25
❑	9	Frank Sanders	.25	.08
❑	10	Rich Gannon	.60	.25
❑	11	Jamal Anderson	.40	.15
❑	12	Curtis Martin	.60	.25
❑	13	Darrell Jackson	.40	.15
❑	14	Micheal Barrow	.25	.08
❑	15	Jeff Wilkins	.25	.08
❑	16	Ricky Williams	.60	.25
❑	17	Brad Johnson	.40	.15
❑	18	Tedy Bruschi	.60	.25
❑	19	Frank Wycheck	.25	.08
❑	20	Byron Chamberlain	.25	.08
❑	21	Terry Glenn	.25	.08
❑	22	James McKnight	.25	.08
❑	23	Thomas Jones	.40	.15
❑	24	Jamie Sharper	.25	.08
❑	25	Trent Green	.40	.15
❑	26	Mike Rucker RC	1.00	.40
❑	27	Mark Brunell	.60	.25
❑	28	Takeo Spikes	.25	.08
❑	29	Dominic Rhodes	.60	.25
❑	30	Jim Miller	.25	.08
❑	31	Corey Bradford	.25	.08
❑	32	Jamir Miller	.25	.08
❑	33	Johnnie Morton	.40	.15
❑	34	Rocket Ismail	.40	.15
❑	35	Mike Anderson	.60	.25
❑	36	James Allen	.40	.15
❑	37	Quincy Carter	.40	.15
❑	38	Germane Crowell	.25	.08
❑	39	Quincy Morgan	.25	.08
❑	40	Kabeer Gbaja-Biamila	.40	.15
❑	41	Reggie Wayne	.60	.25
❑	42	Brian Urlacher	1.00	.40
❑	43	Stacey Mack	.25	.08
❑	44	Justin Smith	.25	.08
❑	45	Snoop Minnis	.25	.08
❑	46	Donald Hayes	.25	.08
❑	47	Jay Fiedler	.40	.15
❑	48	Nate Clements	.25	.08
❑	49	Drew Bledsoe	.75	.30
❑	50	Peter Boulware	.25	.08
❑	51	Lawyer Milloy	.40	.15
❑	52	Michael Pittman	.25	.08
❑	53	Aaron Brooks	.60	.25
❑	54	Maurice Smith	.40	.15
❑	55	Ike Hilliard	.40	.15
❑	56	Derrick Mason	.40	.15
❑	57	LaMont Jordan	.60	.25
❑	58	Charlie Garner	.40	.15
❑	59	Mike Alstott	.60	.25
❑	60	Freddie Mitchell	.40	.15
❑	61	Isaac Bruce	.60	.25
❑	62	Hines Ward	.60	.25
❑	63	John Randle	.25	.08
❑	64	Doug Flutie	.60	.25
❑	65	Terrell Owens	.60	.25
❑	66	Garrison Hearst	.40	.15
❑	67	Rodney Harrison	.25	.08
❑	68	Koren Robinson	.40	.15
❑	69	Amos Zereoue	.60	.25
❑	70	Aeneas Williams	.25	.08
❑	71	Hugh Douglas	.25	.08
❑	72	Jacquez Green	.25	.08
❑	73	Sebastian Janikowski	.25	.08
❑	74	Kevin Dyson	.40	.15
❑	75	Terance Mathis	.25	.08
❑	76	Vinny Testaverde	.40	.15
❑	77	Kwamie Lassiter	.25	.08
❑	78	Ron Dayne	.40	.15
❑	79	Jonathan Ogden	.25	.08
❑	80	Charlie Clemons RC	.25	.08
❑	81	Peter Warrick	.40	.15
❑	82	Adam Vinatieri	.60	.25
❑	83	Ted Washington	.25	.08
❑	84	Randy Moss	1.25	.50
❑	85	Rosevelt Colvin RC	1.00	.40
❑	86	Oronde Gadsden	.40	.15
❑	87	Anthony Henry	.25	.08
❑	88	Priest Holmes	.75	.30
❑	89	Joey Galloway	.40	.15
❑	90	Jimmy Smith	.40	.15
❑	91	Bill Romanowski	.25	.08
❑	92	Chris Claiborne	.40	.15
❑	93	Marvin Harrison	.60	.25
❑	94	Vonnie Holliday	.25	.08
❑	95	Darren Sharper	.25	.08
❑	96	Chad Bratzke	.25	.08
❑	97	James Stewart	.40	.15
❑	98	Fred Taylor	.60	.25
❑	99	Jason Elam	.25	.08
❑	100	Keyshawn Johnson	.60	.25
❑	101	Dexter Coakley	.25	.08
❑	102	Zach Thomas	.60	.25
❑	103	Jamel White	.25	.08
❑	104	Antowain Smith	.40	.15
❑	105	Marty Booker	.25	.08
❑	106	Deuce McAllister	.75	.30
❑	107	Adam Archuleta	.25	.08
❑	108	Rod Smith	.40	.15
❑	109	Tony Boselli	.25	.08
❑	110	Joe Johnson	.25	.08
❑	111	Simeon Rice	.40	.15
❑	112	Cory Schlesinger	.25	.08
❑	113	La'Roi Glover	.25	.08
❑	114	Tiki Barber	.60	.25
❑	115	Michael Westbrook	.25	.08
❑	116	Antonio Freeman	.60	.25
❑	117	Kerry Collins	.40	.15
❑	118	Laveranues Coles	.40	.15
❑	119	Jay Feely	.25	.08
❑	120	Champ Bailey	.40	.15
❑	121	Peyton Manning	1.25	.50
❑	122	Chad Pennington	.75	.30
❑	123	Anthony Dorsett	.25	.08
❑	124	Jamal Lewis	.60	.25
❑	125	Marcus Pollard	.25	.08
❑	126	Charles Woodson	.40	.15
❑	127	Duce Staley	.60	.25
❑	128	Travis Henry	.60	.25
❑	129	Tony Brackens	.25	.08
❑	130	Jeremiah Trotter	.25	.08
❑	131	Jerome Bettis	.60	.25
❑	132	Chad Johnson	.60	.25
❑	133	Lamar Smith	.40	.15
❑	134	Joey Porter	.60	.25
❑	135	Curtis Conway	.25	.08
❑	136	David Terrell	.60	.25
❑	137	Daunte Culpepper	.60	.25
❑	138	Chris Fuamatu-Ma'afala	.25	.08
❑	139	J.J. Stokes	.25	.08
❑	140	Tim Couch	.40	.15
❑	141	Ty Law	.40	.15
❑	142	Vinny Sutherland	.25	.08
❑	143	Trung Canidate	.40	.15
❑	144	Larry Allen	.25	.08
❑	145	Darren Howard	.25	.08
❑	146	Ricky Watters	.40	.15
❑	147	Grant Wistrom	.25	.08
❑	148	Brian Griese	.60	.25
❑	149	Jason Sehorn	.25	.08
❑	150	Marshall Faulk	.60	.25
❑	151	Martin Gramatica	.25	.08
❑	152	Robert Porcher	.25	.08
❑	153	Richie Anderson	.25	.08
❑	154	Derrick Brooks	.60	.25
❑	155	Jevon Kearse	.40	.15
❑	156	Bill Schroeder	.40	.15
❑	157	Marvin Jones	.25	.08
❑	158	Eddie George	.60	.25
❑	159	Keith Brooking	.25	.08
❑	160	Ryan Longwell	.25	.08
❑	161	Brian Dawkins	.40	.15
❑	162	Chris Redman	.25	.08
❑	163	Az-Zahir Hakim	.25	.08
❑	164	James Thrash	.40	.15
❑	165	Rob Johnson	.40	.15
❑	166	Hardy Nickerson	.25	.08
❑	167	Chad Scott	.25	.08
❑	168	Jon Kitna	.40	.15
❑	169	Donnie Edwards	.25	.08
❑	170	Andre Carter	.25	.08
❑	171	Warrick Holdman	.25	.08
❑	172	Jason Taylor	.25	.08
❑	173	Levon Kirkland	.25	.08
❑	174	Mike Brown	.60	.25
❑	175	David Patten	.25	.08
❑	176	Kurt Warner	.60	.25
❑	177	Fred Smoot	.25	.08
❑	178	Dat Nguyen	.25	.08
❑	179	Joe Horn	.40	.15
❑	180	John Lynch	.40	.15
❑	181	Troy Hambrick	.25	.08
❑	182	[illegible]	.25	.08
❑	183	Wesley Walls	.25	.08
❑	184	Deltha O'Neal	.25	.08
❑	185	Joe Jurevicius	.25	.08
❑	186	Steve McNair	.60	.25
❑	187	Scotty Anderson	.25	.08
❑	188	John Abraham	.40	.15
❑	189	Stephen Davis	.40	.15
❑	190	Nate Wayne	.25	.08
❑	191	Corey Simon	.25	.08
❑	192	Joel Makovicka	.25	.08
❑	193	Rob Morris	.25	.08
❑	194	Correll Buckhalter	.40	.15
❑	195	Qadry Ismail	.40	.15
❑	196	Keenan McCardell	.25	.08
❑	197	Jason Gildon	.25	.08
❑	198	Peerless Price	.40	.15
❑	199	Tony Richardson	.25	.08
❑	200	Kevan Barlow	.40	.15
❑	201	Corey Dillon	.40	.15
❑	202	Sam Madison	.25	.08
❑	203	Chad Brown	.25	.08
❑	204	Dez White	.25	.08
❑	205	Troy Brown	.40	.15
❑	206	Orlando Pace	.25	.08
❑	207	Jermaine Lewis	.25	.08
❑	208	Willie Jackson	.25	.08
❑	209	Warrick Dunn	.60	.25
❑	210	James Jackson	.25	.08
❑	211	Sammy Knight	.25	.08
❑	212	Ronde Barber	.25	.08
❑	213	Ed McCaffrey	.60	.25
❑	214	Amani Toomer	.40	.15
❑	215	Rod Gardner	.40	.15
❑	216	Mike McMahon	.60	.25
❑	217	Wayne Chrebet	.40	.15
❑	218	Jake Plummer	.40	.15
❑	219	Bubba Franks	.40	.15
❑	220	Shane Lechler	.40	.15
❑	221	Travis Taylor	.40	.15
❑	222	Edgerrin James	.75	.30
❑	223	David Akers	.25	.08
❑	224	Eric Moulds	.40	.15
❑	225	Mike Vanderjagt	.25	.08
❑	226	Kendrell Bell	.60	.25
❑	227	Darnay Scott	.25	.08
❑	228	Tony Gonzalez	.40	.15
❑	229	Marcellus Wiley	.25	.08
❑	230	Marcus Robinson	.40	.15
❑	231	Muhsin Muhammad	.40	.15
❑	232	Trent Dilfer	.40	.15
❑	233	Kevin Johnson	.40	.15
❑	234	Travis Minor	.25	.08
❑	235	London Fletcher	.25	.08
❑	236	Reggie Swinton	.25	.08
❑	237	Michael Bennett	.40	.15
❑	238	Brett Favre DD	1.50	.60
❑	239	Terrell Davis DD	.60	.25
❑	240	Emmitt Smith DD	1.50	.60
❑	241	Shannon Sharpe DD	.40	.15
❑	242	Cris Carter DD	.60	.25
❑	243	Tim Brown DD	.60	.25
❑	244	Jerry Rice DD	1.25	.50
❑	245	Bruce Smith DD	.40	.15
❑	246	Warren Sapp DD	.40	.15
❑	247	Michael Strahan DD	.40	.15
❑	248	Junior Seau DD	.60	.25
❑	249	Darrell Green DD	.25	.08
❑	250	Rod Woodson DD	.40	.15
❑	251	David Boston BB	.60	.25
❑	252	Michael Vick BB	1.25	.50
❑	253	Anthony Thomas BB	.40	.15
❑	254	Ahman Green BB	.60	.25
❑	255	Chris Chambers BB	.60	.25
❑	256	Tom Brady BB	1.50	.60

❑ 257 Plaxico Burress BB .40 .15
❑ 258 LaDainian Tomlinson BB 1.00 .40
❑ 259 Shaun Alexander BB .75 .30
❑ 260 Torry Holt BB .60 .25
❑ 261 Julius Peppers RC 4.00 1.50
❑ 262 William Green RC 2.00 .75
❑ 263 Joey Harrington RC 2.50 1.00
❑ 264 Jabar Gaffney RC 2.00 .75
❑ 265 T.J. Duckett RC 2.00 .75
❑ 266 Antwaan Randle El RC 2.50 1.00
❑ 267 Javon Walker RC 3.00 1.25
❑ 268 David Carr RC 4.00 1.50
❑ 269 DeShaun Foster RC 2.00 .75
❑ 270 Donte Stallworth RC 3.00 1.25
❑ 271 Antonio Bryant RC 2.00 .75
❑ 272 Clinton Portis RC 6.00 2.50
❑ 273 Josh Reed RC 2.00 .75
❑ 274 Ashley Lelie RC 4.00 1.50
❑ 275 Patrick Ramsey RC 2.00 .75
❑ 276 J.Wells RC/A.Peterson RC 2.00 .75
❑ 277 Q.Jammer RC/R.Williams RC 4.001.50
❑ 278 J.Shockey RC/D.Graham RC 6.002.50
❑ 279 E.Crouch RC/Applewhite RC 2.00 .75
❑ 280 Buchanon RC/Sheppard RC 2.00 .75
❑ 281 K.Hill RC/D.Branch RC 3.00 1.25
❑ 282 R.Sims RC/W.Bryant RC 2.00 .75
❑ 283 J.Scobey RC/Westbrook RC 4.00 1.50
❑ 284 L.Betts RC/O.Easy RC 2.00 .75
❑ 285 A.Davis RC/D.Jones RC 1.50 .60
❑ 286 C.Russell RC/C.Taylor RC 3.00 1.25
❑ 287 McAddley RC/J.McCown RC 2.50 1.00
❑ 288 D.Garrard RC/R.Davey RC 4.00 1.50
❑ 289 M.Walker RC/R.Johnson RC 1.50 .60
❑ 290 L.Staley RC/L.Gordon RC 2.00 .75
❑ 291 R.Caldwell RC/L.Mays RC 2.00 .75
❑ 292 R.Thomas RC/N.Harris RC 2.00 .75
❑ 293 M.Morris RC/J.Stevens RC 2.00 .75
❑ 294 K.Kittner RC/R.Fasani RC 1.50 .60
❑ 295 R.Calmus RC/J.Schifino RC 2.00 .75
❑ 296 T.Carter RC/F.Milons RC 1.50 .60
❑ 297 Wistrom RC/Stephens RC 2.00 .75
❑ 298 M.Williams RC/D.Freeney RC 3.001.25
❑ 299 Hendersn RC/Hayneswrth RC 2.00 .75
❑ 300 N.Davenport RC/C.Nall RC 2.00 .75

2003 Fleer Tradition

❑ COMPLETE SET (300) 40.00 15.00
❑ 1 Aaron Glenn .25 .08
❑ 2 Jerry Rice 1.25 .50
❑ 3 Chad Hutchinson .25 .08
❑ 4 Kris Jenkins .25 .08
❑ 5 Ed Reed .40 .15
❑ 6 Ed McCaffrey .60 .25
❑ 7 Rod Gardner .40 .15
❑ 8 Aaron Brooks .60 .25
❑ 9 Chad Pennington .75 .30
❑ 10 Jevon Kearse .40 .15
❑ 11 Kurt Warner .60 .25
❑ 12 Eddie George .40 .15
❑ 13 Ron Dugans .25 .08
❑ 14 Adam Vinatieri .60 .25
❑ 15 Jimmy Smith .40 .15
❑ 16 Chad Johnson .60 .25
❑ 17 Kyle Brady .25 .08
❑ 18 Eddie Kennison .25 .08
❑ 19 Joe Jurevicius .25 .08
❑ 20 Ronde Barber .25 .08
❑ 21 Adam Archuleta .25 .08
❑ 22 Champ Bailey .40 .15
❑ 23 Joe Horn .40 .15
❑ 24 Ladell Betts .40 .15
❑ 25 Edgerrin James .60 .25
❑ 26 Rosevelt Colvin .25 .08
❑ 27 Ahman Green .60 .25
❑ 28 Joey Porter .60 .25
❑ 29 Charles Woodson .40 .15
❑ 30 Lance Schulters .25 .08
❑ 31 Edgerton Hartwell .25 .08
❑ 32 Joey Galloway .40 .15
❑ 33 Roy Williams .60 .25
❑ 34 Al Wilson .25 .08
❑ 35 Charlie Garner .40 .15
❑ 36 John Lynch .25 .08
❑ 37 La'Roi Glover .25 .08
❑ 38 Emmitt Smith 1.50 .60
❑ 39 Ryan Longwell .25 .08
❑ 40 Alge Crumpler .40 .15
❑ 41 John Abraham .25 .08
❑ 42 Chris Hovan .25 .08
❑ 43 Laveranues Coles .40 .15
❑ 44 Eric Hicks .25 .08
❑ 45 Johnnie Morton .40 .15
❑ 46 Sam Madison .25 .08
❑ 47 Amani Toomer .40 .15
❑ 48 Chris Redman .25 .08
❑ 49 Jon Kitna .40 .15
❑ 50 Leonard Little .25 .08
❑ 51 Eric Moulds .40 .15
❑ 52 Santana Moss .40 .15
❑ 53 Amos Zereoue .40 .15
❑ 54 Jonathan Wells .25 .08
❑ 55 Chris Chambers .60 .25
❑ 56 London Fletcher .25 .08
❑ 57 Frank Wycheck .25 .08
❑ 58 Josh McCown .40 .15
❑ 59 Shannon Sharpe .25 .08
❑ 60 Andre Carter .25 .08
❑ 61 Corey Dillon .40 .15
❑ 62 Josh Reed .40 .15
❑ 63 Marc Boerigter .40 .15
❑ 64 Fred Smoot .25 .08
❑ 65 Shaun Alexander .60 .25
❑ 66 Andre Davis .25 .08
❑ 67 Julian Peterson .25 .08
❑ 68 Corey Bradford .25 .08
❑ 69 Marc Bulger .60 .25
❑ 70 Fred Taylor .60 .25
❑ 71 Junior Seau .60 .25
❑ 72 Simeon Rice .40 .15
❑ 73 Anthony Thomas .40 .15
❑ 74 Correll Buckhalter .40 .15
❑ 75 Justin Smith .25 .08
❑ 76 Marcel Shipp .40 .15
❑ 77 Garrison Hearst .40 .15
❑ 78 Stacey Mack .25 .08
❑ 79 Antowain Smith .40 .15
❑ 80 Kabeer Gbaja-Biamila .40 .15
❑ 81 Curtis Martin .60 .25
❑ 82 Marcellus Wiley .25 .08
❑ 83 Gary Walker .25 .08
❑ 84 Kalimba Edwards .25 .08
❑ 85 Stephen Davis .40 .15
❑ 86 Antwaan Randle El .60 .25
❑ 87 Curtis Conway .25 .08
❑ 88 Keith Brooking .25 .08
❑ 89 Mark Word RC .25 .08
❑ 90 Greg Ellis .25 .08
❑ 91 Steve McNair .60 .25
❑ 92 Ashley Lelie .60 .25
❑ 93 Kelly Holcomb .40 .15
❑ 94 Darrell Jackson .40 .15
❑ 95 Mark Brunell .40 .15
❑ 96 Hugh Douglas .25 .08
❑ 97 Kendrell Bell .40 .15
❑ 98 Steve Smith .60 .25
❑ 99 Bill Schroeder .40 .15
❑ 100 Darren Howard .25 .08
❑ 101 Kevan Barlow .40 .15
❑ 102 Marshall Faulk .60 .25
❑ 103 Ike Hilliard .25 .08
❑ 104 T.J. Duckett .40 .15
❑ 105 Bobby Taylor .25 .08
❑ 106 Kevin Carter .25 .08
❑ 107 Darren Sharper .25 .08
❑ 108 Marty Booker .40 .15
❑ 109 Isaac Bruce .60 .25
❑ 110 Kevin Hardy .25 .08
❑ 111 Tai Streets .25 .08
❑ 112 Brad Johnson .40 .15
❑ 113 Daunte Culpepper .60 .25
❑ 114 Kevin Johnson .40 .15
❑ 115 Matt Hasselbeck .40 .15
❑ 116 Jabar Gaffney .40 .15
❑ 117 Takeo Spikes .25 .08
❑ 118 Brett Favre 1.50 .60
❑ 119 Keyshawn Johnson .60 .25
❑ 120 David Akers .25 .08
❑ 121 Maurice Morris .25 .08
❑ 122 Jake Delhomme .60 .25
❑ 123 Kordell Stewart .40 .15
❑ 124 Terrell Davis .60 .25
❑ 125 Brian Kelly .25 .08
❑ 126 David Terrell .40 .15
❑ 127 Koren Robinson .40 .15
❑ 128 Michael Strahan .40 .15
❑ 129 Jake Plummer .40 .15
❑ 130 Terrell Owens .60 .25
❑ 131 Brian Urlacher 1.00 .40
❑ 132 David Patten .25 .08
❑ 133 Michael Vick 1.50 .60
❑ 134 Jamal Lewis .60 .25
❑ 135 Terry Glenn .25 .08
❑ 136 Brian Simmons .25 .08
❑ 137 David Boston .40 .15
❑ 138 Michael Bennett .40 .15
❑ 139 James Stewart .40 .15
❑ 140 Tiki Barber .60 .25
❑ 141 Brian Griese .60 .25
❑ 142 Deion Branch .60 .25
❑ 143 Mike Peterson .25 .08
❑ 144 James Mungro .25 .08
❑ 145 Tim Couch .25 .08
❑ 146 Brian Dawkins .40 .15
❑ 147 Dennis Northcutt .40 .15
❑ 148 Mike Alstott .60 .25
❑ 149 James Thrash .25 .08
❑ 150 Tim Brown .60 .25
❑ 151 Brian Finneran .25 .08
❑ 152 Derrick Brooks .40 .15
❑ 153 Muhsin Muhammad .40 .15
❑ 154 Jason Elam .25 .08
❑ 155 Tim Dwight .40 .15
❑ 156 Bruce Smith .40 .15
❑ 157 Derrick Mason .40 .15
❑ 158 Napoleon Harris .25 .08
❑ 159 Jason Gildon .25 .08
❑ 160 Todd Heap .40 .15
❑ 161 Aaron Schobel .40 .15
❑ 162 Derrius Thompson .25 .08
❑ 163 Nate Clements .25 .08
❑ 164 Jason McAddley .25 .08
❑ 165 Todd Pinkston .40 .15
❑ 166 Bubba Franks .40 .15
❑ 167 Deuce McAllister .60 .25
❑ 168 Patrick Surtain .25 .08
❑ 169 Javon Walker .40 .15
❑ 170 Tom Brady 1.50 .60
❑ 171 Dexter Coakley .25 .08
❑ 172 Patrick Kerney .25 .08
❑ 173 Jay Fiedler .40 .15
❑ 174 Tommy Maddox .60 .25
❑ 175 Donald Driver .40 .15
❑ 176 Patrick Ramsey .60 .25
❑ 177 Olandis Gary .40 .15
❑ 178 Tony Gonzalez .40 .15
❑ 179 Donnie Edwards .25 .08
❑ 180 Peter Boulware .25 .08
❑ 181 Jeff Blake .25 .08
❑ 182 Torry Holt .60 .25
❑ 183 Donovan McNabb .75 .30
❑ 184 Peter Warrick .25 .08
❑ 185 Jeff Garcia .60 .25
❑ 186 Travis Henry .40 .15
❑ 187 Doug Jolley .25 .08
❑ 188 Peyton Manning 1.00 .40
❑ 189 Jerome Bettis .60 .25
❑ 190 Travis Taylor .40 .15
❑ 191 Drew Brees .60 .25
❑ 192 Phillip Buchanon .25 .08
❑ 193 Jerramy Stevens .25 .08
❑ 194 Trent Green .40 .15
❑ 195 Duce Staley .40 .15
❑ 196 Plaxico Burress .40 .15
❑ 197 Jerry Porter .40 .15
❑ 198 Trevor Pryce .25 .08
❑ 199 Dwight Freeney .40 .15
❑ 200 Quincy Morgan .40 .15
❑ 201 Troy Vincent .25 .08
❑ 202 Randy McMichael .40 .15
❑ 203 Troy Hambrick .25 .08

❑	204 Randy Moss	1.00	.40
❑	205 Troy Brown	.40	.15
❑	206 Ray Lewis	.60	.25
❑	207 Trung Canidate	.40	.15
❑	208 Raynoch Thompson	.25	.08
❑	209 Ty Law	.40	.15
❑	210 Reggie Wayne	.40	.15
❑	211 Warren Sapp	.40	.15
❑	212 Richard Seymour	.25	.08
❑	213 Warrick Dunn	.40	.15
❑	214 Robert Ferguson	.25	.08
❑	215 Wayne Chrebet	.40	.15
❑	216 Rod Coleman RC	.60	.25
❑	217 Will Allen	.25	.08
❑	218 Rod Woodson	.40	.15
❑	219 Zach Thomas	.60	.25
❑	220 Rod Smith	.40	.15
❑	221 Ricky Williams	.60	.25
❑	222 LaDainian Tomlinson	.60	.25
❑	223 Priest Holmes	.75	.30
❑	224 Rich Gannon	.40	.15
❑	225 Drew Bledsoe	.60	.25
❑	226 Kerry Collins	.40	.15
❑	227 Marvin Harrison	.60	.25
❑	228 Hines Ward	.60	.25
❑	229 Peerless Price	.40	.15
❑	230 Jason Taylor	.25	.08
❑	231 Jeremy Shockey	1.00	.40
❑	232 Clinton Portis	1.00	.40
❑	233 Antonio Bryant	.40	.15
❑	234 Donte Stallworth	.60	.25
❑	235 David Carr	1.00	.40
❑	236 Joey Harrington	1.00	.40
❑	237 William Green	.40	.15
❑	238 Julius Peppers	.60	.25
❑	239 Shipp/Thompson/Wilson	.25	.08
❑	240 Vick/Dunn/Finner/Brooking	.75	.30
❑	241 Lewis/Hartwell/Taylor/Reed	.40	.15
❑	242 Bled/Henry/Mould/Fletch	.40	.15
❑	243 Peppers/Smith/Muhammad	.60	.25
❑	244 Booker/Urlacher/Thomas	.60	.25
❑	245 Dillon/Smith/Johnson/Kitna	.60	.25
❑	246 Couch/Green/Morgan/Word	.40	.15
❑	247 Hutchinson/Galloway/Williams/Ellis	.25	.08
❑	248 Portis/Smith/Wilson	.60	.25
❑	249 Harring/Stew/Schr/Edwards	.60	.25
❑	250 Favre/Green/Driver/KGB	.75	.30
❑	251 Carr/Wells/Bradford/Glenn	.60	.25
❑	252 Mann/James/Harr/Freen	.60	.25
❑	253 Brunell/Taylor/Smith/McCree	.25	.08
❑	254 Green/Holmes/Kenn/Hicks	.40	.15
❑	255 Willms/Chamb/Thom/Tayl	.60	.25
❑	256 Culp/Benn/Moss/Williams	.60	.25
❑	257 Brady/Smith/Brown/Vina	1.00	.40
❑	258 Brooks/McAllister/Horn/Howard	.25	.08
❑	259 Collins/Barber/Toomer/Strahan	.60	.25
❑	260 Pennington/Martin Chrebet/Abraham	.40	.15
❑	261 Gannon/Garn/Rice/Woods	.60	.25
❑	262 McNabb/Staley/Pinkston/Taylor	.40	.15
❑	263 Maddox/Zereoue/Ward Gildon/Porter	.40	.15
❑	264 Brees/Tomlinson/Edwards	.60	.25
❑	265 Garcia/Hearst/Owens/Carter	.40	.15
❑	266 Hasselbeck/Alexander Robin/Tongue	.25	.08
❑	267 Bulger/Faulk/Holt/Little	.60	.25
❑	268 B.John/Key.John/S.Rice/Kelly	.40	.15
❑	269 McNair/George/Mason/Schulters	.25	.08
❑	270 Ramsey/Gardner/Smoot	.25	.08
❑	271 Carson Palmer RC	5.00	2.00
❑	272 Kyle Boller RC	1.25	.50
❑	273 Byron Leftwich RC	4.00	1.50
❑	274 Willis McGahee RC	3.00	1.25
❑	275 Larry Johnson RC	5.00	2.50
❑	276 Charles Rogers RC	1.25	.50
❑	277 Andre Johnson RC	2.50	1.00
❑	278 Bryant Johnson RC	1.25	.50
❑	279 Rex Grossman RC	4.00	1.50
❑	280 Taylor Jacobs RC	1.00	.40
❑	281 Rober RC/Sull RC/Will RC	1.25	.50
❑	282 Jopp RC/Davis RC/Rag RC	1.25	.50
❑	283 Witt RC/Clark RC/Smith RC	1.25	.50
❑	284 Edwds RC/Smith RC/Bail RC	1.25	.50
❑	285 SuggsRC/BrownRC/SmithRC	1.25	.50
❑	286 Griff RC/Pinn RC/Askew RC	1.25	.50
❑	287 Farg RC/Gabr RC/Johns RC	1.25	.50
❑	288 Kenn RC/Joseph RC/Warr RC	1.25	.50
❑	289 Sug RC/Hayn RC/McDo RC	2.00	.75
❑	290 Wash RC/Curt RC/Burles RC	1.50	.60
❑	291 Wall RC/Dors RC/Simms RC	2.00	.75
❑	292 Wade RC/Aik RC/Gage RC	1.25	.50
❑	293 McCull RC/Sapp RC/Grah RC	1.25	.50
❑	294 Kelly RC/Gard RC/Tolv RC	1.00	.40
❑	295 Johns RC/Bold RC/Calic RC	3.00	1.25
❑	296 Lloyd RC/McM RC/McD RC	1.25	.50
❑	297 Kels RC/White RC/Doss RC	1.25	.50
❑	298 Newm RC/Truf RC/Wool RC	2.50	1.00
❑	299 Romo RC/King.RC/St.P RC	20.00	10.00
❑	300 Pinn RC/Toef RC/Cobou RC	1.25	.50

2004 Fleer Tradition

❑	COMPLETE SET (360)	100.00	50.00
❑	COMP.SET w/o SP's (330)	30.00	15.00
❑	1 Dolphins TL	.40	.15
❑	2 Bills TL	.40	.15
❑	3 Patriots TL	.60	.25
❑	4 Jets TL	.40	.15
❑	5 Colts TL	.60	.25
❑	6 Jaguars TL	.40	.15
❑	7 Titans TL	.25	.08
❑	8 Texans TL	.40	.15
❑	9 Raiders TL	.60	.25
❑	10 Broncos TL	.40	.15
❑	11 Chiefs TL	.40	.15
❑	12 Chargers TL	.50	.20
❑	13 Steelers TL	.60	.25
❑	14 Browns TL	.25	.08
❑	15 Bengals TL	.40	.15
❑	16 Ravens TL	.40	.15
❑	17 Eagles TL	.40	.15
❑	18 Giants TL	.40	.15
❑	19 Redskins TL	.40	.15
❑	20 Cowboys TL	.40	.15
❑	21 Vikings TL	.60	.25
❑	22 Packers TL	.75	.30
❑	23 Bears TL	.60	.25
❑	24 Lions TL	.40	.15
❑	25 49ers TL	.40	.15
❑	26 Rams TL	.40	.15
❑	27 Seahawks TL	.40	.15
❑	28 Cardinals TL	.25	.08
❑	29 Panthers TL	.40	.15
❑	30 BuccaneersTL	.25	.08
❑	31 Falcons TL	.25	.08
❑	32 Saints TL	.40	.15
❑	33 Anquan Boldin	.60	.25
❑	34 Michael Vick	1.25	.50
❑	35 Kyle Boller	.60	.25
❑	36 Aeneas Williams	.25	.08
❑	37 Jake Delhomme	.60	.25
❑	38 Rex Grossman	.60	.25
❑	39 Carson Palmer	.75	.30
❑	40 Quincy Morgan	.40	.15
❑	41 Terry Glenn	.25	.08
❑	42 Jake Plummer	.40	.15
❑	43 Joey Harrington	.60	.25
❑	44 Brett Favre	1.50	.60
❑	45 Jeff Garcia	.60	.25
❑	46 Peyton Manning	1.00	.40
❑	47 Byron Leftwich	.75	.30
❑	48 Trent Green	.40	.15
❑	49 A.J. Feeley	.60	.25
❑	50 Daunte Culpepper	.60	.25
❑	51 Tom Brady	1.50	.60
❑	52 Aaron Brooks	.40	.15
❑	53 Kerry Collins	.40	.15
❑	54 Chad Pennington	.60	.25
❑	55 Rich Gannon	.40	.15
❑	56 Donovan McNabb	.75	.30
❑	57 Tommy Maddox	.40	.15
❑	58 Drew Brees	.60	.25
❑	59 Terrell Owens	.60	.25
❑	60 Matt Hasselbeck	.40	.15
❑	61 Kurt Warner	.60	.25
❑	62 Brad Johnson	.40	.15
❑	63 Jerome Bettis	.60	.25
❑	64 Keith Bulluck	.25	.08
❑	65 Rod Gardner	.40	.15
❑	66 Eddie George	.40	.15
❑	67 Warren Sapp	.40	.15
❑	68 Marc Bulger	.60	.25
❑	69 Shaun Alexander	.60	.25
❑	70 Tai Streets	.25	.08
❑	71 LaDainian Tomlinson	.75	.30
❑	72 [illegible]	[illegible]	[illegible]
❑	73 Brian Westbrook	.40	.15
❑	74 Jerry Rice	1.25	.50
❑	75 Santana Moss	.40	.15
❑	76 Moe Williams	.25	.08
❑	77 Deuce McAllister	.60	.25
❑	78 Adam Vinatieri	.60	.25
❑	79 Randy Moss	.75	.30
❑	80 Ricky Williams	.60	.25
❑	81 Priest Holmes	.75	.30
❑	82 Jimmy Smith	.40	.15
❑	83 Edgerrin James	.60	.25
❑	84 Andre Johnson	.60	.25
❑	85 Ahman Green	.60	.25
❑	86 Charles Rogers	.40	.15
❑	87 Champ Bailey	.40	.15
❑	88 Roy Williams S	.40	.15
❑	89 Tim Couch	.25	.08
❑	90 Corey Dillon	.40	.15
❑	91 Thomas Jones	.40	.15
❑	92 Stephen Davis	.40	.15
❑	93 Travis Henry	.40	.15
❑	94 Jamal Lewis	.60	.25
❑	95 Warrick Dunn	.40	.15
❑	96 Emmitt Smith	1.25	.50
❑	97 Mark Brunell	.40	.15
❑	98 Willis McGahee	.60	.25
❑	99 Duce Staley	.40	.15
❑	100 Lee Suggs	.60	.25
❑	101 Rod Smith	.40	.15
❑	102 Marvin Harrison	.60	.25
❑	103 Larry Johnson	.75	.30
❑	104 Michael Bennett	.40	.15
❑	105 Donte Stallworth	.40	.15
❑	106 DeShaun Foster	.40	.15
❑	107 Hines Ward	.60	.25
❑	108 T.J. Duckett	.40	.15
❑	109 Brian Urlacher	.75	.30
❑	110 Boss Bailey	.40	.15
❑	111 Tim Brown	.60	.25
❑	112 David Boston	.40	.15
❑	113 Marshall Faulk	.60	.25
❑	114 Jason Witten	.40	.15
❑	115 Richard Seymour	.25	.08
❑	116 Domanick Davis	.60	.25
❑	117 Jon Kitna	.40	.15
❑	118 Ray Lewis	.60	.25
❑	119 Tedy Bruschi	.40	.15
❑	120 Chris Chambers	.40	.15
❑	121 Freddie Mitchell	.40	.15
❑	122 Amani Toomer	.40	.15
❑	123 Curtis Martin	.60	.25
❑	124 Eric Moulds	.40	.15
❑	125 Darrell Jackson	.40	.15
❑	126 Clinton Portis	.60	.25
❑	127 Jay Fiedler	.25	.08
❑	128 Todd Heap	.40	.15
❑	129 Dexter Jackson	.25	.08
❑	130 James Jackson	.25	.08
❑	131 Shannon Sharpe	.40	.15
❑	132 Donald Driver	.40	.15
❑	133 Billy Miller	.25	.08
❑	134 Dante Hall	.60	.25
❑	135 Onterrio Smith	.40	.15
❑	136 Joe Horn	.40	.15
❑	137 Shaun Ellis	.25	.08
❑	138 L.J. Smith	.40	.15
❑	139 Jerry Porter	.40	.15
❑	140 Reggie Wayne	.40	.15
❑	141 Derrick Brooks	.40	.15
❑	142 Terrell Suggs	.40	.15
❑	143 Randy McMichael	.25	.08
❑	144 Mike Alstott	.40	.15
❑	145 Nate Poole RC	.60	.25
❑	146 Chris Brown	.60	.25

❑ 147 Torry Holt .60 .25
❑ 148 Adewale Ogunleye .40 .15
❑ 149 Peter Warrick .40 .15
❑ 150 Alge Crumpler .40 .15
❑ 151 Charlie Garner .40 .15
❑ 152 Jeremy Shockey .60 .25
❑ 153 Simeon Rice .40 .15
❑ 154 Julian Peterson .25 .08
❑ 155 Patrick Ramsey .40 .15
❑ 156 Shawn Springs .25 .08
❑ 157 Marcus Stroud .25 .08
❑ 158 Keyshawn Johnson .40 .15
❑ 159 Steve Smith .60 .25
❑ 160 Ty Law .40 .15
❑ 161 Derrick Mason .40 .15
❑ 162 Josh Reed .25 .08
❑ 163 Fred Smoot .25 .08
❑ 164 Muhsin Muhammad .40 .15
❑ 165 Justin Gage .40 .15
❑ 166 Chad Johnson .60 .25
❑ 167 Dennis Northcutt .25 .08
❑ 168 Joey Galloway .40 .15
❑ 169 Ashley Lelie .40 .15
❑ 170 Casey Fitzsimmons .25 .08
❑ 171 Dwight Freeney .40 .15
❑ 172 Nick Barnett .40 .15
❑ 173 LaBrandon Toefield .25 .08
❑ 174 Jabar Gaffney .40 .15
❑ 175 Tony Gonzalez .40 .15
❑ 176 Zach Thomas .60 .25
❑ 177 Nate Burleson .60 .25
❑ 178 Deion Branch .60 .25
❑ 179 Boo Williams .25 .08
❑ 180 Michael Strahan .40 .15
❑ 181 Anthony Becht .25 .08
❑ 182 Charles Woodson .40 .15
❑ 183 Sheldon Brown .25 .08
❑ 184 Kendrell Bell .40 .15
❑ 185 Kassim Osgood .25 .08
❑ 186 Tony Parrish .25 .08
❑ 187 Marcel Shipp .40 .15
❑ 188 Bobby Engram .25 .08
❑ 189 Keith Brooking .25 .08
❑ 190 Isaac Bruce .40 .15
❑ 191 Travis Taylor .25 .08
❑ 192 Charles Lee .25 .08
❑ 193 Takeo Spikes .25 .08
❑ 194 Justin McCareins .25 .08
❑ 195 Julius Peppers .60 .25
❑ 196 LaVar Arrington 1.25 .50
❑ 197 Dez White .40 .15
❑ 198 Rudi Johnson .40 .15
❑ 199 Andre Davis .25 .08
❑ 200 Quincy Carter .40 .15
❑ 201 Quentin Griffin .60 .25
❑ 202 Dallas Clark .40 .15
❑ 203 Artose Pinner .25 .08
❑ 204 Kevin Johnson .25 .08
❑ 205 Kabeer Gbaja-Biamila .40 .15
❑ 206 Marcus Coleman .25 .08
❑ 207 Johnnie Morton .40 .15
❑ 208 Jason Taylor .25 .08
❑ 209 Kevin Williams .25 .08
❑ 210 David Givens .40 .15
❑ 211 Charles Grant .25 .08
❑ 212 Ike Hilliard .25 .08
❑ 213 Wayne Chrebet .40 .15
❑ 214 Teyo Johnson .25 .08
❑ 215 Brian Dawkins .40 .15
❑ 216 Antwaan Randle El .60 .25
❑ 217 Eric Parker .25 .08
❑ 218 Josh McCown .40 .15
❑ 219 Tim Rattay .25 .08
❑ 220 Brian Finneran .25 .08
❑ 221 Chad Brown .25 .08
❑ 222 Ed Reed .40 .15
❑ 223 Dane Looker .40 .15
❑ 224 Aaron Schobel .40 .15
❑ 225 Joe Jurevicius .25 .08
❑ 226 Ricky Manning .25 .08
❑ 227 Jevon Kearse .40 .15
❑ 228 Laveranues Coles .40 .15
❑ 229 Kelley Washington .25 .08
❑ 230 William Green .40 .15
❑ 231 Terence Newman .40 .15
❑ 232 Bryant Johnson .25 .08
❑ 233 Peerless Price .40 .15
❑ 234 Peter Boulware .40 .15
❑ 235 Drew Bledsoe .60 .25
❑ 236 Kris Jenkins .25 .08
❑ 237 Marty Booker .40 .15
❑ 238 Matt Schobel .25 .08
❑ 239 Earl Little .25 .08
❑ 240 Antonio Bryant .40 .15
❑ 241 Al Wilson .25 .08
❑ 242 Dre Bly .25 .08
❑ 243 Javon Walker .40 .15
❑ 244 David Carr .60 .25
❑ 245 Mike Vanderjagt .25 .08
❑ 246 Fred Taylor .40 .15
❑ 247 Eddie Kennison .25 .08
❑ 248 Patrick Surtain .25 .08
❑ 249 Jim Kleinsasser .25 .08
❑ 250 Daniel Graham .25 .08
❑ 251 Jerome Pathon .25 .08
❑ 252 Tiki Barber .60 .25
❑ 253 John Abraham .25 .08
❑ 254 Justin Fargas .40 .15
❑ 255 Correll Buckhalter .40 .15
❑ 256 Plaxico Burress .40 .15
❑ 257 Quentin Jammer .25 .08
❑ 258 Kevan Barlow .40 .15
❑ 259 Koren Robinson .40 .15
❑ 260 Leonard Little .25 .08
❑ 261 John Lynch .40 .15
❑ 262 Tyrone Calico .40 .15
❑ 263 Taylor Jacobs .40 .15
❑ 264 Joey Porter .40 .15
❑ 265 Freddie Jones .25 .08
❑ 266 Marcus Pollard .25 .08
❑ 267 Mike Peterson .25 .08
❑ 268 Justin Griffith .25 .08
❑ 269 Shawn Bryson .25 .08
❑ 270 Will Allen .25 .08
❑ 271 Antonio Gates .60 .25
❑ 272 Chris McAlister .25 .08
❑ 273 Tony Hollings .25 .08
❑ 274 Cedrick Wilson .25 .08
❑ 275 Adam Archuleta .25 .08
❑ 276 London Fletcher .25 .08
❑ 277 Drew Bennett .40 .15
❑ 278 Rod Smart .25 .08
❑ 279 LaMont Jordan .60 .25
❑ 280 Jerry Azumah .25 .08
❑ 281 Bubba Franks .40 .15
❑ 282 Troy Edwards .25 .08
❑ 283 Willie McGinest .25 .08
❑ 284 Morten Andersen .25 .08
❑ 285 Dat Nguyen .25 .08
❑ 286 Samari Rolle .25 .08
❑ 287 Brian Simmons .25 .08
❑ 288 Chike Okeafor .25 .08
❑ 289 Rodney Harrison .25 .08
❑ 290 Jason Elam .25 .08
❑ 291 Tim Dwight .40 .15
❑ 292 Corey Bradford .25 .08
❑ 293 Charles Tillman .40 .15
❑ 294 Tim Carter .25 .08
❑ 295 Ahmed Plummer .25 .08
❑ 296 Troy Walters .25 .08
❑ 297 Michael Lewis .25 .08
❑ 298 Tory James .25 .08
❑ 299 Doug Flutie .60 .25
❑ 300 Az-Zahir Hakim .25 .08
❑ 301 Itula Mili .25 .08
❑ 302 Jamie Sharper .25 .08
❑ 303 Vonnie Holliday .25 .08
❑ 304 Brian Russell RC .60 .25
❑ 305 Bryan Gilmore .25 .08
❑ 306 Darren Sharper .25 .08
❑ 307 Kyle Brady .25 .08
❑ 308 David Tyree .25 .08
❑ 309 Andre Carter .25 .08
❑ 310 Lawyer Milloy .40 .15
❑ 311 David Terrell .40 .15
❑ 312 Richie Anderson .25 .08
❑ 313 Darren Howard .25 .08
❑ 314 Sebastian Janikowski .25 .08
❑ 315 Kimo von Oelhoffen .60 .25
❑ 316 Donnie Edwards .25 .08
❑ 317 Brandon Lloyd .40 .15
❑ 318 Robert Ferguson .25 .08
❑ 319 Derek Smith .25 .08
❑ 320 Anthony Thomas .40 .15
❑ 321 Ken Hamlin .25 .08
❑ 322 Ronde Barber .25 .08
❑ 323 Erron Kinney .25 .08
❑ 324 Tom Brady AW .60 .25
❑ 325 Peyton Manning AW .60 .25
❑ 326 Steve McNair AW .40 .15
❑ 327 Jamal Lewis AW .40 .15
❑ 328 Ray Lewis AW .40 .15
❑ 329 Anquan Boldin AW .25 .08
❑ 330 Terrell Suggs AW .25 .08
❑ 331 Eli Manning RC 12.00 6.00
❑ 332 Larry Fitzgerald RC 6.00 2.50
❑ 333 Ben Roethlisberger RC 15.00 6.00
❑ 334 Tatum Bell RC 4.00 1.50
❑ 335 Roy Williams RC 5.00 2.00
❑ 336 Drew Henson RC 2.00 .75
❑ 337 Philip Rivers RC 6.00 2.50
❑ 338 Rashaun Woods RC 2.00 .75
❑ 339 Kevin Jones RC 5.00 2.00
❑ 340 Sean Taylor RC 2.00 .75
❑ 341 Steven Jackson RC 6.00 2.50
❑ 342 Kellen Winslow RC 4.00 1.50
❑ 343 Chris Perry RC 3.00 1.25
❑ 344 J.P. Losman RC 4.00 1.50
❑ 345 Greg Jones RC 2.00 .75
❑ 346 Reggie Williams RC 2.50 1.00
❑ 347 Michael Clayton RC 4.00 1.50
❑ 348 Jonathan Vilma RC 2.00 .75
❑ 349 Julius Jones RC 6.00 2.50
❑ 350 Michael Jenkins RC 2.00 .75
❑ 351 E.Manning/Rivers/Roethlis. 25.0012:50
❑ 352 Fitzgerald/Re.Will/Ro.Will. 8.00 3.00
❑ 353 Evans RC/Berr.RC/Ham.RC 4.00 1.50
❑ 354 Ude.RC/Poole RC/Colb.RC 2.50 1.00
❑ 355 Gamb.RC/Rob.RC/Hall RC 3.00 1.25
❑ 356 Trou.RC/Wats.RC/Harts.RC 3.00 1.25
❑ 357 Darl.RC/Morant RC/Wilf.RC 2.50 1.00
❑ 358 McCo.RC/Pick.RC/Sch.RC 5.00 2.00
❑ 359 Bell/Turn.RC/Cobbs RC 5.00 2.00
❑ 360 Moore RC/Wils.RC/Kni.RC 3.00 1.25

2001 Hot Prospects

❑ COMP.SET w/o SP's (100) 25.00 10.00
❑ 1 Aaron Brooks 1.00 .40
❑ 2 Tim Couch .60 .25
❑ 3 Jeff George .60 .25
❑ 4 Brett Favre 3.00 1.25
❑ 5 Donovan McNabb 1.25 .50
❑ 6 Ray Lucas .40 .15
❑ 7 Doug Flutie 1.00 .40
❑ 8 Mark Brunell 1.00 .40
❑ 9 Steve McNair 1.00 .40
❑ 10 Trent Green 1.00 .40
❑ 11 Daunte Culpepper 1.00 .40
❑ 12 Rich Gannon 1.00 .40
❑ 13 Kurt Warner 2.00 .75
❑ 14 Brian Griese 1.00 .40
❑ 15 Kerry Collins .60 .25
❑ 16 Vinny Testaverde .60 .25
❑ 17 David Boston 1.00 .40
❑ 18 Peyton Manning 2.50 1.00
❑ 19 Keyshawn Johnson 1.00 .40
❑ 20 Tim Biakabutuka .60 .25
❑ 22 Emmitt Smith 2.00 .75
❑ 23 Terry Glenn .60 .25
❑ 24 Tony Gonzalez .60 .25
❑ 25 Charlie Garner .60 .25
❑ 26 Lamar Smith .60 .25
❑ 27 Eddie George 1.00 .40
❑ 28 Fred Taylor 1.00 .40
❑ 29 Marvin Harrison 1.00 .40
❑ 30 Terrell Davis 1.00 .40
❑ 31 Marcus Robinson 1.00 .40
❑ 32 Edgerrin James 1.25 .50
❑ 33 Ed McCaffrey 1.00 .40
❑ 34 Ricky Williams 1.00 .40

❑ 36 Jerome Bettis 1.00 .40
❑ 37 Shaun Alexander 1.25 .50
❑ 38 Mike Anderson 1.00 .40
❑ 39 Keenan McCardell .40 .15
❑ 40 Mike Alstott 1.00 .40
❑ 41 Terrell Fletcher .40 .15
❑ 42 Kevin Johnson .60 .25
❑ 43 Wesley Walls .40 .15
❑ 44 Derrick Mason .60 .25
❑ 45 Sammy Morris .40 .15
❑ 46 Joey Galloway .60 .25
❑ 47 Sylvester Morris .40 .15
❑ 48 Stephen Davis 1.00 .40
❑ 49 Terrell Owens 1.00 .40
❑ 50 Troy Edwards .40 .15
❑ 51 Amani Toomer .60 .25
❑ 52 Ray Lewis 1.00 .40
❑ 53 Terance Mathis .60 .25
❑ 54 Brian Urlacher 1.50 .60
❑ 55 Junior Seau 1.00 .40
❑ 56 Rocket Ismail .60 .25
❑ 57 Wayne Chrebet .60 .25
❑ 58 Peter Warrick 1.00 .40
❑ 59 Andre Rison .60 .25
❑ 60 Desmond Howard .40 .15
❑ 61 Eric Moulds .60 .25
❑ 62 Jerry Rice 2.00 .75
❑ 63 Stephen Alexander .40 .15
❑ 64 Isaac Bruce 1.00 .40
❑ 65 Travis Prentice .40 .15
❑ 66 James Stewart .60 .25
❑ 67 Jamal Anderson 1.00 .40
❑ 68 Ricky Watters .40 .15
❑ 69 Jamal Lewis 1.50 .60
❑ 70 Priest Holmes 1.25 .50
❑ 71 Ahman Green 1.00 .40
❑ 72 Marshall Faulk 1.25 .50
❑ 73 Warrick Dunn 1.00 .40
❑ 74 Curtis Martin 1.00 .40
❑ 75 Corey Dillon 1.00 .40
❑ 76 Ron Dayne 1.00 .40
❑ 77 Thomas Jones .60 .25
❑ 78 Duce Staley 1.00 .40
❑ 79 Tiki Barber 1.00 .40
❑ 80 Cris Carter 1.00 .40
❑ 81 Tim Brown 1.00 .40
❑ 82 Jimmy Smith .60 .25
❑ 83 Elvis Grbac .60 .25
❑ 84 Randy Moss 2.00 .75
❑ 85 Tim Dwight 1.00 .40
❑ 86 Antonio Freeman 1.00 .40
❑ 87 Muhsin Muhammad .60 .25
❑ 88 Torry Holt 1.00 .40
❑ 89 Frank Wycheck .40 .15
❑ 90 Jake Plummer .60 .25
❑ 91 Brad Johnson 1.00 .40
❑ 92 Chris Chandler .60 .25
❑ 93 Drew Bledsoe 1.25 .50
❑ 94 Rob Johnson .60 .25
❑ 95 Matt Hasselbeck .60 .25
❑ 96 Jon Kitna .60 .25
❑ 97 Kordell Stewart .60 .25
❑ 98 Charlie Batch 1.00 .40
❑ 99 Cade McNown .40 .15
❑ 100 Jeff Garcia 1.00 .40
❑ 101 Quincy Morgan RC 3.00 1.25
❑ 102 Jesse Palmer RC 3.00 1.25
❑ 103 Reggie Wayne RC 6.00 2.50
❑ 104 Deuce McAllister RC 6.00 2.50
❑ 105 Chad Johnson RC 8.00 3.00
❑ 106 Chris Weinke RC 3.00 1.25
❑ 107 Michael Bennett RC 3.00 1.25
❑ 108 Rod Gardner RC 3.00 1.25
❑ 109 Michael Vick RC 12.00 5.00
❑ 110 Anthony Thomas RC 3.00 1.25
❑ 111 Santana Moss RC 5.00 2.00
❑ 112 Kevan Barlow RC 3.00 1.25
❑ 113 Koren Robinson RC 3.00 1.25
❑ 114 Rudi Johnson RC 6.00 2.50
❑ 115 Josh Heupel RC 3.00 1.25
❑ 116 James Jackson RC 3.00 1.25
❑ 117 Freddie Mitchell RC 3.00 1.25
❑ 118 LaDainian Tomlinson RC 30.00 15.00
❑ 119 Marques Tuiasosopo RC 3.00 1.25
❑ 120 Drew Brees RC 12.00 5.00
❑ 121 David Terrell RC 3.00 1.25
❑ 122 Chris Chambers RC 5.00 2.00
❑ 123 Mike McMahon RC 3.00 1.25
❑ 124 Robert Ferguson RC 3.00 1.25
❑ 125 Justin Smith RC 3.00 1.25
❑ 126 Leonard Davis RC 2.00 .75
❑ 127 Todd Heap RC 3.00 1.25
❑ 128 Dan Morgan RC 3.00 1.25
❑ 129 Gerard Warren RC 3.00 1.25
❑ 130 Travis Henry RC 6.00 2.50
❑ 131 Travis Minor RC 2.00 .75
❑ 132 Richard Seymour RC 3.00 1.25
❑ 133 Quincy Carter RC 3.00 1.25
❑ 134 Snoop Minnis RC 2.00 .75
❑ 135 Sage Rosenfels RC 3.00 1.25
❑ CL1 Checklist .10 .02

2002 Hot Prospects

❑ COMP.SET w/o SP's (80) 25.00 10.00
❑ 1 Donovan McNabb 1.50 .60
❑ 2 Drew Brees 1.25 .50
❑ 3 Curtis Martin 1.25 .50
❑ 4 Priest Holmes 1.50 .60
❑ 5 Quincy Carter .75 .30
❑ 6 Chris Weinke .75 .30
❑ 7 Marshall Faulk 1.25 .50
❑ 8 Jake Plummer .75 .30
❑ 9 Tom Brady 3.00 1.25
❑ 10 Ahman Green 1.25 .50
❑ 11 Brian Urlacher 2.00 .75
❑ 12 Keyshawn Johnson 1.25 .50
❑ 13 Jerome Bettis 1.25 .50
❑ 14 Tiki Barber 1.25 .50
❑ 15 Edgerrin James 1.50 .60
❑ 16 Jamal Lewis 1.25 .50
❑ 17 Terrell Owens 1.25 .50
❑ 18 Joe Horn .75 .30
❑ 19 Daunte Culpepper 1.25 .50
❑ 20 Terrell Davis 1.25 .50
❑ 21 Fred Taylor 1.25 .50
❑ 22 Emmitt Smith 3.00 1.25
❑ 23 Jamal Anderson .75 .30
❑ 24 Garrison Hearst .75 .30
❑ 25 Chad Pennington 1.50 .60
❑ 26 Michael Bennett .75 .30
❑ 27 James Allen .75 .30
❑ 28 Marty Booker .50 .20
❑ 29 Warren Sapp .75 .30
❑ 30 Jerry Rice 2.50 1.00
❑ 31 Antowain Smith .75 .30
❑ 32 Marvin Harrison 1.25 .50
❑ 33 Tim Couch .75 .30
❑ 34 Stephen Davis .75 .30
❑ 35 Kordell Stewart .75 .30
❑ 36 Tony Gonzalez .75 .30
❑ 37 Mike McMahon 1.25 .50
❑ 38 Eric Moulds .75 .30
❑ 39 Kurt Warner 1.25 .50
❑ 40 Ricky Williams 1.25 .50
❑ 41 Michael Strahan .75 .30
❑ 42 Trent Green .75 .30
❑ 43 Brian Griese 1.25 .50
❑ 44 David Boston 1.25 .50
❑ 45 LaDainian Tomlinson 2.00 .75
❑ 46 Tim Brown 1.25 .50
❑ 47 Deuce McAllister 1.50 .60
❑ 48 Jamie Sharper .50 .20
❑ 49 Rod Gardner .75 .30
❑ 50 Isaac Bruce 1.25 .50
❑ 51 Freddie Mitchell .75 .30
❑ 52 Kerry Collins .75 .30
❑ 53 Mark Brunell 1.25 .50
❑ 54 Corey Dillon .75 .30
❑ 55 Steve McNair 1.25 .50
❑ 56 Aaron Brooks 1.25 .50
❑ 57 Chris Chambers 1.25 .50
❑ 58 Bill Schroeder .75 .30
❑ 59 Ray Lewis 1.25 .50
❑ 60 Shaun Alexander 1.50 .60
❑ 61 Kevin Johnson .75 .30
❑ 62 Michael Vick 2.50 1.00
❑ 63 Jeff Garcia 1.25 .50
❑ 64 Laveranues Coles .75 .30
❑ 65 Jimmy Smith .75 .30
❑ 66 Brett Favre 3.00 1.25
❑ 67 Anthony Thomas .75 .30
❑ 68 Torry Holt 1.25 .50
❑ 69 Duce Staley 1.25 .50
❑ 70 Randy Moss 2.50 1.00
❑ 71 Peyton Manning 2.50 1.00
❑ 72 Peter Warrick .75 .30
❑ 73 [illegible]
❑ 74 Plaxico Burress .75 .30
❑ 75 Troy Brown .75 .30
❑ 76 Rod Smith .75 .30
❑ 77 Drew Bledsoe 1.50 .60
❑ 78 Darrell Jackson .75 .30
❑ 79 Rich Gannon 1.25 .50
❑ 80 Jay Fiedler .75 .30
❑ 81 David Carr/250 RC 30.00 12.50
❑ 82 Andre Davis JSY RC 8.00 3.00
❑ 83 Daniel Graham JSY RC 10.00 4.00
❑ 84 Ron Johnson JSY RC 8.00 3.00
❑ 85 Julius Peppers JSY RC 15.00 6.00
❑ 86 Josh Reed JSY RC 10.00 4.00
❑ 87 Travis Stephens JSY RC 8.00 3.00
❑ 88 Mike Williams JSY RC 8.00 3.00
❑ 89 Antonio Bryant JSY RC 10.00 4.00
❑ 90 Eric Crouch JSY RC 10.00 4.00
❑ 91 DeShaun Foster JSY RC 10.00 4.00
❑ 92 Joey Harrington JSY RC 10.00 4.00
❑ 93 Josh McCown JSY RC 10.00 4.00
❑ 94 Patrick Ramsey JSY RC 10.00 4.00
❑ 95 Jeremy Shockey JSY RC 20.00 8.00
❑ 96 Marquise Walker JSY RC 8.00 3.00
❑ 97 Reche Caldwell JSY RC 10.00 4.00
❑ 98 Rohan Davey JSY RC 10.00 4.00
❑ 99 Jabar Gaffney JSY RC 10.00 4.00
❑ 100 David Garrard JSY RC 15.00 6.00
❑ 101 Maurice Morris JSY RC 10.00 4.00
❑ 102 Antwaan Randle El JSY RC 10.00 4.00
❑ 103 Donte Stallworth JSY RC 10.00 4.00
❑ 104 Roy Williams JSY RC 12.00 5.00
❑ 105 Ladell Betts JSY RC 10.00 4.00
❑ 106 Tim Carter JSY RC 8.00 3.00
❑ 107 T.J. Duckett JSY RC 10.00 4.00
❑ 108 William Green JSY RC 10.00 4.00
❑ 109 Ashley Lelie JSY RC 20.00 7.50
❑ 110 Clinton Portis JSY RC 20.00 8.00
❑ 111 Cliff Russell JSY RC 8.00 3.00
❑ 112 Javon Walker JSY RC 10.00 4.00

2003 Hot Prospects

❑ COMP.SET w/o SP's (80) 20.00 7.50
❑ 1 Emmitt Smith 2.50 1.00
❑ 2 Terrell Owens 1.00 .40
❑ 3 Tiki Barber 1.00 .40
❑ 4 Trent Green .60 .25
❑ 5 Quincy Morgan .60 .25
❑ 6 Eric Moulds .60 .25
❑ 7 Simeon Rice .60 .25
❑ 8 Hines Ward 1.00 .40
❑ 9 Michael Bennett .60 .25
❑ 10 Donald Driver .60 .25
❑ 11 Stephen Davis .60 .25
❑ 12 Steve McNair 1.00 .40
❑ 13 David Boston .60 .25
❑ 14 Deuce McAllister 1.00 .40

❑ 15	Marvin Harrison	1.00	.40
❑ 16	Peerless Price	.60	.25
❑ 17	Matt Hasselbeck	.60	.25
❑ 18	Jerry Rice	2.00	.75
❑ 19	Junior Seau	1.00	.40
❑ 20	Clinton Portis	1.50	.60
❑ 21	Fred Taylor	1.00	.40
❑ 22	William Green	.60	.25
❑ 23	Warrick Dunn	.60	.25
❑ 24	Koren Robinson	.60	.25
❑ 25	Jeremy Shockey	1.50	.60
❑ 26	Chris Chambers	1.00	.40
❑ 27	Brett Favre	2.50	1.00
❑ 28	Julius Peppers	1.00	.40
❑ 29	Eddie George	.60	.25
❑ 30	Todd Pinkston	.60	.25
❑ 31	Tom Brady	2.50	1.00
❑ 32	Edgerrin James	1.00	.40
❑ 33	Chad Johnson	1.00	.40
❑ 34	Laveranues Coles	.60	.25
❑ 35	LaDainian Tomlinson	1.00	.40
❑ 36	Priest Holmes	1.25	.50
❑ 37	Shannon Sharpe	.60	.25
❑ 38	Jamal Lewis	1.00	.40
❑ 39	Warren Sapp	.60	.25
❑ 40	Tim Brown	1.00	.40
❑ 41	Kerry Collins	.60	.25
❑ 42	Jimmy Smith	.60	.25
❑ 43	Chad Hutchinson	.60	.25
❑ 44	Marcel Shipp	.60	.25
❑ 45	Jeff Garcia	1.00	.40
❑ 46	Donovan McNabb	1.25	.50
❑ 47	Randy Moss	1.50	.60
❑ 48	Ahman Green	1.00	.40
❑ 49	Travis Henry	.60	.25
❑ 50	Brad Johnson	.60	.25
❑ 51	Tommy Maddox	1.00	.40
❑ 52	Aaron Brooks	1.00	.40
❑ 53	Peyton Manning	1.50	.60
❑ 54	Brian Urlacher	1.50	.60
❑ 55	Rod Gardner	.60	.25
❑ 56	Chad Pennington	1.25	.50
❑ 57	Ricky Williams	1.00	.40
❑ 58	James Stewart	.60	.25
❑ 59	Todd Heap	.60	.25
❑ 60	Marshall Faulk	1.00	.40
❑ 61	Corey Dillon	.60	.25
❑ 62	Michael Vick	2.50	1.00
❑ 63	Shaun Alexander	1.00	.40
❑ 64	Curtis Martin	1.00	.40
❑ 65	Mark Brunell	.60	.25
❑ 66	Joey Harrington	1.50	.60
❑ 67	Drew Bledsoe	1.00	.40
❑ 68	Keyshawn Johnson	1.00	.40
❑ 69	Jerome Bettis	1.00	.40
❑ 70	Daunte Culpepper	1.00	.40
❑ 71	David Carr	1.50	.60
❑ 72	Marty Booker	.60	.25
❑ 73	Patrick Ramsey	1.00	.40
❑ 74	Drew Brees	1.00	.40
❑ 75	Donte Stallworth	1.00	.40
❑ 76	Jake Plummer	.60	.25
❑ 77	Ray Lewis	1.00	.40
❑ 78	Kurt Warner	1.00	.40
❑ 79	Rich Gannon	.60	.25
❑ 80	Tony Gonzalez	.60	.25
❑ 92	Dallas Clark JSY RC	10.00	4.00
❑ 93	Terence Newman JSY RC	15.00	6.00
❑ 94	Rex Grossman JSY RC	25.00	10.00
❑ 95	Kelley Washington JSY RC	10.00	4.00
❑ 96	Kyle Boller JSY RC	8.00	3.00
❑ 97	Carson Palmer JSY RC	30.00	12.50
❑ 98	Charles Rogers JSY RC	8.00	3.00
❑ 99	Chris Simms JSY RC	10.00	4.00
❑ 100	Larry Johnson JSY RC	30.00	15.00
❑ 101	Andre Johnson JSY RC	15.00	6.00
❑ 102	Taylor Jacobs JSY RC	8.00	3.00
❑ 103	Byron Leftwich JSY RC	25.00	10.00
❑ 110	Tyrone Calico RC	5.00	2.00
❑ 111	Billy McMullen RC	4.00	1.50
❑ 112	Jerome McDougle RC	5.00	2.00
❑ 113	Willis McGahee RC	12.00	5.00
❑ 114	Anquan Boldin RC	12.00	5.00
❑ 115	Artose Pinner RC	5.00	2.00
❑ 116	Kevin Williams RC	5.00	2.00
❑ 117	Bethel Johnson RC	5.00	2.00
❑ 118	Quentin Griffin RC	5.00	2.00
❑ 119	Nate Burleson RC	5.00	2.00
❑ 120	DeWayne Robertson RC	5.00	2.00

2004 Hot Prospects

❑	COMP.SET w/o SP's (70)	20.00	7.50
❑	71-94 AU JSY RC ODDS 1:20H, 1:840R		
❑	103-112 RC PRINT RUN 1000 SER. #'d SETS		
❑ 1	Donovan McNabb	1.00	.40
❑ 2	Charlie Garner	.50	.20
❑ 3	Tim Rattay	.30	.10
❑ 4	Drew Brees	.75	.30
❑ 5	Jerry Rice	1.50	.60
❑ 6	Aaron Brooks	.50	.20
❑ 7	Chris Chambers	.50	.20
❑ 8	Byron Leftwich	1.00	.40
❑ 9	Andre Johnson	.75	.30
❑ 10	Edgerrin James	.75	.30
❑ 11	Charles Rogers	.50	.20
❑ 12	Quentin Griffin	.75	.30
❑ 13	Carson Palmer	1.00	.40
❑ 14	Ray Lewis	.75	.30
❑ 15	Clinton Portis	.75	.30
❑ 16	Marc Bulger	.75	.30
❑ 17	Matt Hasselbeck	.50	.20
❑ 18	Plaxico Burress	.50	.20
❑ 19	Priest Holmes	1.00	.40
❑ 20	David Carr	.75	.30
❑ 21	Ahman Green	.75	.30
❑ 22	Roy Williams S	.50	.20
❑ 23	Travis Henry	.50	.20
❑ 24	Michael Vick	1.50	.60
❑ 25	Eddie George	.50	.20
❑ 26	Marshall Faulk	.75	.30
❑ 27	Kevan Barlow	.50	.20
❑ 28	Shaun Alexander	.75	.30
❑ 29	Hines Ward	.75	.30
❑ 30	Anquan Boldin	.75	.30
❑ 31	Chad Pennington	.75	.30
❑ 32	Randy Moss	1.00	.40
❑ 33	Fred Taylor	.50	.20
❑ 34	Marvin Harrison	.75	.30
❑ 35	Joey Harrington	.75	.30
❑ 36	Rich Gannon	.50	.20
❑ 37	Deuce McAllister	.75	.30
❑ 38	Deion Branch	.75	.30
❑ 39	Tony Gonzalez	.50	.20
❑ 40	Brett Favre	2.00	.75
❑ 41	Keyshawn Johnson	.50	.20
❑ 42	Lee Suggs	.75	.30
❑ 43	Jake Delhomme	.75	.30
❑ 44	Rex Grossman	.75	.30
❑ 45	Drew Bledsoe	.75	.30
❑ 46	Warrick Dunn	.50	.20
❑ 47	Steve McNair	.75	.30
❑ 48	Torry Holt	.75	.30
❑ 49	Brian Westbrook	.50	.20
❑ 50	Santana Moss	.50	.20
❑ 51	Jeremy Shockey	.75	.30
❑ 52	Daunte Culpepper	.75	.30
❑ 53	Jeff Garcia	.75	.30
❑ 54	Stephen Davis	.50	.20
❑ 55	Eric Moulds	.50	.20
❑ 56	Emmitt Smith	1.50	.60
❑ 57	Keenan McCardell	.30	.10
❑ 58	LaDainian Tomlinson	1.00	.40
❑ 59	Terrell Owens	.75	.30
❑ 60	Curtis Martin	.75	.30
❑ 61	Joe Horn	.50	.20
❑ 62	Tiki Barber	.75	.30
❑ 63	Tom Brady	2.00	.75
❑ 64	Ricky Williams	.75	.30
❑ 65	Peyton Manning	1.25	.50
❑ 66	Jake Plummer	.50	.20
❑ 67	Chad Johnson	.75	.30
❑ 68	Brian Urlacher	1.00	.40
❑ 69	Jamal Lewis	.75	.30
❑ 70	Laveranues Coles	.50	.20
❑ 71	Tatum Bell JSY AU/350 RC	50.00	25.00
❑ 72	B.Berrian JSY AU/344 RC	50.00	25.00
❑ 73	M.Clayton JSY AU/350 RC	80.00	40.00
❑ 74	Lee Evans JSY AU/350 RC	60.00	30.00
❑ 75	Fitzgerald JSY AU/140 RC	150.00	75.00
❑ 76	Henderson JSY AU/350 RC	40.00	15.00
❑ 77	D.Henson JSY AU/331 RC	30.00	15.00
❑ 78	St.Jackson JSY AU/300 RC	120.00	60.00
❑ 79	M.Jenkins JSY AU/349 RC	40.00	15.00
❑ 80	Greg Jones JSY AU/289 RC	40.00	20.00
❑ 81	Kev.Jones JSY AU/278 RC	80.00	40.00
❑ 82	J.Losman JSY AU/350 RC	60.00	25.00
❑ 83	Eli Manning JSY AU/350 RC	175.00	90.00
❑ 84	Chris Perry JSY AU/350 RC	50.00	20.00
❑ 85	Phil.Rivers JSY AU/350 RC	120.00	60.00
❑ 86	Roethlis.JSY AU/150 RC	250.00	125.00
❑ 87	Reg.Williams JSY AU/350 RC	60.00	25.00
❑ 88	Ro.Williams JSY AU/350 RC	100.00	50.00
❑ 89	Kell.Winslow JSY AU/50 RC	200.00	100.00
❑ 90	R.Woods JSY AU/350 RC	30.00	15.00
❑ 91	Jul.Jones JSY AU/350 RC	100.00	50.00
❑ 93	K.Colbert JSY AU/349 RC	40.00	15.00
❑ 94	M.Schaub JSY AU/120 RC	200.00	100.00
❑ 95	Cedric Cobbs JSY RC	15.00	6.00
❑ 96	Darius Watts JSY RC	15.00	6.00
❑ 97	DeAngelo Hall JSY RC	25.00	10.00
❑ 98	Derrick Hamilton JSY RC	12.00	5.00
❑ 99	Devard Darling JSY RC	15.00	6.00
❑ 100	Ben Troupe JSY RC	15.00	6.00
❑ 101	Mewelde Moore JSY RC	15.00	6.00
❑ 102	Ben Watson JSY RC	15.00	6.00
❑ 103	Sean Taylor RC	5.00	2.00
❑ 104	Ricky Ray RC	4.00	1.50
❑ 105	Carlos Francis RC	4.00	1.50
❑ 106	Samie Parker RC	5.00	2.00
❑ 107	Jerricho Cotchery RC	5.00	2.00
❑ 108	Ernest Wilford RC	5.00	2.00
❑ 109	Craig Krenzel RC	5.00	2.00
❑ 110	Robert Gallery RC	5.00	2.00
❑ 111	Dunta Robinson RC	5.00	2.00
❑ 112	Jonathan Vilma RC	5.00	2.00

2006 Hot Prospects

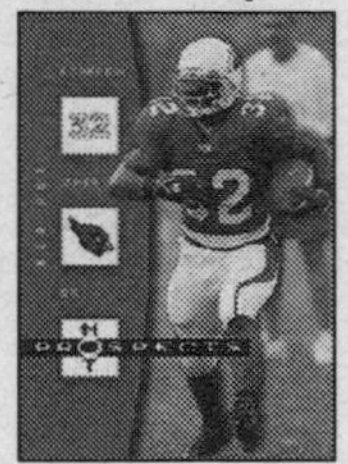

❑ 1	Edgerrin James	.75	.30
❑ 2	Larry Fitzgerald	.75	.30
❑ 3	Anquan Boldin	.50	.20
❑ 4	Michael Vick	.75	.30
❑ 5	Warrick Dunn	.50	.20
❑ 6	Roddy White	.50	.20
❑ 7	Jamal Lewis	.50	.20
❑ 8	Steve McNair	.50	.20
❑ 9	Mark Clayton	.75	.30
❑ 10	Willis McGahee	.75	.30
❑ 11	Lee Evans	.50	.20
❑ 12	J.P. Losman	.50	.20
❑ 13	Jake Delhomme	.50	.20
❑ 14	Steve Smith	.75	.30
❑ 15	DeShaun Foster	.50	.20
❑ 16	Rex Grossman	.75	.30
❑ 17	Thomas Jones	.50	.20
❑ 18	Brian Urlacher	.75	.30
❑ 19	Carson Palmer	.75	.30
❑ 20	Chad Johnson	.50	.20
❑ 21	Rudi Johnson	.50	.20
❑ 22	T.J. Houshmandzadeh	.50	.20
❑ 23	Braylon Edwards	.75	.30
❑ 24	Charlie Frye	.50	.20
❑ 25	Reuben Droughns	.50	.20
❑ 26	Julius Jones	.75	.30

❑ 27 Terrell Owens	.75	.30
❑ 28 Drew Bledsoe	.75	.30
❑ 29 Jake Plummer	.50	.20
❑ 30 Tatum Bell	.50	.20
❑ 31 Javon Walker	.50	.20
❑ 32 Kevin Jones	.75	.30
❑ 33 Roy Williams WR	.75	.30
❑ 34 Mike Williams	.75	.30
❑ 35 Brett Favre	1.50	.60
❑ 36 Donald Driver	.50	.20
❑ 37 Ahman Green	.50	.20
❑ 38 David Carr	.50	.20
❑ 39 Domanick Davis	.50	.20
❑ 40 Andre Johnson	.50	.20
❑ 41 Peyton Manning	[illegible]	[illegible]
❑ 42 Reggie Wayne	.50	.20
❑ 43 Marvin Harrison	.75	.30
❑ 44 Matt Jones	.50	.20
❑ 45 Greg Jones	.40	.15
❑ 46 Byron Leftwich	.50	.20
❑ 47 Larry Johnson	1.00	.40
❑ 48 Trent Green	.50	.20
❑ 49 Eddie Kennison	.40	.15
❑ 50 Tony Gonzalez	.50	.20
❑ 51 Daunte Culpepper	.75	.30
❑ 52 Ronnie Brown	.75	.30
❑ 53 Chris Chambers	.50	.20
❑ 54 Troy Williamson	.50	.20
❑ 55 Chester Taylor	.50	.20
❑ 56 Koren Robinson	.50	.20
❑ 57 Tom Brady	1.25	.50
❑ 58 Corey Dillon	.50	.20
❑ 59 Deion Branch	.50	.20
❑ 60 Drew Brees	.75	.30
❑ 61 Donte Stallworth	.50	.20
❑ 62 Deuce McAllister	.50	.20
❑ 63 Tiki Barber	.75	.30
❑ 64 Eli Manning	1.00	.40
❑ 65 Plaxico Burress	.50	.20
❑ 66 Chad Pennington	.50	.20
❑ 67 Curtis Martin	.75	.30
❑ 68 Justin McCareins	.40	.15
❑ 69 Randy Moss	.75	.30
❑ 70 LaMont Jordan	.50	.20
❑ 71 Aaron Brooks	.50	.20
❑ 72 Jerry Porter	.50	.20
❑ 73 Donovan McNabb	.75	.30
❑ 74 Brian Westbrook	.50	.20
❑ 75 Reggie Brown	.60	.25
❑ 76 Ben Roethlisberger	1.25	.50
❑ 77 Hines Ward	.75	.30
❑ 78 Willie Parker	1.00	.40
❑ 79 LaDainian Tomlinson	1.00	.40
❑ 80 Philip Rivers	.75	.30
❑ 81 Antonio Gates	.75	.30
❑ 82 Alex Smith QB	.75	[illegible]
❑ 83 Frank Gore	.75	.30
❑ 84 Antonio Bryant	.50	.20
❑ 85 Shaun Alexander	.75	.30
❑ 86 Matt Hasselbeck	.50	.20
❑ 87 Nate Burleson	.50	.20
❑ 88 Torry Holt	.50	.20
❑ 89 Marc Bulger	.50	.20
❑ 90 Steven Jackson	.75	.30
❑ 91 Kevin Curtis	.40	.15
❑ 92 Cadillac Williams	.75	.30
❑ 93 Chris Simms	.50	.20
❑ 94 Joey Galloway	.50	.20
❑ 95 Drew Bennett	.40	.15
❑ 96 David Givens	.50	.20
❑ 97 Billy Volek	.50	.20
❑ 98 Clinton Portis	.75	.30
❑ 99 Santana Moss	.50	.20
❑ 100 Antwaan Randle El	.50	.20
❑ 101 Donte Whitner RC	8.00	3.00
❑ 102 Haloti Ngata RC	8.00	3.00
❑ 103 Kamerion Wimbley RC	8.00	3.00
❑ 104 Jason Allen RC	8.00	3.00
❑ 105 Bobby Carpenter RC	8.00	3.00
❑ 106 Antonio Cromartie RC	8.00	3.00
❑ 107 Tamba Hali RC	8.00	3.00
❑ 108 Manny Lawson RC	8.00	3.00
❑ 109 Davin Joseph RC	6.00	2.50
❑ 110 Johnathan Joseph RC	6.00	2.50
❑ 111 John McCargo RC	6.00	2.50
❑ 112 Nick Mangold RC	4.00	1.50
❑ 113 Marcus Vick RC	6.00	2.50
❑ 114 Rocky McIntosh RC	8.00	3.00
❑ 115 Tim Day RC	6.00	2.50
❑ 116 Danieal Manning RC	8.00	3.00
❑ 117 Roman Harper RC	6.00	2.50
❑ 118 Josh Lay RC	4.00	1.50
❑ 119 Chris Gocong RC	6.00	2.50
❑ 120 Greg Blue RC	6.00	2.50
❑ 121 Bernard Pollard RC	6.00	2.50
❑ 122 Richard Marshall RC	6.00	2.50
❑ 123 Tony Scheffler RC	8.00	3.00
❑ 124 Dawan Landry RC	8.00	3.00
❑ 125 Darryl Tapp RC	6.00	2.50
❑ 126 Anthony Schlegel RC	6.00	2.50
❑ 127 Jon Alston RC	8.00	3.00
❑ 128 Pat Watkins RC	8.00	3.00
❑ 129 Anthony Smith RC	10.00	4.00
❑ 130 David Thomas RC	[illegible]	[illegible]
❑ 131 David Pittman RC	6.00	2.50
❑ 132 Frostee Rucker RC	6.00	2.50
❑ 133 Troy Bergeron RC	6.00	2.50
❑ 134 Freddie Keiaho RC	6.00	2.50
❑ 135 Stephen Tulloch RC	6.00	2.50
❑ 136 Gerris Wilkinson RC	4.00	1.50
❑ 137 Eric Smith RC	6.00	2.50
❑ 138 Garrett Mills RC	8.00	3.00
❑ 139 Skyler Green RC	8.00	3.00
❑ 140 Brodie Croyle RC	20.00	8.00
❑ 141 P.J. Daniels RC	6.00	2.50
❑ 142 Marques Hagans RC	6.00	2.50
❑ 143 Jamar Williams RC	6.00	2.50
❑ 144 Ingle Martin RC	8.00	3.00
❑ 145 Charles Spencer RC	4.00	1.50
❑ 146 Andrew Whitworth RC	4.00	1.50
❑ 147 Jeff King RC	6.00	2.50
❑ 148 Taitusi Lutui RC	6.00	2.50
❑ 149 Quinn Sypniewski RC	6.00	2.50
❑ 150 P.J. Pope RC	6.00	2.50
❑ 151 Wali Lundy RC	8.00	3.00
❑ 152 Jonathan Orr RC	6.00	2.50
❑ 153 Jonathan Lewis RC	4.00	1.50
❑ 154 Adam Jennings RC	6.00	2.50
❑ 155 Jeff Webb RC	6.00	2.50
❑ 156 Cedric Humes RC	8.00	3.00
❑ 157 T.J. Williams RC	8.00	3.00
❑ 158 Todd Watkins RC	6.00	2.50
❑ 159 Bennie Brazell RC	6.00	2.50
❑ 160 Marques Colston RC	30.00	12.00
❑ 161 DonTrell Moore AU RC	12.00	5.00
❑ 162 Brad Smith AU RC	15.00	6.00
❑ 163 Gerald Riggs AU RC	15.00	6.00
❑ 164 Chad Greenway AU RC	15.00	6.00
❑ 165 Cory Rodgers AU RC	15.00	6.00
❑ 166 Darrell Hackney AU RC	12.00	5.00
❑ 167 D.J. Shockley AU RC	15.00	6.00
❑ 168 Dominique Byrd AU RC	12.00	5.00
❑ 169 Joseph Addai AU RC	100.00	50.00
❑ 170 Darnell Bing AU RC	15.00	6.00
❑ 171 Mike Bell AU RC	25.00	10.00
❑ 172 Ernie Sims AU RC	20.00	8.00
❑ 173 Brodrick Bunkley AU RC	15.00	6.00
❑ 174 Hank Baskett AU RC	15.00	6.00
❑ 175 Jerome Harrison AU RC	15.00	6.00
❑ 176 Jimmy Williams AU RC	20.00	8.00
❑ 177 D'Brickashaw Ferguson AU RC	15.00	6.00
❑ 178 Josh Betts AU RC	12.00	5.00
❑ 179 Leonard Pope AU RC	15.00	6.00
❑ 180 Terrence Whitehead AU RC	12.00	5.00
❑ 181 Mathias Kiwanuka AU RC	15.00	6.00
❑ 182 Ashton Youboty AU RC	15.00	6.00
❑ 183 DeMeco Ryans AU RC	20.00	8.00
❑ 184 Thomas Howard AU RC	15.00	6.00
❑ 185 Owen Daniels AU RC	20.00	8.00
❑ 186 Reggie McNeal AU RC	12.00	5.00
❑ 187 Tye Hill AU RC	15.00	6.00
❑ 188 Will Blackmon AU RC	12.00	5.00
❑ 189 Winston Justice AU RC	15.00	6.00
❑ 190 Greg Jennings AU RC	40.00	15.00
❑ 191 M.Leinart AU/175 RC	200.00	100.00
❑ 192 V.Young AU/175 RC	250.00	125.00
❑ 193 Jay Cutler AU/175 RC	200.00	100.00
❑ 194 R.Bush AU/175 RC	250.00	125.00
❑ 195 L.Maroney AU/175 RC	120.00	60.00
❑ 196 L.White AU/175 RC	80.00	40.00
❑ 197 DeA.Williams AU/175 RC	100.00	40.00
❑ 198 V.Davis AU/175 RC	80.00	40.00
❑ 199 S.Holmes AU/175 RC	80.00	40.00
❑ 200 Sin.Moss AU/175 RC	40.00	15.00
❑ 201 Jason Avant JSY AU RC	15.00	6.00
❑ 202 Brian Calhoun JSY AU RC	15.00	6.00
❑ 203 Kellen Clemens JSY AU RC	25.00	10.00
❑ 204 Dem.Williams JSY AU RC	15.00	6.00
❑ 205 Br.Williams JSY AU RC	15.00	6.00
❑ 206 Maurice Drew JSY AU RC	50.00	25.00
❑ 207 Travis Wilson JSY AU RC	15.00	6.00
❑ 208 Joe Klopfenstein JSY AU RC	12.00	5.00
❑ 209 Derek Hagan JSY AU RC	15.00	6.00
❑ 210 A.J. Hawk JSY AU RC	50.00	20.00
❑ 211 Michael Huff JSY AU RC	20.00	8.00
❑ 212 T.Jackson JSY AU RC	30.00	12.00
❑ 213 Omar Jacobs JSY AU RC	15.00	6.00
❑ 214 Mario Williams JSY AU RC	25.00	10.00
❑ 215 Marcedes Lewis JSY AU RC	15.00	6.00
❑ 216 B.Marshall JSY AU RC	25.00	10.00
❑ 217 Chad Jackson JSY AU RC	15.00	6.00
❑ 218 Jerious Norwood JSY AU RC	30.00	12.00
❑ 219 M.Robinson JSY AU RC	[illegible]	[illegible]
❑ 220 Maurice Stovall JSY AU RC	15.00	6.00
❑ 221 Leon Washington JSY AU RC	25.00	10.00
❑ 222 Charlie Whitehurst JSY AU RC	15.00	6.00
❑ 223 K.Jennings JSY AU/399 RC	20.00	8.00
❑ 224 M.McNeill JSY AU/399 RC	15.00	6.00

1999 Leaf Certified

❑ COMPLETE SET (225)	200.00	100.00
❑ COMP.SET w/o RCs 175)	40.00	15.00
❑ 1 Simeon Rice	.60	.25
❑ 2 Frank Sanders	.60	.25
❑ 3 Andre Wadsworth	.40	.15
❑ 4 Larry Centers	.40	.15
❑ 5 Byron Hanspard	.40	.15
❑ 6 Terance Mathis	.60	.25
❑ 7 O.J. Santiago	.40	.15
❑ 8 Chris Calloway	.40	.15
❑ 9 Michael Jackson	.40	.15
❑ 10 Rod Woodson	.00	.25
❑ 11 Pat Johnson	.40	.15
❑ 12 Rob Johnson	.60	.25
❑ 13 Andre Reed	.60	.25
❑ 14 Tim Biakabutuka	.60	.25
❑ 15 Rae Carruth	.40	.15
❑ 16 Fred Lane	.40	.15
❑ 17 Muhsin Muhammad	.60	.25
❑ 18 Wesley Walls	.60	.25
❑ 19 Edgar Bennett	.40	.15
❑ 20 Curtis Conway	.60	.25
❑ 21 Bobby Engram	.60	.25
❑ 22 Jeff Blake	.60	.25
❑ 23 Darnay Scott	.40	.15
❑ 24 Ty Detmer	.60	.25
❑ 25 Sedrick Shaw	.40	.15
❑ 26 Leslie Shepherd	.40	.15
❑ 27 Terry Kirby	.40	.15
❑ 28 Chris Warren	.40	.15
❑ 29 Rocket Ismail	.60	.25
❑ 30 Marcus Nash	.40	.15
❑ 31 Neil Smith	.60	.25
❑ 32 Bubby Brister	.40	.15
❑ 33 Brian Griese	1.00	.40
❑ 34 Germane Crowell	.40	.15
❑ 35 Johnnie Morton	.60	.25
❑ 36 Gus Frerotte	.40	.15
❑ 37 Robert Brooks	.60	.25
❑ 38 Mark Chmura	.40	.15
❑ 39 Derrick Mayes	.40	.15
❑ 40 Jerome Pathon	.40	.15
❑ 41 Jimmy Smith	.60	.25
❑ 42 James Stewart	.60	.25
❑ 43 Tavian Banks	.40	.15
❑ 44 Derrick Alexander WR	.60	.25
❑ 45 Kimble Anders	.60	.25
❑ 46 Elvis Grbac	.60	.25
❑ 47 Derrick Thomas	1.00	.40
❑ 48 Byron Bam Morris	.40	.15

☐ 49	Tony Gonzalez	1.00	.40
☐ 50	John Avery	.40	.15
☐ 51	Tyrone Wheatley	.60	.25
☐ 52	Zach Thomas	1.00	.40
☐ 53	Lamar Thomas	.40	.15
☐ 54	Jeff George	.60	.25
☐ 55	John Randle	.60	.25
☐ 56	Jake Reed	.60	.25
☐ 57	Leroy Hoard	.40	.15
☐ 58	Robert Edwards	.40	.15
☐ 59	Ben Coates	.60	.25
☐ 60	Tony Simmons	.40	.15
☐ 61	Shawn Jefferson	.40	.15
☐ 62	Eddie Kennison	.60	.25
☐ 63	Lamar Smith	.60	.25
☐ 64	Tiki Barber	1.00	.40
☐ 65	Kerry Collins	.60	.25
☐ 66	Ike Hilliard	.40	.15
☐ 67	Gary Brown	.40	.15
☐ 68	Joe Jurevicius	.60	.25
☐ 69	Kent Graham	.40	.15
☐ 70	Dedric Ward	.40	.15
☐ 71	Terry Allen	.60	.25
☐ 72	Neil O'Donnell	.60	.25
☐ 73	Desmond Howard	.60	.25
☐ 74	James Jett	.60	.25
☐ 75	Jon Ritchie	.40	.15
☐ 76	Rickey Dudley	.40	.15
☐ 77	Charles Johnson	.40	.15
☐ 78	Chris Fuamatu-Ma'afala	.40	.15
☐ 79	Hines Ward	1.00	.40
☐ 80	Ryan Leaf	1.00	.40
☐ 81	Jim Harbaugh	.60	.25
☐ 82	Junior Seau	1.00	.40
☐ 83	Mikhael Ricks	.40	.15
☐ 84	J.J. Stokes	.60	.25
☐ 85	Ahman Green	1.00	.40
☐ 86	Tony Banks	.60	.25
☐ 87	Robert Holcombe	.40	.15
☐ 88	Az-Zahir Hakim	.40	.15
☐ 89	Greg Hill	.40	.15
☐ 90	Trent Green	1.00	.40
☐ 91	Eric Zeier	.40	.15
☐ 92	Reidel Anthony	.60	.25
☐ 93	Bert Emanuel	.60	.25
☐ 94	Warren Sapp	.40	.15
☐ 95	Kevin Dyson	.60	.25
☐ 96	Yancey Thigpen	.40	.15
☐ 97	Frank Wycheck	.40	.15
☐ 98	Michael Westbrook	.60	.25
☐ 99	Albert Connell	.40	.15
☐ 100	Darrell Green	.40	.15
☐ 101	Rob Moore	.60	.25
☐ 102	Adrian Murrell	.60	.25
☐ 103	Jake Plummer	1.00	.40
☐ 104	Chris Chandler	.60	.25
☐ 105	Jamal Anderson	1.00	.40
☐ 106	Tim Dwight	1.00	.40
☐ 107	Jermaine Lewis	1.00	.40
☐ 108	Priest Holmes	2.50	1.00
☐ 109	Bruce Smith	1.00	.40
☐ 110	Eric Moulds	1.00	.40
☐ 111	Antowain Smith	1.50	.60
☐ 112	Curtis Enis	1.00	.40
☐ 113	Corey Dillon	1.50	.60
☐ 114	Michael Irvin	1.00	.40
☐ 115	Ed McCaffrey	1.00	.40
☐ 116	Shannon Sharpe	1.00	.40
☐ 117	Terrell Davis	1.50	.60
☐ 118	Charlie Batch	1.50	.60
☐ 119	Antonio Freeman	1.00	.40
☐ 120	Dorsey Levens	1.00	.40
☐ 121	Marvin Harrison	1.50	.60
☐ 122	Peyton Manning	5.00	2.00
☐ 123	Keenan McCardell	1.00	.40
☐ 124	Fred Taylor	1.50	.60
☐ 125	Andre Rison	1.00	.40
☐ 126	O.J. McDuffie	1.00	.40
☐ 127	Karim Abdul-Jabbar	1.00	.40
☐ 128	Randy Moss	4.00	1.50
☐ 129	Terry Glenn	1.00	.40
☐ 130	Vinny Testaverde	1.00	.40
☐ 131	Keyshawn Johnson	1.00	.40
☐ 132	Curtis Martin	1.00	.40
☐ 133	Wayne Chrebet	1.00	.40
☐ 134	Napoleon Kaufman	1.00	.40
☐ 135	Charles Woodson	1.00	.40
☐ 136	Duce Staley	1.50	.60
☐ 137	Kordell Stewart	1.00	.40
☐ 138	Terrell Owens	1.50	.60
☐ 139	Ricky Watters	1.00	.40
☐ 140	Joey Galloway	1.00	.40
☐ 141	Jon Kitna	1.00	.40
☐ 142	Isaac Bruce	1.50	.60
☐ 143	Jacquez Green	1.00	.40
☐ 144	Warrick Dunn	1.00	.40
☐ 145	Mike Alstott	1.00	.40
☐ 146	Trent Dilfer	1.00	.40
☐ 147	Steve McNair	1.00	.40
☐ 148	Eddie George	1.50	.60
☐ 149	Skip Hicks	1.00	.40
☐ 150	Brad Johnson	1.50	.60
☐ 151	Doug Flutie	1.50	.60
☐ 152	Thurman Thomas	1.00	.40
☐ 153	Carl Pickens	1.00	.40
☐ 154	Emmitt Smith	5.00	2.00
☐ 155	Troy Aikman	5.00	2.00
☐ 156	Deion Sanders	1.50	.60
☐ 157	John Elway	8.00	3.00
☐ 158	Rod Smith	1.00	.40
☐ 159	Barry Sanders	8.00	3.00
☐ 160	Herman Moore	1.50	.60
☐ 161	Brett Favre	8.00	3.00
☐ 162	Mark Brunell	1.50	.60
☐ 163	Warren Moon	1.50	.60
☐ 164	Dan Marino	8.00	3.00
☐ 165	Randall Cunningham	1.50	.60
☐ 166	Robert Smith	1.50	.60
☐ 167	Cris Carter	1.50	.60
☐ 168	Drew Bledsoe	3.00	1.25
☐ 169	Tim Brown	1.50	.60
☐ 170	Jerome Bettis	1.50	.60
☐ 171	Natrone Means	1.00	.40
☐ 172	Jerry Rice	5.00	2.00
☐ 173	Steve Young	3.00	1.25
☐ 174	Garrison Hearst	1.50	.60
☐ 175	Marshall Faulk	3.00	1.25
☐ 176	David Boston RC	5.00	2.00
☐ 177	Jeff Paulk RC	2.00	.75
☐ 178	Reginald Kelly RC	2.00	.75
☐ 179	Scott Covington RC	5.00	2.00
☐ 180	Chris McAlister RC	3.00	1.25
☐ 181	Shawn Bryson RC	5.00	2.00
☐ 182	Peerless Price RC	5.00	2.00
☐ 183	Cade McNown RC	3.00	1.25
☐ 184	Michael Bishop RC	5.00	2.00
☐ 185	D'Wayne Bates RC	3.00	1.25
☐ 186	Marty Booker RC	5.00	2.00
☐ 187	Akili Smith RC	2.00	.75
☐ 188	Craig Yeast RC	3.00	1.25
☐ 189	Tim Couch RC	5.00	2.00
☐ 190	Kevin Johnson RC	5.00	2.00
☐ 191	Wane McGarity RC	2.00	.75
☐ 192	Olandis Gary RC	5.00	2.00
☐ 193	Travis McGriff RC	2.00	.75
☐ 194	Sedrick Irvin RC	2.00	.75
☐ 195	Chris Claiborne RC	2.00	.75
☐ 196	De'Mond Parker RC	2.00	.75
☐ 197	Dee Miller RC	2.00	.75
☐ 198	Edgerrin James RC	15.00	6.00
☐ 199	Mike Cloud RC	3.00	1.25
☐ 200	Larry Parker RC	5.00	2.00
☐ 201	Cecil Collins RC	2.00	.75
☐ 202	James Johnson RC	3.00	1.25
☐ 203	Rob Konrad RC	5.00	2.00
☐ 204	Daunte Culpepper RC	15.00	6.00
☐ 205	Jim Kleinsasser RC	5.00	2.00
☐ 206	Kevin Faulk RC	5.00	2.00
☐ 207	Andy Katzenmoyer RC	3.00	1.25
☐ 208	Ricky Williams RC	8.00	3.00
☐ 209	Joe Montgomery RC	3.00	1.25
☐ 210	Sean Bennett RC	2.00	.75
☐ 211	Dameane Douglas RC	5.00	2.00
☐ 212	Donovan McNabb RC	20.00	7.50
☐ 213	Na Brown RC	3.00	1.25
☐ 214	Amos Zereoue RC	5.00	2.00
☐ 215	Troy Edwards RC	3.00	1.25
☐ 216	Jermaine Fazande RC	3.00	1.25
☐ 217	Tai Streets RC	5.00	2.00
☐ 218	Brock Huard RC	5.00	2.00
☐ 219	Charlie Rogers RC	3.00	1.25
☐ 220	Karsten Bailey RC	3.00	1.25
☐ 221	Joe Germaine RC	3.00	1.25
☐ 222	Torry Holt RC	10.00	4.00
☐ 223	Shaun King RC	3.00	1.25
☐ 224	Jevon Kearse RC	8.00	3.00
☐ 225	Champ Bailey RC	6.00	2.50

2000 Leaf Certified

☐	COMP.SET w/o RC's (150)	40.00	15.00
☐ 1	Frank Sanders	.40	.15
☐ 2	Rob Moore	.60	.25
☐ 3	Simeon Rice	.60	.25
☐ 4	David Boston	1.00	.40
☐ 5	Tim Dwight	1.00	.40
☐ 6	Jamal Anderson	1.00	.40
☐ 7	Chris Chandler	.40	.15
☐ 8	Terance Mathis	.60	.25
☐ 9	Priest Holmes	1.25	.50
☐ 10	Rod Woodson	.60	.25
☐ 11	Tony Banks	.40	.15
☐ 12	Jermaine Lewis	.40	.15
☐ 13	Shannon Sharpe	.40	.15
☐ 14	Qadry Ismail	.60	.25
☐ 15	Doug Flutie	1.00	.40
☐ 16	Antowain Smith	.60	.25
☐ 17	Peerless Price	.60	.25
☐ 18	Rob Johnson	.40	.15
☐ 19	Muhsin Muhammad	.60	.25
☐ 20	Wesley Walls	.40	.15
☐ 21	Tim Biakabutuka	.40	.15
☐ 22	Steve Beuerlein	.40	.15
☐ 23	Patrick Jeffers	.40	.15
☐ 24	Natrone Means	.40	.15
☐ 25	Curtis Enis	.40	.15
☐ 26	Bobby Engram	.40	.15
☐ 27	Marcus Robinson	1.00	.40
☐ 28	Eddie Kennison	.40	.15
☐ 29	Marty Booker	.60	.25
☐ 30	Darnay Scott	.40	.15
☐ 31	Carl Pickens	.40	.15
☐ 32	Karim Abdul-Jabbar	.40	.15
☐ 33	Errict Rhett	.40	.15
☐ 34	Darrin Chiaverini	.40	.15
☐ 35	Randall Cunningham	.40	.15
☐ 36	Michael Irvin	.40	.15
☐ 37	Rocket Ismail	.40	.15
☐ 38	Ed McCaffrey	1.00	.40
☐ 39	Rod Smith	.40	.15
☐ 40	Herman Moore	.60	.25
☐ 41	Johnnie Morton	.40	.15
☐ 42	James Stewart	.40	.15
☐ 43	Bill Schroeder	.60	.25
☐ 44	Ahman Green	1.00	.40
☐ 45	Terrence Wilkins	.40	.15
☐ 46	Keenan McCardell	.40	.15
☐ 47	Derrick Alexander	.40	.15
☐ 48	Elvis Grbac	.40	.15
☐ 49	Tony Gonzalez	.40	.15
☐ 50	O.J. McDuffie	.40	.15
☐ 51	Tony Martin	.40	.15
☐ 52	James Johnson	.40	.15
☐ 53	Thurman Thomas	.40	.15
☐ 54	Jay Fiedler	1.00	.40
☐ 55	Damon Huard	.40	.15
☐ 56	Leroy Hoard	.40	.15
☐ 57	Terry Glenn	.60	.25
☐ 58	Kevin Faulk	.40	.15
☐ 59	Jeff Blake	.40	.15
☐ 60	Jake Reed	.40	.15
☐ 61	Amani Toomer	.40	.15
☐ 62	Kerry Collins	.40	.15
☐ 63	Ike Hilliard	.40	.15
☐ 64	Joe Montgomery	.40	.15
☐ 65	Vinny Testaverde	.40	.15
☐ 66	Wayne Chrebet	.40	.15
☐ 67	Ray Lucas	.60	.25
☐ 68	Napoleon Kaufman	.60	.25
☐ 69	Charles Woodson	.40	.15

❑ 70 Tyrone Wheatley	.40	.15
❑ 71 Rich Gannon	1.00	.40
❑ 72 Duce Staley	1.00	.40
❑ 73 Kordell Stewart	.60	.25
❑ 74 Jerome Bettis	1.00	.40
❑ 75 Troy Edwards	.40	.15
❑ 76 Junior Seau	1.00	.40
❑ 77 Jim Harbaugh	.40	.15
❑ 78 Curtis Conway	.60	.25
❑ 79 Jermaine Fazande	.40	.15
❑ 80 Terrell Owens	1.00	.40
❑ 81 Charlie Garner	.60	.25
❑ 82 Garrison Hearst	.40	.15
❑ 83 Jeff Garcia	1.00	.40
❑ 84 Derrick Mayes	.40	.15
❑ 85 Az-Zahir Hakim	.40	.15
❑ 86 Mike Alstott	1.00	.40
❑ 87 Warrick Dunn	1.00	.40
❑ 88 Jacquez Green	.40	.15
❑ 89 Warren Sapp	.40	.15
❑ 90 Yancey Thigpen	.40	.15
❑ 91 Kevin Dyson	.40	.15
❑ 92 Frank Wycheck	.40	.15
❑ 93 Jovon Kearse	1.00	.40
❑ 94 Adrian Murrell	.40	.15
❑ 95 Bruce Smith	.40	.15
❑ 96 Michael Westbrook	.40	.15
❑ 97 Albert Connell	.40	.15
❑ 98 Champ Bailey	.60	.25
❑ 99 Jeff George	.40	.15
❑ 100 Deion Sanders	1.00	.40
❑ 101 Jake Plummer	1.00	.40
❑ 102 Eric Moulds	1.50	.60
❑ 103 Cade McNown	.40	.15
❑ 104 Corey Dillon	1.50	.60
❑ 105 Akili Smith	.60	.25
❑ 106 Tim Couch	1.00	.40
❑ 107 Kevin Johnson	1.50	.60
❑ 108 Emmitt Smith	3.00	1.25
❑ 109 Troy Aikman	3.00	1.25
❑ 110 Joey Galloway	1.00	.40
❑ 111 John Elway	5.00	2.00
❑ 112 Terrell Davis	1.00	.40
❑ 113 Olandis Gary	1.50	.60
❑ 114 Brian Griese	1.00	.40
❑ 115 Charlie Batch	1.50	.60
❑ 116 Barry Sanders	4.00	1.50
❑ 117 Germane Crowell	.60	.25
❑ 118 Brett Favre	5.00	2.00
❑ 119 Dorsey Levens	.60	.25
❑ 120 Antonio Freeman	1.50	.60
❑ 121 Peyton Manning	4.00	1.50
❑ 122 Edgerrin James	2.50	1.00
❑ 123 Marvin Harrison	1.50	.60
❑ 124 Mark Brunell	1.00	.40
❑ 125 Fred Taylor	1.00	.40
❑ 126 Jimmy Smith	1.00	.40
❑ 127 Dan Marino	5.00	2.00
❑ 128 Randy Moss	3.00	1.25
❑ 129 Daunte Culpepper	2.00	.75
❑ 130 Cris Carter	1.50	.60
❑ 131 Robert Smith	1.50	.60
❑ 132 Drew Bledsoe	2.00	.75
❑ 133 Ricky Williams	1.00	.40
❑ 134 Curtis Martin	1.50	.60
❑ 135 Tim Brown	1.50	.60
❑ 136 Donovan McNabb	2.50	1.00
❑ 137 Jerry Rice	3.00	1.25
❑ 138 Steve Young	2.00	.75
❑ 139 Jon Kitna	1.50	.60
❑ 140 Ricky Watters	.60	.25
❑ 141 Kurt Warner	3.00	1.25
❑ 142 Marshall Faulk	2.00	.75
❑ 143 Torry Holt	1.50	.60
❑ 144 Isaac Bruce	1.50	.60
❑ 145 Shaun King	.40	.15
❑ 146 Keyshawn Johnson	1.50	.60
❑ 147 Eddie George	1.00	.40
❑ 148 Steve McNair	1.50	.60
❑ 149 Stephen Davis	1.50	.60
❑ 150 Brad Johnson	1.50	.60
❑ 151 Rogers Beckett RC	4.00	1.50
❑ 152 Erik Flowers RC	4.00	1.50
❑ 153 Demario Brown RC	2.50	1.00
❑ 154 Doug Johnson RC	5.00	2.00
❑ 155 Deon Grant RC	4.00	1.50
❑ 156 Ian Gold RC	4.00	1.50
❑ 157 Brian Urlacher RC	20.00	7.50
❑ 158 Frank Murphy RC	2.50	1.00
❑ 159 James Whalen RC	2.50	1.00
❑ 160 JaJuan Dawson RC	2.50	1.00
❑ 161 William Bartee RC	4.00	1.50
❑ 162 Aaron Shea RC	1.00	.40
❑ 163 Deltha O'Neal RC	5.00	2.00
❑ 164 Jarious Jackson RC	4.00	1.50
❑ 165 Muneer Moore RC	2.50	1.00
❑ 166 Hank Poteat RC	4.00	1.50
❑ 167 Jacoby Shepherd RC	2.50	1.00
❑ 168 Ben Kelly RC	2.50	1.00
❑ 169 Orantes Grant RC	2.50	1.00
❑ 170 Chris Hovan RC	4.00	1.50
❑ 171 Leon Murray RC	2.50	1.00
❑ 172 Marc Bulger RC	10.00	4.00
❑ 173 Chad Morton RC	5.00	2.00
❑ 174 Na'il Diggs RC	4.00	1.50
❑ 175 Shaun Ellis RC	5.00	2.00
❑ 176 John Abraham RC	5.00	2.00
❑ 177 Fred Robbins RC	2.50	1.00
❑ 178 Marcus Knight RC	4.00	1.50
❑ 179 Thomas Hamner RC	2.50	1.00
❑ 180 Cornelius Griffin RC	4.00	1.50
❑ 181 Raynoch Thompson RC	4.00	1.50
❑ 182 Paul Smith RC	4.00	1.50
❑ 183 Ahmed Plummer RC	5.00	2.00
❑ 184 John Engelberger RC	4.00	1.50
❑ 185 Darren Howard RC	4.00	1.50
❑ 186 Corey Moore RC	2.50	1.00
❑ 187 Joe Hamilton RC	4.00	1.50
❑ 188 Rob Morris RC	4.00	1.50
❑ 189 Keith Bulluck RC	5.00	2.00
❑ 190 Todd Husak RC	5.00	2.00
❑ 191 Mareno Philyaw RC	3.00	1.25
❑ 192 Kwame Cavil RC	3.00	1.25
❑ 193 Sammy Morris RC	6.00	2.50
❑ 194 Avion Black RC	5.00	2.00
❑ 195 Bashir Yamini RC	3.00	1.25
❑ 196 Curtis Keaton RC	5.00	2.00
❑ 197 Mike Anderson RC	8.00	3.00
❑ 198 Bubba Franks RC	6.00	2.50
❑ 199 Anthony Lucas RC	3.00	1.25
❑ 200 Rondell Mealey RC	3.00	1.25
❑ 201 Terrelle Smith RC	5.00	2.00
❑ 202 Frank Moreau RC	5.00	2.00
❑ 203 Deon Dyer RC	5.00	2.00
❑ 204 Quinton Spotwood RC	3.00	1.25
❑ 205 Troy Walters RC	10.00	4.00
❑ 206 Doug Chapman RC	5.00	2.00
❑ 207 Tom Brady RC	250.00	150.00
❑ 208 Sherrod Gideon RC	3.00	1.25
❑ 209 Ron Dixon RC	5.00	2.00
❑ 210 Anthony Becht RC	6.00	2.50
❑ 211 James Williams RC	5.00	2.00
❑ 212 Sebastian Janikowski RC	6.00	2.50
❑ 213 Corey Simon RC	6.00	2.50
❑ 214 Gari Scott RC	3.00	1.25
❑ 215 Dante Hall RC	12.00	5.00
❑ 216 Tim Rattay RC	6.00	2.50
❑ 217 Chafie Fields RC	3.00	1.25
❑ 218 Trung Canidate RC	5.00	2.00
❑ 219 Chris Coleman RC	6.00	2.50
❑ 220 Erron Kinney RC	6.00	2.50
❑ 221 Thomas Jones RC	15.00	6.00
❑ 222 Travis Taylor RC	10.00	4.00
❑ 223 Chris Redman RC	8.00	3.00
❑ 224 Jamal Lewis RC	25.00	10.00
❑ 225 Dez White RC	10.00	4.00
❑ 226 Peter Warrick RC	10.00	4.00
❑ 227 Ron Dugans RC	8.00	3.00
❑ 228 Courtney Brown RC	10.00	4.00
❑ 229 Travis Prentice RC	8.00	3.00
❑ 230 Dennis Northcutt RC	10.00	4.00
❑ 231 Michael Wiley RC	8.00	3.00
❑ 232 Chris Cole RC	8.00	3.00
❑ 233 Reuben Droughns RC	12.00	5.00
❑ 234 R.Jay Soward RC	8.00	3.00
❑ 235 Shyrone Stith RC	8.00	3.00
❑ 236 Sylvester Morris RC	8.00	3.00
❑ 237 J.R. Redmond RC	8.00	3.00
❑ 238 Ron Dayne RC	10.00	4.00
❑ 239 Chad Pennington RC	25.00	10.00
❑ 240 Laveranues Coles RC	12.00	5.00
❑ 241 Jerry Porter RC	12.00	5.00
❑ 242 Todd Pinkston RC	10.00	4.00
❑ 243 Plaxico Burress RC	20.00	7.50
❑ 244 Danny Farmer RC	8.00	3.00
❑ 245 Tee Martin RC	10.00	4.00
❑ 246 Trevor Gaylor RC	8.00	3.00
❑ 247 Giovanni Carmazzi RC	8.00	3.00
❑ 248 Darrell Jackson RC	20.00	7.50
❑ 249 Shaun Alexander RC	50.00	20.00
❑ 250 Chris Samuels RC	8.00	3.00

2001 Leaf Certified Materials

❑ COMP.SET w/o SP's (100)	30.00	12.50
❑ 1 Aaron Brooks	1.00	.40
❑ 2 Ahman Green	1.00	.40
❑ 3 Akili Smith	.40	.15
❑ 4 Amani Toomer	.60	.25
❑ 5 Antonio Freeman	1.00	.40
❑ 6 Barry Sanders	2.00	.75
❑ 7 Brad Johnson	1.00	.40
❑ 8 Brett Favre	3.00	1.25
❑ 9 Brian Griese	1.00	.40
❑ 10 Brian Urlacher	1.50	.60
❑ 11 Bruce Smith	.40	.15
❑ 12 Cade McNown	.40	.15
❑ 13 Chad Pennington	1.50	.60
❑ 14 Charlie Batch	1.00	.40
❑ 15 Charlie Garner	.60	.25
❑ 16 Corey Dillon	1.00	.40
❑ 17 Cris Carter	1.00	.40
❑ 18 Curtis Martin	1.00	.40
❑ 19 Dan Marino	3.00	1.25
❑ 20 Darrell Jackson	.40	.15
❑ 21 Daunte Culpepper	1.00	.40
❑ 22 David Boston	1.00	.40
❑ 23 Derrick Alexander	.60	.25
❑ 24 Donovan McNabb	1.25	.50
❑ 25 Dorsey Levens	.60	.25
❑ 26 Doug Flutie	1.00	.40
❑ 27 Drew Bledsoe	1.25	.50
❑ 28 Ed McCaffrey	1.00	.40
❑ 29 Eddie George	1.00	.40
❑ 30 Edgerrin James	1.25	.50
❑ 31 Elvis Grbac	.60	.25
❑ 32 Emmitt Smith	2.00	.75
❑ 33 Eric Moulds	1.00	.40
❑ 34 Frank Wycheck	.40	.15
❑ 35 Fred Taylor	1.00	.40
❑ 36 Ike Hilliard	.60	.25
❑ 37 Isaac Bruce	1.00	.40
❑ 38 Jacquez Green	.40	.15
❑ 39 Jake Plummer	.60	.25
❑ 40 Jamal Anderson	1.00	.40
❑ 41 Jamal Lewis	1.50	.60
❑ 42 James Stewart	.60	.25
❑ 43 Jay Fiedler	1.00	.40
❑ 44 Jeff Garcia	1.00	.40
❑ 45 Jeff George	.60	.25
❑ 46 Jerome Bettis	1.00	.40
❑ 47 Jerry Rice	2.00	.75
❑ 48 Jevon Kearse	.60	.25
❑ 49 Jimmy Smith	.60	.25
❑ 50 Joe Horn	.60	.25
❑ 51 Joey Galloway	.60	.25
❑ 52 John Elway	3.00	1.25
❑ 53 Junior Seau	1.00	.40
❑ 54 Keenan McCardell	.40	.15
❑ 55 Kerry Collins	1.00	.40
❑ 56 Keyshawn Johnson	1.00	.40
❑ 57 Kurt Warner	2.00	.75
❑ 58 Lamar Smith	.60	.25
❑ 59 Laveranues Coles	1.00	.40
❑ 60 Marcus Robinson	1.00	.40
❑ 61 Mark Brunell	1.00	.40
❑ 62 Marshall Faulk	1.25	.50
❑ 63 Marvin Harrison	1.00	.40
❑ 64 Matt Hasselbeck	.60	.25

❑ 65 Mike Alstott	1.00	.40
❑ 66 Mike Anderson	1.00	.40
❑ 67 Muhsin Muhammad	.60	.25
❑ 68 Peter Warrick	1.00	.40
❑ 69 Peyton Manning	2.50	1.00
❑ 70 Plaxico Burress	1.00	.40
❑ 71 Randy Moss	2.00	.75
❑ 72 Ray Lewis	1.00	.40
❑ 73 Rich Gannon	1.00	.40
❑ 74 Ricky Watters	.60	.25
❑ 75 Ricky Williams	1.00	.40
❑ 76 Rob Johnson	1.00	.40
❑ 77 Rod Smith	.60	.25
❑ 78 Ron Dayne	1.00	.40
❑ 79 Shannon Sharpe	.60	.25
❑ 80 Shaun Alexander	1.25	.50
❑ 81 Stephen Davis	1.00	.40
❑ 82 Steve McNair	1.00	.40
❑ 83 Steve Young	1.00	.40
❑ 84 Sylvester Morris	.40	.15
❑ 85 Terrell Davis	1.00	.40
❑ 86 Terrell Owens	1.00	.40
❑ 87 Terry Glenn	.60	.25
❑ 88 Thomas Jones	.60	.25
❑ 89 Tiki Barber	1.00	.40
❑ 90 Tim Brown	1.00	.40
❑ 91 Tim Couch	.60	.25
❑ 92 Tony Gonzalez	.60	.25
❑ 93 Torry Holt	1.00	.40
❑ 94 Travis Taylor	.60	.25
❑ 95 Troy Aikman	1.50	.60
❑ 96 Tyrone Wheatley	.60	.25
❑ 97 Vinny Testaverde	.60	.25
❑ 98 Warren Sapp	.60	.25
❑ 99 Warrick Dunn	1.00	.40
❑ 100 Wayne Chrebet	.60	.25
❑ 101 Chris Taylor RC	6.00	2.50
❑ 102 Ken-Yon Rambo RC	6.00	2.50
❑ 103 Correll Buckhalter RC	12.00	5.00
❑ 104 A.J. Feeley RC	10.00	4.00
❑ 105 Josh Booty RC	10.00	4.00
❑ 106 LaMont Jordan RC	25.00	10.00
❑ 107 Alge Crumpler RC	12.00	5.00
❑ 108 Jamal Reynolds RC	10.00	4.00
❑ 109 Nate Clements RC	10.00	4.00
❑ 110 Will Allen RC	6.00	2.50
❑ 111 Santana Moss FF RC	25.00	10.00
❑ 112 Chad Johnson FF RC	50.00	25.00
❑ 113 Chris Chambers FF RC	25.00	10.00
❑ 114 David Terrell FF RC	15.00	6.00
❑ 115 Freddie Mitchell FF RC	15.00	6.00
❑ 116 Koren Robinson FF RC	15.00	6.00
❑ 117 Quincy Morgan FF RC	15.00	6.00
❑ 118 Reggie Wayne FF RC	30.00	12.50
❑ 119 Robert Ferguson FF RC	15.00	6.00
❑ 120 Rod Gardner FF RC	15.00	6.00
❑ 121 Snoop Minnis FF RC	10.00	4.00
❑ 122 Josh Heupel FF RC	15.00	6.00
❑ 123 Anthony Thomas FF RC	15.00	6.00
❑ 124 Deuce McAllister FF RC	30.00	12.50
❑ 125 James Jackson FF RC	15.00	6.00
❑ 126 Travis Minor FF RC	10.00	4.00
❑ 127 Kevan Barlow FF RC	15.00	6.00
❑ 128 LaDain Tomlinson FF RC	100.00	60.00
❑ 129 Todd Heap FF RC	15.00	6.00
❑ 130 Michael Bennett FF RC	15.00	6.00
❑ 131 Rudi Johnson FF RC	30.00	12.50
❑ 132 Travis Henry FF RC	30.00	12.50
❑ 133 Michael Vick FF RC	50.00	20.00
❑ 134 Drew Brees FF RC	50.00	25.00
❑ 135 Chris Weinke FF RC	15.00	6.00
❑ 136 Quincy Carter FF RC	15.00	6.00
❑ 137 Mike McMahon FF RC	15.00	6.00
❑ 138 Jesse Palmer FF RC	15.00	6.00
❑ 139 Marq Tuiasosopo FF RC	15.00	6.00
❑ 140 Dan Morgan FF RC	15.00	6.00
❑ 141 Gerard Warren FF RC	15.00	6.00
❑ 142 Leonard Davis FF RC	10.00	4.00
❑ 143 Andre Carter FF RC	15.00	6.00
❑ 144 Justin Smith FF RC	15.00	6.00
❑ 145 Sage Rosenfels FF RC	15.00	6.00

2002 Leaf Certified

❑ COMP.SET w/o SP's (100)	25.00	10.00
❑ 1 David Boston	1.00	.40
❑ 2 Jake Plummer	.60	.25
❑ 3 Michael Vick	2.00	.75
❑ 4 Jamal Anderson	.60	.25
❑ 5 Chris Redman	.40	.15

❑ 6 Ray Lewis	1.00	.40
❑ 7 Eric Moulds	.60	.25
❑ 8 Travis Henry	1.00	.40
❑ 9 Nate Clements	.40	.15
❑ 10 Chris Weinke	.60	.25
❑ 11 Muhsin Muhammad	.60	.25
❑ 12 Wesley Walls	.40	.15
❑ 13 Anthony Thomas	.60	.25
❑ 14 Brian Urlacher	1.50	.60
❑ 15 Dez White	.40	.15
❑ 16 Corey Dillon	.60	.25
❑ 17 Peter Warrick	.60	.25
❑ 18 Tim Couch	.60	.25
❑ 19 Kevin Johnson	.60	.25
❑ 20 James Jackson	.40	.15
❑ 21 Emmitt Smith	2.50	1.00
❑ 22 Quincy Carter	.60	.25
❑ 23 Brian Griese	1.00	.40
❑ 24 Ed McCaffrey	1.00	.40
❑ 25 Rod Smith	.60	.25
❑ 26 Terrell Davis	1.00	.40
❑ 27 Mike Anderson	1.00	.40
❑ 28 Germane Crowell	.40	.15
❑ 29 James Stewart	.60	.25
❑ 30 Charlie Batch	.60	.25
❑ 31 Antonio Freeman	1.00	.40
❑ 32 Brett Favre	2.50	1.00
❑ 33 Ahman Green	1.00	.40
❑ 34 LeRoy Butler	.40	.15
❑ 35 Edgerrin James	1.25	.50
❑ 36 Marvin Harrison	1.00	.40
❑ 37 Peyton Manning	2.00	.75
❑ 38 Fred Taylor	1.00	.40
❑ 39 Jimmy Smith	.60	.25
❑ 40 Mark Brunell	1.00	.40
❑ 41 Keenan McCardell	.40	.15
❑ 42 Tony Gonzalez	.60	.25
❑ 43 Priest Holmes	1.25	.50
❑ 44 Jay Fiedler	.60	.25
❑ 45 Chris Chambers	1.00	.40
❑ 46 Zach Thomas	1.00	.40
❑ 47 Travis Minor	.40	.15
❑ 48 Cris Carter	1.00	.40
❑ 49 Daunte Culpepper	1.00	.40
❑ 50 Randy Moss	2.00	.75
❑ 51 Drew Bledsoe	1.25	.50
❑ 52 Tom Brady	2.50	1.00
❑ 53 Antowain Smith	.60	.25
❑ 54 Troy Brown	.40	.15
❑ 55 Aaron Brooks	1.00	.40
❑ 56 Ricky Williams	1.00	.40
❑ 57 Ron Dayne	.60	.25
❑ 58 Kerry Collins	.60	.25
❑ 59 Michael Strahan	.60	.25
❑ 60 Amani Toomer	.60	.25
❑ 61 Chad Pennington	1.25	.50
❑ 62 Curtis Martin	1.00	.40
❑ 63 Vinny Testaverde	.60	.25
❑ 64 Wayne Chrebet	.60	.25
❑ 65 Charles Woodson	.60	.25
❑ 66 Rich Gannon	1.00	.40
❑ 67 Tim Brown	1.00	.40
❑ 68 Jerry Rice	2.00	.75
❑ 69 Tyrone Wheatley	.60	.25
❑ 70 Donovan McNabb	1.25	.50
❑ 71 Duce Staley	1.00	.40
❑ 72 Todd Pinkston	.60	.25
❑ 73 Correll Buckhalter	.60	.25
❑ 74 Jerome Bettis	1.00	.40
❑ 75 Kordell Stewart	.60	.25
❑ 76 Plaxico Burress	.60	.25
❑ 77 Hines Ward	1.00	.40
❑ 78 Junior Seau	1.00	.40
❑ 79 LaDainian Tomlinson	1.50	.60
❑ 80 Doug Flutie	1.00	.40
❑ 81 Terrell Owens	1.00	.40
❑ 82 Jeff Garcia	1.00	.40
❑ 83 Ricky Watters	.60	.25
❑ 84 Shaun Alexander	1.25	.50
❑ 85 Koren Robinson	.60	.25
❑ 86 Isaac Bruce	1.00	.40
❑ 87 Kurt Warner	1.00	.40
❑ 88 Marshall Faulk	1.00	.40
❑ 89 Torry Holt	1.00	.40
❑ 90 Keyshawn Johnson	1.00	.40
❑ 91 Mike Alstott	1.00	.40
❑ 92 Warren Sapp	.60	.25
❑ 93 Brad Johnson	.60	.25
❑ 94 Eddie George	1.00	.40
❑ 95 Jevon Kearse	.60	.25
❑ 96 Steve McNair	1.00	.40
❑ 97 Derrick Mason	.60	.25
❑ 98 Frank Wycheck	.40	.15
❑ 99 Champ Bailey	.60	.25
❑ 100 Stephen Davis	.60	.25
❑ 101 Ladell Betts JSY RC	8.00	3.00
❑ 102 Antonio Bryant JSY RC	8.00	3.00
❑ 103 Reche Caldwell JSY RC	8.00	3.00
❑ 104 David Carr JSY RC	15.00	6.00
❑ 105 Tim Carter JSY RC	5.00	2.00
❑ 106 Eric Crouch JSY RC	8.00	3.00
❑ 107 Rohan Davey JSY RC	8.00	3.00
❑ 108 Andre Davis JSY RC	5.00	2.00
❑ 109 T.J. Duckett JSY RC	8.00	3.00
❑ 110 DeShaun Foster JSY RC	8.00	3.00
❑ 111 Jabar Gaffney JSY RC	8.00	3.00
❑ 112 Daniel Graham JSY RC	8.00	3.00
❑ 113 William Green FB RC	8.00	3.00
❑ 114 Joey Harrington JSY RC	10.00	4.00
❑ 115 David Garrard JSY RC	15.00	6.00
❑ 116 Ron Johnson JSY RC	5.00	2.00
❑ 117 Ashley Lelie JSY RC	15.00	6.00
❑ 118 Josh McCown JSY RC	10.00	4.00
❑ 119 Maurice Morris JSY RC	8.00	3.00
❑ 120 Julius Peppers JSY RC	15.00	6.00
❑ 121 Clinton Portis JSY RC	25.00	10.00
❑ 122 Patrick Ramsey JSY RC	8.00	3.00
❑ 123 Antwaan Randle El JSY RC	10.00	4.00
❑ 124 Josh Reed JSY RC	8.00	3.00
❑ 125 Cliff Russell JSY RC	5.00	2.00
❑ 126 Jeremy Shockey JSY RC	25.00	10.00
❑ 127 Donte Stallworth JSY RC	12.00	5.00
❑ 128 Travis Stephens JSY RC	5.00	2.00
❑ 129 Javon Walker JSY RC	12.00	5.00
❑ 130 Marquise Walker JSY RC	5.00	2.00
❑ 131 Roy Williams JSY RC	15.00	6.00
❑ 132 Mike Williams JSY RC	5.00	2.00

2003 Leaf Certified Materials

❑ COMP.SET w/o SP's (150)	30.00	12.50
❑ 1 Jake Plummer	.60	.25
❑ 2 David Boston	.60	.25
❑ 3 MarTay Jenkins	.40	.15
❑ 4 Marcel Shipp	.60	.25
❑ 5 Michael Vick	2.50	1.00
❑ 6 T.J. Duckett	.60	.25
❑ 7 Chris Redman	.40	.15
❑ 8 Ray Lewis	1.00	.40
❑ 9 Jamal Lewis	1.00	.40
❑ 10 Eric Moulds	.60	.25
❑ 11 Nate Clements	.40	.15
❑ 12 Travis Henry	.60	.25

- ❑ 13 Drew Bledsoe 1.00 .40
- ❑ 14 Peerless Price .60 .25
- ❑ 15 Josh Reed .60 .25
- ❑ 16 Wesley Walls .40 .15
- ❑ 17 Muhsin Muhammad .60 .25
- ❑ 18 Julius Peppers 1.00 .40
- ❑ 19 Dez White .40 .15
- ❑ 20 Mike Brown .60 .25
- ❑ 21 Brian Urlacher 1.50 .60
- ❑ 22 Anthony Thomas .60 .25
- ❑ 23 David Terrell .60 .25
- ❑ 24 Corey Dillon .60 .25
- ❑ 25 Peter Warrick .60 .25
- ❑ 26 Josh McCown .60 .25
- ❑ 27 Dennis Northcutt .60 .25
- ❑ 28 Kevin Johnson .60 .25
- ❑ 29 Tim Couch .40 .15
- ❑ 30 Gerard Warren .40 .15
- ❑ 31 William Green .60 .25
- ❑ 32 Antonio Bryant .60 .25
- ❑ 33 Darren Woodson .40 .15
- ❑ 34 Emmitt Smith 2.50 1.00
- ❑ 35 Quincy Carter .60 .25
- ❑ 36 Roy Williams 1.00 .40
- ❑ 37 Brian Griese 1.00 .40
- ❑ 38 Ed McCaffrey 1.00 .40
- ❑ 39 Mike Anderson .60 .25
- ❑ 40 Rod Smith .60 .25
- ❑ 41 Clinton Portis 1.50 .60
- ❑ 42 Ashley Lelie 1.00 .40
- ❑ 43 Cory Schlesinger .40 .15
- ❑ 44 Germane Crowell .40 .15
- ❑ 45 James Stewart .60 .25
- ❑ 46 Scotty Anderson .40 .15
- ❑ 47 Joey Harrington 1.50 .60
- ❑ 48 Brett Favre 2.50 1.00
- ❑ 49 Terry Glenn .40 .15
- ❑ 50 Ahman Green 1.00 .40
- ❑ 51 Donald Driver .60 .25
- ❑ 52 Javon Walker .60 .25
- ❑ 53 David Carr 1.50 .60
- ❑ 54 Ron Dayne .40 .15
- ❑ 55 Terrell Davis 1.00 .40
- ❑ 56 Edgerrin James 1.00 .40
- ❑ 57 Marvin Harrison 1.00 .40
- ❑ 58 Peyton Manning 1.50 .60
- ❑ 59 Fred Taylor 1.00 .40
- ❑ 60 Jimmy Smith .60 .25
- ❑ 61 Kyle Brady .40 .15
- ❑ 62 Mark Brunell .60 .25
- ❑ 63 Tony Gonzalez .60 .25
- ❑ 64 Priest Holmes 1.25 .50
- ❑ 65 Trent Green .60 .25
- ❑ 66 Jason Taylor .40 .15
- ❑ 67 Jay Fiedler .60 .25
- ❑ 68 Zach Thomas 1.00 .40
- ❑ 69 Chris Chambers 1.00 .40
- ❑ 70 Ricky Williams 1.00 .40
- ❑ 71 Randy McMichael .60 .25
- ❑ 72 Daunte Culpepper 1.00 .40
- ❑ 73 Randy Moss 1.50 .60
- ❑ 74 Michael Bennett .60 .25
- ❑ 75 Ty Law .60 .25
- ❑ 76 Tom Brady 2.50 1.00
- ❑ 77 Troy Brown .60 .25
- ❑ 78 Antowain Smith .60 .25
- ❑ 79 Aaron Brooks 1.00 .40
- ❑ 80 Donte Stallworth 1.00 .40
- ❑ 81 Joe Horn .60 .25
- ❑ 82 Deuce McAllister 1.00 .40
- ❑ 83 Amani Toomer .60 .25
- ❑ 84 Kerry Collins .60 .25
- ❑ 85 Michael Strahan .60 .25
- ❑ 86 Tiki Barber 1.00 .40
- ❑ 87 Jeremy Shockey 1.50 .60
- ❑ 88 Chad Pennington 1.25 .50
- ❑ 89 Curtis Martin 1.00 .40
- ❑ 90 Laveranues Coles .60 .25
- ❑ 91 Vinny Testaverde .60 .25
- ❑ 92 Santana Moss .60 .25
- ❑ 93 Charles Woodson .60 .25
- ❑ 94 Sebastian Janikowski .40 .15
- ❑ 95 Tim Brown 1.00 .40
- ❑ 96 Rich Gannon .60 .25
- ❑ 97 Jerry Rice 2.00 .75
- ❑ 98 Donovan McNabb 1.25 .50
- ❑ 99 Duce Staley .60 .25
- ❑ 100 Todd Pinkston .40 .15
- ❑ 101 Chad Lewis .40 .15
- ❑ 102 A.J. Feeley .40 .15
- ❑ 103 Jerome Bettis 1.00 .40
- ❑ 104 Plaxico Burress .60 .25
- ❑ 105 Hines Ward 1.00 .40
- ❑ 106 Antwaan Randle El 1.00 .40
- ❑ 107 Kendrell Bell .60 .25
- ❑ 108 Junior Seau 1.00 .40
- ❑ 109 LaDainian Tomlinson 1.00 .40
- ❑ 110 Doug Flutie 1.00 .40
- ❑ 111 Drew Brees 1.00 .40
- ❑ 112 Terrell Owens 1.00 .40
- ❑ 113 Jeff Garcia 1.00 .40
- ❑ 114 Garrison Hearst .60 .25
- ❑ 115 Koren Robinson .60 .25
- ❑ 116 Shaun Alexander 1.00 .40
- ❑ 117 Isaac Bruce 1.00 .40
- ❑ 118 Kurt Warner 1.00 .40
- ❑ 119 Marshall Faulk 1.00 .40
- ❑ 120 Torry Holt 1.00 .40
- ❑ 121 Keyshawn Johnson 1.00 .40
- ❑ 122 Warren Sapp .60 .25
- ❑ 123 Mike Alstott 1.00 .40
- ❑ 124 Brad Johnson .60 .25
- ❑ 125 Eddie George .60 .25
- ❑ 126 Jevon Kearse .60 .25
- ❑ 127 Steve McNair 1.00 .40
- ❑ 128 Derrick Mason .60 .25
- ❑ 129 Keith Bulluck .40 .15
- ❑ 130 Champ Bailey .60 .25
- ❑ 131 Darrell Green .40 .15
- ❑ 132 Stephen Davis .60 .25
- ❑ 133 Rod Gardner .60 .25
- ❑ 134 Barry Sanders 2.50 1.00
- ❑ 135 Cris Carter 1.00 .40
- ❑ 136 Dan Marino 5.00 2.00
- ❑ 137 Deion Sanders 1.25 .50
- ❑ 138 Jim Kelly 2.00 .75
- ❑ 139 Joe Montana 6.00 2.50
- ❑ 140 John Elway 5.00 2.00
- ❑ 141 Marcus Allen 1.25 .50
- ❑ 142 Reggie White 1.00 .40
- ❑ 143 Sterling Sharpe 1.00 .40
- ❑ 144 Steve Young 1.50 .60
- ❑ 145 Thurman Thomas 1.00 .40
- ❑ 146 Troy Aikman 2.00 .75
- ❑ 147 Warren Moon 1.00 .40
- ❑ 148 Drew Bledsoe 1.00 .40
- ❑ 149 Jerry Rice 2.00 .75
- ❑ 150 Ricky Williams 1.00 .40
- ❑ 151 Carson Palmer JSY RC 30.00 12.50
- ❑ 152 Byron Leftwich JSY RC 25.00 10.00
- ❑ 153 Kyle Boller JSY RC 8.00 3.00
- ❑ 154 Rex Grossman JSY RC 25.00 10.00
- ❑ 155 Dave Ragone JSY RC 8.00 3.00
- ❑ 156 Kliff Kingsbury JSY RC 8.00 3.00
- ❑ 157 Seneca Wallace JSY RC 8.00 3.00
- ❑ 158 Larry Johnson JSY RC 30.00 15.00
- ❑ 159 Willis McGahee JSY RC 20.00 7.50
- ❑ 160 Justin Fargas JSY RC 8.00 3.00
- ❑ 161 Onterrio Smith JSY RC 8.00 3.00
- ❑ 162 Chris Brown JSY RC 8.00 3.00
- ❑ 163 Musa Smith JSY RC 8.00 3.00
- ❑ 164 Artose Pinner JSY RC 8.00 3.00
- ❑ 165 Andre Johnson JSY RC 15.00 6.00
- ❑ 166 Kelley Washington JSY RC 8.00 3.00
- ❑ 167 Taylor Jacobs JSY RC 8.00 3.00
- ❑ 168 Bryant Johnson JSY RC 8.00 3.00
- ❑ 169 Tyrone Calico JSY RC 8.00 3.00
- ❑ 170 Anquan Boldin JSY RC 20.00 7.50
- ❑ 171 Bethel Johnson JSY RC 8.00 3.00
- ❑ 172 Nate Burleson JSY RC 8.00 3.00
- ❑ 173 Kevin Curtis JSY RC 10.00 4.00
- ❑ 174 Dallas Clark JSY RC 8.00 3.00
- ❑ 175 Teyo Johnson JSY RC 8.00 3.00
- ❑ 176 Terrell Suggs JSY RC 12.00 5.00
- ❑ 177 DeWayne Robertson JSY RC 8.003.00
- ❑ 178 Brian St.Pierre JSY RC 8.00 3.00
- ❑ 179 Terence Newman JSY RC 15.00 6.00
- ❑ 180 Marcus Trufant JSY RC 8.00 3.00

2004 Leaf Certified Materials

- ❑ COMP.SET w/o SP's (150) 30.00 12.50
- ❑ 151-200 PRINT RUN 1000 SER.#'d SETS
- ❑ 201-233 PRINT RUN 1250 SER.#'d SETS
- ❑ UNPRICED MIRROR BLACK #'d OF 1
- ❑ UNPRICED MIRROR EMERALD #'d OF 5
- ❑ 1 Anquan Boldin 1.00 .40
- ❑ 2 Emmitt Smith 2.00 .75
- ❑ 3 Josh McCown .60 .25
- ❑ 4 Marcel Shipp .60 .25
- ❑ 5 Michael Vick 2.00 .75
- ❑ 6 Peerless Price .60 .25
- ❑ 7 T.J. Duckett .60 .25
- ❑ 8 Warrick Dunn .60 .25
- ❑ 9 Jamal Lewis 1.00 .40
- ❑ 10 Kyle Boller 1.00 .40
- ❑ 11 Ray Lewis 1.00 .40
- ❑ 12 Terrell Suggs .60 .25
- ❑ 13 Todd Heap .60 .25
- ❑ 14 Drew Bledsoe 1.00 .40
- ❑ 15 Eric Moulds .60 .25
- ❑ 16 Travis Henry .60 .25
- ❑ 17 Julius Peppers 1.00 .40
- ❑ 18 Muhsin Muhammad .60 .25
- ❑ 19 Stephen Davis .60 .25
- ❑ 20 Anthony Thomas .60 .25
- ❑ 21 Brian Urlacher 1.25 .50
- ❑ 22 Rex Grossman 1.00 .40
- ❑ 23 Chad Johnson 1.00 .40
- ❑ 24 Corey Dillon .60 .25
- ❑ 25 Peter Warrick .60 .25
- ❑ 26 Jeff Garcia 1.00 .40
- ❑ 27 Tim Couch .40 .15
- ❑ 28 William Green .60 .25
- ❑ 29 Antonio Bryant .60 .25
- ❑ 30 Keyshawn Johnson .60 .25
- ❑ 31 Quincy Carter .60 .25
- ❑ 32 Roy Williams S .60 .25
- ❑ 33 Terence Newman .60 .25
- ❑ 34 Ashley Lelie .60 .25
- ❑ 35 Ed McCaffrey .60 .25
- ❑ 36 Jake Plummer .60 .25
- ❑ 37 Mike Anderson .60 .25
- ❑ 38 Rod Smith .60 .25
- ❑ 39 Charles Rogers .60 .25
- ❑ 40 Joey Harrington 1.00 .40
- ❑ 41 Ahman Green 1.00 .40
- ❑ 42 Brett Favre 2.50 1.00
- ❑ 43 Donald Driver .60 .25
- ❑ 44 Javon Walker .60 .25
- ❑ 45 Robert Ferguson .40 .15
- ❑ 46 Andre Johnson 1.00 .40
- ❑ 47 David Carr 1.00 .40
- ❑ 48 Edgerrin James 1.00 .40
- ❑ 49 Marvin Harrison 1.00 .40
- ❑ 50 Peyton Manning 1.50 .60
- ❑ 51 Reggie Wayne .60 .25
- ❑ 52 Byron Leftwich 1.25 .50
- ❑ 53 Fred Taylor .60 .25
- ❑ 54 Jimmy Smith .60 .25
- ❑ 55 Dante Hall 1.00 .40
- ❑ 56 Priest Holmes 1.25 .50
- ❑ 57 Tony Gonzalez .60 .25
- ❑ 58 Trent Green .60 .25
- ❑ 59 A.J. Feeley 1.00 .40
- ❑ 60 Chris Chambers .60 .25
- ❑ 61 David Boston .60 .25
- ❑ 62 Jason Taylor .40 .15
- ❑ 63 Jay Fiedler .40 .15
- ❑ 64 Junior Seau 1.00 .40
- ❑ 65 Randy McMichael .40 .15
- ❑ 66 Ricky Williams 1.00 .40
- ❑ 67 Zach Thomas 1.00 .40
- ❑ 68 Daunte Culpepper 1.00 .40
- ❑ 69 Michael Bennett .60 .25
- ❑ 70 Randy Moss 1.25 .50
- ❑ 71 Tom Brady 2.50 1.00
- ❑ 72 Troy Brown .60 .25
- ❑ 73 Ty Law .60 .25
- ❑ 74 Aaron Brooks .60 .25

❑ 75 Deuce McAllister 1.00 .40
❑ 76 Donte Stallworth .60 .25
❑ 77 Amani Toomer .60 .25
❑ 78 Jeremy Shockey 1.00 .40
❑ 79 Kerry Collins .60 .25
❑ 80 Michael Strahan .60 .25
❑ 81 Tiki Barber 1.00 .40
❑ 82 Chad Pennington 1.00 .40
❑ 83 Curtis Martin 1.00 .40
❑ 84 Justin McCareins .40 .15
❑ 85 Santana Moss .60 .25
❑ 86 Charles Woodson .60 .25
❑ 87 Jerry Rice 2.00 .75
❑ 88 Rich Gannon .60 .25
❑ 89 Tim Brown 1.00 .40
❑ 90 Warren Sapp .60 .25
❑ 91 Correll Buckhalter .60 .25
❑ 92 Donovan McNabb 1.25 .50
❑ 93 Freddie Mitchell .60 .25
❑ 94 Jevon Kearse .60 .25
❑ 95 Terrell Owens 1.00 .40
❑ 96 Antwaan Randle El 1.00 .40
❑ 97 Duce Staley .60 .25
❑ 98 Hines Ward 1.00 .40
❑ 99 Jerome Bettis 1.00 .40
❑ 100 Plaxico Burress .60 .25
❑ 101 Doug Flutie 1.00 .40
❑ 102 LaDainian Tomlinson 1.25 .50
❑ 103 Koren Robinson .60 .25
❑ 104 Matt Hasselbeck .60 .25
❑ 105 Shaun Alexander 1.00 .40
❑ 106 Isaac Bruce .60 .25
❑ 107 Kurt Warner 1.00 .40
❑ 108 Marc Bulger 1.00 .40
❑ 109 Marshall Faulk 1.00 .40
❑ 110 Torry Holt 1.00 .40
❑ 111 Brad Johnson .60 .25
❑ 112 Mike Alstott .60 .25
❑ 113 Derrick Mason .60 .25
❑ 114 Drew Bennett .60 .25
❑ 115 Eddie George .60 .25
❑ 116 Frank Wycheck .40 .15
❑ 117 Keith Bulluck .40 .15
❑ 118 Steve McNair 1.00 .40
❑ 119 Tyrone Calico .60 .25
❑ 120 Clinton Portis 1.00 .40
❑ 121 LaVar Arrington 2.00 .75
❑ 122 Laveranues Coles .60 .25
❑ 123 Mark Brunell .60 .25
❑ 124 Patrick Ramsey .60 .25
❑ 125 Rod Gardner .60 .25
❑ 126 Jake Plummer FLB .60 .25
❑ 127 Thomas Jones FLB .60 .25
❑ 128 Priest Holmes FLB 1.25 .50
❑ 129 Jim Kelly FLB 2.00 .75
❑ 130 Doug Flutie FLB 1.00 .40
❑ 131 Walter Payton FLB 6.00 2.50
❑ 132 Troy Aikman FLB 2.50 1.00
❑ 133 John Elway FLB 4.00 1.50
❑ 134 Barry Sanders FLB 3.00 1.25
❑ 135 Mark Brunell FLB .60 .25
❑ 136 Earl Campbell FLB 1.50 .60
❑ 137 Joe Montana FLB 6.00 2.50
❑ 138 Dan Marino FLB 5.00 2.00
❑ 139 Curtis Martin FLB 1.00 .40
❑ 140 Drew Bledsoe FLB 1.00 .40
❑ 141 Ricky Williams FLB 1.00 .40
❑ 142 Junior Seau FLB 1.00 .40
❑ 143 Charlie Garner FLB .60 .25
❑ 144 Jerry Rice FLB 2.00 .75
❑ 145 Ahman Green FLB 1.00 .40
❑ 146 Jerome Bettis FLB 1.00 .40
❑ 147 Trent Green FLB .60 .25
❑ 148 Warrick Dunn FLB .60 .25
❑ 149 Deion Sanders FLB 1.50 .60
❑ 150 Stephen Davis FLB .60 .25
❑ 151 Adimchinobe Echemandu AU RC 10.00 4.00
❑ 152 Ahmad Carroll RC 6.00 2.50
❑ 153 Andy Hall AU RC 10.00 4.00
❑ 154 B.J. Johnson AU RC 10.00 4.00
❑ 155 B.J. Symons AU RC 15.00 6.00
❑ 156 Bradlee Van Pelt AU RC 20.00 8.00
❑ 157 Brandon Miree AU RC 10.00 4.00
❑ 158 Bruce Perry AU RC 15.00 6.00
❑ 159 Carlos Francis AU RC 10.00 4.00
❑ 160 Casey Bramlet AU RC 10.00 4.00
❑ 161 Chris Gamble RC 6.00 2.50
❑ 162 Clarence Moore AU RC 15.00 6.00
❑ 163 Cody Pickett AU RC 15.00 6.00
❑ 164 Craig Krenzel AU RC 15.00 6.00
❑ 165 D.J. Hackett RC 5.00 2.00
❑ 166 D.J. Williams RC 6.00 2.50
❑ 167 Derrick Ward AU RC 15.00 6.00
❑ 168 Drew Carter AU RC 15.00 6.00
❑ 169 Ernest Wilford RC 6.00 2.50
❑ 170 Drew Henson RC 6.00 2.50
❑ 171 Jamaar Taylor AU RC 15.00 6.00
❑ 172 Jared Lorenzen AU RC 10.00 4.00
❑ 173 Jarrett Payton AU RC 15.00 6.00
❑ 174 Jason Babin AU RC EXCH 15.00 6.00
❑ 175 Jeff Smoker AU RC 15.00 6.00
❑ 176 Jeris McIntyre AU RC 10.00 4.00
❑ 177 Jerricho Cotchery RC 6.00 2.50
❑ 178 Jim Sorgi AU RC 15.00 6.00
❑ 179 John Navarre AU RC 15.00 6.00
❑ 180 Patrick Crayton AU RC 15.00 7.50
❑ 181 Johnnie Morant RC 6.00 2.50
❑ 182 Sean Taylor RC 6.00 2.50
❑ 183 Jonathan Vilma RC 6.00 2.50
❑ 184 Josh Harris RC 6.00 2.50
❑ 185 Kenechi Udeze RC 8.00 3.00
❑ 186 Mark Jones AU RC 10.00 4.00
❑ 187 Matt Mauck AU RC 15.00 6.00
❑ 188 Maurice Mann AU RC 10.00 4.00
❑ 189 Michael Turner RC 8.00 3.00
❑ 190 P.K. Sam RC 5.00 2.00
❑ 191 Quincy Wilson RC 5.00 2.00
❑ 192 Ran Carthon AU RC 10.00 4.00
❑ 193 Ryan Krause AU RC 10.00 4.00
❑ 194 Samie Parker RC 6.00 2.50
❑ 195 Sloan Thomas AU RC 10.00 4.00
❑ 196 Tommie Harris RC 6.00 2.50
❑ 197 Triandos Luke AU RC 15.00 6.00
❑ 198 Troy Fleming AU RC 10.00 4.00
❑ 199 Vince Wilfork RC 6.00 2.50
❑ 200 Will Smith RC 6.00 2.50
❑ 201 Larry Fitzgerald JSY RC 20.00 7.50
❑ 202 DeAngelo Hall JSY RC 10.00 4.00
❑ 203 Matt Schaub JSY RC 20.00 7.50
❑ 204 Michael Jenkins JSY RC 8.00 3.00
❑ 205 Devard Darling JSY RC 8.00 3.00
❑ 206 J.P. Losman JSY RC 12.00 5.00
❑ 207 Lee Evans JSY RC 10.00 4.00
❑ 208 Keary Colbert JSY RC 8.00 3.00
❑ 209 Bernard Berrian JSY RC 10.00 4.00
❑ 210 Chris Perry JSY RC 10.00 4.00
❑ 211 Kellen Winslow JSY RC 12.00 5.00
❑ 212 Luke McCown JSY RC 8.00 3.00
❑ 213 Julius Jones JSY RC 20.00 7.50
❑ 214 Darius Watts JSY RC 8.00 3.00
❑ 215 Tatum Bell JSY RC 12.00 5.00
❑ 216 Kevin Jones JSY RC 15.00 6.00
❑ 217 Roy Williams JSY RC 15.00 6.00
❑ 218 Dunta Robinson JSY RC 8.00 3.00
❑ 219 Greg Jones JSY RC 10.00 4.00
❑ 220 Reggie Williams JSY RC 10.00 4.00
❑ 221 Mewelde Moore JSY RC 8.00 3.00
❑ 222 Ben Watson JSY RC 8.00 3.00
❑ 223 Cedric Cobbs JSY RC 8.00 3.00
❑ 224 Devery Henderson JSY RC 8.00 3.00
❑ 225 Eli Manning JSY RC 30.00 15.00
❑ 226 Robert Gallery JSY RC 8.00 3.00
❑ 227 Ben Roethlisberger JSY RC 40.00 15.00
❑ 228 Philip Rivers JSY RC 20.00 10.00
❑ 229 Derrick Hamilton JSY RC 8.00 3.00
❑ 230 Rashaun Woods JSY RC 8.00 3.00
❑ 231 Steven Jackson JSY RC 20.00 7.50
❑ 232 Michael Clayton JSY RC 12.00 5.00
❑ 233 Ben Troupe JSY RC 8.00 3.00

2005 Leaf Certified Materials

❑ COMPLETE SET (229)
❑ COMP.SET w/o RCs (150) 40.00 15.00
❑ 151-200 PRINT RUN 1000 SER.#'d SETS
❑ UNPRICED MIR.BLACK PRINT RUN 1 SET
❑ UNPRICED MIR.EMERALD PRINT RUN 5 SETS
❑ 1 Anquan Boldin .60 .25
❑ 2 Josh McCown .60 .25
❑ 3 Larry Fitzgerald 1.00 .40
❑ 4 Michael Vick 1.50 .60
❑ 5 Peerless Price .50 .20
❑ 6 T.J. Duckett .60 .25
❑ 7 Warrick Dunn .60 .25
❑ 8 Jamal Lewis 1.00 .40
❑ 9 Kyle Boller .60 .25
❑ 10 Todd Heap .60 .25
❑ 11 Ray Lewis 1.00 .40

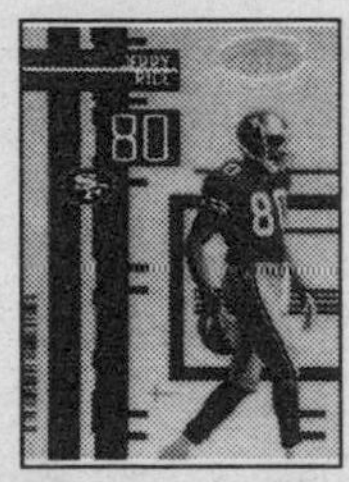

❑ 12 Terrell Suggs .60 .25
❑ 13 Drew Bledsoe 1.00 .40
❑ 14 Eric Moulds .60 .25
❑ 15 J.P. Losman 1.00 .40
❑ 16 Lee Evans .60 .25
❑ 17 Willis McGahee 1.00 .40
❑ 18 DeShaun Foster .60 .25
❑ 19 Jake Delhomme 1.00 .40
❑ 20 Steve Smith .60 .25
❑ 21 Brian Urlacher 1.00 .40
❑ 22 Rex Grossman .60 .25
❑ 23 Carson Palmer 1.00 .40
❑ 24 Chad Johnson 1.00 .40
❑ 25 Rudi Johnson .60 .25
❑ 26 Kellen Winslow Jr. 1.00 .40
❑ 27 Kelly Holcomb .50 .20
❑ 28 Lee Suggs .60 .25
❑ 29 William Green .50 .20
❑ 30 Julius Jones 1.25 .50
❑ 31 Keyshawn Johnson .60 .25
❑ 32 Roy Williams S .60 .25
❑ 33 Terence Newman .50 .20
❑ 34 Ashley Lelie .60 .25
❑ 35 Champ Bailey .60 .25
❑ 36 Darius Watts .60 .25
❑ 37 Jake Plummer .60 .25
❑ 38 Tatum Bell .60 .25
❑ 39 Charles Rogers .60 .25
❑ 40 Joey Harrington 1.00 .40
❑ 41 Kevin Jones 1.00 .40
❑ 42 Roy Williams WR 1.00 .40
❑ 43 Ahman Green 1.00 .40
❑ 44 Brett Favre 2.50 1.00
❑ 45 Javon Walker .60 .25
❑ 46 Robert Ferguson .50 .20
❑ 47 Andre Johnson .60 .25
❑ 48 David Carr 1.00 .40
❑ 49 Domanick Davis .60 .25
❑ 50 Dallas Clark .50 .20
❑ 51 Edgerrin James 1.00 .40
❑ 52 Marvin Harrison 1.00 .40
❑ 53 Peyton Manning 1.50 .60
❑ 54 Reggie Wayne .60 .25
❑ 55 Byron Leftwich 1.00 .40
❑ 56 Fred Taylor .60 .25
❑ 57 Jimmy Smith .60 .25
❑ 58 Reggie Williams .60 .25
❑ 59 Priest Holmes 1.00 .40
❑ 60 Tony Gonzalez .60 .25
❑ 61 Trent Green .60 .25
❑ 62 Chris Chambers .60 .25
❑ 63 Jason Taylor .50 .20
❑ 64 Junior Seau .60 .25
❑ 65 Zach Thomas 1.00 .40
❑ 66 Daunte Culpepper 1.00 .40
❑ 67 Michael Bennett .60 .25
❑ 68 Randy Moss 1.00 .40
❑ 69 Corey Dillon .60 .25
❑ 70 Tom Brady 2.50 1.00
❑ 71 Deion Branch .60 .25
❑ 72 Aaron Brooks .60 .25
❑ 73 Deuce McAllister 1.00 .40
❑ 74 Donte Stallworth .60 .25
❑ 75 Joe Horn .60 .25
❑ 76 Eli Manning 2.00 .75
❑ 77 Jeremy Shockey 1.00 .40
❑ 78 Michael Strahan .60 .25
❑ 79 Tiki Barber 1.00 .40
❑ 80 Anthony Becht .50 .20
❑ 81 Chad Pennington 1.00 .40
❑ 82 Curtis Martin 1.00 .40
❑ 83 Justin McCareins .50 .20

❑ 84 Laveranues Coles	.60	.25
❑ 85 Santana Moss	.60	.25
❑ 86 Shaun Ellis	.50	.20
❑ 87 Jerry Porter	.60	.25
❑ 88 Brian Westbrook	.60	.25
❑ 89 Chad Lewis	.50	.20
❑ 90 Donovan McNabb	1.25	.50
❑ 91 Freddie Mitchell	.50	.20
❑ 92 Hugh Douglas	.50	.20
❑ 93 Jevon Kearse	.60	.25
❑ 94 Terrell Owens	1.00	.40
❑ 95 Todd Pinkston	.50	.20
❑ 96 Antwaan Randle El	.60	.25
❑ 97 Ben Roethlisberger	2.50	1.00
❑ 98 Duce Staley	.60	.25
❑ 99 [illegible]	[illegible]	[illegible]
❑ 100 Jerome Bettis	1.00	.40
❑ 101 Antonio Gates	1.00	.40
❑ 102 Drew Brees	1.00	.40
❑ 103 LaDainian Tomlinson	1.25	.50
❑ 104 Kevan Barlow	.60	.25
❑ 105 Darrell Jackson	.60	.25
❑ 106 Koren Robinson	.60	.25
❑ 107 Matt Hasselbeck	.60	.25
❑ 108 Shaun Alexander	1.25	.50
❑ 109 Marc Bulger	1.00	.40
❑ 110 Steven Jackson	1.25	.50
❑ 111 Torry Holt	1.00	.40
❑ 112 Michael Clayton	1.00	.40
❑ 113 Chris Brown	.60	.25
❑ 114 Drew Bennett	.60	.25
❑ 115 Keith Bulluck	.50	.20
❑ 116 Steve McNair	1.00	.40
❑ 117 Clinton Portis	1.00	.40
❑ 118 LaVar Arrington	1.00	.40
❑ 119 John Riggins	1.25	.50
❑ 120 Sean Taylor	.60	.25
❑ 121 Jake Plummer	.60	.25
❑ 122 Thomas Jones	.60	.25
❑ 123 Doug Flutie	1.00	.40
❑ 124 Walter Payton	4.00	1.50
❑ 125 Corey Dillon	.60	.25
❑ 126 Troy Aikman	1.50	.60
❑ 127 Terrell Davis	1.25	.50
❑ 128 Marshall Faulk	1.00	.40
❑ 129 Dan Marino	3.00	1.25
❑ 130 Thurman Thomas	1.00	.40
❑ 131 Warren Moon	1.00	.40
❑ 132 Curtis Martin	1.00	.40
❑ 133 Drew Bledsoe	1.00	.40
❑ 134 Kerry Collins	.60	.25
❑ 135 Keyshawn Johnson	.60	.25
❑ 136 A.J. Feeley	.60	.25
❑ 137 Duce Staley	.60	.25
❑ 138 Junior Seau	.60	.25
❑ 139 Jerry Rice	2.00	.75
❑ 140 Steve Young	1.50	.60
❑ 141 Jerome Bettis	1.00	.40
❑ 142 Kurt Warner	.60	.25
❑ 143 Trent Green	.60	.25
❑ 144 Keyshawn Johnson	.60	.25
❑ 145 Warren Sapp	.60	.25
❑ 146 Warrick Dunn	.60	.25
❑ 147 Jevon Kearse	.60	.25
❑ 148 Deion Sanders	1.50	.60
❑ 149 Laveranues Coles	.60	.25
❑ 150 Stephen Davis	.60	.25
❑ 151 Cedric Benson RC	12.00	5.00
❑ 152 Mike Williams	5.00	2.00
❑ 153 DeMarcus Ware RC	8.00	3.00
❑ 154 Shawne Merriman RC	8.00	3.00
❑ 155 Thomas Davis RC	5.00	2.00
❑ 156 Derrick Johnson RC	8.00	3.00
❑ 157 Travis Johnson RC	4.00	1.50
❑ 158 David Pollack RC	5.00	2.00
❑ 159 Erasmus James RC	5.00	2.00
❑ 160 Marcus Spears RC	5.00	2.00
❑ 161 Fabian Washington RC	5.00	2.00
❑ 162 Aaron Rodgers RC	15.00	6.00
❑ 163 Marlin Jackson RC	5.00	2.00
❑ 164 Heath Miller RC	10.00	4.00
❑ 165 Matt Roth RC	5.00	2.00
❑ 166 Dan Cody RC	5.00	2.00
❑ 167 Bryant McFadden RC	5.00	2.00
❑ 168 Chris Henry RC	5.00	2.00
❑ 169 David Greene RC	5.00	2.00
❑ 170 Brandon Jones RC	5.00	2.00
❑ 171 Marion Barber RC	8.00	3.00
❑ 172 Brandon Jacobs RC	6.00	2.50
❑ 173 Jerome Mathis RC	5.00	2.00
❑ 174 Craphonso Thorpe RC	4.00	1.50
❑ 175 Alvin Pearman RC	5.00	2.00
❑ 176 Darren Sproles RC	5.00	2.00
❑ 177 Fred Gibson RC	4.00	1.50
❑ 178 Roydell Williams RC	5.00	2.00
❑ 179 Airese Currie RC	5.00	2.00
❑ 180 Damien Nash RC	4.00	1.50
❑ 181 Dan Orlovsky RC	5.00	2.00
❑ 182 Adrian McPherson RC	5.00	2.00
❑ 183 Larry Brackins RC	4.00	1.50
❑ 184 Rasheed Marshall RC	5.00	2.00
❑ 185 Cedric Houston RC	5.00	2.00
❑ 186 Chad Owens RC	5.00	2.00
❑ 187 Tab Perry RC	5.00	2.00
❑ 188 Dante Ridgeway RC	4.00	1.50
❑ 189 Craig Bragg RC	4.00	1.50
❑ 190 Deandra Cobb RC	4.00	1.50
❑ 191 Derek Anderson RC	8.00	3.00
❑ 192 Paris Warren RC	4.00	1.50
❑ 193 Lionel Gates RC	4.00	1.50
❑ 194 Anthony Davis RC	4.00	1.50
❑ 195 Ryan Fitzpatrick RC	5.00	2.00
❑ 196 J.R. Russell RC	4.00	1.50
❑ 197 Jason White RC	5.00	2.00
❑ 198 Kay-Jay Harris RC	4.00	1.50
❑ 199 T.A. McLendon RC	3.00	1.25
❑ 200 Taylor Stubblefield RC	3.00	1.25
❑ 201 Adam Jones JSY/1499 RC	8.00	3.00
❑ 202 Alex Smith QB JSY/499 RC	30.00	12.50
❑ 203 Andrew Walter JSY/1249 RC	8.00	3.00
❑ 204 Antrel Rolle JSY/999 RC	8.00	3.00
❑ 205 Braylon Edwards JSY/499 RC	25.00	10.00
❑ 206 Cadillac Williams JSY/499 RC	30.00	12.50
❑ 207 Carlos Rogers JSY/1499 RC	10.00	4.00
❑ 208 Charlie Frye JSY/1499 RC	10.00	4.00
❑ 209 Ciatrick Fason JSY/1499 RC	8.00	3.00
❑ 210 Courtney Roby JSY/1249 RC	8.00	3.00
❑ 211 Eric Shelton JSY/999 RC	8.00	3.00
❑ 212 Frank Gore JSY/999 RC	12.00	5.00
❑ 213 J.J. Arrington JSY/499 RC	10.00	4.00
❑ 214 Kyle Orton JSY/1499 RC	8.00	3.00
❑ 215 Jason Campbell JSY/749 RC	12.00	5.00
❑ 216 Mark Bradley JSY/999 RC	8.00	3.00
❑ 217 Mark Clayton JSY/499 RC	10.00	4.00
❑ 218 Matt Jones JSY/749 RC	12.00	5.00
❑ 219 Maurice Clarett JSY/999	8.00	3.00
❑ 220 Reggie Brown JSY/999 RC	8.00	3.00
❑ 221 Roddy White JSY/749 RC	8.00	3.00
❑ 222 Ronnie Brown JSY/499 RC	30.00	12.50
❑ 223 Roscoe Parrish JSY/999 RC	8.00	3.00
❑ 224 Ryan Moats JSY/999 RC	8.00	3.00
❑ 225 Stefan LeFors JSY/1499 RC	8.00	3.00
❑ 226 Terrence Murphy JSY/1499 RC	8.00	3.00
❑ 227 Troy Williamson JSY/749 RC	10.00	4.00
❑ 228 Vernand Morency JSY/1499 RC	8.00	3.00
❑ 229 Vincent Jackson JSY/1499 RC	8.00	3.00

2006 Leaf Certified Materials

❑ COMP.SET w/o SP's (150)	40.00	15.00
❑ 1 Anquan Boldin	.60	.25
❑ 2 Edgerrin James	1.00	.40
❑ 3 Kurt Warner	.60	.25
❑ 4 Larry Fitzgerald	1.00	.40
❑ 5 Alge Crumpler	.60	.25
❑ 6 Brian Finneran	.50	.20
❑ 7 Michael Jenkins	.60	.25
❑ 8 Michael Vick	1.00	.40
❑ 9 Warrick Dunn	.60	.25
❑ 10 Derrick Mason	.50	.20
❑ 11 Jamal Lewis	.60	.25
❑ 12 Kyle Boller	.50	.20
❑ 13 Todd Heap	.60	.25
❑ 14 Mark Clayton	1.00	.40
❑ 15 Eric Moulds	.60	.25
❑ 16 J.P. Losman	.60	.25
❑ 17 Josh Reed	.50	.20
❑ 18 Lee Evans	.60	.25
❑ 19 Willis McGahee	1.00	.40
❑ 20 DeShaun Foster	.60	.25
❑ 21 Jake Delhomme	.60	.25
❑ 22 Stephen Davis	.60	.25
❑ 23 Keary Colbert	.50	.20
❑ 24 Steve Smith	1.00	.40
❑ 25 Brian Urlacher	1.00	.40
❑ 26 Cedric Benson	1.00	.40
❑ 27 Muhsin Muhammad	.60	.25
❑ 28 Rex Grossman	1.00	.40
❑ 29 Thomas Jones	.60	.25
❑ 30 Carson Palmer	1.00	.40
❑ 31 Chad Johnson	.60	.25
❑ 32 Rudi Johnson	.60	.25
❑ 33 T.J. Houshmandzadeh	.60	.25
❑ 34 Charlie Frye	.60	.25
❑ 35 Dennis Northcutt	.50	.20
❑ 36 Braylon Edwards	1.00	.40
❑ 37 Reuben Droughns	.60	.25
❑ 38 Drew Bledsoe	1.00	.40
❑ 39 Julius Jones	1.00	.40
❑ 40 Terrell Owens	1.00	.40
❑ 41 Jason Witten	.60	.25
❑ 42 Terry Glenn	.60	.25
❑ 43 Roy Williams S	.60	.25
❑ 44 Jake Plummer	.60	.25
❑ 45 Rod Smith	.60	.25
❑ 46 Tatum Bell	.60	.25
❑ 47 Ashley Lelie	.60	.25
❑ 48 Josh McCown	.60	.25
❑ 49 Kevin Jones	1.00	.40
❑ 50 Mike Williams	1.00	.40
❑ 51 Roy Williams WR	1.00	.40
❑ 52 Ahman Green	.60	.25
❑ 53 Brett Favre	2.00	.75
❑ 54 Aaron Rodgers	1.00	.40
❑ 55 Samkon Gado	.60	.25
❑ 56 Donald Driver	.60	.25
❑ 57 Robert Ferguson	.50	.20
❑ 58 Andre Johnson	.60	.25
❑ 59 David Carr	.60	.25
❑ 60 Domanick Davis	.60	.25
❑ 61 Dallas Clark	.50	.20
❑ 62 Marvin Harrison	1.00	.40
❑ 63 Peyton Manning	1.50	.60
❑ 64 Reggie Wayne	.60	.25
❑ 65 Brandon Stokley	.60	.25
❑ 66 Byron Leftwich	.60	.25
❑ 67 Fred Taylor	.60	.25
❑ 68 Jimmy Smith	.60	.25
❑ 69 Matt Jones	.60	.25
❑ 70 Larry Johnson	1.25	.50
❑ 71 Tony Gonzalez	.60	.25
❑ 72 Trent Green	.60	.25
❑ 73 Eddie Kennison	.50	.20
❑ 74 Samie Parker	.50	.20
❑ 75 Chris Chambers	.60	.25
❑ 76 Daunte Culpepper	1.00	.40
❑ 77 Randy McMichael	.50	.20
❑ 78 Ronnie Brown	1.00	.40
❑ 79 Marty Booker	.50	.20
❑ 80 Zach Thomas	1.00	.40
❑ 81 Brad Johnson	.60	.25
❑ 82 Mewelde Moore	.50	.20
❑ 83 Nate Burleson	.60	.25
❑ 84 Troy Williamson	.60	.25
❑ 85 Deion Branch	.60	.25
❑ 86 Tom Brady	1.50	.60
❑ 87 Corey Dillon	.60	.25
❑ 88 Daniel Graham	.50	.20
❑ 89 Troy Brown	.60	.25
❑ 90 Deuce McAllister	.60	.25
❑ 91 Donte Stallworth	.60	.25
❑ 92 Drew Brees	1.00	.40
❑ 93 Joe Horn	.60	.25
❑ 94 Devery Henderson	.50	.20
❑ 95 Eli Manning	1.25	.50
❑ 96 Jeremy Shockey	1.00	.40
❑ 97 Plaxico Burress	.60	.25
❑ 98 Amani Toomer	.60	.25
❑ 99 Tiki Barber	1.00	.40

❑	100 Chad Pennington	.60	.25
❑	101 Curtis Martin	1.00	.40
❑	102 Laveranues Coles	.60	.25
❑	103 Justin McCareins	.50	.20
❑	104 Jerry Porter	.60	.25
❑	105 LaMont Jordan	.60	.25
❑	106 Doug Gabriel	.50	.20
❑	107 Randy Moss	1.00	.40
❑	108 Brian Westbrook	.60	.25
❑	109 Donovan McNabb	1.00	.40
❑	110 Reggie Brown	.75	.30
❑	111 Chad Lewis	.50	.20
❑	112 Ryan Moats	.50	.20
❑	113 Jevon Kearse	.60	.25
❑	114 Ben Roethlisberger	1.50	.60
❑	115 Heath Miller	.60	.25
❑	116 Hines Ward	1.00	.40
❑	117 Willie Parker	1.25	.50
❑	118 Troy Polamalu	1.25	.50
❑	119 Antonio Gates	1.00	.40
❑	120 Eric Parker	.50	.20
❑	121 Keenan McCardell	.50	.20
❑	122 LaDainian Tomlinson	1.25	.50
❑	123 Philip Rivers	1.00	.40
❑	124 Alex Smith QB	1.00	.40
❑	125 Antonio Bryant	.60	.25
❑	126 Frank Gore	1.00	.40
❑	127 Kevan Barlow	.60	.25
❑	128 Darrell Jackson	.60	.25
❑	129 Jerramy Stevens	.60	.25
❑	130 Matt Hasselbeck	.60	.25
❑	131 Shaun Alexander	1.00	.40
❑	132 Isaac Bruce	.60	.25
❑	133 Marc Bulger	.60	.25
❑	134 Marshall Faulk	.60	.25
❑	135 Steven Jackson	1.00	.40
❑	136 Torry Holt	.60	.25
❑	137 Cadillac Williams	1.00	.40
❑	138 Chris Simms	.60	.25
❑	139 Joey Galloway	.60	.25
❑	140 Michael Clayton	.60	.25
❑	141 Brandon Jones	.50	.20
❑	142 Chris Brown	.60	.25
❑	143 Drew Bennett	.50	.20
❑	144 Tyrone Calico	.50	.20
❑	145 Steve McNair	.60	.25
❑	146 Antwaan Randle El	.60	.25
❑	147 Clinton Portis	1.00	.40
❑	148 Mark Brunell	.60	.25
❑	149 Santana Moss	.60	.25
❑	150 Jason Campbell	.60	.25
❑	151 Brodie Croyle/500 RC	20.00	8.00
❑	152 Greg Jennings/500 RC	15.00	6.00
❑	153 Joseph Addai/500 RC	25.00	10.00
❑	154 Bennie Brazell/1000 RC	4.00	1.50
❑	155 David Thomas/500 RC	8.00	3.00
❑	156 Marques Colston/1000 RC	15.00	6.00
❑	157 Reggie McNeal/500 RC	6.00	2.50
❑	158 D.J. Shockley/1000 RC	5.00	2.00
❑	159 Dominique Byrd/500 RC	6.00	2.50
❑	160 Antonio Cromartie/1000 RC	5.00	2.00
❑	161 Donte Whitner/1000 RC	5.00	2.00
❑	162 Anwar Phillips/1000 RC	4.00	1.50
❑	163 A.J. Nicholson/1000 RC	2.50	1.00
❑	164 De'Arrius Howard/500 RC	8.00	3.00
❑	165 Erik Meyer/500 RC	6.00	2.50
❑	166 Darrell Hackney/1000 RC	4.00	1.50
❑	167 Paul Pinegar/500 RC	6.00	2.50
❑	168 Brandon Kirsch/500 RC	8.00	3.00
❑	169 Quinton Ganther/1000 RC	4.00	1.50
❑	170 Andre Hall/1000 RC	4.00	1.50
❑	171 Derrick Ross/1000 RC	4.00	1.50
❑	172 Mike Bell/1000 RC	5.00	2.00
❑	173 Wendell Mathis/500 RC	6.00	2.50
❑	174 Garrett Mills/500 RC	8.00	3.00
❑	175 David Anderson/1000 RC	4.00	1.50
❑	176 Kevin McMahan/1000 RC	4.00	1.50
❑	177 Martin Nance/1000 RC	4.00	1.50
❑	178 Greg Lee/500 RC	6.00	2.50
❑	179 Anthony Mix/500 RC	6.00	2.50
❑	180 D.Ferguson/500 RC	8.00	3.00
❑	181 Tamba Hali/500 RC	8.00	3.00
❑	182 Haloti Ngata/1000 RC	5.00	2.00
❑	183 Claude Wroten/1000 RC	2.50	1.00
❑	184 Gabe Watson/1000 RC	4.00	1.50
❑	185 D'Qwell Jackson/1000 RC	4.00	1.50
❑	186 Abdul Hodge/500 RC	8.00	3.00
❑	187 Chad Greenway/500 RC	8.00	3.00
❑	188 Bobby Carpenter/1000 RC	5.00	2.00
❑	189 DeMeco Ryans/500 RC	10.00	4.00
❑	190 Rocky McIntosh/500 RC	8.00	3.00
❑	191 Thomas Howard/1000 RC	5.00	2.00
❑	192 Jon Alston/500 RC	8.00	3.00
❑	193 Jimmy Williams/1000 RC	5.00	2.00
❑	194 Ashton Youboty/500 RC	8.00	3.00
❑	195 Alan Zemaitis/1000 RC	5.00	2.00
❑	196 Cedric Griffin/500 RC	6.00	2.50
❑	197 Ko Simpson/1000 RC	4.00	1.50
❑	198 Pat Watkins/500 RC	8.00	3.00
❑	199 Bernard Pollard/1000 RC	4.00	1.50
❑	200 Jay Cutler/500 RC	15.00	6.00
❑	201 Chad Jackson JSY/1400 RC	8.00	3.00
❑	202 L.Maroney JSY/550 RC	20.00	8.00
❑	203 Tar.Jackson JSY/1400 RC	10.00	4.00
❑	204 Michael Huff JSY/1400 RC	8.00	3.00
❑	205 Mario Williams JSY/1400 RC	10.00	4.00
❑	206 Mar.Lewis JSY/1400 RC	8.00	3.00
❑	207 Maurice Drew JSY/1400 RC	15.00	6.00
❑	208 Vince Young JSY/550 RC	25.00	10.00
❑	209 LenDale White JSY/550 RC	12.00	5.00
❑	210 Reggie Bush JSY/550 RC	40.00	15.00
❑	211 Matt Leinart JSY/550 RC	25.00	10.00
❑	212 M.Robinson JSY/1400 RC	8.00	3.00
❑	213 Vernon Davis JSY/550 RC	15.00	6.00
❑	214 Br.Williams JSY/1400 RC	8.00	3.00
❑	215 Derek Hagan JSY/1400 RC	8.00	3.00
❑	216 Jason Avant JSY/1400 RC	8.00	3.00
❑	217 B.Marshall JSY/1400 RC	8.00	3.00
❑	218 Omar Jacobs JSY/1400 RC	8.00	3.00
❑	219 S. Holmes JSY/550 RC	15.00	6.00
❑	220 J.Norwood JSY/1400 RC	10.00	4.00
❑	221 Dem.Williams JSY/1400 RC	8.00	3.00
❑	222 Sinorice Moss JSY/1400 RC	8.00	3.00
❑	223 L.Washington JSY/1400 RC	10.00	4.00
❑	224 Kellen Clemens JSY/900 RC	10.00	4.00
❑	225 A.J. Hawk JSY/550 RC	20.00	8.00
❑	226 Maurice Stovall JSY/1400 RC	8.00	3.00
❑	227 DeA.Williams JSY/550 RC	20.00	8.00
❑	228 C.Whitehurst JSY/1400 RC	6.00	2.50
❑	229 Travis Wilson JSY/1400 RC	8.00	3.00
❑	230 J.Klopfenstein JSY/1400 RC	8.00	3.00
❑	231 Brian Calhoun JSY/1400 RC	8.00	3.00
❑	232 Barry Sanders JSY/150	25.00	10.00
❑	233 Jerry Rice JSY/150	20.00	8.00
❑	234 Dan Marino JSY/150	30.00	12.00
❑	235 Earl Campbell JSY/150	15.00	6.00
❑	236 Jim Brown JSY/100	25.00	10.00
❑	237 Joe Montana JSY/125	25.00	10.00
❑	238 Troy Aikman JSY/150	20.00	8.00
❑	239 Walter Payton JSY/100	40.00	15.00
❑	240 Terry Bradshaw JSY/150	25.00	10.00
❑	241 John Elway JSY/150	25.00	10.00
❑	242 Fred Biletnikoff JSY/100	15.00	6.00
❑	243 Lance Alworth JSY/125	15.00	6.00
❑	244 Ronnie Lott JSY/150	15.00	6.00
❑	245 Yale Lary JSY/125	15.00	6.00
❑	246 Bart Starr JSY/80	30.00	12.00
❑	247 Doak Walker JSY/75	25.00	10.00
❑	248 Gale Sayers JSY/100	20.00	8.00
❑	249 Bo Jackson JSY/150	15.00	6.00
❑	250 Roger Staubach JSY/125	25.00	10.00
❑	251 Dick Butkus JSY/150	20.00	8.00

2000 Leaf Limited

❑	COMP.SET w/o SPs (200)	120.00	60.00
❑	1 Ben Coates	.50	.20
❑	2 Joe Horn	.75	.30
❑	3 Jonathan Linton	.50	.20
❑	4 Derrick Mason	.75	.30
❑	5 Ray Lucas	.75	.30
❑	6 Brock Huard	.75	.30
❑	7 Frank Wycheck	.50	.20
❑	8 Michael Strahan	.75	.30
❑	9 Jessie Armstead	.50	.20
❑	10 Stephen Alexander	.50	.20
❑	11 Larry Centers	.50	.20
❑	12 Michael Pittman	.50	.20
❑	13 Priest Holmes	1.50	.60
❑	14 Jermaine Lewis	.75	.30
❑	15 Jay Riemersma	.50	.20
❑	16 Wesley Walls	.50	.20
❑	17 Curtis Enis	.50	.20
❑	18 Bobby Engram	.75	.30
❑	19 Jim Miller	.50	.20
❑	20 Eddie Kennison	.75	.30
❑	21 Errict Rhett	.50	.20
❑	22 Chris Warren	.50	.20
❑	23 Byron Chamberlain	.50	.20
❑	24 Desmond Howard	.50	.20
❑	25 Lamar Smith	.75	.30
❑	26 Robert Porcher	.50	.20
❑	27 Corey Bradford	.75	.30
❑	28 Donald Driver	1.25	.50
❑	29 Ahman Green	1.25	.50
❑	30 Ken Dilger	.50	.20
❑	31 James McKnight	.75	.30
❑	32 Kimble Anders	.50	.20
❑	33 Zach Thomas	1.25	.50
❑	34 James Johnson	.50	.20
❑	35 Lawyer Milloy	.75	.30
❑	36 Ty Law	.75	.30
❑	37 Willie McGinest	.50	.20
❑	38 Jason Sehorn	.75	.30
❑	39 Andre Rison	.75	.30
❑	40 Rickey Dudley	.50	.20
❑	41 Patrick Jeffers	1.25	.50
❑	42 Darrell Russell	.50	.20
❑	43 Charles Johnson	.75	.30
❑	44 Michael Westbrook	.75	.30
❑	45 Levon Kirkland	.50	.20
❑	46 Ryan Leaf	.75	.30
❑	47 Sean Dawkins	.50	.20
❑	48 Todd Lyght	.50	.20
❑	49 Kevin Carter	.50	.20
❑	50 Neil O'Donnell	.50	.20
❑	51 Randall Cunningham	1.50	.60
❑	52 Oronde Gadsden	1.00	.40
❑	53 O.J. McDuffie	1.00	.40
❑	54 Jake Reed	1.00	.40
❑	55 Brian Mitchell	.60	.25
❑	56 Kordell Stewart	1.00	.40
❑	57 Derrick Mayes	1.00	.40
❑	58 Az-Zahir Hakim	.60	.25
❑	59 Jacquez Green	.60	.25
❑	60 Andre Reed	1.00	.40
❑	61 Deion Sanders	1.50	.60
❑	62 Frank Sanders	1.00	.40
❑	63 Rob Moore	1.00	.40
❑	64 Shawn Jefferson	.60	.25
❑	65 Pat Johnson	.60	.25
❑	66 Peter Boulware	.60	.25
❑	67 Donald Hayes	.60	.25
❑	68 Marty Booker	1.00	.40
❑	69 Leslie Shepherd	.60	.25
❑	70 Jason Tucker	.60	.25
❑	71 Johnnie Morton	1.00	.40
❑	72 Germane Crowell	.60	.25
❑	73 Herman Moore	1.00	.40
❑	74 Bill Schroeder	1.00	.40
❑	75 E.G. Green	.60	.25
❑	76 Jerome Pathon	1.00	.40
❑	77 Tony Brackens	.60	.25
❑	78 Tony Richardson RC	.60	.25
❑	79 Sam Madison	.60	.25
❑	80 Jeff George	1.00	.40
❑	81 Matthew Hatchette	.60	.25
❑	82 Kevin Faulk	1.00	.40
❑	83 Jeff Blake	1.00	.40
❑	84 Ike Hilliard	1.00	.40
❑	85 Napoleon Kaufman	1.00	.40
❑	86 Charles Woodson	1.00	.40
❑	87 Na Brown	.60	.25
❑	88 Hines Ward	1.50	.60
❑	89 Troy Edwards	.60	.25
❑	90 Curtis Conway	1.00	.40
❑	91 Junior Seau	1.50	.60
❑	92 Jim Harbaugh	1.00	.40
❑	93 J.J. Stokes	1.00	.40
❑	94 Jon Kitna	1.50	.60
❑	95 Reidel Anthony	.60	.25

- ❑ 96 Warrick Dunn 1.50 .60
- ❑ 97 Carl Pickens 1.00 .40
- ❑ 98 Yancey Thigpen .60 .25
- ❑ 99 Albert Connell .60 .25
- ❑ 100 Irving Fryar 1.00 .40
- ❑ 101 Qadry Ismail 1.25 .50
- ❑ 102 Shannon Sharpe 1.25 .50
- ❑ 103 Joey Galloway 1.25 .50
- ❑ 104 Ed McCaffrey 2.00 .75
- ❑ 105 Rod Smith 1.25 .50
- ❑ 106 Terrell Owens 2.00 .75
- ❑ 107 Warren Sapp 1.25 .50
- ❑ 108 Jevon Kearse 2.00 .75
- ❑ 109 Bruce Smith 1.25 .50
- ❑ 110 Champ Bailey 1.25 .50
- ❑ 111 David Boston 2.00 .75
- ❑ 112 Tim Dwight 2.00 .75
- ❑ 113 Terance Mathis 1.25 .50
- ❑ 114 Tony Banks 1.25 .50
- ❑ 115 Shawn Bryson .75 .30
- ❑ 116 Peerless Price 1.25 .50
- ❑ 117 Muhsin Muhammad 1.25 .50
- ❑ 118 Tim Biakabutuka 1.25 .50
- ❑ 119 Steve Beuerlein 1.25 .50
- ❑ 120 Corey Dillon 2.00 .75
- ❑ 121 Kevin Johnson 2.00 .75
- ❑ 122 Rocket Ismail 1.25 .50
- ❑ 123 Charlie Batch 2.00 .75
- ❑ 124 James Stewart 1.25 .50
- ❑ 125 Terrence Wilkins .75 .30
- ❑ 126 Keenan McCardell 1.25 .50
- ❑ 127 Mark Brunell 2.00 .75
- ❑ 128 Fred Taylor 2.00 .75
- ❑ 129 Derrick Alexander 1.25 .50
- ❑ 130 Tony Gonzalez 1.25 .50
- ❑ 131 Warren Moon 2.00 .75
- ❑ 132 Thurman Thomas 1.25 .50
- ❑ 133 Tony Martin 1.25 .50
- ❑ 134 Jay Fiedler 2.00 .75
- ❑ 135 John Randle 1.25 .50
- ❑ 136 Troy Brown 1.25 .50
- ❑ 137 Amani Toomer 1.25 .50
- ❑ 138 Kerry Collins 1.25 .50
- ❑ 139 Tiki Barber 2.00 .75
- ❑ 140 Wayne Chrebet 1.25 .50
- ❑ 141 Tyrone Wheatley 1.25 .50
- ❑ 142 Duce Staley 2.00 .75
- ❑ 143 Jermaine Fazande .75 .30
- ❑ 144 Charlie Garner 1.25 .50
- ❑ 145 Torry Holt 2.00 .75
- ❑ 146 Mike Alstott 2.00 .75
- ❑ 147 Shaun King .50 .20
- ❑ 148 Darrell Green .75 .30
- ❑ 149 Brad Johnson 2.00 .75
- ❑ 150 Olandis Gary 2.00 .75
- ❑ 151 Jake Plummer 1.50 .60
- ❑ 152 Chris Chandler 1.50 .60
- ❑ 153 Jamal Anderson 2.50 1.00
- ❑ 154 Eric Moulds 2.50 1.00
- ❑ 155 Doug Flutie 2.50 1.00
- ❑ 156 Rob Johnson 1.50 .60
- ❑ 157 Marcus Robinson 2.50 1.00
- ❑ 158 Cade McNown 1.00 .40
- ❑ 159 Akili Smith 1.00 .40
- ❑ 160 Tim Couch 1.50 .60
- ❑ 161 Emmitt Smith 5.00 2.00
- ❑ 162 Troy Aikman 5.00 2.00
- ❑ 163 Brian Griese 2.50 1.00
- ❑ 164 John Elway 8.00 3.00
- ❑ 165 Terrell Davis 2.50 1.00
- ❑ 166 Dorsey Levens 1.50 .60
- ❑ 167 Antonio Freeman 2.50 1.00
- ❑ 168 Brett Favre 8.00 3.00
- ❑ 169 Marvin Harrison 2.50 1.00
- ❑ 170 Peyton Manning 6.00 2.50
- ❑ 171 Edgerrin James 4.00 1.50
- ❑ 172 Jimmy Smith 1.50 .60
- ❑ 173 Elvis Grbac 1.50 .60
- ❑ 174 Dan Marino 8.00 3.00
- ❑ 175 Randy Moss 5.00 2.00
- ❑ 176 Cris Carter 2.50 1.00
- ❑ 177 Robert Smith 2.50 1.00
- ❑ 178 Daunte Culpepper 3.00 1.25
- ❑ 179 Terry Glenn 1.50 .60
- ❑ 180 Drew Bledsoe 3.00 1.25
- ❑ 181 Ricky Williams 1.25 .50
- ❑ 182 Jake Delhomme RC 8.00 3.00
- ❑ 183 Curtis Martin 2.50 1.00
- ❑ 184 Vinny Testaverde 1.50 .60
- ❑ 185 Tim Brown 2.50 1.00
- ❑ 186 Rich Gannon 2.50 1.00
- ❑ 187 Donovan McNabb 3.00 1.25
- ❑ 188 Jerome Bettis 2.50 1.00
- ❑ 189 Bobby Shaw RC 2.50 1.00
- ❑ 190 Jerry Rice 5.00 2.00
- ❑ 191 Steve Young 3.00 1.25
- ❑ 192 Jeff Garcia 2.50 1.00
- ❑ 193 Ricky Watters 1.00 .40
- ❑ 194 Isaac Bruce 2.50 1.00
- ❑ 195 Marshall Faulk 3.00 1.25
- ❑ 196 Kurt Warner 5.00 2.00
- ❑ 197 Keyshawn Johnson 2.50 1.00
- ❑ 198 Eddie George 2.50 1.00
- ❑ 199 Steve McNair 2.50 1.00
- ❑ 200 Stephen Davis 2.50 1.00
- ❑ 201 Bobby Brooks RC 3.00 1.25
- ❑ 202 Cornelius Griffin RC 4.00 1.50
- ❑ 203 Danny Clark RC 4.00 1.50
- ❑ 204 Pat Dennis RC 3.00 1.25
- ❑ 205 Tommy Hendricks RC 5.00 2.00
- ❑ 206 Fred Jones RC 3.00 1.25
- ❑ 207 Isaiah Kacyvenski RC 3.00 1.25
- ❑ 208 Keith Miller RC 3.00 1.25
- ❑ 209 Andre O' Neal RC 3.00 1.25
- ❑ 210 Justin Snow RC 3.00 1.25
- ❑ 211 Armegis Spearman RC 4.00 1.50
- ❑ 212 Lester Towns RC 3.00 1.25
- ❑ 213 Antonio Wilson RC 3.00 1.25
- ❑ 214 Greg Wesley RC 5.00 2.00
- ❑ 215 Jabari Issa RC 3.00 1.25
- ❑ 216 Darwin Walker RC 3.00 1.25
- ❑ 217 Reggie Grimes RC 3.00 1.25
- ❑ 218 Rian Lindell RC 3.00 1.25
- ❑ 219 Chris Combs RC 3.00 1.25
- ❑ 220 Rashard Anderson RC 4.00 1.50
- ❑ 221 Erik Flowers RC 4.00 1.50
- ❑ 222 Corey Moore RC 3.00 1.25
- ❑ 223 Rob Meier RC 3.00 1.25
- ❑ 224 John Milem RC 3.00 1.25
- ❑ 225 Jeremiah Parker RC 3.00 1.25
- ❑ 226 Neil Rackers RC 5.00 2.00
- ❑ 227 Josh Taves RC 4.00 1.50
- ❑ 228 Mao Tosi RC 3.00 1.25
- ❑ 229 Gary Berry RC 3.00 1.25
- ❑ 230 Matt Bowen RC 3.00 1.25
- ❑ 231 Ralph Brown RC 3.00 1.25
- ❑ 232 Tony Darden RC 3.00 1.25
- ❑ 233 Arturo Freeman RC 3.00 1.25
- ❑ 234 David Gibson RC 3.00 1.25
- ❑ 235 Demario Brown RC 3.00 1.25
- ❑ 236 Deveron Harper RC 3.00 1.25
- ❑ 237 Johnnie Harris RC 3.00 1.25
- ❑ 238 Marcus Knight RC 4.00 1.50
- ❑ 239 Ronnie Heard RC 4.00 1.50
- ❑ 240 Eric Johnson RC 4.00 1.50
- ❑ 241 John Keith RC 3.00 1.25
- ❑ 242 Anthony Malbrough RC 3.00 1.25
- ❑ 243 Anthony Mitchell RC 3.00 1.25
- ❑ 244 Aric Morris RC 3.00 1.25
- ❑ 245 Bobby Myers RC 3.00 1.25
- ❑ 246 Erik Olson RC 3.00 1.25
- ❑ 247 Lewis Sanders RC 3.00 1.25
- ❑ 248 Tony Scott RC 3.00 1.25
- ❑ 249 David Terrell RC 3.00 1.25
- ❑ 250 Travares Tillman RC 3.00 1.25
- ❑ 251 David Stachelski RC 4.00 1.50
- ❑ 252 Darren Howard RC 5.00 2.00
- ❑ 253 Frank Chamberlin RC 4.00 1.50
- ❑ 254 Na'il Diggs RC 5.00 2.00
- ❑ 255 Orantes Grant RC 4.00 1.50
- ❑ 256 Barrett Green RC 4.00 1.50
- ❑ 257 Kory Minor RC 4.00 1.50
- ❑ 258 Deon Grant RC 5.00 2.00
- ❑ 259 Mark Simoneau RC 5.00 2.00
- ❑ 260 Raynoch Thompson RC 5.00 2.00
- ❑ 261 Kenyatta Wright RC 4.00 1.50
- ❑ 262 Marcus Bell LB RC 4.00 1.50
- ❑ 263 Jack Golden RC 4.00 1.50
- ❑ 264 Thomas Hamner RC 4.00 1.50
- ❑ 265 Sekou Sanyika RC 4.00 1.50
- ❑ 266 Marcus Washington RC 5.00 2.00
- ❑ 267 Tim Seder RC 5.00 2.00
- ❑ 268 Paul Edinger RC 6.00 2.50
- ❑ 269 Michael Boireau RC 4.00 1.50
- ❑ 270 Byron Frisch RC 4.00 1.50
- ❑ 271 Ketric Sanford RC 4.00 1.50
- ❑ 272 Frank Murphy RC 4.00 1.50
- ❑ 273 Robaire Smith RC 4.00 1.50
- ❑ 274 Adalius Thomas RC 10.00 4.00
- ❑ 275 William Bartee RC 5.00 2.00
- ❑ 276 Robert Bean RC 5.00 2.00
- ❑ 277 Tyrone Carter RC 6.00 2.50
- ❑ 278 Ike Charlton RC 4.00 1.50
- ❑ 279 Mario Edwards RC 5.00 2.00
- ❑ 280 Dwayne Goodrich RC 4.00 1.50
- ❑ 281 Michael Hawthorne RC 4.00 1.50
- ❑ 282 Kareem Larrimore RC 4.00 1.50
- ❑ 283 Mark Roman RC 5.00 2.00
- ❑ 284 Jacoby Shepherd RC 4.00 1.50
- ❑ 285 Jason Webster RC 4.00 1.50
- ❑ 286 Jimmy Wyrick RC 4.00 1.50
- ❑ 287 Rashidi Barnes RC 4.00 1.50
- ❑ 288 David Barrett RC 4.00 1.50
- ❑ 289 Ainsley Battles RC 4.00 1.50
- ❑ 290 Lamar Chapman RC 4.00 1.50
- ❑ 291 Todd Franz RC 4.00 1.50
- ❑ 292 Michael Green RC 4.00 1.50
- ❑ 293 Antwan Harris RC 4.00 1.50
- ❑ 294 Brandon Jennings RC 4.00 1.50
- ❑ 295 Darrick Vaughn RC 4.00 1.50
- ❑ 296 David Macklin RC 4.00 1.50
- ❑ 297 Bobby Brown RC 4.00 1.50
- ❑ 298 Reggie Stephens RC 4.00 1.50
- ❑ 299 Kenoy Kennedy RC 4.00 1.50
- ❑ 300 Raion Hill RC 4.00 1.50
- ❑ 301 Windrell Hayes RC 8.00 3.00
- ❑ 302 DaShon Polk RC 6.00 2.50
- ❑ 303 Tywan Mitchell RC 8.00 3.00
- ❑ 304 Casey Crawford RC 6.00 2.50
- ❑ 305 Hank Poteat RC 8.00 3.00
- ❑ 306 Mondriel Fulcher RC 6.00 2.50
- ❑ 307 Cory Geason RC 6.00 2.50
- ❑ 308 James Hill RC 6.00 2.50
- ❑ 309 Brian Jennings RC 6.00 2.50
- ❑ 310 John Jones RC 8.00 3.00
- ❑ 311 Anthony Lucas RC 6.00 2.50
- ❑ 312 Mike Leach RC 6.00 2.50
- ❑ 313 Dustin Lyman RC 6.00 2.50
- ❑ 314 Derek Rackley RC 6.00 2.50
- ❑ 315 Sebastian Janikowski RC 10.00 4.00
- ❑ 316 Brad St.Louis RC 6.00 2.50
- ❑ 317 Jay Tant RC 6.00 2.50
- ❑ 318 Austin Wheatley RC 6.00 2.50
- ❑ 319 Jermaine Wiggins RC 10.00 4.00
- ❑ 320 Todd Yoder RC 8.00 3.00
- ❑ 321 Deon Dyer RC 8.00 3.00
- ❑ 322 Jim Finn 6.00 2.50
- ❑ 323 Herbert Goodman RC 8.00 3.00
- ❑ 324 Mike Green RC 8.00 3.00
- ❑ 325 Dante Hall RC 20,00 7.50
- ❑ 326 Thabiti Davis RC 6.00 2.50
- ❑ 327 Kevin Houser RC 8.00 3.00
- ❑ 328 Jonas Lewis RC 6.00 2.50
- ❑ 329 Chad Morton RC 10.00 4.00
- ❑ 330 Patrick Pass RC 8.00 3.00
- ❑ 331 Maurice Smith RC 10.00 4.00
- ❑ 332 Paul Smith RC 8.00 3.00
- ❑ 333 Terrelle Smith RC 8.00 3.00
- ❑ 334 Craig Walendy RC 6.00 2.50
- ❑ 335 Jamel White RC 8.00 3.00
- ❑ 336 Jarious Jackson RC 8.00 3.00
- ❑ 337 Matt Lytle RC 8.00 3.00
- ❑ 338 Ron Powlus RC 10.00 4.00
- ❑ 339 Ian Gold RC 8.00 3.00
- ❑ 340 Brandon Short RC 8.00 3.00
- ❑ 341 T.J. Slaughter RC 6.00 2.50
- ❑ 342 Nate Webster RC 6.00 2.50
- ❑ 343 John Engelberger RC 8.00 3.00
- ❑ 344 Rogers Beckett RC 8.00 3.00
- ❑ 345 Mike Brown RC 15.00 6.00
- ❑ 346 Anthony Wright RC 12.00 5.00
- ❑ 347 Danny Farmer RC 8.00 3.00
- ❑ 348 Clint Stoerner RC 8.00 3.00
- ❑ 349 Julian Peterson RC 10.00 4.00
- ❑ 350 Ahmed Plummer RC 10.00 4.00
- ❑ 351 Avion Black RC 10.00 4.00
- ❑ 352 Kwame Cavil RC 8.00 3.00
- ❑ 353 Chris Cole RC 10.00 4.00
- ❑ 354 Chris Coleman RC 8.00 3.00
- ❑ 355 Trevor Gaylor RC 10.00 4.00
- ❑ 356 Damon Hodge RC 10.00 4.00
- ❑ 357 Darrell Jackson RC 25.00 10.00
- ❑ 358 Reggie Jones RC 8.00 3.00
- ❑ 359 Charles Lee RC 8.00 3.00
- ❑ 360 Jerry Porter RC 15.00 6.00
- ❑ 361 Bobby Shaw 10.00 4.00
- ❑ 362 Ron Dugans RC 8.00 3.00

❑ 363 James Williams RC 10.00 4.00
❑ 364 Bashir Yamini RC 8.00 3.00
❑ 365 Anthony Becht RC 12.00 5.00
❑ 366 Erron Kinney RC 12.00 5.00
❑ 367 Aaron Shea RC 10.00 4.00
❑ 368 Chris Samuels RC 10.00 4.00
❑ 369 Trung Canidate RC 10.00 4.00
❑ 370 Obafemi Ayanbadejo RC 10.00 4.00
❑ 371 Doug Chapman RC 10.00 4.00
❑ 372 Ronney Jenkins RC 10.00 4.00
❑ 373 Curtis Keaton RC 10.00 4.00
❑ 374 Kevin McDougal RC 10.00 4.00
❑ 375 Frank Moreau RC 10.00 4.00
❑ 376 Aaron Stecker RC 12.00 5.00
❑ 377 Shyrone Stith RC 10.00 4.00
❑ 378 Tom Brady RC 400.00 250.00
❑ 379 Giovanni Carmazzi RC 8.00 3.00
❑ 380 Joe Hamilton RC 10.00 4.00
❑ 381 Todd Husak RC 12.00 5.00
❑ 382 Doug Johnson RC 12.00 5.00
❑ 383 Tee Martin RC 12.00 5.00
❑ 384 Chad Pennington RC 60.00 25.00
❑ 385 Tim Rattay RC 12.00 5.00
❑ 386 Chris Redman RC 10.00 4.00
❑ 387 Billy Volek RC 20.00 7.50
❑ 388 Spergon Wynn RC 10.00 4.00
❑ 389 John Abraham RC 12.00 5.00
❑ 390 Keith Bulluck RC 12.00 5.00
❑ 391 Rob Morris RC 10.00 4.00
❑ 392 JaJuan Dawson RC 8.00 3.00
❑ 393 Chris Hovan RC 10.00 4.00
❑ 394 Shaun Ellis RC 12.00 5.00
❑ 395 Deltha O'Neal RC 12.00 5.00
❑ 396 Gari Scott RC 8.00 3.00
❑ 397 Dialleo Burks RC 8.00 3.00
❑ 398 Shockmain Davis RC 8.00 3.00
❑ 399 Brad Hoover RC 10.00 4.00
❑ 400 Brian Finneran RC 12.00 5.00
❑ 401 Sylvester Morris J/FB/750 RC 8.00 3.00
❑ 402 Denn Northcutt J/FB/500 RC 25.00 10.00
❑ 403 Todd Pinkston J/FB/100 RC 20.00 7.50
❑ 404 Larry Foster J/FB/500 RC 20.00 7.50
❑ 405 R.Jay Soward J/FB/1000 RC 12.00 5.00
❑ 406 Travis Taylor J/FB/250 RC 40.00 15.00
❑ 407 Peter Warrick J/FB/1000 RC 20.00 7.50
❑ 408 Dez White J/FB/1000 RC 20.00 7.50
❑ 409 Ron Dayne J/FB/1000 RC 20.00 7.50
❑ 410 Thomas Jones J/FB/500 RC 25.00 10.00
❑ 411 Jamal Lewis J/FB/1000 RC 30.00 12.50
❑ 412 Sammy Morris J/FB/500 RC 25.00 10.00
❑ 413 Travis Prentice J/FB/500 RC 20.00 7.50
❑ 414 J.R. Redmond J/FB/250 RC 25.00 10.00
❑ 415 Michael Wiley FB/1000 RC 12.00 5.00
❑ 416 Laver Coles J/FB/250 RC 40.00 15.00
❑ 417 Bubba Franks J/FB/500 RC 20.00 7.50
❑ 418 Mike Anderson J/FB/250 RC 40.00 20.00
❑ 419 Plaxico Burress J/FB/250 RC 60.00 25.00
❑ 420 Ron Dixon J/FB/1000 RC 12.00 5.00
❑ 421 Troy Walters J/FB/1000 RC 12.00 5.00
❑ 422 Sha Alexander J/FB/1000 RC 50.00 25.00
❑ 423 Brian Urlacher J/FB/1000 RC 40.00 15.00
❑ 424 Corey Simon J/FB/1000 RC 12.00 5.00
❑ 425 Courtney Brown J/FB/500 RC 25.00 10.00

2003 Leaf Limited

❑ COMP.SET w/o SP's (100) 250.00 100.00
❑ 1 Emmitt Smith 10.00 4.00
❑ 2 Michael Vick 10.00 4.00
❑ 3 Peerless Price 2.50 1.00
❑ 4 T.J. Duckett 2.50 1.00
❑ 5 Jamal Lewis 4.00 1.50
❑ 6 Drew Bledsoe 4.00 1.50
❑ 7 Eric Moulds 2.50 1.00
❑ 8 Travis Henry 2.50 1.00
❑ 9 Jim Kelly 8.00 3.00
❑ 10 Julius Peppers 4.00 1.50
❑ 11 Dick Butkus 6.00 2.50
❑ 12 Mike Singletary 4.00 1.50
❑ 13 Walter Payton 15.00 6.00
❑ 14 Anthony Thomas 2.50 1.00
❑ 15 Brian Urlacher 6.00 2.50
❑ 16 Marty Booker 2.50 1.00
❑ 17 Corey Dillon 2.50 1.00
❑ 18 Jim Thorpe 5.00 2.00
❑ 19 Jim Brown 10.00 4.00
❑ 20 Tim Couch 2.50 1.00
❑ 21 William Green 2.50 1.00
❑ 22 Deion Sanders 4.00 1.50
❑ 23 Michael Irvin 4.00 1.50
❑ 24 Roger Staubach 8.00 3.00
❑ 25 Troy Aikman 6.00 2.50
❑ 26 Tony Dorsett 6.00 2.50
❑ 27 Antonio Bryant 2.50 1.00
❑ 28 Clinton Portis 6.00 2.50
❑ 29 Jake Plummer 2.50 1.00
❑ 30 Rod Smith 2.50 1.00
❑ 31 Barry Sanders 8.00 3.00
❑ 32 Doak Walker 4.00 1.50
❑ 33 Joey Harrington 6.00 2.50
❑ 34 Bart Starr 8.00 3.00
❑ 35 Ahman Green 4.00 1.50
❑ 36 Brett Favre 10.00 4.00
❑ 37 Donald Driver 2.50 1.00
❑ 38 David Carr 6.00 2.50
❑ 39 Don Shula 5.00 2.00
❑ 40 Johnny Unitas 8.00 3.00
❑ 41 Edgerrin James 4.00 1.50
❑ 42 Marvin Harrison 4.00 1.50
❑ 43 Peyton Manning 6.00 2.50
❑ 44 Fred Taylor 4.00 1.50
❑ 45 Jimmy Smith 2.50 1.00
❑ 46 Mark Brunell 2.50 1.00
❑ 47 Marcus Allen 4.00 1.50
❑ 48 Priest Holmes 5.00 2.00
❑ 49 Tony Gonzalez 2.50 1.00
❑ 50 Trent Green 2.50 1.00
❑ 51 Dan Marino 12.00 5.00
❑ 52 Bob Griese 5.00 2.00
❑ 53 Chris Chambers 4.00 1.50
❑ 54 Ricky Williams 4.00 1.50
❑ 55 Fran Tarkenton 5.00 2.00
❑ 56 Daunte Culpepper 4.00 1.50
❑ 57 Michael Bennett 2.50 1.00
❑ 58 Randy Moss 6.00 2.50
❑ 59 Tom Brady 10.00 4.00
❑ 60 Aaron Brooks 4.00 1.50
❑ 61 Deuce McAllister 4.00 1.50
❑ 62 Donte Stallworth 4.00 1.50
❑ 63 Mark Bavaro 2.50 1.00
❑ 64 Jeremy Shockey 6.00 2.50
❑ 65 Kerry Collins 2.50 1.00
❑ 66 Tiki Barber 4.00 1.50
❑ 67 Joe Namath 8.00 3.00
❑ 68 Chad Pennington 5.00 2.00
❑ 69 Curtis Martin 4.00 1.50
❑ 70 Jerry Porter 2.50 1.00
❑ 71 Jerry Rice 8.00 3.00
❑ 72 Rich Gannon 2.50 1.00
❑ 73 Tim Brown 4.00 1.50
❑ 74 Donovan McNabb 5.00 2.00
❑ 75 Terry Bradshaw 8.00 3.00
❑ 76 Antwaan Randle El 4.00 1.50
❑ 77 Plaxico Burress 2.50 1.00
❑ 78 Tommy Maddox 4.00 1.50
❑ 79 David Boston 2.50 1.00
❑ 80 Drew Brees 4.00 1.50
❑ 81 LaDainian Tomlinson 4.00 1.50
❑ 82 Joe Montana 20.00 7.50
❑ 83 Steve Young 5.00 2.00
❑ 84 Jeff Garcia 4.00 1.50
❑ 85 Terrell Owens 4.00 1.50
❑ 86 Koren Robinson 2.50 1.00
❑ 87 Matt Hasselbeck 2.50 1.00
❑ 88 Shaun Alexander 4.00 1.50
❑ 89 Isaac Bruce 4.00 1.50
❑ 90 Kurt Warner 4.00 1.50
❑ 91 Marshall Faulk 4.00 1.50
❑ 92 Torry Holt 4.00 1.50
❑ 93 Brad Johnson 2.50 1.00
❑ 94 Keyshawn Johnson 4.00 1.50
❑ 95 Earl Campbell 4.00 1.50
❑ 96 Eddie George 2.50 1.00
❑ 97 Steve McNair 4.00 1.50
❑ 98 John Riggins 6.00 2.50
❑ 99 Laveranues Coles 2.50 1.00
❑ 100 Patrick Ramsey 4.00 1.50
❑ 101 LaTarence Dunbar RC 5.00 2.00
❑ 102 Sam Aiken RC 5.00 2.00
❑ 103 Bobby Wade RC 6.00 2.50
❑ 104 Justin Gage RC 6.00 2.50
❑ 105 Lee Suggs RC 8.00 3.00
❑ 106 Jason Witten RC 12.00 5.00
❑ 107 Quentin Griffin RC 6.00 2.50
❑ 108 Domanick Davis RC 6.00 2.50
❑ 109 LaBrandon Toefield RC 6.00 2.50
❑ 110 J.R. Tolver RC 5.00 2.00
❑ 111 Kliff Kingsbury RC 5.00 2.00
❑ 112 Talman Gardner RC 6.00 2.50
❑ 113 Teyo Johnson RC 6.00 2.50
❑ 114 Billy McMullen RC 5.00 2.00
❑ 115 L.J. Smith RC 6.00 2.50
❑ 116 Brian St.Pierre RC 6.00 2.50
❑ 117 Brandon Lloyd RC 8.00 3.00
❑ 118 Seneca Wallace RC 6.00 2.50
❑ 119 Kevin Curtis RC 8.00 3.00
❑ 120 Shaun McDonald RC 6.00 2.50
❑ 121 Terrell Suggs RC 10.00 4.00
❑ 122 Terence Newman RC 12.00 5.00
❑ 123 Tony Romo RC 60.00 35.00
❑ 124 DeWayne Robertson RC 6.00 2.50
❑ 125 Marcus Trufant RC 6.00 2.50
❑ 126 Artose Pinner AU RC 25.00 10.00
❑ 127 Bryant Johnson AU RC 25.00 10.00
❑ 128 Kelley Washington AU RC 30.00 12.50
❑ 129 Dallas Clark AU RC 25.00 10.00
❑ 130 Onterrio Smith AU RC 25.00 10.00
❑ 131 Tony Hollings AU RC 25.00 10.00
❑ 132 Tyrone Calico AU RC 25.00 10.00
❑ 133 Carson Palmer AU RC 150.00 75.00
❑ 134 Byron Leftwich AU RC 60.00 25.00
❑ 135 Rex Grossman AU RC 60.00 25.00
❑ 136 Kyle Boller AU RC 25.00 10.00
❑ 137 Chris Simms AU RC 50.00 20.00
❑ 138 Dave Ragone AU RC 25.00 10.00
❑ 139 Ken Dorsey AU RC 25.00 10.00
❑ 140 Willis McGahee AU RC 80.00 40.00
❑ 141 Larry Johnson AU RC 120.00 50.00
❑ 142 Musa Smith AU RC 25.00 10.00
❑ 143 Chris Brown AU RC 25.00 10.00
❑ 144 Charles Rogers AU RC 25.00 10.00
❑ 145 Andre Johnson AU RC 60.00 30.00
❑ 146 Taylor Jacobs AU RC 25.00 10.00
❑ 147 Anquan Boldin AU RC 80.00 40.00
❑ 148 Bethel Johnson AU RC 25.00 10.00
❑ 149 Justin Fargas AU RC 30.00 12.50
❑ 150 Nate Burleson AU RC 25.00 10.00

2004 Leaf Limited

❑ 201-233 JSY AU PRINT RUN 150 SETS
❑ 1 A.J. Feeley 4.00 1.50
❑ 2 Aaron Brooks 3.00 1.25
❑ 3 Ahman Green 4.00 1.50
❑ 4 Andre Johnson 4.00 1.50
❑ 5 Anquan Boldin 4.00 1.50
❑ 6 Antwaan Randle El 4.00 1.50
❑ 7 Ashley Lelie 3.00 1.25
❑ 8 Brad Johnson 3.00 1.25
❑ 9 Brett Favre 10.00 4.00
❑ 10 Brian Urlacher 5.00 2.00
❑ 11 Brian Westbrook 3.00 1.25
❑ 12 Byron Leftwich 5.00 2.00
❑ 13 Carson Palmer 5.00 2.00
❑ 14 Chad Johnson 4.00 1.50

❑ 15 Chad Pennington 4.00 1.50
❑ 16 Charlie Garner 3.00 1.25
❑ 17 Charles Rogers 3.00 1.25
❑ 18 Chris Brown 4.00 1.50
❑ 19 Chris Chambers 3.00 1.25
❑ 20 Clinton Portis 4.00 1.50
❑ 21 Corey Dillon 3.00 1.25
❑ 22 Deion Sanders 4.00 1.50
❑ 23 Curtis Martin 4.00 1.50
❑ 24 Daunte Culpepper 4.00 1.50
❑ 25 David Terrell 3.00 1.25
❑ 26 David Carr 4.00 1.50
❑ 27 Deion Branch 4.00 1.50
❑ 28 Derrick Mason 3.00 1.25
❑ 29 DeShaun Foster 3.00 1.25
❑ 30 Deuce McAllister 4.00 1.50
❑ 31 Domanick Davis 4.00 1.50
❑ 32 Donovan McNabb 5.00 2.00
❑ 33 Donte Stallworth 3.00 1.25
❑ 34 Drew Bledsoe 4.00 1.50
❑ 35 Duce Staley 3.00 1.25
❑ 36 Eddie George 3.00 1.25
❑ 37 Edgerrin James 4.00 1.50
❑ 38 Emmitt Smith 8.00 3.00
❑ 39 Eric Moulds 3.00 1.25
❑ 40 Fred Taylor 3.00 1.25
❑ 41 Hines Ward 4.00 1.50
❑ 42 Isaac Bruce 4.00 1.50
❑ 43 Jake Delhomme 4.00 1.50
❑ 44 Jake Plummer 3.00 1.25
❑ 45 Javon Walker 3.00 1.25
❑ 46 Jeff Garcia 4.00 1.50
❑ 47 Jeremy Shockey 4.00 1.50
❑ 48 Jerome Bettis 4.00 1.50
❑ 49 Jerry Porter 3.00 1.25
❑ 50 Jerry Rice 8.00 3.00
❑ 51 Jevon Kearse 3.00 1.25
❑ 52 Jimmy Smith 3.00 1.25
❑ 53 Joe Horn 3.00 1.25
❑ 54 Joey Harrington 4.00 1.50
❑ 55 Josh McCown 3.00 1.25
❑ 56 Kevan Barlow 3.00 1.25
❑ 57 Koren Robinson 3.00 1.25
❑ 58 Kyle Boller 4.00 1.50
❑ 59 LaDainian Tomlinson 5.00 2.00
❑ 60 LaVar Arrington 8.00 3.00
❑ 61 Laveranues Coles 3.00 1.25
❑ 62 Lee Suggs 4.00 1.50
❑ 63 Marc Bulger 4.00 1.50
❑ 64 Mark Brunell 3.00 1.25
❑ 65 Marshall Faulk 4.00 1.50
❑ 66 Marvin Harrison 4.00 1.50
❑ 67 Matt Hasselbeck 3.00 1.25
❑ 68 Michael Bennett 3.00 1.25
❑ 69 Michael Strahan 3.00 1.25
❑ 70 Michael Vick 8.00 3.00
❑ 71 Peerless Price 3.00 1.25
❑ 72 Peter Warrick 3.00 1.25
❑ 73 Peyton Manning 6.00 2.50
❑ 74 Priest Holmes 5.00 2.00
❑ 75 Quentin Griffin 4.00 1.50
❑ 76 Randy Moss 5.00 2.00
❑ 77 Ray Lewis 4.00 1.50
❑ 78 Rex Grossman 4.00 1.50
❑ 79 Lamar Gordon 2.50 1.00
❑ 80 Rod Smith 3.00 1.25
❑ 81 Roy Williams S 3.00 1.25
❑ 82 Rudi Johnson 3.00 1.25
❑ 83 Santana Moss 3.00 1.25
❑ 84 Shaun Alexander 4.00 1.50
❑ 85 Stephen Davis 3.00 1.25
❑ 86 Steve McNair 4.00 1.50
❑ 87 Steve Smith 4.00 1.50
❑ 88 T.J. Duckett 3.00 1.25
❑ 89 Terrell Owens 4.00 1.50
❑ 90 Thomas Jones 3.00 1.25
❑ 91 Tiki Barber 4.00 1.50
❑ 92 Tim Brown 4.00 1.50
❑ 93 Tom Brady 10.00 4.00
❑ 94 Tony Gonzalez 3.00 1.25
❑ 95 Torry Holt 4.00 1.50
❑ 96 Travis Henry 3.00 1.25
❑ 97 Trent Green 3.00 1.25
❑ 98 Warren Sapp 3.00 1.25
❑ 99 William Green 3.00 1.25
❑ 100 Willis McGahee 4.00 1.50
❑ 101 Barry Sanders 8.00 3.00
❑ 102 Bart Starr 10.00 4.00
❑ 103 Bo Jackson 8.00 3.00
❑ 104 Bob Griese 5.00 2.00
❑ 105 Bronko Nagurski 5.00 2.00
❑ 106 Dan Marino 12.00 5.00
❑ 107 Deion Sanders 8.00 3.00
❑ 108 Dick Butkus 8.00 3.00
❑ 109 Doak Walker 5.00 2.00
❑ 110 Don Maynard 4.00 1.50
❑ 111 Don Shula 5.00 2.00
❑ 112 Earl Campbell 5.00 2.00
❑ 113 Fran Tarkenton 6.00 2.50
❑ 114 Franco Harris 6.00 2.50
❑ 115 Fred Biletnikoff 5.00 2.00
❑ 116 Gale Sayers 6.00 2.50
❑ 117 Herman Edwards 4.00 1.50
❑ 118 Jim D[illegible] [illegible] [illegible]
❑ 119 Jim Kelly 6.00 2.50
❑ 120 Jim Thorpe 5.00 2.00
❑ 121 Jimmy Johnson 4.00 1.50
❑ 122 Joe Greene 5.00 2.00
❑ 123 Joe Montana 15.00 6.00
❑ 124 Joe Namath 8.00 3.00
❑ 125 John Elway 8.00 3.00
❑ 126 John Riggins 6.00 2.50
❑ 127 Johnny Unitas 8.00 3.00
❑ 128 Larry Csonka 5.00 2.00
❑ 129 Lawrence Taylor 5.00 2.00
❑ 130 Marcus Allen 5.00 2.00
❑ 131 Mark Bavaro 3.00 1.25
❑ 132 Michael Irvin 5.00 2.00
❑ 133 Mike Ditka 5.00 2.00
❑ 134 Mike Singletary 5.00 2.00
❑ 135 Ozzie Newsome 4.00 1.50
❑ 136 Paul Warfield 4.00 1.50
❑ 137 Randall Cunningham 4.00 1.50
❑ 138 Ray Nitschke 5.00 2.00
❑ 139 Red Grange 6.00 2.50
❑ 140 Reggie White 5.00 2.00
❑ 141 Roger Staubach 8.00 3.00
❑ 142 Sterling Sharpe 4.00 1.50
❑ 143 Steve Largent 5.00 2.00
❑ 144 Terrell Davis 5.00 2.00
❑ 145 Terry Bradshaw 8.00 3.00
❑ 146 Thurman Thomas 4.00 1.50
❑ 147 Tony Dorsett 5.00 2.00
❑ 148 Troy Aikman 6.00 2.50
❑ 149 Walter Payton 15.00 6.00
❑ 150 Warren Moon 4.00 1.50
❑ 151 Ahmad Carroll RC 10.00 4.00
❑ 152 Andy Hall RC 8.00 3.00
❑ 153 Antwan Odom RC 10.00 4.00
❑ 154 B.J. Symons RC 10.00 4.00
❑ 155 Carlos Francis RC 8.00 3.00
❑ 156 Casey Bramlet RC 8.00 3.00
❑ 157 Chris Cooley RC 10.00 4.00
❑ 158 Chris Gamble RC 10.00 4.00
❑ 159 Clarence Moore RC 10.00 4.00
❑ 160 Cody Pickett RC 10.00 4.00
❑ 161 Courtney Watson RC 10.00 4.00
❑ 162 Craig Krenzel RC 10.00 4.00
❑ 163 D.J. Hackett RC 8.00 3.00
❑ 164 D.J. Williams RC 10.00 4.00
❑ 165 Derrick Strait RC 10.00 4.00
❑ 166 Dontarrious Thomas RC 10.00 4.00
❑ 167 Drew Henson RC 10.00 4.00
❑ 168 Ernest Wilford RC 10.00 4.00
❑ 169 Jamaar Taylor RC 10.00 4.00
❑ 170 Jason Babin RC 10.00 4.00
❑ 171 Jeff Smoker RC 10.00 4.00
❑ 172 Jerricho Cotchery RC 10.00 4.00
❑ 173 Jim Sorgi RC 10.00 4.00
❑ 174 Joey Thomas RC 10.00 4.00
❑ 175 John Navarre RC 10.00 4.00
❑ 176 Johnnie Morant RC 10.00 4.00
❑ 177 Jonathan Vilma RC 10.00 4.00
❑ 178 Josh Harris RC 10.00 4.00
❑ 179 Keiwan Ratliff RC 8.00 3.00
❑ 180 Kenechi Udeze RC 10.00 4.00
❑ 181 Kris Wilson RC 10.00 4.00
❑ 182 Marcus Tubbs RC 10.00 4.00
❑ 183 Marquise Hill RC 8.00 3.00
❑ 184 Matt Mauck RC 10.00 4.00
❑ 185 Maurice Mann RC 8.00 3.00
❑ 186 Michael Boulware RC 10.00 4.00
❑ 187 Michael Turner RC 12.00 5.00
❑ 188 P.K. Sam RC 8.00 3.00
❑ 189 Patrick Crayton RC 10.00 4.00
❑ 190 Ricardo Colclough RC 10.00 4.00
❑ 191 Richard Smith RC 8.00 3.00
❑ 192 Samie Parker RC 10.00 4.00
❑ 193 Sean Taylor RC 10.00 4.00
❑ 194 Teddy Lehman RC 10.00 4.00
❑ 195 Thomas Tapeh RC 8.00 3.00
❑ 196 Tommie Harris RC 10.00 4.00
❑ 197 Triandos Luke RC 10.00 4.00
❑ 198 Troy Fleming RC 8.00 3.00
❑ 199 Vince Wilfork RC 10.00 4.00
❑ 200 Will Smith RC 10.00 4.00
❑ 201 Larry Fitzgerald JSY AU RC 100.00 50.00
❑ 202 DeAngelo Hall JSY AU RC 40.00 15.00
❑ 203 Matt Schaub JSY AU RC 100.00 60.00
❑ 204 Michael Jenkins JSY AU RC 30.00 12.50
❑ 205 Devard Darling JSY AU RC 30.00 12.50
❑ 206 J.P. Losman JSY AU RC 50.00 25.00
❑ [illegible]
❑ 208 Keary Colbert JSY AU RC 30.00 12.50
❑ 209 Bernard Berrian JSY AU RC 40.00 20.00
❑ 211 K.Winslow JSY AU RC 60.00 30.00
❑ 212 Luke McCown JSY AU RC 30.00 12.50
❑ 213 Julius Jones JSY AU RC 100.00 40.00
❑ 214 Darius Watts JSY AU RC 30.00 12.50
❑ 215 Tatum Bell JSY AU RC 50.00 25.00
❑ 216 Kevin Jones JSY AU RC 60.00 30.00
❑ 217 Roy Will.WR JSY AU RC 100.00 50.00
❑ 218 Dunta Robinson JSY AU RC 30.00 12.50
❑ 219 Greg Jones JSY AU RC 30.00 12.50
❑ 220 Reggie Williams JSY AU RC 40.00 20.00
❑ 221 Mewelde Moore JSY AU RC 30.00 12.50
❑ 222 Ben Watson JSY AU RC 30.00 12.50
❑ 223 Cedric Cobbs JSY AU RC 30.00 12.50
❑ 224 Devery Henderson JSY AU RC 30.00 12.50
❑ 225 Eli Manning JSY AU RC 175.00 100.00
❑ 226 Robert Gallery JSY AU RC 30.00 12.50
❑ 227 Roethlisberger JSY AU RC 200.00 100.00
❑ 228 Philip Rivers JSY AU RC 120.00 60.00
❑ 229 Derrick Hamilton JSY AU RC 25.00 10.00
❑ 230 Rashaun Woods JSY AU RC 30.00 12.50
❑ 231 Stev.Jackson JSY AU RC 100.00 60.00
❑ 232 Michael Clayton JSY AU RC 60.00 25.00
❑ 233 Ben Troupe JSY AU RC 30.00 12.50

2005 Leaf Limited

❑ 1-150 PRINT RUN 599 SER.#'d SETS
❑ 151-200 ROOKIE PRINT RUN 250
❑ 201-229 JSY AU PRINT RUN 100 SETS
❑ JSY AU EXCH EXPIRATION 6/1/2007
❑ UNPRICED PLATINUM SER.#'d TO 1
❑ 1 Anquan Boldin 3.00 1.25
❑ 2 Kurt Warner 3.00 1.25
❑ 3 Larry Fitzgerald 4.00 1.50
❑ 4 Alge Crumpler 3.00 1.25
❑ 5 Michael Vick 6.00 2.50
❑ 6 Warrick Dunn 3.00 1.25
❑ 7 Jamal Lewis 4.00 1.50
❑ 8 Kyle Boller 3.00 1.25
❑ 9 Ray Lewis 4.00 1.50
❑ 10 Derrick Mason 3.00 1.25
❑ 11 J.P. Losman 4.00 1.50
❑ 12 Lee Evans 3.00 1.25
❑ 13 Willis McGahee 4.00 1.50
❑ 14 DeShaun Foster 3.00 1.25
❑ 15 Jake Delhomme 4.00 1.50
❑ 16 Steve Smith 3.00 1.25
❑ 17 Brian Urlacher 4.00 1.50
❑ 18 Rex Grossman 3.00 1.25
❑ 19 Muhsin Muhammad 3.00 1.25
❑ 20 Carson Palmer 4.00 1.50
❑ 21 Chad Johnson 4.00 1.50
❑ 22 Rudi Johnson 3.00 1.25
❑ 23 Antonio Bryant 2.50 1.00
❑ 24 Lee Suggs 3.00 1.25

❑ 25 Trent Dilfer 3.00 1.25
❑ 26 Drew Bledsoe 4.00 1.50
❑ 27 Julius Jones 5.00 2.00
❑ 28 Keyshawn Johnson 3.00 1.25
❑ 29 Roy Williams S 3.00 1.25
❑ 30 Ashley Lelie 3.00 1.25
❑ 31 Jake Plummer 3.00 1.25
❑ 32 Tatum Bell 3.00 1.25
❑ 33 Rod Smith 3.00 1.25
❑ 34 Joey Harrington 4.00 1.50
❑ 35 Kevin Jones 4.00 1.50
❑ 36 Roy Williams WR 4.00 1.50
❑ 37 Ahman Green 4.00 1.50
❑ 38 Brett Favre 10.00 4.00
❑ 39 Javon Walker 3.00 1.25
❑ 40 Andre Johnson 3.00 1.25
❑ 41 David Carr 4.00 1.50
❑ 42 Domanick Davis 3.00 1.25
❑ 43 Edgerrin James 4.00 1.50
❑ 44 Marvin Harrison 4.00 1.50
❑ 45 Peyton Manning 6.00 2.50
❑ 46 Reggie Wayne 3.00 1.25
❑ 47 Byron Leftwich 4.00 1.50
❑ 48 Fred Taylor 3.00 1.25
❑ 49 Jimmy Smith 3.00 1.25
❑ 50 Priest Holmes 4.00 1.50
❑ 51 Tony Gonzalez 3.00 1.25
❑ 52 Trent Green 3.00 1.25
❑ 53 Chris Chambers 3.00 1.25
❑ 54 Ricky Williams 3.00 1.25
❑ 55 Daunte Culpepper 4.00 1.50
❑ 56 Nate Burleson 3.00 1.25
❑ 57 Michael Bennett 3.00 1.25
❑ 58 Corey Dillon 3.00 1.25
❑ 59 Deion Branch 3.00 1.25
❑ 60 Tom Brady 10.00 4.00
❑ 61 Aaron Brooks 3.00 1.25
❑ 62 Deuce McAllister 4.00 1.50
❑ 63 Joe Horn 3.00 1.25
❑ 64 Eli Manning 8.00 3.00
❑ 65 Jeremy Shockey 4.00 1.50
❑ 66 Plaxico Burress 3.00 1.25
❑ 67 Tiki Barber 4.00 1.50
❑ 68 Chad Pennington 4.00 1.50
❑ 69 Curtis Martin 4.00 1.50
❑ 70 Laveranues Coles 3.00 1.25
❑ 71 Kerry Collins 3.00 1.25
❑ 72 LaMont Jordan 4.00 1.50
❑ 73 Randy Moss 4.00 1.50
❑ 74 Brian Westbrook 3.00 1.25
❑ 75 Donovan McNabb 5.00 2.00
❑ 76 Terrell Owens 4.00 1.50
❑ 77 Ben Roethlisberger 10.00 4.00
❑ 78 Duce Staley 3.00 1.25
❑ 79 Hines Ward 4.00 1.50
❑ 80 Jerome Bettis 4.00 1.50
❑ 81 Antonio Gates 4.00 1.50
❑ 82 Drew Brees 4.00 1.50
❑ 83 LaDainian Tomlinson 5.00 2.00
❑ 84 Brandon Lloyd 2.50 1.00
❑ 85 Kevan Barlow 3.00 1.25
❑ 86 Darrell Jackson 3.00 1.25
❑ 87 Matt Hasselbeck 3.00 1.25
❑ 88 Shaun Alexander 5.00 2.00
❑ 89 Marc Bulger 4.00 1.50
❑ 90 Steven Jackson 5.00 2.00
❑ 91 Torry Holt 4.00 1.50
❑ 92 Brian Griese 3.00 1.25
❑ 93 Michael Clayton 4.00 1.50
❑ 94 Chris Brown 3.00 1.25
❑ 95 Drew Bennett 3.00 1.25
❑ 96 Steve McNair 4.00 1.50
❑ 97 Clinton Portis 4.00 1.50
❑ 98 LaVar Arrington 4.00 1.50
❑ 99 Patrick Ramsey 3.00 1.25
❑ 100 Santana Moss 3.00 1.25
❑ 101 Barry Sanders 8.00 3.00
❑ 102 Bart Starr 8.00 3.00
❑ 103 Bo Jackson 6.00 2.50
❑ 104 Brian Piccolo 6.00 2.50
❑ 105 Bob Griese 5.00 2.00
❑ 106 Dan Fouts 5.00 2.00
❑ 107 Dan Marino 10.00 4.00
❑ 108 Deacon Jones 4.00 1.50
❑ 109 Doak Walker 5.00 2.00
❑ 110 Don Maynard 4.00 1.50
❑ 111 Don Meredith 5.00 2.00
❑ 112 Don Shula 4.00 1.50
❑ 113 Earl Campbell 5.00 2.00
❑ 114 Eric Dickerson 4.00 1.50
❑ 115 Fran Tarkenton 6.00 2.50
❑ 116 Franco Harris 6.00 2.50
❑ 117 Gale Sayers 6.00 2.50
❑ 118 Jack Lambert 6.00 2.50
❑ 119 James Lofton 3.00 1.25
❑ 120 Jim Brown 8.00 3.00
❑ 121 Jim Kelly 6.00 2.50
❑ 122 Jim Thorpe 6.00 2.50
❑ 123 Joe Greene 5.00 2.00
❑ 124 Joe Montana 12.00 5.00
❑ 125 Joe Namath 6.00 2.50
❑ 126 John Elway 8.00 3.00
❑ 127 John Riggins 5.00 2.00
❑ 128 Johnny Unitas 8.00 3.00
❑ 129 Lawrence Taylor 5.00 2.00
❑ 130 Leroy Kelly 4.00 1.50
❑ 131 Marcus Allen 5.00 2.00
❑ 132 Michael Irvin 5.00 2.00
❑ 133 Mike Ditka 5.00 2.00
❑ 134 Mike Singletary 5.00 2.00
❑ 135 Ozzie Newsome 4.00 1.50
❑ 136 Paul Hornung 5.00 2.00
❑ 137 Paul Warfield 4.00 1.50
❑ 138 Randall Cunningham 4.00 1.50
❑ 139 Red Grange 6.00 2.50
❑ 140 Roger Staubach 8.00 3.00
❑ 141 Sammy Baugh 5.00 2.00
❑ 142 Sonny Jurgensen 4.00 1.50
❑ 143 Steve Largent 5.00 2.00
❑ 144 Steve Young 6.00 2.50
❑ 145 Terrell Davis 5.00 2.00
❑ 146 Terry Bradshaw 8.00 3.00
❑ 147 Tony Dorsett 4.00 1.50
❑ 148 Troy Aikman 6.00 2.50
❑ 149 Walter Payton 10.00 4.00
❑ 150 Warren Moon 5.00 2.00
❑ 151 Aaron Rodgers RC 25.00 10.00
❑ 152 Adrian McPherson RC 8.00 3.00
❑ 153 Airese Currie RC 8.00 3.00
❑ 154 Alvin Pearman RC 8.00 3.00
❑ 155 Anthony Davis RC 6.00 2.50
❑ 156 Brandon Jacobs RC 10.00 4.00
❑ 157 Brandon Jones RC 8.00 3.00
❑ 158 Cedric Benson RC 20.00 8.00
❑ 159 Cedric Houston RC 8.00 3.00
❑ 160 Chad Owens RC 8.00 3.00
❑ 161 Chris Henry RC 8.00 3.00
❑ 162 Nate Washington RC 6.00 2.50
❑ 163 Craig Bragg RC 6.00 2.50
❑ 164 Craphonso Thorpe RC 6.00 2.50
❑ 165 Damien Nash RC 6.00 2.50
❑ 166 Dan Orlovsky RC 8.00 3.00
❑ 167 Dante Ridgeway RC 6.00 2.50
❑ 168 Darren Sproles RC 8.00 3.00
❑ 169 David Greene RC 8.00 3.00
❑ 170 David Pollack RC 8.00 3.00
❑ 171 Deandra Cobb RC 6.00 2.50
❑ 172 DeMarcus Ware RC 12.00 5.00
❑ 173 Derek Anderson RC 12.00 5.00
❑ 174 Derrick Johnson RC 12.00 5.00
❑ 175 Erasmus James RC 8.00 3.00
❑ 176 Fabian Washington RC 8.00 3.00
❑ 177 Fred Gibson RC 6.00 2.50
❑ 178 Harry Williams RC 6.00 2.50
❑ 179 Heath Miller RC 15.00 6.00
❑ 180 J.R. Russell RC 6.00 2.50
❑ 181 James Kilian RC 8.00 3.00
❑ 182 Jerome Mathis RC 8.00 3.00
❑ 183 Larry Brackins RC 4.00 1.50
❑ 184 LeRon McCoy RC 6.00 2.50
❑ 185 Lionel Gates RC 6.00 2.50
❑ 186 Marcus Spears RC 8.00 3.00
❑ 187 Marion Barber RC 12.00 5.00
❑ 188 Marlin Jackson RC 8.00 3.00
❑ 189 Matt Cassel RC 12.00 5.00
❑ 190 Mike Williams 8.00 3.00
❑ 191 Noah Herron RC 8.00 3.00
❑ 192 Paris Warren RC 6.00 2.50
❑ 193 Rasheed Marshall RC 8.00 3.00
❑ 194 Roscoe Crosby RC 6.00 2.50
❑ 195 Roydell Williams RC 8.00 3.00
❑ 196 Ryan Fitzpatrick RC 8.00 3.00
❑ 197 Shawne Merriman RC 12.00 5.00
❑ 198 Tab Perry RC 8.00 3.00
❑ 199 Thomas Davis RC 8.00 3.00
❑ 200 Travis Johnson RC 6.00 2.50
❑ 201 Adam Jones JSY AU RC 25.00 10.00
❑ 202 Alex Smith QB JSY AU RC 100.00 40.00
❑ 203 Andrew Walter JSY AU RC 25.00 10.00
❑ 204 Antrel Rolle JSY AU RC 25.00 10.00
❑ 205 Braylon Edwards JSY AU RC 60.00 30.00
❑ 206 Cadillac Williams JSY AU RC 100.00 40.00
❑ 207 Carlos Rogers JSY AU RC 30.00 15.00
❑ 208 Charlie Frye JSY AU RC 30.00 12.50
❑ 209 Ciatrick Fason JSY AU RC 25.00 10.00
❑ 210 Courtney Roby JSY AU RC 25.00 10.00
❑ 211 Eric Shelton JSY AU RC 25.00 10.00
❑ 212 Frank Gore JSY AU RC 80.00 40.00
❑ 213 J.J. Arrington JSY AU RC 30.00 12.50
❑ 214 Kyle Orton JSY AU RC 40.00 15.00
❑ 215 Jason Campbell JSY AU RC 60.00 35.00
❑ 216 Mark Bradley JSY AU RC 30.00 12.50
❑ 217 Mark Clayton JSY AU RC 30.00 12.50
❑ 218 Matt Jones JSY AU RC 60.00 35.00
❑ 219 Maurice Clarett JSY AU 25.00 10.00
❑ 220 Reggie Brown JSY AU RC 30.00 12.50
❑ 221 Ronnie Brown JSY AU RC 100.00 40.00
❑ 222 Roddy White JSY AU RC 25.00 10.00
❑ 223 Ryan Moats JSY AU RC 25.00 10.00
❑ 224 Roscoe Parrish JSY AU RC 25.00 10.00
❑ 225 Stefan LeFors JSY AU RC 25.00 10.00
❑ 226 Terrence Murphy JSY AU RC 25.00 10.00
❑ 227 Troy Williamson JSY AU RC 30.00 12.50
❑ 228 Vernand Morency JSY AU RC 20.00 7.50
❑ 229 Vincent Jackson JSY AU RC 30.00 12.50

2006 Leaf Limited

❑ 1 Alex Smith QB 4.00 1.50
❑ 2 Antonio Bryant 2.50 1.00
❑ 3 Frank Gore 4.00 1.50
❑ 4 Rex Grossman 4.00 1.50
❑ 5 Thomas Jones 2.50 1.00
❑ 6 Cedric Benson 4.00 1.50
❑ 7 Carson Palmer 4.00 1.50
❑ 8 Chad Johnson 2.50 1.00
❑ 9 Rudi Johnson 2.50 1.00
❑ 10 T.J. Houshmandzadeh 2.50 1.00
❑ 11 J.P. Losman 2.50 1.00
❑ 12 Lee Evans 2.50 1.00
❑ 13 Willis McGahee 4.00 1.50
❑ 14 Jake Plummer 2.50 1.00
❑ 15 Javon Walker 2.50 1.00
❑ 16 Rod Smith 2.50 1.00
❑ 17 Tatum Bell 2.50 1.00
❑ 18 Braylon Edwards 4.00 1.50
❑ 19 Charlie Frye 2.50 1.00
❑ 20 Reuben Droughns 2.50 1.00
❑ 21 Cadillac Williams 4.00 1.50
❑ 22 Chris Simms 2.50 1.00
❑ 23 Joey Galloway 2.50 1.00
❑ 24 Anquan Boldin 2.50 1.00
❑ 25 Edgerrin James 4.00 1.50
❑ 26 Kurt Warner 2.50 1.00
❑ 27 Larry Fitzgerald 4.00 1.50
❑ 28 Antonio Gates 4.00 1.50
❑ 29 Keenan McCardell 2.00 .75
❑ 30 LaDainian Tomlinson 5.00 2.00
❑ 31 Philip Rivers 4.00 1.50
❑ 32 Eddie Kennison 2.00 .75
❑ 33 Larry Johnson 5.00 2.00
❑ 34 Priest Holmes 2.50 1.00
❑ 35 Trent Green 2.50 1.00
❑ 36 Tony Gonzalez 2.50 1.00
❑ 37 Dallas Clark 2.00 .75
❑ 38 Marvin Harrison 4.00 1.50
❑ 39 Peyton Manning 6.00 2.50
❑ 40 Reggie Wayne 2.50 1.00
❑ 41 Drew Bledsoe 4.00 1.50
❑ 42 Julius Jones 4.00 1.50
❑ 43 Roy Williams S 2.50 1.00

❑ 44 Terrell Owens 4.00 1.50
❑ 45 Terry Glenn 2.50 1.00
❑ 46 Chris Chambers 2.50 1.00
❑ 47 Daunte Culpepper 4.00 1.50
❑ 48 Marty Booker 2.00 .75
❑ 49 Ronnie Brown 4.00 1.50
❑ 50 Brian Westbrook 2.50 1.00
❑ 51 Donovan McNabb 4.00 1.50
❑ 52 Jevon Kearse 2.50 1.00
❑ 53 Reggie Brown 3.00 1.25
❑ 54 Alge Crumpler 2.50 1.00
❑ 55 Michael Vick 4.00 1.50
❑ 56 Warrick Dunn 2.50 1.00
❑ 57 Eli Manning 5.00 2.00
❑ 58 Jeremy Shockey 4.00 1.50
❑ 59 Plaxico Burress 2.50 1.00
❑ 60 Tiki Barber 4.00 1.50
❑ 61 Byron Leftwich 2.50 1.00
❑ 62 Fred Taylor 2.50 1.00
❑ 63 Jimmy Smith 2.50 1.00
❑ 64 Matt Jones 2.50 1.00
❑ 65 Josh McCown 2.50 1.00
❑ 66 Roy Williams WR 4.00 1.50
❑ 67 Kevin Jones 4.00 1.50
❑ 68 Aaron Rodgers 4.00 1.50
❑ 69 Brett Favre 8.00 3.00
❑ 70 Robert Ferguson 2.00 .75
❑ 71 Samkon Gado 2.50 1.00
❑ 72 Ahman Green 2.50 1.00
❑ 73 DeShaun Foster 2.50 1.00
❑ 74 Jake Delhomme 2.50 1.00
❑ 75 Keary Colbert 2.00 .75
❑ 76 Steve Smith 4.00 1.50
❑ 77 Corey Dillon 2.50 1.00
❑ 78 Deion Branch 2.50 1.00
❑ 79 Tedy Bruschi 4.00 1.50
❑ 80 Tom Brady 6.00 2.50
❑ 81 Jerry Porter 2.50 1.00
❑ 82 Randy Moss 4.00 1.50
❑ 83 LaMont Jordan 2.50 1.00
❑ 84 Isaac Bruce 2.50 1.00
❑ 85 Marc Bulger 2.50 1.00
❑ 86 Steven Jackson 4.00 1.50
❑ 87 Torry Holt 2.50 1.00
❑ 88 Derrick Mason 2.00 .75
❑ 89 Mark Clayton 4.00 1.50
❑ 90 Steve McNair 2.50 1.00
❑ 91 Jamal Lewis 2.50 1.00
❑ 92 Antwaan Randle El 2.50 1.00
❑ 93 Clinton Portis 4.00 1.50
❑ 94 Santana Moss 2.50 1.00
❑ 95 Chad Pennington 2.50 1.00
❑ 96 Laveranues Coles 2.50 1.00
❑ 97 Curtis Martin 4.00 1.50
❑ 98 Mewelde Moore 2.00 .75
❑ 99 Troy Williamson 2.50 1.00
❑ 100 Brad Johnson 2.50 1.00
❑ 101 Darrell Jackson 2.50 1.00
❑ 102 Matt Hasselbeck 2.50 1.00
❑ 103 Nate Burleson 2.50 1.00
❑ 104 Shaun Alexander 4.00 1.50
❑ 105 Ben Roethlisberger 6.00 2.50
❑ 106 Hines Ward 4.00 1.50
❑ 107 Willie Parker 5.00 2.00
❑ 108 Donte Stallworth 2.50 1.00
❑ 109 Drew Brees 4.00 1.50
❑ 110 Deuce McAllister 2.50 1.00
❑ 111 Andre Johnson 2.50 1.00
❑ 112 David Carr 2.50 1.00
❑ 113 Domanick Davis 2.50 1.00
❑ 114 Eric Moulds 2.50 1.00
❑ 115 David Givens 2.50 1.00
❑ 116 Drew Bennett 2.00 .75
❑ 117 Chris Brown 2.50 1.00
❑ 118 Bob Griese 5.00 2.00
❑ 119 Daryle Lamonica 3.00 1.25
❑ 120 Dave Casper 3.00 1.25
❑ 121 Don Meredith 5.00 2.00
❑ 122 Herschel Walker 4.00 1.50
❑ 123 Jack Lambert 5.00 2.00
❑ 124 Jackie Smith 3.00 1.25
❑ 125 Jim Otto 3.00 1.25
❑ 126 John Riggins 5.00 2.00
❑ 127 John Stallworth 4.00 1.50
❑ 128 Lawrence Taylor 5.00 2.00
❑ 129 Lester Hayes 3.00 1.25
❑ 130 L.C. Greenwood 4.00 1.50
❑ 131 Paul Warfield 4.00 1.50
❑ 132 Barry Sanders 8.00 3.00
❑ 133 Bart Starr 8.00 3.00
❑ 134 Billy Sims 4.00 1.50
❑ 135 Bulldog Turner 4.00 1.50
❑ 136 Deion Sanders 6.00 2.50
❑ 137 Dutch Clark 4.00 1.50
❑ 138 Forrest Gregg 3.00 1.25
❑ 139 Gale Sayers 6.00 2.50
❑ 140 Jim Brown 6.00 2.50
❑ 141 Jim Thorpe 6.00 2.50
❑ 142 Joe Montana 10.00 4.00
❑ 143 John Elway 8.00 3.00
❑ 144 Johnny Unitas 8.00 3.00
❑ 145 Lance Alworth 4.00 1.50
❑ 146 Raymond Berry 4.00 1.50
❑ 147 Doak Walker 5.00 2.00
❑ 148 Red Grange 6.00 2.50
❑ 149 Walter Payton 10.00 4.00
❑ 150 Yale Lary 3.00 1.25
❑ 151 Adam Jennings RC 6.00 2.50
❑ 152 Alan Zemaitis RC 8.00 3.00
❑ 153 Patrick Cobbs RC 6.00 2.50
❑ 154 Anthony Schlegel RC 6.00 2.50
❑ 155 Anthony Smith RC 10.00 4.00
❑ 156 Antonio Cromartie RC 8.00 3.00
❑ 157 Ashton Youboty RC 8.00 3.00
❑ 158 Bennie Brazell RC 6.00 2.50
❑ 159 Bernard Pollard RC 6.00 2.50
❑ 160 Brodrick Bunkley RC 8.00 3.00
❑ 161 Calvin Lowry RC 8.00 3.00
❑ 162 Cedric Griffin RC 6.00 2.50
❑ 163 Cedric Humes RC 8.00 3.00
❑ 164 Charles Davis RC 6.00 2.50
❑ 165 Chris Gocong RC 6.00 2.50
❑ 166 Claude Wroten RC 4.00 1.50
❑ 167 Clint Ingram RC 8.00 3.00
❑ 168 D.J. Shockley RC 8.00 3.00
❑ 169 Danieal Manning RC 8.00 3.00
❑ 170 Daniel Bullocks RC 8.00 3.00
❑ 171 Darnell Bing RC 8.00 3.00
❑ 172 Chris Hannon RC 6.00 2.50
❑ 173 Darryl Tapp RC 6.00 2.50
❑ 174 David Anderson RC 6.00 2.50
❑ 175 David Kirtman RC 6.00 2.50
❑ 176 David Pittman RC 6.00 2.50
❑ 177 Davin Joseph RC 6.00 2.50
❑ 178 Sam Hurd RC 12.00 5.00
❑ 179 Delanie Walker RC 6.00 2.50
❑ 180 DeMeco Ryans RC 10.00 4.00
❑ 181 Derrick Ross RC 6.00 2.50
❑ 182 Devin Hester RC 15.00 6.00
❑ 183 Domenik Hixon RC 6.00 2.50
❑ 184 Dominique Byrd RC 6.00 2.50
❑ 185 Donte Whitner RC 8.00 3.00
❑ 186 D'Qwell Jackson RC 6.00 2.50
❑ 187 Dusty Dvoracek RC 8.00 3.00
❑ 188 Eric Smith RC 6.00 2.50
❑ 189 Fred Evans RC 6.00 2.50
❑ 190 Ernie Sims RC 10.00 4.00
❑ 191 Ethan Kilmer RC 8.00 3.00
❑ 192 Freddie Keiaho RC 6.00 2.50
❑ 193 Frostee Rucker RC 6.00 2.50
❑ 194 Gabe Watson RC 6.00 2.50
❑ 195 Garrett Mills RC 8.00 3.00
❑ 196 Dawan Landry RC 8.00 3.00
❑ 197 Gerris Wilkinson RC 4.00 1.50
❑ 198 Jarrad Page RC 8.00 3.00
❑ 199 Haloti Ngata RC 8.00 3.00
❑ 200 Hank Baskett RC 8.00 3.00
❑ 201 Jai Lewis RC 6.00 2.50
❑ 202 Jamar Williams RC 6.00 2.50
❑ 203 James Anderson RC 4.00 1.50
❑ 204 Jason Allen RC 8.00 3.00
❑ 205 Jason Hatcher RC 6.00 2.50
❑ 206 Chris Barclay RC 6.00 2.50
❑ 207 J.D. Runnels RC 6.00 2.50
❑ 208 Jeff King RC 6.00 2.50
❑ 209 Jeffrey Webb RC 6.00 2.50
❑ 210 Jerome Harrison RC 8.00 3.00
❑ 211 Jimmy Williams RC 8.00 3.00
❑ 212 John David Washington RC 6.00 2.50
❑ 213 Jon Alston RC 8.00 3.00
❑ 214 Johnathan Joseph RC 6.00 2.50
❑ 215 Kamerion Wimbley RC 8.00 3.00
❑ 216 Kelly Jennings RC 8.00 3.00
❑ 217 Charles Sharon RC 6.00 2.50
❑ 218 Ko Simpson RC 6.00 2.50
❑ 219 Lawrence Vickers RC 6.00 2.50
❑ 220 Leon Williams RC 6.00 2.50
❑ 221 Leonard Pope RC 8.00 3.00
❑ 222 Marques Colston RC 25.00 10.00
❑ 223 Martin Nance RC 6.00 2.50
❑ 224 Mathias Kiwanuka RC 10.00 4.00
❑ 225 Mike Bell RC 8.00 3.00
❑ 226 Mike Hass RC 8.00 3.00
❑ 227 Miles Austin RC 6.00 2.50
❑ 228 Nate Salley RC 6.00 2.50
❑ 229 Nick Mangold RC 6.00 2.50
❑ 230 Owen Daniels RC 8.00 3.00
❑ 231 Shaun Bodiford RC 6.00 2.50
❑ 232 Quinn Sypniewski RC 6.00 2.50
❑ 233 Quinton Ganther RC 6.00 2.50
❑ 234 Richard Marshall RC 6.00 2.50
❑ 235 Rocky McIntosh RC 8.00 3.00
❑ 236 Roman Harper RC 6.00 2.50
❑ 237 Stephen Tulloch RC 6.00 2.50
❑ 238 Brett Basanez RC 8.00 3.00
❑ 239 Tamba Hali RC 8.00 3.00
❑ 240 Brett Elliott RC 8.00 3.00
❑ 241 Thomas Howard RC 8.00 3.00
❑ 242 Tim Jennings RC 6.00 2.50
❑ 243 Jason Carter RC 6.00 2.50
❑ 244 Todd Watkins RC 6.00 2.50
❑ 245 Tony Scheffler RC 8.00 3.00
❑ 246 Tye Hill RC 8.00 3.00
❑ 247 Victor Adeyanju RC 6.00 2.50
❑ 248 Wendell Mathis RC 6.00 2.50
❑ 249 Will Blackmon RC 6.00 2.50
❑ 250 Willie Reid RC 8.00 3.00
❑ 251 Mario Williams JSY AU RC 30.00 12.00
❑ 252 Reggie Bush JSY AU RC 150.00 75.00
❑ 253 Vince Young JSY AU RC 150.00 75.00
❑ 254 A.J. Hawk JSY AU RC 60.00 25.00
❑ 255 Vernon Davis JSY AU RC 50.00 20.00
❑ 256 Michael Huff JSY AU RC 30.00 12.50
❑ 257 Matt Leinart JSY AU RC 120.00 60.00
❑ 258 Jay Cutler AU RC 120.00 60.00
❑ 259 L.Maroney JSY AU RC 100.00 50.00
❑ 260 Santonio Holmes JSY AU RC 40.00 15.00
❑ 261 DeA.Williams JSY AU RC 80.00 30.00
❑ 262 Marcedes Lewis JSY AU RC 20.00 8.00
❑ 263 Joseph Addai AU RC 100.00 50.00
❑ 264 Chad Jackson JSY AU RC 20.00 8.00
❑ 265 Sinorice Moss JSY AU RC 20.00 8.00
❑ 266 LenDale White JSY AU RC 40.00 20.00
❑ 267 Kellen Clemens JSY AU RC 40.00 20.00
❑ 268 Greg Jennings AU RC 40.00 20.00
❑ 269 Joe Klopfenstein JSY AU RC 15.00 6.00
❑ 270 Maurice Drew JSY AU RC 80.00 30.00
❑ 271 Tarvaris Jackson JSY AU RC 60.00 25.00
❑ 272 Brian Calhoun JSY AU RC 20.00 8.00
❑ 273 Travis Wilson JSY AU RC 20.00 8.00
❑ 274 Jerious Norwood JSY AU RC 50.00 25.00
❑ 275 C.Whitehurst JSY AU RC 20.00 8.00
❑ 276 Derek Hagan JSY AU RC 20.00 8.00
❑ 277 Brandon Williams JSY AU RC 20.00 8.00
❑ 278 Brodie Croyle AU RC 50.00 25.00
❑ 279 Maurice Stovall JSY AU RC 20.00 8.00
❑ 280 Michael Robinson JSY AU RC 20.00 8.00
❑ 281 Jason Avant JSY AU RC 20.00 8.00
❑ 282 Dem.Williams JSY AU RC 20.00 8.00
❑ 283 Leon Washington JSY AU RC 40.00 15.00
❑ 284 Brandon Marshall JSY AU RC 30.00 15.00
❑ 285 Omar Jacobs JSY AU RC 15.00 6.00
❑ 286 Anthony Fasano AU RC 25.00 12.50
❑ 287 Ingle Martin AU RC 20.00 8.00
❑ 288 Reggie McNeal AU RC 15.00 6.00
❑ 289 Brad Smith AU RC 20.00 8.00
❑ 290 Jeremy Bloom AU RC 15.00 6.00
❑ 291 Bruce Gradkowski AU RC 30.00 12.00
❑ 292 P.J. Daniels AU RC 15.00 6.00
❑ 293 Cory Rodgers AU RC 20.00 8.00
❑ 294 Skyler Green AU RC 20.00 8.00
❑ 295 Bobby Carpenter AU RC 20.00 8.00
❑ 296 Arom/Obom/Mix AU/100 25.00 12.50
❑ 297 Hodge/Greenway AU/100 40.00 20.00
❑ 298 M.Will/McCar/Lwsn AU/100 50.00 20.00
❑ 299 Fasano/Stovall AU/50 40.00 20.00
❑ 300 Hawk/Carpenter AU/50 80.00 30.00
❑ 301 Leinart/Bush/Wht AU/25 300.00 150.00
❑ 302 Young/Thomas AU/50 100.00 50.00
❑ 303 Olson/Drew/Lewis AU/100 60.00 35.00
❑ 304 Hagans/Lundy/Ferg AU/100 40.00 20.00
❑ 305 Calhn/Willms/Orr AU/100 40.00 20.00
❑ TC Steve Smith TC/500 6.00 2.50

2007 Leaf Limited

❑ 1 Anquan Boldin 3.00 1.25
❑ 2 Edgerrin James 4.00 1.50

❑ 3 Larry Fitzgerald 3.00 1.25
❑ 4 Matt Leinart 4.00 1.50
❑ 5 Alge Crumpler 3.00 1.25
❑ 6 Warrick Dunn 3.00 1.25
❑ 7 Jerious Norwood 3.00 1.25
❑ 8 Willis McGahee 3.00 1.25
❑ 9 Steve McNair 3.00 1.25
❑ 10 Mark Clayton 3.00 1.25
❑ 11 Anthony Thomas 2.50 1.00
❑ 12 J.P. Losman 3.00 1.25
❑ 13 Lee Evans 3.00 1.25
❑ 14 Jake Delhomme 3.00 1.25
❑ 15 Steve Smith 3.00 1.25
❑ 16 DeAngelo Williams 4.00 1.50
❑ 17 Rex Grossman 3.00 1.25
❑ 18 Cedric Benson 3.00 1.25
❑ 19 Bernard Berrian 2.50 1.00
❑ 20 Carson Palmer 4.00 1.50
❑ 21 Chad Johnson 3.00 1.25
❑ 22 Rudi Johnson 3.00 1.25
❑ 23 T.J. Houshmandzadeh 3.00 1.25
❑ 24 Kellen Winslow 3.00 1.25
❑ 25 Braylon Edwards 3.00 1.25
❑ 26 Jamal Lewis 3.00 1.25
❑ 27 Julius Jones 3.00 1.25
❑ 28 Terrell Owens 4.00 1.50
❑ 29 Tony Romo 8.00 3.00
❑ 30 Jay Cutler 4.00 1.50
❑ 31 Javon Walker 3.00 1.25
❑ 32 Travis Henry 3.00 1.25
❑ 33 Tatum Bell 3.00 1.25
❑ 34 Roy Williams WR 3.00 1.25
❑ 35 Jon Kitna 2.50 1.00
❑ 36 Brett Favre 8.00 3.00
❑ 37 Donald Driver 3.00 1.25
❑ 38 Greg Jennings 3.00 1.25
❑ 39 Matt Schaub 3.00 1.25
❑ 40 Andre Johnson 3.00 1.25
❑ 41 Ahman Green 3.00 1.25
❑ 42 Peyton Manning 6.00 2.50
❑ 43 Marvin Harrison 4.00 1.50
❑ 44 Reggie Wayne 3.00 1.25
❑ 45 Joseph Addai 5.00 2.00
❑ 46 David Garrard 3.00 1.25
❑ 47 Fred Taylor 3.00 1.25
❑ 48 Maurice Jones-Drew 4.00 1.50
❑ 49 Brodie Croyle 4.00 1.50
❑ 50 Larry Johnson 4.00 1.50
❑ 51 Tony Gonzalez 3.00 1.25
❑ 52 Trent Green 3.00 1.25
❑ 53 Ronnie Brown 3.00 1.25
❑ 54 Chris Chambers 3.00 1.25
❑ 55 Tarvaris Jackson 4.00 1.50
❑ 56 Troy Williamson 2.50 1.00
❑ 57 Chester Taylor 2.50 1.00
❑ 58 Tom Brady 8.00 3.00
❑ 59 Randy Moss 4.00 1.50
❑ 60 Laurence Maroney 4.00 1.50
❑ 61 Donte Stallworth 3.00 1.25
❑ 62 Drew Brees 3.00 1.25
❑ 63 Deuce McAllister 3.00 1.25
❑ 64 Reggie Bush 5.00 2.00
❑ 65 Marques Colston 4.00 1.50
❑ 66 Eli Manning 4.00 1.50
❑ 67 Jeremy Shockey 3.00 1.25
❑ 68 Brandon Jacobs 3.00 1.25
❑ 69 Chad Pennington 3.00 1.25
❑ 70 Thomas Jones 3.00 1.25
❑ 71 Laveranues Coles 3.00 1.25
❑ 72 Jerry Porter 3.00 1.25
❑ 73 LaMont Jordan 3.00 1.25
❑ 74 Donovan McNabb 4.00 1.50
❑ 75 Brian Westbrook 3.00 1.25
❑ 76 Reggie Brown 3.00 1.25
❑ 77 Ben Roethlisberger 5.00 2.00
❑ 78 Hines Ward 4.00 1.50
❑ 79 Willie Parker 4.00 1.50
❑ 80 Philip Rivers 4.00 1.50
❑ 81 Antonio Gates 3.00 1.25
❑ 82 LaDainian Tomlinson 5.00 2.00
❑ 83 Alex Smith QB 4.00 1.50
❑ 84 Darrell Jackson 3.00 1.25
❑ 85 Frank Gore 4.00 1.50
❑ 86 Matt Hasselbeck 3.00 1.25
❑ 87 Shaun Alexander 3.00 1.25
❑ 88 Deion Branch 3.00 1.25
❑ 89 Marc Bulger 3.00 1.25
❑ 90 Steven Jackson 4.00 1.50
❑ 91 Torry Holt 3.00 1.25
❑ 92 Jeff Garcia 3.00 1.25
❑ 93 Cadillac Williams 3.00 1.25
❑ 94 Joey Galloway 3.00 1.25
❑ 95 Vince Young 5.00 2.00
❑ 96 Brandon Jones 2.50 1.00
❑ 97 LenDale White 3.00 1.25
❑ 98 Jason Campbell 3.00 1.25
❑ 99 Clinton Portis 3.00 1.25
❑ 100 Santana Moss 3.00 1.25
❑ 101 Alan Page 5.00 2.00
❑ 102 Barry Sanders 12.00 5.00
❑ 103 Bart Starr 12.00 5.00
❑ 104 Bill Dudley 5.00 2.00
❑ 105 Billy Howton 5.00 2.00
❑ 106 Bob Griese 8.00 3.00
❑ 107 Bobby Layne 8.00 3.00
❑ 108 Boyd Dowler 5.00 2.00
❑ 109 Charley Taylor 6.00 2.50
❑ 110 Charley Trippi 5.00 2.00
❑ 111 Charlie Joiner 6.00 2.50
❑ 112 Chuck Bednarik 6.00 2.50
❑ 113 Cris Collinsworth 6.00 2.50
❑ 114 Dan Fouts 8.00 3.00
❑ 115 Dan Hampton 6.00 2.50
❑ 116 Dan Marino 15.00 6.00
❑ 117 Dante Lavelli 5.00 2.00
❑ 118 Darrell Green 6.00 2.50
❑ 119 Daryle Lamonica 5.00 2.00
❑ 120 Deacon Jones 6.00 2.50
❑ 121 Dick Butkus 10.00 4.00
❑ 122 Doak Walker 8.00 3.00
❑ 123 Don Maynard 6.00 2.50
❑ 124 Don Perkins 5.00 2.00
❑ 125 Dutch Clark 6.00 2.50
❑ 126 Earl Campbell 8.00 3.00
❑ 127 Forrest Gregg 5.00 2.00
❑ 128 Fran Tarkenton 10.00 4.00
❑ 129 Franco Harris 8.00 3.00
❑ 130 Fred Biletnikoff 8.00 3.00
❑ 131 Gale Sayers 10.00 4.00
❑ 132 Gene Upshaw 5.00 2.00
❑ 133 George Blanda 6.00 2.50
❑ 134 Harlon Hill 5.00 2.00
❑ 135 Jack Lambert 8.00 3.00
❑ 136 Jack Youngblood 6.00 2.50
❑ 137 James Lofton 5.00 2.00
❑ 138 Jan Stenerud 5.00 2.00
❑ 139 Jethro Pugh 5.00 2.00
❑ 140 Jim Brown 10.00 4.00
❑ 141 Jim Kelly 10.00 4.00
❑ 142 Jim McMahon 10.00 4.00
❑ 143 Jim Otto 5.00 2.00
❑ 144 Jim Thorpe 10.00 4.00
❑ 145 Jimmy Orr 5.00 2.00
❑ 146 Joe Greene 8.00 3.00
❑ 147 Joe Montana 15.00 6.00
❑ 148 Joe Namath 10.00 4.00
❑ 149 Joe Theismann 8.00 3.00
❑ 150 John Elway 12.00 5.00
❑ 151 John Mackey 6.00 2.50
❑ 152 John Riggins 6.00 2.50
❑ 153 John Stallworth 6.00 2.50
❑ 154 Johnny Morris 5.00 2.00
❑ 155 Johnny Unitas 12.00 5.00
❑ 156 Kellen Winslow Sr. 6.00 2.50
❑ 157 Ken Stabler 10.00 4.00
❑ 158 Lance Alworth 6.00 2.50
❑ 159 Larry Csonka 8.00 3.00
❑ 160 Larry Little 5.00 2.00
❑ 161 Lee Roy Selmon 6.00 2.50
❑ 162 Len Dawson 8.00 3.00
❑ 163 Lou Groza 6.00 2.50
❑ 164 Lydell Mitchell 5.00 2.00
❑ 165 Marcus Allen 8.00 3.00
❑ 166 Mark Duper 5.00 2.00
❑ 167 Merlin Olsen 6.00 2.50
❑ 168 Mike Singletary 8.00 3.00
❑ 169 Ollie Matson 6.00 2.50
❑ 170 Otto Graham 6.00 2.50
❑ 171 Ozzie Newsome 6.00 2.50
❑ 172 Paul Hornung 8.00 3.00
❑ 173 Paul Warfield 6.00 2.50
❑ 174 Phil Simms 6.00 2.50
❑ 175 Randall Cunningham 6.00 2.50
❑ 176 Ray Nitschke 8.00 3.00
❑ 177 Raymond Berry 6.00 2.50
❑ 178 Red Grange 10.00 4.00
❑ 179 Rick Casares 5.00 2.00
❑ 180 Ron Mix 5.00 2.00
❑ 181 Roger Craig 6.00 2.50
❑ 182 Roger Staubach 12.00 5.00
❑ 183 Rosey Brown 5.00 2.00
❑ 184 Rosey Grier 5.00 2.00
❑ 185 Ronnie Lott 6.00 2.50
❑ 186 Sam Huff 6.00 2.50
❑ 187 Sammy Baugh 8.00 3.00
❑ 188 Sid Luckman 8.00 3.00
❑ 189 Sonny Jurgensen 6.00 2.50
❑ 190 Sterling Sharpe 6.00 2.50
❑ 191 Steve Largent 8.00 3.00
❑ 192 Steve Young 10.00 4.00
❑ 193 Ted Hendricks 6.00 2.50
❑ 194 Thurman Thomas 6.00 2.50
❑ 195 Tim Brown 8.00 3.00
❑ 196 Tiki Barber 8.00 3.00
❑ 197 Troy Aikman 10.00 4.00
❑ 198 Walter Payton 15.00 6.00
❑ 199 Willie Brown 6.00 2.50
❑ 200 Elroy Hirsch 6.00 2.50
❑ 201 Brandon McDonald RC 6.00 2.50
❑ 202 David Irons RC 6.00 2.50
❑ 203 Fred Bennett RC 6.00 2.50
❑ 204 Nick Graham RC 8.00 3.00
❑ 205 Rashad Barksdale RC 6.00 2.50
❑ 206 Tanard Jackson RC 6.00 2.50
❑ 207 Tarell Brown RC 6.00 2.50
❑ 208 Usama Young RC 8.00 3.00
❑ 209 William Gay RC 8.00 3.00
❑ 210 Jarvis Moss RC 10.00 4.00
❑ 211 Le'Ron McClain RC 8.00 3.00
❑ 212 Kevin Payne RC 6.00 2.50
❑ 213 Adam Hayward RC 8.00 3.00
❑ 214 Brandon Siler RC 8.00 3.00
❑ 215 Chad Nkang RC 6.00 2.50
❑ 216 Clint Session RC 8.00 3.00
❑ 217 Desmond Bishop RC 8.00 3.00
❑ 218 Edmond Miles RC 8.00 3.00
❑ 219 H.B. Blades RC 8.00 3.00
❑ 220 Justin Durant RC 8.00 3.00
❑ 221 Justin Rogers RC 10.00 4.00
❑ 222 Nate Harris RC 8.00 3.00
❑ 223 Quincy Black RC 8.00 3.00
❑ 224 Quinton Culberson RC 6.00 2.50
❑ 225 Ramon Guzman RC 6.00 2.50
❑ 226 Stephen Nicholas RC 8.00 3.00
❑ 227 Tim Shaw RC 8.00 3.00
❑ 228 Tony Taylor RC 8.00 3.00
❑ 229 Zak DeOssie RC 8.00 3.00
❑ 230 Mason Crosby RC 10.00 4.00
❑ 231 Nick Folk RC 10.00 4.00
❑ 232 Matt Gutierrez RC 10.00 4.00
❑ 233 Matt Moore RC 15.00 6.00
❑ 234 Tyler Thigpen RC 10.00 4.00
❑ 235 Clifton Dawson RC 10.00 4.00
❑ 236 Gary Russell RC 10.00 4.00
❑ 237 Kenton Keith RC 10.00 4.00
❑ 238 Pierre Thomas RC 12.00 5.00
❑ 239 Gerald Alexander RC 6.00 2.50
❑ 240 John Wendling RC 8.00 3.00
❑ 241 Eric Frampton RC 8.00 3.00
❑ 242 Eric Weddle RC 8.00 3.00
❑ 243 Daniel Coats RC 8.00 3.00
❑ 244 Michael Matthews RC 8.00 3.00
❑ 245 Biren Ealy RC 8.00 3.00
❑ 246 Bobby Sippio RC 8.00 3.00
❑ 247 Glenn Holt RC 8.00 3.00
❑ 248 John Broussard RC 8.00 3.00
❑ 249 Legedu Naanee RC 8.00 3.00
❑ 250 Syndric Steptoe RC 8.00 3.00
❑ 251 Levi Brown AU RC 12.00 5.00
❑ 252 Jamaal Anderson AU RC 10.00 4.00

❑ 253 Amobi Okoye AU RC 12.00 5.00
❑ 254 Adam Carriker AU RC 10.00 4.00
❑ 255 Darrelle Revis AU RC 12.00 5.00
❑ 256 Michael Griffin AU RC 12.00 5.00
❑ 257 Aaron Ross AU RC 12.00 5.00
❑ 258 Brandon Meriweather AU RC EXCH 12.00 5.00
❑ 259 Jon Beason AU RC 12.00 5.00
❑ 260 Anthony Spencer AU RC 12.00 5.00
❑ 261 Alan Branch AU RC EXCH 10.00 4.00
❑ 262 Chris Houston AU RC 10.00 4.00
❑ 263 LaMarr Woodley AU RC 12.00 5.00
❑ 264 David Harris AU RC 10.00 4.00
❑ 265 Eric Wright AU RC EXCH 12.00 5.00
❑ 266 Josh Wilson AU RC 10.00 4.00
❑ 267 Tim Crowder AU RC 12.00 5.00
❑ 268 Victor Abiamiri AU RC 12.00 5.00
❑ 269 I. Alama-Francis AU RC 12.00 5.00
❑ 270 Dan Bazuin AU RC 10.00 4.00
❑ 271 Sabby Piscitelli AU RC 12.00 5.00
❑ 272 Quentin Moses AU RC 10.00 4.00
❑ 273 Buster Davis AU RC EXCH 10.00 4.00
❑ 274 Marcus McCauley AU RC 10.00 4.00
❑ 275 Matt Spaeth AU RC 12.00 5.00
❑ 276 Demarcus Tank Tyler AU RC EXCH 10.00 4.00
❑ 277 Charles Johnson AU RC EXCH 8.00 3.00
❑ 278 Jonathan Wade AU RC 10.00 4.00
❑ 279 Stewart Bradley AU RC 12.00 5.00
❑ 280 Aaron Rouse AU RC 12.00 5.00
❑ 281 Michael Okwo AU RC 10.00 4.00
❑ 282 Daymeion Hughes AU RC 10.00 4.00
❑ 283 Ray McDonald AU RC 10.00 4.00
❑ 284 Thomas Clayton AU RC EXCH 10.00 4.00
❑ 285 DeShawn Wynn AU RC 12.00 5.00
❑ 286 J. Snelling AU RC EXCH 10.00 4.00
❑ 287 Kenneth Darby AU RC 12.00 5.00
❑ 288 Ahmad Bradshaw AU/291 RC 50.00 25.00
❑ 289 Nate Ilaoa AU/203 RC 12.00 5.00
❑ 290 Joel Filani AU RC 10.00 4.00
❑ 291 Courtney Taylor AU RC 10.00 4.00
❑ 292 Jordan Kent AU/245 RC 10.00 4.00
❑ 293 Dallas Baker AU RC 10.00 4.00
❑ 294 Roy Hall AU RC 12.00 5.00
❑ 295 Chansi Stuckey AU RC EXCH 10.00 4.00
❑ 296 Scott Chandler AU RC 10.00 4.00
❑ 297 Ben Patrick AU RC 10.00 4.00
❑ 298 Chris Leak AU RC 10.00 4.00
❑ 299 Jared Zabransky AU RC EXCH 12.00 5.00
❑ 300 Selvin Young AU/194 RC 25.00 10.00
❑ 301 Adrian Peterson JSY AU RC 300.00 175.00
❑ 302 Anthony Gonzalez JSY AU RC 50.00 25.00
❑ 303 Antonio Pittman JSY AU RC EXCH 15.00 6.00
❑ 304 Aundrae Allison AU RC EXCH 15.00 6.00
❑ 305 Brady Quinn JSY AU RC 150.00 75.00
❑ 306 Br.Jackson JSY AU RC EXCH 25.00 10.00
❑ 307 Brian Leonard JSY AU RC 20.00 8.00
❑ 308 Calvin Johnson JSY AU RC 120.00 60.00
❑ 309 Chris Davis AU RC 15.00 6.00
❑ 310 Chris Henry RB JSY AU RC EXCH 20.00 8.00
❑ 311 Craig Davis JSY AU RC EXCH 20.00 8.00
❑ 312 David Clowney AU RC 20.00 8.00
❑ 313 Drew Stanton JSY AU RC 30.00 15.00
❑ 314 D. Bowe JSY AU RC 50.00 25.00
❑ 315 D. Jarrett JSY AU RC 25.00 10.00
❑ 316 Dwayne Wright AU RC 15.00 6.00
❑ 317 Gaines Adams JSY AU RC 20.00 8.00
❑ 318 Garrett Wolfe JSY AU RC 25.00 10.00
❑ 319 Greg Olsen JSY AU RC 30.00 12.00
❑ 320 Isaiah Stanback AU RC 20.00 8.00
❑ 321 Jacoby Jones AU RC 20.00 8.00
❑ 322 JaMarcus Russell JSY AU RC 120.00 60.00
❑ 323 James Jones AU RC 30.00 12.00
❑ 324 Jason Hill JSY AU RC 20.00 8.00
❑ 325 Jeff Rowe AU RC 15.00 6.00
❑ 326 Joe Thomas JSY AU RC EXCH 20.00 8.00
❑ 327 John Beck JSY AU RC 50.00 25.00
❑ 328 J.Lee Higgins JSY AU RC 15.00 6.00
❑ 329 Jordan Palmer AU RC 20.00 8.00
❑ 330 Kenny Irons JSY AU RC EXCH 20.00 8.00
❑ 331 Kevin Kolb JSY AU RC 60.00 30.00
❑ 332 Kolby Smith AU RC 30.00 12.00
❑ 333 LaRon Landry AU RC 25.00 10.00
❑ 334 Laurent Robinson AU RC 15.00 6.00
❑ 335 Lawrence Timmons AU RC 20.00 8.00
❑ 336 Leon Hall AU RC 15.00 6.00
❑ 337 Lorenzo Booker JSY AU RC 20.00 8.00
❑ 338 Marshawn Lynch JSY AU RC 80.00 40.00
❑ 339 Michael Bush JSY AU RC 30.00 15.00
❑ 340 Mike Walker AU RC 15.00 6.00
❑ 341 Patrick Willis JSY AU RC 50.00 20.00
❑ 342 Paul Posluszny AU RC 25.00 10.00
❑ 343 Paul Williams JSY AU RC 15.00 6.00
❑ 344 Reggie Nelson AU RC 15.00 6.00
❑ 345 Robert Meachem JSY AU RC 20.00 8.00
❑ 346 Ryne Robinson AU RC 15.00 6.00
❑ 347 Sidney Rice JSY AU RC 40.00 20.00
❑ 348 Steve Breaston AU RC 15.00 6.00
❑ 349 Steve Smith USC JSY AU RC 40.00 15.00
❑ 350 Ted Ginn Jr. JSY AU RC 40.00 15.00
❑ 351 Tony Hunt JSY AU RC 20.00 8.00
❑ 352 Trent Edwards JSY AU RC 50.00 20.00
❑ 353 Troy Smith JSY AU RC EXCH 30.00 12.00
❑ 354 Yamon Figurs JSY AU RC 20.00 8.00
❑ 355 Zach Miller AU RC 20.00 8.00

1998 Leaf Rookies and Stars

❑ COMPLETE SET (300) 250.00 125.00
❑ 1 Keyshawn Johnson .60 .25
❑ 2 Marvin Harrison .60 .25
❑ 3 Eddie Kennison .40 .15
❑ 4 Bryant Young .25 .08
❑ 5 Darren Woodson .25 .08
❑ 6 Tyrone Wheatley .40 .15
❑ 7 Michael Westbrook .40 .15
❑ 8 Charles Way .25 .08
❑ 9 Ricky Watters .40 .15
❑ 10 Chris Warren .40 .15
❑ 11 Wesley Walls .40 .15
❑ 12 Tamarick Vanover .25 .08
❑ 13 Zach Thomas .60 .25
❑ 14 Derrick Thomas .60 .25
❑ 15 Yancey Thigpen .25 .08
❑ 16 Vinny Testaverde .40 .15
❑ 17 Dana Stubblefield .25 .08
❑ 18 J.J. Stokes .40 .15
❑ 19 James Stewart .40 .15
❑ 20 Jeff George .40 .15
❑ 21 John Randle .40 .15
❑ 22 Gary Brown .25 .08
❑ 23 Ed McCaffrey .40 .15
❑ 24 James Jett .40 .15
❑ 25 Rob Johnson .40 .15
❑ 26 Daryl Johnston .40 .15
❑ 27 Jermaine Lewis .40 .15
❑ 28 Tony Martin .40 .15
❑ 29 Derrick Mayes .40 .15
❑ 30 Keenan McCardell .40 .15
❑ 31 O.J. McDuffie .40 .15
❑ 32 Chris Chandler .40 .15
❑ 33 Doug Flutie .60 .25
❑ 34 Scott Mitchell .40 .15
❑ 35 Warren Moon .60 .25
❑ 36 Rob Moore .40 .15
❑ 37 Johnnie Morton .40 .15
❑ 38 Neil O'Donnell .40 .15
❑ 39 Rich Gannon .60 .25
❑ 40 Andre Reed .40 .15
❑ 41 Jake Reed .40 .15
❑ 42 Errict Rhett .40 .15
❑ 43 Simeon Rice .40 .15
❑ 44 Andre Rison .40 .15
❑ 45 Eric Moulds .60 .25
❑ 46 Frank Sanders .40 .15
❑ 47 Darnay Scott .40 .15
❑ 48 Junior Seau .60 .25
❑ 49 Shannon Sharpe .40 .15
❑ 50 Bruce Smith .40 .15
❑ 51 Jimmy Smith .40 .15
❑ 52 Robert Smith .60 .25
❑ 53 Derrick Alexander .40 .15
❑ 54 Kimble Anders .40 .15
❑ 55 Jamal Anderson .60 .25
❑ 56 Mario Bates .40 .15
❑ 57 Edgar Bennett .25 .08
❑ 58 Tim Biakabutuka .40 .15
❑ 59 Ki-Jana Carter .25 .08
❑ 60 Larry Centers .25 .08
❑ 61 Mark Chmura .40 .15
❑ 62 Wayne Chrebet .60 .25
❑ 63 Ben Coates .40 .15
❑ 64 Curtis Conway .40 .15
❑ 65 Randall Cunningham .60 .25
❑ 66 Rickey Dudley .25 .08
❑ 67 Bert Emanuel .40 .15
❑ 68 Bobby Engram .40 .15
❑ 69 William Floyd .25 .08
❑ 70 Irving Fryar .40 .15
❑ 71 Elvis Grbac .40 .15
❑ 72 Kevin Greene .40 .15
❑ 73 Jim Harbaugh .40 .15
❑ 74 Raymont Harris .25 .08
❑ 75 Garrison Hearst .60 .25
❑ 76 Greg Hill .25 .08
❑ 77 Desmond Howard .40 .15
❑ 78 Bobby Hoying .40 .15
❑ 79 Michael Jackson .25 .08
❑ 80 Terry Allen .60 .25
❑ 81 Jerome Bettis .60 .25
❑ 82 Jeff Blake .40 .15
❑ 83 Robert Brooks .40 .15
❑ 84 Tim Brown .60 .25
❑ 85 Isaac Bruce .60 .25
❑ 86 Cris Carter .60 .25
❑ 87 Ty Detmer .40 .15
❑ 88 Trent Dilfer .60 .25
❑ 89 Marshall Faulk .75 .30
❑ 90 Antonio Freeman .60 .25
❑ 91 Gus Frerotte .25 .08
❑ 92 Joey Galloway .40 .15
❑ 93 Michael Irvin .60 .25
❑ 94 Brad Johnson .60 .25
❑ 95 Danny Kanell .40 .15
❑ 96 Napoleon Kaufman .60 .25
❑ 97 Dorsey Levens .60 .25
❑ 98 Natrone Means .40 .15
❑ 99 Herman Moore .40 .15
❑ 100 Adrian Murrell .40 .15
❑ 101 Carl Pickens .40 .15
❑ 102 Rod Smith .40 .15
❑ 103 Thurman Thomas .60 .25
❑ 104 Reggie White .60 .25
❑ 105 Jim Druckenmiller .25 .08
❑ 106 Antowain Smith .60 .25
❑ 107 Reidel Anthony .40 .15
❑ 108 Ike Hilliard .40 .15
❑ 109 Rae Carruth .25 .08
❑ 110 Troy Davis .25 .08
❑ 111 Terance Mathis .40 .15
❑ 112 Brett Favre 2.50 1.00
❑ 113 Dan Marino 2.50 1.00
❑ 114 Emmitt Smith 2.00 .75
❑ 115 Barry Sanders 2.00 .75
❑ 116 Eddie George .60 .25
❑ 117 Drew Bledsoe 1.00 .40
❑ 118 Troy Aikman 1.25 .50
❑ 119 Terrell Davis .60 .25
❑ 120 John Elway 2.50 1.00
❑ 121 Mark Brunell .60 .25
❑ 122 Jerry Rice 1.25 .50
❑ 123 Kordell Stewart .60 .25
❑ 124 Steve McNair .60 .25
❑ 125 Curtis Martin .60 .25
❑ 126 Steve Young .75 .30
❑ 127 Kerry Collins .40 .15

❑ 128	Terry Glenn	.60	.25
❑ 129	Deion Sanders	.60	.25
❑ 130	Mike Alstott	.60	.25
❑ 131	Tony Banks	.40	.15
❑ 132	Karim Abdul-Jabbar	.60	.25
❑ 133	Terrell Owens	.60	.25
❑ 134	Yatil Green	.25	.08
❑ 135	Tony Gonzalez	.60	.25
❑ 136	Byron Hanspard	.25	.08
❑ 137	David LaFleur	.25	.08
❑ 138	Danny Wuerffel	.40	.15
❑ 139	Tiki Barber	.60	.25
❑ 140	Peter Boulware	.25	.08
❑ 141	Will Blackwell	.25	.08
❑ 142	Warrick Dunn	.60	.25
❑ 143	Corey Dillon	.60	.25
❑ 144	Jake Plummer	.60	.25
❑ 145	Neil Smith	.40	.15
❑ 146	Charles Johnson	.25	.08
❑ 147	Fred Lane	.25	.08
❑ 148	Dan Wilkinson	.25	.08
❑ 149	Ken Norton Jr.	.25	.08
❑ 150	Stephen Davis	.25	.08
❑ 151	Gilbert Brown	.25	.08
❑ 152	Kenny Bynum RC	.25	.08
❑ 153	Derrick Cullors	.25	.08
❑ 154	Charlie Garner	.40	.15
❑ 155	Jeff Graham	.25	.08
❑ 156	Warren Sapp	.40	.15
❑ 157	Jerald Moore	.25	.08
❑ 158	Sean Dawkins	.25	.08
❑ 159	Charlie Jones	.25	.08
❑ 160	Kevin Lockett	.25	.08
❑ 161	James McKnight	.60	.25
❑ 162	Chris Penn	.25	.08
❑ 163	Leslie Shepherd	.25	.08
❑ 164	Karl Williams	.25	.08
❑ 165	Mark Bruener	.25	.08
❑ 166	Ernie Conwell	.25	.08
❑ 167	Ken Dilger	.25	.08
❑ 168	Troy Drayton	.25	.08
❑ 169	Freddie Jones	.25	.08
❑ 170	Dale Carter	.25	.08
❑ 171	Charles Woodson RC	8.00	3.00
❑ 172	Alonzo Mayes RC	2.50	1.00
❑ 173	Andre Wadsworth RC	4.00	1.50
❑ 174	Grant Wistrom RC	4.00	1.50
❑ 175	Greg Ellis RC	2.50	1.00
❑ 176	Chris Howard RC	2.50	1.00
❑ 177	Keith Brooking RC	6.00	2.50
❑ 178	Takeo Spikes RC	6.00	2.50
❑ 179	Anthony Simmons RC	4.00	1.50
❑ 180	Brian Simmons RC	4.00	1.50
❑ 181	Sam Cowart RC	4.00	1.50
❑ 182	Ken Oxendine RC	2.50	1.00
❑ 183	Vonnie Holliday RC	4.00	1.50
❑ 184	Terry Fair RC	4.00	1.50
❑ 185	Shaun Williams RC	4.00	1.50
❑ 186	Tremayne Stephens RC	2.50	1.00
❑ 187	Duane Starks RC	2.50	1.00
❑ 188	Jason Peter RC	2.50	1.00
❑ 189	Tebucky Jones RC	2.50	1.00
❑ 190	Donovin Darius RC	4.00	1.50
❑ 191	R.W. McQuarters RC	4.00	1.50
❑ 192	Corey Chavous RC	6.00	2.50
❑ 193	Cameron Cleeland RC	2.50	1.00
❑ 194	Stephen Alexander RC	4.00	1.50
❑ 195	Rod Rutledge RC	2.50	1.00
❑ 196	Scott Frost RC	2.50	1.00
❑ 197	Fred Beasley RC	2.50	1.00
❑ 198	Dorian Boose RC	2.50	1.00
❑ 199	Randy Moss RC	30.00	15.00
❑ 200	Jacquez Green RC	4.00	1.50
❑ 201	Marcus Nash RC	2.50	1.00
❑ 202	Hines Ward RC	25.00	12.50
❑ 203	Kevin Dyson RC	6.00	2.50
❑ 204	E.G. Green RC	4.00	1.50
❑ 205	Germane Crowell RC	4.00	1.50
❑ 206	Joe Jurevicius RC	6.00	2.50
❑ 207	Tony Simmons RC	4.00	1.50
❑ 208	Tim Dwight RC	6.00	2.50
❑ 209	Az-Zahir Hakim RC	6.00	2.50
❑ 210	Jerome Pathon RC	6.00	2.50
❑ 211	Pat Johnson RC	4.00	1.50
❑ 212	Mikhael Ricks RC	4.00	1.50
❑ 213	Donald Hayes RC	4.00	1.50
❑ 214	Jammi German RC	2.50	1.00
❑ 215	Larry Shannon RC	2.50	1.00
❑ 216	Brian Alford RC	2.50	1.00
❑ 217	Curtis Enis RC	2.50	1.00
❑ 218	Fred Taylor RC	10.00	4.00
❑ 219	Robert Edwards RC	4.00	1.50
❑ 220	Ahman Green RC	25.00	12.50
❑ 221	Tavian Banks RC	4.00	1.50
❑ 222	Skip Hicks RC	4.00	1.50
❑ 223	Robert Holcombe RC	4.00	1.50
❑ 224	John Avery RC	4.00	1.50
❑ 225	Chris Fuamatu-Ma'afala RC	4.00	1.50
❑ 226	Michael Pittman RC	8.00	4.00
❑ 227	Rashaan Shehee RC	4.00	1.50
❑ 228	Jonathan Linton RC	4.00	1.50
❑ 229	Jon Ritchie RC	4.00	1.50
❑ 230	Chris Floyd RC	2.50	1.00
❑ 231	Wilmont Perry RC	2.50	1.00
❑ 232	Raymond Priester RC	2.50	1.00
❑ 233	Peyton Manning RC	50.00	25.00
❑ 234	Ryan Leaf RC	6.00	2.50
❑ 235	Brian Griese RC	12.00	5.00
❑ 236	Jeff Ogden RC	6.00	2.50
❑ 237	Charlie Batch RC	6.00	2.50
❑ 238	Moses Moreno RC	2.50	1.00
❑ 239	Jonathan Quinn RC	6.00	2.50
❑ 240	Flozell Adams RC	2.50	1.00
❑ 241	Brett Favre PT	12.00	5.00
❑ 242	Dan Marino PT	12.00	5.00
❑ 243	Emmitt Smith PT	10.00	4.00
❑ 244	Barry Sanders PT	10.00	4.00
❑ 245	Eddie George PT	2.50	1.00
❑ 246	Drew Bledsoe PT	5.00	2.00
❑ 247	Troy Aikman PT	6.00	2.50
❑ 248	Terrell Davis PT	2.50	1.00
❑ 249	John Elway PT	12.00	5.00
❑ 250	Carl Pickens PT	2.50	1.00
❑ 251	Jerry Rice PT	6.00	2.50
❑ 252	Kordell Stewart PT	2.50	1.00
❑ 253	Steve McNair PT	2.50	1.00
❑ 254	Curtis Martin PT	2.50	1.00
❑ 255	Steve Young PT	4.00	1.50
❑ 256	Herman Moore PT	2.50	1.00
❑ 257	Dorsey Levens PT	2.50	1.00
❑ 258	Deion Sanders PT	2.50	1.00
❑ 259	Napoleon Kaufman PT	2.50	1.00
❑ 260	Warrick Dunn PT	2.50	1.00
❑ 261	Corey Dillon PT	2.50	1.00
❑ 262	Jerome Bettis PT	2.50	1.00
❑ 263	Tim Brown PT	2.50	1.00
❑ 264	Cris Carter PT	2.50	1.00
❑ 265	Antonio Freeman PT	2.50	1.00
❑ 266	Randy Moss PT	20.00	10.00
❑ 267	Curtis Enis PT	2.50	1.00
❑ 268	Fred Taylor PT	4.00	1.50
❑ 269	Robert Edwards PT	2.50	1.00
❑ 270	Peyton Manning PT	25.00	10.00
❑ 271	Barry Sanders TL	1.00	.40
❑ 272	Eddie George TL	.40	.15
❑ 273	Troy Aikman TL	.60	.25
❑ 274	Mark Brunell TL	.60	.25
❑ 275	Kordell Stewart TL	.60	.25
❑ 276	Tim Biakabutuka TL	.25	.08
❑ 277	Terry Glenn TL	.25	.08
❑ 278	Mike Alstott TL	.25	.08
❑ 279	Tony Banks TL	.25	.08
❑ 280	Karim Abdul-Jabbar TL	.25	.08
❑ 281	Terrell Owens TL	.40	.15
❑ 282	Byron Hanspard TL	.25	.08
❑ 283	Jake Plummer TL	.40	.15
❑ 284	Terry Allen TL	.25	.08
❑ 285	Jeff Blake TL	.25	.08
❑ 286	Brad Johnson TL	.25	.08
❑ 287	Danny Kanell TL	.25	.08
❑ 288	Natrone Means TL	.25	.08
❑ 289	Rod Smith TL	.25	.08
❑ 290	Thurman Thomas TL	.25	.08
❑ 291	Reggie White TL	.25	.08
❑ 292	Troy Davis TL	.25	.08
❑ 293	Curtis Conway TL	.25	.08
❑ 294	Irving Fryar TL	.25	.08
❑ 295	Jim Harbaugh TL	.25	.08
❑ 296	Andre Rison TL	.25	.08
❑ 297	Ricky Watters TL	.25	.08
❑ 298	Keyshawn Johnson TL	.25	.08
❑ 299	Jeff George TL	.25	.08
❑ 300	Marshall Faulk TL	.60	.25

1999 Leaf Rookies and Stars

❑	COMPLETE SET (300)	150.00	75.00
❑	COMP.SET w/o SP's (200)	30.00	15.00
❑ 1	Frank Sanders	.40	.15
❑ 2	Adrian Murrell	.40	.15
❑ 3	Rob Moore	.40	.15
❑ 4	Simeon Rice	.40	.15
❑ 5	Michael Pittman	.25	.08
❑ 6	Jake Plummer	.40	.15
❑ 7	Chris Chandler	.40	.15
❑ 8	Tim Dwight	.40	.15
❑ 9	Chris Calloway	.25	.08
❑ 10	Terance Mathis	.40	.15
❑ 11	Jamal Anderson	.60	.25
❑ 12	Byron Hanspard	.25	.08
❑ 13	O.J. Santiago	.25	.08
❑ 14	Ken Oxendine	.25	.08
❑ 15	Priest Holmes	1.00	.40
❑ 16	Scott Mitchell	.25	.08
❑ 17	Tony Banks	.40	.15
❑ 18	Patrick Johnson	.25	.08
❑ 19	Rod Woodson	.40	.15
❑ 20	Jermaine Lewis	.40	.15
❑ 21	Errict Rhett	.40	.15
❑ 22	Stoney Case	.25	.08
❑ 23	Andre Reed	.40	.15
❑ 24	Eric Moulds	.40	.15
❑ 25	Rob Johnson	.40	.15
❑ 26	Doug Flutie	.60	.25
❑ 27	Bruce Smith	.40	.15
❑ 28	Jay Riemersma	.25	.08
❑ 29	Antowain Smith	.25	.08
❑ 30	Thurman Thomas	.40	.15
❑ 31	Jonathan Linton	.25	.08
❑ 32	Muhsin Muhammad	.40	.15
❑ 33	Rae Carruth	.25	.08
❑ 34	Wesley Walls	.40	.15
❑ 35	Fred Lane	.25	.08
❑ 36	Kevin Greene	.25	.08
❑ 37	Tim Biakabutuka	.40	.15
❑ 38	Curtis Enis	.25	.08
❑ 39	Shane Matthews	.40	.15
❑ 40	Bobby Engram	.40	.15
❑ 41	Curtis Conway	.40	.15
❑ 42	Marcus Robinson	1.25	.50
❑ 43	Darnay Scott	.25	.08
❑ 44	Carl Pickens	.40	.15
❑ 45	Corey Dillon	.60	.25
❑ 46	Jeff Blake	.40	.15
❑ 47	Terry Kirby	.25	.08
❑ 48	Ty Detmer	.40	.15
❑ 49	Leslie Shepherd	.25	.08
❑ 50	Karim Abdul-Jabbar	.40	.15
❑ 51	Emmitt Smith	1.25	.50
❑ 52	Deion Sanders	.60	.25
❑ 53	Michael Irvin	.40	.15
❑ 54	Rocket Ismail	.40	.15
❑ 55	David LaFleur	.25	.08
❑ 56	Troy Aikman	1.25	.50
❑ 57	Ed McCaffrey	.40	.15
❑ 58	Rod Smith	.40	.15
❑ 59	Shannon Sharpe	.40	.15
❑ 60	Brian Griese	.60	.25
❑ 61	John Elway	2.00	.75
❑ 62	Bubby Brister	.25	.08
❑ 63	Neil Smith	.40	.15
❑ 64	Terrell Davis	.60	.25
❑ 65	John Avery	.25	.08
❑ 66	Derek Loville	.25	.08
❑ 67	Ron Rivers	.25	.08
❑ 68	Herman Moore	.40	.15
❑ 69	Johnnie Morton	.40	.15
❑ 70	Charlie Batch	.60	.25
❑ 71	Barry Sanders	2.00	.75
❑ 72	Germane Crowell	.25	.08
❑ 73	Greg Hill	.25	.08

❑ 74 Gus Frerotte	.40	.15
❑ 75 Corey Bradford	.25	.08
❑ 76 Dorsey Levens	.60	.25
❑ 77 Antonio Freeman	.60	.25
❑ 78 Mark Chmura	.25	.08
❑ 79 Brett Favre	2.00	.75
❑ 80 Bill Schroeder	.40	.15
❑ 81 Matt Hasselbeck	.60	.25
❑ 82 E.G. Green	.25	.08
❑ 83 Ken Dilger	.25	.08
❑ 84 Jerome Pathon	.25	.08
❑ 85 Marvin Harrison	.60	.25
❑ 86 Peyton Manning	2.00	.75
❑ 87 Tavian Banks	.25	.08
[illegible]	[illegible]	[illegible]
❑ 89 Mark Brunell	.60	.25
❑ 90 Fred Taylor	.60	.25
❑ 91 Jimmy Smith	.40	.15
❑ 92 James Stewart	.40	.15
❑ 93 Kyle Brady	.25	.08
❑ 94 Derrick Thomas	.60	.25
❑ 95 Rashaan Shehee	.25	.08
❑ 96 Derrick Alexander WR	.40	.15
❑ 97 Byron Bam Morris	.25	.08
❑ 98 Andre Rison	.40	.15
❑ 99 Elvis Grbac	.40	.15
❑ 100 Tony Gonzalez	.60	.25
❑ 101 Donnell Bennett	.25	.08
❑ 102 Warren Moon	.60	.25
❑ 103 Zach Thomas	.60	.25
❑ 104 Oronde Gadsden	.40	.15
❑ 105 Dan Marino	2.00	.75
❑ 106 O.J. McDuffie	.40	.15
❑ 107 Tony Martin	.40	.15
❑ 108 Randy Moss	1.50	.60
❑ 109 Cris Carter	.60	.25
❑ 110 Robert Smith	.60	.25
❑ 111 Randall Cunningham	.60	.25
❑ 112 Jake Reed	.40	.15
❑ 113 John Randle	.40	.15
❑ 114 Leroy Hoard	.25	.08
❑ 115 Jeff George	.40	.15
❑ 116 Ty Law	.40	.15
❑ 117 Shawn Jefferson	.25	.08
❑ 118 Troy Brown	.40	.15
❑ 119 Robert Edwards	.25	.08
❑ 120 Tony Simmons	.25	.08
❑ 121 Terry Glenn	.60	.25
❑ 122 Ben Coates	.40	.15
❑ 123 Drew Bledsoe	.75	.30
❑ 124 Terry Allen	.40	.15
❑ 125 Cameron Cleeland	.25	.08
❑ 126 Eddie Kennison	.40	.15
❑ 127 Amani Toomer	.25	.08
❑ 128 Kerry Collins	.40	.15
❑ 129 Joe Jurevicius	.40	.15
❑ 130 Tiki Barber	.60	.25
❑ 131 Ike Hilliard	.25	.08
❑ 132 Michael Strahan	.40	.15
❑ 133 Gary Brown	.25	.08
❑ 134 Jason Sehorn	.25	.08
❑ 135 Curtis Martin	.60	.25
❑ 136 Vinny Testaverde	.40	.15
❑ 137 Dedric Ward	.25	.08
❑ 138 Keyshawn Johnson	.60	.25
❑ 139 Wayne Chrebet	.40	.15
❑ 140 Tyrone Wheatley	.40	.15
❑ 141 Napoleon Kaufman	.60	.25
❑ 142 Tim Brown	.60	.25
❑ 143 Rickey Dudley	.25	.08
❑ 144 Jon Ritchie	.25	.08
❑ 145 James Jett	.25	.08
❑ 146 Rich Gannon	.60	.25
❑ 147 Charles Woodson	.60	.25
❑ 148 Charles Johnson	.25	.08
❑ 149 Duce Staley	.60	.25
❑ 150 Will Blackwell	.25	.08
❑ 151 Kordell Stewart	.40	.15
❑ 152 Jerome Bettis	.60	.25
❑ 153 Hines Ward	.60	.25
❑ 154 Richard Huntley	.40	.15
❑ 155 Natrone Means	.40	.15
❑ 156 Mikhael Ricks	.25	.08
❑ 157 Junior Seau	.60	.25
❑ 158 Jim Harbaugh	.40	.15
❑ 159 Ryan Leaf	.60	.25
❑ 160 Erik Kramer	.25	.08
❑ 161 Terrell Owens	.60	.25
❑ 162 J.J. Stokes	.40	.15
❑ 163 Lawrence Phillips	.40	.15
❑ 164 Charlie Garner	.40	.15
❑ 165 Jerry Rice	1.25	.50
❑ 166 Garrison Hearst	.40	.15
❑ 167 Steve Young	.75	.30
❑ 168 Derrick Mayes	.40	.15
❑ 169 Ahman Green	.60	.25
❑ 170 Joey Galloway	.40	.15
❑ 171 Ricky Watters	.40	.15
❑ 172 Jon Kitna	.60	.25
❑ 173 Sean Dawkins	.25	.08
❑ 174 Az-Zahir Hakim	.25	.08
❑ 175 Robert Holcombe	.25	.08
❑ 176 Isaac Bruce	.60	.25
[illegible]	[illegible]	[illegible]
❑ 178 Marshall Faulk	.75	.30
❑ 179 Trent Green	.60	.25
❑ 180 Eric Zeier	.40	.15
❑ 181 Bert Emanuel	.40	.15
❑ 182 Jacquez Green	.25	.08
❑ 183 Reidel Anthony	.40	.15
❑ 184 Warren Sapp	.25	.08
❑ 185 Mike Alstott	.60	.25
❑ 186 Warrick Dunn	.60	.25
❑ 187 Trent Dilfer	.60	.25
❑ 188 Neil O'Donnell	.40	.15
❑ 189 Eddie George	.60	.25
❑ 190 Yancey Thigpen	.25	.08
❑ 191 Steve McNair	.60	.25
❑ 192 Kevin Dyson	.40	.15
❑ 193 Frank Wycheck	.25	.08
❑ 194 Stephen Davis	.60	.25
❑ 195 Stephen Alexander	.25	.08
❑ 196 Darrell Green	.25	.08
❑ 197 Skip Hicks	.25	.08
❑ 198 Brad Johnson	.60	.25
❑ 199 Michael Westbrook	.40	.15
❑ 200 Albert Connell	.25	.08
❑ 201 David Boston RC	3.00	1.50
❑ 202 Joel Makovicka RC	3.00	1.50
❑ 203 Chris Greisen RC	2.50	1.25
❑ 204 Jeff Paulk RC	1.50	.75
❑ 205 Reginald Kelly RC	2.50	1.25
❑ 206 Chris McAlister RC	2.50	1.25
❑ 207 Brandon Stokley RC	4.00	1.50
❑ 208 Antoine Winfield RC	2.50	1.25
❑ 209 Bobby Collins RC	1.50	.75
❑ 210 Peerless Price RC	3.00	1.50
❑ 211 Shawn Bryson RC	3.00	1.50
❑ 212 Sheldon Jackson RC	2.50	1.25
❑ 213 Kamil Loud RC	1.50	.75
❑ 214 D'Wayne Bates RC	2.50	1.25
❑ 215 Jerry Azumah RC	2.50	1.25
❑ 216 Marty Booker RC	3.00	1.50
❑ 217 Cade McNown RC	2.50	1.25
❑ 218 James Allen RC	3.00	1.50
❑ 219 Nick Williams RC	2.50	1.25
❑ 220 Akili Smith RC	2.50	1.25
❑ 221 Craig Yeast RC	2.50	1.25
❑ 222 Damon Griffen RC	2.50	1.25
❑ 223 Scott Covington RC	3.00	1.50
❑ 224 Michael Basnight RC	1.50	.75
❑ 225 Ronnie Powell RC	1.50	.75
❑ 226 Rahim Abdullah RC	2.50	1.25
❑ 227 Tim Couch RC	3.00	1.50
❑ 228 Kevin Johnson RC	3.00	1.50
❑ 229 Darrin Chiaverini RC	2.50	1.25
❑ 230 Mark Campbell RC	2.50	1.25
❑ 231 Mike Lucky RC	2.50	1.25
❑ 232 Robert Thomas RC	2.50	1.25
❑ 233 Ebenezer Ekuban RC	2.50	1.25
❑ 234 Dat Nguyen RC	3.00	1.50
❑ 235 Wane McGarity RC	1.50	.75
❑ 236 Jason Tucker RC	2.50	1.25
❑ 237 Olandis Gary RC	3.00	1.50
❑ 238 Al Wilson RC	3.00	1.50
❑ 239 Travis McGriff RC	1.50	.75
❑ 240 Desmond Clark RC	3.00	1.50
❑ 241 Andre Cooper RC	1.50	.75
❑ 242 Chris Watson RC	1.50	.75
❑ 243 Sedrick Irvin RC	1.50	.75
❑ 244 Chris Claiborne RC	1.50	.75
❑ 245 Cory Sauter RC	1.50	.75
❑ 246 Brock Olivo RC	1.50	.75
❑ 247 De'Mond Parker RC	1.50	.75
❑ 248 Aaron Brooks RC	6.00	2.50
❑ 249 Antuan Edwards RC	2.50	1.25
❑ 250 Basil Mitchell RC	1.50	.75
❑ 251 Terrence Wilkins RC	2.50	1.25
❑ 252 Edgerrin James RC	15.00	6.00
❑ 253 Fernando Bryant RC	2.50	1.25
❑ 254 Mike Cloud RC	2.50	1.25
❑ 255 Larry Parker RC	3.00	1.50
❑ 256 Rob Konrad RC	3.00	1.50
❑ 257 Cecil Collins RC	1.50	.75
❑ 258 James Johnson RC	2.50	1.25
❑ 259 Jim Kleinsasser RC	3.00	1.50
❑ 260 Daunte Culpepper RC	15.00	6.00
❑ 261 Michael Bishop RC	3.00	1.50
❑ 262 Andy Katzenmoyer RC	2.50	1.25
❑ 263 Kevin Faulk RC	3.00	1.50
❑ 264 Brett Bech RC	1.50	.75
❑ 265 Ricky Williams RC	8.00	3.00
❑ 266 [illegible] RC	1.50	.75
❑ 267 Joe Montgomery RC	2.50	1.25
❑ 268 Dan Campbell RC	1.50	.75
❑ 269 Ray Lucas RC	3.00	1.50
❑ 270 Scott Dreisbach RC	2.50	1.25
❑ 271 Jed Weaver RC	1.50	.75
❑ 272 Dameane Douglas RC	2.50	1.25
❑ 273 Cecil Martin RC	2.50	1.25
❑ 274 Donovan McNabb RC	20.00	7.50
❑ 275 Na Brown RC	2.50	1.25
❑ 276 Jerame Tuman RC	3.00	1.50
❑ 277 Amos Zereoue RC	3.00	1.50
❑ 278 Troy Edwards RC	2.50	1.25
❑ 279 Jermaine Fazande RC	2.50	1.25
❑ 280 Steve Heiden RC	3.00	1.50
❑ 281 Jeff Garcia RC	20.00	7.50
❑ 282 Terry Jackson RC	2.50	1.25
❑ 283 Charlie Rogers RC	2.50	1.25
❑ 284 Brock Huard RC	3.00	1.50
❑ 285 Karsten Bailey RC	2.50	1.25
❑ 286 Lamar King RC	1.50	.75
❑ 287 Justin Watson RC	1.50	.75
❑ 288 Kurt Warner RC	20.00	7.50
❑ 289 Torry Holt RC	12.00	5.00
❑ 290 Joe Germaine RC	2.50	1.25
❑ 291 Dre' Bly RC	3.00	1.50
❑ 292 Martin Gramatica RC	1.50	.75
❑ 293 Rabih Abdullah RC	2.50	1.25
❑ 294 Shaun King RC	2.50	1.25
❑ 295 Anthony McFarland RC	2.50	1.25
❑ 296 Darnell McDonald RC	2.50	1.25
❑ 297 Kevin Daft RC	2.50	1.25
❑ 298 Jevon Kearse RC	8.00	3.00
❑ 299 Mike Sellers	.25	.08
❑ 300 Champ Bailey RC	6.00	2.50

2000 Leaf Rookies and Stars

❑ COMP.SET w/o SP's (100)	15.00	6.00
❑ 1 Jake Plummer	.40	.15
❑ 2 David Boston	.60	.25
❑ 3 Tim Dwight	.60	.25
❑ 4 Jamal Anderson	.60	.25
❑ 5 Chris Chandler	.40	.15
❑ 6 Tony Banks	.40	.15
❑ 7 Qadry Ismail	.40	.15
❑ 8 Eric Moulds	.60	.25
❑ 9 Doug Flutie	.60	.25
❑ 10 Lamar Smith	.40	.15
❑ 11 Peerless Price	.40	.15
❑ 12 Rob Johnson	.40	.15
❑ 13 Reggie White	.60	.25
❑ 14 Muhsin Muhammad	.40	.15
❑ 15 Steve Beuerlein	.40	.15
❑ 16 Cade McNown	.25	.08
❑ 17 Derrick Alexander	.40	.15
❑ 18 Marcus Robinson	.60	.25

❑	19	Corey Dillon	.60	.25
❑	20	Akili Smith	.25	.08
❑	21	Tim Couch	.40	.15
❑	22	Kevin Johnson	.60	.25
❑	23	Emmitt Smith	1.25	.50
❑	24	Troy Aikman	1.25	.50
❑	25	Joey Galloway	.40	.15
❑	26	Rocket Ismail	.40	.15
❑	27	John Elway	2.00	.75
❑	28	Terrell Davis	.60	.25
❑	29	Brian Griese	.60	.25
❑	30	Olandis Gary	.60	.25
❑	31	Ed McCaffrey	.60	.25
❑	32	Rod Smith	.40	.15
❑	33	Barry Sanders	1.50	.60
❑	34	Charlie Batch	.60	.25
❑	35	Germane Crowell	.25	.08
❑	36	James Stewart	.40	.15
❑	37	Brett Favre	2.00	.75
❑	38	Dorsey Levens	.40	.15
❑	39	Antonio Freeman	.60	.25
❑	40	Peyton Manning	1.50	.60
❑	41	Edgerrin James	1.00	.40
❑	42	Marvin Harrison	.60	.25
❑	43	Fred Taylor	.60	.25
❑	44	Mark Brunell	.60	.25
❑	45	Jimmy Smith	.40	.15
❑	46	Elvis Grbac	.40	.15
❑	47	Tony Gonzalez	.40	.15
❑	48	Dan Marino	2.00	.75
❑	49	Joe Horn	.40	.15
❑	50	Jay Fiedler	.60	.25
❑	51	James Allen	.40	.15
❑	52	Randy Moss	1.25	.50
❑	53	Daunte Culpepper	.75	.30
❑	54	Cris Carter	.60	.25
❑	55	Robert Smith	.60	.25
❑	56	Drew Bledsoe	.75	.30
❑	57	Terry Glenn	.60	.25
❑	58	Ricky Williams	.60	.25
❑	59	Amani Toomer	.40	.15
❑	60	Kerry Collins	.40	.15
❑	61	Curtis Martin	.60	.25
❑	62	Vinny Testaverde	.40	.15
❑	63	Wayne Chrebet	.40	.15
❑	64	Tim Brown	.60	.25
❑	65	Tyrone Wheatley	.40	.15
❑	66	Rich Gannon	.60	.25
❑	67	Donovan McNabb	1.00	.40
❑	68	Duce Staley	.60	.25
❑	69	Jerome Bettis	.60	.25
❑	70	Donald Hayes	.25	.08
❑	71	Junior Seau	.60	.25
❑	72	Jermaine Fazande	.25	.08
❑	73	Jerry Rice	1.25	.50
❑	74	Steve Young	.75	.30
❑	75	Terrell Owens	.60	.25
❑	76	Charlie Garner	.40	.15
❑	77	Jeff Garcia	.60	.25
❑	78	Tim Biakabutuka	.40	.15
❑	79	Tiki Barber	.60	.25
❑	80	Ricky Watters	.40	.15
❑	81	Kurt Warner	1.25	.50
❑	82	Marshall Faulk	.75	.30
❑	83	Isaac Bruce	.60	.25
❑	84	Torry Holt	.60	.25
❑	85	Mike Alstott	.60	.25
❑	86	Warrick Dunn	.60	.25
❑	87	Shaun King	.25	.08
❑	88	Keyshawn Johnson	.60	.25
❑	89	Warren Sapp	.40	.15
❑	90	Eddie George	.60	.25
❑	91	Jevon Kearse	.60	.25
❑	92	Steve McNair	.60	.25
❑	93	Carl Pickens	.40	.15
❑	94	Deion Sanders	.60	.25
❑	95	Stephen Davis	.60	.25
❑	96	Brad Johnson	.60	.25
❑	97	Bruce Smith	.40	.15
❑	98	Michael Westbrook	.40	.15
❑	99	Albert Connell	.25	.08
❑	100	Jeff George	.40	.15
❑	101	Thomas Jones RC	15.00	6.00
❑	102	Bashir Yamini RC	5.00	2.00
❑	103	Jamal Lewis RC	25.00	10.00
❑	104	Travis Taylor RC	10.00	4.00
❑	105	Chris Redman RC	8.00	3.00
❑	106	Avion Black RC	8.00	3.00
❑	107	Sammy Morris RC	10.00	4.00
❑	108	Dez White RC	10.00	4.00
❑	109	Peter Warrick RC	10.00	4.00
❑	110	Ron Dugans RC	5.00	2.00
❑	111	Curtis Keaton RC	8.00	3.00
❑	112	Danny Farmer RC	8.00	3.00
❑	113	Courtney Brown RC	10.00	4.00
❑	114	Dennis Northcutt RC	10.00	4.00
❑	115	Travis Prentice RC	8.00	3.00
❑	116	JaJuan Dawson RC	5.00	2.00
❑	117	Spergon Wynn RC	8.00	3.00
❑	118	Michael Wiley RC	8.00	3.00
❑	119	Chris Cole RC	8.00	3.00
❑	120	Mike Anderson RC	12.00	5.00
❑	121	Muneer Moore RC	5.00	2.00
❑	122	Reuben Droughns RC	12.00	5.00
❑	123	Bubba Franks RC	10.00	4.00
❑	124	Anthony Lucas RC	5.00	2.00
❑	125	Charles Lee RC	5.00	2.00
❑	126	R.Jay Soward RC	8.00	3.00
❑	127	Shyrone Stith RC	8.00	3.00
❑	128	Sylvester Morris RC	8.00	3.00
❑	129	Frank Moreau RC	8.00	3.00
❑	130	Dante Hall RC	20.00	7.50
❑	131	Doug Chapman RC	8.00	3.00
❑	132	Troy Walters RC	10.00	4.00
❑	133	J.R. Redmond RC	8.00	3.00
❑	134	Tom Brady RC	300.00	175.00
❑	135	Terrelle Smith RC	8.00	3.00
❑	136	Chad Morton RC	10.00	4.00
❑	137	Ron Dayne RC	10.00	4.00
❑	138	Ron Dixon RC	8.00	3.00
❑	139	Chad Pennington RC	25.00	10.00
❑	140	Anthony Becht RC	10.00	4.00
❑	141	Laveranues Coles RC	12.00	5.00
❑	142	Windrell Hayes RC	8.00	3.00
❑	143	Sebastian Janikowski RC	10.00	4.00
❑	144	Jerry Porter RC	12.00	5.00
❑	145	Corey Simon RC	10.00	4.00
❑	146	Todd Pinkston RC	10.00	4.00
❑	147	Gari Scott RC	5.00	2.00
❑	148	Plaxico Burress RC	20.00	7.50
❑	149	Tee Martin RC	10.00	4.00
❑	150	Trevor Gaylor RC	8.00	3.00
❑	151	Ronney Jenkins RC	8.00	3.00
❑	152	Giovanni Carmazzi RC	5.00	2.00
❑	153	Tim Rattay RC	10.00	4.00
❑	154	Shaun Alexander RC	40.00	20.00
❑	155	Darrell Jackson RC	15.00	6.00
❑	156	James Williams RC	8.00	3.00
❑	157	Trung Canidate RC	8.00	3.00
❑	158	Joe Hamilton RC	8.00	3.00
❑	159	Erron Kinney RC	10.00	4.00
❑	160	Todd Husak RC	10.00	4.00
❑	161	Raynoch Thompson RC	8.00	3.00
❑	162	Darwin Walker RC	5.00	2.00
❑	163	Jay Tant RC	5.00	2.00
❑	164	Doug Johnson RC	10.00	4.00
❑	165	Robert Bean RC	8.00	3.00
❑	166	Mark Simoneau RC	8.00	3.00
❑	167	John Jones RC	8.00	3.00
❑	168	Obafemi Ayanbadejo RC	8.00	3.00
❑	169	Mike Brown RC	15.00	6.00
❑	170	Shockmain Davis RC	5.00	2.00
❑	171	Erik Flowers RC	8.00	3.00
❑	172	Corey Moore RC	5.00	2.00
❑	173	Drew Haddad RC	5.00	2.00
❑	174	Kwame Cavil RC	5.00	2.00
❑	175	Pat Dennis RC	5.00	2.00
❑	176	Rashard Anderson RC	8.00	3.00
❑	177	Brian Finneran RC	10.00	4.00
❑	178	Na'il Diggs RC	8.00	3.00
❑	179	Marc Bulger RC	20.00	7.50
❑	180	Mondriel Fulcher RC	5.00	2.00
❑	181	Dwayne Carswell	5.00	2.00
❑	182	Brian Urlacher RC	25.00	10.00
❑	183	Paul Edinger RC	10.00	4.00
❑	184	Karon Coleman RC	8.00	3.00
❑	185	Aaron Shea RC	8.00	3.00
❑	186	Fabien Bownes RC	5.00	2.00
❑	187	Damon Hodge RC	8.00	3.00
❑	188	Dwayne Goodrich RC	5.00	2.00
❑	189	Clint Stoerner RC	8.00	3.00
❑	190	James Whalen RC	5.00	2.00
❑	191	Deltha O'Neal RC	10.00	4.00
❑	192	Ian Gold RC	8.00	3.00
❑	193	Kenoy Kennedy RC	5.00	2.00
❑	194	Jarious Jackson RC	8.00	3.00
❑	195	Leroy Fields RC	5.00	2.00
❑	196	Barrett Green RC	5.00	2.00
❑	197	Joey Jamison RC	5.00	2.00
❑	198	Rondell Mealey RC	5.00	2.00
❑	199	Rob Morris RC	8.00	3.00
❑	200	Marcus Washington RC	8.00	3.00
❑	201	Trevor Insley RC	5.00	2.00
❑	202	Jamel White RC	8.00	3.00
❑	203	Kevin McDougal RC	8.00	3.00
❑	204	Ibn Green RC	5.00	2.00
❑	205	T.J. Slaughter RC	5.00	2.00
❑	206	Emanuel Smith RC	5.00	2.00
❑	207	Herbert Goodman RC	8.00	3.00
❑	208	William Bartee RC	8.00	3.00
❑	209	Orantes Grant RC	5.00	2.00
❑	210	Brad Hoover RC	8.00	3.00
❑	211	Deon Dyer RC	8.00	3.00
❑	212	Jonas Lewis RC	5.00	2.00
❑	213	Chris Hovan RC	8.00	3.00
❑	214	Fred Robbins RC	5.00	2.00
❑	215	Michael Boireau RC	5.00	2.00
❑	216	Giles Cole RC	5.00	2.00
❑	217	Dave Stachelski RC	5.00	2.00
❑	218	Patrick Pass RC	8.00	3.00
❑	219	Darren Howard RC	8.00	3.00
❑	220	Austin Wheatley RC	5.00	2.00
❑	221	Kevin Houser RC	8.00	3.00
❑	222	Rian Lindell RC	5.00	2.00
❑	223	Jake Delhomme RC	50.00	25.00
❑	224	Cornelius Griffin RC	8.00	3.00
❑	225	Shaun Ellis RC	10.00	4.00
❑	226	John Abraham RC	10.00	4.00
❑	227	Travares Tillman RC	5.00	2.00
❑	228	Julian Peterson RC	10.00	4.00
❑	229	Marcus Knight RC	8.00	3.00
❑	230	Thomas Hamner RC	5.00	2.00
❑	231	Hank Poteat RC	8.00	3.00
❑	232	Neil Rackers RC	10.00	4.00
❑	233	Bobby Shaw RC	8.00	3.00
❑	234	Rogers Beckett RC	8.00	3.00
❑	235	Reggie Jones RC	5.00	2.00
❑	236	Tim Seder RC	8.00	3.00
❑	237	Durell Price RC	5.00	2.00
❑	238	Ahmed Plummer RC	10.00	4.00
❑	239	John Engelberger RC	8.00	3.00
❑	240	Paul Smith RC	8.00	3.00
❑	241	Chafie Fields RC	5.00	2.00
❑	242	Kevin Feterik RC	5.00	2.00
❑	243	Jacoby Shepherd RC	5.00	2.00
❑	244	Nate Webster RC	5.00	2.00
❑	245	Ketric Sanford RC	5.00	2.00
❑	246	Tavarus Hogans RC	5.00	2.00
❑	247	Keith Bulluck RC	10.00	4.00
❑	248	Mike Green RC	8.00	3.00
❑	249	Chris Coleman RC	10.00	4.00
❑	250	Demario Brown RC	5.00	2.00
❑	251	Billy Volek RC	15.00	6.00
❑	252	Mareno Philyaw RC	5.00	2.00
❑	253	Ethan Howell RC	5.00	2.00
❑	254	Chris Samuels RC	8.00	3.00
❑	255	Brandon Short RC	8.00	3.00
❑	256	Maurice Smith RC	8.00	3.00
❑	257	Frank Murphy RC	5.00	2.00
❑	258	Darrick Vaughn RC	5.00	2.00
❑	259	Payton Williams RC	5.00	2.00
❑	260	JaJuan Seider RC	5.00	2.00
❑	261	Antonio Banks EP RC	2.00	.75
❑	262	Jonathan Brown EP RC	2.00	.75
❑	263	Ontiwaun Carter EP RC	2.00	.75
❑	264	Jeremaine Copeland EP	2.00	.75
❑	265	Ralph Dawkins EP RC	3.00	1.25
❑	266	Marques Douglas EP RC	2.00	.75
❑	267	Kevin Drake EP RC	2.00	.75
❑	268	Damon Dunn EP RC	3.00	1.25
❑	269	Todd Floyd EP RC	2.00	.75
❑	270	Tony Graziani EP	3.00	1.25
❑	271	Derrick Ham EP RC	3.00	1.25
❑	272	Duane Hawthorne EP RC	3.00	1.25
❑	273	Alonzo Johnson EP RC	2.00	.75
❑	274	Mark Kacmarynski EP RC	2.00	.75
❑	275	Eric Kresser EP	2.00	.75
❑	276	Jim Kubiak EP RC	3.00	1.25
❑	277	Blaine McElmurry EP RC	2.00	.75
❑	278	Scott Milanovich EP	3.00	1.25
❑	279	Norman Miller EP RC	2.00	.75
❑	280	Sean Morey EP RC	3.00	1.25
❑	281	Jeff Ogden EP	3.00	1.25
❑	282	Pepe Pearson EP RC	3.00	1.25
❑	283	Ron Powlus EP RC	4.00	1.50
❑	284	Jason Shelley EP RC	2.00	.75
❑	285	Ben Snell EP RC	2.00	.75

❑ 286 Aaron Stecker EP RC	4.00	1.50
❑ 287 L.C. Stevens EP	2.00	.75
❑ 288 Mike Sutton EP RC	2.00	.75
❑ 289 Damian Vaughn EP RC	2.00	.75
❑ 290 Ted White EP	2.00	.75
❑ 291 Marcus Crandell EP RC	3.00	1.25
❑ 292 Darryl Daniel EP RC	3.00	1.25
❑ 293 Jesse Haynes EP	2.00	.75
❑ 294 Matt Lytle EP RC	3.00	1.25
❑ 295 Deon Mitchell EP RC	3.00	1.25
❑ 296 Kendrick Nord EP RC	2.00	.75
❑ 297 Ronnie Powell EP	2.00	.75
❑ 298 Selucio Sanford EP RC	3.00	1.25
❑ 299 Corey Thomas EP	2.00	.75
❑ 300 Vonshon Jackson EP RC	2.00	.75
❑ 301 Michael Vick XRC	50.00	20.00
❑ 302 Drew Brees XRC	40.00	20.00
❑ 303 Quincy Carter XRC	12.00	5.00
❑ 304 Marques Tuiasosopa XRC	15.00	6.00
❑ 305 Chris Weinke XRC	10.00	4.00
❑ 306 LaDainian Tomlinson XRC	100.00	50.00
❑ 307 Deuce McAllister XRC	25.00	10.00
❑ 308 Michael Bennett XRC	10.00	4.00
❑ 309 Anthony Thomas XRC	10.00	4.00
❑ 310 LaMont Jordan XRC	25.00	10.00
❑ 311 David Terrell XRC	12.00	5.00
❑ 312 Koren Robinson XRC	10.00	4.00
❑ 313 Rod Gardner XRC	12.00	5.00
❑ 314 Santana Moss XRC	20.00	7.50
❑ 315 Freddie Mitchell XRC	10.00	4.00
❑ 316 Gerard Warren XRC	10.00	4.00
❑ 317 Justin Smith XRC	10.00	4.00
❑ 318 Richard Seymour XRC	20.00	7.50
❑ 319 Andre Carter XRC	10.00	4.00
❑ 320 Jamal Reynolds XRC	10.00	4.00

2001 Leaf Rookies and Stars

❑ COMP.SET w/o SP's (100)	20.00	7.50
❑ 1 Aaron Brooks	.60	.25
❑ 2 Ahman Green	.60	.25
❑ 3 Antonio Freeman	.60	.25
❑ 4 Brad Johnson	.60	.25
❑ 5 Brett Favre	2.00	.75
❑ 6 Brian Griese	.60	.25
❑ 7 Brian Urlacher	1.00	.40
❑ 8 Bruce Smith	.25	.08
❑ 9 Cade McNown	.25	.08
❑ 10 Chad Pennington	1.00	.40
❑ 11 Champ Bailey	.40	.15
❑ 12 Charles Woodson	.40	.15
❑ 13 Charlie Batch	.60	.25
❑ 14 Charlie Garner	.40	.15
❑ 15 Corey Dillon	.60	.25
❑ 16 Cris Carter	.60	.25
❑ 17 Curtis Martin	.60	.25
❑ 18 Dan Marino	2.50	1.00
❑ 19 Daunte Culpepper	.60	.25
❑ 20 David Boston	.60	.25
❑ 21 Deion Sanders	.60	.25
❑ 22 Donovan McNabb	.75	.30
❑ 23 Doug Flutie	.60	.25
❑ 24 Drew Bledsoe	.75	.30
❑ 25 Duce Staley	.60	.25
❑ 26 Ed McCaffrey	.60	.25
❑ 27 Eddie George	.60	.25
❑ 28 Edgerrin James	.75	.30
❑ 29 Elvis Grbac	.40	.15
❑ 30 Emmitt Smith	1.25	.50
❑ 31 Eric Moulds	.40	.15
❑ 32 Fred Taylor	.60	.25
❑ 33 Germane Crowell	.25	.08
❑ 34 Ike Hilliard	.40	.15
❑ 35 Isaac Bruce	.60	.25
❑ 36 Jake Plummer	.40	.15
❑ 37 Jamal Anderson	.60	.25
❑ 38 Jamal Lewis	1.00	.40
❑ 39 James Allen	.40	.15
❑ 40 James Stewart	.40	.15
❑ 41 Jay Fiedler	.60	.25
❑ 42 Jeff Garcia	.60	.25
❑ 43 Jeff George	.40	.15
❑ 44 Jeff Lewis	.25	.08
❑ 45 Jerome Bettis	.60	.25
❑ 46 Jerry Rice	1.25	.50
❑ 47 Jevon Kearse	.40	.15
❑ 48 Jimmy Smith	.40	.15
❑ 49 Joey Galloway	.40	.15
❑ 50 John Elway	2.50	1.00
❑ 51 Junior Seau	.60	.25
❑ 52 Keenan McCardell	.25	.08
❑ 53 Kerry Collins	.40	.15
❑ 54 Kevin Johnson	.40	.15
❑ 55 Keyshawn Johnson	.60	.25
❑ 56 Kordell Stewart	.40	.15
❑ 57 Kurt Warner	1.25	.50
❑ 58 Lamar Smith	.40	.15
❑ 59 Marcus Robinson	.60	.25
❑ 60 Mark Brunell	.60	.25
❑ 61 Marshall Faulk	.75	.30
❑ 62 Marvin Harrison	.60	.25
❑ 63 Matt Hasselbeck	.40	.15
❑ 64 Mike Alstott	.60	.25
❑ 65 Mike Anderson	.60	.25
❑ 66 Muhsin Muhammad	.40	.15
❑ 67 Peter Warrick	.60	.25
❑ 68 Peyton Manning	1.50	.60
❑ 69 Priest Holmes	.75	.30
❑ 70 Randy Moss	1.25	.50
❑ 71 Ray Lewis	.60	.25
❑ 72 Rich Gannon	.60	.25
❑ 73 Ricky Watters	.40	.15
❑ 74 Ricky Williams	.60	.25
❑ 75 Rob Johnson	.40	.15
❑ 76 Rod Smith	.40	.15
❑ 77 Ron Dayne	.60	.25
❑ 78 Shannon Sharpe	.40	.15
❑ 79 Shaun Alexander	.75	.30
❑ 80 Stephen Davis	.60	.25
❑ 81 Steve McNair	.60	.25
❑ 82 Steve Young	.75	.30
❑ 83 Sylvester Morris	.25	.08
❑ 84 Terrell Davis	.60	.25
❑ 85 Terrell Owens	.60	.25
❑ 86 Thomas Jones	.40	.15
❑ 87 Tim Brown	.60	.25
❑ 88 Tim Couch	.40	.15
❑ 89 Tony Banks	.40	.15
❑ 90 Tony Gonzalez	.40	.15
❑ 91 Torry Holt	.60	.25
❑ 92 Travis Taylor	.40	.15
❑ 93 Trent Green	.60	.25
❑ 94 Troy Aikman	1.00	.40
❑ 95 Tyrone Wheatley	.40	.15
❑ 96 Vinny Testaverde	.40	.15
❑ 97 Warren Sapp	.40	.15
❑ 98 Warrick Dunn	.60	.25
❑ 99 Wayne Chrebet	.40	.15
❑ 100 Zach Thomas	.60	.25
❑ 101 A.J. Feeley RC	6.00	2.50
❑ 102 Josh Booty RC	6.00	2.50
❑ 103 Roderick Robinson RC	4.00	1.50
❑ 104 Renaldo Hill RC	4.00	1.50
❑ 105 Harold Blackmon RC	2.50	1.00
❑ 106 Rudi Johnson RC	10.00	4.00
❑ 107 Curtis Fuller RC	2.50	1.00
❑ 108 Dan Alexander RC	6.00	2.50
❑ 109 Anthony Thomas RPS	6.00	2.50
❑ 110 Travis Minor RPS	3.00	1.25
❑ 111 Heath Evans RC	4.00	1.50
❑ 112 Joe Walker RC	2.50	1.00
❑ 113 Moran Norris RC	2.50	1.00
❑ 114 Quincy Carter RPS	4.00	1.50
❑ 115 Michael Vick RPS	15.00	6.00
❑ 116 Vinny Sutherland RC	4.00	1.50
❑ 117 Scotty Anderson RC	4.00	1.50
❑ 118 Eddie Berlin RC	4.00	1.50
❑ 119 Jonathan Carter RC	4.00	1.50
❑ 120 Monty Beisel RC	6.00	2.50
❑ 121 T.J. Houshmandzadeh RC	8.00	3.00
❑ 122 Rodney Bailey RC	2.50	1.00
❑ 123 Reggie Germany RC	4.00	1.50
❑ 124 Ellis Wyms RC	2.50	1.00
❑ 125 Koren Robinson RPS	6.00	2.50
❑ 126 Antonio Pierce RC	12.00	5.00
❑ 127 Arnold Jackson RC	4.00	1.50
❑ 128 Andre Rone RC	2.50	1.00
❑ 129 Richard Newsome RC	2.50	1.00
❑ 130 Ifeanyi Ohalete RC	2.50	1.00
❑ 131 Dan O'Leary RC	4.00	1.50
❑ 132 Shad Meier RC	4.00	1.50
❑ 133 Jay Feely RC	2.50	1.00
❑ 134 Brandon Manumaleuna RC	4.00	1.50
❑ 135 Riall Johnson RC	2.50	1.00
❑ 136 Snoop Minnis RPS	4.00	1.50
❑ 137 Jermaine Hampton RC	2.50	1.00
❑ 138 Johnny Huggins RC	2.50	1.00
❑ 139 Marcellus Rivers RC	4.00	1.50
❑ 140 Andre Carter RPS	6.00	2.50
❑ 141 Michael Stone RC	2.50	1.00
❑ 142 Tony Dixon RC	4.00	1.50
❑ 143 Bhawoh Jue RC	6.00	2.50
❑ 144 Will Peterson RC	4.00	1.50
❑ 145 Anthony Henry RC	6.00	2.50
❑ 146 Marques Tuiasosopo RPS	4.00	1.50
❑ 147 Reggie Swinton RC	4.00	1.50
❑ 148 Robert Carswell RC	2.50	1.00
❑ 149 Freddie Mitchell RPS	3.00	1.25
❑ 150 Idrees Bashir RC	2.50	1.00
❑ 151 James Boyd RC	2.50	1.00
❑ 152 Chris Chambers RPS	6.00	2.50
❑ 153 Aaron Schobel RC	6.00	2.50
❑ 154 Dominic Raiola RC	2.50	1.00
❑ 155 Derrick Burgess RC	6.00	2.50
❑ 156 DeLawrence Grant RC	2.50	1.00
❑ 157 Karon Riley RC	2.50	1.00
❑ 158 Cedric Scott RC	4.00	1.50
❑ 159 Patrick Washington RC	4.00	1.50
❑ 160 Eric Johnson RC	10.00	4.00
❑ 161 Tevita Ofahengaue RC	2.50	1.00
❑ 162 Chris Cooper RC	4.00	1.50
❑ 163 Fred Wakefield RC	4.00	1.50
❑ 164 Kenny Smith RC	4.00	1.50
❑ 165 Marcus Bell RC	4.00	1.50
❑ 166 Mario Fatafehi RC	4.00	1.50
❑ 167 Anthony Herron RC	2.50	1.00
❑ 168 Joe Tafoya RC	2.50	1.00
❑ 169 Morlon Greenwood RC	4.00	1.50
❑ 170 Orlando Huff RC	2.50	1.00
❑ 171 Carlos Polk RC	2.50	1.00
❑ 172 Edgerton Hartwell RC	2.50	1.00
❑ 173 Zeke Moreno RC	6.00	2.50
❑ 174 Alex Lincoln RC	4.00	1.50
❑ 175 Quinton Caver RC	4.00	1.50
❑ 176 Matt Stewart RC	2.50	1.00
❑ 177 Markus Steele RC	4.00	1.50
❑ 178 Dwight Smith RC	2.50	1.00
❑ 179 Reggie Wayne RPS	8.00	3.00
❑ 180 Jeramotrius Butler RC	4.00	1.50
❑ 181 Jason Doering RC	2.50	1.00
❑ 182 John Howell RC	2.50	1.00
❑ 183 Alvin Porter RC	2.50	1.00
❑ 184 Eric Downing RC	2.50	1.00
❑ 185 John Nix RC	2.50	1.00
❑ 186 Tim Baker RC	2.50	1.00
❑ 187 Robert Garza RC	2.50	1.00
❑ 188 Randy Chevrier RC	2.50	1.00
❑ 189 Drew Brees RPS	12.00	5.00
❑ 190 Shawn Worthen RC	2.50	1.00
❑ 191 Drew Bennett RC	20.00	8.00
❑ 192 Marlon McCree RC	4.00	1.50
❑ 193 David Terrell RPS	4.00	1.50
❑ 194 Jeff Backus RC	4.00	1.50
❑ 195 Otis Leverette RC	2.50	1.00
❑ 196 Jason Glenn RC	6.00	2.50
❑ 197 Rashad Holman RC	2.50	1.00
❑ 198 T.J. Turner RC	2.50	1.00
❑ 199 Lynn Scott RC	6.00	2.50
❑ 200 Bill Gramatica RC	2.50	1.00
❑ 201 Michael Vick RC	30.00	12.50
❑ 202 Drew Brees RC	30.00	12.00
❑ 203 Quincy Carter RC	8.00	3.00
❑ 204 Jesse Palmer RC	8.00	3.00
❑ 205 Mike McMahon RC	8.00	3.00
❑ 206 Dave Dickenson RC	4.00	1.50
❑ 207 Jameel Cook RC	5.00	2.00
❑ 208 Marques Tuiasosopo RC	8.00	3.00
❑ 209 Chris Weinke RC	6.00	2.50
❑ 210 Sage Rosenfels RC	6.00	2.50

❑ 211 Josh Heupel RC 8.00 3.00
❑ 212 LaDainian Tomlinson RC 80.00 40.00
❑ 213 Michael Bennett RC 8.00 3.00
❑ 214 Anthony Thomas RC 8.00 3.00
❑ 215 Travis Henry RC 15.00 6.00
❑ 216 James Jackson RC 6.00 2.50
❑ 217 Correll Buckhalter RC 10.00 4.00
❑ 218 Derrick Blaylock RC 8.00 3.00
❑ 219 Dee Brown RC 8.00 3.00
❑ 220 LeVar Woods RC 5.00 2.00
❑ 221 Deuce McAllister RC 15.00 6.00
❑ 222 LaMont Jordan RC 15.00 6.00
❑ 223 Kevan Barlow RC 8.00 3.00
❑ 224 Travis Minor RC 5.00 2.00
❑ 225 David Terrell RC 8.00 3.00
❑ 226 Koren Robinson RC 8.00 3.00
❑ 227 Rod Gardner RC 8.00 3.00
❑ 228 Santana Moss RC 12.00 5.00
❑ 229 Freddie Mitchell RC 8.00 3.00
❑ 230 Reggie Wayne RC 15.00 6.00
❑ 231 Quincy Morgan RC 8.00 3.00
❑ 232 Chris Chambers RC 12.00 5.00
❑ 233 Steve Smith RC 20.00 10.00
❑ 234 Snoop Minnis RC 5.00 2.00
❑ 235 Justin McCareins RC 8.00 3.00
❑ 236 Onome Ojo RC 5.00 2.00
❑ 237 Damerien McCants RC 5.00 2.00
❑ 238 Mike McMahon RPS 3.00 1.25
❑ 239 Cedrick Wilson RC 8.00 3.00
❑ 240 Kevin Kasper RC 6.00 2.50
❑ 241 Chris Taylor RC 5.00 2.00
❑ 242 Ken-Yon Rambo RC 5.00 2.00
❑ 243 Richmond Flowers RC 5.00 2.00
❑ 244 Andre King RC 5.00 2.00
❑ 245 Boo Williams RC 5.00 2.00
❑ 246 Adrian Wilson RC 5.00 2.00
❑ 247 Cory Bird RC 8.00 3.00
❑ 248 Alex Bannister RC 5.00 2.00
❑ 249 Elvis Joseph RC 5.00 2.00
❑ 250 Chad Johnson RC 20.00 7.50
❑ 251 Robert Ferguson RC 8.00 3.00
❑ 252 David Martin RC 5.00 2.00
❑ 253 Quentin McCord RC 5.00 2.00
❑ 254 Todd Heap RC 8.00 3.00
❑ 255 Alge Crumpler RC 10.00 5.00
❑ 256 Nate Clements RC 8.00 3.00
❑ 257 Will Allen RC 5.00 2.00
❑ 258 Willie Middlebrooks RC 5.00 2.00
❑ 259 Fred Smoot RC 8.00 3.00
❑ 260 Andre Dyson RC 3.00 1.25
❑ 261 Gary Baxter RC 5.00 2.00
❑ 262 Jamar Fletcher RC 5.00 2.00
❑ 263 Ken Lucas RC 5.00 2.00
❑ 264 Tay Cody RC 3.00 1.25
❑ 265 Eric Kelly RC 3.00 1.25
❑ 266 Adam Archuleta RC 8.00 3.00
❑ 267 Derrick Gibson RC 5.00 2.00
❑ 268 Jarrod Cooper RC 8.00 3.00
❑ 269 Hakim Akbar RC 3.00 1.25
❑ 270 Tony Driver RC 5.00 2.00
❑ 271 Justin Smith RC 8.00 3.00
❑ 272 Andre Carter RC 8.00 3.00
❑ 273 Jamal Reynolds RC 8.00 3.00
❑ 274 Gerard Warren RC 8.00 3.00
❑ 275 Richard Seymour RC 8.00 3.00
❑ 276 Damione Lewis RC 5.00 2.00
❑ 277 Casey Hampton RC 5.00 2.00
❑ 278 Marcus Stroud RC 8.00 3.00
❑ 279 Benjamin Gay RC 6.00 2.50
❑ 280 Shaun Rogers RC 8.00 3.00
❑ 281 Dan Morgan RC 8.00 3.00
❑ 282 Kendrell Bell RC 12.00 5.00
❑ 283 Tommy Polley RC 8.00 3.00
❑ 284 Jamie Winborn RC 5.00 2.00
❑ 285 Sedrick Hodge RC 3.00 1.25
❑ 286 Torrance Marshall RC 8.00 3.00
❑ 287 Eric Westmoreland RC 5.00 2.00
❑ 288 Brian Allen RC 3.00 1.25
❑ 289 Brandon Spoon RC 8.00 3.00
❑ 290 Henry Burris RC 5.00 2.00
❑ 291 Leonard Davis RC 5.00 2.00
❑ 292 Kenyatta Walker RC 3.00 1.25
❑ 293 Cedric James RC 5.00 2.00
❑ 294 Sean Brewer RC 3.00 1.25
❑ 295 Jason Brookins RC 6.00 2.50
❑ 296 Kyle Vanden Bosch RC 8.00 3.00
❑ 297 Nick Goings RC 8.00 3.00
❑ 298 Kris Jenkins RC 8.00 3.00
❑ 299 Dominic Rhodes RC 12.00 6.00
❑ 300 Leonard Myers RC 3.00 1.25

2002 Leaf Rookies and Stars

❑ COMPLETE SET (300) 250.00 100.00
❑ COMP.SET w/o SP's (100) 25.00 10.00
❑ 1 Jake Plummer .50 .20
❑ 2 David Boston .75 .30
❑ 3 Thomas Jones .50 .20
❑ 4 Michael Vick 1.50 .60
❑ 5 Warrick Dunn .75 .30
❑ 6 Jamal Lewis .75 .30
❑ 7 Chris Redman .30 .10
❑ 8 Ray Lewis .75 .30
❑ 9 Drew Bledsoe 1.00 .40
❑ 10 Travis Henry .75 .30
❑ 11 Eric Moulds .50 .20
❑ 12 Steve Smith .75 .30
❑ 13 Chris Weinke .50 .20
❑ 14 Lamar Smith .50 .20
❑ 15 Anthony Thomas .50 .20
❑ 16 David Terrell .75 .30
❑ 17 Brian Urlacher 1.25 .50
❑ 18 Corey Dillon .50 .20
❑ 19 Michael Westbrook .50 .20
❑ 20 Peter Warrick .50 .20
❑ 21 Tim Couch .50 .20
❑ 22 James Jackson .50 .20
❑ 23 Kevin Johnson .50 .20
❑ 24 Quincy Carter .50 .20
❑ 25 Joey Galloway .50 .20
❑ 26 Emmitt Smith 2.00 .75
❑ 27 Terrell Davis .75 .30
❑ 28 Brian Griese .75 .30
❑ 29 Ed McCaffrey .75 .30
❑ 30 Rod Smith .50 .20
❑ 31 Mike McMahon .75 .30
❑ 32 Germane Crowell .30 .10
❑ 33 Az-Zahir Hakim .30 .10
❑ 34 Terry Glenn .50 .20
❑ 35 Brett Favre 2.00 .75
❑ 36 Ahman Green .75 .30
❑ 37 James Allen .50 .20
❑ 38 Corey Bradford .30 .10
❑ 39 Peyton Manning 1.50 .60
❑ 40 Edgerrin James 1.00 .40
❑ 41 Marvin Harrison .75 .30
❑ 42 Qadry Ismail .50 .20
❑ 43 Fred Taylor .75 .30
❑ 44 Mark Brunell .75 .30
❑ 45 Jimmy Smith .50 .20
❑ 46 Priest Holmes 1.00 .40
❑ 47 Tony Gonzalez .50 .20
❑ 48 Trent Green .50 .20
❑ 49 Johnnie Morton .50 .20
❑ 50 Chris Chambers .75 .30
❑ 51 Ricky Williams .75 .30
❑ 52 Zach Thomas .75 .30
❑ 53 Randy Moss 1.50 .60
❑ 54 Michael Bennett .50 .20
❑ 55 Derrick Alexander .50 .20
❑ 56 Daunte Culpepper .75 .30
❑ 57 Tom Brady 2.00 .75
❑ 58 Troy Brown .50 .20
❑ 59 Antowain Smith .50 .20
❑ 60 Joe Horn .50 .20
❑ 61 Aaron Brooks .75 .30
❑ 62 Deuce McAllister 1.00 .40
❑ 63 Kerry Collins .50 .20
❑ 64 Amani Toomer .50 .20
❑ 65 Michael Strahan .50 .20
❑ 66 Laveranues Coles .50 .20
❑ 67 Vinny Testaverde .50 .20
❑ 68 Curtis Martin .75 .30
❑ 69 Rich Gannon .75 .30
❑ 70 Tim Brown .75 .30
❑ 71 Jerry Rice 1.50 .60
❑ 72 Donovan McNabb 1.00 .40
❑ 73 Freddie Mitchell .50 .20
❑ 74 Duce Staley .75 .30
❑ 75 Kordell Stewart .50 .20
❑ 76 Jerome Bettis .75 .30
❑ 77 Plaxico Burress .50 .20
❑ 78 Drew Brees .75 .30
❑ 79 LaDainian Tomlinson 1.25 .50
❑ 80 Junior Seau .75 .30
❑ 81 Jeff Garcia .75 .30
❑ 82 Garrison Hearst .50 .20
❑ 83 Terrell Owens .75 .30
❑ 84 Shaun Alexander 1.00 .40
❑ 85 Koren Robinson .50 .20
❑ 86 Kurt Warner .75 .30
❑ 87 Marshall Faulk .75 .30
❑ 88 Isaac Bruce .75 .30
❑ 89 Torry Holt .75 .30
❑ 90 Rob Johnson .50 .20
❑ 91 Brad Johnson .50 .20
❑ 92 Keyshawn Johnson .75 .30
❑ 93 Mike Alstott .75 .30
❑ 94 Eddie George .75 .30
❑ 95 Steve McNair .75 .30
❑ 96 Derrick Mason .50 .20
❑ 97 Jevon Kearse .50 .20
❑ 98 Stephen Davis .50 .20
❑ 99 Sage Rosenfels .30 .10
❑ 100 Rod Gardner .50 .20
❑ 101 Adrian Peterson RC 6.00 2.50
❑ 102 Nick Rolovich RC 4.00 1.50
❑ 103 Lew Thomas RC 2.50 1.00
❑ 104 David Carr RC 10.00 4.00
❑ 105 Daryl Jones RC 4.00 1.50
❑ 106 Brandon Doman RC 4.00 1.50
❑ 107 Ed Reed RC 8.00 3.00
❑ 108 Tellis Redmon RC 4.00 1.50
❑ 109 Andra Davis RC 4.00 1.50
❑ 110 Kendall Newson RC 2.50 1.00
❑ 111 Joe Burns RC 4.00 1.50
❑ 112 Maurice Morris RC 5.00 2.00
❑ 113 Craig Nall RC 5.00 2.00
❑ 114 Phillip Buchanon RC 5.00 2.00
❑ 115 Mike Echols RC 2.50 1.00
❑ 116 Terry Jones Jr. RC 4.00 1.50
❑ 117 Anthony Weaver RC 4.00 1.50
❑ 118 Jeb Putzier RC 5.00 2.00
❑ 119 Tony Fisher RC 5.00 2.00
❑ 120 Joey Harrington RC 6.00 2.50
❑ 121 Lamar Gordon RC 5.00 2.00
❑ 122 Tracey Wistrom RC 4.00 1.50
❑ 123 Ashley Lelie RC 10.00 4.00
❑ 124 Will Witherspoon RC 5.00 2.00
❑ 125 Travis Stephens RC 4.00 1.50
❑ 126 J.T. O'Sullivan RC 4.00 1.50
❑ 127 Brian Westbrook RC 10.00 4.00
❑ 128 James Mungro RC 5.00 2.00
❑ 129 Lamont Thompson RC 4.00 1.50
❑ 130 Jarrod Baxter RC 4.00 1.50
❑ 131 Andre Lott RC 5.00 2.00
❑ 132 Steve Bellisari RC 4.00 1.50
❑ 133 David Garrard RC 10.00 4.00
❑ 134 Michael Lewis RC 5.00 2.00
❑ 135 James Allen RC 2.50 1.00
❑ 136 Bryant McKinnie RC 4.00 1.50
❑ 137 Marques Anderson RC 5.00 2.00
❑ 138 Rohan Davey RC 5.00 2.00
❑ 139 Kyle Johnson RC 2.50 1.00
❑ 140 Dusty Bonner RC 2.50 1.00
❑ 141 DeShaun Foster RC 5.00 2.00
❑ 142 Chad Hutchinson RC 4.00 1.50
❑ 143 Jack Brewer RC 4.00 1.50
❑ 144 Eddie Freeman RC 2.50 1.00
❑ 145 Seth Burford RC 4.00 1.50
❑ 146 Roosevelt Williams RC 2.50 1.00
❑ 147 Jamin Elliott RC 2.50 1.00
❑ 148 Charles Grant RC 5.00 2.00
❑ 149 Jeff Kelly RC 4.00 1.50
❑ 150 Cliff Russell RC 4.00 1.50
❑ 151 Josh Scobey RC 5.00 2.00
❑ 152 Tank Williams RC 4.00 1.50
❑ 153 Larry Tripplett RC 2.50 1.00

❑ 154 Clinton Portis RC	15.00	6.00
❑ 155 Javin Hunter RC	2.50	1.00
❑ 156 Deveren Johnson RC	4.00	1.50
❑ 157 Reche Caldwell RC	5.00	2.00
❑ 158 Ronald Curry RC	5.00	2.00
❑ 159 Chris Hope RC	5.00	2.00
❑ 160 Damien Anderson RC	4.00	1.50
❑ 161 Saleem Rasheed RC	5.00	2.00
❑ 162 Albert Haynesworth RC	4.00	1.50
❑ 163 Bryan Gilmore RC	4.00	1.50
❑ 164 Wes Pate RC	2.50	1.00
❑ 165 Deion Branch RC	8.00	3.00
❑ 166 Ben Leber RC	5.00	2.00
❑ 167 Andre Davis RC	4.00	1.50
❑ 168 Darrell Hill RC	4.00	1.50
❑ 169 Rodney Wright RC	2.50	1.00
❑ 170 Demontray Carter RC	2.50	1.00
❑ 171 Zak Kustok RC	5.00	2.00
❑ 172 James Wofford RC	4.00	1.50
❑ 173 David Priestley RC	4.00	1.50
❑ 174 Donte Stallworth RC	8.00	3.00
❑ 175 Marc Boerigter RC	8.00	3.00
❑ 176 Freddie Milons RC	4.00	1.50
❑ 177 John Simon RC	4.00	1.50
❑ 178 Josh Norman RC	5.00	2.00
❑ 179 Jabar Gaffney RC	5.00	2.00
❑ 180 Doug Jolley RC	5.00	2.00
❑ 181 Preston Parsons RC	2.50	1.00
❑ 182 Chris Baker RC	4.00	1.50
❑ 183 Javon Walker RC	8.00	3.00
❑ 184 Justin Peelle RC	2.50	1.00
❑ 185 Josh Reed RC	5.00	2.00
❑ 186 Omar Easy RC	5.00	2.00
❑ 187 Jerramy Stevens RC	5.00	2.00
❑ 188 Shaun Hill RC	5.00	2.00
❑ 189 David Thornton RC	2.50	1.00
❑ 190 John Henderson RC	5.00	2.00
❑ 191 Verron Haynes RC	5.00	2.00
❑ 192 Dennis Johnson RC	2.50	1.00
❑ 193 Napoleon Harris RC	5.00	2.00
❑ 194 Jonathan Wells RC	5.00	2.00
❑ 195 Howard Green RC	2.50	1.00
❑ 196 Travis Fisher RC	5.00	2.00
❑ 197 Anton Palepoi RC	2.50	1.00
❑ 198 Ed Stansbury RC	2.50	1.00
❑ 199 Josh McCown RC	6.00	2.50
❑ 200 Alex Brown RC	5.00	2.00
❑ 201 Joseph Jefferson RC	4.00	1.50
❑ 202 Julius Peppers RC	10.00	4.00
❑ 203 Larry Ned RC	4.00	1.50
❑ 204 Rock Cartwright RC	6.00	2.50
❑ 205 Kalimba Edwards RC	5.00	2.00
❑ 206 Matt Schobel RC	4.00	1.50
❑ 207 Maurice Jackson RC	2.50	1.00
❑ 208 Kelly Campbell RC	4.00	1.50
❑ 209 Mel Mitchell RC	4.00	1.50
❑ 210 Ken Simonton RC	2.50	1.00
❑ 211 Brian Allen RC	4.00	1.50
❑ 212 Darnell Sanders RC	4.00	1.50
❑ 213 Jesse Chatman RC	5.00	2.00
❑ 214 Keyuo Craver RC	4.00	1.50
❑ 215 Chester Taylor RC	10.00	4.00
❑ 216 Kurt Kittner RC	4.00	1.50
❑ 217 Derek Ross RC	4.00	1.50
❑ 218 Charles Hill RC	2.50	1.00
❑ 219 Jarvis Green RC	4.00	1.50
❑ 220 Mike Jenkins RC	2.50	1.00
❑ 221 Robert Royal RC	5.00	2.00
❑ 222 Ladell Betts RC	5.00	2.00
❑ 223 Antwoine Womack RC	4.00	1.50
❑ 224 Raonall Smith RC	4.00	1.50
❑ 225 Charles Stackhouse RC	4.00	1.50
❑ 226 Quinn Gray RC	2.50	1.00
❑ 227 Lito Sheppard RC	5.00	2.00
❑ 228 Ryan Van Dyke RC	5.00	2.00
❑ 229 Will Overstreet RC	2.50	1.00
❑ 230 Leonard Henry RC	4.00	1.50
❑ 231 Dorsett Davis RC	2.50	1.00
❑ 232 Marquand Manuel RC	2.50	1.00
❑ 233 Luke Staley RC	4.00	1.50
❑ 234 Carlos Hall RC	5.00	2.00
❑ 235 Marcus Brady RC	4.00	1.50
❑ 236 Ryan Denney RC	4.00	1.50
❑ 237 Eric McCoo RC	2.50	1.00
❑ 238 Major Applewhite RC	5.00	2.00
❑ 239 Adam Tate RC	2.50	1.00
❑ 240 Marquise Walker RC	4.00	1.50
❑ 241 John Flowers RC	2.50	1.00
❑ 242 Levar Fisher RC	2.50	1.00
❑ 243 Ricky Williams RC	4.00	1.50
❑ 244 Mike Rumph RC	5.00	2.00
❑ 245 Delvin Joyce RC	4.00	1.50
❑ 246 Bryan Thomas RC	4.00	1.50
❑ 247 Mike Williams RC	4.00	1.50
❑ 248 Sam Brandon RC	4.00	1.50
❑ 249 Eddie Drummond RC	4.00	1.50
❑ 250 Najeh Davenport RC	5.00	2.00
❑ 251 Brian Williams RC	2.50	1.00
❑ 252 Scott Fujita RC	5.00	2.00
❑ 253 Dwight Freeney RC	8.00	3.00
❑ 254 Herb Haygood RC	2.50	1.00
❑ 255 Patrick Ramsey RC	5.00	2.00
❑ 256 Atnaf Harris RC	2.50	1.00
❑ 257 Jason McAddley RC	4.00	1.50
❑ 258 Pete Rebstock RC	2.50	1.00
❑ 259 Quentin Jammer RC	5.00	2.00
❑ 260 Luke Butkus RC	2.50	1.00
❑ 261 Jeremy Allen RC	2.50	1.00
❑ 262 Jake Schifino RC	4.00	1.50
❑ 263 Randy Fasani RC	4.00	1.50
❑ 264 Bryan Fletcher RC	2.50	1.00
❑ 265 Jeremy Shockey RC	15.00	6.00
❑ 266 Kevin Bentley RC	2.50	1.00
❑ 267 Jon McGraw RC	2.50	1.00
❑ 268 Robert Thomas RC	5.00	2.00
❑ 269 Coy Wire RC	5.00	2.00
❑ 270 Brian Poli-Dixon RC	4.00	1.50
❑ 271 Willie Offord RC	4.00	1.50
❑ 272 Rocky Calmus RC	5.00	2.00
❑ 273 Sheldon Brown RC	5.00	2.00
❑ 274 Terry Charles RC	4.00	1.50
❑ 275 Ron Johnson RC	4.00	1.50
❑ 276 Roy Williams RC	10.00	4.00
❑ 277 Sam Simmons RC	2.50	1.00
❑ 278 Andre Goodman RC	5.00	2.00
❑ 279 Ryan Sims RC	5.00	2.00
❑ 280 Antwaan Randle El RC	6.00	2.50
❑ 281 Alan Harper RC	2.50	1.00
❑ 282 Tavon Mason RC	2.50	1.00
❑ 283 Kahlil Hill RC	4.00	1.50
❑ 284 Antonio Bryant RC	5.00	2.00
❑ 285 Akin Ayodele RC	2.50	1.00
❑ 286 T.J. Duckett RC	5.00	2.00
❑ 287 Kenyon Coleman RC	2.50	1.00
❑ 288 Tim Carter RC	4.00	1.50
❑ 289 Lamont Brightful RC	2.50	1.00
❑ 290 Trev Faulk RC	2.50	1.00
❑ 291 Randy McMichael RC	8.00	3.00
❑ 292 Daniel Graham RC	5.00	2.00
❑ 293 Wendell Bryant RC	2.50	1.00
❑ 294 Jamar Martin RC	4.00	1.50
❑ 295 Chris Luzar RC	4.00	1.50
❑ 296 William Green RC	5.00	2.00
❑ 297 Lee Mays RC	4.00	1.50
❑ 298 Eric Crouch RC	5.00	2.00
❑ 299 Steve Smith RC	2.50	1.00
❑ 300 Woody Dantzler RC	4.00	1.50

2003 Leaf Rookies and Stars

❑ COMP.SET w/o SP's (100)	20.00	7.50
❑ 1 Emmitt Smith	2.00	.75
❑ 2 Michael Vick	2.00	.75
❑ 3 Peerless Price	.50	.20
❑ 4 T.J. Duckett	.50	.20
❑ 5 Warrick Dunn	.50	.20
❑ 6 Jamal Lewis	.75	.30
❑ 7 Ray Lewis	.75	.30
❑ 8 Drew Bledsoe	.75	.30
❑ 9 Eric Moulds	.50	.20
❑ 10 Josh Reed	.50	.20
❑ 11 Travis Henry	.50	.20
❑ 12 Julius Peppers	.75	.30
❑ 13 Anthony Thomas	.50	.20
❑ 14 Brian Urlacher	1.25	.50
❑ 15 Marty Booker	.50	.20
❑ 16 Kordell Stewart	.50	.20
❑ 17 Corey Dillon	.50	.20
❑ 18 Chad Johnson	.75	.30
❑ 19 Tim Couch	.30	.10
❑ 20 William Green	.50	.20
❑ 21 Antonio Bryant	.50	.20
❑ 22 Roy Williams	.75	.30
❑ 23 Ashley Lelie	.75	.30
❑ 24 Clinton Portis	1.25	.50
❑ 25 Ed McCaffrey	.75	.30
❑ 26 Jake Plummer	.50	.20
❑ 27 Rod Smith	.50	.20
❑ 28 Joey Harrington	1.25	.50
❑ 29 Ahman Green	.75	.30
❑ 30 Brett Favre	2.00	.75
❑ 31 Donald Driver	.50	.20
❑ 32 Javon Walker	.50	.20
❑ 33 David Carr	1.25	.50
❑ 34 Edgerrin James	.75	.30
❑ 35 Marvin Harrison	.75	.30
❑ 36 Peyton Manning	1.25	.50
❑ 37 Fred Taylor	.75	.30
❑ 38 Jimmy Smith	.50	.20
❑ 39 Mark Brunell	.50	.20
❑ 40 Priest Holmes	1.25	.50
❑ 41 Tony Gonzalez	.50	.20
❑ 42 Trent Green	.50	.20
❑ 43 Chris Chambers	.75	.30
❑ 44 Jay Fiedler	.50	.20
❑ 45 Junior Seau	.75	.30
❑ 46 Ricky Williams	.75	.30
❑ 47 Zach Thomas	.75	.30
❑ 48 Daunte Culpepper	.75	.30
❑ 49 Michael Bennett	.50	.20
❑ 50 Randy Moss	1.25	.50
❑ 51 Tom Brady	2.00	.75
❑ 52 Troy Brown	.50	.20
❑ 53 Aaron Brooks	.75	.30
❑ 54 Deuce McAllister	.75	.30
❑ 55 Donte Stallworth	.75	.30
❑ 56 Joe Horn	.50	.20
❑ 57 Jeremy Shockey	1.25	.50
❑ 58 Kerry Collins	.50	.20
❑ 59 Michael Strahan	.50	.20
❑ 60 Tiki Barber	.75	.30
❑ 61 Chad Pennington	1.00	.40
❑ 62 Curtis Martin	.75	.30
❑ 63 Santana Moss	.50	.20
❑ 64 Charles Woodson	.50	.20
❑ 65 Jerry Rice	1.50	.60
❑ 66 Rich Gannon	.50	.20
❑ 67 Tim Brown	.75	.30
❑ 68 Donovan McNabb	1.00	.40
❑ 69 Antwaan Randle El	.75	.30
❑ 70 Tommy Maddox	.75	.30
❑ 71 Jerome Bettis	.75	.30
❑ 72 Kendrell Bell	.50	.20
❑ 73 Plaxico Burress	.50	.20
❑ 74 David Boston	.50	.20
❑ 75 Drew Brees	.75	.30
❑ 76 LaDainian Tomlinson	.75	.30
❑ 77 Kevan Barlow	.50	.20
❑ 78 Jeff Garcia	.75	.30
❑ 79 Terrell Owens	.75	.30
❑ 80 Matt Hasselbeck	.50	.20
❑ 81 Koren Robinson	.50	.20
❑ 82 Shaun Alexander	.75	.30
❑ 83 Isaac Bruce	.75	.30
❑ 84 Kurt Warner	.75	.30
❑ 85 Marshall Faulk	.75	.30
❑ 86 Torry Holt	.75	.30
❑ 87 Brad Johnson	.50	.20
❑ 88 Keyshawn Johnson	.75	.30
❑ 89 Mike Alstott	.75	.30
❑ 90 Warren Sapp	.50	.20
❑ 91 Eddie George	.50	.20
❑ 92 Jevon Kearse	.50	.20
❑ 93 Steve McNair	.75	.30
❑ 94 Laveranues Coles	.50	.20
❑ 95 Rod Gardner	.50	.20
❑ 96 Patrick Ramsey	.75	.30
❑ 97 Boller/Suggs/Smith CL	.75	.30
❑ 98 R.Grossman/T.Jacobs CL	1.00	.40

❑ 99 A.Boldin/B.Johnson CL .75 .30
❑ 100 T.Calico/C.Brown CL .75 .30
❑ 101 Charles Tillman RC 5.00 2.00
❑ 102 Justin Griffith RC 3.00 1.25
❑ 103 Ovie Mughelli RC 2.00 .75
❑ 104 Chris Edmonds RC 2.00 .75
❑ 105 Jeremi Johnson RC 3.00 1.25
❑ 106 Malaefou MacKenzie RC 2.00 .75
❑ 107 James Lynch RC 3.00 1.25
❑ 108 B.J. Askew RC 4.00 1.50
❑ 109 Andrew Pinnock RC 3.00 1.25
❑ 110 Chris Davis RC 3.00 1.25
❑ 111 Dan Curley RC 2.00 .75
❑ 112 Lenny Walls RC 3.00 1.25
❑ 113 Travis Fisher RC 2.00 .75
❑ 114 Ahmaad Galloway RC 3.00 1.25
❑ 115 Joe Smith RC 4.00 1.50
❑ 116 Reno Mahe RC 4.00 1.50
❑ 117 Torrie Cox RC 3.00 1.25
❑ 118 Kerry Carter RC 3.00 1.25
❑ 119 Dwone Hicks RC 2.00 .75
❑ 120 Cato June RC 5.00 2.00
❑ 121 Terry Pierce RC 3.00 1.25
❑ 122 Eddie Moore RC 3.00 1.25
❑ 123 Mike Seidman RC 2.00 .75
❑ 124 Michael Nattiel RC 4.00 1.50
❑ 125 Casey Fitzsimmons RC 4.00 1.50
❑ 126 George Wrighster RC 3.00 1.25
❑ 127 Mike Pinkard RC 2.00 .75
❑ 128 Donald Lee RC 3.00 1.25
❑ 129 Sean Berton RC 2.00 .75
❑ 130 Soloman Bates RC 2.00 .75
❑ 131 Zach Hilton RC 3.00 1.25
❑ 132 Antonio Gates RC 30.00 15.00
❑ 133 Aaron Walker RC 3.00 1.25
❑ 134 Richard Angulo RC 3.00 1.25
❑ 135 Will Heller RC 3.00 1.25
❑ 136 Theo Sanders RC 2.00 .75
❑ 137 Jimmy Farris RC 3.00 1.25
❑ 138 Ryan Nece RC 4.00 1.50
❑ 139 Antonio Brown RC 2.00 .75
❑ 140 Clarence Coleman RC 2.00 .75
❑ 141 Lawrence Hamilton RC 2.00 .75
❑ 142 C.J. Jones RC 2.00 .75
❑ 143 Frisman Jackson RC 4.00 1.50
❑ 144 Antonio Chatman RC 4.00 1.50
❑ 145 Rocky Boiman RC 3.00 1.25
❑ 146 Tron LaFavor RC 2.00 .75
❑ 147 Derick Armstrong RC 4.00 1.50
❑ 148 J.J. Moses RC 3.00 1.25
❑ 149 Aaron Moorehead RC 4.00 1.50
❑ 150 Brad Pyatt RC 3.00 1.25
❑ 151 Arland Bruce RC 2.00 .75
❑ 152 Chris Horn RC 2.00 .75
❑ 153 Kareem Kelly RC 3.00 1.25
❑ 154 Talman Gardner RC 4.00 1.50
❑ 155 David Tyree RC 3.00 1.25
❑ 156 Willie Ponder RC 2.00 .75
❑ 157 Greg Lewis RC 8.00 3.00
❑ 158 Eric Parker RC 4.00 1.50
❑ 159 Kassim Osgood RC 4.00 1.50
❑ 160 Jason Willis RC 2.00 .75
❑ 161 Akbar Gbaja-Biamila RC 4.00 1.50
❑ 162 Mike Furrey RC 15.00 6.00
❑ 163 Chris Kelsay RC 4.00 1.50
❑ 164 Cory Redding RC 3.00 1.25
❑ 165 Kenny Peterson RC 3.00 1.25
❑ 166 Osi Umenyiora RC 6.00 2.50
❑ 167 Tyler Brayton RC 4.00 1.50
❑ 168 DeWayne White RC 3.00 1.25
❑ 169 Kevin Williams RC 4.00 1.50
❑ 170 Dan Klecko RC 6.00 2.50
❑ 171 Johnathan Sullivan RC 3.00 1.25
❑ 172 William Joseph RC 4.00 1.50
❑ 173 Rien Long RC 2.00 .75
❑ 174 Angelo Crowell RC 3.00 1.25
❑ 175 Chaun Thompson RC 2.00 .75
❑ 176 Bradie James RC 4.00 1.50
❑ 177 Antwan Peek RC 3.00 1.25
❑ 178 Kawika Mitchell RC 3.00 1.25
❑ 179 Cie Grant RC 4.00 1.50
❑ 180 E.J. Henderson RC 4.00 1.50
❑ 181 Victor Hobson RC 4.00 1.50
❑ 182 Alonzo Jackson RC 3.00 1.25
❑ 183 Matt Wilhelm RC 4.00 1.50
❑ 184 Pisa Tinoisamoa RC 4.00 1.50
❑ 185 Ricky Manning RC 4.00 1.50
❑ 186 Dennis Weathersby RC 2.00 .75
❑ 187 Donald Strickland RC 2.00 .75
❑ 188 Asante Samuel RC 10.00 4.00
❑ 189 Eugene Wilson RC 4.00 1.50
❑ 190 Nnamdi Asomugha RC 3.00 1.25
❑ 191 Ike Taylor RC 8.00 3.00
❑ 192 Drayton Florence RC 2.00 .75
❑ 193 DeJuan Groce RC 4.00 1.50
❑ 194 Shane Walton RC 2.00 .75
❑ 195 Terrence Holt RC 3.00 1.25
❑ 196 Rashean Mathis RC 3.00 1.25
❑ 197 Julian Battle RC 3.00 1.25
❑ 198 Hanik Milligan RC 3.00 1.25
❑ 199 Terrence Kiel RC 4.00 1.50
❑ 200 David Kircus RC 4.00 1.50
❑ 201 Lee Suggs RC 6.00 2.50
❑ 202 Charles Rogers RC 6.00 2.50
❑ 203 Brandon Lloyd RC 6.00 2.50
❑ 204 Terrence Edwards RC 5.00 2.00
❑ 205 Tony Romo RC 60.00 35.00
❑ 206 Brooks Bollinger RC 6.00 2.50
❑ 207 Jerome McDougle RC 6.00 2.50
❑ 208 Jimmy Kennedy RC 6.00 2.50
❑ 209 Ken Dorsey RC 6.00 2.50
❑ 210 Kirk Farmer RC 3.00 1.25
❑ 211 Mike Doss RC 6.00 2.50
❑ 212 Chris Simms RC 10.00 4.00
❑ 213 Cecil Sapp RC 5.00 2.00
❑ 214 Justin Gage RC 6.00 2.50
❑ 215 Sam Aiken RC 5.00 2.00
❑ 216 Doug Gabriel RC 6.00 2.50
❑ 217 Jason Witten RC 12.00 5.00
❑ 218 Bennie Joppru RC 6.00 2.50
❑ 219 Jason Gesser RC 6.00 2.50
❑ 220 Brock Forsey RC 6.00 2.50
❑ 221 Quentin Griffin RC 6.00 2.50
❑ 222 Avon Cobourne RC 3.00 1.25
❑ 223 Domanick Davis RC 6.00 2.50
❑ 224 Boss Bailey RC 6.00 2.50
❑ 225 Tony Hollings RC 6.00 2.50
❑ 226 LaBrandon Toefield RC 6.00 2.50
❑ 227 Arlen Harris RC 6.00 2.50
❑ 228 Sultan McCullough RC 5.00 2.00
❑ 229 Visanthe Shiancoe RC 5.00 2.00
❑ 230 L.J. Smith RC 6.00 2.50
❑ 231 LaTarence Dunbar RC 5.00 2.00
❑ 232 Walter Young RC 3.00 1.25
❑ 233 Bobby Wade RC 6.00 2.50
❑ 234 Zuriel Smith RC 3.00 1.25
❑ 235 Adrian Madise RC 5.00 2.00
❑ 236 Ken Hamlin RC 6.00 2.50
❑ 237 Carl Ford RC 3.00 1.25
❑ 238 Cortez Hankton RC 5.00 2.00
❑ 239 J.R. Tolver RC 5.00 2.00
❑ 240 Keenan Howry RC 6.00 2.50
❑ 241 Billy McMullen RC 5.00 2.00
❑ 242 Arnaz Battle RC 6.00 2.50
❑ 243 Shaun McDonald RC 6.00 2.50
❑ 244 Andre Woolfolk RC 6.00 2.50
❑ 245 Sammy Davis RC 6.00 2.50
❑ 246 Calvin Pace RC 5.00 2.00
❑ 247 Michael Haynes RC 6.00 2.50
❑ 248 Ty Warren RC 6.00 2.50
❑ 249 Nick Barnett RC 6.00 2.50
❑ 250 Troy Polamalu RC 30.00 15.00
❑ 251 Carson Palmer JSY RC 30.00 12.50
❑ 252 Byron Leftwich JSY RC 25.00 10.00
❑ 253 Kyle Boller JSY RC 6.00 2.50
❑ 254 Rex Grossman JSY RC 25.00 10.00
❑ 255 Dave Ragone JSY RC 6.00 2.50
❑ 256 Brian St.Pierre JSY RC 6.00 2.50
❑ 257 Kliff Kingsbury JSY RC 6.00 2.50
❑ 258 Seneca Wallace JSY RC 6.00 2.50
❑ 259 Larry Johnson JSY RC 30.00 15.00
❑ 260 Willis McGahee JSY RC 15.00 6.00
❑ 261 Justin Fargas JSY RC 6.00 2.50
❑ 262 Onterrio Smith JSY RC 6.00 2.50
❑ 263 Chris Brown JSY RC 6.00 2.50
❑ 264 Musa Smith JSY RC 6.00 2.50
❑ 265 Artose Pinner JSY RC 6.00 2.50
❑ 266 Andre Johnson JSY RC 15.00 6.00
❑ 267 Kelley Washington JSY RC 8.00 3.00
❑ 268 Taylor Jacobs JSY RC 6.00 2.50
❑ 269 Bryant Johnson JSY RC 6.00 2.50
❑ 270 Tyrone Calico JSY RC 10.00 4.00
❑ 271 Anquan Boldin JSY RC 20.00 7.50
❑ 272 Bethel Johnson JSY RC 6.00 2.50
❑ 273 Nate Burleson JSY RC 6.00 2.50
❑ 274 Kevin Curtis JSY RC 8.00 3.00
❑ 275 Dallas Clark JSY RC 6.00 2.50
❑ 276 Teyo Johnson JSY RC 6.00 2.50
❑ 277 Terrell Suggs JSY RC 10.00 4.00
❑ 278 DeWayne Robertson JSY RC 6.00 2.50
❑ 279 Terence Newman JSY RC 12.00 5.00
❑ 280 Marcus Trufant JSY RC 6.00 2.50
❑ 281 C.Palmer/B.Leftwich JSY 30.00 12.50
❑ 282 K.Boller/D.Ragone JSY 6.00 2.50
❑ 283 R.Grossman/B.St.Pierre JSY 25.00 10.00
❑ 284 K.Kingsbury/S.Wallace JSY 10.00 4.00
❑ 285 L.Johnson/W.McGahee JSY 30.00 12.50
❑ 286 J.Fargas/O.Smith JSY 10.00 4.00
❑ 287 C.Brown/M.Smith JSY 6.00 2.50
❑ 288 A.Pinner/A.Johnson JSY 15.00 6.00
❑ 289 K.Washington/T.Jacobs JSY 10.00 4.00
❑ 290 B.Johnson/T.Calico JSY 12.00 5.00
❑ 291 A.Boldin/B.Johnson JSY 25.00 10.00
❑ 292 N.Burleson/K.Curtis JSY 8.00 3.00
❑ 293 D.Clark/T.Johnson JSY 10.00 4.00
❑ 294 T.Suggs/D.Robertson JSY 10.00 4.00
❑ 295 T.Newman/M.Trufant JSY 12.00 5.00

2004 Leaf Rookies and Stars

❑ COMP.SET w/o SP's (200) 60.00 30.00
❑ COMP.SET w/o RC's (100) 20.00 7.50
❑ 251-283 JSY PRINT RUN 750 SER.#'d SETS
❑ 284-299 PRINT RUN 500 SER.#'d SETS
❑ 1 Anquan Boldin .75 .30
❑ 2 Emmitt Smith 1.50 .60
❑ 3 Josh McCown .50 .20
❑ 4 Michael Vick 1.50 .60
❑ 5 Peerless Price .50 .20
❑ 6 T.J. Duckett .50 .20
❑ 7 Warrick Dunn .50 .20
❑ 8 Jamal Lewis .75 .30
❑ 9 Kyle Boller .75 .30
❑ 10 Ray Lewis .75 .30
❑ 11 Drew Bledsoe .75 .30
❑ 12 Eric Moulds .50 .20
❑ 13 Travis Henry .50 .20
❑ 14 Jake Delhomme .75 .30
❑ 15 Stephen Davis .50 .20
❑ 16 Steve Smith .75 .30
❑ 17 Brian Urlacher 1.00 .40
❑ 18 Rex Grossman .75 .30
❑ 19 Thomas Jones .50 .20
❑ 20 Carson Palmer 1.00 .40
❑ 21 Chad Johnson .75 .30
❑ 22 Rudi Johnson .50 .20
❑ 23 Jeff Garcia .75 .30
❑ 24 William Green .50 .20
❑ 25 Keyshawn Johnson .50 .20
❑ 26 Terence Newman .50 .20
❑ 27 Roy Williams S .50 .20
❑ 28 Jake Plummer .50 .20
❑ 29 Quentin Griffin .75 .30
❑ 30 Rod Smith .50 .20
❑ 31 Charles Rogers .50 .20
❑ 32 Joey Harrington .75 .30
❑ 33 Ahman Green .75 .30
❑ 34 Brett Favre 2.00 .75
❑ 35 Javon Walker .50 .20
❑ 36 Andre Johnson .75 .30
❑ 37 David Carr .75 .30
❑ 38 Domanick Davis .75 .30
❑ 39 Edgerrin James .75 .30
❑ 40 Marvin Harrison .75 .30
❑ 41 Peyton Manning 1.25 .50
❑ 42 Byron Leftwich 1.00 .40
❑ 43 Fred Taylor .50 .20
❑ 44 Jimmy Smith .50 .20
❑ 45 Priest Holmes 1.00 .40

❑ 46 Tony Gonzalez .50 .20
❑ 47 Trent Green .50 .20
❑ 48 A.J. Feeley .75 .30
❑ 49 Chris Chambers .50 .20
❑ 50 Deion Sanders 1.00 .40
❑ 51 Daunte Culpepper .75 .30
❑ 52 Michael Bennett .50 .20
❑ 53 Randy Moss 1.00 .40
❑ 54 Corey Dillon .50 .20
❑ 55 Deion Branch .75 .30
❑ 56 Tom Brady 2.00 .75
❑ 57 Aaron Brooks .50 .20
❑ 58 Deuce McAllister .75 .30
❑ 59 Joe Horn .50 .20
❑ 60 Jeremy Shockey .75 .30
❑ 61 Michael Strahan .50 .20
❑ 62 Tiki Barber .75 .30
❑ 63 Chad Pennington .75 .30
❑ 64 Curtis Martin .75 .30
❑ 65 Santana Moss .50 .20
❑ 66 Jerry Porter .50 .20
❑ 67 Jerry Rice 1.50 .60
❑ 68 Warren Sapp .50 .20
❑ 69 Donovan McNabb 1.00 .40
❑ 70 Jevon Kearse .50 .20
❑ 71 Terrell Owens .75 .30
❑ 72 Duce Staley .50 .20
❑ 73 Hines Ward .75 .30
❑ 74 Jerome Bettis .75 .30
❑ 75 LaDainian Tomlinson 1.00 .40
❑ 76 Kevan Barlow .50 .20
❑ 77 Tim Rattay .50 .20
❑ 78 Koren Robinson .50 .20
❑ 79 Matt Hasselbeck .50 .20
❑ 80 Shaun Alexander .75 .30
❑ 81 Isaac Bruce .50 .20
❑ 82 Marc Bulger .75 .30
❑ 83 Marshall Faulk .75 .30
❑ 84 Torry Holt .75 .30
❑ 85 Brad Johnson .50 .20
❑ 86 Derrick Brooks .50 .20
❑ 87 Chris Brown .75 .30
❑ 88 Derrick Mason .50 .20
❑ 89 Eddie George .50 .20
❑ 90 Steve McNair .75 .30
❑ 91 Clinton Portis .75 .30
❑ 92 LaVar Arrington 1.50 .60
❑ 93 Laveranues Coles .50 .20
❑ 94 Mark Brunell .50 .20
❑ 95 Hall/Schaub/Jenkins CL .75 .30
❑ 96 Losman/L.Evans CL 1.00 .40
❑ 97 Winslow Jr./L.McCown CL 1.50 .60
❑ 98 D.Watts/T.Bell CL .75 .30
❑ 99 K.Jones/Ro.Will. CL 1.25 .50
❑ 100 G.Jones/Re.Will. CL .75 .30
❑ 101 Darnell Dockett RC 3.00 1.25
❑ 102 Karlos Dansby RC 4.00 1.50
❑ 103 Larry Croom RC 3.00 1.25
❑ 104 Chad Lavalais RC 3.00 1.25
❑ 105 Demorrio Williams RC 4.00 1.50
❑ 106 B.J. Sams RC 4.00 1.50
❑ 107 Dwan Edwards RC 2.00 .75
❑ 108 Jason Peters RC 4.00 1.50
❑ 109 Shaud Williams RC 3.00 1.25
❑ 110 Tim Anderson RC 4.00 1.50
❑ 111 Tim Euhus RC 4.00 1.50
❑ 112 Michael Gaines RC 3.00 1.25
❑ 113 Rod Rutherford RC 3.00 1.25
❑ 114 Leon Joe RC 2.00 .75
❑ 115 Nathan Vasher RC 5.00 2.00
❑ 116 Caleb Miller RC 3.00 1.25
❑ 117 Jamall Broussard RC 2.00 .75
❑ 118 Keiwan Ratliff RC 3.00 1.25
❑ 119 Landon Johnson RC 3.00 1.25
❑ 120 Madieu Williams RC 3.00 1.25
❑ 121 Matthias Askew RC 3.00 1.25
❑ 122 Robert Geathers RC 3.00 1.25
❑ 123 Richard Alston RC 3.00 1.25
❑ 124 Bruce Thornton RC 2.00 .75
❑ 125 Patrick Crayton RC 4.00 1.50
❑ 126 Bradlee Van Pelt RC 6.00 2.50
❑ 127 Charlie Adams RC 2.00 .75
❑ 128 Nate Jackson RC 2.00 .75
❑ 129 Roc Alexander RC 2.00 .75
❑ 130 Romar Crenshaw RC 2.00 .75
❑ 131 Keith Smith RC 3.00 1.25
❑ 132 Joey Thomas RC 4.00 1.50
❑ 133 Kelvin Kight RC 2.00 .75
❑ 134 Scott McBrien RC 4.00 1.50
❑ 135 Andrae Thurman RC 2.00 .75
❑ 136 Derick Armstrong 3.00 1.25
❑ 137 Glenn Earl RC 3.00 1.25
❑ 138 Kendrick Starling RC 2.00 .75
❑ 139 Ben Hartsock RC 4.00 1.50
❑ 140 Gilbert Gardner RC 3.00 1.25
❑ 141 Jason David RC 4.00 1.50
❑ 142 Daryl Smith RC 4.00 1.50
❑ 143 Jared Allen RC 4.00 1.50
❑ 144 Jeris McIntyre RC 3.00 1.25
❑ 145 John Booth RC 3.00 1.25
❑ 146 Jonathan Smith RC 3.00 1.25
❑ 147 Junior Siavii RC 4.00 1.50
❑ 148 Keyaron Fox RC 3.00 1.25
❑ 149 Kris Wilson RC 4.00 1.50
❑ 150 Doug Easlick RC 3.00 1.25
❑ 151 Fred Russell RC 4.00 1.50
❑ 152 Tony Bua RC 3.00 1.25
❑ 153 Will Poole RC 4.00 1.50
❑ 154 Ben Nelson RC 2.00 .75
❑ 155 Brook Lognar RC 10.00 4.00
❑ 156 Butchie Wallace RC 3.00 1.25
❑ 157 Darrion Scott RC 4.00 1.50
❑ 158 Dontarrious Thomas RC 4.00 1.50
❑ 159 Richard Owens RC 2.00 .75
❑ 160 Rod Davis RC 2.00 .75
❑ 161 Dexter Reid RC 2.00 .75
❑ 162 Kory Chapman RC 3.00 1.25
❑ 163 Marquise Hill RC 3.00 1.25
❑ 164 Courtney Watson RC 4.00 1.50
❑ 165 Mike Karney RC 3.00 1.25
❑ 166 Gibril Wilson RC 4.00 1.50
❑ 167 Reggie Torbor RC 3.00 1.25
❑ 168 Darrell McClover RC 3.00 1.25
❑ 169 Derrick Strait RC 4.00 1.50
❑ 170 Erik Coleman RC 4.00 1.50
❑ 171 Johnathan Reese RC 2.00 .75
❑ 172 Rashad Washington RC 3.00 1.25
❑ 173 Courtney Anderson RC 3.00 1.25
❑ 174 Stuart Schweigert RC 4.00 1.50
❑ 175 J.R. Reed RC 3.00 1.25
❑ 176 Justin Jenkins RC 3.00 1.25
❑ 177 Matt Ware RC 4.00 1.50
❑ 178 Nate Lawrie RC 3.00 1.25
❑ 179 Thomas Tapeh RC 3.00 1.25
❑ 180 Matt Kranchick RC 4.00 1.50
❑ 181 Willie Parker RC 25.00 12.50
❑ 182 Igor Olshansky RC 4.00 1.50
❑ 183 Ryan Krause RC 3.00 1.25
❑ 184 Shaun Phillips RC 3.00 1.25
❑ 185 Wes Welker RC 12.00 6.00
❑ 186 Richard Seigler RC 3.00 1.25
❑ 187 Shawntae Spencer RC 4.00 1.50
❑ 188 Marcus Tubbs RC 4.00 1.50
❑ 189 Niko Koutouvides RC 3.00 1.25
❑ 190 Brandon Chillar RC 3.00 1.25
❑ 191 Tony Hargrove RC 3.00 1.25
❑ 192 Mark Jones RC 3.00 1.25
❑ 193 Marquis Cooper RC 3.00 1.25
❑ 194 Antwan Odom RC 4.00 1.50
❑ 195 Michael Waddell RC 2.00 .75
❑ 196 Randy Starks RC 3.00 1.25
❑ 197 Rich Gardner RC 3.00 1.25
❑ 198 Travis Laboy RC 4.00 1.50
❑ 199 Vick King RC 3.00 1.25
❑ 200 Chris Cooley RC 4.00 1.50
❑ 201 Adimchinobe Echemandu RC 5.00 2.00
❑ 202 Ahmad Carroll RC 6.00 2.50
❑ 203 Andy Hall RC 5.00 2.00
❑ 204 B.J. Johnson RC 5.00 2.00
❑ 205 B.J. Symons RC 6.00 2.50
❑ 206 Brandon Miree RC 5.00 2.00
❑ 207 Bruce Perry RC 6.00 2.50
❑ 208 Carlos Francis RC 5.00 2.00
❑ 209 Casey Bramlet RC 5.00 2.00
❑ 210 Chris Gamble RC 6.00 2.50
❑ 211 Clarence Moore RC 6.00 2.50
❑ 212 Cody Pickett RC 6.00 2.50
❑ 213 Craig Krenzel RC 6.00 2.50
❑ 214 D.J. Hackett RC 5.00 2.00
❑ 215 D.J. Williams RC 6.00 2.50
❑ 216 Derrick Ward RC 6.00 2.50
❑ 217 Drew Carter RC 6.00 2.50
❑ 218 Drew Henson RC 6.00 2.50
❑ 219 Ernest Wilford RC 6.00 2.50
❑ 220 Jamaar Taylor RC 6.00 2.50
❑ 221 Jared Lorenzen RC 5.00 2.00
❑ 222 Jarrett Payton RC 5.00 2.00
❑ 223 Jason Babin RC 6.00 2.50
❑ 224 Jeff Smoker RC 6.00 2.50
❑ 225 Jerricho Cotchery RC 6.00 2.50
❑ 226 Jim Sorgi RC 6.00 2.50
❑ 227 John Navarre RC 6.00 2.50
❑ 228 Johnnie Morant RC 6.00 2.50
❑ 229 Jonathan Vilma RC 6.00 2.50
❑ 230 Josh Harris RC 6.00 2.50
❑ 231 Kenechi Udeze RC 6.00 2.50
❑ 232 Matt Mauck RC 6.00 2.50
❑ 233 Maurice Mann RC 5.00 2.00
❑ 234 Michael Turner RC 8.00 3.00
❑ 235 P.K. Sam RC 5.00 2.00
❑ 236 Quincy Wilson RC 5.00 2.00
❑ 237 Ran Carthon RC 5.00 2.00
❑ 238 Ricardo Colclough RC 6.00 2.50
❑ 239 Jamie Parker RC 6.00 2.50
❑ 240 Sean Jones RC 5.00 2.00
❑ 241 Sean Taylor RC 6.00 2.50
❑ 242 Sloan Thomas RC 5.00 2.00
❑ 243 Tommie Harris RC 6.00 2.50
❑ 244 Triandos Luke RC 6.00 2.50
❑ 245 Troy Fleming RC 5.00 2.00
❑ 246 Vince Wilfork RC 6.00 2.50
❑ 247 Will Smith RC 6.00 2.50
❑ 248 Michael Boulware RC 6.00 2.50
❑ 249 Richard Smith RC 5.00 2.00
❑ 250 Teddy Lehman RC 6.00 2.50
❑ 251 Larry Fitzgerald JSY RC 20.00 7.50
❑ 252 DeAngelo Hall JSY RC 10.00 4.00
❑ 253 Matt Schaub JSY RC 20.00 7.50
❑ 254 Michael Jenkins JSY RC 8.00 3.00
❑ 255 Devard Darling JSY RC 8.00 3.00
❑ 256 J.P. Losman JSY RC 12.00 5.00
❑ 257 Lee Evans JSY RC 10.00 4.00
❑ 258 Keary Colbert JSY RC 8.00 3.00
❑ 259 Bernard Berrian JSY RC 8.00 3.00
❑ 260 Chris Perry JSY RC 10.00 4.00
❑ 261 Kellen Winslow Jr. JSY RC 12.00 5.00
❑ 262 Luke McCown JSY RC 8.00 3.00
❑ 263 Julius Jones JSY RC 20.00 7.50
❑ 264 Darius Watts JSY RC 8.00 3.00
❑ 265 Tatum Bell JSY RC 12.00 5.00
❑ 266 Kevin Jones JSY RC 15.00 6.00
❑ 267 Roy Williams JSY RC 15.00 6.00
❑ 268 Dunta Robinson JSY RC 8.00 3.00
❑ 269 Greg Jones JSY RC 8.00 3.00
❑ 270 Reggie Williams JSY RC 10.00 4.00
❑ 271 Mewelde Moore JSY RC 8.00 3.00
❑ 272 Ben Watson JSY RC 8.00 3.00
❑ 273 Cedric Cobbs JSY RC 8.00 3.00
❑ 274 Devery Henderson JSY RC 8.00 3.00
❑ 275 Eli Manning JSY RC 30.00 15.00
❑ 276 Robert Gallery JSY RC 8.00 3.00
❑ 277 Ben Roethlisberger JSY RC 40.00 15.00
❑ 278 Philip Rivers JSY RC 20.00 10.00
❑ 279 Derrick Hamilton JSY RC 6.00 2.50
❑ 280 Rashaun Woods JSY RC 8.00 3.00
❑ 281 Steven Jackson JSY RC 20.00 7.50
❑ 282 Michael Clayton JSY RC 12.00 5.00
❑ 283 Ben Troupe JSY RC 8.00 3.00
❑ 284 E.Manning/Rivers JSY 30.00 15.00
❑ 285 Fitzgerald/Ro.Williams JSY 20.00 7.50
❑ 286 Winslow Jr./G.Jones JSY 12.00 5.00
❑ 288 Re.Williams/Darling JSY 8.00 3.00
❑ 289 Roethlisberger/Losman JSY 40.00 15.00
❑ 290 Clayton/Henderson JSY 12.00 5.00
❑ 292 L.Evans/M.Jenkins JSY 12.00 5.00
❑ 293 R.Woods/T.Bell JSY 12.00 5.00
❑ 294 K.Jones/Berrian JSY 20.00 7.50
❑ 295 Watson/Troupe JSY 8.00 3.00
❑ 297 M.Schaub/Hamilton JSY 20.00 7.50
❑ 298 L.McCown/Watts JSY 8.00 3.00
❑ 299 Colbert/Cobbs JSY 8.00 3.00

2005 Leaf Rookies and Stars

❑ COMP.SET w/o RC's (100) 20.00 7.50
❑ 201-250 RC PRINT RUN 799 SER.#'d SETS
❑ 251-279 JSY PRINT RUN 750 SER.#'d SETS
❑ 280-293 JSY DUAL PRINT RUN 500 SER.#'d SETS
❑ 1 Anquan Boldin .50 .20
❑ 2 Kurt Warner .50 .20
❑ 3 Larry Fitzgerald .75 .30
❑ 4 Michael Vick .75 .30
❑ 5 T.J. Duckett .50 .20
❑ 6 Warrick Dunn .50 .20
❑ 7 Jamal Lewis .50 .20
❑ 8 Kyle Boller .50 .20

❑ 9 Ray Lewis	.75	.30
❑ 10 Derrick Mason	.50	.20
❑ 11 J.P. Losman	.75	.30
❑ 12 Lee Evans	.50	.20
❑ 13 Willis McGahee	.75	.30
❑ 14 DeShaun Foster	.50	.20
❑ 15 Jake Delhomme	.75	.30
❑ 16 Steve Smith	.75	.30
❑ 17 Brian Urlacher	.75	.30
❑ 18 Rex Grossman	.75	.30
❑ 19 Muhsin Muhammad	.50	.20
❑ 20 Carson Palmer	.75	.30
❑ 21 Chad Johnson	.50	.20
❑ 22 Rudi Johnson	.50	.20
❑ 23 Lee Suggs	.50	.20
❑ 24 Drew Bledsoe	.75	.30
❑ 25 Julius Jones	1.00	.40
❑ 26 Keyshawn Johnson	.50	.20
❑ 27 Roy Williams S	.50	.20
❑ 28 Ashley Lelie	.50	.20
❑ 29 Jake Plummer	.50	.20
❑ 30 Rod Smith	.50	.20
❑ 31 Tatum Bell	.50	.20
❑ 32 Joey Harrington	.75	.30
❑ 33 Kevin Jones	.75	.30
❑ 34 Roy Williams WR	.75	.30
❑ 35 Ahman Green	.75	.30
❑ 36 Brett Favre	2.00	.75
❑ 37 Javon Walker	.50	.20
❑ 38 Andre Johnson	.50	.20
❑ 39 David Carr	.75	.30
❑ 40 Domanick Davis	.50	.20
❑ 41 Edgerrin James	.75	.30
❑ 42 Marvin Harrison	.75	.30
❑ 43 Peyton Manning	1.25	.50
❑ 44 Reggie Wayne	.50	.20
❑ 45 Byron Leftwich	.75	.30
❑ 46 Fred Taylor	.50	.20
❑ 47 Jimmy Smith	.50	.20
❑ 48 Priest Holmes	.75	.30
❑ 49 Tony Gonzalez	.50	.20
❑ 50 Trent Green	.50	.20
❑ 51 Chris Chambers	.50	.20
❑ 52 Daunte Culpepper	.75	.30
❑ 53 Michael Bennett	.50	.20
❑ 54 Nate Burleson	.50	.20
❑ 55 Corey Dillon	.50	.20
❑ 56 Deion Branch	.50	.20
❑ 57 Tom Brady	1.50	.60
❑ 58 Aaron Brooks	.50	.20
❑ 59 Deuce McAllister	.75	.30
❑ 60 Joe Horn	.50	.20
❑ 61 Eli Manning	1.50	.60
❑ 62 Jeremy Shockey	.75	.30
❑ 63 Tiki Barber	.75	.30
❑ 64 Plaxico Burress	.50	.20
❑ 65 Chad Pennington	.75	.30
❑ 66 Curtis Martin	.75	.30
❑ 67 Laveranues Coles	.50	.20
❑ 68 Jerry Porter	.50	.20
❑ 69 Kerry Collins	.50	.20
❑ 70 LaMont Jordan	.50	.20
❑ 71 Randy Moss	.75	.30
❑ 72 Brian Westbrook	.50	.20
❑ 73 Donovan McNabb	1.00	.40
❑ 74 Terrell Owens	.75	.30
❑ 75 Ben Roethlisberger	2.00	.75
❑ 76 Duce Staley	.50	.20
❑ 77 Hines Ward	.75	.30
❑ 78 Jerome Bettis	.75	.30
❑ 79 Antonio Gates	.75	.30
❑ 80 Drew Brees	.75	.30
❑ 81 LaDainian Tomlinson	1.00	.40
❑ 82 Kevan Barlow	.50	.20
❑ 83 Darrell Jackson	.50	.20
❑ 84 Matt Hasselbeck	.50	.20
❑ 85 Shaun Alexander	.75	.30
❑ 86 Marc Bulger	.75	.30
❑ 87 Steven Jackson	1.00	.40
❑ 88 Torry Holt	.50	.20
❑ 89 Brian Griese	.50	.20
❑ 90 Michael Clayton	.75	.30
❑ 91 Chris Brown	.50	.20
❑ 92 Drew Bennett	.40	.15
❑ 93 Steve McNair	.50	.20
❑ 94 Clinton Portis	.75	.30
❑ 95 LaVar Arrington	.75	.30
❑ 96 Santana Moss	.50	.20
❑ 97 A.Smith QB CL/F.Gore	4.00	1.50
❑ 98 B.Edwards CL/C.Frye	2.00	.75
❑ 99 C.Fason CL/T.Williamson	.75	.30
❑ 100 C.Rogers CL/J.Campbell	1.00	.40
❑ 101 Travis Johnson RC	4.00	1.50
❑ 102 Alex Smith TE RC	5.00	2.00
❑ 103 Channing Crowder RC	5.00	2.00
❑ 104 Craig Bragg RC	4.00	1.50
❑ 105 Darrent Williams RC	5.00	2.00
❑ 106 Derrick Wimbush RC	5.00	2.00
❑ 107 Josh Cribbs RC	5.00	2.00
❑ 108 Luis Castillo RC	5.00	2.00
❑ 109 Matt Roth RC	5.00	2.00
❑ 110 Mike Patterson RC	5.00	2.00
❑ 111 Fred Gibson RC	4.00	1.50
❑ 112 Marcus Spears RC	5.00	2.00
❑ 113 Brodney Pool RC	5.00	2.00
❑ 114 Barrett Ruud RC	5.00	2.00
❑ 115 Stanford Routt RC	4.00	1.50
❑ 116 Josh Bullocks RC	5.00	2.00
❑ 117 Kevin Burnett RC	5.00	2.00
❑ 118 Corey Webster RC	5.00	2.00
❑ 119 Lofa Tatupu RC	6.00	2.50
❑ 120 Mike Nugent RC	5.00	2.00
❑ 121 Jim Leonhard RC	5.00	2.00
❑ 122 Ronald Bartell RC	4.00	1.50
❑ 123 Nick Collins RC	5.00	2.00
❑ 124 Justin Miller RC	4.00	1.50
❑ 125 Jonathan Babineaux RC	4.00	1.50
❑ 126 Kelvin Hayden RC	4.00	1.50
❑ 127 Matt McCoy RC	4.00	1.50
❑ 128 Oshiomogho Atogwe RC	4.00	1.50
❑ 129 Stanley Wilson RC	4.00	1.50
❑ 130 Justin Tuck RC	5.00	2.00
❑ 131 Eric Green RC	2.50	1.00
❑ 132 Karl Paymah RC	5.00	2.00
❑ 133 Kirk Morrison RC	5.00	2.00
❑ 134 Dustin Fox RC	5.00	2.00
❑ 135 Alfred Fincher RC	4.00	1.50
❑ 136 Chris Henry RC	5.00	2.00
❑ 137 Ellis Hobbs RC	5.00	2.00
❑ 138 Scott Starks RC	4.00	1.50
❑ 139 Jordan Beck RC	4.00	1.50
❑ 140 Vincent Burns RC	4.00	1.50
❑ 141 Darryl Blackstock RC	4.00	1.50
❑ 142 Domonique Foxworth RC	5.00	2.00
❑ 143 Leroy Hill RC	5.00	2.00
❑ 144 Cedric Killings RC	4.00	1.50
❑ 145 Leonard Weaver RC	4.00	1.50
❑ 146 Sean Considine RC	5.00	2.00
❑ 147 Antonio Perkins RC	4.00	1.50
❑ 148 Travis Daniels RC	4.00	1.50
❑ 149 Vincent Fuller RC	4.00	1.50
❑ 150 Manuel White RC	4.00	1.50
❑ 151 Kerry Rhodes RC	5.00	2.00
❑ 152 Brady Poppinga RC	5.00	2.00
❑ 153 Chris Canty RC	5.00	2.00
❑ 154 James Sanders RC	5.00	2.00
❑ 155 Matt Giordano RC	5.00	2.00
❑ 156 Boomer Grigsby RC	5.00	2.00
❑ 157 Donte Nicholson RC	5.00	2.00
❑ 158 Jerome Collins RC	4.00	1.50
❑ 159 Trent Cole RC	5.00	2.00
❑ 160 Alphonso Hodge RC	2.50	1.00
❑ 161 Jonathan Welsh RC	4.00	1.50
❑ 162 Adam Seward RC	5.00	2.00
❑ 163 Robert McCune RC	4.00	1.50
❑ 164 Eric King RC	4.00	1.50
❑ 165 Gerald Sensabaugh RC	5.00	2.00
❑ 166 Justin Green RC	5.00	2.00
❑ 167 Jeb Huckeba RC	5.00	2.00
❑ 168 Michael Boley RC	4.00	1.50
❑ 169 Andre Maddox RC	4.00	1.50
❑ 170 Rian Wallace RC	4.00	1.50
❑ 171 Michael Hawkins RC	4.00	1.50
❑ 172 Lance Mitchell RC	4.00	1.50
❑ 173 Ryan Claridge RC	4.00	1.50
❑ 174 James Butler RC	4.00	1.50
❑ 175 Ryan Riddle RC	2.50	1.00
❑ 176 Bo Scaife RC	4.00	1.50
❑ 177 Chris Harris RC	5.00	2.00
❑ 178 C.C. Brown RC	4.00	1.50
❑ 179 Pat Thomas RC	4.00	1.50
❑ 180 Derrick Johnson CB RC	5.00	2.00
❑ 181 Joel Dreessen RC	4.00	1.50
❑ 182 Rick Razzano RC	5.00	2.00
❑ 183 Nehemiah Broughton RC	4.00	1.50
❑ 184 Marcus Maxwell RC	4.00	1.50
❑ 185 Harry Williams RC	4.00	1.50
❑ 186 Patrick Estes RC	4.00	1.50
❑ 187 Billy Bajema RC	4.00	1.50
❑ 188 Madison Hedgecock RC	5.00	2.00
❑ 189 Manuel Wright RC	5.00	2.00
❑ 190 Roscoe Crosby RC	4.00	1.50
❑ 191 Wesley Duke RC	5.00	2.00
❑ 192 Ronnie Cruz RC	4.00	1.50
❑ 193 Adam Bergen RC	5.00	2.00
❑ 194 B.J. Ward RC	4.00	1.50
❑ 195 Stephen Spach RC	4.00	1.50
❑ 196 Marviel Underwood RC	4.00	1.50
❑ 197 John Bronson RC	4.00	1.50
❑ 198 Zak Keasey RC	5.00	2.00
❑ 199 Gregg Guenther RC	4.00	1.50
❑ 200 Jerome Carter RC	4.00	1.50
❑ 201 Aaron Rodgers RC	20.00	7.50
❑ 202 Adrian McPherson RC	6.00	2.50
❑ 203 Alvin Pearman RC	6.00	2.50
❑ 204 Airese Currie RC	6.00	2.50
❑ 205 Anthony Davis RC	5.00	2.00
❑ 206 Brandon Jacobs RC	8.00	3.00
❑ 207 Brandon Jones RC	6.00	2.50
❑ 208 Bryant McFadden RC	6.00	2.50
❑ 209 Cedric Benson RC	15.00	6.00
❑ 210 Cedric Houston RC	6.00	2.50
❑ 211 Chad Owens RC	6.00	2.50
❑ 212 Chris Henry	6.00	2.50
❑ 213 Craphonso Thorpe RC	5.00	2.00
❑ 214 Damien Nash RC	5.00	2.00
❑ 215 Dan Cody RC	6.00	2.50
❑ 216 Dan Orlovsky RC	6.00	2.50
❑ 217 Dante Ridgeway RC	5.00	2.00
❑ 218 Darren Sproles RC	6.00	2.50
❑ 219 David Greene RC	6.00	2.50
❑ 220 David Pollack RC	6.00	2.50
❑ 221 Deandra Cobb RC	5.00	2.00
❑ 222 DeMarcus Ware RC	10.00	4.00
❑ 223 Derek Anderson RC	10.00	4.00
❑ 224 Derrick Johnson RC	10.00	4.00
❑ 225 Fabian Washington RC	6.00	2.50
❑ 226 Roydell Williams RC	6.00	2.50
❑ 227 Heath Miller RC	12.00	5.00
❑ 228 J.R. Russell RC	5.00	2.00
❑ 229 James Kilian RC	6.00	2.50
❑ 230 Jerome Mathis RC	6.00	2.50
❑ 231 Larry Brackins RC	5.00	2.00
❑ 232 LeRon McCoy RC	5.00	2.00
❑ 233 Lionel Gates RC	5.00	2.00
❑ 234 Marion Barber RC	10.00	4.00
❑ 235 Marlin Jackson RC	6.00	2.50
❑ 236 Matt Cassel RC	10.00	4.00
❑ 237 Mike Williams	6.00	2.50
❑ 238 Nate Washington RC	5.00	2.00
❑ 239 Noah Herron RC	6.00	2.50
❑ 240 Fred Amey RC	5.00	2.00
❑ 241 Paris Warren RC	5.00	2.00
❑ 242 Rasheed Marshall RC	6.00	2.50
❑ 243 Ryan Fitzpatrick RC	6.00	2.50
❑ 244 Shaun Cody RC	6.00	2.50
❑ 245 Shawne Merriman RC	10.00	4.00
❑ 246 Tab Perry RC	6.00	2.50
❑ 247 Thomas Davis RC	6.00	2.50
❑ 248 Tyson Thompson RC	8.00	3.00
❑ 249 Chris Carr RC	8.00	3.00
❑ 250 Odell Thurman RC	6.00	2.50
❑ 251 Adam Jones JSY RC	8.00	3.00
❑ 252 Alex Smith QB JSY RC	20.00	7.50
❑ 253 Andrew Walter JSY RC	8.00	3.00
❑ 254 Antrel Rolle JSY RC	8.00	3.00
❑ 255 Braylon Edwards JSY RC	15.00	6.00
❑ 256 Carlos Rogers JSY RC	10.00	4.00
❑ 257 Cadillac Williams JSY RC	25.00	10.00
❑ 258 Charlie Frye JSY RC	8.00	3.00

❑ 259 Ciatrick Fason JSY RC 8.00 3.00
❑ 260 Courtney Roby JSY RC 8.00 3.00
❑ 261 Eric Shelton JSY RC 8.00 3.00
❑ 262 Frank Gore JSY RC 12.00 5.00
❑ 263 J.J. Arrington JSY RC 8.00 3.00
❑ 264 Jason Campbell JSY RC 10.00 4.00
❑ 265 Kyle Orton JSY RC 8.00 3.00
❑ 266 Mark Clayton JSY RC 8.00 3.00
❑ 267 Mark Bradley JSY RC 8.00 3.00
❑ 268 Matt Jones JSY RC 10.00 4.00
❑ 269 Maurice Clarett JSY 8.00 3.00
❑ 270 Reggie Brown JSY RC 8.00 3.00
❑ 271 Roddy White JSY RC 8.00 3.00
❑ 272 Ronnie Brown JSY RC 20.00 7.50
❑ 273 [illegible] Parrish JSY RC 8.00 [illegible]
❑ 274 Ryan Moats JSY RC 8.00 3.00
❑ 275 Stefan LeFors JSY RC 8.00 3.00
❑ 276 Terrence Murphy JSY RC 8.00 3.00
❑ 277 Troy Williamson JSY RC 8.00 3.00
❑ 278 Vernand Morency JSY RC 8.00 3.00
❑ 279 Vincent Jackson JSY RC 8.00 3.00
❑ 280 A.Smith QB J/J.Campbell J 25.00 10.00
❑ 281 R.Brown J/C.Williams J 25.00 10.00
❑ 282 B.Edwards J/T.Williamson J 10.00 4.00
❑ 283 A.Jones J/A.Rolle J 10.00 4.00
❑ 284 R.Parrish J/F.Gore J 15.00 6.00
❑ 285 C.Frye J/A.Walter J 10.00 4.00
❑ 286 J.Arrington J/E.Shelton J 10.00 4.00
❑ 287 C.Rogers J/K.Orton J 10.00 4.00
❑ 288 M.Clayton J/M.Bradley J 10.00 4.00
❑ 289 R.White J/Re.Brown J 10.00 4.00
❑ 290 T.Murphy J/C.Roby J 10.00 4.00
❑ 291 M.Clarett J/C.Fason J 10.00 4.00
❑ 292 R.Moats J/S.LeFors J 10.00 4.00
❑ 293 M.Jones J/V.Jackson J 15.00 6.00

2006 Leaf Rookies and Stars

❑ 1 Anquan Boldin .40 .15
❑ 2 Edgerrin James .60 .25
❑ 3 Kurt Warner .40 .15
❑ 4 Larry Fitzgerald .60 .25
❑ 5 Alge Crumpler .40 .15
❑ 6 Michael Vick .60 .25
❑ 7 Warrick Dunn .40 .15
❑ 8 Derrick Mason .30 .12
❑ 9 Jamal Lewis .40 .15
❑ 10 Mike Anderson .40 .15
❑ 11 Josh Reed .30 .12
❑ 12 Lee Evans .40 .15
❑ 13 Willis McGahee .60 .25
❑ 14 DeShaun Foster .40 .15
❑ 15 Jake Delhomme .40 .15
❑ 16 Keyshawn Johnson .40 .15
❑ 17 Steve Smith .60 .25
❑ 18 Cedric Benson .60 .25
❑ 19 Muhsin Muhammad .40 .15
❑ 20 Rex Grossman .60 .25
❑ 21 Carson Palmer .60 .25
❑ 22 Chad Johnson .40 .15
❑ 23 Rudi Johnson .40 .15
❑ 24 T.J. Houshmandzadeh .40 .15
❑ 25 Charlie Frye .40 .15
❑ 26 Joe Jurevicius .40 .15
❑ 27 Reuben Droughns .40 .15
❑ 28 Drew Bledsoe .60 .25
❑ 29 Julius Jones .60 .25
❑ 30 Terrell Owens .60 .25
❑ 31 Terry Glenn .40 .15
❑ 32 Jake Plummer .40 .15
❑ 33 Rod Smith .40 .15
❑ 34 Tatum Bell .40 .15
❑ 35 Josh McCown .40 .15
❑ 36 Kevin Jones .60 .25
❑ 37 Roy Williams WR .60 .25
❑ 38 Ahman Green .40 .15
❑ 39 Brett Favre 1.25 .50
❑ 40 Donald Driver .40 .15
❑ 41 Robert Ferguson .30 .12
❑ 42 Samkon Gado .40 .15
❑ 43 Andre Johnson .40 .15
❑ 44 David Carr .40 .15
❑ 45 Domanick Davis .40 .15
❑ 46 Eric Moulds .40 .15
❑ 47 Marvin Harrison .60 .25
❑ 48 Peyton Manning 1.00 .40
❑ 49 Reggie Wayne .40 .15
❑ 50 Dallas Clark .30 .12
❑ 51 Fred Taylor .40 .15
❑ 52 Byron Leftwich .40 .15
❑ 53 Jimmy Smith .40 .15
❑ 54 Larry Johnson .75 .30
❑ 55 Tony Gonzalez .40 .15
❑ 56 Trent Green .40 .15
❑ 57 Eddie Kennison .30 .12
❑ 58 Chris Chambers .40 .15
❑ 59 Daunte Culpepper .60 .25
❑ 60 Ronnie Brown .60 .25
❑ 61 Chester Taylor .40 .15
❑ 62 Brad Johnson .40 .15
❑ 63 Deion Branch .40 .15
❑ 64 Corey Dillon .40 .15
❑ 65 Tom Brady 1.00 .40
❑ 66 Deuce McAllister .40 .15
❑ 67 Donte Stallworth .40 .15
❑ 68 Drew Brees .60 .25
❑ 69 Eli Manning .75 .30
❑ 70 Plaxico Burress .40 .15
❑ 71 Tiki Barber .60 .25
❑ 72 Chad Pennington .40 .15
❑ 73 Curtis Martin .60 .25
❑ 74 Laveranues Coles .40 .15
❑ 75 Aaron Brooks .40 .15
❑ 76 LaMont Jordan .40 .15
❑ 77 Randy Moss .60 .25
❑ 78 Brian Westbrook .40 .15
❑ 79 Donovan McNabb .60 .25
❑ 80 Jabar Gaffney .30 .12
❑ 81 Hines Ward .60 .25
❑ 82 Ben Roethlisberger 1.00 .40
❑ 83 Willie Parker .75 .30
❑ 84 Antonio Gates .60 .25
❑ 85 LaDainian Tomlinson .75 .30
❑ 86 Philip Rivers .60 .25
❑ 87 Alex Smith QB .60 .25
❑ 88 Antonio Bryant .40 .15
❑ 89 Kevan Barlow .40 .15
❑ 90 Darrell Jackson .40 .15
❑ 91 Matt Hasselbeck .40 .15
❑ 92 Shaun Alexander .60 .25
❑ 93 Torry Holt .40 .15
❑ 94 Steven Jackson .60 .25
❑ 95 Cadillac Williams .60 .25
❑ 96 Joey Galloway .40 .15
❑ 97 David Givens .40 .15
❑ 98 Drew Bennett .30 .12
❑ 99 Antwaan Randle El .40 .15
❑ 100 Clinton Portis .60 .25
❑ 101 Kamerion Wimbley RC 4.00 1.50
❑ 102 Mathias Kiwanuka RC 5.00 2.00
❑ 103 Reggie McNeal RC 3.00 1.25
❑ 104 Claude Wroten RC 2.00 .75
❑ 105 Gabe Watson RC 3.00 1.25
❑ 106 D'Qwell Jackson RC 3.00 1.25
❑ 107 Todd Watkins RC 3.00 1.25
❑ 108 Bennie Brazell RC 3.00 1.25
❑ 109 David Anderson RC 3.00 1.25
❑ 110 John David Washington RC 3.00 1.25
❑ 111 Marques Hagans RC 3.00 1.25
❑ 112 Kevin Youngblood RC 3.00 1.25
❑ 113 Ben Obomanu RC 3.00 1.25
❑ 114 Jamal Jones RC 3.00 1.25
❑ 115 Nick Mangold RC 3.00 1.25
❑ 116 Davin Joseph RC 3.00 1.25
❑ 117 Erik Meyer RC 3.00 1.25
❑ 118 Taurean Henderson RC 4.00 1.50
❑ 119 A.J. Nicholson RC 2.00 .75
❑ 120 Thomas Howard RC 4.00 1.50
❑ 121 Jon Alston RC 4.00 1.50
❑ 122 Ashton Youboty RC 4.00 1.50
❑ 123 Alan Zemaitis RC 4.00 1.50
❑ 124 Lawrence Vickers RC 3.00 1.25
❑ 125 J.D. Runnels RC 3.00 1.25
❑ 126 Ray Perkins RC 3.00 1.25
❑ 127 Jeff King RC 3.00 1.25
❑ 128 Quinn Sypniewski RC 3.00 1.25
❑ 129 Jason Carter RC 3.00 1.25
❑ 130 Malcolm Floyd RC 4.00 1.50
❑ 131 Mike Jennings RC 3.00 1.25
❑ 132 Chris Gocong RC 3.00 1.25
❑ 133 Frostee Hucker RC 3.00 1.25
❑ 134 Jason Hatcher RC 3.00 1.25
❑ 135 Victor Adeyanju RC 3.00 1.25
❑ 136 Elvis Dumervil RC 2.00 .75
❑ 137 Ray Edwards RC 3.00 1.25
❑ 138 Anthony Schlegel RC 3.00 1.25
❑ 139 Freddie Keiaho RC 3.00 1.25
❑ 140 Gerris Wilkinson RC 2.00 .75
❑ 141 Leon Williams RC 3.00 1.25
❑ 142 Stephen Tulloch RC 3.00 1.25
❑ 143 Jamar Williams RC 3.00 1.25
❑ 144 Clint Ingram RC 4.00 1.50
❑ 145 James Anderson RC 2.00 .75
❑ 146 Darrell Hackney RC 3.00 1.25
❑ 147 Paul Pinegar RC 3.00 1.25
❑ 148 Brandon Kirsch RC 4.00 1.50
❑ 149 Andre Hall RC 3.00 1.25
❑ 150 De'Arrius Howard RC 4.00 1.50
❑ 151 Cedric Humes RC 4.00 1.50
❑ 152 Wendell Mathis RC 3.00 1.25
❑ 153 Gerald Riggs RC 4.00 1.50
❑ 154 Quinton Ganther RC 3.00 1.25
❑ 155 Martin Nance RC 3.00 1.25
❑ 156 Greg Lee RC 3.00 1.25
❑ 157 Jai Lewis RC 3.00 1.25
❑ 158 Cory Rodgers RC 4.00 1.50
❑ 159 Mike Espy RC 4.00 1.50
❑ 160 Chris Barclay RC 3.00 1.25
❑ 161 DeMeco Ryans RC 5.00 2.00
❑ 162 Rocky McIntosh RC 4.00 1.50
❑ 163 David Kirtman RC 3.00 1.25
❑ 164 Skyler Green RC 4.00 1.50
❑ 165 Will Blackmon RC 3.00 1.25
❑ 166 Darryl Tapp RC 3.00 1.25
❑ 167 Dusty Dvoracek RC 4.00 1.50
❑ 168 Richard Marshall RC 3.00 1.25
❑ 169 Tim Jennings RC 3.00 1.25
❑ 170 David Pittman RC 3.00 1.25
❑ 171 DeMario Minter RC 3.00 1.25
❑ 172 Marcus Maxey RC 3.00 1.25
❑ 173 Roman Harper RC 3.00 1.25
❑ 174 Anthony Smith RC 5.00 2.00
❑ 175 Nate Salley RC 3.00 1.25
❑ 176 Mike Hass RC 4.00 1.50
❑ 177 Greg Blue RC 3.00 1.25
❑ 178 Daniel Bullocks RC 4.00 1.50
❑ 179 Danieal Manning RC 4.00 1.50
❑ 180 Calvin Lowry RC 4.00 1.50
❑ 181 Eric Smith RC 3.00 1.25
❑ 182 Jimmy Williams RC 4.00 1.50
❑ 183 Cedric Griffin RC 3.00 1.25
❑ 184 Ko Simpson RC 3.00 1.25
❑ 185 Pat Watkins RC 4.00 1.50
❑ 186 Marcus Vick RC 3.00 1.25
❑ 187 Bernard Pollard RC 3.00 1.25
❑ 188 Darnell Bing RC 4.00 1.50
❑ 189 Cory Ross RC 4.00 1.50
❑ 190 Patrick Cobbs RC 3.00 1.25
❑ 191 Montell Owens RC 3.00 1.25
❑ 192 Chris Hannon RC 3.00 1.25
❑ 193 John Madsen RC 4.00 1.50
❑ 194 Shaun Bodiford RC 3.00 1.25
❑ 195 Fred Evans RC 3.00 1.25
❑ 196 Cletis Gordon RC 2.00 .75
❑ 197 Jarrad Page RC 4.00 1.50
❑ 198 Brett Elliott RC 4.00 1.50
❑ 199 Brett Basanez RC 4.00 1.50
❑ 200 Drew Olson RC 3.00 1.25
❑ 201 Jay Cutler RC 15.00 6.00
❑ 202 Brodie Croyle RC 12.00 5.00
❑ 203 Ingle Martin RC 5.00 2.00
❑ 204 Derrick Ross RC 4.00 1.50
❑ 205 Bruce Gradkowski RC 8.00 3.00
❑ 206 D.J. Shockley RC 5.00 2.00
❑ 207 Joseph Addai RC 15.00 6.00
❑ 208 P.J. Daniels RC 4.00 1.50
❑ 209 Marques Colston RC 20.00 8.00
❑ 210 Jerome Harrison RC 5.00 2.00
❑ 211 Wali Lundy RC 5.00 2.00

- ❑ 212 Mike Bell RC 5.00 2.00
- ❑ 213 Miles Austin RC 4.00 1.50
- ❑ 214 Anthony Fasano RC 5.00 2.00
- ❑ 215 Tony Scheffler RC 5.00 2.00
- ❑ 216 Leonard Pope RC 5.00 2.00
- ❑ 217 David Thomas RC 5.00 2.00
- ❑ 218 Dominique Byrd RC 4.00 1.50
- ❑ 219 Garrett Mills RC 5.00 2.00
- ❑ 220 Hank Baskett RC 5.00 2.00
- ❑ 221 Greg Jennings RC 8.00 3.00
- ❑ 222 Devin Hester RC 10.00 4.00
- ❑ 223 Willie Reid RC 5.00 2.00
- ❑ 224 Brad Smith RC 5.00 2.00
- ❑ 225 Sam Hurd RC 8.00 3.00
- ❑ 226 Owen Daniels RC 5.00 2.00
- ❑ 227 Domenik Hixon RC 4.00 1.50
- ❑ 228 Jeremy Bloom RC 4.00 1.50
- ❑ 229 Dawan Landry RC 5.00 2.00
- ❑ 230 Jonathan Orr RC 4.00 1.50
- ❑ 231 Delanie Walker RC 4.00 1.50
- ❑ 232 Adam Jennings RC 4.00 1.50
- ❑ 233 Jeffrey Webb RC 4.00 1.50
- ❑ 234 Ethan Kilmer RC 5.00 2.00
- ❑ 235 Tye Hill RC 5.00 2.00
- ❑ 236 Jason Allen RC 5.00 2.00
- ❑ 237 Antonio Cromartie RC 5.00 2.00
- ❑ 238 D'Brickashaw Ferguson RC 5.00 2.00
- ❑ 239 Tamba Hali RC 5.00 2.00
- ❑ 240 Haloti Ngata RC 5.00 2.00
- ❑ 241 Brodrick Bunkley RC 5.00 2.00
- ❑ 242 John McCargo RC 4.00 1.50
- ❑ 243 Johnathan Joseph RC 4.00 1.50
- ❑ 244 Kelly Jennings RC 5.00 2.00
- ❑ 245 Donte Whitner RC 5.00 2.00
- ❑ 246 Abdul Hodge RC 5.00 2.00
- ❑ 247 Ernie Sims RC 6.00 2.50
- ❑ 248 Chad Greenway RC 5.00 2.00
- ❑ 249 Bobby Carpenter RC 5.00 2.00
- ❑ 250 Manny Lawson RC 5.00 2.00
- ❑ 251 Matt Leinart JSY/599 RC 20.00 8.00
- ❑ 252 Kellen Clemens JSY RC 8.00 3.00
- ❑ 253 Tarvaris Jackson JSY RC 8.00 3.00
- ❑ 254 Charlie Whitehurst JSY RC 6.00 2.50
- ❑ 255 DeAn.Williams JSY/599 RC 12.00 5.00
- ❑ 256 Maurice Drew JSY RC 10.00 4.00
- ❑ 257 Brian Calhoun JSY RC 6.00 2.50
- ❑ 258 Jerious Norwood JSY RC 10.00 4.00
- ❑ 259 Vernon Davis JSY RC 10.00 4.00
- ❑ 260 Joe Klopfenstein JSY RC 6.00 2.50
- ❑ 261 Sinorice Moss JSY RC 6.00 2.50
- ❑ 262 Derek Hagan JSY RC 6.00 2.50
- ❑ 263 Brandon Williams JSY RC 6.00 2.50
- ❑ 264 Michael Robinson JSY RC 6.00 2.50
- ❑ 265 Jason Avant JSY RC 6.00 2.50
- ❑ 266 Brandon Marshall JSY RC 6.00 2.50
- ❑ 267 Demetrius Williams JSY RC 6.00 2.50
- ❑ 268 Mario Williams JSY RC 8.00 3.00
- ❑ 269 Michael Huff JSY RC 8.00 3.00
- ❑ 270 Chad Jackson JSY RC 6.00 2.50
- ❑ 271 Vince Young JSY AU/249 RC 150.00 90.00
- ❑ 272 Omar Jacobs JSY AU/449 RC 15.00 6.00
- ❑ 273 Reggie Bush JSY AU/99 RC 200.00 100.00
- ❑ 274 L.Maroney JSY AU/99 RC 100.00 50.00
- ❑ 275 LenDale White JSY AU/249 RC 40.00 15.00
- ❑ 276 L.Washington JSY AU/199 RC 30.00 12.00
- ❑ 277 M.Lewis JSY AU/449 RC 15.00 6.00
- ❑ 278 S.Holmes JSY AU/44w9 RC 40.00 15.00
- ❑ 279 Travis Wilson JSY AU/449 RC 12.00 5.00
- ❑ 280 Maurice Stovall JSY AU/99 RC 20.00 8.00
- ❑ 281 A.J. Hawk JSY AU/99 RC 60.00 30.00

2007 Leaf Rookies and Stars

- ❑ 1 Tony Romo 1.50 .60
- ❑ 2 Julius Jones .60 .25
- ❑ 3 Terrell Owens .75 .30
- ❑ 4 Eli Manning .75 .30
- ❑ 5 Plaxico Burress .60 .25
- ❑ 6 Jeremy Shockey .60 .25
- ❑ 7 Brandon Jacobs .60 .25
- ❑ 8 Donovan McNabb .75 .30
- ❑ 9 Brian Westbrook .60 .25
- ❑ 10 Reggie Brown .60 .25
- ❑ 11 Jason Campbell .60 .25
- ❑ 12 Clinton Portis .60 .25
- ❑ 13 Santana Moss .60 .25
- ❑ 14 Rex Grossman .60 .25
- ❑ 15 Cedric Benson .60 .25
- ❑ 16 Muhsin Muhammad .60 .25

- ❑ 17 Jon Kitna .50 .20
- ❑ 18 Roy Williams WR .60 .25
- ❑ 19 Tatum Bell .60 .25
- ❑ 20 Brett Favre 1.50 .60
- ❑ 21 Vernand Morency .60 .25
- ❑ 22 Donald Driver .60 .25
- ❑ 23 Tarvaris Jackson .75 .30
- ❑ 24 Chester Taylor .50 .20
- ❑ 25 Troy Williamson .50 .20
- ❑ 26 Jerious Norwood .60 .25
- ❑ 27 Warrick Dunn .60 .25
- ❑ 28 Alge Crumpler .60 .25
- ❑ 29 Jake Delhomme .60 .25
- ❑ 30 DeShaun Foster .60 .25
- ❑ 31 Steve Smith .60 .25
- ❑ 32 Drew Brees .60 .25
- ❑ 33 Deuce McAllister .60 .25
- ❑ 34 Marques Colston .75 .30
- ❑ 35 Reggie Bush 1.00 .40
- ❑ 36 Jeff Garcia .60 .25
- ❑ 37 Cadillac Williams .60 .25
- ❑ 38 Joey Galloway .60 .25
- ❑ 39 Matt Leinart .75 .30
- ❑ 40 Edgerrin James .75 .30
- ❑ 41 Anquan Boldin .60 .25
- ❑ 42 Larry Fitzgerald .60 .25
- ❑ 43 Marc Bulger .60 .25
- ❑ 44 Steven Jackson .75 .30
- ❑ 45 Torry Holt .60 .25
- ❑ 46 Alex Smith QB .75 .30
- ❑ 47 Frank Gore .75 .30
- ❑ 48 Vernon Davis .60 .25
- ❑ 49 Matt Hasselbeck .60 .25
- ❑ 50 Shaun Alexander .60 .25
- ❑ 51 Deion Branch .60 .25
- ❑ 52 J.P. Losman .60 .25
- ❑ 53 Anthony Thomas .50 .20
- ❑ 54 Lee Evans .60 .25
- ❑ 55 Trent Green .60 .25
- ❑ 56 Ronnie Brown .60 .25
- ❑ 57 Chris Chambers .60 .25
- ❑ 58 Tom Brady 1.50 .60
- ❑ 59 Laurence Maroney .75 .30
- ❑ 60 Randy Moss .75 .30
- ❑ 61 Chad Pennington .60 .25
- ❑ 62 Jerricho Cotchery .50 .20
- ❑ 63 Leon Washington .60 .25
- ❑ 64 Steve McNair .60 .25
- ❑ 65 Willis McGahee .60 .25
- ❑ 66 Mark Clayton .60 .25
- ❑ 67 Carson Palmer .75 .30
- ❑ 68 Rudi Johnson .60 .25
- ❑ 69 Chad Johnson .60 .25
- ❑ 70 T.J. Houshmandzadeh .60 .25
- ❑ 71 Charlie Frye .60 .25
- ❑ 72 Braylon Edwards .60 .25
- ❑ 73 Jamal Lewis .60 .25
- ❑ 74 Ben Roethlisberger 1.00 .40
- ❑ 75 Willie Parker .75 .30
- ❑ 76 Hines Ward .75 .30
- ❑ 77 Ahman Green .60 .25
- ❑ 78 Andre Johnson .60 .25
- ❑ 79 Matt Schaub .60 .25
- ❑ 80 Peyton Manning 1.25 .50
- ❑ 81 Joseph Addai 1.00 .40
- ❑ 82 Marvin Harrison .75 .30
- ❑ 83 Reggie Wayne .60 .25
- ❑ 84 Byron Leftwich .60 .25
- ❑ 85 Fred Taylor .60 .25
- ❑ 86 Maurice Jones-Drew .75 .30
- ❑ 87 Vince Young 1.00 .40
- ❑ 88 LenDale White .60 .25
- ❑ 89 Brandon Jones .50 .20
- ❑ 90 Jay Cutler .75 .30
- ❑ 91 Javon Walker .60 .25
- ❑ 92 Mike Bell .60 .25
- ❑ 93 Larry Johnson .75 .30
- ❑ 94 Tony Gonzalez .60 .25
- ❑ 95 Brodie Croyle .75 .30
- ❑ 96 LaMont Jordan .60 .25
- ❑ 97 Dominic Rhodes .60 .25
- ❑ 98 Philip Rivers .75 .30
- ❑ 99 LaDainian Tomlinson 1.00 .40
- ❑ 100 Antonio Gates .60 .25
- ❑ 101 Drew Brees .60 .25
- ❑ 102 Reggie Bush 1.00 .40
- ❑ 103 Brett Favre 1.50 .60
- ❑ 104 Marvin Harrison .75 .30
- ❑ 105 Eli Manning .75 .30
- ❑ 106 Willie Parker .75 .30
- ❑ 107 Brian Westbrook .60 .25
- ❑ 108 Tom Brady 1.50 .60
- ❑ 109 Jay Cutler .75 .30
- ❑ 110 Rudi Johnson .60 .25
- ❑ 111 J.P. Losman .60 .25
- ❑ 112 Laurence Maroney .75 .30
- ❑ 113 Carson Palmer .75 .30
- ❑ 114 Ben Roethlisberger 1.00 .40
- ❑ 115 Brian Urlacher .75 .30
- ❑ 116 A.J. Davis RC 3.00 1.25
- ❑ 117 Usama Young RC 4.00 1.50
- ❑ 118 Aaron Rouse RC 5.00 2.00
- ❑ 119 Ahmad Bradshaw RC 6.00 2.50
- ❑ 120 Alan Branch RC 4.00 1.50
- ❑ 121 Alonzo Coleman RC 4.00 1.50
- ❑ 122 Amobi Okoye RC 5.00 2.00
- ❑ 123 Anthony Spencer RC 5.00 2.00
- ❑ 124 Deon Anderson RC 4.00 1.50
- ❑ 125 Justin Durant RC 4.00 1.50
- ❑ 126 Brandon Siler RC 4.00 1.50
- ❑ 127 Buster Davis RC 4.00 1.50
- ❑ 128 Charles Johnson RC 3.00 1.25
- ❑ 129 Courtney Taylor RC 4.00 1.50
- ❑ 130 Dallas Baker RC 4.00 1.50
- ❑ 131 Dan Bazuin RC 4.00 1.50
- ❑ 132 Danny Ware RC 5.00 2.00
- ❑ 133 Darius Walker RC 5.00 2.00
- ❑ 134 David Ball RC 3.00 1.25
- ❑ 135 David Harris RC 4.00 1.50
- ❑ 136 David Irons RC 3.00 1.25
- ❑ 137 Daymeion Hughes RC 4.00 1.50
- ❑ 138 Anthony Waters RC 4.00 1.50
- ❑ 139 Antwan Barnes RC 4.00 1.50
- ❑ 140 Eric Frampton RC 4.00 1.50
- ❑ 141 Eric Weddle RC 4.00 1.50
- ❑ 142 Eric Wright RC 5.00 2.00
- ❑ 143 Fred Bennett RC 3.00 1.25
- ❑ 144 Gary Russell RC 5.00 2.00
- ❑ 145 H.B. Blades RC 4.00 1.50
- ❑ 146 Jacoby Jones RC 5.00 2.00
- ❑ 147 Clifton Dawson RC 5.00 2.00
- ❑ 148 Kevin Boss RC 12.00 5.00
- ❑ 149 Jarvis Moss RC 5.00 2.00
- ❑ 150 Gerald Alexander RC 3.00 1.25
- ❑ 151 Jeff Rowe RC 4.00 1.50
- ❑ 152 Tanard Jackson RC 3.00 1.25
- ❑ 153 Joel Filani RC 4.00 1.50
- ❑ 154 Jon Abbate RC 3.00 1.25
- ❑ 155 Jon Beason RC 5.00 2.00
- ❑ 156 Marcus Mason RC 5.00 2.00
- ❑ 157 Jonathan Wade RC 4.00 1.50
- ❑ 158 Dante Rosario RC 4.00 1.50
- ❑ 159 Josh Wilson RC 4.00 1.50
- ❑ 160 Kenneth Darby RC 5.00 2.00
- ❑ 161 Biren Ealy RC 4.00 1.50
- ❑ 162 LaMarr Woodley RC 5.00 2.00
- ❑ 163 Levi Brown RC 5.00 2.00
- ❑ 164 Marcus McCauley RC 4.00 1.50
- ❑ 165 Matt Spaeth RC 5.00 2.00
- ❑ 166 Michael Okwo RC 4.00 1.50
- ❑ 167 Mike Walker RC 4.00 1.50
- ❑ 168 Quentin Moses RC 4.00 1.50
- ❑ 169 Ray McDonald RC 4.00 1.50
- ❑ 170 Reggie Ball RC 4.00 1.50
- ❑ 171 Justin Harrell RC 5.00 2.00
- ❑ 172 Ed Johnson RC 4.00 1.50
- ❑ 173 Rufus Alexander RC 5.00 2.00
- ❑ 174 Ryan McBean RC 5.00 2.00
- ❑ 175 Ryne Robinson RC 4.00 1.50
- ❑ 176 Sabby Piscitelli RC 5.00 2.00
- ❑ 177 Scott Chandler RC 4.00 1.50

❑ 178 Selvin Young RC 6.00 2.50
❑ 179 Steve Breaston RC 4.00 1.50
❑ 180 Stewart Bradley RC 5.00 2.00
❑ 181 Turk McBride RC 4.00 1.50
❑ 182 Demarcus Tank Tyler RC 4.00 1.50
❑ 183 Tim Crowder RC 5.00 2.00
❑ 184 Tim Shaw RC 4.00 1.50
❑ 185 Kenton Keith RC 5.00 2.00
❑ 186 Tyler Palko RC 5.00 2.00
❑ 187 Mason Crosby RC 5.00 2.00
❑ 188 Pierre Thomas RC 6.00 2.50
❑ 189 Victor Abiamiri RC 5.00 2.00
❑ 190 Zak DeOssie RC 4.00 1.50
❑ 191 Tyler Thigpen RC 5.00 2.00
❑ 192 Tony Ugoh RC 4.00 1.50
❑ 193 Michael Allan RC 3.00 1.25
❑ 194 Martrez Milner RC 4.00 1.50
❑ 195 John Broussard RC 4.00 1.50
❑ 196 Roy Hall RC 5.00 2.00
❑ 197 Matt Gutierrez RC 5.00 2.00
❑ 198 Legedu Naanee RC 4.00 1.50
❑ 199 Derek Stanley RC 4.00 1.50
❑ 200 Quincy Black RC 4.00 1.50
❑ 201 Trent Edwards/99 AU RC 60.00 25.00
❑ 202 Marshawn Lynch/99 AU RC 60.00 30.00
❑ 203 Chris Henry/99 AU RC 30.00 12.00
❑ 204 Paul Williams/299 AU RC 15.00 6.00
❑ 205 Sidney Rice/99 AU RC EXCH 50.00 20.00
❑ 206 Adrian Peterson/99 AU RC 350.00 200.00
❑ 207 Drew Stanton/99 AU RC 40.00 15.00
❑ 208 Calvin Johnson/99 AU RC 120.00 60.00
❑ 209 Yamon Figurs/99 AU RC 30.00 12.00
❑ 210 Troy Smith/99 AU RC EXCH 40.00 15.00
❑ 211 Garrett Wolfe/249 AU RC 25.00 10.00
❑ 212 Greg Olsen/99 AU RC 40.00 15.00
❑ 213 Joe Thomas/99 AU RC 30.00 12.00
❑ 214 Brady Quinn/99 AU RC 120.00 60.00
❑ 215 Ted Ginn Jr./99 AU RC EXCH 50.00 20.00
❑ 216 John Beck/99 AU RC 60.00 25.00
❑ 217 Antonio Pittman/99 AU RC EXCH 25.00 10.00
❑ 218 Robert Meachem/99 AU RC 30.00 12.00
❑ 219 J.Russell/99 AU RC EXCH 100.00 50.00
❑ 220 M.Bush/99 AU RC EXCH 40.00 15.00
❑ 221 Kevin Kolb/99 AU RC 50.00 20.00
❑ 222 Tony Hunt/99 AU RC EXCH 30.00 12.00
❑ 223 Patrick Willis/99 AU RC 50.00 25.00
❑ 224 Jason Hill/249 AU RC 20.00 8.00
❑ 225 Brandon Jackson/99 AU RC 40.00 15.00
❑ 226 David Clowney/299 AU RC 20.00 8.00
❑ 227 Kenny Irons/99 AU RC EXCH 30.00 12.00
❑ 228 Leon Hall/99 AU RC EXCH 25.00 10.00
❑ 229 Dwayne Bowe/99 AU RC 60.00 30.00
❑ 230 Kolby Smith/299 AU RC 40.00 20.00
❑ 231 Steve Smith/99 AU RC EXCH 40.00 20.00
❑ 232 Dwayne Jarrett/99 AU RC 40.00 15.00
❑ 233 Lorenzo Booker/99 AU RC 30.00 12.00
❑ 234 Anthony Gonzalez/99 AU RC 50.00 25.00
❑ 235 J.L.Higgins/99 AU RC 25.00 10.00
❑ 236 Isaiah Stanback/299 AU RC 20.00 8.00
❑ 237 L.Landry/249 AU RC EXCH 25.00 10.00
❑ 238 Paul Posluszny/99 AU RC 40.00 15.00
❑ 239 Brian Leonard/99 AU RC 30.00 12.00
❑ 240 G.Adams/99 AU RC EXCH 30.00 12.00
❑ 241 Cra.Davis/249 AU RC EXCH 20.00 8.00
❑ 242 A.Allison/249 AU RC EXCH 15.00 6.00
❑ 243 D.Wynn/299 AU RC EXCH 20.00 8.00
❑ 244 J.Anderson/249 AU RC EXCH 15.00 6.00
❑ 245 Adam Carriker/99 AU RC 25.00 10.00
❑ 246 Darrelle Revis/99 AU RC 30.00 12.00
❑ 247 Lawrence Timmons/99 AU RC 30.00 12.00
❑ 248 Michael Griffin/299 AU RC 20.00 8.00
❑ 249 Aaron Ross/299 AU RC EXCH 20.00 8.00
❑ 250 Reggie Nelson/99 AU RC 25.00 10.00
❑ 251 B.Meriweather/299 AU RC EXCH 20.00 8.00
❑ 252 Zach Miller/99 AU RC 30.00 12.00
❑ 253 Chris Houston/299 AU RC EXCH 15.00 6.00
❑ 254 I.Alama-Francis/299 AU RC EXCH 20.00 8.00
❑ 255 Laurent Robinson/299 AU RC 15.00 6.00
❑ 256 James Jones/246 AU RC 30.00 12.00
❑ 257 D.Wright/299 AU RC EXCH 15.00 6.00
❑ 258 Chris Davis/249 AU RC EXCH 15.00 6.00
❑ 259 Thomas Clayton/299 AU RC 15.00 6.00
❑ 260 Jordan Palmer/99 AU RC 30.00 12.00
❑ 261 Jordan Kent/299 AU RC EXCH 15.00 6.00
❑ 262 Chansi Stuckey/299 AU RC 15.00 6.00
❑ 263 Nate Ilaoa/299 AU RC 20.00 8.00
❑ 264 Chris Leak/99 AU RC 25.00 10.00
❑ 265 J.Zabransky/99 AU RC EXCH 30.00 12.00
❑ 266 Syndric Steptoe/299 AU RC 15.00 6.00

1991 Pacific

❑ COMPLETE SET (660) 15.00 7.50
❑ COMP.SERIES 1 (550) 8.00 4.00
❑ COMP.FACT.SER.1 (550) 10.00 5.00
❑ COMP.SERIES 2 (110) 8.00 4.00
❑ COMP.FACT.SER.2 (110) 12.00 6.00
❑ COMP.CHECKLIST SET (5) 15.00 7.50
❑ 1 Deion Sanders .40 .15
❑ 2 Steve Broussard .05 .01
❑ 3 Aundray Bruce .05 .01
❑ 4 Rick Bryan .05 .01
❑ 5 John Rade .05 .01
❑ 6 Scott Case .05 .01
❑ 7 Tony Casillas .05 .01
❑ 8 Shawn Collins .05 .01
❑ 9 Darion Conner .05 .01
❑ 10 Tory Epps .05 .01
❑ 11 Bill Fralic .05 .01
❑ 12 Mike Gann .05 .01
❑ 13 Tim Green UER .05 .01
❑ 14 Chris Hinton .05 .01
❑ 15 Houston Hoover UER .05 .01
❑ 16 Chris Miller .10 .02
❑ 17 Andre Rison .10 .02
❑ 18 Mike Rozier .05 .01
❑ 19 Jessie Tuggle .05 .01
❑ 20 Don Beebe .05 .01
❑ 21 Ray Bentley .05 .01
❑ 22 Shane Conlan .05 .01
❑ 23 Kent Hull .05 .01
❑ 24 Mark Kelso .05 .01
❑ 25 James Lofton UER .10 .02
❑ 26 Scott Norwood .05 .01
❑ 27 Andre Reed .10 .02
❑ 28 Leonard Smith .05 .01
❑ 29 Bruce Smith .25 .08
❑ 30 Leon Seals .05 .01
❑ 31 Darryl Talley .05 .01
❑ 32 Steve Tasker .10 .02
❑ 33 Thurman Thomas .25 .08
❑ 34 James Williams .05 .01
❑ 35 Will Wolford .05 .01
❑ 36 Frank Reich .10 .02
❑ 37 Jeff Wright RC .05 .01
❑ 38 Neal Anderson .10 .02
❑ 39 Trace Armstrong .05 .01
❑ 40 Johnny Bailey UER .05 .01
❑ 41 Mark Bortz UER .05 .01
❑ 42 Cap Boso RC .05 .01
❑ 43 Kevin Butler .05 .01
❑ 44 Mark Carrier DB .10 .02
❑ 45 Jim Covert .05 .01
❑ 46 Wendell Davis .05 .01
❑ 47 Richard Dent .10 .02
❑ 48 Shaun Gayle .05 .01
❑ 49 Jim Harbaugh .25 .08
❑ 50 Jay Hilgenberg .05 .01
❑ 51 Brad Muster .05 .01
❑ 52 William Perry .10 .02
❑ 53 Mike Singletary UER .10 .02
❑ 54 Peter Tom Willis .05 .01
❑ 55 Donnell Woolford .05 .01
❑ 56 Steve McMichael .10 .02
❑ 57 Eric Ball .05 .01
❑ 58 Lewis Billups .05 .01
❑ 59 Jim Breech .05 .01
❑ 60 James Brooks .10 .02
❑ 61 Eddie Brown .05 .01
❑ 62 Rickey Dixon .05 .01
❑ 63 Boomer Esiason .10 .02
❑ 64 James Francis .05 .01
❑ 65 David Fulcher .05 .01
❑ 66 David Grant .05 .01
❑ 67 Harold Green UER .05 .01
❑ 68 Rodney Holman .05 .01
❑ 69 Stanford Jennings .05 .01
❑ 70A Tim Krumrie ERR .50 .20
❑ 70B Tim Krumrie COR .30 .10
❑ 71 Tim McGee .05 .01
❑ 72 Anthony Munoz .10 .02
❑ 73 Mitchell Price RC .05 .01
❑ 74 Eric Thomas .05 .01
❑ 75 Ickey Woods .05 .01
❑ 76 Mike Baab .05 .01
❑ 77 Thane Gash .05 .01
[illegible]
❑ 79 Mike Johnson .05 .01
❑ 80 Reggie Langhorne .05 .01
❑ 81 Kevin Mack .05 .01
❑ 82 Clay Matthews .10 .02
❑ 83A Eric Metcalf ERR .50 .20
❑ 83B Eric Metcalf COR .30 .10
❑ 84 Frank Minnifield .05 .01
❑ 85 Mike Oliphant .05 .01
❑ 86 Mike Pagel .05 .01
❑ 87 John Talley .05 .01
❑ 88 Lawyer Tillman .05 .01
❑ 89 Gregg Rakoczy UER .05 .01
❑ 90 Bryan Wagner .05 .01
❑ 91 Rob Burnett RC .10 .02
❑ 92 Tommie Agee .05 .01
❑ 93 Troy Aikman UER .75 .30
❑ 94A Bill Bates ERR .50 .20
❑ 94B Bill Bates COR .30 .10
❑ 95 Jack Del Rio .10 .02
❑ 96 Issiac Holt UER .05 .01
❑ 97 Michael Irvin .25 .08
❑ 98 Jim Jeffcoat UER .05 .01
❑ 99 Jimmie Jones .05 .01
❑ 100 Kelvin Martin .05 .01
❑ 101 Nate Newton .10 .02
❑ 102 Danny Noonan .05 .01
❑ 103 Ken Norton Jr. .10 .02
❑ 104 Jay Novacek .25 .08
❑ 105 Mike Saxon .05 .01
❑ 106 Derrick Shepard .05 .01
❑ 107 Emmitt Smith 2.50 1.00
❑ 108 Daniel Stubbs .05 .01
❑ 109 Tony Tolbert .05 .01
❑ 110 Alexander Wright .05 .01
❑ 111 Steve Atwater .05 .01
❑ 112 Melvin Bratton .05 .01
❑ 113 Tyrone Braxton UER .05 .01
❑ 114 Alphonso Carreker .05 .01
❑ 115 John Elway 1.25 .50
❑ 116 Simon Fletcher .05 .01
❑ 117 Bobby Humphrey .05 .01
❑ 118 Mark Jackson .05 .01
❑ 119 Vance Johnson .05 .01
❑ 120 Greg Kragen UER .05 .01
❑ 121 Karl Mecklenburg UER .05 .01
❑ 122A Orsen Mobley ERR .50 .20
❑ 122B Orson Mobley COR .10 .02
❑ 123 Alton Montgomery .05 .01
❑ 124 Ricky Nattiel .05 .01
❑ 125 Steve Sewell .05 .01
❑ 126 Shannon Sharpe .50 .20
❑ 127 Dennis Smith .05 .01
❑ 128A Andre Townsend RC ERR .50 .20
❑ 128B Andre Townsend RC COR .10 .02
❑ 129 Mike Horan .05 .01
❑ 130 Jerry Ball .05 .01
❑ 131 Bennie Blades .05 .01
❑ 132 Lomas Brown .05 .01
❑ 133 Jeff Campbell UER .05 .01
❑ 134 Robert Clark .05 .01
❑ 135 Michael Cofer .05 .01
❑ 136 Dennis Gibson .05 .01
❑ 137 Mel Gray .10 .02
❑ 138 LeRoy Irvin UER .05 .01
❑ 139 George Jamison RC .05 .01
❑ 140 Richard Johnson .05 .01
❑ 141 Eddie Murray .05 .01
❑ 142 Dan Owens .05 .01
❑ 143 Rodney Peete .10 .02
❑ 144 Barry Sanders 1.25 .50
❑ 145 Chris Spielman .10 .02
❑ 146 Marc Spindler .05 .01
❑ 147 Andre Ware .10 .02
❑ 148 William White .05 .01

❑ 149 Tony Bennett .10 .02
❑ 150 Robert Brown .05 .01
❑ 151 LeRoy Butler .10 .02
❑ 152 Anthony Dilweg .05 .01
❑ 153 Michael Haddix .05 .01
❑ 154 Ron Hallstrom .05 .01
❑ 155 Tim Harris .05 .01
❑ 156 Johnny Holland .05 .01
❑ 157 Chris Jacke .05 .01
❑ 158 Perry Kemp .05 .01
❑ 159 Mark Lee .05 .01
❑ 160 Don Majkowski .05 .01
❑ 161 Tony Mandarich UER .05 .01
❑ 162 Mark Murphy .05 .01
❑ 163 Brian Noble .05 .01
❑ 164 Shawn Patterson .05 .01
❑ 165 Jeff Query .05 .01
❑ 166 Sterling Sharpe .25 .08
❑ 167 Darrell Thompson .05 .01
❑ 168 Ed West .05 .01
❑ 169 Ray Childress UER .05 .01
❑ 170A Cris Dishman RC ERR Chris .10 .02
❑ 170B Cris Dishman RC ERR/COR .10 .02
❑ 170C Cris Dishman RC COR .10 .02
❑ 171 Curtis Duncan .05 .01
❑ 172 William Fuller .10 .02
❑ 173 Ernest Givins UER .10 .02
❑ 174 Drew Hill .05 .01
❑ 175A Haywood Jeffires ERR .25 .08
❑ 175B Haywood Jeffires COR .25 .08
❑ 176 Sean Jones .10 .02
❑ 177 Lamar Lathon .05 .01
❑ 178 Bruce Matthews .10 .02
❑ 179 Bubba McDowell .05 .01
❑ 180 Johnny Meads .05 .01
❑ 181 Warren Moon UER .25 .08
❑ 182 Mike Munchak .10 .02
❑ 183 Allen Pinkett .05 .01
❑ 184 Dean Steinkuhler UER .05 .01
❑ 185 Lorenzo White UER .05 .01
❑ 186A John Grimsley ERR .50 .20
❑ 186B John Grimsley COR .10 .02
❑ 187 Pat Beach .05 .01
❑ 188 Albert Bentley .05 .01
❑ 189 Dean Biasucci .05 .01
❑ 190 Duane Bickett .05 .01
❑ 191 Bill Brooks .05 .01
❑ 192 Eugene Daniel .05 .01
❑ 193 Jeff George .25 .08
❑ 194 Jon Hand .05 .01
❑ 195 Jeff Herrod .05 .01
❑ 196A Jessie Hester ERR Jesse .30 .10
❑ 196B Jessie Hester ERR .10 .02
❑ 197 Mike Prior .05 .01
❑ 198 Stacey Simmons .05 .01
❑ 199 Rohn Stark .05 .01
❑ 200 Pat Tomberlin .05 .01
❑ 201 Clarence Verdin .05 .01
❑ 202 Keith Taylor .05 .01
❑ 203 Jack Trudeau .05 .01
❑ 204 Chip Banks .05 .01
❑ 205 John Alt .05 .01
❑ 206 Deron Cherry .05 .01
❑ 207 Steve DeBerg .05 .01
❑ 208 Tim Grunhard .05 .01
❑ 209 Albert Lewis .05 .01
❑ 210 Nick Lowery UER .05 .01
❑ 211 Bill Maas .05 .01
❑ 212 Chris Martin .05 .01
❑ 213 Todd McNair .05 .01
❑ 214 Christian Okoye .05 .01
❑ 215 Stephone Paige .05 .01
❑ 216 Steve Pelluer .05 .01
❑ 217 Kevin Porter .05 .01
❑ 218 Kevin Ross .05 .01
❑ 219 Dan Saleaumua .05 .01
❑ 220 Neil Smith .25 .08
❑ 221 David Szott UER .05 .01
❑ 222 Derrick Thomas .25 .08
❑ 223 Barry Word .05 .01
❑ 224 Percy Snow .05 .01
❑ 225 Marcus Allen .25 .08
❑ 226 Eddie Anderson UER .05 .01
❑ 227 Steve Beuerlein UER .10 .02
❑ 228A Tim Brown ERR NPO .25 .08
❑ 228B Tim Brown COR .25 .08
❑ 229 Scott Davis .05 .01
❑ 230 Mike Dyal .05 .01
❑ 231 Mervyn Fernandez UER .05 .01
❑ 232 Willie Gault UER .05 .01
❑ 233 Ethan Horton UER .05 .01
❑ 234 Bo Jackson UER .30 .10
❑ 235 Howie Long .25 .08
❑ 236 Terry McDaniel .05 .01
❑ 237 Max Montoya .05 .01
❑ 238 Don Mosebar .05 .01
❑ 239 Jay Schroeder .05 .01
❑ 240 Steve Smith .05 .01
❑ 241 Greg Townsend .05 .01
❑ 242 Aaron Wallace .05 .01
❑ 243 Lionel Washington .05 .01
❑ 244A Steve Wisniewski ERR .10 .02
❑ 244B Steve Wisniewski ERR/COR .75 .30
❑ 244C Steve Wisniewski COR .10 .02
❑ 245 Flipper Anderson .05 .01
❑ 246 Latin Berry RC .05 .01
❑ 247 Robert Delpino .05 .01
❑ 248 Marcus Dupree .05 .01
❑ 249 Henry Ellard .10 .02
❑ 250 Jim Everett .10 .02
❑ 251 Cleveland Gary .05 .01
❑ 252 Jerry Gray .05 .01
❑ 253 Kevin Greene .10 .02
❑ 254 Pete Holohan UER .05 .01
❑ 255 Buford McGee .05 .01
❑ 256 Tom Newberry .05 .01
❑ 257A Irv Pankey ERR .50 .20
❑ 257B Irv Pankey COR .10 .02
❑ 258 Jackie Slater .05 .01
❑ 259 Doug Smith .05 .01
❑ 260 Frank Stams .05 .01
❑ 261 Michael Stewart .05 .01
❑ 262 Fred Strickland .05 .01
❑ 263 J.B. Brown UER .05 .01
❑ 264 Mark Clayton .10 .02
❑ 265 Jeff Cross .05 .01
❑ 266 Mark Dennis RC .05 .01
❑ 267 Mark Duper .10 .02
❑ 268 Ferrell Edmunds .05 .01
❑ 269 Dan Marino 1.25 .50
❑ 270 John Offerdahl .05 .01
❑ 271 Louis Oliver .05 .01
❑ 272 Tony Paige .05 .01
❑ 273 Reggie Roby .05 .01
❑ 274 Sammie Smith .05 .01
❑ 275 Keith Sims .05 .01
❑ 276 Brian Sochia .05 .01
❑ 277 Pete Stoyanovich .05 .01
❑ 278 Richmond Webb .05 .01
❑ 279 Jarvis Williams .05 .01
❑ 280 Tim McKyer .05 .01
❑ 281A Jim C. Jensen ERR .50 .20
❑ 281B Jim C. Jensen COR .10 .02
❑ 282 Scott Secules RC .05 .01
❑ 283 Ray Berry .05 .01
❑ 284 Joey Browner UER .05 .01
❑ 285 Anthony Carter .10 .02
❑ 286A Cris Carter ERR Chris .50 .20
❑ 286B Cris Carter ERR/COR Chris 1.50 .60
❑ 286C Cris Carter COR .50 .20
❑ 287 Chris Doleman .05 .01
❑ 288 Mark Dusbabek UER .05 .01
❑ 289 Hassan Jones .05 .01
❑ 290 Steve Jordan .05 .01
❑ 291 Carl Lee .05 .01
❑ 292 Kirk Lowdermilk .05 .01
❑ 293 Randall McDaniel .05 .01
❑ 294 Mike Merriweather .05 .01
❑ 295A Keith Millard UER .20 .07
❑ 295B Keith Millard COR 2.50 1.00
❑ 296 Al Noga UER .05 .01
❑ 297 Scott Studwell UER .05 .01
❑ 298 Henry Thomas .05 .01
❑ 299 Herschel Walker .10 .02
❑ 300 Gary Zimmerman .05 .01
❑ 301 Rich Gannon .25 .08
❑ 302 Wade Wilson UER .10 .02
❑ 303 Vincent Brown .05 .01
❑ 304 Marv Cook .05 .01
❑ 305 Hart Lee Dykes .05 .01
❑ 306 Irving Fryar .10 .02
❑ 307 Tommy Hodson UER .05 .01
❑ 308 Maurice Hurst .05 .01
❑ 309 Ronnie Lippett UER .05 .01
❑ 310 Fred Marion .05 .01
❑ 311 Greg McMurtry .05 .01
❑ 312 Johnny Rembert .05 .01
❑ 313 Chris Singleton .05 .01
❑ 314 Ed Reynolds .05 .01
❑ 315 Andre Tippett .05 .01
❑ 316 Garin Veris .05 .01
❑ 317 Brent Williams .05 .01
❑ 318A John Stephens ERR .10 .02
❑ 318B John Stephens ERR/COR .75 .30
❑ 318C John Stephens COR .10 .02
❑ 319 Sammy Martin .05 .01
❑ 320 Bruce Armstrong .05 .01
❑ 321A Morten Andersen ERR .30 .10
❑ 321B Morten Andersen ERR/COR .75 .30
❑ 321C Morten Andersen COR .10 .02
❑ 322 Gene Atkins UER .05 .01
❑ 323 Vince Buck .05 .01
❑ 324 John Fourcade .05 .01
❑ 325 Kevin Haverdink .05 .01
❑ 326 Bobby Hebert .05 .01
❑ 327 Craig Heyward .10 .02
❑ 328 Dalton Hilliard .05 .01
❑ 329 Rickey Jackson .05 .01
❑ 330A Vaughan Johnson ERR .20 .07
❑ 330B Vaughan Johnson COR 2.50 1.00
❑ 331 Eric Martin .05 .01
❑ 332 Wayne Martin .05 .01
❑ 333 Rueben Mayes UER .05 .01
❑ 334 Sam Mills .05 .01
❑ 335 Brett Perriman .25 .08
❑ 336 Pat Swilling .10 .02
❑ 337 Renaldo Turnbull .05 .01
❑ 338 Lonzell Hill .05 .01
❑ 339 Steve Walsh .05 .01
❑ 340 Carl Banks UER .05 .01
❑ 341 Mark Bavaro UER .05 .01
❑ 342 Maurice Carthon .05 .01
❑ 343 Pat Harlow RC .05 .01
❑ 344 Eric Dorsey .05 .01
❑ 345 John Elliott .05 .01
❑ 346 Rodney Hampton .25 .08
❑ 347 Jeff Hostetler .10 .02
❑ 348 Erik Howard UER .05 .01
❑ 349 Pepper Johnson .05 .01
❑ 350A Sean Landeta ERR .10 .02
❑ 350B Sean Landeta COR .50 .20
❑ 351 Leonard Marshall .05 .01
❑ 352 Dave Meggett .10 .02
❑ 353A Bart Oates ERR .10 .02
❑ 353B Bart Oates ERR/COR .75 .30
❑ 353C Bart Oates COR .10 .02
❑ 354 Gary Reasons .05 .01
❑ 355 Phil Simms .10 .02
❑ 356 Lawrence Taylor .25 .08
❑ 357 Reyna Thompson .05 .01
❑ 358 Brian Williams OL UER .05 .01
❑ 359 Matt Bahr .05 .01
❑ 360 Mark Ingram .10 .02
❑ 361 Brad Baxter .05 .01
❑ 362 Mark Boyer .05 .01
❑ 363 Dennis Byrd .05 .01
❑ 364 Dave Cadigan UER .05 .01
❑ 365 Kyle Clifton .05 .01
❑ 366 James Hasty .05 .01
❑ 367 Joe Kelly UER .05 .01
❑ 368 Jeff Lageman .05 .01
❑ 369 Pat Leahy UER .05 .01
❑ 370 Terance Mathis .10 .02
❑ 371 Erik McMillan .05 .01
❑ 372 Rob Moore .25 .08
❑ 373 Ken O'Brien .05 .01
❑ 374 Tony Stargell .05 .01
❑ 375 Jim Sweeney UER .05 .01
❑ 376 Al Toon .10 .02
❑ 377 Johnny Hector .05 .01
❑ 378 Jeff Criswell .05 .01
❑ 379 Mike Haight RC .05 .01
❑ 380 Troy Benson .05 .01
❑ 381 Eric Allen .05 .01
❑ 382 Fred Barnett .25 .08
❑ 383 Jerome Brown .05 .01
❑ 384 Keith Byars .05 .01
❑ 385 Randall Cunningham .25 .08
❑ 386 Byron Evans .05 .01
❑ 387 Wes Hopkins .05 .01
❑ 388 Keith Jackson .10 .02
❑ 389 Seth Joyner UER .10 .02
❑ 390 Bobby Wilson RC .05 .01
❑ 391 Heath Sherman .05 .01
❑ 392 Clyde Simmons UER .05 .01
❑ 393 Ben Smith .05 .01
❑ 394 Andre Waters .05 .01

❑ 395 Reggie White UER .25 .08
❑ 396 Calvin Williams .10 .02
❑ 397 Al Harris .05 .01
❑ 398 Anthony Toney .05 .01
❑ 399 Mike Quick .05 .01
❑ 400 Anthony Bell .05 .01
❑ 401 Rich Camarillo .05 .01
❑ 402 Roy Green .05 .01
❑ 403 Ken Harvey .10 .02
❑ 404 Eric Hill .05 .01
❑ 405 Garth Jax RC UER .05 .01
❑ 406 Ernie Jones .05 .01
❑ 407A Cedric Mack ERR .20 .07
❑ 407B Cedric Mack COR 2.50 1.00
❑ 408 Dexter Manley .05 .01
❑ 409 Tim McDonald .05 .01
❑ 410 Freddie Joe Nunn .05 .01
❑ 411 Ricky Proehl .05 .01
❑ 412 Moe Gardner RC .05 .01
❑ 413 Timm Rosenbach .05 .01
❑ 414 Luis Sharpe UER .05 .01
❑ 415 Vai Sikahema UER .05 .01
❑ 416 Anthony Thompson .05 .01
❑ 417 Ron Wolfley UER .05 .01
❑ 418 Lonnie Young .05 .01
❑ 419 Gary Anderson K .05 .01
❑ 420 Bubby Brister .05 .01
❑ 421 Thomas Everett .05 .01
❑ 422 Eric Green .05 .01
❑ 423 Delton Hall .05 .01
❑ 424 Bryan Hinkle .05 .01
❑ 425 Merril Hoge .05 .01
❑ 426 Carnell Lake .05 .01
❑ 427 Louis Lipps .05 .01
❑ 428 David Little .05 .01
❑ 429 Greg Lloyd .25 .08
❑ 430 Mike Mularkey .05 .01
❑ 431 Keith Willis UER .05 .01
❑ 432 Dwayne Woodruff .05 .01
❑ 433 Rod Woodson .25 .08
❑ 434 Tim Worley .05 .01
❑ 435 Warren Williams .05 .01
❑ 436 Terry Long UER .05 .01
❑ 437 Martin Bayless .05 .01
❑ 438 Jarrod Bunch RC .05 .01
❑ 439 Marion Butts .10 .02
❑ 440 Gill Byrd UER .05 .01
❑ 441 Arthur Cox .05 .01
❑ 442 John Friesz .25 .08
❑ 443 Leo Goeas .05 .01
❑ 444 Burt Grossman .05 .01
❑ 445 Courtney Hall UER .05 .01
❑ 446 Ronnie Harmon .05 .01
❑ 447 Nate Lewis RC .05 .01
❑ 448 Anthony Miller .10 .02
❑ 449 Leslie O'Neal .10 .02
❑ 450 Gary Plummer .05 .01
❑ 451 Junior Seau .25 .08
❑ 452 Billy Ray Smith .05 .01
❑ 453 Billy Joe Tolliver .05 .01
❑ 454 Broderick Thompson .05 .01
❑ 455 Lee Williams .05 .01
❑ 456 Michael Carter .05 .01
❑ 457 Mike Cofer .05 .01
❑ 458 Kevin Fagan .05 .01
❑ 459 Charles Haley .10 .02
❑ 460 Pierce Holt .05 .01
❑ 461 Johnnie Jackson UER RC .05 .01
❑ 462 Brent Jones .25 .08
❑ 463 Guy McIntyre .05 .01
❑ 464 Joe Montana 1.25 .50
❑ 465A Bubba Paris ERR .10 .02
❑ 465B Bubba Paris ERR/COR .50 .20
❑ 465C Bubba Paris COR .10 .02
❑ 466 Tom Rathman UER .05 .01
❑ 467 Jerry Rice UER .75 .30
❑ 468 Mike Sherrard .05 .01
❑ 469 John Taylor UER .10 .02
❑ 470 Steve Young .75 .30
❑ 471 Dennis Brown .05 .01
❑ 472 Dexter Carter .05 .01
❑ 473 Bill Romanowski .05 .01
❑ 474 Dave Waymer .05 .01
❑ 475 Robert Blackmon .05 .01
❑ 476 Derrick Fenner .05 .01
❑ 477 Nesby Glasgow UER .05 .01
❑ 478 Jacob Green .05 .01
❑ 479 Andy Heck .05 .01
❑ 480 Norm Johnson UER .05 .01
❑ 481 Tommy Kane .05 .01
❑ 482 Cortez Kennedy .25 .08
❑ 483A Dave Krieg ERR .20 .07
❑ 483B Dave Krieg COR 2.50 1.00
❑ 484 Bryan Millard .05 .01
❑ 485 Joe Nash .05 .01
❑ 486 Rufus Porter .05 .01
❑ 487 Eugene Robinson .05 .01
❑ 488 Mike Tice RC .05 .01
❑ 489 Chris Warren .25 .08
❑ 490 John L. Williams UER .05 .01
❑ 491 Terry Wooden .05 .01
❑ 492 Tony Woods .05 .01
❑ 493 Brian Blades .10 .02
❑ 494 Paul Skansi .05 .01
❑ 495 Gary Anderson RB .05 .01
❑ 496 Mark Carrier WR .25 .08
❑ 497 Chris Chandler .25 .08
❑ 498 Steve Christie .05 .01
❑ 499 Reggie Cobb .05 .01
❑ 500 Reuben Davis .05 .01
❑ 501 Willie Drewrey UER .05 .01
❑ 502 Randy Grimes .05 .01
❑ 503 Paul Gruber .05 .01
❑ 504 Wayne Haddix .05 .01
❑ 505 Ron Hall .05 .01
❑ 506 Harry Hamilton .05 .01
❑ 507 Bruce Hill .05 .01
❑ 508 Eugene Marve .05 .01
❑ 509 Keith McCants .05 .01
❑ 510 Winston Moss .05 .01
❑ 511 Kevin Murphy .05 .01
❑ 512 Mark Robinson .05 .01
❑ 513 Vinny Testaverde .10 .02
❑ 514 Broderick Thomas .05 .01
❑ 515A Jeff Bostic UER .10 .02
❑ 515B Jeff Bostic UER .10 .02
❑ 516 Todd Bowles .05 .01
❑ 517 Earnest Byner .05 .01
❑ 518 Gary Clark .25 .08
❑ 519 Craig Erickson RC .25 .08
❑ 520 Darryl Grant .05 .01
❑ 521 Darrell Green .05 .01
❑ 522 Russ Grimm .05 .01
❑ 523 Stan Humphries .25 .08
❑ 524 Joe Jacoby UER .05 .01
❑ 525 Jim Lachey .05 .01
❑ 526 Chip Lohmiller .05 .01
❑ 527 Charles Mann .05 .01
❑ 528 Wilber Marshall .05 .01
❑ 529A Art Monk .10 .02
❑ 529B Art Monk .10 .02
❑ 530 Tracy Rocker .05 .01
❑ 531 Mark Rypien .10 .02
❑ 532 Ricky Sanders UER .05 .01
❑ 533 Alvin Walton UER .05 .01
❑ 534 Todd Marinovich RC UER .05 .01
❑ 535 Mike Dumas RC .05 .01
❑ 536A Russell Maryland RC ERR .25 .08
❑ 536B Russell Maryland RC COR .25 .08
❑ 537 Eric Turner RC UER .10 .02
❑ 538 Ernie Mills RC .10 .02
❑ 539 Ed King RC .05 .01
❑ 540 Mike Stonebreaker .05 .01
❑ 541 Chris Zorich RC .25 .08
❑ 542A Mike Croel RC ERR .05 .01
❑ 542B Mike Croel RC COR .05 .01
❑ 543 Eric Moten RC .05 .01
❑ 544 Dan McGwire RC .05 .01
❑ 545 Keith Cash RC .05 .01
❑ 546 Kenny Walker RC UER .05 .01
❑ 547 Leroy Hoard UER .10 .02
❑ 548 Luis Cristobal UER .05 .01
❑ 549 Stacy Danley .05 .01
❑ 550 Todd Lyght RC .05 .01
❑ 551 Brett Favre RC 8.00 3.00
❑ 552 Mike Pritchard RC .25 .08
❑ 553 Moe Gardner .05 .01
❑ 554 Tim McKyer .05 .01
❑ 555 Erric Pegram RC .25 .08
❑ 556 Norm Johnson .05 .01
❑ 557 Bruce Pickens RC .05 .01
❑ 558 Henry Jones RC .10 .02
❑ 559 Phil Hansen RC .05 .01
❑ 560 Cornelius Bennett .10 .02
❑ 561 Stan Thomas .05 .01
❑ 562 Chris Zorich .10 .02
❑ 563 Anthony Morgan RC .05 .01
❑ 564 Darren Lewis RC .05 .01
❑ 565 Mike Stonebreaker .05 .01
❑ 566 Alfred Williams RC .05 .01
❑ 567 Lamar Rogers RC .05 .01
❑ 568 Erik Wilhelm RC UER .05 .01
❑ 569 Ed King .05 .01
❑ 570 Michael Jackson RC WR .25 .08
❑ 571 James Jones RC DT .05 .01
❑ 572 Russell Maryland .25 .08
❑ 573 Dixon Edwards RC .05 .01
❑ 574 Darrick Brownlow RC .05 .01
❑ 575 Larry Brown RC DB .10 .02
❑ 576 Mike Croel .05 .01
❑ 577 Keith Traylor RC .05 .01
❑ 578 Kenny Walker .05 .01
❑ 579 Reggie Johnson RC .05 .01
❑ 580 Herman Moore RC .25 .08
❑ 581 Kelvin Pritchett RC .10 .02
❑ 582 Kevin Scott RC .05 .01
❑ 583 Vinnie Clark RC .05 .01
❑ 584 Esera Tuaolo RC .05 .01
❑ 585 Don Davey .05 .01
❑ 586 Blair Kiel RC .05 .01
❑ 587 Mike Dumas .05 .01
❑ 588 Darryll Lewis RC .10 .02
❑ 589 John Flannery RC .05 .01
❑ 590 Kevin Donnalley RC .05 .01
❑ 591 Shane Curry .05 .01
❑ 592 Mark Vander Poel RC .05 .01
❑ 593 Dave McCloughan .05 .01
❑ 594 Mel Agee RC .05 .01
❑ 595 Kerry Cash RC .05 .01
❑ 596 Harvey Williams RC .25 .08
❑ 597 Joe Valerio .05 .01
❑ 598 Tim Barnett RC UER .05 .01
❑ 599 Todd Marinovich .10 .02
❑ 600 Nick Bell RC .05 .01
❑ 601 Roger Craig .10 .02
❑ 602 Ronnie Lott .10 .02
❑ 603 Mike Jones RC LB .05 .01
❑ 604 Todd Lyght .05 .01
❑ 605 Roman Phifer RC .05 .01
❑ 606 David Lang RC .05 .01
❑ 607 Aaron Craver RC .05 .01
❑ 608 Mark Higgs RC .05 .01
❑ 609 Chris Green .05 .01
❑ 610 Randy Baldwin RC .05 .01
❑ 611 Pat Harlow .05 .01
❑ 612 Leonard Russell RC .25 .08
❑ 613 Jerome Henderson RC .05 .01
❑ 614 Scott Zolak RC .05 .01
❑ 615 Jon Vaughn RC .05 .01
❑ 616 Harry Colon RC .05 .01
❑ 617 Wesley Carroll RC .05 .01
❑ 618 Quinn Early .10 .02
❑ 619 Reginald Jones RC .05 .01
❑ 620 Jarrod Bunch .05 .01
❑ 621 Kanavis McGhee RC .05 .01
❑ 622 Ed McCaffrey RC 2.00 .75
❑ 623 Browning Nagle RC .05 .01
❑ 624 Mo Lewis RC .10 .02
❑ 625 Blair Thomas .05 .01
❑ 626 Antone Davis RC .05 .01
❑ 627 Jim McMahon .10 .02
❑ 628 Scott Kowalkowski RC .05 .01
❑ 629 Brad Goebel RC .05 .01
❑ 630 William Thomas RC .05 .01
❑ 631 Eric Swann RC .25 .08
❑ 632 Mike Jones DE RC .05 .01
❑ 633 Aeneas Williams RC .25 .08
❑ 634 Dexter Davis RC .05 .01
❑ 635 Tom Tupa UER .05 .01
❑ 636 Johnny Johnson .05 .01
❑ 637 Randal Hill RC .10 .02
❑ 638 Jeff Graham RC WR .25 .08
❑ 639 Ernie Mills .05 .01
❑ 640 Adrian Cooper RC .05 .01
❑ 641 Stanley Richard RC .05 .01
❑ 642 Eric Bieniemy RC .05 .01
❑ 643 Eric Moten .05 .01
❑ 644 Shawn Jefferson RC .10 .02
❑ 645 Ted Washington RC .05 .01
❑ 646 John Johnson RC .05 .01
❑ 647 Dan McGwire .05 .01
❑ 648 Doug Thomas RC .05 .01
❑ 649 David Daniels RC .05 .01
❑ 650 John Kasay RC .10 .02
❑ 651 Jeff Kemp .05 .01
❑ 652 Charles McRae RC .05 .01
❑ 653 Lawrence Dawsey RC .10 .02

❑ 654 Robert Wilson RC	.05	.01
❑ 655 Dexter Manley	.05	.01
❑ 656 Chuck Weatherspoon	.05	.01
❑ 657 Tim Ryan G RC	.05	.01
❑ 658 Bobby Wilson	.05	.01
❑ 659 Ricky Ervins RC	.10	.02
❑ 660 Matt Millen	.10	.02

1992 Pacific

❑ COMPLETE SET (660)	15.00	6.00
❑ COMP.FACT.SET (690)	25.00	10.00
❑ COMP.SERIES 1 (330)	8.00	3.00
❑ COMP.SERIES 2 (330)	8.00	3.00
❑ COMP.CHECKLIST SET (5)	3.00	1.50
❑ 1 Steve Broussard	.05	.01
❑ 2 Darion Conner	.05	.01
❑ 3 Tory Epps	.05	.01
❑ 4 Michael Haynes	.10	.02
❑ 5 Chris Hinton	.05	.01
❑ 6 Mike Kenn	.05	.01
❑ 7 Tim McKyer	.05	.01
❑ 8 Chris Miller	.10	.02
❑ 9 Erric Pegram	.10	.02
❑ 10 Mike Pritchard	.10	.02
❑ 11 Moe Gardner	.05	.01
❑ 12 Tim Green	.05	.01
❑ 13 Norm Johnson	.05	.01
❑ 14 Don Beebe	.05	.01
❑ 15 Cornelius Bennett	.10	.02
❑ 16 Al Edwards	.05	.01
❑ 17 Mark Kelso	.05	.01
❑ 18 James Lofton	.10	.02
❑ 19 Frank Reich	.10	.02
❑ 20 Leon Seals	.05	.01
❑ 21 Darryl Talley	.05	.01
❑ 22 Thurman Thomas	.25	.08
❑ 23 Kent Hull	.05	.01
❑ 24 Jeff Wright	.05	.01
❑ 25 Nate Odomes	.05	.01
❑ 26 Carwell Gardner	.05	.01
❑ 27 Neal Anderson	.05	.01
❑ 28 Mark Carrier DB	.05	.01
❑ 29 Johnny Bailey	.05	.01
❑ 30 Jim Harbaugh	.25	.08
❑ 31 Jay Hilgenberg	.05	.01
❑ 32 William Perry	.10	.02
❑ 33 Wendell Davis	.05	.01
❑ 34 Donnell Woolford	.05	.01
❑ 35 Keith Van Horne	.05	.01
❑ 36 Shaun Gayle	.05	.01
❑ 37 Tom Waddle	.05	.01
❑ 38 Chris Zorich	.10	.02
❑ 39 Tom Thayer	.05	.01
❑ 40 Rickey Dixon	.05	.01
❑ 41 James Francis	.05	.01
❑ 42 David Fulcher	.05	.01
❑ 43 Reggie Rembert	.05	.01
❑ 44 Anthony Munoz	.10	.02
❑ 45 Harold Green	.05	.01
❑ 46 Mitchell Price	.05	.01
❑ 47 Rodney Holman	.05	.01
❑ 48 Bruce Kozerski	.05	.01
❑ 49 Bruce Reimers	.05	.01
❑ 50 Erik Wilhelm	.05	.01
❑ 51 Harlon Barnett	.05	.01
❑ 52 Mike Johnson	.05	.01
❑ 53 Brian Brennan	.05	.01
❑ 54 Ed King	.05	.01
❑ 55 Reggie Langhorne	.05	.01
❑ 56 James Jones DT	.05	.01
❑ 57 Mike Baab	.05	.01
❑ 58 Dan Fike	.05	.01
❑ 59 Frank Minnifield	.05	.01
❑ 60 Clay Matthews	.10	.02
❑ 61 Kevin Mack	.05	.01
❑ 62 Tony Casillas	.05	.01
❑ 63 Jay Novacek	.10	.02
❑ 64 Larry Brown DB	.05	.01
❑ 65 Michael Irvin	.25	.08
❑ 66 Jack Del Rio	.05	.01
❑ 67 Ken Willis	.05	.01
❑ 68 Emmitt Smith	1.50	.60
❑ 69 Alan Veingrad	.05	.01
❑ 70 John Gesek	.05	.01
❑ 71 Steve Beuerlein	.10	.02
❑ 72 Vinson Smith RC	.05	.01
❑ 73 Steve Atwater	.05	.01
❑ 74 Mike Croel	.05	.01
❑ 75 John Elway	1.25	.50
❑ 76 Gaston Green	.05	.01
❑ 77 Mike Horan	.05	.01
❑ 78 Vance Johnson	.05	.01
❑ 79 Karl Mecklenburg	.05	.01
❑ 80 Shannon Sharpe	.25	.08
❑ 81 David Treadwell	.05	.01
❑ 82 Kenny Walker	.05	.01
❑ 83 Greg Lewis	.05	.01
❑ 84 Shawn Moore	.05	.01
❑ 85 Alton Montgomery	.05	.01
❑ 86 Michael Young	.05	.01
❑ 87 Jerry Ball	.05	.01
❑ 88 Bennie Blades	.05	.01
❑ 89 Mel Gray	.10	.02
❑ 90 Herman Moore	.25	.08
❑ 91 Erik Kramer	.10	.02
❑ 92 Willie Green	.05	.01
❑ 93 George Jamison	.05	.01
❑ 94 Chris Spielman	.10	.02
❑ 95 Kelvin Pritchett	.05	.01
❑ 96 William White	.05	.01
❑ 97 Mike Utley	.10	.02
❑ 98 Tony Bennett	.05	.01
❑ 99 LeRoy Butler	.05	.01
❑ 100 Vinnie Clark	.05	.01
❑ 101 Ron Hallstrom	.05	.01
❑ 102 Chris Jacke	.05	.01
❑ 103 Tony Mandarich	.05	.01
❑ 104 Sterling Sharpe	.25	.08
❑ 105 Don Majkowski	.05	.01
❑ 106 Johnny Holland	.05	.01
❑ 107 Esera Tuaolo	.05	.01
❑ 108 Darrell Thompson	.05	.01
❑ 109 Bubba McDowell	.05	.01
❑ 110 Curtis Duncan	.05	.01
❑ 111 Lamar Lathon	.05	.01
❑ 112 Drew Hill	.05	.01
❑ 113 Bruce Matthews	.05	.01
❑ 114 Bo Orlando RC	.05	.01
❑ 115 Don Maggs	.05	.01
❑ 116 Lorenzo White	.05	.01
❑ 117 Ernest Givins	.10	.02
❑ 118 Tony Jones WR	.05	.01
❑ 119 Dean Steinkuhler	.05	.01
❑ 120 Dean Biasucci	.05	.01
❑ 121 Duane Bickett	.05	.01
❑ 122 Bill Brooks	.05	.01
❑ 123 Ken Clark	.05	.01
❑ 124 Jessie Hester	.05	.01
❑ 125 Anthony Johnson	.10	.02
❑ 126 Chip Banks	.05	.01
❑ 127 Mike Prior	.05	.01
❑ 128 Rohn Stark	.05	.01
❑ 129 Jeff Herrod	.05	.01
❑ 130 Clarence Verdin	.05	.01
❑ 131 Tim Manoa	.05	.01
❑ 132 Brian Baldinger RC	.05	.01
❑ 133 Tim Barnett	.05	.01
❑ 134 J.J. Birden	.05	.01
❑ 135 Deron Cherry	.05	.01
❑ 136 Steve DeBerg	.05	.01
❑ 137 Nick Lowery	.05	.01
❑ 138 Todd McNair	.05	.01
❑ 139 Christian Okoye	.05	.01
❑ 140 Mark Vlasic	.05	.01
❑ 141 Dan Saleaumua	.05	.01
❑ 142 Neil Smith	.25	.08
❑ 143 Robb Thomas	.05	.01
❑ 144 Eddie Anderson	.05	.01
❑ 145 Nick Bell	.05	.01
❑ 146 Tim Brown	.25	.08
❑ 147 Roger Craig	.10	.02
❑ 148 Jeff Gossett	.05	.01
❑ 149 Ethan Horton	.05	.01
❑ 150 Jamie Holland	.05	.01
❑ 151 Jeff Jaeger	.05	.01
❑ 152 Todd Marinovich	.05	.01
❑ 153 Marcus Allen	.25	.08
❑ 154 Steve Smith	.05	.01
❑ 155 Flipper Anderson	.05	.01
❑ 156 Robert Delpino	.05	.01
❑ 157 Cleveland Gary	.05	.01
❑ 158 Kevin Greene	.10	.02
❑ 159 Dale Hatcher	.05	.01
❑ 160 Duval Love	.05	.01
❑ 161 Ron Brown	.05	.01
❑ 162 Jackie Slater	.05	.01
❑ 163 Doug Smith	.05	.01
❑ 164 Aaron Cox	.05	.01
❑ 165 Larry Kelm	.05	.01
❑ 166 Mark Clayton	.10	.02
❑ 167 Louis Oliver	.05	.01
❑ 168 Mark Higgs	.05	.01
❑ 169 Aaron Craver	.05	.01
❑ 170 Sammie Smith	.05	.01
❑ 171 Tony Paige	.05	.01
❑ 172 Jeff Cross	.05	.01
❑ 173 David Griggs	.05	.01
❑ 174 Richmond Webb	.05	.01
❑ 175 Vestee Jackson	.05	.01
❑ 176 Jim C. Jensen	.05	.01
❑ 177 Anthony Carter	.10	.02
❑ 178 Cris Carter	.50	.20
❑ 179 Chris Doleman	.05	.01
❑ 180 Rich Gannon	.25	.08
❑ 181 Al Noga	.05	.01
❑ 182 Randall McDaniel	.05	.01
❑ 183 Todd Scott	.05	.01
❑ 184 Henry Thomas	.05	.01
❑ 185 Felix Wright	.05	.01
❑ 186 Gary Zimmerman	.05	.01
❑ 187 Herschel Walker	.10	.02
❑ 188 Vincent Brown	.05	.01
❑ 189 Harry Colon	.05	.01
❑ 190 Irving Fryar	.10	.02
❑ 191 Marv Cook	.05	.01
❑ 192 Leonard Russell	.10	.02
❑ 193 Hugh Millen	.05	.01
❑ 194 Pat Harlow	.05	.01
❑ 195 Jon Vaughn	.05	.01
❑ 196 Ben Coates RC	.75	.30
❑ 197 Johnny Rembert	.05	.01
❑ 198 Greg McMurtry	.05	.01
❑ 199 Morten Andersen	.05	.01
❑ 200 Tommy Barnhardt	.05	.01
❑ 201 Bobby Hebert	.05	.01
❑ 202 Dalton Hilliard	.05	.01
❑ 203 Sam Mills	.05	.01
❑ 204 Pat Swilling	.05	.01
❑ 205 Rickey Jackson	.05	.01
❑ 206 Stan Brock	.05	.01
❑ 207 Reginald Jones	.05	.01
❑ 208 Gill Fenerty	.05	.01
❑ 209 Eric Martin	.05	.01
❑ 210 Matt Bahr	.05	.01
❑ 211 Rodney Hampton	.10	.02
❑ 212 Jeff Hostetler	.10	.02
❑ 213 Pepper Johnson	.05	.01
❑ 214 Leonard Marshall	.05	.01
❑ 215 Doug Riesenberg	.05	.01
❑ 216 Stephen Baker	.05	.01
❑ 217 Mike Fox	.05	.01
❑ 218 Bart Oates	.05	.01
❑ 219 Everson Walls	.05	.01
❑ 220 Gary Reasons	.05	.01
❑ 221 Jeff Lageman	.05	.01
❑ 222 Joe Kelly	.05	.01
❑ 223 Mo Lewis	.05	.01
❑ 224 Tony Stargell	.05	.01
❑ 225 Jim Sweeney	.05	.01
❑ 226 Freeman McNeil	.10	.02
❑ 227 Brian Washington	.05	.01
❑ 228 Johnny Hector	.05	.01
❑ 229 Terance Mathis	.10	.02
❑ 230 Rob Moore	.10	.02
❑ 231 Brad Baxter	.05	.01
❑ 232 Eric Allen	.05	.01
❑ 233 Fred Barnett	.10	.02
❑ 234 Jerome Brown	.05	.01
❑ 235 Keith Byars	.05	.01
❑ 236 William Thomas	.05	.01

❑ 237 Jessie Small .05 .01
❑ 238 Robert Drummond .05 .01
❑ 239 Reggie White .25 .08
❑ 240 James Joseph .05 .01
❑ 241 Brad Goebel .05 .01
❑ 242 Clyde Simmons .05 .01
❑ 243 Rich Camarillo .05 .01
❑ 244 Ken Harvey .05 .01
❑ 245 Garth Jax .05 .01
❑ 246 Johnny Johnson .05 .01
❑ 247 Mike Jones .05 .01
❑ 248 Ernie Jones .05 .01
❑ 249 Tom Tupa .05 .01
❑ 250 Ron Wolfley .05 .01
❑ 251 Luis Sharpe .05 .01
❑ 252 [illegible]
❑ 253 Anthony Thompson .05 .01
❑ 254 Gary Anderson K .05 .01
❑ 255 Dermontti Dawson .05 .01
❑ 256 Jeff Graham .25 .08
❑ 257 Eric Green .05 .01
❑ 258 Louis Lipps .05 .01
❑ 259 Neil O'Donnell .10 .02
❑ 260 Rod Woodson .25 .08
❑ 261 Dwight Stone .05 .01
❑ 262 Aaron Jones .05 .01
❑ 263 Keith Willis .05 .01
❑ 264 Ernie Mills .05 .01
❑ 265 Martin Bayless .05 .01
❑ 266 Rod Bernstine .05 .01
❑ 267 John Carney .05 .01
❑ 268 John Friesz .10 .02
❑ 269 Nate Lewis .05 .01
❑ 270 Shawn Jefferson .05 .01
❑ 271 Burt Grossman .05 .01
❑ 272 Eric Moten .05 .01
❑ 273 Gary Plummer .05 .01
❑ 274 Henry Rolling .05 .01
❑ 275 Steve Hendrickson RC .05 .01
❑ 276 Michael Carter .05 .01
❑ 277 Steve Bono RC .25 .08
❑ 278 Dexter Carter .05 .01
❑ 279 Mike Cofer .05 .01
❑ 280 Charles Haley .10 .02
❑ 281 Tom Rathman .05 .01
❑ 282 Guy McIntyre .05 .01
❑ 283 John Taylor .10 .02
❑ 284 Dave Waymer .05 .01
❑ 285 Steve Wallace .05 .01
❑ 286 Jamie Williams .05 .01
❑ 287 Brian Blades .10 .02
❑ 288 Jeff Bryant .05 .01
❑ 289 Grant Feasel .05 .01
❑ 290 Jacob Green .05 .01
❑ 291 Andy Heck .05 .01
❑ 292 Kelly Stouffer .05 .01
❑ 293 John Kasay .05 .01
❑ 294 Cortez Kennedy .10 .02
❑ 295 Bryan Millard .05 .01
❑ 296 Eugene Robinson .05 .01
❑ 297 Tony Woods .05 .01
❑ 298 Jesse Anderson UER .05 .01
❑ 299 Gary Anderson RB .05 .01
❑ 300 Mark Carrier WR .10 .02
❑ 301 Reggie Cobb .05 .01
❑ 302 Robert Wilson .05 .01
❑ 303 Jesse Solomon .05 .01
❑ 304 Broderick Thomas .05 .01
❑ 305 Lawrence Dawsey .10 .02
❑ 306 Charles McRae .05 .01
❑ 307 Paul Gruber .05 .01
❑ 308 Vinny Testaverde .10 .02
❑ 309 Brian Mitchell .10 .02
❑ 310 Darrell Green .05 .01
❑ 311 Art Monk .10 .02
❑ 312 Russ Grimm .05 .01
❑ 313 Mark Rypien .05 .01
❑ 314 Bobby Wilson .05 .01
❑ 315 Wilber Marshall .05 .01
❑ 316 Gerald Riggs .05 .01
❑ 317 Chip Lohmiller .05 .01
❑ 318 Joe Jacoby .05 .01
❑ 319 Martin Mayhew .05 .01
❑ 320 Amp Lee RC .05 .01
❑ 321 Terrell Buckley RC .05 .01
❑ 322 Tommy Vardell RC .05 .01
❑ 323 Ricardo McDonald RC .05 .01
❑ 324 Joe Bowden RC .05 .01
❑ 325 Darryl Williams RC .05 .01
❑ 326 Carlos Huerta .05 .01
❑ 327 Patrick Rowe RC .05 .01
❑ 328 Siran Stacy RC .05 .01
❑ 329 Dexter McNabb RC .05 .01
❑ 330 Willie Clay RC .05 .01
❑ 331 Oliver Barnett .05 .01
❑ 332 Aundray Bruce .05 .01
❑ 333 Ken Tippins RC .05 .01
❑ 334 Jessie Tuggle .05 .01
❑ 335 Brian Jordan .10 .02
❑ 336 Andre Rison .10 .02
❑ 337 Houston Hoover .05 .01
❑ 338 Bill Fralic .05 .01
❑ 339 Pat Chaffey RC .05 .01
❑ 340 Keith Jones .05 .01
❑ 341 [illegible]
❑ 342 Chris Mohr .05 .01
❑ 343 John Davis .05 .01
❑ 344 Ray Bentley .05 .01
❑ 345 Scott Norwood .05 .01
❑ 346 Shane Conlan .05 .01
❑ 347 Steve Tasker .10 .02
❑ 348 Will Wolford .05 .01
❑ 349 Gary Baldinger RC .05 .01
❑ 350 Kirby Jackson .05 .01
❑ 351 Jamie Mueller .05 .01
❑ 352 Pete Metzelaars .05 .01
❑ 353 Richard Dent .10 .02
❑ 354 Ron Rivera .05 .01
❑ 355 Jim Morrissey .05 .01
❑ 356 John Roper .05 .01
❑ 357 Steve McMichael .10 .02
❑ 358 Ron Morris .05 .01
❑ 359 Darren Lewis .05 .01
❑ 360 Anthony Morgan .05 .01
❑ 361 Stan Thomas .05 .01
❑ 362 James Thornton .05 .01
❑ 363 Brad Muster .05 .01
❑ 364 Tim Krumrie .05 .01
❑ 365 Lee Johnson .05 .01
❑ 366 Eric Ball .05 .01
❑ 367 Alonzo Mitz RC .05 .01
❑ 368 David Grant .05 .01
❑ 369 Lynn James .05 .01
❑ 370 Lewis Billups .05 .01
❑ 371 Jim Breech .05 .01
❑ 372 Alfred Williams .05 .01
❑ 373 Wayne Haddix .05 .01
❑ 374 Tim McGee .05 .01
❑ 375 Michael Jackson .10 .02
❑ 376 Leroy Hoard .10 .02
❑ 377 Tony Jones T .05 .01
❑ 378 Vince Newsome .05 .01
❑ 379 Todd Philcox RC .05 .01
❑ 380 Eric Metcalf .10 .02
❑ 381 John Rienstra .05 .01
❑ 382 Matt Stover .05 .01
❑ 383 Brian Hansen .05 .01
❑ 384 Joe Morris .05 .01
❑ 385 Anthony Pleasant .05 .01
❑ 386 Mark Stepnoski .05 .01
❑ 387 Erik Williams .05 .01
❑ 388 Jimmie Jones .05 .01
❑ 389 Kevin Gogan .05 .01
❑ 390 Manny Hendrix RC .05 .01
❑ 391 Issiac Holt .05 .01
❑ 392 Ken Norton .10 .02
❑ 393 Tommie Agee .05 .01
❑ 394 Alvin Harper .10 .02
❑ 395 Alexander Wright .05 .01
❑ 396 Mike Saxon .05 .01
❑ 397 Michael Brooks .05 .01
❑ 398 Bobby Humphrey .05 .01
❑ 399 Ken Lanier .05 .01
❑ 400 Steve Sewell .05 .01
❑ 401 Robert Perryman .05 .01
❑ 402 Wymon Henderson .05 .01
❑ 403 Keith Kartz .05 .01
❑ 404 Clarence Kay .05 .01
❑ 405 Keith Traylor .05 .01
❑ 406 Doug Widell .05 .01
❑ 407 Dennis Smith .05 .01
❑ 408 Marc Spindler .05 .01
❑ 409 Lomas Brown .05 .01
❑ 410 Robert Clark .05 .01
❑ 411 Eric Andolsek .05 .01
❑ 412 Mike Farr .05 .01
❑ 413 Ray Crockett .05 .01
❑ 414 Jeff Campbell .05 .01
❑ 415 Dan Owens .05 .01
❑ 416 Jim Arnold .05 .01
❑ 417 Barry Sanders 1.25 .50
❑ 418 Eddie Murray .05 .01
❑ 419 Vince Workman .05 .01
❑ 420 Ed West .05 .01
❑ 421 Charles Wilson .05 .01
❑ 422 Perry Kemp .05 .01
❑ 423 Chuck Cecil .05 .01
❑ 424 James Campen .05 .01
❑ 425 Robert Brown .05 .01
❑ 426 Brian Noble .05 .01
❑ 427 Rich Moran .05 .01
❑ 428 Vai Sikahema .05 .01
❑ 429 Allen Rice .05 .01
❑ 430 [illegible]
❑ 431 Warren Moon .25 .08
❑ 432 Greg Montgomery .05 .01
❑ 433 Sean Jones .05 .01
❑ 434 Richard Johnson CB .05 .01
❑ 435 Al Smith .05 .01
❑ 436 Johnny Meads .05 .01
❑ 437 William Fuller .05 .01
❑ 438 Mike Munchak .10 .02
❑ 439 Ray Childress .05 .01
❑ 440 Cody Carlson .05 .01
❑ 441 Scott Radecic .05 .01
❑ 442 Quintus McDonald RC .05 .01
❑ 443 Eugene Daniel .05 .01
❑ 444 Mark Herrmann RC .05 .01
❑ 445 John Baylor RC .05 .01
❑ 446 Dave McCloughan .05 .01
❑ 447 Mark Vander Poel .05 .01
❑ 448 Randy Dixon .05 .01
❑ 449 Keith Taylor .05 .01
❑ 450 Alan Grant .05 .01
❑ 451 Tony Siragusa .05 .01
❑ 452 Rich Baldinger .05 .01
❑ 453 Derrick Thomas .25 .08
❑ 454 Bill Jones RC .05 .01
❑ 455 Troy Stradford .05 .01
❑ 456 Barry Word .05 .01
❑ 457 Tim Grunhard .05 .01
❑ 458 Chris Martin .05 .01
❑ 459 Jayice Pearson RC .05 .01
❑ 460 Dino Hackett .05 .01
❑ 461 David Lutz .05 .01
❑ 462 Albert Lewis .05 .01
❑ 463 Fred Jones RC .05 .01
❑ 464 Winston Moss .05 .01
❑ 465 Sam Graddy RC .05 .01
❑ 466 Steve Wisniewski .05 .01
❑ 467 Jay Schroeder .05 .01
❑ 468 Ronnie Lott .10 .02
❑ 469 Willie Gault .10 .02
❑ 470 Greg Townsend .05 .01
❑ 471 Max Montoya .05 .01
❑ 472 Howie Long .25 .08
❑ 473 Lionel Washington .05 .01
❑ 474 Riki Ellison .05 .01
❑ 475 Tom Newberry .05 .01
❑ 476 Damone Johnson .05 .01
❑ 477 Pat Terrell .05 .01
❑ 478 Marcus Dupree .05 .01
❑ 479 Todd Lyght .05 .01
❑ 480 Buford McGee .05 .01
❑ 481 Bern Brostek .05 .01
❑ 482 Jim Price .05 .01
❑ 483 Robert Young .05 .01
❑ 484 Tony Zendejas .05 .01
❑ 485 Robert Bailey RC .05 .01
❑ 486 Alvin Wright .05 .01
❑ 487 Pat Carter .05 .01
❑ 488 Pete Stoyanovich .05 .01
❑ 489 Reggie Roby .05 .01
❑ 490 Harry Galbreath .05 .01
❑ 491 Mike McGruder RC .05 .01
❑ 492 J.B. Brown .05 .01
❑ 493 E.J. Junior .05 .01
❑ 494 Ferrell Edmunds .05 .01
❑ 495 Scott Secules .05 .01
❑ 496 Greg Baty RC .05 .01
❑ 497 Mike Iaquaniello .05 .01
❑ 498 Keith Sims .05 .01
❑ 499 John Randle .10 .02
❑ 500 Joey Browner .05 .01
❑ 501 Steve Jordan .05 .01
❑ 502 Darrin Nelson .05 .01
❑ 503 Audray McMillian .05 .01

❑ 504	Harry Newsome	.05	.01
❑ 505	Hassan Jones	.05	.01
❑ 506	Ray Berry	.05	.01
❑ 507	Mike Merriweather	.05	.01
❑ 508	Leo Lewis	.05	.01
❑ 509	Tim Irwin	.05	.01
❑ 510	Kirk Lowdermilk	.05	.01
❑ 511	Alfred Anderson	.05	.01
❑ 512	Michael Timpson RC	.05	.01
❑ 513	Jerome Henderson	.05	.01
❑ 514	Andre Tippett	.05	.01
❑ 515	Chris Singleton	.05	.01
❑ 516	John Stephens	.05	.01
❑ 517	Ronnie Lippett	.05	.01
❑ 518	Bruce Armstrong	.05	.01
❑ 519	Marion Hobby RC	.05	.01
❑ 520	Tim Goad	.05	.01
❑ 521	Mickey Washington RC	.05	.01
❑ 522	Fred Smerlas	.05	.01
❑ 523	Wayne Martin	.05	.01
❑ 524	Frank Warren	.05	.01
❑ 525	Floyd Turner	.05	.01
❑ 526	Wesley Carroll	.05	.01
❑ 527	Gene Atkins	.05	.01
❑ 528	Vaughan Johnson	.05	.01
❑ 529	Hoby Brenner	.05	.01
❑ 530	Renaldo Turnbull	.05	.01
❑ 531	Joel Hilgenberg	.05	.01
❑ 532	Craig Heyward	.10	.02
❑ 533	Vince Buck	.05	.01
❑ 534	Jim Dombrowski	.05	.01
❑ 535	Fred McAfee RC	.05	.01
❑ 536	Phil Simms	.10	.02
❑ 537	Lewis Tillman	.05	.01
❑ 538	John Elliott	.05	.01
❑ 539	Dave Meggett	.10	.02
❑ 540	Mark Collins	.05	.01
❑ 541	Ottis Anderson	.10	.02
❑ 542	Bobby Abrams RC	.05	.01
❑ 543	Sean Landeta	.05	.01
❑ 544	Brian Williams OL	.05	.01
❑ 545	Erik Howard	.05	.01
❑ 546	Mark Ingram	.05	.01
❑ 547	Kanavis McGhee	.05	.01
❑ 548	Kyle Clifton	.05	.01
❑ 549	Marvin Washington	.05	.01
❑ 550	Jeff Criswell	.05	.01
❑ 551	Dave Cadigan	.05	.01
❑ 552	Chris Burkett	.05	.01
❑ 553	Erik McMillan	.05	.01
❑ 554	James Hasty	.05	.01
❑ 555	Louie Aguiar RC	.05	.01
❑ 556	Troy Johnson RC	.05	.01
❑ 557	Troy Taylor RC	.05	.01
❑ 558	Pat Kelly RC	.05	.01
❑ 559	Heath Sherman	.05	.01
❑ 560	Roger Ruzek	.05	.01
❑ 561	Andre Waters	.05	.01
❑ 562	Izel Jenkins	.05	.01
❑ 563	Keith Jackson	.10	.02
❑ 564	Byron Evans	.05	.01
❑ 565	Wes Hopkins	.05	.01
❑ 566	Rich Miano	.05	.01
❑ 567	Seth Joyner	.05	.01
❑ 568	Thomas Sanders	.05	.01
❑ 569	David Alexander	.05	.01
❑ 570	Jeff Kemp	.05	.01
❑ 571	Jock Jones RC	.05	.01
❑ 572	Craig Patterson RC	.05	.01
❑ 573	Robert Massey	.05	.01
❑ 574	Bill Lewis	.05	.01
❑ 575	Freddie Joe Nunn	.05	.01
❑ 576	Aeneas Williams	.10	.02
❑ 577	John Jackson WR	.05	.01
❑ 578	Tim McDonald	.05	.01
❑ 579	Michael Zordich RC	.05	.01
❑ 580	Eric Hill	.05	.01
❑ 581	Lorenzo Lynch	.05	.01
❑ 582	Vernice Smith RC	.05	.01
❑ 583	Greg Lloyd	.10	.02
❑ 584	Carnell Lake	.05	.01
❑ 585	Hardy Nickerson	.10	.02
❑ 586	Delton Hall	.05	.01
❑ 587	Gerald Williams	.05	.01
❑ 588	Bryan Hinkle	.05	.01
❑ 589	Barry Foster	.10	.02
❑ 590	Bubby Brister	.10	.02
❑ 591	Rick Strom RC	.05	.01
❑ 592	David Little	.05	.01

❑ 593	Leroy Thompson RC	.05	.01
❑ 594	Eric Bieniemy	.05	.01
❑ 595	Courtney Hall	.05	.01
❑ 596	George Thornton	.05	.01
❑ 597	Donnie Elder	.05	.01
❑ 598	Billy Ray Smith	.05	.01
❑ 599	Gill Byrd	.05	.01
❑ 600	Marion Butts	.05	.01
❑ 601	Ronnie Harmon	.05	.01
❑ 602	Anthony Shelton	.05	.01
❑ 603	Mark May	.05	.01
❑ 604	Craig McEwen RC	.05	.01
❑ 605	Steve Young	.60	.25
❑ 606	Keith Henderson	.05	.01
❑ 607	Pierce Holt	.05	.01
❑ 608	Roy Foster	.05	.01
❑ 609	Don Griffin	.05	.01
❑ 610	Harry Sydney	.05	.01
❑ 611	Todd Bowles	.05	.01
❑ 612	Ted Washington	.05	.01
❑ 613	Johnnie Jackson	.05	.01
❑ 614	Jesse Sapolu	.05	.01
❑ 615	Brent Jones	.10	.02
❑ 616	Travis McNeal	.05	.01
❑ 617	Darrick Brilz RC	.05	.01
❑ 618	Terry Wooden	.05	.01
❑ 619	Tommy Kane	.05	.01
❑ 620	Nesby Glasgow	.05	.01
❑ 621	Dwayne Harper	.05	.01
❑ 622	Rick Tuten	.05	.01
❑ 623	Chris Warren	.10	.02
❑ 624	John L. Williams	.05	.01
❑ 625	Rufus Porter	.05	.01
❑ 626	David Daniels	.05	.01
❑ 627	Keith McCants	.05	.01
❑ 628	Reuben Davis	.05	.01
❑ 629	Mark Royals	.05	.01
❑ 630	Marty Carter RC	.05	.01
❑ 631	Ian Beckles	.05	.01
❑ 632	Ron Hall	.05	.01
❑ 633	Eugene Marve	.05	.01
❑ 634	Willie Drewrey	.05	.01
❑ 635	Tom McHale RC	.05	.01
❑ 636	Kevin Murphy	.05	.01
❑ 637	Robert Hardy RC	.05	.01
❑ 638	Ricky Sanders	.05	.01
❑ 639	Gary Clark	.10	.02
❑ 640	Andre Collins	.05	.01
❑ 641	Brad Edwards	.05	.01
❑ 642	Monte Coleman	.05	.01
❑ 643	Clarence Vaughn RC	.05	.01
❑ 644	Fred Stokes	.05	.01
❑ 645	Charles Mann	.05	.01
❑ 646	Earnest Byner	.05	.01
❑ 647	Jim Lachey	.05	.01
❑ 648	Jeff Bostic	.05	.01
❑ 649	Chris Mims RC	.05	.01
❑ 650	George Williams RC	.05	.01
❑ 651	Ed Cunningham RC	.05	.01
❑ 652	Tony Smith RC WR	.05	.01
❑ 653	Will Furrer RC	.05	.01
❑ 654	Matt Elliott RC	.05	.01
❑ 655	Mike Mooney RC	.05	.01
❑ 656	Eddie Blake RC	.05	.01
❑ 657	Leon Searcy RC	.05	.01
❑ 658	Kevin Turner RC	.05	.01
❑ 659	Keith Hamilton RC	.10	.02
❑ 660	Alan Haller RC	.05	.01

1993 Pacific

❑	COMPLETE SET (440)	20.00	10.00
❑ 1	Emmitt Smith	1.50	.60
❑ 2	Troy Aikman	.75	.30
❑ 3	Larry Brown DB	.05	.01
❑ 4	Tony Casillas	.05	.01
❑ 5	Thomas Everett	.05	.01
❑ 6	Alvin Harper	.10	.02
❑ 7	Michael Irvin	.25	.08
❑ 8	Charles Haley	.10	.02
❑ 9	Leon Lett RC	.10	.02
❑ 10	Kevin Smith	.10	.02
❑ 11	Robert Jones	.05	.01
❑ 12	Jimmy Smith	.25	.08
❑ 13	Derrick Gainer RC	.05	.01
❑ 14	Lin Elliott	.05	.01
❑ 15	William Thomas	.05	.01
❑ 16	Clyde Simmons	.05	.01
❑ 17	Seth Joyner	.05	.01
❑ 18	Randall Cunningham	.25	.08
❑ 19	Byron Evans	.05	.01
❑ 20	Fred Barnett	.10	.02
❑ 21	Calvin Williams	.10	.02
❑ 22	James Joseph	.05	.01
❑ 23	Heath Sherman	.05	.01
❑ 24	Siran Stacy	.05	.01
❑ 25	Andy Harmon	.10	.02
❑ 26	Eric Allen	.05	.01
❑ 27	Herschel Walker	.10	.02
❑ 28	Vai Sikahema	.05	.01
❑ 29	Earnest Byner	.05	.01
❑ 30	Jeff Bostic	.05	.01
❑ 31	Monte Coleman	.05	.01
❑ 32	Ricky Ervins	.05	.01
❑ 33	Darrell Green	.05	.01
❑ 34	Mark Schlereth	.05	.01
❑ 35	Mark Rypien	.05	.01
❑ 36	Art Monk	.10	.02
❑ 37	Brian Mitchell	.10	.02
❑ 38	Chip Lohmiller	.05	.01
❑ 39	Charles Mann	.05	.01
❑ 40	Shane Collins	.05	.01
❑ 41	Jim Lachey	.05	.01
❑ 42	Desmond Howard	.10	.02
❑ 43	Rodney Hampton	.10	.02
❑ 44	Dave Brown RC	.25	.08
❑ 45	Mark Collins	.05	.01
❑ 46	Jarrod Bunch	.05	.01
❑ 47	William Roberts	.05	.01
❑ 48	Sean Landeta	.05	.01
❑ 49	Lawrence Taylor	.25	.08
❑ 50	Ed McCaffrey	.25	.08
❑ 51	Bart Oates	.05	.01
❑ 52	Pepper Johnson	.05	.01
❑ 53	Eric Dorsey	.05	.01
❑ 54	Erik Howard	.05	.01
❑ 55	Phil Simms	.10	.02
❑ 56	Derek Brown TE	.05	.01
❑ 57	Johnny Bailey	.05	.01
❑ 58	Rich Camarillo	.05	.01
❑ 59	Larry Centers RC	.25	.08
❑ 60	Chris Chandler	.10	.02
❑ 61	Randal Hill	.05	.01
❑ 62	Ricky Proehl	.05	.01
❑ 63	Freddie Joe Nunn	.05	.01
❑ 64	Robert Massey	.05	.01
❑ 65	Aeneas Williams	.05	.01
❑ 66	Luis Sharpe	.05	.01
❑ 67	Eric Swann	.10	.02
❑ 68	Timm Rosenbach	.05	.01
❑ 69	Anthony Edwards RC	.05	.01
❑ 70	Greg Davis	.05	.01
❑ 71	Terry Allen	.25	.08
❑ 72	Anthony Carter	.10	.02
❑ 73	Cris Carter	.25	.08
❑ 74	Roger Craig	.10	.02
❑ 75	Jack Del Rio	.05	.01
❑ 76	Chris Doleman	.05	.01
❑ 77	Rich Gannon	.25	.08
❑ 78	Hassan Jones	.05	.01
❑ 79	Steve Jordan	.05	.01
❑ 80	Randall McDaniel	.05	.01
❑ 81	Sean Salisbury	.05	.01
❑ 82	Harry Newsome	.05	.01
❑ 83	Carlos Jenkins	.05	.01
❑ 84	Jake Reed	.25	.08
❑ 85	Edgar Bennett	.25	.08
❑ 86	Tony Bennett	.05	.01
❑ 87	Terrell Buckley	.05	.01
❑ 88	Ty Detmer	.25	.08
❑ 89	Brett Favre	2.00	.75
❑ 90	Chris Jacke	.05	.01

❑ 91	Sterling Sharpe	.25	.08
❑ 92	James Campen	.05	.01
❑ 93	Brian Noble	.05	.01
❑ 94	Lester Archambeau RC	.05	.01
❑ 95	Harry Sydney	.05	.01
❑ 96	Corey Harris	.05	.01
❑ 97	Don Majkowski	.05	.01
❑ 98	Ken Ruettgers	.05	.01
❑ 99	Lomas Brown	.05	.01
❑ 100	Jason Hanson	.05	.01
❑ 101	Robert Porcher	.05	.01
❑ 102	Chris Spielman	.10	.02
❑ 103	Erik Kramer	.10	.02
❑ 104	Tracy Scroggins	.05	.01
❑ 105	Rodney Peete	.05	.01
❑ 106	Barry Sanders	1.25	.50
❑ 107	Herman Moore	.25	.08
❑ 108	Brett Perriman	.25	.08
❑ 109	Mel Gray	.10	.02
❑ 110	Dennis Gibson	.05	.01
❑ 111	Bennie Blades	.05	.01
❑ 112	Andre Ware	.05	.01
❑ 113	Gary Anderson RB	.05	.01
❑ 114	Tyji Armstrong	.05	.01
❑ 115	Reggie Cobb	.05	.01
❑ 116	Marty Carter	.05	.01
❑ 117	Lawrence Dawsey	.05	.01
❑ 118	Steve DeBerg	.05	.01
❑ 119	Ron Hall	.05	.01
❑ 120	Courtney Hawkins	.05	.01
❑ 121	Broderick Thomas	.05	.01
❑ 122	Keith McCants	.05	.01
❑ 123	Bruce Reimers	.05	.01
❑ 124	Darrick Brownlow	.05	.01
❑ 125	Mark Wheeler	.05	.01
❑ 126	Ricky Reynolds	.05	.01
❑ 127	Neal Anderson	.05	.01
❑ 128	Trace Armstrong	.05	.01
❑ 129	Mark Carrier DB	.05	.01
❑ 130	Richard Dent	.10	.02
❑ 131	Wendell Davis	.05	.01
❑ 132	Darren Lewis	.05	.01
❑ 133	Tom Waddle	.05	.01
❑ 134	Jim Harbaugh	.25	.08
❑ 135	Steve McMichael	.10	.02
❑ 136	William Perry	.10	.02
❑ 137	Alonzo Spellman	.05	.01
❑ 138	John Roper	.05	.01
❑ 139	Peter Tom Willis	.05	.01
❑ 140	Dante Jones	.05	.01
❑ 141	Harris Barton	.05	.01
❑ 142	Michael Carter	.05	.01
❑ 143	Eric Davis	.05	.01
❑ 144	Dana Hall	.05	.01
❑ 145	Amp Lee	.05	.01
❑ 146	Don Griffin	.05	.01
❑ 147	Jerry Rice	1.00	.40
❑ 148	Ricky Watters	.25	.08
❑ 149	Steve Young	.75	.30
❑ 150	Bill Romanowski	.05	.01
❑ 151	Klaus Wilmsmeyer	.05	.01
❑ 152	Steve Bono	.10	.02
❑ 153	Tom Rathman	.05	.01
❑ 154	Odessa Turner	.05	.01
❑ 155	Morten Andersen	.05	.01
❑ 156	Richard Cooper	.05	.01
❑ 157	Toi Cook	.05	.01
❑ 158	Quinn Early	.10	.02
❑ 159	Vaughn Dunbar	.05	.01
❑ 160	Rickey Jackson	.05	.01
❑ 161	Wayne Martin	.05	.01
❑ 162	Hoby Brenner	.05	.01
❑ 163	Joel Hilgenberg	.05	.01
❑ 164	Mike Buck	.05	.01
❑ 165	Torrance Small	.05	.01
❑ 166	Eric Martin	.05	.01
❑ 167	Vaughan Johnson	.05	.01
❑ 168	Sam Mills	.05	.01
❑ 169	Steve Broussard	.05	.01
❑ 170	Darion Conner	.05	.01
❑ 171	Drew Hill	.05	.01
❑ 172	Chris Hinton	.05	.01
❑ 173	Chris Miller	.10	.02
❑ 174	Tim McKyer	.05	.01
❑ 175	Norm Johnson	.05	.01
❑ 176	Mike Pritchard	.10	.02
❑ 177	Andre Rison	.10	.02
❑ 178	Deion Sanders	.50	.20
❑ 179	Tony Smith RB	.05	.01
❑ 180	Bruce Pickens	.05	.01
❑ 181	Michael Haynes	.10	.02
❑ 182	Jessie Tuggle	.05	.01
❑ 183	Marc Boutte	.05	.01
❑ 184	Don Bracken	.05	.01
❑ 185	Bern Brostek	.05	.01
❑ 186	Henry Ellard	.10	.02
❑ 187	Jim Everett	.10	.02
❑ 188	Sean Gilbert	.10	.02
❑ 189	Cleveland Gary	.05	.01
❑ 190	Todd Kinchen	.05	.01
❑ 191	Pat Terrell	.05	.01
❑ 192	Jackie Slater	.05	.01
❑ 193	David Lang	.05	.01
❑ 194	Flipper Anderson	.05	.01
❑ 195	Tony Zendejas	.05	.01
❑ 196	Roman Phifer	.05	.01
❑ 197	Steve Christie	.05	.01
❑ 198	Cornelius Bennett	.10	.02
❑ 199	Phil Hansen	.05	.01
❑ 200	Don Beebe	.05	.01
❑ 201	Mark Kelso	.05	.01
❑ 202	Bruce Smith	.25	.08
❑ 203	Darryl Talley	.05	.01
❑ 204	Andre Reed	.10	.02
❑ 205	Mike Lodish	.05	.01
❑ 206	Jim Kelly	.25	.08
❑ 207	Thurman Thomas	.25	.08
❑ 208	Kenneth Davis	.05	.01
❑ 209	Frank Reich	.10	.02
❑ 210	Kent Hull	.05	.01
❑ 211	Marco Coleman	.05	.01
❑ 212	Bryan Cox	.05	.01
❑ 213	Jeff Cross	.05	.01
❑ 214	Mark Higgs	.05	.01
❑ 215	Keith Jackson	.10	.02
❑ 216	Scott Miller	.05	.01
❑ 217	John Offerdahl	.05	.01
❑ 218	Dan Marino	1.50	.60
❑ 219	Keith Sims	.05	.01
❑ 220	Chuck Klingbeil	.05	.01
❑ 221	Troy Vincent	.05	.01
❑ 222	Mike Williams RC WR	.05	.01
❑ 223	Pete Stoyanovich	.05	.01
❑ 224	J.B. Brown	.05	.01
❑ 225	Ashley Ambrose	.05	.01
❑ 226	Jason Belser RC	.05	.01
❑ 227	Jeff George	.25	.08
❑ 228	Quentin Coryatt	.10	.02
❑ 229	Duane Bickett	.05	.01
❑ 230	Steve Emtman	.05	.01
❑ 231	Anthony Johnson	.10	.02
❑ 232	Rohn Stark	.05	.01
❑ 233	Jessie Hester	.05	.01
❑ 234	Reggie Langhorne	.05	.01
❑ 235	Clarence Verdin	.05	.01
❑ 236	Dean Biasucci	.05	.01
❑ 237	Jack Trudeau	.05	.01
❑ 238	Tony Siragusa	.05	.01
❑ 239	Chris Burkett	.05	.01
❑ 240	Brad Baxter	.05	.01
❑ 241	Rob Moore	.10	.02
❑ 242	Browning Nagle	.05	.01
❑ 243	Jim Sweeney	.05	.01
❑ 244	Kurt Barber	.05	.01
❑ 245	Siupeli Malamala RC	.05	.01
❑ 246	Mike Brim	.05	.01
❑ 247	Mo Lewis	.05	.01
❑ 248	Johnny Mitchell	.05	.01
❑ 249	Ken Whisenhunt RC	.30	.10
❑ 250	James Hasty	.05	.01
❑ 251	Kyle Clifton	.05	.01
❑ 252	Terance Mathis	.10	.02
❑ 253	Ray Agnew	.05	.01
❑ 254	Eugene Chung	.05	.01
❑ 255	Marv Cook	.05	.01
❑ 256	Johnny Rembert	.05	.01
❑ 257	Maurice Hurst	.05	.01
❑ 258	Jon Vaughn	.05	.01
❑ 259	Leonard Russell	.10	.02
❑ 260	Pat Harlow	.05	.01
❑ 261	Andre Tippett	.05	.01
❑ 262	Michael Timpson	.05	.01
❑ 263	Greg McMurtry	.05	.01
❑ 264	Chris Singleton	.05	.01
❑ 265	Reggie Redding RC	.05	.01
❑ 266	Walter Stanley	.05	.01
❑ 267	Gary Anderson K	.05	.01
❑ 268	Merril Hoge	.05	.01
❑ 269	Barry Foster	.10	.02
❑ 270	Charles Davenport	.05	.01
❑ 271	Jeff Graham	.10	.02
❑ 272	Adrian Cooper	.05	.01
❑ 273	David Little	.05	.01
❑ 274	Neil O'Donnell	.25	.08
❑ 275	Rod Woodson	.25	.08
❑ 276	Ernie Mills	.05	.01
❑ 277	Dwight Stone	.05	.01
❑ 278	Darren Perry	.05	.01
❑ 279	Dermontti Dawson	.05	.01
❑ 280	Carlton Haselrig	.05	.01
❑ 281	Pat Coleman	.05	.01
❑ 282	Ernest Givins	.10	.02
❑ 283	Warren Moon	.25	.08
❑ 284	Haywood Jeffires	.10	.02
❑ 285	Cody Carlson	.05	.01
❑ 286	Ray Childress	.05	.01
❑ 287	Bruce Matthews	.05	.01
❑ 288	Webster Slaughter	.05	.01
❑ 289	Bo Orlando	.05	.01
❑ 290	Lorenzo White	.05	.01
❑ 291	Eddie Robinson	.05	.01
❑ 292	Bubba McDowell	.05	.01
❑ 293	Bucky Richardson	.05	.01
❑ 294	Sean Jones	.05	.01
❑ 295	David Brandon	.05	.01
❑ 296	Shawn Collins	.05	.01
❑ 297	Lawyer Tillman	.05	.01
❑ 298	Bob Dahl	.05	.01
❑ 299	Kevin Mack	.05	.01
❑ 300	Bernie Kosar	.10	.02
❑ 301	Tommy Vardell	.05	.01
❑ 302	Jay Hilgenberg	.05	.01
❑ 303	Michael Dean Perry	.10	.02
❑ 304	Michael Jackson	.10	.02
❑ 305	Eric Metcalf	.10	.02
❑ 306	Rico Smith RC	.05	.01
❑ 307	Stevon Moore RC	.05	.01
❑ 308	Leroy Hoard	.10	.02
❑ 309	Eric Ball	.05	.01
❑ 310	Derrick Fenner	.05	.01
❑ 311	James Francis	.05	.01
❑ 312	Ricardo McDonald	.05	.01
❑ 313	Tim Krumrie	.05	.01
❑ 314	Carl Pickens	.10	.02
❑ 315	David Klingler	.05	.01
❑ 316	Donald Hollas RC	.05	.01
❑ 317	Harold Green	.05	.01
❑ 318	Daniel Stubbs	.05	.01
❑ 319	Alfred Williams	.05	.01
❑ 320	Darryl Williams	.05	.01
❑ 321	Mike Arthur RC	.05	.01
❑ 322	Leonard Wheeler	.05	.01
❑ 323	Gill Byrd	.05	.01
❑ 324	Eric Bieniemy	.05	.01
❑ 325	Marion Butts	.05	.01
❑ 326	John Carney	.05	.01
❑ 327	Stan Humphries	.10	.02
❑ 328	Ronnie Harmon	.05	.01
❑ 329	Junior Seau	.25	.08
❑ 330	Nate Lewis	.05	.01
❑ 331	Harry Swayne	.05	.01
❑ 332	Leslie O'Neal	.10	.02
❑ 333	Eric Moten	.05	.01
❑ 334	Blaise Winter RC	.05	.01
❑ 335	Anthony Miller	.10	.02
❑ 336	Gary Plummer	.05	.01
❑ 337	Willie Davis	.25	.08
❑ 338	J.J. Birden	.05	.01
❑ 339	Tim Barnett	.05	.01
❑ 340	Dave Krieg	.10	.02
❑ 341	Barry Word	.05	.01
❑ 342	Tracy Simien	.05	.01
❑ 343	Christian Okoye	.05	.01
❑ 344	Todd McNair	.05	.01
❑ 345	Dan Saleaumua	.05	.01
❑ 346	Derrick Thomas	.25	.08
❑ 347	Harvey Williams	.10	.02
❑ 348	Kimble Anders RC	.25	.08
❑ 349	Tim Grunhard	.05	.01
❑ 350	Tony Hargain RC UER	.05	.01
❑ 351	Simon Fletcher	.05	.01
❑ 352	John Elway	1.50	.60
❑ 353	Mike Croel	.05	.01
❑ 354	Steve Atwater	.05	.01
❑ 355	Tommy Maddox	.25	.08
❑ 356	Karl Mecklenburg	.05	.01
❑ 357	Shane Dronett	.05	.01

❑ 358 Kenny Walker	.05	.01
❑ 359 Reggie Rivers RC	.05	.01
❑ 360 Cedric Tillman RC	.05	.01
❑ 361 Arthur Marshall RC	.05	.01
❑ 362 Greg Lewis	.05	.01
❑ 363 Shannon Sharpe	.25	.08
❑ 364 Doug Widell	.05	.01
❑ 365 Todd Marinovich	.05	.01
❑ 366 Nick Bell	.05	.01
❑ 367 Eric Dickerson	.10	.02
❑ 368 Max Montoya	.05	.01
❑ 369 Winston Moss	.05	.01
❑ 370 Howie Long	.25	.08
❑ 371 Willie Gault	.05	.01
❑ 372 Tim Brown	.25	.08
❑ 373 Steve Smith	.05	.01
❑ 374 Steve Wisniewski	.05	.01
❑ 375 Alexander Wright	.05	.01
❑ 376 Ethan Horton	.05	.01
❑ 377 Napoleon McCallum	.05	.01
❑ 378 Terry McDaniel	.05	.01
❑ 379 Patrick Hunter	.05	.01
❑ 380 Robert Blackmon	.05	.01
❑ 381 John Kasay	.05	.01
❑ 382 Cortez Kennedy	.10	.02
❑ 383 Andy Heck	.05	.01
❑ 384 Bill Hitchcock RC	.05	.01
❑ 385 Rick Mirer RC	.25	.08
❑ 386 Jeff Bryant	.05	.01
❑ 387 Eugene Robinson	.05	.01
❑ 388 John L. Williams	.05	.01
❑ 389 Chris Warren	.10	.02
❑ 390 Rufus Porter	.05	.01
❑ 391 Joe Tofflemire RC	.05	.01
❑ 392 Dan McGwire	.05	.01
❑ 393 Boomer Esiason	.10	.02
❑ 394 Brad Muster	.05	.01
❑ 395 James Lofton	.10	.02
❑ 396 Tim McGee	.05	.01
❑ 397 Steve Beuerlein	.10	.02
❑ 398 Gaston Green	.05	.01
❑ 399 Bill Brooks	.05	.01
❑ 400 Ronnie Lott	.10	.02
❑ 401 Jay Schroeder	.05	.01
❑ 402 Marcus Allen	.25	.08
❑ 403 Kevin Greene	.10	.02
❑ 404 Kirk Lowdermilk	.05	.01
❑ 405 Hugh Millen	.05	.01
❑ 406 Pat Swilling	.05	.01
❑ 407 Bobby Hebert	.05	.01
❑ 408 Carl Banks	.05	.01
❑ 409 Jeff Hostetler	.10	.02
❑ 410 Leonard Marshall	.05	.01
❑ 411 Ken O'Brien	.05	.01
❑ 412 Joe Montana	1.50	.60
❑ 413 Reggie White	.25	.08
❑ 414 Gary Clark	.10	.02
❑ 415 Johnny Johnson	.05	.01
❑ 416 Tim McDonald	.05	.01
❑ 417 Pierce Holt	.05	.01
❑ 418 Gino Torretta RC	.10	.02
❑ 419 Glyn Milburn RC	.25	.08
❑ 420 O.J.McDuffie RC	.25	.08
❑ 421 Coleman Rudolph RC	.05	.01
❑ 422 Reggie Brooks RC	.10	.02
❑ 423 Garrison Hearst RC	.60	.25
❑ 424 Leonard Renfro RC	.05	.01
❑ 425 Kevin Williams RC WR	.25	.08
❑ 426 Demetrius DuBose RC	.05	.01
❑ 427 Elvis Grbac RC	1.25	.50
❑ 428 Lincoln Kennedy RC	.05	.01
❑ 429 Carlton Gray RC	.05	.01
❑ 430 Micheal Barrow RC	.25	.08
❑ 431 George Teague RC	.10	.02
❑ 432 Curtis Conway RC	.40	.15
❑ 433 Natrone Means RC	.25	.08
❑ 434 Jerome Bettis RC	5.00	2.00
❑ 435 Drew Bledsoe RC	2.00	.75
❑ 436 Robert Smith RC	1.00	.40
❑ 437 Deon Figures RC	.05	.01
❑ 438 Qadry Ismail RC	.25	.08
❑ 439 Chris Slade RC	.10	.02
❑ 440 Dana Stubblefield RC	.25	.08

1994 Pacific

❑ COMPLETE SET (450)	30.00	15.00
❑ 1 Troy Aikman	1.00	.40
❑ 2 Charles Haley	.10	.02
❑ 3 Alvin Harper	.10	.02

❑ 4 Michael Irvin	.25	.08
❑ 5 Jim Jeffcoat	.05	.01
❑ 6 Daryl Johnston	.10	.02
❑ 7 Robert Jones	.05	.01
❑ 8 Brock Marion RC	.25	.08
❑ 9 Russell Maryland	.05	.01
❑ 10 Ken Norton	.10	.02
❑ 11 Jay Novacek	.10	.02
❑ 12 Emmitt Smith	1.50	.60
❑ 13 Kevin Smith	.05	.01
❑ 14 Tony Tolbert	.05	.01
❑ 15 Kevin Williams WR	.10	.02
❑ 16 Don Beebe	.05	.01
❑ 17 Cornelius Bennett	.10	.02
❑ 18 Bill Brooks	.05	.01
❑ 19 Steve Christie	.05	.01
❑ 20 Russell Copeland	.05	.01
❑ 21 Kenneth Davis	.05	.01
❑ 22 Kent Hull	.05	.01
❑ 23 Jim Kelly	.25	.08
❑ 24 Pete Metzelaars	.05	.01
❑ 25 Andre Reed	.10	.02
❑ 26 Frank Reich	.10	.02
❑ 27 Bruce Smith	.25	.08
❑ 28 Darryl Talley	.05	.01
❑ 29 Steve Tasker	.10	.02
❑ 30 Thurman Thomas	.25	.08
❑ 31 Steve Bono	.10	.02
❑ 32 Dexter Carter	.05	.01
❑ 33 Kevin Fagan	.05	.01
❑ 34 Dana Hall	.05	.01
❑ 35 Brent Jones	.10	.02
❑ 36 Amp Lee	.05	.01
❑ 37 Marc Logan	.05	.01
❑ 38 Tim McDonald	.05	.01
❑ 39 Guy McIntyre	.05	.01
❑ 40 Tom Rathman	.05	.01
❑ 41 Jerry Rice	1.00	.40
❑ 42 Dana Stubblefield	.10	.02
❑ 43 Steve Wallace	.05	.01
❑ 44 Ricky Watters	.10	.02
❑ 45 Steve Young	.75	.30
❑ 46 Marcus Allen	.25	.08
❑ 47 Kimble Anders	.10	.02
❑ 48 Tim Barnett	.05	.01
❑ 49 J.J. Birden	.05	.01
❑ 50 Dale Carter	.05	.01
❑ 51 Jonathan Hayes	.05	.01
❑ 52 Dave Krieg	.10	.02
❑ 53 Albert Lewis	.05	.01
❑ 54 Nick Lowery	.05	.01
❑ 55 Joe Montana	2.00	.75
❑ 56 Neil Smith	.10	.02
❑ 57 John Stephens	.05	.01
❑ 58 Derrick Thomas	.25	.08
❑ 59 Harvey Williams	.10	.02
❑ 60 Micheal Barrow	.05	.01
❑ 61 Gary Brown	.05	.01
❑ 62 Cody Carlson	.05	.01
❑ 63 Ray Childress	.05	.01
❑ 64 Curtis Duncan	.05	.01
❑ 65 Ernest Givins	.10	.02
❑ 66 Haywood Jeffires	.10	.02
❑ 67 Wilber Marshall	.05	.01
❑ 68 Bubba McDowell	.05	.01
❑ 69 Warren Moon	.25	.08
❑ 70 Mike Munchak	.10	.02
❑ 71 Marcus Robertson	.05	.01
❑ 72 Webster Slaughter	.05	.01
❑ 73 Gary Wellman RC	.05	.01
❑ 74 Lorenzo White	.05	.01
❑ 75 Ray Crockett	.05	.01

❑ 76 Jason Hanson	.05	.01
❑ 77 Rodney Holman	.05	.01
❑ 78 George Jamison	.05	.01
❑ 79 Erik Kramer	.10	.02
❑ 80 Ryan McNeil	.05	.01
❑ 81 Derrick Moore	.05	.01
❑ 82 Herman Moore	.25	.08
❑ 83 Rodney Peete	.05	.01
❑ 84 Brett Perriman	.10	.02
❑ 85 Barry Sanders	1.50	.60
❑ 86 Chris Spielman	.10	.02
❑ 87 Pat Swilling	.05	.01
❑ 88 Vernon Turner	.05	.01
❑ 89 Andre Ware	.05	.01
❑ 90 Michael Brooks	.05	.01
❑ 91 Dave Brown	.10	.02
❑ 92 Derek Brown TE	.05	.01
❑ 93 Jarrod Bunch	.05	.01
❑ 94 Chris Calloway	.05	.01
❑ 95 Kent Graham	.10	.02
❑ 96 Rodney Hampton	.10	.02
❑ 97 Mark Jackson	.05	.01
❑ 98 Ed McCaffrey	.25	.08
❑ 99 Dave Meggett	.05	.01
❑ 100 Aaron Pierce	.05	.01
❑ 101 Mike Sherrard	.05	.01
❑ 102 Phil Simms	.10	.02
❑ 103 Lewis Tillman	.05	.01
❑ 104 Eddie Anderson	.05	.01
❑ 105 Patrick Bates	.05	.01
❑ 106 Nick Bell	.05	.01
❑ 107 Tim Brown	.25	.08
❑ 108 Willie Gault	.05	.01
❑ 109 Jeff Gossett	.05	.01
❑ 110 Ethan Horton	.05	.01
❑ 111 Jeff Hostetler	.10	.02
❑ 112 Rocket Ismail	.10	.02
❑ 113 Chester McGlockton	.05	.01
❑ 114 Anthony Smith	.05	.01
❑ 115 Steve Smith	.05	.01
❑ 116 Greg Townsend	.05	.01
❑ 117 Steve Wisniewski	.05	.01
❑ 118 Alexander Wright	.05	.01
❑ 119 Steve Atwater	.05	.01
❑ 120 Rod Bernstine	.05	.01
❑ 121 Mike Croel	.05	.01
❑ 122 Shane Dronett	.05	.01
❑ 123 Jason Elam	.10	.02
❑ 124 John Elway	2.00	.75
❑ 125 Brian Habib	.05	.01
❑ 126 Rondell Jones	.05	.01
❑ 127 Tommy Maddox	.25	.08
❑ 128 Karl Mecklenburg	.05	.01
❑ 129 Glyn Milburn	.10	.02
❑ 130 Derek Russell	.05	.01
❑ 131 Shannon Sharpe	.10	.02
❑ 132 Dennis Smith	.05	.01
❑ 133 Edgar Bennett	.25	.08
❑ 134 Tony Bennett	.05	.01
❑ 135 Robert Brooks	.25	.08
❑ 136 Terrell Buckley	.05	.01
❑ 137 LeRoy Butler	.05	.01
❑ 138 Mark Clayton	.05	.01
❑ 139 Ty Detmer	.10	.02
❑ 140 Brett Favre	2.00	.75
❑ 141 John Jurkovic RC	.10	.02
❑ 142 Bryce Paup	.10	.02
❑ 143 Sterling Sharpe	.10	.02
❑ 144 George Teague	.05	.01
❑ 145 Darrell Thompson	.05	.01
❑ 146 Ed West	.05	.01
❑ 147 Reggie White	.25	.08
❑ 148 Terry Allen	.10	.02
❑ 149 Anthony Carter	.10	.02
❑ 150 Cris Carter	.50	.20
❑ 151 Roger Craig	.10	.02
❑ 152 Jack Del Rio	.05	.01
❑ 153 Chris Doleman	.05	.01
❑ 154 Scottie Graham RC	.10	.02
❑ 155 Eric Guliford RC	.05	.01
❑ 156 Qadry Ismail	.25	.08
❑ 157 Steve Jordan	.05	.01
❑ 158 Randall McDaniel	.05	.01
❑ 159 Jim McMahon	.10	.02
❑ 160 Audray McMillian	.05	.01
❑ 161 Sean Salisbury	.05	.01
❑ 162 Robert Smith	.25	.08
❑ 163 Henry Thomas	.05	.01
❑ 164 Gary Anderson K	.05	.01

❑ 165 Deon Figures .05 .01
❑ 166 Barry Foster .05 .01
❑ 167 Jeff Graham .05 .01
❑ 168 Kevin Greene .10 .02
❑ 169 Dave Hoffman .05 .01
❑ 170 Merril Hoge .05 .01
❑ 171 Gary Jones .05 .01
❑ 172 Greg Lloyd .10 .02
❑ 173 Ernie Mills .05 .01
❑ 174 Neil O'Donnell .25 .08
❑ 175 Darren Perry .05 .01
❑ 176 Leon Searcy .05 .01
❑ 177 Leroy Thompson .05 .01
❑ 178 Willie Williams RC .05 .01
❑ 179 Rod Woodson .10 .02
❑ 180 Keith Byars .05 .01
❑ 181 Marco Coleman .05 .01
❑ 182 Bryan Cox .05 .01
❑ 183 Irving Fryar .10 .02
❑ 184 John Grimsley .05 .01
❑ 185 Mark Higgs .05 .01
❑ 186 Mark Ingram .05 .01
❑ 187 Keith Jackson .05 .01
❑ 188 Terry Kirby .25 .08
❑ 189 Dan Marino 2.00 .75
❑ 190 O.J.McDuffie .25 .08
❑ 191 Scott Mitchell .10 .02
❑ 192 Pete Stoyanovich .05 .01
❑ 193 Troy Vincent .05 .01
❑ 194 Richmond Webb .05 .01
❑ 195 Brad Baxter .05 .01
❑ 196 Chris Burkett .05 .01
❑ 197 Rob Carpenter WR .05 .01
❑ 198 Boomer Esiason .10 .02
❑ 199 Johnny Johnson .05 .01
❑ 200 Jeff Lageman .05 .01
❑ 201 Mo Lewis .05 .01
❑ 202 Ronnie Lott .10 .02
❑ 203 Leonard Marshall .05 .01
❑ 204 Terance Mathis .10 .02
❑ 205 Johnny Mitchell .05 .01
❑ 206 Rob Moore .10 .02
❑ 207 Anthony Prior .05 .01
❑ 208 Blair Thomas .05 .01
❑ 209 Brian Washington .05 .01
❑ 210 Eric Bieniemy .05 .01
❑ 211 Marion Butts .05 .01
❑ 212 Gill Byrd .05 .01
❑ 213 John Carney .05 .01
❑ 214 Darren Carrington .05 .01
❑ 215 John Friesz .10 .02
❑ 216 Ronnie Harmon .05 .01
❑ 217 Stan Humphries .10 .02
❑ 218 Nate Lewis .05 .01
❑ 219 Natrone Means .25 .08
❑ 220 Anthony Miller .10 .02
❑ 221 Chris Mims .05 .01
❑ 222 Eric Moten .05 .01
❑ 223 Leslie O'Neal .05 .01
❑ 224 Junior Seau .25 .08
❑ 225 Morten Andersen .05 .01
❑ 226 Gene Atkins .05 .01
❑ 227 Derek Brown RBK .05 .01
❑ 228 Toi Cook .05 .01
❑ 229 Vaughn Dunbar .05 .01
❑ 230 Quinn Early .10 .02
❑ 231 Reggie Freeman .05 .01
❑ 232 Tyrone Hughes .10 .02
❑ 233 Rickey Jackson .05 .01
❑ 234 Eric Martin .05 .01
❑ 235 Sam Mills .05 .01
❑ 236 Brad Muster .05 .01
❑ 237 Torrance Small .05 .01
❑ 238 Irv Smith .05 .01
❑ 239 Wade Wilson .05 .01
❑ 240 Eric Allen .05 .01
❑ 241 Victor Bailey .05 .01
❑ 242 Fred Barnett .10 .02
❑ 243 Mark Bavaro .05 .01
❑ 244 Bubby Brister .10 .02
❑ 245 Randall Cunningham .25 .08
❑ 246 Antone Davis .05 .01
❑ 247 Britt Hager RC .05 .01
❑ 248 Vaughn Hebron .05 .01
❑ 249 James Joseph .05 .01
❑ 250 Seth Joyner .05 .01
❑ 251 Rich Miano .05 .01
❑ 252 Heath Sherman .05 .01
❑ 253 Clyde Simmons .05 .01
❑ 254 Herschel Walker .10 .02
❑ 255 Calvin Williams .10 .02
❑ 256 Jerry Ball .05 .01
❑ 257 Mark Carrier WR .10 .02
❑ 258 Michael Jackson .10 .02
❑ 259 Mike Johnson .05 .01
❑ 260 James Jones DT .05 .01
❑ 261 Brian Kinchen .05 .01
❑ 262 Clay Matthews .05 .01
❑ 263 Eric Metcalf .10 .02
❑ 264 Stevon Moore .05 .01
❑ 265 Michael Dean Perry .10 .02
❑ 266 Todd Philcox .05 .01
❑ 267 Anthony Pleasant .05 .01
❑ 268 Vinny Testaverde .10 .02
❑ 269 Eric Turner .05 .01
❑ 270 Tommy Vardell .05 .01
❑ 271 Neal Anderson .05 .01
❑ 272 Trace Armstrong .05 .01
❑ 273 Mark Carrier DB .05 .01
❑ 274 Bob Christian .05 .01
❑ 275 Curtis Conway .25 .08
❑ 276 Richard Dent .10 .02
❑ 277 Robert Green .05 .01
❑ 278 Jim Harbaugh .25 .08
❑ 279 Craig Heyward .10 .02
❑ 280 Terry Obee .05 .01
❑ 281 Alonzo Spellman .05 .01
❑ 282 Tom Waddle .05 .01
❑ 283 Peter Tom Willis .05 .01
❑ 284 Donnell Woolford .05 .01
❑ 285 Tim Worley .05 .01
❑ 286 Chris Zorich .05 .01
❑ 287 Steve Broussard .05 .01
❑ 288 Darion Conner .05 .01
❑ 289 Jumpy Geathers .05 .01
❑ 290 Michael Haynes .10 .02
❑ 291 Bobby Hebert .05 .01
❑ 292 Lincoln Kennedy .05 .01
❑ 293 Chris Miller .05 .01
❑ 294 David Mims RC .05 .01
❑ 295 Erric Pegram .05 .01
❑ 296 Mike Pritchard .05 .01
❑ 297 Andre Rison .10 .02
❑ 298 Deion Sanders .50 .20
❑ 299 Chuck Smith .05 .01
❑ 300 Tony Smith RB .05 .01
❑ 301 Johnny Bailey .05 .01
❑ 302 Steve Beuerlein .10 .02
❑ 303 Chuck Cecil .05 .01
❑ 304 Chris Chandler .10 .02
❑ 305 Gary Clark .10 .02
❑ 306 Rick Cunningham RC .05 .01
❑ 307 Ken Harvey .05 .01
❑ 308 Garrison Hearst .25 .08
❑ 309 Randal Hill .05 .01
❑ 310 Robert Massey .05 .01
❑ 311 Ronald Moore .05 .01
❑ 312 Ricky Proehl .05 .01
❑ 313 Eric Swann .10 .02
❑ 314 Aeneas Williams .05 .01
❑ 315 Michael Bates .05 .01
❑ 316 Brian Blades .10 .02
❑ 317 Carlton Gray .05 .01
❑ 318 Paul Green RC .05 .01
❑ 319 Patrick Hunter .05 .01
❑ 320 John Kasay .05 .01
❑ 321 Cortez Kennedy .10 .02
❑ 322 Kelvin Martin .05 .01
❑ 323 Dan McGwire .05 .01
❑ 324 Rick Mirer .25 .08
❑ 325 Eugene Robinson .05 .01
❑ 326 Rick Tuten .05 .01
❑ 327 Chris Warren .10 .02
❑ 328 John L. Williams .05 .01
❑ 329 Reggie Cobb .05 .01
❑ 330 Horace Copeland .05 .01
❑ 331 Lawrence Dawsey .05 .01
❑ 332 Santana Dotson .10 .02
❑ 333 Craig Erickson .05 .01
❑ 334 Ron Hall .05 .01
❑ 335 Courtney Hawkins .05 .01
❑ 336 Keith McCants .05 .01
❑ 337 Hardy Nickerson .10 .02
❑ 338 Mazio Royster RC .05 .01
❑ 339 Broderick Thomas .05 .01
❑ 340 Casey Weldon RC .25 .08
❑ 341 Mark Wheeler .05 .01
❑ 342 Vince Workman .05 .01
❑ 343 Flipper Anderson .05 .01
❑ 344 Jerome Bettis .50 .20
❑ 345 Richard Buchanan .05 .01
❑ 346 Shane Conlan .05 .01
❑ 347 Troy Drayton .05 .01
❑ 348 Henry Ellard .10 .02
❑ 349 Jim Everett .10 .02
❑ 350 Cleveland Gary .05 .01
❑ 351 Sean Gilbert .05 .01
❑ 352 David Lang .05 .01
❑ 353 Todd Lyght .05 .01
❑ 354 T.J. Rubley .05 .01
❑ 355 Jackie Slater .05 .01
❑ 356 Russell White .10 .02
❑ 357 Bruce Armstrong .05 .01
❑ 358 Drew Bledsoe [illegible] [illegible]
❑ 359 Vincent Brisby .10 .02
❑ 360 Vincent Brown .05 .01
❑ 361 Ben Coates .10 .02
❑ 362 Marv Cook .05 .01
❑ 363 Ray Crittenden RC .05 .01
❑ 364 Corey Croom RC .05 .01
❑ 365 Pat Harlow .05 .01
❑ 366 Dion Lambert .05 .01
❑ 367 Greg McMurtry .05 .01
❑ 368 Leonard Russell .05 .01
❑ 369 Scott Secules .05 .01
❑ 370 Chris Slade .05 .01
❑ 371 Michael Timpson .05 .01
❑ 372 Kevin Turner .05 .01
❑ 373 Ashley Ambrose .05 .01
❑ 374 Dean Biasucci .05 .01
❑ 375 Duane Bickett .05 .01
❑ 376 Quentin Coryatt .05 .01
❑ 377 Rodney Culver .05 .01
❑ 378 Sean Dawkins RC .25 .08
❑ 379 Jeff George .25 .08
❑ 380 Jeff Herrod .05 .01
❑ 381 Jessie Hester .05 .01
❑ 382 Anthony Johnson .10 .02
❑ 383 Reggie Langhorne .05 .01
❑ 384 Roosevelt Potts .05 .01
❑ 385 William Schultz RC .05 .01
❑ 386 Rohn Stark .05 .01
❑ 387 Clarence Verdin .05 .01
❑ 388 Carl Banks .05 .01
❑ 389 Reggie Brooks .10 .02
❑ 390 Earnest Byner .05 .01
❑ 391 Tom Carter .05 .01
❑ 392 Cary Conklin .05 .01
❑ 393 Pat Eilers RC .05 .01
❑ 394 Ricky Ervins .05 .01
❑ 395 Rich Gannon .25 .08
❑ 396 Darrell Green .05 .01
❑ 397 Desmond Howard .10 .02
❑ 398 Chip Lohmiller .05 .01
❑ 399 Sterling Palmer RC .05 .01
❑ 400 Mark Rypien .05 .01
❑ 401 Ricky Sanders .05 .01
❑ 402 Johnny Thomas CB .05 .01
❑ 403 John Copeland .05 .01
❑ 404 Derrick Fenner .05 .01
❑ 405 Alex Gordon .05 .01
❑ 406 Harold Green .05 .01
❑ 407 Lance Gunn .05 .01
❑ 408 David Klingler .05 .01
❑ 409 Ricardo McDonald .05 .01
❑ 410 Tim McGee .05 .01
❑ 411 Reggie Rembert .05 .01
❑ 412 Patrick Robinson .05 .01
❑ 413 Jay Schroeder .05 .01
❑ 414 Erik Wilhelm .05 .01
❑ 415 Alfred Williams .05 .01
❑ 416 Darryl Williams .05 .01
❑ 417 Sam Adams RC .10 .02
❑ 418 Mario Bates RC .25 .08
❑ 419 James Bostic RC .25 .08
❑ 420 Bucky Brooks RC .05 .01
❑ 421 Jeff Burris RC .10 .02
❑ 422 Shante Carver RC .05 .01
❑ 423 Jeff Cothran RC .05 .01
❑ 424 Lake Dawson RC .10 .02
❑ 425 Trent Dilfer RC 1.25 .50
❑ 426 Marshall Faulk RC 5.00 2.00
❑ 427 Cory Fleming RC .05 .01
❑ 428 William Floyd RC .25 .08
❑ 429 Glenn Foley RC .25 .08
❑ 430 Rob Fredrickson RC .10 .02
❑ 431 Charlie Garner RC 1.25 .50

❑	432 Greg Hill RC	.25	.08
❑	433 Charles Johnson RC	.25	.08
❑	434 Calvin Jones RC	.05	.01
❑	435 Jimmy Klingler RC	.05	.01
❑	436 Antonio Langham RC	.10	.02
❑	437 Kevin Lee RC	.05	.01
❑	438 Chuck Levy RC	.05	.01
❑	439 Willie McGinest RC	.25	.08
❑	440 Jamir Miller RC	.10	.02
❑	441 Johnnie Morton RC	.50	.20
❑	442 David Palmer RC	.25	.08
❑	443 Errict Rhett RC	.25	.08
❑	444 Corey Sawyer RC	.10	.02
❑	445 Darnay Scott RC	.50	.20
❑	446 Heath Shuler RC	.25	.08
❑	447 Lamar Smith RC	1.25	.50
❑	448 Dan Wilkinson RC	.10	.02
❑	449 Bernard Williams RC	.05	.01
❑	450 Bryant Young RC	.40	.15
❑	P1 Sterling Sharpe Promo	.75	.30

1995 Pacific

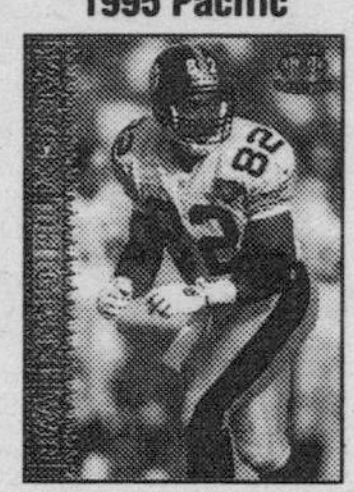

❑	COMPLETE SET (450)	25.00	10.00
❑	1 Randy Baldwin	.10	.02
❑	2 Tommy Barnhardt	.10	.02
❑	3 Tim McKyer	.10	.02
❑	4 Sam Mills	.20	.07
❑	5 Brian O'Neal	.10	.02
❑	6 Frank Reich	.10	.02
❑	7 Jack Trudeau	.10	.02
❑	8 Vernon Turner	.10	.02
❑	9 Kerry Collins RC	1.50	.60
❑	10 Shawn King	.10	.02
❑	11 Steve Beuerlein	.20	.07
❑	12 Derek Brown TE	.10	.02
❑	13 Reggie Clark	.10	.02
❑	14 Reggie Cobb	.10	.02
❑	15 Desmond Howard	.20	.07
❑	16 Jeff Lageman	.10	.02
❑	17 Kelvin Pritchett	.10	.02
❑	18 Cedric Tillman	.10	.02
❑	19 Tony Boselli RC	.30	.10
❑	20 James O. Stewart RC	1.25	.50
❑	21 Eric Davis	.10	.02
❑	22 William Floyd	.20	.07
❑	23 Elvis Grbac	.30	.10
❑	24 Brent Jones	.10	.02
❑	25 Ken Norton, Jr.	.20	.07
❑	26 Bart Oates	.10	.02
❑	27 Jerry Rice	1.00	.40
❑	28 Deion Sanders	.40	.15
❑	29 John Taylor	.10	.02
❑	30 Adam Walker RC	.10	.02
❑	31 Steve Wallace	.10	.02
❑	32 Ricky Watters	.20	.07
❑	33 Lee Woodall	.10	.02
❑	34 Bryant Young	.20	.07
❑	35 Steve Young	.75	.30
❑	36 J.J. Stokes RC	.30	.10
❑	37 Troy Aikman	1.00	.40
❑	38 Larry Allen	.20	.07
❑	39 Chris Boniol RC	.10	.02
❑	40 Lincoln Coleman	.10	.02
❑	41 Charles Haley	.20	.07
❑	42 Alvin Harper	.10	.02
❑	43 Chad Hennings	.20	.07
❑	44 Michael Irvin	.30	.10
❑	45 Daryl Johnston	.20	.07
❑	46 Leon Lett	.10	.02
❑	47 Nate Newton	.20	.07
❑	48 Jay Novacek	.20	.07
❑	49 Emmitt Smith	1.50	.60
❑	50 James Washington	.10	.02
❑	51 Kevin Williams	.20	.07
❑	52 Sherman Williams RC	.10	.02
❑	53 Barry Foster	.20	.07
❑	54 Eric Green	.10	.02
❑	55 Kevin Greene	.20	.07
❑	56 Andre Hastings	.20	.07
❑	57 Charles Johnson	.20	.07
❑	58 Greg Lloyd	.20	.07
❑	59 Ernie Mills	.10	.02
❑	60 Byron Bam Morris	.10	.02
❑	61 Neil O'Donnell	.20	.07
❑	62 Darren Perry	.10	.02
❑	63 Yancey Thigpen RC	.20	.07
❑	64 Mike Tomczak	.10	.02
❑	65 John L. Williams	.10	.02
❑	66 Rod Woodson	.20	.07
❑	67 Mark Bruener RC	.20	.07
❑	68 Kordell Stewart RC	1.50	.60
❑	69 Jeff Brohm RC	.10	.02
❑	70 Andre Coleman	.10	.02
❑	71 Reuben Davis	.10	.02
❑	72 Dennis Gibson	.10	.02
❑	73 Darrien Gordon	.10	.02
❑	74 Stan Humphries	.20	.07
❑	75 Shawn Jefferson	.10	.02
❑	76 Tony Martin	.20	.07
❑	77 Natrone Means	.20	.07
❑	78 Shannon Mitchell RC	.10	.02
❑	79 Leslie O'Neal	.20	.07
❑	80 Alfred Pupunu	.10	.02
❑	81 Stanley Richard	.10	.02
❑	82 Junior Seau	.30	.10
❑	83 Mark Seay	.20	.07
❑	84 Derrick Alexander WR	.30	.10
❑	85 Carl Banks	.10	.02
❑	86 Isaac Booth	.10	.02
❑	87 Rob Burnett	.10	.02
❑	88 Earnest Byner	.10	.02
❑	89 Steve Everitt	.10	.02
❑	90 Leroy Hoard	.10	.02
❑	91 Pepper Johnson	.10	.02
❑	92 Antonio Langham	.10	.02
❑	93 Eric Metcalf	.20	.07
❑	94 Anthony Pleasant	.10	.02
❑	95 Frank Stams	.10	.02
❑	96 Vinny Testaverde	.20	.07
❑	97 Eric Turner	.10	.02
❑	98 Mike Miller RC	.10	.02
❑	99 Craig Powell RC	.10	.02
❑	100 Gene Atkins	.10	.02
❑	101 Aubrey Beavers	.10	.02
❑	102 Tim Bowens	.10	.02
❑	103 Keith Byars	.10	.02
❑	104 Bryan Cox	.10	.02
❑	105 Aaron Craver	.10	.02
❑	106 Jeff Cross	.10	.02
❑	107 Irving Fryar	.20	.07
❑	108 Dan Marino	2.00	.75
❑	109 O.J. McDuffie	.30	.10
❑	110 Bernie Parmalee	.20	.07
❑	111 James Saxon	.10	.02
❑	112 Keith Sims	.10	.02
❑	113 Irving Spikes	.20	.07
❑	114 Pete Mitchell RC	.20	.07
❑	115 Terry Allen	.20	.07
❑	116 Cris Carter	.30	.10
❑	117 Adrian Cooper	.10	.02
❑	118 Bernard Dafney	.10	.02
❑	119 Jack Del Rio	.10	.02
❑	120 Vencie Glenn	.10	.02
❑	121 Qadry Ismail	.20	.07
❑	122 Carlos Jenkins	.10	.02
❑	123 Andrew Jordan	.10	.02
❑	124 Ed McDaniel	.10	.02
❑	125 Warren Moon	.20	.07
❑	126 David Palmer	.20	.07
❑	127 John Randle	.20	.07
❑	128 Jake Reed	.20	.07
❑	129 Derrick Alexander DE RC	.10	.02
❑	130 Chad May RC	.10	.02
❑	131 Korey Stringer RC	.20	.07
❑	132 Bruce Armstrong	.10	.02
❑	133 Drew Bledsoe	.60	.25
❑	134 Vincent Brisby	.10	.02
❑	135 Troy Brown	.30	.10
❑	136 Vincent Brown	.10	.02
❑	137 Marion Butts	.10	.02
❑	138 Ben Coates	.20	.07
❑	139 Ray Crittenden	.10	.02
❑	140 Maurice Hurst	.10	.02
❑	141 Aaron Jones	.10	.02
❑	142 Willie McGinest	.20	.07
❑	143 Marty Moore RC	.30	.10
❑	144 Mike Pitts	.10	.02
❑	145 Leroy Thompson	.10	.02
❑	146 Michael Timpson	.10	.02
❑	147 Bennie Blades	.10	.02
❑	148 Jocelyn Borgella	.10	.02
❑	149 Anthony Carter	.20	.07
❑	150 Willie Clay	.10	.02
❑	151 Mel Gray	.10	.02
❑	152 Mike Johnson	.10	.02
❑	153 Dave Krieg	.10	.02
❑	154 Robert Massey	.10	.02
❑	155 Scott Mitchell	.20	.07
❑	156 Herman Moore	.30	.10
❑	157 Johnnie Morton	.20	.07
❑	158 Barry Sanders	1.50	.60
❑	159 Chris Spielman	.20	.07
❑	160 Broderick Thomas	.10	.02
❑	161 Cory Schlesinger RC	.20	.07
❑	162 Marcus Allen	.30	.10
❑	163 Donnell Bennett	.20	.07
❑	164 J.J. Birden	.10	.02
❑	165 Matt Blundin RC	.10	.02
❑	166 Steve Bono	.20	.07
❑	167 Dale Carter	.20	.07
❑	168 Lake Dawson	.20	.07
❑	169 Ron Dickerson	.10	.02
❑	170 Lin Elliott	.10	.02
❑	171 Jaime Fields	.10	.02
❑	172 Greg Hill	.20	.07
❑	173 Danan Hughes	.10	.02
❑	174 Neil Smith	.20	.07
❑	175 Steve Stenstrom RC	.10	.02
❑	176 Edgar Bennett	.20	.07
❑	177 Robert Brooks	.30	.10
❑	178 Mark Brunell	.60	.25
❑	179 Doug Evans RC	.30	.10
❑	180 Brett Favre	2.00	.75
❑	181 Corey Harris	.10	.02
❑	182 LeShon Johnson	.20	.07
❑	183 Sean Jones	.10	.02
❑	184 Lenny McGill RC	.10	.02
❑	185 Terry Mickens	.10	.02
❑	186 Sterling Sharpe	.20	.07
❑	187 Joe Sims	.10	.02
❑	188 Darrell Thompson	.10	.02
❑	189 Reggie White	.30	.10
❑	190 Craig Newsome RC	.10	.02
❑	191 Tim Brown	.30	.10
❑	192 Vince Evans	.10	.02
❑	193 Rob Fredrickson	.10	.02
❑	194 Andrew Glover RC	.10	.02
❑	195 Jeff Hostetler	.20	.07
❑	196 Rocket Ismail	.20	.07
❑	197 Jeff Jaeger	.10	.02
❑	198 James Jett	.20	.07
❑	199 Chester McGlockton	.20	.07
❑	200 Don Mosebar	.10	.02
❑	201 Tom Rathman	.10	.02
❑	202 Harvey Williams	.10	.02
❑	203 Steve Wisniewski	.10	.02
❑	204 Alexander Wright	.10	.02
❑	205 Napoleon Kaufman RC	1.25	.50
❑	206 Trace Armstrong	.10	.02
❑	207 Curtis Conway	.30	.10
❑	208 Raymont Harris	.10	.02
❑	209 Erik Kramer	.10	.02
❑	210 Nate Lewis	.10	.02
❑	211 Shane Matthews RC	.30	.10
❑	212 John Thierry	.10	.02
❑	213 Lewis Tillman	.10	.02
❑	214 Tom Waddle	.10	.02
❑	215 Steve Walsh	.10	.02
❑	216 James Williams T RC	.10	.02
❑	217 Donnell Woolford	.10	.02
❑	218 Chris Zorich	.10	.02
❑	219 Rashaan Salaam RC	.20	.07
❑	220 John Booty	.10	.02
❑	221 Michael Brooks	.10	.02
❑	222 Dave Brown	.20	.07
❑	223 Chris Calloway	.10	.02
❑	224 Gary Downs	.10	.02
❑	225 Kent Graham	.20	.07
❑	226 Keith Hamilton	.10	.02
❑	227 Rodney Hampton	.20	.07

❑ 228 Brian Kozlowski .10 .02
❑ 229 Thomas Lewis .20 .07
❑ 230 Dave Meggett .10 .02
❑ 231 Aaron Pierce .10 .02
❑ 232 Mike Sherrard .10 .02
❑ 233 Phillippi Sparks .10 .02
❑ 234 Tyrone Wheatley RC 1.25 .50
❑ 235 Trev Alberts .10 .02
❑ 236 Aaron Bailey RC .10 .02
❑ 237 Jason Belser .10 .02
❑ 238 Tony Bennett .10 .02
❑ 239 Kerry Cash .10 .02
❑ 240 Marshall Faulk 1.25 .50
❑ 241 Stephen Grant .10 .02
❑ 242 Jeff Herrod .10 .02
❑ 243 Ronald Humphrey .10 .02
❑ 244 Kirk Lowdermilk .10 .02
❑ 245 Don Majkowski .10 .02
❑ 246 Tony McCoy .10 .02
❑ 247 Floyd Turner .10 .02
❑ 248 Lamont Warren .10 .02
❑ 249 Zack Crockett RC .20 .07
❑ 250 Michael Bankston .10 .02
❑ 251 Larry Centers .20 .07
❑ 252 Gary Clark .10 .02
❑ 253 Ed Cunningham .10 .02
❑ 254 Garrison Hearst .30 .10
❑ 255 Eric Hill .10 .02
❑ 256 Terry Irving .10 .02
❑ 257 Lorenzo Lynch .10 .02
❑ 258 Jamir Miller .10 .02
❑ 259 Ronald Moore .10 .02
❑ 260 Terry Samuels .10 .02
❑ 261 Jay Schroeder .10 .02
❑ 262 Eric Swann .20 .07
❑ 263 Aeneas Williams .10 .02
❑ 264 Frank Sanders RC .30 .10
❑ 265 Morten Andersen .10 .02
❑ 266 Mario Bates .20 .07
❑ 267 Derek Brown RBK .10 .02
❑ 268 Darion Conner .10 .02
❑ 269 Quinn Early .20 .07
❑ 270 Jim Everett .10 .02
❑ 271 Michael Haynes .20 .07
❑ 272 Wayne Martin .10 .02
❑ 273 Derrell Mitchell RC .10 .02
❑ 274 Lorenzo Neal .10 .02
❑ 275 Jimmy Spencer .10 .02
❑ 276 Winfred Tubbs .10 .02
❑ 277 Renaldo Turnbull .10 .02
❑ 278 Jeff Uhlenhake .10 .02
❑ 279 Steve Atwater .10 .02
❑ 280 Keith Burns RC .10 .02
❑ 281 Butler By'Not'e RC .20 .07
❑ 282 Jeff Campbell .10 .02
❑ 283 Derrick Clark RC .10 .02
❑ 284 Shane Dronett .10 .02
❑ 285 Jason Elam .20 .07
❑ 286 John Elway 2.00 .75
❑ 287 Jerry Evans .10 .02
❑ 288 Karl Mecklenburg .10 .02
❑ 289 Glyn Milburn .10 .02
❑ 290 Anthony Miller .20 .07
❑ 291 Tom Rouen .10 .02
❑ 292 Leonard Russell .10 .02
❑ 293 Shannon Sharpe .20 .07
❑ 294 Steve Russ RC .10 .02
❑ 295 Mel Agee .10 .02
❑ 296 Lester Archambeau .10 .02
❑ 297 Bert Emanuel .30 .10
❑ 298 Jeff George .20 .07
❑ 299 Craig Heyward .20 .07
❑ 300 Bobby Hebert .10 .02
❑ 301 D.J. Johnson .10 .02
❑ 302 Mike Kenn .10 .02
❑ 303 Terance Mathis .20 .07
❑ 304 Clay Matthews .20 .07
❑ 305 Erric Pegram .20 .07
❑ 306 Andre Rison .20 .07
❑ 307 Chuck Smith .10 .02
❑ 308 Jessie Tuggle .10 .02
❑ 309 Lorenzo Styles RC .10 .02
❑ 310 Cornelius Bennett .20 .07
❑ 311 Bill Brooks .10 .02
❑ 312 Jeff Burris .10 .02
❑ 313 Carwell Gardner .10 .02
❑ 314 Kent Hull .10 .02
❑ 315 Yonel Jourdain .10 .02
❑ 316 Jim Kelly .30 .10
❑ 317 Vince Marrow .10 .02
❑ 318 Pete Metzelaars .10 .02
❑ 319 Andre Reed .20 .07
❑ 320 Kurt Schulz RC .10 .02
❑ 321 Bruce Smith .30 .10
❑ 322 Darryl Talley .10 .02
❑ 323 Matt Darby .10 .02
❑ 324 Justin Armour RC .10 .02
❑ 325 Todd Collins RC 1.25 .50
❑ 326 David Alexander DE .10 .02
❑ 327 Eric Allen .10 .02
❑ 328 Fred Barnett .20 .07
❑ 329 Randall Cunningham .30 .10
❑ 330 William Fuller .10 .02
❑ 331 Charlie Garner .30 .10
❑ 332 Vaughn Hebron .10 .02
❑ 333 James Joseph .10 .02
❑ 334 Bill Romanowski .10 .02
❑ 335 Ken Rose .10 .02
❑ 336 Jeff Snyder .10 .02
❑ 337 William Thomas .10 .02
❑ 338 Herschel Walker .20 .07
❑ 339 Calvin Williams .20 .07
❑ 340 Dave Barr RC .10 .02
❑ 341 Chidi Ahanotu .10 .02
❑ 342 Barney Bussey .10 .02
❑ 343 Horace Copeland .10 .02
❑ 344 Trent Dilfer .30 .10
❑ 345 Craig Erickson .10 .02
❑ 346 Paul Gruber .10 .02
❑ 347 Courtney Hawkins .10 .02
❑ 348 Lonnie Marts .10 .02
❑ 349 Martin Mayhew .10 .02
❑ 350 Hardy Nickerson .10 .02
❑ 351 Errict Rhett .20 .07
❑ 352 Lamar Thomas .10 .02
❑ 353 Charles Wilson .10 .02
❑ 354 Vince Workman .10 .02
❑ 355 Derrick Brooks RC 1.50 .60
❑ 356 Warren Sapp RC 1.50 .60
❑ 357 Sam Adams .10 .02
❑ 358 Michael Bates .10 .02
❑ 359 Brian Blades .20 .07
❑ 360 Carlton Gray .10 .02
❑ 361 Bill Hitchcock .10 .02
❑ 362 Cortez Kennedy .20 .07
❑ 363 Rick Mirer .20 .07
❑ 364 Eugene Robinson .10 .02
❑ 365 Michael Sinclair .10 .02
❑ 366 Steve Smith .10 .02
❑ 367 Bob Spitulski .10 .02
❑ 368 Rick Tuten .10 .02
❑ 369 Chris Warren .20 .07
❑ 370 Terrence Warren .10 .02
❑ 371 Christian Fauria RC .20 .07
❑ 372 Joey Galloway RC 1.50 .60
❑ 373 Boomer Esiason .20 .07
❑ 374 Aaron Glenn .10 .02
❑ 375 Victor Green RC .10 .02
❑ 376 Johnny Johnson .10 .02
❑ 377 Mo Lewis .10 .02
❑ 378 Ronnie Lott .20 .07
❑ 379 Nick Lowery .10 .02
❑ 380 Johnny Mitchell .10 .02
❑ 381 Rob Moore .20 .07
❑ 382 Adrian Murrell .20 .07
❑ 383 Anthony Prior .10 .02
❑ 384 Brian Washington .10 .02
❑ 385 Matt Willig RC .10 .02
❑ 386 Kyle Brady RC .30 .10
❑ 387 Flipper Anderson .10 .02
❑ 388 Johnny Bailey .10 .02
❑ 389 Jerome Bettis .30 .10
❑ 390 Isaac Bruce .50 .20
❑ 391 Shane Conlan .10 .02
❑ 392 Troy Drayton .10 .02
❑ 393 D'Marco Farr .10 .02
❑ 394 Jessie Hester .10 .02
❑ 395 Todd Kinchen .10 .02
❑ 396 Ron Middleton .10 .02
❑ 397 Chris Miller .10 .02
❑ 398 Marquez Pope .10 .02
❑ 399 Robert Young .10 .02
❑ 400 Tony Zendejas .10 .02
❑ 401 Kevin Carter RC .30 .10
❑ 402 Reggie Brooks .20 .07
❑ 403 Tom Carter .10 .02
❑ 404 Andre Collins .10 .02
❑ 405 Pat Eilers .10 .02
❑ 406 Henry Ellard .20 .07
❑ 407 Ricky Ervins .10 .02
❑ 408 Gus Frerotte .20 .07
❑ 409 Ken Harvey .10 .02
❑ 410 Jim Lachey .10 .02
❑ 411 Brian Mitchell .10 .02
❑ 412 Reggie Roby .10 .02
❑ 413 Heath Shuler .20 .07
❑ 414 Tyronne Stowe .10 .02
❑ 415 Tydus Winans .10 .02
❑ 416 Cory Raymer RC .10 .02
❑ 417 Michael Westbrook RC .30 .10
❑ 418 Jeff Blake RC .75 .30
❑ 419 Steve Broussard .10 .02
❑ 420 Dave Cadigan .10 .02
❑ 421 [illegible]
❑ 422 Derrick Fenner .10 .02
❑ 423 James Francis .10 .02
❑ 424 Lee Johnson .10 .02
❑ 425 Louis Oliver .10 .02
❑ 426 Carl Pickens .20 .07
❑ 427 Jeff Query .10 .02
❑ 428 Corey Sawyer .10 .02
❑ 429 Darnay Scott .20 .07
❑ 430 Dan Wilkinson .20 .07
❑ 431 Alfred Williams .10 .02
❑ 432 Ki-Jana Carter RC .30 .10
❑ 433 David Dunn RC .10 .02
❑ 434 John Walsh RC .10 .02
❑ 435 Gary Brown .10 .02
❑ 436 Pat Carter .10 .02
❑ 437 Ray Childress .10 .02
❑ 438 Ernest Givins .10 .02
❑ 439 Haywood Jeffires .10 .02
❑ 440 Lamar Lathon .10 .02
❑ 441 Bruce Matthews .10 .02
❑ 442 Marcus Robertson .10 .02
❑ 443 Eddie Robinson .10 .02
❑ 444 Malcolm Seabron RC .10 .02
❑ 445 Webster Slaughter .10 .02
❑ 446 Al Smith .10 .02
❑ 447 Billy Joe Tolliver .10 .02
❑ 448 Lorenzo White .10 .02
❑ 449 Steve McNair RC 3.00 1.25
❑ 450 Rodney Thomas RC .20 .07
❑ P1 Natrone Means Promo 1.00 .40
❑ P1J Natrone Means Promo 1.00 .40

1996 Pacific

❑ COMPLETE SET (450) 40.00 20.00
❑ 1 Jeff Feagles .10 .02
❑ 2 Rob Moore .20 .07
❑ 3 Clyde Simmons .10 .02
❑ 4 Mike Buck .10 .02
❑ 5 Aeneas Williams .10 .02
❑ 6 Simeon Rice RC 1.00 .40
❑ 7 Garrison Hearst .20 .07
❑ 8 Eric Swann .10 .02
❑ 9 Dave Krieg .10 .02
❑ 10 Leeland McElroy RC .20 .07
❑ 11 Oscar McBride .10 .02
❑ 12 Frank Sanders .20 .07
❑ 13 Larry Centers .20 .07
❑ 14 Seth Joyner .10 .02
❑ 15 Stevie Anderson .10 .02
❑ 16 Craig Heyward .10 .02
❑ 17 Devin Bush .10 .02
❑ 18 Eric Metcalf .10 .02
❑ 19 Jeff George .20 .07
❑ 20 Richard Huntley RC .20 .07
❑ 21 Jamal Anderson RC .50 .20
❑ 22 Bert Emanuel .20 .07

❑ 23 Terance Mathis .10 .02
❑ 24 Roman Fortin .10 .02
❑ 25 Jessie Tuggle .10 .02
❑ 26 Morten Andersen .10 .02
❑ 27 Chris Doleman .10 .02
❑ 28 D.J. Johnson .10 .02
❑ 29 Kevin Ross .10 .02
❑ 30 Michael Jackson .20 .07
❑ 31 Eric Zeier .10 .02
❑ 32 Jonathan Ogden RC .40 .15
❑ 33 Eric Turner .10 .02
❑ 34 Andre Rison .20 .07
❑ 35 Lorenzo White .10 .02
❑ 36 Earnest Byner .10 .02
❑ 37 Derrick Alexander WR .20 .07
❑ 38 Brian Kinchen .10 .02
❑ 39 Anthony Pleasant .10 .02
❑ 40 Vinny Testaverde .20 .07
❑ 41 Pepper Johnson .10 .02
❑ 42 Frank Hartley .10 .02
❑ 43 Craig Powell .10 .02
❑ 44 Leroy Hoard .10 .02
❑ 45 Kent Hull .10 .02
❑ 46 Bryce Paup .10 .02
❑ 47 Andre Reed .20 .07
❑ 48 Darick Holmes .10 .02
❑ 49 Russell Copeland .10 .02
❑ 50 Jerry Ostroski .10 .02
❑ 51 Chris Green .10 .02
❑ 52 Eric Moulds RC 1.25 .50
❑ 53 Justin Armour .10 .02
❑ 54 Jim Kelly .40 .15
❑ 55 Cornelius Bennett .10 .02
❑ 56 Steve Tasker .10 .02
❑ 57 Thurman Thomas .40 .15
❑ 58 Bruce Smith .20 .07
❑ 59 Todd Collins .20 .07
❑ 60 Shawn King .10 .02
❑ 61 Don Beebe .10 .02
❑ 62 John Kasay .10 .02
❑ 63 Tim McKyer .10 .02
❑ 64 Darion Conner .10 .02
❑ 65 Pete Metzelaars .10 .02
❑ 66 Derrick Moore .10 .02
❑ 67 Blake Brockermeyer .10 .02
❑ 68 Tim Biakabutuka RC .40 .15
❑ 69 Sam Mills .10 .02
❑ 70 Vince Workman .10 .02
❑ 71 Kerry Collins .40 .15
❑ 72 Carlton Bailey .10 .02
❑ 73 Mark Carrier WR .10 .02
❑ 74 Donnell Woolford .10 .02
❑ 75 Walt Harris RC .10 .02
❑ 76 John Thierry .10 .02
❑ 77 Al Fontenot RC .10 .02
❑ 78 Lewis Tillman .10 .02
❑ 79 Curtis Conway .40 .15
❑ 80 Chris Zorich .10 .02
❑ 81 Mark Carrier DB .10 .02
❑ 82 Bobby Engram RC .40 .15
❑ 83 Alonzo Spellman .10 .02
❑ 84 Rashaan Salaam .20 .07
❑ 85 Michael Timpson .10 .02
❑ 86 Nate Lewis .10 .02
❑ 87 James Williams T .10 .02
❑ 88 Jeff Graham .10 .02
❑ 89 Erik Kramer .10 .02
❑ 90 Willie Anderson .10 .02
❑ 91 Tony McGee .10 .02
❑ 92 Marco Battaglia .10 .02
❑ 93 Dan Wilkinson .10 .02
❑ 94 John Walsh .10 .02
❑ 95 Eric Bieniemy .10 .02
❑ 96 Ricardo McDonald .10 .02
❑ 97 Carl Pickens .20 .07
❑ 98 Kevin Sargent .10 .02
❑ 99 David Dunn .10 .02
❑ 100 Jeff Blake .40 .15
❑ 101 Harold Green .10 .02
❑ 102 James Francis .10 .02
❑ 103 John Copeland .10 .02
❑ 104 Darnay Scott .20 .07
❑ 105 Darren Woodson .20 .07
❑ 106 Jay Novacek .10 .02
❑ 107 Charles Haley .20 .07
❑ 108 Mark Tuinei .10 .02
❑ 109 Michael Irvin .40 .15
❑ 110 Troy Aikman 1.00 .40
❑ 111 Chris Boniol .10 .02
❑ 112 Sherman Williams .10 .02
❑ 113 Deion Sanders .60 .25
❑ 114 Emmitt Smith 1.50 .60
❑ 115 Eric Bjornson .10 .02
❑ 116 Nate Newton .10 .02
❑ 117 Larry Allen .10 .02
❑ 118 Kevin Williams .10 .02
❑ 119 Leon Lett .10 .02
❑ 120 John Mobley .10 .02
❑ 121 Anthony Miller .20 .07
❑ 122 Brian Habib .10 .02
❑ 123 Aaron Craver .10 .02
❑ 124 Glyn Milburn .10 .02
❑ 125 Shannon Sharpe .20 .07
❑ 126 Steve Atwater .10 .02
❑ 127 Jason Elam .20 .07
❑ 128 John Elway 2.00 .75
❑ 129 Reggie Rivers .10 .02
❑ 130 Mike Pritchard .10 .02
❑ 131 Vance Johnson .10 .02
❑ 132 Terrell Davis .75 .30
❑ 133 Tyrone Braxton .10 .02
❑ 134 Ed McCaffrey .20 .07
❑ 135 Brett Perriman .10 .02
❑ 136 Chris Spielman .10 .02
❑ 137 Luther Elliss .10 .02
❑ 138 Johnnie Morton .20 .07
❑ 139 Zefross Moss .10 .02
❑ 140 Barry Sanders 1.50 .60
❑ 141 Lomas Brown .10 .02
❑ 142 Cory Schlesinger .10 .02
❑ 143 Jason Hanson .10 .02
❑ 144 Kevin Glover .10 .02
❑ 145 Ron Rivers RC .20 .07
❑ 146 Aubrey Matthews .10 .02
❑ 147 Reggie Brown LB RC .10 .02
❑ 148 Herman Moore .20 .07
❑ 149 Scott Mitchell .20 .07
❑ 150 Brett Favre 2.00 .75
❑ 151 Sean Jones .10 .02
❑ 152 LeRoy Butler .10 .02
❑ 153 Mark Chmura .20 .07
❑ 154 Derrick Mayes RC .40 .15
❑ 155 Mark Ingram .10 .02
❑ 156 Antonio Freeman .40 .15
❑ 157 Chris Darkins RC .10 .02
❑ 158 Robert Brooks .40 .15
❑ 159 William Henderson .40 .15
❑ 160 George Koonce .10 .02
❑ 161 Craig Newsome .10 .02
❑ 162 Darius Holland .10 .02
❑ 163 George Teague .10 .02
❑ 164 Edgar Bennett .20 .07
❑ 165 Reggie White .40 .15
❑ 166 Micheal Barrow .10 .02
❑ 167 Mel Gray .10 .02
❑ 168 Anthony Dorsett .10 .02
❑ 169 Roderick Lewis .10 .02
❑ 170 Henry Ford .10 .02
❑ 171 Mark Stepnoski .10 .02
❑ 172 Chris Sanders .20 .07
❑ 173 Anthony Cook .10 .02
❑ 174 Eddie Robinson .10 .02
❑ 175 Steve McNair .75 .30
❑ 176 Haywood Jeffires .10 .02
❑ 177 Eddie George RC 1.25 .50
❑ 178 Marion Butts .10 .02
❑ 179 Malcolm Seabron .10 .02
❑ 180 Rodney Thomas .10 .02
❑ 181 Ken Dilger .20 .07
❑ 182 Zack Crockett .10 .02
❑ 183 Tony Bennett .10 .02
❑ 184 Quentin Coryatt .10 .02
❑ 185 Marshall Faulk .50 .20
❑ 186 Sean Dawkins .10 .02
❑ 187 Jim Harbaugh .20 .07
❑ 188 Eugene Daniel .10 .02
❑ 189 Roosevelt Potts .10 .02
❑ 190 Lamont Warren .10 .02
❑ 191 Will Wolford .10 .02
❑ 192 Tony Siragusa .10 .02
❑ 193 Aaron Bailey .10 .02
❑ 194 Trev Alberts .10 .02
❑ 195 Kevin Hardy .20 .07
❑ 196 Greg Spann .10 .02
❑ 197 Steve Beuerlein .20 .07
❑ 198 Steve Taneyhill .10 .02
❑ 199 Vaughn Dunbar .10 .02
❑ 200 Mark Brunell .60 .25
❑ 201 Bernard Carter .10 .02
❑ 202 James O. Stewart .20 .07
❑ 203 Tony Boselli .10 .02
❑ 204 Chris Doering .10 .02
❑ 205 Willie Jackson .20 .07
❑ 206 Tony Brackens RC .40 .15
❑ 207 Ernest Givins .10 .02
❑ 208 Le'Shai Maston .10 .02
❑ 209 Pete Mitchell .20 .07
❑ 210 Desmond Howard .20 .07
❑ 211 Vinnie Clark .10 .02
❑ 212 Jeff Lageman .10 .02
❑ 213 Derrick Walker .10 .02
❑ 214 Dan Saleaumua .10 .02
❑ 215 Derrick Thomas .40 .15
❑ 216 Neil Smith .20 .07
❑ 217 Willie Davis .10 .02
❑ 218 Mark Collins .10 .02
❑ 219 Lake Dawson .10 .02
❑ 220 Greg Hill .20 .07
❑ 221 Anthony Davis .10 .02
❑ 222 Kimble Anders .20 .07
❑ 223 Webster Slaughter .10 .02
❑ 224 Tamarick Vanover .20 .07
❑ 225 Marcus Allen .40 .15
❑ 226 Steve Bono .10 .02
❑ 227 Will Shields .10 .02
❑ 228 Karim Abdul-Jabbar RC .40 .15
❑ 229 Tim Bowens .10 .02
❑ 230 Keith Sims .10 .02
❑ 231 Terry Kirby .20 .07
❑ 232 Gene Atkins .10 .02
❑ 233 Dan Marino 2.00 .75
❑ 234 Richmond Webb .10 .02
❑ 235 Gary Clark .10 .02
❑ 236 O.J. McDuffie .20 .07
❑ 237 Marco Coleman .10 .02
❑ 238 Bernie Parmalee .10 .02
❑ 239 Randal Hill .10 .02
❑ 240 Bryan Cox .10 .02
❑ 241 Irving Fryar .20 .07
❑ 242 Derrick Alexander DE .10 .02
❑ 243 Qadry Ismail .20 .07
❑ 244 Warren Moon .20 .07
❑ 245 Cris Carter .40 .15
❑ 246 Chad May .10 .02
❑ 247 Robert Smith .20 .07
❑ 248 Fuad Reveiz .10 .02
❑ 249 Orlando Thomas .10 .02
❑ 250 Chris Hinton .10 .02
❑ 251 Jack Del Rio .10 .02
❑ 252 Moe Williams RB RC 1.00 .40
❑ 253 Roy Barker .10 .02
❑ 254 Jake Reed .20 .07
❑ 255 Adrian Cooper .10 .02
❑ 256 Curtis Martin .75 .30
❑ 257 Ben Coates .20 .07
❑ 258 Drew Bledsoe .60 .25
❑ 259 Maurice Hurst .10 .02
❑ 260 Troy Brown .40 .15
❑ 261 Bruce Armstrong .10 .02
❑ 262 Myron Guyton .10 .02
❑ 263 Dave Meggett .10 .02
❑ 264 Terry Glenn RC 1.00 .40
❑ 265 Chris Slade .10 .02
❑ 266 Vincent Brisby .10 .02
❑ 267 Willie McGinest .10 .02
❑ 268 Vincent Brown .10 .02
❑ 269 Will Moore .10 .02
❑ 270 Jay Barker .10 .02
❑ 271 Ray Zellars .10 .02
❑ 272 Derek Brown RBK .10 .02
❑ 273 William Roaf .10 .02
❑ 274 Quinn Early .10 .02
❑ 275 Michael Haynes .10 .02
❑ 276 Rufus Porter .10 .02
❑ 277 Renaldo Turnbull .10 .02
❑ 278 Wayne Martin .10 .02
❑ 279 Tyrone Hughes .10 .02
❑ 280 Irv Smith .10 .02
❑ 281 Eric Allen .10 .02
❑ 282 Mark Fields .10 .02
❑ 283 Mario Bates .20 .07
❑ 284 Jim Everett .10 .02
❑ 285 Vince Buck .10 .02
❑ 286 Alex Molden RC .10 .02
❑ 287 Tyrone Wheatley .20 .07
❑ 288 Chris Calloway .10 .02
❑ 289 Jessie Armstead .10 .02

❑ 290 Arthur Marshall .10 .02
❑ 291 Aaron Pierce .10 .02
❑ 292 Dave Brown .10 .02
❑ 293 Rodney Hampton .20 .07
❑ 294 Jumbo Elliott .10 .02
❑ 295 Mike Sherrard .10 .02
❑ 296 Howard Cross .10 .02
❑ 297 Michael Brooks .10 .02
❑ 298 Herschel Walker .20 .07
❑ 299 Danny Kanell RC .40 .15
❑ 300 Keith Elias .10 .02
❑ 301 Bobby Houston .10 .02
❑ 302 Dexter Carter .10 .02
❑ 303 Tony Casillas .10 .02
❑ 304 Kyle Brady .10 .02
❑ 305 Glenn Foley .20 .07
❑ 306 Ronald Moore .10 .02
❑ 307 Ryan Yarborough .10 .02
❑ 308 Aaron Glenn .10 .02
❑ 309 Adrian Murrell .20 .07
❑ 310 Boomer Esiason .20 .07
❑ 311 Kyle Clifton .10 .02
❑ 312 Wayne Chrebet .60 .25
❑ 313 Erik Howard .10 .02
❑ 314 Keyshawn Johnson RC 1.00 .40
❑ 315 Marvin Washington .10 .02
❑ 316 Johnny Mitchell .10 .02
❑ 317 Alex Van Dyke RC .20 .07
❑ 318 Billy Joe Hobert .20 .07
❑ 319 Andrew Glover .10 .02
❑ 320 Vince Evans .10 .02
❑ 321 Chester McGlockton .10 .02
❑ 322 Pat Swilling .10 .02
❑ 323 Rocket Ismail .10 .02
❑ 324 Eddie Anderson .10 .02
❑ 325 Rickey Dudley RC .40 .15
❑ 326 Steve Wisniewski .10 .02
❑ 327 Harvey Williams .10 .02
❑ 328 Napoleon Kaufman .40 .15
❑ 329 Tim Brown .40 .15
❑ 330 Jeff Hostetler .10 .02
❑ 331 Anthony Smith .10 .02
❑ 332 Terry McDaniel .10 .02
❑ 333 Charlie Garner .20 .07
❑ 334 Ricky Watters .20 .07
❑ 335 Brian Dawkins RC 1.25 .50
❑ 336 Randall Cunningham .40 .15
❑ 337 Gary Anderson .10 .02
❑ 338 Calvin Williams .10 .02
❑ 339 Chris T. Jones .20 .07
❑ 340 Bobby Hoying RC .40 .15
❑ 341 William Fuller .10 .02
❑ 342 William Thomas .10 .02
❑ 343 Mike Mamula .10 .02
❑ 344 Fred Barnett .10 .02
❑ 345 Rodney Peete .10 .02
❑ 346 Mark McMillian .10 .02
❑ 347 Bobby Taylor .10 .02
❑ 348 Yancey Thigpen .20 .07
❑ 349 Neil O'Donnell .20 .07
❑ 350 Rod Woodson .20 .07
❑ 351 Kordell Stewart .40 .15
❑ 352 Dermontti Dawson .10 .02
❑ 353 Norm Johnson .10 .02
❑ 354 Ernie Mills .10 .02
❑ 355 Byron Bam Morris .10 .02
❑ 356 Mark Bruener .10 .02
❑ 357 Kevin Greene .20 .07
❑ 358 Greg Lloyd .20 .07
❑ 359 Andre Hastings .10 .02
❑ 360 Erric Pegram .10 .02
❑ 361 Carnell Lake .10 .02
❑ 362 Dwayne Harper .10 .02
❑ 363 Ronnie Harmon .10 .02
❑ 364 Leslie O'Neal .10 .02
❑ 365 John Carney .10 .02
❑ 366 Stan Humphries .20 .07
❑ 367 Brian Roche RC .10 .02
❑ 368 Terrell Fletcher .10 .02
❑ 369 Shaun Gayle .10 .02
❑ 370 Alfred Pupunu .10 .02
❑ 371 Shawn Jefferson .10 .02
❑ 372 Junior Seau .40 .15
❑ 373 Mark Seay .10 .02
❑ 374 Aaron Hayden .10 .02
❑ 375 Tony Martin .20 .07
❑ 376 Steve Young .75 .30
❑ 377 J.J. Stokes .40 .15
❑ 378 Jerry Rice 1.00 .40
❑ 379 Derek Loville .10 .02
❑ 380 Lee Woodall .10 .02
❑ 381 Terrell Owens RC 2.50 1.00
❑ 382 Elvis Grbac .20 .07
❑ 383 Ricky Ervins .10 .02
❑ 384 Eric Davis .10 .02
❑ 385 Dana Stubblefield .20 .07
❑ 386 Gary Plummer .10 .02
❑ 387 Tim McDonald .10 .02
❑ 388 William Floyd .20 .07
❑ 389 Ken Norton Jr. .10 .02
❑ 390 Merton Hanks .10 .02
❑ 391 Bart Oates .10 .02
❑ 392 Brent Jones .10 .02
❑ 393 Steve Broussard .10 .02
❑ 394 Robert Blackmon .10 .02
❑ 395 Rick Tuten .10 .02
❑ 396 Pete Kendall .10 .02
❑ 397 John Friesz .10 .02
❑ 398 Terry Wooden .10 .02
❑ 399 Rick Mirer .20 .07
❑ 400 Chris Warren .20 .07
❑ 401 Joey Galloway .40 .15
❑ 402 Howard Ballard .10 .02
❑ 403 Jason Kyle .10 .02
❑ 404 Kevin Mawae .10 .02
❑ 405 Mack Strong .40 .15
❑ 406 Reggie Brown RBK RC .10 .02
❑ 407 Cortez Kennedy .10 .02
❑ 408 Sean Gilbert .10 .02
❑ 409 J.T. Thomas .10 .02
❑ 410 Shane Conlan .10 .02
❑ 411 Johnny Bailey .10 .02
❑ 412 Mark Rypien .10 .02
❑ 413 Leonard Russell .10 .02
❑ 414 Troy Drayton .10 .02
❑ 415 Jerome Bettis .40 .15
❑ 416 Jessie Hester .10 .02
❑ 417 Isaac Bruce .40 .15
❑ 418 Roman Phifer .10 .02
❑ 419 Todd Kinchen .10 .02
❑ 420 Alexander Wright .10 .02
❑ 421 Marcus Jones RC .10 .02
❑ 422 Horace Copeland .10 .02
❑ 423 Eric Curry .10 .02
❑ 424 Courtney Hawkins .10 .02
❑ 425 Alvin Harper .10 .02
❑ 426 Derrick Brooks .40 .15
❑ 427 Errict Rhett .20 .07
❑ 428 Trent Dilfer .40 .15
❑ 429 Hardy Nickerson .10 .02
❑ 430 Brad Culpepper .10 .02
❑ 431 Warren Sapp .10 .02
❑ 432 Reggie Roby .10 .02
❑ 433 Santana Dotson .10 .02
❑ 434 Jerry Ellison .10 .02
❑ 435 Lawrence Dawsey .10 .02
❑ 436 Heath Shuler .20 .07
❑ 437 Stanley Richard .20 .07
❑ 438 Rod Stephens .10 .02
❑ 439 Stephen Davis RC 1.50 .60
❑ 440 Terry Allen .20 .07
❑ 441 Michael Westbrook .40 .15
❑ 442 Ken Harvey .10 .02
❑ 443 Coleman Bell .10 .02
❑ 444 Marvcus Patton .10 .02
❑ 445 Gus Frerotte .20 .07
❑ 446 Leslie Shepherd .10 .02
❑ 447 Tom Carter .10 .02
❑ 448 Brian Mitchell .10 .02
❑ 449 Darrell Green .10 .02
❑ 450A Tony Woods .10 .02
❑ 450B Chris Warren Promo .50 .20
❑ CW1 Chris Warren Promo 1.00 .40

1997 Pacific

❑ COMPLETE SET (450) 30.00 15.00
❑ 1 Lomas Brown .20 .07
❑ 2 Pat Carter .20 .07
❑ 3 Larry Centers .30 .10
❑ 4 Matt Darby .20 .07
❑ 5 Marcus Dowdell .20 .07
❑ 6 Aaron Graham .20 .07
❑ 7 Kent Graham .20 .07
❑ 8 LeShon Johnson .20 .07
❑ 9 Seth Joyner .20 .07
❑ 10 Leeland McElroy .20 .07
❑ 11 Rob Moore .30 .10
❑ 12 Simeon Rice .30 .10
❑ 13 Eric Swann .20 .07
❑ 14 Aeneas Williams .20 .07
❑ 15 Morten Andersen .20 .07
❑ 16 Jamal Anderson .50 .20
❑ 17 Lester Archambeau .20 .07
❑ 18 Cornelius Bennett .20 .07
❑ 19 J.J. Birden .20 .07
❑ 20 Antone Davis .20 .07
❑ 21 Bert Emanuel .30 .10
❑ 22 Travis Hall RC .20 .07
❑ 23 Bobby Hebert .20 .07
❑ 24 Craig Heyward .20 .07
❑ 25 Terance Mathis .30 .10
❑ 26 Tim McKyer .20 .07
❑ 27 Eric Metcalf .30 .10
❑ 28 Jessie Tuggle .20 .07
❑ 29 Derrick Alexander WR .30 .10
❑ 30 Orlando Brown .20 .07
❑ 31 Rob Burnett .20 .07
❑ 32 Earnest Byner .20 .07
❑ 33 Ray Ethridge .20 .07
❑ 34 Steve Everitt .20 .07
❑ 35 Carwell Gardner .20 .07
❑ 36 Michael Jackson .30 .10
❑ 37 Jermaine Lewis .50 .20
❑ 38 Stevon Moore .20 .07
❑ 39 Byron Bam Morris .20 .07
❑ 40 Jonathan Ogden .20 .07
❑ 41 Vinny Testaverde .30 .10
❑ 42 Todd Collins .20 .07
❑ 43 Russell Copeland .20 .07
❑ 44 Quinn Early .20 .07
❑ 45 John Fina .20 .07
❑ 46 Phil Hansen .20 .07
❑ 47 Eric Moulds .50 .20
❑ 48 Bryce Paup .20 .07
❑ 49 Andre Reed .30 .10
❑ 50 Kurt Schulz .20 .07
❑ 51 Bruce Smith .30 .10
❑ 52 Chris Spielman .20 .07
❑ 53 Steve Tasker .20 .07
❑ 54 Thurman Thomas .50 .20
❑ 55 Carlton Bailey .20 .07
❑ 56 Michael Bates .20 .07
❑ 57 Blake Brockermeyer .20 .07
❑ 58 Mark Carrier WR .20 .07
❑ 59 Kerry Collins .50 .20
❑ 60 Eric Davis .20 .07
❑ 61 Kevin Greene .30 .10
❑ 62 Rocket Ismail .30 .10
❑ 63 Anthony Johnson .20 .07
❑ 64 Shawn King .20 .07
❑ 65 Greg Kragen .20 .07
❑ 66 Sam Mills .20 .07
❑ 67 Tyrone Poole .20 .07
❑ 68 Wesley Walls .30 .10
❑ 69 Mark Carrier DB .20 .07
❑ 70 Curtis Conway .30 .10
❑ 71 Bobby Engram .30 .10
❑ 72 Jim Flanigan .20 .07
❑ 73 Al Fontenot .20 .07
❑ 74 Raymont Harris .20 .07
❑ 75 Walt Harris .20 .07
❑ 76 Andy Heck .20 .07
❑ 77 Dave Krieg .20 .07
❑ 78 Rashaan Salaam .20 .07
❑ 79 Vinson Smith .20 .07
❑ 80 Alonzo Spellman .20 .07
❑ 81 Michael Timpson .20 .07
❑ 82 James Williams .20 .07
❑ 83 Ashley Ambrose .20 .07
❑ 84 Eric Bieniemy .20 .07

❑ 85 Jeff Blake .30 .10
❑ 86 Ki-Jana Carter .20 .07
❑ 87 John Copeland .20 .07
❑ 88 David Dunn .20 .07
❑ 89 Jeff Hill .20 .07
❑ 90 Ricardo McDonald .20 .07
❑ 91 Tony McGee .20 .07
❑ 92 Greg Myers .20 .07
❑ 93 Carl Pickens .30 .10
❑ 94 Corey Sawyer .20 .07
❑ 95 Darnay Scott .30 .10
❑ 96 Dan Wilkinson .20 .07
❑ 97 Troy Aikman 1.00 .40
❑ 98 Larry Allen .20 .07
❑ 99 Eric Bjornson .20 .07
❑ 100 Ray Donaldson .20 .07
❑ 101 Michael Irvin .50 .20
❑ 102 Daryl Johnston .30 .10
❑ 103 Nate Newton .20 .07
❑ 104 Deion Sanders .50 .20
❑ 105 Jim Schwantz RC .20 .07
❑ 106 Emmitt Smith 1.50 .60
❑ 107 Broderick Thomas .20 .07
❑ 108 Tony Tolbert .20 .07
❑ 109 Erik Williams .20 .07
❑ 110 Sherman Williams .20 .07
❑ 111 Darren Woodson .20 .07
❑ 112 Steve Atwater .20 .07
❑ 113 Aaron Craver .20 .07
❑ 114 Ray Crockett .20 .07
❑ 115 Terrell Davis .60 .25
❑ 116 Jason Elam .30 .10
❑ 117 John Elway 2.00 .75
❑ 118 Todd Kinchen .20 .07
❑ 119 Ed McCaffrey .30 .10
❑ 120 Anthony Miller .20 .07
❑ 121 John Mobley .20 .07
❑ 122 Michael Dean Perry .20 .07
❑ 123 Reggie Rivers .20 .07
❑ 124 Shannon Sharpe .30 .10
❑ 125 Alfred Williams .20 .07
❑ 126 Reggie Brown LB .30 .10
❑ 127 Luther Elliss .20 .07
❑ 128 Kevin Glover .20 .07
❑ 129 Jason Hanson .20 .07
❑ 130 Pepper Johnson .20 .07
❑ 131 Glyn Milburn .20 .07
❑ 132 Scott Mitchell .30 .10
❑ 133 Herman Moore .30 .10
❑ 134 Johnnie Morton .30 .10
❑ 135 Brett Perriman .20 .07
❑ 136 Robert Porcher .20 .07
❑ 137 Ron Rivers .20 .07
❑ 138 Barry Sanders 1.50 .60
❑ 139 Henry Thomas .20 .07
❑ 140 Don Beebe .20 .07
❑ 141 Edgar Bennett .30 .10
❑ 142 Robert Brooks .30 .10
❑ 143 LeRoy Butler .20 .07
❑ 144 Mark Chmura .30 .10
❑ 145 Brett Favre 2.00 .75
❑ 146 Antonio Freeman .50 .20
❑ 147 Chris Jacke .20 .07
❑ 148 Travis Jervey .30 .10
❑ 149 Sean Jones .20 .07
❑ 150 Dorsey Levens .50 .20
❑ 151 John Michels .20 .07
❑ 152 Craig Newsome .20 .07
❑ 153 Eugene Robinson .20 .07
❑ 154 Reggie White .50 .20
❑ 155 Micheal Barrow .20 .07
❑ 156 Blaine Bishop .20 .07
❑ 157 Chris Chandler .30 .10
❑ 158 Anthony Cook .20 .07
❑ 159 Malcolm Floyd .20 .07
❑ 160 Eddie George .50 .20
❑ 161 Roderick Lewis .20 .07
❑ 162 Steve McNair .60 .25
❑ 163 John Henry Mills RC .20 .07
❑ 164 Derek Russell .20 .07
❑ 165 Chris Sanders .20 .07
❑ 166 Mark Stepnoski .20 .07
❑ 167 Frank Wycheck .20 .07
❑ 168 Robert Young .20 .07
❑ 169 Trev Alberts .20 .07
❑ 170 Aaron Bailey .20 .07
❑ 171 Tony Bennett .20 .07
❑ 172 Ray Buchanan .20 .07
❑ 173 Quentin Coryatt .20 .07
❑ 174 Eugene Daniel .20 .07
❑ 175 Sean Dawkins .20 .07
❑ 176 Ken Dilger .20 .07
❑ 177 Marshall Faulk .60 .25
❑ 178 Jim Harbaugh .30 .10
❑ 179 Marvin Harrison .50 .20
❑ 180 Paul Justin .20 .07
❑ 181 Lamont Warren .20 .07
❑ 182 Bernard Whittington .20 .07
❑ 183 Tony Boselli .20 .07
❑ 184 Tony Brackens .20 .07
❑ 185 Mark Brunell .60 .25
❑ 186 Brian DeMarco .20 .07
❑ 187 Rich Griffith .20 .07
❑ 188 Kevin Hardy .20 .07
❑ 189 Willie Jackson .20 .07
❑ 190 Jeff Lageman .20 .07
❑ 191 Keenan McCardell .30 .10
❑ 192 Natrone Means .30 .10
❑ 193 Pete Mitchell .20 .07
❑ 194 Joel Smeenge .20 .07
❑ 195 Jimmy Smith .30 .10
❑ 196 James O.Stewart .30 .10
❑ 197 Marcus Allen .50 .20
❑ 198 John Alt .20 .07
❑ 199 Kimble Anders .30 .10
❑ 200 Steve Bono .30 .10
❑ 201 Vaughn Booker .20 .07
❑ 202 Dale Carter .20 .07
❑ 203 Mark Collins .20 .07
❑ 204 Greg Hill .20 .07
❑ 205 Joe Horn .50 .20
❑ 206 Dan Saleaumua .20 .07
❑ 207 Will Shields .20 .07
❑ 208 Neil Smith .30 .10
❑ 209 Derrick Thomas .50 .20
❑ 210 Tamarick Vanover .30 .10
❑ 211 Karim Abdul-Jabbar .30 .10
❑ 212 Fred Barnett .20 .07
❑ 213 Tim Bowens .20 .07
❑ 214 Kirby Dar Dar RC .30 .10
❑ 215 Troy Drayton .20 .07
❑ 216 Craig Erickson .20 .07
❑ 217 Daryl Gardener .20 .07
❑ 218 Randal Hill .20 .07
❑ 219 Dan Marino 2.00 .75
❑ 220 O.J. McDuffie .30 .10
❑ 221 Bernie Parmalee .20 .07
❑ 222 Stanley Pritchett .20 .07
❑ 223 Daniel Stubbs .20 .07
❑ 224 Zach Thomas .50 .20
❑ 225 Derrick Alexander DE .20 .07
❑ 226 Cris Carter .50 .20
❑ 227 Jeff Christy .20 .07
❑ 228 Qadry Ismail .30 .10
❑ 229 Brad Johnson .50 .20
❑ 230 Andrew Jordan .20 .07
❑ 231 Randall McDaniel .20 .07
❑ 232 David Palmer .20 .07
❑ 233 John Randle .30 .10
❑ 234 Jake Reed .30 .10
❑ 235 Scott Sisson .20 .07
❑ 236 Korey Stringer .20 .07
❑ 237 Darryl Talley .20 .07
❑ 238 Orlando Thomas .20 .07
❑ 239 Bruce Armstrong .20 .07
❑ 240 Drew Bledsoe .60 .25
❑ 241 Willie Clay .20 .07
❑ 242 Ben Coates .30 .10
❑ 243 Ferric Collons RC .20 .07
❑ 244 Terry Glenn .50 .20
❑ 245 Jerome Henderson .20 .07
❑ 246 Shawn Jefferson .20 .07
❑ 247 Dietrich Jells .20 .07
❑ 248 Ty Law .30 .10
❑ 249 Curtis Martin .60 .25
❑ 250 Willie McGinest .20 .07
❑ 251 Dave Meggett .20 .07
❑ 252 Lawyer Milloy .30 .10
❑ 253 Chris Slade .20 .07
❑ 254 Je'rod Cherry .20 .07
❑ 255 Jim Everett .20 .07
❑ 256 Mark Fields .20 .07
❑ 257 Michael Haynes .20 .07
❑ 258 Tyrone Hughes .20 .07
❑ 259 Haywood Jeffires .20 .07
❑ 260 Wayne Martin .20 .07
❑ 261 Mark McMillian .20 .07
❑ 262 Rufus Porter .20 .07
❑ 263 William Roaf .20 .07
❑ 264 Torrance Small .20 .07
❑ 265 Renaldo Turnbull .20 .07
❑ 266 Ray Zellars .20 .07
❑ 267 Jessie Armstead .20 .07
❑ 268 Chad Bratzke .20 .07
❑ 269 Dave Brown .20 .07
❑ 270 Chris Calloway .20 .07
❑ 271 Howard Cross .20 .07
❑ 272 Lawrence Dawsey .20 .07
❑ 273 Rodney Hampton .30 .10
❑ 274 Danny Kanell .20 .07
❑ 275 Arthur Marshall .20 .07
❑ 276 Aaron Pierce .20 .07
❑ 277 Phillippi Sparks .20 .07
❑ 278 Amani Toomer .30 .10
❑ 279 Charles Way .20 .07
❑ 280 Richie Anderson .30 .10
❑ 281 Fred Baxter .20 .07
❑ 282 Wayne Chrebet .50 .20
❑ 283 Kyle Clifton .20 .07
❑ 284 Jumbo Elliott .20 .07
❑ 285 Aaron Glenn .20 .07
❑ 286 Jeff Graham .20 .07
❑ 287 Bobby Hamilton RC .20 .07
❑ 288 Keyshawn Johnson .50 .20
❑ 289 Adrian Murrell .30 .10
❑ 290 Neil O'Donnell .30 .10
❑ 291 Webster Slaughter .20 .07
❑ 292 Alex Van Dyke .20 .07
❑ 293 Marvin Washington .20 .07
❑ 294 Joe Aska .20 .07
❑ 295 Jerry Ball .20 .07
❑ 296 Tim Brown .50 .20
❑ 297 Rickey Dudley .30 .10
❑ 298 Pat Harlow .20 .07
❑ 299 Nolan Harrison .20 .07
❑ 300 Billy Joe Hobert .30 .10
❑ 301 James Jett .30 .10
❑ 302 Napoleon Kaufman .50 .20
❑ 303 Lincoln Kennedy .20 .07
❑ 304 Albert Lewis .20 .07
❑ 305 Chester McGlockton .20 .07
❑ 306 Pat Swilling .20 .07
❑ 307 Steve Wisniewski .20 .07
❑ 308 Darion Conner .20 .07
❑ 309 Ty Detmer .30 .10
❑ 310 Jason Dunn .20 .07
❑ 311 Irving Fryar .30 .10
❑ 312 James Fuller .20 .07
❑ 313 William Fuller .20 .07
❑ 314 Charlie Garner .30 .10
❑ 315 Bobby Hoying .30 .10
❑ 316 Tom Hutton .20 .07
❑ 317 Chris T. Jones .20 .07
❑ 318 Mike Mamula .20 .07
❑ 319 Mark Seay .20 .07
❑ 320 Bobby Taylor .20 .07
❑ 321 Ricky Watters .30 .10
❑ 322 Jahine Arnold .20 .07
❑ 323 Jerome Bettis .50 .20
❑ 324 Chad Brown .20 .07
❑ 325 Mark Bruener .20 .07
❑ 326 Andre Hastings .20 .07
❑ 327 Norm Johnson .20 .07
❑ 328 Levon Kirkland .20 .07
❑ 329 Carnell Lake .20 .07
❑ 330 Greg Lloyd .20 .07
❑ 331 Ernie Mills .20 .07
❑ 332 Orpheus Roye RC .20 .07
❑ 333 Kordell Stewart .50 .20
❑ 334 Yancey Thigpen .30 .10
❑ 335 Mike Tomczak .20 .07
❑ 336 Rod Woodson .30 .10
❑ 337 Tony Banks .30 .10
❑ 338 Bern Brostek .20 .07
❑ 339 Isaac Bruce .50 .20
❑ 340 Ernie Conwell .20 .07
❑ 341 Keith Crawford .20 .07
❑ 342 Wayne Gandy .20 .07
❑ 343 Harold Green .20 .07
❑ 344 Carlos Jenkins .20 .07
❑ 345 Jimmie Jones .20 .07
❑ 346 Eddie Kennison .30 .10
❑ 347 Todd Lyght .20 .07
❑ 348 Leslie O'Neal .20 .07
❑ 349 Lawrence Phillips .20 .07
❑ 350 Greg Robinson .20 .07
❑ 351 Darren Bennett .20 .07

❑ 352 Lewis Bush .20 .07
❑ 353 Eric Castle .20 .07
❑ 354 Terrell Fletcher .20 .07
❑ 355 Darrien Gordon .20 .07
❑ 356 Kurt Gouveia .20 .07
❑ 357 Aaron Hayden .20 .07
❑ 358 Stan Humphries .30 .10
❑ 359 Tony Martin .30 .10
❑ 360 Vaughn Parker RC .20 .07
❑ 361 Brian Roche .20 .07
❑ 362 Leonard Russell .20 .07
❑ 363 Junior Seau .50 .20
❑ 364 Roy Barker .20 .07
❑ 365 Harris Barton .20 .07
❑ 366 Dexter Carter .20 .07
❑ 367 Chris Doleman .20 .07
❑ 368 Tyronne Drakeford .20 .07
❑ 369 Elvis Grbac .30 .10
❑ 370 Derek Loville .20 .07
❑ 371 Tim McDonald .20 .07
❑ 372 Ken Norton .20 .07
❑ 373 Terrell Owens .60 .25
❑ 374 Gary Plummer .20 .07
❑ 375 Jerry Rice 1.00 .40
❑ 376 Dana Stubblefield .20 .07
❑ 377 Lee Woodall .20 .07
❑ 378 Steve Young .60 .25
❑ 379 Robert Blackmon .20 .07
❑ 380 Brian Blades .20 .07
❑ 381 Carlester Crumpler .20 .07
❑ 382 Christian Fauria .20 .07
❑ 383 John Friesz .20 .07
❑ 384 Joey Galloway .30 .10
❑ 385 Derrick Graham .20 .07
❑ 386 Cortez Kennedy .20 .07
❑ 387 Warren Moon .50 .20
❑ 388 Winston Moss .20 .07
❑ 389 Mike Pritchard .20 .07
❑ 390 Michael Sinclair .20 .07
❑ 391 Lamar Smith .50 .20
❑ 392 Chris Warren .30 .10
❑ 393 Chidi Ahanotu .20 .07
❑ 394 Mike Alstott .50 .20
❑ 395 Reggie Brooks .20 .07
❑ 396 Trent Dilfer .50 .20
❑ 397 Jerry Ellison .20 .07
❑ 398 Paul Gruber .20 .07
❑ 399 Alvin Harper .20 .07
❑ 400 Courtney Hawkins .20 .07
❑ 401 Dave Moore .20 .07
❑ 402 Errict Rhett .20 .07
❑ 403 Warren Sapp .30 .10
❑ 404 Nilo Silvan .20 .07
❑ 405 Regan Upshaw .20 .07
❑ 406 Casey Weldon .20 .07
❑ 407 Terry Allen .50 .20
❑ 408 Jamie Asher .20 .07
❑ 409 Bill Brooks .20 .07
❑ 410 Tom Carter .20 .07
❑ 411 Henry Ellard .20 .07
❑ 412 Gus Frerotte .20 .07
❑ 413 Darrell Green .30 .10
❑ 414 Ken Harvey .20 .07
❑ 415 Tre Johnson .20 .07
❑ 416 Brian Mitchell .20 .07
❑ 417 Rich Owens .20 .07
❑ 418 Heath Shuler .20 .07
❑ 419 Michael Westbrook .30 .10
❑ 420 Tony Woods RC .20 .07
❑ 421 Reidel Anthony RC .50 .20
❑ 422 Darnell Autry RC .30 .10
❑ 423 Tiki Barber RC 3.00 1.25
❑ 424 Pat Barnes RC .50 .20
❑ 425 Terry Battle RC .20 .07
❑ 426 Will Blackwell RC .30 .10
❑ 427 Peter Boulware RC .50 .20
❑ 428 Rae Carruth RC .20 .07
❑ 429 Troy Davis RC .30 .10
❑ 430 Jim Druckenmiller RC .30 .10
❑ 431 Warrick Dunn RC 1.50 .60
❑ 432 Marc Edwards RC .20 .07
❑ 433 James Farrior RC .50 .20
❑ 434 Yatil Green RC .30 .10
❑ 435 Byron Hanspard RC .30 .10
❑ 436 Ike Hilliard RC .75 .30
❑ 437 David LaFleur RC .20 .07
❑ 438 Kevin Lockett RC .30 .10
❑ 439 Sam Madison RC .50 .20
❑ 440 Brian Manning RC .30 .10
❑ 441 Orlando Pace RC .50 .20
❑ 442 Jake Plummer RC 2.50 1.00
❑ 443 Chad Scott RC .30 .10
❑ 444 Sedrick Shaw RC .30 .10
❑ 445 Antowain Smith RC 1.25 .50
❑ 446 Shawn Springs RC .30 .10
❑ 447 Ross Verba RC .20 .07
❑ 448 Bryant Westbrook RC .20 .07
❑ 449 Renaldo Wynn RC .20 .07
❑ 450 Jimmy Johnson CO .30 .10
❑ S1 Mark Brunell Sample 1.00 .40

1998 Pacific

❑ COMPLETE SET (450) 60.00 25.00
❑ 1 Mario Bates .40 .15
❑ 2 Lomas Brown .25 .08
❑ 3 Larry Centers .25 .08
❑ 4 Chris Gedney .25 .08
❑ 5 Terry Irving .25 .08
❑ 6 Tom Knight .25 .08
❑ 7 Eric Metcalf .25 .08
❑ 8 Jamir Miller .25 .08
❑ 9 Rob Moore .40 .15
❑ 10 Joe Nedney .25 .08
❑ 11 Jake Plummer .60 .25
❑ 12 Simeon Rice .40 .15
❑ 13 Frank Sanders .40 .15
❑ 14 Eric Swann .25 .08
❑ 15 Aeneas Williams .25 .08
❑ 16 Morten Andersen .25 .08
❑ 17 Jamal Anderson .60 .25
❑ 18 Michael Booker .25 .08
❑ 19 Keith Brooking RC 1.50 .60
❑ 20 Ray Buchanan .25 .08
❑ 21 Devin Bush .25 .08
❑ 22 Chris Chandler .40 .15
❑ 23 Tony Graziani .25 .08
❑ 24 Harold Green .25 .08
❑ 25 Byron Hanspard .25 .08
❑ 26 Todd Kinchen .25 .08
❑ 27 Tony Martin .40 .15
❑ 28 Terance Mathis .40 .15
❑ 29 Eugene Robinson .25 .08
❑ 30 O.J. Santiago .25 .08
❑ 31 Chuck Smith .25 .08
❑ 32 Jessie Tuggle .25 .08
❑ 33 Bob Whitfield .25 .08
❑ 34 Peter Boulware .25 .08
❑ 35 Jay Graham .25 .08
❑ 36 Eric Green .25 .08
❑ 37 Jim Harbaugh .40 .15
❑ 38 Michael Jackson .25 .08
❑ 39 Jermaine Lewis .40 .15
❑ 40 Ray Lewis .60 .25
❑ 41 Michael McCrary .25 .08
❑ 42 Stevon Moore .25 .08
❑ 43 Jonathan Ogden .25 .08
❑ 44 Errict Rhett .40 .15
❑ 45 Matt Stover .25 .08
❑ 46 Rod Woodson .40 .15
❑ 47 Eric Zeier .40 .15
❑ 48 Ruben Brown .25 .08
❑ 49 Steve Christie .25 .08
❑ 50 Quinn Early .25 .08
❑ 51 John Fina .25 .08
❑ 52 Doug Flutie .60 .25
❑ 53 Phil Hansen .25 .08
❑ 54 Lonnie Johnson .25 .08
❑ 55 Rob Johnson .40 .15
❑ 56 Henry Jones .25 .08
❑ 57 Eric Moulds .60 .25
❑ 58 Andre Reed .40 .15
❑ 59 Antowain Smith .60 .25
❑ 60 Bruce Smith .40 .15
❑ 61 Thurman Thomas .60 .25
❑ 62 Ted Washington .25 .08
❑ 63 Michael Bates .25 .08
❑ 64 Tim Biakabutuka .40 .15
❑ 65 Blake Brockermeyer .25 .08
❑ 66 Mark Carrier .25 .08
❑ 67 Rae Carruth .25 .08
❑ 68 Kerry Collins .40 .15
❑ 69 Doug Evans .25 .08
❑ 70 William Floyd .25 .08
❑ 71 Sean Gilbert .25 .08
❑ 72 Rocket Ismail .25 .08
❑ 73 [illegible]
❑ 74 Fred Lane .25 .08
❑ 75 Lamar Lathon .25 .08
❑ 76 Muhsin Muhammad .40 .15
❑ 77 Wesley Walls .40 .15
❑ 78 Edgar Bennett .25 .08
❑ 79 Tom Carter .25 .08
❑ 80 Curtis Conway .40 .15
❑ 81 Bobby Engram .40 .15
❑ 82 Curtis Enis RC .75 .30
❑ 83 Jim Flanigan .25 .08
❑ 84 Walt Harris .25 .08
❑ 85 Jeff Jaeger .25 .08
❑ 86 Erik Kramer .25 .08
❑ 87 John Mangum .25 .08
❑ 88 Glyn Milburn .25 .08
❑ 89 Barry Minter .25 .08
❑ 90 Chris Penn .25 .08
❑ 91 Todd Sauerbrun .25 .08
❑ 92 James Williams .25 .08
❑ 93 Ashley Ambrose .25 .08
❑ 94 Willie Anderson .25 .08
❑ 95 Eric Bieniemy .25 .08
❑ 96 Jeff Blake .40 .15
❑ 97 Ki-Jana Carter .25 .08
❑ 98 John Copeland .25 .08
❑ 99 Corey Dillon .60 .25
❑ 100 Tony McGee .25 .08
❑ 101 Neil O'Donnell .40 .15
❑ 102 Carl Pickens .40 .15
❑ 103 Kevin Sargent .25 .08
❑ 104 Darnay Scott .40 .15
❑ 105 Takeo Spikes RC 1.50 .60
❑ 106 Troy Aikman 1.25 .50
❑ 107 Larry Allen .25 .08
❑ 108 Eric Bjornson .25 .08
❑ 109 Billy Davis .25 .08
❑ 110 Jason Garrett RC .75 .30
❑ 111 Michael Irvin .60 .25
❑ 112 Daryl Johnston .40 .15
❑ 113 David LaFleur .25 .08
❑ 114 Everett McIver [illegible] [illegible]
❑ 115 Ernie Mills .25 .08
❑ 116 Nate Newton .25 .08
❑ 117 Deion Sanders .60 .25
❑ 118 Emmitt Smith 2.00 .75
❑ 119 Kevin Smith .25 .08
❑ 120 Erik Williams .25 .08
❑ 121 Steve Atwater .25 .08
❑ 122 Tyrone Braxton .25 .08
❑ 123 Ray Crockett .25 .08
❑ 124 Terrell Davis .60 .25
❑ 125 Jason Elam .25 .08
❑ 126 John Elway 2.50 1.00
❑ 127 Willie Green .25 .08
❑ 128 Brian Griese RC 3.00 1.25
❑ 129 Tony Jones .25 .08
❑ 130 Ed McCaffrey .40 .15
❑ 131 John Mobley .25 .08
❑ 132 Tom Nalen .25 .08
❑ 133 Marcus Nash RC .75 .30
❑ 134 Bill Romanowski .25 .08
❑ 135 Shannon Sharpe .40 .15
❑ 136 Neil Smith .40 .15
❑ 137 Rod Smith .40 .15
❑ 138 Keith Traylor .25 .08
❑ 139 Stephen Boyd .25 .08
❑ 140 Mark Carrier DB .25 .08
❑ 141 Charlie Batch RC 1.50 .60
❑ 142 Jason Hanson .25 .08
❑ 143 Scott Mitchell .40 .15
❑ 144 Herman Moore .40 .15
❑ 145 Johnnie Morton .40 .15
❑ 146 Robert Porcher .25 .08
❑ 147 Ron Rivers .25 .08

❑ 148 Barry Sanders 2.00 .75
❑ 149 Tracy Scroggins .25 .08
❑ 150 David Sloan .25 .08
❑ 151 Tommy Vardell .25 .08
❑ 152 Kerwin Waldroup .25 .08
❑ 153 Bryant Westbrook .25 .08
❑ 154 Robert Brooks .40 .15
❑ 155 Gilbert Brown .25 .08
❑ 156 LeRoy Butler .25 .08
❑ 157 Mark Chmura .40 .15
❑ 158 Earl Dotson .25 .08
❑ 159 Santana Dotson .25 .08
❑ 160 Brett Favre 2.50 1.00
❑ 161 Antonio Freeman .60 .25
❑ 162 Raymont Harris .25 .08
❑ 163 William Henderson .40 .15
❑ 164 Vonnie Holliday RC 1.25 .50
❑ 165 George Koonce .25 .08
❑ 166 Dorsey Levens .60 .25
❑ 167 Derrick Mayes .40 .15
❑ 168 Craig Newsome .25 .08
❑ 169 Ross Verba .25 .08
❑ 170 Reggie White .60 .25
❑ 171 Elijah Alexander .25 .08
❑ 172 Aaron Bailey .25 .08
❑ 173 Jason Belser .25 .08
❑ 174 Robert Blackmon .25 .08
❑ 175 Zack Crockett .25 .08
❑ 176 Ken Dilger .25 .08
❑ 177 Marshall Faulk .75 .30
❑ 178 Tarik Glenn .25 .08
❑ 179 Marvin Harrison .60 .25
❑ 180 Tony Mandarich .25 .08
❑ 181 Peyton Manning RC 15.00 6.00
❑ 182 Marcus Pollard .25 .08
❑ 183 Lamont Warren .25 .08
❑ 184 Tavian Banks RC 1.25 .50
❑ 185 Reggie Barlow .25 .08
❑ 186 Tony Boselli .25 .08
❑ 187 Tony Brackens .25 .08
❑ 188 Mark Brunell .60 .25
❑ 189 Kevin Hardy .25 .08
❑ 190 Mike Hollis .25 .08
❑ 191 Jeff Lageman .25 .08
❑ 192 Keenan McCardell .40 .15
❑ 193 Pete Mitchell .25 .08
❑ 194 Bryce Paup .25 .08
❑ 195 Leon Searcy .25 .08
❑ 196 Jimmy Smith .40 .15
❑ 197 James Stewart .40 .15
❑ 198 Fred Taylor RC 2.50 1.00
❑ 199 Renaldo Wynn .25 .08
❑ 200 Derrick Alexander WR .40 .15
❑ 201 Kimble Anders .40 .15
❑ 202 Donnell Bennett .25 .08
❑ 203 Dale Carter .25 .08
❑ 204 Anthony Davis .25 .08
❑ 205 Rich Gannon .60 .25
❑ 206 Tony Gonzalez .60 .25
❑ 207 Elvis Grbac .40 .15
❑ 208 James Hasty .25 .08
❑ 209 Leslie O'Neal .25 .08
❑ 210 Andre Rison .40 .15
❑ 211 Rashaan Shehee RC 1.25 .50
❑ 212 Will Shields .25 .08
❑ 213 Pete Stoyanovich .25 .08
❑ 214 Derrick Thomas .60 .25
❑ 215 Tamarick Vanover .25 .08
❑ 216 Karim Abdul-Jabbar .60 .25
❑ 217 Trace Armstrong .25 .08
❑ 218 John Avery RC 1.25 .50
❑ 219 Tim Bowens .25 .08
❑ 220 Terrell Buckley .25 .08
❑ 221 Troy Drayton .25 .08
❑ 222 Daryl Gardener .25 .08
❑ 223 Damon Huard RC 8.00 3.00
❑ 224 Charles Jordan .25 .08
❑ 225 Dan Marino 2.50 1.00
❑ 226 O.J. McDuffie .40 .15
❑ 227 Bernie Parmalee .25 .08
❑ 228 Stanley Pritchett .25 .08
❑ 229 Derrick Rodgers .25 .08
❑ 230 Lamar Thomas .25 .08
❑ 231 Zach Thomas .60 .25
❑ 232 Richmond Webb .25 .08
❑ 233 Derrick Alexander DE .25 .08
❑ 234 Jerry Ball .25 .08
❑ 235 Cris Carter .60 .25
❑ 236 Randall Cunningham .60 .25
❑ 237 Charles Evans .25 .08
❑ 238 Corey Fuller .25 .08
❑ 239 Andrew Glover .25 .08
❑ 240 Leroy Hoard .25 .08
❑ 241 Brad Johnson .60 .25
❑ 242 Ed McDaniel .25 .08
❑ 243 Randall McDaniel .25 .08
❑ 244 Randy Moss RC 12.00 6.00
❑ 245 John Randle .40 .15
❑ 246 Jake Reed .40 .15
❑ 247 Dwayne Rudd .25 .08
❑ 248 Robert Smith .60 .25
❑ 249 Bruce Armstrong .25 .08
❑ 250 Drew Bledsoe 1.00 .40
❑ 251 Vincent Brisby .25 .08
❑ 252 Tedy Bruschi 1.25 .50
❑ 253 Ben Coates .40 .15
❑ 254 Derrick Cullors .25 .08
❑ 255 Terry Glenn .60 .25
❑ 256 Shawn Jefferson .25 .08
❑ 257 Ted Johnson .25 .08
❑ 258 Ty Law .40 .15
❑ 259 Willie McGinest .25 .08
❑ 260 Lawyer Milloy .40 .15
❑ 261 Sedrick Shaw .25 .08
❑ 262 Chris Slade .25 .08
❑ 263 Troy Davis .25 .08
❑ 264 Mark Fields .25 .08
❑ 265 Andre Hastings .25 .08
❑ 266 Billy Joe Hobert .25 .08
❑ 267 Qadry Ismail .40 .15
❑ 268 Tony Johnson .25 .08
❑ 269 Sammy Knight RC .60 .25
❑ 270 Wayne Martin .25 .08
❑ 271 Chris Naeole .25 .08
❑ 272 Keith Poole .25 .08
❑ 273 William Roaf .25 .08
❑ 274 Pio Sagapolutele .25 .08
❑ 275 Danny Wuerffel .40 .15
❑ 276 Ray Zellars .25 .08
❑ 277 Jessie Armstead .25 .08
❑ 278 Tiki Barber .60 .25
❑ 279 Chris Calloway .25 .08
❑ 280 Percy Ellsworth .25 .08
❑ 281 Sam Garnes RC .75 .30
❑ 282 Kent Graham .25 .08
❑ 283 Ike Hilliard .40 .15
❑ 284 Danny Kanell .40 .15
❑ 285 Corey Miller .25 .08
❑ 286 Phillippi Sparks .25 .08
❑ 287 Michael Strahan .40 .15
❑ 288 Amani Toomer .40 .15
❑ 289 Charles Way .25 .08
❑ 290 Tyrone Wheatley .40 .15
❑ 291 Tito Wooten .25 .08
❑ 292 Kyle Brady .25 .08
❑ 293 Keith Byars .25 .08
❑ 294 Wayne Chrebet .60 .25
❑ 295 John Elliott .25 .08
❑ 296 Glenn Foley .40 .15
❑ 297 Aaron Glenn .25 .08
❑ 298 Keyshawn Johnson .60 .25
❑ 299 Curtis Martin .60 .25
❑ 300 Otis Smith .25 .08
❑ 301 Vinny Testaverde .40 .15
❑ 302 Alex Van Dyke .25 .08
❑ 303 Dedric Ward .25 .08
❑ 304 Greg Biekert .25 .08
❑ 305 Tim Brown .60 .25
❑ 306 Rickey Dudley .25 .08
❑ 307 Jeff George .40 .15
❑ 308 Pat Harlow .25 .08
❑ 309 Desmond Howard .40 .15
❑ 310 James Jett .40 .15
❑ 311 Napoleon Kaufman .60 .25
❑ 312 Lincoln Kennedy .25 .08
❑ 313 Russell Maryland .25 .08
❑ 314 Darrell Russell .25 .08
❑ 315 Eric Turner .25 .08
❑ 316 Steve Wisniewski .25 .08
❑ 317 Charles Woodson RC 2.00 .75
❑ 318 James Darling RC .75 .30
❑ 319 Jason Dunn .25 .08
❑ 320 Irving Fryar .40 .15
❑ 321 Charlie Garner .40 .15
❑ 322 Jeff Graham .25 .08
❑ 323 Bobby Hoying .40 .15
❑ 324 Chad Lewis .40 .15
❑ 325 Rodney Peete .25 .08
❑ 326 Freddie Solomon .25 .08
❑ 327 Duce Staley .75 .30
❑ 328 Bobby Taylor .25 .08
❑ 329 William Thomas .25 .08
❑ 330 Kevin Turner .25 .08
❑ 331 Troy Vincent .25 .08
❑ 332 Jerome Bettis .60 .25
❑ 333 Will Blackwell .25 .08
❑ 334 Mark Bruener .25 .08
❑ 335 Andre Coleman .25 .08
❑ 336 Demontti Dawson .25 .08
❑ 337 Jason Gildon .25 .08
❑ 338 Courtney Hawkins .25 .08
❑ 339 Charles Johnson .25 .08
❑ 340 Levon Kirkland .25 .08
❑ 341 Carnell Lake .25 .08
❑ 342 Tim Lester .25 .08
❑ 343 Joel Steed .25 .08
❑ 344 Kordell Stewart .60 .25
❑ 345 Will Wolford .25 .08
❑ 346 Tony Banks .40 .15
❑ 347 Isaac Bruce .60 .25
❑ 348 Ernie Conwell .25 .08
❑ 349 D'Marco Farr .25 .08
❑ 350 Wayne Gandy .25 .08
❑ 351 Jerome Pathon RC 1.50 .60
❑ 352 Eddie Kennison .40 .15
❑ 353 Amp Lee .25 .08
❑ 354 Keith Lyle .25 .08
❑ 355 Ryan McNeil .25 .08
❑ 356 Jerald Moore .25 .08
❑ 357 Orlando Pace .25 .08
❑ 358 Roman Phifer .25 .08
❑ 359 David Thompson RC .75 .30
❑ 360 Darren Bennett .25 .08
❑ 361 John Carney .25 .08
❑ 362 Marco Coleman .25 .08
❑ 363 Terrell Fletcher .25 .08
❑ 364 William Fuller .25 .08
❑ 365 Charlie Jones .25 .08
❑ 366 Freddie Jones .25 .08
❑ 367 Ryan Leaf RC 1.50 .60
❑ 368 Natrone Means .40 .15
❑ 369 Junior Seau .60 .25
❑ 370 Terrance Shaw .25 .08
❑ 371 Tremayne Stephens RC .75 .30
❑ 372 Bryan Still .25 .08
❑ 373 Aaron Taylor .25 .08
❑ 374 Greg Clark .25 .08
❑ 375 Ty Detmer .40 .15
❑ 376 Jim Druckenmiller .25 .08
❑ 377 Marc Edwards .25 .08
❑ 378 Merton Hanks .25 .08
❑ 379 Garrison Hearst .60 .25
❑ 380 Chuck Levy .25 .08
❑ 381 Ken Norton .25 .08
❑ 382 Terrell Owens .60 .25
❑ 383 Marquez Pope .25 .08
❑ 384 Jerry Rice 1.25 .50
❑ 385 Irv Smith .25 .08
❑ 386 J.J. Stokes .40 .15
❑ 387 Iheanyi Uwaezuoke .25 .08
❑ 388 Bryant Young .25 .08
❑ 389 Steve Young .75 .30
❑ 390 Sam Adams .25 .08
❑ 391 Chad Brown .25 .08
❑ 392 Christian Fauria .25 .08
❑ 393 Joey Galloway .40 .15
❑ 394 Ahman Green RC 8.00 3.00
❑ 395 Walter Jones .25 .08
❑ 396 Cortez Kennedy .25 .08
❑ 397 Jon Kitna .60 .25
❑ 398 James McKnight .60 .25
❑ 399 Warren Moon .60 .25
❑ 400 Mike Pritchard .25 .08
❑ 401 Michael Sinclair .25 .08
❑ 402 Shawn Springs .25 .08
❑ 403 Ricky Watters .40 .15
❑ 404 Darryl Williams .25 .08
❑ 405 Mike Alstott .60 .25
❑ 406 Reidel Anthony .40 .15
❑ 407 Derrick Brooks .60 .25
❑ 408 Brad Culpepper .25 .08
❑ 409 Trent Dilfer .60 .25
❑ 410 Warrick Dunn .60 .25
❑ 411 Bert Emanuel .40 .15
❑ 412 Jacquez Green RC 1.25 .50
❑ 413 Paul Gruber .25 .08
❑ 414 Patrick Hape RC 1.25 .50

No.	Player	Price	Price
415	Dave Moore	.25	.08
416	Hardy Nickerson	.25	.08
417	Warren Sapp	.40	.15
418	Robb Thomas	.25	.08
419	Regan Upshaw	.25	.08
420	Karl Williams	.25	.08
421	Blaine Bishop	.25	.08
422	Anthony Cook	.25	.08
423	Willie Davis	.25	.08
424	Al Del Greco	.25	.08
425	Kevin Dyson	.60	.25
426	Henry Ford	.25	.08
427	Eddie George	.60	.25
428	Jackie Harris	.25	.08
429	Steve McNair	.60	.25
430	Chris Sanders	.25	.08
431	Mark Stepnoski	.25	.08
432	Yancey Thigpen	.25	.08
433	Barron Wortham	.25	.08
434	Frank Wycheck	.25	.08
435	Stephen Alexander RC	1.25	.50
436	Terry Allen	.60	.25
437	Jamie Asher	.25	.08
438	Bob Dahl	.25	.08
439	Stephen Davis	.25	.08
440	Cris Dishman	.25	.08
441	Gus Frerotte	.25	.08
442	Darrell Green	.40	.15
443	Trent Green	.75	.30
444	Ken Harvey	.25	.08
445	Skip Hicks RC	1.25	.50
446	Jeff Hostetler	.25	.08
447	Brian Mitchell	.25	.08
448	Leslie Shepherd	.25	.08
449	Michael Westbrook	.40	.15
450	Dan Wilkinson	.25	.08
S1	Warrick Dunn Sample	1.00	.40

1999 Pacific

No.	Player	Price	Price
	COMPLETE SET (450)	80.00	30.00
1	Mario Bates	.25	.08
2	Larry Centers	.25	.08
3	Chris Gedney	.25	.08
4	Kwamie Lassiter RC	.60	.25
5	Johnny McWilliams	.25	.08
6	Eric Metcalf	.25	.08
7	Rob Moore	.40	.15
8	Adrian Murrell	.40	.15
9	Jake Plummer	.40	.15
10	Simeon Rice	.40	.15
11	Frank Sanders	.40	.15
12	Andre Wadsworth	.25	.08
13	Aeneas Williams	.25	.08
14	M.Pittman/R.Anderson RC	1.25	.50
15	Morten Andersen	.25	.08
16	Jamal Anderson	.60	.25
17	Lester Archambeau	.25	.08
18	Chris Chandler	.40	.15
19	Bob Christian	.25	.08
20	Steve DeBerg	.25	.08
21	Tim Dwight	.60	.25
22	Tony Martin	.40	.15
23	Terance Mathis	.40	.15
24	Eugene Robinson	.25	.08
25	O.J. Santiago	.25	.08
26	Chuck Smith	.25	.08
27	Jessie Tuggle	.25	.08
28	Jammi German/Ken Oxendine	.25	.08
29	Peter Boulware	.25	.08
30	Jay Graham	.25	.08
31	Jim Harbaugh	.40	.15
32	Priest Holmes	1.00	.40
33	Michael Jackson	.25	.08
34	Jermaine Lewis	.40	.15
35	Ray Lewis	.60	.25
36	Michael McCrary	.25	.08
37	Jonathan Ogden	.25	.08
38	Errict Rhett	.25	.08
39	James Roe RC	1.00	.40
40	Floyd Turner	.25	.08
41	Rod Woodson	.40	.15
42	Eric Zeier	.25	.08
43	Wally Richardson/Patrick Johnson	.25	.08
44	Ruben Brown	.25	.08
45	Quinn Early	.25	.08
46	Doug Flutie	.60	.25
47	Sam Gash	.25	.08
48	Phil Hansen	.25	.08
49	Lonnie Johnson	.25	.08
50	Rob Johnson	.40	.15
51	Eric Moulds	.60	.25
52	Andre Reed	.40	.15
53	Jay Riemersma	.25	.08
54	Antowain Smith	.60	.25
55	Bruce Smith	.40	.15
56	Thurman Thomas	.40	.15
57	Ted Washington	.25	.08
58	J.Linton/Kamil Loud RC	1.00	.40
59	Michael Bates	.25	.08
60	Steve Beuerlein	.25	.08
61	Tim Biakabutuka	.40	.15
62	Mark Carrier WR	.25	.08
63	Eric Davis	.25	.08
64	William Floyd	.25	.08
65	Sean Gilbert	.25	.08
66	Kevin Greene	.25	.08
67	Rocket Ismail	.40	.15
68	Anthony Johnson	.25	.08
69	Fred Lane	.25	.08
70	Muhsin Muhammad	.40	.15
71	Winslow Oliver	.25	.08
72	Wesley Walls	.40	.15
73	D.Craig RC/S.Matthews	1.50	.60
74	Edgar Bennett	.25	.08
75	Curtis Conway	.40	.15
76	Bobby Engram	.40	.15
77	Curtis Enis	.25	.08
78	Ty Hallock RC	1.00	.40
79	Walt Harris	.25	.08
80	Jeff Jaeger	.25	.08
81	Erik Kramer	.25	.08
82	Glyn Milburn	.25	.08
83	Chris Penn	.25	.08
84	Steve Stenstrom	.25	.08
85	Ryan Wetnight	.25	.08
86	James Allen RC/Moreno	1.50	.60
87	Ashley Ambrose	.25	.08
88	Brandon Bennett RC	1.00	.40
89	Eric Bieniemy	.25	.08
90	Jeff Blake	.40	.15
91	Corey Dillon	.60	.25
92	Paul Justin	.25	.08
93	Eric Kresser RC	1.00	.40
94	Tremain Mack	.25	.08
95	Tony McGee	.25	.08
96	Neil O'Donnell	.40	.15
97	Carl Pickens	.40	.15
98	Darnay Scott	.25	.08
99	Takeo Spikes	.25	.08
100	Ty Detmer	.25	.08
101	Chris Gardocki	.25	.08
102	Damon Gibson	.25	.08
103	Antonio Langham	.25	.08
104	Jerris McPhail	.25	.08
105	Irv Smith	.25	.08
106	Freddie Solomon	.25	.08
107	S.Milanovich/Fred Brock RC	1.00	.40
108	Troy Aikman	1.25	.50
109	Larry Allen	.25	.08
110	Eric Bjornson	.25	.08
111	Billy Davis	.25	.08
112	Michael Irvin	.40	.15
113	David LaFleur	.25	.08
114	Ernie Mills	.25	.08
115	Nate Newton	.25	.08
116	Deion Sanders	.60	.25
117	Emmitt Smith	1.25	.50
118	Chris Warren	.25	.08
119	Bubby Brister	.40	.15
120	Terrell Davis	.60	.25
121	Jason Elam	.25	.08
122	John Elway	2.00	.75
123	Willie Green	.25	.08
124	Howard Griffith	.25	.08
125	Vaughn Hebron	.25	.08
126	Ed McCaffrey	.40	.15
127	John Mobley	.25	.08
128	Bill Romanowski	.25	.08
129	Shannon Sharpe	.40	.15
130	Neil Smith	.40	.15
131	Rod Smith	.40	.15
132	Brian Griese/M.Nash	.60	.25
133	Charlie Batch	.60	.25
134	Stephen Boyd	.25	.08
135	Mark Carrier DB	.25	.08
136	Germane Crowell	.25	.08
137	Terry Fair	.25	.08
138	Jason Hanson	.25	.08
139	Greg Jeffries RC	1.00	.40
140	Herman Moore	.40	.15
141	Johnnie Morton	.40	.15
142	Robert Porcher	.25	.08
143	Ron Rivers	.25	.08
144	Barry Sanders	2.00	.75
145	Tommy Vardell	.25	.08
146	Bryant Westbrook	.25	.08
147	Robert Brooks	.40	.15
148	LeRoy Butler	.25	.08
149	Mark Chmura	.25	.08
150	Tyrone Davis	.25	.08
151	Brett Favre	2.00	.75
152	Antonio Freeman	.60	.25
153	Raymont Harris	.25	.08
154	Vonnie Holliday	.25	.08
155	Darick Holmes	.25	.08
156	Dorsey Levens	.60	.25
157	Brian Manning	.25	.08
158	Derrick Mayes	.25	.08
159	Roell Preston	.25	.08
160	Jeff Thomason	.25	.08
161	Tyrone Williams	.25	.08
162	C.Bradford/Michael Blair RC	1.50	.60
163	Aaron Bailey	.25	.08
164	Ken Dilger	.25	.08
165	Marshall Faulk	.75	.30
166	E.G. Green	.25	.08
167	Marvin Harrison	.60	.25
168	Craig Heyward	.25	.08
169	Peyton Manning	2.00	.75
170	Jerome Pathon	.40	.15
171	Marcus Pollard	.25	.08
172	Torrance Small	.25	.08
173	Mike Vanderjagt	.25	.08
174	Lamont Warren	.25	.08
175	Tavian Banks	.25	.08
176	Reggie Barlow	.25	.08
177	Tony Boselli	.25	.08
178	Tony Brackens	.25	.08
179	Mark Brunell	.60	.25
180	Kevin Hardy	.25	.08
181	Damon Jones	.25	.08
182	Jamie Martin	.60	.25
183	Keenan McCardell	.40	.15
184	Pete Mitchell	.25	.08
185	Bryce Paup	.25	.08
186	Jimmy Smith	.40	.15
187	Fred Taylor	.60	.25
188	Alvis Whitted/Chris Howard	.25	.08
189	Derrick Alexander WR	.40	.15
190	Kimble Anders	.40	.15
191	Donnell Bennett	.25	.08
192	Dale Carter	.25	.08
193	Rich Gannon	.60	.25
194	Tony Gonzalez	.60	.25
195	Elvis Grbac	.40	.15
196	Joe Horn	.40	.15
197	Kevin Lockett	.25	.08
198	Byron Bam Morris	.25	.08
199	Andre Rison	.40	.15
200	Derrick Thomas	.60	.25
201	Tamarick Vanover	.25	.08
202	Gregory Favors/Rashaan Shehee	.25	.08
203	Karim Abdul-Jabbar	.40	.15
204	Trace Armstrong	.25	.08
205	John Avery	.25	.08
206	Lorenzo Bromell RC	.60	.25
207	Terrell Buckley	.25	.08
208	Oronde Gadsden	.40	.15
209	Sam Madison	.25	.08
210	Dan Marino	2.00	.75

- ❑ 211 O.J. McDuffie .40 .15
- ❑ 212 Ed Perry RC .60 .25
- ❑ 213 Jason Taylor .25 .08
- ❑ 214 Lamar Thomas .25 .08
- ❑ 215 Zach Thomas .60 .25
- ❑ 216 H.Lusk/Nate Jacquet RC 1.00 .40
- ❑ 217 T.Doxzon RC/D.Huard 1.50 .60
- ❑ 218 Gary Anderson .25 .08
- ❑ 219 Cris Carter .60 .25
- ❑ 220 Randall Cunningham .60 .25
- ❑ 221 Andrew Glover .25 .08
- ❑ 222 Matthew Hatchette .25 .08
- ❑ 223 Brad Johnson .60 .25
- ❑ 224 Ed McDaniel .25 .08
- ❑ 225 Randall McDaniel .25 .08
- ❑ 226 Randy Moss 1.50 .60
- ❑ 227 David Palmer .25 .08
- ❑ 228 John Randle .40 .15
- ❑ 229 Jake Reed .40 .15
- ❑ 230 Robert Smith .60 .25
- ❑ 231 Todd Steussie .25 .08
- ❑ 232 S.Colinet RC/K.Mays .25 .08
- ❑ 233 Jay Fiedler RC/T.Bouman RC 6.00 2.50
- ❑ 234 Drew Bledsoe .75 .30
- ❑ 235 Troy Brown .40 .15
- ❑ 236 Ben Coates .40 .15
- ❑ 237 Derrick Cullors .25 .08
- ❑ 238 Robert Edwards .25 .08
- ❑ 239 Terry Glenn .60 .25
- ❑ 240 Shawn Jefferson .25 .08
- ❑ 241 Ty Law .40 .15
- ❑ 242 Lawyer Milloy .40 .15
- ❑ 243 Lovett Purnell RC 1.00 .40
- ❑ 244 Sedrick Shaw .25 .08
- ❑ 245 Tony Simmons .25 .08
- ❑ 246 Chris Slade .25 .08
- ❑ 247 R.Rutledge/Anth.Ladd RC 1.00 .40
- ❑ 248 Chris Floyd/Harold Shaw .25 .08
- ❑ 249 Ink Aleaga RC 1.00 .40
- ❑ 250 Cameron Cleeland .25 .08
- ❑ 251 Kerry Collins .40 .15
- ❑ 252 Troy Davis .25 .08
- ❑ 253 Sean Dawkins .25 .08
- ❑ 254 Mark Fields .25 .08
- ❑ 255 Andre Hastings .25 .08
- ❑ 256 Sammy Knight .25 .08
- ❑ 257 Keith Poole .25 .08
- ❑ 258 William Roaf .25 .08
- ❑ 259 Lamar Smith .40 .15
- ❑ 260 Danny Wuerffel .25 .08
- ❑ 261 Josh Wilcox RC/Brett Bech RC 1.00 .40
- ❑ 262 Chris Bordano RC/W.Perry 1.00 .40
- ❑ 263 Jessie Armstead .25 .08
- ❑ 264 Tiki Barber .60 .25
- ❑ 265 Chad Bratzke .25 .08
- ❑ 266 Gary Brown .25 .08
- ❑ 267 Chris Calloway .25 .08
- ❑ 268 Howard Cross .25 .08
- ❑ 269 Kent Graham .25 .08
- ❑ 270 Ike Hilliard .25 .08
- ❑ 271 Danny Kanell .40 .15
- ❑ 272 Michael Strahan .40 .15
- ❑ 273 Amani Toomer .25 .08
- ❑ 274 Charles Way .25 .08
- ❑ 275 Greg Comella RC/M.Cherry 1.50 .60
- ❑ 276 Kyle Brady .25 .08
- ❑ 277 Keith Byars .25 .08
- ❑ 278 Chad Cascadden .25 .08
- ❑ 279 Wayne Chrebet .40 .15
- ❑ 280 Bryan Cox .25 .08
- ❑ 281 Glenn Foley .40 .15
- ❑ 282 Aaron Glenn .25 .08
- ❑ 283 Keyshawn Johnson .60 .25
- ❑ 284 Leon Johnson .25 .08
- ❑ 285 Mo Lewis .25 .08
- ❑ 286 Curtis Martin .60 .25
- ❑ 287 Otis Smith .25 .08
- ❑ 288 Vinny Testaverde .40 .15
- ❑ 289 Dedric Ward .25 .08
- ❑ 290 Tim Brown .60 .25
- ❑ 291 Rickey Dudley .25 .08
- ❑ 292 Jeff George .40 .15
- ❑ 293 Desmond Howard .40 .15
- ❑ 294 James Jett .40 .15
- ❑ 295 Lance Johnstone .25 .08
- ❑ 296 Randy Jordan .25 .08
- ❑ 297 Napoleon Kaufman .60 .25
- ❑ 298 Lincoln Kennedy .25 .08
- ❑ 299 Terry Mickens .25 .08
- ❑ 300 Darrell Russell .25 .08
- ❑ 301 Harvey Williams .25 .08
- ❑ 302 Ch.Woodson/Ritchie .60 .25
- ❑ 303 Rodney Williams/Jermaine Williams .25 .08
- ❑ 304 Koy Detmer .25 .08
- ❑ 305 Hugh Douglas .25 .08
- ❑ 306 Jason Dunn .25 .08
- ❑ 307 Irving Fryar .40 .15
- ❑ 308 Charlie Garner .40 .15
- ❑ 309 Jeff Graham .25 .08
- ❑ 310 Bobby Hoying .40 .15
- ❑ 311 Rodney Peete .25 .08
- ❑ 312 Allen Rossum .25 .08
- ❑ 313 Duce Staley .60 .25
- ❑ 314 William Thomas .25 .08
- ❑ 315 Kevin Turner .25 .08
- ❑ 316 K.Sinceno RC/C.Walker RC 1.00 .40
- ❑ 317 Jahine Arnold .25 .08
- ❑ 318 Jerome Bettis .60 .25
- ❑ 319 Will Blackwell .25 .08
- ❑ 320 Mark Bruener .25 .08
- ❑ 321 Dermontti Dawson .25 .08
- ❑ 322 Chris Fuamatu-Ma'afala .25 .08
- ❑ 323 Courtney Hawkins .25 .08
- ❑ 324 Richard Huntley .40 .15
- ❑ 325 Charles Johnson .25 .08
- ❑ 326 Levon Kirkland .25 .08
- ❑ 327 Kordell Stewart .40 .15
- ❑ 328 Hines Ward .60 .25
- ❑ 329 Dewayne Washington .25 .08
- ❑ 330 Tony Banks .40 .15
- ❑ 331 Steve Bono .25 .08
- ❑ 332 Isaac Bruce .60 .25
- ❑ 333 June Henley RC 1.25 .50
- ❑ 334 Robert Holcombe .25 .08
- ❑ 335 Mike Jones LB .25 .08
- ❑ 336 Eddie Kennison .40 .15
- ❑ 337 Amp Lee .25 .08
- ❑ 338 Jerald Moore .25 .08
- ❑ 339 Ricky Proehl .25 .08
- ❑ 340 J.T. Thomas .25 .08
- ❑ 341 Derrick Harris/Az-Zahir Hakim .40 .15
- ❑ 342 Roland Williams/Grant Wistrom .25 .08
- ❑ 343 Kurt Warner RC/T.Horne ! 12.00 5.00
- ❑ 344 Terrell Fletcher .25 .08
- ❑ 345 Greg Jackson .25 .08
- ❑ 346 Charlie Jones .25 .08
- ❑ 347 Freddie Jones .25 .08
- ❑ 348 Ryan Leaf .60 .25
- ❑ 349 Natrone Means .40 .15
- ❑ 350 Mikhael Ricks .25 .08
- ❑ 351 Junior Seau .60 .25
- ❑ 352 Bryan Still .25 .08
- ❑ 353 T.Stephens/R.Thelwell RC 1.25 .50
- ❑ 354 Greg Clark .25 .08
- ❑ 355 Marc Edwards .25 .08
- ❑ 356 Merton Hanks .25 .08
- ❑ 357 Garrison Hearst .40 .15
- ❑ 358 R.W. McQuarters .25 .08
- ❑ 359 Ken Norton Jr. .25 .08
- ❑ 360 Terrell Owens .60 .25
- ❑ 361 Jerry Rice 1.25 .50
- ❑ 362 J.J. Stokes .40 .15
- ❑ 363 Bryant Young .25 .08
- ❑ 364 Steve Young .75 .30
- ❑ 365 Chad Brown .25 .08
- ❑ 366 Christian Fauria .25 .08
- ❑ 367 Joey Galloway .40 .15
- ❑ 368 Ahman Green .60 .25
- ❑ 369 Cortez Kennedy .25 .08
- ❑ 370 Jon Kitna .60 .25
- ❑ 371 James McKnight .40 .15
- ❑ 372 Mike Pritchard .25 .08
- ❑ 373 Michael Sinclair .25 .08
- ❑ 374 Shawn Springs .25 .08
- ❑ 375 Ricky Watters .40 .15
- ❑ 376 Darryl Williams .25 .08
- ❑ 377 R.Wilson/K.Joseph RC 1.50 .60
- ❑ 378 Mike Alstott .60 .25
- ❑ 379 Reidel Anthony .40 .15
- ❑ 380 Derrick Brooks .60 .25
- ❑ 381 Trent Dilfer .60 .25
- ❑ 382 Warrick Dunn .60 .25
- ❑ 383 Bert Emanuel .40 .15
- ❑ 384 Jacquez Green .25 .08
- ❑ 385 Patrick Hape .25 .08
- ❑ 386 John Lynch .40 .15
- ❑ 387 Dave Moore .25 .08
- ❑ 388 Hardy Nickerson .25 .08
- ❑ 389 Warren Sapp .40 .15
- ❑ 390 Karl Williams .25 .08
- ❑ 391 Blaine Bishop .25 .08
- ❑ 392 Joe Bowden .25 .08
- ❑ 393 Isaac Byrd RC 1.00 .40
- ❑ 394 Willie Davis .25 .08
- ❑ 395 Al Del Greco .25 .08
- ❑ 396 Kevin Dyson .40 .15
- ❑ 397 Eddie George .60 .25
- ❑ 398 Jackie Harris .25 .08
- ❑ 399 Dave Krieg .25 .08
- ❑ 400 Steve McNair .60 .25
- ❑ 401 Michael Roan .25 .08
- ❑ 402 Yancey Thigpen .25 .08
- ❑ 403 Frank Wycheck .25 .08
- ❑ 404 Derrick Mason/Steve Matthews .40 .15
- ❑ 405 Stephen Alexander .25 .08
- ❑ 406 Terry Allen .40 .15
- ❑ 407 Jamie Asher .25 .08
- ❑ 408 Stephen Davis .60 .25
- ❑ 409 Darrell Green .25 .08
- ❑ 410 Trent Green .60 .25
- ❑ 411 Skip Hicks .25 .08
- ❑ 412 Brian Mitchell .25 .08
- ❑ 413 Leslie Shepherd .25 .08
- ❑ 414 Michael Westbrook .40 .15
- ❑ 415 T.Hardy/Rabih Abdullah RC 1.00 .40
- ❑ 416 C.Thomas RC/M.Quinn RC 1.00 .40
- ❑ 417 J.Quinn/Kelly Holcomb RC 8.00 3.00
- ❑ 418 Brian Alford/Blake Spence 1.00 .40
- ❑ 419 Andy Haase RC/Carlos King 1.00 .40
- ❑ 420 James Thrash RC/K.Hankton 1.50 .60
- ❑ 421 F.Beasley/Itula Mili RC 1.25 .50
- ❑ 422 Champ Bailey RC 2.00 .75
- ❑ 423 D'Wayne Bates RC 1.25 .50
- ❑ 424 Michael Bishop RC 1.50 .60
- ❑ 425 David Boston RC 1.50 .60
- ❑ 426 Shawn Bryson RC 1.50 .60
- ❑ 427 Tim Couch RC 1.50 .60
- ❑ 428 Scott Covington RC 1.50 .60
- ❑ 429 Daunte Culpepper RC 6.00 2.50
- ❑ 430 Autry Denson RC 1.25 .50
- ❑ 431 Troy Edwards RC 1.25 .50
- ❑ 432 Kevin Faulk RC 1.50 .60
- ❑ 433 Joe Germaine RC 1.25 .50
- ❑ 434 Torry Holt RC 4.00 1.50
- ❑ 435 Brock Huard RC 1.50 .60
- ❑ 436 Sedrick Irvin RC 1.00 .40
- ❑ 437 Edgerrin James RC 6.00 2.50
- ❑ 438 Andy Katzenmoyer RC 1.25 .50
- ❑ 439 Shaun King RC 1.25 .50
- ❑ 440 Rob Konrad RC 1.25 .50
- ❑ 441 Donovan McNabb RC 8.00 3.00
- ❑ 442 Cade McNown RC 1.25 .50
- ❑ 443 Billy Miller RC 1.00 .40
- ❑ 444 Dee Miller RC 1.00 .40
- ❑ 445 Sirr Parker RC 1.00 .40
- ❑ 446 Peerless Price RC 1.50 .60
- ❑ 447 Akili Smith RC 1.25 .50
- ❑ 448 Tai Streets RC 1.50 .60
- ❑ 449 Ricky Williams RC 3.00 1.25
- ❑ 450 Amos Zereoue RC 1.50 .60
- ❑ S1 Warrick Dunn Sample .60 .25

2000 Pacific

- ❑ COMPLETE SET (450) 60.00 25.00
- ❑ 1 Mario Bates .25 .08
- ❑ 2 David Boston .60 .25
- ❑ 3 Rob Fredrickson .25 .08
- ❑ 4 Terry Hardy .25 .08
- ❑ 5 Rob Moore .40 .15
- ❑ 6 Adrian Murrell .40 .15

❑ 7 Michael Pittman	.25	.08
❑ 8 Jake Plummer	.40	.15
❑ 9 Simeon Rice	.40	.15
❑ 10 Frank Sanders	.40	.15
❑ 11 Aeneas Williams	.25	.08
❑ 12 M.Cody/A.McCullough	.25	.08
❑ 13 D.McKinley RC/J.Makovicka	.60	.25
❑ 14 Jamal Anderson	.60	.25
❑ 15 Chris Calloway	.25	.08
❑ 16 Chris Chandler	.40	.15
❑ 17 Bob Christian	.25	.08
❑ 18 Tim Dwight	.60	.25
❑ 19 Jammi German	.25	.08
❑ 20 Ronnie Harris	.25	.08
❑ 21 Terance Mathis	.40	.15
❑ 22 Ken Oxendine	.25	.08
❑ 23 O.J. Santiago	.25	.08
❑ 24 Bob Whitfield	.25	.08
❑ 25 E.Baker/R.Kelly	.25	.08
❑ 26 Justin Armour	.25	.08
❑ 27 Tony Banks	.40	.15
❑ 28 Peter Boulware	.25	.08
❑ 29 Stoney Case	.25	.08
❑ 30 Priest Holmes	.75	.30
❑ 31 Qadry Ismail	.40	.15
❑ 32 Patrick Johnson	.25	.08
❑ 33 Michael McCrary	.25	.08
❑ 34 Jonathan Ogden	.25	.08
❑ 35 Errict Rhett	.40	.15
❑ 36 Duane Starks	.25	.08
❑ 37 Doug Flutie	.60	.25
❑ 38 Rob Johnson	.40	.15
❑ 39 Jonathan Linton	.25	.08
❑ 40 Eric Moulds	.60	.25
❑ 41 Peerless Price	.40	.15
❑ 42 Andre Reed	.40	.15
❑ 43 Jay Riemersma	.25	.08
❑ 44 Antowain Smith	.40	.15
❑ 45 Bruce Smith	.40	.15
❑ 46 Thurman Thomas	.40	.15
❑ 47 Kevin Williams	.25	.08
❑ 48 B.Collins/S.Jackson	.25	.08
❑ 49 Michael Bates	.25	.08
❑ 50 Steve Beuerlein	.40	.15
❑ 51 Tim Biakabutuka	.40	.15
❑ 52 Antonio Edwards	.25	.08
❑ 53 Donald Hayes	.25	.08
❑ 54 Patrick Jeffers	.60	.25
❑ 55 Anthony Johnson	.25	.08
❑ 56 Jeff Lewis	.25	.08
❑ 57 Eric Metcalf	.25	.08
❑ 58 Muhsin Muhammad	.40	.15
❑ 59 Jason Peter	.25	.08
❑ 60 Wesley Walls	.25	.08
❑ 61 John Allred	.25	.08
❑ 62 Marty Booker	.40	.15
❑ 63 Curtis Conway	.40	.15
❑ 64 Bobby Engram	.25	.08
❑ 65 Curtis Enis	.25	.08
❑ 66 Shane Matthews	.40	.15
❑ 67 Cade McNown	.25	.08
❑ 68 Glyn Milburn	.25	.08
❑ 69 Jim Miller	.25	.08
❑ 70 Marcus Robinson	.60	.25
❑ 71 Ryan Wetnight	.25	.08
❑ 72 J.Allen/M.Brooks	.40	.15
❑ 73 Jeff Blake	.40	.15
❑ 74 Corey Dillon	.60	.25
❑ 75 Rodney Heath RC	.40	.15
❑ 76 Willie Jackson	.25	.08
❑ 77 Tremain Mack	.25	.08
❑ 78 Tony McGee	.25	.08
❑ 79 Carl Pickens	.40	.15
❑ 80 Darnay Scott	.40	.15
❑ 81 Akili Smith	.25	.08
❑ 82 Takeo Spikes	.25	.08
❑ 83 Craig Yeast	.25	.08
❑ 84 M.Basnight/N.Williams	.25	.08
❑ 85 Karim Abdul-Jabbar	.40	.15
❑ 86 Darrin Chiaverini	.25	.08
❑ 87 Tim Couch	.40	.15
❑ 88 Marc Edwards	.25	.08
❑ 89 Kevin Johnson	.60	.25
❑ 90 Terry Kirby	.25	.08
❑ 91 Daylon McCutcheon	.25	.08
❑ 92 Jamir Miller	.25	.08
❑ 93 Leslie Shepherd	.25	.08
❑ 94 Irv Smith	.25	.08
❑ 95 M.Campbell/J.Dearth	.25	.08

❑ 96 Z.Davis RC/D.Dunn RC	.40	.15
❑ 97 M.Hill/T.Saleh RC	.25	.08
❑ 98 Troy Aikman	1.25	.50
❑ 99 Eric Bjornson	.25	.08
❑ 100 Dexter Coakley	.25	.08
❑ 101 Greg Ellis	.25	.08
❑ 102 Rocket Ismail	.40	.15
❑ 103 David LaFleur	.25	.08
❑ 104 Ernie Mills	.25	.08
❑ 105 Jeff Ogden	.40	.15
❑ 106 R.Neufeld RC/R.Thomas	.40	.15
❑ 107 Deion Sanders	.60	.25
❑ 108 Emmitt Smith	1.25	.50
❑ 109 Chris Warren	.25	.08
❑ 110 M.Lucky/J.Tucker	.25	.08
❑ 111 Byron Chamberlain	.25	.08
❑ 112 Terrell Davis	.60	.25
❑ 113 Jason Elam	.25	.08
❑ 114 Olandis Gary	.60	.25
❑ 115 Brian Griese	.60	.25
❑ 116 Ed McCaffrey	.60	.25
❑ 117 Trevor Pryce	.25	.08
❑ 118 Bill Romanowski	.25	.08
❑ 119 Shannon Sharpe	.40	.15
❑ 120 Rod Smith	.40	.15
❑ 121 Al Wilson	.25	.08
❑ 122 A.Cooper/C.Watson	.25	.08
❑ 123 Charlie Batch	.60	.25
❑ 124 Stephen Boyd	.25	.08
❑ 125 Chris Claiborne	.25	.08
❑ 126 Germane Crowell	.25	.08
❑ 127 Terry Fair	.25	.08
❑ 128 Gus Frerotte	.25	.08
❑ 129 Jason Hanson	.25	.08
❑ 130 Greg Hill	.25	.08
❑ 131 Herman Moore	.40	.15
❑ 132 Johnnie Morton	.40	.15
❑ 133 Barry Sanders	1.50	.60
❑ 134 David Sloan	.25	.08
❑ 135 B.Olivo/C.Sauter	.25	.08
❑ 136 Corey Bradford	.40	.15
❑ 137 Tyrone Davis	.25	.08
❑ 138 Brett Favre	2.00	.75
❑ 139 Antonio Freeman	.60	.25
❑ 140 Vonnie Holliday	.25	.08
❑ 141 Dorsey Levens	.40	.15
❑ 142 Keith McKenzie	.25	.08
❑ 143 Mike McKenzie	.25	.08
❑ 144 Bill Schroeder	.40	.15
❑ 145 Jeff Thomason	.25	.08
❑ 146 Frank Winters	.25	.08
❑ 147 Cornelius Bennett	.25	.08
❑ 148 Tony Blevins RC	.40	.15
❑ 149 Chad Bratzke	.25	.08
❑ 150 Ken Dilger	.25	.08
❑ 151 Tarik Glenn	.25	.08
❑ 152 E.G. Green	.25	.08
❑ 153 Marvin Harrison	.60	.25
❑ 154 Edgerrin James	1.00	.40
❑ 155 Peyton Manning	1.50	.60
❑ 156 Jerome Pathon	.40	.15
❑ 157 Marcus Pollard	.25	.08
❑ 158 Terrence Wilkins	.25	.08
❑ 159 I.Jones RC/P.Shields RC	.60	.25
❑ 160 Reggie Barlow	.25	.08
❑ 161 Aaron Beasley	.25	.08
❑ 162 Tony Boselli	.25	.08
❑ 163 Tony Brackens	.25	.08
❑ 164 Kyle Brady	.25	.08
❑ 165 Mark Brunell	.60	.25
❑ 166 Jay Fiedler	.60	.25
❑ 167 Kevin Hardy	.25	.08
❑ 168 Carnell Lake	.25	.08
❑ 169 Keenan McCardell	.40	.15
❑ 170 Jonathan Quinn	.25	.08
❑ 171 Jimmy Smith	.40	.15
❑ 172 James Stewart	.40	.15
❑ 173 Fred Taylor	.60	.25
❑ 174 L.Jackson RC/S.Mack	.60	.25
❑ 175 Derrick Alexander	.40	.15
❑ 176 Donnell Bennett	.25	.08
❑ 177 Donnie Edwards	.25	.08
❑ 178 Tony Gonzalez	.40	.15
❑ 179 Elvis Grbac	.40	.15
❑ 180 James Hasty	.25	.08
❑ 181 Joe Horn	.40	.15
❑ 182 Lonnie Johnson	.25	.08
❑ 183 Kevin Lockett	.25	.08
❑ 184 Larry Parker	.25	.08

❑ 185 Tony Richardson RC	.40	.15
❑ 186 Rashaan Shehee	.25	.08
❑ 187 Tamarick Vanover	.25	.08
❑ 188 Trace Armstrong	.25	.08
❑ 189 Oronde Gadsden	.40	.15
❑ 190 Damon Huard	.60	.25
❑ 191 Nate Jacquet	.25	.08
❑ 192 James Johnson	.25	.08
❑ 193 Rob Konrad	.25	.08
❑ 194 Sam Madison	.25	.08
❑ 195 Dan Marino	2.00	.75
❑ 196 Tony Martin	.40	.15
❑ 197 O.J. McDuffie	.40	.15
❑ 198 Stanley Pritchett	.25	.08
❑ 199 Tim Ruddy	.25	.08
❑ 200 Patrick Surtain	.25	.08
❑ 201 Zach Thomas	.60	.25
❑ 202 Cris Carter	.60	.25
❑ 203 Duane Clemons	.25	.08
❑ 204 Carlester Crumpler	.25	.08
❑ 205 Daunte Culpepper	.75	.30
❑ 206 Jeff George	.40	.15
❑ 207 Matthew Hatchette	.25	.08
❑ 208 Leroy Hoard	.25	.08
❑ 209 Randy Moss	1.25	.50
❑ 210 John Randle	.40	.15
❑ 211 Jake Reed	.40	.15
❑ 212 Robert Smith	.60	.25
❑ 213 Robert Tate	.25	.08
❑ 214 Terry Allen	.40	.15
❑ 215 Bruce Armstrong	.25	.08
❑ 216 Drew Bledsoe	.75	.30
❑ 217 Ben Coates	.25	.08
❑ 218 Kevin Faulk	.40	.15
❑ 219 Terry Glenn	.40	.15
❑ 220 Shawn Jefferson	.25	.08
❑ 221 Andy Katzenmoyer	.25	.08
❑ 222 Ty Law	.40	.15
❑ 223 Willie McGinest	.25	.08
❑ 224 Lawyer Milloy	.40	.15
❑ 225 Tony Simmons	.25	.08
❑ 226 M.Bishop/S.Morey RC	.40	.15
❑ 227 Cameron Cleeland	.25	.08
❑ 228 Troy Davis	.25	.08
❑ 229 Jake Delhomme RC	3.00	1.25
❑ 230 Andre Hastings	.25	.08
❑ 231 Eddie Kennison	.40	.15
❑ 232 Wilmont Perry	.25	.08
❑ 233 Dino Philyaw	.25	.08
❑ 234 Keith Poole	.25	.08
❑ 235 William Roaf	.25	.08
❑ 236 Billy Joe Tolliver	.25	.08
❑ 237 Fred Weary	.25	.08
❑ 238 Ricky Williams	.60	.25
❑ 239 Franklin RC/M.Powell RC	.60	.25
❑ 240 Jessie Armstead	.25	.08
❑ 241 Tiki Barber	.60	.25
❑ 242 Daniel Campbell	.25	.08
❑ 243 Kerry Collins	.40	.15
❑ 244 Percy Ellsworth	.25	.08
❑ 245 Kent Graham	.25	.08
❑ 246 Ike Hilliard	.40	.15
❑ 247 Cedric Jones	.25	.08
❑ 248 Bashir Levingston RC	.60	.25
❑ 249 Pete Mitchell	.25	.08
❑ 250 Michael Strahan	.40	.15
❑ 251 Amani Toomer	.25	.08
❑ 252 Charles Way	.25	.08
❑ 253 Andre Weathers RC	.40	.15
❑ 254 Richie Anderson	.40	.15
❑ 255 Wayne Chrebet	.40	.15
❑ 256 Marcus Coleman	.25	.08
❑ 257 Bryan Cox	.25	.08
❑ 258 Jason Fabini RC	.40	.15
❑ 259 Robert Farmer RC	.60	.25
❑ 260 Keyshawn Johnson	.60	.25
❑ 261 Ray Lucas	.40	.15
❑ 262 Curtis Martin	.60	.25
❑ 263 Kevin Mawae	.25	.08
❑ 264 Eric Ogbogu	.25	.08
❑ 265 Bernie Parmalee	.25	.08
❑ 266 Vinny Testaverde	.40	.15
❑ 267 Dedric Ward	.25	.08
❑ 268 Eric Barton RC	.40	.15
❑ 269 Tim Brown	.60	.25
❑ 270 Tony Bryant	.25	.08
❑ 271 Rickey Dudley	.25	.08
❑ 272 Rich Gannon	.60	.25
❑ 273 Bobby Hoying	.40	.15

❑ 274 James Jett .25 .08
❑ 275 Napoleon Kaufman .40 .15
❑ 276 Jon Ritchie .25 .08
❑ 277 Darrell Russell .25 .08
❑ 278 Kenny Shedd .25 .08
❑ 279 Marquis Walker RC .40 .15
❑ 280 Tyrone Wheatley .40 .15
❑ 281 Charles Woodson .40 .15
❑ 282 Luther Broughton RC .40 .15
❑ 283 Al Harris RC .25 .08
❑ 284 Greg Jefferson .25 .08
❑ 285 Dietrich Jells .25 .08
❑ 286 Charles Johnson .40 .15
❑ 287 Chad Lewis .25 .08
❑ 288 Mike Mamula .25 .08
❑ 289 Donovan McNabb 1.00 .40
❑ 290 Doug Pederson .25 .08
❑ 291 Allen Rossum .25 .08
❑ 292 Torrance Small .25 .08
❑ 293 Duce Staley .60 .25
❑ 294 Jerome Bettis .60 .25
❑ 295 Kris Brown .25 .08
❑ 296 Mark Bruener .25 .08
❑ 297 Troy Edwards .25 .08
❑ 298 Jason Gildon .25 .08
❑ 299 Richard Huntley .25 .08
❑ 300 Bobby Shaw RC .60 .25
❑ 301 Scott Shields RC .40 .15
❑ 302 Kordell Stewart .40 .15
❑ 303 Hines Ward .60 .25
❑ 304 Amos Zereoue .60 .25
❑ 305 M.Cushing RC/J.Tuman .40 .15
❑ 306 P.Gonzalez/A.Wright RC 1.50 .60
❑ 307 Isaac Bruce .60 .25
❑ 308 Kevin Carter .25 .08
❑ 309 Marshall Faulk .75 .30
❑ 310 London Fletcher RC .40 .15
❑ 311 Joe Germaine .25 .08
❑ 312 Az-Zahir Hakim .40 .15
❑ 313 Torry Holt .60 .25
❑ 314 Tony Horne .25 .08
❑ 315 Mike Jones LB .25 .08
❑ 316 Dexter McCleon RC .60 .25
❑ 317 Orlando Pace .25 .08
❑ 318 Ricky Proehl .25 .08
❑ 319 Kurt Warner 1.25 .50
❑ 320 Roland Williams .25 .08
❑ 321 Grant Wistrom .25 .08
❑ 322 J.Hodgins RC/J.Watson .25 .08
❑ 323 Jermaine Fazande .25 .08
❑ 324 Jeff Graham .25 .08
❑ 325 Jim Harbaugh .40 .15
❑ 326 Raylee Johnson .25 .08
❑ 327 Charlie Jones .25 .08
❑ 328 Freddie Jones .25 .08
❑ 329 Natrone Means .25 .08
❑ 330 Chris Penn .25 .08
❑ 331 Mikhael Ricks .25 .08
❑ 332 Junior Seau .60 .25
❑ 333 R.Davis RC/R.Reed RC .40 .15
❑ 334 Fred Beasley .25 .08
❑ 335 Brentson Buckner .25 .08
❑ 336 Greg Clark .25 .08
❑ 337 Dave Fiore RC .25 .08
❑ 338 Charlie Garner .40 .15
❑ 339 Mark Harris RC .60 .25
❑ 340 Ramos McDonald RC .40 .15
❑ 341 Terrell Owens .60 .25
❑ 342 Jerry Rice 1.25 .50
❑ 343 Lance Schulters .25 .08
❑ 344 J.J. Stokes .40 .15
❑ 345 Bryant Young .25 .08
❑ 346 Steve Young .75 .30
❑ 347 Jeff Garcia .60 .25
❑ 348 Fabien Bownes RC .25 .08
❑ 349 Chad Brown .25 .08
❑ 350 Reggie Brown .25 .08
❑ 351 Sean Dawkins .25 .08
❑ 352 Christian Fauria .25 .08
❑ 353 Ahman Green .60 .25
❑ 354 Walter Jones .25 .08
❑ 355 Cortez Kennedy .25 .08
❑ 356 Jon Kitna .60 .25
❑ 357 Derrick Mayes .40 .15
❑ 358 Charlie Rogers .25 .08
❑ 359 Shawn Springs .25 .08
❑ 360 Ricky Watters .40 .15
❑ 361 Donne Abraham .25 .08
❑ 362 Mike Alstott .60 .25
❑ 363 Reidel Anthony .25 .08
❑ 364 Ronde Barber .25 .08
❑ 365 Derrick Brooks .60 .25
❑ 366 Warrick Dunn .60 .25
❑ 367 Jacquez Green .25 .08
❑ 368 Marcus Jones .25 .08
❑ 369 Shaun King .25 .08
❑ 370 John Lynch .40 .15
❑ 371 Warren Sapp .40 .15
❑ 372 Steve White RC .25 .08
❑ 373 M.Gramatica/K.McLeod RC .40 .15
❑ 374 Blaine Bishop .25 .08
❑ 375 Al Del Greco .25 .08
❑ 376 Kevin Dyson .40 .15
❑ 377 Eddie George .60 .25
❑ 378 Jevon Kearse .60 .25
❑ 379 Derrick Mason .40 .15
❑ 380 Bruce Matthews .25 .08
❑ 381 Steve McNair .60 .25
❑ 382 Neil O'Donnell .25 .08
❑ 383 Yancey Thigpen .25 .08
❑ 384 Frank Wycheck .25 .08
❑ 385 K.Daft/L.Brown .25 .08
❑ 386 Stephen Alexander .25 .08
❑ 387 Champ Bailey .40 .15
❑ 388 Larry Centers .25 .08
❑ 389 Marco Coleman .25 .08
❑ 390 Albert Connell .25 .08
❑ 391 Stephen Davis .60 .25
❑ 392 Irving Fryar .40 .15
❑ 393 Skip Hicks .25 .08
❑ 394 Brad Johnson .60 .25
❑ 395 Michael Westbrook .40 .15
❑ 396 O.Ayanbadejo RC/L.Gordon RC .40 .15
❑ 397 D.Driver/R.Powell .60 .25
❑ 398 T.Bouman/J.Brigham RC .60 .25
❑ 399 B.Huard/S.Bonner .25 .08
❑ 400 M.Sellers/S.George RC .40 .15
❑ 401 Shaun Alexander RC 6.00 2.50
❑ 402 LaVar Arrington RC 5.00 2.00
❑ 403 Tom Brady RC 40.00 20.00
❑ 404 Demario Brown RC .60 .25
❑ 405 Plaxico Burress RC 2.50 1.00
❑ 406 Trung Canidate RC 1.00 .40
❑ 407 Giovanni Carmazzi RC .60 .25
❑ 408 Kwame Cavil RC .60 .25
❑ 409 Chrys Chukwuma RC 1.25 .50
❑ 410 Ron Dayne RC 1.25 .50
❑ 411 Reuben Droughns RC 1.50 .60
❑ 412 Ron Dugans RC .60 .25
❑ 413 Deon Dyer RC 1.00 .40
❑ 414 Danny Farmer RC 1.00 .40
❑ 415 Chafie Fields RC .60 .25
❑ 416 Trevor Gaylor RC 1.00 .40
❑ 417 Sherrod Gideon RC .60 .25
❑ 418 Joey Goodspeed RC .60 .25
❑ 419 Joe Hamilton RC 1.00 .40
❑ 420 Tony Hartley RC .60 .25
❑ 421 Todd Husak RC 1.25 .50
❑ 422 Trevor Insley RC .60 .25
❑ 423 Thomas Jones RC 2.00 .75
❑ 424 Marcus Knight RC 1.00 .40
❑ 425 Jamal Lewis RC 3.00 1.25
❑ 426 Anthony Lucas RC 1.50 .60
❑ 427 Tee Martin RC 1.25 .50
❑ 428 Rondell Mealey RC .60 .25
❑ 429 Sylvester Morris RC 1.00 .40
❑ 430 Chad Morton RC 1.25 .50
❑ 431 Dennis Northcutt RC 1.25 .50
❑ 432 Chad Pennington RC 3.00 1.25
❑ 433 Rodnick Phillips RC .60 .25
❑ 434 Mareno Philyaw RC .60 .25
❑ 435 Jerry Porter RC 1.50 .60
❑ 436 Travis Prentice RC 1.00 .40
❑ 437 Tim Rattay RC 1.25 .50
❑ 438 Chris Redman RC 1.00 .40
❑ 439 J.R. Redmond RC 1.00 .40
❑ 440 Gari Scott RC .60 .25
❑ 441 Keith Smith RC .60 .25
❑ 442 Terrelle Smith RC 1.00 .40
❑ 443 R.Jay Soward RC 1.00 .40
❑ 444 Quinton Spotwood RC .60 .25
❑ 445 Shyrone Stith RC 1.00 .40
❑ 446 Travis Taylor RC 1.25 .50
❑ 447 Troy Walters RC 1.25 .50
❑ 448 Peter Warrick RC 1.25 .50
❑ 449 Dez White RC 1.25 .50
❑ 450 Michael Wiley RC 1.00 .40

2001 Pacific

❑ COMP.SET w/o SP's (450) 50.00 25.00
❑ 1 David Boston .60 .25
❑ 2 Mac Cody .25 .08
❑ 3 Chris Gedney .25 .08
❑ 4 Chris Greisen .25 .08
❑ 5 Terry Hardy .25 .08
❑ 6 MarTay Jenkins .25 .08
❑ 7 Thomas Jones .60 .25
❑ 8 Joel Makovicka .25 .08
❑ 9 Tywan Mitchell .25 .08
❑ 10 Rob Moore .40 .15
❑ 11 Michael Pittman .25 .08
❑ 12 Jake Plummer .40 .15
❑ 13 Frank Sanders .25 .08
❑ 14 Aeneas Williams .25 .08
❑ 15 Jamal Anderson .60 .25
❑ 16 Eugene Baker .25 .08
❑ 17 Chris Chandler .40 .15
❑ 18 Tim Dwight .60 .25
❑ 19 Brian Finneran .25 .08
❑ 20 Jammi German .25 .08
❑ 21 Shawn Jefferson .25 .08
❑ 22 Doug Johnson .25 .08
❑ 23 Danny Kanell .25 .08
❑ 24 Reggie Kelly .25 .08
❑ 25 Terance Mathis .40 .15
❑ 26 Derek Rackley .25 .08
❑ 27 Ron Rivers .25 .08
❑ 28 Maurice Smith .40 .15
❑ 29 Sam Adams .25 .08
❑ 30 Obafemi Ayanbadejo .25 .08
❑ 31 Tony Banks .40 .15
❑ 32 Trent Dilfer .40 .15
❑ 33 Sam Gash .25 .08
❑ 34 Priest Holmes .75 .30
❑ 35 Qadry Ismail .40 .15
❑ 36 Pat Johnson .25 .08
❑ 37 Jamal Lewis 1.00 .40
❑ 38 Jermaine Lewis .25 .08
❑ 39 Ray Lewis .60 .25
❑ 40 Chris Redman .25 .08
❑ 41 Shannon Sharpe .40 .15
❑ 42 Brandon Stokley .40 .15
❑ 43 Travis Taylor .40 .15
❑ 44 Shawn Bryson .25 .08
❑ 45 Kwame Cavil .25 .08
❑ 46 Sam Cowart .25 .08
❑ 47 Doug Flutie .60 .25
❑ 48 Rob Johnson .40 .15
❑ 49 Jonathan Linton .25 .08
❑ 50 Jeremy McDaniel .25 .08
❑ 51 Sammy Morris .25 .08
❑ 52 Eric Moulds .60 .25
❑ 53 Peerless Price .40 .15
❑ 54 Jay Riemersma .25 .08
❑ 55 Antowain Smith .40 .15
❑ 56 Chris Watson .25 .08
❑ 57 Marcellus Wiley .25 .08
❑ 58 Michael Bates .25 .08
❑ 59 Steve Beuerlein .40 .15
❑ 60 Tim Biakabutuka .40 .15
❑ 61 Isaac Byrd .25 .08
❑ 62 Dameyune Craig .25 .08
❑ 63 William Floyd .25 .08
❑ 64 Karl Hankton .25 .08
❑ 65 Donald Hayes .25 .08
❑ 66 Chris Hetherington RC .40 .15
❑ 67 Brad Hoover .25 .08
❑ 68 Patrick Jeffers .60 .25
❑ 69 Muhsin Muhammad .40 .15

❑ 70 Iheanyi Uwaezuoke	.25	.08
❑ 71 Wesley Walls	.25	.08
❑ 72 James Allen	.40	.15
❑ 73 Marlon Barnes	.25	.08
❑ 74 D'Wayne Bates	.25	.08
❑ 75 Marty Booker	.25	.08
❑ 76 Macey Brooks	.25	.08
❑ 77 Bobby Engram	.40	.15
❑ 78 Curtis Enis	.25	.08
❑ 79 Mark Hartsell RC	.40	.15
❑ 80 Eddie Kennison	.25	.08
❑ 81 Shane Matthews	.25	.08
❑ 82 Cade McNown	.25	.08
❑ 83 Jim Miller	.25	.08
❑ 84 Marcus Robinson	.60	.25
❑ 85 Brian Urlacher	1.00	.40
❑ 86 Dez White	.25	.08
❑ 87 Brandon Bennett	.25	.08
❑ 88 Steve Bush RC	.40	.15
❑ 89 Corey Dillon	.60	.25
❑ 90 Ron Dugans	.25	.08
❑ 91 Danny Farmer	.25	.08
❑ 92 Damon Griffin	.25	.08
❑ 93 Clif Groce	.40	.15
❑ 94 Curtis Keaton	.25	.08
❑ 95 Scott Mitchell	.25	.08
❑ 96 Darnay Scott	.40	.15
❑ 97 Akili Smith	.25	.08
❑ 98 Peter Warrick	.60	.25
❑ 99 Nick Williams	.25	.08
❑ 100 Craig Yeast	.25	.08
❑ 101 Bobby Brown	.25	.08
❑ 102 Darrin Chiaverini	.25	.08
❑ 103 Tim Couch	.40	.15
❑ 104 JaJuan Dawson	.25	.08
❑ 105 Marc Edwards	.25	.08
❑ 106 Kevin Johnson	.40	.15
❑ 107 Dennis Northcutt	.40	.15
❑ 108 David Patten	.25	.08
❑ 109 Doug Pederson	.25	.08
❑ 110 Travis Prentice	.25	.08
❑ 111 Errict Rhett	.25	.08
❑ 112 Aaron Shea	.25	.08
❑ 113 Kevin Thompson	.25	.08
❑ 114 Jamel White	.25	.08
❑ 115 Spergon Wynn	.25	.08
❑ 116 Troy Aikman	1.00	.40
❑ 117 Chris Brazzell	.25	.08
❑ 118 Randall Cunningham	.60	.25
❑ 119 Jackie Harris	.25	.08
❑ 120 Damon Hodge	.25	.08
❑ 121 Rocket Ismail	.40	.15
❑ 122 David LaFleur	.25	.08
❑ 123 Wane McGarity	.25	.08
❑ 124 James McKnight	.40	.15
❑ 125 Emmitt Smith	1.25	.50
❑ 126 Clint Stoerner	.25	.08
❑ 127 Jason Tucker	.25	.08
❑ 128 Michael Wiley	.25	.08
❑ 129 Anthony Wright	.25	.08
❑ 130 Mike Anderson	.60	.25
❑ 131 Dwayne Carswell	.25	.08
❑ 132 Byron Chamberlain	.25	.08
❑ 133 Desmond Clark	.25	.08
❑ 134 Chris Cole	.25	.08
❑ 135 KaRon Coleman	.25	.08
❑ 136 Terrell Davis	.60	.25
❑ 137 Gus Frerotte	.40	.15
❑ 138 Olandis Gary	.60	.25
❑ 139 Brian Griese	.60	.25
❑ 140 Howard Griffith	.25	.08
❑ 141 Jarious Jackson	.40	.15
❑ 142 Ed McCaffrey	.60	.25
❑ 143 Scottie Montgomery RC	.40	.15
❑ 144 Rod Smith	.40	.15
❑ 145 Charlie Batch	.60	.25
❑ 146 Stoney Case	.25	.08
❑ 147 Germane Crowell	.25	.08
❑ 148 Larry Foster	.25	.08
❑ 149 Desmond Howard	.25	.08
❑ 150 Sedrick Irvin	.25	.08
❑ 151 Herman Moore	.40	.15
❑ 152 Johnnie Morton	.40	.15
❑ 153 Robert Porcher	.25	.08
❑ 154 Cory Sauter	.25	.08
❑ 155 Cory Schlesinger	.25	.08
❑ 156 David Sloan	.25	.08
❑ 157 Brian Stablein	.25	.08
❑ 158 James Stewart	.40	.15
❑ 159 Corey Bradford	.25	.08
❑ 160 Tyrone Davis	.25	.08
❑ 161 Donald Driver	.40	.15
❑ 162 Brett Favre	2.00	.75
❑ 163 Bubba Franks	.40	.15
❑ 164 Antonio Freeman	.60	.25
❑ 165 Herbert Goodman	.25	.08
❑ 166 Ahman Green	.60	.25
❑ 167 Matt Hasselbeck	.40	.15
❑ 168 William Henderson	.25	.08
❑ 169 Charles Lee	.25	.08
❑ 170 Dorsey Levens	.40	.15
❑ 171 Bill Schroeder	.40	.15
❑ 172 Darren Sharper	.25	.08
❑ 173 Matt Snider	.25	.08
❑ 174 Danny Wuerffel	.25	.08
❑ 175 Ken Dilger	.25	.08
❑ 176 Jim Finn	.25	.08
❑ 177 Lennox Gordon	.25	.08
❑ 178 E.G. Green	.25	.08
❑ 179 Marvin Harrison	.60	.25
❑ 180 Kelly Holcomb	.60	.25
❑ 181 Trevor Insley	.25	.08
❑ 182 Edgerrin James	.75	.30
❑ 183 Peyton Manning	1.50	.60
❑ 184 Kevin McDougal	.25	.08
❑ 185 Jerome Pathon	.40	.15
❑ 186 Marcus Pollard	.25	.08
❑ 187 Justin Snow	.25	.08
❑ 188 Terrence Wilkins	.25	.08
❑ 189 Reggie Barlow	.25	.08
❑ 190 Kyle Brady	.25	.08
❑ 191 Mark Brunell	.60	.25
❑ 192 Kevin Hardy	.25	.08
❑ 193 Anthony Johnson	.25	.08
❑ 194 Stacey Mack	.25	.08
❑ 195 Jamie Martin	.40	.15
❑ 196 Keenan McCardell	.25	.08
❑ 197 Daimon Shelton	.25	.08
❑ 198 Jimmy Smith	.40	.15
❑ 199 R.Jay Soward	.25	.08
❑ 200 Shyrone Stith	.25	.08
❑ 201 Fred Taylor	.60	.25
❑ 202 Alvis Whitted	.25	.08
❑ 203 Jermaine Williams	.25	.08
❑ 204 Derrick Alexander	.40	.15
❑ 205 Kimble Anders	.25	.08
❑ 206 Donnell Bennett	.25	.08
❑ 207 Mike Cloud	.25	.08
❑ 208 Todd Collins	.25	.08
❑ 209 Tony Gonzalez	.40	.15
❑ 210 Elvis Grbac	.40	.15
❑ 211 Dante Hall	.60	.25
❑ 212 Kevin Lockett	.25	.08
❑ 213 Warren Moon	.40	.15
❑ 214 Frank Moreau	.25	.08
❑ 215 Sylvester Morris	.25	.08
❑ 216 Larry Parker	.25	.08
❑ 217 Tony Richardson	.25	.08
❑ 218 Trace Armstrong	.25	.08
❑ 219 Autry Denson	.25	.08
❑ 220 Bert Emanuel	.25	.08
❑ 221 Jay Fiedler	.60	.25
❑ 222 Oronde Gadsden	.40	.15
❑ 223 Damon Huard	.60	.25
❑ 224 James Johnson	.25	.08
❑ 225 Rob Konrad	.25	.08
❑ 226 Tony Martin	.25	.08
❑ 227 O.J. McDuffie	.25	.08
❑ 228 Mike Quinn	.25	.08
❑ 229 Lamar Smith	.25	.08
❑ 230 Jason Taylor	.25	.08
❑ 231 Thurman Thomas	.40	.15
❑ 232 Zach Thomas	.60	.25
❑ 233 Todd Bouman	.40	.15
❑ 234 Bubby Brister	.25	.08
❑ 235 Cris Carter	.60	.25
❑ 236 Daunte Culpepper	.60	.25
❑ 237 John Davis RC	.40	.15
❑ 238 Robert Griffith	.25	.08
❑ 239 Matthew Hatchette	.25	.08
❑ 240 Jim Kleinsasser	.25	.08
❑ 241 Randy Moss	1.25	.50
❑ 242 John Randle	.25	.08
❑ 243 Robert Smith	.60	.25
❑ 244 Chris Walsh RC	.25	.08
❑ 245 Troy Walters	.25	.08
❑ 246 Moe Williams	.40	.15
❑ 247 Michael Bishop	.25	.08
❑ 248 Drew Bledsoe	.75	.30
❑ 249 Troy Brown	.40	.15
❑ 250 Tedy Bruschi	.50	.20
❑ 251 Tony Carter	.25	.08
❑ 252 Shockmain Davis	.25	.08
❑ 253 Kevin Faulk	.40	.15
❑ 254 Terry Glenn	.40	.15
❑ 255 Ty Law	.40	.15
❑ 256 Lawyer Milloy	.40	.15
❑ 257 J.R. Redmond	.25	.08
❑ 258 Harold Shaw	.25	.08
❑ 259 Tony Simmons	.25	.08
❑ 260 Jermaine Wiggins	.40	.15
❑ 261 Jeff Blake	.25	.08
❑ 262 Aaron Brooks	.60	.25
❑ 263 Cam Cleeland	.25	.08
❑ 264 Andrew Glover	.25	.08
❑ 265 La'Roi Glover	.25	.08
❑ 266 Joe Horn	.40	.15
❑ 267 Kevin Houser	.25	.08
❑ 268 Willie Jackson	.25	.08
❑ 269 Jerald Moore	.25	.08
❑ 270 Chad Morton	.25	.08
❑ 271 Keith Poole	.25	.08
❑ 272 Terrelle Smith	.25	.08
❑ 273 Ricky Williams	.60	.25
❑ 274 Robert Wilson	.25	.08
❑ 275 Jessie Armstead	.25	.08
❑ 276 Tiki Barber	.60	.25
❑ 277 Mike Cherry	.25	.08
❑ 278 Kerry Collins	.40	.15
❑ 279 Greg Comella	.25	.08
❑ 280 Thabiti Davis	.25	.08
❑ 281 Ron Dayne	.60	.25
❑ 282 Ron Dixon	.25	.08
❑ 283 Ike Hilliard	.25	.08
❑ 284 Joe Jurevicius	.25	.08
❑ 285 Jason Sehorn	.25	.08
❑ 286 Michael Strahan	.40	.15
❑ 287 Amani Toomer	.25	.08
❑ 288 Craig Walendy	.25	.08
❑ 289 Damon Washington RC	.40	.15
❑ 290 Richie Anderson	.25	.08
❑ 291 Anthony Becht	.25	.08
❑ 292 Wayne Chrebet	.40	.15
❑ 293 Laveranues Coles	.60	.25
❑ 294 Bryan Cox	.25	.08
❑ 295 Marvin Jones	.25	.08
❑ 296 Mo Lewis	.25	.08
❑ 297 Ray Lucas	.25	.08
❑ 298 Curtis Martin	.60	.25
❑ 299 Bernie Parmalee	.25	.08
❑ 300 Chad Pennington	1.00	.40
❑ 301 Jerald Sowell	.25	.08
❑ 302 Dwight Stone	.25	.08
❑ 303 Vinny Testaverde	.40	.15
❑ 304 Dedric Ward	.25	.08
❑ 305 Tim Brown	.60	.25
❑ 306 Zack Crockett	.25	.08
❑ 307 Scott Dreisbach	.25	.08
❑ 308 Rickey Dudley	.25	.08
❑ 309 David Dunn	.25	.08
❑ 310 Mondriel Fulcher	.25	.08
❑ 311 Rich Gannon	.60	.25
❑ 312 James Jett	.25	.08
❑ 313 Randy Jordan	.25	.08
❑ 314 Napoleon Kaufman	.40	.15
❑ 315 Rodney Peete	.25	.08
❑ 316 Jerry Porter	.40	.15
❑ 317 Andre Rison	.40	.15
❑ 318 Tyrone Wheatley	.25	.08
❑ 319 Charles Woodson	.25	.08
❑ 320 Darnell Autry	.25	.08
❑ 321 Na Brown	.25	.08
❑ 322 Hugh Douglas	.25	.08
❑ 323 Charles Johnson	.25	.08
❑ 324 Chad Lewis	.25	.08
❑ 325 Cecil Martin	.25	.08
❑ 326 Donovan McNabb	.75	.30
❑ 327 Brian Mitchell	.25	.08
❑ 328 Todd Pinkston	.25	.08
❑ 329 Ron Powlus	.25	.08
❑ 330 Stanley Pritchett	.25	.08
❑ 331 Torrance Small	.25	.08
❑ 332 Duce Staley	.60	.25
❑ 333 Troy Vincent	.25	.08
❑ 334 Chris Warren	.25	.08
❑ 335 Jerome Bettis	.60	.25
❑ 336 Plaxico Burress	.60	.25

❑	337	Troy Edwards	.25	.08
❑	338	Chris Fuamatu-Ma'afala	.25	.08
❑	339	Cory Geason	.25	.08
❑	340	Kent Graham	.25	.08
❑	341	Courtney Hawkins	.25	.08
❑	342	Richard Huntley	.25	.08
❑	343	Tee Martin	.40	.15
❑	344	Bobby Shaw	.25	.08
❑	345	Kordell Stewart	.40	.15
❑	346	Hines Ward	.60	.25
❑	347	Destry Wright RC	.40	.15
❑	348	Amos Zereoue	.60	.25
❑	349	Isaac Bruce	.60	.25
❑	350	Trung Canidate	.40	.15
❑	351	Marshall Faulk	.75	.30
❑	352	London Fletcher	.25	.08
❑	353	Joe Germaine	.25	.08
❑	354	Trent Green	.60	.25
❑	355	Az-Zahir Hakim	.25	.08
❑	356	James Hodgins	.25	.08
❑	357	Robert Holcombe	.25	.08
❑	358	Torry Holt	.60	.25
❑	359	Tony Horne	.25	.08
❑	360	Ricky Proehl	.25	.08
❑	361	Chris Thomas RC	.40	.15
❑	362	Kurt Warner	1.25	.50
❑	363	Justin Watson	.25	.08
❑	364	Kenny Bynum	.25	.08
❑	365	Robert Chancey	.25	.08
❑	366	Curtis Conway	.40	.15
❑	367	Jermaine Fazande	.25	.08
❑	368	Terrell Fletcher	.25	.08
❑	369	Trevor Gaylor	.25	.08
❑	370	Jeff Graham	.25	.08
❑	371	Jim Harbaugh	.40	.15
❑	372	Rodney Harrison	.25	.08
❑	373	Ronney Jenkins	.25	.08
❑	374	Freddie Jones	.25	.08
❑	375	Reggie Jones	.25	.08
❑	376	Ryan Leaf	.40	.15
❑	377	Junior Seau	.60	.25
❑	378	Fred Beasley	.25	.08
❑	379	Greg Clark	.25	.08
❑	380	Jeff Garcia	.60	.25
❑	381	Charlie Garner	.40	.15
❑	382	Terry Jackson	.25	.08
❑	383	Brian Jennings	.25	.08
❑	384	Travis Jervey	.25	.08
❑	385	Jonas Lewis	.25	.08
❑	386	Terrell Owens	.60	.25
❑	387	Jerry Rice	1.25	.50
❑	388	Paul Smith	.25	.08
❑	389	J.J. Stokes	.40	.15
❑	390	Tai Streets	.25	.08
❑	391	Justin Swift	.25	.08
❑	392	Shaun Alexander	.75	.30
❑	393	Karsten Bailey	.25	.08
❑	394	Chad Brown	.25	.08
❑	395	Sean Dawkins	.25	.08
❑	396	Christian Fauria	.25	.08
❑	397	Brock Huard	.25	.08
❑	398	Darrell Jackson	.25	.08
❑	399	Jon Kitna	.60	.25
❑	400	Derrick Mayes	.25	.08
❑	401	Itula Mili	.25	.08
❑	402	Charlie Rogers	.25	.08
❑	403	Mack Strong	.40	.15
❑	404	Ricky Watters	.25	.08
❑	405	James Williams WR	.25	.08
❑	406	Rabih Abdullah	.25	.08
❑	407	Mike Alstott	.60	.25
❑	408	Reidel Anthony	.25	.08
❑	409	Derrick Brooks	.60	.25
❑	410	Warrick Dunn	.60	.25
❑	411	Jacquez Green	.25	.08
❑	412	Joe Hamilton	.25	.08
❑	413	Keyshawn Johnson	.60	.25
❑	414	Shaun King	.25	.08
❑	415	Charles Kirby RC	.60	.25
❑	416	Warren Sapp	.40	.15
❑	417	Aaron Stecker	.25	.08
❑	418	Todd Yoder	.25	.08
❑	419	Eric Zeier	.25	.08
❑	420	Chris Coleman	.25	.08
❑	421	Kevin Dyson	.40	.15
❑	422	Eddie George	.60	.25
❑	423	Jevon Kearse	.40	.15
❑	424	Erron Kinney	.25	.08
❑	425	Mike Leach	.25	.08
❑	426	Derrick Mason	.40	.15
❑	427	Steve McNair	.60	.25
❑	428	Lorenzo Neal	.25	.08
❑	429	Carl Pickens	.40	.15
❑	430	Chris Sanders	.25	.08
❑	431	Yancey Thigpen	.25	.08
❑	432	Rodney Thomas	.25	.08
❑	433	Frank Wycheck	.25	.08
❑	434	Stephen Alexander	.25	.08
❑	435	Champ Bailey	.40	.15
❑	436	Larry Centers	.25	.08
❑	437	Albert Connell	.25	.08
❑	438	Stephen Davis	.60	.25
❑	439	Zeron Flemister RC	.40	.15
❑	440	Irving Fryar	.40	.15
❑	441	Jeff George	.40	.15
❑	442	Skip Hicks	.25	.08
❑	443	Todd Husak	.25	.08
❑	444	Brad Johnson	.40	.15
❑	445	Adrian Murrell	.25	.08
❑	446	Deion Sanders	.60	.25
❑	447	Mike Sellers	.25	.08
❑	448	Derrius Thompson	.25	.08
❑	449	James Thrash	.40	.15
❑	450	Michael Westbrook	.25	.08
❑	451	Alex Bannister AU/1750 RC	8.00	3.00
❑	452	Kevan Barlow AU/1500 RC	15.00	6.00
❑	453	Drew Brees AU/1000 RC	50.00	25.00
❑	454	Travis Henry AU/1500 RC	25.00	12.50
❑	455	Chad Johnson AU/1750 RC	30.00	12.50
❑	456	M.McMahon AU/1000 RC	10.00	4.00
❑	457	B.Newcombe AU/1750 RC	10.00	4.00
❑	458	Sage Rosenfels AU/1000 RC	20.00	7.50
❑	459	L.Tomlinson AU/1500 RC	120.00	60.00
❑	460	Chris Weinke AU/1000 RC	12.00	5.00
❑	461	Tay Cody RC	2.00	.75
❑	462	Adam Archuleta RC	5.00	2.00
❑	463	Will Allen RC	2.50	1.00
❑	464	Moran Norris RC	2.00	.75
❑	465	Tommy Polley RC	5.00	2.00
❑	466	Ennis Davis RC	2.00	.75
❑	467	Jamar Fletcher RC	2.50	1.00
❑	468	Derrick Gibson RC	2.50	1.00
❑	469	Sedrick Hodge RC	2.00	.75
❑	470	Willie Howard RC	2.50	1.00
❑	471	Steve Hutchinson RC	2.50	1.00
❑	472	Michael Stone RC	2.00	.75
❑	473	Vinny Sutherland/1750 RC	3.00	1.25
❑	474	Joe Tafoya RC	2.00	.75
❑	475	Maurice Williams RC	2.00	.75
❑	476	Pork Chop Womack RC	2.00	.75
❑	477	Chad Ward RC	2.00	.75
❑	478	Scotty Anderson/1750 RC	3.00	1.25
❑	479	Gary Baxter RC	2.50	1.00
❑	480	M.Tuiasosopo/1000 RC	6.00	2.50
❑	481	Tim Hasselbeck/1000 RC	6.00	2.50
❑	482	Clevan Thomas RC	2.00	.75
❑	483	Marcus Stroud RC	5.00	2.00
❑	484	John Schlecht RC	2.00	.75
❑	485	Brandon Spoon RC	5.00	2.00
❑	486	Alex Lincoln RC	2.50	1.00
❑	487	Anthony Thomas/1750 RC	4.00	1.50
❑	488	Freddie Mitchell/1750 RC	4.00	1.50
❑	489	Brian Allen RC	2.50	1.00
❑	490	Zeke Moreno RC	5.00	2.00
❑	491	Tony Driver RC	5.00	2.00
❑	492	Kynan Forney RC	2.00	.75
❑	493	Reggie Wayne/1750 RC	10.00	4.00
❑	494	Larry Casher RC	2.50	1.00
❑	495	Fred Wakefield RC	2.50	1.00
❑	496	Jeff Backus RC	2.50	1.00
❑	497	Jarrod Cooper RC	5.00	2.00
❑	498	Heath Evans RC	5.00	2.00
❑	499	James Jackson/1500 RC	3.00	1.25
❑	500	Jabari Holloway RC	5.00	2.00
❑	501	Quincy Morgan/1750 RC	4.00	1.50
❑	502	Josh Booty/1000 RC	6.00	2.50
❑	503	Ja'Mar Toombs RC	2.50	1.00
❑	504	Jason McKinley/1000 RC	4.00	1.50
❑	505	Reggie White/1500 RC	3.00	1.25
❑	506	Todd Heap/1750 RC	4.00	1.50
❑	507	Rudi Johnson/1500 RC	10.00	4.00
❑	508	Snoop Minnis/1750 RC	3.00	1.25
❑	509	David Terrell/1750 RC	4.00	1.50
❑	510	Torrance Marshall RC	5.00	2.00
❑	511	Michael Bennett/1500 RC	5.00	2.00
❑	512	Chris Chambers/1750 RC	8.00	3.00
❑	513	Ben Leard/1000 RC	4.00	1.50
❑	514	Rod Gardner/1750 RC	4.00	1.50
❑	515	Michael Vick/1000 RC	40.00	15.00
❑	516	Josh Heupel/1000 RC	6.00	2.50
❑	517	Jesse Palmer/1000 RC	6.00	2.50
❑	518	Quincy Carter/1000 RC	6.00	2.50
❑	519	A.J. Feeley/1000 RC	6.00	2.50
❑	520	David Rivers/1000 RC	6.00	2.50
❑	521	Deuce McAllister/1500 RC	12.00	5.00
❑	522	LaMont Jordan/1500 RC	10.00	4.00
❑	523	David Allen/1500 RC	8.00	3.00
❑	524	Correll Buckhalter/1500 RC	12.00	5.00
❑	525	Travis Minor/1500	6.00	2.50
❑	526	Koren Robinson/1750 RC	4.00	1.50
❑	527	Santana Moss/1750 RC	8.00	3.00
❑	528	Robert Ferguson/1750 RC	4.00	1.50
❑	529	T.J.Houshmndzdh/1750 RC	5.00	2.00
❑	530	Cedrick Wilson/1750 RC	4.00	1.50

2002 Pacific

❑		COMPLETE SET (500)	100.00	50.00
❑	1	David Boston	.60	.25
❑	2	Arnold Jackson	.25	.08
❑	3	MarTay Jenkins	.25	.08
❑	4	Thomas Jones	.40	.15
❑	5	Kwamie Lassiter	.25	.08
❑	6	Joel Makovicka	.25	.08
❑	7	Ronald McKinnon	.25	.08
❑	8	Tywan Mitchell	.25	.08
❑	9	Michael Pittman	.25	.08
❑	10	Jake Plummer	.40	.15
❑	11	Frank Sanders	.25	.08
❑	12	Kyle Vanden Bosch	.25	.08
❑	13	Jamal Anderson	.40	.15
❑	14	Keith Brooking	.25	.08
❑	15	Chris Chandler	.40	.15
❑	16	Bob Christian	.25	.08
❑	17	Alge Crumpler	.40	.15
❑	18	Brian Finneran	.25	.08
❑	19	Shawn Jefferson	.25	.08
❑	20	Patrick Kerney	.25	.08
❑	21	Terance Mathis	.25	.08
❑	22	Maurice Smith	.40	.15
❑	23	Rodney Thomas	.25	.08
❑	24	Darrick Vaughn	.25	.08
❑	25	Michael Vick	1.25	.50
❑	26	Sam Adams	.25	.08
❑	27	Terry Allen	.25	.08
❑	28	Obafemi Ayanbadejo	.25	.08
❑	29	Peter Boulware	.25	.08
❑	30	Jason Brookins	.25	.08
❑	31	Randall Cunningham	.60	.25
❑	32	Elvis Grbac	.40	.15
❑	33	Todd Heap	.25	.08
❑	34	Qadry Ismail	.40	.15
❑	35	Jamal Lewis	.60	.25
❑	36	Ray Lewis	.60	.25
❑	37	Chris Redman	.25	.08
❑	38	Shannon Sharpe	.40	.15
❑	39	Brandon Stokley	.40	.15
❑	40	Travis Taylor	.40	.15
❑	41	Moe Williams	.25	.08
❑	42	Rod Woodson	.40	.15
❑	43	Shawn Bryson	.25	.08
❑	44	Larry Centers	.25	.08
❑	45	Nate Clements	.25	.08
❑	46	London Fletcher	.25	.08
❑	47	Reggie Germany	.25	.08
❑	48	Travis Henry	.60	.25
❑	49	Jeremy McDaniel	.25	.08
❑	50	Sammy Morris	.25	.08
❑	51	Eric Moulds	.40	.15
❑	52	Peerless Price	.40	.15
❑	53	Jay Riemersma	.25	.08

❑ 54	Alex Van Pelt	.25	.08
❑ 55	Tim Biakabutuka	.25	.08
❑ 56	Isaac Byrd	.25	.08
❑ 57	Doug Evans	.25	.08
❑ 58	Donald Hayes	.25	.08
❑ 59	Chris Hetherington	.25	.08
❑ 60	Brad Hoover	.25	.08
❑ 61	Richard Huntley	.25	.08
❑ 62	Patrick Jeffers	.25	.08
❑ 63	Matt Lytle	.25	.08
❑ 64	Dan Morgan	.25	.08
❑ 65	Muhsin Muhammad	.40	.15
❑ 66	Mike Rucker RC	1.00	.40
❑ 67	Steve Smith	.60	.25
❑ 68	Wesley Walls	.25	.08
❑ 69	Chris Weinke	.40	.15
❑ 70	James Allen	.40	.15
❑ 71	Fred Baxter	.25	.08
❑ 72	Marty Booker	.25	.08
❑ 73	Mike Brown	.60	.25
❑ 74	Rosevelt Colvin RC	1.00	.40
❑ 75	Phillip Daniels	.25	.08
❑ 76	Leon Johnson	.25	.08
❑ 77	Shane Matthews	.25	.08
❑ 78	Jim Miller	.25	.08
❑ 79	Tony Parrish	.25	.08
❑ 80	Marcus Robinson	.40	.15
❑ 81	David Terrell	.60	.25
❑ 82	Anthony Thomas	.40	.15
❑ 83	Brian Urlacher	1.00	.40
❑ 84	Ted Washington	.25	.08
❑ 85	Dez White	.25	.08
❑ 86	Brandon Bennett	.25	.08
❑ 87	Corey Dillon	.40	.15
❑ 88	Ron Dugans	.25	.08
❑ 89	Danny Farmer	.25	.08
❑ 90	T.J. Houshmandzadeh	.40	.15
❑ 91	Chad Johnson	.60	.25
❑ 92	Curtis Keaton	.25	.08
❑ 93	Jon Kitna	.40	.15
❑ 94	Tony McGee	.25	.08
❑ 95	Lorenzo Neal	.25	.08
❑ 96	Darnay Scott	.25	.08
❑ 97	Akili Smith	.25	.08
❑ 98	Justin Smith	.25	.08
❑ 99	Takeo Spikes	.25	.08
❑ 100	Peter Warrick	.40	.15
❑ 101	Tim Couch	.40	.15
❑ 102	JaJuan Dawson	.25	.08
❑ 103	Benjamin Gay	.40	.15
❑ 104	Anthony Henry	.25	.08
❑ 105	James Jackson	.25	.08
❑ 106	Kevin Johnson	.40	.15
❑ 107	Andre King	.25	.08
❑ 108	Jamir Miller	.25	.08
❑ 109	Quincy Morgan	.25	.08
❑ 110	Dennis Northcutt	.25	.08
❑ 111	O.J. Santiago	.25	.08
❑ 112	Jamel White	.25	.08
❑ 113	Quincy Carter	.40	.15
❑ 114	Darrin Chiaverini	.60	.25
❑ 115	Dexter Coakley	.25	.08
❑ 116	Joey Galloway	.40	.15
❑ 117	Troy Hambrick	.25	.08
❑ 118	Rocket Ismail	.40	.15
❑ 119	Dat Nguyen	.25	.08
❑ 120	Ken-Yon Rambo	.25	.08
❑ 121	Emmitt Smith	1.50	.60
❑ 122	Reggie Swinton	.25	.08
❑ 123	Robert Thomas	.25	.08
❑ 124	Michael Wiley	.25	.08
❑ 125	Anthony Wright	.25	.08
❑ 126	Mike Anderson	.60	.25
❑ 127	Dwayne Carswell	.25	.08
❑ 128	Desmond Clark	.25	.08
❑ 129	Chris Cole	.25	.08
❑ 130	Terrell Davis	.60	.25
❑ 131	Gus Frerotte	.25	.08
❑ 132	Olandis Gary	.40	.15
❑ 133	Brian Griese	.60	.25
❑ 134	Kevin Kasper	.25	.08
❑ 135	Ed McCaffrey	.60	.25
❑ 136	Phil McGeoghan RC	.40	.15
❑ 137	John Mobley	.25	.08
❑ 138	Scottie Montgomery	.25	.08
❑ 139	Deltha O'Neal	.25	.08
❑ 140	Trevor Pryce	.25	.08
❑ 141	Rod Smith	.40	.15
❑ 142	Al Wilson	.25	.08
❑ 143	Scotty Anderson	.25	.08
❑ 144	Charlie Batch	.40	.15
❑ 145	Aveion Cason	.60	.25
❑ 146	Germane Crowell	.25	.08
❑ 147	Reuben Droughns	.60	.25
❑ 148	Bert Emanuel	.25	.08
❑ 149	Larry Foster	.25	.08
❑ 150	Az-Zahir Hakim	.25	.08
❑ 151	Desmond Howard	.25	.08
❑ 152	Mike McMahon	.60	.25
❑ 153	Herman Moore	.40	.15
❑ 154	Johnnie Morton	.40	.15
❑ 155	Robert Porcher	.25	.08
❑ 156	Cory Schlesinger	.25	.08
❑ 157	David Sloan	.25	.08
❑ 158	James Stewart	.40	.15
❑ 159	Lamont Warren	.25	.08
❑ 160	Donald Driver	.40	.15
❑ 161	Brett Favre	1.50	.60
❑ 162	Bubba Franks	.40	.15
❑ 163	Antonio Freeman	.60	.25
❑ 164	Kabeer Gbaja-Biamila	.40	.15
❑ 165	Terry Glenn	.40	.15
❑ 166	Ahman Green	.60	.25
❑ 167	William Henderson	.25	.08
❑ 168	Dorsey Levens	.40	.15
❑ 169	David Martin	.25	.08
❑ 170	Rondell Mealey	.25	.08
❑ 171	Bill Schroeder	.40	.15
❑ 172	Darren Sharper	.25	.08
❑ 173	Avion Black	.25	.08
❑ 174	Tony Boselli	.25	.08
❑ 175	Corey Bradford	.25	.08
❑ 176	Marcus Coleman	.25	.08
❑ 177	Leomont Evans	.25	.08
❑ 178	Aaron Glenn	.25	.08
❑ 179	Trevor Insley	.25	.08
❑ 180	Jermaine Lewis	.25	.08
❑ 181	Anthony Malbrough	.25	.08
❑ 182	Frank Moreau	.25	.08
❑ 183	Mike Quinn	.25	.08
❑ 184	Charlie Rogers	.25	.08
❑ 185	Jamie Sharper	.25	.08
❑ 186	Matt Snider	.25	.08
❑ 187	Gary Walker	.25	.08
❑ 188	Kevin Williams RC	.40	.15
❑ 189	Kailee Wong	.25	.08
❑ 190	Chad Bratzke	.25	.08
❑ 191	Ken Dilger	.25	.08
❑ 192	Marvin Harrison	.60	.25
❑ 193	Edgerrin James	.75	.30
❑ 194	Kevin McDougal	.25	.08
❑ 195	Rob Morris	.25	.08
❑ 196	Jerome Pathon	.25	.08
❑ 197	Marcus Pollard	.25	.08
❑ 198	Dominic Rhodes	.40	.15
❑ 199	Marcus Washington	.25	.08
❑ 200	Reggie Wayne	.60	.25
❑ 201	Terrence Wilkins	.25	.08
❑ 202	Tony Brackens	.25	.08
❑ 203	Kyle Brady	.25	.08
❑ 204	Mark Brunell	.60	.25
❑ 205	Donovin Darius	.25	.08
❑ 206	Sean Dawkins	.25	.08
❑ 207	Damon Gibson	.25	.08
❑ 208	Elvis Joseph	.25	.08
❑ 209	Stacey Mack	.25	.08
❑ 210	Keenan McCardell	.25	.08
❑ 211	Hardy Nickerson	.25	.08
❑ 212	Jonathan Quinn	.25	.08
❑ 213	Micah Ross RC	.25	.08
❑ 214	Jimmy Smith	.40	.15
❑ 215	Fred Taylor	.60	.25
❑ 216	Patrick Washington	.25	.08
❑ 217	Derrick Alexander	.40	.15
❑ 218	Mike Cloud	.25	.08
❑ 219	Donnie Edwards	.25	.08
❑ 220	Tony Gonzalez	.40	.15
❑ 221	Trent Green	.40	.15
❑ 222	Dante Hall	.60	.25
❑ 223	Priest Holmes	.75	.30
❑ 224	Eddie Kennison	.25	.08
❑ 225	Snoop Minnis	.25	.08
❑ 226	Larry Parker	.25	.08
❑ 227	Marvcus Patton	.25	.08
❑ 228	Tony Richardson	.25	.08
❑ 229	Mikhael Ricks	.25	.08
❑ 230	Chris Chambers	.60	.25
❑ 231	Jay Fiedler	.40	.15
❑ 232	Oronde Gadsden	.40	.15
❑ 233	Rob Konrad	.25	.08
❑ 234	Sam Madison	.25	.08
❑ 235	Brock Marion	.25	.08
❑ 236	James McKnight	.25	.08
❑ 237	Travis Minor	.25	.08
❑ 238	Jeff Ogden	.25	.08
❑ 239	Lamar Smith	.40	.15
❑ 240	Jason Taylor	.25	.08
❑ 241	Zach Thomas	.60	.25
❑ 242	Dedric Ward	.25	.08
❑ 243	Ricky Williams	.60	.25
❑ 244	Michael Bennett	.40	.15
❑ 245	Todd Bouman	.25	.08
❑ 246	[illegible]	[illegible]	[illegible]
❑ 247	Byron Chamberlain	.25	.08
❑ 248	Doug Chapman	.25	.08
❑ 249	Kenny Clark RC	.40	.15
❑ 250	Daunte Culpepper	.60	.25
❑ 251	Nate Jacquet	.25	.08
❑ 252	Jim Kleinsasser	.25	.08
❑ 253	Harold Morrow	.25	.08
❑ 254	Randy Moss	1.25	.50
❑ 255	Jake Reed	.25	.08
❑ 256	Spergon Wynn	.25	.08
❑ 257	Drew Bledsoe	.75	.30
❑ 258	Tom Brady	1.50	.60
❑ 259	Troy Brown	.40	.15
❑ 260	Fred Coleman	.25	.08
❑ 261	Marc Edwards	.25	.08
❑ 262	Kevin Faulk	.40	.15
❑ 263	Bobby Hamilton	.25	.08
❑ 264	Ty Law	.40	.15
❑ 265	Lawyer Milloy	.40	.15
❑ 266	David Patten	.25	.08
❑ 267	J.R. Redmond	.25	.08
❑ 268	Antowain Smith	.40	.15
❑ 269	Adam Vinatieri	.60	.25
❑ 270	Jermaine Wiggins	.25	.08
❑ 271	Aaron Brooks	.60	.25
❑ 272	Cam Cleeland	.25	.08
❑ 273	Charlie Clemons RC	.25	.08
❑ 274	James Fenderson RC	.40	.15
❑ 275	La'Roi Glover	.25	.08
❑ 276	Joe Horn	.40	.15
❑ 277	Willie Jackson	.25	.08
❑ 278	Sammy Knight	.25	.08
❑ 279	Michael Lewis	.25	.08
❑ 280	Deuce McAllister	.75	.30
❑ 281	Terrelle Smith	.25	.08
❑ 282	Boo Williams	.25	.08
❑ 283	Robert Wilson	.25	.08
❑ 284	Tiki Barber	.60	.25
❑ 285	Micheal Barrow	.25	.08
❑ 286	Kerry Collins	.40	.15
❑ 287	Greg Comella	.25	.08
❑ 288	Thabiti Davis	.25	.08
❑ 289	Ron Dayne	.40	.15
❑ 290	Ron Dixon	.25	.08
❑ 291	Ike Hilliard	.40	.15
❑ 292	Joe Jurevicius	.25	.08
❑ 293	Michael Strahan	.40	.15
❑ 294	Amani Toomer	.40	.15
❑ 295	Damon Washington	.25	.08
❑ 296	John Abraham	.40	.15
❑ 297	Richie Anderson	.25	.08
❑ 298	Anthony Becht	.25	.08
❑ 299	Wayne Chrebet	.40	.15
❑ 300	Laveranues Coles	.40	.15
❑ 301	James Farrior	.25	.08
❑ 302	Marvin Jones	.25	.08
❑ 303	LaMont Jordan	.60	.25
❑ 304	Curtis Martin	.60	.25
❑ 305	Santana Moss	.60	.25
❑ 306	Chad Pennington	.75	.30
❑ 307	Kevin Swayne	.25	.08
❑ 308	Vinny Testaverde	.40	.15
❑ 309	Craig Yeast	.25	.08
❑ 310	Greg Biekert	.25	.08
❑ 311	Tim Brown	.60	.25
❑ 312	Zack Crockett	.25	.08
❑ 313	Rich Gannon	.60	.25
❑ 314	Charlie Garner	.40	.15
❑ 315	Sebastian Janikowski	.25	.08
❑ 316	Randy Jordan	.25	.08
❑ 317	Terry Kirby	.25	.08
❑ 318	Jerry Porter	.25	.08
❑ 319	Jerry Rice	1.25	.50
❑ 320	Jon Ritchie	.25	.08

❑ 321 Tyrone Wheatley .40 .15
❑ 322 Roland Williams .25 .08
❑ 323 Charles Woodson .40 .15
❑ 324 Correll Buckhalter .40 .15
❑ 325 Brian Dawkins .40 .15
❑ 326 Hugh Douglas .25 .08
❑ 327 A.J. Feeley .60 .25
❑ 328 Chad Lewis .25 .08
❑ 329 Cecil Martin .25 .08
❑ 330 Brian Mitchell .25 .08
❑ 331 Freddie Mitchell .40 .15
❑ 332 Todd Pinkston .40 .15
❑ 333 Rod Smart RC .25 .08
❑ 334 Duce Staley .60 .25
❑ 335 James Thrash .40 .15
❑ 336 Jeremiah Trotter .25 .08
❑ 337 Troy Vincent .25 .08
❑ 338 Kendrell Bell .60 .25
❑ 339 Jerome Bettis .60 .25
❑ 340 Demetrius Brown RC .40 .15
❑ 341 Plaxico Burress .40 .15
❑ 342 Troy Edwards .25 .08
❑ 343 Chris Fuamatu-Ma'afala .25 .08
❑ 344 Jason Gildon .25 .08
❑ 345 Earl Holmes .25 .08
❑ 346 Joey Porter .60 .25
❑ 347 Chad Scott .25 .08
❑ 348 Bobby Shaw .25 .08
❑ 349 Kordell Stewart .40 .15
❑ 350 Hines Ward .60 .25
❑ 351 Amos Zereoue .60 .25
❑ 352 Adam Archuleta .25 .08
❑ 353 Dre' Bly .25 .08
❑ 354 Isaac Bruce .60 .25
❑ 355 Trung Canidate .40 .15
❑ 356 Ernie Conwell .25 .08
❑ 357 Marshall Faulk .60 .25
❑ 358 Torry Holt .60 .25
❑ 359 Leonard Little .25 .08
❑ 360 Yo Murphy .25 .08
❑ 361 Ricky Proehl .25 .08
❑ 362 Kurt Warner .60 .25
❑ 363 Aeneas Williams .25 .08
❑ 364 Drew Brees .60 .25
❑ 365 Curtis Conway .25 .08
❑ 366 Tim Dwight .40 .15
❑ 367 Terrell Fletcher .25 .08
❑ 368 Doug Flutie .60 .25
❑ 369 Jeff Graham .25 .08
❑ 370 Rodney Harrison .25 .08
❑ 371 Ronney Jenkins .25 .08
❑ 372 Raylee Johnson .25 .08
❑ 373 Freddie Jones .25 .08
❑ 374 Ryan McNeil .25 .08
❑ 375 Junior Seau .60 .25
❑ 376 LaDainian Tomlinson 1.00 .40
❑ 377 Marcellus Wiley .25 .08
❑ 378 Kevan Barlow .40 .15
❑ 379 Fred Beasley .25 .08
❑ 380 Zack Bronson RC .40 .15
❑ 381 Andre Carter .25 .08
❑ 382 Jeff Garcia .60 .25
❑ 383 Garrison Hearst .40 .15
❑ 384 Terry Jackson .25 .08
❑ 385 Eric Johnson .40 .15
❑ 386 Saladin McCullough RC .25 .08
❑ 387 Terrell Owens .60 .25
❑ 388 Ahmed Plummer .25 .08
❑ 389 J.J. Stokes .25 .08
❑ 390 Tai Streets .25 .08
❑ 391 Vinny Sutherland .25 .08
❑ 392 Bryant Young .25 .08
❑ 393 Shaun Alexander .75 .30
❑ 394 Chad Brown .25 .08
❑ 395 Kerwin Cook RC .40 .15
❑ 396 Trent Dilfer .40 .15
❑ 397 Bobby Engram .25 .08
❑ 398 Christian Fauria .25 .08
❑ 399 Matt Hasselbeck .40 .15
❑ 400 Darrell Jackson .40 .15
❑ 401 John Randle .25 .08
❑ 402 Koren Robinson .40 .15
❑ 403 Anthony Simmons .25 .08
❑ 404 Mack Strong .40 .15
❑ 405 Ricky Watters .25 .08
❑ 406 James Williams WR .25 .08
❑ 407 Mike Alstott .60 .25
❑ 408 Ronde Barber .25 .08
❑ 409 Derrick Brooks .60 .25
❑ 410 Jameel Cook .25 .08
❑ 411 Warrick Dunn .60 .25
❑ 412 Jacquez Green .25 .08
❑ 413 Brad Johnson .40 .15
❑ 414 Keyshawn Johnson .60 .25
❑ 415 Rob Johnson .40 .15
❑ 416 John Lynch .40 .15
❑ 417 Dave Moore .25 .08
❑ 418 Warren Sapp .40 .15
❑ 419 Aaron Stecker .25 .08
❑ 420 Karl Williams .25 .08
❑ 421 Drew Bennett .60 .25
❑ 422 Eddie Berlin .25 .08
❑ 423 Rafael Cooper RC .40 .15
❑ 424 Kevin Dyson .40 .15
❑ 425 Eddie George .60 .25
❑ 426 Mike Green .25 .08
❑ 427 Skip Hicks .25 .08
❑ 428 Jevon Kearse .40 .15
❑ 429 Erron Kinney .25 .08
❑ 430 Derrick Mason .40 .15
❑ 431 Justin McCareins .40 .15
❑ 432 Steve McNair .60 .25
❑ 433 Neil O'Donnell .25 .08
❑ 434 Frank Wycheck .25 .08
❑ 435 Reidel Anthony .25 .08
❑ 436 Jessie Armstead .25 .08
❑ 437 Champ Bailey .40 .15
❑ 438 Tony Banks .25 .08
❑ 439 Michael Bates .25 .08
❑ 440 Donnell Bennett .25 .08
❑ 441 Ki-Jana Carter .25 .08
❑ 442 Stephen Davis .40 .15
❑ 443 Zeron Flemister .25 .08
❑ 444 Rod Gardner .40 .15
❑ 445 Kevin Lockett .25 .08
❑ 446 Eric Metcalf .25 .08
❑ 447 Sage Rosenfels .25 .08
❑ 448 Fred Smoot .25 .08
❑ 449 Michael Westbrook .25 .08
❑ 450 Danny Wuerffel .25 .08
❑ 451 Jason McAddley RC 1.50 .60
❑ 452 Freddie Milons RC 1.50 .60
❑ 453 Bryan Thomas RC 1.50 .60
❑ 454 Levi Jones RC 1.50 .60
❑ 455 William Green RC 2.00 .75
❑ 456 Luke Staley RC 1.50 .60
❑ 457 Daniel Graham RC 2.00 .75
❑ 458 David Garrard RC 4.00 1.50
❑ 459 Reche Caldwell RC 2.00 .75
❑ 460 Andra Davis RC 1.50 .60
❑ 461 Lito Sheppard RC 2.00 .75
❑ 462 Chris Hope RC 2.00 .75
❑ 463 Javon Walker RC 3.00 1.25
❑ 464 David Carr RC 4.00 1.50
❑ 465 Alan Harper RC 1.00 .40
❑ 466 Adrian Peterson RC 2.50 1.00
❑ 467 Kelly Campbell RC 1.50 .60
❑ 468 Ashley Lelie RC 4.00 1.50
❑ 469 Kurt Kittner RC 1.50 .60
❑ 470 Antwaan Randle El RC 2.50 1.00
❑ 471 Ladell Betts RC 2.00 .75
❑ 472 Josh Reed RC 2.00 .75
❑ 473 Clinton Portis RC 6.00 2.50
❑ 474 Ron Johnson RC 1.50 .60
❑ 475 Eric Crouch RC 2.00 .75
❑ 476 Tracey Wistrom RC 1.50 .60
❑ 477 David Neill RC 1.50 .60
❑ 478 Ronald Curry RC 2.00 .75
❑ 479 Lamar Gordon RC 2.00 .75
❑ 480 Damien Anderson RC 1.50 .60
❑ 481 Napoleon Harris RC 2.00 .75
❑ 482 Zak Kustok RC 2.00 .75
❑ 483 Rocky Calmus RC 2.00 .75
❑ 484 Roy Williams RC 4.00 1.50
❑ 485 Joey Harrington RC 2.50 1.00
❑ 486 Maurice Morris RC 2.00 .75
❑ 487 Antonio Bryant RC 2.00 .75
❑ 488 Josh McCown RC 2.50 1.00
❑ 489 John Henderson RC 2.00 .75
❑ 490 Quentin Jammer RC 2.00 .75
❑ 491 Mike Williams RC 1.50 .60
❑ 492 Patrick Ramsey RC 2.00 .75
❑ 493 Kenyon Coleman RC 1.00 .40
❑ 494 DeShaun Foster RC 2.00 .75
❑ 495 Brian Poli-Dixon RC 1.50 .60
❑ 496 Cliff Russell RC 1.50 .60
❑ 497 Brian Westbrook RC 4.00 1.50
❑ 498 Andre Davis RC 1.50 .60
❑ 499 Larry Tripplett RC 1.00 .40
❑ 500 Lamont Thompson RC 1.50 .60
❑ 501 T.J. Duckett RC 2.00 .75
❑ 502 Dameon Hunter RC 1.00 .40
❑ 503 Javin Hunter RC 1.00 .40
❑ 504 Tellis Redmon RC 1.50 .60
❑ 505 Chester Taylor RC 4.00 1.50
❑ 506 Randy Fasani RC 1.50 .60
❑ 507 Julius Peppers RC 4.00 1.50
❑ 508 Jamin Elliott RC 1.00 .40
❑ 509 Chad Hutchinson RC 1.50 .60
❑ 510 Eddie Drummond RC 1.50 .60
❑ 511 Craig Nall RC 2.00 .75
❑ 512 Jabar Gaffney RC 2.00 .75
❑ 513 Jonathan Wells RC 2.00 .75
❑ 514 Shaun Hill RC 2.00 .75
❑ 515 Deion Branch RC 3.00 1.25
❑ 516 Rohan Davey RC 2.00 .75
❑ 517 J.T. O'Sullivan RC 1.50 .60
❑ 518 Tim Carter RC 1.50 .60
❑ 519 Daryl Jones RC 1.50 .60
❑ 520 Jeremy Shockey RC 6.00 2.50
❑ 521 Seth Burford RC 1.50 .60
❑ 522 Brandon Doman RC 1.50 .60
❑ 523 Jerramy Stevens RC 2.00 .75
❑ 524 Travis Stephens RC 1.50 .60
❑ 525 Marquise Walker RC 1.50 .60

1964 Philadelphia

JIM BROWN

❑ COMPLETE SET (198) 900.00 600.00
❑ WRAPPER (1-CENT) 40.00 30.00
❑ WRAPPER (5-CENT) 20.00 10.00
❑ 1 Raymond Berry ! 20.00 10.00
❑ 2 Tom Gilburg 2.50 1.25
❑ 3 John Mackey RC 30.00 18.00
❑ 4 Gino Marchetti 5.00 2.50
❑ 5 Jim Martin 2.50 1.25
❑ 6 Tom Matte RC 6.00 3.00
❑ 7 Jimmy Orr 3.00 1.50
❑ 8 Jim Parker 4.00 2.00
❑ 9 Bill Pellington 2.50 1.25
❑ 10 Alex Sandusky 2.50 1.25
❑ 11 Dick Szymanski 2.50 1.25
❑ 12 Johnny Unitas 45.00 25.00
❑ 13 Baltimore Colts 3.00 1.50
❑ 14 Colts Play/Don Shula 35.00 20.00
❑ 15 Doug Atkins 5.00 2.50
❑ 16 Ronnie Bull 2.50 1.25
❑ 17 Mike Ditka 40.00 25.00
❑ 18 Joe Fortunato 2.50 1.25
❑ 19 Willie Galimore 3.00 1.50
❑ 20 Joe Marconi 2.50 1.25
❑ 21 Bennie McRae RC 2.50 1.25
❑ 22 Johnny Morris 2.50 1.25
❑ 23 Richie Petitbon 2.50 1.25
❑ 24 Mike Pyle 2.50 1.25
❑ 25 Roosevelt Taylor RC 4.00 2.00
❑ 26 Bill Wade 3.00 1.50
❑ 27 Chicago Bears 3.00 1.50
❑ 28 Bears Play/George Halas 12.00 6.00
❑ 29 Johnny Brewer 2.50 1.25
❑ 30 Jim Brown 90.00 50.00
❑ 31 Gary Collins RC 8.00 4.00
❑ 32 Vince Costello 2.50 1.25
❑ 33 Galen Fiss 2.50 1.25
❑ 34 Bill Glass 2.50 1.25
❑ 35 Ernie Green RC 3.00 1.50
❑ 36 Rich Kreitling 2.50 1.25
❑ 37 John Morrow 2.50 1.25
❑ 38 Frank Ryan 3.00 1.50
❑ 39 Charlie Scales RC 2.50 1.25
❑ 40 Dick Schafrath RC 2.50 1.25

❑ 41 Cleveland Browns	3.00	1.50
❑ 42 Cleveland Browns Play	2.50	1.25
❑ 43 Don Bishop	2.50	1.25
❑ 44 Frank Clarke RC	3.00	1.50
❑ 45 Mike Connelly	2.50	1.25
❑ 46 Lee Folkins	2.50	1.25
❑ 47 Cornell Green RC	8.00	4.00
❑ 48 Bob Lilly	40.00	25.00
❑ 49 Amos Marsh	2.50	1.25
❑ 50 Tommy McDonald	5.00	2.50
❑ 51 Don Meredith	35.00	20.00
❑ 52 Pettis Norman RC	3.00	1.50
❑ 53 Don Perkins	4.00	2.00
❑ 54 Guy Reese	2.50	1.25
❑ 55 Dallas Cowboys	3.00	1.50
❑ 56 Cowboys Play/T.Landry	20.00	12.00
❑ 57 Terry Barr	2.50	1.25
❑ 58 Roger Brown	3.00	1.50
❑ 59 Gail Cogdill	2.50	1.25
❑ 60 John Gordy	2.50	1.25
❑ 61 Dick Lane	4.00	2.00
❑ 62 Yale Lary	4.00	2.00
❑ 63 Dan Lewis	2.50	1.25
❑ 64 Darris McCord	2.50	1.25
❑ 65 Earl Morrall	3.00	1.50
❑ 66 Joe Schmidt	5.00	2.50
❑ 67 Pat Studstill RC	3.00	1.50
❑ 68 Wayne Walker RC	3.00	1.50
❑ 69 Detroit Lions	3.00	1.50
❑ 70 Detroit Lions	2.50	1.25
❑ 71 Herb Adderley RC	35.00	20.00
❑ 72 Willie Davis DE RC	30.00	18.00
❑ 73 Forrest Gregg	5.00	2.50
❑ 74 Paul Hornung	35.00	20.00
❑ 75 Hank Jordan	5.00	2.50
❑ 76 Jerry Kramer	6.00	3.00
❑ 77 Tom Moore	3.00	1.50
❑ 78 Jim Ringo	5.00	2.50
❑ 79 Bart Starr	60.00	35.00
❑ 80 Jim Taylor	25.00	15.00
❑ 81 Jesse Whittenton RC	3.00	1.50
❑ 82 Willie Wood	8.00	4.00
❑ 83 Green Bay Packers	6.00	3.00
❑ 84 Packers Play/Lombardi	35.00	20.00
❑ 85 Jon Arnett	2.50	1.25
❑ 86 Pervis Atkins RC	2.50	1.25
❑ 87 Dick Bass	3.00	1.50
❑ 88 Carroll Dale	4.00	2.00
❑ 89 Roman Gabriel	6.00	3.00
❑ 90 Ed Meador	2.50	1.25
❑ 91 Merlin Olsen RC	50.00	30.00
❑ 92 Jack Pardee RC	4.00	2.00
❑ 93 Jim Phillips	2.50	1.25
❑ 94 Carver Shannon	2.50	1.25
❑ 95 Frank Varrichione	2.50	1.25
❑ 96 Danny Villanueva	2.50	1.25
❑ 97 Los Angeles Rams	3.00	1.50
❑ 98 Los Angeles Rams Play	2.50	1.25
❑ 99 Grady Alderman RC	3.00	1.50
❑ 100 Larry Bowie	2.50	1.25
❑ 101 Bill Brown RC	6.00	3.00
❑ 102 Paul Flatley RC	2.50	1.25
❑ 103 Rip Hawkins	2.50	1.25
❑ 104 Jim Marshall	8.00	4.00
❑ 105 Tommy Mason	3.00	1.50
❑ 106 Jim Prestel	2.50	1.25
❑ 107 Jerry Reichow	2.50	1.25
❑ 108 Ed Sharockman	2.50	1.25
❑ 109 Fran Tarkenton	35.00	20.00
❑ 110 Mick Tingelhoff RC	6.00	3.00
❑ 111 Minnesota Vikings	3.00	1.50
❑ 112 Vikings Play/Van Brock.	4.00	2.00
❑ 113 Erich Barnes	2.50	1.25
❑ 114 Roosevelt Brown	4.00	2.00
❑ 115 Don Chandler	2.50	1.25
❑ 116 Darrell Dess	2.50	1.25
❑ 117 Frank Gifford	35.00	20.00
❑ 118 Dick James	2.50	1.25
❑ 119 Jim Katcavage	2.50	1.25
❑ 120 John Lovetere	2.50	1.25
❑ 121 Dick Lynch RC	3.00	1.50
❑ 122 Jim Patton	2.50	1.25
❑ 123 Del Shofner	2.50	1.25
❑ 124 Y.A.Tittle	20.00	10.00
❑ 125 New York Giants	3.00	1.50
❑ 126 New York Giants Play	2.50	1.25
❑ 127 Sam Baker	2.50	1.25
❑ 128 Maxie Baughan	2.50	1.25
❑ 129 Timmy Brown	3.00	1.50
❑ 130 Mike Clark	2.50	1.25
❑ 131 Irv Cross RC	3.00	1.50
❑ 132 Ted Dean	2.50	1.25
❑ 133 Ron Goodwin	2.50	1.25
❑ 134 King Hill	2.50	1.25
❑ 135 Clarence Peaks	2.50	1.25
❑ 136 Pete Retzlaff	3.00	1.50
❑ 137 Jim Schrader	2.50	1.25
❑ 138 Norm Snead	3.00	1.50
❑ 139 Philadelphia Eagles	3.00	1.50
❑ 140 Philadelphia Eagles Play	2.50	1.25
❑ 141 Gary Ballman RC	2.50	1.25
❑ 142 Charley Bradshaw RC	2.50	1.25
❑ 143 Ed Brown	3.00	1.50
❑ 144 John Henry Johnson	4.00	2.00
❑ 145 Joe Krupa	2.50	1.25
❑ 146 Bill Mack	2.50	1.25
❑ 147 Lou Michaels	2.50	1.25
❑ 148 Buzz Nutter	2.50	1.25
❑ 149 Myron Pottios	2.50	1.25
❑ 150 John Reger	2.50	1.25
❑ 151 Mike Sandusky	2.50	1.25
❑ 152 Clendon Thomas	2.50	1.25
❑ 153 Pittsburgh Steelers	3.00	1.50
❑ 154 Pittsburgh Steelers Play	2.50	1.25
❑ 155 Kermit Alexander RC	3.00	1.50
❑ 156 Bernie Casey	3.00	1.50
❑ 157 Dan Colchico	2.50	1.25
❑ 158 Clyde Conner	2.50	1.25
❑ 159 Tommy Davis	2.50	1.25
❑ 160 Matt Hazeltine	2.50	1.25
❑ 161 Jim Johnson RC	20.00	10.00
❑ 162 Don Lisbon RC	2.50	1.25
❑ 163 Lamar McHan	2.50	1.25
❑ 164 Bob St.Clair	4.00	2.00
❑ 165 J.D. Smith	2.50	1.25
❑ 166 Abe Woodson	2.50	1.25
❑ 167 San Francisco 49ers	3.00	1.50
❑ 168 San Francisco 49ers Play	2.50	1.25
❑ 169 Garland Boyette UER	2.50	1.25
❑ 170 Bobby Joe Conrad	3.00	1.50
❑ 171 Bob DeMarco RC	2.50	1.25
❑ 172 Ken Gray RC	2.50	1.25
❑ 173 Jimmy Hill	2.50	1.25
❑ 174 Charlie Johnson	3.00	1.50
❑ 175 Ernie McMillan	2.50	1.25
❑ 176 Dale Meinert	2.50	1.25
❑ 177 Luke Owens	2.50	1.25
❑ 178 Sonny Randle	2.50	1.25
❑ 179 Joe Robb	2.50	1.25
❑ 180 Bill Stacy	2.50	1.25
❑ 181 St. Louis Cardinals	3.00	1.50
❑ 182 St. Louis Cardinals Play	2.50	1.25
❑ 183 Bill Barnes	2.50	1.25
❑ 184 Don Bosseler	2.50	1.25
❑ 185 Sam Huff	6.00	3.00
❑ 186 Sonny Jurgensen	20.00	10.00
❑ 187 Bob Khayat	2.50	1.25
❑ 188 Riley Mattson	2.50	1.25
❑ 189 Bobby Mitchell	6.00	3.00
❑ 190 John Nisby	2.50	1.25
❑ 191 Vince Promuto	2.50	1.25
❑ 192 Joe Rutgens	2.50	1.25
❑ 193 Lonnie Sanders	2.50	1.25
❑ 194 Jim Steffen	2.50	1.25
❑ 195 Washington Redskins	3.00	1.50
❑ 196 Washington Redskins Play	2.50	1.25
❑ 197 Checklist 1 UER !	30.00	18.00
❑ 198 Checklist 2 UER !	55.00	30.00

1965 Philadelphia

❑ COMPLETE SET (198)	800.00	500.00
❑ WRAPPER (5-CENT)	20.00	10.00
❑ 1 Colts Team !	15.00	7.50
❑ 2 Raymond Berry	10.00	5.00
❑ 3 Bob Boyd DB	2.00	1.00
❑ 4 Wendell Harris	2.00	1.00
❑ 5 Jerry Logan	2.00	1.00
❑ 6 Tony Lorick	2.00	1.00
❑ 7 Lou Michaels	2.00	1.00
❑ 8 Lenny Moore	8.00	4.00
❑ 9 Jimmy Orr	3.00	1.50
❑ 10 Jim Parker	4.00	2.00
❑ 11 Dick Szymanski	2.00	1.00
❑ 12 Johnny Unitas	40.00	25.00
❑ 13 Bob Vogel RC	2.00	1.00
❑ 14 Colts Play/Don Shula	20.00	12.00
❑ 15 Chicago Bears	3.00	1.50
❑ 16 Jon Arnett	2.00	1.00
❑ 17 Doug Atkins	5.00	2.50
❑ 18 Rudy Bukich RC	3.00	1.50
❑ 19 Mike Ditka	40.00	25.00
❑ 20 Dick Evey	2.00	1.00
❑ 21 Joe Fortunato	2.00	1.00
❑ 22 Bobby Joe Green RC	2.00	1.00
❑ 23 Johnny Morris	2.00	1.00
❑ 24 Mike Pyle	2.00	1.00
❑ 25 Roosevelt Taylor	3.00	1.50
❑ 26 Bill Wade	3.00	1.50
❑ 27 Bob Wetoska	2.00	1.00
❑ 28 Bears Play/George Halas	8.00	4.00
❑ 29 Cleveland Browns	3.00	1.50
❑ 30 Walter Beach	2.00	1.00
❑ 31 Jim Brown	80.00	50.00
❑ 32 Gary Collins	3.00	1.50
❑ 33 Bill Glass	2.00	1.00
❑ 34 Ernie Green	2.00	1.00
❑ 35 Jim Houston RC	2.00	1.00
❑ 36 Dick Modzelewski	2.00	1.00
❑ 37 Bernie Parrish	2.00	1.00
❑ 38 Walter Roberts	2.00	1.00
❑ 39 Frank Ryan	3.00	1.50
❑ 40 Dick Schafrath	2.00	1.00
❑ 41 Paul Warfield RC	90.00	50.00
❑ 42 Cleveland Browns	2.00	1.00
❑ 43 Dallas Cowboys	3.00	1.50
❑ 44 Frank Clarke	3.00	1.50
❑ 45 Mike Connelly	2.00	1.00
❑ 46 Buddy Dial	2.00	1.00
❑ 47 Bob Lilly	35.00	20.00
❑ 48 Tony Liscio RC	2.00	1.00
❑ 49 Tommy McDonald	5.00	2.50
❑ 50 Don Meredith	25.00	15.00
❑ 51 Pettis Norman	2.00	1.00
❑ 52 Don Perkins	4.00	2.00
❑ 53 Mel Renfro RC	40.00	25.00
❑ 54 Jim Ridlon	2.00	1.00
❑ 55 Jerry Tubbs	2.00	1.00
❑ 56 Cowboys Play/T.Landry	15.00	7.50
❑ 57 Detroit Lions	3.00	1.50
❑ 58 Terry Barr	2.00	1.00
❑ 59 Roger Brown	2.00	1.00
❑ 60 Gail Cogdill	2.00	1.00
❑ 61 Jim Gibbons	2.00	1.00
❑ 62 John Gordy	2.00	1.00
❑ 63 Yale Lary	4.00	2.00
❑ 64 Dick LeBeau RC	3.00	1.50
❑ 65 Earl Morrall	3.00	1.50
❑ 66 Nick Pietrosante	2.00	1.00
❑ 67 Pat Studstill	2.00	1.00
❑ 68 Wayne Walker	3.00	1.50
❑ 69 Tom Watkins	2.00	1.00
❑ 70 Detroit Lions	3.00	1.50
❑ 71 Green Bay Packers	6.00	3.00
❑ 72 Herb Adderley	8.00	4.00
❑ 73 Willie Davis DE	8.00	4.00
❑ 74 Boyd Dowler	4.00	2.00
❑ 75 Forrest Gregg	5.00	2.50
❑ 76 Paul Hornung	35.00	20.00
❑ 77 Hank Jordan	5.00	2.50
❑ 78 Tom Moore	3.00	1.50
❑ 79 Ray Nitschke	20.00	12.00
❑ 80 Elijah Pitts RC	8.00	4.00
❑ 81 Bart Starr	50.00	30.00
❑ 82 Jim Taylor	20.00	12.00
❑ 83 Willie Wood	6.00	3.00
❑ 84 Packers Play/Lombardi	20.00	12.00
❑ 85 Los Angeles Rams	3.00	1.50
❑ 86 Dick Bass	3.00	1.50
❑ 87 Roman Gabriel	5.00	2.50

❑ 88 Roosevelt Grier	4.00	2.00
❑ 89 Deacon Jones	10.00	5.00
❑ 90 Lamar Lundy RC	4.00	2.00
❑ 91 Marlin McKeever	2.00	1.00
❑ 92 Ed Meador	2.00	1.00
❑ 93 Bill Munson RC	4.00	2.00
❑ 94 Merlin Olsen	15.00	7.50
❑ 95 Bobby Smith	2.00	1.00
❑ 96 Frank Varrichione	2.00	1.00
❑ 97 Ben Wilson	2.00	1.00
❑ 98 Los Angeles Rams	2.00	1.00
❑ 99 Minnesota Vikings	3.00	1.50
❑ 100 Grady Alderman	2.00	1.00
❑ 101 Hal Bedsole RC	2.00	1.00
❑ 102 Bill Brown	3.00	1.50
❑ 103 Bill Butler	2.00	1.00
❑ 104 Fred Cox RC	3.00	1.50
❑ 105 Carl Eller RC	30.00	18.00
❑ 106 Paul Flatley	2.00	1.00
❑ 107 Jim Marshall	6.00	3.00
❑ 108 Tommy Mason	2.00	1.00
❑ 109 George Rose	2.00	1.00
❑ 110 Fran Tarkenton	25.00	15.00
❑ 111 Mick Tingelhoff	3.00	1.50
❑ 112 Vikings Play/Van Brock.	4.00	2.00
❑ 113 New York Giants	3.00	1.50
❑ 114 Erich Barnes	2.00	1.00
❑ 115 Roosevelt Brown	4.00	2.00
❑ 116 Clarence Childs	2.00	1.00
❑ 117 Jerry Hillebrand	2.00	1.00
❑ 118 Greg Larson RC	2.00	1.00
❑ 119 Dick Lynch	2.00	1.00
❑ 120 Joe Morrison RC	4.00	2.00
❑ 121 Lou Slaby	2.00	1.00
❑ 122 Aaron Thomas RC	2.00	1.00
❑ 123 Steve Thurlow	2.00	1.00
❑ 124 Ernie Wheelwright RC	2.00	1.00
❑ 125 Gary Wood RC	3.00	1.50
❑ 126 New York Giants	2.00	1.00
❑ 127 Philadelphia Eagles	3.00	1.50
❑ 128 Sam Baker	2.00	1.00
❑ 129 Maxie Baughan	2.00	1.00
❑ 130 Timmy Brown	3.00	1.50
❑ 131 Jack Concannon RC	2.00	1.00
❑ 132 Irv Cross	3.00	1.50
❑ 133 Earl Gros	2.00	1.00
❑ 134 Dave Lloyd	2.00	1.00
❑ 135 Floyd Peters RC	2.00	1.00
❑ 136 Nate Ramsey	2.00	1.00
❑ 137 Pete Retzlaff	3.00	1.50
❑ 138 Jim Ringo	4.00	2.00
❑ 139 Norm Snead	4.00	2.00
❑ 140 Philadelphia Eagles	2.00	1.00
❑ 141 Pittsburgh Steelers	3.00	1.50
❑ 142 John Baker	2.00	1.00
❑ 143 Gary Ballman	2.00	1.00
❑ 144 Charley Bradshaw	2.00	1.00
❑ 145 Ed Brown	2.00	1.00
❑ 146 Dick Haley	2.00	1.00
❑ 147 John Henry Johnson	4.00	2.00
❑ 148 Brady Keys	2.00	1.00
❑ 149 Ray Lemek	2.00	1.00
❑ 150 Ben McGee	2.00	1.00
❑ 151 Clarence Peaks	2.00	1.00
❑ 152 Myron Pottios	2.00	1.00
❑ 153 Clendon Thomas	2.00	1.00
❑ 154 Pittsburgh Steelers	2.00	1.00
❑ 155 St. Louis Cardinals	3.00	1.50
❑ 156 Jim Bakken RC	3.00	1.50
❑ 157 Joe Childress	2.00	1.00
❑ 158 Bobby Joe Conrad	3.00	1.50
❑ 159 Bob DeMarco	2.00	1.00
❑ 160 Pat Fischer RC	4.00	2.00
❑ 161 Irv Goode	2.00	1.00
❑ 162 Ken Gray	2.00	1.00
❑ 163 Charlie Johnson	3.00	1.50
❑ 164 Bill Koman	2.00	1.00
❑ 165 Dale Meinert	2.00	1.00
❑ 166 Jerry Stovall RC	3.00	1.50
❑ 167 Abe Woodson	2.00	1.00
❑ 168 St. Louis Cardinals	2.00	1.00
❑ 169 San Francisco 49ers	3.00	1.50
❑ 170 Kermit Alexander	2.00	1.00
❑ 171 John Brodie	10.00	5.00
❑ 172 Bernie Casey	3.00	1.50
❑ 173 John David Crow	3.00	1.50
❑ 174 Tommy Davis	2.00	1.00
❑ 175 Matt Hazeltine	2.00	1.00
❑ 176 Jim Johnson	4.00	2.00
❑ 177 Charlie Krueger RC	2.00	1.00
❑ 178 Roland Lakes	2.00	1.00
❑ 179 George Mira RC	3.00	1.50
❑ 180 Dave Parks RC	3.00	1.50
❑ 181 John Thomas RC	2.00	1.00
❑ 182 49ers Play/Christiansen	2.00	1.00
❑ 183 Washington Redskins	3.00	1.50
❑ 184 Pervis Atkins	2.00	1.00
❑ 185 Preston Carpenter	2.00	1.00
❑ 186 Angelo Coia	2.00	1.00
❑ 187 Sam Huff	6.00	3.00
❑ 188 Sonny Jurgensen	15.00	7.50
❑ 189 Paul Krause RC	20.00	12.00
❑ 190 Jim Martin	2.00	1.00
❑ 191 Bobby Mitchell	5.00	2.50
❑ 192 John Nisby	2.00	1.00
❑ 193 John Paluck	2.00	1.00
❑ 194 Vince Promuto	2.00	1.00
❑ 195 Charley Taylor RC	50.00	30.00
❑ 196 Washington Redskins	2.00	1.00
❑ 197 Checklist 1 !	30.00	15.00
❑ 198 Checklist 2 UER !	50.00	25.00

1966 Philadelphia

❑ COMPLETE SET (198)	900.00	600.00
❑ WRAPPER (5-CENT)	20.00	10.00
❑ 1 Falcons Insignia !	12.00	6.00
❑ 2 Larry Benz	2.00	1.00
❑ 3 Dennis Claridge	2.00	1.00
❑ 4 Perry Lee Dunn	2.00	1.00
❑ 5 Dan Grimm	2.00	1.00
❑ 6 Alex Hawkins	2.00	1.00
❑ 7 Ralph Heck	2.00	1.00
❑ 8 Frank Lasky	2.00	1.00
❑ 9 Guy Reese	2.00	1.00
❑ 10 Bob Richards	2.00	1.00
❑ 11 Ron Smith RC	2.00	1.00
❑ 12 Ernie Wheelwright	2.00	1.00
❑ 13 Falcons Roster	3.00	1.50
❑ 14 Baltimore Colts	3.00	1.50
❑ 15 Raymond Berry	8.00	4.00
❑ 16 Bob Boyd DB	2.00	1.00
❑ 17 Jerry Logan	2.00	1.00
❑ 18 John Mackey	6.00	3.00
❑ 19 Tom Matte	4.00	2.00
❑ 20 Lou Michaels	2.00	1.00
❑ 21 Lenny Moore	8.00	4.00
❑ 22 Jimmy Orr	3.00	1.50
❑ 23 Jim Parker	4.00	2.00
❑ 24 Johnny Unitas	40.00	25.00
❑ 25 Bob Vogel	2.00	1.00
❑ 26 Colts Play/Moore/Parker	4.00	2.00
❑ 27 Chicago Bears	3.00	1.50
❑ 28 Doug Atkins	4.00	2.00
❑ 29 Rudy Bukich	2.00	1.00
❑ 30 Ronnie Bull	2.00	1.00
❑ 31 Dick Butkus RC !	250.00	150.00
❑ 32 Mike Ditka	35.00	20.00
❑ 33 Joe Fortunato	2.00	1.00
❑ 34 Bobby Joe Green	2.00	1.00
❑ 35 Roger LeClerc	2.00	1.00
❑ 36 Johnny Morris	2.00	1.00
❑ 37 Mike Pyle	2.00	1.00
❑ 38 Gale Sayers RC !	225.00	125.00
❑ 39 Bears Play/G.Sayers	35.00	20.00
❑ 40 Cleveland Browns	3.00	1.50
❑ 41 Jim Brown	80.00	50.00
❑ 42 Gary Collins	3.00	1.50
❑ 43 Ross Fichtner	2.00	1.00
❑ 44 Ernie Green	2.00	1.00
❑ 45 Gene Hickerson RC	25.00	15.00
❑ 46 Jim Houston	2.00	1.00
❑ 47 John Morrow	2.00	1.00
❑ 48 Walter Roberts	2.00	1.00
❑ 49 Frank Ryan	3.00	1.50
❑ 50 Dick Schafrath	2.00	1.00
❑ 51 Paul Wiggin RC	2.00	1.00
❑ 52 Cleveland Browns	2.00	1.00
❑ 53 Dallas Cowboys	3.00	1.50
❑ 54 George Andrie RC UER	3.00	1.50
❑ 55 Frank Clarke	3.00	1.50
❑ 56 Mike Connelly	2.00	1.00
❑ 57 Cornell Green	4.00	2.00
❑ 58 Bob Hayes RC	50.00	30.00
❑ 59 Chuck Howley RC	18.00	10.00
❑ 60 Bob Lilly	20.00	12.00
❑ 61 Don Meredith	25.00	15.00
❑ 62 Don Perkins	3.00	1.50
❑ 63 Mel Renfro	15.00	7.50
❑ 64 Danny Villanueva	2.00	1.00
❑ 65 Dallas Cowboys	2.00	1.00
❑ 66 Detroit Lions	3.00	1.50
❑ 67 Roger Brown	2.00	1.00
❑ 68 John Gordy	2.00	1.00
❑ 69 Alex Karras	10.00	5.00
❑ 70 Dick LeBeau	2.00	1.00
❑ 71 Amos Marsh	2.00	1.00
❑ 72 Milt Plum	3.00	1.50
❑ 73 Bobby Smith	2.00	1.00
❑ 74 Wayne Rasmussen	2.00	1.00
❑ 75 Pat Studstill	2.00	1.00
❑ 76 Wayne Walker	2.00	1.00
❑ 77 Tom Watkins	2.00	1.00
❑ 78 Detroit Lions	2.00	1.00
❑ 79 Green Bay Packers	6.00	3.00
❑ 80 Herb Adderley	6.00	3.00
❑ 81 Lee Roy Caffey RC	4.00	2.00
❑ 82 Don Chandler	3.00	1.50
❑ 83 Willie Davis DE	6.00	3.00
❑ 84 Boyd Dowler	4.00	2.00
❑ 85 Forrest Gregg	4.00	2.00
❑ 86 Tom Moore	3.00	1.50
❑ 87 Ray Nitschke	15.00	7.50
❑ 88 Bart Starr	50.00	30.00
❑ 89 Jim Taylor	20.00	12.00
❑ 90 Willie Wood	6.00	3.00
❑ 91 Green Bay Packers	2.00	1.00
❑ 92 Los Angeles Rams	3.00	1.50
❑ 93 Willie Brown WR	2.00	1.00
❑ 94 Roman Gabriel/D.Bass	4.00	2.00
❑ 95 Bruce Gossett RC	3.00	1.50
❑ 96 Deacon Jones	6.00	3.00
❑ 97 Tommy McDonald	5.00	2.50
❑ 98 Marlin McKeever	2.00	1.00
❑ 99 Aaron Martin	2.00	1.00
❑ 100 Ed Meador	2.00	1.00
❑ 101 Bill Munson	3.00	1.50
❑ 102 Merlin Olsen	8.00	4.00
❑ 103 Jim Stiger	2.00	1.00
❑ 104 Rams Play/W.Brown	3.00	1.50
❑ 105 Minnesota Vikings	3.00	1.50
❑ 106 Grady Alderman	2.00	1.00
❑ 107 Bill Brown	3.00	1.50
❑ 108 Fred Cox	2.00	1.00
❑ 109 Paul Flatley	2.00	1.00
❑ 110 Rip Hawkins	2.00	1.00
❑ 111 Tommy Mason	2.00	1.00
❑ 112 Ed Sharockman	2.00	1.00
❑ 113 Gordon Smith	2.00	1.00
❑ 114 Fran Tarkenton	30.00	15.00
❑ 115 Mick Tingelhoff	3.00	1.50
❑ 116 Bobby Walden RC**/C	2.00	1.00
❑ 117 Minnesota Vikings	2.00	1.00
❑ 118 New York Giants	3.00	1.50
❑ 119 Roosevelt Brown	4.00	2.00
❑ 120 Henry Carr RC	3.00	1.50
❑ 121 Clarence Childs	2.00	1.00
❑ 122 Tucker Frederickson RC	3.00	1.50
❑ 123 Jerry Hillebrand	2.00	1.00
❑ 124 Greg Larson	2.00	1.00
❑ 125 Spider Lockhart RC	3.00	1.50
❑ 126 Dick Lynch	2.00	1.00
❑ 127 Earl Morrall/Scholtz	3.00	1.50
❑ 128 Joe Morrison	2.00	1.00
❑ 129 Steve Thurlow	2.00	1.00
❑ 130 New York Giants	2.00	1.00
❑ 131 Philadelphia Eagles	3.00	1.50
❑ 132 Sam Baker	2.00	1.00
❑ 133 Maxie Baughan	2.00	1.00
❑ 134 Bob Brown OT RC	12.00	6.00
❑ 135 Timmy Brown	3.00	1.50

❑ 136 Irv Cross 3.00 1.50
❑ 137 Earl Gros 2.00 1.00
❑ 138 Ray Poage 2.00 1.00
❑ 139 Nate Ramsey 2.00 1.00
❑ 140 Pete Retzlaff 3.00 1.50
❑ 141 Jim Ringo 4.00 2.00
❑ 142 Norm Snead 4.00 2.00
❑ 143 Philadelphia Eagles 2.00 1.00
❑ 144 Pittsburgh Steelers 3.00 1.50
❑ 145 Gary Ballman 2.00 1.00
❑ 146 Charley Bradshaw 2.00 1.00
❑ 147 Jim Butler 2.00 1.00
❑ 148 Mike Clark 2.00 1.00
❑ 149 Dick Hoak RC 2.00 1.00
❑ 150 Roy Jefferson RC 3.00 1.50
❑ 151 Frank Lambert 2.00 1.00
❑ 152 Mike Lind 2.00 1.00
❑ 153 Bill Nelsen RC 4.00 2.00
❑ 154 Clarence Peaks 2.00 1.00
❑ 155 Clendon Thomas 2.00 1.00
❑ 156 Pittsburgh Steelers 2.00 1.00
❑ 157 St. Louis Cardinals 3.00 1.50
❑ 158 Jim Bakken 2.00 1.00
❑ 159 Bobby Joe Conrad 3.00 1.50
❑ 160 Willis Crenshaw RC 2.00 1.00
❑ 161 Bob DeMarco 2.00 1.00
❑ 162 Pat Fischer 3.00 1.50
❑ 163 Charlie Johnson 3.00 1.50
❑ 164 Dale Meinert 2.00 1.00
❑ 165 Sonny Randle 2.00 1.00
❑ 166 Sam Silas RC 2.00 1.00
❑ 167 Bill Triplett 2.00 1.00
❑ 168 Larry Wilson 4.00 2.00
❑ 169 St. Louis Cardinals 2.00 1.00
❑ 170 San Francisco 49ers 3.00 1.50
❑ 171 Kermit Alexander 2.00 1.00
❑ 172 Bruce Bosley 2.00 1.00
❑ 173 John Brodie 6.00 3.00
❑ 174 Bernie Casey 3.00 1.50
❑ 175 John David Crow 4.00 2.00
❑ 176 Tommy Davis 2.00 1.00
❑ 177 Jim Johnson 4.00 2.00
❑ 178 Gary Lewis RC 2.00 1.00
❑ 179 Dave Parks 2.00 1.00
❑ 180 Walter Rock RC 3.00 1.50
❑ 181 Ken Willard RC 4.00 2.00
❑ 182 San Francisco 49ers 2.00 1.00
❑ 183 Washington Redskins 3.00 1.50
❑ 184 Rickie Harris 2.00 1.00
❑ 185 Sonny Jurgensen 8.00 4.00
❑ 186 Paul Krause 6.00 3.00
❑ 187 Bobby Mitchell 6.00 3.00
❑ 188 Vince Promuto 2.00 1.00
❑ 189 Pat Richter RC 2.00 1.00
❑ 190 Joe Rutgens 2.00 1.00
❑ 191 Johnny Sample 2.00 1.00
❑ 192 Lonnie Sanders 2.00 1.00
❑ 193 Jim Steffen 2.00 1.00
❑ 194 Charley Taylor 15.00 7.50
❑ 195 Washington Redskins 2.00 1.00
❑ 196 Referee Signals 3.00 1.50
❑ 197 Checklist 1 ! 25.00 12.50
❑ 198 Checklist 2 UER ! 50.00 25.00

1967 Philadelphia

❑ COMPLETE SET (198) 650.00 425.00
❑ WRAPPER (5-CENT) 20.00 10.00
❑ 1 Falcons Team ! 10.00 5.00
❑ 2 Junior Coffey RC 3.00 1.50
❑ 3 Alex Hawkins 2.00 1.00
❑ 4 Randy Johnson RC 3.00 1.50
❑ 5 Lou Kirouac 2.00 1.00
❑ 6 Billy Martin RC 2.00 1.00
❑ 7 Tommy Nobis RC 20.00 10.00
❑ 8 Jerry Richardson RC 4.00 2.00
❑ 9 Marion Rushing 2.00 1.00
❑ 10 Ron Smith 2.00 1.00
❑ 11 Ernie Wheelwright UER 2.00 1.00
❑ 12 Atlanta Falcons 2.00 1.00
❑ 13 Baltimore Colts 3.00 1.50
❑ 14 Raymond Berry UER 7.00 3.50
❑ 15 Bob Boyd DB 2.00 1.00
❑ 16 Ordell Braase RC 2.00 1.00
❑ 17 Alvin Haymond RC 2.00 1.00
❑ 18 Tony Lorick 2.00 1.00
❑ 19 Lenny Lyles 2.00 1.00
❑ 20 John Mackey 5.00 2.50
❑ 21 Tom Matte 3.00 1.50
❑ 22 Lou Michaels 2.00 1.00
❑ 23 Johnny Unitas 40.00 25.00
❑ 24 Baltimore Colts 2.00 1.00
❑ 25 Chicago Bears 3.00 1.50
❑ 26 Rudy Bukich UER 2.00 1.00
❑ 27 Ronnie Bull 2.00 1.00
❑ 28 Dick Butkus 75.00 45.00
❑ 29 Mike Ditka 30.00 18.00
❑ 30 Dick Gordon RC 3.00 1.50
❑ 31 Roger LeClerc 2.00 1.00
❑ 32 Bennie McRae 2.00 1.00
❑ 33 Richie Petitbon 2.00 1.00
❑ 34 Mike Pyle 2.00 1.00
❑ 35 Gale Sayers 75.00 45.00
❑ 36 Chicago Bears 2.00 1.00
❑ 37 Cleveland Browns 3.00 1.50
❑ 38 Johnny Brewer 2.00 1.00
❑ 39 Gary Collins 3.00 1.50
❑ 40 Ross Fichtner 2.00 1.00
❑ 41 Ernie Green 2.00 1.00
❑ 42 Gene Hickerson 5.00 2.50
❑ 43 Leroy Kelly RC 40.00 25.00
❑ 44 Frank Ryan 3.00 1.50
❑ 45 Dick Schafrath 2.00 1.00
❑ 46 Paul Warfield 18.00 10.00
❑ 47 John Wooten 2.00 1.00
❑ 48 Cleveland Browns 2.00 1.00
❑ 49 Dallas Cowboys 3.00 1.50
❑ 50 George Andrie 2.00 1.00
❑ 51 Cornell Green 3.00 1.50
❑ 52 Bob Hayes 20.00 10.00
❑ 53 Chuck Howley 4.00 2.00
❑ 54 Lee Roy Jordan RC 20.00 12.00
❑ 55 Bob Lilly 15.00 7.50
❑ 56 Dave Manders RC 2.00 1.00
❑ 57 Don Meredith 25.00 15.00
❑ 58 Dan Reeves RC 30.00 18.00
❑ 59 Mel Renfro 6.00 3.00
❑ 60 Dallas Cowboys 3.00 1.50
❑ 61 Detroit Lions 3.00 1.50
❑ 62 Roger Brown 3.00 1.50
❑ 63 Gail Cogdill 2.00 1.00
❑ 64 John Gordy 2.00 1.00
❑ 65 Ron Kramer 2.00 1.00
❑ 66 Dick LeBeau 2.00 1.00
❑ 67 Mike Lucci RC 4.00 2.00
❑ 68 Amos Marsh 2.00 1.00
❑ 69 Tom Nowatzke 2.00 1.00
❑ 70 Pat Studstill 2.00 1.00
❑ 71 Karl Sweetan 2.00 1.00
❑ 72 Detroit Lions 2.00 1.00
❑ 73 Green Bay Packers 5.00 2.50
❑ 74 Herb Adderley UER 6.00 3.00
❑ 75 Lee Roy Caffey 3.00 1.50
❑ 76 Willie Davis DE 5.00 2.50
❑ 77 Forrest Gregg 4.00 2.00
❑ 78 Hank Jordan 4.00 2.00
❑ 79 Ray Nitschke 12.00 6.00
❑ 80 Dave Robinson RC 6.00 3.00
❑ 81 Bob Skoronski 3.00 1.50
❑ 82 Bart Starr 50.00 30.00
❑ 83 Willie Wood 5.00 2.50
❑ 84 Green Bay Packers 3.00 1.50
❑ 85 Los Angeles Rams 3.00 1.50
❑ 86 Dick Bass 3.00 1.50
❑ 87 Maxie Baughan 2.00 1.00
❑ 88 Roman Gabriel 4.00 2.00
❑ 89 Bruce Gossett 2.00 1.00
❑ 90 Deacon Jones 5.00 2.50
❑ 91 Tommy McDonald 5.00 2.50
❑ 92 Marlin McKeever 2.00 1.00
❑ 93 Tom Moore 2.00 1.00
❑ 94 Merlin Olsen 6.00 3.00
❑ 95 Clancy Williams 2.00 1.00
❑ 96 Los Angeles Rams 2.00 1.00
❑ 97 Minnesota Vikings 3.00 1.50
❑ 98 Grady Alderman 2.00 1.00
❑ 99 Bill Brown 3.00 1.50
❑ 100 Fred Cox 2.00 1.00
❑ 101 Paul Flatley 2.00 1.00
❑ 102 Dale Hackbart RC 2.00 1.00
❑ 103 Jim Marshall 4.00 2.00
❑ 104 Tommy Mason 2.00 1.00
❑ 105 Milt Sunde RC 2.00 1.00
❑ 106 Fran Tarkenton 20.00 10.00
❑ 107 Mick Tingelhoff 3.00 1.50
❑ 108 Minnesota Vikings 2.00 1.00
❑ 109 New York Giants 3.00 1.50
❑ 110 Henry Carr 2.00 1.00
❑ 111 Clarence Childs 2.00 1.00
❑ 112 Allen Jacobs 2.00 1.00
❑ 113 Homer Jones RC 3.00 1.50
❑ 114 Tom Kennedy 2.00 1.00
❑ 115 Spider Lockhart 2.00 1.00
❑ 116 Joe Morrison 2.00 1.00
❑ 117 Francis Peay 2.00 1.00
❑ 118 Jeff Smith LB 2.00 1.00
❑ 119 Aaron Thomas 2.00 1.00
❑ 120 New York Giants 2.00 1.00
❑ 121 Saints Insignia 3.00 1.50
❑ 122 Charley Bradshaw 2.00 1.00
❑ 123 Paul Hornung 25.00 12.50
❑ 124 Elbert Kimbrough 2.00 1.00
❑ 125 Earl Leggett RC 2.00 1.00
❑ 126 Obert Logan 2.00 1.00
❑ 127 Riley Mattson 2.00 1.00
❑ 128 John Morrow 2.00 1.00
❑ 129 Bob Scholtz 2.00 1.00
❑ 130 Dave Whitsell RC 2.00 1.00
❑ 131 Gary Wood 2.00 1.00
❑ 132 Saints Roster UER 121 3.00 1.50
❑ 133 Philadelphia Eagles 3.00 1.50
❑ 134 Sam Baker 2.00 1.00
❑ 135 Bob Brown OT 5.00 2.00
❑ 136 Timmy Brown 3.00 1.50
❑ 137 Earl Gros 2.00 1.00
❑ 138 Dave Lloyd 2.00 1.00
❑ 139 Floyd Peters 2.00 1.00
❑ 140 Pete Retzlaff 3.00 1.50
❑ 141 Joe Scarpati 2.00 1.00
❑ 142 Norm Snead 3.00 1.50
❑ 143 Jim Skaggs 2.00 1.00
❑ 144 Philadelphia Eagles 2.00 1.00
❑ 145 Pittsburgh Steelers 3.00 1.50
❑ 146 Bill Asbury 2.00 1.00
❑ 147 John Baker 2.00 1.00
❑ 148 Gary Ballman 2.00 1.00
❑ 149 Mike Clark 2.00 1.00
❑ 150 Riley Gunnels 2.00 1.00
❑ 151 John Hilton 2.00 1.00
❑ 152 Roy Jefferson 3.00 1.50
❑ 153 Brady Keys 2.00 1.00
❑ 154 Ben McGee 2.00 1.00
❑ 155 Bill Nelsen 3.00 1.50
❑ 156 Pittsburgh Steelers 2.00 1.00
❑ 157 St. Louis Cardinals 3.00 1.50
❑ 158 Jim Bakken 2.00 1.00
❑ 159 Bobby Joe Conrad 3.00 1.50
❑ 160 Ken Gray 2.00 1.00
❑ 161 Charlie Johnson 3.00 1.50
❑ 162 Joe Robb 2.00 1.00
❑ 163 Johnny Roland RC 3.00 1.50
❑ 164 Roy Shivers 2.00 1.00
❑ 165 Jackie Smith RC 15.00 7.50
❑ 166 Jerry Stovall 2.00 1.00
❑ 167 Larry Wilson 4.00 2.00
❑ 168 St. Louis Cardinals 2.00 1.00
❑ 169 San Francisco 49ers 3.00 1.50
❑ 170 Kermit Alexander 2.00 1.00
❑ 171 Bruce Bosley 2.00 1.00
❑ 172 John Brodie 6.00 3.00
❑ 173 Bernie Casey 3.00 1.50
❑ 174 Tommy Davis 2.00 1.00
❑ 175 Howard Mudd 2.00 1.00
❑ 176 Dave Parks 2.00 1.00
❑ 177 John Thomas 2.00 1.00
❑ 178 Dave Wilcox RC 20.00 10.00
❑ 179 Ken Willard 3.00 1.50
❑ 180 San Francisco 49ers 2.00 1.00
❑ 181 Washington Redskins 3.00 1.50
❑ 182 Charlie Gogolak RC 2.00 1.00
❑ 183 Chris Hanburger RC 5.00 2.50

❑ 184 Len Hauss RC 3.00 1.50
❑ 185 Sonny Jurgensen 7.00 3.50
❑ 186 Bobby Mitchell 5.00 2.50
❑ 187 Brig Owens 2.00 1.00
❑ 188 Jim Shorter 2.00 1.00
❑ 189 Jerry Smith RC 3.00 1.50
❑ 190 Charley Taylor 8.00 4.00
❑ 191 A.D. Whitfield 2.00 1.00
❑ 192 Washington Redskins 2.00 1.00
❑ 193 Browns Play/Leroy Kelly 6.00 3.00
❑ 194 New York Giants PC 2.00 1.00
❑ 195 Atlanta Falcons PC 2.00 1.00
❑ 196 Referee Signals 3.00 1.50
❑ 197 Checklist 1 ! 20.00 12.00
❑ 198 Checklist 2 UER ! 40.00 20.00

1991 Pinnacle

❑ COMPLETE SET (415) 20.00 7.50
❑ 1 Warren Moon .40 .15
❑ 2 Morten Andersen .10 .02
❑ 3 Rohn Stark .10 .02
❑ 4 Mark Bortz .10 .02
❑ 5 Mark Higgs RC .10 .02
❑ 6 Troy Aikman 2.00 .75
❑ 7 John Elway 3.00 1.25
❑ 8 Neal Anderson .20 .07
❑ 9 Chris Doleman .10 .02
❑ 10 Jay Schroeder .10 .02
❑ 11 Sterling Sharpe .40 .15
❑ 12 Steve DeBerg .10 .02
❑ 13 Ronnie Lott .20 .07
❑ 14 Sean Landeta .10 .02
❑ 15 Jim Everett .20 .07
❑ 16 Jim Breech .10 .02
❑ 17 Barry Foster .20 .07
❑ 18 Mike Merriweather .10 .02
❑ 19 Eric Metcalf .20 .07
❑ 20 Mark Carrier DB .20 .07
❑ 21 James Brooks .20 .07
❑ 22 Nate Odomes .10 .02
❑ 23 Rodney Hampton .40 .15
❑ 24 Chris Miller .20 .07
❑ 25 Roger Craig .20 .07
❑ 26 Louis Oliver .10 .02
❑ 27 Allen Pinkett .10 .02
❑ 28 Bubby Brister .10 .02
❑ 29 Reyna Thompson .10 .02
❑ 30 Issiac Holt .10 .02
❑ 31 Steve Broussard .10 .02
❑ 32 Christian Okoye .10 .02
❑ 33 Dave Meggett .20 .07
❑ 34 Andre Reed .20 .07
❑ 35 Shane Conlan .10 .02
❑ 36 Eric Ball .10 .02
❑ 37 Johnny Bailey .10 .02
❑ 38 Don Majkowski .10 .02
❑ 39 Gerald Williams .10 .02
❑ 40 Kevin Mack .10 .02
❑ 41 Jeff Herrod .10 .02
❑ 42 Emmitt Smith 6.00 2.50
❑ 43 Wendell Davis .10 .02
❑ 44 Lorenzo White .10 .02
❑ 45 Andre Rison .20 .07
❑ 46 Jerry Gray .10 .02
❑ 47 Dennis Smith .10 .02
❑ 48 Gaston Green .10 .02
❑ 49 Dermontti Dawson .10 .02
❑ 50 Jeff Hostetler .20 .07
❑ 51 Nick Lowery .10 .02
❑ 52 Merril Hoge .10 .02
❑ 53 Bobby Hebert .10 .02
❑ 54 Scott Case .10 .02
❑ 55 Jack Del Rio .20 .07
❑ 56 Cornelius Bennett .20 .07
❑ 57 Tony Mandarich .10 .02
❑ 58 Bill Brooks .10 .02
❑ 59 Jessie Tuggle .10 .02
❑ 60 Hugh Millen RC .10 .02
❑ 61 Tony Bennett .20 .07
❑ 62 Cris Dishman RC .10 .02
❑ 63 Darryl Henley RC .10 .02
❑ 64 Duane Bickett .10 .02
❑ 65 Jay Hilgenberg .10 .02
❑ 66 Joe Montana 3.00 1.25
❑ 67 Bill Fralic .10 .02
❑ 68 Sam Mills .10 .02
❑ 69 Bruce Armstrong .10 .02
❑ 70 Dan Marino 3.00 1.25
❑ 71 Jim Lachey .10 .02
❑ 72 Rod Woodson .40 .15
❑ 73 Simon Fletcher .10 .02
❑ 74 Bruce Matthews .20 .07
❑ 75 Howie Long .40 .15
❑ 76 John Friesz .40 .15
❑ 77 Karl Mecklenburg .10 .02
❑ 78 John L. Williams UER .10 .02
❑ 79 Rob Burnett RC .20 .07
❑ 80 Anthony Carter .20 .07
❑ 81 Henry Ellard .20 .07
❑ 82 Don Beebe .10 .02
❑ 83 Louis Lipps .10 .02
❑ 84 Greg McMurtry .10 .02
❑ 85 Will Wolford .10 .02
❑ 86 Eric Green .10 .02
❑ 87 Irving Fryar .20 .07
❑ 88 John Offerdahl .10 .02
❑ 89 John Alt .10 .02
❑ 90 Tom Tupa .10 .02
❑ 91 Don Mosebar .10 .02
❑ 92 Jeff George .50 .20
❑ 93 Vinny Testaverde .20 .07
❑ 94 Greg Townsend .10 .02
❑ 95 Derrick Fenner .10 .02
❑ 96 Brian Mitchell .20 .07
❑ 97 Herschel Walker .20 .07
❑ 98 Ricky Proehl .10 .02
❑ 99 Mark Clayton .20 .07
❑ 100 Derrick Thomas .40 .15
❑ 101 Jim Harbaugh .40 .15
❑ 102 Barry Word .10 .02
❑ 103 Jerry Rice 2.00 .75
❑ 104 Keith Byars .10 .02
❑ 105 Marion Butts .20 .07
❑ 106 Rich Moran .10 .02
❑ 107 Thurman Thomas .40 .15
❑ 108 Stephone Paige .10 .02
❑ 109 D.J. Johnson .10 .02
❑ 110 William Perry .20 .07
❑ 111 Haywood Jeffires .20 .07
❑ 112 Rodney Peete .20 .07
❑ 113 Andy Heck .10 .02
❑ 114 Kevin Ross .10 .02
❑ 115 Michael Carter .10 .02
❑ 116 Tim McKyer .10 .02
❑ 117 Kenneth Davis .10 .02
❑ 118 Richmond Webb .10 .02
❑ 119 Rich Camarillo .10 .02
❑ 120 James Francis .10 .02
❑ 121 Craig Heyward .20 .07
❑ 122 Hardy Nickerson .20 .07
❑ 123 Michael Brooks .10 .02
❑ 124 Fred Barnett .40 .15
❑ 125 Cris Carter 1.00 .40
❑ 126 Brian Jordan .20 .07
❑ 127 Pat Leahy .10 .02
❑ 128 Kevin Greene .20 .07
❑ 129 Trace Armstrong .10 .02
❑ 130 Eugene Lockhart .10 .02
❑ 131 Albert Lewis .10 .02
❑ 132 Ernie Jones .10 .02
❑ 133 Eric Martin .10 .02
❑ 134 Anthony Thompson .10 .02
❑ 135 Tim Krumrie .10 .02
❑ 136 James Lofton .20 .07
❑ 137 John Taylor .20 .07
❑ 138 Jeff Cross .10 .02
❑ 139 Tommy Kane .10 .02
❑ 140 Robb Thomas .10 .02
❑ 141 Gary Anderson K .10 .02
❑ 142 Mark Murphy .10 .02
❑ 143 Rickey Jackson .10 .02
❑ 144 Ken O'Brien .10 .02
❑ 145 Ernest Givins .20 .07
❑ 146 Jessie Hester .10 .02
❑ 147 Deion Sanders .75 .30
❑ 148 Keith Henderson RC .10 .02
❑ 149 Chris Singleton .10 .02
❑ 150 Rod Bernstine .10 .02
❑ 151 Quinn Early .20 .07
❑ 152 Boomer Esiason .20 .07
❑ 153 Mike Gann .10 .02
❑ 154 Dino Hackett .10 .02
❑ 155 Perry Kemp .10 .02
❑ 156 Mark Ingram .20 .07
❑ 157 Daryl Johnston .75 .30
❑ 158 Eugene Daniel .10 .02
❑ 159 Dalton Hilliard .10 .02
❑ 160 Rufus Porter .10 .02
❑ 161 Tunch Ilkin .10 .02
❑ 162 James Hasty .10 .02
❑ 163 Keith McKeller .10 .02
❑ 164 Heath Sherman .10 .02
❑ 165 Vai Sikahema .10 .02
❑ 166 Pat Terrell .10 .02
❑ 167 Anthony Munoz .20 .07
❑ 168 Brad Edwards RC .10 .02
❑ 169 Tom Rathman .10 .02
❑ 170 Steve McMichael .20 .07
❑ 171 Vaughan Johnson .10 .02
❑ 172 Nate Lewis RC .10 .02
❑ 173 Mark Rypien .20 .07
❑ 174 Rob Moore .50 .20
❑ 175 Tim Green .10 .02
❑ 176 Tony Casillas .10 .02
❑ 177 Jon Hand .10 .02
❑ 178 Todd McNair .10 .02
❑ 179 Toi Cook RC .10 .02
❑ 180 Eddie Brown .10 .02
❑ 181 Mark Jackson .10 .02
❑ 182 Pete Stoyanovich .10 .02
❑ 183 Bryce Paup RC .40 .15
❑ 184 Anthony Miller .20 .07
❑ 185 Dan Saleaumua .10 .02
❑ 186 Guy McIntyre .10 .02
❑ 187 Broderick Thomas .10 .02
❑ 188 Frank Warren .10 .02
❑ 189 Drew Hill .10 .02
❑ 190 Reggie White .40 .15
❑ 191 Chris Hinton .10 .02
❑ 192 David Little .10 .02
❑ 193 David Fulcher .10 .02
❑ 194 Clarence Verdin .10 .02
❑ 195 Junior Seau .60 .25
❑ 196 Blair Thomas .10 .02
❑ 197 Stan Brock .10 .02
❑ 198 Gary Clark .40 .15
❑ 199 Michael Irvin .40 .15
❑ 200 Ronnie Harmon .10 .02
❑ 201 Steve Young 2.00 .75
❑ 202 Brian Noble .10 .02
❑ 203 Dan Stryzinski .10 .02
❑ 204 Darryl Talley .10 .02
❑ 205 David Alexander .10 .02
❑ 206 Pat Swilling .20 .07
❑ 207 Gary Plummer .10 .02
❑ 208 Robert Delpino .10 .02
❑ 209 Norm Johnson .10 .02
❑ 210 Mike Singletary .20 .07
❑ 211 Anthony Johnson .40 .15
❑ 212 Eric Allen .10 .02
❑ 213 Gill Fenerty .10 .02
❑ 214 Neil Smith .40 .15
❑ 215 Joe Phillips .10 .02
❑ 216 Ottis Anderson .20 .07
❑ 217 LeRoy Butler .20 .07
❑ 218 Ray Childress .10 .02
❑ 219 Rodney Holman .10 .02
❑ 220 Kevin Fagan .10 .02
❑ 221 Bruce Smith .40 .15
❑ 222 Brad Muster .10 .02
❑ 223 Mike Horan .10 .02
❑ 224 Steve Atwater .10 .02
❑ 225 Rich Gannon .50 .20
❑ 226 Anthony Pleasant .10 .02
❑ 227 Steve Jordan .10 .02
❑ 228 Lomas Brown .10 .02
❑ 229 Jackie Slater .10 .02
❑ 230 Brad Baxter .10 .02
❑ 231 Joe Morris .10 .02
❑ 232 Marcus Allen .40 .15

❑ 233 Chris Warren .40 .15
❑ 234 Johnny Johnson .10 .02
❑ 235 Phil Simms .20 .07
❑ 236 Dave Krieg .20 .07
❑ 237 Jim McMahon .20 .07
❑ 238 Richard Dent .20 .07
❑ 239 John Washington RC .10 .02
❑ 240 Sammie Smith .10 .02
❑ 241 Brian Brennan .10 .02
❑ 242 Cortez Kennedy .40 .15
❑ 243 Tim McDonald .10 .02
❑ 244 Charles Haley .20 .07
❑ 245 Joey Browner .10 .02
❑ 246 Eddie Murray .10 .02
❑ 247 Bob Golic .10 .02
❑ 248 Myron Guyton .10 .02
❑ 249 Dennis Byrd .10 .02
❑ 250 Barry Sanders 3.00 1.25
❑ 251 Clay Matthews .20 .07
❑ 252 Pepper Johnson .10 .02
❑ 253 Eric Swann RC .40 .15
❑ 254 Lamar Lathon .10 .02
❑ 255 Andre Tippett .10 .02
❑ 256 Tom Newberry .10 .02
❑ 257 Kyle Clifton .10 .02
❑ 258 Leslie O'Neal .20 .07
❑ 259 Bubba McDowell .10 .02
❑ 260 Scott Davis .10 .02
❑ 261 Wilber Marshall .10 .02
❑ 262 Marv Cook .10 .02
❑ 263 Jeff Lageman .10 .02
❑ 264 Michael Young .10 .02
❑ 265 Gary Zimmerman .10 .02
❑ 266 Mike Munchak .20 .07
❑ 267 David Treadwell .10 .02
❑ 268 Steve Wisniewski .10 .02
❑ 269 Mark Duper .20 .07
❑ 270 Chris Spielman .20 .07
❑ 271 Brett Perriman .40 .15
❑ 272 Lionel Washington .10 .02
❑ 273 Lawrence Taylor .40 .15
❑ 274 Mark Collins .10 .02
❑ 275 Mark Carrier WR .40 .15
❑ 276 Paul Gruber .10 .02
❑ 277 Earnest Byner .10 .02
❑ 278 Andre Collins .10 .02
❑ 279 Reggie Cobb .10 .02
❑ 280 Art Monk .20 .07
❑ 281 Henry Jones RC .20 .07
❑ 282 Mike Pritchard RC .40 .15
❑ 283 Moe Gardner RC .10 .02
❑ 284 Chris Zorich RC .40 .15
❑ 285 Keith Traylor RC .10 .02
❑ 286 Mike Dumas RC .10 .02
❑ 287 Ed King RC .10 .02
❑ 288 Russell Maryland RC .40 .15
❑ 289 Alfred Williams RC .10 .02
❑ 290 Derek Russell RC .10 .02
❑ 291 Vinnie Clark RC .10 .02
❑ 292 Mike Croel RC .10 .02
❑ 293 Todd Marinovich RC .10 .02
❑ 294 Phil Hansen RC .10 .02
❑ 295 Aaron Craver RC .10 .02
❑ 296 Nick Bell RC .10 .02
❑ 297 Kenny Walker RC .10 .02
❑ 298 Roman Phifer RC .10 .02
❑ 299 Kanavis McGhee RC .10 .02
❑ 300 Ricky Ervins RC .20 .07
❑ 301 Jim Price RC .10 .02
❑ 302 John Johnson RC .10 .02
❑ 303 George Thornton RC .10 .02
❑ 304 Huey Richardson RC .10 .02
❑ 305 Harry Colon RC .10 .02
❑ 306 Antone Davis RC .10 .02
❑ 307 Todd Lyght RC .10 .02
❑ 308 Bryan Cox RC .40 .15
❑ 309 Brad Goebel RC .10 .02
❑ 310 Eric Moten RC .10 .02
❑ 311 John Kasay RC .20 .07
❑ 312 Esera Tuaolo RC .10 .02
❑ 313 Bobby Wilson RC .10 .02
❑ 314 Mo Lewis RC .20 .07
❑ 315 Harvey Williams RC .40 .15
❑ 316 Mike Stonebreaker .10 .02
❑ 317 Charles McRae RC .10 .02
❑ 318 John Flannery RC .10 .02
❑ 319 Ted Washington RC .10 .02
❑ 320 Stanley Richard RC .10 .02
❑ 321 Browning Nagle RC .10 .02
❑ 322 Ed McCaffrey RC 5.00 2.00
❑ 323 Jeff Graham RC WR .40 .15
❑ 324 Stan Thomas .10 .02
❑ 325 Lawrence Dawsey RC .20 .07
❑ 326 Eric Bieniemy RC .10 .02
❑ 327 Tim Barnett RC .10 .02
❑ 328 Erric Pegram RC .40 .15
❑ 329 Lamar Rogers RC .10 .02
❑ 330 Ernie Mills RC .20 .07
❑ 331 Pat Harlow RC .10 .02
❑ 332 Greg Lewis RC .10 .02
❑ 333 Jarrod Bunch RC .10 .02
❑ 334 Dan McGwire RC .10 .02
❑ 335 Randal Hill RC .20 .07
❑ 336 Leonard Russell RC .40 .15
❑ 337 Carnell Lake .10 .02
❑ 338 Brian Blades .20 .07
❑ 339 Darrell Green .10 .02
❑ 340 Bobby Humphrey .10 .02
❑ 341 Mervyn Fernandez .10 .02
❑ 342 Ricky Sanders .10 .02
❑ 343 Keith Jackson .20 .07
❑ 344 Carl Banks .10 .02
❑ 345 Bill Byrd .10 .02
❑ 346 Al Toon .20 .07
❑ 347 Stephen Baker .10 .02
❑ 348 Randall Cunningham .40 .15
❑ 349 Flipper Anderson .10 .02
❑ 350 Jay Novacek .40 .15
❑ 351 Steve Young/B.Smith HH .40 .15
❑ 352 Barry Sanders/Browner HH .75 .30
❑ 353 Joe Montana/M.Carrier HH .75 .30
❑ 354 Thurman Thomas/L.Taylor .20 .07
❑ 355 Jerry Rice/Darr.Green HH .50 .20
❑ 356 Warren Moon Tech .20 .07
❑ 357 Anthony Munoz TECH .10 .02
❑ 358 Barry Sanders Tech 1.25 .50
❑ 359 Jerry Rice Tech 1.25 .50
❑ 360 Joey Browner TECH .10 .02
❑ 361 Morten Andersen TECH .10 .02
❑ 362 Sean Landeta TECH .10 .02
❑ 363 Thurman Thomas GW .40 .15
❑ 364 Emmitt Smith GW 3.00 1.25
❑ 365 Gaston Green GW .10 .02
❑ 366 Barry Sanders GW 1.25 .50
❑ 367 Christian Okoye GW .10 .02
❑ 368 Earnest Byner GW .10 .02
❑ 369 Neal Anderson GW .10 .02
❑ 370 Herschel Walker GW .20 .07
❑ 371 Rodney Hampton GW .40 .15
❑ 372 Darryl Talley IDOL .10 .02
❑ 373 Mark Carrier IDOL .10 .02
❑ 374 Jim Breech IDOL .10 .02
❑ 375 R.Hampton/O.Anderson ID .10 .02
❑ 376 Kevin Mack IDOL .10 .02
❑ 377 S.Jordan/O.Robertson ID .10 .02
❑ 378 B.Esiason/B.Jones ID .10 .02
❑ 379 Steve DeBerg IDOL .20 .07
❑ 380 Al Toon IDOL .10 .02
❑ 381 Ronnie Lott/C.Taylor ID .20 .07
❑ 382 Henry Ellard IDOL .10 .02
❑ 383 Troy Aikman/Staubach ID 1.25 .50
❑ 384 T.Thomas/E.Campbell ID .40 .15
❑ 385 Dan Marino/Bradshaw ID 1.50 .60
❑ 386 Howie Long/Joe Greene ID .20 .07
❑ 387 Franco Harris IR .20 .07
❑ 388 Esera Tuaolo .10 .02
❑ 389 Super Bowl XXVI .10 .02
❑ 390 Charles Mann .10 .02
❑ 391 Kenny Walker Succeed .10 .02
❑ 392 Reggie Roby .10 .02
❑ 393 Bruce Pickens RC .10 .02
❑ 394 Ray Childress SIDE .10 .02
❑ 395 Karl Mecklenburg SIDE .10 .02
❑ 396 Dean Biasucci SIDE .10 .02
❑ 397 John Alt SIDE .10 .02
❑ 398 Marcus Allen SL .20 .07
❑ 399 John Offerdahl SIDE .10 .02
❑ 400 Richard Tardits RC SIDE .10 .02
❑ 401 Al Toon SIDE .10 .02
❑ 402 Joey Browner SIDE .10 .02
❑ 403 Spencer Tillman RC SIDE .10 .02
❑ 404 Jay Novacek SIDE .20 .07
❑ 405 Stephen Braggs SIDE .10 .02
❑ 406 Mike Tice RC SIDE .10 .02
❑ 407 Kevin Greene SIDE .20 .07
❑ 408 Reggie White SIDE .20 .07
❑ 409 Brian Noble SIDE .10 .02
❑ 410 Bart Oates SIDE .10 .02
❑ 411 Art Monk SIDE .20 .07
❑ 412 Ron Wolfley SIDE .10 .02
❑ 413 Louis Lipps SIDE .10 .02
❑ 414 Dante Jones RC SIDE .20 .07
❑ 415 Kenneth Davis SIDE .10 .02
❑ P1 Emmitt Smith Promo 25.00 12.50

1992 Pinnacle

❑ COMPLETE SET (360) 25.00 12.50
❑ 1 Reggie White .50 .20
❑ 2 Eric Green .15 .05
❑ 3 Craig Heyward .30 .10
❑ 4 Phil Simms .30 .10
❑ 5 Pepper Johnson .15 .05
❑ 6 Sean Landeta .15 .05
❑ 7 Dino Hackett .15 .05
❑ 8 Andre Ware .15 .05
❑ 9 Ricky Nattiel .15 .05
❑ 10 Jim Price .15 .05
❑ 11 Jim Ritcher .15 .05
❑ 12 Kelly Stouffer .15 .05
❑ 13 Ray Crockett .15 .05
❑ 14 Steve Tasker .30 .10
❑ 15 Barry Sanders 3.00 1.25
❑ 16 Pat Swilling .15 .05
❑ 17 Moe Gardner .15 .05
❑ 18 Steve Young 2.00 .75
❑ 19 Chris Spielman .30 .10
❑ 20 Richard Dent .30 .10
❑ 21 Anthony Munoz .30 .10
❑ 22 Thurman Thomas .50 .20
❑ 23 Ricky Sanders .15 .05
❑ 24 Steve Atwater .15 .05
❑ 25 Tony Tolbert .15 .05
❑ 26 Haywood Jeffires .30 .10
❑ 27 Duane Bickett .15 .05
❑ 28 Tim McDonald .15 .05
❑ 29 Cris Carter .75 .30
❑ 30 Derrick Thomas .50 .20
❑ 31 Hugh Millen .15 .05
❑ 32 Bart Oates .15 .05
❑ 33 Darryl Talley .15 .05
❑ 34 Marion Butts .15 .05
❑ 35 Pete Stoyanovich .15 .05
❑ 36 Ronnie Lott .30 .10
❑ 37 Simon Fletcher .15 .05
❑ 38 Morten Andersen .15 .05
❑ 39 Clyde Simmons .15 .05
❑ 40 Mark Rypien .15 .05
❑ 41 Henry Ellard .30 .10
❑ 42 Michael Irvin .50 .20
❑ 43 Louis Lipps .15 .05
❑ 44 John L. Williams .15 .05
❑ 45 Broderick Thomas .15 .05
❑ 46 Don Majkowski .15 .05
❑ 47 William Perry .30 .10
❑ 48 David Fulcher .15 .05
❑ 49 Tony Bennett .15 .05
❑ 50 Clay Matthews .30 .10
❑ 51 Warren Moon .50 .20
❑ 52 Bruce Armstrong .15 .05
❑ 53 Bill Brooks .15 .05
❑ 54 Greg Townsend .15 .05
❑ 55 Steve Broussard .15 .05
❑ 56 Mel Gray .30 .10
❑ 57 Kevin Mack .15 .05
❑ 58 Emmitt Smith 4.00 2.00
❑ 59 Mike Croel .15 .05
❑ 60 Brian Mitchell .30 .10
❑ 61 Bennie Blades .15 .05
❑ 62 Carnell Lake .15 .05
❑ 63 Cornelius Bennett .30 .10

❑	64	Darrell Thompson	.15	.05
❑	65	Jessie Hester	.15	.05
❑	66	Marv Cook	.15	.05
❑	67	Tim Brown	.50	.20
❑	68	Mark Duper	.15	.05
❑	69	Robert Delpino	.15	.05
❑	70	Eric Martin	.15	.05
❑	71	Wendell Davis	.15	.05
❑	72	Vaughan Johnson	.15	.05
❑	73	Brian Blades	.30	.10
❑	74	Ed King	.15	.05
❑	75	Gaston Green	.15	.05
❑	76	Christian Okoye	.15	.05
❑	77	Rohn Stark	.15	.05
❑	78	Kevin Greene	.30	.10
❑	79	Jay Novacek	.30	.10
❑	80	Chip Lohmiller	.15	.05
❑	81	Cris Dishman	.15	.05
❑	82	Ethan Horton	.15	.05
❑	83	Pat Harlow	.15	.05
❑	84	Mark Ingram	.15	.05
❑	85	Mark Carrier DB	.15	.05
❑	86	Sam Mills	.15	.05
❑	87	Mark Higgs	.15	.05
❑	88	Keith Jackson	.30	.10
❑	89	Gary Anderson K	.15	.05
❑	90	Ken Harvey	.15	.05
❑	91	Anthony Carter	.30	.10
❑	92	Randall McDaniel	.15	.05
❑	93	Johnny Johnson	.15	.05
❑	94	Shane Conlan	.15	.05
❑	95	Sterling Sharpe	.50	.20
❑	96	Guy McIntyre	.15	.05
❑	97	Albert Lewis	.15	.05
❑	98	Chris Doleman	.15	.05
❑	99	Andre Rison	.30	.10
❑	100	Bobby Hebert	.15	.05
❑	101	Dan Owens	.15	.05
❑	102	Rodney Hampton	.30	.10
❑	103	Ernie Jones	.15	.05
❑	104	Reggie Cobb	.15	.05
❑	105	Wilber Marshall	.15	.05
❑	106	Mike Munchak	.30	.10
❑	107	Cortez Kennedy	.30	.10
❑	108	Todd Lyght	.15	.05
❑	109	Burt Grossman	.15	.05
❑	110	Ferrell Edmunds	.15	.05
❑	111	Jim Everett	.30	.10
❑	112	Hardy Nickerson	.30	.10
❑	113	Andre Tippett	.15	.05
❑	114	Ronnie Harmon	.15	.05
❑	115	Andre Waters	.15	.05
❑	116	Ernest Givins	.30	.10
❑	117	Eric Hill	.15	.05
❑	118	Erric Pegram	.30	.10
❑	119	Jarrod Bunch	.15	.05
❑	120	Marcus Allen	.50	.20
❑	121	Barry Foster	.30	.10
❑	122	Kent Hull	.15	.05
❑	123	Neal Anderson	.15	.05
❑	124	Stephen Braggs	.15	.05
❑	125	Nick Lowery	.15	.05
❑	126	Jeff Hostetler	.30	.10
❑	127	Michael Carter	.15	.05
❑	128	Don Warren	.15	.05
❑	129	Brad Baxter	.15	.05
❑	130	John Taylor	.30	.10
❑	131	Harold Green	.15	.05
❑	132	Mike Merriweather	.15	.05
❑	133	Gary Clark	.50	.20
❑	134	Vince Buck	.15	.05
❑	135	Dan Saleaumua	.15	.05
❑	136	Gary Zimmerman	.15	.05
❑	137	Richmond Webb	.15	.05
❑	138	Art Monk	.30	.10
❑	139	Mervyn Fernandez	.15	.05
❑	140	Mark Jackson	.15	.05
❑	141	Freddie Joe Nunn	.15	.05
❑	142	Jeff Lageman	.15	.05
❑	143	Kenny Walker	.15	.05
❑	144	Mark Carrier WR	.30	.10
❑	145	Jon Vaughn	.15	.05
❑	146	Greg Davis	.15	.05
❑	147	Bubby Brister	.15	.05
❑	148	Mo Lewis	.15	.05
❑	149	Howie Long	.50	.20
❑	150	Rod Bernstine	.15	.05
❑	151	Nick Bell	.15	.05
❑	152	Terry Allen	.50	.20
❑	153	William Fuller	.15	.05
❑	154	Dexter Carter	.15	.05
❑	155	Gene Atkins	.15	.05
❑	156	Don Beebe	.15	.05
❑	157	Mark Collins	.15	.05
❑	158	Jerry Ball	.15	.05
❑	159	Fred Barnett	.50	.20
❑	160	Rodney Holman	.15	.05
❑	161	Stephen Baker	.15	.05
❑	162	Jeff Graham	.50	.20
❑	163	Leonard Russell	.30	.10
❑	164	Jeff Gossett	.15	.05
❑	165	Vinny Testaverde	.30	.10
❑	166	Maurice Hurst	.15	.05
❑	167	Louis Oliver	.15	.05
❑	168	Jim Morrissey	.15	.05
❑	169	Greg Kragen	.15	.05
❑	170	Andre Collins	.15	.05
❑	171	Dave Meggett	.30	.10
❑	172	Keith Henderson	.15	.05
❑	173	Vince Newsome	.15	.05
❑	174	Chris Hinton	.15	.05
❑	175	James Hasty	.15	.05
❑	176	John Offerdahl	.15	.05
❑	177	Lomas Brown	.15	.05
❑	178	Neil O'Donnell	.30	.10
❑	179	Leonard Marshall	.15	.05
❑	180	Bubba McDowell	.15	.05
❑	181	Herman Moore	.50	.20
❑	182	Rob Moore	.30	.10
❑	183	Earnest Byner	.15	.05
❑	184	Keith McCants	.15	.05
❑	185	Floyd Turner	.15	.05
❑	186	Steve Jordan	.15	.05
❑	187	Nate Odomes	.15	.05
❑	188	Jeff Herrod	.15	.05
❑	189	Jim Harbaugh	.50	.20
❑	190	Jessie Tuggle	.15	.05
❑	191	Al Smith	.15	.05
❑	192	Lawrence Dawsey	.30	.10
❑	193	Steve Bono RC	.50	.20
❑	194	Greg Lloyd	.30	.10
❑	195	Steve Wisniewski	.15	.05
❑	196	Larry Kelm	.15	.05
❑	197	Tommy Kane	.15	.05
❑	198	Mark Schlereth RC	.15	.05
❑	199	Ray Childress	.15	.05
❑	200	Vincent Brown	.15	.05
❑	201	Rodney Peete	.30	.10
❑	202	Dennis Smith	.15	.05
❑	203	Bruce Matthews	.15	.05
❑	204	Rickey Jackson	.15	.05
❑	205	Eric Allen	.15	.05
❑	206	Rich Camarillo	.15	.05
❑	207	Jim Lachey	.15	.05
❑	208	Kevin Ross	.15	.05
❑	209	Irving Fryar	.30	.10
❑	210	Mark Clayton	.30	.10
❑	211	Keith Byars	.15	.05
❑	212	John Elway	3.00	1.25
❑	213	Harris Barton	.15	.05
❑	214	Aeneas Williams	.30	.10
❑	215	Rich Gannon	.50	.20
❑	216	Toi Cook	.15	.05
❑	217	Rod Woodson	.50	.20
❑	218	Gary Anderson RB	.15	.05
❑	219	Reggie Roby	.15	.05
❑	220	Karl Mecklenburg	.15	.05
❑	221	Rufus Porter	.15	.05
❑	222	Jon Hand	.15	.05
❑	223	Tim Barnett	.15	.05
❑	224	Eric Swann	.30	.10
❑	225	Eugene Robinson	.15	.05
❑	226	Michael Young	.15	.05
❑	227	Frank Warren	.15	.05
❑	228	Mike Kenn	.15	.05
❑	229	Tim Green	.15	.05
❑	230	Barry Word	.15	.05
❑	231	Mike Pritchard	.30	.10
❑	232	John Kasay	.15	.05
❑	233	Derek Russell	.15	.05
❑	234	Jim Breech	.15	.05
❑	235	Pierce Holt	.15	.05
❑	236	Tim Krumrie	.15	.05
❑	237	William Roberts	.15	.05
❑	238	Erik Kramer	.30	.10
❑	239	Brett Perriman	.50	.20
❑	240	Reyna Thompson	.15	.05
❑	241	Chris Miller	.30	.10
❑	242	Drew Hill	.15	.05
❑	243	Curtis Duncan	.15	.05
❑	244	Seth Joyner	.15	.05
❑	245	Ken Norton Jr.	.30	.10
❑	246	Calvin Williams	.30	.10
❑	247	James Joseph	.15	.05
❑	248	Bennie Thompson RC	.15	.05
❑	249	Tunch Ilkin	.15	.05
❑	250	Brad Edwards	.15	.05
❑	251	Jeff Jaeger	.15	.05
❑	252	Gill Byrd	.15	.05
❑	253	Jeff Feagles	.15	.05
❑	254	Jamie Dukes RC	.15	.05
❑	255	Greg McMurtry	.15	.05
❑	256	Anthony Johnson	.30	.10
❑	257	Lamar Lathon	.15	.05
❑	258	John Roper	.15	.05
❑	259	Lorenzo White	.15	.05
❑	260	Brian Noble	.15	.05
❑	261	Chris Singleton	.15	.05
❑	262	Todd Marinovich	.15	.05
❑	263	Jay Hilgenberg	.15	.05
❑	264	Kyle Clifton	.15	.05
❑	265	Tony Casillas	.15	.05
❑	266	James Francis	.15	.05
❑	267	Eddie Anderson	.15	.05
❑	268	Tim Harris	.15	.05
❑	269	James Lofton	.30	.10
❑	270	Jay Schroeder	.15	.05
❑	271	Ed West	.15	.05
❑	272	Don Mosebar	.15	.05
❑	273	Jackie Slater	.15	.05
❑	274	Fred McAfee RC	.15	.05
❑	275	Steve Sewell	.15	.05
❑	276	Charles Mann	.15	.05
❑	277	Ron Hall	.15	.05
❑	278	Darrell Green	.15	.05
❑	279	Jeff Cross	.15	.05
❑	280	Jeff Wright	.15	.05
❑	281	Issiac Holt	.15	.05
❑	282	Dermontti Dawson	.15	.05
❑	283	Michael Haynes	.30	.10
❑	284	Tony Mandarich	.15	.05
❑	285	Leroy Hoard	.30	.10
❑	286	Darryl Henley	.15	.05
❑	287	Tim McGee	.15	.05
❑	288	Willie Gault	.30	.10
❑	289	Dalton Hilliard	.15	.05
❑	290	Tim McKyer	.15	.05
❑	291	Tom Waddle	.15	.05
❑	292	Eric Thomas	.15	.05
❑	293	Herschel Walker	.30	.10
❑	294	Donnell Woolford	.15	.05
❑	295	James Brooks	.30	.10
❑	296	Brad Muster	.15	.05
❑	297	Brent Jones	.30	.10
❑	298	Erik Howard	.15	.05
❑	299	Alvin Harper	.30	.10
❑	300	Joey Browner	.15	.05
❑	301	Jack Del Rio	.15	.05
❑	302	Cleveland Gary	.15	.05
❑	303	Brett Favre	6.00	3.00
❑	304	Freeman McNeil	.15	.05
❑	305	Willie Green	.15	.05
❑	306	Percy Snow	.15	.05
❑	307	Neil Smith	.50	.20
❑	308	Eric Bieniemy	.15	.05
❑	309	Keith Traylor	.15	.05
❑	310	Ernie Mills	.15	.05
❑	311	Will Wolford	.15	.05
❑	312	Robert Young	.15	.05
❑	313	Anthony Smith	.15	.05
❑	314	Robert Porcher RC	.50	.20
❑	315	Leon Searcy RC	.15	.05
❑	316	Amp Lee RC	.15	.05
❑	317	Siran Stacy RC	.15	.05
❑	318	Patrick Rowe RC	.15	.05
❑	319	Chris Mims RC	.15	.05
❑	320	Matt Elliott RC	.15	.05
❑	321	Ricardo McDonald RC	.15	.05
❑	322	Keith Hamilton RC	.30	.10
❑	323	Edgar Bennett RC	.50	.20
❑	324	Chris Hakel RC	.15	.05
❑	325	Dexter McNabb RC	.15	.05
❑	326	Rod Milstead RC	.15	.05
❑	327	Joe Bowden RC	.15	.05
❑	328	Brian Bollinger RC	.15	.05
❑	329	Darryl Williams RC	.15	.05
❑	330	Tommy Vardell RC	.15	.05

❑ 331 Glenn Parker SIDE	.15	.05
❑ 332 Herschel Walker SIDE	.15	.05
❑ 333 Mike Cofer SIDE	.15	.05
❑ 334 Mark Rypien SIDE	.15	.05
❑ 335 Andre Rison GW	.30	.10
❑ 336 Henry Ellard GW	.15	.05
❑ 337 Rob Moore GW	.15	.05
❑ 338 Fred Barnett GW	.15	.05
❑ 339 Mark Clayton GW	.15	.05
❑ 340 Eric Martin GW	.15	.05
❑ 341 Irving Fryar GW	.15	.05
❑ 342 Tim Brown GW	.30	.10
❑ 343 Sterling Sharpe GW	.30	.10
❑ 344 Gary Clark GW	.15	.05
❑ 345 John Mackey HOF	.15	.05
❑ 346 Lem Barney HOF	.15	.05
❑ 347 John Riggins HOF	.30	.10
❑ 348 Marion Butts IDOL	.15	.05
❑ 349 Jeff Lageman IDOL	.15	.05
❑ 350 Eric Green IDOL	.15	.05
❑ 351 Reggie White/Bob.Jones I	.30	.10
❑ 352 Marv Cook IDOL	.15	.05
❑ 353 John Elway/Staubach ID	1.25	.50
❑ 354 Steve Tasker IDOL	.15	.05
❑ 355 Nick Lowery IDOL	.15	.05
❑ 356 Mark Clayton/Warfield ID	.15	.05
❑ 357 Warren Moon/R.Gabriel ID	.30	.10
❑ 358 Eric Metcalf	.30	.10
❑ 359 Charles Haley	.30	.10
❑ 360 Terrell Buckley RC	.15	.05
❑ P1 Promo Panel	5.00	2.00

1993 Pinnacle

❑ COMPLETE SET (360)	20.00	7.50
❑ 1 Brett Favre	3.00	1.25
❑ 2 Tommy Vardell	.10	.02
❑ 3 Jarrod Bunch	.10	.02
❑ 4 Mike Croel	.10	.02
❑ 5 Morten Andersen	.10	.02
❑ 6 Barry Foster	.20	.07
❑ 7 Chris Spielman	.20	.07
❑ 8 Jim Jeffcoat	.10	.02
❑ 9 Ken Ruettgers	.10	.02
❑ 10 Cris Dishman	.10	.02
❑ 11 Ricky Watters	.40	.15
❑ 12 Alfred Williams	.10	.02
❑ 13 Mark Kelso	.10	.02
❑ 14 Moe Gardner	.10	.02
❑ 15 Terry Allen	.40	.15
❑ 16 Willie Gault	.10	.02
❑ 17 Bubba McDowell	.10	.02
❑ 18 Brian Mitchell	.20	.07
❑ 19 Karl Mecklenburg	.10	.02
❑ 20 Jim Everett	.20	.07
❑ 21 Bobby Humphrey	.10	.02
❑ 22 Tim Krumrie	.10	.02
❑ 23 Ken Norton Jr.	.20	.07
❑ 24 Wendell Davis	.10	.02
❑ 25 Brad Baxter	.10	.02
❑ 26 Mel Gray	.20	.07
❑ 27 Jon Vaughn	.10	.02
❑ 28 James Hasty	.10	.02
❑ 29 Chris Warren	.20	.07
❑ 30 Tim Harris	.10	.02
❑ 31 Eric Metcalf	.20	.07
❑ 32 Rob Moore	.20	.07
❑ 33 Charles Haley	.20	.07
❑ 34 Leonard Marshall	.10	.02
❑ 35 Jeff Graham	.20	.07
❑ 36 Eugene Robinson	.10	.02
❑ 37 Darryl Talley	.10	.02
❑ 38 Brent Jones	.20	.07
❑ 39 Reggie Roby	.10	.02
❑ 40 Bruce Armstrong	.10	.02
❑ 41 Audray McMillian	.10	.02
❑ 42 Bern Brostek	.10	.02
❑ 43 Tony Bennett	.10	.02
❑ 44 Albert Lewis	.10	.02
❑ 45 Derrick Thomas	.40	.15
❑ 46 Cris Carter	.40	.15
❑ 47 Richmond Webb	.10	.02
❑ 48 Sean Landeta	.10	.02
❑ 49 Cleveland Gary	.10	.02
❑ 50 Mark Carrier DB	.10	.02
❑ 51 Lawrence Dawsey	.10	.02
❑ 52 Lamar Lathon	.10	.02
❑ 53 Nick Bell	.10	.02
❑ 54 Curtis Duncan	.10	.02
❑ 55 Irving Fryar	.20	.07
❑ 56 Seth Joyner	.10	.02
❑ 57 Jay Novacek	.20	.07
❑ 58 John L. Williams	.10	.02
❑ 59 Amp Lee	.10	.02
❑ 60 Marion Butts	.10	.02
❑ 61 Clyde Simmons	.10	.02
❑ 62 Rich Gannon	.40	.15
❑ 63 Anthony Johnson	.20	.07
❑ 64 Dave Meggett	.10	.02
❑ 65 James Francis	.10	.02
❑ 66 Trace Armstrong	.10	.02
❑ 67 Mo Lewis	.10	.02
❑ 68 Cornelius Bennett	.20	.07
❑ 69 Mark Duper	.10	.02
❑ 70 Frank Reich	.20	.07
❑ 71 Eric Green	.10	.02
❑ 72 Bruce Matthews	.10	.02
❑ 73 Steve Broussard	.10	.02
❑ 74 Anthony Carter	.20	.07
❑ 75 Sterling Sharpe	.40	.15
❑ 76 Mike Kenn	.10	.02
❑ 77 Andre Rison	.20	.07
❑ 78 Todd Marinovich	.10	.02
❑ 79 Vincent Brown	.10	.02
❑ 80 Harold Green	.10	.02
❑ 81 Art Monk	.20	.07
❑ 82 Reggie Cobb	.10	.02
❑ 83 Johnny Johnson	.10	.02
❑ 84 Tommy Kane	.10	.02
❑ 85 Rohn Stark	.10	.02
❑ 86 Steve Tasker	.20	.07
❑ 87 Ronnie Harmon	.10	.02
❑ 88 Pepper Johnson	.10	.02
❑ 89 Hardy Nickerson	.20	.07
❑ 90 Alvin Harper	.20	.07
❑ 91 Louis Oliver	.10	.02
❑ 92 Rod Woodson	.40	.15
❑ 93 Sam Mills	.10	.02
❑ 94 Randall McDaniel	.10	.02
❑ 95 Johnny Holland	.10	.02
❑ 96 Jackie Slater	.10	.02
❑ 97 Don Mosebar	.10	.02
❑ 98 Andre Ware	.10	.02
❑ 99 Kelvin Martin	.10	.02
❑ 100 Emmitt Smith	2.50	1.00
❑ 101 Michael Brooks	.10	.02
❑ 102 Dan Saleaumua	.10	.02
❑ 103 John Elway	2.50	1.00
❑ 104 Henry Jones	.10	.02
❑ 105 William Perry	.20	.07
❑ 106 James Lofton	.20	.07
❑ 107 Carnell Lake	.10	.02
❑ 108 Chip Lohmiller	.10	.02
❑ 109 Andre Tippett	.10	.02
❑ 110 Barry Word	.10	.02
❑ 111 Haywood Jeffires	.20	.07
❑ 112 Kenny Walker	.10	.02
❑ 113 John Randle	.20	.07
❑ 114 Donnell Woolford	.10	.02
❑ 115 Johnny Bailey	.10	.02
❑ 116 Marcus Allen	.40	.15
❑ 117 Mark Jackson	.10	.02
❑ 118 Ray Agnew	.10	.02
❑ 119 Gill Byrd	.10	.02
❑ 120 Kyle Clifton	.10	.02
❑ 121 Marv Cook	.10	.02
❑ 122 Jerry Ball	.10	.02
❑ 123 Steve Jordan	.10	.02
❑ 124 Shannon Sharpe	.40	.15
❑ 125 Brian Blades	.20	.07
❑ 126 Rodney Hampton	.20	.07
❑ 127 Bobby Hebert	.10	.02
❑ 128 Jessie Tuggle	.10	.02
❑ 129 Tom Newberry	.10	.02
❑ 130 Keith McCants	.10	.02
❑ 131 Richard Dent	.20	.07
❑ 132 Herman Moore	.40	.15
❑ 133 Michael Irvin	.40	.15
❑ 134 Ernest Givins	.20	.07
❑ 135 Mark Rypien	.10	.02
❑ 136 Leonard Russell	.20	.07
❑ 137 Reggie White	.40	.15
❑ 138 Thurman Thomas	.40	.15
❑ 139 Nick Lowery	.10	.02
❑ 140 Al Smith	.10	.02
❑ 141 Jackie Harris	.10	.02
❑ 142 Duane Bickett	.10	.02
❑ 143 Lawyer Tillman	.10	.02
❑ 144 Steve Wisniewski	.10	.02
❑ 145 Derrick Fenner	.10	.02
❑ 146 Harris Barton	.10	.02
❑ 147 Rich Camarillo	.10	.02
❑ 148 John Offerdahl	.10	.02
❑ 149 Mike Johnson	.10	.02
❑ 150 Ricky Reynolds	.10	.02
❑ 151 Fred Barnett	.20	.07
❑ 152 Nate Newton	.20	.07
❑ 153 Chris Doleman	.10	.02
❑ 154 Todd Scott	.10	.02
❑ 155 Tim McKyer	.10	.02
❑ 156 Ken Harvey	.10	.02
❑ 157 Jeff Feagles	.10	.02
❑ 158 Vince Workman	.10	.02
❑ 159 Bart Oates	.10	.02
❑ 160 Chris Miller	.20	.07
❑ 161 Pete Stoyanovich	.10	.02
❑ 162 Steve Wallace	.10	.02
❑ 163 Dermontti Dawson	.10	.02
❑ 164 Kenneth Davis	.10	.02
❑ 165 Mike Munchak	.20	.07
❑ 166 George Jamison	.10	.02
❑ 167 Christian Okoye	.10	.02
❑ 168 Chris Hinton	.10	.02
❑ 169 Vaughan Johnson	.10	.02
❑ 170 Gaston Green	.10	.02
❑ 171 Kevin Greene	.20	.07
❑ 172 Rob Burnett	.10	.02
❑ 173 Norm Johnson	.10	.02
❑ 174 Eric Hill	.10	.02
❑ 175 Lomas Brown	.10	.02
❑ 176 Chip Banks	.10	.02
❑ 177 Greg Townsend	.10	.02
❑ 178 David Fulcher	.10	.02
❑ 179 Gary Anderson RB	.10	.02
❑ 180 Brian Washington	.10	.02
❑ 181 Brett Perriman	.40	.15
❑ 182 Chris Chandler	.20	.07
❑ 183 Phil Hansen	.10	.02
❑ 184 Mark Clayton	.10	.02
❑ 185 Frank Warren	.10	.02
❑ 186 Tim Brown	.40	.15
❑ 187 Mark Stepnoski	.10	.02
❑ 188 Bryan Cox	.10	.02
❑ 189 Gary Zimmerman	.10	.02
❑ 190 Neil O'Donnell	.40	.15
❑ 191 Anthony Smith	.10	.02
❑ 192 Craig Heyward	.20	.07
❑ 193 Keith Byars	.10	.02
❑ 194 Sean Salisbury	.10	.02
❑ 195 Todd Lyght	.10	.02
❑ 196 Jessie Hester	.10	.02
❑ 197 Rufus Porter	.10	.02
❑ 198 Steve Christie	.10	.02
❑ 199 Nate Lewis	.10	.02
❑ 200 Barry Sanders	2.00	.75
❑ 201 Michael Haynes	.20	.07
❑ 202 John Taylor	.20	.07
❑ 203 John Friesz	.20	.07
❑ 204 William Fuller	.10	.02
❑ 205 Dennis Smith	.10	.02
❑ 206 Adrian Cooper	.10	.02
❑ 207 Henry Thomas	.10	.02
❑ 208 Gerald Williams	.10	.02
❑ 209 Chris Burkett	.10	.02
❑ 210 Broderick Thomas	.10	.02
❑ 211 Marvin Washington	.10	.02
❑ 212 Bennie Blades	.10	.02
❑ 213 Tony Casillas	.10	.02
❑ 214 Bubby Brister	.10	.02
❑ 215 Don Griffin	.10	.02
❑ 216 Jeff Cross	.10	.02

❑ 217 Derrick Walker	.10	.02
❑ 218 Lorenzo White	.10	.02
❑ 219 Ricky Sanders	.10	.02
❑ 220 Rickey Jackson	.10	.02
❑ 221 Simon Fletcher	.10	.02
❑ 222 Troy Vincent	.10	.02
❑ 223 Gary Clark	.20	.07
❑ 224 Stanley Richard	.10	.02
❑ 225 Dave Krieg	.20	.07
❑ 226 Warren Moon	.40	.15
❑ 227 Reggie Langhorne	.10	.02
❑ 228 Kent Hull	.10	.02
❑ 229 Ferrell Edmunds	.10	.02
❑ 230 Cortez Kennedy	.20	.07
❑ 231 Hugh Millen	.10	.02
❑ 232 Eugene Chung	.10	.02
❑ 233 Rodney Peete	.10	.02
❑ 234 Tom Waddle	.10	.02
❑ 235 David Klingler	.10	.02
❑ 236 Mark Carrier WR	.20	.07
❑ 237 Jay Schroeder	.10	.02
❑ 238 James Jones DT	.10	.02
❑ 239 Phil Simms	.20	.07
❑ 240 Steve Atwater	.10	.02
❑ 241 Jeff Herrod	.10	.02
❑ 242 Dale Carter	.10	.02
❑ 243 Glenn Cadrez RC	.10	.02
❑ 244 Wayne Martin	.10	.02
❑ 245 Willie Davis	.40	.15
❑ 246 Lawrence Taylor	.40	.15
❑ 247 Stan Humphries	.20	.07
❑ 248 Byron Evans	.10	.02
❑ 249 Wilber Marshall	.10	.02
❑ 250 Michael Bankston RC	.10	.02
❑ 251 Steve McMichael	.20	.07
❑ 252 Brad Edwards	.10	.02
❑ 253 Will Wolford	.10	.02
❑ 254 Paul Gruber	.10	.02
❑ 255 Steve Young	1.25	.50
❑ 256 Chuck Cecil	.10	.02
❑ 257 Pierce Holt	.10	.02
❑ 258 Anthony Miller	.20	.07
❑ 259 Carl Banks	.10	.02
❑ 260 Brad Muster	.10	.02
❑ 261 Clay Matthews	.20	.07
❑ 262 Rod Bernstine	.10	.02
❑ 263 Tim Barnett	.10	.02
❑ 264 Greg Lloyd	.20	.07
❑ 265 Sean Jones	.10	.02
❑ 266 J.J. Birden	.10	.02
❑ 267 Tim McDonald	.10	.02
❑ 268 Charles Mann	.10	.02
❑ 269 Bruce Smith	.40	.15
❑ 270 Sean Gilbert	.20	.07
❑ 271 Ricardo McDonald	.10	.02
❑ 272 Jeff Hostetler	.20	.07
❑ 273 Russell Maryland	.10	.02
❑ 274 Dave Brown RC	.40	.15
❑ 275 Ronnie Lott	.20	.07
❑ 276 Jim Kelly	.40	.15
❑ 277 Joe Montana	2.50	1.00
❑ 278 Eric Allen	.10	.02
❑ 279 Browning Nagle	.10	.02
❑ 280 Neal Anderson	.10	.02
❑ 281 Troy Aikman	1.25	.50
❑ 282 Ed McCaffrey	.40	.15
❑ 283 Robert Jones	.10	.02
❑ 284 Dalton Hilliard	.10	.02
❑ 285 Johnny Mitchell	.10	.02
❑ 286 Jay Hilgenberg	.10	.02
❑ 287 Eric Martin	.10	.02
❑ 288 Steve Emtman	.10	.02
❑ 289 Vaughn Dunbar	.10	.02
❑ 290 Mark Wheeler	.10	.02
❑ 291 Leslie O'Neal	.20	.07
❑ 292 Jerry Rice	1.50	.60
❑ 293 Neil Smith	.40	.15
❑ 294 Kerry Cash	.10	.02
❑ 295 Dan McGwire	.10	.02
❑ 296 Carl Pickens	.20	.07
❑ 297 Terrell Buckley	.10	.02
❑ 298 Randall Cunningham	.40	.15
❑ 299 Santana Dotson	.20	.07
❑ 300 Keith Jackson	.20	.07
❑ 301 Jim Lachey	.10	.02
❑ 302 Dan Marino	2.50	1.00
❑ 303 Lee Williams	.10	.02
❑ 304 Burt Grossman	.10	.02
❑ 305 Kevin Mack	.10	.02
❑ 306 Pat Swilling	.10	.02
❑ 307 Arthur Marshall RC	.10	.02
❑ 308 Jim Harbaugh	.40	.15
❑ 309 Kurt Barber	.10	.02
❑ 310 Harvey Williams	.20	.07
❑ 311 Ricky Ervins	.10	.02
❑ 312 Flipper Anderson	.10	.02
❑ 313 Bernie Kosar	.20	.07
❑ 314 Boomer Esiason	.20	.07
❑ 315 Deion Sanders	.75	.30
❑ 316 Ray Childress	.10	.02
❑ 317 Howie Long	.40	.15
❑ 318 Henry Ellard	.20	.07
❑ 319 Marco Coleman	.10	.02
❑ 320 Chris Mims	.10	.02
❑ 321 Quentin Coryatt	.20	.07
❑ 322 Jason Hanson	.10	.02
❑ 323 Ricky Proehl	.10	.02
❑ 324 Randal Hill	.10	.02
❑ 325 Vinny Testaverde	.20	.07
❑ 326 Jeff George	.40	.15
❑ 327 Junior Seau	.40	.15
❑ 328 Earnest Byner	.10	.02
❑ 329 Andre Reed	.20	.07
❑ 330 Phillippi Sparks	.10	.02
❑ 331 Kevin Ross	.10	.02
❑ 332 Clarence Verdin	.10	.02
❑ 333 Darryl Henley	.10	.02
❑ 334 Dana Hall	.10	.02
❑ 335 Greg McMurtry	.10	.02
❑ 336 Ron Hall	.10	.02
❑ 337 Darrell Green	.10	.02
❑ 338 Carlton Bailey	.10	.02
❑ 339 Irv Eatman	.10	.02
❑ 340 Greg Kragen	.10	.02
❑ 341 Wade Wilson	.10	.02
❑ 342 Klaus Wilmsmeyer	.10	.02
❑ 343 Derek Brown TE	.10	.02
❑ 344 Erik Williams	.10	.02
❑ 345 Jim McMahon	.20	.07
❑ 346 Mike Sherrard	.10	.02
❑ 347 Mark Bavaro	.10	.02
❑ 348 Anthony Munoz	.20	.07
❑ 349 Eric Dickerson	.20	.07
❑ 350 Steve Beuerlein	.20	.07
❑ 351 Tim McGee	.10	.02
❑ 352 Terry McDaniel	.10	.02
❑ 353 Dan Fouts HOF	.10	.02
❑ 354 Chuck Noll HOF	.20	.07
❑ 355 Bill Walsh RC HOF	.20	.07
❑ 356 Larry Little HOF	.10	.02
❑ 357 Todd Marinovich HH	.10	.02
❑ 358 Jeff George HH	.40	.15
❑ 359 Bernie Kosar HH	.20	.07
❑ 360 Rob Moore HH	.20	.07
❑ NNO Franco Harris AU/3000	25.00	12.50

1994 Pinnacle

❑ COMPLETE SET (270)	20.00	8.00
❑ 1 Deion Sanders	.50	.20
❑ 2 Eric Metcalf	.20	.07
❑ 3 Barry Sanders	2.00	.75
❑ 4 Ernest Givins	.20	.07
❑ 5 Phil Simms	.20	.07
❑ 6 Rod Woodson	.20	.07
❑ 7 Michael Irvin	.40	.15
❑ 8 Cortez Kennedy	.20	.07
❑ 9 Eric Martin	.10	.02
❑ 10 Jeff Hostetler	.20	.07
❑ 11 Sterling Sharpe	.20	.07
❑ 12 John Elway	2.50	1.00
❑ 13 Neal Anderson	.10	.02
❑ 14 Terry Kirby	.40	.15
❑ 15 Jim Everett	.20	.07
❑ 16 Lawrence Dawsey	.10	.02
❑ 17 Kelvin Martin	.10	.02
❑ 18 Tim McGee	.10	.02
❑ 19 Cris Carter	.50	.20
❑ 20 Ronnie Harmon	.10	.02
❑ 21 Jim Kelly	.40	.15
❑ 22 Steve Young	1.00	.40
❑ 23 Johnny Johnson	.10	.02
❑ 24 Sean Gilbert	.10	.02
❑ 25 Brian Mitchell	.10	.02
❑ 26 Carl Pickens	.20	.07
❑ 27 Tim Brown	.40	.15
❑ 28 Reggie Langhorne	.10	.02
❑ 29 Webster Slaughter	.10	.02
❑ 30 Alvin Harper	.20	.07
❑ 31 Andre Rison	.20	.07
❑ 32 Derrick Thomas	.40	.15
❑ 33 Irving Fryar	.20	.07
❑ 34 Vinny Testaverde	.20	.07
❑ 35 Steve Beuerlein	.20	.07
❑ 36 Brett Favre	2.50	1.00
❑ 37 Barry Foster	.10	.02
❑ 38 Vaughan Johnson	.10	.02
❑ 39 Carlton Bailey	.10	.02
❑ 40 Steve Emtman	.10	.02
❑ 41 Anthony Miller	.20	.07
❑ 42 Jeff Cross	.10	.02
❑ 43 Trace Armstrong	.10	.02
❑ 44 Derek Russell	.10	.02
❑ 45 Vincent Brisby	.20	.07
❑ 46 Mark Jackson	.10	.02
❑ 47 Eugene Robinson	.10	.02
❑ 48 John Friesz	.20	.07
❑ 49 Scott Mitchell	.20	.07
❑ 50 Steve Atwater	.10	.02
❑ 51 Ken Norton	.20	.07
❑ 52 Vincent Brown	.10	.02
❑ 53 Morten Andersen	.10	.02
❑ 54 Gary Anderson K	.10	.02
❑ 55 Eric Curry	.10	.02
❑ 56 Henry Jones	.10	.02
❑ 57 Flipper Anderson	.10	.02
❑ 58 Pat Swilling	.10	.02
❑ 59 Erric Pegram	.10	.02
❑ 60 Bruce Matthews	.10	.02
❑ 61 Willie Davis	.20	.07
❑ 62 O.J.McDuffie	.40	.15
❑ 63 Qadry Ismail	.40	.15
❑ 64 Anthony Smith	.10	.02
❑ 65 Eric Allen	.10	.02
❑ 66 Marion Butts	.10	.02
❑ 67 Chris Miller	.10	.02
❑ 68 Terrell Buckley	.10	.02
❑ 69 Thurman Thomas	.40	.15
❑ 70 Roosevelt Potts	.10	.02
❑ 71 Tony McGee	.10	.02
❑ 72 Jason Hanson	.10	.02
❑ 73 Victor Bailey	.10	.02
❑ 74 Albert Lewis	.10	.02
❑ 75 Nate Odomes	.10	.02
❑ 76 Ben Coates	.20	.07
❑ 77 Warren Moon	.40	.15
❑ 78 Derek Brown RBK	.10	.02
❑ 79 David Klingler	.10	.02
❑ 80 Cleveland Gary	.10	.02
❑ 81 Emmitt Smith	2.00	.75
❑ 82 Jay Novacek	.20	.07
❑ 83 Dana Stubblefield	.20	.07
❑ 84 Michael Brooks	.10	.02
❑ 85 James Jett	.10	.02
❑ 86 J.J. Birden	.10	.02
❑ 87 William Fuller	.10	.02
❑ 88 Glyn Milburn	.20	.07
❑ 89 Tim Worley	.10	.02
❑ 90 Brett Perriman	.20	.07
❑ 91 Randall Cunningham	.40	.15
❑ 92 Drew Bledsoe	1.00	.40
❑ 93 Jerome Bettis	.60	.25
❑ 94 Boomer Esiason	.20	.07
❑ 95 Garrison Hearst	.40	.15
❑ 96 Bruce Smith	.40	.15
❑ 97 Jackie Harris	.10	.02
❑ 98 Jeff George	.40	.15
❑ 99 Tom Waddle	.10	.02
❑ 100 John Copeland	.10	.02
❑ 101 Bobby Hebert	.10	.02

- ❑ 102 Joe Montana 2.50 1.00
- ❑ 103 Herman Moore .40 .15
- ❑ 104 Rick Mirer .40 .15
- ❑ 105 Ricky Watters .20 .07
- ❑ 106 Neil O'Donnell .40 .15
- ❑ 107 Herschel Walker .20 .07
- ❑ 108 Rob Moore .20 .07
- ❑ 109 Reggie Brooks .20 .07
- ❑ 110 Tommy Vardell .10 .02
- ❑ 111 Eric Green .10 .02
- ❑ 112 Stan Humphries .20 .07
- ❑ 113 Greg Robinson .10 .02
- ❑ 114 Eric Swann .20 .07
- ❑ 115 Courtney Hawkins .10 .02
- ❑ [illegible]
- ❑ 117 Steve McMichael .20 .07
- ❑ 118 Gary Brown .10 .02
- ❑ 119 Terry Allen .20 .07
- ❑ 120 Dan Marino 2.50 1.00
- ❑ 121 Gary Clark .20 .07
- ❑ 122 Chris Warren .20 .07
- ❑ 123 Pierce Holt .10 .02
- ❑ 124 Anthony Carter .20 .07
- ❑ 125 Quentin Coryatt .10 .02
- ❑ 126 Harold Green .10 .02
- ❑ 127 Leonard Russell .10 .02
- ❑ 128 Tim McDonald .10 .02
- ❑ 129 Chris Spielman .20 .07
- ❑ 130 Cody Carlson .10 .02
- ❑ 131 Ronald Moore .10 .02
- ❑ 132 Renaldo Turnbull .10 .02
- ❑ 133 Ronnie Lott .20 .07
- ❑ 134 Natrone Means .40 .15
- ❑ 135 Keith Byars .10 .02
- ❑ 136 Henry Ellard .20 .07
- ❑ 137 Steve Jordan .10 .02
- ❑ 138 Calvin Williams .20 .07
- ❑ 139 Brian Blades .20 .07
- ❑ 140 Michael Jackson .20 .07
- ❑ 141 Charles Haley .20 .07
- ❑ 142 Curtis Conway .40 .15
- ❑ 143 Nick Lowery .10 .02
- ❑ 144 Bill Brooks .10 .02
- ❑ 145 Michael Haynes .20 .07
- ❑ 146 Willie Green .10 .02
- ❑ 147 Duane Bickett .10 .02
- ❑ 148 Shannon Sharpe .20 .07
- ❑ 149 Ricky Proehl .10 .02
- ❑ 150 Troy Aikman 1.25 .50
- ❑ 151 Mike Sherrard .10 .02
- ❑ 152 Reggie Cobb .10 .02
- ❑ 153 Norm Johnson .10 .02
- ❑ 154 Neil Smith .20 .07
- ❑ 155 James Francis .10 .02
- ❑ 156 Greg McMurtry .10 .02
- ❑ 157 Greg Townsend .10 [illegible]
- ❑ 158 Mel Gray .10 .02
- ❑ 159 Rocket Ismail .20 .07
- ❑ 160 Leslie O'Neal .10 .02
- ❑ 161 Johnny Mitchell .10 .02
- ❑ 162 Brent Jones .20 .07
- ❑ 163 Chris Doleman .10 .02
- ❑ 164 Seth Joyner .10 .02
- ❑ 165 Marco Coleman .10 .02
- ❑ 166 Mark Higgs .10 .02
- ❑ 167 John L. Williams .10 .02
- ❑ 168 Darrell Green .10 .02
- ❑ 169 Mark Carrier WR .20 .07
- ❑ 170 Reggie White .40 .15
- ❑ 171 Darryl Talley .10 .02
- ❑ 172 Russell Maryland .10 .02
- ❑ 173 Mark Collins .10 .02
- ❑ 174 Chris Jacke .10 .02
- ❑ 175 Richard Dent .20 .07
- ❑ 176 John Taylor .20 .07
- ❑ 177 Rodney Hampton .20 .07
- ❑ 178 Dwight Stone .10 .02
- ❑ 179 Cornelius Bennett .20 .07
- ❑ 180 Cris Dishman .10 .02
- ❑ 181 Jerry Rice 1.25 .50
- ❑ 182 Rod Bernstine .10 .02
- ❑ 183 Keith Hamilton .10 .02
- ❑ 184 Keith Jackson .10 .02
- ❑ 185 Craig Erickson .10 .02
- ❑ 186 Marcus Allen .40 .15
- ❑ 187 Marcus Robertson .10 .02
- ❑ 188 Junior Seau .40 .15
- ❑ 189 LeShon Johnson RC .20 .07
- ❑ 190 Perry Klein RC .10 .02
- ❑ 191 Bryant Young RC .60 .25
- ❑ 192 Byron Bam Morris RC .20 .07
- ❑ 193 Jeff Cothran RC .10 .02
- ❑ 194 Lamar Smith RC 1.50 .60
- ❑ 195 Calvin Jones RC .10 .02
- ❑ 196 James Bostic RC .40 .15
- ❑ 197 Dan Wilkinson RC .20 .07
- ❑ 198 Marshall Faulk RC 6.00 2.50
- ❑ 199 Heath Shuler RC .40 .15
- ❑ 200 Willie McGinest RC .40 .15
- ❑ 201 Trev Alberts RC .20 .07
- ❑ 202 Trent Dilfer RC 1.50 .60
- ❑ 203 Sam Adams RC .20 .07
- ❑ 204 Charles Johnson RC .40 .15
- ❑ [illegible]
- ❑ 206 Thomas Lewis RC .20 .07
- ❑ 207 Greg Hill RC .40 .15
- ❑ 208 William Floyd RC .40 .15
- ❑ 209 Derrick Alexander WR RC .40 .15
- ❑ 210 Darnay Scott RC .75 .30
- ❑ 211 Lake Dawson RC .20 .07
- ❑ 212 Errict Rhett RC .40 .15
- ❑ 213 Kevin Lee RC .10 .02
- ❑ 214 Chuck Levy RC .10 .02
- ❑ 215 David Palmer RC .40 .15
- ❑ 216 Ryan Yarborough RC .10 .02
- ❑ 217 Charlie Garner RC 1.50 .60
- ❑ 218 Mario Bates RC .40 .15
- ❑ 219 Jamir Miller RC .20 .07
- ❑ 220 Bucky Brooks RC .10 .02
- ❑ 221 Donnell Bennett RC .40 .15
- ❑ 222 Kevin Greene .20 .07
- ❑ 223 LeRoy Butler .10 .02
- ❑ 224 Anthony Pleasant .10 .02
- ❑ 225 Steve Christie .10 .02
- ❑ 226 Bill Romanowski .10 .02
- ❑ 227 Darren Carrington .10 .02
- ❑ 228 Chester McGlockton .10 .02
- ❑ 229 Jack Del Rio .10 .02
- ❑ 230 Kevin Smith .10 .02
- ❑ 231 Chris Zorich .10 .02
- ❑ 232 Donnell Woolford .10 .02
- ❑ 233 Tony Casillas .10 .02
- ❑ 234 Terry McDaniel .10 .02
- ❑ 235 Ray Childress .10 .02
- ❑ 236 John Randle .20 .07
- ❑ 237 Clyde Simmons .10 .02
- ❑ 238 Dante Jones .10 .02
- ❑ 239 Karl Mecklenburg .10 .02
- ❑ 240 Daryl Johnston .20 .07
- ❑ 241 Hardy Nickerson .20 .07
- ❑ 242 Jeff Lageman .10 .02
- ❑ 243 Lewis Tillman .10 .02
- ❑ 244 Jim McMahon .20 .07
- ❑ 245 Mike Pritchard .10 .02
- ❑ 246 [illegible] .07
- ❑ 247 Sean Jones .10 .02
- ❑ 248 Stevon Moore .10 .02
- ❑ 249 Pete Metzelaars .10 .02
- ❑ 250 Mike Johnson .10 .02
- ❑ 251 Chris Slade .10 .02
- ❑ 252 Jessie Hester .10 .02
- ❑ 253 Louis Oliver .10 .02
- ❑ 254 Ken Harvey .10 .02
- ❑ 255 Bryan Cox .10 .02
- ❑ 256 Erik Kramer .20 .07
- ❑ 257 Andy Harmon .10 .02
- ❑ 258 Rickey Jackson .10 .02
- ❑ 259 Mark Carrier DB .10 .02
- ❑ 260 Greg Lloyd .20 .07
- ❑ 261 Robert Brooks .40 .15
- ❑ 262 Dave Brown .20 .07
- ❑ 263 Dennis Smith .10 .02
- ❑ 264 Michael Dean Perry .20 .07
- ❑ 265 Dan Saleaumua .10 .02
- ❑ 266 Mo Lewis .10 .02
- ❑ 267 AFC Checklist .10 .02
- ❑ 268 AFC Checklist .10 .02
- ❑ 269 NFC Checklist .10 .02
- ❑ 270 NFC Checklist .10 .02
- ❑ 271SP Jerry Rice TD King SP 8.00 4.00
- ❑ NNO Drew Bledsoe Pin.Passer 40.00 15.00

1995 Pinnacle

- ❑ COMPLETE SET (250) 20.00 8.00
- ❑ 1 Reggie White .40 .15
- ❑ 2 Troy Aikman 1.00 .40
- ❑ 3 Willie Davis .20 .07
- ❑ 4 Jerry Rice 1.00 .40

- ❑ 5 Bruce Smith .40 .15
- ❑ 6 Keith Byars .10 .02
- ❑ 7 Chris Warren .20 .07
- ❑ 8 Erik Kramer .10 .02
- ❑ 9 Leon Lett .10 .02
- ❑ 10 Greg Lloyd .20 .07
- ❑ 11 Jackie Harris .10 .02
- ❑ 12 Irving Fryar .20 .07
- ❑ 13 Rodney Hampton .20 .07
- ❑ 14 Michael Irvin .40 .15
- ❑ 15 Michael Haynes .20 .07
- ❑ 16 Irving Spikes .20 .07
- ❑ 17 Calvin Williams .20 .07
- ❑ 18 Ken Norton Jr. .20 .07
- ❑ 19 Herman Moore .40 .15
- ❑ 20 Lewis Tillman .10 .02
- ❑ 21 Cortez Kennedy .20 .07
- ❑ 22 Dan Marino 2.00 .75
- ❑ 23 Erric Pegram .20 .07
- ❑ 24 Tim Brown .40 .15
- ❑ 25 Jeff Blake RC .75 .30
- ❑ 26 Brett Favre 2.00 .75
- ❑ 27 Garrison Hearst .40 .15
- ❑ 28 Ronnie Harmon .10 .02
- ❑ 29 Qadry Ismail .20 .07
- ❑ 30 Ben Coates .20 .07
- ❑ 31 Deion Sanders .60 .25
- ❑ 32 John Elway 2.00 .75
- ❑ 33 Natrone Means .20 .07
- ❑ 34 Derrick Alexander WR .40 .15
- ❑ 35 Craig Heyward .20 .07
- ❑ 36 Jake Reed .20 .07
- ❑ 37 Steve Walsh .10 .02
- ❑ 38 John Randle .20 .07
- ❑ 39 Barry Sanders 1.50 .60
- ❑ 40 Tydus Winans .10 .02
- ❑ 41 Thomas Lewis .20 .07
- ❑ 42 Jim Kelly .40 .15
- ❑ [illegible]
- ❑ 44 Cris Carter .40 .15
- ❑ 45 Kevin Williams WR .20 .07
- ❑ 46 Dave Meggett .10 .02
- ❑ 47 Pat Swilling .10 .02
- ❑ 48 Neil O'Donnell .20 .07
- ❑ 49 Terance Mathis .20 .07
- ❑ 50 Desmond Howard .20 .07
- ❑ 51 Bryant Young .20 .07
- ❑ 52 Stan Humphries .20 .07
- ❑ 53 Alvin Harper .10 .02
- ❑ 54 Henry Ellard .20 .07
- ❑ 55 Jessie Hester .10 .02
- ❑ 56 Lorenzo White .10 .02
- ❑ 57 John Friesz .20 .07
- ❑ 58 Anthony Smith .10 .02
- ❑ 59 Bert Emanuel .40 .15
- ❑ 60 Gary Clark .10 .02
- ❑ 61 Bill Brooks .10 .02
- ❑ 62 Steve Young .75 .30
- ❑ 63 Jerome Bettis .40 .15
- ❑ 64 John Taylor .10 .02
- ❑ 65 Ricky Proehl .10 .02
- ❑ 66 Junior Seau .40 .15
- ❑ 67 Bubby Brister .10 .02
- ❑ 68 Neil Smith .20 .07
- ❑ 69 Dan McGwire .10 .02
- ❑ 70 Brett Perriman .20 .07
- ❑ 71 Chris Spielman .20 .07
- ❑ 72 Jeff George .20 .07
- ❑ 73 Emmitt Smith 1.00 .40
- ❑ 74 Chris Penn .10 .02
- ❑ 75 Derrick Fenner .10 .02
- ❑ 76 Reggie Brooks .20 .07

❑ 77 Chris Chandler	.20	.07
❑ 78 Rod Woodson	.20	.07
❑ 79 Isaac Bruce	.60	.25
❑ 80 Reggie Cobb	.10	.02
❑ 81 Bryce Paup	.20	.07
❑ 82 Warren Moon	.20	.07
❑ 83 Bryan Reeves	.10	.02
❑ 84 Lake Dawson	.20	.07
❑ 85 Larry Centers	.20	.07
❑ 86 Marshall Faulk	1.25	.50
❑ 87 Jim Harbaugh	.20	.07
❑ 88 Ray Childress	.10	.02
❑ 89 Eric Metcalf	.20	.07
❑ 90 Ernie Mills	.10	.02
❑ 91 Lamar Lathon	.10	.02
❑ 92 Errict Rhett	.20	.07
❑ 93 David Klingler	.20	.07
❑ 94 Vincent Brown	.10	.02
❑ 95 Andre Rison	.20	.07
❑ 96 Brian Mitchell	.10	.02
❑ 97 Mark Rypien	.10	.02
❑ 98 Eugene Robinson	.10	.02
❑ 99 Eric Green	.10	.02
❑ 100 Rocket Ismail	.20	.07
❑ 101 Flipper Anderson	.10	.02
❑ 102 Randall Cunningham	.40	.15
❑ 103 Ricky Watters	.20	.07
❑ 104 Amp Lee	.10	.02
❑ 105 Ernest Givins	.10	.02
❑ 106 Daryl Johnston	.20	.07
❑ 107 Dave Krieg	.10	.02
❑ 108 Dana Stubblefield	.20	.07
❑ 109 Torrance Small	.10	.02
❑ 110 Yancey Thigpen RC	.20	.07
❑ 111 Chester McGlockton	.20	.07
❑ 112 Craig Erickson	.10	.02
❑ 113 Herschel Walker	.20	.07
❑ 114 Mike Sherrard	.10	.02
❑ 115 Tony McGee	.10	.02
❑ 116 Adrian Murrell	.20	.07
❑ 117 Frank Reich	.10	.02
❑ 118 Hardy Nickerson	.10	.02
❑ 119 Andre Reed	.20	.07
❑ 120 Leonard Russell	.10	.02
❑ 121 Eric Allen	.10	.02
❑ 122 Jeff Hostetler	.20	.07
❑ 123 Barry Foster	.20	.07
❑ 124 Anthony Miller	.20	.07
❑ 125 Shawn Jefferson	.10	.02
❑ 126 Richie Anderson RC	.50	.20
❑ 127 Steve Bono	.20	.07
❑ 128 Seth Joyner	.10	.02
❑ 129 Darnay Scott	.20	.07
❑ 130 Johnny Mitchell	.10	.02
❑ 131 Eric Swann	.20	.07
❑ 132 Drew Bledsoe	.60	.25
❑ 133 Marcus Allen	.40	.15
❑ 134 Carl Pickens	.20	.07
❑ 135 Michael Brooks	.10	.02
❑ 136 John L. Williams	.10	.02
❑ 137 Steve Beuerlein	.20	.07
❑ 138 Robert Smith	.40	.15
❑ 139 O.J. McDuffie	.40	.15
❑ 140 Haywood Jeffires	.10	.02
❑ 141 Aeneas Williams	.10	.02
❑ 142 Rick Mirer	.20	.07
❑ 143 William Floyd	.20	.07
❑ 144 Fred Barnett	.20	.07
❑ 145 Leroy Hoard	.10	.02
❑ 146 Terry Kirby	.20	.07
❑ 147 Boomer Esiason	.20	.07
❑ 148 Ken Harvey	.10	.02
❑ 149 Cleveland Gary	.10	.02
❑ 150 Brian Blades	.20	.07
❑ 151 Eric Turner	.10	.02
❑ 152 Vinny Testaverde	.20	.07
❑ 153 Ronald Moore UER	.10	.02
❑ 154 Curtis Conway	.40	.15
❑ 155 Johnnie Morton	.20	.07
❑ 156 Kenneth Davis	.10	.02
❑ 157 Scott Mitchell	.20	.07
❑ 158 Sean Gilbert	.20	.07
❑ 159 Shannon Sharpe	.20	.07
❑ 160 Mark Seay	.20	.07
❑ 161 Cornelius Bennett	.20	.07
❑ 162 Heath Shuler	.20	.07
❑ 163 Byron Bam Morris	.10	.02
❑ 164 Robert Brooks	.40	.15
❑ 165 Glyn Milburn	.10	.02

❑ 166 Gary Brown	.10	.02
❑ 167 Jim Everett	.10	.02
❑ 168 Steve Atwater	.10	.02
❑ 169 Darren Woodson	.20	.07
❑ 170 Mark Ingram	.10	.02
❑ 171 Donnell Woolford	.10	.02
❑ 172 Trent Dilfer	.40	.15
❑ 173 Charlie Garner	.40	.15
❑ 174 Charles Johnson	.20	.07
❑ 175 Mike Pritchard	.10	.02
❑ 176 Derek Brown RBK	.10	.02
❑ 177 Chris Miller	.10	.02
❑ 178 Charles Haley	.20	.07
❑ 179 J.J. Birden	.10	.02
❑ 180 Jeff Graham	.10	.02
❑ 181 Bernie Parmalee	.20	.07
❑ 182 Mark Brunell	.60	.25
❑ 183 Greg Hill	.20	.07
❑ 184 Michael Timpson	.10	.02
❑ 185 Terry Allen	.20	.07
❑ 186 Ricky Ervins	.10	.02
❑ 187 Dave Brown	.20	.07
❑ 188 Dan Wilkinson	.20	.07
❑ 189 Jay Novacek	.20	.07
❑ 190 Harvey Williams	.10	.02
❑ 191 Mario Bates	.20	.07
❑ 192 Steve Young LAW	.50	.20
❑ 193 Joe Montana	2.00	.75
❑ 194 Steve Young PP	.50	.20
❑ 195 Troy Aikman PP	.60	.25
❑ 196 Drew Bledsoe PP	.40	.15
❑ 197 Dan Marino PP	1.00	.40
❑ 198 John Elway PP	1.00	.40
❑ 199 Brett Favre PP	1.00	.40
❑ 200 Heath Shuler PP	.20	.07
❑ 201 Warren Moon PP	.10	.02
❑ 202 Jim Kelly PP	.40	.15
❑ 203 Jeff Hostetler PP	.20	.07
❑ 204 Rick Mirer PP	.20	.07
❑ 205 Dave Brown PP	.20	.07
❑ 206 Randall Cunningham PP	.20	.07
❑ 207 Neil O'Donnell PP	.20	.07
❑ 208 Jim Everett PP	.10	.02
❑ 209 Ki-Jana Carter RC	.40	.15
❑ 210 Steve McNair RC	3.00	1.25
❑ 211 Michael Westbrook RC	.40	.15
❑ 212 Kerry Collins RC	1.50	.60
❑ 213 Joey Galloway RC	1.50	.60
❑ 214 Kyle Brady RC	.40	.15
❑ 215 J.J. Stokes RC	.40	.15
❑ 216 Tyrone Wheatley RC	1.25	.50
❑ 217 Rashaan Salaam RC	.20	.07
❑ 218 Napoleon Kaufman RC	1.25	.50
❑ 219 Frank Sanders RC	.40	.15
❑ 220 Stoney Case RC	.10	.02
❑ 221 Todd Collins RC	1.25	.50
❑ 222 Warren Sapp RC	1.50	.60
❑ 223 Sherman Williams RC	.10	.02
❑ 224 Rob Johnson RC	1.00	.40
❑ 225 Mark Bruener RC	.20	.07
❑ 226 Derrick Brooks RC	1.50	.60
❑ 227 Chad May RC	.10	.02
❑ 228 James A.Stewart RC	.10	.02
❑ 229 Ray Zellars RC	.20	.07
❑ 230 Dave Barr RC	.10	.02
❑ 231 Kordell Stewart RC	1.50	.60
❑ 232 Jimmy Oliver RC	.10	.02
❑ 233 Tony Boselli RC	.40	.15
❑ 234 James O. Stewart RC	1.25	.50
❑ 235 Derrick Alexander DE RC	.10	.02
❑ 236 Lovell Pinkney RC	.10	.02
❑ 237 John Walsh RC	.10	.02
❑ 238 Tyrone Davis RC	.10	.02
❑ 239 Joe Aska RC	.10	.02
❑ 240 Korey Stringer RC	.20	.07
❑ 241 Hugh Douglas RC	.40	.15
❑ 242 Christian Fauria RC	.20	.07
❑ 243 Terrell Fletcher RC	.10	.02
❑ 244 Dan Marino CL	.60	.25
❑ 245 Drew Bledsoe CL	.40	.15
❑ 246 John Elway CL	.40	.15
❑ 247 Emmitt Smith CL	.50	.20
❑ 248 Steve Young CL	.40	.15
❑ 249 Barry Sanders CL	.60	.25
❑ 250 Jerry Rice/Seau CL	.40	.15
❑ 251SP Deion Sanders SP	4.00	1.50

1996 Pinnacle

❑ COMPLETE SET (200)	20.00	8.00
❑ 1 Emmitt Smith	1.50	.60
❑ 2 Robert Brooks	.40	.15
❑ 3 Joey Galloway	.40	.15
❑ 4 Dan Marino	2.00	.75
❑ 5 Frank Sanders	.20	.07
❑ 6 Cris Carter	.40	.15
❑ 7 Jeff Blake	.40	.15
❑ 8 Steve McNair	.75	.30
❑ 9 Tamarick Vanover	.20	.07
❑ 10 Andre Reed	.20	.07
❑ 11 Junior Seau	.40	.15
❑ 12 Alvin Harper	.10	.02
❑ 13 Trent Dilfer	.40	.15
❑ 14 Kordell Stewart	.40	.15
❑ 15 Kyle Brady	.10	.02
❑ 16 Charles Haley	.20	.07
❑ 17 Greg Lloyd	.20	.07
❑ 18 Mario Bates	.20	.07
❑ 19 Shannon Sharpe	.20	.07
❑ 20 Scott Mitchell	.20	.07
❑ 21 Craig Heyward	.10	.02
❑ 22 Marcus Allen	.40	.15
❑ 23 Curtis Martin	.75	.30
❑ 24 Drew Bledsoe	.60	.25
❑ 25 Jerry Rice	1.00	.40
❑ 26 Charlie Garner	.20	.07
❑ 27 Michael Irvin	.40	.15
❑ 28 Curtis Conway	.40	.15
❑ 29 Terrell Davis	.75	.30
❑ 30 Jeff Hostetler	.10	.02
❑ 31 Neil O'Donnell	.20	.07
❑ 32 Errict Rhett	.20	.07
❑ 33 Stan Humphries	.20	.07
❑ 34 Jeff Graham	.10	.02
❑ 35 Floyd Turner	.10	.02
❑ 36 Vincent Brisby	.10	.02
❑ 37 Steve Young	.75	.30
❑ 38 Carl Pickens	.20	.07
❑ 39 Terance Mathis	.10	.02
❑ 40 Brett Favre	2.00	.75
❑ 41 Ki-Jana Carter	.20	.07
❑ 42 Jim Everett	.10	.02
❑ 43 Marshall Faulk	.50	.20
❑ 44 William Floyd	.20	.07
❑ 45 Deion Sanders	.60	.25
❑ 46 Garrison Hearst	.20	.07
❑ 47 Chris Sanders	.20	.07
❑ 48 Isaac Bruce	.40	.15
❑ 49 Natrone Means	.20	.07
❑ 50 Troy Aikman	1.00	.40
❑ 51 Ben Coates	.20	.07
❑ 52 Tony Martin	.20	.07
❑ 53 Rod Woodson	.20	.07
❑ 54 Edgar Bennett	.20	.07
❑ 55 Eric Zeier	.10	.02
❑ 56 Steve Bono	.10	.02
❑ 57 Tim Brown	.40	.15
❑ 58 Kevin Williams	.10	.02
❑ 59 Erik Kramer	.10	.02
❑ 60 Jim Kelly	.40	.15
❑ 61 Larry Centers	.20	.07
❑ 62 Terrell Fletcher	.10	.02
❑ 63 Michael Westbrook	.40	.15
❑ 64 Kerry Collins	.40	.15
❑ 65 Jay Novacek	.10	.02
❑ 66 J.J. Stokes	.40	.15
❑ 67 John Elway	2.00	.75
❑ 68 Jim Harbaugh	.20	.07
❑ 69 Aeneas Williams	.10	.02

❑ 70 Tyrone Wheatley	.20	.07
❑ 71 Chris Warren	.20	.07
❑ 72 Rodney Thomas	.10	.02
❑ 73 Jeff George	.20	.07
❑ 74 Rick Mirer	.20	.07
❑ 75 Yancey Thigpen	.20	.07
❑ 76 Herman Moore	.20	.07
❑ 77 Gus Frerotte	.20	.07
❑ 78 Anthony Miller	.20	.07
❑ 79 Ricky Watters	.20	.07
❑ 80 Sherman Williams	.10	.02
❑ 81 Hardy Nickerson	.10	.02
❑ 82 Henry Ellard	.10	.02
❑ 83 Aaron Craver	.10	.02
❑ 84 Rodney Peete	.10	.02
❑ 85 Eric Metcalf	.10	.02
❑ 86 Brian Blades	.10	.02
❑ 87 Rob Moore	.20	.07
❑ 88 Kimble Anders	.20	.07
❑ 89 Harvey Williams	.10	.02
❑ 90 Thurman Thomas	.40	.15
❑ 91 Dave Brown	.10	.02
❑ 92 Terry Allen	.20	.07
❑ 93 Ken Norton Jr.	.10	.02
❑ 94 Reggie White	.40	.15
❑ 95 Mark Chmura	.20	.07
❑ 96 Bert Emanuel	.20	.07
❑ 97 Brett Perriman	.10	.02
❑ 98 Antonio Freeman	.40	.15
❑ 99 Brian Mitchell	.10	.02
❑ 100 Orlando Thomas	.10	.02
❑ 101 Aaron Hayden	.10	.02
❑ 102 Quinn Early	.10	.02
❑ 103 Lovell Pinkney	.10	.02
❑ 104 Napoleon Kaufman	.40	.15
❑ 105 Daryl Johnston	.20	.07
❑ 106 Steve Tasker	.10	.02
❑ 107 Brent Jones	.10	.02
❑ 108 Mark Brunell	.60	.25
❑ 109 Leslie O'Neal	.10	.02
❑ 110 Irving Fryar	.20	.07
❑ 111 Jim Miller	.40	.15
❑ 112 Sean Dawkins	.10	.02
❑ 113 Boomer Esiason	.20	.07
❑ 114 Heath Shuler	.20	.07
❑ 115 Bruce Smith	.20	.07
❑ 116 Russell Maryland	.10	.02
❑ 117 Jake Reed	.20	.07
❑ 118 O.J. McDuffie	.20	.07
❑ 119 Erik Williams	.10	.02
❑ 120 Willie McGinest	.10	.02
❑ 121 Terry Kirby	.20	.07
❑ 122 Fred Barnett	.10	.02
❑ 123 Andre Hastings	.10	.02
❑ 124 Dale Hellestrae	.10	.02
❑ 125 Darren Woodson	.20	.07
❑ 126 Steve Atwater	.10	.02
❑ 127 Quentin Coryatt	.10	.02
❑ 128 Derrick Thomas	.40	.15
❑ 129 Nate Newton	.10	.02
❑ 130 Kevin Greene	.20	.07
❑ 131 Barry Sanders	1.50	.60
❑ 132 Warren Moon	.20	.07
❑ 133 Rashaan Salaam	.20	.07
❑ 134 Rodney Hampton	.20	.07
❑ 135 James O.Stewart	.20	.07
❑ 136 Erric Pegram	.10	.02
❑ 137 Bryan Cox	.10	.02
❑ 138 Adrian Murrell	.20	.07
❑ 139 Robert Smith	.20	.07
❑ 140 Bernie Parmalee	.10	.02
❑ 141 Bryce Paup	.10	.02
❑ 142 Darick Holmes	.10	.02
❑ 143 Hugh Douglas	.20	.07
❑ 144 Ken Dilger	.20	.07
❑ 145 Derek Loville	.10	.02
❑ 146 Horace Copeland	.10	.02
❑ 147 Wayne Chrebet	.60	.25
❑ 148 Andre Coleman	.10	.02
❑ 149 Greg Hill	.20	.07
❑ 150 Eric Swann	.10	.02
❑ 151 Tyrone Hughes	.10	.02
❑ 152 Ernie Mills	.10	.02
❑ 153 Terry Glenn RC	1.25	.50
❑ 154 Cedric Jones RC	.10	.02
❑ 155 Leeland McElroy RC	.20	.07
❑ 156 Bobby Engram RC	.40	.15
❑ 157 Willie Anderson RC	.10	.02
❑ 158 Mike Alstott RC	1.25	.50

❑ 159 Alex Van Dyke RC	.20	.07
❑ 160 Jeff Lewis RC	.20	.07
❑ 161 Keyshawn Johnson RC	1.25	.50
❑ 162 Regan Upshaw RC	.10	.02
❑ 163 Eric Moulds RC	1.50	.60
❑ 164 Tim Biakabutuka RC	.40	.15
❑ 165 Kevin Hardy RC	.40	.15
❑ 166 Marvin Harrison RC	3.00	1.25
❑ 167 Karim Abdul-Jabbar RC	.40	.15
❑ 168 Tony Brackens RC	.40	.15
❑ 169 Stepfret Williams RC	.20	.07
❑ 170 Eddie George RC	1.50	.60
❑ 171 Lawrence Phillips RC	.40	.15
❑ 172 Danny Kanell RC	.40	.15
❑ 173 Derrick Mayes RC	.40	.15
❑ 174 Daryl Gardener RC	.10	.02
❑ 175 Jonathan Ogden RC	.40	.15
❑ 176 Alex Molden RC	.10	.02
❑ 177 Chris Darkins RC	.10	.02
❑ 178 Stephen Davis RC	2.00	.75
❑ 179 Rickey Dudley RC	.40	.15
❑ 180 Eddie Kennison RC	.40	.15
❑ 181 Simeon Rice RC	1.00	.40
❑ 182 Bobby Hoying RC	.40	.15
❑ 183 Troy Aikman BF6	.50	.20
❑ 184 Emmitt Smith BF6	1.00	.40
❑ 185 Michael Irvin BF6	.20	.07
❑ 186 Deion Sanders BF6	.40	.15
❑ 187 Daryl Johnston BF6	.20	.07
❑ 188 Jay Novacek BF6	.10	.02
❑ 189 Steve Young BF6	.40	.15
❑ 190 Jerry Rice BF6	.50	.20
❑ 191 J.J. Stokes BF6	.40	.15
❑ 192 Ken Norton BF6	.10	.02
❑ 193 William Floyd BF6	.20	.07
❑ 194 Brent Jones BF6	.10	.02
❑ 195 Dan Marino CL	.40	.15
❑ 196 Brett Favre CL	.40	.15
❑ 197 Emmitt Smith CL	.40	.15
❑ 198 Barry Sanders CL	.40	.15
❑ 199 ESmith/Mar/Fav/BSand CL	.40	.15
❑ 200 Brett Favre PackBack	2.00	.75

1997 Pinnacle

❑ COMPLETE SET (200)	20.00	7.50
❑ 1 Brett Favre	2.00	.75
❑ 2 Dan Marino	2.00	.75
❑ 3 Emmitt Smith	1.50	.60
❑ 4 Steve Young	.60	.25
❑ 5 Drew Bledsoe	.60	.25
❑ 6 Eddie George	.50	.20
❑ 7 Barry Sanders	1.50	.60
❑ 8 Jerry Rice	1.00	.40
❑ 9 John Elway	2.00	.75
❑ 10 Troy Aikman	1.00	.40
❑ 11 Kerry Collins	.50	.20
❑ 12 Rick Mirer	.20	.07
❑ 13 Jim Harbaugh	.30	.10
❑ 14 Elvis Grbac	.30	.10
❑ 15 Gus Frerotte	.20	.07
❑ 16 Neil O'Donnell	.30	.10
❑ 17 Jeff George	.30	.10
❑ 18 Kordell Stewart	.50	.20
❑ 19 Junior Seau	.50	.20
❑ 20 Vinny Testaverde	.30	.10
❑ 21 Terry Glenn	.50	.20
❑ 22 Anthony Johnson	.20	.07
❑ 23 Boomer Esiason	.30	.10
❑ 24 Terrell Owens	.60	.25
❑ 25 Natrone Means	.30	.10
❑ 26 Marcus Allen	.50	.20

❑ 27 James Jett	.30	.10
❑ 28 Chris T. Jones	.20	.07
❑ 29 Stan Humphries	.30	.10
❑ 30 Keith Byars	.20	.07
❑ 31 John Friesz	.20	.07
❑ 32 Mike Alstott	.50	.20
❑ 33 Eddie Kennison	.30	.10
❑ 34 Eric Moulds	.50	.20
❑ 35 Frank Sanders	.30	.10
❑ 36 Daryl Johnston	.30	.10
❑ 37 Cris Carter	.50	.20
❑ 38 Errict Rhett	.20	.07
❑ 39 Ben Coates	.30	.10
❑ 40 Shannon Sharpe	.30	.10
❑ 41 Jamal Anderson	.50	.20
❑ 42 Tim Biakabutuka	.30	.10
❑ 43 Jeff Blake	.30	.10
❑ 44 Michael Irvin	.50	.20
❑ 45 Terrell Davis	.60	.25
❑ 46 Byron Bam Morris	.20	.07
❑ 47 Rashaan Salaam	.20	.07
❑ 48 Adrian Murrell	.30	.10
❑ 49 Ty Detmer	.30	.10
❑ 50 Terry Allen	.50	.20
❑ 51 Mark Brunell	.60	.25
❑ 52 O.J. McDuffie	.30	.10
❑ 53 Willie McGinest	.20	.07
❑ 54 Chris Warren	.30	.10
❑ 55 Trent Dilfer	.50	.20
❑ 56 Jerome Bettis	.50	.20
❑ 57 Tamarick Vanover	.30	.10
❑ 58 Ki-Jana Carter	.20	.07
❑ 59 Ray Zellars	.20	.07
❑ 60 J.J. Stokes	.30	.10
❑ 61 Cornelius Bennett	.20	.07
❑ 62 Scott Mitchell	.30	.10
❑ 63 Tyrone Wheatley	.30	.10
❑ 64 Steve McNair	.60	.25
❑ 65 Tony Banks	.30	.10
❑ 66 James O.Stewart	.30	.10
❑ 67 Robert Smith	.30	.10
❑ 68 Thurman Thomas	.50	.20
❑ 69 Mark Chmura	.30	.10
❑ 70 Napoleon Kaufman	.50	.20
❑ 71 Ken Norton	.20	.07
❑ 72 Herschel Walker	.30	.10
❑ 73 Joey Galloway	.30	.10
❑ 74 Neil Smith	.30	.10
❑ 75 Simeon Rice	.30	.10
❑ 76 Michael Jackson	.30	.10
❑ 77 Muhsin Muhammad	.30	.10
❑ 78 Kevin Hardy	.20	.07
❑ 79 Irving Fryar	.30	.10
❑ 80 Jeff Hostetler	.20	.07
❑ 81 Eric Swann	.20	.07
❑ 82 Jim Everett	.20	.07
❑ 83 Karim Abdul-Jabbar	.50	.20
❑ 84 Garrison Hearst	.30	.10
❑ 85 Lawrence Phillips	.20	.07
❑ 86 Bryan Cox	.20	.07
❑ 87 Larry Centers	.30	.10
❑ 88 Wesley Walls	.30	.10
❑ 89 Curtis Conway	.30	.10
❑ 90 Darnay Scott	.30	.10
❑ 91 Anthony Miller	.20	.07
❑ 92 Edgar Bennett	.30	.10
❑ 93 Willie Green	.20	.07
❑ 94 Kent Graham	.20	.07
❑ 95 Dave Brown	.20	.07
❑ 96 Wayne Chrebet	.50	.20
❑ 97 Ricky Watters	.30	.10
❑ 98 Tony Martin	.30	.10
❑ 99 Warren Moon	.50	.20
❑ 100 Curtis Martin	.60	.25
❑ 101 Dorsey Levens	.50	.20
❑ 102 Jim Pyne	.20	.07
❑ 103 Antonio Freeman	.50	.20
❑ 104 Leeland McElroy	.20	.07
❑ 105 Isaac Bruce	.50	.20
❑ 106 Chris Sanders	.20	.07
❑ 107 Tim Brown	.50	.20
❑ 108 Greg Lloyd	.20	.07
❑ 109 Terrell Buckley	.20	.07
❑ 110 Deion Sanders	.50	.20
❑ 111 Carl Pickens	.30	.10
❑ 112 Bobby Engram	.30	.10
❑ 113 Andre Reed	.30	.10
❑ 114 Terance Mathis	.30	.10
❑ 115 Herman Moore	.30	.10

❑	116 Robert Brooks	.30	.10
❑	117 Ken Dilger	.20	.07
❑	118 Keenan McCardell	.30	.10
❑	119 Andre Hastings	.20	.07
❑	120 Willie Davis	.20	.07
❑	121 Bruce Smith	.30	.10
❑	122 Rob Moore	.30	.10
❑	123 Johnnie Morton	.30	.10
❑	124 Sean Dawkins	.20	.07
❑	125 Mario Bates	.20	.07
❑	126 Henry Ellard	.20	.07
❑	127 Derrick Alexander WR	.30	.10
❑	128 Kevin Greene	.30	.10
❑	129 Derrick Thomas	.50	.20
❑	130 Rod Woodson	.30	.10
❑	131 Rodney Hampton	.30	.10
❑	132 Marshall Faulk	.60	.25
❑	133 Michael Westbrook	.30	.10
❑	134 Erik Kramer	.20	.07
❑	135 Todd Collins	.20	.07
❑	136 Bill Romanowski	.20	.07
❑	137 Jake Reed	.30	.10
❑	138 Heath Shuler	.20	.07
❑	139 Keyshawn Johnson	.50	.20
❑	140 Marvin Harrison	.50	.20
❑	141 Andre Rison	.30	.10
❑	142 Zach Thomas	.50	.20
❑	143 Eric Metcalf	.30	.10
❑	144 Amani Toomer	.30	.10
❑	145 Desmond Howard	.30	.10
❑	146 Jimmy Smith	.30	.10
❑	147 Brad Johnson	.50	.20
❑	148 Troy Vincent	.20	.07
❑	149 Bryce Paup	.20	.07
❑	150 Reggie White	.50	.20
❑	151 Jake Plummer RC	2.50	1.00
❑	152 Darnell Autry RC	.30	.10
❑	153 Tiki Barber RC	3.00	1.25
❑	154 Pat Barnes RC	.50	.20
❑	155 Orlando Pace RC	.50	.20
❑	156 Peter Boulware RC	.50	.20
❑	157 Shawn Springs RC	.30	.10
❑	158 Troy Davis RC	.30	.10
❑	159 Ike Hilliard RC	.75	.30
❑	160 Jim Druckenmiller RC	.30	.10
❑	161 Warrick Dunn RC	1.50	.50
❑	162 James Farrior RC	.50	.20
❑	163 Tony Gonzalez RC	1.50	.60
❑	164 Darrell Russell RC	.20	.07
❑	165 Byron Hanspard RC	.30	.10
❑	166 Corey Dillon RC	3.00	1.25
❑	167 Kenny Holmes RC	.50	.20
❑	168 Walter Jones RC	.50	.20
❑	169 Danny Wuerffel RC	.50	.20
❑	170 Tom Knight RC	.20	.07
❑	171 David LaFleur RC	.20	.07
❑	172 Kevin Lockett RC	.30	.10
❑	173 Will Blackwell RC	.30	.10
❑	174 Reidel Anthony RC	.50	.20
❑	175 Dwayne Rudd RC	.50	.20
❑	176 Yatil Green RC	.30	.10
❑	177 Antowain Smith RC	1.25	.50
❑	178 Rae Carruth RC	.20	.07
❑	179 Bryant Westbrook RC	.20	.07
❑	180 Reinard Wilson RC	.30	.10
❑	181 Joey Kent RC	.50	.20
❑	182 Renaldo Wynn RC	.20	.07
❑	183 Brett Favre I	1.00	.40
❑	184 Emmitt Smith I	.75	.30
❑	185 Dan Marino I	1.00	.40
❑	186 Troy Aikman I	.50	.20
❑	187 Jerry Rice I	.50	.20
❑	188 Drew Bledsoe I	.30	.10
❑	189 Eddie George I	.50	.20
❑	190 Terry Glenn I	.30	.10
❑	191 John Elway I	1.00	.40
❑	192 Steve Young I	.30	.10
❑	193 Mark Brunell I	.50	.20
❑	194 Barry Sanders I	.75	.30
❑	195 Kerry Collins I	.30	.10
❑	196 Curtis Martin I	.50	.20
❑	197 Terrell Davis I	.50	.20
❑	198 Bledsoe/KCollins/Marino CL	.50	.20
❑	199 SYoung/Brunell/JGeorge CL	.20	.07
❑	200 Aikman/Elway/Mirer CL	.20	.07

1992 Playoff

❑	COMPLETE SET (150)	25.00	10.00
❑	1 Emmitt Smith	8.00	4.00
❑	2 Steve Young	3.00	1.50
❑	3 Jack Del Rio	.25	.08
❑	4 Bobby Hebert	.25	.08
❑	5 Shannon Sharpe	.75	.30
❑	6 Gary Clark	.75	.30
❑	7 Christian Okoye	.25	.08
❑	8 Ernest Givins	.40	.15
❑	9 Mike Horan	.25	.08
❑	10 Dennis Gentry	.25	.08
❑	11 Michael Irvin	.75	.30
❑	12 Eric Floyd	.25	.08
❑	13 Brent Jones	.40	.15
❑	14 Anthony Carter	.40	.15
❑	15 Tony Martin	.40	.15
❑	16 Greg Lewis UER	.25	.08
❑	17 Todd McNair	.25	.08
❑	18 Earnest Byner	.25	.08
❑	19 Steve Beuerlein	.40	.15
❑	20 Roger Craig	.40	.15
❑	21 Mark Higgs	.25	.08
❑	22 Guy McIntyre	.25	.08
❑	23 Don Warren	.25	.08
❑	24 Alvin Harper	.40	.15
❑	25 Mark Jackson	.25	.08
❑	26 Chris Doleman	.25	.08
❑	27 Jesse Sapolu	.25	.08
❑	28 Tony Tolbert	.25	.08
❑	29 Wendell Davis	.25	.08
❑	30 Dan Saleaumua	.25	.08
❑	31 Jeff Bostic	.25	.08
❑	32 Jay Novacek	.40	.15
❑	33 Cris Carter	1.00	.40
❑	34 Tony Paige	.25	.08
❑	35 Greg Kragen	.25	.08
❑	36 Jeff Dellenbach	.25	.08
❑	37 Keith DeLong	.25	.08
❑	38 Todd Scott	.25	.08
❑	39 Jeff Feagles	.25	.08
❑	40 Mike Saxon	.25	.08
❑	41 Martin Mayhew	.25	.08
❑	42 Steve Bono RC	.75	.30
❑	43 Willie Davis WR RC	.40	.15
❑	44 Mark Stepnoski	.40	.15
❑	45 Harry Newsome	.25	.08
❑	46 Thane Gash	.25	.08
❑	47 Gaston Green	.25	.08
❑	48 James Washington	.25	.08
❑	49 Kenny Walker	.25	.08
❑	50 Jeff Davidson RC	.25	.08
❑	51 Shane Conlan	.25	.08
❑	52 Richard Dent	.40	.15
❑	53 Haywood Jeffires	.40	.15
❑	54 Harry Galbreath	.25	.08
❑	55 Terry Allen	.75	.30
❑	56 Tommy Barnhardt	.25	.08
❑	57 Mike Golic	.25	.08
❑	58 Dalton Hilliard	.25	.08
❑	59 Danny Copeland	.25	.08
❑	60 Jerry Fontenot RC	.25	.08
❑	61 Kelvin Martin	.25	.08
❑	62 Mark Kelso	.25	.08
❑	63 Wymon Henderson	.25	.08
❑	64 Mark Rypien	.25	.08
❑	65 Bobby Humphrey	.25	.08
❑	66 Rich Gannon UER	.75	.30
❑	67 Darren Lewis	.25	.08
❑	68 Barry Foster	.40	.15
❑	69 Ken Norton Jr.	.40	.15
❑	70 James Lofton	.40	.15
❑	71 Trace Armstrong	.25	.08
❑	72 Vestee Jackson	.25	.08
❑	73 Clyde Simmons	.25	.08
❑	74 Brad Muster	.25	.08
❑	75 Cornelius Bennett	.40	.15
❑	76 Mike Merriweather	.25	.08
❑	77 John Elway	4.00	1.50
❑	78 Herschel Walker	.40	.15
❑	79 Hassan Jones UER	.25	.08
❑	80 Jim Harbaugh	.75	.30
❑	81 Issiac Holt	.25	.08
❑	82 David Alexander	.25	.08
❑	83 Brian Mitchell	.40	.15
❑	84 Mark Tuinei	.25	.08
❑	85 Tom Rathman	.25	.08
❑	86 Reggie White	.75	.30
❑	87 William Perry	.40	.15
❑	88 Jeff Wright	.25	.08
❑	89 Keith Kartz	.25	.08
❑	90 Andre Waters	.25	.08
❑	91 Darryl Talley	.25	.08
❑	92 Morten Andersen	.25	.08
❑	93 Tom Waddle	.25	.08
❑	94 Felix Wright UER	.25	.08
❑	95 Keith Jackson	.40	.15
❑	96 Art Monk	.40	.15
❑	97 Seth Joyner	.25	.08
❑	98 Steve McMichael	.40	.15
❑	99 Thurman Thomas	.75	.30
❑	100 Warren Moon	.75	.30
❑	101 Tony Casillas	.25	.08
❑	102 Vance Johnson	.25	.08
❑	103 Doug Dawson RC	.25	.08
❑	104 Bill Maas	.25	.08
❑	105 Mark Clayton	.40	.15
❑	106 Hoby Brenner	.25	.08
❑	107 Gary Anderson K	.25	.08
❑	108 Marc Logan	.25	.08
❑	109 Ricky Sanders	.25	.08
❑	110 Vai Sikahema	.25	.08
❑	111 Neil Smith	.75	.30
❑	112 Cody Carlson	.25	.08
❑	113 Jimmie Jones	.25	.08
❑	114 Pat Swilling	.25	.08
❑	115 Neil O'Donnell	.40	.15
❑	116 Chip Lohmiller	.25	.08
❑	117 Mike Croel	.25	.08
❑	118 Pete Metzelaars	.25	.08
❑	119 Ray Childress	.25	.08
❑	120 Fred Banks	.25	.08
❑	121 Derek Kennard	.25	.08
❑	122 Daryl Johnston	.75	.30
❑	123 Lorenzo White UER	.25	.08
❑	124 Hardy Nickerson	.40	.15
❑	125 Derrick Thomas	.75	.30
❑	126 Steve Walsh	.25	.08
❑	127 Doug Widell	.25	.08
❑	128 Calvin Williams	.40	.15
❑	129 Tim Harris	.25	.08
❑	130 Rod Woodson	.75	.30
❑	131 Craig Heyward	.40	.15
❑	132 Barry Word	.25	.08
❑	133 Mark Duper	.25	.08
❑	134 Tim Johnson	.25	.08
❑	135 John Gesek	.25	.08
❑	136 Steve Jackson	.25	.08
❑	137 Dave Krieg	.40	.15
❑	138 Barry Sanders	4.00	1.50
❑	139 Michael Haynes	.40	.15
❑	140 Eric Metcalf	.40	.15
❑	141 Stan Humphries	.75	.30
❑	142 Sterling Sharpe	.75	.30
❑	143 Todd Marinovich	.25	.08
❑	144 Rodney Hampton	.40	.15
❑	145 Rodney Peete	.40	.15
❑	146 Darryl Williams RC	.25	.08
❑	147 Darren Perry RC	.25	.08
❑	148 Terrell Buckley RC	.25	.08
❑	149 Amp Lee RC	.25	.08
❑	150 Ricky Watters	.75	.30

1993 Playoff

❑ COMPLETE SET (315)	25.00	10.00
❑ 1 Troy Aikman	1.50	.60
❑ 2 Jerry Rice	2.00	.75
❑ 3 Keith Jackson	.20	.07
❑ 4 Sean Gilbert	.20	.07
❑ 5 Jim Kelly	.40	.15
❑ 6 Junior Seau	.40	.15
❑ 7 Deion Sanders	1.00	.40
❑ 8 Joe Montana	3.00	1.25
❑ 9 Terrell Buckley	.10	.02
❑ 10 Emmitt Smith	3.00	1.25
❑ 11 Pete Stoyanovich	.10	.02
❑ 12 Randall Cunningham	.40	.15
❑ 13 Boomer Esiason	.20	.07
❑ 14 Mike Saxon	.10	.02
❑ 15 Chuck Cecil	.10	.02
❑ 16 Vinny Testaverde	.20	.07
❑ 17 Jeff Hostetler	.20	.07
❑ 18 Mark Clayton	.10	.02
❑ 19 Nick Bell	.10	.02
❑ 20 Frank Reich	.20	.07
❑ 21 Henry Ellard	.20	.07
❑ 22 Andre Reed	.20	.07
❑ 23 Mark Ingram	.10	.02
❑ 24 Mike Brim	.10	.02
❑ 25A Bernie Kosar ERR Kozar	.20	.07
❑ 25B Bernie Kosar COR	.20	.07
❑ 26 Jeff George	.40	.15
❑ 27 Tommy Maddox	.40	.15
❑ 28 Kent Graham RC	.40	.15
❑ 29 David Klingler	.10	.02
❑ 30 Robert Delpino	.10	.02
❑ 31 Kevin Fagan	.10	.02
❑ 32 Mark Bavaro	.10	.02
❑ 33 Harold Green	.10	.02
❑ 34 Shawn McCarthy	.10	.02
❑ 35 Ricky Proehl	.10	.02
❑ 36 Eugene Robinson	.10	.02
❑ 37 Phil Simms	.20	.07
❑ 38 David Lang	.10	.02
❑ 39 Santana Dotson	.20	.07
❑ 40 Brett Perriman	.40	.15
❑ 41 Jim Harbaugh	.40	.15
❑ 42 Keith Byars	.10	.02
❑ 43 Quentin Coryatt	.20	.07
❑ 44 Louis Oliver	.10	.02
❑ 45 Howie Long	.40	.15
❑ 46 Mike Sherrard	.10	.02
❑ 47 Earnest Byner	.10	.02
❑ 48 Neil Smith	.40	.15
❑ 49 Audray McMillian	.10	.02
❑ 50 Vaughn Dunbar	.10	.02
❑ 51 Ronnie Lott	.20	.07
❑ 52 Clyde Simmons	.10	.02
❑ 53 Kevin Scott	.10	.02
❑ 54 Bubby Brister	.10	.02
❑ 55 Randal Hill	.10	.02
❑ 56 Pat Swilling	.10	.02
❑ 57 Steve Beuerlein	.20	.07
❑ 58 Gary Clark	.20	.07
❑ 59 Brian Noble	.10	.02
❑ 60 Leslie O'Neal	.20	.07
❑ 61 Vincent Brown	.10	.02
❑ 62 Edgar Bennett	.40	.15
❑ 63 Anthony Carter	.20	.07
❑ 64 Glenn Cadrez RC UER	.10	.02
❑ 65 Dalton Hilliard	.10	.02
❑ 66 James Lofton	.20	.07
❑ 67 Walter Stanley	.10	.02
❑ 68 Tim Harris	.10	.02
❑ 69 Carl Banks	.10	.02
❑ 70 Andre Ware	.10	.02
❑ 71 Karl Mecklenburg	.10	.02
❑ 72 Russell Maryland	.10	.02
❑ 73 Leroy Thompson	.10	.02
❑ 74 Tommy Kane	.10	.02
❑ 75 Dan Marino	3.00	1.25
❑ 76 Darrell Fullington	.10	.02
❑ 77 Jessie Tuggle	.10	.02
❑ 78 Bruce Smith	.40	.15
❑ 79 Neal Anderson	.10	.02
❑ 80 Kevin Mack	.10	.02
❑ 81 Shane Dronett	.10	.02
❑ 82 Nick Lowery	.10	.02
❑ 83 Sheldon White	.10	.02
❑ 84 Flipper Anderson	.10	.02
❑ 85 Jeff Herrod	.10	.02
❑ 86 Dwight Stone	.10	.02
❑ 87 Dave Krieg	.20	.07
❑ 88 Bryan Cox	.10	.02
❑ 89 Greg McMurtry	.10	.02
❑ 90 Rickey Jackson	.10	.02
❑ 91 Ernie Mills	.10	.02
❑ 92 Browning Nagle	.10	.02
❑ 93 John Taylor	.20	.07
❑ 94 Eric Dickerson	.20	.07
❑ 95 Johnny Holland	.10	.02
❑ 96 Anthony Miller	.20	.07
❑ 97 Fred Barnett	.20	.07
❑ 98 Ricky Ervins UER	.10	.02
❑ 99 Leonard Russell	.20	.07
❑ 100 Lawrence Taylor	.40	.15
❑ 101 Tony Casillas	.10	.02
❑ 102 John Elway	3.00	1.25
❑ 103 Bennie Blades	.10	.02
❑ 104 Harry Sydney	.10	.02
❑ 105 Bubba McDowell	.10	.02
❑ 106 Todd McNair	.10	.02
❑ 107 Steve Smith	.10	.02
❑ 108 Jim Everett	.20	.07
❑ 109 Bobby Humphrey	.10	.02
❑ 110 Rich Gannon	.40	.15
❑ 111 Marv Cook	.10	.02
❑ 112 Wayne Martin	.10	.02
❑ 113 Sean Landeta	.10	.02
❑ 114 Brad Baxter UER	.10	.02
❑ 115 Reggie White	.40	.15
❑ 116 Johnny Johnson	.10	.02
❑ 117 Jeff Graham	.20	.07
❑ 118 Darren Carrington RC	.10	.02
❑ 119 Ricky Watters	.40	.15
❑ 120 Art Monk	.20	.07
❑ 121 Cornelius Bennett	.20	.07
❑ 122 Wade Wilson	.10	.02
❑ 123 Daniel Stubbs	.10	.02
❑ 124 Brad Muster	.10	.02
❑ 125 Mike Tomczak	.10	.02
❑ 126 Jay Novacek	.20	.07
❑ 127 Shannon Sharpe	.40	.15
❑ 128 Rodney Peete	.10	.02
❑ 129 Daryl Johnston	.40	.15
❑ 130 Warren Moon	.40	.15
❑ 131 Willie Gault	.10	.02
❑ 132 Tony Martin	.40	.15
❑ 133 Terry Allen	.40	.15
❑ 134 Hugh Millen	.10	.02
❑ 135 Rob Moore	.20	.07
❑ 136 Andy Harmon RC	.20	.07
❑ 137 Kelvin Martin	.10	.02
❑ 138 Rod Woodson	.40	.15
❑ 139 Nate Lewis	.10	.02
❑ 140 Darryl Talley	.10	.02
❑ 141 Guy McIntyre	.10	.02
❑ 142 John L. Williams	.10	.02
❑ 143 Brad Edwards	.10	.02
❑ 144 Trace Armstrong	.10	.02
❑ 145 Kenneth Davis	.10	.02
❑ 146 Clay Matthews	.20	.07
❑ 147 Gaston Green	.10	.02
❑ 148 Chris Spielman	.20	.07
❑ 149 Cody Carlson	.10	.02
❑ 150 Derrick Thomas	.40	.15
❑ 151 Terry McDaniel	.10	.02
❑ 152 Kevin Greene	.20	.07
❑ 153 Roger Craig	.20	.07
❑ 154 Craig Heyward	.20	.07
❑ 155 Rodney Hampton	.20	.07
❑ 156 Heath Sherman	.10	.02
❑ 157 Mark Stepnoski	.10	.02
❑ 158 Chris Chandler	.20	.07
❑ 159 Rod Bernstine	.10	.02
❑ 160 Pierce Holt	.10	.02
❑ 161 Wilber Marshall	.10	.02
❑ 162 Reggie Cobb	.10	.02
❑ 163 Tom Rathman	.10	.02
❑ 164 Michael Haynes	.20	.07
❑ 165 Nate Odomes	.10	.02
❑ 166 Tom Waddle	.10	.02
❑ 167 Eric Ball	.10	.02
❑ 168 Brett Favre UER	4.00	1.50
❑ 169 Michael Jackson	.20	.07
❑ 170 Lorenzo White	.10	.02
❑ 171 Cleveland Gary	.10	.02
❑ 172 Jay Schroeder	.10	.02
❑ 173 Tony Paige	.10	.02
❑ 174 Jack Del Rio	.10	.02
❑ 175 Jon Vaughn	.10	.02
❑ 176 Morten Andersen UER	.10	.02
❑ 177 Chris Burkett	.10	.02
❑ 178 Vai Sikahema	.10	.02
❑ 179 Ronnie Harmon	.10	.02
❑ 180 Amp Lee	.10	.02
❑ 181 Chip Lohmiller	.10	.02
❑ 182 Steve Broussard	.10	.02
❑ 183 Don Beebe	.10	.02
❑ 184 Tommy Vardell	.10	.02
❑ 185 Keith Jennings	.10	.02
❑ 186 Simon Fletcher	.10	.02
❑ 187 Mel Gray	.20	.07
❑ 188 Vince Workman	.10	.02
❑ 189 Haywood Jeffires	.20	.07
❑ 190 Barry Word	.10	.02
❑ 191 Ethan Horton	.10	.02
❑ 192 Mark Higgs	.10	.02
❑ 193 Irving Fryar	.20	.07
❑ 194 Charles Haley	.20	.07
❑ 195 Steve Bono	.20	.07
❑ 196 Mike Golic	.10	.02
❑ 197 Gary Anderson K	.10	.02
❑ 198 Sterling Sharpe	.40	.15
❑ 199 Andre Tippett	.10	.02
❑ 200 Thurman Thomas	.40	.15
❑ 201 Chris Miller	.20	.07
❑ 202 Henry Jones	.10	.02
❑ 203 Mo Lewis	.10	.02
❑ 204 Marion Butts	.10	.02
❑ 205 Mike Johnson	.10	.02
❑ 206 Alvin Harper	.20	.07
❑ 207 Ray Childress	.10	.02
❑ 208 Anthony Johnson	.20	.07
❑ 209 Tony Bennett	.10	.02
❑ 210 Anthony Newman RC	.10	.02
❑ 211 Christian Okoye	.10	.02
❑ 212 Marcus Allen	.40	.15
❑ 213 Jackie Harris	.10	.02
❑ 214 Mark Duper	.10	.02
❑ 215 Cris Carter	.40	.15
❑ 216 John Stephens	.10	.02
❑ 217 Barry Sanders	2.50	1.00
❑ 218A H.Moore ERR Sherman	1.25	.50
❑ 218B Herman Moore COR	2.50	1.00
❑ 219 Marvin Washington	.10	.02
❑ 220 Calvin Williams	.20	.07
❑ 221 John Randle	.20	.07
❑ 222 Marco Coleman	.10	.02
❑ 223 Eric Martin	.10	.02
❑ 224 Dave Meggett	.10	.02
❑ 225 Brian Washington	.10	.02
❑ 226 Barry Foster	.20	.07
❑ 227 Michael Zordich	.10	.02
❑ 228 Stan Humphries	.20	.07
❑ 229 Mike Cofer	.10	.02
❑ 230 Chris Warren	.20	.07
❑ 231 Keith McCants	.10	.02
❑ 232 Mark Rypien	.10	.02
❑ 233 James Francis	.10	.02
❑ 234 Andre Rison	.20	.07
❑ 235 William Perry	.20	.07
❑ 236 Chip Banks	.10	.02
❑ 237 Willie Davis	.40	.15
❑ 238 Chris Doleman	.10	.02
❑ 239 Tim Brown	.40	.15

- ❑ 240 Darren Perry .10 .02
- ❑ 241 Johnny Bailey .10 .02
- ❑ 242 Ernest Givins .20 .07
- ❑ 243 John Carney .10 .02
- ❑ 244 Cortez Kennedy .20 .07
- ❑ 245 Lawrence Dawsey .10 .02
- ❑ 246 Martin Mayhew .10 .02
- ❑ 247 Shane Conlan .10 .02
- ❑ 248 J.J. Birden .10 .02
- ❑ 249 Quinn Early .20 .07
- ❑ 250 Michael Irvin .40 .15
- ❑ 251 Neil O'Donnell .40 .15
- ❑ 252 Stan Gelbaugh .10 .02
- ❑ 253 Drew Hill .10 .02
- ❑ 254 Wendell Davis .10 .02
- ❑ 255 Tim Johnson .10 .02
- ❑ 256 Seth Joyner .10 .02
- ❑ 257 Derrick Fenner .10 .02
- ❑ 258 Steve Young 1.50 .60
- ❑ 259 Jackie Slater .10 .02
- ❑ 260 Eric Metcalf .20 .07
- ❑ 261 Rufus Porter .10 .02
- ❑ 262 Ken Norton Jr. .20 .07
- ❑ 263 Tim McDonald .10 .02
- ❑ 264 Mark Jackson .10 .02
- ❑ 265 Hardy Nickerson .20 .07
- ❑ 266 Anthony Munoz .20 .07
- ❑ 267 Mark Carrier WR .20 .07
- ❑ 268 Mike Pritchard .20 .07
- ❑ 269 Steve Emtman .10 .02
- ❑ 270 Ricky Sanders .10 .02
- ❑ 271 Robert Massey .10 .02
- ❑ 272 Pete Metzelaars .10 .02
- ❑ 273 Reggie Langhorne .10 .02
- ❑ 274 Tim McGee .10 .02
- ❑ 275 Reggie Rivers RC .10 .02
- ❑ 276 Jimmie Jones .10 .02
- ❑ 277 Lorenzo White TB .10 .02
- ❑ 278 Emmitt Smith TB 2.00 .75
- ❑ 279 Thurman Thomas TB .40 .15
- ❑ 280 Barry Sanders TB 1.50 .60
- ❑ 281 Rodney Hampton TB .20 .07
- ❑ 282 Barry Foster TB .20 .07
- ❑ 283 Troy Aikman PC 1.00 .40
- ❑ 284 Michael Irvin PC .20 .07
- ❑ 285 Brett Favre PC 2.50 1.00
- ❑ 286 Sterling Sharpe PC .20 .07
- ❑ 287 Steve Young PC 1.00 .40
- ❑ 288 Jerry Rice PC 1.25 .50
- ❑ 289 Stan Humphries PC .20 .07
- ❑ 290 Anthony Miller PC .20 .07
- ❑ 291 Dan Marino PC 2.00 .75
- ❑ 292 Keith Jackson PC .10 .02
- ❑ 293 Patrick Bates RC .10 .02
- ❑ 294 Jerome Bettis RC 10.00 4.00
- ❑ 295 Drew Bledsoe RC 6.00 2.50
- ❑ 296 Tom Carter RC .20 .07
- ❑ 297 Curtis Conway RC 1.00 .40
- ❑ 298 John Copeland RC .20 .07
- ❑ 299 Eric Curry RC .10 .02
- ❑ 300 Reggie Brooks RC .20 .07
- ❑ 301 Steve Everitt RC .10 .02
- ❑ 302 Deon Figures RC .10 .02
- ❑ 303 Garrison Hearst RC 2.00 .75
- ❑ 304 Qadry Ismail RC UER .40 .15
- ❑ 305 Marvin Jones RC .10 .02
- ❑ 306 Lincoln Kennedy RC .10 .02
- ❑ 307 O.J.McDuffie RC .40 .15
- ❑ 308 Rick Mirer RC .40 .15
- ❑ 309 Wayne Simmons RC .10 .02
- ❑ 310 Irv Smith RC .10 .02
- ❑ 311 Robert Smith RC 3.00 1.25
- ❑ 312 Dana Stubblefield RC .40 .15
- ❑ 313 George Teague RC .20 .07
- ❑ 314 Dan Williams RC .10 .02
- ❑ 315 Kevin Williams RC WR .40 .15
- ❑ NNO Santa Claus 2.00 .75

1994 Playoff

- ❑ COMPLETE SET (336) 30.00 12.50
- ❑ 1 Joe Montana 4.00 1.50
- ❑ 2 Derrick Thomas .50 .20
- ❑ 3 Dan Marino 4.00 1.50
- ❑ 4 Cris Carter .75 .30
- ❑ 5 Boomer Esiason .30 .10
- ❑ 6 Bruce Smith .50 .20
- ❑ 7 Andre Rison .30 .10
- ❑ 8 Curtis Conway .50 .20
- ❑ 9 Michael Irvin .50 .20
- ❑ 10 Shannon Sharpe .30 .10
- ❑ 11 Pat Swilling .15 .05
- ❑ 12 John Parrella .15 .05
- ❑ 13 Mel Gray .15 .05
- ❑ 14 Ray Childress .15 .05
- ❑ 15 Willie Davis .30 .10
- ❑ 16 Rocket Ismail .30 .10
- ❑ 17 Jim Everett .30 .10
- ❑ 18 Mark Higgs .15 .05
- ❑ 19 Trace Armstrong .15 .05
- ❑ 20 Jim Kelly .50 .20
- ❑ 21 Rob Burnett .15 .05
- ❑ 22 Jay Novacek .30 .10
- ❑ 23 Robert Delpino .15 .05
- ❑ 24 Brett Perriman .30 .10
- ❑ 25 Troy Aikman 2.00 .75
- ❑ 26 Reggie White .50 .20
- ❑ 27 Lorenzo White .15 .05
- ❑ 28 Bubba McDowell .15 .05
- ❑ 29 Steve Emtman .15 .05
- ❑ 30 Brett Favre 4.00 1.50
- ❑ 31 Derek Russell .15 .05
- ❑ 32 Jeff Hostetler .30 .10
- ❑ 33 Henry Ellard .30 .10
- ❑ 34 Jack Del Rio .15 .05
- ❑ 35 Mike Saxon .15 .05
- ❑ 36 Rickey Jackson .15 .05
- ❑ 37 Phil Simms .30 .10
- ❑ 38 Quinn Early .30 .10
- ❑ 39 Russell Copeland .15 .05
- ❑ 40 Carl Pickens .30 .10
- ❑ 41 Lance Gunn .15 .05
- ❑ 42 Bernie Kosar .30 .10
- ❑ 43 John Elway 4.00 1.50
- ❑ 44 George Teague .15 .05
- ❑ 45 Nick Lowery .15 .05
- ❑ 46 Haywood Jeffires .30 .10
- ❑ 47 Will Shields .15 .05
- ❑ 48 Daryl Johnston .30 .10
- ❑ 49 Pete Metzelaars .15 .05
- ❑ 50 Warren Moon .50 .20
- ❑ 51 Cornelius Bennett .30 .10
- ❑ 52 Vinny Testaverde .30 .10
- ❑ 53 John Mangum RC .15 .05
- ❑ 54 Tommy Vardell .15 .05
- ❑ 55 Lincoln Coleman RC .15 .05
- ❑ 56 Karl Mecklenburg .15 .05
- ❑ 57 Jackie Harris .15 .05
- ❑ 58 Curtis Duncan .15 .05
- ❑ 59 Quentin Coryatt .15 .05
- ❑ 60 Tim Brown .50 .20
- ❑ 61 Irving Fryar .30 .10
- ❑ 62 Sean Gilbert .15 .05
- ❑ 63 Qadry Ismail .50 .20
- ❑ 64 Irv Smith .15 .05
- ❑ 65 Mark Jackson .15 .05
- ❑ 66 Ronnie Lott .30 .10
- ❑ 67 Henry Jones .15 .05
- ❑ 68 Horace Copeland .15 .05
- ❑ 69 John Copeland .15 .05
- ❑ 70 Mark Carrier WR .30 .10
- ❑ 71 Michael Jackson .30 .10
- ❑ 72 Jason Elam .30 .10
- ❑ 73 Rod Bernstine .15 .05
- ❑ 74 Wayne Simmons .15 .05
- ❑ 75 Cody Carlson .15 .05
- ❑ 76 Alexander Wright .15 .05
- ❑ 77 Shane Conlan .15 .05
- ❑ 78 Keith Jackson .15 .05
- ❑ 79 Sean Salisbury .15 .05
- ❑ 80 Vaughan Johnson .15 .05
- ❑ 81 Rob Moore .30 .10
- ❑ 82 Andre Reed .30 .10
- ❑ 83 David Klingler .15 .05
- ❑ 84 Jim Harbaugh .50 .20
- ❑ 85 John Jett RC .15 .05
- ❑ 86 Sterling Sharpe .30 .10
- ❑ 87 Webster Slaughter .15 .05
- ❑ 88 J.J. Birden .15 .05
- ❑ 89 O.J.McDuffie .50 .20
- ❑ 90 Andre Tippett .15 .05
- ❑ 91 Don Beebe .15 .05
- ❑ 92 Mark Stepnoski .15 .05
- ❑ 93 Neil Smith .30 .10
- ❑ 94 Terry Kirby .50 .20
- ❑ 95 Wade Wilson .15 .05
- ❑ 96 Darryl Talley .15 .05
- ❑ 97 Anthony Smith .15 .05
- ❑ 98 Willie Roaf .15 .05
- ❑ 99 Mo Lewis .15 .05
- ❑ 100 James Washington .15 .05
- ❑ 101 Nate Odomes .15 .05
- ❑ 102 Chris Gedney .15 .05
- ❑ 103 Joe Walter .15 .05
- ❑ 104 Alvin Harper .30 .10
- ❑ 105 Simon Fletcher .15 .05
- ❑ 106 Rodney Peete .15 .05
- ❑ 107 Terrell Buckley .15 .05
- ❑ 108 Jeff George .50 .20
- ❑ 109 James Jett .15 .05
- ❑ 110 Tony Casillas .15 .05
- ❑ 111 Marco Coleman .15 .05
- ❑ 112 Anthony Carter .30 .10
- ❑ 113 Lincoln Kennedy .15 .05
- ❑ 114 Chris Calloway .15 .05
- ❑ 115 Randall Cunningham .50 .20
- ❑ 116 Steve Beuerlein .30 .10
- ❑ 117 Neil O'Donnell .50 .20
- ❑ 118 Stan Humphries .30 .10
- ❑ 119 John Taylor .30 .10
- ❑ 120 Cortez Kennedy .30 .10
- ❑ 121 Santana Dotson .30 .10
- ❑ 122 Thomas Smith .15 .05
- ❑ 123 Kevin Williams WR .30 .10
- ❑ 124 Andre Ware .15 .05
- ❑ 125 Ethan Horton .15 .05
- ❑ 126 Mike Sherrard .15 .05
- ❑ 127 Fred Barnett .30 .10
- ❑ 128 Ricky Proehl .15 .05
- ❑ 129 Kevin Greene .30 .10
- ❑ 130 John Carney .15 .05
- ❑ 131 Tim McDonald .15 .05
- ❑ 132 Rick Mirer .50 .20
- ❑ 133 Blair Thomas .15 .05
- ❑ 134 Hardy Nickerson .30 .10
- ❑ 135 Heath Sherman .15 .05
- ❑ 136 Andre Hastings .30 .10
- ❑ 137 Randal Hill .15 .05
- ❑ 138 Mike Cofer .15 .05
- ❑ 139 Brian Blades .30 .10
- ❑ 140 Earnest Byner .15 .05
- ❑ 141 Bill Bates .30 .10
- ❑ 142 Junior Seau .50 .20
- ❑ 143 Johnny Bailey .15 .05
- ❑ 144 Dwight Stone .15 .05
- ❑ 145 Todd Kelly .15 .05
- ❑ 146 Tyrone Montgomery .15 .05
- ❑ 147 Herschel Walker .30 .10
- ❑ 148 Gary Clark .30 .10
- ❑ 149 Eric Green .15 .05
- ❑ 150 Steve Young 1.50 .60
- ❑ 151 Anthony Miller .30 .10
- ❑ 152 Dana Stubblefield .30 .10
- ❑ 153 Dean Wells RC .15 .05
- ❑ 154 Vincent Brisby .30 .10
- ❑ 155 Chris Chandler .30 .10
- ❑ 156 Clyde Simmons .15 .05
- ❑ 157 Rod Woodson .30 .10
- ❑ 158 Nate Lewis .15 .05
- ❑ 159 Martin Harrison .15 .05
- ❑ 160 Kelvin Martin .15 .05
- ❑ 161 Craig Erickson .15 .05
- ❑ 162 Johnny Mitchell .15 .05
- ❑ 163 Calvin Williams .30 .10
- ❑ 164 Deon Figures .15 .05

❑ 165	Tom Rathman	.15	.05
❑ 166	Rick Hamilton	.15	.05
❑ 167	John L. Williams	.15	.05
❑ 168	Demetrius DuBose	.15	.05
❑ 169	Michael Brooks	.15	.05
❑ 170	Marion Butts	.15	.05
❑ 171	Brent Jones	.30	.10
❑ 172	Bobby Hebert	.15	.05
❑ 173	Brad Edwards	.15	.05
❑ 174	David Wyman	.15	.05
❑ 175	Herman Moore	.50	.20
❑ 176	LeRoy Butler	.15	.05
❑ 177	Reggie Langhorne	.15	.05
❑ 178	Dave Krieg	.30	.10
[illegible]	[illegible]	[illegible]	[illegible]
❑ 180	Erik Kramer	.30	.10
❑ 181	Troy Drayton	.15	.05
❑ 182	Dave Meggett	.15	.05
❑ 183	Eric Allen	.15	.05
❑ 184	Mark Bavaro	.15	.05
❑ 185	Leslie O'Neal	.15	.05
❑ 186	Jerry Rice	2.00	.75
❑ 187	Desmond Howard	.30	.10
❑ 188	Deion Sanders	.75	.30
❑ 189	Bill Maas	.15	.05
❑ 190	Frank Wycheck RC	2.00	.75
❑ 191	Ernest Givins	.30	.10
❑ 192	Terry McDaniel	.15	.05
❑ 193	Bryan Cox	.15	.05
❑ 194	Guy McIntyre	.15	.05
❑ 195	Pierce Holt	.15	.05
❑ 196	Fred Stokes	.15	.05
❑ 197	Mike Pritchard	.15	.05
❑ 198	Terry Obee	.15	.05
❑ 199	Mark Collins	.15	.05
❑ 200	Drew Bledsoe	1.25	.50
❑ 201	Barry Word	.15	.05
❑ 202	Derrick Lassic	.15	.05
❑ 203	Chris Spielman	.30	.10
❑ 204	John Jurkovic RC	.30	.10
❑ 205	Ken Norton Jr.	.30	.10
❑ 206	Dale Carter	.15	.05
❑ 207	Chris Doleman	.15	.05
❑ 208	Keith Hamilton	.15	.05
❑ 209	Andy Harmon	.15	.05
❑ 210	John Friesz	.30	.10
❑ 211	Steve Bono	.30	.10
❑ 212	Mark Rypien	.15	.05
❑ 213	Ricky Sanders	.15	.05
❑ 214	Michael Haynes	.30	.10
❑ 215	Todd McNair	.15	.05
❑ 216	Leon Lett	.15	.05
❑ 217	Scott Mitchell	.30	.10
❑ 218	Mike Morris RC	.15	.05
❑ 219	Darrin Smith	.15	.05
❑ [illegible]	Jim McMahon	[illegible]	.10
❑ 221	Garrison Hearst	.50	.20
❑ 222	Leroy Thompson	.15	.05
❑ 223	Darren Carrington	.15	.05
❑ 224	Pete Stoyanovich	.15	.05
❑ 225	Chris Miller	.15	.05
❑ 226	Bruce Smith SP	.30	.10
❑ 227	Simon Fletcher SP	.15	.05
❑ 228	Reggie White SP	.50	.20
❑ 229	Neil Smith SP	.30	.10
❑ 230	Chris Doleman SP	.15	.05
❑ 231	Keith Hamilton SP	.15	.05
❑ 232	Dana Stubblefield SP	.15	.05
❑ 233	Erric Pegram GA	.15	.05
❑ 234	Thurman Thomas GA	.50	.20
❑ 235	Lewis Tillman GA	.15	.05
❑ 236	Harold Green GA	.15	.05
❑ 237	Eric Metcalf GA	.30	.10
❑ 238	Emmitt Smith GA	3.00	1.25
❑ 239	Glyn Milburn GA	.30	.10
❑ 240	Barry Sanders GA	3.00	1.25
❑ 241	Edgar Bennett GA	.30	.10
❑ 242	Gary Brown GA	.15	.05
❑ 243	Roosevelt Potts GA	.15	.05
❑ 244	Marcus Allen GA	.50	.20
❑ 245	Greg Robinson GA	.15	.05
❑ 246	Jerome Bettis GA	.75	.30
❑ 247	Keith Byars GA	.15	.05
❑ 248	Robert Smith GA	.50	.20
❑ 249	Leonard Russell GA	.15	.05
❑ 250	Derek Brown RBK GA	.15	.05
❑ 251	Rodney Hampton GA	.30	.10

❑ 252	Johnny Johnson GA	.15	.05
❑ 253	Vaughn Hebron GA	.15	.05
❑ 254	Ronald Moore GA	.15	.05
❑ 255	Barry Foster GA	.15	.05
❑ 256	Natrone Means GA	.50	.20
❑ 257	Ricky Watters GA	.30	.10
❑ 258	Chris Warren GA	.50	.20
❑ 259	Vince Workman GA	.15	.05
❑ 260	Reggie Brooks GA	.15	.05
❑ 261	Carolina Panthers	.40	.15
❑ 262	Jacksonville Jaguars	.40	.15
❑ 263	Troy Aikman SB	1.00	.40
❑ 264	Barry Sanders SB	1.50	.60
❑ 265	Emmitt Smith SB	1.50	.60
[illegible]	[illegible]	[illegible]	[illegible]
❑ 267	Jerry Rice SB	1.00	.40
❑ 268	Shannon Sharpe SB	.30	.10
❑ 269	Bob Kratch SB	.15	.05
❑ 270	Howard Ballard SB	.15	.05
❑ 271	Erik Williams SB	.15	.05
❑ 272	Guy McIntyre SB	.15	.05
❑ 273	Kevin Williams WR SB	.30	.10
❑ 274	Mel Gray SB	.15	.05
❑ 275	Eddie Murray SB	.15	.05
❑ 276	Mark Stepnoski SB	.15	.05
❑ 277	Tommy Barnhardt SB	.15	.05
❑ 278	Derrick Thomas SB	.30	.10
❑ 279	Ken Norton Jr. SB	.30	.10
❑ 280	Chris Spielman SB	.15	.05
❑ 281	Deion Sanders SB	.50	.20
❑ 282	Mark Collins SB	.15	.05
❑ 283	Bruce Smith SB	.30	.10
❑ 284	Reggie White SB	.50	.20
❑ 285	Sean Gilbert SB	.15	.05
❑ 286	Cortez Kennedy SB	.30	.10
❑ 287	Steve Atwater SB	.15	.05
❑ 288	Tim McDonald SB	.15	.05
❑ 289	Jerome Bettis SB	.75	.30
❑ 290	Dana Stubblefield SB	.30	.10
❑ 291	Bert Emanuel RC	.50	.20
❑ 292	Jeff Burris RC	.30	.10
❑ 293	Bucky Brooks RC	.15	.05
❑ 294	Dan Wilkinson RC	.30	.10
❑ 295	Darnay Scott RC	1.00	.40
❑ 296	Derrick Alexander WR RC	.50	.20
❑ 297	Antonio Langham RC	.30	.10
❑ 298	Shante Carver RC	.15	.05
❑ 299	Shelby Hill RC	.15	.05
❑ 300	Larry Allen RC	.50	.20
❑ 301	Johnnie Morton RC	2.00	.75
❑ 302	Van Malone RC	.15	.05
❑ 303	Aaron Taylor RC	.15	.05
❑ 304	Marshall Faulk RC	6.00	2.50
❑ 305	Eric Mahlum RC	.15	.05
❑ 306	Trev Alberts RC	.30	.10
❑ 307	Greg Hill RC	.30	.20
❑ 308	Donnell Bennett RC	.50	.20
❑ 309	Rob Fredrickson RC	.30	.10
❑ 310	James Folston RC	.15	.05
❑ 311	Isaac Bruce RC	5.00	2.00
❑ 312	Tim Ruddy RC	.15	.05
❑ 313	Aubrey Beavers RC	.15	.05
❑ 314	David Palmer RC	.50	.20
❑ 315	Dewayne Washington RC	.30	.10
❑ 316	Willie McGinest RC	.50	.20
❑ 317	Mario Bates RC	.50	.20
❑ 318	Kevin Lee RC	.15	.05
❑ 319	Jason Sehorn RC	.75	.30
❑ 320	Thomas Randolph RC	.15	.05
❑ 321	Ryan Yarborough RC	.15	.05
❑ 322	Bernard Williams RC	.15	.05
❑ 323	Chuck Levy RC	.15	.05
❑ 324	Jamir Miller RC	.30	.10
❑ 325	Charles Johnson RC	.50	.20
❑ 326	Bryant Young RC	.75	.30
❑ 327	William Floyd RC	.50	.20
❑ 328	Kevin Mitchell RC	.15	.05
❑ 329	Sam Adams RC	.30	.10
❑ 330	Kevin Mawae RC	.50	.20
❑ 331	Errict Rhett RC	.50	.20
❑ 332	Trent Dilfer RC	1.50	.60
❑ 333	Heath Shuler RC	.50	.20
❑ 334	Aaron Glenn RC	.50	.20
❑ 335	Todd Steussie RC	.30	.10
❑ 336	Toby Wright RC	.15	.05
❑ NNO	Gale Sayers Play.Club	4.00	1.50
❑ NNO	Gale Sayers AUTO	60.00	25.00

1993 Playoff Contenders

❑	COMPLETE SET (150)	20.00	7.50
❑ 1	Brett Favre	3.00	1.50
❑ 2	Thurman Thomas	.40	.15
❑ 3	Barry Word	.10	.02
❑ 4	Herman Moore	.40	.15
❑ 5	Reggie Langhorne	.10	.02
❑ 6	Wilber Marshall	.10	.02
❑ 7	Ricky Watters	.40	.15
❑ 8	Marcus Allen	.40	.15
❑ 9	Jeff Hostetler	.20	.07
❑ 10	Steve Young	1.00	.40
❑ 11	Bobby Hebert	.10	.02
❑ 12	David Klingler	.10	.02
❑ 13	Craig Heyward	.20	.07
❑ 14	Andre Reed	.20	.07
❑ 15	Tommy Vardell	.10	.02
❑ 16	Anthony Carter	.20	.07
❑ 17	Mel Gray	.20	.07
❑ 18	Dan Marino	2.50	1.00
❑ 19	Haywood Jeffires	.20	.07
❑ 20	Joe Montana	2.50	1.00
❑ 21	Tim Brown	.40	.15
❑ 22	Jim McMahon	.20	.07
❑ 23	Scott Mitchell	.40	.15
❑ 24	Rickey Jackson	.10	.02
❑ 25	Troy Aikman	1.50	.60
❑ 26	Rodney Hampton	.20	.07
❑ 27	Fred Barnett	.20	.07
❑ 28	Gary Clark	.20	.07
❑ 29	Barry Foster	.20	.07
❑ 30	Brian Blades	.20	.07
❑ 31	Tim McDonald	.10	.02
❑ 32	Kelvin Martin	.10	.02
❑ 33	Henry Jones	.10	.02
❑ 34	Erric Pegram	.20	.07
❑ 35	Don Beebe	.10	.02
❑ 36	Eric Metcalf	.20	.07
❑ 37	Charles Haley	.20	.07
❑ 38	Robert Delpino	.10	.02
❑ 39	Leonard Russell UER	.20	.07
❑ 40	Jackie Harris	.10	.02
❑ 41	Ernest Givins	.20	.07
❑ 42	Willie Davis	.40	.15
❑ 43	Alexander Wright	.10	.02
❑ 44	Keith Byars	.10	.02
❑ 45	Dave Meggett	.10	.02
❑ 46	Johnny Johnson	.10	.02
❑ 47	Mark Bavaro	.10	.02
❑ 48	Seth Joyner	.10	.02
❑ 49	Junior Seau	.40	.15
❑ 50	Emmitt Smith	2.50	1.25
❑ 51	Shannon Sharpe	.40	.15
❑ 52	Rodney Peete	.10	.02
❑ 53	Andre Rison	.20	.07
❑ 54	Cornelius Bennett	.20	.07
❑ 55	Mark Carrier WR	.20	.07
❑ 56	Mark Clayton	.10	.02
❑ 57	Warren Moon	.40	.15
❑ 58	J.J. Birden	.10	.02
❑ 59	Howie Long	.40	.15
❑ 60	Irving Fryar	.20	.07
❑ 61	Mark Jackson	.10	.02
❑ 62	Eric Martin	.10	.02
❑ 63	Herschel Walker	.20	.07
❑ 64	Cortez Kennedy	.20	.07
❑ 65	Steve Beuerlein	.20	.07
❑ 66	Jim Kelly	.40	.15
❑ 67	Bernie Kosar Cowboys	.20	.07

❑ 68 Pat Swilling	.10	.02
❑ 69 Michael Irvin	.40	.15
❑ 70 Harvey Williams	.20	.07
❑ 71 Steve Smith	.10	.02
❑ 72 Wade Wilson	.10	.02
❑ 73 Phil Simms	.20	.07
❑ 74 Vinny Testaverde	.20	.07
❑ 75 Barry Sanders	2.50	1.00
❑ 76 Ken Norton Jr.	.20	.07
❑ 77 Rod Woodson	.40	.15
❑ 78 Webster Slaughter	.10	.02
❑ 79 Derrick Thomas	.40	.15
❑ 80 Mike Sherrard	.10	.02
❑ 81 Calvin Williams	.20	.07
❑ 82 Jay Novacek	.20	.07
❑ 83 Michael Brooks	.10	.02
❑ 84 Randall Cunningham	.40	.15
❑ 85 Chris Warren	.20	.07
❑ 86 Johnny Mitchell	.10	.02
❑ 87 Jim Harbaugh	.40	.15
❑ 88 Rod Bernstine	.10	.02
❑ 89 John Elway	2.50	1.00
❑ 90 Jerry Rice	1.50	.60
❑ 91 Brent Jones	.20	.07
❑ 92 Cris Carter	.40	.15
❑ 93 Alvin Harper	.20	.07
❑ 94 Horace Copeland RC	.20	.07
❑ 95 Rocket Ismail	.20	.07
❑ 96 Darrin Smith RC	.20	.07
❑ 97 Reggie Brooks RC	.20	.07
❑ 98 Demetrius DuBose RC	.10	.02
❑ 99 Eric Curry RC	.10	.02
❑ 100 Rick Mirer RC	.40	.15
❑ 101 Carlton Gray RC UER	.10	.02
❑ 102 Dana Stubblefield RC	.40	.15
❑ 103 Todd Kelly RC	.10	.02
❑ 104 Natrone Means RC	.40	.15
❑ 105 Darrien Gordon RC	.10	.02
❑ 106 Deon Figures RC	.10	.02
❑ 107 Garrison Hearst RC	1.25	.50
❑ 108 Ronald Moore RC	.20	.07
❑ 109 Leonard Renfro RC	.10	.02
❑ 110 Lester Holmes	.10	.02
❑ 111 Vaughn Hebron RC	.10	.02
❑ 112 Marvin Jones RC	.10	.02
❑ 113 Irv Smith RC	.10	.02
❑ 114 Willie Roaf RC	.20	.07
❑ 115 Derek Brown RC RBK	.20	.07
❑ 116 Vincent Brisby RC	.40	.15
❑ 117 Drew Bledsoe RC	4.00	1.50
❑ 118 Gino Torretta RC	.20	.07
❑ 119 Robert Smith RC	2.00	.75
❑ 120 Qadry Ismail RC	.40	.15
❑ 121 O.J.McDuffie RC	.40	.15
❑ 122 Terry Kirby RC	.40	.15
❑ 123 Troy Drayton RC	.20	.07
❑ 124 Jerome Bettis RC	6.00	2.50
❑ 125 Patrick Bates RC	.10	.02
❑ 126 Roosevelt Potts RC	.10	.02
❑ 127 Tom Carter RC	.20	.07
❑ 128 Patrick Robinson RC	.10	.02
❑ 129 Brad Hopkins RC	.10	.02
❑ 130 George Teague RC	.20	.07
❑ 131 Wayne Simmons RC	.10	.02
❑ 132 Mark Brunell RC	2.50	1.00
❑ 133 Ryan McNeil RC	.40	.15
❑ 134 Dan Williams RC	.10	.02
❑ 135 Glyn Milburn RC	.40	.15
❑ 136 Kevin Williams RC WR	.40	.15
❑ 137 Derrick Lassic RC	.10	.02
❑ 138 Steve Everitt RC	.10	.02
❑ 139 Lance Gunn RC	.10	.02
❑ 140 John Copeland RC	.20	.07
❑ 141 Curtis Conway RC	1.00	.40
❑ 142 Thomas Smith RC	.20	.07
❑ 143 Russell Copeland RC	.20	.07
❑ 144 Lincoln Kennedy RC	.10	.02
❑ 145 Boomer Esiason CL	.10	.02
❑ 146 Neil Smith CL	.10	.02
❑ 147 Jack Del Rio CL	.10	.02
❑ 148 Morten Andersen CL	.10	.02
❑ 149 Sterling Sharpe CL	.20	.07
❑ 150 Reggie White CL	.20	.07

1994 Playoff Contenders

❑ COMPLETE SET (120)	20.00	7.50
❑ 1 Drew Bledsoe	1.00	.40
❑ 2 Barry Sanders	2.50	1.00
❑ 3 Jerry Rice	1.50	.60
❑ 4 Rod Woodson	.20	.07
❑ 5 Irving Fryar	.20	.07
❑ 6 Charles Haley	.20	.07
❑ 7 Chris Warren	.20	.07
❑ 8 Craig Erickson	.10	.02
❑ 9 Eric Metcalf	.20	.07
❑ 10 Marcus Allen	.40	.15
❑ 11 Chris Miller	.10	.02
❑ 12 Andre Rison	.20	.07
❑ 13 Art Monk	.20	.07
❑ 14 Calvin Williams	.20	.07
❑ 15 Shannon Sharpe	.20	.07
❑ 16 Rodney Hampton	.20	.07
❑ 17 Marion Butts	.10	.02
❑ 18 John Jurkovic RC	.20	.07
❑ 19 Jim Kelly	.40	.15
❑ 20 Emmitt Smith	2.50	1.00
❑ 21 Jeff Hostetler	.20	.07
❑ 22 Barry Foster	.10	.02
❑ 23 Boomer Esiason	.20	.07
❑ 24 Jim Harbaugh	.40	.15
❑ 25 Joe Montana	3.00	1.25
❑ 26 Jeff George	.40	.15
❑ 27 Warren Moon	.40	.15
❑ 28 Steve Young	1.25	.50
❑ 29 Randall Cunningham	.40	.15
❑ 30 Shawn Jefferson	.10	.02
❑ 31 Cortez Kennedy	.20	.07
❑ 32 Reggie Brooks	.20	.07
❑ 33 Alvin Harper	.20	.07
❑ 34 Brent Jones	.20	.07
❑ 35 O.J. McDuffie	.40	.15
❑ 36 Jerome Bettis	.60	.25
❑ 37 Daryl Johnston	.20	.07
❑ 38 Herman Moore	.40	.15
❑ 39 Dave Meggett	.10	.02
❑ 40 Reggie White	.40	.15
❑ 41 Junior Seau	.40	.15
❑ 42 Dan Marino	3.00	1.25
❑ 43 Scott Mitchell	.20	.07
❑ 44 John Elway	3.00	1.25
❑ 45 Troy Aikman	1.50	.60
❑ 46 Terry Allen	.20	.07
❑ 47 David Klingler	.10	.02
❑ 48 Stan Humphries	.20	.07
❑ 49 Rick Mirer	.40	.15
❑ 50 Neil O'Donnell	.40	.15
❑ 51 Keith Jackson	.10	.02
❑ 52 Ricky Watters	.20	.07
❑ 53 Dave Brown	.20	.07
❑ 54 Neil Smith	.20	.07
❑ 55 Johnny Mitchell	.10	.02
❑ 56 Jackie Harris	.10	.02
❑ 57 Terry Kirby	.40	.15
❑ 58 Willie Davis	.20	.07
❑ 59 Rob Moore	.20	.07
❑ 60 Nate Newton	.10	.02
❑ 61 Deion Sanders	.75	.30
❑ 62 John Taylor	.20	.07
❑ 63 Sterling Sharpe	.20	.07
❑ 64 Natrone Means	.40	.15
❑ 65 Steve Beuerlein	.20	.07
❑ 66 Erik Kramer	.20	.07
❑ 67 Qadry Ismail	.40	.15
❑ 68 Johnny Johnson	.10	.02
❑ 69 Herschel Walker	.20	.07
❑ 70 Mark Stepnoski	.10	.02
❑ 71 Brett Favre	3.00	1.25
❑ 72 Dana Stubblefield	.20	.07
❑ 73 Bruce Smith	.40	.15
❑ 74 Leroy Hoard	.10	.02
❑ 75 Steve Walsh	.10	.02
❑ 76 Jay Novacek	.20	.07
❑ 77 Derrick Thomas	.40	.15
❑ 78 Keith Byars	.10	.02
❑ 79 Ben Coates	.20	.07
❑ 80 Lorenzo Neal	.10	.02
❑ 81 Ronnie Lott	.20	.07
❑ 82 Tim Brown	.40	.15
❑ 83 Michael Irvin	.40	.15
❑ 84 Ronald Moore	.10	.02
❑ 85 Andre Reed	.20	.07
❑ 86 James Jett	.10	.02
❑ 87 Curtis Conway	.40	.15
❑ 88 Bernie Parmalee RC	.40	.15
❑ 89 Keith Cash	.10	.02
❑ 90 Russell Copeland	.10	.02
❑ 91 Kevin Williams WR	.20	.07
❑ 92 Gary Brown	.10	.02
❑ 93 Thurman Thomas	.40	.15
❑ 94 Jamir Miller RC	.20	.07
❑ 95 Bert Emanuel RC	.40	.15
❑ 96 Bucky Brooks RC	.10	.02
❑ 97 Jeff Burris RC	.20	.07
❑ 98 Antonio Langham RC	.20	.07
❑ 99 Derrick Alexander WR RC	.40	.15
❑ 100 Dan Wilkinson RC	.20	.07
❑ 101 Shante Carver RC	.10	.02
❑ 102 Johnnie Morton RC	2.00	.75
❑ 103 LeShon Johnson RC	.20	.07
❑ 104 Marshall Faulk RC	6.00	2.50
❑ 105 Greg Hill RC	.40	.15
❑ 106 Lake Dawson RC	.20	.07
❑ 107 Irving Spikes RC	.20	.07
❑ 108 David Palmer RC	.40	.15
❑ 109 Willie McGinest RC	.40	.15
❑ 110 Joe Johnson RC	.10	.02
❑ 111 Aaron Glenn RC	.40	.15
❑ 112 Charlie Garner RC	1.50	.60
❑ 113 Charles Johnson RC	.40	.15
❑ 114 Byron Bam Morris RC	.20	.07
❑ 115 Bryant Young RC	.60	.25
❑ 116 William Floyd RC	.40	.15
❑ 117 Trent Dilfer RC	1.50	.60
❑ 118 Errict Rhett RC	.40	.15
❑ 119 Heath Shuler RC	.40	.15
❑ 120 Gus Frerotte RC	.40	.15

1995 Playoff Contenders

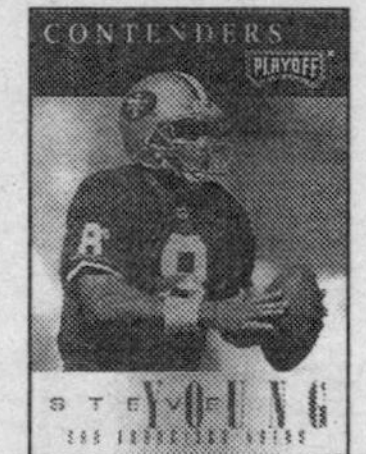

❑ COMPLETE SET (150)	25.00	10.00
❑ 1 Steve Young	1.00	.40
❑ 2 Jeff Blake RC	.75	.30
❑ 3 Rick Mirer	.20	.07
❑ 4 Brett Favre	2.50	1.25
❑ 5 Heath Shuler	.20	.07
❑ 6 Steve Bono	.20	.07
❑ 7 John Elway	2.50	1.00
❑ 8 Troy Aikman	1.25	.50
❑ 9 Rodney Peete	.10	.02
❑ 10 Gus Frerotte	.20	.07
❑ 11 Drew Bledsoe	.75	.30
❑ 12 Jim Kelly	.40	.15
❑ 13 Dan Marino	2.50	1.00
❑ 14 Errict Rhett	.20	.07
❑ 15 Jeff Hostetler	.20	.07
❑ 16 Erik Kramer	.10	.02
❑ 17 Jim Everett	.10	.02

❑ 18 Elvis Grbac	.40	.15
❑ 19 Scott Mitchell	.20	.07
❑ 20 Barry Sanders	2.00	.75
❑ 21 Deion Sanders	.75	.30
❑ 22 Emmitt Smith	2.00	.75
❑ 23 Garrison Hearst	.40	.15
❑ 24 Mario Bates	.20	.07
❑ 25 Mark Brunell	.75	.30
❑ 26 Robert Smith	.40	.15
❑ 27 Rodney Hampton	.20	.07
❑ 28 Marshall Faulk	1.50	.60
❑ 29 Greg Hill	.20	.07
❑ 30 Bernie Parmalee	.20	.07
❑ 31 Natrone Means	.20	.07
❑ 32 Marcus Allen	.40	.15
❑ 33 Byron Bam Morris	.10	.02
❑ 34 Edgar Bennett	.20	.07
❑ 35 Vincent Brisby	.10	.02
❑ 36 Jerome Bettis	.40	.15
❑ 37 Craig Heyward	.20	.07
❑ 38 Anthony Miller	.20	.07
❑ 39 Curtis Conway	.40	.15
❑ 40 William Floyd	.20	.07
❑ 41 Chris Warren	.20	.07
❑ 42 Terry Kirby	.20	.07
❑ 43 Herschel Walker	.20	.07
❑ 44 Eric Metcalf	.20	.07
❑ 45 Darnay Scott	.20	.07
❑ 46 Jackie Harris	.10	.02
❑ 47 Dana Stubblefield	.20	.07
❑ 48 Daryl Johnston	.20	.07
❑ 49 Dave Meggett	.10	.02
❑ 50 Ricky Watters	.20	.07
❑ 51 Ken Norton	.20	.07
❑ 52 Boomer Esiason	.20	.07
❑ 53 Lake Dawson	.20	.07
❑ 54 Eric Green	.10	.02
❑ 55 Junior Seau	.40	.15
❑ 56 Yancey Thigpen RC	.40	.15
❑ 57 James Jett	.20	.07
❑ 58 Leonard Russell	.10	.02
❑ 59 Brent Jones	.10	.02
❑ 60 Trent Dilfer	.40	.15
❑ 61 Terance Mathis	.20	.07
❑ 62 Jeff George	.20	.07
❑ 63 Alvin Harper	.10	.02
❑ 64 Terry Allen	.20	.07
❑ 65 Stan Humphries	.20	.07
❑ 66 Robert Green	.10	.02
❑ 67 Bryce Paup	.20	.07
❑ 68 Tamarick Vanover RC	.40	.15
❑ 69 Desmond Howard	.20	.07
❑ 70 Derek Loville	.10	.02
❑ 71 Dave Brown	.20	.07
❑ 72 Carl Pickens	.20	.07
❑ 73 Gary Clark	.10	.02
❑ 74 Gary Brown	.10	.02
❑ 75 Brett Perriman	.20	.07
❑ 76 Charlie Garner	.40	.15
❑ 77 Ben Coates	.20	.07
❑ 78 Bruce Smith	.40	.15
❑ 79 Erric Pegram	.20	.07
❑ 80 Jerry Rice	1.25	.50
❑ 81 Tim Brown	.40	.15
❑ 82 John Taylor	.10	.02
❑ 83 Will Moore	.10	.02
❑ 84 Jay Novacek	.20	.07
❑ 85 Kevin Williams	.20	.07
❑ 86 Rocket Ismail	.20	.07
❑ 87 Robert Brooks	.40	.15
❑ 88 Michael Irvin	.40	.15
❑ 89 Mark Chmura	.40	.15
❑ 90 Shannon Sharpe	.20	.07
❑ 91 Henry Ellard	.20	.07
❑ 92 Reggie White	.40	.15
❑ 93 Isaac Bruce	.75	.30
❑ 94 Charles Haley	.20	.07
❑ 95 Jake Reed	.20	.07
❑ 96 Pete Metzelaars	.10	.02
❑ 97 Dave Krieg	.10	.02
❑ 98 Tony Martin	.20	.07
❑ 99 Charles Jordan RC	.20	.07
❑ 100 Bert Emanuel	.40	.15
❑ 101 Andre Rison	.20	.07
❑ 102 Jeff Graham	.10	.02
❑ 103 O.J. McDuffie	.40	.15
❑ 104 Randall Cunningham	.40	.15
❑ 105 Harvey Williams	.10	.02
❑ 106 Cris Carter	.40	.15
❑ 107 Irving Fryar	.20	.07
❑ 108 Jim Harbaugh	.20	.07
❑ 109 Bernie Kosar	.10	.02
❑ 110 Charles Johnson	.20	.07
❑ 111 Warren Moon	.20	.07
❑ 112 Neil O'Donnell	.20	.07
❑ 113 Fred Barnett	.20	.07
❑ 114 Herman Moore	.40	.15
❑ 115 Chris Miller	.10	.02
❑ 116 Vinny Testaverde	.20	.07
❑ 117 Craig Erickson	.10	.02
❑ 118 Qadry Ismail	.20	.07
❑ 119 Willie Davis	.20	.07
❑ 120 Michael Jackson	.20	.07
❑ 121 Stoney Case RC	.40	.15
❑ 122 Frank Sanders RC	.40	.15
❑ 123 Todd Collins RC	2.50	1.00
❑ 124 Kerry Collins RC	1.50	.60
❑ 125 Sherman Williams RC	.10	.02
❑ 126 Terrell Davis RC	2.50	1.00
❑ 127 Luther Elliss RC	.10	.02
❑ 128 Steve McNair RC	3.00	1.25
❑ 129 Chris Sanders RC	.40	.15
❑ 130 Ki-Jana Carter RC	.40	.15
❑ 131 Rodney Thomas RC	.40	.15
❑ 132 Tony Boselli RC	.40	.15
❑ 133 Rob Johnson RC	1.00	.40
❑ 134 James O. Stewart RC	1.25	.50
❑ 135 Chad May RC	.10	.02
❑ 136 Eric Bjornson RC	.20	.07
❑ 137 Tyrone Wheatley RC	1.25	.50
❑ 138 Kyle Brady RC	.40	.15
❑ 139 Curtis Martin RC	3.00	1.25
❑ 140 Eric Zeier RC	.40	.15
❑ 141 Ray Zellars RC	.20	.07
❑ 142 Napoleon Kaufman RC	1.25	.50
❑ 143 Mike Mamula RC	.20	.07
❑ 144 Mark Bruener RC	.20	.07
❑ 145 Kordell Stewart RC	1.50	.60
❑ 146 J.J. Stokes RC	.40	.15
❑ 147 Joey Galloway RC	1.50	.60
❑ 148 Warren Sapp RC	1.50	.60
❑ 149 Michael Westbrook RC	.40	.15
❑ 150 Rashaan Salaam RC	.40	.15

1997 Playoff Contenders

❑ COMPLETE SET (150)	40.00	15.00
❑ 1 Kent Graham	.40	.15
❑ 2 Leeland McElroy	.40	.15
❑ 3 Rob Moore	.60	.25
❑ 4 Frank Sanders	.60	.25
❑ 5 Jake Plummer RC	5.00	2.00
❑ 6 Chris Chandler	.60	.25
❑ 7 Bert Emanuel	.60	.25
❑ 8 O.J. Santiago RC	.60	.25
❑ 9 Byron Hanspard RC	.60	.25
❑ 10 Vinny Testaverde	.60	.25
❑ 11 Michael Jackson	.60	.25
❑ 12 Earnest Byner	.40	.15
❑ 13 Jermaine Lewis	1.00	.40
❑ 14 Derrick Alexander WR	.60	.25
❑ 15 Jay Graham RC	.60	.25
❑ 16 Todd Collins	.40	.15
❑ 17 Thurman Thomas	1.00	.40
❑ 18 Bruce Smith	.60	.25
❑ 19 Andre Reed	.60	.25
❑ 20 Quinn Early	.40	.15
❑ 21 Antowain Smith RC	2.50	1.00
❑ 22 Kerry Collins	1.00	.40
❑ 23 Tim Biakabutuka	.60	.25
❑ 24 Anthony Johnson	.40	.15
❑ 25 Wesley Walls	.60	.25
❑ 26 Fred Lane RC	.60	.25
❑ 27 Rae Carruth RC	.40	.15
❑ 28 Raymont Harris	.40	.15
❑ 29 Rick Mirer	.40	.15
❑ 30 Darnell Autry RC	.60	.25
❑ 31 Jeff Blake	.60	.25
❑ 32 Ki-Jana Carter	.40	.15
❑ 33 Carl Pickens	.60	.25
❑ 34 Darnay Scott	.60	.25
❑ 35 Corey Dillon RC	6.00	2.50
❑ 36 Troy Aikman	2.00	.75
❑ 37 Emmitt Smith	3.00	1.25
❑ 38 Michael Irvin	1.00	.40
❑ 39 Deion Sanders	1.00	.40
❑ 40 Anthony Miller	.40	.15
❑ 41 Eric Bjornson	.40	.15
❑ 42 David LaFleur RC	.40	.15
❑ 43 John Elway	4.00	1.50
❑ 44 Terrell Davis	1.25	.50
❑ 45 Shannon Sharpe	.60	.25
❑ 46 Ed McCaffrey	.60	.25
❑ 47 Rod Smith WR	1.00	.40
❑ 48 Scott Mitchell	.60	.25
❑ 49 Barry Sanders	3.00	1.25
❑ 50 Herman Moore	.60	.25
❑ 51 Brett Favre	4.00	1.50
❑ 52 Dorsey Levens	1.00	.40
❑ 53 William Henderson	.60	.25
❑ 54 Derrick Mayes	.60	.25
❑ 55 Antonio Freeman	1.00	.40
❑ 56 Robert Brooks	.60	.25
❑ 57 Mark Chmura	.60	.25
❑ 58 Reggie White	1.00	.40
❑ 59 Darren Sharper RC	1.00	.40
❑ 60 Jim Harbaugh	.60	.25
❑ 61 Marshall Faulk	1.25	.50
❑ 62 Marvin Harrison	1.00	.40
❑ 63 Mark Brunell	1.25	.50
❑ 64 Natrone Means	.60	.25
❑ 65 Jimmy Smith	.60	.25
❑ 66 Keenan McCardell	.60	.25
❑ 67 Elvis Grbac	.60	.25
❑ 68 Greg Hill	.40	.15
❑ 69 Marcus Allen	1.00	.40
❑ 70 Andre Rison	.60	.25
❑ 71 Kimble Anders	.60	.25
❑ 72 Tony Gonzalez RC	3.00	1.25
❑ 73 Pat Barnes RC	1.00	.40
❑ 74 Dan Marino	4.00	1.50
❑ 75 Karim Abdul-Jabbar	.60	.25
❑ 76 Zach Thomas	1.00	.40
❑ 77 O.J. McDuffie	.60	.25
❑ 78 Brian Manning RC	.40	.15
❑ 79 Brad Johnson	1.00	.40
❑ 80 Cris Carter	1.00	.40
❑ 81 Jake Reed	.60	.25
❑ 82 Robert Smith	.60	.25
❑ 83 Drew Bledsoe	1.25	.50
❑ 84 Curtis Martin	1.25	.50
❑ 85 Ben Coates	.60	.25
❑ 86 Terry Glenn	1.00	.40
❑ 87 Shawn Jefferson	.40	.15
❑ 88 Heath Shuler	.40	.15
❑ 89 Mario Bates	.40	.15
❑ 90 Andre Hastings	.40	.15
❑ 91 Troy Davis RC	.60	.25
❑ 92 Danny Wuerffel RC	1.00	.40
❑ 93 Dave Brown	.40	.15
❑ 94 Chris Calloway	.40	.15
❑ 95 Tiki Barber RC	6.00	2.50
❑ 96 Mike Cherry RC	.40	.15
❑ 97 Neil O'Donnell	.60	.25
❑ 98 Keyshawn Johnson	1.00	.40
❑ 99 Adrian Murrell	.60	.25
❑ 100 Wayne Chrebet	1.00	.40
❑ 101 Dedric Ward RC	.60	.25
❑ 102 Leon Johnson RC	.60	.25
❑ 103 Jeff George	.60	.25
❑ 104 Napoleon Kaufman	1.00	.40
❑ 105 Tim Brown	1.00	.40
❑ 106 James Jett	.60	.25
❑ 107 Ty Detmer	.60	.25

108 Ricky Watters	.60	.25
109 Irving Fryar	.60	.25
110 Michael Timpson	.40	.15
111 Chad Lewis RC	2.00	.75
112 Kordell Stewart	1.00	.40
113 Jerome Bettis	1.00	.40
114 Charles Johnson	.60	.25
115 George Jones RC	.60	.25
116 Will Blackwell RC	.60	.25
117 Stan Humphries	.60	.25
118 Junior Seau	1.00	.40
119 Freddie Jones RC	.60	.25
120 Steve Young	1.25	.50
121 Jerry Rice	2.00	.75
122 Garrison Hearst	.60	.25
123 William Floyd	.60	.25
124 Terrell Owens	1.25	.50
125 J.J. Stokes	.60	.25
126 Marc Edwards RC	.40	.15
127 Jim Druckenmiller RC	.60	.25
128 Warren Moon	1.00	.40
129 Chris Warren	.60	.25
130 Joey Galloway	.60	.25
131 Shawn Springs RC	.60	.25
132 Tony Banks	.60	.25
133 Lawrence Phillips	.40	.15
134 Isaac Bruce	1.00	.40
135 Eddie Kennison	.60	.25
136 Orlando Pace RC	1.00	.40
137 Trent Dilfer	1.00	.40
138 Mike Alstott	1.00	.40
139 Horace Copeland	.40	.15
140 Jackie Harris	.40	.15
141 Warrick Dunn RC	3.00	1.25
142 Reidel Anthony RC	1.00	.40
143 Steve McNair	1.25	.50
144 Eddie George	1.00	.40
145 Chris Sanders	.40	.15
146 Gus Frerotte	.40	.15
147 Terry Allen	1.00	.40
148 Henry Ellard	.40	.15
149 Leslie Shepherd	.40	.15
150 Michael Westbrook	.60	.25
S1 Terrell Davis Sample	2.00	.75

1998 Playoff Contenders Ticket

COMP.SET w/o SPs (80)	60.00	25.00
1 Rob Moore	1.25	.50
2 Jake Plummer	2.00	.75
3 Jamal Anderson	2.00	.75
4 Terance Mathis	1.25	.50
5 Priest Holmes RC	50.00	25.00
6 Michael Jackson	.75	.30
7 Eric Zeier	1.25	.50
8 Andre Reed	1.25	.50
9 Antowain Smith	2.00	.75
10 Bruce Smith	1.25	.50
11 Thurman Thomas	2.00	.75
12 Rocket Ismail	.75	.30
13 Wesley Walls	1.25	.50
14 Curtis Conway	1.25	.50
15 Jeff Blake	1.25	.50
16 Corey Dillon	2.00	.75
17 Carl Pickens	1.25	.50
18 Troy Aikman	4.00	1.50
19 Michael Irvin	2.00	.75
20 Ernie Mills	.75	.30
21 Deion Sanders	2.00	.75
22 Emmitt Smith	6.00	2.50
23 Terrell Davis	2.00	.75
24 John Elway	8.00	3.00
25 Neil Smith	1.25	.50
26 Rod Smith WR	1.25	.50
27 Herman Moore	1.25	.50
28 Johnnie Morton	1.25	.50
29 Barry Sanders	6.00	2.50
30 Robert Brooks	1.25	.50
31 Brett Favre	8.00	3.00
32 Antonio Freeman	2.00	.75
33 Dorsey Levens	2.00	.75
34 Reggie White	2.00	.75
35 Marshall Faulk	2.50	1.00
36 Mark Brunell	2.00	.75
37 Jimmy Smith	1.25	.50
38 James Stewart	1.25	.50
39 Donnell Bennett	.75	.30
40 Andre Rison	1.25	.50
41 Derrick Thomas	2.00	.75
42 Karim Abdul-Jabbar	2.00	.75
43 Dan Marino	8.00	3.00
44 Cris Carter	2.00	.75
45 Brad Johnson	2.00	.75
46 Robert Smith	2.00	.75
47 Drew Bledsoe	3.00	1.25
48 Terry Glenn	2.00	.75
49 Lamar Smith	1.25	.50
50 Ike Hilliard	1.25	.50
51 Danny Kanell	1.25	.50
52 Wayne Chrebet	2.00	.75
53 Keyshawn Johnson	2.00	.75
54 Curtis Martin	2.00	.75
55 Tim Brown	2.00	.75
56 Rickey Dudley	.75	.30
57 Jeff George	1.25	.50
58 Napoleon Kaufman	2.00	.75
59 Irving Fryar	1.25	.50
60 Jerome Bettis	2.00	.75
61 Charles Johnson	.75	.30
62 Kordell Stewart	2.00	.75
63 Natrone Means	1.25	.50
64 Bryan Still	.75	.30
65 Garrison Hearst	2.00	.75
66 Jerry Rice	4.00	1.50
67 Steve Young	2.50	1.00
68 Joey Galloway	1.25	.50
69 Warren Moon	2.00	.75
70 Ricky Watters	1.25	.50
71 Isaac Bruce	2.00	.75
72 Mike Alstott	2.00	.75
73 Reidel Anthony	1.25	.50
74 Trent Dilfer	2.00	.75
75 Warrick Dunn	2.00	.75
76 Warren Sapp	1.25	.50
77 Eddie George	2.00	.75
78 Steve McNair	2.00	.75
79 Terry Allen	2.00	.75
80 Gus Frerotte	.75	.30
81 Andre Wadsworth AU/500*	25.00	10.00
82 Tim Dwight AU/500*	40.00	15.00
83 Curtis Enis AU/400*	40.00	15.00
85 Charlie Batch AU/500*	40.00	15.00
86 Germane Crowell AU/500*	25.00	10.00
87 Pey.Manning AU/200*	3000.00	2000.00
88 Jerome Pathon AU/500*	40.00	15.00
89 Fred Taylor AU/500*	120.00	60.00
90 Tavian Banks AU/500*	25.00	10.00
92 Randy Moss AU/300*	750.00	500.00
93 Robert Edwards AU/500*	25.00	10.00
94 Hines Ward AU/500*	250.00	125.00
95 Ryan Leaf AU/200*	60.00	25.00
96 Mikhael Ricks AU/500*	25.00	10.00
97 Ahman Green AU/500*	100.00	50.00
98 Jacquez Green AU/500*	25.00	10.00
99 Kevin Dyson AU/500*	40.00	15.00
100 Skip Hicks AU/500*	25.00	10.00
103 C.Fuamatu-Ma'afala AU/500*	25.00	10.00

1999 Playoff Contenders SSD

COMPLETE SET (200)	2000.00	1000.00
COMP.SET w/o RC/PT's (141)	60.00	25.00
1 Randy Moss	5.00	2.00
2 Randall Cunningham	2.00	.75
3 Cris Carter	2.00	.75

4 Robert Smith	2.00	.75
5 Jake Reed	1.25	.50
6 Albert Connell	.75	.30
7 Jeff George	1.25	.50
8 Brett Favre	6.00	2.50
9 Antonio Freeman	2.00	.75
10 Dorsey Levens	2.00	.75
11 Mark Chmura	1.25	.50
12 Mike Alstott	2.00	.75
13 Warrick Dunn	2.00	.75
14 Trent Dilfer	1.25	.50
15 Jacquez Green	.75	.30
16 Reidel Anthony	.75	.30
17 Warren Sapp	1.25	.50
18 Amani Toomer	.75	.30
19 Curtis Enis	.75	.30
20 Curtis Conway	1.25	.50
21 Bobby Engram	1.25	.50
22 Barry Sanders	6.00	2.50
23 Charlie Batch	2.00	.75
24 Herman Moore	1.25	.50
25 Johnnie Morton	1.25	.50
26 Greg Hill	.75	.30
27 Germane Crowell	.75	.30
28 Kerry Collins	1.25	.50
29 Ike Hilliard	.75	.30
30 Joe Jurevicius	1.25	.50
31 Stephen Davis	2.00	.75
32 Brad Johnson	2.00	.75
33 Skip Hicks	.75	.30
34 Michael Westbrook	1.25	.50
35 Jake Plummer	1.25	.50
36 Adrian Murrell	.75	.30
37 Frank Sanders	1.25	.50
38 Rob Moore	1.25	.50
39 Gary Brown	.75	.30
40 Duce Staley	2.00	.75
41 Charles Johnson	1.25	.50
42 Emmitt Smith	4.00	1.50
43 Troy Aikman	4.00	1.50
44 Michael Irvin	1.25	.50
45 Deion Sanders	2.00	.75
46 Rocket Ismail	1.25	.50
47 Jerry Rice	4.00	1.50
48 Terrell Owens	2.00	.75
49 Steve Young	2.50	1.00
50 Garrison Hearst	1.25	.50
51 J.J. Stokes	1.25	.50
52 Lawrence Phillips	1.25	.50
53 Jamal Anderson	2.00	.75
54 Chris Chandler	1.25	.50
55 Terance Mathis	1.25	.50
56 Tim Dwight	2.00	.75
57 Charlie Garner	1.25	.50
58 Chris Calloway	1.25	.50
59 Eddie Kennison	1.25	.50
60 Billy Joe Hobert	.75	.30
61 Tim Biakabutuka	1.25	.50
62 Muhsin Muhammad	1.25	.50
63 Olandis Gary AU/1825 RC	25.00	10.00
64 Wesley Walls	1.25	.50
65 Isaac Bruce	2.00	.75
66 Marshall Faulk	2.50	1.00
67 Kordell Stewart	1.25	.50
68 Jerome Bettis	2.00	.75
69 Hines Ward	2.00	.75
70 Corey Dillon	2.00	.75
71 Carl Pickens	1.25	.50
72 Darnay Scott	1.25	.50
73 Steve McNair	2.00	.75

❑ 74 Eddie George 2.00 .75
❑ 75 Yancey Thigpen .75 .30
❑ 76 Kevin Dyson 1.25 .50
❑ 77 Fred Taylor 2.00 .75
❑ 78 Mark Brunell 2.00 .75
❑ 79 Jimmy Smith 1.25 .50
❑ 80 Keenan McCardell 1.25 .50
❑ 81 James Stewart 1.25 .50
❑ 82 Jermaine Lewis 1.25 .50
❑ 83 Priest Holmes 3.00 1.25
❑ 84 Stoney Case .75 .30
❑ 85 Errict Rhett 1.25 .50
❑ 86 Bill Schroeder 2.00 .75
❑ 87 Terry Kirby .75 .30
❑ 88 [illegible]
❑ 89 Terrence Wilkins/825 RC 20.00 7.50
❑ 90 Dan Marino 6.00 2.50
❑ 91 O.J. McDuffie 1.25 .50
❑ 92 Karim Abdul-Jabbar 1.25 .50
❑ 93 Zach Thomas 2.00 .75
❑ 94 Terry Allen 1.25 .50
❑ 95 Tony Martin 1.25 .50
❑ 96 Drew Bledsoe 2.50 1.00
❑ 97 Terry Glenn 2.00 .75
❑ 98 Ben Coates 1.25 .50
❑ 99 Tony Simmons .75 .30
❑ 100 Curtis Martin 2.00 .75
❑ 101 Keyshawn Johnson 2.00 .75
❑ 102 Vinny Testaverde 1.25 .50
❑ 103 Wayne Chrebet 2.00 .75
❑ 104 Peyton Manning 6.00 2.50
❑ 105 Marvin Harrison 2.00 .75
❑ 106 E.G. Green .75 .30
❑ 107 Doug Flutie 2.00 .75
❑ 108 Thurman Thomas 1.25 .50
❑ 109 Andre Reed 1.25 .50
❑ 110 Eric Moulds 2.00 .75
❑ 111 Antowain Smith 2.00 .75
❑ 112 Bruce Smith 1.25 .50
❑ 113 Terrell Davis 2.00 .75
❑ 114 John Elway 6.00 2.50
❑ 115 Ed McCaffrey 1.25 .50
❑ 116 Rod Smith 1.25 .50
❑ 117 Shannon Sharpe 1.25 .50
❑ 118 Jeff Garcia AU/325 RC 100.00 50.00
❑ 119 Brian Griese 2.00 .75
❑ 120 Justin Watson/325 RC 25.00 10.00
❑ 121 Bubby Brister 1.25 .50
❑ 122 Ryan Leaf 2.00 .75
❑ 123 Natrone Means 1.25 .50
❑ 124 Mikhael Ricks .75 .30
❑ 125 Junior Seau 2.00 .75
❑ 126 Jim Harbaugh 1.25 .50
❑ 127 Andre Rison 1.25 .50
❑ 128 Elvis Grbac 1.25 .50
❑ 129 [illegible]
❑ 130 Rashaan Shehee .75 .30
❑ 131 Warren Moon 2.00 .75
❑ 132 Tony Gonzalez 2.00 .75
❑ 133 Derrick Alexander 1.25 .50
❑ 134 Jon Kitna 2.00 .75
❑ 135 Ricky Watters 1.25 .50
❑ 136 Joey Galloway 1.25 .50
❑ 137 Ahman Green 2.00 .75
❑ 138 Derrick Mayes 1.25 .50
❑ 139 Tyrone Wheatley 1.25 .50
❑ 140 Napoleon Kaufman 2.00 .75
❑ 141 Tim Brown 2.00 .75
❑ 142 Charles Woodson 2.00 .75
❑ 143 Rich Gannon 2.00 .75
❑ 144 Rickey Dudley .75 .30
❑ 145 Az-Zahir Hakim .75 .30
❑ 146 Kurt Warner AU/1825 RC 50.00 20.00
❑ 147 Sean Bennett AU/1325 RC 15.00 6.00
❑ 148 Bran.Stokley AU/1325 RC 30.00 12.50
❑ 149 Amos Zereoue AU/1325 RC 25.00 10.00
❑ 150 Brock Huard AU/1325 RC 25.00 10.00
❑ 151 Tim Couch AU/1025 RC 30.00 12.50
❑ 152 Ricky Williams AU/725 RC 50.00 20.00
❑ 153 Donov McNabb AU/525 RC 150.00 75.00
❑ 154 Edgerrin James AU/525 RC 100.00 50.00
❑ 155 Torry Holt AU/1025 RC 80.00 40.00
❑ 156 D.Culpepper AU/1025 RC 80.00 30.00
❑ 157 Akili Smith AU/1025 RC 20.00 7.50
❑ 158 Champ Bailey AU/1725 RC 30.00 12.50
❑ 159 Chris Claiborne AU/1825 RC 20.00 7.50
❑ 160A C McAlister No AU/1825 RC 15.00 6.00
❑ 160B Jason Tucker AU/1825 15.00 6.00
❑ 161 Troy Edwards AU/1225 RC 20.00 7.50
❑ 162 Jevon Kearse AU/325 RC 60.00 30.00
❑ 163 Darnell McDonald AU/1825 RC 20.00 7.50
❑ 164 David Boston AU/1025 RC 25.00 10.00
❑ 165 Peerless Price AU/1325 RC 25.00 10.00
❑ 166 C.Collins AU/1025 RC 15.00 6.00
❑ 167 Rob Konrad AU/1325 RC 20.00 7.50
❑ 168 Cade McNown AU/1025 RC 20.00 7.50
❑ 169 Shawn Bryson AU/1825 RC 20.00 7.50
❑ 170 Kevin Faulk AU/1325 RC 25.00 10.00
❑ 171 Corby Jones AU/1825 RC 15.00 6.00
❑ 172A Jam Johnson No AU/1325 RC 15.00 6.00
❑ 172B Patrick Jeffers AU/1325 25.00 10.00
❑ 173 [illegible] AU/1025 RC 20.00 7.50
❑ 174 Sedrick Irvin AU/1825 RC 15.00 6.00
❑ 175 Michael Bishop AU/1825 RC 25.00 10.00
❑ 176 Joe Germaine AU/825 RC 25.00 10.00
❑ 177 De'Mond Parker AU/1325 RC 15.00 6.00
❑ 178A Shaun King No AU/1825 RC 15.00 6.00
❑ 178B Ray Lucas AU/1825 25.00 10.00
❑ 179 D'Wayne Bates AU/1825 RC 20.00 7.50
❑ 180 Tai Streets AU/1825 RC 25.00 10.00
❑ 181 Na Brown AU/1825 RC 20.00 7.50
❑ 182 Desmond Clark AU/1825 RC 20.00 7.50
❑ 183 Jim Kleinsasser AU/1825 RC 20.00 7.50
❑ 184 Kevin Johnson AU/1325 RC 25.00 10.00
❑ 185 Joe Montgomery AU/1325 RC 20.00 7.50
❑ 186 John Elway PT 10.00 4.00
❑ 187 Dan Marino PT 10.00 4.00
❑ 188 Jerry Rice PT 6.00 2.50
❑ 189 Barry Sanders PT 10.00 4.00
❑ 190 Steve Young PT 4.00 1.50
❑ 191 Doug Flutie PT 2.50 1.00
❑ 192 Troy Aikman PT 6.00 2.50
❑ 193 Drew Bledsoe PT 4.00 1.50
❑ 194 Brett Favre PT 10.00 4.00
❑ 195 Randall Cunningham PT 2.50 1.00
❑ 196 Terrell Davis PT 2.50 1.00
❑ 197 Kordell Stewart PT 2.50 1.00
❑ 198 Keyshawn Johnson PT 2.50 1.00
❑ 199 Jake Plummer PT 2.50 1.00
❑ 200 Peyton Manning PT 10.00 4.00
❑ 201 Jay Fiedler/1825 AU 25.00 10.00
❑ 202 Kevin Daft/325 AU 40.00 20.00

2000 Playoff Contenders

❑ COMP.SET w/o SP's (100) 20.00 7.50
❑ 1 David Boston .75 .30
❑ 2 Jake Plummer .50 .20
❑ 3 Chris Chandler .50 .20
❑ 4 Jamal Anderson .75 .30
❑ 5 Tim Dwight .75 .30
❑ 6 Qadry Ismail .50 .20
❑ 7 Tony Banks .50 .20
❑ 8 Lamar Smith .50 .20
❑ 9 Doug Flutie .75 .30
❑ 10 Eric Moulds .75 .30
❑ 11 Peerless Price .50 .20
❑ 12 Rob Johnson .50 .20
❑ 13 Muhsin Muhammad .50 .20
❑ 14 Reggie White .75 .30
❑ 15 Steve Beuerlein .50 .20
❑ 16 Cade McNown .30 .10
❑ 17 Derrick Alexander .50 .20
❑ 18 Marcus Robinson .50 .20
❑ 19 Akili Smith .30 .10
❑ 20 Corey Dillon .75 .30
❑ 21 Kevin Johnson .75 .30
❑ 22 Tim Couch .50 .20
❑ 23 Emmitt Smith 1.50 .60
❑ 24 Joey Galloway .50 .20
❑ 25 Rocket Ismail .50 .20
❑ 26 Troy Aikman 1.50 .60
❑ 27 Brian Griese .75 .30
❑ 28 Ed McCaffrey .75 .30
❑ 29 John Elway 2.50 1.00
❑ 30 Olandis Gary .75 .30
❑ 31 Rod Smith .50 .20
❑ 32 Terrell Davis .75 .30
❑ 33 Charlie Batch .75 .30
❑ 34 Germane Crowell .30 .10
❑ 35 James Stewart .50 .20
❑ 36 Barry Sanders 2.00 .75
❑ 37 Antonio Freeman .75 .30
❑ 38 Brett Favre 2.50 1.00
❑ 39 Dorsey Levens .50 .20
❑ 40 Edgerrin James 1.25 .50
❑ 41 Marvin Harrison .75 .30
❑ 42 Peyton Manning 2.00 .75
❑ 43 Fred Taylor .75 .30
❑ 44 Jimmy Smith .50 .20
❑ 45 Mark Brunell .75 .30
❑ 46 Elvis Grbac .50 .20
❑ 47 Tony Gonzalez .50 .20
❑ 48 Dan Marino 2.50 1.00
❑ 49 Joe Horn .50 .20
❑ 50 Jay Fiedler .75 .30
❑ 51 Thurman Thomas .50 .20
❑ 52 Cris Carter .75 .30
❑ 53 Daunte Culpepper 1.00 .40
❑ 54 Randy Moss 1.50 .60
❑ 55 Robert Smith .75 .30
❑ 56 Drew Bledsoe 1.00 .40
❑ 57 Terry Glenn .50 .20
❑ 58 Ricky Williams .75 .30
❑ 59 Amani Toomer .30 .10
❑ 60 Kerry Collins .50 .20
❑ 61 Curtis Martin .75 .30
❑ 62 Vinny Testaverde .50 .20
❑ 63 Wayne Chrebet .50 .20
❑ 64 Rich Gannon .75 .30
❑ 65 Tim Brown .75 .30
❑ 66 Tyrone Wheatley .50 .20
❑ 67 Donovan McNabb 1.25 .50
❑ 68 Duce Staley .75 .30
❑ 69 Jerome Bettis .75 .30
❑ 70 Jermaine Fazande .30 .10
❑ 71 Junior Seau .75 .30
❑ 72 Donald Hayes .30 .10
❑ 73 Charlie Garner .50 .20
❑ 74 Jeff Garcia .75 .30
❑ 75 Jerry Rice 1.50 .60
❑ 76 Steve Young 1.00 .40
❑ 77 Terrell Owens .75 .30
❑ 78 Tiki Barber .75 .30
❑ 79 Tim Biakabutuka .50 .20
❑ 80 Ricky Watters .50 .20
❑ 81 Isaac Bruce .75 .30
❑ 82 Kurt Warner 1.50 .60
❑ 83 Marshall Faulk 1.00 .40
❑ 84 Torry Holt .75 .30
❑ 85 Keyshawn Johnson .75 .30
❑ 86 Mike Alstott .75 .30
❑ 87 Shaun King .30 .10
❑ 88 Warren Sapp .50 .20
❑ 89 Warrick Dunn .75 .30
❑ 90 Eddie George .75 .30
❑ 91 Jevon Kearse .75 .30
❑ 92 Steve McNair .75 .30
❑ 93 Carl Pickens .50 .20
❑ 94 Albert Connell .30 .10
❑ 95 Brad Johnson .75 .30
❑ 96 Bruce Smith .50 .20
❑ 97 Deion Sanders .75 .30
❑ 98 Jeff George .50 .20
❑ 99 Michael Westbrook .50 .20
❑ 100 Stephen Davis .75 .30
❑ 101 Courtney Brown AU RC 60.00 30.00
❑ 102 Corey Simon AU RC 20.00 7.50
❑ 103 Brian Urlacher AU RC 80.00 40.00
❑ 104 Deon Grant AU RC 15.00 6.00
❑ 105 Peter Warrick AU RC 20.00 7.50
❑ 106 Jamal Lewis AU RC 50.00 25.00
❑ 108 Plaxico Burress AU RC 60.00 30.00
❑ 109 Travis Taylor AU RC 25.00 10.00

❑ 110 Ron Dayne AU RC	40.00	20.00
❑ 111 Bubba Franks AU RC	20.00	7.50
❑ 112 Chad Pennington AU RC	80.00	30.00
❑ 113 Shaun Alexander AU RC	100.00	50.00
❑ 114 Sylvester Morris AU RC	15.00	6.00
❑ 115 Mike Anderson AU RC	30.00	12.50
❑ 116 R.Jay Soward AU RC	15.00	6.00
❑ 117 Trung Canidate AU RC	15.00	6.00
❑ 118 Dennis Northcutt AU RC	20.00	7.50
❑ 119 Todd Pinkston AU RC	20.00	7.50
❑ 120 Jerry Porter AU RC	40.00	15.00
❑ 121 Travis Prentice AU RC	15.00	6.00
❑ 122 Giovanni Carmazzi AU RC	10.00	4.00
❑ 123 Ron Dugans AU RC	10.00	4.00
❑ 124 Dez White AU RC	20.00	7.50
❑ 125 Chris Cole AU RC	15.00	6.00
❑ 126 Ron Dixon AU RC	15.00	6.00
❑ 127 Chris Redman AU RC	15.00	6.00
❑ 128 J.R. Redmond AU RC	20.00	7.50
❑ 129 Laveranues Coles AU RC	30.00	15.00
❑ 130 JaJuan Dawson AU RC	10.00	4.00
❑ 131 Darrell Jackson AU RC	30.00	12.50
❑ 132 Reuben Droughns AU RC	30.00	12.50
❑ 133 Doug Chapman AU RC	15.00	6.00
❑ 134 Curtis Keaton AU RC	15.00	6.00
❑ 135 Gari Scott AU RC	10.00	4.00
❑ 136 Danny Farmer AU RC	15.00	6.00
❑ 137 Trevor Gaylor AU RC	15.00	6.00
❑ 138 Avion Black AU RC	15.00	6.00
❑ 139 Michael Wiley AU RC	15.00	6.00
❑ 140 Sammy Morris AU RC	30.00	15.00
❑ 141 Tee Martin AU RC	20.00	7.50
❑ 142 Troy Walters AU RC	20.00	7.50
❑ 143 Marc Bulger AU RC	50.00	20.00
❑ 144 Tom Brady AU RC	1600.00	1000.00
❑ 145 Todd Husak AU RC	20.00	7.50
❑ 146 Tim Rattay AU RC	20.00	7.50
❑ 147 Jarious Jackson AU RC	15.00	6.00
❑ 148 Joe Hamilton AU RC	15.00	6.00
❑ 149 Shyrone Stith AU RC	15.00	6.00
❑ 150 Kwame Cavil AU RC	10.00	4.00
❑ 151 Antonio Banks ET AU RC	6.00	2.50
❑ 152 Jonathan Brown ET AU RC	6.00	2.50
❑ 153 Ontiwaun Carter ET AU RC	6.00	2.50
❑ 154 Jeremaine Copeland ET	6.00	2.50
❑ 155 Ralph Dawkins ET AU RC	8.00	3.00
❑ 156 Marques Douglas ET AU RC	6.00	2.50
❑ 157 Kevin Drake ET AU RC	6.00	2.50
❑ 158 Damon Dunn ET AU RC	8.00	3.00
❑ 159 Todd Floyd ET AU RC	6.00	2.50
❑ 160 Tony Graziani ET AU	8.00	3.00
❑ 162 Duane Hawthorne ET AU RC	8.00	3.00
❑ 163 Alonzo Johnson ET AU RC	6.00	2.50
❑ 164 Mark Kacmarynski ET AU RC	6.00	2.50
❑ 165 Eric Kresser ET AU	6.00	2.50
❑ 166 Jim Kubiak ET AU RC	8.00	3.00
❑ 167 Blaine McElmurry ET AU RC	6.00	2.50
❑ 168 Scott Milanovich ET AU	10.00	4.00
❑ 169 Norman Miller ET AU RC	6.00	2.50
❑ 170 Sean Morey ET AU RC	8.00	3.00
❑ 171 Jeff Ogden ET AU	8.00	3.00
❑ 172 Pepe Pearson ET AU RC	8.00	3.00
❑ 173 Ron Powlus ET AU RC	10.00	4.00
❑ 174 Jason Shelley ET AU RC	8.00	3.00
❑ 175 Ben Snell ET AU RC	8.00	3.00
❑ 176 Aaron Stecker ET AU RC	8.00	3.00
❑ 177 L.C. Stevens ET AU	6.00	2.50
❑ 178 Mike Sutton ET AU RC	6.00	2.50
❑ 179 Damian Vaughn ET AU RC	6.00	2.50
❑ 180 Ted White ET AU	6.00	2.50
❑ 181 Marcus Crandell ET AU RC	8.00	3.00
❑ 182 Darryl Daniel ET AU RC	8.00	3.00
❑ 183 Jesse Haynes ET AU	6.00	2.50
❑ 184 Matt Lytle ET AU RC	8.00	3.00
❑ 185 Deon Mitchell ET AU RC	8.00	3.00
❑ 186 Kendrick Nord ET AU RC	6.00	2.50
❑ 188 Selucio Sanford ET AU RC	8.00	3.00
❑ 189 Corey Thomas ET AU	6.00	2.50
❑ 190 Vershan Jackson ET AU RC	6.00	2.50
❑ 191 Jake Plummer PT	20.00	7.50
❑ 192 Jim Kelly PT AU	40.00	15.00
❑ 193 Bernie Kosar PT AU	40.00	15.00
❑ 194 Marvin Harrison PT AU	40.00	15.00
❑ 196 Kerry Collins PT AU	30.00	12.50
❑ 197 Kurt Warner PT AU	60.00	25.00
❑ 198 Jevon Kearse PT AU	30.00	12.50
❑ 199 Brad Johnson PT AU	30.00	12.50
❑ 200 Jeff George PT AU	30.00	12.50

2001 Playoff Contenders

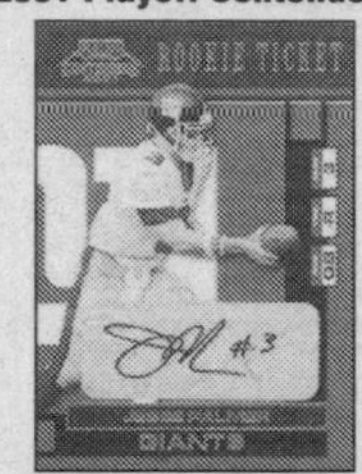

❑ COMP.SET w/o SP's (100)	25.00	10.00
❑ 1 David Boston	1.00	.40
❑ 2 Jake Plummer	.60	.25
❑ 3 Jamal Anderson	1.00	.40
❑ 4 Chris Chandler	.60	.25
❑ 5 Elvis Grbac	.60	.25
❑ 6 Brandon Stokley	.60	.25
❑ 7 Travis Taylor	.60	.25
❑ 8 Ray Lewis	1.00	.40
❑ 9 Rob Johnson	.60	.25
❑ 10 Eric Moulds	.60	.25
❑ 11 Tim Biakabutuka	.60	.25
❑ 12 Muhsin Muhammad	.60	.25
❑ 13 James Allen	.60	.25
❑ 14 Brian Urlacher	1.50	.60
❑ 15 Peter Warrick	1.00	.40
❑ 16 Corey Dillon	1.00	.40
❑ 17 Tim Couch	.60	.25
❑ 18 Kevin Johnson	.60	.25
❑ 19 Rickey Dudley	.40	.10
❑ 20 Emmitt Smith	2.00	.75
❑ 21 Joey Galloway	.60	.25
❑ 22 Brian Griese	1.00	.40
❑ 23 Terrell Davis	1.00	.40
❑ 24 Mike Anderson	1.00	.40
❑ 25 Ed McCaffrey	1.00	.40
❑ 26 Rod Smith	.60	.25
❑ 27 Charlie Batch	1.00	.40
❑ 28 James Stewart	.60	.25
❑ 29 Germane Crowell	.40	.10
❑ 30 Johnnie Morton	.60	.25
❑ 31 Brett Favre	3.00	1.25
❑ 32 Ahman Green	1.00	.40
❑ 33 Antonio Freeman	1.00	.40
❑ 34 Peyton Manning	2.50	1.00
❑ 35 Edgerrin James	1.25	.50
❑ 36 Marvin Harrison	1.00	.40
❑ 37 Jerome Pathon	.60	.25
❑ 38 Mark Brunell	1.00	.40
❑ 39 Fred Taylor	1.00	.40
❑ 40 Keenan McCardell	.40	.10
❑ 41 Jimmy Smith	.60	.25
❑ 42 Trent Green	1.00	.40
❑ 43 Priest Holmes	1.25	.50
❑ 44 Tony Gonzalez	.60	.25
❑ 45 Derrick Alexander	.60	.25
❑ 46 Jay Fiedler	1.00	.40
❑ 47 Lamar Smith	.60	.25
❑ 48 Zach Thomas	1.00	.40
❑ 49 Oronde Gadsden	.60	.25
❑ 50 Daunte Culpepper	1.00	.40
❑ 51 Randy Moss	2.00	.75
❑ 52 Cris Carter	1.00	.40
❑ 53 Drew Bledsoe	1.25	.50
❑ 54 J.R. Redmond	.40	.10
❑ 55 Troy Brown	.60	.25
❑ 56 Aaron Brooks	1.00	.40
❑ 57 Ricky Williams	1.00	.40
❑ 58 Joe Horn	.60	.25
❑ 59 Kerry Collins	.60	.25
❑ 60 Tiki Barber	1.00	.40
❑ 61 Ron Dayne	1.00	.40
❑ 62 Ike Hilliard	.60	.25
❑ 63 Vinny Testaverde	.60	.25
❑ 64 Curtis Martin	1.00	.40
❑ 65 Wayne Chrebet	.60	.25
❑ 66 Laveranues Coles	1.00	.40
❑ 67 Rich Gannon	1.00	.40
❑ 68 Tyrone Wheatley	.60	.25
❑ 69 Tim Brown	1.00	.40
❑ 70 Jerry Rice	2.00	.75
❑ 71 Donovan McNabb	1.25	.50
❑ 72 Duce Staley	1.00	.40
❑ 73 Todd Pinkston	.60	.25
❑ 74 Kordell Stewart	.60	.25
❑ 75 Jerome Bettis	1.00	.40
❑ 76 Plaxico Burress	1.00	.40
❑ 77 Doug Flutie	1.00	.40
❑ 78 Junior Seau	1.00	.40
❑ 79 Jeff Garcia	1.00	.40
❑ 80 Garrison Hearst	.60	.25
❑ 81 Terrell Owens	1.00	.40
❑ 82 Matt Hasselbeck	.60	.25
❑ 83 Ricky Watters	.60	.25
❑ 84 Shaun Alexander	1.25	.50
❑ 85 Darrell Jackson	1.00	.40
❑ 86 Kurt Warner	2.00	.75
❑ 87 Marshall Faulk	1.25	.50
❑ 88 Isaac Bruce	1.00	.40
❑ 89 Torry Holt	1.00	.40
❑ 90 Brad Johnson	1.00	.40
❑ 91 Keyshawn Johnson	1.00	.40
❑ 92 Warrick Dunn	1.00	.40
❑ 93 Warren Sapp	.60	.25
❑ 94 Steve McNair	1.00	.40
❑ 95 Eddie George	1.00	.40
❑ 96 Derrick Mason	.60	.25
❑ 97 Jevon Kearse	.60	.25
❑ 98 Stephen Davis	1.00	.40
❑ 99 Bruce Smith	.60	.25
❑ 100 Michael Westbrook	.60	.25
❑ 101 Adam Archuleta/50 RC	80.00	40.00
❑ 102 Alex Bannister AU RC	15.00	6.00
❑ 103 Alge Crumpler AU RC	30.00	15.00
❑ 104 Andre Carter AU/100 RC	50.00	25.00
❑ 105 Anthony Thomas AU/600 RC	25.00	10.00
❑ 106 Ben Leard AU RC	10.00	4.00
❑ 107 Bobby Newcombe AU RC	15.00	6.00
❑ 108 Brian Allen AU RC	10.00	4.00
❑ 109 Carlos Polk AU RC	10.00	4.00
❑ 110 Casey Hampton No Auto RC	25.00	10.00
❑ 111 Cedric Scott AU RC	10.00	4.00
❑ 112 Cedrick Wilson AU RC	30.00	12.50
❑ 113 Chad Johnson AU RC	135.00	75.00
❑ 114 Chris Chambers AU/170 RC	150.00	75.00
❑ 115 Chris Weinke AU/350 RC	30.00	15.00
❑ 116 Correll Buckhalter AU/590 RC	30.00	12.50
❑ 117 Damione Lewis AU RC	25.00	10.00
❑ 118 Dan Morgan AU RC	40.00	15.00
❑ 119 Daniel Guy AU RC	10.00	4.00
❑ 120 David Allen AU RC	10.00	4.00
❑ 121 David Terrell AU/500 RC	25.00	10.00
❑ 122 Ken Lucas AU/276 RC	10.00	4.00
❑ 123 Deu McAllister AU/500 RC	80.00	40.00
❑ 124 Drew Brees AU/500 RC	200.00	100.00
❑ 125 Eddie Berlin AU RC	10.00	4.00
❑ 126 Boo Williams AU/50 RC	60.00	30.00
❑ 127 Ennis Davis AU RC	10.00	4.00
❑ 128 Freddie Mitchell AU RC	25.00	10.00
❑ 129 Gary Baxter AU RC	15.00	6.00
❑ 130 Gerard Warren AU/200 RC	40.00	15.00
❑ 131 Hakim Akbar AU RC	10.00	4.00
❑ 132 Heath Evans AU RC	10.00	4.00
❑ 133 Jabari Holloway AU RC	15.00	6.00
❑ 134 Jamal Reynolds AU/500 RC	15.00	6.00
❑ 135 James Jackson AU RC	15.00	6.00
❑ 136 Jamie Winborn AU RC	10.00	4.00
❑ 137 Javon Green AU RC	10.00	4.00
❑ 138 Jesse Palmer AU RC	25.00	10.00
❑ 139 Dominic Rhodes AU/300 RC	60.00	30.00
❑ 140 Josh Heupel AU/150 RC	50.00	20.00
❑ 141 Justin Smith AU RC	15.00	6.00
❑ 142 Karon Riley AU RC	10.00	4.00
❑ 143 Keith Adams/50 RC	80.00	40.00
❑ 144 Kendrell Bell AU RC	30.00	15.00
❑ 145 Kenny Smith AU RC	15.00	6.00
❑ 146 Ken. Walker AU/50 RC	80.00	40.00
❑ 147 Ken-Yon Rambo AU RC	10.00	4.00
❑ 148 Kevan Barlow AU RC	30.00	15.00
❑ 149 Koren Robinson AU/400 RC	30.00	12.50
❑ 150 L.Tomlinson AU/600 RC	750.00	450.00
❑ 151 LaMont Jordan AU/50 RC	500.00	350.00

- ❑ 152 Leonard Davis/50 RC 80.00 40.00
- ❑ 153 Marcus Stroud AU RC 25.00 10.00
- ❑ 154 Marques Tuiasosopo AU RC 25.00 10.00
- ❑ 155 Snoop Minnis AU/295 RC 15.00 6.00
- ❑ 156 Michael Bennett AU/600 RC 30.00 15.00
- ❑ 157 Michael Vick AU/327 RC 200.00 100.00
- ❑ 158 Mike McMahon AU/529 RC 30.00 15.00
- ❑ 159 Moran Norris AU RC 10.00 4.00
- ❑ 160 Morlon Greenwood AU RC 10.00 4.00
- ❑ 161 Nate Clements/50 RC 80.00 40.00
- ❑ 162 Quincy Carter AU SP RC 80.00 40.00
- ❑ 163 Quincy Morgan AU RC 25.00 10.00
- ❑ 164 Jamar Fletcher/50 RC 80.00 40.00
- ❑ 165 Reggie Germany AU RC 10.00 4.00
- ❑ 166 [illegible] AU/[illegible] RC 100.00 [illegible]
- ❑ 167 Reggie White AU RC 10.00 4.00
- ❑ 168 Richard Seymour/50 RC 100.00 50.00
- ❑ 169 Robert Carswell/50 RC 60.00 30.00
- ❑ 170 Robert Ferguson AU RC 25.00 10.00
- ❑ 171 Rod Gardner AU/75 RC 120.00 60.00
- ❑ 172 Ronney Daniels AU RC 10.00 4.00
- ❑ 173 Rudi Johnson AU RC 80.00 40.00
- ❑ 174 Sage Rosenfels AU/400 RC 25.00 10.00
- ❑ 175 Santana Moss AU/500 RC 60.00 30.00
- ❑ 176 Shaun Rogers AU RC 25.00 10.00
- ❑ 177 Houshmandzadeh AU RC 50.00 30.00
- ❑ 178 Tim Hasselbeck AU RC 25.00 10.00
- ❑ 179 Todd Heap AU/169 RC 100.00 50.00
- ❑ 180 Tony Stewart AU RC 15.00 6.00
- ❑ 181 Torrance Marshall AU RC 15.00 6.00
- ❑ 182 Travis Henry AU/369 RC 100.00 60.00
- ❑ 183 Travis Minor AU RC 25.00 10.00
- ❑ 184 Vinny Sutherland AU RC 15.00 6.00
- ❑ 185 Will Allen AU RC 15.00 6.00
- ❑ 186 Willie Howard AU RC 10.00 4.00
- ❑ 187 W Middlebrooks/50 RC 60.00 30.00
- ❑ 188 Derrick Blaylock AU/200 RC 60.00 30.00
- ❑ 189 A.J. Feeley AU/200 RC 80.00 30.00
- ❑ 190 Steve Smith AU/300 RC 200.00 100.00
- ❑ 191 Onome Ojo AU/200 RC 15.00 6.00
- ❑ 192 Dee Brown AU/300 RC 25.00 10.00
- ❑ 193 Kevin Kasper AU/200 RC 25.00 10.00
- ❑ 194 Dave Dickenson AU/300 RC 25.00 10.00
- ❑ 195 Chris Barnes AU/200 RC 25.00 10.00
- ❑ 196 Scotty Anderson AU/300 RC 25.00 10.00
- ❑ 197 Chris Taylor AU/300 RC 15.00 6.00
- ❑ 198 Cedric James AU/300 SP RC 25.00 10.00
- ❑ 199 Justin McCareins AU/200 RC 50.00 20.00
- ❑ 200 Tommy Polley AU/200 RC 25.00 10.00

2002 Playoff Contenders

- ❑ COMP.SET w/o SP's (100) 25.00 10.00
- ❑ 1 Drew Bledsoe 1.25 .50
- ❑ 2 Travis Henry 1.00 .40
- ❑ 3 Eric Moulds .60 .25
- ❑ 4 Chris Chambers 1.00 .40
- ❑ 5 Ricky Williams 1.00 .40
- ❑ 6 Zach Thomas 1.00 .40
- ❑ 7 Tom Brady 2.50 1.00
- ❑ 8 Antowain Smith .60 .25
- ❑ 9 Troy Brown .60 .25
- ❑ 10 Curtis Martin 1.00 .40
- ❑ 11 Vinny Testaverde .60 .25
- ❑ 12 Chad Pennington 1.25 .50
- ❑ 13 Jeff Blake .40 .15
- ❑ 14 Jamal Lewis 1.00 .40
- ❑ 15 Ray Lewis 1.00 .40
- ❑ 16 Michael Westbrook .40 .15
- ❑ 17 Corey Dillon .60 .25
- ❑ 18 Peter Warrick .60 .25
- ❑ 19 Tim Couch .60 .25
- ❑ 20 Quincy Morgan .60 .25
- ❑ 21 Kevin Johnson .60 .25
- ❑ 22 Kordell Stewart .60 .25
- ❑ 23 Plaxico Burress .60 .25
- ❑ 24 Jerome Bettis 1.00 .40
- ❑ 25 James Allen .60 .25
- ❑ 26 Corey Bradford .40 .15
- ❑ 27 Mark Brunell 1.00 .40
- ❑ 28 Fred Taylor 1.00 .40
- ❑ 29 Jimmy Smith .60 .25
- ❑ 30 Peyton Manning 2.00 .75
- ❑ 31 Reggie Wayne 1.00 .40
- ❑ [illegible]
- ❑ 33 Edgerrin James 1.25 .50
- ❑ 34 Steve McNair 1.00 .40
- ❑ 35 Eddie George 1.00 .40
- ❑ 36 Jevon Kearse .60 .25
- ❑ 37 Derrick Mason .60 .25
- ❑ 38 Brian Griese 1.00 .40
- ❑ 39 Terrell Davis 1.00 .40
- ❑ 40 Ed McCaffrey 1.00 .40
- ❑ 41 Rod Smith .60 .25
- ❑ 42 Trent Green .60 .25
- ❑ 43 Priest Holmes 1.25 .50
- ❑ 44 Johnnie Morton .60 .25
- ❑ 45 Tony Gonzalez .60 .25
- ❑ 46 Rich Gannon 1.00 .40
- ❑ 47 Tim Brown 1.00 .40
- ❑ 48 Jerry Rice 2.00 .75
- ❑ 49 Charlie Garner .60 .25
- ❑ 50 Drew Brees 1.00 .40
- ❑ 51 LaDainian Tomlinson 1.50 .60
- ❑ 52 Junior Seau 1.00 .40
- ❑ 53 Quincy Carter .60 .25
- ❑ 54 Emmitt Smith 2.50 1.00
- ❑ 55 Joey Galloway .60 .25
- ❑ 56 Kerry Collins .60 .25
- ❑ 57 Tiki Barber 1.00 .40
- ❑ 58 Michael Strahan .60 .25
- ❑ 59 Donovan McNabb 1.25 .50
- ❑ 60 Duce Staley 1.00 .40
- ❑ 61 Antonio Freeman 1.00 .40
- ❑ 62 Derrius Thompson .40 .15
- ❑ 63 Stephen Davis .60 .25
- ❑ 64 Rod Gardner .60 .25
- ❑ 65 Anthony Thomas .60 .25
- ❑ 66 Marty Booker .60 .25
- ❑ 67 Brian Urlacher 1.50 .60
- ❑ 68 James Stewart .60 .25
- ❑ 69 Az-Zahir Hakim .40 .15
- ❑ 70 Brett Favre 2.50 1.00
- ❑ 71 Ahman Green 1.00 .40
- ❑ 72 Donald Driver .60 .25
- ❑ 73 Daunte Culpepper 1.00 .40
- ❑ 74 Michael Bennett .60 .25
- ❑ 75 Randy Moss 2.00 .75
- ❑ 76 Michael Vick 2.00 .75
- ❑ 77 Warrick Dunn 1.00 .40
- ❑ 78 Chris Weinke .60 .25
- ❑ 79 Lamar Smith .60 .25
- ❑ 80 Steve Smith 1.00 .40
- ❑ 81 Aaron Brooks 1.00 .40
- ❑ 82 Deuce McAllister 1.25 .50
- ❑ 83 Joe Horn .60 .25
- ❑ 84 Brad Johnson .60 .25
- ❑ 85 Keyshawn Johnson 1.00 .40
- ❑ 86 Mike Alstott 1.00 .40
- ❑ 87 Warren Sapp .60 .25
- ❑ 88 Jake Plummer .60 .25
- ❑ 89 Thomas Jones .60 .25
- ❑ 90 David Boston 1.00 .40
- ❑ 91 Kurt Warner 1.00 .40
- ❑ 92 Marshall Faulk 1.00 .40
- ❑ 93 Isaac Bruce 1.00 .40
- ❑ 94 Torry Holt 1.00 .40
- ❑ 95 Jeff Garcia 1.00 .40
- ❑ 96 Garrison Hearst .60 .25
- ❑ 97 Kevan Barlow .60 .25
- ❑ 98 Terrell Owens 1.00 .40
- ❑ 99 Trent Dilfer .60 .25
- ❑ 100 Shaun Alexander 1.25 .50
- ❑ 101 Adrian Peterson AU/360 RC 40.00 20.00
- ❑ 102 A.Haynesworth No Auto RC 30.00 12.50
- ❑ 103 Alex Brown AU/410 RC 40.00 20.00
- ❑ 104 Andra Davis AU/510 RC 15.00 6.00
- ❑ 105 Andre Davis AU/360 RC 30.00 12.50
- ❑ 106 Andre Lott AU/750 RC 15.00 6.00
- ❑ 107 Anthony Weaver AU/450 RC 15.00 6.00
- ❑ 108 Antonio Bryant AU/165 RC 50.00 20.00
- ❑ 109 Antw Randle El AU/135 RC 80.00 30.00
- ❑ 110 Ashley Lelie AU/360 RC 30.00 12.50
- ❑ 111 Brian Poli-Dixon AU/460 RC 20.00 7.50
- ❑ 112 Brian Westbrook AU/600 RC 100.00 60.00
- ❑ 113 Bryant McKinnie AU/600 RC 30.00 12.50
- ❑ 114 C Hutchinson AU/450 RC 20.00 7.50
- ❑ 115 Charles Grant AU/450 RC 20.00 7.50
- ❑ 116 Chester Taylor AU/315 RC 50.00 20.00
- ❑ 117 Cliff Russell AU/545 RC 20.00 7.50
- ❑ 118 Clinton Portis AU/360 RC 120.00 60.00
- ❑ 119 [illegible]
- ❑ 120 Damien Anderson AU/460 RC 15.00 6.00
- ❑ 121 Daniel Graham AU/185 RC 50.00 20.00
- ❑ 122 David Carr AU/250 RC 80.00 40.00
- ❑ 123 David Garrard AU/310 RC 100.00 60.00
- ❑ 124 Deion Branch AU/650 RC 50.00 20.00
- ❑ 125 John Simon AU/400 RC 20.00 7.50
- ❑ 126 DeShaun Foster AU/310 RC 60.00 30.00
- ❑ 127 Donte Stallworth AU/302 RC 50.00 20.00
- ❑ 128 Dwight Freeney AU/410 RC 60.00 30.00
- ❑ 129 Ed Reed AU/550 RC 50.00 20.00
- ❑ 130 Eric Crouch AU/280 RC 30.00 12.50
- ❑ 131 Freddie Milons AU/380 RC 20.00 7.50
- ❑ 132 Jabar Gaffney AU/315 RC 30.00 12.50
- ❑ 133 Javon Walker AU/435 RC 60.00 30.00
- ❑ 134 Jeremy Shockey AU/160 RC 200.00 125.00
- ❑ 135 Jerramy Stevens AU/250 RC 30.00 12.50
- ❑ 136 Joey Harrington AU/250 RC 60.00 25.00
- ❑ 137 John Henderson AU/560 RC 30.00 12.50
- ❑ 138 Jonathan Wells AU/485 RC 40.00 15.00
- ❑ 139 Josh McCown AU/595 RC 40.00 20.00
- ❑ 140 Josh Reed AU/290 RC 40.00 15.00
- ❑ 141 Josh Scobey AU/615 RC 15.00 6.00
- ❑ 142 Julius Peppers AU/40 RC 600.00 350.00
- ❑ 143 Kalimba Edwards AU/510 RC 20.00 7.50
- ❑ 144 Kelly Campbell AU/360 RC 30.00 12.50
- ❑ 145 Ken Simonton AU/650 RC 15.00 6.00
- ❑ 146 Keyuo Craver AU/850 RC 15.00 6.00
- ❑ 147 Kahlil Hill AU/850 RC 20.00 7.50
- ❑ 148 Kurt Kittner AU/235 RC 20.00 7.50
- ❑ 149 Ladell Betts AU/600 RC 40.00 20.00
- ❑ 150 Lamar Gordon AU/600 RC 30.00 12.50
- ❑ 151 Levar Fisher AU/760 RC 15.00 6.00
- ❑ 152 Lito Sheppard AU/410 RC 30.00 12.50
- ❑ 153 Luke Staley AU/360 RC 20.00 7.50
- ❑ 154 Marquise Walker AU/330 RC 30.00 12.50
- ❑ 155 Maurice Morris AU/153 RC 60.00 30.00
- ❑ 156 Mike Rumph AU/510 RC 30.00 12.50
- ❑ 157 Mike Williams AU/500 RC 20.00 7.50
- ❑ 158 Najeh Davenport AU/460 RC 30.00 12.50
- ❑ 159 Napoleon Harris AU/900 RC 20.00 7.50
- ❑ 160 Patrick Ramsey AU/375 RC 40.00 15.00
- ❑ 161 Buchanon No AU/310 RC 50.00 20.00
- ❑ 162 Quentin Jammer AU/300 RC 30.00 12.50
- ❑ 163 Randy Fasani AU/500 RC 20.00 7.50
- ❑ 164 Reche Caldwell AU/340 RC 30.00 12.50
- ❑ 165 Robert Thomas AU/460 RC 30.00 12.50
- ❑ 166 Rocky Calmus AU/385 RC 30.00 12.50
- ❑ 167 Rohan Davey AU/295 RC 50.00 20.00
- ❑ 168 Ron Johnson AU/385 RC 20.00 7.50
- ❑ 169 Roy Williams AU/250 RC 80.00 40.00
- ❑ 170 Ryan Sims No AU/360 RC 30.00 12.50
- ❑ 171 Tavon Mason AU/690 RC 15.00 6.00
- ❑ 172 Terry Charles AU/750 RC 15.00 6.00
- ❑ 173 T.J. Duckett AU/335 RC 40.00 15.00
- ❑ 174 Tim Carter AU/600 RC 20.00 7.50
- ❑ 175 Travis Stephens AU/170 RC 50.00 25.00
- ❑ 176 Trev Faulk AU/600 RC 15.00 6.00
- ❑ 177 Wendell Bryant AU/560 RC 15.00 6.00
- ❑ 178 William Green AU/317 RC 30.00 12.50
- ❑ 179 Woody Dantzler AU/185 RC 30.00 12.50
- ❑ 180 Tony Fisher AU/340 RC 30.00 12.50
- ❑ 181 Javin Hunter AU/400 RC 15.00 6.00
- ❑ 182 Daryl Jones AU/400 RC 20.00 7.50
- ❑ 183 Jesse Chatman AU/400 RC 30.00 12.50
- ❑ 184 J.T. O'Sullivan AU/340 RC 20.00 7.50
- ❑ 185 Josh Norman AU/340 RC 30.00 12.50
- ❑ 186 James Mungro AU/100 RC 80.00 40.00

2003 Playoff Contenders

- ❑ COMP.SET w/o SP's (100) 20.00 7.50
- ❑ UNPRICED CHAMPION.TICKET #'d TO 1
- ❑ 1 Roy Williams .75 .30

❑ 2 Antonio Bryant .50 .20
❑ 3 Jeremy Shockey 1.25 .50
❑ 4 Kerry Collins .50 .20
❑ 5 Tiki Barber .75 .30
❑ 6 Michael Strahan .50 .20
❑ 7 Donovan McNabb 1.00 .40
❑ 8 Duce Staley .50 .20
❑ 9 Todd Pinkston .50 .20
❑ 10 Patrick Ramsey .75 .30
❑ 11 Laveranues Coles .50 .20
❑ 12 Rod Gardner .50 .20
❑ 13 Drew Bledsoe .75 .30
❑ 14 Travis Henry .50 .20
❑ 15 Eric Moulds .50 .20
❑ 16 Josh Reed .50 .20
❑ 17 Ricky Williams .75 .30
❑ 18 Jay Fiedler .50 .20
❑ 19 Chris Chambers .75 .30
❑ 20 Zach Thomas .75 .30
❑ 21 Junior Seau .75 .30
❑ 22 Tom Brady 2.00 .75
❑ 23 Troy Brown .50 .20
❑ 24 Chad Pennington 1.00 .40
❑ 25 Curtis Martin .75 .30
❑ 26 Santana Moss .50 .20
❑ 27 Emmitt Smith 2.00 .75
❑ 28 Jeff Garcia .75 .30
❑ 29 Terrell Owens .75 .30
❑ 30 Kevan Barlow .50 .20
❑ 31 Shaun Alexander .75 .30
❑ 32 Matt Hasselbeck .50 .20
❑ 33 Koren Robinson .50 .20
❑ 34 Kurt Warner .75 .30
❑ 35 Marshall Faulk .75 .30
❑ 36 Torry Holt .75 .30
❑ 37 Isaac Bruce .75 .30
❑ 38 Clinton Portis 1.25 .50
❑ 39 Jake Plummer .50 .20
❑ 40 Rod Smith .50 .20
❑ 41 Ed McCaffrey .75 .30
❑ 42 Ashley Lelie .75 .30
❑ 43 Priest Holmes 1.00 .40
❑ 44 Trent Green .50 .20
❑ 45 Tony Gonzalez .50 .20
❑ 46 Jerry Rice 1.50 .60
❑ 47 Rich Gannon .50 .20
❑ 48 Tim Brown .75 .30
❑ 49 Jerry Porter .50 .20
❑ 50 Charles Woodson .50 .20
❑ 51 LaDainian Tomlinson .75 .30
❑ 52 Drew Brees .75 .30
❑ 53 David Boston .50 .20
❑ 54 Brian Urlacher 1.25 .50
❑ 55 Kordell Stewart .50 .20
❑ 56 Marty Booker .50 .20
❑ 57 Joey Harrington 1.25 .50
❑ 58 Brett Favre 2.00 .75
❑ 59 Ahman Green .75 .30
❑ 60 Donald Driver .50 .20
❑ 61 Javon Walker .50 .20
❑ 62 Randy Moss 1.25 .50
❑ 63 Daunte Culpepper .75 .30
❑ 64 Michael Bennett .50 .20
❑ 65 Jamal Lewis .75 .30
❑ 66 Ray Lewis .75 .30
❑ 67 Corey Dillon .50 .20
❑ 68 Chad Johnson .75 .30
❑ 69 William Green .50 .20
❑ 70 Tim Couch .30 .10
❑ 71 Quincy Morgan .50 .20
❑ 72 Plaxico Burress .50 .20
❑ 73 Tommy Maddox .75 .30
❑ 74 Hines Ward .75 .30
❑ 75 Antwaan Randle El .75 .30
❑ 76 Michael Vick 2.00 .75
❑ 77 Peerless Price .50 .20
❑ 78 Warrick Dunn .50 .20
❑ 79 T.J. Duckett .50 .20
❑ 80 Julius Peppers .75 .30
❑ 81 Stephen Davis .50 .20
❑ 82 Deuce McAllister .75 .30
❑ 83 Aaron Brooks .75 .30
❑ 84 Joe Horn .50 .20
❑ 85 Donte Stallworth .75 .30
❑ 86 Mike Alstott .75 .30
❑ 87 Brad Johnson .50 .20
❑ 88 Keyshawn Johnson .75 .30
❑ 89 Warren Sapp .50 .20
❑ 90 David Carr 1.25 .50
❑ 91 Jabar Gaffney .50 .20
❑ 92 Peyton Manning 1.25 .50
❑ 93 Edgerrin James .75 .30
❑ 94 Marvin Harrison .75 .30
❑ 95 Mark Brunell .50 .20
❑ 96 Fred Taylor .75 .30
❑ 97 Jimmy Smith .50 .20
❑ 98 Steve McNair .75 .30
❑ 99 Eddie George .50 .20
❑ 100 Jevon Kearse .50 .20
❑ 101 Lee Suggs AU/499 RC 30.00 15.00
❑ 102 Charles Rogers AU/204 RC 50.00 25.00
❑ 103 Brandon Lloyd AU/589 RC 40.00 20.00
❑ 104 Terrence Edwards AU/399 RC 15.00 6.00
❑ 105 Mike Pinkard AU/849 RC 12.00 5.00
❑ 106 DeWayne White AU/524 RC 12.00 5.00
❑ 107 Jero McDougle AU/339 RC 20.00 7.50
❑ 108 Jimmy Kennedy AU/514 RC 20.00 7.50
❑ 109 William Joseph AU/764 RC 15.00 6.00
❑ 110 E.J. Henderson AU/774 RC 20.00 7.50
❑ 111 Mike Doss AU/574 RC 20.00 7.50
❑ 112A C.Simms Blu AU/310 RC 100.00 40.00
❑ 112B C.Simms Blk AU/79 RC 150.00 75.00
❑ 113 Cecil Sapp AU/474 RC 15.00 6.00
❑ 114 Justin Gage AU/579 RC 20.00 7.50
❑ 115 Sam Aiken AU/664 RC 15.00 6.00
❑ 116 Doug Gabriel AU/389 RC 40.00 20.00
❑ 117 Jason Witten AU/599 RC 80.00 40.00
❑ 118 Bennie Joppru AU/449 RC 20.00 7.50
❑ 119 Chris Kelsay AU/864 RC 15.00 6.00
❑ 120 John.Sullivan/924 RC 10.00 4.00
❑ 121 Kevin Williams AU/764 RC 40.00 20.00
❑ 122 Rien Long AU/849 RC 12.00 5.00
❑ 123 Kenny Peterson/674 RC 15.00 6.00
❑ 124 Boss Bailey AU/564 RC 20.00 7.50
❑ 125 Denn Weathersby AU/774 RC 12.00 5.00
❑ 126A Car.Palmer Blk AU/36 RC 700.00 400.00
❑ 126B Car.Palmer Blu AU/158 RC 500.00 250.00
❑ 127 Byron Leftwich AU/169 RC 150.00 75.00
❑ 128 Kyle Boller AU/439 RC 30.00 12.50
❑ 129 Rex Grossman AU/494 RC 80.00 40.00
❑ 130 Dave Ragone AU/344 RC 20.00 7.50
❑ 131 Brian St.Pierre AU/554 RC 15.00 6.00
❑ 132 Kliff Kingsbury AU/879 RC 20.00 7.50
❑ 133 Seneca Wallace AU/864 RC 30.00 15.00
❑ 134 Larry Johnson AU/344 RC 300.00 175.00
❑ 135 Will McGahee AU/369 RC 100.00 50.00
❑ 136 Justin Fargas AU/354 RC 50.00 25.00
❑ 137 Onterrio Smith AU/414 RC 20.00 7.50
❑ 138 Chris Brown AU/279 RC 50.00 25.00
❑ 139 Musa Smith AU/379 RC 30.00 15.00
❑ 140 Artose Pinner AU/364 RC 20.00 7.50
❑ 141 Andre Johnson AU/199 RC 150.00 75.00
❑ 142 Kell Washington AU/472 RC 30.00 12.50
❑ 143 Taylor Jacobs AU/349 RC 15.00 6.00
❑ 144 Bryant Johnson AU/389 RC 20.00 7.50
❑ 145 Tyrone Calico AU/499 RC 20.00 7.50
❑ 146 Anquan Boldin AU/524 RC 80.00 40.00
❑ 147 Bethel Johnson AU/484 RC 30.00 12.50
❑ 148 Nate Burleson AU/549 RC 30.00 15.00
❑ 149 Kevin Curtis AU/455 RC 35.00 20.00
❑ 150 Dallas Clark AU/539 RC 40.00 20.00
❑ 151 Teyo Johnson AU/389 RC 20.00 7.50
❑ 152 Terrell Suggs AU/564 RC 30.00 15.00
❑ 153 DeWayne Robertson/689 RC 12.00 5.00
❑ 154 Terence Newman AU/364 RC 40.00 20.00
❑ 155 Marcus Trufant AU/739 RC 20.00 7.50
❑ 156 Tony Romo AU/999 RC 400.00 250.00
❑ 157 Brooks Bollinger AU/974 RC 20.00 7.50
❑ 158 Ken Dorsey AU/774 RC 20.00 7.50
❑ 159 Kirk Farmer AU/999 RC 15.00 6.00
❑ 160 Jason Gesser AU/999 RC 15.00 6.00
❑ 161 Brock Forsey AU/999 RC 15.00 6.00
❑ 162 Quentin Griffin AU/999 RC 20.00 7.50
❑ 163 Avon Cobourne AU/974 RC 12.00 5.00
❑ 164 Domanick Davis AU/999 RC 30.00 12.50
❑ 165 Tony Hollings AU/974 RC 20.00 7.50
❑ 166 LaBran.Toefield AU/799 RC 20.00 7.50
❑ 167 Arlen Harris AU/974 RC 20.00 7.50
❑ 168 Sult McCullough AU/989 RC 15.00 6.00
❑ 169 Visant Shiancoe AU/999 RC 12.00 5.00
❑ 170 L.J. Smith AU/974 RC 20.00 7.50
❑ 171 LaTaren Dunbar AU/999 RC 12.00 5.00
❑ 172 Walter Young AU/889 RC 12.00 5.00
❑ 173 Bobby Wade AU/989 RC 15.00 6.00
❑ 174 Zuriel Smith AU/989 RC 12.00 5.00
❑ 175 Adrian Madise AU/999 RC 15.00 6.00
❑ 176 Ken Hamlin AU/989 RC 20.00 7.50
❑ 177 Carl Ford AU/999 RC 12.00 5.00
❑ 178 Cortez Hankton AU/989 RC 15.00 6.00
❑ 179 J.R. Tolver AU/889 RC 15.00 6.00
❑ 180 Keenan Howry AU/999 RC 15.00 6.00
❑ 181 Billy McMullen AU/899 RC 15.00 6.00
❑ 182 Arnaz Battle AU/989 RC 30.00 12.50
❑ 183 Shaun McDonald AU/899 RC 15.00 6.00
❑ 184 Andre Woolfolk AU/989 RC 15.00 6.00
❑ 185 Sammy Davis AU/999 RC 12.00 5.00
❑ 186 Calvin Pace AU/999 RC 12.00 5.00
❑ 187 Michael Haynes AU/999 RC 15.00 6.00
❑ 188 Ty Warren AU/999 RC 15.00 6.00
❑ 189 Nick Barnett AU/999 RC 20.00 7.50
❑ 190 Troy Polamalu AU/989 RC 135.00 75.00
❑ 191 Eric Parker AU/589 RC 25.00 10.00
❑ 192 Justin Griffith AU/589 RC 15.00 6.00
❑ 193 David Tyree AU/599 RC 40.00 25.00
❑ 194 Pisa Tinoisamoa/599 RC 20.00 7.50
❑ 195 Rashean Mathis AU/589 RC 12.00 5.00
❑ 196 Mike Sherman AU/574 RC 30.00 12.50
❑ 197 Dave Wannstedt AU/574 RC 20.00 7.50
❑ 198 Dick Vermeil AU/574 RC 30.00 12.50
❑ 199 Tony Dungy AU/574 RC 80.00 40.00
❑ 200 Mike Martz AU/574 RC 20.00 7.50

2004 Playoff Contenders

❑ COMP.SET w/o SP's (100) 20.00 7.50
❑ AU PRINT RUNS ANNOUNCED BY PLAYOFF
❑ 1 Anquan Boldin .75 .30
❑ 2 Emmitt Smith 1.50 .60
❑ 3 Josh McCown .50 .20
❑ 4 Michael Vick 1.50 .60
❑ 5 Peerless Price .50 .20
❑ 6 T.J. Duckett .50 .20
❑ 7 Warrick Dunn .50 .20
❑ 8 Jamal Lewis .75 .30
❑ 9 Kyle Boller .75 .30
❑ 10 Ray Lewis .75 .30
❑ 11 Drew Bledsoe .75 .30
❑ 12 Eric Moulds .50 .20
❑ 13 Travis Henry .50 .20
❑ 14 Willis McGahee .75 .30
❑ 15 DeShaun Foster .50 .20
❑ 16 Jake Delhomme .75 .30
❑ 17 Stephen Davis .50 .20
❑ 18 Steve Smith .75 .30
❑ 19 Brian Urlacher 1.00 .40
❑ 20 Rex Grossman .75 .30
❑ 21 Thomas Jones .50 .20

❑ 22 Carson Palmer 1.00 .40
❑ 23 Chad Johnson .75 .30
❑ 24 Rudi Johnson .50 .20
❑ 25 Jeff Garcia .75 .30
❑ 26 Lee Suggs .75 .30
❑ 27 William Green .50 .20
❑ 28 Keyshawn Johnson .50 .20
❑ 29 Roy Williams S .50 .20
❑ 30 Eddie George .50 .20
❑ 31 Ashley Lelie .50 .20
❑ 32 Jake Plummer .50 .20
❑ 33 Quentin Griffin .75 .30
❑ 34 Rod Smith .50 .20
❑ 35 Charles Rogers .50 .20
❑ 36 Joey Harrington .75 .30
❑ 37 Ahman Green .75 .30
❑ 38 Brett Favre 2.00 .75
❑ 39 Javon Walker .50 .20
❑ 40 Andre Johnson .75 .30
❑ 41 David Carr .75 .30
❑ 42 Domanick Davis .75 .30
❑ 43 Edgerrin James .75 .30
❑ 44 Marvin Harrison .75 .30
❑ 45 Peyton Manning 1.25 .50
❑ 46 Byron Leftwich 1.00 .40
❑ 47 Fred Taylor .50 .20
❑ 48 Jimmy Smith .50 .20
❑ 49 Priest Holmes 1.00 .40
❑ 50 Tony Gonzalez .50 .20
❑ 51 Trent Green .50 .20
❑ 52 A.J. Feeley .75 .30
❑ 53 Chris Chambers .50 .20
❑ 54 Deion Sanders .75 .30
❑ 55 Daunte Culpepper .75 .30
❑ 56 Michael Bennett .50 .20
❑ 57 Randy Moss 1.00 .40
❑ 58 Corey Dillon .50 .20
❑ 59 Deion Branch .75 .30
❑ 60 Tom Brady 2.00 .75
❑ 61 Aaron Brooks .50 .20
❑ 62 Deuce McAllister .75 .30
❑ 63 Donte Stallworth .50 .20
❑ 64 Joe Horn .50 .20
❑ 65 Amani Toomer .50 .20
❑ 66 Jeremy Shockey .75 .30
❑ 67 Michael Strahan .50 .20
❑ 68 Tiki Barber .75 .30
❑ 69 Chad Pennington .75 .30
❑ 70 Curtis Martin .75 .30
❑ 71 Santana Moss .50 .20
❑ 72 Jerry Porter .50 .20
❑ 73 Jerry Rice 1.50 .60
❑ 74 Warren Sapp .50 .20
❑ 75 Brian Westbrook .50 .20
❑ 76 Donovan McNabb 1.00 .40
❑ 77 Jevon Kearse .50 .20
❑ 78 Terrell Owens .75 .30
❑ 79 Antwaan Randle El .75 .30
❑ 80 Hines Ward .75 .30
❑ 81 Jerome Bettis .75 .30
❑ 82 LaDainian Tomlinson 1.00 .40
❑ 83 Kevan Barlow .50 .20
❑ 84 Tim Rattay .50 .20
❑ 85 Koren Robinson .50 .20
❑ 86 Matt Hasselbeck .50 .20
❑ 87 Shaun Alexander .75 .30
❑ 88 Isaac Bruce .50 .20
❑ 89 Marc Bulger .75 .30
❑ 90 Marshall Faulk .75 .30
❑ 91 Torry Holt .75 .30
❑ 92 Brad Johnson .50 .20
❑ 93 Mike Alstott .50 .20
❑ 94 Chris Brown .75 .30
❑ 95 Derrick Mason .50 .20
❑ 96 Steve McNair .75 .30
❑ 97 Clinton Portis .75 .30
❑ 98 LaVar Arrington 1.50 .60
❑ 99 Laveranues Coles .50 .20
❑ 100 Mark Brunell .50 .20
❑ 101 Adimchinobe Echemandu AU RC 12.00 5.00
❑ 102 Ahmad Carroll AU/574* RC 20.00 8.00
❑ 103 Andy Hall AU RC 15.00 6.00
❑ 104 B.J. Johnson AU RC 12.00 5.00
❑ 105 B.J. Symons AU RC 15.00 6.00
❑ 106 Roethlisberger AU/541* RC 350.00 175.00
❑ 107 Ben Troupe AU/540* RC 20.00 8.00
❑ 108 Ben Watson AU/660* RC 30.00 12.50
❑ 109 Bernard Berrian AU/653* RC 40.00 20.00
❑ 110 Brandon Miree AU RC 12.00 5.00
❑ 111 Bruce Perry AU RC 15.00 6.00
❑ 112 Carlos Francis AU RC 15.00 6.00
❑ 113 Casey Bramlet AU RC 12.00 5.00
❑ 114 Cedric Cobbs AU/630* RC 20.00 8.00
❑ 115 Chris Gamble AU/490* RC 20.00 8.00
❑ 116 Chris Perry AU/478* RC 40.00 15.00
❑ 117 Clarence Moore AU RC 15.00 6.00
❑ 118 Cody Pickett AU RC 15.00 6.00
❑ 119 Craig Krenzel AU RC 20.00 8.00
❑ 120 D.J. Hackett AU/325* RC 35.00 20.00
❑ 121 D.J. Williams AU/490* RC 25.00 12.50
❑ 122 Darius Watts AU RC 15.00 6.00
❑ 123 DeAngelo Hall AU RC 30.00 12.50
❑ 124 Derrick Hamilton AU/373* RC 15.00 6.00
❑ 125 Derrick Ward AU RC 25.00 10.00
❑ 126 Devard Darling AU/325* RC 20.00 8.00
❑ 127 D.Henderson AU/475* RC 30.00 12.50
❑ 128 Drew Carter AU RC 15.00 6.00
❑ 129 Drew Henson AU/415* RC 30.00 12.50
❑ 130 D.Robinson AU/660* RC 25.00 10.00
❑ 131 Eli Manning AU/372* RC 350.00 175.00
❑ 132 Ernest Wilford AU/305* RC 35.00 20.00
❑ 133 Greg Jones AU/553* RC 40.00 15.00
❑ 134 J.P. Losman AU/358* RC 80.00 40.00
❑ 135 Jamaar Taylor AU RC 15.00 6.00
❑ 136 Jared Lorenzen AU RC 15.00 6.00
❑ 137 Jarrett Payton AU RC 15.00 6.00
❑ 138 Jason Babin AU RC 20.00 8.00
❑ 139 Jeff Smoker AU RC 20.00 8.00
❑ 140 J.Cotchery AU/325* RC 30.00 15.00
❑ 141 Jim Sorgi AU RC 20.00 8.00
❑ 142 John Navarre AU RC 20.00 8.00
❑ 143 Johnnie Morant AU/325* RC 30.00 15.00
❑ 144 Jonathan Vilma AU SP RC 30.00 12.50
❑ 145 Josh Harris AU/555* RC 15.00 6.00
❑ 146 Julius Jones AU/252* RC 120.00 60.00
❑ 147 Keary Colbert AU/495* RC 30.00 12.50
❑ 148 Kel.Winslow AU/135* RC 200.00 125.00
❑ 149 Kenechi Udeze AU/475* RC 25.00 12.50
❑ 150 Kevin Jones AU/327* RC 80.00 40.00
❑ 151 L.Fitzgerald AU/50* RC 750.00 400.00
❑ 152 Lee Evans AU/375* RC 50.00 25.00
❑ 153 Luke McCown AU/543* RC 20.00 8.00
❑ 154 Matt Mauck AU RC 15.00 6.00
❑ 155 Matt Schaub AU/367* RC 120.00 60.00
❑ 156 Maurice Mann AU RC 12.00 5.00
❑ 157 Mewelde Moore AU/435* RC 30.00 12.50
❑ 158 Michael Clayton AU/325* RC 80.00 40.00
❑ 159 Michael Jenkins AU/412* RC 40.00 20.00
❑ 160 M.Turner AU/535* RC 120.00 70.00
❑ 161 P.K. Sam AU/300* RC 20.00 8.00
❑ 162 Philip Rivers AU/556* RC 150.00 75.00
❑ 163 Quincy Wilson AU/[illegible]* RC [illegible] [illegible]
❑ 164 Ran Carthon AU RC 12.00 5.00
❑ 165 Rashaun Woods AU RC 15.00 6.00
❑ 166 Re.Williams AU/336* RC 60.00 25.00
❑ 167 R.Colclough AU/640* RC 25.00 10.00
❑ 168 Robert Gallery AU/310* RC 40.00 15.00
❑ 169 Roy Williams AU/564* RC 100.00 50.00
❑ 170 Samie Parker AU/356* RC 30.00 15.00
❑ 171 Sean Jones AU RC 15.00 6.00
❑ 172 S.Taylor/575* RC No Auto 30.00 12.50
❑ 173 Sloan Thomas AU RC 12.00 5.00
❑ 174 Steven Jackson AU/333* RC 175.00 100.00
❑ 175 Tatum Bell AU/539* RC 60.00 25.00
❑ 176 Tommie Harris AU/365* RC 40.00 20.00
❑ 177 Triandos Luke AU RC 15.00 6.00
❑ 178 Troy Fleming AU RC 12.00 5.00
❑ 179 Vince Wilfork AU/315* RC 30.00 15.00
❑ 180 Will Smith AU/565* RC 20.00 8.00
❑ 181 Marcus Tubbs AU RC 15.00 6.00
❑ 182 Michael Boulware AU RC 20.00 8.00
❑ 183 Kris Wilson AU RC 15.00 6.00
❑ 184 Richard Smith AU RC 12.00 5.00
❑ 185 Teddy Lehman AU RC 20.00 8.00
❑ 186 Chris Cooley AU RC 50.00 25.00
❑ 187 Thomas Tapeh AU RC 12.00 5.00
❑ 188A Willie Parker Blk AU RC 150.00 75.00
❑ 188B Willie Parker Blu AU RC 250.00 150.00
❑ 189 Patrick Crayton AU RC 30.00 15.00
❑ 190 Kendrick Starling AU RC 12.00 5.00
❑ 191 B.J. Sams AU RC 15.00 6.00
❑ 192 Derick Armstrong AU RC 12.00 5.00
❑ 193 Wes Welker AU RC 100.00 60.00
❑ 194 Erik Coleman AU RC 15.00 6.00
❑ 195 Gibril Wilson AU RC 20.00 8.00
❑ 196 Andy Reid AU/335* RC 30.00 12.50
❑ 197 Brian Billick AU/585* RC 30.00 12.50
❑ 198 Jeff Fisher AU/585* RC 30.00 15.00
❑ 199 Jon Gruden AU/585* RC 20.00 8.00
❑ 200 Marvin Lewis AU/585* RC 25.00 12.50

2005 Playoff Contenders

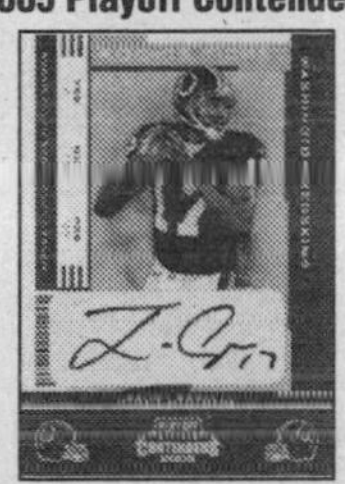

❑ COMP.SET w/o RC's (100) 20.00 7.50
❑ AU PRINT RUNS ANNOUNCED BY PLAYOFF
❑ EXCH EXPIRATION: 8/1/2007
❑ UNPRICED CHAMPION PRINT RUN 1 SET
❑ 1 Anquan Boldin .50 .20
❑ 2 Kurt Warner .50 .20
❑ 3 Larry Fitzgerald .75 .30
❑ 4 Michael Vick 1.25 .50
❑ 5 T.J. Duckett .50 .20
❑ 6 Warrick Dunn .50 .20
❑ 7 Derrick Mason .50 .20
❑ 8 Jamal Lewis .75 .30
❑ 9 Kyle Boller .50 .20
❑ 10 Ray Lewis .75 .30
❑ 11 J.P. Losman .75 .30
❑ 12 Lee Evans .50 .20
❑ 13 Willis McGahee .75 .30
❑ 14 DeShaun Foster .50 .20
❑ 15 Jake Delhomme .75 .30
❑ 16 Steve Smith .50 .20
❑ 17 Brian Urlacher .75 .30
❑ 18 Muhsin Muhammad .50 .20
❑ 19 Rex Grossman .50 .20
❑ 20 Carson Palmer .75 .30
❑ 21 Chad Johnson .75 .30
❑ 22 Rudi Johnson .50 .20
❑ 23 Lee Suggs .50 .20
❑ 24 Trent Dilfer .50 .20
❑ 25 Drew Bledsoe .75 .30
❑ 26 Jason Witten .50 .20
❑ 27 Julius Jones 1.00 .40
❑ 28 Keyshawn Johnson .50 .20
❑ 29 Ashley Lelie .50 .20
❑ 30 Jake Plummer .50 .20
❑ 31 Rod Smith .50 .20
❑ 32 Tatum Bell .50 .20
❑ 33 Joey Harrington .75 .30
❑ 34 Kevin Jones .75 .30
❑ 35 Roy Williams WR .75 .30
❑ 36 Ahman Green .75 .30
❑ 37 Brett Favre 2.00 .75
❑ 38 Javon Walker .50 .20
❑ 39 Andre Johnson .50 .20
❑ 40 David Carr .75 .30
❑ 41 Domanick Davis .50 .20
❑ 42 Edgerrin James .75 .30
❑ 43 Marvin Harrison .75 .30
❑ 44 Peyton Manning 1.25 .50
❑ 45 Reggie Wayne .50 .20
❑ 46 Byron Leftwich .75 .30
❑ 47 Fred Taylor .50 .20
❑ 48 Jimmy Smith .50 .20
❑ 49 Priest Holmes .75 .30
❑ 50 Tony Gonzalez .50 .20
❑ 51 Trent Green .50 .20
❑ 52 Chris Chambers .50 .20
❑ 53 Ricky Williams .50 .20
❑ 54 Daunte Culpepper .75 .30
❑ 55 Michael Bennett .50 .20
❑ 56 Nate Burleson .50 .20
❑ 57 Corey Dillon .50 .20

❑ 58 Deion Branch .50 .20
❑ 59 Tom Brady 2.00 .75
❑ 60 Aaron Brooks .50 .20
❑ 61 Deuce McAllister .75 .30
❑ 62 Joe Horn .50 .20
❑ 63 Eli Manning 1.50 .60
❑ 64 Jeremy Shockey .75 .30
❑ 65 Plaxico Burress .50 .20
❑ 66 Tiki Barber .75 .30
❑ 67 Chad Pennington .75 .30
❑ 68 Curtis Martin .75 .30
❑ 69 Laveranues Coles .50 .20
❑ 70 Kerry Collins .50 .20
❑ 71 LaMont Jordan .75 .30
❑ 72 Randy Moss .75 .30
❑ 73 Brian Westbrook .50 .20
❑ 74 Donovan McNabb 1.00 .40
❑ 75 Terrell Owens .75 .30
❑ 76 Ben Roethlisberger 2.00 .75
❑ 77 Duce Staley .50 .20
❑ 78 Hines Ward .75 .30
❑ 79 Jerome Bettis .75 .30
❑ 80 Antonio Gates .75 .30
❑ 81 Drew Brees .75 .30
❑ 82 LaDainian Tomlinson 1.00 .40
❑ 83 Brandon Lloyd .40 .15
❑ 84 Kevan Barlow .50 .20
❑ 85 Darrell Jackson .50 .20
❑ 86 Matt Hasselbeck .50 .20
❑ 87 Shaun Alexander 1.00 .40
❑ 88 Isaac Bruce .50 .20
❑ 89 Marc Bulger .75 .30
❑ 90 Steven Jackson 1.00 .40
❑ 91 Torry Holt .75 .30
❑ 92 Brian Griese .50 .20
❑ 93 Derrick Brooks .50 .20
❑ 94 Chris Brown .50 .20
❑ 95 Drew Bennett .50 .20
❑ 96 Steve McNair .75 .30
❑ 97 Travis Henry .50 .20
❑ 98 Clinton Portis .75 .30
❑ 99 LaVar Arrington .75 .30
❑ 100 Santana Moss .50 .20
❑ 101 Aaron Rodgers AU/530* RC 150.00 90.00
❑ 102 Adam Jones AU RC 20.00 7.50
❑ 103 A.McPherson AU/365* RC 40.00 20.00
❑ 104 Alvin Pearman AU RC 20.00 7.50
❑ 105 Airese Currie AU RC 20.00 7.50
❑ 106 Alex Smith QB AU/401* RC 100.00 50.00
❑ 107 Andrew Walter AU/99* RC 200.00 100.00
❑ 108 Anthony Davis AU/366* RC 30.00 15.00
❑ 109 Antrel Rolle AU RC 20.00 7.50
❑ 110 Brandon Jacobs AU RC 60.00 35.00
❑ 111 Brandon Jones AU RC 20.00 7.50
❑ 112 Braylon Edwards AU RC 80.00 40.00
❑ 113 Bryant McFadden AU/315* RC 40.00 20.00
❑ 114 Carlos Rogers AU RC 30.00 15.00
❑ 115 Cad.Williams AU/380* RC 100.00 50.00
❑ 116 Cedric Benson AU/289* RC 80.00 40.00
❑ 117 C.Houston AU/116* RC 250.00 150.00
❑ 118 Chad Owens AU RC 20.00 7.50
❑ 119 Charlie Frye AU RC 20.00 8.00
❑ 120 Chris Henry AU RC 50.00 20.00
❑ 121 Ciatrick Fason AU RC 20.00 7.50
❑ 122 Courtney Roby AU RC 20.00 7.50
❑ 123 Craig Bragg AU/425* RC 40.00 20.00
❑ 124 C.Thorpe AU/416* RC 40.00 20.00
❑ 125 Damien Nash AU RC 15.00 6.00
❑ 126 Dan Cody AU/315* RC 40.00 20.00
❑ 127 Dan Orlovsky AU RC 20.00 7.50
❑ 128 Dante Ridgeway AU/373* RC 30.00 15.00
❑ 129 Darren Sproles AU/454* RC 30.00 15.00
❑ 130 David Greene AU RC 20.00 7.50
❑ 131 David Pollack AU RC 20.00 7.50
❑ 132 Deandra Cobb AU/440* RC 30.00 15.00
❑ 133 DeMarcus Ware AU RC 30.00 15.00
❑ 134 Derek Anderson AU/450* RC 100.00 60.00
❑ 135 Derrick Johnson AU RC 40.00 15.00
❑ 136 Erasmus James AU RC 20.00 7.50
❑ 137 Eric Shelton AU RC 20.00 7.50
❑ 138 Fabian Washington AU RC 20.00 7.50
❑ 139 Frank Gore AU RC 100.00 50.00
❑ 140 Fred Gibson AU/476* RC 25.00 10.00
❑ 141 Heath Miller AU/510* RC 50.00 20.00
❑ 142 J.J. Arrington AU/465* RC 25.00 10.00
❑ 143 J.R. Russell AU/489* RC 30.00 15.00
❑ 144 Jason Campbell AU RC 80.00 50.00
❑ 145 Jason White AU RC 15.00 6.00
❑ 146 Jerome Mathis AU/416* RC 30.00 15.00
❑ 147 Josh Davis AU RC 12.00 5.00
❑ 148 Kay-Jay Harris AU RC 12.00 5.00
❑ 149 Kyle Orton AU RC 25.00 10.00
❑ 150 Larry Brackins AU RC 12.00 5.00
❑ 151 Lionel Gates AU/241* RC 40.00 20.00
❑ 152 Marion Barber AU RC 100.00 60.00
❑ 153 Mark Bradley AU RC 25.00 10.00
❑ 154 Mark Clayton AU/494* RC 30.00 12.00
❑ 155 Marlin Jackson AU RC 20.00 7.50
❑ 156 Matt Jones AU/165* RC 80.00 40.00
❑ 157 Matt Roth AU RC 20.00 7.50
❑ 158 Maurice Clarett AU/89* 135.00 75.00
❑ 159 Mike Williams AU/73* 120.00 60.00
❑ 160 Paris Warren AU/241* RC 50.00 25.00
❑ 161 Rasheed Marshall AU RC 15.00 6.00
❑ 162 Reggie Brown AU/528* RC 25.00 10.00
❑ 163 Roddy White AU RC 20.00 7.50
❑ 164 Ronnie Brown AU/550* RC 100.00 50.00
❑ 165 Roscoe Parrish AU RC 20.00 7.50
❑ 166 Royd.Williams AU/491* RC 30.00 15.00
❑ 167 R.Fitzpatrick AU/284* RC 30.00 12.00
❑ 168 Ryan Moats AU RC 30.00 15.00
❑ 169 Shaun Cody AU RC 15.00 6.00
❑ 170 Shawne Merriman AU RC 50.00 25.00
❑ 171 Stefan LeFors AU RC 20.00 7.50
❑ 172 Steve Savoy AU RC 12.00 5.00
❑ 173 T.A. McLendon AU RC 12.00 5.00
❑ 174 Tab Perry AU RC 20.00 7.50
❑ 175 Taylor Stubblefield AU RC 12.00 5.00
❑ 176 Terrence Murphy AU RC 20.00 7.50
❑ 177 Thomas Davis AU RC 15.00 6.00
❑ 178 Travis Johnson AU RC 15.00 6.00
❑ 179 T.Williamson AU/402* RC 25.00 10.00
❑ 180 Vernand Morency AU RC 15.00 6.00
❑ 181 Vincent Jackson AU RC 30.00 15.00
❑ 182 Alex Smith TE AU RC 20.00 7.50
❑ 183 Channing Crowder AU RC 15.00 6.00
❑ 184 Darrent Williams AU RC 40.00 15.00
❑ 185 Derrick Wimbush AU RC 15.00 6.00
❑ 186 James Kilian AU RC 15.00 6.00
❑ 187 Josh Cribbs AU RC 15.00 6.00
❑ 188 LeRon McCoy AU RC 12.00 5.00
❑ 189 Luis Castillo AU RC 20.00 7.50
❑ 190 Matt Cassel AU RC 30.00 15.00
❑ 191 Mike Patterson AU RC 15.00 6.00
❑ 192 Nate Washington AU RC 20.00 7.50
❑ 193 Noah Herron AU RC 20.00 7.50
❑ 194 Fred Amey AU RC 15.00 6.00
❑ 195 Tyson Thompson AU RC 25.00 10.00
❑ 196 Mike Nugent AU RC 15.00 6.00
❑ 197 Odell Thurman AU RC 25.00 10.00
❑ 198 Chris Carr AU RC 20.00 7.50
❑ 199 Bo Scaife AU RC 15.00 6.00
❑ 200 Billy Bajema AU RC 12.00 5.00

2006 Playoff Contenders

❑ COMP.SET w/o RC's (100) 20.00 8.00
❑ 1 Anquan Boldin .50 .20
❑ 2 Edgerrin James .75 .30
❑ 3 Larry Fitzgerald .75 .30
❑ 4 Alge Crumpler .50 .20
❑ 5 Michael Vick .75 .30
❑ 6 Warrick Dunn .50 .20
❑ 7 Steve McNair .50 .20
❑ 8 Mark Clayton .75 .30
❑ 9 Derrick Mason .40 .15
❑ 10 Lee Evans .50 .20
❑ 11 Willis McGahee .75 .30
❑ 12 Jake Delhomme .50 .20
❑ 13 Keyshawn Johnson .50 .20
❑ 14 Steve Smith .75 .30
❑ 15 Cedric Benson .75 .30
❑ 16 Brian Urlacher .75 .30
❑ 17 Thomas Jones .50 .20
❑ 18 Carson Palmer .75 .30
❑ 19 Chad Johnson .50 .20
❑ 20 Rudi Johnson .50 .20
❑ 21 T.J. Houshmandzadeh .50 .20
❑ 22 Charlie Frye .50 .20
❑ 23 Braylon Edwards .75 .30
❑ 24 Reuben Droughns .50 .20
❑ 25 Tony Romo 5.00 2.00
❑ 26 Julius Jones .75 .30
❑ 27 Roy Williams S .50 .20
❑ 28 Terrell Owens .75 .30
❑ 29 Javon Walker .50 .20
❑ 30 Rod Smith .50 .20
❑ 31 Tatum Bell .50 .20
❑ 32 Roy Williams WR .75 .30
❑ 33 Kevin Jones .75 .30
❑ 34 Brett Favre 1.50 .60
❑ 35 Robert Ferguson .40 .15
❑ 36 Samkon Gado .50 .20
❑ 37 Andre Johnson .50 .20
❑ 38 David Carr .50 .20
❑ 39 Domanick Davis .50 .20
❑ 40 Eric Moulds .50 .20
❑ 41 Dallas Clark .40 .15
❑ 42 Marvin Harrison .75 .30
❑ 43 Peyton Manning 1.25 .50
❑ 44 Reggie Wayne .50 .20
❑ 45 Matt Jones .50 .20
❑ 46 Byron Leftwich .50 .20
❑ 47 Fred Taylor .50 .20
❑ 48 Larry Johnson 1.00 .40
❑ 49 Priest Holmes .50 .20
❑ 50 Tony Gonzalez .50 .20
❑ 51 Trent Green .50 .20
❑ 52 Chris Chambers .50 .20
❑ 53 Daunte Culpepper .75 .30
❑ 54 Ronnie Brown .75 .30
❑ 55 Chester Taylor .50 .20
❑ 56 Brad Johnson .50 .20
❑ 57 Corey Dillon .50 .20
❑ 58 Deion Branch .50 .20
❑ 59 Tom Brady 1.25 .50
❑ 60 Tedy Bruschi .75 .30
❑ 61 Deuce McAllister .50 .20
❑ 62 Donte Stallworth .50 .20
❑ 63 Drew Brees .75 .30
❑ 64 Eli Manning 1.00 .40
❑ 65 Jeremy Shockey .75 .30
❑ 66 Tiki Barber .75 .30
❑ 67 Chad Pennington .50 .20
❑ 68 Curtis Martin .75 .30
❑ 69 Laveranues Coles .50 .20
❑ 70 Randy Moss .75 .30
❑ 71 LaMont Jordan .50 .20
❑ 72 Jerry Porter .50 .20
❑ 73 Donovan McNabb .75 .30
❑ 74 Reggie Brown .60 .25
❑ 75 Ben Roethlisberger 1.25 .50
❑ 76 Hines Ward .75 .30
❑ 77 Willie Parker 1.00 .40
❑ 78 Antonio Gates .75 .30
❑ 79 Philip Rivers .75 .30
❑ 80 LaDainian Tomlinson 1.00 .40
❑ 81 Alex Smith QB .75 .30
❑ 82 Antonio Bryant .50 .20
❑ 83 Kevan Barlow .50 .20
❑ 84 Darrell Jackson .50 .20
❑ 85 Matt Hasselbeck .50 .20
❑ 86 Nate Burleson .50 .20
❑ 87 Shaun Alexander .75 .30
❑ 88 Marc Bulger .50 .20
❑ 89 Steven Jackson .75 .30
❑ 90 Isaac Bruce .50 .20
❑ 91 Torry Holt .50 .20
❑ 92 Cadillac Williams .75 .30
❑ 93 Chris Simms .50 .20
❑ 94 Joey Galloway .50 .20
❑ 95 Chris Brown .50 .20
❑ 96 David Givens .50 .20
❑ 97 Drew Bennett .40 .15

❑ 98 Clinton Portis .75 .30
❑ 99 Santana Moss .50 .20
❑ 100 Mark Brunell .50 .20
❑ 101 Malcolm Floyd AU RC 20.00 8.00
❑ 102 Bart Scott AU RC 60.00 30.00
❑ 103 Reggie McNeal AU/457* RC 20.00 8.00
❑ 104 Domenik Hixon AU/586* RC 20.00 8.00
❑ 105 Vince Young AU/487* RC 300.00 150.00
❑ 106 Marcedes Lewis AU RC 20.00 8.00
❑ 107 Wali Lundy AU400* RC EXCH 40.00 15.00
❑ 108 Tarvaris Jackson AU RC 60.00 30.00
❑ 109 Ko Simpson AU RC 15.00 6.00
❑ 110 [illegible] AU RC [illegible]
❑ 111 Anthony Fasano AU RC 20.00 8.00
❑ 112 Joe Klopfenstein AU RC 15.00 6.00
❑ 113 Marques Hagans AU RC 12.00 5.00
❑ 114 Jason Avant AU RC 20.00 8.00
❑ 115 Santonio Holmes AU RC 80.00 40.00
❑ 116 Marcus Vick AU/149* RC 150.00 75.00
❑ 117 Antonio Cromartie AU/322* RC 30.00 15.00
❑ 118 DeAngelo Williams AU RC 100.00 50.00
❑ 119 Laurence Maroney AU RC 150.00 90.00
❑ 120 Daniel Bullocks AU RC 20.00 8.00
❑ 121 Jonathan Orr AU RC 15.00 6.00
❑ 122 Mike Bell AU RC 25.00 10.00
❑ 123 Kellen Clemens AU RC 60.00 30.00
❑ 124 Tim Jennings AU RC 15.00 6.00
❑ 125 Cory Rodgers AU RC 20.00 8.00
❑ 126 Jerome Harrison AU RC 20.00 8.00
❑ 127 Brad Smith AU/570* RC 25.00 10.00
❑ 128 Jeff Webb AU/250* RC EXCH 40.00 20.00
❑ 129 Will Blackmon AU RC 15.00 6.00
❑ 130 Quinton Ganther AU RC 15.00 6.00
❑ 131 Drew Olson AU RC 15.00 6.00
❑ 132 Omar Jacobs AU RC 15.00 6.00
❑ 133 Adam Jennings AU RC 15.00 6.00
❑ 134 Cedric Humes AU RC 20.00 8.00
❑ 135 D.Ross AU/250* RC EXCH 100.00 50.00
❑ 136 Charlie Whitehurst AU RC 30.00 12.50
❑ 137 Bobby Carpenter AU RC 20.00 8.00
❑ 138 Darryl Tapp AU RC 15.00 6.00
❑ 139 A.J. Hawk AU/399* RC 100.00 50.00
❑ 140 Bruce Gradkowski AU RC 30.00 12.00
❑ 141 Chad Greenway AU RC 20.00 8.00
❑ 142 John David Washington AU RC 15.00 6.00
❑ 143 Kamerion Wimbley AU RC 20.00 8.00
❑ 144 LenDale White AU/549* RC 60.00 30.00
❑ 145 Johnathan Joseph AU/549* RC 20.00 8.00
❑ 146 Maurice Drew AU RC 120.00 60.00
❑ 147 Brandon Marshall AU/608* RC 80.00 40.00
❑ 148 Vernon Davis AU/537* RC 80.00 40.00
❑ 149 Joseph Addai AU RC 175.00 90.00
❑ 150 Bennie Brazell AU RC 12.00 5.00
❑ 151 D.J. Shockley AU RC 20.00 8.00
❑ 152 Jay Cutler AU/501* RC 300.00 150.00
❑ 153 Wendell Mathis AU RC 15.00 6.00
❑ 154 Demetrius Williams AU RC 20.00 8.00
❑ 155 Dusty Dvoracek AU RC 20.00 8.00
❑ 156 DeMario Minter AU RC 15.00 6.00
❑ 157 Marcus Maxey AU RC 15.00 6.00
❑ 158 Brodie Croyle AU RC 60.00 30.00
❑ 159 Jeremy Bloom AU/473* RC 40.00 15.00
❑ 160 Todd Watkins AU RC 12.00 5.00
❑ 161 Cory Ross AU RC 20.00 8.00
❑ 162 Tamba Hali AU/500* RC 25.00 10.00
❑ 163 P.J. Daniels AU/555* RC 20.00 8.00
❑ 164 Brandon Williams AU RC 20.00 8.00
❑ 165 Devin Hester AU RC 80.00 40.00
❑ 166 Kelly Jennings AU/393* RC 20.00 8.00
❑ 167 Dawan Landry AU RC 20.00 8.00
❑ 168 Greg Jennings AU RC 40.00 25.00
❑ 169 Mathias Kiwanuka AU RC 25.00 10.00
❑ 170 Leon Washington AU RC 50.00 25.00
❑ 171 Richard Marshall AU RC 15.00 6.00
❑ 172 Haloti Ngata AU RC 20.00 8.00
❑ 173 Sinorice Moss AU RC 25.00 10.00
❑ 174 Greg Blue AU RC 15.00 6.00
❑ 175 Chris Barclay AU RC 15.00 6.00
❑ 176 D'Qwell Jackson AU RC 15.00 6.00
❑ 177 Eric Smith AU RC 12.00 5.00
❑ 178 Ethan Kilmer AU RC 20.00 8.00
❑ 179 Mike Hass AU RC 20.00 8.00
❑ 180 Derek Hagan AU RC 20.00 8.00
❑ 181 Travis Wilson AU RC 20.00 8.00
❑ 182 Reggie Bush AU/645* RC 350.00 200.00
❑ 183 Maurice Stovall AU/579* RC 40.00 20.00
❑ 184 Skyler Green AU RC 15.00 6.00
❑ 185 Calvin Lowry AU RC 15.00 6.00
❑ 186 Jerious Norwood AU RC 60.00 35.00
❑ 187 Brodrick Bunkley AU/518* RC 20.00 8.00
❑ 188 Ernie Sims AU/611* RC 25.00 10.00
❑ 189 Ingle Martin AU RC 20.00 8.00
❑ 190 Anthony Mix AU RC 15.00 6.00
❑ 191 Patrick Cobbs AU RC 15.00 6.00
❑ 192 Delanie Walker AU/212* RC 120.00 60.00
❑ 193 Gabe Watson AU RC 15.00 6.00
❑ 194 Willie Reid AU/515* RC 20.00 8.00
❑ 195 Michael Huff AU RC 30.00 15.00
❑ 196 Mario Williams AU/395* RC 40.00 20.00
❑ 197 [illegible] AU RC [illegible]
❑ 198 David Kirtman AU RC 15.00 6.00
❑ 199 B.Calhoun AU/407* RC EXCH 40.00 15.00
❑ 200 M.Robinson AU/512* RC EXCH 30.00 12.00
❑ 201 D.Ferguson AU/386* RC 30.00 12.00
❑ 202 Donte Whitner AU/518* RC 20.00 8.00
❑ 203 Roman Harper AU RC 15.00 6.00
❑ 204 Manny Lawson AU RC 15.00 6.00
❑ 205 DeMeco Ryans AU RC 30.00 15.00
❑ 206 Anthony Smith AU RC 30.00 15.00
❑ 207 Thomas Howard AU RC 20.00 8.00
❑ 208 John McCargo AU RC 12.00 5.00
❑ 209 David Pittman AU RC 15.00 6.00
❑ 210 Danieal Manning AU RC 20.00 8.00
❑ 211 Nate Salley AU RC 12.00 5.00
❑ 212 Jimmy Williams AU/524* RC 20.00 8.00
❑ 213 Rocky McIntosh AU RC 20.00 8.00
❑ 214 Montell Owens AU RC 12.00 5.00
❑ 215 Devin Aromashodu AU RC 12.00 5.00
❑ 216 Ben Obomanu AU RC 12.00 5.00
❑ 217 David Anderson AU RC 15.00 6.00
❑ 218 Marques Colston AU RC 120.00 60.00
❑ 219 Miles Austin AU RC 20.00 8.00
❑ 220 Tony Scheffler AU/526* RC 40.00 20.00
❑ 221 Leonard Pope AU/495* RC 20.00 8.00
❑ 222 David Thomas AU RC 20.00 8.00
❑ 223 Dominique Byrd AU RC 15.00 6.00
❑ 224 Owen Daniels AU RC 20.00 8.00
❑ 225 Garrett Mills AU RC 15.00 6.00
❑ 226 Hank Baskett AU RC 25.00 12.50
❑ 227 Jason Carter AU RC 15.00 6.00
❑ 228 Sam Hurd AU RC 20.00 8.00
❑ 229 Charles Sharon AU/250* RC 120.00 60.00
❑ 230 Chris Hannon AU RC 12.00 5.00
❑ 231 John Madsen AU RC 20.00 8.00
❑ 232 Shaun Bodiford AU RC 12.00 5.00
❑ 233 Mike Espy AU RC 20.00 8.00
❑ 234 Abdul Hodge AU RC 20.00 8.00
❑ 235 Anthony Montgomery AU RC 15.00 6.00
❑ 236 Matt Leinart AU/567* RC 200.00 100.00
❑ 237 Bernard Pollard AU/307* RC 30.00 15.00
❑ 238 Pat Watkins AU/343* RC 60.00 30.00
❑ 239 Cedric Griffin AU/357* RC 30.00 15.00
❑ 240 A.J. Nicholson AU RC 12.00 5.00
❑ 241 Claude Wroten AU/306* RC 60.00 30.00
❑ 242 Tye Hill AU/368* RC 30.00 12.50

2007 Playoff Contenders

❑ 1 Edgerrin James .75 .30
❑ 2 Larry Fitzgerald .60 .25
❑ 3 Anquan Boldin .60 .25
❑ 4 Matt Leinart .75 .30
❑ 5 Joey Harrington .60 .25
❑ 6 Warrick Dunn .60 .25
❑ 7 Joe Horn .60 .25
❑ 8 Steve McNair .60 .25
❑ 9 Willis McGahee .60 .25
❑ 10 Derrick Mason .50 .20
❑ 11 J.P. Losman .60 .25
❑ 12 Lee Evans .60 .25
❑ 13 Josh Reed .50 .20
❑ 14 Jake Delhomme .60 .25
❑ 15 DeShaun Foster .60 .25
❑ 16 Steve Smith .60 .25
❑ 17 Rex Grossman .60 .25
❑ 18 Bernard Berrian .50 .20
❑ 19 Cedric Benson .60 .25
❑ 20 Carson Palmer .75 .30
❑ 21 Chad Johnson .60 .25
❑ 22 [illegible]
❑ 23 Rudi Johnson .60 .25
❑ 24 Braylon Edwards .60 .25
❑ 25 Kellen Winslow .60 .25
❑ 26 Jamal Lewis .60 .25
❑ 27 Tony Romo 1.50 .60
❑ 28 Terrell Owens .75 .30
❑ 29 Jason Witten .60 .25
❑ 30 Julius Jones .60 .25
❑ 31 Jay Cutler .75 .30
❑ 32 Javon Walker .60 .25
❑ 33 Travis Henry .60 .25
❑ 34 Jon Kitna .50 .20
❑ 35 Roy Williams WR .60 .25
❑ 36 Tatum Bell .60 .25
❑ 37 Brett Favre 1.50 .60
❑ 38 Donald Driver .60 .25
❑ 39 Greg Jennings .60 .25
❑ 40 Matt Schaub .60 .25
❑ 41 Ahman Green .60 .25
❑ 42 Andre Johnson .60 .25
❑ 43 Peyton Manning 1.25 .50
❑ 44 Joseph Addai 1.00 .40
❑ 45 Marvin Harrison .75 .30
❑ 46 Reggie Wayne .60 .25
❑ 47 David Garrard .60 .25
❑ 48 Fred Taylor .60 .25
❑ 49 Maurice Jones-Drew .75 .30
❑ 50 Larry Johnson .75 .30
❑ 51 Damon Huard .60 .25
❑ 52 Tony Gonzalez .60 .25
❑ 53 Trent Green .60 .25
❑ 54 Ronnie Brown .60 .25
❑ 55 Chris Chambers .60 .25
❑ 56 Troy Williamson .50 .20
❑ 57 Tarvaris Jackson .75 .30
❑ 58 Chester Taylor .50 .20
❑ 59 Tom Brady 1.50 .60
❑ 60 Randy Moss .75 .30
❑ 61 Laurence Maroney .75 .30
❑ 62 Drew Brees .60 .25
❑ 63 Deuce McAllister .60 .25
❑ 64 Reggie Bush 1.00 .40
❑ 65 Eli Manning .75 .30
❑ 66 Brandon Jacobs .60 .25
❑ 67 Plaxico Burress .60 .25
❑ 68 Chad Pennington .60 .25
❑ 69 Laveranues Coles .60 .25
❑ 70 Thomas Jones .60 .25
❑ 71 Ronald Curry .60 .25
❑ 72 LaMont Jordan .60 .25
❑ 73 Jerry Porter .60 .25
❑ 74 Donovan McNabb .75 .30
❑ 75 Brian Westbrook .60 .25
❑ 76 Ben Roethlisberger 1.00 .40
❑ 77 Willie Parker .75 .30
❑ 78 Hines Ward .75 .30
❑ 79 LaDainian Tomlinson 1.00 .40
❑ 80 Philip Rivers .75 .30
❑ 81 Antonio Gates .60 .25
❑ 82 Alex Smith QB .75 .30
❑ 83 Frank Gore .75 .30
❑ 84 Darrell Jackson .60 .25
❑ 85 Vernon Davis .60 .25
❑ 86 Deion Branch .60 .25
❑ 87 Matt Hasselbeck .60 .25
❑ 88 Shaun Alexander .60 .25
❑ 89 Marc Bulger .60 .25
❑ 90 Steven Jackson .75 .30
❑ 91 Torry Holt .60 .25
❑ 92 Jeff Garcia .60 .25
❑ 93 Cadillac Williams .60 .25
❑ 94 Joey Galloway .60 .25
❑ 95 Vince Young 1.00 .40
❑ 96 Chris Brown .50 .20

- ❑ 97 Brandon Jones .50 .20
- ❑ 98 Jason Campbell .60 .25
- ❑ 99 Clinton Portis .60 .25
- ❑ 100 Santana Moss .60 .25
- ❑ 101 Aaron Ross AU RC EXCH 30.00 15.00
- ❑ 102 Aaron Rouse AU RC 20.00 8.00
- ❑ 103 Adam Carriker AU/333* RC 40.00 20.00
- ❑ 104 Adrian Peterson AU/355* RC 000.00 300.00
- ❑ 105 A.Bradshaw AU RC EXCH 100.00 60.00
- ❑ 106 Alan Branch AU/326* RC EXCH 25.00 10.00
- ❑ 107 Amobi Okoye AU RC EXCH 20.00 8.00
- ❑ 108 Anthony Gonzalez AU RC 60.00 30.00
- ❑ 109 Anthony Spencer AU RC 20.00 8.00
- ❑ 110 Antonio Pittman AU RC EXCH 25.00 10.00
- ❑ 111 Aundrae Allison AU RC EXCH 20.00 8.00
- ❑ 112 Ben Patrick AU RC 20.00 8.00
- ❑ 113 Biren Ealy AU RC EXCH 20.00 8.00
- ❑ 114 Bobby Sippio AU RC 15.00 6.00
- ❑ 115 Brady Quinn AU/534* RC 200.00100.00
- ❑ 116 Br.Jackson AU RC EXCH 40.00 15.00
- ❑ 117 Brandon Mebane AU RC 15.00 6.00
- ❑ 118 B.Meriweather AU RC EXCH 20.008.00
- ❑ 119 Brandon Siler AU RC 15.00 6.00
- ❑ 120 Brian Leonard AU RC 20.00 8.00
- ❑ 121 Brian Robison AU RC 15.00 6.00
- ❑ 122 Buster Davis AU/246* RC EXCH 40.00 20.00
- ❑ 123 Calvin Johnson AU/525* RC 200.00 100.00
- ❑ 124 Chansi Stuckey AU/502* RC 20.008.00
- ❑ 125 Ch.John AU/303* RC EXCH 80.00 40.00
- ❑ 126 Chris Davis AU RC 15.00 6.00
- ❑ 127 Chris Henry RB AU RC 20.00 8.00
- ❑ 128 Chris Houston AU RC EXCH 15.006.00
- ❑ 129 Clifton Ryan AU RC 15.00 6.00
- ❑ 130 Clifton Dawson AU RC 15.00 6.00
- ❑ 131 Courtney Taylor AU RC 15.00 6.00
- ❑ 132 C.Davis AU RC EXCH 25.00 10.00
- ❑ 133 Dallas Baker AU RC 15.00 6.00
- ❑ 134 Dan Bazuin AU/198* RC 50.00 25.00
- ❑ 135 Daymeion Hughes AU/383* RC 25.00 10.00
- ❑ 136 Dante Rosario AU RC EXCH 20.00 8.00
- ❑ 137 David Irons AU/198* RC 40.00 20.00
- ❑ 138 Darrelle Revis AU/533* RC 20.00 8.00
- ❑ 139 David Clowney AU/410* RC 25.0010.00
- ❑ 140 David Harris AU RC EXCH 15.00 6.00
- ❑ 141 DeShawn Wynn AU/429* RC 40.00 20.00
- ❑ 142 Drew Stanton AU RC 50.00 25.00
- ❑ 143 Dwayne Bowe AU RC 60.00 30.00
- ❑ 144 Dwayne Jarrett AU/484* RC 40.00 20.00
- ❑ 145 Dwayne Wright AU/410* RC 25.00 10.00
- ❑ 146 Ed Johnson AU RC 12.00 5.00
- ❑ 147 Eric Frampton AU/452* RC 20.00 8.00
- ❑ 148 Eric Weddle AU RC 15.00 6.00
- ❑ 149 Eric Wright AU/273* RC EXCH 30.00 15.00
- ❑ 150 Fred Bennett AU RC 12.00 5.00
- ❑ 151 Gaines Adams AU RC EXCH 20.00 8.00
- ❑ 152 Garrett Wolfe AU RC 40.00 15.00
- ❑ 153 Glenn Holt AU RC 15.00 6.00
- ❑ 154 Glenn Martinez AU RC 20.00 8.00
- ❑ 155 Greg Olsen AU RC 30.00 12.00
- ❑ 156 Greg Peterson AU RC 15.00 6.00
- ❑ 157 H.B. Blades AU/383* RC 20.00 8.00
- ❑ 158 I.Alama-Francis AU/222* RC 40.00 20.00
- ❑ 159 Isaiah Stanback AU/510* RC 25.00 10.00
- ❑ 160 Jacoby Jones AU/435* RC 30.00 12.00
- ❑ 161 J.Anderson AU/123* RC SP 120.00 60.00
- ❑ 162 JaMarcus Russell AU RC 175.00 100.00
- ❑ 163 James Jones AU RC 40.00 20.00
- ❑ 164 Zabransky AU/347* RC EXCH 50.00 25.00
- ❑ 165 Jarvis Moss AU/227* RC 60.00 30.00
- ❑ 166 Jason Hill AU RC SP 25.00 10.00
- ❑ 167 Jeff Rowe AU/362* RC 25.00 10.00
- ❑ 168 Joe Thomas AU/129* RC 100.00 60.00
- ❑ 169 Joel Filani AU/483* RC 20.00 8.00
- ❑ 170 John Beck AU RC 80.00 30.00
- ❑ 171 John Broussard AU RC 15.00 6.00
- ❑ 172 Johnnie Lee Higgins AU RC 15.006.00
- ❑ 173 Jon Beason AU RC 20.00 8.00
- ❑ 174 Jonathan Wade AU/365* RC EXCH 20.00 8.00
- ❑ 175 Jordan Kent AU RC 12.00 5.00
- ❑ 176 Josh Wilson AU/501* RC 30.00 15.00
- ❑ 177 Justin Durant AU RC 12.00 5.00
- ❑ 178 Kenneth Darby AU RC 15.00 6.00
- ❑ 179 Kenny Irons AU/50* RC 450.00 300.00
- ❑ 180 Kenton Keith AU RC 25.00 10.00
- ❑ 181 Kevin Kolb AU RC 50.00 25.00
- ❑ 182 Keyunta Dawson AU RC 12.00 5.00
- ❑ 183 Kolby Smith AU/444* RC 50.00 25.00
- ❑ 184 LaMarr Woodley AU RC 25.00 10.00
- ❑ 185 LaRon Landry AU RC EXCH 60.00 30.00
- ❑ 186 Laurent Robinson AU RC 20.00 8.00
- ❑ 187 Lawrence Timmons AU RC 20.00 8.00
- ❑ 188 Legedu Naanee AU RC 15.00 6.00
- ❑ 189 Leon Hall AU RC 15.00 6.00
- ❑ 190 Levi Brown AU/369* RC 20.00 8.00
- ❑ 191 Lorenzo Booker AU RC 25.00 10.00
- ❑ 192 Marcus McCauley AU/386* RC 40.00 20.00
- ❑ 193 Marcus Thomas AU RC 15.00 6.00
- ❑ 194 Marshawn Lynch AU/533* RC 120.00 60.00
- ❑ 195 Martrez Milner AU RC EXCH 20.008.00
- ❑ 196 Mason Crosby AU RC 20.00 8.00
- ❑ 197 Matt Gutierrez AU RC EXCH 25.00 10.00
- ❑ 198 Matt Moore AU RC 40.00 20.00
- ❑ 199 Matt Spaeth AU/237* RC 50.00 25.00
- ❑ 200 Michael Bush AU RC 30.00 12.00
- ❑ 201 Michael Griffin AU RC 15.00 6.00
- ❑ 202 Michael Okwo AU/261* RC 25.0010.00
- ❑ 203 Mike Walker AU/248* RC 50.00 25.00
- ❑ 204 Nick Folk AU RC 30.00 12.00
- ❑ 205 P.Willis AU/239* RC EXCH 120.00 60.00
- ❑ 206 Paul Posluszny AU RC 30.00 12.00
- ❑ 207 Paul Williams AU RC 20.00 8.00
- ❑ 208 Pierre Thomas AU RC 25.00 12.50
- ❑ 209 Quentin Moses AU/498* RC 20.008.00
- ❑ 210 Ray McDonald AU/519* RC 20.00 8.00
- ❑ 211 Reggie Ball AU RC 15.00 6.00
- ❑ 212 Reggie Nelson AU RC 20.00 8.00
- ❑ 213 Robert Meachem AU RC 40.00 20.00
- ❑ 214 Roy Hall AU RC 20.00 8.00
- ❑ 215 Rufus Alexander AU RC 15.00 6.00
- ❑ 216 Ryne Robinson AU/430* RC 25.00 10.00
- ❑ 217 Sabby Piscitelli AU/337* RC 30.0012.00
- ❑ 218 Scott Chandler AU RC 15.00 6.00
- ❑ 219 Selvin Young AU RC EXCH 40.0020.00
- ❑ 220 Sidney Rice AU/529* RC 40.00 20.00
- ❑ 221 Stephen Nicholas AU RC 12.00 5.00
- ❑ 222 Steve Breaston AU/274* RC 30.00 15.00
- ❑ 223 Steve Smith AU/541 RC 40.00 20.00
- ❑ 224 Stewart Bradley AU RC 15.00 6.00
- ❑ 225 Syndric Steptoe AU/149* RC 100.00 50.00
- ❑ 226 Tan.Jackson AU RC EXCH 15.00 6.00
- ❑ 227 Ted Ginn AU/519 RC 60.00 30.00
- ❑ 228 Thomas Clayton AU RC 12.00 5.00
- ❑ 229 Tim Crowder AU/454* RC 20.00 8.00
- ❑ 230 Tim Shaw AU/408* RC 20.00 8.00
- ❑ 231 Tony Hunt AU RC 20.00 8.00
- ❑ 232 Trent Edwards AU RC 80.00 40.00
- ❑ 233 Troy Smith AU RC EXCH 50.00 25.00
- ❑ 234 Turk McBride AU RC 12.00 5.00
- ❑ 235 Tyler Palko AU RC 25.00 10.00
- ❑ 236 Tyler Thigpen AU RC 20.00 8.00
- ❑ 237 Victor Abiamiri AU/449* RC 20.00 8.00
- ❑ 238 Yamon Figurs AU RC 20.00 8.00
- ❑ 239 Zak DeOssie AU RC EXCH 15.00 6.00
- ❑ 240 Zach Miller AU RC 20.00 8.00

2001 Playoff Honors

- ❑ COMP.SET w/o SP's (100) 25.00 10.00
- ❑ 1 Rob Johnson .60 .25
- ❑ 2 Eric Moulds .60 .25
- ❑ 3 Marvin Harrison 1.00 .40
- ❑ 4 Edgerrin James 1.25 .50
- ❑ 5 Peyton Manning 2.50 1.00
- ❑ 6 Jay Fiedler 1.00 .40
- ❑ 7 Lamar Smith .60 .25
- ❑ 8 Zach Thomas 1.00 .40
- ❑ 9 Dan Marino 3.00 1.25
- ❑ 10 Drew Bledsoe 1.25 .50
- ❑ 11 Terry Glenn .60 .25
- ❑ 12 Wayne Chrebet .60 .25
- ❑ 13 Curtis Martin 1.00 .40
- ❑ 14 Chad Pennington 1.50 .60
- ❑ 15 Vinny Testaverde .60 .25
- ❑ 16 Corey Dillon 1.00 .40
- ❑ 17 Jon Kitna 1.00 .40
- ❑ 18 Akili Smith .40 .15
- ❑ 19 Peter Warrick 1.00 .40
- ❑ 20 Kevin Johnson .60 .25
- ❑ 21 Tim Couch .60 .25
- ❑ 22 Eddie George 1.00 .40
- ❑ 23 Steve McNair 1.00 .40
- ❑ 24 Jevon Kearse .60 .25
- ❑ 25 Jerome Bettis 1.00 .40
- ❑ 26 Kordell Stewart .60 .25
- ❑ 27 Plaxico Burress 1.00 .40
- ❑ 28 Mark Brunell 1.00 .40
- ❑ 29 Keenan McCardell .40 .15
- ❑ 30 Jimmy Smith .60 .25
- ❑ 31 Fred Taylor 1.00 .40
- ❑ 32 Elvis Grbac .60 .25
- ❑ 33 Jamal Lewis 1.50 .60
- ❑ 34 Ray Lewis 1.00 .40
- ❑ 35 Mike Anderson 1.00 .40
- ❑ 36 Terrell Davis 1.00 .40
- ❑ 37 John Elway 3.00 1.25
- ❑ 38 Brian Griese 1.00 .40
- ❑ 39 Ed McCaffrey 1.00 .40
- ❑ 40 Tony Gonzalez .60 .25
- ❑ 41 Trent Green 1.00 .40
- ❑ 42 Sylvester Morris .40 .15
- ❑ 43 Tim Brown 1.00 .40
- ❑ 44 Rich Gannon 1.00 .40
- ❑ 45 Charlie Garner .60 .25
- ❑ 46 Tyrone Wheatley .60 .25
- ❑ 47 Charles Woodson .60 .25
- ❑ 48 Tim Dwight 1.00 .40
- ❑ 49 Doug Flutie 1.00 .40
- ❑ 50 Junior Seau 1.00 .40
- ❑ 51 Shaun Alexander 1.25 .50
- ❑ 52 Matt Hasselbeck .60 .25
- ❑ 53 Ricky Watters .60 .25
- ❑ 54 Tony Banks .60 .25
- ❑ 55 Joey Galloway .60 .25
- ❑ 56 Emmitt Smith 2.00 .75
- ❑ 57 Troy Aikman 1.50 .60
- ❑ 58 Kerry Collins .60 .25
- ❑ 59 Ron Dayne 1.00 .40
- ❑ 60 Donovan McNabb 1.25 .50
- ❑ 61 Duce Staley 1.00 .40
- ❑ 62 David Boston 1.00 .40
- ❑ 63 Thomas Jones .60 .25
- ❑ 64 Jake Plummer .60 .25
- ❑ 65 Stephen Davis 1.00 .40
- ❑ 66 Jeff George .60 .25
- ❑ 67 Michael Westbrook .60 .25
- ❑ 68 Deion Sanders 1.00 .40
- ❑ 69 James Allen .60 .25
- ❑ 70 Cade McNown .40 .15
- ❑ 71 Marcus Robinson 1.00 .40
- ❑ 72 Brian Urlacher 1.50 .60
- ❑ 73 Germane Crowell .40 .15
- ❑ 74 Charlie Batch 1.00 .40
- ❑ 75 James Stewart .60 .25
- ❑ 76 Brett Favre 3.00 1.25
- ❑ 77 Antonio Freeman 1.00 .40
- ❑ 78 Ahman Green 1.00 .40
- ❑ 79 Cris Carter 1.00 .40
- ❑ 80 Daunte Culpepper 1.00 .40
- ❑ 81 Randy Moss 2.00 .75
- ❑ 82 Mike Alstott 1.00 .40
- ❑ 83 Warrick Dunn 1.00 .40
- ❑ 84 Brad Johnson 1.00 .40
- ❑ 85 Keyshawn Johnson 1.00 .40
- ❑ 86 Warren Sapp .60 .25
- ❑ 87 Jamal Anderson 1.00 .40
- ❑ 88 Chris Chandler .60 .25
- ❑ 89 Isaac Bruce 1.00 .40
- ❑ 90 Marshall Faulk 1.25 .50
- ❑ 91 Torry Holt 1.00 .40
- ❑ 92 Kurt Warner 2.00 .75
- ❑ 93 Aaron Brooks 1.00 .40
- ❑ 94 Albert Connell .40 .15
- ❑ 95 Ricky Williams 1.00 .40
- ❑ 96 Jeff Garcia 1.00 .40

97	Terrell Owens	1.00	.40
98	Steve Young	1.00	.40
99	Jerry Rice	2.00	.75
100	Jeff Lewis	.40	.15
101	Rashard Casey RC	6.00	2.50
102	A.J. Feeley RC	10.00	4.00
103	Josh Booty RC	10.00	4.00
104	LaMont Jordan RC	20.00	7.50
105	Ben Leard RC	6.00	2.50
106	David Rivers RC	6.00	2.50
107	Tim Hasselbeck RC	10.00	4.00
108	Jason McKinley RC	6.00	2.50
109	Correll Buckhalter RC	12.00	5.00
110	Dan Alexander RC	10.00	4.00
111	Derrick Blaylock RC	10.00	4.00
112	Chris Barnes RC	6.00	2.50
113	Dee Brown RC	10.00	4.00
114	Derek Combs RC	6.00	2.50
115	David Allen RC	6.00	2.50
116	DeAngelo Evans RC	6.00	2.50
117	Reggie White RC	6.00	2.50
118	Heath Evans RC	6.00	2.50
119	George Layne RC	6.00	2.50
120	Moran Norris RC	4.00	1.50
121	Rhawoh Jue RC	10.00	4.00
122	Dustin McClintock RC	6.00	2.50
123	Ja'Mar Toombs RC	6.00	2.50
124	Steve Smith RC	25.00	12.50
125	Milton Wynn RC	6.00	2.50
126	Justin McCareins RC	10.00	4.00
127	Jarrod Cooper RC	10.00	4.00
128	Vinny Sutherland RC	6.00	2.50
129	Alex Bannister RC	6.00	2.50
130	Scotty Anderson RC	6.00	2.50
131	Onome Ojo RC	6.00	2.50
132	Damerien McCants RC	6.00	2.50
133	Eddie Berlin RC	6.00	2.50
134	Jonathan Carter RC	6.00	2.50
135	Bobby Newcombe RC	10.00	4.00
136	Cedrick Wilson RC	10.00	4.00
137	Kevin Kasper RC	10.00	4.00
138	Francis St. Paul RC	6.00	2.50
139	David Martin RC	6.00	2.50
140	T.J. Houshmandzadeh RC	12.00	5.00
141	John Capel RC	6.00	2.50
142	Reggie Germany RC	6.00	2.50
143	Chris Taylor RC	6.00	2.50
144	Ken-Yon Rambo RC	6.00	2.50
145	Richmond Flowers RC	6.00	2.50
146	Quentin McCord RC	6.00	2.50
147	Andre King RC	6.00	2.50
148	Boo Williams RC	6.00	2.50
149	Daniel Guy RC	4.00	1.50
150	Javon Green RC	6.00	2.50
151	Ronney Daniels RC	4.00	1.50
152	Alge Crumpler RC	12.00	6.00
153	Tony Driver RC	6.00	2.50
154	Shad Meier RC	6.00	2.50
155	Jabari Holloway RC	6.00	2.50
156	Ryan Pickett RC	4.00	1.50
157	Cedric James RC	6.00	2.50
158	Tony Stewart RC	10.00	4.00
159	Sean Brewer RC	4.00	1.50
160	Orlando Huff RC	4.00	1.50
161	Nate Clements RC	10.00	4.00
162	Will Allen RC	6.00	2.50
163	Willie Middlebrooks RC	6.00	2.50
164	Jamar Fletcher RC	6.00	2.50
165	Ken Lucas RC	6.00	2.50
166	Fred Smoot RC	10.00	4.00
167	Michael Stone RC	4.00	1.50
168	Tony Dixon RC	6.00	2.50
169	Andre Dyson RC	4.00	1.50
170	Gary Baxter RC	6.00	2.50
171	Adam Archuleta RC	10.00	4.00
172	Derrick Gibson RC	6.00	2.50
173	Edgerton Hartwell RC	4.00	1.50
174	Jamal Reynolds RC	10.00	4.00
175	Richard Seymour RC	10.00	4.00
176	Brandon Manumaleuna RC	6.00	2.50
177	Idrees Bashir RC	4.00	1.50
178	DeLawrence Grant RC	4.00	1.50
179	Karon Riley RC	4.00	1.50
180	Cedric Scott RC	6.00	2.50
181	Damione Lewis RC	6.00	2.50
182	Marcus Stroud RC	10.00	4.00
183	Casey Hampton RC	10.00	4.00
184	Willie Howard RC	6.00	2.50
185	Shaun Rogers RC	10.00	4.00
186	Kenny Smith RC	6.00	2.50
187	Marcus Bell DT RC	6.00	2.50
188	Mario Fatafehi RC	6.00	2.50
189	Kendrell Bell RC	12.00	5.00
190	Tommy Polley RC	10.00	4.00
191	Jamie Winborn RC	6.00	2.50
192	Sedrick Hodge RC	4.00	1.50
193	Torrance Marshall RC	10.00	4.00
194	Eric Westmoreland RC	6.00	2.50
195	Brian Allen RC	4.00	1.50
196	Morlon Greenwood RC	6.00	2.50
197	[illegible]	[illegible]	[illegible]
198	Carlos Polk RC	4.00	1.50
199	Alex Lincoln RC	6.00	2.50
200	Keith Adams RC	4.00	1.50
201	Kevan Barlow JSY RC	10.00	4.00
202	Michael Bennett JSY RC	10.00	4.00
203	Drew Brees JSY RC	30.00	12.00
204	Quincy Carter JSY RC	10.00	4.00
205	Andre Carter JSY RC	10.00	4.00
206	Chris Chambers JSY RC	15.00	6.00
207	Robert Ferguson JSY RC	10.00	4.00
208	Rod Gardner JSY RC	10.00	4.00
210	Travis Henry JSY RC	20.00	7.50
212	Chad Johnson JSY RC	25.00	10.00
213	Rudi Johnson JSY RC	20.00	7.50
214	Sage Rosenfels JSY RC	10.00	4.00
215	Deuce McAllister JSY RC	20.00	7.50
216	Mike McMahon JSY RC	10.00	4.00
217	Snoop Minnis JSY RC	6.00	2.50
218	Travis Minor JSY RC	6.00	2.50
219	Freddie Mitchell JSY RC	10.00	4.00
220	Quincy Morgan JSY RC	10.00	4.00
222	Santana Moss JSY RC	15.00	6.00
223	Jesse Palmer JSY RC	10.00	4.00
224	Koren Robinson JSY RC	10.00	4.00
225	Josh Heupel JSY RC	10.00	4.00
226	Justin Smith JSY RC	10.00	4.00
227	David Terrell JSY RC	10.00	4.00
228	Anthony Thomas JSY RC	10.00	4.00
229	L.Tomlinson JSY RC	60.00	30.00
230	Marques Tuiasosopo JSY RC	10.00	4.00
231	Michael Vick JSY RC	30.00	12.50
232	Gerard Warren JSY RC	10.00	4.00
233	Reggie Wayne JSY RC	20.00	7.50
234	Chris Weinke JSY RC	10.00	4.00
235	Leonard Davis JSY RC	6.00	2.50

2002 Playoff Honors

	COMP.SET w/o SP's (100)	25.00	10.00
1	David Boston	1.00	.40
2	Jake Plummer	.60	.25
3	Warrick Dunn	1.00	.40
4	Michael Vick	2.00	.75
5	Jamal Lewis	1.00	.40
6	Chris Redman	.40	.15
7	Ray Lewis	1.00	.40
8	Drew Bledsoe	1.25	.50
9	Travis Henry	1.00	.40
10	Eric Moulds	.60	.25
11	Lamar Smith	.60	.25
12	Steve Smith	1.00	.40
13	Chris Weinke	.60	.25
14	Chris Chandler	.60	.25
15	David Terrell	1.00	.40
16	Anthony Thomas	.60	.25
17	Brian Urlacher	1.50	.60
18	Corey Dillon	.60	.25
19	Peter Warrick	.60	.25
20	Tim Couch	.60	.25
21	James Jackson	.40	.15
22	Kevin Johnson	.60	.25
23	Quincy Carter	.60	.25
24	Joey Galloway	.60	.25
25	Emmitt Smith	2.50	1.00
26	Terrell Davis	1.00	.40
27	Brian Griese	1.00	.40
28	Rod Smith	.60	.25
29	Germane Crowell	.40	.15
30	Az-Zahir Hakim	.40	.15
31	[illegible]	[illegible]	[illegible]
32	Brett Favre	2.50	1.00
33	Terry Glenn	.60	.25
34	Ahman Green	1.00	.40
35	James Allen	.60	.25
36	Corey Bradford	.40	.15
37	Marvin Harrison	1.00	.40
38	Peyton Manning	2.00	.75
39	Edgerrin James	1.25	.50
40	Reggie Wayne	1.00	.40
41	Mark Brunell	1.00	.40
42	Fred Taylor	1.00	.40
43	Jimmy Smith	.60	.25
44	Tony Gonzalez	.60	.25
45	Trent Green	.60	.25
46	Priest Holmes	1.25	.50
47	Snoop Minnis	.40	.15
48	Chris Chambers	1.00	.40
49	Jay Fiedler	.60	.25
50	Ricky Williams	1.00	.40
51	Zach Thomas	1.00	.40
52	Randy Moss	2.00	.75
53	Daunte Culpepper	1.00	.40
54	Michael Bennett	.60	.25
55	Tom Brady	2.50	1.00
56	Troy Brown	.60	.25
57	Antowain Smith	.60	.25
58	Aaron Brooks	1.00	.40
59	Deuce McAllister	1.00	.40
60	Tiki Barber	1.00	.40
61	Kerry Collins	.60	.25
62	Amani Toomer	.60	.25
63	Michael Strahan	.60	.25
64	Curtis Martin	1.00	.40
65	Vinny Testaverde	.60	.25
66	Chad Pennington	1.25	.50
67	Laveranues Coles	.60	.25
68	Tim Brown	1.00	.40
69	Rich Gannon	1.00	.40
70	Jerry Rice	2.00	.75
71	Donovan McNabb	1.25	.50
72	Freddie Mitchell	[illegible]	[illegible]
73	Duce Staley	1.00	.40
74	Jerome Bettis	1.00	.40
75	Plaxico Burress	.60	.25
76	Kordell Stewart	.60	.25
77	Drew Brees	1.00	.40
78	Doug Flutie	1.00	.40
79	LaDainian Tomlinson	1.50	.60
80	Jeff Garcia	1.00	.40
81	Garrison Hearst	.60	.25
82	Terrell Owens	1.00	.40
83	Shaun Alexander	1.25	.50
84	Trent Dilfer	.60	.25
85	Koren Robinson	.60	.25
86	Isaac Bruce	1.00	.40
87	Marshall Faulk	1.00	.40
88	Torry Holt	1.00	.40
89	Kurt Warner	1.00	.40
90	Mike Alstott	1.00	.40
91	Brad Johnson	.60	.25
92	Keyshawn Johnson	1.00	.40
93	Keenan McCardell	.40	.15
94	Steve McNair	1.00	.40
95	Eddie George	1.00	.40
96	Jevon Kearse	.60	.25
97	Derrick Mason	.60	.25
98	Stephen Davis	.60	.25
99	Sage Rosenfels	.40	.15
100	Rod Gardner	.60	.25
101	Randy Fasani RC	5.00	2.00
102	Kurt Kittner RC	5.00	2.00
103	Brandon Doman RC	5.00	2.00
104	Craig Nall RC	6.00	2.50

❑	105 J.T. O'Sullivan RC	5.00	2.00
❑	106 Seth Burford RC	5.00	2.00
❑	107 Jeff Kelly RC	5.00	2.00
❑	108 Ronald Curry RC	6.00	2.50
❑	109 Wes Pate RC	3.00	1.25
❑	110 Chad Hutchinson RC	5.00	2.00
❑	111 Major Applewhite RC	6.00	2.50
❑	112 Preston Parsons RC	3.00	1.25
❑	113 David Priestley RC	5.00	2.00
❑	114 Lamar Gordon RC	6.00	2.50
❑	115 Brian Westbrook RC	12.00	5.00
❑	116 Jonathan Wells RC	6.00	2.50
❑	117 Omar Easy RC	6.00	2.50
❑	118 Verron Haynes RC	6.00	2.50
❑	119 Josh Scobey RC	6.00	2.50
❑	120 Larry Ned RC	5.00	2.00
❑	121 Adrian Peterson RC	8.00	3.00
❑	122 Brian Allen RC	5.00	2.00
❑	123 Chester Taylor RC	12.00	5.00
❑	124 Luke Staley RC	5.00	2.00
❑	125 Antwoine Womack RC	5.00	2.00
❑	126 Leonard Henry RC	5.00	2.00
❑	127 Jesse Chatman RC	6.00	2.50
❑	128 Damien Anderson RC	5.00	2.00
❑	129 Eric McCoo RC	3.00	1.25
❑	130 Tellis Redmon RC	5.00	2.00
❑	131 Joe Burns RC	5.00	2.00
❑	132 Delvon Flowers RC	5.00	2.00
❑	133 Ken Simonton RC	3.00	1.25
❑	134 Ricky Williams RC	5.00	2.00
❑	135 Dicenzo Miller RC	3.00	1.25
❑	136 James Mungro RC	6.00	2.50
❑	137 Randy McMichael RC	10.00	4.00
❑	138 Deion Branch RC	10.00	4.00
❑	139 Terry Charles RC	5.00	2.00
❑	140 Herb Haygood RC	3.00	1.25
❑	141 Jason McAddley RC	5.00	2.00
❑	142 Jake Schifino RC	5.00	2.00
❑	143 Freddie Milons RC	5.00	2.00
❑	144 Kahlil Hill RC	5.00	2.00
❑	145 Lamont Brightful RC	3.00	1.25
❑	146 Chris Luzar RC	5.00	2.00
❑	147 Daryl Jones RC	5.00	2.00
❑	148 Woody Dantzler RC	5.00	2.00
❑	149 Kelly Campbell RC	5.00	2.00
❑	150 Brian Poli-Dixon RC	5.00	2.00
❑	151 Atrews Bell RC	3.00	1.25
❑	152 Jarrod Baxter RC	5.00	2.00
❑	153 Eddie Drummond RC	5.00	2.00
❑	154 Jerramy Stevens RC	6.00	2.50
❑	155 Doug Jolley RC	6.00	2.50
❑	156 Jamar Martin RC	5.00	2.00
❑	157 Najeh Davenport RC	6.00	2.50
❑	158 Dwight Freeney RC	10.00	4.00
❑	159 Bryan Thomas RC	5.00	2.00
❑	160 Charles Grant RC	6.00	2.50
❑	161 Kalimba Edwards RC	6.00	2.50
❑	162 Ryan Denney RC	5.00	2.00
❑	163 Will Overstreet RC	3.00	1.25
❑	164 Dennis Johnson RC	3.00	1.25
❑	165 Alex Brown RC	6.00	2.50
❑	166 Kenyon Coleman RC	3.00	1.25
❑	167 Ryan Sims RC	6.00	2.50
❑	168 John Henderson RC	6.00	2.50
❑	169 Wendell Bryant RC	3.00	1.25
❑	170 Albert Haynesworth RC	5.00	2.00
❑	171 Larry Tripplett RC	3.00	1.25
❑	172 Eddie Freeman RC	3.00	1.25
❑	173 Anthony Weaver RC	5.00	2.00
❑	174 Quentin Jammer RC	6.00	2.50
❑	175 Phillip Buchanon RC	6.00	2.50
❑	176 Lito Sheppard RC	6.00	2.50
❑	177 Mike Rumph RC	5.00	2.00
❑	178 Roosevelt Williams RC	3.00	1.25
❑	179 Derek Ross RC	5.00	2.00
❑	180 Mike Echols RC	3.00	1.25
❑	181 Keyou Craver RC	5.00	2.00
❑	182 Ed Reed RC	10.00	4.00
❑	183 Lamont Thompson RC	5.00	2.00
❑	184 Tank Williams RC	5.00	2.00
❑	185 Michael Lewis RC	6.00	2.50
❑	186 Napoleon Harris RC	6.00	2.50
❑	187 Robert Thomas RC	6.00	2.50
❑	188 Raonall Smith RC	5.00	2.00
❑	189 Levar Fisher RC	3.00	1.25
❑	190 Rocky Calmus RC	6.00	2.50
❑	191 Andra Davis RC	5.00	2.00
❑	192 Nick Rolovich RC	5.00	2.00
❑	193 Zak Kustok RC	6.00	2.50
❑	194 Dusty Bonner RC	3.00	1.25
❑	195 Tony Fisher RC	6.00	2.50
❑	196 Sam Simmons RC	3.00	1.25
❑	197 Lee Mays RC	5.00	2.00
❑	198 Jamin Elliott RC	3.00	1.25
❑	199 Javin Hunter RC	3.00	1.25
❑	200 Kendall Newson RC	3.00	1.25
❑	201 Ladell Betts JSY RC	10.00	4.00
❑	202 Antonio Bryant JSY RC	10.00	4.00
❑	203 Reche Caldwell JSY RC	10.00	4.00
❑	204 David Carr JSY RC	20.00	7.50
❑	205 Tim Carter JSY RC	8.00	3.00
❑	206 Eric Crouch JSY RC	10.00	4.00
❑	207 Rohan Davey JSY RC	10.00	4.00
❑	208 Andre Davis JSY RC	8.00	3.00
❑	209 T.J. Duckett JSY RC	10.00	4.00
❑	210 DeShaun Foster JSY RC	10.00	4.00
❑	211 Jabar Gaffney JSY RC	10.00	4.00
❑	212 David Garrard JSY RC	20.00	7.50
❑	213 Daniel Graham JSY RC	10.00	4.00
❑	214 William Green JSY RC	10.00	4.00
❑	215 Joey Harrington JSY RC	12.00	5.00
❑	216 Ron Johnson JSY RC	8.00	3.00
❑	217 Ashley Lelie JSY RC	20.00	7.50
❑	218 Josh McCown JSY RC	12.00	5.00
❑	219 Maurice Morris JSY RC	10.00	4.00
❑	220 Julius Peppers JSY RC	20.00	7.50
❑	221 Clinton Portis JSY RC	30.00	12.50
❑	222 Patrick Ramsey JSY RC	10.00	4.00
❑	223 Antwaan Randle El JSY RC	12.00	5.00
❑	224 Josh Reed JSY RC	10.00	4.00
❑	225 Cliff Russell JSY RC	8.00	3.00
❑	226 Jeremy Shockey JSY RC	30.00	12.50
❑	227 Donte Stallworth JSY RC	15.00	6.00
❑	228 Travis Stephens JSY RC	8.00	3.00
❑	229 Javon Walker JSY RC	15.00	6.00
❑	230 Marquise Walker JSY RC	8.00	3.00
❑	231 Roy Williams JSY RC	20.00	7.50
❑	232 Mike Williams JSY RC	8.00	3.00
❑	RWH1 Payton/Smith JSY/250	120.00	50.00
❑	RWH1A Payton/Smith AUTO/22	400.00	200.00

2003 Playoff Honors

❑	COMP.SET w/o SP's (100)	20.00	7.50
❑	1 Aaron Brooks	1.00	.40
❑	2 Ahman Green	1.00	.40
❑	3 Amani Toomer	.60	.25
❑	4 Anthony Thomas	.60	.25
❑	5 Antonio Bryant	.60	.25
❑	6 Antwaan Randle El	1.00	.40
❑	7 Ashley Lelie	1.00	.40
❑	8 Brad Johnson	.60	.25
❑	9 Brett Favre	2.50	1.00
❑	10 Brian Urlacher	1.50	.60
❑	11 Bruce Smith	.60	.25
❑	12 Chad Johnson	1.00	.40
❑	13 Chad Pennington	1.25	.50
❑	14 Charlie Garner	.60	.25
❑	15 Chris Chambers	1.00	.40
❑	16 Clinton Portis	1.50	.60
❑	17 Corey Dillon	.60	.25
❑	18 Curtis Martin	1.00	.40
❑	19 Daunte Culpepper	1.00	.40
❑	20 David Boston	.60	.25
❑	21 David Carr	1.50	.60
❑	22 Deuce McAllister	1.00	.40
❑	23 Donald Driver	.60	.25
❑	24 Donovan McNabb	1.25	.50
❑	25 Donte Stallworth	1.00	.40
❑	26 Drew Bledsoe	1.00	.40
❑	27 Drew Brees	1.00	.40
❑	28 Duce Staley	.60	.25
❑	29 Ed McCaffrey	1.00	.40
❑	30 Eddie George	.60	.25
❑	31 Edgerrin James	1.00	.40
❑	32 Emmitt Smith	2.50	1.00
❑	33 Eric Moulds	.60	.25
❑	34 Fred Taylor	1.00	.40
❑	35 Garrison Hearst	.60	.25
❑	36 Hines Ward	1.00	.40
❑	37 Isaac Bruce	1.00	.40
❑	38 Jabar Gaffney	.60	.25
❑	39 Jake Plummer	.60	.25
❑	40 Jamal Lewis	1.00	.40
❑	41 Jay Fiedler	.60	.25
❑	42 Jeff Garcia	1.00	.40
❑	43 Jeremy Shockey	1.50	.60
❑	44 Jerome Bettis	1.00	.40
❑	45 Jerry Porter	.60	.25
❑	46 Jerry Rice	2.00	.75
❑	47 Jevon Kearse	.60	.25
❑	48 Jimmy Smith	.60	.25
❑	49 Joe Horn	.60	.25
❑	50 Joey Harrington	1.50	.60
❑	51 Josh Reed	.60	.25
❑	52 Julius Peppers	1.00	.40
❑	53 Kendrell Bell	.60	.25
❑	54 Kerry Collins	.60	.25
❑	55 Keyshawn Johnson	1.00	.40
❑	56 Kordell Stewart	.60	.25
❑	57 Koren Robinson	.60	.25
❑	58 Kurt Warner	1.00	.40
❑	59 LaDainian Tomlinson	1.00	.40
❑	60 Laveranues Coles	.60	.25
❑	61 Mark Brunell	.60	.25
❑	62 Marshall Faulk	1.00	.40
❑	63 Marvin Harrison	1.00	.40
❑	64 Matt Hasselbeck	.60	.25
❑	65 Michael Bennett	.60	.25
❑	66 Michael Strahan	.60	.25
❑	67 Michael Vick	2.50	1.00
❑	68 Mike Alstott	1.00	.40
❑	69 Patrick Ramsey	1.00	.40
❑	70 Peerless Price	.60	.25
❑	71 Peyton Manning	1.50	.60
❑	72 Plaxico Burress	.60	.25
❑	73 Priest Holmes	1.25	.50
❑	74 Randy Moss	1.50	.60
❑	75 Ray Lewis	1.00	.40
❑	76 Rich Gannon	.60	.25
❑	77 Ricky Williams	1.00	.40
❑	78 Rod Gardner	.60	.25
❑	79 Rod Smith	.60	.25
❑	80 Roy Williams	1.00	.40
❑	81 Shaun Alexander	1.00	.40
❑	82 Stephen Davis	.60	.25
❑	83 Steve McNair	1.00	.40
❑	84 T.J. Duckett	.60	.25
❑	85 Terrell Owens	1.00	.40
❑	86 Tiki Barber	1.00	.40
❑	87 Tim Brown	1.00	.40
❑	88 Tim Couch	.40	.15
❑	89 Todd Heap	.60	.25
❑	90 Tom Brady	2.50	1.00
❑	91 Tommy Maddox	1.00	.40
❑	92 Tony Gonzalez	.60	.25
❑	93 Torry Holt	1.00	.40
❑	94 Travis Henry	.60	.25
❑	95 Trent Green	.60	.25
❑	96 Troy Brown	.60	.25
❑	97 Warren Sapp	.60	.25
❑	98 Warrick Dunn	.60	.25
❑	99 William Green	.60	.25
❑	100 Zach Thomas	1.00	.40
❑	101 Chris Simms RC	8.00	3.00
❑	102 Brooks Bollinger RC	5.00	2.00
❑	103 Gibran Hamdan RC	2.50	1.00
❑	104 Ken Dorsey RC	5.00	2.00
❑	105 Jason Gesser RC	5.00	2.00
❑	106 Brad Banks RC	4.00	1.50
❑	107 Tony Romo RC	60.00	35.00
❑	108 B.J. Askew RC	5.00	2.00
❑	109 Domanick Davis RC	5.00	2.00

❑ 110 Lee Suggs RC 5.00 2.00
❑ 111 LaBrandon Toefield RC 5.00 2.00
❑ 112 Brock Forsey RC 5.00 2.00
❑ 113 Malaefou MacKenzie RC 2.50 1.00
❑ 114 Andrew Pinnock RC 4.00 1.50
❑ 115 Ahmaad Galloway RC 4.00 1.50
❑ 116 Tony Hollings RC 5.00 2.00
❑ 117 Charles Rogers RC 5.00 2.00
❑ 118 Billy McMullen RC 4.00 1.50
❑ 119 Shaun McDonald RC 5.00 2.00
❑ 120 Brandon Lloyd RC 5.00 2.00
❑ 121 Sam Aiken RC 4.00 1.50
❑ 122 Bobby Wade RC 5.00 2.00
❑ 123 Justin Gage RC 5.00 2.00
❑ 124 Adrian Madise RC 4.00 1.50
❑ 125 Jon Olinger RC. 2.50 1.00
❑ 126 Doug Gabriel RC 5.00 2.00
❑ 127 J.R. Tolver RC 4.00 1.50
❑ 128 David Kircus RC 5.00 2.00
❑ 129 Zuriel Smith RC 2.50 1.00
❑ 130 LaTarence Dunbar RC 4.00 1.50
❑ 131 Arnaz Battle RC 5.00 2.00
❑ 132 Willie Ponder RC 2.50 1.00
❑ 133 Kareem Kelly RC 4.00 1.50
❑ 134 David Tyree RC 4.00 1.50
❑ 135 Keenan Howry RC 5.00 2.00
❑ 136 Taco Wallace RC 4.00 1.50
❑ 137 Walter Young RC 2.50 1.00
❑ 138 Talman Gardner RC 5.00 2.00
❑ 139 DeAndrew Rubin RC 2.50 1.00
❑ 140 Kevin Walter RC 4.00 1.50
❑ 141 Carl Ford RC 2.50 1.00
❑ 142 Travis Anglin RC 2.50 1.00
❑ 143 Ryan Hoag RC 2.50 1.00
❑ 144 Terrence Edwards RC 4.00 1.50
❑ 145 Bennie Joppru RC 5.00 2.00
❑ 146 L.J. Smith RC 5.00 2.00
❑ 147 Jason Witten RC 10.00 4.00
❑ 148 Andre Woolfolk RC 5.00 2.00
❑ 149 Nnamdi Asomugha RC 4.00 1.50
❑ 150 Troy Polamalu RC 25.00 12.50
❑ 151 Nate Hybl RC 10.00 4.00
❑ 152 Curt Anes RC 5.00 2.00
❑ 153 Avon Cobourne RC 5.00 2.00
❑ 154 Cecil Sapp RC 8.00 3.00
❑ 155 Casey Urlacher RC 10.00 4.00
❑ 156 Dwone Hicks RC 5.00 2.00
❑ 157 Jeremi Johnson RC 8.00 3.00
❑ 158 Kirk Farmer RC 8.00 3.00
❑ 159 James MacPherson RC 10.00 4.00
❑ 160 Chris Davis RC 8.00 3.00
❑ 161 Brandon Drumm RC 5.00 2.00
❑ 162 J.T. Wall RC 5.00 2.00
❑ 163 Casey Moore RC 8.00 3.00
❑ 164 Mike Seidman RC 5.00 2.00
❑ 165 Visanthe Shiancoe RC 8.00 3.00
❑ 166 George Wrighster RC 8.00 3.00
❑ 167 Dan Curley RC 5.00 2.00
❑ 168 Donald Lee RC 8.00 3.00
❑ 169 Aaron Walker RC 8.00 3.00
❑ 170 Trent Smith RC 5.00 2.00
❑ 171 Spencer Nead RC 8.00 3.00
❑ 172 Richard Angulo RC 8.00 3.00
❑ 173 Mike Pinkard RC 5.00 2.00
❑ 174 Johnathan Sullivan RC 8.00 3.00
❑ 175 Kevin Williams RC 10.00 4.00
❑ 176 Jimmy Kennedy RC 10.00 4.00
❑ 177 Ty Warren RC 10.00 4.00
❑ 178 William Joseph RC 10.00 4.00
❑ 179 Michael Haynes RC 10.00 4.00
❑ 180 Jerome McDougle RC 10.00 4.00
❑ 181 Calvin Pace RC 8.00 3.00
❑ 182 Tyler Brayton RC 10.00 4.00
❑ 183 Chris Kelsay RC 10.00 4.00
❑ 184 Osi Umenyiora RC 15.00 6.00
❑ 185 Alonzo Jackson RC 8.00 3.00
❑ 186 DeWayne White RC 8.00 3.00
❑ 187 Kenny Peterson RC 8.00 3.00
❑ 188 Nick Barnett RC 10.00 4.00
❑ 189 Boss Bailey RC 10.00 4.00
❑ 190 E.J. Henderson RC 10.00 4.00
❑ 191 Pisa Tinoisamoa RC 10.00 4.00
❑ 192 Sammy Davis RC 10.00 4.00
❑ 193 Charles Tillman RC 12.00 5.00
❑ 194 Eugene Wilson RC 10.00 4.00
❑ 195 Drayton Florence RC 5.00 2.00
❑ 196 Ricky Manning RC 10.00 4.00
❑ 197 Rashean Mathis RC 8.00 3.00
❑ 198 Ken Hamlin RC 10.00 4.00
❑ 199 Mike Doss RC 10.00 4.00
❑ 200 Julian Battle RC 8.00 3.00
❑ 201 Andre Johnson JSY RC 15.00 6.00
❑ 202 Anquan Boldin JSY RC 20.00 10.00
❑ 203 Artose Pinner JSY RC 8.00 3.00
❑ 204 Bethel Johnson JSY RC 8.00 3.00
❑ 205 Brian St.Pierre JSY RC 8.00 3.00
❑ 206 Bryant Johnson JSY RC 8.00 3.00
❑ 207 Byron Leftwich JSY RC 25.00 10.00
❑ 208 Carson Palmer JSY RC 30.00 12.50
❑ 209 Chris Brown JSY RC 8.00 3.00
❑ 210 Dallas Clark JSY RC [illegible] [illegible]
❑ 211 Dave Ragone JSY RC 8.00 3.00
❑ 212 DeWayne Robertson JSY RC 8.003.00
❑ 213 Justin Fargas JSY RC 8.00 3.00
❑ 214 Kelley Washington JSY RC 8.00 3.00
❑ 215 Kevin Curtis JSY RC 10.00 4.00
❑ 216 Kliff Kingsbury JSY RC 6.00 2.50
❑ 217 Kyle Boller JSY RC 8.00 3.00
❑ 218 Larry Johnson JSY RC 30.00 15.00
❑ 219 Marcus Trufant JSY RC 8.00 3.00
❑ 220 Musa Smith JSY RC 8.00 3.00
❑ 221 Nate Burleson JSY RC 8.00 3.00
❑ 222 Onterrio Smith JSY RC 8.00 3.00
❑ 223 Rex Grossman JSY RC 25.00 10.00
❑ 224 Seneca Wallace JSY RC 8.00 3.00
❑ 225 Taylor Jacobs JSY RC 6.00 2.50
❑ 226 Terrell Suggs JSY RC 12.00 5.00
❑ 227 Terence Newman JSY RC 15.00 6.00
❑ 228 Teyo Johnson JSY RC 8.00 3.00
❑ 229 Tyrone Calico JSY RC 8.00 3.00
❑ 230 Willis McGahee JSY RC 20.00 7.50

2004 Playoff Honors

❑ COMP SET w/o SP's (100) 20.00 7.50
❑ 201-233 JSY RC PRINT RUN 750 #'d SETS
❑ 1 Anquan Boldin 1.00 .40
❑ 2 Emmitt Smith 2.00 .75
❑ 3 Josh McCown .60 .25
❑ 4 Michael Vick 2.00 .75
❑ 5 Peerless Price .60 .25
❑ 6 T.J. Duckett .60 .25
❑ 7 Warrick Dunn .60 .25
❑ 8 Jamal Lewis 1.00 .40
❑ 9 Kyle Boller 1.00 .40
❑ 10 Ray Lewis 1.00 .40
❑ 11 Drew Bledsoe 1.00 .40
❑ 12 Eric Moulds .60 .25
❑ 13 Travis Henry .60 .25
❑ 14 DeShaun Foster .60 .25
❑ 15 Jake Delhomme 1.00 .40
❑ 16 Steve Smith 1.00 .40
❑ 17 Stephen Davis .60 .25
❑ 18 Brian Urlacher 1.25 .50
❑ 19 Rex Grossman 1.00 .40
❑ 20 Thomas Jones .60 .25
❑ 21 Carson Palmer 1.25 .50
❑ 22 Chad Johnson 1.00 .40
❑ 23 Rudi Johnson .60 .25
❑ 24 Jeff Garcia 1.00 .40
❑ 25 Lee Suggs 1.00 .40
❑ 26 Keyshawn Johnson .60 .25
❑ 27 Quincy Carter .60 .25
❑ 28 Roy Williams S .60 .25
❑ 29 Jake Plummer .60 .25
❑ 30 Quentin Griffin 1.00 .40
❑ 31 Rod Smith .60 .25
❑ 32 Charles Rogers .60 .25
❑ 33 Joey Harrington 1.00 .40
❑ 34 Ahman Green 1.00 .40
❑ 35 Brett Favre 2.50 1.00
❑ 36 Javon Walker .60 .25
❑ 37 Andre Johnson 1.00 .40
❑ 38 David Carr 1.00 .40
❑ 39 Domanick Davis 1.00 .40
❑ 40 Edgerrin James 1.00 .40
❑ 41 Marvin Harrison 1.00 .40
❑ 42 Peyton Manning 1.50 .60
❑ 43 Byron Leftwich 1.25 .50
❑ 44 Fred Taylor .60 .25
❑ 45 Jimmy Smith [illegible] [illegible]
❑ 46 Priest Holmes 1.25 .50
❑ 47 Tony Gonzalez .60 .25
❑ 48 Trent Green .60 .25
❑ 49 A.J. Feeley 1.00 .40
❑ 50 Chris Chambers .60 .25
❑ 51 Ricky Williams 1.00 .40
❑ 52 Daunte Culpepper 1.00 .40
❑ 53 Michael Bennett .60 .25
❑ 54 Randy Moss 1.25 .50
❑ 55 Corey Dillon .60 .25
❑ 56 Deion Branch 1.00 .40
❑ 57 Tom Brady 2.50 1.00
❑ 58 Aaron Brooks .60 .25
❑ 59 Deuce McAllister 1.00 .40
❑ 60 Joe Horn .60 .25
❑ 61 Jeremy Shockey 1.00 .40
❑ 62 Michael Strahan .60 .25
❑ 63 Tiki Barber 1.00 .40
❑ 64 Chad Pennington 1.00 .40
❑ 65 Curtis Martin 1.00 .40
❑ 66 Santana Moss .60 .25
❑ 67 Jerry Rice 2.00 .75
❑ 68 Justin Fargas .60 .25
❑ 69 Kerry Collins .60 .25
❑ 70 Tim Brown 1.00 .40
❑ 71 Brian Westbrook .60 .25
❑ 72 Donovan McNabb 1.25 .50
❑ 73 Jevon Kearse .60 .25
❑ 74 Terrell Owens 1.00 .40
❑ 75 Duce Staley .60 .25
❑ 76 Hines Ward 1.00 .40
❑ 77 Jerome Bettis 1.00 .40
❑ 78 Tommy Maddox .60 .25
❑ 79 Drew Brees 1.00 .40
❑ 80 LaDainian Tomlinson 1.25 .50
❑ 81 Kevan Barlow .60 .25
❑ 82 Tim Rattay .40 .15
❑ 83 Koren Robinson .60 .25
❑ 84 Matt Hasselbeck .60 .25
❑ 85 Shaun Alexander 1.00 .40
❑ 86 Isaac Bruce .60 .25
❑ 87 Marc Bulger 1.00 .40
❑ 88 Marshall Faulk 1.00 .40
❑ 89 Torry Holt 1.00 .40
❑ 90 Brad Johnson .60 .25
❑ 91 Charlie Garner .60 .25
❑ 92 Keenan McCardell .40 .15
❑ 93 Chris Brown 1.00 .40
❑ 94 Derrick Mason .60 .25
❑ 95 Eddie George .60 .25
❑ 96 Steve McNair 1.00 .40
❑ 97 Clinton Portis 1.00 .40
❑ 98 LaVar Arrington 2.00 .75
❑ 99 Laveranues Coles .60 .25
❑ 100 Mark Brunell .60 .25
❑ 101 Drew Henson RC 5.00 2.00
❑ 102 Craig Krenzel RC 5.00 2.00
❑ 103 Andy Hall RC 4.00 1.50
❑ 104 Josh Harris RC 5.00 2.00
❑ 105 Jim Sorgi RC 5.00 2.00
❑ 106 Jeff Smoker RC 5.00 2.00
❑ 107 John Navarre RC 5.00 2.00
❑ 108 Cody Pickett RC 5.00 2.00
❑ 109 Casey Bramlet RC 4.00 1.50
❑ 110 Matt Mauck RC 5.00 2.00
❑ 111 B.J. Symons RC 5.00 2.00
❑ 112 Bradlee Van Pelt RC 5.00 2.00
❑ 113 Michael Turner RC 6.00 2.50
❑ 114 Troy Fleming RC 4.00 1.50
❑ 115 Adimchinobe Echemandu RC 4.001.50
❑ 116 Quincy Wilson RC 4.00 1.50
❑ 117 Derrick Ward RC 5.00 2.00
❑ 118 Bruce Perry RC 5.00 2.00

❑ 119 Brandon Miree RC 4.00 1.50
❑ 120 Carlos Francis RC 4.00 1.50
❑ 121 Samie Parker RC 5.00 2.00
❑ 122 Jerricho Cotchery RC 5.00 2.00
❑ 123 Ernest Wilford RC 5.00 2.00
❑ 124 Johnnie Morant RC 5.00 2.00
❑ 125 Maurice Mann RC 4.00 1.50
❑ 126 D.J. Hackett RC 4.00 1.50
❑ 127 Drew Carter RC 5.00 2.00
❑ 128 P.K. Sam RC 4.00 1.50
❑ 129 Jamaar Taylor RC 5.00 2.00
❑ 130 Ryan Krause RC 4.00 1.50
❑ 131 Triandos Luke RC 5.00 2.00
❑ 132 Jeris McIntyre RC 4.00 1.50
❑ 133 Clarence Moore RC 5.00 2.00
❑ 134 Mark Jones RC 4.00 1.50
❑ 135 Sloan Thomas RC 4.00 1.50
❑ 136 Jonathan Smith RC 4.00 1.50
❑ 137 Patrick Crayton RC 5.00 2.00
❑ 138 Derek Abney RC 5.00 2.00
❑ 139 Kris Wilson RC 5.00 2.00
❑ 140 Sean Taylor RC 5.00 2.00
❑ 141 Jonathan Vilma RC 5.00 2.00
❑ 142 Tommie Harris RC 5.00 2.00
❑ 143 D.J. Williams RC 5.00 2.00
❑ 144 Will Smith RC 5.00 2.00
❑ 145 Kenechi Udeze RC 5.00 2.00
❑ 146 Vince Wilfork RC 5.00 2.00
❑ 147 Marcus Tubbs RC 5.00 2.00
❑ 148 Ahmad Carroll RC 5.00 2.00
❑ 149 Jason Babin RC 5.00 2.00
❑ 150 Chris Gamble RC 5.00 2.00
❑ 151 Willie Parker RC 35.00 20.00
❑ 152 Darnell Dockett RC 6.00 2.50
❑ 153 Nate Poole RC 4.00 1.50
❑ 154 Matt Kegel RC 8.00 3.00
❑ 155 Kendrick Starling RC 4.00 1.50
❑ 156 Tramon Douglas RC 4.00 1.50
❑ 157 Ryan Dinwiddie RC 6.00 2.50
❑ 158 Brian Gaither RC 4.00 1.50
❑ 159 Ran Carthon RC 6.00 2.50
❑ 160 Derick Armstrong 4.00 1.50
❑ 161 Chris Cooley RC 8.00 3.00
❑ 162 Casey Clausen RC 8.00 3.00
❑ 163 Omar Jenkins RC 4.00 1.50
❑ 164 Justin Jenkins RC 6.00 2.50
❑ 165 Wes Welker RC 25.00 10.00
❑ 166 Terrance Copper RC 6.00 2.50
❑ 167 Jarrett Payton RC 5.00 2.00
❑ 168 Zamir Cobb RC 8.00 3.00
❑ 169 Derrick Knight RC 6.00 2.50
❑ 170 Romby Bryant RC 4.00 1.50
❑ 171 Larry Croom RC 6.00 2.50
❑ 172 Thomas Tapeh RC 6.00 2.50
❑ 173 Brock Lesnar RC 15.00 6.00
❑ 174 Richard Smith RC 6.00 2.50
❑ 175 Ricky Ray RC 6.00 2.50
❑ 176 John Booth RC 4.00 1.50
❑ 177 Huey Whittaker RC 8.00 3.00
❑ 178 Fred Russell RC 8.00 3.00
❑ 179 Ben Hartsock RC 8.00 3.00
❑ 180 Tim Euhus RC 8.00 3.00
❑ 181 Ricardo Colclough RC 8.00 3.00
❑ 182 Keiwan Ratliff RC 6.00 2.50
❑ 183 Shawntae Spencer RC 8.00 3.00
❑ 184 Joey Thomas RC 8.00 3.00
❑ 185 Keith Smith RC 6.00 2.50
❑ 186 Derrick Strait RC 8.00 3.00
❑ 187 Jeremy LeSueur RC 6.00 2.50
❑ 188 Matt Ware RC 8.00 3.00
❑ 189 Rich Gardner RC 6.00 2.50
❑ 190 Daryl Smith RC 8.00 3.00
❑ 191 Dontarrious Thomas RC 8.00 3.00
❑ 192 Courtney Watson RC 8.00 3.00
❑ 193 Karlos Dansby RC 8.00 3.00
❑ 194 Teddy Lehman RC 8.00 3.00
❑ 195 Michael Boulware RC 8.00 3.00
❑ 196 Bob Sanders RC 20.00 8.00
❑ 197 Travis LaBoy RC 8.00 3.00
❑ 198 Antwan Odom RC 8.00 3.00
❑ 199 Marquise Hill RC 6.00 2.50
❑ 200 Terry Johnson RC 6.00 2.50
❑ 201 Larry Fitzgerald JSY RC 15.00 6.00
❑ 202 DeAngelo Hall JSY RC 8.00 3.00
❑ 203 Matt Schaub JSY RC 15.00 6.00
❑ 204 Michael Jenkins JSY RC 6.00 2.50
❑ 205 Devard Darling JSY RC 6.00 2.50
❑ 206 J.P. Losman JSY RC 10.00 4.00
❑ 207 Lee Evans JSY RC 8.00 3.00
❑ 208 Keary Colbert JSY RC 6.00 2.50
❑ 209 Bernard Berrian JSY RC 8.00 3.00
❑ 210 Chris Perry JSY RC 8.00 3.00
❑ 211 Kellen Winslow JSY RC 10.00 4.00
❑ 212 Luke McCown JSY RC 6.00 2.50
❑ 213 Julius Jones JSY RC 15.00 6.00
❑ 214 Darius Watts JSY RC 6.00 2.50
❑ 215 Tatum Bell JSY RC 10.00 4.00
❑ 216 Kevin Jones JSY RC 12.00 5.00
❑ 217 Roy Williams JSY RC 12.00 5.00
❑ 218 Dunta Robinson JSY RC 6.00 2.50
❑ 219 Greg Jones JSY RC 6.00 2.50
❑ 220 Reggie Williams JSY RC 8.00 3.00
❑ 221 Mewelde Moore JSY RC 6.00 2.50
❑ 222 Ben Watson JSY RC 6.00 2.50
❑ 223 Cedric Cobbs JSY RC 6.00 2.50
❑ 224 Devery Henderson JSY RC 6.00 2.50
❑ 225 Eli Manning JSY RC 25.00 12.50
❑ 226 Robert Gallery JSY RC 6.00 2.50
❑ 227 Philip Rivers JSY RC 15.00 7.50
❑ 229 Derrick Hamilton JSY RC 5.00 2.00
❑ 230 Rashaun Woods JSY RC 6.00 2.50
❑ 231 Steven Jackson JSY RC 15.00 6.00
❑ 232 Michael Clayton JSY RC 10.00 4.00
❑ 233 Ben Troupe JSY RC 6.00 2.50
❑ 227 B.Roethlisberger JSY RC 30.00 12.50

2005 Playoff Honors

❑ COMP.SET w/o SP's (100) 20.00 7.50
❑ ROOKIE JSY PRINT RUN 750 SER.#'d SETS
❑ 1 Anquan Boldin .60 .25
❑ 2 Larry Fitzgerald 1.00 .40
❑ 3 Kurt Warner .60 .25
❑ 4 Michael Vick 1.50 .60
❑ 5 Alge Crumpler .60 .25
❑ 6 Warrick Dunn .60 .25
❑ 7 Jamal Lewis 1.00 .40
❑ 8 Kyle Boller .60 .25
❑ 9 Ray Lewis 1.00 .40
❑ 10 Derrick Mason .60 .25
❑ 11 Eric Moulds .60 .25
❑ 12 J.P. Losman 1.00 .40
❑ 13 Willis McGahee 1.00 .40
❑ 14 Jake Delhomme 1.00 .40
❑ 15 Steve Smith .60 .25
❑ 16 DeShaun Foster .60 .25
❑ 17 Rex Grossman .60 .25
❑ 18 Brian Urlacher 1.00 .40
❑ 19 Muhsin Muhammad .60 .25
❑ 20 Carson Palmer 1.00 .40
❑ 21 Chad Johnson 1.00 .40
❑ 22 Rudi Johnson .60 .25
❑ 23 Lee Suggs .60 .25
❑ 24 Trent Dilfer .60 .25
❑ 25 Reuben Droughns .60 .25
❑ 26 Drew Bledsoe 1.00 .40
❑ 27 Julius Jones 1.25 .50
❑ 28 Keyshawn Johnson .60 .25
❑ 29 Roy Williams S .60 .25
❑ 30 Ashley Lelie .60 .25
❑ 31 Jake Plummer .60 .25
❑ 32 Rod Smith .60 .25
❑ 33 Tatum Bell .60 .25
❑ 34 Joey Harrington 1.00 .40
❑ 35 Kevin Jones 1.00 .40
❑ 36 Roy Williams WR 1.00 .40
❑ 37 Ahman Green 1.00 .40
❑ 38 Brett Favre 2.50 1.00
❑ 39 Javon Walker .60 .25
❑ 40 Andre Johnson .60 .25
❑ 41 David Carr 1.00 .40
❑ 42 Domanick Davis .60 .25
❑ 43 Marvin Harrison 1.00 .40
❑ 44 Edgerrin James 1.00 .40
❑ 45 Peyton Manning 1.50 .60
❑ 46 Reggie Wayne .60 .25
❑ 47 Fred Taylor .60 .25
❑ 48 Byron Leftwich 1.00 .40
❑ 49 Jimmy Smith .60 .25
❑ 50 Priest Holmes 1.00 .40
❑ 51 Tony Gonzalez .60 .25
❑ 52 Trent Green .60 .25
❑ 53 A.J. Feeley .60 .25
❑ 54 Chris Chambers .60 .25
❑ 55 Daunte Culpepper 1.00 .40
❑ 56 Nate Burleson .60 .25
❑ 57 Michael Bennett .60 .25
❑ 58 Corey Dillon .60 .25
❑ 59 Deion Branch .60 .25
❑ 60 Tedy Bruschi .60 .25
❑ 61 Tom Brady 2.50 1.00
❑ 62 Aaron Brooks .60 .25
❑ 63 Deuce McAllister 1.00 .40
❑ 64 Joe Horn .60 .25
❑ 65 Eli Manning 2.00 .75
❑ 66 Tiki Barber 1.00 .40
❑ 67 Plaxico Burress .60 .25
❑ 68 Jeremy Shockey 1.00 .40
❑ 69 Chad Pennington 1.00 .40
❑ 70 Curtis Martin 1.00 .40
❑ 71 Laveranues Coles .60 .25
❑ 72 Kerry Collins .60 .25
❑ 73 Randy Moss 1.00 .40
❑ 74 LaMont Jordan 1.00 .40
❑ 75 Brian Westbrook .60 .25
❑ 76 Donovan McNabb 1.25 .50
❑ 77 Terrell Owens 1.00 .40
❑ 78 Ben Roethlisberger 2.50 1.00
❑ 79 Hines Ward 1.00 .40
❑ 80 Duce Staley .60 .25
❑ 81 Jerome Bettis 1.00 .40
❑ 82 Drew Brees 1.00 .40
❑ 83 LaDainian Tomlinson 1.25 .50
❑ 84 Antonio Gates 1.00 .40
❑ 85 Kevan Barlow .60 .25
❑ 86 Brandon Lloyd .50 .20
❑ 87 Darrell Jackson .60 .25
❑ 88 Matt Hasselbeck .60 .25
❑ 89 Shaun Alexander 1.25 .50
❑ 90 Marc Bulger 1.00 .40
❑ 91 Torry Holt 1.00 .40
❑ 92 Steven Jackson 1.25 .50
❑ 93 Brian Griese .60 .25
❑ 94 Michael Clayton 1.00 .40
❑ 95 Drew Bennett .60 .25
❑ 96 Steve McNair 1.00 .40
❑ 97 Chris Brown .60 .25
❑ 98 Clinton Portis 1.00 .40
❑ 99 LaVar Arrington 1.00 .40
❑ 100 Santana Moss .60 .25
❑ 101 Cedric Benson RC 12.00 5.00
❑ 102 Mike Williams 5.00 2.00
❑ 103 DeMarcus Ware RC 8.00 3.00
❑ 104 Shawne Merriman RC 8.00 3.00
❑ 105 Thomas Davis RC 5.00 2.00
❑ 106 Derrick Johnson RC 8.00 3.00
❑ 107 David Pollack RC 5.00 2.00
❑ 108 Erasmus James RC 5.00 2.00
❑ 109 Marcus Spears RC 5.00 2.00
❑ 110 Fabian Washington RC 5.00 2.00
❑ 111 Aaron Rodgers RC 15.00 6.00
❑ 112 Marlin Jackson RC 5.00 2.00
❑ 113 Heath Miller RC 10.00 4.00
❑ 114 Alex Smith TE RC 5.00 2.00
❑ 115 Chris Henry RC 5.00 2.00
❑ 116 David Greene RC 5.00 2.00
❑ 117 Brandon Jones RC 5.00 2.00
❑ 118 Marion Barber RC 8.00 3.00
❑ 119 Brandon Jacobs RC 6.00 2.50
❑ 120 Jerome Mathis RC 5.00 2.00
❑ 121 Craphonso Thorpe RC 4.00 1.50
❑ 122 Manuel White RC 4.00 1.50
❑ 123 Alvin Pearman RC 5.00 2.00
❑ 124 Darren Sproles RC 5.00 2.00

❑ 125 Fred Gibson RC 4.00 1.50
❑ 126 Roydell Williams RC 5.00 2.00
❑ 127 Airese Currie RC 5.00 2.00
❑ 128 Damien Nash RC 4.00 1.50
❑ 129 Dan Orlovsky RC 5.00 2.00
❑ 130 Adrian McPherson RC 5.00 2.00
❑ 131 Larry Brackins RC 4.00 1.50
❑ 132 Rasheed Marshall RC 5.00 2.00
❑ 133 Cedric Houston RC 5.00 2.00
❑ 134 Chad Owens RC 5.00 2.00
❑ 135 Tab Perry RC 5.00 2.00
❑ 136 Dante Ridgeway RC UER 4.00 1.50
❑ 137 Craig Bragg RC 4.00 1.50
❑ 138 Deandra Cobb RC 4.00 1.50
❑ 139 Derek Anderson RC 8.00 3.00
❑ 140 Travis Johnson RC 4.00 1.50
❑ 141 Paris Warren RC 4.00 1.50
❑ 142 LeRon McCoy RC 4.00 1.50
❑ 143 James Kilian RC 5.00 2.00
❑ 144 Matt Cassel RC 8.00 3.00
❑ 145 Lionel Gates RC 4.00 1.50
❑ 146 Harry Williams RC 4.00 1.50
❑ 147 Anthony Davis RC 4.00 1.50
❑ 148 Noah Herron RC 5.00 2.00
❑ 149 Ryan Fitzpatrick RC 5.00 2.00
❑ 150 J.R. Russell RC 4.00 1.50
❑ 151 Cole Magner RC 3.00 1.25
❑ 152 Luis Castillo RC 6.00 2.50
❑ 153 Mike Patterson RC 6.00 2.50
❑ 154 Brodney Pool RC 6.00 2.50
❑ 155 Barrett Ruud RC 6.00 2.50
❑ 156 Shaun Cody RC 6.00 2.50
❑ 157 Stanford Routt RC 5.00 2.00
❑ 158 Josh Bullocks RC 6.00 2.50
❑ 159 Kevin Burnett RC 6.00 2.50
❑ 160 Corey Webster RC 6.00 2.50
❑ 161 Lofa Tatupu RC 8.00 3.00
❑ 162 Matt Roth RC 6.00 2.50
❑ 163 Mike Nugent RC 6.00 2.50
❑ 164 Odell Thurman RC 6.00 2.50
❑ 165 Ronald Bartell RC 5.00 2.00
❑ 166 Nick Collins RC 6.00 2.50
❑ 167 Dan Cody RC 6.00 2.50
❑ 168 Darrent Williams RC 6.00 2.50
❑ 169 Justin Miller RC 5.00 2.00
❑ 170 Jerome Collins RC 5.00 2.00
❑ 171 Justin Green RC 6.00 2.50
❑ 172 Eric Green RC 3.00 1.25
❑ 173 Joel Dreessen RC 5.00 2.00
❑ 174 Bo Scaife RC 5.00 2.00
❑ 175 Antonio Perkins RC 5.00 2.00
❑ 176 Nehemiah Broughton RC 5.00 2.00
❑ 177 Patrick Estes RC 5.00 2.00
❑ 178 Billy Bajema RC 5.00 2.00
❑ 179 Madison Hedgecock RC 6.00 2.50
❑ 180 Roscoe Crosby RC 5.00 2.00
❑ 181 Kendrick Mosley RC 3.00 1.25
❑ 182 Tyson Thompson RC 10.00 4.00
❑ 183 Fred Amey RC 5.00 2.00
❑ 184 Brock Berlin RC 5.00 2.00
❑ 185 Gino Guidugli RC 3.00 1.25
❑ 186 Walter Reyes RC 5.00 2.00
❑ 187 Lydell Ross RC 5.00 2.00
❑ 188 Carlyle Holiday RC 5.00 2.00
❑ 189 Bryan Randall RC 5.00 2.00
❑ 190 Derrick Tinsley RC 5.00 2.00
❑ 191 Ryan Grant RC 225.00 125.00
❑ 192 Bobby Purify RC 5.00 2.00
❑ 193 Leonard Weaver RC 5.00 2.00
❑ 194 Vincent Fuller RC 5.00 2.00
❑ 195 Tony Brown RC 5.00 2.00
❑ 196 Zach Tuiasosopo RC 3.00 1.25
❑ 197 Craig Ochs RC 5.00 2.00
❑ 198 Ruvell Martin RC 8.00 3.00
❑ 199 Manuel Wright RC 6.00 2.50
❑ 200 Travis Daniels RC 5.00 2.00
❑ 201 Adam Jones JSY RC 8.00 3.00
❑ 202 Alex Smith QB JSY RC 20.00 7.50
❑ 203 Andrew Walter JSY RC 8.00 3.00
❑ 204 Antrel Rolle JSY RC 8.00 3.00
❑ 205 Braylon Edwards JSY RC 20.00 7.50
❑ 206 Cadillac Williams JSY RC 20.00 7.50
❑ 207 Carlos Rogers JSY RC 10.00 4.00
❑ 208 Charlie Frye JSY RC 8.00 3.00
❑ 209 Ciatrick Fason JSY RC 8.00 3.00
❑ 210 Courtney Roby JSY RC 8.00 3.00
❑ 211 Eric Shelton JSY RC 8.00 3.00
❑ 212 Frank Gore JSY RC 12.00 5.00
❑ 213 J.J. Arrington JSY RC 8.00 3.00
❑ 214 Jason Campbell JSY RC 10.00 4.00
❑ 215 Kyle Orton JSY RC 8.00 3.00
❑ 216 Mark Bradley JSY RC 8.00 3.00
❑ 217 Mark Clayton JSY RC 8.00 3.00
❑ 218 Matt Jones JSY RC 10.00 4.00
❑ 219 Maurice Clarett JSY 8.00 3.00
❑ 220 Reggie Brown JSY RC 8.00 3.00
❑ 221 Ronnie Brown JSY RC 20.00 7.50
❑ 222 Roddy White JSY RC 8.00 3.00
❑ 223 Ryan Moats JSY RC 8.00 3.00
❑ 224 Roscoe Parrish JSY RC 8.00 3.00
❑ 225 Stefan LeFors JSY RC 8.00 3.00
❑ 226 Terrence Murphy JSY RC 8.00 3.00
❑ 227 Troy Williamson JSY RC 8.00 3.00
❑ 228 Vernand Morency JSY RC 8.00 3.00
❑ 229 Vincent Jackson JSY RC 10.00 4.00

1998 Playoff Prestige Hobby

❑ COMP.HOBBY SET (200) 100.00 40.00
❑ 1 John Elway 8.00 3.00
❑ 2 Steve Atwater .75 .30
❑ 3 Terrell Davis 2.00 .75
❑ 4 Bill Romanowski .75 .30
❑ 5 Rod Smith 1.25 .50
❑ 6 Shannon Sharpe 1.25 .50
❑ 7 Ed McCaffrey 1.25 .50
❑ 8 Neil Smith 1.25 .50
❑ 9 Brett Favre 8.00 3.00
❑ 10 Dorsey Levens 2.00 .75
❑ 11 LeRoy Butler .75 .30
❑ 12 Antonio Freeman 2.00 .75
❑ 13 Robert Brooks 1.25 .50
❑ 14 Mark Chmura 1.25 .50
❑ 15 Gilbert Brown .75 .30
❑ 16 Kordell Stewart 2.00 .75
❑ 17 Jerome Bettis 2.00 .75
❑ 18 Carnell Lake .75 .30
❑ 19 Dermontti Dawson .75 .30
❑ 20 Charles Johnson .75 .30
❑ 21 Greg Lloyd .75 .30
❑ 22 Levon Kirkland .75 .30
❑ 23 Steve Young 2.50 1.00
❑ 24 Jim Druckenmiller .75 .30
❑ 25 Garrison Hearst 2.00 .75
❑ 26 Merton Hanks .75 .30
❑ 27 Ken Norton .75 .30
❑ 28 Jerry Rice 4.00 1.50
❑ 29 Terrell Owens 2.00 .75
❑ 30 J.J. Stokes 1.25 .50
❑ 31 Trent Dilfer 2.00 .75
❑ 32 Warrick Dunn 2.00 .75
❑ 33 Mike Alstott 2.00 .75
❑ 34 Reidel Anthony 1.25 .50
❑ 35 Warren Sapp 1.25 .50
❑ 36 Elvis Grbac 1.25 .50
❑ 37 Kimble Anders 1.25 .50
❑ 38 Ted Popson .75 .30
❑ 39 Derrick Thomas 2.00 .75
❑ 40 Tony Gonzalez 2.00 .75
❑ 41 Andre Rison 1.25 .50
❑ 42 Derrick Alexander 1.25 .50
❑ 43 Brad Johnson 2.00 .75
❑ 44 Robert Smith 2.00 .75
❑ 45 Randall McDaniel .75 .30
❑ 46 Cris Carter 2.00 .75
❑ 47 Jake Reed 1.25 .50
❑ 48 John Randle 1.25 .50
❑ 49 Drew Bledsoe 3.00 1.25
❑ 50 Willie Clay .75 .30
❑ 51 Chris Slade .75 .30
❑ 52 Willie McGinest .75 .30
❑ 53 Shawn Jefferson .75 .30
❑ 54 Ben Coates 1.25 .50
❑ 55 Terry Glenn 2.00 .75
❑ 56 Jason Hanson .75 .30
❑ 57 Scott Mitchell 1.25 .50
❑ 58 Barry Sanders 6.00 2.50
❑ 59 Herman Moore 1.25 .50
❑ 60 Johnnie Morton 1.25 .50
❑ 61 Mark Brunell 2.00 .75
❑ 62 James Stewart 1.25 .50
❑ 63 Tony Boselli .75 .30
❑ 64 Jimmy Smith 1.25 .50
❑ 65 Keenan McCardell 1.25 .50
❑ 66 Dan Marino 8.00 3.00
❑ 67 Troy Drayton .75 .30
❑ 68 Bernie Parmalee .75 .30
❑ 69 Karim Abdul-Jabbar 2.00 .75
❑ 70 Zach Thomas 2.00 .75
❑ 71 O.J. McDuffie 1.25 .50
❑ 72 Tim Bowens .75 .30
❑ 73 Danny Kanell 1.25 .50
❑ 74 Tiki Barber 2.00 .75
❑ 75 Tyrone Wheatley 1.25 .50
❑ 76 Charles Way .75 .30
❑ 77 Jason Sehorn 1.25 .50
❑ 78 Ike Hilliard 1.25 .50
❑ 79 Michael Strahan 1.25 .50
❑ 80 Troy Aikman 4.00 1.50
❑ 81 Deion Sanders 2.00 .75
❑ 82 Emmitt Smith 6.00 2.50
❑ 83 Darron Woodson .75 .30
❑ 84 Daryl Johnston 1.25 .50
❑ 85 Michael Irvin 2.00 .75
❑ 86 David LaFleur .75 .30
❑ 87 Glenn Foley 1.25 .50
❑ 88 Neil O'Donnell 1.25 .50
❑ 89 Keyshawn Johnson 2.00 .75
❑ 90 Aaron Glenn .75 .30
❑ 91 Wayne Chrebet 2.00 .75
❑ 92 Curtis Martin 2.00 .75
❑ 93 Steve McNair 2.00 .75
❑ 94 Eddie George 2.00 .75
❑ 95 Bruce Matthews .75 .30
❑ 96 Frank Wycheck .75 .30
❑ 97 Yancey Thigpen .75 .30
❑ 98 Gus Frerotte .75 .30
❑ 99 Terry Allen 2.00 .75
❑ 100 Michael Westbrook 1.25 .50
❑ 101 Jamie Asher .75 .30
❑ 102 Marshall Faulk 2.50 1.00
❑ 103 Zack Crockett .75 .30
❑ 104 Ken Dilger .75 .30
❑ 105 Marvin Harrison 2.00 .75
❑ 106 Chris Chandler 1.25 .50
❑ 107 Byron Hanspard .75 .30
❑ 108 Jamal Anderson 2.00 .75
❑ 109 Terance Mathis 1.25 .50
❑ 110 Peter Boulware .75 .30
❑ 111 Michael Jackson .75 .30
❑ 112 Jim Harbaugh 1.25 .50
❑ 113 Errict Rhett 1.25 .50
❑ 114 Antowain Smith 2.00 .75
❑ 115 Thurman Thomas 2.00 .75
❑ 116 Bruce Smith 1.25 .50
❑ 117 Doug Flutie 2.00 .75
❑ 118 Rob Johnson 1.25 .50
❑ 119 Kerry Collins 1.25 .50
❑ 120 Fred Lane .75 .30
❑ 121 Wesley Walls 1.25 .50
❑ 122 William Floyd .75 .30
❑ 123 Kevin Greene 1.25 .50
❑ 124 Erik Kramer .75 .30
❑ 125 Darnell Autry .75 .30
❑ 126 Curtis Conway 1.25 .50
❑ 127 Edgar Bennett .75 .30
❑ 128 Jeff Blake 1.25 .50
❑ 129 Corey Dillon 2.00 .75
❑ 130 Carl Pickens 1.25 .50
❑ 131 Darnay Scott 1.25 .50
❑ 132 Jake Plummer 2.00 .75
❑ 133 Larry Centers .75 .30
❑ 134 Frank Sanders 1.25 .50

❑ 135	Rob Moore	1.25	.50
❑ 136	Adrian Murrell	1.25	.50
❑ 137	Troy Davis	.75	.30
❑ 138	Ray Zellars	.75	.30
❑ 139	Willie Roaf	.75	.30
❑ 140	Andre Hastings	.75	.30
❑ 141	Jeff George	1.25	.50
❑ 142	Napoleon Kaufman	2.00	.75
❑ 143	Desmond Howard	1.25	.50
❑ 144	Tim Brown	2.00	.75
❑ 145	James Jett	1.25	.50
❑ 146	Rickey Dudley	.75	.30
❑ 147	Bobby Hoying	1.25	.50
❑ 148	Duce Staley	2.50	1.00
❑ 149	Charlie Garner	1.25	.50
❑ 150	Irving Fryar	1.25	.50
❑ 151	Chris T. Jones	.75	.30
❑ 152	Tony Banks	1.25	.50
❑ 153	Craig Heyward	.75	.30
❑ 154	Isaac Bruce	2.00	.75
❑ 155	Eddie Kennison	1.25	.50
❑ 156	Junior Seau	2.00	.75
❑ 157	Tony Martin	1.25	.50
❑ 158	Freddie Jones	.75	.30
❑ 159	Natrone Means	1.25	.50
❑ 160	Warren Moon	2.00	.75
❑ 161	Steve Broussard	.75	.30
❑ 162	Joey Galloway	1.25	.50
❑ 163	Brian Blades	.75	.30
❑ 164	Ricky Watters	1.25	.50
❑ 165	Peyton Manning RC	25.00	12.50
❑ 166	Ryan Leaf RC	3.00	1.25
❑ 167	Andre Wadsworth RC	2.50	1.00
❑ 168	Charles Woodson RC	4.00	1.50
❑ 169	Curtis Enis RC	1.50	.60
❑ 170	Fred Taylor RC	5.00	2.00
❑ 171	Kevin Dyson RC	3.00	1.25
❑ 172	Robert Edwards RC	2.50	1.00
❑ 173	Randy Moss RC	15.00	7.50
❑ 174	R.W. McQuarters RC	2.50	1.00
❑ 175	John Avery RC	2.50	1.00
❑ 176	Marcus Nash RC	1.50	.60
❑ 177	Jerome Pathon RC	3.00	1.25
❑ 178	Jacquez Green RC	2.50	1.00
❑ 179	Robert Holcombe RC	2.50	1.00
❑ 180	Pat Johnson RC	2.50	1.00
❑ 181	Germane Crowell RC	2.50	1.00
❑ 182	Tony Simmons RC	2.50	1.00
❑ 183	Joe Jurevicius RC	3.00	1.25
❑ 184	Mikhael Ricks RC	2.50	1.00
❑ 185	Charlie Batch RC	3.00	1.25
❑ 186	Jon Ritchie RC	2.50	1.00
❑ 187	Scott Frost RC	1.50	.60
❑ 188	Skip Hicks RC	2.50	1.00
❑ 189	Brian Alford RC	1.50	.60
❑ 190	E.G. Green RC	2.50	1.00
❑ 191	Jammi German RC	1.50	.60
❑ 192	Ahman Green RC	12.00	5.00
❑ 193	Chris Floyd RC	1.50	.60
❑ 194	Larry Shannon RC	1.50	.60
❑ 195	Jonathan Quinn RC	3.00	1.25
❑ 196	Rashaan Shehee RC	2.50	1.00
❑ 197	Brian Griese RC	6.00	2.50
❑ 198	Hines Ward RC	10.00	5.00
❑ 199	Michael Pittman RC	4.00	2.00
❑ 200	Az-Zahir Hakim RC	3.00	1.25

1999 Playoff Prestige EXP

❑	COMPLETE SET (200)	50.00	25.00
❑ 1	Anthony McFarland RC	1.50	.60
❑ 2	Al Wilson RC	1.00	.40
❑ 3	Jevon Kearse RC	2.50	1.00
❑ 4	Aaron Brooks RC	3.00	1.25
❑ 5	Travis McGriff RC	.75	.30
❑ 6	Jeff Paulk RC	.75	.30
❑ 7	Shawn Bryson RC	1.50	.60
❑ 8	Karsten Bailey RC	1.00	.40
❑ 9	Mike Cloud RC	1.00	.40
❑ 10	James Johnson RC	1.00	.40
❑ 11	Tai Streets RC	1.50	.60
❑ 12	Jermaine Fazande RC	1.00	.40
❑ 13	Ebenezer Ekuban RC	1.00	.40
❑ 14	Joe Montgomery RC	1.00	.40
❑ 15	Craig Yeast RC	1.00	.40
❑ 16	Joe Germaine RC	1.00	.40
❑ 17	Andy Katzenmoyer RC	1.00	.40
❑ 18	Kevin Faulk RC	1.50	.60
❑ 19	Chris McAlister RC	1.00	.40
❑ 20	Sedrick Irvin RC	.75	.30
❑ 21	Brock Huard RC	1.50	.60
❑ 22	Cade McNown RC	1.00	.40
❑ 23	Shaun King RC	1.00	.40
❑ 24	Amos Zereoue RC	1.50	.60
❑ 25	Dameane Douglas RC	1.00	.40
❑ 26	D'Wayne Bates RC	1.00	.40
❑ 27	Kevin Johnson RC	1.50	.60
❑ 28	Rob Konrad RC	1.50	.60
❑ 29	Troy Edwards RC	1.00	.40
❑ 30	Peerless Price RC	1.50	.60
❑ 31	Daunte Culpepper RC	6.00	2.50
❑ 32	Akili Smith RC	1.00	.40
❑ 33	David Boston RC	1.50	.60
❑ 34	Chris Claiborne RC	.75	.30
❑ 35	Torry Holt RC	4.00	1.50
❑ 36	Champ Bailey RC	2.00	.75
❑ 37	Edgerrin James RC	6.00	2.50
❑ 38	Donovan McNabb RC	8.00	3.00
❑ 39	Ricky Williams RC	3.00	1.25
❑ 40	Tim Couch RC	1.50	.60
❑ 41	Charles Woodson RP	1.00	.40
❑ 42	Skip Hicks RP	.40	.15
❑ 43	Brian Griese RP	1.00	.40
❑ 44	Tim Dwight RP	1.00	.40
❑ 45	Ryan Leaf RP	.60	.25
❑ 46	Curtis Enis RP	.40	.15
❑ 47	Charlie Batch RP	1.00	.40
❑ 48	Fred Taylor RP	1.00	.40
❑ 49	Peyton Manning RP	1.50	.60
❑ 50	Randy Moss RP	1.25	.50
❑ 51	Jim Harbaugh	.60	.25
❑ 52	Warren Moon	1.00	.40
❑ 53	Jeff George	.60	.25
❑ 54	Rich Gannon	1.00	.40
❑ 55	Scott Mitchell	.40	.15
❑ 56	Kerry Collins	.60	.25
❑ 57	Brad Johnson	1.00	.40
❑ 58	Charles Johnson	.40	.15
❑ 59	Chris Calloway	.40	.15
❑ 60	Tyrone Wheatley	.60	.25
❑ 61	Michael Westbrook	.60	.25
❑ 62	Skip Hicks	.40	.15
❑ 63	Terry Allen	.60	.25
❑ 64	Albert Connell	.40	.15
❑ 65	Kevin Dyson	.60	.25
❑ 66	Frank Wycheck	.40	.15
❑ 67	Yancey Thigpen	.40	.15
❑ 68	Steve McNair	1.00	.40
❑ 69	Eddie George	1.00	.40
❑ 70	Eric Zeier	.40	.15
❑ 71	Jacquez Green	.40	.15
❑ 72	Reidel Anthony	.60	.25
❑ 73	Warren Sapp	.60	.25
❑ 74	Mike Alstott	1.00	.40
❑ 75	Warrick Dunn	1.00	.40
❑ 76	Trent Dilfer	.60	.25
❑ 77	Ahman Green	1.00	.40
❑ 78	Joey Galloway	.60	.25
❑ 79	Ricky Watters	.60	.25
❑ 80	Jon Kitna	1.00	.40
❑ 81	Amp Lee	.40	.15
❑ 82	Isaac Bruce	1.00	.40
❑ 83	Robert Holcombe	.40	.15
❑ 84	Greg Hill	.40	.15
❑ 85	Marshall Faulk	1.25	.50
❑ 86	Trent Green	1.00	.40
❑ 87	J.J. Stokes	.60	.25
❑ 88	Terrell Owens	1.00	.40
❑ 89	Jerry Rice	2.00	.75
❑ 90	Garrison Hearst	.60	.25
❑ 91	Steve Young	1.25	.50
❑ 92	Junior Seau	1.00	.40
❑ 93	Mikhael Ricks	.40	.15
❑ 94	Natrone Means	.60	.25
❑ 95	Ryan Leaf	1.00	.40
❑ 96	Courtney Hawkins	.40	.15
❑ 97	Chris Fuamatu-Ma'afala UER	.40	.15
❑ 98	Jerome Bettis	1.00	.40
❑ 99	Kordell Stewart	.60	.25
❑ 100	Bobby Hoying	.60	.25
❑ 101	Charlie Garner	.60	.25
❑ 102	Duce Staley	1.00	.40
❑ 103	Charles Woodson	1.00	.40
❑ 104	James Jett	.60	.25
❑ 105	Rickey Dudley	.40	.15
❑ 106	Tim Brown	1.00	.40
❑ 107	Napoleon Kaufman	1.00	.40
❑ 108	Wayne Chrebet	.60	.25
❑ 109	Keyshawn Johnson	1.00	.40
❑ 110	Vinny Testaverde	.60	.25
❑ 111	Curtis Martin	1.00	.40
❑ 112	Joe Jurevicius	.60	.25
❑ 113	Tiki Barber	1.00	.40
❑ 114	Ike Hilliard	.40	.15
❑ 115	Kent Graham	.40	.15
❑ 116	Gary Brown	.40	.15
❑ 117	Lamar Smith	.60	.25
❑ 118	Eddie Kennison	.60	.25
❑ 119	Cam Cleeland	.40	.15
❑ 120	Tony Simmons	.40	.15
❑ 121	Ben Coates	.60	.25
❑ 122	Darick Holmes	.40	.15
❑ 123	Terry Glenn	1.00	.40
❑ 124	Drew Bledsoe	1.25	.50
❑ 125	Leroy Hoard	.40	.15
❑ 126	Jake Reed	.60	.25
❑ 127	Randy Moss	2.50	1.00
❑ 128	Cris Carter	1.00	.40
❑ 129	Robert Smith	1.00	.40
❑ 130	Randall Cunningham	1.00	.40
❑ 131	Lamar Thomas	.40	.15
❑ 132	John Avery	.40	.15
❑ 133	O.J. McDuffie	.60	.25
❑ 134	Dan Marino	3.00	1.25
❑ 135	Karim Abdul-Jabbar	.60	.25
❑ 136	Rashaan Shehee	.40	.15
❑ 137	Derrick Alexander WR	.60	.25
❑ 138	Byron Bam Morris	.40	.15
❑ 139	Andre Rison	.60	.25
❑ 140	Elvis Grbac	.60	.25
❑ 141	Tavian Banks	.40	.15
❑ 142	Keenan McCardell	.60	.25
❑ 143	Jimmy Smith	.60	.25
❑ 144	Fred Taylor	1.00	.40
❑ 145	Mark Brunell	1.00	.40
❑ 146	Jerome Pathon	.40	.15
❑ 147	Marvin Harrison	1.00	.40
❑ 148	Peyton Manning	3.00	1.25
❑ 149	Robert Brooks	.60	.25
❑ 150	Mark Chmura	.40	.15
❑ 151	Antonio Freeman	1.00	.40
❑ 152	Dorsey Levens	1.00	.40
❑ 153	Brett Favre	3.00	1.25
❑ 154	Johnnie Morton	.60	.25
❑ 155	Germane Crowell	.40	.15
❑ 156	Barry Sanders	3.00	1.25
❑ 157	Herman Moore	.60	.25
❑ 158	Charlie Batch	1.00	.40
❑ 159	Marcus Nash	.40	.15
❑ 160	Shannon Sharpe	.60	.25
❑ 161	Rod Smith	.60	.25
❑ 162	Ed McCaffrey	.60	.25
❑ 163	Terrell Davis	1.00	.40
❑ 164	John Elway	3.00	1.25
❑ 165	Ernie Mills	.40	.15
❑ 166	Michael Irvin	.60	.25
❑ 167	Deion Sanders	1.00	.40
❑ 168	Emmitt Smith	2.00	.75
❑ 169	Troy Aikman	2.00	.75
❑ 170	Chris Spielman	.40	.15
❑ 171	Terry Kirby	.40	.15
❑ 172	Ty Detmer	.60	.25
❑ 173	Leslie Shepherd	.40	.15

❑ 174 Darnay Scott	.40	.15
❑ 175 Jeff Blake	.60	.25
❑ 176 Carl Pickens	.60	.25
❑ 177 Corey Dillon	1.00	.40
❑ 178 Bobby Engram	.60	.25
❑ 179 Curtis Conway	.60	.25
❑ 180 Curtis Enis	.40	.15
❑ 181 Muhsin Muhammad	.60	.25
❑ 182 Steve Beuerlein	.40	.15
❑ 183 Tim Biakabutuka	.60	.25
❑ 184 Bruce Smith	.60	.25
❑ 185 Andre Reed	.60	.25
❑ 186 Thurman Thomas	.60	.25
❑ 187 Eric Moulds	1.00	.40
❑ 188 Antowain Smith	1.00	.40
❑ 189 Doug Flutie	1.00	.40
❑ 190 Jermaine Lewis	.60	.25
❑ 191 Priest Holmes	1.50	.60
❑ 192 O.J. Santiago	.40	.15
❑ 193 Tim Dwight	1.00	.40
❑ 194 Terance Mathis	.60	.25
❑ 195 Chris Chandler	.60	.25
❑ 196 Jamal Anderson	1.00	.40
❑ 197 Rob Moore	.60	.25
❑ 198 Frank Sanders	.60	.25
❑ 199 Adrian Murrell	.60	.25
❑ 200 Jake Plummer	.60	.25
❑ RR1 Barry Sanders RFR	20.00	7.50

1999 Playoff Prestige SSD

❑ COMPLETE SET (200)	150.00	75.00
❑ COMP.SET w/o SP's (150)	50.00	25.00
❑ 1 Jake Plummer	.75	.30
❑ 2 Adrian Murrell	.75	.30
❑ 3 Frank Sanders	.75	.30
❑ 4 Rob Moore	.75	.30
❑ 5 Jamal Anderson	1.25	.50
❑ 6 Chris Chandler	.75	.30
❑ 7 Terance Mathis	.75	.30
❑ 8 Tim Dwight	1.25	.50
❑ 9 O.J. Santiago	.50	.20
❑ 10 Priest Holmes	2.00	.75
❑ 11 Jermaine Lewis	.75	.30
❑ 12 Doug Flutie	1.25	.50
❑ 13 Antowain Smith	1.25	.50
❑ 14 Eric Moulds	1.25	.50
❑ 15 Thurman Thomas	.75	.30
❑ 16 Andre Reed	.75	.30
❑ 17 Bruce Smith	.75	.30
❑ 18 Tim Biakabutuka	.75	.30
❑ 19 Steve Beuerlein	.50	.20
❑ 20 Muhsin Muhammad	.75	.30
❑ 21 Curtis Enis	.50	.20
❑ 22 Curtis Conway	.75	.30
❑ 23 Bobby Engram	.75	.30
❑ 24 Corey Dillon	1.25	.50
❑ 25 Carl Pickens	.75	.30
❑ 26 Jeff Blake	.75	.30
❑ 27 Darnay Scott	.50	.20
❑ 28 Leslie Shepherd	.50	.20
❑ 29 Ty Detmer	.75	.30
❑ 30 Terry Kirby	.50	.20
❑ 31 Chris Spielman	.50	.20
❑ 32 Troy Aikman	3.00	1.25
❑ 33 Emmitt Smith	3.00	1.25
❑ 34 Deion Sanders	1.25	.50
❑ 35 Michael Irvin	.75	.30
❑ 36 Ernie Mills	.50	.20
❑ 37 John Elway	5.00	2.00
❑ 38 Terrell Davis	1.25	.50
❑ 39 Ed McCaffrey	.75	.30
❑ 40 Rod Smith	.75	.30
❑ 41 Shannon Sharpe	.75	.30
❑ 42 Marcus Nash	.50	.20
❑ 43 Charlie Batch	1.25	.50
❑ 44 Herman Moore	.75	.30
❑ 45 Barry Sanders	5.00	2.00
❑ 46 Germane Crowell	.50	.20
❑ 47 Johnnie Morton	.75	.30
❑ 48 Brett Favre	5.00	2.00
❑ 49 Dorsey Levens	1.25	.50
❑ 50 Antonio Freeman	1.25	.50
❑ 51 Mark Chmura	.50	.20
❑ 52 Robert Brooks	.75	.30
❑ 53 Peyton Manning	5.00	2.00
❑ 54 Marvin Harrison	1.25	.50
❑ 55 Jerome Pathon	.50	.20
❑ 56 Mark Brunell	1.25	.50
❑ 57 Fred Taylor	1.25	.50
❑ 58 Jimmy Smith	.75	.30
❑ 59 Keenan McCardell	.75	.30
❑ 60 Tavian Banks	.50	.20
❑ 61 Elvis Grbac	.75	.30
❑ 62 Andre Rison	.75	.30
❑ 63 Byron Bam Morris	.50	.20
❑ 64 Derrick Alexander WR	.75	.30
❑ 65 Rashaan Shehee	.50	.20
❑ 66 Karim Abdul-Jabbar	.75	.30
❑ 67 Dan Marino	5.00	2.00
❑ 68 O.J. McDuffie	.75	.30
❑ 69 John Avery	.50	.20
❑ 70 Lamar Thomas	.50	.20
❑ 71 Randall Cunningham	1.25	.50
❑ 72 Robert Smith	1.25	.50
❑ 73 Cris Carter	1.25	.50
❑ 74 Randy Moss	4.00	1.50
❑ 75 Jake Reed	.75	.30
❑ 76 Leroy Hoard	.50	.20
❑ 77 Drew Bledsoe	2.00	.75
❑ 78 Terry Glenn	1.25	.50
❑ 79 Darick Holmes	.50	.20
❑ 80 Ben Coates	.75	.30
❑ 81 Tony Simmons	.50	.20
❑ 82 Cam Cleeland	.50	.20
❑ 83 Eddie Kennison	.75	.30
❑ 84 Lamar Smith	.75	.30
❑ 85 Gary Brown	.50	.20
❑ 86 Kent Graham	.50	.20
❑ 87 Ike Hilliard	.50	.20
❑ 88 Tiki Barber	1.25	.50
❑ 89 Joe Jurevicius	.75	.30
❑ 90 Curtis Martin	1.25	.50
❑ 91 Vinny Testaverde	.75	.30
❑ 92 Keyshawn Johnson	1.25	.50
❑ 93 Wayne Chrebet	.75	.30
❑ 94 Napoleon Kaufman	1.25	.50
❑ 95 Tim Brown	1.25	.50
❑ 96 Rickey Dudley	.50	.20
❑ 97 James Jett	.75	.30
❑ 98 Charles Woodson	1.25	.50
❑ 99 Duce Staley	1.25	.50
❑ 100 Charlie Garner	.75	.30
❑ 101 Bobby Hoying	.75	.30
❑ 102 Kordell Stewart	.75	.30
❑ 103 Jerome Bettis	1.25	.50
❑ 104 Chris Fuamatu-Ma'afala	.50	.20
❑ 105 Courtney Hawkins	.50	.20
❑ 106 Ryan Leaf	1.25	.50
❑ 107 Natrone Means	.75	.30
❑ 108 Mikhael Ricks	.50	.20
❑ 109 Junior Seau	1.25	.50
❑ 110 Steve Young	2.00	.75
❑ 111 Garrison Hearst	.75	.30
❑ 112 Jerry Rice	3.00	1.25
❑ 113 Terrell Owens	1.25	.50
❑ 114 J.J. Stokes	.75	.30
❑ 115 Trent Green	1.25	.50
❑ 116 Marshall Faulk	1.50	.60
❑ 117 Greg Hill	.50	.20
❑ 118 Robert Holcombe	.50	.20
❑ 119 Isaac Bruce	1.25	.50
❑ 120 Amp Lee	.50	.20
❑ 121 Jon Kitna	1.25	.50
❑ 122 Ricky Watters	.75	.30
❑ 123 Joey Galloway	.75	.30
❑ 124 Ahman Green	1.25	.50
❑ 125 Trent Dilfer	.75	.30
❑ 126 Warrick Dunn	1.25	.50
❑ 127 Mike Alstott	1.25	.50
❑ 128 Warren Sapp	.75	.30
❑ 129 Reidel Anthony	.75	.30
❑ 130 Jacquez Green	.50	.20
❑ 131 Eric Zeier	.50	.20
❑ 132 Eddie George	1.25	.50
❑ 133 Steve McNair	1.25	.50
❑ 134 Yancey Thigpen	.50	.20
❑ 135 Frank Wycheck	.50	.20
❑ 136 Kevin Dyson	.75	.30
❑ 137 Albert Connell	.50	.20
❑ 138 Terry Allen	.75	.30
❑ 139 Skip Hicks	.50	.20
❑ 140 Michael Westbrook	.75	.30
❑ 141 Tyrone Wheatley	.75	.30
❑ 142 Chris Calloway	.50	.20
❑ 143 Charles Johnson	.50	.20
❑ 144 Brad Johnson	1.25	.50
❑ 145 Kerry Collins	.75	.30
❑ 146 Scott Mitchell	.50	.20
❑ 147 Rich Gannon	1.25	.50
❑ 148 Jeff George	.75	.30
❑ 149 Warren Moon	1.25	.50
❑ 150 Jim Harbaugh	.75	.30
❑ 151 Randy Moss RP	6.00	2.50
❑ 152 Peyton Manning RP	8.00	3.00
❑ 153 Fred Taylor RP	2.50	1.00
❑ 154 Charlie Batch RP	2.50	1.00
❑ 155 Curtis Enis RP	1.50	.60
❑ 156 Ryan Leaf RP	1.50	.60
❑ 157 Tim Dwight RP	1.50	.60
❑ 158 Brian Griese RP	2.50	1.00
❑ 159 Skip Hicks RP	1.50	.60
❑ 160 Charles Woodson RP	2.50	1.00
❑ 161 Tim Couch RC	4.00	1.50
❑ 162 Ricky Williams RC	6.00	2.50
❑ 163 Donovan McNabb RC	15.00	6.00
❑ 164 Edgerrin James RC	12.00	5.00
❑ 165 Champ Bailey RC	5.00	2.00
❑ 166 Torry Holt RC	8.00	3.00
❑ 167 Chris Claiborne RC	2.00	.75
❑ 168 David Boston RC	4.00	1.50
❑ 169 Akili Smith RC	1.50	.60
❑ 170 Daunte Culpepper RC	12.00	5.00
❑ 171 Peerless Price RC	4.00	1.50
❑ 172 Troy Edwards RC	3.00	1.25
❑ 173 Rob Konrad RC	4.00	1.50
❑ 174 Kevin Johnson RC	4.00	1.50
❑ 175 D'Wayne Bates RC	3.00	1.25
❑ 176 Dameane Douglas RC	3.00	1.25
❑ 177 Amos Zereoue RC	4.00	1.50
❑ 178 Shaun King RC	3.00	1.25
❑ 179 Cade McNown RC	3.00	1.25
❑ 180 Brock Huard RC	4.00	1.50
❑ 181 Sedrick Irvin RC	2.00	.75
❑ 182 Chris McAlister RC	3.00	1.25
❑ 183 Kevin Faulk RC	4.00	1.50
❑ 184 Andy Katzenmoyer RC	3.00	1.25
❑ 185 Joe Germaine RC	3.00	1.25
❑ 186 Craig Yeast RC	3.00	1.25
❑ 187 Joe Montgomery RC	3.00	1.25
❑ 188 Ebenezer Ekuban RC	3.00	1.25
❑ 189 Jermaine Fazande RC	3.00	1.25
❑ 190 Tai Streets RC	4.00	1.50
❑ 191 James Johnson RC	3.00	1.25
❑ 192 Mike Cloud RC	3.00	1.25
❑ 193 Karsten Bailey RC	3.00	1.25
❑ 194 Shawn Bryson RC	4.00	1.50
❑ 195 Jeff Paulk RC	2.00	.75
❑ 196 Travis McGriff RC	2.00	.75
❑ 197 Aaron Brooks RC	6.00	2.50
❑ 198 Jevon Kearse RC	6.00	2.50
❑ 199 Al Wilson RC	3.00	1.25
❑ 200 Anthony McFarland RC	4.00	1.50

2000 Playoff Prestige

❑ COMPLETE SET (300)	350.00	175.00
❑ COMP.SET w/o SP's (200)	25.00	10.00
❑ 1 Frank Sanders	.40	.15
❑ 2 Rob Moore	.40	.15
❑ 3 Michael Pittman	.25	.08
❑ 4 Jake Plummer	.40	.15
❑ 5 David Boston	.60	.25
❑ 6 Chris Chandler	.40	.15

❑ 7 Tim Dwight .60 .25
❑ 8 Shawn Jefferson .25 .08
❑ 9 Terance Mathis .40 .15
❑ 10 Jamal Anderson .60 .25
❑ 11 Byron Hanspard .25 .08
❑ 12 Ken Oxendine .25 .08
❑ 13 Priest Holmes .75 .30
❑ 14 Tony Banks .40 .15
❑ 15 Shannon Sharpe .40 .15
❑ 16 Rod Woodson .40 .15
❑ 17 Jermaine Lewis .40 .15
❑ 18 Qadry Ismail .40 .15
❑ 19 Eric Moulds .60 .25
❑ 20 Doug Flutie .60 .25
❑ 21 Jay Riemersma .25 .08
❑ 22 Antowain Smith .40 .15
❑ 23 Jonathan Linton .25 .08
❑ 24 Peerless Price .40 .15
❑ 25 Rob Johnson .40 .15
❑ 26 Muhsin Muhammad .40 .15
❑ 27 Wesley Walls .25 .08
❑ 28 Tim Biakabutuka .40 .15
❑ 29 Steve Beuerlein .40 .15
❑ 30 Patrick Jeffers .60 .25
❑ 31 Natrone Means .25 .08
❑ 32 Curtis Enis .25 .08
❑ 33 Bobby Engram .40 .15
❑ 34 Marcus Robinson .60 .25
❑ 35 Marty Booker .40 .15
❑ 36 Cade McNown .25 .08
❑ 37 Darnay Scott .40 .15
❑ 38 Carl Pickens .40 .15
❑ 39 Corey Dillon .60 .25
❑ 40 Akili Smith .25 .08
❑ 41 Michael Basnight .25 .08
❑ 42 Karim Abdul-Jabbar .40 .15
❑ 43 Tim Couch .40 .15
❑ 44 Kevin Johnson .60 .25
❑ 45 Darrin Chiaverini .25 .08
❑ 46 Errict Rhett .40 .15
❑ 47 Emmitt Smith 1.25 .50
❑ 48 Deion Sanders .60 .25
❑ 49 Michael Irvin .40 .15
❑ 50 Rocket Ismail .40 .15
❑ 51 Troy Aikman 1.25 .50
❑ 52 Jason Tucker .25 .08
❑ 53 Joey Galloway .40 .15
❑ 54 David LaFleur .25 .08
❑ 55 Wane McGarity .25 .08
❑ 56 Ed McCaffrey .60 .25
❑ 57 Rod Smith .40 .15
❑ 58 Brian Griese .60 .25
❑ 59 John Elway 2.00 .75
❑ 60 Gus Frerotte .25 .08
❑ 61 Neil Smith .25 .08
❑ 62 Terrell Davis .60 .25
❑ 63 Olandis Gary .60 .25
❑ 64 Johnnie Morton .40 .15
❑ 65 Charlie Batch .60 .25
❑ 66 Barry Sanders 1.50 .60
❑ 67 James Stewart .40 .15
❑ 68 Germane Crowell .25 .08
❑ 69 Sedrick Irvin .25 .08
❑ 70 Herman Moore .40 .15
❑ 71 Corey Bradford .40 .15
❑ 72 Dorsey Levens .40 .15
❑ 73 Antonio Freeman .60 .25
❑ 74 Brett Favre 2.00 .75
❑ 75 De'Mond Parker .25 .08
❑ 76 Bill Schroeder .40 .15
❑ 77 Donald Driver .60 .25
❑ 78 E.G. Green .25 .08
❑ 79 Marvin Harrison .60 .25
❑ 80 Peyton Manning 1.50 .60
❑ 81 Terrence Wilkins .25 .08
❑ 82 Edgerrin James 1.00 .40
❑ 83 Keenan McCardell .40 .15
❑ 84 Mark Brunell .60 .25
❑ 85 Fred Taylor .60 .25
❑ 86 Jimmy Smith .40 .15
❑ 87 Derrick Alexander .40 .15
❑ 88 Andre Rison .40 .15
❑ 89 Elvis Grbac .40 .15
❑ 90 Tony Gonzalez .40 .15
❑ 91 Donnell Bennett .25 .08
❑ 92 Warren Moon .60 .25
❑ 93 Kimble Anders .25 .08
❑ 94 Tony Richardson RC .40 .15
❑ 95 Jay Fiedler .60 .25
❑ 96 Zach Thomas .60 .25
❑ 97 Oronde Gadsden .40 .15
❑ 98 Dan Marino 2.00 .75
❑ 99 O.J. McDuffie .40 .15
❑ 100 Tony Martin .40 .15
❑ 101 James Johnson .25 .08
❑ 102 Rob Konrad .25 .08
❑ 103 Damon Huard .60 .25
❑ 104 Thurman Thomas .40 .15
❑ 105 Randy Moss 1.25 .50
❑ 106 Cris Carter .60 .25
❑ 107 Robert Smith .60 .25
❑ 108 Randall Cunningham .60 .25
❑ 109 John Randle .40 .15
❑ 110 Leroy Hoard .25 .08
❑ 111 Daunte Culpepper .75 .30
❑ 112 Matthew Hatchette .25 .08
❑ 113 Troy Brown .40 .15
❑ 114 Tony Simmons .25 .08
❑ 115 Terry Glenn .40 .15
❑ 116 Ben Coates .25 .08
❑ 117 Drew Bledsoe .75 .30
❑ 118 Terry Allen .40 .15
❑ 119 Kevin Faulk .25 .08
❑ 120 Ricky Williams .60 .25
❑ 121 Jake Delhomme RC 3.00 1.25
❑ 122 Jake Reed .40 .15
❑ 123 Jeff Blake .40 .15
❑ 124 Amani Toomer .40 .15
❑ 125 Kerry Collins .40 .15
❑ 126 Tiki Barber .60 .25
❑ 127 Ike Hilliard .40 .15
❑ 128 Joe Montgomery .25 .08
❑ 129 Sean Bennett .25 .08
❑ 130 Curtis Martin .60 .25
❑ 131 Vinny Testaverde .40 .15
❑ 132 Wayne Chrebet .40 .15
❑ 133 Ray Lucas .40 .15
❑ 134 Tyrone Wheatley .40 .15
❑ 135 Napoleon Kaufman .40 .15
❑ 136 Tim Brown .60 .25
❑ 137 Rickey Dudley .25 .08
❑ 138 James Jett .25 .08
❑ 139 Rich Gannon .60 .25
❑ 140 Charles Woodson .40 .15
❑ 141 Duce Staley .60 .25
❑ 142 Donovan McNabb 1.00 .40
❑ 143 Na Brown .25 .08
❑ 144 Kordell Stewart .40 .15
❑ 145 Jerome Bettis .60 .25
❑ 146 Hines Ward .60 .25
❑ 147 Troy Edwards .25 .08
❑ 148 Curtis Conway .40 .15
❑ 149 Junior Seau .60 .25
❑ 150 Jim Harbaugh .40 .15
❑ 151 Jermaine Fazande .25 .08
❑ 152 Terrell Owens .60 .25
❑ 153 J.J. Stokes .40 .15
❑ 154 Charlie Garner .40 .15
❑ 155 Jerry Rice 1.25 .50
❑ 156 Garrison Hearst .40 .15
❑ 157 Steve Young .75 .30
❑ 158 Jeff Garcia .60 .25
❑ 159 Derrick Mayes .40 .15
❑ 160 Ahman Green .60 .25
❑ 161 Ricky Watters .40 .15
❑ 162 Jon Kitna .60 .25
❑ 163 Karsten Bailey .25 .08
❑ 164 Sean Dawkins .25 .08
❑ 165 Az-Zahir Hakim .40 .15
❑ 166 Isaac Bruce .60 .25
❑ 167 Marshall Faulk .75 .30
❑ 168 Trent Green .60 .25
❑ 169 Kurt Warner 1.25 .50
❑ 170 Torry Holt .60 .25
❑ 171 Robert Holcombe .25 .08
❑ 172 Kevin Carter .25 .08
❑ 173 Keyshawn Johnson .60 .25
❑ 174 Jacquez Green .25 .08
❑ 175 Reidel Anthony .25 .08
❑ 176 Warren Sapp .40 .15
❑ 177 Mike Alstott .60 .25
❑ 178 Warrick Dunn .60 .25
❑ 179 Trent Dilfer .40 .15
❑ 180 Shaun King .25 .08
❑ 181 Neil O'Donnell .25 .08
❑ 182 Eddie George .60 .25
❑ 183 Yancey Thigpen .25 .08
❑ 184 Steve McNair .60 .25
❑ 185 Kevin Dyson .40 .15
❑ 186 Frank Wycheck .25 .08
❑ 187 Jevon Kearse .60 .25
❑ 188 Adrian Murrell .25 .08
❑ 189 Jeff George .40 .15
❑ 190 Stephen Davis .60 .25
❑ 191 Stephen Alexander .25 .08
❑ 192 Darrell Green .25 .08
❑ 193 Skip Hicks .25 .08
❑ 194 Brad Johnson .60 .25
❑ 195 Michael Westbrook .40 .15
❑ 196 Albert Connell .25 .08
❑ 197 Irving Fryar .40 .15
❑ 198 Bruce Smith .40 .15
❑ 199 Champ Bailey .40 .15
❑ 200 Larry Centers .25 .08
❑ 201 Jake Plummer PP 1.25 .50
❑ 202 Doug Flutie PP 1.25 .50
❑ 203 Eric Moulds PP 1.25 .50
❑ 204 Muhsin Muhammad PP 1.25 .50
❑ 205 Marcus Robinson PP 1.25 .50
❑ 206 Cade McNown PP 1.25 .50
❑ 207 Corey Dillon PP 1.25 .50
❑ 208 Tim Couch PP 1.25 .50
❑ 209 Kevin Johnson PP 1.25 .50
❑ 210 Emmitt Smith PP 3.00 1.25
❑ 211 Troy Aikman PP 3.00 1.25
❑ 212 Brian Griese PP 1.25 .50
❑ 213 Olandis Gary PP 1.25 .50
❑ 214 Germane Crowell PP 1.25 .50
❑ 215 Brett Favre PP 5.00 2.00
❑ 216 Charlie Batch PP 1.25 .50
❑ 217 Antonio Freeman PP 1.25 .50
❑ 218 Dorsey Levens PP 1.25 .50
❑ 219 Peyton Manning PP 4.00 1.50
❑ 220 Edgerrin James PP 2.50 1.00
❑ 221 Marvin Harrison PP 1.25 .50
❑ 222 Fred Taylor PP 1.25 .50
❑ 223 Mark Brunell PP 1.25 .50
❑ 224 Jimmy Smith PP 1.25 .50
❑ 225 Dan Marino PP 5.00 2.00
❑ 226 Randy Moss PP 3.00 1.25
❑ 227 Cris Carter PP 1.25 .50
❑ 228 Robert Smith PP 1.25 .50
❑ 229 Drew Bledsoe PP 2.00 .75
❑ 230 Terry Glenn PP 1.25 .50
❑ 231 Ricky Williams PP 1.25 .50
❑ 232 Amani Toomer PP 1.25 .50
❑ 233 Keyshawn Johnson PP 1.25 .50
❑ 234 Curtis Martin PP 1.25 .50
❑ 235 Ray Lucas PP 1.25 .50
❑ 236 Tim Brown PP 1.25 .50
❑ 237 Duce Staley PP 1.25 .50
❑ 238 Donovan McNabb PP 2.50 1.00
❑ 239 Jerry Rice PP 3.00 1.25
❑ 240 Jon Kitna PP 1.25 .50
❑ 241 Isaac Bruce PP 1.25 .50
❑ 242 Kurt Warner PP 3.00 1.25
❑ 243 Torry Holt PP 1.25 .50
❑ 244 Mike Alstott PP 1.25 .50
❑ 245 Marshall Faulk PP 2.00 .75
❑ 246 Shaun King PP .25 .08
❑ 247 Eddie George PP 1.25 .50
❑ 248 Steve McNair PP 1.25 .50
❑ 249 Stephen Davis PP 1.25 .50
❑ 250 Brad Johnson PP 1.25 .50

Card	Hi	Lo
❑ 251 Rondell Mealey RC	2.50	1.00
❑ 252 Peter Warrick RC	4.00	1.50
❑ 253 Courtney Brown RC	1.25	.50
❑ 254 Plaxico Burress RC	8.00	3.00
❑ 255 Corey Simon RC	1.25	.50
❑ 256 Thomas Jones RC	6.00	2.50
❑ 257 Travis Taylor RC	1.25	.50
❑ 258 Shaun Alexander RC	20.00	7.50
❑ 259 Chris Redman RC	1.25	.50
❑ 260 Chad Pennington RC	10.00	4.00
❑ 261 Jamal Lewis RC	10.00	4.00
❑ 262 Bubba Franks RC	4.00	1.50
❑ 263 Dez White RC	4.00	1.50
❑ 264 Ron Dayne RC	4.00	1.50
❑ 265 Sylvester Morris RC	3.00	1.25
❑ 266 R.Jay Soward RC	3.00	1.25
❑ 267 Sherrod Gideon RC	2.50	1.00
❑ 268 Travis Prentice RC	3.00	1.25
❑ 269 Darrell Jackson RC	8.00	3.00
❑ 270 Giovanni Carmazzi RC	2.50	1.00
❑ 271 Anthony Lucas RC	2.50	1.00
❑ 272 Danny Farmer RC	3.00	1.25
❑ 273 Dennis Northcutt RC	4.00	1.50
❑ 274 Troy Walters RC	4.00	1.50
❑ 275 Laveranues Coles RC	5.00	2.00
❑ 276 Tee Martin RC	4.00	1.50
❑ 277 J.R. Redmond RC	3.00	1.25
❑ 278 Jerry Porter RC	5.00	2.00
❑ 279 Sebastian Janikowski RC	4.00	1.50
❑ 280 Michael Wiley RC	3.00	1.25
❑ 281 Reuben Droughns RC	5.00	2.00
❑ 282 Trung Canidate RC	3.00	1.25
❑ 283 Shyrone Stith RC	3.00	1.25
❑ 284 Trevor Gaylor RC	3.00	1.25
❑ 285 Marc Bulger RC	8.00	3.00
❑ 286 Tom Brady RC	100.00	60.00
❑ 287 Todd Husak RC	4.00	1.50
❑ 288 Jarious Jackson RC	3.00	1.25
❑ 289 Terrelle Smith RC	3.00	1.25
❑ 290 Chad Morton RC	4.00	1.50
❑ 291 Chris Cole RC	4.00	1.50
❑ 292 Kwame Cavil RC	2.50	1.00
❑ 293 JaJuan Dawson RC	2.50	1.00
❑ 294 Curtis Keaton RC	3.00	1.25
❑ 295 Tim Rattay RC	4.00	1.50
❑ 296 Joe Hamilton RC	3.00	1.25
❑ 297 Gari Scott RC	2.50	1.00
❑ 298 Mike Anderson RC	5.00	2.00
❑ 299 Ron Dugans RC	2.50	1.00
❑ 300 Todd Pinkston RC	4.00	1.50

2002 Playoff Prestige

Card	Hi	Lo
❑ COMP.SET w/o SP's (150)	40.00	15.00
❑ 1 David Boston	1.25	.50
❑ 2 MarTay Jenkins	.50	.20
❑ 3 Jake Plummer	.75	.30
❑ 4 Chris Chandler	.75	.30
❑ 5 Jamal Anderson	.75	.30
❑ 6 Michael Vick	2.50	1.00
❑ 7 Maurice Smith	.75	.30
❑ 8 Elvis Grbac	.75	.30
❑ 9 Jamal Lewis	1.25	.50
❑ 10 Todd Heap	.50	.20
❑ 11 Qadry Ismail	.75	.30
❑ 12 Shannon Sharpe	.75	.30
❑ 13 Ray Lewis	1.25	.50
❑ 14 Rod Woodson	.75	.30
❑ 15 Travis Henry	1.25	.50
❑ 16 Rob Johnson	.75	.30
❑ 17 Eric Moulds	.75	.30
❑ 18 Nate Clements	.50	.20
❑ 19 Donald Hayes	.50	.20
❑ 20 Muhsin Muhammad	.75	.30
❑ 21 Steve Smith	1.25	.50
❑ 22 Wesley Walls	.50	.20
❑ 23 Chris Weinke	.75	.30
❑ 24 James Allen	.75	.30
❑ 25 David Terrell	1.25	.50
❑ 26 Anthony Thomas	.75	.30
❑ 27 Dez White	.50	.20
❑ 28 Brian Urlacher	2.00	.75
❑ 29 Mike Brown	1.25	.50
❑ 30 Corey Dillon	.75	.30
❑ 31 Chad Johnson	1.25	.50
❑ 32 Peter Warrick	.75	.30
❑ 33 Justin Smith	.50	.20
❑ 34 Tim Couch	.75	.30
❑ 35 James Jackson	.50	.20
❑ 36 Quincy Morgan	.50	.20
❑ 37 Kevin Johnson	.75	.30
❑ 38 Gerard Warren	.50	.20
❑ 39 Anthony Henry	.50	.20
❑ 40 Quincy Carter	.75	.30
❑ 41 Joey Galloway	.75	.30
❑ 42 Rocket Ismail	.75	.30
❑ 43 Ryan Leaf	.75	.30
❑ 44 Emmitt Smith	3.00	1.25
❑ 45 Troy Hambrick	.50	.20
❑ 46 Mike Anderson	1.25	.50
❑ 47 Terrell Davis	1.25	.50
❑ 48 Brian Griese	1.25	.50
❑ 49 Rod Smith	.75	.30
❑ 50 Ed McCaffrey	1.25	.50
❑ 51 Charlie Batch	.75	.30
❑ 52 Johnnie Morton	.75	.30
❑ 53 Germane Crowell	.50	.20
❑ 54 James Stewart	.75	.30
❑ 55 Shaun Rogers	.50	.20
❑ 56 Brett Favre	3.00	1.25
❑ 57 Antonio Freeman	1.25	.50
❑ 58 Ahman Green	1.25	.50
❑ 59 Bill Schroeder	.75	.30
❑ 60 Kabeer Gbaja-Biamila	.75	.30
❑ 61 Marvin Harrison	1.25	.50
❑ 62 Terrence Wilkins	.50	.20
❑ 63 Dominic Rhodes	.75	.30
❑ 64 Reggie Wayne	1.25	.50
❑ 65 Edgerrin James	1.50	.60
❑ 66 Mark Brunell	1.25	.50
❑ 67 Keenan McCardell	.50	.20
❑ 68 Jimmy Smith	.75	.30
❑ 69 Fred Taylor	1.25	.50
❑ 70 Derrick Alexander	.75	.30
❑ 71 Tony Gonzalez	.75	.30
❑ 72 Trent Green	.75	.30
❑ 73 Priest Holmes	1.50	.60
❑ 74 Snoop Minnis	.50	.20
❑ 75 Chris Chambers	1.25	.50
❑ 76 Jay Fiedler	.75	.30
❑ 77 Travis Minor	.50	.20
❑ 78 Lamar Smith	.75	.30
❑ 79 Zach Thomas	1.25	.50
❑ 80 Michael Bennett	.75	.30
❑ 81 Cris Carter	1.25	.50
❑ 82 Daunte Culpepper	1.25	.50
❑ 83 Randy Moss	2.50	1.00
❑ 84 Drew Bledsoe	1.50	.60
❑ 85 Tom Brady	3.00	1.25
❑ 86 Troy Brown	.75	.30
❑ 87 Antowain Smith	.75	.30
❑ 88 Aaron Brooks	1.25	.50
❑ 89 Joe Horn	.75	.30
❑ 90 Deuce McAllister	1.50	.60
❑ 91 Ricky Williams	1.25	.50
❑ 92 Kerry Collins	.75	.30
❑ 93 Ron Dayne	.75	.30
❑ 94 Michael Strahan	.75	.30
❑ 95 Jason Sehorn	.50	.20
❑ 96 Wayne Chrebet	.75	.30
❑ 97 Laveranues Coles	.75	.30
❑ 98 LaMont Jordan	1.25	.50
❑ 99 Curtis Martin	1.25	.50
❑ 100 Santana Moss	1.25	.50
❑ 101 Vinny Testaverde	.75	.30
❑ 102 Tim Brown	1.25	.50
❑ 103 Jerry Porter	.50	.20
❑ 104 Jerry Rice	2.50	1.00
❑ 105 Charlie Garner	.75	.30
❑ 106 Tyrone Wheatley	.75	.30
❑ 107 Charles Woodson	.75	.30
❑ 108 Correll Buckhalter	.75	.30
❑ 109 Todd Pinkston	.75	.30
❑ 110 Freddie Mitchell	.75	.30
❑ 111 James Thrash	.75	.30
❑ 112 Duce Staley	1.25	.50
❑ 113 Jerome Bettis	1.25	.50
❑ 114 Plaxico Burress	.75	.30
❑ 115 Kordell Stewart	.75	.30
❑ 116 Hines Ward	1.25	.50
❑ 117 Kendrell Bell	1.25	.50
❑ 118 Drew Brees	1.25	.50
❑ 119 Curtis Conway	.50	.20
❑ 120 Doug Flutie	1.25	.50
❑ 121 LaDainian Tomlinson	2.00	.75
❑ 122 Junior Seau	1.25	.50
❑ 123 Kevan Barlow	.75	.30
❑ 124 Jeff Garcia	1.25	.50
❑ 125 Garrison Hearst	.75	.30
❑ 126 Terrell Owens	1.25	.50
❑ 127 Andre Carter	.50	.20
❑ 128 Shaun Alexander	1.50	.60
❑ 129 Matt Hasselbeck	.75	.30
❑ 130 Koren Robinson	.75	.30
❑ 131 Ricky Watters	.75	.30
❑ 132 Isaac Bruce	1.25	.50
❑ 133 Trung Canidate	.75	.30
❑ 134 Marshall Faulk	1.25	.50
❑ 135 Torry Holt	1.25	.50
❑ 136 Kurt Warner	1.25	.50
❑ 137 Mike Alstott	1.25	.50
❑ 138 Warrick Dunn	1.25	.50
❑ 139 Brad Johnson	.75	.30
❑ 140 Keyshawn Johnson	1.25	.50
❑ 141 Warren Sapp	.75	.30
❑ 142 Eddie George	1.25	.50
❑ 143 Derrick Mason	.75	.30
❑ 144 Steve McNair	1.25	.50
❑ 145 Jevon Kearse	.75	.30
❑ 146 Stephen Davis	.75	.30
❑ 147 Rod Gardner	.75	.30
❑ 148 Champ Bailey	.75	.30
❑ 149 Bruce Smith	.50	.20
❑ 150 Houston Texans	1.50	.60
❑ 151 David Carr RC	8.00	3.00
❑ 152 Julius Peppers RC	8.00	3.00
❑ 153 Joey Harrington RC	5.00	2.00
❑ 154 Quentin Jammer RC	4.00	1.50
❑ 155 Ryan Sims RC	4.00	1.50
❑ 156 Bryant McKinnie RC	3.00	1.25
❑ 157 Roy Williams RC	8.00	3.00
❑ 158 John Henderson RC	4.00	1.50
❑ 159 Dwight Freeney RC	6.00	2.50
❑ 160 Wendell Bryant RC	2.00	.75
❑ 161 Donte Stallworth RC	6.00	2.50
❑ 162 Jeremy Shockey RC	12.00	5.00
❑ 163 Albert Haynesworth RC	3.00	1.25
❑ 164 William Green RC	4.00	1.50
❑ 165 Phillip Buchanon RC	4.00	1.50
❑ 166 T.J. Duckett RC	4.00	1.50
❑ 167 Ashley Lelie RC	8.00	3.00
❑ 168 Javon Walker RC	6.00	2.50
❑ 169 Daniel Graham RC	4.00	1.50
❑ 170 Napoleon Harris RC	4.00	1.50
❑ 171 Lito Sheppard RC	4.00	1.50
❑ 172 Robert Thomas RC	4.00	1.50
❑ 173 Patrick Ramsey RC	4.00	1.50
❑ 174 Jabar Gaffney RC	4.00	1.50
❑ 175 DeShaun Foster RC	4.00	1.50
❑ 176 Kalimba Edwards RC	4.00	1.50
❑ 177 Josh Reed RC	4.00	1.50
❑ 178 Larry Tripplett RC	2.00	.75
❑ 179 Andre Davis RC	3.00	1.25
❑ 180 Reche Caldwell RC	4.00	1.50
❑ 181 Levar Fisher RC	2.00	.75
❑ 182 Clinton Portis RC	12.00	5.00
❑ 183 Anthony Weaver RC	3.00	1.25
❑ 184 Maurice Morris RC	4.00	1.50
❑ 185 Ladell Betts RC	4.00	1.50
❑ 186 Antwaan Randle El RC	5.00	2.00
❑ 187 Antonio Bryant RC	4.00	1.50
❑ 188 Rocky Calmus RC	4.00	1.50
❑ 189 Josh McCown RC	5.00	2.00
❑ 190 Lamar Gordon RC	4.00	1.50

❑ 191 Marquise Walker RC	3.00	1.25
❑ 192 Cliff Russell RC	3.00	1.25
❑ 193 Eric Crouch RC	4.00	1.50
❑ 194 Dennis Johnson RC	2.00	.75
❑ 195 Alex Brown RC	4.00	1.50
❑ 196 David Garrard RC	8.00	3.00
❑ 197 Rohan Davey RC	4.00	1.50
❑ 198 Alan Harper RC	2.00	.75
❑ 199 Ron Johnson RC	3.00	1.25
❑ 200 Andra Davis RC	3.00	1.25
❑ 201 Kurt Kittner RC	3.00	1.25
❑ 202 Freddie Milons RC	3.00	1.25
❑ 203 Adrian Peterson RC	5.00	2.00
❑ 204 Luke Staley RC	3.00	1.25
❑ 205 Tracey Wistrom RC	3.00	1.25
❑ 206 Woody Dantzler RC	3.00	1.25
❑ 207 Chad Hutchinson RC	3.00	1.25
❑ 208 Zak Kustok RC	4.00	1.50
❑ 209 Damien Anderson RC	3.00	1.25
❑ 210 James Mungro RC	4.00	1.50
❑ 211 Cortlen Johnson RC	2.00	.75
❑ 212 Demontray Carter RC	2.00	.75
❑ 213 Kelly Campbell RC	3.00	1.25
❑ 214 Brian Poli-Dixon RC	3.00	1.25
❑ 215 Mike Rumph RC	4.00	1.50
❑ 216 Najeh Davenport RC	4.00	1.50

2003 Playoff Prestige

❑ COMP.SET w/o SP's (150)	30.00	12.50
❑ 1 David Boston	.75	.30
❑ 2 Thomas Jones	.75	.30
❑ 3 Jake Plummer	.75	.30
❑ 4 Marcel Shipp	.75	.30
❑ 5 T.J. Duckett	.75	.30
❑ 6 Warrick Dunn	.75	.30
❑ 7 Michael Vick	3.00	1.25
❑ 8 Jeff Blake	.50	.20
❑ 9 Todd Heap	.75	.30
❑ 10 Jamal Lewis	1.25	.50
❑ 11 Ray Lewis	1.25	.50
❑ 12 Drew Bledsoe	1.25	.50
❑ 13 Travis Henry	.75	.30
❑ 14 Eric Moulds	.75	.30
❑ 15 Peerless Price	.75	.30
❑ 16 Josh Reed	.75	.30
❑ 17 DeShaun Foster	.50	.20
❑ 18 Muhsin Muhammad	.75	.30
❑ 19 Steve Smith	1.25	.50
❑ 20 Julius Peppers	1.25	.50
❑ 21 Marty Booker	.75	.30
❑ 22 David Terrell	.75	.30
❑ 23 Anthony Thomas	.75	.30
❑ 24 Brian Urlacher	2.00	.75
❑ 25 Corey Dillon	.75	.30
❑ 26 Chad Johnson	1.25	.50
❑ 27 Jon Kitna	.75	.30
❑ 28 Peter Warrick	.75	.30
❑ 29 Tim Couch	.50	.20
❑ 30 Andre Davis	.50	.20
❑ 31 William Green	.75	.30
❑ 32 Quincy Morgan	.75	.30
❑ 33 Dennis Northcutt	.75	.30
❑ 34 Antonio Bryant	.75	.30
❑ 35 Quincy Carter	.75	.30
❑ 36 Troy Hambrick	.50	.20
❑ 37 Chad Hutchinson	.50	.20
❑ 38 Emmitt Smith	3.00	1.25
❑ 39 Roy Williams	1.25	.50
❑ 40 Brian Griese	1.25	.50
❑ 41 Ashley Lelie	1.25	.50
❑ 42 Ed McCaffrey	.75	.30
❑ 43 Clinton Portis	2.00	.75
❑ 44 Rod Smith	.75	.30
❑ 45 Germane Crowell	.50	.20
❑ 46 Az-Zahir Hakim	.50	.20
❑ 47 Joey Harrington	2.00	.75
❑ 48 James Stewart	.75	.30
❑ 49 Donald Driver	.75	.30
❑ 50 Brett Favre	3.00	1.25
❑ 51 Terry Glenn	.50	.20
❑ 52 Ahman Green	1.25	.50
❑ 53 Javon Walker	.75	.30
❑ 54 Corey Bradford	.50	.20
❑ 55 David Carr	2.00	.75
❑ 56 Jabar Gaffney	.75	.30
❑ 57 Jonathan Wells	.50	.20
❑ 58 Marvin Harrison	1.25	.50
❑ 59 Edgerrin James	1.25	.50
❑ 60 Peyton Manning	2.00	.75
❑ 61 James Mungro	.50	.20
❑ 62 Reggie Wayne	.75	.30
❑ 63 Mark Brunell	.75	.30
❑ 64 David Garrard	.50	.20
❑ 65 Stacey Mack	.50	.20
❑ 66 Jimmy Smith	.75	.30
❑ 67 Fred Taylor	1.25	.50
❑ 68 Marc Boerigter	.75	.30
❑ 69 Tony Gonzalez	.75	.30
❑ 70 Trent Green	.75	.30
❑ 71 Priest Holmes	1.50	.60
❑ 72 Eddie Kennison	.50	.20
❑ 73 Cris Carter	1.25	.50
❑ 74 Chris Chambers	1.25	.50
❑ 75 Jay Fiedler	.75	.30
❑ 76 Randy McMichael	.75	.30
❑ 77 Zach Thomas	.75	.30
❑ 78 Ricky Williams	1.25	.50
❑ 79 Michael Bennett	.75	.30
❑ 80 Todd Bouman	.50	.20
❑ 81 Daunte Culpepper	1.25	.50
❑ 82 Randy Moss	2.00	.75
❑ 83 Tom Brady	3.00	1.25
❑ 84 Deion Branch	1.25	.50
❑ 85 Troy Brown	.75	.30
❑ 86 Kevin Faulk	.50	.20
❑ 87 Antowain Smith	.75	.30
❑ 88 Aaron Brooks	1.25	.50
❑ 89 Joe Horn	.75	.30
❑ 90 Deuce McAllister	1.25	.50
❑ 91 Donte Stallworth	1.25	.50
❑ 92 Tiki Barber	1.25	.50
❑ 93 Kerry Collins	.75	.30
❑ 94 Jeremy Shockey	2.00	.75
❑ 95 Michael Strahan	.75	.30
❑ 96 Amani Toomer	.75	.30
❑ 97 Laveranues Coles	.75	.30
❑ 98 LaMont Jordan	1.25	.50
❑ 99 Curtis Martin	1.25	.50
❑ 100 Santana Moss	.75	.30
❑ 101 Chad Pennington	1.50	.60
❑ 102 Tim Brown	1.25	.50
❑ 103 Rich Gannon	.75	.30
❑ 104 Charlie Garner	.75	.30
❑ 105 Jerry Rice	2.50	1.00
❑ 106 Charles Woodson	.75	.30
❑ 107 Antonio Freeman	.75	.30
❑ 108 Dorsey Levens	.50	.20
❑ 109 Donovan McNabb	1.50	.60
❑ 110 Duce Staley	.75	.30
❑ 111 James Thrash	.50	.20
❑ 112 Jerome Bettis	1.25	.50
❑ 113 Plaxico Burress	.75	.30
❑ 114 Tommy Maddox	1.25	.50
❑ 115 Antwaan Randle El	1.25	.50
❑ 116 Kordell Stewart	.75	.30
❑ 117 Hines Ward	1.25	.50
❑ 118 Drew Brees	1.25	.50
❑ 119 Curtis Conway	.50	.20
❑ 120 Junior Seau	1.25	.50
❑ 121 LaDainian Tomlinson	1.25	.50
❑ 122 Kevan Barlow	.75	.30
❑ 123 Jeff Garcia	1.25	.50
❑ 124 Garrison Hearst	.75	.30
❑ 125 Terrell Owens	1.25	.50
❑ 126 Shaun Alexander	1.25	.50
❑ 127 Trent Dilfer	.75	.30
❑ 128 Darrell Jackson	.75	.30
❑ 129 Maurice Morris	.50	.20
❑ 130 Koren Robinson	.50	.20
❑ 131 Isaac Bruce	1.25	.50
❑ 132 Marc Bulger	1.25	.50
❑ 133 Marshall Faulk	1.25	.50
❑ 134 Torry Holt	1.25	.50
❑ 135 Kurt Warner	1.25	.50
❑ 136 Mike Alstott	1.25	.50
❑ 137 Brad Johnson	.75	.30
❑ 138 Keyshawn Johnson	1.25	.50
❑ 139 Dexter Jackson RC	1.25	.50
❑ 140 Warren Sapp	.75	.30
❑ 141 Kevin Dyson	.75	.30
❑ 142 Eddie George	.75	.30
❑ 143 Jevon Kearse	.75	.30
❑ 144 Derrick Mason	.75	.30
❑ 145 Steve McNair	1.25	.50
❑ 146 Stephen Davis	.75	.30
❑ 147 Rod Gardner	.75	.30
❑ 148 Shane Matthews	.50	.20
❑ 149 Patrick Ramsey	1.25	.50
❑ 150 Derrius Thompson	.50	.20
❑ 151 Byron Leftwich RC	10.00	4.00
❑ 152 Carson Palmer RC	12.00	5.00
❑ 153 Chris Simms RC	5.00	2.00
❑ 154 Kliff Kingsbury RC	2.50	1.00
❑ 155 Dave Ragone RC	3.00	1.25
❑ 156 Jason Gesser RC	3.00	1.25
❑ 157 Ken Dorsey RC	3.00	1.25
❑ 158 Kyle Boller RC	3.00	1.25
❑ 159 Brad Banks RC	2.50	1.00
❑ 160 Rex Grossman RC	10.00	4.00
❑ 161 Seneca Wallace RC	3.00	1.25
❑ 162 Brian St.Pierre RC	3.00	1.25
❑ 163 Larry Johnson RC	12.00	6.00
❑ 164 Earnest Graham RC	3.00	1.25
❑ 165 Musa Smith RC	3.00	1.25
❑ 166 Lee Suggs RC	3.00	1.25
❑ 167 Willis McGahee RC	8.00	3.00
❑ 168 Onterrio Smith RC	3.00	1.25
❑ 170 Sultan McCullough RC	2.50	1.00
❑ 171 Chris Brown RC	3.00	1.25
❑ 172 Justin Fargas RC	3.00	1.25
❑ 173 Avon Cobourne RC	1.50	.60
❑ 174 Dahrran Diedrick RC	3.00	1.25
❑ 175 LaBrandon Toefield RC	3.00	1.25
❑ 176 Artose Pinner RC	3.00	1.25
❑ 177 Quentin Griffin RC	3.00	1.25
❑ 178 ReShard Lee RC	3.00	1.25
❑ 179 Andrew Pinnock RC	2.50	1.00
❑ 180 B.J. Askew RC	3.00	1.25
❑ 181 Andre Johnson RC	6.00	2.50
❑ 182 Brandon Lloyd RC	3.00	1.25
❑ 183 Bryant Johnson RC	3.00	1.25
❑ 184 Charles Rogers RC	3.00	1.25
❑ 185 Doug Gabriel RC	3.00	1.25
❑ 186 Justin Gage RC	3.00	1.25
❑ 187 Kareem Kelly RC	2.50	1.00
❑ 188 Kelley Washington RC	3.00	1.25
❑ 189 Taylor Jacobs RC	2.50	1.00
❑ 190 Terrence Edwards RC	2.50	1.00
❑ 191 Anquan Boldin RC	8.00	3.00
❑ 192 Billy McMullen RC	2.50	1.00
❑ 193 Talman Gardner RC	3.00	1.25
❑ 194 Arnaz Battle RC	3.00	1.25
❑ 195 Sam Aiken RC	2.50	1.00
❑ 196 Bobby Wade RC	3.00	1.25
❑ 197 Mike Bush RC	1.50	.60
❑ 198 Keenan Howry RC	3.00	1.25
❑ 199 Jerel Myers RC	1.50	.60
❑ 200 Dallas Clark RC	3.00	1.25
❑ 201 Mike Pinkard RC	1.50	.60
❑ 202 Teyo Johnson RC	3.00	1.25
❑ 203 Trent Smith RC	2.50	1.00
❑ 204 George Wrighster RC	2.50	1.00
❑ 205 Jason Witten RC	6.00	2.50
❑ 206 Cory Redding RC	2.50	1.00
❑ 207 DeWayne White RC	2.50	1.00
❑ 208 Jerome McDougle RC	3.00	1.25
❑ 209 Michael Haynes RC	3.00	1.25
❑ 210 Chris Kelsay RC	3.00	1.25
❑ 211 Calvin Pace RC	2.50	1.00
❑ 212 Kenny King RC	2.50	1.00
❑ 213 Jimmy Kennedy RC	3.00	1.25
❑ 214 William Joseph RC	3.00	1.25
❑ 215 DeWayne Robertson RC	3.00	1.25

❑ 216 Jarret Johnson RC 2.50 1.00
❑ 217 Rien Long RC 1.50 .60
❑ 218 Boss Bailey RC 3.00 1.25
❑ 219 Terrell Suggs RC 5.00 2.00
❑ 220 Terry Pierce RC 2.50 1.00
❑ 221 Bradie James RC 3.00 1.25
❑ 222 Angelo Crowell RC 2.50 1.00
❑ 223 Andre Woolfolk RC 3.00 1.25
❑ 224 Dennis Weathersby RC 1.50 .60
❑ 225 Marcus Trufant RC 3.00 1.25
❑ 226 Terence Newman RC 6.00 2.50
❑ 227 Ricky Manning RC 3.00 1.25
❑ 228 Mike Doss RC 3.00 1.25
❑ 229 Julian Battle RC 2.50 1.00
❑ 230 Rashean Mathis RC 2.50 1.00

2004 Playoff Prestige

❑ COMP.SET w/o RC's (150) 25.00 10.00
❑ 1 Anquan Boldin 1.00 .40
❑ 2 Emmitt Smith 2.00 .75
❑ 3 Jeff Blake .40 .15
❑ 4 Marcel Shipp .60 .25
❑ 5 Michael Vick 2.00 .75
❑ 6 Peerless Price .60 .25
❑ 7 T.J. Duckett .60 .25
❑ 8 Warrick Dunn .60 .25
❑ 9 Ed Reed .60 .25
❑ 10 Jamal Lewis 1.00 .40
❑ 11 Kyle Boller 1.00 .40
❑ 12 Ray Lewis 1.00 .40
❑ 13 Todd Heap .60 .25
❑ 14 Drew Bledsoe 1.00 .40
❑ 15 Eric Moulds .60 .25
❑ 16 Josh Reed .40 .15
❑ 17 Travis Henry .60 .25
❑ 18 DeShaun Foster .60 .25
❑ 19 Stephen Davis .60 .25
❑ 20 Jake Delhomme 1.00 .40
❑ 21 Julius Peppers 1.00 .40
❑ 22 Steve Smith 1.00 .40
❑ 23 Anthony Thomas .60 .25
❑ 24 Brian Urlacher 1.25 .50
❑ 25 Marty Booker .60 .25
❑ 26 Rex Grossman 1.00 .40
❑ 27 Chad Johnson 1.00 .40
❑ 28 Corey Dillon .60 .25
❑ 29 Carson Palmer 1.25 .50
❑ 30 Peter Warrick .60 .25
❑ 31 Rudi Johnson .60 .25
❑ 32 Andre Davis .40 .15
❑ 33 Quincy Morgan .60 .25
❑ 34 William Green .60 .25
❑ 35 Kelly Holcomb .60 .25
❑ 36 Antonio Bryant .60 .25
❑ 37 Quincy Carter .60 .25
❑ 38 Roy Williams S .60 .25
❑ 39 Terence Newman .60 .25
❑ 40 Terry Glenn .40 .15
❑ 41 Troy Hambrick .40 .15
❑ 42 Ashley Lelie .60 .25
❑ 43 Clinton Portis 1.00 .40
❑ 44 Rod Smith .60 .25
❑ 45 Shannon Sharpe .60 .25
❑ 46 Mike Anderson .60 .25
❑ 47 Jake Plummer .60 .25
❑ 48 Charles Rogers .60 .25
❑ 49 Joey Harrington 1.00 .40
❑ 50 Ahman Green 1.00 .40
❑ 51 Brett Favre 2.50 1.00
❑ 52 Donald Driver .60 .25
❑ 53 Javon Walker .60 .25
❑ 54 Robert Ferguson .40 .15
❑ 55 Andre Johnson 1.00 .40
❑ 56 David Carr 1.00 .40
❑ 57 Domanick Davis 1.00 .40
❑ 58 Jabar Gaffney .60 .25
❑ 59 Dwight Freeney .60 .25
❑ 60 Dallas Clark .60 .25
❑ 61 Edgerrin James 1.00 .40
❑ 62 Marvin Harrison 1.00 .40
❑ 63 Peyton Manning 1.50 .60
❑ 64 Reggie Wayne .60 .25
❑ 65 Byron Leftwich 1.25 .50
❑ 66 Fred Taylor .60 .25
❑ 67 Jimmy Smith .60 .25
❑ 68 Johnnie Morton .60 .25
❑ 69 Priest Holmes 1.25 .50
❑ 70 Tony Gonzalez .60 .25
❑ 71 Trent Green .60 .25
❑ 72 Chris Chambers .60 .25
❑ 73 Jay Fiedler .40 .15
❑ 74 Randy McMichael .40 .15
❑ 75 Ricky Williams 1.00 .40
❑ 76 Zach Thomas 1.00 .40
❑ 77 Daunte Culpepper 1.00 .40
❑ 78 Kelly Campbell .40 .15
❑ 79 Michael Bennett .60 .25
❑ 80 Moe Williams .40 .15
❑ 81 Nate Burleson 1.00 .40
❑ 82 Randy Moss 1.25 .50
❑ 83 Deion Branch 1.00 .40
❑ 84 Kevin Faulk .40 .15
❑ 85 Tom Brady 2.50 1.00
❑ 86 Troy Brown .60 .25
❑ 87 Tedy Bruschi .60 .25
❑ 88 Aaron Brooks .60 .25
❑ 89 Deuce McAllister 1.00 .40
❑ 90 Donte Stallworth .60 .25
❑ 91 Joe Horn .60 .25
❑ 92 Amani Toomer .60 .25
❑ 93 Ike Hilliard .40 .15
❑ 94 Jeremy Shockey 1.00 .40
❑ 95 Kerry Collins .60 .25
❑ 96 Michael Strahan .60 .25
❑ 97 Tiki Barber 1.00 .40
❑ 98 Chad Pennington 1.00 .40
❑ 99 Curtis Martin 1.00 .40
❑ 100 LaMont Jordan 1.00 .40
❑ 101 Santana Moss .60 .25
❑ 102 Charlie Garner .60 .25
❑ 103 Jerry Porter .60 .25
❑ 104 Jerry Rice 2.00 .75
❑ 105 Justin Fargas .60 .25
❑ 106 Rich Gannon .60 .25
❑ 107 Rod Woodson .60 .25
❑ 108 Tim Brown 1.00 .40
❑ 109 Brian Westbrook .60 .25
❑ 110 Correll Buckhalter .60 .25
❑ 111 Donovan McNabb 1.25 .50
❑ 112 Freddie Mitchell .60 .25
❑ 113 James Thrash .40 .15
❑ 114 Amos Zereoue .40 .15
❑ 115 Antwaan Randle El 1.00 .40
❑ 116 Hines Ward 1.00 .40
❑ 117 Joey Porter .60 .25
❑ 118 Kendrell Bell .60 .25
❑ 119 Plaxico Burress .60 .25
❑ 120 David Boston .60 .25
❑ 121 Drew Brees 1.00 .40
❑ 122 LaDainian Tomlinson 1.25 .50
❑ 123 Jeff Garcia 1.00 .40
❑ 124 Kevan Barlow .60 .25
❑ 125 Tai Streets .40 .15
❑ 126 Terrell Owens 1.00 .40
❑ 127 Tim Rattay .40 .15
❑ 128 Darrell Jackson .60 .25
❑ 129 Koren Robinson .60 .25
❑ 130 Matt Hasselbeck .60 .25
❑ 131 Shaun Alexander 1.00 .40
❑ 132 Isaac Bruce .60 .25
❑ 133 Marc Bulger 1.00 .40
❑ 134 Marshall Faulk 1.00 .40
❑ 135 Torry Holt 1.00 .40
❑ 136 Brad Johnson .60 .25
❑ 137 Derrick Brooks .60 .25
❑ 138 Keenan McCardell .40 .15
❑ 139 Keyshawn Johnson .60 .25
❑ 140 Mike Alstott .60 .25
❑ 141 Derrick Mason .60 .25
❑ 142 Drew Bennett .60 .25
❑ 143 Jevon Kearse .60 .25
❑ 144 Justin McCareins .40 .15
❑ 145 Steve McNair 1.00 .40
❑ 146 Tyrone Calico .60 .25
❑ 147 Bruce Smith .60 .25
❑ 148 Laveranues Coles .60 .25
❑ 149 Patrick Ramsey .60 .25
❑ 150 LaVar Arrington 2.00 .75
❑ 151 Eli Manning RC 12.00 6.00
❑ 152 Larry Fitzgerald RC 8.00 3.00
❑ 153 Philip Rivers RC 8.00 3.00
❑ 154 Sean Taylor RC 2.50 1.00
❑ 155 Kellen Winslow RC 5.00 2.00
❑ 156 Roy Williams RC 6.00 2.50
❑ 157 DeAngelo Hall RC 3.00 1.25
❑ 158 Reggie Williams RC 3.00 1.25
❑ 159 Ben Roethlisberger RC 15.00 6.00
❑ 160 Jonathan Vilma RC 2.50 1.00
❑ 161 Lee Evans RC 3.00 1.25
❑ 162 Tommie Harris RC 2.50 1.00
❑ 163 Michael Clayton RC 5.00 2.00
❑ 164 D.J. Williams SP RC 25.00 10.00
❑ 165 Will Smith RC 2.50 1.00
❑ 166 Kenechi Udeze RC 2.50 1.00
❑ 167 Vince Wilfork SP RC 25.00 10.00
❑ 168 J.P. Losman RC 5.00 2.00
❑ 169 Steven Jackson SP RC 50.00 25.00
❑ 170 Ahmad Carroll RC 2.50 1.00
❑ 171 Chris Perry RC 4.00 1.50
❑ 172 Jason Babin SP RC 30.00 15.00
❑ 173 Chris Gamble RC 2.50 1.00
❑ 174 Michael Jenkins RC 2.50 1.00
❑ 175 Kevin Jones RC 6.00 2.50
❑ 176 Rashaun Woods RC 2.50 1.00
❑ 177 Ben Watson RC 2.50 1.00
❑ 178 Karlos Dansby RC 2.50 1.00
❑ 179 Teddy Lehman RC 2.50 1.00
❑ 180 Ricardo Colclough SP RC 30.00 15.00
❑ 181 Daryl Smith RC 2.50 1.00
❑ 182 Ben Troupe RC 2.50 1.00
❑ 183 Tatum Bell RC 5.00 2.00
❑ 184 Julius Jones RC 8.00 3.00
❑ 185 Bob Sanders RC 6.00 2.50
❑ 186 Devery Henderson RC 2.50 1.00
❑ 187 Dwan Edwards RC 1.25 .50
❑ 188 Michael Boulware RC 2.50 1.00
❑ 189 Darius Watts RC 2.50 1.00
❑ 190 Greg Jones RC 2.50 1.00
❑ 191 Antwan Odom RC 2.50 1.00
❑ 192 Sean Jones SP RC 25.00 10.00
❑ 193 Courtney Watson RC 2.50 1.00
❑ 194 Keary Colbert RC 2.50 1.00
❑ 195 Keith Smith RC 2.00 .75
❑ 196 Derrick Strait RC 2.50 1.00
❑ 197 Bernard Berrian RC 3.00 1.25
❑ 198 Devard Darling RC 2.50 1.00
❑ 199 Matt Schaub RC 8.00 3.00
❑ 200 Will Poole RC 2.50 1.00
❑ 201 Samie Parker RC 2.50 1.00
❑ 202 Luke McCown SP RC 30.00 15.00
❑ 203 Jerricho Cotchery RC 2.50 1.00
❑ 204 Mewelde Moore RC 2.50 1.00
❑ 205 Ernest Wilford RC 2.50 1.00
❑ 206 Cedric Cobbs SP RC 30.00 15.00
❑ 207 Johnnie Morant RC 2.50 1.00
❑ 208 Craig Krenzel RC 2.50 1.00
❑ 209 Michael Turner RC 3.00 1.25
❑ 210 D.J. Hackett RC 2.00 .75
❑ 211 P.K. Sam RC 2.00 .75
❑ 212 Josh Harris RC 2.50 1.00
❑ 213 Drew Henson RC 2.50 1.00
❑ 214 Jeff Smoker RC 2.50 1.00
❑ 215 John Navarre RC 2.50 1.00
❑ 216 Cody Pickett RC 2.50 1.00
❑ 217 Quincy Wilson RC 2.00 .75
❑ 218 Derek Abney RC 2.50 1.00
❑ 219 Maurice Clarett SP RC 25.00 10.00
❑ 220 Mike Williams SP RC 15.00 6.00
❑ 221 B.J. Johnson RC 2.00 .75
❑ 222 Brandon Everage RC 2.00 .75
❑ 223 Derek McCoy RC 2.00 .75
❑ 224 Jared Lorenzen RC 2.00 .75
❑ 225 Jarrett Payton RC 2.50 1.00

❑ 226 Jason Fife RC 2.00 .75
❑ 227 Robert Kent RC 1.25 .50

2005 Playoff Prestige

❑ COMP.SET w/o SP's (234) 100.00 50.00
❑ COMP.SET w/o RC's (150) 25.00 10.00
❑ ONE 151-244 DRAFT PICK PER PACK

❑ 1 Anquan Boldin .60 .25
❑ 2 Emmitt Smith 2.00 .75
❑ 3 Josh McCown .60 .25
❑ 4 Larry Fitzgerald 1.00 .40
❑ 5 Michael Vick 1.50 .60
❑ 6 Peerless Price .50 .20
❑ 7 Alge Crumpler .60 .25
❑ 8 T.J. Duckett .60 .25
❑ 9 Warrick Dunn .60 .25
❑ 10 Ed Reed .60 .25
❑ 11 Jamal Lewis 1.00 .40
❑ 12 Kyle Boller .60 .25
❑ 13 Ray Lewis 1.00 .40
❑ 14 Todd Heap .60 .25
❑ 15 Drew Bledsoe 1.00 .40
❑ 16 Eric Moulds .60 .25
❑ 17 Lee Evans .60 .25
❑ 18 Travis Henry .60 .25
❑ 19 Willis McGahee 1.00 .40
❑ 20 Anthony Thomas .60 .25
❑ 21 Brian Urlacher 1.00 .40
❑ 22 Rex Grossman .60 .25
❑ 23 David Terrell .60 .25
❑ 24 Thomas Jones .60 .25
❑ 25 Carson Palmer 1.00 .40
❑ 26 Chad Johnson 1.00 .40
❑ 27 Peter Warrick .50 .20
❑ 28 Rudi Johnson .60 .25
❑ 29 Antonio Bryant .50 .20
❑ 30 William Green .50 .20
❑ 31 Jeff Garcia .60 .25
❑ 32 Kellen Winslow 1.00 .40
❑ 33 Lee Suggs .60 .25
❑ 34 Drew Henson .60 .25
❑ 35 Julius Jones 1.25 .50
❑ 36 Jason Witten .60 .25
❑ 37 Keyshawn Johnson .60 .25
❑ 38 Roy Williams S .60 .25
❑ 39 Ashley Lelie .60 .25
❑ 40 Champ Bailey .60 .25
❑ 41 Jake Plummer .60 .25
❑ 42 Reuben Droughns .60 .25
❑ 43 Rod Smith .60 .25
❑ 44 Charles Rogers .60 .25
❑ 45 Joey Harrington 1.00 .40
❑ 46 Kevin Jones 1.00 .40
❑ 47 Roy Williams WR 1.00 .40
❑ 48 Ahman Green 1.00 .40
❑ 49 Donald Driver .60 .25
❑ 50 Javon Walker .60 .25
❑ 51 Brett Favre 2.50 1.00
❑ 52 Andre Johnson .60 .25
❑ 53 David Carr 1.00 .40
❑ 54 Domanick Davis .60 .25
❑ 55 Jabar Gaffney .50 .20
❑ 56 Edgerrin James 1.00 .40
❑ 57 Marvin Harrison 1.00 .40
❑ 58 Brandon Stokley .60 .25
❑ 59 Peyton Manning 1.50 .60
❑ 60 Reggie Wayne .60 .25
❑ 61 Byron Leftwich 1.00 .40
❑ 62 Fred Taylor .60 .25
❑ 63 Jimmy Smith .60 .25
❑ 64 Priest Holmes 1.00 .40
❑ 65 Tony Gonzalez .60 .25
❑ 66 Johnnie Morton .60 .25
❑ 67 Trent Green .60 .25
❑ 68 Chris Chambers .60 .25
❑ 69 Randy McMichael .50 .20
❑ 70 A.J. Feeley .60 .25
❑ 71 Zach Thomas 1.00 .40
❑ 72 Daunte Culpepper 1.00 .40
❑ 73 Marcus Robinson .60 .25
❑ 74 Mewelde Moore .60 .25
❑ 75 Nate Burleson .60 .25
❑ 76 Onterrio Smith .60 .25
❑ 77 Randy Moss 1.00 .40
❑ 78 Corey Dillon .60 .25
❑ 79 Tom Brady 2.50 1.00
❑ 80 Deion Branch .60 .25
❑ 81 Tedy Bruschi .60 .25
❑ 82 David Givens .60 .25
❑ 83 David Patten .50 .20
❑ 84 Aaron Brooks .60 .25
❑ 85 Deuce McAllister 1.00 .40
❑ 86 Donte Stallworth .60 .25
❑ 87 Joe Horn .60 .25
❑ 88 Eli Manning 2.00 .75
❑ 89 Jeremy Shockey 1.00 .40
❑ 90 Kurt Warner .60 .25
❑ 91 Michael Strahan .60 .25
❑ 92 Tiki Barber 1.00 .40
❑ 93 Amani Toomer .60 .25
❑ 94 Chad Pennington 1.00 .40
❑ 95 Curtis Martin 1.00 .40
❑ 96 Santana Moss .60 .25
❑ 97 Justin McCareins .50 .20
❑ 98 Charles Woodson .60 .25
❑ 99 Kerry Collins .60 .25
❑ 100 Warren Sapp .60 .25
❑ 101 Jerry Porter .60 .25
❑ 102 Donovan McNabb 1.25 .50
❑ 103 Jevon Kearse .60 .25
❑ 104 Terrell Owens 1.00 .40
❑ 105 Brian Westbrook .60 .25
❑ 106 Todd Pinkston .50 .20
❑ 107 Duce Staley .60 .25
❑ 108 Hines Ward 1.00 .40
❑ 109 Jerome Bettis 1.00 .40
❑ 110 Joey Porter .60 .25
❑ 111 Plaxico Burress .60 .25
❑ 112 Ben Roethlisberger 2.50 1.00
❑ 113 Drew Brees 1.00 .40
❑ 114 LaDainian Tomlinson 1.25 .50
❑ 115 Keenan McCardell .50 .20
❑ 116 Philip Rivers 1.00 .40
❑ 117 Antonio Gates 1.00 .40
❑ 118 Eric Johnson .60 .25
❑ 119 Kevan Barlow .60 .25
❑ 120 Brandon Lloyd .50 .20
❑ 121 Tim Rattay .50 .20
❑ 122 Darrell Jackson .60 .25
❑ 123 Koren Robinson .60 .25
❑ 124 Jerry Rice 2.00 .75
❑ 125 Matt Hasselbeck .60 .25
❑ 126 Shaun Alexander 1.25 .50
❑ 127 Isaac Bruce .60 .25
❑ 128 Marc Bulger 1.00 .40
❑ 129 Marshall Faulk 1.00 .40
❑ 130 Steven Jackson 1.25 .50
❑ 131 Torry Holt 1.00 .40
❑ 132 Derrick Brooks .60 .25
❑ 133 Michael Clayton 1.00 .40
❑ 134 Michael Pittman .50 .20
❑ 135 Chris Simms .60 .25
❑ 136 Chris Brown .60 .25
❑ 137 Derrick Mason .60 .25
❑ 138 Drew Bennett .60 .25
❑ 139 Steve McNair 1.00 .40
❑ 140 Clinton Portis 1.00 .40
❑ 141 LaVar Arrington 1.00 .40
❑ 142 Laveranues Coles .60 .25
❑ 143 Patrick Ramsey .60 .25
❑ 144 Rod Gardner .60 .25
❑ 145 DeShaun Foster .60 .25
❑ 146 Stephen Davis .60 .25
❑ 147 Jake Delhomme 1.00 .40
❑ 148 Muhsin Muhammad .60 .25
❑ 149 Steve Smith .60 .25
❑ 150 Keary Colbert .60 .25
❑ 151 Aaron Rodgers SP RC 50.00 20.00
❑ 152 Adrian McPherson SP RC 20.00 8.00
❑ 153 Alex Smith QB RC 10.00 4.00
❑ 154 Andrew Walter RC 2.50 1.00
❑ 155 Brock Berlin RC 2.00 .75
❑ 156 Charlie Frye SP RC 25.00 10.00
❑ 157 Chris Rix RC 2.00 .75
❑ 158 Dan Orlovsky RC 2.50 1.00
❑ 159 Darian Durant RC 2.50 1.00
❑ 160 David Greene RC 2.50 1.00
❑ 161 Derek Anderson RC 4.00 1.50
❑ 162 Gino Guidugli RC 1.25 .50
❑ 163 Jason Campbell RC 4.00 1.50
❑ 164 Jason White RC 2.50 1.00
❑ 165 Kyle Orton RC 2.50 1.00
❑ 166 Matt Jones SP RC 25.00 10.00
❑ 167 Ryan Fitzpatrick RC 2.50 1.00
❑ 168 Stefan LeFors RC 2.50 1.00
❑ 169 Timmy Chang RC 2.00 .75
❑ 170 Alvin Pearman RC 2.50 1.00
❑ 171 Anthony Davis RC 2.00 .75
❑ 172 Brandon Jacobs RC 3.00 1.25
❑ 173 Cadillac Williams RC 10.00 4.00
❑ 174 Cedric Benson RC 6.00 2.50
❑ 175 Cedric Houston RC 2.50 1.00
❑ 176 Ciatrick Fason RC 2.50 1.00
❑ 177 Damien Nash RC 2.00 .75
❑ 178 Darren Sproles RC 2.50 1.00
❑ 179 Eric Shelton SP RC 20.00 8.00
❑ 180 Frank Gore SP RC 40.00 15.00
❑ 181 J.J. Arrington SP RC 25.00 10.00
❑ 182 Kay-Jay Harris RC 2.00 .75
❑ 183 Marion Barber RC 4.00 1.50
❑ 184 Ronnie Brown RC 10.00 4.00
❑ 185 Ryan Moats RC 2.50 1.00
❑ 186 T.A. McLendon RC 1.25 .50
❑ 187 Vernand Morency RC 2.50 1.00
❑ 188 Walter Reyes RC 2.00 .75
❑ 189 Braylon Edwards RC 8.00 3.00
❑ 190 Charles Frederick RC 2.00 .75
❑ 191 Chris Henry RC 2.50 1.00
❑ 192 Courtney Roby RC 2.50 1.00
❑ 193 Craig Bragg RC 2.00 .75
❑ 194 Craphonso Thorpe SP RC 20.00 8.00
❑ 195 Dante Ridgeway RC 2.00 .75
❑ 196 Fred Amey RC 2.00 .75
❑ 197 Fred Gibson RC 2.00 .75
❑ 198 J.R. Russell RC 2.00 .75
❑ 199 Jerome Mathis SP RC 20.00 8.00
❑ 200 Josh Davis RC 2.00 .75
❑ 201 Larry Brackins RC 1.25 .50
❑ 202 Mark Bradley RC 2.50 1.00
❑ 203 Mark Clayton SP RC 25.00 10.00
❑ 204 Mike Williams 2.50 1.00
❑ 205 Reggie Brown RC 2.50 1.00
❑ 206 Roddy White RC 2.50 1.00
❑ 207 Roscoe Parrish RC 2.50 1.00
❑ 208 Roydell Williams RC 2.50 1.00
❑ 209 Steve Savoy RC 1.25 .50
❑ 210 Tab Perry RC 2.50 1.00
❑ 211 Taylor Stubblefield RC 1.25 .50
❑ 212 Terrence Murphy RC 2.50 1.00
❑ 213 Troy Williamson RC 2.50 1.00
❑ 214 Vincent Jackson RC 2.50 1.00
❑ 215 Alex Smith TE RC 2.50 1.00
❑ 216 Heath Miller RC 5.00 2.00
❑ 217 Dan Cody RC 2.50 1.00
❑ 218 David Pollack RC 2.50 1.00
❑ 219 Erasmus James RC 2.50 1.00
❑ 220 Justin Tuck RC 2.50 1.00
❑ 221 Marcus Spears RC 2.50 1.00
❑ 222 Matt Roth RC 2.50 1.00
❑ 223 Anttaj Hawthorne RC 2.00 .75
❑ 224 Mike Patterson RC 2.50 1.00
❑ 225 Shaun Cody RC 2.50 1.00
❑ 226 Travis Johnson RC 2.00 .75
❑ 227 Channing Crowder RC 2.50 1.00
❑ 228 Darryl Blackstock RC 2.00 .75
❑ 229 DeMarcus Ware RC 4.00 1.50
❑ 230 Derrick Johnson RC 4.00 1.50
❑ 231 Kevin Burnett RC 2.50 1.00
❑ 232 Shawne Merriman RC 4.00 1.50
❑ 233 Adam Jones RC 2.50 1.00
❑ 234 Antrel Rolle RC 2.50 1.00
❑ 235 Brandon Browner RC 2.00 .75

❑ 236 Bryant McFadden RC	2.50	1.00
❑ 237 Carlos Rogers RC	3.00	1.25
❑ 238 Corey Webster RC	2.50	1.00
❑ 239 Fabian Washington RC	2.50	1.00
❑ 240 Justin Miller RC	2.00	.75
❑ 241 Marlin Jackson RC	2.50	1.00
❑ 242 Ernest Shazor RC	2.50	1.00
❑ 243 Josh Bullocks RC	2.50	1.00
❑ 244 Thomas Davis RC	2.50	1.00

2006 Playoff Prestige

❑ COMP.SET w/o SP's (239)	100.00	50.00
❑ COMP.SET w/o RC's (150)	25.00	10.00
❑ ONE ROOKIE PER HOBBY PACK		
❑ 1 Anquan Boldin	.60	.25
❑ 2 J.J. Arrington	.60	.25
❑ 3 Josh McCown	.60	.25
❑ 4 Larry Fitzgerald	1.00	.40
❑ 5 Marcel Shipp	.50	.20
❑ 6 Alge Crumpler	.60	.25
❑ 7 Michael Vick	1.00	.40
❑ 8 T.J. Duckett	.60	.25
❑ 9 Warrick Dunn	.60	.25
❑ 10 Michael Jenkins	.60	.25
❑ 11 Derrick Mason	.50	.20
❑ 12 Jamal Lewis	.60	.25
❑ 13 Kyle Boller	.60	.25
❑ 14 Mark Clayton	1.00	.40
❑ 15 Ray Lewis	1.00	.40
❑ 16 Eric Moulds	.60	.25
❑ 17 J.P. Losman	.60	.25
❑ 18 Lee Evans	.60	.25
❑ 19 Willis McGahee	1.00	.40
❑ 20 Jake Delhomme	.60	.25
❑ 21 Julius Peppers	.60	.25
❑ 22 Keary Colbert	.50	.20
❑ 23 Stephen Davis	.60	.25
❑ 24 Steve Smith	1.00	.40
❑ 25 Brian Urlacher	1.00	.40
❑ 26 Cedric Benson	1.00	.40
❑ 27 Kyle Orton	.60	.25
❑ 28 Mark Bradley	.60	.25
❑ 29 Muhsin Muhammad	.60	.25
❑ 30 Thomas Jones	.60	.25
❑ 31 Carson Palmer	1.00	.40
❑ 32 Chad Johnson	.60	.25
❑ 33 Rudi Johnson	.60	.25
❑ 34 T.J. Houshmandzadeh	.60	.25
❑ 35 Braylon Edwards	1.00	.40
❑ 36 Dennis Northcutt	.50	.20
❑ 37 Antonio Bryant	.60	.25
❑ 38 Reuben Droughns	.60	.25
❑ 39 Trent Dilfer	.60	.25
❑ 40 Drew Bledsoe	1.00	.40
❑ 41 Jason Witten	.60	.25
❑ 42 Julius Jones	1.00	.40
❑ 43 Keyshawn Johnson	.60	.25
❑ 44 Roy Williams S	.60	.25
❑ 45 Terry Glenn	.60	.25
❑ 46 Ashley Lelie	.60	.25
❑ 47 Jake Plummer	.60	.25
❑ 48 Mike Anderson	.60	.25
❑ 49 Rod Smith	.60	.25
❑ 50 Tatum Bell	.60	.25
❑ 51 Joey Harrington	.60	.25
❑ 52 Kevin Jones	1.00	.40
❑ 53 Mike Williams	1.00	.40
❑ 54 Roy Williams WR	1.00	.40
❑ 55 Aaron Rodgers	1.00	.40
❑ 56 Brett Favre	2.00	.75
❑ 57 Donald Driver	.60	.25
❑ 58 Javon Walker	.60	.25
❑ 59 Ahman Green	.60	.25
❑ 60 Andre Johnson	.60	.25
❑ 61 Corey Bradford	.50	.20
❑ 62 David Carr	.60	.25
❑ 63 Domanick Davis	.60	.25
❑ 64 Jabar Gaffney	.50	.20
❑ 65 Brandon Stokley	.60	.25
❑ 66 Dallas Clark	.50	.20
❑ 67 Edgerrin James	1.00	.40
❑ 68 Marvin Harrison	1.00	.40
❑ 69 Peyton Manning	1.50	.60
❑ 70 Reggie Wayne	.60	.25
❑ 71 Byron Leftwich	.60	.25
❑ 72 Fred Taylor	.60	.25
❑ 73 Jimmy Smith	.60	.25
❑ 74 Matt Jones	.60	.25
❑ 75 Reggie Williams	.60	.25
❑ 76 Eddie Kennison	.50	.20
❑ 77 Larry Johnson	1.25	.50
❑ 78 Priest Holmes	.60	.25
❑ 79 Tony Gonzalez	.60	.25
❑ 80 Trent Green	.60	.25
❑ 81 Chris Chambers	.60	.25
❑ 82 Marty Booker	.50	.20
❑ 83 Randy McMichael	.50	.20
❑ 84 Ricky Williams	.60	.25
❑ 85 Ronnie Brown	1.00	.40
❑ 86 Zach Thomas	1.00	.40
❑ 87 Daunte Culpepper	1.00	.40
❑ 88 Mewelde Moore	.50	.20
❑ 89 Nate Burleson	.60	.25
❑ 90 Jim Kleinsasser	.50	.20
❑ 91 Corey Dillon	.60	.25
❑ 92 David Givens	.60	.25
❑ 93 Deion Branch	.60	.25
❑ 94 Tedy Bruschi	1.00	.40
❑ 95 Tom Brady	1.50	.60
❑ 96 Aaron Brooks	.60	.25
❑ 97 Deuce McAllister	.60	.25
❑ 98 Donte Stallworth	.60	.25
❑ 99 Joe Horn	.60	.25
❑ 100 Amani Toomer	.60	.25
❑ 101 Eli Manning	1.25	.50
❑ 102 Jeremy Shockey	1.00	.40
❑ 103 Plaxico Burress	.60	.25
❑ 104 Tiki Barber	1.00	.40
❑ 105 Chad Pennington	.60	.25
❑ 106 Curtis Martin	1.00	.40
❑ 107 Justin McCareins	.50	.20
❑ 108 Laveranues Coles	.60	.25
❑ 109 Jerry Porter	.60	.25
❑ 110 Kerry Collins	.60	.25
❑ 111 LaMont Jordan	.60	.25
❑ 112 Randy Moss	1.00	.40
❑ 113 Brian Westbrook	.60	.25
❑ 114 Donovan McNabb	1.00	.40
❑ 115 Terrell Owens	1.00	.40
❑ 116 L.J. Smith	.50	.20
❑ 117 Ben Roethlisberger	1.50	.60
❑ 118 Hines Ward	1.00	.40
❑ 119 Heath Miller	.60	.25
❑ 120 Willie Parker	1.25	.50
❑ 121 Jerome Bettis	1.00	.40
❑ 122 Antonio Gates	1.00	.40
❑ 123 Drew Brees	1.00	.40
❑ 124 Keenan McCardell	.50	.20
❑ 125 LaDainian Tomlinson	1.25	.50
❑ 126 Alex Smith QB	1.00	.40
❑ 127 Brandon Lloyd	.60	.25
❑ 128 Frank Gore	1.00	.40
❑ 129 Kevan Barlow	.60	.25
❑ 130 Darrell Jackson	.60	.25
❑ 131 Joe Jurevicius	.60	.25
❑ 132 Matt Hasselbeck	.60	.25
❑ 133 Shaun Alexander	1.00	.40
❑ 134 Isaac Bruce	.60	.25
❑ 135 Marc Bulger	.60	.25
❑ 136 Marshall Faulk	.60	.25
❑ 137 Steven Jackson	1.00	.40
❑ 138 Torry Holt	.60	.25
❑ 139 Cadillac Williams	1.00	.40
❑ 140 Derrick Brooks	.60	.25
❑ 141 Joey Galloway	.60	.25
❑ 142 Michael Clayton	.60	.25
❑ 143 Brandon Jones	.50	.20
❑ 144 Chris Brown	.60	.25
❑ 145 Steve McNair	.60	.25
❑ 146 Tyrone Calico	.50	.20
❑ 147 Clinton Portis	1.00	.40
❑ 148 Mark Brunell	.60	.25
❑ 149 Santana Moss	.60	.25
❑ 150 David Patten	.50	.20
❑ 151 A.J. Hawk SP RC	40.00	15.00
❑ 152 Abdul Hodge RC	3.00	1.25
❑ 153 Alan Zemaitis RC	3.00	1.25
❑ 154 Andre Hall RC	2.50	1.00
❑ 155 Anthony Fasano RC	3.00	1.25
❑ 156 Ashton Youboty RC	3.00	1.25
❑ 157 Erik Meyer RC	2.50	1.00
❑ 158 Bobby Carpenter RC	3.00	1.25
❑ 159 Brad Smith RC	3.00	1.25
❑ 160 Brandon Kirsch RC	3.00	1.25
❑ 161 Brandon Marshall SP RC	20.00	8.00
❑ 162 Brandon Williams RC	3.00	1.25
❑ 163 Brian Calhoun SP RC	15.00	6.00
❑ 164 Brodie Croyle SP RC	25.00	12.50
❑ 165 Brodrick Bunkley RC	3.00	1.25
❑ 166 Bruce Gradkowski RC	5.00	2.00
❑ 167 Cedric Griffin RC	2.50	1.00
❑ 168 Cedric Humes RC	3.00	1.25
❑ 169 Chad Greenway RC	3.00	1.25
❑ 170 Chad Jackson RC	3.00	1.25
❑ 171 Charlie Whitehurst RC	3.00	1.25
❑ 172 Cory Rodgers RC	3.00	1.25
❑ 173 D.J. Shockley RC	3.00	1.25
❑ 174 Darnell Bing RC	3.00	1.25
❑ 175 Darrell Hackney RC	2.50	1.00
❑ 176 David Thomas SP RC	15.00	6.00
❑ 177 D'Brickashaw Ferguson RC	3.00	1.25
❑ 178 DeAngelo Williams RC	8.00	3.00
❑ 179 Dee Webb RC	2.50	1.00
❑ 180 Delanie Walker RC	2.50	1.00
❑ 181 DeMeco Ryans RC	4.00	1.50
❑ 182 Demetrius Williams RC	3.00	1.25
❑ 183 Derek Hagan RC	3.00	1.25
❑ 184 Devin Aromashodu RC	2.50	1.00
❑ 185 Dominique Byrd RC	2.50	1.00
❑ 186 DonTrell Moore RC	2.50	1.00
❑ 187 D'Qwell Jackson RC	2.50	1.00
❑ 188 Drew Olson RC	2.50	1.00
❑ 189 Eric Winston RC	1.50	.60
❑ 190 Ernie Sims RC	4.00	1.50
❑ 191 Gerald Riggs RC	3.00	1.25
❑ 192 Greg Jennings RC	5.00	2.00
❑ 193 Greg Lee RC	2.50	1.00
❑ 194 Haloti Ngata RC	3.00	1.25
❑ 195 Hank Baskett RC	3.00	1.25
❑ 196 Jason Avant RC	3.00	1.25
❑ 197 Jason Carter RC	2.50	1.00
❑ 198 Jay Cutler RC	10.00	4.00
❑ 199 Jeff Webb RC	2.50	1.00
❑ 200 Jeremy Bloom RC	2.50	1.00
❑ 201 Jerious Norwood RC	5.00	2.00
❑ 202 Jerome Harrison RC	3.00	1.25
❑ 203 Jimmy Williams RC	3.00	1.25
❑ 204 Joe Klopfenstein RC	2.50	1.00
❑ 205 Johnathan Joseph RC	2.50	1.00
❑ 206 Jonathan Orr RC	2.50	1.00
❑ 207 Joseph Addai RC	10.00	4.00
❑ 208 Kai Parham RC	3.00	1.25
❑ 209 Kamerion Wimbley RC	3.00	1.25
❑ 210 Kellen Clemens RC	5.00	2.00
❑ 211 Kelly Jennings RC	3.00	1.25
❑ 212 Ko Simpson RC	2.50	1.00
❑ 213 Laurence Maroney RC	8.00	3.00
❑ 214 Lawrence Vickers RC	2.50	1.00
❑ 215 LenDale White RC	6.00	2.50
❑ 216 Leon Washington RC	5.00	2.00
❑ 217 Leonard Pope RC	3.00	1.25
❑ 218 Marcedes Lewis RC	3.00	1.25
❑ 219 Marcus Vick SP RC	20.00	8.00
❑ 220 Mario Williams RC	5.00	2.00
❑ 221 Martin Nance RC	2.50	1.00
❑ 222 Mathias Kiwanuka RC	4.00	1.50
❑ 223 Matt Leinart RC	10.00	4.00
❑ 224 Maurice Drew SP RC	30.00	15.00
❑ 225 Maurice Stovall SP RC	15.00	6.00
❑ 226 Michael Huff RC	4.00	1.50
❑ 227 Michael Robinson SP RC	15.00	6.00
❑ 228 Mike Hass RC	3.00	1.25
❑ 229 Omar Jacobs RC	2.50	1.00

❑ 230 Paul Pinegar RC	2.50	1.00
❑ 231 Reggie Bush RC	12.00	5.00
❑ 232 Reggie McNeal RC	2.50	1.00
❑ 233 Rodrique Wright RC	1.50	.60
❑ 234 Santonio Holmes RC	6.00	2.50
❑ 235 Sinorice Moss RC	3.00	1.25
❑ 236 Skyler Green RC	3.00	1.25
❑ 237 Tamba Hali RC	3.00	1.25
❑ 238 Tarvaris Jackson RC	5.00	2.00
❑ 239 Taurean Henderson RC	3.00	1.25
❑ 240 Terrence Whitehead RC	2.50	1.00
❑ 241 Tim Day SP RC	15.00	6.00
❑ 242 Todd Watkins RC	2.50	1.00
❑ 243 Travis Wilson RC	3.00	1.25
❑ 244 Tye Hill RC	3.00	1.25
❑ 245 Vernon Davis RC	6.00	2.50
❑ 246 Vince Young RC	12.00	5.00
❑ 247 Wali Lundy RC	2.50	1.00
❑ 248 Wendell Mathis RC	2.50	1.00
❑ 249 Willie Reid SP RC	15.00	6.00
❑ 250 Winston Justice RC	3.00	1.25

2007 Playoff Prestige

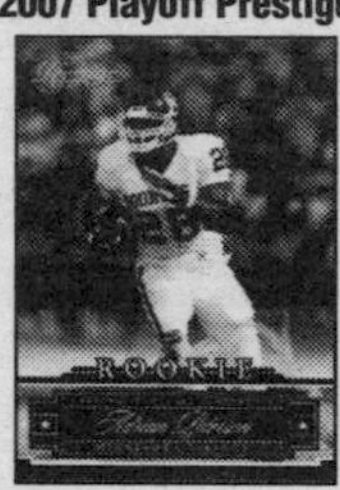

❑ COMPLETE SET (250)	150.00	75.00
❑ COMP.SET w/o RC's (150)	25.00	10.00
❑ 1 Anquan Boldin	.75	.30
❑ 2 Edgerrin James	1.00	.40
❑ 3 Larry Fitzgerald	.75	.30
❑ 4 Matt Leinart	1.00	.40
❑ 5 Alge Crumpler	.75	.30
❑ 6 Michael Vick	1.00	.40
❑ 7 Jerious Norwood	.75	.30
❑ 8 Michael Jenkins	.75	.30
❑ 9 Warrick Dunn	.75	.30
❑ 10 Todd Heap	.60	.25
❑ 11 Jamal Lewis	.75	.30
❑ 12 Mark Clayton	.75	.30
❑ 13 Demetrius Williams	.60	.25
❑ 14 Steve McNair	.75	.30
❑ 15 Ray Lewis	1.00	.40
❑ 16 J.P. Losman	.75	.30
❑ 17 Josh Reed	.60	.25
❑ 18 Lee Evans	.75	.30
❑ 19 Willis McGahee	.75	.30
❑ 20 DeAngelo Williams	1.00	.40
❑ 21 DeShaun Foster	.75	.30
❑ 22 Jake Delhomme	.75	.30
❑ 23 Keyshawn Johnson	.75	.30
❑ 24 Steve Smith	.75	.30
❑ 25 Bernard Berrian	.60	.25
❑ 26 Brian Urlacher	1.00	.40
❑ 27 Cedric Benson	.75	.30
❑ 28 Muhsin Muhammad	.75	.30
❑ 29 Rex Grossman	.75	.30
❑ 30 Thomas Jones	.75	.30
❑ 31 Carson Palmer	1.00	.40
❑ 32 Chad Johnson	.75	.30
❑ 33 Rudi Johnson	.75	.30
❑ 34 T.J. Houshmandzadeh	.75	.30
❑ 35 Braylon Edwards	.75	.30
❑ 36 Kellen Winslow	.75	.30
❑ 37 Charlie Frye	.75	.30
❑ 38 Reuben Droughns	.75	.30
❑ 39 Terry Glenn	.75	.30
❑ 40 Julius Jones	.75	.30
❑ 41 Roy Williams S	.75	.30
❑ 42 Marion Barber	.75	.30
❑ 43 Terrell Owens	1.00	.40
❑ 44 Tony Romo	2.00	.75

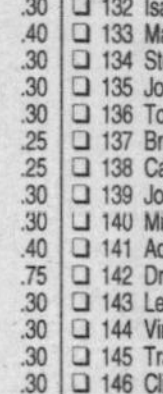

❑ 45 Javon Walker	.75	.30
❑ 46 Jay Cutler	1.00	.40
❑ 47 Mike Bell	.75	.30
❑ 48 Brandon Marshall	.75	.30
❑ 49 Tatum Bell	.75	.30
❑ 50 Jon Kitna	.60	.25
❑ 51 Kevin Jones	.60	.25
❑ 52 Roy Williams WR	.75	.30
❑ 53 Mike Furrey	.75	.30
❑ 54 A.J. Hawk	1.00	.40
❑ 55 Brett Favre	2.00	.75
❑ 56 Donald Driver	.75	.30
❑ 57 Greg Jennings	.75	.30
❑ 58 Ahman Green	.75	.30
❑ 59 Andre Johnson	.75	.30
❑ 60 David Carr	.75	.30
❑ 61 Eric Moulds	.75	.30
❑ 62 Owen Daniels	.60	.25
❑ 63 Wali Lundy	.60	.25
❑ 64 Joseph Addai	1.25	.50
❑ 65 Marvin Harrison	1.00	.40
❑ 66 Peyton Manning	1.50	.60
❑ 67 Reggie Wayne	.75	.30
❑ 68 Dallas Clark	.60	.25
❑ 69 Byron Leftwich	.75	.30
❑ 70 Fred Taylor	.75	.30
❑ 71 Marcedes Lewis	.60	.25
❑ 72 Maurice Jones-Drew	1.00	.40
❑ 73 Reggie Williams	.75	.30
❑ 74 Eddie Kennison	.60	.25
❑ 75 Larry Johnson	1.00	.40
❑ 76 Tony Gonzalez	.75	.30
❑ 77 Trent Green	.75	.30
❑ 78 Chris Chambers	.75	.30
❑ 79 Daunte Culpepper	.75	.30
❑ 80 Marty Booker	.60	.25
❑ 81 Ronnie Brown	.75	.30
❑ 82 Chester Taylor	.60	.25
❑ 83 Tarvaris Jackson	1.00	.40
❑ 84 Troy Williamson	.60	.25
❑ 85 Travis Taylor	.60	.25
❑ 86 Ben Watson	.60	.25
❑ 87 Tom Brady	2.00	.75
❑ 88 Corey Dillon	.75	.30
❑ 89 Laurence Maroney	1.00	.40
❑ 90 Deuce McAllister	.75	.30
❑ 91 Drew Brees	.75	.30
❑ 92 Marques Colston	1.00	.40
❑ 93 Reggie Bush	1.25	.50
❑ 94 Joe Horn	.75	.30
❑ 95 Brandon Jacobs	.75	.30
❑ 96 Eli Manning	1.00	.40
❑ 97 Jeremy Shockey	.75	.30
❑ 98 Plaxico Burress	.75	.30
❑ 99 Chad Pennington	.75	.30
❑ 100 Jerricho Cotchery	.60	.25
❑ 101 Laveranues Coles	.75	.30
❑ 102 Leon Washington	.75	.30
❑ 103 Kevan Barlow	.75	.30
❑ 104 Ronald Curry	.75	.30
❑ 105 LaMont Jordan	.75	.30
❑ 106 John Madsen	.60	.25
❑ 107 Michael Huff	.75	.30
❑ 108 Randy Moss	1.00	.40
❑ 109 Brian Westbrook	.75	.30
❑ 110 Donovan McNabb	1.00	.40
❑ 111 Hank Baskett	.75	.30
❑ 112 Donte Stallworth	.75	.30
❑ 113 Reggie Brown	.75	.30
❑ 114 Ben Roethlisberger	1.25	.50
❑ 115 Hines Ward	1.00	.40
❑ 116 Troy Polamalu	1.00	.40
❑ 117 Willie Parker	1.00	.40
❑ 118 Santonio Holmes	.75	.30
❑ 119 Antonio Gates	.75	.30
❑ 120 LaDainian Tomlinson	1.25	.50
❑ 121 Vincent Jackson	.60	.25
❑ 122 Philip Rivers	1.00	.40
❑ 123 Shawne Merriman	.75	.30
❑ 124 Alex Smith QB	1.00	.40
❑ 125 Antonio Bryant	.75	.30
❑ 126 Frank Gore	1.00	.40
❑ 127 Vernon Davis	.75	.30
❑ 128 Darrell Jackson	.75	.30
❑ 129 Deion Branch	.75	.30
❑ 130 Matt Hasselbeck	.75	.30
❑ 131 Shaun Alexander	.75	.30

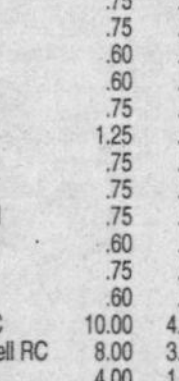

❑ 132 Isaac Bruce	.75	.30
❑ 133 Marc Bulger	.75	.30
❑ 134 Steven Jackson	1.00	.40
❑ 135 Joe Klopfenstein	.60	.25
❑ 136 Torry Holt	.75	.30
❑ 137 Bruce Gradkowski	.75	.30
❑ 138 Cadillac Williams	.75	.30
❑ 139 Joey Galloway	.75	.30
❑ 140 Mike Alstott	.75	.30
❑ 141 Adam Jones	.60	.25
❑ 142 Drew Bennett	.60	.25
❑ 143 LenDale White	.75	.30
❑ 144 Vince Young	1.25	.50
❑ 145 Travis Henry	.75	.30
❑ 146 Clinton Portis	.75	.30
❑ 147 Jason Campbell	.75	.30
❑ 148 Ladell Betts	.60	.25
❑ 149 Santana Moss	.75	.30
❑ 150 Chris Cooley	.60	.25
❑ 151 Brady Quinn RC	10.00	4.00
❑ 152 JaMarcus Russell RC	8.00	3.00
❑ 153 Troy Smith RC	4.00	1.50
❑ 154 Drew Stanton RC	4.00	1.50
❑ 155 Adrian Peterson RC	25.00	10.00
❑ 156 Marshawn Lynch RC	6.00	2.50
❑ 157 Michael Bush RC	4.00	1.50
❑ 158 Kenny Irons SP RC	30.00	12.00
❑ 159 Antonio Pittman RC	2.50	1.00
❑ 160 Tony Hunt RC	3.00	1.25
❑ 161 Darius Walker SP RC	30.00	12.00
❑ 162 DeShawn Wynn RC	3.00	1.25
❑ 163 Calvin Johnson RC	10.00	4.00
❑ 164 Ted Ginn Jr. RC	5.00	2.00
❑ 165 Dwayne Jarrett RC	4.00	1.50
❑ 166 Sidney Rice RC	5.00	2.00
❑ 167 Dwayne Bowe RC	6.00	2.50
❑ 168 Robert Meachem RC	3.00	1.25
❑ 169 Anthony Gonzalez SP RC	50.00	20.00
❑ 170 Craig Buster Davis RC	3.00	1.25
❑ 171 Johnnie Lee Higgins RC	2.50	1.00
❑ 172 Steve Smith USC RC	4.00	1.50
❑ 173 Chansi Stuckey RC	2.50	1.00
❑ 174 David Clowney RC	3.00	1.25
❑ 175 Aundrae Allison RC	2.50	1.00
❑ 176 Jason Hill SP RC	30.00	12.00
❑ 177 Zach Miller RC	3.00	1.25
❑ 178 Greg Olsen RC	4.00	1.50
❑ 179 Gaines Adams RC	3.00	1.25
❑ 180 Jamaal Anderson RC	2.50	1.00
❑ 181 Victor Abiamiri RC	3.00	1.25
❑ 182 Adam Carriker RC	2.50	1.00
❑ 183 LaMarr Woodley RC	3.00	1.25
❑ 184 Quentin Moses RC	2.50	1.00
❑ 185 Charles Johnson RC	2.00	.75
❑ 186 Alan Branch RC	2.50	1.00
❑ 187 Amobi Okoye RC	3.00	1.25
❑ 188 DeMarcus Tank Tyler RC	2.50	1.00
❑ 189 Patrick Willis SP RC	60.00	25.00
❑ 190 Paul Posluszny RC	4.00	1.50
❑ 191 Lawrence Timmons RC	3.00	1.25
❑ 192 Darrelle Revis RC	3.00	1.25
❑ 193 Leon Hall RC	2.50	1.00
❑ 194 Daymeion Hughes RC	2.50	1.00
❑ 195 Chris Houston RC	2.50	1.00
❑ 196 A.J. Davis RC	2.00	.75
❑ 197 Aaron Ross RC	3.00	1.25
❑ 198 LaRon Landry RC	4.00	1.50
❑ 199 Reggie Nelson RC	2.50	1.00
❑ 200 Michael Griffin RC	3.00	1.25
❑ 201 Trent Edwards RC	6.00	2.50
❑ 202 Kevin Kolb RC	5.00	2.00
❑ 203 John Beck RC	6.00	2.50
❑ 204 Kenneth Darby RC	3.00	1.25
❑ 205 Lorenzo Booker RC	3.00	1.25
❑ 206 Jason Snelling RC	2.50	1.00
❑ 207 Selvin Young RC	4.00	1.50
❑ 208 Ahmad Bradshaw RC	4.00	1.50
❑ 209 Brandon Jackson RC	4.00	1.50
❑ 210 Courtney Taylor RC	2.50	1.00
❑ 211 Paul Williams SP RC	25.00	10.00
❑ 212 Rhema McKnight RC	2.50	1.00
❑ 213 David Ball RC	2.00	.75
❑ 214 Syvelle Newton RC	2.50	1.00
❑ 215 Joel Filani RC	2.50	1.00
❑ 216 Chris Davis RC	2.50	1.00
❑ 217 Laurent Robinson RC	2.50	1.00
❑ 218 Jarrett Hicks RC	2.50	1.00

❑ 219 Dallas Baker RC 2.50 1.00
❑ 220 Matt Trannon RC 2.50 1.00
❑ 221 Mike Walker RC 2.50 1.00
❑ 222 Anthony Spencer RC 3.00 1.25
❑ 223 Jarvis Moss RC 3.00 1.25
❑ 224 Tim Crowder RC 3.00 1.25
❑ 225 Brandon Siler RC 2.50 1.00
❑ 226 David Harris RC 2.50 1.00
❑ 227 Buster Davis RC 2.50 1.00
❑ 228 Jon Abbate RC 2.00 .75
❑ 229 Rufus Alexander RC 3.00 1.25
❑ 230 Jon Beason RC 3.00 1.25
❑ 231 Jonathan Wade RC 2.50 1.00
❑ 232 Marcus McCauley RC 2.50 1.00
❑ 233 Tanard Jackson RC 2.00 .75
❑ 234 Kenny Scott RC 2.00 .75
❑ 235 Brandon Meriweather RC 3.00 1.25
❑ 236 Aaron Rouse RC 3.00 1.25
❑ 237 Eric Weddle RC 2.50 1.00
❑ 238 Brian Leonard RC 4.00 1.50
❑ 239 Jared Zabransky SP RC 30.00 12.00
❑ 240 Chris Leak SP RC 25.00 10.00
❑ 241 Jordan Palmer SP RC 30.00 12.00
❑ 242 Garrett Wolfe SP RC 40.00 15.00
❑ 243 Gary Russell RC 3.00 1.25
❑ 244 Isaiah Stanback RC 3.00 1.25
❑ 245 Tyler Palko RC 3.00 1.25
❑ 246 Jeff Rowe RC 2.50 1.00
❑ 247 Kolby Smith RC 4.00 1.50
❑ 248 Dwayne Wright RC 2.50 1.00
❑ 249 Nate Ilaoa RC 3.00 1.25
❑ 250 Steve Breaston RC 2.50 1.00

1989 Pro Set

❑ COMPLETE SET (561) 25.00 10.00
❑ COMP.SERIES 1 (440) 6.00 3.00
❑ COMP.SERIES 2 (100) 20.00 10.00
❑ COMP.FINAL FACT.SET (21) 2.00 [illegible]
❑ 1 Stacey Bailey .10 .02
❑ 2 Aundray Bruce RC .10 .02
❑ 3 Rick Bryan .10 .02
❑ 4 Bobby Butler .10 .02
❑ 5 Scott Case RC .10 .02
❑ 6 Tony Casillas .10 .02
❑ 7 Floyd Dixon .10 .02
❑ 8 Rick Donnelly .10 .02
❑ 9 Bill Fralic .10 .02
❑ 10 Mike Gann .10 .02
❑ 11 Mike Kenn .10 .02
❑ 12 Chris Miller RC .25 .08
❑ 13 John Rade .10 .02
❑ 14 Gerald Riggs UER .15 .05
❑ 15 John Settle RC .10 .02
❑ 16 Marion Campbell CO .10 .02
❑ 17 Cornelius Bennett .15 .05
❑ 18 Derrick Burroughs .10 .02
❑ 19 Shane Conlan .10 .02
❑ 20 Ronnie Harmon .15 .05
❑ 21 Kent Hull RC .10 .02
❑ 22 Jim Kelly .50 .20
❑ 23 Mark Kelso .10 .02
❑ 24 Pete Metzelaars .10 .02
❑ 25 Scott Norwood RC .10 .02
❑ 26 Andre Reed .25 .08
❑ 27 Fred Smerlas .10 .02
❑ 28 Bruce Smith .25 .08
❑ 29 Leonard Smith .10 .02
❑ 30 Art Still .10 .02
❑ 31 Darryl Talley .15 .05
❑ 32 Thurman Thomas RC 1.25 .50
❑ 33 Will Wolford RC .10 .02
❑ 34 Marv Levy CO .10 .02
❑ 35 Neal Anderson .15 .05
❑ 36 Kevin Butler .10 .02
❑ 37 Jim Covert .10 .02
❑ 38 Richard Dent .15 .05
❑ 39 Dave Duerson .10 .02
❑ 40 Dennis Gentry .10 .02
❑ 41 Dan Hampton .15 .05
❑ 42 Jay Hilgenberg .10 .02
❑ 43 Dennis McKinnon UER .10 .02
❑ 44 Jim McMahon .15 .05
❑ 45 Steve McMichael .15 .05
❑ 46 Brad Muster RC .10 .02
❑ 47A William Perry ERR SP 6.00 2.50
❑ 47B Ron Morris RC .10 .02
❑ 48 Ron Rivera .10 .02
❑ 49 Vestee Jackson RC .10 .02
❑ 50 Mike Singletary .15 .05
❑ 51 Mike Tomczak .15 .05
❑ 52 Keith Van Horne RC .10 .02
❑ 53A Mike Ditka CO .25 .08
❑ 53B Mike Ditka CO HOF .25 .08
❑ 54 Lewis Billups .10 .02
❑ 55 James Brooks .15 .05
❑ 56 Eddie Brown .10 .02
❑ 57 Jason Buck RC .10 .02
❑ 58 Boomer Esiason .15 .05
❑ 59 David Fulcher .15 .05
❑ 60A Rodney Holman RC ERR .15 .05
❑ 60B Rodney Holman RC COR .25 .08
❑ 61 Reggie Williams .10 .02
❑ 62 Joe Kelly RC .10 .02
❑ 63 Tim Krumrie .10 .02
❑ 64 Tim McGee .10 .02
❑ 65 Max Montoya .10 .02
❑ 66 Anthony Munoz .15 .05
❑ 67 Jim Skow .10 .02
❑ 68 Eric Thomas RC .10 .02
❑ 69 Leon White .10 .02
❑ 70 Ickey Woods RC .15 .05
❑ 71 Carl Zander .10 .02
❑ 72 Sam Wyche CO .10 .02
❑ 73 Brian Brennan .10 .02
❑ 74 Earnest Byner .10 .02
❑ 75 Hanford Dixon .10 .02
❑ 76 Mike Pagel .10 .02
❑ 77 Bernie Kosar .15 .05
❑ 78 Reggie Langhorne RC .10 .02
❑ 79 Kevin Mack .10 .02
❑ 80 Clay Matthews .15 .05
❑ 81 Gerald McNeil .10 .02
❑ 82 Frank Minnifield .10 .02
❑ 83 Cody Risien .10 .02
❑ 84 Webster Slaughter .15 .05
❑ 85 Felix Wright .10 .02
❑ 86 Bud Carson CO UER .10 .02
❑ 87 Bill Bates .15 .05
❑ 88 Kevin Brooks .10 .02
❑ 89 Michael Irvin RC 1.50 .60
❑ 90 Jim Jeffcoat .10 .02
❑ 91 Ed Too Tall Jones .15 .05
❑ 92 Eugene Lockhart RC .10 .02
❑ 93 Nate Newton RC .15 .05
❑ 94 Danny Noonan .10 .02
❑ 95 Steve Pelluer .10 .02
❑ 96 Herschel Walker .15 .05
❑ 97 Everson Walls .10 .02
❑ 98 Jimmy Johnson RC CO .15 .05
❑ 99 Keith Bishop .10 .02
❑ 100A John Elway DRAFT 6.00 2.50
❑ 100B John Elway TRADE 2.00 .75
❑ 101 Simon Fletcher RC .10 .02
❑ 102 Mike Harden .10 .02
❑ 103 Mike Horan .10 .02
❑ 104 Mark Jackson .10 .02
❑ 105 Vance Johnson .15 .05
❑ 106 Rulon Jones .10 .02
❑ 107 Clarence Kay .10 .02
❑ 108 Karl Mecklenburg .10 .02
❑ 109 Ricky Nattiel .10 .02
❑ 110 Steve Sewell RC .10 .02
❑ 111 Dennis Smith .15 .05
❑ 112 Gerald Willhite .10 .02
❑ 113 Sammy Winder .10 .02
❑ 114 Dan Reeves CO .10 .02
❑ 115 Jim Arnold .10 .02
❑ 116 Jerry Ball RC .10 .02
❑ 117 Bennie Blades RC .10 .02
❑ 118 Lomas Brown .10 .02
❑ 119 Mike Cofer .10 .02
❑ 120 Garry James .10 .02
❑ 121 James Jones FB .10 .02
❑ 122 Chuck Long .10 .02
❑ 123 Pete Mandley .10 .02
❑ 124 Eddie Murray .10 .02
❑ 125 Chris Spielman RC .25 .08
❑ 126 Dennis Gibson .10 .02
❑ 127 Wayne Fontes CO .10 .02
❑ 128 [illegible]
❑ 129 Brent Fullwood RC .10 .02
❑ 130 Mark Cannon .10 .02
❑ 131 Tim Harris .10 .02
❑ 132 Mark Lee .10 .02
❑ 133 Don Majkowski RC .15 .05
❑ 134 Mark Murphy .10 .02
❑ 135 Brian Noble .10 .02
❑ 136 Ken Ruettgers RC .10 .02
❑ 137 Johnny Holland .10 .02
❑ 138 Randy Wright .10 .02
❑ 139 Lindy Infante CO .10 .02
❑ 140 Steve Brown .10 .02
❑ 141 Ray Childress .10 .02
❑ 142 Jeff Donaldson .10 .02
❑ 143 Ernest Givins .15 .05
❑ 144 John Grimsley .10 .02
❑ 145 Alonzo Highsmith .10 .02
❑ 146 Drew Hill .10 .02
❑ 147 Robert Lyles .10 .02
❑ 148 Bruce Matthews RC .75 .30
❑ 149 Warren Moon .25 .08
❑ 150 Mike Munchak .15 .05
❑ 151 Allen Pinkett RC .10 .02
❑ 152 Mike Rozier .10 .02
❑ 153 Tony Zendejas .10 .02
❑ 154 Jerry Glanville CO .10 .02
❑ 155 Albert Bentley .10 .02
❑ 156 Dean Biasucci .10 .02
❑ 157 Duane Bickett .10 .02
❑ 158 Bill Brooks .15 .05
❑ 159 Chris Chandler RC 1.00 .40
❑ 160 Pat Beach .10 .02
❑ 161 Ray Donaldson .10 .02
❑ 162 Jon Hand .10 .02
❑ 163 Chris Hinton .10 .02
❑ 164 Rohn Stark .10 .02
❑ 165 Fredd Young .10 .02
❑ 166 Ron Meyer CO .10 .02
❑ 167 Lloyd Burruss .10 .02
❑ 168 Carlos Carson .10 .02
❑ 169 [illegible]
❑ 170 Irv Eatman .10 .02
❑ 171 Dino Hackett .10 .02
❑ 172 Steve DeBerg .10 .02
❑ 173 Albert Lewis .10 .02
❑ 174 Nick Lowery .10 .02
❑ 175 Bill Maas .10 .02
❑ 176 Christian Okoye .10 .02
❑ 177 Stephone Paige .10 .02
❑ 178 Mark Adickes .10 .02
❑ 179 Kevin Ross RC .15 .05
❑ 180 Neil Smith RC .50 .20
❑ 181 M. Schottenheimer CO .10 .02
❑ 182 Marcus Allen .25 .08
❑ 183 Tim Brown RC 1.50 .60
❑ 184 Willie Gault .15 .05
❑ 185 Bo Jackson .30 .10
❑ 186 Howie Long .25 .08
❑ 187 Vann McElroy .10 .02
❑ 188 Matt Millen .15 .05
❑ 189 Don Mosebar RC .10 .02
❑ 190 Bill Pickel .10 .02
❑ 191 Jerry Robinson UER .10 .02
❑ 192 Jay Schroeder .10 .02
❑ 193A Stacey Toran .10 .02
❑ 193B Stacey Toran .50 .20
❑ 194 Mike Shanahan CO RC .15 .05
❑ 195 Greg Bell .10 .02
❑ 196 Ron Brown .10 .02
❑ 197 Aaron Cox RC .10 .02
❑ 198 Henry Ellard .25 .08
❑ 199 Jim Everett .15 .05
❑ 200 Jerry Gray .10 .02

❑	201	Kevin Greene	.25	.08
❑	202	Pete Holohan	.10	.02
❑	203	LeRoy Irvin	.10	.02
❑	204	Mike Lansford	.10	.02
❑	205	Tom Newberry RC	.10	.02
❑	206	Mel Owens	.10	.02
❑	207	Jackie Slater	.10	.02
❑	208	Doug Smith	.10	.02
❑	209	Mike Wilcher	.10	.02
❑	210	John Robinson CO	.10	.02
❑	211	John Bosa	.10	.02
❑	212	Mark Brown	.10	.02
❑	213	Mark Clayton	.15	.05
❑	214A	Ferrell Edmonds RC ERR	.50	.20
❑	214B	Ferrell Edmunds RC COR	.10	.02
❑	215	Roy Foster	.10	.02
❑	216	Lorenzo Hampton	.10	.02
❑	217	Jim C.Jensen RC UER	.10	.02
❑	218	William Judson	.10	.02
❑	219	Eric Kumerow RC	.10	.02
❑	220	Dan Marino	2.00	.75
❑	221	John Offerdahl	.10	.02
❑	222	Fuad Reveiz	.10	.02
❑	223	Reggie Roby	.10	.02
❑	224	Brian Sochia	.10	.02
❑	225	Don Shula CO RC	.25	.08
❑	226	Alfred Anderson	.10	.02
❑	227	Joey Browner	.10	.02
❑	228	Anthony Carter	.15	.05
❑	229	Chris Doleman	.15	.05
❑	230	Hassan Jones RC	.10	.02
❑	231	Steve Jordan	.10	.02
❑	232	Tommy Kramer	.10	.02
❑	233	Carl Lee RC	.10	.02
❑	234	Kirk Lowdermilk RC	.10	.02
❑	235	Randall McDaniel RC	.25	.08
❑	236	Doug Martin	.10	.02
❑	237	Keith Millard	.10	.02
❑	238	Darrin Nelson	.10	.02
❑	239	Jesse Solomon	.10	.02
❑	240	Scott Studwell	.10	.02
❑	241	Wade Wilson	.15	.05
❑	242	Gary Zimmerman	.10	.02
❑	243	Jerry Burns CO	.10	.02
❑	244	Bruce Armstrong RC	.10	.02
❑	245	Raymond Clayborn	.10	.02
❑	246	Reggie Dupard	.10	.02
❑	247	Tony Eason	.10	.02
❑	248	Sean Farrell	.10	.02
❑	249	Doug Flutie	.75	.25
❑	250	Brent Williams RC	.10	.02
❑	251	Roland James	.10	.02
❑	252	Ronnie Lippett	.10	.02
❑	253	Fred Marion	.10	.02
❑	254	Larry McGrew	.10	.02
❑	255	Stanley Morgan	.10	.02
❑	256	Johnny Rembert RC	.10	.02
❑	257	John Stephens RC	.10	.02
❑	258	Andre Tippett	.10	.02
❑	259	Garin Veris	.10	.02
❑	260A	Raymond Berry CO	.10	.02
❑	260B	Raymond Berry CO HOF	.10	.02
❑	261	Morten Andersen	.10	.02
❑	262	Hoby Brenner	.10	.02
❑	263	Stan Brock	.10	.02
❑	264	Brad Edelman	.10	.02
❑	265	Jumpy Geathers	.10	.02
❑	266A	Bobby Hebert Passers	.50	.20
❑	266B	Bobby Hebert Passes	.10	.02
❑	267	Craig Heyward RC	.25	.08
❑	268	Lonzell Hill	.10	.02
❑	269	Dalton Hilliard	.10	.02
❑	270	Rickey Jackson	.15	.05
❑	271	Steve Korte	.10	.02
❑	272	Eric Martin	.10	.02
❑	273	Rueben Mayes	.10	.02
❑	274	Sam Mills	.15	.05
❑	275	Brett Perriman RC	.25	.08
❑	276	Pat Swilling	.15	.05
❑	277	John Tice	.10	.02
❑	278	Jim Mora CO	.10	.02
❑	279	Eric Moore RC	.10	.02
❑	280	Carl Banks	.10	.02
❑	281	Mark Bavaro	.15	.05
❑	282	Maurice Carthon	.10	.02
❑	283	Mark Collins RC	.10	.02
❑	284	Erik Howard	.10	.02
❑	285	Terry Kinard	.10	.02
❑	286	Sean Landeta	.10	.02
❑	287	Lionel Manuel	.10	.02
❑	288	Leonard Marshall	.10	.02
❑	289	Joe Morris	.10	.02
❑	290	Bart Oates	.10	.02
❑	291	Phil Simms	.15	.05
❑	292	Lawrence Taylor	.25	.08
❑	293	Bill Parcells RC CO	.15	.05
❑	294	Dave Cadigan	.10	.02
❑	295	Kyle Clifton RC	.10	.02
❑	296	Alex Gordon	.10	.02
❑	297	James Hasty RC	.10	.02
❑	298	Johnny Hector	.10	.02
❑	299	Bobby Humphery	.10	.02
❑	300	Pat Leahy	.10	.02
❑	301	Marty Lyons	.10	.02
❑	302	Reggie McElroy RC	.10	.02
❑	303	Erik McMillan RC	.10	.02
❑	304	Freeman McNeil	.10	.02
❑	305	Ken O'Brien	.10	.02
❑	306	Pat Ryan	.10	.02
❑	307	Mickey Shuler	.10	.02
❑	308	Al Toon	.15	.05
❑	309	Jo Jo Townsell	.10	.02
❑	310	Roger Vick	.10	.02
❑	311	Joe Walton CO	.10	.02
❑	312	Jerome Brown	.15	.05
❑	313	Keith Byars	.15	.05
❑	314	Cris Carter RC	1.50	.60
❑	315	Randall Cunningham	.40	.15
❑	316	Terry Hoage	.10	.02
❑	317	Wes Hopkins	.10	.02
❑	318	Keith Jackson RC	.25	.08
❑	319	Mike Quick	.10	.02
❑	320	Mike Reichenbach	.10	.02
❑	321	Dave Rimington	.10	.02
❑	322	John Teltschik	.10	.02
❑	323	Anthony Toney	.10	.02
❑	324	Andre Waters	.10	.02
❑	325	Reggie White	.25	.08
❑	326	Luis Zendejas	.10	.02
❑	327	Buddy Ryan CO	.10	.02
❑	328	Robert Awalt	.10	.02
❑	329	Tim McDonald RC	.15	.05
❑	330	Roy Green	.15	.05
❑	331	Neil Lomax	.10	.02
❑	332	Cedric Mack	.10	.02
❑	333	Stump Mitchell	.10	.02
❑	334	Niko Noga RC	.10	.02
❑	335	Jay Novacek RC	.25	.08
❑	336	Freddie Joe Nunn	.10	.02
❑	337	Luis Sharpe	.10	.02
❑	338	Vai Sikahema	.10	.02
❑	339	J.T. Smith	.10	.02
❑	340	Ron Wolfley	.10	.02
❑	341	Gene Stallings RC CO	.15	.05
❑	342	Gary Anderson K	.10	.02
❑	343	Bubby Brister RC	.25	.08
❑	344	Dermontti Dawson RC	.15	.05
❑	345	Thomas Everett RC	.10	.02
❑	346	Delton Hall RC	.10	.02
❑	347	Bryan Hinkle RC	.10	.02
❑	348	Merril Hoge RC	.10	.02
❑	349	Tunch Ilkin RC	.10	.02
❑	350	Aaron Jones RC	.10	.02
❑	351	Louis Lipps	.15	.05
❑	352	David Little	.10	.02
❑	353	Hardy Nickerson RC	.25	.08
❑	354	Rod Woodson RC	.50	.20
❑	355A	Chuck Noll RC CO 1/3	.15	.05
❑	355B	Chuck Noll RC CO 1/2	.15	.05
❑	356	Gary Anderson RB	.10	.02
❑	357	Rod Bernstine RC	.10	.02
❑	358	Gill Byrd	.10	.02
❑	359	Vencie Glenn	.10	.02
❑	360	Dennis McKnight	.10	.02
❑	361	Lionel James	.10	.02
❑	362	Mark Malone	.10	.02
❑	363A	Anthony Miller RC 14.8	.25	.08
❑	363B	Anthony Miller RC 3	.25	.08
❑	364	Ralf Mojsiejenko	.10	.02
❑	365	Leslie O'Neal	.15	.05
❑	366	Jamie Holland RC	.10	.02
❑	367	Lee Williams	.10	.02
❑	368	Dan Henning CO	.10	.02
❑	369	Harris Barton RC	.10	.02
❑	370	Michael Carter	.10	.02
❑	371	Mike Cofer RC K	.10	.02
❑	372	Roger Craig	.25	.08
❑	373	Riki Ellison RC	.10	.02
❑	374	Jim Fahnhorst	.10	.02
❑	375	John Frank	.10	.02
❑	376	Jeff Fuller	.10	.02
❑	377	Don Griffin	.10	.02
❑	378	Charles Haley	.25	.08
❑	379	Ronnie Lott	.15	.05
❑	380	Tim McKyer	.10	.02
❑	381	Joe Montana	2.00	.75
❑	382	Tom Rathman	.10	.02
❑	383	Jerry Rice	1.50	.60
❑	384	John Taylor RC	.25	.08
❑	385	Keena Turner	.10	.02
❑	386	Michael Walter	.10	.02
❑	387	Bubba Paris	.10	.02
❑	388	Steve Young	1.00	.40
❑	389	George Seifert RC CO	.15	.05
❑	390	Brian Blades RC	.25	.08
❑	391A	B.Bosworth Seattle	.30	.10
❑	391B	B.Bosworth Seahawks	.15	.05
❑	392	Jeff Bryant	.10	.02
❑	393	Jacob Green	.10	.02
❑	394	Norm Johnson	.10	.02
❑	395	Dave Krieg	.15	.05
❑	396	Steve Largent	.25	.08
❑	397	Bryan Millard RC	.10	.02
❑	398	Paul Moyer	.10	.02
❑	399	Joe Nash	.10	.02
❑	400	Rufus Porter RC	.10	.02
❑	401	Eugene Robinson RC	.10	.02
❑	402	Bruce Scholtz	.10	.02
❑	403	Kelly Stouffer RC	.10	.02
❑	404A	Curt Warner 1455	1.25	.50
❑	404B	Curt Warner 6074	.15	.05
❑	405	John L.Williams	.10	.02
❑	406	Tony Woods RC	.10	.02
❑	407	David Wyman	.10	.02
❑	408	Chuck Knox CO	.10	.02
❑	409	Mark Carrier RC WR	.25	.08
❑	410	Randy Grimes	.10	.02
❑	411	Paul Gruber RC	.10	.02
❑	412	Harry Hamilton	.10	.02
❑	413	Ron Holmes	.10	.02
❑	414	Donald Igwebuike	.10	.02
❑	415	Dan Turk	.10	.02
❑	416	Ricky Reynolds	.10	.02
❑	417	Bruce Hill RC	.10	.02
❑	418	Lars Tate	.10	.02
❑	419	Vinny Testaverde	.30	.10
❑	420	James Wilder	.10	.02
❑	421	Ray Perkins CO	.10	.02
❑	422	Jeff Bostic	.10	.02
❑	423	Kelvin Bryant	.10	.02
❑	424	Gary Clark	.25	.08
❑	425	Monte Coleman	.10	.02
❑	426	Darrell Green	.15	.05
❑	427	Joe Jacoby	.10	.02
❑	428	Jim Lachey	.10	.02
❑	429	Charles Mann	.10	.02
❑	430	Dexter Manley	.10	.02
❑	431	Darryl Grant	.10	.02
❑	432	Mark May RC	.10	.02
❑	433	Art Monk	.15	.05
❑	434	Mark Rypien RC	.25	.08
❑	435	Ricky Sanders	.10	.02
❑	436	Alvin Walton RC	.10	.02
❑	437	Don Warren	.10	.02
❑	438	Jamie Morris	.10	.02
❑	439	Doug Williams	.15	.05
❑	440	Joe Gibbs RC CO	.15	.05
❑	441	Marcus Cotton	.10	.02
❑	442	Joel Williams	.10	.02
❑	443	Joe Devlin	.10	.02
❑	444	Robb Riddick	.10	.02
❑	445	William Perry	.15	.05
❑	446	Thomas Sanders RC	.10	.02
❑	447	Brian Blados	.10	.02
❑	448	Cris Collinsworth	.15	.05
❑	449	Stanford Jennings	.10	.02
❑	450	Barry Krauss UER	.10	.02
❑	451	Ozzie Newsome	.15	.05
❑	452	Mike Oliphant RC	.10	.02
❑	453	Tony Dorsett	.25	.08
❑	454	Bruce McNorton	.10	.02

❑ 455 Eric Dickerson	.15	.05
❑ 456 Keith Bostic	.10	.02
❑ 457 Sam Clancy RC	.10	.02
❑ 458 Jack Del Rio RC	.25	.08
❑ 459 Mike Webster	.15	.05
❑ 460 Bob Golic	.10	.02
❑ 461 Otis Wilson	.10	.02
❑ 462 Mike Haynes	.15	.05
❑ 463 Greg Townsend	.10	.02
❑ 464 Mark Duper	.15	.05
❑ 465 E.J. Junior	.10	.02
❑ 466 Troy Stradford	.10	.02
❑ 467 Mike Merriweather	.10	.02
❑ 468 Irving Fryar	.25	.08
[illegible]	[illegible]	[illegible]
❑ 470 Pepper Johnson	.10	.02
❑ 471 Gary Reasons RC	.10	.02
❑ 472 Perry Williams RC	.10	.02
❑ 473 Wesley Walker	.10	.02
❑ 474 Anthony Bell RC	.10	.02
❑ 475 Earl Ferrell	.10	.02
❑ 476 Craig Wolfley	.10	.02
❑ 477 Billy Ray Smith	.10	.02
❑ 478A Jim McMahon NOTR	.15	.05
❑ 478B Jim McMahon TR	.15	.05
❑ 478C Jim McMahon	40.00	15.00
❑ 479 Eric Wright	.10	.02
❑ 480A Earnest Byner NOTR	.10	.02
❑ 480B Earnest Byner TR	.30	.10
❑ 480C Earnest Byner TR	40.00	15.00
❑ 481 Russ Grimm	.10	.02
❑ 482 Wilber Marshall	.10	.02
❑ 483A Gerald Riggs NOTR	.15	.05
❑ 483B Gerald Riggs TR	.30	.10
❑ 483C Gerald Riggs TR	40.00	15.00
❑ 484 Brian Davis RC	.10	.02
❑ 485 Shawn Collins RC	.10	.02
❑ 486 Deion Sanders RC	1.50	.60
❑ 487 Trace Armstrong RC	.10	.02
❑ 488 Donnell Woolford RC	.15	.05
❑ 489 Eric Metcalf RC	.25	.08
❑ 490 Troy Aikman RC	6.00	2.50
❑ 491 Steve Walsh RC	.15	.05
❑ 492 Steve Atwater RC	.25	.08
❑ 493 Bobby Humphrey RC	.10	.02
❑ 494 Barry Sanders RC	8.00	3.00
❑ 495 Tony Mandarich RC	.10	.02
❑ 496 David Williams RC	.10	.02
❑ 497 Andre Rison RC UER	1.00	.40
❑ 498 Derrick Thomas RC	1.50	.60
❑ 499 Cleveland Gary RC	.10	.02
❑ 500 Bill Hawkins RC	.10	.02
❑ 501 Louis Oliver RC	.15	.05
❑ 502 Sammie Smith RC	.10	.02
❑ 503 Hart Lee Dykes RC	.10	.02
❑ [illegible]	[illegible]	.02
❑ 505 Brian Williams OL RC	.10	.02
❑ 506 Jeff Lageman RC	.15	.05
❑ 507 Eric Hill RC	.10	.02
❑ 508 Joe Wolf RC	.10	.02
❑ 509 Timm Rosenbach RC	.10	.02
❑ 510 Tom Ricketts	.10	.02
❑ 511 Tim Worley RC	.10	.02
❑ 512 Burt Grossman RC	.10	.02
❑ 513 Keith DeLong RC	.10	.02
❑ 514 Andy Heck RC	.10	.02
❑ 515 Broderick Thomas RC	.25	.08
❑ 516 Don Beebe RC	.25	.08
❑ 517 James Thornton RC	.10	.02
❑ 518 Eric Kattus	.10	.02
❑ 519 Bruce Kozerski RC	.10	.02
❑ 520 Brian Washington RC	.10	.02
❑ 521 Rodney Peete RC	.50	.20
❑ 522 Erik Affholter RC	.10	.02
❑ 523 Anthony Dilweg RC	.10	.02
❑ 524 O'Brien Alston	.10	.02
❑ 525 Mike Elkins	.10	.02
❑ 526 Jonathan Hayes RC	.10	.02
❑ 527 Terry McDaniel RC	.10	.02
❑ 528 Frank Stams RC	.10	.02
❑ 529 Darryl Ingram RC	.10	.02
❑ 530 Henry Thomas	.10	.02
❑ 531 Eric Coleman DB	.10	.02
❑ 532 Sheldon White RC	.10	.02
❑ 533 Eric Allen RC	.25	.08
❑ 534 Robert Drummond	.10	.02
❑ 535A G.Williams RC bal	10.00	5.00

❑ 535B G.Williams RC w/o scout	.25	.08
❑ 535C G.Williams RC w/scout	.10	.02
❑ 536 Billy Joe Tolliver RC	.10	.02
❑ 537 Daniel Stubbs RC	.10	.02
❑ 538 Wesley Walls RC	.40	.15
❑ 539A James Jefferson RC*ERR	.30	.10
❑ 539B James Jefferson RC*COR	.10	.02
❑ 540 Tracy Rocker	.10	.02
❑ 541 Art Shell CO	.15	.05
❑ 542 Lemuel Stinson RC	.10	.02
❑ 543 Tyrone Braxton RC UER	.10	.02
❑ 544 David Treadwell RC	.10	.02
❑ 545 Flipper Anderson RC	.25	.08
❑ 546 Dave Meggett RC	.25	.08
❑ [illegible]	.10	.02
❑ 548 Carnell Lake RC	.25	.08
❑ 549 Marion Butts RC	.15	.05
❑ 550 Sterling Sharpe RC	1.00	.40
❑ 551 Ezra Johnson	.10	.02
❑ 552 Clarence Verdin RC**	.10	.02
❑ 553 Mervyn Fernandez RC**/C	.10	.02
❑ 554 Ottis Anderson	.15	.05
❑ 555 Gary Hogeboom	.10	.02
❑ 556 Paul Palmer TR	.10	.02
❑ 557 Jesse Solomon TR	.10	.02
❑ 558 Chip Banks TR	.10	.02
❑ 559 Steve Pelluer TR	.10	.02
❑ 560 Darrin Nelson TR	.10	.02
❑ 561 Herschel Walker TR	.15	.05
❑ CC1 Pete Rozelle	.50	.20

1990 Pro Set

❑ COMPLETE SET (801)	25.00	10.00
❑ COMP.SERIES 1 (377)	10.00	4.00
❑ COMP.SERIES 2 (392)	10.00	4.00
❑ COMP.FINAL SERIES (32)	4.00	1.50
❑ COMP.FINAL FACT. (32)	5.00	2.00
❑ 1A [illegible] ROY Hawaii	[illegible]	[illegible]
❑ 1B Barry Sanders ROY	.60	.25
❑ 2A Joe Montana POY 3521 ERR	.50	.20
❑ 2B Joe Montana POY 3130 COR	.50	.20
❑ 3 Lindy Infante UER	.04	.01
❑ 4 Warren Moon MOY UER	.25	.08
❑ 5 Keith Millard	.04	.01
❑ 6 Derrick Thomas D.ROY	.25	.08
❑ 7 Ottis Anderson	.10	.02
❑ 8 Joe Montana LL UER	.50	.20
❑ 9 Christian Okoye	.04	.01
❑ 10 Thurman Thomas LL	.25	.08
❑ 11 Mike Cofer	.04	.01
❑ 12 Dalton Hilliard UER	.04	.01
❑ 13 Sterling Sharpe LL	.25	.08
❑ 14 Rich Camarillo	.04	.01
❑ 15A Walter Stanley LL 87/8	.50	.20
❑ 15B Walter Stanley COR	.04	.01
❑ 16 Rod Woodson	.25	.08
❑ 17 Felix Wright	.04	.01
❑ 18A Chris Doleman ERR	.50	.20
❑ 18B Chris Doleman COR	.50	.20
❑ 19A Andre Ware RC w/o strip	.10	.02
❑ 19B Andre Ware RC w/stripe	.10	.02
❑ 20A Mo Elewonibi RC	.04	.01
❑ 20B Mo Elewonibi RC	.04	.01
❑ 21A Percy Snow	.50	.20
❑ 21B Percy Snow	.04	.01
❑ 22A Anthony Thompson RC w/o	.04	.01
❑ 22B Anthony Thompson RC w/	.04	.01
❑ 23 Buck Buchanan	.04	.01
❑ 24 Bob Griese	.10	.02

❑ 25A Franco Harris ERR	.50	.20
❑ 25B Franco Harris COR	.10	.02
❑ 26 Ted Hendricks	.04	.01
❑ 27A Jack Lambert ERR	.50	.20
❑ 27B Jack Lambert COR	.50	.20
❑ 28 Tom Landry HOF	.10	.02
❑ 29 Bob St.Clair	.04	.01
❑ 30 Aundray Bruce UER	.04	.01
❑ 31 Tony Casillas UER	.04	.01
❑ 32 Shawn Collins	.04	.01
❑ 33 Marcus Cotton	.04	.01
❑ 34 Bill Fralic	.04	.01
❑ 35 Chris Miller	.10	.02
❑ 36 Deion Sanders UER	.50	.20
❑ 37 John Settle	.04	.01
❑ 38 Jerry Glanville CO	.04	.01
❑ 39 Cornelius Bennett	.10	.02
❑ 40 Jim Kelly	.25	.08
❑ 41 Mark Kelso UER	.04	.01
❑ 42 Scott Norwood	.04	.01
❑ 43 Nate Odomes RC	.10	.02
❑ 44 Scott Radecic	.04	.01
❑ 45 Jim Ritcher RC	.04	.01
❑ 46 Leonard Smith	.04	.01
❑ 47 Darryl Talley	.04	.01
❑ 48 Marv Levy CO	.04	.01
❑ 49 Neal Anderson	.10	.02
❑ 50 Kevin Butler	.04	.01
❑ 51 Jim Covert	.04	.01
❑ 52 Richard Dent	.10	.02
❑ 53 Jay Hilgenberg	.04	.01
❑ 54 Steve McMichael	.10	.02
❑ 55 Ron Morris	.04	.01
❑ 56 John Roper	.04	.01
❑ 57 Mike Singletary	.10	.02
❑ 58 Keith Van Horne	.04	.01
❑ 59A Mike Ditka CO	.25	.08
❑ 59B Mike Ditka CO	5.00	2.00
❑ 60 Lewis Billups	.04	.01
❑ 61 Eddie Brown	.04	.01
❑ 62 Jason Buck	.04	.01
❑ 63A Rickey Dixon RC ERR	.50	.20
❑ 63B Rickey Dixon RC COR	.50	.20
❑ 64 Tim McGee	.04	.01
❑ 65 Eric Thomas	.04	.01
❑ 66 Ickey Woods	.04	.01
❑ 67 Carl Zander	.04	.01
❑ 68A Sam Wyche CO ERR	.50	.20
❑ 68B Sam Wyche CO COR	.50	.20
❑ 69 Paul Farren	.04	.01
❑ 70 Thane Gash RC	.04	.01
❑ 71 David Grayson	.04	.01
❑ 72 Bernie Kosar	.10	.02
❑ 73 Reggie Langhorne	.04	.01
❑ 74 Eric Metcalf	.25	.08
❑ 75A Ozzie Newsome ERR	.50	.20
❑ 75B Ozzie Newsome COR	.50	.20
❑ 75C Cody Risien SP	.50	.20
❑ 76 Felix Wright	.04	.01
❑ 77 Bud Carson CO	.04	.01
❑ 78 Troy Aikman	.75	.30
❑ 79 Michael Irvin	.25	.08
❑ 80 Jim Jeffcoat	.04	.01
❑ 81 Crawford Ker	.04	.01
❑ 82 Eugene Lockhart	.04	.01
❑ 83 Kelvin Martin RC	.04	.01
❑ 84 Ken Norton Jr. RC	.25	.08
❑ 85 Jimmy Johnson CO	.10	.02
❑ 86 Steve Atwater	.04	.01
❑ 87 Tyrone Braxton	.04	.01
❑ 88 John Elway	1.25	.50
❑ 89 Simon Fletcher	.04	.01
❑ 90 Ron Holmes	.04	.01
❑ 91 Bobby Humphrey	.04	.01
❑ 92 Vance Johnson	.04	.01
❑ 93 Ricky Nattiel	.04	.01
❑ 94 Dan Reeves CO	.04	.01
❑ 95 Jim Arnold	.04	.01
❑ 96 Jerry Ball	.04	.01
❑ 97 Bennie Blades	.04	.01
❑ 98 Lomas Brown	.04	.01
❑ 99 Michael Cofer	.04	.01
❑ 100 Richard Johnson	.04	.01
❑ 101 Eddie Murray	.04	.01
❑ 102 Barry Sanders	1.25	.50
❑ 103 Chris Spielman	.25	.08
❑ 104 William White RC	.04	.01

❑ 105	Eric Williams RC	.04	.01
❑ 106	Wayne Fontes CO UER	.04	.01
❑ 107	Brent Fullwood	.04	.01
❑ 108	Ron Hallstrom RC	.04	.01
❑ 109	Tim Harris	.04	.01
❑ 110A	Johnny Holland ERR	.50	.20
❑ 110B	Johnny Holland COR	.50	.20
❑ 111A	Perry Kemp ERR	.50	.20
❑ 111B	Perry Kemp COR	.50	.20
❑ 112	Don Majkowski	.04	.01
❑ 113	Mark Murphy	.04	.01
❑ 114A	Sterling Sharpe ERR Gle	.25	.08
❑ 114B	Sterling Sharpe COR Chi	.50	.20
❑ 115	Ed West RC	.04	.01
❑ 116	Lindy Infante CO	.04	.01
❑ 117	Steve Brown	.04	.01
❑ 118	Ray Childress	.04	.01
❑ 119	Ernest Givins	.10	.02
❑ 120	John Grimsley	.04	.01
❑ 121	Alonzo Highsmith	.04	.01
❑ 122	Drew Hill	.04	.01
❑ 123	Bubba McDowell	.04	.01
❑ 124	Dean Steinkuhler	.04	.01
❑ 125	Lorenzo White FPSC	.10	.02
❑ 126	Tony Zendejas	.04	.01
❑ 127	Jack Pardee CO	.04	.01
❑ 128	Albert Bentley	.04	.01
❑ 129	Dean Biasucci	.04	.01
❑ 130	Duane Bickett	.04	.01
❑ 131	Bill Brooks	.04	.01
❑ 132	Jon Hand	.04	.01
❑ 133	Mike Prior	.04	.01
❑ 134A	Andre Rison NOTR	.25	.08
❑ 134B	Andre Rison TR	.25	.08
❑ 134C	Andre Rison TR Lud/back	.25	.08
❑ 135	Rohn Stark	.04	.01
❑ 136	Donnell Thompson	.04	.01
❑ 137	Clarence Verdin	.04	.01
❑ 138	Fredd Young	.04	.01
❑ 139	Ron Meyer CO	.04	.01
❑ 140	John Alt RC	.04	.01
❑ 141	Steve DeBerg	.04	.01
❑ 142	Irv Eatman	.04	.01
❑ 143	Dino Hackett	.04	.01
❑ 144	Nick Lowery	.04	.01
❑ 145	Bill Maas	.04	.01
❑ 146	Stephone Paige	.04	.01
❑ 147	Neil Smith	.25	.08
❑ 148	M. Schottenheimer CO	.04	.01
❑ 149	Steve Beuerlein FPSC	.10	.02
❑ 150	Tim Brown	.25	.08
❑ 151	Mike Dyal	.04	.01
❑ 152A	Mervyn Fernandez ERR	.75	.30
❑ 152B	Mervyn Fernandez COR	.75	.30
❑ 153	Willie Gault	.10	.02
❑ 154	Bob Golic	.04	.01
❑ 155	Bo Jackson	.30	.10
❑ 156	Don Mosebar	.04	.01
❑ 157	Steve Smith	.04	.01
❑ 158	Greg Townsend	.04	.01
❑ 159	Bruce Wilkerson RC	.04	.01
❑ 160	Steve Wisniewski	.10	.02
❑ 161A	Art Shell CO ERR	.50	.20
❑ 161B	Art Shell CO COR	8.00	3.00
❑ 161C	Art Shell CO COR	10.00	4.00
❑ 162	Flipper Anderson	.04	.01
❑ 163	Greg Bell UER	.04	.01
❑ 164	Henry Ellard	.10	.02
❑ 165	Jim Everett	.10	.02
❑ 166	Jerry Gray	.04	.01
❑ 167	Kevin Greene	.10	.02
❑ 168	Pete Holohan	.04	.01
❑ 169	Larry Kelm RC	.04	.01
❑ 170	Tom Newberry	.04	.01
❑ 171	Vince Newsome RC	.04	.01
❑ 172	Irv Pankey	.04	.01
❑ 173	Jackie Slater	.04	.01
❑ 174	Fred Strickland RC	.04	.01
❑ 175	Mike Wilcher UER	.04	.01
❑ 176	John Robinson CO UER	.04	.01
❑ 177	Mark Clayton	.10	.02
❑ 178	Roy Foster	.04	.01
❑ 179	Harry Galbreath RC	.04	.01
❑ 180	Jim C. Jensen	.04	.01
❑ 181	Dan Marino	1.25	.50
❑ 182	Louis Oliver	.04	.01
❑ 183	Sammie Smith	.04	.01
❑ 184	Brian Sochia	.04	.01
❑ 185	Don Shula CO	.10	.02
❑ 186	Joey Browner	.04	.01
❑ 187	Anthony Carter	.10	.02
❑ 188	Chris Doleman	.04	.01
❑ 189	Steve Jordan	.04	.01
❑ 190	Carl Lee	.04	.01
❑ 191	Randall McDaniel	.10	.02
❑ 192	Mike Merriweather	.04	.01
❑ 193	Keith Millard	.04	.01
❑ 194	Al Noga	.04	.01
❑ 195	Scott Studwell	.04	.01
❑ 196	Henry Thomas	.04	.01
❑ 197	Herschel Walker	.10	.02
❑ 198	Wade Wilson	.10	.02
❑ 199	Gary Zimmerman	.04	.01
❑ 200	Jerry Burns CO	.04	.01
❑ 201	Vincent Brown RC	.04	.01
❑ 202	Hart Lee Dykes	.04	.01
❑ 203	Sean Farrell	.04	.01
❑ 204A	Fred Marion belt	250.00	100.00
❑ 204B	Fred Marion no belt	.04	.01
❑ 205	Stanley Morgan UER	.04	.01
❑ 206	Eric Sievers RC	.04	.01
❑ 207	John Stephens	.04	.01
❑ 208	Andre Tippett	.04	.01
❑ 209	Rod Rust CO	.04	.01
❑ 210A	Morten Andersen ERR	.50	.20
❑ 210B	Morten Andersen COR	.50	.20
❑ 211	Brad Edelman	.04	.01
❑ 212	John Fourcade	.04	.01
❑ 213	Dalton Hilliard	.04	.01
❑ 214	Rickey Jackson	.10	.02
❑ 215	Vaughan Johnson	.04	.01
❑ 216A	Eric Martin ERR	.50	.20
❑ 216B	Eric Martin COR	.50	.20
❑ 217	Sam Mills	.10	.02
❑ 218	Pat Swilling UER	.10	.02
❑ 219	Frank Warren RC	.04	.01
❑ 220	Jim Wilks	.04	.01
❑ 221A	Jim Mora CO ERR	.50	.20
❑ 221B	Jim Mora CO COR	.50	.20
❑ 222	Raul Allegre	.04	.01
❑ 223	Carl Banks	.04	.01
❑ 224	John Elliott	.04	.01
❑ 225	Erik Howard	.04	.01
❑ 226	Pepper Johnson	.04	.01
❑ 227	Leonard Marshall UER	.04	.01
❑ 228	Dave Meggett	.10	.02
❑ 229	Bart Oates	.04	.01
❑ 230	Phil Simms	.10	.02
❑ 231	Lawrence Taylor	.25	.08
❑ 232	Bill Parcells CO	.10	.02
❑ 233	Troy Benson	.04	.01
❑ 234	Kyle Clifton UER	.04	.01
❑ 235	Johnny Hector	.04	.01
❑ 236	Jeff Lageman	.04	.01
❑ 237	Pat Leahy	.04	.01
❑ 238	Freeman McNeil	.04	.01
❑ 239	Ken O'Brien	.04	.01
❑ 240	Al Toon	.10	.02
❑ 241	Jo Jo Townsell	.04	.01
❑ 242	Bruce Coslet CO	.04	.01
❑ 243	Eric Allen	.04	.01
❑ 244	Jerome Brown	.04	.01
❑ 245	Keith Byars	.04	.01
❑ 246	Cris Carter	.50	.20
❑ 247	Randall Cunningham	.25	.08
❑ 248	Keith Jackson	.10	.02
❑ 249	Mike Quick	.04	.01
❑ 250	Clyde Simmons	.04	.01
❑ 251	Andre Waters	.04	.01
❑ 252	Reggie White	.25	.08
❑ 253	Buddy Ryan CO	.04	.01
❑ 254	Rich Camarillo	.04	.01
❑ 255	Earl Ferrell	.04	.01
❑ 256	Roy Green	.10	.02
❑ 257	Ken Harvey RC	.25	.08
❑ 258	Ernie Jones RC	.04	.01
❑ 259	Tim McDonald	.04	.01
❑ 260	Timm Rosenbach UER	.04	.01
❑ 261	Luis Sharpe	.04	.01
❑ 262	Vai Sikahema	.04	.01
❑ 263	J.T. Smith	.04	.01
❑ 264	Ron Wolfley UER	.04	.01
❑ 265	Joe Bugel CO	.04	.01
❑ 266	Gary Anderson K	.04	.01
❑ 267	Bubby Brister	.04	.01
❑ 268	Merril Hoge	.04	.01
❑ 269	Carnell Lake	.04	.01
❑ 270	Louis Lipps	.10	.02
❑ 271	David Little	.04	.01
❑ 272	Greg Lloyd	.25	.08
❑ 273	Keith Willis	.04	.01
❑ 274	Tim Worley	.04	.01
❑ 275	Chuck Noll CO	.10	.02
❑ 276	Marion Butts	.10	.02
❑ 277	Gill Byrd	.04	.01
❑ 278	Vencie Glenn UER	.04	.01
❑ 279	Burt Grossman	.04	.01
❑ 280	Gary Plummer	.04	.01
❑ 281	Billy Ray Smith	.04	.01
❑ 282	Billy Joe Tolliver	.04	.01
❑ 283	Dan Henning CO	.04	.01
❑ 284	Harris Barton	.04	.01
❑ 285	Michael Carter	.04	.01
❑ 286	Mike Cofer	.04	.01
❑ 287	Roger Craig	.10	.02
❑ 288	Don Griffin	.04	.01
❑ 289A	Charles Haley ERR	10.00	4.00
❑ 289B	Charles Haley COR 5 fum	.75	.30
❑ 290	Pierce Holt RC	.04	.01
❑ 291	Ronnie Lott	.10	.02
❑ 292	Guy McIntyre	.04	.01
❑ 293	Joe Montana	1.25	.50
❑ 294	Tom Rathman	.04	.01
❑ 295	Jerry Rice	.75	.30
❑ 296	Jesse Sapolu RC	.04	.01
❑ 297	John Taylor	.10	.02
❑ 298	Michael Walter	.04	.01
❑ 299	George Seifert CO	.10	.02
❑ 300	Jeff Bryant	.04	.01
❑ 301	Jacob Green	.04	.01
❑ 302	Norm Johnson UER	.04	.01
❑ 303	Bryan Millard	.04	.01
❑ 304	Joe Nash	.04	.01
❑ 305	Eugene Robinson	.04	.01
❑ 306	John L. Williams	.04	.01
❑ 307	David Wyman	.04	.01
❑ 308	Chuck Knox CO	.04	.01
❑ 309	Mark Carrier WR	.25	.08
❑ 310	Paul Gruber	.04	.01
❑ 311	Harry Hamilton	.04	.01
❑ 312	Bruce Hill	.04	.01
❑ 313	Donald Igwebuike	.04	.01
❑ 314	Kevin Murphy	.04	.01
❑ 315	Ervin Randle	.04	.01
❑ 316	Mark Robinson	.04	.01
❑ 317	Lars Tate	.04	.01
❑ 318	Vinny Testaverde	.10	.02
❑ 319A	Ray Perkins CO ERR	.75	.30
❑ 319B	Ray Perkins CO COR	.04	.01
❑ 320	Earnest Byner	.04	.01
❑ 321	Gary Clark	.25	.08
❑ 322	Darryl Grant	.04	.01
❑ 323	Darrell Green	.10	.02
❑ 324	Jim Lachey	.04	.01
❑ 325	Charles Mann	.04	.01
❑ 326	Wilber Marshall	.04	.01
❑ 327	Ralf Mojsiejenko	.04	.01
❑ 328	Art Monk	.10	.02
❑ 329	Gerald Riggs	.10	.02
❑ 330	Mark Rypien	.10	.02
❑ 331	Ricky Sanders	.04	.01
❑ 332	Alvin Walton	.04	.01
❑ 333	Joe Gibbs CO	.10	.02
❑ 334	Aloha Stadium	.04	.01
❑ 335	Brian Blades PB	.04	.01
❑ 336	James Brooks PB	.04	.01
❑ 337	Shane Conlan PB	.04	.01
❑ 338A	Eric Dickerson PB SP	3.00	1.25
❑ 338B	Lud Denny Promo	200.00	75.00
❑ 339	Ray Donaldson PB	.04	.01
❑ 340	Ferrell Edmunds PB	.04	.01
❑ 341	Boomer Esiason PB	.04	.01
❑ 342	David Fulcher PB	.04	.01
❑ 343A	Chris Hinton PB	8.00	3.00
❑ 343B	Chris Hinton PB	.04	.01
❑ 344	Rodney Holman PB	.04	.01
❑ 345	Kent Hull PB	.04	.01
❑ 346	Tunch Ilkin PB	.04	.01
❑ 347	Mike Johnson PB	.04	.01
❑ 348	Greg Kragen PB	.04	.01
❑ 349	Dave Krieg PB	.10	.02

❑ 350 Albert Lewis PB .04 .01
❑ 351 Howie Long PB .10 .02
❑ 352 Bruce Matthews PB .04 .01
❑ 353 Clay Matthews PB .04 .01
❑ 354 Erik McMillan PB .04 .01
❑ 355 Karl Mecklenburg PB .04 .01
❑ 356 Anthony Miller PB .04 .01
❑ 357 Frank Minnifield PB .04 .01
❑ 358 Max Montoya PB .04 .01
❑ 359 Warren Moon PB .25 .08
❑ 360 Mike Munchak PB .04 .01
❑ 361 Anthony Munoz PB .04 .01
❑ 362 John Offerdahl PB .04 .01
❑ 363 Christian Okoye PB .04 .01
❑ 364 Leslie O'Neal PB [illegible] [illegible]
❑ 365 Rufus Porter PB UER .04 .01
❑ 366 Andre Reed PB .10 .02
❑ 367 Johnny Rembert PB .04 .01
❑ 368 Reggie Roby PB .04 .01
❑ 369 Kevin Ross PB .04 .01
❑ 370 Webster Slaughter PB .04 .01
❑ 371 Bruce Smith PB .10 .02
❑ 372 Dennis Smith PB .04 .01
❑ 373 Derrick Thomas PB .10 .02
❑ 374 Thurman Thomas PB .25 .08
❑ 375 David Treadwell PB .04 .01
❑ 376 Lee Williams PB .04 .01
❑ 377 Rod Woodson PB .10 .02
❑ 378 Bud Carson CO PB .04 .01
❑ 379 Eric Allen PB .04 .01
❑ 380 Neal Anderson PB .10 .02
❑ 381 Jerry Ball PB .04 .01
❑ 382 Joey Browner PB .04 .01
❑ 383 Rich Camarillo PB .04 .01
❑ 384 Mark Carrier WR PB .04 .01
❑ 385 Roger Craig PB .10 .02
❑ 386A Randall Cunningham PB .50 .20
❑ 386B Randall Cunningham PB .50 .20
❑ 387 Chris Doleman PB .04 .01
❑ 388 Henry Ellard PB .04 .01
❑ 389 Bill Fralic PB .04 .01
❑ 390 Brent Fullwood PB .04 .01
❑ 391 Jerry Gray PB .04 .01
❑ 392 Kevin Greene PB .10 .02
❑ 393 Tim Harris PB .04 .01
❑ 394 Jay Hilgenberg PB .04 .01
❑ 395 Dalton Hilliard PB .04 .01
❑ 396 Keith Jackson PB .10 .02
❑ 397 Vaughan Johnson PB .04 .01
❑ 398 Steve Jordan PB .04 .01
❑ 399 Carl Lee PB .04 .01
❑ 400 Ronnie Lott PB .10 .02
❑ 401 Don Majkowski PB .04 .01
❑ 402 Charles Mann PB .04 .01
❑ 403 Randall McDaniel PB .04 .01
❑ 404 Tim McDonald PB .04 .01
❑ 405 Guy McIntyre PB .04 .01
❑ 406 Dave Meggett PB .04 .01
❑ 407 Keith Millard PB .04 .01
❑ 408 Joe Montana PB .50 .20
❑ 409 Eddie Murray PB .04 .01
❑ 410 Tom Newberry PB .04 .01
❑ 411 Jerry Rice PB .50 .20
❑ 412 Mark Rypien PB .04 .01
❑ 413 Barry Sanders PB .60 .25
❑ 414 Luis Sharpe PB .04 .01
❑ 415 Sterling Sharpe PB .04 .01
❑ 416 Mike Singletary PB .10 .02
❑ 417 Jackie Slater PB .04 .01
❑ 418 Doug Smith PB .04 .01
❑ 419 Chris Spielman PB .04 .01
❑ 420 Pat Swilling PB .04 .01
❑ 421 John Taylor PB .04 .01
❑ 422 Lawrence Taylor PB .10 .02
❑ 423 Reggie White PB .10 .02
❑ 424 Ron Wolfley PB .04 .01
❑ 425 Gary Zimmerman PB .04 .01
❑ 426 John Robinson CO PB .04 .01
❑ 427 Scott Case UER .04 .01
❑ 428 Mike Kenn .04 .01
❑ 429 Mike Gann .04 .01
❑ 430 Tim Green RC .04 .01
❑ 431 Michael Haynes RC .25 .08
❑ 432 Jessie Tuggle RC UER .04 .01
❑ 433 John Rade .04 .01
❑ 434 Andre Rison .25 .08
❑ 435 Don Beebe .10 .02
❑ 436 Ray Bentley .04 .01
❑ 437 Shane Conlan .04 .01
❑ 438 Kent Hull .04 .01
❑ 439 Pete Metzelaars .04 .01
❑ 440 Andre Reed UER .25 .08
❑ 441 Frank Reich FPSC .25 .08
❑ 442 Leon Seals RC .04 .01
❑ 443 Bruce Smith .25 .08
❑ 444 Thurman Thomas .25 .08
❑ 445 Will Wolford .04 .01
❑ 446 Trace Armstrong .04 .01
❑ 447 Mark Bortz RC .04 .01
❑ 448 Tom Thayer RC .04 .01
❑ 449A Dan Hampton ERR .50 .20
❑ 449B [illegible]
❑ 450 Shaun Gayle RC .04 .01
❑ 451 Dennis Gentry .04 .01
❑ 452 Jim Harbaugh .25 .08
❑ 453 Vestee Jackson .04 .01
❑ 454 Brad Muster .04 .01
❑ 455 William Perry .10 .02
❑ 456 Ron Rivera .04 .01
❑ 457 James Thornton .04 .01
❑ 458 Mike Tomczak .10 .02
❑ 459 Donnell Woolford .04 .01
❑ 460 Eric Ball .04 .01
❑ 461 James Brooks .10 .02
❑ 462 David Fulcher .04 .01
❑ 463 Boomer Esiason .10 .02
❑ 464 Rodney Holman .04 .01
❑ 465 Bruce Kozerski .04 .01
❑ 466 Tim Krumrie .04 .01
❑ 467 Anthony Munoz .10 .02
❑ 468 Brian Blados .04 .01
❑ 469 Mike Baab .04 .01
❑ 470 Brian Brennan .04 .01
❑ 471 Raymond Clayborn .04 .01
❑ 472 Mike Johnson .04 .01
❑ 473 Kevin Mack .04 .01
❑ 474 Clay Matthews .10 .02
❑ 475 Frank Minnifield .04 .01
❑ 476 Gregg Rakoczy RC .04 .01
❑ 477 Webster Slaughter .10 .02
❑ 478 James Dixon .04 .01
❑ 479 Robert Awalt UER .04 .01
❑ 480 Dennis McKinnon UER .04 .01
❑ 481 Danny Noonan .04 .01
❑ 482 Jesse Solomon .04 .01
❑ 483 Daniel Stubbs UER .04 .01
❑ 484 Steve Walsh .10 .02
❑ 485 Michael Brooks RC .04 .01
❑ 486 Mark Jackson .04 .01
❑ 487 Greg Kragen .04 .01
❑ 488 Ken Lanier RC .04 .01
❑ 489 Karl Mecklenburg .04 .01
❑ 490 Steve [illegible] .04 .01
❑ 491 Dennis Smith .04 .01
❑ 492 David Treadwell .04 .01
❑ 493 Michael Young RC .04 .01
❑ 494 Robert Clark RC .04 .01
❑ 495 Dennis Gibson .04 .01
❑ 496A Kevin Glover RC C/G .50 .20
❑ 496B Kevin Glover RC C .04 .01
❑ 497 Mel Gray .10 .02
❑ 498 Rodney Peete .10 .02
❑ 499 Dave Brown DB .04 .01
❑ 500 Jerry Holmes .04 .01
❑ 501 Chris Jacke .04 .01
❑ 502 Alan Veingrad .04 .01
❑ 503 Mark Lee .04 .01
❑ 504 Tony Mandarich .04 .01
❑ 505 Brian Noble .04 .01
❑ 506 Jeff Query .04 .01
❑ 507 Ken Ruettgers .04 .01
❑ 508 Patrick Allen .04 .01
❑ 509 Curtis Duncan .04 .01
❑ 510 William Fuller .10 .02
❑ 511 Haywood Jeffires RC .25 .08
❑ 512 Sean Jones .10 .02
❑ 513 Terry Kinard .04 .01
❑ 514 Bruce Matthews .10 .02
❑ 515 Gerald McNeil .04 .01
❑ 516 Greg Montgomery RC .04 .01
❑ 517 Warren Moon .25 .08
❑ 518 Mike Munchak .10 .02
❑ 519 Allen Pinkett .04 .01
❑ 520 Pat Beach .04 .01
❑ 521 Eugene Daniel .04 .01
❑ 522 Kevin Call .04 .01
❑ 523 Ray Donaldson .04 .01
❑ 524 Jeff Herrod RC .04 .01
❑ 525 Keith Taylor .04 .01
❑ 526 Jack Trudeau .04 .01
❑ 527 Deron Cherry .04 .01
❑ 528 Jeff Donaldson .04 .01
❑ 529 Albert Lewis .04 .01
❑ 530 Pete Mandley .04 .01
❑ 531 Chris Martin RC .04 .01
❑ 532 Christian Okoye .04 .01
❑ 533 Steve Pelluer .04 .01
❑ 534 Kevin Ross .04 .01
❑ 535 Dan Saleaumua .04 .01
❑ 536 Derrick Thomas .25 .08
❑ 537 Mike Webster .10 .02
❑ 538 Marcus Allen .25 .08
❑ 539 Greg Bell .04 .01
❑ 540 Thomas Benson .04 .01
❑ 541 Ron Brown .04 .01
❑ 542 Scott Davis .04 .01
❑ 543 Riki Ellison .04 .01
❑ 544 Jamie Holland .04 .01
❑ 545 Howie Long .25 .08
❑ 546 Terry McDaniel .04 .01
❑ 547 Max Montoya .04 .01
❑ 548 Jay Schroeder .04 .01
❑ 549 Lionel Washington .04 .01
❑ 550 Robert Delpino FPSC .04 .01
❑ 551 Bobby Humphery .04 .01
❑ 552 Mike Lansford .04 .01
❑ 553 Michael Stewart RC .04 .01
❑ 554 Doug Smith .04 .01
❑ 555 Curt Warner .04 .01
❑ 556 Alvin Wright RC .04 .01
❑ 557 Jeff Cross .04 .01
❑ 558 Jeff Dellenbach RC .04 .01
❑ 559 Mark Duper .10 .02
❑ 560 Ferrell Edmunds .04 .01
❑ 561 Tim McKyer .04 .01
❑ 562 John Offerdahl .04 .01
❑ 563 Reggie Roby .04 .01
❑ 564 Pete Stoyanovich .04 .01
❑ 565 Alfred Anderson .04 .01
❑ 566 Ray Berry .04 .01
❑ 567 Rick Fenney .04 .01
❑ 568 Rich Gannon RC 1.50 .60
❑ 569 Tim Irwin .04 .01
❑ 570 Hassan Jones .04 .01
❑ 571 Cris Carter .50 .20
❑ 572 Kirk Lowdermilk .04 .01
❑ 573 Reggie Rutland RC .04 .01
❑ 574 Ken Stills .04 .01
❑ 575 Bruce Armstrong .04 .01
❑ 576 Irving Fryar .10 .02
❑ 577 Roland James .04 .01
❑ 578 Robert Perryman .04 .01
❑ 579 Cedric Jones .04 .01
❑ 580 Steve Grogan .10 .02
❑ 581 Johnny Rembert .04 .01
❑ 582 Ed Reynolds .04 .01
❑ 583 Brent Williams .04 .01
❑ 584 Marc Wilson .04 .01
❑ 585 Hoby Brenner .04 .01
❑ 586 Stan Brock .04 .01
❑ 587 Jim Dombrowski RC .04 .01
❑ 588 Joel Hilgenberg RC .04 .01
❑ 589 Robert Massey .04 .01
❑ 590 Floyd Turner FPSC .04 .01
❑ 591 Ottis Anderson .10 .02
❑ 592 Mark Bavaro .04 .01
❑ 593 Maurice Carthon .04 .01
❑ 594 Eric Dorsey RC .04 .01
❑ 595 Myron Guyton .04 .01
❑ 596 Jeff Hostetler RC .25 .08
❑ 597 Sean Landeta .04 .01
❑ 598 Lionel Manuel .04 .01
❑ 599 Odessa Turner RC .04 .01
❑ 600 Perry Williams .04 .01
❑ 601 James Hasty .04 .01
❑ 602 Erik McMillan .04 .01
❑ 603 Alex Gordon UER .04 .01
❑ 604 Ron Stallworth .04 .01
❑ 605 Byron Evans RC .04 .01
❑ 606 Ron Heller RC OT .04 .01
❑ 607 Wes Hopkins .04 .01

No.	Card	Price	Price
❑ 608	Mickey Shuler UER	.04	.01
❑ 609	Seth Joyner	.10	.02
❑ 610	Jim McMahon	.10	.02
❑ 611	Mike Pitts	.04	.01
❑ 612	Izel Jenkins RC	.04	.01
❑ 613	Anthony Bell	.04	.01
❑ 614	David Galloway	.04	.01
❑ 615	Eric Hill	.04	.01
❑ 616	Cedric Mack	.04	.01
❑ 617	Freddie Joe Nunn	.04	.01
❑ 618	Tootie Robbins	.04	.01
❑ 619	Tom Tupa RC	.04	.01
❑ 620	Joe Wolf	.04	.01
❑ 621	Dermontti Dawson	.10	.02
❑ 622	Thomas Everett	.04	.01
❑ 623	Tunch Ilkin	.04	.01
❑ 624	Hardy Nickerson	.10	.02
❑ 625	Gerald Williams RC	.04	.01
❑ 626	Rod Woodson	.25	.08
❑ 627A	Rod Bernstine TE	.50	.20
❑ 627B	Rod Bernstine RB	.04	.01
❑ 628	Courtney Hall	.04	.01
❑ 629	Ronnie Harmon	.10	.02
❑ 630A	Anthony Miller WR	.25	.08
❑ 630B	Anthony Miller WR-KR	.10	.02
❑ 631	Joe Phillips	.04	.01
❑ 632A	Leslie O'Neal LB	.15	.05
❑ 632B	Leslie O'Neal COR	.10	.02
❑ 633A	David Richards RC G-T	.15	.05
❑ 633B	David Richards RC G	.15	.05
❑ 634	Mark Vlasic FPSC	.04	.01
❑ 635	Lee Williams	.04	.01
❑ 636	Chet Brooks	.04	.01
❑ 637	Keena Turner	.04	.01
❑ 638	Kevin Fagan RC	.04	.01
❑ 639	Brent Jones RC	.25	.08
❑ 640	Matt Millen	.10	.02
❑ 641	Bubba Paris	.04	.01
❑ 642	Bill Romanowski RC	1.00	.40
❑ 643	Fred Smerlas UER	.04	.01
❑ 644	Dave Waymer	.04	.01
❑ 645	Steve Young	.50	.20
❑ 646	Brian Blades	.10	.02
❑ 647	Andy Heck	.04	.01
❑ 648	Dave Krieg	.10	.02
❑ 649	Rufus Porter	.04	.01
❑ 650	Kelly Stouffer	.04	.01
❑ 651	Tony Woods	.04	.01
❑ 652	Gary Anderson RB	.04	.01
❑ 653	Reuben Davis	.04	.01
❑ 654	Randy Grimes	.04	.01
❑ 655	Ron Hall	.04	.01
❑ 656	Eugene Marve	.04	.01
❑ 657A	Curt Jarvis ERR	.50	.20
❑ 657B	Curt Jarvis COR	10.00	4.00
❑ 658	Ricky Reynolds	.04	.01
❑ 659	Broderick Thomas	.04	.01
❑ 660	Jeff Bostic	.04	.01
❑ 661	Todd Bowles RC	.04	.01
❑ 662	Ravin Caldwell	.04	.01
❑ 663	Russ Grimm UER	.04	.01
❑ 664	Joe Jacoby	.04	.01
❑ 665	Mark May	.04	.01
❑ 666	Walter Stanley	.04	.01
❑ 667	Don Warren	.04	.01
❑ 668	Stan Humphries RC	.25	.08
❑ 669A	Jeff George Illinois SP	1.00	.40
❑ 669B	Jeff George RC	.50	.20
❑ 670	Blair Thomas RC	.10	.02
❑ 671	Cortez Kennedy RC UER	.25	.08
❑ 672	Keith McCants RC	.04	.01
❑ 673	Junior Seau RC	1.25	.50
❑ 674	Mark Carrier RC DB	.25	.08
❑ 675	Andre Ware	.10	.02
❑ 676	Chris Singleton RC UER	.04	.01
❑ 677	Richmond Webb RC	.04	.01
❑ 678	Ray Agnew RC	.04	.01
❑ 679	Anthony Smith RC	.04	.01
❑ 680	James Francis RC	.04	.01
❑ 681	Percy Snow	.04	.01
❑ 682	Renaldo Turnbull RC	.04	.01
❑ 683	Lamar Lathon RC	.10	.02
❑ 684	James Williams DB RC	.04	.01
❑ 685	Emmitt Smith RC	5.00	2.00
❑ 686	Tony Bennett RC	.25	.08
❑ 687	Darrell Thompson RC	.04	.01
❑ 688	Steve Broussard RC	.04	.01
❑ 689	Eric Green RC	.10	.02
❑ 690	Ben Smith RC	.04	.01
❑ 691	Bern Brostek RC UER	.04	.01
❑ 692	Rodney Hampton RC	.25	.08
❑ 693	Dexter Carter RC	.04	.01
❑ 694	Rob Moore RC	.50	.20
❑ 695	Alexander Wright RC	.04	.01
❑ 696	Darion Conner RC	.10	.02
❑ 697	Reggie Rembert RC UER	.04	.01
❑ 698A	Terry Wooden RC 90	.50	.20
❑ 698B	Terry Wooden RC 51	.04	.01
❑ 699	Reggie Cobb RC	.04	.01
❑ 700	Anthony Thompson	.04	.01
❑ 701	Fred Washington RC	.04	.01
❑ 702	Ron Cox RC	.04	.01
❑ 703	Robert Blackmon RC	.04	.01
❑ 704	Dan Owens RC	.04	.01
❑ 705	Anthony Johnson RC	.25	.08
❑ 706	Aaron Wallace RC	.04	.01
❑ 707	Harold Green RC	.25	.08
❑ 708	Keith Sims RC	.04	.01
❑ 709	Tim Grunhard RC	.04	.01
❑ 710	Jeff Alm RC	.04	.01
❑ 711	Carwell Gardner RC	.04	.01
❑ 712	Kenny Davidson RC	.04	.01
❑ 713	Vince Buck RC	.04	.01
❑ 714	Leroy Hoard RC	.25	.08
❑ 715	Andre Collins RC	.04	.01
❑ 716	Dennis Brown RC	.04	.01
❑ 717	LeRoy Butler RC	.25	.08
❑ 718A	Pat Terrell RC 41	.50	.20
❑ 718B	Pat Terrell RC 37	.04	.01
❑ 719	Mike Bellamy RC	.04	.01
❑ 720	Mike Fox RC	.04	.01
❑ 721	Alton Montgomery RC	.04	.01
❑ 722	Eric Davis RC	.10	.02
❑ 723A	Oliver Barnett RC DT	.50	.20
❑ 723B	Oliver Barnett RC NT	.04	.01
❑ 724	Houston Hoover RC	.04	.01
❑ 725	Howard Ballard RC	.04	.01
❑ 726	Keith McKeller RC	.04	.01
❑ 727	Wendell Davis RC	.04	.01
❑ 728	Peter Tom Willis RC	.04	.01
❑ 729	Bernard Clark	.04	.01
❑ 730	Doug Widell RC	.04	.01
❑ 731	Eric Andolsek	.04	.01
❑ 732	Jeff Campbell RC	.04	.01
❑ 733	Marc Spindler RC	.04	.01
❑ 734	Keith Woodside	.04	.01
❑ 735	Willis Peguese RC	.04	.01
❑ 736	Frank Stams	.04	.01
❑ 737	Jeff Uhlenhake	.04	.01
❑ 738	Todd Kalis	.04	.01
❑ 739	Tommy Hodson RC UER	.04	.01
❑ 740	Greg McMurtry RC	.04	.01
❑ 741	Mike Buck RC	.04	.01
❑ 742	Kevin Haverdink UER	.04	.01
❑ 743A	Johnny Bailey RC 46	.10	.02
❑ 743B	Johnny Bailey RC 22	.10	.02
❑ 744A	Eric Moore	.15	.05
❑ 744B	Eric Moore	10.00	4.00
❑ 745	Tony Stargell RC	.04	.01
❑ 746	Fred Barnett RC	.25	.08
❑ 747	Walter Reeves	.04	.01
❑ 748	Derek Hill	.04	.01
❑ 749	Quinn Early	.25	.08
❑ 750	Ronald Lewis	.04	.01
❑ 751	Ken Clark RC	.04	.01
❑ 752	Garry Lewis RC	.04	.01
❑ 753	James Lofton	.10	.02
❑ 754	Steve Tasker UER	.25	.08
❑ 755	Jim Shofner CO	.04	.01
❑ 756	Jimmie Jones RC	.04	.01
❑ 757	Jay Novacek	.25	.08
❑ 758	Jessie Hester RC	.04	.01
❑ 759	Barry Word RC	.04	.01
❑ 760	Eddie Anderson RC	.04	.01
❑ 761	Cleveland Gary	.04	.01
❑ 762	Marcus Dupree RC	.04	.01
❑ 763	David Griggs RC	.04	.01
❑ 764	Rueben Mayes	.04	.01
❑ 765	Stephen Baker FPSC	.04	.01
❑ 766	Reyna Thompson RC UER	.04	.01
❑ 767	Everson Walls	.04	.01
❑ 768	Brad Baxter RC	.04	.01
❑ 769	Steve Walsh	.10	.02
❑ 770	Heath Sherman RC	.04	.01
❑ 771	Johnny Johnson RC	.10	.02
❑ 772A	Dexter Manley ERR	300.00	150.00
❑ 772B	Dexter Manley	.04	.01
❑ 773	Ricky Proehl RC	.25	.08
❑ 774	Frank Cornish	.04	.01
❑ 775	Tommy Kane RC	.04	.01
❑ 776	Derrick Fenner RC	.04	.01
❑ 777	Steve Christie RC	.04	.01
❑ 778	Wayne Haddix RC	.04	.01
❑ 779	Richard Williamson UER	.04	.01
❑ 780	Brian Mitchell RC	.25	.08
❑ 781	American Bowl/London	.04	.01
❑ 782	American Bowl/Berlin	.04	.01
❑ 783	American Bowl/Tokyo	.04	.01
❑ 784	American Bowl/Montreal	.04	.01
❑ 785A	Berlin Wall	.75	.30
❑ 785B	Berlin Wall	.75	.30
❑ 786	Al Davis NEWS	.04	.01
❑ 787	Falcons Back in Black	.04	.01
❑ 788	NFL Goes International	.04	.01
❑ 789	Overseas Appeal	.04	.01
❑ 790	Photo Contest	.04	.01
❑ 791	Photo Contest	.04	.01
❑ 792	Photo Contest	.04	.01
❑ 793	Photo Contest	.04	.01
❑ 794	Barry Sanders PHOTO	.50	.20
❑ 795	Photo Contest	.04	.01
❑ 796	Photo Contest	.04	.01
❑ 797	Photo Contest	.04	.01
❑ 798	Cris Carter PC	.04	.01
❑ 799	Ronnie Lott School	.10	.02
❑ 800D	Mark Carrier DB D-ROY	.10	.02
❑ 800O	Emmitt Smith O-ROY	1.50	.60
❑ 1990	Santa Claus SP	.50	.20
❑ CC2	Paul Tagliabue SP	.40	.15
❑ CC3	Joe Robbie Mem SP	.50	.20
❑ SC	Super Pro SP	.50	.20
❑ SC4	Fred Washington UER	.04	.01
❑ SP1	Payne Stewart SP	1.00	.40
❑ NNO	Lombardi HOLO/10000*	60.00	25.00
❑ NNO	Super Bowl XXIV Logo	.04	.01

1991 Pro Set

No.	Card	Price	Price
❑	COMPLETE SET (850)	20.00	8.00
❑	COMP.SERIES 1 (405)	8.00	3.00
❑	COMP.SERIES 2 (407)	8.00	3.00
❑	COMP.FINAL FACT. (38)	4.00	2.00
❑ 1D	Mark Carrier DB D-ROY	.10	.02
❑ 1O	Emmitt Smith O-ROY	1.25	.50
❑ 3	Joe Montana POY	.50	.20
❑ 4	Art Shell	.10	.02
❑ 5	Mike Singletary	.10	.02
❑ 6	Bruce Smith	.10	.02
❑ 7	Barry Word Comeback	.05	.01
❑ 8A	Jim Kelly LL w/LOGO	.25	.08
❑ 8B	Jim Kelly LL NO LOGO	.25	.08
❑ 8C	Jim Kelly LL Reg NO LOGO	6.00	3.00
❑ 9	Warren Moon LL	.10	.02
❑ 10	Barry Sanders LL	.50	.20
❑ 11	Jerry Rice LL	.40	.15
❑ 12	Jay Novacek	.10	.02
❑ 13	Thurman Thomas LL	.10	.02
❑ 14	Nick Lowery	.05	.01
❑ 15	Mike Horan	.05	.01
❑ 16	Clarence Verdin	.05	.01
❑ 17	Kevin Clark LL RC	.05	.01
❑ 18	Mark Carrier DB LL	.10	.02
❑ 19A	Derrick Thomas LL Bills	20.00	7.50
❑ 19B	Derrick Thomas LL COR	.10	.02

❑ 20 Ottis Anderson ML .10 .02
❑ 21 Roger Craig ML .10 .02
❑ 22 Art Monk ML .10 .02
❑ 23 Chuck Noll ML .10 .02
❑ 24 Randall Cunningham ML .10 .02
❑ 25 Dan Marino ML .50 .20
❑ 26 49ers Road Record ML .05 .01
❑ 27 Earl Campbell HOF .05 .01
❑ 28 John Hannah HOF .05 .01
❑ 29 Stan Jones HOF .05 .01
❑ 30 Tex Schramm HOF .05 .01
❑ 31 Jan Stenerud HOF .05 .01
❑ 32 Russell Maryland RC TW .10 .02
[illegible]
❑ 34 Darryll Lewis RC Thorpe .10 .02
❑ 35 Alfred Williams RC TW .05 .01
❑ 36 Rocket Ismail RC TW 1.00 .40
❑ 37 Ty Detmer RC HH .40 .15
❑ 38 Andre Ware Heisman .10 .02
❑ 39 Barry Sanders HH .50 .20
❑ 40 Tim Brown HH .10 .02
❑ 41 Vinny Testaverde HH .10 .02
❑ 42 Bo Jackson HH .30 .10
❑ 43 Mike Rozier HH .05 .01
❑ 44 Herschel Walker HH .10 .02
❑ 45 Marcus Allen HH .10 .02
❑ 46A James Lofton SB .10 .02
❑ 46B James Lofton SB .10 .02
❑ 47A Bruce Smith SB black ink .10 .02
❑ 47B Bruce Smith SB white ink .10 .02
❑ 48 Myron Guyton SB .05 .01
❑ 49 Stephen Baker SB .05 .01
❑ 50 Mark Ingram SB UER .05 .01
❑ 51 Ottis Anderson SB .10 .02
❑ 52 Thurman Thomas SB .25 .08
❑ 53 Matt Bahr SB .05 .01
❑ 54 Scott Norwood SB .05 .01
❑ 55 Stephen Baker .05 .01
❑ 56 Carl Banks .05 .01
❑ 57 Mark Collins .05 .01
❑ 58 Steve DeOssie .05 .01
❑ 59 Eric Dorsey .05 .01
❑ 60 John Elliott .05 .01
❑ 61 Myron Guyton .05 .01
❑ 62 Rodney Hampton .25 .08
❑ 63 Jeff Hostetler .10 .02
❑ 64 Erik Howard .05 .01
❑ 65 Mark Ingram .10 .02
❑ 66 Greg Jackson RC .05 .01
❑ 67 Leonard Marshall .05 .01
❑ 68 Dave Meggett .10 .02
❑ 69 Eric Moore .05 .01
❑ 70 Bart Oates .05 .01
❑ 71 Gary Reasons .05 .01
❑ 72 Bill Parcells CO .10 .02
❑ 73 Howard Ballard .05 .01
❑ 74A Corn.Bennett w/LOGO .25 .08
❑ 74B Corn.Bennett NO LOGO .05 .01
❑ 75 Shane Conlan .05 .01
❑ 76 Kent Hull .05 .01
❑ 77 Kirby Jackson RC .05 .01
❑ 78A Jim Kelly w/LOGO .60 .25
❑ 78B Jim Kelly NO LOGO .25 .08
❑ 79 Mark Kelso .05 .01
❑ 80 Nate Odomes .05 .01
❑ 81 Andre Reed .10 .02
❑ 82 Jim Ritcher .05 .01
❑ 83 Bruce Smith .25 .08
❑ 84 Darryl Talley .05 .01
❑ 85 Steve Tasker .10 .02
❑ 86 Thurman Thomas .25 .08
❑ 87 James Williams .05 .01
❑ 88 Will Wolford .05 .01
❑ 89 Jeff Wright RC UER .05 .01
❑ 90 Marv Levy CO .05 .01
❑ 91 Steve Broussard .05 .01
❑ 92A Darion Conner ERR '99 10.00 4.00
❑ 92B Darion Conner COR .25 .08
❑ 93 Bill Fralic .05 .01
❑ 94 Tim Green .05 .01
❑ 95 Michael Haynes .25 .08
❑ 96 Chris Hinton .05 .01
❑ 97 Chris Miller UER .10 .02
❑ 98 Deion Sanders UER .40 .15
❑ 99 Jerry Glanville CO .05 .01
❑ 100 Kevin Butler .05 .01
❑ 101 Mark Carrier DB .10 .02
❑ 102 Jim Covert .05 .01
❑ 103 Richard Dent .10 .02
❑ 104 Jim Harbaugh .25 .08
❑ 105 Brad Muster .05 .01
❑ 106 Lemuel Stinson .05 .01
❑ 107 Keith Van Horne .05 .01
❑ 108 Mike Ditka CO UER .25 .08
❑ 109 Lewis Billups .05 .01
❑ 110 James Brooks .10 .02
❑ 111 Boomer Esiason .10 .02
❑ 112 James Francis .05 .01
❑ 113 David Fulcher .05 .01
❑ 114 Rodney Holman .05 .01
[illegible]
❑ 116 Anthony Munoz .10 .02
❑ 117 Sam Wyche CO .05 .01
❑ 118 Paul Farren .05 .01
❑ 119 Thane Gash .05 .01
❑ 120 Mike Johnson .05 .01
❑ 121A Bernie Kosar w/LOGO .10 .02
❑ 121B Bernie Kosar NO LOGO .10 .02
❑ 122 Clay Matthews .10 .02
❑ 123 Eric Metcalf .10 .02
❑ 124 Frank Minnifield .05 .01
❑ 125A Webster Slaughter .10 .02
❑ 125B Webster Slaughter .10 .02
❑ 126 Bill Belichick CO RC 1.50 .60
❑ 127 Tommie Agee .05 .01
❑ 128 Troy Aikman .75 .30
❑ 129 Jack Del Rio .10 .02
❑ 130 John Gesek RC .05 .01
❑ 131 Issiac Holt .05 .01
❑ 132 Michael Irvin .25 .08
❑ 133 Ken Norton .10 .02
❑ 134 Daniel Stubbs .05 .01
❑ 135 Jimmy Johnson CO .10 .02
❑ 136 Steve Atwater .05 .01
❑ 137 Michael Brooks .05 .01
❑ 138 John Elway 1.25 .50
❑ 139 Wymon Henderson .05 .01
❑ 140 Bobby Humphrey .05 .01
❑ 141 Mark Jackson .05 .01
❑ 142 Karl Mecklenburg .05 .01
❑ 143 Doug Widell .05 .01
❑ 144 Dan Reeves CO .05 .01
❑ 145 Eric Andolsek .05 .01
❑ 146 Jerry Ball .05 .01
❑ 147 Bennie Blades .05 .01
❑ 148 Lomas Brown .05 .01
❑ 149 Robert Clark .05 .01
❑ 150 Michael Cofer .05 .01
❑ 151 Dan Owens .05 .01
❑ 152 Rodney Peete .10 .02
❑ 153 Wayne Fontes CO .05 .01
❑ 154 Tim Harris .05 .01
❑ 155 Johnny Holland .05 .01
❑ 156 Don Majkowski .05 .01
❑ 157 Tony Mandarich .05 .01
❑ 158 Mark Murphy .05 .01
❑ 159 Brian Noble .05 .01
❑ 160 Jeff Query .05 .01
❑ 161 Sterling Sharpe .25 .08
❑ 162 Lindy Infante CO .05 .01
❑ 163 Ray Childress .05 .01
❑ 164 Ernest Givins .10 .02
❑ 165 Richard Johnson CB .05 .01
❑ 166 Bruce Matthews .10 .02
❑ 167 Warren Moon .25 .08
❑ 168 Mike Munchak .10 .02
❑ 169 Al Smith .05 .01
❑ 170 Lorenzo White .05 .01
❑ 171 Jack Pardee CO .05 .01
❑ 172 Albert Bentley .05 .01
❑ 173 Duane Bickett .05 .01
❑ 174 Bill Brooks .05 .01
❑ 175A E.Dickerson w/LOGO .40 .15
❑ 175B E.Dickerson NO LOGO 667 1.25 .50
❑ 175C E.Dickerson NO LOGO 677 .25 .08
❑ 176 Ray Donaldson .05 .01
❑ 177 Jeff George .25 .08
❑ 178 Jeff Herrod .05 .01
❑ 179 Clarence Verdin .05 .01
❑ 180 Ron Meyer CO .05 .01
❑ 181 John Alt .05 .01
❑ 182 Steve DeBerg .05 .01
❑ 183 Albert Lewis .05 .01
❑ 184 Nick Lowery UER .05 .01
❑ 185 Christian Okoye .05 .01
❑ 186 Stephone Paige .05 .01
❑ 187 Kevin Porter .05 .01
❑ 188 Derrick Thomas .25 .08
❑ 189 Marty Schottenheimer CO .05 .01
❑ 190 Willie Gault .10 .02
❑ 191 Howie Long .25 .08
❑ 192 Terry McDaniel .05 .01
❑ 193 Jay Schroeder UER .05 .01
❑ 194 Steve Smith .05 .01
❑ 195 Greg Townsend .05 .01
❑ 196 Lionel Washington .05 .01
❑ 197 Steve Wisniewski UER .05 .01
[illegible]
❑ 199 Henry Ellard .10 .02
❑ 200 Jim Everett .10 .02
❑ 201 Jerry Gray .05 .01
❑ 202 Kevin Greene .10 .02
❑ 203 Buford McGee .05 .01
❑ 204 Tom Newberry .05 .01
❑ 205 Frank Stams .05 .01
❑ 206 Alvin Wright .05 .01
❑ 207 John Robinson CO .05 .01
❑ 208 Jeff Cross .05 .01
❑ 209 Mark Duper .10 .02
❑ 210 Dan Marino 1.25 .50
❑ 211A Tim McKyer .10 .02
❑ 211B Tim McKyer TR .25 .08
❑ 212 John Offerdahl .05 .01
❑ 213 Sammie Smith .05 .01
❑ 214 Richmond Webb .05 .01
❑ 215 Jarvis Williams .05 .01
❑ 216 Don Shula CO .10 .02
❑ 217A D.Fullington ERR .10 .02
❑ 217B D.Fullington COR .10 .02
❑ 218 Tim Irwin .05 .01
❑ 219 Mike Merriweather .05 .01
❑ 220 Keith Millard .05 .01
❑ 221 Al Noga .05 .01
❑ 222 Henry Thomas .05 .01
❑ 223 Wade Wilson .10 .02
❑ 224 Gary Zimmerman .05 .01
❑ 225 Jerry Burns CO .05 .01
❑ 226 Bruce Armstrong .05 .01
❑ 227 Marv Cook FPSC .05 .01
❑ 228 Hart Lee Dykes .05 .01
❑ 229 Tommy Hodson .05 .01
❑ 230 Ronnie Lippett .05 .01
❑ 231 Ed Reynolds .05 .01
❑ 232 Chris Singleton .05 .01
❑ 233 John Stephens .05 .01
❑ 234 Dick MacPherson CO .05 .01
❑ 235 Stan Brock .05 .01
❑ 236 Craig Heyward .10 .02
❑ 237 Vaughan Johnson .05 .01
❑ 238 Robert Massey .05 .01
❑ 239 Brett Maxie .05 .01
❑ 240 Rueben Mayes .05 .01
❑ 241 Pat Swilling .10 .02
❑ 242 Renaldo Turnbull .05 .01
❑ 243 Jim Mora CO .05 .01
❑ 244 Kyle Clifton .05 .01
❑ 245 Jeff Criswell .05 .01
❑ 246 James Hasty .05 .01
❑ 247 Erik McMillan .05 .01
❑ 248 Scott Mersereau RC .05 .01
❑ 249 Ken O'Brien .05 .01
❑ 250A Blair Thomas w/LOGO .25 .08
❑ 250B Blair Thomas NO LOGO .10 .02
❑ 251 Al Toon .10 .02
❑ 252 Bruce Coslet CO .05 .01
❑ 253 Eric Allen .05 .01
❑ 254 Fred Barnett .25 .08
❑ 255 Keith Byars .05 .01
❑ 256 Randall Cunningham .25 .08
❑ 257 Seth Joyner .10 .02
❑ 258 Clyde Simmons .05 .01
❑ 259 Jessie Small .05 .01
❑ 260 Andre Waters .05 .01
❑ 261 Rich Kotite CO .05 .01
❑ 262 Roy Green .05 .01
❑ 263 Ernie Jones .05 .01
❑ 264 Tim McDonald .05 .01
❑ 265 Timm Rosenbach .05 .01
❑ 266 Rod Saddler .05 .01
❑ 267 Luis Sharpe .05 .01
❑ 268 Anthony Thompson UER .05 .01

❑ 269 Marcus Turner RC .05 .01
❑ 270 Joe Bugel CO .05 .01
❑ 271 Gary Anderson K .05 .01
❑ 272 Dermontti Dawson .05 .01
❑ 273 Eric Green .05 .01
❑ 274 Merril Hoge .05 .01
❑ 275 Tunch Ilkin .05 .01
❑ 276 D.J. Johnson .05 .01
❑ 277 Louis Lipps .05 .01
❑ 278 Rod Woodson .25 .08
❑ 279 Chuck Noll CO .10 .02
❑ 280 Martin Bayless .05 .01
❑ 281 Marion Butts UER .10 .02
❑ 282 Gill Byrd .05 .01
❑ 283 Burt Grossman .05 .01
❑ 284 Courtney Hall .05 .01
❑ 285 Anthony Miller .10 .02
❑ 286 Leslie O'Neal .10 .02
❑ 287 Billy Joe Tolliver .05 .01
❑ 288 Dan Henning CO .05 .01
❑ 289 Dexter Carter .05 .01
❑ 290 Michael Carter .05 .01
❑ 291 Kevin Fagan .05 .01
❑ 292 Pierce Holt .05 .01
❑ 293 Guy McIntyre .05 .01
❑ 294 Tom Rathman .05 .01
❑ 295 John Taylor .10 .02
❑ 296 Steve Young .75 .30
❑ 297 George Seifert CO .10 .02
❑ 298 Brian Blades .10 .02
❑ 299 Jeff Bryant .05 .01
❑ 300 Norm Johnson .05 .01
❑ 301 Tommy Kane .05 .01
❑ 302 Cortez Kennedy UER .25 .08
❑ 303 Bryan Millard .05 .01
❑ 304 John L. Williams .05 .01
❑ 305 David Wyman .05 .01
❑ 306A Chuck Knox CO w/LOGO .05 .01
❑ 306B Chuck Knox CO NO LOGO .50 .20
❑ 307 Gary Anderson RB .05 .01
❑ 308 Reggie Cobb .05 .01
❑ 309 Randy Grimes .05 .01
❑ 310 Harry Hamilton .05 .01
❑ 311 Bruce Hill .05 .01
❑ 312 Eugene Marve .05 .01
❑ 313 Ervin Randle .05 .01
❑ 314 Vinny Testaverde .10 .02
❑ 315 Richard Williamson CO .05 .01
❑ 316 Earnest Byner .05 .01
❑ 317 Gary Clark .25 .08
❑ 318A Andre Collins .10 .02
❑ 318B Andre Collins .10 .02
❑ 319 Darryl Grant .05 .01
❑ 320 Chip Lohmiller .05 .01
❑ 321 Martin Mayhew .05 .01
❑ 322 Mark Rypien .10 .02
❑ 323 Alvin Walton .05 .01
❑ 324 Joe Gibbs CO UER .10 .02
❑ 325 Jerry Glanville REP .05 .01
❑ 326A J.Elway REP LOGO 4.00 2.00
❑ 326B J.Elway REP NO LOGO 2.00 .75
❑ 327 Boomer Esiason REP .05 .01
❑ 328A Steve Tasker REP 4.00 2.00
❑ 328B Steve Tasker REP 2.00 .75
❑ 329 Jerry Rice REP .40 .15
❑ 330 Jeff Rutledge REP .05 .01
❑ 331 K.C. Defense REP .05 .01
❑ 332 49ers Streak REP .05 .01
❑ 333 Monday Meeting REP .05 .01
❑ 334A R.Cunningham w/LOGO .05 .01
❑ 334B R.Cunningham NO LOGO .05 .01
❑ 335A Bo/Barry REP w/LOGO .50 .20
❑ 335B Bo/Barry REP NO LOGO .50 .20
❑ 336 Lawrence Taylor REP .25 .08
❑ 337 Warren Moon REP .25 .08
❑ 338 Alan Grant REP .05 .01
❑ 339 Todd McNair REP .05 .01
❑ 340A Miami Dolphins REP .05 .01
❑ 340B Miami Dolphins REP .05 .01
❑ 341A Highest Scoring REP 4.00 2.00
❑ 341B Highest Scoring REP 2.00 .75
❑ 342 Matt Bahr REP .05 .01
❑ 343 Robert Tisch NEW .05 .01
❑ 344 Sam Jankovich NEW .05 .01
❑ 345 In-the-Grasp NEW .05 .01
❑ 346 Bo Jackson NEW .10 .02
❑ 347 NFL Teacher of the .05 .01
❑ 348 Ronnie Lott NEW .10 .02
❑ 349 Super Bowl XXV .10 .02
❑ 350 Whitney Houston RC NEW .05 .01
❑ 351 U.S. Troops in .05 .01
❑ 352 Art McNally OFF .05 .01
❑ 353 Dick Jorgensen OFF .05 .01
❑ 354 Jerry Seeman OFF .05 .01
❑ 355 Jim Tunney OFF .05 .01
❑ 356 Gerry Austin OFF .05 .01
❑ 357 Gene Barth OFF .05 .01
❑ 358 Red Cashion OFF .05 .01
❑ 359 Tom Dooley OFF .05 .01
❑ 360 Johnny Grier OFF .05 .01
❑ 361 Pat Haggerty OFF .05 .01
❑ 362 Dale Hamer OFF .05 .01
❑ 363 Dick Hantak OFF .05 .01
❑ 364 Jerry Markbreit OFF .05 .01
❑ 365 Gordon McCarter OFF .05 .01
❑ 366 Bob McElwee OFF .05 .01
❑ 367 Howard Roe OFF .05 .01
❑ 368 Tom White OFF .05 .01
❑ 369 Norm Schachter OFF .05 .01
❑ 370A Warren Moon Crack .25 .08
❑ 370B Warren Moon Crack .25 .08
❑ 371A Boomer Esiason .50 .20
❑ 371B Boomer Esiason .10 .02
❑ 372A Troy Aikman Str.ST .40 .15
❑ 372B Troy Aikman Str.LT .40 .15
❑ 373A Carl Banks .50 .20
❑ 373B Carl Banks .05 .01
❑ 374A Jim Everett .50 .20
❑ 374B Jim Everett .10 .02
❑ 375A Anth.Munoz dificul .10 .02
❑ 375B Anth.Munoz dificil .10 .02
❑ 375C Anth.Munoz large type .10 .02
❑ 375D Anth.Munoz Quedate .10 .02
❑ 376A Ray Childress 1.25 .50
❑ 376B Ray Childress .05 .01
❑ 377A Charles Mann 1.25 .50
❑ 377B Charles Mann .05 .01
❑ 378A Jackie Slater 1.25 .50
❑ 378B Jackie Slater .05 .01
❑ 379 Jerry Rice PB .40 .15
❑ 380 Andre Rison PB .10 .02
❑ 381 Jim Lachey NFC .05 .01
❑ 382 Jackie Slater NFC .05 .01
❑ 383 Randall McDaniel NFC .05 .01
❑ 384 Mark Bortz NFC .05 .01
❑ 385 Jay Hilgenberg NFC .05 .01
❑ 386 Keith Jackson NFC .05 .01
❑ 387 Joe Montana PB .50 .20
❑ 388 Barry Sanders PB .50 .20
❑ 389 Neal Anderson NFC .05 .01
❑ 390 Reggie White NFC .25 .08
❑ 391 Chris Doleman NFC .05 .01
❑ 392 Jerome Brown NFC .05 .01
❑ 393 Charles Haley NFC .05 .01
❑ 394 Lawrence Taylor PB .25 .08
❑ 395 Pepper Johnson NFC .05 .01
❑ 396 Mike Singletary NFC .10 .02
❑ 397 Darrell Green NFC .05 .01
❑ 398 Carl Lee NFC .05 .01
❑ 399 Joey Browner NFC .05 .01
❑ 400 Ronnie Lott NFC .10 .02
❑ 401 Sean Landeta NFC .05 .01
❑ 402 Morten Andersen NFC .05 .01
❑ 403 Mel Gray NFC .05 .01
❑ 404 Reyna Thompson NFC .05 .01
❑ 405 Jimmy Johnson CO NFC .10 .02
❑ 406 Andre Reed AFC .10 .02
❑ 407 Anthony Miller AFC .10 .02
❑ 408 Anthony Munoz AFC .10 .02
❑ 409 Bruce Armstrong AFC .05 .01
❑ 410 Bruce Matthews AFC .05 .01
❑ 411 Mike Munchak AFC .05 .01
❑ 412 Kent Hull AFC .05 .01
❑ 413 Rodney Holman AFC .05 .01
❑ 414 Warren Moon PB .25 .08
❑ 415 Thurman Thomas PB .25 .08
❑ 416 Marion Butts AFC .10 .02
❑ 417 Bruce Smith AFC .10 .02
❑ 418 Greg Townsend AFC .05 .01
❑ 419 Ray Childress AFC .05 .01
❑ 420 Derrick Thomas PB .25 .08
❑ 421 Leslie O'Neal AFC .10 .02
❑ 422 John Offerdahl AFC .05 .01
❑ 423 Shane Conlan AFC .05 .01
❑ 424 Rod Woodson PB .25 .08
❑ 425 Albert Lewis AFC .05 .01
❑ 426 Steve Atwater AFC .05 .01
❑ 427 David Fulcher AFC .05 .01
❑ 428 Rohn Stark AFC .05 .01
❑ 429 Nick Lowery AFC .05 .01
❑ 430 Clarence Verdin AFC .05 .01
❑ 431 Steve Tasker AFC .05 .01
❑ 432 Art Shell CO AFC .10 .02
❑ 433 Scott Case .05 .01
❑ 434 Tory Epps UER .05 .01
❑ 435 Mike Gann UER .05 .01
❑ 436 Brian Jordan FPSC UER .10 .02
❑ 437 Mike Kenn .05 .01
❑ 438 John Rade .05 .01
❑ 439 Andre Rison .10 .02
❑ 440 Mike Rozier .05 .01
❑ 441 Jessie Tuggle .05 .01
❑ 442 Don Beebe .05 .01
❑ 443 John Davis RC .05 .01
❑ 444 James Lofton .10 .02
❑ 445 Keith McKeller .05 .01
❑ 446 Jamie Mueller .05 .01
❑ 447 Scott Norwood .05 .01
❑ 448 Frank Reich .10 .02
❑ 449 Leon Seals .05 .01
❑ 450 Leonard Smith .05 .01
❑ 451 Neal Anderson .10 .02
❑ 452 Trace Armstrong .05 .01
❑ 453 Mark Bortz .05 .01
❑ 454 Wendell Davis .05 .01
❑ 455 Shaun Gayle .05 .01
❑ 456 Jay Hilgenberg .05 .01
❑ 457 Steve McMichael .10 .02
❑ 458 Mike Singletary .10 .02
❑ 459 Donnell Woolford .05 .01
❑ 460 Jim Breech .05 .01
❑ 461 Eddie Brown .05 .01
❑ 462 Barney Bussey RC .05 .01
❑ 463 Bruce Kozerski .05 .01
❑ 464 Tim Krumrie .05 .01
❑ 465 Bruce Reimers .05 .01
❑ 466 Kevin Walker RC .05 .01
❑ 467 Ickey Woods .05 .01
❑ 468 Carl Zander UER .05 .01
❑ 469 Mike Baab .05 .01
❑ 470 Brian Brennan .05 .01
❑ 471 Rob Burnett RC .10 .02
❑ 472 Raymond Clayborn .05 .01
❑ 473 Reggie Langhorne .05 .01
❑ 474 Kevin Mack .05 .01
❑ 475 Anthony Pleasant .05 .01
❑ 476 Joe Morris .05 .01
❑ 477 Dan Fike .05 .01
❑ 478 Ray Horton .05 .01
❑ 479 Jim Jeffcoat .05 .01
❑ 480 Jimmie Jones .05 .01
❑ 481 Kelvin Martin .05 .01
❑ 482 Nate Newton .10 .02
❑ 483 Danny Noonan .05 .01
❑ 484 Jay Novacek .25 .08
❑ 485 Emmitt Smith 2.50 1.00
❑ 486 James Washington RC .05 .01
❑ 487 Simon Fletcher .05 .01
❑ 488 Ron Holmes .05 .01
❑ 489 Mike Horan .05 .01
❑ 490 Vance Johnson .05 .01
❑ 491 Keith Kartz .05 .01
❑ 492 Greg Kragen .05 .01
❑ 493 Ken Lanier .05 .01
❑ 494 Warren Powers .05 .01
❑ 495 Dennis Smith .05 .01
❑ 496 Jeff Campbell .05 .01
❑ 497 Ken Dallafior .05 .01
❑ 498 Dennis Gibson .05 .01
❑ 499 Kevin Glover .05 .01
❑ 500 Mel Gray .10 .02
❑ 501 Eddie Murray .05 .01
❑ 502 Barry Sanders 1.25 .50
❑ 503 Chris Spielman .10 .02
❑ 504 William White .05 .01
❑ 505 Matt Brock RC .05 .01
❑ 506 Robert Brown .05 .01
❑ 507 LeRoy Butler .10 .02
❑ 508 James Campen RC .05 .01
❑ 509 Jerry Holmes .05 .01
❑ 510 Perry Kemp .05 .01

❑ 511 Ken Ruettgers .05 .01
❑ 512 Scott Stephen RC .05 .01
❑ 513 Ed West .05 .01
❑ 514 Cris Dishman RC .05 .01
❑ 515 Curtis Duncan .05 .01
❑ 516 Drew Hill UER .05 .01
❑ 517 Haywood Jeffires .10 .02
❑ 518 Sean Jones .10 .02
❑ 519 Lamar Lathon .05 .01
❑ 520 Don Maggs .05 .01
❑ 521 Bubba McDowell .05 .01
❑ 522 Johnny Meads .05 .01
❑ 523A Chip Banks ERR No Text .50 .20
❑ 523B Chip Banks COR .05 .01
❑ 524 Pat Beach .05 .01
❑ 525 Sam Clancy .05 .01
❑ 526 Eugene Daniel .05 .01
❑ 527 Jon Hand .05 .01
❑ 528 Jessie Hester .05 .01
❑ 529A Mike Prior ERR No Text .50 .20
❑ 529B Mike Prior COR .05 .01
❑ 530 Keith Taylor .05 .01
❑ 531 Donnell Thompson .05 .01
❑ 532 Dino Hackett .05 .01
❑ 533 David Lutz RC .05 .01
❑ 534 Chris Martin .05 .01
❑ 535 Kevin Ross .05 .01
❑ 536 Dan Saleaumua .05 .01
❑ 537 Neil Smith .25 .08
❑ 538 Percy Snow .05 .01
❑ 539 Robb Thomas .05 .01
❑ 540 Barry Word .05 .01
❑ 541 Marcus Allen .25 .08
❑ 542 Eddie Anderson .05 .01
❑ 543 Scott Davis .05 .01
❑ 544 Mervyn Fernandez .05 .01
❑ 545 Ethan Horton .05 .01
❑ 546 Ronnie Lott .10 .02
❑ 547 Don Mosebar .05 .01
❑ 548 Jerry Robinson .05 .01
❑ 549 Aaron Wallace .05 .01
❑ 550 Flipper Anderson .05 .01
❑ 551 Cleveland Gary .05 .01
❑ 552 Damone Johnson RC .05 .01
❑ 553 Duval Love RC .05 .01
❑ 554 Irv Pankey .05 .01
❑ 555 Mike Piel .05 .01
❑ 556 Jackie Slater .05 .01
❑ 557 Michael Stewart .05 .01
❑ 558 Pat Terrell .05 .01
❑ 559 J.B. Brown .05 .01
❑ 560 Mark Clayton .10 .02
❑ 561 Ferrell Edmunds .05 .01
❑ 562 Harry Galbreath .05 .01
❑ 563 David Griggs .05 .01
❑ 564 Jim C. Jensen .05 .01
❑ 565 Louis Oliver .05 .01
❑ 566 Tony Paige .05 .01
❑ 567 Keith Sims .05 .01
❑ 568 Joey Browner .05 .01
❑ 569 Anthony Carter .10 .02
❑ 570 Chris Doleman .05 .01
❑ 571 Rich Gannon UER .25 .08
❑ 572 Hassan Jones .05 .01
❑ 573 Steve Jordan .05 .01
❑ 574 Carl Lee .05 .01
❑ 575 Randall McDaniel .05 .01
❑ 576 Herschel Walker .10 .02
❑ 577 Ray Agnew .05 .01
❑ 578 Vincent Brown .05 .01
❑ 579 Irving Fryar .10 .02
❑ 580 Tim Goad .05 .01
❑ 581 Maurice Hurst .05 .01
❑ 582 Fred Marion .05 .01
❑ 583 Johnny Rembert .05 .01
❑ 584 Andre Tippett .05 .01
❑ 585 Brent Williams .05 .01
❑ 586 Morten Andersen .05 .01
❑ 587 Toi Cook RC .05 .01
❑ 588 Jim Dombrowski .05 .01
❑ 589 Dalton Hilliard .05 .01
❑ 590 Rickey Jackson .05 .01
❑ 591 Eric Martin .05 .01
❑ 592 Sam Mills .05 .01
❑ 593 Bobby Hebert .05 .01
❑ 594 Steve Walsh .05 .01
❑ 595 Ottis Anderson .10 .02
❑ 596 Pepper Johnson .05 .01
❑ 597 Bob Kratch RC .05 .01
❑ 598 Sean Landeta .05 .01
❑ 599 Doug Riesenberg .05 .01
❑ 600 William Roberts .05 .01
❑ 601 Phil Simms .10 .02
❑ 602 Lawrence Taylor .25 .08
❑ 603 Everson Walls .05 .01
❑ 604 Brad Baxter .05 .01
❑ 605 Dennis Byrd .05 .01
❑ 606 Jeff Lageman .05 .01
❑ 607 Pat Leahy .05 .01
❑ 608 Rob Moore .25 .08
❑ 609 Joe Mott .05 .01
❑ 610 Tony Stargell .05 .01
❑ 611 Brian Washington .05 .01
❑ 612 Marvin Washington RC .05 .01
❑ 613 David Alexander .05 .01
❑ 614 Jerome Brown .05 .01
❑ 615 Byron Evans .05 .01
❑ 616 Ron Heller .05 .01
❑ 617 Wes Hopkins .05 .01
❑ 618 Keith Jackson .10 .02
❑ 619 Heath Sherman .05 .01
❑ 620 Reggie White .25 .08
❑ 621 Calvin Williams .10 .02
❑ 622 Ken Harvey .10 .02
❑ 623 Eric Hill .05 .01
❑ 624 Johnny Johnson .05 .01
❑ 625 Freddie Joe Nunn .05 .01
❑ 626 Ricky Proehl .05 .01
❑ 627 Tootie Robbins .05 .01
❑ 628 Jay Taylor .05 .01
❑ 629 Tom Tupa .05 .01
❑ 630 Jim Wahler RC .05 .01
❑ 631 Bubby Brister .05 .01
❑ 632 Thomas Everett .05 .01
❑ 633 Bryan Hinkle .05 .01
❑ 634 Carnell Lake .05 .01
❑ 635 David Little .05 .01
❑ 636 Hardy Nickerson .10 .02
❑ 637 Gerald Williams .05 .01
❑ 638 Keith Willis .05 .01
❑ 639 Tim Worley .05 .01
❑ 640 Rod Bernstine .05 .01
❑ 641 Frank Cornish .05 .01
❑ 642 Gary Plummer .05 .01
❑ 643 Henry Rolling RC .05 .01
❑ 644 Sam Seale .05 .01
❑ 645 Junior Seau .25 .08
❑ 646 Billy Ray Smith .05 .01
❑ 647 Broderick Thompson .05 .01
❑ 648 Derrick Walker RC .05 .01
❑ 649 Todd Bowles .05 .01
❑ 650 Don Griffin .05 .01
❑ 651 Charles Haley .10 .02
❑ 652 Brent Jones UER .10 .02
❑ 653 Joe Montana 1.25 .50
❑ 654 Jerry Rice .75 .30
❑ 655 Bill Romanowski .05 .01
❑ 656 Michael Walter .05 .01
❑ 657 Dave Waymer .05 .01
❑ 658 Jeff Chadwick .05 .01
❑ 659 Derrick Fenner .05 .01
❑ 660 Nesby Glasgow .05 .01
❑ 661 Jacob Green .05 .01
❑ 662 Dwayne Harper RC .05 .01
❑ 663 Andy Heck .05 .01
❑ 664 Dave Krieg .10 .02
❑ 665 Rufus Porter .05 .01
❑ 666 Eugene Robinson .05 .01
❑ 667 Mark Carrier WR .25 .08
❑ 668 Steve Christie .05 .01
❑ 669 Reuben Davis .05 .01
❑ 670 Paul Gruber .05 .01
❑ 671 Wayne Haddix .05 .01
❑ 672 Ron Hall .05 .01
❑ 673 Keith McCants UER .05 .01
❑ 674 Ricky Reynolds .05 .01
❑ 675 Mark Robinson .05 .01
❑ 676 Jeff Bostic .05 .01
❑ 677 Darrell Green .05 .01
❑ 678 Markus Koch .05 .01
❑ 679 Jim Lachey .05 .01
❑ 680 Charles Mann .05 .01
❑ 681 Wilber Marshall .05 .01
❑ 682 Art Monk .10 .02
❑ 683 Gerald Riggs .05 .01
❑ 684 Ricky Sanders .05 .01
❑ 685 Ray Handley NEW .05 .01
❑ 686 NFL announces NEW .05 .01
❑ 687 Miami gets NEW .05 .01
❑ 688 Giants' George Young NEW .05 .01
❑ 689 Five-millionth fan NEW .05 .01
❑ 690 Sports Illustrated NEW .05 .01
❑ 691 American Bowl NEW .05 .01
❑ 692 American Bowl NEW .05 .01
❑ 693 American Bowl NEW .05 .01
❑ 694A Russell Maryland .25 .08
❑ 694B Joe Ferguson LEG .05 .01
❑ 695 Carl Hairston LEG .10 .02
❑ 696 Dan Hampton LEG .10 .02
❑ 697 Mike Haynes LEG .05 .01
❑ 698 Marty Lyons LEG .05 .01
❑ 699 Ozzie Newsome LEGEND .10 .02
❑ 700 Scott Studwell LEG .05 .01
❑ 701 Mike Webster LEG .05 .01
❑ 702 Dwayne Woodruff LEG .05 .01
❑ 703 Larry Kennan CO .05 .01
❑ 704 Stan Gelbaugh RC LL .10 .02
❑ 705 John Brantley LL .05 .01
❑ 706 Danny Lockett LL .05 .01
❑ 707 Anthony Parker RC LL .10 .02
❑ 708 Dan Crossman LL .05 .01
❑ 709 Eric Wilkerson LL .05 .01
❑ 710 Judd Garrett RC LL .05 .01
❑ 711 Tony Baker LL .05 .01
❑ 712 Ran.Cunningham PHOTO .05 .01
❑ 713 2nd Place BW PHOTO .05 .01
❑ 714 3rd Place BW PHOTO .05 .01
❑ 715 1st Place Color PHOTO .05 .01
❑ 716 2nd Place Color PHOTO .05 .01
❑ 717 3rd Place Color PHOTO .05 .01
❑ 718 1st Place Color PHOTO .05 .01
❑ 719 2nd Place Color PHOTO .05 .01
❑ 720 3rd Place Color PHOTO .05 .01
❑ 721 Ray Bentley .05 .01
❑ 722 Earnest Byner .05 .01
❑ 723 Bill Fralic .05 .01
❑ 724 Joe Jacoby .05 .01
❑ 725 Howie Long .25 .08
❑ 726 Dan Marino THINK .50 .20
❑ 727 Ron Rivera .05 .01
❑ 728 Mike Singletary .10 .02
❑ 729 Cornelius Bennett .10 .02
❑ 730 Russell Maryland .25 .08
❑ 731 Eric Turner RC .10 .02
❑ 732 Bruce Pickens RC UER .05 .01
❑ 733 Mike Croel RC .05 .01
❑ 734 Todd Lyght RC .05 .01
❑ 735 Eric Swann RC .25 .08
❑ 736 Charles McRae RC .05 .01
❑ 737 Antone Davis RC .05 .01
❑ 738 Stanley Richard RC .05 .01
❑ 739 Herman Moore RC .25 .08
❑ 740 Pat Harlow RC .05 .01
❑ 741 Alvin Harper RC .25 .08
❑ 742 Mike Pritchard RC .25 .08
❑ 743 Leonard Russell RC .25 .08
❑ 744 Huey Richardson RC .05 .01
❑ 745 Dan McGwire RC .05 .01
❑ 746 Bobby Wilson RC .05 .01
❑ 747 Alfred Williams .05 .01
❑ 748 Vinnie Clark RC .05 .01
❑ 749 Kelvin Pritchett RC .10 .02
❑ 750 Harvey Williams RC .25 .08
❑ 751 Stan Thomas .05 .01
❑ 752 Randal Hill RC .10 .02
❑ 753 Todd Marinovich RC .05 .01
❑ 754 Ted Washington RC .05 .01
❑ 755 Henry Jones RC .10 .02
❑ 756 Jarrod Bunch RC .05 .01
❑ 757 Mike Dumas RC .05 .01
❑ 758 Ed King RC .05 .01
❑ 759 Reggie Johnson RC .05 .01
❑ 760 Roman Phifer RC .05 .01
❑ 761 Mike Jones DE RC .05 .01
❑ 762 Brett Favre RC 8.00 3.00
❑ 763 Browning Nagle RC .05 .01
❑ 764 Esera Tuaolo RC .05 .01
❑ 765 George Thornton RC .05 .01
❑ 766 Dixon Edwards RC .05 .01
❑ 767 Darryll Lewis .10 .02
❑ 768 Eric Bieniemy RC .05 .01

- ❑ 769 Shane Curry .05 .01
- ❑ 770 Jerome Henderson RC .05 .01
- ❑ 771 Wesley Carroll RC .05 .01
- ❑ 772 Nick Bell RC .05 .01
- ❑ 773 John Flannery RC .05 .01
- ❑ 774 Ricky Watters RC 1.50 .60
- ❑ 775 Jeff Graham RC WR .25 .08
- ❑ 776 Eric Moten RC .05 .01
- ❑ 777 Jesse Campbell RC .05 .01
- ❑ 778 Chris Zorich .10 .02
- ❑ 779 Joe Valerio .05 .01
- ❑ 780 Doug Thomas RC .05 .01
- ❑ 781 Lamar Rogers RC UER .05 .01
- ❑ 782 John Johnson RC .05 .01
- ❑ 783 Phil Hansen RC .05 .01
- ❑ 784 Kanavis McGhee RC .05 .01
- ❑ 785 Calvin Stephens RC UER .05 .01
- ❑ 786 James Jones RC DT .05 .01
- ❑ 787 Reggie Barrett .05 .01
- ❑ 788 Aeneas Williams RC .25 .08
- ❑ 789 Aaron Craver RC .05 .01
- ❑ 790 Keith Traylor RC .05 .01
- ❑ 791 Godfrey Myles RC .05 .01
- ❑ 792 Mo Lewis RC .10 .02
- ❑ 793 James Richard RC .05 .01
- ❑ 794 Carlos Jenkins RC .05 .01
- ❑ 795 Lawrence Dawsey RC .10 .02
- ❑ 796 Don Davey .05 .01
- ❑ 797 Jake Reed RC .50 .20
- ❑ 798 Dave McCloughan .05 .01
- ❑ 799 Erik Williams RC .10 .02
- ❑ 800 Steve Jackson RC .05 .01
- ❑ 801 Bob Dahl .05 .01
- ❑ 802 Ernie Mills RC .10 .02
- ❑ 803 David Daniels RC .05 .01
- ❑ 804 Rob Selby RC .05 .01
- ❑ 805 Ricky Ervins RC .10 .02
- ❑ 806 Tim Barnett RC .05 .01
- ❑ 807 Chris Gardocki RC .25 .08
- ❑ 808 Kevin Donnalley RC .05 .01
- ❑ 809 Robert Wilson RC .05 .01
- ❑ 810 Chuck Webb RC .05 .01
- ❑ 811 Darryl Wren RC .05 .01
- ❑ 812 Ed McCaffrey RC 2.00 .75
- ❑ 813 Shula's 300th Victory .05 .01
- ❑ 814 Raiders-49ers sell .05 .01
- ❑ 815 NFL International NEWS .05 .01
- ❑ 816 Moe Gardner RC .05 .01
- ❑ 817 Tim McKyer .05 .01
- ❑ 818 Tom Waddle RC .05 .01
- ❑ 819 Michael Jackson RC WR .25 .08
- ❑ 820 Tony Casillas .05 .01
- ❑ 821 Gaston Green .05 .01
- ❑ 822 Kenny Walker RC .05 .01
- ❑ 823 Willie Green RC .05 .01
- ❑ 824 Erik Kramer RC .25 .08
- ❑ 825 William Fuller .10 .02
- ❑ 826 Allen Pinkett .05 .01
- ❑ 827 Rick Venturi CO .05 .01
- ❑ 828 Bill Maas .05 .01
- ❑ 829 Jeff Jaeger .05 .01
- ❑ 830 Robert Delpino .05 .01
- ❑ 831 Mark Higgs RC .05 .01
- ❑ 832 Reggie Roby .05 .01
- ❑ 833 Terry Allen RC 1.50 .60
- ❑ 834 Cris Carter .50 .20
- ❑ 835 John Randle RC .60 .25
- ❑ 836 Hugh Millen RC .05 .01
- ❑ 837 Jon Vaughn RC .05 .01
- ❑ 838 Gill Fenerty .05 .01
- ❑ 839 Floyd Turner .05 .01
- ❑ 840 Irv Eatman .05 .01
- ❑ 841 Lonnie Young .05 .01
- ❑ 842 Jim McMahon .10 .02
- ❑ 843 Randal Hill .05 .01
- ❑ 844 Barry Foster FPSC .10 .02
- ❑ 845 Neil O'Donnell RC .25 .08
- ❑ 846 John Friesz FPSC .25 .08
- ❑ 847 Broderick Thomas .05 .01
- ❑ 848 Brian Mitchell .10 .02
- ❑ 849 Mike Utley RC .10 .02
- ❑ 850 Mike Croel ROY .05 .01
- ❑ SC1 SB XXVI Theme Art .25 .08
- ❑ SC3 Jim Thorpe Pioneer .75 .30
- ❑ SC4 Otto Graham Pioneer .75 .30
- ❑ SC5 Paul Brown Pioneer .75 .30
- ❑ PSS1 Walter Payton .50 .20
- ❑ PSS2 Red Grange .50 .20
- ❑ MVPC25 Ottis Anderson .25 .08
- ❑ AU336 L.Taylor REP AU/500 175.00 100.00
- ❑ AU394 L.Taylor PB AU/500 175.00 100.00
- ❑ AU699 O.Newsome AU/500 50.00 25.00
- ❑ AU824 Erik Kramer AU 50.00 25.00
- ❑ NNO Mini Pro Set Gazette .25 .08
- ❑ NNO Pro Set Gazette .25 .08
- ❑ NNO Santa Claus .50 .20
- ❑ NNO Super Bowl XXV Art .25 .08
- ❑ NNO Super Bowl XXV Logo .25 .08

1991 Pro Set Platinum

- ❑ COMPLETE SET (315) 10.00 5.00
- ❑ COMP.SERIES 1 (150) 4.00 2.00
- ❑ COMP.SERIES 2 (165) 6.00 3.00
- ❑ 1 Chris Miller .10 .02
- ❑ 2 Andre Rison .25 .08
- ❑ 3 Tim Green .05 .01
- ❑ 4 Jessie Tuggle .05 .01
- ❑ 5 Thurman Thomas .25 .08
- ❑ 6 Darryl Talley .05 .01
- ❑ 7 Kent Hull .05 .01
- ❑ 8 Bruce Smith .25 .08
- ❑ 9 Shane Conlan .05 .01
- ❑ 10 Jim Harbaugh .25 .08
- ❑ 11 Neal Anderson .10 .02
- ❑ 12 Mark Bortz .05 .01
- ❑ 13 Richard Dent .10 .02
- ❑ 14 Steve McMichael .05 .01
- ❑ 15 James Brooks .05 .01
- ❑ 16 Boomer Esiason .10 .02
- ❑ 17 Tim Krumrie .05 .01
- ❑ 18 James Francis .05 .01
- ❑ 19 Lewis Billups .05 .01
- ❑ 20 Eric Metcalf .25 .08
- ❑ 21 Kevin Mack .05 .01
- ❑ 22 Clay Matthews .10 .02
- ❑ 23 Mike Johnson .05 .01
- ❑ 24 Troy Aikman .75 .30
- ❑ 25 Emmitt Smith 2.50 1.00
- ❑ 26 Daniel Stubbs .05 .01
- ❑ 27 Ken Norton .10 .02
- ❑ 28 John Elway 1.25 .50
- ❑ 29 Bobby Humphrey .05 .01
- ❑ 30 Simon Fletcher .05 .01
- ❑ 31 Karl Mecklenburg .05 .01
- ❑ 32 Rodney Peete .10 .02
- ❑ 33 Barry Sanders 1.25 .50
- ❑ 34 Michael Cofer .05 .01
- ❑ 35 Jerry Ball .05 .01
- ❑ 36 Sterling Sharpe .25 .08
- ❑ 37 Tony Mandarich .05 .01
- ❑ 38 Brian Noble .05 .01
- ❑ 39 Tim Harris .05 .01
- ❑ 40 Warren Moon .10 .02
- ❑ 41 Ernest Givins UER .10 .02
- ❑ 42 Mike Munchak .10 .02
- ❑ 43 Sean Jones .10 .02
- ❑ 44 Ray Childress .10 .02
- ❑ 45 Jeff George .25 .08
- ❑ 46 Albert Bentley .05 .01
- ❑ 47 Duane Bickett .05 .01
- ❑ 48 Steve DeBerg .10 .02
- ❑ 49 Christian Okoye .10 .02
- ❑ 50 Neil Smith .25 .08
- ❑ 51 Derrick Thomas .25 .08
- ❑ 52 Willie Gault .10 .02
- ❑ 53 Don Mosebar .05 .01
- ❑ 54 Howie Long .25 .08
- ❑ 55 Greg Townsend .05 .01
- ❑ 56 Terry McDaniel .10 .02
- ❑ 57 Jackie Slater .05 .01
- ❑ 58 Jim Everett .10 .02
- ❑ 59 Cleveland Gary .05 .01
- ❑ 60 Mike Piel .05 .01
- ❑ 61 Jerry Gray .05 .01
- ❑ 62 Dan Marino 1.25 .50
- ❑ 63 Sammie Smith .05 .01
- ❑ 64 Richmond Webb .05 .01
- ❑ 65 Louis Oliver .05 .01
- ❑ 66 Ferrell Edmunds .05 .01
- ❑ 67 Jeff Cross .05 .01
- ❑ 68 Wade Wilson .05 .01
- ❑ 69 Chris Doleman .10 .02
- ❑ 70 Joey Browner .05 .01
- ❑ 71 Keith Millard .05 .01
- ❑ 72 John Stephens .05 .01
- ❑ 73 Andre Tippett .05 .01
- ❑ 74 Brent Williams .05 .01
- ❑ 75 Craig Heyward .10 .02
- ❑ 76 Eric Martin .05 .01
- ❑ 77 Pat Swilling .10 .02
- ❑ 78 Sam Mills .10 .02
- ❑ 79 Jeff Hostetler .10 .02
- ❑ 80 Ottis Anderson .10 .02
- ❑ 81 Lawrence Taylor .25 .08
- ❑ 82 Pepper Johnson .05 .01
- ❑ 83 Blair Thomas .05 .01
- ❑ 84 Al Toon .10 .02
- ❑ 85 Ken O'Brien .05 .01
- ❑ 86 Erik McMillan .05 .01
- ❑ 87 Dennis Byrd .10 .02
- ❑ 88 Randall Cunningham .25 .08
- ❑ 89 Fred Barnett .25 .08
- ❑ 90 Seth Joyner .10 .02
- ❑ 91 Reggie White .25 .08
- ❑ 92 Timm Rosenbach .05 .01
- ❑ 93 Johnny Johnson .05 .01
- ❑ 94 Tim McDonald .05 .01
- ❑ 95 Freddie Joe Nunn .05 .01
- ❑ 96 Bubby Brister .10 .02
- ❑ 97 Gary Anderson K UER .05 .01
- ❑ 98 Merril Hoge .05 .01
- ❑ 99 Keith Willis .05 .01
- ❑ 100 Rod Woodson .25 .08
- ❑ 101 Billy Joe Tolliver .05 .01
- ❑ 102 Marion Butts .10 .02
- ❑ 103 Rod Bernstine .05 .01
- ❑ 104 Lee Williams .05 .01
- ❑ 105 Burt Grossman UER .05 .01
- ❑ 106 Tom Rathman .05 .01
- ❑ 107 John Taylor .10 .02
- ❑ 108 Michael Carter .05 .01
- ❑ 109 Guy McIntyre .05 .01
- ❑ 110 Pierce Holt .05 .01
- ❑ 111 John L. Williams .05 .01
- ❑ 112 Dave Krieg .10 .02
- ❑ 113 Bryan Millard .05 .01
- ❑ 114 Cortez Kennedy .25 .08
- ❑ 115 Derrick Fenner .05 .01
- ❑ 116 Vinny Testaverde .10 .02
- ❑ 117 Reggie Cobb .05 .01
- ❑ 118 Gary Anderson RB .05 .01
- ❑ 119 Bruce Hill .05 .01
- ❑ 120 Wayne Haddix .05 .01
- ❑ 121 Broderick Thomas .05 .01
- ❑ 122 Keith McCants .05 .01
- ❑ 123 Andre Collins .10 .02
- ❑ 124 Earnest Byner .05 .01
- ❑ 125 Jim Lachey .05 .01
- ❑ 126 Mark Rypien .10 .02
- ❑ 127 Charles Mann .05 .01
- ❑ 128 Nick Lowery .05 .01
- ❑ 129 Chip Lohmiller .05 .01
- ❑ 130 Mike Horan .05 .01
- ❑ 131 Rohn Stark .05 .01
- ❑ 132 Sean Landeta .05 .01
- ❑ 133 Clarence Verdin .05 .01
- ❑ 134 Johnny Bailey .05 .01
- ❑ 135 Herschel Walker .10 .02
- ❑ 136 Bo Jackson PP .30 .10
- ❑ 137 Dexter Carter PP .05 .01
- ❑ 138 Warren Moon PP .10 .02
- ❑ 139 Joe Montana PP 1.25 .50
- ❑ 140 Jerry Rice PP .75 .30

❑ 141	Deion Sanders PP	.40	.15
❑ 142	Ronnie Lippett PP	.05	.01
❑ 143	Terance Mathis	.25	.08
❑ 144	Gaston Green PP	.05	.01
❑ 145	Dean Biasucci PP	.05	.01
❑ 146	Charles Haley PP	.10	.02
❑ 147	Derrick Thomas PP	.25	.08
❑ 148	Lawrence Taylor PP	.10	.02
❑ 149	Art Shell CO PP	.10	.02
❑ 150	Bill Parcells CO PP	.10	.02
❑ 151	Steve Broussard	.05	.01
❑ 152	Darion Conner	.05	.01
❑ 153	Bill Fralic	.05	.01
❑ 154	Mike Gann	.05	.01
❑ 155	Tim McKyer	.05	.01
❑ 156	Don Beebe UER	.05	.01
❑ 157	Cornelius Bennett	.10	.02
❑ 158	Andre Reed	.25	.08
❑ 159	Leonard Smith	.05	.01
❑ 160	Will Wolford	.05	.01
❑ 161	Mark Carrier DB	.10	.02
❑ 162	Wendell Davis	.05	.01
❑ 163	Jay Hilgenberg	.05	.01
❑ 164	Brad Muster	.05	.01
❑ 165	Mike Singletary	.10	.02
❑ 166	Eddie Brown	.05	.01
❑ 167	David Fulcher	.05	.01
❑ 168	Rodney Holman	.05	.01
❑ 169	Anthony Munoz	.10	.02
❑ 170	Craig Taylor RC	.05	.01
❑ 171	Mike Baab	.05	.01
❑ 172	David Grayson	.05	.01
❑ 173	Reggie Langhorne	.05	.01
❑ 174	Joe Morris	.05	.01
❑ 175	Kevin Gogan RC	.05	.01
❑ 176	Jack Del Rio	.10	.02
❑ 177	Issiac Holt	.05	.01
❑ 178	Michael Irvin	.25	.08
❑ 179	Jay Novacek	.25	.08
❑ 180	Steve Atwater	.05	.01
❑ 181	Mark Jackson	.05	.01
❑ 182	Ricky Nattiel	.05	.01
❑ 183	Warren Powers	.05	.01
❑ 184	Dennis Smith	.05	.01
❑ 185	Bennie Blades	.05	.01
❑ 186	Lomas Brown UER	.05	.01
❑ 187	Robert Clark UER	.05	.01
❑ 188	Mel Gray	.10	.02
❑ 189	Chris Spielman	.10	.02
❑ 190	Johnny Holland	.05	.01
❑ 191	Don Majkowski	.05	.01
❑ 192	Bryce Paup RC	.25	.08
❑ 193	Darrell Thompson	.05	.01
❑ 194	Ed West UER	.05	.01
❑ 195	Cris Dishman RC	.10	.02
❑ 196	Drew Hill	.10	.02
❑ 197	Bruce Matthews	.10	.02
❑ 198	Bubba McDowell	.05	.01
❑ 199	Allen Pinkett	.05	.01
❑ 200	Bill Brooks	.10	.02
❑ 201	Jeff Herrod	.05	.01
❑ 202	Anthony Johnson	.10	.02
❑ 203	Mike Prior	.05	.01
❑ 204	John Alt	.05	.01
❑ 205	Stephone Paige	.05	.01
❑ 206	Kevin Ross	.05	.01
❑ 207	Dan Saleaumua	.05	.01
❑ 208	Barry Word	.05	.01
❑ 209	Marcus Allen	.25	.08
❑ 210	Roger Craig	.10	.02
❑ 211	Ronnie Lott	.10	.02
❑ 212	Winston Moss	.05	.01
❑ 213	Jay Schroeder	.05	.01
❑ 214	Robert Delpino	.05	.01
❑ 215	Henry Ellard	.10	.02
❑ 216	Kevin Greene	.10	.02
❑ 217	Tom Newberry	.05	.01
❑ 218	Michael Stewart	.05	.01
❑ 219	Mark Duper	.10	.02
❑ 220	Mark Higgs RC	.05	.01
❑ 221	John Offerdahl UER	.05	.01
❑ 222	Keith Sims	.05	.01
❑ 223	Anthony Carter	.10	.02
❑ 224	Cris Carter	.50	.20
❑ 225	Steve Jordan	.05	.01
❑ 226	Randall McDaniel	.05	.01
❑ 227	Al Noga	.05	.01
❑ 228	Ray Agnew	.05	.01
❑ 229	Bruce Armstrong	.05	.01
❑ 230	Irving Fryar	.10	.02
❑ 231	Greg McMurtry	.05	.01
❑ 232	Chris Singleton	.05	.01
❑ 233	Morten Andersen	.05	.01
❑ 234	Vince Buck	.05	.01
❑ 235	Gill Fenerty	.05	.01
❑ 236	Rickey Jackson	.10	.02
❑ 237	Vaughan Johnson	.05	.01
❑ 238	Carl Banks	.05	.01
❑ 239	Mark Collins	.05	.01
❑ 240	Rodney Hampton	.25	.08
❑ 241	Dave Meggett	.10	.02
❑ 242	Bart Oates	.05	.01
❑ 243	Kyle Clifton	.05	.01
❑ 244	Jeff Lageman	.10	.02
❑ 245	Freeman McNeil UER	.10	.02
❑ 246	Rob Moore	.25	.08
❑ 247	Eric Allen	.05	.01
❑ 248	Keith Byars	.10	.02
❑ 249	Keith Jackson	.10	.02
❑ 250	Jim McMahon	.10	.02
❑ 251	Andre Waters	.05	.01
❑ 252	Ken Harvey	.10	.02
❑ 253	Ernie Jones	.05	.01
❑ 254	Luis Sharpe	.05	.01
❑ 255	Anthony Thompson	.05	.01
❑ 256	Tom Tupa	.05	.01
❑ 257	Eric Green	.10	.02
❑ 258	Barry Foster	.10	.02
❑ 259	Bryan Hinkle	.05	.01
❑ 260	Tunch Ilkin	.05	.01
❑ 261	Louis Lipps	.05	.01
❑ 262	Gill Byrd	.05	.01
❑ 263	John Friesz	.10	.02
❑ 264	Anthony Miller	.10	.02
❑ 265	Junior Seau	.25	.08
❑ 266	Ronnie Harmon	.10	.02
❑ 267	Harris Barton	.05	.01
❑ 268	Todd Bowles	.05	.01
❑ 269	Don Griffin	.05	.01
❑ 270	Bill Romanowski	.05	.01
❑ 271	Steve Young	.75	.30
❑ 272	Brian Blades	.10	.02
❑ 273	Jacob Green	.05	.01
❑ 274	Rufus Porter	.05	.01
❑ 275	Eugene Robinson	.05	.01
❑ 276	Mark Carrier WR	.10	.02
❑ 277	Reuben Davis	.05	.01
❑ 278	Paul Gruber	.05	.01
❑ 279	Gary Clark	.25	.08
❑ 280	Darrell Green	.10	.02
❑ 281	Wilber Marshall	.05	.01
❑ 282	Matt Millen	.10	.02
❑ 283	Alvin Walton	.05	.01
❑ 284	Joe Gibbs CO UER	.10	.02
❑ 285	Don Shula CO UER	.10	.02
❑ 286	Larry Brown RC DB	.10	.02
❑ 287	Mike Croel RC	.05	.01
❑ 288	Antone Davis RC	.05	.01
❑ 289	Ricky Ervins RC UER	.10	.02
❑ 290	Brett Favre RC	8.00	3.00
❑ 291	Pat Harlow RC	.05	.01
❑ 292	Michael Jackson RC WR	.25	.08
❑ 293	Henry Jones RC	.10	.02
❑ 294	Aaron Craver RC	.05	.01
❑ 295	Nick Bell RC	.05	.01
❑ 296	Todd Lyght RC	.10	.02
❑ 297	Todd Marinovich RC	.05	.01
❑ 298	Russell Maryland RC	.10	.02
❑ 299	Kanavis McGhee RC	.05	.01
❑ 300	Dan McGwire RC	.10	.02
❑ 301	Charles McRae RC	.05	.01
❑ 302	Eric Moten RC	.05	.01
❑ 303	Jerome Henderson RC	.05	.01
❑ 304	Browning Nagle RC	.05	.01
❑ 305	Mike Pritchard RC	.25	.08
❑ 306	Stanley Richard RC	.10	.02
❑ 307	Randal Hill RC	.10	.02
❑ 308	Leonard Russell RC	.10	.02
❑ 309	Eric Swann RC	.10	.02
❑ 310	Phil Hansen RC	.05	.01
❑ 311	Moe Gardner RC	.05	.01
❑ 312	Jon Vaughn RC	.05	.01
❑ 313	Aeneas Williams RC	.25	.08
❑ 314	Alfred Williams RC	.05	.01
❑ 315	Harvey Williams RC	.25	.08
❑ PM1	Emmitt Smith Plat.	250.00	125.00
❑ PM2	Paul Brown Plat.	60.00	25.00

1992 Pro Set

❑	COMPLETE SET (700)	15.00	6.00
❑	COMP.SERIES 1 (400)	8.00	3.00
❑	COMP.SERIES 2 (300)	8.00	3.00
❑ 1	Mike Croel LL	.05	.01
❑ 2	Thurman Thomas LL	.25	.08
❑ 3	Wayne Fontes CO LL	.05	.01
❑ 4	Anthony Munoz LL	.10	.02
❑ 5	Steve Young LL	.30	.10
❑ 6	Warren Moon LL	.10	.02
❑ 7	Emmitt Smith LL	.60	.25
❑ 8	Haywood Jeffires LL	.05	.01
❑ 9	Marv Cook LL	.05	.01
❑ 10	Michael Irvin LL	.25	.08
❑ 11	Thurman Thomas LL	.25	.08
❑ 12	Chip Lohmiller LL UER	.05	.01
❑ 13	Barry Sanders LL	.50	.20
❑ 14	Reggie Roby LL	.05	.01
❑ 15	Mel Gray LL	.05	.01
❑ 16	Ronnie Lott LL	.10	.02
❑ 17	Pat Swilling LL	.05	.01
❑ 18	Reggie White LL	.10	.02
❑ 19	Haywood Jeffires ML	.05	.01
❑ 20	Pat Leahy MILE	.05	.01
❑ 21	James Lofton MILE	.10	.02
❑ 22	Art Monk MILE	.10	.02
❑ 23	Don Shula MILE	.10	.02
❑ 24A	Nick Lowery MILE ERR	.05	.01
❑ 24B	Nick Lowery MILE COR	.05	.01
❑ 25	John Elway ML	.50	.20
❑ 26	Chicago Bears MILE	.05	.01
❑ 27	Marcus Allen MILE	.10	.02
❑ 28	Terrell Buckley RC	.05	.01
❑ 29	Amp Lee RC	.05	.01
❑ 30	Chris Mims RC	.05	.01
❑ 31	Leon Searcy RC	.05	.01
❑ 32	Jimmy Smith RC	3.00	1.25
❑ 33	Siran Stacy RC	.05	.01
❑ 34	Pete Gogolak INN	.05	.01
❑ 35	Cheerleaders INN	.05	.01
❑ 36	Houston Astrodome INN	.05	.01
❑ 37	Week 1 REPLAY	.05	.01
❑ 38	Week 2 REPLAY	.05	.01
❑ 39	Week 3 REPLAY	.05	.01
❑ 40	Week 4 REPLAY	.05	.01
❑ 41	Week 5 REPLAY	.05	.01
❑ 42	Week 6 REPLAY	.05	.01
❑ 43	Thurman Thomas REP	.10	.02
❑ 44	Week 8 REPLAY	.05	.01
❑ 45	Week 9 REPLAY UER	.05	.01
❑ 46	Week 10 REPLAY	.05	.01
❑ 47	Week 11 REPLAY	.05	.01
❑ 48	Week 12 REPLAY	.05	.01
❑ 49	M.Irvin/S.Beuerlein REP	.10	.02
❑ 50	Week 14 REPLAY	.05	.01
❑ 51	Week 15 REPLAY	.05	.01
❑ 52	Week 16 REPLAY	.05	.01
❑ 53	Week 17 REPLAY	.05	.01
❑ 54	AFC Wild Card REPLAY	.05	.01
❑ 55	AFC Wild Card REPLAY	.05	.01
❑ 56	NFC Wild Card REPLAY	.05	.01
❑ 57	NFC Wild Card REPLAY	.05	.01
❑ 58	AFC Divis. Playoff REPLAY	.05	.01
❑ 59	Thurman Thomas REP	.10	.02
❑ 60	Erik Kramer REP	.05	.01

❑	61	NFC Divis. Playoff REPLAY	.05	.01
❑	62	AFC Championship REPLAY	.05	.01
❑	63	NFC Championship REPLAY	.05	.01
❑	64	Super Bowl XXVI REPLAY	.05	.01
❑	65	Super Bowl XXVI REPLAY	.05	.01
❑	66	Super Bowl XXVI REPLAY	.05	.01
❑	67	Super Bowl XXVI REPLAY	.05	.01
❑	68	Super Bowl XXVI REPLAY	.05	.01
❑	69	Thurman Thomas REP	.10	.02
❑	70	Super Bowl XXVI REPLAY	.05	.01
❑	71	Super Bowl XXVI REPLAY	.05	.01
❑	72	Super Bowl XXVI REPLAY	.05	.01
❑	73	Jeff Bostic	.05	.01
❑	74	Earnest Byner	.05	.01
❑	75	Gary Clark	.25	.08
❑	76	Andre Collins	.05	.01
❑	77	Darrell Green	.05	.01
❑	78	Joe Jacoby	.05	.01
❑	79	Jim Lachey	.05	.01
❑	80	Chip Lohmiller	.05	.01
❑	81	Charles Mann	.05	.01
❑	82	Martin Mayhew	.05	.01
❑	83	Matt Millen	.10	.02
❑	84	Brian Mitchell	.10	.02
❑	85	Art Monk	.10	.02
❑	86	Gerald Riggs	.05	.01
❑	87	Mark Rypien	.05	.01
❑	88	Fred Stokes	.05	.01
❑	89	Bobby Wilson	.05	.01
❑	90	Joe Gibbs CO	.10	.02
❑	91	Howard Ballard	.05	.01
❑	92	Cornelius Bennett UER	.10	.02
❑	93	Kenneth Davis	.05	.01
❑	94	Al Edwards	.05	.01
❑	95	Kent Hull	.05	.01
❑	96	Kirby Jackson	.05	.01
❑	97	Mark Kelso	.05	.01
❑	98	James Lofton	.10	.02
❑	99	Keith McKeller	.05	.01
❑	100	Nate Odomes	.05	.01
❑	101	Jim Ritcher	.05	.01
❑	102	Leon Seals	.05	.01
❑	103	Steve Tasker	.10	.02
❑	104	Darryl Talley	.05	.01
❑	105	Thurman Thomas	.25	.08
❑	106	Will Wolford	.05	.01
❑	107	Jeff Wright	.05	.01
❑	108	Marv Levy CO	.05	.01
❑	109	Darion Conner	.05	.01
❑	110	Bill Fralic	.05	.01
❑	111	Moe Gardner	.05	.01
❑	112	Michael Haynes	.10	.02
❑	113	Chris Miller	.10	.02
❑	114	Erric Pegram	.10	.02
❑	115	Bruce Pickens	.05	.01
❑	116	Andre Rison	.10	.02
❑	117	Jerry Glanville CO	.05	.01
❑	118	Neal Anderson	.05	.01
❑	119	Trace Armstrong	.05	.01
❑	120	Wendell Davis	.05	.01
❑	121	Richard Dent	.10	.02
❑	122	Jay Hilgenberg	.05	.01
❑	123	Lemuel Stinson	.05	.01
❑	124	Stan Thomas	.05	.01
❑	125	Tom Waddle	.05	.01
❑	126	Mike Ditka CO	.25	.08
❑	127	James Brooks	.10	.02
❑	128	Eddie Brown	.05	.01
❑	129	David Fulcher	.05	.01
❑	130	Harold Green	.05	.01
❑	131	Tim Krumrie UER	.05	.01
❑	132	Anthony Munoz	.10	.02
❑	133	Craig Taylor	.05	.01
❑	134	Eric Thomas	.05	.01
❑	135	David Shula RC CO	.05	.01
❑	136	Mike Baab	.05	.01
❑	137	Brian Brennan	.05	.01
❑	138	Michael Jackson	.10	.02
❑	139	James Jones DT UER	.05	.01
❑	140	Ed King	.05	.01
❑	141	Clay Matthews	.10	.02
❑	142	Eric Metcalf	.10	.02
❑	143	Joe Morris	.05	.01
❑	144A	Bill Belichick CO NPO	.25	.08
❑	144B	Bill Belichick CO	.25	.08
❑	145	Steve Beuerlein	.10	.02
❑	146	Larry Brown DB	.05	.01
❑	147	Ray Horton	.05	.01
❑	148	Ken Norton	.10	.02
❑	149	Mike Saxon	.05	.01
❑	150	Emmitt Smith	1.50	.60
❑	151	Mark Stepnoski	.10	.02
❑	152	Alexander Wright	.05	.01
❑	153	Jimmy Johnson CO	.10	.02
❑	154	Mike Croel	.05	.01
❑	155	John Elway	1.25	.50
❑	156	Gaston Green	.05	.01
❑	157	Wymon Henderson	.05	.01
❑	158	Karl Mecklenburg UER	.05	.01
❑	159	Warren Powers	.05	.01
❑	160	Steve Sewell UER	.05	.01
❑	161	Doug Widell	.05	.01
❑	162	Dan Reeves CO	.05	.01
❑	163	Eric Andolsek	.05	.01
❑	164	Jerry Ball	.05	.01
❑	165	Bennie Blades	.05	.01
❑	166	Ray Crockett	.05	.01
❑	167	Willie Green	.05	.01
❑	168	Erik Kramer	.10	.02
❑	169	Barry Sanders	1.25	.50
❑	170	Chris Spielman UER	.05	.01
❑	171	Wayne Fontes CO	.05	.01
❑	172	Vinnie Clark	.05	.01
❑	173	Tony Mandarich	.05	.01
❑	174	Brian Noble	.05	.01
❑	175	Bryce Paup	.25	.08
❑	176	Sterling Sharpe	.25	.08
❑	177	Darrell Thompson	.05	.01
❑	178	Esera Tuaolo UER	.05	.01
❑	179	Ed West	.05	.01
❑	180	Mike Holmgren RC CO	.25	.08
❑	181	Ray Childress	.05	.01
❑	182	Cris Dishman	.05	.01
❑	183	Curtis Duncan	.05	.01
❑	184	William Fuller	.05	.01
❑	185	Lamar Lathon	.05	.01
❑	186	Warren Moon	.25	.08
❑	187	Bo Orlando RC	.05	.01
❑	188	Lorenzo White	.05	.01
❑	189	Jack Pardee CO	.05	.01
❑	190	Chip Banks	.05	.01
❑	191	Dean Biasucci UER	.05	.01
❑	192	Bill Brooks	.05	.01
❑	193	Ray Donaldson	.05	.01
❑	194	Jeff Herrod	.05	.01
❑	195	Mike Prior	.05	.01
❑	196	Mark Vander Poel	.05	.01
❑	197	Clarence Verdin	.05	.01
❑	198	Ted Marchibroda CO	.05	.01
❑	199	John Alt	.05	.01
❑	200	Deron Cherry	.05	.01
❑	201	Steve DeBerg	.05	.01
❑	202	Nick Lowery	.05	.01
❑	203	Neil Smith	.25	.08
❑	204	Derrick Thomas	.25	.08
❑	205	Joe Valerio	.05	.01
❑	206	Barry Word	.05	.01
❑	207	M. Schottenheimer CO	.05	.01
❑	208	Marcus Allen	.25	.08
❑	209	Nick Bell	.05	.01
❑	210	Tim Brown	.25	.08
❑	211	Howie Long	.25	.08
❑	212	Ronnie Lott	.10	.02
❑	213	Todd Marinovich	.05	.01
❑	214	Greg Townsend	.05	.01
❑	215	Steve Wright	.05	.01
❑	216	Art Shell CO	.10	.02
❑	217	Flipper Anderson	.05	.01
❑	218	Robert Delpino	.05	.01
❑	219	Henry Ellard	.10	.02
❑	220	Kevin Greene	.10	.02
❑	221	Todd Lyght	.05	.01
❑	222	Tom Newberry	.05	.01
❑	223	Roman Phifer	.05	.01
❑	224	Michael Stewart	.05	.01
❑	225	Chuck Knox CO	.05	.01
❑	226	Aaron Craver	.05	.01
❑	227	Jeff Cross	.05	.01
❑	228	Mark Duper	.05	.01
❑	229	Ferrell Edmunds	.05	.01
❑	230	Jim C. Jensen	.05	.01
❑	231	Louis Oliver UER	.05	.01
❑	232	Reggie Roby	.05	.01
❑	233	Sammie Smith	.05	.01
❑	234	Don Shula CO	.10	.02
❑	235	Joey Browner	.05	.01
❑	236	Anthony Carter	.10	.02
❑	237	Chris Doleman	.05	.01
❑	238	Steve Jordan	.05	.01
❑	239	Kirk Lowdermilk	.05	.01
❑	240	Henry Thomas	.05	.01
❑	241	Herschel Walker	.10	.02
❑	242	Felix Wright	.05	.01
❑	243	Dennis Green CO RC	.10	.02
❑	244	Ray Agnew	.05	.01
❑	245	Marv Cook	.05	.01
❑	246	Irving Fryar UER	.10	.02
❑	247	Pat Harlow	.05	.01
❑	248	Hugh Millen	.05	.01
❑	249	Leonard Russell	.10	.02
❑	250	Andre Tippett	.05	.01
❑	251	Jon Vaughn	.05	.01
❑	252	Dick MacPherson CO	.05	.01
❑	253	Morten Andersen	.05	.01
❑	254	Bobby Hebert	.05	.01
❑	255	Joel Hilgenberg	.05	.01
❑	256	Vaughan Johnson	.05	.01
❑	257	Sam Mills	.05	.01
❑	258	Pat Swilling	.05	.01
❑	259	Floyd Turner	.05	.01
❑	260	Steve Walsh	.05	.01
❑	261	Jim Mora CO UER	.05	.01
❑	262	Stephen Baker	.05	.01
❑	263	Mark Collins	.05	.01
❑	264	Rodney Hampton	.10	.02
❑	265	Jeff Hostetler	.10	.02
❑	266	Erik Howard	.05	.01
❑	267	Sean Landeta	.05	.01
❑	268	Gary Reasons UER	.05	.01
❑	269	Everson Walls	.05	.01
❑	270	Ray Handley CO	.05	.01
❑	271	Louie Aguiar RC	.05	.01
❑	272	Brad Baxter	.05	.01
❑	273	Chris Burkett	.05	.01
❑	274	Irv Eatman	.05	.01
❑	275	Jeff Lageman	.05	.01
❑	276	Freeman McNeil	.05	.01
❑	277	Rob Moore	.10	.02
❑	278	Lonnie Young	.05	.01
❑	279	Bruce Coslet CO	.05	.01
❑	280	Jerome Brown	.05	.01
❑	281	Keith Byars	.05	.01
❑	282	Bruce Collie UER	.05	.01
❑	283	Keith Jackson	.10	.02
❑	284	James Joseph	.05	.01
❑	285	Seth Joyner	.05	.01
❑	286	Andre Waters	.05	.01
❑	287	Reggie White	.25	.08
❑	288	Rich Kotite CO	.05	.01
❑	289	Rich Camarillo	.05	.01
❑	290	Garth Jax	.05	.01
❑	291	Ernie Jones	.05	.01
❑	292	Tim McDonald	.05	.01
❑	293	Rod Saddler	.05	.01
❑	294	Anthony Thompson UER	.05	.01
❑	295	Tom Tupa UER	.05	.01
❑	296	Ron Wolfley	.05	.01
❑	297	Joe Bugel CO	.05	.01
❑	298	Gary Anderson K	.05	.01
❑	299	Jeff Graham	.25	.08
❑	300	Eric Green	.05	.01
❑	301	Bryan Hinkle	.05	.01
❑	302	Tunch Ilkin	.05	.01
❑	303	Louis Lipps	.05	.01
❑	304	Neil O'Donnell	.10	.02
❑	305	Rod Woodson	.25	.08
❑	306	Bill Cowher CO RC	.75	.30
❑	307	Eric Bieniemy	.05	.01
❑	308	Marion Butts	.05	.01
❑	309	John Friesz	.10	.02
❑	310	Courtney Hall	.05	.01
❑	311	Ronnie Harmon	.05	.01
❑	312	Henry Rolling	.05	.01
❑	313	Billy Ray Smith	.05	.01
❑	314	George Thornton	.05	.01
❑	315	Bobby Ross CO RC	.05	.01
❑	316	Todd Bowles	.05	.01
❑	317	Michael Carter	.05	.01
❑	318	Don Griffin	.05	.01
❑	319	Charles Haley	.10	.02
❑	320	Brent Jones	.10	.02

❑ 321 John Taylor .10 .02
❑ 322 Ted Washington .05 .01
❑ 323 Steve Young .60 .25
❑ 324 George Seifert CO .10 .02
❑ 325 Brian Blades .10 .02
❑ 326 Jacob Green .05 .01
❑ 327 Patrick Hunter .05 .01
❑ 328 Tommy Kane .05 .01
❑ 329 Cortez Kennedy .10 .02
❑ 330 Dave Krieg .10 .02
❑ 331 Rufus Porter .05 .01
❑ 332 John L. Williams .05 .01
❑ 333 Tom Flores CO .05 .01
❑ 334 Gary Anderson RB .05 .01
❑ 335 Mark Carrier WR .10 .02
❑ 336 Reuben Davis .05 .01
❑ 337 Lawrence Dawsey .10 .02
❑ 338 Keith McCants UER .05 .01
❑ 339 Vinny Testaverde .10 .02
❑ 340 Broderick Thomas .05 .01
❑ 341 Robert Wilson .05 .01
❑ 342 Sam Wyche CO .05 .01
❑ 343 1991 Teacher of .05 .01
❑ 344 Owners Reject Instant .05 .01
❑ 345 NFL Experience .05 .01
❑ 346 Chuck Noll Retires .10 .02
❑ 347 Isaac Curtis .05 .01
❑ 348 Michael Irvin/D.Pearson .10 .02
❑ 349 Barry Sanders/B.Sims .50 .20
❑ 350 Todd Marinovich/K.Stable .05 .01
❑ 351 Leonard Russell/C.James .10 .02
❑ 352 Bob Golic .05 .01
❑ 353 Pat Harlow .05 .01
❑ 354 Esera Tuaolo .05 .01
❑ 355 Mark Schlereth RC Envir. .05 .01
❑ 356 Trace Armstrong .05 .01
❑ 357 Eric Bieniemy .05 .01
❑ 358 Bill Romanowski .05 .01
❑ 359 Irv Eatman .05 .01
❑ 360 Jonathan Hayes .05 .01
❑ 361 Atlanta Falcons .05 .01
❑ 362 Chicago Bears .05 .01
❑ 363 Dallas Cowboys .05 .01
❑ 364 Detroit Lions .05 .01
❑ 365 Green Bay Packers .05 .01
❑ 366 Los Angeles Rams .05 .01
❑ 367 Minnesota Vikings .05 .01
❑ 368 New Orleans Saints UER .05 .01
❑ 369 New York Giants .05 .01
❑ 370 Philadelphia Eagles .05 .01
❑ 371 Phoenix Cardinals .05 .01
❑ 372 San Francisco 49ers .05 .01
❑ 373 Tampa Bay Buccaneers .05 .01
❑ 374 Washington Redskins .05 .01
❑ 375 Steve Atwater PB UER .05 .01
❑ 376 Cornelius Bennett PB .10 .02
❑ 377 Tim Brown PB .10 .02
❑ 378 Marion Butts PB .05 .01
❑ 379 Ray Childress PB .05 .01
❑ 380 Mark Clayton PB .05 .01
❑ 381 Marv Cook PB .05 .01
❑ 382 Cris Dishman PB .05 .01
❑ 383 William Fuller PB .05 .01
❑ 384 Gaston Green PB .05 .01
❑ 385 Jeff Jaeger PB .05 .01
❑ 386 Haywood Jeffires PB .10 .02
❑ 387 James Lofton PB .10 .02
❑ 388 Ronnie Lott PB .10 .02
❑ 389 Karl Mecklenburg PB UER .05 .01
❑ 390 Warren Moon PB .10 .02
❑ 391 Anthony Munoz PB .05 .01
❑ 392 Dennis Smith PB .05 .01
❑ 393 Neil Smith PB .10 .02
❑ 394 Darryl Talley PB .05 .01
❑ 395 Derrick Thomas PB .10 .02
❑ 396 Thurman Thomas PB .10 .02
❑ 397 Greg Townsend PB .05 .01
❑ 398 Richmond Webb PB .05 .01
❑ 399 Rod Woodson PB .10 .02
❑ 400 Dan Reeves CO PB .05 .01
❑ 401 Troy Aikman PB .40 .15
❑ 402 Eric Allen PB .05 .01
❑ 403 Bennie Blades PB .05 .01
❑ 404 Lomas Brown PB .05 .01
❑ 405 Mark Carrier DB PB .05 .01
❑ 406 Gary Clark PB .10 .02
❑ 407 Mel Gray PB .05 .01
❑ 408 Darrell Green PB .05 .01
❑ 409 Michael Irvin PB .25 .08
❑ 410 Vaughan Johnson PB .05 .01
❑ 411 Seth Joyner PB .05 .01
❑ 412 Jim Lachey PB .05 .01
❑ 413 Chip Lohmiller PB .05 .01
❑ 414 Charles Mann PB .05 .01
❑ 415 Chris Miller PB .10 .02
❑ 416 Sam Mills PB .05 .01
❑ 417 Bart Oates PB .05 .01
❑ 418 Jerry Rice PB .40 .15
❑ 419 Andre Rison PB .10 .02
❑ 420 Mark Rypien PB .05 .01
❑ 421 Barry Sanders PB .50 .20
❑ 422 Deion Sanders PB .25 .08
❑ 423 Mark Schlereth PB .05 .01
❑ 424 Mike Singletary PB .05 .01
❑ 425 Emmitt Smith PB .60 .25
❑ 426 Pat Swilling PB .05 .01
❑ 427 Reggie White PB .10 .02
❑ 428 Rick Bryan .05 .01
❑ 429 Tim Green .05 .01
❑ 430 Drew Hill .05 .01
❑ 431 Norm Johnson .05 .01
❑ 432 Keith Jones .05 .01
❑ 433 Mike Pritchard .10 .02
❑ 434 Deion Sanders .50 .20
❑ 435 Tony Smith RC RB .05 .01
❑ 436 Jessie Tuggle .05 .01
❑ 437 Steve Christie .05 .01
❑ 438 Shane Conlan .05 .01
❑ 439 Matt Darby RC .05 .01
❑ 440 John Fina RC .05 .01
❑ 441 Henry Jones .05 .01
❑ 442 Jim Kelly .25 .08
❑ 443 Pete Metzelaars .05 .01
❑ 444 Andre Reed .10 .02
❑ 445 Bruce Smith .25 .08
❑ 446 Troy Auzenne RC .05 .01
❑ 447 Mark Carrier DB .05 .01
❑ 448 Will Furrer RC .05 .01
❑ 449 Jim Harbaugh .25 .08
❑ 450 Brad Muster .05 .01
❑ 451 Darren Lewis .05 .01
❑ 452 Mike Singletary .10 .02
❑ 453 Alonzo Spellman RC .10 .02
❑ 454 Chris Zorich .10 .02
❑ 455 Jim Breech .05 .01
❑ 456 Boomer Esiason .10 .02
❑ 457 Derrick Fenner .05 .01
❑ 458 James Francis .05 .01
❑ 459 David Klingler RC .05 .01
❑ 460 Tim McGee .05 .01
❑ 461 Carl Pickens RC .25 .08
❑ 462 Alfred Williams .05 .01
❑ 463 Darryl Williams RC .05 .01
❑ 464 Mark Bavaro .05 .01
❑ 465 Jay Hilgenberg .05 .01
❑ 466 Leroy Hoard .10 .02
❑ 467 Bernie Kosar .10 .02
❑ 468 Michael Dean Perry .10 .02
❑ 469 Todd Philcox RC .05 .01
❑ 470 Patrick Rowe RC .05 .01
❑ 471 Tommy Vardell RC .05 .01
❑ 472 Everson Walls .05 .01
❑ 473 Troy Aikman .75 .30
❑ 474 Kenneth Gant RC .05 .01
❑ 475 Charles Haley .10 .02
❑ 476 Michael Irvin .25 .08
❑ 477 Robert Jones RC .05 .01
❑ 478 Russell Maryland .05 .01
❑ 479 Jay Novacek .10 .02
❑ 480 Kevin Smith RC DB .05 .01
❑ 481 Tony Tolbert .05 .01
❑ 482 Steve Atwater .05 .01
❑ 483 Shane Dronett RC .05 .01
❑ 484 Simon Fletcher .05 .01
❑ 485 Greg Lewis .05 .01
❑ 486 Tommy Maddox RC 2.00 .75
❑ 487 Shannon Sharpe .25 .08
❑ 488 Dennis Smith .05 .01
❑ 489 Sammie Smith .05 .01
❑ 490 Kenny Walker .05 .01
❑ 491 Lomas Brown .05 .01
❑ 492 Mike Farr .05 .01
❑ 493 Mel Gray .10 .02
❑ 494 Jason Hanson RC .10 .02
❑ 495 Herman Moore .25 .08
❑ 496 Rodney Peete .10 .02
❑ 497 Robert Porcher RC .25 .08
❑ 498 Kelvin Pritchett .05 .01
❑ 499 Andre Ware .05 .01
❑ 500 Sanjay Beach RC .05 .01
❑ 501 Edgar Bennett RC .25 .08
❑ 502 Lewis Billups .05 .01
❑ 503 Terrell Buckley .05 .01
❑ 504 Ty Detmer .25 .08
❑ 505 Brett Favre 2.50 1.25
❑ 506 Johnny Holland .05 .01
❑ 507 Dexter McNabb RC .05 .01
❑ 508 Vince Workman .05 .01
❑ 509 Cody Carlson .05 .01
❑ 510 Ernest Givins .10 .02
❑ 511 Jerry Gray .05 .01
❑ 512 Haywood Jeffires .10 .02
❑ 513 Bruce Matthews .05 .01
❑ 514 Bubba McDowell .05 .01
❑ 515 Bucky Richardson RC .05 .01
❑ 516 Webster Slaughter .05 .01
❑ 517 Al Smith .05 .01
❑ 518 Mel Agee .05 .01
❑ 519 Ashley Ambrose RC .25 .08
❑ 520 Kevin Call .05 .01
❑ 521 Ken Clark .05 .01
❑ 522 Quentin Coryatt RC .05 .01
❑ 523 Steve Emtman RC .05 .01
❑ 524 Jeff George .25 .08
❑ 525 Jessie Hester .05 .01
❑ 526 Anthony Johnson .10 .02
❑ 527 Tim Barnett .05 .01
❑ 528 Martin Bayless .05 .01
❑ 529 J.J. Birden .05 .01
❑ 530 Dale Carter RC .10 .02
❑ 531 Dave Krieg .10 .02
❑ 532 Albert Lewis .05 .01
❑ 533 Nick Lowery .05 .01
❑ 534 Christian Okoye .05 .01
❑ 535 Harvey Williams .25 .08
❑ 536 Aundray Bruce .05 .01
❑ 537 Eric Dickerson .10 .02
❑ 538 Willie Gault .10 .02
❑ 539 Ethan Horton .05 .01
❑ 540 Jeff Jaeger .05 .01
❑ 541 Napoleon McCallum .05 .01
❑ 542 Chester McGlockton RC .10 .02
❑ 543 Steve Smith .05 .01
❑ 544 Steve Wisniewski .05 .01
❑ 545 Marc Boutte RC .05 .01
❑ 546 Pat Carter .05 .01
❑ 547 Jim Everett .10 .02
❑ 548 Cleveland Gary .05 .01
❑ 549 Sean Gilbert RC .10 .02
❑ 550 Steve Israel RC .05 .01
❑ 551 Todd Kinchen RC .05 .01
❑ 552 Jackie Slater .05 .01
❑ 553 Tony Zendejas .05 .01
❑ 554 Robert Clark .05 .01
❑ 555 Mark Clayton .10 .02
❑ 556 Marco Coleman RC .05 .01
❑ 557 Bryan Cox .10 .02
❑ 558 Keith Jackson .10 .02
❑ 559 Dan Marino 1.25 .50
❑ 560 John Offerdahl .05 .01
❑ 561 Troy Vincent RC .05 .01
❑ 562 Richmond Webb .05 .01
❑ 563 Terry Allen .25 .08
❑ 564 Cris Carter .50 .20
❑ 565 Roger Craig .10 .02
❑ 566 Rich Gannon .25 .08
❑ 567 Hassan Jones .05 .01
❑ 568 Randall McDaniel .05 .01
❑ 569 Al Noga .05 .01
❑ 570 Todd Scott .05 .01
❑ 571 Van Waiters RC .05 .01
❑ 572 Bruce Armstrong .05 .01
❑ 573 Gene Chilton RC .05 .01
❑ 574 Eugene Chung RC .05 .01
❑ 575 Todd Collins RC .05 .01
❑ 576 Hart Lee Dykes .05 .01
❑ 577 David Howard RC .05 .01
❑ 578 Eugene Lockhart .05 .01
❑ 579 Greg McMurtry .05 .01
❑ 580 Rod Smith DB RC .05 .01
❑ 581 Gene Atkins .05 .01

❑ 582 Vince Buck	.05	.01
❑ 583 Wesley Carroll	.05	.01
❑ 584 Jim Dombrowski	.05	.01
❑ 585 Vaughn Dunbar RC	.05	.01
❑ 586 Craig Heyward	.10	.02
❑ 587 Dalton Hilliard	.05	.01
❑ 588 Wayne Martin	.05	.01
❑ 589 Renaldo Turnbull	.05	.01
❑ 590 Carl Banks	.05	.01
❑ 591 Derek Brown RC TE	.05	.01
❑ 592 Jarrod Bunch	.05	.01
❑ 593 Mark Ingram	.05	.01
❑ 594 Ed McCaffrey	.30	.10
❑ 595 Phil Simms	.10	.02
❑ 596 Phillippi Sparks RC	.05	.01
❑ 597 Lawrence Taylor	.25	.08
❑ 598 Lewis Tillman	.05	.01
❑ 599 Kyle Clifton	.05	.01
❑ 600 Mo Lewis	.05	.01
❑ 601 Terance Mathis	.10	.02
❑ 602 Scott Mersereau	.05	.01
❑ 603 Johnny Mitchell RC	.05	.01
❑ 604 Browning Nagle	.05	.01
❑ 605 Ken O'Brien	.05	.01
❑ 606 Al Toon	.10	.02
❑ 607 Marvin Washington	.05	.01
❑ 608 Eric Allen	.05	.01
❑ 609 Fred Barnett	.25	.08
❑ 610 John Booty	.05	.01
❑ 611 Randall Cunningham	.25	.08
❑ 612 Rich Miano	.05	.01
❑ 613 Clyde Simmons	.05	.01
❑ 614 Siran Stacy	.05	.01
❑ 615 Herschel Walker	.10	.02
❑ 616 Calvin Williams	.10	.02
❑ 617 Chris Chandler	.25	.08
❑ 618 Randal Hill	.05	.01
❑ 619 Johnny Johnson	.05	.01
❑ 620 Lorenzo Lynch	.05	.01
❑ 621 Robert Massey	.05	.01
❑ 622 Ricky Proehl	.05	.01
❑ 623 Timm Rosenbach	.05	.01
❑ 624 Tony Sacca RC	.05	.01
❑ 625 Aeneas Williams UER	.10	.02
❑ 626 Bubby Brister	.05	.01
❑ 627 Barry Foster	.10	.02
❑ 628 Merril Hoge	.05	.01
❑ 629 D.J. Johnson	.05	.01
❑ 630 David Little	.05	.01
❑ 631 Greg Lloyd	.10	.02
❑ 632 Ernie Mills	.05	.01
❑ 633 Leon Searcy RC	.05	.01
❑ 634 Dwight Stone	.05	.01
❑ 635 Sam Anno RC	.05	.01
❑ 636 Burt Grossman	.05	.01
❑ 637 Stan Humphries	.25	.08
❑ 638 Nate Lewis	.05	.01
❑ 639 Anthony Miller	.10	.02
❑ 640 Chris Mims	.25	.08
❑ 641 Marquez Pope RC	.05	.01
❑ 642 Stanley Richard	.05	.01
❑ 643 Junior Seau	.25	.08
❑ 644 Brian Bollinger RC	.05	.01
❑ 645 Steve Bono RC	.25	.08
❑ 646 Dexter Carter	.05	.01
❑ 647 Dana Hall RC	.05	.01
❑ 648 Amp Lee	.05	.01
❑ 649 Joe Montana	1.25	.50
❑ 650 Tom Rathman	.05	.01
❑ 651 Jerry Rice	.75	.30
❑ 652 Ricky Watters	.25	.08
❑ 653 Robert Blackmon	.05	.01
❑ 654 John Kasay	.05	.01
❑ 655 Ronnie Lee RC	.05	.01
❑ 656 Dan McGwire	.05	.01
❑ 657 Ray Roberts RC	.05	.01
❑ 658 Kelly Stouffer	.05	.01
❑ 659 Chris Warren	.25	.08
❑ 660 Tony Woods	.05	.01
❑ 661 David Wyman	.05	.01
❑ 662 Reggie Cobb	.05	.01
❑ 663A Steve DeBerg ERR	.10	.02
❑ 663B Steve DeBerg COR	.10	.02
❑ 664 Santana Dotson RC	.10	.02
❑ 665 Willie Drewery	.05	.01
❑ 666 Paul Gruber	.05	.01
❑ 667 Ron Hall	.05	.01
❑ 668 Courtney Hawkins RC	.10	.02
❑ 669 Charles McRae	.05	.01
❑ 670 Ricky Reynolds	.05	.01
❑ 671 Monte Coleman	.05	.01
❑ 672 Brad Edwards	.05	.01
❑ 673 Jumpy Geathers UER	.05	.01
❑ 674 Kelly Goodburn	.05	.01
❑ 675 Kurt Gouveia	.05	.01
❑ 676 Chris Hakel RC	.05	.01
❑ 677 Wilber Marshall	.05	.01
❑ 678 Ricky Sanders	.05	.01
❑ 679 Mark Schlereth	.05	.01
❑ 680 Buffalo Bills	.05	.01
❑ 681 Cincinnati Bengals	.05	.01
❑ 682 Cleveland Browns	.05	.01
❑ 683 Denver Broncos	.05	.01
❑ 684 Houston Oilers	.05	.01
❑ 685 Indianapolis Colts	.05	.01
❑ 686 Tracy Simien SG	.05	.01
❑ 687 Los Angeles Raiders	.05	.01
❑ 688 Miami Dolphins	.05	.01
❑ 689 New England Patriots	.05	.01
❑ 690 New York Jets	.05	.01
❑ 691 Pittsburgh Steelers	.05	.01
❑ 692 San Diego Chargers	.05	.01
❑ 693 Seattle Seahawks	.05	.01
❑ 694 Play Smart	.05	.01
❑ 695 Hank Williams Jr. NEW	.05	.01
❑ 696 3 Brothers in NFL NEWS	.05	.01
❑ 697 Japan Bowl NEWS	.05	.01
❑ 698 Georgia Dome NEWS	.05	.01
❑ 699 Theme Art NEWS	.05	.01
❑ 700 Mark Rypien SB MVP NEW	.05	.01
❑ AU150 E. Smith AU/1000	120.00	60.00
❑ AU168 Erik Kramer AU/1000	30.00	12.50
❑ NNO E.Smith Power Preview	.75	.30
❑ NNO Santa Claus	.50	.20
❑ SC5 Super Bowl XXVI Logo	.30	.10
❑ P1 Cover Card Promo	1.00	.40

1993 Pro Set

❑ COMPLETE SET (449)	15.00	6.00
❑ 1 Marco Coleman	.05	.01
❑ 2 Steve Young LL	.30	.10
❑ 3 Mike Holmgren	.10	.02
❑ 4 John Elway LL	.75	.30
❑ 5 Steve Young LL	.30	.10
❑ 6 Dan Marino LL	.75	.30
❑ 7 Emmitt Smith LL	.75	.30
❑ 8 Sterling Sharpe LL	.10	.02
❑ 9 Jay Novacek	.10	.02
❑ 10 Sterling Sharpe LL	.10	.02
❑ 11 Thurman Thomas LL	.10	.02
❑ 12 Pete Stoyanovich	.05	.01
❑ 13 Greg Montgomery	.05	.01
❑ 14 Johnny Bailey	.05	.01
❑ 15 Jon Vaughn	.05	.01
❑ 16 Audray McMillian	.05	.01
❑ 17 Clyde Simmons	.05	.01
❑ 18 Cortez Kennedy	.05	.01
❑ 19 AFC Wildcard	.05	.01
❑ 20 AFC Wildcard	.05	.01
❑ 21 NFC Wildcard	.05	.01
❑ 22 NFC Wildcard	.05	.01
❑ 23 AFC Divisional	.05	.01
❑ 24 Dan Marino REP	.75	.30
❑ 25 Troy Aikman REP	.50	.20
❑ 26 Ricky Watters REP	.10	.02
❑ 27 AFC Championship	.05	.01
❑ 28 NFC Championship	.05	.01
❑ 29 Super Bowl XXVIII Logo	.05	.01
❑ 30 Troy Aikman	.75	.30
❑ 31 Thomas Everett	.05	.01
❑ 32 Charles Haley	.10	.02
❑ 33 Alvin Harper	.10	.02
❑ 34 Michael Irvin	.25	.08
❑ 35 Robert Jones	.05	.01
❑ 36 Russell Maryland	.05	.01
❑ 37 Ken Norton	.10	.02
❑ 38 Jay Novacek	.10	.02
❑ 39 Emmitt Smith	1.50	.50
❑ 40 Darrin Smith RC	.10	.02
❑ 41 Mark Stepnoski	.05	.01
❑ 42 Kevin Williams RC WR	.25	.08
❑ 43 Daryl Johnston	.25	.08
❑ 44 Derrick Lassic RC	.05	.01
❑ 45 Don Beebe	.05	.01
❑ 46 Cornelius Bennett	.10	.02
❑ 47 Bill Brooks	.05	.01
❑ 48 Kenneth Davis	.05	.01
❑ 49 Jim Kelly	.25	.08
❑ 50 Andre Reed	.10	.02
❑ 51 Bruce Smith	.25	.08
❑ 52 Thomas Smith RC	.10	.02
❑ 53 Darryl Talley	.05	.01
❑ 54 Thurman Thomas	.25	.08
❑ 55 Russell Copeland RC	.10	.02
❑ 56 Steve Christie	.05	.01
❑ 57 Pete Metzelaars	.05	.01
❑ 58 Frank Reich	.10	.02
❑ 59 Henry Jones	.05	.01
❑ 60 Vinnie Clark	.05	.01
❑ 61 Eric Dickerson	.10	.02
❑ 62 Jumpy Geathers	.05	.01
❑ 63 Roger Harper RC	.05	.01
❑ 64 Michael Haynes	.10	.02
❑ 65 Bobby Hebert	.05	.01
❑ 66 Lincoln Kennedy RC	.05	.01
❑ 67 Chris Miller	.10	.02
❑ 68 Andre Rison	.10	.02
❑ 69 Deion Sanders	.50	.20
❑ 70 Jessie Tuggle	.05	.01
❑ 71 Ron George	.05	.01
❑ 72 Erric Pegram	.10	.02
❑ 73 Melvin Jenkins	.05	.01
❑ 74 Pierce Holt	.05	.01
❑ 75 Neal Anderson	.05	.01
❑ 76 Mark Carrier DB	.05	.01
❑ 77 Curtis Conway RC	.40	.15
❑ 78 Richard Dent	.10	.02
❑ 79 Jim Harbaugh	.25	.08
❑ 80 Craig Heyward	.10	.02
❑ 81 Darren Lewis	.05	.01
❑ 82 Alonzo Spellman	.05	.01
❑ 83 Tom Waddle	.05	.01
❑ 84 Wendell Davis	.05	.01
❑ 85 Chris Zorich	.05	.01
❑ 86 Carl Simpson RC	.05	.01
❑ 87 Chris Gedney RC	.05	.01
❑ 88 Trace Armstrong	.05	.01
❑ 89 Peter Tom Willis	.05	.01
❑ 90 John Copeland RC	.10	.02
❑ 91 Derrick Fenner	.05	.01
❑ 92 James Francis	.05	.01
❑ 93 Harold Green	.05	.01
❑ 94 David Klingler	.05	.01
❑ 95 Tim Krumrie	.05	.01
❑ 96 Tony McGee RC	.10	.02
❑ 97 Carl Pickens	.10	.02
❑ 98 Alfred Williams	.05	.01
❑ 99 Doug Pelfrey RC	.05	.01
❑ 100 Lance Gunn RC	.05	.01
❑ 101 Jay Schroeder	.05	.01
❑ 102 Steve Tovar RC	.05	.01
❑ 103 Jeff Query	.05	.01
❑ 104 Ty Parten RC	.05	.01
❑ 105 Jerry Ball	.05	.01
❑ 106 Mark Carrier WR	.10	.02
❑ 107 Rob Burnett	.05	.01
❑ 108 Michael Jackson	.10	.02
❑ 109 Mike Johnson	.05	.01
❑ 110 Bernie Kosar	.10	.02
❑ 111 Clay Matthews	.10	.02
❑ 112 Eric Metcalf	.10	.02
❑ 113 Michael Dean Perry	.10	.02
❑ 114 Vinny Testaverde	.10	.02

❑ 115	Eric Turner	.05	.01
❑ 116	Tommy Vardell	.05	.01
❑ 117	Leroy Hoard	.10	.02
❑ 118	Steve Everitt RC	.05	.01
❑ 119	Everson Walls	.05	.01
❑ 120	Steve Atwater	.05	.01
❑ 121	Rod Bernstine	.05	.01
❑ 122	Mike Croel	.05	.01
❑ 123	John Elway	1.50	.60
❑ 124	Simon Fletcher	.05	.01
❑ 125	Glyn Milburn RC	.25	.08
❑ 126	Reggie Rivers RC	.05	.01
❑ 127	Shannon Sharpe	.25	.08
❑ 128	Dennis Smith	.05	.01
❑ 129	Dan Williams RC	.05	.01
❑ 130	Rondell Jones RC	.05	.01
❑ 131	Jason Elam RC	.25	.08
❑ 132	Arthur Marshall RC	.05	.01
❑ 133	Gary Zimmerman	.05	.01
❑ 134	Karl Mecklenburg	.05	.01
❑ 135	Bennie Blades	.05	.01
❑ 136	Lomas Brown	.05	.01
❑ 137	Bill Fralic	.05	.01
❑ 138	Mel Gray	.10	.02
❑ 139	Willie Green	.05	.01
❑ 140	Ryan McNeil RC	.25	.08
❑ 141	Rodney Peete	.05	.01
❑ 142	Barry Sanders	1.25	.50
❑ 143	Chris Spielman	.10	.02
❑ 144	Pat Swilling	.05	.01
❑ 145	Andre Ware	.05	.01
❑ 146	Herman Moore	.25	.08
❑ 147	Tim McKyer	.05	.01
❑ 148	Brett Perriman	.25	.08
❑ 149	Antonio London RC	.05	.01
❑ 150	Edgar Bennett	.25	.08
❑ 151	Terrell Buckley	.05	.01
❑ 152	Brett Favre	2.00	.75
❑ 153	Jackie Harris	.05	.01
❑ 154	Johnny Holland	.05	.01
❑ 155	Sterling Sharpe	.25	.08
❑ 156	Tim Hauck	.05	.01
❑ 157	George Teague RC	.10	.02
❑ 158	Reggie White	.25	.08
❑ 159	Mark Clayton	.05	.01
❑ 160	Ty Detmer	.25	.08
❑ 161	Wayne Simmons RC	.05	.01
❑ 162	Mark Brunell RC	1.50	.60
❑ 163	Tony Bennett	.05	.01
❑ 164	Brian Noble	.05	.01
❑ 165	Cody Carlson	.05	.01
❑ 166	Ray Childress	.05	.01
❑ 167	Cris Dishman	.05	.01
❑ 168	Curtis Duncan	.05	.01
❑ 169	Brad Hopkins RC	.05	.01
❑ 170	Haywood Jeffires	.10	.02
❑ 171	Wilber Marshall	.05	.01
❑ 172	Micheal Barrow RC UER	.25	.08
❑ 173	Bubba McDowell	.05	.01
❑ 174	Warren Moon	.25	.08
❑ 175	Webster Slaughter	.05	.01
❑ 176	Travis Hannah RC	.05	.01
❑ 177	Lorenzo White	.05	.01
❑ 178	Ernest Givins UER	.10	.02
❑ 179	Keith McCants	.05	.01
❑ 180	Kerry Cash	.05	.01
❑ 181	Quentin Coryatt	.10	.02
❑ 182	Kirk Lowdermilk	.05	.01
❑ 183	Rodney Culver	.05	.01
❑ 184	Rohn Stark	.05	.01
❑ 185	Steve Emtman	.05	.01
❑ 186	Jeff George	.25	.08
❑ 187	Jeff Herrod	.05	.01
❑ 188	Reggie Langhorne	.05	.01
❑ 189	Roosevelt Potts RC	.05	.01
❑ 190	Jack Trudeau	.05	.01
❑ 191	Will Wolford	.05	.01
❑ 192	Jessie Hester	.05	.01
❑ 193	Anthony Johnson	.10	.02
❑ 194	Ray Buchanan RC	.25	.08
❑ 195	Dale Carter	.05	.01
❑ 196	Willie Davis	.25	.08
❑ 197	John Alt	.05	.01
❑ 198	Joe Montana	1.50	.60
❑ 199	Will Shields RC	.25	.08
❑ 200	Neil Smith	.25	.08
❑ 201	Derrick Thomas	.25	.08
❑ 202	Harvey Williams	.10	.02
❑ 203	Marcus Allen	.25	.08
❑ 204	J.J. Birden	.05	.01
❑ 205	Tim Barnett	.05	.01
❑ 206	Albert Lewis	.05	.01
❑ 207	Nick Lowery	.05	.01
❑ 208	Dave Krieg	.10	.02
❑ 209	Keith Cash	.05	.01
❑ 210	Patrick Bates RC	.05	.01
❑ 211	Nick Bell	.05	.01
❑ 212	Tim Brown	.25	.08
❑ 213	Willie Gault	.05	.01
❑ 214	Ethan Horton	.05	.01
❑ 215	Jeff Hostetler	.10	.02
❑ 216	Howie Long	.25	.08
❑ 217	Greg Townsend	.05	.01
❑ 218	Rocket Ismail	.10	.02
❑ 219	Alexander Wright	.05	.01
❑ 220	Greg Robinson RC	.05	.01
❑ 221	Billy Joe Hobert RC	.25	.08
❑ 222	Steve Wisniewski	.05	.01
❑ 223	Steve Smith	.05	.01
❑ 224	Vince Evans	.05	.01
❑ 225	Flipper Anderson	.05	.01
❑ 226	Jerome Bettis RC	4.00	1.50
❑ 227	Troy Drayton RC	.10	.02
❑ 228	Henry Ellard	.10	.02
❑ 229	Jim Everett	.10	.02
❑ 230	Tony Zendejas	.05	.01
❑ 231	Todd Lyght	.05	.01
❑ 232	Todd Kinchen	.05	.01
❑ 233	Jackie Slater	.05	.01
❑ 234	Fred Stokes	.05	.01
❑ 235	Russell White RC	.10	.02
❑ 236	Cleveland Gary	.05	.01
❑ 237	Sean LaChapelle RC	.05	.01
❑ 238	Steve Israel	.05	.01
❑ 239	Shane Conlan	.05	.01
❑ 240	Keith Byars	.05	.01
❑ 241	Marco Coleman	.05	.01
❑ 242	Bryan Cox	.05	.01
❑ 243	Irving Fryar	.10	.02
❑ 244	Richmond Webb	.05	.01
❑ 245	Mark Higgs	.05	.01
❑ 246	Terry Kirby RC	.25	.08
❑ 247	Mark Ingram	.05	.01
❑ 248	John Offerdahl	.05	.01
❑ 249	Keith Jackson	.10	.02
❑ 250	Dan Marino	1.50	.60
❑ 251	O.J.McDuffie RC	.25	.08
❑ 252	Louis Oliver	.05	.01
❑ 253	Pete Stoyanovich	.05	.01
❑ 254	Troy Vincent	.05	.01
❑ 255	Anthony Carter	.10	.02
❑ 256	Cris Carter	.25	.08
❑ 257	Roger Craig	.10	.02
❑ 258	Jack Del Rio	.05	.01
❑ 259	Chris Doleman	.05	.01
❑ 260	Barry Word	.05	.01
❑ 261	Qadry Ismail RC	.25	.08
❑ 262	Jim McMahon	.10	.02
❑ 263	Robert Smith RC	1.25	.50
❑ 264	Fred Strickland	.05	.01
❑ 265	Randall McDaniel	.05	.01
❑ 266	Carl Lee	.05	.01
❑ 267	Olanda Truitt RC UER	.05	.01
❑ 268	Terry Allen	.25	.08
❑ 269	Audray McMillian	.05	.01
❑ 270	Drew Bledsoe RC	2.50	1.00
❑ 271	Eugene Chung	.05	.01
❑ 272	Marv Cook	.05	.01
❑ 273	Pat Harlow	.05	.01
❑ 274	Greg McMurtry	.05	.01
❑ 275	Leonard Russell	.10	.02
❑ 276	Chris Slade RC	.10	.02
❑ 277	Andre Tippett	.05	.01
❑ 278	Vincent Brisby RC	.25	.08
❑ 279	Ben Coates	.50	.20
❑ 280	Sam Gash RC	.25	.08
❑ 281	Bruce Armstrong	.05	.01
❑ 282	Rod Smith DB	.05	.01
❑ 283	Michael Timpson	.05	.01
❑ 284	Scott Sisson RC	.05	.01
❑ 285	Morten Andersen	.05	.01
❑ 286	Reggie Freeman RC	.05	.01
❑ 287	Dalton Hilliard	.05	.01
❑ 288	Rickey Jackson	.05	.01
❑ 289	Vaughan Johnson	.05	.01
❑ 290	Eric Martin	.05	.01
❑ 291	Sam Mills	.05	.01
❑ 292	Brad Muster	.05	.01
❑ 293	Willie Roaf RC	.10	.02
❑ 294	Irv Smith RC	.05	.01
❑ 295	Wade Wilson	.05	.01
❑ 296	Derek Brown RC RBK	.10	.02
❑ 297	Quinn Early	.10	.02
❑ 298	Steve Walsh	.05	.01
❑ 299	Renaldo Turnbull	.05	.01
❑ 300	Jessie Armstead RC	.10	.02
❑ 301	Carlton Bailey	.05	.01
❑ 302	Michael Brooks	.05	.01
❑ 303	Rodney Hampton	.10	.02
❑ 304	Ed McCaffrey	.25	.08
❑ 305	Dave Meggett	.05	.01
❑ 306	Bart Oates	.05	.01
❑ 307	Mike Sherrard	.05	.01
❑ 308	Phil Simms	.10	.02
❑ 309	Lawrence Taylor	.25	.08
❑ 310	Mark Jackson	.05	.01
❑ 311	Jarrod Bunch	.05	.01
❑ 312	Howard Cross	.05	.01
❑ 313	Michael Strahan RC	1.50	.60
❑ 314	Marcus Buckley RC	.05	.01
❑ 315	Brad Baxter	.05	.01
❑ 316	Adrian Murrell RC	.25	.08
❑ 317	Boomer Esiason	.10	.02
❑ 318	Johnny Johnson	.05	.01
❑ 319	Marvin Jones RC	.05	.01
❑ 320	Jeff Lageman	.05	.01
❑ 321	Ronnie Lott	.10	.02
❑ 322	Leonard Marshall	.05	.01
❑ 323	Johnny Mitchell	.05	.01
❑ 324	Rob Moore	.10	.02
❑ 325	Browning Nagle	.05	.01
❑ 326	Blair Thomas	.05	.01
❑ 327	Brian Washington	.05	.01
❑ 328	Terance Mathis	.10	.02
❑ 329	Kyle Clifton	.05	.01
❑ 330	Eric Allen	.05	.01
❑ 331	Victor Bailey RC	.05	.01
❑ 332	Fred Barnett	.10	.02
❑ 333	Mark Bavaro	.05	.01
❑ 334	Randall Cunningham	.25	.08
❑ 335	Ken O'Brien	.05	.01
❑ 336	Seth Joyner	.05	.01
❑ 337	Leonard Renfro RC	.05	.01
❑ 338	Heath Sherman	.05	.01
❑ 339	Clyde Simmons	.05	.01
❑ 340	Herschel Walker	.10	.02
❑ 341	Calvin Williams	.10	.02
❑ 342	Bubby Brister	.05	.01
❑ 343	Vaughn Hebron RC	.05	.01
❑ 344	Keith Millard	.05	.01
❑ 345	Johnny Bailey	.05	.01
❑ 346	Steve Beuerlein	.10	.02
❑ 347	Chuck Cecil	.05	.01
❑ 348	Larry Centers RC	.25	.08
❑ 349	Chris Chandler	.10	.02
❑ 350	Ernest Dye RC	.05	.01
❑ 351	Garrison Hearst RC	.75	.30
❑ 352	Randal Hill	.05	.01
❑ 353	John Booty	.05	.01
❑ 354	Gary Clark	.10	.02
❑ 355	Ronald Moore RC	.10	.02
❑ 356	Ricky Proehl	.05	.01
❑ 357	Eric Swann	.10	.02
❑ 358	Ken Harvey	.05	.01
❑ 359	Ben Coleman RC	.05	.01
❑ 360	Deon Figures RC	.05	.01
❑ 361	Barry Foster	.10	.02
❑ 362	Jeff Graham	.10	.02
❑ 363	Eric Green	.05	.01
❑ 364	Kevin Greene	.10	.02
❑ 365	Andre Hastings RC	.10	.02
❑ 366	Greg Lloyd	.10	.02
❑ 367	Neil O'Donnell	.25	.08
❑ 368	Dwight Stone	.05	.01
❑ 369	Mike Tomczak	.05	.01
❑ 370	Rod Woodson	.25	.08
❑ 371	Chad Brown RC LB	.10	.02
❑ 372	Ernie Mills	.05	.01
❑ 373	Darren Perry	.05	.01
❑ 374	Leon Searcy	.05	.01
❑ 375	Marion Butts	.05	.01

❑ 376 John Carney .05 .01
❑ 377 Ronnie Harmon .05 .01
❑ 378 Stan Humphries .10 .02
❑ 379 Nate Lewis .05 .01
❑ 380 Natrone Means RC .25 .08
❑ 381 Anthony Miller .10 .02
❑ 382 Chris Mims .05 .01
❑ 383 Leslie O'Neal .10 .02
❑ 384 Joe Cocozzo RC .05 .01
❑ 385 Junior Seau .25 .08
❑ 386 Jerrol Williams .05 .01
❑ 387 John Friesz .10 .02
❑ 388 Darrien Gordon RC .05 .01
❑ 389 Derrick Walker .05 .01
❑ 390 Dana Hall .05 .01
❑ 391 Brent Jones .10 .02
❑ 392 Todd Kelly RC .05 .01
❑ 393 Amp Lee .05 .01
❑ 394 Tim McDonald .05 .01
❑ 395 Jerry Rice 1.00 .40
❑ 396 Dana Stubblefield RC .25 .08
❑ 397 John Taylor .10 .02
❑ 398 Ricky Watters .25 .08
❑ 399 Steve Young .75 .30
❑ 400 Steve Bono .10 .02
❑ 401 Adrian Hardy .05 .01
❑ 402 Tom Rathman .05 .01
❑ 403 Elvis Grbac RC UER 1.50 .60
❑ 404 Bill Romanowski .05 .01
❑ 405 Brian Blades .10 .02
❑ 406 Ferrell Edmunds .05 .01
❑ 407 Carlton Gray RC .05 .01
❑ 408 Cortez Kennedy .10 .02
❑ 409 Kelvin Martin .05 .01
❑ 410 Dan McGwire .05 .01
❑ 411 Rick Mirer RC .25 .08
❑ 412 Rufus Porter .05 .01
❑ 413 Chris Warren .10 .02
❑ 414 Jon Vaughn .05 .01
❑ 415 John L. Williams .05 .01
❑ 416 Eugene Robinson .05 .01
❑ 417 Michael McCrary RC .10 .02
❑ 418 Michael Bates RC .05 .01
❑ 419 Stan Gelbaugh .05 .01
❑ 420 Reggie Cobb .05 .01
❑ 421 Eric Curry RC .05 .01
❑ 422 Lawrence Dawsey .05 .01
❑ 423 Santana Dotson .10 .02
❑ 424 Craig Erickson .10 .02
❑ 425 Ron Hall .05 .01
❑ 426 Courtney Hawkins .05 .01
❑ 427 Broderick Thomas .05 .01
❑ 428 Vince Workman .05 .01
❑ 429 Demetrius DuBose RC .05 .01
❑ 430 Lamar Thomas RC .05 .01
❑ 431 John Lynch RC .60 .25
❑ 432 Hardy Nickerson .10 .02
❑ 433 Horace Copeland RC .10 .02
❑ 434 Steve DeBerg .05 .01
❑ 435 Joe Jacoby .05 .01
❑ 436 Tom Carter RC .10 .02
❑ 437 Andre Collins .05 .01
❑ 438 Darrell Green .05 .01
❑ 439 Desmond Howard .10 .02
❑ 440 Chip Lohmiller .05 .01
❑ 441 Charles Mann .05 .01
❑ 442 Tim McGee .05 .01
❑ 443 Art Monk .10 .02
❑ 444 Mark Rypien .05 .01
❑ 445 Ricky Sanders .05 .01
❑ 446 Brian Mitchell .10 .02
❑ 447 Reggie Brooks RC .10 .02
❑ 448 Carl Banks .05 .01
❑ 449 Cary Conklin .05 .01
❑ NNO Santa Claus 1.50 .60

1989 Score

❑ COMPLETE SET (330) 100.00 50.00
❑ COMP.FACT.SET (330) 100.00 50.00
❑ 1 Joe Montana 4.00 1.50
❑ 2 Bo Jackson .60 .25
❑ 3 Boomer Esiason .20 .07
❑ 4 Roger Craig .50 .20
❑ 5 Ed Too Tall Jones .20 .07
❑ 6 Phil Simms .20 .07
❑ 7 Dan Hampton .20 .07
❑ 8 John Settle RC .10 .02
❑ 9 Bernie Kosar .20 .07
❑ 10 Al Toon .20 .07
❑ 11 Bubby Brister RC 1.00 .40
❑ 12 Mark Clayton .20 .07
❑ 13 Dan Marino 4.00 1.50
❑ 14 Joe Morris .10 .02
❑ 15 Warren Moon .50 .20
❑ 16 Chuck Long .10 .02
❑ 17 Mark Jackson .10 .02
❑ 18 Michael Irvin RC 10.00 4.00
❑ 19 Bruce Smith .50 .20
❑ 20 Anthony Carter .20 .07
❑ 21 Charles Haley .50 .20
❑ 22 Dave Duerson .10 .02
❑ 23 Troy Stradford .10 .02
❑ 24 Freeman McNeil .10 .02
❑ 25 Jerry Gray .10 .02
❑ 26 Bill Maas .10 .02
❑ 27 Chris Chandler RC 4.00 1.50
❑ 28 Tom Newberry RC .10 .02
❑ 29 Albert Lewis .10 .02
❑ 30 Jay Schroeder .10 .02
❑ 31 Dalton Hilliard .10 .02
❑ 32 Tony Eason .10 .02
❑ 33 Rick Donnelly UER .10 .02
❑ 34 Herschel Walker .20 .07
❑ 35 Wesley Walker .10 .02
❑ 36 Chris Doleman .20 .07
❑ 37 Pat Swilling .20 .07
❑ 38 Joey Browner .10 .02
❑ 39 Shane Conlan .10 .02
❑ 40 Mike Tomczak .20 .07
❑ 41 Webster Slaughter .20 .07
❑ 42 Ray Donaldson .10 .02
❑ 43 Christian Okoye .10 .02
❑ 44 John Bosa .10 .02
❑ 45 Aaron Cox RC .10 .02
❑ 46 Bobby Hebert .20 .07
❑ 47 Carl Banks .10 .02
❑ 48 Jeff Fuller .10 .02
❑ 49 Gerald Willhite .10 .02
❑ 50 Mike Singletary .20 .07
❑ 51 Stanley Morgan .10 .02
❑ 52 Mark Bavaro .20 .07
❑ 53 Mickey Shuler .10 .02
❑ 54 Keith Millard .10 .02
❑ 55 Andre Tippett .10 .02
❑ 56 Vance Johnson .20 .07
❑ 57 Bennie Blades RC .20 .07
❑ 58 Tim Harris .10 .02
❑ 59 Hanford Dixon .10 .02
❑ 60 Chris Miller RC 1.00 .40
❑ 61 Cornelius Bennett .50 .20
❑ 62 Neal Anderson .20 .07
❑ 63 Ickey Woods RC UER .50 .20
❑ 64 Gary Anderson RB .10 .02
❑ 65 Vaughan Johnson RC .10 .02
❑ 66 Ronnie Lippett .10 .02
❑ 67 Mike Quick .10 .02
❑ 68 Roy Green .20 .07
❑ 69 Tim Krumrie .10 .02
❑ 70 Mark Malone .10 .02
❑ 71 James Jones FB .10 .02
❑ 72 Cris Carter RC 10.00 4.00
❑ 73 Ricky Nattiel .10 .02
❑ 74 Jim Arnold UER .10 .02
❑ 75 Randall Cunningham 1.00 .40
❑ 76 John L.Williams .10 .02
❑ 77 Paul Gruber RC .10 .02
❑ 78 Rod Woodson RC 3.00 1.25
❑ 79 Ray Childress .10 .02
❑ 80 Doug Williams .20 .07
❑ 81 Deron Cherry .20 .07
❑ 82 John Offerdahl .10 .02
❑ 83 Louis Lipps .20 .07
❑ 84 Neil Lomax .10 .02
❑ 85 Wade Wilson .20 .07
❑ 86 Tim Brown RC 10.00 4.00
❑ 87 Chris Hinton .10 .02
❑ 88 Stump Mitchell .10 .02
❑ 89 Tunch Ilkin RC .10 .02
❑ 90 Steve Pelluer .10 .02
❑ 91 Brian Noble .10 .02
❑ 92 Reggie White .50 .20
❑ 93 Aundray Bruce RC .10 .02
❑ 94 Garry James .10 .02
❑ 95 Drew Hill .10 .02
❑ 96 Anthony Munoz .20 .07
❑ 97 James Wilder .10 .02
❑ 98 Dexter Manley .10 .02
❑ 99 Lee Williams .10 .02
❑ 100 Dave Krieg .20 .07
❑ 101A Keith Jackson RC 84 .50 .20
❑ 101B Keith Jackson RC 88 .50 .20
❑ 102 Luis Sharpe .10 .02
❑ 103 Kevin Greene .50 .20
❑ 104 Duane Bickett .10 .02
❑ 105 Mark Rypien RC .50 .20
❑ 106 Curt Warner .10 .02
❑ 107 Jacob Green .10 .02
❑ 108 Gary Clark .50 .20
❑ 109 Bruce Matthews RC 3.00 1.25
❑ 110 Bill Fralic .10 .02
❑ 111 Bill Bates .20 .07
❑ 112 Jeff Bryant .10 .02
❑ 113 Charles Mann .10 .02
❑ 114 Richard Dent .20 .07
❑ 115 Bruce Hill RC .10 .02
❑ 116 Mark May RC .10 .02
❑ 117 Mark Collins RC .10 .02
❑ 118 Ron Holmes .10 .02
❑ 119 Scott Case RC .10 .02
❑ 120 Tom Rathman .10 .02
❑ 121 Dennis McKinnon .10 .02
❑ 122A Ricky Sanders ERR 46 .25 .08
❑ 122B Ricky Sanders COR 83 .50 .20
❑ 123 Michael Carter .10 .02
❑ 124 Ozzie Newsome .20 .07
❑ 125 Irving Fryar UER .20 .07
❑ 126A Ron Hall RC ERR .25 .08
❑ 126B Ron Hall RC COR .50 .20
❑ 127 Clay Matthews .20 .07
❑ 128 Leonard Marshall .10 .02
❑ 129 Kevin Mack .10 .02
❑ 130 Art Monk .20 .07
❑ 131 Garin Veris .10 .02
❑ 132 Steve Jordan .10 .02
❑ 133 Frank Minnifield .10 .02
❑ 134 Eddie Brown .10 .02
❑ 135 Stacey Bailey .10 .02
❑ 136 Rickey Jackson .20 .07
❑ 137 Henry Ellard .20 .07
❑ 138 Jim Burt .10 .02
❑ 139 Jerome Brown .20 .07
❑ 140 Rodney Holman RC .10 .02
❑ 141 Sammy Winder .10 .02
❑ 142 Marcus Cotton .10 .02
❑ 143 Jim Jeffcoat .10 .02
❑ 144 Rueben Mayes .10 .02
❑ 145 Jim McMahon .20 .07
❑ 146 Reggie Williams .10 .02
❑ 147 John Anderson .10 .02
❑ 148 Harris Barton RC .10 .02
❑ 149 Phillip Epps .10 .02
❑ 150 Jay Hilgenberg .10 .02
❑ 151 Earl Ferrell .10 .02
❑ 152 Andre Reed .50 .20
❑ 153 Dennis Gentry .10 .02
❑ 154 Max Montoya .10 .02
❑ 155 Darrin Nelson .10 .02
❑ 156 Jeff Chadwick .10 .02
❑ 157 James Brooks .20 .07
❑ 158 Keith Bishop .10 .02
❑ 159 Robert Awalt .10 .02
❑ 160 Marty Lyons .10 .02
❑ 161 Johnny Hector .10 .02
❑ 162 Tony Casillas .10 .02

❑ 163 Kyle Clifton RC	.10	.02
❑ 164 Cody Risien	.10	.02
❑ 165 Jamie Holland RC	.10	.02
❑ 166 Merril Hoge RC	.10	.02
❑ 167 Chris Spielman RC	1.00	.40
❑ 168 Carlos Carson	.10	.02
❑ 169 Jerry Ball RC	.10	.02
❑ 170 Don Majkowski RC	.50	.20
❑ 171 Everson Walls	.10	.02
❑ 172 Mike Rozier	.10	.02
❑ 173 Matt Millen	.20	.07
❑ 174 Karl Mecklenburg	.10	.02
❑ 175 Paul Palmer	.10	.02
❑ 176 Brian Blades RC UER	.50	.20
❑ 177 Brent Fullwood RC	.10	.02
❑ 178 Anthony Miller RC	.50	.20
❑ 179 Brian Sochia	.10	.02
❑ 180 Stephen Baker RC	.10	.02
❑ 181 Jesse Solomon	.10	.02
❑ 182 John Grimsley	.10	.02
❑ 183 Timmy Newsome	.10	.02
❑ 184 Steve Sewell RC	.10	.02
❑ 185 Dean Blasucci	.10	.02
❑ 186 Alonzo Highsmith	.10	.02
❑ 187 Randy Grimes	.10	.02
❑ 188A Mark Carrier RC WR ERR	1.00	.40
❑ 188B Mark Carrier RC WR COR	1.00	.40
❑ 189 Vann McElroy	.10	.02
❑ 190 Greg Bell	.10	.02
❑ 191 Quinn Early RC	1.00	.40
❑ 192 Lawrence Taylor	.50	.20
❑ 193 Albert Bentley	.10	.02
❑ 194 Ernest Givins	.20	.07
❑ 195 Jackie Slater	.10	.02
❑ 196 Jim Sweeney	.10	.02
❑ 197 Freddie Joe Nunn	.10	.02
❑ 198 Keith Byars	.20	.07
❑ 199 Hardy Nickerson RC	.50	.20
❑ 200 Steve Beuerlein RC	4.00	1.50
❑ 201 Bruce Armstrong RC	.50	.20
❑ 202 Lionel Manuel	.10	.02
❑ 203 J.T. Smith	.10	.02
❑ 204 Mark Ingram RC	.50	.20
❑ 205 Fred Smerlas	.10	.02
❑ 206 Bryan Hinkle RC	.10	.02
❑ 207 Steve McMichael	.20	.07
❑ 208 Nick Lowery	.10	.02
❑ 209 Jack Trudeau	.10	.02
❑ 210 Lorenzo Hampton	.10	.02
❑ 211 Thurman Thomas RC	8.00	3.00
❑ 212 Steve Young	1.50	.60
❑ 213 James Lofton	.50	.20
❑ 214 Jim Covert	.10	.02
❑ 215 Ronnie Lott	.20	.07
❑ 216 Stephone Paige	.10	.02
❑ 217 Mark Duper	.20	.07
❑ 218A Willie Gault ERR 93	.25	.08
❑ 218B Willie Gault COR 83	.50	.20
❑ 219 Ken Ruettgers RC	.10	.02
❑ 220 Kevin Ross RC	.10	.02
❑ 221 Jerry Rice	3.00	1.50
❑ 222 Billy Ray Smith	.10	.02
❑ 223 Jim Kelly	1.00	.40
❑ 224 Vinny Testaverde	1.00	.40
❑ 225 Steve Largent	.50	.20
❑ 226 Warren Williams RC	.10	.02
❑ 227 Morten Andersen	.10	.02
❑ 228 Bill Brooks	.20	.07
❑ 229 Reggie Langhorne RC	.10	.02
❑ 230 Pepper Johnson	.10	.02
❑ 231 Pat Leahy	.10	.02
❑ 232 Fred Marion	.10	.02
❑ 233 Gary Zimmerman	.10	.02
❑ 234 Marcus Allen	.50	.20
❑ 235 Gaston Green RC	.10	.02
❑ 236 John Stephens RC	.10	.02
❑ 237 Terry Kinard	.10	.02
❑ 238 John Taylor RC	.50	.20
❑ 239 Brian Bosworth	.20	.07
❑ 240 Anthony Toney	.10	.02
❑ 241 Ken O'Brien	.10	.02
❑ 242 Howie Long	.50	.20
❑ 243 Doug Flutie	2.50	1.00
❑ 244 Jim Everett	.50	.20
❑ 245 Broderick Thomas RC	.10	.02
❑ 246 Deion Sanders RC	10.00	4.00
❑ 247 Donnell Woolford RC	.10	.02
❑ 248 Wayne Martin RC	.10	.02
❑ 249 David Williams RC	.10	.02
❑ 250 Bill Hawkins RC	.10	.02
❑ 251 Eric Hill RC	.10	.02
❑ 252 Burt Grossman RC	.10	.02
❑ 253 Tracy Rocker	.10	.02
❑ 254 Steve Wisniewski RC	.50	.20
❑ 255 Jessie Small RC	.10	.02
❑ 256 David Braxton	.10	.02
❑ 257 Barry Sanders RC	40.00	15.00
❑ 258 Derrick Thomas RC	8.00	3.00
❑ 259 Eric Metcalf RC	1.00	.40
❑ 260 Keith DeLong RC	.10	.02
❑ 261 Hart Lee Dykes RC	.10	.02
❑ 262 Sammie Smith RC	.10	.02
❑ 263 Steve Atwater RC	.50	.20
❑ 264 Eric Ball RC	.10	.02
❑ 265 Don Beebe RC	.50	.20
❑ 266 Brian Williams OL RC	.10	.02
❑ 267 Jeff Lageman RC	.10	.02
❑ 268 Tim Worley RC	.10	.02
❑ 269 Tony Mandarich RC	.10	.02
❑ 270 Troy Aikman RC	30.00	12.50
❑ 271 Andy Heck RC	.10	.02
❑ 272 Andre Rison RC	5.00	2.50
❑ 273 AFC Champ/Woods/Esiason	.10	.02
❑ 274 NFC Champ/Joe Montana	1.00	.40
❑ 275 Joe Montana/Jerry Rice	2.00	.75
❑ 276 Rodney Carter	.10	.02
❑ 277 Mark Jackson/V.Johnson/Nattiel	.10	.02
❑ 278 John L. Williams	.10	.02
❑ 279 Joe Montana/Jerry Rice	2.00	.75
❑ 280 Roy Green/Lomax	.10	.02
❑ 281 Ran.Cunningham/K.Jackson	.10	.02
❑ 282 Chris Doleman and	.10	.02
❑ 283 Mark Duper and	.10	.02
❑ 284 Bo Jackson/Marcus Allen	.60	.25
❑ 285 Frank Minnifield AP	.10	.02
❑ 286 Bruce Matthews AP	.40	.15
❑ 287 Joey Browner AP	.10	.02
❑ 288 Jay Hilgenberg AP	.10	.02
❑ 289 Carl Lee RC AP	.10	.02
❑ 290 Scott Norwood AP RC	.10	.02
❑ 291 John Taylor AP	.50	.20
❑ 292 Jerry Rice AP	1.50	.60
❑ 293A Keith Jackson AP 84	.50	.20
❑ 293B Keith Jackson AP 88	.50	.20
❑ 294 Gary Zimmerman AP	.10	.02
❑ 295 Lawrence Taylor AP	.50	.20
❑ 296 Reggie White AP	.50	.20
❑ 297 Roger Craig AP	.20	.07
❑ 298 Boomer Esiason AP	.20	.07
❑ 299 Cornelius Bennett AP	.20	.07
❑ 300 Mike Horan AP	.10	.02
❑ 301 Deron Cherry AP	.10	.02
❑ 302 Tom Newberry AP	.10	.02
❑ 303 Mike Singletary AP	.20	.07
❑ 304 Shane Conlan AP	.10	.02
❑ 305A Tim Brown AP ERR 80	2.00	.75
❑ 305B Tim Brown AP COR 81	2.00	.75
❑ 306 Henry Ellard AP	.20	.07
❑ 307 Bruce Smith AP	.20	.07
❑ 308 Tim Krumrie AP	.10	.02
❑ 309 Anthony Munoz AP	.20	.07
❑ 310 Darrell Green SPD	.10	.02
❑ 311 Anthony Miller SPD	.50	.20
❑ 312 Wesley Walker SPEED	.10	.02
❑ 313 Ron Brown SPEED	.10	.02
❑ 314 Bo Jackson SPD	.60	.25
❑ 315 Phillip Epps SPEED	.10	.02
❑ 316A Eric Thomas RC SPD 31	.25	.08
❑ 316B Eric Thomas RC SPD 22	.50	.20
❑ 317 Herschel Walker SPD	.20	.07
❑ 318 Jacob Green PRED	.10	.02
❑ 319 Andre Tippett PRED	.10	.02
❑ 320 Freddie Joe Nunn PRED	.10	.02
❑ 321 Reggie White PRED	.50	.20
❑ 322 Lawrence Taylor PRED	.50	.20
❑ 323 Greg Townsend PRED	.10	.02
❑ 324 Tim Harris PRED	.10	.02
❑ 325 Bruce Smith PRED	.20	.07
❑ 326 Tony Dorsett RB	.50	.20
❑ 327 Steve Largent RB	.50	.20
❑ 328 Tim Brown RB	2.00	.75
❑ 329 Joe Montana RB	1.50	.60
❑ 330 Tom Landry Tribute	1.00	.40

1990 Score

❑ COMPLETE SET (660)	15.00	6.00
❑ COMP.FACT.SET (665)	20.00	7.50
❑ 1 Joe Montana	1.25	.50
❑ 2 Christian Okoye	.04	.01
❑ 3 Mike Singletary UER	.10	.02
❑ 4 Jim Everett UER	.10	.02
❑ 5 Phil Simms	.10	.02
❑ 6 Brent Fullwood	.04	.01
❑ 7 Bill Fralic	.04	.01
❑ 8 Leslie O'Neal	.10	.02
❑ 9 John Taylor	.25	.08
❑ 10 Bo Jackson	.30	.10
❑ 11 John Stephens	.04	.01
❑ 12 Art Monk	.10	.02
❑ 13 Dan Marino	1.25	.50
❑ 14 John Settle	.04	.01
❑ 15 Don Majkowski	.04	.01
❑ 16 Bruce Smith	.25	.08
❑ 17 Brad Muster	.04	.01
❑ 18 Jason Buck	.04	.01
❑ 19 James Brooks	.10	.02
❑ 20 Barry Sanders	1.25	.50
❑ 21 Troy Aikman	.75	.30
❑ 22 Allen Pinkett	.04	.01
❑ 23 Duane Bickett	.04	.01
❑ 24 Kevin Ross	.04	.01
❑ 25 John Elway	1.25	.50
❑ 26 Jeff Query	.04	.01
❑ 27 Eddie Murray	.04	.01
❑ 28 Richard Dent	.10	.02
❑ 29 Lorenzo White	.04	.01
❑ 30 Eric Metcalf	.25	.08
❑ 31 Jeff Dellenbach RC	.04	.01
❑ 32 Leon White	.04	.01
❑ 33 Jim Jeffcoat	.04	.01
❑ 34 Herschel Walker	.10	.02
❑ 35 Mike Johnson UER	.04	.01
❑ 36 Joe Phillips	.04	.01
❑ 37 Willie Gault	.10	.02
❑ 38 Keith Millard	.04	.01
❑ 39 Fred Marion	.04	.01
❑ 40 Boomer Esiason	.10	.02
❑ 41 Dermontti Dawson	.10	.02
❑ 42 Dino Hackett	.04	.01
❑ 43 Reggie Roby	.04	.01
❑ 44 Roger Vick	.04	.01
❑ 45 Bobby Hebert	.04	.01
❑ 46 Don Beebe	.10	.02
❑ 47 Neal Anderson	.10	.02
❑ 48 Johnny Holland	.04	.01
❑ 49 Bobby Humphery	.04	.01
❑ 50 Lawrence Taylor	.25	.08
❑ 51 Billy Ray Smith	.04	.01
❑ 52 Robert Perryman	.04	.01
❑ 53 Gary Anderson K	.04	.01
❑ 54 Raul Allegre	.04	.01
❑ 55 Pat Swilling	.10	.02
❑ 56 Chris Doleman	.04	.01
❑ 57 Andre Reed	.25	.08
❑ 58 Seth Joyner	.10	.02
❑ 59 Bart Oates	.04	.01
❑ 60 Bernie Kosar	.10	.02
❑ 61 Dave Krieg	.10	.02
❑ 62 Lars Tate	.04	.01
❑ 63 Scott Norwood	.04	.01
❑ 64 Kyle Clifton	.04	.01
❑ 65 Alan Veingrad	.04	.01
❑ 66 Gerald Riggs UER	.10	.02

❑ 67 Tim Worley .04 .01
❑ 68 Rodney Holman .04 .01
❑ 69 Tony Zendejas .04 .01
❑ 70 Chris Miller .25 .08
❑ 71 Wilber Marshall .04 .01
❑ 72 Skip McClendon RC .04 .01
❑ 73 Jim Covert .04 .01
❑ 74 Sam Mills .10 .02
❑ 75 Chris Hinton .04 .01
❑ 76 Irv Eatman .04 .01
❑ 77 Bubba Paris UER .04 .01
❑ 78 John Elliott UER .04 .01
❑ 79 Thomas Everett .04 .01
❑ 80 Steve Smith .04 .01
❑ 81 Jackie Slater .04 .01
❑ 82 Kelvin Martin RC .04 .01
❑ 83 Jo Jo Townsell .04 .01
❑ 84 Jim C. Jensen .04 .01
❑ 85 Bobby Humphrey .04 .01
❑ 86 Mike Dyal .04 .01
❑ 87 Andre Rison UER .25 .08
❑ 88 Brian Sochia .04 .01
❑ 89 Greg Bell .04 .01
❑ 90 Dalton Hilliard .04 .01
❑ 91 Carl Banks .04 .01
❑ 92 Dennis Smith .04 .01
❑ 93 Bruce Matthews .10 .02
❑ 94 Charles Haley .10 .02
❑ 95 Deion Sanders .50 .20
❑ 96 Stephone Paige .04 .01
❑ 97 Marion Butts FSC .10 .02
❑ 98 Howie Long .25 .08
❑ 99 Donald Igwebuike .04 .01
❑ 100 Roger Craig UER .10 .02
❑ 101 Charles Mann .04 .01
❑ 102 Fredd Young .04 .01
❑ 103 Chris Jacke .04 .01
❑ 104 Scott Case .04 .01
❑ 105 Warren Moon .25 .08
❑ 106 Clyde Simmons .04 .01
❑ 107 Steve Atwater .04 .01
❑ 108 Morten Andersen .04 .01
❑ 109 Eugene Marve .04 .01
❑ 110 Thurman Thomas .25 .08
❑ 111 Carnell Lake .04 .01
❑ 112 Jim Kelly .25 .08
❑ 113 Stanford Jennings .04 .01
❑ 114 Jacob Green .04 .01
❑ 115 Karl Mecklenburg .04 .01
❑ 116 Ray Childress .04 .01
❑ 117 Erik McMillan .04 .01
❑ 118 Harry Newsome .04 .01
❑ 119 James Dixon .04 .01
❑ 120 Hassan Jones .04 .01
❑ 121 Eric Allen .04 .01
❑ 122 Felix Wright .04 .01
❑ 123 Merril Hoge .04 .01
❑ 124 Eric Ball .04 .01
❑ 125 Flipper Anderson FSC .04 .01
❑ 126 James Jefferson .04 .01
❑ 127 Tim McDonald .04 .01
❑ 128 Larry Kinnebrew .04 .01
❑ 129 Mark Collins .04 .01
❑ 130 Ickey Woods .04 .01
❑ 131 Jeff Donaldson UER .04 .01
❑ 132 Rich Camarillo .04 .01
❑ 133 Melvin Bratton RC .04 .01
❑ 134A Kevin Butler .35 .12
❑ 134B Kevin Butler .50 .20
❑ 135 Albert Bentley .04 .01
❑ 136A Vai Sikahema .35 .12
❑ 136B Vai Sikahema .50 .20
❑ 137 Todd McNair RC .04 .01
❑ 138 Alonzo Highsmith .04 .01
❑ 139 Brian Blades .10 .02
❑ 140 Jeff Lageman .04 .01
❑ 141 Eric Thomas .04 .01
❑ 142 Derek Hill .04 .01
❑ 143 Rick Fenney .04 .01
❑ 144 Herman Heard .04 .01
❑ 145 Steve Young .50 .20
❑ 146 Kent Hull .04 .01
❑ 147A Joey Browner face left .35 .12
❑ 147B Joey Browner straight .50 .20
❑ 148 Frank Minnifield .04 .01
❑ 149 Robert Massey .04 .01
❑ 150 Dave Meggett .10 .02
❑ 151 Bubba McDowell .04 .01
❑ 152 Rickey Dixon RC .04 .01
❑ 153 Ray Donaldson .04 .01
❑ 154 Alvin Walton .04 .01
❑ 155 Mike Cofer .04 .01
❑ 156 Darryl Talley .04 .01
❑ 157 A.J. Johnson .04 .01
❑ 158 Jerry Gray .04 .01
❑ 159 Keith Byars .04 .01
❑ 160 Andy Heck .04 .01
❑ 161 Mike Munchak .10 .02
❑ 162 Dennis Gentry .04 .01
❑ 163 Timm Rosenbach UER .04 .01
❑ 164 Randall McDaniel .10 .02
❑ 165 Pat Leahy .04 .01
❑ 166 Bubby Brister .04 .01
❑ 167 Aundray Bruce .04 .01
❑ 168 Bill Brooks .04 .01
❑ 169 Eddie Anderson RC .04 .01
❑ 170 Ronnie Lott .10 .02
❑ 171 Jay Hilgenberg .04 .01
❑ 172 Joe Nash .04 .01
❑ 173 Simon Fletcher .04 .01
❑ 174 Shane Conlan .04 .01
❑ 175 Sean Landeta .04 .01
❑ 176 John Alt RC .04 .01
❑ 177 Clay Matthews .10 .02
❑ 178 Anthony Munoz .10 .02
❑ 179 Pete Holohan .04 .01
❑ 180 Robert Awalt .04 .01
❑ 181 Rohn Stark .04 .01
❑ 182 Vance Johnson .04 .01
❑ 183 David Fulcher .04 .01
❑ 184 Robert Delpino FSC .04 .01
❑ 185 Drew Hill .04 .01
❑ 186 Reggie Langhorne UER .04 .01
❑ 187 Lonzell Hill .04 .01
❑ 188 Tom Rathman UER .04 .01
❑ 189 Greg Montgomery RC .04 .01
❑ 190 Leonard Smith .04 .01
❑ 191 Chris Spielman .25 .08
❑ 192 Tom Newberry .04 .01
❑ 193 Cris Carter .50 .20
❑ 194 Kevin Porter RC .04 .01
❑ 195 Donnell Thompson .04 .01
❑ 196 Vaughan Johnson .04 .01
❑ 197 Steve McMichael .10 .02
❑ 198 Jim Sweeney .04 .01
❑ 199 Rich Karlis UER .04 .01
❑ 200 Jerry Rice .75 .30
❑ 201 Dan Hampton UER .10 .02
❑ 202 Jim Lachey .04 .01
❑ 203 Reggie White .25 .08
❑ 204 Jerry Ball .04 .01
❑ 205 Russ Grimm .04 .01
❑ 206 Tim Green RC .04 .01
❑ 207 Shawn Collins .04 .01
❑ 208A R.Mojsiejenko Chargers .15 .05
❑ 208B R.Mojsiejenko Redskins .50 .20
❑ 209 Trace Armstrong .04 .01
❑ 210 Keith Jackson .10 .02
❑ 211 Jamie Holland .04 .01
❑ 212 Mark Clayton .10 .02
❑ 213 Jeff Cross .04 .01
❑ 214 Bob Gagliano .04 .01
❑ 215 Louis Oliver UER .04 .01
❑ 216 Jim Arnold .04 .01
❑ 217 Robert Clark RC .04 .01
❑ 218 Gill Byrd .04 .01
❑ 219 Rodney Peete .10 .02
❑ 220 Anthony Miller .25 .08
❑ 221 Steve Grogan .10 .02
❑ 222 Vince Newsome RC .04 .01
❑ 223 Thomas Benson .04 .01
❑ 224 Kevin Murphy .04 .01
❑ 225 Henry Ellard .10 .02
❑ 226 Richard Johnson .04 .01
❑ 227 Jim Skow .04 .01
❑ 228 Keith Jones .04 .01
❑ 229 Dave Brown DB .04 .01
❑ 230 Marcus Allen .25 .08
❑ 231 Steve Walsh .10 .02
❑ 232 Jim Harbaugh .25 .08
❑ 233 Mel Gray .10 .02
❑ 234 David Treadwell .04 .01
❑ 235 John Offerdahl .04 .01
❑ 236 Gary Reasons .04 .01
❑ 237 Tim Krumrie .04 .01
❑ 238 Dave Duerson .04 .01
❑ 239 Gary Clark UER .25 .08
❑ 240 Mark Jackson .04 .01
❑ 241 Mark Murphy .04 .01
❑ 242 Jerry Holmes .04 .01
❑ 243 Tim McGee .04 .01
❑ 244 Mike Tomczak .10 .02
❑ 245 Sterling Sharpe UER .25 .08
❑ 246 Bennie Blades .04 .01
❑ 247 Ken Harvey RC UER .25 .08
❑ 248 Ron Heller .04 .01
❑ 249 Louis Lipps .10 .02
❑ 250 Wade Wilson .10 .02
❑ 251 Freddie Joe Nunn .04 .01
❑ 252 Jerome Brown UER .04 .01
❑ 253 Myron Guyton .04 .01
❑ 254 Nate Odomes RC .10 .02
❑ 255 Rod Woodson .25 .08
❑ 256 Cornelius Bennett .10 .02
❑ 257 Keith Woodside .04 .01
❑ 258 Jeff Uhlenhake UER .04 .01
❑ 259 Harry Hamilton .04 .01
❑ 260 Mark Bavaro .04 .01
❑ 261 Vinny Testaverde .10 .02
❑ 262 Steve DeBerg .04 .01
❑ 263 Steve Wisniewski UER .10 .02
❑ 264 Pete Mandley .04 .01
❑ 265 Tim Harris .04 .01
❑ 266 Jack Trudeau .04 .01
❑ 267 Mark Kelso .04 .01
❑ 268 Brian Noble .04 .01
❑ 269 Jessie Tuggle RC .04 .01
❑ 270 Ken O'Brien .04 .01
❑ 271 David Little .04 .01
❑ 272 Pete Stoyanovich .04 .01
❑ 273 Odessa Turner RC .04 .01
❑ 274 Anthony Toney .04 .01
❑ 275 Tunch Ilkin .04 .01
❑ 276 Carl Lee .04 .01
❑ 277 Hart Lee Dykes .04 .01
❑ 278 Al Noga .04 .01
❑ 279 Greg Lloyd .25 .08
❑ 280 Billy Joe Tolliver .04 .01
❑ 281 Kirk Lowdermilk .04 .01
❑ 282 Earl Ferrell .04 .01
❑ 283 Eric Sievers RC .04 .01
❑ 284 Steve Jordan .04 .01
❑ 285 Burt Grossman .04 .01
❑ 286 Johnny Rembert .04 .01
❑ 287 Jeff Jaeger RC .04 .01
❑ 288 James Hasty .04 .01
❑ 289 Tony Mandarich DP .04 .01
❑ 290 Chris Singleton RC .04 .01
❑ 291 Lynn James RC .04 .01
❑ 292 Andre Ware RC .25 .08
❑ 293 Ray Agnew RC .04 .01
❑ 294 Joel Smeenge RC .04 .01
❑ 295 Marc Spindler RC .04 .01
❑ 296 Renaldo Turnbull RC .04 .01
❑ 297 Reggie Rembert RC .04 .01
❑ 298 Jeff Alm RC .04 .01
❑ 299 Cortez Kennedy RC .25 .08
❑ 300 Blair Thomas RC .10 .02
❑ 301 Pat Terrell RC .04 .01
❑ 302 Junior Seau RC 1.25 .50
❑ 303 Mo Elewonibi RC .04 .01
❑ 304 Tony Bennett RC .25 .08
❑ 305 Percy Snow RC .04 .01
❑ 306 Richmond Webb RC .04 .01
❑ 307 Rodney Hampton RC .25 .08
❑ 308 Barry Foster RC .25 .08
❑ 309 John Friesz RC .25 .08
❑ 310 Ben Smith RC .04 .01
❑ 311 Joe Montana HG .50 .20
❑ 312 Jim Everett HG .10 .02
❑ 313 Mark Rypien HG .10 .02
❑ 314 Phil Simms HG UER .10 .02
❑ 315 Don Majkowski HG .04 .01
❑ 316 Boomer Esiason HG .04 .01
❑ 317 Warren Moon HG Moon .25 .08
❑ 318 Jim Kelly HG .25 .08
❑ 319 Bernie Kosar HG UER .10 .02
❑ 320 Dan Marino HG UER .50 .20
❑ 321 Christian Okoye GF .04 .01
❑ 322 Thurman Thomas GF .25 .08
❑ 323 James Brooks GF .10 .02

❑ 324	Bobby Humphrey GF	.04	.01
❑ 325	Barry Sanders GF	.60	.25
❑ 326	Neal Anderson GF	.04	.01
❑ 327	Dalton Hilliard GF	.04	.01
❑ 328	Greg Bell GF	.04	.01
❑ 329	Roger Craig GF UER	.10	.02
❑ 330	Bo Jackson GF	.30	.10
❑ 331	Don Warren	.04	.01
❑ 332	Rufus Porter	.04	.01
❑ 333	Sammie Smith	.04	.01
❑ 334	Lewis Tillman	.04	.01
❑ 335	Michael Walter	.04	.01
❑ 336	Marc Logan	.04	.01
❑ 337	Ron Hallstrom RC	.04	.01
❑ [illegible]	[illegible]	[illegible]	[illegible]
❑ 339	Mark Robinson	.04	.01
❑ 340	Frank Reich	.25	.08
❑ 341	Chip Lohmiller FSC	.04	.01
❑ 342	Steve Beuerlein	.10	.02
❑ 343	John L. Williams	.04	.01
❑ 344	Irving Fryar	.25	.08
❑ 345	Anthony Carter	.10	.02
❑ 346	Al Toon	.10	.02
❑ 347	J.T. Smith	.04	.01
❑ 348	Pierce Holt RC	.04	.01
❑ 349	Ferrell Edmunds	.04	.01
❑ 350	Mark Rypien	.10	.02
❑ 351	Paul Gruber	.04	.01
❑ 352	Ernest Givins	.10	.02
❑ 353	Ervin Randle	.04	.01
❑ 354	Guy McIntyre	.04	.01
❑ 355	Webster Slaughter	.10	.02
❑ 356	Reuben Davis	.04	.01
❑ 357	Rickey Jackson	.10	.02
❑ 358	Earnest Byner	.04	.01
❑ 359	Eddie Brown	.04	.01
❑ 360	Troy Stradford	.04	.01
❑ 361	Pepper Johnson	.04	.01
❑ 362	Ravin Caldwell	.04	.01
❑ 363	Chris Mohr RC	.04	.01
❑ 364	Jeff Bryant	.04	.01
❑ 365	Bruce Collie	.04	.01
❑ 366	Courtney Hall	.04	.01
❑ 367	Jerry Olsavsky	.04	.01
❑ 368	David Galloway	.04	.01
❑ 369	Wes Hopkins	.04	.01
❑ 370	Johnny Hector	.04	.01
❑ 371	Clarence Verdin	.04	.01
❑ 372	Nick Lowery	.04	.01
❑ 373	Tim Brown	.25	.08
❑ 374	Kevin Greene	.10	.02
❑ 375	Leonard Marshall	.04	.01
❑ 376	Roland James	.04	.01
❑ 377	Scott Studwell	.04	.01
❑ 378	Jarvis Williams	.04	.01
❑ 379	Mike Saxon	.04	.01
❑ 380	Kevin Mack	.04	.01
❑ 381	Joe Kelly	.04	.01
❑ 382	Tom Thayer RC	.04	.01
❑ 383	Roy Green	.10	.02
❑ 384	Michael Brooks RC	.04	.01
❑ 385	Michael Cofer	.04	.01
❑ 386	Ken Ruettgers	.04	.01
❑ 387	Dean Steinkuhler	.04	.01
❑ 388	Maurice Carthon	.04	.01
❑ 389	Ricky Sanders	.04	.01
❑ 390	Winston Moss RC	.04	.01
❑ 391	Tony Woods	.04	.01
❑ 392	Keith DeLong	.04	.01
❑ 393	David Wyman	.04	.01
❑ 394	Vencie Glenn	.04	.01
❑ 395	Harris Barton	.04	.01
❑ 396	Bryan Hinkle	.04	.01
❑ 397	Derek Kennard	.04	.01
❑ 398	Heath Sherman RC	.04	.01
❑ 399	Troy Benson	.04	.01
❑ 400	Gary Zimmerman	.04	.01
❑ 401	Mark Duper	.10	.02
❑ 402	Eugene Lockhart	.04	.01
❑ 403	Tim Manoa	.04	.01
❑ 404	Reggie Williams	.04	.01
❑ 405	Mark Bortz RC	.04	.01
❑ 406	Mike Kenn	.04	.01
❑ 407	John Grimsley	.04	.01
❑ 408	Bill Romanowski RC	1.00	.40
❑ 409	Perry Kemp	.04	.01
❑ 410	Norm Johnson	.04	.01
❑ 411	Broderick Thomas	.04	.01
❑ 412	Joe Wolf	.04	.01
❑ 413	Andre Waters	.04	.01
❑ 414	Jason Staurovsky	.04	.01
❑ 415	Eric Martin	.04	.01
❑ 416	Joe Prokop	.04	.01
❑ 417	Steve Sewell	.04	.01
❑ 418	Cedric Jones	.04	.01
❑ 419	Alphonso Carreker	.04	.01
❑ 420	Keith Willis	.04	.01
❑ 421	Bobby Butler	.04	.01
❑ 422	John Roper	.04	.01
❑ 423	Tim Spencer	.04	.01
❑ 424	Jesse Sapolu RC	.04	.01
❑ [illegible]	[illegible]	[illegible]	[illegible]
❑ 426	Doug Smith	.04	.01
❑ 427	William Howard	.04	.01
❑ 428	Keith Van Horne	.04	.01
❑ 429	Tony Jordan	.04	.01
❑ 430	Mervyn Fernandez	.04	.01
❑ 431	Shaun Gayle RC	.04	.01
❑ 432	Ricky Nattiel	.04	.01
❑ 433	Albert Lewis	.04	.01
❑ 434	Fred Banks RC	.04	.01
❑ 435	Henry Thomas	.04	.01
❑ 436	Chet Brooks	.04	.01
❑ 437	Mark Ingram	.10	.02
❑ 438	Jeff Gossett	.04	.01
❑ 439	Mike Wilcher	.04	.01
❑ 440	Deron Cherry UER	.04	.01
❑ 441	Mike Rozier	.04	.01
❑ 442	Jon Hand	.04	.01
❑ 443	Ozzie Newsome	.10	.02
❑ 444	Sammy Martin	.04	.01
❑ 445	Luis Sharpe	.04	.01
❑ 446	Lee Williams	.04	.01
❑ 447	Chris Martin RC	.04	.01
❑ 448	Kevin Fagan RC	.04	.01
❑ 449	Gene Lang	.04	.01
❑ 450	Greg Townsend	.04	.01
❑ 451	Robert Lyles	.04	.01
❑ 452	Eric Hill	.04	.01
❑ 453	John Teltschik	.04	.01
❑ 454	Vestee Jackson	.04	.01
❑ 455	Bruce Reimers	.04	.01
❑ 456	Butch Rolle RC	.04	.01
❑ 457	Lawyer Tillman	.04	.01
❑ 458	Andre Tippett	.04	.01
❑ 459	James Thornton	.04	.01
❑ 460	Randy Grimes	.04	.01
❑ 461	Larry Roberts	.04	.01
❑ 462	Ron Holmes	.04	.01
❑ 463	Mike Wise DE	.04	.01
❑ 464	Danny Copeland RC	.04	.01
❑ 465	Bruce Wilkerson RC	.04	.01
❑ 466	Mike Quick	.04	.01
❑ 467	Mickey Shuler	.04	.01
❑ 468	Mike Prior	.04	.01
❑ 469	Ron Rivera	.04	.01
❑ 470	Dean Biasucci	.04	.01
❑ 471	Perry Williams	.04	.01
❑ 472	Darren Comeaux UER	.04	.01
❑ 473	Freeman McNeil	.04	.01
❑ 474	Tyrone Braxton	.04	.01
❑ 475	Jay Schroeder	.04	.01
❑ 476	Naz Worthen	.04	.01
❑ 477	Lionel Washington	.04	.01
❑ 478	Carl Zander	.04	.01
❑ 479	Al(Bubba) Baker	.10	.02
❑ 480	Mike Merriweather	.04	.01
❑ 481	Mike Gann	.04	.01
❑ 482	Brent Williams	.04	.01
❑ 483	Eugene Robinson	.04	.01
❑ 484	Ray Horton	.04	.01
❑ 485	Bruce Armstrong	.04	.01
❑ 486	John Fourcade	.04	.01
❑ 487	Lewis Billups	.04	.01
❑ 488	Scott Davis	.04	.01
❑ 489	Kenneth Sims	.04	.01
❑ 490	Chris Chandler	.25	.08
❑ 491	Mark Lee	.04	.01
❑ 492	Johnny Meads	.04	.01
❑ 493	Tim Irwin	.04	.01
❑ 494	E.J. Junior	.04	.01
❑ 495	Hardy Nickerson	.10	.02
❑ 496	Rob McGovern	.04	.01
❑ 497	Fred Strickland RC	.04	.01
❑ 498	Reggie Rutland RC	.04	.01
❑ 499	Mel Owens	.04	.01
❑ 500	Derrick Thomas	.25	.08
❑ 501	Jerrol Williams	.04	.01
❑ 502	Maurice Hurst RC	.04	.01
❑ 503	Larry Kelm RC	.04	.01
❑ 504	Herman Fontenot	.04	.01
❑ 505	Pat Beach	.04	.01
❑ 506	Haywood Jeffires RC	.25	.08
❑ 507	Neil Smith	.25	.08
❑ 508	Cleveland Gary FSC	.04	.01
❑ 509	William Perry	.10	.02
❑ 510	Michael Carter	.04	.01
❑ 511	Walker Lee Ashley	.04	.01
❑ [illegible]	[illegible]	[illegible]	[illegible]
❑ 513	Danny Villa RC	.04	.01
❑ 514	Matt Millen	.10	.02
❑ 515	Don Griffin	.04	.01
❑ 516	Jonathan Hayes	.04	.01
❑ 517	Gerald Williams RC	.04	.01
❑ 518	Scott Fulhage	.04	.01
❑ 519	Irv Pankey	.04	.01
❑ 520	Randy Dixon RC	.04	.01
❑ 521	Terry McDaniel	.04	.01
❑ 522	Dan Saleaumua	.04	.01
❑ 523	Darrin Nelson	.04	.01
❑ 524	Leonard Griffin	.04	.01
❑ 525	Michael Ball RC	.04	.01
❑ 526	Ernie Jones RC	.04	.01
❑ 527	Tony Eason UER	.04	.01
❑ 528	Ed Reynolds	.04	.01
❑ 529	Gary Hogeboom	.04	.01
❑ 530	Don Mosebar	.04	.01
❑ 531	Ottis Anderson	.10	.02
❑ 532	Bucky Scribner	.04	.01
❑ 533	Aaron Cox	.04	.01
❑ 534	Sean Jones	.10	.02
❑ 535	Doug Flutie	.50	.20
❑ 536	Leo Lewis	.04	.01
❑ 537	Art Still	.04	.01
❑ 538	Matt Bahr	.04	.01
❑ 539	Keena Turner	.04	.01
❑ 540	Sammy Winder	.04	.01
❑ 541	Mike Webster	.10	.02
❑ 542	Doug Riesenberg RC	.04	.01
❑ 543	Dan Fike	.04	.01
❑ 544	Clarence Kay	.04	.01
❑ 545	Jim Burt	.04	.01
❑ 546	Mike Horan	.04	.01
❑ 547	Al Harris	.04	.01
❑ 548	Maury Buford	.04	.01
❑ 549	Jerry Robinson	.04	.01
❑ 550	Tracy Rocker	.04	.01
❑ 551	Karl Mecklenburg CC	.04	.01
❑ 552	Lawrence Taylor CC	.25	.08
❑ 553	Derrick Thomas CC	.25	.08
❑ 554	Mike Singletary CC	.10	.02
❑ 555	Tim Harris CC	.04	.01
❑ 556	Jerry Rice RM	.50	.20
❑ 557	Art Monk RM	.10	.02
❑ 558	Mark Carrier WR RM	.10	.02
❑ 559	Andre Reed RM	.10	.02
❑ 560	Sterling Sharpe RM	.25	.08
❑ 561	Herschel Walker GF	.10	.02
❑ 562	Ottis Anderson GF	.10	.02
❑ 563	Randall Cunningham HG	.10	.02
❑ 564	John Elway HG	.50	.20
❑ 565	David Fulcher AP	.04	.01
❑ 566	Ronnie Lott AP	.10	.02
❑ 567	Jerry Gray AP	.04	.01
❑ 568	Albert Lewis AP	.04	.01
❑ 569	Karl Mecklenburg AP	.04	.01
❑ 570	Mike Singletary AP	.10	.02
❑ 571	Lawrence Taylor AP	.25	.08
❑ 572	Tim Harris AP	.04	.01
❑ 573	Keith Millard AP	.04	.01
❑ 574	Reggie White AP	.25	.08
❑ 575	Chris Doleman AP	.04	.01
❑ 576	Dave Meggett AP	.10	.02
❑ 577	Rod Woodson AP	.25	.08
❑ 578	Sean Landeta AP	.04	.01
❑ 579	Eddie Murray AP	.04	.01
❑ 580	Barry Sanders AP	.60	.25
❑ 581	Christian Okoye AP	.04	.01
❑ 582	Joe Montana AP	.50	.20
❑ 583	Jay Hilgenberg AP	.04	.01
❑ 584	Bruce Matthews AP	.10	.02

❑ 585 Tom Newberry AP	.04	.01
❑ 586 Gary Zimmerman AP	.04	.01
❑ 587 Anthony Munoz AP	.10	.02
❑ 588 Keith Jackson AP	.10	.02
❑ 589 Sterling Sharpe AP	.25	.08
❑ 590 Jerry Rice AP	.50	.20
❑ 591 Bo Jackson RB	.30	.10
❑ 592 Steve Largent RB	.25	.08
❑ 593 Flipper Anderson RB	.04	.01
❑ 594 Joe Montana RB	.50	.20
❑ 595 Franco Harris HOF	.10	.02
❑ 596 Bob St. Clair HOF	.04	.01
❑ 597 Tom Landry HOF	.10	.02
❑ 598 Jack Lambert HOF	.10	.02
❑ 599 Ted Hendricks HOF	.04	.01
❑ 600A Buck Buchanan HOF ERR 83	.10	.02
❑ 600B Buck Buchanan HOF COR 63	.10	.02
❑ 601 Bob Griese HOF	.10	.02
❑ 602 Super Bowl Wrap	.04	.01
❑ 603A Vince Lombardi w/o logo	.20	.07
❑ 603B Vince Lombardi Curt.logo	.20	.07
❑ 604 Mark Carrier WR UER	.10	.02
❑ 605 Randall Cunningham	.25	.08
❑ 606 Percy Snow C90	.04	.01
❑ 607 Andre Ware C90	.25	.08
❑ 608 Blair Thomas C90	.10	.02
❑ 609 Eric Green C90	.04	.01
❑ 610 Reggie Rembert C90	.04	.01
❑ 611 Richmond Webb C90	.04	.01
❑ 612 Bern Brostek C90	.04	.01
❑ 613 James Williams C90	.04	.01
❑ 614 Mark Carrier DB C90	.10	.02
❑ 615 Renaldo Turnbull C90	.04	.01
❑ 616 Cortez Kennedy C90	.10	.02
❑ 617 Keith McCants C90	.04	.01
❑ 618 Anthony Thompson RC	.04	.01
❑ 619 LeRoy Butler RC	.25	.08
❑ 620 Aaron Wallace RC	.04	.01
❑ 621 Alexander Wright RC	.04	.01
❑ 622 Keith McCants RC	.04	.01
❑ 623 Jimmie Jones RC	.04	.01
❑ 624 Anthony Johnson RC	.25	.08
❑ 625 Fred Washington RC	.04	.01
❑ 626 Mike Bellamy RC	.04	.01
❑ 627 Mark Carrier DB RC	.25	.08
❑ 628 Harold Green RC	.25	.08
❑ 629 Eric Green RC	.10	.02
❑ 630 Andre Collins RC	.04	.01
❑ 631 Lamar Lathon RC	.10	.02
❑ 632 Terry Wooden RC	.04	.01
❑ 633 Jesse Anderson RC	.04	.01
❑ 634 Jeff George RC	.50	.20
❑ 635 Carwell Gardner RC	.04	.01
❑ 636 Darrell Thompson RC	.04	.01
❑ 637 Vince Buck RC	.04	.01
❑ 638 Mike Jones TE RC	.04	.01
❑ 639 Charles Arbuckle RC	.04	.01
❑ 640 Dennis Brown RC	.04	.01
❑ 641 James Williams DB RC	.04	.01
❑ 642 Bern Brostek RC	.04	.01
❑ 643 Darion Conner RC	.10	.02
❑ 644 Mike Fox RC	.04	.01
❑ 645 Cary Conklin RC	.04	.01
❑ 646 Tim Grunhard RC	.04	.01
❑ 647 Ron Cox RC	.04	.01
❑ 648 Keith Sims RC	.04	.01
❑ 649 Alton Montgomery RC	.04	.01
❑ 650 Greg McMurtry RC	.04	.01
❑ 651 Scott Mitchell RC	.25	.08
❑ 652 Tim Ryan DE RC	.04	.01
❑ 653 Jeff Mills RC	.04	.01
❑ 654 Ricky Proehl RC	.25	.08
❑ 655 Steve Broussard RC	.04	.01
❑ 656 Peter Tom Willis RC	.04	.01
❑ 657 Dexter Carter RC	.04	.01
❑ 658 Tony Casillas	.04	.01
❑ 659 Joe Morris	.04	.01
❑ 660 Greg Kragen	.04	.01
❑ B1 Matt Stover FF	.25	.08
❑ B2 Demetrius Davis	.04	.01
❑ B3 Ken McMichel	.04	.01
❑ B4 Judd Garrett FF	.04	.01
❑ B5 Elliott Searcy	.04	.01

1990 Score Supplemental

❑ COMP.FACT.SET (110)	80.00	40.00
❑ 1T Marcus Dupree RC**	.15	.05
❑ 2T Jerry Kauric	.15	.05
❑ 3T Everson Walls	.15	.05
❑ 4T Elliott Smith	.15	.05
❑ 5T Donald Evans RC UER	.30	.10
❑ 6T Jerry Holmes	.15	.05
❑ 7T Dan Stryzinski RC	.15	.05
❑ 8T Gerald McNeil	.15	.05
❑ 9T Rick Tuten RC	.15	.05
❑ 10T Mickey Shuler	.15	.05
❑ 11T Jay Novacek	.60	.25
❑ 12T Eric Williams RC	.15	.05
❑ 13T Stanley Morgan	.15	.05
❑ 14T Wayne Haddix RC	.15	.05
❑ 15T Gary Anderson RB	.15	.05
❑ 16T Stan Humphries RC	.60	.25
❑ 17T Raymond Clayborn	.15	.05
❑ 18T Mark Boyer RC	.15	.05
❑ 19T Dave Waymer	.15	.05
❑ 20T Andre Rison	.60	.25
❑ 21T Daniel Stubbs	.15	.05
❑ 22T Mike Rozier	.15	.05
❑ 23T Damian Johnson	.15	.05
❑ 24T Don Smith RBK RC	.15	.05
❑ 25T Max Montoya	.15	.05
❑ 26T Terry Kinard	.15	.05
❑ 27T Herb Welch	.15	.05
❑ 28T Cliff Odom	.15	.05
❑ 29T John Kidd	.15	.05
❑ 30T Barry Word RC	.15	.05
❑ 31T Rich Karlis	.15	.05
❑ 32T Mike Baab	.15	.05
❑ 33T Ronnie Harmon	.30	.10
❑ 34T Jeff Donaldson	.15	.05
❑ 35T Riki Ellison	.15	.05
❑ 36T Steve Walsh	.30	.10
❑ 37T Bill Lewis RC	.15	.05
❑ 38T Tim McKyer	.15	.05
❑ 39T James Wilder	.15	.05
❑ 40T Tony Paige	.15	.05
❑ 41T Derrick Fenner RC	.15	.05
❑ 42T Thane Gash RC	.15	.05
❑ 43T Dave Duerson	.15	.05
❑ 44T Clarence Weathers	.15	.05
❑ 45T Matt Bahr	.15	.05
❑ 46T Alonzo Highsmith	.15	.05
❑ 47T Joe Kelly	.15	.05
❑ 48T Chris Hinton	.15	.05
❑ 49T Bobby Humphery	.15	.05
❑ 50T Greg Bell	.15	.05
❑ 51T Fred Smerlas	.15	.05
❑ 52T Walter Stanley	.15	.05
❑ 53T Jim Skow	.15	.05
❑ 54T Renaldo Turnbull	.15	.05
❑ 55T Bern Brostek	.15	.05
❑ 56T Charles Wilson RC	.15	.05
❑ 57T Keith McCants	.15	.05
❑ 58T Alexander Wright	.30	.10
❑ 59T Ian Beckles RC	.15	.05
❑ 60T Eric Davis RC	.30	.10
❑ 61T Chris Singleton	.15	.05
❑ 62T Rob Moore RC	2.50	1.00
❑ 63T Darion Conner	.30	.10
❑ 64T Tim Grunhard	.15	.05
❑ 65T Junior Seau	6.00	2.50
❑ 66T Tony Stargell RC	.15	.05
❑ 67T Anthony Thompson	.15	.05
❑ 68T Cortez Kennedy	.60	.25
❑ 69T Darrell Thompson	.15	.05
❑ 70T Calvin Williams RC	.60	.25
❑ 71T Rodney Hampton	.60	.25
❑ 72T Terry Wooden	.15	.05
❑ 73T Leo Goeas RC	.15	.05
❑ 74T Ken Willis	.15	.05
❑ 75T Ricky Proehl	.60	.25
❑ 76T Steve Christie RC	.15	.05
❑ 77T Andre Ware	.60	.25
❑ 78T Jeff George	2.50	1.00
❑ 79T Walter Wilson	.15	.05
❑ 80T Johnny Bailey RC	.15	.05
❑ 81T Harold Green	.30	.10
❑ 82T Mark Carrier DB	.60	.25
❑ 83T Frank Cornish	.15	.05
❑ 84T James Williams	.15	.05
❑ 85T James Francis RC	.15	.05
❑ 86T Percy Snow	.15	.05
❑ 87T Anthony Johnson	.60	.25
❑ 88T Tim Ryan DE	.15	.05
❑ 89T Dan Owens RC	.15	.05
❑ 90T Aaron Wallace RC	.15	.05
❑ 91T Steve Broussard	.15	.05
❑ 92T Eric Green	.15	.05
❑ 93T Blair Thomas	.30	.10
❑ 94T Robert Blackmon RC	.15	.05
❑ 95T Alan Grant RC	.15	.05
❑ 96T Andre Collins	.15	.05
❑ 97T Dexter Carter	.15	.05
❑ 98T Reggie Cobb RC	.15	.05
❑ 99T Dennis Brown	.15	.05
❑ 100T Kenny Davidson RC	.15	.05
❑ 101T Emmitt Smith RC	60.00	30.00
❑ 102T Jeff Alm	.15	.05
❑ 103T Alton Montgomery	.15	.05
❑ 104T Tony Bennett	.60	.25
❑ 105T Johnny Johnson RC	.30	.10
❑ 106T Leroy Hoard RC	.60	.25
❑ 107T Ray Agnew	.15	.05
❑ 108T Richmond Webb	.15	.05
❑ 109T Keith Sims	.15	.05
❑ 110T Barry Foster	.60	.25

1991 Score

❑ COMPLETE SET (686)	20.00	7.50
❑ COMP.FACT.SET (690)	25.00	12.50
❑ 1 Joe Montana	1.25	.50
❑ 2 Eric Allen	.05	.01
❑ 3 Rohn Stark	.05	.01
❑ 4 Frank Reich	.10	.02
❑ 5 Derrick Thomas	.25	.08
❑ 6 Mike Singletary	.10	.02
❑ 7 Boomer Esiason	.10	.02
❑ 8 Matt Millen	.10	.02
❑ 9 Chris Spielman	.10	.02
❑ 10 Gerald McNeil	.05	.01
❑ 11 Nick Lowery	.05	.01
❑ 12 Randall Cunningham	.25	.08
❑ 13 Marion Butts	.10	.02
❑ 14 Tim Brown	.25	.08
❑ 15 Emmitt Smith	2.50	1.00
❑ 16 Rich Camarillo	.05	.01
❑ 17 Mike Merriweather	.05	.01
❑ 18 Derrick Fenner	.05	.01
❑ 19 Clay Matthews	.10	.02
❑ 20 Barry Sanders	1.25	.50
❑ 21 James Brooks	.10	.02
❑ 22 Alton Montgomery	.05	.01
❑ 23 Steve Atwater	.05	.01
❑ 24 Ron Morris	.05	.01
❑ 25 Brad Muster	.05	.01
❑ 26 Andre Rison	.10	.02

❑ 27 Brian Brennan .05 .01
❑ 28 Leonard Smith .05 .01
❑ 29 Kevin Butler .05 .01
❑ 30 Tim Harris .05 .01
❑ 31 Jay Novacek .25 .08
❑ 32 Eddie Murray .05 .01
❑ 33 Keith Woodside .05 .01
❑ 34 Ray Crockett RC .05 .01
❑ 35 Eugene Lockhart .05 .01
❑ 36 Bill Romanowski .05 .01
❑ 37 Eddie Brown .05 .01
❑ 38 Eugene Daniel .05 .01
❑ 39 Scott Fulhage .05 .01
❑ 40 Harold Green .10 .02
❑ [illegible]
❑ 42 Sterling Sharpe .25 .08
❑ 43 Mel Gray .10 .02
❑ 44 Jerry Holmes .05 .01
❑ 45 Allen Pinkett .05 .01
❑ 46 Warren Powers .05 .01
❑ 47 Rodney Peete .10 .02
❑ 48 Lorenzo White .05 .01
❑ 49 Dan Owens .05 .01
❑ 50 James Francis .05 .01
❑ 51 Ken Norton .10 .02
❑ 52 Ed West .05 .01
❑ 53 Andre Reed .10 .02
❑ 54 John Grimsley .05 .01
❑ 55 Michael Cofer .05 .01
❑ 56 Chris Doleman .05 .01
❑ 57 Pat Swilling .10 .02
❑ 58 Jessie Tuggle .05 .01
❑ 59 Mike Johnson .05 .01
❑ 60 Steve Walsh .05 .01
❑ 61 Sam Mills .05 .01
❑ 62 Don Mosebar .05 .01
❑ 63 Jay Hilgenberg .05 .01
❑ 64 Cleveland Gary .05 .01
❑ 65 Andre Tippett .05 .01
❑ 66 Tom Newberry .05 .01
❑ 67 Maurice Hurst .05 .01
❑ 68 Louis Oliver .05 .01
❑ 69 Fred Marion .05 .01
❑ 70 Christian Okoye .05 .01
❑ 71 Marv Cook FSC .05 .01
❑ 72 Darryl Talley .05 .01
❑ 73 Rick Fenney .05 .01
❑ 74 Kelvin Martin .05 .01
❑ 75 Howie Long .25 .08
❑ 76 Steve Wisniewski .05 .01
❑ 77 Karl Mecklenburg .05 .01
❑ 78 Dan Saleaumua .05 .01
❑ 79 Ray Childress .05 .01
❑ 80 Henry Ellard .10 .02
❑ 81 Ernest Givins UER .10 .02
❑ 82 Ferrell Edmunds .05 .01
❑ 83 Steve Jordan .05 .01
❑ 84 Tony Mandarich .05 .01
❑ 85 Eric Martin .05 .01
❑ 86 Rich Gannon FSC .25 .08
❑ 87 Irving Fryar .10 .02
❑ 88 Tom Rathman .05 .01
❑ 89 Dan Hampton .10 .02
❑ 90 Barry Word .05 .01
❑ 91 Kevin Greene .10 .02
❑ 92 Sean Landeta .05 .01
❑ 93 Trace Armstrong .05 .01
❑ 94 Dennis Byrd .05 .01
❑ 95 Timm Rosenbach .05 .01
❑ 96 Anthony Toney .05 .01
❑ 97 Tim Krumrie .05 .01
❑ 98 Jerry Ball .05 .01
❑ 99 Tim Green .05 .01
❑ 100 Bo Jackson .30 .10
❑ 101 Myron Guyton .05 .01
❑ 102 Mike Mularkey .05 .01
❑ 103 Jerry Gray .05 .01
❑ 104 Scott Stephen RC .05 .01
❑ 105 Anthony Bell .05 .01
❑ 106 Lomas Brown .05 .01
❑ 107 David Little .05 .01
❑ 108 Brad Baxter FSC .05 .01
❑ 109 Freddie Joe Nunn .05 .01
❑ 110 Dave Meggett .10 .02
❑ 111 Mark Rypien .10 .02
❑ 112 Warren Williams .05 .01
❑ 113 Ron Rivera .05 .01
❑ 114 Terance Mathis .10 .02
❑ 115 Anthony Munoz .10 .02
❑ 116 Jeff Bryant .05 .01
❑ 117 Issiac Holt .05 .01
❑ 118 Steve Sewell .05 .01
❑ 119 Tim Newton .05 .01
❑ 120 Emile Harry .05 .01
❑ 121 Gary Anderson K .05 .01
❑ 122 Mark Lee .05 .01
❑ 123 Alfred Anderson .05 .01
❑ 124 Anthony Blaylock .05 .01
❑ 125 Earnest Byner .05 .01
❑ 126 Bill Maas .05 .01
❑ 127 Keith Taylor .05 .01
❑ [illegible]
❑ 129 Bob Golic .05 .01
❑ 130 Bart Oates .05 .01
❑ 131 Jim Arnold .05 .01
❑ 132 Jeff Herrod .05 .01
❑ 183 Bruce Armstrong .05 .01
❑ 134 Craig Heyward .10 .02
❑ 135 Joey Browner .05 .01
❑ 136 Darren Comeaux .05 .01
❑ 137 Pat Beach .05 .01
❑ 138 Dalton Hilliard .05 .01
❑ 139 David Treadwell .05 .01
❑ 140 Gary Anderson RB .05 .01
❑ 141 Eugene Robinson .05 .01
❑ 142 Scott Case .05 .01
❑ 143 Paul Farren .05 .01
❑ 144 Gill Fenerty .05 .01
❑ 145 Tim Irwin .05 .01
❑ 146 Norm Johnson .05 .01
❑ 147 Willie Gault .10 .02
❑ 148 Clarence Verdin .05 .01
❑ 149 Jeff Uhlenhake .05 .01
❑ 150 Erik McMillan .05 .01
❑ 151 Kevin Ross .05 .01
❑ 152 Pepper Johnson .05 .01
❑ 153 Bryan Hinkle .05 .01
❑ 154 Gary Clark .25 .08
❑ 155 Robert Delpino .05 .01
❑ 156 Doug Smith .05 .01
❑ 157 Chris Martin .05 .01
❑ 158 Ray Berry .05 .01
❑ 159 Steve Christie .05 .01
❑ 160 Don Smith RB .05 .01
❑ 161 Greg McMurtry .05 .01
❑ 162 Jack Del Rio .10 .02
❑ 163 Floyd Dixon .05 .01
❑ 164 Buford McGee .05 .01
❑ 165 Brett Maxie .05 .01
❑ 166 Morten Andersen .05 .01
❑ 167 Kent Hull .05 .01
❑ 168 Skip McClendon .05 .01
❑ 169 Keith Sims .05 .01
❑ 170 Leonard Marshall .05 .01
❑ 171 Tony Woods .05 .01
❑ 172 Byron Evans .05 .01
❑ 173 Rob Burnett RC .10 .02
❑ 174 Tory Epps .05 .01
❑ 175 Toi Cook RC .05 .01
❑ 176 John Elliott .05 .01
❑ 177 Tommie Agee .05 .01
❑ 178 Keith Van Horne .05 .01
❑ 179 Dennis Smith .05 .01
❑ 180 James Lofton .10 .02
❑ 181 Art Monk .10 .02
❑ 182 Anthony Carter .10 .02
❑ 183 Louis Lipps .05 .01
❑ 184 Bruce Hill .05 .01
❑ 185 Michael Young .05 .01
❑ 186 Eric Green .05 .01
❑ 187 Barney Bussey RC .05 .01
❑ 188 Curtis Duncan .05 .01
❑ 189 Robert Awalt .05 .01
❑ 190 Johnny Johnson .05 .01
❑ 191 Jeff Cross .05 .01
❑ 192 Keith McKeller .05 .01
❑ 193 Robert Brown .05 .01
❑ 194 Vincent Brown .05 .01
❑ 195 Calvin Williams .10 .02
❑ 196 Sean Jones .10 .02
❑ 197 Willie Drewrey .05 .01
❑ 198 Bubba McDowell .05 .01
❑ 199 Al Noga .05 .01
❑ 200 Ronnie Lott .10 .02
❑ 201 Warren Moon .25 .08
❑ 202 Chris Hinton .05 .01
❑ 203 Jim Sweeney .05 .01
❑ 204 Wayne Haddix .05 .01
❑ 205 Tim Jorden RC .05 .01
❑ 206 Marvin Allen .05 .01
❑ 207 Jim Morrissey RC .05 .01
❑ 208 Ben Smith .05 .01
❑ 209 William White .05 .01
❑ 210 Jim C. Jensen .05 .01
❑ 211 Doug Reed .05 .01
❑ 212 Ethan Horton .05 .01
❑ 213 Chris Jacke .05 .01
❑ 214 Johnny Hector .05 .01
❑ [illegible]
❑ 216 Roy Green .05 .01
❑ 217 Dean Steinkuhler .05 .01
❑ 218 Cedric Mack .05 .01
❑ 219 Chris Miller .10 .02
❑ 220 Keith Byars .05 .01
❑ 221 Lewis Billups .05 .01
❑ 222 Roger Craig .10 .02
❑ 223 Shaun Gayle .05 .01
❑ 224 Mike Rozier .05 .01
❑ 225 Troy Aikman .75 .30
❑ 226 Bobby Humphrey .05 .01
❑ 227 Eugene Marve .05 .01
❑ 228 Michael Carter .05 .01
❑ 229 Richard Johnson CB RC .05 .01
❑ 230 Billy Joe Tolliver .05 .01
❑ 231 Mark Murphy .05 .01
❑ 232 John L. Williams .05 .01
❑ 233 Ronnie Harmon .05 .01
❑ 234 Thurman Thomas .25 .08
❑ 235 Martin Mayhew .05 .01
❑ 236 Richmond Webb .05 .01
❑ 237 Gerald Riggs UER .10 .02
❑ 238 Mike Prior .05 .01
❑ 239 Mike Gann .05 .01
❑ 240 Alvin Walton .05 .01
❑ 241 Tim McGee .05 .01
❑ 242 Bruce Matthews .10 .02
❑ 243 Johnny Holland .05 .01
❑ 244 Martin Bayless .05 .01
❑ 245 Eric Metcalf .10 .02
❑ 246 John Alt .05 .01
❑ 247 Max Montoya .05 .01
❑ 248 Rod Bernstine .05 .01
❑ 249 Paul Gruber .05 .01
❑ 250 Charles Haley .10 .02
❑ 251 Scott Norwood .05 .01
❑ 252 Michael Haddix .05 .01
❑ 253 Ricky Sanders .05 .01
❑ 254 Ervin Randle .05 .01
❑ 255 Duane Bickett .05 .01
❑ 256 Mike Munchak .10 .02
❑ 257 Keith Jones .05 .01
❑ 258 Riki Ellison .05 .01
❑ 259 Vince Newsome .05 .01
❑ 260 Lee Williams .05 .01
❑ 261 Steve Smith .05 .01
❑ 262 Sam Clancy .05 .01
❑ 263 Pierce Holt .05 .01
❑ 264 Jim Harbaugh .25 .08
❑ 265 Dino Hackett .05 .01
❑ 266 Andy Heck .05 .01
❑ 267 Leo Goeas .05 .01
❑ 268 Russ Grimm .05 .01
❑ 269 Gill Byrd .05 .01
❑ 270 Neal Anderson .10 .02
❑ 271 Jackie Slater .05 .01
❑ 272 Joe Nash .05 .01
❑ 273 Todd Bowles .05 .01
❑ 274 D.J. Dozier .05 .01
❑ 275 Kevin Fagan .05 .01
❑ 276 Don Warren .05 .01
❑ 277 Jim Jeffcoat .05 .01
❑ 278 Bruce Smith .25 .08
❑ 279 Cortez Kennedy .25 .08
❑ 280 Thane Gash .05 .01
❑ 281 Perry Kemp .05 .01
❑ 282 John Taylor .10 .02
❑ 283 Stephone Paige .05 .01
❑ 284 Paul Skansi .05 .01
❑ 285 Shawn Collins .05 .01
❑ 286 Mervyn Fernandez .05 .01
❑ 287 Daniel Stubbs .05 .01

❑ 288	Chip Lohmiller	.05	.01
❑ 289	Brian Blades	.10	.02
❑ 290	Mark Carrier WR	.25	.08
❑ 291	Carl Zander	.05	.01
❑ 292	David Wyman	.05	.01
❑ 293	Jeff Bostic	.05	.01
❑ 294	Irv Pankey	.05	.01
❑ 295	Keith Millard	.05	.01
❑ 296	Jamie Mueller	.05	.01
❑ 297	Bill Fralic	.05	.01
❑ 298	Wendell Davis FSC	.05	.01
❑ 299	Ken Clarke	.05	.01
❑ 300	Wymon Henderson	.05	.01
❑ 301	Jeff Campbell	.05	.01
❑ 302	Cody Carlson RC	.05	.01
❑ 303	Matt Brock RC	.05	.01
❑ 304	Maurice Carthon	.05	.01
❑ 305	Scott Mersereau RC	.05	.01
❑ 306	Steve Wright RC	.05	.01
❑ 307	J.B. Brown	.05	.01
❑ 308	Ricky Reynolds	.05	.01
❑ 309	Darryl Pollard	.05	.01
❑ 310	Donald Evans	.05	.01
❑ 311	Nick Bell RC	.05	.01
❑ 312	Pat Harlow RC	.05	.01
❑ 313	Dan McGwire RC	.05	.01
❑ 314	Mike Dumas RC	.05	.01
❑ 315	Mike Croel RC	.05	.01
❑ 316	Chris Smith RC	.05	.01
❑ 317	Kenny Walker RC	.05	.01
❑ 318	Todd Lyght RC	.05	.01
❑ 319	Mike Stonebreaker	.05	.01
❑ 320	Randall Cunningham 90	.10	.02
❑ 321	Terance Mathis 90	.25	.08
❑ 322	Gaston Green 90	.05	.01
❑ 323	Johnny Bailey 90	.05	.01
❑ 324	Donnie Elder 90	.05	.01
❑ 325	Dwight Stone 90 UER	.05	.01
❑ 326	J.J.Birden RC 90	.10	.02
❑ 327	Alexander Wright 90	.05	.01
❑ 328	Eric Metcalf 90	.10	.02
❑ 329	Andre Rison TL	.10	.02
❑ 330	Warren Moon TL UER	.10	.02
❑ 331	Steve Tasker DT	.05	.01
❑ 332	Mel Gray DT	.10	.02
❑ 333	Nick Lowery DT	.05	.01
❑ 334	Sean Landeta DT	.05	.01
❑ 335	David Fulcher DT	.05	.01
❑ 336	Joey Browner DT	.05	.01
❑ 337	Albert Lewis DT	.05	.01
❑ 338	Rod Woodson DT	.10	.02
❑ 339	Shane Conlan DT	.05	.01
❑ 340	Pepper Johnson DT	.05	.01
❑ 341	Chris Spielman DT	.05	.01
❑ 342	Derrick Thomas DT	.10	.02
❑ 343	Ray Childress DT	.05	.01
❑ 344	Reggie White DT	.10	.02
❑ 345	Bruce Smith DT	.10	.02
❑ 346	Darrell Green	.05	.01
❑ 347	Ray Bentley	.05	.01
❑ 348	Herschel Walker	.10	.02
❑ 349	Rodney Holman	.05	.01
❑ 350	Al Toon	.10	.02
❑ 351	Harry Hamilton	.05	.01
❑ 352	Albert Lewis	.05	.01
❑ 353	Renaldo Turnbull	.05	.01
❑ 354	Junior Seau	.25	.08
❑ 355	Merril Hoge	.05	.01
❑ 356	Shane Conlan	.05	.01
❑ 357	Jay Schroeder	.05	.01
❑ 358	Steve Broussard	.05	.01
❑ 359	Mark Bavaro	.05	.01
❑ 360	Jim Lachey	.05	.01
❑ 361	Greg Townsend	.05	.01
❑ 362	Dave Krieg	.10	.02
❑ 363	Jessie Hester	.05	.01
❑ 364	Steve Tasker	.10	.02
❑ 365	Ron Hall	.05	.01
❑ 366	Pat Leahy	.05	.01
❑ 367	Jim Everett	.10	.02
❑ 368	Felix Wright	.05	.01
❑ 369	Ricky Proehl	.05	.01
❑ 370	Anthony Miller	.10	.02
❑ 371	Keith Jackson	.10	.02
❑ 372	Pete Stoyanovich	.05	.01
❑ 373	Tommy Kane	.05	.01
❑ 374	Richard Johnson	.05	.01
❑ 375	Randall McDaniel	.05	.01
❑ 376	John Stephens	.05	.01
❑ 377	Haywood Jeffires	.10	.02
❑ 378	Rodney Hampton	.25	.08
❑ 379	Tim Grunhard	.05	.01
❑ 380	Jerry Rice	.75	.30
❑ 381	Ken Harvey	.10	.02
❑ 382	Vaughan Johnson	.05	.01
❑ 383	J.T. Smith	.05	.01
❑ 384	Carnell Lake	.05	.01
❑ 385	Dan Marino	1.25	.50
❑ 386	Kyle Clifton	.05	.01
❑ 387	Wilber Marshall	.05	.01
❑ 388	Pete Holohan	.05	.01
❑ 389	Gary Plummer	.05	.01
❑ 390	William Perry	.10	.02
❑ 391	Mark Robinson	.05	.01
❑ 392	Nate Odomes	.05	.01
❑ 393	Ickey Woods	.05	.01
❑ 394	Reyna Thompson	.05	.01
❑ 395	Deion Sanders	.40	.15
❑ 396	Harris Barton	.05	.01
❑ 397	Sammie Smith	.05	.01
❑ 398	Vinny Testaverde	.10	.02
❑ 399	Ray Donaldson	.05	.01
❑ 400	Tim McKyer	.05	.01
❑ 401	Nesby Glasgow	.05	.01
❑ 402	Brent Williams	.05	.01
❑ 403	Rob Moore	.25	.08
❑ 404	Bubby Brister	.05	.01
❑ 405	David Fulcher	.05	.01
❑ 406	Reggie Cobb	.05	.01
❑ 407	Jerome Brown	.05	.01
❑ 408	Erik Howard	.05	.01
❑ 409	Tony Paige	.05	.01
❑ 410	John Elway	1.25	.50
❑ 411	Charles Mann	.05	.01
❑ 412	Luis Sharpe	.05	.01
❑ 413	Hassan Jones	.05	.01
❑ 414	Frank Minnifield	.05	.01
❑ 415	Steve DeBerg	.05	.01
❑ 416	Mark Carrier DB	.10	.02
❑ 417	Brian Jordan FSC	.10	.02
❑ 418	Reggie Langhorne	.05	.01
❑ 419	Don Majkowski	.05	.01
❑ 420	Marcus Allen	.25	.08
❑ 421	Michael Brooks	.05	.01
❑ 422	Vai Sikahema	.05	.01
❑ 423	Dermontti Dawson	.05	.01
❑ 424	Jacob Green	.05	.01
❑ 425	Flipper Anderson	.05	.01
❑ 426	Bill Brooks	.05	.01
❑ 427	Keith McCants	.05	.01
❑ 428	Ken O'Brien	.05	.01
❑ 429	Fred Barnett FSC	.25	.08
❑ 430	Mark Duper	.10	.02
❑ 431	Mark Kelso	.05	.01
❑ 432	Leslie O'Neal	.10	.02
❑ 433	Ottis Anderson	.10	.02
❑ 434	Jesse Sapolu	.05	.01
❑ 435	Gary Zimmerman	.05	.01
❑ 436	Kevin Porter	.05	.01
❑ 437	Anthony Thompson	.05	.01
❑ 438	Robert Clark	.05	.01
❑ 439	Chris Warren	.25	.08
❑ 440	Gerald Williams	.05	.01
❑ 441	Jim Skow	.05	.01
❑ 442	Rick Donnelly	.05	.01
❑ 443	Guy McIntyre	.05	.01
❑ 444	Jeff Lageman	.05	.01
❑ 445	John Offerdahl	.05	.01
❑ 446	Clyde Simmons	.05	.01
❑ 447	John Kidd	.05	.01
❑ 448	Chip Banks	.05	.01
❑ 449	Johnny Meads	.05	.01
❑ 450	Rickey Jackson	.05	.01
❑ 451	Lee Johnson	.05	.01
❑ 452	Michael Irvin	.25	.08
❑ 453	Leon Seals	.05	.01
❑ 454	Darrell Thompson	.05	.01
❑ 455	Everson Walls	.05	.01
❑ 456	LeRoy Butler	.10	.02
❑ 457	Marcus Dupree	.05	.01
❑ 458	Kirk Lowdermilk	.05	.01
❑ 459	Chris Singleton	.05	.01
❑ 460	Seth Joyner	.10	.02
❑ 461	Rueben Mayes UER	.05	.01
❑ 462	Ernie Jones	.05	.01
❑ 463	Greg Kragen	.05	.01
❑ 464	Bennie Blades	.05	.01
❑ 465	Mark Bortz	.05	.01
❑ 466	Tony Stargell	.05	.01
❑ 467	Mike Cofer	.05	.01
❑ 468	Randy Grimes	.05	.01
❑ 469	Tim Worley	.05	.01
❑ 470	Kevin Mack	.05	.01
❑ 471	Wes Hopkins	.05	.01
❑ 472	Will Wolford	.05	.01
❑ 473	Sam Seale	.05	.01
❑ 474	Jim Ritcher	.05	.01
❑ 475	Jeff Hostetler FSC	.25	.08
❑ 476	Mitchell Price RC	.05	.01
❑ 477	Ken Lanier	.05	.01
❑ 478	Naz Worthen	.05	.01
❑ 479	Ed Reynolds	.05	.01
❑ 480	Mark Clayton	.10	.02
❑ 481	Matt Bahr	.05	.01
❑ 482	Gary Reasons	.05	.01
❑ 483	David Szott	.05	.01
❑ 484	Barry Foster	.10	.02
❑ 485	Bruce Reimers	.05	.01
❑ 486	Dean Biasucci	.05	.01
❑ 487	Cris Carter	.50	.20
❑ 488	Albert Bentley	.05	.01
❑ 489	Robert Massey	.05	.01
❑ 490	Al Smith	.05	.01
❑ 491	Greg Lloyd	.25	.08
❑ 492	Steve McMichael UER	.10	.02
❑ 493	Jeff Wright RC	.05	.01
❑ 494	Scott Davis	.05	.01
❑ 495	Freeman McNeil	.05	.01
❑ 496	Simon Fletcher	.05	.01
❑ 497	Terry McDaniel	.05	.01
❑ 498	Heath Sherman	.05	.01
❑ 499	Jeff Jaeger	.05	.01
❑ 500	Mark Collins	.05	.01
❑ 501	Tim Goad	.05	.01
❑ 502	Jeff George	.25	.08
❑ 503	Jimmie Jones	.05	.01
❑ 504	Henry Thomas	.05	.01
❑ 505	Steve Young	.75	.30
❑ 506	William Roberts	.05	.01
❑ 507	Neil Smith	.25	.08
❑ 508	Mike Saxon	.05	.01
❑ 509	Johnny Bailey	.05	.01
❑ 510	Broderick Thomas	.05	.01
❑ 511	Wade Wilson	.10	.02
❑ 512	Hart Lee Dykes	.05	.01
❑ 513	Hardy Nickerson	.10	.02
❑ 514	Tim McDonald	.05	.01
❑ 515	Frank Cornish	.05	.01
❑ 516	Jarvis Williams	.05	.01
❑ 517	Carl Lee	.05	.01
❑ 518	Carl Banks	.05	.01
❑ 519	Mike Golic	.05	.01
❑ 520	Brian Noble	.05	.01
❑ 521	James Hasty	.05	.01
❑ 522	Bubba Paris	.05	.01
❑ 523	Kevin Walker RC	.05	.01
❑ 524	William Fuller	.10	.02
❑ 525	Eddie Anderson	.05	.01
❑ 526	Roger Ruzek	.05	.01
❑ 527	Robert Blackmon	.05	.01
❑ 528	Vince Buck	.05	.01
❑ 529	Lawrence Taylor	.25	.08
❑ 530	Reggie Roby	.05	.01
❑ 531	Doug Riesenberg	.05	.01
❑ 532	Joe Jacoby	.05	.01
❑ 533	Kirby Jackson RC	.05	.01
❑ 534	Robb Thomas	.05	.01
❑ 535	Don Griffin	.05	.01
❑ 536	Andre Waters	.05	.01
❑ 537	Marc Logan	.05	.01
❑ 538	James Thornton	.05	.01
❑ 539	Ray Agnew	.05	.01
❑ 540	Frank Stams	.05	.01
❑ 541	Brett Perriman	.25	.08
❑ 542	Andre Ware	.10	.02
❑ 543	Kevin Haverdink	.05	.01
❑ 544	Greg Jackson RC	.05	.01
❑ 545	Tunch Ilkin	.05	.01
❑ 546	Dexter Carter	.05	.01
❑ 547	Rod Woodson	.25	.08
❑ 548	Donnell Woolford	.05	.01

❑ 549 Mark Boyer .05 .01
❑ 550 Jeff Query .05 .01
❑ 551 Burt Grossman .05 .01
❑ 552 Mike Kenn .05 .01
❑ 553 Richard Dent .10 .02
❑ 554 Gaston Green .05 .01
❑ 555 Phil Simms .10 .02
❑ 556 Brent Jones .25 .08
❑ 557 Ronnie Lippett .05 .01
❑ 558 Mike Horan .05 .01
❑ 559 Danny Noonan .05 .01
❑ 560 Reggie White .25 .08
❑ 561 Rufus Porter .05 .01
❑ 562 Aaron Wallace .05 .01
❑ 563 Vance Johnson .05 .01
❑ 564A Aaron Craver RC ERR .05 .01
❑ 564B Aaron Craver RC COR .05 .01
❑ 565A Russell Maryland RC ERR .25 .08
❑ 565B Russell Maryland RC COR .25 .08
❑ 566 Paul Justin RC .05 .01
❑ 567 Walter Dean .05 .01
❑ 568 Herman Moore RC .25 .08
❑ 569 Bill Musgrave RC .05 .01
❑ 570 Rob Carpenter RC WR .05 .01
❑ 571 Greg Lewis RC .05 .01
❑ 572 Ed King RC .05 .01
❑ 573 Ernie Mills RC .10 .02
❑ 574 Jake Reed RC .50 .20
❑ 575 Ricky Watters RC 1.50 .60
❑ 576 Derek Russell RC .05 .01
❑ 577 Shawn Moore RC .05 .01
❑ 578 Eric Bieniemy RC .05 .01
❑ 579 Chris Zorich RC .25 .08
❑ 580 Scott Miller .05 .01
❑ 581 Jarrod Bunch RC .05 .01
❑ 582 Ricky Ervins RC .10 .02
❑ 583 Browning Nagle RC .05 .01
❑ 584 Eric Turner RC .10 .02
❑ 585 William Thomas RC .05 .01
❑ 586 Stanley Richard RC .05 .01
❑ 587 Adrian Cooper RC .05 .01
❑ 588 Harvey Williams RC .25 .08
❑ 589 Alvin Harper RC .25 .08
❑ 590 John Carney .05 .01
❑ 591 Mark Vander Poel RC .05 .01
❑ 592 Mike Pritchard RC .25 .08
❑ 593 Eric Moten RC .05 .01
❑ 594 Moe Gardner RC .05 .01
❑ 595 Wesley Carroll RC .05 .01
❑ 596 Eric Swann RC .25 .08
❑ 597 Joe Kelly .05 .01
❑ 598 Steve Jackson RC .05 .01
❑ 599 Kelvin Pritchett RC .10 .02
❑ 600 Jesse Campbell RC .05 .01
❑ 601 Darryll Lewis RC UER .10 .02
❑ 602 Howard Griffith .05 .01
❑ 603 Blaise Bryant .05 .01
❑ 604 Vinnie Clark RC .05 .01
❑ 605 Mel Agee RC .05 .01
❑ 606 Bobby Wilson RC .05 .01
❑ 607 Kevin Donnalley RC .05 .01
❑ 608 Randal Hill RC .10 .02
❑ 609 Stan Thomas .05 .01
❑ 610 Mike Heldt .05 .01
❑ 611 Brett Favre RC 8.00 3.00
❑ 612 Lawrence Dawsey RC UER .10 .02
❑ 613 Dennis Gibson .05 .01
❑ 614 Dean Dingman .05 .01
❑ 615 Bruce Pickens RC .05 .01
❑ 616 Todd Marinovich RC .05 .01
❑ 617 Gene Atkins .05 .01
❑ 618 Marcus Dupree .05 .01
❑ 619 Warren Moon Man of Year .10 .02
❑ 620 Joe Montana TM .50 .20
❑ 621 Neal Anderson MVP .05 .01
❑ 622 James Brooks MVP .10 .02
❑ 623 Thurman Thomas TM .10 .02
❑ 624 Bobby Humphrey MVP .05 .01
❑ 625 Kevin Mack MVP .05 .01
❑ 626 Mark Carrier WR MVP .05 .01
❑ 627 Johnny Johnson TM .05 .01
❑ 628 Marion Butts MVP .10 .02
❑ 629 Steve DeBerg MVP .05 .01
❑ 630 Jeff George TM .10 .02
❑ 631 Troy Aikman TM .40 .15
❑ 632 Dan Marino TM .50 .20
❑ 633 Randall Cunningham TM .10 .02
❑ 634 Andre Rison TM .10 .02
❑ 635 Pepper Johnson MVP .05 .01
❑ 636 Pat Leahy MVP .05 .01
❑ 637 Barry Sanders TM .50 .20
❑ 638 Warren Moon TM .10 .02
❑ 639 Sterling Sharpe TM .05 .01
❑ 640 Bruce Armstrong MVP .05 .01
❑ 641 Bo Jackson TM .10 .02
❑ 642 Henry Ellard MVP .10 .02
❑ 643 Earnest Byner MVP .05 .01
❑ 644 Pat Swilling MVP .05 .01
❑ 645 John L. Williams MVP .05 .01
❑ 646 Rod Woodson TM .10 .02
❑ 647 Chris Doleman MVP .05 .01
❑ 648 [illegible]
❑ 649 Erik McMillan CC .05 .01
❑ 650 David Fulcher CC .05 .01
❑ 651A Ronnie Lott CC ERR .10 .02
❑ 651B Ronnie Lott CC COR .10 .02
❑ 652 Louis Oliver CC .05 .01
❑ 653 Mark Robinson CC .05 .01
❑ 654 Dennis Smith CC .05 .01
❑ 655 Reggie White SA ERR .10 .02
❑ 656 Charles Haley SA .05 .01
❑ 657 Leslie O'Neal SA .10 .02
❑ 658 Kevin Greene SA .10 .02
❑ 659 Dennis Byrd SA .05 .01
❑ 660 Bruce Smith SA .10 .02
❑ 661 Derrick Thomas SACK .10 .02
❑ 662 Steve DeBerg TL .05 .01
❑ 663 Barry Sanders TL .50 .20
❑ 664 Thurman Thomas TL .10 .02
❑ 665 Jerry Rice TL .40 .15
❑ 666 Derrick Thomas TL .10 .02
❑ 667 Bruce Smith TL .10 .02
❑ 668 Mark Carrier DB TL .05 .01
❑ 669 Richard Johnson CB TL .05 .01
❑ 670 Jan Stenerud HOF .05 .01
❑ 671 Stan Jones HOF .05 .01
❑ 672 John Hannah HOF .05 .01
❑ 673 Tex Schramm HOF .05 .01
❑ 674 Earl Campbell HOF .25 .08
❑ 675 Emmitt Smith/Carrier ROY .75 .30
❑ 676 Warren Moon DT .10 .02
❑ 677 Barry Sanders DT .50 .20
❑ 678 Thurman Thomas DT .25 .08
❑ 679 Andre Reed DT .10 .02
❑ 680 Andre Rison DT .10 .02
❑ 681 Keith Jackson DT .05 .01
❑ 682 Bruce Armstrong DT .05 .01
❑ 683 Jim Lachey DT .05 .01
❑ 684 Bruce Matthews DT .05 .01
❑ 685 Mike Munchak DT .05 .01
❑ 686 Don Mosebar DT .05 .01
❑ B1 Jeff Hostetler BONUS SB .25 .08
❑ B2 Matt Bahr SB .05 .01
❑ B3 Ottis Anderson SB .10 .02
❑ B4 Ottis Anderson SB .10 .02

1992 Score

❑ COMPLETE SET (550) 25.00 12.50
❑ 1 Barry Sanders 2.00 .75
❑ 2 Pat Swilling .05 .01
❑ 3 Moe Gardner .05 .01
❑ 4 Steve Young 1.00 .40
❑ 5 Chris Spielman .10 .02
❑ 6 Richard Dent .10 .02
❑ 7 Anthony Munoz .10 .02
❑ 8 Martin Mayhew .05 .01
❑ 9 Terry McDaniel .05 .01
❑ 10 Thurman Thomas .25 .08
❑ 11 Ricky Sanders .05 .01
❑ 12 Steve Atwater .05 .01
❑ 13 Tony Tolbert .05 .01
❑ 14 Vince Workman .05 .01
❑ 15 Haywood Jeffires .10 .02
❑ 16 Duane Bickett .05 .01
❑ 17 Jeff Uhlenhake .05 .01
❑ 18 Tim McDonald .05 .01
❑ 19 Cris Carter .50 .20
❑ 20 Derrick Thomas .25 .08
❑ 21 Hugh Millen .05 .01
❑ 22 Bart Oates .05 .01
❑ 23 [illegible]
❑ 24 Jerrol Williams .05 .01
❑ 25 Reggie White .25 .08
❑ 26 Marion Butts .05 .01
❑ 27 Jim Sweeney .05 .01
❑ 28 Tom Newberry .05 .01
❑ 29 Pete Stoyanovich .05 .01
❑ 30 Ronnie Lott .10 .02
❑ 31 Simon Fletcher .05 .01
❑ 32 Dino Hackett .05 .01
❑ 33 Morten Andersen .05 .01
❑ 34 Clyde Simmons .05 .01
❑ 35 Mark Rypien .05 .01
❑ 36 Greg Montgomery .05 .01
❑ 37 Nate Lewis .05 .01
❑ 38 Henry Ellard .10 .02
❑ 39 Luis Sharpe .05 .01
❑ 40 Michael Irvin .25 .08
❑ 41 Louis Lipps .05 .01
❑ 42 John L. Williams .05 .01
❑ 43 Broderick Thomas .05 .01
❑ 44 Michael Haynes .10 .02
❑ 45 Don Majkowski .05 .01
❑ 46 William Perry .10 .02
❑ 47 David Fulcher .05 .01
❑ 48 Tony Bennett .05 .01
❑ 49 Clay Matthews .10 .02
❑ 50 Warren Moon .25 .08
❑ 51 Bruce Armstrong .05 .01
❑ 52 Harry Newsome .05 .01
❑ 53 Bill Brooks .05 .01
❑ 54 Greg Townsend .05 .01
❑ 55 Tom Rathman .05 .01
❑ 56 Sean Landeta .05 .01
❑ 57 Kyle Clifton .05 .01
❑ 58 Steve Broussard .05 .01
❑ 59 Mark Carrier WR .10 .02
❑ 60 Mel Gray .10 .02
❑ 61 Tim Krumrie .05 .01
❑ 62 Rufus Porter .05 .01
❑ 63 Kevin Mack .05 .01
❑ 64 Todd Bowles .05 .01
❑ 65 Emmitt Smith 2.50 1.25
❑ 66 Mike Croel .05 .01
❑ 67 Brian Mitchell .10 .02
❑ 68 Bennie Blades .05 .01
❑ 69 Carnell Lake .05 .01
❑ 70 Cornelius Bennett .10 .02
❑ 71 Darrell Thompson .05 .01
❑ 72 Wes Hopkins .05 .01
❑ 73 Jessie Hester .05 .01
❑ 74 Irv Eatman .05 .01
❑ 75 Marv Cook .05 .01
❑ 76 Tim Brown .25 .08
❑ 77 Pepper Johnson .05 .01
❑ 78 Mark Duper .05 .01
❑ 79 Robert Delpino .05 .01
❑ 80 Charles Mann .05 .01
❑ 81 Brian Jordan .10 .02
❑ 82 Wendell Davis .05 .01
❑ 83 Lee Johnson .05 .01
❑ 84 Ricky Reynolds .05 .01
❑ 85 Vaughan Johnson .05 .01
❑ 86 Brian Blades .10 .02
❑ 87 Sam Seale .05 .01
❑ 88 Ed King .05 .01
❑ 89 Gaston Green .05 .01
❑ 90 Christian Okoye .05 .01
❑ 91 Chris Jacke .05 .01
❑ 92 Rohn Stark .05 .01
❑ 93 Kevin Greene .10 .02
❑ 94 Jay Novacek .10 .02
❑ 95 Chip Lohmiller .05 .01

❑	96	Cris Dishman	.05	.01
❑	97	Ethan Horton	.05	.01
❑	98	Pat Harlow	.05	.01
❑	99	Mark Ingram	.05	.01
❑	100	Mark Carrier DB	.05	.01
❑	101	Deron Cherry	.05	.01
❑	102	Sam Mills	.05	.01
❑	103	Mark Higgs	.05	.01
❑	104	Keith Jackson	.10	.02
❑	105	Steve Tasker	.10	.02
❑	106	Ken Harvey	.05	.01
❑	107	Bryan Hinkle	.05	.01
❑	108	Anthony Carter	.10	.02
❑	109	Johnny Hector	.05	.01
❑	110	Randall McDaniel	.05	.01
❑	111	Johnny Johnson	.05	.01
❑	112	Shane Conlan	.05	.01
❑	113	Ray Horton	.05	.01
❑	114	Sterling Sharpe	.25	.08
❑	115	Guy McIntyre	.05	.01
❑	116	Tom Waddle	.05	.01
❑	117	Albert Lewis	.05	.01
❑	118	Riki Ellison	.05	.01
❑	119	Chris Doleman	.05	.01
❑	120	Andre Rison	.10	.02
❑	121	Bobby Hebert	.05	.01
❑	122	Dan Owens	.05	.01
❑	123	Rodney Hampton	.10	.02
❑	124	Ron Holmes	.05	.01
❑	125	Ernie Jones	.05	.01
❑	126	Michael Carter	.05	.01
❑	127	Reggie Cobb	.05	.01
❑	128	Esera Tuaolo	.05	.01
❑	129	Wilber Marshall	.05	.01
❑	130	Mike Munchak	.10	.02
❑	131	Cortez Kennedy	.10	.02
❑	132	Lamar Lathon	.05	.01
❑	133	Todd Lyght	.05	.01
❑	134	Jeff Feagles	.05	.01
❑	135	Burt Grossman	.05	.01
❑	136	Mike Cofer	.05	.01
❑	137	Frank Warren	.05	.01
❑	138	Jarvis Williams	.05	.01
❑	139	Eddie Brown	.05	.01
❑	140	John Elliott	.05	.01
❑	141	Jim Everett	.10	.02
❑	142	Hardy Nickerson	.10	.02
❑	143	Eddie Murray	.05	.01
❑	144	Andre Tippett	.05	.01
❑	145	Heath Sherman	.05	.01
❑	146	Ronnie Harmon	.05	.01
❑	147	Eric Metcalf	.10	.02
❑	148	Tony Martin	.10	.02
❑	149	Chris Burkett	.05	.01
❑	150	Andre Waters	.05	.01
❑	151	Ray Donaldson	.05	.01
❑	152	Paul Gruber	.05	.01
❑	153	Chris Singleton	.05	.01
❑	154	Clarence Kay	.05	.01
❑	155	Ernest Givins	.10	.02
❑	156	Eric Hill	.05	.01
❑	157	Jesse Sapolu	.05	.01
❑	158	Jack Del Rio	.05	.01
❑	159	Erric Pegram	.10	.02
❑	160	Joey Browner	.05	.01
❑	161	Marcus Allen	.25	.08
❑	162	Eric Moten	.05	.01
❑	163	Donnell Thompson	.05	.01
❑	164	Chuck Cecil	.05	.01
❑	165	Matt Millen	.10	.02
❑	166	Barry Foster	.10	.02
❑	167	Kent Hull	.05	.01
❑	168	Tony Jones WR	.05	.01
❑	169	Mike Prior	.05	.01
❑	170	Neal Anderson	.05	.01
❑	171	Roger Craig	.10	.02
❑	172	Felix Wright	.05	.01
❑	173	James Francis	.05	.01
❑	174	Eugene Lockhart	.05	.01
❑	175	Dalton Hilliard	.05	.01
❑	176	Nick Lowery	.05	.01
❑	177	Tim McKyer	.05	.01
❑	178	Lorenzo White	.05	.01
❑	179	Jeff Hostetler	.10	.02
❑	180	Jackie Harris RC	.25	.08
❑	181	Ken Norton	.10	.02
❑	182	Flipper Anderson	.05	.01
❑	183	Don Warren	.05	.01
❑	184	Brad Baxter	.05	.01
❑	185	John Taylor	.10	.02
❑	186	Harold Green	.05	.01
❑	187	James Washington	.05	.01
❑	188	Aaron Craver	.05	.01
❑	189	Mike Merriweather	.05	.01
❑	190	Gary Clark	.25	.08
❑	191	Vince Buck	.05	.01
❑	192	Cleveland Gary	.05	.01
❑	193	Dan Saleaumua	.05	.01
❑	194	Gary Zimmerman	.05	.01
❑	195	Richmond Webb	.05	.01
❑	196	Gary Plummer	.05	.01
❑	197	Willie Green	.05	.01
❑	198	Chris Warren	.25	.08
❑	199	Mike Pritchard	.10	.02
❑	200	Art Monk	.10	.02
❑	201	Matt Stover	.05	.01
❑	202	Tim Grunhard	.05	.01
❑	203	Mervyn Fernandez	.05	.01
❑	204	Mark Jackson	.05	.01
❑	205	Freddie Joe Nunn	.05	.01
❑	206	Stan Thomas	.05	.01
❑	207	Keith McKeller	.05	.01
❑	208	Jeff Lageman	.05	.01
❑	209	Kenny Walker	.05	.01
❑	210	Dave Krieg	.10	.02
❑	211	Dean Biasucci	.05	.01
❑	212	Herman Moore	.25	.08
❑	213	Jon Vaughn	.05	.01
❑	214	Howard Cross	.05	.01
❑	215	Greg Davis	.05	.01
❑	216	Bubby Brister	.05	.01
❑	217	John Kasay	.05	.01
❑	218	Ron Hall	.05	.01
❑	219	Mo Lewis	.05	.01
❑	220	Eric Green	.05	.01
❑	221	Scott Case	.05	.01
❑	222	Sean Jones	.05	.01
❑	223	Winston Moss	.05	.01
❑	224	Reggie Langhorne	.05	.01
❑	225	Greg Lewis	.05	.01
❑	226	Todd McNair	.05	.01
❑	227	Rod Bernstine	.05	.01
❑	228	Joe Jacoby	.05	.01
❑	229	Brad Muster	.05	.01
❑	230	Nick Bell	.05	.01
❑	231	Terry Allen	.25	.08
❑	232	Cliff Odom	.05	.01
❑	233	Brian Hansen	.05	.01
❑	234	William Fuller	.05	.01
❑	235	Issiac Holt	.05	.01
❑	236	Dexter Carter	.05	.01
❑	237	Gene Atkins	.05	.01
❑	238	Pat Beach	.05	.01
❑	239	Tim McGee	.05	.01
❑	240	Dermontti Dawson	.05	.01
❑	241	Dan Fike	.05	.01
❑	242	Don Beebe	.05	.01
❑	243	Jeff Bostic	.05	.01
❑	244	Mark Collins	.05	.01
❑	245	Steve Sewell	.05	.01
❑	246	Steve Walsh	.05	.01
❑	247	Erik Kramer	.10	.02
❑	248	Scott Norwood	.05	.01
❑	249	Jesse Solomon	.05	.01
❑	250	Jerry Ball	.05	.01
❑	251	Eugene Daniel	.05	.01
❑	252	Michael Stewart	.05	.01
❑	253	Fred Barnett	.25	.08
❑	254	Rodney Holman	.05	.01
❑	255	Stephen Baker	.05	.01
❑	256	Don Griffin	.05	.01
❑	257	Will Wolford	.05	.01
❑	258	Perry Kemp	.05	.01
❑	259	Leonard Russell	.10	.02
❑	260	Jeff Gossett	.05	.01
❑	261	Dwayne Harper	.05	.01
❑	262	Vinny Testaverde	.10	.02
❑	263	Maurice Hurst	.05	.01
❑	264	Tony Casillas	.05	.01
❑	265	Louis Oliver	.05	.01
❑	266	Jim Morrissey	.05	.01
❑	267	Kenneth Davis	.05	.01
❑	268	John Alt	.05	.01
❑	269	Michael Zordich RC	.05	.01
❑	270	Brian Brennan	.05	.01
❑	271	Greg Kragen	.05	.01
❑	272	Andre Collins	.05	.01
❑	273	Dave Meggett	.10	.02
❑	274	Scott Fulhage	.05	.01
❑	275	Tony Zendejas	.05	.01
❑	276	Herschel Walker	.10	.02
❑	277	Keith Henderson	.05	.01
❑	278	Johnny Bailey	.05	.01
❑	279	Vince Newsome	.05	.01
❑	280	Chris Hinton	.05	.01
❑	281	Robert Blackmon	.05	.01
❑	282	James Hasty	.05	.01
❑	283	John Offerdahl	.05	.01
❑	284	Wesley Carroll	.05	.01
❑	285	Lomas Brown	.05	.01
❑	286	Neil O'Donnell	.10	.02
❑	287	Kevin Porter	.05	.01
❑	288	Lionel Washington	.05	.01
❑	289	Carlton Bailey RC	.05	.01
❑	290	Leonard Marshall	.05	.01
❑	291	John Carney	.05	.01
❑	292	Bubba McDowell	.05	.01
❑	293	Nate Newton	.05	.01
❑	294	Dave Waymer	.05	.01
❑	295	Rob Moore	.10	.02
❑	296	Earnest Byner	.05	.01
❑	297	Jason Staurovsky	.05	.01
❑	298	Keith McCants	.05	.01
❑	299	Floyd Turner	.05	.01
❑	300	Steve Jordan	.05	.01
❑	301	Nate Odomes	.05	.01
❑	302	Gerald Riggs	.05	.01
❑	303	Marvin Washington	.05	.01
❑	304	Anthony Thompson	.05	.01
❑	305	Steve DeBerg	.05	.01
❑	306	Jim Harbaugh	.25	.08
❑	307	Larry Brown DB	.05	.01
❑	308	Roger Ruzek	.05	.01
❑	309	Jessie Tuggle	.05	.01
❑	310	Al Smith	.05	.01
❑	311	Mark Kelso	.05	.01
❑	312	Lawrence Dawsey	.10	.02
❑	313	Steve Bono RC	.25	.08
❑	314	Greg Lloyd	.10	.02
❑	315	Steve Wisniewski	.05	.01
❑	316	Gill Fenerty	.05	.01
❑	317	Mark Stepnoski	.10	.02
❑	318	Derek Russell	.05	.01
❑	319	Chris Martin	.05	.01
❑	320	Shaun Gayle	.05	.01
❑	321	Bob Golic	.05	.01
❑	322	Larry Kelm	.05	.01
❑	323	Mike Brim RC	.05	.01
❑	324	Tommy Kane	.05	.01
❑	325	Mark Schlereth RC	.05	.01
❑	326	Ray Childress	.05	.01
❑	327	Richard Brown RC	.05	.01
❑	328	Vincent Brown	.05	.01
❑	329	Mike Farr UER	.05	.01
❑	330	Eric Swann	.10	.02
❑	331	Bill Fralic	.05	.01
❑	332	Rodney Peete	.10	.02
❑	333	Jerry Gray	.05	.01
❑	334	Ray Berry	.05	.01
❑	335	Dennis Smith	.05	.01
❑	336	Jeff Herrod	.05	.01
❑	337	Tony Mandarich	.05	.01
❑	338	Matt Bahr	.05	.01
❑	339	Mike Saxon	.05	.01
❑	340	Bruce Matthews	.05	.01
❑	341	Rickey Jackson	.05	.01
❑	342	Eric Allen	.05	.01
❑	343	Lonnie Young	.05	.01
❑	344	Steve McMichael	.10	.02
❑	345	Willie Gault	.10	.02
❑	346	Barry Word	.05	.01
❑	347	Rich Camarillo	.05	.01
❑	348	Bill Romanowski	.05	.01
❑	349	Jim Lachey	.05	.01
❑	350	Jim Ritcher	.05	.01
❑	351	Irving Fryar	.10	.02
❑	352	Gary Anderson K	.05	.01
❑	353	Henry Rolling	.05	.01
❑	354	Mark Bortz	.05	.01
❑	355	Mark Clayton	.10	.02
❑	356	Keith Woodside	.05	.01

❑ 357 Jonathan Hayes .05 .01
❑ 358 Derrick Fenner .05 .01
❑ 359 Keith Byars .05 .01
❑ 360 Drew Hill .05 .01
❑ 361 Harris Barton .05 .01
❑ 362 John Kidd .05 .01
❑ 363 Aeneas Williams .10 .02
❑ 364 Brian Washington .05 .01
❑ 365 John Stephens .05 .01
❑ 366 Norm Johnson .05 .01
❑ 367 Darryl Henley .05 .01
❑ 368 William White .05 .01
❑ 369 Mark Murphy .05 .01
❑ 370 Myron Guyton .05 .01
❑ 371 Leon Seals .05 .01
❑ 372 Rich Gannon .25 .08
❑ 373 Toi Cook .05 .01
❑ 374 Anthony Johnson .10 .02
❑ 375 Rod Woodson .25 .08
❑ 376 Alexander Wright .05 .01
❑ 377 Kevin Butler .05 .01
❑ 378 Neil Smith .25 .08
❑ 379 Gary Anderson RB .05 .01
❑ 380 Reggie Roby .05 .01
❑ 381 Jeff Bryant .05 .01
❑ 382 Ray Crockett .05 .01
❑ 383 Richard Johnson CB .05 .01
❑ 384 Hassan Jones .05 .01
❑ 385 Karl Mecklenburg .05 .01
❑ 386 Jeff Jaeger .05 .01
❑ 387 Keith Willis .05 .01
❑ 388 Phil Simms .10 .02
❑ 389 Kevin Ross .05 .01
❑ 390 Chris Miller .10 .02
❑ 391 Brian Noble .05 .01
❑ 392 Jamie Dukes RC .05 .01
❑ 393 George Jamison .05 .01
❑ 394 Rickey Dixon .05 .01
❑ 395 Carl Lee .05 .01
❑ 396 Jon Hand .05 .01
❑ 397 Kirby Jackson .05 .01
❑ 398 Pat Terrell .05 .01
❑ 399 Howie Long .25 .08
❑ 400 Michael Young .05 .01
❑ 401 Keith Sims .05 .01
❑ 402 Tommy Barnhardt .05 .01
❑ 403 Greg McMurtry .05 .01
❑ 404 Keith Van Horne .05 .01
❑ 405 Seth Joyner .05 .01
❑ 406 Jim Jeffcoat .05 .01
❑ 407 Courtney Hall .05 .01
❑ 408 Tony Covington .05 .01
❑ 409 Jacob Green .05 .01
❑ 410 Charles Haley .10 .02
❑ 411 Darryl Talley .05 .01
❑ 412 Jeff Cross .05 .01
❑ 413 John Elway 2.00 .75
❑ 414 Donald Evans .05 .01
❑ 415 Jackie Slater .05 .01
❑ 416 John Friesz .10 .02
❑ 417 Anthony Smith .05 .01
❑ 418 Gill Byrd .05 .01
❑ 419 Willie Drewrey .05 .01
❑ 420 Jay Hilgenberg .05 .01
❑ 421 David Treadwell .05 .01
❑ 422 Curtis Duncan .05 .01
❑ 423 Sammie Smith .05 .01
❑ 424 Henry Thomas .05 .01
❑ 425 James Lofton .10 .02
❑ 426 Fred Marion .05 .01
❑ 427 Bryce Paup .25 .08
❑ 428 Michael Timpson RC .05 .01
❑ 429 Reyna Thompson .05 .01
❑ 430 Mike Kenn .05 .01
❑ 431 Bill Maas .05 .01
❑ 432 Quinn Early .10 .02
❑ 433 Everson Walls .05 .01
❑ 434 Jimmie Jones .05 .01
❑ 435 Dwight Stone .05 .01
❑ 436 Harry Colon .05 .01
❑ 437 Don Mosebar .05 .01
❑ 438 Calvin Williams .10 .02
❑ 439 Tom Tupa .05 .01
❑ 440 Darrell Green .05 .01
❑ 441 Eric Thomas .05 .01
❑ 442 Terry Wooden .05 .01
❑ 443 Brett Perriman .25 .08
❑ 444 Todd Marinovich .05 .01
❑ 445 Jim Breech .05 .01
❑ 446 Eddie Anderson .05 .01
❑ 447 Jay Schroeder .05 .01
❑ 448 William Roberts .05 .01
❑ 449 Brad Edwards .05 .01
❑ 450 Tunch Ilkin .05 .01
❑ 451 Ivy Joe Hunter RC .05 .01
❑ 452 Robert Clark .05 .01
❑ 453 Tim Barnett .05 .01
❑ 454 Jarrod Bunch .05 .01
❑ 455 Tim Harris .05 .01
❑ 456 James Brooks .10 .02
❑ 457 Trace Armstrong .05 .01
❑ 458 Michael Brooks .05 .01
❑ 459 Andy Heck .05 .01
❑ 460 Greg Jackson .05 .01
❑ 461 Vance Johnson .05 .01
❑ 462 Kirk Lowdermilk .05 .01
❑ 463 Erik McMillan .05 .01
❑ 464 Scott Mersereau .05 .01
❑ 465 Jeff Wright .05 .01
❑ 466 Mike Tomczak .05 .01
❑ 467 David Alexander .05 .01
❑ 468 Bryan Millard .05 .01
❑ 469 John Randle .10 .02
❑ 470 Joel Hilgenberg .05 .01
❑ 471 Bennie Thompson RC .05 .01
❑ 472 Freeman McNeil .05 .01
❑ 473 Terry Orr RC .05 .01
❑ 474 Mike Horan .05 .01
❑ 475 Leroy Hoard .10 .02
❑ 476 Patrick Rowe RC .05 .01
❑ 477 Siran Stacy RC .05 .01
❑ 478 Amp Lee RC .05 .01
❑ 479 Eddie Blake RC .05 .01
❑ 480 Joe Bowden RC .05 .01
❑ 481 Rod Milstead RC .05 .01
❑ 482 Keith Hamilton RC .10 .02
❑ 483 Darryl Williams RC .05 .01
❑ 484 Robert Porcher RC .25 .08
❑ 485 Ed Cunningham RC .05 .01
❑ 486 Chris Mims RC .05 .01
❑ 487 Chris Hakel RC .05 .01
❑ 488 Jimmy Smith RC 4.00 1.50
❑ 489 Todd Harrison RC .05 .01
❑ 490 Edgar Bennett RC .25 .08
❑ 491 Dexter McNabb RC .05 .01
❑ 492 Leon Searcy RC .05 .01
❑ 493 Tommy Vardell RC .05 .01
❑ 494 Terrell Buckley RC .05 .01
❑ 495 Kevin Turner RC .05 .01
❑ 496 Russ Campbell RC .05 .01
❑ 497 Torrance Small RC .10 .02
❑ 498 Nate Turner RC .05 .01
❑ 499 Cornelius Benton RC .05 .01
❑ 500 Matt Elliott RC .05 .01
❑ 501 Robert Stewart RC .05 .01
❑ 502 Muhammad Shamsid-Deen RC .05 .01
❑ 503 George Williams RC .05 .01
❑ 504 Pumpy Tudors RC .05 .01
❑ 505 Matt LaBounty RC .05 .01
❑ 506 Darryl Hardy RC .05 .01
❑ 507 Derrick Moore RC .10 .02
❑ 508 Willie Clay RC .05 .01
❑ 509 Bob Whitfield RC .05 .01
❑ 510 Ricardo McDonald RC .05 .01
❑ 511 Carlos Huerta RC .05 .01
❑ 512 Selwyn Jones RC .05 .01
❑ 513 Steve Gordon RC .05 .01
❑ 514 Bob Meeks RC .05 .01
❑ 515 Bennie Blades CC .05 .01
❑ 516 Andre Waters CC .05 .01
❑ 517 Bubba McDowell CC .05 .01
❑ 518 Kevin Porter CC .05 .01
❑ 519 Carnell Lake CC .05 .01
❑ 520 Leonard Russell ROY .10 .02
❑ 521 Mike Croel ROY .05 .01
❑ 522 Lawrence Dawsey ROY .05 .01
❑ 523 Moe Gardner ROY .05 .01
❑ 524 Steve Broussard LBM .05 .01
❑ 525 Dave Meggett LBM .05 .01
❑ 526 Darrell Green LBM .05 .01
❑ 527 Tony Jones WR LBM .05 .01
❑ 528 Barry Sanders LBM 1.00 .40
❑ 529 Pat Swilling SA .05 .01
❑ 530 Reggie White SA .10 .02
❑ 531 William Fuller SA .05 .01
❑ 532 Simon Fletcher SA .05 .01
❑ 533 Derrick Thomas SA .10 .02
❑ 534 Mark Rypien MOY .05 .01
❑ 535 John Mackey HOF .05 .01
❑ 536 John Riggins HOF .10 .02
❑ 537 Lem Barney HOF .05 .01
❑ 538 Shawn McCarthy RC 90 .05 .01
❑ 539 Al Edwards 90 .05 .01
❑ 540 Alexander Wright 90 .05 .01
❑ 541 Ray Crockett 90 .05 .01
❑ 542 Steve Young/J.Taylor 90 .25 .08
❑ 543 Nate Lewis 90 .05 .01
❑ 544 Dexter Carter 90 .05 .01
❑ 545 Reggie Rutland 90 .05 .01
❑ 546 Jon Vaughn 90 .05 .01
❑ 547 Chris Martin 90 .05 .01
❑ 548 Warren Moon HL .10 .02
❑ 549 Super Bowl Highlights .05 .01
❑ 550 Robb Thomas .05 .01
❑ NNO Dick Butkus Promo 8.00 4.00

1993 Score

❑ COMPLETE SET (440) 15.00 6.00
❑ 1 Barry Sanders 1.25 .50
❑ 2 Moe Gardner .05 .01
❑ 3 Ricky Watters .25 .08
❑ 4 Todd Lyght .05 .01
❑ 5 Rodney Hampton .10 .02
❑ 6 Curtis Duncan .05 .01
❑ 7 Barry Word .05 .01
❑ 8 Reggie Cobb .05 .01
❑ 9 Mike Kenn .05 .01
❑ 10 Michael Irvin .25 .08
❑ 11 Bryan Cox .05 .01
❑ 12 Chris Doleman .05 .01
❑ 13 Rod Woodson .25 .08
❑ 14 Emmitt Smith 1.50 .60
❑ 15 Pete Stoyanovich .05 .01
❑ 16 Steve Young .75 .30
❑ 17 Randall McDaniel .05 .01
❑ 18 Cortez Kennedy .10 .02
❑ 19 Mel Gray .10 .02
❑ 20 Barry Foster .10 .02
❑ 21 Tim Brown .25 .08
❑ 22 Todd McNair .05 .01
❑ 23 Anthony Johnson .10 .02
❑ 24 Nate Odomes .05 .01
❑ 25 Brett Favre 2.00 .75
❑ 26 Jack Del Rio .05 .01
❑ 27 Terry McDaniel .05 .01
❑ 28 Haywood Jeffires .10 .02
❑ 29 Jay Novacek .10 .02
❑ 30 Wilber Marshall .05 .01
❑ 31 Richmond Webb .05 .01
❑ 32 Steve Atwater .05 .01
❑ 33 James Lofton .10 .02
❑ 34 Harold Green .05 .01
❑ 35 Eric Metcalf .10 .02
❑ 36 Bruce Matthews .05 .01
❑ 37 Albert Lewis .05 .01
❑ 38 Jeff Herrod .05 .01
❑ 39 Vince Workman .05 .01
❑ 40 John Elway 1.50 .60
❑ 41 Brett Perriman .25 .08
❑ 42 Jon Vaughn .05 .01
❑ 43 Terry Allen .25 .08
❑ 44 Clyde Simmons .05 .01
❑ 45 Bennie Thompson .05 .01

❑ 46 Wendell Davis .05 .01
❑ 47 Bobby Hebert .05 .01
❑ 48 John Offerdahl .05 .01
❑ 49 Jeff Graham .10 .02
❑ 50 Steve Wisniewski .05 .01
❑ 51 Louis Oliver .05 .01
❑ 52 Rohn Stark .05 .01
❑ 53 Cleveland Gary .05 .01
❑ 54 John Randle .10 .02
❑ 55 Jim Everett .10 .02
❑ 56 Donnell Woolford .05 .01
❑ 57 Pepper Johnson .05 .01
❑ 58 Irving Fryar .10 .02
❑ 59 Greg Townsend .05 .01
❑ 60 Chris Burkett .05 .01
❑ 61 Johnny Johnson .05 .01
❑ 62 Ronnie Harmon .05 .01
❑ 63 Don Griffin .05 .01
❑ 64 Wayne Martin .05 .01
❑ 65 John L. Williams .05 .01
❑ 66 Brad Edwards .05 .01
❑ 67 Toi Cook .05 .01
❑ 68 Lawrence Dawsey .05 .01
❑ 69 Johnny Bailey .05 .01
❑ 70 Mike Brim .05 .01
❑ 71 Andre Rison .10 .02
❑ 72 Cornelius Bennett .10 .02
❑ 73 Brad Muster .05 .01
❑ 74 Broderick Thomas .05 .01
❑ 75 Tom Waddle .05 .01
❑ 76 Paul Gruber .05 .01
❑ 77 Jackie Harris .05 .01
❑ 78 Kenneth Davis .05 .01
❑ 79 Norm Johnson .05 .01
❑ 80 Jim Jeffcoat .05 .01
❑ 81 Chris Warren .10 .02
❑ 82 Greg Kragen .05 .01
❑ 83 Ricky Reynolds .05 .01
❑ 84 Hardy Nickerson .10 .02
❑ 85 Brian Mitchell .10 .02
❑ 86 Rufus Porter .05 .01
❑ 87 Greg Jackson .05 .01
❑ 88 Seth Joyner .05 .01
❑ 89 Tim Grunhard .05 .01
❑ 90 Tim Harris .05 .01
❑ 91 Sterling Sharpe .25 .08
❑ 92 Daniel Stubbs .05 .01
❑ 93 Rob Burnett .05 .01
❑ 94 Rich Camarillo .05 .01
❑ 95 Al Smith .05 .01
❑ 96 Thurman Thomas .25 .08
❑ 97 Morten Andersen .05 .01
❑ 98 Reggie White .25 .08
❑ 99 Gill Byrd .05 .01
❑ 100 Pierce Holt .05 .01
❑ 101 Tim McGee .05 .01
❑ 102 Rickey Jackson .05 .01
❑ 103 Vince Newsome .05 .01
❑ 104 Chris Spielman .10 .02
❑ 105 Tim McDonald .05 .01
❑ 106 James Francis .05 .01
❑ 107 Andre Tippett .05 .01
❑ 108 Sam Mills .05 .01
❑ 109 Hugh Millen .05 .01
❑ 110 Brad Baxter .05 .01
❑ 111 Ricky Sanders .05 .01
❑ 112 Marion Butts .05 .01
❑ 113 Fred Barnett .10 .02
❑ 114 Wade Wilson .05 .01
❑ 115 Dave Meggett .05 .01
❑ 116 Kevin Greene .10 .02
❑ 117 Reggie Langhorne .05 .01
❑ 118 Simon Fletcher .05 .01
❑ 119 Tommy Vardell .05 .01
❑ 120 Darion Conner .05 .01
❑ 121 Darren Lewis .05 .01
❑ 122 Charles Mann .05 .01
❑ 123 David Fulcher .05 .01
❑ 124 Tommy Kane .05 .01
❑ 125 Richard Brown .05 .01
❑ 126 Nate Lewis .05 .01
❑ 127 Tony Tolbert .05 .01
❑ 128 Greg Lloyd .10 .02
❑ 129 Herman Moore .25 .08
❑ 130 Robert Massey .05 .01
❑ 131 Chris Jacke .05 .01
❑ 132 Keith Byars .05 .01
❑ 133 William Fuller .05 .01
❑ 134 Rob Moore .10 .02
❑ 135 Duane Bickett .05 .01
❑ 136 Jarrod Bunch .05 .01
❑ 137 Ethan Horton .05 .01
❑ 138 Leonard Russell .10 .02
❑ 139 Darryl Henley .05 .01
❑ 140 Tony Bennett .05 .01
❑ 141 Harry Newsome .05 .01
❑ 142 Kelvin Martin .05 .01
❑ 143 Audray McMillian .05 .01
❑ 144 Chip Lohmiller .05 .01
❑ 145 Henry Jones .05 .01
❑ 146 Rod Bernstine .05 .01
❑ 147 Darryl Talley .05 .01
❑ 148 Clarence Verdin .05 .01
❑ 149 Derrick Thomas .25 .08
❑ 150 Raleigh McKenzie .05 .01
❑ 151 Phil Hansen .05 .01
❑ 152 Lin Elliott RC .05 .01
❑ 153 Chip Banks .05 .01
❑ 154 Shannon Sharpe .25 .08
❑ 155 David Williams .05 .01
❑ 156 Gaston Green .05 .01
❑ 157 Trace Armstrong .05 .01
❑ 158 Todd Scott .05 .01
❑ 159 Stan Humphries .10 .02
❑ 160 Christian Okoye .05 .01
❑ 161 Dennis Smith .05 .01
❑ 162 Derek Kennard .05 .01
❑ 163 Melvin Jenkins .05 .01
❑ 164 Tommy Barnhardt .05 .01
❑ 165 Eugene Robinson .05 .01
❑ 166 Tom Rathman .05 .01
❑ 167 Chris Chandler .10 .02
❑ 168 Steve Broussard .05 .01
❑ 169 Wymon Henderson .05 .01
❑ 170 Bryce Paup .10 .02
❑ 171 Kent Hull .05 .01
❑ 172 Willie Davis .25 .08
❑ 173 Richard Dent .10 .02
❑ 174 Rodney Peete .05 .01
❑ 175 Clay Matthews .10 .02
❑ 176 Erik Williams .05 .01
❑ 177 Mike Cofer .05 .01
❑ 178 Mark Kelso .05 .01
❑ 179 Kurt Gouveia .05 .01
❑ 180 Keith McCants .05 .01
❑ 181 Jim Arnold .05 .01
❑ 182 Sean Jones .05 .01
❑ 183 Chuck Cecil .05 .01
❑ 184 Mark Rypien .05 .01
❑ 185 William Perry .10 .02
❑ 186 Mark Jackson .05 .01
❑ 187 Jim Dombrowski .05 .01
❑ 188 Heath Sherman .05 .01
❑ 189 Bubba McDowell .05 .01
❑ 190 Fuad Reveiz .05 .01
❑ 191 Darren Perry .05 .01
❑ 192 Karl Mecklenburg .05 .01
❑ 193 Frank Reich .10 .02
❑ 194 Tony Casillas .05 .01
❑ 195 Jerry Ball .05 .01
❑ 196 Jessie Hester .05 .01
❑ 197 David Lang .05 .01
❑ 198 Sean Landeta .05 .01
❑ 199 Jerry Gray .05 .01
❑ 200 Mark Higgs .05 .01
❑ 201 Bruce Armstrong .05 .01
❑ 202 Vaughan Johnson .05 .01
❑ 203 Calvin Williams .10 .02
❑ 204 Leonard Marshall .05 .01
❑ 205 Mike Munchak .10 .02
❑ 206 Kevin Ross .05 .01
❑ 207 Daryl Johnston .25 .08
❑ 208 Jay Schroeder .05 .01
❑ 209 Mo Lewis .05 .01
❑ 210 Carlton Haselrig .05 .01
❑ 211 Cris Carter .25 .08
❑ 212 Marv Cook .05 .01
❑ 213 Mark Duper .05 .01
❑ 214 Jackie Slater .05 .01
❑ 215 Mike Prior .05 .01
❑ 216 Warren Moon .25 .08
❑ 217 Mike Saxon .05 .01
❑ 218 Derrick Fenner .05 .01
❑ 219 Brian Washington .05 .01
❑ 220 Jessie Tuggle .05 .01
❑ 221 Jeff Hostetler .10 .02
❑ 222 Deion Sanders .50 .20
❑ 223 Neal Anderson .05 .01
❑ 224 Kevin Mack .05 .01
❑ 225 Tommy Maddox .25 .08
❑ 226 Neil Smith .25 .08
❑ 227 Ronnie Lott .10 .02
❑ 228 Flipper Anderson .05 .01
❑ 229 Keith Jackson .10 .02
❑ 230 Pat Swilling .05 .01
❑ 231 Carl Banks .05 .01
❑ 232 Eric Allen .05 .01
❑ 233 Randal Hill .05 .01
❑ 234 Burt Grossman .05 .01
❑ 235 Jerry Rice 1.00 .40
❑ 236 Santana Dotson .10 .02
❑ 237 Andre Reed .10 .02
❑ 238 Troy Aikman .75 .30
❑ 239 Ray Childress .05 .01
❑ 240 Phil Simms .10 .02
❑ 241 Steve McMichael .10 .02
❑ 242 Browning Nagle .05 .01
❑ 243 Anthony Miller .10 .02
❑ 244 Earnest Byner .05 .01
❑ 245 Jay Hilgenberg .05 .01
❑ 246 Jeff George .25 .08
❑ 247 Marco Coleman .05 .01
❑ 248 Mark Carrier DB .05 .01
❑ 249 Howie Long .25 .08
❑ 250 Ed McCaffrey .25 .08
❑ 251 Jim Kelly .25 .08
❑ 252 Henry Ellard .10 .02
❑ 253 Joe Montana 1.50 .60
❑ 254 Dale Carter .05 .01
❑ 255 Boomer Esiason .10 .02
❑ 256 Gary Clark .10 .02
❑ 257 Carl Pickens .10 .02
❑ 258 Dave Krieg .10 .02
❑ 259 Russell Maryland .05 .01
❑ 260 Randall Cunningham .25 .08
❑ 261 Leslie O'Neal .10 .02
❑ 262 Vinny Testaverde .10 .02
❑ 263 Ricky Ervins .05 .01
❑ 264 Chris Mims .05 .01
❑ 265 Dan Marino 1.50 .60
❑ 266 Eric Martin .05 .01
❑ 267 Bruce Smith .25 .08
❑ 268 Jim Harbaugh .25 .08
❑ 269 Steve Emtman .05 .01
❑ 270 Ricky Proehl .05 .01
❑ 271 Vaughn Dunbar .05 .01
❑ 272 Junior Seau .25 .08
❑ 273 Sean Gilbert .10 .02
❑ 274 Jim Lachey .05 .01
❑ 275 Dalton Hilliard .05 .01
❑ 276 David Klingler .05 .01
❑ 277 Robert Jones .05 .01
❑ 278 David Treadwell .05 .01
❑ 279 Tracy Scroggins .05 .01
❑ 280 Terrell Buckley .05 .01
❑ 281 Quentin Coryatt .10 .02
❑ 282 Jason Hanson .05 .01
❑ 283 Shane Conlan .05 .01
❑ 284 Guy McIntyre .05 .01
❑ 285 Gary Zimmerman .05 .01
❑ 286 Marty Carter .05 .01
❑ 287 Jim Sweeney .05 .01
❑ 288 Arthur Marshall RC .05 .01
❑ 289 Eugene Chung .05 .01
❑ 290 Mike Pritchard .10 .02
❑ 291 Jim Ritcher .05 .01
❑ 292 Todd Marinovich .05 .01
❑ 293 Courtney Hall .05 .01
❑ 294 Mark Collins .05 .01
❑ 295 Troy Auzenne .05 .01
❑ 296 Aeneas Williams .05 .01
❑ 297 Andy Heck .05 .01
❑ 298 Shaun Gayle .05 .01
❑ 299 Kevin Fagan .05 .01
❑ 300 Carnell Lake .05 .01
❑ 301 Bernie Kosar .10 .02
❑ 302 Maurice Hurst .05 .01
❑ 303 Mike Merriweather .05 .01
❑ 304 Reggie Roby .05 .01
❑ 305 Darryl Williams .05 .01
❑ 306 Jerome Bettis RC 5.00 2.50

- ❑ 307 Curtis Conway RC .40 .15
- ❑ 308 Drew Bledsoe RC 2.50 1.00
- ❑ 309 John Copeland RC .10 .02
- ❑ 310 Eric Curry RC .05 .01
- ❑ 311 Lincoln Kennedy RC .05 .01
- ❑ 312 Dan Williams RC .05 .01
- ❑ 313 Patrick Bates RC .05 .01
- ❑ 314 Tom Carter RC .10 .02
- ❑ 315 Garrison Hearst RC .75 .30
- ❑ 316 Joel Hilgenberg .05 .01
- ❑ 317 Harris Barton .05 .01
- ❑ 318 Jeff Lageman .05 .01
- ❑ 319 Charles Mincy RC .05 .01
- ❑ 320 Ricardo McDonald .05 .01
- ❑ 321 Lorenzo White .05 .01
- ❑ 322 Troy Vincent .05 .01
- ❑ 323 Bennie Blades .05 .01
- ❑ 324 Dana Hall .05 .01
- ❑ 325 Ken Norton Jr. .10 .02
- ❑ 326 Will Wolford .05 .01
- ❑ 327 Neil O'Donnell .25 .08
- ❑ 328 Tracy Simien .05 .01
- ❑ 329 Darrell Green .05 .01
- ❑ 330 Kyle Clifton .05 .01
- ❑ 331 Elbert Shelley RC .05 .01
- ❑ 332 Jeff Wright .05 .01
- ❑ 333 Mike Johnson .05 .01
- ❑ 334 John Gesek .05 .01
- ❑ 335 Michael Brooks .05 .01
- ❑ 336 George Jamison .05 .01
- ❑ 337 Johnny Holland .05 .01
- ❑ 338 Lamar Lathon .05 .01
- ❑ 339 Bern Brostek .05 .01
- ❑ 340 Steve Jordan .05 .01
- ❑ 341 Gene Atkins .05 .01
- ❑ 342 Aaron Wallace .05 .01
- ❑ 343 Adrian Cooper .05 .01
- ❑ 344 Amp Lee .05 .01
- ❑ 345 Vincent Brown .05 .01
- ❑ 346 James Hasty .05 .01
- ❑ 347 Ron Hall .05 .01
- ❑ 348 Matt Elliott .05 .01
- ❑ 349 Tim Krumrie .05 .01
- ❑ 350 Mark Stepnoski .05 .01
- ❑ 351 Matt Stover .05 .01
- ❑ 352 James Washington .05 .01
- ❑ 353 Marc Spindler .05 .01
- ❑ 354 Frank Warren .05 .01
- ❑ 355 Vai Sikahema .05 .01
- ❑ 356 Dan Saleaumua .05 .01
- ❑ 357 Mark Clayton .05 .01
- ❑ 358 Brent Jones .10 .02
- ❑ 359 Andy Harmon RC .10 .02
- ❑ 360 Anthony Parker .05 .01
- ❑ 361 Chris Hinton .05 .01
- ❑ 362 Greg Montgomery .05 .01
- ❑ 363 Greg McMurtry .05 .01
- ❑ 364 Craig Heyward .10 .02
- ❑ 365 D.J. Johnson .05 .01
- ❑ 366 Bill Romanowski .05 .01
- ❑ 367 Steve Christie .05 .01
- ❑ 368 Art Monk .10 .02
- ❑ 369 Howard Ballard .05 .01
- ❑ 370 Andre Collins .05 .01
- ❑ 371 Alvin Harper .10 .02
- ❑ 372 Blaise Winter RC .05 .01
- ❑ 373 Al Del Greco .05 .01
- ❑ 374 Eric Green .05 .01
- ❑ 375 Chris Mohr .05 .01
- ❑ 376 Tom Newberry .05 .01
- ❑ 377 Cris Dishman .05 .01
- ❑ 378 Jumpy Geathers .05 .01
- ❑ 379 Don Mosebar .05 .01
- ❑ 380 Andre Ware .05 .01
- ❑ 381 Marvin Washington .05 .01
- ❑ 382 Bobby Humphrey .05 .01
- ❑ 383 Marc Logan .05 .01
- ❑ 384 Lomas Brown .05 .01
- ❑ 385 Steve Tasker .10 .02
- ❑ 386 Chris Miller .10 .02
- ❑ 387 Tony Paige .05 .01
- ❑ 388 Charles Haley .10 .02
- ❑ 389 Rich Moran .05 .01
- ❑ 390 Mike Sherrard .05 .01
- ❑ 391 Nick Lowery .05 .01
- ❑ 392 Henry Thomas .05 .01
- ❑ 393 Keith Sims .05 .01
- ❑ 394 Thomas Everett .05 .01
- ❑ 395 Steve Wallace .05 .01
- ❑ 396 John Carney .05 .01
- ❑ 397 Tim Johnson .05 .01
- ❑ 398 Jeff Gossett .05 .01
- ❑ 399 Anthony Smith .05 .01
- ❑ 400 Kelvin Pritchett .05 .01
- ❑ 401 Dermontti Dawson .05 .01
- ❑ 402 Alfred Williams .05 .01
- ❑ 403 Michael Haynes .10 .02
- ❑ 404 Bart Oates .05 .01
- ❑ 405 Ken Lanier .05 .01
- ❑ 406 Vencie Glenn .05 .01
- ❑ 407 John Taylor .10 .02
- ❑ 408 Nate Newton .10 .02
- ❑ 409 Mark Carrier WR .10 .02
- ❑ 410 Ken Harvey .05 .01
- ❑ 411 Troy Aikman SB .40 .15
- ❑ 412 Charles Haley SB .05 .01
- ❑ 413 Warren Moon/Jeffires DT .10 .02
- ❑ 414 Henry Jones DT .05 .01
- ❑ 415 Rickey Jackson DT .05 .01
- ❑ 416 Clyde Simmons DT .05 .01
- ❑ 417 Dale Carter ROY .05 .01
- ❑ 418 Carl Pickens ROY .10 .02
- ❑ 419 Vaughn Dunbar ROY .05 .01
- ❑ 420 Santana Dotson ROY .05 .01
- ❑ 421 Steve Emtman 90 .05 .01
- ❑ 422 Louis Oliver 90 .05 .01
- ❑ 423 Carl Pickens 90 .10 .02
- ❑ 424 Eddie Anderson 90 .05 .01
- ❑ 425 Deion Sanders 90 .25 .08
- ❑ 426 Jon Vaughn 90 .05 .01
- ❑ 427 Darren Lewis 90 .05 .01
- ❑ 428 Kevin Ross 90 .05 .01
- ❑ 429 David Brandon 90 .05 .01
- ❑ 430 Dave Meggett 90 .05 .01
- ❑ 431 Jerry Rice HL .50 .20
- ❑ 432 Sterling Sharpe HL .10 .02
- ❑ 433 Art Monk HL .05 .01
- ❑ 434 James Lofton HL .05 .01
- ❑ 435 Lawrence Taylor .10 .02
- ❑ 436 Bill Walsh RC HOF .10 .02
- ❑ 437 Chuck Noll HOF .10 .02
- ❑ 438 Dan Fouts HOF .05 .01
- ❑ 439 Larry Little HOF .05 .01
- ❑ 440 Steve Young MOY .40 .15
- ❑ NNO Dick Butkus AU/3000 40.00 25.00

1994 Score

- ❑ COMPLETE SET (330) 12.00 5.00
- ❑ 1 Barry Sanders 1.25 .50
- ❑ 2 Troy Aikman .75 .30
- ❑ 3 Sterling Sharpe .10 .02
- ❑ 4 Deion Sanders .50 .20
- ❑ 5 Bruce Smith .25 .08
- ❑ 6 Eric Metcalf .10 .02
- ❑ 7 John Elway 1.50 .60
- ❑ 8 Bruce Matthews .05 .01
- ❑ 9 Rickey Jackson .05 .01
- ❑ 10 Cortez Kennedy .10 .02
- ❑ 11 Jerry Rice .75 .30
- ❑ 12 Stanley Richard .05 .01
- ❑ 13 Rod Woodson .10 .02
- ❑ 14 Eric Swann .10 .02
- ❑ 15 Eric Allen .05 .01
- ❑ 16 Richard Dent .10 .02
- ❑ 17 Carl Pickens .10 .02
- ❑ 18 Rohn Stark .05 .01
- ❑ 19 Marcus Allen .25 .08
- ❑ 20 Steve Wisniewski .05 .01
- ❑ 21 Jerome Bettis .50 .20
- ❑ 22 Darrell Green .05 .01
- ❑ 23 Lawrence Dawsey .05 .01
- ❑ 24 Larry Centers .25 .08
- ❑ 25 Steve Jordan .05 .01
- ❑ 26 Johnny Johnson .05 .01
- ❑ 27 Phil Simms .10 .02
- ❑ 28 Bruce Armstrong .05 .01
- ❑ 29 Willie Roaf .05 .01
- ❑ 30 Andre Rison .10 .02
- ❑ 31 Henry Jones .05 .01
- ❑ 32 Warren Moon .25 .08
- ❑ 33 Sean Gilbert .05 .01
- ❑ 34 [illegible] .10 .02
- ❑ 35 Seth Joyner .05 .01
- ❑ 36 Ronnie Harmon .05 .01
- ❑ 37 Quentin Coryatt .05 .01
- ❑ 38 Ricky Sanders .05 .01
- ❑ 39 Gerald Williams .05 .01
- ❑ 40 Emmitt Smith 1.00 .40
- ❑ 41 Jason Hanson .05 .01
- ❑ 42 Kevin Smith .05 .01
- ❑ 43 Irving Fryar .10 .02
- ❑ 44 Boomer Esiason .10 .02
- ❑ 45 Darryl Talley .05 .01
- ❑ 46 Paul Gruber .05 .01
- ❑ 47 Anthony Smith .05 .01
- ❑ 48 John Copeland .05 .01
- ❑ 49 Michael Jackson .10 .02
- ❑ 50 Shannon Sharpe .10 .02
- ❑ 51 Reggie White .25 .08
- ❑ 52 Andre Collins .05 .01
- ❑ 53 Jack Del Rio .05 .01
- ❑ 54 John Elliott .05 .01
- ❑ 55 Kevin Greene .10 .02
- ❑ 56 Steve Young .60 .25
- ❑ 57 Errict Pegram .05 .01
- ❑ 58 Donnell Woolford .05 .01
- ❑ 59 Darryl Williams .05 .01
- ❑ 60 Michael Irvin .25 .08
- ❑ 61 Mel Gray .05 .01
- ❑ 62 Greg Montgomery .05 .01
- ❑ 63 Neil Smith .10 .02
- ❑ 64 Andy Harmon .05 .01
- ❑ 65 Dan Marino 1.50 .60
- ❑ 66 Leonard Russell .05 .01
- ❑ 67 Joe Montana 1.50 .60
- ❑ 68 John Taylor .10 .02
- ❑ 69 Cris Dishman .05 .01
- ❑ 70 Cornelius Bennett .10 .02
- ❑ 71 Harold Green .05 .01
- ❑ 72 Anthony Pleasant .05 .01
- ❑ 73 Dennis Smith .05 .01
- ❑ 74 Bryce Paup .10 .02
- ❑ 75 Jeff George .25 .08
- ❑ 76 Henry Ellard .10 .02
- ❑ 77 Randall McDaniel .05 .01
- ❑ 78 Derek Brown RBK .05 .01
- ❑ 79 Johnny Mitchell .05 .01
- ❑ 80 Leroy Thompson .05 .01
- ❑ 81 Junior Seau .25 .08
- ❑ 82 Kelvin Martin .05 .01
- ❑ 83 Guy McIntyre .05 .01
- ❑ 84 Elbert Shelley .05 .01
- ❑ 85 Louis Oliver .05 .01
- ❑ 86 Tommy Vardell .05 .01
- ❑ 87 Jeff Herrod .05 .01
- ❑ 88 Edgar Bennett .25 .08
- ❑ 89 Reggie Langhorne .05 .01
- ❑ 90 Terry Kirby .25 .08
- ❑ 91 Marcus Robertson .05 .01
- ❑ 92 Mark Collins .05 .01
- ❑ 93 Calvin Williams .10 .02
- ❑ 94 Barry Foster .05 .01
- ❑ 95 Brent Jones .10 .02
- ❑ 96 Reggie Cobb .05 .01
- ❑ 97 Ray Childress .05 .01
- ❑ 98 Chris Miller .05 .01
- ❑ 99 John Carney .05 .01
- ❑ 100 Ricky Proehl .05 .01
- ❑ 101 Renaldo Turnbull .05 .01
- ❑ 102 John Randle .10 .02
- ❑ 103 Flipper Anderson .05 .01
- ❑ 104 Scottie Graham RC .10 .02
- ❑ 105 Webster Slaughter .05 .01

❑ 106 Tyrone Hughes .10 .02
❑ 107 Ken Norton Jr. .10 .02
❑ 108 Jim Kelly .25 .08
❑ 109 Michael Haynes .10 .02
❑ 110 Mark Carrier DB .05 .01
❑ 111 Eddie Murray .05 .01
❑ 112 Glyn Milburn .10 .02
❑ 113 Jackie Harris .05 .01
❑ 114 Dean Biasucci .05 .01
❑ 115 Tim Brown .25 .08
❑ 116 Mark Higgs .05 .01
❑ 117 Steve Emtman .05 .01
❑ 118 Clay Matthews .05 .01
❑ 119 Clyde Simmons .05 .01
❑ 120 Howard Ballard .05 .01
❑ 121 Ricky Watters .10 .02
❑ 122 William Fuller .05 .01
❑ 123 Robert Brooks .25 .08
❑ 124 Brian Blades .10 .02
❑ 125 Leslie O'Neal .05 .01
❑ 126 Gary Clark .10 .02
❑ 127 Jim Sweeney .05 .01
❑ 128 Vaughan Johnson .05 .01
❑ 129 Gary Brown .05 .01
❑ 130 Todd Lyght .05 .01
❑ 131 Nick Lowery .05 .01
❑ 132 Ernest Givins .10 .02
❑ 133 Lomas Brown .05 .01
❑ 134 Craig Erickson .05 .01
❑ 135 James Francis .05 .01
❑ 136 Andre Reed .10 .02
❑ 137 Jim Everett .10 .02
❑ 138 Nate Odomes .05 .01
❑ 139 Tom Waddle .05 .01
❑ 140 Stevon Moore .05 .01
❑ 141 Rod Bernstine .05 .01
❑ 142 Brett Favre 1.50 .60
❑ 143 Roosevelt Potts .05 .01
❑ 144 Chester McGlockton .05 .01
❑ 145 LeRoy Butler .05 .01
❑ 146 Charles Haley .10 .02
❑ 147 Rodney Hampton .10 .02
❑ 148 George Teague .05 .01
❑ 149 Gary Anderson K .05 .01
❑ 150 Mark Stepnoski .05 .01
❑ 151 Courtney Hawkins .05 .01
❑ 152 Tim Grunhard .05 .01
❑ 153 David Klingler .05 .01
❑ 154 Erik Williams .05 .01
❑ 155 Herman Moore .25 .08
❑ 156 Daryl Johnston .10 .02
❑ 157 Chris Zorich .05 .01
❑ 158 Shane Conlan .05 .01
❑ 159 Santana Dotson .10 .02
❑ 160 Sam Mills .05 .01
❑ 161 Ronnie Lott .10 .02
❑ 162 Jesse Sapolu .05 .01
❑ 163 Marion Butts .05 .01
❑ 164 Eugene Robinson .05 .01
❑ 165 Mark Schlereth .05 .01
❑ 166 John L. Williams .05 .01
❑ 167 Anthony Miller .10 .02
❑ 168 Rich Camarillo .05 .01
❑ 169 Jeff Lageman .05 .01
❑ 170 Michael Brooks .05 .01
❑ 171 Scott Mitchell .10 .02
❑ 172 Duane Bickett .05 .01
❑ 173 Willie Davis .10 .02
❑ 174 Maurice Hurst .05 .01
❑ 175 Brett Perriman .10 .02
❑ 176 Jay Novacek .10 .02
❑ 177 Terry Allen .10 .02
❑ 178 Pete Metzelaars .05 .01
❑ 179 Erik Kramer .10 .02
❑ 180 Neal Anderson .05 .01
❑ 181 Ethan Horton .05 .01
❑ 182 Tony Bennett .05 .01
❑ 183 Gary Zimmerman .05 .01
❑ 184 Jeff Hostetler .10 .02
❑ 185 Jeff Cross .05 .01
❑ 186 Vincent Brown .05 .01
❑ 187 Herschel Walker .10 .02
❑ 188 Courtney Hall .05 .01
❑ 189 Norm Johnson .05 .01
❑ 190 Hardy Nickerson .10 .02
❑ 191 Greg Townsend .05 .01
❑ 192 Mike Munchak .10 .02
❑ 193 Dante Jones .05 .01
❑ 194 Vinny Testaverde .10 .02
❑ 195 Vance Johnson .05 .01
❑ 196 Chris Jacke .05 .01
❑ 197 Will Wolford .05 .01
❑ 198 Terry McDaniel .05 .01
❑ 199 Bryan Cox .05 .01
❑ 200 Nate Newton .05 .01
❑ 201 Keith Byars .05 .01
❑ 202 Neil O'Donnell .25 .08
❑ 203 Harris Barton .05 .01
❑ 204 Thurman Thomas .25 .08
❑ 205 Jeff Query .05 .01
❑ 206 Russell Maryland .05 .01
❑ 207 Pat Swilling .05 .01
❑ 208 Haywood Jeffires .10 .02
❑ 209 John Alt .05 .01
❑ 210 O.J.McDuffie .25 .08
❑ 211 Keith Sims .05 .01
❑ 212 Eric Martin .05 .01
❑ 213 Kyle Clifton .05 .01
❑ 214 Luis Sharpe .05 .01
❑ 215 Thomas Everett .05 .01
❑ 216 Chris Warren .10 .02
❑ 217 Chris Doleman .05 .01
❑ 218 Tony Jones T .05 .01
❑ 219 Karl Mecklenburg .05 .01
❑ 220 Rob Moore .10 .02
❑ 221 Jessie Hester .05 .01
❑ 222 Jeff Jaeger .05 .01
❑ 223 Keith Jackson .05 .01
❑ 224 Mo Lewis .05 .01
❑ 225 Mike Horan .05 .01
❑ 226 Eric Green .05 .01
❑ 227 Jim Ritcher .05 .01
❑ 228 Eric Curry .05 .01
❑ 229 Stan Humphries .10 .02
❑ 230 Mike Johnson .05 .01
❑ 231 Alvin Harper .10 .02
❑ 232 Bennie Blades .05 .01
❑ 233 Cris Carter .50 .20
❑ 234 Morten Andersen .05 .01
❑ 235 Brian Washington .05 .01
❑ 236 Eric Hill .05 .01
❑ 237 Natrone Means .25 .08
❑ 238 Carlton Bailey .05 .01
❑ 239 Anthony Carter .10 .02
❑ 240 Jessie Tuggle .05 .01
❑ 241 Tim Irwin .05 .01
❑ 242 Mark Carrier WR .10 .02
❑ 243 Steve Atwater .05 .01
❑ 244 Sean Jones .05 .01
❑ 245 Bernie Kosar .10 .02
❑ 246 Richmond Webb .05 .01
❑ 247 Dave Meggett .05 .01
❑ 248 Vincent Brisby .10 .02
❑ 249 Fred Barnett .10 .02
❑ 250 Greg Lloyd .10 .02
❑ 251 Tim McDonald .05 .01
❑ 252 Mike Pritchard .05 .01
❑ 253 Greg Robinson .05 .01
❑ 254 Tony McGee .05 .01
❑ 255 Chris Spielman .10 .02
❑ 256 Keith Loneker RC .05 .01
❑ 257 Derrick Thomas .25 .08
❑ 258 Wayne Martin .05 .01
❑ 259 Art Monk .10 .02
❑ 260 Andy Heck .05 .01
❑ 261 Chip Lohmiller .05 .01
❑ 262 Simon Fletcher .05 .01
❑ 263 Ricky Reynolds .05 .01
❑ 264 Chris Hinton .05 .01
❑ 265 Ronald Moore .05 .01
❑ 266 Rocket Ismail .10 .02
❑ 267 Pete Stoyanovich .05 .01
❑ 268 Mark Jackson .05 .01
❑ 269 Randall Cunningham .25 .08
❑ 270 Dermontti Dawson .05 .01
❑ 271 Bill Romanowski .05 .01
❑ 272 Tim Johnson .05 .01
❑ 273 Steve Tasker .10 .02
❑ 274 Keith Hamilton .05 .01
❑ 275 Pierce Holt .05 .01
❑ 276 Heath Shuler RC .25 .08
❑ 277 Marshall Faulk RC 5.00 2.00
❑ 278 Charles Johnson RC .25 .08
❑ 279 Sam Adams RC .10 .02
❑ 280 Trev Alberts RC .10 .02
❑ 281 Derrick Alexander WR RC .25 .08
❑ 282 Bryant Young RC .40 .15
❑ 283 Greg Hill RC .25 .08
❑ 284 Darnay Scott RC .50 .20
❑ 285 Willie McGinest RC .25 .08
❑ 286 Thomas Randolph RC .05 .01
❑ 287 Errict Rhett RC .25 .08
❑ 288 Lamar Smith RC 1.25 .50
❑ 289 William Floyd RC .25 .08
❑ 290 Johnnie Morton RC .50 .20
❑ 291 Jamir Miller RC .10 .02
❑ 292 David Palmer RC .25 .08
❑ 293 Dan Wilkinson RC .10 .02
❑ 294 Trent Dilfer RC 1.25 .50
❑ 295 Antonio Langham RC .10 .02
❑ 296 Chuck Levy RC .05 .01
❑ 297 John Thierry RC .05 .01
❑ 298 Kevin Lee RC .05 .01
❑ 299 Aaron Glenn RC .25 .08
❑ 300 Charlie Garner RC 1.25 .50
❑ 301 Lonnie Johnson RC .05 .01
❑ 302 LeShon Johnson RC .10 .02
❑ 303 Thomas Lewis RC .10 .02
❑ 304 Ryan Yarborough RC .05 .01
❑ 305 Mario Bates RC .25 .08
❑ 306 Buffalo Bills TC .05 .01
❑ 307 Cincinnati Bengals TC .05 .01
❑ 308 Cleveland Browns TC .05 .01
❑ 309 Denver Broncos TC .05 .01
❑ 310 Houston Oilers TC .05 .01
❑ 311 Indianapolis Colts TC .05 .01
❑ 312 Kansas City Chiefs TC .05 .01
❑ 313 Los Angeles Raiders TC .05 .01
❑ 314 Miami Dolphins TC .05 .01
❑ 315 New England Patriots TC .05 .01
❑ 316 New York Jets TC .05 .01
❑ 317 Pittsburgh Steelers TC .05 .01
❑ 318 San Diego Charges TC .05 .01
❑ 319 Seattle Seahawks TC .05 .01
❑ 320 Garrison Hearst FF .25 .08
❑ 321 Drew Bledsoe FF .75 .30
❑ 322 Tyrone Hughes FF .10 .02
❑ 323 James Jett FF .05 .01
❑ 324 Tom Carter FF .05 .01
❑ 325 Reggie Brooks FF .05 .01
❑ 326 Dana Stubblefield FF .10 .02
❑ 327 Jerome Bettis FF .25 .08
❑ 328 Chris Slade FF .05 .01
❑ 329 Rick Mirer FF .25 .08
❑ 330 Emmitt Smith MVP .50 .20

1995 Score

❑ COMPLETE SET (275) 15.00 6.00
❑ 1 Steve Young .60 .25
❑ 2 Barry Sanders 1.25 .50
❑ 3 Jerry Rice .75 .30
❑ 4 Marshall Faulk 1.00 .40
❑ 5 Terance Mathis .10 .02
❑ 6 Rod Woodson .10 .02
❑ 7 Seth Joyner .05 .01
❑ 8 Michael Timpson .05 .01
❑ 9 Deion Sanders .50 .20
❑ 10 Emmitt Smith 1.25 .50
❑ 11 Cris Carter .25 .08
❑ 12 Jake Reed .10 .02
❑ 13 Reggie White .25 .08
❑ 14 Shannon Sharpe .10 .02
❑ 15 Troy Aikman .75 .30

❑	16	Andre Reed	.10	.02
❑	17	Tyrone Hughes	.10	.02
❑	18	Sterling Sharpe	.10	.02
❑	19	Jerome Bettis	.25	.08
❑	20	Irving Fryar	.10	.02
❑	21	Warren Moon	.10	.02
❑	22	Ben Coates	.10	.02
❑	23	Frank Reich	.05	.01
❑	24	Henry Ellard	.10	.02
❑	25	Steve Atwater	.05	.01
❑	26	Willie Davis	.10	.02
❑	27	Michael Irvin	.25	.08
❑	28	Harvey Williams	.05	.01
❑	29	Aeneas Williams	.05	.01
❑	30	Errict Rhett	.10	.02
❑	31	Lorenzo White	.05	.01
❑	32	John Elway	1.50	.60
❑	33	Rodney Hampton	.10	.02
❑	34	Webster Slaughter	.05	.01
❑	35	Eric Turner	.05	.01
❑	36	Dan Marino	1.50	.60
❑	37	Daryl Johnston	.10	.02
❑	38	Bruce Smith	.25	.08
❑	39	Ronald Moore	.05	.01
❑	40	Larry Centers	.10	.02
❑	41	Curtis Conway	.25	.08
❑	42	Drew Bledsoe	.50	.20
❑	43	Quinn Early	.10	.02
❑	44	Marcus Allen	.25	.08
❑	45	Andre Rison	.10	.02
❑	46	Jeff Blake RC	.50	.20
❑	47	Barry Foster	.10	.02
❑	48	Antonio Langham	.05	.01
❑	49	Herman Moore	.25	.08
❑	50	Flipper Anderson	.05	.01
❑	51	Rick Mirer	.10	.02
❑	52	Jay Novacek	.10	.02
❑	53	Tim Bowens	.05	.01
❑	54	Carl Pickens	.10	.02
❑	55	Lewis Tillman	.05	.01
❑	56	Lawrence Dawsey	.05	.01
❑	57	Leroy Hoard	.05	.01
❑	58	Steve Broussard	.05	.01
❑	59	Dave Krieg	.05	.01
❑	60	John Taylor	.05	.01
❑	61	Johnny Mitchell	.05	.01
❑	62	Jessie Hester	.05	.01
❑	63	Johnny Bailey	.05	.01
❑	64	Brett Favre	1.50	.60
❑	65	Bryce Paup	.10	.02
❑	66	J.J. Birden	.05	.01
❑	67	Steve Tasker	.10	.02
❑	68	Edgar Bennett	.10	.02
❑	69	Ray Buchanan	.05	.01
❑	70	Brent Jones	.05	.01
❑	71	Dave Meggett	.05	.01
❑	72	Jeff Graham	.05	.01
❑	73	Michael Brooks	.05	.01
❑	74	Ricky Ervins	.05	.01
❑	75	Chris Warren	.10	.02
❑	76	Natrone Means	.10	.02
❑	77	Tim Brown	.25	.08
❑	78	Jim Everett	.05	.01
❑	79	Chris Calloway	.05	.01
❑	80	John L. Williams	.05	.01
❑	81	Chris Chandler	.10	.02
❑	82	Tim McDonald	.05	.01
❑	83	Calvin Williams	.10	.02
❑	84	Tony McGee	.05	.01
❑	85	Erik Kramer	.05	.01
❑	86	Eric Green	.05	.01
❑	87	Nate Newton	.10	.02
❑	88	Leonard Russell	.05	.01
❑	89	Jeff George	.10	.02
❑	90	Raymont Harris	.05	.01
❑	91	Darnay Scott	.10	.02
❑	92	Brian Mitchell	.05	.01
❑	93	Craig Erickson	.05	.01
❑	94	Cortez Kennedy	.10	.02
❑	95	Derrick Alexander WR	.25	.08
❑	96	Charles Haley	.10	.02
❑	97	Randall Cunningham	.25	.08
❑	98	Haywood Jeffires	.05	.01
❑	99	Ronnie Harmon	.05	.01
❑	100	Dale Carter	.10	.02
❑	101	Dave Brown	.10	.02
❑	102	Michael Haynes	.10	.02
❑	103	Johnny Johnson	.05	.01
❑	104	William Floyd	.10	.02
❑	105	Jeff Hostetler	.10	.02
❑	106	Bernie Parmalee	.10	.02
❑	107	Mo Lewis	.05	.01
❑	108	Byron Bam Morris	.05	.01
❑	109	Vincent Brisby	.05	.01
❑	110	John Randle	.10	.02
❑	111	Steve Walsh	.05	.01
❑	112	Terry Allen	.10	.02
❑	113	Greg Lloyd	.10	.02
❑	114	Merton Hanks	.05	.01
❑	115	Mel Gray	.05	.01
❑	116	Jim Kelly	.25	.08
❑	117	Don Beebe	.05	.01
❑	118	Floyd Turner	.05	.01
❑	119	Neil Smith	.10	.02
❑	120	Keith Byars	.05	.01
❑	121	Rocket Ismail	.10	.02
❑	122	Leslie O'Neal	.10	.02
❑	123	Mike Sherrard	.05	.01
❑	124	Marion Butts	.05	.01
❑	125	Andre Coleman	.05	.01
❑	126	Charles Johnson	.10	.02
❑	127	Derrick Fenner	.05	.01
❑	128	Vinny Testaverde	.10	.02
❑	129	Chris Spielman	.10	.02
❑	130	Bert Emanuel	.25	.08
❑	131	Craig Heyward	.10	.02
❑	132	Anthony Miller	.10	.02
❑	133	Rob Moore	.10	.02
❑	134	Gary Brown	.05	.01
❑	135	David Klingler	.10	.02
❑	136	Sean Dawkins	.10	.02
❑	137	Terry McDaniel	.05	.01
❑	138	Fred Barnett	.10	.02
❑	139	Bryan Cox	.05	.01
❑	140	Andrew Jordan	.05	.01
❑	141	Leroy Thompson	.05	.01
❑	142	Richmond Webb	.05	.01
❑	143	Kimble Anders	.10	.02
❑	144	Mario Bates	.10	.02
❑	145	Irv Smith	.05	.01
❑	146	Carnell Lake	.05	.01
❑	147	Mark Seay	.10	.02
❑	148	Dana Stubblefield	.10	.02
❑	149	Kelvin Martin	.05	.01
❑	150	Pete Metzelaars	.05	.01
❑	151	Roosevelt Potts	.05	.01
❑	152	Bubby Brister	.05	.01
❑	153	Trent Dilfer	.25	.08
❑	154	Ricky Proehl	.05	.01
❑	155	Aaron Glenn	.05	.01
❑	156	Eric Metcalf	.10	.02
❑	157	Kevin Williams WR	.10	.02
❑	158	Charlie Garner	.25	.08
❑	159	Glyn Milburn	.05	.01
❑	160	Fuad Reveiz	.05	.01
❑	161	Brett Perriman	.10	.02
❑	162	Neil O'Donnell	.10	.02
❑	163	Tony Martin	.10	.02
❑	164	Sam Adams	.05	.01
❑	165	John Friesz	.10	.02
❑	166	Bryant Young	.10	.02
❑	167	Junior Seau	.25	.08
❑	168	Ken Harvey	.05	.01
❑	169	Bill Brooks	.05	.01
❑	170	Eugene Robinson	.05	.01
❑	171	Ricky Sanders	.10	.02
❑	172	Rodney Peete	.05	.01
❑	173	Boomer Esiason	.10	.02
❑	174	Reggie Roby	.05	.01
❑	175	Michael Jackson	.10	.02
❑	176	Gus Frerotte	.10	.02
❑	177	Terry Kirby	.10	.02
❑	178	Jessie Tuggle	.05	.01
❑	179	Courtney Hawkins	.05	.01
❑	180	Heath Shuler	.10	.02
❑	181	Jack Del Rio	.05	.01
❑	182	O.J. McDuffie	.25	.08
❑	183	Ricky Watters	.10	.02
❑	184	Willie Roaf	.05	.01
❑	185	Glenn Foley	.05	.01
❑	186	Blair Thomas	.05	.01
❑	187	Darren Woodson	.10	.02
❑	188	Kevin Greene	.10	.02
❑	189	Jeff Burris	.05	.01
❑	190	Jay Schroeder	.05	.01
❑	191	Stan Humphries	.10	.02
❑	192	Irving Spikes	.10	.02
❑	193	Jim Harbaugh	.10	.02
❑	194	Robert Brooks	.25	.08
❑	195	Greg Hill	.10	.02
❑	196	Herschel Walker	.10	.02
❑	197	Brian Blades	.10	.02
❑	198	Mark Ingram	.05	.01
❑	199	Kevin Turner	.05	.01
❑	200	Lake Dawson	.10	.02
❑	201	Alvin Harper	.05	.01
❑	202	Derek Brown RBK	.05	.01
❑	203	Qadry Ismail	.10	.02
❑	204	Reggie Brooks	.10	.02
❑	205	Steve Young SS	.30	.10
❑	206	Emmitt Smith SS	.60	.25
❑	207	Stan Humphries SS	.05	.01
❑	208	Barry Sanders SS	.60	.25
❑	209	Marshall Faulk SS	.40	.15
❑	210	Drew Bledsoe SS	.25	.08
❑	211	Jerry Rice SS	.40	.15
❑	212	Tim Brown SS	.10	.02
❑	213	Cris Carter SS	.25	.08
❑	214	Dan Marino SS	.75	.30
❑	215	Troy Aikman SS	.40	.15
❑	216	Jerome Bettis SS	.10	.02
❑	217	Deion Sanders SS	.25	.08
❑	218	Junior Seau SS	.10	.02
❑	219	John Elway SS	.75	.30
❑	220	Warren Moon SS	.05	.01
❑	221	Sterling Sharpe SS	.10	.02
❑	222	Marcus Allen SS	.25	.08
❑	223	Michael Irvin SS	.10	.02
❑	224	Brett Favre SS	.75	.30
❑	225	Rodney Hampton SS	.05	.01
❑	226	Dave Brown SS	.10	.02
❑	227	Ben Coates SS	.10	.02
❑	228	Jim Kelly SS	.25	.08
❑	229	Heath Shuler SS	.10	.02
❑	230	Herman Moore SS	.25	.08
❑	231	Jeff Hostetler SS	.10	.02
❑	232	Rick Mirer SS	.10	.02
❑	233	Byron Bam Morris SS	.05	.01
❑	234	Terance Mathis SS	.05	.01
❑	235	John Elway/B.Sanders CL	.40	.15
❑	236	Troy Aikman CL	.25	.08
❑	237	Jerry Rice CL	.25	.08
❑	238	Emmitt Smith CL	.50	.20
❑	239	Steve Young CL	.25	.08
❑	240	Drew Bledsoe CL	.25	.08
❑	241	Marshall Faulk CL	.25	.08
❑	242	Dan Marino CL	.40	.15
❑	243	Junior Seau CL	.10	.02
❑	244	Ray Zellars RC	.10	.02
❑	245	Rob Johnson RC	.75	.30
❑	246	Tony Boselli RC	.25	.08
❑	247	Kevin Carter RC	.25	.08
❑	248	Steve McNair RC	2.50	1.00
❑	249	Tyrone Wheatley RC	.75	.30
❑	250	Steve Stenstrom RC	.05	.01
❑	251	Stoney Case RC	.05	.01
❑	252	Rodney Thomas RC	.10	.02
❑	253	Michael Westbrook RC	.25	.08
❑	254	Derrick Alexander DE RC	.05	.01
❑	255	Kyle Brady RC	.25	.08
❑	256	Kerry Collins RC	1.25	.50
❑	257	Rashaan Salaam RC	.10	.02
❑	258	Frank Sanders RC	.25	.08
❑	259	John Walsh RC	.05	.01
❑	260	Sherman Williams RC	.05	.01
❑	261	Ki-Jana Carter RC	.25	.08
❑	262	Jack Jackson RC	.05	.01
❑	263	J.J. Stokes RC	.25	.08
❑	264	Kordell Stewart RC	1.25	.50
❑	265	Dave Barr RC	.05	.01
❑	266	Eddie Goines RC	.05	.01
❑	267	Warren Sapp RC	1.25	.50
❑	268	James O. Stewart RC	.75	.30
❑	269	Joey Galloway RC	1.25	.50
❑	270	Tyrone Davis RC	.05	.01
❑	271	Napoleon Kaufman RC	1.00	.40
❑	272	Mark Bruener RC	.10	.02
❑	273	Todd Collins RC	.75	.30
❑	274	Billy Williams RC	.05	.01
❑	275	James A.Stewart RC	.05	.01

❑ P264 Kordell Stewart PROMO	2.50	1.00
❑ AD3 Steve Young	3.00	1.25

1996 Score

❑ COMPLETE SET (275)	20.00	7.50
❑ 1 Emmitt Smith	1.25	.50
❑ 2 Flipper Anderson	.10	.02
❑ 3 Kordell Stewart	.40	.15
❑ 4 Bruce Smith	.20	.07
❑ 5 Marshall Faulk	.50	.20
❑ 6 William Floyd	.20	.07
❑ 7 Darren Woodson	.20	.07
❑ 8 Lake Dawson	.10	.02
❑ 9 Terry Allen	.20	.07
❑ 10 Ki-Jana Carter	.20	.07
❑ 11 Tony Boselli	.10	.02
❑ 12 Christian Fauria	.10	.02
❑ 13 Jeff George	.20	.07
❑ 14 Dan Marino	1.50	.60
❑ 15 Rodney Thomas	.10	.02
❑ 16 Anthony Miller	.20	.07
❑ 17 Chris Sanders	.20	.07
❑ 18 Natrone Means	.20	.07
❑ 19 Curtis Conway	.40	.15
❑ 20 Ben Coates	.20	.07
❑ 21 Alvin Harper	.10	.02
❑ 22 Frank Sanders	.20	.07
❑ 23 Boomer Esiason	.20	.07
❑ 24 Lovell Pinkney	.10	.02
❑ 25 Troy Aikman	.75	.30
❑ 26 Quinn Early	.10	.02
❑ 27 Adrian Murrell	.20	.07
❑ 28 Chris Spielman	.10	.02
❑ 29 Tyrone Wheatley	.20	.07
❑ 30 Tim Brown	.40	.15
❑ 31 Erik Kramer	.10	.02
❑ 32 Warren Moon	.20	.07
❑ 33 Jimmy Oliver	.10	.02
❑ 34 Herman Moore	.20	.07
❑ 35 Quentin Coryatt	.10	.02
❑ 36 Heath Shuler	.20	.07
❑ 37 Jim Kelly	.40	.15
❑ 38 Mike Morris	.10	.02
❑ 39 Harvey Williams	.10	.02
❑ 40 Vinny Testaverde	.20	.07
❑ 41 Steve McNair	.60	.25
❑ 42 Jerry Rice	.75	.30
❑ 43 Darick Holmes	.10	.02
❑ 44 Kyle Brady	.10	.02
❑ 45 Greg Lloyd	.20	.07
❑ 46 Kerry Collins	.40	.15
❑ 47 Willie McGinest	.10	.02
❑ 48 Isaac Bruce	.40	.15
❑ 49 Carnell Lake	.10	.02
❑ 50 Charles Haley	.20	.07
❑ 51 Troy Vincent	.10	.02
❑ 52 Randall Cunningham	.40	.15
❑ 53 Rashaan Salaam	.20	.07
❑ 54 Willie Jackson	.20	.07
❑ 55 Chris Warren	.20	.07
❑ 56 Michael Irvin	.40	.15
❑ 57 Mario Bates	.20	.07
❑ 58 Warren Sapp	.10	.02
❑ 59 John Elway	1.50	.60
❑ 60 Shannon Sharpe	.20	.07
❑ 61 Cornelius Bennett	.10	.02
❑ 62 Robert Brooks	.40	.15
❑ 63 Rodney Hampton	.20	.07
❑ 64 Ken Norton Jr.	.10	.02
❑ 65 Bryce Paup	.10	.02
❑ 66 Eric Swann	.10	.02
❑ 67 Rodney Peete	.10	.02
❑ 68 Larry Centers	.20	.07
❑ 69 Lamont Warren	.10	.02
❑ 70 Jay Novacek	.10	.02
❑ 71 Cris Carter	.40	.15
❑ 72 Terrell Fletcher	.10	.02
❑ 73 Andre Rison	.20	.07
❑ 74 Ricky Watters	.20	.07
❑ 75 Napoleon Kaufman	.40	.15
❑ 76 Reggie White	.40	.15
❑ 77 Yancey Thigpen	.20	.07
❑ 78 Terry Kirby	.20	.07
❑ 79 Deion Sanders	.40	.15
❑ 80 Irving Fryar	.20	.07
❑ 81 Marcus Allen	.40	.15
❑ 82 Carl Pickens	.20	.07
❑ 83 Drew Bledsoe	.50	.20
❑ 84 Eric Metcalf	.10	.02
❑ 85 Robert Smith	.20	.07
❑ 86 Tamarick Vanover	.20	.07
❑ 87 Henry Ellard	.10	.02
❑ 88 Kevin Greene	.20	.07
❑ 89 Mark Brunell	.50	.20
❑ 90 Terrell Davis	.60	.25
❑ 91 Brian Mitchell	.10	.02
❑ 92 Aaron Bailey	.10	.02
❑ 93 Rocket Ismail	.10	.02
❑ 94 Dave Brown	.10	.02
❑ 95 Rod Woodson	.20	.07
❑ 96 Sean Gilbert	.10	.02
❑ 97 Mark Seay	.10	.02
❑ 98 Zack Crockett	.10	.02
❑ 99 Scott Mitchell	.20	.07
❑ 100 Eric Pegram	.10	.02
❑ 101 David Palmer	.10	.02
❑ 102 Vincent Brisby	.10	.02
❑ 103 Brett Perriman	.10	.02
❑ 104 Jim Everett	.10	.02
❑ 105 Tony Martin	.20	.07
❑ 106 Desmond Howard	.20	.07
❑ 107 Stan Humphries	.20	.07
❑ 108 Bill Brooks	.10	.02
❑ 109 Neil Smith	.20	.07
❑ 110 Michael Westbrook	.40	.15
❑ 111 Herschel Walker	.20	.07
❑ 112 Andre Coleman	.10	.02
❑ 113 Derrick Alexander WR	.20	.07
❑ 114 Jeff Blake	.40	.15
❑ 115 Sherman Williams	.10	.02
❑ 116 James O.Stewart	.20	.07
❑ 117 Hardy Nickerson	.10	.02
❑ 118 Elvis Grbac	.20	.07
❑ 119 Brett Favre	1.50	.60
❑ 120 Mike Sherrard	.10	.02
❑ 121 Edgar Bennett	.20	.07
❑ 122 Calvin Williams	.10	.02
❑ 123 Brian Blades	.10	.02
❑ 124 Jeff Graham	.10	.02
❑ 125 Gary Brown	.10	.02
❑ 126 Bernie Parmalee	.10	.02
❑ 127 Kimble Anders	.20	.07
❑ 128 Hugh Douglas	.20	.07
❑ 129 James A.Stewart	.10	.02
❑ 130 Eric Bjornson	.10	.02
❑ 131 Ken Dilger	.20	.07
❑ 132 Jerome Bettis	.40	.15
❑ 133 Cortez Kennedy	.10	.02
❑ 134 Bryan Cox	.10	.02
❑ 135 Darnay Scott	.20	.07
❑ 136 Bert Emanuel	.20	.07
❑ 137 Steve Bono	.10	.02
❑ 138 Charles Johnson	.10	.02
❑ 139 Glyn Milburn	.10	.02
❑ 140 Derrick Alexander DE	.10	.02
❑ 141 Dave Meggett	.10	.02
❑ 142 Trent Dilfer	.40	.15
❑ 143 Eric Zeier	.10	.02
❑ 144 Jim Harbaugh	.20	.07
❑ 145 Antonio Freeman	.40	.15
❑ 146 Orlando Thomas	.10	.02
❑ 147 Russell Maryland	.10	.02
❑ 148 Chad May	.10	.02
❑ 149 Craig Heyward	.10	.02
❑ 150 Aeneas Williams	.10	.02
❑ 151 Kevin Williams WR	.10	.02
❑ 152 Charlie Garner	.20	.07
❑ 153 J.J. Stokes	.40	.15
❑ 154 Stoney Case	.10	.02
❑ 155 Mark Chmura	.20	.07
❑ 156 Mark Bruener	.10	.02
❑ 157 Derek Loville	.10	.02
❑ 158 Justin Armour	.10	.02
❑ 159 Brent Jones	.10	.02
❑ 160 Aaron Craver	.10	.02
❑ 161 Terance Mathis	.10	.02
❑ 162 Chris Zorich	.10	.02
❑ 163 Glenn Foley	.20	.07
❑ 164 Johnny Mitchell	.10	.02
❑ 165 Junior Seau	.40	.15
❑ 166 Willie Davis	.10	.02
❑ 167 Rick Mirer	.20	.07
❑ 168 Mike Jones LB	.10	.02
❑ 169 Greg Hill	.20	.07
❑ 170 Steve Tasker	.10	.02
❑ 171 Tony Bennett	.10	.02
❑ 172 Jeff Hostetler	.10	.02
❑ 173 Dave Krieg	.10	.02
❑ 174 Mark Carrier WR	.10	.02
❑ 175 Michael Haynes	.10	.02
❑ 176 Chris Chandler	.20	.07
❑ 177 Ernie Mills	.10	.02
❑ 178 Jake Reed	.20	.07
❑ 179 Errict Rhett	.20	.07
❑ 180 Garrison Hearst	.20	.07
❑ 181 Derrick Thomas	.40	.15
❑ 182 Aaron Hayden RC	.10	.02
❑ 183 Jackie Harris	.10	.02
❑ 184 Curtis Martin	.60	.25
❑ 185 Neil O'Donnell	.20	.07
❑ 186 Derrick Moore	.10	.02
❑ 187 Steve Young	.60	.25
❑ 188 Pat Swilling	.10	.02
❑ 189 Amp Lee	.10	.02
❑ 190 Rob Johnson	.40	.15
❑ 191 Todd Collins	.20	.07
❑ 192 J.J. Birden	.10	.02
❑ 193 O.J. McDuffie	.20	.07
❑ 194 Shawn Jefferson	.10	.02
❑ 195 Sean Dawkins	.10	.02
❑ 196 Fred Barnett	.10	.02
❑ 197 Roosevelt Potts	.10	.02
❑ 198 Rob Moore	.20	.07
❑ 199 Kevin Miniefield	.10	.02
❑ 200 Barry Sanders	1.25	.50
❑ 201 Floyd Turner	.10	.02
❑ 202 Wayne Chrebet	.60	.25
❑ 203 Andre Reed	.20	.07
❑ 204 Tyrone Hughes	.10	.02
❑ 205 Keenan McCardell	.40	.15
❑ 206 Gus Frerotte	.20	.07
❑ 207 Daryl Johnston	.20	.07
❑ 208 Steve Broussard	.10	.02
❑ 209 Steve Atwater	.10	.02
❑ 210 Thurman Thomas	.40	.15
❑ 211 Andre Hastings	.10	.02
❑ 212 Joey Galloway	.40	.15
❑ 213 Kevin Carter	.10	.02
❑ 214 Keyshawn Johnson RC	1.00	.40
❑ 215 Tony Brackens RC	.40	.15
❑ 216 Stepfret Williams RC	.20	.07
❑ 217 Mike Alstott RC	1.00	.40
❑ 218 Terry Glenn RC	1.00	.40
❑ 219 Tim Biakabutuka RC	.40	.15
❑ 220 Eric Moulds RC	1.25	.50
❑ 221 Jeff Lewis RC	.20	.07
❑ 222 Bobby Engram RC	.40	.15
❑ 223 Cedric Jones RC	.10	.02
❑ 224 Stanley Pritchett RC	.20	.07
❑ 225 Kevin Hardy RC	.40	.15
❑ 226 Alex Van Dyke RC	.20	.07
❑ 227 Willie Anderson RC	.10	.02
❑ 228 Regan Upshaw RC	.10	.02
❑ 229 Leeland McElroy RC	.20	.07
❑ 230 Marvin Harrison RC	2.50	1.00
❑ 231 Eddie George RC	1.25	.50
❑ 232 Lawrence Phillips RC	.40	.15
❑ 233 Daryl Gardener RC	.10	.02
❑ 234 Alex Molden RC	.10	.02
❑ 235 Derrick Mayes RC	.40	.15
❑ 236 John Mobley RC	.10	.02
❑ 237 Israel Ifeanyi RC	.10	.02
❑ 238 Pete Kendall RC	.10	.02

❑ 239 Danny Kanell RC .40 .15
❑ 240 Jonathan Ogden RC .40 .15
❑ 241 Reggie Brown LB RC .10 .02
❑ 242 Marcus Jones RC .10 .02
❑ 243 Jon Stark RC .10 .02
❑ 244 Barry Sanders SE .60 .25
❑ 245 Brett Favre SE .75 .30
❑ 246 John Elway SE .75 .30
❑ 247 Dan Marino SE .75 .30
❑ 248 Drew Bledsoe SE .40 .15
❑ 249 Michael Irvin SE .20 .07
❑ 250 Troy Aikman SE .40 .15
❑ 251 Emmitt Smith SE .50 .20
❑ 252 Steve Young SE .40 .15
❑ 253 Jerry Rice SE .40 .15
❑ 254 Jeff Blake SE .20 .07
❑ 255 Tim Brown SE .20 .07
❑ 256 Eric Metcalf SE .10 .02
❑ 257 Rodney Hampton SE .10 .02
❑ 258 Scott Mitchell SE .10 .02
❑ 259 Garrison Hearst SE .20 .07
❑ 260 Larry Centers SE .20 .07
❑ 261 Neil O'Donnell SE .20 .07
❑ 262 Orlando Thomas SE .10 .02
❑ 263 Hugh Douglas SE .10 .02
❑ 264 Bill Brooks SE .10 .02
❑ 265 Harvey Williams SE .10 .02
❑ 266 Charles Haley SE .20 .07
❑ 267 Greg Lloyd SE .20 .07
❑ 268 Daryl Johnston SE .20 .07
❑ 269 Dan Marino CL .40 .15
❑ 270 Jeff Blake CL .20 .07
❑ 271 John Elway CL .40 .15
❑ 272 Emmitt Smith CL .40 .15
❑ 273 Brett Favre CL .40 .15
❑ 274 Jerry Rice CL .40 .15
❑ 275 Five Star Players CL .40 .15
❑ P1 Barry Sanders Promo 2.00 .75

1997 Score

❑ COMPLETE SET (330) 25.00 10.00
❑ 1 John Elway 2.00 .75
❑ 2 Drew Bledsoe .60 .25
❑ 3 Brett Favre 2.00 .75
❑ 4 Emmitt Smith 1.50 .60
❑ 5 Kerry Collins .50 .20
❑ 6 Jerry Rice 1.00 .40
❑ 7 Kordell Stewart .50 .20
❑ 8 Barry Sanders 1.50 .60
❑ 9 Dan Marino 2.00 .75
❑ 10 Steve Young .60 .25
❑ 11 Erik Kramer .20 .07
❑ 12 Warren Moon .50 .20
❑ 13 Chris Calloway .20 .07
❑ 14 Doug Evans .20 .07
❑ 15 Darren Woodson .20 .07
❑ 16 Alonzo Spellman .20 .07
❑ 17 Greg Hill .20 .07
❑ 18 Aaron Craver .20 .07
❑ 19 Jeff Hostetler .20 .07
❑ 20 William Thomas .20 .07
❑ 21 Marco Coleman .20 .07
❑ 22 Wayne Simmons .20 .07
❑ 23 Donnell Woolford .20 .07
❑ 24 Vinny Testaverde .30 .10
❑ 25 Ed McCaffrey .30 .10
❑ 26 Jim Everett .20 .07
❑ 27 Gilbert Brown .30 .10
❑ 28 Jason Dunn .20 .07
❑ 29 Stanley Pritchett .20 .07
❑ 30 Joey Galloway .30 .10
❑ 31 Amani Toomer .30 .10
❑ 32 Chris Penn .20 .07
❑ 33 Aeneas Williams .20 .07
❑ 34 Bobby Taylor .20 .07
❑ 35 Bryan Still .20 .07
❑ 36 Ty Law .30 .10
❑ 37 Shannon Sharpe .30 .10
❑ 38 Marty Carter .20 .07
❑ 39 Sam Mills .20 .07
❑ 40 William Floyd .30 .10
❑ 41 Brad Johnson .50 .20
❑ 42 Sean Dawkins .20 .07
❑ 43 Michael Irvin .50 .20
❑ 44 Jeff George .30 .10
❑ 45 Brent Jones .30 .10
❑ 46 Mark Brunell .60 .25
❑ 47 Rob Moore .30 .10
❑ 48 Hardy Nickerson .20 .07
❑ 49 Chris Chandler .30 .10
❑ 50 Willie Anderson .20 .07
❑ 51 Isaac Bruce .50 .20
❑ 52 Natrone Means .30 .10
❑ 53 Tony Banks .30 .10
❑ 54 Marshall Faulk .60 .25
❑ 55 Michael Westbrook .30 .10
❑ 56 Bruce Smith .30 .10
❑ 57 Jamal Anderson .50 .20
❑ 58 Jackie Harris .20 .07
❑ 59 Sean Gilbert .20 .07
❑ 60 Ki-Jana Carter .20 .07
❑ 61 Eric Moulds .50 .20
❑ 62 James O.Stewart .30 .10
❑ 63 Jeff Blake .30 .10
❑ 64 O.J. McDuffie .30 .10
❑ 65 Neil Smith .30 .10
❑ 66 Kevin Smith .20 .07
❑ 67 Terry Allen .50 .20
❑ 68 Sean LaChapelle .20 .07
❑ 69 Rashaan Salaam .20 .07
❑ 70 Jeff Graham .20 .07
❑ 71 Mark Carrier WR .20 .07
❑ 72 Allen Aldridge .20 .07
❑ 73 Keenan McCardell .30 .10
❑ 74 Willie McGinest .20 .07
❑ 75 Napoleon Kaufman .50 .20
❑ 76 Jerris McPhail .20 .07
❑ 77 Eric Swann .20 .07
❑ 78 Kimble Anders .30 .10
❑ 79 Charles Johnson .30 .10
❑ 80 Bryan Cox .20 .07
❑ 81 Johnnie Morton .30 .10
❑ 82 Andre Rison .30 .10
❑ 83 Corey Miller .20 .07
❑ 84 Troy Drayton .20 .07
❑ 85 Jim Harbaugh .30 .10
❑ 86 Wesley Walls .30 .10
❑ 87 Bryce Paup .20 .07
❑ 88 Curtis Martin .60 .25
❑ 89 Michael Sinclair .20 .07
❑ 90 Chris T. Jones .20 .07
❑ 91 Jake Reed .30 .10
❑ 92 LeRoy Butler .20 .07
❑ 93 Reggie Tongue .20 .07
❑ 94 Bert Emanuel .30 .10
❑ 95 Stan Humphries .30 .10
❑ 96 Neil O'Donnell .30 .10
❑ 97 Troy Vincent .20 .07
❑ 98 Mike Alstott .50 .20
❑ 99 Chad Cota .20 .07
❑ 100 Marvin Harrison .50 .20
❑ 101 Terrell Owens .60 .25
❑ 102 Dave Brown .20 .07
❑ 103 Harvey Williams .20 .07
❑ 104 Desmond Howard .30 .10
❑ 105 Carl Pickens .30 .10
❑ 106 Kent Graham .20 .07
❑ 107 Michael Bates .20 .07
❑ 108 Terrell Davis .60 .25
❑ 109 Marcus Allen .50 .20
❑ 110 Ray Zellars .20 .07
❑ 111 Chris Warren .30 .10
❑ 112 Phillippi Sparks .20 .07
❑ 113 Craig Erickson .20 .07
❑ 114 Eddie George .50 .20
❑ 115 Daryl Johnston .30 .10
❑ 116 Ricky Watters .30 .10
❑ 117 Tedy Bruschi 1.00 .40
❑ 118 Mike Mamula .20 .07
❑ 119 Ken Harvey .20 .07
❑ 120 John Randle .30 .10
❑ 121 Mark Chmura .30 .10
❑ 122 Sam Gash .20 .07
❑ 123 John Kasay .20 .07
❑ 124 Barry Minter .20 .07
❑ 125 Raymont Harris .20 .07
❑ 126 Derrick Thomas .50 .20
❑ 127 Trent Dilfer .50 .20
❑ 128 Carnell Lake .20 .07
❑ 129 Brian Dawkins .50 .20
❑ 130 Tyronne Drakeford .20 .07
❑ 131 Daryl Gardener .20 .07
❑ 132 Fred Strickland .20 .07
❑ 133 Kevin Hardy .20 .07
❑ 134 Winslow Oliver .20 .07
❑ 135 Herman Moore .30 .10
❑ 136 Keith Byars .20 .07
❑ 137 Harold Green .20 .07
❑ 138 Ty Detmer .30 .10
❑ 139 Lamar Thomas .20 .07
❑ 140 Elvis Grbac .30 .10
❑ 141 Edgar Bennett .30 .10
❑ 142 Cornelius Bennett .20 .07
❑ 143 Tony Tolbert .20 .07
❑ 144 James Hasty .20 .07
❑ 145 Ben Coates .30 .10
❑ 146 Errict Rhett .20 .07
❑ 147 Jason Sehorn .30 .10
❑ 148 Michael Jackson .30 .10
❑ 149 John Mobley .20 .07
❑ 150 Walt Harris .20 .07
❑ 151 Terry Kirby .30 .10
❑ 152 Devin Wyman .20 .07
❑ 153 Ray Crockett .20 .07
❑ 154 Quinn Early .20 .07
❑ 155 Rodney Thomas .20 .07
❑ 156 Mark Seay .20 .07
❑ 157 Derrick Alexander WR .30 .10
❑ 158 Lamar Lathon .20 .07
❑ 159 Anthony Miller .20 .07
❑ 160 Shawn Wooden RC .20 .07
❑ 161 Antonio Freeman .50 .20
❑ 162 Cortez Kennedy .20 .07
❑ 163 Rickey Dudley .30 .10
❑ 164 Tony Carter .20 .07
❑ 165 Kevin Williams .20 .07
❑ 166 Reggie White .50 .20
❑ 167 Tim Bowens .20 .07
❑ 168 Roy Barker .20 .07
❑ 169 Adrian Murrell .30 .10
❑ 170 Anthony Johnson .20 .07
❑ 171 Terry Glenn .50 .20
❑ 172 Jeff Lewis .20 .07
❑ 173 Dorsey Levens .50 .20
❑ 174 Willie Jackson .20 .07
❑ 175 Willie Clay .20 .07
❑ 176 Richmond Webb .20 .07
❑ 177 Shawn Lee .20 .07
❑ 178 Joe Aska .20 .07
❑ 179 Rod Woodson .30 .10
❑ 180 Jim Schwantz RC .20 .07
❑ 181 Alfred Williams .20 .07
❑ 182 Ferric Collons .20 .07
❑ 183 Ken Norton Jr. .20 .07
❑ 184 Rick Mirer .20 .07
❑ 185 Leeland McElroy .20 .07
❑ 186 Rodney Hampton .30 .10
❑ 187 Ted Popson .20 .07
❑ 188 Fred Barnett .20 .07
❑ 189 Junior Seau .50 .20
❑ 190 Micheal Barrow .20 .07
❑ 191 Corey Widmer .20 .07
❑ 192 Rodney Peete .20 .07
❑ 193 Rod Smith WR .50 .20
❑ 194 Muhsin Muhammad .30 .10
❑ 195 Keith Jackson .20 .07
❑ 196 Jimmy Smith .30 .10
❑ 197 Dave Meggett .20 .07
❑ 198 Lawrence Phillips .20 .07
❑ 199 Chad Brown .20 .07
❑ 200 Darrin Smith .20 .07
❑ 201 Larry Centers .30 .10
❑ 202 Kevin Greene .30 .10

❑ 203 Sherman Williams	.20	.07
❑ 204 Chris Sanders	.20	.07
❑ 205 Shawn Jefferson	.20	.07
❑ 206 Thurman Thomas	.50	.20
❑ 207 Keyshawn Johnson	.50	.20
❑ 208 Bryant Young	.20	.07
❑ 209 Tim Biakabutuka	.30	.10
❑ 210 Troy Aikman	1.00	.40
❑ 211 Quentin Coryatt	.20	.07
❑ 212 Karim Abdul-Jabbar	.50	.20
❑ 213 Brian Blades	.20	.07
❑ 214 Ray Farmer	.20	.07
❑ 215 Simeon Rice	.30	.10
❑ 216 Tyrone Braxton	.20	.07
❑ 217 Jerome Woods	.20	.07
❑ 218 Charles Way	.30	.10
❑ 219 Garrison Hearst	.30	.10
❑ 220 Bobby Engram	.30	.10
❑ 221 Billy Davis RC	.20	.07
❑ 222 Ken Dilger	.20	.07
❑ 223 Robert Smith	.30	.10
❑ 224 John Friesz	.20	.07
❑ 225 Charlie Garner	.30	.10
❑ 226 Jerome Bettis	.50	.20
❑ 227 Darnay Scott	.30	.10
❑ 228 Terance Mathis	.30	.10
❑ 229 Brian Williams LB	.20	.07
❑ 230 Cris Carter	.50	.20
❑ 231 Michael Haynes	.20	.07
❑ 232 Cedric Jones	.20	.07
❑ 233 Danny Kanell	.30	.10
❑ 234 Deion Sanders	.50	.20
❑ 235 Steve Atwater	.20	.07
❑ 236 Jonathan Ogden	.20	.07
❑ 237 Lake Dawson	.20	.07
❑ 238 Eric Allen	.20	.07
❑ 239 Eddie Kennison	.30	.10
❑ 240 Irving Fryar	.30	.10
❑ 241 Michael Strahan	.30	.10
❑ 242 Steve McNair	.60	.25
❑ 243 Terrell Buckley	.20	.07
❑ 244 Merton Hanks	.20	.07
❑ 245 Jessie Armstead	.20	.07
❑ 246 Dana Stubblefield	.20	.07
❑ 247 Brett Perriman	.20	.07
❑ 248 Mark Collins	.20	.07
❑ 249 Willie Roaf	.20	.07
❑ 250 Gus Frerotte	.20	.07
❑ 251 William Fuller	.20	.07
❑ 252 Tamarick Vanover	.30	.10
❑ 253 Scott Mitchell	.30	.10
❑ 254 Eric Metcalf	.30	.10
❑ 255 Herschel Walker	.30	.10
❑ 256 Robert Brooks	.30	.10
❑ 257 Zach Thomas	.50	.20
❑ 258 Alvin Harper	.20	.07
❑ 259 Wayne Chrebet	.50	.20
❑ 260 Bill Romanowski	.20	.07
❑ 261 Willie Green	.20	.07
❑ 262 Dale Carter	.20	.07
❑ 263 Chris Slade	.20	.07
❑ 264 J.J. Stokes	.30	.10
❑ 265 Tim Brown	.50	.20
❑ 266 Eric Davis	.20	.07
❑ 267 Mark Carrier DB	.20	.07
❑ 268 Tony Martin	.30	.10
❑ 269 Tyrone Wheatley	.30	.10
❑ 270 Eugene Robinson	.20	.07
❑ 271 Curtis Conway	.30	.10
❑ 272 Michael Timpson	.20	.07
❑ 273 Orlando Pace RC	.50	.20
❑ 274 Tiki Barber RC	3.00	1.25
❑ 275 Byron Hanspard RC	.30	.10
❑ 276 Warrick Dunn RC	1.50	.60
❑ 277 Rae Carruth RC	.20	.07
❑ 278 Bryant Westbrook RC	.20	.07
❑ 279 Antowain Smith RC	1.25	.50
❑ 280 Peter Boulware RC	.50	.20
❑ 281 Reidel Anthony RC	.50	.20
❑ 282 Troy Davis RC	.30	.10
❑ 283 Jake Plummer RC	2.50	1.00
❑ 284 Chris Canty RC	.20	.07
❑ 285 Dwayne Rudd RC	.50	.20
❑ 286 Ike Hilliard RC	.75	.30
❑ 287 Reinard Wilson RC	.30	.10
❑ 288 Corey Dillon RC	3.00	1.25
❑ 289 Tony Gonzalez RC	1.50	.60
❑ 290 Darnell Autry RC	.30	.10
❑ 291 Kevin Lockett RC	.30	.10
❑ 292 Darrell Russell RC	.20	.07
❑ 293 Jim Druckenmiller RC	.30	.10
❑ 294 Shon Mitchell RC	.20	.07
❑ 295 Joey Kent RC	.50	.20
❑ 296 Shawn Springs RC	.30	.10
❑ 297 James Farrior RC	.50	.20
❑ 298 Sedrick Shaw RC	.30	.10
❑ 299 Marcus Harris RC	.20	.07
❑ 300 Danny Wuerffel RC	.50	.20
❑ 301 Marc Edwards RC	.20	.07
❑ 302 Michael Booker RC	.20	.07
❑ 303 David LaFleur RC	.20	.07
❑ 304 Mike Adams WR RC	.20	.07
❑ 305 Pat Barnes RC	.50	.20
❑ 306 George Jones RC	.30	.10
❑ 307 Yatil Green RC	.30	.10
❑ 308 Drew Bledsoe TBP	.50	.20
❑ 309 Troy Aikman TBP	.50	.20
❑ 310 Terrell Davis TBP	.30	.10
❑ 311 Jim Everett TBP	.20	.07
❑ 312 John Elway TBP	1.00	.40
❑ 313 Barry Sanders TBP	.75	.30
❑ 314 Jim Harbaugh TBP	.30	.10
❑ 315 Steve Young TBP	.50	.20
❑ 316 Dan Marino TBP	1.00	.40
❑ 317 Michael Irvin TBP	.50	.20
❑ 318 Emmitt Smith TBP	.75	.30
❑ 319 Jeff Hostetler TBP	.20	.07
❑ 320 Mark Brunell TBP	.50	.20
❑ 321 Jeff Blake TBP	.50	.20
❑ 322 Scott Mitchell TBP	.20	.07
❑ 323 Boomer Esiason TBP	.30	.10
❑ 324 Jerome Bettis TBP	.50	.20
❑ 325 Warren Moon TBP	.30	.10
❑ 326 Neil O'Donnell TBP	.30	.10
❑ 327 Jim Kelly TBP	.50	.20
❑ 328 Dan Marino CL	.50	.20
❑ 329 John Elway CL	.50	.20
❑ 330 Drew Bledsoe CL	.30	.10
❑ P1 Troy Aikman Promo	1.00	.40
❑ P2 Brett Favre Promo	2.00	.75
❑ P3 Dan Marino Promo	2.00	.75
❑ P4 Barry Sanders Promo	1.50	.60

1998 Score

❑ COMPLETE SET (270)	40.00	15.00
❑ 1 John Elway	2.00	.75
❑ 2 Kordell Stewart	.50	.20
❑ 3 Warrick Dunn	.50	.20
❑ 4 Brad Johnson	.50	.20
❑ 5 Kerry Collins	.30	.10
❑ 6 Danny Kanell	.30	.10
❑ 7 Emmitt Smith	1.50	.60
❑ 8 Jamal Anderson	.50	.20
❑ 9 Jim Harbaugh	.30	.10
❑ 10 Tony Martin	.30	.10
❑ 11 Rod Smith	.30	.10
❑ 12 Dorsey Levens	.50	.20
❑ 13 Steve McNair	.50	.20
❑ 14 Derrick Thomas	.50	.20
❑ 15 Rob Moore	.30	.10
❑ 16 Peter Boulware	.20	.07
❑ 17 Terry Allen	.50	.20
❑ 18 Joey Galloway	.30	.10
❑ 19 Jerome Bettis	.50	.20
❑ 20 Carl Pickens	.30	.10
❑ 21 Napoleon Kaufman	.50	.20
❑ 22 Troy Aikman	1.00	.40
❑ 23 Curtis Conway	.30	.10
❑ 24 Adrian Murrell	.30	.10
❑ 25 Elvis Grbac	.30	.10
❑ 26 Garrison Hearst	.50	.20
❑ 27 Chris Sanders	.20	.07
❑ 28 Scott Mitchell	.30	.10
❑ 29 Junior Seau	.50	.20
❑ 30 Chris Chandler	.30	.10
❑ 31 Kevin Hardy	.20	.07
❑ 32 Terrell Davis	.50	.20
❑ 33 Keyshawn Johnson	.50	.20
❑ 34 Natrone Means	.30	.10
❑ 35 Antowain Smith	.50	.20
❑ 36 Jake Plummer	.50	.20
❑ 37 Isaac Bruce	.50	.20
❑ 38 Tony Banks	.30	.10
❑ 39 Reidel Anthony	.30	.10
❑ 40 Darren Woodson	.20	.07
❑ 41 Corey Dillon	.50	.20
❑ 42 Antonio Freeman	.50	.20
❑ 43 Eddie George	.50	.20
❑ 44 Yancey Thigpen	.20	.07
❑ 45 Tim Brown	.50	.20
❑ 46 Wayne Chrebet	.50	.20
❑ 47 Andre Rison	.30	.10
❑ 48 Michael Strahan	.30	.10
❑ 49 Deion Sanders	.50	.20
❑ 50 Eric Moulds	.50	.20
❑ 51 Mark Brunell	.50	.20
❑ 52 Rae Carruth	.20	.07
❑ 53 Warren Sapp	.30	.10
❑ 54 Mark Chmura	.30	.10
❑ 55 Darrell Green	.30	.10
❑ 56 Quinn Early	.20	.07
❑ 57 Barry Sanders	1.50	.60
❑ 58 Neil O'Donnell	.30	.10
❑ 59 Tony Brackens	.20	.07
❑ 60 Willie Davis	.20	.07
❑ 61 Shannon Sharpe	.30	.10
❑ 62 Shawn Springs	.20	.07
❑ 63 Tony Gonzalez	.50	.20
❑ 64 Rodney Thomas	.20	.07
❑ 65 Terance Mathis	.30	.10
❑ 66 Brett Favre	2.00	.75
❑ 67 Eric Swann	.20	.07
❑ 68 Kevin Turner	.20	.07
❑ 69 Tyrone Wheatley	.30	.10
❑ 70 Trent Dilfer	.50	.20
❑ 71 Bryan Cox	.20	.07
❑ 72 Lake Dawson	.20	.07
❑ 73 Will Blackwell	.20	.07
❑ 74 Fred Lane	.20	.07
❑ 75 Ty Detmer	.30	.10
❑ 76 Eddie Kennison	.30	.10
❑ 77 Jimmy Smith	.30	.10
❑ 78 Chris Calloway	.20	.07
❑ 79 Shawn Jefferson	.20	.07
❑ 80 Dan Marino	2.00	.75
❑ 81 LeRoy Butler	.20	.07
❑ 82 William Roaf	.20	.07
❑ 83 Rick Mirer	.20	.07
❑ 84 Dermontti Dawson	.20	.07
❑ 85 Errict Rhett	.30	.10
❑ 86 Lamar Thomas	.20	.07
❑ 87 Lamar Lathon	.20	.07
❑ 88 John Randle	.30	.10
❑ 89 Darryl Williams	.20	.07
❑ 90 Keenan McCardell	.30	.10
❑ 91 Erik Kramer	.20	.07
❑ 92 Ken Dilger	.20	.07
❑ 93 Dave Meggett	.20	.07
❑ 94 Jeff Blake	.30	.10
❑ 95 Ed McCaffrey	.30	.10
❑ 96 Charles Johnson	.20	.07
❑ 97 Irving Spikes	.20	.07
❑ 98 Mike Alstott	.50	.20
❑ 99 Vincent Brisby	.20	.07
❑ 100 Michael Westbrook	.30	.10
❑ 101 Rickey Dudley	.20	.07
❑ 102 Bert Emanuel	.30	.10
❑ 103 Daryl Johnston	.30	.10
❑ 104 Lawrence Phillips	.20	.07
❑ 105 Eric Bieniemy	.20	.07
❑ 106 Bryant Westbrook	.20	.07
❑ 107 Rob Johnson	.30	.10
❑ 108 Ray Zellars	.20	.07

❑ 109 Anthony Johnson	.20	.07
❑ 110 Reggie White	.50	.20
❑ 111 Wesley Walls	.30	.10
❑ 112 Amani Toomer	.30	.10
❑ 113 Gary Brown	.20	.07
❑ 114 Brian Blades	.20	.07
❑ 115 Alex Van Dyke	.20	.07
❑ 116 Michael Haynes	.20	.07
❑ 117 Jessie Armstead	.20	.07
❑ 118 James Jett	.30	.10
❑ 119 Troy Drayton	.20	.07
❑ 120 Craig Heyward	.20	.07
❑ 121 Steve Atwater	.20	.07
❑ 122 Tiki Barber	.50	.20
❑ 123 Karim Abdul-Jabbar	.50	.20
❑ 124 Kimble Anders	.30	.10
❑ 125 Frank Sanders	.30	.10
❑ 126 David Sloan	.20	.07
❑ 127 Andre Hastings	.20	.07
❑ 128 Vinny Testaverde	.30	.10
❑ 129 Robert Smith	.50	.20
❑ 130 Horace Copeland	.20	.07
❑ 131 Larry Centers	.20	.07
❑ 132 J.J. Stokes	.30	.10
❑ 133 Ike Hilliard	.30	.10
❑ 134 Muhsin Muhammad	.30	.10
❑ 135 Sean Dawkins	.20	.07
❑ 136 Raymont Harris	.20	.07
❑ 137 Lamar Smith	.30	.10
❑ 138 David Palmer	.20	.07
❑ 139 Steve Young	.60	.25
❑ 140 Bryan Still	.20	.07
❑ 141 Keith Byars	.20	.07
❑ 142 Cris Carter	.50	.20
❑ 143 Charlie Garner	.30	.10
❑ 144 Drew Bledsoe	.75	.30
❑ 145 Simeon Rice	.30	.10
❑ 146 Merton Hanks	.20	.07
❑ 147 Aeneas Williams	.20	.07
❑ 148 Rodney Hampton	.30	.10
❑ 149 Zach Thomas	.50	.20
❑ 150 Mark Bruener	.20	.07
❑ 151 Jason Dunn	.20	.07
❑ 152 Danny Wuerffel	.30	.10
❑ 153 Jim Druckenmiller	.20	.07
❑ 154 Greg Hill	.20	.07
❑ 155 Earnest Byner	.20	.07
❑ 156 Greg Lloyd	.20	.07
❑ 157 John Mobley	.20	.07
❑ 158 Tim Biakabutuka	.30	.10
❑ 159 Terrell Owens	.50	.20
❑ 160 O.J. McDuffie	.30	.10
❑ 161 Glenn Foley	.30	.10
❑ 162 Derrick Brooks	.50	.20
❑ 163 Dave Brown	.20	.07
❑ 164 Ki-Jana Carter	.20	.07
❑ 165 Bobby Hoying	.30	.10
❑ 166 Randal Hill	.20	.07
❑ 167 Michael Irvin	.50	.20
❑ 168 Bruce Smith	.30	.10
❑ 169 Troy Davis	.20	.07
❑ 170 Derrick Mayes	.30	.10
❑ 171 Henry Ellard	.30	.10
❑ 172 Dana Stubblefield	.20	.07
❑ 173 Willie McGinest	.20	.07
❑ 174 Leeland McElroy	.20	.07
❑ 175 Edgar Bennett	.20	.07
❑ 176 Robert Porcher	.20	.07
❑ 177 Randall Cunningham	.50	.20
❑ 178 Jim Everett	.20	.07
❑ 179 Jake Reed	.30	.10
❑ 180 Quentin Coryatt	.20	.07
❑ 181 William Floyd	.20	.07
❑ 182 Jason Sehorn	.30	.10
❑ 183 Carnell Lake	.20	.07
❑ 184 Dexter Coakley	.20	.07
❑ 185 Derrick Alexander WR	.30	.10
❑ 186 Johnnie Morton	.30	.10
❑ 187 Irving Fryar	.30	.10
❑ 188 Warren Moon	.50	.20
❑ 189 Todd Collins	.20	.07
❑ 190 Ken Norton Jr.	.20	.07
❑ 191 Terry Glenn	.50	.20
❑ 192 Rashaan Salaam	.20	.07
❑ 193 Jerry Rice	1.00	.40
❑ 194 James O.Stewart	.30	.10
❑ 195 David LaFleur	.20	.07
❑ 196 Eric Green	.20	.07
❑ 197 Gus Frerotte	.20	.07
❑ 198 Willie Green	.20	.07
❑ 199 Marshall Faulk	.60	.25
❑ 200 Brett Perriman	.20	.07
❑ 201 Darnay Scott	.30	.10
❑ 202 Marvin Harrison	.50	.20
❑ 203 Joe Aska	.20	.07
❑ 204 Darrien Gordon	.20	.07
❑ 205 Herman Moore	.30	.10
❑ 206 Curtis Martin	.50	.20
❑ 207 Derek Loville	.20	.07
❑ 208 Dale Carter	.20	.07
❑ 209 Heath Shuler	.20	.07
❑ 210 Jonathan Ogden	.20	.07
❑ 211 Leslie Shepherd	.20	.07
❑ 212 Tony Boselli	.20	.07
❑ 213 Eric Metcalf	.20	.07
❑ 214 Neil Smith	.30	.10
❑ 215 Anthony Miller	.20	.07
❑ 216 Jeff George	.30	.10
❑ 217 Charles Way	.20	.07
❑ 218 Mario Bates	.30	.10
❑ 219 Ben Coates	.30	.10
❑ 220 Michael Jackson	.20	.07
❑ 221 Thurman Thomas	.50	.20
❑ 222 Kyle Brady	.20	.07
❑ 223 Marcus Allen	.50	.20
❑ 224 Robert Brooks	.30	.10
❑ 225 Yatil Green	.20	.07
❑ 226 Byron Hanspard	.20	.07
❑ 227 Andre Reed	.30	.10
❑ 228 Chris Warren	.30	.10
❑ 229 Jackie Harris	.20	.07
❑ 230 Ricky Watters	.30	.10
❑ 231 Bobby Engram	.30	.10
❑ 232 Tamarick Vanover	.20	.07
❑ 233 Peyton Manning RC	15.00	6.00
❑ 234 Curtis Enis RC	.75	.30
❑ 235 Randy Moss RC	10.00	5.00
❑ 236 Charles Woodson RC	1.50	.60
❑ 237 Robert Edwards RC	1.00	.40
❑ 238 Jacquez Green RC	1.00	.40
❑ 239 Keith Brooking RC	1.50	.60
❑ 240 Jerome Pathon RC	1.50	.60
❑ 241 Kevin Dyson RC	1.50	.60
❑ 242 Fred Taylor RC	2.00	.75
❑ 243 Tavian Banks RC	1.00	.40
❑ 244 Marcus Nash RC	.75	.30
❑ 245 Brian Griese RC	2.50	1.00
❑ 246 Andre Wadsworth RC	1.00	.40
❑ 247 Ahman Green RC	6.00	2.50
❑ 248 Joe Jurevicius RC	1.50	.60
❑ 249 Germane Crowell RC	1.00	.40
❑ 250 Skip Hicks RC	1.00	.40
❑ 251 Ryan Leaf RC	1.50	.60
❑ 252 Hines Ward RC	6.00	2.50
❑ 253 John Elway OS	1.00	.40
❑ 254 Mark Brunell OS	.50	.20
❑ 255 Brett Favre OS	1.00	.40
❑ 256 Troy Aikman OS	.50	.20
❑ 257 Warrick Dunn OS	.30	.10
❑ 258 Barry Sanders OS	.75	.30
❑ 259 Eddie George OS	.50	.20
❑ 260 Kordell Stewart OS	.50	.20
❑ 261 Emmitt Smith OS	.75	.30
❑ 262 Steve Young OS	.50	.20
❑ 263 Terrell Davis OS	.50	.20
❑ 264 Dorsey Levens OS	.30	.10
❑ 265 Dan Marino OS	1.00	.40
❑ 266 Jerry Rice OS	.50	.20
❑ 267 Drew Bledsoe OS	.50	.20
❑ 268 Brett Favre CL	.60	.25
❑ 269 Barry Sanders CL	.50	.20
❑ 270 Terrell Davis CL	.50	.20
❑ 251AU Ryan Leaf AUTO	40.00	15.00

1999 Score

❑ COMPLETE SET (275)	60.00	25.00
❑ COMP.SET w/o SP's (220)	15.00	6.00
❑ 1 Randy Moss	1.50	.60
❑ 2 Randall Cunningham	.60	.25
❑ 3 Cris Carter	.60	.25
❑ 4 Robert Smith	.60	.25
❑ 5 Jake Reed	.40	.15
❑ 6 Leroy Hoard	.25	.08
❑ 7 John Randle	.40	.15
❑ 8 Brett Favre	2.00	.75
❑ 9 Antonio Freeman	.60	.25
❑ 10 Dorsey Levens	.60	.25
❑ 11 Robert Brooks	.40	.15
❑ 12 Derrick Mayes	.40	.15
❑ 13 Mark Chmura	.40	.15
❑ 14 Darick Holmes	.25	.08
❑ 15 Vonnie Holliday	.25	.08
❑ 16 Mike Alstott	.60	.25
❑ 17 Warrick Dunn	.60	.25
❑ 18 Trent Dilfer	.40	.15
❑ 19 Jacquez Green	.25	.08
❑ 20 Reidel Anthony	.40	.15
❑ 21 Warren Sapp	.40	.15
❑ 22 Bert Emanuel	.40	.15
❑ 23 Curtis Enis	.25	.08
❑ 24 Curtis Conway	.40	.15
❑ 25 Bobby Engram	.40	.15
❑ 26 Erik Kramer	.40	.15
❑ 27 Moses Moreno	.25	.08
❑ 28 Edgar Bennett	.25	.08
❑ 29 Barry Sanders	2.00	.75
❑ 30 Charlie Batch	.60	.25
❑ 31 Herman Moore	.40	.15
❑ 32 Johnnie Morton	.40	.15
❑ 33 Germane Crowell	.25	.08
❑ 34 Terry Fair	.25	.08
❑ 35 Gary Brown	.25	.08
❑ 36 Kent Graham	.25	.08
❑ 37 Kerry Collins	.40	.15
❑ 38 Charles Way	.25	.08
❑ 39 Tiki Barber	.60	.25
❑ 40 Ike Hilliard	.25	.08
❑ 41 Joe Jurevicius	.40	.15
❑ 42 Michael Strahan	.40	.15
❑ 43 Jason Sehorn	.25	.08
❑ 44 Brad Johnson	.60	.25
❑ 45 Terry Allen	.40	.15
❑ 46 Skip Hicks	[illegible]	[illegible]
❑ 47 Michael Westbrook	.40	.15
❑ 48 Leslie Shepherd	.25	.08
❑ 49 Stephen Alexander	.25	.08
❑ 50 Albert Connell	.25	.08
❑ 51 Darrell Green	.40	.15
❑ 52 Jake Plummer	.40	.15
❑ 53 Adrian Murrell	.40	.15
❑ 54 Frank Sanders	.40	.15
❑ 55 Rob Moore	.40	.15
❑ 56 Larry Centers	.25	.08
❑ 57 Simeon Rice	.40	.15
❑ 58 Andre Wadsworth	.25	.08
❑ 59 Duce Staley	.60	.25
❑ 60 Charles Johnson	.25	.08
❑ 61 Charlie Garner	.40	.15
❑ 62 Bobby Hoying	.40	.15
❑ 63 Daryl Johnston	.40	.15
❑ 64 Emmitt Smith	1.25	.50
❑ 65 Troy Aikman	1.25	.50
❑ 66 Michael Irvin	.40	.15
❑ 67 Deion Sanders	.60	.25
❑ 68 Chris Warren	.25	.08
❑ 69 Darren Woodson	.25	.08
❑ 70 Rod Woodson	.40	.15
❑ 71 Travis Jervey	.25	.08
❑ 72 Jerry Rice	1.25	.50
❑ 73 Terrell Owens	.60	.25
❑ 74 Steve Young	.75	.30
❑ 75 Garrison Hearst	.40	.15
❑ 76 J.J. Stokes	.40	.15
❑ 77 Ken Norton	.25	.08

❑ 78	R.W. McQuarters	.25	.08
❑ 79	Bryant Young	.25	.08
❑ 80	Jamal Anderson	.60	.25
❑ 81	Chris Chandler	.40	.15
❑ 82	Terance Mathis	.40	.15
❑ 83	Tim Dwight	.60	.25
❑ 84	O.J. Santiago	.25	.08
❑ 85	Chris Calloway	.25	.08
❑ 86	Keith Brooking	.25	.08
❑ 87	Eddie Kennison	.40	.15
❑ 88	Willie Roaf	.25	.08
❑ 89	Cam Cleeland	.25	.08
❑ 90	Lamar Smith	.40	.15
❑ 91	Sean Dawkins	.25	.08
❑ 92	Tim Biakabutuka	.40	.15
❑ 93	Muhsin Muhammad	.40	.15
❑ 94	Steve Beuerlein	.25	.08
❑ 95	Rae Carruth	.25	.08
❑ 96	Wesley Walls	.40	.15
❑ 97	Kevin Greene	.40	.15
❑ 98	Trent Green	.60	.25
❑ 99	Tony Banks	.40	.15
❑ 100	Greg Hill	.25	.08
❑ 101	Robert Holcombe	.25	.08
❑ 102	Isaac Bruce	.60	.25
❑ 103	Amp Lee	.25	.08
❑ 104	Az-Zahir Hakim	.25	.08
❑ 105	Warren Moon	.60	.25
❑ 106	Jeff George	.40	.15
❑ 107	Rocket Ismail	.40	.15
❑ 108	Kordell Stewart	.40	.15
❑ 109	Jerome Bettis	.60	.25
❑ 110	Courtney Hawkins	.25	.08
❑ 111	Chris Fuamatu-Ma'afala	.25	.08
❑ 112	Levon Kirkland	.25	.08
❑ 113	Hines Ward	.60	.25
❑ 114	Will Blackwell	.25	.08
❑ 115	Corey Dillon	.60	.25
❑ 116	Carl Pickens	.40	.15
❑ 117	Neil O'Donnell	.40	.15
❑ 118	Jeff Blake	.40	.15
❑ 119	Darnay Scott	.25	.08
❑ 120	Takeo Spikes	.25	.08
❑ 121	Steve McNair	.60	.25
❑ 122	Frank Wycheck	.25	.08
❑ 123	Eddie George	.60	.25
❑ 124	Chris Sanders	.25	.08
❑ 125	Yancey Thigpen	.25	.08
❑ 126	Kevin Dyson	.40	.15
❑ 127	Blaine Bishop	.25	.08
❑ 128	Fred Taylor	.60	.25
❑ 129	Mark Brunell	.60	.25
❑ 130	Jimmy Smith	.40	.15
❑ 131	Keenan McCardell	.40	.15
❑ 132	Kyle Brady	.25	.08
❑ 133	Tavian Banks	.25	.08
❑ 134	James Stewart	.40	.15
❑ 135	Kevin Hardy	.25	.08
❑ 136	Jonathan Quinn	.25	.08
❑ 137	Jermaine Lewis	.40	.15
❑ 138	Priest Holmes	1.00	.40
❑ 139	Scott Mitchell	.40	.15
❑ 140	Eric Zeier	.40	.15
❑ 141	Patrick Johnson	.25	.08
❑ 142	Ray Lewis	.60	.25
❑ 143	Terry Kirby	.25	.08
❑ 144	Ty Detmer	.25	.08
❑ 145	Irv Smith	.25	.08
❑ 146	Chris Spielman	.25	.08
❑ 147	Antonio Langham	.25	.08
❑ 148	Dan Marino	2.00	.75
❑ 149	O.J. McDuffie	.40	.15
❑ 150	Oronde Gadsden	.40	.15
❑ 151	Karim Abdul-Jabbar	.40	.15
❑ 152	Yatil Green	.25	.08
❑ 153	Zach Thomas	.60	.25
❑ 154	John Avery	.25	.08
❑ 155	Lamar Thomas	.25	.08
❑ 156	Drew Bledsoe	.75	.30
❑ 157	Terry Glenn	.60	.25
❑ 158	Ben Coates	.40	.15
❑ 159	Shawn Jefferson	.25	.08
❑ 160	Sedrick Shaw	.25	.08
❑ 161	Tony Simmons	.25	.08
❑ 162	Ty Law	.40	.15
❑ 163	Robert Edwards	.25	.08
❑ 164	Curtis Martin	.60	.25
❑ 165	Keyshawn Johnson	.60	.25
❑ 166	Vinny Testaverde	.40	.15
❑ 167	Aaron Glenn	.25	.08
❑ 168	Wayne Chrebet	.40	.15
❑ 169	Dedric Ward	.25	.08
❑ 170	Peyton Manning	2.00	.75
❑ 171	Marshall Faulk	.75	.30
❑ 172	Marvin Harrison	.60	.25
❑ 173	Jerome Pathon	.25	.08
❑ 174	Ken Dilger	.25	.08
❑ 175	E.G. Green	.25	.08
❑ 176	Doug Flutie	.60	.25
❑ 177	Thurman Thomas	.40	.15
❑ 178	Andre Reed	.40	.15
❑ 179	Eric Moulds	.60	.25
❑ 180	Antowain Smith	.60	.25
❑ 181	Bruce Smith	.40	.15
❑ 182	Rob Johnson	.40	.15
❑ 183	Terrell Davis	.60	.25
❑ 184	John Elway	2.00	.75
❑ 185	Ed McCaffrey	.40	.15
❑ 186	Rod Smith	.40	.15
❑ 187	Shannon Sharpe	.40	.15
❑ 188	Marcus Nash	.25	.08
❑ 189	Brian Griese	.60	.25
❑ 190	Neil Smith	.40	.15
❑ 191	Bubby Brister	.25	.08
❑ 192	Ryan Leaf	.60	.25
❑ 193	Natrone Means	.40	.15
❑ 194	Mikhael Ricks	.25	.08
❑ 195	Junior Seau	.60	.25
❑ 196	Jim Harbaugh	.40	.15
❑ 197	Bryan Still	.25	.08
❑ 198	Freddie Jones	.25	.08
❑ 199	Andre Rison	.40	.15
❑ 200	Elvis Grbac	.40	.15
❑ 201	Byron Bam Morris	.25	.08
❑ 202	Rashaan Shehee	.25	.08
❑ 203	Kimble Anders	.40	.15
❑ 204	Donnell Bennett	.25	.08
❑ 205	Tony Gonzalez	.60	.25
❑ 206	Derrick Alexander WR	.40	.15
❑ 207	Jon Kitna	.60	.25
❑ 208	Ricky Watters	.40	.15
❑ 209	Joey Galloway	.40	.15
❑ 210	Ahman Green	.60	.25
❑ 211	Shawn Springs	.25	.08
❑ 212	Michael Sinclair	.25	.08
❑ 213	Napoleon Kaufman	.60	.25
❑ 214	Tim Brown	.60	.25
❑ 215	Charles Woodson	.60	.25
❑ 216	Harvey Williams	.25	.08
❑ 217	Jon Ritchie	.25	.08
❑ 218	Rich Gannon	.60	.25
❑ 219	Rickey Dudley	.25	.08
❑ 220	James Jett	.40	.15
❑ 221	Tim Couch RC	3.00	1.25
❑ 222	Ricky Williams RC	4.00	1.50
❑ 223	Donovan McNabb RC	10.00	4.00
❑ 224	Edgerrin James RC	8.00	3.00
❑ 225	Torry Holt RC	6.00	2.50
❑ 226	Daunte Culpepper RC	8.00	3.00
❑ 227	Akili Smith RC	2.00	.75
❑ 228	Champ Bailey RC	4.00	1.50
❑ 229	Chris Claiborne RC	1.25	.50
❑ 230	Chris McAlister RC	2.00	.75
❑ 231	Troy Edwards RC	2.00	.75
❑ 232	Jevon Kearse RC	5.00	2.00
❑ 233	Shaun King RC	2.00	.75
❑ 234	David Boston RC	3.00	1.25
❑ 235	Peerless Price RC	3.00	1.25
❑ 236	Cecil Collins RC	1.25	.50
❑ 237	Rob Konrad RC	2.00	.75
❑ 238	Cade McNown UER RC	2.00	.75
❑ 239	Shawn Bryson RC	3.00	1.25
❑ 240	Kevin Faulk RC	3.00	1.25
❑ 241	Scott Covington RC	3.00	1.25
❑ 242	James Johnson RC	2.00	.75
❑ 243	Mike Cloud RC	2.00	.75
❑ 244	Aaron Brooks RC	4.00	1.50
❑ 245	Sedrick Irvin RC	1.25	.50
❑ 246	Amos Zereoue RC	3.00	1.25
❑ 247	Jermaine Fazande RC	2.00	.75
❑ 248	Joe Germaine RC	2.00	.75
❑ 249	Brock Huard RC	3.00	1.25
❑ 250	Craig Yeast RC	2.00	.75
❑ 251	Travis McGriff RC	1.25	.50
❑ 252	D'Wayne Bates RC	2.00	.75
❑ 253	Na Brown RC	2.00	.75
❑ 254	Tai Streets RC	3.00	1.25
❑ 255	Andy Katzenmoyer RC	2.00	.75
❑ 256	Kevin Johnson RC	3.00	1.25
❑ 257	Joe Montgomery RC	2.00	.75
❑ 258	Karsten Bailey RC	2.00	.75
❑ 259	De'Mond Parker RC	1.25	.50
❑ 260	Reginald Kelly RC	1.25	.50
❑ 261	Eddie George AP	1.50	.60
❑ 262	Jamal Anderson AP	1.50	.60
❑ 263	Barry Sanders AP	6.00	2.50
❑ 264	Fred Taylor AP	1.50	.60
❑ 265	Keyshawn Johnson AP	1.50	.60
❑ 266	Jerry Rice AP	4.00	1.50
❑ 267	Doug Flutie AP	1.50	.60
❑ 268	Deion Sanders AP	1.50	.60
❑ 269	Randall Cunningham AP	1.50	.60
❑ 270	Steve Young AP	2.50	1.00
❑ 271	J.Elway/T.Davis GC	5.00	2.00
❑ 272	P.Manning/M.Faulk GC	5.00	2.00
❑ 273	B.Favre/A.Freeman GC	6.00	2.50
❑ 274	T.Aikman/E.Smith GC	4.00	1.50
❑ 275	C.Carter/R.Moss GC	4.00	1.50

1999 Score Supplemental

❑	COMPLETE SET (110)	25.00	10.00
❑	COMP.FACT.SET (110)	30.00	12.50
❑ S1	Chris Greisen RC	1.00	.40
❑ S2	Sherdrick Bonner RC	.60	.25
❑ S3	Joel Makovicka RC	1.50	.60
❑ S4	Andy McCullough RC	.60	.25
❑ S5	Jeff Paulk RC	.60	.25
❑ S6	Brandon Stokley RC	2.00	.75
❑ S7	Sheldon Jackson RC	1.00	.40
❑ S8	Bobby Collins RC	.60	.25
❑ S9	Kamil Loud RC	.60	.25
❑ S10	Antoine Winfield RC	1.00	.40
❑ S11	Jerry Azumah RC	1.00	.40
❑ S12	James Allen RC	1.50	.60
❑ S13	Nick Williams RC	1.00	.40
❑ S14	Michael Basnight RC	.60	.25
❑ S15	Damon Griffin RC	1.00	.40
❑ S16	Ronnie Powell RC	.60	.25
❑ S17	Darrin Chiaverini RC	1.00	.40
❑ S18	Mark Campbell RC	1.00	.40
❑ S19	Mike Lucky RC	1.00	.40
❑ S20	Wane McGarity RC	.60	.25
❑ S21	Jason Tucker RC	1.00	.40
❑ S22	Ebenezer Ekuban RC	1.00	.40
❑ S23	Robert Thomas RC	1.00	.40
❑ S24	Dat Nguyen RC	1.00	.40
❑ S25	Olandis Gary RC	1.50	.60
❑ S26	Desmond Clark RC	1.50	.60
❑ S27	Andre Cooper RC	.60	.25
❑ S28	Chris Watson RC	.60	.25
❑ S29	Al Wilson RC	1.50	.60
❑ S30	Cory Sauter RC	.60	.25
❑ S31	Brock Olivo RC	.60	.25
❑ S32	Basil Mitchell RC	.60	.25
❑ S33	Matt Snider RC	.60	.25
❑ S34	Antuan Edwards RC	1.00	.40
❑ S35	Mike McKenzie RC	1.00	.40
❑ S36	Terrence Wilkins RC	1.00	.40
❑ S37	Fernando Bryant RC	1.00	.40
❑ S38	Larry Parker RC	1.50	.60
❑ S39	Autry Denson RC	1.00	.40
❑ S40	Jim Kleinsasser RC	1.50	.60
❑ S41	Michael Bishop RC	1.50	.60

❑	S42	Andy Katzenmoyer	.25	.08
❑	S43	Brett Bech RC	.60	.25
❑	S44	Sean Bennett RC	.60	.25
❑	S45	Dan Campbell RC	.60	.25
❑	S46	Ray Lucas RC	1.50	.60
❑	S47	Scott Dreisbach RC	1.00	.40
❑	S48	Cecil Martin RC	1.00	.40
❑	S49	Dameane Douglas RC	1.00	.40
❑	S50	Jed Weaver RC	1.00	.40
❑	S51	Jerame Tuman RC	1.50	.60
❑	S52	Steve Heiden RC	1.50	.60
❑	S53	Jeff Garcia RC	4.00	1.50
❑	S54	Terry Jackson RC	1.00	.40
❑	S55	Charlie Rogers RC	1.00	.40
❑	S56	Lamar King RC	1.00	.40
❑	S57	Kurt Warner RC	8.00	3.00
❑	S58	Dre' Bly RC	1.50	.60
❑	S59	Justin Watson RC	.60	.25
❑	S60	Rabih Abdullah RC	1.00	.40
❑	S61	Martin Gramatica RC	.60	.25
❑	S62	Darnell McDonald RC	1.00	.40
❑	S63	Anthony McFarland RC	1.00	.40
❑	S64	Larry Brown TE RC	.60	.25
❑	S65	Kevin Daft RC	1.00	.40
❑	S66	Mike Sellers	.15	.05
❑	S67	Ken Oxendine	.15	.05
❑	S68	Errict Rhett	.25	.08
❑	S69	Stoney Case	.15	.05
❑	S70	Jonathan Linton	.15	.05
❑	S71	Marcus Robinson	1.00	.40
❑	S72	Shane Matthews	.25	.08
❑	S73	Cade McNown	1.00	.40
❑	S74	Akili Smith	.15	.05
❑	S75	Karim Abdul-Jabbar	.25	.08
❑	S76	Tim Couch	1.50	.60
❑	S77	Kevin Johnson	.40	.15
❑	S78	Ron Rivers	.15	.05
❑	S79	Bill Schroeder	.40	.15
❑	S80	Edgerrin James	2.50	1.00
❑	S81	Cecil Collins	.75	.30
❑	S82	Matthew Hatchette	.15	.05
❑	S83	Daunte Culpepper	2.50	1.00
❑	S84	Ricky Williams	1.25	.50
❑	S85	Tyrone Wheatley	.40	.15
❑	S86	Donovan McNabb	3.00	1.25
❑	S87	Marshall Faulk	.50	.20
❑	S88	Torry Holt	2.00	.75
❑	S89	Stephen Davis	.40	.15
❑	S90	Brad Johnson	.40	.15
❑	S91	Jake Plummer SS	.25	.08
❑	S92	Emmitt Smith SS	.75	.30
❑	S93	Troy Aikman SS	.75	.30
❑	S94	John Elway SS	1.25	.50
❑	S95	Terrell Davis SS	.40	.15
❑	S96	Barry Sanders SS	1.25	.50
❑	S97	Brett Favre SS	1.25	.50
❑	S98	Antonio Freeman SS	.40	.15
❑	S99	Peyton Manning SS	1.25	.50
❑	S100	Fred Taylor SS	.40	.15
❑	S101	Mark Brunell SS	.40	.15
❑	S102	Dan Marino SS	1.25	.50
❑	S103	Randy Moss SS	1.00	.40
❑	S104	Cris Carter SS	.40	.15
❑	S105	Drew Bledsoe SS	.50	.20
❑	S106	Terry Glenn SS	.40	.15
❑	S107	Keyshawn Johnson SS	.40	.15
❑	S108	Jerry Rice SS	.75	.30
❑	S109	Steve Young SS	.50	.20
❑	S110	Eddie George SS	.40	.15

2000 Score

❑		COMP.SET w/o SP's (220)	20.00	7.50
❑	1	Michael Pittman	.25	.08
❑	2	Jake Plummer	.40	.15
❑	3	Rob Moore	.40	.15
❑	4	David Boston	.60	.25
❑	5	Frank Sanders	.40	.15
❑	6	Jamal Anderson	.60	.25
❑	7	Chris Chandler	.40	.15
❑	8	Tim Dwight	.60	.25
❑	9	Terance Mathis	.40	.15
❑	10	Shawn Jefferson	.25	.08
❑	11	Ashley Ambrose	.25	.08
❑	12	Peter Boulware	.25	.08
❑	13	Priest Holmes	.75	.30
❑	14	Tony Banks	.40	.15
❑	15	Qadry Ismail	.40	.15
❑	16	Shannon Sharpe	.40	.15
❑	17	Rod Woodson	.40	.15
❑	18	Matt Stover	.25	.08
❑	19	Michael McCrary	.25	.08
❑	20	Doug Flutie	.60	.25
❑	21	Rob Johnson	.40	.15
❑	22	Eric Moulds	.60	.25
❑	23	Peerless Price	.40	.15
❑	24	Jonathan Linton	.25	.08
❑	25	Antowain Smith	.40	.15
❑	26	Jay Riemersma	.25	.08
❑	27	Muhsin Muhammad	.40	.15
❑	28	Tim Biakabutuka	.40	.15
❑	29	Patrick Jeffers	.60	.25
❑	30	Wesley Walls	.25	.08
❑	31	Steve Beuerlein	.40	.15
❑	32	John Kasay	.25	.08
❑	33	Curtis Enis	.25	.08
❑	34	Cade McNown	.25	.08
❑	35	Marcus Robinson	.60	.25
❑	36	Bobby Engram	.25	.08
❑	37	Eddie Kennison	.25	.08
❑	38	Akili Smith	.25	.08
❑	39	Carl Pickens	.40	.15
❑	40	Corey Dillon	.60	.25
❑	41	Darnay Scott	.40	.15
❑	42	Errict Rhett	.40	.15
❑	43	Karim Abdul-Jabbar	.40	.15
❑	44	Tim Couch	.40	.15
❑	45	Kevin Johnson	.60	.25
❑	46	Darrin Chiaverini	.25	.08
❑	47	Terry Kirby	.25	.08
❑	48	Jason Tucker	.25	.08
❑	49	Rocket Ismail	.40	.15
❑	50	Joey Galloway	.40	.15
❑	51	Michael Irvin	.40	.15
❑	52	Troy Aikman	1.25	.50
❑	53	Emmitt Smith	1.25	.50
❑	54	David LaFleur	.25	.08
❑	55	Trevor Pryce	.25	.08
❑	56	Brian Griese	.60	.25
❑	57	Olandis Gary	.60	.25
❑	58	Terrell Davis	.60	.25
❑	59	Rod Smith	.40	.15
❑	60	Ed McCaffrey	.60	.25
❑	61	Gus Frerotte	.25	.08
❑	62	Jason Elam	.25	.08
❑	63	Kavika Pittman	.25	.08
❑	64	James Stewart	.40	.15
❑	65	Charlie Batch	.60	.25
❑	66	Johnnie Morton	.40	.15
❑	67	Herman Moore	.40	.15
❑	68	Germane Crowell	.25	.08
❑	69	Barry Sanders	1.50	.60
❑	70	Chris Claiborne	.25	.08
❑	71	Brett Favre	2.00	.75
❑	72	Antonio Freeman	.60	.25
❑	73	Dorsey Levens	.40	.15
❑	74	De'Mond Parker	.25	.08
❑	75	Corey Bradford	.40	.15
❑	76	Basil Mitchell	.25	.08
❑	77	Bill Schroeder	.40	.15
❑	78	Peyton Manning	1.50	.60
❑	79	Marvin Harrison	.60	.25
❑	80	Terrence Wilkins	.25	.08
❑	81	Edgerrin James	1.00	.40
❑	82	E.G. Green	.25	.08
❑	83	Chad Bratzke	.25	.08
❑	84	Mark Brunell	.60	.25
❑	85	Fred Taylor	.60	.25
❑	86	Jimmy Smith	.40	.15
❑	87	Keenan McCardell	.40	.15
❑	88	Kevin Hardy	.25	.08
❑	89	Aaron Beasley	.25	.08
❑	90	Elvis Grbac	.40	.15
❑	91	Derrick Alexander	.40	.15
❑	92	Tony Gonzalez	.40	.15
❑	93	Donnell Bennett	.25	.08
❑	94	Warren Moon	.60	.25
❑	95	Andre Rison	.40	.15
❑	96	James Hasty	.25	.08
❑	97	Dan Marino	2.00	.75
❑	98	Thurman Thomas	.40	.15
❑	99	James Johnson	.25	.08
❑	100	O.J. McDuffie	.40	.15
❑	101	Tony Martin	.40	.15
❑	102	Oronde Gadsden	.40	.15
❑	103	Zach Thomas	.60	.25
❑	104	Sam Madison	.25	.08
❑	105	Jay Fiedler	.60	.25
❑	106	Damon Huard	.60	.25
❑	107	Robert Smith	.60	.25
❑	108	Leroy Hoard	.25	.08
❑	109	Randy Moss	1.25	.50
❑	110	Cris Carter	.60	.25
❑	111	Daunte Culpepper	.75	.30
❑	112	John Randle	.40	.15
❑	113	Randall Cunningham	.60	.25
❑	114	Gary Anderson	.25	.08
❑	115	Drew Bledsoe DP	.75	.30
❑	116	Terry Glenn	.40	.15
❑	117	Kevin Faulk	.40	.15
❑	118	Terry Allen SP	15.00	7.50
❑	119	Adam Vinatieri	.60	.25
❑	120	Ty Law	.40	.15
❑	121	Lawyer Milloy	.40	.15
❑	122	Troy Brown	.40	.15
❑	123	Ben Coates	.25	.08
❑	124	Cam Cleeland	.25	.08
❑	125	Jeff Blake	.40	.15
❑	126	Ricky Williams	.60	.25
❑	127	Jake Reed	.40	.15
❑	128	Jake Delhomme RC	2.50	1.00
❑	129	Andrew Glover	.25	.08
❑	130	Keith Poole	.25	.08
❑	131	Joe Horn	.40	.15
❑	132	Kerry Collins	.40	.15
❑	133	Joe Montgomery	.25	.08
❑	134	Sean Bennett	.25	.08
❑	135	Amani Toomer	.25	.08
❑	136	Ike Hilliard	.40	.15
❑	137	Joe Jurevicius	.25	.08
❑	138	Tiki Barber	.60	.25
❑	139	Victor Green	.25	.08
❑	140	Ray Lucas	.40	.15
❑	141	Vinny Testaverde	.40	.15
❑	142	Curtis Martin	.60	.25
❑	143	Wayne Chrebet	.40	.15
❑	144	Tyrone Wheatley	.40	.15
❑	145	Rich Gannon	.60	.25
❑	146	Napoleon Kaufman	.40	.15
❑	147	Tim Brown	.25	.08
❑	148	Rickey Dudley	.25	.08
❑	149	Charles Woodson	.60	.25
❑	150	James Jett	.25	.08
❑	151	Duce Staley	.60	.25
❑	152	Charles Johnson	.40	.15
❑	153	Donovan McNabb	1.00	.40
❑	154	Troy Vincent	.25	.08
❑	155	Troy Edwards	.25	.08
❑	156	Jerome Bettis	.60	.25
❑	157	Kordell Stewart	.40	.15
❑	158	Richard Huntley	.25	.08
❑	159	Hines Ward	.60	.25
❑	160	Levon Kirkland	.25	.08
❑	161	Ryan Leaf	.40	.15
❑	162	Jim Harbaugh	.40	.15
❑	163	Jermaine Fazande	.25	.08
❑	164	Natrone Means	.25	.08
❑	165	Junior Seau	.60	.25
❑	166	Curtis Conway	.40	.15
❑	167	Freddie Jones	.25	.08
❑	168	Jeff Graham	.25	.08
❑	169	Terrell Owens	.60	.25
❑	170	Jeff Garcia	.60	.25
❑	171	Jerry Rice	1.25	.50
❑	172	Steve Young	.75	.30

❑ 173	Garrison Hearst	.40	.15
❑ 174	Charlie Garner	.40	.15
❑ 175	Fred Beasley	.25	.08
❑ 176	Bryant Young	.25	.08
❑ 177	Derrick Mayes	.40	.15
❑ 178	Sean Dawkins	.25	.08
❑ 179	Jon Kitna	.60	.25
❑ 180	Ricky Watters	.40	.15
❑ 181	Charlie Rogers	.25	.08
❑ 182	Kurt Warner	1.25	.50
❑ 183	Marshall Faulk	.75	.30
❑ 184	Isaac Bruce	.60	.25
❑ 185	Az-Zahir Hakim	.40	.15
❑ 186	Trent Green	.60	.25
❑ 187	Jeff Wilkins	.25	.08
❑ 188	Torry Holt	.60	.25
❑ 189	London Fletcher RC	.40	.15
❑ 190	Robert Holcombe	.25	.08
❑ 191	Todd Lyght	.25	.08
❑ 192	Keyshawn Johnson	.60	.25
❑ 193	Derrick Brooks	.60	.25
❑ 194	Warren Sapp	.40	.15
❑ 195	Shaun King	.25	.08
❑ 196	Warrick Dunn	.60	.25
❑ 197	Mike Alstott	.60	.25
❑ 198	Jacquez Green	.25	.08
❑ 199	Reidel Anthony	.25	.08
❑ 200	Martin Gramatica	.25	.08
❑ 201	Donnie Abraham	.25	.08
❑ 202	Steve McNair	.60	.25
❑ 203	Eddie George	.60	.25
❑ 204	Jevon Kearse	.60	.25
❑ 205	Frank Wycheck	.25	.08
❑ 206	Kevin Dyson	.40	.15
❑ 207	Yancey Thigpen	.25	.08
❑ 208	Al Del Greco	.25	.08
❑ 209	Jeff George	.40	.15
❑ 210	Adrian Murrell	.40	.15
❑ 211	Brad Johnson	.60	.25
❑ 212	Stephen Davis	.60	.25
❑ 213	Stephen Alexander	.25	.08
❑ 214	Michael Westbrook	.40	.15
❑ 215	Darrell Green	.25	.08
❑ 216	Champ Bailey	.60	.25
❑ 217	Albert Connell	.25	.08
❑ 218	Larry Centers	.25	.08
❑ 219	Bruce Smith	.40	.15
❑ 220	Deion Sanders	.60	.25
❑ 221	Ricky Williams SS	.60	.25
❑ 222	Edgerrin James SS	1.00	.40
❑ 223	Tim Couch SS	.40	.15
❑ 224	Cade McNown SS	.30	.10
❑ 225	Olandis Gary SS	.75	.30
❑ 226	Torry Holt SS	.75	.30
❑ 227	Donovan McNabb SS	1.00	.40
❑ 228	Shaun King SS	.25	.08
❑ 229	Kevin Johnson SS	.75	.30
❑ 230	Kurt Warner SS	1.50	.60
❑ 231	Tony Gonzalez AP	.50	.20
❑ 232	Frank Wycheck AP	.30	.10
❑ 233	Eddie George AP	.75	.30
❑ 234	Mark Brunell AP	.75	.30
❑ 235	Corey Dillon AP	.75	.30
❑ 236	Peyton Manning AP	2.00	.75
❑ 237	Keyshawn Johnson AP	.75	.30
❑ 238	Rich Gannon AP	.75	.30
❑ 239	Terry Glenn AP	.50	.20
❑ 240	Tony Brackens AP	.30	.10
❑ 241	Edgerrin James AP	1.00	.40
❑ 242	Tim Brown AP	.75	.30
❑ 243	Michael Strahan AP	.50	.20
❑ 244	Kurt Warner AP	1.50	.60
❑ 245	Brad Johnson AP	.75	.30
❑ 246	Aeneas Williams AP	.30	.10
❑ 247	Marshall Faulk AP	1.00	.40
❑ 248	Dexter Coakley AP	.30	.10
❑ 249	Warren Sapp AP	.50	.20
❑ 250	Mike Alstott AP	.75	.30
❑ 251	David Sloan AP	.30	.10
❑ 252	Cris Carter AP	.75	.30
❑ 253	Muhsin Muhammad AP	.30	.10
❑ 254	Isaac Bruce AP	.75	.30
❑ 255	Wesley Walls AP	.30	.10
❑ 256	Steve Beuerlein LL	.50	.20
❑ 257	Kurt Warner LL	1.50	.60
❑ 258	Peyton Manning LL	2.00	.75
❑ 259	Brad Johnson LL	.75	.30
❑ 260	Edgerrin James LL	1.00	.40
❑ 261	Curtis Martin LL	.75	.30
❑ 262	Stephen Davis LL	.75	.30
❑ 263	Emmitt Smith LL	1.50	.60
❑ 264	Marvin Harrison LL	.75	.30
❑ 265	Jimmy Smith LL	.50	.20
❑ 266	Randy Moss LL	1.50	.60
❑ 267	Marcus Robinson LL	.75	.30
❑ 268	Kevin Carter LL	.30	.10
❑ 269	Simeon Rice LL	.50	.20
❑ 270	Robert Porcher LL	.30	.10
❑ 271	Jevon Kearse LL	.75	.30
❑ 272	Mike Vanderjagt LL	.30	.10
❑ 273	Olindo Mare LL	.30	.10
❑ 274	Todd Peterson LL	.30	.10
❑ 275	Mike Hollis LL	.30	.10
❑ 276	Mike Anderson RC/500	30.00	12.50
❑ 277	Peter Warrick RC	2.00	.75
❑ 278	Courtney Brown RC	.75	.30
❑ 279	Plaxico Burress RC	4.00	1.50
❑ 280	Corey Simon RC	.75	.30
❑ 281	Thomas Jones RC	3.00	1.25
❑ 282	Travis Taylor RC	.75	.30
❑ 283	Shaun Alexander RC	10.00	4.00
❑ 284	Patrick Pass RC/500	20.00	7.50
❑ 285	Chris Redman RC	.50	.20
❑ 286	Chad Pennington RC	5.00	2.00
❑ 287	Jamal Lewis RC	5.00	2.00
❑ 288	Brian Urlacher RC	8.00	3.00
❑ 289	Bubba Franks RC	2.00	.75
❑ 290	Dez White RC	2.00	.75
❑ 291	Frank Moreau RC/500	20.00	7.50
❑ 292	Ron Dayne RC	2.00	.75
❑ 293	Sylvester Morris RC	.50	.20
❑ 294	R.Jay Soward RC	1.50	.60
❑ 295	Curtis Keaton RC	1.50	.60
❑ 296	Spergon Wynn RC/500	20.00	7.50
❑ 297	Rondell Mealey RC	1.50	.60
❑ 298	Travis Prentice RC	1.50	.60
❑ 299	Darrell Jackson RC	4.00	1.50
❑ 300	Giovanni Carmazzi RC	1.50	.60
❑ 301	Anthony Lucas RC	1.50	.60
❑ 302	Danny Farmer RC	1.50	.60
❑ 303	Dennis Northcutt RC	2.00	.75
❑ 304	Troy Walters RC	2.00	.75
❑ 305	Laveranues Coles RC	2.50	1.00
❑ 306	Kwame Cavil RC	1.50	.60
❑ 307	Tee Martin RC	2.00	.75
❑ 308	J.R. Redmond RC	1.50	.60
❑ 309	Tim Rattay RC	2.00	.75
❑ 310	Jerry Porter RC	2.50	1.00
❑ 311	Michael Wiley RC	1.50	.60
❑ 312	Reuben Droughns RC	2.50	1.00
❑ 313	Trung Canidate RC	1.50	.60
❑ 314	Shyrone Stith RC	1.50	.60
❑ 315	Marc Bulger RC	4.00	1.50
❑ 316	Tom Brady RC	40.00	20.00
❑ 317	Doug Johnson RC	2.00	.75
❑ 318	Todd Husak RC	2.00	.75
❑ 319	Gari Scott RC	1.50	.60
❑ 320	Windrell Hayes RC/500	20.00	7.50
❑ 321	Chris Cole RC	1.50	.60
❑ 322	Sammy Morris RC	2.00	.75
❑ 323	Trevor Gaylor RC	1.50	.60
❑ 324	Jarious Jackson RC	1.50	.60
❑ 325	Doug Chapman RC/500	20.00	7.50
❑ 326	Ron Dugans RC	1.50	.60
❑ 327	Ron Dixon RC/500	20.00	7.50
❑ 328	Joe Hamilton RC	1.50	.60
❑ 329	Todd Pinkston RC	2.00	.75
❑ 330	Chad Morton RC	2.00	.75

2001 Score

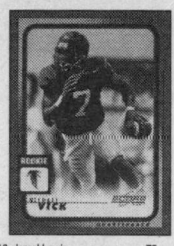

❑	COMPLETE SET (330)	80.00	40.00
❑	COMP.SET w/o SP's (220)	25.00	10.00
❑ 1	David Boston	.50	.20
❑ 2	Frank Sanders	.20	.07
❑ 3	Jake Plummer	.30	.10
❑ 4	Michael Pittman	.20	.07
❑ 5	Rob Moore	.30	.10
❑ 6	Thomas Jones	.30	.10
❑ 7	Chris Chandler	.30	.10
❑ 8	Doug Johnson	.20	.07
❑ 9	Jamal Anderson	.50	.20
❑ 10	Tim Dwight	.50	.20
❑ 11	Brandon Stokley	.30	.10
❑ 12	Chris Redman	.20	.07
❑ 13	Jamal Lewis	.75	.30
❑ 14	Qadry Ismail	.30	.10
❑ 15	Ray Lewis	.50	.20
❑ 16	Rod Woodson	.30	.10
❑ 17	Shannon Sharpe	.30	.10
❑ 18	Travis Taylor	.30	.10
❑ 19	Trent Dilfer	.30	.10
❑ 20	Elvis Grbac	.30	.10
❑ 21	Eric Moulds	.30	.10
❑ 22	Jay Riemersma	.20	.07
❑ 23	Peerless Price	.30	.10
❑ 24	Rob Johnson	.30	.10
❑ 25	Sam Cowart	.20	.07
❑ 26	Sammy Morris	.20	.07
❑ 27	Shawn Bryson	.20	.07
❑ 28	Donald Hayes	.20	.07
❑ 29	Muhsin Muhammad	.30	.10
❑ 30	Patrick Jeffers	.30	.10
❑ 31	Reggie White DE	.50	.20
❑ 32	Steve Beuerlein	.30	.10
❑ 33	Tim Biakabutuka	.30	.10
❑ 34	Wesley Walls	.20	.07
❑ 35	Brian Urlacher	.75	.30
❑ 36	Cade McNown	.20	.07
❑ 37	Dez White	.20	.07
❑ 38	James Allen	.30	.10
❑ 39	Marcus Robinson	.50	.20
❑ 40	Marty Booker	.20	.07
❑ 41	Akili Smith	.20	.07
❑ 42	Corey Dillon	.50	.20
❑ 43	Danny Farmer	.20	.07
❑ 44	Peter Warrick	.50	.20
❑ 45	Ron Dugans	.20	.07
❑ 46	Takeo Spikes	.20	.07
❑ 47	Courtney Brown	.30	.10
❑ 48	Dennis Northcutt	.30	.10
❑ 49	JaJuan Dawson	.20	.07
❑ 50	Kevin Johnson	.30	.10
❑ 51	Tim Couch	.30	.10
❑ 52	Travis Prentice	.20	.07
❑ 53	Anthony Wright	.20	.07
❑ 54	Emmitt Smith	1.00	.40
❑ 55	James McKnight	.30	.10
❑ 56	Joey Galloway	.30	.10
❑ 57	Rocket Ismail	.30	.10
❑ 58	Randall Cunningham	.50	.20
❑ 59	Troy Aikman	.75	.30
❑ 60	Brian Griese	.50	.20
❑ 61	Ed McCaffrey	.50	.20
❑ 62	Gus Frerotte	.20	.07
❑ 63	John Elway	1.50	.60
❑ 64	Mike Anderson	.50	.20
❑ 65	Olandis Gary	.30	.10
❑ 66	Rod Smith	.30	.10
❑ 67	Terrell Davis	.50	.20
❑ 68	Barry Sanders	1.00	.40
❑ 69	Charlie Batch	.50	.20
❑ 70	Germane Crowell	.20	.07
❑ 71	Herman Moore	.30	.10
❑ 72	James Stewart	.30	.10
❑ 73	Johnnie Morton	.30	.10
❑ 74	Robert Porcher	.20	.07
❑ 75	Jim Harbaugh	.30	.10
❑ 76	Ahman Green	.50	.20
❑ 77	Antonio Freeman	.50	.20
❑ 78	Bill Schroeder	.30	.10
❑ 79	Brett Favre	1.50	.60
❑ 80	Bubba Franks	.30	.10
❑ 81	Dorsey Levens	.30	.10
❑ 82	E.G. Green	.20	.07

❑ 83	Edgerrin James	.60	.25
❑ 84	Jerome Pathon	.30	.10
❑ 85	Ken Dilger	.20	.07
❑ 86	Marcus Pollard	.20	.07
❑ 87	Marvin Harrison	.50	.20
❑ 88	Peyton Manning	1.25	.50
❑ 89	Terrence Wilkins	.20	.07
❑ 90	Fred Taylor	.50	.20
❑ 91	Hardy Nickerson	.20	.07
❑ 92	Jimmy Smith	.30	.10
❑ 93	Keenan McCardell	.20	.07
❑ 94	Kyle Brady	.20	.07
❑ 95	Mark Brunell	.50	.20
❑ 96	Tony Brackens	.20	.07
❑ 97	Derrick Alexander	.30	.10
❑ 98	Sylvester Morris	.20	.07
❑ 99	Tony Gonzalez	.30	.10
❑ 100	Tony Richardson	.20	.07
❑ 101	Kimble Anders	.20	.07
❑ 102	Warren Moon	.50	.20
❑ 103	Dan Marino	1.50	.60
❑ 104	Jay Fiedler	.50	.20
❑ 105	Lamar Smith	.30	.10
❑ 106	O.J. McDuffie	.20	.07
❑ 107	Oronde Gadsden	.30	.10
❑ 108	Sam Madison	.20	.07
❑ 109	Thurman Thomas	.20	.07
❑ 110	Tony Martin	.20	.07
❑ 111	Zach Thomas	.50	.20
❑ 112	Cris Carter	.50	.20
❑ 113	Daunte Culpepper	.50	.20
❑ 114	Matthew Hatchette	.20	.07
❑ 115	Randy Moss	1.00	.40
❑ 116	Robert Smith	.50	.20
❑ 117	Drew Bledsoe	.60	.25
❑ 118	J.R. Redmond	.20	.07
❑ 119	Kevin Faulk	.30	.10
❑ 120	Michael Bishop	.20	.07
❑ 121	Terry Glenn	.30	.10
❑ 122	Troy Brown	.30	.10
❑ 123	Ty Law	.30	.10
❑ 124	Aaron Brooks	.50	.20
❑ 125	Darren Howard	.20	.07
❑ 126	Jake Reed	.30	.10
❑ 127	Jeff Blake	.30	.10
❑ 128	Joe Horn	.30	.10
❑ 129	La'Roi Glover	.20	.07
❑ 130	Ricky Williams	.50	.20
❑ 131	Willie Jackson	.20	.07
❑ 132	Albert Connell	.20	.07
❑ 133	Amani Toomer	.20	.07
❑ 134	Ike Hilliard	.30	.10
❑ 135	Jason Sehorn	.20	.07
❑ 136	Jessie Armstead	.20	.07
❑ 137	Kerry Collins	.30	.10
❑ 138	Michael Strahan	.30	.10
❑ 139	Ron Dayne	.50	.20
❑ 140	Ron Dixon	.20	.07
❑ 141	Tiki Barber	.50	.20
❑ 142	Anthony Becht	.20	.07
❑ 143	Chad Pennington	.75	.30
❑ 144	Curtis Martin	.50	.20
❑ 145	Dedric Ward	.20	.07
❑ 146	Laveranues Coles	.50	.20
❑ 147	Vinny Testaverde	.30	.10
❑ 148	Wayne Chrebet	.30	.10
❑ 149	Andre Rison	.30	.10
❑ 150	Charles Woodson	.30	.10
❑ 151	Darrell Russell	.20	.07
❑ 152	Napoleon Kaufman	.30	.10
❑ 153	Rich Gannon	.50	.20
❑ 154	Tim Brown	.50	.20
❑ 155	Tyrone Wheatley	.30	.10
❑ 156	Chad Lewis	.20	.07
❑ 157	Charles Johnson	.20	.07
❑ 158	Donovan McNabb	.60	.25
❑ 159	Duce Staley	.50	.20
❑ 160	Hugh Douglas	.20	.07
❑ 161	Na Brown	.20	.07
❑ 162	Todd Pinkston	.20	.07
❑ 163	James Thrash	.30	.10
❑ 164	Bobby Shaw	.20	.07
❑ 165	Hines Ward	.50	.20
❑ 166	Jerome Bettis	.50	.20
❑ 167	Kordell Stewart	.30	.10
❑ 168	Levon Kirkland	.20	.07
❑ 169	Plaxico Burress	.50	.20
❑ 170	Richard Huntley	.20	.07
❑ 171	Troy Edwards	.20	.07
❑ 172	Jeff Graham	.20	.07
❑ 173	Junior Seau	.50	.20
❑ 174	Doug Flutie	.50	.20
❑ 175	Charlie Garner	.30	.10
❑ 176	Jeff Garcia	.50	.20
❑ 177	Jerry Rice	1.00	.40
❑ 178	Steve Young	.50	.20
❑ 179	Terrell Owens	.50	.20
❑ 180	Brock Huard	.20	.07
❑ 181	Darrell Jackson	.50	.20
❑ 182	Derrick Mayes	.30	.10
❑ 183	Ricky Watters	.30	.10
❑ 184	Shaun Alexander	.60	.25
❑ 185	Matt Hasselbeck	[illegible]	.10
❑ 186	John Randle	.30	.10
❑ 187	Az-Zahir Hakim	.20	.07
❑ 188	Isaac Bruce	.50	.20
❑ 189	Kurt Warner	1.00	.40
❑ 190	Marshall Faulk	.60	.25
❑ 191	Torry Holt	.50	.20
❑ 192	Trent Green	.50	.20
❑ 193	Derrick Brooks	.60	.20
❑ 194	Jacquez Green	.20	.07
❑ 195	John Lynch	.30	.10
❑ 196	Keyshawn Johnson	.50	.20
❑ 197	Mike Alstott	.50	.20
❑ 198	Reidel Anthony	.20	.07
❑ 199	Shaun King	.20	.07
❑ 200	Warren Sapp	.30	.10
❑ 201	Warrick Dunn	.50	.20
❑ 202	Ryan Leaf	.30	.10
❑ 203	Carl Pickens	.20	.07
❑ 204	Derrick Mason	.30	.10
❑ 205	Eddie George	.50	.20
❑ 206	Frank Wycheck	.20	.07
❑ 207	Jevon Kearse	.30	.10
❑ 208	Neil O'Donnell	.20	.07
❑ 209	Steve McNair	.50	.20
❑ 210	Yancey Thigpen	.20	.07
❑ 211	Andre Reed	.30	.10
❑ 212	Brad Johnson	.50	.20
❑ 213	Bruce Smith	.30	.10
❑ 214	Champ Bailey	.50	.20
❑ 215	Darrell Green	.20	.07
❑ 216	Deion Sanders	.50	.20
❑ 217	Irving Fryar	.30	.10
❑ 218	Jeff George	.30	.10
❑ 219	Michael Westbrook	.30	.10
❑ 220	Stephen Davis	.50	.20
❑ 221	Terrell Owens AP	1.00	.40
❑ 222	Peyton Manning AP	2.50	1.00
❑ 223	Stephen Davis AP	1.00	.40
❑ 224	Marvin Harrison AP	1.00	.40
❑ 225	Donovan McNabb AP	1.25	.50
❑ 226	Edgerrin James AP	1.25	.50
❑ 227	Eric Moulds AP	.60	.25
❑ 228	Daunte Culpepper AP	1.00	.40
❑ 229	Eddie George AP	1.00	.40
❑ 230	Cris Carter AP	1.00	.40
❑ 231	Rich Gannon AP	1.00	.40
❑ 232	Jeff Garcia AP	1.00	.40
❑ 233	Jimmy Smith AP	.60	.25
❑ 234	Tony Gonzalez AP	.60	.25
❑ 235	Torry Holt AP	1.00	.40
❑ 236	Jevon Kearse AP	.60	.25
❑ 237	Ray Lewis AP	1.00	.40
❑ 238	Warren Sapp AP	.60	.25
❑ 239	Brian Urlacher AP	1.50	.60
❑ 240	Champ Bailey AP	.60	.25
❑ 241	Peyton Manning LL	2.50	1.00
❑ 242	Jeff Garcia LL	1.00	.40
❑ 243	Elvis Grbac LL	.60	.25
❑ 244	Daunte Culpepper LL	1.00	.40
❑ 245	Brett Favre LL	3.00	1.25
❑ 246	Edgerrin James LL	1.25	.50
❑ 247	Robert Smith LL	.60	.25
❑ 248	Eddie George LL	1.00	.40
❑ 249	Mike Anderson LL	1.00	.40
❑ 250	Corey Dillon LL	1.00	.40
❑ 251	Torry Holt LL	1.00	.40
❑ 252	Rod Smith LL	.60	.25
❑ 253	Isaac Bruce LL	1.00	.40
❑ 254	Terrell Owens LL	1.00	.40
❑ 255	Randy Moss LL	2.00	.75
❑ 256	La'Roi Glover LL	.40	.15
❑ 257	Trace Armstrong LL	.40	.15
❑ 258	Warren Sapp LL	.60	.25
❑ 259	Hugh Douglas LL	.40	.15
❑ 260	Jason Taylor LL	.40	.15
❑ 261	Mike Anderson SS	1.00	.40
❑ 262	Jamal Lewis SS	1.25	.50
❑ 263	Sylvester Morris SS	.40	.15
❑ 264	Darrell Jackson SS	1.00	.40
❑ 265	Peter Warrick SS	1.00	.40
❑ 266	Ron Dayne SS	1.00	.40
❑ 267	Shaun Alexander SS	1.25	.50
❑ 268	Plaxico Burress SS	1.00	.40
❑ 269	Brian Urlacher SS	1.50	.60
❑ 270	Courtney Brown SS	.60	.25
❑ 271	Michael Vick RC	8.00	3.00
❑ 272	Drew Brees RC	[illegible]	[illegible]
❑ 273	Chris Weinke RC	1.00	.40
❑ 274	Quincy Carter RC	2.00	.75
❑ 275	Sage Rosenfels RC	1.00	.40
❑ 276	Josh Heupel RC	2.00	.75
❑ 277	David Rivers RC	1.25	.50
❑ 278	Ben Leard RC	1.25	.50
❑ 279	Marques Tuiasosopo RC	2.00	.75
❑ 280	Mike McMahon RC	2.00	.75
❑ 281	Deuce McAllister RC	4.00	1.50
❑ 282	LaMont Jordan RC	4.00	1.50
❑ 283	LaDainian Tomlinson RC	20.00	8.00
❑ 284	James Jackson RC	2.00	.75
❑ 285	Anthony Thomas RC	2.00	.75
❑ 286	Travis Henry RC	4.00	1.50
❑ 287	Travis Minor RC	1.25	.50
❑ 288	Rudi Johnson RC	4.00	1.50
❑ 289	Michael Bennett RC	2.00	.75
❑ 290	Kevan Barlow RC	2.00	.75
❑ 291	Reggie White RC	1.25	.50
❑ 292	Moran Norris RC	.75	.30
❑ 293	Ja'Mar Toombs RC	1.25	.50
❑ 294	Heath Evans RC	1.25	.50
❑ 295	David Terrell RC	2.00	.75
❑ 296	Santana Moss RC	3.00	1.25
❑ 297	Rod Gardner RC	2.00	.75
❑ 298	Quincy Morgan RC	2.00	.75
❑ 299	Freddie Mitchell RC	2.00	.75
❑ 300	Boo Williams RC	1.25	.50
❑ 301	Reggie Wayne RC	4.00	1.50
❑ 302	Ronney Daniels RC	.75	.30
❑ 303	Bobby Newcombe RC	1.25	.50
❑ 304	Vinny Sutherland RC	1.25	.50
❑ 305	Cedrick Wilson RC	2.00	.75
❑ 306	Robert Ferguson RC	2.00	.75
❑ 307	Ken-Yon Rambo RC	1.25	.50
❑ 308	Alex Bannister RC	1.25	.50
❑ 309	Koren Robinson RC	2.00	.75
❑ 310	Chad Johnson RC	5.00	2.00
❑ 311	Chris Chambers RC	3.00	1.25
❑ 312	Javon Green RC	1.25	.50
❑ 313	Snoop Minnis RC	1.25	.50
❑ 314	Scotty Anderson RC	1.25	.50
❑ 315	Todd Heap RC	2.00	.75
❑ 316	Alge Crumpler RC	2.50	1.00
❑ 317	Marcellus Rivers RC	1.25	.50
❑ 318	Rashon Burns RC	.75	.30
❑ 319	Jamal Reynolds RC	2.00	.75
❑ 320	Andre Carter RC	2.00	.75
❑ 321	Justin Smith RC	2.00	.75
❑ 322	Gerard Warren RC	2.00	.75
❑ 323	Tommy Polley RC	2.00	.75
❑ 324	Dan Morgan RC	1.00	.40
❑ 325	Torrance Marshall RC	2.00	.75
❑ 326	Correll Buckhalter RC	2.50	1.00
❑ 327	Derrick Gibson RC	1.25	.50
❑ 328	Adam Archuleta RC	2.00	.75
❑ 329	Jamar Fletcher RC	1.25	.50
❑ 330	Nate Clements RC	2.00	.75

2002 Score

❑	COMPLETE SET (330)	50.00	20.00
❑ 1	David Boston	.50	.20
❑ 2	Arnold Jackson	.20	.07
❑ 3	MarTay Jenkins	.20	.07
❑ 4	Thomas Jones	.30	.10
❑ 5	Kwamie Lassiter	.20	.07
❑ 6	Michael Pittman	.20	.07
❑ 7	Jake Plummer	.30	.10
❑ 8	Chris Chandler	.30	.10
❑ 9	Alge Crumpler	.30	.10
❑ 10	Terance Mathis	.20	.07

❑ 11 Maurice Smith .30 .10
❑ 12 Ray Buchanan .20 .07
❑ 13 Jamal Anderson .30 .10
❑ 14 Keith Brooking .20 .07
❑ 15 Michael Vick 1.00 .40
❑ 16 Obafemi Ayanbadejo .20 .07
❑ 17 Jason Brookins .20 .07
❑ 18 Randall Cunningham .20 .07
❑ 19 Elvis Grbac .30 .10
❑ 20 Todd Heap .20 .07
❑ 21 Qadry Ismail .30 .10
❑ 22 Shannon Sharpe .30 .10
❑ 23 Travis Taylor .30 .10
❑ 24 Ray Lewis .50 .20
❑ 25 Jamal Lewis .50 .20
❑ 26 Larry Centers .20 .07
❑ 27 Rob Johnson .30 .10
❑ 28 Shawn Bryson .20 .07
❑ 29 Eric Moulds .30 .10
❑ 30 Peerless Price .30 .10
❑ 31 Nate Clements .20 .07
❑ 32 Travis Henry .50 .20
❑ 33 Isaac Byrd .20 .07
❑ 34 Nick Goings .20 .07
❑ 35 Donald Hayes .20 .07
❑ 36 Richard Huntley .20 .07
❑ 37 Muhsin Muhammad .30 .10
❑ 38 Steve Smith .50 .20
❑ 39 Wesley Walls .20 .07
❑ 40 Chris Weinke .30 .10
❑ 41 James Allen .30 .10
❑ 42 Marty Booker .20 .07
❑ 43 Jim Miller .20 .07
❑ 44 David Terrell .50 .20
❑ 45 Dez White .20 .07
❑ 46 Brian Urlacher .75 .30
❑ 47 Mike Brown .50 .20
❑ 48 Anthony Thomas .30 .10
❑ 49 T.J. Houshmandzadeh .30 .10
❑ 50 Chad Johnson .50 .20
❑ 51 Darnay Scott .20 .07
❑ 52 Peter Warrick .30 .10
❑ 53 Akili Smith .20 .07
❑ 54 Jon Kitna .30 .10
❑ 55 Justin Smith .20 .07
❑ 56 Corey Dillon .30 .10
❑ 57 Benjamin Gay .30 .10
❑ 58 Kevin Johnson .30 .10
❑ 59 Quincy Morgan .20 .07
❑ 60 James Jackson .20 .07
❑ 61 Anthony Henry .20 .07
❑ 62 Gerard Warren .20 .07
❑ 63 Jamir Miller .20 .07
❑ 64 Tim Couch .30 .10
❑ 65 Quincy Carter .30 .10
❑ 66 Joey Galloway .30 .10
❑ 67 Troy Hambrick .20 .07
❑ 68 Rocket Ismail .30 .10
❑ 69 Dexter Coakley .20 .07
❑ 70 Darren Woodson .20 .07
❑ 71 Emmitt Smith 1.25 .50
❑ 72 Mike Anderson .50 .20
❑ 73 Terrell Davis .50 .20
❑ 74 Kevin Kasper .20 .07
❑ 75 Rod Smith .30 .10
❑ 76 Ed McCaffrey .50 .20
❑ 77 Olandis Gary .30 .10
❑ 78 Dwayne Carswell .20 .07
❑ 79 Deltha O'Neal .20 .07
❑ 80 Brian Griese .50 .20
❑ 81 Scotty Anderson .20 .07
❑ 82 Johnnie Morton .30 .10
❑ 83 Cory Schlesinger .20 .07
❑ 84 James Stewart .30 .10
❑ 85 Shaun Rogers .20 .07
❑ 86 Mike McMahon .50 .20
❑ 87 Charlie Batch .30 .10
❑ 88 Robert Porcher .20 .07
❑ 89 Bubba Franks .30 .10
❑ 90 Robert Ferguson .20 .07
❑ 91 Antonio Freeman .50 .20
❑ 92 Ahman Green .50 .20
❑ 93 Bill Schroeder .30 .10
❑ 94 Kabeer Gbaja-Biamila .30 .10
❑ 95 Jamal Reynolds .20 .07
❑ 96 Darren Sharper .20 .07
❑ 97 Brett Favre 1.25 .50
❑ 98 Marvin Harrison .50 .20
❑ 99 Dominic Rhodes .30 .10
❑ 100 Edgerrin James .60 .25
❑ 101 Reggie Wayne .50 .20
❑ 102 Terrence Wilkins .20 .07
❑ 103 Ken Dilger .20 .07
❑ 104 Peyton Manning 1.00 .40
❑ 105 Elvis Joseph .20 .07
❑ 106 Stacey Mack .20 .07
❑ 107 Fred Taylor .50 .20
❑ 108 Keenan McCardell .20 .07
❑ 109 Jimmy Smith .30 .10
❑ 110 Mark Brunell .50 .20
❑ 111 Derrick Alexander .30 .10
❑ 112 Tony Gonzalez .30 .10
❑ 113 Trent Green .30 .10
❑ 114 Snoop Minnis .20 .07
❑ 115 Priest Holmes .60 .25
❑ 116 Chris Chambers .50 .20
❑ 117 Jay Fiedler .30 .10
❑ 118 Oronde Gadsden .30 .10
❑ 119 Travis Minor .20 .07
❑ 120 Lamar Smith .30 .10
❑ 121 Zach Thomas .50 .20
❑ 122 Michael Bennett .30 .10
❑ 123 Todd Bouman .20 .07
❑ 124 Cris Carter .50 .20
❑ 125 Byron Chamberlain .20 .07
❑ 126 Randy Moss 1.00 .40
❑ 127 Jake Reed .30 .10
❑ 128 Daunte Culpepper .50 .20
❑ 129 Drew Bledsoe .50 .20
❑ 130 Troy Brown .30 .10
❑ 131 David Patten .20 .07
❑ 132 J.R. Redmond .20 .07
❑ 133 Antowain Smith .30 .10
❑ 134 Ty Law .30 .10
❑ 135 Richard Seymour .20 .07
❑ 136 Adam Vinatieri .50 .20
❑ 137 Tom Brady 1.25 .50
❑ 138 Joe Horn .30 .10
❑ 139 Willie Jackson .20 .07
❑ 140 Deuce McAllister .60 .25
❑ 141 Boo Williams .20 .07
❑ 142 Ricky Williams .50 .20
❑ 143 La'Roi Glover .20 .07
❑ 144 Sammy Knight .20 .07
❑ 145 Aaron Brooks .50 .20
❑ 146 Tiki Barber .50 .20
❑ 147 Ron Dayne .30 .10
❑ 148 Ike Hilliard .30 .10
❑ 149 Amani Toomer .30 .10
❑ 150 Will Allen .20 .07
❑ 151 Michael Strahan .30 .10
❑ 152 Jason Sehorn .20 .07
❑ 153 Kerry Collins .30 .10
❑ 154 Anthony Becht .20 .07
❑ 155 Wayne Chrebet .30 .10
❑ 156 Laveranues Coles .30 .10
❑ 157 LaMont Jordan .50 .20
❑ 158 Santana Moss .50 .20
❑ 159 Chad Pennington .60 .25
❑ 160 John Abraham .30 .10
❑ 161 Vinny Testaverde .30 .10
❑ 162 Curtis Martin .50 .20
❑ 163 Tim Brown .50 .20
❑ 164 Rich Gannon .50 .20
❑ 165 Charlie Garner .30 .10
❑ 166 Jerry Porter .20 .07
❑ 167 Marques Tuiasosopo .30 .10
❑ 168 Tyrone Wheatley .30 .10
❑ 169 Charles Woodson .30 .10
❑ 170 Jerry Rice 1.00 .40
❑ 171 Correll Buckhalter .30 .10
❑ 172 Chad Lewis .20 .07
❑ 173 Brian Mitchell .20 .07
❑ 174 Freddie Mitchell .30 .10
❑ 175 Todd Pinkston .30 .10
❑ 176 Duce Staley .50 .20
❑ 177 Tony Stewart .20 .07
❑ 178 James Thrash .30 .10
❑ 179 Hugh Douglas .20 .07
❑ 180 Donovan McNabb .60 .25
❑ 181 Plaxico Burress .30 .10
❑ 182 Chris Fuamatu-Ma'afala .20 .07
❑ 183 Kordell Stewart .30 .10
❑ 184 Hines Ward .50 .20
❑ 185 Amos Zereoue .50 .20
❑ 186 Kendrell Bell .50 .20
❑ 187 Casey Hampton .20 .07
❑ 188 Jerome Bettis .50 .20
❑ 189 Drew Brees .50 .20
❑ 190 Curtis Conway .20 .07
❑ 191 Tim Dwight .30 .10
❑ 192 Doug Flutie .50 .20
❑ 193 Junior Seau .50 .20
❑ 194 Marcellus Wiley .20 .07
❑ 195 Ryan McNeil .20 .07
❑ 196 Jeff Graham .20 .07
❑ 197 LaDainian Tomlinson .75 .30
❑ 198 Kevan Barlow .30 .10
❑ 199 Garrison Hearst .30 .10
❑ 200 Eric Johnson .30 .10
❑ 201 Terrell Owens .50 .20
❑ 202 J.J. Stokes .30 .10
❑ 203 Andre Carter .20 .07
❑ 204 Jeff Garcia .50 .20
❑ 205 Trent Dilfer .30 .10
❑ 206 Matt Hasselbeck .30 .10
❑ 207 Darrell Jackson .30 .10
❑ 208 Koren Robinson .30 .10
❑ 209 Ricky Watters .30 .10
❑ 210 John Randle .20 .07
❑ 211 Shaun Alexander .60 .25
❑ 212 Isaac Bruce .50 .20
❑ 213 Trung Canidate .30 .10
❑ 214 Marshall Faulk .50 .20
❑ 215 Az-Zahir Hakim .20 .07
❑ 216 Torry Holt .50 .20
❑ 217 Yo Murphy .20 .07
❑ 218 Ricky Proehl .20 .07
❑ 219 Adam Archuleta .20 .07
❑ 220 Dre Bly .20 .07
❑ 221 London Fletcher .20 .07
❑ 222 Tommy Polley .20 .07
❑ 223 Aeneas Williams .20 .07
❑ 224 Kurt Warner .50 .20
❑ 225 Mike Alstott .50 .20
❑ 226 Warrick Dunn .50 .20
❑ 227 Jacquez Green .20 .07
❑ 228 Derrick Brooks .50 .20
❑ 229 John Lynch .30 .10
❑ 230 Warren Sapp .30 .10
❑ 231 Ronde Barber .20 .07
❑ 232 Brad Johnson .30 .10
❑ 233 Keyshawn Johnson .50 .20
❑ 234 Drew Bennett .50 .20
❑ 235 Kevin Dyson .30 .10
❑ 236 Eddie George .50 .20
❑ 237 Derrick Mason .30 .10
❑ 238 Justin McCareins .30 .10
❑ 239 Frank Wycheck .20 .07
❑ 240 Jevon Kearse .30 .10
❑ 241 Samari Rolle .20 .07
❑ 242 Steve McNair .50 .20
❑ 243 Tony Banks .20 .07
❑ 244 Stephen Davis .30 .10
❑ 245 Michael Westbrook .20 .07
❑ 246 Champ Bailey .30 .10
❑ 247 Darrell Green .20 .07
❑ 248 Bruce Smith .20 .07
❑ 249 Fred Smoot .20 .07
❑ 250 Rod Gardner .30 .10
❑ 251 David Carr RC 2.50 1.00
❑ 252 Joey Harrington RC 1.50 .60
❑ 253 Patrick Ramsey RC 1.25 .50
❑ 254 Kurt Kittner RC .60 .25

❑	255 Eric Crouch RC	1.25	.50
❑	256 Josh McCown RC	1.50	.60
❑	257 David Garrard RC	2.50	1.00
❑	258 Rohan Davey RC	1.25	.50
❑	259 Ronald Curry RC	1.25	.50
❑	260 Chad Hutchinson RC	.60	.25
❑	261 William Green RC	1.25	.50
❑	262 T.J. Duckett RC	1.25	.50
❑	263 Clinton Portis RC	4.00	1.50
❑	264 DeShaun Foster RC	1.25	.50
❑	265 Luke Staley RC	.60	.25
❑	266 Wes Pate RC	.50	.20
❑	267 Travis Stephens RC	.60	.25
❑	268 Adrian Peterson RC	1.50	.60
❑	269 Zak Kustok RC	1.25	.50
❑	270 Maurice Morris RC	1.25	.50
❑	271 Lamar Gordon RC	1.25	.50
❑	272 Chester Taylor RC	2.50	1.00
❑	273 Najeh Davenport RC	1.25	.50
❑	274 Ladell Betts RC	1.25	.50
❑	275 Ashley Lelie RC	2.50	1.00
❑	276 Josh Reed RC	1.25	.50
❑	277 Cliff Russell RC	.60	.25
❑	278 Javon Walker RC	2.00	.75
❑	279 Ron Johnson RC	.60	.25
❑	280 Antwaan Randle El RC	1.50	.60
❑	281 Andre Davis RC	.60	.25
❑	282 Marquise Walker RC	.60	.25
❑	283 Kelly Campbell RC	.60	.25
❑	284 Tavon Mason RC	.50	.20
❑	285 Antonio Bryant RC	1.25	.50
❑	286 Jabar Gaffney RC	1.25	.50
❑	287 Donte Stallworth RC	2.00	.75
❑	288 Tim Carter RC	.60	.25
❑	289 Reche Caldwell RC	1.25	.50
❑	290 Freddie Milons RC	.60	.25
❑	291 Brian Poli-Dixon RC	.60	.25
❑	292 Brian Westbrook RC	2.50	1.00
❑	293 Josh Scobey RC	1.25	.50
❑	294 Jeremy Shockey RC	4.00	1.50
❑	295 Daniel Graham RC	1.25	.50
❑	296 Deion Branch RC	2.00	.75
❑	297 Julius Peppers RC	2.50	1.00
❑	298 Kalimba Edwards RC	1.25	.50
❑	299 Dwight Freeney RC	2.00	.75
❑	300 Terry Charles RC	.60	.25
❑	301 Alex Brown RC	1.25	.50
❑	302 Jason McAddley RC	.60	.25
❑	303 Michael Lewis RC	1.25	.50
❑	304 Dennis Johnson RC	.50	.20
❑	305 Albert Haynesworth RC	.60	.25
❑	306 Ryan Sims RC	1.25	.50
❑	307 Larry Tripplett RC	.50	.20
❑	308 Anthony Weaver RC	.60	.25
❑	309 Wendell Bryant RC	.50	.20
❑	310 John Henderson RC	1.25	.50
❑	311 Alan Harper RC	.50	.20
❑	312 Napoleon Harris RC	1.25	.50
❑	313 Bryan Thomas RC	.60	.25
❑	314 Andra Davis RC	.60	.25
❑	315 Levar Fisher RC	.50	.20
❑	316 Woody Dantzler RC	.60	.25
❑	317 Robert Thomas RC	1.25	.50
❑	318 Quentin Jammer RC	1.25	.50
❑	319 Lito Sheppard RC	1.25	.50
❑	320 Travis Fisher RC	1.25	.50
❑	321 Roy Williams RC	2.50	1.00
❑	322 Phillip Buchanon RC	1.25	.50
❑	323 Joseph Jefferson RC	.60	.25
❑	324 Ed Reed RC	2.00	.75
❑	325 Lamont Thompson RC	.60	.25
❑	326 Raonall Smith RC	.60	.25
❑	327 Mike Rumph RC	1.25	.50
❑	328 Rocky Calmus RC	1.25	.50
❑	329 Bryant McKinnie RC	.60	.25
❑	330 Mike Williams RC	.60	.25

2003 Score

❑	COMPLETE SET (327)	50.00	20.00
❑	1 Jeff Blake	.20	.08
❑	2 Todd Heap	.30	.10
❑	3 Ron Johnson	.20	.08
❑	4 Jamal Lewis	.50	.20
❑	5 Ray Lewis	.50	.20
❑	6 Chris Redman	.20	.08
❑	7 Ed Reed	.30	.10
❑	8 Travis Taylor	.20	.08
❑	9 Anthony Weaver	.20	.08
❑	10 Drew Bledsoe	.50	.20
❑	11 Larry Centers	.20	.08
❑	12 Nate Clements	.20	.08
❑	13 Travis Henry	.30	.10
❑	14 Eric Moulds	.30	.10
❑	15 Peerless Price	.30	.10
❑	16 Josh Reed	.30	.10
❑	17 Coy Wire	.20	.08
❑	18 Corey Dillon	.30	.10
❑	19 T.J. Houshmandzadeh	.20	.08
❑	20 Chad Johnson	.50	.20
❑	21 Jon Kitna	.30	.10
❑	22 Lorenzo Neal	.20	.08
❑	23 Peter Warrick	.30	.10
❑	24 Nicolas Luchey RC	.20	.08
❑	25 Tim Couch	.20	.08
❑	26 Andre Davis	.20	.08
❑	27 William Green	.30	.10
❑	28 Kevin Johnson	.30	.10
❑	29 Quincy Morgan	.30	.10
❑	30 Dennis Northcutt	.30	.10
❑	31 Jamel White	.20	.08
❑	32 Mike Anderson	.30	.10
❑	33 Steve Beuerlein	.20	.08
❑	34 Jason Elam	.20	.08
❑	35 Olandis Gary	.30	.10
❑	36 Brian Griese	.50	.20
❑	37 Ashley Lelie	.50	.20
❑	38 Ed McCaffrey	.30	.10
❑	39 Clinton Portis	.75	.30
❑	40 Shannon Sharpe	.30	.10
❑	41 Rod Smith	.30	.10
❑	42 James Allen	.30	.10
❑	43 Corey Bradford	.20	.08
❑	44 David Carr	.75	.30
❑	45 JaJuan Dawson	.20	.08
❑	46 Jabar Gaffney	.30	.10
❑	47 Aaron Glenn	.20	.08
❑	48 Billy Miller	.20	.08
❑	49 Jonathan Wells	.20	.08
❑	50 Dwight Freeney	.30	.10
❑	51 Marvin Harrison	.50	.20
❑	52 Qadry Ismail	.30	.10
❑	53 Edgerrin James	.50	.20
❑	54 Peyton Manning	.75	.30
❑	55 James Mungro	.20	.08
❑	56 Marcus Pollard	.20	.08
❑	57 Reggie Wayne	.30	.10
❑	58 Kyle Brady	.20	.08
❑	59 Mark Brunell	.30	.10
❑	60 David Garrard	.20	.08
❑	61 John Henderson	.20	.08
❑	62 Stacey Mack	.20	.08
❑	63 Jimmy Smith	.30	.10
❑	64 Fred Taylor	.50	.20
❑	65 Marc Boerigter	.30	.10
❑	66 Tony Gonzalez	.30	.10
❑	67 Trent Green	.30	.10
❑	68 Priest Holmes	.60	.25
❑	69 Eddie Kennison	.20	.08
❑	70 Snoop Minnis	.20	.08
❑	71 Johnnie Morton	.30	.10
❑	72 Cris Carter	.50	.20
❑	73 Chris Chambers	.50	.20
❑	74 Robert Edwards	.20	.08
❑	75 Jay Fiedler	.30	.10
❑	76 Ray Lucas	.20	.08
❑	77 Randy McMichael	.30	.10
❑	78 Travis Minor	.20	.08
❑	79 Zach Thomas	.30	.10
❑	80 Ricky Williams	.50	.20
❑	81 Tom Brady	1.25	.50
❑	82 Deion Branch	.50	.20
❑	83 Troy Brown	.30	.10
❑	84 Tedy Bruschi	.50	.20
❑	85 Kevin Faulk	.20	.08
❑	86 Daniel Graham	.20	.08
❑	87 David Patten	.20	.08
❑	88 Antowain Smith	.30	.10
❑	89 Adam Vinatieri	.50	.20
❑	90 Donnie Abraham	.20	.08
❑	91 Anthony Becht	.20	.08
❑	92 Wayne Chrebet	.30	.10
❑	93 Laveranues Coles	.30	.10
❑	94 LaMont Jordan	.50	.20
❑	95 Curtis Martin	.50	.20
❑	96 Chad Morton	.20	.08
❑	97 Santana Moss	.30	.10
❑	98 Chad Pennington	.60	.25
❑	99 Vinny Testaverde	.30	.10
❑	100 Tim Brown	.50	.20
❑	101 Phillip Buchanon	.20	.08
❑	102 Rich Gannon	.30	.10
❑	103 Charlie Garner	.30	.10
❑	104 Doug Jolley	.20	.08
❑	105 Jerry Porter	.30	.10
❑	106 Jerry Rice	1.00	.40
❑	107 Marques Tuiasosopo	.30	.10
❑	108 Charles Woodson	.30	.10
❑	109 Rod Woodson	.30	.10
❑	110 Kendrell Bell	.30	.10
❑	111 Jerome Bettis	.50	.20
❑	112 Plaxico Burress	.30	.10
❑	113 Tommy Maddox	.50	.20
❑	114 Joey Porter	.50	.20
❑	115 Antwaan Randle El	.50	.20
❑	116 Kordell Stewart	.30	.10
❑	117 Hines Ward	.50	.20
❑	118 Amos Zereoue	.30	.10
❑	119 Drew Brees	.50	.20
❑	120 Reche Caldwell	.20	.08
❑	121 Curtis Conway	.20	.08
❑	122 Tim Dwight	.30	.10
❑	123 Doug Flutie	.50	.20
❑	124 Quentin Jammer	.20	.08
❑	125 Ben Leber	.20	.08
❑	126 Josh Norman	.20	.08
❑	127 Junior Seau	.50	.20
❑	128 LaDainian Tomlinson	.50	.20
❑	129 Keith Bulluck	.20	.08
❑	130 Rocky Calmus	.20	.08
❑	131 Kevin Carter	.20	.08
❑	132 Kevin Dyson	.30	.10
❑	133 Eddie George	.30	.10
❑	134 Albert Haynesworth	.20	.08
❑	135 Jevon Kearse	.30	.10
❑	136 Derrick Mason	.30	.10
❑	137 Justin McCareins	.20	.08
❑	138 Steve McNair	.50	.20
❑	139 Frank Wycheck	.20	.08
❑	140 David Boston	.30	.10
❑	141 MarTay Jenkins	.20	.08
❑	142 Freddie Jones	.20	.08
❑	143 Thomas Jones	.30	.10
❑	144 Jason McAddley	.20	.08
❑	145 Josh McCown	.30	.10
❑	146 Jake Plummer	.30	.10
❑	147 Marcel Shipp	.30	.10
❑	148 Alge Crumpler	.30	.10
❑	149 T.J. Duckett	.30	.10
❑	150 Warrick Dunn	.30	.10
❑	151 Brian Finneran	.20	.08
❑	152 Trevor Gaylor	.20	.08
❑	153 Shawn Jefferson	.20	.08
❑	154 Michael Vick	1.25	.50
❑	155 Randy Fasani	.20	.08
❑	156 DeShaun Foster	.20	.08
❑	157 Muhsin Muhammad	.30	.10
❑	158 Rodney Peete	.20	.08
❑	159 Julius Peppers	.50	.20
❑	160 Lamar Smith	.20	.08
❑	161 Steve Smith	.50	.20
❑	162 Chris Weinke	.30	.10
❑	163 Wesley Walls	.20	.08
❑	164 Marty Booker	.30	.10
❑	165 Mike Brown	.30	.10

❑	166	Chris Chandler	.20	.08
❑	167	Jim Miller	.20	.08
❑	168	Marcus Robinson	.30	.10
❑	169	David Terrell	.30	.10
❑	170	Anthony Thomas	.30	.10
❑	171	Brian Urlacher	.75	.30
❑	172	Dez White	.20	.08
❑	173	Antonio Bryant	.30	.10
❑	174	Quincy Carter	.30	.10
❑	175	Dexter Coakley	.20	.08
❑	176	Joey Galloway	.30	.10
❑	177	La'Roi Glover	.20	.08
❑	178	Troy Hambrick	.20	.08
❑	179	Chad Hutchinson	.20	.08
❑	180	Rocket Ismail	.30	.10
❑	181	Emmitt Smith	1.25	.50
❑	182	Roy Williams	.50	.20
❑	183	Scotty Anderson	.20	.08
❑	184	Germane Crowell	.20	.08
❑	185	Az-Zahir Hakim	.20	.08
❑	186	Joey Harrington	.75	.30
❑	187	Cory Schlesinger	.20	.08
❑	188	Bill Schroeder	.30	.10
❑	189	James Stewart	.30	.10
❑	190	Marques Anderson	.20	.08
❑	191	Najeh Davenport	.20	.08
❑	192	Donald Driver	.30	.10
❑	193	Brett Favre	1.25	.50
❑	194	Bubba Franks	.30	.10
❑	195	Terry Glenn	.20	.08
❑	196	Ahman Green	.50	.20
❑	197	Darren Sharper	.20	.08
❑	198	Javon Walker	.30	.10
❑	199	D'Wayne Bates	.20	.08
❑	200	Michael Bennett	.30	.10
❑	201	Todd Bouman	.20	.08
❑	202	Byron Chamberlain	.20	.08
❑	203	Daunte Culpepper	.50	.20
❑	204	Randy Moss	.75	.30
❑	205	Kelly Campbell	.30	.10
❑	206	Aaron Brooks	.50	.20
❑	207	Charles Grant	.20	.08
❑	208	Joe Horn	.30	.10
❑	209	Michael Lewis	.20	.08
❑	210	Deuce McAllister	.50	.20
❑	211	Jerome Pathon	.30	.10
❑	212	Donte Stallworth	.50	.20
❑	213	Boo Williams	.20	.08
❑	214	Tiki Barber	.50	.20
❑	215	Tim Carter	.30	.10
❑	216	Kerry Collins	.30	.10
❑	217	Ron Dayne	.20	.08
❑	218	Jesse Palmer	.20	.08
❑	219	Will Peterson	.20	.08
❑	220	Jason Sehorn	.20	.08
❑	221	Jeremy Shockey	.75	.30
❑	222	Michael Strahan	.30	.10
❑	223	Amani Toomer	.30	.10
❑	224	Koy Detmer	.20	.08
❑	225	Antonio Freeman	.30	.10
❑	226	Dorsey Levens	.20	.08
❑	227	Chad Lewis	.20	.08
❑	228	Donovan McNabb	.60	.25
❑	229	Freddie Mitchell	.30	.10
❑	230	Duce Staley	.30	.10
❑	231	James Thrash	.20	.08
❑	232	Brian Westbrook	.30	.10
❑	233	Kevan Barlow	.30	.10
❑	234	Andre Carter	.20	.08
❑	235	Jeff Garcia	.50	.20
❑	236	Garrison Hearst	.30	.10
❑	237	Eric Johnson	.30	.10
❑	238	Terrell Owens	.50	.20
❑	239	Jamal Robertson	.30	.10
❑	240	Tai Streets	.20	.08
❑	241	Shaun Alexander	.50	.20
❑	242	Trent Dilfer	.30	.10
❑	243	Bobby Engram	.20	.08
❑	244	Matt Hasselbeck	.30	.10
❑	245	Darrell Jackson	.30	.10
❑	246	Maurice Morris	.20	.08
❑	247	Koren Robinson	.20	.08
❑	248	Jerramy Stevens	.20	.08
❑	249	Isaac Bruce	.50	.20
❑	250	Marc Bulger	.50	.20
❑	251	Marshall Faulk	.50	.20
❑	252	Lamar Gordon	.20	.08
❑	253	Torry Holt	.50	.20
❑	254	Ricky Proehl	.20	.08
❑	255	Kurt Warner	.50	.20
❑	256	Aeneas Williams	.20	.08
❑	257	Mike Alstott	.50	.20
❑	258	Ken Dilger	.20	.08
❑	259	Brad Johnson	.30	.10
❑	260	Keyshawn Johnson	.50	.20
❑	261	Rob Johnson	.30	.10
❑	262	John Lynch	.30	.10
❑	263	Keenan McCardell	.20	.08
❑	264	Michael Pittman	.20	.08
❑	265	Warren Sapp	.30	.10
❑	266	Marquise Walker	.20	.08
❑	267	Champ Bailey	.30	.10
❑	268	Stephen Davis	.30	.10
❑	269	Rod Gardner	.30	.10
❑	270	Darrell Green	.20	.08
❑	271	Shane Matthews	.20	.08
❑	272	Darnerien McCants	.20	.08
❑	273	Patrick Ramsey	.50	.20
❑	274	Bruce Smith	.30	.10
❑	275	Kenny Watson	.20	.08
❑	276	Carson Palmer RC	5.00	2.00
❑	277	Byron Leftwich RC	4.00	1.50
❑	278	Kyle Boller RC	1.25	.50
❑	279	Chris Simms RC	2.00	.75
❑	280	Dave Ragone RC	1.25	.50
❑	281	Rex Grossman RC	4.00	1.50
❑	282	Brian St.Pierre RC	1.25	.50
❑	283	Larry Johnson RC	5.00	2.50
❑	284	Lee Suggs RC	1.25	.50
❑	285	Justin Fargas RC	1.25	.50
❑	286	Onterrio Smith RC	1.25	.50
❑	287	Willis McGahee RC	3.00	1.25
❑	288	Chris Brown RC	1.25	.50
❑	289	Musa Smith RC	1.25	.50
❑	290	Artose Pinner RC	1.25	.50
❑	291	Cecil Sapp RC	1.00	.40
❑	292	Derek Watson SP RC		
❑	293	LaBrandon Toefield RC	1.25	.50
❑	294	Charles Rogers RC	1.25	.50
❑	295	Andre Johnson RC	2.50	1.00
❑	296	Taylor Jacobs RC	1.00	.40
❑	297	Bryant Johnson RC	1.25	.50
❑	298	Kelley Washington RC	1.25	.50
❑	299	Brandon Lloyd RC	1.25	.50
❑	300	Justin Gage RC	1.25	.50
❑	301	Tyrone Calico RC	1.25	.50
❑	302	Kevin Curtis RC	1.50	.60
❑	303	Sam Aiken RC	1.00	.40
❑	304	Doug Gabriel RC	1.25	.50
❑	305	Talman Gardner RC	1.25	.50
❑	306	Jason Witten RC	2.50	1.00
❑	307	Mike Pinkard RC	.60	.25
❑	308	Teyo Johnson RC	1.25	.50
❑	309	Bennie Joppru RC	1.25	.50
❑	310	Dallas Clark RC	1.25	.50
❑	311	Terrell Suggs RC	2.00	.75
❑	312	Chris Kelsay RC	1.25	.50
❑	313	Jerome McDougle RC	1.25	.50
❑	314	Andrew Williams RC	1.00	.40
❑	315	Michael Haynes RC	1.25	.50
❑	316	Jimmy Kennedy RC	1.25	.50
❑	317	Kevin Williams RC	1.25	.50
❑	318	Ken Dorsey RC	1.25	.50
❑	319	William Joseph RC	1.25	.50
❑	320	Kenny Peterson RC	1.00	.40
❑	321	Rien Long RC	.60	.25
❑	322	Boss Bailey RC	1.25	.50
❑	323	E.J. Henderson SP RC		
❑	324	Terence Newman RC	2.50	1.00
❑	325	Marcus Trufant RC	1.25	.50
❑	326	Andre Woolfolk RC	1.25	.50
❑	327	Dennis Weathersby RC	.60	.25
❑	328	Eugene Wilson SP RC		
❑	329	Mike Doss RC	1.25	.50
❑	330	Rashean Mathis RC	1.00	.40

2004 Score

❑		COMPLETE SET (440)	80.00	40.00
❑	1	Emmitt Smith	1.00	.40
❑	2	Anquan Boldin	.50	.20
❑	3	Bryant Johnson	.20	.07
❑	4	Marcel Shipp	.30	.10
❑	5	Josh McCown	.30	.10
❑	6	Dexter Jackson	.20	.07
❑	7	Bertrand Berry	.20	.07
❑	8	Freddie Jones	.20	.07
❑	9	Duane Starks	.20	.07
❑	10	Michael Vick	1.00	.40
❑	11	T.J. Duckett	.30	.10
❑	12	Warrick Dunn	.30	.10
❑	13	Peerless Price	.30	.10
❑	14	Alge Crumpler	.30	.10
❑	15	Brian Finneran	.20	.07
❑	16	Jason Webster	.20	.07
❑	17	Dez White	.30	.10
❑	18	Keith Brooking	.20	.07
❑	19	Rod Coleman	.20	.07
❑	20	Jamal Lewis	.50	.20
❑	21	Kyle Boller	.50	.20
❑	22	Todd Heap	.30	.10
❑	23	Jonathan Ogden	.20	.07
❑	24	Travis Taylor	.20	.07
❑	25	Ray Lewis	.50	.20
❑	26	Peter Boulware	.30	.10
❑	27	Terrell Suggs	.30	.10
❑	28	Chris McAlister	.20	.07
❑	29	Ed Reed	.30	.10
❑	30	Drew Bledsoe	.50	.20
❑	31	Travis Henry	.30	.10
❑	32	Eric Moulds	.30	.10
❑	33	Josh Reed	.20	.07
❑	34	Willis McGahee	.50	.20
❑	35	Takeo Spikes	.20	.07
❑	36	Lawyer Milloy	.30	.10
❑	37	Troy Vincent	.20	.07
❑	38	Sam Adams	.20	.07
❑	39	Nate Clements	.20	.07
❑	40	Jake Delhomme	.50	.20
❑	41	Stephen Davis	.30	.10
❑	42	DeShaun Foster	.30	.10
❑	43	Muhsin Muhammad	.30	.10
❑	44	Steve Smith	.50	.20
❑	45	Ricky Proehl	.20	.07
❑	46	Julius Peppers	.50	.20
❑	47	Kris Jenkins	.20	.07
❑	48	Dan Morgan	.20	.07
❑	49	Ricky Manning	.20	.07
❑	50	Brad Hoover	.20	.07
❑	51	Carson Palmer	.60	.25
❑	52	Rudi Johnson	.30	.10
❑	53	Corey Dillon	.30	.10
❑	54	Chad Johnson	.50	.20
❑	55	Peter Warrick	.30	.10
❑	56	Kelley Washington	.20	.07
❑	57	Kevin Hardy	.20	.07
❑	58	Tory James	.20	.07
❑	59	Ickey Woods	.50	.20
❑	60	Anthony Thomas	.30	.10
❑	61	Thomas Jones	.30	.10
❑	62	Rex Grossman	.50	.20
❑	63	Marty Booker	.30	.10
❑	64	Justin Gage	.30	.10
❑	65	David Terrell	.30	.10
❑	66	Brian Urlacher	.60	.25
❑	67	Mike Brown	.20	.07
❑	68	Charles Tillman	.30	.10
❑	69	Jeff Garcia	.50	.20
❑	70	Lee Suggs	.50	.20
❑	71	William Green	.30	.10
❑	72	Kelly Holcomb	.30	.10
❑	73	Quincy Morgan	.30	.10
❑	74	Andre Davis	.20	.07
❑	75	Dennis Northcutt	.20	.07
❑	76	Gerard Warren	.20	.07

❑	77	Courtney Brown	.30	.10
❑	78	Joey Harrington	.50	.20
❑	79	Shawn Bryson	.20	.07
❑	80	Charles Rogers	.30	.10
❑	81	Mikhael Ricks	.20	.07
❑	82	Artose Pinner	.20	.07
❑	83	Az-Zahir Hakim	.20	.07
❑	84	Dre Bly	.20	.07
❑	85	Fernando Bryant	.20	.07
❑	86	Boss Bailey	.30	.10
❑	87	Tai Streets	.20	.07
❑	88	Jake Plummer	.30	.10
❑	89	Quentin Griffin	.50	.20
❑	90	Mike Anderson	.30	.10
❑	91	[illegible]	[illegible]	.10
❑	92	Rod Smith	.30	.10
❑	93	Ashley Lelie	.30	.10
❑	94	Shannon Sharpe	.30	.10
❑	95	Al Wilson	.20	.07
❑	96	Champ Bailey	.30	.10
❑	97	Jason Elam	.20	.07
❑	98	John Lynch	.30	.10
❑	99	Quincy Carter	.30	.10
❑	100	Antonio Bryant	.30	.10
❑	101	Terry Glenn	.20	.07
❑	102	Keyshawn Johnson	.30	.10
❑	103	Jason Witten	.30	.10
❑	104	La'Roi Glover	.20	.07
❑	105	Dat Nguyen	.20	.07
❑	106	Dexter Coakley	.20	.07
❑	107	Terence Newman	.30	.10
❑	108	Darren Woodson	.20	.07
❑	109	Roy Williams S	.30	.10
❑	110	Brett Favre	1.25	.50
❑	111	Ahman Green	.50	.20
❑	112	Najeh Davenport	.20	.07
❑	113	Donald Driver	.30	.10
❑	114	Robert Ferguson	.20	.07
❑	115	Javon Walker	.30	.10
❑	116	Bubba Franks	.30	.10
❑	117	Kabeer Gbaja-Biamila	.30	.10
❑	118	Darren Sharper	.20	.07
❑	119	Mike McKenzie	.20	.07
❑	120	Nick Barnett	.30	.10
❑	121	David Carr	.50	.20
❑	122	Domanick Davis	.50	.20
❑	123	Andre Johnson	.50	.20
❑	124	Corey Bradford	.20	.07
❑	125	Jabar Gaffney	.30	.10
❑	126	Billy Miller	.20	.07
❑	127	Gary Walker	.20	.07
❑	128	Jamie Sharper	.20	.07
❑	129	Aaron Glenn	.20	.07
❑	130	Robaire Smith	.20	.07
❑	131	Peyton Manning	.75	.30
❑	132	Edgerrin James	.50	[illegible]
❑	133	Dominic Rhodes	.30	.10
❑	134	Marvin Harrison	.50	.20
❑	135	Reggie Wayne	.30	.10
❑	136	Brandon Stokley	.30	.10
❑	137	Marcus Pollard	.20	.07
❑	138	Dallas Clark	.30	.10
❑	139	Mike Vanderjagt	.20	.07
❑	140	Dwight Freeney	.30	.10
❑	141	Mike Doss	.20	.07
❑	142	Byron Leftwich	.60	.25
❑	143	Fred Taylor	.30	.10
❑	144	LaBrandon Toefield	.20	.07
❑	145	Jimmy Smith	.30	.10
❑	146	Kevin Johnson	.20	.07
❑	147	Marcus Stroud	.20	.07
❑	148	John Henderson	.20	.07
❑	149	Donovin Darius	.20	.07
❑	150	Deon Grant	.20	.07
❑	151	Rashean Mathis	.20	.07
❑	152	Trent Green	.30	.10
❑	153	Priest Holmes	.60	.25
❑	154	Johnnie Morton	.30	.10
❑	155	Eddie Kennison	.20	.07
❑	156	Marc Boerigter	.30	.10
❑	157	Tony Gonzalez	.30	.10
❑	158	Dante Hall	.50	.20
❑	159	Tony Richardson	.20	.07
❑	160	Gary Stills	.20	.07
❑	161	Daunte Culpepper	.50	.20
❑	162	Michael Bennett	.30	.10
❑	163	Moe Williams	.20	.07
❑	164	Onterrio Smith	.30	.10
❑	165	Jim Kleinsasser	.20	.07
❑	166	Antoine Winfield	.20	.07
❑	167	Nate Burleson	.50	.20
❑	168	Randy Moss	.60	.25
❑	169	Marcus Robinson	.30	.10
❑	170	Chris Hovan	.20	.07
❑	171	Brian Russell RC	.50	.20
❑	172	A.J. Feeley	.50	.20
❑	173	Jay Fiedler	.20	.07
❑	174	Ricky Williams	.50	.20
❑	175	Chris Chambers	.30	.10
❑	176	David Boston	.30	.10
❑	177	Randy McMichael	.20	.07
❑	178	Jason Taylor	.20	.07
❑	179	Adewale Ogunleye	.30	.10
❑	180	Zach Thomas	.50	.20
❑	181	Junior Seau	.50	.20
❑	182	Patrick Surtain	.20	.07
❑	183	Tom Brady	1.25	.50
❑	184	Kevin Faulk	.20	.07
❑	185	Troy Brown	.30	.10
❑	186	Deion Branch	.50	.20
❑	187	David Givens	.30	.10
❑	188	Dethel Johnson	.30	.10
❑	189	Richard Seymour	.20	.07
❑	190	Tedy Bruschi	.30	.10
❑	191	Ty Law	.30	.10
❑	192	Rodney Harrison	.20	.07
❑	193	Willie McGinest	.20	.07
❑	194	Adam Vinatieri	.60	.20
❑	195	Aaron Brooks	.30	.10
❑	196	Deuce McAllister	.50	.20
❑	197	Joe Horn	.30	.10
❑	198	Donte Stallworth	.30	.10
❑	199	Jerome Pathon	.20	.07
❑	200	Boo Williams	.20	.07
❑	201	Charles Grant	.20	.07
❑	202	Darren Howard	.20	.07
❑	203	Michael Lewis	.20	.07
❑	204	Johnathan Sullivan	.20	.07
❑	205	LeCharles Bentley RC	.20	.07
❑	206	Kerry Collins	.30	.10
❑	207	Tiki Barber	.50	.20
❑	208	Amani Toomer	.30	.10
❑	209	Ike Hilliard	.20	.07
❑	210	Tim Carter	.20	.07
❑	211	Jeremy Shockey	.50	.20
❑	212	Michael Strahan	.30	.10
❑	213	Will Allen	.20	.07
❑	214	Will Peterson	.20	.07
❑	215	William Joseph	.20	.07
❑	216	Chad Pennington	.50	.20
❑	217	Curtis Martin	.50	.20
❑	218	LaMont Jordan	.50	.20
❑	219	Santana Moss	.30	.10
❑	220	Justin McCareins	.20	.07
❑	221	Wayne Chrebet	.30	.10
❑	222	Anthony Becht	.20	.07
❑	223	Shaun Ellis	.20	.07
❑	224	John Abraham	.20	.07
❑	225	DeWayne Robertson	.20	.07
❑	226	Rich Gannon	.30	.10
❑	227	Justin Fargas	.30	.10
❑	228	Tyrone Wheatley	.20	.07
❑	229	Jerry Rice	1.00	.40
❑	230	Tim Brown	.50	.20
❑	231	Jerry Porter	.30	.10
❑	232	Teyo Johnson	.20	.07
❑	233	Charles Woodson	.30	.10
❑	234	Phillip Buchanon	.20	.07
❑	235	Rod Woodson	.30	.10
❑	236	Warren Sapp	.30	.10
❑	237	Donovan McNabb	.60	.25
❑	238	Brian Westbrook	.30	.10
❑	239	Correll Buckhalter	.30	.10
❑	240	Chad Lewis	.20	.07
❑	241	L.J. Smith	.30	.10
❑	242	Terrell Owens	.50	.20
❑	243	Todd Pinkston	.20	.07
❑	244	Freddie Mitchell	.30	.10
❑	245	Jevon Kearse	.30	.10
❑	246	Brian Dawkins	.30	.10
❑	247	Corey Simon	.30	.10
❑	248	Tommy Maddox	.30	.10
❑	249	Duce Staley	.30	.10
❑	250	Jerome Bettis	.50	.20
❑	251	Hines Ward	.50	.20
❑	252	Plaxico Burress	.30	.10
❑	253	Antwaan Randle El	.50	.20
❑	254	Kendrell Bell	.30	.10
❑	255	Joey Porter	.30	.10
❑	256	Alan Faneca	.50	.20
❑	257	Casey Hampton	.20	.07
❑	258	Drew Brees	.50	.20
❑	259	Doug Flutie	.50	.20
❑	260	LaDainian Tomlinson	.60	.25
❑	261	Reche Caldwell	.20	.07
❑	262	Tim Dwight	.30	.10
❑	263	Eric Parker	.20	.07
❑	264	Kevin Dyson	.20	.07
❑	265	Antonio Gates	.50	.20
❑	266	Quentin Jammer	.20	.07
❑	267	Zeke Moreno	.20	.07
❑	268	Tim Rattay	.20	.07
❑	269	Kevan Barlow	.30	.10
❑	270	Cedrick Wilson	.20	.07
❑	271	Brandon Lloyd	.30	.10
❑	272	Fred Beasley	.20	.07
❑	273	Andre Carter	.20	.07
❑	274	Julian Peterson	.20	.07
❑	275	Ahmed Plummer	.20	.07
❑	276	Tony Parrish	.20	.07
❑	277	Bryant Young	.20	.07
❑	278	Matt Hasselbeck	.30	.10
❑	279	Shaun Alexander	.50	.20
❑	280	Maurice Morris	.20	.07
❑	281	Koren Robinson	.30	.10
❑	282	Darrell Jackson	.30	.10
❑	283	Bobby Engram	.20	.07
❑	284	Grant Wistrom	.20	.07
❑	285	Chad Brown	.20	.07
❑	286	Marcus Trufant	.20	.07
❑	287	Bobby Taylor	.20	.07
❑	288	Marc Bulger	.50	.20
❑	289	Kurt Warner	.50	.20
❑	290	Marshall Faulk	.50	.20
❑	291	Lamar Gordon	.20	.07
❑	292	Torry Holt	.50	.20
❑	293	Isaac Bruce	.30	.10
❑	294	Leonard Little	.20	.07
❑	295	Aeneas Williams	.20	.07
❑	296	Orlando Pace	.20	.07
❑	297	Tommy Polley	.20	.07
❑	298	Pisa Tinoisamoa	.20	.07
❑	299	Brad Johnson	.30	.10
❑	300	Michael Pittman	.20	.07
❑	301	Charlie Garner	.30	.10
❑	302	Mike Alstott	.30	.10
❑	303	Keenan McCardell	.20	.07
❑	304	Joey Galloway	.30	.10
❑	305	Joe Jurevicius	.20	.07
❑	306	Anthony McFarland	.20	.07
❑	307	Derrick Brooks	.30	.10
❑	308	Ronde Barber	.20	.07
❑	309	Shelton Quarles	.20	.07
❑	310	Steve McNair	.50	.20
❑	311	Eddie George	.30	.10
❑	312	Chris Brown	.50	.20
❑	313	Derrick Mason	.30	.10
❑	314	Tyrone Calico	.30	.10
❑	315	Drew Bennett	.30	.10
❑	316	Kevin Carter	.20	.07
❑	317	Keith Bulluck	.20	.07
❑	318	Samari Rolle	.20	.07
❑	319	Albert Haynesworth	.20	.07
❑	320	Erron Kinney	.20	.07
❑	321	Mark Brunell	.30	.10
❑	322	Patrick Ramsey	.30	.10
❑	323	Laveranues Coles	.30	.10
❑	324	Rod Gardner	.30	.10
❑	325	Darnerien McCants	.20	.07
❑	326	Clinton Portis	.50	.20
❑	327	LaVar Arrington	1.00	.40
❑	328	Shawn Springs	.20	.07
❑	329	Fred Smoot	.20	.07
❑	330	James Thrash	.20	.07
❑	331	Marvin Harrison PB	.30	.10
❑	332	Steve McNair PB	.30	.10
❑	333	Ray Lewis PB	.30	.10
❑	334	Trent Green PB	.20	.07
❑	335	Peyton Manning PB	.50	.20
❑	336	Priest Holmes PB	.50	.20
❑	337	Clinton Portis PB	.50	.20

❑ 338 Torry Holt PB	.30	.10
❑ 339 Anquan Boldin PB	.20	.07
❑ 340 Daunte Culpepper PB	.30	.10
❑ 341 Ahman Green PB	.30	.10
❑ 342 Brian Urlacher PB	.50	.20
❑ 343 Donovan McNabb PB	.50	.20
❑ 344 Marc Bulger PB	.30	.10
❑ 345 Shaun Alexander PB	.30	.10
❑ 346 Peyton Manning LL	.50	.20
❑ 347 Daunte Culpepper LL	.30	.10
❑ 348 Brett Favre LL	.50	.20
❑ 349 Steve McNair LL	.30	.10
❑ 350 Tom Brady LL	.50	.20
❑ 351 Jamal Lewis LL	.30	.10
❑ 352 Deuce McAllister LL	.30	.10
❑ 353 Clinton Portis LL	.50	.20
❑ 354 Ahman Green LL	.30	.10
❑ 355 LaDainian Tomlinson LL	.40	.15
❑ 356 Torry Holt LL	.30	.10
❑ 357 Anquan Boldin LL	.20	.07
❑ 358 Randy Moss LL	.50	.20
❑ 359 Chad Johnson LL	.30	.10
❑ 360 Marvin Harrison LL	.30	.10
❑ 361 Peyton Manning HL	.50	.20
❑ 362 Jamal Lewis HL	.30	.10
❑ 363 Ray Lewis HL	.30	.10
❑ 364 Anquan Boldin HL	.20	.07
❑ 365 Terrell Suggs HL	.20	.07
❑ 366 Jamal Lewis HL	.30	.10
❑ 367 Priest Holmes HL	.50	.20
❑ 368 Tom Brady HL	.50	.20
❑ 369 Marc Bulger HL	.30	.10
❑ 370 Steve McNair HL	.30	.10
❑ 371 Eli Manning RC	10.00	5.00
❑ 372 Robert Gallery RC	1.25	.50
❑ 373 Larry Fitzgerald RC	4.00	1.50
❑ 374 Philip Rivers RC	4.00	1.50
❑ 375 Sean Taylor RC	1.25	.50
❑ 376 Kellen Winslow RC	2.50	1.00
❑ 377 Roy Williams RC	3.00	1.25
❑ 378 DeAngelo Hall RC	1.50	.60
❑ 379 Reggie Williams RC	1.50	.60
❑ 380 Dunta Robinson RC	1.25	.50
❑ 381 Ben Roethlisberger RC	10.00	4.00
❑ 382 Jonathan Vilma RC	1.25	.50
❑ 383 Lee Evans RC	1.50	.60
❑ 384 Tommie Harris RC	1.25	.50
❑ 385 Michael Clayton RC	2.50	1.00
❑ 386 D.J. Williams RC	1.25	.50
❑ 387 Will Smith RC	1.25	.50
❑ 388 Kenechi Udeze RC	1.25	.50
❑ 389 Vince Wilfork RC	1.25	.50
❑ 390 J.P. Losman RC	2.50	1.00
❑ 391 Marcus Tubbs RC	1.25	.50
❑ 392 Steven Jackson RC	4.00	1.50
❑ 393 Ahmad Carroll RC	1.25	.50
❑ 394 Chris Perry RC	1.50	.60
❑ 395 Jason Babin RC	1.25	.50
❑ 396 Chris Gamble RC	1.25	.50
❑ 397 Michael Jenkins RC	1.25	.50
❑ 398 Kevin Jones RC	3.00	1.25
❑ 399 Rashaun Woods RC	1.25	.50
❑ 400 Ben Watson RC	1.25	.50
❑ 401 Karlos Dansby RC	1.25	.50
❑ 402 Igor Olshansky RC	1.25	.50
❑ 403 Junior Siavii RC	1.25	.50
❑ 404 Teddy Lehman RC	1.25	.50
❑ 405 Ricardo Colclough RC	1.25	.50
❑ 406 Daryl Smith RC	1.25	.50
❑ 407 Ben Troupe RC	1.25	.50
❑ 408 Tatum Bell RC	2.50	1.00
❑ 409 Travis LaBoy RC	1.25	.50
❑ 410 Julius Jones RC	4.00	1.50
❑ 411 Mewelde Moore RC	1.25	.50
❑ 412 Drew Henson RC	1.25	.50
❑ 413 Dontarrious Thomas RC	1.25	.50
❑ 414 Keiwan Ratliff RC	1.00	.40
❑ 415 Devery Henderson RC	1.25	.50
❑ 416 Dwan Edwards RC	.60	.25
❑ 417 Michael Boulware RC	1.25	.50
❑ 418 Darius Watts RC	1.25	.50
❑ 419 Greg Jones RC	1.25	.50
❑ 420 Madieu Williams RC	1.00	.40
❑ 421 Antwan Odom RC	1.25	.50
❑ 422 Shawntae Spencer RC	1.25	.50
❑ 423 Sean Jones RC	1.00	.40
❑ 424 Courtney Watson RC	1.25	.50
❑ 425 Kris Wilson RC	1.25	.50
❑ 426 Keary Colbert RC	1.25	.50
❑ 427 Marquise Hill RC	1.00	.40
❑ 428 Darnell Dockett RC	1.00	.40
❑ 429 Stuart Schweigert RC	1.25	.50
❑ 430 Ben Hartsock RC	1.25	.50
❑ 431 Joey Thomas RC	1.25	.50
❑ 432 Randy Starks RC	1.00	.40
❑ 433 Keith Smith RC	1.00	.40
❑ 434 Derrick Hamilton RC	1.00	.40
❑ 435 Bernard Berrian RC	1.50	.60
❑ 436 Chris Cooley RC	1.25	.50
❑ 437 Devard Darling RC	1.25	.50
❑ 438 Matt Schaub RC	4.00	1.50
❑ 439 Luke McCown RC	1.25	.50
❑ 440 Cedric Cobbs RC	1.25	.50

2005 Score

❑ COMPLETE SET (385)	80.00	40.00
❑ ONE ROOKIE PER PACK		
❑ 1 Anquan Boldin	.30	.10
❑ 2 Bertrand Berry	.25	.08
❑ 3 Bryant Johnson	.25	.08
❑ 4 Darnell Dockett	.25	.08
❑ 5 Freddie Jones	.25	.08
❑ 6 Josh McCown	.30	.10
❑ 7 Karlos Dansby	.25	.08
❑ 8 Larry Fitzgerald	.50	.20
❑ 9 Alge Crumpler	.30	.10
❑ 10 DeAngelo Hall	.30	.10
❑ 11 Keith Brooking	.25	.08
❑ 12 Michael Jenkins	.30	.10
❑ 13 Michael Vick	.75	.30
❑ 14 Peerless Price	.25	.08
❑ 15 Rod Coleman	.25	.08
❑ 16 T.J. Duckett	.30	.10
❑ 17 Warrick Dunn	.30	.10
❑ 18 Chris McAlister	.25	.08
❑ 19 Clarence Moore	.25	.08
❑ 20 Ed Reed	.30	.10
❑ 21 Jamal Lewis	.50	.20
❑ 22 Jonathan Ogden	.25	.08
❑ 23 Kyle Boller	.30	.10
❑ 24 Peter Boulware	.25	.08
❑ 25 Ray Lewis	.50	.20
❑ 26 Terrell Suggs	.30	.10
❑ 27 Todd Heap	.30	.10
❑ 28 Drew Bledsoe	.50	.20
❑ 29 Eric Moulds	.30	.10
❑ 30 Josh Reed	.25	.08
❑ 31 Lee Evans	.30	.10
❑ 32 Nate Clements	.25	.08
❑ 33 Takeo Spikes	.25	.08
❑ 34 Travis Henry	.30	.10
❑ 35 Willis McGahee	.50	.20
❑ 36 Dan Morgan	.25	.08
❑ 37 DeShaun Foster	.30	.10
❑ 38 Jake Delhomme	.50	.20
❑ 39 Julius Peppers	.30	.10
❑ 40 Keary Colbert	.30	.10
❑ 41 Kris Jenkins	.25	.08
❑ 42 Muhsin Muhammad	.30	.10
❑ 43 Nick Goings	.25	.08
❑ 44 Stephen Davis	.30	.10
❑ 45 Steve Smith	.30	.10
❑ 46 Anthony Thomas	.30	.10
❑ 47 Adewale Ogunleye	.25	.08
❑ 48 Bernard Berrian	.25	.08
❑ 49 Brian Urlacher	.50	.20
❑ 50 David Terrell	.30	.10
❑ 51 Mike Brown	.25	.08
❑ 52 Rex Grossman	.30	.10
❑ 53 Thomas Jones	.30	.10
❑ 54 Tommie Harris	.25	.08
❑ 55 Carson Palmer	.50	.20
❑ 56 Chad Johnson	.50	.20
❑ 57 Chris Perry	.30	.10
❑ 58 Kelley Washington	.25	.08
❑ 59 Madieu Williams	.25	.08
❑ 60 Peter Warrick	.25	.08
❑ 61 Rudi Johnson	.30	.10
❑ 62 T.J. Houshmandzadeh	.25	.08
❑ 63 Tory James	.25	.08
❑ 64 Andre Davis	.25	.08
❑ 65 Antonio Bryant	.25	.08
❑ 66 Dennis Northcutt	.25	.08
❑ 67 Gerard Warren	.25	.08
❑ 68 Jeff Garcia	.30	.10
❑ 69 Kellen Winslow Jr.	.50	.20
❑ 70 Lee Suggs	.30	.10
❑ 71 William Green	.25	.08
❑ 72 Drew Henson	.30	.10
❑ 73 Jason Witten	.30	.10
❑ 74 Julius Jones	.60	.25
❑ 75 Keyshawn Johnson	.30	.10
❑ 76 La'Roi Glover	.25	.08
❑ 77 J.P. Losman	.50	.20
❑ 78 Roy Williams S	.30	.10
❑ 79 Terence Newman	.25	.08
❑ 80 Terry Glenn	.25	.08
❑ 81 Al Wilson	.25	.08
❑ 82 Ashley Lelie	.30	.10
❑ 83 Champ Bailey	.30	.10
❑ 84 D.J. Williams	.25	.08
❑ 85 Jake Plummer	.30	.10
❑ 86 Jason Elam	.25	.08
❑ 87 John Lynch	.30	.10
❑ 88 Reuben Droughns	.30	.10
❑ 89 Rod Smith	.30	.10
❑ 90 Tatum Bell	.30	.10
❑ 91 Trent Dilfer	.30	.10
❑ 92 Charles Rogers	.30	.10
❑ 93 Dre' Bly	.25	.08
❑ 94 Joey Harrington	.50	.20
❑ 95 Kevin Jones	.50	.20
❑ 96 Roy Williams WR	.50	.20
❑ 97 Shawn Bryson	.25	.08
❑ 98 Tai Streets	.25	.08
❑ 99 Teddy Lehman	.25	.08
❑ 100 Ahman Green	.50	.20
❑ 101 Brett Favre	1.25	.50
❑ 102 Bubba Franks	.30	.10
❑ 103 Darren Sharper	.25	.08
❑ 104 Donald Driver	.30	.10
❑ 105 Javon Walker	.30	.10
❑ 106 Najeh Davenport	.25	.08
❑ 107 Nick Barnett	.25	.08
❑ 108 Robert Ferguson	.25	.08
❑ 109 Aaron Glenn	.25	.08
❑ 110 Andre Johnson	.30	.10
❑ 111 Corey Bradford	.25	.08
❑ 112 David Carr	.50	.20
❑ 113 Domanick Davis	.30	.10
❑ 114 Dunta Robinson	.30	.10
❑ 115 Jabar Gaffney	.25	.08
❑ 116 Jamie Sharper	.25	.08
❑ 117 Jason Babin	.25	.08
❑ 118 Brandon Stokley	.30	.10
❑ 119 Dallas Clark	.25	.08
❑ 120 Dwight Freeney	.30	.10
❑ 121 Edgerrin James	.50	.20
❑ 122 Marcus Pollard	.25	.08
❑ 123 Marvin Harrison	.50	.20
❑ 124 Peyton Manning	.75	.30
❑ 125 Reggie Wayne	.30	.10
❑ 126 Robert Mathis RC	1.25	.50
❑ 127 Byron Leftwich	.50	.20
❑ 128 Daryl Smith	.25	.08
❑ 129 Donovan Darius	.25	.08
❑ 130 Ernest Wilford	.25	.08
❑ 131 Fred Taylor	.30	.10
❑ 132 Jimmy Smith	.30	.10
❑ 133 John Henderson	.25	.08
❑ 134 Marcus Stroud	.25	.08
❑ 135 Reggie Williams	.30	.10
❑ 136 Dante Hall	.30	.10

❑	137 Eddie Kennison	.25	.08
❑	138 Jared Allen	.30	.10
❑	139 Johnnie Morton	.30	.10
❑	140 Larry Johnson	.50	.20
❑	141 Priest Holmes	.50	.20
❑	142 Samie Parker	.25	.08
❑	143 Tony Gonzalez	.30	.10
❑	144 Trent Green	.30	.10
❑	145 A.J. Feeley	.30	.10
❑	146 Chris Chambers	.30	.10
❑	147 Jason Taylor	.25	.08
❑	148 Junior Seau	.30	.10
❑	149 Marty Booker	.30	.10
❑	150 Patrick Surtain	.25	.08
❑	151 Randy McMichael	.25	.08
❑	152 Sammy Morris	.25	.08
❑	153 Zach Thomas	.50	.20
❑	154 Daunte Culpepper	.50	.20
❑	155 Jim Kleinsasser	.25	.08
❑	156 Kelly Campbell	.25	.08
❑	157 Kevin Williams	.25	.08
❑	158 Marcus Robinson	.30	.10
❑	159 Mewelde Moore	.30	.10
❑	160 Michael Bennett	.30	.10
❑	161 Nate Burleson	.30	.10
❑	162 Onterrio Smith	.30	.10
❑	163 Randy Moss	.50	.20
❑	164 Adam Vinatieri	.50	.20
❑	165 Corey Dillon	.30	.10
❑	166 David Givens	.30	.10
❑	167 David Patten	.25	.08
❑	168 Deion Branch	.30	.10
❑	169 Mike Vrabel	.30	.10
❑	170 Richard Seymour	.30	.10
❑	171 Tedy Bruschi	.30	.10
❑	172 Tom Brady	1.25	.50
❑	173 Troy Brown	.30	.10
❑	174 Ty Law	.30	.10
❑	175 Aaron Brooks	.30	.10
❑	176 Charles Grant	.25	.08
❑	177 Deuce McAllister	.50	.20
❑	178 Devery Henderson	.25	.08
❑	179 Donte Stallworth	.30	.10
❑	180 Jerome Pathon	.25	.08
❑	181 Joe Horn	.30	.10
❑	182 Will Smith	.25	.08
❑	183 Amani Toomer	.30	.10
❑	184 Eli Manning	1.00	.40
❑	185 Gibril Wilson	.25	.08
❑	186 Ike Hilliard	.30	.10
❑	187 Jeremy Shockey	.50	.20
❑	188 Michael Strahan	.30	.10
❑	189 Tiki Barber	.50	.20
❑	190 Jamaar Taylor	.25	.08
❑	191 Tim Carter	.25	.08
❑	192 Chad Pennington	.50	.20
❑	193 DeWayne Robertson	.25	.08
❑	194 Curtis Martin	.50	.20
❑	195 John Abraham	.25	.08
❑	196 Jonathan Vilma	.30	.10
❑	197 Justin McCareins	.25	.08
❑	198 LaMont Jordan	.50	.20
❑	199 Santana Moss	.30	.10
❑	200 Shaun Ellis	.25	.08
❑	201 Wayne Chrebet	.30	.10
❑	202 Charles Woodson	.30	.10
❑	203 Doug Jolley	.25	.08
❑	204 Jerry Porter	.30	.10
❑	205 Justin Fargas	.25	.08
❑	206 Kerry Collins	.30	.10
❑	207 Robert Gallery	.30	.10
❑	208 Ronald Curry	.30	.10
❑	209 Sebastian Janikowski	.25	.08
❑	210 Tyrone Wheatley	.25	.08
❑	211 Warren Sapp	.30	.10
❑	212 Brian Dawkins	.30	.10
❑	213 Brian Westbrook	.30	.10
❑	214 Chad Lewis	.25	.08
❑	215 Corey Simon	.25	.08
❑	216 Donovan McNabb	.60	.25
❑	217 Freddie Mitchell	.25	.08
❑	218 Jevon Kearse	.30	.10
❑	219 L.J. Smith	.25	.08
❑	220 Lito Sheppard	.25	.08
❑	221 Terrell Owens	.50	.20
❑	222 Todd Pinkston	.25	.08
❑	223 Alan Faneca	.50	.20
❑	224 Antwaan Randle El	.30	.10
❑	225 Ben Roethlisberger	1.25	.50
❑	226 Duce Staley	.30	.10
❑	227 Hines Ward	.50	.20
❑	228 James Farrior	.25	.08
❑	229 Jerome Bettis	.50	.20
❑	230 Joey Porter	.30	.10
❑	231 Kendrell Bell	.30	.10
❑	232 Plaxico Burress	.30	.10
❑	233 Troy Polamalu	.75	.30
❑	234 Antonio Gates	.50	.20
❑	235 Reche Caldwell	.25	.08
❑	236 Doug Flutie	.50	.20
❑	237 Drew Brees	.50	.20
❑	238 Eric Parker	.25	.08
❑	239 Keenan McCardell	.25	.08
❑	240 LaDainian Tomlinson	.60	.25
❑	241 Philip Rivers	.50	.20
❑	242 Quentin Jammer	.25	.08
❑	243 Tim Dwight	.25	.08
❑	244 Brandon Lloyd	.25	.08
❑	245 Bryant Young	.25	.08
❑	246 Cedrick Wilson	.25	.08
❑	247 Eric Johnson	.30	.10
❑	248 Julian Peterson	.25	.08
❑	249 Kevan Barlow	.30	.10
❑	250 Rashaun Woods	.30	.10
❑	251 Maurice Hicks RC	.50	.20
❑	252 Tim Rattay	.25	.08
❑	253 Bobby Engram	.25	.08
❑	254 Chad Brown	.25	.08
❑	255 Darrell Jackson	.30	.10
❑	256 Grant Wistrom	.25	.08
❑	257 Jerramy Stevens	.25	.08
❑	258 Koren Robinson	.30	.10
❑	259 Marcus Trufant	.25	.08
❑	260 Matt Hasselbeck	.30	.10
❑	261 Michael Boulware	.25	.08
❑	262 Shaun Alexander	.60	.25
❑	263 Isaac Bruce	.30	.10
❑	264 Leonard Little	.25	.08
❑	265 Marc Bulger	.50	.20
❑	266 Marshall Faulk	.50	.20
❑	267 Orlando Pace	.25	.08
❑	268 Pisa Tinoisamoa	.25	.08
❑	269 Shaun McDonald	.25	.08
❑	270 Steven Jackson	.60	.25
❑	271 Torry Holt	.50	.20
❑	272 Anthony McFarland	.25	.08
❑	273 Brian Griese	.30	.10
❑	274 Charlie Garner	.30	.10
❑	275 Derrick Brooks	.30	.10
❑	276 Joe Jurevicius	.25	.08
❑	277 Joey Galloway	.30	.10
❑	278 Michael Clayton	.50	.20
❑	279 Michael Pittman	.25	.08
❑	280 Mike Alstott	.30	.10
❑	281 Ronde Barber	.25	.08
❑	282 Albert Haynesworth	.25	.08
❑	283 Ben Troupe	.25	.08
❑	284 Billy Volek	.30	.10
❑	285 Chris Brown	.30	.10
❑	286 Derrick Mason	.30	.10
❑	287 Drew Bennett	.30	.10
❑	288 Keith Bulluck	.25	.08
❑	289 Kevin Carter	.25	.08
❑	290 Samari Rolle	.25	.08
❑	291 Steve McNair	.50	.20
❑	292 Tyrone Calico	.30	.10
❑	293 Chris Cooley	.30	.10
❑	294 Clinton Portis	.50	.20
❑	295 Fred Smoot	.25	.08
❑	296 LaVar Arrington	.50	.20
❑	297 Laveranues Coles	.30	.10
❑	298 Patrick Ramsey	.30	.10
❑	299 Rod Gardner	.30	.10
❑	300 Sean Taylor	.30	.10
❑	301 Michael Vick PB	.50	.20
❑	302 Daunte Culpepper PB	.30	.10
❑	303 Donovan McNabb PB	.50	.20
❑	304 Brian Westbrook PB	.25	.08
❑	305 Tiki Barber PB	.30	.10
❑	306 Ahman Green PB	.30	.10
❑	307 Joe Horn PB	.25	.08
❑	308 Javon Walker PB	.25	.08
❑	309 Torry Holt PB	.30	.10
❑	310 Muhsin Muhammad PB	.25	.08
❑	311 Jason Witten PB	.25	.08
❑	312 Alge Crumpler PB	.25	.08
❑	313 Peyton Manning PB	.50	.20
❑	314 Tom Brady PB	.50	.20
❑	315 Drew Brees PB	.30	.10
❑	316 LaDainian Tomlinson PB	.50	.20
❑	317 Rudi Johnson PB	.25	.08
❑	318 Jerome Bettis PB	.30	.10
❑	319 Marvin Harrison PB	.30	.10
❑	320 Hines Ward PB	.30	.10
❑	321 Andre Johnson PB	.25	.08
❑	322 Chad Johnson PB	.30	.10
❑	323 Tony Gonzalez PB	.25	.08
❑	324 Adam Vinatieri PB	.30	.10
❑	325 David Akers PB	.25	.08
❑	326 Takeo Spikes PB	.25	.08
❑	327 Joey Porter PB	.25	.08
❑	328 Tedy Bruschi PB	.30	.10
❑	329 Ed Reed PB	.30	.10
❑	330 Terrell Owens PB	.30	.10
❑	331 Alex Smith QB RC	4.00	1.50
❑	332 Ronnie Brown RC	4.00	1.50
❑	333 Braylon Edwards RC	3.00	1.25
❑	334 Cedric Benson RC	2.50	1.00
❑	335 Cadillac Williams RC	4.00	1.50
❑	336 Adam Jones RC	1.00	.40
❑	337 Troy Williamson RC	1.00	.40
❑	338 Antrel Rolle RC	1.00	.40
❑	339 Carlos Rogers RC	1.25	.50
❑	340 Mike Williams	1.00	.40
❑	341 DeMarcus Ware RC	1.50	.60
❑	342 Shawne Merriman RC	1.50	.60
❑	343 Thomas Davis RC	1.00	.40
❑	344 Derrick Johnson RC	1.50	.60
❑	345 Travis Johnson RC	1.00	.40
❑	346 David Pollack RC	1.00	.40
❑	347 Erasmus James RC	1.00	.40
❑	348 Marcus Spears RC	1.00	.40
❑	349 Matt Jones RC	1.50	.60
❑	350 Mark Clayton RC	1.00	.40
❑	351 Fabian Washington RC	1.00	.40
❑	352 Aaron Rodgers RC	3.00	1.25
❑	353 Jason Campbell RC	1.50	.60
❑	354 Roddy White RC	1.00	.40
❑	355 Marlin Jackson RC	1.00	.40
❑	356 Heath Miller RC	2.00	.75
❑	357 Mike Patterson RC	1.00	.40
❑	358 Reggie Brown RC	1.00	.40
❑	359 Shaun Cody RC	1.00	.40
❑	360 Mark Bradley RC	1.00	.40
❑	361 J.J. Arrington RC	1.00	.40
❑	362 Dan Cody RC	1.00	.40
❑	363 Eric Shelton RC	1.00	.40
❑	364 Roscoe Parrish RC	1.00	.40
❑	365 Terrence Murphy RC	1.00	.40
❑	366 Vincent Jackson RC	1.00	.40
❑	367 Frank Gore RC	2.00	.75
❑	368 Charlie Frye RC	1.00	.40
❑	369 Courtney Roby RC	1.00	.40
❑	370 Andrew Walter RC	1.00	.40
❑	371 Vernand Morency RC	1.00	.40
❑	372 Ryan Moats RC	1.00	.40
❑	373 Chris Henry RC	1.00	.40
❑	374 David Greene RC	1.00	.40
❑	375 Brandon Jones RC	1.00	.40
❑	376 Maurice Clarett	1.00	.40
❑	377 Kyle Orton RC	1.00	.40
❑	378 Marion Barber RC	1.50	.60
❑	379 Brandon Jacobs RC	1.25	.50
❑	380 Ciatrick Fason RC	1.00	.40
❑	381 Jerome Mathis RC	1.00	.40
❑	382 Craphonso Thorpe RC	1.00	.40
❑	383 Stefan LeFors RC	1.00	.40
❑	384 Darren Sproles RC	1.00	.40
❑	385 Fred Gibson RC	1.00	.40

2006 Score

❑	1 Kurt Warner	.30	.12
❑	2 J.J. Arrington	.30	.12
❑	3 Anquan Boldin	.30	.12
❑	4 Larry Fitzgerald	.50	.20
❑	5 Marcel Shipp	.25	.10
❑	6 Bryant Johnson	.25	.10
❑	7 Bertrand Berry	.25	.10
❑	8 John Navarre	.25	.10
❑	9A Michael Vick	.50	.20
❑	10 Warrick Dunn	.30	.12

Card	Player	Mint	Ex
❑ 11	Roddy White	.30	.12
❑ 12	Alge Crumpler	.30	.12
❑ 13A	T.J. Duckett	.30	.12
❑ 14	Michael Jenkins	.30	.12
❑ 15	DeAngelo Hall	.30	.12
❑ 16	Brian Finneran	.25	.10
❑ 17	Kyle Boller	.25	.10
❑ 18	Jamal Lewis	.30	.12
❑ 19A	Chester Taylor	.30	.12
❑ 20	Derrick Mason	.25	.10
❑ 21	Mark Clayton	.50	.20
❑ 22	Todd Heap	.30	.12
❑ 23	Ray Lewis	.50	.20
❑ 24	Devard Darling	.25	.10
❑ 25	J.P. Losman	.30	.12
❑ 26	Willis McGahee	.50	.20
❑ 27	Lee Evans	.30	.12
❑ 28A	Eric Moulds	.30	.12
❑ 29A	Lawyer Milloy	.25	.10
❑ 30	Josh Reed	.25	.10
❑ 31	Kelly Holcomb	.25	.10
❑ 32	Jake Delhomme	.30	.12
❑ 33	DeShaun Foster	.30	.12
❑ 34	Steve Smith	.50	.20
❑ 35	Julius Peppers	.30	.12
❑ 36	Drew Carter	.25	.10
❑ 37	Chris Gamble	.25	.10
❑ 38	Stephen Davis	.30	.12
❑ 39	Keary Colbert	.25	.10
❑ 40	Nick Goings	.25	.10
❑ 41	Eric Shelton	.25	.10
❑ 42	Rex Grossman	.50	.20
❑ 43	Thomas Jones	.30	.12
❑ 44	Cedric Benson	.50	.20
❑ 45	Muhsin Muhammad	.30	.12
❑ 46	Brian Urlacher	.50	.20
❑ 47	Mark Bradley	.30	.12
❑ 48	Kyle Orton	.30	.12
❑ 49	Tommie Harris	.25	.10
❑ 50	Adrian Peterson	.25	.10
❑ 51	Bernard Berrian	.25	.10
❑ 52	Justin Gage	.25	.10
❑ 53	Carson Palmer	.50	.20
❑ 54	Rudi Johnson	.30	.12
❑ 55	Chad Johnson	.30	.12
❑ 56	T.J. Houshmandzadeh	.30	.12
❑ 57	Chris Henry	.25	.10
❑ 58	Chris Perry	.30	.12
❑ 59A	Jon Kitna	.25	.10
❑ 60	Deltha O'Neal	.25	.10
❑ 61	Charlie Frye	.30	.12
❑ 62	Reuben Droughns	.30	.12
❑ 63	Braylon Edwards	.50	.20
❑ 64	Kellen Winslow	.50	.20
❑ 65A	Antonio Bryant	.30	.12
❑ 66A	Trent Dilfer	.30	.12
❑ 67	Dennis Northcutt	.25	.10
❑ 68	Drew Bledsoe	.50	.20
❑ 69	Julius Jones	.50	.20
❑ 70	Marion Barber	.30	.12
❑ 71	Terry Glenn	.30	.12
❑ 72A	Keyshawn Johnson	.30	.12
❑ 73	Roy Williams S	.30	.12
❑ 74	Jason Witten	.30	.12
❑ 75	Terence Newman	.25	.10
❑ 76	Drew Henson	.25	.10
❑ 77	Patrick Crayton	.25	.10
❑ 78	Jake Plummer	.30	.12
❑ 79A	Mike Anderson	.30	.12
❑ 80	Tatum Bell	.30	.12
❑ 81A	Ashley Lelie	.30	.12
❑ 82	Rod Smith	.30	.12
❑ 83	D.J. Williams	.25	.10
❑ 84	Darius Watts	.25	.10
❑ 85	Ron Dayne	.30	.12
❑ 86A	Jeb Putzier	.25	.10
❑ 87A	Joey Harrington	.30	.12
❑ 88	Kevin Jones	.50	.20
❑ 89	Roy Williams WR	.50	.20
❑ 90	Mike Williams	.50	.20
❑ 91	Charles Rogers	.30	.12
❑ 92	Teddy Lehman	.25	.10
❑ 93	Marcus Pollard	.25	.10
❑ 94	Artose Pinner	.25	.10
❑ 95	Brett Favre	1.00	.40
❑ 96	Ahman Green	.30	.12
❑ 97	Najeh Davenport	.25	.10
❑ 98	Samkon Gado	.30	.12
❑ 99A	Javon Walker	.30	.12
❑ 100	Donald Driver	.30	.12
❑ 101	Aaron Rodgers	.50	.20
❑ 102	Robert Ferguson	.25	.10
❑ 103	David Carr	.30	.12
❑ 104	Domanick Davis	.30	.12
❑ 105	Andre Johnson	.30	.12
❑ 106A	Jabar Gaffney	.25	.10
❑ 107	Jonathan Wells	.25	.10
❑ 108	Vernand Morency	.30	.12
❑ 109A	Corey Bradford	.25	.10
❑ 110	Jerome Mathis	.25	.10
❑ 111A	Peyton Manning	.75	.30
❑ 112A	Edgerrin James	.50	.20
❑ 113	Marvin Harrison	.50	.20
❑ 114	Reggie Wayne	.30	.12
❑ 115	Dwight Freeney	.30	.12
❑ 116	Dallas Clark	.25	.10
❑ 117	Dominic Rhodes	.30	.12
❑ 118	Jim Sorgi	.25	.10
❑ 119	Brandon Stokley	.30	.12
❑ 120	Bob Sanders	.30	.12
❑ 121	Mike Doss	.25	.10
❑ 122	Marlin Jackson	.25	.10
❑ 123	Byron Leftwich	.30	.12
❑ 124	Fred Taylor	.30	.12
❑ 125	Jimmy Smith	.30	.12
❑ 126	Matt Jones	.30	.12
❑ 127	Ernest Wilford	.25	.10
❑ 128	Greg Jones	.25	.10
❑ 129	Mike Peterson	.25	.10
❑ 130	Reggie Williams	.30	.12
❑ 131	Rashean Mathis	.25	.10
❑ 132	Trent Green	.30	.12
❑ 133	Larry Johnson	.60	.25
❑ 134	Priest Holmes	.30	.12
❑ 135	Eddie Kennison	.25	.10
❑ 136	Tony Gonzalez	.30	.12
❑ 137	Kendrell Bell	.25	.10
❑ 138	Samie Parker	.25	.10
❑ 139	Dante Hall	.30	.12
❑ 140A	Tony Richardson	.25	.10
❑ 141A	Gus Frerotte	.25	.10
❑ 142	Ronnie Brown	.50	.20
❑ 143A	Neil Rackers	.25	.10
❑ 144	Chris Chambers	.30	.12
❑ 145	Zach Thomas	.50	.20
❑ 146	Cliff Russell	.25	.10
❑ 147A	David Boston	.25	.10
❑ 148	Wes Welker	.50	.20
❑ 149	Marty Booker	.25	.10
❑ 150	Randy McMichael	.25	.10
❑ 151A	Daunte Culpepper	.50	.20
❑ 152	Mewelde Moore	.25	.10
❑ 153A	Nate Burleson	.30	.12
❑ 154	Troy Williamson	.30	.12
❑ 155	Koren Robinson	.30	.12
❑ 156	Erasmus James	.25	.10
❑ 157	Marcus Robinson	.30	.12
❑ 158	E.J. Henderson	.25	.10
❑ 159	Brad Johnson	.30	.12
❑ 160A	Michael Bennett	.25	.10
❑ 161	Travis Taylor	.25	.10
❑ 162	Tom Brady	.75	.30
❑ 163	Corey Dillon	.30	.12
❑ 164	Deion Branch	.30	.12
❑ 165	Tedy Bruschi	.50	.20
❑ 166	Ben Watson	.25	.10
❑ 167	Daniel Graham	.25	.10
❑ 168A	Bethel Johnson	.25	.10
❑ 169	Kevin Faulk	.25	.10
❑ 170A	David Givens	.30	.12
❑ 171	Troy Brown	.30	.12
❑ 172A	Aaron Brooks	.30	.12
❑ 173	Deuce McAllister	.30	.12
❑ 174	Joe Horn	.30	.12
❑ 175A	Donte Stallworth	.30	.12
❑ 176A	Antowain Smith	.25	.10
❑ 177	Devery Henderson	.25	.10
❑ 178	Eli Manning	.60	.25
❑ 179	Tiki Barber	.50	.20
❑ 180	Plaxico Burress	.30	.12
❑ 181	Jeremy Shockey	.50	.20
❑ 182A	Osi Umenyiora	.25	.10
❑ 183	Gibril Wilson	.25	.10
❑ 184	Brandon Jacobs	.30	.12
❑ 185	Michael Strahan	.30	.12
❑ 186A	Will Allen	.25	.10
❑ 187	Amani Toomer	.30	.12
❑ 188	Chad Pennington	.30	.12
❑ 189	Curtis Martin	.50	.20
❑ 190	Laveranues Coles	.30	.12
❑ 191	Jonathan Vilma	.30	.12
❑ 192A	Ty Law	.30	.12
❑ 193	Cedric Houston	.25	.10
❑ 194	Justin McCareins	.25	.10
❑ 195	Jerald Sowell	.25	.10
❑ 196	Josh Brown	.25	.10
❑ 197	LaMont Jordan	.30	.12
❑ 198	Randy Moss	.50	.20
❑ 199	Jerry Porter	.30	.12
❑ 200	Doug Gabriel	.25	.10
❑ 201	Johnnie Morant	.25	.10
❑ 202	Zack Crockett	.25	.10
❑ 203A	Derrick Burgess	.25	.10
❑ 204	Donovan McNabb	.50	.20
❑ 205	Brian Westbrook	.30	.12
❑ 206	Reggie Brown	.40	.15
❑ 207A	Terrell Owens	.50	.20
❑ 208	Ryan Moats	.25	.10
❑ 209	Correll Buckhalter	.30	.12
❑ 210	Jevon Kearse	.30	.12
❑ 211	L.J. Smith	.25	.10
❑ 212	Lamar Gordon	.25	.10
❑ 213	Greg Lewis	.25	.10
❑ 214	Ben Roethlisberger	.75	.30
❑ 215	Willie Parker	.60	.25
❑ 216	Jerome Bettis	.50	.20
❑ 217	Hines Ward	.50	.20
❑ 218	Troy Polamalu	.60	.25
❑ 219	Heath Miller	.30	.12
❑ 220A	Antwaan Randle El	.30	.12
❑ 221	Duce Staley	.30	.12
❑ 222	Cedrick Wilson	.25	.10
❑ 223	James Farrior	.25	.10
❑ 224A	Drew Brees	.50	.20
❑ 225	LaDainian Tomlinson	.60	.25
❑ 226	Keenan McCardell	.25	.10
❑ 227	Antonio Gates	.50	.20
❑ 228	Shawne Merriman	.30	.12
❑ 229	Philip Rivers	.50	.20
❑ 230	Vincent Jackson	.25	.10
❑ 231	Donnie Edwards	.25	.10
❑ 232	Eric Parker	.25	.10
❑ 233A	Reche Caldwell	.25	.10
❑ 234	Alex Smith QB	.50	.20
❑ 235	Frank Gore	.50	.20
❑ 236A	Brandon Lloyd	.30	.12
❑ 237A	Kevan Barlow	.30	.12
❑ 238A	Rashaun Woods	.25	.10
❑ 239	Arnaz Battle	.25	.10
❑ 240	Matt Hasselbeck	.30	.12
❑ 241	Shaun Alexander	.50	.20
❑ 242	Darrell Jackson	.30	.12
❑ 243	Jerramy Stevens	.30	.12
❑ 244	Lofa Tatupu	.30	.12
❑ 245	D.J. Hackett	.25	.10
❑ 246	Bobby Engram	.25	.10
❑ 247A	Joe Jurevicius	.30	.12
❑ 248	Maurice Morris	.25	.10
❑ 249	Marc Bulger	.30	.12
❑ 250	Steven Jackson	.50	.20
❑ 251	Torry Holt	.30	.12
❑ 252	Isaac Bruce	.30	.12
❑ 253	Kevin Curtis	.25	.10
❑ 254	Marshall Faulk	.30	.12

❑ 255 Shaun McDonald .25 .10
❑ 256 Chris Simms .30 .12
❑ 257 Cadillac Williams .50 .20
❑ 258 Joey Galloway .30 .12
❑ 259 Michael Clayton .30 .12
❑ 260 Derrick Brooks .30 .12
❑ 261 Ronde Barber .25 .10
❑ 262 Michael Pittman .25 .10
❑ 263 Alex Smith TE .25 .10
❑ 264 Simeon Rice .25 .10
❑ 265A Steve McNair .30 .12
❑ 266 Chris Brown .30 .12
❑ 267 Drew Bennett .25 .10
❑ 268 Brandon Jones .25 .10
❑ [illegible]
❑ 270 Keith Bulluck .25 .10
❑ 271 Ben Troupe .25 .10
❑ 272 Jarrett Payton .25 .10
❑ 273 Tyrone Calico .25 .10
❑ 274 Bobby Wade .25 .10
❑ 275 Troy Fleming .25 .10
❑ 276 Mark Brunell .30 .12
❑ 277 Clinton Portis .50 .20
❑ 278 Santana Moss .30 .12
❑ 279 Jason Campbell .30 .12
❑ 280 Chris Cooley .25 .10
❑ 281 Carlos Rogers .25 .10
❑ 282 Ladell Betts .25 .10
❑ 283A Patrick Ramsey .30 .12
❑ 284 Taylor Jacobs .25 .10
❑ 285 James Thrash .25 .10
❑ 286 Adrian Wilson .25 .10
❑ 287 London Fletcher .25 .10
❑ 288 Lance Briggs .30 .12
❑ 289 Robert Mathis .25 .10
❑ 290 Rod Coleman .25 .10
❑ 291 Bart Scott RC 1.50 .60
❑ 292 Brian Moorman RC .40 .15
❑ 293 Shayne Graham RC .40 .15
❑ 294 Kevin Kaesviharn RC .40 .15
❑ 295 Leigh Bodden RC .40 .15
❑ 296 Lousaka Polite RC .40 .15
❑ 297 Todd Devoe RC .75 .30
❑ 298 Scottie Vines .40 .15
❑ 299 Cullen Jenkins RC .40 .15
❑ 300 Donovan Morgan RC .40 .15
❑ 301 C.C. Brown .40 .15
❑ 302 Demarcus Faggins RC .40 .15
❑ 303 Shantee Orr RC .40 .15
❑ 304 Vashon Pearson RC .40 .15
❑ 305 Reggie Hayward RC .40 .15
❑ 306 Paul Spicer RC .40 .15
❑ 307A Kenny Wright Jaguars RC .40 .15
❑ 308 Rich Alexis RC .40 .15
❑ 309 Terrence Melton RC .40 .15
❑ 310 Willie Whitehead RC .40 .15
❑ 311A Kendrick Clancy Giants RC .40 .15
❑ 312 Mark Brown RC .40 .15
❑ 313 Tommy Kelly RC .40 .15
❑ 314 Josh Parry RC .40 .15
❑ 315 Malcolm Floyd RC .75 .30
❑ 316 Mike Adams RC .40 .15
❑ 317 Ben Emanuel RC .40 .15
❑ 318 Brandon Moore RC .40 .15
❑ 319 Chartric Darby RC .40 .15
❑ 320 Bryce Fisher RC .40 .15
❑ 321 D.D. Lewis RC .40 .15
❑ 322 Jimmy Williams DB RC .40 .15
❑ 323A Robert Pollard portrait RC .40 .15
❑ 324A Chris Johnson Rams RC .40 .15
❑ 325 Edell Shepherd RC .40 .15
❑ 326 O.J. Small RC .40 .15
❑ 327A Brad Kassell Titans RC .40 .15
❑ 328 M.Leinart/R.Bush 2.50 1.00
❑ 329 M.Leinart/V.Young 2.50 1.00
❑ 330 White/Leinart/Bush 2.50 1.00
❑ 331 Matt Leinart RC 4.00 1.50
❑ 332A Chad Greenway RC 1.25 .50
❑ 333A Devin Aromashodu RC 1.00 .40
❑ 334 DeAngelo Williams RC 3.00 1.25
❑ 335 Travis Wilson RC 1.25 .50
❑ 336 Leon Washington RC 2.00 .75
❑ 337 Maurice Stovall RC 1.25 .50
❑ 338 Michael Huff SP RC 1.50 .60
❑ 339 Charlie Whitehurst RC 1.25 .50
❑ 340 Vince Young RC 5.00 2.00
❑ 341 Jerious Norwood RC 2.00 .75
❑ 342A D'Brickashaw Ferguson RC 1.25 .50
❑ 343A Taurean Henderson RC 1.25 .50
❑ 344A Dominique Byrd RC 1.00 .40
❑ 345 Sinorice Moss SP RC 1.25 .50
❑ 346A Martin Nance RC 1.00 .40
❑ 347 Vernon Davis RC 2.50 1.00
❑ 348 Ko Simpson RC 1.00 .40
❑ 349A Jerome Harrison RC 1.25 .50
❑ 350A Jay Cutler RC 4.00 1.50
❑ 351A Alan Zemaitis RC 1.25 .50
❑ 352A Haloti Ngata SP RC 1.25 .50
❑ 353A Greg Lee RC 1.00 .40
❑ 354 Laurence Maroney RC 3.00 1.25
❑ 355A Bobby Carpenter SP RC 1.25 .50
❑ [illegible] 1.00 .40
❑ 357 Marcedes Lewis RC 1.25 .50
❑ 358A Brodrick Bunkley SP RC 1.25 .50
❑ 359A Todd Watkins RC 1.00 .40
❑ 360 Reggie Bush RC 5.00 2.00
❑ 361A Jimmy Williams RC 1.25 .50
❑ 362 Maurice Drew RC 3.00 1.25
❑ 363 Mario Williams RC 2.00 .75
❑ 364 Derek Hagan RC 1.25 .50
❑ 365 Santonio Holmes RC 2.50 1.00
❑ 366A Tye Hill RC 1.25 .50
❑ 367 Jason Avant RC 1.25 .50
❑ 368A Tamba Hali SP RC 1.25 .50
❑ 369 Joe Klopfenstein RC 1.00 .40
❑ 370 LenDale White RC 2.50 1.00
❑ 371A DeMeco Ryans RC 1.50 .60
❑ 372A Bruce Gradkowski SP RC 2.00 .75
❑ 373 A.J. Hawk RC 2.50 1.00
❑ 374A Gabe Watson RC 1.00 .40
❑ 375A Devin Hester SP RC 2.50 1.00
❑ 376 Demetrius Williams SP RC 1.25 .50
❑ 377A Joseph Addai RC 4.00 1.50
❑ 377B Joseph Addai 4.00 1.50
❑ 378A Leonard Pope RC 1.25 .50
❑ 379 Omar Jacobs RC 1.00 .40
❑ 380A Brad Smith SP RC 1.25 .50
❑ 381 Michael Robinson RC 1.25 .50
❑ 382A Brodie Croyle RC 3.00 1.25
❑ 383A Anthony Fasano RC 1.25 .50
❑ 384 Brian Calhoun RC 1.25 .50
❑ 385 Chad Jackson RC 1.25 .50
❑ 386 Drew Olson RC 1.00 .40
❑ 387 Greg Jennings RC 2.00 .75
❑ 388 Andre Hall RC 1.00 .40
❑ 389 Mike Espy RC 1.25 .50
❑ 390 Tim Day RC 1.00 .40
❑ 391 Brandon Williams RC 1.25 .50
❑ 392 Mark Anderson RC 3.00 1.25
❑ 393 DonTrell Moore RC 1.25 .50
❑ 394 Kellen Clemens RC 2.00 .75
❑ 395 Ernie Sims RC 1.50 .60
❑ 396 [illegible] RC 1.00 [illegible]
❑ 397 Brandon Kirsch RC 1.25 .50
❑ 398 Tony Scheffler RC 1.25 .50
❑ 399 Kelly Jennings RC 1.25 .50
❑ 400 Manny Lawson RC 1.25 .50
❑ 401 Terrence Whitehead RC 1.00 .40
❑ 402 Marcus Vick RC 1.00 .40
❑ 403 De'Arrius Howard RC 1.25 .50
❑ 404 Wendell Mathis RC 1.00 .40
❑ 405 Abdul Hodge RC 1.25 .50
❑ 406 Owen Daniels RC 1.25 .50
❑ 407 Mike Hass RC 1.25 .50
❑ 408 Brett Elliott RC 1.25 .50
❑ 409 Kamerion Wimbley RC 1.25 .50
❑ 410 Jeremy Bloom RC 1.00 .40
❑ 411 D.J. Shockley RC 1.25 .50
❑ 412 Darnell Bing RC 1.25 .50
❑ 413 Miles Austin RC 1.00 .40
❑ 414 D'Qwell Jackson RC 1.00 .40
❑ 415 Tarvaris Jackson RC 2.00 .75
❑ 416 Mathias Kiwanuka RC 1.50 .60
❑ 417 Mike Bell RC 1.25 .50
❑ 418 Paul Pinegar RC 1.00 .40
❑ 419 David Thomas RC 1.25 .50
❑ 420 Hank Baskett RC 1.25 .50
❑ 421 P.J. Daniels RC 1.00 .40
❑ 422 Jon Alston RC 1.25 .50
❑ 423 Reggie McNeal RC 1.00 .40
❑ 424 Brandon Marshall RC 1.25 .50
❑ 425 Gerald Riggs RC 1.25 .50
❑ 426 Delanie Walker RC 1.00 .40
❑ 427 Erik Meyer RC 1.00 .40
❑ 428 Jeff Webb RC 1.00 .40
❑ 429 Skyler Green RC 1.25 .50
❑ 430 Thomas Howard RC 1.25 .50
❑ 431 Ashton Youboty RC 1.25 .50
❑ 432 Cedric Griffin RC 1.00 .40
❑ 433 Donte Whitner RC 1.25 .50
❑ 434 Jason Allen RC 1.25 .50
❑ 435 Pat Watkins RC 1.25 .50
❑ 436 Rocky McIntosh RC 1.25 .50
❑ 437 Ingle Martin RC 1.25 .50
❑ 438 John David Washington RC 1.00 .40
❑ 439 Cory Rodgers RC 1.25 .50
❑ 440 Willie Reid RC 1.25 .50

2007 Score

❑ 1 Tony Romo 1.00 .40
❑ 2 Julius Jones .40 .15
❑ 3 Terry Glenn .40 .15
❑ 4 Terrell Owens .50 .20
❑ 5 Jason Witten .40 .15
❑ 6 Marion Barber .40 .15
❑ 7 Patrick Crayton .30 .12
❑ 8 Bradie James .30 .12
❑ 9 DeMarcus Ware .40 .15
❑ 10 Roy Williams S .40 .15
❑ 11 Eli Manning .50 .20
❑ 12 Plaxico Burress .40 .15
❑ 13 Jeremy Shockey .40 .15
❑ 14 Brandon Jacobs .40 .15
❑ 15 Sinorice Moss .40 .15
❑ 16 Antonio Pierce .30 .12
❑ 17 David Tyree .30 .12
❑ 18 Donovan McNabb .50 .20
❑ 19 Brian Westbrook .40 .15
❑ 20 Reggie Brown .40 .15
❑ 21 L.J. Smith .30 .12
❑ 22 Hank Baskett .40 .15
❑ 23 Jeremiah Trotter .30 .12
❑ 24 Trent Cole .30 .12
❑ 25 Lito Sheppard .30 .12
❑ 26 Jason Campbell .40 .15
❑ 27 Clinton Portis .40 .15
❑ 28 Santana Moss .40 .15
❑ 29 Brandon Lloyd .40 .15
❑ 30 Chris Cooley .30 .12
❑ 31 Sean Taylor .30 .12
❑ 32 Lemar Marshall .30 .12
❑ 33 Ladell Betts .30 .12
❑ 34 London Fletcher .30 .12
❑ 35 Rex Grossman .40 .15
❑ 36 Cedric Benson .40 .15
❑ 37 Muhsin Muhammad .40 .15
❑ 38 Bernard Berrian .30 .12
❑ 39 Desmond Clark .30 .12
❑ 40 Lance Briggs .30 .12
❑ 41 Robbie Gould .30 .12
❑ 42 Devin Hester .50 .20
❑ 43 Mark Anderson .40 .15
❑ 44 Brian Urlacher .50 .20
❑ 45 Jon Kitna .30 .12
❑ 46 Kevin Jones .30 .12
❑ 47 Roy Williams WR .40 .15
❑ 48 Mike Furrey .40 .15
❑ 49 Cory Redding .30 .12
❑ 50 Ernie Sims .30 .12
❑ 51 Tatum Bell .40 .15
❑ 52 Brian Calhoun .30 .12
❑ 53 Brett Favre 1.00 .40
❑ 54 Vernand Morency .40 .15

❑ 55 Donald Driver	.40	.15
❑ 56 Greg Jennings	.40	.15
❑ 57 Aaron Kampman	.40	.15
❑ 58 Charles Woodson	.40	.15
❑ 59 A.J. Hawk	.50	.20
❑ 60 Nick Barnett	.30	.12
❑ 61 Aaron Rodgers	.50	.20
❑ 62 Tarvaris Jackson	.50	.20
❑ 63 Chester Taylor	.30	.12
❑ 64 Troy Williamson	.30	.12
❑ 65 Jim Kleinsasser	.30	.12
❑ 66 Dwight Smith	.30	.12
❑ 67 Antoine Winfield	.30	.12
❑ 68 E.J. Henderson	.30	.12
❑ 69 Mewelde Moore	.30	.12
❑ 70 Michael Vick	.50	.20
❑ 71 Warrick Dunn	.40	.15
❑ 72 Joe Horn	.40	.15
❑ 73 Michael Jenkins	.40	.15
❑ 74 Alge Crumpler	.40	.15
❑ 75 DeAngelo Hall	.40	.15
❑ 76 Keith Brooking	.30	.12
❑ 77 Lawyer Milloy	.30	.12
❑ 78 Jerious Norwood	.40	.15
❑ 79 Matt Schaub	.40	.15
❑ 80 Jake Delhomme	.40	.15
❑ 81 DeShaun Foster	.40	.15
❑ 82 Steve Smith	.40	.15
❑ 83 Keyshawn Johnson	.40	.15
❑ 84 Julius Peppers	.40	.15
❑ 85 DeAngelo Williams	.50	.20
❑ 86 Chris Draft	.30	.12
❑ 87 Drew Brees	.40	.15
❑ 88 Deuce McAllister	.40	.15
❑ 89 Scott Fujita	.30	.12
❑ 90 Marques Colston	.50	.20
❑ 91 Terrance Copper	.30	.12
❑ 92 Will Smith	.30	.12
❑ 93 Charles Grant	.30	.12
❑ 94 Devery Henderson	.30	.12
❑ 95 Reggie Bush	.60	.25
❑ 96 Jeff Garcia	.40	.15
❑ 97 Cadillac Williams	.40	.15
❑ 98 Joey Galloway	.40	.15
❑ 99 Michael Clayton	.40	.15
❑ 100 Alex Smith TE	.30	.12
❑ 101 Ronde Barber	.30	.12
❑ 102 Jermaine Phillips	.30	.12
❑ 103 Derrick Brooks	.40	.15
❑ 104 Matt Leinart	.50	.20
❑ 105 Edgerrin James	.50	.20
❑ 106 Anquan Boldin	.40	.15
❑ 107 Larry Fitzgerald	.40	.15
❑ 108 Neil Rackers	.30	.12
❑ 109 Adrian Wilson	.30	.12
❑ 110 Karlos Dansby	.30	.12
❑ 111 Chike Okeafor	.30	.12
❑ 112 Marc Bulger	.40	.15
❑ 113 Steven Jackson	.50	.20
❑ 114 Torry Holt	.40	.15
❑ 115 Isaac Bruce	.40	.15
❑ 116 Joe Klopfenstein	.30	.12
❑ 117 Randy McMichael	.30	.12
❑ 118 Will Witherspoon	.30	.12
❑ 119 Drew Bennett	.30	.12
❑ 120 Alex Smith QB	.50	.20
❑ 121 Frank Gore	.50	.20
❑ 122 Arnaz Battle	.30	.12
❑ 123 Ashley Lelie	.40	.15
❑ 124 Vernon Davis	.40	.15
❑ 125 Walt Harris	.30	.12
❑ 126 Brandon Moore	.30	.12
❑ 127 Nate Clements	.30	.12
❑ 128 Matt Hasselbeck	.40	.15
❑ 129 Shaun Alexander	.40	.15
❑ 130 Deion Branch	.40	.15
❑ 131 Darrell Jackson	.40	.15
❑ 132 Nate Burleson	.30	.12
❑ 133 Julian Peterson	.30	.12
❑ 134 Lofa Tatupu	.40	.15
❑ 135 Mack Strong	.30	.12
❑ 136 Josh Brown	.30	.12
❑ 137 J.P. Losman	.40	.15
❑ 138 Anthony Thomas	.30	.12
❑ 139 Lee Evans	.40	.15
❑ 140 Josh Reed	.30	.12
❑ 141 Roscoe Parrish	.30	.12
❑ 142 Aaron Schobel	.30	.12
❑ 143 Donte Whitner	.30	.12
❑ 144 Shaud Williams	.30	.12
❑ 145 Daunte Culpepper	.40	.15
❑ 146 Ronnie Brown	.40	.15
❑ 147 Chris Chambers	.40	.15
❑ 148 Marty Booker	.30	.12
❑ 149 Derek Hagan	.30	.12
❑ 150 Jason Taylor	.30	.12
❑ 151 Vonnie Holliday	.30	.12
❑ 152 Zach Thomas	.40	.15
❑ 153 Channing Crowder	.30	.12
❑ 154 Joey Porter	.30	.12
❑ 155 Tom Brady	1.00	.40
❑ 156 Laurence Maroney	.50	.20
❑ 157 Chad Jackson	.30	.12
❑ 158 Wes Welker	.50	.20
❑ 159 Ben Watson	.30	.12
❑ 160 Donte Stallworth	.40	.15
❑ 161 Rosevelt Colvin	.30	.12
❑ 162 Ty Warren	.30	.12
❑ 163 Asante Samuel	.30	.12
❑ 164 Adalius Thomas	.30	.12
❑ 165 Tedy Bruschi	.50	.20
❑ 166 Chad Pennington	.40	.15
❑ 167 Thomas Jones	.40	.15
❑ 168 Laveranues Coles	.40	.15
❑ 169 Jerricho Cotchery	.30	.12
❑ 170 Chris Baker	.30	.12
❑ 171 Bryan Thomas	.30	.12
❑ 172 Leon Washington	.40	.15
❑ 173 Jonathan Vilma	.40	.15
❑ 174 Eric Barton	.30	.12
❑ 175 Erik Coleman	.30	.12
❑ 176 Steve McNair	.40	.15
❑ 177 Willis McGahee	.40	.15
❑ 178 Derrick Mason	.30	.12
❑ 179 Demetrius Williams	.30	.12
❑ 180 Todd Heap	.30	.12
❑ 181 Ray Lewis	.50	.20
❑ 182 Trevor Pryce	.30	.12
❑ 183 Bart Scott	.40	.15
❑ 184 Terrell Suggs	.30	.12
❑ 185 Mark Clayton	.40	.15
❑ 186 Carson Palmer	.50	.20
❑ 187 Rudi Johnson	.40	.15
❑ 188 Chad Johnson	.40	.15
❑ 189 T.J. Houshmandzadeh	.40	.15
❑ 190 Robert Geathers	.30	.12
❑ 191 Justin Smith	.30	.12
❑ 192 Tory James	.30	.12
❑ 193 Landon Johnson	.30	.12
❑ 194 Shayne Graham	.30	.12
❑ 195 Charlie Frye	.40	.15
❑ 196 Reuben Droughns	.40	.15
❑ 197 Braylon Edwards	.40	.15
❑ 198 Travis Wilson	.30	.12
❑ 199 Kellen Winslow	.40	.15
❑ 200 Kamerion Wimbley	.30	.12
❑ 201 Sean Jones	.30	.12
❑ 202 Andra Davis	.30	.12
❑ 203 Jamal Lewis	.40	.15
❑ 204 Ben Roethlisberger	.60	.25
❑ 205 Willie Parker	.50	.20
❑ 206 Hines Ward	.50	.20
❑ 207 Santonio Holmes	.40	.15
❑ 208 Heath Miller	.30	.12
❑ 209 Troy Polamalu	.50	.20
❑ 210 James Farrior	.30	.12
❑ 211 Cedrick Wilson	.30	.12
❑ 212 Dunta Robinson	.30	.12
❑ 213 Ahman Green	.40	.15
❑ 214 Andre Johnson	.40	.15
❑ 215 Jerome Mathis	.30	.12
❑ 216 Owen Daniels	.30	.12
❑ 217 DeMeco Ryans	.40	.15
❑ 218 Wali Lundy	.30	.12
❑ 219 Mario Williams	.40	.15
❑ 220 Peyton Manning	.75	.30
❑ 221 Joseph Addai	.60	.25
❑ 222 Marvin Harrison	.50	.20
❑ 223 Reggie Wayne	.40	.15
❑ 224 Dallas Clark	.30	.12
❑ 225 Robert Mathis	.30	.12
❑ 226 Cato June	.30	.12
❑ 227 Adam Vinatieri	.40	.15
❑ 228 Bob Sanders	.40	.15
❑ 229 Dwight Freeney	.40	.15
❑ 230 Byron Leftwich	.40	.15
❑ 231 Fred Taylor	.40	.15
❑ 232 Matt Jones	.40	.15
❑ 233 Reggie Williams	.40	.15
❑ 234 Marcedes Lewis	.30	.12
❑ 235 Bobby McCray	.30	.12
❑ 236 Rashean Mathis	.30	.12
❑ 237 Maurice Jones-Drew	.50	.20
❑ 238 Ernest Wilford	.30	.12
❑ 239 Daryl Smith	.30	.12
❑ 240 Vince Young	.60	.25
❑ 241 LenDale White	.40	.15
❑ 242 Brandon Jones	.30	.12
❑ 243 Bo Scaife	.30	.12
❑ 244 Keith Bulluck	.30	.12
❑ 245 Chris Hope	.30	.12
❑ 246 Kyle Vanden Bosch	.30	.12
❑ 247 Roydell Williams	.30	.12
❑ 248 Jay Cutler	.50	.20
❑ 249 Travis Henry	.40	.15
❑ 250 Javon Walker	.40	.15
❑ 251 Rod Smith	.40	.15
❑ 252 Tony Scheffler	.30	.12
❑ 253 Elvis Dumervil	.30	.12
❑ 254 Champ Bailey	.40	.15
❑ 255 Mike Bell	.40	.15
❑ 256 Brandon Marshall	.40	.15
❑ 257 Al Wilson	.30	.12
❑ 258 Trent Green	.40	.15
❑ 259 Larry Johnson	.50	.20
❑ 260 Eddie Kennison	.30	.12
❑ 261 Samie Parker	.30	.12
❑ 262 Tony Gonzalez	.40	.15
❑ 263 Jared Allen	.30	.12
❑ 264 Kawika Mitchell	.30	.12
❑ 265 Tamba Hali	.30	.12
❑ 266 Dante Hall	.40	.15
❑ 267 Brodie Croyle	.50	.20
❑ 268 Andrew Walter	.30	.12
❑ 269 LaMont Jordan	.40	.15
❑ 270 Dominic Rhodes	.40	.15
❑ 271 Randy Moss	.50	.20
❑ 272 Ronald Curry	.40	.15
❑ 273 Courtney Anderson	.30	.12
❑ 274 Derrick Burgess	.30	.12
❑ 275 Warren Sapp	.40	.15
❑ 276 Michael Huff	.40	.15
❑ 277 Thomas Howard	.30	.12
❑ 278 Kirk Morrison	.30	.12
❑ 279 Philip Rivers	.50	.20
❑ 280 LaDainian Tomlinson	.60	.25
❑ 281 Vincent Jackson	.30	.12
❑ 282 Lorenzo Neal	.30	.12
❑ 283 Antonio Gates	.40	.15
❑ 284 Shawne Merriman	.40	.15
❑ 285 Shaun Phillips	.30	.12
❑ 286 Michael Turner	.40	.15
❑ 287 Jamal Williams	.30	.12
❑ 288 Nate Kaeding	.30	.12
❑ 289 Michael Okwo RC	1.00	.40
❑ 290 Gary Russell RC	1.25	.50
❑ 291 Josh Wilson RC	1.00	.40
❑ 292 Thomas Clayton RC	1.00	.40
❑ 293 Jerard Rabb RC	1.00	.40
❑ 294 Roy Hall RC	1.25	.50
❑ 295 LaMarr Woodley RC	1.25	.50
❑ 296 Eric Wright RC	1.25	.50
❑ 297 Dan Bazuin RC	1.00	.40
❑ 298 A.J. Davis RC	.75	.30
❑ 299 Buster Davis RC	1.00	.40
❑ 300 Stewart Bradley RC	1.25	.50
❑ 301 Toby Korrodi RC	1.00	.40
❑ 302 Marcus McCauley RC	1.00	.40
❑ 303 Demarcus Tank Tyler RC	1.00	.40
❑ 304 Jon Abbate RC	.75	.30
❑ 305 Ikaika Alama-Francis RC	1.25	.50
❑ 306 Tim Crowder RC	1.25	.50
❑ 307 D'Juan Woods RC	1.00	.40
❑ 308 Tim Shaw RC	1.00	.40
❑ 309 Fred Bennett RC	.75	.30
❑ 310 Victor Abiamiri RC	1.25	.50
❑ 311 Eric Weddle RC	1.00	.40
❑ 312 Danny Ware RC	1.25	.50
❑ 313 Quentin Moses RC	1.00	.40
❑ 314 Ryan McBean RC	1.25	.50
❑ 315 David Harris RC	1.00	.40

❑ 316 David Irons RC .75 .30
❑ 317 Syndric Steptoe RC 1.00 .40
❑ 318 Eric Frampton RC 1.00 .40
❑ 319 Jemalle Cornelius RC 1.00 .40
❑ 320 Earl Everett RC 1.00 .40
❑ 321 Alonzo Coleman RC 1.00 .40
❑ 322 Josh Gattis RC .75 .30
❑ 323 Zak DeOssie RC 1.00 .40
❑ 324 Jon Beason RC 1.25 .50
❑ 325 Joe Staley RC 1.00 .40
❑ 326 Aaron Rouse RC 1.25 .50
❑ 327 Reggie Ball RC 1.00 .40
❑ 328 Rufus Alexander RC 1.25 .50
❑ 329 Daymeion Hughes RC 1.00 .40
❑ [illegible]
❑ [illegible]
❑ 332 Paul Williams RC 1.00 .40
❑ 333 Kenny Irons RC 1.25 .50
❑ 334 Chris Davis RC 1.00 .40
❑ 335 Darius Walker RC 1.25 .50
❑ 336 Dwayne Bowe RC 2.50 1.00
❑ 337 Isaiah Stanback RC 1.25 .50
❑ 338 Leon Hall RC 1.00 .40
❑ 339 Sidney Rice RC 2.00 .75
❑ 340 Amobi Okoye RC 1.25 .50
❑ 341 Adrian Peterson RC 10.00 4.00
❑ 342 LaRon Landry RC 1.50 .60
❑ 343 Lorenzo Booker RC 1.25 .50
❑ 344 Craig Buster Davis RC 1.25 .50
❑ 345 Mike Walker RC 1.00 .40
❑ 346 Zach Miller RC 1.25 .50
❑ 347 Levi Brown RC 1.25 .50
❑ 348 Brian Leonard RC 1.50 .60
❑ 349 Aundrae Allison RC 1.00 .40
❑ 350 Brandon Siler RC 1.00 .40
❑ 351 Calvin Johnson RC 4.00 1.50
❑ 352 Gaines Adams RC 1.25 .50
❑ 353 Anthony Gonzalez RC 2.00 .75
❑ 354 John Beck RC 2.50 1.00
❑ 355 Joe Thomas RC 1.25 .50
❑ 356 Michael Bush RC 1.50 .60
❑ 357 Courtney Taylor RC 1.00 .40
❑ 358 Lawrence Timmons RC 1.25 .50
❑ 359 Drew Stanton RC 1.50 .60
❑ 360 Chansi Stuckey RC 1.00 .40
❑ 361 Greg Olsen RC 1.50 .60
❑ 362 Rhema McKnight RC 1.00 .40
❑ 363 Antonio Pittman RC 1.00 .40
❑ 364 Kevin Kolb RC 2.00 .75
❑ 365 Alan Branch RC 1.00 .40
❑ 366 Robert Meachem RC 1.25 .50
❑ 367 Troy Smith RC 1.50 .60
❑ 368 Jamaal Anderson RC 1.00 .40
❑ 369 Tony Hunt RC 1.25 .50
❑ 370 David Clowney RC 1.25 .50
❑ 371 Brady Quinn RC [illegible] [illegible]
❑ 372 Michael Griffin RC 1.25 .50
❑ 373 Jared Zabransky RC 1.25 .50
❑ 374 Jason Hill RC 1.25 .50
❑ 375 Trent Edwards RC 2.50 1.00
❑ 376 Dwayne Jarrett RC 1.50 .60
❑ 377 DeShawn Wynn RC 1.25 .50
❑ 378 Patrick Willis RC 2.50 1.00
❑ 379 Steve Smith USC RC 1.50 .60
❑ 380 David Ball RC .75 .30
❑ 381 Marshawn Lynch RC 2.50 1.00
❑ 382 Paul Posluszny RC 1.50 .60
❑ 383 Johnnie Lee Higgins RC 1.00 .40
❑ 384 Kolby Smith RC 1.50 .60
❑ 385 Ted Ginn Jr. RC 2.00 .75
❑ 386 Adam Carriker RC 1.00 .40
❑ 387 Tyler Palko RC 1.25 .50
❑ 388 Joel Filani RC 1.00 .40
❑ 389 Garrett Wolfe RC 1.50 .60
❑ 390 Ryne Robinson RC 1.00 .40
❑ 391 Reggie Nelson RC 1.00 .40
❑ 392 Dallas Baker RC 1.00 .40
❑ 393 Dwayne Wright RC 1.00 .40
❑ 394 Scott Chandler RC 1.00 .40
❑ 395 Jordan Kent RC 1.00 .40
❑ 396 Jarvis Moss RC 1.25 .50
❑ 397 Jonathan Wade RC 1.00 .40
❑ 398 Ben Grubbs RC 1.00 .40
❑ 399 Jason Snelling RC 1.00 .40
❑ 400 Jeff Rowe RC 1.00 .40
❑ 401 Aaron Ross RC 1.25 .50
❑ 402 Daniel Sepulveda RC .75 .30
❑ 403 Chris Henry RC 1.25 .50
❑ 404 James Jones RC 2.00 .75
❑ 405 Matt Spaeth RC 1.25 .50
❑ 406 Brandon Meriweather RC 1.25 .50
❑ 407 Nate Ilaoa RC 1.25 .50
❑ 408 Mason Crosby RC 1.00 .40
❑ 409 Ray McDonald RC 1.00 .40
❑ 410 Chris Leak RC 1.00 .40
❑ 411 Darrelle Revis RC 1.25 .50
❑ 412 Ahmad Bradshaw RC 1.50 .60
❑ 413 Tyler Thigpen RC 1.25 .50
❑ 414 Justise Hairston RC 1.00 .40
❑ 415 Charles Johnson RC .75 .30
❑ 416 Anthony Spencer RC 1.25 .50
❑ [illegible]
❑ [illegible]
❑ 419 Steve Breaston RC 1.00 .40
❑ 420 Ben Patrick RC 1.00 .40
❑ 421 Chris Houston RC 1.00 .40
❑ 422 Jordan Palmer RC 1.25 .50
❑ 423 Laurent Robinson RC 1.00 .40
❑ 424 Selvin Young RC 1.50 .60
❑ 425 Justin Harrell RC 1.25 .50
❑ 426 Sabby Piscitelli RC 1.25 .50
❑ 427 Yamon Figurs RC 1.25 .50
❑ 428 Brandon Jackson RC 1.50 .60
❑ 429 Jacoby Jones RC 1.25 .50
❑ 430 H.B. Blades RC 1.00 .40
❑ 431 Tanard Jackson RC .75 .30
❑ 432 Matt Gutierrez RC 1.25 .50
❑ 433 Matt Moore RC 2.00 .75
❑ 434 Clifton Dawson RC 1.25 .50
❑ 435 Marcus Mason RC 1.25 .50
❑ 436 Pierre Thomas RC 1.25 .50
❑ 437 Dante Rosario RC 1.00 .40
❑ 438 Biren Ealy RC 1.00 .40
❑ 439 John Broussard RC 1.00 .40
❑ 440 Kenton Keith RC 1.25 .50

1993 Select

❑ COMPLETE SET (200) 20.00 7.50
❑ 1 Steve Young 2.00 .75
❑ 2 Andre Reed .40 .15
❑ 3 Deion Sanders 1.25 .50
❑ 4 Harold Green .20 .07
❑ 5 Wendell Davis .20 .07
❑ 6 Mike Johnson .20 .07
❑ 7 Troy Aikman 2.00 .75
❑ 8 Johnny Mitchell .20 .07
❑ 9 Dale Carter .20 .07
❑ 10 Bruce Matthews .20 .07
❑ 11 Terrell Buckley .20 .07
❑ 12 Steve Emtman .20 .07
❑ 13 Neil Smith .75 .30
❑ 14 Tim Brown .75 .30
❑ 15 Chris Doleman .20 .07
❑ 16 Dan Marino 4.00 1.50
❑ 17 Terry McDaniel .20 .07
❑ 18 Neal Anderson .20 .07
❑ 19 Phil Simms .40 .15
❑ 20 Jeff Lageman .20 .07
❑ 21 Jerry Rice 2.50 1.00
❑ 22 Dermontti Dawson .20 .07
❑ 23 Reggie Cobb .20 .07
❑ 24 Junior Seau .75 .30
❑ 25 Darrell Green .20 .07
❑ 26 Chris Warren .40 .15
❑ 27 Randall Cunningham .75 .30
❑ 28 Bruce Smith .75 .30
❑ 29 Bryan Cox .20 .07
❑ 30 David Klingler .20 .07
❑ 31 Chip Lohmiller .20 .07
❑ 32 Eric Metcalf .40 .15
❑ 33 Ken Norton Jr. .40 .15
❑ 34 John Elway 4.00 1.50
❑ 35 Harris Barton .20 .07
❑ 36 Tim Barnett .20 .07
❑ 37 Rodney Hampton .40 .15
❑ 38 Desmond Howard .40 .15
❑ 39 Tom Rathman .20 .07
❑ 40 Derrick Thomas .75 .30
❑ 41 Randal Hill .20 .07
❑ 42 Steve Wisniewski .20 .07
❑ [illegible]
❑ 44 Darryl Talley [illegible] [illegible]
❑ 45 Shane Conlan .20 .07
❑ 46 Anthony Miller .40 .15
❑ 47 Randall McDaniel .20 .07
❑ 48 Rod Woodson .75 .30
❑ 49 Eric Martin .20 .07
❑ 50 Ronnie Lott .40 .15
❑ 51 Chris Spielman .40 .15
❑ 52 Vincent Brown .20 .07
❑ 53 Donnell Woolford .20 .07
❑ 54 Richmond Webb .20 .07
❑ 55 Emmitt Smith 3.00 1.25
❑ 56 Haywood Jeffires .40 .15
❑ 57 Jim Kelly .75 .30
❑ 58 James Francis .20 .07
❑ 59 Steve Wallace .20 .07
❑ 60 Jarrod Bunch .20 .07
❑ 61 Lawrence Dawsey .20 .07
❑ 62 Steve Atwater .20 .07
❑ 63 Art Monk .40 .15
❑ 64 Eric Green .20 .07
❑ 65 Lawrence Taylor .75 .30
❑ 66 Ronnie Harmon .20 .07
❑ 67 Fred Barnett .40 .15
❑ 68 Cortez Kennedy .40 .15
❑ 69 Mark Collins .20 .07
❑ 70 Howie Long .75 .30
❑ 71 Jackie Harris .20 .07
❑ 72 Irving Fryar .40 .15
❑ 73 Jim Everett .40 .15
❑ 74 Troy Vincent .20 .07
❑ 75 Cris Carter .75 .30
❑ 76 Boomer Esiason .40 .15
❑ 77 Sam Mills .20 .07
❑ 78 Lorenzo White .20 .07
❑ 79 Andre Rison .40 .15
❑ 80 Quentin Coryatt .40 .15
❑ 81 Steve McMichael .40 .15
❑ 82 Nick Lowery .20 .07
❑ 83 Michael Irvin .75 .30
❑ 84 Thurman Thomas [illegible] [illegible]
❑ 85 Bill Romanowski .20 .07
❑ 86 Carl Pickens .40 .15
❑ 87 Tim McDonald .20 .07
❑ 88 Bernie Kosar .40 .15
❑ 89 Greg Lloyd .40 .15
❑ 90 Barry Sanders 3.00 1.25
❑ 91 Shannon Sharpe .75 .30
❑ 92 Henry Thomas .20 .07
❑ 93 Barry Foster .40 .15
❑ 94 Antone Davis .20 .07
❑ 95 Stan Humphries .40 .15
❑ 96 Eric Swann .40 .15
❑ 97 Mike Pritchard .40 .15
❑ 98 Reggie White .75 .30
❑ 99 Jeff Hostetler .40 .15
❑ 100 Flipper Anderson .20 .07
❑ 101 Gary Clark .40 .15
❑ 102 Morten Andersen .20 .07
❑ 103 Leonard Russell .40 .15
❑ 104 Chris Hinton .20 .07
❑ 105 John Stephens .20 .07
❑ 106 Byron Evans .20 .07
❑ 107 Warren Moon .75 .30
❑ 108 Marv Cook .20 .07
❑ 109 Carlton Gray RC .20 .07
❑ 110 Jay Novacek .40 .15
❑ 111 Gary Anderson K .20 .07
❑ 112 Andre Tippett .20 .07
❑ 113 Cornelius Bennett .40 .15
❑ 114 Clyde Simmons .20 .07
❑ 115 Jeff George .75 .30

❑ 116 Audray McMillian	.20	.07
❑ 117 Mark Carrier WR	.40	.15
❑ 118 Vaughan Johnson	.20	.07
❑ 119 Kevin Greene	.40	.15
❑ 120 John Taylor	.40	.15
❑ 121 Jerry Ball	.20	.07
❑ 122 Pat Swilling	.20	.07
❑ 123 George Teague RC	.40	.15
❑ 124 Ricky Reynolds	.20	.07
❑ 125 Marcus Allen	.75	.30
❑ 126 Henry Jones	.20	.07
❑ 127 Ricky Watters	.75	.30
❑ 128 Leon Searcy	.20	.07
❑ 129 Chris Miller	.40	.15
❑ 130 Jim Harbaugh	.75	.30
❑ 131 Luis Sharpe	.20	.07
❑ 132 Simon Fletcher	.20	.07
❑ 133 Eric Allen	.20	.07
❑ 134 Carlton Haselrig	.20	.07
❑ 135 Harvey Williams	.40	.15
❑ 136 Leslie O'Neal	.40	.15
❑ 137 Sterling Sharpe	.75	.30
❑ 138 Tim Harris	.20	.07
❑ 139 Mark Rypien	.20	.07
❑ 140 Harry Galbreath	.20	.07
❑ 141 Sean Gilbert	.40	.15
❑ 142 Keith Jackson	.40	.15
❑ 143 Mark Clayton	.20	.07
❑ 144 Guy McIntyre	.20	.07
❑ 145 Jessie Tuggle	.20	.07
❑ 146 Leonard Marshall	.20	.07
❑ 147 Willie Davis	.75	.30
❑ 148 Herman Moore	.75	.30
❑ 149 Charles Haley	.40	.15
❑ 150 Amp Lee	.20	.07
❑ 151 Gary Zimmerman	.20	.07
❑ 152 Bennie Blades	.20	.07
❑ 153 Pierce Holt	.20	.07
❑ 154 Edgar Bennett	.75	.30
❑ 155 Joe Montana	4.00	1.50
❑ 156 Ted Washington	.20	.07
❑ 157 Hardy Nickerson	.40	.15
❑ 158 Rohn Stark	.20	.07
❑ 159 Brent Jones	.40	.15
❑ 160 Eugene Robinson	.20	.07
❑ 161 Pepper Johnson	.20	.07
❑ 162 Dan Saleaumua	.20	.07
❑ 163 Seth Joyner	.20	.07
❑ 164 Bruce Armstrong	.20	.07
❑ 165 Mike Munchak	.40	.15
❑ 166 Drew Bledsoe RC	5.00	2.00
❑ 167 Curtis Conway RC	1.25	.50
❑ 168 Lincoln Kennedy RC	.20	.07
❑ 169 Dana Stubblefield RC	.75	.30
❑ 170 Wayne Simmons RC	.20	.07
❑ 171 Garrison Hearst RC	2.00	.75
❑ 172 Jerome Bettis RC	8.00	3.00
❑ 173 Eric Curry RC	.20	.07
❑ 174 Natrone Means RC	.75	.30
❑ 175 Glyn Milburn RC	.75	.30
❑ 176 Marvin Jones RC	.20	.07
❑ 177 O.J.McDuffie RC	.75	.30
❑ 178 Dan Williams RC	.20	.07
❑ 179 Rick Mirer RC	.75	.30
❑ 180 John Copeland RC	.40	.15
❑ 181 Willie Roaf RC	.40	.15
❑ 182 Patrick Bates RC	.20	.07
❑ 183 Troy Drayton RC	.40	.15
❑ 184 Vincent Brisby RC	.75	.30
❑ 185 Irv Smith RC	.20	.07
❑ 186 Marion Butts	.20	.07
❑ 187 Wayne Martin	.20	.07
❑ 188 Brian Blades	.40	.15
❑ 189 Mel Gray	.40	.15
❑ 190 Mark Stepnoski	.20	.07
❑ 191 Ernest Givins	.40	.15
❑ 192 Steve Tasker	.40	.15
❑ 193 Tim Grunhard	.20	.07
❑ 194 Stanley Richard	.20	.07
❑ 195 Jeff Wright	.20	.07
❑ 196 Rodney Peete	.20	.07
❑ 197 Tunch Ilkin	.20	.07
❑ 198 Rich Camarillo	.20	.07
❑ 199 Erik Williams	.20	.07
❑ 200 Pete Stoyanovich	.20	.07
❑ S21 Jerry Rice SAMPLE	2.50	1.00

1994 Select

❑ COMPLETE SET (225)	15.00	6.00
❑ 1 Emmitt Smith	2.50	1.00
❑ 2 Bruce Smith	.40	.15
❑ 3 Randall McDaniel	.10	.02
❑ 4 Drew Bledsoe	1.25	.50
❑ 5 Rod Woodson	.20	.07
❑ 6 Richard Dent	.20	.07
❑ 7 Norm Johnson	.10	.02
❑ 8 Jim Everett	.20	.07
❑ 9 Harold Green	.10	.02
❑ 10 John Elway	3.00	1.25
❑ 11 Barry Sanders	2.50	1.00
❑ 12 Sterling Sharpe	.20	.07
❑ 13 Marcus Robertson	.10	.02
❑ 14 Steve Wisniewski	.10	.02
❑ 15 Irving Fryar	.20	.07
❑ 16 Tyrone Hughes	.20	.07
❑ 17 Garrison Hearst	.40	.15
❑ 18 Randall Cunningham	.40	.15
❑ 19 Junior Seau	.40	.15
❑ 20 Rick Mirer	.40	.15
❑ 21 Jerry Rice	1.50	.60
❑ 22 Eric Metcalf	.20	.07
❑ 23 Roosevelt Potts	.10	.02
❑ 24 Neil Smith	.20	.07
❑ 25 Jerome Bettis	.75	.30
❑ 26 Keith Hamilton	.10	.02
❑ 27 Hardy Nickerson	.20	.07
❑ 28 Steve Tasker	.20	.07
❑ 29 Johnny Johnson	.10	.02
❑ 30 Tom Carter	.10	.02
❑ 31 Andre Rison	.20	.07
❑ 32 Cortez Kennedy	.20	.07
❑ 33 Mark Carrier DB	.10	.02
❑ 34 Shannon Sharpe	.20	.07
❑ 35 Eric Swann	.20	.07
❑ 36 Steve Young	1.25	.50
❑ 37 Johnny Mitchell	.10	.02
❑ 38 Dermontti Dawson	.10	.02
❑ 39 Mike Johnson	.10	.02
❑ 40 Troy Aikman	1.50	.60
❑ 41 Pierce Holt	.10	.02
❑ 42 Derrick Thomas	.40	.15
❑ 43 Reggie Cobb	.10	.02
❑ 44 Michael Jackson	.20	.07
❑ 45 Lomas Brown	.10	.02
❑ 46 Jeff Hostetler	.20	.07
❑ 47 Pete Stoyanovich	.10	.02
❑ 48 Reggie White	.40	.15
❑ 49 Quentin Coryatt	.10	.02
❑ 50 Cris Carter	.75	.30
❑ 51 Sean Gilbert	.10	.02
❑ 52 Chris Slade	.10	.02
❑ 53 Ronnie Harmon	.10	.02
❑ 54 Renaldo Turnbull	.10	.02
❑ 55 Fred Barnett	.20	.07
❑ 56 John Elliott	.10	.02
❑ 57 Deion Sanders	.75	.30
❑ 58 John Carney	.10	.02
❑ 59 Louis Oliver	.10	.02
❑ 60 Greg Lloyd	.20	.07
❑ 61 Chris Hinton	.10	.02
❑ 62 Ronald Moore	.10	.02
❑ 63 Vincent Brown	.10	.02
❑ 64 Tony McGee	.10	.02
❑ 65 Erik Williams	.10	.02
❑ 66 Thurman Thomas	.40	.15
❑ 67 Neil O'Donnell	.40	.15
❑ 68 Scott Mitchell	.20	.07
❑ 69 Keith Byars	.10	.02
❑ 70 Henry Ellard	.20	.07
❑ 71 Chris Spielman	.20	.07
❑ 72 LeRoy Butler	.10	.02
❑ 73 Tim Brown	.40	.15
❑ 74 Darrell Green	.10	.02
❑ 75 Bruce Matthews	.10	.02
❑ 76 Stan Humphries	.20	.07
❑ 77 Will Wolford	.10	.02
❑ 78 John Taylor	.20	.07
❑ 79 Joe Montana	3.00	1.25
❑ 80 Chris Warren	.20	.07
❑ 81 Michael Brooks	.10	.02
❑ 82 Vance Johnson	.10	.02
❑ 83 Rob Moore	.20	.07
❑ 84 Herschel Walker	.20	.07
❑ 85 Alvin Harper	.20	.07
❑ 86 Wayne Martin	.10	.02
❑ 87 Leslie O'Neal	.10	.02
❑ 88 Flipper Anderson	.10	.02
❑ 89 Tommy Vardell	.10	.02
❑ 90 Mike Sherrard	.10	.02
❑ 91 Chris Jacke	.10	.02
❑ 92 Jim Kelly	.40	.15
❑ 93 Jeff Graham	.10	.02
❑ 94 Bryan Cox	.10	.02
❑ 95 Michael Irvin	.40	.15
❑ 96 Jeff Lageman	.10	.02
❑ 97 Webster Slaughter	.10	.02
❑ 98 Eugene Robinson	.10	.02
❑ 99 Vencie Glenn	.10	.02
❑ 100 Sean Jones	.10	.02
❑ 101 Calvin Williams	.20	.07
❑ 102 Jim Harbaugh	.40	.15
❑ 103 Eric Curry	.10	.02
❑ 104 Terry Allen	.20	.07
❑ 105 Darryl Williams	.10	.02
❑ 106 Gary Clark	.20	.07
❑ 107 Marcus Allen	.40	.15
❑ 108 Chip Lohmiller	.10	.02
❑ 109 Vaughan Johnson	.10	.02
❑ 110 Herman Moore	.40	.15
❑ 111 Barry Foster	.10	.02
❑ 112 Rocket Ismail	.20	.07
❑ 113 Erric Pegram	.10	.02
❑ 114 Anthony Miller	.20	.07
❑ 115 Shane Conlan	.10	.02
❑ 116 David Klingler	.10	.02
❑ 117 Mark Collins	.10	.02
❑ 118 Tony Bennett	.10	.02
❑ 119 Donnell Woolford	.10	.02
❑ 120 Reggie Brooks	.20	.07
❑ 121 Sam Mills	.10	.02
❑ 122 Greg Montgomery	.10	.02
❑ 123 Kevin Greene	.20	.07
❑ 124 Terry McDaniel	.10	.02
❑ 125 Henry Jones	.10	.02
❑ 126 Ricky Watters	.20	.07
❑ 127 Dan Marino	3.00	1.25
❑ 128 Steve Atwater	.10	.02
❑ 129 Ricky Proehl	.10	.02
❑ 130 Ernest Givins	.20	.07
❑ 131 John L. Williams	.10	.02
❑ 132 John Randle	.20	.07
❑ 133 Jay Novacek	.20	.07
❑ 134 Boomer Esiason	.20	.07
❑ 135 Jessie Hester	.10	.02
❑ 136 Courtney Hawkins	.10	.02
❑ 137 Ben Coates	.20	.07
❑ 138 Stevon Moore	.10	.02
❑ 139 Eric Allen	.10	.02
❑ 140 Jessie Tuggle	.10	.02
❑ 141 Marion Butts	.10	.02
❑ 142 Brett Favre	3.00	1.25
❑ 143 Andre Reed	.20	.07
❑ 144 Rodney Hampton	.20	.07
❑ 145 Keith Sims	.10	.02
❑ 146 Derek Brown RBK	.10	.02
❑ 147 Eric Green	.10	.02
❑ 148 Greg Robinson	.10	.02
❑ 149 Nate Newton	.10	.02
❑ 150 Mark Higgs	.10	.02
❑ 151 Nick Lowery	.10	.02
❑ 152 Craig Erickson	.10	.02
❑ 153 Anthony Carter	.20	.07
❑ 154 Simon Fletcher	.10	.02

❑ 155 Ronnie Lott	.20	.07
❑ 156 Gary Brown	.10	.02
❑ 157 Brent Jones	.20	.07
❑ 158 Jim Sweeney	.10	.02
❑ 159 Robert Brooks	.40	.15
❑ 160 Keith Jackson	.10	.02
❑ 161 Daryl Johnston	.20	.07
❑ 162 Tom Waddle	.10	.02
❑ 163 Eric Martin	.10	.02
❑ 164 Cornelius Bennett	.20	.07
❑ 165 Tim McDonald	.10	.02
❑ 166 Chris Doleman	.10	.02
❑ 167 Gary Zimmerman	.10	.02
❑ 168 Al Smith	.10	.02
❑ 169 Mark Carrier WR	.20	.07
❑ 170 Harris Barton	.10	.02
❑ 171 Ray Childress	.10	.02
❑ 172 Darryl Talley	.10	.02
❑ 173 James Jett	.10	.02
❑ 174 Mark Stepnoski	.10	.02
❑ 175 Jeff Query	.10	.02
❑ 176 Charles Haley	.20	.07
❑ 177 Rod Bernstine	.10	.02
❑ 178 Richmond Webb	.10	.02
❑ 179 Rich Camarillo	.10	.02
❑ 180 Pat Swilling	.10	.02
❑ 181 Chris Miller	.10	.02
❑ 182 Mike Pritchard	.10	.02
❑ 183 Checklist NFC	.10	.02
❑ 184 Natrone Means	.40	.15
❑ 185 Erik Kramer	.20	.07
❑ 186 Clyde Simmons	.10	.02
❑ 187 Checklist AFC/NFC	.10	.02
❑ 188 Warren Moon	.40	.15
❑ 189 Michael Haynes	.20	.07
❑ 190 Terry Kirby	.40	.15
❑ 191 Brian Blades	.20	.07
❑ 192 Haywood Jeffires	.20	.07
❑ 193 Thomas Everett	.10	.02
❑ 194 Morten Andersen	.10	.02
❑ 195 Dana Stubblefield	.20	.07
❑ 196 Ken Norton	.20	.07
❑ 197 Art Monk	.20	.07
❑ 198 Seth Joyner	.10	.02
❑ 199 Heath Shuler RC	.40	.15
❑ 200 Marshall Faulk RC	6.00	2.50
❑ 201 Charles Johnson RC	.40	.15
❑ 202 Derrick Alexander WR RC	.40	.15
❑ 203 Greg Hill RC	.40	.15
❑ 204 Darnay Scott RC	1.00	.40
❑ 205 Willie McGinest RC	.40	.15
❑ 206 Thomas Randolph RC	.10	.02
❑ 207 Errict Rhett RC	.40	.15
❑ 208 William Floyd RC	.40	.15
❑ 209 Johnnie Morton RC	2.00	.75
❑ 210 David Palmer RC	.40	.15
❑ 211 Dan Wilkinson RC	.20	.07
❑ 212 Trent Dilfer RC	1.25	.50
❑ 213 Antonio Langham RC	.20	.07
❑ 214 Chuck Levy RC	.10	.02
❑ 215 John Thierry RC	.10	.02
❑ 216 Kevin Lee RC	.10	.02
❑ 217 Aaron Glenn RC	.40	.15
❑ 218 Charlie Garner RC	1.50	.60
❑ 219 Jeff Burris RC	.20	.07
❑ 220 LeShon Johnson RC	.20	.07
❑ 221 Thomas Lewis RC	.20	.07
❑ 222 Ryan Yarborough RC	.10	.02
❑ 223 Mario Bates RC	.40	.15
❑ 224 Checklist NFC/AFC	.10	.02
❑ 225 Checklist AFC	.10	.02
❑ SR1 Marshall Faulk SR	40.00	15.00
❑ SR2 Dan Wilkinson SR	8.00	3.00

1996 Select

❑ COMPLETE SET (200)	20.00	8.00
❑ 1 Troy Aikman	1.00	.40
❑ 2 Marshall Faulk	.50	.20
❑ 3 Kordell Stewart	.40	.15
❑ 4 Larry Centers	.20	.07
❑ 5 Tamarick Vanover	.20	.07
❑ 6 Ken Norton Jr.	.10	.02
❑ 7 Steve Tasker	.10	.02
❑ 8 Dan Marino	2.00	.75
❑ 9 Heath Shuler	.20	.07
❑ 10 Anthony Miller	.20	.07
❑ 11 Mario Bates	.20	.07
❑ 12 Natrone Means	.20	.07
❑ 13 Darren Woodson	.20	.07
❑ 14 Chris Sanders	.20	.07
❑ 15 Chris Warren	.20	.07
❑ 16 Eric Metcalf	.10	.02
❑ 17 Quentin Coryatt	.10	.02
❑ 18 Jeff Hostetler	.10	.02
❑ 19 Brett Favre	2.00	.75
❑ 20 Curtis Martin	.75	.30
❑ 21 Floyd Turner	.10	.02
❑ 22 Curtis Conway	.40	.15
❑ 23 Orlando Thomas	.10	.02
❑ 24 Lee Woodall	.10	.02
❑ 25 Darick Holmes	.10	.02
❑ 26 Marcus Allen	.40	.15
❑ 27 Ricky Watters	.20	.07
❑ 28 Herman Moore	.20	.07
❑ 29 Rodney Hampton	.20	.07
❑ 30 Alvin Harper	.10	.02
❑ 31 Jeff Blake	.40	.15
❑ 32 Wayne Chrebet	.60	.25
❑ 33 Jerry Rice	1.00	.40
❑ 34 Dave Krieg	.10	.02
❑ 35 Mark Brunell	.60	.25
❑ 36 Terry Allen	.20	.07
❑ 37 Emmitt Smith	1.50	.60
❑ 38 Bryan Cox	.10	.02
❑ 39 Tony Martin	.20	.07
❑ 40 John Elway	2.00	.75
❑ 41 Warren Moon	.20	.07
❑ 42 Yancey Thigpen	.20	.07
❑ 43 Jeff George	.20	.07
❑ 44 Rodney Thomas	.10	.02
❑ 45 Joey Galloway	.40	.15
❑ 46 Jim Kelly	.40	.15
❑ 47 Drew Bledsoe	.60	.25
❑ 48 Greg Lloyd	.20	.07
❑ 49 Michael Irvin	.40	.15
❑ 50 Quinn Early	.10	.02
❑ 51 Brent Jones	.10	.02
❑ 52 Rashaan Salaam	.20	.07
❑ 53 James O.Stewart	.20	.07
❑ 54 Gus Frerotte	.20	.07
❑ 55 Edgar Bennett	.20	.07
❑ 56 Lamont Warren	.10	.02
❑ 57 Napoleon Kaufman	.40	.15
❑ 58 Kevin Williams	.10	.02
❑ 59 Irving Fryar	.20	.07
❑ 60 Trent Dilfer	.40	.15
❑ 61 Eric Zeier	.10	.02
❑ 62 Tyrone Wheatley	.20	.07
❑ 63 Isaac Bruce	.40	.15
❑ 64 Terrell Davis	.75	.30
❑ 65 Lake Dawson	.10	.02
❑ 66 Carnell Lake	.10	.02
❑ 67 Kerry Collins	.40	.15
❑ 68 Kyle Brady	.10	.02
❑ 69 Rodney Peete	.10	.02
❑ 70 Carl Pickens	.20	.07
❑ 71 Robert Smith	.20	.07
❑ 72 Rod Woodson	.20	.07
❑ 73 Deion Sanders	.60	.25
❑ 74 Sean Dawkins	.10	.02
❑ 75 William Floyd	.20	.07
❑ 76 Barry Sanders	1.50	.60
❑ 77 Ben Coates	.20	.07
❑ 78 Neil O'Donnell	.20	.07
❑ 79 Bill Brooks	.10	.02
❑ 80 Steve Bono	.10	.02
❑ 81 Jay Novacek	.10	.02
❑ 82 Bernie Parmalee	.10	.02
❑ 83 Derek Loville	.10	.02
❑ 84 Frank Sanders	.20	.07
❑ 85 Robert Brooks	.40	.15
❑ 86 Jim Harbaugh	.20	.07
❑ 87 Rick Mirer	.20	.07
❑ 88 Craig Heyward	.10	.02
❑ 89 Greg Hill	.20	.07
❑ 90 Andre Coleman	.10	.02
❑ 91 Shannon Sharpe	.20	.07
❑ 92 Hugh Douglas	.20	.07
❑ 93 Andre Hastings	.10	.02
❑ 94 Bryce Paup	.10	.02
❑ 95 Jim Everett	.10	.02
❑ 96 Brian Mitchell	.10	.02
❑ 97 Jeff Graham	.10	.02
❑ 98 Steve McNair	.75	.30
❑ 99 Charlie Garner	.20	.07
❑ 100 Willie McGinest	.10	.02
❑ 101 Harvey Williams	.10	.02
❑ 102 Daryl Johnston	.20	.07
❑ 103 Cris Carter	.40	.15
❑ 104 J.J. Stokes	.40	.15
❑ 105 Garrison Hearst	.20	.07
❑ 106 Mark Chmura	.20	.07
❑ 107 Derrick Thomas	.40	.15
❑ 108 Errict Rhett	.20	.07
❑ 109 Terance Mathis	.10	.02
❑ 110 Dave Brown	.10	.02
❑ 111 Erric Pegram	.10	.02
❑ 112 Scott Mitchell	.20	.07
❑ 113 Aaron Bailey	.10	.02
❑ 114 Stan Humphries	.20	.07
❑ 115 Bruce Smith	.20	.07
❑ 116 Rob Johnson	.40	.15
❑ 117 O.J. McDuffie	.20	.07
❑ 118 Brian Blades	.10	.02
❑ 119 Steve Atwater	.10	.02
❑ 120 Tyrone Hughes	.10	.02
❑ 121 Michael Westbrook	.40	.15
❑ 122 Ki-Jana Carter	.20	.07
❑ 123 Adrian Murrell	.20	.07
❑ 124 Steve Young	.75	.30
❑ 125 Charles Haley	.20	.07
❑ 126 Vincent Brisby	.10	.02
❑ 127 Jerome Bettis	.40	.15
❑ 128 Erik Kramer	.10	.02
❑ 129 Roosevelt Potts	.10	.02
❑ 130 Tim Brown	.40	.15
❑ 131 Reggie White	.40	.15
❑ 132 Jake Reed	.20	.07
❑ 133 Junior Seau	.40	.15
❑ 134 Stoney Case	.10	.02
❑ 135 Kimble Anders	.20	.07
❑ 136 Brett Perriman	.10	.02
❑ 137 Todd Collins	.20	.07
❑ 138 Sherman Williams	.10	.02
❑ 139 Hardy Nickerson	.10	.02
❑ 140 Ernie Mills	.10	.02
❑ 141 Glyn Milburn	.10	.02
❑ 142 Terry Kirby	.20	.07
❑ 143 Bert Emanuel	.20	.07
❑ 144 Aeneas Williams	.10	.02
❑ 145 Aaron Craver	.10	.02
❑ 146 Jackie Harris	.10	.02
❑ 147 Thurman Thomas	.40	.15
❑ 148 Aaron Hayden RC	.10	.02
❑ 149 Antonio Freeman	.40	.15
❑ 150 Kevin Greene	.20	.07
❑ 151 Kevin Hardy RC	.40	.15
❑ 152 Eric Moulds RC	1.50	.60
❑ 153 Tim Biakabutuka RC	.40	.15
❑ 154 Keyshawn Johnson RC	1.25	.50
❑ 155 Jeff Lewis RC	.20	.07
❑ 156 Stepfret Williams RC	.20	.07
❑ 157 Tony Brackens RC	.40	.15
❑ 158 Mike Alstott RC	1.25	.50
❑ 159 Willie Anderson RC	.10	.02
❑ 160 Marvin Harrison RC	3.00	1.25
❑ 161 Regan Upshaw RC	.10	.02
❑ 162 Bobby Engram RC	.40	.15
❑ 163 Leeland McElroy RC	.20	.07
❑ 164 Alex Van Dyke RC	.20	.07
❑ 165 Stanley Pritchett RC	.20	.07
❑ 166 Cedric Jones RC	.10	.02
❑ 167 Terry Glenn RC	1.25	.50
❑ 168 Eddie George RC	1.50	.60

❑ 169 Lawrence Phillips RC .40 .15
❑ 170 Jonathan Ogden RC .40 .15
❑ 171 Danny Kanell RC .40 .15
❑ 172 Alex Molden RC .10 .02
❑ 173 Daryl Gardener RC .10 .02
❑ 174 Derrick Mayes RC .40 .15
❑ 175 Marco Battaglia RC .10 .02
❑ 176 Jon Stark RC .10 .02
❑ 177 Karim Abdul-Jabbar RC .40 .15
❑ 178 Stephen Davis RC 2.00 .75
❑ 179 Rickey Dudley RC .40 .15
❑ 180 Eddie Kennison RC .40 .15
❑ 181 Barry Sanders FF .75 .30
❑ 182 Brett Favre FF 1.00 .40
❑ 183 John Elway FF 1.00 .40
❑ 184 Steve Young FF .40 .15
❑ 185 Michael Irvin FF .20 .07
❑ 186 Jerry Rice FF .50 .20
❑ 187 Emmitt Smith FF .75 .30
❑ 188 Isaac Bruce FF .40 .15
❑ 189 Chris Warren FF .20 .07
❑ 190 Errict Rhett FF .20 .07
❑ 191 Herman Moore FF .20 .07
❑ 192 Carl Pickens FF .20 .07
❑ 193 Cris Carter FF .40 .15
❑ 194 Terrell Davis FF .40 .15
❑ 195 Rodney Thomas FF .10 .02
❑ 196 Dan Marino CL .40 .15
❑ 197 Drew Bledsoe CL .20 .07
❑ 198 Emmitt Smith CL .40 .15
❑ 199 Jerry Rice CL .40 .15
❑ 200 Barry Sanders/Elway CL .40 .15

2001 Select

❑ COMP.SET w/o SPs (220) 30.00 12.50
❑ 1 David Boston .75 .30
❑ 2 Frank Sanders .30 .10
❑ 3 Jake Plummer .50 .20
❑ 4 Michael Pittman .30 .10
❑ 5 Rob Moore .50 .20
❑ 6 Thomas Jones .50 .20
❑ 7 Chris Chandler .50 .20
❑ 8 Doug Johnson .30 .10
❑ 9 Jamal Anderson .75 .30
❑ 10 Tim Dwight .75 .30
❑ 11 Brandon Stokley .50 .20
❑ 12 Chris Redman .30 .10
❑ 13 Jamal Lewis 1.25 .50
❑ 14 Qadry Ismail .50 .20
❑ 15 Ray Lewis .75 .30
❑ 16 Rod Woodson .50 .20
❑ 17 Shannon Sharpe .50 .20
❑ 18 Travis Taylor .50 .20
❑ 19 Trent Dilfer .50 .20
❑ 20 Elvis Grbac .50 .20
❑ 21 Eric Moulds .50 .20
❑ 22 Jay Riemersma .30 .10
❑ 23 Peerless Price .50 .20
❑ 24 Rob Johnson .50 .20
❑ 25 Sam Cowart .30 .10
❑ 26 Sammy Morris .30 .10
❑ 27 Shawn Bryson .30 .10
❑ 28 Donald Hayes .30 .10
❑ 29 Muhsin Muhammad .50 .20
❑ 30 Patrick Jeffers .50 .20
❑ 31 Reggie White DE .75 .30
❑ 32 Steve Beuerlein .50 .20
❑ 33 Tim Biakabutuka .50 .20
❑ 34 Wesley Walls .30 .10
❑ 35 Brian Urlacher 1.25 .50
❑ 36 Cade McNown .30 .10
❑ 37 Dez White .30 .10
❑ 38 James Allen .50 .20
❑ 39 Marcus Robinson .75 .30
❑ 40 Marty Booker .30 .10
❑ 41 Akili Smith .30 .10
❑ 42 Corey Dillon .75 .30
❑ 43 Danny Farmer .30 .10
❑ 44 Peter Warrick .75 .30
❑ 45 Ron Dugans .30 .10
❑ 46 Takeo Spikes .30 .10
❑ 47 Courtney Brown .50 .20
❑ 48 Dennis Northcutt .50 .20
❑ 49 JaJuan Dawson .30 .10
❑ 50 Kevin Johnson .50 .20
❑ 51 Tim Couch .50 .20
❑ 52 Travis Prentice .30 .10
❑ 53 Anthony Wright .30 .10
❑ 54 Emmitt Smith 1.50 .60
❑ 55 James McKnight .50 .20
❑ 56 Joey Galloway .50 .20
❑ 57 Rocket Ismail .50 .20
❑ 58 Randall Cunningham .75 .30
❑ 59 Troy Aikman 1.25 .50
❑ 60 Brian Griese .75 .30
❑ 61 Ed McCaffrey .75 .30
❑ 62 Gus Frerotte .30 .10
❑ 63 John Elway 2.50 1.00
❑ 64 Mike Anderson .75 .30
❑ 65 Olandis Gary .50 .20
❑ 66 Rod Smith .50 .20
❑ 67 Terrell Davis .75 .30
❑ 68 Barry Sanders 1.50 .60
❑ 69 Charlie Batch .75 .30
❑ 70 Germane Crowell .30 .10
❑ 71 Herman Moore .50 .20
❑ 72 James Stewart .50 .20
❑ 73 Johnnie Morton .50 .20
❑ 74 Robert Porcher .30 .10
❑ 75 Jim Harbaugh .50 .20
❑ 76 Ahman Green .75 .30
❑ 77 Antonio Freeman .75 .30
❑ 78 Bill Schroeder .50 .20
❑ 79 Brett Favre 2.50 1.00
❑ 80 Bubba Franks .50 .20
❑ 81 Dorsey Levens .50 .20
❑ 82 E.G. Green .30 .10
❑ 83 Edgerrin James 1.00 .40
❑ 84 Jerome Pathon .50 .20
❑ 85 Ken Dilger .30 .10
❑ 86 Marcus Pollard .30 .10
❑ 87 Marvin Harrison .75 .30
❑ 88 Peyton Manning 2.00 .75
❑ 89 Terrence Wilkins .30 .10
❑ 90 Fred Taylor .75 .30
❑ 91 Hardy Nickerson .30 .10
❑ 92 Jimmy Smith .50 .20
❑ 93 Keenan McCardell .30 .10
❑ 94 Kyle Brady .30 .10
❑ 95 Mark Brunell .75 .30
❑ 96 Tony Brackens .30 .10
❑ 97 Derrick Alexander WR .50 .20
❑ 98 Sylvester Morris .30 .10
❑ 99 Tony Gonzalez .50 .20
❑ 100 Tony Richardson .30 .10
❑ 101 Kimble Anders .30 .10
❑ 102 Warren Moon .75 .30
❑ 103 Dan Marino 2.50 1.00
❑ 104 Jay Fiedler .75 .30
❑ 105 Lamar Smith .50 .20
❑ 106 O.J. McDuffie .30 .10
❑ 107 Oronde Gadsden .50 .20
❑ 108 Sam Madison .30 .10
❑ 109 Thurman Thomas .50 .20
❑ 110 Tony Martin .30 .10
❑ 111 Zach Thomas .75 .30
❑ 112 Cris Carter .75 .30
❑ 113 Daunte Culpepper .75 .30
❑ 114 Matthew Hatchette .30 .10
❑ 115 Randy Moss 1.50 .60
❑ 116 Robert Smith .75 .30
❑ 117 Drew Bledsoe 1.00 .40
❑ 118 J.R. Redmond .30 .10
❑ 119 Kevin Faulk .50 .20
❑ 120 Michael Bishop .30 .10
❑ 121 Terry Glenn .50 .20
❑ 122 Troy Brown .50 .20
❑ 123 Ty Law .50 .20
❑ 124 Aaron Brooks .75 .30
❑ 125 Darren Howard .30 .10
❑ 126 Jake Reed .50 .20
❑ 127 Jeff Blake .50 .20
❑ 128 Joe Horn .50 .20
❑ 129 La'Roi Glover .30 .10
❑ 130 Ricky Williams .75 .30
❑ 131 Willie Jackson .30 .10
❑ 132 Albert Connell .30 .10
❑ 133 Amani Toomer .50 .20
❑ 134 Ike Hilliard .50 .20
❑ 135 Jason Sehorn .30 .10
❑ 136 Jessie Armstead .30 .10
❑ 137 Kerry Collins .50 .20
❑ 138 Michael Strahan .50 .20
❑ 139 Ron Dayne .75 .30
❑ 140 Ron Dixon .30 .10
❑ 141 Tiki Barber .75 .30
❑ 142 Anthony Becht .30 .10
❑ 143 Chad Pennington 1.25 .50
❑ 144 Curtis Martin .75 .30
❑ 145 Dedric Ward .30 .10
❑ 146 Laveranues Coles .75 .30
❑ 147 Vinny Testaverde .50 .20
❑ 148 Wayne Chrebet .50 .20
❑ 149 Andre Rison .50 .20
❑ 150 Charles Woodson .50 .20
❑ 151 Darrell Russell .30 .10
❑ 152 Napoleon Kaufman .50 .20
❑ 153 Rich Gannon .75 .30
❑ 154 Tim Brown .75 .30
❑ 155 Tyrone Wheatley .50 .20
❑ 156 Chad Lewis .30 .10
❑ 157 Charles Johnson .30 .10
❑ 158 Donovan McNabb 1.00 .40
❑ 159 Duce Staley .75 .30
❑ 160 Hugh Douglas .30 .10
❑ 161 Na Brown .30 .10
❑ 162 Todd Pinkston .30 .10
❑ 163 James Thrash .50 .20
❑ 164 Bobby Shaw .30 .10
❑ 165 Hines Ward .75 .30
❑ 166 Jerome Bettis .75 .30
❑ 167 Kordell Stewart .50 .20
❑ 168 Levon Kirkland .30 .10
❑ 169 Plaxico Burress .75 .30
❑ 170 Richard Huntley .30 .10
❑ 171 Troy Edwards .30 .10
❑ 172 Jeff Graham .30 .10
❑ 173 Junior Seau .75 .30
❑ 174 Doug Flutie .75 .30
❑ 175 Charlie Garner .50 .20
❑ 176 Jeff Garcia .75 .30
❑ 177 Jerry Rice 1.50 .60
❑ 178 Steve Young 1.00 .40
❑ 179 Terrell Owens .75 .30
❑ 180 Brock Huard .30 .10
❑ 181 Darrell Jackson .75 .30
❑ 182 Derrick Mayes .30 .10
❑ 183 Ricky Watters .50 .20
❑ 184 Shaun Alexander 1.00 .40
❑ 185 Matt Hasselbeck .50 .20
❑ 186 John Randle .50 .20
❑ 187 Az-Zahir Hakim .30 .10
❑ 188 Isaac Bruce .75 .30
❑ 189 Kurt Warner 1.50 .60
❑ 190 Marshall Faulk 1.00 .40
❑ 191 Torry Holt .75 .30
❑ 192 Trent Green .75 .30
❑ 193 Derrick Brooks .75 .30
❑ 194 Jacquez Green .30 .10
❑ 195 John Lynch .50 .20
❑ 196 Keyshawn Johnson .75 .30
❑ 197 Mike Alstott .75 .30
❑ 198 Reidel Anthony .30 .10
❑ 199 Shaun King .30 .10
❑ 200 Warren Sapp .50 .20
❑ 201 Warrick Dunn .75 .30
❑ 202 Ryan Leaf .50 .20
❑ 203 Carl Pickens .30 .10
❑ 204 Derrick Mason .50 .20
❑ 205 Eddie George .75 .30
❑ 206 Frank Wycheck .30 .10
❑ 207 Jevon Kearse .50 .20
❑ 208 Neil O'Donnell .30 .10

❑ 209 Steve McNair .75 .30
❑ 210 Yancey Thigpen .30 .10
❑ 211 Andre Reed .50 .20
❑ 212 Brad Johnson .75 .30
❑ 213 Bruce Smith .50 .20
❑ 214 Champ Bailey .75 .30
❑ 215 Darrell Green .30 .10
❑ 216 Deion Sanders .75 .30
❑ 217 Irving Fryar .50 .20
❑ 218 Jeff George .50 .20
❑ 219 Michael Westbrook .50 .20
❑ 220 Stephen Davis .75 .30
❑ 221 Terrell Owens AP 2.00 .75
❑ 222 Peyton Manning AP 6.00 2.50
❑ 223 Stephen Davis AP 2.00 .75
[illegible]
❑ 225 Donovan McNabb AP 3.00 1.25
❑ 226 Edgerrin James AP 3.00 1.25
❑ 227 Eric Moulds AP 1.25 .50
❑ 228 Daunte Culpepper AP 2.00 .75
❑ 229 Eddie George AP 2.00 .75
❑ 230 Cris Carter AP 2.00 .75
❑ 231 Rich Gannon AP 2.00 .75
❑ 232 Jeff Garcia AP 2.00 .75
❑ 233 Jimmy Smith AP 1.25 .50
❑ 234 Tony Gonzalez AP 1.25 .50
❑ 235 Torry Holt AP 2.00 .75
❑ 236 Jevon Kearse AP 1.25 .50
❑ 237 Ray Lewis AP 2.00 .75
❑ 238 Warren Sapp AP 1.25 .50
❑ 239 Brian Urlacher AP 4.00 1.50
❑ 240 Champ Bailey AP 1.25 .50
❑ 241 Peyton Manning LL 6.00 2.50
❑ 242 Jeff Garcia LL 2.00 .75
❑ 243 Elvis Grbac LL 1.25 .50
❑ 244 Daunte Culpepper LL 2.00 .75
❑ 245 Brett Favre LL 8.00 3.00
❑ 246 Edgerrin James LL 3.00 1.25
❑ 247 Robert Smith LL 1.25 .50
❑ 248 Eddie George LL 2.00 .75
❑ 249 Mike Anderson LL 2.00 .75
❑ 250 Corey Dillon LL 2.00 .75
❑ 251 Torry Holt LL 2.00 .75
❑ 252 Rod Smith LL 1.25 .50
❑ 253 Isaac Bruce LL 2.00 .75
❑ 254 Terrell Owens LL 2.00 .75
❑ 255 Randy Moss LL 5.00 2.00
❑ 256 La'Roi Glover LL .75 .30
❑ 257 Trace Armstrong LL .75 .30
❑ 258 Warren Sapp LL 1.25 .50
❑ 259 Hugh Douglas LL .75 .30
❑ 260 Jason Taylor LL .75 .30
❑ 261 Mike Anderson SS 2.00 .75
❑ 262 Jamal Lewis SS 3.00 1.25
❑ 263 Sylvester Morris SS .75 .30
❑ 264 Darrell Jackson SS 2.00 .75
[illegible]
❑ 266 Ron Dayne SS 2.00 .75
❑ 267 Shaun Alexander SS 3.00 1.25
❑ 268 Plaxico Burress SS 2.00 .75
❑ 269 Brian Urlacher SS 4.00 1.50
❑ 270 Courtney Brown SS 1.25 .50
❑ 271 Michael Vick RC 40.00 15.00
❑ 272 Drew Brees RC 40.00 20.00
❑ 273 Chris Weinke RC 12.00 5.00
❑ 274 Quincy Carter RC 12.00 5.00
❑ 275 Sage Rosenfels RC 12.00 5.00
❑ 276 Josh Heupel RC 12.00 5.00
❑ 277 David Rivers RC 8.00 3.00
❑ 278 Ben Leard RC 8.00 3.00
❑ 279 Marques Tuiasosopo RC 12.00 5.00
❑ 280 Mike McMahon RC 12.00 5.00
❑ 281 Deuce McAllister RC 25.00 10.00
❑ 282 LaMont Jordan RC 25.00 10.00
❑ 283 LaDainian Tomlinson RC 80.00 40.00
❑ 284 James Jackson RC 12.00 5.00
❑ 285 Anthony Thomas RC 12.00 5.00
❑ 286 Travis Henry RC 25.00 10.00
❑ 287 Travis Minor RC 8.00 3.00
❑ 288 Rudi Johnson RC 25.00 10.00
❑ 289 Michael Bennett RC 12.00 5.00
❑ 290 Kevan Barlow RC 12.00 5.00
❑ 291 Reggie White RC 8.00 3.00
❑ 292 Moran Norris RC 5.00 2.00
❑ 293 Ja'Mar Toombs RC 8.00 3.00
❑ 294 Heath Evans RC 8.00 3.00
❑ 295 David Terrell RC 12.00 5.00

❑ 296 Santana Moss RC 20.00 7.50
❑ 297 Rod Gardner RC 12.00 5.00
❑ 298 Quincy Morgan RC 12.00 5.00
❑ 299 Freddie Mitchell RC 12.00 5.00
❑ 300 Boo Williams RC 8.00 3.00
❑ 301 Reggie Wayne RC 25.00 10.00
❑ 302 Ronney Daniels RC 5.00 2.00
❑ 303 Bobby Newcombe RC 8.00 3.00
❑ 304 Vinny Sutherland RC 8.00 3.00
❑ 305 Cedrick Wilson RC 12.00 5.00
❑ 306 Robert Ferguson RC 12.00 5.00
❑ 307 Ken-Yon Rambo RC 8.00 3.00
❑ 308 Alex Bannister RC 8.00 3.00
❑ 309 Koren Robinson RC 12.00 5.00
❑ 310 Chad Johnson RC 30.00 12.50
[illegible]
❑ 312 Javon Green RC 8.00 3.00
❑ 313 Snoop Minnis RC 8.00 3.00
❑ 314 Scotty Anderson RC 8.00 3.00
❑ 315 Todd Heap RC 12.00 5.00
❑ 316 Alge Crumpler RC 15.00 6.00
❑ 317 Marcellus Rivers RC 8.00 3.00
❑ 318 Rashon Burns RC 5.00 2.00
❑ 319 Jamal Reynolds RC 12.00 5.00
❑ 320 Andre Carter RC 12.00 5.00
❑ 321 Justin Smith RC 12.00 5.00
❑ 322 Gerard Warren RC 12.00 5.00
❑ 323 Tommy Polley RC 12.00 5.00
❑ 324 Dan Morgan RC 12.00 5.00
❑ 325 Torrance Marshall RC 12.00 5.00
❑ 326 Correll Buckhalter RC 15.00 6.00
❑ 327 Derrick Gibson RC 8.00 3.00
❑ 328 Adam Archuleta RC 12.00 5.00
❑ 329 Jamar Fletcher RC 8.00 3.00
❑ 330 Nate Clements RC 12.00 5.00

2006 Select

❑ COMP.SET w/o RC's (330) 50.00 25.00
❑ 331-430 RC PRINT RUN 599 SETS
❑ 1 Kurt Warner .50 .20
❑ 2 J.J. Arrington .50 .20
❑ 3 Anquan Boldin .50 .20
❑ 4 Larry Fitzgerald .75 .30
❑ 5 Marcel Shipp .40 .15
❑ 6 Bryant Johnson .40 .15
❑ 7 Bertrand Berry .40 .15
❑ 8 John Navarre .40 .15
❑ 9 Michael Vick .75 .30
❑ 10 Warrick Dunn .50 .20
❑ 11 Roddy White .50 .20
❑ 12 Alge Crumpler .50 .20
❑ 13 T.J. Duckett .50 .20
❑ 14 Michael Jenkins .50 .20
❑ 15 DeAngelo Hall .50 .20
❑ 16 Brian Finneran .40 .15
❑ 17 Kyle Boller .40 .15
❑ 18 Jamal Lewis .50 .20
❑ 19 Chester Taylor .50 .20
❑ 20 Derrick Mason .40 .15
❑ 21 Mark Clayton .75 .30
❑ 22 Todd Heap .50 .20
❑ 23 Ray Lewis .75 .30
❑ 24 Devard Darling .40 .15
❑ 25 J.P. Losman .50 .20
❑ 26 Willis McGahee .75 .30
❑ 27 Lee Evans .50 .20
❑ 28 Eric Moulds .50 .20
❑ 29 Lawyer Milloy .40 .15
❑ 30 Josh Reed .40 .15

❑ 31 Kelly Holcomb .40 .15
❑ 32 Jake Delhomme .50 .20
❑ 33 DeShaun Foster .50 .20
❑ 34 Steve Smith .75 .30
❑ 35 Julius Peppers .50 .20
❑ 36 Drew Carter .40 .15
❑ 37 Chris Gamble .40 .15
❑ 38 Stephen Davis .50 .20
❑ 39 Keary Colbert .40 .15
❑ 40 Nick Goings .40 .15
❑ 41 Eric Shelton .40 .15
❑ 42 Rex Grossman .75 .30
❑ 43 Thomas Jones .50 .20
❑ 44 Cedric Benson .75 .30
❑ 45 Muhsin Muhammad .50 .20
[illegible]
❑ 47 Mark Bradley .50 .20
❑ 48 Kyle Orton .50 .20
❑ 49 Tommie Harris .40 .15
❑ 50 Adrian Peterson .40 .15
❑ 51 Bernard Berrian .40 .15
❑ 52 Justin Gage .40 .15
❑ 53 Carson Palmer .75 .30
❑ 54 Rudi Johnson .50 .20
❑ 55 Chad Johnson .50 .20
❑ 56 T.J. Houshmandzadeh .50 .20
❑ 57 Chris Henry .40 .15
❑ 58 Chris Perry .50 .20
❑ 59 Jon Kitna .40 .15
❑ 60 Deltha O'Neal .40 .15
❑ 61 Charlie Frye .50 .20
❑ 62 Reuben Droughns .50 .20
❑ 63 Braylon Edwards .75 .30
❑ 64 Kellen Winslow .75 .30
❑ 65 Antonio Bryant .50 .20
❑ 66 Trent Dilfer .50 .20
❑ 67 Dennis Northcutt .40 .15
❑ 68 Drew Bledsoe .75 .30
❑ 69 Julius Jones .75 .30
❑ 70 Marion Barber .50 .20
❑ 71 Terry Glenn .50 .20
❑ 72 Keyshawn Johnson .50 .20
❑ 73 Roy Williams S .50 .20
❑ 74 Jason Witten .50 .20
❑ 75 Terence Newman .40 .15
❑ 76 Drew Henson .40 .15
❑ 77 Patrick Crayton .40 .15
❑ 78 Jake Plummer .50 .20
❑ 79 Mike Anderson .50 .20
❑ 80 Tatum Bell .50 .20
❑ 81 Ashley Lelie .50 .20
❑ 82 Rod Smith .50 .20
❑ 83 D.J. Williams .40 .15
❑ 84 Darius Watts .40 .15
❑ 85 Ron Dayne .50 .20
❑ 86 Jeb Putzier .40 .15
[illegible]
❑ 88 Kevin Jones .75 .30
❑ 89 Roy Williams WR .75 .30
❑ 90 Mike Williams .75 .30
❑ 91 Charles Rogers .50 .20
❑ 92 Teddy Lehman .40 .15
❑ 93 Marcus Pollard .40 .15
❑ 94 Artose Pinner .40 .15
❑ 95 Brett Favre 1.50 .60
❑ 96 Ahman Green .50 .20
❑ 97 Najeh Davenport .40 .15
❑ 98 Samkon Gado .50 .20
❑ 99 Javon Walker .50 .20
❑ 100 Donald Driver .50 .20
❑ 101 Aaron Rodgers .75 .30
❑ 102 Robert Ferguson .40 .15
❑ 103 David Carr .50 .20
❑ 104 Domanick Davis .50 .20
❑ 105 Andre Johnson .50 .20
❑ 106 Jabar Gaffney .40 .15
❑ 107 Jonathan Wells .40 .15
❑ 108 Vernand Morency .50 .20
❑ 109 Corey Bradford .40 .15
❑ 110 Jerome Mathis .40 .15
❑ 111 Peyton Manning 1.25 .50
❑ 112 Edgerrin James .75 .30
❑ 113 Marvin Harrison .75 .30
❑ 114 Reggie Wayne .50 .20
❑ 115 Dwight Freeney .50 .20
❑ 116 Dallas Clark .40 .15
❑ 117 Dominic Rhodes .50 .20

❑ 118 Jim Sorgi .40 .15
❑ 119 Brandon Stokley .50 .20
❑ 120 Bob Sanders .50 .20
❑ 121 Mike Doss .40 .15
❑ 122 Marlin Jackson .40 .15
❑ 123 Byron Leftwich .50 .20
❑ 124 Fred Taylor .50 .20
❑ 125 Jimmy Smith .50 .20
❑ 126 Matt Jones .50 .20
❑ 127 Ernest Wilford .40 .15
❑ 128 Greg Jones .40 .15
❑ 129 Mike Peterson .40 .15
❑ 130 Reggie Williams .50 .20
❑ 131 Rashean Mathis .40 .15
❑ 132 Trent Green .50 .20
❑ 133 Larry Johnson 1.00 .40
❑ 134 Priest Holmes .50 .20
❑ 135 Eddie Kennison .40 .15
❑ 136 Tony Gonzalez .50 .20
❑ 137 Kendrell Bell .40 .15
❑ 138 Samie Parker .40 .15
❑ 139 Dante Hall .50 .20
❑ 140 Tony Richardson .40 .15
❑ 141 Gus Frerotte .40 .15
❑ 142 Ronnie Brown .75 .30
❑ 143 Neil Rackers .40 .15
❑ 144 Chris Chambers .50 .20
❑ 145 Zach Thomas .75 .30
❑ 146 Cliff Russell .40 .15
❑ 147 David Boston .40 .15
❑ 148 Wes Welker .75 .30
❑ 149 Marty Booker .40 .15
❑ 150 Randy McMichael .40 .15
❑ 151 Daunte Culpepper .75 .30
❑ 152 Mewelde Moore .40 .15
❑ 153 Nate Burleson .50 .20
❑ 154 Troy Williamson .50 .20
❑ 155 Koren Robinson .50 .20
❑ 156 Erasmus James .40 .15
❑ 157 Marcus Robinson .50 .20
❑ 158 E.J. Henderson .40 .15
❑ 159 Brad Johnson .50 .20
❑ 160 Michael Bennett .40 .15
❑ 161 Travis Taylor .40 .15
❑ 162 Tom Brady 1.25 .50
❑ 163 Corey Dillon .50 .20
❑ 164 Deion Branch .50 .20
❑ 165 Tedy Bruschi .75 .30
❑ 166 Ben Watson .40 .15
❑ 167 Daniel Graham .40 .15
❑ 168 Bethel Johnson .40 .15
❑ 169 Kevin Faulk .40 .15
❑ 170 David Givens .50 .20
❑ 171 Troy Brown .50 .20
❑ 172 Aaron Brooks .50 .20
❑ 173 Deuce McAllister .50 .20
❑ 174 Joe Horn .50 .20
❑ 175 Donte Stallworth .50 .20
❑ 176 Antowain Smith .40 .15
❑ 177 Devery Henderson .40 .15
❑ 178 Eli Manning 1.00 .40
❑ 179 Tiki Barber .75 .30
❑ 180 Plaxico Burress .50 .20
❑ 181 Jeremy Shockey .75 .30
❑ 182 Osi Umenyiora .40 .15
❑ 183 Gibril Wilson .40 .15
❑ 184 Brandon Jacobs .50 .20
❑ 185 Michael Strahan .50 .20
❑ 186 Will Allen .40 .15
❑ 187 Amani Toomer .50 .20
❑ 188 Chad Pennington .50 .20
❑ 189 Curtis Martin .75 .30
❑ 190 Laveranues Coles .50 .20
❑ 191 Jonathan Vilma .50 .20
❑ 192 Ty Law .50 .20
❑ 193 Cedric Houston .40 .15
❑ 194 Justin McCareins .40 .15
❑ 195 Jerald Sowell .40 .15
❑ 196 Josh Brown .40 .15
❑ 197 LaMont Jordan .50 .20
❑ 198 Randy Moss .75 .30
❑ 199 Jerry Porter .50 .20
❑ 200 Doug Gabriel .40 .15
❑ 201 Johnnie Morant .40 .15
❑ 202 Zack Crockett .40 .15
❑ 203 Derrick Burgess .40 .15
❑ 204 Donovan McNabb .75 .30
❑ 205 Brian Westbrook .50 .20
❑ 206 Reggie Brown .60 .25
❑ 207 Terrell Owens .75 .30
❑ 208 Ryan Moats .40 .15
❑ 209 Correll Buckhalter .50 .20
❑ 210 Jevon Kearse .50 .20
❑ 211 L.J. Smith .40 .15
❑ 212 Lamar Gordon .40 .15
❑ 213 Greg Lewis .40 .15
❑ 214 Ben Roethlisberger 1.25 .50
❑ 215 Willie Parker 1.00 .40
❑ 216 Jerome Bettis .75 .30
❑ 217 Hines Ward .75 .30
❑ 218 Troy Polamalu 1.00 .40
❑ 219 Heath Miller .50 .20
❑ 220 Antwaan Randle El .50 .20
❑ 221 Duce Staley .50 .20
❑ 222 Cedrick Wilson .40 .15
❑ 223 James Farrior .40 .15
❑ 224 Drew Brees .75 .30
❑ 225 LaDainian Tomlinson 1.00 .40
❑ 226 Keenan McCardell .40 .15
❑ 227 Antonio Gates .75 .30
❑ 228 Shawne Merriman .50 .20
❑ 229 Philip Rivers .75 .30
❑ 230 Vincent Jackson .40 .15
❑ 231 Donnie Edwards .40 .15
❑ 232 Eric Parker .40 .15
❑ 233 Reche Caldwell .40 .15
❑ 234 Alex Smith QB .75 .30
❑ 235 Frank Gore .75 .30
❑ 236 Brandon Lloyd .50 .20
❑ 237 Kevan Barlow .50 .20
❑ 238 Rashaun Woods .40 .15
❑ 239 Arnaz Battle .40 .15
❑ 240 Matt Hasselbeck .50 .20
❑ 241 Shaun Alexander .75 .30
❑ 242 Darrell Jackson .50 .20
❑ 243 Jerramy Stevens .50 .20
❑ 244 Lofa Tatupu .50 .20
❑ 245 D.J. Hackett .40 .15
❑ 246 Bobby Engram .40 .15
❑ 247 Joe Jurevicius .50 .20
❑ 248 Maurice Morris .40 .15
❑ 249 Marc Bulger .50 .20
❑ 250 Steven Jackson .75 .30
❑ 251 Torry Holt .50 .20
❑ 252 Isaac Bruce .50 .20
❑ 253 Kevin Curtis .40 .15
❑ 254 Marshall Faulk .50 .20
❑ 255 Shaun McDonald .40 .15
❑ 256 Chris Simms .50 .20
❑ 257 Cadillac Williams .75 .30
❑ 258 Joey Galloway .50 .20
❑ 259 Michael Clayton .50 .20
❑ 260 Derrick Brooks .50 .20
❑ 261 Ronde Barber .40 .15
❑ 262 Michael Pittman .40 .15
❑ 263 Alex Smith TE .40 .15
❑ 264 Simeon Rice .40 .15
❑ 265 Steve McNair .50 .20
❑ 266 Chris Brown .50 .20
❑ 267 Drew Bennett .40 .15
❑ 268 Brandon Jones .40 .15
❑ 269 Adam Jones .40 .15
❑ 270 Keith Bulluck .40 .15
❑ 271 Ben Troupe .40 .15
❑ 272 Jarrett Payton .40 .15
❑ 273 Tyrone Calico .40 .15
❑ 274 Bobby Wade .40 .15
❑ 275 Troy Fleming .40 .15
❑ 276 Mark Brunell .50 .20
❑ 277 Clinton Portis .75 .30
❑ 278 Santana Moss .50 .20
❑ 279 Jason Campbell .50 .20
❑ 280 Chris Cooley .40 .15
❑ 281 Carlos Rogers .40 .15
❑ 282 Ladell Betts .40 .15
❑ 283 Patrick Ramsey .50 .20
❑ 284 Taylor Jacobs .40 .15
❑ 285 James Thrash .40 .15
❑ 286 Adrian Wilson .40 .15
❑ 287 London Fletcher .40 .15
❑ 288 Lance Briggs .50 .20
❑ 289 Robert Mathis .40 .15
❑ 290 Rod Coleman .40 .15
❑ 291 Bart Scott RC 2.50 1.00
❑ 292 Brian Moorman RC .60 .25
❑ 293 Shayne Graham RC .60 .25
❑ 294 Kevin Kaesviharn RC .60 .25
❑ 295 Leigh Bodden RC .60 .25
❑ 296 Lousaka Polite RC .60 .25
❑ 297 Todd Devoe RC 1.25 .50
❑ 298 Scottie Vines .60 .25
❑ 299 Cullen Jenkins RC .60 .25
❑ 300 Donovan Morgan RC .60 .25
❑ 301 C.C. Brown .60 .25
❑ 302 Demarcus Faggins RC .60 .25
❑ 303 Shantee Orr RC .60 .25
❑ 304 Vashon Pearson RC .60 .25
❑ 305 Reggie Hayward RC .60 .25
❑ 306 Paul Spicer RC .60 .25
❑ 307 Kenny Wright RC .60 .25
❑ 308 Rich Alexis RC .60 .25
❑ 309 Terrence Melton RC .60 .25
❑ 310 Willie Whitehead RC .60 .25
❑ 311 Kendrick Clancy RC .60 .25
❑ 312 Mark Brown RC .60 .25
❑ 313 Tommy Kelly .60 .25
❑ 314 Josh Parry RC .60 .25
❑ 315 Malcolm Floyd RC 1.25 .50
❑ 316 Mike Adams RC .60 .25
❑ 317 Ben Emanuel RC .60 .25
❑ 318 Brandon Moore RC .60 .25
❑ 319 Chartric Darby RC .60 .25
❑ 320 Bryce Fisher RC .60 .25
❑ 321 D.D. Lewis RC .60 .25
❑ 322 Jimmy Williams DB RC .60 .25
❑ 323 Robert Pollard RC .60 .25
❑ 324 Chris Johnson RC .60 .25
❑ 325 Edell Shepherd RC .60 .25
❑ 326 O.J. Small RC .60 .25
❑ 327 Brad Kassell RC .60 .25
❑ 328 M.Leinart/R.Bush 4.00 1.50
❑ 329 M.Leinart/V.Young 4.00 1.50
❑ 330 White/Leinart/Bush 4.00 1.50
❑ 331 Matt Leinart RC 20.00 8.00
❑ 332 Chad Greenway RC 6.00 2.50
❑ 333 Devin Aromashodu RC 5.00 2.00
❑ 334 DeAngelo Williams RC 15.00 6.00
❑ 335 Travis Wilson RC 6.00 2.50
❑ 336 Leon Washington RC 10.00 4.00
❑ 337 Maurice Stovall RC 6.00 2.50
❑ 338 Michael Huff RC 8.00 3.00
❑ 339 Charlie Whitehurst RC 6.00 2.50
❑ 340 Vince Young RC 25.00 10.00
❑ 341 Jerious Norwood RC 10.00 4.00
❑ 342 D'Brickashaw Ferguson RC 6.00 2.50
❑ 343 Taurean Henderson RC 6.00 2.50
❑ 344 Dominique Byrd RC 5.00 2.00
❑ 345 Sinorice Moss RC 6.00 2.50
❑ 346 Martin Nance RC 5.00 2.00
❑ 347 Vernon Davis RC 12.00 5.00
❑ 348 Ko Simpson RC 5.00 2.00
❑ 349 Jerome Harrison RC 6.00 2.50
❑ 350 Jay Cutler RC 20.00 8.00
❑ 351 Alan Zemaitis RC 6.00 2.50
❑ 352 Haloti Ngata RC 6.00 2.50
❑ 353 Greg Lee RC 5.00 2.00
❑ 354 Laurence Maroney RC 15.00 6.00
❑ 355 Bobby Carpenter RC 6.00 2.50
❑ 356 Jonathan Orr RC 5.00 2.00
❑ 357 Marcedes Lewis RC 6.00 2.50
❑ 358 Brodrick Bunkley RC 6.00 2.50
❑ 359 Todd Watkins RC 5.00 2.00
❑ 360 Reggie Bush RC 50.00 20.00
❑ 361 Jimmy Williams RC 6.00 2.50
❑ 362 Maurice Drew RC 15.00 6.00
❑ 363 Mario Williams RC 10.00 4.00
❑ 364 Derek Hagan RC 6.00 2.50
❑ 365 Santonio Holmes RC 12.00 5.00
❑ 366 Tye Hill RC 6.00 2.50
❑ 367 Jason Avant RC 6.00 2.50
❑ 368 Tamba Hali RC 6.00 2.50
❑ 369 Joe Klopfenstein RC 5.00 2.00
❑ 370 LenDale White RC 12.00 5.00
❑ 371 DeMeco Ryans RC 8.00 3.00
❑ 372 Bruce Gradkowski RC 10.00 4.00
❑ 373 A.J. Hawk RC 12.00 5.00
❑ 374 Gabe Watson RC 5.00 2.00
❑ 375 Devin Hester RC 12.00 5.00
❑ 376 Demetrius Williams RC 6.00 2.50
❑ 377 Joseph Addai RC 20.00 8.00
❑ 378 Leonard Pope RC 6.00 2.50

❑ 379 Omar Jacobs RC 5.00 2.00
❑ 380 Brad Smith RC 6.00 2.50
❑ 381 Michael Robinson RC 6.00 2.50
❑ 382 Brodie Croyle RC 15.00 6.00
❑ 383 Anthony Fasano RC 6.00 2.50
❑ 384 Brian Calhoun RC 6.00 2.50
❑ 385 Chad Jackson RC 6.00 2.50
❑ 386 Drew Olson RC 5.00 2.00
❑ 387 Greg Jennings RC 12.00 5.00
❑ 388 Andre Hall RC 5.00 2.00
❑ 389 Ryan Gilbert RC 5.00 2.00
❑ 390 Tim Day RC 5.00 2.00
❑ 391 Brandon Williams RC 6.00 2.50
❑ 392 Mark Anderson RC 15.00 6.00
❑ 393 DonTrell Moore RC 5.00 2.00
❑ 394 [illegible] 10.00 4.00
❑ 395 Ernie Sims RC 8.00 3.00
❑ 396 Cedric Humes RC 6.00 2.50
❑ 397 Brandon Kirsch RC 6.00 2.50
❑ 398 Tony Scheffler RC 6.00 2.50
❑ 399 Kelly Jennings RC 6.00 2.50
❑ 400 Manny Lawson RC 6.00 2.50
❑ 401 Terrence Whitehead RC 5.00 2.00
❑ 402 Marcus Vick RC 5.00 2.00
❑ 403 De'Arrius Howard RC 6.00 2.50
❑ 404 Wendell Mathis RC 5.00 2.00
❑ 405 Abdul Hodge RC 6.00 2.50
❑ 406 Owen Daniels RC 6.00 2.50
❑ 407 Mike Hass RC 6.00 2.50
❑ 408 Brett Elliott RC 6.00 2.50
❑ 409 Kamerion Wimbley RC 6.00 2.50
❑ 410 Jeremy Bloom RC 5.00 2.00
❑ 411 D.J. Shockley RC 6.00 2.50
❑ 412 Darrell Bing RC 6.00 2.50
❑ 413 Miles Austin RC 5.00 2.00
❑ 414 D'Qwell Jackson RC 5.00 2.00
❑ 415 Tarvaris Jackson RC 10.00 4.00
❑ 416 Mathias Kiwanuka RC 8.00 3.00
❑ 417 Mike Bell RC 6.00 2.50
❑ 418 Paul Pinegar RC 5.00 2.00
❑ 419 David Thomas RC 6.00 2.50
❑ 420 Hank Baskett RC 6.00 2.50
❑ 421 P.J. Daniels RC 5.00 2.00
❑ 422 Jon Alston RC 6.00 2.50
❑ 423 Reggie McNeal RC 5.00 2.00
❑ 424 Brandon Marshall RC 6.00 2.50
❑ 425 Gerald Riggs RC 6.00 2.50
❑ 426 Delanie Walker RC 5.00 2.00
❑ 427 Erik Meyer RC 5.00 2.00
❑ 428 Jeff Webb RC 5.00 2.00
❑ 429 Skyler Green RC 6.00 2.50
❑ 430 Thomas Howard RC 6.00 2.50

2007 Select

❑ 1 Tony Romo 1.50 .60
❑ 2 Julius Jones .60 .25
❑ 3 Terry Glenn .60 .25
❑ 4 Terrell Owens .75 .30
❑ 5 Jason Witten .60 .25
❑ 6 Marion Barber .60 .25
❑ 7 Patrick Crayton .50 .20
❑ 8 Bradie James .50 .20
❑ 9 DeMarcus Ware .60 .25
❑ 10 Roy Williams S .60 .25
❑ 11 Eli Manning .75 .30
❑ 12 Plaxico Burress .60 .25
❑ 13 Jeremy Shockey .60 .25
❑ 14 Brandon Jacobs .60 .25
❑ 15 Sinorice Moss .60 .25
❑ 16 Antonio Pierce .50 .20
❑ 17 David Tyree .50 .20
❑ 18 Donovan McNabb .75 .30
❑ 19 Brian Westbrook .60 .25
❑ 20 Reggie Brown .60 .25
❑ 21 L.J. Smith .50 .20
❑ 22 Hank Baskett .60 .25
❑ 23 Jeremiah Trotter .50 .20
❑ 24 Trent Cole .50 .20
❑ 25 Lito Sheppard .50 .20
❑ 26 Jason Campbell .60 .25
❑ 27 Clinton Portis .60 .25
❑ 28 Santana Moss .60 .25
❑ 29 Brandon Lloyd .60 .25
❑ 30 Chris Cooley .50 .20
❑ 31 Sean Taylor .50 .20
❑ 32 Lemar Marshall .50 .20
❑ 33 Ladell Betts .50 .20
❑ 34 London Fletcher .50 .20
❑ 35 Rex Grossman .60 .25
❑ 36 Cedric Benson .60 .25
❑ 37 Muhsin Muhammad .60 .25
❑ 38 Bernard Berrian .50 .20
❑ 39 Desmond Clark .50 .20
❑ 40 Lance Briggs .50 .20
❑ 41 Robbie Gould .50 .20
❑ 42 Devin Hester .75 .30
❑ 43 Mark Anderson .60 .25
❑ 44 Brian Urlacher .75 .30
❑ 45 Jon Kitna .50 .20
❑ 46 Kevin Jones .50 .20
❑ 47 Roy Williams WR .60 .25
❑ 48 Mike Furrey .60 .25
❑ 49 Cory Redding .50 .20
❑ 50 Ernie Sims .50 .20
❑ 51 Tatum Bell .60 .25
❑ 52 Brian Calhoun .50 .20
❑ 53 Brett Favre 1.50 .60
❑ 54 Vernand Morency .60 .25
❑ 55 Donald Driver .60 .25
❑ 56 Greg Jennings .60 .25
❑ 57 Aaron Kampman .60 .25
❑ 58 Charles Woodson .60 .25
❑ 59 A.J. Hawk .75 .30
❑ 60 Nick Barnett .50 .20
❑ 61 Aaron Rodgers .75 .30
❑ 62 Tarvaris Jackson .75 .30
❑ 63 Chester Taylor .50 .20
❑ 64 Troy Williamson .50 .20
❑ 65 Jim Kleinsasser .50 .20
❑ 66 Dwight Smith .50 .20
❑ 67 Antoine Winfield .50 .20
❑ 68 E.J. Henderson .50 .20
❑ 69 Mewelde Moore .50 .20
❑ 70 Michael Vick .75 .30
❑ 71 Warrick Dunn .60 .25
❑ 72 Joe Horn .60 .25
❑ 73 Michael Jenkins .60 .25
❑ 74 Alge Crumpler .60 .25
❑ 75 DeAngelo Hall .60 .25
❑ 76 Keith Brooking .50 .20
❑ 77 Lawyer Milloy .50 .20
❑ 78 Jerious Norwood .60 .25
❑ 79 Matt Schaub .60 .25
❑ 80 Jake Delhomme .60 .25
❑ 81 DeShaun Foster .60 .25
❑ 82 Steve Smith .60 .25
❑ 83 Keyshawn Johnson .60 .25
❑ 84 Julius Peppers .60 .25
❑ 85 DeAngelo Williams .75 .30
❑ 86 Chris Draft .50 .20
❑ 87 Drew Brees .60 .25
❑ 88 Deuce McAllister .60 .25
❑ 89 Scott Fujita .50 .20
❑ 90 Marques Colston .75 .30
❑ 91 Terrance Copper .50 .20
❑ 92 Will Smith .50 .20
❑ 93 Charles Grant .50 .20
❑ 94 Devery Henderson .50 .20
❑ 95 Reggie Bush 1.00 .40
❑ 96 Jeff Garcia .60 .25
❑ 97 Cadillac Williams .60 .25
❑ 98 Joey Galloway .60 .25
❑ 99 Michael Clayton .60 .25
❑ 100 Alex Smith TE .50 .20
❑ 101 Ronde Barber .50 .20
❑ 102 Jermaine Phillips .50 .20
❑ 103 Derrick Brooks .60 .25
❑ 104 Matt Leinart .75 .30
❑ 105 Edgerrin James .75 .30
❑ 106 Anquan Boldin .60 .25
❑ 107 Larry Fitzgerald .60 .25
❑ 108 Neil Rackers .50 .20
❑ 109 Adrian Wilson .50 .20
❑ 110 Karlos Dansby .50 .20
❑ 111 Chike Okeafor .50 .20
❑ 112 Marc Bulger .60 .25
❑ 113 Steven Jackson .75 .30
❑ 114 Torry Holt .60 .25
❑ 115 Isaac Bruce .60 .25
❑ 116 Joe Klopfenstein .50 .20
❑ 117 Randy McMichael .50 .20
❑ 118 Will Witherspoon .50 .20
❑ 119 Drew Bennett .50 .20
❑ 120 Alex Smith QB .75 .30
❑ 121 Frank Gore .75 .30
❑ 122 Arnaz Battle .50 .20
❑ 123 Ashley Lelie .60 .25
❑ 124 Vernon Davis .60 .25
❑ 125 Walt Harris .50 .20
❑ 126 Brandon Moore .50 .20
❑ 127 Nate Clements .50 .20
❑ 128 Matt Hasselbeck .60 .25
❑ 129 Shaun Alexander .60 .25
❑ 130 Deion Branch .60 .25
❑ 131 Darrell Jackson .60 .25
❑ 132 Nate Burleson .50 .20
❑ 133 Julian Peterson .50 .20
❑ 134 Lofa Tatupu .60 .25
❑ 135 Mack Strong .50 .20
❑ 136 Josh Brown .50 .20
❑ 137 J.P. Losman .60 .25
❑ 138 Anthony Thomas .50 .20
❑ 139 Lee Evans .60 .25
❑ 140 Josh Reed .50 .20
❑ 141 Roscoe Parrish .50 .20
❑ 142 Aaron Schobel .50 .20
❑ 143 Donte Whitner .50 .20
❑ 144 Shaud Williams .50 .20
❑ 145 Daunte Culpepper .60 .25
❑ 146 Ronnie Brown .60 .25
❑ 147 Chris Chambers .60 .25
❑ 148 Marty Booker .50 .20
❑ 149 Derek Hagan .50 .20
❑ 150 Jason Taylor .50 .20
❑ 151 Vonnie Holliday .50 .20
❑ 152 Zach Thomas .60 .25
❑ 153 Channing Crowder .50 .20
❑ 154 Joey Porter .50 .20
❑ 155 Tom Brady 1.50 .60
❑ 156 Laurence Maroney .75 .30
❑ 157 Chad Jackson .50 .20
❑ 158 Wes Welker .75 .30
❑ 159 Ben Watson .50 .20
❑ 160 Donte Stallworth .60 .25
❑ 161 Rosevelt Colvin .50 .20
❑ 162 Ty Warren .50 .20
❑ 163 Asante Samuel .50 .20
❑ 164 Adalius Thomas .50 .20
❑ 165 Tedy Bruschi .75 .30
❑ 166 Chad Pennington .60 .25
❑ 167 Thomas Jones .60 .25
❑ 168 Laveranues Coles .60 .25
❑ 169 Jerricho Cotchery .50 .20
❑ 170 Chris Baker .50 .20
❑ 171 Bryan Thomas .50 .20
❑ 172 Leon Washington .60 .25
❑ 173 Jonathan Vilma .60 .25
❑ 174 Eric Barton .50 .20
❑ 175 Erik Coleman .50 .20
❑ 176 Steve McNair .60 .25
❑ 177 Willis McGahee .60 .25
❑ 178 Derrick Mason .50 .20
❑ 179 Demetrius Williams .50 .20
❑ 180 Todd Heap .50 .20
❑ 181 Ray Lewis .75 .30
❑ 182 Trevor Pryce .50 .20
❑ 183 Bart Scott .60 .25
❑ 184 Terrell Suggs .50 .20
❑ 185 Mark Clayton .60 .25
❑ 186 Carson Palmer .75 .30
❑ 187 Rudi Johnson .60 .25
❑ 188 Chad Johnson .60 .25
❑ 189 T.J. Houshmandzadeh .60 .25

❑	190	Robert Geathers	.50	.20
❑	191	Justin Smith	.50	.20
❑	192	Tory James	.50	.20
❑	193	Landon Johnson	.50	.20
❑	194	Shayne Graham	.50	.20
❑	195	Charlie Frye	.60	.25
❑	196	Reuben Droughns	.60	.25
❑	197	Braylon Edwards	.60	.25
❑	198	Travis Wilson	.50	.20
❑	199	Kellen Winslow	.60	.25
❑	200	Kamerion Wimbley	.50	.20
❑	201	Sean Jones	.50	.20
❑	202	Andra Davis	.50	.20
❑	203	Jamal Lewis	.60	.25
❑	204	Ben Roethlisberger	1.00	.40
❑	205	Willie Parker	.75	.30
❑	206	Hines Ward	.75	.30
❑	207	Santonio Holmes	.60	.25
❑	208	Heath Miller	.50	.20
❑	209	Troy Polamalu	.75	.30
❑	210	James Farrior	.50	.20
❑	211	Cedrick Wilson	.50	.20
❑	212	Dunta Robinson	.50	.20
❑	213	Ahman Green	.60	.25
❑	214	Andre Johnson	.60	.25
❑	215	Jerome Mathis	.50	.20
❑	216	Owen Daniels	.50	.20
❑	217	DeMeco Ryans	.60	.25
❑	218	Wali Lundy	.50	.20
❑	219	Mario Williams	.60	.25
❑	220	Peyton Manning	1.25	.50
❑	221	Joseph Addai	1.00	.40
❑	222	Marvin Harrison	.75	.30
❑	223	Reggie Wayne	.60	.25
❑	224	Dallas Clark	.50	.20
❑	225	Robert Mathis	.50	.20
❑	226	Cato June	.50	.20
❑	227	Adam Vinatieri	.60	.25
❑	228	Bob Sanders	.60	.25
❑	229	Dwight Freeney	.60	.25
❑	230	Byron Leftwich	.60	.25
❑	231	Fred Taylor	.60	.25
❑	232	Matt Jones	.60	.25
❑	233	Reggie Williams	.60	.25
❑	234	Marcedes Lewis	.50	.20
❑	235	Bobby McCray	.50	.20
❑	236	Rashean Mathis	.50	.20
❑	237	Maurice Jones-Drew	.75	.30
❑	238	Ernest Wilford	.50	.20
❑	239	Daryl Smith	.50	.20
❑	240	Vince Young	1.00	.40
❑	241	LenDale White	.60	.25
❑	242	Brandon Jones	.50	.20
❑	243	Bo Scaife	.50	.20
❑	244	Keith Bulluck	.50	.20
❑	245	Chris Hope	.50	.20
❑	246	Kyle Vanden Bosch	.50	.20
❑	247	Roydell Williams	.50	.20
❑	248	Jay Cutler	.75	.30
❑	249	Travis Henry	.60	.25
❑	250	Javon Walker	.60	.25
❑	251	Rod Smith	.60	.25
❑	252	Tony Scheffler	.50	.20
❑	253	Elvis Dumervil	.50	.20
❑	254	Champ Bailey	.60	.25
❑	255	Mike Bell	.60	.25
❑	256	Brandon Marshall	.60	.25
❑	257	Al Wilson	.50	.20
❑	258	Trent Green	.60	.25
❑	259	Larry Johnson	.75	.30
❑	260	Eddie Kennison	.50	.20
❑	261	Samie Parker	.50	.20
❑	262	Tony Gonzalez	.60	.25
❑	263	Jared Allen	.50	.20
❑	264	Kawika Mitchell	.50	.20
❑	265	Tamba Hali	.50	.20
❑	266	Dante Hall	.60	.25
❑	267	Brodie Croyle	.75	.30
❑	268	Andrew Walter	.50	.20
❑	269	LaMont Jordan	.60	.25
❑	270	Dominic Rhodes	.60	.25
❑	271	Randy Moss	.75	.30
❑	272	Ronald Curry	.60	.25
❑	273	Courtney Anderson	.50	.20
❑	274	Derrick Burgess	.50	.20
❑	275	Warren Sapp	.60	.25
❑	276	Michael Huff	.60	.25
❑	277	Thomas Howard	.50	.20
❑	278	Kirk Morrison	.50	.20
❑	279	Philip Rivers	.75	.30
❑	280	LaDainian Tomlinson	1.00	.40
❑	281	Vincent Jackson	.50	.20
❑	282	Lorenzo Neal	.50	.20
❑	283	Antonio Gates	.60	.25
❑	284	Shawne Merriman	.60	.25
❑	285	Shaun Phillips	.50	.20
❑	286	Michael Turner	.60	.25
❑	287	Jamal Williams	.50	.20
❑	288	Nate Kaeding	.50	.20
❑	289	Michael Okwo RC	1.50	.60
❑	290	Gary Russell RC	2.00	.75
❑	291	Josh Wilson RC	1.50	.60
❑	292	Thomas Clayton RC	1.50	.60
❑	293	Jerard Rabb RC	1.50	.60
❑	294	Roy Hall RC	2.00	.75
❑	295	LaMarr Woodley RC	2.00	.75
❑	296	Eric Wright RC	2.00	.75
❑	297	Dan Bazuin RC	1.50	.60
❑	298	A.J. Davis RC	1.25	.50
❑	299	Buster Davis RC	1.50	.60
❑	300	Stewart Bradley RC	2.00	.75
❑	301	Toby Korrodi RC	1.50	.60
❑	302	Marcus McCauley RC	1.50	.60
❑	303	DeMarcus Tank Tyler RC	1.50	.60
❑	304	Jon Abbate RC	1.25	.50
❑	305	Ikaika Alama-Francis RC	2.00	.75
❑	306	Tim Crowder RC	2.00	.75
❑	307	D'Juan Woods RC	1.50	.60
❑	308	Tim Shaw RC	1.50	.60
❑	309	Fred Bennett RC	1.25	.50
❑	310	Victor Abiamiri RC	2.00	.75
❑	311	Eric Weddle RC	1.50	.60
❑	312	Danny Ware RC	2.00	.75
❑	313	Quentin Moses RC	1.50	.60
❑	314	Ryan McBean RC	2.00	.75
❑	315	David Harris RC	1.50	.60
❑	316	David Irons RC	1.25	.50
❑	317	Syndric Steptoe RC	1.50	.60
❑	318	Eric Frampton RC	1.50	.60
❑	319	Jemalle Cornelius RC	1.50	.60
❑	320	Earl Everett RC	1.50	.60
❑	321	Alonzo Coleman RC	1.50	.60
❑	322	Josh Gattis RC	1.25	.50
❑	323	Zak DeOssie RC	1.50	.60
❑	324	Jon Beason RC	2.00	.75
❑	325	Joe Staley RC	1.50	.60
❑	326	Aaron Rouse RC	2.00	.75
❑	327	Reggie Ball RC	1.50	.60
❑	328	Rufus Alexander RC	2.00	.75
❑	329	Daymeion Hughes RC	1.50	.60
❑	330	Justin Durant RC	1.50	.60
❑	331	JaMarcus Russell RC	15,00	6.00
❑	332	Paul Williams RC	5.00	2.00
❑	333	Kenny Irons RC	6.00	2.50
❑	334	Chris Davis RC	5.00	2.00
❑	335	Darius Walker RC	6.00	2.50
❑	336	Dwayne Bowe RC	12.00	5.00
❑	337	Isaiah Stanback RC	6.00	2.50
❑	338	Leon Hall RC	5.00	2.00
❑	339	Sidney Rice RC	10.00	4.00
❑	340	Amobi Okoye RC	6.00	2.50
❑	341	Adrian Peterson RC	50.00	20.00
❑	342	LaRon Landry RC	8.00	3.00
❑	343	Lorenzo Booker RC	6.00	2.50
❑	344	Craig Buster Davis RC	6.00	2.50
❑	345	Mike Walker RC	5.00	2.00
❑	346	Zach Miller RC	6.00	2.50
❑	347	Levi Brown RC	6.00	2.50
❑	348	Brian Leonard RC	8.00	3.00
❑	349	Aundrae Allison RC	5.00	2.00
❑	350	Brandon Siler RC	5.00	2.00
❑	351	Calvin Johnson RC	20.00	8.00
❑	352	Gaines Adams RC	6.00	2.50
❑	353	Anthony Gonzalez RC	10.00	4.00
❑	354	John Beck RC	12.00	5.00
❑	355	Joe Thomas RC	6.00	2.50
❑	356	Michael Bush RC	8.00	3.00
❑	357	Courtney Taylor RC	5.00	2.00
❑	358	Lawrence Timmons RC	6.00	2.50
❑	359	Drew Stanton RC	8.00	3.00
❑	360	Chansi Stuckey RC	5.00	2.00
❑	361	Greg Olsen RC	8.00	3.00
❑	362	Rhema McKnight RC	5.00	2.00
❑	363	Antonio Pittman RC	5.00	2.00
❑	364	Kevin Kolb RC	10.00	4.00
❑	365	Alan Branch RC	5.00	2.00
❑	366	Robert Meachem RC	6.00	2.50
❑	367	Troy Smith RC	8.00	3.00
❑	368	Jamaal Anderson RC	5.00	2.00
❑	369	Tony Hunt RC	6.00	2.50
❑	370	David Clowney RC	6.00	2.50
❑	371	Brady Quinn RC	20.00	8.00
❑	372	Michael Griffin RC	6.00	2.50
❑	373	Jared Zabransky RC	6.00	2.50
❑	374	Jason Hill RC	6.00	2.50
❑	375	Trent Edwards RC	12.00	5.00
❑	376	Dwayne Jarrett RC	8.00	3.00
❑	377	DeShawn Wynn RC	6.00	2.50
❑	378	Patrick Willis RC	12.00	5.00
❑	379	Steve Smith USC RC	8.00	3.00
❑	380	David Ball RC	4.00	1.50
❑	381	Marshawn Lynch RC	12.00	5.00
❑	382	Paul Posluszny RC	8.00	3.00
❑	383	Johnnie Lee Higgins RC	5.00	2.00
❑	384	Kolby Smith RC	8.00	3.00
❑	385	Ted Ginn Jr. RC	10.00	4.00
❑	386	Adam Carriker RC	5.00	2.00
❑	387	Tyler Palko RC	6.00	2.50
❑	388	Joel Filani RC	5.00	2.00
❑	389	Garrett Wolfe RC	8.00	3.00
❑	390	Ryne Robinson RC	5.00	2.00
❑	391	Reggie Nelson RC	5.00	2.00
❑	392	Dallas Baker RC	5.00	2.00
❑	393	Dwayne Wright RC	5.00	2.00
❑	394	Scott Chandler RC	5.00	2.00
❑	395	Jordan Kent RC	5.00	2.00
❑	396	Jarvis Moss RC	6.00	2.50
❑	397	Jonathan Wade RC	5.00	2.00
❑	398	Ben Grubbs RC	5.00	2.00
❑	399	Jason Snelling RC	5.00	2.00
❑	400	Jeff Rowe RC	5.00	2.00
❑	401	Aaron Ross RC	6.00	2.50
❑	402	Jarrett Hicks RC	5.00	2.00
❑	403	Chris Henry RC	6.00	2.50
❑	404	James Jones RC	10.00	4.00
❑	405	Matt Spaeth RC	6.00	2.50
❑	406	Brandon Meriweather RC	6.00	2.50
❑	407	Nate Ilaoa RC	6.00	2.50
❑	408	Brandon Myles RC	5.00	2.00
❑	409	Ray McDonald RC	5.00	2.00
❑	410	Chris Leak RC	5.00	2.00
❑	411	Darrelle Revis RC	6.00	2.50
❑	412	Ahmad Bradshaw RC	8.00	3.00
❑	413	Tyler Thigpen RC	6.00	2.50
❑	414	Justise Hairston RC	5.00	2.00
❑	415	Charles Johnson RC	4.00	1.50
❑	416	Anthony Spencer RC	6.00	2.50
❑	417	Legedu Naanee RC	5.00	2.00
❑	418	Kenneth Darby RC	6.00	2.50
❑	419	Steve Breaston RC	5.00	2.00
❑	420	Ben Patrick RC	5.00	2.00
❑	421	Chris Houston RC	5.00	2.00
❑	422	Jordan Palmer RC	6.00	2.50
❑	423	Laurent Robinson RC	5.00	2.00
❑	424	Selvin Young RC	8.00	3.00
❑	425	Justin Harrell RC	6.00	2.50
❑	426	Sabby Piscitelli RC	6.00	2.50
❑	427	Yamon Figurs RC	6.00	2.50
❑	428	Brandon Jackson RC	8.00	3.00
❑	429	Jacoby Jones RC	6.00	2.50
❑	430	H.B. Blades RC	5.00	2.00

1995 Select Certified

Card	Mint	Exc
❑ COMPLETE SET (135)	40.00	15.00
❑ 1 Marshall Faulk	4.00	1.50
❑ 2 Heath Shuler	.50	.20
❑ 3 Garrison Hearst	1.00	.40
❑ 4 Errict Rhett	.50	.20
❑ 5 Jeff George	.50	.20
❑ 6 Jerome Bettis	1.00	.40
❑ 7 Jim Kelly	1.00	.40
❑ 8 Rick Mirer	.50	.20
❑ 9 Willie Davis	.50	.20
❑ 10 Steve Young	2.50	1.00
❑ 11 Erik Kramer	.25	.08
❑ 12 Natrone Means	.50	.20
❑ 13 Jeff Blake RC	3.00	1.25
❑ 14 Neil O'Donnell	.50	.20
❑ 15 [illegible]	[illegible]	[illegible]
❑ 16 Randall Cunningham	1.00	.40
❑ 17 Emmitt Smith	5.00	2.00
❑ 18 Tim Brown	1.00	.40
❑ 19 Shannon Sharpe	.50	.20
❑ 20 Boomer Esiason	.50	.20
❑ 21 Barry Sanders	5.00	2.00
❑ 22 Rodney Hampton	.50	.20
❑ 23 Robert Brooks	1.00	.40
❑ 24 Jim Everett	.25	.08
❑ 25 Gary Brown	.25	.08
❑ 26 Drew Bledsoe	1.25	.50
❑ 27 Desmond Howard	.50	.20
❑ 28 Cris Carter	1.00	.40
❑ 29 Marcus Allen	1.00	.40
❑ 30 Dan Marino	6.00	2.50
❑ 31 Warren Moon	.50	.20
❑ 32 Dave Krieg	.25	.08
❑ 33 Ben Coates	.50	.20
❑ 34 Terance Mathis	.50	.20
❑ 35 Mario Bates	.50	.20
❑ 36 Andre Reed	.50	.20
❑ 37 Dave Brown	.50	.20
❑ 38 Jeff Graham	.25	.08
❑ 39 Johnny Mitchell	.25	.08
❑ 40 Carl Pickens	.50	.20
❑ 41 Jeff Hostetler	.50	.20
❑ 42 Vinny Testaverde	.50	.20
❑ 43 Ricky Watters	.50	.20
❑ 44 Troy Aikman	3.00	1.25
❑ 45 Byron Bam Morris	.25	.08
❑ 46 John Elway	6.00	2.50
❑ 47 Junior Seau	1.00	.40
❑ 48 Scott Mitchell	.50	.20
❑ 49 Jerry Rice	3.00	1.25
❑ 50 Brett Favre	6.00	2.50
❑ 51 Chris Warren	.50	.20
❑ 52 Chris Chandler	.50	.20
❑ 53 Lorenzo White	.25	.08
❑ 54 Craig Erickson	.25	.08
❑ 55 Alvin Harper	.25	.08
❑ 56 Steve Beuerlein	[illegible]	[illegible]
❑ 57 Edgar Bennett	.50	.20
❑ 58 Steve Bono	.50	.20
❑ 59 Eric Green	.25	.08
❑ 60 Jake Reed	.50	.20
❑ 61 Terry Kirby	.50	.20
❑ 62 Vincent Brisby	.25	.08
❑ 63 Lake Dawson	.50	.20
❑ 64 Torrance Small	.25	.08
❑ 65 Mark Brunell	1.25	.50
❑ 66 Haywood Jeffires	.25	.08
❑ 67 Flipper Anderson	.25	.08
❑ 68 Ronald Moore	.25	.08
❑ 69 LeShon Johnson	.50	.20
❑ 70 Rocket Ismail	.50	.20
❑ 71 Herman Moore	1.00	.40
❑ 72 Charlie Garner	1.00	.40
❑ 73 Anthony Miller	.50	.20
❑ 74 Greg Lloyd	.50	.20
❑ 75 Michael Irvin	1.00	.40
❑ 76 Stan Humphries	.50	.20
❑ 77 Leroy Hoard	.25	.08
❑ 78 Deion Sanders Mail Out	3.00	1.25
❑ 79 Darnay Scott	.50	.20
❑ 80 Chris Miller	.25	.08
❑ 81 Curtis Conway	1.00	.40
❑ 82 Trent Dilfer	1.00	.40
❑ 83 Bruce Smith	1.00	.40
❑ 84 Reggie Brooks	.50	.20
❑ 85 Frank Reich	.25	.08
❑ 86 Henry Ellard	.50	.20
❑ 87 Eric Metcalf	.50	.20
❑ 88 Sean Gilbert	.50	.20
❑ 89 Larry Centers	.50	.20
❑ 90 Ricky Ervins	.25	.08
❑ 91 Craig Heyward	.50	.20
❑ 92 Rod Woodson	.50	.20
❑ 93 Steve Walsh	.25	.08
❑ 94 Fred Barnett	.50	.20
❑ 95 William Floyd	.50	.20
❑ 96 Harvey Williams	.25	.08
❑ 97 Greg Hill	.50	.20
❑ 98 Irving Fryar	.50	.20
❑ 99 Kevin Williams WR	.50	.20
❑ 100 Herschel Walker	.50	.20
❑ 101 Sean Dawkins	.50	.20
❑ 102 Michael Haynes	[illegible]	[illegible]
❑ 103 Reggie White	1.00	.40
❑ 104 Robert Smith	1.00	.40
❑ 105 Todd Collins RC	6.00	2.50
❑ 106 Michael Westbrook RC	2.00	.75
❑ 107 Frank Sanders RC	2.00	.75
❑ 108 Christian Fauria RC	1.00	.40
❑ 109 Stoney Case RC	.50	.20
❑ 110 Jimmy Oliver RC	.50	.20
❑ 111 Mark Bruener RC	1.00	.40
❑ 112 Rodney Thomas RC	1.00	.40
❑ 113 Chris T.Jones RC	.50	.20
❑ 114 James A.Stewart RC	.50	.20
❑ 115 Kevin Carter RC	2.00	.75
❑ 116 Eric Zeier RC	2.00	.75
❑ 117 Curtis Martin RC	15.00	6.00
❑ 118 James O. Stewart RC	5.00	2.00
❑ 119 Joe Aska RC	.50	.20
❑ 120 Ken Dilger RC	2.00	.75
❑ 121 Tyrone Wheatley RC	5.00	2.00
❑ 122 Ray Zellars RC	1.00	.40
❑ 123 Kyle Brady RC	2.00	.75
❑ 124 Chad May RC	.50	.20
❑ 125 Napoleon Kaufman RC	5.00	2.00
❑ 126 Terrell Davis RC	12.00	5.00
❑ 127 Warren Sapp RC	6.00	2.50
❑ 128 Sherman Williams RC	.50	.20
❑ 129 Kordell Stewart RC	8.00	3.00
❑ 130 Ki-Jana Carter RC	2.00	.75
❑ 131 Terrell Fletcher RC	.50	.20
❑ 132 Rashaan Salaam RC	1.00	.40
❑ 133 J.J. Stokes RC	2.00	.75
❑ 134 Kerry Collins RC	8.00	3.00
❑ 135 Joey Galloway RC	8.00	3.00
❑ P7 Dan Marino Promo	5.00	2.00
❑ P10 Steve Young Promo	2.00	.75
❑ P44 Troy Aikman Promo	2.50	1.00

1996 Select Certified

Card	Mint	Exc
❑ COMPLETE SET (125)	50.00	20.00
❑ 1 Isaac Bruce	.75	.30
❑ 2 Rick Mirer	.40	.15
❑ 3 Jake Reed	.40	.15
❑ 4 Reggie White	.75	.30
❑ 5 Harvey Williams	.20	.07
❑ 6 Jim Everett	.20	.07
❑ 7 Tony Martin	.40	.15
❑ 8 Craig Heyward	.20	.07
❑ 9 Tamarick Vanover	.40	.15
❑ 10 Hugh Douglas	.40	.15
❑ 11 Erik Kramer	.20	.07
❑ 12 Charlie Garner	.40	.15
❑ 13 Erric Pegram	.20	.07
❑ 14 Scott Mitchell	.40	.15
❑ 15 Michael Westbrook	.75	.30
❑ 16 Robert Smith	.40	.15
❑ 17 Kerry Collins	.75	.30
❑ 18 Derek Loville	.20	.07
❑ 19 Jeff Blake	.75	.30
❑ 20 Terry Kirby	.40	.15
❑ 21 Bruce Smith	.40	.15
❑ 22 Stan Humphries	.40	.15
❑ 23 Rodney Thomas	.20	.07
❑ 24 Wayne Chrebet	1.00	.40
❑ 25 Napoleon Kaufman	.75	.30
❑ 26 Marshall Faulk	1.00	.40
❑ 27 Emmitt Smith	3.00	1.25
❑ 28 Natrone Means	.40	.15
❑ 29 Neil O'Donnell	.40	.15
❑ 30 Warren Moon	.40	.15
❑ 31 Junior Seau	.75	.30
❑ 32 Chris Sanders	.40	.15
❑ 33 Barry Sanders	3.00	1.25
❑ 34 Jeff Graham	.20	.07
❑ 35 Kordell Stewart	.75	.30
❑ 36 Jim Harbaugh	.40	.15
❑ 37 Chris Warren	.40	.15
❑ 38 Cris Carter	.75	.30
❑ 39 J.J. Stokes	.75	.30
❑ 40 Tyrone Wheatley	.40	.15
❑ 41 Terrell Davis	1.50	.60
❑ 42 Mark Brunell	1.25	.50
❑ 43 Steve Young	1.50	.60
❑ 44 Rodney Hampton	.40	.15
❑ 45 Drew Bledsoe	1.25	.50
❑ 46 Larry Centers	.40	.15
❑ 47 Ken Norton Jr.	.20	.07
❑ 48 Deion Sanders	1.25	.50
❑ 49 Alvin Harper	.20	.07
❑ 50 Trent Dilfer	.75	.30
❑ 51 Steve McNair	1.50	.60
❑ 52 Robert Brooks	.75	.30
❑ 53 Edgar Bennett	.40	.15
❑ 54 Troy Aikman	2.00	.75
❑ 55 Dan Marino	4.00	1.50
❑ 56 Steve Bono	.20	.07
❑ 57 Marcus Allen	.75	.30
❑ 58 Rodney Peete	.20	.07
❑ 59 Ben Coates	.40	.15
❑ 60 Yancey Thigpen	.40	.15
❑ 61 Tim Brown	.75	.30
❑ 62 Jerry Rice	2.00	.75
❑ 63 Quinn Early	.20	.07
❑ 64 Ricky Watters	.40	.15
❑ 65 Thurman Thomas	.75	.30
❑ 66 Greg Lloyd	.40	.15
❑ 67 Eric Metcalf	.20	.07
❑ 68 Jeff George	.40	.15
❑ 69 John Elway	4.00	1.50
❑ 70 Frank Sanders	.40	.15
❑ 71 Curtis Conway	.75	.30
❑ 72 Greg Hill	.40	.15
❑ 73 Darick Holmes	.20	.07
❑ 74 Herman Moore	.40	.15
❑ 75 Carl Pickens	.40	.15
❑ 76 Eric Zeier	.20	.07
❑ 77 Curtis Martin	1.50	.60
❑ 78 Rashaan Salaam	.40	.15
❑ 79 Joey Galloway	.75	.30
❑ 80 Jeff Hostetler	.20	.07
❑ 81 Jim Kelly	.75	.30
❑ 82 Dave Brown	.20	.07
❑ 83 Sean Dawkins	.20	.07
❑ 84 Michael Irvin	.75	.30
❑ 85 Brett Favre	4.00	1.50
❑ 86 Cedric Jones RC	.25	.08
❑ 87 Jeff Lewis RC	.50	.20
❑ 88 Alex Van Dyke RC	.50	.20
❑ 89 Regan Upshaw RC	.25	.08
❑ 90 Karim Abdul-Jabbar RC	1.00	.40
❑ 91 Marvin Harrison RC	12.00	5.00
❑ 92 Stephen Davis RC	8.00	3.00
❑ 93 Terry Glenn RC	4.00	1.50
❑ 94 Kevin Hardy RC	1.00	.40
❑ 95 Stanley Pritchett RC	.25	.08
❑ 96 Willie Anderson RC	.25	.08
❑ 97 Lawrence Phillips RC	.50	.20
❑ 98 Bobby Hoying RC	1.00	.40
❑ 99 Amani Toomer RC	4.00	1.50
❑ 100 Eddie George RC	6.00	2.50
❑ 101 Stepfret Williams RC	.25	.08

❑ 102	Eric Moulds RC	5.00	2.00
❑ 103	Simeon Rice RC	2.50	1.00
❑ 104	John Mobley RC	.25	.08
❑ 105	Keyshawn Johnson RC	4.00	1.50
❑ 106	Daryl Gardener RC	.25	.08
❑ 107	Tony Banks RC	1.00	.40
❑ 108	Bobby Engram RC	1.00	.40
❑ 109	Jonathan Ogden RC	1.00	.40
❑ 110	Eddie Kennison RC	1.00	.40
❑ 111	Danny Kanell RC	1.00	.40
❑ 112	Tony Brackens RC	1.00	.40
❑ 113	Tim Biakabutuka RC	1.00	.40
❑ 114	Leeland McElroy RC	.50	.20
❑ 115	Rickey Dudley RC	1.00	.40
❑ 116	Troy Aikman SS	1.00	.40
❑ 117	Brett Favre SS	2.00	.75
❑ 118	Drew Bledsoe SS	.75	.30
❑ 119	Steve Young SS	.75	.30
❑ 120	Kerry Collins SS	.75	.30
❑ 121	John Elway SS	2.00	.75
❑ 122	Dan Marino SS	2.00	.75
❑ 123	Kordell Stewart SS	.75	.30
❑ 124	Jeff Blake SS	.40	.15
❑ 125	Jim Harbaugh SS	.40	.15

1993 SP

❑	COMPLETE SET (270)	60.00	25.00
❑ 1	Curtis Conway FOIL RC	4.00	1.50
❑ 2	John Copeland FOIL RC	.75	.30
❑ 3	Kevin Williams RC WR FOIL	1.50	.60
❑ 4	Dan Williams FOIL RC	.75	.30
❑ 5	Patrick Bates FOIL RC	.75	.30
❑ 6	Jerome Bettis FOIL RC	25.00	15.00
❑ 7	O.J.McDuffie FOIL RC	3.00	1.25
❑ 8	Robert Smith FOIL RC	8.00	3.00
❑ 9	Drew Bledsoe FOIL RC	30.00	12.50
❑ 10	Irv Smith FOIL RC	.75	.30
❑ 11	Marvin Jones FOIL RC	.75	.30
❑ 12	Victor Bailey FOIL RC	.75	.30
❑ 13	Garrison Hearst FOIL RC	8.00	3.00
❑ 14	Natrone Means FOIL RC	3.00	1.25
❑ 15	Todd Kelly FOIL RC	.75	.30
❑ 16	Rick Mirer FOIL RC	3.00	1.25
❑ 17	Eric Curry FOIL RC	.75	.30
❑ 18	Reggie Brooks FOIL RC	1.50	.60
❑ 19	Eric Dickerson	.50	.20
❑ 20	Roger Harper RC	.30	.10
❑ 21	Michael Haynes	.50	.20
❑ 22	Bobby Hebert	.30	.10
❑ 23	Lincoln Kennedy RC	.30	.10
❑ 24	Chris Miller	.50	.20
❑ 25	Mike Pritchard	.50	.20
❑ 26	Andre Rison	.50	.20
❑ 27	Deion Sanders	1.50	.60
❑ 28	Cornelius Bennett	.50	.20
❑ 29	Kenneth Davis	.30	.10
❑ 30	Henry Jones	.30	.10
❑ 31	Jim Kelly	1.00	.40
❑ 32	John Parrella RC	.30	.10
❑ 33	Andre Reed	.50	.20
❑ 34	Bruce Smith	1.00	.40
❑ 35	Thomas Smith RC	.50	.20
❑ 36	Thurman Thomas	1.00	.40
❑ 37	Neal Anderson	.30	.10
❑ 38	Myron Baker RC	.30	.10
❑ 39	Mark Carrier DB	.30	.10
❑ 40	Richard Dent	.50	.20
❑ 41	Chris Gedney RC	.30	.10
❑ 42	Jim Harbaugh	1.00	.40
❑ 43	Craig Heyward	.50	.20
❑ 44	Carl Simpson RC	.30	.10
❑ 45	Alonzo Spellman	.30	.10
❑ 46	Derrick Fenner	.30	.10
❑ 47	Harold Green	.30	.10
❑ 48	David Klingler	.30	.10
❑ 49	Ricardo McDonald	.30	.10
❑ 50	Tony McGee RC	.50	.20
❑ 51	Carl Pickens	.50	.20
❑ 52	Steve Tovar RC	.30	.10
❑ 53	Alfred Williams	.30	.10
❑ 54	Darryl Williams	.30	.10
❑ 55	Jerry Ball	.30	.10
❑ 56	Mike Caldwell RC	.30	.10
❑ 57	Mark Carrier WR	.50	.20
❑ 58	Steve Everitt RC	.30	.10
❑ 59	Dan Footman RC	.30	.10
❑ 60	Pepper Johnson	.30	.10
❑ 61	Bernie Kosar	.50	.20
❑ 62	Eric Metcalf	.50	.20
❑ 63	Michael Dean Perry	.50	.20
❑ 64	Troy Aikman	2.50	1.25
❑ 65	Charles Haley	.50	.20
❑ 66	Michael Irvin	1.00	.40
❑ 67	Robert Jones	.30	.10
❑ 68	Derrick Lassic RC	.30	.10
❑ 69	Russell Maryland	.30	.10
❑ 70	Ken Norton Jr.	.50	.20
❑ 71	Darrin Smith RC	.50	.20
❑ 72	Emmitt Smith	5.00	2.50
❑ 73	Steve Atwater	.30	.10
❑ 74	Rod Bernstine	.30	.10
❑ 75	Jason Elam RC	1.00	.40
❑ 76	John Elway	5.00	2.00
❑ 77	Simon Fletcher	.30	.10
❑ 78	Tommy Maddox	1.00	.40
❑ 79	Glyn Milburn RC	1.00	.40
❑ 80	Derek Russell	.30	.10
❑ 81	Shannon Sharpe	1.00	.40
❑ 82	Bennie Blades	.30	.10
❑ 83	Willie Green	.30	.10
❑ 84	Antonio London RC	.30	.10
❑ 85	Ryan McNeil RC	1.00	.40
❑ 86	Herman Moore	1.00	.40
❑ 87	Rodney Peete	.30	.10
❑ 88	Barry Sanders	4.00	1.50
❑ 89	Chris Spielman	.50	.20
❑ 90	Pat Swilling	.30	.10
❑ 91	Mark Brunell RC	15.00	6.00
❑ 92	Terrell Buckley	.30	.10
❑ 93	Brett Favre	6.00	3.00
❑ 94	Jackie Harris	.30	.10
❑ 95	Sterling Sharpe	1.00	.40
❑ 96	John Stephens	.30	.10
❑ 97	Wayne Simmons RC	.30	.10
❑ 98	George Teague RC	.50	.20
❑ 99	Reggie White	1.00	.40
❑ 100	Micheal Barrow RC	1.00	.40
❑ 101	Cody Carlson	.30	.10
❑ 102	Ray Childress	.30	.10
❑ 103	Brad Hopkins RC	.30	.10
❑ 104	Haywood Jeffires	.50	.20
❑ 105	Wilber Marshall	.30	.10
❑ 106	Warren Moon	1.00	.40
❑ 107	Webster Slaughter	.30	.10
❑ 108	Lorenzo White	.30	.10
❑ 109	John Baylor	.30	.10
❑ 110	Duane Bickett	.30	.10
❑ 111	Quentin Coryatt	.50	.20
❑ 112	Steve Emtman	.30	.10
❑ 113	Jeff George	1.00	.40
❑ 114	Jessie Hester	.30	.10
❑ 115	Anthony Johnson	.50	.20
❑ 116	Reggie Langhorne	.30	.10
❑ 117	Roosevelt Potts RC	.30	.10
❑ 118	Marcus Allen	1.00	.40
❑ 119	J.J. Birden	.30	.10
❑ 120	Willie Davis	1.00	.40
❑ 121	Jaime Fields RC	.30	.10
❑ 122	Joe Montana	5.00	2.00
❑ 123	Will Shields RC	1.00	.40
❑ 124	Neil Smith	1.00	.40
❑ 125	Derrick Thomas	1.00	.40
❑ 126	Harvey Williams	.50	.20
❑ 127	Tim Brown	1.00	.40
❑ 128	Billy Joe Hobert RC	1.00	.40
❑ 129	Jeff Hostetler	.50	.20
❑ 130	Ethan Horton	.30	.10
❑ 131	Rocket Ismail	.50	.20
❑ 132	Howie Long	1.00	.40
❑ 133	Terry McDaniel	.30	.10
❑ 134	Greg Robinson RC	.30	.10
❑ 135	Anthony Smith	.30	.10
❑ 136	Flipper Anderson	.30	.10
❑ 137	Marc Boutte	.30	.10
❑ 138	Shane Conlan	.30	.10
❑ 139	Troy Drayton RC	.50	.20
❑ 140	Henry Ellard	.50	.20
❑ 141	Jim Everett	.50	.20
❑ 142	Cleveland Gary	.30	.10
❑ 143	Sean Gilbert	.50	.20
❑ 144	Robert Young	.30	.10
❑ 145	Marco Coleman	.30	.10
❑ 146	Bryan Cox	.30	.10
❑ 147	Irving Fryar	.50	.20
❑ 148	Keith Jackson	.50	.20
❑ 149	Terry Kirby RC	1.00	.40
❑ 150	Dan Marino	5.00	2.00
❑ 151	Scott Mitchell	1.00	.40
❑ 152	Louis Oliver	.30	.10
❑ 153	Troy Vincent	.30	.10
❑ 154	Anthony Carter	.50	.20
❑ 155	Cris Carter	1.00	.40
❑ 156	Roger Craig	.50	.20
❑ 157	Chris Doleman	.30	.10
❑ 158	Qadry Ismail RC	2.00	.75
❑ 159	Steve Jordan	.30	.10
❑ 160	Randall McDaniel	.30	.10
❑ 161	Audray McMillian	.30	.10
❑ 162	Barry Word	.30	.10
❑ 163	Vincent Brown	.30	.10
❑ 164	Marv Cook	.30	.10
❑ 165	Sam Gash RC	1.00	.40
❑ 166	Pat Harlow	.30	.10
❑ 167	Greg McMurtry	.30	.10
❑ 168	Todd Rucci RC	.30	.10
❑ 169	Leonard Russell	.50	.20
❑ 170	Scott Sisson RC	.30	.10
❑ 171	Chris Slade RC	.50	.20
❑ 172	Morten Andersen	.30	.10
❑ 173	Derek Brown RC RBK	.50	.20
❑ 174	Reggie Freeman RC	.30	.10
❑ 175	Rickey Jackson	.30	.10
❑ 176	Eric Martin	.30	.10
❑ 177	Wayne Martin	.30	.10
❑ 178	Brad Muster	.30	.10
❑ 179	Willie Roaf RC	.50	.20
❑ 180	Renaldo Turnbull	.30	.10
❑ 181	Derek Brown TE	.30	.10
❑ 182	Marcus Buckley RC	.30	.10
❑ 183	Jarrod Bunch	.30	.10
❑ 184	Rodney Hampton	.50	.20
❑ 185	Ed McCaffrey	1.00	.40
❑ 186	Kanavis McGhee	.30	.10
❑ 187	Mike Sherrard	.30	.10
❑ 188	Phil Simms	.50	.20
❑ 189	Lawrence Taylor	1.00	.40
❑ 190	Kurt Barber	.30	.10
❑ 191	Boomer Esiason	.50	.20
❑ 192	Johnny Johnson	.30	.10
❑ 193	Ronnie Lott	.50	.20
❑ 194	Johnny Mitchell	.30	.10
❑ 195	Rob Moore	.50	.20
❑ 196	Adrian Murrell RC	1.00	.40
❑ 197	Browning Nagle	.30	.10
❑ 198	Marvin Washington	.30	.10
❑ 199	Eric Allen	.30	.10
❑ 200	Fred Barnett	.50	.20
❑ 201	Randall Cunningham	1.00	.40
❑ 202	Byron Evans	.30	.10
❑ 203	Tim Harris	.30	.10
❑ 204	Seth Joyner	.30	.10
❑ 205	Leonard Renfro RC	.30	.10
❑ 206	Heath Sherman	.30	.10
❑ 207	Clyde Simmons	.30	.10
❑ 208	Johnny Bailey	.30	.10
❑ 209	Steve Beuerlein	.50	.20
❑ 210	Chuck Cecil	.30	.10
❑ 211	Larry Centers RC	1.00	.40
❑ 212	Gary Clark	.50	.20
❑ 213	Ernest Dye RC	.30	.10
❑ 214	Ken Harvey	.30	.10
❑ 215	Randal Hill	.30	.10
❑ 216	Ricky Proehl	.30	.10

- ❑ 217 Deon Figures RC .30 .10
- ❑ 218 Barry Foster .50 .20
- ❑ 219 Eric Green .30 .10
- ❑ 220 Kevin Greene .50 .20
- ❑ 221 Carlton Haselrig .30 .10
- ❑ 222 Andre Hastings RC .50 .20
- ❑ 223 Greg Lloyd .50 .20
- ❑ 224 Neil O'Donnell 1.00 .40
- ❑ 225 Rod Woodson 1.00 .40
- ❑ 226 Marion Butts .30 .10
- ❑ 227 Darren Carrington RC .30 .10
- ❑ 228 Darrien Gordon RC .30 .10
- ❑ 229 Ronnie Harmon .30 .10
- ❑ 230 Stan Humphries .50 .20
- ❑ 231 Anthony Miller .50 .20
- ❑ 232 Chris Mims .30 .10
- ❑ 233 Leslie O'Neal .50 .20
- ❑ 234 Junior Seau 1.00 .40
- ❑ 235 Dana Hall .30 .10
- ❑ 236 Adrian Hardy .30 .10
- ❑ 237 Brent Jones .50 .20
- ❑ 238 Tim McDonald .30 .10
- ❑ 239 Tom Rathman .30 .10
- ❑ 240 Jerry Rice 3.00 1.50
- ❑ 241 Dana Stubblefield RC 1.00 .40
- ❑ 242 Ricky Watters 1.00 .40
- ❑ 243 Steve Young 2.50 1.25
- ❑ 244 Brian Blades .50 .20
- ❑ 245 Ferrell Edmunds .30 .10
- ❑ 246 Carlton Gray RC .30 .10
- ❑ 247 Cortez Kennedy .50 .20
- ❑ 248 Kelvin Martin .30 .10
- ❑ 249 Dan McGwire .30 .10
- ❑ 250 Jon Vaughn .30 .10
- ❑ 251 Chris Warren .50 .20
- ❑ 252 John L. Williams .30 .10
- ❑ 253 Reggie Cobb .30 .10
- ❑ 254 Horace Copeland RC .50 .20
- ❑ 255 Lawrence Dawsey .30 .10
- ❑ 256 Demetrius DuBose RC .30 .10
- ❑ 257 Craig Erickson .50 .20
- ❑ 258 Courtney Hawkins .30 .10
- ❑ 259 John Lynch RC 8.00 3.00
- ❑ 260 Hardy Nickerson .50 .20
- ❑ 261 Lamar Thomas RC .30 .10
- ❑ 262 Carl Banks .30 .10
- ❑ 263 Tom Carter RC .50 .20
- ❑ 264 Brad Edwards .30 .10
- ❑ 265 Kurt Gouveia .30 .10
- ❑ 266 Desmond Howard .50 .20
- ❑ 267 Charles Mann .30 .10
- ❑ 268 Art Monk .50 .20
- ❑ 269 Mark Rypien .30 .10
- ❑ 270 Ricky Sanders .30 .10
- ❑ P1 Joe Montana Promo 5.00 2.00

1994 SP

- ❑ COMPLETE SET (200) 50.00 25.00
- ❑ 1 Dan Wilkinson FOIL RC 1.25 .50
- ❑ 2 Heath Shuler FOIL RC .75 .30
- ❑ 3 Marshall Faulk FOIL RC 15.00 6.00
- ❑ 4 Willie McGinest FOIL RC 2.00 .75
- ❑ 5 Trent Dilfer FOIL RC 5.00 2.00
- ❑ 6 Bryant Young FOIL RC 2.00 .75
- ❑ 7 Antonio Langham FOIL RC .40 .15
- ❑ 8 John Thierry FOIL RC .40 .15
- ❑ 9 Aaron Glenn FOIL RC 1.25 .50
- ❑ 10 Charles Johnson FOIL RC 1.25 .50
- ❑ 11 Dewayne Washington FOIL RC .40 .15
- ❑ 12 Johnnie Morton FOIL RC 3.00 1.25
- ❑ 13 Greg Hill FOIL RC .75 .30
- ❑ 14 William Floyd FOIL RC .75 .30
- ❑ 15 Derrick Alexander WR FOIL RC 1.25 .50
- ❑ 16 Darnay Scott FOIL RC 1.25 .50
- ❑ 17 Errict Rhett FOIL RC 1.25 .50
- ❑ 18 Charlie Garner FOIL RC 3.00 1.25
- ❑ 19 Thomas Lewis FOIL RC .40 .15
- ❑ 20 David Palmer FOIL RC 1.25 .50
- ❑ 21 Andre Reed .30 .10
- ❑ 22 Thurman Thomas .50 .20
- ❑ 23 Bruce Smith .50 .20
- ❑ 24 Jim Kelly .50 .20
- ❑ 25 Cornelius Bennett .30 .10
- ❑ 26 Bucky Brooks RC .15 .05
- ❑ 27 Jeff Burris RC .30 .10
- ❑ 28 Jim Harbaugh .50 .20
- ❑ 29 Tony Bennett .15 .05
- ❑ 30 Quentin Coryatt .15 .05
- ❑ 31 Floyd Turner .15 .05
- ❑ 32 Roosevelt Potts .15 .05
- ❑ 33 Jeff Herrod .15 .05
- ❑ 34 Irving Fryar .30 .10
- ❑ 35 Bryan Cox .15 .05
- ❑ 36 Dan Marino 4.00 1.50
- ❑ 37 Terry Kirby .50 .20
- ❑ 38 Michael Stewart .15 .05
- ❑ 39 Bernie Kosar .30 .10
- ❑ 40 Aubrey Beavers RC .15 .05
- ❑ 41 Vincent Brisby .30 .10
- ❑ 42 Ben Coates .30 .10
- ❑ 43 Drew Bledsoe 2.00 .75
- ❑ 44 Marion Butts .15 .05
- ❑ 45 Chris Slade .15 .05
- ❑ 46 Michael Timpson .15 .05
- ❑ 47 Ray Crittenden RC .15 .05
- ❑ 48 Rob Moore .30 .10
- ❑ 49 Johnny Mitchell .15 .05
- ❑ 50 Art Monk .30 .10
- ❑ 51 Boomer Esiason .30 .10
- ❑ 52 Ronnie Lott .30 .10
- ❑ 53 Ryan Yarborough RC .15 .05
- ❑ 54 Carl Pickens .30 .10
- ❑ 55 David Klingler .15 .05
- ❑ 56 Harold Green .15 .05
- ❑ 57 John Copeland .15 .05
- ❑ 58 Louis Oliver .15 .05
- ❑ 59 Corey Sawyer .30 .10
- ❑ 60 Michael Jackson .30 .10
- ❑ 61 Mark Rypien .15 .05
- ❑ 62 Vinny Testaverde .30 .10
- ❑ 63 Eric Metcalf .30 .10
- ❑ 64 Eric Turner .15 .05
- ❑ 65 Haywood Jeffires .30 .10
- ❑ 66 Micheal Barrow .15 .05
- ❑ 67 Cody Carlson .15 .05
- ❑ 68 Gary Brown .15 .05
- ❑ 69 Bucky Richardson .15 .05
- ❑ 70 Al Smith .15 .05
- ❑ 71 Eric Green .15 .05
- ❑ 72 Neil O'Donnell .50 .20
- ❑ 73 Barry Foster .15 .05
- ❑ 74 Greg Lloyd .30 .10
- ❑ 75 Rod Woodson .30 .10
- ❑ 76 Byron Bam Morris RC .30 .10
- ❑ 77 John L. Williams .15 .05
- ❑ 78 Anthony Miller .30 .10
- ❑ 79 Mike Pritchard .15 .05
- ❑ 80 John Elway 4.00 1.50
- ❑ 81 Shannon Sharpe .30 .10
- ❑ 82 Steve Atwater .15 .05
- ❑ 83 Simon Fletcher .15 .05
- ❑ 84 Glyn Milburn .30 .10
- ❑ 85 Mark Collins .15 .05
- ❑ 86 Keith Cash .15 .05
- ❑ 87 Willie Davis .30 .10
- ❑ 88 Joe Montana 4.00 1.50
- ❑ 89 Marcus Allen .50 .20
- ❑ 90 Neil Smith .30 .10
- ❑ 91 Derrick Thomas .50 .20
- ❑ 92 Tim Brown .50 .20
- ❑ 93 Jeff Hostetler .30 .10
- ❑ 94 Terry McDaniel .15 .05
- ❑ 95 Rocket Ismail .30 .10
- ❑ 96 Rob Fredrickson RC .30 .10
- ❑ 97 Harvey Williams .30 .10
- ❑ 98 Steve Wisniewski .15 .05
- ❑ 99 Stan Humphries .30 .10
- ❑ 100 Natrone Means .50 .20
- ❑ 101 Leslie O'Neal .15 .05
- ❑ 102 Junior Seau .50 .20
- ❑ 103 Ronnie Harmon .15 .05
- ❑ 104 Shawn Jefferson .15 .05
- ❑ 105 Howard Ballard .15 .05
- ❑ 106 Rick Mirer .50 .20
- ❑ 107 Cortez Kennedy .30 .10
- ❑ 108 Chris Warren .30 .10
- ❑ 109 Brian Blades .30 .10
- ❑ 110 Sam Adams RC .30 .10
- ❑ 111 Gary Clark .30 .10
- ❑ 112 Steve Beuerlein .30 .10
- ❑ 113 Ronald Moore .15 .05
- ❑ 114 Eric Swann .30 .10
- ❑ 115 Clyde Simmons .15 .05
- ❑ 116 Seth Joyner .15 .05
- ❑ 117 Troy Aikman 2.00 .75
- ❑ 118 Charles Haley .30 .10
- ❑ 119 Alvin Harper .30 .10
- ❑ 120 Michael Irvin .50 .20
- ❑ 121 Daryl Johnston .30 .10
- ❑ 122 Emmitt Smith 3.00 1.25
- ❑ 123 Shante Carver RC .15 .05
- ❑ 124 Dave Brown .30 .10
- ❑ 125 Rodney Hampton .30 .10
- ❑ 126 Dave Meggett .15 .05
- ❑ 127 Chris Calloway .15 .05
- ❑ 128 Mike Sherrard .15 .05
- ❑ 129 Carlton Bailey .15 .05
- ❑ 130 Randall Cunningham .50 .20
- ❑ 131 William Fuller .15 .05
- ❑ 132 Eric Allen .15 .05
- ❑ 133 Calvin Williams .30 .10
- ❑ 134 Herschel Walker .30 .10
- ❑ 135 Bernard Williams RC .15 .05
- ❑ 136 Henry Ellard .30 .10
- ❑ 137 Ethan Horton .15 .05
- ❑ 138 Desmond Howard .30 .10
- ❑ 139 Reggie Brooks .30 .10
- ❑ 140 John Friesz .30 .10
- ❑ 141 Tom Carter .15 .05
- ❑ 142 Terry Allen .30 .10
- ❑ 143 Adrian Cooper .15 .05
- ❑ 144 Qadry Ismail .50 .20
- ❑ 145 Warren Moon .50 .20
- ❑ 146 Henry Thomas .15 .05
- ❑ 147 Todd Steussie RC .30 .10
- ❑ 148 Cris Carter .75 .30
- ❑ 149 Andy Heck .15 .05
- ❑ 150 Curtis Conway .50 .20
- ❑ 151 Erik Kramer .30 .10
- ❑ 152 Lewis Tillman .15 .05
- ❑ 153 Dante Jones .15 .05
- ❑ 154 Alonzo Spellman .15 .05
- ❑ 155 Herman Moore .50 .20
- ❑ 156 Broderick Thomas .15 .05
- ❑ 157 Scott Mitchell .30 .10
- ❑ 158 Barry Sanders 3.00 1.25
- ❑ 159 Chris Spielman .30 .10
- ❑ 160 Pat Swilling .15 .05
- ❑ 161 Bennie Blades .15 .05
- ❑ 162 Sterling Sharpe .30 .10
- ❑ 163 Brett Favre 4.00 1.50
- ❑ 164 Reggie Cobb .15 .05
- ❑ 165 Reggie White .50 .20
- ❑ 166 Sean Jones .15 .05
- ❑ 167 George Teague .15 .05
- ❑ 168 LeShon Johnson RC .30 .10
- ❑ 169 Courtney Hawkins .15 .05
- ❑ 170 Jackie Harris .15 .05
- ❑ 171 Craig Erickson .15 .05
- ❑ 172 Santana Dotson .30 .10
- ❑ 173 Eric Curry .15 .05
- ❑ 174 Hardy Nickerson .30 .10
- ❑ 175 Derek Brown RBK .15 .05
- ❑ 176 Jim Everett .30 .10
- ❑ 177 Michael Haynes .30 .10
- ❑ 178 Tyrone Hughes .30 .10
- ❑ 179 Wayne Martin .15 .05
- ❑ 180 Willie Roaf .15 .05
- ❑ 181 Irv Smith .15 .05
- ❑ 182 Jeff George .50 .20
- ❑ 183 Andre Rison .30 .10
- ❑ 184 Erric Pegram .15 .05
- ❑ 185 Bert Emanuel RC 1.00 .40

❑ 186 Chris Doleman .15 .05
❑ 187 Ron George .15 .05
❑ 188 Chris Miller .15 .05
❑ 189 Troy Drayton .15 .05
❑ 190 Chris Chandler .30 .10
❑ 191 Jerome Bettis 1.00 .40
❑ 192 Jimmie Jones .15 .05
❑ 193 Sean Gilbert .15 .05
❑ 194 Jerry Rice 2.00 .75
❑ 195 Brent Jones .30 .10
❑ 196 Deion Sanders 1.00 .40
❑ 197 Steve Young 1.50 .60
❑ 198 Ricky Watters .30 .10
❑ 199 Dana Stubblefield .30 .10
❑ 200 Ken Norton Jr. .30 .10
❑ RB1 Dan Marino RB 25.00 10.00
❑ RB2 Jerry Rice RB 25.00 12.50
❑ P16 Joe Montana Promo 4.00 1.50

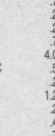

1995 SP

❑ COMPLETE SET (200) 50.00 20.00
❑ 1 Ki-Jana Carter FOIL RC 2.00 .75
❑ 2 Eric Zeier FOIL RC 2.00 .75
❑ 3 Steve McNair FOIL RC 10.00 4.00
❑ 4 Michael Westbrook FOIL RC 2.00 .75
❑ 5 Kerry Collins FOIL RC 5.00 2.00
❑ 6 Joey Galloway FOIL RC 5.00 2.00
❑ 7 Kevin Carter FOIL RC 2.00 .75
❑ 8 Mike Mamula RC .50 .20
❑ 9 Kyle Brady FOIL RC 2.00 .75
❑ 10 J.J. Stokes FOIL RC 2.00 .75
❑ 11 Tyrone Poole RC 2.00 .75
❑ 12 Rashaan Salaam FOIL RC 1.00 .40
❑ 13 Sherman Williams FOIL RC .50 .20
❑ 14 Luther Elliss RC .50 .20
❑ 15 James O. Stewart FOIL RC 3.00 1.25
❑ 16 Tamarick Vanover FOIL RC 2.00 .75
❑ 17 Napoleon Kaufman FOIL RC 3.00 1.25
❑ 18 Curtis Martin FOIL RC 12.00 6.00
❑ 19 Tyrone Wheatley FOIL RC 3.00 1.25
❑ 20 Frank Sanders FOIL RC 2.00 .75
❑ 21 Devin Bush .20 .07
❑ 22 Terance Mathis .40 .15
❑ 23 Bert Emanuel .75 .30
❑ 24 Eric Metcalf .40 .15
❑ 25 Craig Heyward .40 .15
❑ 26 Jeff George .40 .15
❑ 27 Mark Carrier WR .40 .15
❑ 28 Pete Metzelaars .20 .07
❑ 29 Frank Reich .20 .07
❑ 30 Sam Mills .40 .15
❑ 31 John Kasay .20 .07
❑ 32 Willie Green .40 .15
❑ 33 Jeff Graham .20 .07
❑ 34 Curtis Conway .75 .30
❑ 35 Steve Walsh .20 .07
❑ 36 Erik Kramer .20 .07
❑ 37 Michael Timpson .20 .07
❑ 38 Mark Carrier DB .20 .07
❑ 39 Troy Aikman 2.00 .75
❑ 40 Michael Irvin .75 .30
❑ 41 Charles Haley .40 .15
❑ 42 Deion Sanders 1.25 .50
❑ 43 Jay Novacek .40 .15
❑ 44 Emmitt Smith 3.00 1.25
❑ 45 Herman Moore .75 .30
❑ 46 Scott Mitchell UER .40 .15
❑ 47 Bennie Blades .20 .07
❑ 48 Johnnie Morton .40 .15

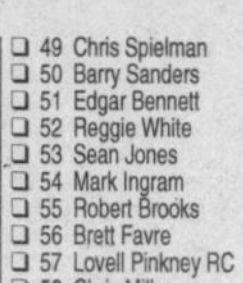
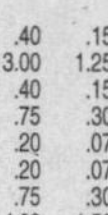

❑ 49 Chris Spielman .40 .15
❑ 50 Barry Sanders 3.00 1.25
❑ 51 Edgar Bennett .40 .15
❑ 52 Reggie White .75 .30
❑ 53 Sean Jones .20 .07
❑ 54 Mark Ingram .20 .07
❑ 55 Robert Brooks .75 .30
❑ 56 Brett Favre 4.00 1.50
❑ 57 Lovell Pinkney RC .50 .20
❑ 58 Chris Miller .20 .07
❑ 59 Isaac Bruce 1.25 .50
❑ 60 Roman Phifer .20 .07
❑ 61 Sean Gilbert .40 .15
❑ 62 Jerome Bettis .75 .30
❑ 63 Derrick Alexander DE RC .50 .20
❑ 64 Cris Carter .75 .30
❑ 65 Jake Reed .40 .15
❑ 66 Robert Smith .75 .30
❑ 67 David Palmer .40 .15
❑ 68 Warren Moon .40 .15
❑ 69 Ray Zellars RC 1.00 .40
❑ 70 Jim Everett .20 .07
❑ 71 Michael Haynes .40 .15
❑ 72 Quinn Early .40 .15
❑ 73 Willie Roaf .20 .07
❑ 74 Mario Bates .40 .15
❑ 75 Mike Sherrard .20 .07
❑ 76 Chris Calloway .20 .07
❑ 77 Dave Brown .40 .15
❑ 78 Thomas Lewis .40 .15
❑ 79 Herschel Walker .40 .15
❑ 80 Rodney Hampton .40 .15
❑ 81 Fred Barnett .40 .15
❑ 82 Calvin Williams .40 .15
❑ 83 Randall Cunningham .75 .30
❑ 84 Charlie Garner .75 .30
❑ 85 Bobby Taylor RC 3.00 1.25
❑ 86 Ricky Watters .40 .15
❑ 87 Dave Krieg .20 .07
❑ 88 Rob Moore .40 .15
❑ 89 Eric Swann .40 .15
❑ 90 Clyde Simmons .20 .07
❑ 91 Seth Joyner .20 .07
❑ 92 Garrison Hearst .75 .30
❑ 93 Jerry Rice 2.00 .75
❑ 94 Bryant Young .40 .15
❑ 95 Brent Jones .20 .07
❑ 96 Ken Norton .40 .15
❑ 97 William Floyd .40 .15
❑ 98 Steve Young 1.50 .60
❑ 99 Warren Sapp RC 5.00 2.00
❑ 100 Trent Dilfer .75 .30
❑ 101 Alvin Harper .20 .07
❑ 102 Hardy Nickerson .20 .07
❑ 103 Derrick Brooks RC 5.00 2.00
❑ 104 Errict Rhett .40 .15
❑ 105 Henry Ellard .40 .15
❑ 106 Ken Harvey .20 .07
❑ 107 Gus Frerotte .40 .15
❑ 108 Brian Mitchell .20 .07
❑ 109 Terry Allen .40 .15
❑ 110 Heath Shuler .40 .15
❑ 111 Jim Kelly .75 .30
❑ 112 Andre Reed .40 .15
❑ 113 Bruce Smith .75 .30
❑ 114 Darick Holmes RC 1.00 .40
❑ 115 Bryce Paup .40 .15
❑ 116 Cornelius Bennett .40 .15
❑ 117 Carl Pickens .40 .15
❑ 118 Darnay Scott .40 .15
❑ 119 Jeff Blake RC 2.00 .75
❑ 120 Steve Tovar .20 .07
❑ 121 Tony McGee .20 .07
❑ 122 Dan Wilkinson .40 .15
❑ 123 Craig Powell RC .20 .07
❑ 124 Vinny Testaverde .40 .15
❑ 125 Eric Turner .20 .07
❑ 126 Leroy Hoard .20 .07
❑ 127 Lorenzo White .20 .07
❑ 128 Andre Rison .40 .15
❑ 129 Shannon Sharpe .40 .15
❑ 130 Terrell Davis RC 8.00 3.00
❑ 131 Anthony Miller .40 .15
❑ 132 Mike Pritchard .20 .07
❑ 133 Steve Atwater .20 .07
❑ 134 John Elway 4.00 1.50
❑ 135 Haywood Jeffires .20 .07

❑ 136 Gary Brown .20 .07
❑ 137 Al Smith .20 .07
❑ 138 Rodney Thomas RC 1.00 .40
❑ 139 Chris Chandler .40 .15
❑ 140 Mel Gray .20 .07
❑ 141 Craig Erickson .20 .07
❑ 142 Sean Dawkins .40 .15
❑ 143 Ken Dilger RC 2.00 .75
❑ 144 Ellis Johnson RC .50 .20
❑ 145 Quentin Coryatt .40 .15
❑ 146 Marshall Faulk 2.50 1.00
❑ 147 Tony Boselli RC 2.00 .75
❑ 148 Rob Johnson RC 3.00 1.25
❑ 149 Desmond Howard .40 .15
❑ 150 Steve Beuerlein .40 .15
❑ 151 Reggie Cobb .20 .07
❑ 152 Jeff Lageman .20 .07
❑ 153 Willie Davis .40 .15
❑ 154 Marcus Allen .75 .30
❑ 155 Neil Smith .40 .15
❑ 156 Greg Hill .40 .15
❑ 157 Steve Bono .40 .15
❑ 158 Derrick Thomas .75 .30
❑ 159 Jeff Hostetler .40 .15
❑ 160 Harvey Williams .20 .07
❑ 161 Rocket Ismail .40 .15
❑ 162 Chester McGlockton .40 .15
❑ 163 Terry McDaniel .20 .07
❑ 164 Tim Brown .75 .30
❑ 165 Terry Kirby .40 .15
❑ 166 Irving Fryar .40 .15
❑ 167 O.J. McDuffie .75 .30
❑ 168 Bryan Cox .20 .07
❑ 169 Eric Green .20 .07
❑ 170 Dan Marino 4.00 1.50
❑ 171 Ben Coates .40 .15
❑ 172 Vincent Brisby .20 .07
❑ 173 Chris Slade .20 .07
❑ 174 Ty Law RC 4.00 1.50
❑ 175 Vincent Brown .20 .07
❑ 176 Drew Bledsoe 1.25 .50
❑ 177 Johnny Mitchell .20 .07
❑ 178 Boomer Esiason .40 .15
❑ 179 Wayne Chrebet RC 6.00 3.00
❑ 180 Mo Lewis .20 .07
❑ 181 Ronald Moore .20 .07
❑ 182 Aaron Glenn .20 .07
❑ 183 Mark Bruener RC 1.00 .40
❑ 184 Neil O'Donnell .40 .15
❑ 185 Charles Johnson .40 .15
❑ 186 Greg Lloyd .40 .15
❑ 187 Rod Woodson .40 .15
❑ 188 Byron Bam Morris .20 .07
❑ 189 Terrell Fletcher RC .50 .20
❑ 190 Terrance Shaw RC UER .50 .20
❑ 191 Stan Humphries .40 .15
❑ 192 Junior Seau .75 .30
❑ 193 Leslie O'Neal .40 .15
❑ 194 Natrone Means .40 .15
❑ 195 Christian Fauria RC 1.00 .40
❑ 196 Rick Mirer .40 .15
❑ 197 Sam Adams .20 .07
❑ 198 Cortez Kennedy .40 .15
❑ 199 Eugene Robinson .20 .07
❑ 200 Chris Warren .40 .15
❑ DM1 Dan Marino Tribute 20.00 7.50
❑ JM1 Joe Montana Salute 20.00 7.50
❑ JMAP Joe Montana Promo 4.00 1.50
❑ NNO Dan Marino TRI Jumbo 25.00 10.00
❑ NNO Joe Montana SAL Jumbo 25.00 10.00
❑ P113 Dan Marino Promo 3.00 1.25

1996 SP

❑ COMPLETE SET (188) 100.00 40.00
❑ 1 Keyshawn Johnson RC 8.00 4.00
❑ 2 Kevin Hardy RC .75 .30
❑ 3 Simeon Rice RC 3.00 1.25
❑ 4 Jonathan Ogden RC 1.25 .50
❑ 5 Eddie George RC 10.00 4.00
❑ 6 Terry Glenn RC 6.00 2.50
❑ 7 Terrell Owens RC 25.00 12.50
❑ 8 Tim Biakabutuka RC 2.00 .75
❑ 9 Lawrence Phillips RC .75 .30
❑ 10 Alex Molden RC .40 .15
❑ 11 Regan Upshaw RC .40 .15
❑ 12 Rickey Dudley RC 1.25 .50
❑ 13 Duane Clemons RC .40 .15

❑ 14 John Mobley RC .75 .30
❑ 15 Eddie Kennison RC 2.00 .75
❑ 16 Karim Abdul-Jabbar RC 1.25 .50
❑ 17 Eric Moulds RC 8.00 3.00
❑ 18 Marvin Harrison RC 20.00 10.00
❑ 19 Stepfret Williams RC .40 .15
❑ 20 Stephen Davis RC 12.00 5.00
❑ 21 Deion Sanders 1.25 .50
❑ 22 Emmitt Smith 3.00 1.25
❑ 23 Troy Aikman 2.00 .75
❑ 24 Michael Irvin .75 .30
❑ 25 Herschel Walker .40 .15
❑ 26 Kavika Pittman RC .20 .07
❑ 27 Andre Hastings .20 .07
❑ 28 Jerome Bettis .75 .30
❑ 29 Mike Tomczak .20 .07
❑ 30 Kordell Stewart .75 .30
❑ 31 Charles Johnson .20 .07
❑ 32 Greg Lloyd .40 .15
❑ 33 Brett Favre 4.00 1.50
❑ 34 Mark Chmura .40 .15
❑ 35 Edgar Bennett .40 .15
❑ 36 Robert Brooks .40 .15
❑ 37 Craig Newsome .20 .07
❑ 38 Reggie White .75 .30
❑ 39 Jim Harbaugh .40 .15
❑ 40 Marshall Faulk 1.00 .40
❑ 41 Sean Dawkins .20 .07
❑ 42 Quentin Coryatt .20 .07
❑ 43 Ray Buchanan .20 .07
❑ 44 Ken Dilger .40 .15
❑ 45 Jerry Rice 2.00 .75
❑ 46 J.J. Stokes .75 .30
❑ 47 Steve Young 1.50 .60
❑ 48 Derek Loville .20 .07
❑ 49 Terry Kirby .40 .15
❑ 50 Ken Norton .20 .07
❑ 51 Tamarick Vanover .40 .15
❑ 52 Marcus Allen .75 .30
❑ 53 Steve Bono .20 .07
❑ 54 Neil Smith .40 .15
❑ 55 Derrick Thomas .75 .30
❑ 56 Dale Carter .20 .07
❑ 57 Terance Mathis .20 .07
❑ 58 Eric Metcalf .20 .07
❑ 59 Jamal Anderson RC 1.50 .60
❑ 60 Bert Emanuel .40 .15
❑ 61 Craig Heyward .20 .07
❑ 62 Cornelius Bennett .20 .07
❑ 63 Tony Martin .40 .15
❑ 64 Stan Humphries .40 .15
❑ 65 Andre Coleman .20 .07
❑ 66 Junior Seau .75 .30
❑ 67 Terrell Fletcher .20 .07
❑ 68 John Carney .20 .07
❑ 69 Charlie Jones RC .40 .15
❑ 70 Ricky Watters .40 .15
❑ 71 Charlie Garner .40 .15
❑ 72 Bobby Hoying RC .75 .30
❑ 73 Jason Dunn RC .40 .15
❑ 74 Bobby Taylor .20 .07
❑ 75 Irving Fryar .40 .15
❑ 76 Jim Kelly .75 .30
❑ 77 Thurman Thomas .75 .30
❑ 78 Bruce Smith .40 .15
❑ 79 Bryce Paup .20 .07
❑ 80 Darick Holmes .20 .07
❑ 81 Andre Reed .40 .15
❑ 82 Glyn Milburn .20 .07
❑ 83 Brett Perriman .20 .07
❑ 84 Herman Moore .40 .15
❑ 85 Scott Mitchell .40 .15
❑ 86 Barry Sanders 3.00 1.25
❑ 87 Johnnie Morton .40 .15
❑ 88 Dan Marino 4.00 1.50
❑ 89 O.J. McDuffie .40 .15
❑ 90 Stanley Pritchett RC .20 .07
❑ 91 Zach Thomas RC 4.00 1.50
❑ 92 Daryl Gardener RC .20 .07
❑ 93 Rashaan Salaam .40 .15
❑ 94 Erik Kramer .20 .07
❑ 95 Curtis Conway .75 .30
❑ 96 Bobby Engram RC .75 .30
❑ 97 Walt Harris RC .20 .07
❑ 98 Bryan Cox .20 .07
❑ 99 John Elway 4.00 1.50
❑ 100 Terrell Davis 1.50 .60
❑ 101 Anthony Miller .40 .15
❑ 102 Shannon Sharpe .40 .15
❑ 103 Tory James RC .75 .30
❑ 104 Jeff Lewis RC .40 .15
❑ 105 Joey Galloway .75 .30
❑ 106 Chris Warren .40 .15
❑ 107 Rick Mirer .40 .15
❑ 108 Cortez Kennedy .20 .07
❑ 109 Michael Sinclair .20 .07
❑ 110 John Friesz .20 .07
❑ 111 Warren Moon .40 .15
❑ 112 Cris Carter .75 .30
❑ 113 Jake Reed .40 .15
❑ 114 Robert Smith .40 .15
❑ 115 John Randle .40 .15
❑ 116 Orlando Thomas .20 .07
❑ 117 Jeff Hostetler .20 .07
❑ 118 Tim Brown .75 .30
❑ 119 Joe Aska .20 .07
❑ 120 Napoleon Kaufman .75 .30
❑ 121 Terry McDaniel .20 .07
❑ 122 Harvey Williams .20 .07
❑ 123 Trent Dilfer .75 .30
❑ 124 Reggie Brooks .20 .07
❑ 125 Alvin Harper .20 .07
❑ 126 Mike Alstott RC 5.00 2.00
❑ 127 Hardy Nickerson .20 .07
❑ 128 Mario Bates .40 .15
❑ 129 Jim Everett .20 .07
❑ 130 Tyrone Hughes .20 .07
❑ 131 Michael Haynes .20 .07
❑ 132 Eric Allen .20 .07
❑ 133 Isaac Bruce .75 .30
❑ 134 Kevin Carter .20 .07
❑ 135 Leslie O'Neal .20 .07
❑ 136 Tony Banks RC .75 .30
❑ 137 Chris Chandler .40 .15
❑ 138 Steve McNair 1.50 .60
❑ 139 Chris Sanders .40 .15
❑ 140 Ronnie Harmon .20 .07
❑ 141 Willie Davis .20 .07
❑ 142 Michael Westbrook .75 .30
❑ 143 Terry Allen .40 .15
❑ 144 Brian Mitchell .20 .07
❑ 145 Henry Ellard .20 .07
❑ 146 Gus Frerotte .40 .15
❑ 147 Kerry Collins .75 .30
❑ 148 Sam Mills .20 .07
❑ 149 Wesley Walls .40 .15
❑ 150 Kevin Greene .40 .15
❑ 151 Muhsin Muhammad RC 5.00 2.00
❑ 152 Winslow Oliver .20 .07
❑ 153 Jeff Blake .75 .30
❑ 154 Carl Pickens .40 .15
❑ 155 Darnay Scott .40 .15
❑ 156 Garrison Hearst .40 .15
❑ 157 Marco Battaglia RC .20 .07
❑ 158 Drew Bledsoe 1.25 .50
❑ 159 Curtis Martin 1.50 .60
❑ 160 Shawn Jefferson .20 .07
❑ 161 Ben Coates .40 .15
❑ 162 Lawyer Milloy RC 2.50 1.00
❑ 163 Tyrone Wheatley .40 .15
❑ 164 Rodney Hampton .40 .15
❑ 165 Chris Calloway .20 .07
❑ 166 Dave Brown .20 .07
❑ 167 Amani Toomer RC 5.00 2.00
❑ 168 Vinny Testaverde .40 .15
❑ 169 Michael Jackson .40 .15
❑ 170 Eric Turner .20 .07
❑ 171 DeRon Jenkins .20 .07
❑ 172 Jermaine Lewis RC .75 .30
❑ 173 Frank Sanders .40 .15
❑ 174 Rob Moore .40 .15
❑ 175 Kent Graham .20 .07
❑ 176 Leeland McElroy RC .40 .15
❑ 177 Larry Centers .40 .15
❑ 178 Eric Swann .20 .07
❑ 179 Mark Brunell 1.25 .50
❑ 180 Willie Jackson .40 .15
❑ 181 James O. Stewart .40 .15
❑ 182 Natrone Means .40 .15
❑ 183 Tony Brackens RC .75 .30
❑ 184 Adrian Murrell .40 .15
❑ 185 Neil O'Donnell .40 .15
❑ 186 Hugh Douglas .40 .15
❑ 187 Wayne Chrebet 1.00 .40
❑ 188 Alex Van Dyke RC .40 .15
❑ SP13 Dan Marino Promo 3.00 1.25

1997 SP Authentic

❑ COMPLETE SET (198) 100.00 50.00
❑ 1 Orlando Pace RC 2.00 .75
❑ 2 Darrell Russell RC .50 .20
❑ 3 Shawn Springs RC 1.00 .40
❑ 4 Peter Boulware RC 4.00 1.50
❑ 5 Bryant Westbrook RC 1.00 .40
❑ 6 Walter Jones RC 2.00 .75
❑ 7 Ike Hilliard RC 4.00 1.50
❑ 8 James Farrior RC 3.00 1.25
❑ 9 Tom Knight RC .50 .20
❑ 10 Warrick Dunn RC 15.00 6.00
❑ 11 Tony Gonzalez RC 15.00 6.00
❑ 12 Reinard Wilson RC 1.00 .40
❑ 13 Yatil Green RC 1.00 .40
❑ 14 Reidel Anthony RC 2.00 .75
❑ 15 Kenny Holmes RC .50 .20
❑ 16 Dwayne Rudd RC .50 .20
❑ 17 Renaldo Wynn RC .50 .20
❑ 18 David LaFleur RC .50 .20
❑ 19 Antowain Smith RC 6.00 2.50
❑ 20 Jim Druckenmiller RC 1.00 .40
❑ 21 Rae Carruth RC .50 .20
❑ 22 Byron Hanspard RC 1.00 .40
❑ 23 Jake Plummer RC 12.00 5.00
❑ 24 Joey Kent RC 1.00 .40
❑ 25 Corey Dillon RC 10.00 4.00
❑ 26 Danny Wuerffel RC 5.00 2.00
❑ 27 Will Blackwell RC .50 .20
❑ 28 Troy Davis RC 1.00 .40
❑ 29 Darnell Autry RC 1.00 .40
❑ 30 Pat Barnes RC 1.00 .40
❑ 31 Kent Graham .50 .20
❑ 32 Simeon Rice .75 .30
❑ 33 Frank Sanders .75 .30
❑ 34 Rob Moore .75 .30
❑ 35 Eric Swann .50 .20
❑ 36 Chris Chandler .75 .30
❑ 37 Jamal Anderson 1.25 .50
❑ 38 Terance Mathis .75 .30
❑ 39 Bert Emanuel .75 .30
❑ 40 Michael Booker .50 .20
❑ 41 Vinny Testaverde .75 .30
❑ 42 Byron Bam Morris .50 .20
❑ 43 Michael Jackson .75 .30
❑ 44 Derrick Alexander WR .75 .30
❑ 45 Jamie Sharper RC 2.00 .75
❑ 46 Kim Herring RC .50 .20
❑ 47 Todd Collins .50 .20

❑ 48 Thurman Thomas 1.25 .50
❑ 49 Andre Reed .75 .30
❑ 50 Quinn Early .50 .20
❑ 51 Bryce Paup .50 .20
❑ 52 Lonnie Johnson .50 .20
❑ 53 Kerry Collins 1.25 .50
❑ 54 Anthony Johnson .50 .20
❑ 55 Tim Biakabutuka .75 .30
❑ 56 Muhsin Muhammad .75 .30
❑ 57 Sam Mills .50 .20
❑ 58 Wesley Walls .75 .30
❑ 59 Rick Mirer .50 .20
❑ 60 Raymont Harris .50 .20
❑ 61 Curtis Conway .75 .30
❑ 62 Bobby Engram .75 .30
❑ 63 Bryan Cox .50 .20
❑ 64 John Allred RC .50 .20
❑ 65 Jeff Blake .75 .30
❑ 66 Ki-Jana Carter .50 .20
❑ 67 Darnay Scott .75 .30
❑ 68 Carl Pickens .75 .30
❑ 69 Dan Wilkinson .50 .20
❑ 70 Troy Aikman 2.50 1.25
❑ 71 Emmitt Smith 4.00 2.00
❑ 72 Michael Irvin 1.25 .50
❑ 73 Deion Sanders 1.25 .50
❑ 74 Anthony Miller .50 .20
❑ 75 Antonio Anderson RC .50 .20
❑ 76 John Elway 5.00 2.00
❑ 77 Terrell Davis 1.50 .60
❑ 78 Rod Smith WR 1.25 .50
❑ 79 Shannon Sharpe .75 .30
❑ 80 Neil Smith .75 .30
❑ 81 Trevor Pryce RC 2.00 .75
❑ 82 Scott Mitchell .75 .30
❑ 83 Barry Sanders 4.00 1.50
❑ 84 Herman Moore .75 .30
❑ 85 Johnnie Morton .75 .30
❑ 86 Matt Russell RC .50 .20
❑ 87 Brett Favre 5.00 2.50
❑ 88 Edgar Bennett .75 .30
❑ 89 Robert Brooks .75 .30
❑ 90 Antonio Freeman 1.25 .50
❑ 91 Reggie White 1.25 .50
❑ 92 Craig Newsome .50 .20
❑ 93 Jim Harbaugh .75 .30
❑ 94 Marshall Faulk 1.50 .60
❑ 95 Sean Dawkins .50 .20
❑ 96 Marvin Harrison 1.25 .50
❑ 97 Quentin Coryatt .50 .20
❑ 98 Tarik Glenn RC 1.00 .40
❑ 99 Mark Brunell 1.50 .60
❑ 100 Natrone Means .75 .30
❑ 101 Keenan McCardell .75 .30
❑ 102 Jimmy Smith .75 .30
❑ 103 Tony Brackens .50 .20
❑ 104 Kevin Hardy .50 .20
❑ 105 Elvis Grbac .75 .30
❑ 106 Marcus Allen 1.25 .50
❑ 107 Greg Hill .50 .20
❑ 108 Derrick Thomas 1.25 .50
❑ 109 Dale Carter .50 .20
❑ 110 Dan Marino 5.00 2.00
❑ 111 Karim Abdul-Jabbar .75 .30
❑ 112 Brian Manning RC .50 .20
❑ 113 Daryl Gardener .50 .20
❑ 114 Troy Drayton .50 .20
❑ 115 Zach Thomas 1.25 .50
❑ 116 Jason Taylor RC 12.00 5.00
❑ 117 Brad Johnson 1.25 .50
❑ 118 Robert Smith .75 .30
❑ 119 John Randle .75 .30
❑ 120 Cris Carter 1.25 .50
❑ 121 Jake Reed .75 .30
❑ 122 Randall Cunningham 1.25 .50
❑ 123 Drew Bledsoe 1.50 .60
❑ 124 Curtis Martin 1.50 .60
❑ 125 Terry Glenn 1.25 .50
❑ 126 Willie McGinest .50 .20
❑ 127 Chris Canty RC .50 .20
❑ 128 Sedrick Shaw RC 1.00 .40
❑ 129 Heath Shuler .50 .20
❑ 130 Mario Bates .50 .20
❑ 131 Ray Zellars .50 .20
❑ 132 Andre Hastings .50 .20
❑ 133 Dave Brown .50 .20
❑ 134 Tyrone Wheatley .75 .30
❑ 135 Rodney Hampton .75 .30
❑ 136 Chris Calloway .50 .20
❑ 137 Tiki Barber RC 30.00 15.00
❑ 138 Neil O'Donnell .75 .30
❑ 139 Adrian Murrell .75 .30
❑ 140 Wayne Chrebet 1.25 .50
❑ 141 Keyshawn Johnson 1.25 .50
❑ 142 Hugh Douglas .50 .20
❑ 143 Jeff George .75 .30
❑ 144 Napoleon Kaufman 1.25 .50
❑ 145 Tim Brown 1.25 .50
❑ 146 Desmond Howard .75 .30
❑ 147 Rickey Dudley .75 .30
❑ 148 Terry McDaniel .50 .20
❑ 149 Ty Detmer .75 .30
❑ 150 Ricky Watters .75 .30
❑ 151 Chris T. Jones .50 .20
❑ 152 Irving Fryar .75 .30
❑ 153 Mike Mamula .50 .20
❑ 154 Jon Harris RC .50 .20
❑ 155 Kordell Stewart 1.25 .50
❑ 156 Jerome Bettis 1.25 .50
❑ 157 Charles Johnson .75 .30
❑ 158 Greg Lloyd .50 .20
❑ 159 George Jones RC .50 .20
❑ 160 Terrell Fletcher .50 .20
❑ 161 Stan Humphries .75 .30
❑ 162 Tony Martin .75 .30
❑ 163 Eric Metcalf .75 .30
❑ 164 Junior Seau 1.25 .50
❑ 165 Rod Woodson .75 .30
❑ 166 Steve Young 1.50 .60
❑ 167 Terry Kirby .75 .30
❑ 168 Garrison Hearst .75 .30
❑ 169 Jerry Rice 2.50 1.25
❑ 170 Ken Norton .50 .20
❑ 171 Kevin Greene .75 .30
❑ 172 Lamar Smith 1.25 .50
❑ 173 Warren Moon 1.25 .50
❑ 174 Chris Warren .75 .30
❑ 175 Cortez Kennedy .50 .20
❑ 176 Joey Galloway .75 .30
❑ 177 Tony Banks .75 .30
❑ 178 Isaac Bruce 1.25 .50
❑ 179 Eddie Kennison .75 .30
❑ 180 Kevin Carter .50 .20
❑ 181 Craig Heyward .50 .20
❑ 182 Trent Dilfer 1.25 .50
❑ 183 Errict Rhett .50 .20
❑ 184 Mike Alstott 1.25 .50
❑ 185 Hardy Nickerson .50 .20
❑ 186 Ronde Barber RC 10.00 4.00
❑ 187 Steve McNair 1.50 .60
❑ 188 Eddie George 1.25 .50
❑ 189 Chris Sanders .50 .20
❑ 190 Blaine Bishop .50 .20
❑ 191 Derrick Mason RC 12.00 5.00
❑ 192 Gus Frerotte .50 .20
❑ 193 Terry Allen 1.25 .50
❑ 194 Brian Mitchell .50 .20
❑ 195 Alvin Harper .50 .20
❑ 196 Jeff Hostetler .50 .20
❑ 197 Leslie Shepherd .50 .20
❑ 198 Stephen Davis 1.25 .50
❑ A1 Aikman Audio Blue 4.00 1.50
❑ A2 Aikman Audio Pro Bowl 10.00 4.00
❑ A3 Aikman Audio White/500 30.00 15.00

1998 SP Authentic

❑ COMP.SET w/o SP's (84) 40.00 20.00
❑ *HAND NUMBERED RCs: .5X TO .8X
❑ 1 Andre Wadsworth RC 25.00 10.00
❑ 2 Corey Chavous RC 40.00 15.00
❑ 3 Keith Brooking RC 40.00 15.00
❑ 4 Duane Starks RC 15.00 7.50
❑ 5 Pat Johnson RC 25.00 10.00
❑ 6 Jason Peter RC 15.00 7.50
❑ 7 Curtis Enis RC 15.00 7.50
❑ 8 Takeo Spikes RC 40.00 15.00
❑ 9 Greg Ellis RC 15.00 7.50
❑ 10 Marcus Nash RC 15.00 7.50
❑ 11 Brian Griese RC 50.00 20.00
❑ 12 Germane Crowell RC 25.00 10.00
❑ 13 Vonnie Holliday RC 25.00 10.00
❑ 14 Peyton Manning RC 800.00 450.00
❑ 15 Jerome Pathon RC 25.00 10.00
❑ 16 Fred Taylor RC 50.00 25.00
❑ 17 John Avery RC 25.00 10.00
❑ 18 Randy Moss RC 350.00 200.00
❑ 19 Robert Edwards RC 15.00 7.50
❑ 20 Tony Simmons RC 25.00 10.00
❑ 21 Shaun Williams RC 25.00 10.00
❑ 22 Joe Jurevicius RC 40.00 15.00
❑ 23 Charles Woodson RC 50.00 20.00
❑ 24 Tra Thomas RC 15.00 7.50
❑ 25 Grant Wistrom RC 25.00 10.00
❑ 26 Ryan Leaf RC 40.00 15.00
❑ 27 Ahman Green RC 80.00 30.00
❑ 28 Jacquez Green RC 25.00 10.00
❑ 29 Kevin Dyson RC 40.00 15.00
❑ 30 Stephen Alexander RC 25.00 10.00
❑ 31 John Elway TW 20.00 7.50
❑ 32 Jerry Rice TW 12.00 5.00
❑ 33 Emmitt Smith TW 20.00 7.50
❑ 34 Steve Young TW 8.00 3.00
❑ 35 Jerome Bettis TW 6.00 2.50
❑ 36 Deion Sanders TW 6.00 2.50
❑ 37 Andre Rison TW 4.00 1.50
❑ 38 Warren Moon TW 6.00 2.50
❑ 39 Mark Brunell TW 6.00 2.50
❑ 40 Ricky Watters TW 4.00 1.50
❑ 41 Dan Marino TW 25.00 10.00
❑ 42 Brett Favre TW 25.00 10.00
❑ 43 Jake Plummer 1.00 .40
❑ 44 Adrian Murrell .60 .25
❑ 45 Eric Swann .40 .15
❑ 46 Jamal Anderson 1.00 .40
❑ 47 Chris Chandler .60 .25
❑ 48 Jim Harbaugh .60 .25
❑ 49 Michael Jackson .40 .15
❑ 50 Jermaine Lewis .60 .25
❑ 51 Rob Johnson .60 .25
❑ 52 Antowain Smith 1.00 .40
❑ 53 Thurman Thomas 1.00 .40
❑ 54 Kerry Collins .60 .25
❑ 55 Fred Lane .40 .15
❑ 56 Rae Carruth .40 .15
❑ 57 Erik Kramer .40 .15
❑ 58 Curtis Conway .60 .25
❑ 59 Corey Dillon 1.00 .40
❑ 60 Neil O'Donnell .60 .25
❑ 61 Carl Pickens .60 .25
❑ 62 Troy Aikman 2.00 .75
❑ 63 Emmitt Smith 3.00 1.25
❑ 64 Deion Sanders 1.00 .40
❑ 65 Terrell Davis 1.00 .40
❑ 66 John Elway 4.00 1.50
❑ 67 Rod Smith .60 .25
❑ 68 Scott Mitchell .60 .25
❑ 69 Barry Sanders 3.00 1.25
❑ 70 Herman Moore .60 .25
❑ 71 Brett Favre 4.00 1.50
❑ 72 Dorsey Levens 1.00 .40
❑ 73 Antonio Freeman 1.00 .40
❑ 74 Marshall Faulk 1.25 .50
❑ 75 Marvin Harrison 1.00 .40
❑ 76 Mark Brunell 1.00 .40
❑ 77 Keenan McCardell .60 .25
❑ 78 Jimmy Smith .60 .25
❑ 79 Andre Rison .60 .25
❑ 80 Elvis Grbac .60 .25
❑ 81 Derrick Alexander .60 .25
❑ 82 Dan Marino 4.00 1.50
❑ 83 Karim Abdul-Jabbar 1.00 .40
❑ 84 O.J. McDuffie .60 .25
❑ 85 Brad Johnson 1.00 .40

❑ 86 Cris Carter 1.00 .40
❑ 87 Robert Smith 1.00 .40
❑ 88 Drew Bledsoe 1.50 .60
❑ 89 Terry Glenn 1.00 .40
❑ 90 Ben Coates .60 .25
❑ 91 Lamar Smith .60 .25
❑ 92 Danny Wuerffel .60 .25
❑ 93 Tiki Barber 1.00 .40
❑ 94 Danny Kanell .60 .25
❑ 95 Ike Hilliard .60 .25
❑ 96 Curtis Martin 1.00 .40
❑ 97 Keyshawn Johnson 1.00 .40
❑ 98 Glenn Foley .60 .25
❑ 99 Jeff George .60 .25
❑ 100 Tim Brown 1.00 .40
❑ 101 Napoleon Kaufman 1.00 .40
❑ 102 Bobby Hoying .60 .25
❑ 103 Charlie Garner .60 .25
❑ 104 Irving Fryar .60 .25
❑ 105 Kordell Stewart 1.00 .40
❑ 106 Jerome Bettis 1.00 .40
❑ 107 Charles Johnson .40 .15
❑ 108 Tony Banks .60 .25
❑ 109 Isaac Bruce 1.00 .40
❑ 110 Natrone Means .60 .25
❑ 111 Junior Seau 1.00 .40
❑ 112 Steve Young 1.25 .50
❑ 113 Jerry Rice 2.00 .75
❑ 114 Garrison Hearst 1.00 .40
❑ 115 Ricky Watters .60 .25
❑ 116 Warren Moon 1.00 .40
❑ 117 Joey Galloway .60 .25
❑ 118 Trent Dilfer 1.00 .40
❑ 119 Warrick Dunn 1.25 .50
❑ 120 Mike Alstott 1.00 .40
❑ 121 Steve McNair 1.00 .40
❑ 122 Eddie George 1.00 .40
❑ 123 Yancey Thigpen .40 .15
❑ 124 Gus Frerotte .40 .15
❑ 125 Terry Allen 1.00 .40
❑ 126 Michael Westbrook .60 .25
❑ AE13 Dan Marino SAMPLE 2.00 .75

1999 SP Authentic

❑ COMP.SET w/o SPs (90) 35.00 15.00
❑ *HAND NUMBERED RCs: .5X TO .8X
❑ 1 Jake Plummer .60 .25
❑ 2 Adrian Murrell .60 .25
❑ 3 Frank Sanders .60 .25
❑ 4 Jamal Anderson 1.00 .40
❑ 5 Chris Chandler .60 .25
❑ 6 Terance Mathis .60 .25
❑ 7 Priest Holmes 1.50 .60
❑ 8 Jermaine Lewis .60 .25
❑ 9 Antowain Smith 1.00 .40
❑ 10 Doug Flutie 1.00 .40
❑ 11 Eric Moulds 1.00 .40
❑ 12 Muhsin Muhammad .60 .25
❑ 13 Tim Biakabutuka .60 .25
❑ 14 Wesley Walls .60 .25
❑ 15 Curtis Enis .40 .15
❑ 16 Bobby Engram .60 .25
❑ 17 Corey Dillon 1.00 .40
❑ 18 Darnay Scott .60 .25
❑ 19 Terry Kirby .40 .15
❑ 20 Ty Detmer .60 .25
❑ 21 Troy Aikman 2.00 .75
❑ 22 Michael Irvin .60 .25
❑ 23 Emmitt Smith 2.00 .75
❑ 24 Terrell Davis 1.00 .40
❑ 25 Brian Griese 1.00 .40
❑ 26 Rod Smith .60 .25
❑ 27 Shannon Sharpe .60 .25
❑ 28 Barry Sanders 3.00 1.25
❑ 29 Charlie Batch 1.00 .40
❑ 30 Herman Moore .60 .25
❑ 31 Johnnie Morton .60 .25
❑ 32 Brett Favre 3.00 1.25
❑ 33 Antonio Freeman 1.00 .40
❑ 34 Dorsey Levens 1.00 .40
❑ 35 Mark Chmura .60 .25
❑ 36 Peyton Manning 3.00 1.25
❑ 37 Marvin Harrison 1.00 .40
❑ 38 Mark Brunell 1.00 .40
❑ 39 Fred Taylor 1.00 .40
❑ 40 Jimmy Smith .60 .25
❑ 41 Elvis Grbac .60 .25
❑ 42 Andre Rison .60 .25
❑ 43 Dan Marino 3.00 1.25
❑ 44 O.J. McDuffie .60 .25
❑ 45 Yatil Green .40 .15
❑ 46 Randall Cunningham 1.00 .40
❑ 47 Randy Moss 3.00 1.25
❑ 48 Robert Smith 1.00 .40
❑ 49 Cris Carter 1.00 .40
❑ 50 Drew Bledsoe 1.25 .50
❑ 51 Ben Coates .40 .15
❑ 52 Terry Glenn 1.00 .40
❑ 53 Eddie Kennison .60 .25
❑ 54 Cam Cleeland .40 .15
❑ 55 Ike Hilliard .60 .25
❑ 56 Gary Brown .40 .15
❑ 57 Kerry Collins .60 .25
❑ 58 Vinny Testaverde .60 .25
❑ 59 Keyshawn Johnson 1.00 .40
❑ 60 Wayne Chrebet 1.00 .40
❑ 61 Curtis Martin 1.00 .40
❑ 62 Tim Brown 1.00 .40
❑ 63 Napoleon Kaufman 1.00 .40
❑ 64 Charles Woodson 1.00 .40
❑ 65 Duce Staley 1.00 .40
❑ 66 Charles Johnson .60 .25
❑ 67 Kordell Stewart .60 .25
❑ 68 Jerome Bettis 1.00 .40
❑ 69 Marshall Faulk 1.25 .50
❑ 70 Isaac Bruce 1.00 .40
❑ 71 Trent Green 1.00 .40
❑ 72 Jim Harbaugh .60 .25
❑ 73 Junior Seau 1.00 .40
❑ 74 Natrone Means .60 .25
❑ 75 Steve Young 1.25 .50
❑ 76 Jerry Rice 2.00 .75
❑ 77 Terrell Owens 1.00 .40
❑ 78 Lawrence Phillips .60 .25
❑ 79 Joey Galloway .60 .25
❑ 80 Ricky Watters .60 .25
❑ 81 Jon Kitna 1.00 .40
❑ 82 Warrick Dunn 1.00 .40
❑ 83 Trent Dilfer .60 .25
❑ 84 Mike Alstott 1.00 .40
❑ 85 Eddie George 1.00 .40
❑ 86 Steve McNair 1.00 .40
❑ 87 Yancey Thigpen .40 .15
❑ 88 Brad Johnson 1.00 .40
❑ 89 Skip Hicks .40 .15
❑ 90 Michael Westbrook .60 .25
❑ 91 Ricky Williams RC 40.00 15.00
❑ 92 Tim Couch RC 25.00 10.00
❑ 93 Akili Smith RC 20.00 7.50
❑ 94 Edgerrin James RC 80.00 30.00
❑ 95 Donovan McNabb RC 100.00 40.00
❑ 96 Torry Holt RC 60.00 30.00
❑ 97 Cade McNown RC 20.00 7.50
❑ 98 Shaun King RC 20.00 7.50
❑ 99 Daunte Culpepper RC 60.00 25.00
❑ 100 Brock Huard RC 25.00 10.00
❑ 101 Chris Claiborne RC 12.00 5.00
❑ 102 James Johnson RC 20.00 7.50
❑ 103 Rob Konrad RC 25.00 10.00
❑ 104 Peerless Price RC 25.00 10.00
❑ 105 Kevin Faulk RC 25.00 10.00
❑ 106 Andy Katzenmoyer RC 20.00 7.50
❑ 107 Troy Edwards RC 20.00 7.50
❑ 108 Kevin Johnson RC 25.00 10.00
❑ 109 Mike Cloud RC 20.00 7.50
❑ 110 David Boston RC 25.00 10.00
❑ 111 Champ Bailey RC 30.00 12.50
❑ 112 D'Wayne Bates RC 20.00 7.50
❑ 113 Joe Germaine RC 20.00 7.50
❑ 114 Antoine Winfield RC 20.00 7.50
❑ 115 Fernando Bryant RC 20.00 7.50
❑ 116 Jevon Kearse RC 40.00 15.00
❑ 117 Chris McAlister RC 20.00 7.50
❑ 118 Brandon Stokley RC 25.00 10.00
❑ 119 Karsten Bailey RC 20.00 7.50
❑ 120 Daylon McCutcheon RC 20.00 7.50
❑ 121 Jermaine Fazande RC 20.00 7.50
❑ 122 Joel Makovicka RC 25.00 10.00
❑ 123 Ebenezer Ekuban RC 20.00 7.50
❑ 124 Joe Montgomery RC 20.00 7.50
❑ 125 Sean Bennett RC 12.00 5.00
❑ 126 Na Brown RC 20.00 7.50
❑ 127 De'Mond Parker RC 12.00 5.00
❑ 128 Sedrick Irvin RC 12.00 5.00
❑ 129 Terry Jackson RC 20.00 7.50
❑ 130 Jeff Paulk RC 12.00 5.00
❑ 131 Cecil Collins RC 12.00 5.00
❑ 132 Bobby Collins RC 12.00 5.00
❑ 133 Amos Zereoue RC 25.00 10.00
❑ 134 Travis McGriff RC 12.00 5.00
❑ 135 Larry Parker RC 25.00 10.00
❑ 136 Wane McGarity RC 12.00 5.00
❑ 137 Cecil Martin RC 20.00 7.50
❑ 138 Al Wilson RC 20.00 7.50
❑ 139 Jim Kleinsasser RC 20.00 7.50
❑ 140 Dat Nguyen RC 20.00 7.50
❑ 141 Marty Booker RC 25.00 10.00
❑ 142 Reginald Kelly RC 12.00 5.00
❑ 143 Scott Covington RC 25.00 10.00
❑ 144 Antuan Edwards RC 20.00 7.50
❑ 145 Craig Yeast RC 20.00 7.50
❑ WPA W.Payton AU/100 600.00 400.00
❑ WPSP W.Payton Jsy AU/34 1500.00 1000.00

2000 SP Authentic

❑ COMP.SET w/o SP's (90) 15.00 6.00
❑ 1 Jake Plummer .60 .25
❑ 2 David Boston 1.00 .40
❑ 3 Frank Sanders .60 .25
❑ 4 Chris Chandler .60 .25
❑ 5 Jamal Anderson 1.00 .40
❑ 6 Shawn Jefferson .40 .15
❑ 7 Tony Banks .60 .25
❑ 8 Shannon Sharpe .60 .25
❑ 9 Rob Johnson .60 .25
❑ 10 Antowain Smith .60 .25
❑ 11 Muhsin Muhammad .60 .25
❑ 12 Steve Beuerlein .60 .25
❑ 13 Cade McNown .40 .15
❑ 14 Curtis Enis .40 .15
❑ 15 Marcus Robinson 1.00 .40
❑ 16 Akili Smith .40 .15
❑ 17 Corey Dillon 1.00 .40
❑ 18 Tim Couch .60 .25
❑ 19 Kevin Johnson 1.00 .40
❑ 20 Errict Rhett .40 .15
❑ 21 Troy Aikman 2.00 .75
❑ 22 Emmitt Smith 2.50 1.00
❑ 23 Rocket Ismail .60 .25
❑ 24 Joey Galloway .60 .25
❑ 25 Terrell Davis 1.00 .40
❑ 26 Olandis Gary 1.00 .40
❑ 27 Ed McCaffrey 1.00 .40
❑ 28 Brian Griese 1.00 .40

❑ 29 Charlie Batch 1.00 .40
❑ 30 Germane Crowell .40 .15
❑ 31 James O. Stewart .60 .25
❑ 32 Brett Favre 3.00 1.25
❑ 33 Antonio Freeman 1.00 .40
❑ 34 Dorsey Levens .60 .25
❑ 35 Peyton Manning 2.50 1.00
❑ 36 Edgerrin James 1.50 .60
❑ 37 Marvin Harrison 1.00 .40
❑ 38 Mark Brunell 1.00 .40
❑ 39 Fred Taylor 1.00 .40
❑ 40 Jimmy Smith .60 .25
❑ 41 Elvis Grbac .60 .25
❑ 42 Tony Gonzalez .60 .25
❑ 43 James Johnson .40 .15
❑ 44 Oronde Gadsden .60 .25
❑ 45 Damon Huard 1.00 .40
❑ 46 Randy Moss 2.00 .75
❑ 47 Cris Carter 1.00 .40
❑ 48 Daunte Culpepper 1.25 .50
❑ 49 Drew Bledsoe 1.25 .50
❑ 50 Terry Glenn .60 .25
❑ 51 Ricky Williams 1.00 .40
❑ 52 Jeff Blake .60 .25
❑ 53 Keith Poole .40 .15
❑ 54 Kerry Collins .60 .25
❑ 55 Amani Toomer .60 .25
❑ 56 Ike Hilliard .60 .25
❑ 57 Wayne Chrebet .60 .25
❑ 58 Curtis Martin 1.00 .40
❑ 59 Vinny Testaverde .60 .25
❑ 60 Tim Brown 1.00 .40
❑ 61 Rich Gannon 1.00 .40
❑ 62 Tyrone Wheatley .60 .25
❑ 63 Duce Staley 1.00 .40
❑ 64 Donovan McNabb 1.50 .60
❑ 65 Troy Edwards .40 .15
❑ 66 Jerome Bettis 1.00 .40
❑ 67 Kordell Stewart .60 .25
❑ 68 Marshall Faulk 1.25 .50
❑ 69 Kurt Warner 1.50 .60
❑ 70 Isaac Bruce 1.00 .40
❑ 71 Torry Holt 1.00 .40
❑ 72 Ryan Leaf .60 .25
❑ 73 Jim Harbaugh .60 .25
❑ 74 Jermaine Fazande .40 .15
❑ 75 Jerry Rice 2.00 .75
❑ 76 Terrell Owens 1.00 .40
❑ 77 Jeff Garcia 1.00 .40
❑ 78 Ricky Watters .60 .25
❑ 79 Jon Kitna 1.00 .40
❑ 80 Derrick Mayes .60 .25
❑ 81 Shaun King .40 .15
❑ 82 Mike Alstott 1.00 .40
❑ 83 Keyshawn Johnson 1.00 .40
❑ 84 Warrick Dunn 1.00 .40
❑ 85 Eddie George 1.00 .40
❑ 86 Steve McNair 1.00 .40
❑ 87 Jevon Kearse 1.00 .40
❑ 88 Brad Johnson 1.00 .40
❑ 89 Stephen Davis 1.00 .40
❑ 90 Michael Westbrook .60 .25
❑ 91 Anthony Lucas RC 10.00 4.00
❑ 92 Avion Black RC 15.00 6.00
❑ 93 Dante Hall RC 40.00 15.00
❑ 94 Darrell Jackson RC 30.00 12.50
❑ 95 Deltha O'Neal RC 20.00 7.50
❑ 96 Erron Kinney RC 20.00 7.50
❑ 97 Doug Chapman RC 15.00 6.00
❑ 98 Frank Murphy RC 10.00 4.00
❑ 99 Gari Scott RC 10.00 4.00
❑ 100 Giovanni Carmazzi RC 10.00 4.00
❑ 101 JaJuan Dawson RC 10.00 4.00
❑ 102 Jarious Jackson RC 15.00 6.00
❑ 103 Rashard Anderson RC 15.00 6.00
❑ 104 Michael Wiley RC 15.00 6.00
❑ 105 Spergon Wynn RC 15.00 6.00
❑ 106 Muneer Moore RC 10.00 4.00
❑ 107 Ahmed Plummer RC 20.00 7.50
❑ 108 Chad Morton RC 20.00 7.50
❑ 109 Rob Morris RC 15.00 6.00
❑ 110 Ron Dixon RC 15.00 6.00
❑ 111 Rondell Mealey RC 10.00 4.00
❑ 112 Sebastian Janikowski RC 20.00 7.50
❑ 113 Shaun Ellis RC 20.00 7.50
❑ 114 Rogers Beckett RC 15.00 6.00
❑ 115 Shyrone Stith RC 15.00 6.00
❑ 116 Tim Rattay RC 20.00 7.50
❑ 117 Todd Husak RC 20.00 7.50
❑ 118 Tom Brady RC 1600.00 1000.00
❑ 119 Trevor Gaylor RC 15.00 6.00
❑ 120 Windrell Hayes RC 15.00 6.00
❑ 121 Anthony Becht RC 20.00 7.50
❑ 122 Brian Urlacher RC 80.00 40.00
❑ 123 Bubba Franks RC 20.00 7.50
❑ 124 Chad Pennington RC 80.00 30.00
❑ 125 Chris Redman RC 15.00 6.00
❑ 126 Corey Simon RC 20.00 7.50
❑ 127 Curtis Keaton RC 15.00 6.00
❑ 128 Danny Farmer RC 15.00 6.00
❑ 129 Dennis Northcutt RC 20.00 7.50
❑ 130 Dez White RC 20.00 7.50
❑ 131 J.R. Redmond RC 15.00 6.00
❑ 132 Jamal Lewis RC 80.00 30.00
❑ 133 Jerry Porter RC 50.00 20.00
❑ 134 Joe Hamilton RC 15.00 6.00
❑ 135 Laveranues Coles RC 40.00 15.00
❑ 136 R.Jay Soward RC 15.00 6.00
❑ 137 Reuben Droughns RC 40.00 15.00
❑ 138 Ron Dayne RC 30.00 12.50
❑ 139 Ron Dugans RC 10.00 4.00
❑ 140 Shaun Alexander RC 150.00 75.00
❑ 141 Sylvester Morris RC 15.00 6.00
❑ 142 Tee Martin RC 20.00 7.50
❑ 143 Thomas Jones RC 40.00 15.00
❑ 144 Todd Pinkston RC 20.00 7.50
❑ 145 Travis Prentice RC 15.00 6.00
❑ 146 Travis Taylor RC 20.00 7.50
❑ 147 Trung Canidate RC 15.00 6.00
❑ 148 Courtney Brown RC 20.00 7.50
❑ 149 Plaxico Burress RC 50.00 20.00
❑ 150 Peter Warrick RC 20.00 7.50
❑ 151 Billy Volek RC 50.00 20.00
❑ 152 Bobby Shaw RC 10.00 4.00
❑ 153 Brad Hoover RC 15.00 6.00
❑ 154 Brian Finneran RC 20.00 7.50
❑ 155 Charles Lee RC 10.00 4.00
❑ 156 Chris Cole RC 10.00 4.00
❑ 157 Clint Stoerner RC 15.00 6.00
❑ 158 Doug Johnson RC 20.00 7.50
❑ 159 Frank Moreau RC 15.00 6.00
❑ 160 Jake Delhomme RC 80.00 40.00
❑ 161 KaRon Coleman RC 10.00 4.00
❑ 162 Kevin McDougal RC 10.00 4.00
❑ 163 Larry Foster RC 10.00 4.00
❑ 164 Mike Anderson RC 25.00 10.00
❑ 165 Patrick Pass RC 10.00 4.00
❑ 166 Reggie Jones RC 10.00 4.00
❑ 167 Sammy Morris RC 20.00 10.00
❑ 168 Shockmain Davis RC 10.00 4.00
❑ 169 Terrelle Smith RC 10.00 4.00
❑ 170 Ronney Jenkins RC 10.00 4.00
❑ 171 Troy Walters RC 15.00 6.00

2001 SP Authentic

❑ COMP.SET w/o SP's (90) 20.00 7.50
❑ *SINGLE COLOR SWATCH: .3X TO .8X
❑ 1 Jake Plummer .60 .25
❑ 2 Thomas Jones .60 .25
❑ 3 Frank Sanders .40 .15
❑ 4 Jamal Anderson 1.00 .40
❑ 5 Chris Chandler .60 .25
❑ 6 Tony Martin .60 .25
❑ 7 Jamal Lewis 1.25 .50
❑ 8 Elvis Grbac .60 .25
❑ 9 Travis Taylor .60 .25
❑ 10 Peerless Price .60 .25
❑ 11 Rob Johnson .60 .25
❑ 12 Eric Moulds .60 .25
❑ 13 Muhsin Muhammad .60 .25
❑ 14 Isaac Byrd .40 .15
❑ 15 Wesley Walls .40 .15
❑ 16 James Allen .60 .25
❑ 17 Marcus Robinson 1.00 .40
❑ 18 Brian Urlacher 1.25 .50
❑ 19 Jon Kitna .00 .25
❑ 20 Peter Warrick 1.00 .40
❑ 21 Corey Dillon 1.00 .40
❑ 22 Kevin Johnson .60 .25
❑ 23 JaJuan Dawson .40 .15
❑ 24 Tim Couch .60 .25
❑ 25 Rocket Ismail .60 .25
❑ 26 Emmitt Smith 2.00 .75
❑ 27 Joey Galloway .60 .25
❑ 28 Terrell Davis 1.00 .40
❑ 29 Mike Anderson 1.00 .40
❑ 30 Brian Griese 1.00 .40
❑ 31 Ed McCaffrey 1.00 .40
❑ 32 Charlie Batch 1.00 .40
❑ 33 James O. Stewart .60 .25
❑ 34 Johnnie Morton .60 .25
❑ 35 Brett Favre 3.00 1.25
❑ 36 Antonio Freeman 1.00 .40
❑ 37 Bill Schroeder .40 .15
❑ 38 Ahman Green 1.00 .40
❑ 39 Peyton Manning 2.50 1.00
❑ 40 Edgerrin James 1.25 .50
❑ 41 Marvin Harrison 1.00 .40
❑ 42 Mark Brunell 1.00 .40
❑ 43 Fred Taylor 1.00 .40
❑ 44 Jimmy Smith .60 .25
❑ 45 Tony Gonzalez .60 .25
❑ 46 Trent Green 1.00 .40
❑ 47 Oronde Gadsden .60 .25
❑ 48 Jay Fiedler 1.00 .40
❑ 49 Lamar Smith .60 .25
❑ 50 Randy Moss 2.00 .75
❑ 51 Cris Carter 1.00 .40
❑ 52 Daunte Culpepper 1.00 .40
❑ 53 Drew Bledsoe 1.25 .50
❑ 54 Terry Glenn .60 .25
❑ 55 Antowain Smith .60 .25
❑ 56 Ricky Williams 1.00 .40
❑ 57 Joe Horn .60 .25
❑ 58 Aaron Brooks 1.00 .40
❑ 59 Kerry Collins .60 .25
❑ 60 Tiki Barber 1.00 .40
❑ 61 Ron Dayne 1.00 .40
❑ 62 Vinny Testaverde .60 .25
❑ 63 Wayne Chrebet .60 .25
❑ 64 Curtis Martin 1.00 .40
❑ 65 Tim Brown 1.00 .40
❑ 66 Rich Gannon 1.00 .40
❑ 67 Jerry Rice 2.00 .75
❑ 68 Duce Staley 1.00 .40
❑ 69 Donovan McNabb 1.25 .50
❑ 70 Kordell Stewart .60 .25
❑ 71 Jerome Bettis 1.00 .40
❑ 72 Marshall Faulk 1.25 .50
❑ 73 Kurt Warner 1.50 .60
❑ 74 Isaac Bruce 1.00 .40
❑ 75 Doug Flutie 1.00 .40
❑ 76 Junior Seau 1.00 .40
❑ 77 Jeff Garcia 1.00 .40
❑ 78 Garrison Hearst .60 .25
❑ 79 Terrell Owens 1.00 .40
❑ 80 Ricky Watters .60 .25
❑ 81 Matt Hasselbeck .60 .25
❑ 82 Brad Johnson 1.00 .40
❑ 83 Warrick Dunn 1.00 .40
❑ 84 Mike Alstott 1.00 .40
❑ 85 Kevin Dyson .60 .25
❑ 86 Eddie George 1.00 .40
❑ 87 Steve McNair 1.00 .40
❑ 88 Champ Bailey .60 .25
❑ 89 Michael Westbrook .60 .25
❑ 90 Stephen Davis 1.00 .40
❑ 91 Michael Vick JSY AU RC 600.00 300.00
❑ 92 Rod Gardner JSY AU RC 60.00 30.00
❑ 93 Freddie Mitchell JSY AU RC 60.00 25.00
❑ 94 Koren Robinson JSY/500 RC 50.00 20.00
❑ 95 David Terrell JSY/500 RC 25.00 10.00
❑ 96 Michael Bennett JSY RC 40.00 15.00

❑ 97 Robert Ferguson JSY RC 40.00 15.00
❑ 98 Deuce McAllister JSY RC 80.00 40.00
❑ 99 Travis Henry JSY RC 80.00 40.00
❑ 100 Andre Carter JSY RC 25.00 10.00
❑ 101 Drew Brees JSY RC 150.00 75.00
❑ 102 Santana Moss JSY/500 RC 80.00 40.00
❑ 103 Chris Weinke JSY/390 RC 40.00 15.00
❑ 104 Chad Johnson JSY/160 RC 400.00 250.00
❑ 105 Reggie Wayne JSY RC 100.00 60.00
❑ 106 Kevan Barlow JSY/500 RC 40.00 15.00
❑ 107 Chr Chambers JSY/500 RC 80.00 40.00
❑ 108 Todd Heap JSY/500 RC 80.00 30.00
❑ 109 A Thomas JSY/500 RC 30.00 12.50
❑ 110 James Jackson JSY/500 RC 25.00 10.00
[illegible]
❑ 112 Mike McMahon JSY RC 25.00 10.00
❑ 113 Josh Heupel JSY RC 30.00 12.00
❑ 114 Travis Minor JSY/500 RC 30.00 12.50
❑ 115 Quincy Morgan JSY/500 RC 30.00 12.50
❑ 116 Dan Morgan JSY/500 RC 30.00 12.50
❑ 117 Jesse Palmer JSY/500 RC 50.00 20.00
❑ 118 Sage Rosenfels JSY/300 RC 50.00 20.00
❑ 119 Marq Tuiasosopo JSY RC 25.00 10.00
❑ 120 L.Tomlinson JSY/500 RC 800.00 450.00
❑ 123 Alge Crumpler AU RC 30.00 15.00
❑ 124 Arnold Jackson AU RC 20.00 7.50
❑ 125 Bobby Newcombe AU RC 20.00 7.50
❑ 126 Brand Manumaleuna AU RC 20.00 7.50
❑ 127 Cedrick Wilson AU RC 35.00 20.00
❑ 128 Brian Allen AU RC 15.00 6.00
❑ 129 Dee Brown AU RC 25.00 10.00
❑ 130 Damerien McCants AU RC 20.00 7.50
❑ 131 Dave Dickenson AU RC 20.00 7.50
❑ 132 Derrick Blaylock AU RC 40.00 20.00
❑ 133 Eddie Berlin AU RC 20.00 7.50
❑ 134 Francis St.Paul AU RC 20.00 7.50
❑ 135 Jamar Fletcher AU RC 20.00 7.50
❑ 136 Josh Booty AU RC 25.00 10.00
❑ 137 Scotty Anderson AU RC 20.00 7.50
❑ 138 Ken-Yon Rambo AU RC 20.00 7.50
❑ 139 Kenyatta Walker AU RC 15.00 6.00
❑ 140 Kevin Kasper AU RC 25.00 10.00
❑ 141 Snoop Minnis AU RC 20.00 7.50
❑ 142 Houshmandzadeh AU RC 60.00 35.00
❑ 143 Quincy Carter AU RC 25.00 10.00
❑ 144 Ronney Daniels AU RC 15.00 6.00
❑ 145 Sedrick Hodge AU RC 15.00 6.00
❑ 146 Steve Smith AU RC 135.00 75.00
❑ 147 Tim Hasselbeck AU RC 25.00 10.00
❑ 148 Vinny Sutherland AU RC 20.00 7.50
❑ 149 Richard Seymour AU RC 60.00 30.00
❑ 150 Jamie Winborn AU 20.00 7.50
❑ 151 Gerard Warren RC 12.00 5.00
❑ 152 Justin Smith RC 12.00 5.00
❑ 153 David Martin RC 10.00 4.00
❑ 154 Jamal Reynolds RC 12.00 5.00
❑ 155 Dominic Rhodes RC 20.00 10.00
❑ 156 Nate Clements RC 12.00 5.00
❑ 157 Michael Lewis RC 12.00 5.00
❑ 158 Andre King RC 10.00 4.00
❑ 159 Benjamin Gay RC 12.00 5.00
❑ 160 Correll Buckhalter RC 30.00 15.00
❑ 161 Roderick Robinson RC 10.00 4.00
❑ 162 Moran Norris RC 8.00 3.00
❑ 163 Onome Ojo RC 10.00 4.00
❑ 164 Will Allen RC 10.00 4.00
❑ 165 Jonathan Carter RC 10.00 4.00
❑ 166 LaMont Jordan RC 40.00 15.00
❑ 167 DeLawrence Grant RC 8.00 3.00
❑ 168 Derrick Gibson RC 10.00 4.00
❑ 169 A.J. Feeley RC 20.00 7.50
❑ 170 Tim Baker RC 8.00 3.00
❑ 171 Kendrell Bell RC 25.00 10.00
❑ 172 Zeke Moreno RC 12.00 5.00
❑ 173 Carlos Polk RC 8.00 3.00
❑ 174 Ken Lucas RC 10.00 4.00
❑ 175 Heath Evans RC 10.00 4.00
❑ 176 Elvis Joseph RC 10.00 4.00
❑ 177 Damione Lewis RC 10.00 4.00
❑ 178 Tommy Polley RC 12.00 5.00
❑ 179 Fred Smoot RC 12.00 5.00
❑ 180 Jason Brookins RC 12.00 5.00
❑ 181 Nick Goings RC 12.00 5.00
❑ 182 Drew Bennett RC 25.00 10.00
❑ 183 Justin McCareins RC 15.00 6.00
❑ 184 Kabeer Gbaja-Biamila RC 25.00 10.00
❑ 185 Edgerton Hartwell RC 8.00 3.00
❑ 186 Robert Carswell RC 8.00 3.00
❑ 187 Aaron Schobel RC 12.00 5.00
❑ 188 Dan Alexander RC 12.00 5.00
❑ 189 Jamie Winborn RC 10.00 4.00
❑ 190 Karon Riley RC 8.00 3.00
❑ EG Eddie George SAMPLE 3.00 1.50

2002 SP Authentic

❑ COMP.SET w/o SP's (90) 25.00 10.00
❑ 1 Tom Brady 2.00 .75
❑ 2 Antowain Smith .60 .25
❑ 3 Troy Brown .60 .25
❑ 4 Kurt Warner 1.00 .40
❑ 5 Marshall Faulk 1.00 .40
❑ 6 Isaac Bruce 1.00 .40
❑ 7 Kordell Stewart .60 .25
❑ 8 Jerome Bettis 1.00 .40
❑ 9 Plaxico Burress .60 .25
❑ 10 Hines Ward 1.00 .40
❑ 11 Donovan McNabb 1.25 .50
❑ 12 Duce Staley 1.00 .40
❑ 13 Dorsey Levens .60 .25
❑ 14 Antonio Freeman 1.00 .40
❑ 15 Jerry Rice 2.00 .75
❑ 16 Rich Gannon 1.00 .40
❑ 17 Tim Brown 1.00 .40
❑ 18 Jim Miller .60 .25
❑ 19 Marty Booker .60 .25
❑ 20 Brian Urlacher 1.25 .50
❑ 21 Jamal Lewis 1.00 .40
❑ 22 Chris Redman .40 .15
❑ 23 Ray Lewis 1.00 .40
❑ 24 Brett Favre 2.50 1.00
❑ 25 Ahman Green 1.00 .40
❑ 26 Terry Glenn .60 .25
❑ 27 Keyshawn Johnson 1.00 .40
❑ 28 Keenan McCardell .40 .15
❑ 29 Michael Pittman .40 .15
❑ 30 Curtis Martin 1.00 .40
❑ 31 Vinny Testaverde .60 .25
❑ 32 Chad Pennington 1.25 .50
❑ 33 Wayne Chrebet .60 .25
❑ 34 Terrell Owens 1.00 .40
❑ 35 Garrison Hearst .60 .25
❑ 36 Jay Fiedler .60 .25
❑ 37 Ricky Williams 1.00 .40
❑ 38 Chris Chambers 1.00 .40
❑ 39 Shaun Alexander 1.25 .50
❑ 40 Darrell Jackson .60 .25
❑ 41 Drew Bledsoe 1.25 .50
❑ 42 Travis Henry 1.00 .40
❑ 43 Eric Moulds .60 .25
❑ 44 Stephen Davis .60 .25
❑ 45 Rod Gardner .60 .25
❑ 46 Brian Griese 1.00 .40
❑ 47 Olandis Gary .60 .25
❑ 48 Shannon Sharpe .60 .25
❑ 49 Tim Couch .60 .25
❑ 50 Kevin Johnson .60 .25
❑ 51 Steve McNair 1.00 .40
❑ 52 Eddie George 1.00 .40
❑ 53 Aaron Brooks 1.00 .40
❑ 54 Deuce McAllister 1.25 .50
❑ 55 Joe Horn .60 .25
❑ 56 Michael Vick 1.50 .60
❑ 57 Warrick Dunn 1.00 .40
❑ 58 Kerry Collins .60 .25
❑ 59 Tiki Barber 1.00 .40
❑ 60 Amani Toomer .60 .25
❑ 61 Jake Plummer .60 .25
❑ 62 David Boston 1.00 .40
❑ 63 Thomas Jones .60 .25
❑ 64 Edgerrin James 1.25 .50
❑ 65 Marvin Harrison 1.00 .40
❑ 66 Mark Brunell 1.00 .40
❑ 67 Jimmy Smith .60 .25
❑ 68 Fred Taylor 1.00 .40
❑ 69 Corey Dillon .60 .25
❑ 70 Jon Kitna .60 .25
❑ 71 Michael Westbrook .40 .15
❑ 72 Trent Green .60 .25
❑ 73 Priest Holmes 1.25 .50
❑ 74 Tony Gonzalez .60 .25
❑ 75 Daunte Culpepper 1.00 .40
❑ 76 Michael Bennett .60 .25
❑ 77 Randy Moss 1.50 .60
❑ 78 Drew Brees 1.00 .40
❑ 79 Curtis Conway .40 .15
❑ 80 Junior Seau 1.00 .40
❑ 81 Quincy Carter .60 .25
❑ 82 Emmitt Smith 2.50 1.00
❑ 83 Joey Galloway .60 .25
❑ 84 Cory Schlesinger .40 .15
❑ 85 James Stewart .60 .25
❑ 86 Az-Zahir Hakim .40 .15
❑ 87 Rodney Peete .60 .25
❑ 88 Lamar Smith .60 .25
❑ 89 Corey Bradford .40 .15
❑ 90 Jermaine Lewis .40 .15
❑ 91 Peyton Manning AU 120.00 60.00
❑ 92 Anthony Thomas AU 25.00 12.50
❑ 93 LaDainian Tomlinson AU 80.00 40.00
❑ 94 Jeff Garcia AU 25.00 10.00
❑ 95 Kurt Warner SC 3.00 1.25
❑ 96 Brett Favre SC 8.00 3.00
❑ 97 Michael Vick SC 6.00 2.50
❑ 98 Donovan McNabb SC 4.00 1.50
❑ 99 Daunte Culpepper SC 3.00 1.25
❑ 100 Tom Brady SC 8.00 3.00
❑ 101 Drew Brees SC 3.00 1.25
❑ 102 Kordell Stewart SC 2.00 .75
❑ 103 Steve McNair SC 3.00 1.25
❑ 104 Peyton Manning SC 6.00 2.50
❑ 105 Mark Brunell SC 3.00 1.25
❑ 106 Jeff Garcia SC 3.00 1.25
❑ 107 Aaron Brooks SC 3.00 1.25
❑ 108 Rich Gannon SC 3.00 1.25
❑ 109 Tim Couch SC 2.00 .75
❑ 110 Jake Plummer SC 3.00 1.25
❑ 111 Drew Bledsoe SC 4.00 1.50
❑ 112 Brian Griese SC 3.00 1.25
❑ 113 Quincy Carter SC 2.00 .75
❑ 114 Vinny Testaverde SC 2.00 .75
❑ 115 Chad Pennington SC 4.00 1.50
❑ 116 Brad Johnson SC 2.00 .75
❑ 117 Trent Dilfer SC 2.00 .75
❑ 118 Jim Miller SC 2.00 .75
❑ 119 Tommy Maddox SC 8.00 3.00
❑ 120 Trent Green SC 2.00 .75
❑ 121 Rodney Peete SC 2.00 .75
❑ 122 Jay Fiedler SC 2.00 .75
❑ 123 Kerry Collins SC 2.00 .75
❑ 124 Chris Redman SC 2.00 .75
❑ 125 Marshall Faulk SS 4.00 1.50
❑ 126 Donovan McNabb SS 5.00 2.00
❑ 127 Michael Vick SS 8.00 3.00
❑ 128 Brett Favre SS 10.00 4.00
❑ 129 Peyton Manning SS 8.00 3.00
❑ 130 Kurt Warner SS 4.00 1.50
❑ 131 Curtis Martin SS 4.00 1.50
❑ 132 Randy Moss SS 8.00 3.00
❑ 133 Edgerrin James SS 5.00 2.00
❑ 134 Jerome Bettis SS 4.00 1.50
❑ 135 Emmitt Smith SS 10.00 4.00
❑ 136 LaDainian Tomlinson SS 6.00 2.50
❑ 137 Jeff Garcia SS 4.00 1.50
❑ 138 Kordell Stewart SS 2.50 1.00
❑ 139 Anthony Thomas SS 2.50 1.00
❑ 140 Tom Brady SS 10.00 4.00
❑ 141 Daunte Culpepper SS 4.00 1.50
❑ 142 Drew Bledsoe SS 5.00 2.00
❑ 143 Ricky Williams SS 4.00 1.50
❑ 144 Warrick Dunn SS 4.00 1.50
❑ 145 Steve McNair SS 4.00 1.50
❑ 146 Rich Gannon SS 4.00 1.50
❑ 147 Jake Plummer SS 2.50 1.00

❑ 148 Jerry Rice SS	8.00	3.00
❑ 149 Mark Brunell SS	4.00	1.50
❑ 150 Brian Griese SS	4.00	1.50
❑ 151 Eddie George SS	4.00	1.50
❑ 152 Tim Couch SS	2.50	1.00
❑ 153 Keyshawn Johnson SS	4.00	1.50
❑ 154 Shannon Sharpe SS	2.50	1.00
❑ 155 Phillip Buchanon RC	12.00	5.00
❑ 156 Brian Allen RC	10.00	4.00
❑ 157 Brian Westbrook RC	40.00	20.00
❑ 158 Lito Sheppard RC	12.00	5.00
❑ 159 Daryl Jones RC	10.00	4.00
❑ 160 Javin Hunter RC	6.00	2.50
❑ 161 Derrick Lewis RC	6.00	2.50
❑ 162 Javon Walker RC	30.00	15.00
❑ 163 Tank Williams RC	10.00	4.00
❑ 164 Shaun Hill RC	12.00	5.00
❑ 165 Napoleon Harris RC	12.00	5.00
❑ 166 Herb Haygood RC	6.00	2.50
❑ 167 Jake Schifino RC	10.00	4.00
❑ 168 Quentin Jammer RC	12.00	5.00
❑ 169 Jason McAddley RC	10.00	4.00
❑ 170 Jerramy Stevens RC	12.00	5.00
❑ 171 Jesse Chatman RC	12.00	5.00
❑ 172 Larry Ned RC	10.00	4.00
❑ 173 Najeh Davenport RC	12.00	5.00
❑ 174 Lamont Thompson RC	10.00	4.00
❑ 175 Darrell Hill RC	10.00	4.00
❑ 176 Ryan Sims RC	12.00	5.00
❑ 177 Ryan Denney RC	10.00	4.00
❑ 178 Jamin Elliott RC	6.00	2.50
❑ 179 Sam Simmons RC	6.00	2.50
❑ 180 Seth Burford RC	10.00	4.00
❑ 181 Tellis Redmon RC	10.00	4.00
❑ 182 Ben Leber RC	12.00	5.00
❑ 183 Kendall Newson RC	6.00	2.50
❑ 184 Marques Anderson RC	12.00	5.00
❑ 185 Adrian Peterson AU RC	25.00	10.00
❑ 186 Haynesworth AU RC EXCH		
❑ 187 Antwoine Womack AU RC	20.00	7.50
❑ 188 Brandon Doman AU RC	20.00	7.50
❑ 189 Craig Nall AU RC	30.00	12.50
❑ 190 Chad Hutchinson AU RC	20.00	7.50
❑ 191 Chester Taylor AU RC	40.00	20.00
❑ 192 Damien Anderson AU RC	20.00	7.50
❑ 193 Deion Branch AU RC	50.00	25.00
❑ 194 Dusty Bonner AU RC	15.00	6.00
❑ 195 Ed Reed AU RC	50.00	20.00
❑ 196 Eric McCoo AU RC	15.00	6.00
❑ 197 J.T. O'Sullivan AU RC	20.00	7.50
❑ 198 Kalimba Edwards AU RC	25.00	10.00
❑ 199 Jonathan Wells AU RC	25.00	10.00
❑ 200 Josh Scobey AU RC	20.00	7.50
❑ 201 Kelly Campbell AU RC	30.00	15.00
❑ 202 Kurt Kittner AU RC	20.00	7.50
❑ 203 Lamar Gordon AU RC	25.00	10.00
❑ 204 Lee Mays AU RC	20.00	7.50
❑ 205 Leonard Henry AU RC	20.00	7.50
❑ 206 Luke Staley AU RC	20.00	7.50
❑ 207 Justin Peelle AU RC	15.00	6.00
❑ 208 Randy Fasani AU RC	20.00	7.50
❑ 209 Ricky Williams AU RC	25.00	10.00
❑ 210 Ronald Curry AU RC	30.00	15.00
❑ 211 Travis Stephens AU RC	20.00	7.50
❑ 212 Wendell Bryant AU RC	15.00	6.00
❑ 213 Woody Dantzler AU RC	20.00	7.50
❑ 214 Kahlil Hill AU RC	20.00	7.50
❑ 215 Donte Stallworth JSY RC	50.00	20.00
❑ 216 Joey Harrington AU/280 RC	60.00	30.00
❑ 217 Cliff Russell JSY RC	30.00	12.50
❑ 218 Clinton Portis JSY RC	100.00	40.00
❑ 219 Daniel Graham JSY RC	30.00	15.00
❑ 220 David Garrard JSY RC	60.00	35.00
❑ 221 DeShaun Foster JSY RC	50.00	25.00
❑ 222 Julius Peppers JSY RC	50.00	25.00
❑ 223 Jeremy Shockey JSY RC	60.00	30.00
❑ 224 Patrick Ramsey JSY RC	30.00	12.50
❑ 225 Josh Reed JSY RC	30.00	12.50
❑ 226 LaDell Betts JSY RC	30.00	12.50
❑ 227 Mike Williams JSY/350 RC	30.00	12.50
❑ 228 Reche Caldwell JSY RC	30.00	12.50
❑ 229 Rohan Davey JSY RC	30.00	12.50
❑ 230 Ron Johnson JSY RC	30.00	12.50
❑ 231 Roy Williams JSY/350 RC	60.00	25.00
❑ 232 T.J. Duckett JSY RC	30.00	12.50
❑ 233 Tim Carter JSY RC	30.00	12.50
❑ 234 William Green JSY RC	30.00	12.50
❑ 235 Randle El JSY AU RC	80.00	40.00
❑ 237 David Carr JSY AU RC	120.00	60.00
❑ 238 Andre Davis JSY AU RC	40.00	20.00
❑ 239 Eric Crouch JSY AU RC	50.00	20.00
❑ 240 Antonio Bryant JSY AU RC	40.00	15.00
❑ 241 Jabar Gaffney JSY AU RC	40.00	15.00
❑ 242 Marquise Walker JSY AU RC	40.00	20.00
❑ 243 Maurice Morris JSY AU RC	50.00	25.00
❑ 244 Josh McCown JSY AU RC	80.00	30.00
❑ AP1 Walter Payton AU/34	750.00	500.00
❑ SW1 Walter Payton JSY/150	120.00	50.00
❑ SW1 W.Payton Gold JSY/34	200.00	100.00
❑ SCPS Payt/Smith JSY/250	120.00	60.00
❑ SCPSG Payt/Smith Gld JSY/34	300.00	175.00

2003 SP Authentic

❑ COMP.SET w/o SP's (90)	20.00	7.50
❑ 1 Donovan McNabb	1.25	.50
❑ 2 Tim Couch	.40	.15
❑ 3 Joey Harrington	1.25	.50
❑ 4 Brett Favre	2.50	1.00
❑ 5 Jeff Garcia	1.00	.40
❑ 6 Kerry Collins	.60	.25
❑ 7 Michael Vick	2.00	.75
❑ 8 David Carr	1.25	.50
❑ 9 Steve McNair	1.00	.40
❑ 10 Chad Pennington	1.25	.50
❑ 11 Patrick Ramsey	1.00	.40
❑ 12 Rich Gannon	.60	.25
❑ 13 Kurt Warner	1.00	.40
❑ 14 Brad Johnson	.60	.25
❑ 15 Jay Fiedler	.60	.25
❑ 16 Jake Plummer	.60	.25
❑ 17 Mark Brunell	.60	.25
❑ 18 Peyton Manning	1.50	.60
❑ 19 Brian Griese	1.00	.40
❑ 20 Kordell Stewart	.60	.25
❑ 21 Kelly Holcomb	.60	.25
❑ 22 Josh McCown	.60	.25
❑ 23 Matt Hasselbeck	.60	.25
❑ 24 Marc Bulger	1.00	.40
❑ 25 Chris Redman	.40	.15
❑ 26 Rodney Peete	.60	.25
❑ 27 Jake Delhomme	1.00	.40
❑ 28 Jon Kitna	.60	.25
❑ 29 Trent Green	.60	.25
❑ 30 Quincy Carter	.60	.25
❑ 31 Chad Hutchinson	.40	.15
❑ 32 Edgerrin James	1.00	.40
❑ 33 Deuce McAllister	1.00	.40
❑ 34 Ricky Williams	1.00	.40
❑ 35 Priest Holmes	1.25	.50
❑ 36 Curtis Martin	1.00	.40
❑ 37 Shaun Alexander	1.00	.40
❑ 38 Eddie George	.60	.25
❑ 39 Marshall Faulk	1.00	.40
❑ 40 Garrison Hearst	.60	.25
❑ 41 Ahman Green	1.00	.40
❑ 42 Corey Dillon	.60	.25
❑ 43 Jamal Lewis	1.00	.40
❑ 44 William Green	.60	.25
❑ 45 Travis Henry	.60	.25
❑ 46 Mike Alstott	1.00	.40
❑ 47 Amos Zereoue	.60	.25
❑ 48 Stephen Davis	.60	.25
❑ 49 Duce Staley	.60	.25
❑ 50 Fred Taylor	1.00	.40
❑ 51 Anthony Thomas	.60	.25
❑ 52 Charlie Garner	.60	.25
❑ 53 Kevan Barlow	.60	.25
❑ 54 Brian Urlacher	1.25	.50
❑ 55 Junior Seau	1.00	.40
❑ 56 Zach Thomas	1.00	.40
❑ 57 Ray Lewis	1.00	.40
❑ 58 Jerry Porter	.60	.25
❑ 59 Marty Booker	.60	.25
❑ 60 Javon Walker	.60	.25
❑ 61 Donald Driver	.60	.25
❑ 62 Amani Toomer	.60	.25
❑ 63 Peerless Price	.60	.25
❑ 64 Santana Moss	.60	.25
❑ 65 Laveranues Coles	.60	.25
❑ 66 Troy Brown	.60	.25
❑ 67 Chris Chambers	1.00	.40
❑ 68 Rod Smith	.60	.25
❑ 69 Ashley Lelie	1.00	.40
❑ 70 Plaxico Burress	.60	.25
❑ 71 Keyshawn Johnson	1.00	.40
❑ 72 Isaac Bruce	1.00	.40
❑ 73 Torry Holt	1.00	.40
❑ 74 Koren Robinson	.60	.25
❑ 75 Derrick Mason	.60	.25
❑ 76 Kevin Johnson	.60	.25
❑ 77 Andre' Davis	.40	.15
❑ 78 Antonio Bryant	.60	.25
❑ 79 Eric Moulds	.60	.25
❑ 80 Jerry Rice	2.00	.75
❑ 81 Tim Brown	1.00	.40
❑ 82 Antwaan Randle El	1.00	.40
❑ 83 Donte Stallworth	1.00	.40
❑ 84 Randy Moss	1.50	.60
❑ 85 Chad Johnson	1.00	.40
❑ 86 Hines Ward	1.00	.40
❑ 87 Rod Gardner	.60	.25
❑ 88 Marvin Harrison	1.00	.40
❑ 89 David Boston	.60	.25
❑ 90 Julius Peppers	1.00	.40
❑ 91 Dewayne White RC	5.00	2.00
❑ 92 Casey Fitzsimmons RC	6.00	2.50
❑ 93 Aaron Moorehead RC	6.00	2.50
❑ 94 Jimmy Farris RC	5.00	2.00
❑ 95 Eric Parker RC	6.00	2.50
❑ 96 Michael Haynes RC	6.00	2.50
❑ 97 J.J. Moses RC	5.00	2.00
❑ 98 Ken Hamlin RC	6.00	2.50
❑ 99 William Joseph RC	6.00	2.50
❑ 100 Alonzo Jackson RC	5.00	2.00
❑ 101 Tyler Brayton RC	6.00	2.50
❑ 102 Eddie Moore RC	5.00	2.00
❑ 103 Cleo Lemon RC	15.00	7.50
❑ 104 Arlen Harris RC	6.00	2.50
❑ 105 Cortez Hankton RC	5.00	2.00
❑ 106 Angelo Crowell RC	5.00	2.00
❑ 107 Johnathan Sullivan RC	5.00	2.00
❑ 108 Pisa Tinoisamoa RC	6.00	2.50
❑ 109 Boss Bailey RC	6.00	2.50
❑ 110 Tommy Jones RC	3.00	1.25
❑ 111 E.J. Henderson RC	6.00	2.50
❑ 112 Jimmy Kennedy RC	6.00	2.50
❑ 113 Nnamdi Asomugha RC	5.00	2.00
❑ 114 Hanik Milligan RC	5.00	2.00
❑ 115 Sammy Davis RC	6.00	2.50
❑ 116 Drayton Florence RC	3.00	1.25
❑ 117 Andre Woolfolk RC	6.00	2.50
❑ 118 Dennis Weathersby RC	3.00	1.25
❑ 119 Mike Doss RC	6.00	2.50
❑ 120 Troy Polamalu RC	30.00	18.00
❑ 121 Clinton Portis SS	6.00	2.50
❑ 122 Daunte Culpepper SS	5.00	2.00
❑ 123 Jeremy Shockey SS	6.00	2.50
❑ 124 Drew Brees SS	5.00	2.00
❑ 125 Marshall Faulk SS	5.00	2.00
❑ 126 Emmitt Smith SS	10.00	4.00
❑ 127 Terrell Owens SS	5.00	2.00
❑ 128 Ricky Williams SS	5.00	2.00
❑ 129 Deuce McAllister SS	5.00	2.00
❑ 130 Ahman Green SS	5.00	2.00
❑ 131 Chad Pennington SS	5.00	2.00
❑ 132 Plaxico Burress SS	5.00	2.00
❑ 133 Steve McNair SS	5.00	2.00
❑ 134 Keyshawn Johnson SS	5.00	2.00
❑ 135 Jeff Garcia SS	5.00	2.00
❑ 136 Drew Bledsoe SS	5.00	2.00
❑ 137 Jerry Rice SS	8.00	3.00
❑ 138 Randy Moss SS	6.00	2.50
❑ 139 David Carr SS	6.00	2.50

❑ 140 Joey Harrington SS 6.00 2.50
❑ 141 Michael Vick SS 10.00 4.00
❑ 142 Tom Brady SS 10.00 4.00
❑ 143 Brian Urlacher SS 6.00 2.50
❑ 144 Brett Favre SS 10.00 4.00
❑ 145 Kurt Warner SS 5.00 2.00
❑ 146 LaDainian Tomlinson SS 5.00 2.00
❑ 147 Aaron Brooks SS 5.00 2.00
❑ 148 Edgerrin James SS 5.00 2.00
❑ 149 Peyton Manning SS 6.00 2.50
❑ 150 Donovan McNabb SS 5.00 2.00
❑ 151 Jason Gesser RC 12.00 5.00
❑ 152 Ken Dorsey RC 12.00 5.00
❑ 153 Jason Johnson RC 6.00 2.50
❑ 154 Avon Cobourne RC [illegible] [illegible]
❑ 155 Andrew Pinnock RC 10.00 4.00
❑ 156 Kirk Farmer RC 6.00 2.50
❑ 157 Reno Mahe RC 12.00 5.00
❑ 158 Lon Sheriff RC 6.00 2.50
❑ 159 Marquel Blackwell RC 6.00 2.50
❑ 160 Quentin Griffin RC 12.00 5.00
❑ 161 Rashean Mathis RC 10.00 4.00
❑ 162 Lee Suggs RC 15.00 6.00
❑ 163 Jeremi Johnson RC 10.00 4.00
❑ 164 Ovie Mughelli RC 6.00 2.50
❑ 165 Nick Barnett RC 15.00 6.00
❑ 166 Brock Forsey RC 12.00 5.00
❑ 167 Malaefou MacKenzie RC 6.00 2.50
❑ 168 Ahmaad Galloway RC 10.00 4.00
❑ 169 Cecil Sapp RC 10.00 4.00
❑ 170 Kerry Carter RC 10.00 4.00
❑ 171 Dahrran Diedrick RC 12.00 5.00
❑ 171A Terrence Edwards RC 10.00 4.00
❑ 172 Jeffrey Reynolds RC 6.00 2.50
❑ 173 Sultan McCullough RC 10.00 4.00
❑ 174 Brandon Drumm RC 6.00 2.50
❑ 175 Casey Moore RC 10.00 4.00
❑ 176 Gerald Hayes RC 6.00 2.50
❑ 178 Jamal Burke RC 6.00 2.50
❑ 179 Antonio Chatman RC 12.00 5.00
❑ 180 Reggie Newhouse RC 10.00 4.00
❑ 181 Chris Horn RC 6.00 2.50
❑ 182 Denero Marriott RC 6.00 2.50
❑ 183 DeAndrew Rubin RC 6.00 2.50
❑ 184 Taco Wallace RC 10.00 4.00
❑ 185 Doug Gabriel RC 12.00 5.00
❑ 186 Willie Ponder RC 6.00 2.50
❑ 187 David Tyree RC 10.00 4.00
❑ 188 Kevin Walter RC 10.00 4.00
❑ 189 Zuriel Smith RC 6.00 2.50
❑ 190 Keenan Howry RC 12.00 5.00
❑ 191 C.J. Jones RC 6.00 2.50
❑ 192 Arnaz Battle RC 12.00 5.00
❑ 193 Walter Young RC 6.00 2.50
❑ 194 Anthony Adams RC 10.00 4.00
❑ 195 Jerome McDougle RC 12.00 5.00
❑ 196 Will Hollor RC 10.00 4.00
❑ 197 Cecil Moore RC 6.00 2.50
❑ 198 Mike Seidman RC 6.00 2.50
❑ 199 Jason Witten RC 30.00 15.00
❑ 200 L.J. Smith RC 12.00 5.00
❑ 201 Bennie Joppru RC 12.00 5.00
❑ 202 Donald Lee RC 10.00 4.00
❑ 203 Aaron Walker RC 10.00 4.00
❑ 204 Antonio Brown RC 6.00 2.50
❑ 205 George Wrighster RC 10.00 4.00
❑ 206 Danny Curley RC 6.00 2.50
❑ 207 Mike Banks RC 6.00 2.50
❑ 208 Mike Pinkard RC 6.00 2.50
❑ 209 Ryan Hoag RC 6.00 2.50
❑ 210 Brad Pyatt RC 10.00 4.00
❑ 211 Charles Rogers RC 12.00 5.00
❑ 212 Chris Simms AU/250 RC 150.00 75.00
❑ 213 Nate Hybl AU RC 20.00 7.50
❑ 214 Brandon Lloyd AU RC 50.00 20.00
❑ 215 ReShard Lee AU RC 20.00 7.50
❑ 216 Dwone Hicks AU RC 12.00 5.00
❑ 217 Tony Romo AU RC 400.00 250.00
❑ 218 Brett Engemann AU RC 12.00 5.00
❑ 219 Nick Maddox AU RC 12.00 5.00
❑ 220 James MacPherson AU RC 12.00 5.00
❑ 221 Juston Wood AU RC 12.00 5.00
❑ 222 Adrian Madise AU RC 15.00 6.00
❑ 223 Shaun McDonald AU RC 20.00 7.50
❑ 224 Carl Ford AU RC 12.00 5.00
❑ 225 Vishante Shiancoe AU RC 15.00 6.00
❑ 226 Gibran Hamdan AU RC 12.00 5.00
❑ 227 Brooks Bollinger AU RC 20.00 7.50
❑ 228 B.J. Askew AU RC 20.00 7.50
❑ 229 Domanick Davis AU RC 30.00 12.50
❑ 230 LaBrandon Toefield AU RC 20.00 7.50
❑ 231 Bobby Wade AU RC 20.00 7.50
❑ 232 Justin Gage AU RC 20.00 7.50
❑ 233 Billy McMullen AU RC 15.00 6.00
❑ 234 David Kircus AU RC 25.00 10.00
❑ 235 J.R. Tolver AU RC 15.00 6.00
❑ 236 Sam Aiken AU RC 15.00 6.00
❑ 237 LaTarence Dunbar AU RC 15.00 6.00
❑ 238 Kassim Osgood AU RC 20.00 7.50
❑ 239 Tony Hollings AU RC 20.00 7.50
❑ 240 Justin Griffith AU RC 15.00 6.00
❑ 241 Brian St.Pierre JSY RC [illegible] [illegible]
❑ 242 Kevin Curtis JSY RC 30.00 12.50
❑ 243 Dallas Clark JSY RC 40.00 15.00
❑ 244 Willis McGahee JSY RC 80.00 30.00
❑ 245 Terence Newman JSY RC 30.00 15.00
❑ 246 Justin Fargas JSY AU RC 40.00 20.00
❑ 247 Artose Pinner JSY RC 30.00 12.50
❑ 248 Kelley Washington JSY RC 40.00 15.00
❑ 249 DeWayne Robertson JSY RC 25.00 10.00
❑ 250 Nate Burleson JSY RC 30.00 12.50
❑ 251 Kliff Kingsbury JSY RC 25.00 10.00
❑ 252 Bethel Johnson JSY RC 30.00 12.50
❑ 253 Anquan Boldin JSY RC 60.00 30.00
❑ 254 Bryant Johnson JSY AU RC 40.00 20.00
❑ 255 Terrell Suggs JSY AU RC 60.00 30.00
❑ 256 Musa Smith JSY RC 30.00 12.50
❑ 257 Chris Brown JSY RC 30.00 12.50
❑ 258 Marcus Trufant JSY RC 30.00 12.50
❑ 259 Teyo Johnson JSY RC 30.00 12.50
❑ 260 Tyrone Calico JSY RC 40.00 15.00
❑ 261 Dave Ragone JSY AU RC 40.00 20.00
❑ 262 Kyle Boller JSY AU RC 50.00 25.00
❑ 263 Onterrio Smith JSY AU RC 40.00 20.00
❑ 264 Rex Grossman JSY RC 80.00 30.00
❑ 265 Larry Johnson JSY RC 120.00 60.00
❑ 266 Seneca Wallace JSY AU RC 80.00 40.00
❑ 268 Taylor Jacobs JSY AU RC 40.00 20.00
❑ 269 Byron Leftwich JSY AU RC 175.00 90.00
❑ 270 Carson Palmer JSY AU RC 700.00 400.00

2004 SP Authentic

❑ COMP.SET w/o SP's (90) 25.00 10.00
❑ 151-185 AU RC PRINT RUN 990 SER.#'d SETS
❑ 186-200 JSY AU RC PRINT RUN 799
❑ 201-206 JSY AU RC PRINT RUN 499
❑ 207-216 JSY AU RC PRINT RUN 299
❑ 1 Josh McCown .60 .25
❑ 2 Anquan Boldin 1.00 .40
❑ 3 Michael Vick 2.00 .75
❑ 4 Peerless Price .60 .25
❑ 5 Todd Heap .60 .25
❑ 6 Kyle Boller 1.00 .40
❑ 7 Jamal Lewis 1.00 .40
❑ 8 Drew Bledsoe 1.00 .40
❑ 9 Travis Henry .60 .25
❑ 10 Eric Moulds .60 .25
❑ 11 Steve Smith 1.00 .40
❑ 12 Stephen Davis .60 .25
❑ 13 Jake Delhomme 1.00 .40
❑ 14 Rex Grossman 1.00 .40
❑ 15 Brian Urlacher 1.25 .50
❑ 16 Thomas Jones .60 .25
❑ 17 Chad Johnson 1.00 .40
❑ 18 Rudi Johnson .60 .25
❑ 19 Carson Palmer 1.25 .50
❑ 20 William Green .60 .25
❑ 21 Andre Davis .40 .15
❑ 22 Jeff Garcia 1.00 .40
❑ 23 Roy Williams S .60 .25
❑ 24 Eddie George .60 .25
❑ 25 Keyshawn Johnson .60 .25
❑ 26 Ashley Lelie .60 .25
❑ 27 Jake Plummer .60 .25
❑ 28 Champ Bailey .60 .25
❑ 29 Charles Rogers .60 .25
❑ 30 Joey Harrington 1.00 .40
❑ 31 Ahman Green 1.00 .40
❑ 32 Brett Favre 2.50 1.00
❑ 33 Javon Walker .60 .25
❑ 34 [illegible]
❑ 35 Domanick Davis 1.00 .40
❑ 36 Andre Johnson 1.00 .40
❑ 37 Marvin Harrison 1.00 .40
❑ 38 Edgerrin James 1.00 .40
❑ 39 Peyton Manning 1.50 .60
❑ 40 Byron Leftwich 1.25 .50
❑ 41 Fred Taylor .60 .25
❑ 42 Trent Green .60 .25
❑ 43 Tony Gonzalez .60 .25
❑ 44 Priest Holmes 1.25 .50
❑ 45 Ricky Williams 1.00 .40
❑ 46 Chris Chambers .60 .25
❑ 47 Jay Fiedler .40 .15
❑ 48 Daunte Culpepper 1.00 .40
❑ 49 Randy Moss 1.25 .50
❑ 50 Onterrio Smith .60 .25
❑ 51 Tom Brady 2.50 1.00
❑ 52 Troy Brown .60 .25
❑ 53 Corey Dillon .60 .25
❑ 54 Deuce McAllister 1.00 .40
❑ 55 Aaron Brooks .60 .25
❑ 56 Joe Horn .60 .25
❑ 57 Amani Toomer .60 .25
❑ 58 Kurt Warner 1.00 .40
❑ 59 Jeremy Shockey 1.00 .40
❑ 60 Chad Pennington 1.00 .40
❑ 61 Santana Moss .60 .25
❑ 62 Curtis Martin 1.00 .40
❑ 63 Rich Gannon .60 .25
❑ 64 Jerry Rice 2.00 .75
❑ 65 Jerry Porter .60 .25
❑ 66 Terrell Owens 1.00 .40
❑ 67 Jevon Kearse .60 .25
❑ 68 Donovan McNabb 1.25 .50
❑ 69 Hines Ward 1.00 .40
❑ 70 Plaxico Burress .60 .25
❑ 71 Tommy Maddox .60 .25
❑ 72 Drew Brees 1.00 .40
❑ 73 LaDainian Tomlinson 1.25 .50
❑ 74 Tim Rattay .40 .15
❑ 75 Brandon Lloyd [illegible] [illegible]
❑ 76 Kevan Barlow .60 .25
❑ 77 Shaun Alexander 1.00 .40
❑ 78 Koren Robinson .60 .25
❑ 79 Matt Hasselbeck .60 .25
❑ 80 Marshall Faulk 1.00 .40
❑ 81 Torry Holt 1.00 .40
❑ 82 Marc Bulger 1.00 .40
❑ 83 Brad Johnson .60 .25
❑ 84 Joey Galloway .60 .25
❑ 85 Steve McNair 1.00 .40
❑ 86 Derrick Mason .60 .25
❑ 87 Chris Brown 1.00 .40
❑ 88 Mark Brunell .60 .25
❑ 89 Laveranues Coles .60 .25
❑ 90 Clinton Portis 1.00 .40
❑ 91 Triandos Luke RC 8.00 3.00
❑ 92 Keith Smith RC 6.00 2.50
❑ 93 Shaun Phillips RC 6.00 2.50
❑ 94 D.J. Williams RC 8.00 3.00
❑ 95 Keiwan Ratliff RC 6.00 2.50
❑ 96 Madieu Williams RC 6.00 2.50
❑ 97 Chris Cooley RC 8.00 3.00
❑ 98 Stuart Schweigert RC 8.00 3.00
❑ 99 Sloan Thomas RC 6.00 2.50
❑ 100 Chad Lavalais RC 6.00 2.50
❑ 101 Jared Allen RC 12.00 5.00
❑ 102 Brian Jones RC 6.00 2.50
❑ 103 Matt Ware RC 8.00 3.00
❑ 104 Daryl Smith RC 8.00 3.00
❑ 105 J.R. Reed RC 6.00 2.50
❑ 106 D.J. Hackett RC 6.00 2.50

❑ 107 Jeris McIntyre RC	6.00	2.50
❑ 108 Dexter Reid RC	4.00	1.50
❑ 109 Courtney Anderson RC	6.00	2.50
❑ 110 Courtney Watson RC	8.00	3.00
❑ 111 Larry Croom RC	6.00	2.50
❑ 112 Jonathan Smith RC	6.00	2.50
❑ 113 Vernon Carey RC	6.00	2.50
❑ 114 Michael Gaines RC	6.00	2.50
❑ 115 Chris Snee RC	6.00	2.50
❑ 116 Nathan Vasher RC	10.00	4.00
❑ 117 Teddy Lehman RC	8.00	3.00
❑ 118 Marcus Tubbs RC	8.00	3.00
❑ 119 Ben Utecht RC	4.00	1.50
❑ 120 Maurice Mann RC	6.00	2.50
❑ 121 Thomas Tapeh RC	6.00	2.50
❑ 122 Will Allen RC	8.00	3.00
❑ 123 Demorrio Williams RC	8.00	3.00
❑ 124 Ran Carthon RC	6.00	2.50
❑ 125 Tim Euhus RC	8.00	3.00
❑ 126 Bradlee Van Pelt RC	8.00	3.00
❑ 127 Patrick Crayton RC	10.00	5.00
❑ 128 Ryan Krause RC	6.00	2.50
❑ 129 Joey Thomas RC	8.00	3.00
❑ 130 Antwan Odom RC	8.00	3.00
❑ 131 Karlos Dansby RC	8.00	3.00
❑ 132 Junior Siavii RC	8.00	3.00
❑ 133 Jamaar Taylor RC	8.00	3.00
❑ 134 Kendrick Starling RC	4.00	1.50
❑ 135 Wes Welker RC	35.00	20.00
❑ 136 Igor Olshansky RC	8.00	3.00
❑ 137 Mark Jones RC	6.00	2.50
❑ 138 Bruce Thornton RC	4.00	1.50
❑ 139 Michael Boulware RC	8.00	3.00
❑ 140 Matt Mauck RC	8.00	3.00
❑ 141 Clarence Moore RC	8.00	3.00
❑ 142 Derrick Strait RC	8.00	3.00
❑ 143 Jarrett Payton RC	8.00	3.00
❑ 144 Dontarrious Thomas RC	8.00	3.00
❑ 145 Shawntae Spencer RC	8.00	3.00
❑ 146 Bob Sanders RC	20.00	10.00
❑ 147 Darnell Dockett RC	6.00	2.50
❑ 148 Sean Taylor RC	8.00	3.00
❑ 149 Jason Babin RC	8.00	3.00
❑ 150 Ricardo Colclough RC	8.00	3.00
❑ 151 Brandon Chillar AU RC	15.00	6.00
❑ 152 Clarence Farmer AU RC	15.00	6.00
❑ 153 B.J. Symons AU RC	20.00	7.50
❑ 154 John Navarre AU RC	20.00	7.50
❑ 155 P.K. Sam AU RC EXCH	20.00	7.50
❑ 156 Casey Clausen AU RC	20.00	7.50
❑ 157 Drew Henson AU RC	20.00	7.50
❑ 158 Kris Wilson AU RC	20.00	7.50
❑ 159 Vince Wilfork AU RC	25.00	10.00
❑ 160 Michael Turner AU RC	80.00	40.00
❑ 161 Jonathan Vilma AU RC	30.00	12.50
❑ 162 Samie Parker AU RC	20.00	7.50
❑ 163 B.J. Sams AU RC	20.00	7.50
❑ 164 A.Echemandu AU RC	15.00	6.00
❑ 165 Ernest Wilford AU RC	20.00	7.50
❑ 166 Troy Fleming AU RC	20.00	7.50
❑ 167 Tommie Harris AU RC	25.00	12.50
❑ 168 Jammal Lord AU RC	20.00	7.50
❑ 169 Kenechi Udeze AU RC	20.00	7.50
❑ 170 Chris Gamble AU RC	25.00	10.00
❑ 171 Carlos Francis AU RC	15.00	6.00
❑ 172 Mewelde Moore AU RC	20.00	7.50
❑ 173 Jared Lorenzen AU RC	15.00	6.00
❑ 174 Jeff Smoker AU RC	20.00	7.50
❑ 175 Ben Hartsock AU RC	20.00	7.50
❑ 176 Jerricho Cotchery AU RC	20.00	7.50
❑ 177 Josh Harris AU RC	20.00	7.50
❑ 178 Cody Pickett AU RC	20.00	7.50
❑ 179 Quincy Wilson AU RC	15.00	6.00
❑ 180 Will Smith AU RC	20.00	7.50
❑ 181 Ahmad Carroll AU RC	25.00	10.00
❑ 182 B.J. Johnson AU RC	15.00	6.00
❑ 183 Dunta Robinson AU RC	25.00	10.00
❑ 184 Craig Krenzel AU RC	20.00	7.50
❑ 185 Johnnie Morant AU RC	20.00	7.50
❑ 186 Cedric Cobbs JSY AU RC	50.00	20.00
❑ 187 Matt Schaub JSY AU RC	200.00	100.00
❑ 188 Bernard Berrian JSY AU RC	100.00	50.00
❑ 189 Devard Darling JSY AU RC	50.00	20.00
❑ 190 Ben Watson JSY AU RC	60.00	30.00
❑ 191 Darius Watts JSY AU RC	50.00	20.00
❑ 192 DeAngelo Hall JSY AU RC	60.00	30.00
❑ 193 Ben Troupe JSY AU RC	50.00	20.00
❑ 194 Mich Jenkins JSY AU RC	50.00	20.00
❑ 195 Keary Colbert JSY AU RC	50.00	20.00
❑ 196 Robert Gallery JSY AU RC	50.00	20.00
❑ 197 Greg Jones JSY AU RC	60.00	30.00
❑ 198 Mich.Clayton JSY AU RC	80.00	40.00
❑ 199 Luke McCown JSY AU RC	50.00	20.00
❑ 200 Derrick Hamilton JSY AU RC	50.00	20.00
❑ 201 Ras.Woods JSY AU RC	50.00	20.00
❑ 202 Chris Perry JSY AU RC	80.00	30.00
❑ 203 D.Henderson JSY AU RC	60.00	30.00
❑ 204 Tatum Bell JSY AU RC	60.00	25.00
❑ 205 Lee Evans JSY AU RC	100.00	50.00
❑ 206 J.P. Losman JSY AU RC	120.00	60.00
❑ 207 Kel.Winslow JSY AU RC	120.00	60.00
❑ 208 Reg.Williams JSY AU RC	80.00	40.00
❑ 209 Julius Jones JSY AU RC	250.00	125.00
❑ 210 S.Jackson JSY AU RC	400.00	250.00
❑ 211 Kevin Jones JSY AU RC	150.00	75.00
❑ 212 Roy Williams JSY AU RC	250.00	125.00
❑ 213 Roethlisberger JSY AU RC	500.00	250.00
❑ 214 Philip Rivers JSY AU RC	400.00	200.00
❑ 215 L.Fitzgerald JSY AU RC	250.00	125.00
❑ 216 Eli Manning JSY AU RC	500.00	300.00

2005 SP Authentic

❑ COMP.SET w/o RC's (90)	25.00	10.00
❑ 91-180 PRINT RUN 750 SER.#'d SETS		
❑ 181-220/254-257 PRINT RUN 850 SETS		
❑ 221-253 PRINT RUN 99-899 SER.#'d SETS		
❑ UNPRICED NFL LOGO PATCHES #'d TO 1		
❑ EXCH EXPIRATION:12/20/2008		
❑ 1 Kurt Warner	.60	.25
❑ 2 Larry Fitzgerald	1.00	.40
❑ 3 Anquan Boldin	.60	.25
❑ 4 Michael Vick	1.50	.60
❑ 5 Alge Crumpler	.60	.25
❑ 6 Warrick Dunn	.60	.25
❑ 7 Kyle Boller	.60	.25
❑ 8 Jamal Lewis	1.00	.40
❑ 9 J.P. Losman	1.00	.40
❑ 10 Willis McGahee	1.00	.40
❑ 11 Lee Evans	.60	.25
❑ 12 Jake Delhomme	1.00	.40
❑ 13 DeShaun Foster	.60	.25
❑ 14 Muhsin Muhammad	.60	.25
❑ 15 Walter Payton	4.00	1.50
❑ 16 Brian Urlacher	1.00	.40
❑ 17 Carson Palmer	1.00	.40
❑ 18 Rudi Johnson	.60	.25
❑ 19 Chad Johnson	1.00	.40
❑ 20 Lee Suggs	.60	.25
❑ 21 Antonio Bryant	.50	.20
❑ 22 Julius Jones	1.25	.50
❑ 23 Drew Bledsoe	1.00	.40
❑ 24 Keyshawn Johnson	.60	.25
❑ 25 Tatum Bell	.60	.25
❑ 26 Jake Plummer	.60	.25
❑ 27 Roy Williams WR	1.00	.40
❑ 28 Kevin Jones	1.00	.40
❑ 29 Jeff Garcia	.60	.25
❑ 30 Brett Favre	2.50	1.00
❑ 31 Ahman Green	1.00	.40
❑ 32 Javon Walker	.60	.25
❑ 33 David Carr	1.00	.40
❑ 34 Andre Johnson	.60	.25
❑ 35 Domanick Davis	.60	.25
❑ 36 Peyton Manning	1.50	.60
❑ 37 Edgerrin James	1.00	.40
❑ 38 Reggie Wayne	.60	.25
❑ 39 Byron Leftwich	1.00	.40
❑ 40 Fred Taylor	.60	.25
❑ 41 Jimmy Smith	.60	.25
❑ 42 Priest Holmes	1.00	.40
❑ 43 Larry Johnson	1.00	.40
❑ 44 Trent Green	.60	.25
❑ 45 Randy McMichael	.50	.20
❑ 46 Chris Chambers	.60	.25
❑ 47 Ricky Williams	.60	.25
❑ 48 Daunte Culpepper	1.00	.40
❑ 49 Nate Burleson	.60	.25
❑ 50 Tom Brady	2.50	1.00
❑ 51 Corey Dillon	.60	.25
❑ 52 David Givens	.60	.25
❑ 53 Aaron Brooks	.60	.25
❑ 54 Deuce McAllister	1.00	.40
❑ 55 Joe Horn	.60	.25
❑ 56 Eli Manning	2.00	.75
❑ 57 Jeremy Shockey	1.00	.40
❑ 58 Tiki Barber	1.00	.40
❑ 59 Chad Pennington	1.00	.40
❑ 60 Santana Moss	.60	.25
❑ 61 Curtis Martin	1.00	.40
❑ 62 Randy Moss	1.00	.40
❑ 63 LaMont Jordan	1.00	.40
❑ 64 Kerry Collins	.60	.25
❑ 65 Donovan McNabb	1.25	.50
❑ 66 Brian Westbrook	.60	.25
❑ 67 Terrell Owens	1.00	.40
❑ 68 Ben Roethlisberger	2.50	1.00
❑ 69 Hines Ward	1.00	.40
❑ 70 Jerome Bettis	1.00	.40
❑ 71 Drew Brees	1.00	.40
❑ 72 Antonio Gates	1.00	.40
❑ 73 LaDainian Tomlinson	1.25	.50
❑ 74 Kevan Barlow	.60	.25
❑ 75 Brandon Lloyd	.50	.20
❑ 76 Matt Hasselbeck	.60	.25
❑ 77 Shaun Alexander	1.25	.50
❑ 78 Darrell Jackson	.60	.25
❑ 79 Marc Bulger	1.00	.40
❑ 80 Steven Jackson	1.25	.50
❑ 81 Torry Holt	1.00	.40
❑ 82 Brian Griese	.60	.25
❑ 83 Michael Clayton	1.00	.40
❑ 84 Michael Pittman	.50	.20
❑ 85 Steve McNair	1.00	.40
❑ 86 Drew Bennett	.60	.25
❑ 87 Chris Brown	.60	.25
❑ 88 Clinton Portis	1.00	.40
❑ 89 Patrick Ramsey	.60	.25
❑ 90 Laveranues Coles	.60	.25
❑ 91 Nehemiah Broughton RC	6.00	2.50
❑ 92 Madison Hedgecock RC	8.00	3.00
❑ 93 Damien Nash RC	6.00	2.50
❑ 94 Michael Boley RC	6.00	2.50
❑ 95 Lionel Gates RC	6.00	2.50
❑ 96 Noah Herron RC	8.00	3.00
❑ 97 Bo Scaife RC	6.00	2.50
❑ 98 Joel Dreessen RC	6.00	2.50
❑ 99 Rasheed Marshall RC	8.00	3.00
❑ 100 Andre Maddox RC	6.00	2.50
❑ 101 Tab Perry RC	8.00	3.00
❑ 102 Dante Ridgeway RC	6.00	2.50
❑ 103 Patrick Estes RC	6.00	2.50
❑ 104 Billy Bajema RC	6.00	2.50
❑ 105 Paris Warren RC	6.00	2.50
❑ 106 LeRon McCoy RC	6.00	2.50
❑ 107 Adam Bergen RC	8.00	3.00
❑ 108 Manuel White RC	6.00	2.50
❑ 109 Stephen Spach RC	6.00	2.50
❑ 110 Donte Nicholson RC	8.00	3.00
❑ 111 Brodney Pool RC	8.00	3.00
❑ 112 Stanford Routt RC	6.00	2.50
❑ 113 Josh Bullocks RC	8.00	3.00
❑ 114 Ronald Bartell RC	6.00	2.50
❑ 115 Nick Collins RC	8.00	3.00
❑ 116 Darrent Williams RC	8.00	3.00
❑ 117 Justin Miller RC	6.00	2.50
❑ 118 Kelvin Hayden RC	6.00	2.50
❑ 119 Bryant McFadden RC	8.00	3.00
❑ 120 Oshiomogho Atogwe RC	6.00	2.50
❑ 121 Stanley Wilson RC	6.00	2.50
❑ 122 Eric Green RC	4.00	1.50
❑ 123 Michael Hawkins RC	6.00	2.50
❑ 124 Marcus Spears RC	8.00	3.00
❑ 125 Ellis Hobbs RC	8.00	3.00

❑ 126 Scott Starks RC 6.00 2.50
❑ 127 Domonique Foxworth RC 8.00 3.00
❑ 128 Sean Considine RC 8.00 3.00
❑ 129 James Sanders RC 8.00 3.00
❑ 130 Travis Daniels RC 6.00 2.50
❑ 131 Vincent Fuller RC 6.00 2.50
❑ 132 Marviel Underwood RC 6.00 2.50
❑ 133 Jerome Carter RC 6.00 2.50
❑ 134 Kerry Rhodes RC 8.00 3.00
❑ 135 Fred Amey RC 6.00 2.50
❑ 136 Eric King RC 6.00 2.50
❑ 137 Derrick Johnson CB RC 8.00 3.00
❑ 138 Luis Castillo RC 8.00 3.00
❑ 139 Shaun Cody RC 8.00 3.00
❑ 140 Matt Roth RC 8.00 3.00
❑ 141 Jonathan Babineaux RC 6.00 2.50
❑ 142 Justin Tuck RC 8.00 3.00
❑ 143 Sione Pouha RC 8.00 3.00
❑ 144 Daven Holly RC 8.00 3.00
❑ 145 Vincent Burns RC 6.00 2.50
❑ 146 Derrick Johnson RC 12.00 5.00
❑ 147 Lofa Tatupu RC 12.00 5.00
❑ 148 Odell Thurman RC 8.00 3.00
❑ 149 Rick Razzano RC 8.00 3.00
❑ 150 Channing Crowder RC 8.00 3.00
❑ 151 Kirk Morrison RC 8.00 3.00
❑ 152 Alfred Fincher RC 6.00 2.50
❑ 153 Jordan Beck RC 6.00 2.50
❑ 154 Darryl Blackstock RC 6.00 2.50
❑ 155 Leroy Hill RC 8.00 3.00
❑ 156 Jammal Brown RC 8.00 3.00
❑ 157 Alex Barron RC 4.00 1.50
❑ 158 Chris Spencer RC 8.00 3.00
❑ 159 Logan Mankins RC 8.00 3.00
❑ 160 David Baas RC 6.00 2.50
❑ 161 Michael Roos RC 4.00 1.50
❑ 162 Kurt Campbell RC 6.00 2.50
❑ 163 Khalif Barnes RC 6.00 2.50
❑ 164 Antonio Perkins RC 6.00 2.50
❑ 165 Vonta Leach RC 8.00 3.00
❑ 166 Brady Poppinga RC 8.00 3.00
❑ 167 Trent Cole RC 8.00 3.00
❑ 168 Dave Rayner RC 6.00 2.50
❑ 169 Bill Swancutt RC 6.00 2.50
❑ 170 Eric Moore RC 6.00 2.50
❑ 171 Justin Green RC 8.00 3.00
❑ 172 Shaun Suisham RC 6.00 2.50
❑ 173 C.J. Mosley RC 6.00 2.50
❑ 174 Ryan Riddle RC 4.00 1.50
❑ 175 Darrell Shropshire RC 6.00 2.50
❑ 176 Boomer Grigsby RC 8.00 3.00
❑ 177 Rian Wallace RC 6.00 2.50
❑ 178 Lance Mitchell RC 6.00 2.50
❑ 179 Nick Speegle RC 6.00 2.50
❑ 180 Tyson Thompson RC 10.00 4.00
❑ 181 Dan Orlovsky AU RC 15.00 6.00
❑ 182 Anthony Davis AU RC 12.00 6.00
❑ 183 Kay-Jay Harris AU RC 12.00 5.00
❑ 184 Walter Reyes AU RC 12.00 5.00
❑ 185 Darren Sproles AU RC 20.00 8.00
❑ 186 Marlin Jackson AU RC 15.00 6.00
❑ 187 Corey Webster AU RC 15.00 6.00
❑ 188 Marion Barber AU RC 80.00 40.00
❑ 189 Chris Henry AU RC EXCH 20.00 7.50
❑ 190 Derek Anderson AU RC 100.00 60.00
❑ 191 David Pollack AU RC EXCH 15.00 6.00
❑ 192 Anttaj Hawthorne AU RC 12.00 5.00
❑ 193 David Greene AU RC 15.00 6.00
❑ 194 Erasmus James AU RC 15.00 6.00
❑ 195 Ryan Fitzpatrick AU RC 15.00 6.00
❑ 196 Derrick Johnson AU 25.00 10.00
❑ 197 Barrett Ruud AU RC 15.00 6.00
❑ 198 Kevin Burnett AU RC 15.00 6.00
❑ 199 C.Houston AU RC EXCH 20.00 10.00
❑ 200 J.R. Russell AU RC 12.00 5.00
❑ 201 Larry Brackins AU RC 12.00 5.00
❑ 202 Thomas Davis AU RC 15.00 6.00
❑ 203 Fred Gibson AU RC 12.00 5.00
❑ 204 Craphonso Thorpe AU RC 12.00 5.00
❑ 205 Brandon Jacobs AU RC 60.00 35.00
❑ 206 Taylor Stubblefield AU RC 10.00 4.00
❑ 207 Shawne Merriman AU RC 50.00 25.00
❑ 208 Travis Johnson AU RC 12.00 5.00
❑ 209 Adrian McPherson AU RC 15.00 6.00
❑ 210 Brandon Jones AU RC 15.00 6.00
❑ 211 Jerome Mathis AU RC 15.00 6.00
❑ 212 Alex Smith TE AU RC 15.00 6.00
❑ 213 Fabian Washington AU RC 15.00 6.00
❑ 214 Mike Nugent AU RC 15.00 6.00
❑ 215 Chase Lyman AU RC 12.00 5.00
❑ 216 Roydell Williams AU RC 15.00 6.00
❑ 217 Matt Cassel AU RC 30.00 15.00
❑ 218 Alvin Pearman AU RC 15.00 6.00
❑ 219 DeMarcus Ware AU RC 40.00 20.00
❑ 220 Mike Patterson AU RC 15.00 6.00
❑ 221 C.Roby JSY/899 AU RC 50.00 20.00
❑ 222 E.Shelton JSY/899 AU RC 50.00 20.00
❑ 223 S.LeFors JSY/899 AU RC 50.00 20.00
❑ 224 Frank Gore JSY/899 AU RC 150.00 75.00
❑ 225 Ryan Moats JSY/899 AU RC 50.00 25.00
❑ 226 A.Walter JSY/899 AU RC 50.00 20.00
❑ 227 A.Jones JSY/899 AU RC 50.00 20.00
❑ 228 C.Rogers JSY/699 AU RC 50.00 20.00
❑ 229 T.Murphy JSY/899 AU RC 50.00 20.00
❑ 230 Kyle Orton JSY/699 AU RC 50.00 20.00
❑ 231 C.Fason JSY/699 AU RC 50.00 25.00
❑ 232 V.Morency JSY/699 AU RC 60.00 30.00
❑ 233 R.Parrish JSY/699 AU RC 50.00 20.00
❑ 234 V.Jackson JSY/699 AU RC 60.00 30.00
❑ 235 M.Bradley JSY/699 AU RC 60.00 30.00
❑ 236 Ro.Brown JSY/500 AU RC 60.00 25.00
❑ 237 Ro.White JSY/499 AU RC 60.00 30.00
❑ 238 M.Clayton JSY/499 AU RC 60.00 25.00
❑ 239 Antrel Rolle JSY/499 AU RC 50.00 20.00
❑ 240 Maurice Clarett JSY/499 AU 50.00 20.00
❑ 241 J.Arrington JSY/699 AU RC 50.00 20.00
❑ 242 Matt Jones JSY/399 AU RC 60.00 25.00
❑ 243 Ro.Brown JSY/299 AU RC 250.00 125.00
❑ 244 C.Frye JSY/499 AU RC 50.00 20.00
❑ 245 J.Campbell JSY/299 AU RC 175.00 100.00
❑ 246 T.Willmsn JSY/299 AU RC 80.00 30.00
❑ 247 B.Edwrd JSY/299 AU RC 150.00 90.00
❑ 248 A.Smith QB JSY/299 AU RC 250.00 125.00
❑ 249 C.Wllms JSY/299 AU RC 250.00 125.00
❑ 250 H.Miller JSY/299 AU RC 80.00 40.00
❑ 251 C.Benson JSY/99 AU RC 250.00 125.00
❑ 252 A.Rodgers JSY/99 AU RC 400.00 250.00
❑ 253 M.Williams JSY/99 AU 100.00 40.00
❑ 254 Chris Carr AU RC 20.00 7.50
❑ 255 Deandra Cobb AU RC 12.00 5.00
❑ 256 James Kilian AU RC 15.00 6.00
❑ 257 Airese Currie AU RC 15.00 6.00

2006 SP Authentic

❑ 1 Edgerrin James 1.00 .40
❑ 2 Larry Fitzgerald 1.00 .40
❑ 3 Anquan Boldin .60 .25
❑ 4 Michael Vick 1.00 .40
❑ 5 Warrick Dunn .60 .25
❑ 6 Alge Crumpler .60 .25
❑ 7 Steve McNair .60 .25
❑ 8 Jamal Lewis .60 .25
❑ 9 Derrick Mason .50 .20
❑ 10 Willis McGahee 1.00 .40
❑ 11 Lee Evans .60 .25
❑ 12 Jake Delhomme .60 .25
❑ 13 Steve Smith 1.00 .40
❑ 14 DeShaun Foster .60 .25
❑ 15 Rex Grossman 1.00 .40
❑ 16 Thomas Jones .60 .25
❑ 17 Brian Urlacher 1.00 .40
❑ 18 Carson Palmer 1.00 .40
❑ 19 Chad Johnson .60 .25
❑ 20 Rudi Johnson .60 .25
❑ 21 Charlie Frye .60 .25
❑ 22 Braylon Edwards 1.00 .40
❑ 23 Reuben Droughns .60 .25
❑ 24 Drew Bledsoe 1.00 .40
❑ 25 Terrell Owens 1.00 .40
❑ 26 Julius Jones 1.00 .40
❑ 27 Jake Plummer .60 .25
❑ 28 Tatum Bell .60 .25
❑ 29 Javon Walker .60 .25
❑ 30 Kevin Jones 1.00 .40
❑ 31 Roy Williams WR 1.00 .40
❑ 32 Brett Favre 2.00 .75
❑ 33 Donald Driver .60 .25
❑ 34 David Carr .60 .25
❑ 35 Ron Dayne .60 .25
❑ 36 Andre Johnson .60 .25
❑ 37 Peyton Manning 1.50 .60
❑ 38 Marvin Harrison 1.00 .40
❑ 39 Reggie Wayne .60 .25
❑ 40 Byron Leftwich .60 .25
❑ 41 Fred Taylor .60 .25
❑ 42 Matt Jones .60 .25
❑ 43 Trent Green .60 .25
❑ 44 Larry Johnson 1.25 .50
❑ 45 Tony Gonzalez .60 .25
❑ 46 Daunte Culpepper 1.00 .40
❑ 47 Ronnie Brown 1.00 .40
❑ 48 Chris Chambers .60 .25
❑ 49 Chester Taylor .60 .25
❑ 50 Troy Williamson .60 .25
❑ 51 Tom Brady 1.50 .60
❑ 52 Corey Dillon .60 .25
❑ 53 Troy Brown .60 .25
❑ 54 Drew Brees 1.00 .40
❑ 55 Deuce McAllister .60 .25
❑ 56 Joe Horn .60 .25
❑ 57 Eli Manning 1.25 .50
❑ 58 Tiki Barber 1.00 .40
❑ 59 Plaxico Burress .60 .25
❑ 60 Laveranues Coles .60 .25
❑ 61 Chad Pennington .60 .25
❑ 62 Aaron Brooks .60 .25
❑ 63 Randy Moss 1.00 .40
❑ 64 LaMont Jordan .60 .25
❑ 65 Donovan McNabb 1.00 .40
❑ 66 Brian Westbrook .60 .25
❑ 67 Ben Roethlisberger 1.50 .60
❑ 68 Willie Parker 1.25 .50
❑ 69 Hines Ward 1.00 .40
❑ 70 Philip Rivers 1.00 .40
❑ 71 LaDainian Tomlinson 1.25 .50
❑ 72 Antonio Gates 1.00 .40
❑ 73 Alex Smith QB 1.00 .40
❑ 74 Frank Gore 1.00 .40
❑ 75 Antonio Bryant .60 .25
❑ 76 Matt Hasselbeck .60 .25
❑ 77 Shaun Alexander 1.00 .40
❑ 78 Darrell Jackson .60 .25
❑ 79 Marc Bulger .60 .25
❑ 80 Steven Jackson 1.00 .40
❑ 81 Torry Holt .60 .25
❑ 82 Chris Simms .60 .25
❑ 83 Cadillac Williams 1.00 .40
❑ 84 Joey Galloway .60 .25
❑ 85 Travis Henry .60 .25
❑ 86 Drew Bennett .50 .20
❑ 87 David Givens .60 .25
❑ 88 Mark Brunell .60 .25
❑ 89 Clinton Portis 1.00 .40
❑ 90 Santana Moss .60 .25
❑ 91 Bernard Pollard RC 10.00 4.00
❑ 92 Brodie Croyle RC 40.00 20.00
❑ 93 Cedric Griffin RC 10.00 4.00
❑ 94 Marques Colston RC 50.00 20.00
❑ 95 Daniel Bullocks RC 12.00 5.00
❑ 96 Darryl Tapp RC 10.00 4.00
❑ 97 David Thomas RC 12.00 5.00
❑ 98 Montell Owens RC 10.00 4.00
❑ 99 DeMeco Ryans RC 15.00 6.00
❑ 100 Devin Hester RC 25.00 10.00
❑ 101 Donte Whitner RC 12.00 5.00
❑ 102 D'Qwell Jackson RC 10.00 4.00
❑ 103 Patrick Cobbs RC 10.00 4.00
❑ 104 Haloti Ngata RC 12.00 5.00
❑ 105 Lawrence Vickers RC 10.00 4.00
❑ 106 Jeff King RC 10.00 4.00
❑ 107 Jeremy Bloom RC 10.00 4.00
❑ 108 Johnathan Joseph RC 10.00 4.00
❑ 109 DeDe Dorsey RC 10.00 4.00

❑ 110 Marcus Vick RC 10.00 4.00
❑ 111 Bobby Carpenter RC 12.00 5.00
❑ 112 Manny Lawson RC 12.00 5.00
❑ 113 Nick Mangold RC 10.00 4.00
❑ 114 Quinn Sypniewski RC 10.00 4.00
❑ 115 Richard Marshall RC 10.00 4.00
❑ 116 Rocky McIntosh RC 12.00 5.00
❑ 117 Roman Harper RC 10.00 4.00
❑ 118 Tamba Hali RC 12.00 5.00
❑ 119 Tony Scheffler RC 12.00 5.00
❑ 120 Wali Lundy RC 12.00 5.00
❑ 121 A.J. Nicholson RC 5.00 2.00
❑ 122 Abdul Hodge RC 10.00 4.00
❑ 123 Adam Jennings RC 8.00 3.00
❑ 124 Alan Zemaitis RC 10.00 4.00
❑ 125 Andrew Whitworth RC 5.00 2.00
❑ 126 Anthony Schlegel RC 8.00 3.00
❑ 127 Anthony Smith RC 12.00 5.00
❑ 128 Antoine Bethea RC 12.00 5.00
❑ 129 Barry Cofield RC 10.00 4.00
❑ 130 Brandon Johnson RC 8.00 3.00
❑ 131 Calvin Lowry RC 10.00 4.00
❑ 132 Shaun Bodiford RC 8.00 3.00
❑ 133 Charlie Peprah RC 8.00 3.00
❑ 134 Claude Wroten RC 5.00 2.00
❑ 135 Clint Ingram RC 10.00 4.00
❑ 136 Cortland Finnegan RC 10.00 4.00
❑ 137 Daryn Colledge RC 10.00 4.00
❑ 138 David Anderson RC 8.00 3.00
❑ 139 David Kirtman RC 8.00 3.00
❑ 140 Boone Stutz RC 8.00 3.00
❑ 141 Delanie Walker RC 8.00 3.00
❑ 142 Sam Hurd RC 15.00 6.00
❑ 143 Derrick Martin RC 8.00 3.00
❑ 144 Willie Andrews RC 8.00 3.00
❑ 145 Dusty Dvoracek RC 10.00 4.00
❑ 146 Elvis Dumervil RC 5.00 2.00
❑ 147 Eric Smith RC 8.00 3.00
❑ 148 Freddie Keiaho RC 8.00 3.00
❑ 149 Gabe Watson RC 8.00 3.00
❑ 150 Gerris Wilkinson RC 5.00 2.00
❑ 151 Greg Blue RC 8.00 3.00
❑ 152 Guy Whimper RC 5.00 2.00
❑ 153 Jamar Williams RC 8.00 3.00
❑ 154 James Anderson RC 5.00 2.00
❑ 155 Jason Spitz RC 10.00 4.00
❑ 156 Jeff Webb RC 8.00 3.00
❑ 157 Jeremy Mincey RC 8.00 3.00
❑ 158 Jeremy Trueblood RC 8.00 3.00
❑ 159 Omar Gaither RC 8.00 3.00
❑ 160 Jon Alston RC 10.00 4.00
❑ 161 Julian Jenkins RC 8.00 3.00
❑ 162 Keith Ellison RC 8.00 3.00
❑ 163 Kevin McMahan RC 8.00 3.00
❑ 164 Kyle Williams RC 10.00 4.00
❑ 165 Leon Williams RC 8.00 3.00
❑ 166 Mark Anderson RC 15.00 6.00
❑ 167 LaJuan Ramsey RC 10.00 4.00
❑ 168 Nate Salley RC 8.00 3.00
❑ 169 Rob Ninkovich RC 8.00 3.00
❑ 170 Parys Haralson RC 8.00 3.00
❑ 171 Pat Watkins RC 10.00 4.00
❑ 172 Paul McQuistan RC 5.00 2.00
❑ 173 Rashad Butler RC 5.00 2.00
❑ 174 Ray Edwards RC 8.00 3.00
❑ 175 Reed Doughty RC 8.00 3.00
❑ 176 Ronnie Prude RC 8.00 3.00
❑ 177 Stephen Tulloch RC 8.00 3.00
❑ 178 Tim Jennings RC 8.00 3.00
❑ 179 Jarrad Page RC 10.00 4.00
❑ 180 Victor Adeyanju RC 8.00 3.00
❑ 181 Andre Hall AU RC 12.00 5.00
❑ 182 Anthony Fasano AU RC 15.00 6.00
❑ 183 Antonio Cromartie AU RC 20.00 10.00
❑ 184 Ashton Youboty AU RC 12.00 5.00
❑ 185 Kamerion Wimbley AU RC 15.00 6.00
❑ 186 Brad Smith AU RC 15.00 6.00
❑ 187 Brodrick Bunkley AU RC 12.00 5.00
❑ 188 Bruce Gradkowski AU RC 25.00 10.00
❑ 189 Chad Greenway AU RC 15.00 6.00
❑ 190 Cory Rodgers AU RC 12.00 5.00
❑ 191 D.J. Shockley AU RC 15.00 6.00
❑ 192 Danieal Manning AU RC 15.00 6.00
❑ 193 Darrell Bing AU RC 12.00 5.00
❑ 194 Darrell Hackney AU RC 12.00 5.00
❑ 195 D.Ferguson AU RC EXCH 15.00 6.00
❑ 196 Dominique Byrd AU RC 12.00 5.00
❑ 197 Drew Olson AU RC 12.00 5.00
❑ 198 Ernie Sims AU RC 15.00 6.00
❑ 199 Garrett Mills AU/99 RC 100.00 50.00
❑ 200 Gerald Riggs AU RC 12.00 5.00
❑ 201 Greg Jennings AU RC 40.00 20.00
❑ 202 Greg Lee AU RC 12.00 5.00
❑ 203 Hank Baskett AU RC 20.00 8.00
❑ 204 Ingle Martin AU RC 15.00 6.00
❑ 205 Jason Allen AU RC 12.00 5.00
❑ 206 Jerome Harrison AU RC 15.00 6.00
❑ 207 Jimmy Williams AU RC 15.00 6.00
❑ 208 John McCargo AU RC 10.00 4.00
❑ 209 Josh Betts AU RC 12.00 5.00
❑ 210 Leonard Pope AU RC 15.00 6.00
❑ 211 Marques Hagans AU RC 12.00 5.00
❑ 212 Martin Nance AU RC 12.00 5.00
❑ 213 Mathias Kiwanuka AU RC 20.00 8.00
❑ 214 Mike Bell AU RC 15.00 6.00
❑ 215 Mike Hass AU RC 15.00 6.00
❑ 216 Owen Daniels AU RC 15.00 6.00
❑ 217 P.J. Daniels AU RC 12.00 5.00
❑ 218 Reggie McNeal AU RC 12.00 5.00
❑ 219 Skyler Green AU RC 12.00 5.00
❑ 220 Terrence Whitehead AU RC 12.00 5.00
❑ 221 Thomas Howard AU RC 12.00 5.00
❑ 222 Tye Hill AU RC 12.00 5.00
❑ 223 Will Blackmon AU RC 12.00 5.00
❑ 224 Willie Reid AU RC 15.00 6.00
❑ 225 Winston Justice AU RC 15.00 6.00
❑ 226 Jay Cutler AU/99 RC 1200.00 600.00
❑ 227 J. Addai AU/99 RC 600.00 350.00
❑ 228 Br.Williams JSY/999 AU RC 40.00 15.00
❑ 229 B.Calhoun JSY/999 AU RC 40.00 15.00
❑ 230 Ch.Jackson JSY/699 AU RC 50.00 25.00
❑ 231 C.Whitehurst JSY/999 AU RC 40.00 15.00
❑ 232 DeA.Williams JSY/175 AU RC 400.00 200.00
❑ 233 Dem.Williams JSY/999 AU RC 40.00 15.00
❑ 234 Derek Hagan JSY/999 AU RC 40.00 15.00
❑ 235 Jason Avant JSY/999 AU RC 40.00 15.00
❑ 236 J.Norwood JSY/999 AU RC 120.00 60.00
❑ 237 J.Klopfenstein JSY/999 AU RC 30.00 12.00
❑ 238 K.Clemens JSY/999 AU RC 100.00 40.00
❑ 239 K.Jennings JSY/199 AU RC 80.00 40.00
❑ 240 L.Maroney JSY/999 AU RC 200.00 100.00
❑ 241 L.White JSY/999 AU RC 200.00 100.00
❑ 242 L.Washington JSY/999 AU RC 60.00 30.00
❑ 243 M.Lewis JSY/999 AU RC 40.00 15.00
❑ 244 M.McNeill JSY/260 AU RC 60.00 30.00
❑ 245 Ma.Williams JSY/699 AU RC 60.00 30.00
❑ 246 Matt Leinart JSY/299 AU RC 500.00 250.00
❑ 247 M.Drew JSY/999 AU RC 200.00 100.00
❑ 248 M.Stovall JSY/999 AU RC 40.00 15.00
❑ 249 Michael Huff JSY/999 AU RC 50.00 20.00
❑ 250 M.Robinson JSY/999 AU RC 40.00 15.00
❑ 251 Omar Jacobs/750 RC 10.00 4.00
❑ 252 Reggie Bush JSY/299 AU RC 600.00 300.00
❑ 253 S.Holmes JSY/399 AU RC 150.00 75.00
❑ 254 Sinorice Moss JSY/99 AU RC 150.00 75.00
❑ 255 T.Jackson JSY/999 AU RC 100.00 50.00
❑ 256 Travis Wilson JSY/999 AU RC 40.00 15.00
❑ 257 V.Davis JSY/699 AU RC 100.00 50.00
❑ 258 Vince Young JSY/270 AU RC 600.00 300.00
❑ 259 A.J. Hawk JSY/399 AU RC 100.00 50.00
❑ 260 B.Marshall JSY/999 AU RC 80.00 40.00

2007 SP Authentic

❑ 1 Ahman Green .75 .30
❑ 2 A.J. Hawk 1.00 .40
❑ 3 Alex Smith QB 1.00 .40
❑ 4 Andre Johnson .75 .30
❑ 5 Antonio Gates .75 .30
❑ 6 Ben Roethlisberger 1.25 .50
❑ 7 Bernard Berrian .60 .25
❑ 8 Brandon Jacobs .75 .30
❑ 9 Braylon Edwards .75 .30
❑ 10 Brett Favre 2.00 .75
❑ 11 Brian Urlacher 1.00 .40
❑ 12 Brian Westbrook .75 .30
❑ 13 Brodie Croyle 1.00 .40
❑ 14 Byron Leftwich .75 .30
❑ 15 Cadillac Williams .75 .30
❑ 16 Carson Palmer 1.00 .40
❑ 17 Cedric Benson .75 .30
❑ 18 Chad Johnson .75 .30
❑ 19 Chad Pennington .75 .30
❑ 20 Champ Bailey .75 .30
❑ 21 Derek Anderson .75 .30
❑ 22 Chester Taylor .60 .25
❑ 23 Chris Brown .60 .25
❑ 24 Chris Chambers .75 .30
❑ 25 Clinton Portis .75 .30
❑ 26 Darrell Jackson .75 .30
❑ 27 Deuce McAllister .75 .30
❑ 28 Dominic Rhodes .75 .30
❑ 29 Donald Driver .75 .30
❑ 30 Donovan McNabb 1.00 .40
❑ 31 Donte Stallworth .75 .30
❑ 32 Drew Brees .75 .30
❑ 33 Edgerrin James 1.00 .40
❑ 34 Eli Manning 1.00 .40
❑ 35 Frank Gore 1.00 .40
❑ 36 Fred Taylor .75 .30
❑ 37 Greg Jennings .75 .30
❑ 38 Hines Ward 1.00 .40
❑ 39 Jake Delhomme .75 .30
❑ 40 Jamal Lewis .75 .30
❑ 41 Jason Campbell .75 .30
❑ 42 Jason Taylor .60 .25
❑ 43 Jason Witten .75 .30
❑ 44 Javon Walker .75 .30
❑ 45 Jay Cutler 1.00 .40
❑ 46 Jerious Norwood .75 .30
❑ 47 Jerry Porter .75 .30
❑ 48 Jon Kitna .60 .25
❑ 49 Joseph Addai 1.25 .50
❑ 50 Julius Jones .75 .30
❑ 51 LaDainian Tomlinson 1.25 .50
❑ 52 Larry Johnson 1.00 .40
❑ 53 Larry Fitzgerald .75 .30
❑ 54 Laurence Maroney 1.00 .40
❑ 55 Marc Bulger .75 .30
❑ 56 Marion Barber .75 .30
❑ 57 Mark Clayton .75 .30
❑ 58 Marques Colston 1.00 .40
❑ 59 Marvin Harrison 1.00 .40
❑ 60 Matt Hasselbeck .75 .30
❑ 61 Matt Jones .75 .30
❑ 62 Matt Leinart 1.00 .40
❑ 63 Matt Schaub .75 .30
❑ 64 Maurice Jones-Drew 1.00 .40
❑ 65 Jeff Garcia .75 .30
❑ 66 Mike Alstott .75 .30
❑ 67 David Garrard .75 .30
❑ 68 Peyton Manning 1.50 .60
❑ 69 Philip Rivers 1.00 .40
❑ 70 Plaxico Burress .75 .30
❑ 71 Randy Moss 1.00 .40
❑ 72 Reggie Brown .75 .30
❑ 73 Reggie Bush 1.25 .50
❑ 74 Reggie Wayne .75 .30
❑ 75 Rex Grossman .75 .30
❑ 76 Ronnie Brown .75 .30
❑ 77 Roy Williams S .75 .30
❑ 78 Roy Williams WR .75 .30
❑ 79 Rudi Johnson .75 .30
❑ 80 Shaun Alexander .75 .30
❑ 81 Shawne Merriman .75 .30
❑ 82 Steven Jackson 1.00 .40
❑ 83 Steve McNair .75 .30
❑ 84 Steve Smith .75 .30
❑ 85 T.J. Houshmandzadeh .75 .30
❑ 86 Tarvaris Jackson 1.00 .40
❑ 87 Tedy Bruschi 1.00 .40
❑ 88 Terrell Owens 1.00 .40
❑ 89 Thomas Jones .75 .30
❑ 90 Tom Brady 2.00 .75

	Card	Hi	Lo
❑	91 Torry Holt	.75	.30
❑	92 Travis Henry	.75	.30
❑	93 Trent Green	.75	.30
❑	94 Vince Young	1.25	.50
❑	95 Vincent Jackson	.60	.25
❑	96 Walter Jones	.60	.25
❑	97 Warrick Dunn	.75	.30
❑	98 Willie Parker	1.00	.40
❑	99 Willis McGahee	.75	.30
❑	100 Tony Romo	2.00	.75
❑	101 Deon Anderson RC	8.00	3.00
❑	102 Ben Patrick RC	8.00	3.00
❑	103 Reagan Mauia RC	6.00	2.50
❑	104 Derek Schouman RC	8.00	3.00
❑	105 Keyunta Dawson RC	8.00	3.00
❑	106 Usama Young RC	8.00	3.00
❑	107 Syndric Steptoe RC	8.00	3.00
❑	108 Martrez Milner RC	8.00	3.00
❑	109 Brandon McDonald RC	6.00	2.50
❑	110 Jason Snelling RC	8.00	3.00
❑	111 Derek Stanley RC	8.00	3.00
❑	112 Ed Johnson RC	8.00	3.00
❑	113 Jacob Bender RC	6.00	2.50
❑	114 Charles Ali RC	8.00	3.00
❑	115 Tanard Jackson RC	6.00	2.50
❑	116 Paul Soliai RC	6.00	2.50
❑	117 Marvin White RC	6.00	2.50
❑	118 Jared Gaither RC	6.00	2.50
❑	119 Baraka Atkins RC	6.00	2.50
❑	120 Marcus Thomas RC	8.00	3.00
❑	121 Fred Bennett RC	6.00	2.50
❑	122 Dashon Goldson RC	6.00	2.50
❑	123 Kareem Brown RC	8.00	3.00
❑	124 Courtney Bryan RC	6.00	2.50
❑	125 Joe Cohen RC	6.00	2.50
❑	126 Jay Richardson RC	8.00	3.00
❑	127 Greg Peterson RC	8.00	3.00
❑	128 Dallas Sartz RC	8.00	3.00
❑	129 Brandon Harrison RC	6.00	2.50
❑	130 Tarell Brown RC	6.00	2.50
❑	131 Matt Gutierrez RC	10.00	4.00
❑	132 Edmond Miles RC	8.00	3.00
❑	133 Clifton Ryan RC	8.00	3.00
❑	134 Antwan Barnes RC	8.00	3.00
❑	135 Tim Shaw RC	8.00	3.00
❑	136 Eric Frampton RC	8.00	3.00
❑	137 William Gay RC	8.00	3.00
❑	138 Nick Graham RC	8.00	3.00
❑	139 Matt Toeaina RC	8.00	3.00
❑	140 John Wendling RC	8.00	3.00
❑	141 Mason Crosby RC	10.00	4.00
❑	142 C.J. Wallace RC	8.00	3.00
❑	143 Prescott Burgess RC	8.00	3.00
❑	144 Oscar Lua RC	8.00	3.00
❑	145 Chase Pittman RC	8.00	3.00
❑	146 Zachary Diles RC	8.00	3.00
❑	147 Kelvin Smith RC	8.00	3.00
❑	148 Marvin Mitchell RC	8.00	3.00
❑	149 Trumaine McBride RC	8.00	3.00
❑	150 Edgar Jones RC	8.00	3.00
❑	151 Abraham Wright RC	6.00	2.50
❑	152 Nick Folk RC	10.00	4.00
❑	153 Brandon Siler RC	8.00	3.00
❑	154 Clint Session RC	8.00	3.00
❑	155 Nedu Ndukwe RC	10.00	4.00
❑	156 C.J. Wilson RC	8.00	3.00
❑	157 Desmond Bishop RC	8.00	3.00
❑	158 Melvin Bullitt RC	8.00	3.00
❑	159 Courtney Brown RC	8.00	3.00
❑	160 Troy Smith RC	15.00	6.00
❑	161 Levi Brown RC	10.00	4.00
❑	162 Justin Harrell RC	10.00	4.00
❑	163 Jarvis Moss RC	10.00	4.00
❑	164 Aaron Ross RC	10.00	4.00
❑	165 Jon Beason RC	10.00	4.00
❑	166 Anthony Spencer RC	10.00	4.00
❑	167 Joe Staley RC	8.00	3.00
❑	168 Ben Grubbs RC	8.00	3.00
❑	169 Arron Sears RC	8.00	3.00
❑	170 Eric Weddle RC	8.00	3.00
❑	171 Justin Blalock RC	6.00	2.50
❑	172 Chris Houston RC	8.00	3.00
❑	173 David Harris RC	8.00	3.00
❑	174 Justin Durant RC	8.00	3.00
❑	175 Turk McBride RC	8.00	3.00
❑	176 Josh Wilson RC	8.00	3.00
❑	177 Tim Crowder RC	10.00	4.00
❑	178 Victor Abiamiri RC	10.00	4.00
❑	179 Ikaika Alama-Francis RC	10.00	4.00
❑	180 Ryan Kalil RC	8.00	3.00
❑	181 Samson Satele RC	6.00	2.50
❑	182 Gerald Alexander RC	6.00	2.50
❑	183 Corey Graham RC	6.00	2.50
❑	184 Sabby Piscitelli RC	10.00	4.00
❑	185 Quincy Black RC	8.00	3.00
❑	186 Daniel Coats RC	8.00	3.00
❑	187 Tony Ugoh RC	8.00	3.00
❑	188 David Jones RC	6.00	2.50
❑	189 DeMarcus Tank Tyler RC	8.00	3.00
❑	190 Chad Nkang RC	6.00	2.50
❑	191 Jonathan Wade RC	[illegible]	[illegible]
❑	192 Brandon Mebane RC	8.00	3.00
❑	193 Stewart Bradley RC	10.00	4.00
❑	194 Aaron Rouse RC	10.00	4.00
❑	195 Michael Okwo RC	8.00	3.00
❑	196 Anthony Waters RC	8.00	3.00
❑	197 Ray McDonald RC	8.00	3.00
❑	198 Clifton Dawson RC	10.00	4.00
❑	199 Brian Robison RC	10.00	4.00
❑	200 Jay Moore RC	8.00	3.00
❑	201 Dante Rosario AU RC	12.00	5.00
❑	202 Ahmad Bradshaw AU RC	60.00	30.00
❑	203 Roy Hall AU RC	15.00	6.00
❑	204 Aundrae Allison AU RC	12.00	5.00
❑	205 Brent Celek AU RC	12.00	5.00
❑	206 Chansi Stuckey AU RC	12.00	5.00
❑	207 Courtney Taylor AU RC	12.00	5.00
❑	208 Dallas Baker AU RC	12.00	5.00
❑	209 Darius Walker AU RC	15.00	6.00
❑	210 David Ball AU RC	10.00	4.00
❑	211 David Clowney AU RC	15.00	6.00
❑	212 David Irons AU RC	10.00	4.00
❑	213 Daymeion Hughes AU RC	12.00	5.00
❑	214 DeShawn Wynn AU RC	15.00	6.00
❑	215 Jordan Kent AU RC	12.00	5.00
❑	216 Dwayne Wright AU RC	12.00	5.00
❑	217 Eric Wright AU RC	15.00	6.00
❑	218 Gary Russell AU RC EXCH	15.00	6.00
❑	219 Mike Walker AU RC	12.00	5.00
❑	220 Isaiah Stanback AU RC	15.00	6.00
❑	221 Jamaal Anderson AU RC	12.00	5.00
❑	222 Jared Zabransky AU RC	15.00	6.00
❑	223 Jeff Rowe AU RC	12.00	5.00
❑	224 Joel Filani AU RC	12.00	5.00
❑	225 Jordan Palmer AU RC	15.00	6.00
❑	226 Kenneth Darby AU RC	15.00	6.00
❑	227 Kolby Smith AU RC	25.00	10.00
❑	228 Thomas Clayton AU RC	12.00	5.00
❑	229 Steve Breaston AU RC	12.00	5.00
❑	230 James Jones AU RC	25.00	10.00
❑	231 Marcus McCauley AU RC	12.00	5.00
❑	232 Alan Branch AU RC	12.00	5.00
❑	233 Michael Griffin AU RC	15.00	6.00
❑	234 Paul Posluszny AU RC	20.00	8.00
❑	235 Quentin Moses AU RC	12.00	5.00
❑	236 Lawrence Timmons AU RC	15.00	6.00
❑	237 Scott Chandler AU RC	12.00	5.00
❑	238 Jacoby Jones AU RC	15.00	6.00
❑	239 Tyler Thigpen AU RC	15.00	6.00
❑	240 Laurent Robinson AU RC	12.00	5.00
❑	241 John Broussard AU RC	12.00	5.00
❑	242 Zach Miller AU RC	15.00	6.00
❑	243 Matt Spaeth AU RC	15.00	6.00
❑	244 Rync Robinson AU RC EXCH	12.00	5.00
❑	245 Danny Ware AU RC	15.00	6.00
❑	246 Legedu Naanee AU RC	12.00	5.00
❑	247 Le'Ron McClain AU RC	12.00	5.00
❑	248 Kevin Boss AU RC	30.00	15.00
❑	249 Orenthal O'Neal AU RC	10.00	4.00
❑	250 Amobi Okoye AU RC	15.00	6.00
❑	251 Darrelle Revis AU RC	25.00	10.00
❑	252 LaRon Landry AU RC	30.00	12.00
❑	253 Chris Leak AU RC	20.00	8.00
❑	254 Craig Davis AU RC	25.00	10.00
❑	255 Leon Hall AU RC	20.00	8.00
❑	256 Reggie Nelson AU RC	20.00	8.00
❑	257 Adam Carriker AU RC	20.00	8.00
❑	258 H.B. Blades AU RC	20.00	8.00
❑	259 LaMarr Woodley AU RC	30.00	12.00
❑	260 Korey Hall AU RC	20.00	8.00
❑	261 Rhema McKnight AU RC	20.00	8.00
❑	262 Brandon Meriweather AU RC	25.00	10.00
❑	263 Matt Moore AU RC	60.00	30.00
❑	264 Selvin Young AU RC EXCH	50.00	25.00
❑	265 Tyler Palko AU RC	25.00	10.00
❑	266 Anthony Gonzalez JSY AU RC	60.00	30.00
❑	267 Antonio Pittman JSY AU RC	30.00	12.00
❑	268 Br.Jackson JSY AU RC	50.00	20.00
❑	269 Brian Leonard JSY AU RC	40.00	15.00
❑	270 Chris Henry JSY AU RC	40.00	15.00
❑	271 Drew Stanton JSY AU RC	80.00	30.00
❑	273 Garrett Wolfe JSY AU RC	50.00	20.00
❑	274 Greg Olsen JSY AU RC	50.00	20.00
❑	275 Jason Hill JSY AU RC	40.00	15.00
❑	276 Joe Thomas JSY AU RC	40.00	15.00
❑	277 John Beck JSY AU RC	100.00	50.00
❑	278 J.Lee Higgins JSY AU RC	30.00	12.00
❑	[illegible]	[illegible]	10.00
❑	280 Kevin Kolb JSY AU RC	100.00	50.00
❑	281 Lorenzo Booker JSY AU RC	50.00	20.00
❑	282 Michael Bush JSY AU RC	60.00	30.00
❑	283 Patrick Willis JSY AU RC	80.00	40.00
❑	284 Paul Williams JSY AU RC	30.00	12.00
❑	285 Steve Smith JSY AU RC	60.00	30.00
❑	286 Tony Hunt JSY AU RC	40.00	15.00
❑	287 Trent Edwards JSY AU RC	100.00	50.00
❑	288 Yamon Figurs JSY AU RC	40.00	15.00
❑	289 Adrian Peterson JSY AU RC	800.00	450.00
❑	290 Brady Quinn JSY AU RC	300.00	150.00
❑	291 Calvin Johnson JSY AU RC	250.00	125.00
❑	292 J.Russell JSY AU RC EXCH	250.00	150.00
❑	293 Marshawn Lynch JSY AU RC	250.00	125.00
❑	294 Dwayne Bowe JSY AU RC	120.00	60.00
❑	295 S.Rice JSY AU RC EXCH	80.00	40.00
❑	296 Robert Meachem JSY AU RC	60.00	30.00
❑	297 Dwayne Jarrett JSY AU RC	60.00	30.00
❑	298 Ted Ginn JSY AU RC	100.00	50.00

1999 SPx

	Card	Hi	Lo
❑	COMPLETE SET (135)	2000.00	1000.00
❑	COMP SET w/o SP's (90)	25.00	12.50
❑	*HAND NUMBERED RCs: .5X TO .8X		
❑	1 Jake Plummer	1.00	.40
❑	2 Adrian Murrell	1.00	.40
❑	3 Frank Sanders	1.00	.40
❑	4 Jamal Anderson	1.50	.60
❑	5 Chris Chandler	1.00	.40
❑	6 Terance Mathis	1.00	.40
❑	7 Tony Banks	1.00	.40
❑	8 Priest Holmes	2.50	1.00
❑	9 Jermaine Lewis	1.00	.40
❑	10 Antowain Smith	1.50	.60
❑	11 Doug Flutie	1.50	.60
❑	12 Eric Moulds	1.50	.60
❑	13 Tim Biakabutuka	1.00	.40
❑	14 Steve Beuerlein	1.00	.40
❑	15 Muhsin Muhammad	1.00	.40
❑	16 Bobby Engram	1.00	.40
❑	17 Curtis Conway	1.00	.40
❑	18 Curtis Enis	.60	.25
❑	19 Corey Dillon	1.50	.60
❑	20 Jeff Blake	1.00	.40
❑	21 Carl Pickens	1.00	.40
❑	22 Ty Detmer	1.00	.40
❑	23 Terry Kirby	.60	.25
❑	24 Leslie Shepherd	.60	.25
❑	25 Troy Aikman	3.00	1.25
❑	26 Emmitt Smith	3.00	1.25
❑	27 Deion Sanders	1.50	.60
❑	28 Terrell Davis	1.50	.60
❑	29 Rod Smith	1.00	.40
❑	30 Bubby Brister	1.00	.40
❑	31 Barry Sanders	5.00	2.00

Card	Player	Price 1	Price 2
❑ 32	Herman Moore	1.00	.40
❑ 33	Charlie Batch	1.50	.60
❑ 34	Brett Favre	5.00	2.00
❑ 35	Antonio Freeman	1.50	.60
❑ 36	Dorsey Levens	1.50	.60
❑ 37	Peyton Manning	5.00	2.00
❑ 38	Marvin Harrison	1.50	.60
❑ 39	Jerome Pathon	.60	.25
❑ 40	Mark Brunell	1.50	.60
❑ 41	Jimmy Smith	1.00	.40
❑ 42	Fred Taylor	1.50	.60
❑ 43	Elvis Grbac	1.00	.40
❑ 44	Andre Rison	1.00	.40
❑ 45	Warren Moon	1.50	.60
❑ 46	Dan Marino	5.00	2.00
❑ 47	Karim Abdul-Jabbar	1.00	.40
❑ 48	O.J. McDuffie	1.00	.40
❑ 49	Randall Cunningham	1.50	.60
❑ 50	Robert Smith	1.50	.60
❑ 51	Randy Moss	4.00	1.50
❑ 52	Drew Bledsoe	2.00	.75
❑ 53	Terry Glenn	1.50	.60
❑ 54	Tony Simmons	.60	.25
❑ 55	Danny Wuerffel	.60	.25
❑ 56	Cam Cleeland	.60	.25
❑ 57	Kerry Collins	1.00	.40
❑ 58	Gary Brown	.60	.25
❑ 59	Ike Hilliard	.60	.25
❑ 60	Vinny Testaverde	1.00	.40
❑ 61	Curtis Martin	1.50	.60
❑ 62	Keyshawn Johnson	1.50	.60
❑ 63	Rich Gannon	1.50	.60
❑ 64	Napoleon Kaufman	1.50	.60
❑ 65	Tim Brown	1.50	.60
❑ 66	Duce Staley	1.50	.60
❑ 67	Doug Pederson	.60	.25
❑ 68	Charles Johnson	.60	.25
❑ 69	Kordell Stewart	1.00	.40
❑ 70	Jerome Bettis	1.50	.60
❑ 71	Trent Green	1.50	.60
❑ 72	Marshall Faulk	2.00	.75
❑ 73	Ryan Leaf	1.50	.60
❑ 74	Natrone Means	1.00	.40
❑ 75	Jim Harbaugh	1.00	.40
❑ 76	Steve Young	2.00	.75
❑ 77	Garrison Hearst	1.00	.40
❑ 78	Jerry Rice	3.00	1.25
❑ 79	Terrell Owens	1.50	.60
❑ 80	Ricky Watters	1.00	.40
❑ 81	Joey Galloway	1.00	.40
❑ 82	Jon Kitna	1.50	.60
❑ 83	Warrick Dunn	1.50	.60
❑ 84	Trent Dilfer	1.00	.40
❑ 85	Mike Alstott	1.50	.60
❑ 86	Steve McNair	1.50	.60
❑ 87	Eddie George	1.50	.60
❑ 88	Yancey Thigpen	.60	.25
❑ 89	Skip Hicks	.60	.25
❑ 90	Michael Westbrook	1.00	.40
❑ 91	Amos Zereoue RC	15.00	6.00
❑ 92	Chris Claiborne AU RC	25.00	10.00
❑ 93	Scott Covington RC	15.00	6.00
❑ 94	Jeff Paulk RC	10.00	4.00
❑ 95	Brandon Stokley AU RC	40.00	15.00
❑ 96	Antoine Winfield RC	12.00	5.00
❑ 97	Reginald Kelly RC	10.00	4.00
❑ 98	Jermaine Fazande AU RC	15.00	6.00
❑ 99	Andy Katzenmoyer RC	12.00	5.00
❑ 100	Craig Yeast RC	12.00	5.00
❑ 101	Joe Montgomery RC	12.00	5.00
❑ 102	Darrin Chiaverini RC	12.00	5.00
❑ 103	Travis McGriff RC	10.00	4.00
❑ 104	Jevon Kearse RC	30.00	12.50
❑ 105	Joel Makovicka AU RC	15.00	6.00
❑ 106	Aaron Brooks RC	20.00	8.00
❑ 107	Chris McAlister RC	12.00	5.00
❑ 108	Jim Kleinsasser RC	15.00	6.00
❑ 109	Ebenezer Ekuban RC	12.00	5.00
❑ 110	Karsten Bailey RC	12.00	5.00
❑ 111	Sedrick Irvin AU RC	12.00	5.00
❑ 112	D'Wayne Bates AU RC	12.00	5.00
❑ 113	Joe Germaine AU RC	15.00	6.00
❑ 114	Cecil Collins AU RC	15.00	6.00
❑ 115	Mike Cloud RC	12.00	5.00
❑ 116	James Johnson RC	12.00	5.00
❑ 117	Champ Bailey AU RC	40.00	15.00
❑ 118	Rob Konrad RC	15.00	6.00
❑ 119	Peerless Price AU RC	30.00	12.50
❑ 120	Kevin Faulk AU RC	25.00	10.00
❑ 121	Dameane Douglas RC	10.00	4.00
❑ 122	Kevin Johnson AU RC	15.00	6.00
❑ 123	Troy Edwards AU RC	25.00	10.00
❑ 124	Edgerrin James AU RC	100.00	50.00
❑ 125	David Boston AU RC	25.00	10.00
❑ 126	Michael Bishop AU RC	25.00	10.00
❑ 127	Shaun King AU RC SP	50.00	25.00
❑ 127X	Shaun King EXCH	10.00	4.00
❑ 128	Brock Huard AU RC	15.00	6.00
❑ 129	Torry Holt AU RC	60.00	30.00
❑ 130	Cade McNown AU/500 RC	40.00	15.00
❑ 131	Tim Couch AU/500 RC	40.00	15.00
❑ 132	Donovan McNabb AU RC	120.00	60.00
❑ 132X	Donovan McNabb EXCH	5.00	2.00
❑ 133	Akili Smith AU/500 RC	40.00	15.00
❑ 134	D.Culpepper AU/500 RC	150.00	75.00
❑ 135	Ricky Williams AU/500 RC	60.00	30.00
❑ S8	Troy Aikman Sample	2.00	.75

2000 SPx

Card	Player	Price 1	Price 2
❑	COMP.SET w/o SP's (90)	20.00	7.50
❑ 1	Jake Plummer	.60	.25
❑ 2	David Boston	1.00	.40
❑ 3	Frank Sanders	.60	.25
❑ 4	Chris Chandler	.60	.25
❑ 5	Jamal Anderson	1.00	.40
❑ 6	Shawn Jefferson	.40	.15
❑ 7	Qadry Ismail	.60	.25
❑ 8	Tony Banks	.60	.25
❑ 9	Shannon Sharpe	.60	.25
❑ 10	Rob Johnson	.60	.25
❑ 11	Eric Moulds	1.00	.40
❑ 12	Muhsin Muhammad	.60	.25
❑ 13	Steve Beuerlein	.40	.15
❑ 14	Cade McNown	.40	.15
❑ 15	Marcus Robinson	1.00	.40
❑ 16	Akili Smith	.40	.15
❑ 17	Corey Dillon	1.00	.40
❑ 18	Darnay Scott	.60	.25
❑ 19	Tim Couch	.60	.25
❑ 20	Kevin Johnson	1.00	.40
❑ 21	Errict Rhett	.40	.15
❑ 22	Troy Aikman	2.00	.75
❑ 23	Emmitt Smith	2.00	.75
❑ 24	Joey Galloway	.60	.25
❑ 25	Terrell Davis	1.00	.40
❑ 26	Olandis Gary	1.00	.40
❑ 27	Brian Griese	1.00	.40
❑ 28	Charlie Batch	1.00	.40
❑ 29	Germane Crowell	.40	.15
❑ 30	James Stewart	.60	.25
❑ 31	Brett Favre	3.00	1.25
❑ 32	Antonio Freeman	1.00	.40
❑ 33	Dorsey Levens	.60	.25
❑ 34	Peyton Manning	2.50	1.00
❑ 35	Edgerrin James	1.50	.60
❑ 36	Marvin Harrison	1.00	.40
❑ 37	Mark Brunell	1.00	.40
❑ 38	Fred Taylor	1.00	.40
❑ 39	Jimmy Smith	.60	.25
❑ 40	Keenan McCardell	.60	.25
❑ 41	Elvis Grbac	.60	.25
❑ 42	Tony Gonzalez	.60	.25
❑ 43	Tony Martin	.60	.25
❑ 44	Jay Fiedler	1.00	.40
❑ 45	Damon Huard	1.00	.40
❑ 46	Randy Moss	2.00	.75
❑ 47	Robert Smith	1.00	.40
❑ 48	Cris Carter	1.00	.40
❑ 49	Daunte Culpepper	1.25	.50
❑ 50	Drew Bledsoe	1.25	.50
❑ 51	Terry Glenn	.60	.25
❑ 52	Ricky Williams	1.00	.40
❑ 53	Jeff Blake	.60	.25
❑ 54	Keith Poole	.40	.15
❑ 55	Kerry Collins	.60	.25
❑ 56	Amani Toomer	.60	.25
❑ 57	Ike Hilliard	.60	.25
❑ 58	Ray Lucas	.60	.25
❑ 59	Curtis Martin	1.00	.40
❑ 60	Vinny Testaverde	.60	.25
❑ 61	Tim Brown	1.00	.40
❑ 62	Rich Gannon	1.00	.40
❑ 63	Tyrone Wheatley	.60	.25
❑ 64	Napoleon Kaufman	.60	.25
❑ 65	Duce Staley	1.00	.40
❑ 66	Donovan McNabb	1.50	.60
❑ 67	Troy Edwards	.40	.15
❑ 68	Jerome Bettis	1.00	.40
❑ 69	Kordell Stewart	.60	.25
❑ 70	Marshall Faulk	1.25	.50
❑ 71	Kurt Warner	1.50	.60
❑ 72	Isaac Bruce	1.00	.40
❑ 73	Torry Holt	1.00	.40
❑ 74	Ryan Leaf	.60	.25
❑ 75	Jim Harbaugh	.60	.25
❑ 76	Jerry Rice	2.00	.75
❑ 77	Terrell Owens	1.00	.40
❑ 78	Jeff Garcia	1.00	.40
❑ 79	Ricky Watters	.60	.25
❑ 80	Jon Kitna	1.00	.40
❑ 81	Derrick Mayes	.60	.25
❑ 82	Shaun King	.40	.15
❑ 83	Mike Alstott	1.00	.40
❑ 84	Keyshawn Johnson	1.00	.40
❑ 85	Eddie George	1.00	.40
❑ 86	Steve McNair	1.00	.40
❑ 87	Jevon Kearse	1.00	.40
❑ 88	Brad Johnson	1.00	.40
❑ 89	Stephen Davis	1.00	.40
❑ 90	Michael Westbrook	.60	.25
❑ 91	Anthony Lucas RC	8.00	3.00
❑ 92	Avion Black RC	12.00	5.00
❑ 93	Corey Moore RC	8.00	3.00
❑ 94	Chris Cole RC	12.00	5.00
❑ 95	Chris Hovan RC	12.00	5.00
❑ 96	Dante Hall RC	30.00	12.50
❑ 97	Darrell Jackson RC	30.00	12.50
❑ 98	Deltha O'Neal RC	15.00	6.00
❑ 99	Doug Chapman RC	12.00	5.00
❑ 100	Doug Johnson RC	15.00	6.00
❑ 101	Erron Kinney RC	15.00	6.00
❑ 102	Frank Moreau RC	12.00	5.00
❑ 103	Patrick Pass RC	12.00	5.00
❑ 104	Gari Scott RC	8.00	3.00
❑ 105	Giovanni Carmazzi RC	8.00	3.00
❑ 106	JaJuan Dawson RC	8.00	3.00
❑ 107	James Williams RC	12.00	5.00
❑ 108	Jarious Jackson RC	12.00	5.00
❑ 109	John Abraham RC	20.00	7.50
❑ 110	Keith Bulluck RC	15.00	6.00
❑ 111	Jonas Lewis RC	8.00	3.00
❑ 112	Mike Green RC	12.00	5.00
❑ 113	Ronney Jenkins RC	12.00	5.00
❑ 114	Michael Wiley RC	12.00	5.00
❑ 115	Mike Anderson RC	20.00	10.00
❑ 116	Mareno Philyaw RC	8.00	3.00
❑ 117	Muneer Moore RC	8.00	3.00
❑ 118	Paul Smith RC	12.00	5.00
❑ 119	Raynoch Thompson RC	12.00	5.00
❑ 120	Rob Morris RC	12.00	5.00
❑ 121	Ron Dixon RC	12.00	5.00
❑ 122	Rondell Mealey RC	8.00	3.00
❑ 123	Sebastian Janikowski RC	15.00	6.00
❑ 124	Shaun Ellis RC	15.00	6.00
❑ 125	Charles Lee RC	12.00	5.00
❑ 126	Shyrone Stith RC	12.00	5.00
❑ 127	Thomas Hamner RC	8.00	3.00
❑ 128	Tim Rattay RC	15.00	6.00
❑ 129	Todd Husak RC	15.00	6.00
❑ 130	Tom Brady RC	700.00	500.00
❑ 131	Trevor Gaylor RC	12.00	5.00
❑ 132	Windrell Hayes RC	12.00	5.00
❑ 133	Anthony Becht JSY AU RC	25.00	10.00

❑ 134 Brian Urlacher JSY AU RC 135.00 75.00
❑ 135 Bubba Franks JSY AU RC 30.00 12.50
❑ 136 C Pennington JSY AU RC 60.00 30.00
❑ 137 Chr Redman JSY AU RC 25.00 10.00
❑ 138 Corey Simon JSY AU RC 30.00 12.50
❑ 139 Curtis Keaton JSY AU RC 25.00 10.00
❑ 140 Danny Farmer JSY AU RC 25.00 10.00
❑ 141 Den Northcutt JSY AU RC 30.00 12.50
❑ 142 Dez White JSY AU RC 30.00 12.50
❑ 143 J.R. Redmond JSY AU SP RC 25.00 10.00
❑ 144 Jamal Lewis JSY AU RC 50.00 25.00
❑ 145 Jerry Porter JSY AU RC 50.00 20.00
❑ 146 Joe Hamilton EXCH 3.00 1.25
❑ 147 Laver Coles JSY AU RC 40.00 20.00
❑ 148 R.Jay Soward JSY AU RC 25.00 10.00
❑ 149 Reu Droughns JSY AU RC 40.00 15.00
❑ 150 Ron Dayne JSY AU RC 40.00 15.00
❑ 151 Ron Dugans JSY AU RC 20.00 7.50
❑ 152 Sha Alexander JSY AU RC 120.00 60.00
❑ 153 Sylvester Morris JSY AU RC 25.00 10.00
❑ 154 Tee Martin JSY AU RC 30.00 12.50
❑ 155 Th.Jones JSY AU RC SP 150.00 75.00
❑ 156 Todd Pinkston JSY AU RC 30.00 12.50
❑ 157 Travis Prentice JSY AU RC 25.00 10.00
❑ 158 Travis Taylor JSY AU SP RC 40.00 15.00
❑ 159 Trung Canidate JSY AU RC 25.00 10.00
❑ 160 Courtney Brown JSY AU RC 30.00 12.50
❑ 161 Peter Warrick JSY AU RC 30.00 12.50
❑ 162 Plaxico Burress JSY AU RC 100.00 60.00
❑ S1 Peyton Manning Sample 4.00 1.50

2001 SPx

❑ COMP.SET w/o SP's (90) 20.00 7.50
❑ 1 Jake Plummer .60 .25
❑ 2 David Boston 1.00 .40
❑ 3 Jamal Anderson 1.00 .40
❑ 4 Chris Chandler .60 .25
❑ 5 Tony Martin .60 .25
❑ 6 Elvis Grbac .60 .25
❑ 7 Qadry Ismail .60 .25
❑ 8 Ray Lewis 1.00 .40
❑ 9 Rob Johnson .60 .25
❑ 10 Shawn Bryson .40 .15
❑ 11 Eric Moulds .60 .25
❑ 12 Tim Biakabutuka .60 .25
❑ 13 Jeff Lewis .40 .15
❑ 14 Muhsin Muhammad .60 .25
❑ 15 Shane Matthews .40 .15
❑ 16 Marcus Robinson 1.00 .40
❑ 17 Brian Urlacher 1.50 .60
❑ 18 Jon Kitna .40 .15
❑ 19 Peter Warrick 1.00 .40
❑ 20 Corey Dillon 1.00 .40
❑ 21 Tim Couch .60 .25
❑ 22 Travis Prentice .40 .15
❑ 23 Kevin Johnson .60 .25
❑ 24 Rocket Ismail .60 .25
❑ 25 Emmitt Smith 2.00 .75
❑ 26 Joey Galloway .60 .25
❑ 27 Terrell Davis 1.00 .40
❑ 28 Brian Griese 1.00 .40
❑ 29 Rod Smith .60 .25
❑ 30 Ed McCaffrey 1.00 .40
❑ 31 Charlie Batch 1.00 .40
❑ 32 Germane Crowell .40 .15
❑ 33 James O. Stewart .60 .25
❑ 34 Brett Favre 3.00 1.25
❑ 35 Antonio Freeman 1.00 .40
❑ 36 Ahman Green 1.00 .40
❑ 37 Peyton Manning 2.50 1.00
❑ 38 Edgerrin James 1.25 .50
❑ 39 Marvin Harrison 1.00 .40
❑ 40 Mark Brunell 1.00 .40
❑ 41 Fred Taylor 1.00 .40
❑ 42 Jimmy Smith .60 .25
❑ 43 Tony Gonzalez .60 .25
❑ 44 Trent Green 1.00 .40
❑ 45 Priest Holmes 1.25 .50
❑ 46 Lamar Smith .60 .25
❑ 47 Jay Fiedler 1.00 .40
❑ 48 Oronde Gadsden .60 .25
❑ 49 Daunte Culpepper 1.00 .40
❑ 50 Randy Moss [illegible] [illegible]
❑ 51 Cris Carter 1.00 .40
❑ 52 Drew Bledsoe 1.25 .50
❑ 53 Troy Brown .60 .25
❑ 54 Ricky Williams 1.00 .40
❑ 55 Joe Horn .60 .25
❑ 56 Aaron Brooks 1.00 .40
❑ 57 Albert Connell .40 .15
❑ 58 Kerry Collins .60 .25
❑ 59 Tiki Barber 1.00 .40
❑ 60 Ron Dayne 1.00 .40
❑ 61 Vinny Testaverde .60 .25
❑ 62 Wayne Chrebet .60 .25
❑ 63 Curtis Martin 1.00 .40
❑ 64 Tim Brown 1.00 .40
❑ 65 Jerry Rice 2.00 .75
❑ 66 Rich Gannon 1.00 .40
❑ 67 Duce Staley 1.00 .40
❑ 68 Donovan McNabb 1.25 .50
❑ 69 Kordell Stewart .60 .25
❑ 70 Jerome Bettis 1.00 .40
❑ 71 Marshall Faulk 1.25 .50
❑ 72 Kurt Warner 2.00 .75
❑ 73 Isaac Bruce 1.00 .40
❑ 74 Torry Holt 1.00 .40
❑ 75 Doug Flutie 1.00 .40
❑ 76 Junior Seau 1.00 .40
❑ 77 Jeff Garcia 1.00 .40
❑ 78 Garrison Hearst .60 .25
❑ 79 Terrell Owens 1.00 .40
❑ 80 Ricky Watters .60 .25
❑ 81 Matt Hasselbeck .60 .25
❑ 82 Brad Johnson 1.00 .40
❑ 83 Keyshawn Johnson 1.00 .40
❑ 84 Warrick Dunn 1.00 .40
❑ 85 Mike Alstott 1.00 .40
❑ 86 Kevin Dyson .60 .25
❑ 87 Eddie George 1.00 .40
❑ 88 Steve McNair 1.00 .40
❑ 89 Michael Westbrook .60 .25
❑ 90 Stephen Davis 1.00 .40
❑ 91B D McAllister JSY AU/250 RC 100.00 50.00
❑ 91G D McAllister JSY AU/250 RC 100.00 50.00
❑ 92B Fr Mitchell JSY AU/250 RC 30.00 12.50
❑ 92G Fr Mitchell JSY AU/250 RC 30.00 12.50
❑ 93B Koren Robinson/999 RC 10.00 4.00
❑ 93G Koren Robinson/999 RC 10.00 4.00
❑ 94B David Terrell/999 RC 10.00 4.00
❑ 94G David Terrell/999 RC 10.00 4.00
❑ 95B M Vick JSY AU/250 RC 120.00 50.00
❑ 95G M Vick JSY AU/250 RC 120.00 50.00
❑ 96B M Bennett JSY AU/550 RC 30.00 12.50
❑ 96G M Bennett JSY AU/550 RC 30.00 12.50
❑ 97B Robert Ferguson/999 RC 10.00 4.00
❑ 97G Robert Ferguson/999 RC 10.00 4.00
❑ 98B Rod Gardner/999 RC 10.00 4.00
❑ 98G Rod Gardner/999 RC 10.00 4.00
❑ 99B Travis Henry JSY AU/550 RC 60.00 30.00
❑ 99G Travis Henry JSY AU/550 RC 60.00 30.00
❑ 100B C Johnson JSY AU/550 RC 100.00 60.00
❑ 100G C Johnson JSY AU/550 RC 100.00 60.00
❑ 101B D.Brees JSY AU/250 RC 175.00 100.00
❑ 101G D.Brees JSY AU/250 RC 175.00 100.00
❑ 102B S Moss JSY AU/550 RC 50.00 25.00
❑ 102G S Moss JSY AU/550 RC 50.00 25.00
❑ 103B C Weinke JSY AU/550 RC 25.00 10.00
❑ 103G C Weinke JSY AU/550 RC 25.00 10.00
❑ 104B R Seymour JSY AU/900 RC 40.00 20.00
❑ 104G R Seymour JSY AU/900 RC 40.00 20.00
❑ 105B Reggie Wayne/999 RC 25.00 10.00
❑ 105G Reggie Wayne/999 RC 25.00 10.00
❑ 106B K Barlow JSY AU/550 RC 30.00 12.50
❑ 106G K Barlow JSY AU/550 RC 30.00 12.50
❑ 107B Chambers JSY AU/900 RC 50.00 25.00
❑ 107G Chambers JSY AU/900 RC 50.00 25.00
❑ 108B Todd Heap JSY AU/900 RC 30.00 12.50
❑ 108G Todd Heap JSY AU/900 RC 30.00 12.50
❑ 109B A Thomas JSY AU/550 RC 30.00 12.50
❑ 109G A Thomas JSY AU/550 RC 30.00 12.50
❑ 110B J Jackson JSY AU/550 RC 25.00 10.00
❑ 110G J Jackson JSY AU/550 RC 25.00 10.00
❑ 111B R Johnson JSY AU/900 RC 80.00 40.00
❑ 111G R.Johnson JSY AU/900 RC 80.00 40.00
❑ 112B McMahon JSY AU/900 RC 25.00 10.00
❑ 112G McMahon JSY AU/900 RC 25.00 10.00
❑ 113B J.Heupel JSY AU/900 RC 100.00 50.00
❑ 113G J.Heupel JSY AU/900 RC 100.00 50.00
❑ [illegible] 10.00
❑ 114G T Minor JSY AU/900 RC 25.00 10.00
❑ 115B Quincy Morgan/999 RC 10.00 4.00
❑ 115G Quincy Morgan/999 RC 10.00 4.00
❑ 116B D Morgan JSY AU/900 RC 20.00 10.00
❑ 116G D Morgan JSY AU/900 RC 20.00 10.00
❑ 117B J Palmer JSY AU/900 RC 25.00 10.00
❑ 117G J Palmer JSY AU/900 RC 25.00 10.00
❑ 118B S Rosenfels JSY AU/900 RC 25.00 10.00
❑ 118G S Rosenfels JSY AU/900 RC 25.00 10.00
❑ 119B Tuiasosopo JSY AU/900 RC 30.00 12.50
❑ 119G Tuiasosopo JSY AU/900 RC 30.00 12.50
❑ 120B Damerien McCants/999 RC 6.00 2.50
❑ 120G Damerien McCants/999 RC 6.00 2.50
❑ 121B Snoop Minnis/999 RC 6.00 2.50
❑ 121G Snoop Minnis/999 RC 6.00 2.50
❑ 122B L.Tomlinson JSY/250 RC 200.00 100.00
❑ 122G L.Tomlinson JSY/250 RC 250.00 125.00
❑ 123B Quincy Carter/999 RC 10.00 4.00
❑ 123G Quincy Carter/999 RC 10.00 4.00
❑ 124B Arnold Jackson/999 RC 6.00 2.50
❑ 124G Arnold Jackson/999 RC 6.00 2.50
❑ 125B Justin McCareins/999 RC 10.00 4.00
❑ 125G Justin McCareins/999 RC 10.00 4.00
❑ 126B Eddie Berlin/999 RC 6.00 2.50
❑ 126G Eddie Berlin/999 RC 6.00 2.50
❑ 127B Quentin McCord/999 RC 6.00 2.50
❑ 127G Quentin McCord/999 RC 6.00 2.50
❑ 128B Vinny Sutherland/999 RC 6.00 2.50
❑ 128G Vinny Sutherland/999 RC 6.00 2.50
❑ 129B Willie Middlebrooks/999 RC 6.00 2.50
❑ 129G Willie Middlebrooks/999 RC 6.00 2.50
❑ 130B Dan Alexander/999 RC 10.00 4.00
❑ 130G Dan Alexander/999 RC 10.00 4.00
❑ 131B Dee Brown/999 RC 10.00 4.00
❑ 131G Dee Brown/999 RC 10.00 4.00
❑ 132B Andre Carter/999 RC 10.00 4.00
❑ 132G Andre Carter/999 RC 10.00 4.00
❑ 133B Justin Smith/999 RC 10.00 4.00
❑ 133G Justin Smith/999 RC 10.00 4.00
❑ 134B Houshmandzadeh/999 RC 12.00 5.00
❑ 134G Houshmandzadeh/999 RC 12.00 5.00
❑ 135B Andre King/999 RC 6.00 2.50
❑ 135G Andre King/999 RC 6.00 2.50
❑ 136B Nick Goings/999 RC 10.00 4.00
❑ 136G Nick Goings/999 RC 10.00 4.00
❑ 137B Scotty Anderson/999 RC 6.00 2.50
❑ 137G Scotty Anderson/999 RC 6.00 2.50
❑ 138B David Martin/999 RC 6.00 2.50
❑ 138G David Martin/999 RC 6.00 2.50
❑ 139B Derrick Blaylock/999 RC 12.00 5.00
❑ 139G Derrick Blaylock/999 RC 12.00 5.00
❑ 140B Onome Ojo/999 RC 6.00 2.50
❑ 140G Onome Ojo/999 RC 6.00 2.50
❑ 141B Jonathan Carter/999 RC 6.00 2.50
❑ 141G Jonathan Carter/999 RC 6.00 2.50
❑ 142B LaMont Jordan/999 RC 20.00 7.50
❑ 142G LaMont Jordan/999 RC 20.00 7.50
❑ 143B Dominic Rhodes/999 RC 15.00 6.00
❑ 143G Dominic Rhodes/999 RC 15.00 6.00
❑ 145B A.J. Feeley/999 RC 10.00 4.00
❑ 145G A.J. Feeley/999 RC 10.00 4.00
❑ 146B Correll Buckhalter/999 RC 12.00 5.00
❑ 146G Correll Buckhalter/999 RC 12.00 5.00
❑ 147B Steve Smith/999 RC 25.00 12.50
❑ 147G Steve Smith/999 RC 25.00 12.50
❑ 148B Dave Dickenson/999 RC 6.00 2.50
❑ 148G Dave Dickenson/999 RC 6.00 2.50
❑ 149B Cedrick Wilson/999 RC 10.00 4.00
❑ 149G Cedrick Wilson/999 RC 10.00 4.00
❑ 150B Jamie Winborn/999 RC 6.00 2.50
❑ 150G Jamie Winborn/999 RC 6.00 2.50
❑ 151B Alex Bannister/999 RC 6.00 2.50
❑ 151G Alex Bannister/999 RC 6.00 2.50

❑ 152B Heath Evans/999 RC 6.00 2.50
❑ 152G Heath Evans/999 RC 6.00 2.50
❑ 153B Josh Booty/999 RC 10.00 4.00
❑ 153G Josh Booty/999 RC 10.00 4.00
❑ 154B Adam Archuleta/999 RC 10.00 4.00
❑ 154G Adam Archuleta/999 RC 10.00 4.00
❑ 155B Francis St.Paul/999 RC 6.00 2.50
❑ 155G Francis St.Paul/999 RC 6.00 2.50
❑ 156B Andre Dyson/999 RC 4.00 1.50
❑ 156G Andre Dyson/999 RC 4.00 1.50
❑ RM Randy Moss SAMPLE 2.00 .75

2002 SPx

❑ COMP.SET w/o SP's (90) 20.00 7.50
❑ 1 Drew Bledsoe 1.25 .50
❑ 2 Peerless Price .60 .25
❑ 3 Travis Henry 1.00 .40
❑ 4 Ricky Williams 1.00 .40
❑ 5 Jay Fiedler .60 .25
❑ 6 Tom Brady 2.50 1.00
❑ 7 Troy Brown .60 .25
❑ 8 Antowain Smith .60 .25
❑ 9 Santana Moss 1.00 .40
❑ 10 Curtis Martin 1.00 .40
❑ 11 Vinny Testaverde .60 .25
❑ 12 Jamal Lewis 1.00 .40
❑ 13 Chris Redman .40 .15
❑ 14 Travis Taylor .60 .25
❑ 15 Corey Dillon .60 .25
❑ 16 T.J. Houshmandzadeh .60 .25
❑ 17 Peter Warrick .60 .25
❑ 18 Courtney Brown .60 .25
❑ 19 Kevin Johnson .60 .25
❑ 20 Tim Couch .60 .25
❑ 21 Hines Ward 1.00 .40
❑ 22 Jerome Bettis 1.00 .40
❑ 23 Kordell Stewart .60 .25
❑ 24 Corey Bradford .40 .15
❑ 25 Jermaine Lewis .40 .15
❑ 26 Edgerrin James 1.25 .50
❑ 27 Marvin Harrison 1.00 .40
❑ 28 Peyton Manning 2.00 .75
❑ 29 Jimmy Smith .60 .25
❑ 30 Mark Brunell 1.00 .40
❑ 31 Fred Taylor 1.00 .40
❑ 32 Eddie George 1.00 .40
❑ 33 Steve McNair 1.00 .40
❑ 34 Brian Griese 1.00 .40
❑ 35 Shannon Sharpe .60 .25
❑ 36 Rod Smith .60 .25
❑ 37 Trent Green .60 .25
❑ 38 Johnnie Morton .60 .25
❑ 39 Priest Holmes 1.25 .50
❑ 40 Jerry Rice 2.00 .75
❑ 41 Rich Gannon 1.00 .40
❑ 42 Tim Brown 1.00 .40
❑ 43 Drew Brees 1.00 .40
❑ 44 Junior Seau 1.00 .40
❑ 45 LaDainian Tomlinson 1.50 .60
❑ 46 Emmitt Smith 2.50 1.00
❑ 47 Quincy Carter .60 .25
❑ 48 Rocket Ismail .60 .25
❑ 49 Amani Toomer .60 .25
❑ 50 Kerry Collins .60 .25
❑ 51 Ron Dayne .60 .25
❑ 52 Donovan McNabb 1.25 .50
❑ 53 Duce Staley 1.00 .40
❑ 54 Antonio Freeman 1.00 .40
❑ 55 Rod Gardner .60 .25
❑ 56 Stephen Davis .60 .25
❑ 57 Brian Urlacher 1.50 .60
❑ 58 Anthony Thomas .60 .25
❑ 59 Jim Miller .60 .25
❑ 60 Marty Booker .60 .25
❑ 61 Az-Zahir Hakim .40 .15
❑ 62 James Stewart .60 .25
❑ 63 Ahman Green 1.00 .40
❑ 64 Brett Favre 2.50 1.00
❑ 65 Robert Ferguson .40 .15
❑ 66 Terry Glenn .60 .25
❑ 67 Randy Moss 2.00 .75
❑ 68 Daunte Culpepper 1.00 .40
❑ 69 Michael Bennett .60 .25
❑ 70 Michael Vick 2.00 .75
❑ 71 Warrick Dunn 1.00 .40
❑ 72 Rodney Peete .60 .25
❑ 73 Muhsin Muhammad .60 .25
❑ 74 Aaron Brooks 1.00 .40
❑ 75 Deuce McAllister 1.25 .50
❑ 76 Keyshawn Johnson 1.00 .40
❑ 77 Michael Pittman .40 .15
❑ 78 Brad Johnson .60 .25
❑ 79 Thomas Jones .60 .25
❑ 80 David Boston 1.00 .40
❑ 81 Jake Plummer .60 .25
❑ 82 Terrell Owens 1.00 .40
❑ 83 Garrison Hearst .60 .25
❑ 84 Jeff Garcia 1.00 .40
❑ 85 Darrell Jackson .60 .25
❑ 86 Shaun Alexander 1.25 .50
❑ 87 Trent Dilfer .60 .25
❑ 88 Isaac Bruce 1.00 .40
❑ 89 Kurt Warner 1.00 .40
❑ 90 Marshall Faulk 1.00 .40
❑ 91 Saleem Rasheed RC 10.00 4.00
❑ 92 Jason McAddley RC 8.00 3.00
❑ 93 Brandon Doman RC 8.00 3.00
❑ 94 Mike Rumph RC 10.00 4.00
❑ 95 Wendell Bryant RC 5.00 2.00
❑ 96 Bryan Thomas RC 8.00 3.00
❑ 97 Anthony Weaver RC 8.00 3.00
❑ 98 Chester Taylor RC 20.00 7.50
❑ 99 Ed Reed RC 15.00 6.00
❑ 100 Lamar Gordon RC 10.00 4.00
❑ 101 Tellis Redmon RC 8.00 3.00
❑ 102 Ben Leber RC 10.00 4.00
❑ 103 Javin Hunter RC 5.00 2.00
❑ 104 Javon Walker RC 20.00 7.50
❑ 105 Shaun Hill RC 10.00 4.00
❑ 106 Raonall Smith RC 8.00 3.00
❑ 107 Darrell Hill RC 8.00 3.00
❑ 108 Kalimba Edwards RC 10.00 4.00
❑ 109 Robert Thomas RC 10.00 4.00
❑ 110 Craig Nall RC 10.00 4.00
❑ 111 Marques Anderson RC 10.00 4.00
❑ 112 Najeh Davenport RC 10.00 4.00
❑ 113 Jonathan Wells RC 10.00 4.00
❑ 114 Dwight Freeney RC 20.00 7.50
❑ 115 Larry Tripplett RC 5.00 2.00
❑ 116 T.J. Duckett RC 10.00 4.00
❑ 117 John Henderson RC 10.00 4.00
❑ 118 Albert Haynesworth RC 8.00 3.00
❑ 119 Tank Williams RC 8.00 3.00
❑ 120 Ryan Sims RC 10.00 4.00
❑ 121 Leonard Henry RC 8.00 3.00
❑ 122 Clinton Portis RC 50.00 20.00
❑ 123 Josh Reed RC 10.00 4.00
❑ 124 Chad Hutchinson RC 8.00 3.00
❑ 125 Deion Branch RC 20.00 7.50
❑ 126 Rocky Calmus RC 10.00 4.00
❑ 127 Donte Stallworth RC 20.00 7.50
❑ 128 Daryl Jones RC 8.00 3.00
❑ 129 Joey Harrington RC 15.00 6.00
❑ 130 Napoleon Harris RC 10.00 4.00
❑ 131 Phillip Buchanon RC 10.00 4.00
❑ 132 Patrick Ramsey RC 10.00 4.00
❑ 133 Brian Westbrook RC 20.00 10.00
❑ 134 Freddie Milons RC 8.00 3.00
❑ 135 Lito Sheppard RC 10.00 4.00
❑ 136 Michael Lewis RC 10.00 4.00
❑ 137 Jamin Elliott RC 5.00 2.00
❑ 138 Lee Mays RC 10.00 4.00
❑ 139 Verron Haynes RC 10.00 4.00
❑ 140 Jesse Chatman RC 10.00 4.00
❑ 141 Quentin Jammer RC 10.00 4.00
❑ 142 Seth Burford RC 8.00 3.00
❑ 143 Julius Peppers RC 20.00 7.50
❑ 144 William Green RC 10.00 4.00
❑ 145 DeShaun Foster RC 10.00 4.00
❑ 146 Daniel Graham RC 10.00 4.00
❑ 147 David Garrard RC 20.00 10.00
❑ 148 Reche Caldwell RC 10.00 4.00
❑ 149 Randy Fasani RC 8.00 3.00
❑ 150 J.T. O'Sullivan RC 8.00 3.00
❑ 151 Josh McCown JSY AU RC 40.00 15.00
❑ 152 Kurt Kittner JSY AU RC 20.00 7.50
❑ 153 Kahlil Hill JSY AU RC 15.00 6.00
❑ 154 Ladell Betts JSY AU RC 40.00 20.00
❑ 155 Ron Johnson JSY AU RC 15.00 6.00
❑ 156 Maurice Morris JSY AU RC 25.0010.00
❑ 157 Andre Davis JSY AU RC 25.00 10.00
❑ 158 Antonio Bryant JSY AU RC 20.00 8.00
❑ 159 Roy Williams JSY AU RC 40.00 15.00
❑ 160 Lam Thompson JSY AU RC 15.006.00
❑ 161 Cliff Russell JSY AU RC 15.00 6.00
❑ 162 Woody Dantzler JSY AU RC 15.006.00
❑ 163 Travis Stephens JSY AU RC 15.006.00
❑ 164 Tony Fisher JSY AU RC 20.00 7.50
❑ 165 Eric McCoo JSY AU RC 15.00 6.00
❑ 166 Eric Crouch JSY AU RC 25.00 10.00
❑ 167 Rohan Davey JSY AU RC 20.00 7.50
❑ 168 Marquise Walker JSY AU RC 15.006.00
❑ 169 Jeremy Shockey JSY RC 50.00 20.00
❑ 170 Tim Carter JSY AU RC 20.00 7.50
❑ 171 Atrews Bell JSY AU RC 15.00 6.00
❑ 172 Ant Randle El JSY AU RC 50.00 20.00
❑ 173 Ricky Williams JSY AU RC 25.0010.00
❑ 174 Mike Williams JSY AU 15.00 6.00
❑ 175 Adrian Peterson JSY AU RC 40.00 15.00
❑ 176 Jab Gaffney JSY AU/650 RC 25.00 10.00
❑ 177 Ashley Lelie JSY AU/250 RC 30.00 12.50
❑ 178 David Carr JSY AU/250 RC 80.0040.00

2003 SPx

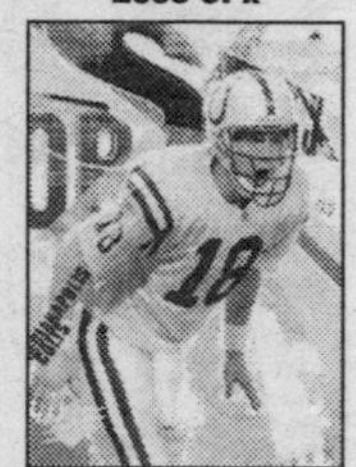

❑ COMP.SET w/o SP's (110) 25.00 10.00
❑ 1 Peyton Manning 1.50 .60
❑ 2 Aaron Brooks 1.00 .40
❑ 3 Joey Harrington 1.50 .60
❑ 4 Tim Couch .40 .15
❑ 5 Jeff Garcia 1.00 .40
❑ 6 Jay Fiedler .60 .25
❑ 7 Chad Hutchinson .40 .15
❑ 8 Tommy Maddox 1.00 .40
❑ 9 Drew Brees 1.00 .40
❑ 10 Trent Green .60 .25
❑ 11 Patrick Ramsey 1.00 .40
❑ 12 Daunte Culpepper 1.00 .40
❑ 13 Kurt Warner 1.00 .40
❑ 14 Brad Johnson .60 .25
❑ 15 Rich Gannon .60 .25
❑ 16 Jake Plummer .60 .25
❑ 17 Steve McNair 1.00 .40
❑ 18 Mark Brunell .60 .25
❑ 19 Drew Bledsoe 1.00 .40
❑ 20 Kordell Stewart .60 .25
❑ 21 Kelly Holcomb .60 .25
❑ 22 Josh McCown .60 .25
❑ 23 Matt Hasselbeck .60 .25
❑ 24 Marc Bulger 1.00 .40
❑ 25 Chris Redman .40 .15
❑ 26 Rodney Peete .60 .25
❑ 27 Jake Delhomme 1.00 .40
❑ 28 Jon Kitna .60 .25
❑ 29 Kerry Collins .60 .25
❑ 30 Quincy Carter .60 .25

❑ 31 Ricky Williams 1.00 .40
❑ 32 Clinton Portis 1.50 .60
❑ 33 Deuce McAllister 1.00 .40
❑ 34 Ahman Green 1.00 .40
❑ 35 Priest Holmes 1.25 .50
❑ 36 Curtis Martin 1.00 .40
❑ 37 Michael Bennett .60 .25
❑ 38 Eddie George .60 .25
❑ 39 Marshall Faulk 1.00 .40
❑ 40 Garrison Hearst .60 .25
❑ 41 Shaun Alexander 1.00 .40
❑ 42 Corey Dillon .60 .25
❑ 43 Jamal Lewis 1.00 .40
❑ 44 William Green .60 .25
❑ 45 Travis Henry .60 .25
❑ 46 Randy Moss 1.50 .60
❑ 47 Terrell Owens 1.00 .40
❑ 48 Peerless Price .60 .25
❑ 49 David Boston .60 .25
❑ 50 Eric Moulds .60 .25
❑ 51 Marvin Harrison 1.00 .40
❑ 52 Laveranues Coles .60 .25
❑ 53 Santana Moss .60 .25
❑ 54 Troy Brown .60 .25
❑ 55 Chris Chambers 1.00 .40
❑ 56 Tim Brown 1.00 .40
❑ 57 Rod Smith .60 .25
❑ 58 Hines Ward 1.00 .40
❑ 59 Keyshawn Johnson 1.00 .40
❑ 60 Isaac Bruce 1.00 .40
❑ 61 Torry Holt 1.00 .40
❑ 62 Koren Robinson .60 .25
❑ 63 Chad Johnson 1.00 .40
❑ 64 Derrick Mason .60 .25
❑ 65 Antonio Bryant .60 .25
❑ 66 Kevin Johnson .60 .25
❑ 67 Todd Heap .60 .25
❑ 68 Tony Gonzalez .60 .25
❑ 69 Jeremy Shockey 1.50 .60
❑ 70 Brian Urlacher 1.50 .60
❑ 71 Emmitt Smith/500 20.00 7.50
❑ 72 Edgerrin James/500 10.00 4.00
❑ 73 LaDainian Tomlinson/500 8.00 3.00
❑ 74 Brett Favre/500 20.00 7.50
❑ 75 Donovan McNabb/500 10.00 4.00
❑ 76 Tom Brady/500 20.00 7.50
❑ 77 Michael Vick/500 20.00 7.50
❑ 78 David Carr/500 12.00 5.00
❑ 79 Jerry Rice/500 15.00 6.00
❑ 80 Chad Pennington/500 10.00 4.00
❑ 81 Joey Harrington XCT 1.50 .60
❑ 82 Clinton Portis XCT 1.50 .60
❑ 83 Jeremy Shockey XCT 1.50 .60
❑ 84 David Boston XCT .60 .25
❑ 85 Marshall Faulk XCT 1.00 .40
❑ 86 Emmitt Smith XCT 2.50 1.00
❑ 87 Terrell Owens XCT 1.00 .40
❑ 88 Randy Moss XCT 1.50 .60
❑ 89 Deuce McAllister XCT 1.00 .40
❑ 90 Ahman Green XCT 1.00 .40
❑ 91 Peerless Price XCT .60 .25
❑ 92 Plaxico Burress XCT .60 .25
❑ 93 Marvin Harrison XCT 1.00 .40
❑ 94 Keyshawn Johnson XCT 1.00 .40
❑ 95 Laveranues Coles XCT .60 .25
❑ 96 Drew Bledsoe XCT 1.00 .40
❑ 97 Eric Moulds XCT .60 .25
❑ 98 Chad Pennington XCT 1.25 .50
❑ 99 Jerry Rice XCT 2.00 .75
❑ 100 David Carr XCT 1.50 .60
❑ 101 Michael Vick XCT 2.50 1.00
❑ 102 Tom Brady XCT 2.50 1.00
❑ 103 Donovan McNabb XCT 1.25 .50
❑ 104 Brett Favre XCT 2.50 1.00
❑ 105 Kurt Warner XCT 1.00 .40
❑ 106 LaDainian Tomlinson XCT 1.00 .40
❑ 107 Drew Brees XCT 1.00 .40
❑ 108 Edgerrin James XCT 1.00 .40
❑ 109 Peyton Manning XCT 1.50 .60
❑ 110 Ricky Williams XCT 1.00 .40
❑ 111 Brooks Bollinger RC 10.00 4.00
❑ 112 Gibran Hamden RC 5.00 2.00
❑ 113 Jason Johnson RC 5.00 2.00
❑ 114 Tony Romo RC 75.00 40.00
❑ 115 Juston Wood RC 5.00 2.00
❑ 116 Kirk Farmer RC 5.00 2.00
❑ 117 Kliff Kingsbury RC 8.00 3.00
❑ 118 Jason Gesser RC 10.00 4.00
❑ 119 Brad Banks RC 8.00 3.00
❑ 120 Rob Adamson RC 5.00 2.00
❑ 121 Ken Dorsey RC 10.00 4.00
❑ 122 Curt Anes RC 5.00 2.00
❑ 123 George Wrighster RC 8.00 3.00
❑ 124 Brett Engemann RC 5.00 2.00
❑ 125 Aaron Walker RC 8.00 3.00
❑ 126 Nate Hybl RC 10.00 4.00
❑ 127 Chris Simms RC 15.00 6.00
❑ 128 Marquel Blackwell RC 5.00 2.00
❑ 129 Domanick Davis RC 10.00 4.00
❑ 130 Quentin Griffin RC 10.00 4.00
❑ 131 B.J. Askew RC 10.00 4.00
❑ 132 Earnest Graham RC 10.00 4.00
❑ 133 Sultan McCullough RC 8.00 3.00
❑ 134 Dahrran Diedrick RC 10.00 4.00
❑ 135 Cecil Sapp RC 8.00 3.00
❑ 136 LaBrandon Toefield RC 10.00 4.00
❑ 137 ReShard Lee RC 10.00 4.00
❑ 138 Dwone Hicks RC 5.00 2.00
❑ 139 Brock Forsey RC 10.00 4.00
❑ 140 Bethel Johnson RC 10.00 4.00
❑ 141 Andrew Pinnock RC 8.00 3.00
❑ 142 Ahmaad Galloway RC 8.00 3.00
❑ 143 J.T. Wall RC 5.00 2.00
❑ 144 Tom Lopienski RC 8.00 3.00
❑ 145 Justin Griffith RC 8.00 3.00
❑ 146 Lee Suggs RC 10.00 4.00
❑ 147 Nick Maddox RC 5.00 2.00
❑ 148 Jeremi Johnson RC 8.00 3.00
❑ 149 Doug Gabriel RC 10.00 4.00
❑ 150 Bobby Wade RC 10.00 4.00
❑ 151 Justin Gage RC 10.00 4.00
❑ 152 Arnaz Battle RC 10.00 4.00
❑ 153 Brandon Lloyd RC 10.00 4.00
❑ 154 Talman Gardner RC 10.00 4.00
❑ 155 Kareem Kelly RC 8.00 3.00
❑ 156 Billy McMullen RC 8.00 3.00
❑ 157 Antwone Savage RC 5.00 2.00
❑ 158 J.R. Tolver RC 8.00 3.00
❑ 159 Kassim Osgood RC 10.00 4.00
❑ 160 Shaun McDonald RC 10.00 4.00
❑ 161 Sam Aiken RC 8.00 3.00
❑ 162 Adrian Madise RC 8.00 3.00
❑ 163 Charles Rogers RC 10.00 4.00
❑ 164 David Kircus RC 10.00 4.00
❑ 165 Zuriel Smith RC 5.00 2.00
❑ 166 LaTarence Dunbar RC 8.00 3.00
❑ 167 Willie Ponder RC 8.00 3.00
❑ 168 David Tyree RC 5.00 2.00
❑ 169 Kevin Walter RC 8.00 3.00
❑ 170 Keenan Howry RC 10.00 4.00
❑ 171 Walter Young RC 5.00 2.00
❑ 172 DeAndrew Rubin RC 5.00 2.00
❑ 173 Carl Ford RC 5.00 2.00
❑ 174 Taco Wallace RC 8.00 3.00
❑ 175 Travis Anglin RC 5.00 2.00
❑ 176 Ryan Hoag RC 5.00 2.00
❑ 177 Ronald Bellamy RC 8.00 3.00
❑ 178 Terrence Edwards RC 8.00 3.00
❑ 179 Jerel Myers RC 5.00 2.00
❑ 180 Mike Bush RC 8.00 3.00
❑ 181 Dan Curley RC 5.00 2.00
❑ 182 Carl Morris RC 5.00 2.00
❑ 183 Reggie Newhouse RC 8.00 3.00
❑ 184 Troy Polamalu RC 40.00 20.00
❑ 185 Cecil Moore RC 5.00 2.00
❑ 186 Bennie Joppru RC 10.00 4.00
❑ 187 Donald Lee RC 8.00 3.00
❑ 188 Jason Witten RC 20.00 10.00
❑ 189 Mike Seidman RC 5.00 2.00
❑ 190 Vishante Shiancoe RC 8.00 3.00
❑ 191 Anquan Boldin JSY AU RC 50.00 20.00
❑ 192 Kyle Boller JSY AU/450 RC 40.00 15.00
❑ 193 Chris Brown JSY AU RC 40.00 15.00
❑ 194 Nate Burleson JSY AU RC 30.00 12.50
❑ 195 Tyro Calico JSY AU/450 RC 40.00 15.00
❑ 196 Dallas Clark JSY AU RC 40.00 20.00
❑ 197 Kevin Curtis JSY AU RC 40.00 20.00
❑ 198 Kliff Kingsbury JSY AU RC 25.00 10.00
❑ 199 Justin Fargas JSY AU RC 40.00 15.00
❑ 200 Grossman JSY AU/450 RC 100.00 40.00
❑ 201 Taylor Jacobs JSY AU RC 25.00 10.00
❑ 202 An.Johnson JSY AU/250 RC 150.00 75.00
❑ 203 Malae MacKenzie JSY AU RC 15.00 6.00
❑ 204 Bryant Johnson JSY AU RC 30.00 12.50
❑ 205 Larry Johnson JSY AU RC 120.00 60.00
❑ 206 T Johnson JSY AU/450 RC 50.00 25.00
❑ 207 Leftwich JSY AU/250 RC 100.00 40.00
❑ 208 McGahee JSY AU/450 RC 120.00 50.00
❑ 210 C.Palmer JSY AU/250 RC 300.00 150.00
❑ 211 Artose Pinner JSY AU RC 30.00 12.50
❑ 212 Dave Ragone JSY AU RC 30.00 12.50
❑ 213 Terrell Suggs JSY AU RC 40.00 15.00
❑ 215 Onterio Smith JSY AU RC 30.00 12.50
❑ 216 Musa Smith JSY AU RC 30.00 12.50
❑ 217 Brian St.Pierre JSY AU RC 30.00 12.50
❑ 218 Marcus Trufant JSY AU RC 30.00 12.50
❑ 219 Seneca Wallace JSY AU RC 30.00 12.50
❑ 220 Kell Washington JSY AU RC 40.00 15.00

2004 SPx

❑ COMP.SET w/o SP's (100) 30.00 15.00
❑ 191-221 JSY AU RC #'d TO 1499 UNLESS NOTED
❑ 1 Anquan Boldin 1.00 .40
❑ 2 Marcel Shipp .60 .25
❑ 3 Josh McCown .60 .25
❑ 4 Peerless Price .60 .25
❑ 5 Michael Vick 2.00 .75
❑ 6 T.J. Duckett .60 .25
❑ 7 Kyle Boller 1.00 .40
❑ 8 Todd Heap .60 .25
❑ 9 Jamal Lewis 1.00 .40
❑ 10 Travis Henry .60 .25
❑ 11 Drew Bledsoe 1.00 .40
❑ 12 Eric Moulds .60 .25
❑ 13 Jake Delhomme 1.00 .40
❑ 14 Steve Smith 1.00 .40
❑ 15 Stephen Davis .60 .25
❑ 16 Brian Urlacher 1.25 .50
❑ 17 Rex Grossman 1.00 .40
❑ 18 Thomas Jones .60 .25
❑ 19 Chad Johnson 1.00 .40
❑ 20 Carson Palmer 1.25 .50
❑ 21 Rudi Johnson .60 .25
❑ 22 William Green .60 .25
❑ 23 Jeff Garcia 1.00 .40
❑ 24 Andre Davis .40 .15
❑ 25 Roy Williams S .60 .25
❑ 26 Eddie George .60 .25
❑ 27 Keyshawn Johnson .60 .25
❑ 28 Jake Plummer .60 .25
❑ 29 Ashley Lelie .60 .25
❑ 30 Quentin Griffin 1.00 .40
❑ 31 Charles Rogers .60 .25
❑ 32 Olandis Gary .40 .15
❑ 33 Joey Harrington 1.00 .40
❑ 34 Brett Favre 2.50 1.00
❑ 35 Javon Walker .60 .25
❑ 36 Ahman Green 1.00 .40
❑ 37 Andre Johnson 1.00 .40
❑ 38 Domanick Davis 1.00 .40
❑ 39 David Carr 1.00 .40
❑ 40 Peyton Manning 1.50 .60
❑ 41 Edgerrin James 1.00 .40
❑ 42 Marvin Harrison 1.00 .40
❑ 43 Byron Leftwich 1.25 .50
❑ 44 Jimmy Smith .60 .25
❑ 45 Fred Taylor .60 .25
❑ 46 Trent Green .60 .25
❑ 47 Priest Holmes 1.25 .50
❑ 48 Dante Hall 1.00 .40
❑ 49 Tony Gonzalez .60 .25
❑ 50 A.J. Feeley 1.00 .40

❑ 51	Marty Booker	.60	.25
❑ 52	Chris Chambers	.60	.25
❑ 53	Zach Thomas	1.00	.40
❑ 54	Randy Moss	1.25	.50
❑ 55	Daunte Culpepper	1.00	.40
❑ 56	Onterrio Smith	.60	.25
❑ 57	Troy Brown	.60	.25
❑ 58	Corey Dillon	.60	.25
❑ 59	Tom Brady	2.50	1.00
❑ 60	Deuce McAllister	1.00	.40
❑ 61	Joe Horn	.60	.25
❑ 62	Aaron Brooks	.60	.25
❑ 63	Jeremy Shockey	1.00	.40
❑ 64	Kurt Warner	1.00	.40
❑ 65	Tiki Barber	1.00	.40
❑ 66	Chad Pennington	1.00	.40
❑ 67	Curtis Martin	1.00	.40
❑ 68	Santana Moss	.60	.25
❑ 69	Rich Gannon	.60	.25
❑ 70	Jerry Rice	2.00	.75
❑ 71	Warren Sapp	.60	.25
❑ 72	Donovan McNabb	1.25	.50
❑ 73	Terrell Owens	1.00	.40
❑ 74	Jevon Kearse	.60	.25
❑ 75	Brian Westbrook	.60	.25
❑ 76	Hines Ward	1.00	.40
❑ 77	Duce Staley	.60	.25
❑ 78	Tommy Maddox	.60	.25
❑ 79	LaDainian Tomlinson	1.25	.50
❑ 80	Drew Brees	1.00	.40
❑ 81	Tim Rattay	.40	.15
❑ 82	Kevan Barlow	.60	.25
❑ 83	Brandon Lloyd	.60	.25
❑ 84	Shaun Alexander	1.00	.40
❑ 85	Matt Hasselbeck	.60	.25
❑ 86	Koren Robinson	.60	.25
❑ 87	Marc Bulger	1.00	.40
❑ 88	Marshall Faulk	1.00	.40
❑ 89	Torry Holt	1.00	.40
❑ 90	Isaac Bruce	.60	.25
❑ 91	Brad Johnson	.60	.25
❑ 92	Keenan McCardell	.40	.15
❑ 93	Derrick Brooks	.60	.25
❑ 94	Steve McNair	1.00	.40
❑ 95	Chris Brown	1.00	.40
❑ 96	Derrick Mason	.60	.25
❑ 97	Clinton Portis	1.00	.40
❑ 98	Mark Brunell	.60	.25
❑ 99	Laveranues Coles	.60	.25
❑ 100	LaVar Arrington	2.00	.75
❑ 101	B.J. Johnson RC	8.00	3.00
❑ 102	Craig Krenzel RC	10.00	4.00
❑ 103	Will Smith RC	10.00	4.00
❑ 104	Jamaar Taylor RC	10.00	4.00
❑ 105	Tommie Harris RC	10.00	4.00
❑ 106	Shawn Andrews RC	10.00	4.00
❑ 107	Kendrick Starling RC	5.00	2.00
❑ 108	Jeris McIntyre RC	8.00	3.00
❑ 109	Jason Babin RC	10.00	4.00
❑ 110	Marcus Tubbs RC	10.00	4.00
❑ 111	Triandos Luke RC	10.00	4.00
❑ 112	Karlos Dansby RC	10.00	4.00
❑ 113	Vernon Carey RC	8.00	3.00
❑ 114	Ryan Krause RC	8.00	3.00
❑ 115	Daryl Smith RC	10.00	4.00
❑ 116	Ricardo Colclough RC	10.00	4.00
❑ 117	Michael Boulware RC	10.00	4.00
❑ 118	Chris Cooley RC	10.00	4.00
❑ 119	Tank Johnson RC	8.00	3.00
❑ 120	Marquise Hill RC	8.00	3.00
❑ 121	Teddy Lehman RC	10.00	4.00
❑ 122	Antwan Odom RC	10.00	4.00
❑ 123	Sean Jones RC	8.00	3.00
❑ 124	Junior Siavii RC	10.00	4.00
❑ 125	Joey Thomas RC	10.00	4.00
❑ 126	Shawntae Spencer RC	10.00	4.00
❑ 127	Dontarrious Thomas RC	10.00	4.00
❑ 128	Travis LaBoy RC	10.00	4.00
❑ 129	Justin Jenkins RC	8.00	3.00
❑ 130	Dwan Edwards RC	5.00	2.00
❑ 131	Derrick Strait RC	10.00	4.00
❑ 132	Matt Ware RC	10.00	4.00
❑ 133	Jared Lorenzen RC	8.00	3.00
❑ 134	Demorrio Williams RC	10.00	4.00
❑ 135	Bob Sanders RC	20.00	10.00
❑ 136	Justin Smiley RC	10.00	4.00
❑ 137	Casey Bramlet RC	8.00	3.00

❑ 138	Jake Grove RC	5.00	2.00
❑ 139	Thomas Tapeh RC	8.00	3.00
❑ 140	Igor Olshansky RC	10.00	4.00
❑ 141	Stuart Schweigert RC	10.00	4.00
❑ 142	Cody Pickett RC	10.00	4.00
❑ 143	Derrick Ward RC	10.00	4.00
❑ 144	Gilbert Gardner RC	8.00	3.00
❑ 145	D.J. Hackett RC	8.00	3.00
❑ 146	Marquis Cooper RC	8.00	3.00
❑ 147	Courtney Watson RC	10.00	4.00
❑ 148	Jim Sorgi RC	10.00	4.00
❑ 149	Caleb Miller RC	8.00	3.00
❑ 150	Casey Clausen RC	10.00	4.00
❑ 151	Jammal Lord RC	10.00	4.00
❑ 152	Sloan Thomas RC	8.00	3.00
❑ 153	Keyaron Fox RC	8.00	3.00
❑ 154	Adimchinobe Echemandu RC	8.00	3.00
❑ 155	Ryan Dinwiddie RC	8.00	3.00
❑ 156	Kris Wilson RC	10.00	4.00
❑ 157	D.J. Williams RC	12.00	5.00
❑ 158	Tim Euhus RC	10.00	4.00
❑ 159	Bradlee Van Pelt RC	12.00	5.00
❑ 160	Keiwan Ratliff RC	8.00	3.00
❑ 161	Darnell Dockett RC	8.00	3.00
❑ 162	Troy Fleming RC	8.00	3.00
❑ 163	Tramon Douglas RC	5.00	2.00
❑ 164	Jeremy LeSueur RC	8.00	3.00
❑ 165	Matt Mauck RC	10.00	4.00
❑ 166	Sean Taylor RC	12.00	5.00
❑ 167	B.J. Symons RC	12.00	5.00
❑ 168	Quincy Wilson RC	10.00	4.00
❑ 169	Ernest Wilford RC	12.00	5.00
❑ 170	Jerricho Cotchery RC	12.00	5.00
❑ 171	Michael Turner RC	15.00	6.00
❑ 172	Samie Parker RC	12.00	5.00
❑ 173	Andy Hall RC	10.00	4.00
❑ 174	Keith Smith RC	10.00	4.00
❑ 175	Josh Harris RC	12.00	5.00
❑ 176	Maurice Mann RC	10.00	4.00
❑ 177	Jonathan Vilma RC	12.00	5.00
❑ 178	Jeff Smoker RC	12.00	5.00
❑ 179	Ben Hartsock RC	12.00	5.00
❑ 180	Chris Gamble RC	12.00	5.00
❑ 181	Derrick Hamilton RC	10.00	4.00
❑ 182	John Navarre RC	12.00	5.00
❑ 183	P.K. Sam RC	10.00	4.00
❑ 184	Kenechi Udeze RC	12.00	5.00
❑ 185	Mewelde Moore RC	12.00	5.00
❑ 186	Carlos Francis RC	10.00	4.00
❑ 187	Dunta Robinson RC	12.00	5.00
❑ 188	Johnnie Morant RC	12.00	5.00
❑ 189	Ahmad Carroll RC	12.00	5.00
❑ 190	Vince Wilfork RC	12.00	5.00
❑ 191	Tatum Bell JSY AU RC	40.00	20.00
❑ 192	Cedric Cobbs JSY AU RC	20.00	7.50
❑ 193	Darius Watts JSY AU RC	20.00	7.50
❑ 194	Jul.Jones JSY AU/375 RC	100.00	40.00
❑ 195	Robert Gallery JSY AU RC	20.00	7.50
❑ 196	DeAngelo Hall JSY AU RC	30.00	12.50
❑ 197	Ben Watson JSY AU RC	25.00	10.00
❑ 198	Ben Troupe JSY AU RC	20.00	7.50
❑ 199	Matt Schaub JSY AU RC	60.00	35.00
❑ 200	Michael Jenkins JSY AU RC	25.00	10.00
❑ 201	Luke McCown JSY AU RC	20.00	7.50
❑ 202	Devery Henderson JSY AU RC	20.00	7.50
❑ 203	Bernard Berrian JSY AU RC	30.00	15.00
❑ 204	Keary Colbert JSY AU RC	20.00	7.50
❑ 205	Devard Darling JSY AU RC	20.00	7.50
❑ 206	Lee Evans JSY AU RC	30.00	15.00
❑ 207	Greg Jones JSY AU RC	25.00	12.50
❑ 208	Mich.Clayton JSY AU RC	40.00	15.00
❑ 209	Re.Williams JSY AU RC	25.00	10.00
❑ 210	C.Perry JSY AU/799 RC	25.00	10.00
❑ 211	Rash.Woods JSY AU RC	20.00	7.50
❑ 212	J.P. Losman JSY AU RC	40.00	15.00
❑ 213	Kevin Jones JSY AU RC	40.00	20.00
❑ 214	K.Winslow JSY AU/375 RC	50.00	25.00
❑ 215	S.Jackson JSY AU/375 RC	150.00	75.00
❑ 216	Hamilton JSY AU RC EXCH	15.00	6.00
❑ 217	Ro.Will.JSY AU/375 RC	100.00	40.00
❑ 218	P.Rivers JSY AU/375 RC	120.00	60.00
❑ 219	Fitzgerald JSY AU/100 RC	200.00	100.00
❑ 220	Roethlis.JSY AU/375 RC	300.00	150.00
❑ 221	Manning JSY AU/375 RC	250.00	150.00

2005 SPx

❑ COMP.SET w/o SP's (100) 30.00 15.00
❑ 101-170 RC PRINT RUN 1199 SER.#'d SETS
❑ 171-200 RC PRINT RUN 499 SER.#'d SETS
❑ EXCH EXPIRATION: 10/25/2008
❑ JSY AU RC PRINT RUN 1275 UNLESS NOTED
❑ UNPRICED NFL LOGO AUTOS #'d OF 1

❑ 1	Larry Fitzgerald	1.00	.40
❑ 2	Anquan Boldin	.60	.25
❑ 3	Josh McCown	.60	.25
❑ 4	Michael Vick	1.50	.60
❑ 5	Alge Crumpler	.60	.25
❑ 6	Peerless Price	.50	.20
❑ 7	Ray Lewis	1.00	.40
❑ 8	Jamal Lewis	1.00	.40
❑ 9	Kyle Boller	.60	.25
❑ 10	J.P. Losman	1.00	.40
❑ 11	Willis McGahee	1.00	.40
❑ 12	Eric Moulds	.60	.25
❑ 13	Jake Delhomme	1.00	.40
❑ 14	DeShaun Foster	.60	.25
❑ 15	Steve Smith	.60	.25
❑ 16	Brian Urlacher	1.00	.40
❑ 17	Rex Grossman	.60	.25
❑ 18	Muhsin Muhammad	.60	.25
❑ 19	Carson Palmer	1.00	.40
❑ 20	Rudi Johnson	.60	.25
❑ 21	Chad Johnson	1.00	.40
❑ 22	Julius Jones	1.25	.50
❑ 23	Keyshawn Johnson	.60	.25
❑ 24	Roy Williams S	.60	.25
❑ 25	Tatum Bell	.60	.25
❑ 26	Jake Plummer	.60	.25
❑ 27	Ashley Lelie	.60	.25
❑ 28	Roy Williams WR	1.00	.40
❑ 29	Kevin Jones	1.00	.40
❑ 30	Joey Harrington	1.00	.40
❑ 31	Brett Favre	2.50	1.00
❑ 32	Ahman Green	1.00	.40
❑ 33	Javon Walker	.60	.25
❑ 34	David Carr	1.00	.40
❑ 35	Andre Johnson	.60	.25
❑ 36	Domanick Davis	.60	.25
❑ 37	Peyton Manning	1.50	.60
❑ 38	Reggie Wayne	.60	.25
❑ 39	Edgerrin James	1.00	.40
❑ 40	Marvin Harrison	1.00	.40
❑ 41	Byron Leftwich	1.00	.40
❑ 42	Fred Taylor	.60	.25
❑ 43	Jimmy Smith	.60	.25
❑ 44	Priest Holmes	1.00	.40
❑ 45	Larry Johnson	1.00	.40
❑ 46	Trent Green	.60	.25
❑ 47	A.J. Feeley	.60	.25
❑ 48	Chris Chambers	.60	.25
❑ 49	Randy McMichael	.50	.20
❑ 50	Daunte Culpepper	1.00	.40
❑ 51	Nate Burleson	.60	.25
❑ 52	Michael Bennett	.60	.25
❑ 53	Tom Brady	2.50	1.00
❑ 54	Corey Dillon	.60	.25
❑ 55	Deion Branch	.60	.25
❑ 56	David Givens	.60	.25
❑ 57	Aaron Brooks	.60	.25
❑ 58	Deuce McAllister	1.00	.40
❑ 59	Joe Horn	.60	.25
❑ 60	Eli Manning	2.00	.75
❑ 61	Jeremy Shockey	1.00	.40
❑ 62	Tiki Barber	1.00	.40

- ❑ 63 Chad Pennington 1.00 .40
- ❑ 64 Curtis Martin 1.00 .40
- ❑ 65 Laveranues Coles .60 .25
- ❑ 66 Kerry Collins .60 .25
- ❑ 67 Jerry Porter .60 .25
- ❑ 68 Randy Moss 1.00 .40
- ❑ 69 Donovan McNabb 1.25 .50
- ❑ 70 Terrell Owens 1.00 .40
- ❑ 71 Brian Dawkins .60 .25
- ❑ 72 Brian Westbrook .60 .25
- ❑ 73 Ben Roethlisberger 2.50 1.00
- ❑ 74 Jerome Bettis 1.00 .40
- ❑ [illegible]
- ❑ 76 Duce Staley .60 .25
- ❑ 77 Drew Brees 1.00 .40
- ❑ 78 LaDainian Tomlinson 1.25 .50
- ❑ 79 Antonio Gates 1.00 .40
- ❑ 80 Eric Parker .50 .20
- ❑ 81 Tim Rattay .50 .20
- ❑ 82 Kevan Barlow .60 .25
- ❑ 83 Eric Johnson .60 .25
- ❑ 84 Shaun Alexander 1.25 .50
- ❑ 85 Darrell Jackson .60 .25
- ❑ 86 Matt Hasselbeck .60 .25
- ❑ 87 Marc Bulger 1.00 .40
- ❑ 88 Steven Jackson 1.25 .50
- ❑ 89 Marshall Faulk 1.00 .40
- ❑ 90 Torry Holt 1.00 .40
- ❑ 91 Michael Pittman .50 .20
- ❑ 92 Brian Griese .60 .25
- ❑ 93 Michael Clayton 1.00 .40
- ❑ 94 Steve McNair 1.00 .40
- ❑ 95 Drew Bennett .60 .25
- ❑ 96 Billy Volek .60 .25
- ❑ 97 Chris Brown .60 .25
- ❑ 98 Clinton Portis 1.00 .40
- ❑ 99 Patrick Ramsey .60 .25
- ❑ 100 Santana Moss .60 .25
- ❑ 101 Matt Jones RC 12.00 5.00
- ❑ 102 Jonathan Babineaux RC 6.00 2.50
- ❑ 103 Darrent Williams RC 8.00 3.00
- ❑ 104 Timmy Chang RC 6.00 2.50
- ❑ 105 Kelvin Hayden RC 6.00 2.50
- ❑ 106 Paris Warren RC 6.00 2.50
- ❑ 107 Stanley Wilson RC 6.00 2.50
- ❑ 108 Walter Reyes RC 6.00 2.50
- ❑ 109 Roydell Williams RC 8.00 3.00
- ❑ 110 Chase Lyman RC 6.00 2.50
- ❑ 111 Anthony Davis RC 6.00 2.50
- ❑ 112 Rasheed Marshall RC 8.00 3.00
- ❑ 113 Jerome Carter RC 6.00 2.50
- ❑ 114 Mike Nugent RC 8.00 3.00
- ❑ 115 Brodney Pool RC 8.00 3.00
- ❑ 116 Sean Considine RC 8.00 3.00
- ❑ 117 Chris Rix RC 6.00 2.50
- ❑ 118 Donte Nicholson RC 8.00 3.00
- ❑ 119 Dustin Fox RC 8.00 3.00
- ❑ 120 Oshiomogho Atogwe RC 6.00 2.50
- ❑ 121 Vincent Fuller RC 6.00 2.50
- ❑ 122 Josh Bullocks RC 8.00 3.00
- ❑ 123 Ronald Bartell RC 6.00 2.50
- ❑ 124 Brock Berlin RC 6.00 2.50
- ❑ 125 Fabian Washington RC 8.00 3.00
- ❑ 126 Domonique Foxworth RC 8.00 3.00
- ❑ 127 Bryant McFadden RC 8.00 3.00
- ❑ 128 Marlin Jackson RC 8.00 3.00
- ❑ 129 Eric Green RC 4.00 1.50
- ❑ 130 Justin Miller RC 6.00 2.50
- ❑ 131 Lofa Tatupu RC 10.00 4.00
- ❑ 132 Justin Tuck RC 8.00 3.00
- ❑ 133 Kurt Campbell RC 6.00 2.50
- ❑ 134 Darryl Blackstock RC 6.00 2.50
- ❑ 135 Kevin Burnett RC 8.00 3.00
- ❑ 136 Marviel Underwood RC 6.00 2.50
- ❑ 137 Kirk Morrison RC 8.00 3.00
- ❑ 138 Alfred Fincher RC 6.00 2.50
- ❑ 139 Lance Mitchell RC 6.00 2.50
- ❑ 140 Barrett Ruud RC 8.00 3.00
- ❑ 141 David Pollack RC 6.00 2.50
- ❑ 142 Bill Swancutt RC 6.00 2.50
- ❑ 143 DeMarcus Ware RC 12.00 5.00
- ❑ 144 Steve Savoy RC 4.00 1.50
- ❑ 145 Matt Roth RC 8.00 3.00
- ❑ 146 Shaun Cody RC 8.00 3.00
- ❑ 147 Dan Cody RC 8.00 3.00
- ❑ 148 Jordan Beck RC 6.00 2.50
- ❑ 149 Kevin Everett RC 8.00 3.00
- ❑ 150 Anttaj Hawthorne RC 6.00 2.50
- ❑ 151 Mike Patterson RC 8.00 3.00
- ❑ 152 Jerome Collins RC 6.00 2.50
- ❑ 153 Dante Ridgeway RC 6.00 2.50
- ❑ 154 Bryan Randall RC 6.00 2.50
- ❑ 155 Marcus Maxwell RC 6.00 2.50
- ❑ 156 Airese Currie RC 8.00 3.00
- ❑ 157 Chad Owens RC 8.00 3.00
- ❑ 158 Brandon Jacobs RC 10.00 4.00
- ❑ 159 Manuel White RC 6.00 2.50
- ❑ 160 Ellis Hobbs RC 8.00 3.00
- ❑ 161 Lionel Gates RC 6.00 2.50
- ❑ [illegible]
- ❑ 163 Noah Herron RC 8.00 3.00
- ❑ 164 Kay-Jay Harris RC 6.00 2.50
- ❑ 165 T.A. McLendon RC 4.00 1.50
- ❑ 166 Kerry Rhodes RC 8.00 3.00
- ❑ 167 Nick Collins RC 8.00 3.00
- ❑ 168 Eric Moore RC 6.00 2.50
- ❑ 169 Harry Williams RC 6.00 2.50
- ❑ 170 Luis Castillo RC 8.00 3.00
- ❑ 171 James Killian RC 10.00 4.00
- ❑ 172 Matt Cassel RC 15.00 6.00
- ❑ 173 Alvin Pearman RC 10.00 4.00
- ❑ 174 Dan Orlovsky RC 10.00 4.00
- ❑ 175 Damien Nash RC 8.00 3.00
- ❑ 176 Jason White RC 10.00 4.00
- ❑ 177 Craig Bragg RC 8.00 3.00
- ❑ 178 Craphonso Thorpe RC 8.00 3.00
- ❑ 179 Derrick Johnson RC 15.00 6.00
- ❑ 180 Derek Anderson RC 15.00 6.00
- ❑ 181 Darren Sproles RC 10.00 4.00
- ❑ 182 Cedric Houston RC 10.00 4.00
- ❑ 183 Jerome Mathis RC 10.00 4.00
- ❑ 184 Larry Brackins RC 8.00 3.00
- ❑ 185 Fred Gibson RC 8.00 3.00
- ❑ 186 J.R. Russell RC 8.00 3.00
- ❑ 187 Alex Smith TE RC 10.00 4.00
- ❑ 188 Deandra Cobb RC 8.00 3.00
- ❑ 189 Tab Perry RC 10.00 4.00
- ❑ 190 Travis Johnson RC 8.00 3.00
- ❑ 191A Marion Barber RC 15.00 6.00
- ❑ 191B Andrew Walter JSY AU RC 30.00 12.00
- ❑ 192A Erasmus James RC 10.00 4.00
- ❑ 192B V.Morency JSY AU RC 30.00 12.00
- ❑ 193A Marcus Spears RC 8.00 3.00
- ❑ 193B Antrel Rolle JSY AU RC 25.00 10.00
- ❑ 194A Channing Crowder RC 10.00 4.00
- ❑ 194B Adam Jones JSY AU RC 25.00 10.00
- ❑ 195A Odell Thurman RC 8.00 3.00
- ❑ 195B M.Clarett JSY AU/250 40.00 15.00
- ❑ 196A Shawne Merriman RC 15.00 6.00
- ❑ 196B Mark Bradley JSY AU RC 25.00 10.00
- ❑ 197A Adrian McPherson RC 10.00 4.00
- ❑ 197B Eric Shelton JSY AU RC 25.00 10.00
- ❑ 198A Chris Henry RC 10.00 4.00
- ❑ 198B Kyle Orton JSY AU RC 30.00 12.00
- ❑ 199A Thomas Davis RC 10.00 4.00
- ❑ 199B Ryan Moats JSY AU RC 25.00 10.00
- ❑ 200A Corey Webster RC 10.00 4.00
- ❑ 200B Frank Gore JSY AU RC 80.00 40.00
- ❑ 201 J.J. Arrington JSY AU RC 25.00 10.00
- ❑ 202 M.Williams JSY AU/250 30.00 12.00
- ❑ 203 V.Jackson JSY AU RC 30.00 12.00
- ❑ 204 Stefan LeFors JSY AU RC 25.00 10.00
- ❑ 206 T.Murphy JSY AU RC 25.00 10.00
- ❑ 207 Courtney Roby JSY AU RC 25.00 10.00
- ❑ 208 Carlos Rogers JSY AU RC 30.00 12.00
- ❑ 209 Charlie Frye JSY AU RC 25.00 10.00
- ❑ 210 Mark Clayton JSY AU RC 25.00 10.00
- ❑ 211 Roddy White JSY AU RC 25.00 10.00
- ❑ 212 Jason Campbell JSY AU RC 50.00 25.00
- ❑ 213 Roscoe Parrish JSY AU RC 25.00 10.00
- ❑ 214 Reggie Brown JSY AU RC 25.00 10.00
- ❑ 215 H.Miller JSY AU RC EXCH 40.00 20.00
- ❑ 216 Williamson JSY AU/250 RC 80.00 30.00
- ❑ 217 Ciatrick Fason JSY AU RC 25.00 10.00
- ❑ 218 C.Benson JSY AU/150 RC 200.00 100.00
- ❑ 219 B.Edwards JSY AU/250 RC 120.00 60.00
- ❑ 220 Ro.Brown JSY AU/250 RC 150.00 75.00
- ❑ 221 C.Williams JSY AU/250 RC 150.00 75.00
- ❑ 222 A.Smith QB JSY AU/250 RC 150.00 75.00
- ❑ 223 A.Rodgers JSY AU/250 RC 150.00 90.00

2006 SPx

- ❑ COMP.SET w/o RC's (90) 30.00 12.50
- ❑ 91-180 ROOKIE PRINT RUN 1299
- ❑ 181-187 RC JSY AU PRINT RUN 399
- ❑ 181-187 RC JSY AU PRINT RUN 1650
- ❑ 1 Edgerrin James 1.00 .40
- ❑ 2 Kurt Warner .60 .25
- ❑ 3 Larry Fitzgerald 1.00 .40
- ❑ 4 Michael Vick 1.00 .40
- ❑ 5 Warrick Dunn .60 .25
- ❑ 6 Michael Jenkins .60 .25
- ❑ 7 Jamal Lewis .60 .25
- ❑ 8 Kyle Boller .50 .20
- ❑ 9 Derrick Mason .50 .20
- ❑ 10 Willis McGahee 1.00 .40
- ❑ 11 Lee Evans .60 .25
- ❑ 12 Jake Delhomme .60 .25
- ❑ 13 Steve Smith 1.00 .40
- ❑ 14 DeShaun Foster .60 .25
- ❑ 15 Rex Grossman 1.00 .40
- ❑ 16 Muhsin Muhammad .60 .25
- ❑ 17 Thomas Jones .60 .25
- ❑ 18 Carson Palmer 1.00 .40
- ❑ 19 Chad Johnson .60 .25
- ❑ 20 Rudi Johnson .60 .25
- ❑ 21 Charlie Frye .60 .25
- ❑ 22 Reuben Droughns .60 .25
- ❑ 23 Braylon Edwards 1.00 .40
- ❑ 24 Drew Bledsoe 1.00 .40
- ❑ 25 Terrell Owens 1.00 .40
- ❑ 26 Julius Jones 1.00 .40
- ❑ 27 Jake Plummer .60 .25
- ❑ 28 Tatum Bell .60 .25
- ❑ 29 Rod Smith .60 .25
- ❑ 30 Kevin Jones 1.00 .40
- ❑ 31 Roy Williams WR 1.00 .40
- ❑ 32 Brett Favre 2.00 .75
- ❑ 33 Ahman Green .60 .25
- ❑ 34 Donald Driver .60 .25
- ❑ 35 David Carr .60 .25
- ❑ 36 Andre Johnson .60 .25
- ❑ 37 Peyton Manning 1.50 .60
- ❑ 38 Marvin Harrison 1.00 .40
- ❑ 39 Reggie Wayne .60 .25
- ❑ 40 Byron Leftwich .60 .25
- ❑ 41 Fred Taylor .60 .25
- ❑ 42 Ernest Wilford .50 .20
- ❑ 43 Larry Johnson 1.25 .50
- ❑ 44 Trent Green .60 .25
- ❑ 45 Tony Gonzalez .60 .25
- ❑ 46 Daunte Culpepper 1.00 .40
- ❑ 47 Ronnie Brown 1.00 .40
- ❑ 48 Chris Chambers .60 .25
- ❑ 49 Troy Williamson .60 .25
- ❑ 50 Chester Taylor .60 .25
- ❑ 51 Brad Johnson .60 .25
- ❑ 52 Tom Brady 1.50 .60
- ❑ 53 Deion Branch .60 .25
- ❑ 54 Corey Dillon .60 .25
- ❑ 55 Drew Brees 1.00 .40
- ❑ 56 Deuce McAllister .60 .25
- ❑ 57 Donte Stallworth .60 .25
- ❑ 58 Eli Manning 1.25 .50
- ❑ 59 Tiki Barber 1.00 .40
- ❑ 60 Plaxico Burress .60 .25
- ❑ 61 Chad Pennington .60 .25
- ❑ 62 Curtis Martin 1.00 .40
- ❑ 63 Randy Moss 1.00 .40
- ❑ 64 LaMont Jordan .60 .25

❑ 65 Aaron Brooks .60 .25
❑ 66 Donovan McNabb 1.00 .40
❑ 67 Brian Westbrook .60 .25
❑ 68 Ben Roethlisberger 1.50 .60
❑ 69 Hines Ward 1.00 .40
❑ 70 Willie Parker 1.25 .50
❑ 71 LaDainian Tomlinson 1.25 .50
❑ 72 Philip Rivers 1.00 .40
❑ 73 Antonio Gates 1.00 .40
❑ 74 Alex Smith QB 1.00 .40
❑ 75 Antonio Bryant .60 .25
❑ 76 Frank Gore 1.00 .40
❑ 77 Shaun Alexander 1.00 .40
❑ 78 Matt Hasselbeck .60 .25
❑ 79 Nate Burleson .60 .25
❑ 80 Marc Bulger .60 .25
❑ 81 Steven Jackson 1.00 .40
❑ 82 Torry Holt .60 .25
❑ 83 Cadillac Williams 1.00 .40
❑ 84 Joey Galloway .60 .25
❑ 85 Chris Simms .60 .25
❑ 86 Billy Volek .60 .25
❑ 87 Drew Bennett .50 .20
❑ 88 Clinton Portis 1.00 .40
❑ 89 Santana Moss .60 .25
❑ 90 Mark Brunell .60 .25
❑ 91 Haloti Ngata RC 10.00 4.00
❑ 92 Willie Reid RC 10.00 4.00
❑ 93 Kamerion Wimbley RC 10.00 4.00
❑ 94 Donte Whitner RC 10.00 4.00
❑ 95 Ethan Kilmer RC 10.00 4.00
❑ 96 Johnathan Joseph RC 8.00 3.00
❑ 97 Brodie Croyle RC 25.00 10.00
❑ 98 Bobby Carpenter RC 10.00 4.00
❑ 99 Antonio Cromartie RC 10.00 4.00
❑ 100 Eric Winston RC 5.00 2.00
❑ 101 Nick Mangold RC 5.00 2.00
❑ 102 Manny Lawson RC 10.00 4.00
❑ 103 Claude Wroten RC 5.00 2.00
❑ 104 D'Qwell Jackson RC 8.00 3.00
❑ 105 Richard Marshall RC 8.00 3.00
❑ 106 Tamba Hali RC 10.00 4.00
❑ 107 Ko Simpson RC 8.00 3.00
❑ 108 Danieal Manning RC 10.00 4.00
❑ 109 Gabe Watson RC 8.00 3.00
❑ 110 Kevin McMahan RC 8.00 3.00
❑ 111 Jai Lewis RC 8.00 3.00
❑ 112 Darryl Tapp RC 8.00 3.00
❑ 113 John McCargo RC 8.00 3.00
❑ 114 Jeff King RC 8.00 3.00
❑ 115 Charles Davis RC 8.00 3.00
❑ 116 Calvin Lowry RC 10.00 4.00
❑ 117 Delanie Walker RC 8.00 3.00
❑ 118 Roman Harper RC 8.00 3.00
❑ 119 Nate Salley RC 8.00 3.00
❑ 120 Cooper Wallace RC 8.00 3.00
❑ 121 Bernard Pollard RC 8.00 3.00
❑ 122 Derrick Ross RC 8.00 3.00
❑ 123 Ingle Martin RC 10.00 4.00
❑ 124 Wali Lundy RC 10.00 4.00
❑ 125 Marcus Vick RC 8.00 3.00
❑ 126 Cedric Humes RC 10.00 4.00
❑ 127 Marques Hagans RC 8.00 3.00
❑ 128 Taurean Henderson RC 10.00 4.00
❑ 129 Marques Colston RC 40.00 15.00
❑ 130 Devin Aromashodu RC 8.00 3.00
❑ 131 Jonathan Orr RC 8.00 3.00
❑ 132 Skyler Green RC 10.00 4.00
❑ 133 Jeff Webb RC 8.00 3.00
❑ 134 Jon Alston RC 10.00 4.00
❑ 135 Daniel Bullocks RC 10.00 4.00
❑ 136 Anthony Schlegel RC 8.00 3.00
❑ 137 Adam Jennings RC 8.00 3.00
❑ 138 Gerris Wilkinson RC 5.00 2.00
❑ 139 James Anderson RC 5.00 2.00
❑ 140 Owen Daniels RC 10.00 4.00
❑ 141 Ray Edwards RC 8.00 3.00
❑ 142 Chris Gocong RC 8.00 3.00
❑ 143 Babatunde Oshinowo RC 8.00 3.00
❑ 144 Marvin Philip RC 10.00 4.00
❑ 145 Stanley McClover RC 8.00 3.00
❑ 146 DeMeco Ryans RC 12.00 5.00
❑ 147 Tony Scheffler RC 10.00 4.00
❑ 148 T.J. Williams RC 10.00 4.00
❑ 149 P.J. Daniels RC 8.00 3.00
❑ 150 Bennie Brazell RC 8.00 3.00
❑ 151 Will Blackmon RC 8.00 3.00

❑ 152 Bruce Gradkowski RC 15.00 6.00
❑ 153 Drew Olson RC 8.00 3.00
❑ 154 Darnell Bing RC 10.00 4.00
❑ 155 Darrell Hackney RC 8.00 3.00
❑ 156 Cory Rodgers RC 10.00 4.00
❑ 157 DonTrell Moore RC 8.00 3.00
❑ 158 Ernie Sims RC 12.00 5.00
❑ 159 Jay Cutler RC 30.00 12.00
❑ 160 D.J. Shockley RC 10.00 4.00
❑ 161 Martin Nance RC 8.00 3.00
❑ 162 Joseph Addai RC 30.00 12.00
❑ 163 Leonard Pope RC 10.00 4.00
❑ 164 Anthony Fasano RC 10.00 4.00
❑ 165 Mathias Kiwanuka RC 12.00 5.00
❑ 166 Greg Jennings RC 15.00 6.00
❑ 167 Greg Lee RC 8.00 3.00
❑ 168 Jerome Harrison RC 10.00 4.00
❑ 169 Jimmy Williams RC 10.00 4.00
❑ 170 Josh Betts RC 8.00 3.00
❑ 171 Ashton Youboty RC 10.00 4.00
❑ 172 Terrence Whitehead RC 8.00 3.00
❑ 173 Brad Smith RC 10.00 4.00
❑ 174 D'Brickashaw Ferguson RC 10.00 4.00
❑ 175 Mike Hass RC 10.00 4.00
❑ 176 Reggie McNeal RC 8.00 3.00
❑ 177 Dominique Byrd RC 8.00 3.00
❑ 178 Winston Justice RC 10.00 4.00
❑ 179 Chad Greenway RC 10.00 4.00
❑ 180 Tye Hill RC 10.00 4.00
❑ 181 Chad Jackson JSY AU RC 50.00 20.00
❑ 182 DeA.Williams JSY AU RC 120.00 60.00
❑ 183 Vince Young JSY AU RC 300.00 150.00
❑ 184 S.Holmes JSY AU RC 100.00 40.00
❑ 185 Sinorice Moss JSY AU RC 40.00 15.00
❑ 186 Matt Leinart JSY AU RC 200.00 100.00
❑ 187 Reggie Bush JSY AU RC 350.00 200.00
❑ 188 LenDale White JSY AU RC 50.00 20.00
❑ 189 Vernon Davis JSY AU RC 40.00 20.00
❑ 190 L.Maroney JSY AU RC 100.00 50.00
❑ 191 A.J. Hawk JSY AU RC 80.00 30.00
❑ 192 Marcus McNeill JSY AU RC 15.00 6.00
❑ 193 Kelly Jennings JSY AU RC 20.00 8.00
❑ 194 B.Williams JSY AU RC 20.00 8.00
❑ 195 Brian Calhoun JSY AU RC 20.00 8.00
❑ 196 Travis Wilson JSY AU RC 20.00 8.00
❑ 197 C.Whitehurst JSY AU RC 20.00 8.00
❑ 198 Omar Jacobs JSY AU RC 15.00 6.00
❑ 199 J.Klopfenstein JSY AU RC 15.00 6.00
❑ 200 Derek Hagan JSY AU RC 20.00 8.00
❑ 201 Michael Huff JSY AU RC 25.00 10.00
❑ 202 Maurice Stovall JSY AU RC 20.00 8.00
❑ 203 Maurice Drew JSY AU RC 60.00 30.00
❑ 204 Jason Avant JSY AU RC 20.00 8.00
❑ 205 K.Clemens JSY AU RC 30.00 12.00
❑ 206 J.Norwood JSY AU RC 50.00 25.00
❑ 207 T.Jackson JSY AU RC 40.00 20.00
❑ 208 B.Marshall JSY AU RC 30.00 15.00
❑ 209 Dem.Williams JSY AU RC 20.00 8.00
❑ 210 L.Washington JSY AU RC 40.00 20.00
❑ 211 M.Robinson JSY AU RC 20.00 8.00
❑ 212 Marcedes Lewis JSY AU RC 20.00 8.00
❑ 213 Mario Williams JSY AU RC 30.00 12.00

2007 SPx

❑ 1 Matt Leinart 1.25 .50
❑ 2 Anquan Boldin 1.00 .40
❑ 3 Larry Fitzgerald 1.00 .40
❑ 4 Edgerrin James 1.25 .50
❑ 5 Michael Vick 1.25 .50
❑ 6 Warrick Dunn 1.00 .40
❑ 7 DeAngelo Hall 1.00 .40
❑ 8 Steve McNair 1.00 .40
❑ 9 Willis McGahee 1.00 .40
❑ 10 Ray Lewis 1.25 .50
❑ 11 J.P. Losman 1.00 .40
❑ 12 Lee Evans 1.00 .40
❑ 13 Anthony Thomas .75 .30
❑ 14 Jake Delhomme 1.00 .40
❑ 15 Steve Smith 1.00 .40
❑ 16 DeAngelo Williams 1.25 .50
❑ 17 Brian Urlacher 1.25 .50
❑ 18 Cedric Benson 1.00 .40
❑ 19 Rex Grossman 1.00 .40
❑ 20 Carson Palmer 1.25 .50
❑ 21 Chad Johnson 1.00 .40
❑ 22 Rudi Johnson 1.00 .40
❑ 23 Charlie Frye 1.00 .40
❑ 24 Braylon Edwards 1.00 .40
❑ 25 Jamal Lewis 1.00 .40
❑ 26 Tony Romo 2.50 1.00
❑ 27 Terrell Owens 1.25 .50
❑ 28 Julius Jones 1.00 .40
❑ 29 Marion Barber 1.00 .40
❑ 30 Jay Cutler 1.25 .50
❑ 31 Javon Walker 1.00 .40
❑ 32 Travis Henry 1.00 .40
❑ 33 Roy Williams WR 1.00 .40
❑ 34 Mike Furrey 1.00 .40
❑ 35 Tatum Bell 1.00 .40
❑ 36 Greg Jennings 1.00 .40
❑ 37 Brett Favre 2.50 1.00
❑ 38 A.J. Hawk 1.25 .50
❑ 39 Matt Schaub 1.00 .40
❑ 40 Andre Johnson 1.00 .40
❑ 41 Ahman Green 1.00 .40
❑ 42 Peyton Manning 2.00 .75
❑ 43 Marvin Harrison 1.25 .50
❑ 44 Reggie Wayne 1.00 .40
❑ 45 Joseph Addai 1.50 .60
❑ 46 Fred Taylor 1.00 .40
❑ 47 Maurice Jones-Drew 1.25 .50
❑ 48 Byron Leftwich 1.00 .40
❑ 49 Damon Huard .75 .30
❑ 50 Larry Johnson 1.25 .50
❑ 51 Tony Gonzalez 1.00 .40
❑ 52 Zach Thomas 1.00 .40
❑ 53 Ronnie Brown 1.00 .40
❑ 54 Chris Chambers 1.00 .40
❑ 55 Tarvaris Jackson 1.25 .50
❑ 56 Chester Taylor .75 .30
❑ 57 Troy Williamson .75 .30
❑ 58 Tom Brady 2.50 1.00
❑ 59 Donte Stallworth 1.00 .40
❑ 60 Laurence Maroney 1.25 .50
❑ 61 Reggie Bush 1.50 .60
❑ 62 Deuce McAllister 1.00 .40
❑ 63 Drew Brees 1.00 .40
❑ 64 Marques Colston 1.25 .50
❑ 65 Eli Manning 1.25 .50
❑ 66 Plaxico Burress 1.00 .40
❑ 67 Brandon Jacobs 1.00 .40
❑ 68 Chad Pennington 1.00 .40
❑ 69 Thomas Jones 1.00 .40
❑ 70 Laveranues Coles 1.00 .40
❑ 71 LaMont Jordan 1.00 .40
❑ 72 Randy Moss 1.25 .50
❑ 73 Nnamdi Asomugha .75 .30
❑ 74 Donovan McNabb 1.25 .50
❑ 75 Brian Westbrook 1.00 .40
❑ 76 Reggie Brown 1.00 .40
❑ 77 Ben Roethlisberger 1.50 .60
❑ 78 Hines Ward 1.25 .50
❑ 79 Willie Parker 1.25 .50
❑ 80 LaDainian Tomlinson 1.50 .60
❑ 81 Philip Rivers 1.25 .50
❑ 82 Antonio Gates 1.00 .40
❑ 83 Frank Gore 1.25 .50
❑ 84 Alex Smith QB 1.25 .50
❑ 85 Ashley Lelie 1.00 .40
❑ 86 Matt Hasselbeck 1.00 .40
❑ 87 Shaun Alexander 1.00 .40
❑ 88 Deion Branch 1.00 .40
❑ 89 Marc Bulger 1.00 .40
❑ 90 Torry Holt 1.00 .40
❑ 91 Steven Jackson 1.25 .50
❑ 92 Cadillac Williams 1.00 .40

❑ 93	Chris Simms	.75	.30
❑ 94	Joey Galloway	1.00	.40
❑ 95	Vince Young	1.50	.60
❑ 96	David Givens	.75	.30
❑ 97	LenDale White	1.00	.40
❑ 98	Jason Campbell	1.00	.40
❑ 99	Santana Moss	1.00	.40
❑ 100	Clinton Portis	1.00	.40
❑ 101	Levi Brown RC	10.00	4.00
❑ 102	Adam Carriker RC	8.00	3.00
❑ 103	Jarvis Moss RC	10.00	4.00
❑ 104	Aaron Ross RC	10.00	4.00
❑ 105	Chris Houston RC	8.00	3.00
[illegible]	[illegible]	[illegible]	[illegible]
❑ 107	Justin Harrell RC	10.00	4.00
❑ 108	Joe Staley RC	8.00	3.00
❑ 109	Jon Beason RC	10.00	4.00
❑ 110	Anthony Spencer RC	10.00	4.00
❑ 111	Ben Grubbs RC	8.00	3.00
❑ 112	Charles Johnson RC	6.00	2.50
❑ 113	Marcus McCauley RC	8.00	3.00
❑ 114	Justin Blalock RC	6.00	2.50
❑ 115	Tim Crowder RC	10.00	4.00
❑ 116	Brandon Meriweather RC	10.00	4.00
❑ 117	Arron Sears RC	8.00	3.00
❑ 118	Zach Miller RC	10.00	4.00
❑ 119	Turk McBride RC	8.00	3.00
❑ 120	Ryan Kalil RC	8.00	3.00
❑ 121	Tony Ugoh RC	8.00	3.00
❑ 122	David Harris RC	8.00	3.00
❑ 123	Jonathan Wade RC	8.00	3.00
❑ 124	Josh Wilson RC	8.00	3.00
❑ 125	Demarcus Tank Tyler RC	8.00	3.00
❑ 126	Tanard Jackson RC	6.00	2.50
❑ 127	Jordan Kent RC	8.00	3.00
❑ 128	Ray McDonald RC	8.00	3.00
❑ 129	Quentin Moses RC	8.00	3.00
❑ 130	Eric Weddle RC	8.00	3.00
❑ 131	Victor Abiamiri RC	10.00	4.00
❑ 132	Josh Beekman RC	6.00	2.50
❑ 133	Brandon Siler RC	8.00	3.00
❑ 134	Aundrae Allison RC	8.00	3.00
❑ 135	Ben Patrick RC	8.00	3.00
❑ 136	Chris Davis RC	8.00	3.00
❑ 137	A.J. Davis RC	6.00	2.50
❑ 138	Scott Chandler RC	8.00	3.00
❑ 139	Mason Crosby RC	10.00	4.00
❑ 140	Zak DeOssie RC	8.00	3.00
❑ 141	Matt Spaeth RC	10.00	4.00
❑ 142	James Jones RC	15.00	6.00
❑ 143	Mike Walker RC	8.00	3.00
❑ 144	Martrez Milner RC	8.00	3.00
❑ 145	Michael Okwo RC	8.00	3.00
❑ 146	Steve Breaston RC	8.00	3.00
❑ 147	Isaiah Stanback RC	10.00	4.00
❑ 148	Laurent Robinson RC	8.00	3.00
❑ 149	Brandon Mebane RC	8.00	3.00
❑ 150	Quinn Pitcock RC	8.00	3.00
❑ 151	Roy Hall RC	10.00	4.00
❑ 152	Buster Davis RC	8.00	3.00
❑ 153	Alan Branch RC	8.00	3.00
❑ 154	Josh Gattis RC	6.00	2.50
❑ 155	Aaron Rouse RC	10.00	4.00
❑ 156	Tim Shaw RC	8.00	3.00
❑ 157	Sabby Piscitelli RC	10.00	4.00
❑ 158	Rufus Alexander RC	10.00	4.00
❑ 159	Marcus Thomas RC	8.00	3.00
❑ 160	Tarell Brown RC	6.00	2.50
❑ 161	Chris Leak AU RC	15.00	6.00
❑ 162	Amobi Okoye AU RC	20.00	8.00
❑ 163	Tyler Palko AU RC	20.00	8.00
❑ 164	Craig Buster Davis AU RC	20.00	8.00
❑ 165	Courtney Taylor AU RC	15.00	6.00
❑ 166	Tyrone Moss AU RC	12.00	5.00
❑ 167	Darrelle Revis AU RC	20.00	8.00
❑ 168	David Ball AU RC	12.00	5.00
❑ 169	David Clowney AU RC	20.00	8.00
❑ 170	Daymeion Hughes AU RC	15.00	6.00
❑ 171	DeShawn Wynn AU RC	20.00	8.00
❑ 172	Drew Tate AU RC	15.00	6.00
❑ 173	Dwayne Wright AU RC	15.00	6.00
❑ 174	Eric Wright AU RC	20.00	8.00
❑ 175	Kenneth Darby AU RC	20.00	8.00
❑ 176	H.B. Blades AU RC	15.00	6.00
❑ 177	Jamaal Anderson AU RC	15.00	6.00
❑ 178	Jared Zabransky AU RC	20.00	8.00
❑ 179	Rhema McKnight AU RC	15.00	6.00
❑ 180	Jeff Rowe AU RC	15.00	6.00
❑ 181	LaRon Landry AU RC	25.00	10.00
❑ 182	Jordan Palmer AU RC	20.00	8.00
❑ 183	Kolby Smith AU RC	30.00	15.00
❑ 184	LaMarr Woodley AU RC	20.00	8.00
❑ 185	Lawrence Timmons AU RC	20.00	8.00
❑ 186	Leon Hall AU RC	15.00	6.00
❑ 187	Matt Moore AU RC	40.00	20.00
❑ 188	Gary Russell AU RC	20.00	8.00
❑ 189	Paul Posluszny AU RC	25.00	10.00
❑ 190	Reggie Nelson AU RC	15.00	6.00
❑ 191	Antonio Pittman JSY AU RC	20.00	8.00
❑ 192	A.Gonzalez JSY AU/399 RC	50.00	25.00
[illegible]	[illegible]	[illegible]	[illegible]
❑ 194	Brandon Jackson JSY AU RC	80.00	40.00
❑ 195	Brian Leonard JSY AU RC	30.00	12.00
❑ 196	J.Higgins JSY AU RC	20.00	8.00
❑ 197	Chris Henry RB JSY AU RC	25.00	10.00
❑ 198	Patrick Willis JSY AU RC	50.00	20.00
❑ 199	Drew Stanton JSY AU RC	50.00	20.00
❑ 200	D.Bowe JSY AU/399 RC	60.00	25.00
❑ 201	Greg Olsen JSY AU RC	40.00	20.00
❑ 202	John Beck JSY AU RC	60.00	30.00
❑ 203	Jason Hill JSY AU RC	25.00	10.00
❑ 204	Paul Williams JSY AU RC	20.00	8.00
❑ 205	Joe Thomas JSY AU RC	30.00	12.50
❑ 206	Lorenzo Booker JSY AU RC	30.00	12.50
❑ 207	Yamon Figurs JSY AU RC	25.00	10.00
❑ 208	Kenny Irons JSY AU RC	25.00	10.00
❑ 209	Kevin Kolb JSY AU/399 RC	40.00	20.00
❑ 210	Garrett Wolfe JSY AU RC	30.00	12.00
❑ 211	Michael Bush JSY AU RC	40.00	20.00
❑ 212	H.Meachem JSY AU/399 RC	30.00	12.00
❑ 213	Sidney Rice JSY AU/399 RC	50.00	20.00
❑ 214	Steve Smith JSY AU RC	30.00	15.00
❑ 215	Tony Hunt JSY AU RC	25.00	10.00
❑ 217	T.Edwards JSY AU/399 RC	60.00	25.00
❑ 218	A.Peterson JSY AU/299 RC	450.00	250.00
❑ 219	B.Quinn JSY AU/299 RC	200.00	100.00
❑ 220	Ca.Johnson JSY AU/299 RC	200.00	75.00
❑ 221	D.Jarrett JSY AU/299 RC	60.00	30.00
❑ 222	J.Russell JSY AU/299 RC	200.00	100.00
❑ 223	M.Lynch JSY AU/299 RC	120.00	60.00
❑ 224	Ted Ginn Jr. JSY AU/299 RC	60.00	30.00

1991 Stadium Club

❑	COMPLETE SET (500)	60.00	30.00
❑ 1	Pepper Johnson	.20	.07
❑ 2	Emmitt Smith	5.00	2.00
❑ 3	Deion Sanders	1.50	.60
❑ 4	Andre Collins	.20	.07
❑ 5	Eric Metcalf	.40	.15
❑ 6	Richard Dent	.40	.15
❑ 7	Eric Martin	.20	.07
❑ 8	Marcus Allen	.75	.30
❑ 9	Gary Anderson K	.20	.07
❑ 10	Joey Browner	.20	.07
❑ 11	Lorenzo White	.20	.07
❑ 12	Bruce Smith	.75	.30
❑ 13	Mark Boyer	.20	.07
❑ 14	Mike Piel	.20	.07
❑ 15	Albert Bentley	.20	.07
❑ 16	Bennie Blades	.20	.07
❑ 17	Jason Staurovsky	.20	.07
❑ 18	Anthony Toney	.20	.07
❑ 19	Dave Krieg	.40	.15
❑ 20	Harvey Williams RC	.75	.30
❑ 21	Bubba Paris	.20	.07
❑ 22	Tim McGee	.20	.07
❑ 23	Brian Noble	.20	.07
❑ 24	Vinny Testaverde	.40	.15
❑ 25	Doug Widell	.20	.07
❑ 26	John Jackson WR RC	.20	.07
❑ 27	Marion Butts	.40	.15
❑ 28	Deron Cherry	.20	.07
❑ 29	Don Warren	.20	.07
❑ 30	Rod Woodson	.75	.30
❑ 31	Mike Baab	.20	.07
❑ 32	Greg Jackson RC	.20	.07
❑ 33	Jerry Robinson	.20	.07
❑ 34	Dalton Hilliard	.20	.07
❑ 35	Brian Jordan	.40	.15
❑ 36	James Thornton UER	.20	.07
❑ 37	Michael Irvin	.75	.30
❑ 38	Billy Joe Tolliver	.20	.07
❑ 39	Jeff Herrod	.20	.07
❑ 40	Scott Norwood	.20	.07
❑ 41	Ferrell Edmunds	.20	.07
❑ 42	Andre Waters	.20	.07
❑ 43	Kevin Glover	.20	.07
❑ 44	Ray Berry	.20	.07
❑ 45	Timm Rosenbach	.20	.07
❑ 46	Reuben Davis	.20	.07
❑ 47	Charles Wilson	.20	.07
❑ 48	Todd Marinovich RC	.20	.07
❑ 49	Harris Barton	.20	.07
❑ 50	Jim Breech	.20	.07
❑ 51	Ron Holmes	.20	.07
❑ 52	Chris Singleton	.20	.07
❑ 53	Pat Leahy	.20	.07
❑ 54	Tom Newberry	.20	.07
❑ 55	Greg Montgomery	.20	.07
❑ 56	Robert Blackmon	.20	.07
❑ 57	Jay Hilgenberg	.20	.07
❑ 58	Rodney Hampton	.75	.30
❑ 59	Brett Perriman	.75	.30
❑ 60	Ricky Watters RC	6.00	2.50
❑ 61	Howie Long	.75	.30
❑ 62	Frank Cornish	.20	.07
❑ 63	Chris Miller	.40	.15
❑ 64	Keith Taylor	.20	.07
❑ 65	Tony Paige	.20	.07
❑ 66	Gary Zimmerman	.20	.07
❑ 67	Mark Royals RC	.20	.07
❑ 68	Ernie Jones	.20	.07
❑ 69	David Grant	.20	.07
❑ 70	Shane Conlan	.20	.07
❑ 71	Jerry Rice	2.50	1.00
❑ 72	Christian Okoye	.20	.07
❑ 73	Eddie Murray	.20	.07
❑ 74	Reggie White	.75	.30
❑ 75	Jeff Graham RC WR	1.00	.40
❑ 76	Mark Jackson	.20	.07
❑ 77	David Grayson	.20	.07
❑ 78	Dan Stryzinski	.20	.07
❑ 79	Sterling Sharpe	.75	.30
❑ 80	Cleveland Gary	.20	.07
❑ 81	Johnny Meads	.20	.07
❑ 82	Howard Cross	.20	.07
❑ 83	Ken O'Brien	.20	.07
❑ 84	Brian Blades	.40	.15
❑ 85	Ethan Horton	.20	.07
❑ 86	Bruce Armstrong	.20	.07
❑ 87	James Washington RC	.20	.07
❑ 88	Eugene Daniel	.20	.07
❑ 89	James Lofton	.40	.15
❑ 90	Louis Oliver	.20	.07
❑ 91	Boomer Esiason	.40	.15
❑ 92	Seth Joyner	.40	.15
❑ 93	Mark Carrier WR	.75	.30
❑ 94	Brett Favre RC UER	50.00	35.00
❑ 95	Lee Williams	.20	.07
❑ 96	Neal Anderson	.40	.15
❑ 97	Brent Jones	.75	.30
❑ 98	John Alt	.20	.07
❑ 99	Rodney Peete	.40	.15
❑ 100	Steve Broussard	.20	.07
❑ 101	Cedric Mack	.20	.07
❑ 102	Pat Swilling	.40	.15
❑ 103	Stan Humphries	.75	.30
❑ 104	Darrell Thompson	.20	.07
❑ 105	Reggie Langhorne	.20	.07
❑ 106	Kenny Davidson	.20	.07
❑ 107	Jim Everett	.40	.15
❑ 108	Keith Millard	.20	.07
❑ 109	Garry Lewis	.20	.07

❑ 110 Jeff Hostetler .40 .15
❑ 111 Lamar Lathon .20 .07
❑ 112 Johnny Bailey .20 .07
❑ 113 Cornelius Bennett .40 .15
❑ 114 Travis McNeal .20 .07
❑ 115 Jeff Lageman .20 .07
❑ 116 Nick Bell RC .20 .07
❑ 117 Calvin Williams .40 .15
❑ 118 Shawn Lee RC .20 .07
❑ 119 Anthony Munoz .40 .15
❑ 120 Jay Novacek .75 .30
❑ 121 Kevin Fagan .20 .07
❑ 122 Leo Goeas .20 .07
❑ 123 Vance Johnson .20 .07
❑ 124 Brent Williams .20 .07
❑ 125 Clarence Verdin .20 .07
❑ 126 Luis Sharpe .20 .07
❑ 127 Darrell Green .20 .07
❑ 128 Barry Word .20 .07
❑ 129 Steve Walsh .20 .07
❑ 130 Bryan Hinkle .20 .07
❑ 131 Ed West .20 .07
❑ 132 Jeff Campbell .20 .07
❑ 133 Dennis Byrd .20 .07
❑ 134 Nate Odomes .20 .07
❑ 135 Trace Armstrong .20 .07
❑ 136 Jarvis Williams .20 .07
❑ 137 Warren Moon .75 .30
❑ 138 Eric Moten RC .20 .07
❑ 139 Tony Woods .20 .07
❑ 140 Phil Simms .40 .15
❑ 141 Ricky Reynolds .20 .07
❑ 142 Frank Stams .20 .07
❑ 143 Kevin Mack .20 .07
❑ 144 Wade Wilson .40 .15
❑ 145 Shawn Collins .20 .07
❑ 146 Roger Craig .40 .15
❑ 147 Jeff Feagles RC .20 .07
❑ 148 Norm Johnson .20 .07
❑ 149 Terance Mathis .40 .15
❑ 150 Reggie Cobb .20 .07
❑ 151 Chip Banks .20 .07
❑ 152 Darryl Pollard .20 .07
❑ 153 Karl Mecklenburg .20 .07
❑ 154 Ricky Proehl .20 .07
❑ 155 Pete Stoyanovich .20 .07
❑ 156 John Stephens .20 .07
❑ 157 Ron Morris .20 .07
❑ 158 Steve DeBerg .20 .07
❑ 159 Mike Munchak .40 .15
❑ 160 Brett Maxie .20 .07
❑ 161 Don Beebe .20 .07
❑ 162 Martin Mayhew .20 .07
❑ 163 Merril Hoge .20 .07
❑ 164 Kelvin Pritchett RC .40 .15
❑ 165 Jim Jeffcoat .20 .07
❑ 166 Myron Guyton .20 .07
❑ 167 Ickey Woods .20 .07
❑ 168 Andre Ware .40 .15
❑ 169 Gary Plummer .20 .07
❑ 170 Henry Ellard .40 .15
❑ 171 Scott Davis .20 .07
❑ 172 Randall McDaniel .20 .07
❑ 173 Randal Hill RC .40 .15
❑ 174 Anthony Bell .20 .07
❑ 175 Gary Anderson RB .20 .07
❑ 176 Byron Evans .20 .07
❑ 177 Tony Mandarich .20 .07
❑ 178 Jeff George 1.00 .40
❑ 179 Art Monk .40 .15
❑ 180 Mike Kenn .20 .07
❑ 181 Sean Landeta .20 .07
❑ 182 Shaun Gayle .20 .07
❑ 183 Michael Carter .20 .07
❑ 184 Robb Thomas .20 .07
❑ 185 Richmond Webb .20 .07
❑ 186 Carnell Lake .20 .07
❑ 187 Rueben Mayes .20 .07
❑ 188 Issiac Holt .20 .07
❑ 189 Leon Seals .20 .07
❑ 190 Al Smith .20 .07
❑ 191 Steve Atwater .20 .07
❑ 192 Greg McMurtry .20 .07
❑ 193 Al Toon .40 .15
❑ 194 Cortez Kennedy .75 .30
❑ 195 Gill Byrd .20 .07
❑ 196 Carl Zander .20 .07
❑ 197 Robert Brown .20 .07
❑ 198 Buford McGee .20 .07
❑ 199 Mervyn Fernandez .20 .07
❑ 200 Mike Dumas RC .20 .07
❑ 201 Rob Burnett RC .40 .15
❑ 202 Brian Mitchell .40 .15
❑ 203 Randall Cunningham .75 .30
❑ 204 Sammie Smith .20 .07
❑ 205 Ken Clarke .20 .07
❑ 206 Floyd Dixon .20 .07
❑ 207 Ken Norton .40 .15
❑ 208 Tony Siragusa RC .40 .15
❑ 209 Louis Lipps .20 .07
❑ 210 Chris Martin .20 .07
❑ 211 Jamie Mueller .20 .07
❑ 212 Dave Waymer .20 .07
❑ 213 Donnell Woolford .20 .07
❑ 214 Paul Gruber .20 .07
❑ 215 Ken Harvey .40 .15
❑ 216 Henry Jones RC .40 .15
❑ 217 Tommy Barnhardt RC .20 .07
❑ 218 Arthur Cox .20 .07
❑ 219 Pat Terrell .20 .07
❑ 220 Curtis Duncan .20 .07
❑ 221 Jeff Jaeger .20 .07
❑ 222 Scott Stephen RC .20 .07
❑ 223 Rob Moore 1.00 .40
❑ 224 Chris Hinton .20 .07
❑ 225 Marv Cook .20 .07
❑ 226 Patrick Hunter RC .20 .07
❑ 227 Earnest Byner .20 .07
❑ 228 Troy Aikman 3.00 1.25
❑ 229 Kevin Walker RC .20 .07
❑ 230 Keith Jackson .40 .15
❑ 231 Russell Maryland RC .75 .30
❑ 232 Charles Haley .40 .15
❑ 233 Nick Lowery .20 .07
❑ 234 Erik Howard .20 .07
❑ 235 Leonard Smith .20 .07
❑ 236 Tim Irwin .20 .07
❑ 237 Simon Fletcher .20 .07
❑ 238 Thomas Everett .20 .07
❑ 239 Reggie Roby .20 .07
❑ 240 Leroy Hoard .40 .15
❑ 241 Wayne Haddix .20 .07
❑ 242 Gary Clark .75 .30
❑ 243 Eric Andolsek .20 .07
❑ 244 Jim Wahler RC .20 .07
❑ 245 Vaughan Johnson .20 .07
❑ 246 Kevin Butler .20 .07
❑ 247 Steve Tasker .40 .15
❑ 248 LeRoy Butler .40 .15
❑ 249 Darion Conner .20 .07
❑ 250 Eric Turner RC .40 .15
❑ 251 Kevin Ross .20 .07
❑ 252 Stephen Baker .20 .07
❑ 253 Harold Green .40 .15
❑ 254 Rohn Stark .20 .07
❑ 255 Joe Nash .20 .07
❑ 256 Jesse Sapolu .20 .07
❑ 257 Willie Gault .40 .15
❑ 258 Jerome Brown .20 .07
❑ 259 Ken Willis .20 .07
❑ 260 Courtney Hall .20 .07
❑ 261 Hart Lee Dykes .20 .07
❑ 262 William Fuller .40 .15
❑ 263 Stan Thomas .20 .07
❑ 264 Dan Marino 4.00 1.50
❑ 265 Ron Cox .20 .07
❑ 266 Eric Green .20 .07
❑ 267 Anthony Carter .40 .15
❑ 268 Jerry Ball .20 .07
❑ 269 Ron Hall .20 .07
❑ 270 Dennis Smith .20 .07
❑ 271 Eric Hill .20 .07
❑ 272 Dan McGwire RC .20 .07
❑ 273 Lewis Billups UER .20 .07
❑ 274 Rickey Jackson .20 .07
❑ 275 Jim Sweeney .20 .07
❑ 276 Pat Beach .20 .07
❑ 277 Kevin Porter .20 .07
❑ 278 Mike Sherrard .20 .07
❑ 279 Andy Heck .20 .07
❑ 280 Ron Brown .20 .07
❑ 281 Lawrence Taylor .75 .30
❑ 282 Anthony Pleasant .20 .07
❑ 283 Wes Hopkins .20 .07
❑ 284 Jim Lachey .20 .07
❑ 285 Tim Harris .20 .07
❑ 286 Tory Epps .20 .07
❑ 287 Wendell Davis .20 .07
❑ 288 Bubba McDowell .20 .07
❑ 289 Bubby Brister .20 .07
❑ 290 Chris Zorich RC .75 .30
❑ 291 Mike Merriweather .20 .07
❑ 292 Burt Grossman .20 .07
❑ 293 Erik McMillan .20 .07
❑ 294 John Elway 4.00 1.50
❑ 295 Toi Cook RC .20 .07
❑ 296 Tom Rathman .20 .07
❑ 297 Matt Bahr .20 .07
❑ 298 Chris Spielman .40 .15
❑ 299 F.J.Nunn w/Aikman/Emmitt .40 .15
❑ 300 Jim C. Jensen .20 .07
❑ 301 David Fulcher UER .20 .07
❑ 302 Tommy Hodson .20 .07
❑ 303 Stephone Paige .20 .07
❑ 304 Greg Townsend .20 .07
❑ 305 Dean Biasucci .20 .07
❑ 306 Jimmie Jones .20 .07
❑ 307 Eugene Marve .20 .07
❑ 308 Flipper Anderson .20 .07
❑ 309 Darryl Talley .20 .07
❑ 310 Mike Croel RC .20 .07
❑ 311 Thane Gash .20 .07
❑ 312 Perry Kemp .20 .07
❑ 313 Heath Sherman .20 .07
❑ 314 Mike Singletary .40 .15
❑ 315 Chip Lohmiller .20 .07
❑ 316 Tunch Ilkin .20 .07
❑ 317 Junior Seau 1.25 .50
❑ 318 Mike Gann .20 .07
❑ 319 Tim McDonald .20 .07
❑ 320 Kyle Clifton .20 .07
❑ 321 Dan Owens .20 .07
❑ 322 Tim Grunhard .20 .07
❑ 323 Stan Brock .20 .07
❑ 324 Rodney Holman .20 .07
❑ 325 Mark Ingram .40 .15
❑ 326 Browning Nagle RC .20 .07
❑ 327 Joe Montana 5.00 2.00
❑ 328 Carl Lee .20 .07
❑ 329 John L. Williams .20 .07
❑ 330 David Griggs .20 .07
❑ 331 Clarence Kay .20 .07
❑ 332 Irving Fryar .40 .15
❑ 333 Doug Smith DT RC** .40 .15
❑ 334 Kent Hull .20 .07
❑ 335 Mike Wilcher .20 .07
❑ 336 Ray Donaldson .20 .07
❑ 337 Mark Carrier DB UER .20 .07
❑ 338 Kelvin Martin .20 .07
❑ 339 Keith Byars .20 .07
❑ 340 Wilber Marshall .20 .07
❑ 341 Ronnie Lott .40 .15
❑ 342 Blair Thomas .20 .07
❑ 343 Ronnie Harmon .20 .07
❑ 344 Brian Brennan .20 .07
❑ 345 Charles McRae RC .20 .07
❑ 346 Michael Cofer .20 .07
❑ 347 Keith Willis .20 .07
❑ 348 Bruce Kozerski .20 .07
❑ 349 Dave Meggett .40 .15
❑ 350 John Taylor .40 .15
❑ 351 Johnny Holland .20 .07
❑ 352 Steve Christie .20 .07
❑ 353 Ricky Ervins RC .40 .15
❑ 354 Robert Massey .20 .07
❑ 355 Derrick Thomas .75 .30
❑ 356 Tommy Kane .20 .07
❑ 357 Melvin Bratton .20 .07
❑ 358 Bruce Matthews .40 .15
❑ 359 Mark Duper .40 .15
❑ 360 Jeff Wright RC .20 .07
❑ 361 Barry Sanders 4.00 1.50
❑ 362 Chuck Webb RC .20 .07
❑ 363 Darryl Grant .20 .07
❑ 364 William Roberts .20 .07
❑ 365 Reggie Rutland .20 .07
❑ 366 Clay Matthews .40 .15
❑ 367 Anthony Miller .40 .15
❑ 368 Mike Prior .20 .07
❑ 369 Jessie Tuggle .20 .07
❑ 370 Brad Muster .20 .07

	#	Player	Price	Price
❑	371	Jay Schroeder	.20	.07
❑	372	Greg Lloyd	.75	.30
❑	373	Mike Cofer	.20	.07
❑	374	James Brooks	.40	.15
❑	375	Danny Noonan UER	.20	.07
❑	376	Latin Berry RC	.20	.07
❑	377	Brad Baxter	.20	.07
❑	378	Godfrey Myles RC	.20	.07
❑	379	Morten Andersen	.20	.07
❑	380	Keith Woodside	.20	.07
❑	381	Bobby Humphrey	.20	.07
❑	382	Mike Golic	.20	.07
❑	383	Keith McCants	.20	.07
❑	384	[illegible]	[illegible]	[illegible]
❑	385	Mark Clayton	.40	.15
❑	386	Neil Smith	.75	.30
❑	387	Bryan Millard	.20	.07
❑	388	Mel Gray UER	.40	.15
❑	389	Ernest Givins	.40	.15
❑	390	Reyna Thompson	.20	.07
❑	391	Eric Bieniemy RC	.20	.07
❑	392	Jon Hand	.20	.07
❑	393	Mark Rypien	.40	.15
❑	394	Bill Romanowski	.20	.07
❑	395	Thurman Thomas	.75	.30
❑	396	Jim Harbaugh	.75	.30
❑	397	Don Mosebar	.20	.07
❑	398	Andre Rison	.40	.15
❑	399	Mike Johnson	.20	.07
❑	400	Dermontti Dawson	.20	.07
❑	401	Herschel Walker	.40	.15
❑	402	Joe Prokop	.20	.07
❑	403	Eddie Brown	.20	.07
❑	404	Nate Newton	.40	.15
❑	405	Damone Johnson RC	.20	.07
❑	406	Jessie Hester	.20	.07
❑	407	Jim Arnold	.20	.07
❑	408	Ray Agnew	.20	.07
❑	409	Michael Brooks	.20	.07
❑	410	Keith Sims	.20	.07
❑	411	Carl Banks	.20	.07
❑	412	Jonathan Hayes	.20	.07
❑	413	Richard Johnson CB RC	.20	.07
❑	414	Darryll Lewis RC	.40	.15
❑	415	Jeff Bryant	.20	.07
❑	416	Leslie O'Neal	.40	.15
❑	417	Andre Reed	.40	.15
❑	418	Charles Mann	.20	.07
❑	419	Keith DeLong	.20	.07
❑	420	Bruce Hill	.20	.07
❑	421	Matt Brock RC	.20	.07
❑	422	Johnny Johnson	.20	.07
❑	423	Mark Bortz	.20	.07
❑	424	Ben Smith	.20	.07
❑	425	Jeff Cross	.20	.07
❑	426	Irv Pankey	.20	.07
❑	427	Hassan Jones	.20	.07
❑	428	Andre Tippett	.20	.07
❑	429	Tim Worley	.20	.07
❑	430	Daniel Stubbs	.20	.07
❑	431	Max Montoya	.20	.07
❑	432	Jumbo Elliott	.20	.07
❑	433	Duane Bickett	.20	.07
❑	434	Nate Lewis RC	.20	.07
❑	435	Leonard Russell RC	.75	.30
❑	436	Hoby Brenner	.20	.07
❑	437	Ricky Sanders	.20	.07
❑	438	Pierce Holt	.20	.07
❑	439	Derrick Fenner	.20	.07
❑	440	Drew Hill	.20	.07
❑	441	Will Wolford	.20	.07
❑	442	Albert Lewis	.20	.07
❑	443	James Francis	.20	.07
❑	444	Chris Jacke	.20	.07
❑	445	Mike Farr	.20	.07
❑	446	Stephen Braggs	.20	.07
❑	447	Michael Haynes	.75	.30
❑	448	Freeman McNeil UER	.20	.07
❑	449	Kevin Donnalley RC	.20	.07
❑	450	John Offerdahl	.20	.07
❑	451	Eric Allen	.20	.07
❑	452	Keith McKeller	.20	.07
❑	453	Kevin Greene	.40	.15
❑	454	Ronnie Lippett	.20	.07
❑	455	Ray Childress	.20	.07
❑	456	Mike Saxon	.20	.07
❑	457	Mark Robinson	.20	.07

	#	Player	Price	Price
❑	458	Greg Kragen	.20	.07
❑	459	Steve Jordan	.20	.07
❑	460	John Johnson RC	.20	.07
❑	461	Sam Mills	.20	.07
❑	462	Bo Jackson	1.00	.40
❑	463	Mark Collins	.20	.07
❑	464	Percy Snow	.20	.07
❑	465	Jeff Bostic	.20	.07
❑	466	Jacob Green	.20	.07
❑	467	Dexter Carter	.20	.07
❑	468	Rich Camarillo	.20	.07
❑	469	Bill Brooks	.20	.07
❑	470	John Carney	.20	.07
❑	471	Don Majkowski	[illegible]	[illegible]
❑	472	Ralph Tamm RC	.20	.07
❑	473	Fred Barnett	.75	.30
❑	474	Jim Covert	.20	.07
❑	475	Kenneth Davis	.20	.07
❑	476	Jerry Gray	.20	.07
❑	477	Broderick Thomas	.20	.07
❑	478	Chris Doleman	.20	.07
❑	479	Haywood Jeffires	.40	.15
❑	480	Craig Heyward	.40	.15
❑	481	Markus Koch	.20	.07
❑	482	Tim Krumrie	.20	.07
❑	483	Robert Clark	.20	.07
❑	484	Mike Rozier	.20	.07
❑	485	Danny Villa	.20	.07
❑	486	Gerald Williams	.20	.07
❑	487	Steve Wisniewski	.20	.07
❑	488	J.B. Brown	.20	.07
❑	489	Eugene Robinson	.20	.07
❑	490	Ottis Anderson	.40	.15
❑	491	Tony Stargell	.20	.07
❑	492	Jack Del Rio	.40	.15
❑	493	Lamar Rogers RC	.20	.07
❑	494	Ricky Nattiel	.20	.07
❑	495	Dan Saleaumua	.20	.07
❑	496	Checklist 1-100	.20	.07
❑	497	Checklist 101-200	.20	.07
❑	498	Checklist 201-300	.20	.07
❑	499	Checklist 301-400	.20	.07
❑	500	Checklist 401-500	.20	.07

1992 Stadium Club

	#	Player	Price	Price
❑		COMPLETE SET (700)	200.00	100.00
❑		COMP.SERIES 1 (300)	15.00	6.00
❑		COMP.SERIES 2 (300)	15.00	6.00
❑		COMP.HIGH SER.(100)	175.00	100.00
❑	1	Mark Rypien	.10	.02
❑	2	Carlton Bailey RC	.10	.02
❑	3	Kevin Glover	.10	.02
❑	4	Vance Johnson	.10	.02
❑	5	Jim Jeffcoat	.10	.02
❑	6	Dan Saleaumua	.10	.02
❑	7	Darion Conner	.10	.02
❑	8	Don Maggs	.10	.02
❑	9	Richard Dent	.15	.05
❑	10	Mark Murphy	.10	.02
❑	11	Wesley Carroll	.10	.02
❑	12	Chris Burkett	.10	.02
❑	13	Steve Wallace	.10	.02
❑	14	Jacob Green	.10	.02
❑	15	Roger Ruzek	.10	.02
❑	16	J.B. Brown	.10	.02
❑	17	Dave Meggett	.15	.05
❑	18	D.J. Johnson	.10	.02
❑	19	Rich Gannon	.30	.10
❑	20	Kevin Mack	.10	.02
❑	21A	Reggie Cobb ERR	.10	.02
❑	21B	Reggie Cobb COR	.10	.02
❑	22	Nate Lewis	.10	.02
❑	23	Doug Smith	.10	.02
❑	24	Irving Fryar	.15	.05
❑	25	Anthony Thompson	.10	.02
❑	26	Duane Bickett	.10	.02
❑	27	Don Majkowski	.10	.02
❑	28	Mark Schlereth RC	.10	.02
❑	29	Melvin Jenkins	.10	.02
❑	30	Michael Haynes	.15	.05
❑	31	Greg Lewis	.10	.02
❑	32	Kenneth Davis	.10	.02
❑	33	Derrick Thomas	.30	.10
❑	34	David Williams	.10	.02
❑	35	Neal Anderson	.10	.02
❑	36	Andre Collins	.10	.02
❑	37	Jesse Solomon	.10	.02
❑	38	Barry Sanders	2.50	1.00
❑	39	Jeff Gossett	.10	.02
❑	40	Rickey Jackson	.10	.02
❑	41	Ray Berry	.10	.02
❑	42	Leroy Hoard	.15	.05
❑	43	Eric Thomas	.10	.02
❑	44	Brian Washington	.10	.02
❑	45	Pat Terrell	.10	.02
❑	46	Eugene Robinson	.10	.02
❑	47	Luis Sharpe	.10	.02
❑	48	Jerome Brown	.10	.02
❑	49	Mark Collins	.10	.02
❑	50	Johnny Holland	.10	.02
❑	51	Tony Paige	.10	.02
❑	52	Willie Green	.10	.02
❑	53	Steve Atwater	.10	.02
❑	54	Brad Muster	.10	.02
❑	55	Cris Dishman	.10	.02
❑	56	Eddie Anderson	.10	.02
❑	57	Sam Mills	.10	.02
❑	58	Donald Evans	.10	.02
❑	59	Jon Vaughn	.10	.02
❑	60	Marion Butts	.10	.02
❑	61	Rodney Holman	.10	.02
❑	62	Dwayne White RC	.10	.02
❑	63	Martin Mayhew	.10	.02
❑	64	Jonathan Hayes	.10	.02
❑	65	Andre Rison	.15	.05
❑	66	Calvin Williams	.15	.05
❑	67	James Washington	.10	.02
❑	68	Tim Harris	.10	.02
❑	69	Jim Ritcher	.10	.02
❑	70	Johnny Johnson	.10	.02
❑	71	John Offerdahl	.10	.02
❑	72	Herschel Walker	.15	.05
❑	73	Perry Kemp	.10	.02
❑	74	Erik Howard	.10	.02
❑	75	Lamar Lathon	.10	.02
❑	76	Greg Kragen	.10	.02
❑	77	Jay Schroeder	.10	.02
❑	78	Jim Arnold	.10	.02
❑	79	Chris Miller	.15	.05
❑	80	Deron Cherry	.10	.02
❑	81	Jim Harbaugh	.30	.10
❑	82	Gill Fenerty	.10	.02
❑	83	Fred Stokes	.10	.02
❑	84	Roman Phifer	.10	.02
❑	85	Clyde Simmons	.10	.02
❑	86	Vince Newsome	.10	.02
❑	87	Lawrence Dawsey	.15	.05
❑	88	Eddie Brown	.10	.02
❑	89	Greg Montgomery	.10	.02
❑	90	Jeff Lageman	.10	.02
❑	91	Terry Wooden	.10	.02
❑	92	Nate Newton	.10	.02
❑	93	David Richards	.10	.02
❑	94	Derek Russell	.10	.02
❑	95	Steve Jordan	.10	.02
❑	96	Hugh Millen	.10	.02
❑	97	Mark Duper	.10	.02
❑	98	Sean Landeta	.10	.02
❑	99	James Thornton	.10	.02
❑	100	Darrell Green	.10	.02
❑	101	Harris Barton	.10	.02
❑	102	John Alt	.10	.02
❑	103	Mike Farr	.10	.02
❑	104	Bob Golic	.10	.02
❑	105	Gene Atkins	.10	.02
❑	106	Gary Anderson K	.10	.02

❑	107 Norm Johnson	.10	.02
❑	108 Eugene Daniel	.10	.02
❑	109 Kent Hull	.10	.02
❑	110 John Elway	2.50	1.00
❑	111 Rich Camarillo	.10	.02
❑	112 Charles Wilson	.10	.02
❑	113 Matt Bahr	.10	.02
❑	114 Mark Carrier WR	.15	.05
❑	115 Richmond Webb	.10	.02
❑	116 Charles Mann	.10	.02
❑	117 Tim McGee	.10	.02
❑	118 Wes Hopkins	.10	.02
❑	119 Mo Lewis	.10	.02
❑	120 Warren Moon	.30	.10
❑	121 Damone Johnson	.10	.02
❑	122 Kevin Gogan	.10	.02
❑	123 Joey Browner	.10	.02
❑	124 Tommy Kane	.10	.02
❑	125 Vincent Brown	.10	.02
❑	126 Barry Word	.10	.02
❑	127 Michael Brooks	.10	.02
❑	128 Jumbo Elliott	.10	.02
❑	129 Marcus Allen	.30	.10
❑	130 Tom Waddle	.10	.02
❑	131 Jim Dombrowski	.10	.02
❑	132 Aeneas Williams	.15	.05
❑	133 Clay Matthews	.15	.05
❑	134 Thurman Thomas	.30	.10
❑	135 Dean Biasucci	.10	.02
❑	136 Moe Gardner	.10	.02
❑	137 James Campen	.10	.02
❑	138 Tim Johnson	.10	.02
❑	139 Erik Kramer	.15	.05
❑	140 Keith McCants	.10	.02
❑	141 John Carney	.10	.02
❑	142 Tunch Ilkin	.10	.02
❑	143 Louis Oliver	.10	.02
❑	144 Bill Maas	.10	.02
❑	145 Wendell Davis	.10	.02
❑	146 Pepper Johnson	.10	.02
❑	147 Howie Long	.30	.10
❑	148 Brett Maxie	.10	.02
❑	149 Tony Casillas	.10	.02
❑	150 Michael Carter	.10	.02
❑	151 Byron Evans	.10	.02
❑	152 Lorenzo White	.10	.02
❑	153 Larry Kelm	.10	.02
❑	154 Andy Heck	.10	.02
❑	155 Harry Newsome	.10	.02
❑	156 Chris Singleton	.10	.02
❑	157 Mike Kenn	.10	.02
❑	158 Jeff Faulkner	.10	.02
❑	159 Ken Lanier	.10	.02
❑	160 Darryl Talley	.10	.02
❑	161 Louie Aguiar RC	.10	.02
❑	162 Danny Copeland	.10	.02
❑	163 Kevin Porter	.10	.02
❑	164 Trace Armstrong	.10	.02
❑	165 Dermontti Dawson	.10	.02
❑	166 Fred McAfee RC	.10	.02
❑	167 Ronnie Lott	.15	.05
❑	168 Tony Mandarich	.10	.02
❑	169 Howard Cross	.10	.02
❑	170 Vestee Jackson	.10	.02
❑	171 Jeff Herrod	.10	.02
❑	172 Randy Hilliard RC	.10	.02
❑	173 Robert Wilson	.10	.02
❑	174 Joe Walter RC	.10	.02
❑	175 Chris Spielman	.15	.05
❑	176 Darryl Henley	.10	.02
❑	177 Jay Hilgenberg	.10	.02
❑	178 John Kidd	.10	.02
❑	179 Doug Widell	.10	.02
❑	180 Seth Joyner	.10	.02
❑	181 Nick Bell	.10	.02
❑	182 Don Griffin	.10	.02
❑	183 Johnny Meads	.10	.02
❑	184 Jeff Bostic	.10	.02
❑	185 Johnny Hector	.10	.02
❑	186 Jessie Tuggle	.10	.02
❑	187 Robb Thomas	.10	.02
❑	188 Shane Conlan	.10	.02
❑	189 Michael Zordich RC	.10	.02
❑	190 Emmitt Smith	3.00	1.50
❑	191 Robert Blackmon	.10	.02
❑	192 Carl Lee	.10	.02
❑	193 Harry Galbreath	.10	.02
❑	194 Ed King	.10	.02
❑	195 Stan Thomas	.10	.02
❑	196 Andre Waters	.10	.02
❑	197 Pat Harlow	.10	.02
❑	198 Zefross Moss	.10	.02
❑	199 Bobby Hebert	.10	.02
❑	200 Doug Riesenberg	.10	.02
❑	201 Mike Croel	.10	.02
❑	202 Jeff Jaeger	.10	.02
❑	203 Gary Plummer	.10	.02
❑	204 Chris Jacke	.10	.02
❑	205 Neil O'Donnell	.15	.05
❑	206 Mark Bortz	.10	.02
❑	207 Tim Barnett	.10	.02
❑	208 Jerry Ball	.10	.02
❑	209 Chip Lohmiller	.10	.02
❑	210 Jim Everett	.15	.05
❑	211 Tim McKyer	.10	.02
❑	212 Aaron Craver	.10	.02
❑	213 John L. Williams	.10	.02
❑	214 Simon Fletcher	.10	.02
❑	215 Walter Reeves	.10	.02
❑	216 Terance Mathis	.15	.05
❑	217 Mike Pitts	.10	.02
❑	218 Bruce Matthews	.10	.02
❑	219 Howard Ballard	.10	.02
❑	220 Leonard Russell	.15	.05
❑	221 Michael Stewart	.10	.02
❑	222 Mike Merriweather	.10	.02
❑	223 Ricky Sanders	.10	.02
❑	224 Ray Horton	.10	.02
❑	225 Michael Jackson	.15	.05
❑	226 Bill Romanowski	.10	.02
❑	227 Steve McMichael UER	.15	.05
❑	228 Chris Martin	.10	.02
❑	229 Tim Green	.10	.02
❑	230 Karl Mecklenburg	.10	.02
❑	231 Felix Wright	.10	.02
❑	232 Charles McRae	.10	.02
❑	233 Pete Stoyanovich	.10	.02
❑	234 Stephen Baker	.10	.02
❑	235 Herman Moore	.30	.10
❑	236 Terry McDaniel	.10	.02
❑	237 Dalton Hilliard	.10	.02
❑	238 Gill Byrd	.10	.02
❑	239 Leon Seals	.10	.02
❑	240 Rod Woodson	.30	.10
❑	241 Curtis Duncan	.10	.02
❑	242 Keith Jackson	.15	.05
❑	243 Mark Stepnoski	.15	.05
❑	244 Art Monk	.15	.05
❑	245 Matt Stover	.10	.02
❑	246 John Roper	.10	.02
❑	247 Rodney Hampton	.15	.05
❑	248 Steve Wisniewski	.10	.02
❑	249 Bryan Millard	.10	.02
❑	250 Todd Lyght	.10	.02
❑	251 Marvin Washington	.10	.02
❑	252 Eric Swann	.15	.05
❑	253 Bruce Kozerski	.10	.02
❑	254 Jon Hand	.10	.02
❑	255 Scott Fulhage	.10	.02
❑	256 Chuck Cecil	.10	.02
❑	257 Eric Martin	.10	.02
❑	258 Eric Metcalf	.15	.05
❑	259 T.J. Turner	.10	.02
❑	260 Kirk Lowdermilk	.10	.02
❑	261 Keith McKeller	.10	.02
❑	262 Wymon Henderson	.10	.02
❑	263 David Alexander	.10	.02
❑	264 George Jamison	.10	.02
❑	265 Ken Norton Jr.	.15	.05
❑	266 Jim Lachey	.10	.02
❑	267 Bo Orlando RC	.10	.02
❑	268 Nick Lowery	.10	.02
❑	269 Keith Van Horne	.10	.02
❑	270 Dwight Stone	.10	.02
❑	271 Keith DeLong	.10	.02
❑	272 James Francis	.10	.02
❑	273 Greg McMurtry	.10	.02
❑	274 Ethan Horton	.10	.02
❑	275 Stan Brock	.10	.02
❑	276 Ken Harvey	.10	.02
❑	277 Ronnie Harmon	.10	.02
❑	278 Mike Pritchard	.15	.05
❑	279 Kyle Clifton	.10	.02
❑	280 Anthony Johnson	.15	.05
❑	281 Esera Tuaolo	.10	.02
❑	282 Vernon Turner	.10	.02
❑	283 David Griggs	.10	.02
❑	284 Dino Hackett	.10	.02
❑	285 Carwell Gardner	.10	.02
❑	286 Ron Hall	.10	.02
❑	287 Reggie White	.30	.10
❑	288 Checklist 1-100	.10	.02
❑	289 Checklist 101-200	.10	.02
❑	290 Checklist 201-300	.10	.02
❑	291 Mark Clayton MC	.10	.02
❑	292 Pat Swilling MC	.10	.02
❑	293 Ernest Givins MC	.10	.02
❑	294 Broderick Thomas MC	.10	.02
❑	295 John Friesz MC	.10	.02
❑	296 Cornelius Bennett MC	.10	.02
❑	297 Anthony Carter MC	.15	.05
❑	298 Earnest Byner MC	.10	.02
❑	299 Michael Irvin MC	.30	.10
❑	300 Cortez Kennedy MC	.10	.02
❑	301 Barry Sanders MC	1.50	.60
❑	302 Mike Croel MC	.10	.02
❑	303 Emmitt Smith MC	2.00	.75
❑	304 Leonard Russell MC	.10	.02
❑	305 Neal Anderson MC	.10	.02
❑	306 Derrick Thomas MC	.15	.05
❑	307 Mark Rypien MC	.10	.02
❑	308 Reggie White MC	.15	.05
❑	309 Rod Woodson MC	.15	.05
❑	310 Rodney Hampton MC	.15	.05
❑	311 Carnell Lake	.10	.02
❑	312 Robert Delpino	.10	.02
❑	313 Brian Blades	.15	.05
❑	314 Marc Spindler	.10	.02
❑	315 Scott Norwood	.10	.02
❑	316 Frank Warren	.10	.02
❑	317 David Treadwell	.10	.02
❑	318 Steve Broussard	.10	.02
❑	319 Lorenzo Lynch	.10	.02
❑	320 Ray Agnew	.10	.02
❑	321 Derrick Walker	.10	.02
❑	322 Vinson Smith RC	.10	.02
❑	323 Gary Clark	.30	.10
❑	324 Charles Haley	.15	.05
❑	325 Keith Byars	.10	.02
❑	326 Winston Moss	.10	.02
❑	327 Paul McJulien RC UER	.10	.02
❑	328 Tony Covington	.10	.02
❑	329 Mark Carrier DB	.10	.02
❑	330 Mark Tuinei	.10	.02
❑	331 Tracy Simien RC	.10	.02
❑	332 Jeff Wright	.10	.02
❑	333 Bryan Cox	.15	.05
❑	334 Lonnie Young	.10	.02
❑	335 Clarence Verdin	.10	.02
❑	336 Dan Fike	.10	.02
❑	337 Steve Sewell	.10	.02
❑	338 Gary Zimmerman	.10	.02
❑	339 Barney Bussey	.10	.02
❑	340 William Perry	.15	.05
❑	341 Jeff Hostetler	.15	.05
❑	342 Doug Smith	.10	.02
❑	343 Cleveland Gary	.10	.02
❑	344 Todd Marinovich	.10	.02
❑	345 Rich Moran	.10	.02
❑	346 Tony Woods	.10	.02
❑	347 Vaughan Johnson	.10	.02
❑	348 Marv Cook	.10	.02
❑	349 Pierce Holt	.10	.02
❑	350 Gerald Williams	.10	.02
❑	351 Kevin Butler	.10	.02
❑	352 William White	.10	.02
❑	353 Henry Rolling	.10	.02
❑	354 James Joseph	.10	.02
❑	355 Vinny Testaverde	.15	.05
❑	356 Scott Radecic	.10	.02
❑	357 Lee Johnson	.10	.02
❑	358 Steve Tasker	.15	.05
❑	359 David Lutz	.10	.02
❑	360 Audray McMillian UER	.10	.02
❑	361 Brad Baxter	.10	.02
❑	362 Mark Dennis	.10	.02
❑	363 Erric Pegram	.15	.05
❑	364 Sean Jones	.10	.02
❑	365 William Roberts	.10	.02
❑	366 Steve Young	1.00	.40
❑	367 Joe Jacoby	.10	.02

❑ 368	Richard Brown RC	.10	.02
❑ 369	Keith Kartz	.10	.02
❑ 370	Freddie Joe Nunn	.10	.02
❑ 371	Darren Comeaux	.10	.02
❑ 372	Larry Brown DB	.10	.02
❑ 373	Haywood Jeffires	.15	.05
❑ 374	Tom Newberry	.10	.02
❑ 375	Steve Bono RC	.30	.10
❑ 376	Kevin Ross	.10	.02
❑ 377	Kelvin Pritchett	.10	.02
❑ 378	Jessie Hester	.10	.02
❑ 379	Mitchell Price	.10	.02
❑ 380	Barry Foster	.15	.05
❑ 381	Reyna Thompson	.10	.02
❑ 382	Cris Carter	.75	.30
❑ 383	Lemuel Stinson	.10	.02
❑ 384	Rod Bernstine	.10	.02
❑ 385	James Lofton	.15	.05
❑ 386	Kevin Murphy	.10	.02
❑ 387	Greg Townsend	.10	.02
❑ 388	Edgar Bennett RC	.30	.10
❑ 389	Rob Moore	.15	.05
❑ 390	Eugene Lockhart	.10	.02
❑ 391	Bern Brostek	.10	.02
❑ 392	Craig Heyward	.15	.05
❑ 393	Ferrell Edmunds	.10	.02
❑ 394	John Kasay	.10	.02
❑ 395	Jesse Sapolu	.10	.02
❑ 396	Jim Breech	.10	.02
❑ 397	Neil Smith	.30	.10
❑ 398	Bryce Paup	.30	.10
❑ 399	Tony Tolbert	.10	.02
❑ 400	Bubby Brister	.10	.02
❑ 401	Dennis Smith	.10	.02
❑ 402	Dan Owens	.10	.02
❑ 403	Steve Beuerlein	.15	.05
❑ 404	Rick Tuten	.10	.02
❑ 405	Eric Allen	.10	.02
❑ 406	Eric Hill	.10	.02
❑ 407	Don Warren	.10	.02
❑ 408	Greg Jackson	.10	.02
❑ 409	Chris Doleman	.10	.02
❑ 410	Anthony Munoz	.15	.05
❑ 411	Michael Young	.10	.02
❑ 412	Cornelius Bennett	.15	.05
❑ 413	Ray Childress	.10	.02
❑ 414	Kevin Call	.10	.02
❑ 415	Burt Grossman	.10	.02
❑ 416	Scott Miller	.10	.02
❑ 417	Tim Newton	.10	.02
❑ 418	Robert Young	.10	.02
❑ 419	Tommy Vardell RC	.10	.02
❑ 420	Michael Walter	.10	.02
❑ 421	Chris Port RC	.10	.02
❑ 422	Carlton Haselrig RC	.10	.02
❑ 423	Rodney Peete	.15	.05
❑ 424	Scott Stephen	.10	.02
❑ 425	Chris Warren	.30	.10
❑ 426	Scott Galbraith RC	.10	.02
❑ 427	Fuad Reveiz UER	.10	.02
❑ 428	Irv Eatman	.10	.02
❑ 429	David Szott	.10	.02
❑ 430	Brent Williams	.10	.02
❑ 431	Mike Horan	.10	.02
❑ 432	Brent Jones	.15	.05
❑ 433	Paul Gruber	.10	.02
❑ 434	Carlos Huerta	.10	.02
❑ 435	Scott Case	.10	.02
❑ 436	Greg Davis	.10	.02
❑ 437	Ken Clarke	.10	.02
❑ 438	Alfred Williams	.10	.02
❑ 439	Jim C. Jensen	.10	.02
❑ 440	Louis Lipps	.10	.02
❑ 441	Larry Roberts	.10	.02
❑ 442	James Jones DT	.10	.02
❑ 443	Don Mosebar	.10	.02
❑ 444	Quinn Early	.15	.05
❑ 445	Robert Brown	.10	.02
❑ 446	Tom Thayer	.10	.02
❑ 447	Michael Irvin	.30	.10
❑ 448	Jarrod Bunch	.10	.02
❑ 449	Riki Ellison	.10	.02
❑ 450	Joe Phillips	.10	.02
❑ 451	Ernest Givins	.15	.05
❑ 452	Glenn Parker	.10	.02
❑ 453	Brett Perriman UER	.30	.10
❑ 454	Jayice Pearson RC	.10	.02

❑ 455	Mark Jackson	.10	.02
❑ 456	Siran Stacy RC	.10	.02
❑ 457	Rufus Porter	.10	.02
❑ 458	Michael Ball	.10	.02
❑ 459	Craig Taylor	.10	.02
❑ 460	George Thomas RC	.10	.02
❑ 461	Alvin Wright	.10	.02
❑ 462	Ron Hallstrom	.10	.02
❑ 463	Mike Mooney RC	.10	.02
❑ 464	Dexter Carter	.10	.02
❑ 465	Marty Carter RC	.10	.02
❑ 466	Pat Swilling	.10	.02
❑ 467	Mike Golic	.10	.02
❑ 468	Reggie Roby	.10	.02
❑ 469	Randall McDaniel	.10	.02
❑ 470	John Stephens	.10	.02
❑ 471	Ricardo McDonald RC	.10	.02
❑ 472	Wilber Marshall	.10	.02
❑ 473	Jim Sweeney	.10	.02
❑ 474	Ernie Jones	.10	.02
❑ 475	Bennie Blades	.10	.02
❑ 476	Don Beebe	.10	.02
❑ 477	Grant Feasel	.10	.02
❑ 478	Ernie Mills	.10	.02
❑ 479	Tony Jones T	.10	.02
❑ 480	Jeff Uhlenhake	.10	.02
❑ 481	Gaston Green	.10	.02
❑ 482	John Taylor	.15	.05
❑ 483	Anthony Smith	.10	.02
❑ 484	Tony Bennett	.10	.02
❑ 485	David Brandon RC	.10	.02
❑ 486	Shawn Jefferson	.10	.02
❑ 487	Christian Okoye	.10	.02
❑ 488	Leonard Marshall	.10	.02
❑ 489	Jay Novacek	.15	.05
❑ 490	Harold Green	.10	.02
❑ 491	Bubba McDowell	.10	.02
❑ 492	Gary Anderson RB	.10	.02
❑ 493	Terrell Buckley RC	.10	.02
❑ 494	Jamie Dukes RC	.10	.02
❑ 495	Morten Andersen	.10	.02
❑ 496	Henry Thomas	.10	.02
❑ 497	Bill Lewis	.10	.02
❑ 498	Jeff Cross	.10	.02
❑ 499	Hardy Nickerson	.15	.05
❑ 500	Henry Ellard	.15	.05
❑ 501	Joe Bowden RC	.10	.02
❑ 502	Brian Noble	.10	.02
❑ 503	Mike Cofer	.10	.02
❑ 504	Jeff Bryant	.10	.02
❑ 505	Lomas Brown	.10	.02
❑ 506	Chip Banks	.10	.02
❑ 507	Keith Traylor	.10	.02
❑ 508	Mark Kelso	.10	.02
❑ 509	Dexter McNabb RC	.10	.02
❑ 510	Gene Chilton RC	.10	.02
❑ 511	George Thornton	.10	.02
❑ 512	Jeff Criswell	.10	.02
❑ 513	Brad Edwards	.10	.02
❑ 514	Ron Heller	.10	.02
❑ 515	Tim Brown	.30	.10
❑ 516	Keith Hamilton RC	.15	.05
❑ 517	Mark Higgs	.10	.02
❑ 518	Tommy Barnhardt	.10	.02
❑ 519	Brian Jordan	.15	.05
❑ 520	Ray Crockett	.10	.02
❑ 521	Karl Wilson	.10	.02
❑ 522	Ricky Reynolds	.10	.02
❑ 523	Max Montoya	.10	.02
❑ 524	David Little	.10	.02
❑ 525	Alonzo Mitz RC	.10	.02
❑ 526	Darryll Lewis	.10	.02
❑ 527	Keith Henderson	.10	.02
❑ 528	LeRoy Butler	.10	.02
❑ 529	Rob Burnett	.10	.02
❑ 530	Chris Chandler	.30	.10
❑ 531	Maury Buford	.10	.02
❑ 532	Mark Ingram	.10	.02
❑ 533	Mike Saxon	.10	.02
❑ 534	Bill Fralic	.10	.02
❑ 535	Craig Patterson RC	.10	.02
❑ 536	John Randle	.15	.05
❑ 537	Dwayne Harper	.10	.02
❑ 538	Chris Hakel RC	.10	.02
❑ 539	Maurice Hurst	.10	.02
❑ 540	Warren Powers UER	.10	.02
❑ 541	Will Wolford	.10	.02

❑ 542	Dennis Gibson	.10	.02
❑ 543	Jackie Slater	.10	.02
❑ 544	Floyd Turner	.10	.02
❑ 545	Guy McIntyre	.10	.02
❑ 546	Eric Green	.10	.02
❑ 547	Rohn Stark	.10	.02
❑ 548	William Fuller	.10	.02
❑ 549	Alvin Harper	.15	.05
❑ 550	Mark Clayton	.15	.05
❑ 551	Natu Tuatagaloa RC	.10	.02
❑ 552	Fred Barnett	.30	.10
❑ 553	Bob Whitfield RC	.10	.02
❑ 554	Courtney Hall	.10	.02
❑ 555	Brian Mitchell	.15	.05
❑ 556	Patrick Hunter	.10	.02
❑ 557	Rick Bryan	.10	.02
❑ 558	Anthony Carter	.15	.05
❑ 559	Jim Wahler	.10	.02
❑ 560	Joe Morris	.10	.02
❑ 561	Tony Zendejas	.10	.02
❑ 562	Mervyn Fernandez	.10	.02
❑ 563	Jamie Williams	.10	.02
❑ 564	Darrell Thompson	.10	.02
❑ 565	Adrian Cooper	.10	.02
❑ 566	Chris Goode	.10	.02
❑ 567	Jeff Davidson RC	.10	.02
❑ 568	James Hasty	.10	.02
❑ 569	Chris Mims RC	.10	.02
❑ 570	Ray Seals RC	.10	.02
❑ 571	Myron Guyton	.10	.02
❑ 572	Todd McNair	.10	.02
❑ 573	Andre Tippett	.10	.02
❑ 574	Kirby Jackson	.10	.02
❑ 575	Mel Gray	.15	.05
❑ 576	Stephone Paige	.10	.02
❑ 577	Scott Davis	.10	.02
❑ 578	John Gesek	.10	.02
❑ 579	Earnest Byner	.10	.02
❑ 580	John Friesz	.15	.05
❑ 581	Al Smith	.10	.02
❑ 582	Flipper Anderson	.10	.02
❑ 583	Amp Lee RC	.10	.02
❑ 584	Greg Lloyd	.15	.05
❑ 585	Cortez Kennedy	.15	.05
❑ 586	Keith Sims	.10	.02
❑ 587	Terry Allen	.30	.10
❑ 588	David Fulcher	.10	.02
❑ 589	Chris Hinton	.10	.02
❑ 590	Tim McDonald	.10	.02
❑ 591	Bruce Armstrong	.10	.02
❑ 592	Sterling Sharpe	.30	.10
❑ 593	Tom Rathman	.10	.02
❑ 594	Bill Brooks	.10	.02
❑ 595	Broderick Thomas	.10	.02
❑ 596	Jim Wilks	.10	.02
❑ 597	Tyrone Braxton UER	.10	.02
❑ 598	Checklist 301-400 UER	.10	.02
❑ 599	Checklist 401-500	.10	.02
❑ 600	Checklist 501-600	.10	.02
❑ 601	Andre Reed MC	.75	.30
❑ 602	Troy Aikman MC	4.00	2.00
❑ 603	Dan Marino MC	6.00	2.50
❑ 604	Randall Cunningham MC	.75	.30
❑ 605	Jim Kelly MC	1.50	.60
❑ 606	Deion Sanders MC	2.00	.75
❑ 607	Junior Seau MC	1.50	.60
❑ 608	Jerry Rice MC	4.00	2.00
❑ 609	Bruce Smith MC	.75	.30
❑ 610	Lawrence Taylor MC	1.50	.60
❑ 611	Todd Collins RC	.50	.20
❑ 612	Ty Detmer	1.50	.60
❑ 613	Browning Nagle	.50	.20
❑ 614	Tony Sacca RC UER	.50	.20
❑ 615	Boomer Esiason	.75	.30
❑ 616	Billy Joe Tolliver	.50	.20
❑ 617	Leslie O'Neal	.75	.30
❑ 618	Mark Wheeler RC	.50	.20
❑ 619	Eric Dickerson	.75	.30
❑ 620	Phil Simms	.75	.30
❑ 621	Troy Vincent RC	.50	.20
❑ 622	Jason Hanson RC	.75	.30
❑ 623	Andre Reed	.75	.30
❑ 624	Russell Maryland	.50	.20
❑ 625	Steve Emtman RC	.50	.20
❑ 626	Sean Gilbert RC	.75	.30
❑ 627	Dana Hall RC	.50	.20
❑ 628	Dan McGwire	.50	.20

❑	629 Lewis Billups	.50	.20
❑	630 Darryl Williams RC	.50	.20
❑	631 Dwayne Sabb RC	.50	.20
❑	632 Mark Royals	.50	.20
❑	633 Cary Conklin	.50	.20
❑	634 Al Toon	.75	.30
❑	635 Junior Seau	1.50	.60
❑	636 Greg Skrepenak RC UER 60	.50	.20
❑	637 Deion Sanders	3.00	1.50
❑	638 Steve DeOssie	.50	.20
❑	639 Randall Cunningham	1.50	.60
❑	640 Jim Kelly	1.50	.60
❑	641 Michael Brandon RC	.50	.20
❑	642 Clayton Holmes RC	.50	.20
❑	643 Webster Slaughter	.50	.20
❑	644 Ricky Proehl	.50	.20
❑	645 Jerry Rice	5.00	2.50
❑	646 Carl Banks	.50	.20
❑	647 J.J.Birden	.50	.20
❑	648 Tracy Scroggins RC	.50	.20
❑	649 Alonzo Spellman RC	.75	.30
❑	650 Joe Montana	8.00	3.00
❑	651 Courtney Hawkins RC	.75	.30
❑	652 Corey Widmer RC	.50	.20
❑	653 Robert Brooks RC	4.00	1.50
❑	654 Darren Woodson RC	1.50	.60
❑	655 Derrick Fenner	.50	.20
❑	656 Steve Christie	.50	.20
❑	657 Chester McGlockton RC	.75	.30
❑	658 Steve Israel RC	.50	.20
❑	659 Robert Harris RC	.50	.20
❑	660 Dan Marino	8.00	3.00
❑	661 Ed McCaffrey	5.00	2.00
❑	662 Johnny Mitchell RC	.50	.20
❑	663 Timm Rosenbach	.50	.20
❑	664 Anthony Miller	.75	.30
❑	665 Merril Hoge	.50	.20
❑	666 Eugene Chung RC	.50	.20
❑	667 Rueben Mayes	.50	.20
❑	668 Martin Bayless	.50	.20
❑	669 Ashley Ambrose RC	1.50	.60
❑	670 Michael Cofer UER	.50	.20
❑	671 Shane Dronett RC	.50	.20
❑	672 Bernie Kosar	.75	.30
❑	673 Mike Singletary	.75	.30
❑	674 Mike Lodish RC	.50	.20
❑	675 Phillippi Sparks RC	.50	.20
❑	676 Joel Steed RC	.50	.20
❑	677 Kevin Fagan	.50	.20
❑	678 Randal Hill	.50	.20
❑	679 Ken O'Brien	.50	.20
❑	680 Lawrence Taylor	1.50	.60
❑	681 Harvey Williams	1.50	.60
❑	682 Quentin Coryatt RC	.50	.20
❑	683 Brett Favre	150.00	90.00
❑	684 Robert Jones RC	.50	.20
❑	685 Michael Dean Perry	.75	.30
❑	686 Bruce Smith	1.50	.60
❑	687 Troy Auzenne RC	.50	.20
❑	688 Thomas McLemore RC	.50	.20
❑	689 Dale Carter RC	.75	.30
❑	690 Marc Boutte RC	.50	.20
❑	691 Jeff George	1.50	.60
❑	692 Dion Lambert RC	.50	.20
❑	693 Vaughn Dunbar RC	.50	.20
❑	694 Derek Brown TE RC	.50	.20
❑	695 Troy Aikman	5.00	2.50
❑	696 John Fina RC	.50	.20
❑	697 Kevin Smith RC DB	.50	.20
❑	698 Corey Miller RC	.50	.20
❑	699 Lance Olberding RC	.50	.20
❑	700 Checklist 601-700 UER	.50	.20
❑	P1 Promo Sheet Natl.	10.00	4.00
❑	P2 Promo Sheet Diam.Day	12.00	5.00

1993 Stadium Club

❑	COMPLETE SET (550)	40.00	15.00
❑	COMP.SERIES 1 (250)	25.00	10.00
❑	COMP.SERIES 2 (250)	15.00	6.00
❑	COMP.HIGH SERIES (50)	8.00	4.00
❑	COMP.HIGH FACT.SET (51)	12.00	5.00
❑	1 Sterling Sharpe	.20	.07
❑	2 Chris Burkett	.10	.02
❑	3 Santana Dotson	.20	.07
❑	4 Michael Jackson	.20	.07
❑	5 Neal Anderson	.10	.02
❑	6 Bryan Cox	.10	.02

❑	7 Dennis Gibson	.10	.02
❑	8 Jeff Graham	.20	.07
❑	9 Roger Ruzek	.10	.02
❑	10 Duane Bickett	.10	.02
❑	11 Charles Mann	.10	.02
❑	12 Tommy Maddox	.40	.15
❑	13 Vaughn Dunbar	.10	.02
❑	14 Gary Plummer	.10	.02
❑	15 Chris Miller	.20	.07
❑	16 Chris Warren	.20	.07
❑	17 Alvin Harper	.20	.07
❑	18 Eric Dickerson	.20	.07
❑	19 Mike Jones	.10	.02
❑	20 Ernest Givins	.20	.07
❑	21 Natrone Means RC	.40	.15
❑	22 Doug Riesenberg	.10	.02
❑	23 Barry Word	.10	.02
❑	24 Sean Salisbury	.10	.02
❑	25 Derrick Fenner	.10	.02
❑	26 David Howard	.10	.02
❑	27 Mark Kelso	.10	.02
❑	28 Todd Lyght	.10	.02
❑	29 Dana Hall	.10	.02
❑	30 Eric Metcalf	.20	.07
❑	31 Jason Hanson	.10	.02
❑	32 Dwight Stone	.10	.02
❑	33 Johnny Mitchell	.10	.02
❑	34 Reggie Roby	.10	.02
❑	35 Terrell Buckley	.10	.02
❑	36 Steve McMichael	.20	.07
❑	37 Marty Carter	.10	.02
❑	38 Seth Joyner	.10	.02
❑	39 Rohn Stark	.10	.02
❑	40 Eric Curry RC	.10	.02
❑	41 Tommy Barnhardt	.10	.02
❑	42 Karl Mecklenburg	.10	.02
❑	43 Darion Conner	.10	.02
❑	44 Ronnie Harmon	.10	.02
❑	45 Cortez Kennedy	.20	.07
❑	46 Tim Brown	.40	.15
❑	47 Bill Lewis	.10	.02
❑	48 Randall McDaniel	.10	.02
❑	49 Curtis Duncan	.10	.02
❑	50 Troy Aikman	1.50	.60
❑	51 David Klingler	.10	.02
❑	52 Brent Jones	.20	.07
❑	53 Dave Krieg	.20	.07
❑	54 Bruce Smith	.40	.15
❑	55 Vincent Brown	.10	.02
❑	56 O.J.McDuffie RC	.40	.15
❑	57 Cleveland Gary	.10	.02
❑	58 Larry Centers RC	.40	.15
❑	59 Pepper Johnson	.10	.02
❑	60 Dan Marino	3.00	1.25
❑	61 Robert Porcher	.10	.02
❑	62 Jim Harbaugh	.40	.15
❑	63 Sam Mills	.10	.02
❑	64 Gary Anderson RB	.10	.02
❑	65 Neil O'Donnell	.20	.07
❑	66 Keith Byars	.10	.02
❑	67 Jeff Herrod	.10	.02
❑	68 Marion Butts	.10	.02
❑	69 Terry McDaniel	.10	.02
❑	70 John Elway	3.00	1.25
❑	71 Steve Broussard	.10	.02
❑	72 Kelvin Martin	.10	.02
❑	73 Tom Carter RC	.20	.07
❑	74 Bryce Paup	.20	.07
❑	75 Jim Kelly UER	.20	.07
❑	76 Bill Romanowski	.10	.02
❑	77 Andre Collins	.10	.02
❑	78 Mike Farr	.10	.02
❑	79 Henry Ellard	.20	.07
❑	80 Dale Carter	.10	.02
❑	81 Johnny Bailey	.10	.02
❑	82 Garrison Hearst RC	1.50	.60
❑	83 Brent Williams	.10	.02
❑	84 Ricardo McDonald	.10	.02
❑	85 Emmitt Smith	3.00	1.50
❑	86 Vai Sikahema	.10	.02
❑	87 Jackie Harris	.10	.02
❑	88 Alonzo Spellman	.10	.02
❑	89 Mark Wheeler	.10	.02
❑	90 Dalton Hilliard	.10	.02
❑	91 Mark Higgs	.10	.02
❑	92 Aaron Wallace	.10	.02
❑	93 Earnest Byner	.10	.02
❑	94 Stanley Richard	.10	.02
❑	95 Cris Carter	.40	.15
❑	96 Bobby Houston RC	.10	.02
❑	97 Craig Heyward	.20	.07
❑	98 Bernie Kosar	.20	.07
❑	99 Mike Croel	.10	.02
❑	100 Deion Sanders	1.00	.40
❑	101 Warren Moon	.20	.07
❑	102 Christian Okoye	.10	.02
❑	103 Ricky Watters	.40	.15
❑	104 Eric Swann	.20	.07
❑	105 Rodney Hampton	.20	.07
❑	106 Daryl Johnston	.20	.07
❑	107 Andre Reed	.20	.07
❑	108 Jerome Bettis RC	8.00	4.00
❑	109 Eugene Daniel	.10	.02
❑	110 Leonard Russell	.20	.07
❑	111 Darryl Williams	.10	.02
❑	112 Rod Woodson	.40	.15
❑	113 Boomer Esiason	.20	.07
❑	114 James Hasty	.10	.02
❑	115 Marc Boutte	.10	.02
❑	116 Tom Waddle	.10	.02
❑	117 Lawrence Dawsey	.10	.02
❑	118 Mark Collins	.10	.02
❑	119 Willie Gault	.10	.02
❑	120 Barry Sanders	2.50	1.00
❑	121 Leroy Hoard	.20	.07
❑	122 Anthony Munoz	.20	.07
❑	123 Jesse Sapolu	.10	.02
❑	124 Art Monk	.20	.07
❑	125 Randal Hill	.10	.02
❑	126 John Offerdahl	.10	.02
❑	127 Carlos Jenkins	.10	.02
❑	128 Al Smith	.10	.02
❑	129 Michael Irvin	.40	.15
❑	130 Kenneth Davis	.10	.02
❑	131 Curtis Conway RC	.75	.30
❑	132 Steve Atwater	.10	.02
❑	133 Neil Smith	.40	.15
❑	134 Steve Everitt RC	.10	.02
❑	135 Chris Mims	.10	.02
❑	136 Rickey Jackson	.10	.02
❑	137 Edgar Bennett	.40	.15
❑	138 Mike Pritchard	.20	.07
❑	139 Richard Dent	.20	.07
❑	140 Barry Foster	.20	.07
❑	141 Eugene Robinson	.10	.02
❑	142 Jackie Slater	.10	.02
❑	143 Paul Gruber	.10	.02
❑	144 Rob Moore	.20	.07
❑	145 Robert Smith RC	2.50	1.00
❑	146 Lorenzo White	.10	.02
❑	147 Tommy Vardell	.10	.02
❑	148 Dave Meggett	.10	.02
❑	149 Vince Workman	.10	.02
❑	150 Terry Allen	.40	.15
❑	151 Howie Long	.40	.15
❑	152 Charles Haley	.20	.07
❑	153 Pete Metzelaars	.10	.02
❑	154 John Copeland RC	.20	.07
❑	155 Aeneas Williams	.10	.02
❑	156 Ricky Sanders	.10	.02
❑	157 Andre Ware	.10	.02
❑	158 Tony Paige	.10	.02
❑	159 Jerome Henderson	.10	.02
❑	160 Harold Green	.10	.02
❑	161 Wymon Henderson	.10	.02
❑	162 Andre Rison	.20	.07
❑	163 Donald Evans	.10	.02

❑ 164 Todd Scott	.10	.02
❑ 165 Steve Emtman	.10	.02
❑ 166 William Fuller	.10	.02
❑ 167 Michael Dean Perry	.20	.07
❑ 168 Randall Cunningham	.40	.15
❑ 169 Toi Cook	.10	.02
❑ 170 Browning Nagle	.10	.02
❑ 171 Darryl Henley	.10	.02
❑ 172 George Teague RC	.20	.07
❑ 173 Derrick Thomas	.40	.15
❑ 174 Jay Novacek	.20	.07
❑ 175 Mark Carrier DB	.10	.02
❑ 176 Kevin Fagan	.10	.02
❑ 177 Nate Lewis	.10	.02
❑ 178 Courtney Hawkins	.10	.02
❑ 179 Robert Blackmon	.10	.02
❑ 180 Rick Mirer RC	.40	.15
❑ 181 Mike Lodish	.10	.02
❑ 182 Jarrod Bunch	.10	.02
❑ 183 Anthony Smith	.10	.02
❑ 184 Brian Noble	.10	.02
❑ 185 Eric Bieniemy	.10	.02
❑ 186 Keith Jackson	.20	.07
❑ 187 Eric Martin	.10	.02
❑ 188 Vance Johnson	.10	.02
❑ 189 Kevin Mack	.10	.02
❑ 190 Rich Camarillo	.10	.02
❑ 191 Ashley Ambrose	.10	.02
❑ 192 Ray Childress	.10	.02
❑ 193 Jim Arnold	.10	.02
❑ 194 Ricky Ervins	.10	.02
❑ 195 Gary Anderson K	.10	.02
❑ 196 Eric Allen	.10	.02
❑ 197 Roger Craig	.20	.07
❑ 198 Jon Vaughn	.10	.02
❑ 199 Tim McDonald	.10	.02
❑ 200 Broderick Thomas	.10	.02
❑ 201 Jessie Tuggle	.10	.02
❑ 202 Alonzo Mitz	.10	.02
❑ 203 Harvey Williams	.20	.07
❑ 204 Russell Maryland	.10	.02
❑ 205 Marvin Washington	.10	.02
❑ 206 Jim Everett	.20	.07
❑ 207 Trace Armstrong	.10	.02
❑ 208 Steve Young	1.50	.60
❑ 209 Tony Woods	.10	.02
❑ 210 Brett Favre	4.00	2.00
❑ 211 Nate Odomes	.10	.02
❑ 212 Ricky Proehl	.10	.02
❑ 213 Jim Dombrowski	.10	.02
❑ 214 Anthony Carter	.20	.07
❑ 215 Tracy Simien	.10	.02
❑ 216 Clay Matthews	.20	.07
❑ 217 Patrick Bates RC	.10	.02
❑ 218 Jeff George	.40	.15
❑ 219 David Fulcher	.10	.02
❑ 220 Phil Simms	.20	.07
❑ 221 Eugene Chung	.10	.02
❑ 222 Reggie Cobb	.10	.02
❑ 223 Jim Sweeney	.10	.02
❑ 224 Greg Lloyd	.20	.07
❑ 225 Sean Jones	.10	.02
❑ 226 Marvin Jones RC	.10	.02
❑ 227 Bill Brooks	.10	.02
❑ 228 Moe Gardner	.10	.02
❑ 229 Louis Oliver	.10	.02
❑ 230 Flipper Anderson	.10	.02
❑ 231 Marc Spindler	.10	.02
❑ 232 Jerry Rice	2.00	.75
❑ 233 Chip Lohmiller	.10	.02
❑ 234 Nolan Harrison	.10	.02
❑ 235 Heath Sherman	.10	.02
❑ 236 Reyna Thompson	.10	.02
❑ 237 Derrick Walker	.10	.02
❑ 238 Rufus Porter	.10	.02
❑ 239 Checklist 1-125	.10	.02
❑ 240 Checklist 126-250	.10	.02
❑ 241 John Elway MC	1.50	.60
❑ 242 Troy Aikman MC	.75	.30
❑ 243 Steve Emtman MC	.10	.02
❑ 244 Ricky Watters MC	.20	.07
❑ 245 Barry Foster MC	.10	.02
❑ 246 Dan Marino MC	1.50	.60
❑ 247 Reggie White MC	.20	.07
❑ 248 Thurman Thomas MC	.20	.07
❑ 249 Broderick Thomas MC	.10	.02
❑ 250 Joe Montana MC	1.50	.60
❑ 251 Tim Goad	.10	.02
❑ 252 Joe Nash	.10	.02
❑ 253 Anthony Johnson	.20	.07
❑ 254 Carl Pickens	.20	.07
❑ 255 Steve Beuerlein	.20	.07
❑ 256 Anthony Newman	.10	.02
❑ 257 Corey Miller	.10	.02
❑ 258 Steve DeBerg	.10	.02
❑ 259 Johnny Holland	.10	.02
❑ 260 Jerry Ball	.10	.02
❑ 261 Siupeli Malamala RC	.10	.02
❑ 262 Steve Wisniewski	.10	.02
❑ 263 Kelvin Pritchett	.10	.02
❑ 264 Chris Gardocki	.10	.02
❑ 265 Henry Thomas	.10	.02
❑ 266 Arthur Marshall RC	.10	.02
❑ 267 Quinn Early	.20	.07
❑ 268 Jonathan Hayes	.10	.02
❑ 269 Erric Pegram	.20	.07
❑ 270 Clyde Simmons	.10	.02
❑ 271 Eric Moten	.10	.02
❑ 272 Brian Mitchell	.20	.07
❑ 273 Adrian Cooper	.10	.02
❑ 274 Gaston Green	.10	.02
❑ 275 John Taylor	.20	.07
❑ 276 Jeff Uhlenhake	.10	.02
❑ 277 Phil Hansen	.10	.02
❑ 278A Kev.Williams RC WR ERR	.40	.15
❑ 278B Kev.Williams RC WR COR	.40	.15
❑ 279 Robert Massey	.10	.02
❑ 280A Drew Bledsoe RC ERR	10.00	4.00
❑ 280B Drew Bledsoe RC COR	5.00	2.00
❑ 281 Walter Reeves	.10	.02
❑ 282A Carlton Gray RC ERR	.25	.08
❑ 282B Carlton Gray RC COR	.15	.05
❑ 283 Derek Brown TE	.10	.02
❑ 284 Martin Mayhew	.10	.02
❑ 285 Sean Gilbert	.20	.07
❑ 286 Jessie Hester	.10	.02
❑ 287 Mark Clayton	.10	.02
❑ 288 Blair Thomas	.10	.02
❑ 289 J.J. Birden	.10	.02
❑ 290 Shannon Sharpe	.40	.15
❑ 291 Richard Fain RC	.10	.02
❑ 292 Gene Atkins	.10	.02
❑ 293 Burt Grossman	.10	.02
❑ 294 Chris Doleman	.10	.02
❑ 295 Pat Swilling	.10	.02
❑ 296 Mike Kenn	.10	.02
❑ 297 Merril Hoge	.10	.02
❑ 298 Don Mosebar	.10	.02
❑ 299 Kevin Smith	.20	.07
❑ 300 Darrell Green	.10	.02
❑ 301A Dan Footman RC ERR	.25	.08
❑ 301B Dan Footman RC COR	.15	.05
❑ 302 Vestee Jackson	.10	.02
❑ 303 Carwell Gardner	.10	.02
❑ 304 Amp Lee	.10	.02
❑ 305 Bruce Matthews	.10	.02
❑ 306 Antone Davis	.10	.02
❑ 307 Dean Biasucci	.10	.02
❑ 308 Maurice Hurst	.10	.02
❑ 309 John Kasay	.10	.02
❑ 310 Lawrence Taylor	.20	.07
❑ 311 Ken Harvey	.10	.02
❑ 312 Willie Davis	.20	.07
❑ 313 Tony Bennett	.10	.02
❑ 314 Jay Schroeder	.10	.02
❑ 315 Darren Perry	.10	.02
❑ 316A Troy Drayton RC ERR	.25	.08
❑ 316B Troy Drayton RC COR	.15	.05
❑ 317A Dan Williams RC ERR	.25	.08
❑ 317B Dan Williams RC COR	.15	.05
❑ 318 Michael Haynes	.20	.07
❑ 319 Renaldo Turnbull	.10	.02
❑ 320 Junior Seau	.40	.15
❑ 321 Ray Crockett	.10	.02
❑ 322 Will Furrer	.10	.02
❑ 323 Byron Evans	.10	.02
❑ 324 Jim McMahon	.20	.07
❑ 325 Robert Jones	.10	.02
❑ 326 Eric Davis	.10	.02
❑ 327 Jeff Cross	.10	.02
❑ 328 Kyle Clifton	.10	.02
❑ 329 Haywood Jeffires	.20	.07
❑ 330 Jeff Hostetler	.20	.07
❑ 331 Darryl Talley	.10	.02
❑ 332 Keith McCants	.10	.02
❑ 333 Mo Lewis	.10	.02
❑ 334 Matt Stover	.10	.02
❑ 335 Ferrell Edmunds	.10	.02
❑ 336 Matt Brock	.10	.02
❑ 337 Ernie Mills	.10	.02
❑ 338 Shane Dronett	.10	.02
❑ 339 Brad Muster	.10	.02
❑ 340 Jesse Solomon	.10	.02
❑ 341 John Randle	.20	.07
❑ 342 Chris Spielman	.20	.07
❑ 343 David Whitmore	.10	.02
❑ 344 Glenn Parker	.10	.02
❑ 345 Marco Coleman	.10	.02
❑ 346 Kenneth Gant	.10	.02
❑ 347 Cris Dishman	.10	.02
❑ 348 Kenny Walker	.10	.02
❑ 349A Roosevelt Potts RC ERR	.25	.08
❑ 349B Roosevelt Potts RC COR	.15	.05
❑ 350 Reggie White	.40	.15
❑ 351 Gerald Robinson	.10	.02
❑ 352 Mark Rypien	.10	.02
❑ 353 Stan Humphries	.20	.07
❑ 354 Chris Singleton	.10	.02
❑ 355 Herschel Walker	.20	.07
❑ 356 Ron Hall	.10	.02
❑ 357 Ethan Horton	.10	.02
❑ 358 Anthony Pleasant	.10	.02
❑ 359A Thomas Smith RC ERR	.25	.08
❑ 359B Thomas Smith RC COR	.15	.05
❑ 360 Audray McMillian	.10	.02
❑ 361 D.J. Johnson	.10	.02
❑ 362 Ron Heller	.10	.02
❑ 363 Bern Brostek	.10	.02
❑ 364 Ronnie Lott	.20	.07
❑ 365 Reggie Johnson	.10	.02
❑ 366 Lin Elliott	.10	.02
❑ 367 Lemuel Stinson	.10	.02
❑ 368 William White	.10	.02
❑ 369 Ernie Jones	.10	.02
❑ 370 Tom Rathman	.10	.02
❑ 371 Tommy Kane	.10	.02
❑ 372 David Brandon	.10	.02
❑ 373 Lee Johnson	.10	.02
❑ 374 Wade Wilson	.10	.02
❑ 375 Nick Lowery	.10	.02
❑ 376 Bubba McDowell	.10	.02
❑ 377A Wayne Simmons RC ERR	.25	.08
❑ 377B Wayne Simmons RC COR	.15	.05
❑ 378 Calvin Williams	.20	.07
❑ 379 Courtney Hall	.10	.02
❑ 380 Troy Vincent	.10	.02
❑ 381 Tim McGee	.10	.02
❑ 382 Russell Freeman RC	.10	.02
❑ 383 Steve Tasker	.20	.07
❑ 384A Michael Strahan RC ERR	3.00	1.25
❑ 384B Michael Strahan RC COR	3.00	1.25
❑ 385 Greg Skrepenak	.10	.02
❑ 386 Jake Reed	.20	.07
❑ 387 Pete Stoyanovich	.10	.02
❑ 388 Levon Kirkland	.10	.02
❑ 389 Mel Gray	.20	.07
❑ 390 Brian Washington	.10	.02
❑ 391 Don Griffin	.10	.02
❑ 392 Desmond Howard	.20	.07
❑ 393 Luis Sharpe	.10	.02
❑ 394 Mike Johnson	.10	.02
❑ 395 Andre Tippett	.10	.02
❑ 396 Donnell Woolford	.10	.02
❑ 397A Demetrius DuBose RC ERR	.25	.08
❑ 397B Demetrius DuBose RC COR	.15	.05
❑ 398 Pat Terrell	.10	.02
❑ 399 Todd McNair	.10	.02
❑ 400 Ken Norton	.20	.07
❑ 401 Keith Hamilton	.10	.02
❑ 402 Andy Heck	.10	.02
❑ 403 Jeff Gossett	.10	.02
❑ 404 Dexter McNabb	.10	.02
❑ 405 Richmond Webb	.10	.02
❑ 406 Irving Fryar	.20	.07
❑ 407 Brian Hansen	.10	.02
❑ 408 David Little	.10	.02
❑ 409A Glyn Milburn RC ERR	.40	.15
❑ 409B Glyn Milburn RC COR	.20	.07
❑ 410 Doug Dawson	.10	.02
❑ 411 Scott Mersereau	.10	.02
❑ 412 Don Beebe	.10	.02

❑ 413 Vaughan Johnson .10 .02
❑ 414 Jack Del Rio .10 .02
❑ 415A Darrien Gordon RC ERR .25 .08
❑ 415B Darrien Gordon RC COR .15 .05
❑ 416 Mark Schlereth .10 .02
❑ 417 Lomas Brown .10 .02
❑ 418 William Thomas .10 .02
❑ 419 James Francis .10 .02
❑ 420 Quentin Coryatt .20 .07
❑ 421 Tyji Armstrong .10 .02
❑ 422 Hugh Millen .10 .02
❑ 423 Adrian White RC .10 .02
❑ 424 Eddie Anderson .10 .02
❑ 425 Mark Ingram .10 .02
❑ 426 Ken O'Brien .10 .02
❑ 427 Simon Fletcher .10 .02
❑ 428 Tim McKyer .10 .02
❑ 429 Leonard Marshall .10 .02
❑ 430 Eric Green .10 .02
❑ 431 Leonard Harris .10 .02
❑ 432 Darin Jordan RC .10 .02
❑ 433 Erik Howard .10 .02
❑ 434 David Lang .10 .02
❑ 435 Eric Turner .10 .02
❑ 436 Michael Cofer .10 .02
❑ 437 Jeff Bryant .10 .02
❑ 438 Charles McRae .10 .02
❑ 439 Henry Jones .10 .02
❑ 440 Joe Montana 3.00 1.25
❑ 441 Morten Andersen .10 .02
❑ 442 Jeff Jaeger .10 .02
❑ 443 Leslie O'Neal .20 .07
❑ 444 LeRoy Butler .10 .02
❑ 445 Steve Jordan .10 .02
❑ 446 Brad Edwards .10 .02
❑ 447 J.B. Brown .10 .02
❑ 448 Kerry Cash .10 .02
❑ 449 Mark Tuinei .10 .02
❑ 450 Rodney Peete .10 .02
❑ 451 Sheldon White .10 .02
❑ 452 Wesley Carroll .10 .02
❑ 453 Brad Baxter .10 .02
❑ 454 Mike Pitts .10 .02
❑ 455 Greg Montgomery .10 .02
❑ 456 Kenny Davidson .10 .02
❑ 457 Scott Fulhage .10 .02
❑ 458 Greg Townsend .10 .02
❑ 459 Rod Bernstine .10 .02
❑ 460 Gary Clark .20 .07
❑ 461 Hardy Nickerson .20 .07
❑ 462 Sean Landeta .10 .02
❑ 463 Rob Burnett .10 .02
❑ 464 Fred Barnett .20 .07
❑ 465 John L. Williams .10 .02
❑ 466 Anthony Miller .20 .07
❑ 467 Roman Phifer .10 .02
❑ 468 Rich Moran .10 .02
❑ 469A Willie Roaf RC ERR .25 .08
❑ 469B Willie Roaf RC COR .15 .05
❑ 470 William Perry .20 .07
❑ 471 Marcus Allen .40 .15
❑ 472 Carl Lee .10 .02
❑ 473 Kurt Gouveia .10 .02
❑ 474 Jarvis Williams .10 .02
❑ 475 Alfred Williams .10 .02
❑ 476 Mark Stepnoski .10 .02
❑ 477 Steve Wallace .10 .02
❑ 478 Pat Harlow .10 .02
❑ 479 Chip Banks .10 .02
❑ 480 Cornelius Bennett .20 .07
❑ 481A Ryan McNeil RC ERR .15 .05
❑ 481B Ryan McNeil RC COR .40 .15
❑ 482 Norm Johnson .10 .02
❑ 483 Dermontti Dawson .10 .02
❑ 484 Dwayne White .10 .02
❑ 485 Derek Russell .10 .02
❑ 486 Lionel Washington .10 .02
❑ 487 Eric Hill .10 .02
❑ 488 Micheal Barrow RC .40 .15
❑ 489 Checklist 251-375 UER .10 .02
❑ 490 Checklist 376-500 UER .10 .02
❑ 491 Emmitt Smith MC 1.50 .60
❑ 492 Derrick Thomas MC .20 .07
❑ 493 Deion Sanders MC .40 .15
❑ 494 Randall Cunningham MC .20 .07
❑ 495 Sterling Sharpe MC .20 .07
❑ 496 Barry Sanders MC 1.25 .50
❑ 497 Thurman Thomas MC .20 .07
❑ 498 Brett Favre MC 2.00 .75
❑ 499 Vaughan Johnson MC .10 .02
❑ 500 Steve Young MC .75 .30
❑ 501 Marvin Jones MC .10 .02
❑ 502 Reggie Brooks RC MC .20 .07
❑ 503 Eric Curry MC .10 .02
❑ 504 Drew Bledsoe MC 2.00 .75
❑ 505 Glyn Milburn MC .20 .07
❑ 506 Jerome Bettis MC 4.00 1.50
❑ 507 Robert Smith MC 1.00 .40
❑ 508 Dana Stubblefield RC MC .40 .15
❑ 509 Tom Carter MC .20 .07
❑ 510 Rick Mirer MC .40 .15
❑ 511 Russell Copeland RC .20 .07
❑ 512 Deon Figures RC .10 .02
❑ 513 Tony McGee RC .20 .07
❑ 514 Derrick Lassic RC .10 .02
❑ 515 Everett Lindsay RC .10 .02
❑ 516 Derek Brown RC RBK .10 .02
❑ 517 Harold Alexander RC .10 .02
❑ 518 Tom Scott OL RC .10 .02
❑ 519 Elvis Grbac RC 3.00 1.25
❑ 520 Terry Kirby RC .40 .15
❑ 521 Doug Pelfrey RC .10 .02
❑ 522 Horace Copeland RC .20 .07
❑ 523 Irv Smith RC .10 .02
❑ 524 Lincoln Kennedy RC .10 .02
❑ 525 Jason Elam RC .40 .15
❑ 526 Qadry Ismail RC .40 .15
❑ 527 Artie Smith RC .10 .02
❑ 528 Tyrone Hughes RC .20 .07
❑ 529 Lance Gunn RC .10 .02
❑ 530 Vincent Brisby RC .40 .15
❑ 531 Patrick Robinson RC .10 .02
❑ 532 Rocket Ismail .20 .07
❑ 533 Willie Beamon RC .10 .02
❑ 534 Vaughn Hebron RC .10 .02
❑ 535 Darren Drozdov RC .40 .15
❑ 536 James Jett RC .40 .15
❑ 537 Michael Bates RC .10 .02
❑ 538 Tom Rouen RC .10 .02
❑ 539 Michael Husted RC .10 .02
❑ 540 Greg Robinson RC .10 .02
❑ 541 Carl Banks .10 .02
❑ 542 Kevin Greene .20 .07
❑ 543 Scott Mitchell .40 .15
❑ 544 Michael Brooks .10 .02
❑ 545 Shane Conlan .10 .02
❑ 546 Vinny Testaverde .20 .07
❑ 547 Robert Delpino .10 .02
❑ 548 Bill Fralic .10 .02
❑ 549 Carlton Bailey .10 .02
❑ 550 Johnny Johnson .10 .02
❑ NNO Jerry Rice RB 10.00 4.00
❑ P1 Promo Sheet 5.00 2.00

1994 Stadium Club

❑ COMPLETE SET (630) 60.00 25.00
❑ COMP.SERIES 1 (270) 25.00 10.00
❑ COMP.SERIES 2 (270) 25.00 10.00
❑ COMP.HIGH SERIES (90) 10.00 5.00
❑ 1 Dan Wilkinson RC .20 .07
❑ 2 Chip Lohmiller .10 .02
❑ 3 Roosevelt Potts .10 .02
❑ 4 Martin Mayhew .10 .02
❑ 5 Shane Conlan .10 .02
❑ 6 Sam Adams RC .20 .07
❑ 7 Mike Kenn .10 .02
❑ 8 Tim Goad .10 .02
❑ 9 Tony Jones T .10 .02
❑ 10 Ronald Moore .10 .02
❑ 11 Mark Bortz .10 .02
❑ 12 Darren Carrington .10 .02
❑ 13 Eric Martin .10 .02
❑ 14 Eric Allen .10 .02
❑ 15 Aaron Glenn RC .40 .15
❑ 16 Bryan Cox .10 .02
❑ 17 Levon Kirkland .10 .02
❑ 18 Qadry Ismail .40 .15
❑ 19 Shane Dronett .10 .02
❑ 20 Chris Spielman .20 .07
❑ 21 Rob Fredrickson RC .20 .07
❑ 22 Wayne Simmons .10 .02
❑ 23 Glenn Montgomery .10 .02
❑ 24 Jason Sehorn RC .60 .25
❑ 25 Nick Lowery .10 .02
❑ 26 Dennis Brown .10 .02
❑ 27 Kenneth Davis .10 .02
❑ 28 Shante Carver RC .10 .02
❑ 29 Ryan Yarborough RC .10 .02
❑ 30 Cortez Kennedy .20 .07
❑ 31 Anthony Pleasant .10 .02
❑ 32 Jessie Tuggle .10 .02
❑ 33 Herschel Walker .20 .07
❑ 34 Andre Collins .10 .02
❑ 35 William Floyd RC .40 .15
❑ 36 Harold Green .10 .02
❑ 37 Courtney Hawkins .10 .02
❑ 38 Curtis Conway .40 .15
❑ 39 Ben Coates .20 .07
❑ 40 Natrone Means .40 .15
❑ 41 Eric Hill .10 .02
❑ 42 Keith Kartz .10 .02
❑ 43 Alexander Wright .10 .02
❑ 44 Willie Roaf .10 .02
❑ 45 Vencie Glenn .10 .02
❑ 46 Ronnie Lott .20 .07
❑ 47 George Koonce .10 .02
❑ 48 Rod Woodson .20 .07
❑ 49 Tim Grunhard .10 .02
❑ 50 Cody Carlson .10 .02
❑ 51 Bryant Young RC .60 .25
❑ 52 Jay Novacek .20 .07
❑ 53 Darryl Talley .10 .02
❑ 54 Harry Colon .10 .02
❑ 55 Dave Meggett .10 .02
❑ 56 Aubrey Beavers RC .10 .02
❑ 57 James Folston .10 .02
❑ 58 Willie Davis .20 .07
❑ 59 Jason Elam .20 .07
❑ 60 Eric Metcalf .20 .07
❑ 61 Bruce Armstrong .10 .02
❑ 62 Ron Heller .10 .02
❑ 63 LeRoy Butler .10 .02
❑ 64 Terry Obee .10 .02
❑ 65 Kurt Gouveia .10 .02
❑ 66 Pierce Holt .10 .02
❑ 67 David Alexander .10 .02
❑ 68 Deral Boykin .10 .02
❑ 69 Carl Pickens .20 .07
❑ 70 Broderick Thomas .10 .02
❑ 71 Barry Sanders CT 1.25 .50
❑ 72 Qadry Ismail CT .40 .15
❑ 73 Thurman Thomas CT .40 .15
❑ 74 Junior Seau .40 .15
❑ 75 Vinny Testaverde .20 .07
❑ 76 Tyrone Hughes .20 .07
❑ 77 Nate Newton .10 .02
❑ 78 Eric Swann .20 .07
❑ 79 Brad Baxter .10 .02
❑ 80 Dana Stubblefield .20 .07
❑ 81 Jumbo Elliott .10 .02
❑ 82 Steve Wisniewski .10 .02
❑ 83 Eddie Robinson .10 .02
❑ 84 Isaac Davis .10 .02
❑ 85 Cris Carter .60 .25
❑ 86 Mel Gray .10 .02
❑ 87 Cornelius Bennett .20 .07
❑ 88 Neil O'Donnell .40 .15
❑ 89 Jon Hand .10 .02
❑ 90 John Elway 3.00 1.25
❑ 91 Bill Hitchcock .10 .02
❑ 92 Neil Smith .20 .07
❑ 93 Joe Johnson RC .10 .02
❑ 94 Edgar Bennett .40 .15

❑ 95 Vincent Brown	.10	.02
❑ 96 Tommy Vardell	.10	.02
❑ 97 Donnell Woolford	.10	.02
❑ 98 Lincoln Kennedy	.10	.02
❑ 99 O.J.McDuffie	.40	.15
❑ 100 Heath Shuler RC	.40	.15
❑ 101 Jerry Rice BO	.75	.30
❑ 102 Erik Williams BO	.10	.02
❑ 103 Randall McDaniel BO	.10	.02
❑ 104 Dermontti Dawson BO	.10	.02
❑ 105 Nate Newton BO	.10	.02
❑ 106 Harris Barton BO	.10	.02
❑ 107 Shannon Sharpe BO	.20	.07
❑ 108 Sterling Sharpe BO	.20	.07
❑ 109 Steve Young BO	.60	.25
❑ 110 Emmitt Smith BO	1.25	.50
❑ 111 Thurman Thomas BO	.40	.15
❑ 112 Kyle Clifton	.10	.02
❑ 113 Desmond Howard	.20	.07
❑ 114 Quinn Early	.20	.07
❑ 115 David Klingler	.10	.02
❑ 116 Bern Brostek	.10	.02
❑ 117 Gary Clark	.20	.07
❑ 118 Courtney Hall	.10	.02
❑ 119 Joe King	.10	.02
❑ 120 Quentin Coryatt	.10	.02
❑ 121 Johnnie Morton RC	2.00	.75
❑ 122 Andre Reed	.20	.07
❑ 123 Eric Davis	.10	.02
❑ 124 Jack Del Rio	.10	.02
❑ 125 Greg Lloyd	.20	.07
❑ 126 Bubba McDowell	.10	.02
❑ 127 Mark Jackson	.10	.02
❑ 128 Jeff Jaeger	.10	.02
❑ 129 Chris Warren	.20	.07
❑ 130 Tom Waddle	.10	.02
❑ 131 Tony Smith RB	.10	.02
❑ 132 Todd Collins	.10	.02
❑ 133 Mark Bavaro	.10	.02
❑ 134 Joe Phillips	.10	.02
❑ 135 Chris Jacke	.10	.02
❑ 136 Glyn Milburn	.20	.07
❑ 137 Keith Jackson	.10	.02
❑ 138 Steve Tovar	.10	.02
❑ 139 Tim Johnson	.10	.02
❑ 140 Brian Washington	.10	.02
❑ 141 Troy Drayton	.10	.02
❑ 142 Dewayne Washington RC	.20	.07
❑ 143 Erik Williams	.10	.02
❑ 144 Eric Turner	.10	.02
❑ 145 John Taylor	.20	.07
❑ 146 Richard Cooper	.10	.02
❑ 147 Van Malone	.10	.02
❑ 148 Tim Ruddy RC	.10	.02
❑ 149 Henry Jones	.10	.02
❑ 150 Tim Brown	.40	.15
❑ 151 Stan Humphries	.20	.07
❑ 152 Harry Newsome	.10	.02
❑ 153 Craig Erickson	.10	.02
❑ 154 Gary Anderson K	.10	.02
❑ 155 Ray Childress	.10	.02
❑ 156 Howard Cross	.10	.02
❑ 157 Heath Sherman	.10	.02
❑ 158 Terrell Buckley	.10	.02
❑ 159 J.B. Brown	.10	.02
❑ 160 Joe Montana	3.00	1.25
❑ 161 David Wyman	.10	.02
❑ 162 Norm Johnson	.10	.02
❑ 163 Rod Stephens	.10	.02
❑ 164 Willie McGinest RC	.40	.15
❑ 165 Barry Sanders	2.50	1.00
❑ 166 Marc Logan	.10	.02
❑ 167 Anthony Newman	.10	.02
❑ 168 Russell Maryland	.10	.02
❑ 169 Luis Sharpe	.10	.02
❑ 170 Jim Kelly	.40	.15
❑ 171 Tre Johnson RC	.10	.02
❑ 172 Johnny Mitchell	.10	.02
❑ 173 David Palmer RC	.40	.15
❑ 174 Bob Dahl	.10	.02
❑ 175 Aaron Wallace	.10	.02
❑ 176 Chris Gardocki	.10	.02
❑ 177 Hardy Nickerson	.20	.07
❑ 178 Jeff Query	.10	.02
❑ 179 Leslie O'Neal	.10	.02
❑ 180 Kevin Greene	.20	.07
❑ 181 Alonzo Spellman	.10	.02
❑ 182 Reggie Brooks	.20	.07
❑ 183 Dana Stubblefield	.20	.07
❑ 184 Tyrone Hughes	.20	.07
❑ 185 Drew Bledsoe GE	.40	.15
❑ 186 Ronald Moore GE	.10	.02
❑ 187 Jason Elam GE	.10	.02
❑ 188 Rick Mirer GE	.40	.15
❑ 189 Willie Roaf GE	.10	.02
❑ 190 Jerome Bettis GE	.40	.15
❑ 191 Brad Hopkins	.10	.02
❑ 192 Derek Brown RBK	.10	.02
❑ 193 Nolan Harrison	.10	.02
❑ 194 John Randle	.20	.07
❑ 195 Carlton Bailey	.10	.02
❑ 196 Kevin Williams WR	.20	.07
❑ 197 Greg Hill RC	.40	.15
❑ 198 Mark McMillian	.10	.02
❑ 199 Brad Edwards	.10	.02
❑ 200 Dan Marino	3.00	1.25
❑ 201 Ricky Watters	.20	.07
❑ 202 George Teague	.10	.02
❑ 203 Steve Beuerlein	.20	.07
❑ 204 Jeff Burris RC	.20	.07
❑ 205 Steve Atwater	.10	.02
❑ 206 John Thierry RC	.10	.02
❑ 207 Patrick Hunter	.10	.02
❑ 208 Wayne Gandy	.10	.02
❑ 209 Derrick Moore	.10	.02
❑ 210 Phil Simms	.20	.07
❑ 211 Kirk Lowdermilk	.10	.02
❑ 212 Patrick Robinson	.10	.02
❑ 213 Kevin Mitchell	.10	.02
❑ 214 Jonathan Hayes	.10	.02
❑ 215 Michael Dean Perry	.20	.07
❑ 216 John Fina	.10	.02
❑ 217 Anthony Smith	.10	.02
❑ 218 Paul Gruber	.10	.02
❑ 219 Carnell Lake	.10	.02
❑ 220 Carl Lee	.10	.02
❑ 221 Steve Christie	.10	.02
❑ 222 Greg Montgomery	.10	.02
❑ 223 Reggie Brooks	.20	.07
❑ 224 Derrick Thomas	.40	.15
❑ 225 Eric Metcalf	.20	.07
❑ 226 Michael Haynes	.20	.07
❑ 227 Bobby Hebert	.10	.02
❑ 228 Tyrone Hughes	.20	.07
❑ 229 Donald Frank	.10	.02
❑ 230 Vaughan Johnson	.10	.02
❑ 231 Eric Thomas	.10	.02
❑ 232 Ernest Givins	.20	.07
❑ 233 Charles Haley	.20	.07
❑ 234 Darrell Green	.10	.02
❑ 235 Harold Alexander	.10	.02
❑ 236 Dwayne Sabb	.10	.02
❑ 237 Harris Barton	.10	.02
❑ 238 Randall Cunningham	.40	.15
❑ 239 Ray Buchanan	.10	.02
❑ 240 Sterling Sharpe	.20	.07
❑ 241 Chris Mims	.10	.02
❑ 242 Mark Carrier DB	.10	.02
❑ 243 Ricky Proehl	.10	.02
❑ 244 Michael Brooks	.10	.02
❑ 245 Sean Gilbert	.10	.02
❑ 246 David Lutz	.10	.02
❑ 247 Kelvin Martin	.10	.02
❑ 248 Scottie Graham RC	.20	.07
❑ 249 Irving Fryar	.20	.07
❑ 250 Ricardo McDonald	.10	.02
❑ 251 Marvcus Patton	.10	.02
❑ 252 Errict Rhett RC	.40	.15
❑ 253 Winston Moss	.10	.02
❑ 254 Rod Bernstine	.10	.02
❑ 255 Terry Wooden	.10	.02
❑ 256 Antonio Langham RC	.20	.07
❑ 257 Tommy Barnhardt	.10	.02
❑ 258 Marvin Washington	.10	.02
❑ 259 Bo Orlando	.10	.02
❑ 260 Marcus Allen	.40	.15
❑ 261 Mario Bates RC	.40	.15
❑ 262 Marco Coleman	.10	.02
❑ 263 Doug Riesenberg	.10	.02
❑ 264 Jesse Sapolu	.10	.02
❑ 265 Dermontti Dawson	.10	.02
❑ 266 Fernando Smith RC	.10	.02
❑ 267 David Szott	.10	.02
❑ 268 Steve Christie	.10	.02
❑ 269 Bruce Matthews	.10	.02
❑ 270 Michael Irvin	.40	.15
❑ 271 Seth Joyner	.10	.02
❑ 272 Santana Dotson	.20	.07
❑ 273 Vincent Brisby	.20	.07
❑ 274 Rohn Stark	.10	.02
❑ 275 John Copeland	.10	.02
❑ 276 Toby Wright	.10	.02
❑ 277 David Griggs	.10	.02
❑ 278 Aaron Taylor	.10	.02
❑ 279 Chris Doleman	.10	.02
❑ 280 Reggie Brooks	.20	.07
❑ 281 Flipper Anderson	.10	.02
❑ 282 Alvin Harper	.20	.07
❑ 283 Chris Hinton	.10	.02
❑ 284 Kelvin Pritchett	.10	.02
❑ 285 Russell Copeland	.10	.02
❑ 286 Dwight Stone	.10	.02
❑ 287 Jeff Gossett	.10	.02
❑ 288 Larry Allen RC	.40	.15
❑ 289 Kevin Mawae RC	.40	.15
❑ 290 Mark Collins	.10	.02
❑ 291 Chris Zorich	.10	.02
❑ 292 Vince Buck	.10	.02
❑ 293 Gene Atkins	.10	.02
❑ 294 Webster Slaughter	.10	.02
❑ 295 Steve Young	1.25	.50
❑ 296 Dan Williams	.10	.02
❑ 297 Jessie Armstead	.10	.02
❑ 298 Victor Bailey	.10	.02
❑ 299 John Carney	.10	.02
❑ 300 Emmitt Smith	2.50	1.00
❑ 301 Bucky Brooks RC	.10	.02
❑ 302 Mo Lewis	.10	.02
❑ 303 Eugene Daniel	.10	.02
❑ 304 Tyji Armstrong	.10	.02
❑ 305 Eugene Chung	.10	.02
❑ 306 Rocket Ismail	.20	.07
❑ 307 Sean Jones	.10	.02
❑ 308 Rick Cunningham	.10	.02
❑ 309 Ken Harvey	.10	.02
❑ 310 Jeff George	.40	.15
❑ 311 Jon Vaughn	.10	.02
❑ 312 Roy Barker RC	.10	.02
❑ 313 Micheal Barrow	.10	.02
❑ 314 Ryan McNeil	.10	.02
❑ 315 Pete Stoyanovich	.10	.02
❑ 316 Darryl Williams	.10	.02
❑ 317 Renaldo Turnbull	.10	.02
❑ 318 Eric Green	.10	.02
❑ 319 Nate Lewis	.10	.02
❑ 320 Mike Flores	.10	.02
❑ 321 Derek Russell	.10	.02
❑ 322 Marcus Spears RC	.10	.02
❑ 323 Corey Miller	.10	.02
❑ 324 Derrick Thomas	.40	.15
❑ 325 Steve Everitt	.10	.02
❑ 326 Brent Jones	.20	.07
❑ 327 Marshall Faulk RC	6.00	2.50
❑ 328 Don Beebe	.10	.02
❑ 329 Harry Swayne	.10	.02
❑ 330 Boomer Esiason	.20	.07
❑ 331 Don Mosebar	.10	.02
❑ 332 Isaac Bruce RC	5.00	2.00
❑ 333 Rickey Jackson	.10	.02
❑ 334 Daryl Johnston	.20	.07
❑ 335 Lorenzo Lynch	.10	.02
❑ 336 Brian Blades	.20	.07
❑ 337 Michael Timpson	.10	.02
❑ 338 Reggie Cobb	.10	.02
❑ 339 Joe Walter	.10	.02
❑ 340 Barry Foster	.10	.02
❑ 341 Richmond Webb	.10	.02
❑ 342 Pat Swilling	.10	.02
❑ 343 Shaun Gayle	.10	.02
❑ 344 Reggie Roby	.10	.02
❑ 345 Chris Calloway	.10	.02
❑ 346 Doug Dawson	.10	.02
❑ 347 Rob Burnett	.10	.02
❑ 348 Dana Hall	.10	.02
❑ 349 Horace Copeland	.10	.02
❑ 350 Shannon Sharpe	.20	.07
❑ 351 Rich Miano	.10	.02
❑ 352 Henry Thomas	.10	.02
❑ 353 Dan Saleaumua	.10	.02
❑ 354 Kevin Ross	.10	.02
❑ 355 Morten Andersen	.10	.02

❑	356	Anthony Blaylock	.10	.02
❑	357	Stanley Richard	.10	.02
❑	358	Albert Lewis	.10	.02
❑	359	Darren Woodson	.20	.07
❑	360	Drew Bledsoe	1.00	.40
❑	361	Eric Mahlum	.10	.02
❑	362	Trent Dilfer RC	1.50	.60
❑	363	William Roberts	.10	.02
❑	364	Robert Brooks	.40	.15
❑	365	Jason Hanson	.10	.02
❑	366	Troy Vincent	.10	.02
❑	367	William Thomas	.10	.02
❑	368	Lonnie Johnson RC	.10	.02
❑	369	Jamir Miller RC	.20	.07
❑	370	Michael Jackson	.20	.07
❑	371	Charlie Ward CT RC	.40	.15
❑	372	Shannon Sharpe CT	.20	.07
❑	373	Jackie Slater CT	.10	.02
❑	374	Steve Young CT	.60	.25
❑	375	Bobby Wilson	.10	.02
❑	376	Paul Frase	.10	.02
❑	377	Dale Carter	.10	.02
❑	378	Robert Delpino	.10	.02
❑	379	Bert Emanuel RC	.40	.15
❑	380	Rick Mirer	.40	.15
❑	381	Carlos Jenkins	.10	.02
❑	382	Gary Brown	.10	.02
❑	383	Doug Pelfrey	.10	.02
❑	384	Dexter Carter	.10	.02
❑	385	Chris Miller	.10	.02
❑	386	Charles Johnson RC	.40	.15
❑	387	James Joseph	.10	.02
❑	388	Darrin Smith	.10	.02
❑	389	James Jett	.10	.02
❑	390	Junior Seau	.40	.15
❑	391	Chris Slade	.10	.02
❑	392	Jim Harbaugh	.40	.15
❑	393	Herman Moore	.40	.15
❑	394	Thomas Randolph RC	.10	.02
❑	395	Lamar Thomas	.10	.02
❑	396	Reggie Rivers	.10	.02
❑	397	Larry Centers	.40	.15
❑	398	Chad Brown	.10	.02
❑	399	Terry Kirby	.40	.15
❑	400	Bruce Smith	.40	.15
❑	401	Keenan McCardell RC	2.00	.75
❑	402	Tim McDonald	.10	.02
❑	403	Robert Smith	.40	.15
❑	404	Matt Brock	.10	.02
❑	405	Tony McGee	.10	.02
❑	406	Ethan Horton	.10	.02
❑	407	Michael Haynes	.20	.07
❑	408	Steve Jackson	.10	.02
❑	409	Erik Kramer	.20	.07
❑	410	Jerome Bettis	.60	.25
❑	411	D.J. Johnson	.10	.02
❑	412	John Alt	.10	.02
❑	413	Jeff Lageman	.10	.02
❑	414	Rick Tuten	.10	.02
❑	415	Jeff Robinson	.10	.02
❑	416	Kevin Lee RC	.10	.02
❑	417	Thomas Lewis RC	.20	.07
❑	418	Kerry Cash	.10	.02
❑	419	Chuck Levy RC	.10	.02
❑	420	Mark Ingram	.10	.02
❑	421	Dennis Gibson	.10	.02
❑	422	Tyronne Drakeford	.10	.02
❑	423	James Washington	.10	.02
❑	424	Dante Jones	.10	.02
❑	425	Eugene Robinson	.10	.02
❑	426	Johnny Johnson	.10	.02
❑	427	Brian Mitchell	.10	.02
❑	428	Charles Mincy	.10	.02
❑	429	Mark Carrier WR	.20	.07
❑	430	Vince Workman	.10	.02
❑	431	James Francis	.10	.02
❑	432	Clay Matthews	.10	.02
❑	433	Randall McDaniel	.10	.02
❑	434	Brad Ottis	.10	.02
❑	435	Bruce Smith	.40	.15
❑	436	Cortez Kennedy BD	.10	.02
❑	437	John Randle BD	.20	.07
❑	438	Neil Smith BD	.20	.07
❑	439	Cornelius Bennett BD	.20	.07
❑	440	Junior Seau BD	.20	.07
❑	441	Derrick Thomas BD	.20	.07
❑	442	Rod Woodson BD	.20	.07
❑	443	Terry McDaniel BD	.10	.02
❑	444	Tim McDonald BD	.10	.02
❑	445	Mark Carrier DB BD	.10	.02
❑	446	Irv Smith	.10	.02
❑	447	Steve Wallace	.10	.02
❑	448	Cris Dishman	.10	.02
❑	449	Bill Brooks	.10	.02
❑	450	Jeff Hostetler	.20	.07
❑	451	Brentson Buckner RC	.10	.02
❑	452	Ken Ruettgers	.10	.02
❑	453	Marc Boutte	.10	.02
❑	454	John Offerdahl	.10	.02
❑	455	Allen Aldridge	.10	.02
❑	456	Steve Emtman	.10	.02
❑	457	Andre Rison	.20	.07
❑	458	Shawn Jefferson	.10	.02
❑	459	Todd Steussie RC	.20	.07
❑	460	Scott Mitchell	.20	.07
❑	461	Tom Carter	.10	.02
❑	462	Donnell Bennett RC	.40	.15
❑	463	James Jones DT	.10	.02
❑	464	Antone Davis	.10	.02
❑	465	Jim Everett	.20	.07
❑	466	Tony Tolbert	.10	.02
❑	467	Merril Hoge	.10	.02
❑	468	Michael Bates	.10	.02
❑	469	Phil Hansen	.10	.02
❑	470	Rodney Hampton	.20	.07
❑	471	Aeneas Williams	.10	.02
❑	472	Al Del Greco	.10	.02
❑	473	Todd Lyght	.10	.02
❑	474	Joel Steed	.10	.02
❑	475	Merton Hanks	.20	.07
❑	476	Tony Stargell	.10	.02
❑	477	Greg Robinson	.10	.02
❑	478	Roger Duffy	.10	.02
❑	479	Simon Fletcher	.10	.02
❑	480	Reggie White	.40	.15
❑	481	Lee Johnson	.10	.02
❑	482	Wayne Martin	.10	.02
❑	483	Thurman Thomas	.40	.15
❑	484	Warren Moon	.40	.15
❑	485	Sam Rogers RC	.10	.02
❑	486	Erric Pegram	.10	.02
❑	487	Will Wolford	.10	.02
❑	488	Duane Young	.10	.02
❑	489	Keith Hamilton	.10	.02
❑	490	Haywood Jeffires	.20	.07
❑	491	Trace Armstrong	.10	.02
❑	492	J.J. Birden	.10	.02
❑	493	Ricky Ervins	.10	.02
❑	494	Robert Blackmon	.10	.02
❑	495	William Perry	.20	.07
❑	496	Robert Massey	.10	.02
❑	497	Jim Jeffcoat	.10	.02
❑	498	Pat Harlow	.10	.02
❑	499	Jeff Cross	.10	.02
❑	500	Jerry Rice	1.50	.60
❑	501	Darnay Scott RC	1.00	.40
❑	502	Clyde Simmons	.10	.02
❑	503	Henry Rolling	.10	.02
❑	504	James Hasty	.10	.02
❑	505	Leroy Thompson	.10	.02
❑	506	Darrell Thompson	.10	.02
❑	507	Tim Bowens RC	.20	.07
❑	508	Gerald Perry	.10	.02
❑	509	Mike Croel	.10	.02
❑	510	Sam Mills	.10	.02
❑	511	Steve Young RZ	.60	.25
❑	512	Hardy Nickerson RZ	.20	.07
❑	513	Cris Carter RZ	.20	.07
❑	514	Boomer Esiason RZ	.10	.02
❑	515	Bruce Smith RZ	.20	.07
❑	516	Emmitt Smith RZ	1.25	.50
❑	517	Eugene Robinson RZ	.10	.02
❑	518	Gary Brown RZ	.10	.02
❑	519	Jerry Rice RZ	.75	.30
❑	520	Troy Aikman RZ	.75	.30
❑	521	Marcus Allen RZ	.20	.07
❑	522	Junior Seau RZ	.20	.07
❑	523	Sterling Sharpe RZ	.20	.07
❑	524	Dana Stubblefield RZ	.20	.07
❑	525	Tom Carter RZ	.10	.02
❑	526	Pete Metzelaars	.10	.02
❑	527	Russell Freeman	.10	.02
❑	528	Keith Cash	.10	.02
❑	529	Willie Drewrey	.10	.02
❑	530	Randal Hill	.10	.02
❑	531	Pepper Johnson	.10	.02
❑	532	Rob Moore	.20	.07
❑	533	Todd Kelly	.10	.02
❑	534	Keith Byars	.10	.02
❑	535	Mike Fox	.10	.02
❑	536	Brett Favre	3.00	1.25
❑	537	Terry McDaniel	.10	.02
❑	538	Darren Perry	.10	.02
❑	539	Maurice Hurst	.10	.02
❑	540	Troy Aikman	1.50	.60
❑	541	Junior Seau	.40	.15
❑	542	Steve Broussard	.10	.02
❑	543	Lorenzo White	.10	.02
❑	544	Terry McDaniel	.10	.02
❑	545	Henry Thomas	.10	.02
❑	546	Tyrone Hughes	.20	.07
❑	547	Mark Collins	.10	.02
❑	548	Gary Anderson K	.10	.02
❑	549	Darrell Green	.10	.02
❑	550	Jerry Rice	1.25	.50
❑	551	Cornelius Bennett	.20	.07
❑	552	Aeneas Williams	.10	.02
❑	553	Eric Metcalf	.20	.07
❑	554	Jumbo Elliott	.10	.02
❑	555	Mo Lewis	.10	.02
❑	556	Darren Carrington	.10	.02
❑	557	Kevin Greene	.20	.07
❑	558	John Elway	2.50	1.00
❑	559	Eugene Robinson	.10	.02
❑	560	Drew Bledsoe	.75	.30
❑	561	Fred Barnett	.20	.07
❑	562	Bernie Parmalee RC	.40	.15
❑	563	Bryce Paup	.20	.07
❑	564	Donnell Woolford	.10	.02
❑	565	Terance Mathis	.20	.07
❑	566	Santana Dotson	.20	.07
❑	567	Randall McDaniel	.10	.02
❑	568	Stanley Richard	.10	.02
❑	569	Brian Blades	.20	.07
❑	570	Jerome Bettis	.50	.20
❑	571	Neil Smith	.20	.07
❑	572	Andre Reed	.20	.07
❑	573	Michael Bankston	.10	.02
❑	574	Dana Stubblefield	.20	.07
❑	575	Rod Woodson	.20	.07
❑	576	Ken Harvey	.10	.02
❑	577	Andre Rison	.20	.07
❑	578	Darion Conner	.10	.02
❑	579	Michael Strahan	.40	.15
❑	580	Barry Sanders	2.00	.75
❑	581	Pepper Johnson	.10	.02
❑	582	Lewis Tillman	.10	.02
❑	583	Jeff George	.40	.15
❑	584	Michael Haynes	.20	.07
❑	585	Herschel Walker	.20	.07
❑	586	Tim Brown	.40	.15
❑	587	Jim Kelly	.40	.15
❑	588	Ricky Watters	.20	.07
❑	589	Randall Cunningham	.40	.15
❑	590	Troy Aikman	1.25	.50
❑	591	Ken Norton Jr.	.20	.07
❑	592	Cortez Kennedy	.20	.07
❑	593	Ricky Ervins	.10	.02
❑	594	Cris Carter	.50	.20
❑	595	Sterling Sharpe	.20	.07
❑	596	John Randle	.20	.07
❑	597	Shannon Sharpe	.20	.07
❑	598	Ray Crittenden RC	.10	.02
❑	599	Barry Foster	.10	.02
❑	600	Deion Sanders	.60	.25
❑	601	Seth Joyner	.10	.02
❑	602	Chris Warren	.20	.07
❑	603	Tom Rathman	.10	.02
❑	604	Brett Favre	2.50	1.00
❑	605	Marshall Faulk	2.00	.75
❑	606	Terry Allen	.20	.07
❑	607	Ben Coates	.20	.07
❑	608	Brian Washington	.10	.02
❑	609	Henry Ellard	.20	.07
❑	610	Dave Meggett	.10	.02
❑	611	Stan Humphries	.20	.07
❑	612	Warren Moon	.40	.15
❑	613	Marcus Allen	.40	.15
❑	614	Ed McDaniel	.10	.02
❑	615	Joe Montana	2.50	1.00
❑	616	Jeff Hostetler	.20	.07

❑ 617	Johnny Johnson	.10	.02
❑ 618	Andre Coleman RC	.10	.02
❑ 619	Willie Davis	.20	.07
❑ 620	Rick Mirer	.40	.15
❑ 621	Dan Marino	2.50	1.00
❑ 622	Rob Moore	.20	.07
❑ 623	Byron Bam Morris RC	.20	.07
❑ 624	Natrone Means	.40	.15
❑ 625	Steve Young	.75	.30
❑ 626	Jim Everett	.20	.07
❑ 627	Michael Brooks	.10	.02
❑ 628	Dermontti Dawson	.10	.02
❑ 629	Reggie White	.40	.15
❑ 630	Emmitt Smith	1.50	.60
❑ [illegible]	Micheal Barrow [illegible]	4.00	2.00
❑ NNO	Checklist Card 1	.10	.02
❑ NNO	Checklist Card 2	.10	.02
❑ NNO	Checklist Card 3	.10	.02

1995 Stadium Club

❑	COMPLETE SET (450)	60.00	25.00
❑	COMP.SERIES 1 (225)	30.00	12.50
❑	COMP.SERIES 2 (225)	30.00	12.50
❑ 1	Steve Young	1.25	.50
❑ 2	Stan Humphries	.20	.07
❑ 3	Chris Boniol RC	.10	.02
❑ 4	Darren Perry	.10	.02
❑ 5	Vinny Testaverde	.20	.07
❑ 6	Aubrey Beavers	.10	.02
❑ 7	Dewayne Washington	.20	.07
❑ 8	Marion Butts	.10	.02
❑ 9	George Koonce	.10	.02
❑ 10	Joe Cain	.10	.02
❑ 11	Mike Johnson	.10	.02
❑ 12	Dale Carter	.20	.07
❑ 13	Greg Biekert	.10	.02
❑ 14	Aaron Pierce	.10	.02
❑ 15	Aeneas Williams	.10	.02
❑ 16	Stephen Grant RC	.10	.02
❑ 17	Henry Jones	.10	.02
❑ 18	James Williams LB	.10	.02
❑ 19	Andy Harmon	.10	.02
❑ 20	Anthony Miller	.20	.07
❑ 21	Kevin Ross	.10	.02
❑ 22	Erik Howard	.10	.02
❑ 23	Brian Blades	.20	.07
❑ 24	Trent Dilfer	.40	.15
❑ 25	Roman Phifer	.10	.02
❑ 26	Bruce Kozerski	.10	.02
❑ 27	Henry Ellard	.20	.07
❑ 28	Rich Camarillo	.10	.02
❑ 29	Richmond Webb	.10	.02
❑ 30	George Teague	.10	.02
❑ 31	Antonio Langham	.10	.02
❑ 32	Barry Foster	.20	.07
❑ 33	Bruce Armstrong	.10	.02
❑ 34	Tim McDonald	.10	.02
❑ 35	James Harris DE	.10	.02
❑ 36	Lomas Brown	.10	.02
❑ 37	Jay Novacek	.20	.07
❑ 38	John Thierry	.10	.02
❑ 39	John Elliott	.10	.02
❑ 40	Terry McDaniel	.10	.02
❑ 41	Shawn Lee	.10	.02
❑ 42	Shane Dronett	.10	.02
❑ 43	Cornelius Bennett	.20	.07
❑ 44	Steve Bono	.20	.07
❑ 45	Byron Evans	.10	.02
❑ 46	Eugene Robinson	.10	.02
❑ 47	Tony Bennett	.10	.02
❑ 48	Michael Bankston	.10	.02
❑ 49	Willie Roaf	.10	.02
❑ 50	Bobby Houston	.10	.02
❑ 51	Ken Harvey	.10	.02
❑ 52	Bruce Matthews	.10	.02
❑ 53	Lincoln Kennedy	.10	.02
❑ 54	Todd Lyght	.10	.02
❑ 55	Paul Gruber	.10	.02
❑ 56	Corey Sawyer	.10	.02
❑ 57	Myron Guyton	.10	.02
❑ 58	John Jackson T	.10	.02
❑ 59	Sean Jones	.10	.02
❑ 60	Pepper Johnson	.10	.02
❑ 61	Steve Walsh	.10	.02
❑ 62	Corey Miller	.10	.02
❑ 63	Fuad Reveiz	.10	.02
❑ 64	Rickey Jackson	.10	.02
❑ 65	Scott Mitchell	.20	.07
❑ 66	Michael Irvin	.40	.15
❑ 67	Andre Reed	.20	.07
❑ 68	Mark Seay	.20	.07
❑ 69	Keith Byars	.10	.02
❑ 70	Marcus Allen	.40	.15
❑ 71	Shannon Sharpe	.20	.07
❑ 72	Eric Hill	.10	.02
❑ 73	James Washington	.10	.02
❑ 74	Greg Jackson	.10	.02
❑ 75	Chris Warren	.20	.07
❑ 76	Will Wolford	.10	.02
❑ 77	Anthony Smith	.10	.02
❑ 78	Cris Dishman	.10	.02
❑ 79	Carl Pickens	.20	.07
❑ 80	Tyrone Hughes	.20	.07
❑ 81	Chris Miller	.10	.02
❑ 82	Clay Matthews	.20	.07
❑ 83	Lonnie Marts	.10	.02
❑ 84	Jerome Henderson	.10	.02
❑ 85	Ben Coates	.20	.07
❑ 86	Deon Figures	.10	.02
❑ 87	Anthony Pleasant	.10	.02
❑ 88	Guy McIntyre	.10	.02
❑ 89	Jake Reed	.20	.07
❑ 90	Rodney Hampton	.20	.07
❑ 91	Santana Dotson	.10	.02
❑ 92	Jeff Blackshear	.10	.02
❑ 93	Willie Clay	.10	.02
❑ 94	Nate Newton	.20	.07
❑ 95	Bucky Brooks	.10	.02
❑ 96	Lamar Lathon	.10	.02
❑ 97	Tim Grunhard	.10	.02
❑ 98	Harris Barton	.10	.02
❑ 99	Brian Mitchell	.10	.02
❑ 100	Natrone Means	.20	.07
❑ 101	Sean Dawkins	.20	.07
❑ 102	Chris Slade	.10	.02
❑ 103	Tom Rathman	.10	.02
❑ 104	Fred Barnett	.20	.07
❑ 105	Gary Brown	.10	.02
❑ 106	Leonard Russell	.10	.02
❑ 107	Alfred Williams	.10	.02
❑ 108	Kelvin Martin	.10	.02
❑ 109	Alexander Wright	.10	.02
❑ 110	O.J. McDuffie	.40	.15
❑ 111	Mario Bates	.20	.07
❑ 112	Tony Casillas	.10	.02
❑ 113	Michael Timpson	.10	.02
❑ 114	Robert Brooks	.40	.15
❑ 115	Rob Burnett	.10	.02
❑ 116	Mark Collins	.10	.02
❑ 117	Chris Calloway	.10	.02
❑ 118	Courtney Hawkins	.10	.02
❑ 119	Marvcus Patton	.10	.02
❑ 120	Greg Lloyd	.20	.07
❑ 121	Ryan McNeil	.10	.02
❑ 122	Gary Plummer	.10	.02
❑ 123	Dwayne Sabb	.10	.02
❑ 124	Jessie Hester	.10	.02
❑ 125	Terance Mathis	.20	.07
❑ 126	Steve Atwater	.10	.02
❑ 127	Lorenzo Lynch	.10	.02
❑ 128	James Francis	.10	.02
❑ 129	John Fina	.10	.02
❑ 130	Emmitt Smith	2.50	1.25
❑ 131	Bryan Cox	.10	.02
❑ 132	Robert Blackmon	.10	.02
❑ 133	Kenny Davidson	.10	.02

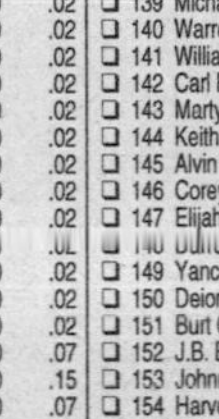

❑ 134	Eugene Daniel	.10	.02
❑ 135	Vince Buck	.10	.02
❑ 136	Leslie O'Neal	.20	.07
❑ 137	James Jett	.20	.07
❑ 138	Johnny Johnson	.10	.02
❑ 139	Michael Zordich	.10	.02
❑ 140	Warren Moon	.20	.07
❑ 141	William White	.10	.02
❑ 142	Carl Banks	.10	.02
❑ 143	Marty Carter	.10	.02
❑ 144	Keith Hamilton	.10	.02
❑ 145	Alvin Harper	.10	.02
❑ 146	Corey Harris	.10	.02
❑ 147	Elijah Alexander RC	.10	.02
❑ 148	[illegible]	[illegible]	[illegible]
❑ 149	Yancey Thigpen RC	.20	.07
❑ 150	Deion Sanders	1.00	.40
❑ 151	Burt Grossman	.10	.02
❑ 152	J.B. Brown	.10	.02
❑ 153	Johnny Bailey	.10	.02
❑ 154	Harvey Williams	.10	.02
❑ 155	Jeff Blake RC	1.00	.40
❑ 156	Al Smith	.10	.02
❑ 157	Chris Doleman	.10	.02
❑ 158	Garrison Hearst	.40	.15
❑ 159	Bryce Paup	.20	.07
❑ 160	Herman Moore	.40	.15
❑ 161	Cortez Kennedy	.20	.07
❑ 162	Marquez Pope	.10	.02
❑ 163	Quinn Early	.20	.07
❑ 164	Broderick Thomas	.10	.02
❑ 165	Jeff Herrod	.10	.02
❑ 166	Robert Jones	.10	.02
❑ 167	Mo Lewis	.10	.02
❑ 168	Ray Crittenden	.10	.02
❑ 169	Raymont Harris	.10	.02
❑ 170	Bruce Smith	.40	.15
❑ 171	Dana Stubblefield	.20	.07
❑ 172	Charles Haley	.20	.07
❑ 173	Charles Johnson	.20	.07
❑ 174	Shawn Jefferson	.10	.02
❑ 175	Leroy Hoard	.10	.02
❑ 176	Bernie Parmalee	.20	.07
❑ 177	Scottie Graham	.20	.07
❑ 178	Edgar Bennett	.20	.07
❑ 179	Aubrey Matthews	.10	.02
❑ 180	Don Beebe	.10	.02
❑ 181	Eric Swann EC SP	.30	.10
❑ 182	Jeff George EC SP	.30	.10
❑ 183	Jim Kelly EC SP	.60	.25
❑ 184	Sam Mills EC SP	.30	.10
❑ 185	Mark Carrier DB EC SP	.20	.07
❑ 186	Dan Wilkinson EC SP	.30	.10
❑ 187	Eric Turner EC SP	.20	.07
❑ 188	Troy Aikman EC SP	2.00	.75
❑ 189	John Elway EC SP	4.00	1.50
❑ 190	Barry Sanders EC SP	3.00	1.25
❑ 191	Brett Favre EC SP	4.00	2.00
❑ 192	Micheal Barrow EC SP	.20	.07
❑ 193	Marshall Faulk EC SP	2.50	1.00
❑ 194	Steve Beuerlein EC SP	.30	.10
❑ 195	Neil Smith EC SP	.30	.10
❑ 196	Jeff Hostetler EC SP	.30	.10
❑ 197	Jerome Bettis EC SP	.60	.25
❑ 198	Dan Marino EC SP	4.00	1.50
❑ 199	Cris Carter EC SP	.60	.25
❑ 200	Drew Bledsoe EC SP	1.00	.40
❑ 201	Jim Everett EC SP	.20	.07
❑ 202	Dave Brown EC SP	.30	.10
❑ 203	Boomer Esiason EC SP	.30	.10
❑ 204	Randall Cunningham EC SP	.30	.10
❑ 205	Rod Woodson EC SP	.30	.10
❑ 206	Junior Seau EC SP	.60	.25
❑ 207	Jerry Rice EC SP	2.00	.75
❑ 208	Rick Mirer EC SP	.30	.10
❑ 209	Errict Rhett EC SP	.30	.10
❑ 210	Heath Shuler EC SP	.30	.10
❑ 211	Bobby Taylor SP RC	.60	.25
❑ 212	Jesse James SP RC	.20	.07
❑ 213	Devin Bush SP RC	.20	.07
❑ 214	Luther Elliss SP RC	.20	.07
❑ 215	Kerry Collins RC SP	2.00	.75
❑ 216	Derr.Alexander DE SP RC	.20	.07
❑ 217	Rashaan Salaam RC SP	.30	.10
❑ 218	J.J. Stokes RC SP	.60	.25
❑ 219	Todd Collins RC SP	2.00	.75
❑ 220	Ki-Jana Carter RC SP	.60	.25

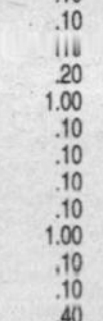

❑ 221 Kyle Brady RC SP .60 .25
❑ 222 Kevin Carter RC SP .60 .25
❑ 223 Tony Boselli RC SP .60 .25
❑ 224 Scott Gragg SP RC .20 .07
❑ 225 Warren Sapp RC SP 2.00 .75
❑ 226 Ricky Reynolds .10 .02
❑ 227 Roosevelt Potts .10 .02
❑ 228 Jessie Tuggle .10 .02
❑ 229 Anthony Newman .10 .02
❑ 230 Randall Cunningham .40 .15
❑ 231 Jason Elam .20 .07
❑ 232 Darnay Scott .20 .07
❑ 233 Tom Carter .10 .02
❑ 234 Micheal Barrow .10 .02
❑ 235 Steve Tasker .20 .07
❑ 236 Howard Cross .10 .02
❑ 237 Charles Wilson .10 .02
❑ 238 Rob Fredrickson .10 .02
❑ 239 Russell Maryland .10 .02
❑ 240 Dan Marino 3.00 1.25
❑ 241 Rafael Robinson .10 .02
❑ 242 Ed McDaniel .10 .02
❑ 243 Brett Perriman .20 .07
❑ 244 Chuck Levy .10 .02
❑ 245 Errict Rhett .20 .07
❑ 246 Tracy Simien .10 .02
❑ 247 Steve Everitt .10 .02
❑ 248 John Jurkovic .10 .02
❑ 249 Johnny Mitchell .10 .02
❑ 250 Mark Carrier DB .10 .02
❑ 251 Merton Hanks .10 .02
❑ 252 Joe Johnson .10 .02
❑ 253 Andre Coleman .10 .02
❑ 254 Ray Buchanan .10 .02
❑ 255 Jeff George .20 .07
❑ 256 Shane Conlan .10 .02
❑ 257 Gus Frerotte .20 .07
❑ 258 Doug Pelfrey .10 .02
❑ 259 Glenn Montgomery .10 .02
❑ 260 John Elway 3.00 1.25
❑ 261 Larry Centers .20 .07
❑ 262 Calvin Williams .20 .07
❑ 263 Gene Atkins .10 .02
❑ 264 Tim Brown .40 .15
❑ 265 Leon Lett .10 .02
❑ 266 Martin Mayhew .10 .02
❑ 267 Arthur Marshall .10 .02
❑ 268 Maurice Hurst .10 .02
❑ 269 Greg Hill .20 .07
❑ 270 Junior Seau .40 .15
❑ 271 Rick Mirer .20 .07
❑ 272 Jack Del Rio .10 .02
❑ 273 Lewis Tillman .10 .02
❑ 274 Renaldo Turnbull .10 .02
❑ 275 Dan Footman .10 .02
❑ 276 John Taylor .10 .02
❑ 277 Russell Copeland .10 .02
❑ 278 Tracy Scroggins .10 .02
❑ 279 Lou Benfatti .10 .02
❑ 280 Rod Woodson .20 .07
❑ 281 Troy Drayton .10 .02
❑ 282 Quentin Coryatt .20 .07
❑ 283 Craig Heyward .20 .07
❑ 284 Jeff Cross .10 .02
❑ 285 Hardy Nickerson .10 .02
❑ 286 Dorsey Levens .75 .30
❑ 287 Derek Russell .10 .02
❑ 288 Seth Joyner .10 .02
❑ 289 Kimble Anders .20 .07
❑ 290 Drew Bledsoe .75 .30
❑ 291 Bryant Young .20 .07
❑ 292 Chris Zorich .10 .02
❑ 293 Michael Strahan .40 .15
❑ 294 Kevin Greene .20 .07
❑ 295 Aaron Glenn .10 .02
❑ 296 Jimmy Spencer RC .10 .02
❑ 297 Eric Turner .10 .02
❑ 298 William Thomas .10 .02
❑ 299 Dan Wilkinson .20 .07
❑ 300 Troy Aikman 1.50 .60
❑ 301 Terry Wooden .10 .02
❑ 302 Heath Shuler .20 .07
❑ 303 Jeff Burris .10 .02
❑ 304 Mark Stepnoski .10 .02
❑ 305 Chris Mims .10 .02
❑ 306 Todd Steussie .10 .02
❑ 307 Johnnie Morton .20 .07
❑ 308 Darryl Talley .10 .02
❑ 309 Nolan Harrison .10 .02
❑ 310 Dave Brown .20 .07
❑ 311 Brent Jones .10 .02
❑ 312 Curtis Conway .40 .15
❑ 313 Ronald Humphrey .10 .02
❑ 314 Richie Anderson RC .50 .20
❑ 315 Jim Everett .10 .02
❑ 316 Willie Davis .20 .07
❑ 317 Ed Cunningham .10 .02
❑ 318 Willie McGinest .20 .07
❑ 319 Sean Gilbert .20 .07
❑ 320 Brett Favre 3.00 1.50
❑ 321 Bennie Thompson .10 .02
❑ 322 Neil O'Donnell .20 .07
❑ 323 Vince Workman .10 .02
❑ 324 Terry Kirby .20 .07
❑ 325 Simon Fletcher .10 .02
❑ 326 Ricardo McDonald .10 .02
❑ 327 Duane Young .10 .02
❑ 328 Jim Harbaugh .20 .07
❑ 329 D.J. Johnson .10 .02
❑ 330 Boomer Esiason .20 .07
❑ 331 Donnell Woolford .10 .02
❑ 332 Mike Sherrard .10 .02
❑ 333 Tyrone Legette .10 .02
❑ 334 Larry Brown DB .10 .02
❑ 335 William Floyd .20 .07
❑ 336 Reggie Brooks .20 .07
❑ 337 Patrick Bates .10 .02
❑ 338 Jim Jeffcoat .10 .02
❑ 339 Ray Childress .10 .02
❑ 340 Cris Carter .40 .15
❑ 341 Charlie Garner .40 .15
❑ 342 Bill Hitchcock .10 .02
❑ 343 Levon Kirkland .10 .02
❑ 344 Robert Porcher .10 .02
❑ 345 Darryl Williams .10 .02
❑ 346 Vincent Brisby .10 .02
❑ 347 Kenyon Rasheed .10 .02
❑ 348 Floyd Turner .10 .02
❑ 349 Bob Whitfield .10 .02
❑ 350 Jerome Bettis .40 .15
❑ 351 Brad Baxter .10 .02
❑ 352 Darrin Smith .10 .02
❑ 353 Lamar Thomas .10 .02
❑ 354 Lorenzo Neal .10 .02
❑ 355 Erik Kramer .10 .02
❑ 356 Dwayne Harper .10 .02
❑ 357 Doug Evans RC .40 .15
❑ 358 Jeff Feagles .10 .02
❑ 359 Ray Crockett .10 .02
❑ 360 Neil Smith .20 .07
❑ 361 Troy Vincent .10 .02
❑ 362 Don Griffin .10 .02
❑ 363 Michael Brooks .10 .02
❑ 364 Carlton Gray .10 .02
❑ 365 Thomas Smith .10 .02
❑ 366 Ken Norton .20 .07
❑ 367 Tony McGee .10 .02
❑ 368 Eric Metcalf .20 .07
❑ 369 Mel Gray .10 .02
❑ 370 Barry Sanders 2.50 1.00
❑ 371 Rocket Ismail .20 .07
❑ 372 Chad Brown .20 .07
❑ 373 Qadry Ismail .20 .07
❑ 374 Anthony Prior .10 .02
❑ 375 Kevin Lee .10 .02
❑ 376 Robert Young .10 .02
❑ 377 Kevin Williams WR .20 .07
❑ 378 Tydus Winans .10 .02
❑ 379 Ricky Watters .20 .07
❑ 380 Jim Kelly .40 .15
❑ 381 Eric Swann .20 .07
❑ 382 Mike Pritchard .10 .02
❑ 383 Derek Brown RBK .10 .02
❑ 384 Dennis Gibson .10 .02
❑ 385 Byron Bam Morris .10 .02
❑ 386 Reggie White .40 .15
❑ 387 Jeff Graham .10 .02
❑ 388 Marshall Faulk 2.00 .75
❑ 389 Joe Phillips .10 .02
❑ 390 Jeff Hostetler .20 .07
❑ 391 Irving Fryar .20 .07
❑ 392 Stevon Moore .10 .02
❑ 393 Bert Emanuel .40 .15
❑ 394 Leon Searcy .10 .02
❑ 395 Robert Smith .40 .15
❑ 396 Michael Bates .10 .02
❑ 397 Thomas Lewis .20 .07
❑ 398 Joe Bowden .10 .02
❑ 399 Steve Tovar .10 .02
❑ 400 Jerry Rice 1.50 .60
❑ 401 Toby Wright .10 .02
❑ 402 Daryl Johnston .20 .07
❑ 403 Vincent Brown .10 .02
❑ 404 Marvin Washington .10 .02
❑ 405 Chris Spielman .20 .07
❑ 406 Willie Jackson ET SP .30 .10
❑ 407 Harry Boatswain ET SP .20 .07
❑ 408 Kelvin Pritchett ET SP .20 .07
❑ 409 Dave Widell ET SP .20 .07
❑ 410 Frank Reich ET SP .20 .07
❑ 411 Corey Mayfield ET SP RC .20 .07
❑ 412 Pete Metzelaars ET SP .20 .07
❑ 413 Keith Goganious ET SP .20 .07
❑ 414 John Kasay ET SP .20 .07
❑ 415 Ernest Givins ET SP .20 .07
❑ 416 Randy Baldwin ET SP .20 .07
❑ 417 Shawn Bouwens ET SP .20 .07
❑ 418 Mike Fox ET SP .20 .07
❑ 419 Mark Carrier WR ET SP .30 .10
❑ 420 Steve Beuerlein ET SP .30 .10
❑ 421 Steve Lofton ET SP .20 .07
❑ 422 Jeff Lageman ET SP .20 .07
❑ 423 Paul Butcher ET SP .20 .07
❑ 424 Mark Brunell ET SP 1.00 .40
❑ 425 Vernon Turner ET SP .20 .07
❑ 426 Tim McKyer ET SP .20 .07
❑ 427 James Williams ET SP .20 .07
❑ 428 Tommy Barnhardt ET SP .20 .07
❑ 429 Rogerick Green ET SP .20 .07
❑ 430 Desmond Howard ET SP .30 .10
❑ 431 Darion Conner ET SP .20 .07
❑ 432 Reggie Clark ET SP .20 .07
❑ 433 Eric Guliford ET SP .20 .07
❑ 434 Rob Johnson ET RC SP 1.25 .50
❑ 435 Sam Mills ET SP .30 .10
❑ 436 Kordell Stewart RC SP 2.00 .75
❑ 437 James O. Stewart RC SP 1.50 .60
❑ 438 Zach Wiegert SP .20 .07
❑ 439 Ellis Johnson RC SP .20 .07
❑ 440 Matt O'Dwyer RC SP .20 .07
❑ 441 Anthony Cook RC SP .20 .07
❑ 442 Ron Davis RC SP .20 .07
❑ 443 Chris Hudson RC SP .20 .07
❑ 444 Hugh Douglas RC SP .60 .25
❑ 445 Tyrone Poole RC SP .60 .25
❑ 446 Korey Stringer RC SP .30 .10
❑ 447 Ruben Brown RC SP .60 .25
❑ 448 Brian DeMarco RC SP .20 .07
❑ 449 Michael Westbrook RC SP .60 .25
❑ 450 Steve McNair RC SP 4.00 1.50

1996 Stadium Club

❑ COMPLETE SET (360) 60.00 30.00
❑ COMP.SERIES 1 (180) 30.00 15.00
❑ COMP.SERIES 2 (180) 30.00 15.00
❑ 1 Kyle Brady .10 .02
❑ 2 Mickey Washington .10 .02
❑ 3 Seth Joyner .10 .02
❑ 4 Vinny Testaverde .25 .08
❑ 5 Thomas Randolph .10 .02
❑ 6 Heath Shuler .25 .08
❑ 7 Ty Law .50 .20
❑ 8 Blake Brockermeyer .10 .02

❑	9	Darryll Lewis	.10	.02
❑	10	Jeff Blake	.50	.20
❑	11	Tyrone Hughes	.10	.02
❑	12	Horace Copeland	.10	.02
❑	13	Roman Phifer	.10	.02
❑	14	Eugene Robinson	.10	.02
❑	15	Anthony Miller	.25	.08
❑	16	Robert Smith	.25	.08
❑	17	Chester McGlockton	.10	.02
❑	18	Marty Carter	.10	.02
❑	19	Scott Mitchell	.25	.08
❑	20	O.J. McDuffie	.25	.08
❑	21	Stan Humphries	.25	.08
❑	22	Eugene Daniel	.10	.02
❑	23	Devin Bush	.10	.02
❑	24	Darick Holmes	.10	.02
❑	25	Ricky Watters	.25	.08
❑	26	J.J. Stokes	.50	.20
❑	27	George Koonce	.10	.02
❑	28	Tamarick Vanover	.25	.08
❑	29	Yancey Thigpen	.25	.08
❑	30	Troy Aikman	1.25	.50
❑	31	Rashaan Salaam	.25	.08
❑	32	Anthony Cook	.10	.02
❑	33	Tim McKyer	.10	.02
❑	34	Dale Carter	.10	.02
❑	35	Marvin Washington	.10	.02
❑	36	Terry Allen	.25	.08
❑	37	Keith Goganious	.10	.02
❑	38	Pepper Johnson	.10	.02
❑	39	Dave Brown	.10	.02
❑	40	Levon Kirkland	.10	.02
❑	41	Ken Dilger	.25	.08
❑	42	Harvey Williams	.10	.02
❑	43	Robert Blackmon	.10	.02
❑	44	Kevin Carter	.10	.02
❑	45	Warren Moon	.25	.08
❑	46	Allen Aldridge	.10	.02
❑	47	Terance Mathis	.10	.02
❑	48	Junior Seau	.50	.20
❑	49	William Fuller	.10	.02
❑	50	Lee Woodall	.10	.02
❑	51	Aeneas Williams	.10	.02
❑	52	Thomas Smith	.10	.02
❑	53	Chris Slade	.10	.02
❑	54	Eric Allen	.10	.02
❑	55	David Sloan	.10	.02
❑	56	Hardy Nickerson	.10	.02
❑	57	Michael Irvin	.50	.20
❑	58	Corey Sawyer	.10	.02
❑	59	Eric Green	.10	.02
❑	60	Reggie White	.50	.20
❑	61	Isaac Bruce	.50	.20
❑	62	Darrell Green	.10	.02
❑	63	Aaron Glenn	.10	.02
❑	64	Mark Brunell	.75	.30
❑	65	Mark Carrier WR	.10	.02
❑	66	Mel Gray	.10	.02
❑	67	Phillippi Sparks	.10	.02
❑	68	Ernie Mills	.10	.02
❑	69	Rick Mirer	.25	.08
❑	70	Neil Smith	.25	.08
❑	71	Terry McDaniel	.10	.02
❑	72	Terrell Davis	1.00	.40
❑	73	Alonzo Spellman	.10	.02
❑	74	Jessie Tuggle	.10	.02
❑	75	Terry Kirby	.25	.08
❑	76	David Palmer	.10	.02
❑	77	Calvin Williams	.10	.02
❑	78	Shaun Gayle	.10	.02
❑	79	Bryant Young	.25	.08
❑	80	Jim Harbaugh	.25	.08
❑	81	Michael Jackson	.25	.08
❑	82	Dave Meggett	.10	.02
❑	83	Henry Thomas	.10	.02
❑	84	Jim Kelly	.50	.20
❑	85	Frank Sanders	.25	.08
❑	86	Daryl Johnston	.25	.08
❑	87	Alvin Harper	.10	.02
❑	88	John Copeland	.10	.02
❑	89	Mark Chmura	.25	.08
❑	90	Jim Everett	.10	.02
❑	91	Bobby Houston	.10	.02
❑	92	Willie Jackson	.25	.08
❑	93	Carlton Bailey	.10	.02
❑	94	Todd Lyght	.10	.02
❑	95	Ken Harvey	.10	.02
❑	96	Erric Pegram	.10	.02
❑	97	Anthony Smith	.10	.02
❑	98	Kimble Anders	.25	.08
❑	99	Steve McNair	1.00	.40
❑	100	Jeff George	.25	.08
❑	101	Michael Timpson	.10	.02
❑	102	Brent Jones	.10	.02
❑	103	Mike Mamula	.10	.02
❑	104	Jeff Cross	.10	.02
❑	105	Craig Newsome	.10	.02
❑	106	Howard Cross	.10	.02
❑	107	Terry Wooden	.10	.02
❑	108	Randall McDaniel	.10	.02
❑	109	Andre Reed	.25	.08
❑	110	Steve Atwater	.10	.02
❑	111	Larry Centers	.25	.08
❑	112	Tony Bennett	.10	.02
❑	113	Drew Bledsoe	.75	.30
❑	114	Terrell Fletcher	.10	.02
❑	115	Warren Sapp	.10	.02
❑	116	Deion Sanders	.75	.30
❑	117	Bryce Paup	.10	.02
❑	118	Mario Bates	.25	.08
❑	119	Steve Tovar	.10	.02
❑	120	Barry Sanders	2.00	.75
❑	121	Tony Boselli	.10	.02
❑	122	Micheal Barrow	.10	.02
❑	123	Sam Mills	.10	.02
❑	124	Tim Brown	.50	.20
❑	125	Darren Perry	.10	.02
❑	126	Brian Blades	.10	.02
❑	127	Tyrone Wheatley	.25	.08
❑	128	Derrick Thomas	.50	.20
❑	129	Edgar Bennett	.25	.08
❑	130	Cris Carter	.50	.20
❑	131	Stephen Grant	.10	.02
❑	132	Kevin Williams	.10	.02
❑	133	Darnay Scott	.25	.08
❑	134	Rod Stephens	.10	.02
❑	135	Ken Norton	.10	.02
❑	136	Tim Biakabutuka SP RC	.50	.20
❑	137	Willie Anderson SP RC	.10	.02
❑	138	Lawrence Phillips SP RC	.50	.20
❑	139	Jonathan Ogden SP RC	.50	.20
❑	140	Simeon Rice SP RC	1.25	.50
❑	141	Alex Van Dyke SP RC	.25	.08
❑	142	Jerome Woods SP RC	.10	.02
❑	143	Eric Moulds SP RC	2.00	.75
❑	144	Mike Alstott SP RC	1.50	.60
❑	145	Marvin Harrison SP RC	4.00	1.50
❑	146	Duane Clemons SP RC	.10	.02
❑	147	Regan Upshaw SP RC	.10	.02
❑	148	Eddie Kennison SP RC	.50	.20
❑	149	John Mobley SP RC	.10	.02
❑	150	Keyshawn Johnson SP RC	1.50	.60
❑	151	Marco Battaglia SP RC	.10	.02
❑	152	Rickey Dudley SP RC	.50	.20
❑	153	Kevin Hardy SP RC	.50	.20
❑	154	Curtis Martin SM SP	1.00	.40
❑	155	Dan Marino SM SP	2.50	1.00
❑	156	Rashaan Salaam SM SP	.25	.08
❑	157	Joey Galloway SM SP	.50	.20
❑	158	John Elway SM SP	2.50	1.00
❑	159	Marshall Faulk SM SP	.60	.25
❑	160	Jerry Rice SM SP	1.25	.50
❑	161	Darren Bennett SM SP	.10	.02
❑	162	Tamarick Vanover SM SP	.25	.08
❑	163	Orlando Thomas SM SP	.10	.02
❑	164	Jim Kelly SM SP	.50	.20
❑	165	Larry Brown SM SP	.10	.02
❑	166	Errict Rhett SM SP	.25	.08
❑	167	Warren Moon SM SP	.10	.02
❑	168	Hugh Douglas SM SP	.10	.02
❑	169	Jim Everett SM SP	.10	.02
❑	170	AFC Championship Game SP	.10	.02
❑	171	Larry Centers SM SP	.25	.08
❑	172	Marcus Allen GM SP	.50	.20
❑	173	Morten Andersen GM SP	.10	.02
❑	174	Brett Favre GM SP	2.50	1.00
❑	175	Jerry Rice GM SP	1.25	.50
❑	176	Glyn Milburn GM SP	.10	.02
❑	177	Thurman Thomas GM SP	.25	.08
❑	178	Michael Irvin GM SP	.25	.08
❑	179	Barry Sanders GM SP	2.00	.75
❑	180	Dan Marino GM SP	2.50	1.00
❑	181	Joey Galloway	.50	.20
❑	182	Dwayne Harper	.10	.02
❑	183	Antonio Langham	.10	.02
❑	184	Chris Zorich	.10	.02
❑	185	Willie McGinest	.10	.02
❑	186	Wayne Chrebet	.75	.30
❑	187	Dermontti Dawson	.10	.02
❑	188	Charlie Garner	.25	.08
❑	189	Quentin Coryatt	.10	.02
❑	190	Rodney Hampton	.25	.08
❑	191	Kelvin Pritchett	.10	.02
❑	192	Willie Green	.10	.02
❑	193	Garrison Hearst	.25	.08
❑	194	Tracy Scroggins	.10	.02
❑	195	Rocket Ismail	.10	.02
❑	196	Michael Westbrook	.50	.20
❑	197	Troy Drayton	.10	.02
❑	198	Rob Fredrickson	.10	.02
❑	199	Sean Lumpkin	.10	.02
❑	200	John Elway	2.50	1.00
❑	201	Bernie Parmalee	.10	.02
❑	202	Chris Chandler	.25	.08
❑	203	Lake Dawson	.10	.02
❑	204	Orlando Thomas	.10	.02
❑	205	Carl Pickens	.25	.08
❑	206	Kurt Schulz	.10	.02
❑	207	Clay Matthews	.10	.02
❑	208	Winston Moss	.10	.02
❑	209	Sean Dawkins	.10	.02
❑	210	Emmitt Smith	2.00	.75
❑	211	Mark Carrier DB	.10	.02
❑	212	Clyde Simmons	.10	.02
❑	213	Derrick Brooks	.50	.20
❑	214	William Floyd	.25	.08
❑	215	Aaron Hayden	.10	.02
❑	216	Brian DeMarco	.10	.02
❑	217	Ben Coates	.25	.08
❑	218	Renaldo Turnbull	.10	.02
❑	219	Adrian Murrell	.25	.08
❑	220	Marcus Allen	.50	.20
❑	221	Brett Maxie	.10	.02
❑	222	Trev Alberts	.10	.02
❑	223	Darren Woodson	.25	.08
❑	224	Brian Mitchell	.10	.02
❑	225	Michael Haynes	.10	.02
❑	226	Sean Jones	.10	.02
❑	227	Eric Zeier	.10	.02
❑	228	Herman Moore	.25	.08
❑	229	Shane Conlan	.10	.02
❑	230	Chris Warren	.25	.08
❑	231	Dana Stubblefield	.25	.08
❑	232	Andre Coleman	.10	.02
❑	233	Kordell Stewart UER	.50	.20
❑	234	Ray Crockett	.10	.02
❑	235	Craig Heyward	.10	.02
❑	236	Mike Fox	.10	.02
❑	237	Derek Brown RBK	.10	.02
❑	238	Thomas Lewis	.10	.02
❑	239	Hugh Douglas	.25	.08
❑	240	Tom Carter	.10	.02
❑	241	Toby Wright	.10	.02
❑	242	Jason Belser	.10	.02
❑	243	Rodney Peete	.10	.02
❑	244	Napoleon Kaufman	.50	.20
❑	245	Merton Hanks	.10	.02
❑	246	Harry Colon	.10	.02
❑	247	Greg Hill	.25	.08
❑	248	Vincent Brisby	.10	.02
❑	249	Eric Hill	.10	.02
❑	250	Brett Favre	2.50	1.00
❑	251	Leroy Hoard	.10	.02
❑	252	Eric Guliford	.10	.02
❑	253	Stanley Richard	.25	.08
❑	254	Carlos Jenkins	.10	.02
❑	255	D'Marco Farr	.10	.02
❑	256	Carlton Gray	.10	.02
❑	257	Derek Loville	.10	.02
❑	258	Ray Buchanan	.10	.02
❑	259	Jake Reed	.25	.08
❑	260	Dan Marino	2.50	1.00
❑	261	Brad Baxter	.10	.02
❑	262	Pat Swilling	.10	.02
❑	263	Andy Harmon	.10	.02
❑	264	Harold Green	.10	.02
❑	265	Shannon Sharpe	.25	.08
❑	266	Erik Kramer	.10	.02
❑	267	Lamar Lathon	.10	.02
❑	268	Stevon Moore	.10	.02
❑	269	Tony Martin	.25	.08

❑ 270 Bruce Smith .25 .08
❑ 271 James Washington .10 .02
❑ 272 Tyrone Poole .10 .02
❑ 273 Eric Swann .10 .02
❑ 274 Dexter Carter .10 .02
❑ 275 Greg Lloyd .25 .08
❑ 276 Michael Zordich .10 .02
❑ 277 Steve Wisniewski .10 .02
❑ 278 Chris Calloway .10 .02
❑ 279 Irv Smith .10 .02
❑ 280 Steve Young 1.00 .40
❑ 281 James O.Stewart .25 .08
❑ 282 Blaine Bishop .10 .02
❑ 283 Rob Moore .25 .08
❑ 284 Eric Metcalf .10 .02
❑ 285 Kerry Collins .50 .20
❑ 286 Dan Wilkinson .10 .02
❑ 287 Curtis Conway .50 .20
❑ 288 Jay Novacek .10 .02
❑ 289 Henry Ellard .10 .02
❑ 290 Curtis Martin 1.00 .40
❑ 291 Brett Perriman .10 .02
❑ 292 Jeff Lageman .10 .02
❑ 293 Trent Dilfer .50 .20
❑ 294 Cortez Kennedy .10 .02
❑ 295 Jeff Hostetler .10 .02
❑ 296 Mark Fields .10 .02
❑ 297 Qadry Ismail .25 .08
❑ 298 Steve Bono .10 .02
❑ 299 Tony Tolbert .10 .02
❑ 300 Jerry Rice 1.25 .50
❑ 301 Marvcus Patton .10 .02
❑ 302 Robert Brooks .50 .20
❑ 303 Terry Ray RC .10 .02
❑ 304 John Thierry .10 .02
❑ 305 Errict Rhett .25 .08
❑ 306 Ricardo McDonald .10 .02
❑ 307 Antonio London .10 .02
❑ 308 Lonnie Johnson .10 .02
❑ 309 Mark Collins .10 .02
❑ 310 Marshall Faulk .60 .25
❑ 311 Anthony Pleasant .10 .02
❑ 312 Howard Griffith .10 .02
❑ 313 Roosevelt Potts .10 .02
❑ 314 Jim Flanigan .10 .02
❑ 315 Omar Ellison RC .10 .02
❑ 316 Boomer Esiason SP .25 .08
❑ 317 Leslie O'Neal SP .10 .02
❑ 318 Jerome Bettis SP .50 .20
❑ 319 Larry Brown SP .10 .02
❑ 320 Neil O'Donnell SP .25 .08
❑ 321 Andre Rison SP .25 .08
❑ 322 Cornelius Bennett SP .10 .02
❑ 323 Quinn Early SP .10 .02
❑ 324 Bryan Cox SP .10 .02
❑ 325 Irving Fryar SP .25 .08
❑ 326 Eddie Robinson SP .10 .02
❑ 327 Chris Doleman SP .10 .02
❑ 328 Sean Gilbert SP .10 .02
❑ 329 Steve Walsh SP .10 .02
❑ 330 Kevin Greene SP .25 .08
❑ 331 Chris Spielman SP .10 .02
❑ 332 Jeff Graham SP .10 .02
❑ 333 Anthony Dorsett SP RC .10 .02
❑ 334 Amani Toomer SP RC 1.50 .60
❑ 335 Walt Harris SP RC .10 .02
❑ 336 Ray Mickens SP RC .10 .02
❑ 337 Danny Kanell SP RC .50 .20
❑ 338 Daryl Gardener SP RC .10 .02
❑ 339 Jonathan Ogden SP .25 .08
❑ 340 Eddie George SP RC 2.00 .75
❑ 341 Jeff Lewis SP RC .25 .08
❑ 342 Terrell Owens SP RC 4.00 1.50
❑ 343 Brian Dawkins SP RC 2.00 .75
❑ 344 Tim Biakabutuka SP .50 .20
❑ 345 Marvin Harrison SP 1.50 .60
❑ 346 Lawyer Milloy SP RC .60 .25
❑ 347 Eric Moulds SP .75 .30
❑ 348 Alex Van Dyke SP .25 .08
❑ 349 John Mobley SP .10 .02
❑ 350 Kevin Hardy SP .50 .20
❑ 351 Ray Lewis SP RC 5.00 2.00
❑ 352 Lawrence Phillips SP .50 .20
❑ 353 Stepfret Williams SP RC .25 .08
❑ 354 Bobby Engram SP RC .50 .20
❑ 355 Leeland McElroy SP RC .25 .08
❑ 356 Marco Battaglia SP .10 .02
❑ 357 Rickey Dudley SP .50 .20
❑ 358 Bobby Hoying SP RC .50 .20
❑ 359 Cedric Jones SP RC .10 .02
❑ 360 Keyshawn Johnson SP .50 .20
❑ P19 Scott Mitchell Prototype .50 .20
❑ P31 Rashaan Salaam Prototype .75 .30
❑ P56 Hardy Nickerson Prototype .50 .20
❑ NNO Checklist Card .10 .02

1997 Stadium Club

❑ COMPLETE SET (340) 60.00 25.00
❑ COMP.SERIES 1 (170) 30.00 15.00
❑ COMP.SERIES 2 (170) 30.00 15.00
❑ 1 Junior Seau .75 .30
❑ 2 Michael Irvin .75 .30
❑ 3 Marcus Allen .75 .30
❑ 4 Dale Carter .30 .10
❑ 5 Darnell Autry RC .50 .20
❑ 6 Isaac Bruce .75 .30
❑ 7 Darrell Green .50 .20
❑ 8 Joey Galloway .50 .20
❑ 9 Steve Atwater .30 .10
❑ 10 Kordell Stewart .75 .30
❑ 11 Tony Brackens .30 .10
❑ 12 Gus Frerotte .30 .10
❑ 13 Henry Ellard .30 .10
❑ 14 Charles Way .50 .20
❑ 15 Jim Druckenmiller RC .50 .20
❑ 16 Orlando Thomas .30 .10
❑ 17 Terrell Davis 1.00 .40
❑ 18 Jim Schwantz .30 .10
❑ 19 Derrick Thomas .75 .30
❑ 20 Curtis Martin 1.00 .40
❑ 21 Deion Sanders .75 .30
❑ 22 Bruce Smith .50 .20
❑ 23 Jake Reed .50 .20
❑ 24 Leeland McElroy .30 .10
❑ 25 Jerome Bettis .75 .30
❑ 26 Neil Smith .50 .20
❑ 27 Terry Allen .75 .30
❑ 28 Gilbert Brown .50 .20
❑ 29 Steve McNair 1.00 .40
❑ 30 Kerry Collins .75 .30
❑ 31 Thurman Thomas .75 .30
❑ 32 Kenny Holmes RC .75 .30
❑ 33 Karim Abdul-Jabbar .75 .30
❑ 34 Steve Young 1.00 .40
❑ 35 Jerry Rice 1.50 .60
❑ 36 Jeff George .50 .20
❑ 37 Errict Rhett .30 .10
❑ 38 Mike Alstott .75 .30
❑ 39 Tim Brown .75 .30
❑ 40 Keyshawn Johnson .75 .30
❑ 41 Jim Harbaugh .50 .20
❑ 42 Kevin Hardy .30 .10
❑ 43 Kevin Greene .50 .20
❑ 44 Eric Metcalf .50 .20
❑ 45 Troy Aikman 1.50 .60
❑ 46 Marshall Faulk 1.00 .40
❑ 47 Shannon Sharpe .50 .20
❑ 48 Warren Moon .75 .30
❑ 49 Mark Brunell 1.00 .40
❑ 50 Dan Marino 3.00 1.25
❑ 51 Byron Hanspard RC .50 .20
❑ 52 Chris Chandler .50 .20
❑ 53 Wayne Chrebet .75 .30
❑ 54 Antonio Langham .30 .10
❑ 55 Barry Sanders 2.50 1.00
❑ 56 Curtis Conway .50 .20
❑ 57 Ricky Watters .50 .20
❑ 58 William Thomas .30 .10
❑ 59 Chris Warren .50 .20
❑ 60 Terry Glenn .75 .30
❑ 61 Peter Boulware RC .75 .30
❑ 62 Chad Cota .30 .10
❑ 63 Eddie Kennison .50 .20
❑ 64 Lamar Smith .75 .30
❑ 65 Brett Favre 3.00 1.50
❑ 66 Michael Westbrook .50 .20
❑ 67 Larry Centers .50 .20
❑ 68 Trent Dilfer .75 .30
❑ 69 Stevon Moore .30 .10
❑ 70 John Elway 3.00 1.25
❑ 71 Bryce Paup .30 .10
❑ 72 Quentin Coryatt .30 .10
❑ 73 Rashaan Salaam .30 .10
❑ 74 Thomas Lewis .30 .10
❑ 75 Drew Bledsoe 1.00 .40
❑ 76 Cris Carter .75 .30
❑ 77 Joe Bowden .30 .10
❑ 78 Allen Aldridge .30 .10
❑ 79 Zach Thomas .75 .30
❑ 80 Emmitt Smith 2.50 1.00
❑ 81 Daryl Johnston .50 .20
❑ 82 Vinny Testaverde .50 .20
❑ 83 James O.Stewart .50 .20
❑ 84 Edgar Bennett .50 .20
❑ 85 Shawn Springs RC .50 .20
❑ 86 Elvis Grbac .50 .20
❑ 87 Levon Kirkland .30 .10
❑ 88 Jeff Graham .30 .10
❑ 89 Terrell Fletcher .30 .10
❑ 90 Eddie George .75 .30
❑ 91 Jessie Tuggle .30 .10
❑ 92 Terrell Owens 1.00 .40
❑ 93 Wayne Martin .30 .10
❑ 94 Dwayne Harper .30 .10
❑ 95 Mark Collins .30 .10
❑ 96 Marvcus Patton .30 .10
❑ 97 Napoleon Kaufman .75 .30
❑ 98 Keenan McCardell .50 .20
❑ 99 Ty Detmer .50 .20
❑ 100 Reggie White .75 .30
❑ 101 William Floyd .50 .20
❑ 102 Scott Mitchell .50 .20
❑ 103 Robert Blackmon .30 .10
❑ 104 Dan Wilkinson .30 .10
❑ 105 Warren Sapp .50 .20
❑ 106 Dave Meggett .30 .10
❑ 107 Brian Mitchell .30 .10
❑ 108 Tyrone Poole .30 .10
❑ 109 Derrick Alexander WR .50 .20
❑ 110 David Palmer .30 .10
❑ 111 James Farrior RC .75 .30
❑ 112 Chad Brown .30 .10
❑ 113 Marty Carter .30 .10
❑ 114 Lawrence Phillips .30 .10
❑ 115 Wesley Walls .50 .20
❑ 116 John Friesz .30 .10
❑ 117 Roman Phifer .30 .10
❑ 118 Jason Sehorn .50 .20
❑ 119 Henry Thomas .30 .10
❑ 120 Natrone Means .50 .20
❑ 121 Ty Law .50 .20
❑ 122 Tony Gonzalez RC 3.00 1.25
❑ 123 Kevin Williams .30 .10
❑ 124 Regan Upshaw .30 .10
❑ 125 Antonio Freeman .75 .30
❑ 126 Jessie Armstead .30 .10
❑ 127 Pat Barnes RC .75 .30
❑ 128 Charlie Garner .50 .20
❑ 129 Irving Fryar .50 .20
❑ 130 Rickey Dudley .50 .20
❑ 131 Rodney Harrison RC 1.50 .60
❑ 132 Brent Jones .50 .20
❑ 133 Neil O'Donnell .50 .20
❑ 134 Darryll Lewis .30 .10
❑ 135 Jason Belser .30 .10
❑ 136 Mark Chmura .50 .20
❑ 137 Seth Joyner .30 .10
❑ 138 Herschel Walker .50 .20
❑ 139 Santana Dotson .30 .10
❑ 140 Carl Pickens .50 .20
❑ 141 Terance Mathis .50 .20
❑ 142 Walt Harris .30 .10
❑ 143 John Mobley .30 .10

❑ 144 Gabe Northern .30 .10
❑ 145 Herman Moore .50 .20
❑ 146 Michael Jackson .50 .20
❑ 147 Chris Sanders .30 .10
❑ 148 LeShon Johnson .30 .10
❑ 149 Darrell Russell RC .30 .10
❑ 150 Winslow Oliver .30 .10
❑ 151 Tamarick Vanover .50 .20
❑ 152 Tony Martin .50 .20
❑ 153 Lamar Lathon .30 .10
❑ 154 Ray Mickens .30 .10
❑ 155 Derrick Brooks .75 .30
❑ 156 Warrick Dunn RC 3.00 1.25
❑ 157 Tim McDonald .30 .10
❑ 158 Keith Lyle .30 .10
❑ 159 Terry McDaniel .30 .10
❑ 160 Andre Hastings .30 .10
❑ 161 Phillippi Sparks .30 .10
❑ 162 Tedy Bruschi 1.50 .60
❑ 163 Bryant Westbrook RC .30 .10
❑ 164 Victor Green .30 .10
❑ 165 Jimmy Smith .50 .20
❑ 166 Greg Biekert .30 .10
❑ 167 Frank Sanders .50 .20
❑ 168 Chris Doleman .30 .10
❑ 169 Phil Hansen .30 .10
❑ 170 Walter Jones RC .75 .30
❑ 171 Mark Carrier WR .30 .10
❑ 172 Greg Hill .30 .10
❑ 173 Erik Kramer .30 .10
❑ 174 Chris Spielman .30 .10
❑ 175 Tom Knight RC .30 .10
❑ 176 Sam Mills .30 .10
❑ 177 Robert Smith .50 .20
❑ 178 Dorsey Levens .75 .30
❑ 179 Chris Slade .30 .10
❑ 180 Troy Vincent .30 .10
❑ 181 Mario Bates .30 .10
❑ 182 Ed McCaffrey .50 .20
❑ 183 Mike Mamula .30 .10
❑ 184 Chad Hennings .30 .10
❑ 185 Stan Humphries .50 .20
❑ 186 Reinard Wilson RC .50 .20
❑ 187 Kevin Carter .30 .10
❑ 188 Qadry Ismail .50 .20
❑ 189 Cortez Kennedy .30 .10
❑ 190 Eric Swann .30 .10
❑ 191 Corey Dillon RC 6.00 2.50
❑ 192 Renaldo Wynn .30 .10
❑ 193 Bobby Hebert .30 .10
❑ 194 Fred Barnett .30 .10
❑ 195 Ray Lewis 1.25 .50
❑ 196 Robert Jones .30 .10
❑ 197 Brian Williams .30 .10
❑ 198 Willie McGinest .30 .10
❑ 199 Jake Plummer RC 5.00 2.00
❑ 200 Aeneas Williams .30 .10
❑ 201 Ashley Ambrose .30 .10
❑ 202 Cornelius Bennett .30 .10
❑ 203 Mo Lewis .30 .10
❑ 204 James Hasty .30 .10
❑ 205 Carnell Lake .30 .10
❑ 206 Heath Shuler .30 .10
❑ 207 Dana Stubblefield .30 .10
❑ 208 Corey Miller .30 .10
❑ 209 Ike Hilliard RC 1.25 .50
❑ 210 Bryant Young .30 .10
❑ 211 Hardy Nickerson .30 .10
❑ 212 Blaine Bishop .30 .10
❑ 213 Marcus Robertson .30 .10
❑ 214 Tony Bennett .30 .10
❑ 215 Kent Graham .30 .10
❑ 216 Steve Bono .50 .20
❑ 217 Will Blackwell RC .50 .20
❑ 218 Tyrone Braxton .30 .10
❑ 219 Eric Moulds .75 .30
❑ 220 Rod Woodson .50 .20
❑ 221 Anthony Johnson .30 .10
❑ 222 Willie Davis .30 .10
❑ 223 Darrin Smith .30 .10
❑ 224 Rick Mirer .30 .10
❑ 225 Marvin Harrison .75 .30
❑ 226 Terrell Buckley .30 .10
❑ 227 Joe Aska .30 .10
❑ 228 Yatil Green RC .50 .20
❑ 229 William Fuller .30 .10
❑ 230 Eddie Robinson .30 .10
❑ 231 Brian Blades .30 .10
❑ 232 Michael Sinclair .30 .10
❑ 233 Ken Harvey .30 .10
❑ 234 Harvey Williams .30 .10
❑ 235 Simeon Rice .50 .20
❑ 236 Chris T. Jones .30 .10
❑ 237 Bert Emanuel .50 .20
❑ 238 Corey Sawyer .30 .10
❑ 239 Chris Calloway .30 .10
❑ 240 Jeff Blake .50 .20
❑ 241 Alonzo Spellman .30 .10
❑ 242 Bryan Cox .30 .10
❑ 243 Antowain Smith RC 2.50 1.00
❑ 244 Tim Biakabutuka .50 .20
❑ 245 Ray Crockett .30 .10
❑ 246 Dwayne Rudd .30 .10
❑ 247 Glyn Milburn .30 .10
❑ 248 Gary Plummer .30 .10
❑ 249 O.J. McDuffie .50 .20
❑ 250 Willie Clay .30 .10
❑ 251 Jim Everett .30 .10
❑ 252 Eugene Daniel .30 .10
❑ 253 Corey Widmer .30 .10
❑ 254 Mel Gray .30 .10
❑ 255 Ken Norton .30 .10
❑ 256 Johnnie Morton .50 .20
❑ 257 Courtney Hawkins .30 .10
❑ 258 Ricardo McDonald .30 .10
❑ 259 Todd Lyght .30 .10
❑ 260 Micheal Barrow .30 .10
❑ 261 Aaron Glenn .30 .10
❑ 262 Jeff Herrod .30 .10
❑ 263 Troy Davis RC .50 .20
❑ 264 Eric Hill .30 .10
❑ 265 Darrien Gordon .30 .10
❑ 266 Lake Dawson .30 .10
❑ 267 John Randle .50 .20
❑ 268 Henry Jones .30 .10
❑ 269 Mickey Washington .30 .10
❑ 270 Amani Toomer .50 .20
❑ 271 Steve Grant .30 .10
❑ 272 Adrian Murrell .50 .20
❑ 273 Derrick Witherspoon .30 .10
❑ 274 Albert Lewis .30 .10
❑ 275 Ben Coates .50 .20
❑ 276 Reidel Anthony RC .75 .30
❑ 277 Jim Schwantz .30 .10
❑ 278 Aaron Hayden .30 .10
❑ 279 Ryan McNeil .30 .10
❑ 280 LeRoy Butler .30 .10
❑ 281 Craig Newsome .30 .10
❑ 282 Bill Romanowski .30 .10
❑ 283 Michael Bankston .30 .10
❑ 284 Kevin Smith .30 .10
❑ 285 Byron Bam Morris .30 .10
❑ 286 Darnay Scott .50 .20
❑ 287 David LaFleur RC .30 .10
❑ 288 Randall Cunningham .75 .30
❑ 289 Eric Davis .30 .10
❑ 290 Todd Collins .30 .10
❑ 291 Steve Tovar .30 .10
❑ 292 Jermaine Lewis .75 .30
❑ 293 Alfred Williams .30 .10
❑ 294 Brad Johnson .75 .30
❑ 295 Charles Johnson .50 .20
❑ 296 Ted Johnson .30 .10
❑ 297 Morton Hanks .30 .10
❑ 298 Andre Coleman .30 .10
❑ 299 Keith Jackson .30 .10
❑ 300 Terry Kirby .50 .20
❑ 301 Tony Banks .50 .20
❑ 302 Terrance Shaw .30 .10
❑ 303 Bobby Engram .50 .20
❑ 304 Hugh Douglas .30 .10
❑ 305 Lawyer Milloy .50 .20
❑ 306 James Jett .50 .20
❑ 307 Joey Kent RC .75 .30
❑ 308 Rodney Hampton .50 .20
❑ 309 Dewayne Washington .30 .10
❑ 310 Kevin Lockett RC .50 .20
❑ 311 Ki-Jana Carter .30 .10
❑ 312 Jeff Lageman .30 .10
❑ 313 Don Beebe .30 .10
❑ 314 Willie Williams .30 .10
❑ 315 Tyrone Wheatley .50 .20
❑ 316 Leslie O'Neal .30 .10
❑ 317 Quinn Early .30 .10
❑ 318 Sean Gilbert .30 .10
❑ 319 Tim Bowens .30 .10
❑ 320 Sean Dawkins .30 .10
❑ 321 Ken Dilger .30 .10
❑ 322 George Koonce .30 .10
❑ 323 Jevon Langford .30 .10
❑ 324 Mike Caldwell .30 .10
❑ 325 Orlando Pace RC .75 .30
❑ 326 Garrison Hearst .50 .20
❑ 327 Mike Tomczak .30 .10
❑ 328 Rob Moore .50 .20
❑ 329 Andre Reed .50 .20
❑ 330 Kimble Anders .50 .20
❑ 331 Qadry Ismail .50 .20
❑ 332 Eric Allen .30 .10
❑ 333 Dave Brown .30 .10
❑ 334 Bennie Blades .30 .10
❑ 335 Jamal Anderson .75 .30
❑ 336 John Lynch .50 .20
❑ 337 Tyrone Hughes .30 .10
❑ 338 Ronnie Harmon .30 .10
❑ 339 Rae Carruth RC .30 .10
❑ 340 Robert Brooks .50 .20
❑ P1 Junior Seau Prototype .50 .20
❑ P20 Curtis Martin Prototype 1.00 .40
❑ P21 Deion Sanders Prototype .50 .20
❑ P30 Kerry Collins Prototype .75 .30
❑ P47 Shannon Sharpe Prototype .50 .20
❑ P84 Edgar Bennett Prototype .50 .20

1998 Stadium Club

❑ COMPLETE SET (195) 60.00 25.00
❑ 1 Barry Sanders 2.50 1.00
❑ 2 Tony Martin .50 .20
❑ 3 Fred Lane .30 .10
❑ 4 Darren Woodson .30 .10
❑ 5 Andre Reed .50 .20
❑ 6 Blaine Bishop .30 .10
❑ 7 Robert Brooks .50 .20
❑ 8 Tony Banks .50 .20
❑ 9 Charles Way .30 .10
❑ 10 Mark Brunell .75 .30
❑ 11 Darrell Green .50 .20
❑ 12 Aeneas Williams .30 .10
❑ 13 Rob Johnson .50 .20
❑ 14 Deion Sanders .75 .30
❑ 15 Marshall Faulk 1.00 .40
❑ 16 Stephen Boyd .30 .10
❑ 17 Adrian Murrell .50 .20
❑ 18 Wayne Chrebet .75 .30
❑ 19 Michael Sinclair .30 .10
❑ 20 Dan Marino 3.00 1.25
❑ 21 Willie Davis .30 .10
❑ 22 Chris Warren .50 .20
❑ 23 John Mobley .30 .10
❑ 24 Shannon Sharpe .50 .20
❑ 25 Thurman Thomas .75 .30
❑ 26 Corey Dillon .75 .30
❑ 27 Zach Thomas .75 .30
❑ 28 James Jett .50 .20
❑ 29 Eric Metcalf .30 .10
❑ 30 Drew Bledsoe 1.25 .50
❑ 31 Scott Greene .30 .10
❑ 32 Simeon Rice .50 .20
❑ 33 Robert Smith .75 .30
❑ 34 Keenan McCardell .50 .20
❑ 35 Jessie Armstead .30 .10
❑ 36 Jerry Rice 1.50 .60
❑ 37 Eric Green .30 .10

❑	38	Terrell Owens	.75	.30
❑	39	Tim Brown	.75	.30
❑	40	Vinny Testaverde	.50	.20
❑	41	Brian Stablein	.30	.10
❑	42	Bert Emanuel	.50	.20
❑	43	Terry Glenn	.75	.30
❑	44	Chad Cota	.30	.10
❑	45	Jermaine Lewis	.50	.20
❑	46	Derrick Thomas	.75	.30
❑	47	O.J. McDuffie	.50	.20
❑	48	Frank Wycheck	.30	.10
❑	49	Steve Broussard	.30	.10
❑	50	Terrell Davis	.75	.30
❑	51	Eric Allen	.30	.10
❑	52	Napoleon Kaufman	.75	.30
❑	53	Dan Wilkinson	.30	.10
❑	54	Kerry Collins	.50	.20
❑	55	Frank Sanders	.50	.20
❑	56	Jeff Burris	.30	.10
❑	57	Michael Westbrook	.50	.20
❑	58	Michael McCrary	.30	.10
❑	59	Bobby Hoying	.50	.20
❑	60	Jerome Bettis	.75	.30
❑	61	Amp Lee	.30	.10
❑	62	Levon Kirkland	.30	.10
❑	63	Dana Stubblefield	.30	.10
❑	64	Terance Mathis	.50	.20
❑	65	Mark Chmura	.50	.20
❑	66	Bryant Westbrook	.30	.10
❑	67	Rod Smith	.50	.20
❑	68	Derrick Alexander	.50	.20
❑	69	Jason Taylor	.50	.20
❑	70	Eddie George	.75	.30
❑	71	Elvis Grbac	.50	.20
❑	72	Junior Seau	.75	.30
❑	73	Marvin Harrison	.75	.30
❑	74	Neil O'Donnell	.50	.20
❑	75	Johnnie Morton	.50	.20
❑	76	John Randle	.50	.20
❑	77	Danny Kanell	.50	.20
❑	78	Charlie Garner	.50	.20
❑	79	J.J. Stokes	.50	.20
❑	80	Troy Aikman	1.50	.60
❑	81	Gus Frerotte	.30	.10
❑	82	Jake Plummer	.75	.30
❑	83	Andre Hastings	.30	.10
❑	84	Steve Atwater	.30	.10
❑	85	Larry Centers	.30	.10
❑	86	Kevin Hardy	.30	.10
❑	87	Willie McGinest	.30	.10
❑	88	Joey Galloway	.50	.20
❑	89	Charles Johnson	.30	.10
❑	90	Warrick Dunn	.75	.30
❑	91	Derrick Rodgers	.30	.10
❑	92	Aaron Glenn	.30	.10
❑	93	Shawn Jefferson	.30	.10
❑	94	Antonio Freeman	.75	.30
❑	95	Jake Reed	.50	.20
❑	96	Reidel Anthony	.50	.20
❑	97	Cris Dishman	.30	.10
❑	98	Jason Sehorn	.50	.20
❑	99	Herman Moore	.50	.20
❑	100	John Elway	3.00	1.25
❑	101	Brad Johnson	.75	.30
❑	102	Jeff George	.50	.20
❑	103	Emmitt Smith	2.50	1.00
❑	104	Steve McNair	.75	.30
❑	105	Ed McCaffrey	.50	.20
❑	106	Errict Rhett	.50	.20
❑	107	Dorsey Levens	.75	.30
❑	108	Michael Jackson	.30	.10
❑	109	Carl Pickens	.50	.20
❑	110	James Stewart	.50	.20
❑	111	Karim Abdul-Jabbar	.75	.30
❑	112	Jim Harbaugh	.50	.20
❑	113	Yancey Thigpen	.30	.10
❑	114	Chad Brown	.30	.10
❑	115	Chris Sanders	.30	.10
❑	116	Cris Carter	.75	.30
❑	117	Glenn Foley	.50	.20
❑	118	Ben Coates	.50	.20
❑	119	Jamal Anderson	.75	.30
❑	120	Steve Young	1.00	.40
❑	121	Scott Mitchell	.50	.20
❑	122	Rob Moore	.50	.20
❑	123	Bobby Engram	.50	.20
❑	124	Rod Woodson	.50	.20
❑	125	Terry Allen	.75	.30
❑	126	Warren Sapp	.50	.20
❑	127	Irving Fryar	.50	.20
❑	128	Isaac Bruce	.75	.30
❑	129	Rae Carruth	.30	.10
❑	130	Sean Dawkins	.30	.10
❑	131	Andre Rison	.50	.20
❑	132	Kevin Greene	.50	.20
❑	133	Warren Moon	.75	.30
❑	134	Keyshawn Johnson	.75	.30
❑	135	Jay Graham	.30	.10
❑	136	Mike Alstott	.75	.30
❑	137	Peter Boulware	.30	.10
❑	138	Doug Evans	.30	.10
❑	139	Jimmy Smith	.50	.20
❑	140	Kordell Stewart	.75	.30
❑	141	Tamarick Vanover	.30	.10
❑	142	Chris Slade	.30	.10
❑	143	Freddie Jones	.30	.10
❑	144	Erik Kramer	.30	.10
❑	145	Ricky Watters	.50	.20
❑	146	Chris Chandler	.50	.20
❑	147	Garrison Hearst	.75	.30
❑	148	Trent Dilfer	.75	.30
❑	149	Bruce Smith	.50	.20
❑	150	Brett Favre	3.00	1.25
❑	151	Will Blackwell	.30	.10
❑	152	Rickey Dudley	.30	.10
❑	153	Natrone Means	.50	.20
❑	154	Curtis Conway	.50	.20
❑	155	Tony Gonzalez	.75	.30
❑	156	Jeff Blake	.50	.20
❑	157	Michael Irvin	.75	.30
❑	158	Curtis Martin	.75	.30
❑	159	Tim McDonald	.30	.10
❑	160	Wesley Walls	.50	.20
❑	161	Michael Strahan	.50	.20
❑	162	Reggie White	.75	.30
❑	163	Jeff Graham	.30	.10
❑	164	Ray Lewis	.75	.30
❑	165	Antowain Smith	.75	.30
❑	166	Ryan Leaf RC	2.50	1.00
❑	167	Jerome Pathon RC	2.50	1.00
❑	168	Duane Starks RC	1.25	.50
❑	169	Brian Simmons RC	2.00	.75
❑	170	Pat Johnson RC	2.00	.75
❑	171	Keith Brooking RC	2.50	1.00
❑	172	Kevin Dyson RC	2.50	1.00
❑	173	Robert Edwards RC	2.00	.75
❑	174	Grant Wistrom RC	2.00	.75
❑	175	Curtis Enis RC	1.25	.50
❑	176	John Avery RC	2.00	.75
❑	177	Jason Peter RC	1.25	.50
❑	178	Brian Griese RC	5.00	2.00
❑	179	Tavian Banks RC	2.00	.75
❑	180	Andre Wadsworth RC	2.00	.75
❑	181	Skip Hicks RC	2.00	.75
❑	182	Hines Ward RC	10.00	5.00
❑	183	Greg Ellis RC	1.25	.50
❑	184	Robert Holcombe RC	2.00	.75
❑	185	Joe Jurevicius RC	2.50	1.00
❑	186	Takeo Spikes RC	2.50	1.00
❑	187	Ahman Green RC	12.00	5.00
❑	188	Jacquez Green RC	2.00	.75
❑	189	Randy Moss RC	15.00	7.50
❑	190	Charles Woodson RC	3.00	1.25
❑	191	Fred Taylor RC	4.00	1.50
❑	192	Marcus Nash RC	1.25	.50
❑	193	Germane Crowell RC	2.00	.75
❑	194	Tim Dwight RC	2.50	1.00
❑	195	Peyton Manning RC	25.00	12.50

1999 Stadium Club

❑		COMPLETE SET (200)	60.00	25.00
❑		COMP.SET w/o SP's (175)	20.00	7.50
❑		UNPRICED 1/1 PRESS PLATES EXIST		
❑		FOUR DIFF.PP's PRODUCED PER CARD		
❑	1	Dan Marino	2.50	1.00
❑	2	Andre Reed	.50	.20
❑	3	Michael Westbrook	.50	.20
❑	4	Isaac Bruce	.75	.30
❑	5	Curtis Martin	.75	.30
❑	6	Courtney Hawkins	.30	.10
❑	7	Charles Way	.30	.10
❑	8	Terrell Owens	.75	.30
❑	9	Warrick Dunn	.75	.30
❑	10	Jake Plummer	.50	.20
❑	11	Chad Brown	.30	.10
❑	12	Yancey Thigpen	.30	.10
❑	13	Lamar Thomas	.30	.10
❑	14	Keenan McCardell	.50	.20
❑	15	Shannon Sharpe	.50	.20
❑	16	Robert Brooks	.50	.20
❑	17	Cameron Cleeland	.30	.10
❑	18	Derrick Thomas	.75	.30
❑	19	Mark Brunell	.75	.30
❑	20	Jamal Anderson	.75	.30
❑	21	Germane Crowell	.30	.10
❑	22	Rod Smith	.50	.20
❑	23	Ty Law	.50	.20
❑	24	Cris Carter	.75	.30
❑	25	Terrell Davis	.75	.30
❑	26	Takeo Spikes	.30	.10
❑	27	Tim Biakabutuka	.50	.20
❑	28	Jermaine Lewis	.50	.20
❑	29	Adrian Murrell	.50	.20
❑	30	Doug Flutie	.75	.30
❑	31	Curtis Enis	.30	.10
❑	32	Skip Hicks	.30	.10
❑	33	Steve McNair	.75	.30
❑	34	Charles Woodson	.75	.30
❑	35	Jessie Armstead	.30	.10
❑	36	Shawn Springs	.30	.10
❑	37	Levon Kirkland	.30	.10
❑	38	Freddie Jones	.30	.10
❑	39	Warren Sapp	.30	.10
❑	40	Emmitt Smith	1.50	.60
❑	41	Reidel Anthony	.50	.20
❑	42	Tony Simmons	.30	.10
❑	43	Andre Hastings	.30	.10
❑	44	Byron Bam Morris	.30	.10
❑	45	Jimmy Smith	.50	.20
❑	46	Antonio Freeman	.75	.30
❑	47	Herman Moore	.50	.20
❑	48	Muhsin Muhammad	.50	.20
❑	49	Chris Chandler	.50	.20
❑	50	John Elway	2.50	1.00
❑	51	Aeneas Williams	.30	.10
❑	52	Bobby Engram	.50	.20
❑	53	Keith Poole	.30	.10
❑	54	Zach Thomas	.75	.30
❑	55	Mike Alstott	.75	.30
❑	56	Junior Seau	.75	.30
❑	57	Aaron Glenn	.30	.10
❑	58	Darrell Green	.30	.10
❑	59	Thurman Thomas	.50	.20
❑	60	Troy Aikman	1.50	.60
❑	61	Bill Romanowski	.30	.10
❑	62	Wesley Walls	.50	.20
❑	63	Andre Wadsworth	.30	.10
❑	64	Robert Smith	.75	.30
❑	65	Elvis Grbac	.50	.20
❑	66	Terry Fair	.30	.10
❑	67	Ben Coates	.50	.20
❑	68	Bert Emanuel	.50	.20
❑	69	Jacquez Green	.30	.10
❑	70	Barry Sanders	2.50	1.00
❑	71	James Jett	.50	.20
❑	72	Gary Brown	.30	.10
❑	73	Stephen Alexander	.30	.10
❑	74	Wayne Chrebet	.50	.20
❑	75	Drew Bledsoe	1.00	.40
❑	76	John Lynch	.50	.20
❑	77	Jake Reed	.50	.20
❑	78	Marvin Harrison	.75	.30
❑	79	Johnnie Morton	.50	.20
❑	80	Brett Favre	2.50	1.00

- ❑ 81 Charlie Batch .75 .30
- ❑ 82 Antowain Smith .75 .30
- ❑ 83 Mikhael Ricks .30 .10
- ❑ 84 Derrick Mayes .30 .10
- ❑ 85 John Mobley .30 .10
- ❑ 86 Ernie Mills .30 .10
- ❑ 87 Jeff Blake .50 .20
- ❑ 88 Curtis Conway .50 .20
- ❑ 89 Bruce Smith .50 .20
- ❑ 90 Peyton Manning 2.50 1.00
- ❑ 91 Tyrone Davis .30 .10
- ❑ 92 Ray Buchanan .30 .10
- ❑ 93 Tim Dwight .75 .30
- [illegible]
- ❑ 95 Vonnie Holliday .30 .10
- ❑ 96 Jon Kitna .75 .30
- ❑ 97 Trent Dilfer .50 .20
- ❑ 98 Jerome Bettis .75 .30
- ❑ 99 Dedric Ward .30 .10
- ❑ 100 Fred Taylor .75 .30
- ❑ 101 Ike Hilliard .30 .10
- ❑ 102 Frank Wycheck .30 .10
- ❑ 103 Eric Moulds .75 .30
- ❑ 104 Rob Moore .50 .20
- ❑ 105 Ed McCaffrey .50 .20
- ❑ 106 Carl Pickens .50 .20
- ❑ 107 Priest Holmes 1.25 .50
- ❑ 108 Kevin Hardy .30 .10
- ❑ 109 Terry Glenn .75 .30
- ❑ 110 Keyshawn Johnson .75 .30
- ❑ 111 Karim Abdul-Jabbar .50 .20
- ❑ 112 Stephen Boyd .30 .10
- ❑ 113 Ahman Green .75 .30
- ❑ 114 Duce Staley .75 .30
- ❑ 115 Vinny Testaverde .50 .20
- ❑ 116 Napoleon Kaufman .75 .30
- ❑ 117 Frank Sanders .50 .20
- ❑ 118 Peter Boulware .30 .10
- ❑ 119 Kevin Greene .30 .10
- ❑ 120 Steve Young 1.00 .40
- ❑ 121 Darnay Scott .30 .10
- ❑ 122 Deion Sanders .75 .30
- ❑ 123 Corey Dillon .75 .30
- ❑ 124 Randall Cunningham .75 .30
- ❑ 125 Eddie George .75 .30
- ❑ 126 Derrick Alexander .30 .10
- ❑ 127 Mark Chmura .30 .10
- ❑ 128 Michael Sinclair .30 .10
- ❑ 129 Rickey Dudley .30 .10
- ❑ 130 Joey Galloway .50 .20
- ❑ 131 Michael Strahan .50 .20
- ❑ 132 Ricky Proehl .30 .10
- ❑ 133 Natrone Means .50 .20
- ❑ 134 Dorsey Levens .75 .30
- ❑ 135 Andre Rison .50 .20
- ❑ 136 Alonzo Mayes .30 .10
- ❑ 137 John Randle .50 .20
- ❑ 138 Terance Mathis .50 .20
- ❑ 139 Rae Carruth .30 .10
- ❑ 140 Jerry Rice 1.50 .60
- ❑ 141 Michael Irvin .50 .20
- ❑ 142 Oronde Gadsden .50 .20
- ❑ 143 Jerome Pathon .30 .10
- ❑ 144 Ricky Watters .50 .20
- ❑ 145 J.J. Stokes .50 .20
- ❑ 146 Kordell Stewart .50 .20
- ❑ 147 Tim Brown .75 .30
- ❑ 148 Garrison Hearst .50 .20
- ❑ 149 Tony Gonzalez .75 .30
- ❑ 150 Randy Moss 2.00 .75
- ❑ 151 Daunte Culpepper RC 6.00 2.50
- ❑ 152 Amos Zereoue RC 2.00 .75
- ❑ 153 Champ Bailey RC 2.50 1.00
- ❑ 154 Peerless Price RC 2.00 .75
- ❑ 155 Edgerrin James RC 6.00 2.50
- ❑ 156 Joe Germaine RC 1.50 .60
- ❑ 157 David Boston RC 2.00 .75
- ❑ 158 Kevin Faulk RC 2.00 .75
- ❑ 159 Troy Edwards RC 1.50 .60
- ❑ 160 Akili Smith RC 1.50 .60
- ❑ 161 Kevin Johnson RC 2.00 .75
- ❑ 162 Rob Konrad RC 1.50 .60
- ❑ 163 Shaun King RC 1.50 .60
- ❑ 164 James Johnson RC 1.50 .60
- ❑ 165 Donovan McNabb RC 8.00 3.00
- ❑ 166 Torry Holt RC 4.00 1.50
- ❑ 167 Mike Cloud RC 1.50 .60
- ❑ 168 Sedrick Irvin RC 1.00 .40
- ❑ 169 Cade McNown RC 1.50 .60
- ❑ 170 Ricky Williams RC 3.00 1.25
- ❑ 171 Karsten Bailey RC 1.50 .60
- ❑ 172 Cecil Collins RC 1.00 .40
- ❑ 173 Brock Huard RC 2.00 .75
- ❑ 174 D'Wayne Bates RC 1.50 .60
- ❑ 175 Tim Couch RC 2.00 .75
- ❑ 176 Torrance Small .30 .10
- ❑ 177 Warren Moon .75 .30
- ❑ 178 Rocket Ismail .50 .20
- ❑ 179 Marshall Faulk 1.00 .40
- ❑ 180 Trent Green .75 .30
- [illegible]
- ❑ 182 Pete Mitchell .30 .10
- ❑ 183 Jeff Graham .30 .10
- ❑ 184 Eddie Kennison .50 .20
- ❑ 185 Kerry Collins .50 .20
- ❑ 186 Eric Green .30 .10
- ❑ 187 Kyle Brady .30 .10
- ❑ 188 Tony Martin .50 .20
- ❑ 189 Jim Harbaugh .50 .20
- ❑ 190 Erik Kramer .30 .10
- ❑ 191 Steve Atwater .30 .10
- ❑ 192 Chad Bratzke .30 .10
- ❑ 193 Charles Johnson .30 .10
- ❑ 194 Damon Gibson .30 .10
- ❑ 195 Jeff George .50 .20
- ❑ 196 Scott Mitchell .30 .10
- ❑ 197 Terry Kirby .30 .10
- ❑ 198 Rich Gannon .75 .30
- ❑ 199 Chris Spielman .30 .10
- ❑ 200 Brad Johnson .75 .30
- ❑ PP4 Emmitt Smith PROMO 3.00 1.25

2000 Stadium Club

- ❑ COMPLETE SET (175) 50.00 20.00
- ❑ COMP.SET w/o SP's (150) 20.00 7.50
- ❑ 1 Peyton Manning 1.50 .60
- ❑ 2 Pete Mitchell .25 .08
- ❑ 3 Napoleon Kaufman .40 .15
- ❑ 4 Mikhael Ricks .25 .08
- ❑ 5 Mike Alstott .60 .25
- ❑ 6 Brad Johnson .60 .25
- ❑ 7 Tony Gonzalez .40 .15
- ❑ 8 Germane Crowell .25 .08
- ❑ 9 Marcus Robinson .60 .25
- ❑ 10 Stephen Davis .60 .25
- ❑ 11 Terance Mathis .40 .15
- ❑ 12 Jake Plummer .40 .15
- ❑ 13 Qadry Ismail .40 .15
- ❑ 14 Cade McNown .25 .08
- ❑ 15 Zach Thomas .60 .25
- ❑ 16 Curtis Martin .60 .25
- ❑ 17 Torrance Small .25 .08
- ❑ 18 Steve McNair .60 .25
- ❑ 19 Jim Harbaugh .40 .15
- ❑ 20 Keyshawn Johnson .60 .25
- ❑ 21 Antonio Freeman .60 .25
- ❑ 22 Ed McCaffrey .60 .25
- ❑ 23 Elvis Grbac .40 .15
- ❑ 24 Peerless Price .40 .15
- ❑ 25 Jerome Bettis .60 .25
- ❑ 26 Yancey Thigpen .25 .08
- ❑ 27 Jake Delhomme RC 3.00 1.25
- ❑ 28 Keith Poole .25 .08
- ❑ 29 Carl Pickens .40 .15
- ❑ 30 Jerry Rice 1.25 .50
- ❑ 31 Rob Moore .40 .15
- ❑ 32 Reidel Anthony .25 .08
- ❑ 33 Jimmy Smith .40 .15
- ❑ 34 Ray Lucas .40 .15
- ❑ 35 Troy Aikman 1.25 .50
- ❑ 36 Steve Beuerlein .40 .15
- ❑ 37 Charlie Batch .60 .25
- ❑ 38 Derrick Mayes .40 .15
- ❑ 39 Tim Brown .60 .25
- ❑ 40 Eddie George .60 .25
- ❑ 41 O.J. McDuffie .40 .15
- ❑ 42 Ike Hilliard .40 .15
- ❑ 43 Bill Schroeder .40 .15
- ❑ 44 Jim Miller .25 .08
- [illegible]
- ❑ 46 Fred Taylor .60 .25
- ❑ 47 Ricky Watters .40 .15
- ❑ 48 Tyrone Wheatley .40 .15
- ❑ 49 Bruce Smith .40 .15
- ❑ 50 Marshall Faulk .75 .30
- ❑ 51 Kevin Carter .25 .08
- ❑ 52 Champ Bailey .40 .15
- ❑ 53 Troy Edwards .25 .08
- ❑ 54 Doug Flutie .60 .25
- ❑ 55 Charles Johnson .40 .15
- ❑ 56 Michael Westbrook .40 .15
- ❑ 57 Frank Wycheck .25 .08
- ❑ 58 Drew Bledsoe .75 .30
- ❑ 59 Terrence Wilkins .25 .08
- ❑ 60 Ricky Williams .60 .25
- ❑ 61 Rod Smith .40 .15
- ❑ 62 Errict Rhett .40 .15
- ❑ 63 Vinny Testaverde .40 .15
- ❑ 64 Jacquez Green .25 .08
- ❑ 65 Curtis Conway .40 .15
- ❑ 66 Wayne Chrebet .40 .15
- ❑ 67 Albert Connell .25 .08
- ❑ 68 Kordell Stewart .40 .15
- ❑ 69 Bert Emanuel .25 .08
- ❑ 70 Randy Moss 1.25 .50
- ❑ 71 Akili Smith .25 .08
- ❑ 72 Brian Griese .60 .25
- ❑ 73 Frank Sanders .40 .15
- ❑ 74 Wesley Walls .25 .08
- ❑ 75 Michael Pittman .25 .08
- ❑ 76 Steve Young .75 .30
- ❑ 77 Jevon Kearse .60 .25
- ❑ 78 Az-Zahir Hakim .40 .15
- ❑ 79 James Stewart .40 .15
- ❑ 80 Brett Favre 2.00 .75
- ❑ 81 Dan Marino 2.00 .75
- ❑ 82 Joe Horn .40 .15
- ❑ 83 Mark Brunell .60 .25
- ❑ 84 Eddie Kennison .40 .15
- ❑ 85 Deion Sanders .60 .25
- ❑ 86 Priest Holmes .75 .30
- ❑ 87 Terry Glenn .40 .15
- ❑ 88 Olandis Gary .60 .25
- ❑ 89 Patrick Jeffers .60 .25
- ❑ 90 Emmitt Smith 1.25 .50
- ❑ 91 J.J. Stokes .40 .15
- ❑ 92 Warrick Dunn .60 .25
- ❑ 93 Damon Huard .60 .25
- ❑ 94 Herman Moore .40 .15
- ❑ 95 Corey Dillon .60 .25
- ❑ 96 Joey Galloway .40 .15
- ❑ 97 Jamal Anderson .60 .25
- ❑ 98 Junior Seau .60 .25
- ❑ 99 Robert Smith .60 .25
- ❑ 100 Edgerrin James 1.00 .40
- ❑ 101 Derrick Alexander .40 .15
- ❑ 102 Johnnie Morton .40 .15
- ❑ 103 Sean Dawkins .25 .08
- ❑ 104 Derrick Brooks .60 .25
- ❑ 105 Rickey Dudley .25 .08
- ❑ 106 Keenan McCardell .40 .15
- ❑ 107 Kerry Collins .40 .15
- ❑ 108 Kevin Johnson .60 .25
- ❑ 109 Eric Moulds .60 .25
- ❑ 110 Terrell Davis .60 .25
- ❑ 111 Shawn Jefferson .25 .08
- ❑ 112 Donovan McNabb 1.00 .40
- ❑ 113 Torry Holt .60 .25
- ❑ 114 Marvin Harrison .60 .25
- ❑ 115 Amani Toomer .40 .15
- ❑ 116 Tony Martin .40 .15
- ❑ 117 Curtis Enis .25 .08
- ❑ 118 Tiki Barber .60 .25

❑ 119 Freddie Jones	.25	.08
❑ 120 Muhsin Muhammad	.40	.15
❑ 121 Shaun King	.25	.08
❑ 122 Isaac Bruce	.60	.25
❑ 123 Duce Staley	.60	.25
❑ 124 Hardy Nickerson	.25	.08
❑ 125 Corey Bradford	.40	.15
❑ 126 Kevin Hardy	.25	.08
❑ 127 Hines Ward	.60	.25
❑ 128 Charlie Garner	.40	.15
❑ 129 Warren Sapp	.40	.15
❑ 130 Tim Couch	.40	.15
❑ 131 Kevin Dyson	.40	.15
❑ 132 Rocket Ismail	.40	.15
❑ 133 Tim Dwight	.60	.25
❑ 134 Darnay Scott	.40	.15
❑ 135 Jeff George	.40	.15
❑ 136 Dorsey Levens	.40	.15
❑ 137 Jeff Blake	.40	.15
❑ 138 Jon Kitna	.60	.25
❑ 139 Rich Gannon	.60	.25
❑ 140 Cris Carter	.60	.25
❑ 141 Jeff Graham	.25	.08
❑ 142 James Johnson	.25	.08
❑ 143 Tim Biakabutuka	.40	.15
❑ 144 Bobby Engram	.40	.15
❑ 145 Tony Banks	.40	.15
❑ 146 Shannon Sharpe	.40	.15
❑ 147 Antowain Smith	.40	.15
❑ 148 Terrell Owens	.60	.25
❑ 149 Rob Johnson	.40	.15
❑ 150 Kurt Warner	1.25	.50
❑ 151 Thomas Jones RC	4.00	1.50
❑ 152 Chad Pennington RC	6.00	2.50
❑ 153 Ron Dayne RC	2.50	1.00
❑ 154 Tee Martin RC	2.50	1.00
❑ 155 Reuben Droughns RC	3.00	1.25
❑ 156 Jerry Porter RC	3.00	1.25
❑ 157 R.Jay Soward RC	2.00	.75
❑ 158 Sylvester Morris RC	2.00	.75
❑ 159 Todd Pinkston RC	2.50	1.00
❑ 160 Courtney Brown RC	2.50	1.00
❑ 161 Travis Taylor RC	2.50	1.00
❑ 162 Ron Dugans RC	2.00	.75
❑ 163 Laveranues Coles RC	3.00	1.25
❑ 164 Joe Hamilton RC	2.00	.75
❑ 165 Curtis Keaton RC	2.00	.75
❑ 166 Bubba Franks RC	2.50	1.00
❑ 167 Dennis Northcutt RC	2.50	1.00
❑ 168 Chris Redman RC	2.00	.75
❑ 169 Travis Prentice RC	2.00	.75
❑ 170 Shaun Alexander RC	12.00	5.00
❑ 171 Jamal Lewis RC	6.00	2.50
❑ 172 Peter Warrick RC	2.50	1.00
❑ 173 J.R. Redmond RC	2.00	.75
❑ 174 Trung Canidate RC	2.00	.75
❑ 175 Plaxico Burress RC	5.00	2.00

2001 Stadium Club

❑ COMPLETE SET (175)	120.00	60.00
❑ COMP.SET w/o SPs (125)	20.00	7.50
❑ 1 Peyton Manning	1.50	.60
❑ 2 Akili Smith	.25	.08
❑ 3 Brian Griese	.60	.25
❑ 4 Wayne Chrebet	.40	.15
❑ 5 Oronde Gadsden	.40	.15
❑ 6 Marvin Harrison	.60	.25
❑ 7 Charles Johnson	.25	.08
❑ 8 Jay Fiedler	.60	.25
❑ 9 Kerry Collins	.40	.15
❑ 10 Troy Aikman	1.00	.40
❑ 11 Donovan McNabb	.75	.30
❑ 12 Ike Hilliard	.40	.15
❑ 13 Warrick Dunn	.60	.25
❑ 14 Derrick Alexander	.40	.15
❑ 15 Jake Plummer	.40	.15
❑ 16 Corey Dillon	.60	.25
❑ 17 Ahman Green	.60	.25
❑ 18 Keenan McCardell	.25	.08
❑ 19 Derrick Mason	.40	.15
❑ 20 Jerry Rice	1.25	.50
❑ 21 Emmitt Smith	1.25	.50
❑ 22 Dedric Ward	.25	.08
❑ 23 Jamal Anderson	.60	.25
❑ 24 Charlie Garner	.40	.15
❑ 25 Vinny Testaverde	.40	.15
❑ 26 Shaun Alexander	.75	.30
❑ 27 Terry Glenn	.40	.15
❑ 28 Cade McNown	.25	.08
❑ 29 Germane Crowell	.25	.08
❑ 30 Jeff Graham	.25	.08
❑ 31 Rich Gannon	.60	.25
❑ 32 Jevon Kearse	.40	.15
❑ 33 Shannon Sharpe	.40	.15
❑ 34 Marcus Robinson	.60	.25
❑ 35 Rod Smith	.40	.15
❑ 36 Curtis Martin	.60	.25
❑ 37 Robert Smith	.60	.25
❑ 38 Marshall Faulk	.75	.30
❑ 39 Tony Richardson	.25	.08
❑ 40 Travis Prentice	.25	.08
❑ 41 Edgerrin James	.75	.30
❑ 42 Duce Staley	.60	.25
❑ 43 Keyshawn Johnson	.60	.25
❑ 44 Joe Horn	.40	.15
❑ 45 Shawn Bryson	.25	.08
❑ 46 Ray Lewis	.60	.25
❑ 47 Fred Taylor	.60	.25
❑ 48 Jeff George	.40	.15
❑ 49 Sean Dawkins	.25	.08
❑ 50 Daunte Culpepper	.60	.25
❑ 51 Chris Chandler	.40	.15
❑ 52 Tim Couch	.40	.15
❑ 53 Trent Dilfer	.40	.15
❑ 54 Steve McNair	.60	.25
❑ 55 Kordell Stewart	.40	.15
❑ 56 Aaron Brooks	.60	.25
❑ 57 Michael Pittman	.25	.08
❑ 58 Bill Schroeder	.40	.15
❑ 59 Junior Seau	.60	.25
❑ 60 Kurt Warner	1.25	.50
❑ 61 Drew Bledsoe	.75	.30
❑ 62 Steve Beuerlein	.40	.15
❑ 63 Mike Anderson	.60	.25
❑ 64 Brad Johnson	.60	.25
❑ 65 Tim Brown	.60	.25
❑ 66 Qadry Ismail	.40	.15
❑ 67 Doug Flutie	.60	.25
❑ 68 Terrell Owens	.60	.25
❑ 69 Rocket Ismail	.40	.15
❑ 70 Charlie Batch	.60	.25
❑ 71 Jerome Pathon	.40	.15
❑ 72 Peter Warrick	.60	.25
❑ 73 Hines Ward	.60	.25
❑ 74 Ron Dayne	.60	.25
❑ 75 Lamar Smith	.40	.15
❑ 76 Amani Toomer	.40	.15
❑ 77 Joey Galloway	.40	.15
❑ 78 James Allen	.40	.15
❑ 79 Isaac Bruce	.60	.25
❑ 80 David Boston	.60	.25
❑ 81 James Thrash	.40	.15
❑ 82 Tony Gonzalez	.40	.15
❑ 83 Jason Taylor	.25	.08
❑ 84 Ricky Watters	.40	.15
❑ 85 Terance Mathis	.40	.15
❑ 86 Troy Brown	.40	.15
❑ 87 Mark Brunell	.60	.25
❑ 88 Rob Johnson	.40	.15
❑ 89 Freddie Jones	.25	.08
❑ 90 Eddie George	.60	.25
❑ 91 Tiki Barber	.60	.25
❑ 92 Donald Hayes	.25	.08
❑ 93 Muhsin Muhammad	.40	.15
❑ 94 Johnnie Morton	.40	.15
❑ 95 Warren Sapp	.40	.15
❑ 96 Bobby Shaw	.25	.08
❑ 97 Randy Moss	1.25	.50
❑ 98 Jerome Bettis	.60	.25
❑ 99 Antonio Freeman	.60	.25
❑ 100 Jamal Lewis	1.00	.40
❑ 101 Andre Rison	.40	.15
❑ 102 Kevin Faulk	.40	.15
❑ 103 Jon Kitna	.60	.25
❑ 104 Shawn Jefferson	.25	.08
❑ 105 Kevin Johnson	.40	.15
❑ 106 Torry Holt	.60	.25
❑ 107 Cris Carter	.60	.25
❑ 108 Chad Lewis	.25	.08
❑ 109 Stephen Davis	.60	.25
❑ 110 Jeff Blake	.40	.15
❑ 111 Elvis Grbac	.40	.15
❑ 112 Ed McCaffrey	.60	.25
❑ 113 Tim Biakabutuka	.40	.15
❑ 114 Trent Green	.60	.25
❑ 115 Jeff Garcia	.60	.25
❑ 116 Jacquez Green	.25	.08
❑ 117 Shaun King	.25	.08
❑ 118 Jimmy Smith	.40	.15
❑ 119 James Stewart	.40	.15
❑ 120 Brian Urlacher	1.00	.40
❑ 121 Tyrone Wheatley	.40	.15
❑ 122 J.R. Redmond	.25	.08
❑ 123 Eric Moulds	.40	.15
❑ 124 Ricky Williams	.60	.25
❑ 125 Brett Favre	2.00	.75
❑ 126 Koren Robinson RC	2.50	1.00
❑ 127 Richard Seymour RC	2.50	1.00
❑ 128 Jamal Reynolds RC	2.50	1.00
❑ 129 Kevin Kasper RC	2.50	1.00
❑ 130 LaMont Jordan RC	5.00	2.00
❑ 131 Reggie Wayne RC	5.00	2.00
❑ 132 Travis Henry RC	5.00	2.00
❑ 133 Alge Crumpler RC	3.00	1.25
❑ 134 Quincy Carter RC	2.50	1.00
❑ 135 Michael Bennett RC	2.50	1.00
❑ 136 Jamie Winborn RC	1.50	.60
❑ 137 Josh Heupel RC	2.50	1.00
❑ 138 Will Allen RC	1.50	.60
❑ 139 Scotty Anderson RC	1.50	.60
❑ 140 LaDainian Tomlinson RC	25.00	10.00
❑ 141 Freddie Mitchell RC	2.50	1.00
❑ 142 Gerard Warren RC	2.50	1.00
❑ 143 Chad Johnson RC	6.00	2.50
❑ 144 Todd Heap RC	2.50	1.00
❑ 145 Leonard Davis RC	1.50	.60
❑ 146 Kevan Barlow RC	2.50	1.00
❑ 147 Correll Buckhalter RC	3.00	1.25
❑ 148 Fred Smoot RC	2.50	1.00
❑ 149 Steve Smith RC	6.00	3.00
❑ 150 David Terrell RC	2.50	1.00
❑ 151 Chris Chambers RC	4.00	1.50
❑ 152 Mike McMahon RC	2.50	1.00
❑ 153 Rudi Johnson RC	5.00	2.00
❑ 154 Marques Tuiasosopo RC	2.50	1.00
❑ 155 Deuce McAllister RC	5.00	2.00
❑ 156 Marcus Stroud RC	2.50	1.00
❑ 157 Bobby Newcombe RC	1.50	.60
❑ 158 Rod Gardner RC	2.50	1.00
❑ 159 Drew Brees RC	8.00	3.00
❑ 160 Jesse Palmer RC	2.50	1.00
❑ 161 Derrick Gibson RC	1.50	.60
❑ 162 James Jackson RC	2.50	1.00
❑ 163 Dan Morgan RC	2.50	1.00
❑ 164 Michael Vick RC	8.00	3.00
❑ 165 Snoop Minnis RC	1.50	.60
❑ 166 Anthony Thomas RC	2.50	1.00
❑ 167 Andre Carter RC	2.50	1.00
❑ 168 Travis Minor RC	1.50	.60
❑ 169 Quincy Morgan RC	2.50	1.00
❑ 170 Justin Smith RC	2.50	1.00
❑ 171 Tay Cody RC	1.00	.40
❑ 172 Santana Moss RC	4.00	1.50
❑ 173 Sage Rosenfels RC	2.50	1.00
❑ 174 Robert Ferguson RC	2.50	1.00
❑ 175 Chris Weinke RC	2.50	1.00

2002 Stadium Club

❑ COMP.SET w/o SP's (125)	25.00	10.00
❑ 1 Randy Moss	1.25	.50
❑ 2 Kordell Stewart	.40	.15
❑ 3 Marvin Harrison	.60	.25
❑ 4 Chris Weinke	.40	.15

❑	5 James Allen	.40	.15
❑	6 Michael Pittman	.25	.08
❑	7 Quincy Carter	.40	.15
❑	8 Mike Anderson	.60	.25
❑	9 Mike McMahon	.60	.25
❑	10 Chris Chambers	.60	.25
❑	11 Laveranues Coles	.40	.15
❑	12 Curtis Conway	.25	.08
❑	13 Brad Johnson	.40	.15
❑	14 Shaun Alexander	.75	.30
❑	15 Jerry Rice	1.25	.50
❑	16 Rod Gardner	.40	.15
❑	17 Derrick Mason	.40	.15
❑	18 Tom Brady	1.50	.60
❑	19 Jimmy Smith	.40	.15
❑	20 Tim Couch	.40	.15
❑	21 Jim Miller	.25	.08
❑	22 Eric Moulds	.40	.15
❑	23 Michael Vick	1.25	.50
❑	24 Jon Kitna	.40	.15
❑	25 Johnnie Morton	.40	.15
❑	26 Priest Holmes	.75	.30
❑	27 Aaron Brooks	.60	.25
❑	28 Duce Staley	.60	.25
❑	29 LaDainian Tomlinson	1.00	.40
❑	30 Lamar Smith	.40	.15
❑	31 Rod Smith	.40	.15
❑	32 Richard Huntley	.25	.08
❑	33 Antonio Freeman	.60	.25
❑	34 Amani Toomer	.40	.15
❑	35 Hines Ward	.60	.25
❑	36 Marshall Faulk	.60	.25
❑	37 Steve McNair	.60	.25
❑	38 Tim Brown	.60	.25
❑	39 Curtis Martin	.60	.25
❑	40 Kevin Johnson	.40	.15
❑	41 Rob Johnson	.40	.15
❑	42 Qadry Ismail	.40	.15
❑	43 Daunte Culpepper	.60	.25
❑	44 Willie Jackson	.25	.08
❑	45 Jeff Garcia	.60	.25
❑	46 Matt Hasselbeck	.40	.15
❑	47 Corey Bradford	.25	.08
❑	48 Snoop Minnis	.25	.08
❑	49 Ron Dayne	.40	.15
❑	50 Peyton Manning	1.25	.50
❑	51 Drew Bledsoe	.75	.30
❑	52 Terry Glenn	.40	.15
❑	53 Warrick Dunn	.60	.25
❑	54 Mark Brunell	.60	.25
❑	55 James Stewart	.40	.15
❑	56 Muhsin Muhammad	.40	.15
❑	57 Jake Plummer	.40	.15
❑	58 Terance Mathis	.25	.08
❑	59 Rocket Ismail	.40	.15
❑	60 Joe Horn	.40	.15
❑	61 Wayne Chrebet	.40	.15
❑	62 James Thrash	.40	.15
❑	63 Stephen Davis	.40	.15
❑	64 Isaac Bruce	.60	.25
❑	65 Peter Warrick	.40	.15
❑	66 Anthony Thomas	.40	.15
❑	67 Maurice Smith	.40	.15
❑	68 Tony Gonzalez	.40	.15
❑	69 Michael Bennett	.40	.15
❑	70 Ike Hilliard	.40	.15
❑	71 Plaxico Burress	.40	.15
❑	72 Darrell Jackson	.40	.15
❑	73 Kevan Barlow	.40	.15
❑	74 Ray Lewis	.60	.25
❑	75 Emmitt Smith	1.50	.60
❑	76 Bill Schroeder	.40	.15
❑	77 Az-Zahir Hakim	.25	.08
❑	78 Troy Brown	.40	.15
❑	79 Keyshawn Johnson	.60	.25
❑	80 Tim Dwight	.40	.15
❑	81 Peerless Price	.40	.15
❑	82 Marty Booker	.25	.08
❑	83 Terrell Davis	.60	.25
❑	84 Dominic Rhodes	.40	.15
❑	85 Jay Fiedler	.40	.15
❑	86 Rich Gannon	.60	.25
❑	87 Terrell Owens	.60	.25
❑	88 Donald Hayes	.25	.08
❑	89 Thomas Jones	.40	.15
❑	90 Ricky Williams	.60	.25
❑	91 Donovan McNabb	.75	.30
❑	92 Eddie George	.60	.25
❑	93 Germane Crowell	.25	.08
❑	94 David Terrell	.60	.25
❑	95 Alex Van Pelt	.25	.08
❑	96 Antowain Smith	.40	.15
❑	97 Jerome Bettis	.60	.25
❑	98 Mike Alstott	.60	.25
❑	99 Doug Flutie	.60	.25
❑	100 Kurt Warner	.60	.25
❑	101 Cris Carter	.60	.25
❑	102 Oronde Gadsden	.40	.15
❑	103 Ahman Green	.60	.25
❑	104 Corey Dillon	.40	.15
❑	105 Marcus Robinson	.40	.15
❑	106 Shannon Sharpe	.40	.15
❑	107 Kerry Collins	.40	.15
❑	108 Garrison Hearst	.40	.15
❑	109 David Boston	.60	.25
❑	110 Travis Henry	.60	.25
❑	111 James Jackson	.25	.08
❑	112 Fred Taylor	.60	.25
❑	113 Edgerrin James	.75	.30
❑	114 Vinny Testaverde	.40	.15
❑	115 Todd Pinkston	.40	.15
❑	116 Koren Robinson	.40	.15
❑	117 Torry Holt	.60	.25
❑	118 Brian Griese	.60	.25
❑	119 Trent Green	.40	.15
❑	120 James McKnight	.25	.08
❑	121 Charlie Garner	.40	.15
❑	122 Tiki Barber	.60	.25
❑	123 Joey Galloway	.40	.15
❑	124 Quincy Morgan	.25	.08
❑	125 Brett Favre	1.50	.60
❑	126 Joey Harrington RC	4.00	1.50
❑	127 Ashley Lelie RC	6.00	2.50
❑	128 Terry Charles RC	2.50	1.00
❑	129 Charles Grant RC	[illegible]	1.00
❑	130 Levar Fisher RC	1.50	.60
❑	131 Larry Tripplett RC	1.50	.60
❑	132 Quentin Jammer RC	3.00	1.25
❑	133 Ron Johnson RC	2.50	1.00
❑	134 Maurice Morris RC	3.00	1.25
❑	135 Roy Williams RC	6.00	2.50
❑	136 Kurt Kittner RC	2.50	1.00
❑	137 Dennis Johnson RC	1.50	.60
❑	138 Seth Burford RC	2.50	1.00
❑	139 Michael Lewis RC	3.00	1.25
❑	140 William Green RC	3.00	1.25
❑	141 Rohan Davey RC	3.00	1.25
❑	142 Rocky Calmus RC	3.00	1.25
❑	143 Robert Thomas RC	3.00	1.25
❑	144 Travis Stephens RC	2.50	1.00
❑	145 Ladell Betts RC	3.00	1.25
❑	146 Daniel Graham RC	3.00	1.25
❑	147 Chester Taylor RC	6.00	2.50
❑	148 Tim Carter RC	2.50	1.00
❑	149 Lito Sheppard RC	3.00	1.25
❑	150 David Carr RC	6.00	2.50
❑	151 Alex Brown RC	3.00	1.25
❑	152 John Henderson RC	3.00	1.25
❑	153 Jamar Martin RC	2.50	1.00
❑	154 Raonall Smith RC	2.50	1.00
❑	155 Leonard Henry RC	2.50	1.00
❑	156 T.J. Duckett RC	3.00	1.25
❑	157 Patrick Ramsey RC	3.00	1.25
❑	158 Antwaan Randle El RC	4.00	1.50
❑	159 Luke Staley RC	2.50	1.00
❑	160 Jon McGraw RC	1.50	.60
❑	161 Phillip Buchanon RC	3.00	1.25
❑	162 Dwight Freeney RC	5.00	2.00
❑	163 Mike Rumph RC	3.00	1.25
❑	164 Albert Haynesworth RC	2.50	1.00
❑	165 Antonio Bryant RC	3.00	1.25
❑	166 Josh Reed RC	3.00	1.25
❑	167 Eric Crouch RC	3.00	1.25
❑	168 Reche Caldwell RC	3.00	1.25
❑	169 Adrian Peterson RC	4.00	1.50
❑	170 Jonathan Wells RC	3.00	1.25
❑	171 Wendell Bryant RC	1.50	.60
❑	172 Tellis Redmon RC	2.50	1.00
❑	173 Josh McCown RC	4.00	1.50
❑	174 DeShaun Foster RC	3.00	1.25
❑	175 Cliff Russell RC	2.50	1.00
❑	176 David Garrard RC	6.00	2.50
❑	177 Brian Westbrook RC	6.00	2.50
❑	178 Anthony Weaver RC	2.50	1.00
❑	179 Bryan Thomas RC	2.50	1.00
❑	180 Kalimba Edwards RC	3.00	1.25
❑	181 Javon Walker RC	5.00	2.00
❑	182 Marquise Walker RC	2.50	1.00
❑	183 Deion Branch RC	5.00	2.00
❑	184 Lamar Gordon RC	3.00	1.25
❑	185 Jeremy Shockey RC	10.00	4.00
❑	186 Clinton Portis RC	10.00	4.00
❑	187 Napoleon Harris RC	3.00	1.25
❑	188 Freddie Milons RC	2.50	1.00
❑	189 Julius Peppers RC	6.00	2.50
❑	190 Andre Davis RC	2.50	1.00
❑	191 Travis Fisher RC	3.00	1.25
❑	192 Chad Hutchinson RC	2.50	1.00
❑	193 Najeh Davenport RC	3.00	1.25
❑	194 Ed Reed RC	5.00	2.00
❑	195 Donte Stallworth RC	5.00	2.00
❑	196 Brandon Doman RC	2.50	1.00
❑	197 Zak Kustok RC	3.00	1.25
❑	198 Randy Fasani RC	2.50	1.00
❑	199 J.T. O'Sullivan RC	2.50	1.00
❑	200 Jabar Gaffney RC	3.00	1.25

1955 Topps All American

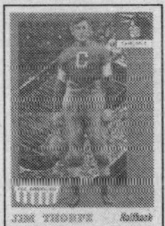

❑	COMPLETE SET (100)	3800.00	2800.00
❑	WRAPPER (1-CENT)	300.00	250.00
❑	WRAPPER (5-CENT)	250.00	200.00
❑	1 Herman Hickman RC !	125.00	65.00
❑	2 John Kimbrough	18.00	10.00
❑	3 Ed Weir	18.00	10.00
❑	4 Erny Pinckert	18.00	10.00
❑	5 Bobby Grayson	18.00	10.00
❑	6 Nile Kinnick RC UER	135.00	75.00
❑	7 Andy Bershak	18.00	10.00
❑	8 George Cafego RC	18.00	10.00
❑	9 Tom Hamilton SP	30.00	20.00
❑	10 Bill Dudley	40.00	25.00
❑	11 Bobby Dodd SP	30.00	20.00
❑	12 Otto Graham	200.00	100.00
❑	13 Aaron Rosenberg	18.00	10.00
❑	14A Gay.Tinsley RC ERR	100.00	50.00
❑	14B Gay.Tinsley RC COR	25.00	15.00
❑	15 Ed Kaw SP	30.00	20.00
❑	16 Knute Rockne	275.00	175.00
❑	17 Bob Reynolds HB	18.00	10.00
❑	18 Pudg.Heffelfinger RC SP	40.00	25.00
❑	19 Bruce Smith	35.00	20.00
❑	20 Sammy Baugh	200.00	125.00
❑	21A W.White RC SP ERR	250.00	150.00
❑	21B W.White RC SP COR	100.00	60.00
❑	22 Brick Muller	18.00	10.00
❑	23 Dick Kazmaier RC	25.00	15.00

❑ 24 Ken Strong 50.00 30.00
❑ 25 Casimir Myslinski SP 30.00 20.00
❑ 26 Larry Kelley RC SP 40.00 25.00
❑ 27 Red Grange UER 300.00 200.00
❑ 28 Mel Hein RC SP 75.00 40.00
❑ 29 Leo Nomellini SP 100.00 60.00
❑ 30 Wes Fesler 18.00 10.00
❑ 31 George Sauer Sr. RC 25.00 15.00
❑ 32 Hank Foldberg 18.00 10.00
❑ 33 Bob Higgins 18.00 10.00
❑ 34 Davey O'Brien RC 50.00 30.00
❑ 35 Tom Harmon RC SP 100.00 60.00
❑ 36 Turk Edwards SP 60.00 35.00
❑ 37 Jim Thorpe 400.00 275.00
❑ 38 Amos A. Stagg RC 75.00 40.00
❑ 39 Jerome Holland RC 25.00 15.00
❑ 40 Donn Moomaw 18.00 10.00
❑ 41 Joseph Alexander SP 30.00 20.00
❑ 42 Eddie Tryon RC SP 40.00 25.00
❑ 43 George Savitsky 18.00 10.00
❑ 44 Ed Garbisch 18.00 10.00
❑ 45 Elmer Oliphant 18.00 10.00
❑ 46 Arnold Lassman 18.00 10.00
❑ 47 Bo McMillin RC 25.00 15.00
❑ 48 Ed Widseth 18.00 10.00
❑ 49 Don Gordon Zimmerman 18.00 10.00
❑ 50 Ken Kavanaugh 25.00 15.00
❑ 51 Duane Purvis SP 30.00 20.00
❑ 52 Johnny Lujack 90.00 50.00
❑ 53 John F. Green 18.00 10.00
❑ 54 Edwin Dooley SP 30.00 20.00
❑ 55 Frank Merritt SP 30.00 20.00
❑ 56 Ernie Nevers RC 125.00 75.00
❑ 57 Vic Hanson SP 30.00 20.00
❑ 58 Ed Franco 18.00 10.00
❑ 59 Doc Blanchard RC 50.00 30.00
❑ 60 Dan Hill 18.00 10.00
❑ 61 Charles Brickley SP 30.00 20.00
❑ 62 Harry Newman 18.00 10.00
❑ 63 Charlie Justice 35.00 20.00
❑ 64 Benny Friedman RC 30.00 18.00
❑ 65 Joe Donchess SP 30.00 20.00
❑ 66 Bruiser Kinard RC 35.00 20.00
❑ 67 Frankie Albert 25.00 15.00
❑ 68 Four Horsemen RC SP 500.00 325.00
❑ 69 Frank Sinkwich RC 25.00 15.00
❑ 70 Bill Daddio 18.00 10.00
❑ 71 Bobby Wilson 18.00 10.00
❑ 72 Chub Peabody 18.00 10.00
❑ 73 Paul Governali 25.00 15.00
❑ 74 Gene McEver 18.00 10.00
❑ 75 Hugh Gallarneau 18.00 10.00
❑ 76 Angelo Bertelli RC 25.00 15.00
❑ 77 Bowden Wyatt SP 30.00 20.00
❑ 78 Jay Berwanger RC 35.00 20.00
❑ 79 Pug Lund 18.00 10.00
❑ 80 Bennie Oosterbaan 18.00 10.00
❑ 81 Cotton Warburton 18.00 10.00
❑ 82 Alex Wojciechowicz 35.00 20.00
❑ 83 Ted Coy SP 30.00 20.00
❑ 84 Ace Parker RC SP 50.00 30.00
❑ 85 Sid Luckman 150.00 90.00
❑ 86 Albie Booth SP 30.00 20.00
❑ 87 Adolph Schultz SP 30.00 20.00
❑ 88 Ralph Kercheval 18.00 10.00
❑ 89 Marshall Goldberg 25.00 15.00
❑ 90 Charlie O'Rourke 18.00 10.00
❑ 91 Bob Odell UER 18.00 10.00
❑ 92 Biggie Munn 18.00 10.00
❑ 93 Willie Heston SP 40.00 25.00
❑ 94 Joe Bernard SP 40.00 25.00
❑ 95 Chris Cagle SP 40.00 25.00
❑ 96 Bill Hollenback SP 40.00 25.00
❑ 97 Don Hutson RC SP 225.00 150.00
❑ 98 Beattie Feathers SP 100.00 60.00
❑ 99 Don Whitmire SP 40.00 25.00
❑ 100 Fats Henry RC SP ! 200.00 100.00

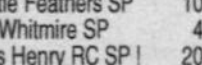

❑ COMPLETE SET (120) 1800.00 1200.00
❑ WRAPPER (1-CENT) 250.00 200.00
❑ WRAPPER (5-CENT) 50.00 40.00
❑ 1 Johnny Carson SP ! 80.00 40.00
❑ 2 Gordy Soltau 6.00 3.50
❑ 3 Frank Varrichione 6.00 3.50
❑ 4 Eddie Bell 6.00 3.50
❑ 5 Alex Webster RC 12.00 6.00

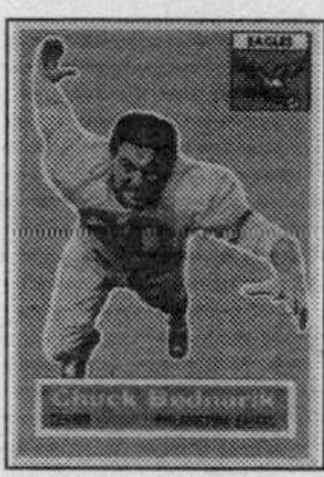

❑ 6 Norm Van Brocklin 30.00 18.00
❑ 7 Green Bay Packers 25.00 15.00
❑ 8 Lou Creekmur 15.00 7.50
❑ 9 Lou Groza 25.00 15.00
❑ 10 Tom Bienemann SP 25.00 15.00
❑ 11 George Blanda 50.00 30.00
❑ 12 Alan Ameche 12.00 6.00
❑ 13 Vic Janowicz SP 45.00 25.00
❑ 14 Dick Moegle 8.00 4.00
❑ 15 Fran Rogel 6.00 3.50
❑ 16 Harold Giancanelli 6.00 3.50
❑ 17 Emlen Tunnell 15.00 7.50
❑ 18 Tank Younger 12.00 6.00
❑ 19 Billy Howton 8.00 4.00
❑ 20 Jack Christiansen 15.00 7.50
❑ 21 Darrel Brewster 6.00 3.50
❑ 22 Chicago Cardinals SP 100.00 60.00
❑ 23 Ed Brown 8.00 4.00
❑ 24 Joe Campanella 6.00 3.50
❑ 25 Leon Heath SP 22.00 12.00
❑ 26 San Francisco 49ers 18.00 10.00
❑ 27 Dick Flanagan 6.00 3.50
❑ 28 Chuck Bednarik 25.00 15.00
❑ 29 Kyle Rote 12.00 6.00
❑ 30 Les Richter 8.00 4.00
❑ 31 Howard Ferguson 6.00 3.50
❑ 32 Dorne Dibble 6.00 3.50
❑ 33 Kenny Konz 6.00 3.50
❑ 34 Dave Mann SP 25.00 15.00
❑ 35 Rick Casares 12.00 6.00
❑ 36 Art Donovan 30.00 18.00
❑ 37 Chuck Drazenovich SP 22.00 12.00
❑ 38 Joe Arenas 6.00 3.50
❑ 39 Lynn Chandnois 6.00 3.50
❑ 40 Philadelphia Eagles 18.00 10.00
❑ 41 Roosevelt Brown RC 35.00 20.00
❑ 42 Tom Fears 25.00 15.00
❑ 43 Gary Knafelc 6.00 3.50
❑ 44 Joe Schmidt RC 50.00 30.00
❑ 45 Cleveland Browns 18.00 10.00
❑ 46 Len Teeuws RC SP 25.00 15.00
❑ 47 Bill George RC 30.00 18.00
❑ 48 Baltimore Colts 18.00 10.00
❑ 49 Eddie LeBaron SP 45.00 25.00
❑ 50 Hugh McElhenny 30.00 18.00
❑ 51 Ted Marchibroda 12.00 6.00
❑ 52 Adrian Burk 6.00 3.50
❑ 53 Frank Gifford 60.00 35.00
❑ 54 Charley Toogood 6.00 3.50
❑ 55 Tobin Rote 8.00 4.00
❑ 56 Bill Stits 6.00 3.50
❑ 57 Don Colo 6.00 3.50
❑ 58 Ollie Matson SP 75.00 40.00
❑ 59 Harlon Hill 8.00 4.00
❑ 60 Lenny Moore RC ! 90.00 50.00
❑ 61 Wash.Redskins SP 90.00 50.00
❑ 62 Billy Wilson 6.00 3.50
❑ 63 Pittsburgh Steelers 18.00 10.00
❑ 64 Bob Pellegrini 6.00 3.50
❑ 65 Ken MacAfee E 6.00 3.50
❑ 66 Willard Sherman 6.00 3.50
❑ 67 Roger Zatkoff 6.00 3.50
❑ 68 Dave Middleton 6.00 3.50
❑ 69 Ray Renfro 8.00 4.00
❑ 70 Don Stonesifer SP 25.00 15.00
❑ 71 Stan Jones RC 30.00 18.00
❑ 72 Jim Mutscheller 6.00 3.50
❑ 73 Volney Peters SP 22.00 12.00
❑ 74 Leo Nomellini 20.00 12.00
❑ 75 Ray Mathews 6.00 3.50
❑ 76 Dick Bielski 6.00 3.50
❑ 77 Charley Conerly 25.00 15.00
❑ 78 Elroy Hirsch 30.00 18.00
❑ 79 Bill Forester RC 8.00 4.00
❑ 80 Jim Doran 6.00 3.50
❑ 81 Fred Morrison 6.00 3.50
❑ 82 Jack Simmons SP 25.00 15.00
❑ 83 Bill McColl 6.00 3.50
❑ 84 Bert Hechichar 6.00 3.50
❑ 85 Joe Scudero SP 22.00 12.00
❑ 86 Y.A.Tittle 50.00 30.00
❑ 87 Ernie Stautner 20.00 12.00
❑ 88 Norm Willey 6.00 3.50
❑ 89 Bob Schnelker 6.00 3.50
❑ 90 Dan Towler 12.00 6.00
❑ 91 John Martinkovic 6.00 3.50
❑ 92 Detroit Lions 18.00 10.00
❑ 93 George Ratterman 8.00 4.00
❑ 94 Chuck Ulrich SP 25.00 15.00
❑ 95 Bobby Watkins 6.00 3.50
❑ 96 Buddy Young 12.00 6.00
❑ 97 Billy Wells SP 22.00 12.00
❑ 98 Bob Toneff 6.00 3.50
❑ 99 Bill McPeak 6.00 3.50
❑ 100 Bobby Thomason 6.00 3.50
❑ 101 Roosevelt Grier RC 40.00 25.00
❑ 102 Ron Waller 6.00 3.50
❑ 103 Bobby Dillon 6.00 3.50
❑ 104 Leon Hart 12.00 6.00
❑ 105 Mike McCormack 15.00 7.50
❑ 106 John Olszewski SP 25.00 15.00
❑ 107 Bill Wightkin 6.00 3.50
❑ 108 George Shaw RC 8.00 4.00
❑ 109 Dale Atkeson SP 22.00 12.00
❑ 110 Joe Perry 25.00 15.00
❑ 111 Dale Dodrill 6.00 3.50
❑ 112 Tom Scott 6.00 3.50
❑ 113 New York Giants 18.00 10.00
❑ 114 Los Angeles Rams 18.00 10.00
❑ 115 Al Carmichael 6.00 3.50
❑ 116 Bobby Layne 50.00 30.00
❑ 117 Ed Modzelewski 6.00 3.50
❑ 118 Lamar McHan RC SP 25.00 15.00
❑ 119 Chicago Bears 18.00 10.00
❑ 120 Billy Vessels RC ! 40.00 20.00

1957 Topps

❑ COMPLETE SET (154) 2200.00 1600.00
❑ COMMON CARD (1-88) 4.00 2.50
❑ COMMON CARD (89-154) 10.00 5.00
❑ WRAPPER (1-CENT) 50.00 30.00
❑ WRAPPER (5-CENT) 75.00 50.00
❑ 1 Eddie LeBaron ! 50.00 30.00
❑ 2 Pete Retzlaff RC 15.00 7.50
❑ 3 Mike McCormack 12.00 6.00
❑ 4 Lou Baldacci 4.00 2.50
❑ 5 Gino Marchetti 20.00 10.00
❑ 6 Leo Nomellini 20.00 10.00
❑ 7 Bobby Watkins 4.00 2.50
❑ 8 Dave Middleton 4.00 2.50
❑ 9 Bobby Dillon 4.00 2.50
❑ 10 Les Richter 6.00 3.50
❑ 11 Roosevelt Brown 20.00 10.00
❑ 12 Lavern Torgeson RC 4.00 2.50
❑ 13 Dick Bielski 4.00 2.50
❑ 14 Pat Summerall 20.00 10.00
❑ 15 Jack Butler RC 10.00 5.00
❑ 16 John Henry Johnson 15.00 7.50
❑ 17 Art Spinney 4.00 2.50

Card	Player	NRMT	VG-E
❑ 18	Bob St. Clair	12.00	6.00
❑ 19	Perry Jeter	4.00	2.50
❑ 20	Lou Creekmur	12.00	6.00
❑ 21	Dave Hanner	6.00	3.50
❑ 22	Norm Van Brocklin	30.00	18.00
❑ 23	Don Chandler RC	10.00	5.00
❑ 24	Al Dorow	4.00	2.50
❑ 25	Tom Scott	4.00	2.50
❑ 26	Ollie Matson	20.00	12.00
❑ 27	Fran Rogel	4.00	2.50
❑ 28	Lou Groza	25.00	15.00
❑ 29	Billy Vessels	6.00	3.50
❑ 30	Y.A.Tittle	40.00	25.00
❑ 31	George Blanda	40.00	25.00
❑ 32	Bobby Layne	40.00	25.00
❑ 33	Billy Howton	6.00	3.50
❑ 34	Bill Wade	10.00	5.00
❑ 35	Emlen Tunnell	15.00	7.50
❑ 36	Leo Elter	4.00	2.50
❑ 37	Clarence Peaks RC	6.00	3.50
❑ 38	Don Stonesifer	4.00	2.50
❑ 39	George Tarasovic	4.00	2.50
❑ 40	Darrel Brewster	4.00	2.50
❑ 41	Bert Rechichar	4.00	2.50
❑ 42	Billy Wilson	4.00	2.50
❑ 43	Ed Brown	6.00	3.50
❑ 44	Gene Gedman	4.00	2.50
❑ 45	Gary Knafelc	4.00	2.50
❑ 46	Elroy Hirsch	30.00	18.00
❑ 47	Don Heinrich	6.00	3.50
❑ 48	Gene Brito	4.00	2.50
❑ 49	Chuck Bednarik	25.00	15.00
❑ 50	Dave Mann	4.00	2.50
❑ 51	Bill McPeak	4.00	2.50
❑ 52	Kenny Konz	4.00	2.50
❑ 53	Alan Ameche	10.00	5.00
❑ 54	Gordy Soltau	4.00	2.50
❑ 55	Rick Casares	6.00	3.50
❑ 56	Charlie Ane	4.00	2.50
❑ 57	Al Carmichael	4.00	2.50
❑ 58A	Willard Sherman ERR	300.00	175.00
❑ 58B	Willard Sherman COR	4.00	2.50
❑ 59	Kyle Rote	10.00	5.00
❑ 60	Chuck Drazenovich	4.00	2.50
❑ 61	Bobby Walston	4.00	2.50
❑ 62	John Olszewski	4.00	2.50
❑ 63	Ray Mathews	4.00	2.50
❑ 64	Maurice Bassett	4.00	2.50
❑ 65	Art Donovan	25.00	15.00
❑ 66	Joe Arenas	4.00	2.50
❑ 67	Harlon Hill	6.00	3.50
❑ 68	Yale Lary	12.00	6.00
❑ 69	Bill Forester	6.00	3.50
❑ 70	Bob Boyd	4.00	2.50
❑ 71	Andy Robustelli	20.00	12.00
❑ 72	Sam Baker RC	6.00	3.50
❑ 73	Bob Pellegrini	4.00	2.50
❑ 74	Leo Sanford	4.00	2.50
❑ 75	Sid Watson	4.00	2.50
❑ 76	Ray Renfro	6.00	3.50
❑ 77	Carl Taseff	4.00	2.50
❑ 78	Clyde Conner	4.00	2.50
❑ 79	J.C. Caroline	4.00	2.50
❑ 80	Howard Cassady RC	15.00	7.50
❑ 81	Tobin Rote	6.00	3.50
❑ 82	Ron Waller	4.00	2.50
❑ 83	Jim Patton RC	6.00	3.50
❑ 84	Volney Peters	4.00	2.50
❑ 85	Dick Lane RC	50.00	30.00
❑ 86	Royce Womble	4.00	2.50
❑ 87	Duane Putnam RC	6.00	3.50
❑ 88	Frank Gifford !	60.00	30.00
❑ 89	Steve Meilinger	10.00	5.00
❑ 90	Buck Lansford	10.00	5.00
❑ 91	Lindon Crow DP	8.00	4.00
❑ 92	Ernie Stautner DP	25.00	12.50
❑ 93	Preston Carpenter RC DP	8.00	4.00
❑ 94	Raymond Berry RC	135.00	75.00
❑ 95	Hugh McElhenny	30.00	18.00
❑ 96	Stan Jones	25.00	15.00
❑ 97	Dorne Dibble	10.00	5.00
❑ 98	Joe Scudero DP	8.00	4.00
❑ 99	Eddie Bell	10.00	5.00
❑ 100	Joe Childress DP	8.00	4.00
❑ 101	Elbert Nickel	12.00	6.00
❑ 102	Walt Michaels	12.00	6.00
❑ 103	Jim Mutscheller DP	8.00	4.00
❑ 104	Earl Morrall RC	50.00	30.00
❑ 105	Larry Strickland	10.00	5.00
❑ 106	Jack Christiansen	15.00	7.50
❑ 107	Fred Cone DP	8.00	4.00
❑ 108	Bud McFadin RC	12.00	6.00
❑ 109	Charley Conerly	30.00	18.00
❑ 110	Tom Runnels DP	8.00	4.00
❑ 111	Ken Keller DP	8.00	4.00
❑ 112	James Root	10.00	5.00
❑ 113	Ted Marchibroda DP	10.00	5.00
❑ 114	Don Paul DB	10.00	5.00
❑ 115	George Shaw	12.00	6.00
❑ 116	Dick Moegle	12.00	6.00
❑ 117	Don Bingham	10.00	5.00
❑ 118	Leon Hart	14.00	7.00
❑ 119	Bart Starr RC	450.00	300.00
❑ 120	Paul Miller DP	8.00	4.00
❑ 121	Alex Webster	12.00	6.00
❑ 122	Ray Wietecha DP	8.00	4.00
❑ 123	Johnny Carson	10.00	5.00
❑ 124	Tom. McDonald RC DP	30.00	18.00
❑ 125	Jerry Tubbs RC	12.00	6.00
❑ 126	Jack Scarbath	10.00	5.00
❑ 127	Ed Modzelewski DP	8.00	4.00
❑ 128	Lenny Moore	50.00	30.00
❑ 129	Joe Perry DP	25.00	15.00
❑ 130	Bill Wightkin	10.00	5.00
❑ 131	Jim Doran	10.00	5.00
❑ 132	Howard Ferguson UER	10.00	5.00
❑ 133	Tom Wilson	10.00	5.00
❑ 134	Dick James	10.00	5.00
❑ 135	Jimmy Harris	10.00	5.00
❑ 136	Chuck Ulrich	10.00	5.00
❑ 137	Lynn Chandnois	10.00	5.00
❑ 138	Johnny Unitas RC DP	450.00	300.00
❑ 139	Jim Ridlon DP	8.00	4.00
❑ 140	Zeke Bratkowski DP	10.00	5.00
❑ 141	Ray Krouse	10.00	5.00
❑ 142	John Martinkovic	10.00	5.00
❑ 143	Jim Cason DP	8.00	4.00
❑ 144	Ken MacAfee E	10.00	5.00
❑ 145	Sid Youngelman RC	12.00	6.00
❑ 146	Paul Larson	10.00	5.00
❑ 147	Len Ford	30.00	18.00
❑ 148	Bob Toneff DP	8.00	4.00
❑ 149	Ronnie Knox DP	8.00	4.00
❑ 150	Jim David RC	12.00	6.00
❑ 151	Paul Hornung RC	400.00	250.00
❑ 152	Tank Younger	14.00	7.00
❑ 153	Bill Svoboda DP	8.00	4.00
❑ 154	Fred Morrison !	70.00	35.00
❑ NNO1	Checklist Bazooka SP!	750.00	500.00
❑ NNO2	Checklist Blony SP	750.00	500.00

1958 Topps

Card	Player	NRMT	VG-E
❑	COMPLETE SET (132)	1250.00	850.00
❑	WRAPPER (1-CENT)	60.00	35.00
❑	WRAPPER (5-CENT)	125.00	75.00
❑ 1	Gene Filipski RC !	15.00	7.50
❑ 2	Bobby Layne	35.00	20.00
❑ 3	Joe Schmidt	12.00	6.00
❑ 4	Bill Barnes	4.00	2.00
❑ 5	Milt Plum RC	8.00	4.00
❑ 6	Billy Howton UER	5.00	2.50
❑ 7	Howard Cassady	5.00	2.50
❑ 8	Jim Dooley	4.00	2.00
❑ 9	Cleveland Browns	6.00	3.00
❑ 10	Lenny Moore	25.00	12.50
❑ 11	Darrel Brewster	4.00	2.00
❑ 12	Alan Ameche	8.00	4.00
❑ 13	Jim David	4.00	2.00
❑ 14	Jim Mutscheller	4.00	2.00
❑ 15	Andy Robustelli	10.00	5.00
❑ 16	Gino Marchetti	12.00	6.00
❑ 17	Ray Renfro	5.00	2.50
❑ 18	Yale Lary	8.00	4.00
❑ 19	Gary Glick	4.00	2.00
❑ 20	Jon Arnett RC	8.00	4.00
❑ 21	Bob Boyd	4.00	2.00
❑ 22	Johnny Unitas UER	135.00	75.00
❑ 23	Zeke Bratkowski	5.00	2.50
❑ 24	Sid Youngelman UER	4.00	2.00
❑ 25	Leo Elter	4.00	2.00
❑ 26	Kenny Konz	4.00	2.00
❑ 27	Washington Redskins	6.00	3.00
❑ 28	Carl Brettschneider	4.00	2.00
❑ 29	Chicago Bears	6.00	3.00
❑ 30	Alex Webster	5.00	2.50
❑ 31	Al Carmichael	4.00	2.00
❑ 32	Bobby Dillon	4.00	2.00
❑ 33	Steve Meilinger	4.00	2.00
❑ 34	Sam Baker	4.00	2.00
❑ 35	Chuck Bednarik	15.00	7.50
❑ 36	Bert Vic Zucco	4.00	2.00
❑ 37	George Tarasovic	4.00	2.00
❑ 38	Bill Wade	8.00	4.00
❑ 39	Dick Stanfel	5.00	2.50
❑ 40	Jerry Norton	4.00	2.00
❑ 41	San Francisco 49ers	6.00	3.00
❑ 42	Emlen Tunnell	10.00	5.00
❑ 43	Jim Doran	4.00	2.00
❑ 44	Ted Marchibroda	8.00	4.00
❑ 45	Chet Hanulak	4.00	2.00
❑ 46	Dale Dodrill	4.00	2.00
❑ 47	Johnny Carson	4.00	2.00
❑ 48	Dick Deschaine	4.00	2.00
❑ 49	Billy Wells UER	4.00	2.00
❑ 50	Larry Morris	4.00	2.00
❑ 51	Jack McClairen	4.00	2.00
❑ 52	Lou Groza	15.00	7.50
❑ 53	Rick Casares	5.00	2.50
❑ 54	Don Chandler	5.00	2.50
❑ 55	Duane Putnam	4.00	2.00
❑ 56	Gary Knafelc	4.00	2.00
❑ 57	Earl Morrall	10.00	5.00
❑ 58	Ron Kramer RC	5.00	2.50
❑ 59	Mike McCormack	8.00	4.00
❑ 60	Gern Nagler	4.00	2.00
❑ 61	New York Giants	6.00	3.00
❑ 62	Jim Brown RC !	500.00	350.00
❑ 63	Joe Marconi RC	4.00	2.00
❑ 64	R.C. Owens RC UER	5.00	2.50
❑ 65	Jimmy Carr RC	5.00	2.50
❑ 66	Bart Starr UER	150.00	90.00
❑ 67	Tom Wilson	4.00	2.00
❑ 68	Lamar McHan	4.00	2.00
❑ 69	Chicago Cardinals	6.00	3.00
❑ 70	Jack Christiansen	8.00	4.00
❑ 71	Don McIlhenny RC	4.00	2.00
❑ 72	Ron Waller	4.00	2.00
❑ 73	Frank Gifford	50.00	25.00
❑ 74	Bert Rechichar	4.00	2.00
❑ 75	John Henry Johnson	10.00	5.00
❑ 76	Jack Butler	5.00	2.50
❑ 77	Frank Varrichione	4.00	2.00
❑ 78	Ray Mathews	4.00	2.00
❑ 79	Marv Matuszak UER	4.00	2.00
❑ 80	Harlon Hill UER	4.00	2.00
❑ 81	Lou Creekmur	8.00	4.00
❑ 82	Woodley Lewis UER	4.00	2.00
❑ 83	Don Heinrich	4.00	2.00
❑ 84	Charley Conerly	15.00	7.50
❑ 85	Los Angeles Rams	6.00	3.00
❑ 86	Y.A.Tittle	30.00	18.00
❑ 87	Bobby Walston	4.00	2.00
❑ 88	Earl Putman	4.00	2.00
❑ 89	Leo Nomellini	15.00	7.50
❑ 90	Sonny Jurgensen RC	100.00	60.00
❑ 91	Don Paul DB	4.00	2.00
❑ 92	Paige Cothren	4.00	2.00
❑ 93	Joe Perry	15.00	7.50
❑ 94	Tobin Rote	5.00	2.50
❑ 95	Billy Wilson	4.00	2.00
❑ 96	Green Bay Packers	6.00	3.00
❑ 97	Lavern Torgeson	4.00	2.00
❑ 98	Milt Davis	4.00	2.00

99 Larry Strickland	4.00	2.00
100 Matt Hazeltine RC	5.00	2.50
101 Walt Yowarsky	4.00	2.00
102 Roosevelt Brown	8.00	4.00
103 Jim Ringo	10.00	5.00
104 Joe Krupa	4.00	2.00
105 Les Richter	5.00	2.50
106 Art Donovan	20.00	12.00
107 John Olszewski	4.00	2.00
108 Ken Keller	4.00	2.00
109 Philadelphia Eagles	6.00	3.00
110 Baltimore Colts	6.00	3.00
111 Dick Bielski	4.00	2.00
112 Eddie LeBaron	8.00	4.00
113 Gene Brito	4.00	2.00
114 Willie Galimore RC	8.00	4.00
115 Detroit Lions	6.00	3.00
116 Pittsburgh Steelers	6.00	3.00
117 L.G. Dupre	5.00	2.50
118 Babe Parilli	5.00	2.50
119 Bill George	10.00	5.00
120 Raymond Berry	40.00	25.00
121 Jim Podoley UER	4.00	2.00
122 Hugh McElhenny	15.00	7.50
123 Ed Brown	5.00	2.50
124 Dick Moegle	5.00	2.50
125 Tom Scott	4.00	2.00
126 Tommy McDonald	12.00	6.00
127 Ollie Matson	20.00	10.00
128 Preston Carpenter	4.00	2.00
129 George Blanda	30.00	18.00
130 Gordy Soltau	4.00	2.00
131 Dick Nolan RC	5.00	2.50
132 Don Bosseler RC !	20.00	10.00

1959 Topps

COMPLETE SET (176)	900.00	600.00
COMMON CARD (1-88)	3.00	1.50
COMMON CARD (89-176)	2.00	1.00
WRAPPER (1-CENT)	90.00	50.00
WRAPPER (1-CENT, REP)	80.00	50.00
WRAPPER (5-CENT)	80.00	50.00
1 Johnny Unitas !	150.00	90.00
2 Gene Brito	3.00	1.50
3 Detroit Lions	6.00	3.00
4 Max McGee RC	15.00	7.50
5 Hugh McElhenny	15.00	7.50
6 Joe Schmidt	8.00	4.00
7 Kyle Rote	6.00	3.00
8 Clarence Peaks	3.00	1.50
9 Pittsburgh Steelers	3.50	1.75
10 Jim Brown	150.00	90.00
11 Ray Mathews	3.00	1.50
12 Bobby Dillon	3.00	1.50
13 Joe Childress	3.00	1.50
14 Terry Barr RC	3.00	1.50
15 Del Shofner RC	4.00	2.00
16 Bob Pellegrini UER	3.00	1.50
17 Baltimore Colts	6.00	3.00
18 Preston Carpenter	3.00	1.50
19 Leo Nomellini	10.00	5.00
20 Frank Gifford	40.00	25.00
21 Charlie Ane	3.00	1.50
22 Jack Butler	3.00	1.50
23 Bart Starr	60.00	35.00
24 Chicago Cardinals	3.50	1.75
25 Bill Barnes	3.00	1.50
26 Walt Michaels	4.00	2.00
27 Clyde Conner UER	3.00	1.50
28 Paige Cothren	3.00	1.50
29 Roosevelt Grier	6.00	3.00
30 Alan Ameche	6.00	3.00
31 Philadelphia Eagles	6.00	3.00
32 Dick Nolan	4.00	2.00
33 R.C. Owens	4.00	2.00
34 Dale Dodrill	3.00	1.50
35 Gene Gedman	3.00	1.50
36 Gene Lipscomb RC	10.00	5.00
37 Ray Renfro	4.00	2.00
38 Cleveland Browns	3.50	1.75
39 Bill Forester	4.00	2.00
40 Bobby Layne	25.00	15.00
41 Pat Summerall	10.00	5.00
42 Jerry Mertens	3.00	1.50
43 Steve Myhra	3.00	1.50
44 John Henry Johnson	8.00	4.00
45 Woodley Lewis UER	3.00	1.50
46 Green Bay Packers	8.00	4.00
47 Don Owens UER	3.00	1.50
48 Ed Beatty	3.00	1.50
49 Don Chandler	3.00	1.50
50 Ollie Matson	12.00	6.00
51 Sam Huff RC	50.00	30.00
52 Tom Miner	3.00	1.50
53 New York Giants	3.50	1.75
54 Kenny Konz	3.00	1.50
55 Raymond Berry	20.00	10.00
56 Howard Ferguson UER	3.00	1.50
57 Chuck Ulrich	3.00	1.50
58 Bob St.Clair	6.00	3.00
59 Don Burroughs RC	3.00	1.50
60 Lou Groza	15.00	7.50
61 San Francisco 49ers	6.00	3.00
62 Andy Nelson	3.00	1.50
63 Harold Bradley	3.00	1.50
64 Dave Hanner	4.00	2.00
65 Charley Conerly	10.00	5.00
66 Gene Cronin RC	3.00	1.50
67 Duane Putnam	3.00	1.50
68 Baltimore Colts	3.50	1.75
69 Ernie Stautner	8.00	4.00
70 Jon Arnett	4.00	2.00
71 Ken Panfil	3.00	1.50
72 Matt Hazeltine	3.00	1.50
73 Harley Sewell	3.00	1.50
74 Mike McCormack	6.00	3.00
75 Jim Ringo	8.00	4.00
76 Los Angeles Rams	6.00	3.00
77 Bob Gain RC	3.00	1.50
78 Buzz Nutter	3.00	1.50
79 Jerry Norton	3.00	1.50
80 Joe Perry	12.00	6.00
81 Carl Brettschneider	3.00	1.50
82 Paul Hornung	60.00	30.00
83 Philadelphia Eagles	3.50	1.75
84 Les Richter	4.00	2.00
85 Howard Cassady	4.00	2.00
86 Art Donovan	15.00	7.50
87 Jim Patton	4.00	2.00
88 Pete Retzlaff	4.00	2.00
89 Jim Mutscheller	2.00	1.00
90 Zeke Bratkowski	3.00	1.50
91 Washington Redskins	4.00	2.00
92 Art Hunter	2.00	1.00
93 Gern Nagler	2.00	1.00
94 Chuck Weber	2.00	1.00
95 Lew Carpenter RC	3.00	1.50
96 Stan Jones	5.00	2.50
97 Ralph Guglielmi UER	3.00	1.50
98 Green Bay Packers	4.00	2.00
99 Ray Wietecha	2.00	1.00
100 Lenny Moore	12.00	6.00
101 Jim Ray Smith RC UER	3.00	1.50
102 Abe Woodson RC	3.00	1.50
103 Alex Karras RC	40.00	25.00
104 Chicago Bears	4.00	2.00
105 John David Crow RC	12.00	6.00
106 Joe Fortunato RC	2.00	1.00
107 Babe Parilli	3.00	1.50
108 Proverb Jacobs	2.00	1.00
109 Gino Marchetti	8.00	4.00
110 Bill Wade	3.00	1.50
111 San Francisco 49ers	3.00	1.50
112 Karl Rubke	2.00	1.00
113 Dave Middleton UER	2.00	1.00
114 Roosevelt Brown	5.00	2.50
115 John Olszewski	2.00	1.00
116 Jerry Kramer RC	30.00	18.00
117 King Hill RC	3.00	1.50
118 Chicago Cardinals	4.00	2.00
119 Frank Varrichione	2.00	1.00
120 Rick Casares	3.00	1.50
121 George Strugar	2.00	1.00
122 Bill Glass RC	3.00	1.50
123 Don Bosseler	2.00	1.00
124 John Reger	2.00	1.00
125 Jim Ninowski RC	2.00	1.00
126 Los Angeles Rams	3.00	1.50
127 Willard Sherman	2.00	1.00
128 Bob Schnelker	2.00	1.00
129 Ollie Spencer	2.00	1.00
130 Y.A.Tittle	25.00	15.00
131 Yale Lary	5.00	2.50
132 Jim Parker RC	25.00	12.50
133 New York Giants	4.00	2.00
134 Jim Schrader	2.00	1.00
135 M.C. Reynolds	2.00	1.00
136 Mike Sandusky	2.00	1.00
137 Ed Brown	3.00	1.50
138 Al Barry	2.00	1.00
139 Detroit Lions	3.00	1.50
140 Bobby Mitchell RC	35.00	20.00
141 Larry Morris	2.00	1.00
142 Jim Phillips RC	3.00	1.50
143 Jim David	2.00	1.00
144 Joe Krupa	2.00	1.00
145 Willie Galimore	3.00	1.50
146 Pittsburgh Steelers	4.00	2.00
147 Andy Robustelli	8.00	4.00
148 Billy Wilson	2.00	1.00
149 Leo Sanford	2.00	1.00
150 Eddie LeBaron	5.00	2.50
151 Bill McColl	2.00	1.00
152 Buck Lansford UER	2.00	1.00
153 Chicago Bears	3.00	1.50
154 Leo Sugar	2.00	1.00
155 Jim Taylor RC UER	35.00	20.00
156 Lindon Crow	2.00	1.00
157 Jack McClairen	2.00	1.00
158 Vince Costello RC UER	2.00	1.00
159 Stan Wallace	2.00	1.00
160 Mel Triplett RC	2.00	1.00
161 Cleveland Browns	4.00	2.00
162 Dan Currie RC	3.00	1.50
163 L.G. Dupre UER	3.00	1.50
164 John Morrow UER	2.00	1.00
165 Jim Podoley	2.00	1.00
166 Bruce Bosley RC	2.00	1.00
167 Harlon Hill	2.00	1.00
168 Washington Redskins	3.00	1.50
169 Junior Wren	2.00	1.00
170 Tobin Rote	3.00	1.50
171 Art Spinney	2.00	1.00
172 Chuck Drazenovich UER	2.00	1.00
173 Bobby Joe Conrad RC	3.00	1.50
174 Jesse Richardson	2.00	1.00
175 Sam Baker	2.00	1.00
176 Tom Tracy RC !	8.00	4.00

1960 Topps

COMPLETE SET (132)	600.00	400.00
WRAPPER (1-CENT)	80.00	50.00
WRAPPER (1-CENT, REP)	300.00	150.00
WRAPPER (5-CENT)	80.00	50.00
1 Johnny Unitas !	80.00	40.00

❑ 2 Alan Ameche 4.00 2.00
❑ 3 Lenny Moore 10.00 5.00
❑ 4 Raymond Berry 12.00 6.00
❑ 5 Jim Parker 8.00 4.00
❑ 6 George Preas 2.50 1.25
❑ 7 Art Spinney 2.50 1.25
❑ 8 Bill Pellington RC 3.00 1.50
❑ 9 Johnny Sample RC 3.00 1.50
❑ 10 Gene Lipscomb 3.00 1.50
❑ 11 Baltimore Colts 3.00 1.50
❑ 12 Ed Brown 3.00 1.50
❑ 13 Rick Casares 3.00 1.50
❑ 14 Willie Galimore [illegible] 1.50
❑ 15 Jim Dooley 2.50 1.25
❑ 16 Harlon Hill UER 2.50 1.25
❑ 17 Stan Jones 4.00 2.00
❑ 18 Bill George 4.00 2.00
❑ 19 Erich Barnes RC 3.00 1.50
❑ 20 Doug Atkins 6.00 3.00
❑ 21 Chicago Bears 3.00 1.50
❑ 22 Milt Plum 3.00 1.50
❑ 23 Jim Brown 100.00 [illegible]
❑ 24 Sam Baker 2.50 1.25
❑ 25 Bobby Mitchell 10.00 5.00
❑ 26 Ray Renfro 3.00 1.50
❑ 27 Billy Howton 3.00 1.50
❑ 28 Jim Ray Smith 2.50 1.25
❑ 29 Jim Shofner RC 3.00 1.50
❑ 30 Bob Gain 2.50 1.25
❑ 31 Cleveland Browns 3.00 1.50
❑ 32 Don Heinrich 2.50 1.25
❑ 33 Ed Modzelewski UER 2.50 1.25
❑ 34 Fred Cone 2.50 1.25
❑ 35 L.G. Dupre 3.00 1.50
❑ 36 Dick Bielski 2.50 1.25
❑ 37 Charlie Ane UER 2.50 1.25
❑ 38 Jerry Tubbs 3.00 1.50
❑ 39 Doyle Nix 2.50 1.25
❑ 40 Ray Krouse 2.50 1.25
❑ 41 Earl Morrall 4.00 2.00
❑ 42 Howard Cassady 3.00 1.50
❑ 43 Dave Middleton 2.50 1.25
❑ 44 Jim Gibbons RC 3.00 1.50
❑ 45 Darris McCord 2.50 1.25
❑ 46 Joe Schmidt 6.00 3.00
❑ 47 Terry Barr 2.50 1.25
❑ 48 Yale Lary 4.00 2.00
❑ 49 Gil Mains 2.50 1.25
❑ 50 Detroit Lions 3.00 1.50
❑ 51 Bart Starr 45.00 30.00
❑ 52 Jim Taylor UER 8.00 4.00
❑ 53 Lew Carpenter 3.00 1.50
❑ 54 Paul Hornung 45.00 30.00
❑ 55 Max McGee 4.00 2.00
❑ 56 Forrest Gregg RC 40.00 25.00
❑ 57 Jim Ringo 5.00 2.50
❑ 58 Bill Forester 3.00 1.50
❑ 59 Dave Hanner 3.00 1.50
❑ 60 Green Bay Packers 8.00 4.00
❑ 61 Bill Wade 3.00 1.50
❑ 62 Frank Ryan RC 4.00 2.00
❑ 63 Ollie Matson 10.00 5.00
❑ 64 Jon Arnett 3.00 1.50
❑ 65 Del Shofner 3.00 1.50
❑ 66 Jim Phillips 2.50 1.25
❑ 67 Art Hunter 2.50 1.25
❑ 68 Les Richter 3.00 1.50
❑ 69 Lou Michaels RC 3.00 1.50
❑ 70 John Baker 2.50 1.25
❑ 71 Los Angeles Rams 3.00 1.50
❑ 72 Charley Conerly 8.00 4.00
❑ 73 Mel Triplett 2.50 1.25
❑ 74 Frank Gifford 35.00 20.00
❑ 75 Alex Webster 3.00 1.50
❑ 76 Bob Schnelker 2.50 1.25
❑ 77 Pat Summerall 8.00 4.00
❑ 78 Roosevelt Brown 4.00 2.00
❑ 79 Jim Patton 2.50 1.25
❑ 80 Sam Huff 20.00 10.00
❑ 81 Andy Robustelli 6.00 3.00
❑ 82 New York Giants 3.00 1.50
❑ 83 Clarence Peaks 2.50 1.25
❑ 84 Bill Barnes 2.50 1.25
❑ 85 Pete Retzlaff 3.00 1.50
❑ 86 Bobby Walston 2.50 1.25
❑ 87 Chuck Bednarik UER 8.00 4.00
❑ 88 Bob Pellegrini 2.50 1.25
❑ 89 Tom Brookshier RC 3.00 1.50
❑ 90 Marion Campbell 3.00 1.50
❑ 91 Jesse Richardson 2.50 1.25
❑ 92 Philadelphia Eagles 3.00 1.50
❑ 93 Bobby Layne 30.00 18.00
❑ 94 John Henry Johnson 6.00 3.00
❑ 95 Tom Tracy UER 3.00 1.50
❑ 96 Preston Carpenter 2.50 1.25
❑ 97 Frank Varrichione UER 2.50 1.25
❑ 98 John Nisby 2.50 1.25
❑ 99 Dean Derby 2.50 1.25
❑ 100 George Tarasovic 2.50 1.25
❑ 101 [illegible] [illegible] [illegible]
❑ 102 Pittsburgh Steelers 3.00 1.50
❑ 103 King Hill 2.50 1.25
❑ 104 Mal Hammack 2.50 1.25
❑ 105 John David Crow 3.00 1.50
❑ 106 Bobby Joe Conrad 3.00 1.50
❑ 107 Woodley Lewis 2.50 1.25
❑ 108 Don Gillis 2.50 1.25
❑ 109 Carl Brettschneider 2.50 1.25
❑ 110 Leo Sugar 2.50 1.25
❑ 111 Frank Fuller 2.50 1.25
❑ 112 St. Louis Cardinals 3.00 1.50
❑ 113 Y.A.Tittle 30.00 18.00
❑ 114 Joe Perry 8.00 4.00
❑ 115 J.D.Smith RC 3.00 1.50
❑ 116 Hugh McElhenny 8.00 4.00
❑ 117 Billy Wilson 2.50 1.25
❑ 118 Bob St.Clair 4.00 2.00
❑ 119 Matt Hazeltine 2.50 1.25
❑ 120 Abe Woodson 2.50 1.25
❑ 121 Leo Nomellini 5.00 2.50
❑ 122 San Francisco 49ers 3.00 1.50
❑ 123 Ralph Guglielmi UER 2.50 1.25
❑ 124 Don Bosseler 2.50 1.25
❑ 125 John Olszewski 2.50 1.25
❑ 126 Bill Anderson UER 2.50 1.25
❑ 127 Joe Walton RC 3.00 1.50
❑ 128 Jim Schrader 2.50 1.25
❑ 129 Ralph Felton 2.50 1.25
❑ 130 Gary Glick 2.50 1.25
❑ 131 Bob Toneff 2.50 1.25
❑ 132 Redskins Team ! 30.00 18.00

1961 Topps

ALAN AMECHE

❑ COMPLETE SET (198) 1000.00 650.00
❑ COMMON CARD (1-132) 2.50 1.25
❑ COMMON CARD (133-198) 3.00 1.50
❑ WRAPPER (1-CENT) 350.00 200.00
❑ WRAPPER (1-CENT, REP) 200.00 125.00
❑ WRAPPER (5-CENT) 100.00 60.00
❑ 1 Johnny Unitas 100.00 50.00
❑ 2 Lenny Moore 12.00 6.00
❑ 3 Alan Ameche 4.00 2.00
❑ 4 Raymond Berry 12.00 6.00
❑ 5 Jim Mutscheller 2.50 1.25
❑ 6 Jim Parker 5.00 2.50
❑ 7 Gino Marchetti 6.00 3.00
❑ 8 Gene Lipscomb 4.00 2.00
❑ 9 Baltimore Colts 3.00 1.50
❑ 10 Bill Wade 3.00 1.50
❑ 11 Johnny Morris RC 6.00 3.00
❑ 12 Rick Casares 3.00 1.50
❑ 13 Harlon Hill 2.50 1.25
❑ 14 Stan Jones 4.00 2.00
❑ 15 Doug Atkins 5.00 2.50
❑ 16 Bill George 4.00 2.00
❑ 17 J.C. Caroline 2.50 1.25
❑ 18 Chicago Bears 3.00 1.50
❑ 19 Eddie LeBaron IA 3.00 1.50
❑ 20 Eddie LeBaron 3.00 1.50
❑ 21 Don McIlhenny 2.50 1.25
❑ 22 L.G. Dupre 3.00 1.50
❑ 23 Jim Doran 2.50 1.25
❑ 24 Billy Howton 3.00 1.50
❑ 25 Buzz Guy 2.50 1.25
❑ 26 Jack Patera RC 2.50 1.25
❑ 27 Tom Franckhauser RC 2.50 1.25
❑ 28 Cowboys Team 15.00 7.50
❑ 29 Jim Ninowski 2.50 1.25
❑ [illegible]
❑ 31 Nick Pietrosante RC 3.00 1.50
❑ 32 Gail Cogdill RC 3.00 1.50
❑ 33 Jim Gibbons 2.50 1.25
❑ 34 Jim Martin 2.50 1.25
❑ 35 Alex Karras 15.00 7.50
❑ 36 Joe Schmidt 5.00 2.50
❑ 37 Detroit Lions 3.00 1.50
❑ 38 Paul Hornung IA 18.00 9.00
❑ 39 Bart Starr 40.00 25.00
❑ 40 Paul Hornung 40.00 25.00
❑ 41 Jim Taylor 35.00 20.00
❑ 42 Max McGee 4.00 2.00
❑ 43 Boyd Dowler RC 8.00 4.00
❑ 44 Jim Ringo 5.00 2.50
❑ 45 Hank Jordan RC 30.00 18.00
❑ 46 Bill Forester 3.00 1.50
❑ 47 Green Bay Packers 15.00 7.50
❑ 48 Frank Ryan 3.00 1.50
❑ 49 Jon Arnett 3.00 1.50
❑ 50 Ollie Matson 8.00 4.00
❑ 51 Jim Phillips 2.50 1.25
❑ 52 Del Shofner 3.00 1.50
❑ 53 Art Hunter 2.50 1.25
❑ 54 Gene Brito 2.50 1.25
❑ 55 Lindon Crow 2.50 1.25
❑ 56 Los Angeles Rams 3.00 1.50
❑ 57 Johnny Unitas IA 25.00 15.00
❑ 58 Y.A.Tittle 30.00 18.00
❑ 59 John Brodie RC 40.00 25.00
❑ 60 J.D. Smith 2.50 1.25
❑ 61 R.C. Owens 3.00 1.50
❑ 62 Clyde Conner 2.50 1.25
❑ 63 Bob St.Clair 4.00 2.00
❑ 64 Leo Nomellini 6.00 3.00
❑ 65 Abe Woodson 2.50 1.25
❑ 66 San Francisco 49ers 3.00 1.50
❑ 67 Checklist Card 40.00 25.00
❑ 68 Milt Plum 3.00 1.50
❑ 69 Ray Renfro 3.00 1.50
❑ 70 Bobby Mitchell 8.00 4.00
❑ 71 Jim Brown 100.00 70.00
❑ 72 Mike McCormack 4.00 2.00
❑ 73 Jim Ray Smith 2.50 1.25
❑ 74 Sam Baker 2.50 1.25
❑ 75 Walt Michaels 3.00 1.50
❑ 76 Cleveland Browns 3.00 1.50
❑ 77 Jim Brown IA 35.00 20.00
❑ 78 George Shaw 2.50 1.25
❑ 79 Hugh McElhenny 8.00 4.00
❑ 80 Clancy Osborne 2.50 1.25
❑ 81 Dave Middleton 2.50 1.25
❑ 82 Frank Youso 2.50 1.25
❑ 83 Don Joyce 2.50 1.25
❑ 84 Ed Culpepper 2.50 1.25
❑ 85 Charley Conerly 8.00 4.00
❑ 86 Mel Triplett 2.50 1.25
❑ 87 Kyle Rote 3.00 1.50
❑ 88 Roosevelt Brown 4.00 2.00
❑ 89 Ray Wietecha 2.50 1.25
❑ 90 Andy Robustelli 5.00 2.50
❑ 91 Sam Huff 8.00 4.00
❑ 92 Jim Patton 2.50 1.25
❑ 93 New York Giants 3.00 1.50
❑ 94 Charley Conerly IA 6.00 3.00
❑ 95 Sonny Jurgensen 25.00 15.00
❑ 96 Tommy McDonald 5.00 2.50
❑ 97 Bill Barnes 2.50 1.25
❑ 98 Bobby Walston 2.50 1.25
❑ 99 Pete Retzlaff 3.00 1.50
❑ 100 Jim McCusker 2.50 1.25
❑ 101 Chuck Bednarik 8.00 4.00
❑ 102 Tom Brookshier 3.00 1.50
❑ 103 Philadelphia Eagles 3.00 1.50
❑ 104 Bobby Layne 30.00 18.00

❑ 105 John Henry Johnson	4.00	2.00
❑ 106 Tom Tracy	3.00	1.50
❑ 107 Buddy Dial RC	2.50	1.25
❑ 108 Jimmy Orr RC	4.00	2.00
❑ 109 Mike Sandusky	2.50	1.25
❑ 110 John Reger	2.50	1.25
❑ 111 Junior Wren	2.50	1.25
❑ 112 Pittsburgh Steelers	3.00	1.50
❑ 113 Bobby Layne IA	10.00	5.00
❑ 114 John Roach	2.50	1.25
❑ 115 Sam Etcheverry RC	3.00	1.50
❑ 116 John David Crow	3.00	1.50
❑ 117 Mal Hammack	2.50	1.25
❑ 118 Sonny Randle RC	3.00	1.50
❑ 119 Leo Sugar	2.50	1.25
❑ 120 Jerry Norton	2.50	1.25
❑ 121 St. Louis Cardinals	3.00	1.50
❑ 122 Checklist Card	50.00	30.00
❑ 123 Ralph Guglielmi	2.50	1.25
❑ 124 Dick James	2.50	1.25
❑ 125 Don Bosseler	2.50	1.25
❑ 126 Joe Walton	2.50	1.25
❑ 127 Bill Anderson	2.50	1.25
❑ 128 Vince Promuto RC	2.50	1.25
❑ 129 Bob Toneff	2.50	1.25
❑ 130 John Paluck	2.50	1.25
❑ 131 Washington Redskins	3.00	1.50
❑ 132 Milt Plum IA !	2.50	1.25
❑ 133 Abner Haynes !	8.00	4.00
❑ 134 Mel Branch UER	4.00	2.00
❑ 135 Jerry Cornelison UER	3.00	1.50
❑ 136 Bill Krisher	3.00	1.50
❑ 137 Paul Miller	3.00	1.50
❑ 138 Jack Spikes	4.00	2.00
❑ 139 Johnny Robinson RC	8.00	4.00
❑ 140 Cotton Davidson RC	4.00	2.00
❑ 141 Dave Smith RB	3.00	1.50
❑ 142 Bill Groman	3.00	1.50
❑ 143 Rich Michael	3.00	1.50
❑ 144 Mike Dukes	3.00	1.50
❑ 145 George Blanda	25.00	15.00
❑ 146 Billy Cannon	6.00	3.00
❑ 147 Dennit Morris	3.00	1.50
❑ 148 Jacky Lee UER	4.00	2.00
❑ 149 Al Dorow	3.00	1.50
❑ 150 Don Maynard RC	50.00	25.00
❑ 151 Art Powell RC	8.00	4.00
❑ 152 Sid Youngelman	3.00	1.50
❑ 153 Bob Mischak	3.00	1.50
❑ 154 Larry Grantham	3.00	1.50
❑ 155 Tom Saidock	3.00	1.50
❑ 156 Roger Donnahoo	3.00	1.50
❑ 157 Laverne Torczon	3.00	1.50
❑ 158 Archie Matsos RC	4.00	2.00
❑ 159 Elbert Dubenion	4.00	2.00
❑ 160 Wray Carlton RC	4.00	2.00
❑ 161 Rich McCabe	3.00	1.50
❑ 162 Ken Rice	3.00	1.50
❑ 163 Art Baker RC	3.00	1.50
❑ 164 Tom Rychlec	3.00	1.50
❑ 165 Mack Yoho	3.00	1.50
❑ 166 Jack Kemp	100.00	50.00
❑ 167 Paul Lowe	6.00	3.00
❑ 168 Ron Mix	10.00	5.00
❑ 169 Paul Maguire UER	6.00	3.00
❑ 170 Volney Peters	3.00	1.50
❑ 171 Ernie Wright RC	4.00	2.00
❑ 172 Ron Nery RC	3.00	1.50
❑ 173 Dave Kocourek RC	4.00	2.00
❑ 174 Jim Colclough	3.00	1.50
❑ 175 Babe Parilli	4.00	2.00
❑ 176 Billy Lott	3.00	1.50
❑ 177 Fred Bruney	3.00	1.50
❑ 178 Ross O'Hanley	3.00	1.50
❑ 179 Walt Cudzik	3.00	1.50
❑ 180 Charley Leo	3.00	1.50
❑ 181 Bob Dee	3.00	1.50
❑ 182 Jim Otto RC	40.00	25.00
❑ 183 Eddie Macon	3.00	1.50
❑ 184 Dick Christy	3.00	1.50
❑ 185 Alan Miller	3.00	1.50
❑ 186 Tom Flores RC	20.00	10.00
❑ 187 Joe Cannavino	3.00	1.50
❑ 188 Don Manoukian	3.00	1.50
❑ 189 Bob Coolbaugh	3.00	1.50
❑ 190 Lionel Taylor RC	8.00	4.00
❑ 191 Bud McFadin	3.00	1.50
❑ 192 Goose Gonsoulin RC	6.00	3.00
❑ 193 Frank Tripucka	4.00	2.00
❑ 194 Gene Mingo RC	4.00	2.00
❑ 195 Eldon Danenhauer	3.00	1.50
❑ 196 Bob McNamara	3.00	1.50
❑ 197 Dave Rolle UER	3.00	1.50
❑ 198 Checklist UER !	100.00	60.00

1962 Topps

❑ COMPLETE SET (176)	2000.00	1200.00
❑ WRAPPER (1-CENT)	250.00	175.00
❑ WRAPPER (5-CENT,STARS)	50.00	25.00
❑ WRAPPER (5-CENT,BUCKS)	40.00	25.00
❑ 1 Johnny Unitas !	200.00	125.00
❑ 2 Lenny Moore	12.00	6.00
❑ 3 Alex Hawkins RC SP	10.00	5.00
❑ 4 Joe Perry	8.00	4.00
❑ 5 Raymond Berry SP	40.00	25.00
❑ 6 Steve Myhra	4.00	2.00
❑ 7 Tom Gilburg SP	8.00	4.00
❑ 8 Gino Marchetti	8.00	4.00
❑ 9 Bill Pellington	4.00	2.00
❑ 10 Andy Nelson	4.00	2.00
❑ 11 Wendell Harris SP	8.00	4.00
❑ 12 Baltimore Colts	6.00	3.00
❑ 13 Bill Wade SP	10.00	5.00
❑ 14 Willie Galimore	5.00	2.50
❑ 15 Johnny Morris SP	8.00	4.00
❑ 16 Rick Casares	5.00	2.50
❑ 17 Mike Ditka RC	300.00	175.00
❑ 18 Stan Jones	6.00	3.00
❑ 19 Roger LeClerc	4.00	2.00
❑ 20 Angelo Coia	4.00	2.00
❑ 21 Doug Atkins	7.00	3.50
❑ 22 Bill George	6.00	3.00
❑ 23 Richie Petitbon RC	5.00	2.50
❑ 24 Ronnie Bull RC SP	8.00	4.00
❑ 25 Chicago Bears	6.00	3.00
❑ 26 Howard Cassady	5.00	2.50
❑ 27 Ray Renfro SP	10.00	5.00
❑ 28 Jim Brown	175.00	100.00
❑ 29 Rich Kreitling	4.00	2.00
❑ 30 Jim Ray Smith	4.00	2.00
❑ 31 John Morrow	4.00	2.00
❑ 32 Lou Groza	15.00	7.50
❑ 33 Bob Gain	4.00	2.00
❑ 34 Bernie Parrish	4.00	2.00
❑ 35 Jim Shofner	4.00	2.00
❑ 36 Ernie Davis RC SP	150.00	90.00
❑ 37 Cleveland Browns	6.00	3.00
❑ 38 Eddie LeBaron	5.00	2.50
❑ 39 Don Meredith SP	100.00	60.00
❑ 40 J.W. Lockett SP	8.00	4.00
❑ 41 Don Perkins RC	10.00	5.00
❑ 42 Billy Howton	5.00	2.50
❑ 43 Dick Bielski	4.00	2.00
❑ 44 Mike Connelly RC	4.00	2.00
❑ 45 Jerry Tubbs SP	8.00	4.00
❑ 46 Don Bishop SP	8.00	4.00
❑ 47 Dick Moegle	4.00	2.00
❑ 48 Bobby Plummer SP	8.00	4.00
❑ 49 Cowboys Team	20.00	12.00
❑ 50 Milt Plum	5.00	2.50
❑ 51 Dan Lewis	4.00	2.00
❑ 52 Nick Pietrosante SP	8.00	4.00
❑ 53 Gail Cogdill	4.00	2.00
❑ 54 Jim Gibbons	4.00	2.00
❑ 55 Jim Martin	4.00	2.00
❑ 56 Yale Lary	6.00	3.00
❑ 57 Darris McCord	4.00	2.00
❑ 58 Alex Karras	25.00	15.00
❑ 59 Joe Schmidt	7.00	3.50
❑ 60 Dick Lane	6.00	3.00
❑ 61 John Lomakoski SP	8.00	4.00
❑ 62 Detroit Lions SP	18.00	10.00
❑ 63 Bart Starr SP	125.00	75.00
❑ 64 Paul Hornung SP	100.00	60.00
❑ 65 Tom Moore SP	12.00	6.00
❑ 66 Jim Taylor SP	50.00	30.00
❑ 67 Max McGee SP	12.00	6.00
❑ 68 Jim Ringo SP	15.00	7.50
❑ 69 Fuzzy Thurston RC SP	25.00	15.00
❑ 70 Forrest Gregg	7.00	3.50
❑ 71 Boyd Dowler	6.00	3.00
❑ 72 Hank Jordan SP	15.00	7.50
❑ 73 Bill Forester SP	10.00	5.00
❑ 74 Earl Gros SP	8.00	4.00
❑ 75 Packers Team SP	35.00	20.00
❑ 76 Checklist SP	80.00	45.00
❑ 77 Zeke Bratkowski SP	10.00	5.00
❑ 78 Jon Arnett SP	10.00	5.00
❑ 79 Ollie Matson SP	35.00	20.00
❑ 80 Dick Bass SP	10.00	5.00
❑ 81 Jim Phillips	4.00	2.00
❑ 82 Carroll Dale RC	5.00	2.50
❑ 83 Frank Varrichione	4.00	2.00
❑ 84 Art Hunter	4.00	2.00
❑ 85 Danny Villanueva RC	4.00	2.00
❑ 86 Les Richter SP	8.00	4.00
❑ 87 Lindon Crow	4.00	2.00
❑ 88 Roman Gabriel RC SP	60.00	35.00
❑ 89 Los Angeles Rams SP	18.00	10.00
❑ 90 Fran Tarkenton RC SP	225.00	125.00
❑ 91 Jerry Reichow SP	8.00	4.00
❑ 92 Hugh McElhenny SP	30.00	18.00
❑ 93 Mel Triplett SP	8.00	4.00
❑ 94 Tommy Mason RC SP	12.00	6.00
❑ 95 Dave Middleton SP	8.00	4.00
❑ 96 Frank Youso SP	8.00	4.00
❑ 97 Mike Mercer SP	8.00	4.00
❑ 98 Rip Hawkins SP	8.00	4.00
❑ 99 Cliff Livingston SP	8.00	4.00
❑ 100 Roy Winston RC SP	8.00	4.00
❑ 101 Vikings Team SP	25.00	15.00
❑ 102 Y.A.Tittle	40.00	25.00
❑ 103 Joe Walton	4.00	2.00
❑ 104 Frank Gifford	50.00	30.00
❑ 105 Alex Webster	5.00	2.50
❑ 106 Del Shofner	5.00	2.50
❑ 107 Don Chandler	4.00	2.00
❑ 108 Andy Robustelli	7.00	3.50
❑ 109 Jim Katcavage RC	5.00	2.50
❑ 110 Sam Huff SP	40.00	25.00
❑ 111 Erich Barnes	4.00	2.00
❑ 112 Jim Patton	4.00	2.00
❑ 113 Jerry Hillebrand SP	8.00	4.00
❑ 114 New York Giants	6.00	3.00
❑ 115 Sonny Jurgensen	40.00	25.00
❑ 116 Tommy McDonald	8.00	4.00
❑ 117 Ted Dean SP	8.00	4.00
❑ 118 Clarence Peaks	4.00	2.00
❑ 119 Bobby Walston	4.00	2.00
❑ 120 Pete Retzlaff SP	10.00	5.00
❑ 121 Jim Schrader SP	8.00	4.00
❑ 122 J.D. Smith T	4.00	2.00
❑ 123 King Hill	4.00	2.00
❑ 124 Maxie Baughan	5.00	2.50
❑ 125 Pete Case SP	8.00	4.00
❑ 126 Philadelphia Eagles	6.00	3.00
❑ 127 Bobby Layne	40.00	25.00
❑ 128 Tom Tracy	5.00	2.50
❑ 129 John Henry Johnson	6.00	3.00
❑ 130 Buddy Dial SP	10.00	5.00
❑ 131 Preston Carpenter	4.00	2.00
❑ 132 Lou Michaels SP	8.00	4.00
❑ 133 Gene Lipscomb SP	10.00	5.00
❑ 134 Ernie Stautner SP	20.00	12.00
❑ 135 John Reger SP	8.00	4.00
❑ 136 Myron Pottios RC	4.00	2.00
❑ 137 Bob Ferguson SP	8.00	4.00
❑ 138 Pittsburgh Steelers SP	18.00	10.00
❑ 139 Sam Etcheverry	5.00	2.50
❑ 140 John David Crow SP	10.00	5.00
❑ 141 Bobby Joe Conrad SP	10.00	5.00
❑ 142 Prentice Gautt RC SP	8.00	4.00
❑ 143 Frank Mestnik	4.00	2.00

❑ 144 Sonny Randle 5.00 2.50
❑ 145 Gerry Perry UER 4.00 2.00
❑ 146 Jerry Norton 4.00 2.00
❑ 147 Jimmy Hill 4.00 2.00
❑ 148 Bill Stacy 4.00 2.00
❑ 149 Fate Echols SP 8.00 4.00
❑ 150 St. Louis Cardinals 6.00 3.00
❑ 151 Billy Kilmer RC 35.00 20.00
❑ 152 John Brodie 18.00 10.00
❑ 153 J.D. Smith RB 5.00 2.50
❑ 154 C.R. Roberts SP 8.00 4.00
❑ 155 Monty Stickles 4.00 2.00
❑ 156 Clyde Conner UER 4.00 2.00
❑ [illegible]
❑ 158 Tommy Davis RC 4.00 2.00
❑ 159 Leo Nomellini 8.00 4.00
❑ 160 Matt Hazeltine 4.00 2.00
❑ 161 Abe Woodson 4.00 2.00
❑ 162 Dave Baker 4.00 2.00
❑ 163 San Francisco 49ers 6.00 3.00
❑ 164 Norm Snead RC SP 30.00 18.00
❑ 165 Dick James 5.00 2.50
❑ 166 Bobby Mitchell 8.00 4.00
❑ 167 Sam Horner 4.00 2.00
❑ 168 Bill Barnes 4.00 2.00
❑ 169 Bill Anderson 4.00 2.00
❑ 170 Fred Dugan 4.00 2.00
❑ 171 John Aveni SP 8.00 4.00
❑ 172 Bob Toneff 4.00 2.00
❑ 173 Jim Kerr 4.00 2.00
❑ 174 Leroy Jackson SP 8.00 4.00
❑ 175 Washington Redskins 6.00 3.00
❑ 176 Checklist ! 100.00 60.00

1963 Topps

❑ COMPLETE SET (170) 1350.00 850.00
❑ WRAPPER (1-CENT) 450.00 300.00
❑ WRAPPER (5-CENT) 80.00 50.00
❑ 1 Johnny Unitas ! 135.00 75.00
❑ 2 Lenny Moore 8.00 4.00
❑ 3 Jimmy Orr 3.00 1.50
❑ 4 Raymond Berry 8.00 4.00
❑ 5 Jim Parker 5.00 2.50
❑ 6 Alex Sandusky 2.50 1.25
❑ 7 Dick Szymanski RC 2.50 1.25
❑ 8 Gino Marchetti 6.00 3.00
❑ 9 Billy Ray Smith RC 3.00 1.50
❑ 10 Bill Pellington 2.50 1.25
❑ 11 Bob Boyd RC DB 2.50 1.25
❑ 12 Baltimore Colts SP 10.00 5.00
❑ 13 Frank Ryan SP 8.00 4.00
❑ 14 Jim Brown SP 200.00 100.00
❑ 15 Ray Renfro SP 8.00 4.00
❑ 16 Rich Kreitling SP 6.00 3.50
❑ 17 Mike McCormack SP 10.00 5.00
❑ 18 Jim Ray Smith SP 6.00 3.50
❑ 19 Lou Groza SP 25.00 15.00
❑ 20 Bill Glass SP 6.00 3.50
❑ 21 Galen Fiss SP 6.00 3.50
❑ 22 Don Fleming RC SP 8.00 4.00
❑ 23 Bob Gain SP 6.00 3.50
❑ 24 Cleveland Browns SP 10.00 5.00
❑ 25 Milt Plum 3.00 1.50
❑ 26 Dan Lewis 2.50 1.25
❑ 27 Nick Pietrosante 2.50 1.25
❑ 28 Gail Cogdill 2.50 1.25
❑ 29 Harley Sewell 2.50 1.25
❑ 30 Jim Gibbons 2.50 1.25
❑ 31 Carl Brettschneider 2.50 1.25
❑ 32 Dick Lane 5.00 2.50
❑ 33 Yale Lary 5.00 2.50
❑ 34 Roger Brown RC 3.00 1.50
❑ 35 Joe Schmidt 6.00 3.00
❑ 36 Detroit Lions SP 10.00 5.00
❑ 37 Roman Gabriel 8.00 4.00
❑ 38 Zeke Bratkowski 3.00 1.50
❑ 39 Dick Bass 3.00 1.50
❑ 40 Jon Arnett 3.00 1.50
❑ 41 Jim Phillips 2.50 1.25
❑ 42 Frank Varrichione 2.50 1.25
❑ 43 Danny Villanueva 2.50 1.25
❑ 44 Deacon Jones RC 50.00 30.00
❑ 45 [illegible]
❑ 46 Marlin McKeever 2.50 1.25
❑ 47 Ed Meador RC 2.50 1.25
❑ 48 Los Angeles Rams 4.00 2.00
❑ 49 Y.A.Tittle SP 50.00 30.00
❑ 50 Del Shofner SP 6.00 3.50
❑ 51 Alex Webster SP 8.00 4.00
❑ 52 Phil King SP 6.00 3.50
❑ 53 Jack Stroud SP 6.00 3.50
❑ 54 Darrell Dess SP 6.00 3.50
❑ 55 Jim Katcavage SP 6.00 3.50
❑ 56 Roosevelt Grier SP 10.00 5.00
❑ 57 Erich Barnes SP 6.00 3.50
❑ 58 Jim Patton SP 6.00 3.50
❑ 59 Sam Huff SP 20.00 12.00
❑ 60 New York Giants 4.00 2.00
❑ 61 Bill Wade 3.00 1.50
❑ 62 Mike Ditka 60.00 35.00
❑ 63 Johnny Morris 2.50 1.25
❑ 64 Roger LeClerc 2.50 1.25
❑ 65 Roger Davis RC 2.50 1.25
❑ 66 Joe Marconi 2.50 1.25
❑ 67 Herman Lee 2.50 1.25
❑ 68 Doug Atkins 6.00 3.00
❑ 69 Joe Fortunato 2.50 1.25
❑ 70 Bill George 5.00 2.50
❑ 71 Richie Petitbon 3.00 1.50
❑ 72 Bears Team SP 10.00 5.00
❑ 73 Eddie LeBaron SP 10.00 5.00
❑ 74 Don Meredith SP 60.00 35.00
❑ 75 Don Perkins SP 10.00 5.00
❑ 76 Amos Marsh SP 6.00 3.50
❑ 77 Billy Howton SP 8.00 4.00
❑ 78 Andy Cvercko SP 6.00 3.50
❑ 79 Sam Baker SP 6.00 3.50
❑ 80 Jerry Tubbs SP 6.00 3.50
❑ 81 Don Bishop SP 6.00 3.50
❑ 82 Bob Lilly RC SP 175.00 100.00
❑ 83 Jerry Norton SP 6.00 3.50
❑ 84 Cowboys Team SP 20.00 12.00
❑ 85 Checklist 25.00 15.00
❑ 86 Bart Starr 75.00 40.00
❑ 87 Jim Taylor 30.00 18.00
❑ 88 Boyd Dowler 5.00 2.50
❑ 89 Forrest Gregg 6.00 3.00
❑ 90 Fuzzy Thurston 6.00 3.00
❑ 91 Jim Ringo 6.00 3.00
❑ 92 Ron Kramer 3.00 1.50
❑ 93 Hank Jordan 6.00 3.00
❑ 94 Bill Forester 3.00 1.50
❑ 95 Willie Wood RC 40.00 25.00
❑ 96 Ray Nitschke RC 125.00 75.00
❑ 97 Green Bay Packers 15.00 7.50
❑ 98 Fran Tarkenton 60.00 35.00
❑ 99 Tommy Mason 3.00 1.50
❑ 100 Mel Triplett 2.50 1.25
❑ 101 Jerry Reichow 2.50 1.25
❑ 102 Frank Youso 2.50 1.25
❑ 103 Hugh McElhenny 8.00 4.00
❑ 104 Gerald Huth 2.50 1.25
❑ 105 Ed Sharockman 2.50 1.25
❑ 106 Rip Hawkins 2.50 1.25
❑ 107 Jim Marshall RC 35.00 20.00
❑ 108 Jim Prestel 2.50 1.25
❑ 109 Minnesota Vikings 4.00 2.00
❑ 110 Sonny Jurgensen SP 25.00 15.00
❑ 111 Timmy Brown RC SP 10.00 5.00
❑ 112 Tommy McDonald SP 15.00 7.50
❑ 113 Clarence Peaks SP 6.00 3.50
❑ 114 Pete Retzlaff SP 8.00 4.00
❑ 115 Jim Schrader SP 6.00 3.50
❑ 116 Jim McCusker SP 6.00 3.50
❑ 117 Don Burroughs SP 6.00 3.50
❑ 118 Maxie Baughan SP 6.00 3.50
❑ 119 Riley Gunnels SP 6.00 3.50
❑ 120 Jimmy Carr SP 6.00 3.50
❑ 121 Philadelphia Eagles SP 10.00 5.00
❑ 122 Ed Brown SP 8.00 4.00
❑ 123 John H.Johnson SP 15.00 7.50
❑ 124 Buddy Dial SP 6.00 3.50
❑ 125 Bill Red Mack SP 6.00 3.50
❑ 126 Preston Carpenter SP 6.00 3.50
❑ 127 Ray Lemek SP 6.00 3.50
❑ 128 Buzz Nutter SP 6.00 3.50
❑ 129 Ernie Stautner SP 15.00 7.50
❑ 130 Lou Michaels SP 6.00 3.50
❑ 131 Clendon Thomas RC SP 6.00 3.50
❑ 132 Tom Bettis SP 6.00 3.50
❑ 133 Pittsburgh Steelers SP 10.00 5.00
❑ 134 John Brodie 8.00 4.00
❑ 135 J.D. Smith 2.50 1.25
❑ 136 Billy Kilmer 5.00 2.50
❑ 137 Bernie Casey RC 3.00 1.50
❑ 138 Tommy Davis 2.50 1.25
❑ 139 Ted Connolly 2.50 1.25
❑ 140 Bob St.Clair 5.00 2.50
❑ 141 Abe Woodson 2.50 1.25
❑ 142 Matt Hazeltine 2.50 1.25
❑ 143 Leo Nomellini 6.00 3.00
❑ 144 Dan Colchico 2.50 1.25
❑ 145 San Francisco 49ers SP 10.00 5.00
❑ 146 Charlie Johnson RC 8.00 4.00
❑ 147 John David Crow 3.00 1.50
❑ 148 Bobby Joe Conrad 3.00 1.50
❑ 149 Sonny Randle 2.50 1.25
❑ 150 Prentice Gautt 2.50 1.25
❑ 151 Taz Anderson 2.50 1.25
❑ 152 Ernie McMillan RC 3.00 1.50
❑ 153 Jimmy Hill 2.50 1.25
❑ 154 Bill Koman 2.50 1.25
❑ 155 Larry Wilson RC 20.00 12.00
❑ 156 Don Owens 2.50 1.25
❑ 157 St. Louis Cardinals SP 10.00 5.00
❑ 158 Norm Snead SP 10.00 5.00
❑ 159 Bobby Mitchell SP 15.00 7.50
❑ 160 Bill Barnes SP 6.00 3.50
❑ 161 Fred Dugan SP 6.00 3.50
❑ 162 Don Bosseler SP 6.00 3.50
❑ 163 John Nisby SP 6.00 3.50
❑ 164 Riley Mattson SP 6.00 3.50
❑ 165 Bob Toneff SP 6.00 3.50
❑ 166 Rod Breedlove SP 6.00 3.50
❑ 167 Dick James SP 6.00 3.50
❑ 168 Claude Crabb SP 6.00 3.50
❑ 169 Washington Redskins SP 10.00 5.00
❑ 170 Checklist UER ! 50.00 30.00

1964 Topps

❑ COMPLETE SET (176) 1500.00 1000.00
❑ WRAPPER (1-CENT) 40.00 30.00
❑ WRAPPER (5-CENT, PENN) 125.00 75.00
❑ WRAP. (5-CENT, 8-CARD) 150.00 90.00
❑ 1 Tommy Addison SP ! 30.00 15.00
❑ 2 Houston Antwine RC 4.00 2.00
❑ 3 Nick Buoniconti 25.00 15.00
❑ 4 Ron Burton SP 10.00 5.00
❑ 5 Gino Cappelletti 5.00 2.50
❑ 6 Jim Colclough SP 6.00 3.00
❑ 7 Bob Dee SP 6.00 3.00
❑ 8 Larry Eisenhauer 4.00 2.00
❑ 9 Dick Felt SP 6.00 3.00
❑ 10 Larry Garron 4.00 2.00
❑ 11 Art Graham 4.00 2.00

Card	NrMt	VG-E
❑ 12 Ron Hall DB	4.00	2.00
❑ 13 Charles Long	4.00	2.00
❑ 14 Don McKinnon	4.00	2.00
❑ 15 Don Oakes SP	6.00	3.00
❑ 16 Ross O'Hanley SP	6.00	3.00
❑ 17 Babe Parilli SP	10.00	5.00
❑ 18 Jesse Richardson SP	6.00	3.00
❑ 19 Jack Rudolph SP	6.00	3.00
❑ 20 Don Webb RC	4.00	2.00
❑ 21 Boston Patriots	6.00	3.00
❑ 22 Ray Abruzzese	4.00	2.00
❑ 23 Stew Barber RC	4.00	2.00
❑ 24 Dave Behrman	4.00	2.00
❑ 25 Al Bemiller	4.00	2.00
❑ 26 Elbert Dubenion SP	10.00	5.00
❑ 27 Jim Dunaway RC SP	6.00	3.00
❑ 28 Booker Edgerson SP	6.00	3.00
❑ 29 Cookie Gilchrist SP	25.00	15.00
❑ 30 Jack Kemp SP	120.00	60.00
❑ 31 Daryle Lamonica RC	75.00	40.00
❑ 32 Bill Miller	4.00	2.00
❑ 33 Herb Paterra RC	4.00	2.00
❑ 34 Ken Rice SP	6.00	3.00
❑ 35 Ed Rutkowski	4.00	2.00
❑ 36 George Saimes RC	4.00	2.00
❑ 37 Tom Sestak	4.00	2.00
❑ 38 Billy Shaw SP	15.00	7.50
❑ 39 Mike Stratton	5.00	2.50
❑ 40 Gene Sykes	4.00	2.00
❑ 41 John Tracey SP	6.00	3.00
❑ 42 Sid Youngelman SP	6.00	3.00
❑ 43 Buffalo Bills	6.00	3.00
❑ 44 Eldon Danenhauer SP	6.00	3.00
❑ 45 Jim Fraser SP	6.00	3.00
❑ 46 Chuck Gavin SP	6.00	3.00
❑ 47 Goose Gonsoulin SP	10.00	5.00
❑ 48 Ernie Barnes RC	4.00	2.00
❑ 49 Tom Janik	4.00	2.00
❑ 50 Billy Joe RC	5.00	2.50
❑ 51 Ike Lassiter RC	4.00	2.00
❑ 52 John McCormick QB SP	6.00	3.00
❑ 53 Bud McFadin SP	6.00	3.00
❑ 54 Gene Mingo SP	6.00	3.00
❑ 55 Charlie Mitchell	4.00	2.00
❑ 56 John Nocera SP	6.00	3.00
❑ 57 Tom Nomina	4.00	2.00
❑ 58 Harold Olson SP	6.00	3.00
❑ 59 Bob Scarpitto	4.00	2.00
❑ 60 John Sklopan	4.00	2.00
❑ 61 Mickey Slaughter	4.00	2.00
❑ 62 Don Stone	4.00	2.00
❑ 63 Jerry Sturm	4.00	2.00
❑ 64 Lionel Taylor SP	12.00	6.00
❑ 65 Broncos Team SP	20.00	10.00
❑ 66 Scott Appleton RC	4.00	2.00
❑ 67 Tony Banfield SP	6.00	3.00
❑ 68 George Blanda SP	75.00	40.00
❑ 69 Billy Cannon	6.00	3.00
❑ 70 Doug Cline SP	6.00	3.00
❑ 71 Gary Cutsinger SP	6.00	3.00
❑ 72 Willard Dewveall SP	6.00	3.00
❑ 73 Don Floyd SP	6.00	3.00
❑ 74 Freddy Glick SP	6.00	3.00
❑ 75 Charlie Hennigan SP	10.00	5.00
❑ 76 Ed Husmann SP	6.00	3.00
❑ 77 Bobby Jancik SP	6.00	3.00
❑ 78 Jacky Lee SP	10.00	5.00
❑ 79 Bob McLeod SP	6.00	3.00
❑ 80 Rich Michael SP	6.00	3.00
❑ 81 Larry Onesti RC	4.00	2.00
❑ 82 Checklist Card UER	60.00	30.00
❑ 83 Bob Schmidt SP	6.00	3.00
❑ 84 Walt Suggs SP	6.00	3.00
❑ 85 Bob Talamini SP	6.00	3.00
❑ 86 Charley Tolar SP	6.00	3.00
❑ 87 Don Trull RC	4.00	2.00
❑ 88 Houston Oilers	6.00	3.00
❑ 89 Fred Arbanas	4.00	2.00
❑ 90 Bobby Bell RC	40.00	25.00
❑ 91 Mel Branch SP	10.00	5.00
❑ 92 Buck Buchanan RC	40.00	25.00
❑ 93 Ed Budde RC	4.00	2.00
❑ 94 Chris Burford SP	10.00	5.00
❑ 95 Walt Corey RC	5.00	2.50
❑ 96 Len Dawson SP	75.00	40.00
❑ 97 Dave Grayson RC	4.00	2.00
❑ 98 Abner Haynes	6.00	3.00
❑ 99 Sherrill Headrick SP	10.00	5.00
❑ 100 E.J. Holub	4.00	2.00
❑ 101 Bobby Hunt RC	4.00	2.00
❑ 102 Frank Jackson SP	6.00	3.00
❑ 103 Curtis McClinton	5.00	2.50
❑ 104 Jerry Mays SP	10.00	5.00
❑ 105 Johnny Robinson SP	12.00	6.00
❑ 106 Jack Spikes SP	6.00	3.00
❑ 107 Smokey Stover SP	6.00	3.00
❑ 108 Jim Tyrer RC	8.00	4.00
❑ 109 Duane Wood SP	6.00	3.00
❑ 110 Kansas City Chiefs	6.00	3.00
❑ 111 Dick Christy SP	6.00	3.00
❑ 112 Dan Ficca SP	6.00	3.00
❑ 113 Larry Grantham	4.00	2.00
❑ 114 Curley Johnson SP	6.00	3.00
❑ 115 Gene Heeter	4.00	2.00
❑ 116 Jack Klotz	4.00	2.00
❑ 117 Pete Liske RC	5.00	2.50
❑ 118 Bob McAdam	4.00	2.00
❑ 119 Dee Mackey SP	6.00	3.00
❑ 120 Bill Mathis SP	10.00	5.00
❑ 121 Don Maynard	35.00	20.00
❑ 122 Dainard Paulson SP	6.00	3.00
❑ 123 Gerry Philbin RC	5.00	2.50
❑ 124 Mark Smolinski SP	6.00	3.00
❑ 125 Matt Snell RC	20.00	10.00
❑ 126 Mike Taliaferro	4.00	2.00
❑ 127 Bake Turner RC SP	10.00	5.00
❑ 128 Jeff Ware	4.00	2.00
❑ 129 Clyde Washington	4.00	2.00
❑ 130 Dick Wood RC	4.00	2.00
❑ 131 New York Jets	6.00	3.00
❑ 132 Dalva Allen SP	6.00	3.00
❑ 133 Dan Birdwell	4.00	2.00
❑ 134 Dave Costa RC	4.00	2.00
❑ 135 Dobie Craig	4.00	2.00
❑ 136 Clem Daniels	5.00	2.50
❑ 137 Cotton Davidson SP	10.00	5.00
❑ 138 Claude Gibson	4.00	2.00
❑ 139 Tom Flores SP	15.00	7.50
❑ 140 Wayne Hawkins SP	6.00	3.00
❑ 141 Ken Herock	4.00	2.00
❑ 142 Jon Jelacic SP	6.00	3.00
❑ 143 Joe Krakoski	4.00	2.00
❑ 144 Archie Matsos SP	6.00	3.00
❑ 145 Mike Mercer	4.00	2.00
❑ 146 Alan Miller SP	6.00	3.00
❑ 147 Bob Mischak SP	6.00	3.00
❑ 148 Jim Otto SP	30.00	18.00
❑ 149 Clancy Osborne SP	6.00	3.00
❑ 150 Art Powell SP	12.00	6.00
❑ 151 Bo Roberson	4.00	2.00
❑ 152 Fred Williamson SP	30.00	18.00
❑ 153 Oakland Raiders	6.00	3.00
❑ 154 Chuck Allen RC SP	10.00	5.00
❑ 155 Lance Alworth	50.00	30.00
❑ 156 George Blair	4.00	2.00
❑ 157 Earl Faison	4.00	2.00
❑ 158 Sam Gruneisen	4.00	2.00
❑ 159 John Hadl RC	40.00	25.00
❑ 160 Dick Harris SP	6.00	3.00
❑ 161 Emil Karas SP	6.00	3.00
❑ 162 Dave Kocourek SP	6.00	3.00
❑ 163 Ernie Ladd	8.00	4.00
❑ 164 Keith Lincoln	6.00	3.00
❑ 165 Paul Lowe SP	12.00	6.00
❑ 166 Charley McNeil	4.00	2.00
❑ 167 Jacque MacKinnon SP RC	6.00	3.00
❑ 168 Ron Mix SP	20.00	10.00
❑ 169 Don Norton SP	6.00	3.00
❑ 170 Don Rogers SP	6.00	3.00
❑ 171 Tobin Rote SP	10.00	5.00
❑ 172 Henry Schmidt SP RC	6.00	3.00
❑ 173 Bud Whitehead	4.00	2.00
❑ 174 Ernie Wright SP	10.00	5.00
❑ 175 San Diego Chargers	6.00	3.00
❑ 176 Checklist SP UER !	160.00	80.00

1965 Topps

Card	NrMt	VG-E
❑ COMPLETE SET (176)	4000.00	2500.00
❑ WRAPPER (5-CENT)	150.00	90.00
❑ 1 Tommy Addison SP !	35.00	20.00
❑ 2 Houston Antwine SP	12.00	7.00
❑ 3 Nick Buoniconti SP	30.00	18.00
❑ 4 Ron Burton SP	20.00	10.00
❑ 5 Gino Cappelletti SP	20.00	10.00
❑ 6 Jim Colclough	7.00	3.50
❑ 7 Bob Dee SP	12.00	7.00
❑ 8 Larry Eisenhauer	7.00	3.50
❑ 9 J.D. Garrett	7.00	3.50
❑ 10 Larry Garron	7.00	3.50
❑ 11 Art Graham SP	12.00	7.00
❑ 12 Ron Hall DB	7.00	3.50
❑ 13 Charles Long	7.00	3.50
❑ 14 Jon Morris RC	10.00	5.00
❑ 15 Billy Neighbors SP	12.00	7.00
❑ 16 Ross O'Hanley	7.00	3.50
❑ 17 Babe Parilli SP	20.00	10.00
❑ 18 Tony Romeo SP	12.00	7.00
❑ 19 Jack Rudolph SP	12.00	7.00
❑ 20 Bob Schmidt	7.00	3.50
❑ 21 Don Webb SP	12.00	7.00
❑ 22 Jim Whalen SP	12.00	7.00
❑ 23 Stew Barber	7.00	3.50
❑ 24 Glenn Bass SP	12.00	7.00
❑ 25 Al Bemiller SP	12.00	7.00
❑ 26 Wray Carlton SP	12.00	7.00
❑ 27 Tom Day	7.00	3.50
❑ 28 Elbert Dubenion SP	15.00	7.50
❑ 29 Jim Dunaway	7.00	3.50
❑ 30 Pete Gogolak RC SP	20.00	10.00
❑ 31 Dick Hudson SP	12.00	7.00
❑ 32 Harry Jacobs SP	12.00	7.00
❑ 33 Billy Joe SP	15.00	7.50
❑ 34 Tom Keating RC SP	12.00	7.00
❑ 35 Jack Kemp SP !	150.00	75.00
❑ 36 Daryle Lamonica SP	50.00	30.00
❑ 37 Paul Maguire SP	20.00	10.00
❑ 38 Ron McDole RC SP	12.00	7.00
❑ 39 George Saimes SP	12.00	7.00
❑ 40 Tom Sestak SP	12.00	7.00
❑ 41 Billy Shaw SP	20.00	10.00
❑ 42 Mike Stratton SP	12.00	7.00
❑ 43 John Tracey SP	12.00	7.00
❑ 44 Ernie Warlick	7.00	3.50
❑ 45 Odell Barry	7.00	3.50
❑ 46 Willie Brown RC SP	100.00	60.00
❑ 47 Gerry Bussell SP	12.00	7.00
❑ 48 Eldon Danenhauer SP	12.00	7.00
❑ 49 Al Denson SP	12.00	7.00
❑ 50 Hewritt Dixon RC SP	15.00	7.50
❑ 51 Cookie Gilchrist SP	30.00	18.00
❑ 52 Goose Gonsoulin SP	15.00	7.50
❑ 53 Abner Haynes SP	20.00	10.00
❑ 54 Jerry Hopkins	7.00	3.50
❑ 55 Ray Jacobs SP	12.00	7.00
❑ 56 Jacky Lee SP	15.00	7.50
❑ 57 John McCormick QB	7.00	3.50
❑ 58 Bob McCullough SP	12.00	7.00
❑ 59 John McGeever	7.00	3.50
❑ 60 Charlie Mitchell SP	12.00	7.00
❑ 61 Jim Perkins SP	12.00	7.00
❑ 62 Bob Scarpitto SP	12.00	7.00
❑ 63 Mickey Slaughter SP	12.00	7.00
❑ 64 Jerry Sturm SP	12.00	7.00
❑ 65 Lionel Taylor SP	20.00	10.00
❑ 66 Scott Appleton SP	12.00	7.00
❑ 67 Johnny Baker SP	12.00	7.00
❑ 68 Sonny Bishop SP	12.00	7.00
❑ 69 George Blanda SP	125.00	75.00
❑ 70 Sid Blanks SP	12.00	7.00
❑ 71 Ode Burrell SP	12.00	7.00
❑ 72 Doug Cline SP	12.00	7.00
❑ 73 Willard Dewveall	7.00	3.50
❑ 74 Larry Elkins RC	7.00	3.50
❑ 75 Don Floyd SP	12.00	7.00

❑ 76 Freddy Glick 7.00 3.50
❑ 77 Tom Goode SP 12.00 7.00
❑ 78 Charlie Hennigan SP 20.00 10.00
❑ 79 Ed Husmann 7.00 3.50
❑ 80 Bobby Jancik SP 12.00 7.00
❑ 81 Bud McFadin SP 12.00 7.00
❑ 82 Bob McLeod SP 12.00 7.00
❑ 83 Jim Norton SP 12.00 7.00
❑ 84 Walt Suggs 7.00 3.50
❑ 85 Bob Talamini 7.00 3.50
❑ 86 Charley Tolar SP 12.00 7.00
❑ 87 Checklist SP ! 175.00 100.00
❑ 88 Don Trull SP 12.00 7.00
❑ 89 Fred Arbanas SP 12.00 7.00
❑ 90 Pete Beathard RC SP 12.00 7.00
❑ 91 Bobby Bell SP 40.00 25.00
❑ 92 Mel Branch SP 12.00 7.00
❑ 93 Tommy Brooker SP 12.00 7.00
❑ 94 Buck Buchanan SP 35.00 20.00
❑ 95 Ed Budde SP 12.00 7.00
❑ 96 Chris Burford SP 12.00 7.00
❑ 97 Walt Corey 7.00 3.50
❑ 98 Jerry Cornelison 7.00 3.50
❑ 99 Len Dawson SP 100.00 60.00
❑ 100 Jon Gilliam SP 12.00 7.00
❑ 101 Sherrill Headrick SP UER 12.00 7.00
❑ 102 Dave Hill SP 12.00 7.00
❑ 103 E.J. Holub SP 12.00 7.00
❑ 104 Bobby Hunt SP 12.00 7.00
❑ 105 Frank Jackson SP 12.00 7.00
❑ 106 Jerry Mays 10.00 5.00
❑ 107 Curtis McClinton SP 15.00 7.50
❑ 108 Bobby Ply SP 12.00 7.00
❑ 109 Johnny Robinson SP 15.00 7.50
❑ 110 Jim Tyrer SP 12.00 7.00
❑ 111 Bill Baird SP 12.00 7.00
❑ 112 Ralph Baker RC SP 12.00 7.00
❑ 113 Sam DeLuca SP 12.00 7.00
❑ 114 Larry Grantham SP 15.00 7.50
❑ 115 Gene Heeter SP 12.00 7.00
❑ 116 Winston Hill RC SP 20.00 10.00
❑ 117 John Huarte RC SP 30.00 18.00
❑ 118 Cosmo Iacavazzi SP 12.00 7.00
❑ 119 Curley Johnson SP 12.00 7.00
❑ 120 Dee Mackey UER 7.00 3.50
❑ 121 Don Maynard 50.00 30.00
❑ 122 Joe Namath RC SP ! 1800.00 1200.00
❑ 123 Dainard Paulson 7.00 3.50
❑ 124 Gerry Philbin SP 12.00 7.00
❑ 125 Sherman Plunkett RC SP 15.00 7.50
❑ 126 Mark Smolinski 7.00 3.50
❑ 127 Matt Snell SP 30.00 18.00
❑ 128 Mike Taliaferro SP 12.00 7.00
❑ 129 Bake Turner SP 12.00 7.00
❑ 130 Clyde Washington SP 12.00 7.00
❑ 131 Verlon Biggs RC SP 12.00 7.00
❑ 132 Dalva Allen 7.00 3.50
❑ 133 Fred Biletnikoff RC SP 225.00 150.00
❑ 134 Billy Cannon SP 20.00 10.00
❑ 135 Dave Costa SP 12.00 7.00
❑ 136 Clem Daniels SP 15.00 7.50
❑ 137 Ben Davidson RC SP 60.00 35.00
❑ 138 Cotton Davidson SP 15.00 7.50
❑ 139 Tom Flores SP 20.00 10.00
❑ 140 Claude Gibson 7.00 3.50
❑ 141 Wayne Hawkins 7.00 3.50
❑ 142 Archie Matsos SP 12.00 7.00
❑ 143 Mike Mercer SP 12.00 7.00
❑ 144 Bob Mischak SP 12.00 7.00
❑ 145 Jim Otto 30.00 18.00
❑ 146 Art Powell UER 10.00 5.00
❑ 147 Warren Powers DB SP 12.00 7.00
❑ 148 Ken Rice SP 12.00 7.00
❑ 149 Bo Roberson SP 12.00 7.00
❑ 150 Harry Schuh RC 7.00 3.50
❑ 151 Larry Todd SP 12.00 7.00
❑ 152 Fred Williamson SP 30.00 15.00
❑ 153 J.R. Williamson 7.00 3.50
❑ 154 Chuck Allen 10.00 5.00
❑ 155 Lance Alworth 75.00 50.00
❑ 156 Frank Buncom 7.00 3.50
❑ 157 Steve DeLong RC SP 12.00 7.00
❑ 158 Earl Faison SP 15.00 7.50
❑ 159 Kenny Graham SP 12.00 7.00
❑ 160 George Gross SP 12.00 7.00
❑ 161 John Hadl SP 35.00 20.00
❑ 162 Emil Karas SP 12.00 7.00
❑ 163 Dave Kocourek SP 12.00 7.00
❑ 164 Ernie Ladd SP 20.00 10.00
❑ 165 Keith Lincoln SP 20.00 10.00
❑ 166 Paul Lowe SP 20.00 10.00
❑ 167 Jacque MacKinnon 7.00 3.50
❑ 168 Ron Mix 20.00 12.00
❑ 169 Don Norton SP 12.00 7.00
❑ 170 Bob Petrich 7.00 3.50
❑ 171 Rick Redman SP 12.00 7.00
❑ 172 Pat Shea 7.00 3.50
❑ 173 Walt Sweeney RC SP 15.00 7.50
❑ 174 Dick Westmoreland RC 7.00 3.50
❑ 175 Ernie Wright SP 20.00 10.00
❑ 176 Checklist SP ! 225.00 125.00

1966 Topps

❑ COMPLETE SET (132) 1500.00 950.00
❑ WRAPPER (5-CENT) 60.00 30.00
❑ 1 Tommy Addison ! 20.00 10.00
❑ 2 Houston Antwine 5.00 3.00
❑ 3 Nick Buoniconti 10.00 5.00
❑ 4 Gino Cappelletti 7.00 3.50
❑ 5 Bob Dee 5.00 3.00
❑ 6 Larry Garron 5.00 3.00
❑ 7 Art Graham 5.00 3.00
❑ 8 Ron Hall DB 5.00 3.00
❑ 9 Charles Long 5.00 3.00
❑ 10 Jon Morris 5.00 3.00
❑ 11 Don Oakes 5.00 3.00
❑ 12 Babe Parilli 7.00 3.50
❑ 13 Don Webb 5.00 3.00
❑ 14 Jim Whalen 5.00 3.00
❑ 15 Funny Ring Checklist ! 300.00 200.00
❑ 16 Stew Barber 5.00 3.00
❑ 17 Glenn Bass 5.00 3.00
❑ 18 Dave Behrman 5.00 3.00
❑ 19 Al Bemiller 5.00 3.00
❑ 20 Butch Byrd RC 7.00 3.50
❑ 21 Wray Carlton 5.00 3.00
❑ 22 Tom Day 5.00 3.00
❑ 23 Elbert Dubenion 7.00 3.50
❑ 24 Jim Dunaway 5.00 3.00
❑ 25 Dick Hudson 5.00 3.00
❑ 26 Jack Kemp 150.00 75.00
❑ 27 Daryle Lamonica 20.00 12.00
❑ 28 Tom Sestak 5.00 3.00
❑ 29 Billy Shaw 10.00 5.00
❑ 30 Mike Stratton 5.00 3.00
❑ 31 Eldon Danenhauer 5.00 3.00
❑ 32 Cookie Gilchrist 10.00 5.00
❑ 33 Goose Gonsoulin 7.00 3.50
❑ 34 Wendell Hayes RC 10.00 5.00
❑ 35 Abner Haynes 10.00 5.00
❑ 36 Jerry Hopkins 5.00 3.00
❑ 37 Ray Jacobs 5.00 3.00
❑ 38 Charlie Janerette 5.00 3.00
❑ 39 Ray Kubala 5.00 3.00
❑ 40 John McCormick QB 5.00 3.00
❑ 41 Leroy Moore 5.00 3.00
❑ 42 Bob Scarpitto 5.00 3.00
❑ 43 Mickey Slaughter 5.00 3.00
❑ 44 Jerry Sturm 5.00 3.00
❑ 45 Lionel Taylor 10.00 5.00
❑ 46 Scott Appleton 5.00 3.00
❑ 47 Johnny Baker 5.00 3.00
❑ 48 George Blanda 35.00 20.00
❑ 49 Sid Blanks 5.00 3.00
❑ 50 Danny Brabham 5.00 3.00
❑ 51 Ode Burrell 5.00 3.00
❑ 52 Gary Cutsinger 5.00 3.00
❑ 53 Larry Elkins 5.00 3.00
❑ 54 Don Floyd 5.00 3.00
❑ 55 Willie Frazier RC 7.00 3.50
❑ 56 Freddy Glick 5.00 3.00
❑ 57 Charlie Hennigan 7.00 3.50
❑ 58 Bobby Jancik 5.00 3.00
❑ 59 Rich Michael 5.00 3.00
❑ 60 Don Trull 5.00 3.00
❑ 61 Checklist 55.00 30.00
❑ 62 Fred Arbanas 5.00 3.00
❑ 63 Pete Beathard 5.00 3.00
❑ 64 Bobby Bell 10.00 5.00
❑ 65 Ed Budde 5.00 3.00
❑ 66 Chris Burford 5.00 3.00
❑ 67 Len Dawson 40.00 25.00
❑ 68 Jon Gilliam 5.00 3.00
❑ 69 Sherrill Headrick 5.00 3.00
❑ 70 E.J. Holub UER 5.00 3.00
❑ 71 Bobby Hunt 5.00 3.00
❑ 72 Curtis McClinton 7.00 3.50
❑ 73 Jerry Mays 5.00 3.00
❑ 74 Johnny Robinson 7.00 3.50
❑ 75 Otis Taylor RC 25.00 15.00
❑ 76 Tom Erlandson 7.00 3.50
❑ 77 Norm Evans RC 10.00 5.00
❑ 78 Tom Goode 7.00 3.50
❑ 79 Mike Hudock 7.00 3.50
❑ 80 Frank Jackson 7.00 3.50
❑ 81 Billy Joe 7.00 3.50
❑ 82 Dave Kocourek 7.00 3.50
❑ 83 Bo Roberson 7.00 3.50
❑ 84 Jack Spikes 7.00 3.50
❑ 85 Jim Warren RC 7.00 3.50
❑ 86 Willie West RC 7.00 3.50
❑ 87 Dick Westmoreland 7.00 3.50
❑ 88 Eddie Wilson 7.00 3.50
❑ 89 Dick Wood 7.00 3.50
❑ 90 Verlon Biggs 7.00 3.50
❑ 91 Sam DeLuca 5.00 3.00
❑ 92 Winston Hill 5.00 3.00
❑ 93 Dee Mackey 5.00 3.00
❑ 94 Bill Mathis 5.00 3.00
❑ 95 Don Maynard 30.00 18.00
❑ 96 Joe Namath 250.00 150.00
❑ 97 Dainard Paulson 5.00 3.00
❑ 98 Gerry Philbin 7.00 3.50
❑ 99 Sherman Plunkett 5.00 3.00
❑ 100 Paul Rochester 5.00 3.00
❑ 101 George Sauer Jr. RC 15.00 7.50
❑ 102 Matt Snell 10.00 5.00
❑ 103 Jim Turner RC 7.00 3.50
❑ 104 Fred Biletnikoff UER 50.00 30.00
❑ 105 Bill Budness 5.00 3.00
❑ 106 Billy Cannon 10.00 5.00
❑ 107 Clem Daniels 7.00 3.50
❑ 108 Ben Davidson 15.00 7.50
❑ 109 Cotton Davidson 7.00 3.50
❑ 110 Claude Gibson 5.00 3.00
❑ 111 Wayne Hawkins 5.00 3.00
❑ 112 Ken Herock 5.00 3.00
❑ 113 Bob Mischak 5.00 3.00
❑ 114 Gus Otto 5.00 3.00
❑ 115 Jim Otto 20.00 12.00
❑ 116 Art Powell 10.00 5.00
❑ 117 Harry Schuh 5.00 3.00
❑ 118 Chuck Allen 5.00 3.00
❑ 119 Lance Alworth 40.00 25.00
❑ 120 Frank Buncom 5.00 3.00
❑ 121 Steve DeLong 5.00 3.00
❑ 122 John Farris 5.00 3.00
❑ 123 Kenny Graham 5.00 3.00
❑ 124 Sam Gruneisen 5.00 3.00
❑ 125 John Hadl 10.00 5.00
❑ 126 Walt Sweeney 5.00 3.00
❑ 127 Keith Lincoln 10.00 5.00
❑ 128 Ron Mix 10.00 5.00
❑ 129 Don Norton 5.00 3.00
❑ 130 Pat Shea 5.00 3.00
❑ 131 Ernie Wright 10.00 5.00
❑ 132 Checklist ! 100.00 50.00

1967 Topps

❑ COMPLETE SET (132) 700.00 400.00
❑ WRAPPER (5-CENT) 60.00 30.00
❑ 1 John Huarte ! 18.00 10.00
❑ 2 Babe Parilli 4.00 2.00
❑ 3 Gino Cappelletti 4.00 2.00

❑ 4 Larry Garron 3.00 1.50
❑ 5 Tommy Addison 3.00 1.50
❑ 6 Jon Morris 3.00 1.50
❑ 7 Houston Antwine 3.00 1.50
❑ 8 Don Oakes 3.00 1.50
❑ 9 Larry Eisenhauer 3.00 1.50
❑ 10 Jim Hunt 3.00 1.50
❑ 11 Jim Whalen 3.00 1.50
❑ 12 Art Graham 3.00 1.50
❑ 13 Nick Buoniconti 6.00 3.00
❑ 14 Bob Dee 3.00 1.50
❑ 15 Keith Lincoln 6.00 3.00
❑ 16 Tom Flores 4.00 2.00
❑ 17 Art Powell 4.00 2.00
❑ 18 Stew Barber 3.00 1.50
❑ 19 Wray Carlton 3.00 1.50
❑ 20 Elbert Dubenion 4.00 2.00
❑ 21 Jim Dunaway 3.00 1.50
❑ 22 Dick Hudson 3.00 1.50
❑ 23 Harry Jacobs 3.00 1.50
❑ 24 Jack Kemp 80.00 40.00
❑ 25 Ron McDole 3.00 1.50
❑ 26 George Saimes 3.00 1.50
❑ 27 Tom Sestak 3.00 1.50
❑ 28 Billy Shaw 6.00 3.00
❑ 29 Mike Stratton 3.00 1.50
❑ 30 Nemiah Wilson RC 3.00 1.50
❑ 31 John McCormick QB 3.00 1.50
❑ 32 Rex Mirich 3.00 1.50
❑ 33 Dave Costa 3.00 1.50
❑ 34 Goose Gonsoulin 4.00 2.00
❑ 35 Abner Haynes 6.00 3.00
❑ 36 Wendell Hayes 4.00 2.00
❑ 37 Archie Matsos 3.00 1.50
❑ 38 John Bramlett 3.00 1.50
❑ 39 Jerry Sturm 3.00 1.50
❑ 40 Max Leetzow 3.00 1.50
❑ 41 Bob Scarpitto 3.00 1.50
❑ 42 Lionel Taylor 6.00 3.00
❑ 43 Al Denson 3.00 1.50
❑ 44 Miller Farr RC 3.00 1.50
❑ 45 Don Trull 3.00 1.50
❑ 46 Jacky Lee 4.00 2.00
❑ 47 Bobby Jancik 3.00 1.50
❑ 48 Ode Burrell 3.00 1.50
❑ 49 Larry Elkins 3.00 1.50
❑ 50 W.K. Hicks 3.00 1.50
❑ 51 Sid Blanks 3.00 1.50
❑ 52 Jim Norton 3.00 1.50
❑ 53 Bobby Maples RC 3.00 1.50
❑ 54 Bob Talamini 3.00 1.50
❑ 55 Walt Suggs 3.00 1.50
❑ 56 Gary Cutsinger 3.00 1.50
❑ 57 Danny Brabham 3.00 1.50
❑ 58 Ernie Ladd 6.00 3.00
❑ 59 Checklist 50.00 25.00
❑ 60 Pete Beathard 3.00 1.50
❑ 61 Len Dawson 30.00 18.00
❑ 62 Bobby Hunt 3.00 1.50
❑ 63 Bert Coan 3.00 1.50
❑ 64 Curtis McClinton 4.00 2.00
❑ 65 Johnny Robinson 4.00 2.00
❑ 66 E.J. Holub 3.00 1.50
❑ 67 Jerry Mays 3.00 1.50
❑ 68 Jim Tyrer 4.00 2.00
❑ 69 Bobby Bell 6.00 3.00
❑ 70 Fred Arbanas 3.00 1.50
❑ 71 Buck Buchanan 6.00 3.00
❑ 72 Chris Burford 3.00 1.50
❑ 73 Otis Taylor 6.00 3.00
❑ 74 Cookie Gilchrist 8.00 4.00
❑ 75 Earl Faison 3.00 1.50
❑ 76 George Wilson Jr. 4.00 2.00
❑ 77 Rick Norton 3.00 1.50
❑ 78 Frank Jackson 4.00 2.00
❑ 79 Joe Auer 3.00 1.50
❑ 80 Willie West 3.00 1.50
❑ 81 Jim Warren 3.00 1.50
❑ 82 Wahoo McDaniel RC 50.00 30.00
❑ 83 Ernie Park 3.00 1.50
❑ 84 Billy Neighbors 3.00 1.50
❑ 85 Norm Evans 4.00 2.00
❑ 86 Tom Nomina 3.00 1.50
❑ 87 Rich Zecher 3.00 1.50
❑ 88 Dave Kocourek 3.00 1.50
❑ 89 Bill Baird 3.00 1.50
❑ 90 Ralph Baker 3.00 1.50
❑ 91 Verlon Biggs 3.00 1.50
❑ 92 Sam DeLuca 3.00 1.50
❑ 93 Larry Grantham 4.00 2.00
❑ 94 Jim Harris 3.00 1.50
❑ 95 Winston Hill 3.00 1.50
❑ 96 Bill Mathis 3.00 1.50
❑ 97 Don Maynard 20.00 12.00
❑ 98 Joe Namath 150.00 75.00
❑ 99 Gerry Philbin 4.00 2.00
❑ 100 Paul Rochester 3.00 1.50
❑ 101 George Sauer Jr. 4.00 2.00
❑ 102 Matt Snell 6.00 3.00
❑ 103 Daryle Lamonica 10.00 5.00
❑ 104 Glenn Bass 3.00 1.50
❑ 105 Jim Otto 6.00 3.00
❑ 106 Fred Biletnikoff 30.00 18.00
❑ 107 Cotton Davidson 4.00 2.00
❑ 108 Larry Todd 3.00 1.50
❑ 109 Billy Cannon 6.00 3.00
❑ 110 Clem Daniels 4.00 2.00
❑ 111 Dave Grayson 3.00 1.50
❑ 112 Kent McCloughan RC 3.00 1.50
❑ 113 Bob Svihus 3.00 1.50
❑ 114 Ike Lassiter 3.00 1.50
❑ 115 Harry Schuh 3.00 1.50
❑ 116 Ben Davidson 8.00 4.00
❑ 117 Tom Day 3.00 1.50
❑ 118 Scott Appleton 3.00 1.50
❑ 119 Steve Tensi RC 3.00 1.50
❑ 120 John Hadl 6.00 3.00
❑ 121 Paul Lowe 4.00 2.00
❑ 122 Jim Allison 3.00 1.50
❑ 123 Lance Alworth 35.00 20.00
❑ 124 Jacque MacKinnon 3.00 1.50
❑ 125 Ron Mix 6.00 3.00
❑ 126 Bob Petrich 3.00 1.50
❑ 127 Howard Kindig 3.00 1.50
❑ 128 Steve DeLong 3.00 1.50
❑ 129 Chuck Allen 3.00 1.50
❑ 130 Frank Buncom 3.00 1.50
❑ 131 Speedy Duncan RC 4.00 2.00
❑ 132 Checklist ! 70.00 35.00

1968 Topps

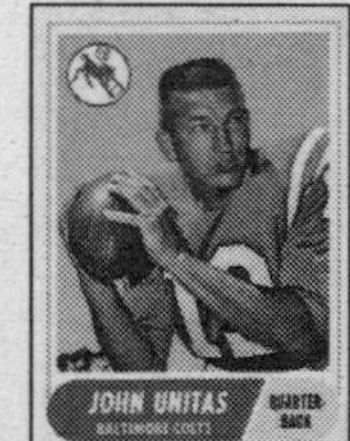

❑ COMPLETE SET (219) 550.00 350.00
❑ COMMON CARD (1-131) 1.50 .75
❑ COMMON CARD (132-219) 2.00 1.00
❑ WRAPPER (5-CENT, SER.1) 20.00 10.00
❑ WRAPPER (5-CENT, SER.2) 30.00 20.00
❑ 1 Bart Starr ! 40.00 25.00
❑ 2 Dick Bass 2.00 1.00
❑ 3 Grady Alderman 1.50 .75
❑ 4 Obert Logan 1.50 .75
❑ 5 Ernie Koy RC 2.00 1.00
❑ 6 Don Hultz 1.50 .75
❑ 7 Earl Gros 1.50 .75
❑ 8 Jim Bakken 1.50 .75
❑ 9 George Mira 2.00 1.00
❑ 10 Carl Kammerer 1.50 .75
❑ 11 Willie Frazier 1.50 .75
❑ 12 Kent McCloughan UER 1.50 .75
❑ 13 George Sauer Jr. 2.00 1.00
❑ 14 Jack Clancy 1.50 .75
❑ 15 Jim Tyrer 2.00 1.00
❑ 16 Bobby Maples 1.50 .75
❑ 17 Bo Hickey 1.50 .75
❑ 18 Frank Buncom 1.50 .75
❑ 19 Keith Lincoln 2.00 1.00
❑ 20 Jim Whalen 1.50 .75
❑ 21 Junior Coffey 1.50 .75
❑ 22 Billy Ray Smith 1.50 .75
❑ 23 Johnny Morris 1.50 .75
❑ 24 Ernie Green 1.50 .75
❑ 25 Don Meredith 25.00 15.00
❑ 26 Wayne Walker 1.50 .75
❑ 27 Carroll Dale 2.00 1.00
❑ 28 Bernie Casey 2.00 1.00
❑ 29 Dave Osborn RC 2.00 1.00
❑ 30 Ray Poage 1.50 .75
❑ 31 Homer Jones 1.50 .75
❑ 32 Sam Baker 1.50 .75
❑ 33 Bill Saul 1.50 .75
❑ 34 Ken Willard 2.00 1.00
❑ 35 Bobby Mitchell 4.00 2.00
❑ 36 Gary Garrison RC 2.00 1.00
❑ 37 Billy Cannon 2.00 1.00
❑ 38 Ralph Baker 1.50 .75
❑ 39 Howard Twilley RC 4.00 2.00
❑ 40 Wendell Hayes 2.00 1.00
❑ 41 Jim Norton 1.50 .75
❑ 42 Tom Beer 1.50 .75
❑ 43 Chris Burford 1.50 .75
❑ 44 Stew Barber 1.50 .75
❑ 45 Leroy Mitchell UER 1.50 .75
❑ 46 Dan Grimm 1.50 .75
❑ 47 Jerry Logan 1.50 .75
❑ 48 Andy Livingston 1.50 .75
❑ 49 Paul Warfield 15.00 7.50
❑ 50 Don Perkins 3.00 1.50
❑ 51 Ron Kramer 1.50 .75
❑ 52 Bob Jeter RC 2.00 1.00
❑ 53 Les Josephson RC 2.00 1.00
❑ 54 Bobby Walden 1.50 .75
❑ 55 Checklist 15.00 7.50
❑ 56 Walter Roberts 1.50 .75
❑ 57 Henry Carr 1.50 .75
❑ 58 Gary Ballman 1.50 .75
❑ 59 J.R. Wilburn 1.50 .75
❑ 60 Jim Hart RC 10.00 5.00
❑ 61 Jim Johnson 3.00 1.50
❑ 62 Chris Hanburger 2.00 1.00
❑ 63 John Hadl 3.00 1.50
❑ 64 Hewritt Dixon 2.00 1.00
❑ 65 Joe Namath 80.00 50.00
❑ 66 Jim Warren 1.50 .75
❑ 67 Curtis McClinton 2.00 1.00
❑ 68 Bob Talamini 1.50 .75
❑ 69 Steve Tensi 1.50 .75
❑ 70 Dick Van Raaphorst UER 1.50 .75
❑ 71 Art Powell 2.00 1.00
❑ 72 Jim Nance RC 4.00 2.00
❑ 73 Bob Riggle 1.50 .75
❑ 74 John Mackey 5.00 2.50
❑ 75 Gale Sayers 40.00 25.00
❑ 76 Gene Hickerson 2.50 1.25
❑ 77 Dan Reeves 10.00 5.00
❑ 78 Tom Nowatzke 1.50 .75
❑ 79 Elijah Pitts 3.00 1.50
❑ 80 Lamar Lundy 2.00 1.00
❑ 81 Paul Flatley 1.50 .75
❑ 82 Dave Whitsell 1.50 .75
❑ 83 Spider Lockhart 2.00 1.00
❑ 84 Dave Lloyd 1.50 .75
❑ 85 Roy Jefferson 2.00 1.00
❑ 86 Jackie Smith 6.00 3.00
❑ 87 John David Crow 2.00 1.00
❑ 88 Sonny Jurgensen 6.00 3.00
❑ 89 Ron Mix 3.00 1.50
❑ 90 Clem Daniels 2.00 1.00

❑ 91 Cornell Gordon 1.50 .75
❑ 92 Tom Goode 1.50 .75
❑ 93 Bobby Bell 3.00 1.50
❑ 94 Walt Suggs 1.50 .75
❑ 95 Eric Crabtree 1.50 .75
❑ 96 Sherrill Headrick 1.50 .75
❑ 97 Wray Carlton 1.50 .75
❑ 98 Gino Cappelletti 2.00 1.00
❑ 99 Tommy McDonald 4.00 2.00
❑ 100 Johnny Unitas 35.00 20.00
❑ 101 Richie Petitbon 1.50 .75
❑ 102 Erich Barnes 1.50 .75
❑ 103 Bob Hayes 8.00 4.00
❑ 104 Milt Plum 2.00 1.00
❑ 105 Boyd Dowler 2.00 1.00
❑ 106 Ed Meador 1.50 .75
❑ 107 Fred Cox 1.50 .75
❑ 108 Steve Stonebreaker RC 1.50 .75
❑ 109 Aaron Thomas 1.50 .75
❑ 110 Norm Snead 2.00 1.00
❑ 111 Paul Martha RC 1.50 .75
❑ 112 Jerry Stovall 1.50 .75
❑ 113 Kay McFarland 1.50 .75
❑ 114 Pat Richter 1.50 .75
❑ 115 Rick Redman 1.50 .75
❑ 116 Tom Keating 1.50 .75
❑ 117 Matt Snell 2.00 1.00
❑ 118 Dick Westmoreland 1.50 .75
❑ 119 Jerry Mays 1.50 .75
❑ 120 Sid Blanks 1.50 .75
❑ 121 Al Denson 1.50 .75
❑ 122 Bobby Hunt 1.50 .75
❑ 123 Mike Mercer 1.50 .75
❑ 124 Nick Buoniconti 3.00 1.50
❑ 125 Ron Vanderkelen RC 1.50 .75
❑ 126 Ordell Braase 1.50 .75
❑ 127 Dick Butkus 45.00 30.00
❑ 128 Gary Collins 2.00 1.00
❑ 129 Mel Renfro 6.00 3.00
❑ 130 Alex Karras 5.00 2.50
❑ 131 Herb Adderley ! 5.00 2.50
❑ 132 Roman Gabriel ! 4.00 2.00
❑ 133 Bill Brown 2.50 1.25
❑ 134 Kent Kramer 2.00 1.00
❑ 135 Tucker Frederickson 2.50 1.25
❑ 136 Nate Ramsey 2.00 1.00
❑ 137 Marv Woodson 2.00 1.00
❑ 138 Ken Gray 2.00 1.00
❑ 139 John Brodie 5.00 2.50
❑ 140 Jerry Smith 2.00 1.00
❑ 141 Brad Hubbert 2.00 1.00
❑ 142 George Blanda 20.00 10.00
❑ 143 Pete Lammons RC 2.00 1.00
❑ 144 Doug Moreau 2.00 1.00
❑ 145 E.J. Holub 2.00 1.00
❑ 146 Ode Burrell 2.00 1.00
❑ 147 Bob Scarpitto 2.00 1.00
❑ 148 Andre White 2.00 1.00
❑ 149 Jack Kemp 50.00 30.00
❑ 150 Art Graham 2.00 1.00
❑ 151 Tommy Nobis 6.00 3.00
❑ 152 Willie Richardson RC 2.50 1.25
❑ 153 Jack Concannon 2.00 1.00
❑ 154 Bill Glass 2.00 1.00
❑ 155 Craig Morton RC 10.00 5.00
❑ 156 Pat Studstill 2.00 1.00
❑ 157 Ray Nitschke 10.00 5.00
❑ 158 Roger Brown 2.00 1.00
❑ 159 Joe Kapp RC 5.00 2.50
❑ 160 Jim Taylor 15.00 7.50
❑ 161 Fran Tarkenton 20.00 10.00
❑ 162 Mike Ditka 30.00 18.00
❑ 163 Andy Russell RC 6.00 3.00
❑ 164 Larry Wilson 4.00 2.00
❑ 165 Tommy Davis 2.00 1.00
❑ 166 Paul Krause 4.00 2.00
❑ 167 Speedy Duncan 2.00 1.00
❑ 168 Fred Biletnikoff 15.00 7.50
❑ 169 Don Maynard 10.00 5.00
❑ 170 Frank Emanuel 2.00 1.00
❑ 171 Len Dawson 15.00 7.50
❑ 172 Miller Farr 2.00 1.00
❑ 173 Floyd Little RC 20.00 10.00
❑ 174 Lonnie Wright 2.00 1.00
❑ 175 Paul Costa 2.00 1.00
❑ 176 Don Trull 2.00 1.00
❑ 177 Jerry Simmons 2.00 1.00
❑ 178 Tom Matte 2.50 1.25
❑ 179 Bennie McRae 2.00 1.00
❑ 180 Jim Kanicki 2.00 1.00
❑ 181 Bob Lilly 15.00 7.50
❑ 182 Tom Watkins 2.00 1.00
❑ 183 Jim Grabowski RC 4.00 2.00
❑ 184 Jack Snow RC 4.00 2.00
❑ 185 Gary Cuozzo RC 2.50 1.25
❑ 186 Billy Kilmer 4.00 2.00
❑ 187 Jim Katcavage 2.00 1.00
❑ 188 Floyd Peters 2.00 1.00
❑ 189 Bill Nelsen 2.50 1.25
❑ 190 Bobby Joe Conrad 2.50 1.25
❑ 191 Kermit Alexander 2.00 1.00
❑ 192 Charley Taylor UER 6.00 3.00
❑ 193 Lance Alworth 20.00 10.00
❑ 194 Daryle Lamonica 5.00 2.50
❑ 195 Al Atkinson 2.00 1.00
❑ 196 Bob Griese RC 90.00 50.00
❑ 197 Buck Buchanan 4.00 2.00
❑ 198 Pete Beathard 2.00 1.00
❑ 199 Nemiah Wilson 2.00 1.00
❑ 200 Ernie Wright 2.00 1.00
❑ 201 George Saimes 2.00 1.00
❑ 202 John Charles 2.00 1.00
❑ 203 Randy Johnson 2.00 1.00
❑ 204 Tony Lorick 2.00 1.00
❑ 205 Dick Evey 2.00 1.00
❑ 206 Leroy Kelly 10.00 5.00
❑ 207 Lee Roy Jordan 6.00 3.00
❑ 208 Jim Gibbons 2.00 1.00
❑ 209 Donny Anderson RC 4.00 2.00
❑ 210 Maxie Baughan 2.00 1.00
❑ 211 Joe Morrison 2.00 1.00
❑ 212 Jim Snowden 2.00 1.00
❑ 213 Lenny Lyles 2.00 1.00
❑ 214 Bobby Joe Green 2.00 1.00
❑ 215 Frank Ryan 2.50 1.25
❑ 216 Cornell Green 2.50 1.25
❑ 217 Karl Sweetan 2.00 1.00
❑ 218 Dave Williams 2.00 1.00
❑ 219A Checklist Green ! 18.00 10.00
❑ 219B Checklist Blue ! 20.00 12.00

1969 Topps

❑ COMPLETE SET (263) 550.00 350.00
❑ COMMON CARD (1-132) 1.50 .75
❑ COMMON CARD (133-263) 2.00 1.00
❑ WRAPPER (5-CENT) 30.00 15.00
❑ 1 Leroy Kelly ! 20.00 10.00
❑ 2 Paul Flatley 1.50 .75
❑ 3 Jim Cadile 1.50 .75
❑ 4 Erich Barnes 1.50 .75
❑ 5 Willie Richardson 1.50 .75
❑ 6 Bob Hayes 5.00 2.50
❑ 7 Bob Jeter 1.50 .75
❑ 8 Jim Colclough 1.50 .75
❑ 9 Sherrill Headrick 1.50 .75
❑ 10 Jim Dunaway 1.50 .75
❑ 11 Bill Munson 2.00 1.00
❑ 12 Jack Pardee 2.00 1.00
❑ 13 Jim Lindsey 1.50 .75
❑ 14 Dave Whitsell 1.50 .75
❑ 15 Tucker Frederickson 1.50 .75
❑ 16 Alvin Haymond 2.00 1.00
❑ 17 Andy Russell 2.00 1.00
❑ 18 Tom Beer 1.50 .75
❑ 19 Bobby Maples 1.50 .75
❑ 20 Len Dawson 8.00 4.00
❑ 21 Willis Crenshaw 1.50 .75
❑ 22 Tommy Davis 1.50 .75
❑ 23 Rickie Harris 1.50 .75
❑ 24 Jerry Simmons 1.50 .75
❑ 25 Johnny Unitas 40.00 25.00
❑ 26 Brian Piccolo RC UER 80.00 50.00
❑ 27 Bob Matheson 1.50 .75
❑ 28 Howard Twilley 2.00 1.00
❑ 29 Jim Turner 2.00 1.00
❑ 30 Pete Banaszak RC 2.00 1.00
❑ 31 Lance Rentzel RC 2.00 1.00
❑ 32 Bill Triplett 1.50 .75
❑ 33 Boyd Dowler 2.00 1.00
❑ 34 Merlin Olsen 5.00 2.50
❑ 35 Joe Kapp 3.00 1.50
❑ 36 Dan Abramowicz RC 4.00 2.00
❑ 37 Spider Lockhart 2.00 1.00
❑ 38 Tom Day 1.50 .75
❑ 39 Art Graham 1.50 .75
❑ 40 Bob Cappadona 1.50 .75
❑ 41 Gary Ballman 1.50 .75
❑ 42 Clendon Thomas 1.50 .75
❑ 43 Jackie Smith 4.00 2.00
❑ 44 Dave Wilcox 3.00 1.50
❑ 45 Jerry Smith 1.50 .75
❑ 46 Dan Grimm 1.50 .75
❑ 47 Tom Matte 2.00 1.00
❑ 48 John Stofa 1.50 .75
❑ 49 Rex Mirich 1.50 .75
❑ 50 Miller Farr 1.50 .75
❑ 51 Gale Sayers 40.00 25.00
❑ 52 Bill Nelsen 2.00 1.00
❑ 53 Bob Lilly 6.00 3.00
❑ 54 Wayne Walker 1.50 .75
❑ 55 Ray Nitschke 5.00 2.50
❑ 56 Ed Meador 1.50 .75
❑ 57 Lonnie Warwick 1.50 .75
❑ 58 Wendell Hayes 1.50 .75
❑ 59 Dick Anderson RC 5.00 2.50
❑ 60 Don Maynard 6.00 3.00
❑ 61 Tony Lorick 1.50 .75
❑ 62 Pete Gogolak 1.50 .75
❑ 63 Nate Ramsey 1.50 .75
❑ 64 Dick Shiner 1.50 .75
❑ 65 Larry Wilson UER 3.00 1.50
❑ 66 Ken Willard 2.00 1.00
❑ 67 Charley Taylor 5.00 2.50
❑ 68 Billy Cannon 2.00 1.00
❑ 69 Lance Alworth 8.00 4.00
❑ 70 Jim Nance 2.00 1.00
❑ 71 Nick Rassas 1.50 .75
❑ 72 Lenny Lyles 1.50 .75
❑ 73 Bennie McRae 1.50 .75
❑ 74 Bill Glass 1.50 .75
❑ 75 Don Meredith 25.00 15.00
❑ 76 Dick LeBeau 1.50 .75
❑ 77 Carroll Dale 2.00 1.00
❑ 78 Ron McDole 1.50 .75
❑ 79 Charley King 1.50 .75
❑ 80 Checklist UER 15.00 7.50
❑ 81 Dick Bass 2.00 1.00
❑ 82 Roy Winston 1.50 .75
❑ 83 Don McCall 1.50 .75
❑ 84 Jim Katcavage 2.00 1.00
❑ 85 Norm Snead 2.00 1.00
❑ 86 Earl Gros 1.50 .75
❑ 87 Don Brumm 1.50 .75
❑ 88 Sonny Bishop 1.50 .75
❑ 89 Fred Arbanas 1.50 .75
❑ 90 Karl Noonan 1.50 .75
❑ 91 Dick Witcher 1.50 .75
❑ 92 Vince Promuto 1.50 .75
❑ 93 Tommy Nobis 4.00 2.00
❑ 94 Jerry Hill 1.50 .75
❑ 95 Ed O'Bradovich RC 1.50 .75
❑ 96 Ernie Kellerman 1.50 .75
❑ 97 Chuck Howley 2.00 1.00
❑ 98 Hewritt Dixon 1.50 .75
❑ 99 Ron Mix 3.00 1.50
❑ 100 Joe Namath 75.00 40.00
❑ 101 Billy Gambrell 1.50 .75
❑ 102 Elijah Pitts 2.00 1.00
❑ 103 Billy Truax RC 2.00 1.00
❑ 104 Ed Sharockman 1.50 .75
❑ 105 Doug Atkins 3.00 1.50
❑ 106 Greg Larson 1.50 .75
❑ 107 Israel Lang 1.50 .75

	Card	Price 1	Price 2
❑	108 Houston Antwine	1.50	.75
❑	109 Paul Guidry	1.50	.75
❑	110 Al Denson	1.50	.75
❑	111 Roy Jefferson	2.00	1.00
❑	112 Chuck Latourette	1.50	.75
❑	113 Jim Johnson	3.00	1.50
❑	114 Bobby Mitchell	4.00	2.00
❑	115 Randy Johnson	1.50	.75
❑	116 Lou Michaels	1.50	.75
❑	117 Rudy Kuechenberg	1.50	.75
❑	118 Walt Suggs	1.50	.75
❑	119 Goldie Sellers	1.50	.75
❑	120 Larry Csonka RC !	75.00	40.00
❑	121 Jim Houston	1.50	.75
❑	122 Craig Baynham	1.50	.75
❑	123 Alex Karras	5.00	2.50
❑	124 Jim Grabowski	2.00	1.00
❑	125 Roman Gabriel	3.00	1.50
❑	126 Larry Bowie	1.50	.75
❑	127 Dave Parks	2.00	1.00
❑	128 Ben Davidson	3.00	1.50
❑	129 Steve DeLong	1.50	.75
❑	130 Fred Hill	1.50	.75
❑	131 Ernie Koy	2.00	1.00
❑	132A Checklist no border !	15.00	7.50
❑	132B Checklist bordered !	20.00	10.00
❑	133 Dick Hoak	2.00	1.00
❑	134 Larry Stallings RC	2.00	1.00
❑	135 Clifton McNeil RC	2.00	1.00
❑	136 Walter Rock	2.00	1.00
❑	137 Billy Lothridge	2.00	1.00
❑	138 Bob Vogel	2.00	1.00
❑	139 Dick Butkus	40.00	25.00
❑	140 Frank Ryan	2.50	1.25
❑	141 Larry Garron	2.00	1.00
❑	142 George Saimes	2.00	1.00
❑	143 Frank Buncom	2.00	1.00
❑	144 Don Perkins	2.50	1.25
❑	145 Johnnie Robinson UER	2.00	1.00
❑	146 Lee Roy Caffey	2.50	1.25
❑	147 Bernie Casey	2.50	1.25
❑	148 Billy Martin E	2.00	1.00
❑	149 Gene Howard	2.00	1.00
❑	150 Fran Tarkenton	20.00	10.00
❑	151 Eric Crabtree	2.00	1.00
❑	152 W.K. Hicks	2.00	1.00
❑	153 Bobby Bell	4.00	2.00
❑	154 Sam Baker	2.00	1.00
❑	155 Marv Woodson	2.00	1.00
❑	156 Dave Williams	2.00	1.00
❑	157 Bruce Bosley UER	2.00	1.00
❑	158 Carl Kammerer	2.00	1.00
❑	159 Jim Burson	2.00	1.00
❑	160 Roy Hilton	2.00	1.00
❑	161 Bob Griese	25.00	15.00
❑	162 Bob Talamini	2.00	1.00
❑	163 Jim Otto	4.00	2.00
❑	164 Ronnie Bull	2.00	1.00
❑	165 Walter Johnson RC	2.00	1.00
❑	166 Lee Roy Jordan	4.00	2.00
❑	167 Mike Lucci	2.50	1.25
❑	168 Willie Wood	4.00	2.00
❑	169 Maxie Baughan	2.00	1.00
❑	170 Bill Brown	2.50	1.25
❑	171 John Hadl	4.00	2.00
❑	172 Gino Cappelletti	2.50	1.25
❑	173 George Butch Byrd	2.50	1.25
❑	174 Steve Stonebreaker	2.00	1.00
❑	175 Joe Morrison	2.00	1.00
❑	176 Joe Scarpati	2.00	1.00
❑	177 Bobby Walden	2.00	1.00
❑	178 Roy Shivers	2.00	1.00
❑	179 Kermit Alexander	2.00	1.00
❑	180 Pat Richter	2.00	1.00
❑	181 Pete Perreault	2.00	1.00
❑	182 Pete Duranko	2.00	1.00
❑	183 Leroy Mitchell	2.00	1.00
❑	184 Jim Simon	2.00	1.00
❑	185 Billy Ray Smith	2.00	1.00
❑	186 Jack Concannon	2.00	1.00
❑	187 Ben Davis	2.00	1.00
❑	188 Mike Clark	2.00	1.00
❑	189 Jim Gibbons	2.00	1.00
❑	190 Dave Robinson	2.50	1.25
❑	191 Otis Taylor	2.50	1.25
❑	192 Nick Buoniconti	4.00	2.00
❑	193 Matt Snell	2.50	1.25
❑	194 Bruce Gossett	2.00	1.00
❑	195 Mick Tingelhoff	2.50	1.25
❑	196 Earl Leggett	2.00	1.00
❑	197 Pete Case	2.00	1.00
❑	198 Tom Woodeshick RC	2.00	1.00
❑	199 Ken Kortas	2.00	1.00
❑	200 Jim Hart	4.00	2.00
❑	201 Fred Biletnikoff	10.00	5.00
❑	202 Jacque MacKinnon	2.00	1.00
❑	203 Jim Whalen	2.00	1.00
❑	204 Matt Hazeltine	2.00	1.00
❑	205 Charlie Gogolak	2.00	1.00
❑	206 Ray Ogden	2.00	1.00
❑	207 John Mackey	4.00	2.00
❑	208 Roosevelt Taylor	2.00	1.00
❑	209 Gene Hickerson	2.50	1.25
❑	210 Dave Edwards RC	2.50	1.25
❑	211 Tom Sestak	2.00	1.00
❑	212 Ernie Wright	2.00	1.00
❑	213 Dave Costa	2.00	1.00
❑	214 Tom Vaughn	2.00	1.00
❑	215 Bart Starr	35.00	20.00
❑	216 Les Josephson	2.00	1.00
❑	217 Fred Cox	2.00	1.00
❑	218 Mike Tilleman	2.00	1.00
❑	219 Darrell Dess	2.00	1.00
❑	220 Dave Lloyd	2.00	1.00
❑	221 Pete Beathard	2.00	1.00
❑	222 Buck Buchanan	4.00	2.00
❑	223 Frank Emanuel	2.00	1.00
❑	224 Paul Martha	2.00	1.00
❑	225 Johnny Roland	2.00	1.00
❑	226 Gary Lewis	2.00	1.00
❑	227 Sonny Jurgensen UER	6.00	3.00
❑	228 Jim Butler	2.00	1.00
❑	229 Mike Curtis RC	6.00	3.00
❑	230 Richie Petitbon	2.00	1.00
❑	231 George Sauer Jr.	2.50	1.25
❑	232 George Blanda	20.00	10.00
❑	233 Gary Garrison	2.00	1.00
❑	234 Gary Collins	2.50	1.25
❑	235 Craig Morton	4.00	2.00
❑	236 Tom Nowatzke	2.00	1.00
❑	237 Donny Anderson	2.50	1.25
❑	238 Deacon Jones	4.00	2.00
❑	239 Grady Alderman	2.00	1.00
❑	240 Billy Kilmer	4.00	2.00
❑	241 Mike Taliaferro	2.00	1.00
❑	242 Stew Barber	2.00	1.00
❑	243 Bobby Hunt	2.00	1.00
❑	244 Homer Jones	2.00	1.00
❑	245 Bob Brown OT	4.00	2.00
❑	246 Bill Asbury	2.00	1.00
❑	247 Charlie Johnson	2.50	1.25
❑	248 Chris Hanburger	2.50	1.25
❑	249 John Brodie	6.00	3.00
❑	250 Earl Morrall	2.50	1.25
❑	251 Floyd Little	5.00	2.50
❑	252 Jerrel Wilson RC	2.00	1.00
❑	253 Jim Keyes	2.00	1.00
❑	254 Mel Renfro	4.00	2.00
❑	255 Herb Adderley	4.00	2.00
❑	256 Jack Snow	2.50	1.25
❑	257 Charlie Durkee	2.00	1.00
❑	258 Charlie Harper	2.00	1.00
❑	259 J.R. Wilburn	2.00	1.00
❑	260 Charlie Krueger	2.00	1.00
❑	261 Pete Jacques	2.00	1.00
❑	262 Gerry Philbin	2.00	1.00
❑	263 Daryle Lamonica !	10.00	5.00

1970 Topps

	Card	Price 1	Price 2
❑	COMPLETE SET (263)	475.00	300.00
❑	COMMON CARD (1-132)	1.00	.40
❑	COMMON CARD (133-263)	1.25	.50
❑	WRAPPER (10-CENT)	12.00	8.00
❑	1 Len Dawson UER !	20.00	12.00
❑	2 Doug Hart	1.00	.40
❑	3 Verlon Biggs	1.00	.40
❑	4 Ralph Neely RC	1.50	.60
❑	5 Harmon Wages	1.00	.40
❑	6 Dan Conners	1.00	.40
❑	7 Gino Cappelletti	1.50	.60
❑	8 Erich Barnes	1.00	.40
❑	9 Checklist	10.00	5.00
❑	10 Bob Griese	15.00	7.50
❑	11 Ed Flanagan	1.00	.40
❑	12 George Seals	1.00	.40
❑	13 Harry Jacobs	1.00	.40
❑	14 Mike Haffner	1.00	.40
❑	15 Bob Vogel	1.00	.40
❑	16 Bill Peterson	1.00	.40
❑	17 Spider Lockhart	1.00	.40
❑	18 Billy Truax	1.00	.40
❑	19 Jim Beirne	1.00	.40
❑	20 Leroy Kelly	6.00	3.00
❑	21 Dave Lloyd	1.00	.40
❑	22 Mike Tilleman	1.00	.40
❑	23 Gary Garrison	1.00	.40
❑	24 Larry Brown RC	8.00	4.00
❑	25 Jan Stenerud RC	12.00	6.00
❑	26 Rolf Krueger	1.00	.40
❑	27 Roland Lakes	1.00	.40
❑	28 Dick Hoak	1.00	.40
❑	29 Gene Washington Vik RC	2.50	1.25
❑	30 Bart Starr	20.00	10.00
❑	31 Dave Grayson	1.00	.40
❑	32 Jerry Rush	1.00	.40
❑	33 Len St. Jean	1.00	.40
❑	34 Randy Edmunds	1.00	.40
❑	35 Matt Snell	1.50	.60
❑	36 Paul Costa	1.00	.40
❑	37 Mike Pyle	1.00	.40
❑	38 Roy Hilton	1.00	.40
❑	39 Steve Tensi	1.00	.40
❑	40 Tommy Nobis	2.50	1.25
❑	41 Pete Case	1.00	.40
❑	42 Andy Rice	1.00	.40
❑	43 Elvin Bethea RC	8.00	4.00
❑	44 Jack Snow	1.50	.60
❑	45 Mel Renfro	2.50	1.25
❑	46 Andy Livingston	1.00	.40
❑	47 Gary Ballman	1.00	.40
❑	48 Bob DeMarco	1.00	.40
❑	49 Steve DeLong	1.00	.40
❑	50 Daryle Lamonica	4.00	2.00
❑	51 Jim Lynch RC	1.00	.40
❑	52 Mel Farr RC	1.00	.40
❑	53 Bob Long RC	1.00	.40
❑	54 John Elliott	1.00	.40
❑	55 Ray Nitschke	5.00	2.50
❑	56 Jim Shorter	1.00	.40
❑	57 Dave Wilcox	2.50	1.25
❑	58 Eric Crabtree	1.00	.40
❑	59 Alan Page RC	30.00	15.00
❑	60 Jim Nance	1.50	.60
❑	61 Glen Ray Hines	1.00	.40
❑	62 John Mackey	2.50	1.25
❑	63 Ron McDole	1.00	.40
❑	64 Tom Beier	1.00	.40
❑	65 Bill Nelsen	1.50	.60
❑	66 Paul Flatley	1.00	.40
❑	67 Sam Brunelli	1.00	.40
❑	68 Jack Pardee	1.50	.60
❑	69 Brig Owens	1.00	.40
❑	70 Gale Sayers	25.00	12.50
❑	71 Lee Roy Jordan	2.50	1.25
❑	72 Harold Jackson RC	5.00	2.50
❑	73 John Hadl	2.50	1.25
❑	74 Dave Parks	1.00	.40
❑	75 Lem Barney RC	14.00	7.00
❑	76 Johnny Roland	1.00	.40
❑	77 Ed Budde	1.00	.40
❑	78 Ben McGee	1.00	.40
❑	79 Ken Bowman	1.00	.40
❑	80 Fran Tarkenton	15.00	7.50
❑	81 G.Washington 49er RC	5.00	2.50

❑ 82 Larry Grantham 1.00 .40
❑ 83 Bill Brown 1.50 .60
❑ 84 John Charles 1.00 .40
❑ 85 Fred Biletnikoff 7.00 3.50
❑ 86 Royce Berry 1.00 .40
❑ 87 Bob Lilly 5.00 2.50
❑ 88 Earl Morrall 1.50 .60
❑ 89 Jerry LeVias RC 1.50 .60
❑ 90 O.J. Simpson RC 80.00 40.00
❑ 91 Mike Howell 1.00 .40
❑ 92 Ken Gray 1.00 .40
❑ 93 Chris Hanburger 1.00 .40
❑ 94 Larry Seiple RC 1.00 .40
❑ 95 Rich Jackson RC 1.00 .40
❑ [illegible] 1.00 .40
❑ 97 Dick Post RC 1.50 .60
❑ 98 Ben Hawkins RC 1.00 .40
❑ 99 Ken Reaves 1.00 .40
❑ 100 Roman Gabriel 2.50 1.25
❑ 101 Dave Rowe 1.00 .40
❑ 102 Dave Robinson 1.00 .40
❑ 103 Otis Taylor 1.50 .60
❑ 104 Jim Turner 1.00 .40
❑ 105 Joe Morrison 1.00 .40
❑ 106 Dick Evey 1.00 .40
❑ 107 Ray Mansfield 1.00 .40
❑ 108 Grady Alderman 1.00 .40
❑ 109 Bruce Gossett 1.00 .40
❑ 110 Bob Trumpy RC 4.00 2.00
❑ 111 Jim Hunt 1.00 .40
❑ 112 Larry Stallings 1.00 .40
❑ 113A Lance Rentzel Red 1.50 .60
❑ 113B Lance Rentzel Black 1.50 .60
❑ 114 Bubba Smith RC 25.00 12.50
❑ 115 Norm Snead 1.50 .60
❑ 116 Jim Otto 2.50 1.25
❑ 117 Bo Scott RC 1.00 .40
❑ 118 Rick Redman 1.00 .40
❑ 119 George Butch Byrd 1.00 .40
❑ 120 George Webster RC 1.50 .60
❑ 121 Chuck Walton RC 1.00 .40
❑ 122 Dave Costa 1.00 .40
❑ 123 Al Dodd 1.00 .40
❑ 124 Len Hauss 1.00 .40
❑ 125 Deacon Jones 2.50 1.25
❑ 126 Randy Johnson 1.00 .40
❑ 127 Ralph Heck 1.00 .40
❑ 128 Emerson Boozer RC 1.50 .60
❑ 129 Johnny Robinson 1.50 .60
❑ 130 John Brodie 5.00 2.50
❑ 131 Gale Gillingham RC 1.00 .40
❑ 132 Checklist DP 6.00 3.00
❑ 133 Chuck Walker 1.25 .50
❑ 134 Bennie McRae 1.25 .50
❑ 135 Paul Warfield 7.00 3.50
❑ 136 Dan Darragh 1.25 .50
❑ 137 Paul Robinson RC 1.25 .50
❑ 138 Ed Philpott 1.25 .50
❑ 139 Craig Morton 3.00 1.50
❑ 140 Tom Dempsey RC 2.00 .75
❑ 141 Al Nelson 1.25 .50
❑ 142 Tom Matte 2.00 .75
❑ 143 Dick Schafrath 1.25 .50
❑ 144 Willie Brown 4.00 2.00
❑ 145 Charley Taylor UER 5.00 2.50
❑ 146 John Huard 1.25 .50
❑ 147 Dave Osborn 1.25 .50
❑ 148 Gene Mingo 1.25 .50
❑ 149 Larry Hand 1.25 .50
❑ 150 Joe Namath 50.00 25.00
❑ 151 Tom Mack RC 10.00 5.00
❑ 152 Kenny Graham 1.25 .50
❑ 153 Don Herrmann 1.25 .50
❑ 154 Bobby Bell 3.00 1.50
❑ 155 Hoyle Granger 1.25 .50
❑ 156 Claude Humphrey RC 4.00 1.50
❑ 157 Clifton McNeil 1.25 .50
❑ 158 Mick Tingelhoff 2.00 .75
❑ 159 Don Horn RC 1.25 .50
❑ 160 Larry Wilson 3.00 1.50
❑ 161 Tom Neville 1.25 .50
❑ 162 Larry Csonka 20.00 10.00
❑ 163 Doug Buffone RC 1.25 .50
❑ 164 Cornell Green 2.00 .75
❑ 165 Haven Moses RC 2.00 .75
❑ 166 Billy Kilmer 3.00 1.50
❑ 167 Tim Rossovich RC 1.25 .50
❑ 168 Bill Bergey RC 4.00 2.00
❑ 169 Gary Collins 2.00 .75
❑ 170 Floyd Little 3.00 1.50
❑ 171 Tom Keating 1.25 .50
❑ 172 Pat Fischer 1.25 .50
❑ 173 Walt Sweeney 1.25 .50
❑ 174 Greg Larson 1.25 .50
❑ 175 Carl Eller 3.00 1.50
❑ 176 George Sauer Jr. 2.00 .75
❑ 177 Jim Hart 3.00 1.50
❑ 178 Bob Brown OT 3.00 1.50
❑ 179 Mike Garrett RC 2.00 .75
❑ 180 Johnny Unitas 25.00 15.00
❑ 181 Tom Regner 1.25 .50
❑ 182 Bob Jeter 1.25 .50
❑ 183 Gail Cogdill 1.25 .50
❑ 184 Earl Gros 1.25 .50
❑ 185 Dennis Partee 1.25 .50
❑ 186 Charlie Krueger 1.25 .50
❑ 187 Martin Baccaglio 1.25 .50
❑ 188 Charles Long 1.25 .50
❑ 189 Bob Hayes 4.00 2.00
❑ 190 Dick Butkus 25.00 12.50
❑ 191 Al Bemiller 1.25 .50
❑ 192 Dick Westmoreland 1.25 .50
❑ 193 Joe Scarpati 1.25 .50
❑ 194 Ron Snidow 1.25 .50
❑ 195 Earl McCullouch RC 1.25 .50
❑ 196 Jake Kupp 1.25 .50
❑ 197 Bob Lurtsema 1.25 .50
❑ 198 Mike Current 1.25 .50
❑ 199 Charlie Smith RB 1.25 .50
❑ 200 Sonny Jurgensen 6.00 3.00
❑ 201 Mike Curtis 2.00 .75
❑ 202 Aaron Brown RC 1.25 .50
❑ 203 Richie Petitbon 1.25 .50
❑ 204 Walt Suggs 1.25 .50
❑ 205 Roy Jefferson 1.25 .50
❑ 206 Russ Washington RC 1.25 .50
❑ 207 Woody Peoples RC 1.25 .50
❑ 208 Dave Williams 1.25 .50
❑ 209 John Zook RC 1.25 .50
❑ 210 Tom Woodeshick 1.25 .50
❑ 211 Howard Fest 1.25 .50
❑ 212 Jack Concannon 1.25 .50
❑ 213 Jim Marshall 3.00 1.50
❑ 214 Jon Morris 1.25 .50
❑ 215 Dan Abramowicz 2.00 .75
❑ 216 Paul Martha 1.25 .50
❑ 217 Ken Willard 1.25 .50
❑ 218 Walter Rock 1.25 .50
❑ 219 Garland Boyette 1.25 .50
❑ 220 Buck Buchanan 3.00 1.50
❑ 221 Bill Munson 2.00 .75
❑ 222 David Lee RC 1.25 .50
❑ 223 Karl Noonan 1.25 .50
❑ 224 Harry Schuh 1.25 .50
❑ 225 Jackie Smith 3.00 1.50
❑ 226 Gerry Philbin 1.25 .50
❑ 227 Ernie Koy 1.25 .50
❑ 228 Chuck Howley 2.00 .75
❑ 229 Billy Shaw 3.00 1.50
❑ 230 Jerry Hillebrand 1.25 .50
❑ 231 Bill Thompson RC 2.00 .75
❑ 232 Carroll Dale 2.00 .75
❑ 233 Gene Hickerson 2.50 1.00
❑ 234 Jim Butler 1.25 .50
❑ 235 Greg Cook RC 1.25 .50
❑ 236 Lee Roy Caffey 1.25 .50
❑ 237 Merlin Olsen 4.00 2.00
❑ 238 Fred Cox 1.25 .50
❑ 239 Nate Ramsey 1.25 .50
❑ 240 Lance Alworth 7.00 3.50
❑ 241 Chuck Hinton 1.25 .50
❑ 242 Jerry Smith 1.25 .50
❑ 243 Tony Baker FB 1.25 .50
❑ 244 Nick Buoniconti 3.00 1.50
❑ 245 Jim Johnson 3.00 1.50
❑ 246 Willie Richardson 1.25 .50
❑ 247 Fred Dryer RC 10.00 5.00
❑ 248 Bobby Maples 1.25 .50
❑ 249 Alex Karras 4.00 2.00
❑ 250 Joe Kapp 2.00 .75
❑ 251 Ben Davidson 3.00 1.50
❑ 252 Mike Stratton 1.25 .50
❑ 253 Les Josephson 1.25 .50
❑ 254 Don Maynard 6.00 3.00
❑ 255 Houston Antwine 1.25 .50
❑ 256 Mac Percival RC 1.25 .50
❑ 257 George Goeddeke 1.25 .50
❑ 258 Homer Jones 1.25 .50
❑ 259 Bob Berry 1.25 .50
❑ 260A Calvin Hill RC Red 15.00 7.50
❑ 260B Calvin Hill RC Black 20.00 10.00
❑ 261 Willie Wood 3.00 1.50
❑ 262 Ed Weisacosky 1.25 .50
❑ 263 Jim Tyrer ! 3.00 1.50

1971 Topps

❑ COMPLETE SET (263) 500.00 300.00
❑ COMMON CARD (1-132) .75 .30
❑ COMMON CARD (133-263) 1.00 .40
❑ 1 Johnny Unitas ! 30.00 15.00
❑ 2 Jim Butler .75 .30
❑ 3 Marty Schottenheimer RC 12.00 6.00
❑ 4 Joe O'Donnell .75 .30
❑ 5 Tom Dempsey 1.25 .50
❑ 6 Chuck Allen .75 .30
❑ 7 Ernie Kellerman .75 .30
❑ 8 Walt Garrison RC 2.00 .75
❑ 9 Bill Van Heusen .75 .30
❑ 10 Lance Alworth 8.00 4.00
❑ 11 Greg Landry RC 2.00 .75
❑ 12 Larry Krause .75 .30
❑ 13 Buck Buchanan 2.00 .75
❑ 14 Roy Gerela RC 1.25 .50
❑ 15 Clifton McNeil .75 .30
❑ 16 Bob Brown OT 2.00 .75
❑ 17 Lloyd Mumphord .75 .30
❑ 18 Gary Cuozzo .75 .30
❑ 19 Don Maynard 5.00 2.50
❑ 20 Larry Wilson 2.00 .75
❑ 21 Charlie Smith RB .75 .30
❑ 22 Ken Avery .75 .30
❑ 23 Billy Walik .75 .30
❑ 24 Jim Johnson 2.00 .75
❑ 25 Dick Butkus 25.00 12.50
❑ 26 Charley Taylor UER 4.00 2.00
❑ 27 Checklist UER 8.00 4.00
❑ 28 Lionel Aldridge RC .75 .30
❑ 29 Billy Lothridge .75 .30
❑ 30 Terry Hanratty RC 1.25 .50
❑ 31 Lee Roy Jordan 2.00 .75
❑ 32 Rick Volk RC .75 .30
❑ 33 Howard Kindig .75 .30
❑ 34 Carl Garrett RC .75 .30
❑ 35 Bobby Bell 2.00 .75
❑ 36 Gene Hickerson 1.50 .60
❑ 37 Dave Parks .75 .30
❑ 38 Paul Martha .75 .30
❑ 39 George Blanda 15.00 7.50
❑ 40 Tom Woodeshick .75 .30
❑ 41 Alex Karras 3.00 1.50
❑ 42 Rick Redman .75 .30
❑ 43 Zeke Moore .75 .30
❑ 44 Jack Snow 1.25 .50
❑ 45 Larry Csonka 15.00 7.50
❑ 46 Karl Kassulke .75 .30
❑ 47 Jim Hart 2.00 .75
❑ 48 Al Atkinson .75 .30
❑ 49 Horst Muhlmann RC .75 .30
❑ 50 Sonny Jurgensen 5.00 2.50
❑ 51 Ron Johnson RC 1.25 .50
❑ 52 Cas Banaszek .75 .30
❑ 53 Bubba Smith 8.00 4.00
❑ 54 Bobby Douglass RC 1.25 .50

❑ 55 Willie Wood 2.00 .75
❑ 56 Bake Turner .75 .30
❑ 57 Mike Morgan LB .75 .30
❑ 58 George Butch Byrd 1.25 .50
❑ 59 Don Horn .75 .30
❑ 60 Tommy Nobis 2.00 .75
❑ 61 Jan Stenerud 4.00 2.00
❑ 62 Altie Taylor RC .75 .30
❑ 63 Gary Pettigrew .75 .30
❑ 64 Spike Jones RC .75 .30
❑ 65 Duane Thomas RC 2.00 .75
❑ 66 Marty Domres RC .75 .30
❑ 67 Dick Anderson 1.25 .50
❑ 68 Ken Iman .75 .30
❑ 69 Miller Farr .75 .30
❑ 70 Daryle Lamonica 3.00 1.50
❑ 71 Alan Page 12.00 6.00
❑ 72 Pat Matson .75 .30
❑ 73 Emerson Boozer .75 .30
❑ 74 Pat Fischer .75 .30
❑ 75 Gary Collins 1.25 .50
❑ 76 John Fuqua RC 1.25 .50
❑ 77 Bruce Gossett .75 .30
❑ 78 Ed O'Bradovich .75 .30
❑ 79 Bob Tucker RC 1.25 .50
❑ 80 Mike Curtis 1.25 .50
❑ 81 Rich Jackson .75 .30
❑ 82 Tom Janik .75 .30
❑ 83 Gale Gillingham .75 .30
❑ 84 Jim Mitchell TE .75 .30
❑ 85 Charlie Johnson 1.25 .50
❑ 86 Edgar Chandler .75 .30
❑ 87 Cyril Pinder .75 .30
❑ 88 Johnny Robinson 1.25 .50
❑ 89 Ralph Neely .75 .30
❑ 90 Dan Abramowicz .75 .30
❑ 91 Mercury Morris RC 5.00 2.50
❑ 92 Steve DeLong .75 .30
❑ 93 Larry Stallings .75 .30
❑ 94 Tom Mack 2.00 .75
❑ 95 Hewritt Dixon .75 .30
❑ 96 Fred Cox .75 .30
❑ 97 Chris Hanburger .75 .30
❑ 98 Gerry Philbin .75 .30
❑ 99 Ernie Wright .75 .30
❑ 100 John Brodie 4.00 2.00
❑ 101 Tucker Frederickson .75 .30
❑ 102 Bobby Walden .75 .30
❑ 103 Dick Gordon .75 .30
❑ 104 Walter Johnson .75 .30
❑ 105 Mike Lucci 1.25 .50
❑ 106 Checklist DP 6.00 3.00
❑ 107 Ron Berger .75 .30
❑ 108 Dan Sullivan .75 .30
❑ 109 George Kunz RC .75 .30
❑ 110 Floyd Little 2.00 .75
❑ 111 Zeke Bratkowski 1.25 .50
❑ 112 Haven Moses 1.25 .50
❑ 113 Ken Houston RC 15.00 7.50
❑ 114 Willie Lanier RC 15.00 7.50
❑ 115 Larry Brown 2.00 .75
❑ 116 Tim Rossovich .75 .30
❑ 117 Errol Linden .75 .30
❑ 118 Mel Renfro 2.00 .75
❑ 119 Mike Garrett .75 .30
❑ 120 Fran Tarkenton 15.00 7.50
❑ 121 Garo Yepremian RC 2.00 .75
❑ 122 Glen Condren .75 .30
❑ 123 Johnny Roland .75 .30
❑ 124 Dave Herman .75 .30
❑ 125 Merlin Olsen 3.00 1.50
❑ 126 Doug Buffone .75 .30
❑ 127 Earl McCullouch .75 .30
❑ 128 Spider Lockhart .75 .30
❑ 129 Ken Willard .75 .30
❑ 130 Gene Washington Vik .75 .30
❑ 131 Mike Phipps RC 1.25 .50
❑ 132 Andy Russell 1.25 .50
❑ 133 Ray Nitschke ! 4.00 2.00
❑ 134 Jerry Logan 1.00 .40
❑ 135 MacArthur Lane RC 1.50 .60
❑ 136 Jim Turner 1.00 .40
❑ 137 Kent McCloughan 1.00 .40
❑ 138 Paul Guidry 1.00 .40
❑ 139 Otis Taylor 1.50 .60
❑ 140 Virgil Carter RC 1.00 .40
❑ 141 Joe Dawkins 1.00 .40
❑ 142 Steve Preece 1.00 .40
❑ 143 Mike Bragg RC 1.00 .40
❑ 144 Bob Lilly 5.00 2.50
❑ 145 Joe Kapp 1.50 .60
❑ 146 Al Dodd 1.00 .40
❑ 147 Nick Buoniconti 2.50 1.25
❑ 148 Speedy Duncan 1.00 .40
❑ 149 Cedrick Hardman RC 1.00 .40
❑ 150 Gale Sayers 25.00 12.50
❑ 151 Jim Otto 2.50 1.25
❑ 152 Billy Truax 1.00 .40
❑ 153 John Elliott 1.00 .40
❑ 154 Dick LeBeau 1.00 .40
❑ 155 Bill Bergey 1.50 .60
❑ 156 Terry Bradshaw RC ! 200.00 125.00
❑ 157 Leroy Kelly 6.00 3.00
❑ 158 Paul Krause 2.50 1.25
❑ 159 Ted Vactor 1.00 .40
❑ 160 Bob Griese 15.00 7.50
❑ 161 Ernie McMillan 1.00 .40
❑ 162 Donny Anderson 1.50 .60
❑ 163 John Pitts 1.00 .40
❑ 164 Dave Costa 1.00 .40
❑ 165 Gene Washington 49er 1.50 .60
❑ 166 John Zook 1.00 .40
❑ 167 Pete Gogolak 1.00 .40
❑ 168 Erich Barnes 1.00 .40
❑ 169 Alvin Reed 1.00 .40
❑ 170 Jim Nance 1.50 .60
❑ 171 Craig Morton 2.50 1.25
❑ 172 Gary Garrison 1.00 .40
❑ 173 Joe Scarpati 1.00 .40
❑ 174 Adrian Young UER 1.00 .40
❑ 175 John Mackey 2.50 1.25
❑ 176 Mac Percival 1.00 .40
❑ 177 Preston Pearson RC 4.00 2.00
❑ 178 Fred Biletnikoff 8.00 4.00
❑ 179 Mike Battle RC 1.00 .40
❑ 180 Len Dawson 8.00 4.00
❑ 181 Les Josephson 1.00 .40
❑ 182 Royce Berry 1.00 .40
❑ 183 Herman Weaver 1.00 .40
❑ 184 Norm Snead 1.50 .60
❑ 185 Sam Brunelli 1.00 .40
❑ 186 Jim Kiick RC 5.00 2.50
❑ 187 Austin Denney 1.00 .40
❑ 188 Roger Wehrli RC 12.00 6.00
❑ 189 Dave Wilcox 2.50 1.25
❑ 190 Bob Hayes 2.50 1.25
❑ 191 Joe Morrison 1.00 .40
❑ 192 Manny Sistrunk 1.00 .40
❑ 193 Don Cockroft RC 1.00 .40
❑ 194 Lee Bouggess 1.00 .40
❑ 195 Bob Berry 1.00 .40
❑ 196 Ron Sellers 1.00 .40
❑ 197 George Webster 1.00 .40
❑ 198 Hoyle Granger 1.00 .40
❑ 199 Bob Vogel 1.00 .40
❑ 200 Bart Starr 20.00 10.00
❑ 201 Mike Mercer 1.00 .40
❑ 202 Dave Smith WR 1.00 .40
❑ 203 Lee Roy Caffey 1.00 .40
❑ 204 Mick Tingelhoff 1.50 .60
❑ 205 Matt Snell 1.50 .60
❑ 206 Jim Tyrer 1.00 .40
❑ 207 Willie Brown 2.50 1.25
❑ 208 Bob Johnson RC 1.00 .40
❑ 209 Deacon Jones 2.50 1.25
❑ 210 Charlie Sanders RC 5.00 2.00
❑ 211 Jake Scott RC 6.00 3.00
❑ 212 Bob Anderson RC 1.00 .40
❑ 213 Charlie Krueger 1.00 .40
❑ 214 Jim Bakken 1.00 .40
❑ 215 Harold Jackson 1.50 .60
❑ 216 Bill Brundige 1.00 .40
❑ 217 Calvin Hill 5.00 2.50
❑ 218 Claude Humphrey 1.00 .40
❑ 219 Glen Ray Hines 1.00 .40
❑ 220 Bill Nelsen 1.50 .60
❑ 221 Roy Hilton 1.00 .40
❑ 222 Don Herrmann 1.00 .40
❑ 223 John Bramlett 1.00 .40
❑ 224 Ken Ellis 1.00 .40
❑ 225 Dave Osborn 1.50 .60
❑ 226 Edd Hargett RC 1.00 .40
❑ 227 Gene Mingo 1.00 .40
❑ 228 Larry Grantham 1.00 .40
❑ 229 Dick Post 1.00 .40
❑ 230 Roman Gabriel 2.50 1.25
❑ 231 Mike Eischeid 1.00 .40
❑ 232 Jim Lynch 1.00 .40
❑ 233 Lemar Parrish RC 1.50 .60
❑ 234 Cecil Turner 1.00 .40
❑ 235 Dennis Shaw RC 1.00 .40
❑ 236 Mel Farr 1.00 .40
❑ 237 Curt Knight 1.00 .40
❑ 238 Chuck Howley 1.50 .60
❑ 239 Bruce Taylor RC 1.00 .40
❑ 240 Jerry LeVias 1.00 .40
❑ 241 Bob Lurtsema 1.00 .40
❑ 242 Earl Morrall 1.50 .60
❑ 243 Kermit Alexander 1.00 .40
❑ 244 Jackie Smith 2.50 1.25
❑ 245 Joe Greene RC 50.00 30.00
❑ 246 Harmon Wages 1.00 .40
❑ 247 Errol Mann 1.00 .40
❑ 248 Mike McCoy DT RC 1.00 .40
❑ 249 Milt Morin RC 1.00 .40
❑ 250 Joe Namath 60.00 35.00
❑ 251 Jackie Burkett 1.00 .40
❑ 252 Steve Chomyszak 1.00 .40
❑ 253 Ed Sharockman 1.00 .40
❑ 254 Robert Holmes RC 1.00 .40
❑ 255 John Hadl 2.50 1.25
❑ 256 Cornell Gordon 1.00 .40
❑ 257 Mark Moseley RC 1.50 .60
❑ 258 Gus Otto 1.00 .40
❑ 259 Mike Taliaferro 1.00 .40
❑ 260 O.J.Simpson 25.00 12.50
❑ 261 Paul Warfield 8.00 4.00
❑ 262 Jack Concannon 1.00 .40
❑ 263 Tom Matte ! 2.50 1.25

1972 Topps

❑ COMPLETE SET (351) 2500.00 1500.00
❑ COMMON CARD (1-132) .50 .25
❑ COMMON CARD (133-263) .60 .30
❑ COMMON CARD (264-351) 18.00 10.00
❑ WRAPPER (10-CENT) 10.00 6.00
❑ WRAPPER SER.3 (10-CENT) 20.00 15.00
❑ 1 L.Csonka/Litt/Hubb LL 4.00 2.00
❑ 2 NFC Rushing Leaders .50 .25
❑ 3 B.Griese/Dawson/Cart LL 2.00 .75
❑ 4 R.Staubach/Lan/Kil LL 5.00 2.50
❑ 5 AFC Receiving Leaders 1.00 .40
❑ 6 NFC Receiving Leaders .50 .25
❑ 7 Yepre/Stener/O'Brien LL .50 .25
❑ 8 NFC Scoring Leaders .50 .25
❑ 9 Jim Kiick 2.00 .75
❑ 10 Otis Taylor 1.00 .40
❑ 11 Bobby Joe Green .50 .25
❑ 12 Ken Ellis .50 .25
❑ 13 John Riggins RC 20.00 10.00
❑ 14 Dave Parks .50 .25
❑ 15 John Hadl 2.00 .75
❑ 16 Ron Hornsby .50 .25
❑ 17 Chip Myers RC .50 .25
❑ 18 Billy Kilmer 2.00 .75
❑ 19 Fred Hoaglin .50 .25
❑ 20 Carl Eller 2.00 .75
❑ 21 Steve Zabel .50 .25
❑ 22 Vic Washington RC .50 .25
❑ 23 Len St. Jean .50 .25
❑ 24 Bill Thompson .50 .25
❑ 25 Steve Owens RC 2.00 .75
❑ 26 Ken Burrough RC 1.00 .40

❑	27	Mike Clark	.50	.25
❑	28	Willie Brown	2.00	.75
❑	29	Checklist	6.00	3.00
❑	30	Marlin Briscoe RC	.50	.25
❑	31	Jerry Logan	.50	.25
❑	32	Donny Anderson	1.00	.40
❑	33	Rich McGeorge	.50	.25
❑	34	Charlie Durkee	.50	.25
❑	35	Willie Lanier	4.00	2.00
❑	36	Chris Farasopoulos	.50	.25
❑	37	Ron Shanklin RC	.50	.25
❑	38	Forrest Blue RC	.50	.25
❑	39	Ken Reaves	.50	.25
❑	40	Roman Gabriel	[illegible]	[illegible]
❑	41	Mac Percival	.50	.25
❑	42	Lem Barney	3.00	1.50
❑	43	Nick Buoniconti	2.00	.75
❑	44	Charlie Gogolak	.50	.25
❑	45	Bill Bradley RC	1.00	.40
❑	46	Joe Jones DE	.50	.25
❑	47	Dave Williams	.50	.25
❑	48	Pete Athas	.50	.25
❑	49	Virgil Carter	.50	.25
❑	50	Floyd Little	2.00	.75
❑	51	Curt Knight	.50	.25
❑	52	Bobby Maples	.50	.25
❑	53	Charlie West	.50	.25
❑	54	Marv Hubbard RC	1.00	.40
❑	55	Archie Manning RC	20.00	10.00
❑	56	Jim O'Brien RC	1.00	.40
❑	57	Wayne Patrick	.50	.25
❑	58	Ken Bowman	.50	.25
❑	59	Roger Wehrli	1.25	.50
❑	60	Charlie Sanders	1.25	.50
❑	61	Jan Stenerud	2.00	.75
❑	62	Willie Ellison	.50	.25
❑	63	Walt Sweeney	.50	.25
❑	64	Ron Smith	.50	.25
❑	65	Jim Plunkett RC	20.00	10.00
❑	66	Herb Adderley UER	2.00	.75
❑	67	Mike Reid RC	2.00	.75
❑	68	Richard Caster RC	1.00	.40
❑	69	Dave Wilcox	2.00	.75
❑	70	Leroy Kelly	3.00	1.50
❑	71	Bob Lee RC	.50	.25
❑	72	Verlon Biggs	.50	.25
❑	73	Henry Allison	.50	.25
❑	74	Steve Ramsey	.50	.25
❑	75	Claude Humphrey	1.00	.40
❑	76	Bob Grim RC	.50	.25
❑	77	John Fuqua	1.00	.40
❑	78	Ken Houston	4.00	2.00
❑	79	Checklist DP	5.00	2.50
❑	80	Bob Griese	8.00	4.00
❑	81	Lance Rentzel	1.00	.40
❑	82	Ed Podolak RC	1.00	.40
❑	83	Ike Hill	.50	.25
❑	84	George Farmer	.50	.25
❑	85	John Brockington RC	2.00	.75
❑	86	Jim Otto	2.00	.75
❑	87	Richard Neal	.50	.25
❑	88	Jim Hart	2.00	.75
❑	89	Bob Babich	.50	.25
❑	90	Gene Washington 49er	1.00	.40
❑	91	John Zook	.50	.25
❑	92	Bobby Duhon	.50	.25
❑	93	Ted Hendricks RC	15.00	7.50
❑	94	Rockne Freitas	.50	.25
❑	95	Larry Brown	2.00	.75
❑	96	Mike Phipps	1.00	.40
❑	97	Julius Adams	.50	.25
❑	98	Dick Anderson	1.00	.40
❑	99	Fred Willis	.50	.25
❑	100	Joe Namath	35.00	20.00
❑	101	L.C.Greenwood RC	15.00	7.50
❑	102	Mark Nordquist	.50	.25
❑	103	Robert Holmes	.50	.25
❑	104	Ron Yary RC	5.00	2.00
❑	105	Bob Hayes	2.00	.75
❑	106	Lyle Alzado RC	15.00	7.50
❑	107	Bob Berry	.50	.25
❑	108	Phil Villapiano RC	1.00	.40
❑	109	Dave Elmendorf	.50	.25
❑	110	Gale Sayers	20.00	10.00
❑	111	Jim Tyrer	.50	.25
❑	112	Mel Gray RC	2.00	.75
❑	113	Gerry Philbin	.50	.25
❑	114	Bob James	.50	.25
❑	115	Garo Yepremian	1.00	.40
❑	116	Dave Robinson	1.00	.40
❑	117	Jeff Queen	.50	.25
❑	118	Norm Snead	1.00	.40
❑	119	Jim Nance IA	1.00	.40
❑	120	Terry Bradshaw IA	15.00	7.50
❑	121	Jim Kiick IA	1.00	.40
❑	122	Roger Staubach IA	20.00	12.00
❑	123	Bo Scott IA	.50	.25
❑	124	John Brodie IA	2.00	.75
❑	125	Rick Volk IA	.50	.25
❑	126	John Riggins IA	6.00	3.00
❑	[illegible]	[illegible]	[illegible]	[illegible]
❑	128	Roman Gabriel IA	1.00	.40
❑	129	Calvin Hill IA	1.00	.40
❑	130	Bill Nelsen IA	.50	.25
❑	131	Tom Matte IA	1.00	.40
❑	132	Bob Griese IA	4.00	2.00
❑	133	AFC Semi-Final	1.00	.40
❑	134	NFC Semi-Final	1.00	.40
❑	135	AFC Semi-Final	1.00	.40
❑	136	NFC Semi-Final	1.00	.40
❑	137	AFC Title Game/Unitas	3.00	1.50
❑	138	NFC Title Game/Bob Lilly	2.00	.75
❑	139	Super Bowl VI/Staubach	5.00	2.50
❑	140	Larry Csonka	8.00	4.00
❑	141	Rick Volk	.60	.30
❑	142	Roy Jefferson	1.00	.40
❑	143	Raymond Chester RC	1.00	.40
❑	144	Bobby Douglass	.60	.30
❑	145	Bob Lilly	5.00	2.50
❑	146	Harold Jackson	1.00	.40
❑	147	Pete Gogolak	.60	.30
❑	148	Art Malone	.60	.30
❑	149	Ed Flanagan	.60	.30
❑	150	Terry Bradshaw	40.00	25.00
❑	151	MacArthur Lane	1.00	.40
❑	152	Jack Snow	1.00	.40
❑	153	Al Beauchamp	.60	.30
❑	154	Bob Anderson	.60	.30
❑	155	Ted Kwalick RC	.60	.30
❑	156	Dan Pastorini RC	2.00	.75
❑	157	Emmitt Thomas RC	15.00	7.50
❑	158	Randy Vataha RC	.60	.30
❑	159	Al Atkinson	.60	.30
❑	160	O.J.Simpson	15.00	7.50
❑	161	Jackie Smith	2.00	.75
❑	162	Ernie Kellerman	.60	.30
❑	163	Dennis Partee	.60	.30
❑	164	Jake Kupp	.60	.30
❑	165	Johnny Unitas	20.00	10.00
❑	166	Clint Jones RC	.60	.30
❑	167	Paul Warfield	6.00	3.00
❑	168	Roland McDole	.60	.30
❑	169	Daryle Lamonica	2.00	.75
❑	170	Dick Butkus	15.00	7.50
❑	171	Jim Butler	.60	.30
❑	172	Mike McCoy DT	.60	.30
❑	173	Dave Smith WR	.60	.30
❑	174	Greg Landry	1.00	.40
❑	175	Tom Dempsey	1.00	.40
❑	176	John Charles	.60	.30
❑	177	Bobby Bell	2.00	.75
❑	178	Don Horn	.60	.30
❑	179	Bob Trumpy	2.00	.75
❑	180	Duane Thomas	1.00	.40
❑	181	Merlin Olsen	3.00	1.50
❑	182	Dave Herman	.60	.30
❑	183	Jim Nance	1.00	.40
❑	184	Pete Beathard	.60	.30
❑	185	Bob Tucker	.60	.30
❑	186	Gene Upshaw RC	15.00	7.50
❑	187	Bo Scott	.60	.30
❑	188	J.D.Hill RC	.60	.30
❑	189	Bruce Gossett	.60	.30
❑	190	Bubba Smith	4.00	2.00
❑	191	Edd Hargett	.60	.30
❑	192	Gary Garrison	.60	.30
❑	193	Jake Scott	1.00	.40
❑	194	Fred Cox	.60	.30
❑	195	Sonny Jurgensen	4.00	2.00
❑	196	Greg Brezina RC	.60	.30
❑	197	Ed O'Bradovich	.60	.30
❑	198	John Rowser	.60	.30
❑	199	Altie Taylor UER	.60	.30
❑	200	Roger Staubach RC !	175.00	100.00
❑	201	Leroy Keyes RC	.60	.30
❑	202	Garland Boyette	.60	.30
❑	203	Tom Beer	.60	.30
❑	204	Buck Buchanan	2.00	.75
❑	205	Larry Wilson	2.00	.75
❑	206	Scott Hunter RC	.60	.30
❑	207	Ron Johnson	.60	.30
❑	208	Sam Brunelli	.60	.30
❑	209	Deacon Jones	2.00	.75
❑	210	Fred Biletnikoff	6.00	3.00
❑	211	Bill Nelsen	1.00	.40
❑	212	George Nock	.60	.30
❑	213	Dan Abramowicz	1.00	.40
❑	214	[illegible]	[illegible]	.30
❑	215	Isiah Robertson RC	1.00	.40
❑	216	Tom Matte	1.00	.40
❑	217	Pat Fischer	.60	.30
❑	218	Gene Washington Vik	.60	.30
❑	219	Paul Robinson	.60	.30
❑	220	John Brodie	4.00	2.00
❑	221	Manny Fernandez RC	1.00	.40
❑	222	Errol Mann	.60	.30
❑	223	Dick Gordon	.60	.30
❑	224	Calvin Hill	2.00	.75
❑	225	Fran Tarkenton	12.00	6.00
❑	226	Jim Turner	.60	.30
❑	227	Jim Mitchell TE	.60	.30
❑	228	Pete Liske	.60	.30
❑	229	Carl Garrett	.60	.30
❑	230	Joe Greene	20.00	10.00
❑	231	Gale Gillingham	.60	.30
❑	232	Norm Bulaich RC	1.00	.40
❑	233	Spider Lockhart	.60	.30
❑	234	Ken Willard	.60	.30
❑	235	George Blanda	12.00	6.00
❑	236	Wayne Mulligan	.60	.30
❑	237	Dave Lewis	.60	.30
❑	238	Dennis Shaw	.60	.30
❑	239	Fair Hooker	.60	.30
❑	240	Larry Little RC	15.00	7.50
❑	241	Mike Garrett	.60	.30
❑	242	Glen Ray Hines	.60	.30
❑	243	Myron Pottios	.60	.30
❑	244	Charlie Joiner RC	20.00	10.00
❑	245	Len Dawson	6.00	3.00
❑	246	W.K. Hicks	.60	.30
❑	247	Les Josephson	.60	.30
❑	248	Lance Alworth UER	6.00	3.00
❑	249	Frank Nunley	.60	.30
❑	250	Mel Farr IA	.60	.30
❑	251	Johnny Unitas IA	8.00	4.00
❑	252	George Farmer IA	.60	.30
❑	253	Duane Thomas IA	1.00	.40
❑	254	John Hadl IA	2.00	.75
❑	255	Vic Washington IA	.60	.30
❑	256	Don Horn IA	.60	.30
❑	257	L.C.Greenwood IA	2.00	.75
❑	258	Bob Lee IA	.60	.30
❑	259	Larry Csonka IA	4.00	2.00
❑	260	Mike McCoy DT IA	.60	.30
❑	261	Greg Landry IA	1.00	.40
❑	262	Ray May IA	.60	.30
❑	263	Bobby Douglass IA	.60	.30
❑	264	Charlie Sanders AP !	30.00	15.00
❑	265	Ron Yary AP	30.00	15.00
❑	266	Rayfield Wright AP	40.00	20.00
❑	267	Larry Little AP	35.00	20.00
❑	268	John Niland AP	30.00	15.00
❑	269	Forrest Blue AP	30.00	15.00
❑	270	Otis Taylor AP	30.00	15.00
❑	271	Paul Warfield AP	50.00	30.00
❑	272	Bob Griese AP	70.00	40.00
❑	273	John Brockington AP	30.00	15.00
❑	274	Floyd Little AP	30.00	15.00
❑	275	Garo Yepremian AP	30.00	15.00
❑	276	Jerrel Wilson AP	18.00	10.00
❑	277	Carl Eller AP	30.00	15.00
❑	278	Bubba Smith AP	40.00	25.00
❑	279	Alan Page AP	40.00	25.00
❑	280	Bob Lilly AP	60.00	30.00
❑	281	Ted Hendricks AP	50.00	30.00
❑	282	Dave Wilcox AP	30.00	15.00
❑	283	Willie Lanier AP	35.00	20.00
❑	284	Jim Johnson AP	30.00	15.00
❑	285	Willie Brown AP	35.00	20.00
❑	286	Bill Bradley AP	30.00	15.00
❑	287	Ken Houston AP	35.00	20.00

❑ 288 Mel Farr	18.00	10.00
❑ 289 Kermit Alexander	18.00	10.00
❑ 290 John Gilliam RC	25.00	12.50
❑ 291 Steve Spurrier RC	100.00	50.00
❑ 292 Walter Johnson	18.00	10.00
❑ 293 Jack Pardee	25.00	12.50
❑ 294 Checklist UER	80.00	50.00
❑ 295 Winston Hill	18.00	10.00
❑ 296 Hugo Hollas	18.00	10.00
❑ 297 Ray May RC	18.00	10.00
❑ 298 Jim Bakken	18.00	10.00
❑ 299 Larry Carwell	18.00	10.00
❑ 300 Alan Page	50.00	30.00
❑ 301 Walt Garrison	25.00	12.50
❑ 302 Mike Lucci	25.00	12.50
❑ 303 Nemiah Wilson	18.00	10.00
❑ 304 Carroll Dale	25.00	12.50
❑ 305 Jim Kanicki	18.00	10.00
❑ 306 Preston Pearson	30.00	15.00
❑ 307 Lemar Parrish	25.00	12.50
❑ 308 Earl Morrall	25.00	12.50
❑ 309 Tommy Nobis	25.00	12.50
❑ 310 Rich Jackson	18.00	10.00
❑ 311 Doug Cunningham	18.00	10.00
❑ 312 Jim Marsalis	18.00	10.00
❑ 313 Jim Beirne	18.00	10.00
❑ 314 Tom McNeill	18.00	10.00
❑ 315 Milt Morin	18.00	10.00
❑ 316 Rayfield Wright RC	40.00	20.00
❑ 317 Jerry LeVias	25.00	12.50
❑ 318 Travis Williams RC	25.00	12.50
❑ 319 Edgar Chandler	18.00	10.00
❑ 320 Bob Wallace	18.00	10.00
❑ 321 Delles Howell	18.00	10.00
❑ 322 Emerson Boozer	25.00	12.50
❑ 323 George Atkinson RC	25.00	12.50
❑ 324 Mike Montler	18.00	10.00
❑ 325 Randy Johnson	18.00	10.00
❑ 326 Mike Curtis UER	25.00	12.50
❑ 327 Miller Farr	18.00	10.00
❑ 328 Horst Muhlmann	18.00	10.00
❑ 329 John Niland RC	25.00	12.50
❑ 330 Andy Russell	30.00	15.00
❑ 331 Mercury Morris	40.00	25.00
❑ 332 Jim Johnson	30.00	15.00
❑ 333 Jerrel Wilson	18.00	10.00
❑ 334 Charley Taylor	40.00	25.00
❑ 335 Dick LeBeau	18.00	10.00
❑ 336 Jim Marshall	30.00	15.00
❑ 337 Tom Mack	30.00	15.00
❑ 338 Steve Spurrier IA	60.00	30.00
❑ 339 Floyd Little IA	25.00	12.50
❑ 340 Len Dawson IA	40.00	25.00
❑ 341 Dick Butkus IA	70.00	40.00
❑ 342 Larry Brown IA	25.00	12.50
❑ 343 Joe Namath IA	150.00	75.00
❑ 344 Jim Turner IA	18.00	10.00
❑ 345 Doug Cunningham IA	18.00	10.00
❑ 346 Edd Hargett IA	18.00	10.00
❑ 347 Steve Owens IA	18.00	10.00
❑ 348 George Blanda IA	50.00	30.00
❑ 349 Ed Podolak IA	18.00	10.00
❑ 350 Rich Jackson IA	18.00	10.00
❑ 351 Ken Willard IA !	40.00	25.00

1973 Topps

❑ COMPLETE SET (528)	400.00	200.00
❑ 1 Simpson/L.Brown LL	8.00	3.00
❑ 2 Passing Leaders	1.00	.40
❑ 3 Jackson/Biletnikoff LL	1.50	.60
❑ 4 Scoring Leaders	.50	.25
❑ 5 Interception Leaders	.50	.25
❑ 6 Punting Leaders	.50	.25
❑ 7 Bob Trumpy	1.50	.60
❑ 8 Mel Tom	.50	.25
❑ 9 Clarence Ellis	.50	.25
❑ 10 John Niland	.50	.25
❑ 11 Randy Jackson	.50	.25
❑ 12 Greg Landry	1.50	.60
❑ 13 Cid Edwards	.50	.25
❑ 14 Phil Olsen	.50	.25
❑ 15 Terry Bradshaw	25.00	15.00
❑ 16 Al Cowlings RC	1.50	.60
❑ 17 Walker Gillette	.50	.25
❑ 18 Bob Atkins	.50	.25
❑ 19 Diron Talbert RC	.50	.25
❑ 20 Jim Johnson	1.50	.60
❑ 21 Howard Twilley	1.00	.40
❑ 22 Dick Enderle	.50	.25
❑ 23 Wayne Colman	.50	.25
❑ 24 John Schmitt	.50	.25
❑ 25 George Blanda	10.00	5.00
❑ 26 Milt Morin	.50	.25
❑ 27 Mike Current	.50	.25
❑ 28 Rex Kern RC	.50	.25
❑ 29 MacArthur Lane	1.00	.40
❑ 30 Alan Page	3.00	1.50
❑ 31 Randy Vataha	.50	.25
❑ 32 Jim Kearney	.50	.25
❑ 33 Steve Smith T	.50	.25
❑ 34 Ken Anderson RC	15.00	7.50
❑ 35 Calvin Hill	1.50	.60
❑ 36 Andy Maurer	.50	.25
❑ 37 Joe Taylor	.50	.25
❑ 38 Deacon Jones	1.50	.60
❑ 39 Mike Weger	.50	.25
❑ 40 Roy Gerela	1.00	.40
❑ 41 Les Josephson	.50	.25
❑ 42 Dave Washington	.50	.25
❑ 43 Bill Curry RC	1.00	.40
❑ 44 Fred Heron	.50	.25
❑ 45 John Brodie	3.00	1.50
❑ 46 Roy Winston	.50	.25
❑ 47 Mike Bragg	.50	.25
❑ 48 Mercury Morris	1.50	.60
❑ 49 Jim Files	.50	.25
❑ 50 Gene Upshaw	3.00	1.50
❑ 51 Hugo Hollas	.50	.25
❑ 52 Rod Sherman	.50	.25
❑ 53 Ron Snidow	.50	.25
❑ 54 Steve Tannen RC	.50	.25
❑ 55 Jim Carter RC	.50	.25
❑ 56 Lydell Mitchell RC	1.50	.60
❑ 57 Jack Rudnay RC	.50	.25
❑ 58 Halvor Hagen	.50	.25
❑ 59 Tom Dempsey	1.00	.40
❑ 60 Fran Tarkenton	10.00	5.00
❑ 61 Lance Alworth	5.00	2.50
❑ 62 Vern Holland	.50	.25
❑ 63 Steve DeLong	.50	.25
❑ 64 Art Malone	.50	.25
❑ 65 Isiah Robertson	1.00	.40
❑ 66 Jerry Rush	.50	.25
❑ 67 Bryant Salter	.50	.25
❑ 68 Checklist 1-132	5.00	2.50
❑ 69 J.D. Hill	.50	.25
❑ 70 Forrest Blue	.50	.25
❑ 71 Myron Pottios	.50	.25
❑ 72 Norm Thompson RC	.50	.25
❑ 73 Paul Robinson	.50	.25
❑ 74 Larry Grantham	.50	.25
❑ 75 Manny Fernandez	1.00	.40
❑ 76 Kent Nix	.50	.25
❑ 77 Art Shell RC	15.00	7.50
❑ 78 George Saimes	.50	.25
❑ 79 Don Cockroft	.50	.25
❑ 80 Bob Tucker	1.00	.40
❑ 81 Don McCauley RC	.50	.25
❑ 82 Bob Brown DT	.50	.25
❑ 83 Larry Carwell	.50	.25
❑ 84 Mo Moorman	.50	.25
❑ 85 John Gilliam	1.00	.40
❑ 86 Wade Key	.50	.25
❑ 87 Ross Brupbacher	.50	.25
❑ 88 Dave Lewis	.50	.25
❑ 89 Franco Harris RC	50.00	25.00
❑ 90 Tom Mack	1.50	.60
❑ 91 Mike Tilleman	.50	.25
❑ 92 Carl Mauck	.50	.25
❑ 93 Larry Hand	.50	.25
❑ 94 Dave Foley RC	.50	.25
❑ 95 Frank Nunley	.50	.25
❑ 96 John Charles	.50	.25
❑ 97 Jim Bakken	.50	.25
❑ 98 Pat Fischer	1.00	.40
❑ 99 Randy Rasmussen	.50	.25
❑ 100 Larry Csonka	6.00	3.00
❑ 101 Mike Siani RC	.50	.25
❑ 102 Tom Roussel	.50	.25
❑ 103 Clarence Scott RC	1.00	.40
❑ 104 Charlie Johnson	1.00	.40
❑ 105 Rick Volk	.50	.25
❑ 106 Willie Young	.50	.25
❑ 107 Emmitt Thomas	1.00	.40
❑ 108 Jon Morris	.50	.25
❑ 109 Clarence Williams	.50	.25
❑ 110 Rayfield Wright	1.00	.40
❑ 111 Norm Bulaich	.50	.25
❑ 112 Mike Eischeid	.50	.25
❑ 113 Speedy Thomas	.50	.25
❑ 114 Glen Holloway	.50	.25
❑ 115 Jack Ham RC	30.00	15.00
❑ 116 Jim Nettles	.50	.25
❑ 117 Errol Mann	.50	.25
❑ 118 John Mackey	1.50	.60
❑ 119 George Kunz	.50	.25
❑ 120 Bob James	.50	.25
❑ 121 Garland Boyette	.50	.25
❑ 122 Mel Phillips	.50	.25
❑ 123 Johnny Roland	.50	.25
❑ 124 Doug Swift	.50	.25
❑ 125 Archie Manning	4.00	2.00
❑ 126 Dave Herman	.50	.25
❑ 127 Carleton Oats	.50	.25
❑ 128 Bill Van Heusen	.50	.25
❑ 129 Rich Jackson	.50	.25
❑ 130 Len Hauss	1.00	.40
❑ 131 Billy Parks RC	.50	.25
❑ 132 Ray May	.50	.25
❑ 133 NFC Semi/Staubach	5.00	2.00
❑ 134 AFC Semi/Immac.Rec.	2.50	1.00
❑ 135 NFC Semi-Final	1.00	.40
❑ 136 AFC Semi/L.Csonka	2.00	.75
❑ 137 NFC Title Game/Kilmer	1.50	.60
❑ 138 AFC Title Game	1.00	.40
❑ 139 Super Bowl VII	1.50	.60
❑ 140 Dwight White RC	5.00	2.00
❑ 141 Jim Marsalis	.50	.25
❑ 142 Doug Van Horn	.50	.25
❑ 143 Al Matthews	.50	.25
❑ 144 Bob Windsor	.50	.25
❑ 145 Dave Hampton RC	.50	.25
❑ 146 Horst Muhlmann	.50	.25
❑ 147 Wally Hilgenberg RC	.50	.25
❑ 148 Ron Smith	.50	.25
❑ 149 Coy Bacon RC	1.00	.40
❑ 150 Winston Hill	.50	.25
❑ 151 Ron Jessie RC	1.00	.40
❑ 152 Ken Iman	.50	.25
❑ 153 Ron Saul	.50	.25
❑ 154 Jim Braxton RC	1.00	.40
❑ 155 Bubba Smith	2.50	1.25
❑ 156 Gary Cuozzo	1.00	.40
❑ 157 Charlie Krueger	1.00	.40
❑ 158 Tim Foley RC	1.00	.40
❑ 159 Lee Roy Jordan	1.50	.60
❑ 160 Bob Brown OT	1.50	.60
❑ 161 Margene Adkins	.50	.25
❑ 162 Ron Widby	.50	.25
❑ 163 Jim Houston	.50	.25
❑ 164 Joe Dawkins	.50	.25
❑ 165 L.C.Greenwood	4.00	2.00
❑ 166 Richmond Flowers RC	.50	.25
❑ 167 Curley Culp RC	1.50	.60
❑ 168 Len St. Jean	.50	.25
❑ 169 Walter Rock	.50	.25
❑ 170 Bill Bradley	1.00	.40
❑ 171 Ken Riley RC	1.50	.60
❑ 172 Rich Coady	.50	.25
❑ 173 Don Hansen	.50	.25
❑ 174 Lionel Aldridge	.50	.25
❑ 175 Don Maynard	4.00	2.00
❑ 176 Dave Osborn	1.00	.40

❑ 177	Jim Bailey	.50	.25
❑ 178	John Pitts	.50	.25
❑ 179	Dave Parks	.50	.25
❑ 180	Chester Marcol RC	.50	.25
❑ 181	Len Rohde	.50	.25
❑ 182	Jeff Staggs	.50	.25
❑ 183	Gene Hickerson	1.25	.50
❑ 184	Charlie Evans	.50	.25
❑ 185	Mel Renfro	1.50	.60
❑ 186	Marvin Upshaw	.50	.25
❑ 187	George Atkinson	1.00	.40
❑ 188	Norm Evans	1.00	.40
❑ 189	Steve Ramsey	.50	.25
❑ 190	Dave Chapple	.50	.25
❑ 191	Gerry Mullins	.50	.25
❑ 192	John Didion	.50	.25
❑ 193	Bob Gladieux	.50	.25
❑ 194	Don Hultz	.50	.25
❑ 195	Mike Lucci	.50	.25
❑ 196	John Wilbur	.50	.25
❑ 197	George Farmer	.50	.25
❑ 198	Tommy Casanova RC	1.00	.40
❑ 199	Russ Washington	.50	.25
❑ 200	Claude Humphrey	1.50	.60
❑ 201	Pat Hughes	.50	.25
❑ 202	Zeke Moore	.50	.25
❑ 203	Chip Glass	.50	.25
❑ 204	Glenn Ressler	.50	.25
❑ 205	Willie Ellison	1.00	.40
❑ 206	John Leypoldt	.50	.25
❑ 207	Johnny Fuller	.50	.25
❑ 208	Bill Hayhoe	.50	.25
❑ 209	Ed Bell	.50	.25
❑ 210	Willie Brown	1.50	.60
❑ 211	Carl Eller	1.50	.60
❑ 212	Mark Nordquist	.50	.25
❑ 213	Larry Willingham	.50	.25
❑ 214	Nick Buoniconti	1.50	.60
❑ 215	John Hadl	1.50	.60
❑ 216	Jethro Pugh RC	1.50	.60
❑ 217	Leroy Mitchell	.50	.25
❑ 218	Billy Newsome	.50	.25
❑ 219	John McMakin	.50	.25
❑ 220	Larry Brown	1.50	.60
❑ 221	Clarence Scott RC	.50	.25
❑ 222	Paul Naumoff	.50	.25
❑ 223	Ted Fritsch Jr.	.50	.25
❑ 224	Checklist 133-264	5.00	2.50
❑ 225	Dan Pastorini	1.50	.60
❑ 226	Joe Beauchamp UER	.50	.25
❑ 227	Pat Matson	.50	.25
❑ 228	Tony McGee DT	.50	.25
❑ 229	Mike Phipps	1.00	.40
❑ 230	Harold Jackson	1.50	.60
❑ 231	Willie Williams	.50	.25
❑ 232	Spike Jones	.50	.25
❑ 233	Jim Tyrer	.50	.25
❑ 234	Roy Hilton	.50	.25
❑ 235	Phil Villapiano	1.00	.40
❑ 236	Charley Taylor UER	3.00	1.50
❑ 237	Malcolm Snider	.50	.25
❑ 238	Vic Washington	.50	.25
❑ 239	Grady Alderman	.50	.25
❑ 240	Dick Anderson	1.00	.40
❑ 241	Ron Yankowski	.50	.25
❑ 242	Billy Masters	.50	.25
❑ 243	Herb Adderley	1.50	.60
❑ 244	David Ray	.50	.25
❑ 245	John Riggins	8.00	4.00
❑ 246	Mike Wagner RC	3.00	1.25
❑ 247	Don Morrison	.50	.25
❑ 248	Earl McCullouch	.50	.25
❑ 249	Dennis Wirgowski	.50	.25
❑ 250	Chris Hanburger	1.00	.40
❑ 251	Pat Sullivan RC	1.50	.60
❑ 252	Walt Sweeney	.50	.25
❑ 253	Willie Alexander	.50	.25
❑ 254	Doug Dressler	.50	.25
❑ 255	Walter Johnson	.50	.25
❑ 256	Ron Hornsby	.50	.25
❑ 257	Ben Hawkins	.50	.25
❑ 258	Donnie Green RC	.50	.25
❑ 259	Fred Hoaglin	.50	.25
❑ 260	Jerrel Wilson	.50	.25
❑ 261	Horace Jones	.50	.25
❑ 262	Woody Peoples	.50	.25
❑ 263	Jim Hill RC	.50	.25
❑ 264	John Fuqua	.50	.25
❑ 265	Donny Anderson KP	1.00	.40
❑ 266	Roman Gabriel KP	1.50	.60
❑ 267	Mike Garrett KP	1.00	.40
❑ 268	Rufus Mayes RC	.50	.25
❑ 269	Chip Myrtle	.50	.25
❑ 270	Bill Stanfill RC	1.00	.40
❑ 271	Clint Jones	.50	.25
❑ 272	Miller Farr	.50	.25
❑ 273	Harry Schuh	.50	.25
❑ 274	Bob Hayes	1.50	.60
❑ 275	Bobby Douglass	1.00	.40
❑ 276	Gus Hollomon	.50	.25
❑ 277	Del Williams	.50	.25
❑ 278	[illegible]	[illegible]	[illegible]
❑ 279	Herman Weaver	.50	.25
❑ 280	Joe Greene	8.00	4.00
❑ 281	Wes Chesson	.50	.25
❑ 282	Charlie Harraway	.50	.25
❑ 283	Paul Guidry	.50	.25
❑ 284	Terry Owens RC	.50	.25
❑ 285	Jan Stenerud	1.50	.60
❑ 286	Pete Athas	.50	.25
❑ 287	Dale Lindsey	.50	.25
❑ 288	Jack Tatum RC	15.00	6.00
❑ 289	Floyd Little	1.50	.60
❑ 290	Bob Johnson	.50	.25
❑ 291	Tommy Hart RC	.50	.25
❑ 292	Tom Mitchell	.50	.25
❑ 293	Walt Patulski RC	.50	.25
❑ 294	Jim Skaggs	.50	.25
❑ 295	Bob Griese	6.00	3.00
❑ 296	Mike McCoy DT	.50	.25
❑ 297	Mel Gray	1.00	.40
❑ 298	Bobby Bryant	.50	.25
❑ 299	Blaine Nye RC	.50	.25
❑ 300	Dick Butkus	12.00	6.00
❑ 301	Charlie Cowan RC	.50	.25
❑ 302	Mark Lomas	.50	.25
❑ 303	Josh Ashton	.50	.25
❑ 304	Happy Feller	.50	.25
❑ 305	Ron Shanklin	.50	.25
❑ 306	Wayne Rasmussen	.50	.25
❑ 307	Jerry Smith	.50	.25
❑ 308	Ken Reaves	.50	.25
❑ 309	Ron East	.50	.25
❑ 310	Otis Taylor	1.50	.60
❑ 311	John Garlington	.50	.25
❑ 312	Lyle Alzado	4.00	2.00
❑ 313	Remi Prudhomme	.50	.25
❑ 314	Cornelius Johnson	.50	.25
❑ 315	Lemar Parrish	1.00	.40
❑ 316	Jim Kiick	1.50	.60
❑ 317	Steve Zabel	.50	.25
❑ 318	Alden Roche	.50	.25
❑ 319	Tom Blanchard	.50	.25
❑ 320	Fred Biletnikoff	4.00	2.00
❑ 321	Ralph Neely	1.00	.40
❑ 322	Dan Dierdorf RC	20.00	7.50
❑ 323	Richard Caster	1.00	.40
❑ 324	Gene Howard	.50	.25
❑ 325	Elvin Bethea	1.50	.60
❑ 326	Carl Garrett	1.00	.40
❑ 327	Ron Billingsley	.50	.25
❑ 328	Charlie West	.50	.25
❑ 329	Tom Neville	.50	.25
❑ 330	Ted Kwalick	1.00	.40
❑ 331	Rudy Redmond	.50	.25
❑ 332	Henry Davis	.50	.25
❑ 333	John Zook	.50	.25
❑ 334	Jim Turner	.50	.25
❑ 335	Len Dawson	5.00	2.50
❑ 336	Bob Chandler RC	1.00	.40
❑ 337	Al Beauchamp	.50	.25
❑ 338	Tom Matte	1.00	.40
❑ 339	Paul Laaveg	.50	.25
❑ 340	Ken Ellis	.50	.25
❑ 341	Jim Langer RC	10.00	5.00
❑ 342	Ron Porter	.50	.25
❑ 343	Jack Youngblood RC	15.00	7.50
❑ 344	Cornell Green	1.50	.60
❑ 345	Marv Hubbard	1.00	.40
❑ 346	Bruce Taylor	.50	.25
❑ 347	Sam Havrilak	.50	.25
❑ 348	Walt Sumner	.50	.25
❑ 349	Steve O'Neal	.50	.25
❑ 350	Ron Johnson	1.00	.40
❑ 351	Rockne Freitas	.50	.25
❑ 352	Larry Stallings	.50	.25
❑ 353	Jim Cadile	.50	.25
❑ 354	Ken Burrough	1.00	.40
❑ 355	Jim Plunkett	4.00	2.00
❑ 356	Dave Long	.50	.25
❑ 357	Ralph Anderson	.50	.25
❑ 358	Checklist 265-396	5.00	2.50
❑ 359	Gene Washington Vik	1.00	.40
❑ 360	Dave Wilcox	1.50	.60
❑ 361	Paul Smith	.50	.25
❑ 362	Alvin Wyatt	.50	.25
❑ 363	Charlie Smith RB	.50	.25
❑ 364	Royce Berry	.50	.25
❑ 365	Dave Elmendorf	.50	.25
❑ 366	Scott Hunter	1.00	.40
❑ 367	Bob Kuechenberg RC	3.00	1.25
❑ 368	Pete Gogolak	.50	.25
❑ 369	Dave Edwards	.50	.25
❑ 370	Lem Barney	2.50	1.25
❑ 371	Verlon Biggs	.50	.25
❑ 372	John Reaves RC	.50	.25
❑ 373	Ed Podolak	1.00	.40
❑ 374	Chris Farasopoulos	.50	.25
❑ 375	Gary Garrison	.50	.25
❑ 376	Tom Funchess	.50	.25
❑ 377	Bobby Joe Green	.50	.25
❑ 378	Don Brumm	.50	.25
❑ 379	Jim O'Brien	.50	.25
❑ 380	Paul Krause	1.50	.60
❑ 381	Leroy Kelly	2.50	1.25
❑ 382	Ray Mansfield	.50	.25
❑ 383	Dan Abramowicz	1.00	.40
❑ 384	John Outlaw RC	.50	.25
❑ 385	Tommy Nobis	1.50	.60
❑ 386	Tom Domres	.50	.25
❑ 387	Ken Willard	.50	.25
❑ 388	Mike Stratton	.50	.25
❑ 389	Fred Dryer	2.50	1.25
❑ 390	Jake Scott	1.50	.60
❑ 391	Rich Houston	.50	.25
❑ 392	Virgil Carter	.50	.25
❑ 393	Tody Smith	.50	.25
❑ 394	Ernie Calloway	.50	.25
❑ 395	Charlie Sanders	1.25	.50
❑ 396	Fred Willis	.50	.25
❑ 397	Curt Knight	.50	.25
❑ 398	Nemiah Wilson	.50	.25
❑ 399	Carroll Dale	1.00	.40
❑ 400	Joe Namath	30.00	15.00
❑ 401	Wayne Mulligan	.50	.25
❑ 402	Jim Harrison	.50	.25
❑ 403	Tim Rossovich	.50	.25
❑ 404	David Lee	.50	.25
❑ 405	Frank Pitts	.50	.25
❑ 406	Jim Marshall	1.50	.60
❑ 407	Bob Brown TE	.50	.25
❑ 408	John Rowser	.50	.25
❑ 409	Mike Montler	.50	.25
❑ 410	Willie Lanier	1.50	.60
❑ 411	Bill Bell K	.50	.25
❑ 412	Cedrick Hardman	.50	.25
❑ 413	Bob Anderson	.50	.25
❑ 414	Earl Morrall	1.50	.60
❑ 415	Ken Houston	1.50	.60
❑ 416	Jack Snow	1.00	.40
❑ 417	Dick Cunningham	.50	.25
❑ 418	Greg Larson	.50	.25
❑ 419	Mike Bass	1.00	.40
❑ 420	Mike Reid	1.50	.60
❑ 421	Walt Garrison	1.50	.60
❑ 422	Pete Liske	.50	.25
❑ 423	Jim Yarbrough	.50	.25
❑ 424	Rich McGeorge	.50	.25
❑ 425	Bobby Howfield	.50	.25
❑ 426	Pete Banaszak	.50	.25
❑ 427	Willie Holman	.50	.25
❑ 428	Dale Hackbart	.50	.25
❑ 429	Fair Hooker	.50	.25
❑ 430	Ted Hendricks	5.00	2.50
❑ 431	Mike Garrett	1.00	.40
❑ 432	Glen Ray Hines	.50	.25
❑ 433	Fred Cox	.50	.25
❑ 434	Bobby Walden	.50	.25
❑ 435	Bobby Bell	1.50	.60
❑ 436	Dave Rowe	.50	.25
❑ 437	Bob Berry	.50	.25

❑ 438	Bill Thompson	.50	.25
❑ 439	Jim Beirne	.50	.25
❑ 440	Larry Little	3.00	1.50
❑ 441	Rocky Thompson	.50	.25
❑ 442	Brig Owens	.50	.25
❑ 443	Richard Neal	.50	.25
❑ 444	Al Nelson	.50	.25
❑ 445	Chip Myers	.50	.25
❑ 446	Ken Bowman	.50	.25
❑ 447	Jim Purnell	.50	.25
❑ 448	Altie Taylor	.50	.25
❑ 449	Linzy Cole	.50	.25
❑ 450	Bob Lilly	5.00	2.50
❑ 451	Charlie Ford	.50	.25
❑ 452	Milt Sunde	.50	.25
❑ 453	Doug Wyatt	.50	.25
❑ 454	Don Nottingham RC	1.00	.40
❑ 455	Johnny Unitas	15.00	7.50
❑ 456	Frank Lewis RC	1.00	.40
❑ 457	Roger Wehrli	1.00	.40
❑ 458	Jim Cheyunski	.50	.25
❑ 459	Jerry Sherk RC	1.00	.40
❑ 460	Gene Washington 49er	1.00	.40
❑ 461	Jim Otto	1.50	.60
❑ 462	Ed Budde	.50	.25
❑ 463	Jim Mitchell TE	1.00	.40
❑ 464	Emerson Boozer	1.00	.40
❑ 465	Garo Yepremian	1.50	.60
❑ 466	Pete Duranko	.50	.25
❑ 467	Charlie Joiner	8.00	4.00
❑ 468	Spider Lockhart	1.00	.40
❑ 469	Marty Domres	.50	.25
❑ 470	John Brockington	1.50	.60
❑ 471	Ed Flanagan	.50	.25
❑ 472	Roy Jefferson	1.00	.40
❑ 473	Julian Fagan	.50	.25
❑ 474	Bill Brown	1.00	.40
❑ 475	Roger Staubach	30.00	15.00
❑ 476	Jan White RC	.50	.25
❑ 477	Pat Holmes	.50	.25
❑ 478	Bob DeMarco	.50	.25
❑ 479	Merlin Olsen	2.50	1.25
❑ 480	Andy Russell	1.50	.60
❑ 481	Steve Spurrier	20.00	10.00
❑ 482	Nate Ramsey	.50	.25
❑ 483	Dennis Partee	.50	.25
❑ 484	Jerry Simmons	.50	.25
❑ 485	Donny Anderson	1.50	.60
❑ 486	Ralph Baker	.50	.25
❑ 487	Ken Stabler RC !	60.00	35.00
❑ 488	Ernie McMillan	.50	.25
❑ 489	Ken Burrow	.50	.25
❑ 490	Jack Gregory RC	.50	.25
❑ 491	Larry Seiple	1.00	.40
❑ 492	Mick Tingelhoff	1.00	.40
❑ 493	Craig Morton	1.50	.60
❑ 494	Cecil Turner	.50	.25
❑ 495	Steve Owens	1.50	.60
❑ 496	Rickie Harris	.50	.25
❑ 497	Buck Buchanan	1.50	.60
❑ 498	Checklist 397-528	5.00	2.50
❑ 499	Billy Kilmer	1.50	.60
❑ 500	O.J.Simpson	15.00	7.50
❑ 501	Bruce Gossett	.50	.25
❑ 502	Art Thoms RC	.50	.25
❑ 503	Larry Kaminski	.50	.25
❑ 504	Larry Smith RB	.50	.25
❑ 505	Bruce Van Dyke	.50	.25
❑ 506	Alvin Reed	.50	.25
❑ 507	Delles Howell	.50	.25
❑ 508	Leroy Keyes	.50	.25
❑ 509	Bo Scott	1.00	.40
❑ 510	Ron Yary	1.50	.60
❑ 511	Paul Warfield	5.00	2.50
❑ 512	Mac Percival	.50	.25
❑ 513	Essex Johnson	.50	.25
❑ 514	Jackie Smith	1.50	.60
❑ 515	Norm Snead	1.50	.60
❑ 516	Charlie Stukes	.50	.25
❑ 517	Reggie Rucker RC	1.00	.40
❑ 518	Bill Sandeman UER	.50	.25
❑ 519	Mel Farr	1.00	.40
❑ 520	Raymond Chester	1.00	.40
❑ 521	Fred Carr RC	1.00	.40
❑ 522	Jerry LeVias	1.00	.40
❑ 523	Jim Strong	.50	.25
❑ 524	Roland McDole	.50	.25
❑ 525	Dennis Shaw	.50	.25
❑ 526	Dave Manders	.50	.25
❑ 527	Skip Vanderbundt	.50	.25
❑ 528	Mike Sensibaugh RC !	1.50	.60

1974 Topps

❑	COMPLETE SET (528)	300.00	175.00
❑ 1	O.J.Simpson RB UER	20.00	10.00
❑ 2	Blaine Nye	.40	.20
❑ 3	Don Hansen	.40	.20
❑ 4	Ken Bowman	.40	.20
❑ 5	Carl Eller	1.50	.60
❑ 6	Jerry Smith	.40	.20
❑ 7	Ed Podolak	.40	.20
❑ 8	Mel Gray	1.50	.60
❑ 9	Pat Matson	.40	.20
❑ 10	Floyd Little	1.50	.60
❑ 11	Frank Pitts	.40	.20
❑ 12	Vern Den Herder RC	.75	.30
❑ 13	John Fuqua	.75	.30
❑ 14	Jack Tatum	2.00	.75
❑ 15	Winston Hill	.40	.20
❑ 16	John Beasley	.40	.20
❑ 17	David Lee	.40	.20
❑ 18	Rich Coady	.40	.20
❑ 19	Ken Willard	.40	.20
❑ 20	Coy Bacon	.75	.30
❑ 21	Ben Hawkins	.40	.20
❑ 22	Paul Guidry	.40	.20
❑ 23	Norm Snead HOR	.75	.30
❑ 24	Jim Yarbrough	.40	.20
❑ 25	Jack Reynolds RC	3.00	1.25
❑ 26	Josh Ashton	.40	.20
❑ 27	Donnie Green	.40	.20
❑ 28	Bob Hayes	1.50	.60
❑ 29	John Zook	.40	.20
❑ 30	Bobby Bryant	.40	.20
❑ 31	Scott Hunter	.75	.30
❑ 32	Dan Dierdorf	6.00	3.00
❑ 33	Curt Knight	.40	.20
❑ 34	Elmo Wright RC	.40	.20
❑ 35	Essex Johnson	.40	.20
❑ 36	Walt Sumner	.40	.20
❑ 37	Marv Montgomery	.40	.20
❑ 38	Tim Foley	.75	.30
❑ 39	Mike Siani	.40	.20
❑ 40	Joe Greene	6.00	3.00
❑ 41	Bobby Howfield	.40	.20
❑ 42	Del Williams	.40	.20
❑ 43	Don McCauley	.40	.20
❑ 44	Randy Jackson	.40	.20
❑ 45	Ron Smith	.40	.20
❑ 46	Gene Washington 49er	.75	.30
❑ 47	Po James	.40	.20
❑ 48	Solomon Freelon	.40	.20
❑ 49	Bob Windsor HOR	.40	.20
❑ 50	John Hadl	1.50	.60
❑ 51	Greg Larson	.40	.20
❑ 52	Steve Owens	.75	.30
❑ 53	Jim Cheyunski	.40	.20
❑ 54	Rayfield Wright	.75	.30
❑ 55	Dave Hampton	.40	.20
❑ 56	Ron Widby	.40	.20
❑ 57	Milt Sunde	.40	.20
❑ 58	Billy Kilmer	1.50	.60
❑ 59	Bobby Bell	1.50	.60
❑ 60	Jim Bakken	.40	.20
❑ 61	Rufus Mayes	.40	.20
❑ 62	Vic Washington	.40	.20
❑ 63	Gene Washington Vik	.75	.30
❑ 64	Clarence Scott	.40	.20
❑ 65	Gene Upshaw	2.00	.75
❑ 66	Larry Seiple	.75	.30
❑ 67	John McMakin	.40	.20
❑ 68	Ralph Baker	.40	.20
❑ 69	Lydell Mitchell	.75	.30
❑ 70	Archie Manning	2.50	1.25
❑ 71	George Farmer	.40	.20
❑ 72	Ron East	.40	.20
❑ 73	Al Nelson	.40	.20
❑ 74	Pat Hughes	.40	.20
❑ 75	Fred Willis	.40	.20
❑ 76	Larry Walton	.40	.20
❑ 77	Tom Neville	.40	.20
❑ 78	Ted Kwalick	.40	.20
❑ 79	Walt Patulski	.40	.20
❑ 80	John Niland	.40	.20
❑ 81	Ted Fritsch Jr.	.40	.20
❑ 82	Paul Krause	1.50	.60
❑ 83	Jack Snow	.75	.30
❑ 84	Mike Bass	.40	.20
❑ 85	Jim Tyrer	.40	.20
❑ 86	Ron Yankowski	.40	.20
❑ 87	Mike Phipps	.75	.30
❑ 88	Al Beauchamp	.40	.20
❑ 89	Riley Odoms RC	1.50	.60
❑ 90	MacArthur Lane	.40	.20
❑ 91	Art Thoms	.40	.20
❑ 92	Marlin Briscoe	.40	.20
❑ 93	Bruce Van Dyke	.40	.20
❑ 94	Tom Myers RC	.40	.20
❑ 95	Calvin Hill	1.50	.60
❑ 96	Bruce Laird	.40	.20
❑ 97	Tony McGee DT	.40	.20
❑ 98	Len Rohde	.40	.20
❑ 99	Tom McNeill	.40	.20
❑ 100	Delles Howell	.40	.20
❑ 101	Gary Garrison	.40	.20
❑ 102	Dan Goich	.40	.20
❑ 103	Len St. Jean	.40	.20
❑ 104	Zeke Moore	.40	.20
❑ 105	Ahmad Rashad RC	20.00	10.00
❑ 106	Mel Renfro	1.50	.60
❑ 107	Jim Mitchell TE	.40	.20
❑ 108	Ed Budde	.40	.20
❑ 109	Harry Schuh	.40	.20
❑ 110	Greg Pruitt RC	4.00	2.00
❑ 111	Ed Flanagan	.40	.20
❑ 112	Larry Stallings	.40	.20
❑ 113	Chuck Foreman RC	4.00	2.00
❑ 114	Royce Berry	.40	.20
❑ 115	Gale Gillingham	.40	.20
❑ 116	Charlie Johnson HOR	1.50	.60
❑ 117	Checklist 1-132 UER	4.00	2.00
❑ 118	Bill Butler	.40	.20
❑ 119	Roy Jefferson	.75	.30
❑ 120	Bobby Douglass	.75	.30
❑ 121	Harold Carmichael RC	12.00	6.00
❑ 122	George Kunz AP	.40	.20
❑ 123	Larry Little	2.00	.75
❑ 124	Forrest Blue AP	.40	.20
❑ 125	Ron Yary	1.50	.60
❑ 126	Tom Mack AP	1.50	.60
❑ 127	Bob Tucker AP	.75	.30
❑ 128	Paul Warfield	4.00	2.00
❑ 129	Fran Tarkenton	10.00	5.00
❑ 130	O.J.Simpson	12.00	6.00
❑ 131	Larry Csonka	6.00	3.00
❑ 132	Bruce Gossett AP	.40	.20
❑ 133	Bill Stanfill AP	.75	.30
❑ 134	Alan Page	2.50	1.25
❑ 135	Paul Smith AP	.40	.20
❑ 136	Claude Humphrey AP	.75	.30
❑ 137	Jack Ham	10.00	5.00
❑ 138	Lee Roy Jordan	1.50	.60
❑ 139	Phil Villapiano AP	.75	.30
❑ 140	Ken Ellis AP	.40	.20
❑ 141	Willie Brown	1.50	.60
❑ 142	Dick Anderson AP	.75	.30
❑ 143	Bill Bradley AP	.75	.30
❑ 144	Jerrel Wilson AP	.40	.20
❑ 145	Reggie Rucker	.75	.30
❑ 146	Marty Domres	.40	.20
❑ 147	Bob Kowalkowski	.40	.20
❑ 148	John Matuszak RC	6.00	2.50
❑ 149	Mike Adamle RC	.75	.30

❑ 150 Johnny Unitas 15.00 7.50
❑ 151 Charlie Ford .40 .20
❑ 152 Bob Klein RC .40 .20
❑ 153 Jim Merlo .40 .20
❑ 154 Willie Young .40 .20
❑ 155 Donny Anderson .75 .30
❑ 156 Brig Owens .40 .20
❑ 157 Bruce Jarvis .40 .20
❑ 158 Ron Carpenter RC .40 .20
❑ 159 Don Cockroft .40 .20
❑ 160 Tommy Nobis 1.50 .60
❑ 161 Craig Morton 1.50 .60
❑ 162 Jon Staggers .40 .20
❑ 163 Mike Eischeid .40 .20
❑ 164 Jerry Sisemore RC [illegible] [illegible]
❑ 165 Cedrick Hardman .40 .20
❑ 166 Bill Thompson .75 .30
❑ 167 Jim Lynch .75 .30
❑ 168 Bob Moore .40 .20
❑ 169 Glen Edwards .40 .20
❑ 170 Mercury Morris 1.50 .60
❑ 171 Julius Adams .40 .20
❑ 172 Cotton Speyrer .40 .20
❑ 173 Bill Munson .75 .30
❑ 174 Benny Johnson .40 .20
❑ 175 Burgess Owens RC .40 .20
❑ 176 Cid Edwards .40 .20
❑ 177 Doug Buffone .40 .20
❑ 178 Charlie Cowan .40 .20
❑ 179 Bob Newland .40 .20
❑ 180 Ron Johnson .75 .30
❑ 181 Bob Rowe .40 .20
❑ 182 Len Hauss .40 .20
❑ 183 Joe DeLamielleure RC 8.00 3.00
❑ 184 Sherman White RC .40 .20
❑ 185 Fair Hooker .40 .20
❑ 186 Nick Mike-Mayor .40 .20
❑ 187 Ralph Neely .40 .20
❑ 188 Rich McGeorge .40 .20
❑ 189 Ed Marinaro RC 4.00 1.50
❑ 190 Dave Wilcox 1.50 .60
❑ 191 Joe Owens RC .40 .20
❑ 192 Bill Van Heusen .40 .20
❑ 193 Jim Kearney .40 .20
❑ 194 Otis Sistrunk RC 1.50 .60
❑ 195 Ron Shanklin .40 .20
❑ 196 Bill Lenkaitis .40 .20
❑ 197 Tom Drougas .40 .20
❑ 198 Larry Hand .40 .20
❑ 199 Mack Alston .40 .20
❑ 200 Bob Griese 6.00 3.00
❑ 201 Earlie Thomas .40 .20
❑ 202 Carl Gersbach .40 .20
❑ 203 Jim Harrison .40 .20
❑ 204 Jake Kupp .40 .20
❑ 205 Merlin Olsen 2.00 .75
❑ 206 Spider Lockhart .75 .30
❑ 207 Walker Gillette .40 .20
❑ 208 Verlon Biggs .40 .20
❑ 209 Bob James .40 .20
❑ 210 Bob Trumpy 1.50 .60
❑ 211 Jerry Sherk .40 .20
❑ 212 Andy Maurer .40 .20
❑ 213 Fred Carr .40 .20
❑ 214 Mick Tingelhoff .75 .30
❑ 215 Steve Spurrier 15.00 7.50
❑ 216 Richard Harris .40 .20
❑ 217 Charlie Greer .40 .20
❑ 218 Buck Buchanan 1.50 .60
❑ 219 Ray Guy RC 10.00 5.00
❑ 220 Franco Harris 12.00 6.00
❑ 221 Darryl Stingley RC 1.50 .60
❑ 222 Rex Kern .40 .20
❑ 223 Toni Fritsch .75 .30
❑ 224 Levi Johnson .40 .20
❑ 225 Bob Kuechenberg .75 .30
❑ 226 Elvin Bethea 1.50 .60
❑ 227 Al Woodall RC .75 .30
❑ 228 Terry Owens .40 .20
❑ 229 Bivian Lee .40 .20
❑ 230 Dick Butkus 10.00 5.00
❑ 231 Jim Bertelsen RC .75 .30
❑ 232 John Mendenhall RC .40 .20
❑ 233 Conrad Dobler RC 1.50 .60
❑ 234 J.D. Hill .75 .30
❑ 235 Ken Houston 1.50 .60
❑ 236 Dave Lewis .40 .20
❑ 237 John Garlington .40 .20
❑ 238 Bill Sandeman .40 .20
❑ 239 Alden Roche .40 .20
❑ 240 John Gilliam .75 .30
❑ 241 Bruce Taylor .40 .20
❑ 242 Vern Winfield .40 .20
❑ 243 Bobby Maples .40 .20
❑ 244 Wendell Hayes .40 .20
❑ 245 George Blanda 8.00 4.00
❑ 246 Dwight White .75 .30
❑ 247 Sandy Durko .40 .20
❑ 248 Tom Mitchell .40 .20
❑ 249 Chuck Walton .40 .20
❑ 250 Bob Lilly 4.00 2.00
❑ 251 [illegible] [illegible] [illegible]
❑ 252 Lynn Dickey RC 1.50 .60
❑ 253 Jerome Barkum RC .40 .20
❑ 254 Clint Jones .40 .20
❑ 255 Billy Newsome .40 .20
❑ 256 Bob Asher .40 .20
❑ 257 Joe Scibelli .40 .20
❑ 258 Tom Blanchard .40 .20
❑ 259 Norm Thompson .40 .20
❑ 260 Larry Brown 1.50 .60
❑ 261 Paul Seymour .40 .20
❑ 262 Checklist 133-264 4.00 2.00
❑ 263 Doug Dieken RC .40 .20
❑ 264 Lemar Parrish .75 .30
❑ 265 Bob Lee UER .40 .20
❑ 266 Bob Brown DT .40 .20
❑ 267 Roy Winston .40 .20
❑ 268 Randy Beisler .40 .20
❑ 269 Joe Dawkins .40 .20
❑ 270 Tom Dempsey .75 .30
❑ 271 Jack Rudnay .40 .20
❑ 272 Art Shell 5.00 2.50
❑ 273 Mike Wagner .75 .30
❑ 274 Rick Cash .40 .20
❑ 275 Greg Landry 1.50 .60
❑ 276 Glenn Ressler .40 .20
❑ 277 Billy Joe DuPree RC 3.00 1.25
❑ 278 Norm Evans .40 .20
❑ 279 Billy Parks .40 .20
❑ 280 John Riggins 6.00 3.00
❑ 281 Lionel Aldridge .40 .20
❑ 282 Steve O'Neal .40 .20
❑ 283 Craig Clemons .40 .20
❑ 284 Willie Williams .40 .20
❑ 285 Isiah Robertson .75 .30
❑ 286 Dennis Shaw .40 .20
❑ 287 Bill Brundige .40 .20
❑ 288 John Leypoldt .40 .20
❑ 289 John DeMarie .40 .20
❑ 290 Mike Reid 1.50 .60
❑ 291 Greg Brezina .40 .20
❑ 292 Willie Buchanon RC .40 .20
❑ 293 Dave Osborn .75 .30
❑ 294 Mel Phillips .40 .20
❑ 295 Haven Moses .75 .30
❑ 296 Wade Key .40 .20
❑ 297 Marvin Upshaw .40 .20
❑ 298 Ray Mansfield .40 .20
❑ 299 Edgar Chandler .40 .20
❑ 300 Marv Hubbard .75 .30
❑ 301 Herman Weaver .40 .20
❑ 302 Jim Bailey .40 .20
❑ 303 D.D.Lewis RC 1.50 .60
❑ 304 Ken Burrough .75 .30
❑ 305 Jake Scott 1.50 .60
❑ 306 Randy Rasmussen .40 .20
❑ 307 Pettis Norman .40 .20
❑ 308 Carl Johnson .40 .20
❑ 309 Joe Taylor .40 .20
❑ 310 Pete Gogolak .40 .20
❑ 311 Tony Baker FB .40 .20
❑ 312 John Richardson .40 .20
❑ 313 Dave Robinson .75 .30
❑ 314 Reggie McKenzie RC 1.50 .60
❑ 315 Isaac Curtis RC 1.50 .60
❑ 316 Thom Darden .40 .20
❑ 317 Ken Reaves .40 .20
❑ 318 Malcolm Snider .40 .20
❑ 319 Jeff Siemon RC .75 .30
❑ 320 Dan Abramowicz .75 .30
❑ 321 Lyle Alzado 2.00 .75
❑ 322 John Reaves .40 .20
❑ 323 Morris Stroud .40 .20
❑ 324 Bobby Walden .40 .20
❑ 325 Randy Vataha .40 .20
❑ 326 Nemiah Wilson .40 .20
❑ 327 Paul Naumoff .40 .20
❑ 328 O.J.Simpson/Brock. LL 3.00 1.50
❑ 329 R.Staubach/Stabler LL 5.00 2.50
❑ 330 Harold Carmichael/Wil LL 1.50 .60
❑ 331 Scoring Leaders .75 .30
❑ 332 Interception Leaders .75 .30
❑ 333 Punting Leaders .75 .30
❑ 334 Dennis Nelson .40 .20
❑ 335 Walt Garrison .75 .30
❑ 336 Tody Smith .40 .20
❑ 337 Ed Bell .40 .20
❑ 338 Bryant Salter .40 .20
❑ 339 Wayne Colman .40 .20
❑ 340 Garo Yepremian .75 .30
❑ 341 Bob Newton .40 .20
❑ 342 Vince Clements RC .40 .20
❑ 343 Ken Iman .40 .20
❑ 344 Jim Tolbert .40 .20
❑ 345 Chris Hanburger .75 .30
❑ 346 Dave Foley .40 .20
❑ 347 Tommy Casanova .75 .30
❑ 348 John James .40 .20
❑ 349 Clarence Williams .40 .20
❑ 350 Leroy Kelly 1.50 .60
❑ 351 Stu Voigt RC .75 .30
❑ 352 Skip Vanderbundt .40 .20
❑ 353 Pete Duranko .40 .20
❑ 354 John Outlaw .40 .20
❑ 355 Jan Stenerud 1.50 .60
❑ 356 Barry Pearson .40 .20
❑ 357 Brian Dowling RC .40 .20
❑ 358 Dan Conners .40 .20
❑ 359 Bob Bell .40 .20
❑ 360 Rick Volk .40 .20
❑ 361 Pat Toomay .75 .30
❑ 362 Bob Gresham .40 .20
❑ 363 John Schmitt .40 .20
❑ 364 Mel Rogers .40 .20
❑ 365 Manny Fernandez .75 .30
❑ 366 Ernie Jackson .40 .20
❑ 367 Gary Huff RC .75 .30
❑ 368 Bob Grim .40 .20
❑ 369 Ernie McMillan .40 .20
❑ 370 Dave Elmendorf .40 .20
❑ 371 Mike Bragg .40 .20
❑ 372 John Skorupan .40 .20
❑ 373 Howard Fest .40 .20
❑ 374 Jerry Tagge RC .75 .30
❑ 375 Art Malone .40 .20
❑ 376 Bob Babich .40 .20
❑ 377 Jim Marshall 1.50 .60
❑ 378 Bob Hoskins .40 .20
❑ 379 Don Zimmerman .40 .20
❑ 380 Ray May .40 .20
❑ 381 Emmitt Thomas .75 .30
❑ 382 Terry Hanratty .75 .30
❑ 383 John Hannah RC 15.00 7.50
❑ 384 George Atkinson .40 .20
❑ 385 Ted Hendricks 3.00 1.50
❑ 386 Jim O'Brien .40 .20
❑ 387 Jethro Pugh .75 .30
❑ 388 Elbert Drungo .40 .20
❑ 389 Richard Caster .75 .30
❑ 390 Deacon Jones 1.50 .60
❑ 391 Checklist 265-396 4.00 2.00
❑ 392 Jess Phillips .40 .20
❑ 393 Garry Lyle UER .40 .20
❑ 394 Jim Files .40 .20
❑ 395 Jim Hart 1.50 .60
❑ 396 Dave Chapple .40 .20
❑ 397 Jim Langer 2.00 .75
❑ 398 John Wilbur .40 .20
❑ 399 Dwight Harrison .40 .20
❑ 400 John Brockington .75 .30
❑ 401 Ken Anderson 6.00 3.00
❑ 402 Mike Tilleman .40 .20
❑ 403 Charlie Hall .40 .20
❑ 404 Tommy Hart .40 .20
❑ 405 Norm Bulaich .75 .30
❑ 406 Jim Turner .40 .20
❑ 407 Mo Moorman .40 .20
❑ 408 Ralph Anderson .40 .20
❑ 409 Jim Otto 1.50 .60
❑ 410 Andy Russell 1.50 .60

❑ 411 Glenn Doughty .40 .20
❑ 412 Altie Taylor .40 .20
❑ 413 Marv Bateman .40 .20
❑ 414 Willie Alexander .40 .20
❑ 415 Bill Zapalac RC .40 .20
❑ 416 Russ Washington .40 .20
❑ 417 Joe Federspiel .40 .20
❑ 418 Craig Cotton .40 .20
❑ 419 Randy Johnson .40 .20
❑ 420 Harold Jackson 1.50 .60
❑ 421 Roger Wehrli 1.00 .40
❑ 422 Charlie Harraway .40 .20
❑ 423 Spike Jones .40 .20
❑ 424 Bob Johnson .40 .20
❑ 425 Mike McCoy DT .40 .20
❑ 426 Dennis Havig .40 .20
❑ 427 Bob McKay RC .40 .20
❑ 428 Steve Zabel .40 .20
❑ 429 Horace Jones .40 .20
❑ 430 Jim Johnson 1.50 .60
❑ 431 Roy Gerela .75 .30
❑ 432 Tom Graham RC .40 .20
❑ 433 Curley Culp .75 .30
❑ 434 Ken Mendenhall .40 .20
❑ 435 Jim Plunkett 2.50 1.25
❑ 436 Julian Fagan .40 .20
❑ 437 Mike Garrett .75 .30
❑ 438 Bobby Joe Green .40 .20
❑ 439 Jack Gregory .40 .20
❑ 440 Charlie Sanders 1.00 .40
❑ 441 Bill Curry .75 .30
❑ 442 Bob Pollard .40 .20
❑ 443 David Ray .40 .20
❑ 444 Terry Metcalf RC 3.00 1.50
❑ 445 Pat Fischer .75 .30
❑ 446 Bob Chandler .75 .30
❑ 447 Bill Bergey .75 .30
❑ 448 Walter Johnson .40 .20
❑ 449 Charle Young RC 1.50 .60
❑ 450 Chester Marcol .40 .20
❑ 451 Ken Stabler 20.00 10.00
❑ 452 Preston Pearson 1.50 .60
❑ 453 Mike Current .40 .20
❑ 454 Ron Bolton .40 .20
❑ 455 Mark Lomas .40 .20
❑ 456 Raymond Chester .75 .30
❑ 457 Jerry LeVias .75 .30
❑ 458 Skip Butler .40 .20
❑ 459 Mike Livingston RC .40 .20
❑ 460 AFC Semi-Final .75 .30
❑ 461 NFC Semi/Staubach 4.00 2.00
❑ 462 Playoff Champs/Stabler 3.00 1.50
❑ 463 SB VIII/L.Csonka 2.00 .75
❑ 464 Wayne Mulligan .40 .20
❑ 465 Horst Muhlmann .40 .20
❑ 466 Milt Morin .40 .20
❑ 467 Don Parish .40 .20
❑ 468 Richard Neal .40 .20
❑ 469 Ron Jessie .75 .30
❑ 470 Terry Bradshaw 25.00 12.50
❑ 471 Fred Dryer 1.50 .60
❑ 472 Jim Carter .40 .20
❑ 473 Ken Burrow .40 .20
❑ 474 Wally Chambers RC .75 .30
❑ 475 Dan Pastorini 1.50 .60
❑ 476 Don Morrison .40 .20
❑ 477 Carl Mauck .40 .20
❑ 478 Larry Cole RC .75 .30
❑ 479 Jim Kiick 1.50 .60
❑ 480 Willie Lanier 1.50 .60
❑ 481 Don Herrmann .75 .30
❑ 482 George Hunt .40 .20
❑ 483 Bob Howard RC .40 .20
❑ 484 Myron Pottios .40 .20
❑ 485 Jackie Smith 1.50 .60
❑ 486 Vern Holland .40 .20
❑ 487 Jim Braxton .40 .20
❑ 488 Joe Reed .40 .20
❑ 489 Wally Hilgenberg .40 .20
❑ 490 Fred Biletnikoff 4.00 2.00
❑ 491 Bob DeMarco .40 .20
❑ 492 Mark Nordquist .40 .20
❑ 493 Larry Brooks .40 .20
❑ 494 Pete Athas .40 .20
❑ 495 Emerson Boozer .75 .30
❑ 496 L.C.Greenwood 2.00 .75
❑ 497 Rockne Freitas .40 .20
❑ 498 Checklist 397-528 UER 4.00 2.00
❑ 499 Joe Schmiesing .40 .20
❑ 500 Roger Staubach 25.00 12.50
❑ 501 Al Cowlings UER .75 .30
❑ 502 Sam Cunningham RC 1.50 .60
❑ 503 Dennis Partee .40 .20
❑ 504 John Didion .40 .20
❑ 505 Nick Buoniconti 1.50 .60
❑ 506 Carl Garrett .75 .30
❑ 507 Doug Van Horn .40 .20
❑ 508 Jamie Rivers .40 .20
❑ 509 Jack Youngblood 4.00 2.00
❑ 510 Charley Taylor UER 2.50 1.25
❑ 511 Ken Riley 1.50 .60
❑ 512 Joe Ferguson RC 3.00 1.25
❑ 513 Bill Lueck .40 .20
❑ 514 Ray Brown DB RC .40 .20
❑ 515 Fred Cox .40 .20
❑ 516 Joe Jones DE .40 .20
❑ 517 Larry Schreiber .40 .20
❑ 518 Dennis Wirgowski .40 .20
❑ 519 Leroy Mitchell .40 .20
❑ 520 Otis Taylor 1.50 .60
❑ 521 Henry Davis .40 .20
❑ 522 Bruce Barnes .40 .20
❑ 523 Charlie Smith RB .40 .20
❑ 524 Bert Jones RC 5.00 2.00
❑ 525 Lem Barney 2.00 .75
❑ 526 John Fitzgerald RC .40 .20
❑ 527 Tom Funchess .40 .20
❑ 528 Steve Tannen 1.50 .60

1975 Topps

❑ COMPLETE SET (528) 300.00 175.00
❑ 1 McCutcheon/Armstrong LL 1.50 .60
❑ 2 Jurgensen/K.Anderson LL 1.50 .60
❑ 3 Receiving Leaders 1.50 .60
❑ 4 Scoring Leaders .75 .30
❑ 5 Interception Leaders .75 .30
❑ 6 Punting Leaders 1.50 .60
❑ 7 George Blanda HL 5.00 2.50
❑ 8 George Blanda 5.00 2.50
❑ 9 Ralph Baker .30 .15
❑ 10 Don Woods .30 .15
❑ 11 Bob Asher .30 .15
❑ 12 Mel Blount RC 20.00 10.00
❑ 13 Sam Cunningham .75 .30
❑ 14 Jackie Smith 1.50 .60
❑ 15 Greg Landry .75 .30
❑ 16 Buck Buchanan 1.50 .60
❑ 17 Haven Moses .75 .30
❑ 18 Clarence Ellis .30 .15
❑ 19 Jim Carter .30 .15
❑ 20 Charley Taylor UER 2.00 .75
❑ 21 Jess Phillips .30 .15
❑ 22 Larry Seiple .30 .15
❑ 23 Doug Dieken .30 .15
❑ 24 Ron Saul .30 .15
❑ 25 Isaac Curtis 1.50 .60
❑ 26 Gary Larsen RC .30 .15
❑ 27 Bruce Jarvis .30 .15
❑ 28 Steve Zabel .30 .15
❑ 29 John Mendenhall .30 .15
❑ 30 Rick Volk .30 .15
❑ 31 Checklist 1-132 4.00 2.00
❑ 32 Dan Abramowicz .75 .30
❑ 33 Bubba Smith 1.50 .60
❑ 34 David Ray .30 .15
❑ 35 Dan Dierdorf 4.00 2.00
❑ 36 Randy Rasmussen .30 .15
❑ 37 Bob Howard .30 .15
❑ 38 Gary Huff .75 .30
❑ 39 Rocky Bleier RC 20.00 10.00
❑ 40 Mel Gray .75 .30
❑ 41 Tony McGee DT .30 .15
❑ 42 Larry Hand .30 .15
❑ 43 Wendell Hayes .30 .15
❑ 44 Doug Wilkerson RC .30 .15
❑ 45 Paul Smith .30 .15
❑ 46 Dave Robinson .75 .30
❑ 47 Bivian Lee .30 .15
❑ 48 Jim Mandich RC .75 .30
❑ 49 Greg Pruitt 1.50 .60
❑ 50 Dan Pastorini 1.50 .60
❑ 51 Ron Pritchard .30 .15
❑ 52 Dan Conners .30 .15
❑ 53 Fred Cox .30 .15
❑ 54 Tony Greene .30 .15
❑ 55 Craig Morton 1.50 .60
❑ 56 Jerry Sisemore .30 .15
❑ 57 Glenn Doughty .30 .15
❑ 58 Larry Schreiber .30 .15
❑ 59 Charlie Waters RC 4.00 2.00
❑ 60 Jack Youngblood 1.50 .60
❑ 61 Bill Lenkaitis .30 .15
❑ 62 Greg Brezina .30 .15
❑ 63 Bob Pollard .30 .15
❑ 64 Mack Alston .30 .15
❑ 65 Drew Pearson RC 20.00 10.00
❑ 66 Charlie Stukes .30 .15
❑ 67 Emerson Boozer .75 .30
❑ 68 Dennis Partee .30 .15
❑ 69 Bob Newton .30 .15
❑ 70 Jack Tatum 1.50 .60
❑ 71 Frank Lewis .30 .15
❑ 72 Bob Young .30 .15
❑ 73 Julius Adams .30 .15
❑ 74 Paul Naumoff .30 .15
❑ 75 Otis Taylor 1.50 .60
❑ 76 Dave Hampton .30 .15
❑ 77 Mike Current .30 .15
❑ 78 Brig Owens .30 .15
❑ 79 Bobby Scott .30 .15
❑ 80 Harold Carmichael 3.00 1.50
❑ 81 Bill Stanfill .30 .15
❑ 82 Bob Babich .30 .15
❑ 83 Vic Washington .30 .15
❑ 84 Mick Tingelhoff .75 .30
❑ 85 Bob Trumpy 1.50 .60
❑ 86 Earl Edwards .30 .15
❑ 87 Ron Hornsby .30 .15
❑ 88 Don McCauley .30 .15
❑ 89 Jim Johnson 1.50 .60
❑ 90 Andy Russell .75 .30
❑ 91 Cornell Green 1.50 .60
❑ 92 Charlie Cowan .30 .15
❑ 93 Jon Staggers .30 .15
❑ 94 Billy Newsome .30 .15
❑ 95 Willie Brown 1.50 .60
❑ 96 Carl Mauck .30 .15
❑ 97 Doug Buffone .30 .15
❑ 98 Preston Pearson .75 .30
❑ 99 Jim Bakken .30 .15
❑ 100 Bob Griese 5.00 2.50
❑ 101 Bob Windsor .30 .15
❑ 102 Rockne Freitas .30 .15
❑ 103 Jim Marsalis .30 .15
❑ 104 Bill Thompson .75 .30
❑ 105 Ken Burrow .30 .15
❑ 106 Diron Talbert .30 .15
❑ 107 Joe Federspiel .30 .15
❑ 108 Norm Bulaich .75 .30
❑ 109 Bob DeMarco .30 .15
❑ 110 Tom Wittum .30 .15
❑ 111 Larry Hefner .30 .15
❑ 112 Tody Smith .30 .15
❑ 113 Stu Voigt .30 .15
❑ 114 Horst Muhlmann .30 .15
❑ 115 Ahmad Rashad 6.00 3.00
❑ 116 Joe Dawkins .30 .15
❑ 117 George Kunz .30 .15
❑ 118 D.D.Lewis .75 .30
❑ 119 Levi Johnson .30 .15
❑ 120 Len Dawson 4.00 2.00
❑ 121 Jim Bertelsen .30 .15
❑ 122 Ed Bell .30 .15

❑ 123 Art Thoms .30 .15
❑ 124 Joe Beauchamp .30 .15
❑ 125 Jack Ham 6.00 3.00
❑ 126 Carl Garrett .30 .15
❑ 127 Roger Finnie .30 .15
❑ 128 Howard Twilley .75 .30
❑ 129 Bruce Barnes .30 .15
❑ 130 Nate Wright .30 .15
❑ 131 Jerry Tagge .30 .15
❑ 132 Floyd Little 1.50 .60
❑ 133 John Zook .30 .15
❑ 134 Len Hauss .30 .15
❑ 135 Archie Manning 1.50 .60
❑ 136 Po James .30 .15
❑ 137 Walt Sumner .30 .15
❑ 138 Randy Beisler .30 .15
❑ 139 Willie Alexander .30 .15
❑ 140 Garo Yepremian .75 .30
❑ 141 Chip Myers .30 .15
❑ 142 Jim Braxton .30 .15
❑ 143 Doug Van Horn .30 .15
❑ 144 Stan White .30 .15
❑ 145 Roger Staubach 20.00 10.00
❑ 146 Herman Weaver .30 .15
❑ 147 Marvin Upshaw .30 .15
❑ 148 Bob Klein .30 .15
❑ 149 Earlie Thomas .30 .15
❑ 150 John Brockington .75 .30
❑ 151 Mike Siani .30 .15
❑ 152 Sam Davis RC .30 .15
❑ 153 Mike Wagner .75 .30
❑ 154 Larry Stallings .30 .15
❑ 155 Wally Chambers .30 .15
❑ 156 Randy Vataha .30 .15
❑ 157 Jim Marshall 1.50 .60
❑ 158 Jim Turner .30 .15
❑ 159 Walt Sweeney .30 .15
❑ 160 Ken Anderson 4.00 2.00
❑ 161 Ray Brown DB .30 .15
❑ 162 John Didion .30 .15
❑ 163 Tom Dempsey .30 .15
❑ 164 Clarence Scott .30 .15
❑ 165 Gene Washington 49er .75 .30
❑ 166 Willie Rodgers RC .30 .15
❑ 167 Doug Swift .30 .15
❑ 168 Rufus Mayes .30 .15
❑ 169 Marv Bateman .30 .15
❑ 170 Lydell Mitchell .75 .30
❑ 171 Ron Smith .30 .15
❑ 172 Bill Munson .75 .30
❑ 173 Bob Grim .30 .15
❑ 174 Ed Budde .30 .15
❑ 175 Bob Lilly UER 4.00 2.00
❑ 176 Jim Youngblood RC 1.50 .60
❑ 177 Steve Tannen .30 .15
❑ 178 Rich McGeorge .30 .15
❑ 179 Jim Tyrer .30 .15
❑ 180 Forrest Blue .30 .15
❑ 181 Jerry LeVias .75 .30
❑ 182 Joe Gilliam RC 1.50 .60
❑ 183 Jim Otis RC .75 .30
❑ 184 Mel Tom .30 .15
❑ 185 Paul Seymour .30 .15
❑ 186 George Webster .30 .15
❑ 187 Pete Duranko .30 .15
❑ 188 Essex Johnson .30 .15
❑ 189 Bob Lee .75 .30
❑ 190 Gene Upshaw 1.50 .60
❑ 191 Tom Myers .30 .15
❑ 192 Don Zimmerman .30 .15
❑ 193 John Garlington .30 .15
❑ 194 Skip Butler .30 .15
❑ 195 Tom Mitchell .30 .15
❑ 196 Jim Langer 1.50 .60
❑ 197 Ron Carpenter .30 .15
❑ 198 Dave Foley .30 .15
❑ 199 Bert Jones 1.50 .60
❑ 200 Larry Brown .75 .30
❑ 201 Biletnikoff/C.Taylor AP 2.00 .75
❑ 202 All Pro Tackles .30 .15
❑ 203 L.Little/T.Mack AP 1.50 .60
❑ 204 All Pro Centers .30 .15
❑ 205 Hannah/Gillingham AP 1.50 .60
❑ 206 Dan Dierdorf/W.Hill AP 1.50 .60
❑ 207 All Pro Tight Ends .75 .30
❑ 208 F.Tarkenton/Stabler AP 4.00 2.00
❑ 209 Simpson/McCutch. AP 3.00 1.50
❑ 210 All Pro Backs .75 .30
❑ 211 All Pro Receivers .75 .30
❑ 212 All Pro Kickers .30 .15
❑ 213 Youngblood/Bethea AP 1.50 .60
❑ 214 All Pro Tackles .75 .30
❑ 215 M.Olsen/M.Reid AP 1.50 .60
❑ 216 Carl Eller/L.Alzado AP 1.50 .60
❑ 217 Hendricks/Villapiano AP 1.50 .60
❑ 218 Willie Lanier/Jordan AP 1.50 .60
❑ 219 All Pro Linebackers .75 .30
❑ 220 All Pro Cornerbacks .30 .15
❑ 221 All Pro Cornerbacks .30 .15
❑ 222 K.Houston/D.Anderson AP .75 .30
❑ 223 Cliff Harris/J.Tatum AP 1.50 .60
❑ 224 All Pro Punters .75 .30
❑ 225 All Pro Returners .75 .30
❑ 226 Ted Kwalick .30 .15
❑ 227 Spider Lockhart .75 .30
❑ 228 Mike Livingston .30 .15
❑ 229 Larry Cole .30 .15
❑ 230 Gary Garrison .30 .15
❑ 231 Larry Brooks .30 .15
❑ 232 Bobby Howfield .30 .15
❑ 233 Fred Carr .30 .15
❑ 234 Norm Evans .30 .15
❑ 235 Dwight White .75 .30
❑ 236 Conrad Dobler .75 .30
❑ 237 Garry Lyle .30 .15
❑ 238 Darryl Stingley 1.50 .60
❑ 239 Tom Graham .30 .15
❑ 240 Chuck Foreman 1.50 .60
❑ 241 Ken Riley .75 .30
❑ 242 Don Morrison .30 .15
❑ 243 Lynn Dickey .75 .30
❑ 244 Don Cockroft .30 .15
❑ 245 Claude Humphrey .75 .30
❑ 246 John Skorupan .30 .15
❑ 247 Raymond Chester .75 .30
❑ 248 Cas Banaszek .30 .15
❑ 249 Art Malone .30 .15
❑ 250 Ed Flanagan .30 .15
❑ 251 Checklist 133-264 4.00 2.00
❑ 252 Nemiah Wilson .30 .15
❑ 253 Ron Jessie .30 .15
❑ 254 Jim Lynch .30 .15
❑ 255 Bob Tucker .75 .30
❑ 256 Terry Owens .30 .15
❑ 257 John Fitzgerald .30 .15
❑ 258 Jack Snow .75 .30
❑ 259 Garry Puetz .30 .15
❑ 260 Mike Phipps .75 .30
❑ 261 Al Matthews .30 .15
❑ 262 Bob Kuechenberg .30 .15
❑ 263 Ron Yankowski .30 .15
❑ 264 Ron Shanklin .30 .15
❑ 265 Bobby Douglass .75 .30
❑ 266 Josh Ashton .30 .15
❑ 267 Bill Van Heusen .30 .15
❑ 268 Jeff Siemon .30 .15
❑ 269 Bob Newland .30 .15
❑ 270 Gale Gillingham .30 .15
❑ 271 Zeke Moore .30 .15
❑ 272 Mike Tilleman .30 .15
❑ 273 John Leypoldt .30 .15
❑ 274 Ken Mendenhall .30 .15
❑ 275 Norm Snead .75 .30
❑ 276 Bill Bradley .75 .30
❑ 277 Jerry Smith .30 .15
❑ 278 Clarence Davis .30 .15
❑ 279 Jim Yarbrough .30 .15
❑ 280 Lemar Parrish .30 .15
❑ 281 Bobby Bell 1.50 .60
❑ 282 Lynn Swann RC UER ! 60.00 30.00
❑ 283 John Hicks .30 .15
❑ 284 Coy Bacon .75 .30
❑ 285 Lee Roy Jordan 1.50 .60
❑ 286 Willie Buchanon .30 .15
❑ 287 Al Woodall .30 .15
❑ 288 Reggie Rucker .75 .30
❑ 289 John Schmitt .30 .15
❑ 290 Carl Eller 1.50 .60
❑ 291 Jake Scott .75 .30
❑ 292 Donny Anderson .75 .30
❑ 293 Charley Wade .30 .15
❑ 294 John Tanner .30 .15
❑ 295 Charlie Johnson .75 .30
❑ 296 Tom Blanchard .30 .15
❑ 297 Curley Culp .75 .30
❑ 298 Jeff Van Note RC .75 .30
❑ 299 Bob James .30 .15
❑ 300 Franco Harris 8.00 4.00
❑ 301 Tim Berra .75 .30
❑ 302 Bruce Gossett .30 .15
❑ 303 Verlon Biggs .30 .15
❑ 304 Bob Kowalkowski .30 .15
❑ 305 Marv Hubbard .30 .15
❑ 306 Ken Avery .30 .15
❑ 307 Mike Adamle .30 .15
❑ 308 Don Herrmann .30 .15
❑ 309 Chris Fletcher .30 .15
❑ 310 Roman Gabriel 1.50 .60
❑ 311 Billy Joe DuPree 1.50 .60
❑ 312 Fred Dryer 1.50 .60
❑ 313 John Riggins 5.00 2.50
❑ 314 Bob McKay .30 .15
❑ 315 Ted Hendricks 1.50 .60
❑ 316 Bobby Bryant .30 .15
❑ 317 Don Nottingham .30 .15
❑ 318 John Hannah 4.00 2.00
❑ 319 Rich Coady .30 .15
❑ 320 Phil Villapiano .75 .30
❑ 321 Jim Plunkett 1.50 .60
❑ 322 Lyle Alzado 1.50 .60
❑ 323 Ernie Jackson .30 .15
❑ 324 Billy Parks .30 .15
❑ 325 Willie Lanier 1.50 .60
❑ 326 John James .30 .15
❑ 327 Joe Ferguson .75 .30
❑ 328 Ernie Holmes RC 1.50 .60
❑ 329 Bruce Laird .30 .15
❑ 330 Chester Marcol .30 .15
❑ 331 Dave Wilcox 1.50 .60
❑ 332 Pat Fischer .75 .30
❑ 333 Steve Owens .75 .30
❑ 334 Royce Berry .30 .15
❑ 335 Russ Washington .30 .15
❑ 336 Walker Gillette .30 .15
❑ 337 Mark Nordquist .30 .15
❑ 338 James Harris RC 1.50 .60
❑ 339 Warren Koegel .30 .15
❑ 340 Emmitt Thomas .75 .30
❑ 341 Walt Garrison .75 .30
❑ 342 Thom Darden .30 .15
❑ 343 Mike Eischeid .30 .15
❑ 344 Ernie McMillan .30 .15
❑ 345 Nick Buoniconti 1.50 .60
❑ 346 George Farmer .30 .15
❑ 347 Sam Adams OL .30 .15
❑ 348 Larry Cipa .30 .15
❑ 349 Bob Moore .30 .15
❑ 350 Otis Armstrong RC 1.50 .60
❑ 351 George Blanda RB 3.00 1.50
❑ 352 Fred Cox RB .75 .30
❑ 353 Tom Dempsey RB .75 .30
❑ 354 Ken Houston RB 1.50 .60
❑ 355 O.J.Simpson RB 5.00 2.50
❑ 356 Ron Smith RB .75 .30
❑ 357 Bob Atkins .30 .15
❑ 358 Pat Sullivan .75 .30
❑ 359 Joe DeLamielleure 2.50 1.00
❑ 360 Lawr. McCutcheon RC 1.50 .60
❑ 361 David Lee .30 .15
❑ 362 Mike McCoy DT .30 .15
❑ 363 Skip Vanderbundt .30 .15
❑ 364 Mark Moseley .75 .30
❑ 365 Lem Barney 1.50 .60
❑ 366 Doug Dressler .30 .15
❑ 367 Dan Fouts RC 40.00 20.00
❑ 368 Bob Hyland .30 .15
❑ 369 John Outlaw .30 .15
❑ 370 Roy Gerela .30 .15
❑ 371 Isiah Robertson .75 .30
❑ 372 Jerome Barkum .30 .15
❑ 373 Ed Podolak .30 .15
❑ 374 Milt Morin .30 .15
❑ 375 John Niland .30 .15
❑ 376 Checklist 265-396 UER 4.00 2.00
❑ 377 Ken Iman .30 .15
❑ 378 Manny Fernandez .75 .30
❑ 379 Dave Gallagher .30 .15
❑ 380 Ken Stabler 15.00 7.50
❑ 381 Mack Herron .30 .15
❑ 382 Bill McClard .30 .15
❑ 383 Ray May .30 .15

❑ 384 Don Hansen .30 .15
❑ 385 Elvin Bethea 1.50 .60
❑ 386 Joe Scibelli .30 .15
❑ 387 Neal Craig .30 .15
❑ 388 Marty Domres .30 .15
❑ 389 Ken Ellis .30 .15
❑ 390 Charle Young .75 .30
❑ 391 Tommy Hart .30 .15
❑ 392 Moses Denson .30 .15
❑ 393 Larry Walton .30 .15
❑ 394 Dave Green .30 .15
❑ 395 Ron Johnson .75 .30
❑ 396 Ed Bradley RC .30 .15
❑ 397 J.T. Thomas .30 .15
❑ 398 Jim Bailey .30 .15
❑ 399 Barry Pearson .30 .15
❑ 400 Fran Tarkenton 8.00 4.00
❑ 401 Jack Rudnay .30 .15
❑ 402 Rayfield Wright .75 .30
❑ 403 Roger Wehrli 1.00 .40
❑ 404 Vern Den Herder .30 .15
❑ 405 Fred Biletnikoff 3.00 1.50
❑ 406 Ken Grandberry .30 .15
❑ 407 Bob Adams .30 .15
❑ 408 Jim Merlo .30 .15
❑ 409 John Pitts .30 .15
❑ 410 Dave Osborn .75 .30
❑ 411 Dennis Havig .30 .15
❑ 412 Bob Johnson .30 .15
❑ 413 Ken Burrough UER .75 .30
❑ 414 Jim Cheyunski .30 .15
❑ 415 MacArthur Lane .30 .15
❑ 416 Joe Theismann RC 25.00 12.50
❑ 417 Mike Boryla RC .30 .15
❑ 418 Bruce Taylor .30 .15
❑ 419 Chris Hanburger .75 .30
❑ 420 Tom Mack 1.50 .60
❑ 421 Errol Mann .30 .15
❑ 422 Jack Gregory .30 .15
❑ 423 Harrison Davis .30 .15
❑ 424 Burgess Owens .30 .15
❑ 425 Joe Greene 5.00 2.50
❑ 426 Morris Stroud .30 .15
❑ 427 John DeMarie .30 .15
❑ 428 Mel Renfro 1.50 .60
❑ 429 Cid Edwards .30 .15
❑ 430 Mike Reid 1.50 .60
❑ 431 Jack Mildren RC .30 .15
❑ 432 Jerry Simmons .30 .15
❑ 433 Ron Yary 1.50 .60
❑ 434 Howard Stevens .30 .15
❑ 435 Ray Guy 2.00 .75
❑ 436 Tommy Nobis 1.50 .60
❑ 437 Solomon Freelon .30 .15
❑ 438 J.D. Hill .75 .30
❑ 439 Toni Linhart .30 .15
❑ 440 Dick Anderson .75 .30
❑ 441 Guy Morriss .30 .15
❑ 442 Bob Hoskins .30 .15
❑ 443 John Hadl 1.50 .60
❑ 444 Roy Jefferson .30 .15
❑ 445 Charlie Sanders 1.00 .40
❑ 446 Pat Curran .30 .15
❑ 447 David Knight .30 .15
❑ 448 Bob Brown DT .30 .15
❑ 449 Pete Gogolak .30 .15
❑ 450 Terry Metcalf 1.50 .60
❑ 451 Bill Bergey 1.50 .60
❑ 452 Dan Abramowicz HL .75 .30
❑ 453 Otis Armstrong HL .75 .30
❑ 454 Cliff Branch HL 1.50 .60
❑ 455 John James HL .30 .15
❑ 456 Lydell Mitchell HL .75 .30
❑ 457 Lemar Parrish HL .75 .30
❑ 458 Ken Stabler HL 5.00 2.50
❑ 459 Lynn Swann HL 8.00 4.00
❑ 460 Emmitt Thomas HL .30 .15
❑ 461 Terry Bradshaw 20.00 10.00
❑ 462 Jerrel Wilson .30 .15
❑ 463 Walter Johnson .30 .15
❑ 464 Golden Richards .75 .30
❑ 465 Tommy Casanova .75 .30
❑ 466 Randy Jackson .30 .15
❑ 467 Ron Bolton .30 .15
❑ 468 Joe Owens .30 .15
❑ 469 Wally Hilgenberg .30 .15
❑ 470 Riley Odoms .75 .30
❑ 471 Otis Sistrunk .75 .30
❑ 472 Eddie Ray .30 .15
❑ 473 Reggie McKenzie .75 .30
❑ 474 Elbert Drungo .30 .15
❑ 475 Mercury Morris 1.50 .60
❑ 476 Dan Dickel .30 .15
❑ 477 Merritt Kersey .30 .15
❑ 478 Mike Holmes .30 .15
❑ 479 Clarence Williams .30 .15
❑ 480 Billy Kilmer 1.50 .60
❑ 481 Altie Taylor .30 .15
❑ 482 Dave Elmendorf .30 .15
❑ 483 Bob Rowe .30 .15
❑ 484 Pete Athas .30 .15
❑ 485 Winston Hill .30 .15
❑ 486 Bo Matthews .30 .15
❑ 487 Earl Thomas .30 .15
❑ 488 Jan Stenerud 1.50 .60
❑ 489 Steve Holden .30 .15
❑ 490 Cliff Harris RC 5.00 2.50
❑ 491 Boobie Clark RC .75 .30
❑ 492 Joe Taylor .30 .15
❑ 493 Tom Neville .30 .15
❑ 494 Wayne Colman .30 .15
❑ 495 Jim Mitchell TE .30 .15
❑ 496 Paul Krause 1.50 .60
❑ 497 Jim Otto 1.50 .60
❑ 498 John Rowser .30 .15
❑ 499 Larry Little 1.50 .60
❑ 500 O.J.Simpson 10.00 5.00
❑ 501 John Dutton RC 1.50 .60
❑ 502 Pat Hughes .30 .15
❑ 503 Malcolm Snider .30 .15
❑ 504 Fred Willis .30 .15
❑ 505 Harold Jackson 1.50 .60
❑ 506 Mike Bragg .30 .15
❑ 507 Jerry Sherk .75 .30
❑ 508 Mirro Roder .30 .15
❑ 509 Tom Sullivan .30 .15
❑ 510 Jim Hart 1.50 .60
❑ 511 Cedrick Hardman .30 .15
❑ 512 Blaine Nye .30 .15
❑ 513 Elmo Wright .30 .15
❑ 514 Herb Orvis .30 .15
❑ 515 Richard Caster .75 .30
❑ 516 Doug Kotar RC .30 .15
❑ 517 Checklist 397-528 4.00 2.00
❑ 518 Jesse Freitas .30 .15
❑ 519 Ken Houston 1.50 .60
❑ 520 Alan Page 1.50 .60
❑ 521 Tim Foley .75 .30
❑ 522 Bill Olds .30 .15
❑ 523 Bobby Maples .30 .15
❑ 524 Cliff Branch RC 15.00 7.50
❑ 525 Merlin Olsen 1.50 .60
❑ 526 AFC Champs/Brad./Harris 4.00 2.00
❑ 527 NFC Champs/Foreman 1.50 .60
❑ 528 Super Bowl IX/Bradshaw 5.00 2.50

1976 Topps

❑ COMPLETE SET (528) 350.00 200.00
❑ 1 George Blanda RB ! 5.00 2.50
❑ 2 Neal Colzie RB .75 .30
❑ 3 Chuck Foreman RB .75 .30
❑ 4 Jim Marshall RB .75 .30
❑ 5 Terry Metcalf RB .75 .30
❑ 6 O.J.Simpson RB 3.00 1.50
❑ 7 Fran Tarkenton RB 3.00 1.50
❑ 8 Charley Taylor RB 1.50 .60
❑ 9 Ernie Holmes .75 .30
❑ 10 Ken Anderson 1.50 .60
❑ 11 Bobby Bryant .30 .15
❑ 12 Jerry Smith .75 .30
❑ 13 David Lee .30 .15
❑ 14 Robert Newhouse RC 1.50 .60
❑ 15 Vern Den Herder .30 .15
❑ 16 John Hannah 1.50 .60
❑ 17 J.D. Hill .75 .30
❑ 18 James Harris .75 .30
❑ 19 Willie Buchanon .30 .15
❑ 20 Charle Young .75 .30
❑ 21 Jim Yarbrough .30 .15
❑ 22 Ronnie Coleman .30 .15
❑ 23 Don Cockroft .30 .15
❑ 24 Willie Lanier 1.50 .60
❑ 25 Fred Biletnikoff 3.00 1.50
❑ 26 Ron Yankowski .30 .15
❑ 27 Spider Lockhart .30 .15
❑ 28 Bob Johnson .30 .15
❑ 29 J.T. Thomas .30 .15
❑ 30 Ron Yary 1.50 .60
❑ 31 Brad Dusek RC .30 .15
❑ 32 Raymond Chester .75 .30
❑ 33 Larry Little 1.50 .60
❑ 34 Pat Leahy RC 1.50 .60
❑ 35 Steve Bartkowski RC 4.00 2.00
❑ 36 Tom Myers .30 .15
❑ 37 Bill Van Heusen .30 .15
❑ 38 Russ Washington .30 .15
❑ 39 Tom Sullivan .30 .15
❑ 40 Curley Culp .75 .30
❑ 41 Johnnie Gray .30 .15
❑ 42 Bob Klein .30 .15
❑ 43 Lem Barney 1.50 .60
❑ 44 Harvey Martin RC 6.00 3.00
❑ 45 Reggie Rucker .75 .30
❑ 46 Neil Clabo .30 .15
❑ 47 Ray Hamilton .30 .15
❑ 48 Joe Ferguson .75 .30
❑ 49 Ed Podolak .30 .15
❑ 50 Ray Guy 1.50 .60
❑ 51 Glen Edwards .30 .15
❑ 52 Jim LeClair .30 .15
❑ 53 Mike Barnes .30 .15
❑ 54 Nat Moore RC 1.50 .60
❑ 55 Billy Kilmer 1.50 .60
❑ 56 Larry Stallings .30 .15
❑ 57 Jack Gregory .30 .15
❑ 58 Steve Mike-Mayer .30 .15
❑ 59 Virgil Livers .30 .15
❑ 60 Jerry Sherk .75 .30
❑ 61 Guy Morriss .30 .15
❑ 62 Barty Smith .30 .15
❑ 63 Jerome Barkum .30 .15
❑ 64 Ira Gordon .30 .15
❑ 65 Paul Krause 1.50 .60
❑ 66 John McMakin .30 .15
❑ 67 Checklist 1-132 3.00 1.50
❑ 68 Charlie Johnson UER .75 .30
❑ 69 Tommy Nobis 1.50 .60
❑ 70 Lydell Mitchell .75 .30
❑ 71 Vern Holland .30 .15
❑ 72 Tim Foley .75 .30
❑ 73 Golden Richards .75 .30
❑ 74 Bryant Salter .30 .15
❑ 75 Terry Bradshaw 20.00 10.00
❑ 76 Ted Hendricks 1.50 .60
❑ 77 Rich Saul RC .30 .15
❑ 78 John Smith RC .30 .15
❑ 79 Altie Taylor .30 .15
❑ 80 Cedrick Hardman .30 .15
❑ 81 Ken Payne .30 .15
❑ 82 Zeke Moore .30 .15
❑ 83 Alvin Maxson .30 .15
❑ 84 Wally Hilgenberg .30 .15
❑ 85 John Niland .30 .15
❑ 86 Mike Sensibaugh .30 .15
❑ 87 Ron Johnson .75 .30
❑ 88 Winston Hill .30 .15
❑ 89 Charlie Joiner 4.00 2.00
❑ 90 Roger Wehrli .75 .30
❑ 91 Mike Bragg .30 .15
❑ 92 Dan Dickel .30 .15
❑ 93 Earl Morrall .75 .30
❑ 94 Pat Toomay .30 .15
❑ 95 Gary Garrison .30 .15

❑ 96	Ken Geddes	.30	.15
❑ 97	Mike Current	.30	.15
❑ 98	Bob Avellini RC	.75	.30
❑ 99	Dave Pureifory	.30	.15
❑ 100	Franco Harris	8.00	4.00
❑ 101	Randy Logan	.30	.15
❑ 102	John Fitzgerald	.30	.15
❑ 103	Gregg Bingham RC	.75	.30
❑ 104	Jim Plunkett	1.50	.60
❑ 105	Carl Eller	1.50	.60
❑ 106	Larry Walton	.30	.15
❑ 107	Clarence Scott	.30	.15
❑ 108	Skip Vanderbundt	.30	.15
❑ 109	Boobie Clark	.75	.30
❑ 110	Tom Mack	1.50	.60
❑ 111	Bruce Laird	.30	.15
❑ 112	Dave Dalby RC	.30	.15
❑ 113	John Leypoldt	.30	.15
❑ 114	Barry Pearson	.30	.15
❑ 115	Larry Brown	.75	.30
❑ 116	Jackie Smith	1.50	.60
❑ 117	Pat Hughes	.30	.15
❑ 118	Al Woodall	.30	.15
❑ 119	John Zook	.30	.15
❑ 120	Jake Scott	.75	.30
❑ 121	Rich Glover	.30	.15
❑ 122	Ernie Jackson	.30	.15
❑ 123	Otis Armstrong	1.50	.60
❑ 124	Bob Grim	.30	.15
❑ 125	Jeff Siemon	.75	.30
❑ 126	Harold Hart	.30	.15
❑ 127	John DeMarie	.30	.15
❑ 128	Dan Fouts	12.00	6.00
❑ 129	Jim Kearney	.30	.15
❑ 130	John Dutton	.75	.30
❑ 131	Calvin Hill	1.50	.60
❑ 132	Toni Fritsch	.30	.15
❑ 133	Ron Jessie	.30	.15
❑ 134	Don Nottingham	.30	.15
❑ 135	Lemar Parrish	.30	.15
❑ 136	Russ Francis RC	1.50	.60
❑ 137	Joe Reed	.30	.15
❑ 138	C.L. Whittington	.30	.15
❑ 139	Otis Sistrunk	.75	.30
❑ 140	Lynn Swann	20.00	10.00
❑ 141	Jim Carter	.30	.15
❑ 142	Mike Montler	.30	.15
❑ 143	Walter Johnson	.30	.15
❑ 144	Doug Kotar	.30	.15
❑ 145	Roman Gabriel	1.50	.60
❑ 146	Billy Newsome	.30	.15
❑ 147	Ed Bradley	.30	.15
❑ 148	Walter Payton RC	250.00	125.00
❑ 149	Johnny Fuller	.30	.15
❑ 150	Alan Page	1.50	.60
❑ 151	Frank Grant	.30	.15
❑ 152	Dave Green	.30	.15
❑ 153	Nelson Munsey	.30	.15
❑ 154	Jim Mandich	.30	.15
❑ 155	Lawrence McCutcheon	1.50	.60
❑ 156	Steve Ramsey	.30	.15
❑ 157	Ed Flanagan	.30	.15
❑ 158	Randy White RC	20.00	10.00
❑ 159	Gerry Mullins	.30	.15
❑ 160	Jan Stenerud	1.50	.60
❑ 161	Steve Odom	.30	.15
❑ 162	Roger Finnie	.30	.15
❑ 163	Norm Snead	.75	.30
❑ 164	Jeff Van Note	.75	.30
❑ 165	Bill Bergey	1.50	.60
❑ 166	Allen Carter	.30	.15
❑ 167	Steve Holden	.30	.15
❑ 168	Sherman White	.30	.15
❑ 169	Bob Berry	.30	.15
❑ 170	Ken Houston	1.50	.60
❑ 171	Bill Olds	.30	.15
❑ 172	Larry Seiple	.30	.15
❑ 173	Cliff Branch	4.00	2.00
❑ 174	Reggie McKenzie	.75	.30
❑ 175	Dan Pastorini	1.50	.60
❑ 176	Paul Naumoff	.30	.15
❑ 177	Checklist 133-264	3.00	1.50
❑ 178	Durwood Keeton	.30	.15
❑ 179	Earl Thomas	.30	.15
❑ 180	L.C.Greenwood	1.50	.60
❑ 181	John Outlaw	.30	.15
❑ 182	Frank Nunley	.30	.15
❑ 183	Dave Jennings RC	.75	.30
❑ 184	MacArthur Lane	.30	.15
❑ 185	Chester Marcol	.30	.15
❑ 186	J.J. Jones	.30	.15
❑ 187	Tom DeLeone	.30	.15
❑ 188	Steve Zabel	.30	.15
❑ 189	Ken Johnson DT	.30	.15
❑ 190	Rayfield Wright	.75	.30
❑ 191	Brent McClanahan	.30	.15
❑ 192	Pat Fischer	.75	.30
❑ 193	Roger Carr RC	.75	.30
❑ 194	Manny Fernandez	.75	.30
❑ 195	Roy Gerela	.30	.15
❑ 196	Dave Elmendorf	.30	.15
❑ 197	Bob Kowalkowski	.30	.15
❑ 198	Phil Villapiano	.75	.30
❑ 199	Will Wynn	.30	.15
❑ 200	Terry Metcalf	1.50	.60
❑ 201	Tarkenton/Anderson LL	2.00	.75
❑ 202	Receiving Leaders	.75	.30
❑ 203	O.J.Simpson/J.Otis LL	2.50	1.25
❑ 204	Simpson/Foreman LL	2.50	1.25
❑ 205	M.Blount/P.Krause LL	1.50	.60
❑ 206	Punting Leaders	.75	.30
❑ 207	Ken Ellis	.30	.15
❑ 208	Ron Saul	.30	.15
❑ 209	Toni Linhart	.30	.15
❑ 210	Jim Langer	1.50	.60
❑ 211	Jeff Wright S	.30	.15
❑ 212	Moses Denson	.30	.15
❑ 213	Earl Edwards	.30	.15
❑ 214	Walker Gillette	.30	.15
❑ 215	Bob Trumpy	.75	.30
❑ 216	Emmitt Thomas	.75	.30
❑ 217	Lyle Alzado	1.50	.60
❑ 218	Carl Garrett	.75	.30
❑ 219	Van Green	.30	.15
❑ 220	Jack Lambert RC	35.00	20.00
❑ 221	Spike Jones	.30	.15
❑ 222	John Hadl	1.50	.60
❑ 223	Billy Johnson RC	1.50	.60
❑ 224	Tony McGee DT	.30	.15
❑ 225	Preston Pearson	.75	.30
❑ 226	Isiah Robertson	.75	.30
❑ 227	Errol Mann	.30	.15
❑ 228	Paul Seal	.30	.15
❑ 229	Roland Harper RC	.30	.15
❑ 230	Ed White RC	.75	.30
❑ 231	Joe Theismann	6.00	3.00
❑ 232	Jim Cheyunski	.30	.15
❑ 233	Bill Stanfill	.75	.30
❑ 234	Marv Hubbard	.30	.15
❑ 235	Tommy Casanova	.75	.30
❑ 236	Bob Hyland	.30	.15
❑ 237	Jesse Freitas	.30	.15
❑ 238	Norm Thompson	.30	.15
❑ 239	Charlie Smith WR	.30	.15
❑ 240	John James	.30	.15
❑ 241	Alden Roche	.30	.15
❑ 242	Gordon Jolley	.30	.15
❑ 243	Larry Ely	.30	.15
❑ 244	Richard Caster	.30	.15
❑ 245	Joe Greene	5.00	2.00
❑ 246	Larry Schreiber	.30	.15
❑ 247	Terry Schmidt	.30	.15
❑ 248	Jerrel Wilson	.30	.15
❑ 249	Marty Domres	.30	.15
❑ 250	Isaac Curtis	.75	.30
❑ 251	Harold McLinton	.30	.15
❑ 252	Fred Dryer	1.50	.60
❑ 253	Bill Lenkaitis	.30	.15
❑ 254	Don Hardeman	.30	.15
❑ 255	Bob Griese	4.00	2.00
❑ 256	Oscar Roan RC	.30	.15
❑ 257	Randy Gradishar RC	2.50	1.25
❑ 258	Bob Thomas RC	.30	.15
❑ 259	Joe Owens	.30	.15
❑ 260	Cliff Harris	1.50	.60
❑ 261	Frank Lewis	.30	.15
❑ 262	Mike McCoy DT	.30	.15
❑ 263	Rickey Young RC	.30	.15
❑ 264	Brian Kelley RC	.30	.15
❑ 265	Charlie Sanders	.75	.30
❑ 266	Jim Hart	1.50	.60
❑ 267	Greg Gantt	.30	.15
❑ 268	John Ward	.30	.15
❑ 269	Al Beauchamp	.30	.15
❑ 270	Jack Tatum	1.50	.60
❑ 271	Jim Lash	.30	.15
❑ 272	Diron Talbert	.30	.15
❑ 273	Checklist 265-396	3.00	1.50
❑ 274	Steve Spurrier	8.00	3.00
❑ 275	Greg Pruitt	1.50	.60
❑ 276	Jim Mitchell TE	.30	.15
❑ 277	Jack Rudnay	.30	.15
❑ 278	Freddie Solomon RC	.75	.30
❑ 279	Frank LeMaster	.30	.15
❑ 280	Wally Chambers	.30	.15
❑ 281	Mike Collier	.30	.15
❑ 282	Clarence Williams	.30	.15
❑ 283	Mitch Hoopes	.30	.15
❑ 284	Ron Bolton	.30	.15
❑ 285	Harold Jackson	1.50	.60
❑ 286	Greg Landry	.75	.30
❑ 287	Tony Greene	.30	.15
❑ 288	Howard Stevens	.30	.15
❑ 289	Roy Jefferson	.30	.15
❑ 290	Jim Bakken	.30	.15
❑ 291	Doug Sutherland	.30	.15
❑ 292	Marvin Cobb RC	.30	.15
❑ 293	Mack Alston	.30	.15
❑ 294	Rod McNeill	.30	.15
❑ 295	Gene Upshaw	1.50	.60
❑ 296	Dave Gallagher	.30	.15
❑ 297	Larry Ball	.30	.15
❑ 298	Ron Howard	.30	.15
❑ 299	Don Strock RC	1.50	.60
❑ 300	O.J.Simpson	8.00	4.00
❑ 301	Ray Mansfield	.30	.15
❑ 302	Larry Marshall	.30	.15
❑ 303	Dick Himes	.30	.15
❑ 304	Ray Wersching RC	.30	.15
❑ 305	John Riggins	4.00	2.00
❑ 306	Bob Parsons	.30	.15
❑ 307	Ray Brown DB	.30	.15
❑ 308	Len Dawson	3.00	1.50
❑ 309	Andy Maurer	.30	.15
❑ 310	Jack Youngblood	1.50	.60
❑ 311	Essex Johnson	.30	.15
❑ 312	Stan White	.30	.15
❑ 313	Drew Pearson	5.00	2.00
❑ 314	Rockne Freitas	.30	.15
❑ 315	Mercury Morris	1.50	.60
❑ 316	Willie Alexander	.30	.15
❑ 317	Paul Warfield	3.00	1.50
❑ 318	Bob Chandler	.75	.30
❑ 319	Bobby Walden	.30	.15
❑ 320	Riley Odoms	.75	.30
❑ 321	Mike Boryla	.30	.15
❑ 322	Bruce Van Dyke	.30	.15
❑ 323	Pete Banaszak	.30	.15
❑ 324	Darryl Stingley	1.50	.60
❑ 325	John Mendenhall	.30	.15
❑ 326	Dan Dierdorf	2.00	.75
❑ 327	Bruce Taylor	.30	.15
❑ 328	Don McCauley	.30	.15
❑ 329	John Reaves UER	.30	.15
❑ 330	Chris Hanburger	.75	.30
❑ 331	NFC Champs/Staubach	3.00	1.50
❑ 332	AFC Champs/F.Harris	2.00	.75
❑ 333	Super Bowl X/Bradshaw	2.50	1.25
❑ 334	Godwin Turk	.30	.15
❑ 335	Dick Anderson	.75	.30
❑ 336	Woody Green	.30	.15
❑ 337	Pat Curran	.30	.15
❑ 338	Council Rudolph	.30	.15
❑ 339	Joe Lavender	.30	.15
❑ 340	John Gilliam	.75	.30
❑ 341	Steve Furness RC	.75	.30
❑ 342	D.D. Lewis	.75	.30
❑ 343	Duane Carrell	.30	.15
❑ 344	Jon Morris	.30	.15
❑ 345	John Brockington	.75	.30
❑ 346	Mike Phipps	.75	.30
❑ 347	Lyle Blackwood RC	.30	.15
❑ 348	Julius Adams	.30	.15
❑ 349	Terry Hermeling	.30	.15
❑ 350	Rolland Lawrence RC	.30	.15
❑ 351	Glenn Doughty	.30	.15
❑ 352	Doug Swift	.30	.15
❑ 353	Mike Strachan	.30	.15
❑ 354	Craig Morton	1.50	.60
❑ 355	George Blanda	5.00	2.50
❑ 356	Garry Puetz	.30	.15

❑	357 Carl Mauck	.30	.15
❑	358 Walt Patulski	.30	.15
❑	359 Stu Voigt	.30	.15
❑	360 Fred Carr	.30	.15
❑	361 Po James	.30	.15
❑	362 Otis Taylor	1.50	.60
❑	363 Jeff West	.30	.15
❑	364 Gary Huff	.75	.30
❑	365 Dwight White	.75	.30
❑	366 Dan Ryczek	.30	.15
❑	367 Jon Keyworth RC	.30	.15
❑	368 Mel Renfro	1.50	.60
❑	369 Bruce Coslet RC	1.50	.60
❑	370 Len Hauss	.30	.15
❑	371 Rick Volk	.30	.15
❑	372 Howard Twilley	.75	.30
❑	373 Cullen Bryant RC	.75	.30
❑	374 Bob Babich	.30	.15
❑	375 Herman Weaver	.30	.15
❑	376 Steve Grogan RC	3.00	1.25
❑	377 Bubba Smith	1.50	.60
❑	378 Burgess Owens	.30	.15
❑	379 Al Matthews	.30	.15
❑	380 Art Shell	1.50	.60
❑	381 Larry Brown	.30	.15
❑	382 Horst Muhlmann	.30	.15
❑	383 Ahmad Rashad	2.50	1.25
❑	384 Bobby Maples	.30	.15
❑	385 Jim Marshall	1.50	.60
❑	386 Joe Dawkins	.30	.15
❑	387 Dennis Partee	.30	.15
❑	388 Eddie McMillan RC	.30	.15
❑	389 Randy Johnson	.30	.15
❑	390 Bob Kuechenberg	.30	.15
❑	391 Rufus Mayes	.30	.15
❑	392 Lloyd Mumphord	.30	.15
❑	393 Ike Harris	.30	.15
❑	394 Dave Hampton	.30	.15
❑	395 Roger Staubach	20.00	10.00
❑	396 Doug Buffone	.30	.15
❑	397 Howard Fest	.30	.15
❑	398 Wayne Mulligan	.30	.15
❑	399 Bill Bradley	.75	.30
❑	400 Chuck Foreman	1.50	.60
❑	401 Jack Snow	.75	.30
❑	402 Bob Howard	.30	.15
❑	403 John Matuszak	1.50	.60
❑	404 Bill Munson	.75	.30
❑	405 Andy Russell	.75	.30
❑	406 Skip Butler	.30	.15
❑	407 Hugh McKinnis	.30	.15
❑	408 Bob Penchion	.30	.15
❑	409 Mike Bass	.30	.15
❑	410 George Kunz	.30	.15
❑	411 Ron Pritchard	.30	.15
❑	412 Barry Smith	.30	.15
❑	413 Norm Bulaich	.30	.15
❑	414 Marv Bateman	.30	.15
❑	415 Ken Stabler	12.00	6.00
❑	416 Conrad Dobler	.75	.30
❑	417 Bob Tucker	.75	.30
❑	418 Gene Washington 49er	.75	.30
❑	419 Ed Marinaro	1.50	.60
❑	420 Jack Ham	4.00	2.00
❑	421 Jim Turner	.30	.15
❑	422 Chris Fletcher	.30	.15
❑	423 Carl Barzilauskas	.30	.15
❑	424 Robert Brazile RC	1.50	.60
❑	425 Harold Carmichael	2.00	.75
❑	426 Ron Jaworski RC	5.00	2.00
❑	427 Ed Too Tall Jones RC	20.00	10.00
❑	428 Larry McCarren	.30	.15
❑	429 Mike Thomas RC	.30	.15
❑	430 Joe DeLamielleure	1.50	.60
❑	431 Tom Blanchard	.30	.15
❑	432 Ron Carpenter	.30	.15
❑	433 Levi Johnson	.30	.15
❑	434 Sam Cunningham	.75	.30
❑	435 Garo Yepremian	.75	.30
❑	436 Mike Livingston	.30	.15
❑	437 Larry Csonka	4.00	2.00
❑	438 Doug Dieken	.75	.30
❑	439 Bill Lueck	.30	.15
❑	440 Tom MacLeod	.30	.15
❑	441 Mick Tingelhoff	.75	.30
❑	442 Terry Hanratty	.75	.30
❑	443 Mike Siani	.30	.15
❑	444 Dwight Harrison	.30	.15
❑	445 Jim Otis	.75	.30
❑	446 Jack Reynolds	.75	.30
❑	447 Jean Fugett RC	.75	.30
❑	448 Dave Beverly	.30	.15
❑	449 Bernard Jackson RC	.30	.15
❑	450 Charley Taylor	2.00	.75
❑	451 Atlanta Falcons CL	2.00	.75
❑	452 Baltimore Colts CL	2.00	.75
❑	453 Buffalo Bills CL	2.00	.75
❑	454 Chicago Bears CL	2.00	.75
❑	455 Cincinnati Bengals CL	2.00	.75
❑	456 Cleveland Browns CL	2.00	.75
❑	457 Dallas Cowboys CL	2.00	.75
❑	458 Denver Broncos CL UER	2.00	.75
❑	459 Detroit Lions CL	2.00	.75
❑	460 Green Bay Packers CL	2.00	.75
❑	461 Houston Oilers CL	2.00	.75
❑	462 Kansas City Chiefs CL	2.00	.75
❑	463 Los Angeles Rams CL	2.00	.75
❑	464 Miami Dolphins CL	2.00	.75
❑	465 Minnesota Vikings CL	2.00	.75
❑	466 New England Patriots CL	2.00	.75
❑	467 New Orleans Saints CL	2.00	.75
❑	468 New York Giants CL	2.00	.75
❑	469 New York Jets CL	2.00	.75
❑	470 Oakland Raiders CL	2.00	.75
❑	471 Philadelphia Eagles CL	2.00	.75
❑	472 Pittsburgh Steelers CL	2.00	.75
❑	473 St. Louis Cardinals CL	2.00	.75
❑	474 San Diego Chargers CL	2.00	.75
❑	475 San Francisco 49ers CL	2.00	.75
❑	476 Seattle Seahawks CL	2.00	.75
❑	477 Tampa Bay Buccaneers CL	2.00	.75
❑	478 Washington Redskins CL	2.00	.75
❑	479 Fred Cox	.30	.15
❑	480 Mel Blount	6.00	3.00
❑	481 John Bunting RC	.75	.30
❑	482 Ken Mendenhall	.30	.15
❑	483 Will Harrell	.30	.15
❑	484 Marlin Briscoe	.30	.15
❑	485 Archie Manning	1.50	.60
❑	486 Tody Smith	.30	.15
❑	487 George Hunt	.30	.15
❑	488 Roscoe Word	.30	.15
❑	489 Paul Seymour	.30	.15
❑	490 Lee Roy Jordan	1.50	.60
❑	491 Chip Myers	.30	.15
❑	492 Norm Evans	.30	.15
❑	493 Jim Bertelsen	.30	.15
❑	494 Mark Moseley	.75	.30
❑	495 George Buehler	.30	.15
❑	496 Charlie Hall	.30	.15
❑	497 Marvin Upshaw	.30	.15
❑	498 Tom Banks RC	.30	.15
❑	499 Randy Vataha	.30	.15
❑	500 Fran Tarkenton	6.00	3.00
❑	501 Mike Wagner	.75	.30
❑	502 Art Malone	.30	.15
❑	503 Fred Cook	.30	.15
❑	504 Rich McGeorge	.30	.15
❑	505 Ken Burrough	.75	.30
❑	506 Nick Mike-Mayer	.30	.15
❑	507 Checklist 397-528	3.00	1.50
❑	508 Steve Owens	.75	.30
❑	509 Brad Van Pelt RC	.30	.15
❑	510 Ken Riley	.75	.30
❑	511 Art Thoms	.30	.15
❑	512 Ed Bell	.30	.15
❑	513 Tom Wittum	.30	.15
❑	514 Jim Braxton	.30	.15
❑	515 Nick Buoniconti	1.50	.60
❑	516 Brian Sipe RC	6.00	2.50
❑	517 Jim Lynch	.30	.15
❑	518 Prentice McCray	.30	.15
❑	519 Tom Dempsey	.30	.15
❑	520 Mel Gray	.75	.30
❑	521 Nate Wright	.30	.15
❑	522 Rocky Bleier	6.00	3.00
❑	523 Dennis Johnson RC	.30	.15
❑	524 Jerry Sisemore	.30	.15
❑	525 Bert Jones	.30	.15
❑	526 Perry Smith	.30	.15
❑	527 Blaine Nye	.30	.15
❑	528 Bob Moore !	1.50	.60

1977 Topps

❑	COMPLETE SET (528)	250.00	125.00
❑	1 K.Stabler/J.Harris LL !	2.50	1.25
❑	2 Drew Pearson/M.Lane LL	1.00	.40
❑	3 W.Payton/Simpson LL	10.00	5.00
❑	4 Scoring Leaders	.50	.20
❑	5 Interception Leaders	.50	.20
❑	6 Punting Leaders	.25	.10
❑	7 Mike Phipps	.50	.20
❑	8 Rick Volk	.25	.10
❑	9 Steve Furness	.50	.20
❑	10 Isaac Curtis	.50	.20
❑	11 Nate Wright	.50	.20
❑	12 Jean Fugett	.25	.10
❑	13 Ken Mendenhall	.25	.10
❑	14 Sam Adams OL	.25	.10
❑	15 Charlie Waters	1.00	.40
❑	16 Bill Stanfill	.25	.10
❑	17 John Holland	.25	.10
❑	18 Pat Haden RC	2.00	.75
❑	19 Bob Young	.25	.10
❑	20 Wally Chambers	.25	.10
❑	21 Lawrence Gaines	.25	.10
❑	22 Larry McCarren	.25	.10
❑	23 Horst Muhlmann	.25	.10
❑	24 Phil Villapiano	.50	.20
❑	25 Greg Pruitt	.50	.20
❑	26 Ron Howard	.25	.10
❑	27 Craig Morton	1.00	.40
❑	28 Rufus Mayes	.25	.10
❑	29 Lee Roy Selmon RC UER	12.00	6.00
❑	30 Ed White	.50	.20
❑	31 Harold McLinton	.25	.10
❑	32 Glenn Doughty	.25	.10
❑	33 Bob Kuechenberg	1.00	.40
❑	34 Duane Carrell	.25	.10
❑	35 Riley Odoms	.25	.10
❑	36 Bobby Scott	.25	.10
❑	37 Nick Mike-Mayer	.25	.10
❑	38 Bill Lenkaitis	.25	.10
❑	39 Roland Harper	.50	.20
❑	40 Tommy Hart	.25	.10
❑	41 Mike Sensibaugh	.25	.10
❑	42 Rusty Jackson	.25	.10
❑	43 Levi Johnson	.25	.10
❑	44 Mike McCoy DT	.25	.10
❑	45 Roger Staubach	20.00	10.00
❑	46 Fred Cox	.25	.10
❑	47 Bob Babich	.25	.10
❑	48 Reggie McKenzie	.50	.20
❑	49 Dave Jennings	.25	.10
❑	50 Mike Haynes RC	10.00	4.00
❑	51 Larry Brown	.50	.20
❑	52 Marvin Cobb	.25	.10
❑	53 Fred Cook	.25	.10
❑	54 Freddie Solomon	.50	.20
❑	55 John Riggins	2.50	1.25
❑	56 John Bunting	.50	.20
❑	57 Ray Wersching	.50	.20
❑	58 Mike Livingston	.25	.10
❑	59 Billy Johnson	.50	.20
❑	60 Mike Wagner	.25	.10
❑	61 Waymond Bryant	.25	.10
❑	62 Jim Otis	.50	.20
❑	63 Ed Galigher	.25	.10
❑	64 Randy Vataha	.25	.10
❑	65 Jim Zorn RC	4.00	1.50
❑	66 Jon Keyworth	.25	.10
❑	67 Checklist 1-132	2.00	.75

❑ 68 Henry Childs .25 .10
❑ 69 Thom Darden .25 .10
❑ 70 George Kunz .25 .10
❑ 71 Lenvil Elliott .25 .10
❑ 72 Curtis Johnson .25 .10
❑ 73 Doug Van Horn .25 .10
❑ 74 Joe Theismann 4.00 2.00
❑ 75 Dwight White .50 .20
❑ 76 Scott Laidlaw .25 .10
❑ 77 Monte Johnson .25 .10
❑ 78 Dave Beverly .25 .10
❑ 79 Jim Mitchell TE .25 .10
❑ 80 Jack Youngblood 1.00 .40
❑ 81 Mel Gray .50 .20
❑ [illegible]
❑ 83 John Hadl .50 .20
❑ 84 Matt Blair RC 1.00 .40
❑ 85 Charlie Sanders .60 .25
❑ 86 Noah Jackson .25 .10
❑ 87 Ed Marinaro .50 .20
❑ 88 Bob Howard .25 .10
❑ 89 John McDaniel .25 .10
❑ 90 Dan Dierdorf 1.50 .60
❑ 91 Mark Moseley .50 .20
❑ 92 Cleo Miller .25 .10
❑ 93 Andre Tillman .25 .10
❑ 94 Bruce Taylor .25 .10
❑ 95 Bert Jones 1.00 .40
❑ 96 Anthony Davis RC 1.00 .40
❑ 97 Don Goode .25 .10
❑ 98 Ray Rhodes RC 6.00 3.00
❑ 99 Mike Webster RC 12.00 6.00
❑ 100 O.J.Simpson 6.00 3.00
❑ 101 Doug Plank RC .25 .10
❑ 102 Efren Herrera .50 .20
❑ 103 Charlie Smith WR .25 .10
❑ 104 Carlos Brown RC 1.00 .40
❑ 105 Jim Marshall 1.00 .40
❑ 106 Paul Naumoff .25 .10
❑ 107 Walter White .25 .10
❑ 108 John Cappelletti RC 3.00 1.25
❑ 109 Chip Myers .25 .10
❑ 110 Ken Stabler 10.00 5.00
❑ 111 Joe Ehrmann .25 .10
❑ 112 Rick Engles .25 .10
❑ 113 Jack Dolbin RC .25 .10
❑ 114 Ron Bolton .25 .10
❑ 115 Mike Thomas .25 .10
❑ 116 Mike Fuller .25 .10
❑ 117 John Hill .25 .10
❑ 118 Richard Todd RC 1.00 .40
❑ 119 Duriel Harris RC 1.00 .40
❑ 120 John James .25 .10
❑ 121 Lionel Antoine .25 .10
❑ 122 John Skorupan .25 .10
❑ 123 Skip Butler .25 .10
❑ 124 Bob Tucker .25 .10
❑ 125 Paul Krause 1.00 .40
❑ 126 Dave Hampton .25 .10
❑ 127 Tom Wittum .25 .10
❑ 128 Gary Huff .50 .20
❑ 129 Emmitt Thomas .25 .10
❑ 130 Drew Pearson 2.00 .75
❑ 131 Ron Saul .25 .10
❑ 132 Steve Niehaus .25 .10
❑ 133 Fred Carr 1.00 .40
❑ 134 Norm Bulaich .25 .10
❑ 135 Bob Trumpy .50 .20
❑ 136 Greg Landry .50 .20
❑ 137 George Buehler .25 .10
❑ 138 Reggie Rucker .50 .20
❑ 139 Julius Adams .25 .10
❑ 140 Jack Ham 2.50 1.25
❑ 141 Wayne Morris RC .25 .10
❑ 142 Marv Bateman .25 .10
❑ 143 Bobby Maples .25 .10
❑ 144 Harold Carmichael 1.00 .40
❑ 145 Bob Avellini .50 .20
❑ 146 Harry Carson RC 3.00 1.50
❑ 147 Lawrence Pillers .25 .10
❑ 148 Ed Williams RC .25 .10
❑ 149 Dan Pastorini .50 .20
❑ 150 Ron Yary 1.00 .40
❑ 151 Joe Lavender .25 .10
❑ 152 Pat McInally RC .50 .20
❑ 153 Lloyd Mumphord .25 .10
❑ 154 Cullen Bryant .50 .20
❑ 155 Willie Lanier 1.00 .40
❑ 156 Gene Washington 49er .50 .20
❑ 157 Scott Hunter .25 .10
❑ 158 Jim Merlo .25 .10
❑ 159 Randy Grossman .50 .20
❑ 160 Blaine Nye .25 .10
❑ 161 Ike Harris .25 .10
❑ 162 Doug Dieken .25 .10
❑ 163 Guy Morriss .25 .10
❑ 164 Bob Parsons .25 .10
❑ 165 Steve Grogan 1.00 .40
❑ 166 John Brockington .50 .20
❑ 167 Charlie Joiner 2.50 1.25
❑ 168 Ron Carpenter .25 .10
❑ [illegible]
❑ 170 Chris Hanburger .25 .10
❑ 171 Roosevelt Leaks RC .50 .20
❑ 172 Larry Little 1.00 .40
❑ 173 John Matuszak .50 .20
❑ 174 Joe Ferguson .50 .20
❑ 175 Brad Van Pelt .50 .20
❑ 176 Dexter Bussey RC .50 .20
❑ 177 Steve Largent RC 40.00 20.00
❑ 178 Dewey Selmon .50 .20
❑ 179 Randy Gradishar 1.00 .40
❑ 180 Mel Blount 3.00 1.50
❑ 181 Dan Neal .25 .10
❑ 182 Rich Szaro .25 .10
❑ 183 Mike Boryla .25 .10
❑ 184 Steve Jones .25 .10
❑ 185 Paul Warfield 2.50 1.25
❑ 186 Greg Buttle RC .25 .10
❑ 187 Rich McGeorge .25 .10
❑ 188 Leon Gray RC .50 .20
❑ 189 John Shinners .25 .10
❑ 190 Toni Linhart .25 .10
❑ 191 Robert Miller .25 .10
❑ 192 Jake Scott .25 .10
❑ 193 Jon Morris .25 .10
❑ 194 Randy Crowder .25 .10
❑ 195 Lynn Swann UER 18.00 10.00
❑ 196 Marsh White .25 .10
❑ 197 Rod Perry RC 1.00 .40
❑ 198 Willie Hall .25 .10
❑ 199 Mike Hartenstine .25 .10
❑ 200 Jim Bakken .25 .10
❑ 201 Atlanta Falcons CL UER 1.25 .50
❑ 202 Baltimore Colts CL 1.25 .50
❑ 203 Buffalo Bills CL 1.25 .50
❑ 204 Chicago Bears CL 1.25 .50
❑ 205 Cincinnati Bengals CL 1.25 .50
❑ 206 Cleveland Browns CL 1.25 .50
❑ 207 Dallas Cowboys CL 1.25 .50
❑ 208 Denver Broncos CL 1.25 .50
❑ 209 Detroit Lions CL 1.25 .50
❑ 210 Green Bay Packers CL 1.25 .50
❑ 211 Houston Oilers CL 1.25 .50
❑ 212 Kansas City Chiefs CL 1.25 .50
❑ 213 Los Angeles Rams CL 1.25 .50
❑ 214 Miami Dolphins CL 1.25 .50
❑ 215 Minnesota Vikings CL 1.25 .50
❑ 216 New England Patriots CL 1.25 .50
❑ 217 New Orleans Saints CL 1.25 .50
❑ 218 New York Giants CL 1.25 .50
❑ 219 New York Jets CL 1.25 .50
❑ 220 Oakland Raiders CL 1.25 .50
❑ 221 Philadelphia Eagles CL 1.25 .50
❑ 222 Pittsburgh Steelers CL 1.25 .50
❑ 223 St. Louis Cardinals CL 1.25 .50
❑ 224 San Diego Chargers CL 1.25 .50
❑ 225 San Francisco 49ers CL 1.25 .50
❑ 226 Seattle Seahawks CL 1.25 .50
❑ 227 Tampa Bay Buccaneers CL 1.25 .50
❑ 228 Washington Redskins CL 1.25 .50
❑ 229 Sam Cunningham .50 .20
❑ 230 Alan Page 1.00 .40
❑ 231 Eddie Brown S .25 .10
❑ 232 Stan White .25 .10
❑ 233 Vern Den Herder .25 .10
❑ 234 Clarence Davis .25 .10
❑ 235 Ken Anderson 1.00 .40
❑ 236 Karl Chandler .25 .10
❑ 237 Will Harrell .25 .10
❑ 238 Clarence Scott .25 .10
❑ 239 Bo Rather .25 .10
❑ 240 Robert Brazile .50 .20
❑ 241 Bob Bell .25 .10
❑ 242 Rolland Lawrence .25 .10
❑ 243 Tom Sullivan .25 .10
❑ 244 Larry Brunson .25 .10
❑ 245 Terry Bradshaw 20.00 10.00
❑ 246 Rich Saul .25 .10
❑ 247 Cleveland Elam .25 .10
❑ 248 Don Woods .25 .10
❑ 249 Bruce Laird .25 .10
❑ 250 Coy Bacon .50 .20
❑ 251 Russ Francis 1.00 .40
❑ 252 Jim Braxton .25 .10
❑ 253 Perry Smith .25 .10
❑ 254 Jerome Barkum .25 .10
❑ 255 Garo Yepremian .50 .20
❑ [illegible]
❑ 257 Tony Galbreath RC .50 .20
❑ 258 Troy Archer .25 .10
❑ 259 Brian Sipe 1.00 .40
❑ 260 Billy Joe DuPree .50 .20
❑ 261 Bobby Walden .25 .10
❑ 262 Larry Marshall .25 .10
❑ 263 Ted Fritsch Jr. .25 .10
❑ 264 Larry Hand .25 .10
❑ 265 Tom Mack 1.00 .40
❑ 266 Ed Bradley .25 .10
❑ 267 Pat Leahy .50 .20
❑ 268 Louis Carter .25 .10
❑ 269 Archie Griffin RC 6.00 3.00
❑ 270 Art Shell 1.00 .40
❑ 271 Stu Voigt .25 .10
❑ 272 Prentice McCray .25 .10
❑ 273 MacArthur Lane .25 .10
❑ 274 Dan Fouts 6.00 3.00
❑ 275 Charle Young .50 .20
❑ 276 Wilbur Jackson RC .25 .10
❑ 277 John Hicks .25 .10
❑ 278 Nat Moore 1.00 .40
❑ 279 Virgil Livers .25 .10
❑ 280 Curley Culp .50 .20
❑ 281 Rocky Bleier 2.50 1.25
❑ 282 John Zook .25 .10
❑ 283 Tom DeLeone .25 .10
❑ 284 Danny White RC 10.00 5.00
❑ 285 Otis Armstrong .50 .20
❑ 286 Larry Walton .25 .10
❑ 287 Jim Carter .25 .10
❑ 288 Don McCauley .25 .10
❑ 289 Frank Grant .25 .10
❑ 290 Roger Wehrli .60 .25
❑ 291 Mick Tingelhoff .50 .20
❑ 292 Bernard Jackson .25 .10
❑ 293 Tom Owen RC .25 .10
❑ 294 Mike Esposito .25 .10
❑ 295 Fred Biletnikoff 2.50 1.25
❑ 296 Revie Sorey RC .25 .10
❑ 297 John McMakin .25 .10
❑ 298 Dan Ryczek .25 .10
❑ 299 Wayne Moore .25 .10
❑ 300 Franco Harris 4.00 2.00
❑ 301 Rick Upchurch RC 1.00 .40
❑ 302 Jim Stienke .25 .10
❑ 303 Charlie Davis .25 .10
❑ 304 Don Cockroft .25 .10
❑ 305 Ken Burrough .50 .20
❑ 306 Clark Gaines .25 .10
❑ 307 Bobby Douglass .25 .10
❑ 308 Ralph Perretta .25 .10
❑ 309 Wally Hilgenberg .25 .10
❑ 310 Monte Jackson RC .50 .20
❑ 311 Chris Bahr RC .50 .20
❑ 312 Jim Cheyunski .25 .10
❑ 313 Mike Patrick .25 .10
❑ 314 Ed Too Tall Jones 5.00 2.50
❑ 315 Bill Bradley .25 .10
❑ 316 Benny Malone .25 .10
❑ 317 Paul Seymour .25 .10
❑ 318 Jim Laslavic .25 .10
❑ 319 Frank Lewis .50 .20
❑ 320 Ray Guy 1.00 .40
❑ 321 Allan Ellis .25 .10
❑ 322 Conrad Dobler .50 .20
❑ 323 Chester Marcol .25 .10
❑ 324 Doug Kotar .25 .10
❑ 325 Lemar Parrish .50 .20
❑ 326 Steve Holden .25 .10
❑ 327 Jeff Van Note .50 .20
❑ 328 Howard Stevens .25 .10

❑ 329 Brad Dusek .50 .20
❑ 330 Joe DeLamielleure 1.00 .40
❑ 331 Jim Plunkett 1.00 .40
❑ 332 Checklist 265-396 2.00 .75
❑ 333 Lou Piccone .25 .10
❑ 334 Ray Hamilton .25 .10
❑ 335 Jan Stenerud 1.00 .40
❑ 336 Jeris White .25 .10
❑ 337 Sherman Smith RC .25 .10
❑ 338 Dave Green .25 .10
❑ 339 Terry Schmidt .25 .10
❑ 340 Sammie White RC 1.00 .40
❑ 341 Jon Kolb RC .25 .10
❑ 342 Randy White 8.00 4.00
❑ 343 Bob Klein .25 .10
❑ 344 Bob Kowalkowski .25 .10
❑ 345 Terry Metcalf .50 .20
❑ 346 Joe Danelo .25 .10
❑ 347 Ken Payne .25 .10
❑ 348 Neal Craig .25 .10
❑ 349 Dennis Johnson .25 .10
❑ 350 Bill Bergey .50 .20
❑ 351 Raymond Chester .25 .10
❑ 352 Bob Matheson .25 .10
❑ 353 Mike Kadish .25 .10
❑ 354 Mark Van Eeghen RC 1.00 .40
❑ 355 L.C.Greenwood 1.00 .40
❑ 356 Sam Hunt .25 .10
❑ 357 Darrell Austin .25 .10
❑ 358 Jim Turner .25 .10
❑ 359 Ahmad Rashad 2.00 .75
❑ 360 Walter Payton 40.00 15.00
❑ 361 Mark Arneson .25 .10
❑ 362 Jerrel Wilson .25 .10
❑ 363 Steve Bartkowski 1.00 .40
❑ 364 John Watson .25 .10
❑ 365 Ken Riley .50 .20
❑ 366 Gregg Bingham .25 .10
❑ 367 Golden Richards .50 .20
❑ 368 Clyde Powers .25 .10
❑ 369 Diron Talbert .25 .10
❑ 370 Lydell Mitchell .50 .20
❑ 371 Bob Jackson .25 .10
❑ 372 Jim Mandich .25 .10
❑ 373 Frank LeMaster .25 .10
❑ 374 Benny Ricardo .25 .10
❑ 375 Lawrence McCutcheon .50 .20
❑ 376 Lynn Dickey .50 .20
❑ 377 Phil Wise .25 .10
❑ 378 Tony McGee DT .25 .10
❑ 379 Norm Thompson .25 .10
❑ 380 Dave Casper RC 4.00 1.50
❑ 381 Glen Edwards .25 .10
❑ 382 Bob Thomas .25 .10
❑ 383 Bob Chandler .50 .20
❑ 384 Rickey Young .50 .20
❑ 385 Carl Eller 1.00 .40
❑ 386 Lyle Alzado 1.00 .40
❑ 387 John Leypoldt .25 .10
❑ 388 Gordon Bell .25 .10
❑ 389 Mike Bragg .25 .10
❑ 390 Jim Langer 1.00 .40
❑ 391 Vern Holland .25 .10
❑ 392 Nelson Munsey .25 .10
❑ 393 Mack Mitchell .25 .10
❑ 394 Tony Adams RC .25 .10
❑ 395 Preston Pearson .50 .20
❑ 396 Emanuel Zanders .25 .10
❑ 397 Vince Papale RC 20.00 8.00
❑ 398 Joe Fields RC .50 .20
❑ 399 Craig Clemons .25 .10
❑ 400 Fran Tarkenton 5.00 2.50
❑ 401 Andy Johnson .25 .10
❑ 402 Willie Buchanon .25 .10
❑ 403 Pat Curran .25 .10
❑ 404 Ray Jarvis .25 .10
❑ 405 Joe Greene 2.50 1.25
❑ 406 Bill Simpson .25 .10
❑ 407 Ronnie Coleman .25 .10
❑ 408 J.K. McKay RC .50 .20
❑ 409 Pat Fischer .50 .20
❑ 410 John Dutton .50 .20
❑ 411 Boobie Clark .25 .10
❑ 412 Pat Tilley RC 1.00 .40
❑ 413 Don Strock .50 .20
❑ 414 Brian Kelley .25 .10
❑ 415 Gene Upshaw 1.00 .40
❑ 416 Mike Montler .25 .10
❑ 417 Checklist 397-528 2.00 .75
❑ 418 John Gilliam .25 .10
❑ 419 Brent McClanahan .25 .10
❑ 420 Jerry Sherk .25 .10
❑ 421 Roy Gerela .25 .10
❑ 422 Tim Fox .50 .20
❑ 423 John Ebersole .25 .10
❑ 424 James Scott RC .25 .10
❑ 425 Delvin Williams RC .50 .20
❑ 426 Spike Jones .25 .10
❑ 427 Harvey Martin 1.00 .40
❑ 428 Don Herrmann .25 .10
❑ 429 Calvin Hill .50 .20
❑ 430 Isiah Robertson .25 .10
❑ 431 Tony Greene .25 .10
❑ 432 Bob Johnson .25 .10
❑ 433 Lem Barney 1.00 .40
❑ 434 Eric Torkelson .25 .10
❑ 435 John Mendenhall .25 .10
❑ 436 Larry Seiple .50 .20
❑ 437 Art Kuehn .25 .10
❑ 438 John Vella .25 .10
❑ 439 Greg Latta .25 .10
❑ 440 Roger Carr .50 .20
❑ 441 Doug Sutherland .25 .10
❑ 442 Mike Kruczek RC .25 .10
❑ 443 Steve Zabel .25 .10
❑ 444 Mike Pruitt RC 1.00 .40
❑ 445 Harold Jackson .50 .20
❑ 446 George Jakowenko .25 .10
❑ 447 John Fitzgerald .25 .10
❑ 448 Carey Joyce .25 .10
❑ 449 Jim LeClair .25 .10
❑ 450 Ken Houston 1.00 .40
❑ 451 Steve Grogan RB .50 .20
❑ 452 Jim Marshall RB .50 .20
❑ 453 O.J.Simpson RB 2.50 1.25
❑ 454 Fran Tarkenton RB 3.00 1.50
❑ 455 Jim Zorn RB .50 .20
❑ 456 Robert Pratt .25 .10
❑ 457 Walker Gillette .25 .10
❑ 458 Charlie Hall .25 .10
❑ 459 Robert Newhouse .50 .20
❑ 460 John Hannah 1.00 .40
❑ 461 Ken Reaves .25 .10
❑ 462 Herman Weaver .25 .10
❑ 463 James Harris .50 .20
❑ 464 Howard Twilley .50 .20
❑ 465 Jeff Siemon .50 .20
❑ 466 John Outlaw .25 .10
❑ 467 Chuck Muncie RC 1.00 .40
❑ 468 Bob Moore .25 .10
❑ 469 Robert Woods .25 .10
❑ 470 Cliff Branch 2.00 .75
❑ 471 Johnnie Gray .25 .10
❑ 472 Don Hardeman .25 .10
❑ 473 Steve Ramsey .25 .10
❑ 474 Steve Mike-Mayer .25 .10
❑ 475 Gary Garrison .25 .10
❑ 476 Walter Johnson .25 .10
❑ 477 Neil Clabo .25 .10
❑ 478 Len Hauss .25 .10
❑ 479 Darryl Stingley .50 .20
❑ 480 Jack Lambert 8.00 4.00
❑ 481 Mike Adamle .50 .20
❑ 482 David Lee .25 .10
❑ 483 Tom Mullen .25 .10
❑ 484 Claude Humphrey .25 .10
❑ 485 Jim Hart 1.00 .40
❑ 486 Bobby Thompson RB .25 .10
❑ 487 Jack Rudnay .25 .10
❑ 488 Rich Sowells .25 .10
❑ 489 Reuben Gant .25 .10
❑ 490 Cliff Harris 1.00 .40
❑ 491 Bob Brown DT .25 .10
❑ 492 Don Nottingham .25 .10
❑ 493 Ron Jessie .25 .10
❑ 494 Otis Sistrunk .50 .20
❑ 495 Billy Kilmer .50 .20
❑ 496 Oscar Roan .25 .10
❑ 497 Bill Van Heusen .25 .10
❑ 498 Randy Logan .25 .10
❑ 499 John Smith .25 .10
❑ 500 Chuck Foreman .50 .20
❑ 501 J.T. Thomas .25 .10
❑ 502 Steve Schubert .25 .10
❑ 503 Mike Barnes .25 .10
❑ 504 J.V. Cain .25 .10
❑ 505 Larry Csonka 3.00 1.50
❑ 506 Elvin Bethea 1.00 .40
❑ 507 Ray Easterling .25 .10
❑ 508 Joe Reed .25 .10
❑ 509 Steve Odom .25 .10
❑ 510 Tommy Casanova .25 .10
❑ 511 Dave Dalby .25 .10
❑ 512 Richard Caster .25 .10
❑ 513 Fred Dryer 1.00 .40
❑ 514 Jeff Kinney .25 .10
❑ 515 Bob Griese 3.00 1.50
❑ 516 Butch Johnson RC 1.00 .40
❑ 517 Gerald Irons .25 .10
❑ 518 Don Calhoun .25 .10
❑ 519 Jack Gregory .25 .10
❑ 520 Tom Banks .25 .10
❑ 521 Bobby Bryant .25 .10
❑ 522 Reggie Harrison .25 .10
❑ 523 Terry Hermeling .25 .10
❑ 524 David Taylor .25 .10
❑ 525 Brian Baschnagel RC .50 .20
❑ 526 AFC Champ/Stabler 1.00 .40
❑ 527 NFC Championship .50 .20
❑ 528 Super Bowl XI 1.00 .40

1978 Topps

❑ COMPLETE SET (528) 150.00 80.00
❑ 1 Gary Huff HL ! 1.00 .40
❑ 2 Craig Morton HL 1.00 .40
❑ 3 Walter Payton HL 8.00 3.00
❑ 4 O.J.Simpson HL 2.00 .75
❑ 5 Fran Tarkenton HL 2.00 .75
❑ 6 Bob Thomas HL .20 .07
❑ 7 Joe Pisarcik .50 .20
❑ 8 Skip Thomas .20 .07
❑ 9 Roosevelt Leaks .20 .07
❑ 10 Ken Houston 1.00 .40
❑ 11 Tom Blanchard .20 .07
❑ 12 Jim Turner .20 .07
❑ 13 Tom DeLeone .20 .07
❑ 14 Jim LeClair .20 .07
❑ 15 Bob Avellini .50 .20
❑ 16 Tony McGee DT .20 .07
❑ 17 James Harris .50 .20
❑ 18 Terry Nelson .20 .07
❑ 19 Rocky Bleier 2.00 .75
❑ 20 Joe DeLamielleure 1.00 .40
❑ 21 Richard Caster .20 .07
❑ 22 A.J.Duhe RC 1.00 .40
❑ 23 John Outlaw .20 .07
❑ 24 Danny White 1.25 .50
❑ 25 Larry Csonka 2.50 1.00
❑ 26 David Hill RC .50 .20
❑ 27 Mark Arneson .20 .07
❑ 28 Jack Tatum .50 .20
❑ 29 Norm Thompson .20 .07
❑ 30 Sammie White .50 .20
❑ 31 Dennis Johnson .20 .07
❑ 32 Robin Earl .20 .07
❑ 33 Don Cockroft .20 .07
❑ 34 Bob Johnson .20 .07
❑ 35 John Hannah 1.00 .40
❑ 36 Scott Hunter .20 .07
❑ 37 Ken Burrough .50 .20
❑ 38 Wilbur Jackson .50 .20
❑ 39 Rich McGeorge .20 .07
❑ 40 Lyle Alzado 1.00 .40

❑ 41	John Ebersole	.20	.07
❑ 42	Gary Green RC	.20	.07
❑ 43	Art Kuehn	.20	.07
❑ 44	Glen Edwards	.50	.20
❑ 45	Lawrence McCutcheon	.50	.20
❑ 46	Duriel Harris	.20	.07
❑ 47	Rich Szaro	.20	.07
❑ 48	Mike Washington	.20	.07
❑ 49	Stan White	.20	.07
❑ 50	Dave Casper	1.00	.40
❑ 51	Len Hauss	.20	.07
❑ 52	James Scott	.20	.07
❑ 53	Brian Sipe	1.00	.40
❑ 54	Gary Shirk	.20	.07
❑ 55	[illegible]	1.00	[illegible]
❑ 56	Mike Patrick	.20	.07
❑ 57	Mario Clark	.20	.07
❑ 58	Jeff Siemon	.20	.07
❑ 59	Steve Mike-Mayer	.20	.07
❑ 60	Randy White	4.00	2.00
❑ 61	Darrell Austin	.20	.07
❑ 62	Tom Sullivan	.20	.07
❑ 63	Johnny Rodgers RC	1.00	.40
❑ 64	Ken Reaves	.20	.07
❑ 65	Terry Bradshaw	12.00	6.00
❑ 66	Fred Steinfort	.20	.07
❑ 67	Curley Culp	.50	.20
❑ 68	Ted Hendricks	1.00	.40
❑ 69	Raymond Chester	.20	.07
❑ 70	Jim Langer	1.00	.40
❑ 71	Calvin Hill	.50	.20
❑ 72	Mike Hartenstine	.20	.07
❑ 73	Gerald Irons	.20	.07
❑ 74	Billy Brooks	.50	.20
❑ 75	John Mendenhall	.20	.07
❑ 76	Andy Johnson	.20	.07
❑ 77	Tom Wittum	.20	.07
❑ 78	Lynn Dickey	.50	.20
❑ 79	Carl Eller	1.00	.40
❑ 80	Tom Mack	1.00	.40
❑ 81	Clark Gaines	.20	.07
❑ 82	Lem Barney	1.00	.40
❑ 83	Mike Montler	.20	.07
❑ 84	Jon Kolb	.20	.07
❑ 85	Bob Chandler	.50	.20
❑ 86	Robert Newhouse	.50	.20
❑ 87	Frank LeMaster	.20	.07
❑ 88	Jeff West	.20	.07
❑ 89	Lyle Blackwood	.50	.20
❑ 90	Gene Upshaw	1.00	.40
❑ 91	Frank Grant	.20	.07
❑ 92	Tom Hicks	.20	.07
❑ 93	Mike Pruitt	.50	.20
❑ 94	Chris Bahr	.20	.07
❑ 95	Russ Francis	.50	.20
❑ 96	Norris Thomas	.20	.07
❑ 97	Gary Barbaro RC	.50	.20
❑ 98	Jim Merlo	.20	.07
❑ 99	Karl Chandler	.20	.07
❑ 100	Fran Tarkenton	4.00	1.50
❑ 101	Abdul Salaam	.20	.07
❑ 102	Marv Kellum	.20	.07
❑ 103	Herman Weaver	.20	.07
❑ 104	Roy Gerela	.20	.07
❑ 105	Harold Jackson	.50	.20
❑ 106	Dewey Selmon	.50	.20
❑ 107	Checklist 1-132	1.00	.40
❑ 108	Clarence Davis	.20	.07
❑ 109	Robert Pratt	.20	.07
❑ 110	Harvey Martin	1.00	.40
❑ 111	Brad Dusek	.20	.07
❑ 112	Greg Latta	.20	.07
❑ 113	Tony Peters	.20	.07
❑ 114	Jim Braxton	.20	.07
❑ 115	Ken Riley	.50	.20
❑ 116	Steve Nelson	.20	.07
❑ 117	Rick Upchurch	.50	.20
❑ 118	Spike Jones	.20	.07
❑ 119	Doug Kotar	.20	.07
❑ 120	Bob Griese	2.50	1.00
❑ 121	Burgess Owens	.20	.07
❑ 122	Rolf Benirschke RC	.50	.20
❑ 123	Haskel Stanback RC	.20	.07
❑ 124	J.T. Thomas	.20	.07
❑ 125	Ahmad Rashad	1.50	.60
❑ 126	Rick Kane	.20	.07
❑ 127	Elvin Bethea	1.00	.40
❑ 128	Dave Dalby	.20	.07
❑ 129	Mike Barnes	.20	.07
❑ 130	Isiah Robertson	.20	.07
❑ 131	Jim Plunkett	1.00	.40
❑ 132	Allan Ellis	.20	.07
❑ 133	Mike Bragg	.20	.07
❑ 134	Bob Jackson	.20	.07
❑ 135	Coy Bacon	.20	.07
❑ 136	John Smith	.20	.07
❑ 137	Chuck Muncie	.50	.20
❑ 138	Johnnie Gray	.20	.07
❑ 139	Jimmy Robinson	.20	.07
❑ 140	Tom Banks	.20	.07
❑ 141	Marvin Powell RC	[illegible]	.07
❑ 142	Jerrel Wilson	.20	.07
❑ 143	Ron Howard	.20	.07
❑ 144	Rob Lytle RC	.50	.20
❑ 145	L.C.Greenwood	1.00	.40
❑ 146	Morris Owens	.20	.07
❑ 147	Joe Reed	.20	.07
❑ 148	Mike Kadish	.20	.07
❑ 149	Phil Villapiano	.50	.20
❑ 150	Lydell Mitchell	.50	.20
❑ 151	Randy Logan	.20	.07
❑ 152	Mike Williams RC	.20	.07
❑ 153	Jeff Van Note	.50	.20
❑ 154	Steve Schubert	.20	.07
❑ 155	Billy Kilmer	.50	.20
❑ 156	Boobie Clark	.20	.07
❑ 157	Charlie Hall	.20	.07
❑ 158	Raymond Clayborn RC	1.00	.40
❑ 159	Jack Gregory	.20	.07
❑ 160	Cliff Harris	1.00	.40
❑ 161	Joe Fields	.20	.07
❑ 162	Don Nottingham	.20	.07
❑ 163	Ed White	.50	.20
❑ 164	Toni Fritsch	.20	.07
❑ 165	Jack Lambert	4.00	2.00
❑ 166	NFC Champs/Staubach	1.50	.60
❑ 167	AFC Champs/Lytle	.50	.20
❑ 168	Super Bowl XII/Dorsett	3.00	1.50
❑ 169	Neal Colzie RC	.20	.07
❑ 170	Cleveland Elam	.20	.07
❑ 171	David Lee	.20	.07
❑ 172	Jim Otis	.20	.07
❑ 173	Archie Manning	1.00	.40
❑ 174	Jim Carter	.20	.07
❑ 175	Jean Fugett	.20	.07
❑ 176	Willie Parker C	.20	.07
❑ 177	Haven Moses	.50	.20
❑ 178	Horace King RC	.20	.07
❑ 179	Bob Thomas	.20	.07
❑ 180	Monte Jackson	.20	.07
❑ 181	Steve Zabel	.20	.07
❑ 182	John Fitzgerald	.20	.07
❑ 183	Mike Livingston	.20	.07
❑ 184	Larry Poole	.20	.07
❑ 185	Isaac Curtis	.50	.20
❑ 186	Chuck Ramsey	.20	.07
❑ 187	Bob Klein	.20	.07
❑ 188	Ray Rhodes	1.00	.40
❑ 189	Otis Sistrunk	.50	.20
❑ 190	Bill Bergey	.50	.20
❑ 191	Sherman Smith	.50	.20
❑ 192	Dave Green	.20	.07
❑ 193	Carl Mauck	.20	.07
❑ 194	Reggie Harrison	.20	.07
❑ 195	Roger Carr	.50	.20
❑ 196	Steve Bartkowski	1.00	.40
❑ 197	Ray Wersching	.20	.07
❑ 198	Willie Buchanon	.20	.07
❑ 199	Neil Clabo	.20	.07
❑ 200	Walter Payton UER	25.00	12.50
❑ 201	Sam Adams OL	.20	.07
❑ 202	Larry Gordon	.20	.07
❑ 203	Pat Tilley	.50	.20
❑ 204	Mack Mitchell	.20	.07
❑ 205	Ken Anderson	1.00	.40
❑ 206	Scott Dierking	.20	.07
❑ 207	Jack Rudnay	.20	.07
❑ 208	Jim Stienke	.20	.07
❑ 209	Bill Simpson	.20	.07
❑ 210	Errol Mann	.20	.07
❑ 211	Bucky Dilts	.20	.07
❑ 212	Reuben Gant	.20	.07
❑ 213	Thomas Henderson RC	1.50	.60
❑ 214	Steve Furness	.50	.20
❑ 215	John Riggins	2.00	.75
❑ 216	Keith Krepfle RC	.20	.07
❑ 217	Fred Dean RC	10.00	5.00
❑ 218	Emanuel Zanders	.20	.07
❑ 219	Don Testerman	.20	.07
❑ 220	George Kunz	.20	.07
❑ 221	Darryl Stingley	.50	.20
❑ 222	Ken Sanders	.20	.07
❑ 223	Gary Huff	.20	.07
❑ 224	Gregg Bingham	.20	.07
❑ 225	Jerry Sherk	.20	.07
❑ 226	Doug Plank	.20	.07
❑ 227	Ed Taylor	.20	.07
❑ 228	[illegible]	[illegible]	.07
❑ 229	Reggie Williams RC	1.00	.40
❑ 230	Claude Humphrey	.20	.07
❑ 231	Randy Cross RC	2.00	.75
❑ 232	Jim Hart	1.00	.40
❑ 233	Bobby Bryant	.20	.07
❑ 234	Larry Brown	.20	.07
❑ 235	Mark Van Eeghen	.50	.20
❑ 236	Terry Hermeling	.20	.07
❑ 237	Steve Odom	.20	.07
❑ 238	Jan Stenerud	1.00	.40
❑ 239	Andre Tillman	.20	.07
❑ 240	Tom Jackson RC	5.00	2.00
❑ 241	Ken Mendenhall	.20	.07
❑ 242	Tim Fox	.20	.07
❑ 243	Don Herrmann	.20	.07
❑ 244	Eddie McMillan	.20	.07
❑ 245	Greg Pruitt	.50	.20
❑ 246	J.K. McKay	.20	.07
❑ 247	Larry Keller	.20	.07
❑ 248	Dave Jennings	.50	.20
❑ 249	Bo Harris	.20	.07
❑ 250	Revie Sorey	.20	.07
❑ 251	Tony Greene	.20	.07
❑ 252	Butch Johnson	.50	.20
❑ 253	Paul Naumoff	.20	.07
❑ 254	Rickey Young	.50	.20
❑ 255	Dwight White	.50	.20
❑ 256	Joe Lavender	.20	.07
❑ 257	Checklist 133-264	1.00	.40
❑ 258	Ronnie Coleman	.20	.07
❑ 259	Charlie Smith WR	.20	.07
❑ 260	Ray Guy	1.00	.40
❑ 261	David Taylor	.20	.07
❑ 262	Bill Lenkaitis	.20	.07
❑ 263	Jim Mitchell TE	.20	.07
❑ 264	Delvin Williams	.20	.07
❑ 265	Jack Youngblood	1.00	.40
❑ 266	Chuck Crist	.20	.07
❑ 267	Richard Todd	.50	.20
❑ 268	Dave Logan RC	1.00	.40
❑ 269	Rufus Mayes	[illegible]	.07
❑ 270	Brad Van Pelt	.20	.07
❑ 271	Chester Marcol	.20	.07
❑ 272	J.V. Cain	.20	.07
❑ 273	Larry Seiple	.20	.07
❑ 274	Brent McClanahan	.20	.07
❑ 275	Mike Wagner	.20	.07
❑ 276	Diron Talbert	.20	.07
❑ 277	Brian Baschnagel	.20	.07
❑ 278	Ed Podolak	.20	.07
❑ 279	Don Goode	.20	.07
❑ 280	John Dutton	.50	.20
❑ 281	Don Calhoun	.20	.07
❑ 282	Monte Johnson	.20	.07
❑ 283	Ron Jessie	.20	.07
❑ 284	Jon Morris	.20	.07
❑ 285	Riley Odoms	.20	.07
❑ 286	Marv Bateman	.20	.07
❑ 287	Joe Klecko RC	1.00	.40
❑ 288	Oliver Davis	.20	.07
❑ 289	John McDaniel	.20	.07
❑ 290	Roger Staubach	12.00	6.00
❑ 291	Brian Kelley	.20	.07
❑ 292	Mike Hogan	.20	.07
❑ 293	John Leypoldt	.20	.07
❑ 294	Jack Novak	.20	.07
❑ 295	Joe Greene	2.00	.75
❑ 296	John Hill	.20	.07
❑ 297	Danny Buggs	.20	.07
❑ 298	Ted Albrecht	.20	.07
❑ 299	Nelson Munsey	.20	.07
❑ 300	Chuck Foreman	.50	.20
❑ 301	Dan Pastorini	.50	.20

❑ 302 Tommy Hart	.20	.07
❑ 303 Dave Beverly	.20	.07
❑ 304 Tony Reed RC	.50	.20
❑ 305 Cliff Branch	1.50	.60
❑ 306 Clarence Duren	.20	.07
❑ 307 Randy Rasmussen	.20	.07
❑ 308 Oscar Roan	.20	.07
❑ 309 Lenvil Elliott	.20	.07
❑ 310 Dan Dierdorf	1.00	.40
❑ 311 Johnny Perkins	.20	.07
❑ 312 Rafael Septien RC	.50	.20
❑ 313 Terry Beeson	.20	.07
❑ 314 Lee Roy Selmon	2.00	.75
❑ 315 Tony Dorsett RC	40.00	25.00
❑ 316 Greg Landry	.50	.20
❑ 317 Jake Scott	.20	.07
❑ 318 Dan Peiffer	.20	.07
❑ 319 John Bunting	.50	.20
❑ 320 John Stallworth RC	20.00	10.00
❑ 321 Bob Howard	.20	.07
❑ 322 Larry Little	1.00	.40
❑ 323 Reggie McKenzie	.50	.20
❑ 324 Duane Carrell	.20	.07
❑ 325 Ed Simonini	.20	.07
❑ 326 John Vella	.20	.07
❑ 327 Wesley Walker RC	3.00	1.50
❑ 328 Jon Keyworth	.20	.07
❑ 329 Ron Bolton	.20	.07
❑ 330 Tommy Casanova	.20	.07
❑ 331 R.Staubach/B.Griese LL	4.00	2.00
❑ 332 A.Rashad/Mitchell LL	1.00	.40
❑ 333 W.Payton/VanEeghenLL	3.00	1.25
❑ 334 W.Payton/E.Mann LL	3.00	1.25
❑ 335 Interception Leaders	.20	.07
❑ 336 Punting Leaders	.50	.20
❑ 337 Robert Brazile	.50	.20
❑ 338 Charlie Joiner	1.50	.60
❑ 339 Joe Ferguson	.50	.20
❑ 340 Bill Thompson	.20	.07
❑ 341 Sam Cunningham	.50	.20
❑ 342 Curtis Johnson	.20	.07
❑ 343 Jim Marshall	1.00	.40
❑ 344 Charlie Sanders	.50	.20
❑ 345 Willie Hall	.20	.07
❑ 346 Pat Haden	1.00	.40
❑ 347 Jim Bakken	.20	.07
❑ 348 Bruce Taylor	.20	.07
❑ 349 Barty Smith	.20	.07
❑ 350 Drew Pearson	1.50	.60
❑ 351 Mike Webster	2.50	1.00
❑ 352 Bobby Hammond	.20	.07
❑ 353 Dave Mays	.20	.07
❑ 354 Pat McInally	.20	.07
❑ 355 Toni Linhart	.20	.07
❑ 356 Larry Hand	.20	.07
❑ 357 Ted Fritsch Jr.	.20	.07
❑ 358 Larry Marshall	.20	.07
❑ 359 Waymond Bryant	.20	.07
❑ 360 Louie Kelcher RC	.50	.20
❑ 361 Stanley Morgan RC	2.00	.75
❑ 362 Bruce Harper RC	.50	.20
❑ 363 Bernard Jackson	.20	.07
❑ 364 Walter White	.20	.07
❑ 365 Ken Stabler	8.00	4.00
❑ 366 Fred Dryer	1.00	.40
❑ 367 Ike Harris	.20	.07
❑ 368 Norm Bulaich	.20	.07
❑ 369 Merv Krakau	.20	.07
❑ 370 John James	.20	.07
❑ 371 Bennie Cunningham RC	.20	.07
❑ 372 Doug Van Horn	.20	.07
❑ 373 Thom Darden	.20	.07
❑ 374 Eddie Edwards RC	.20	.07
❑ 375 Mike Thomas	.20	.07
❑ 376 Fred Cook	.20	.07
❑ 377 Mike Phipps	.50	.20
❑ 378 Paul Krause	1.00	.40
❑ 379 Harold Carmichael	1.00	.40
❑ 380 Mike Haynes	1.00	.40
❑ 381 Wayne Morris	.20	.07
❑ 382 Greg Buttle	.20	.07
❑ 383 Jim Zorn	1.00	.40
❑ 384 Jack Dolbin	.20	.07
❑ 385 Charlie Waters	.50	.20
❑ 386 Dan Ryczek	.20	.07
❑ 387 Joe Washington RC	1.00	.40
❑ 388 Checklist 265-396	1.00	.40
❑ 389 James Hunter	.20	.07
❑ 390 Billy Johnson	.50	.20
❑ 391 Jim Allen RC	.20	.07
❑ 392 George Buehler	.20	.07
❑ 393 Harry Carson	1.00	.40
❑ 394 Cleo Miller	.20	.07
❑ 395 Gary Burley	.20	.07
❑ 396 Mark Moseley	.50	.20
❑ 397 Virgil Livers	.20	.07
❑ 398 Joe Ehrmann	.20	.07
❑ 399 Freddie Solomon	.20	.07
❑ 400 O.J.Simpson	4.00	2.00
❑ 401 Julius Adams	.20	.07
❑ 402 Artimus Parker	.20	.07
❑ 403 Gene Washington 49er	.50	.20
❑ 404 Herman Edwards	.50	.20
❑ 405 Craig Morton	1.00	.40
❑ 406 Alan Page	1.00	.40
❑ 407 Larry McCarren	.20	.07
❑ 408 Tony Galbreath	.50	.20
❑ 409 Roman Gabriel	1.00	.40
❑ 410 Efren Herrera	.20	.07
❑ 411 Jim Smith RC	1.00	.40
❑ 412 Bill Bryant	.20	.07
❑ 413 Doug Dieken	.20	.07
❑ 414 Marvin Cobb	.20	.07
❑ 415 Fred Biletnikoff	2.00	.75
❑ 416 Joe Theismann	2.50	1.00
❑ 417 Roland Harper	.20	.07
❑ 418 Derrel Luce	.20	.07
❑ 419 Ralph Perretta	.20	.07
❑ 420 Louis Wright RC	1.00	.40
❑ 421 Prentice McCray	.20	.07
❑ 422 Garry Puetz	.20	.07
❑ 423 Alfred Jenkins RC	1.00	.40
❑ 424 Paul Seymour	.20	.07
❑ 425 Garo Yepremian	.50	.20
❑ 426 Emmitt Thomas	.20	.07
❑ 427 Dexter Bussey	.20	.07
❑ 428 John Sanders	.20	.07
❑ 429 Ed Too Tall Jones	2.00	.75
❑ 430 Ron Yary	1.00	.40
❑ 431 Frank Lewis	.50	.20
❑ 432 Jerry Golsteyn	.20	.07
❑ 433 Clarence Scott	.20	.07
❑ 434 Pete Johnson RC	1.00	.40
❑ 435 Charle Young	.50	.20
❑ 436 Harold McLinton	.20	.07
❑ 437 Noah Jackson	.20	.07
❑ 438 Bruce Laird	.20	.07
❑ 439 John Matuszak	.50	.20
❑ 440 Nat Moore	.50	.20
❑ 441 Leon Gray	.20	.07
❑ 442 Jerome Barkum	.20	.07
❑ 443 Steve Largent	12.00	6.00
❑ 444 John Zook	.20	.07
❑ 445 Preston Pearson	.50	.20
❑ 446 Conrad Dobler	.50	.20
❑ 447 Wilbur Summers	.20	.07
❑ 448 Lou Piccone	.20	.07
❑ 449 Ron Jaworski	1.00	.40
❑ 450 Jack Ham	1.50	.60
❑ 451 Mick Tingelhoff	.50	.20
❑ 452 Clyde Powers	.20	.07
❑ 453 John Cappelletti	1.00	.40
❑ 454 Dick Ambrose	.20	.07
❑ 455 Lemar Parrish	.20	.07
❑ 456 Ron Saul	.20	.07
❑ 457 Bob Parsons	.20	.07
❑ 458 Glenn Doughty	.20	.07
❑ 459 Don Woods	.20	.07
❑ 460 Art Shell	1.00	.40
❑ 461 Sam Hunt	.20	.07
❑ 462 Lawrence Pillers	.20	.07
❑ 463 Henry Childs	.20	.07
❑ 464 Roger Wehrli	.50	.20
❑ 465 Otis Armstrong	.50	.20
❑ 466 Bob Baumhower RC	2.00	.75
❑ 467 Ray Jarvis	.20	.07
❑ 468 Guy Morriss	.20	.07
❑ 469 Matt Blair	.50	.20
❑ 470 Billy Joe DuPree	.50	.20
❑ 471 Roland Hooks	.20	.07
❑ 472 Joe Danelo	.20	.07
❑ 473 Reggie Rucker	.50	.20
❑ 474 Vern Holland	.20	.07
❑ 475 Mel Blount	1.50	.60
❑ 476 Eddie Brown S	.20	.07
❑ 477 Bo Rather	.20	.07
❑ 478 Don McCauley	.20	.07
❑ 479 Glen Walker	.20	.07
❑ 480 Randy Gradishar	1.00	.40
❑ 481 Dave Rowe	.20	.07
❑ 482 Pat Leahy	.50	.20
❑ 483 Mike Fuller	.20	.07
❑ 484 David Lewis RC	.20	.07
❑ 485 Steve Grogan	1.00	.40
❑ 486 Mel Gray	.50	.20
❑ 487 Eddie Payton RC	.50	.20
❑ 488 Checklist 397-528	1.00	.40
❑ 489 Stu Voigt	.20	.07
❑ 490 Rolland Lawrence	.20	.07
❑ 491 Nick Mike-Mayer	.20	.07
❑ 492 Troy Archer	.20	.07
❑ 493 Benny Malone	.20	.07
❑ 494 Golden Richards	.50	.20
❑ 495 Chris Hanburger	.20	.07
❑ 496 Dwight Harrison	.20	.07
❑ 497 Gary Fencik RC	1.00	.40
❑ 498 Rich Saul	.20	.07
❑ 499 Dan Fouts	4.00	2.00
❑ 500 Franco Harris	4.00	2.00
❑ 501 Atlanta Falcons TL	.75	.30
❑ 502 Baltimore Colts TL	.75	.30
❑ 503 Bills TL/O.J.Simpson	1.50	.60
❑ 504 Bears TL/Walter Payton	2.00	.75
❑ 505 Bengals TL/Reg.Williams	.75	.30
❑ 506 Cleveland Browns TL	.75	.30
❑ 507 Cowboys TL/T.Dorsett	2.50	1.00
❑ 508 Denver Broncos TL	1.00	.40
❑ 509 Detroit Lions TL	.75	.30
❑ 510 Green Bay Packers TL	1.00	.40
❑ 511 Houston Oilers TL	.75	.30
❑ 512 Kansas City Chiefs TL	.75	.30
❑ 513 Los Angeles Rams TL	.75	.30
❑ 514 Miami Dolphins TL	1.00	.40
❑ 515 Minnesota Vikings TL	.75	.30
❑ 516 New England Patriots TL	.75	.30
❑ 517 New Orleans Saints TL	.75	.30
❑ 518 New York Giants TL	.75	.30
❑ 519 Jets TL/Wesley Walker	.75	.30
❑ 520 Oakland Raiders TL	1.00	.40
❑ 521 Philadelphia Eagles TL	.75	.30
❑ 522 Steelers TL/Harris/Blount	1.00	.40
❑ 523 St.Louis Cardinals TL	.75	.30
❑ 524 San Diego Chargers TL	1.00	.40
❑ 525 San Francisco 49ers TL	.75	.30
❑ 526 Seahawks TL/S.Largent	1.50	.60
❑ 527 Tampa Bay Bucs TL	.75	.30
❑ 528 Redskins TL/Ken Houston	1.00	.40

1979 Topps

❑ COMPLETE SET (528)	150.00	75.00
❑ 1 Staubach/Bradshaw LL	8.00	4.00
❑ 2 S.Largent/R.Young LL	1.00	.40
❑ 3 E.Campbell/W.Payton LL	8.00	4.00
❑ 4 Scoring Leaders	.20	.07
❑ 5 Interception Leaders	.20	.07
❑ 6 Punting Leaders	.20	.07
❑ 7 Johnny Perkins	.20	.07
❑ 8 Charles Phillips	.20	.07
❑ 9 Derrel Luce	.20	.07
❑ 10 John Riggins	1.25	.50
❑ 11 Chester Marcol	.20	.07
❑ 12 Bernard Jackson	.20	.07
❑ 13 Dave Logan	.20	.07

❑ 14	Bo Harris	.20	.07
❑ 15	Alan Page	1.00	.40
❑ 16	John Smith	.20	.07
❑ 17	Dwight McDonald	.20	.07
❑ 18	John Cappelletti	.50	.20
❑ 19	Steelers TL/Harris/Dungy	12.00	5.00
❑ 20	Bill Bergey	.50	.20
❑ 21	Jerome Barkum	.20	.07
❑ 22	Larry Csonka	2.50	1.00
❑ 23	Joe Ferguson	.50	.20
❑ 24	Ed Too Tall Jones	1.25	.50
❑ 25	Dave Jennings	.50	.20
❑ 26	Horace King	.20	.07
[illegible]	[illegible]	[illegible]	[illegible]
❑ 28	Morris Bradshaw	.20	.07
❑ 29	Joe Ehrmann	.20	.07
❑ 30	Ahmad Rashad	1.00	.40
❑ 31	Joe Lavender	.20	.07
❑ 32	Dan Neal	.20	.07
❑ 33	Johnny Evans	.20	.07
❑ 34	Pete Johnson	.50	.20
❑ 35	Mike Haynes	1.00	.40
❑ 36	Tim Mazzetti	.20	.07
❑ 37	Mike Barber RC	.20	.07
❑ 38	49ers TL/O.J.Simpson	1.50	.60
❑ 39	Bill Gregory	.20	.07
❑ 40	Randy Gradishar	1.00	.40
❑ 41	Richard Todd	.50	.20
❑ 42	Henry Marshall	.20	.07
❑ 43	John Hill	.20	.07
❑ 44	Sidney Thornton	.20	.07
❑ 45	Ron Jessie	.20	.07
❑ 46	Bob Baumhower	.50	.20
❑ 47	Johnnie Gray	.20	.07
❑ 48	Doug Williams RC	6.00	3.00
❑ 49	Don McCauley	.20	.07
❑ 50	Ray Guy	.50	.20
❑ 51	Bob Klein	.20	.07
❑ 52	Golden Richards	.20	.07
❑ 53	Mark Miller QB	.20	.07
❑ 54	John Sanders	.20	.07
❑ 55	Gary Burley	.20	.07
❑ 56	Steve Nelson	.20	.07
❑ 57	Buffalo Bills TL	.75	.30
❑ 58	Bobby Bryant	.20	.07
❑ 59	Rick Kane	.20	.07
❑ 60	Larry Little	1.00	.40
❑ 61	Ted Fritsch Jr.	.20	.07
❑ 62	Larry Mallory	.20	.07
❑ 63	Marvin Powell	.20	.07
❑ 64	Jim Hart	1.00	.40
❑ 65	Joe Greene	1.50	.60
❑ 66	Walter White	.20	.07
❑ 67	Gregg Bingham	.20	.07
❑ 68	Errol Mann	.20	.07
❑ 69	Bruce Laird	.20	.07
❑ 70	Drew Pearson	1.00	.40
❑ 71	Steve Bartkowski	1.00	.40
❑ 72	Ted Albrecht	.20	.07
❑ 73	Charlie Hall	.20	.07
❑ 74	Pat McInally	.20	.07
❑ 75	Bubba Baker RC	1.00	.40
❑ 76	New England Pats TL	.75	.30
❑ 77	Steve DeBerg RC	2.00	.75
❑ 78	John Yarno	.20	.07
❑ 79	Stu Voigt	.20	.07
❑ 80	Frank Corral AP	.20	.07
❑ 81	Troy Archer	.20	.07
❑ 82	Bruce Harper	.20	.07
❑ 83	Tom Jackson	1.50	.60
❑ 84	Larry Brown	.50	.20
❑ 85	Wilbert Montgomery RC	1.00	.40
❑ 86	Butch Johnson	.50	.20
❑ 87	Mike Kadish	.20	.07
❑ 88	Ralph Perretta	.20	.07
❑ 89	David Lee	.20	.07
❑ 90	Mark Van Eeghen	.50	.20
❑ 91	John McDaniel	.20	.07
❑ 92	Gary Fencik	.50	.20
❑ 93	Mack Mitchell	.20	.07
❑ 94	Cincinnati Bengals TL/Jauron	1.00	.40
❑ 95	Steve Grogan	1.00	.40
❑ 96	Garo Yepremian	.50	.20
❑ 97	Barty Smith	.20	.07
❑ 98	Frank Reed	.20	.07
❑ 99	Jim Clack	.20	.07
❑ 100	Chuck Foreman	.50	.20
❑ 101	Joe Klecko	1.00	.40
❑ 102	Pat Tilley	.50	.20
❑ 103	Conrad Dobler	.50	.20
❑ 104	Craig Colquitt	.20	.07
❑ 105	Dan Pastorini	.50	.20
❑ 106	Rod Perry AP	.20	.07
❑ 107	Nick Mike-Mayer	.20	.07
❑ 108	John Matuszak	.50	.20
❑ 109	David Taylor	.20	.07
❑ 110	Billy Joe DuPree	.50	.20
❑ 111	Harold McLinton	.20	.07
❑ 112	Virgil Livers	.20	.07
❑ 113	Cleveland Browns TL	.75	.30
[illegible]	[illegible]	[illegible]	[illegible]
❑ 115	Ken Anderson	1.00	.40
❑ 116	Bill Lenkaitis	.20	.07
❑ 117	Bucky Dilts	.20	.07
❑ 118	Tony Greene	.20	.07
❑ 119	Bobby Hammond	.20	.07
❑ 120	Nat Moore	.50	.20
❑ 121	Pat Leahy	.50	.20
❑ 122	James Harris	.50	.20
❑ 123	Lee Roy Selmon	1.25	.50
❑ 124	Bennie Cunningham	.50	.20
❑ 125	Matt Blair AP	.50	.20
❑ 126	Jim Allen	.20	.07
❑ 127	Alfred Jenkins	.50	.20
❑ 128	Arthur Whittington	.20	.07
❑ 129	Norm Thompson	.20	.07
❑ 130	Pat Haden	1.00	.40
❑ 131	Freddie Solomon	.20	.07
❑ 132	Bears TL/W.Payton	2.00	.75
❑ 133	Mark Moseley	.20	.07
❑ 134	Cleo Miller	.20	.07
❑ 135	Ross Browner RC	.50	.20
❑ 136	Don Calhoun	.20	.07
❑ 137	David Whitehurst	.20	.07
❑ 138	Terry Beeson	.20	.07
❑ 139	Ken Stone	.20	.07
❑ 140	Brad Van Pelt AP	.20	.07
❑ 141	Wesley Walker	1.00	.40
❑ 142	Jan Stenerud	1.00	.40
❑ 143	Henry Childs	.20	.07
❑ 144	Otis Armstrong	1.00	.40
❑ 145	Dwight White	.50	.20
❑ 146	Steve Wilson	.20	.07
❑ 147	Tom Skladany RC	.20	.07
❑ 148	Lou Piccone	.20	.07
❑ 149	Monte Johnson	.20	.07
❑ 150	Joe Washington	.50	.20
❑ 151	Eagles TL/W.Montgomery	.75	.30
❑ 152	Fred Dean	.20	.07
❑ 153	Rolland Lawrence	.20	.07
❑ 154	Brian Baschnagel	.20	.07
❑ 155	Joe Theismann	[illegible]	.75
❑ 156	Marvin Cobb	.20	.07
❑ 157	Dick Ambrose	.20	.07
❑ 158	Mike Patrick	.20	.07
❑ 159	Gary Shirk	.20	.07
❑ 160	Tony Dorsett	12.00	6.00
❑ 161	Greg Buttle	.20	.07
❑ 162	A.J. Duhe	.50	.20
❑ 163	Mick Tingelhoff	.50	.20
❑ 164	Ken Burrough	.50	.20
❑ 165	Mike Wagner	.20	.07
❑ 166	AFC Champs/F.Harris	1.00	.40
❑ 167	NFC Championship	.50	.20
❑ 168	Super Bowl XIII/Harris	1.25	.50
❑ 169	Raiders TL/Ted Hendricks	1.00	.40
❑ 170	O.J.Simpson	4.00	1.50
❑ 171	Doug Nettles	.20	.07
❑ 172	Dan Dierdorf	1.00	.40
❑ 173	Dave Beverly	.20	.07
❑ 174	Jim Zorn	1.00	.40
❑ 175	Mike Thomas	.20	.07
❑ 176	John Outlaw	.20	.07
❑ 177	Jim Turner	.20	.07
❑ 178	Freddie Scott	.20	.07
❑ 179	Mike Phipps	.50	.20
❑ 180	Jack Youngblood	1.00	.40
❑ 181	Sam Hunt	.20	.07
❑ 182	Tony Hill RC	1.00	.40
❑ 183	Gary Barbaro	.20	.07
❑ 184	Archie Griffin	.50	.20
❑ 185	Jerry Sherk	.20	.07
❑ 186	Bobby Jackson	.20	.07
❑ 187	Don Woods	.20	.07
❑ 188	New York Giants TL	.75	.30
❑ 189	Raymond Chester	.20	.07
❑ 190	Joe DeLamielleure AP	1.00	.40
❑ 191	Tony Galbreath	.50	.20
❑ 192	Robert Brazile AP	.50	.20
❑ 193	Neil O'Donoghue	.20	.07
❑ 194	Mike Webster	1.00	.40
❑ 195	Ed Simonini	.20	.07
❑ 196	Benny Malone	.20	.07
❑ 197	Tom Wittum	.20	.07
❑ 198	Steve Largent	8.00	4.00
❑ 199	Tommy Hart	.20	.07
❑ 200	Fran Tarkenton	3.00	1.50
[illegible]	[illegible]	[illegible]	[illegible]
❑ 202	Leroy Harris	.20	.07
❑ 203	Eric Williams LB	.20	.07
❑ 204	Thom Darden AP	.20	.07
❑ 205	Ken Riley	.50	.20
❑ 206	Clark Gaines	.20	.07
❑ 207	Kansas City Chiefs TL	.75	.30
❑ 208	Joe Danelo	.20	.07
❑ 209	Glen Walker	.20	.07
❑ 210	Art Shell	1.00	.40
❑ 211	Jon Keyworth	.20	.07
❑ 212	Herman Edwards	.20	.07
❑ 213	John Fitzgerald	.20	.07
❑ 214	Jim Smith	.50	.20
❑ 215	Coy Bacon	.50	.20
❑ 216	Dennis Johnson RBK RC	.20	.07
❑ 217	John Jefferson RC	3.00	1.50
❑ 218	Gary Weaver	.20	.07
❑ 219	Tom Blanchard	.20	.07
❑ 220	Bert Jones	1.00	.40
❑ 221	Stanley Morgan	1.00	.40
❑ 222	James Hunter	.20	.07
❑ 223	Jim O'Bradovich	.20	.07
❑ 224	Carl Mauck	.20	.07
❑ 225	Chris Bahr	.20	.07
❑ 226	Jets TL/Wesley Walker	.75	.30
❑ 227	Roland Harper	.20	.07
❑ 228	Randy Dean	.20	.07
❑ 229	Bob Jackson	.20	.07
❑ 230	Sammie White	.50	.20
❑ 231	Mike Dawson	.20	.07
❑ 232	Checklist 133-264	1.00	.40
❑ 233	Ken MacAfee RC	.20	.07
❑ 234	Jon Kolb AP	.20	.07
❑ 235	Willie Hall	.20	.07
❑ 236	Ron Saul AP	.20	.07
❑ 237	Haskel Stanback	.20	.07
❑ 238	Zenon Andrusyshyn	.20	.07
❑ 239	Norris Thomas	.20	.07
❑ 240	Rick Upchurch	.50	.20
❑ 241	Robert Pratt	.20	.07
❑ 242	Julius Adams	.20	.07
❑ 243	Rich McGeorge	.20	.07
❑ 244	Seahawks TL/S.Largent	1.25	.50
❑ 245	Blair Bush RC	.20	.07
❑ 246	Billy Johnson	.50	.20
❑ 247	Randy Rasmussen	.20	.07
❑ 248	Brian Kelley	.20	.07
❑ 249	Mike Pruitt	.50	.20
❑ 250	Harold Carmichael	1.00	.40
❑ 251	Mike Hartenstine	.20	.07
❑ 252	Robert Newhouse	.50	.20
❑ 253	Gary Danielson RC	1.00	.40
❑ 254	Mike Fuller	.20	.07
❑ 255	L.C.Greenwood	1.00	.40
❑ 256	Lemar Parrish	.20	.07
❑ 257	Ike Harris	.20	.07
❑ 258	Ricky Bell RC	1.00	.40
❑ 259	Willie Parker C	.20	.07
❑ 260	Gene Upshaw	1.00	.40
❑ 261	Glenn Doughty	.20	.07
❑ 262	Steve Zabel	.20	.07
❑ 263	Atlanta Falcons TL	.75	.30
❑ 264	Ray Wersching	.20	.07
❑ 265	Lawrence McCutcheon	.50	.20
❑ 266	Willie Buchanon AP	.20	.07
❑ 267	Matt Robinson	.20	.07
❑ 268	Reggie Rucker	.50	.20
❑ 269	Doug Van Horn	.20	.07
❑ 270	Lydell Mitchell	.50	.20
❑ 271	Vern Holland	.20	.07
❑ 272	Eason Ramson	.20	.07
❑ 273	Steve Towle	.20	.07
❑ 274	Jim Marshall	1.00	.40

❑ 275 Mel Blount 1.25 .50
❑ 276 Bob Kuziel .20 .07
❑ 277 James Scott .20 .07
❑ 278 Tony Reed .20 .07
❑ 279 Dave Green .20 .07
❑ 280 Toni Linhart .20 .07
❑ 281 Andy Johnson .20 .07
❑ 282 Los Angeles Rams TL .75 .30
❑ 283 Phil Villapiano .50 .20
❑ 284 Dexter Bussey .20 .07
❑ 285 Craig Morton 1.00 .40
❑ 286 Guy Morriss .20 .07
❑ 287 Lawrence Pillers .20 .07
❑ 288 Gerald Irons .20 .07
❑ 289 Scott Perry .20 .07
❑ 290 Randy White 2.00 .75
❑ 291 Jack Gregory .20 .07
❑ 292 Bob Chandler .20 .07
❑ 293 Rich Szaro .20 .07
❑ 294 Sherman Smith .20 .07
❑ 295 Tom Banks AP .20 .07
❑ 296 Revie Sorey AP .20 .07
❑ 297 Ricky Thompson .20 .07
❑ 298 Ron Yary 1.00 .40
❑ 299 Lyle Blackwood .20 .07
❑ 300 Franco Harris 2.50 1.25
❑ 301 Oilers TL/E.Campbell 3.00 1.50
❑ 302 Scott Bull .20 .07
❑ 303 Dewey Selmon .50 .20
❑ 304 Jack Rudnay .20 .07
❑ 305 Fred Biletnikoff 2.00 .75
❑ 306 Jeff West .20 .07
❑ 307 Shafer Suggs .20 .07
❑ 308 Ozzie Newsome RC 12.00 6.00
❑ 309 Boobie Clark .20 .07
❑ 310 James Lofton RC 12.00 6.00
❑ 311 Joe Pisarcik .20 .07
❑ 312 Bill Simpson AP .20 .07
❑ 313 Haven Moses .50 .20
❑ 314 Jim Merlo .20 .07
❑ 315 Preston Pearson .50 .20
❑ 316 Larry Tearry .20 .07
❑ 317 Tom Dempsey .20 .07
❑ 318 Greg Latta .20 .07
❑ 319 Redskins TL/John Riggins 1.50 .60
❑ 320 Jack Ham 1.25 .50
❑ 321 Harold Jackson .50 .20
❑ 322 George Roberts .20 .07
❑ 323 Ron Jaworski 1.00 .40
❑ 324 Jim Otis .20 .07
❑ 325 Roger Carr .50 .20
❑ 326 Jack Tatum .50 .20
❑ 327 Derrick Gaffney .20 .07
❑ 328 Reggie Williams 1.00 .40
❑ 329 Doug Dieken .20 .07
❑ 330 Efren Herrera .20 .07
❑ 331 Earl Campbell RB 6.00 3.00
❑ 332 Tony Galbreath RB .20 .07
❑ 333 Bruce Harper RB .20 .07
❑ 334 John James RB .20 .07
❑ 335 Walter Payton RB 4.00 1.50
❑ 336 Rickey Young RB .20 .07
❑ 337 Jeff Van Note .50 .20
❑ 338 Chargers TL/J.Jefferson 1.00 .40
❑ 339 Stan Walters RC .20 .07
❑ 340 Louis Wright .50 .20
❑ 341 Horace Ivory .20 .07
❑ 342 Andre Tillman .20 .07
❑ 343 Greg Coleman RC .20 .07
❑ 344 Doug English RC 1.00 .40
❑ 345 Ted Hendricks 1.00 .40
❑ 346 Rich Saul .20 .07
❑ 347 Mel Gray .50 .20
❑ 348 Toni Fritsch .20 .07
❑ 349 Cornell Webster .20 .07
❑ 350 Ken Houston 1.00 .40
❑ 351 Ron Johnson DB RC .50 .20
❑ 352 Doug Kotar .20 .07
❑ 353 Brian Sipe 1.00 .40
❑ 354 Billy Brooks .20 .07
❑ 355 John Dutton .50 .20
❑ 356 Don Goode .20 .07
❑ 357 Detroit Lions TL .75 .30
❑ 358 Reuben Gant .20 .07
❑ 359 Bob Parsons .20 .07
❑ 360 Cliff Harris 1.00 .40
❑ 361 Raymond Clayborn .50 .20
❑ 362 Scott Dierking .20 .07
❑ 363 Bill Bryan .20 .07
❑ 364 Mike Livingston .20 .07
❑ 365 Otis Sistrunk .50 .20
❑ 366 Charle Young .50 .20
❑ 367 Keith Wortman .20 .07
❑ 368 Checklist 265-396 1.00 .40
❑ 369 Mike Michel .20 .07
❑ 370 Delvin Williams AP .20 .07
❑ 371 Steve Furness .50 .20
❑ 372 Emery Moorehead .20 .07
❑ 373 Clarence Scott .20 .07
❑ 374 Rufus Mayes .20 .07
❑ 375 Chris Hanburger .20 .07
❑ 376 Baltimore Colts TL .75 .30
❑ 377 Bob Avellini .50 .20
❑ 378 Jeff Siemon .20 .07
❑ 379 Roland Hooks .20 .07
❑ 380 Russ Francis .50 .20
❑ 381 Roger Wehrli .50 .20
❑ 382 Joe Fields .20 .07
❑ 383 Archie Manning 1.00 .40
❑ 384 Rob Lytle .20 .07
❑ 385 Thomas Henderson .50 .20
❑ 386 Morris Owens .20 .07
❑ 387 Dan Fouts 3.00 1.50
❑ 388 Chuck Crist .20 .07
❑ 389 Ed O'Neil .20 .07
❑ 390 Earl Campbell RC 30.00 15.00
❑ 391 Randy Grossman .20 .07
❑ 392 Monte Jackson .20 .07
❑ 393 John Mendenhall .20 .07
❑ 394 Miami Dolphins TL 1.00 .40
❑ 395 Isaac Curtis .50 .20
❑ 396 Mike Bragg .20 .07
❑ 397 Doug Plank .20 .07
❑ 398 Mike Barnes .20 .07
❑ 399 Calvin Hill .50 .20
❑ 400 Roger Staubach 10.00 5.00
❑ 401 Doug Beaudoin .20 .07
❑ 402 Chuck Ramsey .20 .07
❑ 403 Mike Hogan .20 .07
❑ 404 Mario Clark .20 .07
❑ 405 Riley Odoms .20 .07
❑ 406 Carl Eller 1.00 .40
❑ 407 Packers TL/J.Lofton 1.50 .60
❑ 408 Mark Arneson .20 .07
❑ 409 Vince Ferragamo RC 1.00 .40
❑ 410 Cleveland Elam .20 .07
❑ 411 Donnie Shell RC 4.00 1.50
❑ 412 Ray Rhodes 1.00 .40
❑ 413 Don Cockroft .20 .07
❑ 414 Don Bass .50 .20
❑ 415 Cliff Branch 1.00 .40
❑ 416 Diron Talbert .20 .07
❑ 417 Tom Hicks .20 .07
❑ 418 Roosevelt Leaks .20 .07
❑ 419 Charlie Joiner 1.00 .40
❑ 420 Lyle Alzado 1.00 .40
❑ 421 Sam Cunningham .50 .20
❑ 422 Larry Keller .20 .07
❑ 423 Jim Mitchell TE .20 .07
❑ 424 Randy Logan .20 .07
❑ 425 Jim Langer 1.00 .40
❑ 426 Gary Green .20 .07
❑ 427 Luther Blue .20 .07
❑ 428 Dennis Johnson .20 .07
❑ 429 Danny White 1.00 .40
❑ 430 Roy Gerela .20 .07
❑ 431 Jimmy Robinson .20 .07
❑ 432 Minnesota Vikings TL .75 .30
❑ 433 Oliver Davis .20 .07
❑ 434 Lenvil Elliott .20 .07
❑ 435 Willie Miller RC .20 .07
❑ 436 Brad Dusek .20 .07
❑ 437 Bob Thomas .20 .07
❑ 438 Ken Mendenhall .20 .07
❑ 439 Clarence Davis .20 .07
❑ 440 Bob Griese 2.50 1.00
❑ 441 Tony McGee DT .20 .07
❑ 442 Ed Taylor .20 .07
❑ 443 Ron Howard .20 .07
❑ 444 Wayne Morris .20 .07
❑ 445 Charlie Waters .50 .20
❑ 446 Rick Danmeier .20 .07
❑ 447 Paul Naumoff .20 .07
❑ 448 Keith Krepfle .20 .07
❑ 449 Rusty Jackson .20 .07
❑ 450 John Stallworth 4.00 2.00
❑ 451 New Orleans Saints TL .75 .30
❑ 452 Ron Mikolajczyk .20 .07
❑ 453 Fred Dryer 1.00 .40
❑ 454 Jim LeClair .20 .07
❑ 455 Greg Pruitt .50 .20
❑ 456 Jake Scott .20 .07
❑ 457 Steve Schubert .20 .07
❑ 458 George Kunz .20 .07
❑ 459 Mike Williams .20 .07
❑ 460 Dave Casper AP 1.00 .40
❑ 461 Sam Adams OL .20 .07
❑ 462 Abdul Salaam .20 .07
❑ 463 Terdell Middleton .50 .20
❑ 464 Mike Wood .20 .07
❑ 465 Bill Thompson AP .20 .07
❑ 466 Larry Gordon .20 .07
❑ 467 Benny Ricardo .20 .07
❑ 468 Reggie McKenzie .50 .20
❑ 469 Cowboys TL/T.Dorsett 1.50 .60
❑ 470 Rickey Young .50 .20
❑ 471 Charlie Smith WR .20 .07
❑ 472 Al Dixon .20 .07
❑ 473 Tom DeLeone .20 .07
❑ 474 Louis Breeden .50 .20
❑ 475 Jack Lambert 2.00 .75
❑ 476 Terry Hermeling .20 .07
❑ 477 J.K. McKay .20 .07
❑ 478 Stan White .20 .07
❑ 479 Terry Nelson .20 .07
❑ 480 Walter Payton 20.00 10.00
❑ 481 Dave Dalby .20 .07
❑ 482 Burgess Owens .20 .07
❑ 483 Rolf Benirschke .20 .07
❑ 484 Jack Dolbin .20 .07
❑ 485 John Hannah 1.00 .40
❑ 486 Checklist 397-528 1.00 .40
❑ 487 Greg Landry .50 .20
❑ 488 St. Louis Cardinals TL .75 .30
❑ 489 Paul Krause 1.00 .40
❑ 490 John James .20 .07
❑ 491 Merv Krakau .20 .07
❑ 492 Dan Doornink .20 .07
❑ 493 Curtis Johnson .20 .07
❑ 494 Rafael Septien .20 .07
❑ 495 Jean Fugett .20 .07
❑ 496 Frank LeMaster .20 .07
❑ 497 Allan Ellis .20 .07
❑ 498 Billy Waddy RC .50 .20
❑ 499 Hank Bauer .20 .07
❑ 500 Terry Bradshaw UER 10.00 5.00
❑ 501 Larry McCarren .20 .07
❑ 502 Fred Cook .20 .07
❑ 503 Chuck Muncie .50 .20
❑ 504 Herman Weaver .20 .07
❑ 505 Eddie Edwards .20 .07
❑ 506 Tony Peters .20 .07
❑ 507 Denver Broncos TL .75 .30
❑ 508 Jimbo Elrod .20 .07
❑ 509 David Hill .20 .07
❑ 510 Harvey Martin .50 .20
❑ 511 Terry Miller .50 .20
❑ 512 June Jones RC .50 .20
❑ 513 Randy Cross 1.00 .40
❑ 514 Duriel Harris .20 .07
❑ 515 Harry Carson 1.00 .40
❑ 516 Tim Fox .20 .07
❑ 517 John Zook .20 .07
❑ 518 Bob Tucker .20 .07
❑ 519 Kevin Long RC .20 .07
❑ 520 Ken Stabler 6.00 3.00
❑ 521 John Bunting .50 .20
❑ 522 Rocky Bleier 1.25 .50
❑ 523 Noah Jackson .20 .07
❑ 524 Cliff Parsley .20 .07
❑ 525 Louie Kelcher AP .50 .20
❑ 526 Bucs TL/Ricky Bell .75 .30
❑ 527 Bob Brudzinski RC .20 .07
❑ 528 Danny Buggs .20 .07

1980 Topps

❑ COMPLETE SET (528) 75.00 40.00
❑ 1 Ottis Anderson RB 1.00 .40
❑ 2 Harold Carmichael RB 1.00 .40
❑ 3 Dan Fouts RB 1.00 .40
❑ 4 Paul Krause RB .50 .20

❑ 5 Rick Upchurch RB	.50	.20
❑ 6 Garo Yepremian RB	.20	.07
❑ 7 Harold Jackson	.50	.20
❑ 8 Mike Williams	.20	.07
❑ 9 Calvin Hill	.50	.20
❑ 10 Jack Ham	1.00	.40
❑ 11 Dan Melville	.20	.07
❑ 12 Matt Robinson	.20	.07
❑ 13 Billy Campfield	.20	.07
❑ 14 Phil Tabor	.20	.07
❑ 15 Randy Hughes UER	.20	.07
❑ 16 Andre Tillman	.20	.07
❑ 17 Isaac Curtis	.50	.20
❑ 18 Charley Hannah	.20	.07
❑ 19 Redskins TL/J.Riggins	1.00	.40
❑ 20 Jim Zorn	.50	.20
❑ 21 Brian Baschnagel	.20	.07
❑ 22 Jon Keyworth	.20	.07
❑ 23 Phil Villapiano	.20	.07
❑ 24 Richard Osborne	.20	.07
❑ 25 Rich Saul AP	.20	.07
❑ 26 Doug Beaudoin	.20	.07
❑ 27 Cleveland Elam	.20	.07
❑ 28 Charlie Joiner	1.00	.40
❑ 29 Dick Ambrose	.20	.07
❑ 30 Mike Reinfeldt RC	.20	.07
❑ 31 Matt Bahr RC	1.00	.40
❑ 32 Keith Krepfle	.20	.07
❑ 33 Herb Scott	.20	.07
❑ 34 Doug Kotar	.20	.07
❑ 35 Bob Griese	1.50	.60
❑ 36 Jerry Butler RC	1.00	.40
❑ 37 Rolland Lawrence	.20	.07
❑ 38 Gary Weaver	.20	.07
❑ 39 Chiefs TL/J.T.Smith	.50	.20
❑ 40 Chuck Muncie	.50	.20
❑ 41 Mike Hartenstine	.20	.07
❑ 42 Sammie White	.50	.20
❑ 43 Ken Clark	.20	.07
❑ 44 Clarence Harmon	.20	.07
❑ 45 Bert Jones	1.00	.40
❑ 46 Mike Washington	.20	.07
❑ 47 Joe Fields	.20	.07
❑ 48 Mike Wood	.20	.07
❑ 49 Oliver Davis	.20	.07
❑ 50 Stan Walters AP	.20	.07
❑ 51 Riley Odoms	.20	.07
❑ 52 Steve Pisarkiewicz	.20	.07
❑ 53 Tony Hill	1.00	.40
❑ 54 Scott Perry	.20	.07
❑ 55 George Martin RC	.20	.07
❑ 56 George Roberts	.20	.07
❑ 57 Seahawks TL/S. Largent	1.00	.40
❑ 58 Billy Johnson	.50	.20
❑ 59 Reuben Gant	.20	.07
❑ 60 Dennis Harrah RC	.20	.07
❑ 61 Rocky Bleier	1.00	.40
❑ 62 Sam Hunt	.20	.07
❑ 63 Allan Ellis	.20	.07
❑ 64 Ricky Thompson	.20	.07
❑ 65 Ken Stabler	4.00	2.00
❑ 66 Dexter Bussey	.20	.07
❑ 67 Ken Mendenhall	.20	.07
❑ 68 Woodrow Lowe	.20	.07
❑ 69 Thom Darden	.20	.07
❑ 70 Randy White	1.50	.60
❑ 71 Ken MacAfee	.20	.07
❑ 72 Ron Jaworski	1.00	.40
❑ 73 William Andrews RC	1.00	.40
❑ 74 Jimmy Robinson	.20	.07
❑ 75 Roger Wehrli AP	.40	.15
❑ 76 Dolphins TL/L.Csonka	1.00	.40
❑ 77 Jack Rudnay	.20	.07
❑ 78 James Lofton	2.00	.75
❑ 79 Robert Brazile	.50	.20
❑ 80 Russ Francis	.50	.20
❑ 81 Ricky Bell	1.00	.40
❑ 82 Bob Avellini	.50	.20
❑ 83 Bobby Jackson	.20	.07
❑ 84 Mike Bragg	.20	.07
❑ 85 Cliff Branch	1.00	.40
❑ 86 Blair Bush	.20	.07
❑ 87 Sherman Smith	.20	.07
❑ 88 Glen Edwards	.20	.07
❑ 89 Don Cockroft	.20	.07
❑ 90 Louis Wright	.50	.20
❑ 91 Randy Grossman	.20	.07
❑ 92 Carl Hairston RC	1.00	.40
❑ 93 Archie Manning	1.00	.40
❑ 94 New York Giants TL	.50	.20
❑ 95 Preston Pearson	.50	.20
❑ 96 Rusty Chambers	.20	.07
❑ 97 Greg Coleman	.20	.07
❑ 98 Charle Young	.20	.07
❑ 99 Matt Cavanaugh RC	.50	.20
❑ 100 Jesse Baker	.20	.07
❑ 101 Doug Plank	.20	.07
❑ 102 Checklist 1-132	.75	.30
❑ 103 Luther Bradley RC	.20	.07
❑ 104 Bob Kuziel	.20	.07
❑ 105 Craig Morton	.50	.20
❑ 106 Sherman White	.20	.07
❑ 107 Jim Breech RC	.50	.20
❑ 108 Hank Bauer	.20	.07
❑ 109 Tom Blanchard	.20	.07
❑ 110 Ozzie Newsome	2.00	.75
❑ 111 Steve Furness	.20	.07
❑ 112 Frank LeMaster	.20	.07
❑ 113 Cowboys TL/T.Dorsett	1.00	.40
❑ 114 Doug Van Horn	.20	.07
❑ 115 Delvin Williams	.20	.07
❑ 116 Lyle Blackwood	.20	.07
❑ 117 Derrick Gaffney	.20	.07
❑ 118 Cornell Webster	.20	.07
❑ 119 Sam Cunningham	.50	.20
❑ 120 Jim Youngblood AP	.50	.20
❑ 121 Bob Thomas	.20	.07
❑ 122 Jack Thompson RC	.50	.20
❑ 123 Randy Cross	1.00	.40
❑ 124 Karl Lorch RC	.20	.07
❑ 125 Mel Gray	.20	.07
❑ 126 John James	.20	.07
❑ 127 Terdell Middleton	.20	.07
❑ 128 Leroy Jones	.20	.07
❑ 129 Tom DeLeone	.20	.07
❑ 130 John Stallworth	1.50	.60
❑ 131 Jimmie Giles RC	.50	.20
❑ 132 Philadelphia Eagles TL	1.00	.40
❑ 133 Gary Green	.20	.07
❑ 134 John Dutton	.50	.20
❑ 135 Harry Carson	1.00	.40
❑ 136 Bob Kuechenberg	.50	.20
❑ 137 Ike Harris	.20	.07
❑ 138 Tommy Kramer RC	1.00	.40
❑ 139 Sam Adams OL	.20	.07
❑ 140 Doug English	.50	.20
❑ 141 Steve Schubert	.20	.07
❑ 142 Rusty Jackson	.20	.07
❑ 143 Reese McCall	.20	.07
❑ 144 Scott Dierking	.20	.07
❑ 145 Ken Houston	1.00	.40
❑ 146 Bob Martin	.20	.07
❑ 147 Sam McCullum	.20	.07
❑ 148 Tom Banks	.20	.07
❑ 149 Willie Buchanon	.20	.07
❑ 150 Greg Pruitt	.50	.20
❑ 151 Denver Broncos TL	1.00	.40
❑ 152 Don Smith RC	.20	.07
❑ 153 Pete Johnson	.50	.20
❑ 154 Charlie Smith WR	.20	.07
❑ 155 Mel Blount	1.00	.40
❑ 156 John Mendenhall	.20	.07
❑ 157 Danny White	1.00	.40
❑ 158 Jimmy Cefalo RC	.50	.20
❑ 159 Richard Bishop AP	.20	.07
❑ 160 Walter Payton	12.00	6.00
❑ 161 Dave Dalby	.20	.07
❑ 162 Preston Dennard	.20	.07
❑ 163 Johnnie Gray	.20	.07
❑ 164 Russell Erxleben	.20	.07
❑ 165 Toni Fritsch AP	.20	.07
❑ 166 Terry Hermeling	.20	.07
❑ 167 Roland Hooks	.20	.07
❑ 168 Roger Carr	.20	.07
❑ 169 San Diego Chargers TL	1.00	.40
❑ 170 Ottis Anderson RC	4.00	1.50
❑ 171 Brian Sipe	1.00	.40
❑ 172 Leonard Thompson	.20	.07
❑ 173 Tony Reed	.20	.07
❑ 174 Bob Tucker	.20	.07
❑ 175 Joe Greene	1.00	.40
❑ 176 Jack Dolbin	.20	.07
❑ 177 Chuck Ramsey	.20	.07
❑ 178 Paul Hofer	.20	.07
❑ 179 Randy Logan	.20	.07
❑ 180 David Lewis AP	.20	.07
❑ 181 Durlel Harris	.20	.07
❑ 182 June Jones	.50	.20
❑ 183 Larry McCarren	.20	.07
❑ 184 Ken Johnson RB	.20	.07
❑ 185 Charlie Waters	.50	.20
❑ 186 Noah Jackson	.20	.07
❑ 187 Reggie Williams	.50	.20
❑ 188 New England Patriots TL	.50	.20
❑ 189 Carl Eller	1.00	.40
❑ 190 Ed White AP	.20	.07
❑ 191 Mario Clark	.20	.07
❑ 192 Roosevelt Leaks	.20	.07
❑ 193 Ted McKnight	.20	.07
❑ 194 Danny Buggs	.20	.07
❑ 195 Lester Hayes RC	2.00	.75
❑ 196 Clarence Scott	.20	.07
❑ 197 Saints TL/Wes Chandler	.50	.20
❑ 198 Richard Caster	.20	.07
❑ 199 Louie Giammona	.20	.07
❑ 200 Terry Bradshaw	8.00	3.00
❑ 201 Ed Newman	.20	.07
❑ 202 Fred Dryer	1.00	.40
❑ 203 Dennis Franks	.20	.07
❑ 204 Bob Breunig RC	.50	.20
❑ 205 Alan Page	1.00	.40
❑ 206 Earnest Gray RC	.20	.07
❑ 207 Vikings TL/A.Rashad	1.00	.40
❑ 208 Horace Ivory	.20	.07
❑ 209 Isaac Hagins	.20	.07
❑ 210 Gary Johnson AP	.20	.07
❑ 211 Kevin Long	.20	.07
❑ 212 Bill Thompson	.20	.07
❑ 213 Don Bass	.20	.07
❑ 214 George Starke RC	.20	.07
❑ 215 Efren Herrera	.20	.07
❑ 216 Theo Bell	.20	.07
❑ 217 Monte Jackson	.20	.07
❑ 218 Reggie McKenzie	.20	.07
❑ 219 Bucky Dilts	.20	.07
❑ 220 Lyle Alzado	1.00	.40
❑ 221 Tim Foley	.20	.07
❑ 222 Mark Arneson	.20	.07
❑ 223 Fred Quillan	.20	.07
❑ 224 Benny Ricardo	.20	.07
❑ 225 Phil Simms RC	12.00	6.00
❑ 226 Bears TL/Walter Payton	1.25	.50
❑ 227 Max Runager	.20	.07
❑ 228 Barty Smith	.20	.07
❑ 229 Jay Saldi	.50	.20
❑ 230 John Hannah	1.00	.40
❑ 231 Tim Wilson	.20	.07
❑ 232 Jeff Van Note	.20	.07
❑ 233 Henry Marshall	.20	.07
❑ 234 Diron Talbert	.20	.07
❑ 235 Garo Yepremian	.50	.20
❑ 236 Larry Brown	.20	.07
❑ 237 Clarence Williams RB	.20	.07
❑ 238 Burgess Owens	.20	.07
❑ 239 Vince Ferragamo	.50	.20
❑ 240 Rickey Young	.20	.07
❑ 241 Dave Logan	.20	.07
❑ 242 Larry Gordon	.20	.07
❑ 243 Terry Miller	.20	.07
❑ 244 Baltimore Colts TL	1.00	.40
❑ 245 Steve DeBerg	1.00	.40
❑ 246 Checklist 133-264	.75	.30
❑ 247 Greg Latta	.20	.07
❑ 248 Raymond Clayborn	.50	.20

❑ 249 Jim Clack .20 .07
❑ 250 Drew Pearson 1.00 .40
❑ 251 John Bunting .50 .20
❑ 252 Rob Lytle .20 .07
❑ 253 Jim Hart 1.00 .40
❑ 254 John McDaniel .20 .07
❑ 255 Dave Pear AP .20 .07
❑ 256 Donnie Shell 1.00 .40
❑ 257 Dan Doornink .20 .07
❑ 258 Wallace Francis RC 1.00 .40
❑ 259 Dave Beverly .20 .07
❑ 260 Lee Roy Selmon 1.00 .40
❑ 261 Doug Dieken .20 .07
❑ 262 Gary Davis .20 .07
❑ 263 Bob Rush .20 .07
❑ 264 Buffalo Bills TL .50 .20
❑ 265 Greg Landry .50 .20
❑ 266 Jan Stenerud 1.00 .40
❑ 267 Tom Hicks .20 .07
❑ 268 Pat McInally .20 .07
❑ 269 Tim Fox .20 .07
❑ 270 Harvey Martin .50 .20
❑ 271 Dan Lloyd .20 .07
❑ 272 Mike Barber .20 .07
❑ 273 Wendell Tyler RC 1.00 .40
❑ 274 Jeff Komlo .20 .07
❑ 275 Wes Chandler RC 1.00 .40
❑ 276 Brad Dusek .20 .07
❑ 277 Charlie Johnson NT .20 .07
❑ 278 Dennis Swilley .20 .07
❑ 279 Johnny Evans .20 .07
❑ 280 Jack Lambert 1.50 .60
❑ 281 Vern Den Herder .20 .07
❑ 282 Tampa Bay Bucs TL 1.00 .40
❑ 283 Bob Klein .20 .07
❑ 284 Jim Turner .20 .07
❑ 285 Marvin Powell AP .50 .20
❑ 286 Aaron Kyle .20 .07
❑ 287 Dan Neal .20 .07
❑ 288 Wayne Morris .20 .07
❑ 289 Steve Bartkowski .50 .20
❑ 290 Dave Jennings AP .50 .20
❑ 291 John Smith .20 .07
❑ 292 Bill Gregory .20 .07
❑ 293 Frank Lewis .20 .07
❑ 294 Fred Cook .20 .07
❑ 295 David Hill AP .20 .07
❑ 296 Wade Key .20 .07
❑ 297 Sidney Thornton .20 .07
❑ 298 Charlie Hall .20 .07
❑ 299 Joe Lavender .20 .07
❑ 300 Tom Rafferty RC .20 .07
❑ 301 Mike Renfro RC .50 .20
❑ 302 Wilbur Jackson .50 .20
❑ 303 Packers TL/J.Lofton 1.00 .40
❑ 304 Henry Childs .20 .07
❑ 305 Russ Washington AP .20 .07
❑ 306 Jim LeClair .20 .07
❑ 307 Tommy Hart .20 .07
❑ 308 Gary Barbaro .20 .07
❑ 309 Billy Taylor .20 .07
❑ 310 Ray Guy .50 .20
❑ 311 Don Hasselbeck RC .50 .20
❑ 312 Doug Williams 1.00 .40
❑ 313 Nick Mike-Mayer .20 .07
❑ 314 Don McCauley .20 .07
❑ 315 Wesley Walker 1.00 .40
❑ 316 Dan Dierdorf 1.00 .40
❑ 317 Dave Brown DB RC .50 .20
❑ 318 Leroy Harris .20 .07
❑ 319 Steelers TL/Harris/Lambrt 1.00 .40
❑ 320 Mark Moseley AP UER .20 .07
❑ 321 Mark Dennard .20 .07
❑ 322 Terry Nelson .20 .07
❑ 323 Tom Jackson 1.00 .40
❑ 324 Rick Kane .20 .07
❑ 325 Jerry Sherk .20 .07
❑ 326 Ray Preston .20 .07
❑ 327 Golden Richards .20 .07
❑ 328 Randy Dean .20 .07
❑ 329 Rick Danmeier .20 .07
❑ 330 Tony Dorsett 6.00 3.00
❑ 331 R.Staubach/Fouts LL 3.00 1.50
❑ 332 Receiving Leaders .50 .20
❑ 333 Sacks Leaders 1.00 .40
❑ 334 Scoring Leaders 1.00 .40
❑ 335 Interception Leaders 1.00 .40
❑ 336 Punting Leaders 1.00 .40
❑ 337 Freddie Solomon .20 .07
❑ 338 Cincinnati Bengals TL/Jauron 1.00 .40
❑ 339 Ken Stone .20 .07
❑ 340 Greg Buttle AP .20 .07
❑ 341 Bob Baumhower .50 .20
❑ 342 Billy Waddy .20 .07
❑ 343 Cliff Parsley .20 .07
❑ 344 Walter White .20 .07
❑ 345 Mike Thomas .20 .07
❑ 346 Neil O'Donoghue .20 .07
❑ 347 Freddie Scott .20 .07
❑ 348 Joe Ferguson .50 .20
❑ 349 Doug Nettles .20 .07
❑ 350 Mike Webster 1.00 .40
❑ 351 Ron Saul .20 .07
❑ 352 Julius Adams .20 .07
❑ 353 Rafael Septien .20 .07
❑ 354 Cleo Miller .20 .07
❑ 355 Keith Simpson AP .20 .07
❑ 356 Johnny Perkins .20 .07
❑ 357 Jerry Sisemore .20 .07
❑ 358 Arthur Whittington .20 .07
❑ 359 Cardinals TL/Anderson 1.00 .40
❑ 360 Rick Upchurch .50 .20
❑ 361 Kim Bokamper RC .20 .07
❑ 362 Roland Harper .20 .07
❑ 363 Pat Leahy .20 .07
❑ 364 Louis Breeden .20 .07
❑ 365 John Jefferson 1.00 .40
❑ 366 Jerry Eckwood .20 .07
❑ 367 David Whitehurst .20 .07
❑ 368 Willie Parker C .20 .07
❑ 369 Ed Simonini .20 .07
❑ 370 Jack Youngblood 1.00 .40
❑ 371 Don Warren RC 1.00 .40
❑ 372 Andy Johnson .20 .07
❑ 373 D.D. Lewis .50 .20
❑ 374A B.Reece RC ERR 1.00 .40
❑ 374B Beasley Reece RC COR .50 .20
❑ 375 L.C.Greenwood 1.00 .40
❑ 376 Cleveland Browns TL .50 .20
❑ 377 Herman Edwards .20 .07
❑ 378 Rob Carpenter RC RB .20 .07
❑ 379 Herman Weaver .20 .07
❑ 380 Gary Fencik .20 .07
❑ 381 Don Strock .50 .20
❑ 382 Art Shell 1.00 .40
❑ 383 Tim Mazzetti .20 .07
❑ 384 Bruce Harper .20 .07
❑ 385 Al (Bubba) Baker .50 .20
❑ 386 Conrad Dobler .20 .07
❑ 387 Stu Voigt .20 .07
❑ 388 Ken Anderson 1.00 .40
❑ 389 Pat Tilley .20 .07
❑ 390 John Riggins 1.00 .40
❑ 391 Checklist 265-396 .75 .30
❑ 392 Fred Dean .20 .07
❑ 393 Benny Barnes RC .20 .07
❑ 394 Los Angeles Rams TL .50 .20
❑ 395 Brad Van Pelt .20 .07
❑ 396 Eddie Hare .20 .07
❑ 397 John Sciarra RC .20 .07
❑ 398 Bob Jackson .20 .07
❑ 399 John Yarno .20 .07
❑ 400 Franco Harris 2.00 .75
❑ 401 Ray Wersching .20 .07
❑ 402 Virgil Livers .20 .07
❑ 403 Raymond Chester .20 .07
❑ 404 Leon Gray .20 .07
❑ 405 Richard Todd .50 .20
❑ 406 Larry Little 1.00 .40
❑ 407 Ted Fritsch Jr. .20 .07
❑ 408 Larry Mucker .20 .07
❑ 409 Jim Allen .20 .07
❑ 410 Randy Gradishar 1.00 .40
❑ 411 Atlanta Falcons TL 1.00 .40
❑ 412 Louie Kelcher .50 .20
❑ 413 Robert Newhouse .50 .20
❑ 414 Gary Shirk .20 .07
❑ 415 Mike Haynes 1.00 .40
❑ 416 Craig Colquitt .20 .07
❑ 417 Lou Piccone .20 .07
❑ 418 Clay Matthews RC 2.50 1.00
❑ 419 Marvin Cobb .20 .07
❑ 420 Harold Carmichael 1.00 .40
❑ 421 Uwe Von Schamann .50 .20
❑ 422 Mike Phipps .50 .20
❑ 423 Nolan Cromwell RC 1.00 .40
❑ 424 Glenn Doughty .20 .07
❑ 425 Bob Young AP .20 .07
❑ 426 Tony Galbreath .20 .07
❑ 427 Luke Prestridge RC .20 .07
❑ 428 Terry Beeson .20 .07
❑ 429 Jack Tatum .50 .20
❑ 430 Lemar Parrish AP .20 .07
❑ 431 Chester Marcol .20 .07
❑ 432 Houston Oilers TL 1.00 .40
❑ 433 John Fitzgerald .20 .07
❑ 434 Gary Jeter RC .50 .20
❑ 435 Steve Grogan 1.00 .40
❑ 436 Jon Kolb UER .20 .07
❑ 437 Jim O'Bradovich UER .20 .07
❑ 438 Gerald Irons .20 .07
❑ 439 Jeff West .20 .07
❑ 440 Wilbert Montgomery .50 .20
❑ 441 Norris Thomas .20 .07
❑ 442 James Scott .20 .07
❑ 443 Curtis Brown .20 .07
❑ 444 Ken Fantetti .20 .07
❑ 445 Pat Haden 1.00 .40
❑ 446 Carl Mauck .20 .07
❑ 447 Bruce Laird .20 .07
❑ 448 Otis Armstrong .20 .07
❑ 449 Gene Upshaw 1.00 .40
❑ 450 Steve Largent 6.00 3.00
❑ 451 Benny Malone .20 .07
❑ 452 Steve Nelson .20 .07
❑ 453 Mark Cotney .20 .07
❑ 454 Joe Danelo .20 .07
❑ 455 Billy Joe DuPree .50 .20
❑ 456 Ron Johnson DB .20 .07
❑ 457 Archie Griffin .50 .20
❑ 458 Reggie Rucker .20 .07
❑ 459 Claude Humphrey .20 .07
❑ 460 Lydell Mitchell .50 .20
❑ 461 Steve Towle .20 .07
❑ 462 Revie Sorey .20 .07
❑ 463 Tom Skladany .20 .07
❑ 464 Clark Gaines .20 .07
❑ 465 Frank Corral .20 .07
❑ 466 Steve Fuller RC .50 .20
❑ 467 Ahmad Rashad 1.00 .40
❑ 468 Oakland Raiders TL 1.00 .40
❑ 469 Brian Peets .20 .07
❑ 470 Pat Donovan RC .50 .20
❑ 471 Ken Burrough .20 .07
❑ 472 Don Calhoun .20 .07
❑ 473 Bill Bryan .20 .07
❑ 474 Terry Jackson .20 .07
❑ 475 Joe Theismann 1.25 .50
❑ 476 Jim Smith .50 .20
❑ 477 Joe DeLamielleure 1.00 .40
❑ 478 Mike Pruitt AP .50 .20
❑ 479 Steve Mike-Mayer .20 .07
❑ 480 Bill Bergey .50 .20
❑ 481 Mike Fuller .20 .07
❑ 482 Bob Parsons .20 .07
❑ 483 Billy Brooks .20 .07
❑ 484 Jerome Barkum .20 .07
❑ 485 Larry Csonka 1.50 .60
❑ 486 John Hill .20 .07
❑ 487 Mike Dawson .20 .07
❑ 488 Detroit Lions TL .50 .20
❑ 489 Ted Hendricks 1.00 .40
❑ 490 Dan Pastorini .50 .20
❑ 491 Stanley Morgan 1.00 .40
❑ 492 AFC Champs/Bleier 1.00 .40
❑ 493 NFC Champs/Ferragamo .50 .20
❑ 494 Super Bowl XIV 1.00 .40
❑ 495 Dwight White .50 .20
❑ 496 Haven Moses .20 .07
❑ 497 Guy Morriss .20 .07
❑ 498 Dewey Selmon .50 .20
❑ 499 Dave Butz RC 1.00 .40
❑ 500 Chuck Foreman .50 .20
❑ 501 Chris Bahr .20 .07
❑ 502 Mark Miller QB .20 .07
❑ 503 Tony Greene .20 .07
❑ 504 Brian Kelley .20 .07
❑ 505 Joe Washington .50 .20
❑ 506 Butch Johnson .50 .20
❑ 507 New York Jets TL .50 .20
❑ 508 Steve Little .20 .07

❑ 509	Checklist 397-528	.75	.30
❑ 510	Mark Van Eeghen	.20	.07
❑ 511	Gary Danielson	.50	.20
❑ 512	Manu Tuiasosopo	.20	.07
❑ 513	Paul Coffman RC	.50	.20
❑ 514	Cullen Bryant	.20	.07
❑ 515	Nat Moore	.50	.20
❑ 516	Bill Lenkaitis	.20	.07
❑ 517	Lynn Cain RC	.20	.07
❑ 518	Gregg Bingham	.20	.07
❑ 519	Ted Albrecht	.20	.07
❑ 520	Dan Fouts	2.00	.75
❑ 521	Bernard Jackson	.20	.07
❑ 522	Coy Bacon	.20	.07
❑ 523	Tony Franklin RC	.50	.20
❑ 524	Bo Harris	.20	.07
❑ 525	Bob Grupp AP	.20	.07
❑ 526	San Francisco 49ers TL	1.00	.40
❑ 527	Steve Wilson	.20	.07
❑ 528	Bennie Cunningham	.50	.20

1981 Topps

❑	COMPLETE SET (528)	200.00	100.00
❑ 1	Ron Jaworski/B.Sipe LL	.75	.30
❑ 2	K.Winslow/Cooper LL	.75	.30
❑ 3	Sack Leaders	.40	.15
❑ 4	Scoring Leaders	.15	.05
❑ 5	Interception Leaders	.40	.15
❑ 6	Punting Leaders	.15	.05
❑ 7	Don Calhoun	.15	.05
❑ 8	Jack Tatum	.40	.15
❑ 9	Reggie Rucker	.15	.05
❑ 10	Mike Webster	.75	.30
❑ 11	Vince Evans RC	.75	.30
❑ 12	Ottis Anderson SA	.75	.30
❑ 13	Leroy Harris	.15	.05
❑ 14	Gordon King	.15	.05
❑ 15	Harvey Martin	.40	.15
❑ 16	Johnny Lam Jones RC	.40	.15
❑ 17	Ken Greene	.15	.05
❑ 18	Frank Lewis	.15	.05
❑ 19	Seahawks TL/Largent	.75	.30
❑ 20	Lester Hayes	.75	.30
❑ 21	Uwe Von Schamann	.15	.05
❑ 22	Joe Washington	.15	.05
❑ 23	Louie Kelcher	.15	.05
❑ 24	Willie Miller	.15	.05
❑ 25	Steve Grogan	.75	.30
❑ 26	John Hill	.15	.05
❑ 27	Stan White	.15	.05
❑ 28	William Andrews SA	.40	.15
❑ 29	Clarence Scott	.15	.05
❑ 30	Leon Gray AP	.15	.05
❑ 31	Craig Colquitt	.15	.05
❑ 32	Doug Williams	.75	.30
❑ 33	Bob Breunig	.40	.15
❑ 34	Billy Taylor	.15	.05
❑ 35	Harold Carmichael	.75	.30
❑ 36	Ray Wersching	.15	.05
❑ 37	Dennis Johnson LB RC	.15	.05
❑ 38	Archie Griffin	.40	.15
❑ 39	Los Angeles Rams TL	.40	.15
❑ 40	Gary Fencik	.40	.15
❑ 41	Lynn Dickey	.15	.05
❑ 42	Steve Bartkowski SA	.40	.15
❑ 43	Art Shell	.75	.30
❑ 44	Wilbur Jackson	.15	.05
❑ 45	Frank Corral	.15	.05
❑ 46	Ted McKnight	.15	.05
❑ 47	Joe Klecko	.40	.15
❑ 48	Dan Doornink	.15	.05
❑ 49	Doug Dieken	.15	.05
❑ 50	Jerry Robinson RC	.40	.15
❑ 51	Wallace Francis	.15	.05
❑ 52	Dave Preston RC	.15	.05
❑ 53	Jay Saldi	.15	.05
❑ 54	Rush Brown	.15	.05
❑ 55	Phil Simms	3.00	1.50
❑ 56	Nick Mike-Mayer	.15	.05
❑ 57	Redskins TL/A.Monk	2.00	.75
❑ 58	Mike Renfro	.15	.05
❑ 59	Ted Brown SA	.15	.05
❑ 60	Steve Nelson	.15	.05
❑ 61	Sidney Thornton	.15	.05
❑ 62	Kent Hill	.15	.05
❑ 63	Don Bessillieu	.15	.05
❑ 64	Fred Cook	.15	.05
❑ 65	Raymond Chester	.15	.05
❑ 66	Rick Kane	.15	.05
❑ 67	Mike Fuller	.15	.05
❑ 68	Dewey Selmon	.40	.15
❑ 69	Charles White RC	.75	.30
❑ 70	Jeff Van Note	.15	.05
❑ 71	Robert Newhouse	.40	.15
❑ 72	Roynell Young RC	.15	.05
❑ 73	Lynn Cain SA	.15	.05
❑ 74	Mike Friede	.15	.05
❑ 75	Earl Cooper RC	.15	.05
❑ 76	New Orleans Saints TL	.40	.15
❑ 77	Rick Danmeier	.15	.05
❑ 78	Darrol Ray	.15	.05
❑ 79	Gregg Bingham	.15	.05
❑ 80	John Hannah	.75	.30
❑ 81	Jack Thompson	.40	.15
❑ 82	Rick Upchurch	.40	.15
❑ 83	Mike Butler	.15	.05
❑ 84	Don Warren	.15	.05
❑ 85	Mark Van Eeghen	.15	.05
❑ 86	J.T.Smith RC	.75	.30
❑ 87	Herman Weaver	.15	.05
❑ 88	Terry Bradshaw SA	2.00	.75
❑ 89	Charlie Hall	.15	.05
❑ 90	Donnie Shell	.75	.30
❑ 91	Ike Harris	.15	.05
❑ 92	Charlie Johnson NT	.15	.05
❑ 93	Rickey Watts	.15	.05
❑ 94	New England Patriots TL	.75	.30
❑ 95	Drew Pearson	.75	.30
❑ 96	Neil O'Donoghue	.15	.05
❑ 97	Conrad Dobler	.15	.05
❑ 98	Jewerl Thomas RC	.15	.05
❑ 99	Mike Barber	.15	.05
❑ 100	Billy Sims RC	3.00	1.25
❑ 101	Vern Den Herder	.15	.05
❑ 102	Greg Landry	.40	.15
❑ 103	Joe Cribbs SA	.40	.15
❑ 104	Mark Murphy S RC	.15	.05
❑ 105	Chuck Muncie	.40	.15
❑ 106	Alfred Jackson	.40	.15
❑ 107	Chris Bahr	.15	.05
❑ 108	Gordon Jones	.15	.05
❑ 109	Willie Harper RC	.15	.05
❑ 110	Dave Jennings	.15	.05
❑ 111	Bennie Cunningham	.15	.05
❑ 112	Jerry Sisemore	.15	.05
❑ 113	Cleveland Browns TL	.75	.30
❑ 114	Rickey Young	.15	.05
❑ 115	Ken Anderson	.75	.30
❑ 116	Randy Gradishar	.75	.30
❑ 117	Eddie Lee Ivery RC	.15	.05
❑ 118	Wesley Walker	.75	.30
❑ 119	Chuck Foreman	.40	.15
❑ 120	Nolan Cromwell UER	.40	.15
❑ 121	Curtis Dickey SA	.15	.05
❑ 122	Wayne Morris	.15	.05
❑ 123	Greg Stemrick	.15	.05
❑ 124	Coy Bacon	.15	.05
❑ 125	Jim Zorn	.40	.15
❑ 126	Henry Childs	.15	.05
❑ 127	Checklist 1-132	.75	.30
❑ 128	Len Walterscheid	.15	.05
❑ 129	Johnny Evans	.15	.05
❑ 130	Gary Barbaro	.15	.05
❑ 131	Jim Smith	.15	.05
❑ 132	New York Jets TL	.40	.15
❑ 133	Curtis Brown	.15	.05
❑ 134	D.D. Lewis	.15	.05
❑ 135	Jim Plunkett	.75	.30
❑ 136	Nat Moore	.40	.15
❑ 137	Don McCauley	.15	.05
❑ 138	Tony Dorsett SA	.75	.30
❑ 139	Julius Adams	.15	.05
❑ 140	Ahmad Rashad	.75	.30
❑ 141	Rich Saul	.15	.05
❑ 142	Ken Fantetti	.15	.05
❑ 143	Kenny Johnson	.15	.05
❑ 144	Clark Gaines	.15	.05
❑ 145	Mark Moseley	.15	.05
❑ 146	Vernon Perry RC	.15	.05
❑ 147	Jerry Eckwood	.15	.05
❑ 148	Freddie Coleman	.15	.05
❑ 149	Jerry Sherk	.15	.05
❑ 150	Kellen Winslow RC	8.00	4.00
❑ 151	Packers TL/Lofton	.75	.30
❑ 152	Ross Browner	.15	.05
❑ 153	Dan Fouts SA	.75	.30
❑ 154	Woody Peoples	.15	.05
❑ 155	Jack Lambert	1.00	.40
❑ 156	Mike Dennis	.15	.05
❑ 157	Rafael Septien	.15	.05
❑ 158	Archie Manning	.75	.30
❑ 159	Don Hasselbeck	.15	.05
❑ 160	Alan Page	.75	.30
❑ 161	Arthur Whittington	.15	.05
❑ 162	Billy Waddy	.15	.05
❑ 163	Horace Belton	.15	.05
❑ 164	Luke Prestridge	.15	.05
❑ 165	Joe Theismann	.75	.30
❑ 166	Morris Towns	.15	.05
❑ 167	Dave Brown DB	.15	.05
❑ 168	Ezra Johnson	.15	.05
❑ 169	Tampa Bay Bucs TL	.15	.05
❑ 170	Joe DeLamielleure	.75	.30
❑ 171	Earnest Gray SA	.15	.05
❑ 172	Mike Thomas	.15	.05
❑ 173	Jim Haslett RC	2.00	.75
❑ 174	David Woodley RC	.40	.15
❑ 175	Al(Bubba) Baker	.40	.15
❑ 176	Nesby Glasgow RC	.15	.05
❑ 177	Pat Leahy	.15	.05
❑ 178	Tom Brahaney	.15	.05
❑ 179	Herman Edwards	.15	.05
❑ 180	Junior Miller RC	.15	.05
❑ 181	Richard Wood RC	.15	.05
❑ 182	Lenvil Elliott	.15	.05
❑ 183	Sammie White	.40	.15
❑ 184	Russell Erxleben	.15	.05
❑ 185	Ed Too Tall Jones	.75	.30
❑ 186	Ray Guy SA	.40	.15
❑ 187	Haven Moses	.15	.05
❑ 188	New York Giants TL	.40	.15
❑ 189	David Whitehurst	.15	.05
❑ 190	John Jefferson	.75	.30
❑ 191	Terry Beeson	.15	.05
❑ 192	Dan Ross RC	.40	.15
❑ 193	Dave Williams RB RC	.15	.05
❑ 194	Art Monk RC	15.00	7.50
❑ 195	Roger Wehrli	.40	.15
❑ 196	Ricky Feacher	.15	.05
❑ 197	Miami Dolphins TL	.75	.30
❑ 198	Carl Roaches RC	.15	.05
❑ 199	Billy Campfield	.15	.05
❑ 200	Ted Hendricks	.75	.30
❑ 201	Fred Smerlas RC	.75	.30
❑ 202	Walter Payton SA	3.00	1.25
❑ 203	Luther Bradley	.15	.05
❑ 204	Herb Scott	.15	.05
❑ 205	Jack Youngblood	.75	.30
❑ 206	Danny Pittman	.15	.05
❑ 207	Houston Oilers TL	.40	.15
❑ 208	Vagas Ferguson RC	.40	.15
❑ 209	Mark Dennard	.15	.05
❑ 210	Lemar Parrish	.15	.05
❑ 211	Bruce Harper	.15	.05
❑ 212	Ed Simonini	.15	.05
❑ 213	Nick Lowery RC	.75	.30
❑ 214	Kevin House RC	.40	.15
❑ 215	Mike Kenn RC	.75	.30
❑ 216	Joe Montana RC	150.00	75.00
❑ 217	Joe Senser	.15	.05
❑ 218	Lester Hayes SA	.40	.15
❑ 219	Gene Upshaw	.75	.30
❑ 220	Franco Harris	1.25	.50

❑	221	Ron Bolton	.15	.05
❑	222	Charles Alexander RC	.40	.15
❑	223	Matt Robinson	.15	.05
❑	224	Ray Oldham	.15	.05
❑	225	George Martin	.15	.05
❑	226	Buffalo Bills TL	.75	.30
❑	227	Tony Franklin	.15	.05
❑	228	George Cumby	.15	.05
❑	229	Butch Johnson	.40	.15
❑	230	Mike Haynes	.75	.30
❑	231	Rob Carpenter	.40	.15
❑	232	Steve Fuller	.40	.15
❑	233	John Sawyer	.15	.05
❑	234	Kenny King SA	.15	.05
❑	235	Jack Ham	.75	.30
❑	236	Jimmy Rogers	.15	.05
❑	237	Bob Parsons	.15	.05
❑	238	Marty Lyons RC	.75	.30
❑	239	Pat Tilley	.15	.05
❑	240	Dennis Harrah	.15	.05
❑	241	Thom Darden	.15	.05
❑	242	Rolf Benirschke	.15	.05
❑	243	Gerald Small	.15	.05
❑	244	Atlanta Falcons TL	.75	.30
❑	245	Roger Carr	.15	.05
❑	246	Sherman White	.15	.05
❑	247	Ted Brown	.15	.05
❑	248	Matt Cavanaugh	.40	.15
❑	249	John Dutton	.15	.05
❑	250	Bill Bergey	.40	.15
❑	251	Jim Allen	.15	.05
❑	252	Mike Nelms SA	.15	.05
❑	253	Tom Blanchard	.15	.05
❑	254	Ricky Thompson	.15	.05
❑	255	John Matuszak	.40	.15
❑	256	Randy Grossman	.15	.05
❑	257	Ray Griffin RC	.15	.05
❑	258	Lynn Cain	.15	.05
❑	259	Checklist 133-264	.75	.30
❑	260	Mike Pruitt	.40	.15
❑	261	Chris Ward RC	.15	.05
❑	262	Fred Steinfort	.15	.05
❑	263	James Owens	.15	.05
❑	264	Bears TL/Payton/Hampton	1.50	.60
❑	265	Dan Fouts	1.50	.60
❑	266	Arnold Morgado	.15	.05
❑	267	John Jefferson SA	.75	.30
❑	268	Bill Lenkaitis	.15	.05
❑	269	James Jones COW	.15	.05
❑	270	Brad Van Pelt	.15	.05
❑	271	Steve Largent	2.50	1.25
❑	272	Elvin Bethea	.75	.30
❑	273	Cullen Bryant	.15	.05
❑	274	Gary Danielson	.40	.15
❑	275	Tony Galbreath	.15	.05
❑	276	Dave Butz	.15	.05
❑	277	Steve Mike-Mayer	.15	.05
❑	278	Ron Johnson DB	.15	.05
❑	279	Tom DeLeone	.15	.05
❑	280	Ron Jaworski	.75	.30
❑	281	Mel Gray	.15	.05
❑	282	San Diego Chargers TL	.75	.30
❑	283	Mark Brammer RC	.15	.05
❑	284	Alfred Jenkins SA	.40	.15
❑	285	Greg Buttle	.15	.05
❑	286	Randy Hughes	.15	.05
❑	287	Delvin Williams	.15	.05
❑	288	Brian Baschnagel	.15	.05
❑	289	Gary Jeter	.15	.05
❑	290	Stanley Morgan	.75	.30
❑	291	Gerry Ellis	.15	.05
❑	292	Al Richardson	.15	.05
❑	293	Jimmie Giles	.40	.15
❑	294	Dave Jennings SA	.15	.05
❑	295	Wilbert Montgomery	.40	.15
❑	296	Dave Pureifory	.15	.05
❑	297	Greg Hawthorne	.15	.05
❑	298	Dick Ambrose	.15	.05
❑	299	Terry Hermeling	.15	.05
❑	300	Danny White	.75	.30
❑	301	Ken Burrough	.15	.05
❑	302	Paul Hofer	.15	.05
❑	303	Denver Broncos TL	.75	.30
❑	304	Eddie Payton	.40	.15
❑	305	Isaac Curtis	.40	.15
❑	306	Benny Ricardo	.15	.05
❑	307	Riley Odoms	.15	.05
❑	308	Bob Chandler	.15	.05
❑	309	Larry Heater	.15	.05
❑	310	Art Still RC	.75	.30
❑	311	Harold Jackson	.40	.15
❑	312	Charlie Joiner SA	.75	.30
❑	313	Jeff Nixon	.15	.05
❑	314	Aundra Thompson	.15	.05
❑	315	Richard Todd	.40	.15
❑	316	Dan Hampton RC	3.00	1.25
❑	317	Doug Marsh	.15	.05
❑	318	Louie Giammona	.15	.05
❑	319	49ers TL/Dwight Clark	.75	.30
❑	320	Manu Tuiasosopo	.15	.05
❑	321	Rich Milot	.15	.05
❑	322	Mike Guman RC	.15	.05
❑	323	Bob Kuechenberg	.40	.15
❑	324	Tom Skladany	.15	.05
❑	325	Dave Logan	.15	.05
❑	326	Bruce Laird	.15	.05
❑	327	James Jones COW SA	.15	.05
❑	328	Joe Danelo	.15	.05
❑	329	Kenny King RC	.40	.15
❑	330	Pat Donovan	.15	.05
❑	331	Earl Cooper RB	.40	.15
❑	332	John Jefferson RB	.75	.30
❑	333	Kenny King RB	.40	.15
❑	334	Rod Martin RB	.40	.15
❑	335	Jim Plunkett RB	.75	.30
❑	336	Bill Thompson RB	.40	.15
❑	337	John Cappelletti	.40	.15
❑	338	Lions TL/Billy Sims	.75	.30
❑	339	Don Smith	.15	.05
❑	340	Rod Perry	.15	.05
❑	341	David Lewis	.15	.05
❑	342	Mark Gastineau RC	1.00	.40
❑	343	Steve Largent SA	.75	.30
❑	344	Charle Young	.15	.05
❑	345	Toni Fritsch	.15	.05
❑	346	Matt Blair	.40	.15
❑	347	Don Bass	.15	.05
❑	348	Jim Jensen RC	.40	.15
❑	349	Karl Lorch	.15	.05
❑	350	Brian Sipe	.40	.15
❑	351	Theo Bell	.15	.05
❑	352	Sam Adams OL	.15	.05
❑	353	Paul Coffman	.15	.05
❑	354	Eric Harris	.15	.05
❑	355	Tony Hill	.40	.15
❑	356	J.T. Turner	.15	.05
❑	357	Frank LeMaster	.15	.05
❑	358	Jim Jodat	.15	.05
❑	359	Raiders TL/Hendricks	.75	.30
❑	360	Joe Cribbs RC	.75	.30
❑	361	James Lofton SA	.75	.30
❑	362	Dexter Bussey	.15	.05
❑	363	Bobby Jackson	.15	.05
❑	364	Steve DeBerg	.75	.30
❑	365	Ottis Anderson	1.00	.40
❑	366	Tom Myers	.15	.05
❑	367	John James	.15	.05
❑	368	Reese McCall	.15	.05
❑	369	Jack Reynolds	.40	.15
❑	370	Gary Johnson	.15	.05
❑	371	Jimmy Cefalo	.15	.05
❑	372	Horace Ivory	.15	.05
❑	373	Garo Yepremian	.15	.05
❑	374	Brian Kelley	.15	.05
❑	375	Terry Bradshaw	6.00	2.50
❑	376	Cowboys TL/Tony Dorsett	.75	.30
❑	377	Randy Logan	.15	.05
❑	378	Tim Wilson	.15	.05
❑	379	Archie Manning SA	.75	.30
❑	380	Revie Sorey	.15	.05
❑	381	Randy Holloway	.15	.05
❑	382	Henry Lawrence	.15	.05
❑	383	Pat McInally	.15	.05
❑	384	Kevin Long	.15	.05
❑	385	Louis Wright	.40	.15
❑	386	Leonard Thompson	.15	.05
❑	387	Jan Stenerud	.40	.15
❑	388	Raymond Butler RC	.15	.05
❑	389	Checklist 265-396	.75	.30
❑	390	Steve Bartkowski	.40	.15
❑	391	Clarence Harmon	.15	.05
❑	392	Wilbert Montgomery SA	.40	.15
❑	393	Billy Joe DuPree	.40	.15
❑	394	Kansas City Chiefs TL	.40	.15
❑	395	Earnest Gray	.15	.05
❑	396	Ray Hamilton	.15	.05
❑	397	Brenard Wilson	.15	.05
❑	398	Calvin Hill	.75	.30
❑	399	Robin Cole	.15	.05
❑	400	Walter Payton	12.00	6.00
❑	401	Jim Hart	.75	.30
❑	402	Ron Yary	.75	.30
❑	403	Cliff Branch	.75	.30
❑	404	Roland Hooks	.15	.05
❑	405	Ken Stabler	3.00	1.50
❑	406	Chuck Ramsey	.15	.05
❑	407	Mike Nelms RC	.15	.05
❑	408	Ron Jaworski SA	.40	.15
❑	409	James Hunter	.15	.05
❑	410	Lee Roy Selmon	.75	.30
❑	411	Baltimore Colts TL	.40	.15
❑	412	Henry Marshall	.15	.05
❑	413	Preston Pearson	.40	.15
❑	414	Richard Bishop	.15	.05
❑	415	Greg Pruitt	.40	.15
❑	416	Matt Bahr	.40	.15
❑	417	Tom Mullady	.15	.05
❑	418	Glen Edwards	.15	.05
❑	419	Sam McCullum	.15	.05
❑	420	Stan Walters	.15	.05
❑	421	George Roberts	.15	.05
❑	422	Dwight Clark RC	5.00	2.00
❑	423	Pat Thomas RC	.15	.05
❑	424	Bruce Harper SA	.15	.05
❑	425	Craig Morton	.40	.15
❑	426	Derrick Gaffney	.15	.05
❑	427	Pete Johnson	.15	.05
❑	428	Wes Chandler	.75	.30
❑	429	Burgess Owens	.15	.05
❑	430	James Lofton	2.00	.75
❑	431	Tony Reed	.15	.05
❑	432	Vikings TL/A.Rashad	.75	.30
❑	433	Ron Springs RC	.40	.15
❑	434	Tim Fox	.15	.05
❑	435	Ozzie Newsome	2.00	.75
❑	436	Steve Furness	.15	.05
❑	437	Will Lewis	.15	.05
❑	438	Mike Hartenstine	.15	.05
❑	439	John Bunting	.15	.05
❑	440	Eddie Murray RC	.75	.30
❑	441	Mike Pruitt SA	.40	.15
❑	442	Larry Swider	.15	.05
❑	443	Steve Freeman	.15	.05
❑	444	Bruce Hardy RC	.15	.05
❑	445	Pat Haden	.40	.15
❑	446	Curtis Dickey RC	.15	.05
❑	447	Doug Wilkerson	.15	.05
❑	448	Alfred Jenkins	.40	.15
❑	449	Dave Dalby	.15	.05
❑	450	Robert Brazile	.15	.05
❑	451	Bobby Hammond	.15	.05
❑	452	Raymond Clayborn	.15	.05
❑	453	Jim Miller P RC	.15	.05
❑	454	Roy Simmons	.15	.05
❑	455	Charlie Waters	.40	.15
❑	456	Ricky Bell	.75	.30
❑	457	Ahmad Rashad SA	.75	.30
❑	458	Don Cockroft	.15	.05
❑	459	Keith Krepfle	.15	.05
❑	460	Marvin Powell	.15	.05
❑	461	Tommy Kramer	.75	.30
❑	462	Jim LeClair	.15	.05
❑	463	Freddie Scott	.15	.05
❑	464	Rob Lytle	.15	.05
❑	465	Johnnie Gray	.15	.05
❑	466	Doug France RC	.15	.05
❑	467	Carlos Carson RC	.40	.15
❑	468	Cardinals TL/O.Anderson	.75	.30
❑	469	Efren Herrera	.15	.05
❑	470	Randy White	1.00	.40
❑	471	Richard Caster	.15	.05
❑	472	Andy Johnson	.15	.05
❑	473	Billy Sims SA	.75	.30
❑	474	Joe Lavender	.15	.05
❑	475	Harry Carson	.40	.15
❑	476	John Stallworth	1.00	.40
❑	477	Bob Thomas	.15	.05
❑	478	Keith Wright RC	.15	.05
❑	479	Ken Stone	.15	.05
❑	480	Carl Hairston	.40	.15
❑	481	Reggie McKenzie	.15	.05

❑ 482 Bob Griese	1.50	.60
❑ 483 Mike Bragg	.15	.05
❑ 484 Scott Dierking	.15	.05
❑ 485 David Hill	.15	.05
❑ 486 Brian Sipe SA	.40	.15
❑ 487 Rod Martin RC	.40	.15
❑ 488 Cincinnati Bengals TL	.40	.15
❑ 489 Preston Dennard	.15	.05
❑ 490 John Smith	.15	.05
❑ 491 Mike Reinfeldt	.15	.05
❑ 492 NFC Champs/Jaworski	.75	.30
❑ 493 AFC Champs/Plunkett	.75	.30
❑ 494 Super Bowl XV/J.Plunkett	.75	.30
❑ 495 Joe Greene	.75	.30
[illegible]	[illegible]	[illegible]
❑ 497 Rolland Lawrence	.15	.05
❑ 498 Al(Bubba) Baker SA	.40	.15
❑ 499 Brad Dusek	.15	.05
❑ 500 Tony Dorsett	4.00	2.00
❑ 501 Robin Earl	.15	.05
❑ 502 Theotis Brown RC	.15	.05
❑ 503 Joe Ferguson	.40	.15
❑ 504 Beasley Reece	.15	.05
❑ 505 Lyle Alzado	.75	.30
❑ 506 Tony Nathan RC	.75	.30
❑ 507 Philadelphia Eagles TL	.40	.15
❑ 508 Herb Orvis	.15	.05
❑ 509 Clarence Williams RB	.15	.05
❑ 510 Ray Guy	.40	.15
❑ 511 Jeff Komlo	.15	.05
❑ 512 Freddie Solomon SA	.15	.05
❑ 513 Tim Mazzetti	.15	.05
❑ 514 Elvis Peacock RC	.15	.05
❑ 515 Russ Francis	.40	.15
❑ 516 Roland Harper	.15	.05
❑ 517 Checklist 397-528	.75	.30
❑ 518 Billy Johnson	.40	.15
❑ 519 Dan Dierdorf	.75	.30
❑ 520 Fred Dean	.15	.05
❑ 521 Jerry Butler	.15	.05
❑ 522 Ron Saul	.15	.05
❑ 523 Charlie Smith WR	.15	.05
❑ 524 Kellen Winslow SA	3.00	1.50
❑ 525 Bert Jones	.75	.30
❑ 526 Steelers TL/Fr.Harris	.75	.30
❑ 527 Duriel Harris	.15	.05
❑ 528 William Andrews	.75	.30

1982 Topps

❑ COMPLETE SET (528)	80.00	40.00
❑ 1 Ken Anderson RB	.75	.30
❑ 2 Dan Fouts RB	.75	.30
❑ 3 LeRoy Irvin RB	.15	.05
❑ 4 Stump Mitchell RB	.15	.05
❑ 5 George Rogers RB	.75	.30
❑ 6 Dan Ross RB	.15	.05
❑ 7 AFC Champs/K.Anderson	.75	.30
❑ 8 NFC Champs/E.Cooper	.75	.30
❑ 9 Super Bowl XVI/A.Munoz	.75	.30
❑ 10 Baltimore Colts TL	.15	.05
❑ 11 Raymond Butler	.15	.05
❑ 12 Roger Carr	.15	.05
❑ 13 Curtis Dickey	.40	.15
❑ 14 Zachary Dixon	.15	.05
❑ 15 Nesby Glasgow	.15	.05
❑ 16 Bert Jones	.75	.30
❑ 17 Bruce Laird	.15	.05
❑ 18 Reese McCall	.15	.05
❑ 19 Randy McMillan	.15	.05
❑ 20 Ed Simonini	.15	.05
❑ 21 Buffalo Bills TL	.40	.15
❑ 22 Mark Brammer	.15	.05
❑ 23 Curtis Brown	.15	.05
❑ 24 Jerry Butler	.15	.05
❑ 25 Mario Clark	.15	.05
❑ 26 Joe Cribbs	.40	.15
❑ 27 Joe Cribbs IA	.40	.15
❑ 28 Joe Ferguson	.40	.15
❑ 29 Jim Haslett	.75	.30
❑ 30 Frank Lewis	.15	.05
❑ 31 Frank Lewis IA	.15	.05
❑ 32 Shane Nelson	.15	.05
❑ 33 Charles Romes	.15	.05
❑ 34 Bill Simpson	.15	.05
❑ 35 Fred Smerlas	.15	.05
❑ 36 Bengals TL/C.Collinswort	.40	.15
❑ 37 Charles Alexander	.15	.05
❑ 38 Ken Anderson	.75	.30
❑ 39 Ken Anderson IA	.75	.30
❑ 40 Jim Breech	.15	.05
❑ 41 Jim Breech IA	.15	.05
❑ 42 Louie Breeden	.15	.05
❑ 43 Ross Browner	.15	.05
❑ 44 Cris Collinsworth RC	2.00	.75
❑ 45 Cris Collinsworth IA	.75	.30
❑ 46 Isaac Curtis	.15	.05
❑ 47 Pete Johnson	.15	.05
❑ 48 Pete Johnson IA	.15	.05
❑ 49 Steve Kreider	.15	.05
❑ 50 Pat McInally	.15	.05
❑ 51 Anthony Munoz RC	8.00	4.00
❑ 52 Dan Ross	.15	.05
❑ 53 David Verser RC	.15	.05
❑ 54 Reggie Williams	.40	.15
❑ 55 Browns TL/O.Newsome	.40	.15
❑ 56 Lyle Alzado	.75	.30
❑ 57 Dick Ambrose	.15	.05
❑ 58 Ron Bolton	.15	.05
❑ 59 Steve Cox	.15	.05
❑ 60 Joe DeLamielleure	.75	.30
❑ 61 Tom DeLeone	.15	.05
❑ 62 Doug Dieken	.15	.05
❑ 63 Ricky Feacher	.15	.05
❑ 64 Don Goode	.15	.05
❑ 65 Robert L.Jackson RC	.15	.05
❑ 66 Dave Logan	.15	.05
❑ 67 Ozzie Newsome	1.00	.40
❑ 68 Ozzie Newsome IA	.75	.30
❑ 69 Greg Pruitt	.40	.15
❑ 70 Mike Pruitt	.40	.15
❑ 71 Mike Pruitt IA	.40	.15
❑ 72 Reggie Rucker	.15	.05
❑ 73 Clarence Scott	.15	.05
❑ 74 Brian Sipe	.40	.15
❑ 75 Charles White	.40	.15
❑ 76 Denver Broncos TL	.40	.15
❑ 77 Rubin Carter	.15	.05
❑ 78 Steve Foley	.15	.05
❑ 79 Randy Gradishar	.40	.15
❑ 80 Tom Jackson	.75	.30
❑ 81 Craig Morton	.40	.15
❑ 82 Craig Morton IA	.40	.15
❑ 83 Riley Odoms	.15	.05
❑ 84 Rick Parros	.15	.05
❑ 85 Dave Preston	.15	.05
❑ 86 Tony Reed	.15	.05
❑ 87 Bob Swenson RC	.15	.05
❑ 88 Bill Thompson	.15	.05
❑ 89 Rick Upchurch	.40	.15
❑ 90 Steve Watson RC	.40	.15
❑ 91 Steve Watson IA	.15	.05
❑ 92 Houston Oilers TL	.15	.05
❑ 93 Mike Barber	.15	.05
❑ 94 Elvin Bethea	.75	.30
❑ 95 Gregg Bingham	.15	.05
❑ 96 Robert Brazile	.15	.05
❑ 97 Ken Burrough	.15	.05
❑ 98 Toni Fritsch	.15	.05
❑ 99 Leon Gray	.15	.05
❑ 100 Gifford Nielsen RC	.40	.15
❑ 101 Vernon Perry	.15	.05
❑ 102 Mike Reinfeldt	.15	.05
❑ 103 Mike Renfro	.15	.05
❑ 104 Carl Roaches	.15	.05
❑ 105 Ken Stabler	2.00	.75
❑ 106 Greg Stemrick	.15	.05
❑ 107 J.C. Wilson	.15	.05
❑ 108 Tim Wilson	.15	.05
❑ 109 Kansas City Chiefs TL	.15	.05
❑ 110 Gary Barbaro	.15	.05
❑ 111 Brad Budde RC	.15	.05
❑ 112 Joe Delaney RC	.75	.30
❑ 113 Joe Delaney IA	.40	.15
❑ 114 Steve Fuller	.15	.05
❑ 115 Gary Green	.15	.05
❑ 116 James Hadnot	.15	.05
❑ 117 Eric Harris	.15	.05
❑ 118 Billy Jackson	.15	.05
❑ 119 Bill Kenney RC	.15	.05
❑ 120 Nick Lowery	.75	.30
❑ 121 Nick Lowery IA	.40	.15
❑ 122 Henry Marshall	.15	.05
❑ 123 J.T.Smith	.40	.15
❑ 124 Art Still	.15	.05
❑ 125 Miami Dolphins TL	.40	.15
❑ 126 Bob Baumhower	.40	.15
❑ 127 Glenn Blackwood RC	.15	.05
❑ 128 Jimmy Cefalo	.15	.05
❑ 129 A.J. Duhe	.40	.15
❑ 130 Andra Franklin RC	.15	.05
❑ 131 Duriel Harris	.15	.05
❑ 132 Nat Moore	.40	.15
❑ 133 Tony Nathan	.40	.15
❑ 134 Ed Newman	.15	.05
❑ 135 Earnie Rhone	.15	.05
❑ 136 Don Strock	.15	.05
❑ 137 Tommy Vigorito	.15	.05
❑ 138 Uwe Von Schamann	.15	.05
❑ 139 Uwe Von Schamann IA	.15	.05
❑ 140 David Woodley	.40	.15
❑ 141 New England Pats TL	.40	.15
❑ 142 Julius Adams	.15	.05
❑ 143 Richard Bishop	.15	.05
❑ 144 Matt Cavanaugh	.15	.05
❑ 145 Raymond Clayborn	.15	.05
❑ 146 Tony Collins RC	.15	.05
❑ 147 Vagas Ferguson	.15	.05
❑ 148 Tim Fox	.15	.05
❑ 149 Steve Grogan	.40	.15
❑ 150 John Hannah	.75	.30
❑ 151 John Hannah IA	.40	.15
❑ 152 Don Hasselbeck	.15	.05
❑ 153 Mike Haynes	.40	.15
❑ 154 Harold Jackson	.40	.15
❑ 155 Andy Johnson	.15	.05
❑ 156 Stanley Morgan	.40	.15
❑ 157 Stanley Morgan IA	.40	.15
❑ 158 Steve Nelson	.15	.05
❑ 159 Rod Shoate	.15	.05
❑ 160 Jets TL/F.McNeil	.40	.15
❑ 161 Dan Alexander RC	.15	.05
❑ 162 Mike Augustyniak	.15	.05
❑ 163 Jerome Barkum	.15	.05
❑ 164 Greg Buttle	.15	.05
❑ 165 Scott Dierking	.15	.05
❑ 166 Joe Fields	.15	.05
❑ 167 Mark Gastineau	.40	.15
❑ 168 Mark Gastineau IA	.40	.15
❑ 169 Bruce Harper	.15	.05
❑ 170 Johnny Lam Jones	.15	.05
❑ 171 Joe Klecko	.40	.15
❑ 172 Joe Klecko IA	.40	.15
❑ 173 Pat Leahy	.40	.15
❑ 174 Pat Leahy IA	.15	.05
❑ 175 Marty Lyons	.40	.15
❑ 176 Freeman McNeil RC	.75	.30
❑ 177 Marvin Powell	.15	.05
❑ 178 Chuck Ramsey	.15	.05
❑ 179 Darrol Ray	.15	.05
❑ 180 Abdul Salaam	.15	.05
❑ 181 Richard Todd	.40	.15
❑ 182 Richard Todd IA	.40	.15
❑ 183 Wesley Walker	.40	.15
❑ 184 Chris Ward	.15	.05
❑ 185 Oakland Raiders TL	.40	.15
❑ 186 Cliff Branch	.75	.30
❑ 187 Bob Chandler	.15	.05
❑ 188 Ray Guy	.40	.15
❑ 189 Lester Hayes	.40	.15
❑ 190 Ted Hendricks	.75	.30
❑ 191 Monte Jackson	.15	.05
❑ 192 Derrick Jensen	.15	.05
❑ 193 Kenny King	.15	.05

❑ 194 Rod Martin .15 .05
❑ 195 John Matuszak .40 .15
❑ 196 Matt Millen RC 1.50 .60
❑ 197 Derrick Ramsey .15 .05
❑ 198 Art Shell .75 .30
❑ 199 Mark Van Eeghen .15 .05
❑ 200 Arthur Whittington .15 .05
❑ 201 Marc Wilson RC .40 .15
❑ 202 Steelers TL/Fr.Harris .75 .30
❑ 203 Mel Blount .75 .30
❑ 204 Terry Bradshaw 5.00 2.00
❑ 205 Terry Bradshaw IA 1.25 .50
❑ 206 Craig Colquitt .15 .05
❑ 207 Bennie Cunningham .15 .05
❑ 208 Russell Davis RC .15 .05
❑ 209 Gary Dunn .15 .05
❑ 210 Jack Ham .75 .30
❑ 211 Franco Harris 1.00 .40
❑ 212 Franco Harris IA .75 .30
❑ 213 Jack Lambert .75 .30
❑ 214 Jack Lambert IA .75 .30
❑ 215 Mark Malone RC .75 .30
❑ 216 Frank Pollard RC .15 .05
❑ 217 Donnie Shell .75 .30
❑ 218 Jim Smith .15 .05
❑ 219 John Stallworth .75 .30
❑ 220 John Stallworth IA .75 .30
❑ 221 David Trout .15 .05
❑ 222 Mike Webster .75 .30
❑ 223 San Diego Chargers TL .75 .30
❑ 224 Rolf Benirschke .15 .05
❑ 225 Rolf Benirschke IA .15 .05
❑ 226 James Brooks RC .75 .30
❑ 227 Willie Buchanon .15 .05
❑ 228 Wes Chandler .75 .30
❑ 229 Wes Chandler IA .40 .15
❑ 230 Dan Fouts 1.00 .40
❑ 231 Dan Fouts IA .75 .30
❑ 232 Gary Johnson .15 .05
❑ 233 Charlie Joiner .75 .30
❑ 234 Charlie Joiner IA .75 .30
❑ 235 Louie Kelcher .15 .05
❑ 236 Chuck Muncie .40 .15
❑ 237 Chuck Muncie IA .15 .05
❑ 238 George Roberts .15 .05
❑ 239 Ed White .15 .05
❑ 240 Doug Wilkerson .15 .05
❑ 241 Kellen Winslow 2.00 .75
❑ 242 Kellen Winslow IA .75 .30
❑ 243 Seahawks TL/S.Largent .75 .30
❑ 244 Theotis Brown .15 .05
❑ 245 Dan Doornink .15 .05
❑ 246 John Harris .15 .05
❑ 247 Efren Herrera .15 .05
❑ 248 David Hughes .15 .05
❑ 249 Steve Largent 2.00 .75
❑ 250 Steve Largent IA .75 .30
❑ 251 Sam McCullum .15 .05
❑ 252 Sherman Smith .15 .05
❑ 253 Manu Tuiasosopo .15 .05
❑ 254 John Yarno .15 .05
❑ 255 Jim Zorn .40 .15
❑ 256 Jim Zorn IA .40 .15
❑ 257 J.Montana/Anderson LL 4.00 2.00
❑ 258 Kellen Winslow/Clark LL .75 .30
❑ 259 QB Sack Leaders .15 .05
❑ 260 Scoring Leaders .40 .15
❑ 261 Interception Leaders .40 .15
❑ 262 Punting Leaders .15 .05
❑ 263 Brothers: Bahr .15 .05
❑ 264 Brothers: Blackwood .40 .15
❑ 265 Brothers: Brock .15 .05
❑ 266 Brothers: Griffin .40 .15
❑ 267 Brothers: Hannah .75 .30
❑ 268 Brothers: Jackson .15 .05
❑ 269 Walter/Eddie Payton 1.00 .40
❑ 270 Brothers: Selmon .75 .30
❑ 271 Atlanta Falcons TL .40 .15
❑ 272 William Andrews .40 .15
❑ 273 William Andrews IA .40 .15
❑ 274 Steve Bartkowski .40 .15
❑ 275 Steve Bartkowski IA .40 .15
❑ 276 Bobby Butler RC .15 .05
❑ 277 Lynn Cain .15 .05
❑ 278 Wallace Francis .15 .05
❑ 279 Alfred Jackson .15 .05
❑ 280 John James .15 .05
❑ 281 Alfred Jenkins .15 .05
❑ 282 Alfred Jenkins IA .15 .05
❑ 283 Kenny Johnson .15 .05
❑ 284 Mike Kenn .75 .30
❑ 285 Fulton Kuykendall .15 .05
❑ 286 Mick Luckhurst RC .15 .05
❑ 287 Mick Luckhurst IA .15 .05
❑ 288 Junior Miller .15 .05
❑ 289 Al Richardson .15 .05
❑ 290 R.C.Thielemann RC .15 .05
❑ 291 Jeff Van Note .15 .05
❑ 292 Bears TL/Walter Payton .75 .30
❑ 293 Brian Baschnagel .15 .05
❑ 294 Robin Earl .15 .05
❑ 295 Vince Evans .40 .15
❑ 296 Gary Fencik .15 .05
❑ 297 Dan Hampton .75 .30
❑ 298 Noah Jackson .15 .05
❑ 299 Ken Margerum .15 .05
❑ 300 Jim Osborne .15 .05
❑ 301 Bob Parsons .15 .05
❑ 302 Walter Payton 10.00 4.00
❑ 303 Walter Payton IA 3.00 1.25
❑ 304 Revie Sorey .15 .05
❑ 305 Matt Suhey RC .75 .30
❑ 306 Rickey Watts .15 .05
❑ 307 Cowboys TL/Dorsett .75 .30
❑ 308 Bob Breunig .15 .05
❑ 309 Doug Cosbie RC .15 .05
❑ 310 Pat Donovan .15 .05
❑ 311 Tony Dorsett 1.50 .60
❑ 312 Tony Dorsett IA .75 .30
❑ 313 Michael Downs RC .15 .05
❑ 314 Billy Joe DuPree .40 .15
❑ 315 John Dutton .15 .05
❑ 316 Tony Hill .40 .15
❑ 317 Butch Johnson .40 .15
❑ 318 Ed Too Tall Jones .75 .30
❑ 319 James Jones COW .15 .05
❑ 320 Harvey Martin .40 .15
❑ 321 Drew Pearson .75 .30
❑ 322 Herb Scott .15 .05
❑ 323 Rafael Septien .15 .05
❑ 324 Rafael Septien IA .15 .05
❑ 325 Ron Springs .40 .15
❑ 326 Dennis Thurman RC .15 .05
❑ 327 Everson Walls RC .75 .30
❑ 328 Everson Walls IA .75 .30
❑ 329 Danny White .75 .30
❑ 330 Danny White IA .40 .15
❑ 331 Randy White .75 .30
❑ 332 Randy White IA .75 .30
❑ 333 Detroit Lions TL .40 .15
❑ 334 Jim Allen .15 .05
❑ 335 Al(Bubba) Baker .40 .15
❑ 336 Dexter Bussey .15 .05
❑ 337 Doug English .40 .15
❑ 338 Ken Fantetti .15 .05
❑ 339 William Gay .15 .05
❑ 340 David Hill .15 .05
❑ 341 Eric Hipple RC .15 .05
❑ 342 Rick Kane .15 .05
❑ 343 Eddie Murray .75 .30
❑ 344 Eddie Murray IA .40 .15
❑ 345 Ray Oldham .15 .05
❑ 346 Dave Pureifory .15 .05
❑ 347 Freddie Scott .15 .05
❑ 348 Freddie Scott IA .15 .05
❑ 349 Billy Sims .75 .30
❑ 350 Billy Sims IA .75 .30
❑ 351 Tom Skladany .15 .05
❑ 352 Leonard Thompson .15 .05
❑ 353 Stan White .15 .05
❑ 354 Packers TL/Lofton .75 .30
❑ 355 Paul Coffman .15 .05
❑ 356 George Cumby .15 .05
❑ 357 Lynn Dickey .15 .05
❑ 358 Lynn Dickey IA .15 .05
❑ 359 Gerry Ellis .15 .05
❑ 360 Maurice Harvey .15 .05
❑ 361 Harlan Huckleby .15 .05
❑ 362 John Jefferson .75 .30
❑ 363 Mark Lee RC .15 .05
❑ 364 James Lofton 1.00 .40
❑ 365 James Lofton IA .75 .30
❑ 366 Jan Stenerud .40 .15
❑ 367 Jan Stenerud IA .40 .15
❑ 368 Rich Wingo .15 .05
❑ 369 Los Angeles Rams TL .40 .15
❑ 370 Frank Corral .15 .05
❑ 371 Nolan Cromwell .40 .15
❑ 372 Nolan Cromwell IA .40 .15
❑ 373 Preston Dennard .15 .05
❑ 374 Mike Fanning .15 .05
❑ 375 Doug France .15 .05
❑ 376 Mike Guman .15 .05
❑ 377 Pat Haden .40 .15
❑ 378 Dennis Harrah .15 .05
❑ 379 Drew Hill RC .75 .30
❑ 380 LeRoy Irvin RC .15 .05
❑ 381 Cody Jones .15 .05
❑ 382 Rod Perry .15 .05
❑ 383 Rich Saul .15 .05
❑ 384 Pat Thomas .15 .05
❑ 385 Wendell Tyler .40 .15
❑ 386 Wendell Tyler IA .40 .15
❑ 387 Billy Waddy .15 .05
❑ 388 Jack Youngblood .75 .30
❑ 389 Minnesota Vikings TL .15 .05
❑ 390 Matt Blair .15 .05
❑ 391 Ted Brown .15 .05
❑ 392 Ted Brown IA .15 .05
❑ 393 Rick Danmeier .15 .05
❑ 394 Tommy Kramer .40 .15
❑ 395 Mark Mullaney .15 .05
❑ 396 Eddie Payton .15 .05
❑ 397 Ahmad Rashad .75 .30
❑ 398 Joe Senser .15 .05
❑ 399 Joe Senser IA .15 .05
❑ 400 Sammie White .40 .15
❑ 401 Sammie White IA .15 .05
❑ 402 Ron Yary .75 .30
❑ 403 Rickey Young .15 .05
❑ 404 Saints TL/Ric.Jackson .40 .15
❑ 405 Russell Erxleben .15 .05
❑ 406 Elois Grooms .15 .05
❑ 407 Jack Holmes .15 .05
❑ 408 Archie Manning .75 .30
❑ 409 Derland Moore .15 .05
❑ 410 George Rogers RC .75 .30
❑ 411 George Rogers IA .75 .30
❑ 412 Toussaint Tyler .15 .05
❑ 413 Dave Waymer RC .15 .05
❑ 414 Wayne Wilson .15 .05
❑ 415 New York Giants TL .15 .05
❑ 416 Scott Brunner RC .15 .05
❑ 417 Rob Carpenter .15 .05
❑ 418 Harry Carson .40 .15
❑ 419 Bill Currier .15 .05
❑ 420 Joe Danelo .15 .05
❑ 421 Joe Danelo IA .15 .05
❑ 422 Mark Haynes RC .15 .05
❑ 423 Terry Jackson .15 .05
❑ 424 Dave Jennings .15 .05
❑ 425 Gary Jeter .15 .05
❑ 426 Brian Kelley .15 .05
❑ 427 George Martin .15 .05
❑ 428 Curtis McGriff .15 .05
❑ 429 Bill Neill .15 .05
❑ 430 Johnny Perkins .15 .05
❑ 431 Beasley Reece .15 .05
❑ 432 Gary Shirk .15 .05
❑ 433 Phil Simms 2.00 .75
❑ 434 Lawrence Taylor RC 20.00 7.50
❑ 435 Lawrence Taylor IA 10.00 4.00
❑ 436 Brad Van Pelt .15 .05
❑ 437 Philadelphia Eagles TL .40 .15
❑ 438 John Bunting .15 .05
❑ 439 Billy Campfield .15 .05
❑ 440 Harold Carmichael .75 .30
❑ 441 Harold Carmichael IA .75 .30
❑ 442 Herman Edwards .15 .05
❑ 443 Tony Franklin .15 .05
❑ 444 Tony Franklin IA .15 .05
❑ 445 Carl Hairston .15 .05
❑ 446 Dennis Harrison .15 .05
❑ 447 Ron Jaworski .75 .30
❑ 448 Charlie Johnson NT .15 .05
❑ 449 Keith Krepfle .15 .05
❑ 450 Frank LeMaster .15 .05
❑ 451 Randy Logan .15 .05
❑ 452 Wilbert Montgomery .40 .15
❑ 453 Wilbert Montgomery IA .40 .15
❑ 454 Hubie Oliver .15 .05

❑ 455 Jerry Robinson .15 .05
❑ 456 Jerry Robinson IA .15 .05
❑ 457 Jerry Sisemore .15 .05
❑ 458 Charlie Smith WR .15 .05
❑ 459 Stan Walters .15 .05
❑ 460 Brenard Wilson .15 .05
❑ 461 Roynell Young .15 .05
❑ 462 Cardinals TL/O.Anderson .40 .15
❑ 463 Ottis Anderson .75 .30
❑ 464 Ottis Anderson IA .75 .30
❑ 465 Carl Birdsong .15 .05
❑ 466 Rush Brown .15 .05
❑ 467 Mel Gray .40 .15
❑ [illegible]
❑ 469 Jim Hart .75 .30
❑ 470 E.J.Junior RC .40 .15
❑ 471 Neil Lomax RC .75 .30
❑ 472 Stump Mitchell RC .75 .30
❑ 473 Wayne Morris .15 .05
❑ 474 Neil O'Donoghue .15 .05
❑ 475 Pat Tilley .15 .05
❑ 476 Pat Tilley IA .15 .05
❑ 477 49ers TL/Dwight Clark .40 .15
❑ 478 Dwight Clark .75 .30
❑ 479 Dwight Clark IA .75 .30
❑ 480 Earl Cooper .15 .05
❑ 481 Randy Cross .40 .15
❑ 482 Johnny Davis RC .15 .05
❑ 483 Fred Dean .15 .05
❑ 484 Fred Dean IA .15 .05
❑ 485 Dwight Hicks RC .75 .30
❑ 486 Ronnie Lott RC 20.00 7.50
❑ 487 Ronnie Lott IA 8.00 3.00
❑ 488 Joe Montana 20.00 7.50
❑ 489 Joe Montana IA 12.00 5.00
❑ 490 Ricky Patton .15 .05
❑ 491 Jack Reynolds .40 .15
❑ 492 Freddie Solomon .15 .05
❑ 493 Ray Wersching .15 .05
❑ 494 Charle Young .15 .05
❑ 495 Tampa Bay Bucs TL .40 .15
❑ 496 Cedric Brown .15 .05
❑ 497 Neal Colzie .15 .05
❑ 498 Jerry Eckwood .15 .05
❑ 499 Jimmie Giles .40 .15
❑ 500 Hugh Green RC .75 .30
❑ 501 Kevin House .15 .05
❑ 502 Kevin House IA .15 .05
❑ 503 Cecil Johnson .15 .05
❑ 504 James Owens .15 .05
❑ 505 Lee Roy Selmon .75 .30
❑ 506 Mike Washington .15 .05
❑ 507 James Wilder RC .40 .15
❑ 508 Doug Williams .40 .15
❑ 509 [illegible] TL/Monk [illegible] [illegible]
❑ 510 Perry Brooks .15 .05
❑ 511 Dave Butz .40 .15
❑ 512 Wilbur Jackson .15 .05
❑ 513 Joe Lavender .15 .05
❑ 514 Terry Metcalf .40 .15
❑ 515 Art Monk 3.00 1.25
❑ 516 Mark Moseley .15 .05
❑ 517 Mark Murphy .15 .05
❑ 518 Mike Nelms .15 .05
❑ 519 Lemar Parrish .15 .05
❑ 520 John Riggins .75 .30
❑ 521 Joe Theismann .75 .30
❑ 522 Ricky Thompson .15 .05
❑ 523 Don Warren UER .15 .05
❑ 524 Joe Washington .40 .15
❑ 525 Checklist 1-132 .50 .20
❑ 526 Checklist 133-264 .50 .20
❑ 527 Checklist 265-396 .50 .20
❑ 528 Checklist 397-528 .50 .20

1983 Topps

❑ COMPLETE SET (396) 60.00 30.00
❑ 1 Ken Anderson RB .60 .25
❑ 2 Tony Dorsett RB .60 .25
❑ 3 Dan Fouts RB .60 .25
❑ 4 Joe Montana RB 3.00 1.50
❑ 5 Mark Moseley RB .30 .10
❑ 6 Mike Nelms RB .10 .02
❑ 7 Darrol Ray RB .10 .02
❑ 8 John Riggins RB .60 .25
❑ 9 Fulton Walker RB .10 .02
❑ 10 NFC Champs/Riggins .60 .25

❑ 11 AFC Championship .30 .10
❑ 12 Super Bowl XVII/J.Riggins .10 .02
❑ 13 Atlanta Falcons TL .30 .10
❑ 14 William Andrews DP .30 .10
❑ 15 Steve Bartkowski .30 .10
❑ 16 Bobby Butler .10 .02
❑ 17 Buddy Curry .10 .02
❑ 18 Alfred Jackson DP .10 .02
❑ 19 Alfred Jenkins .10 .02
❑ 20 Kenny Johnson .10 .02
❑ 21 Mike Kenn .10 .02
❑ 22 Mick Luckhurst .10 .02
❑ 23 Junior Miller .10 .02
❑ 24 Al Richardson .10 .02
❑ 25 Gerald Riggs RC DP .30 .10
❑ 26 R.C. Thielemann .10 .02
❑ 27 Jeff Van Note .10 .02
❑ 28 Bears TL/W.Payton 1.00 .40
❑ 29 Brian Baschnagel .10 .02
❑ 30 Dan Hampton .60 .25
❑ 31 Mike Hartenstine .10 .02
❑ 32 Noah Jackson .10 .02
❑ 33 Jim McMahon RC 8.00 4.00
❑ 34 Emery Moorehead DP .10 .02
❑ 35 Bob Parsons .10 .02
❑ 36 Walter Payton 6.00 3.00
❑ 37 Terry Schmidt .10 .02
❑ 38 Mike Singletary RC 8.00 4.00
❑ 39 Matt Suhey DP .30 .10
❑ 40 Rickey Watts DP .10 .02
❑ 41 Otis Wilson RC DP .30 .10
❑ 42 Cowboys TL/Tony Dorsett .60 .25
❑ 43 Bob Breunig .30 .10
❑ 44 Doug Cosbie .10 .02
❑ 45 Pat Donovan .10 .02
❑ 46 Tony Dorsett DP 1.00 .40
❑ 47 Tony Hill .30 .10
❑ 48 Butch Johnson DP .30 .10
❑ 49 Ed Too Tall Jones DP .60 .25
❑ 50 Harvey Martin DP .30 .10
❑ 51 Drew Pearson .60 .25
❑ 52 Rafael Septien .10 .02
❑ 53 Ron Springs DP .10 .02
❑ 54 Dennis Thurman .10 .02
❑ 55 Everson Walls .30 .10
❑ 56 Danny White DP .60 .25
❑ 57 Randy White .60 .25
❑ 58 Detroit Lions TL .30 .10
❑ 59 Al(Bubba) Baker DP .30 .10
❑ 60 Dexter Bussey DP .10 .02
❑ 61 Gary Danielson DP .10 .02
❑ 62 Keith Dorney DP .10 .02
❑ 63 Doug English .10 .02
❑ 64 Ken Fantetti DP .10 .02
❑ 65 Alvin Hall DP .10 .02
❑ 66 David Hill DP .10 .02
❑ 67 Eric Hipple .10 .02
❑ 68 Eddie Murray DP .30 .10
❑ 69 Freddie Scott .10 .02
❑ 70 Billy Sims DP .30 .10
❑ 71 Tom Skladany DP .10 .02
❑ 72 Leonard Thompson DP .10 .02
❑ 73 Bobby Watkins .10 .02
❑ 74 Green Bay Packers TL .10 .02
❑ 75 John Anderson .10 .02
❑ 76 Paul Coffman .10 .02
❑ 77 Lynn Dickey .10 .02
❑ 78 Mike Douglass DP .10 .02
❑ 79 Eddie Lee Ivery .10 .02
❑ 80 John Jefferson DP .60 .25
❑ 81 Ezra Johnson .10 .02
❑ 82 Mark Lee .10 .02
❑ 83 James Lofton .60 .25
❑ 84 Larry McCarren .10 .02
❑ 85 Jan Stenerud DP .30 .10
❑ 86 Los Angeles Rams TL .10 .02
❑ 87 Bill Bain DP .10 .02
❑ 88 Nolan Cromwell .30 .10
❑ 89 Preston Dennard .10 .02
❑ 90 Vince Ferragamo DP .30 .10
❑ 91 Mike Guman .10 .02
❑ 92 Kent Hill .10 .02
❑ 93 Mike Lansford RC DP .10 .02
❑ [illegible]
❑ 95 Pat Thomas DP .10 .02
❑ 96 Jack Youngblood .60 .25
❑ 97 Minnesota Vikings TL .10 .02
❑ 98 Matt Blair .10 .02
❑ 99 Ted Brown .10 .02
❑ 100 Greg Coleman .10 .02
❑ 101 Randy Holloway .10 .02
❑ 102 Tommy Kramer .30 .10
❑ 103 Doug Martin DP .10 .02
❑ 104 Mark Mullaney .10 .02
❑ 105 Joe Senser .10 .02
❑ 106 Willie Teal DP .10 .02
❑ 107 Sammie White .30 .10
❑ 108 Rickey Young .10 .02
❑ 109 New Orleans Saints TL .30 .10
❑ 110 Stan Brock RC .10 .02
❑ 111 Bruce Clark RC .10 .02
❑ 112 Russell Erxleben DP .10 .02
❑ 113 Russell Gary .10 .02
❑ 114 Jeff Groth DP .10 .02
❑ 115 John Hill DP .10 .02
❑ 116 Derland Moore .10 .02
❑ 117 George Rogers .30 .10
❑ 118 Ken Stabler 1.50 .60
❑ 119 Wayne Wilson .10 .02
❑ 120 New York Giants TL .10 .02
❑ 121 Scott Brunner .10 .02
❑ 122 Rob Carpenter .10 .02
❑ 123 Harry Carson .30 .10
❑ 124 Joe Danelo DP .10 .02
❑ 125 Earnest Gray .10 .02
❑ 126 Mark Haynes DP .30 .10
❑ 127 Terry Jackson .10 .02
❑ 128 Dave Jennings .10 .02
❑ 129 Brian Kelley .10 .02
❑ 130 George Martin .10 .02
❑ 131 Tom Mullady .10 .02
❑ 132 Johnny Perkins .10 .02
❑ 133 Lawrence Taylor 5.00 2.00
❑ 134 Brad Van Pelt .10 .02
❑ 135 Butch Woolfolk DP RC .10 .02
❑ 136 Philadelphia Eagles TL .30 .10
❑ 137 Harold Carmichael .60 .25
❑ 138 Herman Edwards .10 .02
❑ 139 Tony Franklin DP .10 .02
❑ 140 Carl Hairston DP .10 .02
❑ 141 Dennis Harrison DP .10 .02
❑ 142 Ron Jaworski DP .30 .10
❑ 143 Frank LeMaster .10 .02
❑ 144 Wilbert Montgomery DP .30 .10
❑ 145 Guy Morriss .10 .02
❑ 146 Jerry Robinson .10 .02
❑ 147 Max Runager .10 .02
❑ 148 Ron Smith DP RC .10 .02
❑ 149 John Spagnola .10 .02
❑ 150 Stan Walters DP .10 .02
❑ 151 Roynell Young DP .10 .02
❑ 152 Cardinals TL/O.Anderson .30 .10
❑ 153 Ottis Anderson .60 .25
❑ 154 Carl Birdsong .10 .02
❑ 155 Dan Dierdorf DP .60 .25
❑ 156 Roy Green RC .60 .25
❑ 157 Elois Grooms .10 .02
❑ 158 Neil Lomax DP .30 .10
❑ 159 Wayne Morris .10 .02
❑ 160 Tootie Robbins RC .10 .02
❑ 161 Luis Sharpe RC .10 .02
❑ 162 Pat Tilley .10 .02
❑ 163 San Francisco 49ers TL .10 .02
❑ 164 Dwight Clark .60 .25
❑ 165 Randy Cross .30 .10
❑ 166 Russ Francis .30 .10
❑ 167 Dwight Hicks .10 .02

❑ 168 Ronnie Lott 2.50 1.25
❑ 169 Joe Montana DP 10.00 4.00
❑ 170 Jeff Moore .10 .02
❑ 171 Renaldo Nehemiah RC DP .60 .25
❑ 172 Freddie Solomon .10 .02
❑ 173 Ray Wersching DP .10 .02
❑ 174 Tampa Bay Bucs TL .10 .02
❑ 175 Cedric Brown .10 .02
❑ 176 Bill Capece .10 .02
❑ 177 Neal Colzie .10 .02
❑ 178 Jimmie Giles .10 .02
❑ 179 Hugh Green .30 .10
❑ 180 Kevin House DP .10 .02
❑ 181 James Owens .10 .02
❑ 182 Lee Roy Selmon .60 .25
❑ 183 Mike Washington .10 .02
❑ 184 James Wilder .10 .02
❑ 185 Doug Williams DP .30 .10
❑ 186 Redskins TL/John Riggins .60 .25
❑ 187 Jeff Bostic RC DP 1.00 .40
❑ 188 Charlie Brown RC .30 .10
❑ 189 Vernon Dean DP RC .10 .02
❑ 190 Joe Jacoby RC 2.00 .75
❑ 191 Dexter Manley RC .30 .10
❑ 192 Rich Milot .10 .02
❑ 193 Art Monk DP 1.00 .40
❑ 194 Mark Moseley DP .10 .02
❑ 195 Mike Nelms .10 .02
❑ 196 Neal Olkewicz DP .10 .02
❑ 197 Tony Peters .10 .02
❑ 198 John Riggins DP .60 .25
❑ 199 Joe Theismann .60 .25
❑ 200 Don Warren .10 .02
❑ 201 Jeris White DP .10 .02
❑ 202 J.Theismann/K.Anderson LL .60 .25
❑ 203 Receiving Leaders .30 .10
❑ 204 Tony Dorsett/F.McNeil LL .60 .25
❑ 205 M.Allen/W.Tyler LL 1.25 .50
❑ 206 Interception Leaders .30 .10
❑ 207 Punting Leaders .10 .02
❑ 208 Baltimore Colts TL .10 .02
❑ 209 Matt Bouza .10 .02
❑ 210 Johnie Cooks RC DP .10 .02
❑ 211 Curtis Dickey .10 .02
❑ 212 Nesby Glasgow DP .10 .02
❑ 213 Derrick Hatchett .10 .02
❑ 214 Randy McMillan .10 .02
❑ 215 Mike Pagel RC .30 .10
❑ 216 Rohn Stark RC DP .30 .10
❑ 217 Donnell Thompson RC DP .10 .02
❑ 218 Leo Wisniewski DP .10 .02
❑ 219 Buffalo Bills TL .30 .10
❑ 220 Curtis Brown .10 .02
❑ 221 Jerry Butler .10 .02
❑ 222 Greg Cater DP .10 .02
❑ 223 Joe Cribbs .30 .10
❑ 224 Joe Ferguson .30 .10
❑ 225 Roosevelt Leaks .10 .02
❑ 226 Frank Lewis .10 .02
❑ 227 Eugene Marve RC .10 .02
❑ 228 Fred Smerlas DP .10 .02
❑ 229 Ben Williams DP .10 .02
❑ 230 Cincinnati Bengals TL .10 .02
❑ 231 Charles Alexander .10 .02
❑ 232 Ken Anderson DP .60 .25
❑ 233 Jim Breech DP .10 .02
❑ 234 Ross Browner .10 .02
❑ 235 Cris Collinsworth DP .60 .25
❑ 236 Isaac Curtis .10 .02
❑ 237 Pete Johnson .10 .02
❑ 238 Steve Kreider DP .10 .02
❑ 239 Max Montoya RC DP .10 .02
❑ 240 Anthony Munoz 1.00 .40
❑ 241 Ken Riley .10 .02
❑ 242 Dan Ross .10 .02
❑ 243 Reggie Williams .30 .10
❑ 244 Cleveland Browns TL .30 .10
❑ 245 Chip Banks RC DP .30 .10
❑ 246 Tom Cousineau RC DP .30 .10
❑ 247 Joe DeLamielleure DP .30 .10
❑ 248 Doug Dieken DP .10 .02
❑ 249 Hanford Dixon RC .10 .02
❑ 250 Ricky Feacher DP .10 .02
❑ 251 Lawrence Johnson DP .10 .02
❑ 252 Dave Logan DP .10 .02
❑ 253 Paul McDonald DP .10 .02
❑ 254 Ozzie Newsome DP .60 .25
❑ 255 Mike Pruitt .30 .10
❑ 256 Clarence Scott DP .10 .02
❑ 257 Brian Sipe DP .30 .10
❑ 258 Dwight Walker DP .10 .02
❑ 259 Charles White .30 .10
❑ 260 Denver Broncos TL .10 .02
❑ 261 Steve DeBerg DP .30 .10
❑ 262 Randy Gradishar DP .30 .10
❑ 263 Rulon Jones RC DP .10 .02
❑ 264 Rich Karlis DP .10 .02
❑ 265 Don Latimer .10 .02
❑ 266 Rick Parros DP .10 .02
❑ 267 Luke Prestridge .10 .02
❑ 268 Rick Upchurch .30 .10
❑ 269 Steve Watson DP .10 .02
❑ 270 Gerald Willhite DP .10 .02
❑ 271 Houston Oilers TL .10 .02
❑ 272 Harold Bailey .10 .02
❑ 273 Jesse Baker DP .10 .02
❑ 274 Gregg Bingham DP .10 .02
❑ 275 Robert Brazile DP .10 .02
❑ 276 Donnie Craft .10 .02
❑ 277 Daryl Hunt .10 .02
❑ 278 Archie Manning DP .30 .10
❑ 279 Gifford Nielsen .10 .02
❑ 280 Mike Renfro .10 .02
❑ 281 Carl Roaches DP .10 .02
❑ 282 Kansas City Chiefs TL .30 .10
❑ 283 Gary Barbaro .10 .02
❑ 284 Joe Delaney .10 .02
❑ 285 Jeff Gossett RC .60 .25
❑ 286 Gary Green DP .10 .02
❑ 287 Eric Harris DP .10 .02
❑ 288 Billy Jackson DP .10 .02
❑ 289 Bill Kenney DP .10 .02
❑ 290 Nick Lowery .60 .25
❑ 291 Henry Marshall .10 .02
❑ 292 Art Still DP .10 .02
❑ 293 Raiders TL/M.Allen 2.00 .75
❑ 294 Marcus Allen RC DP 15.00 6.00
❑ 295 Lyle Alzado .60 .25
❑ 296 Chris Bahr DP .10 .02
❑ 297 Cliff Branch .60 .25
❑ 298 Todd Christensen RC .75 .30
❑ 299 Ray Guy .30 .10
❑ 300 Frank Hawkins DP .10 .02
❑ 301 Lester Hayes DP .10 .02
❑ 302 Ted Hendricks DP .60 .25
❑ 303 Kenny King DP .10 .02
❑ 304 Rod Martin .10 .02
❑ 305 Matt Millen DP .60 .25
❑ 306 Burgess Owens .10 .02
❑ 307 Jim Plunkett .60 .25
❑ 308 Miami Dolphins TL .30 .10
❑ 309 Bob Baumhower .10 .02
❑ 310 Glenn Blackwood .10 .02
❑ 311 Lyle Blackwood DP .10 .02
❑ 312 A.J. Duhe .10 .02
❑ 313 Andra Franklin .10 .02
❑ 314 Duriel Harris .10 .02
❑ 315 Bob Kuechenberg DP .30 .10
❑ 316 Don McNeal .10 .02
❑ 317 Tony Nathan .30 .10
❑ 318 Ed Newman .10 .02
❑ 319 Earnie Rhone DP .10 .02
❑ 320 Joe Rose DP .10 .02
❑ 321 Don Strock DP .10 .02
❑ 322 Uwe Von Schamann .10 .02
❑ 323 David Woodley DP .30 .10
❑ 324 New England Pats TL .10 .02
❑ 325 Julius Adams .10 .02
❑ 326 Pete Brock .10 .02
❑ 327 Rich Camarillo RC DP .10 .02
❑ 328 Tony Collins DP .10 .02
❑ 329 Steve Grogan .30 .10
❑ 330 John Hannah .60 .25
❑ 331 Don Hasselbeck .10 .02
❑ 332 Mike Haynes .30 .10
❑ 333 Roland James RC .10 .02
❑ 334A Stanley Morgan ERR IL .60 .25
❑ 334B Stanley Morgan COR .30 .10
❑ 335 Steve Nelson .10 .02
❑ 336 Kenneth Sims DP .10 .02
❑ 337 Mark Van Eeghen .30 .10
❑ 338 New York Jets TL .30 .10
❑ 339 Greg Buttle .10 .02
❑ 340 Joe Fields .10 .02
❑ 341 Mark Gastineau DP .30 .10
❑ 342 Bruce Harper .10 .02
❑ 343 Bobby Jackson .10 .02
❑ 344 Bobby Jones .10 .02
❑ 345 Johnny Lam Jones DP .10 .02
❑ 346 Joe Klecko .30 .10
❑ 347 Marty Lyons .10 .02
❑ 348 Freeman McNeil .60 .25
❑ 349 Lance Mehl RC .10 .02
❑ 350 Marvin Powell DP .10 .02
❑ 351 Darrol Ray DP .10 .02
❑ 352 Abdul Salaam .10 .02
❑ 353 Richard Todd .30 .10
❑ 354 Wesley Walker .30 .10
❑ 355 Steelers TL/Franco Harris .60 .25
❑ 356 Gary Anderson K RC DP 6.00 3.00
❑ 357 Mel Blount DP .60 .25
❑ 358 Terry Bradshaw DP 1.50 .60
❑ 359 Larry Brown .10 .02
❑ 360 Bennie Cunningham .10 .02
❑ 361 Gary Dunn .10 .02
❑ 362 Franco Harris .75 .30
❑ 363 Jack Lambert .60 .25
❑ 364 Frank Pollard .10 .02
❑ 365 Donnie Shell .30 .10
❑ 366 John Stallworth .60 .25
❑ 367 Loren Toews .10 .02
❑ 368 Mike Webster DP .60 .25
❑ 369 Dwayne Woodruff RC .10 .02
❑ 370 San Diego Chargers TL .30 .10
❑ 371 Rolf Benirschke DP .10 .02
❑ 372 James Brooks .60 .25
❑ 373 Wes Chandler .30 .10
❑ 374 Dan Fouts DP .60 .25
❑ 375 Tim Fox .10 .02
❑ 376 Gary Johnson .10 .02
❑ 377 Charlie Joiner DP .60 .25
❑ 378 Louie Kelcher .10 .02
❑ 379 Chuck Muncie .10 .02
❑ 380 Cliff Thrift .10 .02
❑ 381 Doug Wilkerson .10 .02
❑ 382 Kellen Winslow .75 .30
❑ 383 Seattle Seahawks TL .10 .02
❑ 384 Kenny Easley RC .60 .25
❑ 385 Jacob Green RC .30 .10
❑ 386 John Harris .10 .02
❑ 387 Michael Jackson .10 .02
❑ 388 Norm Johnson RC .10 .02
❑ 389 Steve Largent 1.25 .50
❑ 390 Keith Simpson .10 .02
❑ 391 Sherman Smith .10 .02
❑ 392 Jeff West DP .10 .02
❑ 393 Jim Zorn DP .30 .10
❑ 394 Checklist 1-132 .50 .20
❑ 395 Checklist 133-264 .50 .20
❑ 396 Checklist 265-396 .50 .20

1984 Topps

❑ COMPLETE SET (396) 200.00 100.00
❑ COMP.FACT.SET (396) 350.00 200.00
❑ 1 Eric Dickerson RB .50 .20
❑ 2 Ali Haji-Sheikh RB .25 .08
❑ 3 Franco Harris RB .50 .20
❑ 4 Mark Moseley RB .25 .08
❑ 5 John Riggins RB .50 .20
❑ 6 Jan Stenerud RB .25 .08
❑ 7 AFC Champs/M.Allen .50 .20
❑ 8 NFC Champs/Riggins .25 .08
❑ 9 Super Bowl XVIII/Allen UER .50 .20

❑ 10 Indianapolis Colts TL	.10	.02
❑ 11 Raul Allegre RC	.10	.02
❑ 12 Curtis Dickey	.25	.08
❑ 13 Ray Donaldson RC	.25	.08
❑ 14 Nesby Glasgow	.10	.02
❑ 15 Chris Hinton RC	.50	.20
❑ 16 Vernon Maxwell RC	.10	.02
❑ 17 Randy McMillan	.10	.02
❑ 18 Mike Pagel	.25	.08
❑ 19 Rohn Stark	.25	.08
❑ 20 Leo Wisniewski	.10	.02
❑ 21 Buffalo Bills TL	.25	.08
❑ 22 Jerry Butler	.10	.02
❑ 23 Joe Danelo	.10	.02
❑ 24 Joe Ferguson	.25	.08
❑ 25 Steve Freeman	.10	.02
❑ 26 Roosevelt Leaks	.25	.08
❑ 27 Frank Lewis	.10	.02
❑ 28 Eugene Marve	.10	.02
❑ 29 Booker Moore	.10	.02
❑ 30 Fred Smerlas	.10	.02
❑ 31 Ben Williams	.25	.08
❑ 32 Cincinnati Bengals TL	.25	.08
❑ 33 Charles Alexander	.10	.02
❑ 34 Ken Anderson	.50	.20
❑ 35 Ken Anderson IR	.50	.20
❑ 36 Jim Breech	.10	.02
❑ 37 Cris Collinsworth	.50	.20
❑ 38 Cris Collinsworth IR	.50	.20
❑ 39 Isaac Curtis	.25	.08
❑ 40 Eddie Edwards	.10	.02
❑ 41 Ray Horton RC	.10	.02
❑ 42 Pete Johnson	.25	.08
❑ 43 Steve Kreider	.10	.02
❑ 44 Max Montoya	.10	.02
❑ 45 Anthony Munoz	.50	.20
❑ 46 Reggie Williams	.25	.08
❑ 47 Cleveland Browns TL	.25	.08
❑ 48 Matt Bahr	.25	.08
❑ 49 Chip Banks	.10	.02
❑ 50 Tom Cousineau	.10	.02
❑ 51 Joe DeLamielleure	.50	.20
❑ 52 Doug Dieken	.10	.02
❑ 53 Bob Golic RC	.50	.20
❑ 54 Bobby Jones	.10	.02
❑ 55 Dave Logan	.10	.02
❑ 56 Clay Matthews	.50	.20
❑ 57 Paul McDonald	.10	.02
❑ 58 Ozzie Newsome	.50	.20
❑ 59 Ozzie Newsome IR	.50	.20
❑ 60 Mike Pruitt	.25	.08
❑ 61 Denver Broncos TL	.25	.08
❑ 62 Barney Chavous RC	.10	.02
❑ 63 John Elway RC !	80.00	30.00
❑ 64 Steve Foley	.10	.02
❑ 65 Tom Jackson	.50	.20
❑ 66 Rich Karlis	.10	.02
❑ 67 Luke Prestridge	.10	.02
❑ 68 Zach Thomas WR	.10	.02
❑ 69 Rick Upchurch	.25	.08
❑ 70 Steve Watson	.25	.08
❑ 71 Sammy Winder RC	.25	.08
❑ 72 Louis Wright	.25	.08
❑ 73 Houston Oilers TL	.10	.02
❑ 74 Jesse Baker	.10	.02
❑ 75 Gregg Bingham	.10	.02
❑ 76 Robert Brazile	.25	.08
❑ 77 Steve Brown RC	.10	.02
❑ 78 Chris Dressel	.10	.02
❑ 79 Doug France	.10	.02
❑ 80 Florian Kempf	.10	.02
❑ 81 Carl Roaches	.25	.08
❑ 82 Tim Smith WR RC	.25	.08
❑ 83 Willie Tullis	.10	.02
❑ 84 Kansas City Chiefs TL	.10	.02
❑ 85 Mike Bell RC	.10	.02
❑ 86 Theotis Brown	.10	.02
❑ 87 Carlos Carson	.50	.20
❑ 88 Carlos Carson IR	.25	.08
❑ 89 Deron Cherry RC	.25	.08
❑ 90 Gary Green	.10	.02
❑ 91 Billy Jackson	.10	.02
❑ 92 Bill Kenney	.25	.08
❑ 93 Bill Kenney IR	.25	.08
❑ 94 Nick Lowery	.50	.20
❑ 95 Henry Marshall	.10	.02
❑ 96 Art Still	.10	.02
❑ 97 Los Angeles Raiders TL	.25	.08
❑ 98 Marcus Allen	5.00	2.50
❑ 99 Marcus Allen IR	2.50	1.00
❑ 100 Lyle Alzado	.25	.08
❑ 101 Lyle Alzado IR	.25	.08
❑ 102 Chris Bahr	.10	.02
❑ 103 Malcolm Barnwell RC	.10	.02
❑ 104 Cliff Branch	.50	.20
❑ 105 Todd Christensen	.50	.20
❑ 106 Todd Christensen IR	.50	.20
❑ 107 Ray Guy	.50	.20
❑ 108 Frank Hawkins	.10	.02
❑ 109 Lester Hayes	.25	.08
❑ 110 Ted Hendricks	.50	.20
❑ 111 Howie Long RC	15.00	6.00
❑ 112 Rod Martin	.25	.08
❑ 113 Vann McElroy RC	.10	.02
❑ 114 Jim Plunkett	.50	.20
❑ 115 Greg Pruitt	.25	.08
❑ 116 Dolphins TL/M.Duper	.50	.20
❑ 117 Bob Baumhower	.10	.02
❑ 118 Doug Betters RC	.10	.02
❑ 119 A.J. Duhe	.10	.02
❑ 120 Mark Duper RC	.50	.20
❑ 121 Andra Franklin	.10	.02
❑ 122 William Judson	.10	.02
❑ 123 Dan Marino RC !	80.00	30.00
❑ 124 Dan Marino IR	12.00	5.00
❑ 125 Nat Moore	.25	.08
❑ 126 Ed Newman	.10	.02
❑ 127 Reggie Roby RC	.25	.08
❑ 128 Gerald Small	.10	.02
❑ 129 Dwight Stephenson RC	5.00	2.00
❑ 130 Uwe Von Schamann	.10	.02
❑ 131 New England Pats TL	.10	.02
❑ 132 Rich Camarillo	.25	.08
❑ 133 Tony Collins	.25	.08
❑ 134 Tony Collins IR	.10	.02
❑ 135 Bob Cryder	.10	.02
❑ 136 Steve Grogan	.25	.08
❑ 137 John Hannah	.50	.20
❑ 138 Brian Holloway RC	.10	.02
❑ 139 Roland James	.10	.02
❑ 140 Stanley Morgan	.25	.08
❑ 141 Rick Sanford	.10	.02
❑ 142 Mosi Tatupu RC	.10	.02
❑ 143 Andre Tippett RC	5.00	2.00
❑ 144 New York Jets TL	.25	.08
❑ 145 Jerome Barkum	.10	.02
❑ 146 Mark Gastineau	.25	.08
❑ 147 Mark Gastineau IR	.25	.08
❑ 148 Bruce Harper	.10	.02
❑ 149 Johnny Lam Jones	.10	.02
❑ 150 Joe Klecko	.25	.08
❑ 151 Pat Leahy	.10	.02
❑ 152 Freeman McNeil	.25	.08
❑ 153 Lance Mehl	.10	.02
❑ 154 Marvin Powell	.25	.08
❑ 155 Darrol Ray	.10	.02
❑ 156 Pat Ryan RC	.10	.02
❑ 157 Kirk Springs	.10	.02
❑ 158 Wesley Walker	.25	.08
❑ 159 Steelers TL/F.Harris	.50	.20
❑ 160 Walter Abercrombie RC	.25	.08
❑ 161 Gary Anderson K	.50	.20
❑ 162 Terry Bradshaw	2.00	.75
❑ 163 Craig Colquitt	.10	.02
❑ 164 Bennie Cunningham	.10	.02
❑ 165 Franco Harris	.50	.20
❑ 166 Franco Harris IR	.50	.20
❑ 167 Jack Lambert	.50	.20
❑ 168 Jack Lambert IR	.50	.20
❑ 169 Frank Pollard	.10	.02
❑ 170 Donnie Shell	.25	.08
❑ 171 Mike Webster	.25	.08
❑ 172 Keith Willis RC	.10	.02
❑ 173 Rick Woods	.10	.02
❑ 174 Chargers TL/K.Winslow	.50	.20
❑ 175 Rolf Benirschke	.10	.02
❑ 176 James Brooks	.25	.08
❑ 177 Maury Buford	.10	.02
❑ 178 Wes Chandler	.25	.08
❑ 179 Dan Fouts	.60	.25
❑ 180 Dan Fouts IR	.50	.20
❑ 181 Charlie Joiner	.50	.20
❑ 182 Linden King	.10	.02
❑ 183 Chuck Muncie	.25	.08
❑ 184 Billy Ray Smith RC	.50	.20
❑ 185 Danny Walters RC	.10	.02
❑ 186 Kellen Winslow	.60	.25
❑ 187 Kellen Winslow IR	.50	.20
❑ 188 Seahawks TL/C.Warner	.50	.20
❑ 189 Steve August	.10	.02
❑ 190 Dave Brown DB	.10	.02
❑ 191 Zachary Dixon	.10	.02
❑ 192 Kenny Easley	.25	.08
❑ 193 Jacob Green	.10	.02
❑ 194 Norm Johnson	.25	.08
❑ 195 Dave Krieg RC	1.50	.60
❑ 196 Steve Largent	1.00	.40
❑ 197 Steve Largent IR	.50	.20
❑ 198 Curt Warner RC	.50	.20
❑ 199 Curt Warner IR	.50	.20
❑ 200 Jeff West	.10	.02
❑ 201 Charle Young	.10	.02
❑ 202 D.Marino/Bartkow. LL	6.00	2.50
❑ 203 Receiving Leaders	.25	.08
❑ 204 Eric Dickerson/Warner LL	.50	.20
❑ 205 Scoring Leaders	.10	.02
❑ 206 Interception Leaders	.10	.02
❑ 207 Punting Leaders	.10	.02
❑ 208 Atlanta Falcons TL	.25	.08
❑ 209 William Andrews	.25	.08
❑ 210 William Andrews IR	.25	.08
❑ 211 Stacey Bailey RC	.10	.02
❑ 212 Steve Bartkowski	.50	.20
❑ 213 Steve Bartkowski IR	.25	.08
❑ 214 Ralph Giacomarro	.10	.02
❑ 215 Billy Johnson	.25	.08
❑ 216 Mike Kenn	.25	.08
❑ 217 Mick Luckhurst	.10	.02
❑ 218 Gerald Riggs	.50	.20
❑ 219 R.C. Thielemann	.10	.02
❑ 220 Jeff Van Note	.25	.08
❑ 221 Bears TL/W.Payton	.75	.30
❑ 222 Jim Covert RC	.50	.20
❑ 223 Leslie Frazier	.10	.02
❑ 224 Willie Gault RC	.50	.20
❑ 225 Mike Hartenstine	.10	.02
❑ 226 Noah Jackson UER	.10	.02
❑ 227 Jim McMahon	1.25	.50
❑ 228 Walter Payton	6.00	2.50
❑ 229 Walter Payton IR	1.25	.50
❑ 230 Mike Richardson RC	.10	.02
❑ 231 Terry Schmidt	.10	.02
❑ 232 Mike Singletary	1.25	.50
❑ 233 Matt Suhey	.25	.08
❑ 234 Bob Thomas	.10	.02
❑ 235 Cowboys TL/T.Dorsett	.50	.20
❑ 236 Bob Breunig	.10	.02
❑ 237 Doug Cosbie	.25	.08
❑ 238 Tony Dorsett	1.00	.40
❑ 239 Tony Dorsett IR	.50	.20
❑ 240 John Dutton	.10	.02
❑ 241 Tony Hill	.25	.08
❑ 242 Ed Too Tall Jones	.50	.20
❑ 243 Drew Pearson	.50	.20
❑ 244 Rafael Septien	.10	.02
❑ 245 Ron Springs	.25	.08
❑ 246 Dennis Thurman	.10	.02
❑ 247 Everson Walls	.10	.02
❑ 248 Danny White	.50	.20
❑ 249 Randy White	.50	.20
❑ 250 Detroit Lions TL	.25	.08
❑ 251 Jeff Chadwick RC	.25	.08
❑ 252 Garry Cobb	.10	.02
❑ 253 Doug English	.25	.08
❑ 254 William Gay	.10	.02
❑ 255 Eric Hipple	.25	.08
❑ 256 James Jones FB RC	.25	.08
❑ 257 Bruce McNorton	.10	.02
❑ 258 Eddie Murray	.25	.08
❑ 259 Ulysses Norris	.10	.02
❑ 260 Billy Sims	.50	.20
❑ 261 Billy Sims IR	.25	.08
❑ 262 Leonard Thompson	.10	.02
❑ 263 Packers TL/J.Lofton	.50	.20
❑ 264 John Anderson	.10	.02
❑ 265 Paul Coffman	.25	.08
❑ 266 Lynn Dickey	.25	.08
❑ 267 Gerry Ellis	.10	.02
❑ 268 John Jefferson	.50	.20
❑ 269 John Jefferson IR	.50	.20
❑ 270 Ezra Johnson	.10	.02

❑	271 Tim Lewis RC	.10	.02
❑	272 James Lofton	.50	.20
❑	273 James Lofton IR	.50	.20
❑	274 Larry McCarren	.10	.02
❑	275 Jan Stenerud	.25	.08
❑	276 Rams TL/E.Dickerson	.50	.20
❑	277 Mike Barber	.10	.02
❑	278 Jim Collins	.10	.02
❑	279 Nolan Cromwell	.25	.08
❑	280 Eric Dickerson RC	10.00	4.00
❑	281 Eric Dickerson IR	2.00	.75
❑	282 George Farmer South.	.10	.02
❑	283 Vince Ferragamo	.25	.08
❑	284 Kent Hill	.10	.02
❑	285 John Misko	.10	.02
❑	286 Jackie Slater RC	4.00	1.50
❑	287 Jack Youngblood	.25	.08
❑	288 Minnesota Vikings TL	.10	.02
❑	289 Ted Brown	.25	.08
❑	290 Greg Coleman	.10	.02
❑	291 Steve Dils	.10	.02
❑	292 Tony Galbreath	.10	.02
❑	293 Tommy Kramer	.25	.08
❑	294 Doug Martin	.10	.02
❑	295 Darrin Nelson RC	.25	.08
❑	296 Benny Ricardo	.10	.02
❑	297 John Swain	.10	.02
❑	298 John Turner	.10	.02
❑	299 New Orleans Saints TL	.25	.08
❑	300 Morten Andersen RC	1.50	.60
❑	301 Russell Erxleben	.10	.02
❑	302 Jeff Groth	.10	.02
❑	303 Rickey Jackson RC	.50	.20
❑	304 Johnnie Poe RC	.10	.02
❑	305 George Rogers	.25	.08
❑	306 Richard Todd	.25	.08
❑	307 Jim Wilks RC	.10	.02
❑	308 Dave Wilson RC	.10	.02
❑	309 Wayne Wilson	.10	.02
❑	310 New York Giants TL	.10	.02
❑	311 Leon Bright	.10	.02
❑	312 Scott Brunner	.10	.02
❑	313 Rob Carpenter	.10	.02
❑	314 Harry Carson	.25	.08
❑	315 Earnest Gray	.10	.02
❑	316 Ali Haji-Sheikh RC	.10	.02
❑	317 Mark Haynes	.25	.08
❑	318 Dave Jennings	.10	.02
❑	319 Brian Kelley	.10	.02
❑	320 Phil Simms	.75	.30
❑	321 Lawrence Taylor	3.00	1.50
❑	322 Lawrence Taylor IR	1.50	.60
❑	323 Brad Van Pelt	.10	.02
❑	324 Butch Woolfolk	.10	.02
❑	325 Eagles TL/M.Quick	.25	.08
❑	326 Harold Carmichael	.25	.08
❑	327 Herman Edwards	.10	.02
❑	328 Michael Haddix RC	.10	.02
❑	329 Dennis Harrison	.10	.02
❑	330 Ron Jaworski	.25	.08
❑	331 Wilbert Montgomery	.25	.08
❑	332 Hubie Oliver	.10	.02
❑	333 Mike Quick RC	.50	.20
❑	334 Jerry Robinson	.10	.02
❑	335 Max Runager	.10	.02
❑	336 Michael Williams	.10	.02
❑	337 Cardinals TL/O.Anderson	.25	.08
❑	338 Ottis Anderson	.50	.20
❑	339 Al(Bubba) Baker	.25	.08
❑	340 Carl Birdsong	.10	.02
❑	341 David Galloway	.10	.02
❑	342 Roy Green	.25	.08
❑	343 Roy Green IR	.25	.08
❑	344 Curtis Greer RC	.10	.02
❑	345 Neil Lomax	.25	.08
❑	346 Doug Marsh	.10	.02
❑	347 Stump Mitchell	.25	.08
❑	348 Lionel Washington RC	.25	.08
❑	349 49ers TL/D.Clark	.25	.08
❑	350 Dwaine Board	.10	.02
❑	351 Dwight Clark	.50	.20
❑	352 Dwight Clark IR	.25	.08
❑	353 Roger Craig RC !	3.00	1.25
❑	354 Fred Dean	.25	.08
❑	355 Fred Dean IR w/Marino	.50	.20
❑	356 Dwight Hicks	.25	.08
❑	357 Ronnie Lott	1.50	.60
❑	358 Joe Montana	10.00	4.00
❑	359 Joe Montana IR	3.00	1.50
❑	360 Freddie Solomon	.10	.02
❑	361 Wendell Tyler	.10	.02
❑	362 Ray Wersching	.10	.02
❑	363 Eric Wright RC	.25	.08
❑	364 Tampa Bay Bucs TL	.10	.02
❑	365 Gerald Carter	.10	.02
❑	366 Hugh Green	.25	.08
❑	367 Kevin House	.25	.08
❑	368 Michael Morton RC	.10	.02
❑	369 James Owens	.10	.02
❑	370 Booker Reese	.10	.02
❑	371 Lee Roy Selmon	.50	.20
❑	372 Jack Thompson	.25	.08
❑	373 James Wilder	.25	.08
❑	374 Steve Wilson	.10	.02
❑	375 Redskins TL/J.Riggins	.50	.20
❑	376 Jeff Bostic	.10	.02
❑	377 Charlie Brown	.50	.20
❑	378 Charlie Brown IR	.25	.08
❑	379 Dave Butz	.25	.08
❑	380 Darrell Green RC	12.00	6.00
❑	381 Russ Grimm RC	1.00	.40
❑	382 Joe Jacoby	.25	.08
❑	383 Dexter Manley	.25	.08
❑	384 Art Monk	1.00	.40
❑	385 Mark Moseley	.25	.08
❑	386 Mark Murphy	.10	.02
❑	387 Mike Nelms	.10	.02
❑	388 John Riggins	.50	.20
❑	389 John Riggins IR	.50	.20
❑	390 Joe Theismann	.50	.20
❑	391 Joe Theismann IR	.50	.20
❑	392 Don Warren	.25	.08
❑	393 Joe Washington	.25	.08
❑	394 Checklist 1-132	.30	.10
❑	395 Checklist 133-264	.30	.10
❑	396 Checklist 265-396	.30	.10

1984 Topps USFL

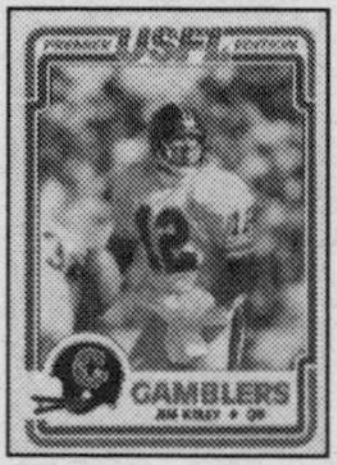

❑	COMP.FACT.SET (132)	300.00	150.00
❑	COMPLETE SET (132)	300.00	150.00
❑	1 Luther Bradley	2.00	.75
❑	2 Frank Corral	2.00	.75
❑	3 Trumaine Johnson	2.00	.75
❑	4 Greg Landry	2.50	1.25
❑	5 Kit Lathrop	2.00	.75
❑	6 Kevin Long	2.00	.75
❑	7 Tim Spencer	2.00	.75
❑	8 Stan White	2.00	.75
❑	9 Buddy Aydelette	2.00	.75
❑	10 Tom Banks	2.00	.75
❑	11 Fred Bohannon	2.00	.75
❑	12 Joe Cribbs	4.00	2.00
❑	13 Joey Jones	2.00	.75
❑	14 Scott Norwood XRC	2.50	1.25
❑	15 Jim Smith	2.50	1.25
❑	16 Cliff Stoudt	4.00	2.00
❑	17 Vince Evans	4.00	2.00
❑	18 Vagas Ferguson	2.00	.75
❑	19 John Gillen	2.00	.75
❑	20 Kris Haines	2.00	.75
❑	21 Glenn Hyde	2.00	.75
❑	22 Mark Keel	2.00	.75
❑	23 Gary Lewis XRC	2.00	.75
❑	24 Doug Plank	2.00	.75
❑	25 Neil Balholm	2.00	.75
❑	26 David Dumars	2.00	.75
❑	27 David Martin XRC	2.00	.75
❑	28 Craig Penrose	2.00	.75
❑	29 Dave Stalls	2.00	.75
❑	30 Harry Sydney XRC	2.00	.75
❑	31 Vincent White	2.00	.75
❑	32 George Yarno	2.00	.75
❑	33 Kiki DeAyala	2.00	.75
❑	34 Sam Harrell	2.00	.75
❑	35 Mike Hawkins	2.00	.75
❑	36 Jim Kelly XRC	80.00	40.00
❑	37 Mark Rush	2.00	.75
❑	38 Ricky Sanders XRC	6.00	3.00
❑	39 Paul Bergmann	2.00	.75
❑	40 Tom Dinkel	2.00	.75
❑	41 Wyatt Henderson	2.00	.75
❑	42 Vaughan Johnson XRC	2.50	1.25
❑	43 Willie McClendon Geor.	2.00	.75
❑	44 Matt Robinson	2.00	.75
❑	45 George Achica	2.00	.75
❑	46 Mark Adickes	2.00	.75
❑	47 Howard Carson	2.00	.75
❑	48 Kevin Nelson	2.00	.75
❑	49 Jeff Partridge	2.00	.75
❑	50 Jo Jo Townsell	2.50	1.25
❑	51 Eddie Weaver	2.00	.75
❑	52 Steve Young XRC	120.00	60.00
❑	53 Derrick Crawford	2.00	.75
❑	54 Walter Lewis	2.00	.75
❑	55 Phil McKinnely	2.00	.75
❑	56 Vic Minore	2.00	.75
❑	57 Gary Shirk	2.00	.75
❑	58 Reggie White XRC	60.00	30.00
❑	59 Anthony Carter XRC	12.00	5.00
❑	60 John Corker	2.00	.75
❑	61 David Greenwood	2.00	.75
❑	62 Bobby Hebert XRC	4.00	2.00
❑	63 Derek Holloway	2.00	.75
❑	64 Ken Lacy	2.00	.75
❑	65 Tyrone McGriff	2.00	.75
❑	66 Ray Pinney	2.00	.75
❑	67 Gary Barbaro	2.00	.75
❑	68 Sam Bowers	2.00	.75
❑	69 Clarence Collins	2.00	.75
❑	70 Willie Harper	2.00	.75
❑	71 Jim LeClair	2.00	.75
❑	72 Bobby Leopold XRC	2.00	.75
❑	73 Brian Sipe	4.00	2.00
❑	74 Herschel Walker XRC	25.00	12.50
❑	75 Junior Ah You XRC	2.00	.75
❑	76 Marcus Dupree XRC	6.00	2.50
❑	77 Marcus Marek	2.00	.75
❑	78 Tim Mazzetti	2.00	.75
❑	79 Mike Robinson XRC	2.00	.75
❑	80 Dan Ross	4.00	2.00
❑	81 Mark Schellen	2.00	.75
❑	82 Johnnie Walton	2.00	.75
❑	83 Gordon Banks	2.00	.75
❑	84 Fred Besana	2.00	.75
❑	85 Dave Browning	2.00	.75
❑	86 Eric Jordan	2.00	.75
❑	87 Frank Manumaleuga	2.00	.75
❑	88 Gary Plummer XRC	4.00	2.00
❑	89 Stan Talley	2.00	.75
❑	90 Arthur Whittington	2.00	.75
❑	91 Terry Beeson	2.00	.75
❑	92 Mel Gray	4.00	2.00
❑	93 Mike Katolin	2.00	.75
❑	94 Dewey McClain	2.00	.75
❑	95 Sidney Thornton	2.00	.75
❑	96 Doug Williams	4.00	2.00
❑	97 Kelvin Bryant XRC	4.00	2.00
❑	98 John Bunting	2.00	.75
❑	99 Irv Eatman XRC	2.50	1.25
❑	100 Scott Fitzkee	2.00	.75
❑	101 Chuck Fusina	2.00	.75
❑	102 Sean Landeta XRC	2.50	1.25
❑	103 David Trout	2.00	.75
❑	104 Scott Woerner	2.00	.75
❑	105 Glenn Carano	2.00	.75
❑	106 Ron Crosby	2.00	.75
❑	107 Jerry Holmes	2.00	.75
❑	108 Bruce Huther	2.00	.75
❑	109 Mike Rozier XRC	4.00	2.00
❑	110 Larry Swider	2.00	.75
❑	111 Danny Buggs	2.00	.75
❑	112 Putt Choate	2.00	.75
❑	113 Rich Garza	2.00	.75

❑ 114	Joey Hackett	2.00	.75
❑ 115	Rick Neuheisel XRC	4.00	2.00
❑ 116	Mike St. Clair	2.00	.75
❑ 117	Gary Anderson XRC RB	4.00	2.00
❑ 118	Zenon Andrusyshyn	2.00	.75
❑ 119	Doug Beaudoin	2.00	.75
❑ 120	Mike Butler	2.00	.75
❑ 121	Willie Gillespie	2.00	.75
❑ 122	Fred Nordgren	2.00	.75
❑ 123	John Reaves	2.00	.75
❑ 124	Eric Truvillion	2.00	.75
❑ 125	Reggie Collier	2.00	.75
❑ 126	Mike Guess	2.00	.75
❑ 127	Mike Hohensee	2.00	.75
❑ 128	[illegible]	[illegible]	[illegible]
❑ 129	Eric Robinson	2.00	.75
❑ 130	Billy Taylor	2.00	.75
❑ 131	Joey Walters	2.00	.75
❑ 132	Checklist 1-132	2.50	1.25

1985 Topps

❑	COMPLETE SET (396)	60.00	35.00
❑	COMP.FACT.SET (396)	75.00	40.00
❑ 1	Mark Clayton RB	.50	.20
❑ 2	Eric Dickerson RB	.50	.20
❑ 3	Charlie Joiner RB	.50	.20
❑ 4	Dan Marino RB	6.00	3.00
❑ 5	Art Monk RB	.50	.20
❑ 6	Walter Payton RB	1.00	.40
❑ 7	NFC Champs/Suhey	.25	.08
❑ 8	AFC Championship	.25	.08
❑ 9	Super Bowl XIX	.25	.08
❑ 10	Atlanta Falcons TL	.10	.02
❑ 11	William Andrews	.25	.08
❑ 12	Stacey Bailey	.10	.02
❑ 13	Steve Bartkowski	.50	.20
❑ 14	Rick Bryan RC	.10	.02
❑ 15	Alfred Jackson	.10	.02
❑ 16	Kenny Johnson	.10	.02
❑ 17	Mike Kenn	.10	.02
❑ 18	Mike Pitts RC	.10	.02
❑ 19	Gerald Riggs	.25	.08
❑ 20	Sylvester Stamps	.10	.02
❑ 21	R.C. Thielemann	.10	.02
❑ 22	Bears TL/W.Payton	.75	.30
❑ 23	Todd Bell RC	.10	.02
❑ 24	Richard Dent RC	4.00	1.50
❑ 25	Gary Fencik	.25	.08
❑ 26	Dave Finzer	.10	.02
❑ 27	Leslie Frazier	.10	.02
❑ 28	Steve Fuller	.25	.08
❑ 29	Willie Gault	.50	.20
❑ 30	Dan Hampton	.50	.20
❑ 31	Jim McMahon	.75	.30
❑ 32	Steve McMichael RC	.50	.20
❑ 33	Walter Payton	6.00	2.50
❑ 34	Mike Singletary	.75	.30
❑ 35	Matt Suhey	.10	.02
❑ 36	Bob Thomas	.10	.02
❑ 37	Cowboys TL/Dorsett	.50	.20
❑ 38	Bill Bates RC	1.00	.40
❑ 39	Doug Cosbie	.25	.08
❑ 40	Tony Dorsett	.75	.30
❑ 41	Michael Downs	.10	.02
❑ 42	Mike Hegman RC UER	.10	.02
❑ 43	Tony Hill	.25	.08
❑ 44	Gary Hogeboom RC	.10	.02
❑ 45	Jim Jeffcoat RC	.50	.20
❑ 46	Ed Too Tall Jones	.50	.20
❑ 47	Mike Renfro	.10	.02
❑ 48	Rafael Septien	.10	.02
❑ 49	Dennis Thurman	.10	.02
❑ 50	Everson Walls	.25	.08
❑ 51	Danny White	.50	.20
❑ 52	Randy White	.50	.20
❑ 53	Detroit Lions TL	.10	.02
❑ 54	Jeff Chadwick	.10	.02
❑ 55	Michael Cofer RC	.10	.02
❑ 56	Gary Danielson	.10	.02
❑ 57	Keith Dorney	.10	.02
❑ 58	Doug English	.25	.08
❑ 59	William Gay	.10	.02
❑ 60	Ken Jenkins	.10	.02
❑ 61	[illegible]	[illegible]	[illegible]
❑ 62	Eddie Murray	.25	.08
❑ 63	Billy Sims	.50	.20
❑ 64	Leonard Thompson	.10	.02
❑ 65	Bobby Watkins	.10	.02
❑ 66	Green Bay Packers TL	.25	.08
❑ 67	Paul Coffman	.10	.02
❑ 68	Lynn Dickey	.25	.08
❑ 69	Mike Douglass	.10	.02
❑ 70	Tom Flynn RC	.10	.02
❑ 71	Eddie Lee Ivery	.10	.02
❑ 72	Ezra Johnson	.10	.02
❑ 73	Mark Lee	.10	.02
❑ 74	Tim Lewis	.10	.02
❑ 75	James Lofton	.50	.20
❑ 76	Bucky Scribner	.10	.02
❑ 77	Rams TL/Dickerson	.50	.20
❑ 78	Nolan Cromwell	.25	.08
❑ 79	Eric Dickerson	1.25	.50
❑ 80	Henry Ellard RC	2.50	1.00
❑ 81	Kent Hill	.10	.02
❑ 82	LeRoy Irvin	.25	.08
❑ 83	Jeff Kemp RC	.25	.08
❑ 84	Mike Lansford	.10	.02
❑ 85	Barry Redden	.10	.02
❑ 86	Jackie Slater	.50	.20
❑ 87	Doug Smith C RC	.25	.08
❑ 88	Jack Youngblood	.25	.08
❑ 89	Minnesota Vikings TL	.10	.02
❑ 90	Alfred Anderson RC	.10	.02
❑ 91	Ted Brown	.25	.08
❑ 92	Greg Coleman	.10	.02
❑ 93	Tommy Hannon	.10	.02
❑ 94	Tommy Kramer	.25	.08
❑ 95	Leo Lewis RC	.25	.08
❑ 96	Doug Martin	.10	.02
❑ 97	Darrin Nelson	.25	.08
❑ 98	Jan Stenerud	.25	.08
❑ 99	Sammie White	.25	.08
❑ 100	New Orleans Saints TL	.10	.02
❑ 101	Morten Andersen	.50	.20
❑ 102	Hoby Brenner RC	.25	.08
❑ 103	Bruce Clark	.10	.02
❑ 104	Hokie Gajan	.10	.02
❑ 105	Brian Hansen RC	.10	.02
❑ 106	Rickey Jackson	.50	.20
❑ 107	George Rogers	.25	.08
❑ 108	Dave Wilson	.10	.02
❑ 109	Tyrone Young	.10	.02
❑ 110	New York Giants TL	.10	.02
❑ 111	Carl Banks RC	.50	.20
❑ 112	Jim Burt RC	.50	.20
❑ 113	Rob Carpenter	.10	.02
❑ 114	Harry Carson	.25	.08
❑ 115	Earnest Gray	.10	.02
❑ 116	Ali Haji-Sheikh	.10	.02
❑ 117	Mark Haynes	.25	.08
❑ 118	Bobby Johnson	.10	.02
❑ 119	Lionel Manuel RC	.25	.08
❑ 120	Joe Morris RC	.50	.20
❑ 121	Zeke Mowatt RC	.25	.08
❑ 122	Jeff Rutledge RC	.10	.02
❑ 123	Phil Simms	.50	.20
❑ 124	Lawrence Taylor	1.50	.60
❑ 125	Philadelphia Eagles TL	.10	.02
❑ 126	Greg Brown	.10	.02
❑ 127	Ray Ellis	.10	.02
❑ 128	Dennis Harrison	.10	.02
❑ 129	Wes Hopkins RC	.25	.08
❑ 130	Mike Horan RC	.10	.02
❑ 131	Kenny Jackson RC	.10	.02
❑ 132	Ron Jaworski	.25	.08
❑ 133	Paul McFadden	.10	.02
❑ 134	Wilbert Montgomery	.25	.08
❑ 135	Mike Quick	.50	.20
❑ 136	John Spagnola	.10	.02
❑ 137	St.Louis Cardinals TL	.10	.02
❑ 138	Ottis Anderson	.50	.20
❑ 139	Al(Bubba) Baker	.25	.08
❑ 140	Roy Green	.25	.08
❑ 141	Curtis Greer	.10	.02
❑ 142	E.J.Junior	.10	.02
❑ 143	Neil Lomax	.25	.08
❑ 144	Stump Mitchell	.25	.08
❑ 145	Neil O'Donoghue	.10	.02
❑ 146	Pat Tilley	.10	.02
❑ 147	Lionel Washington	.10	.02
❑ 148	[illegible]	[illegible]	[illegible]
❑ 149	Dwaine Board	.10	.02
❑ 150	Dwight Clark	.50	.20
❑ 151	Roger Craig	1.00	.40
❑ 152	Randy Cross	.25	.08
❑ 153	Fred Dean	.25	.08
❑ 154	Keith Fahnhorst RC	.10	.02
❑ 155	Dwight Hicks	.10	.02
❑ 156	Ronnie Lott	.50	.20
❑ 157	Joe Montana	10.00	4.00
❑ 158	Renaldo Nehemiah	.25	.08
❑ 159	Fred Quillan	.10	.02
❑ 160	Jack Reynolds	.10	.02
❑ 161	Freddie Solomon	.10	.02
❑ 162	Keena Turner RC	.10	.02
❑ 163	Wendell Tyler	.10	.02
❑ 164	Ray Wersching	.10	.02
❑ 165	Carlton Williamson	.10	.02
❑ 166	Tampa Bay Bucs TL	.25	.08
❑ 167	Gerald Carter	.10	.02
❑ 168	Mark Cotney	.10	.02
❑ 169	Steve DeBerg	.50	.20
❑ 170	Sean Farrell RC	.10	.02
❑ 171	Hugh Green	.25	.08
❑ 172	Kevin House	.25	.08
❑ 173	David Logan	.10	.02
❑ 174	Michael Morton	.10	.02
❑ 175	Lee Roy Selmon	.50	.20
❑ 176	James Wilder	.10	.02
❑ 177	Redskins TL/J.Riggins	.50	.20
❑ 178	Charlie Brown	.10	.02
❑ 179	Monte Coleman RC	.25	.08
❑ 180	Vernon Dean	.10	.02
❑ 181	Darrell Green	.50	.20
❑ 182	Russ Grimm	.25	.08
❑ 183	Joe Jacoby	.25	.08
❑ 184	Dexter Manley	.25	.08
❑ 185	Art Monk	.50	.20
❑ 186	Mark Moseley	.25	.08
❑ 187	Calvin Muhammad	.10	.02
❑ 188	Mike Nelms	.10	.02
❑ 189	John Riggins	.50	.20
❑ 190	Joe Theismann	.50	.20
❑ 191	Joe Washington	.25	.08
❑ 192	D.Marino/Montana LL	10.00	4.00
❑ 193	Art Monk/O.Newsome LL	.25	.08
❑ 194	E.Dickerson/Jackson LL	.50	.20
❑ 195	Scoring Leaders	.10	.02
❑ 196	Interception Leaders	.10	.02
❑ 197	Punting Leaders	.10	.02
❑ 198	Bills TL/Greg Bell	.10	.02
❑ 199	Greg Bell RC	.25	.08
❑ 200	Preston Dennard	.10	.02
❑ 201	Joe Ferguson	.25	.08
❑ 202	Byron Franklin	.10	.02
❑ 203	Steve Freeman	.10	.02
❑ 204	Jim Haslett	.25	.08
❑ 205	Charles Romes	.10	.02
❑ 206	Fred Smerlas	.10	.02
❑ 207	Darryl Talley RC	.50	.20
❑ 208	Van Williams	.10	.02
❑ 209	Cincinnati Bengals TL	.25	.08
❑ 210	Ken Anderson	.50	.20
❑ 211	Jim Breech	.10	.02
❑ 212	Louis Breeden	.10	.02
❑ 213	James Brooks	.25	.08
❑ 214	Ross Browner	.25	.08
❑ 215	Eddie Edwards	.10	.02
❑ 216	M.L. Harris	.10	.02
❑ 217	Bobby Kemp	.10	.02
❑ 218	Larry Kinnebrew RC	.10	.02
❑ 219	Anthony Munoz	.50	.20
❑ 220	Reggie Williams	.25	.08

❑	221 Cleveland Browns TL	.10	.02
❑	222 Matt Bahr	.25	.08
❑	223 Chip Banks	.10	.02
❑	224 Reggie Camp	.10	.02
❑	225 Tom Cousineau	.10	.02
❑	226 Joe DeLamielleure	.50	.20
❑	227 Ricky Feacher	.10	.02
❑	228 Boyce Green RC	.10	.02
❑	229 Al Gross	.10	.02
❑	230 Clay Matthews	.50	.20
❑	231 Paul McDonald	.10	.02
❑	232 Ozzie Newsome	.50	.20
❑	233 Mike Pruitt	.25	.08
❑	234 Don Rogers DB	.10	.02
❑	235 Broncos TL/J.Elway	2.50	1.00
❑	236 Rubin Carter	.10	.02
❑	237 Barney Chavous	.10	.02
❑	238 John Elway	12.00	5.00
❑	239 Steve Foley	.10	.02
❑	240 Mike Harden RC	.10	.02
❑	241 Tom Jackson	.50	.20
❑	242 Butch Johnson	.10	.02
❑	243 Rulon Jones	.10	.02
❑	244 Rich Karlis	.10	.02
❑	245 Steve Watson	.25	.08
❑	246 Gerald Willhite	.10	.02
❑	247 Sammy Winder	.25	.08
❑	248 Houston Oilers TL	.10	.02
❑	249 Jesse Baker	.10	.02
❑	250 Carter Hartwig	.10	.02
❑	251 Warren Moon RC	15.00	6.00
❑	252 Larry Moriarty RC	.10	.02
❑	253 Mike Munchak RC	3.00	1.25
❑	254 Carl Roaches	.10	.02
❑	255 Tim Smith	.25	.08
❑	256 Willie Tullis	.10	.02
❑	257 Jamie Williams RC	.10	.02
❑	258 Indianapolis Colts TL	.10	.02
❑	259 Raymond Butler	.10	.02
❑	260 Johnie Cooks	.10	.02
❑	261 Eugene Daniel RC	.10	.02
❑	262 Curtis Dickey	.25	.08
❑	263 Chris Hinton	.25	.08
❑	264 Vernon Maxwell	.10	.02
❑	265 Randy McMillan	.10	.02
❑	266 Art Schlichter RC	.50	.20
❑	267 Rohn Stark	.25	.08
❑	268 Leo Wisniewski	.10	.02
❑	269 Kansas City Chiefs TL	.10	.02
❑	270 Jim Arnold	.10	.02
❑	271 Mike Bell	.10	.02
❑	272 Todd Blackledge RC	.25	.08
❑	273 Carlos Carson	.25	.08
❑	274 Deron Cherry	.25	.08
❑	275 Herman Heard RC	.10	.02
❑	276 Bill Kenney	.25	.08
❑	277 Nick Lowery	.50	.20
❑	278 Bill Maas RC	.10	.02
❑	279 Henry Marshall	.10	.02
❑	280 Art Still	.10	.02
❑	281 Raiders TL/M.Allen	.50	.20
❑	282 Marcus Allen	2.50	1.00
❑	283 Lyle Alzado	.25	.08
❑	284 Chris Bahr	.10	.02
❑	285 Malcolm Barnwell	.10	.02
❑	286 Cliff Branch	.50	.20
❑	287 Todd Christensen	.50	.20
❑	288 Ray Guy	.50	.20
❑	289 Lester Hayes	.25	.08
❑	290 Mike Haynes	.25	.08
❑	291 Henry Lawrence	.10	.02
❑	292 Howie Long	2.00	.75
❑	293 Rod Martin	.25	.08
❑	294 Vann McElroy	.10	.02
❑	295 Matt Millen	.25	.08
❑	296 Bill Pickel RC	.10	.02
❑	297 Jim Plunkett	.50	.20
❑	298 Dokie Williams RC	.10	.02
❑	299 Marc Wilson	.25	.08
❑	300 Dolphins TL/Duper	.25	.08
❑	301 Bob Baumhower	.10	.02
❑	302 Doug Betters	.10	.02
❑	303 Glenn Blackwood	.25	.08
❑	304 Lyle Blackwood	.25	.08
❑	305 Kim Bokamper	.10	.02
❑	306 Charles Bowser RC	.10	.02
❑	307 Jimmy Cefalo	.10	.02
❑	308 Mark Clayton RC	.75	.30
❑	309 A.J. Duhe	.10	.02
❑	310 Mark Duper	.50	.20
❑	311 Andra Franklin	.10	.02
❑	312 Bruce Hardy	.10	.02
❑	313 Pete Johnson	.25	.08
❑	314 Dan Marino	12.00	5.00
❑	315 Tony Nathan	.25	.08
❑	316 Ed Newman	.10	.02
❑	317 Reggie Roby	.50	.20
❑	318 Dwight Stephenson	1.00	.40
❑	319 Uwe Von Schamann	.10	.02
❑	320 New England Pats TL	.10	.02
❑	321 Raymond Clayborn	.25	.08
❑	322 Tony Collins	.25	.08
❑	323 Tony Eason RC	.50	.20
❑	324 Tony Franklin	.10	.02
❑	325 Irving Fryar RC	5.00	2.00
❑	326 John Hannah	.50	.20
❑	327 Brian Holloway	.10	.02
❑	328 Craig James RC	.75	.30
❑	329 Stanley Morgan	.25	.08
❑	330 Steve Nelson	.10	.02
❑	331 Derrick Ramsey	.10	.02
❑	332 Stephen Starring RC	.25	.08
❑	333 Mosi Tatupu	.10	.02
❑	334 Andre Tippett	.50	.20
❑	335 New York Jets TL	.25	.08
❑	336 Russell Carter RC	.10	.02
❑	337 Mark Gastineau	.25	.08
❑	338 Bruce Harper	.10	.02
❑	339 Bobby Humphery RC	.10	.02
❑	340 Johnny Lam Jones	.10	.02
❑	341 Joe Klecko	.25	.08
❑	342 Pat Leahy	.10	.02
❑	343 Marty Lyons	.25	.08
❑	344 Freeman McNeil	.25	.08
❑	345 Lance Mehl	.10	.02
❑	346 Ken O'Brien RC	.50	.20
❑	347 Marvin Powell	.10	.02
❑	348 Pat Ryan	.10	.02
❑	349 Mickey Shuler RC	.10	.02
❑	350 Wesley Walker	.25	.08
❑	351 Pittsburgh Steelers TL	.25	.08
❑	352 Walter Abercrombie	.10	.02
❑	353 Gary Anderson K	.25	.08
❑	354 Robin Cole	.10	.02
❑	355 Bennie Cunningham	.10	.02
❑	356 Rich Erenberg	.10	.02
❑	357 Jack Lambert	.50	.20
❑	358 Louis Lipps RC	.50	.20
❑	359 Mark Malone	.25	.08
❑	360 Mike Merriweather RC	.10	.02
❑	361 Frank Pollard	.10	.02
❑	362 Donnie Shell	.25	.08
❑	363 John Stallworth	.50	.20
❑	364 Sam Washington	.10	.02
❑	365 Mike Webster	.25	.08
❑	366 Dwayne Woodruff	.10	.02
❑	367 San Diego Chargers TL	.10	.02
❑	368 Rolf Benirschke	.10	.02
❑	369 Gill Byrd RC	.50	.20
❑	370 Wes Chandler	.25	.08
❑	371 Bobby Duckworth	.10	.02
❑	372 Dan Fouts	.50	.20
❑	373 Mike Green	.10	.02
❑	374 Pete Holohan RC	.10	.02
❑	375 Earnest Jackson RC	.25	.08
❑	376 Lionel James RC	.25	.08
❑	377 Charlie Joiner	.50	.20
❑	378 Billy Ray Smith	.25	.08
❑	379 Kellen Winslow	.50	.20
❑	380 Seattle Seahawks TL	.25	.08
❑	381 Dave Brown DB	.10	.02
❑	382 Jeff Bryant	.10	.02
❑	383 Dan Doornink	.10	.02
❑	384 Kenny Easley	.25	.08
❑	385 Jacob Green	.25	.08
❑	386 David Hughes	.10	.02
❑	387 Norm Johnson	.10	.02
❑	388 Dave Krieg	.50	.20
❑	389 Steve Largent	1.00	.40
❑	390 Joe Nash RC	.10	.02
❑	391 Daryl Turner RC	.10	.02
❑	392 Curt Warner	.50	.20
❑	393 Fredd Young RC	.25	.08
❑	394 Checklist 1-132	.25	.08
❑	395 Checklist 133-264	.25	.08
❑	396 Checklist 265-396	.25	.08

1985 Topps USFL

❑	COMP.FACT.SET (132)	120.00	60.00
❑	COMPLETE SET (132)	120.00	60.00
❑	1 Case DeBruijn	.50	.20
❑	2 Mike Katolin	.50	.20
❑	3 Bruce Laird	.50	.20
❑	4 Kit Lathrop	.50	.20
❑	5 Kevin Long	.50	.20
❑	6 Karl Lorch	.50	.20
❑	7 Dave Tipton DT	.50	.20
❑	8 Doug Williams	2.00	.75
❑	9 Luis Zendejas XRC	.50	.20
❑	10 Kelvin Bryant	1.00	.40
❑	11 Willie Collier	.50	.20
❑	12 Irv Eatman	.50	.20
❑	13 Scott Fitzkee	.50	.20
❑	14 William Fuller XRC	3.00	1.25
❑	15 Chuck Fusina	.50	.20
❑	16 Pete Kugler	.50	.20
❑	17 Garcia Lane	.50	.20
❑	18 Mike Lush	.50	.20
❑	19 Sam Mills XRC	5.00	2.00
❑	20 Buddy Aydelette	.50	.20
❑	21 Joe Cribbs	2.00	.75
❑	22 David Dumars	.50	.20
❑	23 Robin Earl	.50	.20
❑	24 Joey Jones	.50	.20
❑	25 Leon Perry RB	.50	.20
❑	26 Dave Pureifory	.50	.20
❑	27 Bill Roe	.50	.20
❑	28 Doug Smith DT XRC	2.00	.75
❑	29 Cliff Stoudt	1.00	.40
❑	30 Jeff Delaney	.50	.20
❑	31 Vince Evans	1.00	.40
❑	32 Leonard Harris XRC	.50	.20
❑	33 Bill Johnson RB	.50	.20
❑	34 Marc Lewis XRC	.50	.20
❑	35 David Martin	.50	.20
❑	36 Bruce Thornton	.50	.20
❑	37 Craig Walls	.50	.20
❑	38 Vincent White	.50	.20
❑	39 Luther Bradley	.50	.20
❑	40 Pete Catan	.50	.20
❑	41 Kiki DeAyala	.50	.20
❑	42 Toni Fritsch	.50	.20
❑	43 Sam Harrell	.50	.20
❑	44 Richard Johnson WR XRC	1.00	.40
❑	45 Jim Kelly	20.00	10.00
❑	46 Gerald McNeil XRC	.50	.20
❑	47 Clarence Verdin XRC	2.00	.75
❑	48 Dale Walters	.50	.20
❑	49 Gary Clark XRC	6.00	2.50
❑	50 Tom Dinkel	.50	.20
❑	51 Mike Edwards LB	.50	.20
❑	52 Brian Franco	.50	.20
❑	53 Bob Gruber	.50	.20
❑	54 Robbie Mahfouz	.50	.20
❑	55 Mike Rozier	2.00	.75
❑	56 Brian Sipe	1.00	.40
❑	57 J.T. Turner	.50	.20
❑	58 Howard Carson	.50	.20
❑	59 Wymon Henderson XRC	.50	.20
❑	60 Kevin Nelson	.50	.20
❑	61 Jeff Partridge	.50	.20
❑	62 Ben Rudolph	.50	.20
❑	63 Jo Jo Townsell	1.00	.40

❑ 64 Eddie Weaver .50 .20
❑ 65 Steve Young 30.00 15.00
❑ 66 Tony Zendejas XRC 1.00 .40
❑ 67 Mossy Cade .50 .20
❑ 68 Leonard Coleman XRC .50 .20
❑ 69 John Corker .50 .20
❑ 70 Derrick Crawford .50 .20
❑ 71 Art Kuehn .50 .20
❑ 72 Walter Lewis .50 .20
❑ 73 Tyrone McGriff .50 .20
❑ 74 Tim Spencer 1.00 .40
❑ 75 Reggie White 25.00 12.50
❑ 76 Gizmo Williams XRC 2.00 .75
❑ 77 [illegible] .50 .20
❑ 78 Maurice Carthon XRC 2.00 .75
❑ 79 Clarence Collins .50 .20
❑ 80 Doug Flutie XRC 30.00 12.50
❑ 81 Freddie Gilbert DE .50 .20
❑ 82 Kerry Justin .50 .20
❑ 83 Dave Lapham .50 .20
❑ 84 Rick Partridge .50 .20
❑ 85 Roger Ruzek XRC 1.00 .40
❑ 86 Herschel Walker 8.00 3.00
❑ 87 Gordon Banks .50 .20
❑ 88 Monte Bennett .50 .20
❑ 89 Albert Bentley XRC 1.00 .40
❑ 90 Novo Bojovic .50 .20
❑ 91 Dave Browning .50 .20
❑ 92 Anthony Carter 2.00 .75
❑ 93 Bobby Hebert 2.00 .75
❑ 94 Ray Pinney .50 .20
❑ 95 Stan Talley .50 .20
❑ 96 Ruben Vaughan .50 .20
❑ 97 Curtis Bledsoe .50 .20
❑ 98 Reggie Collier .50 .20
❑ 99 Jerry Doerger .50 .20
❑ 100 Jerry Golsteyn .50 .20
❑ 101 Bob Niziolek .50 .20
❑ 102 Joel Patten .50 .20
❑ 103 Ricky Simmons .50 .20
❑ 104 Joey Walters .50 .20
❑ 105 Marcus Dupree 1.00 .40
❑ 106 Jeff Gossett 1.00 .40
❑ 107 Frank Lockett .50 .20
❑ 108 Marcus Marek .50 .20
❑ 109 Kenny Neil .50 .20
❑ 110 Robert Pennywell .50 .20
❑ 111 Matt Robinson .50 .20
❑ 112 Dan Ross 1.00 .40
❑ 113 Doug Woodward .50 .20
❑ 114 Danny Buggs .50 .20
❑ 115 Putt Choate .50 .20
❑ 116 Greg Fields .50 .20
❑ 117 Ken Hartley .50 .20
❑ 118 Nick Mike Mayer .50 .20
❑ 119 Rick Neuheisel 2.00 .75
❑ 120 Peter Raeford .50 .20
❑ 121 Gary Worthy .50 .20
❑ 122 Gary Anderson RB 1.00 .40
❑ 123 Zenon Andrusyshyn .50 .20
❑ 124 Greg Boone .50 .20
❑ 125 Mike Butler .50 .20
❑ 126 Mike Clark .50 .20
❑ 127 Willie Gillespie .50 .20
❑ 128 James Harrell .50 .20
❑ 129 Marvin Harvey .50 .20
❑ 130 John Reaves 1.00 .40
❑ 131 Eric Truvillion .50 .20
❑ 132 Checklist 1-132 1.00 .40

1986 Topps

❑ COMPLETE SET (396) 120.00 60.00
❑ COMP.FACT.SET (396) 225.00 150.00
❑ 1 Marcus Allen RB .75 .30
❑ 2 Eric Dickerson RB .50 .20
❑ 3 Lionel James RB .10 .02
❑ 4 Steve Largent RB .50 .20
❑ 5 George Martin RB .10 .02
❑ 6 Stephone Paige RB .10 .02
❑ 7 Walter Payton RB .75 .30
❑ 8 Super Bowl XX .25 .08
❑ 9 Bears TL/W.Payton .60 .25
❑ 10 Jim McMahon .50 .20
❑ 11 Walter Payton 5.00 2.00
❑ 12 Matt Suhey .10 .02
❑ 13 Willie Gault .25 .08
❑ 14 Dennis McKinnon RC .10 .02

❑ 15 Emery Moorehead .10 .02
❑ 16 Jim Covert .25 .08
❑ 17 Jay Hilgenberg RC .50 .20
❑ 18 Kevin Butler RC .25 .08
❑ 19 Richard Dent .75 .30
❑ 20 William Perry RC .50 .20
❑ 21 Steve McMichael .50 .20
❑ 22 Dan Hampton .50 .20
❑ 23 Otis Wilson .10 .02
❑ 24 Mike Singletary .60 .25
❑ 25 Wilber Marshall RC .50 .20
❑ 26 Leslie Frazier .10 .02
❑ 27 Dave Duerson RC .10 .02
❑ 28 Gary Fencik .10 .02
❑ 29 Patriots TL .50 .20
❑ 30 Tony Eason .10 .02
❑ 31 Steve Grogan .25 .08
❑ 32 Craig James .50 .20
❑ 33 Tony Collins .10 .02
❑ 34 Irving Fryar 1.25 .50
❑ 35 Brian Holloway .10 .02
❑ 36 John Hannah .50 .20
❑ 37 Tony Franklin .10 .02
❑ 38 Garin Veris RC .10 .02
❑ 39 Andre Tippett .25 .08
❑ 40 Steve Nelson .10 .02
❑ 41 Raymond Clayborn .10 .02
❑ 42 Fred Marion RC .10 .02
❑ 43 Rich Camarillo .10 .02
❑ 44 Dolphins TL/D.Marino 2.00 .75
❑ 45 Dan Marino 8.00 4.00
❑ 46 Tony Nathan .25 .08
❑ 47 Ron Davenport RC .10 .02
❑ 48 Mark Duper .50 .20
❑ 49 Mark Clayton .50 .20
❑ 50 Nat Moore .25 .08
❑ 51 Bruce Hardy .10 .02
❑ 52 Roy Foster .10 .02
❑ 53 Dwight Stephenson .75 .30
❑ 54 Fuad Reveiz RC .25 .08
❑ 55 Bob Baumhower .10 .02
❑ 56 Mike Charles .10 .02
❑ 57 Hugh Green .25 .08
❑ 58 Glenn Blackwood .10 .02
❑ 59 Reggie Roby .25 .08
❑ 60 Raiders TL/M.Allen .50 .20
❑ 61 Marc Wilson .10 .02
❑ 62 Marcus Allen 1.50 .60
❑ 63 Dokie Williams .10 .02
❑ 64 Todd Christensen .50 .20
❑ 65 Chris Bahr .10 .02
❑ 66 Fulton Walker .10 .02
❑ 67 Howie Long 1.25 .50
❑ 68 Bill Pickel .10 .02
❑ 69 Ray Guy .50 .20
❑ 70 Greg Townsend RC .50 .20
❑ 71 Rod Martin .25 .08
❑ 72 Matt Millen .25 .08
❑ 73 Mike Haynes .25 .08
❑ 74 Lester Hayes .25 .08
❑ 75 Vann McElroy .10 .02
❑ 76 Rams TL/ Dickerson .50 .20
❑ 77 Dieter Brock RC .25 .08
❑ 78 Eric Dickerson .75 .30
❑ 79 Henry Ellard 1.00 .40
❑ 80 Ron Brown RC .25 .08
❑ 81 Tony Hunter RC .10 .02
❑ 82 Kent Hill AP .10 .02
❑ 83 Doug Smith .10 .02
❑ 84 Dennis Harrah .10 .02
❑ 85 Jackie Slater .50 .20
❑ 86 Mike Lansford .10 .02
❑ 87 Gary Jeter .10 .02
❑ 88 Mike Wilcher .10 .02
❑ 89 Jim Collins .10 .02
❑ 90 LeRoy Irvin .25 .08
❑ 91 Gary Green .10 .02
❑ 92 Nolan Cromwell .25 .08
❑ 93 Dale Hatcher RC .10 .02
❑ 94 Jets TL .25 .08
❑ 95 Ken O'Brien .50 .20
❑ 96 Freeman McNeil .25 .08
❑ 97 Tony Paige RC .10 .02
❑ 98 Johnny Lam Jones .10 .02
❑ 99 Wesley Walker .25 .08
❑ 100 Kurt Sohn .10 .02
❑ 101 Al Toon RC .50 .20
❑ 102 Mickey Shuler .10 .02
❑ 103 Marvin Powell .10 .02
❑ 104 Pat Leahy .10 .02
❑ 105 Mark Gastineau .25 .08
❑ 106 Joe Klecko .25 .08
❑ 107 Marty Lyons .10 .02
❑ 108 Lance Mehl .10 .02
❑ 109 Bobby Jackson .10 .02
❑ 110 Dave Jennings .10 .02
❑ 111 Broncos TL .25 .08
❑ 112 John Elway 8.00 4.00
❑ 113 Sammy Winder .25 .08
❑ 114 Gerald Willhite .10 .02
❑ 115 Steve Watson .10 .02
❑ 116 Vance Johnson RC .50 .20
❑ 117 Rich Karlis .10 .02
❑ 118 Rulon Jones .10 .02
❑ 119 Karl Mecklenburg RC .50 .20
❑ 120 Louis Wright .10 .02
❑ 121 Mike Harden .10 .02
❑ 122 Dennis Smith RC .50 .20
❑ 123 Steve Foley .10 .02
❑ 124 Cowboys TL .25 .08
❑ 125 Danny White .50 .20
❑ 126 Tony Dorsett .60 .25
❑ 127 Timmy Newsome .10 .02
❑ 128 Mike Renfro .10 .02
❑ 129 Tony Hill .25 .08
❑ 130 Doug Cosbie .25 .08
❑ 131 Rafael Septien .10 .02
❑ 132 Ed Too Tall Jones .50 .20
❑ 133 Randy White .50 .20
❑ 134 Jim Jeffcoat .50 .20
❑ 135 Everson Walls .25 .08
❑ 136 Dennis Thurman .10 .02
❑ 137 Giants TL .25 .08
❑ 138 Phil Simms .50 .20
❑ 139 Joe Morris .50 .20
❑ 140 George Adams RC .10 .02
❑ 141 Lionel Manuel .25 .08
❑ 142 Bobby Johnson .10 .02
❑ 143 Phil McConkey RC .25 .08
❑ 144 Mark Bavaro RC .50 .20
❑ 145 Zeke Mowatt .10 .02
❑ 146 Brad Benson RC .10 .02
❑ 147 Bart Oates RC .25 .08
❑ 148 Leonard Marshall RC .50 .20
❑ 149 Jim Burt .25 .08
❑ 150 George Martin .10 .02
❑ 151 Lawrence Taylor 1.25 .50
❑ 152 Harry Carson .25 .08
❑ 153 Elvis Patterson RC .10 .02
❑ 154 Sean Landeta RC .25 .08
❑ 155 49ers TL/Roger Craig .50 .20
❑ 156 Joe Montana 8.00 4.00
❑ 157 Roger Craig .50 .20
❑ 158 Wendell Tyler .10 .02
❑ 159 Carl Monroe .10 .02
❑ 160 Dwight Clark .25 .08
❑ 161 Jerry Rice RC ! 80.00 40.00
❑ 162 Randy Cross .25 .08
❑ 163 Keith Fahnhorst .10 .02
❑ 164 Jeff Stover .10 .02
❑ 165 Michael Carter RC .10 .02
❑ 166 Dwaine Board .10 .02
❑ 167 Eric Wright .25 .08
❑ 168 Ronnie Lott .75 .30
❑ 169 Carlton Williamson .10 .02
❑ 170 Redskins TL .25 .08
❑ 171 Joe Theismann .50 .20

❑	172 Jay Schroeder RC	.50	.20
❑	173 George Rogers	.25	.08
❑	174 Ken Jenkins	.10	.02
❑	175 Art Monk	.50	.20
❑	176 Gary Clark RC	2.00	.75
❑	177 Joe Jacoby	.25	.08
❑	178 Russ Grimm	.25	.08
❑	179 Mark Moseley	.10	.02
❑	180 Dexter Manley	.25	.08
❑	181 Charles Mann RC	.50	.20
❑	182 Vernon Dean	.10	.02
❑	183 Raphel Cherry RC	.10	.02
❑	184 Curtis Jordan	.10	.02
❑	185 Browns TL/Kosar	.50	.20
❑	186 Gary Danielson	.25	.08
❑	187 Bernie Kosar RC	3.00	1.25
❑	188 Kevin Mack RC	.50	.20
❑	189 Earnest Byner RC	.75	.30
❑	190 Glen Young	.10	.02
❑	191 Ozzie Newsome	.50	.20
❑	192 Mike Baab	.10	.02
❑	193 Cody Risien	.25	.08
❑	194 Bob Golic	.25	.08
❑	195 Reggie Camp	.10	.02
❑	196 Chip Banks	.25	.08
❑	197 Tom Cousineau	.10	.02
❑	198 Frank Minnifield RC	.10	.02
❑	199 Al Gross	.10	.02
❑	200 Seahawks TL	.25	.08
❑	201 Dave Krieg	.50	.20
❑	202 Curt Warner	.25	.08
❑	203 Steve Largent	.60	.25
❑	204 Norm Johnson	.10	.02
❑	205 Daryl Turner	.10	.02
❑	206 Jacob Green	.10	.02
❑	207 Joe Nash	.10	.02
❑	208 Jeff Bryant	.10	.02
❑	209 Randy Edwards	.10	.02
❑	210 Fredd Young	.10	.02
❑	211 Kenny Easley	.10	.02
❑	212 John Harris	.10	.02
❑	213 Packers TL	.10	.02
❑	214 Lynn Dickey	.25	.08
❑	215 Gerry Ellis	.10	.02
❑	216 Eddie Lee Ivery	.10	.02
❑	217 Jessie Clark	.10	.02
❑	218 James Lofton	.50	.20
❑	219 Paul Coffman	.10	.02
❑	220 Alphonso Carreker	.10	.02
❑	221 Ezra Johnson	.10	.02
❑	222 Mike Douglass	.10	.02
❑	223 Tim Lewis	.10	.02
❑	224 Mark Murphy RC CB	.10	.02
❑	225 Joe Montana/K.O'Brien LL	1.00	.40
❑	226 Receiving Leaders	.25	.08
❑	227 Marcus Allen/G.Riggs LL	.50	.20
❑	228 Scoring Leaders	.25	.08
❑	229 Interception Leaders	.10	.02
❑	230 Chargers TL/Dan Fouts	.50	.20
❑	231 Dan Fouts	.50	.20
❑	232 Lionel James	.10	.02
❑	233 Gary Anderson RB RC	.50	.20
❑	234 Tim Spencer RC	.25	.08
❑	235 Wes Chandler	.25	.08
❑	236 Charlie Joiner	.50	.20
❑	237 Kellen Winslow	.50	.20
❑	238 Jim Lachey RC	.50	.20
❑	239 Bob Thomas	.10	.02
❑	240 Jeffery Dale	.10	.02
❑	241 Ralf Mojsiejenko	.10	.02
❑	242 Lions TL	.10	.02
❑	243 Eric Hipple	.10	.02
❑	244 Billy Sims	.25	.08
❑	245 James Jones FB	.10	.02
❑	246 Pete Mandley RC	.10	.02
❑	247 Leonard Thompson	.10	.02
❑	248 Lomas Brown RC	.25	.08
❑	249 Eddie Murray	.25	.08
❑	250 Curtis Green	.10	.02
❑	251 William Gay	.10	.02
❑	252 Jimmy Williams	.10	.02
❑	253 Bobby Watkins	.10	.02
❑	254 Bengals TL/B.Esiason	.50	.20
❑	255 Boomer Esiason RC	5.00	2.00
❑	256 James Brooks	.25	.08
❑	257 Larry Kinnebrew	.10	.02
❑	258 Cris Collinsworth	.25	.08
❑	259 Mike Martin	.10	.02
❑	260 Eddie Brown RC	.50	.20
❑	261 Anthony Munoz	.50	.20
❑	262 Jim Breech	.10	.02
❑	263 Ross Browner	.25	.08
❑	264 Carl Zander	.10	.02
❑	265 James Griffin	.10	.02
❑	266 Robert Jackson	.10	.02
❑	267 Pat McInally	.10	.02
❑	268 Eagles TL	.50	.20
❑	269 Ron Jaworski	.25	.08
❑	270 Earnest Jackson	.25	.08
❑	271 Mike Quick	.25	.08
❑	272 John Spagnola	.10	.02
❑	273 Mark Dennard	.10	.02
❑	274 Paul McFadden	.10	.02
❑	275 Reggie White RC	20.00	7.50
❑	276 Greg Brown	.10	.02
❑	277 Herman Edwards	.10	.02
❑	278 Roynell Young	.10	.02
❑	279 Wes Hopkins	.10	.02
❑	280 Steelers TL	.25	.08
❑	281 Mark Malone	.25	.08
❑	282 Frank Pollard	.10	.02
❑	283 Walter Abercrombie	.10	.02
❑	284 Louis Lipps	.50	.20
❑	285 John Stallworth	.50	.20
❑	286 Mike Webster	.25	.08
❑	287 Gary Anderson K	.25	.08
❑	288 Keith Willis	.10	.02
❑	289 Mike Merriweather	.10	.02
❑	290 Dwayne Woodruff	.10	.02
❑	291 Donnie Shell	.25	.08
❑	292 Vikings TL	.25	.08
❑	293 Tommy Kramer	.25	.08
❑	294 Darrin Nelson	.10	.02
❑	295 Ted Brown	.25	.08
❑	296 Buster Rhymes	.10	.02
❑	297 Anthony Carter RC	1.00	.40
❑	298 Steve Jordan RC	.50	.20
❑	299 Keith Millard RC	.50	.20
❑	300 Joey Browner RC	.50	.20
❑	301 John Turner	.10	.02
❑	302 Greg Coleman	.10	.02
❑	303 Chiefs TL	.10	.02
❑	304 Bill Kenney	.10	.02
❑	305 Herman Heard	.10	.02
❑	306 Stephone Paige RC	.50	.20
❑	307 Carlos Carson	.25	.08
❑	308 Nick Lowery	.25	.08
❑	309 Mike Bell	.10	.02
❑	310 Bill Maas	.10	.02
❑	311 Art Still	.10	.02
❑	312 Albert Lewis RC	.50	.20
❑	313 Deron Cherry	.25	.08
❑	314 Colts TL	.10	.02
❑	315 Mike Pagel	.10	.02
❑	316 Randy McMillan	.10	.02
❑	317 Albert Bentley RC	.25	.08
❑	318 George Wonsley RC	.10	.02
❑	319 Robbie Martin	.10	.02
❑	320 Pat Beach	.10	.02
❑	321 Chris Hinton	.25	.08
❑	322 Duane Bickett RC	.50	.20
❑	323 Eugene Daniel	.10	.02
❑	324 Cliff Odom RC	.10	.02
❑	325 Rohn Stark	.25	.08
❑	326 Cardinals TL	.10	.02
❑	327 Neil Lomax	.25	.08
❑	328 Stump Mitchell	.25	.08
❑	329 Ottis Anderson	.50	.20
❑	330 J.T.Smith	.25	.08
❑	331 Pat Tilley	.10	.02
❑	332 Roy Green	.25	.08
❑	333 Lance Smith RC	.10	.02
❑	334 Curtis Greer	.10	.02
❑	335 Freddie Joe Nunn RC	.25	.08
❑	336 E.J. Junior	.25	.08
❑	337 Lonnie Young RC	.10	.02
❑	338 Saints TL	.10	.02
❑	339 Bobby Hebert RC	.50	.20
❑	340 Dave Wilson	.10	.02
❑	341 Wayne Wilson	.10	.02
❑	342 Hoby Brenner	.10	.02
❑	343 Stan Brock	.25	.08
❑	344 Morten Andersen	.50	.20
❑	345 Bruce Clark	.10	.02
❑	346 Rickey Jackson	.50	.20
❑	347 Dave Waymer	.10	.02
❑	348 Brian Hansen	.10	.02
❑	349 Oilers TL/W.Moon	.50	.20
❑	350 Warren Moon	3.00	1.50
❑	351 Mike Rozier RC	.50	.20
❑	352 Butch Woolfolk	.10	.02
❑	353 Drew Hill	.50	.20
❑	354 Willie Drewrey RC	.10	.02
❑	355 Tim Smith	.25	.08
❑	356 Mike Munchak	.50	.20
❑	357 Ray Childress RC	.50	.20
❑	358 Frank Bush	.10	.02
❑	359 Steve Brown	.10	.02
❑	360 Falcons TL	.10	.02
❑	361 David Archer RC	.50	.20
❑	362 Gerald Riggs	.25	.08
❑	363 William Andrews	.25	.08
❑	364 Billy Johnson	.25	.08
❑	365 Arthur Cox	.10	.02
❑	366 Mike Kenn	.10	.02
❑	367 Bill Fralic RC	.25	.08
❑	368 Mick Luckhurst	.10	.02
❑	369 Rick Bryan	.10	.02
❑	370 Bobby Butler	.10	.02
❑	371 Rick Donnelly RC	.10	.02
❑	372 Buccaneers TL	.10	.02
❑	373 Steve DeBerg	.50	.20
❑	374 Steve Young RC	20.00	10.00
❑	375 James Wilder	.10	.02
❑	376 Kevin House	.10	.02
❑	377 Gerald Carter	.10	.02
❑	378 Jimmie Giles	.25	.08
❑	379 Sean Farrell	.10	.02
❑	380 Donald Igwebuike	.10	.02
❑	381 David Logan	.10	.02
❑	382 Jeremiah Castille RC	.10	.02
❑	383 Bills TL	.10	.02
❑	384 Bruce Mathison RC	.10	.02
❑	385 Joe Cribbs	.25	.08
❑	386 Greg Bell	.25	.08
❑	387 Jerry Butler	.10	.02
❑	388 Andre Reed RC	6.00	2.50
❑	389 Bruce Smith RC	5.00	2.00
❑	390 Fred Smerlas	.10	.02
❑	391 Darryl Talley	.50	.20
❑	392 Jim Haslett	.25	.08
❑	393 Charles Romes	.10	.02
❑	394 Checklist 1-132	.20	.07
❑	395 Checklist 133-264	.20	.07
❑	396 Checklist 265-396	.20	.07

1987 Topps

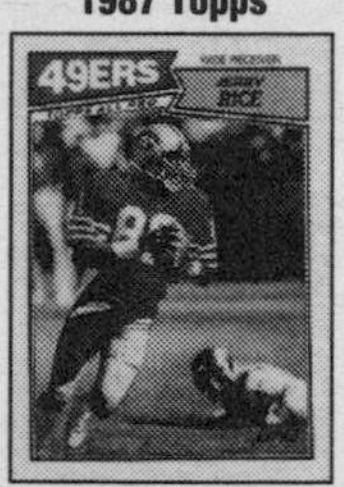

❑	COMPLETE SET (396)	30.00	15.00
❑	COMP.FACT.SET (396)	80.00	50.00
❑	1 Super Bowl XXI	.50	.20
❑	2 Todd Christensen RB	.25	.08
❑	3 Dave Jennings RB	.10	.02
❑	4 Charlie Joiner RB	.50	.20
❑	5 Steve Largent RB	.50	.20
❑	6 Dan Marino RB	2.00	.75
❑	7 Donnie Shell RB	.25	.08
❑	8 Phil Simms RB	.50	.20
❑	9 New York Giants TL	.25	.08
❑	10 Phil Simms	.50	.20
❑	11 Joe Morris	.25	.08
❑	12 Maurice Carthon RC	.50	.20
❑	13 Lee Rouson	.10	.02
❑	14 Bobby Johnson	.10	.02

❑ 15	Lionel Manuel	.10	.02
❑ 16	Phil McConkey	.10	.02
❑ 17	Mark Bavaro	.50	.20
❑ 18	Zeke Mowatt	.10	.02
❑ 19	Raul Allegre	.10	.02
❑ 20	Sean Landeta	.10	.02
❑ 21	Brad Benson	.10	.02
❑ 22	Jim Burt	.10	.02
❑ 23	Leonard Marshall	.50	.20
❑ 24	Carl Banks	.50	.20
❑ 25	Harry Carson	.10	.02
❑ 26	Lawrence Taylor	.75	.30
❑ 27	Terry Kinard RC	.10	.02
❑ 28	Vance Johnson RC	.50	.20
❑ 29	Erik Howard RC	.10	.02
❑ 30	Broncos TL	.10	.02
❑ 31	John Elway	6.00	2.50
❑ 32	Gerald Willhite	.10	.02
❑ 33	Sammy Winder	.25	.08
❑ 34	Ken Bell	.10	.02
❑ 35	Steve Watson	.10	.02
❑ 36	Rich Karlis	.10	.02
❑ 37	Keith Bishop	.10	.02
❑ 38	Rulon Jones	.10	.02
❑ 39	Karl Mecklenburg	.50	.20
❑ 40	Louis Wright	.10	.02
❑ 41	Mike Harden	.10	.02
❑ 42	Dennis Smith	.25	.08
❑ 43	Bears TL/W.Payton	.50	.20
❑ 44	Jim McMahon	.50	.20
❑ 45	Doug Flutie RC	8.00	3.00
❑ 46	Walter Payton	4.00	1.50
❑ 47	Matt Suhey	.10	.02
❑ 48	Willie Gault	.25	.08
❑ 49	Dennis Gentry RC	.10	.02
❑ 50	Kevin Butler	.10	.02
❑ 51	Jim Covert	.10	.02
❑ 52	Jay Hilgenberg	.25	.08
❑ 53	Dan Hampton	.50	.20
❑ 54	Steve McMichael	.50	.20
❑ 55	William Perry	.50	.20
❑ 56	Richard Dent	.50	.20
❑ 57	Otis Wilson	.10	.02
❑ 58	Mike Singletary	.50	.20
❑ 59	Wilber Marshall	.50	.20
❑ 60	Mike Richardson	.10	.02
❑ 61	Dave Duerson	.10	.02
❑ 62	Gary Fencik	.10	.02
❑ 63	Redskins TL	.25	.08
❑ 64	Jay Schroeder	.25	.08
❑ 65	George Rogers	.25	.08
❑ 66	Kelvin Bryant RC	.25	.08
❑ 67	Ken Jenkins	.10	.02
❑ 68	Gary Clark	.50	.20
❑ 69	Art Monk	.50	.20
❑ 70	Clint Didier RC	.10	.02
❑ 71	Steve Cox	.10	.02
❑ 72	Joe Jacoby	.10	.02
❑ 73	Russ Grimm	.10	.02
❑ 74	Charles Mann	.25	.08
❑ 75	Dave Butz	.10	.02
❑ 76	Dexter Manley	.25	.08
❑ 77	Darrell Green	.50	.20
❑ 78	Curtis Jordan	.10	.02
❑ 79	Browns TL	.10	.02
❑ 80	Bernie Kosar	.50	.20
❑ 81	Curtis Dickey	.10	.02
❑ 82	Kevin Mack	.25	.08
❑ 83	Herman Fontenot	.10	.02
❑ 84	Brian Brennan RC	.10	.02
❑ 85	Ozzie Newsome	.50	.20
❑ 86	Jeff Gossett	.25	.08
❑ 87	Cody Risien	.10	.02
❑ 88	Reggie Camp	.10	.02
❑ 89	Bob Golic	.10	.02
❑ 90	Carl Hairston	.10	.02
❑ 91	Chip Banks	.10	.02
❑ 92	Frank Minnifield	.10	.02
❑ 93	Hanford Dixon	.10	.02
❑ 94	Gerald McNeil RC	.10	.02
❑ 95	Dave Puzzuoli	.10	.02
❑ 96	Patriots TL	.10	.02
❑ 97	Tony Eason	.25	.08
❑ 98	Craig James	.25	.08
❑ 99	Tony Collins	.25	.08
❑ 100	Mosi Tatupu	.10	.02
❑ 101	Stanley Morgan	.25	.08
❑ 102	Irving Fryar	.50	.20
❑ 103	Stephen Starring	.10	.02
❑ 104	Tony Franklin	.10	.02
❑ 105	Rich Camarillo	.10	.02
❑ 106	Garin Veris	.10	.02
❑ 107	Andre Tippett	.25	.08
❑ 108	Don Blackmon	.10	.02
❑ 109	Ronnie Lippett RC	.10	.02
❑ 110	Raymond Clayborn	.10	.02
❑ 111	49ers TL/R.Craig	.25	.08
❑ 112	Joe Montana	6.00	2.50
❑ 113	Roger Craig	.50	.20
❑ 114	Joe Cribbs	.25	.08
❑ 115	Jerry Rice	6.00	2.50
❑ 116	Dwight Clark	.25	.08
❑ 117	Ray Wersching	.10	.02
❑ 118	Max Runager	.10	.02
❑ 119	Jeff Stover	.10	.02
❑ 120	Dwaine Board	.10	.02
❑ 121	Tim McKyer RC	.25	.08
❑ 122	Don Griffin RC	.25	.08
❑ 123	Ronnie Lott	.50	.20
❑ 124	Tom Holmoe	.10	.02
❑ 125	Charles Haley RC	2.00	.75
❑ 126	Jets TL	.10	.02
❑ 127	Ken O'Brien	.25	.08
❑ 128	Pat Ryan	.10	.02
❑ 129	Freeman McNeil	.25	.08
❑ 130	Johnny Hector RC	.10	.02
❑ 131	Al Toon	.50	.20
❑ 132	Wesley Walker	.25	.08
❑ 133	Mickey Shuler	.10	.02
❑ 134	Pat Leahy	.10	.02
❑ 135	Mark Gastineau	.25	.08
❑ 136	Joe Klecko	.25	.08
❑ 137	Marty Lyons	.10	.02
❑ 138	Bob Crable	.10	.02
❑ 139	Lance Mehl	.10	.02
❑ 140	Dave Jennings	.10	.02
❑ 141	Harry Hamilton RC	.10	.02
❑ 142	Lester Lyles	.10	.02
❑ 143	Bobby Humphery UER	.10	.02
❑ 144	Rams TL/E.Dickerson	.50	.20
❑ 145	Jim Everett RC	1.25	.50
❑ 146	Eric Dickerson	.50	.20
❑ 147	Barry Redden	.10	.02
❑ 148	Ron Brown	.25	.08
❑ 149	Kevin House	.10	.02
❑ 150	Henry Ellard	.50	.20
❑ 151	Doug Smith	.10	.02
❑ 152	Dennis Harrah	.10	.02
❑ 153	Jackie Slater	.25	.08
❑ 154	Gary Jeter	.10	.02
❑ 155	Carl Ekern	.10	.02
❑ 156	Mike Wilcher	.10	.02
❑ 157	Jerry Gray RC	.10	.02
❑ 158	LeRoy Irvin	.10	.02
❑ 159	Nolan Cromwell	.25	.08
❑ 160	Chiefs TL	.10	.02
❑ 161	Bill Kenney	.10	.02
❑ 162	Stephone Paige	.25	.08
❑ 163	Henry Marshall	.10	.02
❑ 164	Carlos Carson	.10	.02
❑ 165	Nick Lowery	.25	.08
❑ 166	Irv Eatman RC	.10	.02
❑ 167	Brad Budde	.10	.02
❑ 168	Art Still	.10	.02
❑ 169	Bill Maas	.10	.02
❑ 170	Lloyd Burruss RC	.10	.02
❑ 171	Deron Cherry	.10	.02
❑ 172	Seahawks TL	.25	.08
❑ 173	Dave Krieg	.50	.20
❑ 174	Curt Warner	.25	.08
❑ 175	John L.Williams RC	.50	.20
❑ 176	Bobby Joe Edmonds RC	.25	.08
❑ 177	Steve Largent	.60	.25
❑ 178	Bruce Scholtz	.10	.02
❑ 179	Norm Johnson	.10	.02
❑ 180	Jacob Green	.10	.02
❑ 181	Fredd Young	.10	.02
❑ 182	Dave Brown DB	.10	.02
❑ 183	Kenny Easley	.10	.02
❑ 184	Bengals TL	.25	.08
❑ 185	Boomer Esiason	.50	.20
❑ 186	James Brooks	.25	.08
❑ 187	Larry Kinnebrew	.10	.02
❑ 188	Cris Collinsworth	.25	.08
❑ 189	Eddie Brown	.50	.20
❑ 190	Tim McGee RC	.50	.20
❑ 191	Jim Breech	.10	.02
❑ 192	Anthony Munoz	.50	.20
❑ 193	Max Montoya	.10	.02
❑ 194	Eddie Edwards	.10	.02
❑ 195	Ross Browner	.25	.08
❑ 196	Emanuel King	.10	.02
❑ 197	Louis Breeden	.10	.02
❑ 198	Vikings TL	.10	.02
❑ 199	Tommy Kramer	.25	.08
❑ 200	Darrin Nelson	.10	.02
❑ 201	Allen Rice	.10	.02
❑ 202	Anthony Carter	.50	.20
❑ 203	Leo Lewis	.10	.02
❑ 204	Steve Jordan	.50	.20
❑ 205	Chuck Nelson RC	.10	.02
❑ 206	Greg Coleman	.10	.02
❑ 207	Gary Zimmerman RC	2.50	1.00
❑ 208	Doug Martin	.10	.02
❑ 209	Keith Millard	.10	.02
❑ 210	Issiac Holt RC	.10	.02
❑ 211	Joey Browner	.25	.08
❑ 212	Rufus Bess	.10	.02
❑ 213	Raiders TL/M.Allen	.50	.20
❑ 214	Jim Plunkett	.50	.20
❑ 215	Marcus Allen	1.00	.40
❑ 216	Napoleon McCallum RC	.25	.08
❑ 217	Dokie Williams	.10	.02
❑ 218	Todd Christensen	.50	.20
❑ 219	Chris Bahr	.10	.02
❑ 220	Howie Long	.60	.25
❑ 221	Bill Pickel	.10	.02
❑ 222	Sean Jones RC	.50	.20
❑ 223	Lester Hayes	.25	.08
❑ 224	Mike Haynes	.25	.08
❑ 225	Vann McElroy	.10	.02
❑ 226	Fulton Walker	.10	.02
❑ 227	Dan Marino/T.Kramer LL	1.25	.50
❑ 228	J.Rice/Christensen LL	1.25	.50
❑ 229	Eric Dickerson/Warner LL	.50	.20
❑ 230	Scoring Leaders	.10	.02
❑ 231	Interception Leaders	.50	.20
❑ 232	Dolphins TL	.25	.08
❑ 233	Dan Marino	6.00	2.50
❑ 234	Lorenzo Hampton RC	.10	.02
❑ 235	Tony Nathan	.25	.08
❑ 236	Mark Duper	.50	.20
❑ 237	Mark Clayton	.50	.20
❑ 238	Nat Moore	.25	.08
❑ 239	Bruce Hardy	.10	.02
❑ 240	Reggie Roby	.25	.08
❑ 241	Roy Foster	.10	.02
❑ 242	Dwight Stephenson	.50	.20
❑ 243	Hugh Green	.10	.02
❑ 244	John Offerdahl RC	.50	.20
❑ 245	Mark Brown	.10	.02
❑ 246	Doug Betters	.10	.02
❑ 247	Bob Baumhower	.10	.02
❑ 248	Falcons TL	.10	.02
❑ 249	David Archer	.50	.20
❑ 250	Gerald Riggs	.25	.08
❑ 251	William Andrews	.25	.08
❑ 252	Charlie Brown	.10	.02
❑ 253	Arthur Cox	.10	.02
❑ 254	Rick Donnelly	.10	.02
❑ 255	Bill Fralic	.10	.02
❑ 256	Mike Gann RC	.10	.02
❑ 257	Rick Bryan	.10	.02
❑ 258	Bret Clark	.10	.02
❑ 259	Mike Pitts	.10	.02
❑ 260	Cowboys TL/T.Dorsett	.50	.20
❑ 261	Danny White	.50	.20
❑ 262	Steve Pelluer RC	.10	.02
❑ 263	Tony Dorsett UER	.50	.20
❑ 264	Herschel Walker RC	2.50	1.00
❑ 265	Timmy Newsome	.10	.02
❑ 266	Tony Hill	.25	.08
❑ 267	Mike Sherrard RC	.50	.20
❑ 268	Jim Jeffcoat	.50	.20
❑ 269	Ron Fellows	.10	.02
❑ 270	Bill Bates	.50	.20
❑ 271	Michael Downs	.10	.02
❑ 272	Saints TL/B.Hebert	.25	.08
❑ 273	Dave Wilson	.10	.02
❑ 274	Rueben Mayes RC UER	.10	.02
❑ 275	Hoby Brenner	.10	.02

- ❑ 276 Eric Martin RC .50 .20
- ❑ 277 Morten Andersen .25 .08
- ❑ 278 Brian Hansen .10 .02
- ❑ 279 Rickey Jackson .50 .20
- ❑ 280 Dave Waymer .10 .02
- ❑ 281 Bruce Clark .10 .02
- ❑ 282 Jumpy Geathers RC .25 .08
- ❑ 283 Steelers TL .25 .08
- ❑ 284 Mark Malone .25 .08
- ❑ 285 Earnest Jackson .10 .02
- ❑ 286 Walter Abercrombie .10 .02
- ❑ 287 Louis Lipps .25 .08
- ❑ 288 John Stallworth UER .50 .20
- ❑ 289 Gary Anderson K .10 .02
- ❑ 290 Keith Willis .10 .02
- ❑ 291 Mike Merriweather .10 .02
- ❑ 292 Lupe Sanchez .10 .02
- ❑ 293 Donnie Shell .25 .08
- ❑ 294 Eagles TL/K.Byars .50 .20
- ❑ 295 Mike Reichenbach .10 .02
- ❑ 296 Randall Cunningham RC 6.00 3.00
- ❑ 297 Keith Byars RC .75 .30
- ❑ 298 Mike Quick .25 .08
- ❑ 299 Kenny Jackson .10 .02
- ❑ 300 John Teltschik RC .10 .02
- ❑ 301 Reggie White 3.00 1.50
- ❑ 302 Ken Clarke .10 .02
- ❑ 303 Greg Brown .10 .02
- ❑ 304 Roynell Young .10 .02
- ❑ 305 Andre Waters RC .50 .20
- ❑ 306 Oilers TL/W.Moon .50 .20
- ❑ 307 Warren Moon 1.50 .60
- ❑ 308 Mike Rozier .25 .08
- ❑ 309 Drew Hill .25 .08
- ❑ 310 Ernest Givins RC .50 .20
- ❑ 311 Lee Johnson RC .10 .02
- ❑ 312 Kent Hill .10 .02
- ❑ 313 Dean Steinkuhler RC .25 .08
- ❑ 314 Ray Childress .50 .20
- ❑ 315 John Grimsley RC .10 .02
- ❑ 316 Jesse Baker .10 .02
- ❑ 317 Lions TL .10 .02
- ❑ 318 Chuck Long RC .25 .08
- ❑ 319 James Jones FB .10 .02
- ❑ 320 Garry James .10 .02
- ❑ 321 Jeff Chadwick .10 .02
- ❑ 322 Leonard Thompson .10 .02
- ❑ 323 Pete Mandley .10 .02
- ❑ 324 Jimmie Giles .25 .08
- ❑ 325 Herman Hunter .10 .02
- ❑ 326 Keith Ferguson .10 .02
- ❑ 327 Devon Mitchell .10 .02
- ❑ 328 Cardinals TL .10 .02
- ❑ 329 Neil Lomax .25 .08
- ❑ 330 Stump Mitchell .10 .02
- ❑ 331 Earl Ferrell .10 .02
- ❑ 332 Vai Sikahema RC .25 .08
- ❑ 333 Ron Wolfley RC .10 .02
- ❑ 334 J.T.Smith .25 .08
- ❑ 335 Roy Green .25 .08
- ❑ 336 Al(Bubba) Baker .10 .02
- ❑ 337 Freddie Joe Nunn .10 .02
- ❑ 338 Cedric Mack .10 .02
- ❑ 339 Chargers TL .25 .08
- ❑ 340 Dan Fouts .50 .20
- ❑ 341 Gary Anderson RB UER .50 .20
- ❑ 342 Wes Chandler .25 .08
- ❑ 343 Kellen Winslow .50 .20
- ❑ 344 Ralf Mojsiejenko .10 .02
- ❑ 345 Rolf Benirschke .10 .02
- ❑ 346 Lee Williams RC .25 .08
- ❑ 347 Leslie O'Neal RC 1.00 .40
- ❑ 348 Billy Ray Smith .25 .08
- ❑ 349 Gill Byrd .25 .08
- ❑ 350 Packers TL .10 .02
- ❑ 351 Randy Wright .10 .02
- ❑ 352 Kenneth Davis RC .50 .20
- ❑ 353 Gerry Ellis .10 .02
- ❑ 354 James Lofton .50 .20
- ❑ 355 Phillip Epps RC .10 .02
- ❑ 356 Walter Stanley RC .10 .02
- ❑ 357 Eddie Lee Ivery .10 .02
- ❑ 358 Tim Harris RC .50 .20
- ❑ 359 Mark Lee UER .10 .02
- ❑ 360 Mossy Cade .10 .02
- ❑ 361 Bills TL/J.Kelly 1.00 .40
- ❑ 362 Jim Kelly RC 10.00 4.00
- ❑ 363 Robb Riddick RC .10 .02
- ❑ 364 Greg Bell .10 .02
- ❑ 365 Andre Reed 1.25 .50
- ❑ 366 Pete Metzelaars RC .50 .20
- ❑ 367 Sean McNanie .10 .02
- ❑ 368 Fred Smerlas .10 .02
- ❑ 369 Bruce Smith 1.50 .60
- ❑ 370 Darryl Talley .25 .08
- ❑ 371 Charles Romes .10 .02
- ❑ 372 Colts TL .10 .02
- ❑ 373 Jack Trudeau RC .25 .08
- ❑ 374 Gary Hogeboom .10 .02
- ❑ 375 Randy McMillan .10 .02
- ❑ 376 Albert Bentley .10 .02
- ❑ 377 Matt Bouza .10 .02
- ❑ 378 Bill Brooks RC .75 .30
- ❑ 379 Rohn Stark .10 .02
- ❑ 380 Chris Hinton .10 .02
- ❑ 381 Ray Donaldson .10 .02
- ❑ 382 Jon Hand RC .10 .02
- ❑ 383 Buccaneers TL .10 .02
- ❑ 384 Steve Young 5.00 2.00
- ❑ 385 James Wilder .10 .02
- ❑ 386 Frank Garcia .10 .02
- ❑ 387 Gerald Carter .10 .02
- ❑ 388 Phil Freeman .10 .02
- ❑ 389 Calvin Magee .10 .02
- ❑ 390 Donald Igwebuike .10 .02
- ❑ 391 David Logan .10 .02
- ❑ 392 Jeff Davis .10 .02
- ❑ 393 Chris Washington .10 .02
- ❑ 394 Checklist 1-132 .10 .02
- ❑ 395 Checklist 133-264 .10 .02
- ❑ 396 Checklist 265-396 .10 .02

1988 Topps

- ❑ COMPLETE SET (396) 20.00 7.50
- ❑ COMP.FACT.SET (396) 30.00 15.00
- ❑ 1 Super Bowl XXII .20 .07
- ❑ 2 Vencie Glenn RB .05 .01
- ❑ 3 Steve Largent RB .40 .15
- ❑ 4 Joe Montana RB .75 .30
- ❑ 5 Walter Payton RB .40 .15
- ❑ 6 Jerry Rice RB .75 .30
- ❑ 7 Redskins TL .20 .07
- ❑ 8 Doug Williams .20 .07
- ❑ 9 George Rogers .20 .07
- ❑ 10 Kelvin Bryant .20 .07
- ❑ 11 Timmy Smith SR .20 .07
- ❑ 12 Art Monk .40 .15
- ❑ 13 Gary Clark .40 .15
- ❑ 14 Ricky Sanders RC .40 .15
- ❑ 15 Steve Cox .05 .01
- ❑ 16 Joe Jacoby .05 .01
- ❑ 17 Charles Mann .20 .07
- ❑ 18 Dave Butz .05 .01
- ❑ 19 Darrell Green .20 .07
- ❑ 20 Dexter Manley .05 .01
- ❑ 21 Barry Wilburn .05 .01
- ❑ 22 Broncos TL .05 .01
- ❑ 23 John Elway 2.00 .75
- ❑ 24 Sammy Winder .05 .01
- ❑ 25 Vance Johnson .20 .07
- ❑ 26 Mark Jackson RC .40 .15
- ❑ 27 Ricky Nattiel RC .05 .01
- ❑ 28 Clarence Kay .05 .01
- ❑ 29 Rich Karlis .05 .01
- ❑ 30 Keith Bishop .05 .01
- ❑ 31 Mike Horan .05 .01
- ❑ 32 Rulon Jones .05 .01
- ❑ 33 Karl Mecklenburg .20 .07
- ❑ 34 Jim Ryan .05 .01
- ❑ 35 Mark Haynes .20 .07
- ❑ 36 Mike Harden .05 .01
- ❑ 37 49ers TL .40 .15
- ❑ 38 Joe Montana 2.00 .75
- ❑ 39 Steve Young 1.00 .40
- ❑ 40 Roger Craig .20 .07
- ❑ 41 Tom Rathman RC .40 .15
- ❑ 42 Joe Cribbs .20 .07
- ❑ 43 Jerry Rice 2.00 .75
- ❑ 44 Mike Wilson RC .05 .01
- ❑ 45 Ron Heller TE RC .05 .01
- ❑ 46 Ray Wersching .05 .01
- ❑ 47 Michael Carter .05 .01
- ❑ 48 Dwaine Board .05 .01
- ❑ 49 Michael Walter .05 .01
- ❑ 50 Don Griffin .05 .01
- ❑ 51 Ronnie Lott .40 .15
- ❑ 52 Charles Haley .40 .15
- ❑ 53 Dana McLemore .05 .01
- ❑ 54 Saints TL .20 .07
- ❑ 55 Bobby Hebert .20 .07
- ❑ 56 Rueben Mayes .05 .01
- ❑ 57 Dalton Hilliard RC .05 .01
- ❑ 58 Eric Martin .20 .07
- ❑ 59 John Tice RC .05 .01
- ❑ 60 Brad Edelman .05 .01
- ❑ 61 Morten Andersen .20 .07
- ❑ 62 Brian Hansen .05 .01
- ❑ 63 Mel Gray RC .40 .15
- ❑ 64 Rickey Jackson .20 .07
- ❑ 65 Sam Mills RC .75 .30
- ❑ 66 Pat Swilling RC .40 .15
- ❑ 67 Dave Waymer .05 .01
- ❑ 68 Bears TL .20 .07
- ❑ 69 Jim McMahon .40 .15
- ❑ 70 Mike Tomczak RC .05 .01
- ❑ 71 Neal Anderson RC .40 .15
- ❑ 72 Willie Gault .20 .07
- ❑ 73 Dennis Gentry .05 .01
- ❑ 74 Dennis McKinnon .05 .01
- ❑ 75 Kevin Butler .05 .01
- ❑ 76 Jim Covert .05 .01
- ❑ 77 Jay Hilgenberg .05 .01
- ❑ 78 Steve McMichael .20 .07
- ❑ 79 William Perry .20 .07
- ❑ 80 Richard Dent .40 .15
- ❑ 81 Ron Rivera RC .05 .01
- ❑ 82 Mike Singletary .40 .15
- ❑ 83 Dan Hampton .40 .15
- ❑ 84 Dave Duerson .05 .01
- ❑ 85 Browns TL .20 .07
- ❑ 86 Bernie Kosar .40 .15
- ❑ 87 Earnest Byner .40 .15
- ❑ 88 Kevin Mack .20 .07
- ❑ 89 Webster Slaughter RC .40 .15
- ❑ 90 Gerald McNeil .05 .01
- ❑ 91 Brian Brennan .05 .01
- ❑ 92 Ozzie Newsome .40 .15
- ❑ 93 Cody Risien .05 .01
- ❑ 94 Bob Golic .05 .01
- ❑ 95 Carl Hairston .05 .01
- ❑ 96 Mike Johnson RC .05 .01
- ❑ 97 Clay Matthews .20 .07
- ❑ 98 Frank Minnifield .05 .01
- ❑ 99 Hanford Dixon .05 .01
- ❑ 100 Dave Puzzuoli .05 .01
- ❑ 101 Felix Wright RC .05 .01
- ❑ 102 Oilers TL/Moon .40 .15
- ❑ 103 Warren Moon .50 .20
- ❑ 104 Mike Rozier .05 .01
- ❑ 105 Alonzo Highsmith RC .20 .07
- ❑ 106 Drew Hill .20 .07
- ❑ 107 Ernest Givins .40 .15
- ❑ 108 Curtis Duncan RC .40 .15
- ❑ 109 Tony Zendejas RC .05 .01
- ❑ 110 Mike Munchak .40 .15
- ❑ 111 Kent Hill .05 .01
- ❑ 112 Ray Childress .20 .07
- ❑ 113 Al Smith RC .20 .07
- ❑ 114 Keith Bostic RC .05 .01
- ❑ 115 Jeff Donaldson .05 .01
- ❑ 116 Colts TL/Dickerson .40 .15
- ❑ 117 Jack Trudeau .05 .01
- ❑ 118 Eric Dickerson .40 .15

❑	119	Albert Bentley	.05	.01
❑	120	Matt Bouza	.05	.01
❑	121	Bill Brooks	.40	.15
❑	122	Dean Biasucci RC	.05	.01
❑	123	Chris Hinton	.05	.01
❑	124	Ray Donaldson	.05	.01
❑	125	Ron Solt RC	.05	.01
❑	126	Donnell Thompson	.05	.01
❑	127	Barry Krauss RC	.05	.01
❑	128	Duane Bickett	.05	.01
❑	129	Mike Prior RC	.05	.01
❑	130	Seahawks TL	.20	.07
❑	131	Dave Krieg	.20	.07
❑	132	Curt Warner	.20	.07
❑	133	John L. Williams	.40	.15
❑	134	Bobby Joe Edmonds	.05	.01
❑	135	Steve Largent	.40	.15
❑	136	Raymond Butler	.05	.01
❑	137	Norm Johnson	.05	.01
❑	138	Ruben Rodriguez	.05	.01
❑	139	Blair Bush	.05	.01
❑	140	Jacob Green	.05	.01
❑	141	Joe Nash	.05	.01
❑	142	Jeff Bryant	.05	.01
❑	143	Fredd Young	.05	.01
❑	144	Brian Bosworth RC	1.50	.60
❑	145	Kenny Easley	.05	.01
❑	146	Vikings TL	.20	.07
❑	147	Wade Wilson RC	.40	.15
❑	148	Tommy Kramer	.20	.07
❑	149	Darrin Nelson	.05	.01
❑	150	D.J.Dozier RC	.20	.07
❑	151	Anthony Carter	.20	.07
❑	152	Leo Lewis	.05	.01
❑	153	Steve Jordan	.20	.07
❑	154	Gary Zimmerman	.05	.01
❑	155	Chuck Nelson	.05	.01
❑	156	Henry Thomas RC	.40	.15
❑	157	Chris Doleman RC	.40	.15
❑	158	Scott Studwell RC	.05	.01
❑	159	Jesse Solomon RC	.05	.01
❑	160	Joey Browner	.05	.01
❑	161	Neal Guggemos	.05	.01
❑	162	Steelers TL	.20	.07
❑	163	Mark Malone	.05	.01
❑	164	Walter Abercrombie	.05	.01
❑	165	Earnest Jackson	.05	.01
❑	166	Frank Pollard	.05	.01
❑	167	Dwight Stone RC	.20	.07
❑	168	Gary Anderson K	.05	.01
❑	169	Harry Newsome RC	.05	.01
❑	170	Keith Willis	.05	.01
❑	171	Keith Gary	.05	.01
❑	172	David Little RC	.20	.07
❑	173	Mike Merriweather	.05	.01
❑	174	Dwayne Woodruff	.05	.01
❑	175	Patriots TL	.40	.15
❑	176	Steve Grogan	.20	.07
❑	177	Tony Eason	.20	.07
❑	178	Tony Collins	.20	.07
❑	179	Mosi Tatupu	.05	.01
❑	180	Stanley Morgan	.20	.07
❑	181	Irving Fryar	.40	.15
❑	182	Stephen Starring	.05	.01
❑	183	Tony Franklin	.05	.01
❑	184	Rich Camarillo	.05	.01
❑	185	Garin Veris	.05	.01
❑	186	Andre Tippett	.20	.07
❑	187	Ronnie Lippett	.05	.01
❑	188	Fred Marion	.05	.01
❑	189	Dolphins TL/D.Marino	.75	.30
❑	190	Dan Marino	2.00	.75
❑	191	Troy Stradford RC	.20	.07
❑	192	Lorenzo Hampton	.05	.01
❑	193	Mark Duper	.20	.07
❑	194	Mark Clayton	.20	.07
❑	195	Reggie Roby	.20	.07
❑	196	Dwight Stephenson	.40	.15
❑	197	T.J. Turner RC	.05	.01
❑	198	John Bosa RC	.05	.01
❑	199	Jackie Shipp	.05	.01
❑	200	John Offerdahl	.20	.07
❑	201	Mark Brown	.05	.01
❑	202	Paul Lankford	.05	.01
❑	203	Chargers TL	.40	.15
❑	204	Tim Spencer	.05	.01
❑	205	Gary Anderson RB	.20	.07
❑	206	Curtis Adams	.05	.01
❑	207	Lionel James	.05	.01
❑	208	Chip Banks	.05	.01
❑	209	Kellen Winslow	.40	.15
❑	210	Ralf Mojsiejenko	.05	.01
❑	211	Jim Lachey	.20	.07
❑	212	Lee Williams	.05	.01
❑	213	Billy Ray Smith	.05	.01
❑	214	Vencie Glenn RC	.20	.07
❑	215	J.Montana/B.Kosar LL	.50	.20
❑	216	Receiving Leaders	.20	.07
❑	217	Eric Dickerson/C.White L	.20	.07
❑	218	Jerry Rice/J.Breech LL	.40	.15
❑	219	Interception Leaders	.05	.01
❑	220	Bills TL/Jim Kelly	.40	.15
❑	221	Jim Kelly	.75	.30
❑	222	Ronnie Harmon RC	.40	.15
❑	223	Robb Riddick	.05	.01
❑	224	Andre Reed	.40	.15
❑	225	Chris Burkett RC	.05	.01
❑	226	Pete Metzelaars	.40	.15
❑	227	Bruce Smith	.50	.20
❑	228	Darryl Talley	.20	.07
❑	229	Eugene Marve	.05	.01
❑	230	Cornelius Bennett RC	.75	.30
❑	231	Mark Kelso RC	.05	.01
❑	232	Shane Conlan RC	.40	.15
❑	233	Eagles TL/R.Cunningham	.40	.15
❑	234	Randall Cunningham	1.00	.40
❑	235	Keith Byars	.40	.15
❑	236	Anthony Toney RC	.05	.01
❑	237	Mike Quick	.20	.07
❑	238	Kenny Jackson	.05	.01
❑	239	John Spagnola	.05	.01
❑	240	Paul McFadden	.05	.01
❑	241	Reggie White	.60	.25
❑	242	Ken Clarke	.05	.01
❑	243	Mike Pitts	.05	.01
❑	244	Clyde Simmons RC	.40	.15
❑	245	Seth Joyner RC	.40	.15
❑	246	Andre Waters	.40	.15
❑	247	Jerome Brown RC	.40	.15
❑	248	Cardinals TL	.05	.01
❑	249	Neil Lomax	.20	.07
❑	250	Stump Mitchell	.05	.01
❑	251	Earl Ferrell	.05	.01
❑	252	Vai Sikahema	.05	.01
❑	253	J.T. Smith	.20	.07
❑	254	Roy Green	.20	.07
❑	255	Robert Awalt RC	.20	.07
❑	256	Freddie Joe Nunn	.05	.01
❑	257	Leonard Smith RC	.05	.01
❑	258	Travis Curtis	.05	.01
❑	259	Cowboys TL/H.Walker	.40	.15
❑	260	Danny White	.40	.15
❑	261	Herschel Walker	.40	.15
❑	262	Tony Dorsett	.40	.15
❑	263	Doug Cosbie	.05	.01
❑	264	Roger Ruzek RC	.20	.07
❑	265	Darryl Clack	.05	.01
❑	266	Ed Too Tall Jones	.40	.15
❑	267	Jim Jeffcoat	.05	.01
❑	268	Everson Walls	.05	.01
❑	269	Bill Bates	.20	.07
❑	270	Michael Downs	.05	.01
❑	271	Giants TL	.20	.07
❑	272	Phil Simms	.40	.15
❑	273	Joe Morris	.20	.07
❑	274	Lee Rouson	.05	.01
❑	275	George Adams	.05	.01
❑	276	Lionel Manuel	.05	.01
❑	277	Mark Bavaro	.20	.07
❑	278	Raul Allegre	.05	.01
❑	279	Sean Landeta	.05	.01
❑	280	Erik Howard	.05	.01
❑	281	Leonard Marshall	.20	.07
❑	282	Carl Banks	.20	.07
❑	283	Pepper Johnson	.20	.07
❑	284	Harry Carson	.20	.07
❑	285	Lawrence Taylor	.40	.15
❑	286	Terry Kinard	.05	.01
❑	287	Rams TL/Everett	.40	.15
❑	288	Jim Everett	.40	.15
❑	289	Charles White	.20	.07
❑	290	Ron Brown	.20	.07
❑	291	Henry Ellard	.40	.15
❑	292	Mike Lansford	.05	.01
❑	293	Dale Hatcher	.05	.01
❑	294	Doug Smith	.05	.01
❑	295	Jackie Slater	.20	.07
❑	296	Jim Collins	.05	.01
❑	297	Jerry Gray	.05	.01
❑	298	LeRoy Irvin	.05	.01
❑	299	Nolan Cromwell	.20	.07
❑	300	Kevin Greene RC	1.25	.50
❑	301	Jets TL	.20	.07
❑	302	Ken O'Brien	.20	.07
❑	303	Freeman McNeil	.20	.07
❑	304	Johnny Hector	.05	.01
❑	305	Al Toon	.20	.07
❑	306	Jo Jo Townsell RC	[illegible]	[illegible]
❑	307	Mickey Shuler	.05	.01
❑	308	Pat Leahy	.05	.01
❑	309	Roger Vick	.05	.01
❑	310	Alex Gordon RC	.05	.01
❑	311	Troy Benson	.05	.01
❑	312	Bob Crable	.05	.01
❑	313	Harry Hamilton	.05	.01
❑	314	Packers TL	.05	.01
❑	315	Randy Wright	.05	.01
❑	316	Kenneth Davis	.20	.07
❑	317	Phillip Epps	.05	.01
❑	318	Walter Stanley	.05	.01
❑	319	Frankie Neal	.05	.01
❑	320	Don Bracken	.05	.01
❑	321	Brian Noble RC	.20	.07
❑	322	Johnny Holland RC	.20	.07
❑	323	Tim Harris	.20	.07
❑	324	Mark Murphy	.05	.01
❑	325	Raiders TL/B.Jackson	.50	.20
❑	326	Marc Wilson	.05	.01
❑	327	Bo Jackson RC	5.00	2.00
❑	328	Marcus Allen	.40	.15
❑	329	James Lofton	.40	.15
❑	330	Todd Christensen	.20	.07
❑	331	Chris Bahr	.05	.01
❑	332	Stan Talley	.05	.01
❑	333	Howie Long	.40	.15
❑	334	Sean Jones	.40	.15
❑	335	Matt Millen	.20	.07
❑	336	Stacey Toran	.05	.01
❑	337	Vann McElroy	.05	.01
❑	338	Greg Townsend	.20	.07
❑	339	Bengals TL/Esiason	.40	.15
❑	340	Boomer Esiason	.40	.15
❑	341	Larry Kinnebrew	.05	.01
❑	342	Stanford Jennings RC	.05	.01
❑	343	Eddie Brown	.20	.07
❑	344	Jim Breech	.05	.01
❑	345	Anthony Munoz	.40	.15
❑	346	Scott Fulhage RC	.05	.01
❑	347	Tim Krumrie RC	.05	.01
❑	348	Reggie Williams	.20	.07
❑	349	David Fulcher RC	.05	.01
❑	350	Buccaneers TL	.05	.01
❑	351	Frank Garcia	.05	.01
❑	352	Vinny Testaverde RC	4.00	1.50
❑	353	James Wilder	.05	.01
❑	354	Jeff Smith RBK	.05	.01
❑	355	Gerald Carter	.05	.01
❑	356	Calvin Magee	.05	.01
❑	357	Donald Igwebuike	.05	.01
❑	358	Ron Holmes RC	.05	.01
❑	359	Chris Washington	.05	.01
❑	360	Ervin Randle	.05	.01
❑	361	Chiefs TL	.05	.01
❑	362	Bill Kenney	.05	.01
❑	363	Christian Okoye RC	.40	.15
❑	364	Paul Palmer	.05	.01
❑	365	Stephone Paige	.20	.07
❑	366	Carlos Carson	.05	.01
❑	367	Kelly Goodburn RC	.05	.01
❑	368	Bill Maas	.05	.01
❑	369	Mike Bell	.05	.01
❑	370	Dino Hackett RC	.05	.01
❑	371	Deron Cherry	.05	.01
❑	372	Lions TL	.05	.01
❑	373	Chuck Long	.20	.07
❑	374	Garry James	.05	.01
❑	375	James Jones FB	.05	.01
❑	376	Pete Mandley	.05	.01
❑	377	Gary Lee RC	.05	.01
❑	378	Eddie Murray	.05	.01
❑	379	Jim Arnold	.05	.01

❑ 380 Dennis Gibson RC .05 .01
❑ 381 Michael Cofer LB .05 .01
❑ 382 James Griffin .05 .01
❑ 383 Falcons TL .05 .01
❑ 384 Scott Campbell .05 .01
❑ 385 Gerald Riggs .20 .07
❑ 386 Floyd Dixon RC .05 .01
❑ 387 Rick Donnelly .05 .01
❑ 388 Bill Fralic .20 .07
❑ 389 Major Everett .05 .01
❑ 390 Mike Gann .05 .01
❑ 391 Tony Casillas RC .20 .07
❑ 392 Rick Bryan .05 .01
❑ 393 John Rade RC .05 .01
❑ 394 Checklist 1-132 .05 .01
❑ 395 Checklist 133-264 .05 .01
❑ 396 Checklist 265-396 .05 .01

1989 Topps

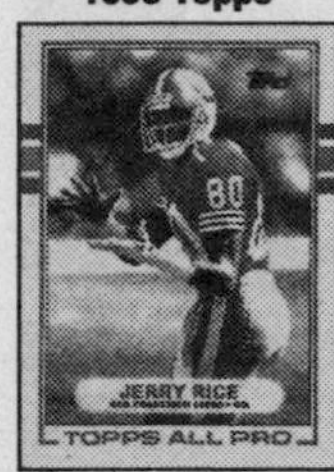

❑ COMPLETE SET (396) 20.00 7.50
❑ COMP.FACT.SET (396) 25.00 10.00
❑ 1 Super Bowl XXIII/Montana .50 .20
❑ 2 Tim Brown RB .50 .20
❑ 3 Eric Dickerson RB .10 .02
❑ 4 Steve Largent RB .25 .08
❑ 5 Dan Marino RB .75 .30
❑ 6 49ers TL/Montana .50 .20
❑ 7 Jerry Rice 1.50 .60
❑ 8 Roger Craig .25 .08
❑ 9 Ronnie Lott .10 .02
❑ 10 Michael Carter .05 .01
❑ 11 Charles Haley .25 .08
❑ 12 Joe Montana 2.00 .75
❑ 13 John Taylor RC .10 .02
❑ 14 Michael Walter .05 .01
❑ 15 Mike Cofer K RC .05 .01
❑ 16 Tom Rathman .05 .01
❑ 17 Daniel Stubbs RC .05 .01
❑ 18 Keena Turner .05 .01
❑ 19 Tim McKyer .05 .01
❑ 20 Larry Roberts .05 .01
❑ 21 Jeff Fuller .05 .01
❑ 22 Bubba Paris .05 .01
❑ 23 Bengals Team UER .10 .02
❑ 24 Eddie Brown .05 .01
❑ 25 Boomer Esiason .10 .02
❑ 26 Tim Krumrie .05 .01
❑ 27 Ickey Woods RC .10 .02
❑ 28 Anthony Munoz .10 .02
❑ 29 Tim McGee .05 .01
❑ 30 Max Montoya .05 .01
❑ 31 David Grant .05 .01
❑ 32 Rodney Holman RC .05 .01
❑ 33 David Fulcher .10 .02
❑ 34 Jim Skow .05 .01
❑ 35 James Brooks .10 .02
❑ 36 Reggie Williams .05 .01
❑ 37 Eric Thomas RC .05 .01
❑ 38 Stanford Jennings .05 .01
❑ 39 Jim Breech .05 .01
❑ 40 Bills TL/Jim Kelly .25 .08
❑ 41 Shane Conlan .05 .01
❑ 42 Scott Norwood RC .05 .01
❑ 43 Cornelius Bennett .10 .02
❑ 44 Bruce Smith .25 .08
❑ 45 Thurman Thomas RC 1.25 .50
❑ 46 Jim Kelly .50 .20
❑ 47 John Kidd .05 .01
❑ 48 Kent Hull RC .05 .01
❑ 49 Art Still .05 .01
❑ 50 Fred Smerlas .05 .01
❑ 51A Derrick Burroughs .05 .01
❑ 51B Derrick Burroughs .05 .01
❑ 52 Andre Reed .25 .08
❑ 53 Robb Riddick .05 .01
❑ 54 Chris Burkett .05 .01
❑ 55 Ronnie Harmon .10 .02
❑ 56 Mark Kelso UER .05 .01
❑ 57 Bears Team .05 .01
❑ 58 Mike Singletary .10 .02
❑ 59 Jay Hilgenberg UER .05 .01
❑ 60 Richard Dent .10 .02
❑ 61 Ron Rivera .05 .01
❑ 62 Jim McMahon .10 .02
❑ 63 Mike Tomczak .10 .02
❑ 64 Neal Anderson .10 .02
❑ 65 Dennis Gentry .05 .01
❑ 66 Dan Hampton .10 .02
❑ 67 David Tate .05 .01
❑ 68 Thomas Sanders RC .05 .01
❑ 69 Steve McMichael .10 .02
❑ 70 Dennis McKinnon .05 .01
❑ 71 Brad Muster RC .05 .01
❑ 72 Vestee Jackson RC .05 .01
❑ 73 Dave Duerson .05 .01
❑ 74 Vikings Team .05 .01
❑ 75 Joey Browner .05 .01
❑ 76 Carl Lee RC .05 .01
❑ 77 Gary Zimmerman .05 .01
❑ 78 Hassan Jones RC .05 .01
❑ 79 Anthony Carter .10 .02
❑ 80 Ray Berry .05 .01
❑ 81 Steve Jordan .05 .01
❑ 82 Issiac Holt .05 .01
❑ 83 Wade Wilson .10 .02
❑ 84 Chris Doleman .10 .02
❑ 85 Alfred Anderson .05 .01
❑ 86 Keith Millard .05 .01
❑ 87 Darrin Nelson .05 .01
❑ 88 D.J. Dozier .05 .01
❑ 89 Scott Studwell .05 .01
❑ 90 Oilers Team .05 .01
❑ 91 Bruce Matthews RC .75 .30
❑ 92 Curtis Duncan .05 .01
❑ 93 Warren Moon .25 .08
❑ 94 Johnny Meads RC .05 .01
❑ 95 Drew Hill .05 .01
❑ 96 Alonzo Highsmith .05 .01
❑ 97 Mike Munchak .10 .02
❑ 98 Mike Rozier .05 .01
❑ 99 Tony Zendejas .05 .01
❑ 100 Jeff Donaldson .05 .01
❑ 101 Ray Childress .05 .01
❑ 102 Sean Jones .10 .02
❑ 103 Ernest Givins .10 .02
❑ 104 William Fuller RC .25 .08
❑ 105 Allen Pinkett RC .05 .01
❑ 106 Eagles TL/R.Cunningham .10 .02
❑ 107 Keith Jackson RC .25 .08
❑ 108 Reggie White .25 .08
❑ 109 Clyde Simmons .10 .02
❑ 110 John Teltschik .05 .01
❑ 111 Wes Hopkins .05 .01
❑ 112 Keith Byars .10 .02
❑ 113 Jerome Brown .10 .02
❑ 114 Mike Quick .05 .01
❑ 115 Randall Cunningham .40 .15
❑ 116 Anthony Toney .05 .01
❑ 117 Ron Johnson WR .05 .01
❑ 118 Terry Hoage .05 .01
❑ 119 Seth Joyner .10 .02
❑ 120 Eric Allen RC .25 .08
❑ 121 Cris Carter RC 1.50 .60
❑ 122 Rams Team .05 .01
❑ 123 Tom Newberry RC .05 .01
❑ 124 Pete Holohan .05 .01
❑ 125 Robert Delpino RC UER .05 .01
❑ 126 Carl Ekern .05 .01
❑ 127 Greg Bell .05 .01
❑ 128 Mike Lansford .05 .01
❑ 129 Jim Everett .10 .02
❑ 130 Mike Wilcher .05 .01
❑ 131 Jerry Gray .05 .01
❑ 132 Dale Hatcher .05 .01
❑ 133 Doug Smith .05 .01
❑ 134 Kevin Greene .25 .08
❑ 135 Jackie Slater .05 .01
❑ 136 Aaron Cox RC .05 .01
❑ 137 Henry Ellard .25 .08
❑ 138 Browns Team .10 .02
❑ 139 Frank Minnifield .05 .01
❑ 140 Webster Slaughter .10 .02
❑ 141 Bernie Kosar .10 .02
❑ 142 Charles Buchanan .05 .01
❑ 143 Clay Matthews .10 .02
❑ 144 Reggie Langhorne RC .05 .01
❑ 145 Hanford Dixon .05 .01
❑ 146 Brian Brennan .05 .01
❑ 147 Earnest Byner .05 .01
❑ 148 Michael Dean Perry RC .10 .02
❑ 149 Kevin Mack .05 .01
❑ 150 Matt Bahr .05 .01
❑ 151 Ozzie Newsome .10 .02
❑ 152 Saints Team .10 .02
❑ 153 Morten Andersen .05 .01
❑ 154 Pat Swilling .10 .02
❑ 155 Sam Mills .10 .02
❑ 156 Lonzell Hill .05 .01
❑ 157 Dalton Hilliard .05 .01
❑ 158 Craig Heyward RC .10 .02
❑ 159 Vaughan Johnson RC .05 .01
❑ 160 Rueben Mayes .05 .01
❑ 161 Gene Atkins RC .05 .01
❑ 162 Bobby Hebert .10 .02
❑ 163 Rickey Jackson .10 .02
❑ 164 Eric Martin .05 .01
❑ 165 Giants Team .05 .01
❑ 166 Lawrence Taylor .25 .08
❑ 167 Bart Oates .05 .01
❑ 168 Carl Banks .05 .01
❑ 169 Eric Moore RC .05 .01
❑ 170 Sheldon White RC .05 .01
❑ 171 Mark Collins RC .05 .01
❑ 172 Phil Simms .10 .02
❑ 173 Jim Burt .05 .01
❑ 174 Stephen Baker RC .10 .02
❑ 175 Mark Bavaro .10 .02
❑ 176 Pepper Johnson .05 .01
❑ 177 Lionel Manuel .05 .01
❑ 178 Joe Morris .05 .01
❑ 179 Jumbo Elliott RC .05 .01
❑ 180 Gary Reasons RC .05 .01
❑ 181 Seahawks Team .10 .02
❑ 182 Brian Blades RC .25 .08
❑ 183 Steve Largent .25 .08
❑ 184 Rufus Porter RC .05 .01
❑ 185 Ruben Rodriguez .05 .01
❑ 186 Curt Warner .05 .01
❑ 187 Paul Moyer .05 .01
❑ 188 Dave Krieg .10 .02
❑ 189 Jacob Green .05 .01
❑ 190 John L.Williams .05 .01
❑ 191 Eugene Robinson RC .05 .01
❑ 192 Brian Bosworth .10 .02
❑ 193 Patriots Team .05 .01
❑ 194 John Stephens RC .05 .01
❑ 195 Robert Perryman RC .05 .01
❑ 196 Andre Tippett .05 .01
❑ 197 Fred Marion .05 .01
❑ 198 Doug Flutie 1.00 .40
❑ 199 Stanley Morgan .05 .01
❑ 200 Johnny Rembert RC .05 .01
❑ 201 Tony Eason .05 .01
❑ 202 Marvin Allen .05 .01
❑ 203 Raymond Clayborn .05 .01
❑ 204 Irving Fryar .25 .08
❑ 205 Colts Team .05 .01
❑ 206 Eric Dickerson .10 .02
❑ 207 Chris Hinton .05 .01
❑ 208 Duane Bickett .05 .01
❑ 209 Chris Chandler RC 1.00 .40
❑ 210 Jon Hand .05 .01
❑ 211 Ray Donaldson .05 .01
❑ 212 Dean Biasucci .05 .01
❑ 213 Bill Brooks .10 .02
❑ 214 Chris Goode RC .05 .01
❑ 215 Clarence Verdin RC .05 .01
❑ 216 Albert Bentley .05 .01
❑ 217 Passing Leaders .10 .02
❑ 218 Receiving Leaders .10 .02
❑ 219 Eric Dickerson/Walker LL .10 .02
❑ 220 Scoring Leaders .05 .01
❑ 221 Interception Leaders .05 .01

❑ 222	Jets Team	.05	.01
❑ 223	Erik McMillan RC	.05	.01
❑ 224	James Hasty RC	.05	.01
❑ 225	Al Toon	.10	.02
❑ 226	John Booty RC	.05	.01
❑ 227	Johnny Hector	.05	.01
❑ 228	Ken O'Brien	.05	.01
❑ 229	Marty Lyons	.05	.01
❑ 230	Mickey Shuler	.05	.01
❑ 231	Robin Cole	.05	.01
❑ 232	Freeman McNeil	.05	.01
❑ 233	Marion Barber RC	.05	.01
❑ 234	Jo Jo Townsell	.05	.01
❑ 235	Wesley Walker	.05	.01
❑ 236	Roger Vick	.05	.01
❑ 237	Pat Leahy	.05	.01
❑ 238	Broncos TL/Elway	.50	.20
❑ 239	Mike Horan	.05	.01
❑ 240	Tony Dorsett	.25	.08
❑ 241	John Elway	2.00	.75
❑ 242	Mark Jackson	.05	.01
❑ 243	Sammy Winder	.05	.01
❑ 244	Rich Karlis	.05	.01
❑ 245	Vance Johnson	.10	.02
❑ 246	Steve Sewell RC	.05	.01
❑ 247	Karl Mecklenburg UER	.05	.01
❑ 248	Rulon Jones	.05	.01
❑ 249	Simon Fletcher RC	.05	.01
❑ 250	Redskins Team	.10	.02
❑ 251	Chip Lohmiller RC	.05	.01
❑ 252	Jamie Morris	.05	.01
❑ 253	Mark Rypien RC UER	.10	.02
❑ 254	Barry Wilburn	.05	.01
❑ 255	Mark May RC	.05	.01
❑ 256	Wilber Marshall	.05	.01
❑ 257	Charles Mann	.05	.01
❑ 258	Gary Clark	.25	.08
❑ 259	Doug Williams	.10	.02
❑ 260	Art Monk	.10	.02
❑ 261	Kelvin Bryant	.05	.01
❑ 262	Dexter Manley	.05	.01
❑ 263	Ricky Sanders	.05	.01
❑ 264	Raiders Team	.25	.08
❑ 265	Tim Brown RC	1.50	.60
❑ 266	Jay Schroeder	.05	.01
❑ 267	Marcus Allen	.25	.08
❑ 268	Mike Haynes	.10	.02
❑ 269	Bo Jackson	.30	.10
❑ 270	Steve Beuerlein RC	.60	.25
❑ 271	Vann McElroy	.05	.01
❑ 272	Willie Gault	.10	.02
❑ 273	Howie Long	.25	.08
❑ 274	Greg Townsend	.05	.01
❑ 275	Mike Wise DE	.05	.01
❑ 276	Cardinals Team	.05	.01
❑ 277	Luis Sharpe	.05	.01
❑ 278	Scott Dill	.05	.01
❑ 279	Vai Sikahema	.05	.01
❑ 280	Ron Wolfley	.05	.01
❑ 281	David Galloway	.05	.01
❑ 282	Jay Novacek RC	.25	.08
❑ 283	Neil Lomax	.05	.01
❑ 284	Robert Awalt	.05	.01
❑ 285	Cedric Mack	.05	.01
❑ 286	Freddie Joe Nunn	.05	.01
❑ 287	J.T. Smith	.05	.01
❑ 288	Stump Mitchell	.05	.01
❑ 289	Roy Green	.10	.02
❑ 290	Dolphins TL/Marino	.50	.20
❑ 291	Jarvis Williams RC	.05	.01
❑ 292	Troy Stradford	.05	.01
❑ 293	Dan Marino	2.00	.75
❑ 294	T.J. Turner	.05	.01
❑ 295	John Offerdahl	.05	.01
❑ 296	Ferrell Edmunds RC	.05	.01
❑ 297	Scott Schwedes	.05	.01
❑ 298	Lorenzo Hampton	.05	.01
❑ 299	Jim C.Jensen RC	.05	.01
❑ 300	Brian Sochia	.05	.01
❑ 301	Reggie Roby	.05	.01
❑ 302	Mark Clayton	.10	.02
❑ 303	Chargers Team	.05	.01
❑ 304	Lee Williams	.05	.01
❑ 305	Gary Plummer RC	.05	.01
❑ 306	Gary Anderson RB	.05	.01
❑ 307	Gill Byrd	.05	.01
❑ 308	Jamie Holland RC	.05	.01
❑ 309	Billy Ray Smith	.05	.01
❑ 310	Lionel James	.05	.01
❑ 311	Mark Vlasic RC	.05	.01
❑ 312	Curtis Adams	.05	.01
❑ 313	Anthony Miller RC	.25	.08
❑ 314	Steelers Team	.05	.01
❑ 315	Bubby Brister RC	.25	.08
❑ 316	David Little	.05	.01
❑ 317	Tunch Ilkin RC	.05	.01
❑ 318	Louis Lipps	.10	.02
❑ 319	Warren Williams RC	.05	.01
❑ 320	Dwight Stone	.10	.02
❑ 321	Merril Hoge RC	.05	.01
❑ 322	Thomas Everett RC	.05	.01
❑ 323	Rod Woodson RC	.50	.20
❑ 324	Gary Anderson K	.05	.01
❑ 325	Buccaneers Team	.05	.01
❑ 326	Donnie Elder	.05	.01
❑ 327	Vinny Testaverde	.30	.10
❑ 328	Harry Hamilton	.05	.01
❑ 329	James Wilder	.05	.01
❑ 330	Lars Tate	.05	.01
❑ 331	Mark Carrier RC WR	.25	.08
❑ 332	Bruce Hill RC	.05	.01
❑ 333	Paul Gruber RC	.05	.01
❑ 334	Ricky Reynolds	.05	.01
❑ 335	Eugene Marve	.05	.01
❑ 336	Falcons Team	.05	.01
❑ 337	Aundray Bruce RC	.05	.01
❑ 338	John Rade	.05	.01
❑ 339	Scott Case RC	.05	.01
❑ 340	Robert Moore	.05	.01
❑ 341	Chris Miller RC	.25	.08
❑ 342	Gerald Riggs	.10	.02
❑ 343	Gene Lang	.05	.01
❑ 344	Marcus Cotton	.05	.01
❑ 345	Rick Donnelly	.05	.01
❑ 346	John Settle RC	.05	.01
❑ 347	Bill Fralic	.05	.01
❑ 348	Chiefs Team	.05	.01
❑ 349	Steve DeBerg	.05	.01
❑ 350	Mike Stensrud	.05	.01
❑ 351	Dino Hackett	.05	.01
❑ 352	Deron Cherry	.10	.02
❑ 353	Christian Okoye	.05	.01
❑ 354	Bill Maas	.05	.01
❑ 355	Carlos Carson	.05	.01
❑ 356	Albert Lewis	.05	.01
❑ 357	Paul Palmer	.05	.01
❑ 358	Nick Lowery	.05	.01
❑ 359	Stephone Paige	.05	.01
❑ 360	Lions Team	.05	.01
❑ 361	Chris Spielman RC	.25	.08
❑ 362	Jim Arnold	.05	.01
❑ 363	Devon Mitchell	.05	.01
❑ 364	Mike Cofer	.05	.01
❑ 365	Bennie Blades RC	.05	.01
❑ 366	James Jones FB	.05	.01
❑ 367	Garry James	.05	.01
❑ 368	Pete Mandley	.05	.01
❑ 369	Keith Ferguson	.05	.01
❑ 370	Dennis Gibson	.05	.01
❑ 371	Packers Team UER	.05	.01
❑ 372	Brent Fullwood RC	.05	.01
❑ 373	Don Majkowski RC	.10	.02
❑ 374	Tim Harris	.05	.01
❑ 375	Keith Woodside RC	.05	.01
❑ 376	Mark Murphy	.05	.01
❑ 377	Dave Brown DB	.05	.01
❑ 378	Perry Kemp RC	.05	.01
❑ 379	Sterling Sharpe RC	.75	.30
❑ 380	Chuck Cecil RC	.05	.01
❑ 381	Walter Stanley	.05	.01
❑ 382	Cowboys Team	.05	.01
❑ 383	Michael Irvin RC	1.50	.60
❑ 384	Bill Bates	.10	.02
❑ 385	Herschel Walker	.25	.08
❑ 386	Darryl Clack	.05	.01
❑ 387	Danny Noonan	.05	.01
❑ 388	Eugene Lockhart RC	.05	.01
❑ 389	Ed Too Tall Jones	.10	.02
❑ 390	Steve Pelluer	.05	.01
❑ 391	Ray Alexander	.05	.01
❑ 392	Nate Newton RC	.10	.02
❑ 393	Garry Cobb	.05	.01
❑ 394	Checklist 1-132	.05	.01
❑ 395	Checklist 133-264	.05	.01
❑ 396	Checklist 265-396	.05	.01

1989 Topps Traded

❑	COMP.FACT.SET (132)	15.00	6.00
❑ 1T	Eric Ball RC	.05	.01
❑ 2T	Tony Mandarich RC	.05	.01
❑ 3T	Shawn Collins RC	.05	.01
❑ 4T	Ray Bentley RC	.05	.01
❑ 5T	Tony Casillas	.05	.01
❑ 6T	Al Del Greco RC	.05	.01
❑ 7T	Dan Saleaumua RC	.10	.02
❑ 8T	Keith Bishop	.05	.01
❑ 9T	Rodney Peete RC	.60	.25
❑ 10T	Lorenzo White RC	.25	.08
❑ 11T	Steve Smith RC	.10	.02
❑ 12T	Pete Mandley	.05	.01
❑ 13T	Mervyn Fernandez RC**/C	.05	.01
❑ 14T	Flipper Anderson RC	.25	.08
❑ 15T	Louis Oliver RC	.10	.02
❑ 16T	Rick Fenney	.05	.01
❑ 17T	Gary Jeter	.05	.01
❑ 18T	Greg Cox	.05	.01
❑ 19T	Bubba McDowell RC	.10	.02
❑ 20T	Ron Heller	.05	.01
❑ 21T	Tim McDonald RC	.05	.01
❑ 22T	Jerrol Williams RC	.05	.01
❑ 23T	Marion Butts RC	.10	.02
❑ 24T	Steve Young	.75	.30
❑ 25T	Mike Merriweather	.05	.01
❑ 26T	Richard Johnson	.05	.01
❑ 27T	Gerald Riggs	.10	.02
❑ 28T	Dave Waymer	.05	.01
❑ 29T	Issiac Holt	.05	.01
❑ 30T	Deion Sanders RC	1.50	.60
❑ 31T	Todd Blackledge	.05	.01
❑ 32T	Jeff Cross RC	.05	.01
❑ 33T	Steve Wisniewski RC	.10	.02
❑ 34T	Ron Brown	.10	.02
❑ 35T	Rod Bernstine RC	.05	.01
❑ 36T	Jeff Uhlenhake RC	.05	.01
❑ 37T	Donnell Woolford RC	.25	.08
❑ 38T	Bob Gagliano RC	.05	.01
❑ 39T	Ezra Johnson	.05	.01
❑ 40T	Ron Jaworski	.05	.01
❑ 41T	Lawyer Tillman RC	.05	.01
❑ 42T	Lorenzo Lynch RC	.05	.01
❑ 43T	Mike Alexander	.05	.01
❑ 44T	Tim Worley RC	.05	.01
❑ 45T	Guy Bingham	.05	.01
❑ 46T	Cleveland Gary RC	.05	.01
❑ 47T	Danny Peebles	.05	.01
❑ 48T	Clarence Weathers RC	.05	.01
❑ 49T	Jeff Lageman RC	.25	.08
❑ 50T	Eric Metcalf RC	.25	.08
❑ 51T	Myron Guyton RC	.05	.01
❑ 52T	Steve Atwater RC	.05	.01
❑ 53T	John Fourcade RC	.05	.01
❑ 54T	Randall McDaniel RC	.25	.08
❑ 55T	Al Noga RC	.05	.01
❑ 56T	Sammie Smith RC	.10	.02
❑ 57T	Jesse Solomon	.05	.01
❑ 58T	Greg Kragen RC	.05	.01
❑ 59T	Don Beebe RC	.25	.08
❑ 60T	Hart Lee Dykes RC	.10	.02
❑ 61T	Trace Armstrong RC	.10	.02
❑ 62T	Steve Pelluer	.05	.01
❑ 63T	Barry Krauss	.05	.01
❑ 64T	Kevin Murphy RC	.05	.01

❑ 65T Steve Tasker RC .25 .08
❑ 66T Jessie Small RC .05 .01
❑ 67T Dave Meggett RC .25 .08
❑ 68T Dean Hamel .05 .01
❑ 69T Jim Covert .05 .01
❑ 70T Troy Aikman RC 5.00 2.00
❑ 71T Raul Allegre .05 .01
❑ 72T Chris Jacke RC .10 .02
❑ 73T Leslie O'Neal .10 .02
❑ 74T Keith Taylor RC .05 .01
❑ 75T Steve Walsh RC .25 .08
❑ 76T Tracy Rocker .05 .01
❑ 77T Robert Massey RC .10 .02
❑ 78T Bryan Wagner .05 .01
❑ 79T Steve DeOssie .05 .01
❑ 80T Carnell Lake RC .25 .08
❑ 81T Frank Reich RC .25 .08
❑ 82T Tyrone Braxton RC .05 .01
❑ 83T Barry Sanders RC 6.00 2.50
❑ 84T Pete Stoyanovich RC .10 .02
❑ 85T Paul Palmer .05 .01
❑ 86T Billy Joe Tolliver RC .05 .01
❑ 87T Eric Hill RC .10 .02
❑ 88T Gerald McNeil .05 .01
❑ 89T Bill Hawkins RC .05 .01
❑ 90T Derrick Thomas RC 1.25 .50
❑ 91T Jim Harbaugh RC .75 .30
❑ 92T Brian Williams OL RC .05 .01
❑ 93T Jack Trudeau .05 .01
❑ 94T Leonard Smith .05 .01
❑ 95T Gary Hogeboom .05 .01
❑ 96T A.J.Johnson RC .05 .01
❑ 97T Jim McMahon .10 .02
❑ 98T David Williams RC .05 .01
❑ 99T Rohn Stark .05 .01
❑ 100T Sean Landeta .05 .01
❑ 101T Tim Johnson RC .05 .01
❑ 102T Andre Rison RC .75 .30
❑ 103T Earnest Byner .10 .02
❑ 104T Don McPherson RC .05 .01
❑ 105T Zefross Moss RC .05 .01
❑ 106T Frank Stams RC .05 .01
❑ 107T Courtney Hall RC .10 .02
❑ 108T Marc Logan RC .05 .01
❑ 109T James Lofton .25 .08
❑ 110T Lewis Tillman RC .10 .02
❑ 111T Irv Pankey RC .05 .01
❑ 112T Ralf Mojsiejenko .05 .01
❑ 113T Bobby Humphrey RC .05 .01
❑ 114T Chris Burkett .05 .01
❑ 115T Greg Lloyd RC .25 .08
❑ 116T Matt Millen .10 .02
❑ 117T Carl Zander .05 .01
❑ 118T Wayne Martin RC .25 .08
❑ 119T Mike Saxon .05 .01
❑ 120T Herschel Walker .10 .02
❑ 121T Andy Heck RC .05 .01
❑ 122T Mark Robinson .05 .01
❑ 123T Keith Van Horne RC .05 .01
❑ 124T Ricky Hunley .05 .01
❑ 125T Timm Rosenbach RC .10 .02
❑ 126T Steve Grogan .10 .02
❑ 127T Stephen Braggs RC .05 .01
❑ 128T Terry Long .05 .01
❑ 129T Evan Cooper .05 .01
❑ 130T Robert Lyles .05 .01
❑ 131T Mike Webster .10 .02
❑ 132T Checklist 1-132 .05 .01

1990 Topps

❑ COMPLETE SET (528) 25.00 10.00
❑ COMP.FACT.SET (528) 30.00 12.50
❑ 1 Joe Montana RB .50 .20
❑ 2 Flipper Anderson RB .05 .01
❑ 3 Troy Aikman RB .40 .15
❑ 4 Kevin Butler RB .05 .01
❑ 5 Super Bowl XXIV .05 .01
❑ 6 Dexter Carter RC .05 .01
❑ 7 Matt Millen .10 .02
❑ 8 Jerry Rice .75 .30
❑ 9 Ronnie Lott .10 .02
❑ 10 John Taylor .10 .02
❑ 11 Guy McIntyre .05 .01
❑ 12 Roger Craig .10 .02
❑ 13 Joe Montana 1.25 .50
❑ 14 Brent Jones RC .25 .08
❑ 15 Tom Rathman .05 .01
❑ 16 Harris Barton .05 .01
❑ 17 Charles Haley .10 .02
❑ 18 Pierce Holt RC .05 .01
❑ 19 Michael Carter .05 .01
❑ 20 Chet Brooks .05 .01
❑ 21 Eric Wright .05 .01
❑ 22 Mike Cofer .05 .01
❑ 23 Jim Fahnhorst .05 .01
❑ 24 Keena Turner .05 .01
❑ 25 Don Griffin .05 .01
❑ 26 Kevin Fagan RC .05 .01
❑ 27 Bubba Paris .05 .01
❑ 28 Barry Sanders/C.Okoye LL .50 .20
❑ 29 Steve Atwater .05 .01
❑ 30 Tyrone Braxton .05 .01
❑ 31 Ron Holmes .05 .01
❑ 32 Bobby Humphrey .05 .01
❑ 33 Greg Kragen .05 .01
❑ 34 David Treadwell .05 .01
❑ 35 Karl Mecklenburg .05 .01
❑ 36 Dennis Smith .05 .01
❑ 37 John Elway 1.25 .50
❑ 38 Vance Johnson .05 .01
❑ 39 Simon Fletcher UER .05 .01
❑ 40 Jim Juriga .05 .01
❑ 41 Mark Jackson .05 .01
❑ 42 Melvin Bratton RC .05 .01
❑ 43 Wymon Henderson RC .05 .01
❑ 44 Ken Bell .05 .01
❑ 45 Sammy Winder .05 .01
❑ 46 Alphonso Carreker .05 .01
❑ 47 Orson Mobley RC .05 .01
❑ 48 Rodney Hampton RC .25 .08
❑ 49 Dave Meggett .10 .02
❑ 50 Myron Guyton .05 .01
❑ 51 Phil Simms .10 .02
❑ 52 Lawrence Taylor .25 .08
❑ 53 Carl Banks .05 .01
❑ 54 Pepper Johnson .05 .01
❑ 55 Leonard Marshall .05 .01
❑ 56 Mark Collins .05 .01
❑ 57 Erik Howard .05 .01
❑ 58 Eric Dorsey RC .05 .01
❑ 59 Ottis Anderson .10 .02
❑ 60 Mark Bavaro .05 .01
❑ 61 Odessa Turner RC .05 .01
❑ 62 Gary Reasons .05 .01
❑ 63 Maurice Carthon .05 .01
❑ 64 Lionel Manuel .05 .01
❑ 65 Sean Landeta .05 .01
❑ 66 Perry Williams .05 .01
❑ 67 Pat Terrell RC .05 .01
❑ 68 Flipper Anderson .05 .01
❑ 69 Jackie Slater .05 .01
❑ 70 Tom Newberry .05 .01
❑ 71 Jerry Gray .05 .01
❑ 72 Henry Ellard .10 .02
❑ 73 Doug Smith .05 .01
❑ 74 Kevin Greene .10 .02
❑ 75 Jim Everett .10 .02
❑ 76 Mike Lansford .05 .01
❑ 77 Greg Bell .05 .01
❑ 78 Pete Holohan .05 .01
❑ 79 Robert Delpino .05 .01
❑ 80 Mike Wilcher .05 .01
❑ 81 Mike Piel .05 .01
❑ 82 Mel Owens .05 .01
❑ 83 Michael Stewart RC .05 .01
❑ 84 Ben Smith RC .05 .01
❑ 85 Keith Jackson .10 .02
❑ 86 Reggie White .25 .08
❑ 87 Eric Allen .05 .01
❑ 88 Jerome Brown .05 .01
❑ 89 Robert Drummond .05 .01
❑ 90 Anthony Toney .05 .01
❑ 91 Keith Byars .05 .01
❑ 92 Cris Carter .50 .20
❑ 93 Randall Cunningham .25 .08
❑ 94 Ron Johnson WR .05 .01
❑ 95 Mike Quick .05 .01
❑ 96 Clyde Simmons .05 .01
❑ 97 Mike Pitts .05 .01
❑ 98 Izel Jenkins RC .05 .01
❑ 99 Seth Joyner .10 .02
❑ 100 Mike Schad .05 .01
❑ 101 Wes Hopkins .05 .01
❑ 102 Kirk Lowdermilk .05 .01
❑ 103 Rick Fenney .05 .01
❑ 104 Randall McDaniel .10 .02
❑ 105 Herschel Walker .10 .02
❑ 106 Al Noga .05 .01
❑ 107 Gary Zimmerman .05 .01
❑ 108 Chris Doleman .05 .01
❑ 109 Keith Millard .05 .01
❑ 110 Carl Lee .05 .01
❑ 111 Joey Browner .05 .01
❑ 112 Steve Jordan .05 .01
❑ 113 Reggie Rutland RC .05 .01
❑ 114 Wade Wilson .10 .02
❑ 115 Anthony Carter .10 .02
❑ 116 Rich Karlis .05 .01
❑ 117 Hassan Jones .05 .01
❑ 118 Henry Thomas .05 .01
❑ 119 Scott Studwell .05 .01
❑ 120 Ralf Mojsiejenko .05 .01
❑ 121 Earnest Byner .05 .01
❑ 122 Gerald Riggs .10 .02
❑ 123 Tracy Rocker .05 .01
❑ 124 A.J. Johnson .05 .01
❑ 125 Charles Mann .05 .01
❑ 126 Art Monk .10 .02
❑ 127 Ricky Sanders .05 .01
❑ 128 Gary Clark .25 .08
❑ 129 Jim Lachey .05 .01
❑ 130 Martin Mayhew RC .05 .01
❑ 131 Ravin Caldwell .05 .01
❑ 132 Don Warren .05 .01
❑ 133 Mark Rypien .10 .02
❑ 134 Ed Simmons RC .05 .01
❑ 135 Darryl Grant .05 .01
❑ 136 Darrell Green .10 .02
❑ 137 Chip Lohmiller .05 .01
❑ 138 Tony Bennett RC .25 .08
❑ 139 Tony Mandarich .05 .01
❑ 140 Sterling Sharpe .25 .08
❑ 141 Tim Harris .05 .01
❑ 142 Don Majkowski .05 .01
❑ 143 Rich Moran RC .05 .01
❑ 144 Jeff Query .05 .01
❑ 145 Brent Fullwood .05 .01
❑ 146 Chris Jacke .05 .01
❑ 147 Keith Woodside .05 .01
❑ 148 Perry Kemp .05 .01
❑ 149 Herman Fontenot .05 .01
❑ 150 Dave Brown DB .05 .01
❑ 151 Brian Noble .05 .01
❑ 152 Johnny Holland .05 .01
❑ 153 Mark Murphy .05 .01
❑ 154 Bob Nelson NT .05 .01
❑ 155 Darrell Thompson RC .05 .01
❑ 156 Lawyer Tillman .05 .01
❑ 157 Eric Metcalf .25 .08
❑ 158 Webster Slaughter .10 .02
❑ 159 Frank Minnifield .05 .01
❑ 160 Brian Brennan .05 .01
❑ 161 Thane Gash RC .05 .01
❑ 162 Robert Banks DE .05 .01
❑ 163 Bernie Kosar .10 .02
❑ 164 David Grayson .05 .01
❑ 165 Kevin Mack .05 .01
❑ 166 Mike Johnson .05 .01
❑ 167 Tim Manoa .05 .01
❑ 168 Ozzie Newsome .10 .02
❑ 169 Felix Wright .05 .01
❑ 170A Al Baker Orng. .10 .02
❑ 170B Al Baker Wht. .10 .02
❑ 171 Reggie Langhorne .05 .01

❑ 172	Clay Matthews	.10	.02
❑ 173	Andrew Stewart	.05	.01
❑ 174	Barry Foster RC	.25	.08
❑ 175	Tim Worley	.05	.01
❑ 176	Tim Johnson	.05	.01
❑ 177	Carnell Lake	.05	.01
❑ 178	Greg Lloyd	.25	.08
❑ 179	Rod Woodson	.25	.08
❑ 180	Tunch Ilkin	.05	.01
❑ 181	Dermontti Dawson	.10	.02
❑ 182	Gary Anderson K	.05	.01
❑ 183	Bubby Brister	.05	.01
❑ 184	Louis Lipps	.10	.02
❑ 185	Merril Hoge	.05	.01
❑ 186	Mike Mularkey	.05	.01
❑ 187	Derek Hill	.05	.01
❑ 188	Rodney Carter	.05	.01
❑ 189	Dwayne Woodruff	.05	.01
❑ 190	Keith Willis	.05	.01
❑ 191	Jerry Olsavsky	.05	.01
❑ 192	Mark Stock	.05	.01
❑ 193	Sacks Leaders	.05	.01
❑ 194	Leonard Smith	.05	.01
❑ 195	Darryl Talley	.05	.01
❑ 196	Mark Kelso	.05	.01
❑ 197	Kent Hull	.05	.01
❑ 198	Nate Odomes RC	.10	.02
❑ 199	Pete Metzelaars	.05	.01
❑ 200	Don Beebe	.10	.02
❑ 201	Ray Bentley	.05	.01
❑ 202	Steve Tasker	.10	.02
❑ 203	Scott Norwood	.05	.01
❑ 204	Andre Reed	.25	.08
❑ 205	Bruce Smith	.25	.08
❑ 206	Thurman Thomas	.25	.08
❑ 207	Jim Kelly	.25	.08
❑ 208	Cornelius Bennett	.10	.02
❑ 209	Shane Conlan	.05	.01
❑ 210	Larry Kinnebrew	.05	.01
❑ 211	Jeff Alm RC	.05	.01
❑ 212	Robert Lyles	.05	.01
❑ 213	Bubba McDowell	.05	.01
❑ 214	Mike Munchak	.10	.02
❑ 215	Bruce Matthews	.10	.02
❑ 216	Warren Moon	.25	.08
❑ 217	Drew Hill	.05	.01
❑ 218	Ray Childress	.05	.01
❑ 219	Steve Brown	.05	.01
❑ 220	Alonzo Highsmith	.05	.01
❑ 221	Allen Pinkett	.05	.01
❑ 222	Sean Jones	.10	.02
❑ 223	Johnny Meads	.05	.01
❑ 224	John Grimsley	.05	.01
❑ 225	Haywood Jeffires RC	.25	.08
❑ 226	Curtis Duncan	.05	.01
❑ 227	Greg Montgomery RC	.05	.01
❑ 228	Ernest Givins	.10	.02
❑ 229	Joe Montana/B.Esiason LL	.30	.10
❑ 230	Robert Massey	.05	.01
❑ 231	John Fourcade	.05	.01
❑ 232	Dalton Hilliard	.05	.01
❑ 233	Vaughan Johnson	.05	.01
❑ 234	Hoby Brenner	.05	.01
❑ 235	Pat Swilling	.10	.02
❑ 236	Kevin Haverdink	.05	.01
❑ 237	Bobby Hebert	.05	.01
❑ 238	Sam Mills	.10	.02
❑ 239	Eric Martin	.05	.01
❑ 240	Lonzell Hill	.05	.01
❑ 241	Steve Trapilo	.05	.01
❑ 242	Rickey Jackson	.10	.02
❑ 243	Craig Heyward	.10	.02
❑ 244	Rueben Mayes	.05	.01
❑ 245	Morten Andersen	.05	.01
❑ 246	Percy Snow RC	.05	.01
❑ 247	Pete Mandley	.05	.01
❑ 248	Derrick Thomas	.25	.08
❑ 249	Dan Saleaumua	.05	.01
❑ 250	Todd McNair RC	.05	.01
❑ 251	Leonard Griffin	.05	.01
❑ 252	Jonathan Hayes	.05	.01
❑ 253	Christian Okoye	.05	.01
❑ 254	Albert Lewis	.05	.01
❑ 255	Nick Lowery	.05	.01
❑ 256	Kevin Ross	.05	.01
❑ 257	Steve DeBerg UER	.05	.01
❑ 258	Stephone Paige	.05	.01
❑ 259	James Saxon RC	.05	.01
❑ 260	Herman Heard	.05	.01
❑ 261	Deron Cherry	.05	.01
❑ 262	Dino Hackett	.05	.01
❑ 263	Neil Smith	.25	.08
❑ 264	Steve Pelluer	.05	.01
❑ 265	Eric Thomas	.05	.01
❑ 266	Eric Ball	.05	.01
❑ 267	Leon White	.05	.01
❑ 268	Tim Krumrie	.05	.01
❑ 269	Jason Buck	.05	.01
❑ 270	Boomer Esiason	.10	.02
❑ 271	Carl Zander	.05	.01
❑ 272	Eddie Brown	.05	.01
❑ 273	David Fulcher	.05	.01
❑ 274	Tim McGee	.05	.01
❑ 275	James Brooks	.10	.02
❑ 276	Rickey Dixon RC	.05	.01
❑ 277	Ickey Woods	.05	.01
❑ 278	Anthony Munoz	.10	.02
❑ 279	Rodney Holman	.05	.01
❑ 280	Mike Alexander	.05	.01
❑ 281	Mervyn Fernandez	.05	.01
❑ 282	Steve Wisniewski	.10	.02
❑ 283	Steve Smith	.05	.01
❑ 284	Howie Long	.25	.08
❑ 285	Bo Jackson	.30	.10
❑ 286	Mike Dyal	.05	.01
❑ 287	Thomas Benson	.05	.01
❑ 288	Willie Gault	.10	.02
❑ 289	Marcus Allen	.25	.08
❑ 290	Greg Townsend	.05	.01
❑ 291	Steve Beuerlein	.10	.02
❑ 292	Scott Davis	.05	.01
❑ 293	Eddie Anderson RC	.05	.01
❑ 294	Terry McDaniel	.05	.01
❑ 295	Tim Brown	.25	.08
❑ 296	Bob Golic	.05	.01
❑ 297	Jeff Jaeger RC	.05	.01
❑ 298	Jeff George RC	.50	.20
❑ 299	Chip Banks	.05	.01
❑ 300	Andre Rison UER	.25	.08
❑ 301	Rohn Stark	.05	.01
❑ 302	Keith Taylor	.05	.01
❑ 303	Jack Trudeau	.05	.01
❑ 304	Chris Hinton	.05	.01
❑ 305	Ray Donaldson	.05	.01
❑ 306	Jeff Herrod RC	.05	.01
❑ 307	Clarence Verdin	.05	.01
❑ 308	Jon Hand	.05	.01
❑ 309	Bill Brooks	.05	.01
❑ 310	Albert Bentley	.05	.01
❑ 311	Mike Prior	.05	.01
❑ 312	Pat Beach	.05	.01
❑ 313	Eugene Daniel	.05	.01
❑ 314	Duane Bickett	.05	.01
❑ 315	Dean Biasucci	.05	.01
❑ 316	Richmond Webb RC	.05	.01
❑ 317	Jeff Cross	.05	.01
❑ 318	Louis Oliver	.05	.01
❑ 319	Sammie Smith	.05	.01
❑ 320	Pete Stoyanovich	.05	.01
❑ 321	John Offerdahl	.05	.01
❑ 322	Ferrell Edmunds	.05	.01
❑ 323	Dan Marino	1.25	.50
❑ 324	Andre Brown	.05	.01
❑ 325	Reggie Roby	.05	.01
❑ 326	Jarvis Williams	.05	.01
❑ 327	Roy Foster	.05	.01
❑ 328	Mark Clayton	.10	.02
❑ 329	Brian Sochia	.05	.01
❑ 330	Mark Duper	.10	.02
❑ 331	T.J. Turner	.05	.01
❑ 332	Jeff Uhlenhake	.05	.01
❑ 333	Jim C.Jensen	.05	.01
❑ 334	Cortez Kennedy RC	.25	.08
❑ 335	Andy Heck	.05	.01
❑ 336	Rufus Porter	.05	.01
❑ 337	Brian Blades	.10	.02
❑ 338	Dave Krieg	.10	.02
❑ 339	John L. Williams	.05	.01
❑ 340	David Wyman	.05	.01
❑ 341	Paul Skansi RC	.05	.01
❑ 342	Eugene Robinson	.05	.01
❑ 343	Joe Nash	.05	.01
❑ 344	Jacob Green	.05	.01
❑ 345	Jeff Bryant	.05	.01
❑ 346	Ruben Rodriguez	.05	.01
❑ 347	Norm Johnson	.05	.01
❑ 348	Darren Comeaux	.05	.01
❑ 349	Andre Ware RC	.10	.02
❑ 350	Richard Johnson	.05	.01
❑ 351	Rodney Peete	.10	.02
❑ 352	Barry Sanders	1.25	.50
❑ 353	Chris Spielman	.25	.08
❑ 354	Eddie Murray	.05	.01
❑ 355	Jerry Ball	.05	.01
❑ 356	Mel Gray	.10	.02
❑ 357	Eric Williams RC	.05	.01
❑ 358	Robert Clark RC	.05	.01
❑ 359	Jason Phillips	.05	.01
❑ 360	Terry Taylor RC	.05	.01
❑ 361	Bennie Blades	.05	.01
❑ 362	Michael Cofer	.05	.01
❑ 363	Jim Arnold	.05	.01
❑ 364	Marc Spindler RC	.05	.01
❑ 365	Jim Covert	.05	.01
❑ 366	Jim Harbaugh	.25	.08
❑ 367	Neal Anderson	.10	.02
❑ 368	Mike Singletary	.10	.02
❑ 369	John Roper	.05	.01
❑ 370	Steve McMichael	.10	.02
❑ 371	Dennis Gentry	.05	.01
❑ 372	Brad Muster	.05	.01
❑ 373	Ron Morris	.05	.01
❑ 374	James Thornton	.05	.01
❑ 375	Kevin Butler	.05	.01
❑ 376	Richard Dent	.10	.02
❑ 377	Dan Hampton	.10	.02
❑ 378	Jay Hilgenberg	.05	.01
❑ 379	Donnell Woolford	.05	.01
❑ 380	Trace Armstrong	.05	.01
❑ 381	Junior Seau RC	1.25	.50
❑ 382	Rod Bernstine	.05	.01
❑ 383	Marion Butts	.10	.02
❑ 384	Burt Grossman	.05	.01
❑ 385	Darrin Nelson	.05	.01
❑ 386	Leslie O'Neal	.10	.02
❑ 387	Billy Joe Tolliver	.05	.01
❑ 388	Courtney Hall	.05	.01
❑ 389	Lee Williams	.05	.01
❑ 390	Anthony Miller	.25	.08
❑ 391	Gill Byrd	.05	.01
❑ 392	Wayne Walker WR	.05	.01
❑ 393	Billy Ray Smith	.05	.01
❑ 394	Vencie Glenn	.05	.01
❑ 395	Tim Spencer	.05	.01
❑ 396	Gary Plummer	.05	.01
❑ 397	Arthur Cox	.05	.01
❑ 398	Jamie Holland	.05	.01
❑ 399	Keith McCants RC	.05	.01
❑ 400	Kevin Murphy	.05	.01
❑ 401	Danny Peebles	.05	.01
❑ 402	Mark Robinson	.05	.01
❑ 403	Broderick Thomas	.05	.01
❑ 404	Ron Hall	.05	.01
❑ 405	Mark Carrier WR	.25	.08
❑ 406	Paul Gruber	.05	.01
❑ 407	Vinny Testaverde	.10	.02
❑ 408	Bruce Hill	.05	.01
❑ 409	Lars Tate	.05	.01
❑ 410	Harry Hamilton	.05	.01
❑ 411	Ricky Reynolds	.05	.01
❑ 412	Donald Igwebuike	.05	.01
❑ 413	Reuben Davis	.05	.01
❑ 414	William Howard	.05	.01
❑ 415	Winston Moss RC	.05	.01
❑ 416	Chris Singleton RC	.05	.01
❑ 417	Hart Lee Dykes	.05	.01
❑ 418	Steve Grogan	.10	.02
❑ 419	Bruce Armstrong	.05	.01
❑ 420	Robert Perryman	.05	.01
❑ 421	Andre Tippett	.05	.01
❑ 422	Sammy Martin	.05	.01
❑ 423	Stanley Morgan	.05	.01
❑ 424	Cedric Jones	.05	.01
❑ 425	Sean Farrell	.05	.01
❑ 426	Marc Wilson	.05	.01
❑ 427	John Stephens	.05	.01
❑ 428	Eric Sievers RC	.05	.01
❑ 429	Maurice Hurst RC	.05	.01
❑ 430	Johnny Rembert	.05	.01
❑ 431	Jerry Rice/Andre Reed LL	.30	.10
❑ 432	Eric Hill	.05	.01

❑ 433 Gary Hogeboom .05 .01
❑ 434 Timm Rosenbach UER .05 .01
❑ 435 Tim McDonald .05 .01
❑ 436 Rich Camarillo .05 .01
❑ 437 Luis Sharpe .05 .01
❑ 438 J.T. Smith .05 .01
❑ 439 Roy Green .10 .02
❑ 440 Ernie Jones RC .05 .01
❑ 441 Robert Awalt .05 .01
❑ 442 Vai Sikahema .05 .01
❑ 443 Joe Wolf .05 .01
❑ 444 Stump Mitchell .05 .01
❑ 445 David Galloway .05 .01
❑ 446 Ron Wolfley .05 .01
❑ 447 Freddie Joe Nunn .05 .01
❑ 448 Blair Thomas RC .10 .02
❑ 449 Jeff Lageman .05 .01
❑ 450 Tony Eason .05 .01
❑ 451 Erik McMillan .05 .01
❑ 452 Jim Sweeney .05 .01
❑ 453 Ken O'Brien .05 .01
❑ 454 Johnny Hector .05 .01
❑ 455 Jo Jo Townsell .05 .01
❑ 456 Roger Vick .05 .01
❑ 457 James Hasty .05 .01
❑ 458 Dennis Byrd RC .10 .02
❑ 459 Ron Stallworth .05 .01
❑ 460 Mickey Shuler .05 .01
❑ 461 Bobby Humphery .05 .01
❑ 462 Kyle Clifton .05 .01
❑ 463 Al Toon .10 .02
❑ 464 Freeman McNeil .05 .01
❑ 465 Pat Leahy .05 .01
❑ 466 Scott Case .05 .01
❑ 467 Shawn Collins .05 .01
❑ 468 Floyd Dixon .05 .01
❑ 469 Deion Sanders .50 .20
❑ 470 Tony Casillas .05 .01
❑ 471 Michael Haynes RC .25 .08
❑ 472 Chris Miller .25 .08
❑ 473 John Settle .05 .01
❑ 474 Aundray Bruce .05 .01
❑ 475 Gene Lang .05 .01
❑ 476 Tim Gordon RC .05 .01
❑ 477 Scott Fulhage .05 .01
❑ 478 Bill Fralic .05 .01
❑ 479 Jessie Tuggle RC .05 .01
❑ 480 Marcus Cotton .05 .01
❑ 481 Steve Walsh .10 .02
❑ 482 Troy Aikman .75 .30
❑ 483 Ray Horton .05 .01
❑ 484 Tony Tolbert RC .10 .02
❑ 485 Steve Folsom .05 .01
❑ 486 Ken Norton Jr. RC .25 .08
❑ 487 Kelvin Martin RC .05 .01
❑ 488 Jack Del Rio .10 .02
❑ 489 Daryl Johnston RC 1.00 .40
❑ 490 Bill Bates .10 .02
❑ 491 Jim Jeffcoat .05 .01
❑ 492 Vince Albritton .05 .01
❑ 493 Eugene Lockhart .05 .01
❑ 494 Mike Saxon .05 .01
❑ 495 James Dixon .05 .01
❑ 496 Willie Broughton .05 .01
❑ 497 Checklist 1-132 .05 .01
❑ 498 Checklist 133-264 .05 .01
❑ 499 Checklist 265-396 .05 .01
❑ 500 Checklist 397-528 .05 .01
❑ 501 Bears Team .10 .02
❑ 502 Bengals Team .05 .01
❑ 503 Bills Team .05 .01
❑ 504 Broncos Team .05 .01
❑ 505 Browns Team .05 .01
❑ 506 Buccaneers Team .05 .01
❑ 507 Cardinals Team .05 .01
❑ 508 Chargers Team .05 .01
❑ 509 Chiefs Team .05 .01
❑ 510 Colts Team .05 .01
❑ 511 Cowboys TL/Aikman .30 .10
❑ 512 Dolphins Team .05 .01
❑ 513 Eagles Team .05 .01
❑ 514 Falcons Team .05 .01
❑ 515 49ers TL/Montana/Craig .30 .10
❑ 516 Giants Team .05 .01
❑ 517 Jets Team .05 .01
❑ 518 Lions Team .05 .01
❑ 519 Oilers TL/Moon .10 .02
❑ 520 Packers Team .05 .01
❑ 521 Patriots Team .05 .01
❑ 522 Raiders TL/Bo Jackson .10 .02
❑ 523 Rams Team .05 .01
❑ 524 Redskins Team .05 .01
❑ 525 Saints Team .05 .01
❑ 526 Seahawks Team .05 .01
❑ 527 Steelers Team .05 .01
❑ 528 Vikings Team .05 .01

1990 Topps Traded

❑ COMP.FACT.SET (132) 15.00 6.00
❑ 1T Gerald McNeil .05 .01
❑ 2T Andre Rison .25 .08
❑ 3T Steve Walsh .25 .08
❑ 4T Lorenzo White .10 .02
❑ 5T Max Montoya .05 .01
❑ 6T William Roberts RC .05 .01
❑ 7T Alonzo Highsmith .05 .01
❑ 8T Chris Hinton .10 .02
❑ 9T Stanley Morgan .10 .02
❑ 10T Mickey Shuler .05 .01
❑ 11T Bobby Humphery .05 .01
❑ 12T Gary Anderson RB .05 .01
❑ 13T Mike Tomczak .10 .02
❑ 14T Anthony Pleasant RC .10 .02
❑ 15T Walter Stanley .05 .01
❑ 16T Greg Bell .05 .01
❑ 17T Tony Martin RC .75 .30
❑ 18T Terry Kinard .05 .01
❑ 19T Cris Carter .50 .20
❑ 20T James Wilder .05 .01
❑ 21T Jerry Kauric .05 .01
❑ 22T Irving Fryar .25 .08
❑ 23T Ken Harvey RC .25 .08
❑ 24T James Williams DB RC .05 .01
❑ 25T Ron Cox RC .05 .01
❑ 26T Andre Ware .25 .08
❑ 27T Emmitt Smith RC 12.00 5.00
❑ 28T Junior Seau .75 .30
❑ 29T Mark Carrier RC DB .25 .08
❑ 30T Rodney Hampton .25 .08
❑ 31T Rob Moore RC .50 .20
❑ 32T Bern Brostek RC .05 .01
❑ 33T Dexter Carter .10 .02
❑ 34T Blair Thomas .10 .02
❑ 35T Harold Green RC .25 .08
❑ 36T Darrell Thompson .05 .01
❑ 37T Eric Green RC .25 .08
❑ 38T Renaldo Turnbull RC .25 .08
❑ 39T Leroy Hoard RC .25 .08
❑ 40T Anthony Thompson RC .10 .02
❑ 41T Jeff George .25 .08
❑ 42T Alexander Wright RC .05 .01
❑ 43T Richmond Webb .05 .01
❑ 44T Cortez Kennedy .25 .08
❑ 45T Ray Agnew RC .05 .01
❑ 46T Percy Snow .05 .01
❑ 47T Chris Singleton .05 .01
❑ 48T James Francis RC .10 .02
❑ 49T Tony Bennett .10 .02
❑ 50T Reggie Cobb RC .10 .02
❑ 51T Barry Foster .25 .08
❑ 52T Ben Smith .05 .01
❑ 53T Anthony Smith RC .25 .08
❑ 54T Steve Christie RC .05 .01
❑ 55T Johnny Bailey RC .10 .02
❑ 56T Alan Grant RC .05 .01
❑ 57T Eric Floyd RC .05 .01
❑ 58T Robert Blackmon RC .05 .01
❑ 59T Brent Williams .05 .01
❑ 60T Raymond Clayborn .05 .01
❑ 61T Dave Duerson .05 .01
❑ 62T Derrick Fenner RC .10 .02
❑ 63T Ken Willis .05 .01
❑ 64T Brad Baxter RC .10 .02
❑ 65T Tony Paige .05 .01
❑ 66T Jay Schroeder .05 .01
❑ 67T Jim Breech .05 .01
❑ 68T Barry Word RC .10 .02
❑ 69T Anthony Dilweg FTC .05 .01
❑ 70T Rich Gannon RC 2.00 .75
❑ 71T Stan Humphries RC .25 .08
❑ 72T Jay Novacek .25 .08
❑ 73T Tommy Kane RC .05 .01
❑ 74T Everson Walls .05 .01
❑ 75T Mike Rozier .10 .02
❑ 76T Robb Thomas .05 .01
❑ 77T Terance Mathis RC .75 .30
❑ 78T LeRoy Irvin .05 .01
❑ 79T Jeff Donaldson .05 .01
❑ 80T Ethan Horton RC .10 .02
❑ 81T J.B.Brown RC .05 .01
❑ 82T Joe Kelly .05 .01
❑ 83T John Carney RC .05 .01
❑ 84T Dan Stryzinski RC .05 .01
❑ 85T John Kidd .05 .01
❑ 86T Al Smith .10 .02
❑ 87T Travis McNeal .05 .01
❑ 88T Reyna Thompson RC .05 .01
❑ 89T Rick Donnelly .05 .01
❑ 90T Marv Cook RC .10 .02
❑ 91T Mike Farr RC .05 .01
❑ 92T Daniel Stubbs .05 .01
❑ 93T Jeff Campbell RC .05 .01
❑ 94T Tim McKyer .05 .01
❑ 95T Ian Beckles RC .05 .01
❑ 96T Lemuel Stinson .05 .01
❑ 97T Frank Cornish .05 .01
❑ 98T Riki Ellison .05 .01
❑ 99T Jamie Mueller RC .05 .01
❑ 100T Brian Hansen .05 .01
❑ 101T Warren Powers RC .05 .01
❑ 102T Howard Cross RC .05 .01
❑ 103T Tim Grunhard RC .05 .01
❑ 104T Johnny Johnson RC .25 .08
❑ 105T Calvin Williams RC .25 .08
❑ 106T Keith McCants .05 .01
❑ 107T Lamar Lathon RC .10 .02
❑ 108T Steve Broussard RC .10 .02
❑ 109T Glenn Parker RC .05 .01
❑ 110T Alton Montgomery RC .05 .01
❑ 111T Jim McMahon .10 .02
❑ 112T Aaron Wallace RC .05 .01
❑ 113T Keith Sims RC .05 .01
❑ 114T Ervin Randle .05 .01
❑ 115T Walter Wilson .05 .01
❑ 116T Terry Wooden RC .05 .01
❑ 117T Bernard Clark .05 .01
❑ 118T Tony Stargell RC .05 .01
❑ 119T Jimmie Jones RC .05 .01
❑ 120T Andre Collins RC .10 .02
❑ 121T Ricky Proehl RC .25 .08
❑ 122T Darion Conner RC .10 .02
❑ 123T Jeff Rutledge .05 .01
❑ 124T Heath Sherman RC .10 .02
❑ 125T Tommie Agee RC .05 .01
❑ 126T Tory Epps RC .05 .01
❑ 127T Tommy Hodson RC .05 .01
❑ 128T Jessie Hester RC .05 .01
❑ 129T Alfred Oglesby RC .05 .01
❑ 130T Chris Chandler .25 .08
❑ 131T Fred Barnett RC .25 .08
❑ 132T Checklist 1-132 .05 .01

1991 Topps

❑ COMPLETE SET (660)	20.00	10.00
❑ COMP.FACT.SET (660)	30.00	15.00
❑ 1 Super Bowl XXV	.05	.01
❑ 2 Roger Craig HL	.10	.02
❑ 3 Derrick Thomas HL	.10	.02
❑ 4 Pete Stoyanovich HL	.05	.01
❑ 5 Ottis Anderson HL	.10	.02
❑ 6 Jerry Rice HL	.50	.20
❑ 7 Warren Moon HL	.10	.02
❑ 8 Warren Moon/J.Everett LL	.10	.02
❑ 9 B.Sanders/T.Thomas LL	.40	.15
❑ 10 J.Rice/H.Jeffires LL	.30	.10
❑ 11 M.Carrier DB/R.Johnson DB LL	.05	.01
❑ 12 Derrick Thomas/C.Haley L	.10	.02
❑ 13 Jumbo Elliott	.05	.01
❑ 14 Leonard Marshall	.05	.01
❑ 15 William Roberts	.05	.01
❑ 16 Lawrence Taylor	.25	.08
❑ 17 Mark Ingram	.10	.02
❑ 18 Rodney Hampton	.25	.08
❑ 19 Carl Banks	.05	.01
❑ 20 Ottis Anderson	.10	.02
❑ 21 Mark Collins	.05	.01
❑ 22 Pepper Johnson	.05	.01
❑ 23 Dave Meggett	.10	.02
❑ 24 Reyna Thompson	.05	.01
❑ 25 Stephen Baker	.05	.01
❑ 26 Mike Fox	.05	.01
❑ 27 Maurice Carthon UER	.05	.01
❑ 28 Jeff Hostetler	.25	.08
❑ 29 Greg Jackson RC	.05	.01
❑ 30 Sean Landeta	.05	.01
❑ 31 Bart Oates	.05	.01
❑ 32 Phil Simms	.10	.02
❑ 33 Erik Howard	.05	.01
❑ 34 Myron Guyton	.05	.01
❑ 35 Mark Bavaro	.05	.01
❑ 36 Jarrod Bunch RC	.05	.01
❑ 37 Will Wolford	.05	.01
❑ 38 Ray Bentley	.05	.01
❑ 39 Nate Odomes	.05	.01
❑ 40 Scott Norwood	.05	.01
❑ 41 Darryl Talley	.05	.01
❑ 42 Carwell Gardner	.05	.01
❑ 43 James Lofton	.10	.02
❑ 44 Shane Conlan	.05	.01
❑ 45 Steve Tasker	.10	.02
❑ 46 James Williams	.05	.01
❑ 47 Kent Hull	.05	.01
❑ 48 Al Edwards	.05	.01
❑ 49 Frank Reich	.10	.02
❑ 50 Leon Seals	.05	.01
❑ 51 Keith McKeller	.05	.01
❑ 52 Thurman Thomas	.25	.08
❑ 53 Leonard Smith	.05	.01
❑ 54 Andre Reed	.10	.02
❑ 55 Kenneth Davis	.05	.01
❑ 56 Jeff Wright RC	.05	.01
❑ 57 Jamie Mueller	.05	.01
❑ 58 Jim Ritcher	.05	.01
❑ 59 Bruce Smith	.25	.08
❑ 60 Ted Washington RC	.05	.01
❑ 61 Guy McIntyre	.05	.01
❑ 62 Michael Carter	.05	.01
❑ 63 Pierce Holt	.05	.01
❑ 64 Darryl Pollard	.05	.01
❑ 65 Mike Sherrard	.05	.01
❑ 66 Dexter Carter	.05	.01
❑ 67 Bubba Paris	.05	.01
❑ 68 Harry Sydney	.05	.01
❑ 69 Tom Rathman	.05	.01
❑ 70 Jesse Sapolu	.05	.01
❑ 71 Mike Cofer	.05	.01
❑ 72 Keith DeLong	.05	.01
❑ 73 Joe Montana	1.25	.50
❑ 74 Bill Romanowski	.05	.01
❑ 75 John Taylor	.10	.02
❑ 76 Brent Jones	.25	.08
❑ 77 Harris Barton	.05	.01
❑ 78 Charles Haley	.10	.02
❑ 79 Eric Davis	.05	.01
❑ 80 Kevin Fagan	.05	.01
❑ 81 Jerry Rice	.75	.30
❑ 82 Dave Waymer	.05	.01
❑ 83 Todd Marinovich RC	.05	.01
❑ 84 Steve Smith	.05	.01
❑ 85 Tim Brown	.25	.08
❑ 86 Ethan Horton	.05	.01
❑ 87 Marcus Allen	.25	.08
❑ 88 Terry McDaniel	.05	.01
❑ 89 Thomas Benson	.05	.01
❑ 90 Roger Craig	.10	.02
❑ 91 Don Mosebar	.05	.01
❑ 92 Aaron Wallace	.05	.01
❑ 93 Eddie Anderson	.05	.01
❑ 94 Willie Gault	.10	.02
❑ 95 Howie Long	.25	.08
❑ 96 Jay Schroeder	.05	.01
❑ 97 Ronnie Lott	.10	.02
❑ 98 Bob Golic	.05	.01
❑ 99 Bo Jackson	.30	.10
❑ 100 Max Montoya	.05	.01
❑ 101 Scott Davis	.05	.01
❑ 102 Greg Townsend	.05	.01
❑ 103 Garry Lewis	.05	.01
❑ 104 Mervyn Fernandez	.05	.01
❑ 105 Steve Wisniewski UER	.05	.01
❑ 106 Jeff Jaeger	.05	.01
❑ 107 Nick Bell RC	.05	.01
❑ 108 Mark Dennis RC	.05	.01
❑ 109 Jarvis Williams	.05	.01
❑ 110 Mark Clayton	.10	.02
❑ 111 Harry Galbreath	.05	.01
❑ 112 Dan Marino	1.25	.50
❑ 113 Louis Oliver	.05	.01
❑ 114 Pete Stoyanovich	.05	.01
❑ 115 Ferrell Edmunds	.05	.01
❑ 116 Jeff Cross	.05	.01
❑ 117 Richmond Webb	.05	.01
❑ 118 Jim C. Jensen	.05	.01
❑ 119 Keith Sims	.05	.01
❑ 120 Mark Duper	.10	.02
❑ 121 Shawn Lee RC	.05	.01
❑ 122 Reggie Roby	.05	.01
❑ 123 Jeff Uhlenhake	.05	.01
❑ 124 Sammie Smith	.05	.01
❑ 125 John Offerdahl	.05	.01
❑ 126 Hugh Green	.05	.01
❑ 127 Tony Paige	.05	.01
❑ 128 David Griggs	.05	.01
❑ 129 J.B. Brown	.05	.01
❑ 130 Harvey Williams RC	.25	.08
❑ 131 John Alt	.05	.01
❑ 132 Albert Lewis	.05	.01
❑ 133 Robb Thomas	.05	.01
❑ 134 Neil Smith	.25	.08
❑ 135 Stephone Paige	.05	.01
❑ 136 Nick Lowery	.05	.01
❑ 137 Steve DeBerg	.05	.01
❑ 138 Rich Baldinger RC	.05	.01
❑ 139 Percy Snow	.05	.01
❑ 140 Kevin Porter	.05	.01
❑ 141 Chris Martin	.05	.01
❑ 142 Deron Cherry	.05	.01
❑ 143 Derrick Thomas	.25	.08
❑ 144 Tim Grunhard	.05	.01
❑ 145 Todd McNair	.05	.01
❑ 146 David Szott	.05	.01
❑ 147 Dan Saleaumua	.05	.01
❑ 148 Jonathan Hayes	.05	.01
❑ 149 Christian Okoye	.05	.01
❑ 150 Dino Hackett	.05	.01
❑ 151 Bryan Barker RC	.05	.01
❑ 152 Kevin Ross	.05	.01
❑ 153 Barry Word	.05	.01
❑ 154 Stan Thomas	.05	.01
❑ 155 Brad Muster	.05	.01
❑ 156 Donnell Woolford	.05	.01
❑ 157 Neal Anderson	.10	.02
❑ 158 Jim Covert	.05	.01
❑ 159 Jim Harbaugh	.25	.08
❑ 160 Shaun Gayle	.05	.01
❑ 161 William Perry	.10	.02
❑ 162 Ron Morris	.05	.01
❑ 163 Mark Bortz	.05	.01
❑ 164 James Thornton	.05	.01
❑ 165 Ron Rivera	.05	.01
❑ 166 Kevin Butler	.05	.01
❑ 167 Jay Hilgenberg	.05	.01
❑ 168 Peter Tom Willis	.05	.01
❑ 169 Johnny Bailey	.05	.01
❑ 170 Ron Cox	.05	.01
❑ 171 Keith Van Horne	.05	.01
❑ 172 Mark Carrier DB	.10	.02
❑ 173 Richard Dent	.10	.02
❑ 174 Wendell Davis	.05	.01
❑ 175 Trace Armstrong	.05	.01
❑ 176 Mike Singletary	.10	.02
❑ 177 Chris Zorich RC	.25	.08
❑ 178 Gerald Riggs	.05	.01
❑ 179 Jeff Bostic	.05	.01
❑ 180 Kurt Gouveia RC	.05	.01
❑ 181 Stan Humphries	.25	.08
❑ 182 Chip Lohmiller	.05	.01
❑ 183 Raleigh McKenzie RC	.05	.01
❑ 184 Alvin Walton	.05	.01
❑ 185 Earnest Byner	.05	.01
❑ 186 Markus Koch	.05	.01
❑ 187 Art Monk	.10	.02
❑ 188 Ed Simmons	.05	.01
❑ 189 Bobby Wilson RC	.05	.01
❑ 190 Charles Mann	.05	.01
❑ 191 Darrell Green	.05	.01
❑ 192 Mark Rypien	.10	.02
❑ 193 Ricky Sanders	.05	.01
❑ 194 Jim Lachey	.05	.01
❑ 195 Martin Mayhew	.05	.01
❑ 196 Gary Clark	.25	.08
❑ 197 Wilber Marshall	.05	.01
❑ 198 Darryl Grant	.05	.01
❑ 199 Don Warren	.05	.01
❑ 200 Ricky Ervins RC UER	.10	.02
❑ 201 Eric Allen	.05	.01
❑ 202 Anthony Toney	.05	.01
❑ 203 Ben Smith UER	.05	.01
❑ 204 David Alexander	.05	.01
❑ 205 Jerome Brown	.05	.01
❑ 206 Mike Golic	.05	.01
❑ 207 Roger Ruzek	.05	.01
❑ 208 Andre Waters	.05	.01
❑ 209 Fred Barnett	.25	.08
❑ 210 Randall Cunningham	.25	.08
❑ 211 Mike Schad	.05	.01
❑ 212 Reggie White	.25	.08
❑ 213 Mike Bellamy	.05	.01
❑ 214 Jeff Feagles RC	.05	.01
❑ 215 Wes Hopkins	.05	.01
❑ 216 Clyde Simmons	.05	.01
❑ 217 Keith Byars	.05	.01
❑ 218 Seth Joyner	.10	.02
❑ 219 Byron Evans	.05	.01
❑ 220 Keith Jackson	.10	.02
❑ 221 Calvin Williams	.10	.02
❑ 222 Mike Dumas RC	.05	.01
❑ 223 Ray Childress	.05	.01
❑ 224 Ernest Givins	.10	.02
❑ 225 Lamar Lathon	.05	.01
❑ 226 Greg Montgomery	.05	.01
❑ 227 Mike Munchak	.10	.02
❑ 228 Al Smith	.05	.01
❑ 229 Bubba McDowell	.05	.01
❑ 230 Haywood Jeffires	.10	.02
❑ 231 Drew Hill	.05	.01

232	William Fuller	.10	.02
233	Warren Moon	.25	.08
234	Doug Smith DT RC	.10	.02
235	Cris Dishman RC	.05	.01
236	Teddy Garcia RC	.05	.01
237	Richard Johnson CB RC	.05	.01
238	Bruce Matthews	.10	.02
239	Gerald McNeil	.05	.01
240	Johnny Meads	.05	.01
241	Curtis Duncan	.05	.01
242	Sean Jones	.10	.02
243	Lorenzo White	.05	.01
244	Rob Carpenter RC WR	.05	.01
245	Bruce Reimers	.05	.01
246	Ickey Woods	.05	.01
247	Lewis Billups	.05	.01
248	Boomer Esiason	.10	.02
249	Tim Krumrie	.05	.01
250	David Fulcher	.05	.01
251	Jim Breech	.05	.01
252	Mitchell Price RC	.05	.01
253	Carl Zander	.05	.01
254	Barney Bussey RC	.05	.01
255	Leon White	.05	.01
256	Eddie Brown	.05	.01
257	James Francis	.05	.01
258	Harold Green	.10	.02
259	Anthony Munoz	.10	.02
260	James Brooks	.10	.02
261	Kevin Walker RC UER	.05	.01
262	Bruce Kozerski	.05	.01
263	David Grant	.05	.01
264	Tim McGee	.05	.01
265	Rodney Holman	.05	.01
266	Dan McGwire RC	.05	.01
267	Andy Heck	.05	.01
268	Dave Krieg	.10	.02
269	David Wyman	.05	.01
270	Robert Blackmon	.05	.01
271	Grant Feasel	.05	.01
272	Patrick Hunter RC	.05	.01
273	Travis McNeal	.05	.01
274	John L. Williams	.05	.01
275	Tony Woods	.05	.01
276	Derrick Fenner	.05	.01
277	Jacob Green	.05	.01
278	Brian Blades	.10	.02
279	Eugene Robinson	.05	.01
280	Terry Wooden	.05	.01
281	Jeff Bryant	.05	.01
282	Norm Johnson	.05	.01
283	Joe Nash UER	.05	.01
284	Rick Donnelly	.05	.01
285	Chris Warren	.25	.08
286	Tommy Kane	.05	.01
287	Cortez Kennedy	.25	.08
288	Ernie Mills RC	.10	.02
289	Dermontti Dawson	.05	.01
290	Tunch Ilkin	.05	.01
291	Tim Worley	.05	.01
292	David Little	.05	.01
293	Gary Anderson K	.05	.01
294	Chris Calloway	.05	.01
295	Carnell Lake	.05	.01
296	Dan Stryzinski	.05	.01
297	Rod Woodson	.25	.08
298	John Jackson T RC	.05	.01
299	Bubby Brister	.05	.01
300	Thomas Everett	.05	.01
301	Merril Hoge	.05	.01
302	Eric Green	.05	.01
303	Greg Lloyd	.25	.08
304	Gerald Williams	.05	.01
305	Bryan Hinkle	.05	.01
306	Keith Willis	.05	.01
307	Louis Lipps	.05	.01
308	Donald Evans	.05	.01
309	D.J. Johnson	.05	.01
310	Wesley Carroll RC	.05	.01
311	Eric Martin	.05	.01
312	Brett Maxie	.05	.01
313	Rickey Jackson	.05	.01
314	Robert Massey	.05	.01
315	Pat Swilling	.10	.02
316	Morten Andersen	.05	.01
317	Toi Cook RC	.05	.01
318	Sam Mills	.05	.01
319	Steve Walsh	.05	.01
320	Tommy Barnhardt RC	.05	.01
321	Vince Buck	.05	.01
322	Joel Hilgenberg	.05	.01
323	Rueben Mayes	.05	.01
324	Renaldo Turnbull	.05	.01
325	Brett Perriman	.25	.08
326	Vaughan Johnson	.05	.01
327	Gill Fenerty	.05	.01
328	Stan Brock	.05	.01
329	Dalton Hilliard	.05	.01
330	Hoby Brenner	.05	.01
331	Craig Heyward	.10	.02
332	Jon Hand	.05	.01
333	Duane Bickett	.05	.01
334	Jessie Hester	.05	.01
335	Rohn Stark	.05	.01
336	Zefross Moss	.05	.01
337	Bill Brooks	.05	.01
338	Clarence Verdin	.05	.01
339	Mike Prior	.05	.01
340	Chip Banks	.05	.01
341	Dean Biasucci	.05	.01
342	Ray Donaldson	.05	.01
343	Jeff Herrod	.05	.01
344	Donnell Thompson	.05	.01
345	Chris Goode	.05	.01
346	Eugene Daniel	.05	.01
347	Pat Beach	.05	.01
348	Keith Taylor	.05	.01
349	Jeff George	.25	.08
350	Tony Siragusa RC	.10	.02
351	Randy Dixon	.05	.01
352	Albert Bentley	.05	.01
353	Russell Maryland RC	.25	.08
354	Mike Saxon	.05	.01
355	Godfrey Myles RC UER	.05	.01
356	Mark Stepnoski RC	.10	.02
357	James Washington RC	.05	.01
358	Jay Novacek	.25	.08
359	Kelvin Martin	.05	.01
360	Emmitt Smith UER	2.50	1.00
361	Jim Jeffcoat	.05	.01
362	Alexander Wright	.05	.01
363	James Dixon UER	.05	.01
364	Alonzo Highsmith	.05	.01
365	Daniel Stubbs	.05	.01
366	Jack Del Rio	.10	.02
367	Mark Tuinei RC	.05	.01
368	Michael Irvin	.25	.08
369	John Gesek RC	.05	.01
370	Ken Willis	.05	.01
371	Troy Aikman	.75	.30
372	Jimmie Jones	.05	.01
373	Nate Newton	.10	.02
374	Issiac Holt	.05	.01
375	Alvin Harper RC	.25	.08
376	Todd Kalis	.05	.01
377	Wade Wilson	.10	.02
378	Joey Browner	.05	.01
379	Chris Doleman	.05	.01
380	Hassan Jones	.05	.01
381	Henry Thomas	.05	.01
382	Darrell Fullington	.05	.01
383	Steve Jordan	.05	.01
384	Gary Zimmerman	.05	.01
385	Ray Berry	.05	.01
386	Cris Carter	.50	.20
387	Mike Merriweather	.05	.01
388	Carl Lee	.05	.01
389	Keith Millard	.05	.01
390	Reggie Rutland	.05	.01
391	Anthony Carter	.10	.02
392	Mark Dusbabek	.05	.01
393	Kirk Lowdermilk	.05	.01
394	Al Noga UER	.05	.01
395	Herschel Walker	.10	.02
396	Randall McDaniel	.05	.01
397	Herman Moore RC	.25	.08
398	Eddie Murray	.05	.01
399	Lomas Brown	.05	.01
400	Marc Spindler	.05	.01
401	Bennie Blades	.05	.01
402	Kevin Glover	.05	.01
403	Aubrey Matthews RC	.05	.01
404	Michael Cofer	.05	.01
405	Robert Clark	.05	.01
406	Eric Andolsek	.05	.01
407	William White	.05	.01
408	Rodney Peete	.10	.02
409	Mel Gray	.10	.02
410	Jim Arnold	.05	.01
411	Jeff Campbell	.05	.01
412	Chris Spielman	.10	.02
413	Jerry Ball	.05	.01
414	Dan Owens	.05	.01
415	Barry Sanders	1.25	.50
416	Andre Ware	.10	.02
417	Stanley Richard RC	.05	.01
418	Gill Byrd	.05	.01
419	John Kidd	.05	.01
420	Sam Seale	.05	.01
421	Gary Plummer	.05	.01
422	Anthony Miller	.10	.02
423	Ronnie Harmon	.05	.01
424	Frank Cornish	.05	.01
425	Marion Butts	.10	.02
426	Leo Goeas	.05	.01
427	Junior Seau	.25	.08
428	Courtney Hall	.05	.01
429	Leslie O'Neal	.10	.02
430	Martin Bayless	.05	.01
431	John Carney	.05	.01
432	Lee Williams	.05	.01
433	Arthur Cox	.05	.01
434	Burt Grossman	.05	.01
435	Nate Lewis RC	.05	.01
436	Rod Bernstine	.05	.01
437	Henry Rolling RC	.05	.01
438	Billy Joe Tolliver	.05	.01
439	Vinnie Clark RC	.05	.01
440	Brian Noble	.05	.01
441	Charles Wilson	.05	.01
442	Don Majkowski	.05	.01
443	Tim Harris	.05	.01
444	Scott Stephen RC	.05	.01
445	Perry Kemp	.05	.01
446	Darrell Thompson	.05	.01
447	Chris Jacke	.05	.01
448	Mark Murphy	.05	.01
449	Ed West	.05	.01
450	LeRoy Butler	.10	.02
451	Keith Woodside	.05	.01
452	Tony Bennett	.10	.02
453	Mark Lee	.05	.01
454	James Campen RC	.05	.01
455	Robert Brown	.05	.01
456	Sterling Sharpe	.25	.08
457A	T.Mandarich ERR Bronc.	2.50	1.25
457B	T.Mandarich COR Packers	.05	.01
458	Johnny Holland	.05	.01
459	Matt Brock RC	.05	.01
460A	Esera Tuaolo RC ERR	.05	.01
460B	Esera Tuaolo RC COR	.05	.01
461	Freeman McNeil	.05	.01
462	Terance Mathis UER 460	.25	.08
463	Rob Moore	.25	.08
464	Darrell Davis RC	.05	.01
465	Chris Burkett	.05	.01
466	Jeff Criswell	.05	.01
467	Tony Stargell	.05	.01
468	Ken O'Brien	.05	.01
469	Erik McMillan	.05	.01
470	Jeff Lageman UER	.05	.01
471	Pat Leahy	.05	.01
472	Dennis Byrd	.05	.01
473	Jim Sweeney	.05	.01
474	Brad Baxter	.05	.01
475	Joe Kelly	.05	.01
476	Al Toon	.10	.02
477	Joe Prokop	.05	.01
478	Mark Boyer	.05	.01
479	Kyle Clifton	.05	.01
480	James Hasty	.05	.01
481	Browning Nagle RC	.05	.01

❑ 482	Gary Anderson RB	.05	.01
❑ 483	Mark Carrier WR	.25	.08
❑ 484	Ricky Reynolds	.05	.01
❑ 485	Bruce Hill	.05	.01
❑ 486	Steve Christie	.05	.01
❑ 487	Paul Gruber	.05	.01
❑ 488	Jesse Anderson	.05	.01
❑ 489	Reggie Cobb	.05	.01
❑ 490	Harry Hamilton	.05	.01
❑ 491	Vinny Testaverde	.10	.02
❑ 492	Mark Royals RC	.05	.01
❑ 493	Keith McCants	.05	.01
❑ 494	Ron Hall	.05	.01
❑ 495	Ian Beckles	.05	.01
❑ 496	Mark Robinson	.05	.01
❑ 497	Reuben Davis	.05	.01
❑ 498	Wayne Haddix	.05	.01
❑ 499	Kevin Murphy	.05	.01
❑ 500	Eugene Marve	.05	.01
❑ 501	Broderick Thomas	.05	.01
❑ 502	Eric Swann RC UER	.25	.08
❑ 503	Ernie Jones	.05	.01
❑ 504	Rich Camarillo	.05	.01
❑ 505	Tim McDonald	.05	.01
❑ 506	Freddie Joe Nunn	.05	.01
❑ 507	Tim Jorden RC	.05	.01
❑ 508	Johnny Johnson	.05	.01
❑ 509	Eric Hill	.05	.01
❑ 510	Derek Kennard	.05	.01
❑ 511	Ricky Proehl	.05	.01
❑ 512	Bill Lewis	.05	.01
❑ 513	Roy Green	.05	.01
❑ 514	Anthony Bell	.05	.01
❑ 515	Timm Rosenbach	.05	.01
❑ 516	Jim Wahler RC	.05	.01
❑ 517	Anthony Thompson	.05	.01
❑ 518	Ken Harvey	.10	.02
❑ 519	Luis Sharpe	.05	.01
❑ 520	Walter Reeves	.05	.01
❑ 521	Lonnie Young	.05	.01
❑ 522	Rod Saddler	.05	.01
❑ 523	Todd Lyght RC	.05	.01
❑ 524	Alvin Wright	.05	.01
❑ 525	Flipper Anderson	.05	.01
❑ 526	Jackie Slater	.05	.01
❑ 527	Damone Johnson RC	.05	.01
❑ 528	Cleveland Gary	.05	.01
❑ 529	Mike Piel	.05	.01
❑ 530	Buford McGee	.05	.01
❑ 531	Michael Stewart	.05	.01
❑ 532	Jim Everett	.10	.02
❑ 533	Mike Wilcher	.05	.01
❑ 534	Irv Pankey	.05	.01
❑ 535	Bern Brostek	.05	.01
❑ 536	Henry Ellard	.10	.02
❑ 537	Doug Smith	.05	.01
❑ 538	Larry Kelm	.05	.01
❑ 539	Pat Terrell	.05	.01
❑ 540	Tom Newberry	.05	.01
❑ 541	Jerry Gray	.05	.01
❑ 542	Kevin Greene	.10	.02
❑ 543	Duval Love RC	.05	.01
❑ 544	Frank Stams	.05	.01
❑ 545	Mike Croel RC	.05	.01
❑ 546	Mark Jackson	.05	.01
❑ 547	Greg Kragen	.05	.01
❑ 548	Karl Mecklenburg	.05	.01
❑ 549	Simon Fletcher	.05	.01
❑ 550	Bobby Humphrey	.05	.01
❑ 551	Ken Lanier	.05	.01
❑ 552	Vance Johnson	.05	.01
❑ 553	Ron Holmes	.05	.01
❑ 554	John Elway	1.25	.50
❑ 555	Melvin Bratton	.05	.01
❑ 556	Dennis Smith	.05	.01
❑ 557	Ricky Nattiel	.05	.01
❑ 558	Clarence Kay	.05	.01
❑ 559	Michael Brooks	.05	.01
❑ 560	Mike Horan	.05	.01
❑ 561	Warren Powers	.05	.01
❑ 562	Keith Kartz	.05	.01
❑ 563	Shannon Sharpe	.50	.20
❑ 564	Wymon Henderson	.05	.01
❑ 565	Steve Atwater	.05	.01
❑ 566	David Treadwell	.05	.01
❑ 567	Bruce Pickens RC	.05	.01
❑ 568	Jessie Tuggle	.05	.01
❑ 569	Chris Hinton	.05	.01
❑ 570	Keith Jones	.05	.01
❑ 571	Bill Fralic	.05	.01
❑ 572	Mike Rozier	.05	.01
❑ 573	Scott Fulhage	.05	.01
❑ 574	Floyd Dixon	.05	.01
❑ 575	Andre Rison	.10	.02
❑ 576	Darion Conner	.05	.01
❑ 577	Brian Jordan	.10	.02
❑ 578	Michael Haynes	.25	.08
❑ 579	Oliver Barnett	.05	.01
❑ 580	Shawn Collins	.05	.01
❑ 581	Tim Green	.05	.01
❑ 582	Deion Sanders	.40	.15
❑ 583	Mike Kenn	.05	.01
❑ 584	Mike Gann	.05	.01
❑ 585	Chris Miller	.10	.02
❑ 586	Tory Epps	.05	.01
❑ 587	Steve Broussard	.05	.01
❑ 588	Gary Wilkins	.05	.01
❑ 589	Eric Turner RC	.10	.02
❑ 590	Thane Gash	.05	.01
❑ 591	Clay Matthews	.10	.02
❑ 592	Mike Johnson	.05	.01
❑ 593	Raymond Clayborn	.05	.01
❑ 594	Leroy Hoard	.10	.02
❑ 595	Reggie Langhorne	.05	.01
❑ 596	Mike Baab	.05	.01
❑ 597	Anthony Pleasant	.05	.01
❑ 598	David Grayson	.05	.01
❑ 599	Rob Burnett RC	.10	.02
❑ 600	Frank Minnifield	.05	.01
❑ 601	Gregg Rakoczy	.05	.01
❑ 602	Eric Metcalf UER	.25	.08
❑ 603	Paul Farren	.05	.01
❑ 604	Brian Brennan	.05	.01
❑ 605	Tony Jones T RC	.05	.01
❑ 606	Stephen Braggs	.05	.01
❑ 607	Kevin Mack	.05	.01
❑ 608	Pat Harlow RC	.05	.01
❑ 609	Marv Cook	.05	.01
❑ 610	John Stephens	.05	.01
❑ 611	Ed Reynolds	.05	.01
❑ 612	Tim Goad	.05	.01
❑ 613	Chris Singleton	.05	.01
❑ 614	Bruce Armstrong	.05	.01
❑ 615	Tommy Hodson	.05	.01
❑ 616	Sammy Martin	.05	.01
❑ 617	Andre Tippett	.05	.01
❑ 618	Johnny Rembert	.05	.01
❑ 619	Maurice Hurst	.05	.01
❑ 620	Vincent Brown	.05	.01
❑ 621	Ray Agnew	.05	.01
❑ 622	Ronnie Lippett	.05	.01
❑ 623	Greg McMurtry	.05	.01
❑ 624	Brent Williams	.05	.01
❑ 625	Jason Staurovsky	.05	.01
❑ 626	Marvin Allen	.05	.01
❑ 627	Hart Lee Dykes	.05	.01
❑ 628	Atlanta Falcons	.05	.01
❑ 629	Buffalo Bills	.05	.01
❑ 630	Chicago Bears	.10	.02
❑ 631	Cincinnati Bengals	.05	.01
❑ 632	Cleveland Browns	.05	.01
❑ 633	Dallas Cowboys	.05	.01
❑ 634	Denver Broncos	.05	.01
❑ 635	Detroit Lions	.05	.01
❑ 636	Green Bay Packers	.05	.01
❑ 637	Oilers TL/Warren Moon	.10	.02
❑ 638	Colts TL/Jeff George	.05	.01
❑ 639	Kansas City Chiefs	.05	.01
❑ 640	Los Angeles Raiders	.10	.02
❑ 641	Los Angeles Rams	.05	.01
❑ 642	Miami Dolphins	.05	.01
❑ 643	Minnesota Vikings	.10	.02
❑ 644	New Eng. Patriots	.05	.01
❑ 645	New Orleans Saints	.05	.01
❑ 646	New York Giants	.05	.01
❑ 647	New York Jets	.05	.01
❑ 648	Eagles TL/R.Cunningham	.05	.01
❑ 649	Phoenix Cardinals	.05	.01
❑ 650	Pittsburgh Steelers	.05	.01
❑ 651	San Diego Chargers	.05	.01
❑ 652	San Francisco 49ers	.05	.01
❑ 653	Seattle Seahawks	.05	.01
❑ 654	Tampa Bay Buccaneers	.05	.01
❑ 655	Washington Redskins	.05	.01
❑ 656	Checklist 1-132	.05	.01
❑ 657	Checklist 132-264	.05	.01
❑ 658	Checklist 265-396	.05	.01
❑ 659	Checklist 397-528	.05	.01
❑ 660	Checklist 529-660	.05	.01

1992 Topps

❑	COMPLETE SET (759)	50.00	25.00
❑	COMP.FACT.SET (680)	80.00	40.00
❑	COMP.SERIES 1 (330)	20.00	10.00
❑	COMP.SERIES 2 (330)	20.00	10.00
❑	COMP.HIGH SER.(00)	10.00	5.00
❑	COMP.FACT.HIGH SET (113)	12.00	5.00
❑ 1	Tim McGee	.05	.01
❑ 2	Rich Camarillo	.05	.01
❑ 3	Anthony Johnson	.10	.02
❑ 4	Larry Kelm	.05	.01
❑ 5	Irving Fryar	.10	.02
❑ 6	Joey Browner	.05	.01
❑ 7	Michael Walter	.05	.01
❑ 8	Cortez Kennedy	.10	.02
❑ 9	Reyna Thompson	.05	.01
❑ 10	John Friesz	.10	.02
❑ 11	Leroy Hoard	.10	.02
❑ 12	Steve McMichael	.10	.02
❑ 13	Marvin Washington	.05	.01
❑ 14	Clyde Simmons	.05	.01
❑ 15	Stephone Paige	.05	.01
❑ 16	Mike Utley	.10	.02
❑ 17	Tunch Ilkin	.05	.01
❑ 18	Lawrence Dawsey	.10	.02
❑ 19	Vance Johnson	.05	.01
❑ 20	Bryce Paup	.25	.08
❑ 21	Jeff Wright	.05	.01
❑ 22	Gill Fenerty	.05	.01
❑ 23	Lamar Lathon	.05	.01
❑ 24	Danny Copeland	.05	.01
❑ 25	Marcus Allen	.25	.08
❑ 26	Tim Green	.05	.01
❑ 27	Pete Stoyanovich	.05	.01
❑ 28	Alvin Harper	.10	.02
❑ 29	Roy Foster	.05	.01
❑ 30	Eugene Daniel	.05	.01
❑ 31	Luis Sharpe	.05	.01
❑ 32	Terry Wooden	.05	.01
❑ 33	Jim Breech	.05	.01
❑ 34	Randy Hilliard RC	.05	.01
❑ 35	Roman Phifer	.05	.01
❑ 36	Erik Howard	.05	.01
❑ 37	Chris Singleton	.05	.01
❑ 38	Matt Stover	.05	.01
❑ 39	Tim Irwin	.05	.01
❑ 40	Karl Mecklenburg	.05	.01
❑ 41	Joe Phillips	.05	.01
❑ 42	Bill Jones RC	.05	.01
❑ 43	Mark Carrier DB	.05	.01
❑ 44	George Jamison	.05	.01
❑ 45	Rob Taylor	.05	.01
❑ 46	Jeff Jaeger	.05	.01
❑ 47	Don Majkowski	.05	.01
❑ 48	Al Edwards	.05	.01

❑	49	Curtis Duncan	.05	.01
❑	50	Sam Mills	.05	.01
❑	51	Terance Mathis	.10	.02
❑	52	Brian Mitchell	.10	.02
❑	53	Mike Pritchard	.10	.02
❑	54	Calvin Williams	.10	.02
❑	55	Hardy Nickerson	.10	.02
❑	56	Nate Newton	.05	.01
❑	57	Steve Wallace	.05	.01
❑	58	John Offerdahl	.05	.01
❑	59	Aeneas Williams	.10	.02
❑	60	Lee Johnson	.05	.01
❑	61	Ricardo McDonald RC	.05	.01
❑	62	David Richards	.05	.01
❑	63	Paul Gruber	.05	.01
❑	64	Greg McMurtry	.05	.01
❑	65	Jay Hilgenberg	.05	.01
❑	66	Tim Grunhard	.05	.01
❑	67	Dwayne White RC	.05	.01
❑	68	Don Beebe	.05	.01
❑	69	Simon Fletcher	.05	.01
❑	70	Warren Moon	.25	.08
❑	71	Chris Jacke	.05	.01
❑	72	Steve Wisniewski UER	.05	.01
❑	73	Mike Cofer	.05	.01
❑	74	Tim Johnson UER	.05	.01
❑	75	T.J. Turner	.05	.01
❑	76	Scott Case	.05	.01
❑	77	Michael Jackson	.10	.02
❑	78	Jon Hand	.05	.01
❑	79	Stan Brock	.05	.01
❑	80	Robert Blackmon	.05	.01
❑	81	D.J. Johnson	.05	.01
❑	82	Damone Johnson	.05	.01
❑	83	Marc Spindler	.05	.01
❑	84	Larry Brown DB	.05	.01
❑	85	Ray Berry	.05	.01
❑	86	Andre Waters	.05	.01
❑	87	Carlos Huerta	.05	.01
❑	88	Brad Muster	.05	.01
❑	89	Chuck Cecil	.05	.01
❑	90	Nick Lowery	.05	.01
❑	91	Cornelius Bennett	.10	.02
❑	92	Jessie Tuggle	.05	.01
❑	93	Mark Schlereth RC	.05	.01
❑	94	Vestee Jackson	.05	.01
❑	95	Eric Bieniemy	.05	.01
❑	96	Jeff Hostetler	.10	.02
❑	97	Ken Lanier	.05	.01
❑	98	Wayne Haddix	.05	.01
❑	99	Lorenzo White	.05	.01
❑	100	Mervyn Fernandez	.05	.01
❑	101	Brent Williams	.05	.01
❑	102	Ian Beckles	.05	.01
❑	103	Harris Barton	.05	.01
❑	104	Edgar Bennett RC	.25	.08
❑	105	Mike Pitts	.05	.01
❑	106	Fuad Reveiz	.05	.01
❑	107	Vernon Turner	.05	.01
❑	108	Tracy Hayworth RC	.05	.01
❑	109	Checklist 1-110	.05	.01
❑	110	Tom Waddle	.05	.01
❑	111	Fred Stokes	.05	.01
❑	112	Howard Ballard	.05	.01
❑	113	David Szott	.05	.01
❑	114	Tim McKyer	.05	.01
❑	115	Kyle Clifton	.05	.01
❑	116	Tony Bennett	.05	.01
❑	117	Joel Hilgenberg	.05	.01
❑	118	Dwayne Harper	.05	.01
❑	119	Mike Baab	.05	.01
❑	120	Mark Clayton	.10	.02
❑	121	Eric Swann	.10	.02
❑	122	Neil O'Donnell	.10	.02
❑	123	Mike Munchak	.10	.02
❑	124	Howie Long	.25	.08
❑	125	John Elway	1.25	.50
❑	126	Joe Prokop	.05	.01
❑	127	Pepper Johnson	.05	.01
❑	128	Richard Dent	.10	.02
❑	129	Robert Porcher RC	.25	.08
❑	130	Earnest Byner	.05	.01
❑	131	Kent Hull	.05	.01
❑	132	Mike Merriweather	.05	.01
❑	133	Scott Fulhage	.05	.01
❑	134	Kevin Porter	.05	.01
❑	135	Tony Casillas	.05	.01
❑	136	Dean Biasucci	.05	.01
❑	137	Ben Smith	.05	.01
❑	138	Bruce Kozerski	.05	.01
❑	139	Jeff Campbell	.05	.01
❑	140	Kevin Greene	.10	.02
❑	141	Gary Plummer	.05	.01
❑	142	Vincent Brown	.05	.01
❑	143	Ron Hall	.05	.01
❑	144	Louie Aguiar RC	.05	.01
❑	145	Mark Duper	.05	.01
❑	146	Jesse Sapolu	.05	.01
❑	147	Jeff Gossett	.05	.01
❑	148	Brian Noble	.05	.01
❑	149	Derek Russell	.05	.01
❑	150	Carlton Bailey RC	.05	.01
❑	151	Kelly Goodburn	.05	.01
❑	152	Audray McMillian UER	.05	.01
❑	153	Neal Anderson	.05	.01
❑	154	Bill Maas	.05	.01
❑	155	Rickey Jackson	.05	.01
❑	156	Chris Miller	.10	.02
❑	157	Darren Comeaux	.05	.01
❑	158	David Williams	.05	.01
❑	159	Rich Gannon	.25	.08
❑	160	Kevin Mack	.05	.01
❑	161	Jim Arnold	.05	.01
❑	162	Reggie White	.25	.08
❑	163	Leonard Russell	.10	.02
❑	164	Doug Smith	.05	.01
❑	165	Tony Mandarich	.05	.01
❑	166	Greg Lloyd	.10	.02
❑	167	Jumbo Elliott	.05	.01
❑	168	Jonathan Hayes	.05	.01
❑	169	Jim Ritcher	.05	.01
❑	170	Mike Kenn	.05	.01
❑	171	James Washington	.05	.01
❑	172	Tim Harris	.05	.01
❑	173	James Thornton	.05	.01
❑	174	John Brandes RC	.05	.01
❑	175	Fred McAfee RC	.05	.01
❑	176	Henry Rolling	.05	.01
❑	177	Tony Paige	.05	.01
❑	178	Jay Schroeder	.05	.01
❑	179	Jeff Herrod	.05	.01
❑	180	Emmitt Smith	1.50	.60
❑	181	Wymon Henderson	.05	.01
❑	182	Rob Moore	.10	.02
❑	183	Robert Wilson	.05	.01
❑	184	Michael Zordich RC	.05	.01
❑	185	Jim Harbaugh	.25	.08
❑	186	Vince Workman	.05	.01
❑	187	Ernest Givins	.10	.02
❑	188	Herschel Walker	.10	.02
❑	189	Dan Fike	.05	.01
❑	190	Seth Joyner	.05	.01
❑	191	Steve Young	.60	.25
❑	192	Dennis Gibson	.05	.01
❑	193	Darryl Talley	.05	.01
❑	194	Emile Harry	.05	.01
❑	195	Bill Fralic	.05	.01
❑	196	Michael Stewart	.05	.01
❑	197	James Francis	.05	.01
❑	198	Jerome Henderson	.05	.01
❑	199	John L. Williams	.05	.01
❑	200	Rod Woodson	.25	.08
❑	201	Mike Farr	.05	.01
❑	202	Greg Montgomery	.05	.01
❑	203	Andre Collins	.05	.01
❑	204	Scott Miller	.05	.01
❑	205	Clay Matthews	.10	.02
❑	206	Ethan Horton	.05	.01
❑	207	Rich Miano	.05	.01
❑	208	Chris Mims RC	.05	.01
❑	209	Anthony Morgan	.05	.01
❑	210	Rodney Hampton	.10	.02
❑	211	Chris Hinton	.05	.01
❑	212	Esera Tuaolo	.05	.01
❑	213	Shane Conlan	.05	.01
❑	214	John Carney	.05	.01
❑	215	Kenny Walker	.05	.01
❑	216	Scott Radecic	.05	.01
❑	217	Chris Martin	.05	.01
❑	218	Checklist 111-220 UER	.05	.01
❑	219	Wesley Carroll	.05	.01
❑	220	Bill Romanowski	.05	.01
❑	221	Reggie Cobb	.05	.01
❑	222	Alfred Anderson	.05	.01
❑	223	Cleveland Gary	.05	.01
❑	224	Eddie Blake RC	.05	.01
❑	225	Chris Spielman	.10	.02
❑	226	John Roper	.05	.01
❑	227	George Thomas RC	.05	.01
❑	228	Jeff Faulkner	.05	.01
❑	229	Chip Lohmiller UER	.05	.01
❑	230	Hugh Millen	.05	.01
❑	231	Ray Horton	.05	.01
❑	232	James Campen	.05	.01
❑	233	Howard Cross	.05	.01
❑	234	Keith McKeller	.05	.01
❑	235	Dino Hackett	.05	.01
❑	236	Jerome Brown	.05	.01
❑	237	Andy Heck	.05	.01
❑	238	Rodney Holman	.05	.01
❑	239	Bruce Matthews	.05	.01
❑	240	Jeff Lageman	.05	.01
❑	241	Bobby Hebert	.05	.01
❑	242	Gary Anderson K	.05	.01
❑	243	Mark Bortz	.05	.01
❑	244	Rich Moran	.05	.01
❑	245	Jeff Uhlenhake	.05	.01
❑	246	Ricky Sanders	.05	.01
❑	247	Clarence Kay	.05	.01
❑	248	Ed King	.05	.01
❑	249	Eddie Anderson	.05	.01
❑	250	Amp Lee RC	.05	.01
❑	251	Norm Johnson	.05	.01
❑	252	Michael Carter	.05	.01
❑	253	Felix Wright	.05	.01
❑	254	Leon Seals	.05	.01
❑	255	Nate Lewis	.05	.01
❑	256	Kevin Call	.05	.01
❑	257	Darryl Henley	.05	.01
❑	258	Jon Vaughn	.05	.01
❑	259	Matt Bahr	.05	.01
❑	260	Johnny Johnson	.05	.01
❑	261	Ken Norton	.10	.02
❑	262	Wendell Davis	.05	.01
❑	263	Eugene Robinson	.05	.01
❑	264	David Treadwell	.05	.01
❑	265	Michael Haynes	.10	.02
❑	266	Robb Thomas	.05	.01
❑	267	Nate Odomes	.05	.01
❑	268	Martin Mayhew	.05	.01
❑	269	Perry Kemp	.05	.01
❑	270	Jerry Ball	.05	.01
❑	271	Tommy Vardell RC	.05	.01
❑	272	Ernie Mills	.05	.01
❑	273	Mo Lewis	.05	.01
❑	274	Roger Ruzek	.05	.01
❑	275	Steve Smith	.05	.01
❑	276	Bo Orlando RC	.05	.01
❑	277	Louis Oliver	.05	.01
❑	278	Toi Cook	.05	.01
❑	279	Eddie Brown	.05	.01
❑	280	Keith McCants	.05	.01
❑	281	Rob Burnett	.05	.01
❑	282	Keith DeLong	.05	.01
❑	283	Stan Thomas UER	.05	.01
❑	284	Robert Brown	.05	.01
❑	285	John Alt	.05	.01
❑	286	Randy Dixon	.05	.01
❑	287	Siran Stacy RC	.05	.01
❑	288	Ray Agnew	.05	.01
❑	289	Darion Conner	.05	.01
❑	290	Kirk Lowdermilk	.05	.01
❑	291	Greg Jackson	.05	.01
❑	292	Ken Harvey	.05	.01
❑	293	Jacob Green	.05	.01
❑	294	Mark Tuinei	.05	.01
❑	295	Mark Rypien	.05	.01
❑	296	Gerald Robinson RC	.05	.01
❑	297	Broderick Thompson	.05	.01
❑	298	Doug Widell	.05	.01
❑	299	Carwell Gardner	.05	.01
❑	300	Barry Sanders	1.25	.50

❑ 301 Eric Metcalf .10 .02
❑ 302 Eric Thomas .05 .01
❑ 303 Terrell Buckley RC .05 .01
❑ 304 Byron Evans .05 .01
❑ 305 Johnny Hector .05 .01
❑ 306 Steve Broussard .05 .01
❑ 307 Gene Atkins .05 .01
❑ 308 Terry McDaniel .05 .01
❑ 309 Charles McRae .05 .01
❑ 310 Jim Lachey .05 .01
❑ 311 Pat Harlow .05 .01
❑ 312 Kevin Butler .05 .01
❑ 313 Scott Stephen .05 .01
[illegible]
❑ 315 Johnny Meads .05 .01
❑ 316 Checklist 221-330 .05 .01
❑ 317 Aaron Craver .05 .01
❑ 318 Michael Brooks .05 .01
❑ 319 Guy McIntyre .05 .01
❑ 320 Thurman Thomas .25 .08
❑ 321 Courtney Hall .05 .01
❑ 322 Dan Saleaumua .05 .01
❑ 323 Vinson Smith RC .05 .01
❑ 324 Steve Jordan .05 .01
❑ 325 Walter Reeves .05 .01
❑ 326 Erik Kramer .10 .02
❑ 327 Duane Bickett .05 .01
❑ 328 Tom Newberry .05 .01
❑ 329 John Kasay .05 .01
❑ 330 Dave Meggett .10 .02
❑ 331 Kevin Ross .05 .01
❑ 332 Keith Hamilton RC .10 .02
❑ 333 Dwight Stone .05 .01
❑ 334 Mel Gray .10 .02
❑ 335 Harry Galbreath .05 .01
❑ 336 William Perry .10 .02
❑ 337 Brian Blades .10 .02
❑ 338 Randall McDaniel .05 .01
❑ 339 Pat Coleman RC .05 .01
❑ 340 Michael Irvin .25 .08
❑ 341 Checklist 331-440 .05 .01
❑ 342 Chris Mohr .05 .01
❑ 343 Greg Davis .05 .01
❑ 344 Dave Cadigan .05 .01
❑ 345 Art Monk .10 .02
❑ 346 Tim Goad .05 .01
❑ 347 Vinnie Clark .05 .01
❑ 348 David Fulcher .05 .01
❑ 349 Craig Heyward .10 .02
❑ 350 Ronnie Lott .10 .02
❑ 351 Dexter Carter .05 .01
❑ 352 Mark Jackson .05 .01
❑ 353 Brian Jordan .10 .02
❑ 354 Ray Donaldson .05 .01
❑ 355 Jim Price .05 .01
❑ 356 Rod Bernstine .05 .01
❑ 357 Tony Mayberry RC .05 .01
❑ 358 Richard Brown RC .05 .01
❑ 359 David Alexander .05 .01
❑ 360 Haywood Jeffires .10 .02
❑ 361 Henry Thomas .05 .01
❑ 362 Jeff Graham .25 .08
❑ 363 Don Warren .05 .01
❑ 364 Scott Davis .05 .01
❑ 365 Harlon Barnett .05 .01
❑ 366 Mark Collins .05 .01
❑ 367 Rick Tuten .05 .01
❑ 368 Lonnie Marts RC .05 .01
❑ 369 Dennis Smith .05 .01
❑ 370 Steve Tasker .10 .02
❑ 371 Robert Massey .05 .01
❑ 372 Ricky Reynolds .05 .01
❑ 373 Alvin Wright .05 .01
❑ 374 Kelvin Martin .05 .01
❑ 375 Vince Buck .05 .01
❑ 376 John Kidd .05 .01
❑ 377 William White .05 .01
❑ 378 Bryan Cox .10 .02
❑ 379 Jamie Dukes RC .05 .01
❑ 380 Anthony Munoz .10 .02
❑ 381 Mark Gunn RC .05 .01
❑ 382 Keith Henderson .05 .01
❑ 383 Charles Wilson .05 .01
❑ 384 Shawn McCarthy RC .05 .01
❑ 385 Ernie Jones .05 .01
❑ 386 Nick Bell .05 .01
❑ 387 Derrick Walker .05 .01
❑ 388 Mark Stepnoski .10 .02
❑ 389 Broderick Thomas .05 .01
❑ 390 Reggie Roby .05 .01
❑ 391 Bubba McDowell .05 .01
❑ 392 Eric Martin .05 .01
❑ 393 Toby Caston RC .05 .01
❑ 394 Bern Brostek .05 .01
❑ 395 Christian Okoye .05 .01
❑ 396 Frank Minnifield .05 .01
❑ 397 Mike Golic .05 .01
[illegible]
❑ 399 Michael Ball .05 .01
❑ 400 Mike Croel .05 .01
❑ 401 Maury Buford .05 .01
❑ 402 Jeff Bostic UER .05 .01
❑ 403 Sean Landeta .05 .01
❑ 404 Terry Allen .25 .08
❑ 405 Donald Evans .05 .01
❑ 406 Don Mosebar .05 .01
❑ 407 D.J. Dozier .05 .01
❑ 408 Bruce Pickens .05 .01
❑ 409 Jim Dombrowski .05 .01
❑ 410 Deron Cherry .05 .01
❑ 411 Richard Johnson CB .05 .01
❑ 412 Alexander Wright .05 .01
❑ 413 Tom Rathman .05 .01
❑ 414 Mark Dennis .05 .01
❑ 415 Phil Hansen .05 .01
❑ 416 Lonnie Young .05 .01
❑ 417 Burt Grossman .05 .01
❑ 418 Tony Covington .05 .01
❑ 419 John Stephens .05 .01
❑ 420 Jim Everett .10 .02
❑ 421 Johnny Holland .05 .01
❑ 422 Mike Barber RC WR .05 .01
❑ 423 Carl Lee .05 .01
❑ 424 Craig Patterson RC .05 .01
❑ 425 Greg Townsend .05 .01
❑ 426 Brett Perriman .25 .08
❑ 427 Morten Andersen .05 .01
❑ 428 John Gesek .05 .01
❑ 429 Bryan Barker .05 .01
❑ 430 John Taylor .10 .02
❑ 431 Donnell Woolford .05 .01
❑ 432 Ron Holmes .05 .01
❑ 433 Lee Williams .05 .01
❑ 434 Alfred Oglesby .05 .01
❑ 435 Jarrod Bunch .05 .01
❑ 436 Carlton Haselrig RC .05 .01
❑ 437 Rufus Porter .05 .01
❑ 438 Rohn Stark .05 .01
❑ 439 Tony Jones T .05 .01
❑ 440 Andre Rison .10 .02
❑ 441 Eric Hill .05 .01
❑ 442 Jesse Solomon .05 .01
❑ 443 Jackie Slater .05 .01
❑ 444 Donnie Elder .05 .01
❑ 445 Brett Maxie .05 .01
❑ 446 Max Montoya .05 .01
❑ 447 Will Wolford .05 .01
❑ 448 Craig Taylor .05 .01
❑ 449 Jimmie Jones .05 .01
❑ 450 Anthony Carter .10 .02
❑ 451 Brian Bollinger RC .05 .01
❑ 452 Checklist 441-550 .05 .01
❑ 453 Brad Edwards .05 .01
❑ 454 Gene Chilton RC .05 .01
❑ 455 Eric Allen .05 .01
❑ 456 William Roberts .05 .01
❑ 457 Eric Green .05 .01
❑ 458 Irv Eatman .05 .01
❑ 459 Derrick Thomas .25 .08
❑ 460 Tommy Kane .05 .01
❑ 461 LeRoy Butler .05 .01
❑ 462 Oliver Barnett .05 .01
❑ 463 Anthony Smith .05 .01
❑ 464 Cris Dishman .05 .01
❑ 465 Pat Terrell .05 .01
❑ 466 Greg Kragen .05 .01
❑ 467 Rodney Peete .10 .02
❑ 468 Willie Drewrey .05 .01
❑ 469 Jim Wilks .05 .01
❑ 470 Vince Newsome .05 .01
❑ 471 Chris Gardocki .05 .01
❑ 472 Chris Chandler .25 .08
❑ 473 George Thornton .05 .01
❑ 474 Albert Lewis .05 .01
❑ 475 Kevin Glover .05 .01
❑ 476 Joe Bowden RC .05 .01
❑ 477 Harry Sydney .05 .01
❑ 478 Bob Golic .05 .01
❑ 479 Tony Zendejas .05 .01
❑ 480 Brad Baxter .05 .01
❑ 481 Steve Beuerlein .10 .02
[illegible]
❑ 483 Drew Hill .05 .01
❑ 484 Bryan Millard .05 .01
❑ 485 Mark Kelso .05 .01
❑ 486 David Grant .05 .01
❑ 487 Gary Zimmerman .05 .01
❑ 488 Leonard Marshall .05 .01
❑ 489 Keith Jackson .10 .02
❑ 490 Sterling Sharpe .25 .08
❑ 491 Ferrell Edmunds .05 .01
❑ 492 Wilber Marshall .05 .01
❑ 493 Charles Haley .10 .02
❑ 494 Riki Ellison .05 .01
❑ 495 Bill Brooks .05 .01
❑ 496 Bill Hawkins .05 .01
❑ 497 Erik Williams .05 .01
❑ 498 Leon Searcy RC .05 .01
❑ 499 Mike Horan .05 .01
❑ 500 Pat Swilling .05 .01
❑ 501 Maurice Hurst .05 .01
❑ 502 William Fuller .05 .01
❑ 503 Tim Newton .05 .01
❑ 504 Lorenzo Lynch .05 .01
❑ 505 Tim Barnett .05 .01
❑ 506 Tom Thayer .05 .01
❑ 507 Chris Burkett .05 .01
❑ 508 Ronnie Harmon .05 .01
❑ 509 James Brooks .10 .02
❑ 510 Bennie Blades .05 .01
❑ 511 Roger Craig .10 .02
❑ 512 Tony Woods .05 .01
❑ 513 Greg Lewis .05 .01
❑ 514 Erric Pegram .10 .02
❑ 515 Elvis Patterson .05 .01
❑ 516 Jeff Cross .05 .01
❑ 517 Myron Guyton .05 .01
❑ 518 Jay Novacek .10 .02
❑ 519 Leo Barker RC .05 .01
❑ 520 Keith Byars .05 .01
❑ 521 Dalton Hilliard .05 .01
❑ 522 Tod Washington .05 .01
❑ 523 Dexter McNabb RC .05 .01
❑ 524 Frank Reich .10 .02
❑ 525 Henry Ellard .10 .02
❑ 526 Barry Foster .10 .02
❑ 527 Barry Word .05 .01
❑ 528 Gary Anderson RB .05 .01
❑ 529 Reggie Rutland .05 .01
❑ 530 Stephen Baker .05 .01
❑ 531 John Flannery .05 .01
❑ 532 Steve Wright .05 .01
❑ 533 Eric Sanders .05 .01
❑ 534 Bob Whitfield RC .05 .01
❑ 535 Gaston Green .05 .01
❑ 536 Anthony Pleasant .05 .01
❑ 537 Jeff Bryant .05 .01
❑ 538 Jarvis Williams .05 .01
❑ 539 Jim Morrissey .05 .01
❑ 540 Andre Tippett .05 .01
❑ 541 Gill Byrd .05 .01
❑ 542 Raleigh McKenzie .05 .01
❑ 543 Jim Sweeney .05 .01
❑ 544 David Lutz .05 .01
❑ 545 Wayne Martin .05 .01
❑ 546 Karl Wilson .05 .01
❑ 547 Pierce Holt .05 .01
❑ 548 Doug Smith .05 .01
❑ 549 Nolan Harrison RC .05 .01
❑ 550 Freddie Joe Nunn .05 .01
❑ 551 Eric Moore .05 .01
❑ 552 Cris Carter .50 .20

❑ 553 Kevin Gogan .05 .01
❑ 554 Harold Green .05 .01
❑ 555 Kenneth Davis .05 .01
❑ 556 Travis McNeal .05 .01
❑ 557 Jim C. Jensen .05 .01
❑ 558 Willie Green .05 .01
❑ 559 Scott Galbraith RC .05 .01
❑ 560 Louis Lipps .05 .01
❑ 561 Matt Brock .05 .01
❑ 562 Mike Prior .05 .01
❑ 563 Checklist 551-660 .05 .01
❑ 564 Robert Delpino .05 .01
❑ 565 Vinny Testaverde .10 .02
❑ 566 Willie Gault .10 .02
❑ 567 Quinn Early .10 .02
❑ 568 Eric Moten .05 .01
❑ 569 Lance Smith .05 .01
❑ 570 Darrell Green .05 .01
❑ 571 Moe Gardner .05 .01
❑ 572 Steve Atwater .05 .01
❑ 573 Ray Childress .05 .01
❑ 574 Dave Krieg .10 .02
❑ 575 Bruce Armstrong .05 .01
❑ 576 Fred Barnett .25 .08
❑ 577 Don Griffin .05 .01
❑ 578 David Brandon RC .05 .01
❑ 579 Robert Young .05 .01
❑ 580 Keith Van Horne .05 .01
❑ 581 Jeff Criswell .05 .01
❑ 582 Lewis Tillman .05 .01
❑ 583 Bubby Brister .05 .01
❑ 584 Aaron Wallace .05 .01
❑ 585 Chris Doleman .05 .01
❑ 586 Marty Carter RC .05 .01
❑ 587 Chris Warren .25 .08
❑ 588 David Griggs .05 .01
❑ 589 Darrell Thompson .05 .01
❑ 590 Marion Butts .05 .01
❑ 591 Scott Norwood .05 .01
❑ 592 Lomas Brown .05 .01
❑ 593 Daryl Johnston .25 .08
❑ 594 Alonzo Mitz RC .05 .01
❑ 595 Tommy Barnhardt .05 .01
❑ 596 Tim Jorden .05 .01
❑ 597 Neil Smith .25 .08
❑ 598 Todd Marinovich .05 .01
❑ 599 Sean Jones .05 .01
❑ 600 Clarence Verdin .05 .01
❑ 601 Trace Armstrong .05 .01
❑ 602 Steve Bono RC .25 .08
❑ 603 Mark Ingram .05 .01
❑ 604 Flipper Anderson .05 .01
❑ 605 James Jones DT .05 .01
❑ 606 Al Noga .05 .01
❑ 607 Rick Bryan .05 .01
❑ 608 Eugene Lockhart .05 .01
❑ 609 Charles Mann .05 .01
❑ 610 James Hasty .05 .01
❑ 611 Jeff Feagles .05 .01
❑ 612 Tim Brown .25 .08
❑ 613 David Little .05 .01
❑ 614 Keith Sims .05 .01
❑ 615 Kevin Murphy .05 .01
❑ 616 Ray Crockett .05 .01
❑ 617 Jim Jeffcoat .05 .01
❑ 618 Patrick Hunter .05 .01
❑ 619 Keith Kartz .05 .01
❑ 620 Peter Tom Willis .05 .01
❑ 621 Vaughan Johnson .05 .01
❑ 622 Shawn Jefferson .05 .01
❑ 623 Anthony Thompson .05 .01
❑ 624 John Rienstra .05 .01
❑ 625 Don Maggs .05 .01
❑ 626 Todd Lyght .05 .01
❑ 627 Brent Jones .10 .02
❑ 628 Todd McNair .05 .01
❑ 629 Winston Moss .05 .01
❑ 630 Mark Carrier WR .10 .02
❑ 631 Dan Owens .05 .01
❑ 632 Sammie Smith UER .05 .01
❑ 633 James Lofton .10 .02
❑ 634 Paul McJulien RC .05 .01
❑ 635 Tony Tolbert .05 .01
❑ 636 Carnell Lake .05 .01
❑ 637 Gary Clark .25 .08
❑ 638 Brian Washington .05 .01
❑ 639 Jessie Hester .05 .01
❑ 640 Doug Riesenberg .05 .01
❑ 641 Joe Walter RC .05 .01
❑ 642 John Rade .05 .01
❑ 643 Wes Hopkins .05 .01
❑ 644 Kelly Stouffer .05 .01
❑ 645 Marv Cook .05 .01
❑ 646 Ken Clarke .05 .01
❑ 647 Bobby Humphrey UER .05 .01
❑ 648 Tim McDonald .05 .01
❑ 649 Donald Frank RC .05 .01
❑ 650 Richmond Webb .05 .01
❑ 651 Lemuel Stinson .05 .01
❑ 652 Merton Hanks .10 .02
❑ 653 Frank Warren .05 .01
❑ 654 Thomas Benson .05 .01
❑ 655 Al Smith .05 .01
❑ 656 Steve DeBerg .05 .01
❑ 657 Jayice Pearson RC .05 .01
❑ 658 Joe Morris .05 .01
❑ 659 Fred Strickland .05 .01
❑ 660 Kelvin Pritchett .05 .01
❑ 661 Lewis Billups .05 .01
❑ 662 Todd Collins RC .05 .01
❑ 663 Corey Miller RC .05 .01
❑ 664 Levon Kirkland RC .05 .01
❑ 665 Jerry Rice .75 .30
❑ 666 Mike Lodish RC .05 .01
❑ 667 Chuck Smith RC .05 .01
❑ 668 Lance Olberding RC .05 .01
❑ 669 Kevin Smith RC DB .05 .01
❑ 670 Dale Carter RC .10 .02
❑ 671 Sean Gilbert RC .10 .02
❑ 672 Ken O'Brien .05 .01
❑ 673 Ricky Proehl .05 .01
❑ 674 Junior Seau .25 .08
❑ 675 Courtney Hawkins RC .10 .02
❑ 676 Eddie Robinson RC .05 .01
❑ 677 Tommy Jeter RC .05 .01
❑ 678 Jeff George .25 .08
❑ 679 Cary Conklin .05 .01
❑ 680 Rueben Mayes .05 .01
❑ 681 Sean Lumpkin RC .05 .01
❑ 682 Dan Marino 1.25 .50
❑ 683 Ed McDaniel RC .05 .01
❑ 684 Greg Skrepenak RC .05 .01
❑ 685 Tracy Scroggins RC .05 .01
❑ 686 Tommy Maddox RC 2.00 .75
❑ 687 Mike Singletary .10 .02
❑ 688 Patrick Rowe RC .05 .01
❑ 689 Phillippi Sparks RC .05 .01
❑ 690 Joel Steed RC .05 .01
❑ 691 Kevin Fagan .05 .01
❑ 692 Deion Sanders .50 .20
❑ 693 Bruce Smith .25 .08
❑ 694 David Klingler RC .05 .01
❑ 695 Clayton Holmes RC .05 .01
❑ 696 Brett Favre 6.00 2.50
❑ 697 Marc Boutte RC .05 .01
❑ 698 Dwayne Sabb RC .05 .01
❑ 699 Ed McCaffrey .30 .10
❑ 700 Randall Cunningham .25 .08
❑ 701 Quentin Coryatt RC .05 .01
❑ 702 Bernie Kosar .10 .02
❑ 703 Vaughn Dunbar RC .05 .01
❑ 704 Browning Nagle .05 .01
❑ 705 Mark Wheeler RC .05 .01
❑ 706 Paul Siever RC .05 .01
❑ 707 Anthony Miller .10 .02
❑ 708 Corey Widmer RC .05 .01
❑ 709 Eric Dickerson .10 .02
❑ 710 Martin Bayless .05 .01
❑ 711 Jason Hanson RC .10 .02
❑ 712 Michael Dean Perry .10 .02
❑ 713 Billy Joe Tolliver UER .05 .01
❑ 714 Chad Hennings RC .10 .02
❑ 715 Bucky Richardson RC .05 .01
❑ 716 Steve Israel RC .05 .01
❑ 717 Robert Harris RC .05 .01
❑ 718 Timm Rosenbach .05 .01
❑ 719 Joe Montana 1.25 .50
❑ 720 Derek Brown TE RC .05 .01
❑ 721 Robert Brooks RC .75 .30
❑ 722 Boomer Esiason .10 .02
❑ 723 Troy Auzenne RC .05 .01
❑ 724 John Fina RC .05 .01
❑ 725 Chris Crooms RC .05 .01
❑ 726 Eugene Chung RC .05 .01
❑ 727 Darren Woodson RC .25 .08
❑ 728 Leslie O'Neal .10 .02
❑ 729 Dan McGwire .05 .01
❑ 730 Al Toon .10 .02
❑ 731 Michael Brandon RC .05 .01
❑ 732 Steve DeOssie .05 .01
❑ 733 Jim Kelly .25 .08
❑ 734 Webster Slaughter .05 .01
❑ 735 Tony Smith RBK RC .05 .01
❑ 736 Shane Collins RC .05 .01
❑ 737 Randal Hill .05 .01
❑ 738 Chris Holder RC .05 .01
❑ 739 Russell Maryland .05 .01
❑ 740 Carl Pickens RC .25 .08
❑ 741 Andre Reed .10 .02
❑ 742 Steve Emtman RC .05 .01
❑ 743 Carl Banks .05 .01
❑ 744 Troy Aikman .75 .30
❑ 745 Mark Royals .05 .01
❑ 746 J.J.Birden .05 .01
❑ 747 Michael Cofer .05 .01
❑ 748 Darryl Ashmore RC .05 .01
❑ 749 Dion Lambert RC .05 .01
❑ 750 Phil Simms .10 .02
❑ 751 Reggie E.White RC .05 .01
❑ 752 Harvey Williams .25 .08
❑ 753 Ty Detmer .25 .08
❑ 754 Tony Brooks RC .05 .01
❑ 755 Steve Christie .05 .01
❑ 756 Lawrence Taylor .25 .08
❑ 757 Merril Hoge .05 .01
❑ 758 Robert Jones RC .05 .01
❑ 759 Checklist 661-759 .05 .01

1993 Topps

❑ COMPLETE SET (660) 40.00 20.00
❑ COMP.FACT.SET (673) 125.00 75.00
❑ COMP.SERIES 1 (330) 15.00 6.00
❑ COMP.SERIES 2 (330) 10.00 5.00
❑ 1 Art Monk RB .05 .01
❑ 2 Jerry Rice RB .50 .20
❑ 3 Stanley Richard .05 .01
❑ 4 Ron Hall .05 .01
❑ 5 Daryl Johnston .25 .08
❑ 6 Wendell Davis .05 .01
❑ 7 Vaughn Dunbar .05 .01
❑ 8 Mike Jones .05 .01
❑ 9 Anthony Johnson .10 .02
❑ 10 Chris Miller .10 .02
❑ 11 Kyle Clifton .05 .01
❑ 12 Curtis Conway RC .40 .15
❑ 13 Lionel Washington .05 .01
❑ 14 Reggie Johnson .05 .01
❑ 15 David Little .05 .01
❑ 16 Nick Lowery .05 .01
❑ 17 Darryl Williams .05 .01
❑ 18 Brent Jones .10 .02
❑ 19 Bruce Matthews .05 .01
❑ 20 Heath Sherman .05 .01
❑ 21 John Kasay UER .05 .01
❑ 22 Troy Drayton RC .10 .02

❑ 23	Eric Metcalf	.10	.02
❑ 24	Andre Tippett	.05	.01
❑ 25	Rodney Hampton	.10	.02
❑ 26	Henry Jones	.05	.01
❑ 27	Jim Everett	.10	.02
❑ 28	Steve Jordan	.05	.01
❑ 29	LeRoy Butler	.05	.01
❑ 30	Troy Vincent	.05	.01
❑ 31	Nate Lewis	.05	.01
❑ 32	Rickey Jackson	.05	.01
❑ 33	Darion Conner	.05	.01
❑ 34	Tom Carter RC	.10	.02
❑ 35	Jeff George	.25	.08
❑ 36	Larry Centers RC	.25	.08
❑ 37	Reggie Cobb	.05	.01
❑ 38	Mike Saxon	.05	.01
❑ 39	Brad Baxter	.05	.01
❑ 40	Reggie White	.25	.08
❑ 41	Haywood Jeffires	.10	.02
❑ 42	Alfred Williams	.05	.01
❑ 43	Aaron Wallace	.05	.01
❑ 44	Tracy Simien	.05	.01
❑ 45	Pat Harlow	.05	.01
❑ 46	D.J. Johnson	.05	.01
❑ 47	Don Griffin	.05	.01
❑ 48	Flipper Anderson	.05	.01
❑ 49	Keith Kartz	.05	.01
❑ 50	Bernie Kosar	.10	.02
❑ 51	Kent Hull	.05	.01
❑ 52	Erik Howard	.05	.01
❑ 53	Pierce Holt	.05	.01
❑ 54	Dwayne Harper	.05	.01
❑ 55	Bennie Blades	.05	.01
❑ 56	Mark Duper	.05	.01
❑ 57	Brian Noble	.05	.01
❑ 58	Jeff Feagles	.05	.01
❑ 59	Michael Haynes	.10	.02
❑ 60	Junior Seau	.25	.08
❑ 61	Gary Anderson RB	.05	.01
❑ 62	Jon Hand	.05	.01
❑ 63	Lin Elliott RC	.05	.01
❑ 64	Dana Stubblefield RC	.25	.08
❑ 65	Vaughan Johnson	.05	.01
❑ 66	Mo Lewis	.05	.01
❑ 67	Aeneas Williams	.05	.01
❑ 68	David Fulcher	.05	.01
❑ 69	Chip Lohmiller	.05	.01
❑ 70	Greg Townsend	.05	.01
❑ 71	Simon Fletcher	.05	.01
❑ 72	Sean Salisbury	.05	.01
❑ 73	Christian Okoye	.05	.01
❑ 74	Jim Arnold	.05	.01
❑ 75	Bruce Smith	.25	.08
❑ 76	Fred Barnett	.10	.02
❑ 77	Bill Romanowski	.05	.01
❑ 78	Dermontti Dawson	.05	.01
❑ 79	Bern Brostek	.05	.01
❑ 80	Warren Moon	.25	.08
❑ 81	Bill Fralic	.05	.01
❑ 82	Lomas Brown FP	.05	.01
❑ 83	Duane Bickett FP	.05	.01
❑ 84	Neil Smith FP	.10	.02
❑ 85	Reggie White FP	.10	.02
❑ 86	Tim McDonald FP	.05	.01
❑ 87	Leslie O'Neal FP	.05	.01
❑ 88	Steve Young FP	.40	.15
❑ 89	Paul Gruber FP	.05	.01
❑ 90	Wilber Marshall FP	.05	.01
❑ 91	Trace Armstrong	.05	.01
❑ 92	Bobby Houston RC	.05	.01
❑ 93	George Thornton	.05	.01
❑ 94	Keith McCants	.05	.01
❑ 95	Ricky Sanders	.05	.01
❑ 96	Jackie Harris	.05	.01
❑ 97	Todd Marinovich	.05	.01
❑ 98	Henry Thomas	.05	.01
❑ 99	Jeff Wright	.05	.01
❑ 100	John Elway	1.50	.60
❑ 101	Garrison Hearst RC	.75	.30
❑ 102	Roy Foster	.05	.01
❑ 103	David Lang	.05	.01
❑ 104	Matt Stover	.05	.01
❑ 105	Lawrence Taylor	.25	.08
❑ 106	Pete Stoyanovich	.05	.01
❑ 107	Jessie Tuggle	.05	.01
❑ 108	William White	.05	.01
❑ 109	Andy Harmon RC	.10	.02
❑ 110	John L. Williams	.05	.01
❑ 111	Jon Vaughn	.05	.01
❑ 112	John Alt	.05	.01
❑ 113	Chris Jacke	.05	.01
❑ 114	Jim Breech	.05	.01
❑ 115	Eric Martin	.05	.01
❑ 116	Derrick Walker	.05	.01
❑ 117	Ricky Ervins	.05	.01
❑ 118	Roger Craig	.10	.02
❑ 119	Jeff Gossett	.05	.01
❑ 120	Emmitt Smith	1.50	.60
❑ 121	Bob Whitfield	.05	.01
❑ 122	Alonzo Spellman	.05	.01
❑ 123	David Klingler	.05	.01
❑ 124	Tommy Maddox	.25	.08
❑ 125	Robert Porcher	.05	.01
❑ 126	Edgar Bennett	.25	.08
❑ 127	Harvey Williams	.10	.02
❑ 128	Dave Brown RC	.25	.08
❑ 129	Johnny Mitchell	.05	.01
❑ 130	Drew Bledsoe RC	2.50	1.00
❑ 131	Zefross Moss	.05	.01
❑ 132	Nate Odomes	.05	.01
❑ 133	Rufus Porter	.05	.01
❑ 134	Jackie Slater	.05	.01
❑ 135	Steve Young	.75	.30
❑ 136	Chris Calloway	.10	.02
❑ 137	Steve Atwater	.05	.01
❑ 138	Mark Carrier DB	.05	.01
❑ 139	Marvin Washington	.05	.01
❑ 140	Barry Foster	.10	.02
❑ 141	Ricky Reynolds	.05	.01
❑ 142	Bubba McDowell	.05	.01
❑ 143	Dan Footman RC	.05	.01
❑ 144	Richmond Webb	.05	.01
❑ 145	Mike Pritchard	.10	.02
❑ 146	Chris Spielman	.10	.02
❑ 147	Dave Krieg	.10	.02
❑ 148	Nick Bell	.05	.01
❑ 149	Vincent Brown	.05	.01
❑ 150	Seth Joyner	.05	.01
❑ 151	Tommy Kane	.05	.01
❑ 152	Carlton Gray RC	.05	.01
❑ 153	Harry Newsome	.05	.01
❑ 154	Rohn Stark	.05	.01
❑ 155	Shannon Sharpe	.25	.08
❑ 156	Charles Haley	.10	.02
❑ 157	Cornelius Bennett	.10	.02
❑ 158	Doug Riesenberg	.05	.01
❑ 159	Amp Lee	.05	.01
❑ 160	Sterling Sharpe UER	.25	.08
❑ 161	Alonzo Mitz	.05	.01
❑ 162	Pat Terrell	.05	.01
❑ 163	Mark Schlereth	.05	.01
❑ 164	Gary Anderson K	.05	.01
❑ 165	Quinn Early	.10	.02
❑ 166	Jerome Bettis RC	5.00	2.50
❑ 167	Lawrence Dawsey	.05	.01
❑ 168	Derrick Thomas	.25	.08
❑ 169	Rodney Peete	.05	.01
❑ 170	Jim Kelly	.25	.08
❑ 171	Deion Sanders TL	.25	.08
❑ 172	Richard Dent TL	.05	.01
❑ 173	Emmitt Smith TL	.75	.30
❑ 174	Barry Sanders TL	.60	.25
❑ 175	Sterling Sharpe TL	.10	.02
❑ 176	Cleveland Gary TL	.05	.01
❑ 177	Terry Allen TL	.10	.02
❑ 178	Vaughan Johnson TL	.05	.01
❑ 179	Rodney Hampton TL	.05	.01
❑ 180	Randall Cunningham TL	.10	.02
❑ 181	Ricky Proehl TL	.05	.01
❑ 182	Jerry Rice TL	.50	.20
❑ 183	Reggie Cobb TL	.05	.01
❑ 184	Earnest Byner TL	.05	.01
❑ 185	Jeff Lageman	.05	.01
❑ 186	Carlos Jenkins	.05	.01
❑ 187	G.Hearst/Dye/Moore/Cole.	.40	.15
❑ 188	Todd Lyght	.05	.01
❑ 189	Carl Simpson RC	.05	.01
❑ 190	Barry Sanders	1.25	.50
❑ 191	Jim Harbaugh	.25	.08
❑ 192	Roger Ruzek	.05	.01
❑ 193	Brent Williams	.05	.01
❑ 194	Chip Banks	.05	.01
❑ 195	Mike Croel	.05	.01
❑ 196	Marion Butts	.05	.01
❑ 197	James Washington	.05	.01
❑ 198	John Offerdahl	.05	.01
❑ 199	Tom Rathman	.05	.01
❑ 200	Joe Montana	1.50	.60
❑ 201	Pepper Johnson	.05	.01
❑ 202	Cris Dishman	.05	.01
❑ 203	Adrian White RC	.05	.01
❑ 204	Reggie Brooks RC	.10	.02
❑ 205	Cortez Kennedy	.10	.02
❑ 206	Robert Massey	.05	.01
❑ 207	Tol Cook	.05	.01
❑ 208	Harry Sydney	.05	.01
❑ 209	Lincoln Kennedy RC	.05	.01
❑ 210	Randall McDaniel	.05	.01
❑ 211	Eugene Daniel	.05	.01
❑ 212	Rob Burnett	.05	.01
❑ 213	Steve Broussard	.05	.01
❑ 214	Brian Washington	.05	.01
❑ 215	Leonard Renfro RC	.05	.01
❑ 216	Audray McMillian LL	.05	.01
❑ 217	Sterling Sharpe/Miller L	.05	.01
❑ 218	Clyde Simmons LL	.05	.01
❑ 219	Emmitt Smith/B.Foster LL	.40	.15
❑ 220	Steve Young/W.Moon LL	.25	.08
❑ 221	Mel Gray	.10	.02
❑ 222	Luis Sharpe	.05	.01
❑ 223	Eric Moten	.05	.01
❑ 224	Albert Lewis	.05	.01
❑ 225	Alvin Harper	.10	.02
❑ 226	Steve Wallace	.05	.01
❑ 227	Mark Higgs	.05	.01
❑ 228	Eugene Lockhart	.05	.01
❑ 229	Sean Jones	.05	.01
❑ 230	J.Lynch RC/Thom/DuBose	.60	.25
❑ 231	Jimmy Williams	.05	.01
❑ 232	Demetrius DuBose RC	.05	.01
❑ 233	John Roper	.05	.01
❑ 234	Keith Hamilton	.05	.01
❑ 235	Donald Evans	.05	.01
❑ 236	Kenneth Davis	.05	.01
❑ 237	John Copeland RC	.10	.02
❑ 238	Leonard Russell	.10	.02
❑ 239	Ken Harvey	.05	.01
❑ 240	Dale Carter	.05	.01
❑ 241	Anthony Pleasant	.05	.01
❑ 242	Darrell Green	.05	.01
❑ 243	Natrone Means RC	.25	.08
❑ 244	Rob Moore	.10	.02
❑ 245	Chris Doleman	.05	.01
❑ 246	J.B. Brown	.05	.01
❑ 247	Ray Crockett	.05	.01
❑ 248	John Taylor	.10	.02
❑ 249	Russell Maryland	.05	.01
❑ 250	Brett Favre	2.00	.75
❑ 251	Carl Pickens	.10	.02
❑ 252	Andy Heck	.05	.01
❑ 253	Jerome Henderson	.05	.01
❑ 254	Deion Sanders	.50	.20
❑ 255	Steve Emtman	.05	.01
❑ 256	Calvin Williams	.10	.02
❑ 257	Sean Gilbert	.10	.02
❑ 258	Don Beebe	.05	.01
❑ 259	Robert Smith RC	1.25	.50
❑ 260	Robert Blackmon	.05	.01
❑ 261	Jim Kelly TL	.10	.02
❑ 262	Harold Green TL UER	.05	.01
❑ 263	Clay Matthews TL	.05	.01
❑ 264	John Elway TL	.75	.30
❑ 265	Warren Moon TL	.10	.02
❑ 266	Jeff George TL	.10	.02
❑ 267	Derrick Thomas TL	.10	.02
❑ 268	Howie Long TL	.05	.01
❑ 269	Dan Marino TL	.75	.30
❑ 270	Jon Vaughn TL	.05	.01
❑ 271	Chris Burkett TL	.05	.01
❑ 272	Barry Foster TL	.05	.01
❑ 273	Marion Butts TL	.05	.01
❑ 274	Chris Warren TL	.05	.01

❑ 275 M.Strahan RC/M.Buck. 2.00 .75
❑ 276 Tony Casillas .05 .01
❑ 277 Jarrod Bunch .05 .01
❑ 278 Eric Green .05 .01
❑ 279 Stan Brock .05 .01
❑ 280 Chester McGlockton .10 .02
❑ 281 Ricky Watters .25 .08
❑ 282 Dan Saleaumua .05 .01
❑ 283 Rich Camarillo .05 .01
❑ 284 Cris Carter .25 .08
❑ 285 Rick Mirer RC .25 .08
❑ 286 Matt Brock .05 .01
❑ 287 Burt Grossman .05 .01
❑ 288 Andre Collins .05 .01
❑ 289 Mark Jackson .05 .01
❑ 290 Dan Marino 1.50 .60
❑ 291 Cornelius Bennett FG .05 .01
❑ 292 Steve Atwater FG .05 .01
❑ 293 Bryan Cox FG .05 .01
❑ 294 Sam Mills FG .05 .01
❑ 295 Pepper Johnson FG .05 .01
❑ 296 Seth Joyner FG .05 .01
❑ 297 Chris Spielman FG .05 .01
❑ 298 Junior Seau FG .10 .02
❑ 299 Cortez Kennedy FG .05 .01
❑ 300 Broderick Thomas FG .05 .01
❑ 301 Todd McNair .05 .01
❑ 302 Nate Newton .10 .02
❑ 303 Michael Walter .05 .01
❑ 304 Clyde Simmons .05 .01
❑ 305 Ernie Mills .05 .01
❑ 306 Steve Wisniewski .05 .01
❑ 307 Coleman Rudolph RC .05 .01
❑ 308 Thurman Thomas .25 .08
❑ 309 Reggie Roby .05 .01
❑ 310 Eric Swann .10 .02
❑ 311 Mark Wheeler .05 .01
❑ 312 Jeff Herrod .05 .01
❑ 313 Leroy Hoard .10 .02
❑ 314 Patrick Bates RC .05 .01
❑ 315 Earnest Byner .05 .01
❑ 316 Dave Meggett .05 .01
❑ 317 George Teague RC .10 .02
❑ 318 Ray Childress .05 .01
❑ 319 Mike Kenn .05 .01
❑ 320 Jason Hanson .05 .01
❑ 321 Gary Clark .10 .02
❑ 322 Chris Gardocki .05 .01
❑ 323 Ken Norton .10 .02
❑ 324 Eric Curry RC .05 .01
❑ 325 Byron Evans .05 .01
❑ 326 O.J.McDuffie RC .25 .08
❑ 327 Dwight Stone .05 .01
❑ 328 Tommy Barnhardt .05 .01
❑ 329 Checklist 1-165 .05 .01
❑ 330 Checklist 166-329 .05 .01
❑ 331 Erik Williams .05 .01
❑ 332 Phil Hansen .05 .01
❑ 333 Martin Harrison RC .05 .01
❑ 334 Mark Ingram .05 .01
❑ 335 Mark Rypien .05 .01
❑ 336 Anthony Miller .10 .02
❑ 337 Antone Davis .05 .01
❑ 338 Mike Munchak .10 .02
❑ 339 Wayne Martin .05 .01
❑ 340 Joe Montana 1.50 .60
❑ 341 Deon Figures RC .05 .01
❑ 342 Ed McDaniel .05 .01
❑ 343 Chris Burkett .05 .01
❑ 344 Tony Smith RB .05 .01
❑ 345 James Lofton .10 .02
❑ 346 Courtney Hawkins .05 .01
❑ 347 Dennis Smith .05 .01
❑ 348 Anthony Morgan .05 .01
❑ 349 Chris Goode .05 .01
❑ 350 Phil Simms .10 .02
❑ 351 Patrick Hunter .05 .01
❑ 352 Brett Perriman .25 .08
❑ 353 Corey Miller .05 .01
❑ 354 Harry Galbreath .05 .01
❑ 355 Mark Carrier WR .10 .02
❑ 356 Troy Drayton .10 .02
❑ 357 Greg Davis .05 .01
❑ 358 Tim Krumrie .05 .01
❑ 359 Tim McDonald .05 .01
❑ 360 Webster Slaughter .05 .01
❑ 361 Steve Christie .05 .01
❑ 362 Courtney Hall .05 .01
❑ 363 Charles Mann .05 .01
❑ 364 Vestee Jackson .05 .01
❑ 365 Robert Jones .05 .01
❑ 366 Rich Miano .05 .01
❑ 367 Morten Andersen .05 .01
❑ 368 Jeff Graham .10 .02
❑ 369 Martin Mayhew .05 .01
❑ 370 Anthony Carter .10 .02
❑ 371 Greg Kragen .05 .01
❑ 372 Ron Cox .05 .01
❑ 373 Perry Williams .05 .01
❑ 374 Willie Gault .05 .01
❑ 375 Chris Warren .10 .02
❑ 376 Reyna Thompson .05 .01
❑ 377 Bennie Thompson .05 .01
❑ 378 Kevin Mack .05 .01
❑ 379 Clarence Verdin .05 .01
❑ 380 Marc Boutte .05 .01
❑ 381 Marvin Jones RC .05 .01
❑ 382 Greg Jackson .05 .01
❑ 383 Steve Bono .10 .02
❑ 384 Terrell Buckley .05 .01
❑ 385 Garrison Hearst .25 .08
❑ 386 Mike Brim .05 .01
❑ 387 Jesse Sapolu .05 .01
❑ 388 Carl Lee .05 .01
❑ 389 Jeff Cross .05 .01
❑ 390 Karl Mecklenburg .05 .01
❑ 391 Chad Hennings .05 .01
❑ 392 Oliver Barnett .05 .01
❑ 393 Dalton Hilliard .05 .01
❑ 394 Broderick Thompson .05 .01
❑ 395 Rocket Ismail .10 .02
❑ 396 John Kidd .05 .01
❑ 397 Eddie Anderson .05 .01
❑ 398 Lamar Lathon .05 .01
❑ 399 Darren Perry .05 .01
❑ 400 Drew Bledsoe 1.25 .50
❑ 401 Ferrell Edmunds .05 .01
❑ 402 Lomas Brown .05 .01
❑ 403 Drew Hill .05 .01
❑ 404 David Whitmore .05 .01
❑ 405 Mike Johnson .05 .01
❑ 406 Paul Gruber .05 .01
❑ 407 Kirk Lowdermilk .05 .01
❑ 408 Curtis Conway .25 .08
❑ 409 Bryce Paup .10 .02
❑ 410 Boomer Esiason .10 .02
❑ 411 Jay Schroeder .05 .01
❑ 412 Anthony Newman .05 .01
❑ 413 Ernie Jones .05 .01
❑ 414 Carlton Bailey .05 .01
❑ 415 Kenneth Gant .05 .01
❑ 416 Todd Scott .05 .01
❑ 417 Anthony Smith .05 .01
❑ 418 Erik McMillan .05 .01
❑ 419 Ronnie Harmon .05 .01
❑ 420 Andre Reed .10 .02
❑ 421 Wymon Henderson .05 .01
❑ 422 Carnell Lake .05 .01
❑ 423 Al Noga .05 .01
❑ 424 Curtis Duncan .05 .01
❑ 425 Mike Gann .05 .01
❑ 426 Eugene Robinson .05 .01
❑ 427 Scott Mersereau .05 .01
❑ 428 Chris Singleton .05 .01
❑ 429 Gerald Robinson .05 .01
❑ 430 Pat Swilling .05 .01
❑ 431 Ed McCaffrey .25 .08
❑ 432 Neal Anderson .05 .01
❑ 433 Joe Phillips .05 .01
❑ 434 Jerry Ball .05 .01
❑ 435 Tyronne Stowe .05 .01
❑ 436 Dana Stubblefield .25 .08
❑ 437 Eric Curry .05 .01
❑ 438 Derrick Fenner .05 .01
❑ 439 Mark Clayton .05 .01
❑ 440 Quentin Coryatt .10 .02
❑ 441 Willie Roaf RC .10 .02
❑ 442 Ernest Dye .05 .01
❑ 443 Jeff Jaeger .05 .01
❑ 444 Stan Humphries .10 .02
❑ 445 Johnny Johnson .05 .01
❑ 446 Larry Brown DB .05 .01
❑ 447 Kurt Gouveia .05 .01
❑ 448 Qadry Ismail RC .25 .08
❑ 449 Dan Footman .05 .01
❑ 450 Tom Waddle .05 .01
❑ 451 Kelvin Martin .05 .01
❑ 452 Kanavis McGhee .05 .01
❑ 453 Herman Moore .25 .08
❑ 454 Jesse Solomon .05 .01
❑ 455 Shane Conlan .05 .01
❑ 456 Joel Steed .05 .01
❑ 457 Charles Arbuckle .05 .01
❑ 458 Shane Dronett .05 .01
❑ 459 Steve Tasker .10 .02
❑ 460 Herschel Walker .10 .02
❑ 461 Willie Davis .25 .08
❑ 462 Al Smith .05 .01
❑ 463 O.J.McDuffie .25 .08
❑ 464 Kevin Fagan .05 .01
❑ 465 Hardy Nickerson .10 .02
❑ 466 Leonard Marshall .05 .01
❑ 467 John Baylor .05 .01
❑ 468 Jay Novacek .10 .02
❑ 469 Wayne Simmons RC .05 .01
❑ 470 Tommy Vardell .05 .01
❑ 471 Cleveland Gary .05 .01
❑ 472 Mark Collins .05 .01
❑ 473 Craig Heyward .10 .02
❑ 474 John Copeland UER .10 .02
❑ 475 Jeff Hostetler .10 .02
❑ 476 Brian Mitchell .10 .02
❑ 477 Natrone Means .25 .08
❑ 478 Brad Muster .05 .01
❑ 479 David Lutz .05 .01
❑ 480 Andre Rison .10 .02
❑ 481 Michael Zordich .05 .01
❑ 482 Jim McMahon .10 .02
❑ 483 Carlton Gray .05 .01
❑ 484 Chris Mohr .05 .01
❑ 485 Ernest Givins .10 .02
❑ 486 Tony Tolbert .05 .01
❑ 487 Vai Sikahema .05 .01
❑ 488 Larry Webster .05 .01
❑ 489 James Hasty .05 .01
❑ 490 Reggie White .25 .08
❑ 491 Reggie Rivers RC .05 .01
❑ 492 Roman Phifer .05 .01
❑ 493 Levon Kirkland .05 .01
❑ 494 Demetrius DuBose .05 .01
❑ 495 William Perry .10 .02
❑ 496 Clay Matthews .10 .02
❑ 497 Aaron Jones .05 .01
❑ 498 Jack Trudeau .05 .01
❑ 499 Michael Brooks .05 .01
❑ 500 Jerry Rice 1.00 .40
❑ 501 Lonnie Marts .05 .01
❑ 502 Tim McGee .05 .01
❑ 503 Kelvin Pritchett .05 .01
❑ 504 Bobby Hebert .05 .01
❑ 505 Audray McMillian .05 .01
❑ 506 Chuck Cecil .05 .01
❑ 507 Leonard Renfro .05 .01
❑ 508 Ethan Horton .05 .01
❑ 509 Kevin Smith .10 .02
❑ 510 Louis Oliver .05 .01
❑ 511 John Stephens .05 .01
❑ 512 Browning Nagle .05 .01
❑ 513 Ricardo McDonald .05 .01
❑ 514 Leslie O'Neal .10 .02
❑ 515 Lorenzo White .05 .01
❑ 516 Thomas Smith RC .10 .02
❑ 517 Tony Woods .05 .01
❑ 518 Darryl Henley .05 .01
❑ 519 Robert Delpino .05 .01
❑ 520 Rod Woodson .25 .08
❑ 521 Phillippi Sparks .05 .01
❑ 522 Jessie Hester .05 .01
❑ 523 Shaun Gayle .05 .01
❑ 524 Brad Edwards .05 .01
❑ 525 Randall Cunningham .25 .08
❑ 526 Marv Cook .05 .01

❑ 527 Dennis Gibson	.05	.01
❑ 528 Erric Pegram	.10	.02
❑ 529 Terry McDaniel	.05	.01
❑ 530 Troy Aikman	.75	.30
❑ 531 Irving Fryar	.10	.02
❑ 532 Blair Thomas	.05	.01
❑ 533 Jim Wilks	.05	.01
❑ 534 Michael Jackson	.10	.02
❑ 535 Eric Davis	.05	.01
❑ 536 James Campen	.05	.01
❑ 537 Steve Beuerlein	.10	.02
❑ 538 Robert Smith	.50	.20
❑ 539 J.J. Birden	.05	.01
[illegible]	[illegible]	[illegible]
❑ 541 Darryl Talley	.05	.01
❑ 542 Russell Freeman RC	.05	.01
❑ 543 David Alexander	.05	.01
❑ 544 Chris Mims	.05	.01
❑ 545 Coleman Rudolph	.05	.01
❑ 546 Steve McMichael	.10	.02
❑ 547 David Williams	.05	.01
❑ 548 Chris Hinton	.05	.01
❑ 549 Jim Jeffcoat	.05	.01
❑ 550 Howie Long	.25	.08
❑ 551 Roosevelt Potts RC	.05	.01
❑ 552 Bryan Cox	.05	.01
❑ 553 David Richards UER	.05	.01
❑ 554 Reggie Brooks	.10	.02
❑ 555 Neil O'Donnell	.25	.08
❑ 556 Irv Smith RC	.05	.01
❑ 557 Henry Ellard	.10	.02
❑ 558 Steve DeBerg	.05	.01
❑ 559 Jim Sweeney	.05	.01
❑ 560 Harold Green	.05	.01
❑ 561 Darrell Thompson	.05	.01
❑ 562 Vinny Testaverde	.10	.02
❑ 563 Bubby Brister	.05	.01
❑ 564 Sean Landeta	.05	.01
❑ 565 Neil Smith	.25	.08
❑ 566 Craig Erickson	.10	.02
❑ 567 Jim Ritcher	.05	.01
❑ 568 Don Mosebar	.05	.01
❑ 569 John Gesek	.05	.01
❑ 570 Gary Plummer	.05	.01
❑ 571 Norm Johnson	.05	.01
❑ 572 Ron Heller	.05	.01
❑ 573 Carl Simpson	.05	.01
❑ 574 Greg Montgomery	.05	.01
❑ 575 Dana Hall	.05	.01
❑ 576 Vencie Glenn	.05	.01
❑ 577 Dean Biasucci	.05	.01
❑ 578 Rod Bernstine UER	.05	.01
❑ 579 Randal Hill	.05	.01
❑ 580 Sam Mills	.05	.01
❑ 581 Santana Dotson	.10	.02
❑ 582 Greg Lloyd	.10	.02
❑ 583 Eric Thomas	.05	.01
❑ 584 Henry Rolling	.05	.01
❑ 585 Tony Bennett	.05	.01
❑ 586 Sheldon White	.05	.01
❑ 587 Mark Kelso	.05	.01
❑ 588 Marc Spindler	.05	.01
❑ 589 Greg McMurtry	.05	.01
❑ 590 Art Monk	.10	.02
❑ 591 Marco Coleman	.05	.01
❑ 592 Tony Jones T	.05	.01
❑ 593 Melvin Jenkins	.05	.01
❑ 594 Kevin Ross	.05	.01
❑ 595 William Fuller	.05	.01
❑ 596 James Joseph	.05	.01
❑ 597 Lamar McGriggs RC	.05	.01
❑ 598 Gill Byrd	.05	.01
❑ 599 Alexander Wright	.05	.01
❑ 600 Rick Mirer	.25	.08
❑ 601 Richard Dent	.10	.02
❑ 602 Thomas Everett	.05	.01
❑ 603 Jack Del Rio	.05	.01
❑ 604 Jerome Bettis	2.50	1.00
❑ 605 Ronnie Lott	.10	.02
❑ 606 Marty Carter	.05	.01
❑ 607 Arthur Marshall RC	.05	.01
❑ 608 Lee Johnson	.05	.01
❑ 609 Bruce Armstrong	.05	.01
❑ 610 Ricky Proehl	.05	.01
❑ 611 Will Wolford	.05	.01
❑ 612 Mike Prior	.05	.01
❑ 613 George Jamison	.05	.01
❑ 614 Gene Atkins	.05	.01
❑ 615 Merril Hoge	.05	.01
❑ 616 Desmond Howard	.10	.02
❑ 617 Jarvis Williams	.05	.01
❑ 618 Marcus Allen	.25	.08
❑ 619 Gary Brown	.05	.01
❑ 620 Bill Brooks	.05	.01
❑ 621 Eric Allen	.05	.01
❑ 622 Todd Kelly	.05	.01
❑ 623 Michael Dean Perry	.10	.02
[illegible]	[illegible]	[illegible]
❑ 625 Mike Sherrard	.05	.01
❑ 626 Jeff Bryant	.05	.01
❑ 627 Eric Bieniemy	.05	.01
❑ 628 Tim Brown	.25	.08
❑ 629 Troy Auzenne	.05	.01
❑ 630 Michael Irvin	.25	.08
❑ 631 Maurice Hurst	.05	.01
❑ 632 Duane Bickett	.05	.01
❑ 633 George Teague	.10	.02
❑ 634 Vince Workman	.05	.01
❑ 635 Renaldo Turnbull	.05	.01
❑ 636 Johnny Bailey	.05	.01
❑ 637 Dan Williams RC	.05	.01
❑ 638 James Thornton	.05	.01
❑ 639 Terry Allen	.25	.08
❑ 640 Kevin Greene	.10	.02
❑ 641 Tony Zendejas	.05	.01
❑ 642 Scott Kowalkowski RC	.05	.01
❑ 643 Jeff Query UER	.05	.01
❑ 644 Brian Blades	.10	.02
❑ 645 Keith Jackson	.10	.02
❑ 646 Monte Coleman	.05	.01
❑ 647 Guy McIntyre	.05	.01
❑ 648 Barry Word	.05	.01
❑ 649 Steve Everitt RC	.05	.01
❑ 650 Patrick Bates	.05	.01
❑ 651 Marcus Robertson RC	.05	.01
❑ 652 John Carney	.05	.01
❑ 653 Derek Brown TE	.05	.01
❑ 654 Carwell Gardner	.05	.01
❑ 655 Moe Gardner	.05	.01
❑ 656 Andre Ware	.05	.01
❑ 657 Keith Van Horne	.05	.01
❑ 658 Hugh Millen	.05	.01
❑ 659 Checklist 330-495	.05	.01
❑ 660 Checklist 496-660	.05	.01

1994 Topps

❑ COMPLETE SET (660)	80.00	40.00
❑ COMP.FACT.SET	80.00	45.00
❑ COMP.SERIES 1 (330)	25.00	12.50
❑ COMP.SERIES 2 (330)	25.00	12.50
❑ 1 Emmitt Smith	1.50	.60
❑ 2 Russell Copeland	.05	.01
❑ 3 Jesse Sapolu	.05	.01
❑ 4 David Szott	.05	.01
❑ 5 Rodney Hampton	.10	.02
❑ 6 Bubba McDowell	.05	.01
❑ 7 Bryce Paup	.10	.02
❑ 8 Winston Moss	.05	.01
❑ 9 Brett Perriman	.10	.02
❑ 10 Rod Woodson	.10	.02
❑ 11 John Randle	.10	.02
❑ 12 David Wyman	.05	.01
❑ 13 Jeff Cross	.05	.01
❑ 14 Richard Cooper	.05	.01
❑ 15 Johnny Mitchell	.05	.01
❑ 16 David Alexander	.05	.01
❑ 17 Ronnie Harmon	.05	.01
❑ 18 Tyronne Stowe UER	.05	.01
❑ 19 Chris Zorich	.05	.01
❑ 20 Rob Burnett	.05	.01
❑ 21 Harold Alexander	.05	.01
❑ 22 Rod Stephens	.05	.01
❑ 23 Mark Wheeler	.05	.01
❑ 24 Dwayne Sabb	.05	.01
[illegible]	[illegible]	[illegible]
❑ 26 Kurt Gouveia	.05	.01
❑ 27 Warren Moon	.25	.08
❑ 28 Jeff Query	.05	.01
❑ 29 Chuck Levy RC	.05	.01
❑ 30 Bruce Smith	.25	.08
❑ 31 Doug Riesenberg	.05	.01
❑ 32 Willie Drewrey	.05	.01
❑ 33 Nate Newton UER	.05	.01
❑ 34 James Jett	.05	.01
❑ 35 George Teague	.05	.01
❑ 36 Marc Spindler	.05	.01
❑ 37 Jack Del Rio	.05	.01
❑ 38 Dale Carter	.05	.01
❑ 39 Steve Atwater	.05	.01
❑ 40 Herschel Walker	.10	.02
❑ 41 James Hasty	.05	.01
❑ 42 Seth Joyner	.05	.01
❑ 43 Keith Jackson	.05	.01
❑ 44 Tommy Vardell	.05	.01
❑ 45 Antonio Langham RC	.10	.02
❑ 46 Derek Brown RBK	.05	.01
❑ 47 John Wojciechowski	.05	.01
❑ 48 Horace Copeland	.05	.01
❑ 49 Luis Sharpe	.05	.01
❑ 50 Pat Harlow	.05	.01
❑ 51 David Palmer RC	.25	.08
❑ 52 Tony Smith RB	.05	.01
❑ 53 Tim Johnson	.05	.01
❑ 54 Anthony Newman	.05	.01
❑ 55 Terry Wooden	.05	.01
❑ 56 Derrick Fenner	.05	.01
❑ 57 Mike Fox	.05	.01
❑ 58 Brad Hopkins	.05	.01
❑ 59 Daryl Johnston UER	.10	.02
❑ 60 Steve Young	.75	.30
❑ 61 Scottie Graham RC	.10	.02
❑ 62 Nolan Harrison	.05	.01
❑ 63 David Richards	.05	.01
❑ 64 [illegible]	.05	.01
❑ 65 Hardy Nickerson	.10	.02
❑ 66 Heath Sherman	.05	.01
❑ 67 Irving Fryar	.10	.02
❑ 68 Ray Buchanan UER	.05	.01
❑ 69 Jay Taylor	.05	.01
❑ 70 Shannon Sharpe	.10	.02
❑ 71 Vinny Testaverde	.10	.02
❑ 72 Renaldo Turnbull	.05	.01
❑ 73 Dwight Stone	.05	.01
❑ 74 Willie McGinest RC	.25	.08
❑ 75 Darrell Green	.05	.01
❑ 76 Kyle Clifton	.05	.01
❑ 77 Leo Goeas	.05	.01
❑ 78 Ken Ruettgers	.05	.01
❑ 79 Craig Heyward	.10	.02
❑ 80 Andre Rison	.10	.02
❑ 81 Chris Mims	.05	.01
❑ 82 Gary Clark	.10	.02
❑ 83 Ricardo McDonald	.05	.01
❑ 84 Patrick Hunter	.05	.01
❑ 85 Bruce Matthews	.05	.01
❑ 86 Russell Maryland	.05	.01
❑ 87 Gary Anderson K	.05	.01
❑ 88 Brad Edwards	.05	.01
❑ 89 Carlton Bailey	.05	.01
❑ 90 Qadry Ismail	.25	.08
❑ 91 Terry McDaniel	.05	.01
❑ 92 Willie Green	.05	.01
❑ 93 Cornelius Bennett	.10	.02
❑ 94 Paul Gruber	.05	.01
❑ 95 Pete Stoyanovich	.05	.01

96	Merton Hanks	.10	.02
97	Tre Johnson RC	.05	.01
98	Jonathan Hayes	.05	.01
99	Jason Elam	.10	.02
100	Jerome Bettis	.50	.20
101	Ronnie Lott	.10	.02
102	Maurice Hurst	.05	.01
103	Kirk Lowdermilk	.05	.01
104	Tony Jones T	.05	.01
105	Steve Beuerlein	.10	.02
106	Isaac Davis RC	.05	.01
107	Vaughan Johnson	.05	.01
108	Terrell Buckley	.05	.01
109	Pierce Holt	.05	.01
110	Alonzo Spellman	.05	.01
111	Patrick Robinson	.05	.01
112	Cortez Kennedy	.10	.02
113	Kevin Williams WR	.10	.02
114	Danny Copeland	.05	.01
115	Chris Doleman	.05	.01
116	Jerry Rice LL	.50	.20
117	Neil Smith LL	.10	.02
118	Emmitt Smith LL	.75	.30
119	E.Robinson/Odomes LL	.05	.01
120	Steve Young LL	.25	.08
121	Carnell Lake	.05	.01
122	Ernest Givins UER	.10	.02
123	Henry Jones	.05	.01
124	Michael Brooks	.05	.01
125	Jason Hanson	.05	.01
126	Andy Harmon	.05	.01
127	Errict Rhett RC	.25	.08
128	Harris Barton	.05	.01
129	Greg Robinson	.05	.01
130	Derrick Thomas	.25	.08
131	Keith Kartz	.05	.01
132	Lincoln Kennedy	.05	.01
133	Leslie O'Neal	.05	.01
134	Tim Goad	.05	.01
135	Rohn Stark	.05	.01
136	O.J.McDuffie	.25	.08
137	Donnell Woolford	.05	.01
138	Jamir Miller RC	.10	.02
139	Eric Thomas UER	.05	.01
140	Willie Roaf	.05	.01
141	Wayne Gandy RC	.05	.01
142	Mike Brim	.05	.01
143	Kelvin Martin	.05	.01
144	Edgar Bennett	.25	.08
145	Michael Dean Perry	.10	.02
146	Shante Carver RC	.05	.01
147	Jessie Armstead UER	.05	.01
148	Mo Elewonibi	.05	.01
149	Dana Stubblefield	.10	.02
150	Cody Carlson	.05	.01
151	Vencie Glenn	.05	.01
152	Levon Kirkland	.05	.01
153	Derrick Moore	.05	.01
154	John Fina	.05	.01
155	Jeff Hostetler	.10	.02
156	Courtney Hawkins	.05	.01
157	Todd Collins	.05	.01
158	Neil Smith	.10	.02
159	Simon Fletcher	.05	.01
160	Dan Marino	2.00	.75
161	Sam Adams RC	.10	.02
162	Marvin Washington	.05	.01
163	John Copeland	.05	.01
164	Eugene Robinson	.05	.01
165	Mark Carrier DB	.05	.01
166	Mike Kenn	.05	.01
167	Tyrone Hughes	.10	.02
168	Darren Carrington	.05	.01
169	Shane Conlan	.05	.01
170	Ricky Proehl	.05	.01
171	Jeff Herrod	.05	.01
172	Mark Carrier WR	.10	.02
173	George Koonce	.05	.01
174	Desmond Howard	.10	.02
175	Dave Meggett	.05	.01
176	Charles Haley	.10	.02
177	Steve Wisniewski	.05	.01
178	Dermontti Dawson	.05	.01
179	Tim McDonald	.05	.01
180	Broderick Thomas	.05	.01
181	Bernard Dafney	.05	.01
182	Bo Orlando	.05	.01
183	Andre Reed	.10	.02
184	Randall Cunningham	.25	.08
185	Chris Spielman	.10	.02
186	Keith Byars	.05	.01
187	Ben Coates	.10	.02
188	Tracy Simien	.05	.01
189	Carl Pickens	.10	.02
190	Reggie White	.25	.08
191	Norm Johnson	.05	.01
192	Brian Washington	.05	.01
193	Stan Humphries	.10	.02
194	Fred Stokes	.05	.01
195	Dan Williams	.05	.01
196	John Elway TOG	.75	.30
197	Eric Allen TOG	.05	.01
198	Hardy Nickerson TOG	.10	.02
199	Jerome Bettis TOG	.25	.08
200	Troy Aikman TOG	.50	.20
201	Thurman Thomas TOG	.10	.02
202	Cornelius Bennett TOG UER	.10	.02
203	Michael Irvin TOG	.10	.02
204	Jim Kelly TOG	.10	.02
205	Junior Seau TOG	.10	.02
206	Heath Shuler RC UER	.25	.08
207	Howard Cross UER	.05	.01
208	Pat Swilling	.05	.01
209	Pete Metzelaars	.05	.01
210	Tony McGee	.05	.01
211	Neil O'Donnell	.25	.08
212	Eugene Chung	.05	.01
213	J.B. Brown	.05	.01
214	Marcus Allen	.25	.08
215	Harry Newsome	.05	.01
216	Greg Hill RC	.25	.08
217	Ryan Yarborough	.05	.01
218	Marty Carter	.05	.01
219	Bern Brostek	.05	.01
220	Boomer Esiason	.10	.02
221	Vince Buck	.05	.01
222	Jim Jeffcoat	.05	.01
223	Bob Dahl	.05	.01
224	Marion Butts	.05	.01
225	Ronald Moore	.05	.01
226	Robert Blackmon	.05	.01
227	Curtis Conway	.25	.08
228	Jon Hand	.05	.01
229	Shane Dronett	.05	.01
230	Erik Williams UER	.05	.01
231	Dennis Brown	.05	.01
232	Ray Childress	.05	.01
233	Johnnie Morton RC	.50	.20
234	Kent Hull	.05	.01
235	John Elliott	.05	.01
236	Ron Heller	.05	.01
237	J.J. Birden	.05	.01
238	Thomas Randolph RC	.05	.01
239	Chip Lohmiller	.05	.01
240	Tim Brown	.25	.08
241	Steve Tovar	.05	.01
242	Moe Gardner	.05	.01
243	Vincent Brown	.05	.01
244	Tony Zendejas	.05	.01
245	Eric Allen	.05	.01
246	Joe King RC	.05	.01
247	Mo Lewis	.05	.01
248	Rod Bernstine	.05	.01
249	Tom Waddle	.05	.01
250	Junior Seau	.25	.08
251	Eric Metcalf	.10	.02
252	Cris Carter	.50	.20
253	Bill Hitchcock	.05	.01
254	Zefross Moss	.05	.01
255	Morten Andersen	.05	.01
256	Keith Rucker RC	.05	.01
257	Chris Jacke	.05	.01
258	Richmond Webb	.05	.01
259	Herman Moore	.25	.08
260	Phil Simms	.10	.02
261	Mark Tuinei	.05	.01
262	Don Beebe	.05	.01
263	Marc Logan	.05	.01
264	Willie Davis	.10	.02
265	David Klingler	.05	.01
266	Martin Mayhew UER	.05	.01
267	Mark Bavaro	.05	.01
268	Greg Lloyd	.10	.02
269	Al Del Greco	.05	.01
270	Reggie Brooks	.10	.02
271	Greg Townsend	.05	.01
272	Rohn Stark CAL	.05	.01
273	Marcus Allen CAL	.10	.02
274	Ronnie Lott CAL	.10	.02
275	Dan Marino CAL	.75	.30
276	Sean Gilbert	.05	.01
277	LeRoy Butler	.05	.01
278	Troy Auzenne	.05	.01
279	Eric Swann	.10	.02
280	Quentin Coryatt	.05	.01
281	Anthony Pleasant	.05	.01
282	Brad Baxter	.05	.01
283	Carl Lee	.05	.01
284	Courtney Hall	.05	.01
285	Quinn Early	.10	.02
286	Eddie Robinson	.05	.01
287	Marco Coleman	.05	.01
288	Harold Green	.05	.01
289	Santana Dotson	.10	.02
290	Robert Porcher	.05	.01
291	Joe Phillips	.05	.01
292	Mark McMillian	.05	.01
293	Eric Davis	.05	.01
294	Mark Jackson	.05	.01
295	Darryl Talley	.05	.01
296	Curtis Duncan	.05	.01
297	Bruce Armstrong	.05	.01
298	Eric Hill	.05	.01
299	Andre Collins	.05	.01
300	Jay Novacek	.10	.02
301	Roosevelt Potts	.05	.01
302	Eric Martin	.05	.01
303	Chris Warren	.10	.02
304	Deral Boykin RC	.05	.01
305	Jessie Tuggle	.05	.01
306	Glyn Milburn	.10	.02
307	Terry Obee	.05	.01
308	Eric Turner	.05	.01
309	Dewayne Washington RC	.10	.02
310	Sterling Sharpe	.10	.02
311	Jeff Gossett	.05	.01
312	John Carney	.05	.01
313	Aaron Glenn RC	.25	.08
314	Nick Lowery	.05	.01
315	Thurman Thomas	.25	.08
316	Troy Aikman MG	.50	.20
317	Thurman Thomas MG	.10	.02
318	Michael Irvin MG	.10	.02
319	Steve Beuerlein MG	.10	.02
320	Jerry Rice	1.00	.40
321	Alexander Wright	.05	.01
322	Michael Bates	.05	.01
323	Greg Davis	.05	.01
324	Mark Bortz	.05	.01
325	Kevin Greene	.10	.02
326	Wayne Simmons	.05	.01
327	Wayne Martin	.05	.01
328	Michael Irvin UER	.25	.08
329	Checklist Card	.05	.01
330	Checklist Card	.05	.01
331	Doug Pelfrey	.05	.01
332	Myron Guyton	.05	.01
333	Howard Ballard	.05	.01
334	Ricky Ervins	.05	.01
335	Steve Emtman	.05	.01
336	Eric Curry	.05	.01
337	Bert Emanuel RC	.25	.08
338	Darryl Ashmore	.05	.01
339	Stevon Moore	.05	.01
340	Garrison Hearst	.25	.08
341	Vance Johnson	.05	.01
342	Anthony Johnson	.10	.02
343	Merril Hoge	.05	.01
344	William Thomas	.05	.01
345	Scott Mitchell	.10	.02
346	Jim Everett	.10	.02
347	Ray Crockett	.05	.01

❑ 348 Bryan Cox .05 .01
❑ 349 Charles Johnson RC .25 .08
❑ 350 Randall McDaniel .05 .01
❑ 351 Micheal Barrow .05 .01
❑ 352 Darrell Thompson .05 .01
❑ 353 Kevin Gogan .05 .01
❑ 354 Brad Daluiso .05 .01
❑ 355 Mark Collins .05 .01
❑ 356 Bryant Young RC .40 .15
❑ 357 Steve Christie .05 .01
❑ 358 Derek Kennard .05 .01
❑ 359 Jon Vaughn .05 .01
❑ 360 Drew Bledsoe 3X .75 .30
❑ 361 Randy Baldwin .05 .01
❑ 362 Kevin Ross .05 .01
❑ 363 Reuben Davis .05 .01
❑ 364 Chris Miller .05 .01
❑ 365 Tim McGee .05 .01
❑ 366 Tony Woods .05 .01
❑ 367 Dean Biasucci .05 .01
❑ 368 George Jamison .05 .01
❑ 369 Lorenzo Lynch .05 .01
❑ 370 Johnny Johnson .05 .01
❑ 371 Greg Kragen .05 .01
❑ 372 Vinson Smith .05 .01
❑ 373 Vince Workman .05 .01
❑ 374 Allen Aldridge .05 .01
❑ 375 Terry Kirby .25 .08
❑ 376 Mario Bates RC .25 .08
❑ 377 Dixon Edwards .05 .01
❑ 378 Leon Searcy .05 .01
❑ 379 Eric Guliford RC .05 .01
❑ 380 Gary Brown .05 .01
❑ 381 Phil Hansen .05 .01
❑ 382 Keith Hamilton .05 .01
❑ 383 John Alt .05 .01
❑ 384 John Taylor .10 .02
❑ 385 Reggie Cobb .05 .01
❑ 386 Rob Fredrickson RC .10 .02
❑ 387 Pepper Johnson .05 .01
❑ 388 Kevin Lee RC .05 .01
❑ 389 Stanley Richard .05 .01
❑ 390 Jackie Slater .05 .01
❑ 391 Darrick Brilz .05 .01
❑ 392 John Gesek .05 .01
❑ 393 Kelvin Pritchett .05 .01
❑ 394 Aeneas Williams .05 .01
❑ 395 Henry Ford .05 .01
❑ 396 Eric Mahlum .05 .01
❑ 397 Tom Rouen .05 .01
❑ 398 Vinnie Clark .05 .01
❑ 399 Jim Sweeney .05 .01
❑ 400 Troy Aikman 1.00 .40
❑ 401 Toi Cook .05 .01
❑ 402 Dan Saleaumua .05 .01
❑ 403 Andy Heck .05 .01
❑ 404 Deon Figures .05 .01
❑ 405 Henry Thomas .05 .01
❑ 406 Glenn Montgomery .05 .01
❑ 407 Trent Dilfer RC 1.00 .40
❑ 408 Eddie Murray .05 .01
❑ 409 Gene Atkins .05 .01
❑ 410 Mike Sherrard .05 .01
❑ 411 Don Mosebar .05 .01
❑ 412 Thomas Smith .05 .01
❑ 413 Ken Norton Jr. .10 .02
❑ 414 Robert Brooks .25 .08
❑ 415 Jeff Lageman .05 .01
❑ 416 Tony Siragusa .05 .01
❑ 417 Brian Blades .10 .02
❑ 418 Matt Stover .05 .01
❑ 419 Jesse Solomon .05 .01
❑ 420 Reggie Roby .05 .01
❑ 421 Shawn Jefferson .05 .01
❑ 422 Marc Boutte .05 .01
❑ 423 William White .05 .01
❑ 424 Clyde Simmons .05 .01
❑ 425 Anthony Miller .10 .02
❑ 426 Brent Jones .10 .02
❑ 427 Tim Grunhard .05 .01
❑ 428 Alfred Williams .05 .01
❑ 429 Roy Barker RC .05 .01
❑ 430 Dante Jones .05 .01
❑ 431 Leroy Thompson .05 .01
❑ 432 Marcus Robertson .05 .01
❑ 433 Thomas Lewis RC .10 .02
❑ 434 Sean Jones .05 .01
❑ 435 Michael Haynes .10 .02
❑ 436 Albert Lewis .05 .01
❑ 437 Tim Bowens RC .10 .02
❑ 438 Marvcus Patton .05 .01
❑ 439 Rich Miano .05 .01
❑ 440 Craig Erickson .05 .01
❑ 441 Larry Allen RC .25 .08
❑ 442 Fernando Smith .05 .01
❑ 443 D.J. Johnson .05 .01
❑ 444 Leonard Russell .05 .01
❑ 445 Marshall Faulk RC 5.00 2.00
❑ 446 Najee Mustafaa .05 .01
❑ 447 Brian Hansen .05 .01
❑ 448 Isaac Bruce RC 4.00 2.00
❑ 449 Kevin Scott .05 .01
❑ 450 Natrone Means UER .25 .08
❑ 451 Tracy Rogers RC .05 .01
❑ 452 Mike Croel .05 .01
❑ 453 Anthony Edwards .05 .01
❑ 454 Brentson Buckner RC .05 .01
❑ 455 Tom Carter .05 .01
❑ 456 Burt Grossman .05 .01
❑ 457 Jimmy Spencer RC .05 .01
❑ 458 Rocket Ismail .10 .02
❑ 459 Fred Strickland .05 .01
❑ 460 Jeff Burris RC .10 .02
❑ 461 Adrian Hardy .05 .01
❑ 462 Lamar McGriggs .05 .01
❑ 463 Webster Slaughter .05 .01
❑ 464 Demetrius DuBose .05 .01
❑ 465 Dave Brown .10 .02
❑ 466 Kenneth Gant .05 .01
❑ 467 Erik Kramer .10 .02
❑ 468 Mark Ingram .05 .01
❑ 469 Roman Phifer .05 .01
❑ 470 Steve Young .50 .20
❑ 471 Nick Lowery .05 .01
❑ 472 Irving Fryar .10 .02
❑ 473 Art Monk .10 .02
❑ 474 Mel Gray .05 .01
❑ 475 Reggie White .25 .08
❑ 476 Eric Ball .05 .01
❑ 477 Dwayne Harper .05 .01
❑ 478 Will Shields .05 .01
❑ 479 Roger Harper .05 .01
❑ 480 Rick Mirer .25 .08
❑ 481 Vincent Brisby .10 .02
❑ 482 John Jurkovic RC .10 .02
❑ 483 Michael Jackson .10 .02
❑ 484 Ed Cunningham .05 .01
❑ 485 Brad Ottis .05 .01
❑ 486 Sterling Palmer RC .05 .01
❑ 487 Tony Bennett .05 .01
❑ 488 Mike Pritchard .05 .01
❑ 489 Bucky Brooks RC .05 .01
❑ 490 Troy Vincent .05 .01
❑ 491 Eric Green .05 .01
❑ 492 Van Malone .05 .01
❑ 493 Marcus Spears RC .05 .01
❑ 494 Brian Williams OL .05 .01
❑ 495 Robert Smith .25 .08
❑ 496 Haywood Jeffires .10 .02
❑ 497 Darrin Smith .05 .01
❑ 498 Tommy Barnhardt .05 .01
❑ 499 Anthony Smith .05 .01
❑ 500 Ricky Watters .10 .02
❑ 501 Antone Davis .05 .01
❑ 502 David Braxton .05 .01
❑ 503 Donnell Bennett RC .25 .08
❑ 504 Donald Evans .05 .01
❑ 505 Lewis Tillman .05 .01
❑ 506 Lance Smith .05 .01
❑ 507 Aaron Taylor .05 .01
❑ 508 Ricky Sanders .05 .01
❑ 509 Dennis Smith .05 .01
❑ 510 Barry Foster .05 .01
❑ 511 Stan Brock .05 .01
❑ 512 Henry Rolling .05 .01
❑ 513 Walter Reeves .05 .01
❑ 514 John Booty .05 .01
❑ 515 Kenneth Davis .05 .01
❑ 516 Cris Dishman .05 .01
❑ 517 Bill Lewis .05 .01
❑ 518 Jeff Bryant .05 .01
❑ 519 Brian Mitchell .05 .01
❑ 520 Joe Montana 2.00 .75
❑ 521 Keith Sims .05 .01
❑ 522 Harry Colon .05 .01
❑ 523 Leon Lett .05 .01
❑ 524 Carlos Jenkins .05 .01
❑ 525 Victor Bailey .05 .01
❑ 526 Harvey Williams .10 .02
❑ 527 Irv Smith .05 .01
❑ 528 Jason Sehorn RC .40 .15
❑ 529 John Thierry RC .05 .01
❑ 530 Brett Favre 2.00 .75
❑ 531 Sean Dawkins RC .25 .08
❑ 532 Erric Pegram .05 .01
❑ 533 Jimmy Williams .05 .01
❑ 534 Michael Timpson .05 .01
❑ 535 Flipper Anderson .05 .01
❑ 536 John Parrella .05 .01
❑ 537 Freddie Joe Nunn .05 .01
❑ 538 Doug Dawson .05 .01
❑ 539 Michael Stewart .05 .01
❑ 540 John Elway 2.00 .75
❑ 541 Ronnie Lott .10 .02
❑ 542 Barry Sanders TOG .75 .30
❑ 543 Andre Reed TOG .10 .02
❑ 544 Deion Sanders TOG .25 .08
❑ 545 Dan Marino TOG .75 .30
❑ 546 Carlton Bailey TOG .05 .01
❑ 547 Emmitt Smith TOG .75 .30
❑ 548 Alvin Harper TOG .10 .02
❑ 549 Eric Metcalf TOG .10 .02
❑ 550 Jerry Rice TOG .50 .20
❑ 551 Derrick Thomas TOG .25 .08
❑ 552 Mark Collins TOG .05 .01
❑ 553 Eric Turner TOG .05 .01
❑ 554 Sterling Sharpe TOG .10 .02
❑ 555 Steve Young TOG .25 .08
❑ 556 Darnay Scott RC .50 .20
❑ 557 Joel Steed .05 .01
❑ 558 Dennis Gibson .05 .01
❑ 559 Charles Mincy .05 .01
❑ 560 Rickey Jackson .05 .01
❑ 561 Dave Cadigan .05 .01
❑ 562 Rick Tuten .05 .01
❑ 563 Mike Caldwell .05 .01
❑ 564 Todd Steussie RC .10 .02
❑ 565 Kevin Smith .05 .01
❑ 566 Arthur Marshall .05 .01
❑ 567 Aaron Wallace .05 .01
❑ 568 Calvin Williams .10 .02
❑ 569 Todd Kelly .05 .01
❑ 570 Barry Sanders 1.50 .60
❑ 571 Shaun Gayle .05 .01
❑ 572 Will Wolford .05 .01
❑ 573 Ethan Horton .05 .01
❑ 574 Chris Slade .05 .01
❑ 575 Jeff Wright .05 .01
❑ 576 Toby Wright .05 .01
❑ 577 Lamar Thomas .05 .01
❑ 578 Chris Singleton .05 .01
❑ 579 Ed West .05 .01
❑ 580 Jeff George .25 .08
❑ 581 Kevin Mitchell .05 .01
❑ 582 Chad Brown .05 .01
❑ 583 Rich Camarillo .05 .01
❑ 584 Gary Zimmerman .05 .01
❑ 585 Randal Hill .05 .01
❑ 586 Keith Cash .05 .01
❑ 587 Sam Mills .05 .01
❑ 588 Shawn Lee .05 .01
❑ 589 Kent Graham .10 .02
❑ 590 Steve Everitt .05 .01
❑ 591 Rob Moore .10 .02
❑ 592 Kevin Mawae RC .25 .08
❑ 593 Jerry Ball .05 .01
❑ 594 Larry Brown DB .05 .01
❑ 595 Tim Krumrie .05 .01
❑ 596 Aubrey Beavers RC .05 .01
❑ 597 Chris Hinton .05 .01
❑ 598 Greg Montgomery .05 .01
❑ 599 Jimmie Jones .05 .01

❑ 600 Jim Kelly .25 .08
❑ 601 Joe Johnson RC .05 .01
❑ 602 Tim Irwin .05 .01
❑ 603 Steve Jackson .05 .01
❑ 604 James Williams RC LB .05 .01
❑ 605 Blair Thomas .05 .01
❑ 606 Danan Hughes .05 .01
❑ 607 Russell Freeman .05 .01
❑ 608 Andre Hastings .10 .02
❑ 609 Ken Harvey .05 .01
❑ 610 Jim Harbaugh .25 .08
❑ 611 Emmitt Smith MG .75 .30
❑ 612 Andre Rison MG .10 .02
❑ 613 Steve Young MG .25 .08
❑ 614 Anthony Miller MG .05 .01
❑ 615 Barry Sanders MG .75 .30
❑ 616 Bernie Kosar .10 .02
❑ 617 Chris Gardocki .05 .01
❑ 618 William Floyd RC .25 .08
❑ 619 Matt Brock .05 .01
❑ 620 Dan Wilkinson RC .10 .02
❑ 621 Tony Meola RC .10 .02
❑ 622 Tony Tolbert .05 .01
❑ 623 Mike Zandofsky .05 .01
❑ 624 William Fuller .05 .01
❑ 625 Steve Jordan .05 .01
❑ 626 Mike Johnson .05 .01
❑ 627 Ferrell Edmunds .05 .01
❑ 628 Gene Williams .05 .01
❑ 629 Willie Beamon .05 .01
❑ 630 Gerald Perry .05 .01
❑ 631 John Baylor .05 .01
❑ 632 Carwell Gardner .05 .01
❑ 633 Thomas Everett .05 .01
❑ 634 Lamar Lathon .05 .01
❑ 635 Michael Bankston .05 .01
❑ 636 Ray Crittenden RC .05 .01
❑ 637 Kimble Anders .10 .02
❑ 638 Robert Delpino .05 .01
❑ 639 Darren Perry .05 .01
❑ 640 Byron Evans .05 .01
❑ 641 Mark Higgs .05 .01
❑ 642 Lorenzo Neal .05 .01
❑ 643 Henry Ellard .10 .02
❑ 644 Trace Armstrong .05 .01
❑ 645 Greg McMurtry .05 .01
❑ 646 Steve McMichael .10 .02
❑ 647 Terance Mathis .10 .02
❑ 648 Eric Bieniemy .05 .01
❑ 649 Bobby Houston .05 .01
❑ 650 Alvin Harper .10 .02
❑ 651 James Folston RC .05 .01
❑ 652 Mel Gray .05 .01
❑ 653 Adrian Cooper .05 .01
❑ 654 Dexter Carter .05 .01
❑ 655 Don Griffin .05 .01
❑ 656 Corey Widmer .05 .01
❑ 657 Lee Johnson .05 .01
❑ 658 Nate Odomes .05 .01
❑ 659 Checklist Card .05 .01
❑ 660 Checklist Card .05 .01
❑ P1 Promo Sheet 4.00 1.50
❑ P2 Promo Sheet Special Effects 4.00 1.50

1995 Topps

❑ COMPLETE SET (468) 40.00 15.00
❑ COMP.FACT.SET (478) 50.00 25.00
❑ COMP.SERIES 1 (248) 20.00 7.50
❑ COMP.SERIES 2 (220) 20.00 7.50
❑ 1 Barry Sanders TYC .75 .30
❑ 2 Chris Warren TYC .20 .07
❑ 3 Jerry Rice TYC .50 .20
❑ 4 Emmitt Smith TYC .75 .30
❑ 5 Henry Ellard TYC .20 .07
❑ 6 Natrone Means TYC .20 .07
❑ 7 Terance Mathis TYC .20 .07
❑ 8 Tim Brown TYC .20 .07
❑ 9 Andre Reed TYC .20 .07
❑ 10 Marshall Faulk TYC .60 .25
❑ 11 Irving Fryar TYC .20 .07
❑ 12 Cris Carter TYC .30 .10
❑ 13 Michael Irvin TYC .30 .10
❑ 14 Jake Reed TYC .20 .07
❑ 15 Ben Coates TYC .20 .07
❑ 16 Herman Moore TYC .30 .10
❑ 17 Carl Pickens TYC .20 .07
❑ 18 Fred Barnett TYC .20 .07
❑ 19 Sterling Sharpe TYC .20 .07
❑ 20 Anthony Miller TYC .20 .07
❑ 21 Thurman Thomas TYC .30 .10
❑ 22 Andre Rison TYC .20 .07
❑ 23 Brian Blades TYC .20 .07
❑ 24 Rodney Hampton TYC .20 .07
❑ 25 Terry Allen TYC .20 .07
❑ 26 Jerome Bettis TYC .30 .10
❑ 27 Errict Rhett TYC .20 .07
❑ 28 Rob Moore TYC .20 .07
❑ 29 Shannon Sharpe TYC .20 .07
❑ 30 Drew Bledsoe TYC .30 .10
❑ 31 Dan Marino TYC 1.00 .40
❑ 32 Warren Moon TYC .20 .07
❑ 33 Steve Young TYC .40 .15
❑ 34 Brett Favre TYC 1.00 .40
❑ 35 Jim Everett TYC .10 .02
❑ 36 Jeff George TYC .20 .07
❑ 37 John Elway TYC 1.00 .40
❑ 38 Jeff Hostetler TYC .20 .07
❑ 39 Randall Cunningham TYC .30 .10
❑ 40 Stan Humphries TYC .20 .07
❑ 41 Jim Kelly TYC .30 .10
❑ 42 Tommy Barnhardt .10 .02
❑ 43 Bob Whitfield .10 .02
❑ 44 William Thomas .10 .02
❑ 45 Glyn Milburn .10 .02
❑ 46 Steve Christie .10 .02
❑ 47 Kevin Mawae .10 .02
❑ 48 Vencie Glenn .10 .02
❑ 49 Eric Curry .10 .02
❑ 50 Jeff Hostetler .20 .07
❑ 51 Tyronne Stowe .10 .02
❑ 52 Steve Jackson .10 .02
❑ 53 Ben Coleman .10 .02
❑ 54 Brad Baxter .10 .02
❑ 55 Darryl Williams .10 .02
❑ 56 Troy Drayton .10 .02
❑ 57 George Teague .10 .02
❑ 58 Calvin Williams .20 .07
❑ 59 Jeff Cross .10 .02
❑ 60 Leroy Hoard .10 .02
❑ 61 John Carney .10 .02
❑ 62 Daryl Johnston .20 .07
❑ 63 Jim Jeffcoat .10 .02
❑ 64 Matt Stover .10 .02
❑ 65 LeRoy Butler .10 .02
❑ 66 Curtis Conway .30 .10
❑ 67 O.J. McDuffie .30 .10
❑ 68 Robert Massey .10 .02
❑ 69 Ed McDaniel .10 .02
❑ 70 William Floyd .20 .07
❑ 71 Willie Davis .20 .07
❑ 72 William Roberts .10 .02
❑ 73 Chester McGlockton .20 .07
❑ 74 D.J. Johnson .10 .02
❑ 75 Rondell Jones .10 .02
❑ 76 Morten Andersen .10 .02
❑ 77 Glenn Parker .10 .02
❑ 78 William Fuller .10 .02
❑ 79 Ray Buchanan .10 .02
❑ 80 Maurice Hurst .10 .02
❑ 81 Wayne Gandy .10 .02
❑ 82 Marcus Turner .10 .02
❑ 83 Greg Davis .10 .02
❑ 84 Terry Wooden .10 .02
❑ 85 Thomas Everett .10 .02
❑ 86 Steve Broussard .10 .02
❑ 87 Tom Carter .10 .02
❑ 88 Glenn Montgomery .10 .02
❑ 89 Larry Allen .20 .07
❑ 90 Donnell Woolford .10 .02
❑ 91 John Alt .10 .02
❑ 92 Phil Hansen .10 .02
❑ 93 Seth Joyner .10 .02
❑ 94 Michael Brooks .10 .02
❑ 95 Randall McDaniel .10 .02
❑ 96 Tydus Winans .10 .02
❑ 97 Rob Fredrickson .10 .02
❑ 98 Ray Crockett .10 .02
❑ 99 Courtney Hall .10 .02
❑ 100 Merton Hanks .10 .02
❑ 101 Aaron Glenn .10 .02
❑ 102 Roosevelt Potts .10 .02
❑ 103 Leon Lett .10 .02
❑ 104 Jessie Tuggle .10 .02
❑ 105 Martin Mayhew .10 .02
❑ 106 Willie Roaf .10 .02
❑ 107 Todd Lyght .10 .02
❑ 108 Ernest Givins .10 .02
❑ 109 Tony McGee .10 .02
❑ 110 Barry Sanders 1.50 .60
❑ 111 Dermontti Dawson .20 .07
❑ 112 Rick Tuten .10 .02
❑ 113 Vincent Brisby .10 .02
❑ 114 Charlie Garner .30 .10
❑ 115 Irving Fryar .20 .07
❑ 116 Stevon Moore .10 .02
❑ 117 Matt Darby .10 .02
❑ 118 Howard Cross .10 .02
❑ 119 John Gesek .10 .02
❑ 120 Jack Del Rio .10 .02
❑ 121 Marcus Allen .30 .10
❑ 122 Torrance Small .10 .02
❑ 123 Chris Mims .10 .02
❑ 124 Don Mosebar .10 .02
❑ 125 Carl Pickens .20 .07
❑ 126 Tom Rouen .10 .02
❑ 127 Garrison Hearst .30 .10
❑ 128 Charles Johnson .20 .07
❑ 129 Derek Brown RBK .10 .02
❑ 130 Troy Aikman 1.00 .40
❑ 131 Troy Vincent .10 .02
❑ 132 Ken Ruettgers .10 .02
❑ 133 Michael Jackson .20 .07
❑ 134 Dennis Gibson .10 .02
❑ 135 Brett Perriman .20 .07
❑ 136 Jeff Graham .10 .02
❑ 137 Chad Brown .20 .07
❑ 138 Ken Norton Jr. .20 .07
❑ 139 Chris Slade .10 .02
❑ 140 Dave Brown .20 .07
❑ 141 Bert Emanuel .30 .10
❑ 142 Renaldo Turnbull .10 .02
❑ 143 Jim Harbaugh .20 .07
❑ 144 Micheal Barrow .10 .02
❑ 145 Vincent Brown .10 .02
❑ 146 Bryant Young .20 .07
❑ 147 Boomer Esiason .20 .07
❑ 148 Sean Gilbert .20 .07
❑ 149 Greg Truitt .10 .02
❑ 150 Rod Woodson .20 .07
❑ 151 Robert Porcher .10 .02
❑ 152 Joe Phillips .10 .02
❑ 153 Gary Zimmerman .10 .02
❑ 154 Bruce Smith .30 .10
❑ 155 Randall Cunningham .30 .10
❑ 156 Fred Strickland .10 .02
❑ 157 Derrick Alexander WR .30 .10
❑ 158 James Williams LB .10 .02
❑ 159 Scott Dill .10 .02
❑ 160 Tim Bowens .10 .02
❑ 161 Floyd Turner .10 .02
❑ 162 Ronnie Harmon .10 .02
❑ 163 Wayne Martin .10 .02
❑ 164 John Randle .20 .07
❑ 165 Larry Centers .20 .07
❑ 166 Larry Brown DB .10 .02

❑ 167	Albert Lewis	.10	.02
❑ 168	Michael Strahan	.30	.10
❑ 169	Reggie Brooks	.20	.07
❑ 170	Craig Heyward	.20	.07
❑ 171	Pat Harlow	.10	.02
❑ 172	Eugene Robinson	.10	.02
❑ 173	Shane Conlan	.10	.02
❑ 174	Bennie Blades	.10	.02
❑ 175	Neil O'Donnell	.20	.07
❑ 176	Steve Tovar	.10	.02
❑ 177	Donald Evans	.10	.02
❑ 178	Brent Jones	.10	.02
❑ 179	Ray Childress	.10	.02
[illegible]	[illegible]	[illegible]	[illegible]
❑ 181	David Alexander	.10	.02
❑ 182	Greg Hill	.20	.07
❑ 183	Vinny Testaverde	.20	.07
❑ 184	Jeff Burris	.10	.02
❑ 185	Hardy Nickerson	.10	.02
❑ 186	Terry Kirby	.20	.07
❑ 187	Kirk Lowdermilk	.10	.02
❑ 188	Eric Swann	.20	.07
❑ 189	Chris Zorich	.10	.02
❑ 190	Simon Fletcher	.10	.02
❑ 191	Qadry Ismail	.20	.07
❑ 192	Heath Shuler	.20	.07
❑ 193	Michael Haynes	.20	.07
❑ 194	Mike Sherrard	.10	.02
❑ 195	Nolan Harrison	.10	.02
❑ 196	Marcus Robertson	.10	.02
❑ 197	Kevin Williams WR	.20	.07
❑ 198	Moe Gardner	.10	.02
❑ 199	Rick Mirer	.20	.07
❑ 200	Junior Seau	.30	.10
❑ 201	Byron Bam Morris	.10	.02
❑ 202	Willie McGinest	.20	.07
❑ 203	Chris Spielman	.20	.07
❑ 204	Darnay Scott	.20	.07
❑ 205	Jesse Sapolu	.10	.02
❑ 206	Marvin Washington	.10	.02
❑ 207	Anthony Newman	.10	.02
❑ 208	Cortez Kennedy	.20	.07
❑ 209	Quentin Coryatt	.20	.07
❑ 210	Neil Smith	.20	.07
❑ 211	Keith Sims	.10	.02
❑ 212	Sean Jones	.10	.02
❑ 213	Tony Jones T	.10	.02
❑ 214	Lewis Tillman	.10	.02
❑ 215	Darren Woodson	.20	.07
❑ 216	Jason Hanson	.10	.02
❑ 217	John Taylor	.10	.02
❑ 218	Shawn Lee	.10	.02
❑ 219	Kevin Greene	.20	.07
❑ 220	Jerry Rice	1.00	.40
❑ 221	Ki-Jana Carter RC	.30	.10
❑ 222	Tony Boselli RC	.30	.10
❑ 223	Michael Westbrook RC	.30	.10
❑ 224	Kerry Collins RC	1.25	.50
❑ 225	Kevin Carter RC	.30	.10
❑ 226	Kyle Brady RC	.30	.10
❑ 227	J.J. Stokes RC	.30	.10
❑ 228	Derrick Alexander DE RC	.10	.02
❑ 229	Warren Sapp RC	1.50	.60
❑ 230	Ruben Brown RC	.30	.10
❑ 231	Hugh Douglas RC	.30	.10
❑ 232	Luther Elliss RC	.10	.02
❑ 233	Rashaan Salaam RC	.20	.07
❑ 234	Tyrone Poole RC	.30	.10
❑ 235	Korey Stringer RC	.20	.07
❑ 236	Devin Bush RC	.10	.02
❑ 237	Cory Raymer RC	.10	.02
❑ 238	Zach Wiegert RC	.10	.02
❑ 239	Ron Davis RC	.10	.02
❑ 240	Todd Collins RC	1.25	.50
❑ 241	Bobby Taylor RC	.30	.10
❑ 242	Patrick Riley RC	.10	.02
❑ 243	Scott Gragg	.10	.02
❑ 244	Marvcus Patton	.10	.02
❑ 245	Alvin Harper	.10	.02
❑ 246	Ricky Watters	.20	.07
❑ 247	Checklist 1	.10	.02
❑ 248	Checklist 2	.10	.02
❑ 249	Terance Mathis	.20	.07
❑ 250	Mark Carrier DB	.10	.02
❑ 251	Elijah Alexander	.10	.02
❑ 252	George Koonce	.10	.02
❑ 253	Tony Bennett	.10	.02
❑ 254	Steve Wisniewski	.10	.02
❑ 255	Bernie Parmalee	.20	.07
❑ 256	Dwayne Sabb	.10	.02
❑ 257	Lorenzo Neal	.10	.02
❑ 258	Corey Miller	.10	.02
❑ 259	Fred Barnett	.20	.07
❑ 260	Greg Lloyd	.20	.07
❑ 261	Robert Blackmon	.10	.02
❑ 262	Ken Harvey	.10	.02
❑ 263	Eric Hill	.10	.02
[illegible]	[illegible]	[illegible]	[illegible]
❑ 265	Jeff Blake RC	.75	.30
❑ 266	Carl Banks	.10	.02
❑ 267	Jay Novacek	.20	.07
❑ 268	Mel Gray	.10	.02
❑ 269	Kimble Anders	.20	.07
❑ 270	Cris Carter	.30	.10
❑ 271	Johnny Mitchell	.10	.02
❑ 272	Shawn Jefferson	.10	.02
❑ 273	Doug Brien	.10	.02
❑ 274	Sean Landeta	.10	.02
❑ 275	Scott Mitchell	.20	.07
❑ 276	Charles Wilson	.10	.02
❑ 277	Anthony Smith	.10	.02
❑ 278	Anthony Miller	.20	.07
❑ 279	Steve Walsh	.10	.02
❑ 280	Drew Bledsoe	.60	.25
❑ 281	Jamir Miller	.10	.02
❑ 282	Robert Brooks	.30	.10
❑ 283	Sean Lumpkin	.10	.02
❑ 284	Bryan Cox	.10	.02
❑ 285	Byron Evans	.10	.02
❑ 286	Chris Doleman	.10	.02
❑ 287	Anthony Pleasant	.10	.02
❑ 288	Stephen Grant RC	.10	.02
❑ 289	Doug Riesenberg	.10	.02
❑ 290	Natrone Means	.20	.07
❑ 291	Henry Thomas	.10	.02
❑ 292	Mike Pritchard	.10	.02
❑ 293	Courtney Hawkins	.10	.02
❑ 294	Bill Bates	.20	.07
❑ 295	Jerome Bettis	.30	.10
❑ 296	Russell Maryland	.10	.02
❑ 297	Stanley Richard	.10	.02
❑ 298	William White	.10	.02
❑ 299	Dan Wilkinson	.20	.07
❑ 300	Steve Young	.75	.30
❑ 301	Gary Brown	.10	.02
❑ 302	Jake Reed	.20	.07
❑ 303	Carlton Gray	.10	.02
❑ 304	Levon Kirkland	.10	.02
❑ 305	Shannon Sharpe	.20	.07
❑ 306	Luis Sharpe	.10	.02
❑ 307	Marshall Faulk	1.25	.50
❑ 308	Stan Humphries	.20	.07
❑ 309	Chris Calloway	.10	.02
❑ 310	Tim Brown	.30	.10
❑ 311	Steve Everitt	.10	.02
❑ 312	Raymont Harris	.10	.02
❑ 313	Tim McDonald	.10	.02
❑ 314	Trent Dilfer	.30	.10
❑ 315	Jim Everett	.10	.02
❑ 316	Ray Crittenden	.10	.02
❑ 317	Jim Kelly	.30	.10
❑ 318	Andre Reed	.20	.07
❑ 319	Chris Miller	.10	.02
❑ 320	Bobby Houston	.10	.02
❑ 321	Charles Haley	.20	.07
❑ 322	James Francis	.10	.02
❑ 323	Bernard Williams	.10	.02
❑ 324	Michael Bates	.10	.02
❑ 325	Brian Mitchell	.10	.02
❑ 326	Mike Johnson	.10	.02
❑ 327	Eric Bieniemy	.10	.02
❑ 328	Aubrey Beavers	.10	.02
❑ 329	Dale Carter	.20	.07
❑ 330	Emmitt Smith	1.50	.60
❑ 331	Darren Perry	.10	.02
❑ 332	Marquez Pope	.10	.02
❑ 333	Clyde Simmons	.10	.02
❑ 334	Corey Croom	.10	.02
❑ 335	Thomas Randolph	.10	.02
❑ 336	Harvey Williams	.10	.02
❑ 337	Michael Timpson	.10	.02
❑ 338	Eugene Daniel	.10	.02
❑ 339	Shane Dronett	.10	.02
❑ 340	Eric Turner	.10	.02
❑ 341	Eric Metcalf	.20	.07
❑ 342	Leslie O'Neal	.20	.07
❑ 343	Mark Wheeler	.10	.02
❑ 344	Mark Pike	.10	.02
❑ 345	Brett Favre	2.00	.75
❑ 346	Johnny Bailey	.10	.02
❑ 347	Henry Ellard	.20	.07
[illegible]	[illegible]	[illegible]	[illegible]
❑ 349	Henry Jones	.10	.02
❑ 350	Dan Marino	2.00	.75
❑ 351	Lake Dawson	.20	.07
❑ 352	Mark McMillian	.10	.02
❑ 353	Deion Sanders	.60	.25
❑ 354	Antonio London	.10	.02
❑ 355	Cris Dishman	.10	.02
❑ 356	Ricardo McDonald	.10	.02
❑ 357	Dexter Carter	.10	.02
❑ 358	Kevin Smith	.10	.02
❑ 359	Yancey Thigpen RC	.20	.07
❑ 360	Chris Warren	.20	.07
❑ 361	Quinn Early	.20	.07
❑ 362	John Mangum	.10	.02
❑ 363	Santana Dotson	.10	.02
❑ 364	Rocket Ismail	.20	.07
❑ 365	Aeneas Williams	.10	.02
❑ 366	Dan Williams	.10	.02
❑ 367	Sean Dawkins	.20	.07
❑ 368	Pepper Johnson	.10	.02
❑ 369	Roman Phifer	.10	.02
❑ 370	Rodney Hampton	.20	.07
❑ 371	Darrell Green	.10	.02
❑ 372	Michael Zordich	.10	.02
❑ 373	Andre Coleman	.10	.02
❑ 374	Wayne Simmons	.10	.02
❑ 375	Michael Irvin	.30	.10
❑ 376	Clay Matthews	.20	.07
❑ 377	Dewayne Washington	.20	.07
❑ 378	Keith Byars	.10	.02
❑ 379	Todd Collins LB	.30	.10
❑ 380	Mark Collins	.10	.02
❑ 381	Joel Steed	.10	.02
❑ 382	Bart Oates	.10	.02
❑ 383	Al Smith	.10	.02
❑ 384	Rafael Robinson	.10	.02
❑ 385	Mo Lewis	.10	.02
❑ 386	Aubrey Matthews	.10	.02
❑ 387	Corey Sawyer	.10	.02
❑ 388	Bucky Brooks	.10	.02
❑ 389	Erik Kramer	.10	.02
❑ 390	Tyrone Hughes	.20	.07
❑ 391	Terry McDaniel	.10	.02
❑ 392	Craig Erickson	.10	.02
❑ 393	Mike Flores	.10	.02
❑ 394	Harry Swayne	.10	.02
❑ 395	Irving Spikes	.20	.07
❑ 396	Lorenzo Lynch	.10	.02
❑ 397	Antonio Langham	.10	.02
❑ 398	Edgar Bennett	.20	.07
❑ 399	Thomas Lewis	.20	.07
❑ 400	John Elway	2.00	.75
❑ 401	Jeff George	.20	.07
❑ 402	Errict Rhett	.20	.07
❑ 403	Bill Romanowski	.10	.02
❑ 404	Alexander Wright	.10	.02
❑ 405	Warren Moon	.20	.07
❑ 406	Eddie Robinson	.10	.02
❑ 407	John Copeland	.10	.02
❑ 408	Robert Jones	.10	.02
❑ 409	Steve Bono	.20	.07
❑ 410	Cornelius Bennett	.20	.07
❑ 411	Ben Coates	.20	.07
❑ 412	Dana Stubblefield	.20	.07
❑ 413	Darryl Talley	.10	.02
❑ 414	Brian Blades	.20	.07
❑ 415	Herman Moore	.30	.10
❑ 416	Nick Lowery	.10	.02
❑ 417	Donnell Bennett	.20	.07
❑ 418	Van Malone	.10	.02

❑ 419 Pete Stoyanovich .10 .02
❑ 420 Joe Montana 2.00 .75
❑ 421 Steve Young .50 .20
❑ 422 Steve Young .50 .20
❑ 423 Steve Young .50 .20
❑ 424 Steve Young .50 .20
❑ 425 Steve Young .50 .20
❑ 426 Rod Stephens .10 .02
❑ 427 Ellis Johnson RC UER .10 .02
❑ 428 Kordell Stewart RC 1.25 .50
❑ 429 James O. Stewart RC 1.00 .40
❑ 430 Steve McNair RC 2.50 1.00
❑ 431 Brian DeMarco .20 .07
❑ 432 Matt O'Dwyer .10 .02
❑ 433 Lorenzo Styles RC .10 .02
❑ 434 Anthony Cook RC .10 .02
❑ 435 Jesse James .10 .02
❑ 436 Darryl Pounds RC .10 .02
❑ 437 Derrick Graham .10 .02
❑ 438 Vernon Turner .10 .02
❑ 439 Carlton Bailey .10 .02
❑ 440 Darion Conner .10 .02
❑ 441 Randy Baldwin .10 .02
❑ 442 Tim McKyer .10 .02
❑ 443 Sam Mills .20 .07
❑ 444 Bob Christian .10 .02
❑ 445 Steve Lofton .10 .02
❑ 446 Lamar Lathon .10 .02
❑ 447 Tony Smith RB .10 .02
❑ 448 Don Beebe .10 .02
❑ 449 Barry Foster .20 .07
❑ 450 Frank Reich .10 .02
❑ 451 Pete Metzelaars .10 .02
❑ 452 Reggie Cobb .10 .02
❑ 453 Jeff Lageman .10 .02
❑ 454 Derek Brown TE .10 .02
❑ 455 Desmond Howard .20 .07
❑ 456 Vinnie Clark .10 .02
❑ 457 Keith Goganious .10 .02
❑ 458 Shawn Bouwens .10 .02
❑ 459 Rob Johnson RC .75 .30
❑ 460 Steve Beuerlein .20 .07
❑ 461 Mark Brunell .60 .25
❑ 462 Harry Colon .10 .02
❑ 463 Chris Hudson .10 .02
❑ 464 Darren Carrington .10 .02
❑ 465 Ernest Givins .10 .02
❑ 466 Kelvin Pritchett .10 .02
❑ 467 Checklist (249-358) .10 .02
❑ 468 Checklist (358-468) .10 .02

1996 Topps

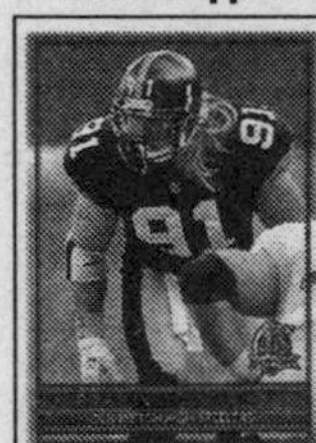

❑ COMPLETE SET (440) 40.00 20.00
❑ COMP.FACT.SET (448) 60.00 35.00
❑ COMP.CER.FACT.SET (445) 40.00 20.00
❑ 1 Troy Aikman 1.00 .40
❑ 2 Kevin Greene .20 .07
❑ 3 Robert Brooks .30 .10
❑ 4 Eugene Daniel .10 .02
❑ 5 Rodney Peete .10 .02
❑ 6 James Hasty .10 .02
❑ 7 Tim McDonald .10 .02
❑ 8 Darick Holmes .10 .02
❑ 9 Morten Andersen .10 .02
❑ 10 Junior Seau .30 .10
❑ 11 Brett Perriman .10 .02
❑ 12 Eric Green .10 .02
❑ 13 Jim Flanigan .10 .02
❑ 14 Cortez Kennedy .10 .02
❑ 15 Orlando Thomas .10 .02
❑ 16 Anthony Miller .20 .07
❑ 17 Sean Gilbert .10 .02
❑ 18 Rob Fredrickson .10 .02
❑ 19 Willie Green .10 .02
❑ 20 Jeff Blake .30 .10
❑ 21 Trent Dilfer .30 .10
❑ 22 Chris Chandler .20 .07
❑ 23 Renaldo Turnbull .10 .02
❑ 24 Dave Meggett .10 .02
❑ 25 Heath Shuler .20 .07
❑ 26 Michael Jackson .20 .07
❑ 27 Thomas Randolph .10 .02
❑ 28 Keith Goganious .10 .02
❑ 29 Seth Joyner .10 .02
❑ 30 Wayne Chrebet .60 .25
❑ 31 Craig Newsome .10 .02
❑ 32 William Fuller .10 .02
❑ 33 Merton Hanks .10 .02
❑ 34 Dale Carter .10 .02
❑ 35 Quentin Coryatt .10 .02
❑ 36 Robert Jones .10 .02
❑ 37 Eric Metcalf .10 .02
❑ 38 Byron Bam Morris .10 .02
❑ 39 Bill Brooks .10 .02
❑ 40 Barry Sanders 1.50 .60
❑ 41 Michael Haynes .10 .02
❑ 42 Joey Galloway .30 .10
❑ 43 Robert Smith .20 .07
❑ 44 John Thierry .10 .02
❑ 45 Bryan Cox .10 .02
❑ 46 Anthony Parker .10 .02
❑ 47 Harvey Williams .10 .02
❑ 48 Terrell Davis .75 .30
❑ 49 Darnay Scott .20 .07
❑ 50 Kerry Collins .30 .10
❑ 51 Cris Dishman .10 .02
❑ 52 Dwayne Harper .10 .02
❑ 53 Warren Sapp .10 .02
❑ 54 Will Moore .10 .02
❑ 55 Earnest Byner .10 .02
❑ 56 Aaron Glenn .10 .02
❑ 57 Michael Westbrook .30 .10
❑ 58 Vencie Glenn .10 .02
❑ 59 Rob Moore .20 .07
❑ 60 Mark Brunell .60 .25
❑ 61 Craig Heyward .10 .02
❑ 62 Eric Allen .10 .02
❑ 63 Bill Romanowski .10 .02
❑ 64 Dana Stubblefield .20 .07
❑ 65 Steve Bono .10 .02
❑ 66 George Koonce .10 .02
❑ 67 Larry Brown .10 .02
❑ 68 Warren Moon .20 .07
❑ 69 Erric Pegram .10 .02
❑ 70 Jim Kelly .30 .10
❑ 71 Jason Belser .10 .02
❑ 72 Henry Thomas .10 .02
❑ 73 Mark Carrier DB .10 .02
❑ 74 Terry Wooden .10 .02
❑ 75 Terry McDaniel .10 .02
❑ 76 O.J. McDuffie .20 .07
❑ 77 Dan Wilkinson .10 .02
❑ 78 Blake Brockermeyer .10 .02
❑ 79 Micheal Barrow .10 .02
❑ 80 Dave Brown .10 .02
❑ 81 Todd Lyght .10 .02
❑ 82 Henry Ellard .10 .02
❑ 83 Jeff Lageman .10 .02
❑ 84 Anthony Pleasant .10 .02
❑ 85 Aeneas Williams .10 .02
❑ 86 Vincent Brisby .10 .02
❑ 87 Terrell Fletcher .10 .02
❑ 88 Brad Baxter .10 .02
❑ 89 Shannon Sharpe .20 .07
❑ 90 Errict Rhett .20 .07
❑ 91 Michael Zordich .10 .02
❑ 92 Dan Saleaumua .10 .02
❑ 93 Devin Bush .10 .02
❑ 94 Wayne Simmons .10 .02
❑ 95 Tyrone Hughes .10 .02
❑ 96 John Randle .20 .07
❑ 97 Tony Tolbert .10 .02
❑ 98 Yancey Thigpen .20 .07
❑ 99 J.J. Stokes .30 .10
❑ 100 Marshall Faulk .40 .15
❑ 101 Barry Minter .10 .02
❑ 102 Glenn Foley .20 .07
❑ 103 Chester McGlockton .10 .02
❑ 104 Carlton Gray .10 .02
❑ 105 Terry Kirby .20 .07
❑ 106 Darryll Lewis .10 .02
❑ 107 Thomas Smith .10 .02
❑ 108 Mike Fox .10 .02
❑ 109 Antonio Langham .10 .02
❑ 110 Drew Bledsoe .60 .25
❑ 111 Troy Drayton .10 .02
❑ 112 Marvcus Patton .10 .02
❑ 113 Tyrone Wheatley .20 .07
❑ 114 Desmond Howard .20 .07
❑ 115 Johnny Mitchell .10 .02
❑ 116 Dave Krieg .10 .02
❑ 117 Natrone Means .20 .07
❑ 118 Herman Moore .20 .07
❑ 119 Darren Woodson .20 .07
❑ 120 Ricky Watters .20 .07
❑ 121 Emmitt Smith TYC .75 .30
❑ 122 Barry Sanders TYC .75 .30
❑ 123 Curtis Martin TYC .30 .10
❑ 124 Chris Warren TYC .20 .07
❑ 125 Terry Allen TYC .20 .07
❑ 126 Ricky Watters TYC .20 .07
❑ 127 Errict Rhett TYC .20 .07
❑ 128 Rodney Hampton TYC .10 .02
❑ 129 Terrell Davis TYC .30 .10
❑ 130 Harvey Williams TYC .10 .02
❑ 131 Craig Heyward TYC .10 .02
❑ 132 Marshall Faulk TYC .30 .10
❑ 133 Rashaan Salaam TYC .20 .07
❑ 134 Garrison Hearst TYC .20 .07
❑ 135 Edgar Bennett TYC .20 .07
❑ 136 Thurman Thomas TYC .20 .07
❑ 137 Brian Washington .10 .02
❑ 138 Derek Loville .10 .02
❑ 139 Curtis Conway .30 .10
❑ 140 Isaac Bruce .30 .10
❑ 141 Ricardo McDonald .10 .02
❑ 142 Bruce Armstrong .10 .02
❑ 143 Will Wolford .10 .02
❑ 144 Thurman Thomas .30 .10
❑ 145 Mel Gray .10 .02
❑ 146 Napoleon Kaufman .30 .10
❑ 147 Terry Allen .20 .07
❑ 148 Chris Calloway .10 .02
❑ 149 Harry Colon .10 .02
❑ 150 Pepper Johnson .10 .02
❑ 151 Marco Coleman .10 .02
❑ 152 Shawn Jefferson .10 .02
❑ 153 Larry Centers .20 .07
❑ 154 Lamar Lathon .10 .02
❑ 155 Mark Chmura .20 .07
❑ 156 Dermontti Dawson .10 .02
❑ 157 Alvin Harper .10 .02
❑ 158 Randall McDaniel .10 .02
❑ 159 Allen Aldridge .10 .02
❑ 160 Chris Warren .20 .07
❑ 161 Jessie Tuggle .10 .02
❑ 162 Sean Lumpkin .10 .02
❑ 163 Bobby Houston .10 .02
❑ 164 Dexter Carter .10 .02
❑ 165 Erik Kramer .10 .02
❑ 166 Brock Marion .10 .02
❑ 167 Toby Wright .10 .02
❑ 168 John Copeland .10 .02
❑ 169 Sean Dawkins .10 .02
❑ 170 Tim Brown .30 .10
❑ 171 Darion Conner .10 .02
❑ 172 Aaron Hayden RC .10 .02
❑ 173 Charlie Garner .20 .07
❑ 174 Anthony Cook .10 .02
❑ 175 Derrick Thomas .30 .10
❑ 176 Willie McGinest .10 .02
❑ 177 Thomas Lewis .10 .02
❑ 178 Sherman Williams .10 .02
❑ 179 Cornelius Bennett .10 .02
❑ 180 Frank Sanders .30 .10

❑ 181 Leroy Hoard .10 .02
❑ 182 Bernie Parmalee .10 .02
❑ 183 Sterling Palmer .10 .02
❑ 184 Kelvin Pritchett .10 .02
❑ 185 Kordell Stewart .30 .10
❑ 186 Brent Jones .10 .02
❑ 187 Robert Blackmon .10 .02
❑ 188 Adrian Murrell .20 .07
❑ 189 Edgar Bennett .20 .07
❑ 190 Rashaan Salaam .20 .07
❑ 191 Ellis Johnson .10 .02
❑ 192 Andre Coleman .10 .02
❑ 193 Will Shields .10 .02
❑ 194 Derrick Brooks .30 .10
❑ 195 Carl Pickens .20 .07
❑ 196 Carlton Bailey .10 .02
❑ 197 Terance Mathis .20 .07
❑ 198 Carlos Jenkins .10 .02
❑ 199 Derrick Alexander .10 .02
❑ 200 Deion Sanders .60 .25
❑ 201 Glyn Milburn .10 .02
❑ 202 Chris Sanders .20 .07
❑ 203 Rocket Ismail .10 .02
❑ 204 Fred Barnett .10 .02
❑ 205 Quinn Early .10 .02
❑ 206 Henry Jones .10 .02
❑ 207 Herschel Walker .20 .07
❑ 208 James Washington .10 .02
❑ 209 Lee Woodall .10 .02
❑ 210 Neil Smith .20 .07
❑ 211 Tony Bennett .10 .02
❑ 212 Ernie Mills .10 .02
❑ 213 Clyde Simmons .10 .02
❑ 214 Chris Slade .10 .02
❑ 215 Tony Boselli .10 .02
❑ 216 Ryan McNeil .10 .02
❑ 217 Rob Burnett .10 .02
❑ 218 Stan Humphries .20 .07
❑ 219 Rick Mirer .20 .07
❑ 220 Troy Vincent .10 .02
❑ 221 Sean Jones .10 .02
❑ 222 Marty Carter .10 .02
❑ 223 Boomer Esiason .20 .07
❑ 224 Charles Haley .20 .07
❑ 225 Sam Mills .10 .02
❑ 226 Greg Biekert .10 .02
❑ 227 Bryant Young .20 .07
❑ 228 Ken Dilger .20 .07
❑ 229 Levon Kirkland .10 .02
❑ 230 Brian Mitchell .10 .02
❑ 231 Hardy Nickerson .10 .02
❑ 232 Elvis Grbac .20 .07
❑ 233 Kurt Schulz .10 .02
❑ 234 Chris Doleman .10 .02
❑ 235 Tamarick Vanover .20 .07
❑ 236 Jesse Campbell .10 .02
❑ 237 William Thomas .10 .02
❑ 238 Shane Conlan .10 .02
❑ 239 Jason Elam .20 .07
❑ 240 Steve McNair .75 .30
❑ 241 Jerry Rice TYC .50 .20
❑ 242 Isaac Bruce TYC .30 .10
❑ 243 Herman Moore TYC .20 .07
❑ 244 Michael Irvin TYC .20 .07
❑ 245 Robert Brooks TYC .30 .10
❑ 246 Brett Perriman TYC .10 .02
❑ 247 Cris Carter TYC .30 .10
❑ 248 Tim Brown TYC .20 .07
❑ 249 Yancey Thigpen TYC .20 .07
❑ 250 Jeff Graham TYC .10 .02
❑ 251 Carl Pickens TYC .20 .07
❑ 252 Tony Martin TYC .10 .02
❑ 253 Eric Metcalf TYC .10 .02
❑ 254 Jake Reed TYC .20 .07
❑ 255 Quinn Early TYC .10 .02
❑ 256 Anthony Miller TYC .20 .07
❑ 257 Joey Galloway TYC .30 .10
❑ 258 Bert Emanuel TYC .20 .07
❑ 259 Terance Mathis TYC .10 .02
❑ 260 Curtis Conway TYC .20 .07
❑ 261 Henry Ellard TYC .10 .02
❑ 262 Mark Carrier TYC .10 .02
❑ 263 Brian Blades TYC .10 .02
❑ 264 William Roaf .10 .02
❑ 265 Ed McDaniel .10 .02
❑ 266 Nate Newton .10 .02
❑ 267 Brett Maxie .10 .02
❑ 268 Anthony Smith .10 .02
❑ 269 Mickey Washington .10 .02
❑ 270 Jerry Rice 1.00 .40
❑ 271 Shaun Gayle .10 .02
❑ 272 Gilbert Brown RC .30 .10
❑ 273 Mark Bruener .10 .02
❑ 274 Eugene Robinson .10 .02
❑ 275 Marvin Washington .10 .02
❑ 276 Keith Sims .10 .02
❑ 277 Ashley Ambrose .10 .02
❑ 278 Garrison Hearst .20 .07
❑ 279 Donnell Woolford .10 .02
❑ 280 Cris Carter .30 .10
❑ 281 Curtis Martin .75 .30
❑ 282 Scott Mitchell .20 .07
❑ 283 Stevon Moore .10 .02
❑ 284 Roman Phifer .10 .02
❑ 285 Ken Harvey .10 .02
❑ 286 Rodney Hampton .20 .07
❑ 287 Willie Davis .10 .02
❑ 288 Yonel Jourdain .10 .02
❑ 289 Brian DeMarco .10 .02
❑ 290 Reggie White .30 .10
❑ 291 Kevin Williams .10 .02
❑ 292 Gary Plummer .10 .02
❑ 293 Terrance Shaw .10 .02
❑ 294 Calvin Williams .10 .02
❑ 295 Eddie Robinson .10 .02
❑ 296 Tony McGee .10 .02
❑ 297 Clay Matthews .10 .02
❑ 298 Joe Cain .10 .02
❑ 299 Tim McKyer .10 .02
❑ 300 Greg Lloyd .20 .07
❑ 301 Steve Wisniewski .10 .02
❑ 302 Ray Buchanan .10 .02
❑ 303 Lake Dawson .10 .02
❑ 304 Kevin Carter .10 .02
❑ 305 Phillippi Sparks .10 .02
❑ 306 Emmitt Smith 1.50 .60
❑ 307 Ruben Brown .10 .02
❑ 308 Tom Carter .10 .02
❑ 309 William Floyd .20 .07
❑ 310 Jim Everett .10 .02
❑ 311 Vincent Brown .10 .02
❑ 312 Dennis Gibson .10 .02
❑ 313 Lorenzo Lynch .10 .02
❑ 314 Corey Harris .10 .02
❑ 315 James O.Stewart .20 .07
❑ 316 Kyle Brady .10 .02
❑ 317 Irving Fryar .20 .07
❑ 318 Jake Reed .20 .07
❑ 319 Vinny Testaverde .20 .07
❑ 320 John Elway 2.00 .75
❑ 321 Tracy Scroggins .10 .02
❑ 322 Chris Spielman .10 .02
❑ 323 Horace Copeland .10 .02
❑ 324 Chris Zorich .10 .02
❑ 325 Mike Mamula .10 .02
❑ 326 Henry Ford .10 .02
❑ 327 Steve Walsh .10 .02
❑ 328 Stanley Richard .20 .07
❑ 329 Mike Jones .10 .02
❑ 330 Jim Harbaugh .20 .07
❑ 331 Darren Perry .10 .02
❑ 332 Ken Norton .10 .02
❑ 333 Kimble Anders .20 .07
❑ 334 Harold Green .10 .02
❑ 335 Tyrone Poole .10 .02
❑ 336 Mark Fields .10 .02
❑ 337 Darren Bennett .10 .02
❑ 338 Mike Sherrard .10 .02
❑ 339 Terry Ray RC .10 .02
❑ 340 Bruce Smith .20 .07
❑ 341 Daryl Johnston .20 .07
❑ 342 Vinnie Clark .10 .02
❑ 343 Mike Caldwell .10 .02
❑ 344 Vinson Smith .10 .02
❑ 345 Mo Lewis .10 .02
❑ 346 Brian Blades .10 .02
❑ 347 Rod Stephens .10 .02
❑ 348 David Palmer .10 .02
❑ 349 Blaine Bishop .10 .02
❑ 350 Jeff George .20 .07
❑ 351 George Teague .10 .02
❑ 352 Jeff Hostetler .10 .02
❑ 353 Michael Strahan .20 .07
❑ 354 Eric Davis .10 .02
❑ 355 Jerome Bettis .30 .10
❑ 356 Irv Smith .10 .02
❑ 357 Jeff Herrod .10 .02
❑ 358 Jay Novacek .10 .02
❑ 359 Bryce Paup .10 .02
❑ 360 Neil O'Donnell .20 .07
❑ 361 Eric Swann .10 .02
❑ 362 Corey Sawyer .10 .02
❑ 363 Ty Law .30 .10
❑ 364 Bo Orlando .10 .02
❑ 365 Marcus Allen .30 .10
❑ 366 Mark McMillian .10 .02
❑ 367 Mark Carrier WR .10 .02
❑ 368 Jackie Harris .10 .02
❑ 369 Steve Atwater .10 .02
❑ 370 Steve Young .75 .30
❑ 371 Brett Favre TYC 1.00 .40
❑ 372 Scott Mitchell TYC .10 .02
❑ 373 Warren Moon TYC .10 .02
❑ 374 Jeff George TYC .20 .07
❑ 375 Jim Everett TYC .10 .02
❑ 376 John Elway TYC 1.00 .40
❑ 377 Erik Kramer TYC .10 .02
❑ 378 Jeff Blake TYC .20 .07
❑ 379 Dan Marino TYC 1.00 .40
❑ 380 Dave Krieg TYC .10 .02
❑ 381 Drew Bledsoe TYC .30 .10
❑ 382 Stan Humphries TYC .10 .02
❑ 383 Troy Aikman TYC .50 .20
❑ 384 Steve Young TYC .30 .10
❑ 385 Jim Kelly TYC .30 .10
❑ 386 Steve Bono TYC .10 .02
❑ 387 David Sloan .10 .02
❑ 388 Jeff Graham .10 .02
❑ 389 Hugh Douglas .20 .07
❑ 390 Dan Marino 2.00 .75
❑ 391 Winston Moss .10 .02
❑ 392 Darrell Green .10 .02
❑ 393 Mark Stepnoski .10 .02
❑ 394 Bert Emanuel .20 .07
❑ 395 Eric Zeier .10 .02
❑ 396 Willie Jackson .20 .07
❑ 397 Qadry Ismail .20 .07
❑ 398 Michael Brooks .10 .02
❑ 399 D'Marco Farr .10 .02
❑ 400 Brett Favre 2.00 .75
❑ 401 Carnell Lake .10 .02
❑ 402 Pat Swilling .10 .02
❑ 403 Stephen Grant .10 .02
❑ 404 Steve Tasker .10 .02
❑ 405 Ben Coates .20 .07
❑ 406 Steve Tovar .10 .02
❑ 407 Tony Martin .20 .07
❑ 408 Greg Hill .20 .07
❑ 409 Eric Guliford .10 .02
❑ 410 Michael Irvin .30 .10
❑ 411 Eric Hill .10 .02
❑ 412 Mario Bates .20 .07
❑ 413 Brian Stablein RC .10 .02
❑ 414 Marcus Jones RC .10 .02
❑ 415 Reggie Brown LB RC .10 .02
❑ 416 Lawrence Phillips RC .30 .10
❑ 417 Alex Van Dyke RC .20 .07
❑ 418 Daryl Gardener RC .10 .02
❑ 419 Mike Alstott RC 1.00 .40
❑ 420 Kevin Hardy RC .30 .10
❑ 421 Rickey Dudley RC .30 .10
❑ 422 Jerome Woods RC .10 .02
❑ 423 Eric Moulds RC 1.25 .50
❑ 424 Cedric Jones RC .10 .02
❑ 425 Simeon Rice RC .75 .30
❑ 426 Marvin Harrison RC 2.50 1.00
❑ 427 Tim Biakabutuka RC .30 .10
❑ 428 Duane Clemons RC .10 .02
❑ 429 Alex Molden RC .10 .02
❑ 430 Keyshawn Johnson RC 1.00 .40
❑ 431 Willie Anderson RC .10 .02
❑ 432 John Mobley RC .10 .02

❑ 433 Leeland McElroy RC .20 .07
❑ 434 Regan Upshaw RC .10 .02
❑ 435 Eddie George RC 1.25 .50
❑ 436 Jonathan Ogden RC .30 .10
❑ 437 Eddie Kennison RC .30 .10
❑ 438 Jermane Mayberry RC .10 .02
❑ 439 Checklist 1 of 2 .10 .02
❑ 440 Checklist 2 of 2 .10 .02
❑ P1 Joe Namath/Steve Young Promo 15.00 7.50
❑ P1R Joe Namath Promo 20.00 10.00
Steve Young

1997 Topps

❑ COMPLETE SET (415) 40.00 20.00
❑ COMP.FACT.SET (424) 70.00 40.00
❑ 1 Brett Favre 2.00 .75
❑ 2 Lawyer Milloy .30 .10
❑ 3 Tim Biakabutuka .30 .10
❑ 4 Clyde Simmons .20 .07
❑ 5 Deion Sanders .50 .20
❑ 6 Anthony Miller .20 .07
❑ 7 Marquez Pope .20 .07
❑ 8 Mike Tomczak .20 .07
❑ 9 William Thomas .20 .07
❑ 10 Marshall Faulk .60 .25
❑ 11 John Randle .30 .10
❑ 12 Jim Kelly .50 .20
❑ 13 Steve Bono .30 .10
❑ 14 Rod Stephens .20 .07
❑ 15 Stan Humphries .20 .07
❑ 16 Terrell Buckley .20 .07
❑ 17 Ki-Jana Carter .20 .07
❑ 18 Marcus Robertson .20 .07
❑ 19 Corey Harris .20 .07
❑ 20 Rashaan Salaam .20 .07
❑ 21 Rickey Dudley .30 .10
❑ 22 Jamir Miller .20 .07
❑ 23 Martin Mayhew .20 .07
❑ 24 Jason Sehorn .30 .10
❑ 25 Isaac Bruce .50 .20
❑ 26 Johnnie Morton .30 .10
❑ 27 Antonio Langham .20 .07
❑ 28 Cornelius Bennett .20 .07
❑ 29 Joe Johnson .20 .07
❑ 30 Keyshawn Johnson .50 .20
❑ 31 Willie Green .20 .07
❑ 32 Craig Newsome .20 .07
❑ 33 Brock Marion .20 .07
❑ 34 Corey Fuller .20 .07
❑ 35 Ben Coates .30 .10
❑ 36 Ty Detmer .30 .10
❑ 37 Charles Johnson .30 .10
❑ 38 Willie Jackson .20 .07
❑ 39 Tyronne Drakeford .20 .07
❑ 40 Gus Frerotte .20 .07
❑ 41 Robert Blackmon .20 .07
❑ 42 Andre Coleman .20 .07
❑ 43 Mario Bates .20 .07
❑ 44 Chris Calloway .20 .07
❑ 45 Terry McDaniel .20 .07
❑ 46 Anthony Davis .20 .07
❑ 47 Stanley Pritchett .20 .07
❑ 48 Ray Buchanan .20 .07
❑ 49 Chris Chandler .30 .10
❑ 50 Ashley Ambrose .20 .07
❑ 51 Tyrone Braxton .20 .07
❑ 52 Pepper Johnson .20 .07
❑ 53 Frank Sanders .30 .10
❑ 54 Clay Matthews .20 .07
❑ 55 Bruce Smith .30 .10
❑ 56 Jermaine Lewis .50 .20
❑ 57 Mark Carrier WR UER .20 .07
❑ 58 Jeff Graham .20 .07
❑ 59 Keith Lyle .20 .07
❑ 60 Trent Dilfer .50 .20
❑ 61 Trace Armstrong .20 .07
❑ 62 Jeff Herrod .20 .07
❑ 63 Tyrone Wheatley .30 .10
❑ 64 Torrance Small .20 .07
❑ 65 Chris Warren .30 .10
❑ 66 Terry Kirby .30 .10
❑ 67 Erric Pegram .20 .07
❑ 68 Sean Gilbert .20 .07
❑ 69 Greg Biekert .20 .07
❑ 70 Ricky Watters .30 .10
❑ 71 Chris Hudson .20 .07
❑ 72 Tamarick Vanover .30 .10
❑ 73 Orlando Thomas .20 .07
❑ 74 Jimmy Spencer .20 .07
❑ 75 John Mobley .20 .07
❑ 76 Henry Thomas .20 .07
❑ 77 Santana Dotson .20 .07
❑ 78 Boomer Esiason .30 .10
❑ 79 Bobby Hebert .20 .07
❑ 80 Kerry Collins .50 .20
❑ 81 Bobby Engram .30 .10
❑ 82 Kevin Smith .20 .07
❑ 83 Rick Mirer .20 .07
❑ 84 Ted Johnson .20 .07
❑ 85 Derrick Alexander WR .30 .10
❑ 86 Hugh Douglas .20 .07
❑ 87 Rodney Harrison RC 1.00 .40
❑ 88 Roman Phifer .20 .07
❑ 89 Warren Moon .50 .20
❑ 90 Thurman Thomas .50 .20
❑ 91 Michael McCrary .20 .07
❑ 92 Dana Stubblefield .20 .07
❑ 93 Andre Hastings UER .20 .07
❑ 94 William Fuller .20 .07
❑ 95 Jeff Hostetler .20 .07
❑ 96 Danny Kanell .20 .07
❑ 97 Mark Fields .20 .07
❑ 98 Eddie Robinson .20 .07
❑ 99 Daryl Gardener .20 .07
❑ 100 Drew Bledsoe .60 .25
❑ 101 Winslow Oliver .20 .07
❑ 102 Raymont Harris .20 .07
❑ 103 LeShon Johnson .20 .07
❑ 104 Byron Bam Morris .20 .07
❑ 105 Herman Moore .30 .10
❑ 106 Keith Jackson .20 .07
❑ 107 Chris Penn .20 .07
❑ 108 Robert Griffith RC .20 .07
❑ 109 Jeff Burris .20 .07
❑ 110 Troy Aikman 1.00 .40
❑ 111 Allen Aldridge .20 .07
❑ 112 Mel Gray .20 .07
❑ 113 Aaron Bailey .20 .07
❑ 114 Michael Strahan .30 .10
❑ 115 Adrian Murrell .30 .10
❑ 116 Chris Mims .20 .07
❑ 117 Robert Jones .20 .07
❑ 118 Derrick Brooks .50 .20
❑ 119 Tom Carter .20 .07
❑ 120 Carl Pickens .30 .10
❑ 121 Tony Brackens .20 .07
❑ 122 O.J. McDuffie .30 .10
❑ 123 Napoleon Kaufman .50 .20
❑ 124 Chris T. Jones .20 .07
❑ 125 Kordell Stewart .50 .20
❑ 126 Ray Zellars .20 .07
❑ 127 Jessie Tuggle .20 .07
❑ 128 Greg Kragen .20 .07
❑ 129 Brett Perriman .20 .07
❑ 130 Steve Young .60 .25
❑ 131 Willie Clay .20 .07
❑ 132 Kimble Anders .30 .10
❑ 133 Eugene Daniel .20 .07
❑ 134 Jevon Langford .20 .07
❑ 135 Shannon Sharpe .30 .10
❑ 136 Wayne Simmons .20 .07
❑ 137 Leeland McElroy .20 .07
❑ 138 Mike Caldwell .20 .07
❑ 139 Eric Moulds .50 .20
❑ 140 Eddie George .50 .20
❑ 141 Jamal Anderson .50 .20
❑ 142 Michael Timpson .20 .07
❑ 143 Tony Tolbert .20 .07
❑ 144 Robert Smith .30 .10
❑ 145 Mike Alstott .50 .20
❑ 146 Gary Jones .20 .07
❑ 147 Terrance Shaw .20 .07
❑ 148 Carlton Gray .20 .07
❑ 149 Kevin Carter .20 .07
❑ 150 Darrell Green .30 .10
❑ 151 David Dunn .20 .07
❑ 152 Ken Norton .20 .07
❑ 153 Chad Brown .20 .07
❑ 154 Pat Swilling .20 .07
❑ 155 Irving Fryar .30 .10
❑ 156 Michael Haynes .20 .07
❑ 157 Shawn Jefferson .20 .07
❑ 158 Stephen Grant .20 .07
❑ 159 James O.Stewart .30 .10
❑ 160 Derrick Thomas .50 .20
❑ 161 Tim Bowens .20 .07
❑ 162 Dixon Edwards .20 .07
❑ 163 Micheal Barrow .20 .07
❑ 164 Antonio Freeman .50 .20
❑ 165 Terrell Davis .60 .25
❑ 166 Henry Ellard .30 .10
❑ 167 Daryl Johnston .30 .10
❑ 168 Bryan Cox .20 .07
❑ 169 Chad Cota .20 .07
❑ 170 Vinny Testaverde .30 .10
❑ 171 Andre Reed .30 .10
❑ 172 Larry Centers .30 .10
❑ 173 Craig Heyward .20 .07
❑ 174 Glyn Milburn .20 .07
❑ 175 Hardy Nickerson .20 .07
❑ 176 Corey Miller .20 .07
❑ 177 Bobby Houston .20 .07
❑ 178 Marco Coleman .20 .07
❑ 179 Winston Moss .20 .07
❑ 180 Tony Banks .30 .10
❑ 181 Jeff Lageman .20 .07
❑ 182 Jason Belser .20 .07
❑ 183 James Jett .30 .10
❑ 184 Wayne Martin .20 .07
❑ 185 Dave Meggett .20 .07
❑ 186 Terrell Owens .60 .25
❑ 187 Willie Williams .20 .07
❑ 188 Eric Turner .20 .07
❑ 189 Chuck Smith .20 .07
❑ 190 Simeon Rice .30 .10
❑ 191 Kevin Greene .30 .10
❑ 192 Lance Johnstone .20 .07
❑ 193 Marty Carter .20 .07
❑ 194 Ricardo McDonald .20 .07
❑ 195 Michael Irvin .50 .20
❑ 196 George Koonce .20 .07
❑ 197 Robert Porcher .20 .07
❑ 198 Mark Collins .20 .07
❑ 199 Louis Oliver .20 .07
❑ 200 John Elway 2.00 .75
❑ 201 Jake Reed .30 .10
❑ 202 Rodney Hampton .30 .10
❑ 203 Aaron Glenn .20 .07
❑ 204 Mike Mamula .20 .07
❑ 205 Terry Allen .50 .20
❑ 206 John Lynch .30 .10
❑ 207 Todd Lyght .20 .07
❑ 208 Dean Wells .20 .07
❑ 209 Aaron Hayden .20 .07
❑ 210 Blaine Bishop .20 .07
❑ 211 Bert Emanuel .30 .10
❑ 212 Mark Carrier DB UER .20 .07
❑ 213 Dale Carter .20 .07
❑ 214 Jimmy Smith .30 .10
❑ 215 Jim Harbaugh .30 .10
❑ 216 Jeff George .30 .10
❑ 217 Anthony Newman .20 .07
❑ 218 Ty Law .30 .10
❑ 219 Brent Jones .20 .07
❑ 220 Emmitt Smith 1.50 .60
❑ 221 Bennie Blades .20 .07

❑ 222 Alfred Williams .20 .07
❑ 223 Eugene Robinson .20 .07
❑ 224 Fred Barnett .20 .07
❑ 225 Errict Rhett .20 .07
❑ 226 Leslie O'Neal .20 .07
❑ 227 Michael Sinclair .20 .07
❑ 228 Marvcus Patton .20 .07
❑ 229 Darrien Gordon .20 .07
❑ 230 Jerome Bettis .50 .20
❑ 231 Troy Vincent .20 .07
❑ 232 Ray Mickens .20 .07
❑ 233 Lonnie Johnson .20 .07
❑ 234 Charles Way .20 .07
❑ 235 Chris Sanders .20 .07
❑ 236 Bracy Walker .20 .07
❑ 237 Dave Krieg UER .20 .07
❑ 238 Kent Graham .20 .07
❑ 239 Ray Lewis .75 .30
❑ 240 Cris Carter .50 .20
❑ 241 Elvis Grbac .30 .10
❑ 242 Eric Davis .20 .07
❑ 243 Harvey Williams .20 .07
❑ 244 Eric Allen .20 .07
❑ 245 Bryant Young .20 .07
❑ 246 Terrell Fletcher .20 .07
❑ 247 Darren Perry .20 .07
❑ 248 Ken Harvey .20 .07
❑ 249 Marvin Washington .20 .07
❑ 250 Marcus Allen .50 .20
❑ 251 Darrin Smith .20 .07
❑ 252 James Francis .20 .07
❑ 253 Michael Jackson .30 .10
❑ 254 Ryan McNeil .20 .07
❑ 255 Mark Chmura .30 .10
❑ 256 Keenan McCardell .30 .10
❑ 257 Tony Bennett .20 .07
❑ 258 Irving Spikes .20 .07
❑ 259 Jason Dunn .20 .07
❑ 260 Joey Galloway .30 .10
❑ 261 Eddie Kennison .30 .10
❑ 262 Lonnie Marts .20 .07
❑ 263 Thomas Lewis .20 .07
❑ 264 Tedy Bruschi 1.00 .40
❑ 265 Steve Atwater .20 .07
❑ 266 Dorsey Levens .50 .20
❑ 267 Kurt Schulz .20 .07
❑ 268 Rob Moore .30 .10
❑ 269 Walt Harris .20 .07
❑ 270 Steve McNair .60 .25
❑ 271 Bill Romanowski .20 .07
❑ 272 Sean Dawkins .20 .07
❑ 273 Don Beebe .20 .07
❑ 274 Fernando Smith .20 .07
❑ 275 Willie McGinest .20 .07
❑ 276 Levon Kirkland .20 .07
❑ 277 Tony Martin .30 .10
❑ 278 Warren Sapp .30 .10
❑ 279 Lamar Smith .50 .20
❑ 280 Mark Brunell .60 .25
❑ 281 Jim Everett .20 .07
❑ 282 Victor Green .20 .07
❑ 283 Mike Jones .20 .07
❑ 284 Charlie Garner .30 .10
❑ 285 Karim Abdul-Jabbar .30 .10
❑ 286 Michael Westbrook .30 .10
❑ 287 Lawrence Phillips .20 .07
❑ 288 Amani Toomer .30 .10
❑ 289 Neil Smith .30 .10
❑ 290 Barry Sanders 1.50 .60
❑ 291 Willie Davis .20 .07
❑ 292 Bo Orlando .20 .07
❑ 293 Alonzo Spellman .20 .07
❑ 294 Eric Hill .20 .07
❑ 295 Wesley Walls .30 .10
❑ 296 Todd Collins .20 .07
❑ 297 Stevon Moore .20 .07
❑ 298 Eric Metcalf .30 .10
❑ 299 Darren Woodson .20 .07
❑ 300 Jerry Rice 1.00 .40
❑ 301 Scott Mitchell .30 .10
❑ 302 Ray Crockett .20 .07
❑ 303 Jim Schwantz RC UER .20 .07
❑ 304 Steve Tovar .20 .07
❑ 305 Terance Mathis .30 .10
❑ 306 Earnest Byner .20 .07
❑ 307 Chris Spielman .20 .07
❑ 308 Curtis Conway .30 .10
❑ 309 Cris Dishman .20 .07
❑ 310 Marvin Harrison .50 .20
❑ 311 Sam Mills .20 .07
❑ 312 Brent Alexander RC .20 .07
❑ 313 Shawn Wooden RC .20 .07
❑ 314 Dewayne Washington .20 .07
❑ 315 Terry Glenn .50 .20
❑ 316 Winfred Tubbs .20 .07
❑ 317 Dave Brown .20 .07
❑ 318 Neil O'Donnell .30 .10
❑ 319 Anthony Parker .20 .07
❑ 320 Junior Seau .50 .20
❑ 321 Brian Mitchell .20 .07
❑ 322 Regan Upshaw .20 .07
❑ 323 Darryl Williams .20 .07
❑ 324 Chris Doleman .20 .07
❑ 325 Rod Woodson .30 .10
❑ 326 Derrick Witherspoon .20 .07
❑ 327 Chester McGlockton .20 .07
❑ 328 Mickey Washington .20 .07
❑ 329 Greg Hill .20 .07
❑ 330 Reggie White .50 .20
❑ 331 John Copeland .20 .07
❑ 332 Doug Evans .20 .07
❑ 333 Lamar Lathon .20 .07
❑ 334 Mark Maddox .20 .07
❑ 335 Natrone Means .30 .10
❑ 336 Corey Widmer .20 .07
❑ 337 Terry Wooden .20 .07
❑ 338 Merton Hanks .20 .07
❑ 339 Cortez Kennedy .20 .07
❑ 340 Tyrone Hughes .20 .07
❑ 341 Tim Brown .50 .20
❑ 342 John Jurkovic .20 .07
❑ 343 Carnell Lake .20 .07
❑ 344 Stanley Richard .20 .07
❑ 345 Darryll Lewis .20 .07
❑ 346 Dan Wilkinson .20 .07
❑ 347 Broderick Thomas .20 .07
❑ 348 Brian Williams .20 .07
❑ 349 Eric Swann .20 .07
❑ 350 Dan Marino 2.00 .75
❑ 351 Anthony Johnson .20 .07
❑ 352 Joe Cain .20 .07
❑ 353 Quinn Early .20 .07
❑ 354 Seth Joyner .20 .07
❑ 355 Garrison Hearst .30 .10
❑ 356 Edgar Bennett .30 .10
❑ 357 Brian Washington .20 .07
❑ 358 Kevin Hardy .20 .07
❑ 359 Quentin Coryatt .20 .07
❑ 360 Tim McDonald .20 .07
❑ 361 Brian Blades .20 .07
❑ 362 Courtney Hawkins .20 .07
❑ 363 Ray Farmer .20 .07
❑ 364 Jessie Armstead .20 .07
❑ 365 Curtis Martin .60 .25
❑ 366 Zach Thomas .50 .20
❑ 367 Frank Wycheck .30 .10
❑ 368 Darnay Scott .30 .10
❑ 369 Percy Ellsworth RC .20 .07
❑ 370 Desmond Howard .30 .10
❑ 371 Aeneas Williams .20 .07
❑ 372 Bryce Paup .20 .07
❑ 373 Michael Bates .20 .07
❑ 374 Brad Johnson .50 .20
❑ 375 Jeff Blake .30 .10
❑ 376 Donnell Woolford UER .20 .07
❑ 377 Mo Lewis .20 .07
❑ 378 Phillippi Sparks .20 .07
❑ 379 Michael Bankston .20 .07
❑ 380 LeRoy Butler .20 .07
❑ 381 Tyrone Poole .20 .07
❑ 382 Wayne Chrebet .50 .20
❑ 383 Chris Slade .20 .07
❑ 384 Checklist 1 (1-208) .20 .07
❑ 385 Checklist 2 (209-415) .20 .07
❑ 386 Will Blackwell RC SP .30 .10
❑ 387 Tom Knight RC SP .20 .07
❑ 388 Darnell Autry RC SP .50 .20
❑ 389 Bryant Westbrook RC SP .20 .07
❑ 390 David LaFleur RC SP .30 .10
❑ 391 Antowain Smith RC SP 2.50 1.00
❑ 392 Kevin Lockett RC SP .50 .20
❑ 393 Rae Carruth RC SP .30 .10
❑ 394 Renaldo Wynn RC SP .30 .10
❑ 395 Jim Druckenmiller RC SP .50 .20
❑ 396 Kenny Holmes RC SP .75 .30
❑ 397 Shawn Springs RC SP .50 .20
❑ 398 Troy Davis RC SP .50 .20
❑ 399 Dwayne Rudd RC SP .75 .30
❑ 400 Orlando Pace RC SP .75 .30
❑ 401 Byron Hanspard RC SP .50 .20
❑ 402 Corey Dillon RC SP 6.00 2.50
❑ 403 Walter Jones RC SP [illegible] [illegible]
❑ 404 Reidel Anthony RC SP .75 .30
❑ 405 Peter Boulware RC SP .75 .30
❑ 406 Reinard Wilson RC SP .50 .20
❑ 407 Pat Barnes RC SP .75 .30
❑ 408 Yatil Green RC SP .75 .30
❑ 409 Joey Kent RC SP .75 .30
❑ 410 Ike Hilliard RC SP 1.50 .60
❑ 411 Jake Plummer SP RC 5.00 2.00
❑ 412 Darrell Russell RC SP .30 .10
❑ 413 James Farrior RC SP .75 .30
❑ 414 Tony Gonzalez RC SP 3.00 1.25
❑ 415 Warrick Dunn RC SP 3.00 1.25
❑ P40 Gus Frerotte PROMO .25 .10
❑ P170 Vinny Testaverde PROMO .25 .10
❑ P240 Cris Carter PROMO .40 .15
❑ P250 Marcus Allen PROMO .40 .15
❑ P285 Karim Abdul-Jabbar PROMO .25 .10
❑ P356 Edgar Bennett PROMO .25 .10

1998 Topps

❑ COMPLETE SET (360) 60.00 30.00
❑ COMP FACT SET (365) 80.00 40.00
❑ 1 Barry Sanders 1.50 .60
❑ 2 Derrick Rodgers .20 .07
❑ 3 Chris Calloway .20 .07
❑ 4 Bruce Armstrong .20 .07
❑ 5 Horace Copeland .20 .07
❑ 6 Chad Brown .20 .07
❑ 7 Ken Harvey .20 .07
❑ 8 Levon Kirkland .20 .07
❑ 9 Glenn Foley .30 .10
❑ 10 Corey Dillon .50 .20
❑ 11 Sean Dawkins .20 .07
❑ 12 Curtis Conway .30 .10
❑ 13 Chris Chandler .30 .10
❑ 14 Kerry Collins .30 .10
❑ 15 Jonathan Ogden .20 .07
❑ 16 Sam Shade .20 .07
❑ 17 Vaughn Hebron .20 .07
❑ 18 Quentin Coryatt .20 .07
❑ 19 Jerris McPhail .20 .07
❑ 20 Warrick Dunn .50 .20
❑ 21 Wayne Martin .20 .07
❑ 22 Chad Lewis .30 .10
❑ 23 Danny Kanell .30 .10
❑ 24 Shawn Springs .20 .07
❑ 25 Emmitt Smith 1.50 .60
❑ 26 Todd Lyght .20 .07
❑ 27 Donnie Edwards .20 .07
❑ 28 Charlie Jones .20 .07
❑ 29 Willie McGinest .20 .07
❑ 30 Steve Young .60 .25
❑ 31 Darrell Russell .20 .07

❑ 32 Gary Anderson	.20	.07
❑ 33 Stanley Richard	.20	.07
❑ 34 Leslie O'Neal	.20	.07
❑ 35 Dermontti Dawson	.20	.07
❑ 36 Jeff Brady	.20	.07
❑ 37 Kimble Anders	.30	.10
❑ 38 Glyn Milburn	.20	.07
❑ 39 Greg Hill	.20	.07
❑ 40 Freddie Jones	.20	.07
❑ 41 Bobby Engram	.30	.10
❑ 42 Aeneas Williams	.20	.07
❑ 43 Antowain Smith	.50	.20
❑ 44 Reggie White	.50	.20
❑ 45 Rae Carruth	.20	.07
❑ 46 Leon Johnson	.20	.07
❑ 47 Bryant Young	.20	.07
❑ 48 Jamie Asher	.20	.07
❑ 49 Hardy Nickerson	.20	.07
❑ 50 Jerome Bettis	.50	.20
❑ 51 Michael Strahan	.30	.10
❑ 52 John Randle	.30	.10
❑ 53 Kevin Hardy	.20	.07
❑ 54 Eric Bjornson	.20	.07
❑ 55 Morten Andersen UER	.20	.07
❑ 56 Larry Centers	.20	.07
❑ 57 Bryce Paup	.20	.07
❑ 58 John Mobley	.20	.07
❑ 59 Michael Bates	.20	.07
❑ 60 Tim Brown	.50	.20
❑ 61 Doug Evans	.20	.07
❑ 62 Will Shields	.20	.07
❑ 63 Jeff Graham	.20	.07
❑ 64 Henry Jones	.20	.07
❑ 65 Steve Broussard	.20	.07
❑ 66 Blaine Bishop	.20	.07
❑ 67 Ernie Conwell	.20	.07
❑ 68 Heath Shuler	.20	.07
❑ 69 Eric Metcalf	.20	.07
❑ 70 Terry Glenn	.50	.20
❑ 71 James Hasty	.20	.07
❑ 72 Robert Porcher	.20	.07
❑ 73 Keenan McCardell	.30	.10
❑ 74 Tyrone Hughes	.20	.07
❑ 75 Troy Aikman	1.00	.40
❑ 76 Peter Boulware	.20	.07
❑ 77 Rob Johnson	.30	.10
❑ 78 Erik Kramer	.20	.07
❑ 79 Kevin Smith	.20	.07
❑ 80 Andre Rison	.30	.10
❑ 81 Jim Harbaugh	.30	.10
❑ 82 Chris Hudson	.20	.07
❑ 83 Ray Zellars	.20	.07
❑ 84 Jeff George	.30	.10
❑ 85 Willie Davis	.20	.07
❑ 86 Jason Gildon	.20	.07
❑ 87 Robert Brooks	.30	.10
❑ 88 Chad Cota	.20	.07
❑ 89 Simeon Rice	.30	.10
❑ 90 Mark Brunell	.50	.20
❑ 91 Jay Graham	.20	.07
❑ 92 Scott Greene	.20	.07
❑ 93 Jeff Blake	.30	.10
❑ 94 Jason Belser	.20	.07
❑ 95 Derrick Alexander DE	.20	.07
❑ 96 Ty Law	.30	.10
❑ 97 Charles Johnson	.20	.07
❑ 98 James Jett	.30	.10
❑ 99 Darrell Green	.30	.10
❑ 100 Brett Favre	2.00	.75
❑ 101 George Jones	.20	.07
❑ 102 Derrick Mason	.30	.10
❑ 103 Sam Adams	.20	.07
❑ 104 Lawrence Phillips	.20	.07
❑ 105 Randal Hill	.20	.07
❑ 106 John Mangum	.20	.07
❑ 107 Natrone Means	.30	.10
❑ 108 Bill Romanowski	.20	.07
❑ 109 Terance Mathis	.30	.10
❑ 110 Bruce Smith	.30	.10
❑ 111 Pete Mitchell	.20	.07
❑ 112 Duane Clemons	.20	.07
❑ 113 Willie Clay	.20	.07
❑ 114 Eric Allen	.20	.07
❑ 115 Troy Drayton	.20	.07
❑ 116 Derrick Thomas	.50	.20
❑ 117 Charles Way	.20	.07
❑ 118 Wayne Chrebet	.50	.20
❑ 119 Bobby Hoying	.30	.10
❑ 120 Michael Jackson	.20	.07
❑ 121 Gary Zimmerman	.20	.07
❑ 122 Yancey Thigpen	.20	.07
❑ 123 Dana Stubblefield	.20	.07
❑ 124 Keith Lyle	.20	.07
❑ 125 Marco Coleman	.20	.07
❑ 126 Karl Williams	.20	.07
❑ 127 Stephen Davis	.20	.07
❑ 128 Chris Sanders	.20	.07
❑ 129 Cris Dishman	.20	.07
❑ 130 Jake Plummer	.50	.20
❑ 131 Darryl Williams	.20	.07
❑ 132 Merton Hanks	.20	.07
❑ 133 Torrance Small	.20	.07
❑ 134 Aaron Glenn	.20	.07
❑ 135 Chester McGlockton	.20	.07
❑ 136 William Thomas	.20	.07
❑ 137 Kordell Stewart	.50	.20
❑ 138 Jason Taylor	.30	.10
❑ 139 Lake Dawson	.20	.07
❑ 140 Carl Pickens	.30	.10
❑ 141 Eugene Robinson	.20	.07
❑ 142 Ed McCaffrey	.30	.10
❑ 143 Lamar Lathon	.20	.07
❑ 144 Ray Buchanan	.20	.07
❑ 145 Thurman Thomas	.50	.20
❑ 146 Andre Reed	.30	.10
❑ 147 Wesley Walls	.30	.10
❑ 148 Rob Moore	.30	.10
❑ 149 Darren Woodson	.20	.07
❑ 150 Eddie George	.50	.20
❑ 151 Michael Irvin	.50	.20
❑ 152 Johnnie Morton	.30	.10
❑ 153 Ken Dilger	.20	.07
❑ 154 Tony Boselli	.20	.07
❑ 155 Randall McDaniel	.20	.07
❑ 156 Mark Fields	.20	.07
❑ 157 Phillippi Sparks	.20	.07
❑ 158 Troy Davis	.20	.07
❑ 159 Troy Vincent	.20	.07
❑ 160 Cris Carter	.50	.20
❑ 161 Amp Lee	.20	.07
❑ 162 Will Blackwell	.20	.07
❑ 163 Chad Scott	.20	.07
❑ 164 Henry Ellard	.30	.10
❑ 165 Robert Jones	.20	.07
❑ 166 Garrison Hearst	.50	.20
❑ 167 James McKnight	.50	.20
❑ 168 Rodney Harrison	.30	.10
❑ 169 Adrian Murrell	.30	.10
❑ 170 Rod Smith WR	.30	.10
❑ 171 Desmond Howard	.30	.10
❑ 172 Ben Coates	.30	.10
❑ 173 David Palmer	.20	.07
❑ 174 Zach Thomas	.50	.20
❑ 175 Dale Carter	.20	.07
❑ 176 Mark Chmura	.30	.10
❑ 177 Elvis Grbac	.30	.10
❑ 178 Jason Hanson	.20	.07
❑ 179 Walt Harris	.20	.07
❑ 180 Ricky Watters	.30	.10
❑ 181 Ray Lewis	.50	.20
❑ 182 Lonnie Johnson	.20	.07
❑ 183 Marvin Harrison	.50	.20
❑ 184 Dorsey Levens	.50	.20
❑ 185 Tony Gonzalez	.50	.20
❑ 186 Andre Hastings	.20	.07
❑ 187 Kevin Turner	.20	.07
❑ 188 Mo Lewis	.20	.07
❑ 189 Jason Sehorn	.30	.10
❑ 190 Drew Bledsoe	.75	.30
❑ 191 Michael Sinclair	.20	.07
❑ 192 William Floyd	.20	.07
❑ 193 Kenny Holmes	.20	.07
❑ 194 Marvcus Patton	.20	.07
❑ 195 Warren Sapp	.30	.10
❑ 196 Junior Seau	.50	.20
❑ 197 Ryan McNeil	.20	.07
❑ 198 Tyrone Wheatley	.30	.10
❑ 199 Robert Smith	.50	.20
❑ 200 Terrell Davis	.50	.20
❑ 201 Brett Perriman	.20	.07
❑ 202 Tamarick Vanover	.20	.07
❑ 203 Stephen Boyd	.20	.07
❑ 204 Zack Crockett	.20	.07
❑ 205 Sherman Williams	.20	.07
❑ 206 Neil Smith	.30	.10
❑ 207 Jermaine Lewis	.30	.10
❑ 208 Kevin Williams	.20	.07
❑ 209 Byron Hanspard	.20	.07
❑ 210 Warren Moon	.50	.20
❑ 211 Tony McGee	.20	.07
❑ 212 Raymont Harris	.20	.07
❑ 213 Eric Davis	.20	.07
❑ 214 Darrien Gordon	.20	.07
❑ 215 James Stewart	.30	.10
❑ 216 Derrick Mayes	.30	.10
❑ 217 Brad Johnson	.50	.20
❑ 218 Karim Abdul-Jabbar UER	.50	.20
❑ 219 Hugh Douglas	.20	.07
❑ 220 Terry Allen	.50	.20
❑ 221 Rhett Hall	.20	.07
❑ 222 Terrell Fletcher	.20	.07
❑ 223 Carnell Lake	.20	.07
❑ 224 Darryll Lewis	.20	.07
❑ 225 Chris Slade	.20	.07
❑ 226 Michael Westbrook	.30	.10
❑ 227 Willie Williams	.20	.07
❑ 228 Tony Banks	.30	.10
❑ 229 Keyshawn Johnson	.50	.20
❑ 230 Mike Alstott	.50	.20
❑ 231 Tiki Barber	.50	.20
❑ 232 Jake Reed	.30	.10
❑ 233 Eric Swann	.20	.07
❑ 234 Eric Moulds	.50	.20
❑ 235 Vinny Testaverde	.30	.10
❑ 236 Jessie Tuggle	.20	.07
❑ 237 Ryan Wetnight RC	.20	.07
❑ 238 Tyrone Poole	.20	.07
❑ 239 Bryant Westbrook	.20	.07
❑ 240 Steve McNair	.50	.20
❑ 241 Jimmy Smith	.30	.10
❑ 242 Dewayne Washington	.20	.07
❑ 243 Robert Harris	.20	.07
❑ 244 Rod Woodson	.30	.10
❑ 245 Reidel Anthony	.30	.10
❑ 246 Jessie Armstead	.20	.07
❑ 247 O.J. McDuffie	.30	.10
❑ 248 Carlton Gray	.20	.07
❑ 249 LeRoy Butler	.20	.07
❑ 250 Jerry Rice	1.00	.40
❑ 251 Frank Sanders	.30	.10
❑ 252 Todd Collins	.20	.07
❑ 253 Fred Lane	.20	.07
❑ 254 David Dunn	.20	.07
❑ 255 Micheal Barrow	.20	.07
❑ 256 Luther Elliss	.20	.07
❑ 257 Scott Mitchell	.30	.10
❑ 258 Dave Meggett	.20	.07
❑ 259 Rickey Dudley	.20	.07
❑ 260 Isaac Bruce	.50	.20
❑ 261 Tony Martin	.30	.10
❑ 262 Leslie Shepherd	.20	.07
❑ 263 Derrick Brooks	.50	.20
❑ 264 Greg Lloyd	.20	.07
❑ 265 Terrell Buckley	.20	.07
❑ 266 Antonio Freeman	.50	.20
❑ 267 Tony Brackens	.20	.07
❑ 268 Mark McMillian	.20	.07
❑ 269 Dexter Coakley	.20	.07
❑ 270 Dan Marino	2.00	.75
❑ 271 Bryan Cox	.20	.07
❑ 272 Leeland McElroy	.20	.07
❑ 273 Jeff Burris	.20	.07
❑ 274 Eric Green	.20	.07
❑ 275 Darnay Scott	.30	.10
❑ 276 Greg Clark	.20	.07
❑ 277 Mario Bates	.30	.10
❑ 278 Eric Turner	.20	.07
❑ 279 Neil O'Donnell	.30	.10
❑ 280 Herman Moore	.30	.10
❑ 281 Gary Brown	.20	.07
❑ 282 Terrell Owens	.50	.20
❑ 283 Frank Wycheck	.20	.07

❑ 284 Trent Dilfer .50 .20
❑ 285 Curtis Martin .50 .20
❑ 286 Ricky Proehl .20 .07
❑ 287 Steve Atwater .20 .07
❑ 288 Aaron Bailey .20 .07
❑ 289 William Henderson .30 .10
❑ 290 Marcus Allen .50 .20
❑ 291 Tom Knight .20 .07
❑ 292 Quinn Early .20 .07
❑ 293 Michael McCrary .20 .07
❑ 294 Bert Emanuel .30 .10
❑ 295 Tom Carter .20 .07
❑ 296 Kevin Glover .20 .07
❑ 297 [illegible]
❑ 298 Harvey Williams .20 .07
❑ 299 Chris Warren .30 .10
❑ 300 John Elway 2.00 .75
❑ 301 Eddie Kennison .30 .10
❑ 302 Gus Frerotte .20 .07
❑ 303 Regan Upshaw .20 .07
❑ 304 Kevin Gogan .20 .07
❑ 305 Napoleon Kaufman .50 .20
❑ 306 Charlie Garner .30 .10
❑ 307 Shawn Jefferson .20 .07
❑ 308 Tommy Vardell .20 .07
❑ 309 Mike Hollis .20 .07
❑ 310 Irving Fryar .30 .10
❑ 311 Shannon Sharpe .30 .10
❑ 312 Byron Bam Morris .20 .07
❑ 313 Jamal Anderson .50 .20
❑ 314 Chris Gedney .20 .07
❑ 315 Chris Spielman .20 .07
❑ 316 Derrick Alexander WR .30 .10
❑ 317 O.J. Santiago .20 .07
❑ 318 Anthony Miller .20 .07
❑ 319 Ki-Jana Carter .20 .07
❑ 320 Deion Sanders .50 .20
❑ 321 Joey Galloway .30 .10
❑ 322 J.J. Stokes .30 .10
❑ 323 Rodney Thomas .20 .07
❑ 324 John Lynch .30 .10
❑ 325 Mike Pritchard .20 .07
❑ 326 Terrance Shaw .20 .07
❑ 327 Ted Johnson .20 .07
❑ 328 Ashley Ambrose .20 .07
❑ 329 Checklist 1 .20 .07
❑ 330 Checklist 2 .20 .07
❑ 331 Jerome Pathon RC 2.50 1.00
❑ 332 Ryan Leaf RC 2.50 1.00
❑ 333 Duane Starks RC 1.25 .50
❑ 334 Brian Simmons RC 2.00 .75
❑ 335 Keith Brooking RC 2.50 1.00
❑ 336 Robert Edwards RC 2.00 .75
❑ 337 Curtis Enis RC 1.25 .50
❑ 338 John Avery RC 2.00 .75
❑ 339 Fred Taylor RC 4.00 1.50
❑ 340 Germane Crowell RC 2.00 .75
❑ 341 Hines Ward RC 10.00 4.00
❑ 342 Marcus Nash RC 1.25 .50
❑ 343 Jacquez Green RC 2.00 .75
❑ 344 Joe Jurevicius RC 2.50 1.00
❑ 345 Greg Ellis RC 1.25 .50
❑ 346 Brian Griese RC 5.00 2.00
❑ 347 Tavian Banks RC 2.00 .75
❑ 348 Robert Holcombe RC 2.00 .75
❑ 349 Skip Hicks RC 2.00 .75
❑ 350 Ahman Green RC 12.00 5.00
❑ 351 Takeo Spikes RC 2.50 1.00
❑ 352 Randy Moss RC 15.00 7.50
❑ 353 Andre Wadsworth RC 2.00 .75
❑ 354 Jason Peter RC 1.25 .50
❑ 355 Grant Wistrom RC 2.00 .75
❑ 356 Charles Woodson RC 3.00 1.25
❑ 357 Kevin Dyson RC 2.50 1.00
❑ 358 Pat Johnson RC 2.00 .75
❑ 359 Tim Dwight RC 2.50 1.00
❑ 360 Peyton Manning RC 25.00 12.50
❑ P1 Robert Tisch 5.00 2.00

1999 Topps

❑ COMPLETE SET (357) 50.00 20.00
❑ COMP.SET w/o SP's (330) 20.00 10.00
❑ 1 Terrell Davis .60 .25
❑ 2 Adrian Murrell .40 .15
❑ 3 Ernie Mills .25 .08
❑ 4 Jimmy Hitchcock .25 .08
❑ 5 Charlie Garner .40 .15
❑ 6 Blaine Bishop .25 .08
❑ 7 Junior Seau .60 .25
❑ 8 Andre Rison .40 .15
❑ 9 Jake Reed .40 .15
❑ 10 Cris Carter .60 .25
❑ 11 Torrance Small .25 .08
❑ 12 Ronald McKinnon .25 .08
❑ 13 Tyrone Davis .25 .08
❑ 14 Warren Moon .60 .25
❑ 15 Joe Johnson .25 .08
❑ 16 Bert Emanuel .40 .15
❑ 17 Brad Culpepper .25 .08
❑ 18 Henry Jones .25 .08
❑ 19 Jonathan Ogden .25 .08
❑ 20 Terrell Owens .60 .25
❑ 21 Derrick Mason .40 .15
❑ 22 Jon Ritchie .25 .08
❑ 23 Eric Metcalf .25 .08
❑ 24 Kevin Carter .25 .08
❑ 25 Fred Taylor .60 .25
❑ 26 DeWayne Washington .25 .08
❑ 27 William Thomas .25 .08
❑ 28 Rocket Ismail .40 .15
❑ 29 Jason Taylor .25 .08
❑ 30 Doug Flutie .60 .25
❑ 31 Michael Sinclair .25 .08
❑ 32 Yancey Thigpen .25 .08
❑ 33 Darnay Scott .25 .08
❑ 34 Amani Toomer .25 .08
❑ 35 Edgar Bennett .25 .08
❑ 36 LeRoy Butler .25 .08
❑ 37 Jessie Tuggle .25 .08
❑ 38 Andrew Glover .25 .08
❑ 39 Tim McDonald .25 .08
❑ 40 Marshall Faulk .75 .30
❑ 41 Ray Mickens .25 .08
❑ 42 Kimble Anders .40 .15
❑ 43 Trent Green .60 .25
❑ 44 Dermontti Dawson .25 .08
❑ 45 Greg Ellis .25 .08
❑ 46 Hugh Douglas .25 .08
❑ 47 Amp Lee .25 .08
❑ 48 Lamar Thomas .25 .08
❑ 49 Curtis Conway .40 .15
❑ 50 Emmitt Smith 1.25 .50
❑ 51 Elvis Grbac .40 .15
❑ 52 Tony Simmons .25 .08
❑ 53 Darrin Smith .25 .08
❑ 54 Donovin Darius .25 .08
❑ 55 Corey Chavous .25 .08
❑ 56 Phillippi Sparks .25 .08
❑ 57 Luther Elliss .25 .08
❑ 58 Tim Dwight .60 .25
❑ 59 Andre Hastings .25 .08
❑ 60 Dan Marino 2.00 .75
❑ 61 Micheal Barrow .25 .08
❑ 62 Corey Fuller .25 .08
❑ 63 Bill Romanowski .25 .08
❑ 64 Derrick Rodgers .40 .15
❑ 65 Natrone Means .40 .15
❑ 66 Peter Boulware .25 .08
❑ 67 Brian Mitchell .25 .08
❑ 68 Cornelius Bennett .25 .08
❑ 69 Dedric Ward .25 .08
❑ 70 Drew Bledsoe .75 .30
❑ 71 Freddie Jones .25 .08
❑ 72 Derrick Thomas .60 .25
❑ 73 Willie Davis .25 .08
❑ 74 Larry Centers .25 .08
❑ 75 Mark Brunell .60 .25
❑ 76 Chuck Smith .25 .08
❑ 77 Desmond Howard .40 .15
❑ 78 Sedrick Shaw .25 .08
❑ 79 Tiki Barber .60 .25
❑ 80 Curtis Martin .60 .25
❑ 81 Barry Minter .25 .08
❑ 82 Skip Hicks .25 .08
❑ 83 [illegible]
❑ 84 Ed McCaffrey .40 .15
❑ 85 Terrell Buckley .25 .08
❑ 86 Charlie Jones .25 .08
❑ 87 Pete Mitchell .25 .08
❑ 88 La'Roi Glover RC .60 .25
❑ 89 Eric Davis .25 .08
❑ 90 John Elway 2.00 .75
❑ 91 Kavika Pittman .25 .08
❑ 92 Fred Lane .25 .08
❑ 93 Warren Sapp .25 .08
❑ 94 Lorenzo Bromell RC .60 .25
❑ 95 Lawyer Milloy .40 .15
❑ 96 Aeneas Williams .25 .08
❑ 97 Michael McCrary .25 .08
❑ 98 Rickey Dudley .25 .08
❑ 99 Bryce Paup .25 .08
❑ 100 Jamal Anderson .60 .25
❑ 101 D'Marco Farr .25 .08
❑ 102 Johnnie Morton .40 .15
❑ 103 Jeff Graham .25 .08
❑ 104 Sam Cowart .25 .08
❑ 105 Bryant Young .25 .08
❑ 106 Jermaine Lewis .40 .15
❑ 107 Chad Bratzke .25 .08
❑ 108 Jeff Burris .25 .08
❑ 109 Roell Preston .25 .08
❑ 110 Vinny Testaverde .40 .15
❑ 111 Ruben Brown .25 .08
❑ 112 Darryll Lewis .25 .08
❑ 113 Billy Davis .25 .08
❑ 114 Bryant Westbrook .25 .08
❑ 115 Stephen Alexander .25 .08
❑ 116 Terrell Fletcher .25 .08
❑ 117 Terry Glenn .60 .25
❑ 118 Rod Smith .40 .15
❑ 119 Carl Pickens .40 .15
❑ 120 Tim Brown .60 .25
❑ 121 Mikhael Ricks .25 .08
❑ 122 Jason Gildon .25 .08
❑ 123 Charles Way .25 .08
❑ 124 Rob Moore .40 .15
❑ 125 Jerome Bettis .60 .25
❑ 126 Kerry Collins .40 .15
❑ 127 Bruce Smith .40 .15
❑ 128 James Hasty .25 .08
❑ 129 Ken Norton Jr. .25 .08
❑ 130 Charles Woodson .60 .25
❑ 131 Tony McGee .25 .08
❑ 132 Kevin Turner .25 .08
❑ 133 Jerome Pathon .25 .08
❑ 134 Garrison Hearst .40 .15
❑ 135 Craig Newsome .25 .08
❑ 136 Hardy Nickerson .25 .08
❑ 137 Ray Lewis .60 .25
❑ 138 Derrick Alexander .25 .08
❑ 139 Phil Hansen .25 .08
❑ 140 Joey Galloway .40 .15
❑ 141 Oronde Gadsden .40 .15
❑ 142 Herman Moore .40 .15
❑ 143 Bobby Taylor .25 .08
❑ 144 Mario Bates .25 .08
❑ 145 Kevin Dyson .40 .15
❑ 146 Aaron Glenn .25 .08
❑ 147 Ed McDaniel .25 .08
❑ 148 Terry Allen .40 .15
❑ 149 Ike Hilliard .25 .08
❑ 150 Steve Young .75 .30
❑ 151 Eugene Robinson .25 .08
❑ 152 John Mobley .25 .08
❑ 153 Kevin Hardy .25 .08

❑	154 Lance Johnstone	.25	.08
❑	155 Willie McGinest	.25	.08
❑	156 Gary Anderson	.25	.08
❑	157 Dexter Coakley	.25	.08
❑	158 Mark Fields	.25	.08
❑	159 Steve McNair	.60	.25
❑	160 Corey Dillon	.60	.25
❑	161 Zach Thomas	.60	.25
❑	162 Kent Graham	.25	.08
❑	163 Tony Parrish	.25	.08
❑	164 Sam Gash	.25	.08
❑	165 Kyle Brady	.25	.08
❑	166 Donnell Bennett	.25	.08
❑	167 Tony Martin	.40	.15
❑	168 Michael Bates	.25	.08
❑	169 Bobby Engram	.40	.15
❑	170 Jimmy Smith	.40	.15
❑	171 Vonnie Holliday	.25	.08
❑	172 Simeon Rice	.40	.15
❑	173 Kevin Greene	.25	.08
❑	174 Mike Alstott	.60	.25
❑	175 Eddie George	.60	.25
❑	176 Michael Jackson	.25	.08
❑	177 Neil O'Donnell	.40	.15
❑	178 Sean Dawkins	.25	.08
❑	179 Courtney Hawkins	.25	.08
❑	180 Michael Irvin	.40	.15
❑	181 Thurman Thomas	.40	.15
❑	182 Cam Cleeland	.25	.08
❑	183 Ellis Johnson	.25	.08
❑	184 Will Blackwell	.25	.08
❑	185 Ty Law	.40	.15
❑	186 Merton Hanks	.25	.08
❑	187 Dan Wilkinson	.25	.08
❑	188 Andre Wadsworth	.25	.08
❑	189 Troy Vincent	.25	.08
❑	190 Frank Sanders	.40	.15
❑	191 Stephen Boyd	.25	.08
❑	192 Jason Elam	.25	.08
❑	193 Kordell Stewart	.40	.15
❑	194 Ted Johnson	.25	.08
❑	195 Glyn Milburn	.25	.08
❑	196 Gary Brown	.25	.08
❑	197 Travis Hall	.25	.08
❑	198 John Randle	.40	.15
❑	199 Jay Riemersma	.25	.08
❑	200 Barry Sanders	2.00	.75
❑	201 Chris Spielman	.25	.08
❑	202 Rod Woodson	.40	.15
❑	203 Darrell Russell	.25	.08
❑	204 Tony Boselli	.25	.08
❑	205 Darren Woodson	.25	.08
❑	206 Muhsin Muhammad	.40	.15
❑	207 Jim Harbaugh	.40	.15
❑	208 Isaac Bruce	.60	.25
❑	209 Mo Lewis	.25	.08
❑	210 Dorsey Levens	.60	.25
❑	211 Frank Wycheck	.25	.08
❑	212 Napoleon Kaufman	.60	.25
❑	213 Walt Harris	.25	.08
❑	214 Leon Lett	.25	.08
❑	215 Karim Abdul-Jabbar	.40	.15
❑	216 Carnell Lake	.25	.08
❑	217 Byron Bam Morris	.25	.08
❑	218 John Avery	.25	.08
❑	219 Chris Slade	.25	.08
❑	220 Robert Smith	.60	.25
❑	221 Mike Pritchard	.25	.08
❑	222 Ty Detmer	.40	.15
❑	223 Randall Cunningham	.60	.25
❑	224 Alonzo Mayes	.25	.08
❑	225 Jake Plummer	.40	.15
❑	226 Derrick Mayes	.25	.08
❑	227 Jeff Brady	.25	.08
❑	228 John Lynch	.40	.15
❑	229 Steve Atwater	.25	.08
❑	230 Warrick Dunn	.60	.25
❑	231 Shawn Jefferson	.25	.08
❑	232 Erik Kramer	.25	.08
❑	233 Ken Dilger	.25	.08
❑	234 Ryan Leaf	.60	.25
❑	235 Ray Buchanan	.25	.08
❑	236 Kevin Williams	.25	.08
❑	237 Ricky Watters	.40	.15
❑	238 Dwayne Rudd	.25	.08
❑	239 Duce Staley	.60	.25
❑	240 Charlie Batch	.60	.25
❑	241 Tim Biakabutuka	.40	.15
❑	242 Tony Gonzalez	.60	.25
❑	243 Bryan Still	.25	.08
❑	244 Donnie Edwards	.25	.08
❑	245 Troy Aikman	1.25	.50
❑	246 Tony Banks	.40	.15
❑	247 Curtis Enis	.25	.08
❑	248 Chris Chandler	.40	.15
❑	249 James Jett	.40	.15
❑	250 Brett Favre	2.00	.75
❑	251 Keith Poole	.25	.08
❑	252 Ricky Proehl	.25	.08
❑	253 Shannon Sharpe	.40	.15
❑	254 Robert Jones	.25	.08
❑	255 Chad Brown	.25	.08
❑	256 Ben Coates	.40	.15
❑	257 Jacquez Green	.25	.08
❑	258 Jessie Armstead	.25	.08
❑	259 Dale Carter	.25	.08
❑	260 Antowain Smith	.60	.25
❑	261 Mark Chmura	.25	.08
❑	262 Michael Westbrook	.40	.15
❑	263 Marvin Harrison	.60	.25
❑	264 Darrien Gordon	.25	.08
❑	265 Rodney Harrison	.25	.08
❑	266 Charles Johnson	.25	.08
❑	267 Roman Phifer	.25	.08
❑	268 Reidel Anthony	.40	.15
❑	269 Jerry Rice	1.25	.50
❑	270 Eric Moulds	.60	.25
❑	271 Robert Porcher	.25	.08
❑	272 Deion Sanders	.60	.25
❑	273 Germane Crowell	.25	.08
❑	274 Randy Moss	1.50	.60
❑	275 Antonio Freeman	.60	.25
❑	276 Trent Dilfer	.40	.15
❑	277 Eric Turner	.25	.08
❑	278 Jeff George	.40	.15
❑	279 Levon Kirkland	.25	.08
❑	280 O.J. McDuffie	.40	.15
❑	281 Takeo Spikes	.25	.08
❑	282 Jim Flanigan	.25	.08
❑	283 Chris Warren	.25	.08
❑	284 J.J. Stokes	.40	.15
❑	285 Bryan Cox	.25	.08
❑	286 Sam Madison	.25	.08
❑	287 Priest Holmes	1.00	.40
❑	288 Keenan McCardell	.40	.15
❑	289 Michael Strahan	.40	.15
❑	290 Robert Edwards	.25	.08
❑	291 Tommy Vardell	.25	.08
❑	292 Wayne Chrebet	.40	.15
❑	293 Chris Calloway	.25	.08
❑	294 Wesley Walls	.40	.15
❑	295 Derrick Brooks	.60	.25
❑	296 Trace Armstrong	.25	.08
❑	297 Brian Simmons	.25	.08
❑	298 Darrell Green	.25	.08
❑	299 Robert Brooks	.40	.15
❑	300 Peyton Manning	2.00	.75
❑	301 Dana Stubblefield	.25	.08
❑	302 Shawn Springs	.25	.08
❑	303 Leslie Shepherd	.25	.08
❑	304 Ken Harvey	.25	.08
❑	305 Jon Kitna	.60	.25
❑	306 Terance Mathis	.40	.15
❑	307 Andre Reed	.40	.15
❑	308 Jackie Harris	.25	.08
❑	309 Rich Gannon	.60	.25
❑	310 Keyshawn Johnson	.60	.25
❑	311 Victor Green	.25	.08
❑	312 Eric Allen	.25	.08
❑	313 Terry Fair	.25	.08
❑	314 Jason Elam SH	.25	.08
❑	315 Garrison Hearst SH	.40	.15
❑	316 Jake Plummer SH	.40	.15
❑	317 Randall Cunningham SH	.60	.25
❑	318 Randy Moss SH	.75	.30
❑	319 Jamal Anderson SH	.60	.25
❑	320 John Elway SH	1.00	.40
❑	321 Doug Flutie SH	.40	.15
❑	322 Emmitt Smith SH	.75	.30
❑	323 Terrell Davis SH	.60	.25
❑	324 Jerris McPhail	.25	.08
❑	325 Damon Gibson	.25	.08
❑	326 Jim Pyne	.25	.08
❑	327 Antonio Langham	.25	.08
❑	328 Freddie Solomon	.25	.08
❑	329 Ricky Williams RC	4.00	1.50
❑	330 Daunte Culpepper RC	8.00	3.00
❑	331 Chris Claiborne RC	1.25	.50
❑	332 Amos Zereoue RC	2.50	1.00
❑	333 Chris McAlister RC	2.00	.75
❑	334 Kevin Faulk RC	2.50	1.00
❑	335 James Johnson RC	2.00	.75
❑	336 Mike Cloud RC	2.00	.75
❑	337 Jevon Kearse RC	4.00	1.50
❑	338 Akili Smith RC	2.00	.75
❑	339 Edgerrin James RC	8.00	3.00
❑	340 Cecil Collins RC	1.25	.50
❑	341 Donovan McNabb RC	10.00	4.00
❑	342 Kevin Johnson RC	2.50	1.00
❑	343 Torry Holt RC	5.00	2.00
❑	344 Rob Konrad RC	1.25	.50
❑	345 Tim Couch RC	2.50	1.00
❑	346 David Boston RC	2.50	1.00
❑	347 Karsten Bailey RC	2.00	.75
❑	348 Troy Edwards RC	2.00	.75
❑	349 Sedrick Irvin RC	1.25	.50
❑	350 Shaun King RC	2.00	.75
❑	351 Peerless Price RC	2.50	1.00
❑	352 Brock Huard RC	2.50	1.00
❑	353 Cade McNown RC	2.00	.75
❑	354 Champ Bailey RC	3.00	1.25
❑	355 D'Wayne Bates RC	2.00	.75
❑	356 Checklist Card	.25	.08
❑	357 Checklist Card	.25	.08

2000 Topps

❑	COMPLETE SET (400)	60.00	25.00
❑	COMP.SET w/o SP's (360)	20.00	7.50
❑	SBMVP STATED ODDS 1:1287 HTA		
❑	1 Kurt Warner	1.25	.50
❑	2 Darrell Russell	.25	.08
❑	3 Tai Streets	.25	.08
❑	4 Bryant Young	.25	.08
❑	5 Kent Graham	.25	.08
❑	6 Shawn Jefferson	.25	.08
❑	7 Wesley Walls	.25	.08
❑	8 Jessie Armstead	.25	.08
❑	9 Dedric Ward	.25	.08
❑	10 Emmitt Smith	1.25	.50
❑	11 James Stewart	.40	.15
❑	12 Frank Sanders	.25	.08
❑	13 Ray Buchanan	.25	.08
❑	14 Olindo Mare	.25	.08
❑	15 Andre Reed	.40	.15
❑	16 Curtis Conway	.40	.15
❑	17 Patrick Jeffers	.60	.25
❑	18 Greg Hill	.25	.08
❑	19 John Unitas	.60	.25
❑	20 Brett Favre	2.00	.75
❑	21 Jerome Pathon	.40	.15
❑	22 Jason Tucker	.25	.08
❑	23 Charles Johnson	.40	.15
❑	24 Brian Mitchell	.25	.08
❑	25 Billy Miller	.25	.08
❑	26 Jay Fiedler	.60	.25

❑ 27	Marcus Pollard	.25	.08
❑ 28	De'Mond Parker	.25	.08
❑ 29	Leslie Shepherd	.25	.08
❑ 30	Fred Taylor	.60	.25
❑ 31	Michael Pittman	.25	.08
❑ 32	Ricky Watters	.40	.15
❑ 33	Derrick Brooks	.60	.25
❑ 34	Junior Seau	.60	.25
❑ 35	Troy Vincent	.25	.08
❑ 36	Eric Allen	.25	.08
❑ 37	Pete Mitchell	.25	.08
❑ 38	Tony Simmons	.25	.08
❑ 39	Az-Zahir Hakim	.40	.15
❑ 40	Dan Marino	2.00	.75
❑ 41	Mac Cody	.25	.08
❑ 42	Scott Dreisbach	.25	.08
❑ 43	Al Wilson	.25	.08
❑ 44	Luther Broughton RC	.40	.15
❑ 45	Wane McGarity	.25	.08
❑ 46	Stephen Boyd	.25	.08
❑ 47	Michael Strahan	.40	.15
❑ 48	Chris Chandler	.40	.15
❑ 49	Tony Martin	.40	.15
❑ 50	Edgerrin James	1.00	.40
❑ 51	John Randle	.40	.15
❑ 52	Warrick Dunn	.60	.25
❑ 53	Elvis Grbac	.40	.15
❑ 54	Champ Bailey	.40	.15
❑ 55	Kyle Brady	.25	.08
❑ 56	John Lynch	.40	.15
❑ 57	Kevin Carter	.25	.08
❑ 58	Mike Pritchard	.25	.08
❑ 59	Deon Mitchell RC	.40	.15
❑ 60	Randy Moss	1.25	.50
❑ 61	Jermaine Fazande	.25	.08
❑ 62	Donovan McNabb	1.00	.40
❑ 63	Richard Huntley	.25	.08
❑ 64	Rich Gannon	.60	.25
❑ 65	Aaron Glenn	.25	.08
❑ 66	Amani Toomer	.25	.08
❑ 67	Andre Hastings	.25	.08
❑ 68	Ricky Williams	.60	.25
❑ 69	Sam Madison	.25	.08
❑ 70	Drew Bledsoe	.75	.30
❑ 71	Eric Moulds	.60	.25
❑ 72	Justin Armour	.25	.08
❑ 73	Jamal Anderson	.60	.25
❑ 74	Mario Bates	.25	.08
❑ 75	Sam Gash	.25	.08
❑ 76	Macey Brooks	.25	.08
❑ 77	Tremain Mack	.25	.08
❑ 78	David LaFleur	.25	.08
❑ 79	Dexter Coakley	.25	.08
❑ 80	Cris Carter	.60	.25
❑ 81	Byron Chamberlain	.25	.08
❑ 82	David Sloan	.25	.08
❑ 83	Mike Devlin RC	.25	.08
❑ 84	Jimmy Smith	.40	.15
❑ 85	Derrick Alexander	.40	.15
❑ 86	Damon Huard	.60	.25
❑ 87	Jake Reed	.40	.15
❑ 88	Darrell Green	.25	.08
❑ 89	Derrick Mason	.40	.15
❑ 90	Curtis Martin	.60	.25
❑ 91	Donnie Abraham	.25	.08
❑ 92	D'Marco Farr	.25	.08
❑ 93	Ahman Green	.60	.25
❑ 94	Shane Matthews	.40	.15
❑ 95	Torrance Small	.25	.08
❑ 96	Duce Staley	.60	.25
❑ 97	Jon Ritchie	.25	.08
❑ 98	Victor Green	.25	.08
❑ 99	Kerry Collins	.40	.15
❑ 100	Peyton Manning	1.50	.60
❑ 101	Ben Coates	.25	.08
❑ 102	Thurman Thomas	.40	.15
❑ 103	Cornelius Bennett	.25	.08
❑ 104	Terance Mathis	.40	.15
❑ 105	Adrian Murrell	.40	.15
❑ 106	Donald Hayes	.25	.08
❑ 107	Terry Kirby	.25	.08
❑ 108	James Allen	.40	.15
❑ 109	Ty Law	.40	.15
❑ 110	Tim Brown	.60	.25
❑ 111	Chad Bratzke	.25	.08
❑ 112	Deion Sanders	.60	.25
❑ 113	James Johnson	.25	.08
❑ 114	Tony Richardson RC	.40	.15
❑ 115	Tony Brackens	.25	.08
❑ 116	Ken Dilger	.25	.08
❑ 117	Albert Connell	.25	.08
❑ 118	Neil O'Donnell	.25	.08
❑ 119	Selucio Sanford EP RC	.60	.25
❑ 120	Steve Young	.75	.30
❑ 121	Tony Horne	.25	.08
❑ 122	Charlie Rogers	.25	.08
❑ 123	J.J. Stokes	.40	.15
❑ 124	[illegible]	[illegible]	[illegible]
❑ 125	Jeff Graham	.25	.08
❑ 126	Ike Hilliard	.40	.15
❑ 127	Ray Lucas	.40	.15
❑ 128	Terry Glenn	.40	.15
❑ 129	Rickey Dudley	.25	.08
❑ 130	Joey Galloway	.40	.15
❑ 131	Brian Dawkins	.60	.25
❑ 132	Rob Moore	.40	.15
❑ 133	Bob Christian	.25	.08
❑ 134	Anthony Wright RC	2.00	.75
❑ 135	Antowain Smith	.40	.15
❑ 136	Kevin Johnson	.60	.25
❑ 137	Scott Covington	.25	.08
❑ 138	D'Wayne Bates	.25	.08
❑ 139	Sam Cowart	.25	.08
❑ 140	Isaac Bruce	.60	.25
❑ 141	Tony McGee	.25	.08
❑ 142	Dale Carter	.25	.08
❑ 143	Matt Hasselbeck	.40	.15
❑ 144	Torry Holt	.60	.25
❑ 145	Daunte Culpepper	.75	.30
❑ 146	Yatil Green	.25	.08
❑ 147	Chris Howard	.25	.08
❑ 148	Irving Fryar	.40	.15
❑ 149	Derrick Mayes	.40	.15
❑ 150	Warren Sapp	.40	.15
❑ 151	Ricky Proehl	.25	.08
❑ 152	Eric Kresser EP	.50	.20
❑ 153	Jeff Garcia	.60	.25
❑ 154	Freddie Jones	.25	.08
❑ 155	Mike Cloud	.25	.08
❑ 156	Wayne Chrebet	.40	.15
❑ 157	Joe Montgomery	.25	.08
❑ 158	Shannon Sharpe	.40	.15
❑ 159	Eddie Kennison	.25	.08
❑ 160	Eddie George	.60	.25
❑ 161	Jay Riemersma	.25	.08
❑ 162	Peter Boulware	.25	.08
❑ 163	Aeneas Williams	.25	.08
❑ 164	Jim Miller	.25	.08
❑ 165	Jamir Miller	.25	.08
❑ 166	Tim Biakabutuka	.40	.15
❑ 167	Kordell Stewart	.40	.15
❑ 168	Charlie Garner	.40	.15
❑ 169	Germane Crowell	.25	.08
❑ 170	Stephen Davis	.60	.25
❑ 171	Jeff George	.40	.15
❑ 172	Mark Brunell	.60	.25
❑ 173	Stephen Alexander	.25	.08
❑ 174	Mike Alstott	.60	.25
❑ 175	Terry Allen	.40	.15
❑ 176	Ed McCaffrey	.60	.25
❑ 177	Bobby Engram	.25	.08
❑ 178	Andre Cooper	.25	.08
❑ 179	Kevin Faulk	.25	.08
❑ 180	Errict Rhett	.40	.15
❑ 181	Jammi German	.25	.08
❑ 182	Oronde Gadsden	.40	.15
❑ 183	Jevon Kearse	.60	.25
❑ 184	Herman Moore	.40	.15
❑ 185	Terrence Wilkins	.25	.08
❑ 186	Rocket Ismail	.40	.15
❑ 187	Patrick Johnson	.25	.08
❑ 188	Simeon Rice	.40	.15
❑ 189	Mo Lewis	.25	.08
❑ 190	Qadry Ismail	.40	.15
❑ 191	Terry Jackson	.25	.08
❑ 192	Rashaan Shehee	.25	.08
❑ 193	Charles Woodson	.40	.15
❑ 194	Akili Smith	.25	.08
❑ 195	Yancey Thigpen	.25	.08
❑ 196	Michael Westbrook	.40	.15
❑ 197	Donnell Bennett	.25	.08
❑ 198	Sedrick Irvin	.25	.08
❑ 199	Keenan McCardell	.40	.15
❑ 200	Marshall Faulk	.75	.30
❑ 201	Jeff Blake	.40	.15
❑ 202	Rob Johnson	.40	.15
❑ 203	Vinny Testaverde	.40	.15
❑ 204	Andy Katzenmoyer	.25	.08
❑ 205	Michael Basnight	.25	.08
❑ 206	Lance Schulters	.25	.08
❑ 207	Shaun King	.25	.08
❑ 208	[illegible]	[illegible]	[illegible]
❑ 209	Skip Hicks	.25	.08
❑ 210	Jake Plummer	.40	.15
❑ 211	Leroy Hoard	.25	.08
❑ 212	Reggie Barlow	.25	.08
❑ 213	E.G. Green	.25	.08
❑ 214	Fred Lane	.25	.08
❑ 215	Antonio Freeman	.60	.25
❑ 216	Grant Wistrom	.25	.08
❑ 217	Kevin Dyson	.40	.15
❑ 218	Mikhael Ricks	.25	.08
❑ 219	Rod Woodson	.40	.15
❑ 220	Tim Dwight	.60	.25
❑ 221	Darnay Scott	.40	.15
❑ 222	Curtis Enis	.25	.08
❑ 223	Sean Bennett	.25	.08
❑ 224	Napoleon Kaufman	.40	.15
❑ 225	Jonathan Linton	.25	.08
❑ 226	Jim Harbaugh	.40	.15
❑ 227	Hardy Nickerson	.25	.08
❑ 228	Todd Lyght	.25	.08
❑ 229	Dorsey Levens	.40	.15
❑ 230	Steve Beuerlein	.40	.15
❑ 231	Marty Booker	.40	.15
❑ 232	Andre Wadsworth	.25	.08
❑ 233	James Hasty	.25	.08
❑ 234	Shawn Bryson	.25	.08
❑ 235	Larry Centers	.25	.08
❑ 236	Charlie Batch	.60	.25
❑ 237	Steve McNair	.60	.25
❑ 238	Darrin Chiaverini	.25	.08
❑ 239	Jerome Bettis	.60	.25
❑ 240	Muhsin Muhammad	.40	.15
❑ 241	Terrell Fletcher	.25	.08
❑ 242	Jon Kitna	.60	.25
❑ 243	Frank Wycheck	.25	.08
❑ 244	Tony Gonzalez	.40	.15
❑ 245	Ron Rivers	.25	.08
❑ 246	Olandis Gary	.60	.25
❑ 247	Jermaine Lewis	.25	.08
❑ 248	Joe Jurevicius	.25	.08
❑ 249	Richie Anderson	.40	.15
❑ 250	Marcus Robinson	.60	.25
❑ 251	Shawn Springs	.25	.08
❑ 252	William Floyd	.25	.08
❑ 253	Bobby Shaw RC	.60	.25
❑ 254	Glyn Milburn	.25	.08
❑ 255	Brian Griese	.60	.25
❑ 256	Donnie Edwards	.25	.08
❑ 257	Joe Horn	.40	.15
❑ 258	Cameron Cleeland	.25	.08
❑ 259	Glenn Foley	.25	.08
❑ 260	Corey Dillon	.60	.25
❑ 261	Troy Brown	.40	.15
❑ 262	Stoney Case	.25	.08
❑ 263	Kevin Williams	.25	.08
❑ 264	London Fletcher RC	.40	.15
❑ 265	O.J. McDuffie	.40	.15
❑ 266	Jonathan Quinn	.25	.08
❑ 267	Trent Dilfer	.40	.15
❑ 268	Dameyune Craig	.25	.08
❑ 269	Terrell Owens	.60	.25
❑ 270	Tim Couch	.40	.15
❑ 271	Dameane Douglas	.25	.08
❑ 272	Moses Moreno	.25	.08
❑ 273	Bruce Smith	.40	.15
❑ 274	Peerless Price	.40	.15
❑ 275	Sam Garnes	.25	.08
❑ 276	Natrone Means	.25	.08
❑ 277	Na Brown	.25	.08
❑ 278	Dave Moore	.25	.08

❑ 279 Chris Sanders .25 .08
❑ 280 Troy Aikman 1.25 .50
❑ 281 Cecil Collins .25 .08
❑ 282 Matthew Hatchette .25 .08
❑ 283 Bill Romanowski .25 .08
❑ 284 Basil Mitchell .25 .08
❑ 285 Tony Banks .40 .15
❑ 286 Jake Delhomme RC 3.00 1.25
❑ 287 Keyshawn Johnson .60 .25
❑ 288 Dexter McCleon RC .60 .25
❑ 289 Corey Bradford .40 .15
❑ 290 Terrell Davis .60 .25
❑ 291 Johnnie Morton .40 .15
❑ 292 Kevin Lockett .25 .08
❑ 293 Robert Smith .60 .25
❑ 294 Jeff Lewis .25 .08
❑ 295 Wali Rainer .25 .08
❑ 296 Troy Edwards .25 .08
❑ 297 Keith Poole .25 .08
❑ 298 Priest Holmes .75 .30
❑ 299 David Boston .60 .25
❑ 300 Marvin Harrison .60 .25
❑ 301 Levon Kirkland .25 .08
❑ 302 Robert Holcombe .25 .08
❑ 303 Autry Denson .25 .08
❑ 304 Kevin Hardy .25 .08
❑ 305 Rod Smith .40 .15
❑ 306 Robert Porcher .25 .08
❑ 307 Cade McNown .25 .08
❑ 308 Craig Yeast .25 .08
❑ 309 Doug Flutie .60 .25
❑ 310 Jerry Rice 1.25 .50
❑ 311 Brad Johnson .60 .25
❑ 312 Tiki Barber .60 .25
❑ 313 Will Blackwell .25 .08
❑ 314 Sean Dawkins .25 .08
❑ 315 Jacquez Green .25 .08
❑ 316 Zach Thomas .60 .25
❑ 317 Gus Frerotte .25 .08
❑ 318 Chris Warren .25 .08
❑ 319 Carl Pickens .40 .15
❑ 320 Tyrone Wheatley HL .25 .08
❑ 321 Kurt Warner HL .60 .25
❑ 322 Dan Marino HL 1.00 .40
❑ 323 Cris Carter HL .40 .15
❑ 324 Brett Favre HL 1.00 .40
❑ 325 Marshall Faulk HL .60 .25
❑ 326 Jevon Kearse HL .40 .15
❑ 327 Edgerrin James HL .60 .25
❑ 328 Emmitt Smith HL .60 .25
❑ 329 Andre Reed HL .25 .08
❑ 330 K.Dyson/F.Wycheck HL .25 .08
❑ 331 Olindo Mare MM .25 .08
❑ 332 Marcus Coleman MM .25 .08
❑ 333 James Johnson MM .25 .08
❑ 334 Ray Lucas MM .40 .15
❑ 335 Dedric Ward MM .25 .08
❑ 336 Richie Cunningham MM .25 .08
❑ 337 James Hasty MM .25 .08
❑ 338 Sedrick Shaw MM .25 .08
❑ 339 Kurt Warner MM .60 .25
❑ 340 Marshall Faulk MM .60 .25
❑ 341 Brian Shay EP .50 .20
❑ 342 L.C. Stevens EP .50 .20
❑ 343 Corey Thomas EP .50 .20
❑ 344 Scott Milanovich EP .60 .25
❑ 345 Pat Barnes EP .60 .25
❑ 346 Danny Wuerffel EP .60 .25
❑ 347 Kevin Daft EP .50 .20
❑ 348 Ron Powlus EP RC 1.00 .40
❑ 349 Tony Graziani EP .60 .25
❑ 350 Norman Miller EP RC .50 .20
❑ 351 Cory Sauter EP .50 .20
❑ 352 Marcus Crandell EP RC .60 .25
❑ 353 Sean Morey EP RC .60 .25
❑ 354 Jeff Ogden EP .60 .25
❑ 355 Ted White EP .50 .20
❑ 356 Jim Kubiak EP RC .60 .25
❑ 357 Aaron Stecker EP RC 1.00 .40
❑ 358 Ronnie Powell EP .50 .20
❑ 359 Matt Lytle EP RC .60 .25
❑ 360 Kendrick Nord EP RC .50 .20
❑ 361 Tim Rattay RC 2.50 1.00
❑ 362 Rob Morris RC 2.50 1.00
❑ 363 Chris Samuels RC 2.00 .75
❑ 364 Todd Husak RC 2.50 1.00
❑ 365 Ahmed Plummer RC 2.50 1.00
❑ 366 Frank Murphy RC 2.00 .75
❑ 367 Michael Wiley RC 2.50 1.00
❑ 368 Giovanni Carmazzi RC 2.00 .75
❑ 369 Anthony Becht RC 2.50 1.00
❑ 370 John Abraham RC 2.50 1.00
❑ 371 Shaun Alexander RC 12.00 5.00
❑ 372 Thomas Jones RC 4.00 1.50
❑ 373 Courtney Brown RC 1.00 .40
❑ 374 Curtis Keaton RC 2.00 .75
❑ 375 Jerry Porter RC 3.00 1.25
❑ 376 Corey Simon RC 1.00 .40
❑ 377 Dez White RC 2.50 1.00
❑ 378 Jamal Lewis RC 6.00 2.50
❑ 379 Ron Dayne RC 2.50 1.00
❑ 380 R.Jay Soward RC 2.50 1.00
❑ 381 Tee Martin RC 2.50 1.00
❑ 382 Shaun Ellis RC 2.50 1.00
❑ 383 Brian Urlacher RC 10.00 4.00
❑ 384 Reuben Droughns RC 4.00 1.50
❑ 385 Travis Taylor RC 1.00 .40
❑ 386 Plaxico Burress RC 5.00 2.00
❑ 387 Chad Pennington RC 6.00 2.50
❑ 388 Sylvester Morris RC 2.50 1.00
❑ 389 Ron Dugans RC 2.00 .75
❑ 390 Joe Hamilton RC 2.50 1.00
❑ 391 Chris Redman RC .60 .25
❑ 392 Trung Canidate RC 2.50 1.00
❑ 393 J.R. Redmond RC 2.50 1.00
❑ 394 Danny Farmer RC 2.50 1.00
❑ 395 Todd Pinkston RC 2.50 1.00
❑ 396 Dennis Northcutt RC 2.50 1.00
❑ 397 Laveranues Coles RC 3.00 1.25
❑ 398 Bubba Franks RC 2.50 1.00
❑ 399 Travis Prentice RC 2.50 1.00
❑ 400 Peter Warrick RC 2.50 1.00
❑ SBMVP Kurt Warner FB AU 120.00 50.00

2001 Topps

❑ COMPLETE SET (385) 75.00 45.00
❑ 1 Marshall Faulk .75 .30
❑ 2 Lawyer Milloy .40 .15
❑ 3 Rich Gannon .60 .25
❑ 4 Rod Smith .40 .15
❑ 5 David Boston .60 .25
❑ 6 Jeremy McDaniel .25 .08
❑ 7 Joey Galloway .40 .15
❑ 8 Ron Dixon .25 .08
❑ 9 Terrell Fletcher .25 .08
❑ 10 Deion Sanders .60 .25
❑ 11 Jevon Kearse .40 .15
❑ 12 Charles Woodson .40 .15
❑ 13 Brian Walker .25 .08
❑ 14 Mike Peterson .25 .08
❑ 15 Marcus Robinson .60 .25
❑ 16 Duane Starks .25 .08
❑ 17 KaRon Coleman .25 .08
❑ 18 Randy Moss 1.25 .50
❑ 19 Reggie Jones .25 .08
❑ 20 Derrick Brooks .60 .25
❑ 21 Eddie George .60 .25
❑ 22 Wayne Chrebet .40 .15
❑ 23 Kevin Hardy .25 .08
❑ 24 Bill Schroeder .40 .15
❑ 25 Doug Flutie .60 .25
❑ 26 Tim Dwight .60 .25
❑ 27 Eddie Kennison .40 .15
❑ 28 Reggie Kelly .25 .08
❑ 29 Ricky Watters .40 .15
❑ 30 Stephen Alexander .25 .08
❑ 31 Az-Zahir Hakim .25 .08
❑ 32 Henri Crockett .25 .08
❑ 33 Joe Horn .40 .15
❑ 34 Danny Farmer .25 .08
❑ 35 Shannon Sharpe .40 .15
❑ 36 Brad Hoover .25 .08
❑ 37 David Patten .25 .08
❑ 38 Kevin Faulk .40 .15
❑ 39 Freddie Jones .25 .08
❑ 40 Michael Westbrook .40 .15
❑ 41 Jacquez Green .25 .08
❑ 42 Torrance Small .25 .08
❑ 43 Terrence Wilkins .25 .08
❑ 44 Brett Favre 2.00 .75
❑ 45 Tony Banks .40 .15
❑ 46 Johnnie Morton .40 .15
❑ 47 Jimmy Smith .40 .15
❑ 48 Jerry Rice 1.25 .50
❑ 49 Jeff George .40 .15
❑ 50 Ray Lewis .60 .25
❑ 51 Joe Johnson .25 .08
❑ 52 Rocket Ismail .40 .15
❑ 53 Muhsin Muhammad .40 .15
❑ 54 Ken Dilger .25 .08
❑ 55 Ike Hilliard .40 .15
❑ 56 Joey Porter RC 8.00 3.00
❑ 57 Shaun Alexander .75 .30
❑ 58 Jeff Garcia .60 .25
❑ 59 Jay Fiedler .60 .25
❑ 60 Wane McGarity .25 .08
❑ 61 Steve Beuerlein .25 .08
❑ 62 Tywan Mitchell .25 .08
❑ 63 Travis Prentice .25 .08
❑ 64 Robert Griffith .25 .08
❑ 65 Napoleon Kaufman .25 .08
❑ 66 Randall Godfrey .25 .08
❑ 67 Junior Seau .60 .25
❑ 68 Willie Jackson .25 .08
❑ 69 Larry Foster .25 .08
❑ 70 Brandon Stokley .40 .15
❑ 71 Hugh Douglas .25 .08
❑ 72 James Thrash .40 .15
❑ 73 Vinny Testaverde .40 .15
❑ 74 Leslie Shepherd .25 .08
❑ 75 Terrell Davis .60 .25
❑ 76 Jake Plummer .40 .15
❑ 77 Corey Dillon .60 .25
❑ 78 Ron Dayne .60 .25
❑ 79 Brock Huard .25 .08
❑ 80 Todd Husak .25 .08
❑ 81 Richard Huntley .25 .08
❑ 82 Shaun Ellis .25 .08
❑ 83 Kyle Brady .25 .08
❑ 84 Corey Bradford .25 .08
❑ 85 Eric Moulds .40 .15
❑ 86 Brian Finneran .25 .08
❑ 87 Antonio Freeman .60 .25
❑ 88 Terry Glenn .25 .08
❑ 89 Tai Streets .25 .08
❑ 90 Chris Sanders .25 .08
❑ 91 Sylvester Morris .25 .08
❑ 92 Peter Warrick .60 .25
❑ 93 Chris Greisen .25 .08
❑ 94 Cade McNown .25 .08
❑ 95 Jerome Pathon .40 .15
❑ 96 John Randle .25 .08
❑ 97 Curtis Conway .40 .15
❑ 98 Keyshawn Johnson .60 .25
❑ 99 Trent Green .60 .25
❑ 100 Mike Anderson .60 .25
❑ 101 Jeff Blake .40 .15
❑ 102 Tee Martin .40 .15
❑ 103 Darrell Jackson .60 .25
❑ 104 Mark Brunell .60 .25
❑ 105 Charlie Batch .60 .25
❑ 106 Wesley Walls .25 .08
❑ 107 Edgerrin James .75 .30
❑ 108 Robert Wilson .25 .08
❑ 109 Donovan McNabb .75 .30

❑ 110	Champ Bailey	.40	.15
❑ 111	Isaac Bruce	.60	.25
❑ 112	Michael Strahan	.40	.15
❑ 113	Donnie Edwards	.25	.08
❑ 114	Randall Cunningham	.60	.25
❑ 115	Germane Crowell	.25	.08
❑ 116	Jermaine Lewis	.25	.08
❑ 117	Dennis McKinley	.25	.08
❑ 118	Ryan Leaf	.40	.15
❑ 119	Samari Rolle	.25	.08
❑ 120	Daunte Culpepper	.60	.25
❑ 121	Tim Couch	.40	.15
❑ 122	Greg Biekert	.25	.08
❑ [illegible]	[illegible]	[illegible]	[illegible]
❑ 124	Richie Anderson	.25	.08
❑ 125	Trace Armstrong	.25	.08
❑ 126	Bernardo Harris	.25	.08
❑ 127	Kwame Cavil	.25	.08
❑ 128	James Allen	.40	.15
❑ 129	Anthony Becht	.25	.08
❑ 130	Tiki Barber	.60	.25
❑ 131	Brad Johnson	.60	.25
❑ 132	Tyrone Wheatley	.40	.15
❑ 133	Kurt Warner	1.25	.50
❑ 134	Desmond Howard	.25	.08
❑ 135	Thomas Jones	.40	.15
❑ 136	Peyton Manning	1.50	.60
❑ 137	Tony Richardson	.25	.08
❑ 138	Chris Chandler	.40	.15
❑ 139	Plaxico Burress	.60	.25
❑ 140	J.R. Redmond	.25	.08
❑ 141	Fred Taylor	.60	.25
❑ 142	Akili Smith	.25	.08
❑ 143	Sammy Morris	.25	.08
❑ 144	Jessie Armstead	.25	.08
❑ 145	Charlie Garner	.40	.15
❑ 146	Steve McNair	.60	.25
❑ 147	Charles Johnson	.25	.08
❑ 148	Troy Aikman	1.00	.40
❑ 149	Kevin Johnson	.40	.15
❑ 150	Brian Urlacher	1.00	.40
❑ 151	Travis Taylor	.40	.15
❑ 152	Aaron Shea	.25	.08
❑ 153	Mike Cloud	.25	.08
❑ 154	Donald Driver	.40	.15
❑ 155	Chad Pennington	1.00	.40
❑ 156	Troy Edwards	.25	.08
❑ 157	Reidel Anthony	.25	.08
❑ 158	Michael Bishop	.25	.08
❑ 159	Mo Lewis	.25	.08
❑ 160	Damon Huard	.25	.08
❑ 161	James McKnight	.40	.15
❑ 162	Craig Yeast	.25	.08
❑ 163	Michael Pittman	.25	.08
❑ 164	Robert Smith	.40	.15
❑ 165	Terrelle Smith	.25	.08
❑ 166	Jeremiah Trotter	.40	.15
❑ 167	Amani Toomer	.25	.08
❑ 168	JaJuan Dawson	.25	.08
❑ 169	Tim Biakabutuka	.40	.15
❑ 170	Oronde Gadsden	.40	.15
❑ 171	Ray Lucas	.25	.08
❑ 172	Jermaine Fazande	.25	.08
❑ 173	Todd Bouman	.40	.15
❑ 174	Frank Wycheck	.25	.08
❑ 175	Hines Ward	.60	.25
❑ 176	Ahman Green	.60	.25
❑ 177	Kaseem Sinceno	.25	.08
❑ 178	Jamal Anderson	.60	.25
❑ 179	Jay Riemersma	.25	.08
❑ 180	Jarious Jackson	.40	.15
❑ 181	Andre Rison	.40	.15
❑ 182	Jerome Bettis	.60	.25
❑ 183	Blaine Bishop	.25	.08
❑ 184	Dorsey Levens	.25	.08
❑ 185	James Stewart	.40	.15
❑ 186	Chad Lewis	.25	.08
❑ 187	Justin Watson	.25	.08
❑ 188	Warren Sapp	.40	.15
❑ 189	Rod Woodson	.40	.15
❑ 190	Ricky Williams	.60	.25
❑ 191	Marty Booker	.25	.08
❑ 192	MarTay Jenkins	.25	.08
❑ 193	Peerless Price	.40	.15
❑ 194	Tony Gonzalez	.40	.15
❑ 195	Jon Kitna	.40	.15
❑ 196	Stephen Davis	.60	.25
❑ 197	Curtis Martin	.60	.25
❑ 198	Matt Hasselbeck	.40	.15
❑ 199	Pat Johnson	.25	.08
❑ 200	Emmitt Smith	1.25	.50
❑ 201	Doug Johnson	.25	.08
❑ 202	Autry Denson	.25	.08
❑ 203	Troy Brown	.40	.15
❑ 204	Jeff Graham	.25	.08
❑ 205	Corey Simon	.40	.15
❑ 206	Jamel White	.25	.08
❑ [illegible]	[illegible]	[illegible]	[illegible]
❑ 208	Frank Sanders	.25	.08
❑ 209	Al Wilson	.25	.08
❑ 210	Jason Sehorn	.25	.08
❑ 211	Shaun King	.25	.08
❑ 212	Torry Holt	.60	.25
❑ 213	Kordell Stewart	.40	.15
❑ 214	Keenan McCardell	.25	.08
❑ 215	Dedric Ward	.25	.08
❑ 216	Michael Wiley	.25	.08
❑ 217	Rob Johnson	.40	.15
❑ 218	Jamal Lewis	1.00	.40
❑ 219	Herman Moore	.40	.15
❑ 220	Ron Dugans	.25	.08
❑ 221	Jason Taylor	.25	.08
❑ 222	Charles Lee	.25	.08
❑ 223	J.J. Stokes	.40	.15
❑ 224	Albert Connell	.25	.08
❑ 225	Keith Poole	.25	.08
❑ 226	Elvis Grbac	.40	.15
❑ 227	Shawn Jefferson	.25	.08
❑ 228	Jackie Harris	.25	.08
❑ 229	Derrick Alexander	.40	.15
❑ 230	Darnell Autry	.25	.08
❑ 231	Bobby Shaw	.25	.08
❑ 232	Aaron Brooks	.60	.25
❑ 233	Cris Carter	.60	.25
❑ 234	Desmond Clark	.25	.08
❑ 235	Spergon Wynn	.25	.08
❑ 236	Qadry Ismail	.40	.15
❑ 237	Sam Cowart	.25	.08
❑ 238	Zach Thomas	.60	.25
❑ 239	Drew Bledsoe	.75	.30
❑ 240	Ronney Jenkins	.25	.08
❑ 241	Keith Mitchell RC	.25	.08
❑ 242	Laveranues Coles	.60	.25
❑ 243	Marcus Pollard	.25	.08
❑ 244	Darren Sharper	.25	.08
❑ 245	Donald Hayes	.25	.08
❑ 246	Brian Griese	.60	.25
❑ 247	Frank Moreau	.25	.08
❑ 248	Bruce Smith	.25	.08
❑ 249	Fred Beasley	.25	.08
❑ 250	Mike Alstott	.60	.25
❑ 251	Trent Dilfer	.40	.15
❑ 252	Terance Mathis	.40	.15
❑ 253	Shawn Bryson	.25	.08
❑ 254	Dennis Northcutt	.40	.15
❑ 255	Brandon Bennett	.25	.08
❑ 256	Stacey Mack	.25	.08
❑ 257	Tim Brown	.60	.25
❑ 258	Duce Staley	.60	.25
❑ 259	Sean Dawkins	.25	.08
❑ 260	Ricky Proehl	.25	.08
❑ 261	Chris Fuamatu-ma'afala	.25	.08
❑ 262	La'Roi Glover	.25	.08
❑ 263	Bubba Franks	.40	.15
❑ 264	Kevin Lockett	.25	.08
❑ 265	Lamar Smith	.40	.15
❑ 266	Priest Holmes	.75	.30
❑ 267	Macey Brooks	.25	.08
❑ 268	Anthony Wright	.25	.08
❑ 269	Ed McCaffrey	.60	.25
❑ 270	Joe Jurevicius	.25	.08
❑ 271	Terrell Owens	.60	.25
❑ 272	Tony Simmons	.25	.08
❑ 273	Itula Mili	.25	.08
❑ 274	Chad Morton	.25	.08
❑ 275	Marvin Harrison	.60	.25
❑ 276	Jason Gildon	.25	.08
❑ 277	Derrick Mason	.40	.15
❑ 278	Greg Clark	.25	.08
❑ 279	Casey Crawford	.25	.08
❑ 280	Kerry Collins	.40	.15
❑ 281	Terrell Owens	.60	.25
❑ 282	Marshall Faulk	.60	.25
❑ 283	Mike Anderson	.40	.15
❑ 284	Cris Carter	.40	.15
❑ 285	Corey Dillon	.40	.15
❑ 286	Daunte Culpepper	.60	.25
❑ 287	Peyton Manning	.75	.30
❑ 288	Torry Holt	.60	.25
❑ 289	Marvin Harrison	.40	.15
❑ 290	Edgerrin James	.75	.30
❑ [illegible]	[illegible]	[illegible]	[illegible]
❑ 292	John Lynch	.40	.15
❑ 293	Sam Madison	.25	.08
❑ 294	Stephen Boyd	.25	.08
❑ 295	Tony Siragusa	.25	.08
❑ 296	Robert Porcher	.25	.08
❑ 297	Donnell Bennett	.25	.08
❑ 298	Hardy Nickerson	.25	.08
❑ 299	Jonathan Quinn	.25	.08
❑ 300	Rob Morris	.25	.08
❑ 301	E.G. Green	.25	.08
❑ 302	David Sloan	.25	.08
❑ 303	Jason Tucker	.25	.08
❑ 304	Darrin Chiaverini	.25	.08
❑ 305	Wali Rainer	.25	.08
❑ 306	Jerry Azumah	.25	.08
❑ 307	Jonathan Linton	.25	.08
❑ 308	Dameyune Craig	.25	.08
❑ 309	Courtney Brown	.25	.08
❑ 310	Jammi German	.25	.08
❑ 311	Michael Vick RC	5.00	2.00
❑ 312	Jamar Fletcher RC	.75	.30
❑ 313	Will Allen RC	.75	.30
❑ 314	Jamal Reynolds RC	1.25	.50
❑ 315	Quincy Morgan RC	1.25	.50
❑ 316	Eric Kelly RC	.50	.20
❑ 317	Michael Stone RC	.50	.20
❑ 318	Rod Gardner RC	1.25	.50
❑ 319	Ken-Yon Rambo RC	.75	.30
❑ 320	Eric Westmoreland RC	.75	.30
❑ 321	Steve Smith RC	3.00	1.50
❑ 322	George Layne RC	.75	.30
❑ 323	Justin McCareins RC	1.25	.50
❑ 324	Adam Archuleta RC	1.25	.50
❑ 325	Justin Smith RC	1.25	.50
❑ 326	David Terrell RC	1.25	.50
❑ 327	Correll Buckhalter RC	1.50	.60
❑ 328	Drew Brees RC	5.00	2.00
❑ 329	Chris Barnes RC	.75	.30
❑ 330	Santana Moss RC	2.00	.75
❑ 331	Josh Heupel RC	1.25	.50
❑ 332	Cedrick Wilson RC	1.25	.50
❑ 333	Gerard Warren RC	1.25	.50
❑ 334	Jamie Henderson RC	.75	.30
❑ 335	Onomo Ojo RC	.75	.30
❑ 336	Marcus Stroud RC	1.25	.50
❑ 337	Quincy Carter RC	1.25	.50
❑ 338	Koren Robinson RC	1.25	.50
❑ 339	Ryan Pickett RC	.50	.20
❑ 340	Chad Johnson RC	3.00	1.25
❑ 341	Nate Clements RC	1.25	.50
❑ 342	Jesse Palmer RC	1.25	.50
❑ 343	Snoop Minnis RC	.75	.30
❑ 344	Reggie Wayne RC	2.50	1.00
❑ 345	Kevin Kasper RC	1.25	.50
❑ 346	Will Peterson RC	.75	.30
❑ 347	Marques Tuiasosopo RC	1.25	.50
❑ 348	Sage Rosenfels RC	1.25	.50
❑ 349	Dan Alexander RC	1.25	.50
❑ 350	LaDainian Tomlinson RC	25.00	10.00
❑ 351	Dan Morgan RC	1.25	.50
❑ 352	Scotty Anderson RC	.75	.30
❑ 353	Deuce McAllister RC	2.50	1.00
❑ 354	Todd Heap RC	1.25	.50
❑ 355	Tony Dixon RC	.75	.30
❑ 356	Chris Chambers RC	2.00	.75
❑ 357	Eddie Berlin RC	.75	.30
❑ 358	Anthony Thomas RC	1.25	.50
❑ 359	James Jackson RC	1.25	.50
❑ 360	Richard Seymour RC	1.25	.50
❑ 361	Andre Carter RC	1.25	.50

- ❑ 362 Bobby Newcombe RC .75 .30
- ❑ 363 Robert Ferguson RC 1.25 .50
- ❑ 364 Jonathan Carter RC .75 .30
- ❑ 365 Damione Lewis RC .75 .30
- ❑ 366 Damerien McCants RC .75 .30
- ❑ 367 Tim Hasselbeck RC 1.25 .50
- ❑ 368 Derrick Gibson RC .75 .30
- ❑ 369 Rudi Johnson RC 2.50 1.00
- ❑ 370 Alge Crumpler RC 1.50 .60
- ❑ 371 Derrick Blaylock RC 1.25 .50
- ❑ 372 Moran Norris RC .50 .20
- ❑ 373 Travis Minor RC .75 .30
- ❑ 374 LaMont Jordan RC 2.50 1.00
- ❑ 375 Kevan Barlow RC 1.25 .50
- ❑ 376 Freddie Mitchell RC 1.25 .50
- ❑ 377 Shaun Rogers RC 1.25 .50
- ❑ 378 Tay Cody RC .50 .20
- ❑ 379 Travis Henry RC 2.50 1.00
- ❑ 380 Chris Weinke RC 1.25 .50
- ❑ 381 Willie Middlebrooks RC .75 .30
- ❑ 382 Rashard Casey RC .75 .30
- ❑ 383 Mike McMahon RC 1.25 .50
- ❑ 384 Michael Bennett RC 1.25 .50
- ❑ 385 Jabari Holloway RC .75 .30
- ❑ SBMVP Ray Lewis FB AU 250.00 125.00

2002 Topps

- ❑ COMPLETE SET (385) 50.00 20.00
- ❑ 1 Kurt Warner .60 .25
- ❑ 2 Jeff Graham .25 .08
- ❑ 3 Todd Bouman .25 .08
- ❑ 4 Duce Staley .60 .25
- ❑ 5 Jon Kitna .40 .15
- ❑ 6 Shannon Sharpe .40 .15
- ❑ 7 Darrell Jackson .40 .15
- ❑ 8 Michael Pittman .25 .08
- ❑ 9 Tony Gonzalez .40 .15
- ❑ 10 Wayne Chrebet .40 .15
- ❑ 11 Jevon Kearse .40 .15
- ❑ 12 Bill Schroeder .40 .15
- ❑ 13 Jeremy McDaniel .25 .08
- ❑ 14 Todd Pinkston .40 .15
- ❑ 15 Maurice Smith .40 .15
- ❑ 16 Charlie Batch .40 .15
- ❑ 17 Olandis Gary .40 .15
- ❑ 18 Ron Dugans .25 .08
- ❑ 19 Brian Urlacher 1.00 .40
- ❑ 20 Amani Toomer .40 .15
- ❑ 21 Tim Couch .40 .15
- ❑ 22 Derrick Brooks .60 .25
- ❑ 23 Frank Sanders .25 .08
- ❑ 24 James Williams .25 .08
- ❑ 25 Lamar Smith .40 .15
- ❑ 26 Darrick Vaughn .25 .08
- ❑ 27 Cris Carter .60 .25
- ❑ 28 Roland Williams .25 .08
- ❑ 29 Bobby Shaw .25 .08
- ❑ 30 Jerome Pathon .40 .15
- ❑ 31 Rod Woodson .40 .15
- ❑ 32 Ronney Jenkins .25 .08
- ❑ 33 Chris Chandler .40 .15
- ❑ 34 Dez White .25 .08
- ❑ 35 Rod Smith .40 .15
- ❑ 36 Troy Brown .40 .15
- ❑ 37 JaJuan Dawson .25 .08
- ❑ 38 Reidel Anthony .25 .08
- ❑ 39 Mike Green .25 .08
- ❑ 40 Steve Smith .60 .25
- ❑ 41 Willie Jackson .25 .08
- ❑ 42 MarTay Jenkins .25 .08
- ❑ 43 Reggie Germany .25 .08
- ❑ 44 Desmond Howard .25 .08
- ❑ 45 Fred Taylor .60 .25
- ❑ 46 Scotty Anderson .25 .08
- ❑ 47 John Lynch .40 .15
- ❑ 48 Amos Zereoue .60 .25
- ❑ 49 Darnay Scott .25 .08
- ❑ 50 Anthony Thomas .40 .15
- ❑ 51 Jeff Garcia .60 .25
- ❑ 52 Charlie Garner .40 .15
- ❑ 53 Drew Bledsoe .60 .25
- ❑ 54 Donnie Edwards .25 .08
- ❑ 55 Corey Bradford .25 .08
- ❑ 56 Desmond Clark .25 .08
- ❑ 57 Courtney Brown .40 .15
- ❑ 58 Wesley Walls .25 .08
- ❑ 59 Chad Brown .25 .08
- ❑ 60 Shawn Jefferson .25 .08
- ❑ 61 Corey Dillon .40 .15
- ❑ 62 Johnnie Morton .40 .15
- ❑ 63 Marcus Pollard .25 .08
- ❑ 64 Jason Taylor .25 .08
- ❑ 65 Kevin Faulk .40 .15
- ❑ 66 Shane Matthews .25 .08
- ❑ 67 Hines Ward .60 .25
- ❑ 68 Garrison Hearst .40 .15
- ❑ 69 Trung Canidate .40 .15
- ❑ 70 Tony Banks .25 .08
- ❑ 71 Matt Hasselbeck .40 .15
- ❑ 72 Correll Buckhalter .40 .15
- ❑ 73 Ron Dayne .40 .15
- ❑ 74 Zach Thomas .60 .25
- ❑ 75 Emmitt Smith 1.50 .60
- ❑ 76 Peter Warrick .40 .15
- ❑ 77 Rob Johnson .40 .15
- ❑ 78 Michael Strahan .40 .15
- ❑ 79 Ray Lewis .60 .25
- ❑ 80 Jamir Miller .25 .08
- ❑ 81 Brian Griese .60 .25
- ❑ 82 Stacey Mack .25 .08
- ❑ 83 Michael Bennett .40 .15
- ❑ 84 Ricky Williams 1.00 .40
- ❑ 85 Jamal Lewis .60 .25
- ❑ 86 Doug Flutie .60 .25
- ❑ 87 Jonathan Quinn .25 .08
- ❑ 88 Mike Alstott .60 .25
- ❑ 89 Samari Rolle .25 .08
- ❑ 90 LaMont Jordan .60 .25
- ❑ 91 Dominic Rhodes .40 .15
- ❑ 92 Quincy Carter .40 .15
- ❑ 93 Marcus Robinson .40 .15
- ❑ 94 Travis Henry .60 .25
- ❑ 95 Jason Brookins .25 .08
- ❑ 96 Nick Goings .25 .08
- ❑ 97 Brian Finneran .25 .08
- ❑ 98 Dorsey Levens .40 .15
- ❑ 99 Reggie Swinton .25 .08
- ❑ 100 Chris Chambers .60 .25
- ❑ 101 Kordell Stewart .40 .15
- ❑ 102 Tai Streets .25 .08
- ❑ 103 Chris Redman .25 .08
- ❑ 104 Jacquez Green .25 .08
- ❑ 105 Rod Gardner .40 .15
- ❑ 106 Kevin Kasper .25 .08
- ❑ 107 Anthony Henry .25 .08
- ❑ 108 Dan Morgan .25 .08
- ❑ 109 Ronald McKinnon .25 .08
- ❑ 110 Qadry Ismail .40 .15
- ❑ 111 Chad Johnson .60 .25
- ❑ 112 James Stewart .40 .15
- ❑ 113 Terrence Wilkins .25 .08
- ❑ 114 Joey Galloway .40 .15
- ❑ 115 Deuce McAllister .75 .30
- ❑ 116 Joe Jurevicius .25 .08
- ❑ 117 Tyrone Wheatley .40 .15
- ❑ 118 Jason Gildon .25 .08
- ❑ 119 LaDainian Tomlinson 1.00 .40
- ❑ 120 Grant Wistrom .25 .08
- ❑ 121 Eddie George .60 .25
- ❑ 122 Laveranues Coles .40 .15
- ❑ 123 Antowain Smith .40 .15
- ❑ 124 Larry Parker .25 .08
- ❑ 125 Bubba Franks .40 .15
- ❑ 126 Troy Hambrick .25 .08
- ❑ 127 Jamal Reynolds .25 .08
- ❑ 128 Doug Chapman .25 .08
- ❑ 129 Freddie Mitchell .40 .15
- ❑ 130 Tim Dwight .40 .15
- ❑ 131 Erron Kinney .25 .08
- ❑ 132 James Allen .40 .15
- ❑ 133 Eric Moulds .40 .15
- ❑ 134 Keenan McCardell .25 .08
- ❑ 135 David Sloan .25 .08
- ❑ 136 Dennis Northcutt .40 .15
- ❑ 137 Kevan Barlow .40 .15
- ❑ 138 Bobby Engram .25 .08
- ❑ 139 Champ Bailey .40 .15
- ❑ 140 Donald Hayes .25 .08
- ❑ 141 Brandon Bennett .25 .08
- ❑ 142 Deltha O'Neal .25 .08
- ❑ 143 James Jackson .25 .08
- ❑ 144 Shaun Rogers .25 .08
- ❑ 145 Joe Johnson .25 .08
- ❑ 146 Ricky Watters .40 .15
- ❑ 147 Warrick Dunn .60 .25
- ❑ 148 Steve McNair .60 .25
- ❑ 149 Marvin Harrison .60 .25
- ❑ 150 Kendrell Bell .60 .25
- ❑ 151 Jim Miller .25 .08
- ❑ 152 Terry Allen .25 .08
- ❑ 153 Jake Plummer .40 .15
- ❑ 154 James McKnight .25 .08
- ❑ 155 Curtis Martin .60 .25
- ❑ 156 Keyshawn Johnson .60 .25
- ❑ 157 Kevin Lockett .25 .08
- ❑ 158 Jeremiah Trotter .25 .08
- ❑ 159 Derrick Alexander .40 .15
- ❑ 160 Brandon Stokley .40 .15
- ❑ 161 J.J. Stokes .40 .15
- ❑ 162 Drew Bennett .60 .25
- ❑ 163 Drew Brees .60 .25
- ❑ 164 Tim Brown .60 .25
- ❑ 165 Daunte Culpepper .60 .25
- ❑ 166 Rocket Ismail .40 .15
- ❑ 167 Alex Van Pelt .40 .15
- ❑ 168 Arnold Jackson .25 .08
- ❑ 169 Oronde Gadsden .40 .15
- ❑ 170 Isaac Bruce .60 .25
- ❑ 171 Warren Sapp .40 .15
- ❑ 172 Michael Westbrook .25 .08
- ❑ 173 John Abraham .40 .15
- ❑ 174 Jessie Armstead .25 .08
- ❑ 175 Brock Marion .25 .08
- ❑ 176 Brett Favre 1.50 .60
- ❑ 177 Benjamin Gay .40 .15
- ❑ 178 Muhsin Muhammad .40 .15
- ❑ 179 Reggie Wayne .60 .25
- ❑ 180 Kailee Wong .25 .08
- ❑ 181 Rich Gannon .60 .25
- ❑ 182 Chris Fuamatu-Ma'afala .25 .08
- ❑ 183 Shaun Alexander .75 .30
- ❑ 184 Kevin Dyson .40 .15
- ❑ 185 Kwamie Lassiter .25 .08
- ❑ 186 Elvis Joseph .25 .08
- ❑ 187 Trent Dilfer .40 .15
- ❑ 188 Marty Booker .25 .08
- ❑ 189 Travis Taylor .40 .15
- ❑ 190 Michael Vick 1.25 .50
- ❑ 191 Mike McMahon .60 .25
- ❑ 192 Jay Fiedler .40 .15
- ❑ 193 Zack Bronson .25 .08
- ❑ 194 Derrick Mason .40 .15
- ❑ 195 Anthony Becht .25 .08
- ❑ 196 Ahman Green .60 .25
- ❑ 197 Alge Crumpler .40 .15
- ❑ 198 Thomas Jones .40 .15
- ❑ 199 Tiki Barber .60 .25
- ❑ 200 Donovan McNabb .75 .30
- ❑ 201 Andre Carter .25 .08
- ❑ 202 Stephen Davis .40 .15
- ❑ 203 Troy Edwards .25 .08
- ❑ 204 Lawyer Milloy .40 .15
- ❑ 205 Peyton Manning 1.25 .50
- ❑ 206 James Farrior .25 .08
- ❑ 207 Gerard Warren .25 .08

❑ 208	Peerless Price	.40	.15
❑ 209	Avion Black	.25	.08
❑ 210	Marcellus Wiley	.25	.08
❑ 211	Torry Holt	.60	.25
❑ 212	A.J. Feeley	.60	.25
❑ 213	Travis Minor	.25	.08
❑ 214	Darren Sharper	.25	.08
❑ 215	Jerry Porter	.25	.08
❑ 216	Randall Cunningham	.25	.08
❑ 217	Chris Weinke	.40	.15
❑ 218	Mike Anderson	.60	.25
❑ 219	Snoop Minnis	.25	.08
❑ 220	David Martin	.25	.08
❑ 221	Vinny Sutherland	[illegible]	[illegible]
❑ 222	Ki-Jana Carter	.25	.08
❑ 223	Kevin Swayne	.25	.08
❑ 224	Mark Brunell	.60	.25
❑ 225	Quincy Morgan	.25	.08
❑ 226	David Terrell	.60	.25
❑ 227	Terance Mathis	.25	.08
❑ 228	Frank Wycheck	.25	.08
❑ 229	Az-Zahir Hakim	.25	.08
❑ 230	Freddie Jones	.25	.08
❑ 231	Jerry Rice	1.25	.50
❑ 232	Ike Hilliard	.40	.15
❑ 233	Terrell Davis	.60	.25
❑ 234	Shawn Bryson	.25	.08
❑ 235	David Boston	.60	.25
❑ 236	Edgerrin James	.75	.30
❑ 237	Trent Green	.40	.15
❑ 238	Charlie Rogers	.25	.08
❑ 239	Vinny Testaverde	.40	.15
❑ 240	Koren Robinson	.40	.15
❑ 241	Ronde Barber	.25	.08
❑ 242	Dwayne Carswell	.25	.08
❑ 243	Dedric Ward	.25	.08
❑ 244	Richard Huntley	.25	.08
❑ 245	Jamal Anderson	.40	.15
❑ 246	Ryan Leaf	.40	.15
❑ 247	Priest Holmes	.75	.30
❑ 248	Tom Brady	1.50	.60
❑ 249	Charles Woodson	.40	.15
❑ 250	Jerome Bettis	.60	.25
❑ 251	Tommy Polley	.25	.08
❑ 252	Anthony Wright	.25	.08
❑ 253	Chad Pennington	.75	.30
❑ 254	David Patten	.25	.08
❑ 255	Antonio Freeman	.60	.25
❑ 256	Jamel White	.25	.08
❑ 257	Jermaine Lewis	.25	.08
❑ 258	Aaron Brooks	.60	.25
❑ 259	Ron Dixon	.25	.08
❑ 260	James Thrash	.40	.15
❑ 261	Junior Seau	.60	.25
❑ 262	Byron Chamberlain	.25	.08
❑ 263	Ed McCaffrey	.60	.25
❑ 264	Nate Clements	.25	.08
❑ 265	Tony Martin	.40	.15
❑ 266	Germane Crowell	.25	.08
❑ 267	Terrell Owens	.60	.25
❑ 268	Marshall Faulk	.60	.25
❑ 269	Dat Nguyen	.25	.08
❑ 270	Elvis Grbac	.40	.15
❑ 271	Dante Hall	.60	.25
❑ 272	Sylvester Morris	.25	.08
❑ 273	Mike Brown	.60	.25
❑ 274	Kevin Johnson	.40	.15
❑ 275	Jimmy Smith	.40	.15
❑ 276	Randy Moss	1.25	.50
❑ 277	Kerry Collins	.40	.15
❑ 278	Santana Moss	.60	.25
❑ 279	Plaxico Burress	.40	.15
❑ 280	Brad Johnson	.40	.15
❑ 281	Curtis Conway	.25	.08
❑ 282	Eric Johnson	.40	.15
❑ 283	Joe Horn	.40	.15
❑ 284	Peter Boulware	.25	.08
❑ 285	Larry Foster	.25	.08
❑ 286	Nate Jacquet	.25	.08
❑ 287	Terry Glenn	.40	.15
❑ 288	Jarious Jackson	.25	.08
❑ 289	Hugh Douglas	.25	.08
❑ 290	Chad Lewis	.25	.08
❑ 291	Ahman Green WW	.40	.15
❑ 292	Peyton Manning WW	.60	.25
❑ 293	Kurt Warner WW	.40	.15
❑ 294	Daunte Culpepper WW	.60	.25
❑ 295	Tom Brady WW	.75	.30
❑ 296	Rod Gardner WW	.25	.08
❑ 297	Corey Dillon WW	.40	.15
❑ 298	Priest Holmes WW	.50	.20
❑ 299	Shaun Alexander WW	.50	.20
❑ 300	Randy Moss WW	.60	.25
❑ 301	Eric Moulds WW	.25	.08
❑ 302	Brett Favre WW	.75	.30
❑ 303	Todd Bouman WW	.25	.08
❑ 304	Dominic Rhodes WW	.40	.15
❑ 305	Marvin Harrison WW	.40	.15
❑ 306	Torry Holt WW	.60	.25
❑ 307	Derrick Mason WW	.25	.08
❑ 308	Jerry Rice WW	.60	.25
❑ 309	Donovan McNabb WW	.40	.15
❑ 310	Marshall Faulk WW	.40	.15
❑ 311	David Carr RC	2.50	1.00
❑ 312	Quentin Jammer RC	1.25	.50
❑ 313	Mike Williams RC	1.00	.40
❑ 314	Rocky Calmus RC	1.25	.50
❑ 315	Travis Fisher RC	1.25	.50
❑ 316	Dwight Freeney RC	2.00	.75
❑ 317	Jeremy Shockey RC	4.00	1.50
❑ 318	Marquise Walker RC	1.00	.40
❑ 319	Eric Crouch RC	1.25	.50
❑ 320	DeShaun Foster RC	1.25	.50
❑ 321	Roy Williams RC	2.50	1.00
❑ 322	Andre Davis RC	1.00	.40
❑ 323	Alex Brown RC	1.25	.50
❑ 324	Michael Lewis RC	1.25	.50
❑ 325	Terry Charles RC	1.00	.40
❑ 326	Clinton Portis RC	4.00	1.50
❑ 327	Dennis Johnson RC	.60	.25
❑ 328	Lito Sheppard RC	1.25	.50
❑ 329	Ryan Sims RC	1.25	.50
❑ 330	Raonall Smith RC	1.00	.40
❑ 331	Albert Haynesworth RC	1.00	.40
❑ 332	Eddie Freeman RC	.60	.25
❑ 333	Levi Jones RC	1.00	.40
❑ 334	Josh McCown RC	1.50	.60
❑ 335	Cliff Russell RC	1.00	.40
❑ 336	Maurice Morris RC	1.25	.50
❑ 337	Antwaan Randle El RC	1.50	.60
❑ 338	Ladell Betts RC	1.25	.50
❑ 339	Daniel Graham RC	1.25	.50
❑ 340	David Garrard RC	2.50	1.00
❑ 341	Antonio Bryant RC	1.25	.50
❑ 342	Patrick Ramsey RC	1.25	.50
❑ 343	Kelly Campbell RC	1.00	.40
❑ 344	Will Overstreet RC	[illegible]	[illegible]
❑ 345	Ryan Denney RC	1.00	.40
❑ 346	John Henderson RC	1.25	.50
❑ 347	Freddie Milons RC	1.00	.40
❑ 348	Tim Carter RC	1.00	.40
❑ 349	Kurt Kittner RC	1.00	.40
❑ 350	Joey Harrington RC	1.50	.60
❑ 351	Ricky Williams RC	1.25	.50
❑ 352	Bryant McKinnie RC	1.00	.40
❑ 353	Ed Reed RC	2.00	.75
❑ 354	Josh Reed RC	1.25	.50
❑ 355	Seth Burford RC	1.00	.40
❑ 356	Javon Walker RC	2.00	.75
❑ 357	Jamar Martin RC	1.00	.40
❑ 358	Leonard Henry RC	1.00	.40
❑ 359	Julius Peppers RC	2.50	1.00
❑ 360	Jabar Gaffney RC	1.25	.50
❑ 361	Kalimba Edwards RC	1.25	.50
❑ 362	Napoleon Harris RC	1.25	.50
❑ 363	Ashley Lelie RC	2.50	1.00
❑ 364	Anthony Weaver RC	1.00	.40
❑ 365	Bryan Thomas RC	1.00	.40
❑ 366	Wendell Bryant RC	.60	.25
❑ 367	Damien Anderson RC	1.00	.40
❑ 368	Travis Stephens RC	1.00	.40
❑ 369	Rohan Davey RC	1.25	.50
❑ 370	Mike Pearson RC	.60	.25
❑ 371	Marc Colombo RC	.60	.25
❑ 372	Phillip Buchanon RC	1.25	.50
❑ 373	T.J. Duckett RC	1.25	.50
❑ 374	Ron Johnson RC	1.00	.40
❑ 375	Larry Tripplett RC	.60	.25
❑ 376	Randy Fasani RC	1.00	.40
❑ 377	Keyuo Craver RC	1.00	.40
❑ 378	Marquand Manuel RC	.60	.25
❑ 379	Jonathan Wells RC	1.25	.50
❑ 380	Reche Caldwell RC	1.25	.50
❑ 381	Luke Staley RC	1.00	.40
❑ 382	Donte Stallworth RC	2.00	.75
❑ 383	Levar Fisher RC	.60	.25
❑ 384	Lamar Gordon RC	1.25	.50
❑ 385	William Green RC	1.25	.50
❑ SBMVP	Tom Brady FB AU/150	500.00	350.00

2003 Topps

❑	COMPLETE SET (385)	60.00	25.00
❑ 1	Michael Vick	1.50	.60
❑ 2	Wesley Walls	.25	.08
❑ 3	Josh Reed	.40	.15
❑ 4	Josh McCown	.40	.15
❑ 5	James Stewart	.40	.15
❑ 6	Deltha O'Neal	.25	.08
❑ 7	Quincy Morgan	.40	.15
❑ 8	Tony Fisher	.25	.08
❑ 9	Corey Bradford	.25	.08
❑ 10	Byron Chamberlain	.25	.08
❑ 11	James McKnight	.25	.08
❑ 12	Fred Taylor	.60	.25
❑ 13	David Patten	.25	.08
❑ 14	Jerome Bettis	.60	.25
❑ 15	Jerry Porter	.40	.15
❑ 16	Anthony Becht	.25	.08
❑ 17	Steve McNair	.60	.25
❑ 18	Stephen Davis	.40	.15
❑ 19	Terrence Wilkins	.25	.08
❑ 20	Jamie Martin	.25	.08
❑ 21	Tai Streets	.25	.08
❑ 22	Frank Wycheck	.25	.08
❑ 23	Sammy Knight	.25	.08
❑ 24	Marcus Pollard	.25	.08
❑ 25	Jamie Sharper	.25	.08
❑ 26	T.J. Houshmandzadeh	.25	.08
❑ 27	Javin Hunter	.25	.08
❑ 28	Alge Crumpler	.40	.15
❑ 29	Chris Weinke	.40	.15
❑ 30	David Terrell	.40	.15
❑ 31	Troy Hambrick	.25	.08
❑ 32	Bubba Franks	.40	.15
❑ 33	Todd Bouman	.25	.08
❑ 34	Trent Green	.40	.15
❑ 35	Mark Brunell	.40	.15
❑ 36	James Thrash	.25	.08
❑ 37	Donnie Edwards	.25	.08
❑ 38	Mike Alstott	.60	.25
❑ 39	Bobby Engram	.25	.08
❑ 40	Deuce McAllister	.60	.25
❑ 41	Santana Moss	.40	.15
❑ 42	Kordell Stewart	.40	.15
❑ 43	Jason Taylor	.25	.08
❑ 44	Corey Dillon	.40	.15
❑ 45	Damien Anderson	.25	.08
❑ 46	Rodney Peete	.25	.08
❑ 47	Jeff Blake	.25	.08
❑ 48	Mike McMahon	.40	.15
❑ 49	Ed McCaffrey	.60	.25
❑ 50	Priest Holmes	.75	.30
❑ 51	Moe Williams	.25	.08
❑ 52	Brian Dawkins	.40	.15
❑ 53	Tim Brown	.60	.25

❑ 54 Curtis Martin .60 .25
❑ 55 Charles Stackhouse .25 .08
❑ 56 Derrius Thompson .25 .08
❑ 57 John Simon .25 .08
❑ 58 Joe Jurevicius .25 .08
❑ 59 Jonathan Wells .25 .08
❑ 60 William Green .40 .15
❑ 61 Ken-Yon Rambo .25 .08
❑ 62 Frank Sanders .25 .08
❑ 63 Chester Taylor .25 .08
❑ 64 Keith Brooking .25 .08
❑ 65 Bill Schroeder .40 .15
❑ 66 Travis Minor .25 .08
❑ 67 Eric Parker RC .60 .25
❑ 68 Phillip Buchanon .25 .08
❑ 69 Amos Zereoue .40 .15
❑ 70 Warren Sapp .40 .15
❑ 71 Ladell Betts .40 .15
❑ 72 Lamar Gordon .25 .08
❑ 73 Koren Robinson .25 .08
❑ 74 Ron Dayne .25 .08
❑ 75 Donovan McNabb .75 .30
❑ 76 Edgerrin James .60 .25
❑ 77 Stacey Mack .25 .08
❑ 78 Justin Smith .25 .08
❑ 79 Kelly Holcomb .40 .15
❑ 80 Thomas Jones .40 .15
❑ 81 Randy McMichael .40 .15
❑ 82 Daunte Culpepper .60 .25
❑ 83 Tommy Maddox .60 .25
❑ 84 Tyrone Wheatley .25 .08
❑ 85 Kevin Dyson .40 .15
❑ 86 Rod Gardner .40 .15
❑ 87 Wayne Chrebet .40 .15
❑ 88 Marc Boerigter .40 .15
❑ 89 Darnay Scott .25 .08
❑ 90 T.J. Duckett .40 .15
❑ 91 Marcel Shipp .40 .15
❑ 92 Ross Tucker .25 .08
❑ 93 Drew Bledsoe .60 .25
❑ 94 Scotty Anderson .25 .08
❑ 95 Rod Smith .40 .15
❑ 96 Jim Kleinsasser .25 .08
❑ 97 Peyton Manning 1.00 .40
❑ 98 Junior Seau .60 .25
❑ 99 Darrell Jackson .40 .15
❑ 100 Brett Favre 1.50 .60
❑ 101 Ashley Lelie .60 .25
❑ 102 Jajuan Dawson .25 .08
❑ 103 Kyle Brady .25 .08
❑ 104 Kevin Faulk .25 .08
❑ 105 Jeremy Shockey 1.00 .40
❑ 106 Hines Ward .60 .25
❑ 107 Jeff Garcia .60 .25
❑ 108 Shane Matthews .25 .08
❑ 109 Jevon Kearse .40 .15
❑ 110 Eddie Kennison .25 .08
❑ 111 Quincy Carter .40 .15
❑ 112 Brian Urlacher 1.00 .40
❑ 113 Charlie Rogers .25 .08
❑ 114 Robert Ferguson .25 .08
❑ 115 Christian Fauria .25 .08
❑ 116 Brian Westbrook .40 .15
❑ 117 Antwaan Randle El .60 .25
❑ 118 Eddie George .40 .15
❑ 119 Derrick Brooks .40 .15
❑ 120 Isaac Bruce .60 .25
❑ 121 Joe Horn .40 .15
❑ 122 Jermaine Lewis .25 .08
❑ 123 Jon Kitna .40 .15
❑ 124 David Boston .40 .15
❑ 125 Todd Heap .40 .15
❑ 126 Lamar Smith .25 .08
❑ 127 Marcus Robinson .40 .15
❑ 128 Germane Crowell .25 .08
❑ 129 Kevin Johnson .40 .15
❑ 130 Cris Carter .60 .25
❑ 131 Drew Brees .60 .25
❑ 132 Champ Bailey .40 .15
❑ 133 Brian Finneran .25 .08
❑ 134 Mike Anderson .60 .25
❑ 135 Derek Ross .25 .08
❑ 136 Javon Walker .40 .15
❑ 137 D'Wayne Bates .25 .08
❑ 138 Chad Lewis .25 .08
❑ 139 Charlie Garner .40 .15
❑ 140 Laveranues Coles .40 .15
❑ 141 Ron Dixon .25 .08
❑ 142 Rob Johnson .40 .15
❑ 143 Shaun Alexander .60 .25
❑ 144 Kevan Barlow .40 .15
❑ 145 Aaron Brooks .60 .25
❑ 146 Jay Foreman .25 .08
❑ 147 Mike Peterson .25 .08
❑ 148 Brandon Bennett .25 .08
❑ 149 Jake Plummer .40 .15
❑ 150 Emmitt Smith 1.50 .60
❑ 151 Mikhael Ricks .25 .08
❑ 152 Terry Glenn .25 .08
❑ 153 Michael Bennett .40 .15
❑ 154 Deion Branch .60 .25
❑ 155 Justin McCareins .25 .08
❑ 156 Keyshawn Johnson .60 .25
❑ 157 Marc Bulger .60 .25
❑ 158 Matt Hasselbeck .40 .15
❑ 159 Garrison Hearst .40 .15
❑ 160 Jamel White .25 .08
❑ 161 Doug Johnson .25 .08
❑ 162 Larry Centers .25 .08
❑ 163 Dee Brown .25 .08
❑ 164 Dez White .25 .08
❑ 165 Brian Griese .60 .25
❑ 166 Johnnie Morton .40 .15
❑ 167 Oronde Gadsden .25 .08
❑ 168 Chad Morton .25 .08
❑ 169 Rod Woodson .40 .15
❑ 170 Ricky Proehl .25 .08
❑ 171 Tim Dwight .40 .15
❑ 172 Patrick Ramsey .60 .25
❑ 173 Donald Driver .40 .15
❑ 174 Joey Harrington 1.00 .40
❑ 175 Ricky Williams .60 .25
❑ 176 David Givens .60 .25
❑ 177 Antonio Freeman .40 .15
❑ 178 Dwight Freeney .40 .15
❑ 179 Jabar Gaffney .40 .15
❑ 180 Leon Johnson .25 .08
❑ 181 Freddie Jones .25 .08
❑ 182 Ron Johnson .25 .08
❑ 183 Duce Staley .40 .15
❑ 184 Charles Woodson .40 .15
❑ 185 Trung Canidate .40 .15
❑ 186 Jerome Pathon .25 .08
❑ 187 Jimmy Smith .40 .15
❑ 188 Reggie Wayne .40 .15
❑ 189 Chad Johnson .60 .25
❑ 190 Steve Beuerlein .25 .08
❑ 191 Joey Galloway .40 .15
❑ 192 Chris Walsh .25 .08
❑ 193 Ty Law .40 .15
❑ 194 Ike Hilliard .25 .08
❑ 195 Curtis Conway .25 .08
❑ 196 Kenny Watson .25 .08
❑ 197 Brad Johnson .40 .15
❑ 198 Shawn Jefferson .25 .08
❑ 199 Jamal Lewis .60 .25
❑ 200 Terrell Owens .60 .25
❑ 201 Todd Pinkston .40 .15
❑ 202 Maurice Morris .25 .08
❑ 203 Dante Hall .60 .25
❑ 204 Jeremiah Trotter UER .25 .08
❑ 205 Keenan McCardell .25 .08
❑ 206 Antonio Bryant .40 .15
❑ 207 Trevor Gaylor .25 .08
❑ 208 Eric Moulds .40 .15
❑ 209 Jim Miller .25 .08
❑ 210 Kabeer Gbaja-Biamila .40 .15
❑ 211 James Mungro .25 .08
❑ 212 Troy Brown .40 .15
❑ 213 J.J. Stokes .40 .15
❑ 214 Rich Gannon .40 .15
❑ 215 Chad Pennington .75 .30
❑ 216 Michael Strahan .40 .15
❑ 217 David Garrard .25 .08
❑ 218 Chris Chambers .60 .25
❑ 219 Antowain Smith .40 .15
❑ 220 Olandis Gary .40 .15
❑ 221 Jason McAddley .25 .08
❑ 222 Brandon Stokley .40 .15
❑ 223 Derrick Alexander .25 .08
❑ 224 Hugh Douglas .25 .08
❑ 225 Danny Wuerffel .25 .08
❑ 226 Derrick Mason .40 .15
❑ 227 Michael Pittman .25 .08
❑ 228 Torry Holt .60 .25
❑ 229 Bobby Shaw .25 .08
❑ 230 Tony Gonzalez .40 .15
❑ 231 Ed Hartwell .25 .08
❑ 232 Kris Mangum RC .40 .15
❑ 233 Martay Jenkins .25 .08
❑ 234 Marty Booker .40 .15
❑ 235 London Fletcher .25 .08
❑ 236 Shannon Sharpe .40 .15
❑ 237 Zach Thomas .60 .25
❑ 238 Plaxico Burress .60 .25
❑ 239 Trent Dilfer .40 .15
❑ 240 Kurt Warner .60 .25
❑ 241 Vinny Testaverde .40 .15
❑ 242 Al Wilson .25 .08
❑ 243 Chris Redman .25 .08
❑ 244 Warrick Dunn .40 .15
❑ 245 Jay Fiedler .40 .15
❑ 246 A.J. Feeley .25 .08
❑ 247 LaMont Jordan .60 .25
❑ 248 Kerry Collins .40 .15
❑ 249 Michael Lewis .25 .08
❑ 250 Jerry Rice 1.25 .50
❑ 251 Simeon Rice .40 .15
❑ 252 Reche Caldwell .25 .08
❑ 253 Randy Moss 1.00 .40
❑ 254 Az-Zahir Hakim .25 .08
❑ 255 Nate Wayne .25 .08
❑ 256 James Allen .40 .15
❑ 257 Qadry Ismail .40 .15
❑ 258 Tom Brady 1.50 .60
❑ 259 Brian Kelly .25 .08
❑ 260 Ray Lucas .25 .08
❑ 261 Amani Toomer .40 .15
❑ 262 Travis Henry .40 .15
❑ 263 Chris Chandler .25 .08
❑ 264 Peter Warrick .40 .15
❑ 265 Ray Lewis .60 .25
❑ 266 Sam Cowart .25 .08
❑ 267 Donte Stallworth .60 .25
❑ 268 David Carr 1.00 .40
❑ 269 Andre Davis .25 .08
❑ 270 Jake Delhomme .60 .25
❑ 271 Travis Taylor .40 .15
❑ 272 Steve Smith .60 .25
❑ 273 Tiki Barber .60 .25
❑ 274 Chad Hutchinson .25 .08
❑ 275 Marshall Faulk .60 .25
❑ 276 Chris Claiborne .25 .08
❑ 277 Billy Miller .25 .08
❑ 278 Peerless Price .40 .15
❑ 279 Ed Reed .40 .15
❑ 280 Ahman Green .60 .25
❑ 281 Roy Williams .60 .25
❑ 282 Dennis Northcutt .25 .08
❑ 283 Julius Peppers .60 .25
❑ 284 John Davis .25 .08
❑ 285 LaDainian Tomlinson .60 .25
❑ 286 Muhsin Muhammad .40 .15
❑ 287 Tim Couch .25 .08
❑ 288 Clinton Portis 1.00 .40
❑ 289 Anthony Thomas .40 .15
❑ 290 Marvin Harrison .60 .25
❑ 291 Priest Holmes WW .40 .15
❑ 292 Drew Bledsoe WW .40 .15
❑ 293 Tom Brady WW .60 .25
❑ 294 Shaun Alexander WW .25 .08
❑ 295 Brett Favre WW .60 .25
❑ 296 Travis Henry WW .25 .08
❑ 297 Marshall Faulk WW .40 .15
❑ 298 Terrell Owens WW .25 .08
❑ 299 Jeff Garcia WW .25 .08
❑ 300 Plaxico Burress WW .25 .08
❑ 301 Donovan McNabb WW .40 .15
❑ 302 Ricky Williams WW .40 .15
❑ 303 Michael Vick WW .75 .30
❑ 304 Steve Smith WW .40 .15
❑ 305 Marvin Harrison WW .25 .08

- ❑ 306 Chad Pennington WW .40 .15
- ❑ 307 Jeremy Shockey WW .60 .25
- ❑ 308 Tommy Maddox WW .25 .08
- ❑ 309 Steve McNair WW .25 .08
- ❑ 310 Rich Gannon WW .25 .08
- ❑ 311 Carson Palmer RC 6.00 2.50
- ❑ 312 Keenan Howry RC 1.25 .50
- ❑ 313 Michael Haynes RC 1.25 .50
- ❑ 314 Terrell Suggs RC 2.00 .75
- ❑ 315 Rashean Mathis RC 1.00 .40
- ❑ 316 Chris Kelsay RC 1.25 .50
- ❑ 317 Brad Banks RC 1.00 .40
- ❑ 318 Jordan Gross RC 1.00 .40
- ❑ 319 Lee Suggs RC 1.25 .50
- ❑ [illegible] [illegible] RC 1.00 .40
- ❑ 321 William Joseph RC 1.25 .50
- ❑ 322 Kelley Washington RC 1.25 .50
- ❑ 323 Jerome McDougle RC 1.25 .50
- ❑ 324 Osi Umenyiora RC 2.00 .75
- ❑ 325 Chris Simms RC 2.00 .75
- ❑ 326 Alonzo Jackson RC 1.00 .40
- ❑ 327 L.J. Smith RC 1.25 .50
- ❑ 328 Mike Doss RC 1.25 .50
- ❑ 329 Bobby Wade RC 1.25 .50
- ❑ 330 Ken Hamlin RC 1.25 .50
- ❑ 331 Brandon Lloyd RC 1.25 .50
- ❑ 332 Justin Fargas RC 1.25 .50
- ❑ 333 DeWayne Robertson RC 1.25 .50
- ❑ 334 Bryant Johnson RC 1.25 .50
- ❑ 335 Boss Bailey RC 1.25 .50
- ❑ 336 Onterrio Smith RC 1.25 .50
- ❑ 337 Doug Gabriel RC 1.25 .50
- ❑ 338 Jimmy Kennedy RC 1.25 .50
- ❑ 339 B.J. Askew RC 1.25 .50
- ❑ 340 Taylor Jacobs RC 1.00 .40
- ❑ 341 Dallas Clark RC 1.25 .50
- ❑ 342 DeWayne White RC 1.00 .40
- ❑ 343 Arnaz Battle RC 1.25 .50
- ❑ 344 Kareem Kelly RC 1.00 .40
- ❑ 345 Terry Pierce RC 1.00 .40
- ❑ 346 Billy McMullen RC 1.00 .40
- ❑ 347 Talman Gardner RC 1.25 .50
- ❑ 348 Anquan Boldin RC 3.00 1.25
- ❑ 349 Travis Anglin RC .60 .25
- ❑ 350 Byron Leftwich RC 4.00 1.50
- ❑ 351 Marcus Trufant RC 1.25 .50
- ❑ 352 Sam Aiken RC 1.00 .40
- ❑ 353 LaBrandon Toefield RC 1.25 .50
- ❑ 354 J.R. Tolver RC 1.00 .40
- ❑ 355 Charles Rogers RC 1.25 .50
- ❑ 356 Chaun Thompson RC .60 .25
- ❑ 357 Chris Brown RC 1.25 .50
- ❑ 358 Justin Gage RC 1.25 .50
- ❑ 359 Kevin Williams RC 1.25 .50
- ❑ 360 Willis McGahee RC 3.00 1.25
- ❑ 361 Victor Hobson RC 1.25 .50
- ❑ 362 Brian St.Pierre RC 1.25 .50
- ❑ 363 Nate Burleson RC 1.25 .50
- ❑ 364 Calvin Pace RC 1.00 .40
- ❑ 365 Larry Johnson RC 6.00 2.50
- ❑ 366 Andre Woolfolk RC 1.25 .50
- ❑ 367 Tyrone Calico RC 1.25 .50
- ❑ 368 Seneca Wallace RC 1.25 .50
- ❑ 369 Domanick Davis RC 1.25 .50
- ❑ 370 Rex Grossman RC 4.00 1.50
- ❑ 371 Artose Pinner RC 1.25 .50
- ❑ 372 Jason Witten RC 2.50 1.00
- ❑ 373 Bennie Joppru RC 1.25 .50
- ❑ 374 Bethel Johnson RC 1.25 .50
- ❑ 375 Kyle Boller RC 1.25 .50
- ❑ 376 Shaun McDonald RC 1.25 .50
- ❑ 377 Musa Smith RC 1.25 .50
- ❑ 378 Ken Dorsey RC 1.25 .50
- ❑ 379 Johnathan Sullivan RC 1.00 .40
- ❑ 380 Andre Johnson RC 2.50 1.00
- ❑ 381 Nick Barnett RC 1.25 .50
- ❑ 382 Teyo Johnson RC 1.25 .50
- ❑ 383 Terence Newman RC 2.50 1.00
- ❑ 384 Kevin Curtis RC 1.50 .60
- ❑ 385 Dave Ragone RC 1.25 .50
- ❑ MVP Dex.Jackson FB AU/250 120.00 50.00
- ❑ RH Dexter Jackson RH 2.00 .75
- ❑ RHA Dexter Jackson RH AU 150.00 75.00

2004 Topps

- ❑ COMPLETE SET (385) 60.00 30.00
- ❑ RH38 STATED ODDS 1:36 H/HTA/R
- ❑ RH38A ODDS 1:13,494H, 1:3895HTA
- ❑ SBMVP ODDS 1:35,787H,1:10,710HTA,1:33,084R
- ❑ 1 Peyton Manning 1.00 .40
- ❑ 2 Curtis Conway .25 .08
- ❑ 3 Tim Brown .60 .25
- ❑ 4 David Givens .40 .15
- ❑ 5 Dorsey Levens .25 .08
- ❑ 6 Jamal Robertson .25 .08
- ❑ 7 Doug Flutie .60 .25
- ❑ 8 Lamar Gordon .25 .08
- ❑ 9 Leonard Little .25 .08
- ❑ 10 Patrick Ramsey .40 .15
- ❑ 11 Justin McCareins .25 .08
- ❑ 12 Charles Lee .25 .08
- ❑ 13 Matt Hasselbeck .40 .15
- ❑ 14 Chris Chambers .40 .15
- ❑ 15 Derrick Blaylock .40 .15
- ❑ 16 Shannon Sharpe .40 .15
- ❑ 17 Bubba Franks .40 .15
- ❑ 18 London Fletcher .25 .08
- ❑ 19 Eric Moulds .40 .15
- ❑ 20 Anquan Boldin .60 .25
- ❑ 21 Brian Urlacher .75 .30
- ❑ 22 Stephen Davis .40 .15
- ❑ 23 Mikhael Ricks .25 .08
- ❑ 24 Jason Taylor .25 .08
- ❑ 25 Michael Vick 1.25 .50
- ❑ 26 Dante Hall .60 .25
- ❑ 27 Marcus Pollard .25 .08
- ❑ 28 Rick Mirer .25 .08
- ❑ 29 David Tyree .25 .08
- ❑ 30 Chad Pennington .60 .25
- ❑ 31 Kevan Barlow .40 .15
- ❑ 32 James Farrior .25 .08
- ❑ 33 James Thrash .25 .08
- ❑ 34 Damerien McCants .25 .08
- ❑ 35 L.J. Smith .40 .15
- ❑ 36 Tommy Maddox .40 .15
- ❑ 37 Tedy Bruschi .40 .15
- ❑ 38 Moe Williams .25 .08
- ❑ 39 Todd Bouman .25 .08
- ❑ 40 Domanick Davis .60 .25
- ❑ 41 Dwight Freeney .40 .15
- ❑ 42 Kyle Brady .25 .08
- ❑ 43 LaVar Arrington 1.25 .50
- ❑ 44 Troy Hambrick .25 .08
- ❑ 45 Jake Plummer .40 .15
- ❑ 46 Freddie Jones .25 .08
- ❑ 47 Chester Taylor .25 .08
- ❑ 48 Willis McGahee .60 .25
- ❑ 49 Bobby Wade .25 .08
- ❑ 50 Steve McNair .60 .25
- ❑ 51 Joe Jurevicius .25 .08
- ❑ 52 Ladell Betts .25 .08
- ❑ 53 LaMont Jordan .60 .25
- ❑ 54 Kerry Collins .40 .15
- ❑ 55 Hines Ward .60 .25
- ❑ 56 Scott Fujita .25 .08
- ❑ 57 Kevin Johnson .25 .08
- ❑ 58 Troy Brown .40 .15
- ❑ 59 Jerome Pathon .25 .08
- ❑ 60 Andre Johnson .60 .25
- ❑ 61 DeShaun Foster .40 .15
- ❑ 62 Terrell Suggs .40 .15
- ❑ 63 Marcel Shipp .40 .15
- ❑ 64 Allen Rossum .25 .08
- ❑ 65 Kyle Boller .60 .25
- ❑ 66 Terence Newman .40 .15
- ❑ 67 Javon Walker .40 .15
- ❑ 68 Shawn Bryson .25 .08
- ❑ 69 Travis Minor .25 .08
- ❑ 70 Terrell Owens .60 .25
- ❑ 71 Kassim Osgood .25 .08
- ❑ 72 Bobby Engram .25 .08
- ❑ 73 Drew Bennett .40 .15
- ❑ 74 Rock Cartwright .25 .08
- ❑ 75 Ahman Green .60 .25
- ❑ 76 Steve Beuerlein .25 .08
- ❑ 77 Takeo Spikes .25 .08
- ❑ 78 Dez White .40 .15
- ❑ 79 Tim Couch .25 .08
- ❑ 80 Travis Henry .40 .15
- ❑ 81 T.J. Duckett .40 .15
- ❑ 82 LaBrandon Toefield .25 .08
- ❑ 83 Randy McMichael .25 .08
- ❑ 84 Jonathan Carter [illegible] [illegible]
- ❑ 85 Jerry Rice 1.25 .50
- ❑ 86 Maurice Morris .25 .08
- ❑ 87 Kurt Warner .60 .25
- ❑ 88 Josh Scobey .25 .08
- ❑ 89 Travis Taylor .25 .08
- ❑ 90 Fred Taylor .40 .15
- ❑ 91 Zach Thomas .60 .25
- ❑ 92 Kelly Campbell .25 .08
- ❑ 93 Tim Carter .25 .08
- ❑ 94 Marques Tuiasosopo .40 .15
- ❑ 95 Laveranues Coles .40 .15
- ❑ 96 Chris Brown .60 .25
- ❑ 97 Thomas Jones .40 .15
- ❑ 98 Dane Looker .40 .15
- ❑ 99 Ross Tucker .25 .08
- ❑ 100 Priest Holmes .75 .30
- ❑ 101 Troy Walters .25 .08
- ❑ 102 Jamie Sharper .25 .08
- ❑ 103 Quincy Morgan .40 .15
- ❑ 104 Aveion Cason .25 .08
- ❑ 105 Joey Galloway .40 .15
- ❑ 106 Bill Schroeder .25 .08
- ❑ 107 Tony Fisher .25 .08
- ❑ 108 Adewale Ogunleye .40 .15
- ❑ 109 Justin Fargas .40 .15
- ❑ 110 Daunte Culpepper .60 .25
- ❑ 111 Donnie Edwards .25 .08
- ❑ 112 Jed Weaver .25 .08
- ❑ 113 Arlen Harris .25 .08
- ❑ 114 Keenan McCardell .25 .08
- ❑ 115 Chad Johnson .60 .25
- ❑ 116 Marty Booker .40 .15
- ❑ 117 Anthony Wright .25 .08
- ❑ 118 Brian Finneran .25 .08
- ❑ 119 Robert Ferguson .25 .08
- ❑ 120 Ricky Williams .60 .25
- ❑ 121 Shaun Ellis .25 .08
- ❑ 122 Brian Westbrook .40 .15
- ❑ 123 Sam Cowart .25 .08
- ❑ 124 Tim Rattay .25 .08
- ❑ 125 LaDainian Tomlinson .75 .30
- ❑ 126 Simeon Rice .40 .15
- ❑ 127 Jason Witten .40 .15
- ❑ 128 Lee Suggs .60 .25
- ❑ 129 Keith Brooking .25 .08
- ❑ 130 Rex Grossman .60 .25
- ❑ 131 Kelley Washington .25 .08
- ❑ 132 Antonio Bryant .40 .15
- ❑ 133 Dallas Clark .40 .15
- ❑ 134 Stacey Mack .25 .08
- ❑ 135 Charles Rogers .40 .15
- ❑ 136 Donte' Stallworth .40 .15
- ❑ 137 Deion Branch .60 .25
- ❑ 138 Nate Burleson .60 .25
- ❑ 139 Ike Hilliard .25 .08
- ❑ 140 Randy Moss .75 .30
- ❑ 141 Michael Strahan .40 .15
- ❑ 142 John Abraham .25 .08
- ❑ 143 Tim Dwight .40 .15
- ❑ 144 Isaac Bruce .40 .15
- ❑ 145 Brad Johnson .40 .15

❑ 146 Trung Canidate .25 .08
❑ 147 Warrick Dunn .40 .15
❑ 148 Josh McCown .40 .15
❑ 149 Muhsin Muhammad .40 .15
❑ 150 Donovan McNabb .75 .30
❑ 151 Tai Streets .25 .08
❑ 152 Antonio Gates .60 .25
❑ 153 Antwaan Randle El .60 .25
❑ 154 Doug Jolley .25 .08
❑ 155 Shaun Alexander .60 .25
❑ 156 William Green .40 .15
❑ 157 Carson Palmer .75 .30
❑ 158 Quentin Griffin .60 .25
❑ 159 Az-Zahir Hakim .25 .08
❑ 160 Edgerrin James .60 .25
❑ 161 Gus Frerotte .25 .08
❑ 162 Brandon Lloyd .40 .15
❑ 163 Brian Griese .40 .15
❑ 164 Boo Williams .25 .08
❑ 165 Santana Moss .40 .15
❑ 166 Tyrone Wheatley .25 .08
❑ 167 Eric Parker .25 .08
❑ 168 Amos Zereoue .25 .08
❑ 169 Itula Mili .25 .08
❑ 170 Marshall Faulk .60 .25
❑ 171 Tyrone Calico .40 .15
❑ 172 Tim Hasselbeck .25 .08
❑ 173 Anthony Becht .25 .08
❑ 174 Larry Johnson .75 .30
❑ 175 Marvin Harrison .60 .25
❑ 176 Tony Gonzalez .40 .15
❑ 177 Wayne Chrebet .40 .15
❑ 178 Mike Barrow .25 .08
❑ 179 Bethel Johnson .40 .15
❑ 180 Deuce McAllister .60 .25
❑ 181 Drew Brees .60 .25
❑ 182 Teyo Johnson .25 .08
❑ 183 Garrison Hearst .40 .15
❑ 184 Todd Pinkston .25 .08
❑ 185 Jeff Garcia .60 .25
❑ 186 Darrell Jackson .40 .15
❑ 187 Billy Volek .60 .25
❑ 188 Ray Lewis .60 .25
❑ 189 Ricky Proehl .25 .08
❑ 190 Rudi Johnson .40 .15
❑ 191 Emmitt Smith 1.25 .50
❑ 192 Cedrick Wilson .25 .08
❑ 193 Julius Peppers .60 .25
❑ 194 Peter Warrick .40 .15
❑ 195 Trent Green .40 .15
❑ 196 Derrius Thompson .25 .08
❑ 197 Onterrio Smith .40 .15
❑ 198 Jerome Bettis .60 .25
❑ 199 Keyshawn Johnson .40 .15
❑ 200 Jamal Lewis .60 .25
❑ 201 Alge Crumpler .40 .15
❑ 202 Justin Gage .40 .15
❑ 203 Mike Rucker .25 .08
❑ 204 Michael Bennett .40 .15
❑ 205 Jimmy Smith .40 .15
❑ 206 Ricky Williams TT .25 .08
❑ 207 Corey Bradford .25 .08
❑ 208 Jerry Porter .40 .15
❑ 209 Erron Kinney .25 .08
❑ 210 Marc Bulger .60 .25
❑ 211 Jeff Blake .25 .08
❑ 212 Terry Jones .25 .08
❑ 213 Kordell Stewart .40 .15
❑ 214 Andra Davis .25 .08
❑ 215 David Carr .60 .25
❑ 216 Nick Barnett .40 .15
❑ 217 Mark Brunell .40 .15
❑ 218 Daniel Graham .25 .08
❑ 219 Jim Kleinsasser .25 .08
❑ 220 Aaron Brooks .40 .15
❑ 221 Plaxico Burress .40 .15
❑ 222 Correll Buckhalter .40 .15
❑ 223 Jevon Kearse .40 .15
❑ 224 Michael Pittman .25 .08
❑ 225 Clinton Portis .60 .25
❑ 226 Corey Dillon .40 .15
❑ 227 Steve Smith .60 .25
❑ 228 David Thornton .25 .08
❑ 229 Eddie Kennison .25 .08
❑ 230 Amani Toomer .40 .15
❑ 231 Artose Pinner .25 .08
❑ 232 Kelly Holcomb .40 .15
❑ 233 Jay Fiedler .25 .08
❑ 234 Ernie Conwell .25 .08
❑ 235 Torry Holt .60 .25
❑ 236 Eddie George .40 .15
❑ 237 Jeremy Shockey .60 .25
❑ 238 Troy Edwards .25 .08
❑ 239 Antowain Smith .40 .15
❑ 240 Jon Kitna .40 .15
❑ 241 Bryant Johnson .25 .08
❑ 242 Todd Heap .40 .15
❑ 243 Doug Johnson .25 .08
❑ 244 Ashley Lelie .40 .15
❑ 245 Byron Leftwich .75 .30
❑ 246 Shawn Barber .25 .08
❑ 247 Duce Staley .40 .15
❑ 248 Rod Gardner .40 .15
❑ 249 Warren Sapp .40 .15
❑ 250 Brett Favre 1.50 .60
❑ 251 Olandis Gary .25 .08
❑ 252 Reggie Wayne .40 .15
❑ 253 Billy Miller .25 .08
❑ 254 Johnnie Morton .40 .15
❑ 255 Joe Horn .40 .15
❑ 256 Curtis Martin .60 .25
❑ 257 Freddie Mitchell .40 .15
❑ 258 Charlie Garner .40 .15
❑ 259 Marcus Robinson .40 .15
❑ 260 Derrick Mason .40 .15
❑ 261 Bobby Shaw .25 .08
❑ 262 Desmond Clark .25 .08
❑ 263 James Jackson .25 .08
❑ 264 Josh Reed .25 .08
❑ 265 David Boston .40 .15
❑ 266 Drew Bledsoe .60 .25
❑ 267 Brock Forsey .25 .08
❑ 268 Dat Nguyen .25 .08
❑ 269 Mike Anderson .40 .15
❑ 270 Anthony Thomas .40 .15
❑ 271 Najeh Davenport .25 .08
❑ 272 Jabar Gaffney .40 .15
❑ 273 Tiki Barber .60 .25
❑ 274 Rich Gannon .40 .15
❑ 275 Tom Brady 1.50 .60
❑ 276 Terry Glenn .25 .08
❑ 277 Dennis Northcutt .25 .08
❑ 278 A.J. Feeley .60 .25
❑ 279 Peerless Price .40 .15
❑ 280 Jake Delhomme .60 .25
❑ 281 Kevin Faulk .25 .08
❑ 282 Quincy Carter .40 .15
❑ 283 Andre' Davis .25 .08
❑ 284 Tony Hollings .25 .08
❑ 285 Joey Harrington .60 .25
❑ 286 Richie Anderson .25 .08
❑ 287 Donald Driver .40 .15
❑ 288 Koren Robinson .40 .15
❑ 289 Tony Banks .25 .08
❑ 290 Rod Smith .40 .15
❑ 291 Anquan Boldin WW .25 .08
❑ 292 Jamal Lewis WW .40 .15
❑ 293 Priest Holmes WW .60 .25
❑ 294 Peyton Manning WW .60 .25
❑ 295 Marvin Harrison WW .40 .15
❑ 296 Steve McNair WW .40 .15
❑ 297 Travis Henry WW .25 .08
❑ 298 Torry Holt WW .40 .15
❑ 299 Tom Brady WW .60 .25
❑ 300 Ahman Green WW .40 .15
❑ 301 Donovan McNabb WW .60 .25
❑ 302 Deuce McAllister WW .40 .15
❑ 303 Domanick Davis WW .40 .15
❑ 304 Clinton Portis WW .60 .25
❑ 305 Rudi Johnson WW .25 .08
❑ 306 Brett Favre WW .60 .25
❑ 307 LaDainian Tomlinson WW .50 .20
❑ 308 Steve Smith WW .40 .15
❑ 309 Edgerrin James WW .40 .15
❑ 310 Ty Law WW .25 .08
❑ 311 Ben Roethlisberger RC 15.00 6.00
❑ 312 Ahmad Carroll RC 1.50 .60
❑ 313 Johnnie Morant RC 1.50 .60
❑ 314 Greg Jones RC 1.50 .60
❑ 315 Michael Clayton RC 3.00 1.25
❑ 316 Josh Harris RC 1.50 .60
❑ 317 Tatum Bell RC 3.00 1.25
❑ 318 Robert Gallery RC 1.50 .60
❑ 319 B.J. Symons RC 1.50 .60
❑ 320 Roy Williams RC 4.00 1.50
❑ 321 DeAngelo Hall RC 2.00 .75
❑ 322 Jeff Smoker RC 1.50 .60
❑ 323 Lee Evans RC 2.00 .75
❑ 324 Michael Jenkins RC 1.50 .60
❑ 325 Steven Jackson RC 5.00 2.00
❑ 326 Will Smith RC 1.50 .60
❑ 327 Vince Wilfork RC 1.50 .60
❑ 328 Ben Troupe RC 1.50 .60
❑ 329 Chris Gamble RC 1.50 .60
❑ 330 Kevin Jones RC 4.00 1.50
❑ 331 Jonathan Vilma RC 1.50 .60
❑ 332 Dontarrious Thomas RC 1.50 .60
❑ 333 Michael Boulware RC 1.50 .60
❑ 334 Mewelde Moore RC 1.50 .60
❑ 335 Drew Henson RC 1.50 .60
❑ 336 D.J. Williams RC 1.50 .60
❑ 337 Ernest Wilford RC 1.50 .60
❑ 338 John Navarre RC 1.50 .60
❑ 339 Jerricho Cotchery RC 1.50 .60
❑ 340 Derrick Hamilton RC 1.25 .50
❑ 341 Carlos Francis RC 1.25 .50
❑ 342 Ben Watson RC 1.50 .60
❑ 343 Reggie Williams RC 2.00 .75
❑ 344 Devard Darling RC 1.50 .60
❑ 345 Chris Perry RC 2.00 .75
❑ 346 Derrick Strait RC 1.50 .60
❑ 347 Sean Taylor RC 1.50 .60
❑ 348 Michael Turner RC 2.00 .75
❑ 349 Keary Colbert RC 1.50 .60
❑ 350 Eli Manning RC 12.00 6.00
❑ 351 Julius Jones RC 5.00 2.00
❑ 352 Jason Babin RC 1.50 .60
❑ 353 Cody Pickett RC 1.50 .60
❑ 354 Kenechi Udeze RC 1.50 .60
❑ 355 Rashaun Woods RC 1.50 .60
❑ 356 Matt Schaub RC 5.00 2.00
❑ 357 Tommie Harris RC 1.50 .60
❑ 358 Dwan Edwards RC .75 .30
❑ 359 Shawn Andrews RC 1.50 .60
❑ 360 Larry Fitzgerald RC 5.00 2.00
❑ 361 P.K. Sam RC 1.25 .50
❑ 362 Teddy Lehman RC 1.50 .60
❑ 363 Darius Watts RC 1.50 .60
❑ 364 D.J. Hackett RC 1.25 .50
❑ 365 Cedric Cobbs RC 1.50 .60
❑ 366 Antwan Odom RC 1.50 .60
❑ 367 Marquise Hill RC 1.25 .50
❑ 368 Luke McCown RC 1.50 .60
❑ 369 Triandos Luke RC 1.50 .60
❑ 370 Kellen Winslow RC 3.00 1.25
❑ 371 Derek Abney RC 1.50 .60
❑ 372 Chris Cooley RC 1.50 .60
❑ 373 Dunta Robinson RC 1.50 .60
❑ 374 Sean Jones RC 1.25 .50
❑ 375 Philip Rivers RC 5.00 2.00
❑ 376 Craig Krenzel RC 1.50 .60
❑ 377 Daryl Smith RC 1.50 .60
❑ 378 Samie Parker RC 1.50 .60
❑ 379 Ben Hartsock RC 1.50 .60
❑ 380 J.P. Losman RC 3.00 1.25
❑ 381 Karlos Dansby RC 1.50 .60
❑ 382 Ricardo Colclough RC 1.50 .60
❑ 383 Bernard Berrian RC 2.00 .75
❑ 384 Junior Siavii RC 1.50 .60
❑ 385 Devery Henderson RC 1.50 .60
❑ TB38 Tom Brady RH 6.00 2.50
❑ RHTBR2 Tom Brady RH AU 500.00 300.00
❑ SBMVP Tom Brady FB AU/99 500.00350.00

2005 Topps

❑ COMP.COWBOYS SET (445) 50.00 25.00
❑ COMP.EAGLES SET (445) 50.00 25.00
❑ COMP.FACT.SET (445) 50.00 25.00
❑ COMP.PACKERS SET (445) 50.00 25.00
❑ COMP.RAIDERS SET (445) 50.00 25.00
❑ COMP.SB XL SET (445) 80.00 50.00
❑ COMPLETE SET (440) 50.00 25.00

❑ RH39 STATED ODDS 1:275 HOB/HTA/RET
❑ RH39A 1:62,233H, 1:15,547HTA, 1:51,346R
❑ SBMVP 1:27,629H, 1:7774HTA, 1:43,632R
❑ UNPRICED PLATINUM PRINT RUN 1 SET

❑	1	Brian Westbrook	.40	.15
❑	2	Tim Rattay	.30	.10
❑	3	Domanick Davis	.40	.15
❑	4	Lee Suggs	.40	.15
❑	5	Keith Brooking	.30	.10
❑	6	Rex Grossman	.40	.15
❑	7	Chad Johnson	.60	.25
❑	8	Willis McGahee	.60	.25
❑	9	Eli Manning	1.25	.50
❑	10	Tom Brady	1.50	.60
❑	11	Ray Lewis	.60	.25
❑	12	Terence Newman	.30	.10
❑	13	Daunte Culpepper	.60	.25
❑	14	Marvin Harrison	.60	.25
❑	15	Greg Jones	.30	.10
❑	16	Anquan Boldin	.40	.15
❑	17	Julius Peppers	.40	.15
❑	18	Kevin Jones	.60	.25
❑	19	Javon Walker	.40	.15
❑	20	Michael Lewis	.30	.10
❑	21	Jamaar Taylor	.30	.10
❑	22	Hines Ward	.60	.25
❑	23	Drew Brees	.60	.25
❑	24	Marcus Trufant	.30	.10
❑	25	Derrick Brooks	.40	.15
❑	26	Sean Taylor	.40	.15
❑	27	Derrius Thompson	.30	.10
❑	28	Nick Barnett	.30	.10
❑	29	Dante Hall	.40	.15
❑	30	Mike Cloud	.30	.10
❑	31	Jake Plummer	.40	.15
❑	32	Donte Stallworth	.40	.15
❑	33	Shaun Ellis	.30	.10
❑	34	Jeremy Shockey	.60	.25
❑	35	Teyo Johnson	.30	.10
❑	36	Adam Archuleta	.30	.10
❑	37	Darius Watts	.40	.15
❑	38	Michael Pittman	.30	.10
❑	39	Drew Bennett	.40	.15
❑	40	Aaron Stecker	.30	.10
❑	41	Artose Pinner	.30	.10
❑	42	Dane Looker	.30	.10
❑	43	Jeff Garcia	.40	.15
❑	44	Travis Taylor	.30	.10
❑	45	Najeh Davenport	.30	.10
❑	46	Walter Jones	.30	.10
❑	47	Donnie Edwards	.30	.10
❑	48	Terrell Owens	.60	.25
❑	49	Matt Birk	.30	.10
❑	50	Chris Baker	.30	.10
❑	51	Brandon Lloyd	.30	.10
❑	52	Marshall Faulk	.60	.25
❑	53	Jonathan Vilma	.40	.15
❑	54	Dallas Clark	.30	.10
❑	55	David Carr	.60	.25
❑	56	Jerricho Cotchery	.30	.10
❑	57	Deuce McAllister	.60	.25
❑	58	Donald Driver	.40	.15
❑	59	Jeff Smoker	.40	.15
❑	60	Champ Bailey	.40	.15
❑	61	Jason Witten	.40	.15
❑	62	T.J. Houshmandzadeh	.30	.10
❑	63	Jay Fiedler	.30	.10
❑	64	Philip Rivers	.60	.25
❑	65	Jake Delhomme	.60	.25
❑	66	Terrence McGee RC	.60	.25
❑	67	Chester Taylor	.40	.15
❑	68	Tommy Maddox	.30	.10
❑	69	Bryant Johnson	.30	.10
❑	70	Justin Gage	.30	.10
❑	71	Troy Hambrick	.30	.10
❑	72	Kerry Collins	.40	.15
❑	73	Jeb Putzier	.30	.10
❑	74	Keary Colbert	.40	.15
❑	75	Jason Elam	.30	.10
❑	76	Jerramy Stevens	.30	.10
❑	77	Clinton Portis	.60	.25
❑	78	Sam Aiken	.30	.10
❑	79	Trent Green	.40	.15
❑	80	Dat Nguyen	.30	.10
❑	81	Ladell Betts	.30	.10
❑	82	Peter Warrick	.30	.10
❑	83	Dominic Rhodes	.30	.10
❑	84	Jason Taylor	.30	.10
❑	85	Antwaan Randle El	.40	.15
❑	86	Michael Jenkins	.40	.15
❑	87	Adam Vinatieri	.60	.25
❑	88	Mark Brunell	.40	.15
❑	89	Brian Finneran	.30	.10
❑	90	Ernie Conwell	.30	.10
❑	91	Chad Pennington	.60	.25
❑	92	Dan Morgan	.30	.10
❑	93	Kelly Holcomb	.30	.10
❑	94	Ronde Barber	.30	.10
❑	95	Torry Holt	.60	.25
❑	96	Bubba Franks	.40	.15
❑	97	Keyshawn Johnson	.40	.15
❑	98	J.P. Losman	.60	.25
❑	99	Ed Reed	.40	.15
❑	100	Chris McAlister	.30	.10
❑	101	Jamie Sharper	.30	.10
❑	102	Chad Lewis	.30	.10
❑	103	Chris Brown	.40	.15
❑	104	Marc Boerigter	.40	.15
❑	105	Zach Thomas	.60	.25
❑	106	Byron Leftwich	.60	.25
❑	107	Tatum Bell	.40	.15
❑	108	Tai Streets	.30	.10
❑	109	Tory James	.30	.10
❑	110	Cedrick Wilson	.30	.10
❑	111	Darrell Jackson	.40	.15
❑	112	Ben Roethlisberger	1.50	.60
❑	113	Quentin Jammer	.30	.10
❑	114	Maurice Morris	.30	.10
❑	115	Simeon Rice	.40	.15
❑	116	Tyrone Calico	.40	.15
❑	117	Patrick Ramsey	.40	.15
❑	118	Marcus Robinson	.40	.15
❑	119	Reggie Wayne	.40	.15
❑	120	Kevin Faulk	.30	.10
❑	121	Nate Burleson	.40	.15
❑	122	Aaron Brooks	.40	.15
❑	123	Willie Roaf	.30	.10
❑	124	Fred Taylor	.40	.15
❑	125	Dwight Freeney	.40	.15
❑	126	Olin Kreutz	.30	.10
❑	127	Dunta Robinson	.40	.15
❑	128	Warren Sapp	.40	.15
❑	129	Chris Perry	.40	.15
❑	130	Desmond Clark	.30	.10
❑	131	Takeo Spikes	.30	.10
❑	132	B.J. Sams	.30	.10
❑	133	Bertrand Berry	.30	.10
❑	134	Drew Henson	.40	.15
❑	135	Robert Ferguson	.30	.10
❑	136	Julius Jones	.75	.30
❑	137	Jeremiah Trotter	.30	.10
❑	138	Chris Simms	.40	.15
❑	139	Damerien McCants	.30	.10
❑	140	Robert Gallery	.40	.15
❑	141	Michael Strahan	.40	.15
❑	142	Reggie Williams	.40	.15
❑	143	Tony Gonzalez	.40	.15
❑	144	Priest Holmes	.60	.25
❑	145	Luke McCown	.30	.10
❑	146	Allen Rossum	.30	.10
❑	147	Eric Moulds	.40	.15
❑	148	Jonathan Wells	.30	.10
❑	149	Randy McMichael	.30	.10
❑	150	John Abraham	.30	.10
❑	151	Doug Gabriel	.30	.10
❑	152	Tiki Barber	.60	.25
❑	153	Marcel Shipp	.30	.10
❑	154	LaDainian Tomlinson	.75	.30
❑	155	Richard Seymour	.40	.15
❑	156	Mike Vanderjagt	.30	.10
❑	157	Roy Williams WR	.60	.25
❑	158	William Green	.30	.10
❑	159	DeAngelo Hall	.40	.15
❑	160	Josh McCown	.40	.15
❑	161	[illegible]	[illegible]	[illegible]
❑	162	Brian Dawkins	.40	.15
❑	163	Lee Evans	.40	.15
❑	164	Nick Goings	.30	.10
❑	165	Carson Palmer	.60	.25
❑	166	Charles Woodson	.40	.15
❑	167	Keenan McCardell	.30	.10
❑	168	Kevan Barlow	.40	.15
❑	169	Matt Hasselbeck	.40	.15
❑	170	Steven Jackson	.75	.30
❑	171	Ben Troupe	.30	.10
❑	172	Jamal Lewis	.60	.25
❑	173	Sammy Morris	.30	.10
❑	174	Troy Polamalu	1.00	.40
❑	175	Donovan McNabb	.75	.30
❑	176	Curtis Martin	.60	.25
❑	177	David Givens	.40	.15
❑	178	Kenechi Udeze	.30	.10
❑	179	A.J. Feeley	.40	.15
❑	180	Eddie Kennison	.30	.10
❑	181	LaBrandon Toefield	.30	.10
❑	182	Jabar Gaffney	.30	.10
❑	183	Bethel Johnson	.30	.10
❑	184	Eddie Drummond	.30	.10
❑	185	Rod Smith	.40	.15
❑	186	La'Roi Glover	.30	.10
❑	187	Onterrio Smith	.40	.15
❑	188	Antonio Bryant	.30	.10
❑	189	Lee Mays	.30	.10
❑	190	Michael Vick	1.00	.40
❑	191	Samie Parker	.30	.10
❑	192	London Fletcher	.30	.10
❑	193	DeShaun Foster	.40	.15
❑	194	Rashaun Woods	.40	.15
❑	195	Marc Bulger	.60	.25
❑	196	Adrian Peterson	.30	.10
❑	197	Justin McCareins	.30	.10
❑	198	Corey Dillon	.40	.15
❑	199	James Farrior	.30	.10
❑	200	Antonio Gates	.60	.25
❑	201	Todd Pinkston	.30	.10
❑	202	Randy Hymes	.30	.10
❑	203	Peyton Manning	1.00	.40
❑	204	Ahman Green	.60	.25
❑	205	Charles Rogers	.40	.15
❑	206	John Lynch	.40	.15
❑	207	Larry Fitzgerald	.60	.25
❑	208	Jonathan Ogden	.30	.10
❑	209	Michael Bennett	.40	.15
❑	210	DeWayne Robertson	.30	.10
❑	211	Justin Fargas	.30	.10
❑	212	Duce Staley	.40	.15
❑	213	Koren Robinson	.40	.15
❑	214	Billy Volek	.40	.15
❑	215	Laveranues Coles	.40	.15
❑	216	Michael Clayton	.60	.25
❑	217	Amani Toomer	.40	.15
❑	218	Thomas Jones	.40	.15
❑	219	Todd Heap	.40	.15
❑	220	Ken Lucas	.30	.10
❑	221	Donovin Darius	.30	.10
❑	222	Ashley Lelie	.40	.15
❑	223	Warrick Dunn	.40	.15
❑	224	Doug Jolley	.30	.10
❑	225	Jimmy Smith	.40	.15
❑	226	Quentin Griffin	.40	.15
❑	227	Isaac Bruce	.40	.15
❑	228	Ronald Curry	.40	.15
❑	229	Corey Bradford	.30	.10
❑	230	LaVar Arrington	.60	.25
❑	231	William Henderson	.30	.10

❑ 232 Brandon Stokley .40 .15
❑ 233 Alge Crumpler .40 .15
❑ 234 Joe Horn .40 .15
❑ 235 Bernard Berrian .30 .10
❑ 236 Michael Boulware .30 .10
❑ 237 Brett Favre 1.50 .60
❑ 238 Dennis Northcutt .30 .10
❑ 239 Muhsin Muhammad .40 .15
❑ 240 Shawn Springs .30 .10
❑ 241 Kelly Campbell .30 .10
❑ 242 Johnnie Morton .40 .15
❑ 243 Derrick Blaylock .30 .10
❑ 244 Chris Chambers .40 .15
❑ 245 Joey Harrington .60 .25
❑ 246 Brian Urlacher .60 .25
❑ 247 T.J. Duckett .40 .15
❑ 248 Quincy Morgan .30 .10
❑ 249 Darren Sharper .30 .10
❑ 250 L.J. Smith .30 .10
❑ 251 Steve McNair .60 .25
❑ 252 Eric Parker .30 .10
❑ 253 Jerome Bettis .60 .25
❑ 254 LaMont Jordan .60 .25
❑ 255 Tedy Bruschi .40 .15
❑ 256 Ernest Wilford .30 .10
❑ 257 Reuben Droughns .40 .15
❑ 258 Lito Sheppard .30 .10
❑ 259 Steve Smith .40 .15
❑ 260 Shaun Alexander .60 .25
❑ 261 Kevin Curtis .40 .15
❑ 262 Drew Bledsoe .60 .25
❑ 263 Derrick Mason .40 .15
❑ 264 Jevon Kearse .40 .15
❑ 265 Jerry Porter .40 .15
❑ 266 Edgerrin James .60 .25
❑ 267 Santana Moss .40 .15
❑ 268 Kyle Boller .40 .15
❑ 269 Travis Henry .40 .15
❑ 270 Stephen Davis .40 .15
❑ 271 Gibril Wilson .30 .10
❑ 272 Plaxico Burress .40 .15
❑ 273 Deion Branch .40 .15
❑ 274 Larry Johnson .60 .25
❑ 275 Rudi Johnson .40 .15
❑ 276 Andre Johnson .40 .15
❑ 277 David Akers .30 .10
❑ 278 Randy Moss .60 .25
❑ 279 Roy Williams S .40 .15
❑ 280 Antoine Winfield .30 .10
❑ 281 Antonio Pierce .30 .10
❑ 282 Keith Bulluck .30 .10
❑ 283 Correll Buckhalter .40 .15
❑ 284 Troy Vincent .30 .10
❑ 285 D.J. Williams .30 .10
❑ 286 Matt Schaub .40 .15
❑ 287 Clarence Moore .30 .10
❑ 288 Billy Miller .30 .10
❑ 289 Terrence Holt .30 .10
❑ 290 Tony Hollings .30 .10
❑ 291 E.J. Henderson .30 .10
❑ 292 Fred Smoot .30 .10
❑ 293 Patrick Crayton .30 .10
❑ 294 Mike Alstott .40 .15
❑ 295 Mewelde Moore .40 .15
❑ 296 Shawn Bryson .30 .10
❑ 297 David Garrard .30 .10
❑ 298 Kurt Warner .40 .15
❑ 299 Nate Clements .30 .10
❑ 300 Kellen Winslow .60 .25
❑ 301 Eric Johnson .40 .15
❑ 302 Peerless Price .30 .10
❑ 303 Joey Galloway .40 .15
❑ 304 Sebastian Janikowski .30 .10
❑ 305 Jason McAddley .30 .10
❑ 306 Chris Gamble .40 .15
❑ 307 Brian Griese .40 .15
❑ 308 Greg Lewis .60 .25
❑ 309 Wes Welker .30 .10
❑ 310 Jesse Chatman .30 .10
❑ 311 Curtis Martin LL .40 .15
❑ 312 Daunte Culpepper LL .40 .15
❑ 313 Muhsin Muhammad LL .30 .10
❑ 314 Shaun Alexander LL .60 .25
❑ 315 Trent Green LL .30 .10
❑ 316 Joe Horn LL .30 .10
❑ 317 Corey Dillon LL .30 .10
❑ 318 Peyton Manning LL .60 .25
❑ 319 Javon Walker LL .30 .10
❑ 320 Edgerrin James LL .40 .15
❑ 321 Jake Scott GM .30 .10
❑ 322 John Elway GM 1.00 .40
❑ 323 Dwight Clark GM .40 .15
❑ 324 Lawrence Taylor GM .60 .25
❑ 325 Joe Namath GM .75 .30
❑ 326 Richard Dent GM .40 .15
❑ 327 Peyton Manning GM .60 .25
❑ 328 Don Maynard GM .30 .10
❑ 329 Joe Greene GM .60 .25
❑ 330 Roger Staubach GM .75 .30
❑ 331 Daunte Culpepper AP .40 .15
❑ 332 Peyton Manning AP .60 .25
❑ 333 Tiki Barber AP .40 .15
❑ 334 Antonio Gates AP .40 .15
❑ 335 Marvin Harrison AP .40 .15
❑ 336 Lito Sheppard AP .30 .10
❑ 337 LaDainian Tomlinson AP .60 .25
❑ 338 Muhsin Muhammad AP .30 .10
❑ 339 Allen Rossum AP .30 .10
❑ 340 Dwight Freeney AP .40 .15
❑ 341 Jerome Bettis AP .40 .15
❑ 342 Alge Crumpler AP .30 .10
❑ 343 Ed Reed AP .30 .10
❑ 344 Ronde Barber AP .30 .10
❑ 345 Takeo Spikes AP .30 .10
❑ 346 Rudi Johnson AP .30 .10
❑ 347 Adam Vinatieri AP .40 .15
❑ 348 Torry Holt AP .40 .15
❑ 349 Chad Johnson AP .40 .15
❑ 350 Brian Westbrook AP .30 .10
❑ 351 Michael Vick AP .60 .25
❑ 352 Tom Brady AP .60 .25
❑ 353 Donovan McNabb AP .60 .25
❑ 354 Ahman Green AP .40 .15
❑ 355 Andre Johnson AP .30 .10
❑ 356 Drew Brees AP .40 .15
❑ 357 Hines Ward AP .40 .15
❑ 358 Deion Branch PH .30 .10
❑ 359 Philadelphia Eagles PH .60 .25
❑ 360 Tom Brady PH .60 .25
❑ 361 Taylor Stubblefield RC .75 .30
❑ 362 Dan Cody RC 1.50 .60
❑ 363 Ryan Claridge RC 1.25 .50
❑ 364 David Pollack RC 1.50 .60
❑ 365 Craig Bragg RC 1.25 .50
❑ 366 Alvin Pearman RC 1.50 .60
❑ 367 Marcus Maxwell RC 1.25 .50
❑ 368 Brock Berlin RC 1.25 .50
❑ 369 Khalif Barnes RC 1.25 .50
❑ 370 Eric King RC 1.25 .50
❑ 371 Alex Smith TE RC 1.50 .60
❑ 372 Dante Ridgeway RC 1.25 .50
❑ 373 Shaun Cody RC 1.50 .60
❑ 374 Donte Nicholson RC 1.50 .60
❑ 375 DeMarcus Ware RC 2.50 1.00
❑ 376 Lionel Gates RC 1.25 .50
❑ 377 Fabian Washington RC 1.50 .60
❑ 378 Brandon Jacobs RC 2.00 .75
❑ 379 Noah Herron RC 1.50 .60
❑ 380 Derrick Johnson RC 2.50 1.00
❑ 381 J.R. Russell RC 1.25 .50
❑ 382 Adrian McPherson RC 1.50 .60
❑ 383 Marcus Spears RC 1.50 .60
❑ 384 Justin Miller RC 1.25 .50
❑ 385 Marion Barber RC 2.50 1.00
❑ 386 Anthony Davis RC 1.25 .50
❑ 387 Chad Owens RC 1.50 .60
❑ 388 Craphonso Thorpe RC 1.25 .50
❑ 389 Travis Johnson RC 1.25 .50
❑ 390 Erasmus James RC 1.50 .60
❑ 391 Mike Patterson RC 1.50 .60
❑ 392 Alphonso Hodge RC .75 .30
❑ 393 Airese Currie RC 1.50 .60
❑ 394 Justin Tuck RC 1.50 .60
❑ 395 Dan Orlovsky RC 1.50 .60
❑ 396 Thomas Davis RC 1.50 .60
❑ 397 Derek Anderson RC 2.50 1.00
❑ 398 Matt Roth RC 1.50 .60
❑ 399 Darryl Blackstock RC 1.25 .50
❑ 400 Chris Henry RC 1.50 .60
❑ 401 Rasheed Marshall RC 1.50 .60
❑ 402 Anttaj Hawthorne RC 1.25 .50
❑ 403 Bryant McFadden RC 1.50 .60
❑ 404 Darren Sproles RC 1.50 .60
❑ 405 Oshiomogho Atogwe RC 1.25 .50
❑ 406 Fred Gibson RC 1.25 .50
❑ 407 J.J. Arrington RC 1.50 .60
❑ 408 Cedric Benson RC 4.00 1.50
❑ 409 Mark Bradley RC 1.50 .60
❑ 410 Reggie Brown RC 1.50 .60
❑ 411 Ronnie Brown RC 6.00 2.50
❑ 412 Jason Campbell RC 2.50 1.00
❑ 413 Maurice Clarett 1.50 .60
❑ 414 Mark Clayton RC 1.50 .60
❑ 415 Braylon Edwards RC 5.00 2.00
❑ 416 Ciatrick Fason RC 1.50 .60
❑ 417 Charlie Frye RC 1.50 .60
❑ 418 Frank Gore RC 3.00 1.25
❑ 419 David Greene RC 1.50 .60
❑ 420 Vincent Jackson RC 1.50 .60
❑ 421 Adam Jones RC 1.50 .60
❑ 422 Matt Jones RC 2.50 1.00
❑ 423 Stefan LeFors RC 1.50 .60
❑ 424 Heath Miller RC 3.00 1.25
❑ 425 Ryan Moats RC 1.50 .60
❑ 426 Vernand Morency RC 1.50 .60
❑ 427 Terrence Murphy RC 1.50 .60
❑ 428 Kyle Orton RC 1.50 .60
❑ 429 Roscoe Parrish RC 1.50 .60
❑ 430 Courtney Roby RC 1.50 .60
❑ 431 Aaron Rodgers RC 5.00 2.00
❑ 432 Carlos Rogers RC 2.00 .75
❑ 433 Antrel Rolle RC 1.50 .60
❑ 434 Eric Shelton RC 1.50 .60
❑ 435 Alex Smith QB RC 6.00 2.50
❑ 436 Andrew Walter RC 1.50 .60
❑ 437 Roddy White RC 1.50 .60
❑ 438 Cadillac Williams RC 6.00 2.50
❑ 439 Mike Williams 1.50 .60
❑ 440 Troy Williamson RC 1.50 .60
❑ RHDB Deion Branch RH 5.00 2.00
❑ RHDBA Deion Branch RH AU 350.00 200.00
❑ SBMVP D.Branch FB AU/200 150.00 60.00

2006 Topps

❑ COMPLETE SET (385) 50.00 25.00
❑ 1 Jonathan Vilma .40 .15
❑ 2 Mewelde Moore .30 .10
❑ 3 Shaun McDonald .30 .10
❑ 4 Marcus Pollard .30 .10
❑ 5 Marcus Robinson .40 .15
❑ 6 David Garrard .30 .12
❑ 7 Chris Gamble .30 .12
❑ 8 Rex Grossman .60 .25
❑ 9 Lee Suggs .30 .12
❑ 10 Steve McNair .40 .15
❑ 11 Chester Taylor .40 .15
❑ 12 Randy Moss .60 .25
❑ 13 Jeremy Shockey .60 .25
❑ 14 Tedy Bruschi .60 .25
❑ 15 Walter Jones .30 .12
❑ 16 Troy Polamalu .75 .30
❑ 17 Ladell Betts .30 .12
❑ 18 DeMarcus Ware .40 .15
❑ 19 Erron Kinney .30 .12
❑ 20 Trent Cole .30 .12

21	Charlie Adams	.30	.12
22	Brandon Jacobs	.40	.15
23	Nathan Vasher	.30	.12
24	Shawne Merriman	.40	.15
25	Drew Carter	.30	.12
26	Clinton Portis	.60	.25
27	Alex Brown	.30	.12
28	Osi Umenyiora	.30	.12
29	Willie Parker	.75	.30
30	Lofa Tatupu	.40	.15
31	Odell Thurman	.30	.12
32	Scottie Vines	.30	.12
33	Sam Gado	.40	.15
34	Todd DeVoe	.60	.25
35	Keith Brooking	[illegible]	.12
36	Eddie Kennison	.30	.12
37	Mike Williams	.60	.25
38	Adam Jones	.30	.12
39	Charlie Frye	.40	.15
40	Reggie Wayne	.40	.15
41	Donte Stallworth	.40	.15
42	Vincent Jackson	.30	.12
43	Alex Smith QB	.60	.25
44	Greg Lewis	.30	.12
45	Billy Volek	.40	.15
46	Domonique Foxworth	.30	.12
47	Terrell Owens	.60	.25
48	Josh McCown	.40	.15
49	Simeon Rice	.30	.10
50	Curtis Martin	.60	.25
51	Peyton Manning	1.00	.40
52	Nick Barnett	.30	.10
53	Marion Barber	.40	.15
54	Chris McAlister	.30	.10
55	Jerramy Stevens	.40	.15
56	Jerome Bettis	.60	.25
57	Chris Brown	.40	.15
58	LeRon McCoy	.30	.10
59	John Abraham	.30	.10
60	LaMont Jordan	.40	.15
61	Jason Taylor	.30	.10
62	Michael Clayton	.40	.15
63	Jake Plummer	.40	.15
64	Travis Taylor	.30	.10
65	Samie Parker	.30	.10
66	Carlos Rogers	.30	.10
67	Kevin Faulk	.30	.10
68	Alvin Pearman	.30	.10
69	Derrick Johnson	.40	.15
70	Cedric Benson	.60	.25
71	J.P. Losman	.40	.15
72	Julius Peppers	.40	.15
73	DeAngelo Hall	.40	.15
74	Joey Galloway	.40	.15
75	Marcus Trufant	.30	.10
76	Frisman Jackson	.30	.10
77	Jason Campbell	.40	.15
78	Ron Dayne	.40	.15
79	Ashley Lelie	.40	.15
80	Drew Bennett	.30	.10
81	Brandon Lloyd	.40	.15
82	Trent Dilfer	.40	.15
83	Marty Booker	.30	.10
84	Aaron Rodgers	.60	.25
85	Deltha O'Neal	.30	.10
86	Jon Kitna	.30	.12
87	Doug Gabriel	.30	.10
88	Keenan McCardell	.30	.10
89	Brian Griese	.40	.15
90	Michael Jenkins	.40	.15
91	Brian Westbrook	.40	.15
92	Terrence Holt	.30	.10
93	Justin Gage	.30	.10
94	Shayne Graham	.30	.10
95	D.J. Hackett	.30	.10
96	Kevan Barlow	.40	.15
97	Bob Sanders	.40	.15
98	Charles Rogers	.40	.15
99	Kevin Curtis	.30	.10
100	LaDainian Tomlinson	.75	.30
101	Plaxico Burress	.40	.15
102	Kyle Boller	.30	.10
103	Donald Driver	.40	.15
104	Jerome Mathis	.30	.10
105	Takeo Spikes	.30	.10
106	Tony Gonzalez	.40	.15
107	Keary Colbert	.30	.10
108	Derrick Burgess	.30	.10
109	T.J. Duckett	.40	.15
110	Chris Chambers	.40	.15
111	Cadillac Williams	.60	.25
112	Jerricho Cotchery	.30	.10
113	Ernest Wilford	.30	.10
114	Torry Holt	.40	.15
115	Corey Dillon	.40	.15
116	Chris Simms	.40	.15
117	Philip Rivers	.60	.25
118	LaVar Arrington	.60	.25
119	Andrew Walter	.40	.15
120	Joe Jurevicius	.40	.15
121	Kyle Vanden Bosch	.30	.10
122	London Fletcher	.30	.10
123	Deuce McAllister	.40	.15
124	Cedrick Wilson	.30	.10
125	Jason Witten	.40	.15
126	Troy Williamson	.40	.15
127	Dominic Rhodes	.40	.15
128	Koren Robinson	.40	.15
129	Eli Manning	.75	.30
130	Brian Finneran	.30	.10
131	Fabian Washington	.30	.10
132	Michael Boulware	.30	.10
133	Bernard Berrian	.30	.10
134	Stephen Davis	.40	.15
135	Reggie Brown	.50	.20
136	Chad Johnson	.40	.15
137	Ronnie Brown	.60	.25
138	Amani Toomer	.40	.15
139	Deion Branch	.40	.15
140	Darren Sproles	.30	.10
141	L.J. Smith	.30	.10
142	Arnaz Battle	.30	.10
143	Jerry Porter	.40	.15
144	Terry Glenn	.50	.20
145	Mike Vrabel	.40	.15
146	Chad Pennington	.40	.15
147	Allen Rossum	.30	.10
148	Greg Jones	.30	.10
149	Jake Delhomme	.40	.15
150	Tom Brady	1.00	.40
151	Neil Rackers	.30	.10
152	Charles Woodson	.40	.15
153	Carson Palmer	.60	.25
154	Kerry Collins	.40	.15
155	Brian Urlacher	.60	.25
156	Kevin Jones	.60	.25
157	Eric Parker	.30	.10
158	Daniel Graham	.30	.10
159	Dallas Clark	.30	.10
160	Matt Schaub	.40	.15
161	Drew Brees	.60	.25
162	Andre Johnson	.40	.15
163	Ray Lewis	.60	.25
164	Cato June	.40	.15
165	J.J. Arrington	.40	.15
166	Warren Sapp	.40	.15
167	T.J. Houshmandzadeh	.50	.20
168	Donnie Edwards	.30	.10
169	Thomas Jones	.40	.15
170	Mark Clayton	.60	.25
171	Kyle Orton	.40	.15
172	Najeh Davenport	.30	.10
173	Dan Morgan	.30	.10
174	David Pollack	.30	.10
175	D.J. Williams	.30	.10
176	Julius Jones	.60	.25
177	Roy Williams WR	.60	.25
178	Willis McGahee	.60	.25
179	Keyshawn Johnson	.40	.15
180	Dennis Northcutt	.30	.10
181	Courtney Roby	.30	.10
182	Jonathan Ogden	.30	.10
183	Kellen Winslow	.60	.25
184	Matt Jones	.40	.15
185	Robert Gallery	.30	.10
186	Mike Anderson	.40	.15
187	Frank Gore	.60	.25
188	Jimmy Smith	.40	.15
189	Antonio Pierce	.30	.10
190	Todd Heap	.40	.15
191	Champ Bailey	.40	.15
192	Roddy White	.40	.15
193	Rod Smith	.40	.15
194	Brian Dawkins	.40	.15
195	Larry Johnson	.75	.30
196	Ed Reed	.40	.15
197	Marc Bulger	.40	.15
198	Zach Thomas	.60	.25
199	Cedric Houston	.30	.10
200	Brett Favre	1.50	.60
201	Mark Brunell	.40	.15
202	Edgerrin James	.60	.25
203	Ronald Curry	.40	.15
204	Antonio Gates	.60	.25
205	Roscoe Parrish	.30	.10
206	Steve Smith	.60	.25
207	Reuben Droughns	.40	.15
208	Michael Vick	.60	.25
209	Chris Cooley	.30	.10
210	Chris Perry	.40	.15
211	Muhsin Muhammad	.40	.15
212	Trent Green	.40	.15
213	Matt Hasselbeck	.40	.15
214	Ben Roethlisberger	1.00	.40
215	Tyrone Calico	.30	.10
216	Jamal Lewis	.40	.15
217	Antwaan Randle El	.40	.15
218	Byron Leftwich	.40	.15
219	Priest Holmes	.40	.15
220	Anquan Boldin	.40	.15
221	Drew Bledsoe	.60	.25
222	Randy McMichael	.30	.10
223	Tatum Bell	.40	.15
224	Daunte Culpepper	[illegible]	.25
225	David Carr	.40	.15
226	Mark Bradley	.40	.15
227	Lee Evans	.40	.15
228	Domanick Davis	.40	.15
229	Robert Ferguson	.30	.10
230	Peter Warrick	.30	.10
231	Heath Miller	.40	.15
232	Derrick Brooks	.40	.15
233	Isaac Bruce	.40	.15
234	Aaron Brooks	.40	.15
235	Nate Burleson	.40	.15
236	Braylon Edwards	.60	.25
237	Ben Watson	.30	.10
238	Hines Ward	.60	.25
239	Shaun Alexander	.60	.25
240	Kurt Warner	.40	.15
241	Warrick Dunn	.40	.15
242	Rodney Harrison	[illegible]	.10
243	Dante Hall	.40	.15
244	Tiki Barber	.60	.25
245	Santana Moss	.40	.15
246	Fred Taylor	.40	.15
247	Laveranues Coles	.40	.15
248	Darren Sharper	.30	.10
249	Brandon Stokley	.40	.15
250	Alge Crumpler	.40	.15
251	Derrick Mason	.30	.10
252	Antonio Bryant	.40	.15
253	Antrel Rolle	.30	.10
254	Eric Moulds	.40	.15
255	Bubba Franks	.30	.10
256	Joe Horn	.40	.15
257	Dunta Robinson	.40	.15
258	Larry Fitzgerald	.60	.25
259	Roy Williams S	.40	.15
260	Javon Walker	.40	.15
261	Alex Smith TE	.30	.10
262	Travis Henry	.40	.15
263	Luke McCown	.30	.10
264	James Farrior	.30	.10
265	Darrell Jackson	.40	.15
266	Marvin Harrison	.60	.25
267	Patrick Ramsey	.40	.15
268	Ernie Conwell	.30	.10
269	Ahman Green	.40	.15
270	Ryan Moats	.30	.10
271	Donovan McNabb	.60	.25
272	Steven Jackson	.60	.25

❑ 273 Ronde Barber .30 .10
❑ 274 Michael Strahan .40 .15
❑ 275 Dwight Freeney .40 .15
❑ 276 DeShaun Foster .40 .15
❑ 277 Terence Newman .30 .10
❑ 278 Rudi Johnson .40 .15
❑ 279 Shaun Alexander LL .40 .15
❑ 280 Tom Brady LL .60 .25
❑ 281 Steve Smith LL .40 .15
❑ 282 Tiki Barber LL .40 .15
❑ 283 Trent Green LL .25 .10
❑ 284 Santana Moss LL .25 .10
❑ 285 Larry Johnson LL .50 .20
❑ 286 Brett Favre LL 1.00 .40
❑ 287 Chad Johnson AP .25 .10
❑ 288 Peyton Manning AP .60 .25
❑ 289 Matt Hasselbeck AP .25 .10
❑ 290 Edgerrin James AP .40 .15
❑ 291 Shaun Alexander AP .40 .15
❑ 292 Larry Johnson AP .50 .20
❑ 293 Tiki Barber AP .40 .15
❑ 294 Marvin Harrison AP .40 .15
❑ 295 Santana Moss AP .25 .10
❑ 296 Chad Johnson AP .25 .10
❑ 297 Alge Crumpler AP .25 .10
❑ 298 LaDainian Tomlinson AP .50 .20
❑ 299 Derrick Brooks AP .25 .10
❑ 300 Antonio Gates AP .40 .15
❑ 301 Steve Smith AP .40 .15
❑ 302 Shawne Merriman AP .25 .10
❑ 303 Michael Vick AP .40 .15
❑ 304 Tony Gonzalez AP .25 .10
❑ 305 Jake Delhomme AP .25 .10
❑ 306 Steve McNair AP .25 .10
❑ 307 Larry Fitzgerald AP .40 .15
❑ 308 Ben Roethlisberger HL .60 .25
❑ 309 Seattle Seahawks HL .60 .25
❑ 310 Pittsburgh Steelers HL .60 .25
❑ 311 Tamba Hali RC 1.50 .60
❑ 312 Haloti Ngata RC 1.50 .60
❑ 313 Mike Hass RC 1.50 .60
❑ 314 Manny Lawson RC 1.50 .60
❑ 315 Reggie McNeal RC 1.25 .50
❑ 316 Kelly Jennings RC 1.50 .60
❑ 317 Jason Allen RC 1.50 .60
❑ 318 Joe Klopfenstein RC 1.25 .50
❑ 319 Willie Reid RC 1.50 .60
❑ 320 Brad Smith RC 1.50 .60
❑ 321 Bruce Gradkowski RC 2.50 1.00
❑ 322 Ashton Youboty RC 1.50 .60
❑ 323 Abdul Hodge RC 1.50 .60
❑ 324 P.J. Daniels RC 1.25 .50
❑ 325 D'Qwell Jackson RC 1.25 .50
❑ 326 Johnathan Joseph RC 1.25 .50
❑ 327 Antonio Cromartie RC 1.50 .60
❑ 328 Elvis Dumervil RC .75 .30
❑ 329 Tye Hill RC 1.50 .60
❑ 330 Mathias Kiwanuka RC 2.00 .75
❑ 331 Leonard Pope RC 1.50 .60
❑ 332 DeMeco Ryans RC 2.00 .75
❑ 333 Brodrick Bunkley RC 1.50 .60
❑ 334 Devin Hester RC 3.00 1.25
❑ 335 Thomas Howard RC 1.50 .60
❑ 336 Cory Rodgers RC 1.50 .60
❑ 337 Ernie Sims RC 2.00 .75
❑ 338 Todd Watkins RC 1.25 .50
❑ 339 Rocky McIntosh RC 1.50 .60
❑ 340 Donte Whitner RC 1.50 .60
❑ 341 Anthony Schlegel RC 1.25 .50
❑ 342 Kamerion Wimbley RC 1.50 .60
❑ 343 Wali Lundy RC 1.50 .60
❑ 344 Bobby Carpenter RC 1.50 .60
❑ 345 Jimmy Williams RC 1.50 .60
❑ 346 Michael Robinson RC 1.50 .60
❑ 347 Brandon Williams RC 1.50 .60
❑ 348 Skyler Green RC 1.50 .60
❑ 349 Jerious Norwood RC 2.50 1.00
❑ 350 Travis Wilson RC 1.50 .60
❑ 351 Mario Williams RC 2.50 1.00
❑ 352 Santonio Holmes RC 3.00 1.25
❑ 353 Vince Young RC 6.00 2.50
❑ 354 Matt Leinart RC 5.00 2.00
❑ 355 D'Brickashaw Ferguson RC 1.50 .60
❑ 356 Michael Huff RC 2.00 .75
❑ 357 Chad Greenway RC 1.50 .60
❑ 358 Chad Jackson RC 1.50 .60
❑ 359A Reggie Bush RC 6.00 2.50
❑ 359B Reggie Bush RC 6.00 2.50
❑ 360 A.J. Hawk RC 3.00 1.25
❑ 361 DeAngelo Williams RC 4.00 1.50
❑ 362 Derek Hagan RC 1.50 .60
❑ 363 Vernon Davis RC 3.00 1.25
❑ 364 Joseph Addai RC 5.00 2.00
❑ 365 Jay Cutler RC 5.00 2.00
❑ 366 Jason Avant RC 1.50 .60
❑ 367 Brian Calhoun RC 1.50 .60
❑ 368 LenDale White RC 3.00 1.25
❑ 369 Greg Jennings RC 2.50 1.00
❑ 370 Charlie Whitehurst RC 1.50 .60
❑ 371 Sinorice Moss RC 1.50 .60
❑ 372 Maurice Stovall RC 1.50 .60
❑ 373 Laurence Maroney RC 4.00 1.50
❑ 374 Brodie Croyle RC 4.00 1.50
❑ 375 Demetrius Williams RC 1.50 .60
❑ 376 Jerome Harrison RC 1.50 .60
❑ 377 Maurice Drew RC 4.00 1.50
❑ 378 Kellen Clemens RC 2.50 1.00
❑ 379 Marcedes Lewis RC 1.50 .60
❑ 380 Leon Washington RC 2.50 1.00
❑ 381 Anthony Fasano RC 1.50 .60
❑ 382 Jeremy Bloom RC 1.25 .50
❑ 383 Omar Jacobs RC 1.25 .50
❑ 384 Tarvaris Jackson RC 2.50 1.00
❑ 385 Brandon Marshall RC 1.50 .60

2007 Topps

❑ COMPLETE SET (440) 50.00 25.00
❑ 1 Matt Leinart .60 .25
❑ 2 Kurt Warner .50 .20
❑ 3 Matt Schaub .50 .20
❑ 4 Michael Vick .60 .25
❑ 5 Kyle Boller .40 .15
❑ 6 Steve McNair .50 .20
❑ 7 J.P. Losman .50 .20
❑ 8 Jake Delhomme .50 .20
❑ 9 Rex Grossman .50 .20
❑ 10 Brian Griese .50 .20
❑ 11 Carson Palmer .60 .25
❑ 12 Charlie Frye .50 .20
❑ 13 Drew Bledsoe .60 .25
❑ 14 Tony Romo 1.25 .50
❑ 15 Joey Harrington .50 .20
❑ 16 Jay Cutler .60 .25
❑ 17 Jon Kitna .40 .15
❑ 18 Aaron Rodgers .60 .25
❑ 19 Brett Favre 1.25 .50
❑ 20 David Carr .50 .20
❑ 21 Peyton Manning 1.00 .40
❑ 22 David Garrard .50 .20
❑ 23 Byron Leftwich .50 .20
❑ 24 Trent Green .50 .20
❑ 25 Damon Huard .40 .15
❑ 26 Daunte Culpepper .50 .20
❑ 27 Tarvaris Jackson .60 .25
❑ 28 Tom Brady 1.25 .50
❑ 29 Drew Brees .50 .20
❑ 30 Eli Manning .60 .25
❑ 31 Chad Pennington .50 .20
❑ 32 Andrew Walter .40 .15
❑ 33 Aaron Brooks .40 .15
❑ 34 Donovan McNabb .60 .25
❑ 35 Jeff Garcia .50 .20
❑ 36 Ben Roethlisberger .75 .30
❑ 37 Philip Rivers .60 .25
❑ 38 Alex Smith QB .60 .25
❑ 39 Matt Hasselbeck .50 .20
❑ 40 Seneca Wallace .40 .15
❑ 41 Marc Bulger .50 .20
❑ 42 Chris Simms .40 .15
❑ 43 Bruce Gradkowski .50 .20
❑ 44 Vince Young .75 .30
❑ 45 Jason Campbell .50 .20
❑ 46 Jared Lorenzen .40 .15
❑ 47 Mark Brunell .50 .20
❑ 48 J.J. Arrington .50 .20
❑ 49 Edgerrin James .60 .25
❑ 50 Jerious Norwood .50 .20
❑ 51 Warrick Dunn .50 .20
❑ 52 Mike Anderson .50 .20
❑ 53 Jamal Lewis .50 .20
❑ 54 Willis McGahee .50 .20
❑ 55 DeShaun Foster .50 .20
❑ 56 DeAngelo Williams .60 .25
❑ 57 Cedric Benson .50 .20
❑ 58 Thomas Jones .50 .20
❑ 59 Chris Perry .40 .15
❑ 60 Rudi Johnson .50 .20
❑ 61 Reuben Droughns .50 .20
❑ 62 Jerome Harrison .40 .15
❑ 63 Marion Barber .50 .20
❑ 64 Julius Jones .50 .20
❑ 65 Tatum Bell .50 .20
❑ 66 Mike Bell .50 .20
❑ 67 Kevin Jones .40 .15
❑ 68 Brian Calhoun .40 .15
❑ 69 Ahman Green .50 .20
❑ 70 Vernand Morency .50 .20
❑ 71 Ron Dayne .50 .20
❑ 72 Wali Lundy .40 .15
❑ 73 Dominic Rhodes .50 .20
❑ 74 Joseph Addai .75 .30
❑ 75 Fred Taylor .50 .20
❑ 76 Maurice Jones-Drew .60 .25
❑ 77 Larry Johnson .60 .25
❑ 78 Sammy Morris .40 .15
❑ 79 Ronnie Brown .50 .20
❑ 80 Mewelde Moore .40 .15
❑ 81 Chester Taylor .40 .15
❑ 82 Kevin Faulk .40 .15
❑ 83 Corey Dillon .50 .20
❑ 84 Laurence Maroney .60 .25
❑ 85 Deuce McAllister .50 .20
❑ 86 Reggie Bush .75 .30
❑ 87 Brandon Jacobs .50 .20
❑ 88 Anthony Thomas .40 .15
❑ 89 Cedric Houston .40 .15
❑ 90 Leon Washington .50 .20
❑ 91 Kevan Barlow .50 .20
❑ 92 LaMont Jordan .50 .20
❑ 93 Justin Fargas .40 .15
❑ 94 Brian Westbrook .50 .20
❑ 95 Correll Buckhalter .50 .20
❑ 96 Willie Parker .60 .25
❑ 97 Najeh Davenport .40 .15
❑ 98 LaDainian Tomlinson .75 .30
❑ 99 Darren Sproles .40 .15
❑ 100 Frank Gore .60 .25
❑ 101 Michael Robinson .50 .20
❑ 102 Shaun Alexander .50 .20
❑ 103 Maurice Morris .40 .15
❑ 104 Steven Jackson .60 .25
❑ 105 Stephen Davis .50 .20
❑ 106 Cadillac Williams .50 .20
❑ 107 Travis Henry .50 .20
❑ 108 LenDale White .50 .20
❑ 109 Ladell Betts .40 .15
❑ 110 Clinton Portis .50 .20
❑ 111 Michael Turner .50 .20
❑ 112 T.J. Duckett .40 .15
❑ 113 Anquan Boldin .50 .20
❑ 114 Larry Fitzgerald .50 .20
❑ 115 Bryant Johnson .40 .15
❑ 116 Michael Jenkins .50 .20
❑ 117 Ashley Lelie .50 .20
❑ 118 Roddy White .50 .20

❑ 119 Mark Clayton	.50	.20
❑ 120 Derrick Mason	.40	.15
❑ 121 Demetrius Williams	.40	.15
❑ 122 Peerless Price	.40	.15
❑ 123 Lee Evans	.50	.20
❑ 124 Drew Carter	.40	.15
❑ 125 Keyshawn Johnson	.50	.20
❑ 126 Steve Smith	.50	.20
❑ 127 Bernard Berrian	.40	.15
❑ 128 Mark Bradley	.40	.15
❑ 129 Muhsin Muhammad	.50	.20
❑ 130 Chad Johnson	.50	.20
❑ 131 T.J. Houshmandzadeh	.50	.20
[illegible]	[illegible]	[illegible]
❑ 133 Joe Jurevicius	.40	.15
❑ 134 Braylon Edwards	.50	.20
❑ 135 Terrell Owens	.60	.25
❑ 136 Terry Glenn	.50	.20
❑ 137 Skyler Green	.40	.15
❑ 138 Rod Smith	.50	.20
❑ 139 Javon Walker	.50	.20
❑ 140 Brandon Marshall	.50	.20
❑ 141 Mike Furrey	.50	.20
❑ 142 Mike Williams	.40	.15
❑ 143 Roy Williams WR	.50	.20
❑ 144 Donald Driver	.50	.20
❑ 145 Greg Jennings	.50	.20
❑ 146 Andre Johnson	.50	.20
❑ 147 Eric Moulds	.50	.20
❑ 148 Reggie Wayne	.50	.20
❑ 149 Marvin Harrison	.60	.25
❑ 150 Ernest Wilford	.40	.15
❑ 151 Matt Jones	.50	.20
❑ 152 Reggie Williams	.50	.20
❑ 153 Eddie Kennison	.40	.15
❑ 154 Samie Parker	.40	.15
❑ 155 Marty Booker	.40	.15
❑ 156 Chris Chambers	.50	.20
❑ 157 Wes Welker	.60	.25
❑ 158 Travis Taylor	.40	.15
❑ 159 Troy Williamson	.40	.15
❑ 160 Reche Caldwell	.40	.15
❑ 161 Chad Jackson	.40	.15
❑ 162 Devery Henderson	.40	.15
❑ 163 Joe Horn	.50	.20
❑ 164 Marques Colston	.60	.25
❑ 165 Plaxico Burress	.50	.20
❑ 166 Amani Toomer	.50	.20
❑ 167 Sinorice Moss	.50	.20
❑ 168 Jerricho Cotchery	.40	.15
❑ 169 Laveranues Coles	.50	.20
❑ 170 Randy Moss	.60	.25
❑ 171 Ronald Curry	.50	.20
❑ 172 Donte Stallworth	.50	.20
❑ 173 Reggie Brown	.50	.20
❑ 174 Hines Ward	.60	.25
❑ 175 Nate Washington	.40	.15
❑ 176 Santonio Holmes	.50	.20
❑ 177 Keenan McCardell	.40	.15
❑ 178 Eric Parker	.40	.15
❑ 179 Arnaz Battle	.40	.15
❑ 180 Antonio Bryant	.50	.20
❑ 181 D.J. Hackett	.40	.15
❑ 182 Deion Branch	.50	.20
❑ 183 Darrell Jackson	.50	.20
❑ 184 Kevin Curtis	.40	.15
❑ 185 Torry Holt	.50	.20
❑ 186 Isaac Bruce	.50	.20
❑ 187 Michael Clayton	.50	.20
❑ 188 Joey Galloway	.50	.20
❑ 189 Drew Bennett	.40	.15
❑ 190 Bobby Wade	.40	.15
❑ 191 Antwaan Randle El	.40	.15
❑ 192 Santana Moss	.50	.20
❑ 193 Roscoe Parrish	.40	.15
❑ 194 Leonard Pope	.40	.15
❑ 195 Alge Crumpler	.50	.20
❑ 196 Todd Heap	.40	.15
❑ 197 Desmond Clark	.40	.15
❑ 198 Kellen Winslow	.50	.20
❑ 199 Jason Witten	.50	.20
❑ 200 Marcus Pollard	.40	.15
❑ 201 Bubba Franks	.40	.15
❑ 202 Dallas Clark	.40	.15
❑ 203 George Wrighster	.40	.15
❑ 204 Tony Gonzalez	.50	.20
❑ 205 Randy McMichael	.40	.15
❑ 206 Jermaine Wiggins	.40	.15
❑ 207 Ben Watson	.40	.15
❑ 208 Ernie Conwell	.40	.15
❑ 209 Jeremy Shockey	.50	.20
❑ 210 L.J. Smith	.40	.15
❑ 211 Heath Miller	.40	.15
❑ 212 Antonio Gates	.50	.20
❑ 213 Vernon Davis	.50	.20
❑ 214 Jerramy Stevens	.40	.15
❑ 215 Joe Klopfenstein	.40	.15
[illegible]	[illegible]	[illegible]
❑ 217 Bo Scaife	.40	.15
❑ 218 Anthony Fasano	.40	.15
❑ 219 Chris Cooley	.40	.15
❑ 220 Robbie Gould	.40	.15
❑ 221 Adam Vinatieri	.50	.20
❑ 222 Devin Hester	.60	.25
❑ 223 Justin Miller	.40	.15
❑ 224 Sean Taylor	.40	.15
❑ 225 DeAngelo Hall	.50	.20
❑ 226 Chris McAlister	.40	.15
❑ 227 Nate Clements	.40	.15
❑ 228 Chris Gamble	.40	.15
❑ 229 Ricky Manning	.40	.15
❑ 230 Charles Tillman	.40	.15
❑ 231 Deltha O'Neal	.40	.15
❑ 232 Terence Newman	.40	.15
❑ 233 Champ Bailey	.50	.20
❑ 234 Charles Woodson	.50	.20
❑ 235 Dunta Robinson	.40	.15
❑ 236 Rashean Mathis	.40	.15
❑ 237 Antoine Winfield	.40	.15
❑ 238 Asante Samuel	.40	.15
❑ 239 Nnamdi Asomugha	.40	.15
❑ 240 Lito Sheppard	.40	.15
❑ 241 Walt Harris	.40	.15
❑ 242 Tye Hill	.40	.15
❑ 243 Ronde Barber	.40	.15
❑ 244 Quentin Jammer	.40	.15
❑ 245 Ed Reed	.50	.20
❑ 246 Roy Williams S	.50	.20
❑ 247 Troy Polamalu	.60	.25
❑ 248 Brian Dawkins	.50	.20
❑ 249 Terrell Suggs	.40	.15
❑ 250 Aaron Schobel	.40	.15
❑ 251 Julius Peppers	.50	.20
❑ 252 Alex Brown	.40	.15
❑ 253 Kamerion Wimbley	.40	.15
❑ 254 DeMarcus Ware	.50	.20
❑ 255 Elvis Dumervil	.40	.15
❑ 256 Mario Williams	.50	.20
❑ 257 Dwight Freeney	.50	.20
❑ 258 Tamba Hali	.40	.15
❑ 259 Jason Taylor	.40	.15
❑ 260 Michael Strahan	.50	.20
❑ 261 Aaron Kampman	.50	.20
❑ 262 Derrick Burgess	.40	.15
❑ 263 Leonard Little	.40	.15
❑ 264 Ty Warren	.40	.15
❑ 265 Warren Sapp	.50	.20
❑ 266 Luis Castillo	.40	.15
❑ 267 Keith Brooking	.40	.15
❑ 268 Ray Lewis	.60	.25
❑ 269 London Fletcher	.40	.15
❑ 270 Brian Urlacher	.60	.25
❑ 271 Ernie Sims	.40	.15
❑ 272 A.J. Hawk	.60	.25
❑ 273 DeMeco Ryans	.50	.20
❑ 274 Cato June	.40	.15
❑ 275 Derrick Johnson LB	.40	.15
❑ 276 Zach Thomas	.50	.20
❑ 277 Antonio Pierce	.40	.15
❑ 278 Jonathan Vilma	.50	.20
❑ 279 James Farrior	.40	.15
❑ 280 Shawne Merriman	.50	.20
❑ 281 Lofa Tatupu	.50	.20
❑ 282 Derrick Brooks	.50	.20
❑ 283 Jonathan Ogden	.40	.15
❑ 284 Steve Hutchinson	.40	.15
❑ 285 Walter Jones	.40	.15
❑ 286 JaMarcus Russell RC	4.00	1.50
❑ 287 Brady Quinn RC	5.00	2.00
❑ 288 Drew Stanton RC	2.00	.75
❑ 289 Troy Smith RC	2.00	.75
❑ 290 Kevin Kolb RC	2.50	1.00
❑ 291 Trent Edwards RC	3.00	1.25
❑ 292 John Beck RC	3.00	1.25
❑ 293 Jordan Palmer RC	1.50	.60
❑ 294 Chris Leak RC	1.25	.50
❑ 295 Isaiah Stanback RC	1.50	.60
❑ 296 Tyler Palko RC	1.50	.60
❑ 297 Jared Zabransky RC	1.50	.60
❑ 298 Jeff Rowe RC	1.25	.50
❑ 299 Zac Taylor RC	1.50	.60
[illegible]	[illegible]	[illegible]
❑ 301 Adrian Peterson RC	12.00	5.00
❑ 302 Marshawn Lynch RC	3.00	1.25
❑ 303 Brandon Jackson RC	2.00	.75
❑ 304 Michael Bush RC	2.00	.75
❑ 305 Kenny Irons RC	1.50	.60
❑ 306 Antonio Pittman RC	1.25	.50
❑ 307 Tony Hunt RC	1.50	.60
❑ 308 Darius Walker RC	1.50	.60
❑ 309 Dwayne Wright RC	1.25	.50
❑ 310 Lorenzo Booker RC	1.50	.60
❑ 311 Kenneth Darby RC	1.50	.60
❑ 312 Chris Henry RC	1.50	.60
❑ 313 Selvin Young RC	2.00	.75
❑ 314 Brian Leonard RC	2.00	.75
❑ 315 Ahmad Bradshaw RC	2.00	.75
❑ 316 Gary Russell RC	1.50	.60
❑ 317 Kolby Smith RC	2.00	.75
❑ 318 Thomas Clayton RC	1.25	.50
❑ 319 Garrett Wolfe RC	2.00	.75
❑ 320 Calvin Johnson RC	5.00	2.00
❑ 321 Ted Ginn Jr. RC	2.50	1.00
❑ 322 Dwayne Jarrett RC	2.00	.75
❑ 323 Dwayne Bowe RC	3.00	1.25
❑ 324 Sidney Rice RC	2.50	1.00
❑ 325 Robert Meachem RC	1.50	.60
❑ 326 Anthony Gonzalez RC	2.50	1.00
❑ 327 Craig Buster Davis RC	1.50	.60
❑ 328 Aundrae Allison RC	1.25	.50
❑ 329 Chansi Stuckey RC	1.25	.50
❑ 330 David Clowney RC	1.50	.60
❑ 331 Steve Smith USC RC	2.00	.75
❑ 332 Courtney Taylor RC	1.25	.50
❑ 333 Paul Williams RC	1.25	.50
❑ 334 Johnnie Lee Higgins RC	1.25	.50
❑ 335 Rhema McKnight RC	1.25	.50
❑ 336 Jason Hill RC	1.50	.60
❑ 337 Dallas Baker RC	1.25	.50
❑ 338 Greg Olsen RC	2.00	.75
❑ 339 Yamon Figurs RC	1.50	.60
❑ 340 Scott Chandler RC	1.25	.50
❑ 341 Matt Spaeth RC	1.50	.60
❑ 342 Ben Patrick RC	1.25	.50
❑ 343 Clark Harris RC	1.50	.60
❑ 344 Martrez Milner RC	1.25	.50
❑ 345 Joe Newton RC	1.25	.50
❑ 346 Alan Branch RC	1.25	.50
❑ 347 Amobi Okoye RC	1.50	.60
❑ 348 DeMarcus Tank Tyler RC	1.25	.50
❑ 349 Justin Harrell RC	1.50	.60
❑ 350 Brandon Mebane RC	1.25	.50
❑ 351 Gaines Adams RC	1.50	.60
❑ 352 Jamaal Anderson RC	1.25	.50
❑ 353 Adam Carriker RC	1.25	.50
❑ 354 Jarvis Moss RC	1.50	.60
❑ 355 Charles Johnson RC	1.00	.40
❑ 356 Anthony Spencer RC	1.50	.60
❑ 357 Quentin Moses RC	1.25	.50
❑ 358 LaMarr Woodley RC	1.50	.60
❑ 359 Victor Abiamiri RC	1.50	.60
❑ 360 Ray McDonald RC	1.25	.50
❑ 361 Tim Crowder RC	1.50	.60
❑ 362 Patrick Willis RC	3.00	1.25
❑ 363 Brandon Siler RC	1.25	.50
❑ 364 David Harris RC	1.25	.50
❑ 365 Buster Davis RC	1.25	.50
❑ 366 Lawrence Timmons RC	1.50	.60
❑ 367 Paul Posluszny RC	2.00	.75
❑ 368 Jon Beason RC	1.50	.60
❑ 369 Rufus Alexander RC	1.50	.60
❑ 370 Earl Everett RC	1.25	.50

❑ 371 Stewart Bradley RC 1.50 .60
❑ 372 Prescott Burgess RC 1.25 .50
❑ 373 Leon Hall RC 1.25 .50
❑ 374 Darrelle Revis RC 1.50 .60
❑ 375 Aaron Ross RC 1.50 .60
❑ 376 Daymeion Hughes RC 1.25 .50
❑ 377 Marcus McCauley RC 1.25 .50
❑ 378 Chris Houston RC 1.25 .50
❑ 379 Tanard Jackson RC 1.00 .40
❑ 380 Jonathan Wade RC 1.25 .50
❑ 381 Josh Wilson RC 1.25 .50
❑ 382 Eric Wright RC 1.50 .60
❑ 383 A.J. Davis RC 1.00 .40
❑ 384 David Irons RC 1.00 .40
❑ 385 LaRon Landry RC 2.00 .75
❑ 386 Reggie Nelson RC 1.25 .50
❑ 387 Michael Griffin RC 1.50 .60
❑ 388 Brandon Meriweather RC 1.50 .60
❑ 389 Eric Weddle RC 1.25 .50
❑ 390 Aaron Rouse RC 1.50 .60
❑ 391 Josh Gattis RC 1.00 .40
❑ 392 Joe Thomas RC 1.50 .60
❑ 393 Levi Brown RC 1.50 .60
❑ 394 Tony Ugoh RC 1.25 .50
❑ 395 Ryan Kalil RC 1.25 .50
❑ 396 Peyton Manning LL .75 .30
❑ 397 Marc Bulger LL .40 .15
❑ 398 LaDainian Tomlinson LL .60 .25
❑ 399 Larry Johnson LL .50 .20
❑ 400 Frank Gore LL .50 .20
❑ 401 Chad Johnson LL .40 .15
❑ 402 Marvin Harrison LL .50 .20
❑ 403 Reggie Wayne LL .40 .15
❑ 404 LaDainian Tomlinson LL .60 .25
❑ 405 Peyton Manning PB .75 .30
❑ 406 Marvin Harrison PB .50 .20
❑ 407 LaDainian Tomlinson PB .60 .25
❑ 408 Reggie Wayne PB .40 .15
❑ 409 Antonio Gates PB .40 .15
❑ 410 Jeff Saturday PB .30 .12
❑ 411 Jason Taylor PB .30 .12
❑ 412 Shawne Merriman PB .40 .15
❑ 413 Champ Bailey PB .40 .15
❑ 414 Troy Polamalu PB .50 .20
❑ 415 Drew Brees PB .40 .15
❑ 416 Frank Gore PB .50 .20
❑ 417 Tony Gonzalez PB .40 .15
❑ 418 Steve Smith PB .40 .15
❑ 419 Walter Jones PB .30 .12
❑ 420 Devin Hester PB .50 .20
❑ 421 Julius Peppers PB .40 .15
❑ 422 Tony Romo PB 1.00 .40
❑ 423 Ronde Barber PB .30 .12
❑ 424 Larry Johnson PB .50 .20
❑ 425 LaDainian Tomlinson MVP .60 .25
❑ 426 Vince Young OROY .60 .25
❑ 427 DeMeco Ryans DROY .40 .15
❑ 428 P.Manning/R.Wayne PSH .75 .30
❑ 429 Drew Brees LL .40 .15
❑ 430 Asante Samuel PSH .30 .12
❑ 431 New Orleans Saints PSH .40 .15
❑ 432 Reggie Bush PSH .60 .25
❑ 433 Peyton Manning PSH .75 .30
❑ 434 Robbie Gould PSH .30 .12
❑ 435 T.Jones/C.Benson PSH .40 .15
❑ 436 Joseph Addai PSH .60 .25
❑ 437 Tom Brady PSH 1.00 .40
❑ 438 Colts Defense PSH .40 .15
❑ 439 Adam Vinatieri PSH .40 .15
❑ 440 Devin Hester PSH .50 .20
❑ RH41 Peyton Manning RH 6.00 2.50
❑ RH41A Peyton Manning RH AU 350.00 250.00
❑ SBMVP P.Manning MVP FB/25 200.00 125.00

1996 Topps Chrome

❑ COMPLETE SET (165) 100.00 40.00
❑ 1 Troy Aikman 2.50 1.00
❑ 2 Kevin Greene .50 .20
❑ 3 Robert Brooks 1.00 .40
❑ 4 Junior Seau 1.00 .40
❑ 5 Brett Perriman .20 .07
❑ 6 Cortez Kennedy .20 .07
❑ 7 Orlando Thomas .20 .07
❑ 8 Anthony Miller .50 .20

❑ 9 Jeff Blake 1.00 .40
❑ 10 Trent Dilfer 1.00 .40
❑ 11 Heath Shuler .50 .20
❑ 12 Michael Jackson .50 .20
❑ 13 Merton Hanks .20 .07
❑ 14 Dale Carter .20 .07
❑ 15 Eric Metcalf .20 .07
❑ 16 Barry Sanders 4.00 1.50
❑ 17 Joey Galloway 1.00 .40
❑ 18 Bryan Cox .20 .07
❑ 19 Harvey Williams .20 .07
❑ 20 Terrell Davis 1.50 .60
❑ 21 Darnay Scott .50 .20
❑ 22 Kerry Collins 1.00 .40
❑ 23 Warren Sapp .20 .07
❑ 24 Michael Westbrook 1.00 .40
❑ 25 Mark Brunell 1.50 .60
❑ 26 Craig Heyward .20 .07
❑ 27 Eric Allen .20 .07
❑ 28 Dana Stubblefield .50 .20
❑ 29 Steve Bono .20 .07
❑ 30 Larry Brown .20 .07
❑ 31 Warren Moon .50 .20
❑ 32 Jim Kelly 1.00 .40
❑ 33 Terry McDaniel .20 .07
❑ 34 Dan Wilkinson .20 .07
❑ 35 Dave Brown .20 .07
❑ 36 Todd Lyght .20 .07
❑ 37 Aeneas Williams .20 .07
❑ 38 Shannon Sharpe .50 .20
❑ 39 Errict Rhett .50 .20
❑ 40 Yancey Thigpen .50 .20
❑ 41 J.J. Stokes 1.00 .40
❑ 42 Marshall Faulk 1.25 .50
❑ 43 Chester McGlockton .20 .07
❑ 44 Darryll Lewis .20 .07
❑ 45 Drew Bledsoe 1.50 .60
❑ 46 Tyrone Wheatley .50 .20
❑ 47 Herman Moore .50 .20
❑ 48 Darren Woodson .50 .20
❑ 49 Ricky Watters .50 .20
❑ 50 Emmitt Smith TYC 1.50 .60
❑ 51 Barry Sanders TYC 1.50 .60
❑ 52 Curtis Martin TYC 1.00 .40
❑ 53 Chris Warren TYC .50 .20
❑ 54 Errict Rhett TYC .50 .20
❑ 55 Rodney Hampton TYC .20 .07
❑ 56 Terrell Davis TYC 1.00 .40
❑ 57 Marshall Faulk TYC 1.00 .40
❑ 58 Rashaan Salaam TYC .50 .20
❑ 59 Curtis Conway 1.00 .40
❑ 60 Isaac Bruce 1.00 .40
❑ 61 Thurman Thomas 1.00 .40
❑ 62 Terry Allen .50 .20
❑ 63 Lamar Lathon .20 .07
❑ 64 Mark Chmura .50 .20
❑ 65 Chris Warren .50 .20
❑ 66 Jessie Tuggle .20 .07
❑ 67 Erik Kramer .20 .07
❑ 68 Tim Brown 1.00 .40
❑ 69 Derrick Thomas 1.00 .40
❑ 70 Willie McGinest .20 .07
❑ 71 Frank Sanders .50 .20
❑ 72 Bernie Parmalee .20 .07
❑ 73 Kordell Stewart 1.00 .40
❑ 74 Brent Jones .20 .07
❑ 75 Edgar Bennett .50 .20
❑ 76 Rashaan Salaam .50 .20
❑ 77 Carl Pickens .50 .20
❑ 78 Terance Mathis .20 .07
❑ 79 Deion Sanders 1.25 .50
❑ 80 Glyn Milburn .20 .07
❑ 81 Lee Woodall .20 .07
❑ 82 Neil Smith .50 .20
❑ 83 Stan Humphries .50 .20
❑ 84 Rick Mirer .50 .20
❑ 85 Troy Vincent .20 .07
❑ 86 Sam Mills .20 .07
❑ 87 Brian Mitchell .20 .07
❑ 88 Hardy Nickerson .20 .07
❑ 89 Tamarick Vanover .50 .20
❑ 90 Steve McNair 1.50 .60
❑ 91 Jerry Rice TYC 1.00 .40
❑ 92 Isaac Bruce TYC 1.00 .40
❑ 93 Herman Moore TYC .50 .20
❑ 94 Cris Carter TYC 1.00 .40
❑ 95 Tim Brown TYC .50 .20
❑ 96 Carl Pickens TYC .50 .20
❑ 97 Joey Galloway TYC 1.00 .40
❑ 98 Jerry Rice 2.50 1.00
❑ 99 Cris Carter 1.00 .40
❑ 100 Curtis Martin 1.50 .60
❑ 101 Scott Mitchell .50 .20
❑ 102 Ken Harvey .20 .07
❑ 103 Rodney Hampton .50 .20
❑ 104 Reggie White 1.00 .40
❑ 105 Eddie Robinson .20 .07
❑ 106 Greg Lloyd .50 .20
❑ 107 Phillippi Sparks .20 .07
❑ 108 Emmitt Smith 4.00 1.50
❑ 109 Tom Carter .20 .07
❑ 110 Jim Everett .20 .07
❑ 111 James O.Stewart .50 .20
❑ 112 Kyle Brady .20 .07
❑ 113 Irving Fryar .50 .20
❑ 114 Vinny Testaverde .50 .20
❑ 115 John Elway 5.00 2.00
❑ 116 Chris Spielman .20 .07
❑ 117 Mike Mamula .20 .07
❑ 118 Jim Harbaugh .50 .20
❑ 119 Ken Norton .20 .07
❑ 120 Bruce Smith .50 .20
❑ 121 Daryl Johnston .50 .20
❑ 122 Blaine Bishop .20 .07
❑ 123 Jeff George .50 .20
❑ 124 Jeff Hostetler .20 .07
❑ 125 Jerome Bettis 1.00 .40
❑ 126 Jay Novacek .20 .07
❑ 127 Bryce Paup .20 .07
❑ 128 Neil O'Donnell .50 .20
❑ 129 Marcus Allen 1.00 .40
❑ 130 Steve Young 1.50 .60
❑ 131 Brett Favre TYC 2.00 .75
❑ 132 Scott Mitchell TYC .20 .07
❑ 133 John Elway TYC 2.00 .75
❑ 134 Jeff Blake TYC .50 .20
❑ 135 Dan Marino TYC 2.00 .75
❑ 136 Drew Bledsoe TYC 1.00 .40
❑ 137 Troy Aikman TYC 1.00 .40
❑ 138 Steve Young TYC 1.00 .40
❑ 139 Jim Kelly TYC 1.00 .40
❑ 140 Jeff Graham .20 .07
❑ 141 Hugh Douglas .50 .20
❑ 142 Dan Marino 5.00 2.00
❑ 143 Darrell Green .20 .07
❑ 144 Eric Zeier .20 .07
❑ 145 Brett Favre 5.00 2.00
❑ 146 Carnell Lake .20 .07
❑ 147 Ben Coates .50 .20
❑ 148 Tony Martin .50 .20
❑ 149 Michael Irvin 1.00 .40
❑ 150 Lawrence Phillips RC 1.00 .40
❑ 151 Alex Van Dyke RC 1.50 .60
❑ 152 Kevin Hardy RC 1.50 .60
❑ 153 Rickey Dudley RC 5.00 2.00
❑ 154 Eric Moulds RC 10.00 5.00
❑ 155 Simeon Rice RC 4.00 1.50
❑ 156 Marvin Harrison RC 30.00 15.00
❑ 157 Tim Biakabutuka RC 4.00 1.50
❑ 158 Duane Clemons RC 1.00 .40
❑ 159 Keyshawn Johnson RC 12.00 5.00

❑ 160 John Mobley RC 1.50 .60
❑ 161 Leeland McElroy RC 1.50 .60
❑ 162 Eddie George RC 12.00 6.00
❑ 163 Jonathan Ogden RC 2.00 .75
❑ 164 Eddie Kennison RC 5.00 2.00
❑ 165 Checklist .20 .07

1997 Topps Chrome

❑ COMPLETE SET (165) 60.00 30.00
❑ 1 Brett Favre 6.00 2.50
❑ 2 Tim Biakabutuka 1.00 .40
❑ 3 Deion Sanders 1.50 .60
❑ 4 Marshall Faulk 2.00 .75
❑ 5 John Randle 1.00 .40
❑ 6 Stan Humphries 1.00 .40
❑ 7 Ki-Jana Carter .60 .25
❑ 8 Rashaan Salaam .60 .25
❑ 9 Rickey Dudley 1.00 .40
❑ 10 Isaac Bruce 1.50 .60
❑ 11 Keyshawn Johnson 1.50 .60
❑ 12 Ben Coates 1.00 .40
❑ 13 Ty Detmer 1.00 .40
❑ 14 Gus Frerotte .60 .25
❑ 15 Mario Bates .60 .25
❑ 16 Chris Calloway .60 .25
❑ 17 Frank Sanders 1.00 .40
❑ 18 Bruce Smith 1.00 .40
❑ 19 Jeff Graham .60 .25
❑ 20 Trent Dilfer 1.50 .60
❑ 21 Tyrone Wheatley 1.00 .40
❑ 22 Chris Warren 1.00 .40
❑ 23 Terry Kirby 1.00 .40
❑ 24 Tony Gonzalez RC 8.00 3.00
❑ 25 Ricky Watters 1.00 .40
❑ 26 Tamarick Vanover 1.00 .40
❑ 27 Kerry Collins 1.50 .60
❑ 28 Bobby Engram 1.00 .40
❑ 29 Derrick Alexander WR 1.00 .40
❑ 30 Hugh Douglas .60 .25
❑ 31 Thurman Thomas 1.50 .60
❑ 32 Drew Bledsoe 2.00 .75
❑ 33 LeShon Johnson .60 .25
❑ 34 Byron Bam Morris .60 .25
❑ 35 Herman Moore 1.00 .40
❑ 36 Troy Aikman 3.00 1.25
❑ 37 Mel Gray .60 .25
❑ 38 Adrian Murrell 1.00 .40
❑ 39 Carl Pickens 1.00 .40
❑ 40 Tony Brackens .60 .25
❑ 41 O.J. McDuffie 1.00 .40
❑ 42 Napoleon Kaufman 1.50 .60
❑ 43 Chris T. Jones .60 .25
❑ 44 Kordell Stewart 1.50 .60
❑ 45 Steve Young 2.00 .75
❑ 46 Shannon Sharpe 1.00 .40
❑ 47 Leeland McElroy .60 .25
❑ 48 Eric Moulds 1.50 .60
❑ 49 Eddie George 1.50 .60
❑ 50 Jamal Anderson 1.50 .60
❑ 51 Robert Smith 1.00 .40
❑ 52 Mike Alstott 1.50 .60
❑ 53 Darrell Green 1.00 .40
❑ 54 Irving Fryar 1.00 .40
❑ 55 Derrick Thomas 1.50 .60
❑ 56 Antonio Freeman 1.50 .60
❑ 57 Terrell Davis 2.00 .75
❑ 58 Henry Ellard .60 .25
❑ 59 Daryl Johnston 1.00 .40
❑ 60 Bryan Cox .60 .25
❑ 61 Vinny Testaverde 1.00 .40
❑ 62 Andre Reed 1.00 .40
❑ 63 Larry Centers 1.00 .40
❑ 64 Hardy Nickerson .60 .25
❑ 65 Tony Banks 1.00 .40
❑ 66 Dave Meggett .60 .25
❑ 67 Simeon Rice 1.00 .40
❑ 68 Warrick Dunn RC 10.00 4.00
❑ 69 Michael Irvin 1.50 .60
❑ 70 John Elway 6.00 2.50
❑ 71 Jake Reed 1.00 .40
❑ 72 Rodney Hampton 1.00 .40
❑ 73 Aaron Glenn .60 .25
❑ 74 Terry Allen 1.50 .60
❑ 75 Blaine Bishop .60 .25
❑ 76 Bert Emanuel 1.00 .40
❑ 77 Mark Carrier WR .60 .25
❑ 78 Jimmy Smith 1.00 .40
❑ 79 Jim Harbaugh 1.00 .40
❑ 80 Brent Jones 1.00 .40
❑ 81 Emmitt Smith 5.00 2.00
❑ 82 Fred Barnett .60 .25
❑ 83 Errict Rhett .60 .25
❑ 84 Michael Sinclair .60 .25
❑ 85 Jerome Bettis 1.50 .60
❑ 86 Chris Sanders .60 .25
❑ 87 Kent Graham .60 .25
❑ 88 Cris Carter 1.50 .60
❑ 89 Harvey Williams .60 .25
❑ 90 Eric Allen .60 .25
❑ 91 Bryant Young .60 .25
❑ 92 Marcus Allen 1.50 .60
❑ 93 Michael Jackson 1.00 .40
❑ 94 Mark Chmura 1.00 .40
❑ 95 Keenan McCardell 1.00 .40
❑ 96 Joey Galloway 1.00 .40
❑ 97 Eddie Kennison 1.00 .40
❑ 98 Steve Atwater .60 .25
❑ 99 Dorsey Levens 1.50 .60
❑ 100 Rob Moore 1.00 .40
❑ 101 Steve McNair 2.00 .75
❑ 102 Sean Dawkins .60 .25
❑ 103 Don Beebe .60 .25
❑ 104 Willie McGinest .60 .25
❑ 105 Tony Martin 1.00 .40
❑ 106 Mark Brunell 2.00 .75
❑ 107 Karim Abdul-Jabbar 1.50 .60
❑ 108 Michael Westbrook 1.00 .40
❑ 109 Lawrence Phillips .60 .25
❑ 110 Barry Sanders 5.00 2.00
❑ 111 Willie Davis .60 .25
❑ 112 Wesley Walls 1.00 .40
❑ 113 Todd Collins .60 .25
❑ 114 Jerry Rice 3.00 1.25
❑ 115 Scott Mitchell 1.00 .40
❑ 116 Terance Mathis 1.00 .40
❑ 117 Chris Spielman .60 .25
❑ 118 Curtis Conway 1.00 .40
❑ 119 Marvin Harrison 1.50 .60
❑ 120 Terry Glenn 1.50 .60
❑ 121 Dave Brown .60 .25
❑ 122 Neil O'Donnell 1.00 .40
❑ 123 Junior Seau 1.50 .60
❑ 124 Reggie White 1.50 .60
❑ 125 Lamar Lathon .60 .25
❑ 126 Natrone Means 1.00 .40
❑ 127 Tim Brown 1.50 .60
❑ 128 Eric Swann .60 .25
❑ 129 Dan Marino 6.00 2.50
❑ 130 Anthony Johnson .60 .25
❑ 131 Edgar Bennett 1.00 .40
❑ 132 Kevin Hardy .60 .25
❑ 133 Brian Blades .60 .25
❑ 134 Curtis Martin 2.00 .75
❑ 135 Zach Thomas 1.50 .60
❑ 136 Darnay Scott 1.00 .40
❑ 137 Desmond Howard 1.00 .40
❑ 138 Aeneas Williams .60 .25
❑ 139 Bryce Paup .60 .25
❑ 140 Brad Johnson 1.50 .60
❑ 141 Jeff Blake 1.00 .40
❑ 142 Wayne Chrebet 1.50 .60
❑ 143 Will Blackwell RC 1.25 .50
❑ 144 Tom Knight RC .60 .25
❑ 145 Darnell Autry RC 1.00 .40
❑ 146 Bryant Westbrook RC .60 .25
❑ 147 David LaFleur RC .75 .30
❑ 148 Antowain Smith RC 8.00 3.00
❑ 149 Rae Carruth RC .75 .30
❑ 150 Jim Druckenmiller RC 1.00 .40
❑ 151 Shawn Springs RC .75 .30
❑ 152 Troy Davis RC 1.25 .50
❑ 153 Orlando Pace RC 2.00 .75
❑ 154 Byron Hanspard RC 1.25 .50
❑ 155 Corey Dillon RC 10.00 4.00
❑ 156 [illegible] [illegible] [illegible]
❑ 157 Peter Boulware RC 2.00 .75
❑ 158 Reinard Wilson RC 1.25 .50
❑ 159 Pat Barnes RC 2.00 .75
❑ 160 Joey Kent RC 2.00 .75
❑ 161 Ike Hilliard RC 3.00 1.25
❑ 162 Jake Plummer RC 8.00 3.00
❑ 163 Darrell Russell RC .75 .30
❑ 164 Checklist Card .60 .25
❑ 165 Checklist Card .60 .25

1998 Topps Chrome

❑ COMPLETE SET (165) 120.00 50.00
❑ 1 Barry Sanders 4.00 1.50
❑ 2 Duane Starks RC 2.00 .75
❑ 3 J.J. Stokes .75 .30
❑ 4 Joey Galloway .75 .30
❑ 5 Deion Sanders 1.25 .50
❑ 6 Anthony Miller .50 .20
❑ 7 Jamal Anderson 1.25 .50
❑ 8 Shannon Sharpe .75 .30
❑ 9 Irving Fryar .75 .30
❑ 10 Curtis Martin 1.25 .50
❑ 11 Shawn Jefferson .50 .20
❑ 12 Charlie Garner .75 .30
❑ 13 Robert Edwards RC 3.00 1.25
❑ 14 Napoleon Kaufman 1.25 .50
❑ 15 Gus Frerotte .50 .20
❑ 16 John Elway 5.00 2.00
❑ 17 Jerome Pathon RC 4.00 1.50
❑ 18 Marshall Faulk 1.50 .60
❑ 19 Michael McCrary .50 .20
❑ 20 Marcus Allen 1.25 .50
❑ 21 Trent Dilfer 1.25 .50
❑ 22 Frank Wycheck .50 .20
❑ 23 Terrell Owens 1.25 .50
❑ 24 Herman Moore .75 .30
❑ 25 Neil O'Donnell .75 .30
❑ 26 Darnay Scott .75 .30
❑ 27 Keith Brooking RC 4.00 1.50
❑ 28 Eric Green .50 .20
❑ 29 Dan Marino 5.00 2.00
❑ 30 Antonio Freeman 1.25 .50
❑ 31 Tony Martin .75 .30
❑ 32 Isaac Bruce 1.25 .50
❑ 33 Rickey Dudley .50 .20
❑ 34 Scott Mitchell .75 .30
❑ 35 Randy Moss RC 25.00 12.50
❑ 36 Fred Lane .50 .20
❑ 37 Frank Sanders .75 .30
❑ 38 Jerry Rice 2.50 1.00
❑ 39 O.J. McDuffie .75 .30
❑ 40 Jessie Armstead .50 .20
❑ 41 Reidel Anthony .75 .30

❑ 42	Steve McNair	1.25	.50
❑ 43	Jake Reed	.75	.30
❑ 44	Charles Woodson RC	5.00	2.00
❑ 45	Tiki Barber	1.25	.50
❑ 46	Mike Alstott	1.25	.50
❑ 47	Keyshawn Johnson	1.25	.50
❑ 48	Tony Banks	.75	.30
❑ 49	Michael Westbrook	.75	.30
❑ 50	Chris Slade	.50	.20
❑ 51	Terry Allen	1.25	.50
❑ 52	Karim Abdul-Jabbar	1.25	.50
❑ 53	Brad Johnson	1.25	.50
❑ 54	Tony McGee	.50	.20
❑ 55	Kevin Dyson RC	4.00	1.50
❑ 56	Warren Moon	1.25	.50
❑ 57	Byron Hanspard	.50	.20
❑ 58	Jermaine Lewis	.75	.30
❑ 59	Neil Smith	.75	.30
❑ 60	Tamarick Vanover	.50	.20
❑ 61	Terrell Davis	1.25	.50
❑ 62	Robert Smith	1.25	.50
❑ 63	Junior Seau	1.25	.50
❑ 64	Warren Sapp	.75	.30
❑ 65	Michael Sinclair	.50	.20
❑ 66	Ryan Leaf RC	4.00	1.50
❑ 67	Drew Bledsoe	2.00	.75
❑ 68	Jason Sehorn	.75	.30
❑ 69	Andre Hastings	.50	.20
❑ 70	Tony Gonzalez	1.25	.50
❑ 71	Dorsey Levens	1.25	.50
❑ 72	Ray Lewis	1.25	.50
❑ 73	Grant Wistrom RC	3.00	1.25
❑ 74	Elvis Grbac	.75	.30
❑ 75	Mark Chmura	.75	.30
❑ 76	Zach Thomas	1.25	.50
❑ 77	Ben Coates	.75	.30
❑ 78	Rod Smith WR	.75	.30
❑ 79	Andre Wadsworth RC	3.00	1.25
❑ 80	Garrison Hearst	1.25	.50
❑ 81	Will Blackwell	.50	.20
❑ 82	Cris Carter	1.25	.50
❑ 83	Mark Fields	.50	.20
❑ 84	Ken Dilger	.50	.20
❑ 85	Johnnie Morton	.75	.30
❑ 86	Michael Irvin	1.25	.50
❑ 87	Eddie George	1.25	.50
❑ 88	Rob Moore	.75	.30
❑ 89	Takeo Spikes RC	4.00	1.50
❑ 90	Wesley Walls	.75	.30
❑ 91	Andre Reed	.75	.30
❑ 92	Thurman Thomas	1.25	.50
❑ 93	Ed McCaffrey	.75	.30
❑ 94	Carl Pickens	.75	.30
❑ 95	Jason Taylor	.75	.30
❑ 96	Kordell Stewart	1.25	.50
❑ 97	Greg Ellis RC	2.00	.75
❑ 98	Aaron Glenn	.50	.20
❑ 99	Jake Plummer	1.25	.50
❑ 100	Checklist	.50	.20
❑ 101	Chris Sanders	.50	.20
❑ 102	Michael Jackson	.50	.20
❑ 103	Bobby Hoying	.75	.30
❑ 104	Wayne Chrebet	1.25	.50
❑ 105	Charles Way	.50	.20
❑ 106	Derrick Thomas	1.25	.50
❑ 107	Troy Drayton	.50	.20
❑ 108	Robert Holcombe RC	3.00	1.25
❑ 109	Pete Mitchell	.50	.20
❑ 110	Bruce Smith	.75	.30
❑ 111	Terance Mathis	.75	.30
❑ 112	Lawrence Phillips	.50	.20
❑ 113	Brett Favre	5.00	2.00
❑ 114	Darrell Green	.75	.30
❑ 115	Charles Johnson	.50	.20
❑ 116	Jeff Blake	.75	.30
❑ 117	Mark Brunell	1.25	.50
❑ 118	Simeon Rice	.75	.30
❑ 119	Robert Brooks	.75	.30
❑ 120	Jacquez Green RC	3.00	1.25
❑ 121	Willie Davis	.50	.20
❑ 122	Jeff George	.75	.30
❑ 123	Andre Rison	.75	.30
❑ 124	Erik Kramer	.50	.20
❑ 125	Peter Boulware	.50	.20
❑ 126	Marcus Nash RC	2.00	.75
❑ 127	Troy Aikman	2.50	1.00
❑ 128	Keenan McCardell	.75	.30
❑ 129	Bryant Westbrook	.50	.20
❑ 130	Terry Glenn	1.25	.50
❑ 131	Blaine Bishop	.50	.20
❑ 132	Tim Brown	1.25	.50
❑ 133	Brian Griese RC	8.00	3.00
❑ 134	John Mobley	.50	.20
❑ 135	Larry Centers	.50	.20
❑ 136	Eric Bjornson	.50	.20
❑ 137	Kevin Hardy	.50	.20
❑ 138	John Randle	.75	.30
❑ 139	Michael Strahan	.75	.30
❑ 140	Jerome Bettis	1.25	.50
❑ 141	Rae Carruth	.50	.20
❑ 142	Reggie White	1.25	.50
❑ 143	Antowain Smith	1.25	.50
❑ 144	Aeneas Williams	.50	.20
❑ 145	Bobby Engram	.75	.30
❑ 146	Germane Crowell RC	3.00	1.25
❑ 147	Freddie Jones	.50	.20
❑ 148	Kimble Anders	.75	.30
❑ 149	Steve Young	1.50	.60
❑ 150	Willie McGinest	.50	.20
❑ 151	Emmitt Smith	4.00	1.50
❑ 152	Fred Taylor RC	6.00	2.50
❑ 153	Danny Kanell	.75	.30
❑ 154	Warrick Dunn	1.25	.50
❑ 155	Kerry Collins	.75	.30
❑ 156	Chris Chandler	.75	.30
❑ 157	Curtis Conway	.75	.30
❑ 158	Curtis Enis RC	2.00	.75
❑ 159	Corey Dillon	1.25	.50
❑ 160	Glenn Foley	.75	.30
❑ 161	Marvin Harrison	1.25	.50
❑ 162	Chad Brown	.50	.20
❑ 163	Derrick Rodgers	.50	.20
❑ 164	Levon Kirkland	.50	.20
❑ 165	Peyton Manning RC	50.00	25.00

1999 Topps Chrome

❑	COMPLETE SET (165)	150.00	60.00
❑	COMP.SET w/o SP's (135)	50.00	25.00
❑ 1	Randy Moss	3.00	1.25
❑ 2	Keyshawn Johnson	1.25	.50
❑ 3	Priest Holmes	2.00	.75
❑ 4	Warren Moon	1.25	.50
❑ 5	Joey Galloway	.75	.30
❑ 6	Zach Thomas	1.25	.50
❑ 7	Cam Cleeland	.50	.20
❑ 8	Jim Harbaugh	.75	.30
❑ 9	Napoleon Kaufman	1.25	.50
❑ 10	Fred Taylor	1.25	.50
❑ 11	Mark Brunell	1.25	.50
❑ 12	Shannon Sharpe	.75	.30
❑ 13	Jacquez Green	.50	.20
❑ 14	Adrian Murrell	.75	.30
❑ 15	Cris Carter	1.25	.50
❑ 16	Jerome Pathon	.50	.20
❑ 17	Drew Bledsoe	1.50	.60
❑ 18	Curtis Martin	1.25	.50
❑ 19	Johnnie Morton	.75	.30
❑ 20	Doug Flutie	1.25	.50
❑ 21	Carl Pickens	.75	.30
❑ 22	Jerome Bettis	1.25	.50
❑ 23	Derrick Alexander	.50	.20
❑ 24	Antowain Smith	1.25	.50
❑ 25	Barry Sanders	4.00	1.50
❑ 26	Reidel Anthony	.75	.30
❑ 27	Wayne Chrebet	.75	.30
❑ 28	Terance Mathis	.75	.30
❑ 29	Shawn Springs	.50	.20
❑ 30	Emmitt Smith	2.50	1.00
❑ 31	Robert Smith	1.25	.50
❑ 32	Charles Johnson	.50	.20
❑ 33	Mike Alstott	1.25	.50
❑ 34	Ike Hilliard	.50	.20
❑ 35	Ricky Watters	.75	.30
❑ 36	Charles Woodson	1.25	.50
❑ 37	Rod Smith	.75	.30
❑ 38	Pete Mitchell	.50	.20
❑ 39	Derrick Thomas	1.25	.50
❑ 40	Dan Marino	4.00	1.50
❑ 41	Darnay Scott	.50	.20
❑ 42	Jake Reed	.75	.30
❑ 43	Chris Chandler	.75	.30
❑ 44	Dorsey Levens	1.25	.50
❑ 45	Kordell Stewart	.75	.30
❑ 46	Eddie George	1.25	.50
❑ 47	Corey Dillon	1.25	.50
❑ 48	Rich Gannon	1.25	.50
❑ 49	Chris Spielman	.50	.20
❑ 50	Jerry Rice	2.50	1.00
❑ 51	Trent Dilfer	.75	.30
❑ 52	Mark Chmura	.50	.20
❑ 53	Jimmy Smith	.75	.30
❑ 54	Isaac Bruce	1.25	.50
❑ 55	Karim Abdul-Jabbar	.75	.30
❑ 56	Sedrick Shaw	.50	.20
❑ 57	Jake Plummer	.75	.30
❑ 58	Tony Gonzalez	1.25	.50
❑ 59	Ben Coates	.75	.30
❑ 60	John Elway	4.00	1.50
❑ 61	Bruce Smith	.75	.30
❑ 62	Tim Brown	1.25	.50
❑ 63	Tim Dwight	1.25	.50
❑ 64	Yancey Thigpen	.50	.20
❑ 65	Terrell Owens	1.25	.50
❑ 66	Kyle Brady	.50	.20
❑ 67	Tony Martin	.75	.30
❑ 68	Michael Strahan	.75	.30
❑ 69	Deion Sanders	1.25	.50
❑ 70	Steve Young	1.50	.60
❑ 71	Dale Carter	.50	.20
❑ 72	Ty Law	.75	.30
❑ 73	Frank Wycheck	.50	.20
❑ 74	Marshall Faulk	1.50	.60
❑ 75	Vinny Testaverde	.75	.30
❑ 76	Chad Brown	.50	.20
❑ 77	Natrone Means	.75	.30
❑ 78	Bert Emanuel	.75	.30
❑ 79	Kerry Collins	.75	.30
❑ 80	Randall Cunningham	1.25	.50
❑ 81	Garrison Hearst	.75	.30
❑ 82	Curtis Enis	.50	.20
❑ 83	Steve Atwater	.50	.20
❑ 84	Kevin Greene	.50	.20
❑ 85	Steve McNair	1.25	.50
❑ 86	Andre Reed	.75	.30
❑ 87	J.J. Stokes	.75	.30
❑ 88	Eric Moulds	1.25	.50
❑ 89	Marvin Harrison	1.25	.50
❑ 90	Troy Aikman	2.50	1.00
❑ 91	Herman Moore	.75	.30
❑ 92	Michael Irvin	.75	.30
❑ 93	Frank Sanders	.75	.30
❑ 94	Duce Staley	1.25	.50
❑ 95	James Jett	.75	.30
❑ 96	Ricky Proehl	.50	.20
❑ 97	Andre Rison	.75	.30
❑ 98	Leslie Shepherd	.50	.20
❑ 99	Trent Green	1.25	.50
❑ 100	Terrell Davis	1.25	.50
❑ 101	Freddie Jones	.50	.20
❑ 102	Skip Hicks	.50	.20
❑ 103	Jeff Graham	.50	.20
❑ 104	Rob Moore	.75	.30
❑ 105	Torrance Small	.50	.20
❑ 106	Antonio Freeman	1.25	.50
❑ 107	Robert Brooks	.75	.30

❑ 108 Jon Kitna 1.25 .50
❑ 109 Curtis Conway .75 .30
❑ 110 Brett Favre 4.00 1.50
❑ 111 Warrick Dunn 1.25 .50
❑ 112 Elvis Grbac .75 .30
❑ 113 Corey Fuller .50 .20
❑ 114 Rickey Dudley .50 .20
❑ 115 Jamal Anderson 1.25 .50
❑ 116 Terry Glenn 1.25 .50
❑ 117 Rocket Ismail .75 .30
❑ 118 John Randle .75 .30
❑ 119 Chris Calloway .50 .20
❑ 120 Peyton Manning 4.00 1.50
❑ [illegible]
❑ 122 O.J. McDuffie .75 .30
❑ 123 Ed McCaffrey .75 .30
❑ 124 Charlie Batch 1.25 .50
❑ 125 Jason Elam SH .50 .20
❑ 126 Randy Moss SH 1.50 .60
❑ 127 John Elway SH 2.00 .75
❑ 128 Emmitt Smith SH 1.25 .50
❑ 129 Terrell Davis SH 1.25 .50
❑ 130 Jerris McPhail .50 .20
❑ 131 Damon Gibson .50 .20
❑ 132 Jim Pyne .50 .20
❑ 133 Antonio Langham .50 .20
❑ 134 Freddie Solomon .50 .20
❑ 135 Ricky Williams RC 10.00 4.00
❑ 136 Daunte Culpepper RC 25.00 10.00
❑ 137 Chris Claiborne RC 2.00 .75
❑ 138 Amos Zereoue RC 5.00 2.00
❑ 139 Chris McAlister RC 4.00 1.50
❑ 140 Kevin Faulk RC 5.00 2.00
❑ 141 James Johnson RC 4.00 1.50
❑ 142 Mike Cloud RC 4.00 1.50
❑ 143 Jevon Kearse RC 10.00 4.00
❑ 144 Akili Smith RC 4.00 1.50
❑ 145 Edgerrin James RC 20.00 10.00
❑ 146 Cecil Collins RC 2.00 .75
❑ 147 Donovan McNabb RC 25.00 12.50
❑ 148 Kevin Johnson RC 5.00 2.00
❑ 149 Torry Holt RC 15.00 6.00
❑ 150 Rob Konrad RC 5.00 2.00
❑ 151 Tim Couch RC 5.00 2.00
❑ 152 David Boston RC 5.00 2.00
❑ 153 Karsten Bailey RC 4.00 1.50
❑ 154 Troy Edwards RC 4.00 1.50
❑ 155 Sedrick Irvin RC 2.00 .75
❑ 156 Shaun King RC 4.00 1.50
❑ 157 Peerless Price RC 5.00 2.00
❑ 158 Brock Huard RC 5.00 2.00
❑ 159 Cade McNown RC 4.00 1.50
❑ 160 Champ Bailey RC 8.00 3.00
❑ 161 D'Wayne Bates RC 4.00 1.50
❑ 162 Joe Germaine RC 4.00 1.50
❑ 163 Andy Katzenmoyer RC 4.00 1.50
❑ 164 Antoine Winfield RC 4.00 1.50
❑ 165 Checklist Card .50 .20

2000 Topps Chrome

❑ COMPLETE SET (270) 800.00 400.00
❑ COMP.SET w/o SPs (180) 50.00 25.00
❑ 1 Daunte Culpepper 1.50 .60
❑ 2 Troy Edwards .40 .15
❑ 3 Terrell Owens 1.25 .50
❑ 4 Ricky Proehl .40 .15
❑ 5 Shaun King .40 .15
❑ 6 Jeff George .60 .25
❑ 7 Champ Bailey .60 .25
❑ 8 Amani Toomer .40 .15
❑ 9 Stephen Boyd .40 .15
❑ 10 Thurman Thomas .60 .25
❑ 11 Patrick Jeffers 1.25 .50
❑ 12 Jake Plummer .60 .25
❑ 13 Peter Boulware .40 .15
❑ 14 Darrin Chiaverini .40 .15
❑ 15 Olandis Gary 1.25 .50
❑ 16 Peyton Manning 3.00 1.25
❑ 17 Joe Horn .60 .25
❑ 18 Wayne Chrebet .60 .25
❑ [illegible]
❑ 20 Kurt Warner 2.50 1.00
❑ 21 Mike Alstott 1.25 .50
❑ 22 Stephen Davis 1.25 .50
❑ 23 Tim Brown 1.25 .50
❑ 24 Damon Huard 1.25 .50
❑ 25 Terry Glenn .60 .25
❑ 26 Ricky Williams 1.25 .50
❑ 27 Tim Dwight 1.25 .50
❑ 28 Jay Riemersma .40 .15
❑ 29 Carl Pickens .60 .25
❑ 30 Brett Favre 4.00 1.50
❑ 31 Oronde Gadsden .60 .25
❑ 32 Steve McNair 1.25 .50
❑ 33 Michael Pittman .40 .15
❑ 34 Emmitt Smith 2.50 1.00
❑ 35 Mark Brunell 1.25 .50
❑ 36 Ed McCaffrey 1.25 .50
❑ 37 Tyrone Wheatley .60 .25
❑ 38 Sean Dawkins .40 .15
❑ 39 Jevon Kearse 1.25 .50
❑ 40 Tai Streets .40 .15
❑ 41 Keyshawn Johnson 1.25 .50
❑ 42 Germane Crowell .40 .15
❑ 43 Yatil Green .40 .15
❑ 44 Anthony Wright RC 4.00 1.50
❑ 45 Jerry Rice 2.50 1.00
❑ 46 Az-Zahir Hakim .60 .25
❑ 47 Stephen Alexander .40 .15
❑ 48 Zach Thomas 1.25 .50
❑ 49 Tony Simmons .40 .15
❑ 50 Jessie Armstead .40 .15
❑ 51 Kordell Stewart .60 .25
❑ 52 Cade McNown .40 .15
❑ 53 Tony Gonzalez .60 .25
❑ 54 John Randle .60 .25
❑ 55 Donovan McNabb 2.00 .75
❑ 56 Warrick Dunn 1.25 .50
❑ 57 Dorsey Levens .60 .25
❑ 58 Errict Rhett .60 .25
❑ 59 Priest Holmes 1.50 .60
❑ 60 Terrell Davis 1.25 .50
❑ 61 Natrone Means .40 .15
❑ 62 Brad Johnson 1.25 .50
❑ 63 Rickey Dudley .40 .15
❑ 64 Moses Moreno .40 .15
❑ 65 Randy Moss 2.50 1.00
❑ 66 Joe Montgomery .40 .15
❑ 67 Johnnie Morton .60 .25
❑ 68 Peerless Price .60 .25
❑ 69 Rocket Ismail .60 .25
❑ 70 David Boston 1.25 .50
❑ 71 Fred Taylor 1.25 .50
❑ 72 Jermaine Fazande .40 .15
❑ 73 Elvis Grbac .60 .25
❑ 74 Derrick Mayes .60 .25
❑ 75 Yancey Thigpen .40 .15
❑ 76 Ike Hilliard .60 .25
❑ 77 Muhsin Muhammad .60 .25
❑ 78 Shawn Jefferson .40 .15
❑ 79 Rod Smith .60 .25
❑ 80 Darnay Scott .60 .25
❑ 81 Cam Cleeland .40 .15
❑ 82 Steve Young 1.50 .60
❑ 83 E.G. Green .40 .15
❑ 84 Robert Smith 1.25 .50
❑ 85 Jermaine Lewis .60 .25
❑ 86 Tim Biakabutuka .60 .25
❑ 87 Jerome Pathon .60 .25
❑ 88 Kent Graham .40 .15
❑ 89 Bruce Smith .60 .25
❑ 90 Isaac Bruce 1.25 .50
❑ 91 Curtis Enis .40 .15
❑ 92 Bert Emanuel .40 .15
❑ 93 Keith Poole .40 .15
❑ 94 Troy Aikman 2.50 1.00
❑ 95 Rich Gannon 1.25 .50
❑ 96 Michael Westbrook .60 .25
❑ 97 Albert Connell .40 .15
❑ 98 James Johnson .40 .15
❑ 99 Jeff Blake .60 .25
❑ 100 Joey Galloway .60 .25
❑ 101 Rob Moore .60 .25
❑ 102 Chris Chandler .60 .25
❑ [illegible]
❑ 104 Eddie Kennison .60 .25
❑ 105 Kevin Hardy .40 .15
❑ 106 Napoleon Kaufman .60 .25
❑ 107 Kevin Dyson .60 .25
❑ 108 Keenan McCardell .60 .25
❑ 109 Drew Bledsoe 1.50 .60
❑ 110 Kevin Johnson 1.25 .50
❑ 111 Terance Mathis .60 .25
❑ 112 Gus Frerotte .40 .15
❑ 113 Matthew Hatchette .40 .15
❑ 114 Herman Moore .60 .25
❑ 115 Curtis Martin 1.25 .50
❑ 116 Jacquez Green .40 .15
❑ 117 Jake Reed .60 .25
❑ 118 Antonio Freeman 1.25 .50
❑ 119 Jim Miller .40 .15
❑ 120 Frank Sanders .60 .25
❑ 121 Brian Griese 1.25 .50
❑ 122 Troy Brown .60 .25
❑ 123 Jeff Graham .40 .15
❑ 124 Marshall Faulk 1.50 .60
❑ 125 Vinny Testaverde .60 .25
❑ 126 Frank Wycheck .40 .15
❑ 127 Kerry Collins .60 .25
❑ 128 Jay Fiedler 1.25 .50
❑ 129 Cris Carter 1.25 .50
❑ 130 Jason Tucker .40 .15
❑ 131 Antowain Smith .60 .25
❑ 132 Tony Banks .60 .25
❑ 133 Terrence Wilkins .40 .15
❑ 134 Tony Martin .60 .25
❑ 135 Richard Huntley .40 .15
❑ 136 J.J. Stokes .60 .25
❑ 137 Ricky Watters .60 .25
❑ 138 Pete Mitchell .40 .15
❑ 139 Jimmy Smith .60 .25
❑ 140 Doug Flutie 1.25 .50
❑ 141 Corey Bradford .60 .25
❑ 142 Curtis Conway .60 .25
❑ 143 Pete Mitchell .40 .15
❑ 144 Torry Holt 1.25 .50
❑ 145 Warren Sapp .60 .25
❑ 146 Duce Staley 1.25 .50
❑ 147 Mikhael Ricks .40 .15
❑ 148 Edgerrin James 2.00 .75
❑ 149 Charlie Batch 1.25 .50
❑ 150 Rob Johnson .60 .25
❑ 151 Jamal Anderson 1.25 .50
❑ 152 Tim Couch .60 .25
❑ 153 O.J. McDuffie .60 .25
❑ 154 Charles Woodson .60 .25
❑ 155 Jake Delhomme RC 12.00 5.00
❑ 156 Eddie George 1.25 .50
❑ 157 Jim Harbaugh .60 .25
❑ 158 Jon Kitna 1.25 .50
❑ 159 Derrick Alexander .60 .25
❑ 160 Marvin Harrison 1.25 .50
❑ 161 James Stewart .60 .25
❑ 162 Qadry Ismail .60 .25
❑ 163 Wesley Walls .40 .15
❑ 164 Steve Beuerlein .60 .25
❑ 165 Marcus Robinson 1.25 .50
❑ 166 Bill Schroeder .60 .25
❑ 167 Charles Johnson .60 .25
❑ 168 Charlie Garner .60 .25
❑ 169 Eric Moulds 1.25 .50
❑ 170 Jerome Bettis 1.25 .50
❑ 171 Tai Streets .40 .15
❑ 172 Akili Smith .40 .15
❑ 173 Jonathan Linton .40 .15

❑ 174 Corey Dillon	1.25	.50
❑ 175 Junior Seau	1.25	.50
❑ 176 Jonathan Quinn	.40	.15
❑ 177 Bobby Engram	.40	.15
❑ 178 Shannon Sharpe	.60	.25
❑ 179 Michael Basnight	.40	.15
❑ 180 Sedrick Irvin	.40	.15
❑ 181 Sammy Morris RC	12.00	5.00
❑ 182 Ron Dixon RC	10.00	4.00
❑ 183 Trevor Gaylor RC	10.00	4.00
❑ 184 Chris Cole RC	8.00	3.00
❑ 185 Deltha O'Neal RC	15.00	6.00
❑ 186 Sebastian Janikowski RC	15.00	6.00
❑ 187 Kwame Cavil RC	8.00	3.00
❑ 188 Chad Morton RC	15.00	6.00
❑ 189 Terrelle Smith RC	10.00	4.00
❑ 190 Frank Moreau RC	10.00	4.00
❑ 191 Kurt Warner HL	1.50	.60
❑ 192 Dan Marino HL	2.50	1.00
❑ 193 Cris Carter HL	.60	.25
❑ 194 Brett Favre HL	2.50	1.00
❑ 195 Marshall Faulk HL	1.25	.50
❑ 196 Jevon Kearse HL	.60	.25
❑ 197 Edgerrin James HL	1.50	.60
❑ 198 Emmitt Smith HL	1.50	.60
❑ 199 Andre Reed HL	.40	.15
❑ 200 K.Dyson/F.Wycheck HL	.40	.15
❑ 201 Olindo Mare MM	.40	.15
❑ 202 Marcus Coleman MM	.40	.15
❑ 203 James Johnson MM	.40	.15
❑ 204 Ray Lucas MM	.60	.25
❑ 205 Dedric Ward MM	.40	.15
❑ 206 Richie Cunningham MM	.40	.15
❑ 207 James Hasty MM	.40	.15
❑ 208 Sedrick Shaw MM	.40	.15
❑ 209 Kurt Warner MM	1.50	.60
❑ 210 Marshall Faulk MM	1.25	.50
❑ 211 Brian Shay EP	1.00	.40
❑ 212 L.C. Stevens EP	1.00	.40
❑ 213 Corey Thomas EP	1.00	.40
❑ 214 Scott Milanovich EP	1.50	.60
❑ 215 Pat Barnes EP	1.50	.60
❑ 216 Danny Wuerffel EP	1.50	.60
❑ 217 Kevin Daft EP	1.00	.40
❑ 218 Ron Powlus EP RC	2.00	.75
❑ 219 Eric Kresser EP	1.00	.40
❑ 220 Norman Miller EP RC	1.00	.40
❑ 221 Cory Sauter EP	1.00	.40
❑ 222 Marcus Crandell EP RC	1.50	.60
❑ 223 Sean Morey EP RC	1.50	.60
❑ 224 Jeff Ogden EP	1.50	.60
❑ 225 Ted White EP	1.00	.40
❑ 226 Jim Kubiak EP RC	1.50	.60
❑ 227 Aaron Stecker EP RC	2.00	.75
❑ 228 Ronnie Powell EP	1.00	.40
❑ 229 Matt Lytle EP RC	1.50	.60
❑ 230 Kendrick Nord EP RC	1.00	.40
❑ 231 Tim Rattay RC	15.00	6.00
❑ 232 Rob Morris RC	10.00	4.00
❑ 233 Chris Samuels RC	10.00	4.00
❑ 234 Todd Husak RC	15.00	6.00
❑ 235 Ahmed Plummer RC	15.00	6.00
❑ 236 Frank Murphy RC	8.00	3.00
❑ 237 Michael Wiley RC	10.00	4.00
❑ 238 Giovanni Carmazzi RC	8.00	3.00
❑ 239 Anthony Becht RC	15.00	6.00
❑ 240 John Abraham RC	20.00	7.50
❑ 241 Shaun Alexander RC	60.00	25.00
❑ 242 Thomas Jones RC	30.00	12.50
❑ 243 Courtney Brown RC	15.00	6.00
❑ 244 Curtis Keaton RC	10.00	4.00
❑ 245 Jerry Porter RC	25.00	10.00
❑ 246 Corey Simon RC	15.00	6.00
❑ 247 Dez White RC	15.00	6.00
❑ 248 Jamal Lewis RC	30.00	12.50
❑ 249 Ron Dayne RC	15.00	6.00
❑ 250 R.Jay Soward RC	10.00	4.00
❑ 251 Tee Martin RC	15.00	0.00
❑ 252 Shaun Ellis RC	15.00	6.00
❑ 253 Brian Urlacher RC	50.00	20.00
❑ 254 Reuben Droughns RC	15.00	6.00
❑ 255 Travis Taylor RC	15.00	6.00
❑ 256 Plaxico Burress RC	30.00	12.50
❑ 257 Chad Pennington RC	30.00	12.50
❑ 258 Sylvester Morris RC	10.00	4.00
❑ 259 Ron Dugans RC	8.00	3.00
❑ 260 Joe Hamilton RC	10.00	4.00
❑ 261 Chris Redman RC	10.00	4.00
❑ 262 Trung Canidate RC	10.00	4.00
❑ 263 J.R. Redmond RC	10.00	4.00
❑ 264 Danny Farmer RC	10.00	4.00
❑ 265 Todd Pinkston RC	15.00	6.00
❑ 266 Dennis Northcutt RC	15.00	6.00
❑ 267 Laveranues Coles RC	20.00	7.50
❑ 268 Bubba Franks RC	15.00	6.00
❑ 269 Travis Prentice RC	10.00	4.00
❑ 270 Peter Warrick RC	15.00	6.00

2001 Topps Chrome

❑ COMP.SET w/o SP's (210)	50.00	20.00
❑ 1 Randy Moss	2.50	1.00
❑ 2 Desmond Howard	.50	.20
❑ 3 Shawn Bryson	.50	.20
❑ 4 Lamar Smith	.75	.30
❑ 5 Peter Warrick	1.25	.50
❑ 6 Hines Ward	1.25	.50
❑ 7 J.R. Redmond	.50	.20
❑ 8 Reidel Anthony	.50	.20
❑ 9 Rich Gannon	1.25	.50
❑ 10 Ed McCaffrey	1.25	.50
❑ 11 Jamel White	.50	.20
❑ 12 Michael Pittman	.50	.20
❑ 13 Rob Johnson	.75	.30
❑ 14 Tim Couch	.75	.30
❑ 15 Stephen Alexander	.50	.20
❑ 16 Ricky Watters	.75	.30
❑ 17 Kerry Collins	.75	.30
❑ 18 Ricky Williams	1.25	.50
❑ 19 Joey Galloway	.75	.30
❑ 20 Chris Chandler	.75	.30
❑ 21 Marty Booker	.50	.20
❑ 22 Mark Brunell	1.25	.50
❑ 23 Antonio Freeman	1.25	.50
❑ 24 Richie Anderson	.50	.20
❑ 25 Amani Toomer	.75	.30
❑ 26 Trent Green	1.25	.50
❑ 27 Terrell Fletcher	.50	.20
❑ 28 Kevin Lockett	.50	.20
❑ 29 Ron Dixon	.50	.20
❑ 30 Charlie Batch	1.25	.50
❑ 31 Oronde Gadsden	.75	.30
❑ 32 Dorsey Levens	.75	.30
❑ 33 Jamal Lewis	2.00	.75
❑ 34 Craig Yeast	.50	.20
❑ 35 Muhsin Muhammad	.75	.30
❑ 36 Willie Jackson	.50	.20
❑ 37 Isaac Bruce	1.25	.50
❑ 38 Frank Wycheck	.50	.20
❑ 39 Troy Brown	.75	.30
❑ 40 Anthony Wright	.50	.20
❑ 41 Zach Thomas	1.25	.50
❑ 42 Qadry Ismail	.75	.30
❑ 43 Jake Plummer	.75	.30
❑ 44 Keenan McCardell	.50	.20
❑ 45 Charles Johnson	.50	.20
❑ 46 Brett Favre	4.00	1.50
❑ 47 Jacquez Green	.50	.20
❑ 48 Matt Hasselbeck	.75	.30
❑ 49 Tiki Barber	1.25	.50
❑ 50 Jeff Garcia	1.25	.50
❑ 51 Shawn Jefferson	.50	.20
❑ 52 Kevin Johnson	.75	.30
❑ 53 Terrence Wilkins	.50	.20
❑ 54 Mike Anderson	1.25	.50
❑ 55 Tim Brown	1.25	.50
❑ 56 Champ Bailey	1.25	.50
❑ 57 Jimmy Smith	.75	.30
❑ 58 Trent Dilfer	.75	.30
❑ 59 James Allen	.75	.30
❑ 60 David Boston	1.25	.50
❑ 61 Jeremiah Trotter	.75	.30
❑ 62 Freddie Jones	.50	.20
❑ 63 Deion Sanders	1.25	.50
❑ 64 Darrell Jackson	1.25	.50
❑ 65 David Patten	.50	.20
❑ 66 Jeremy McDaniel	.50	.20
❑ 67 Jay Fiedler	1.25	.50
❑ 68 Chad Lewis	.50	.20
❑ 69 Rocket Ismail	.75	.30
❑ 70 Cade McNown	.50	.20
❑ 71 Jevon Kearse	.75	.30
❑ 72 Jermaine Fazande	.50	.20
❑ 73 Junior Seau	1.25	.50
❑ 74 Rod Smith	.75	.30
❑ 75 Jermaine Lewis	.50	.20
❑ 76 Dennis Northcutt	.75	.30
❑ 77 Charlie Garner	.75	.30
❑ 78 Charles Woodson	.75	.30
❑ 79 Wayne Chrebet	.75	.30
❑ 80 Ahman Green	1.25	.50
❑ 81 Donald Hayes	.50	.20
❑ 82 Terance Mathis	.50	.20
❑ 83 Warrick Dunn	1.25	.50
❑ 84 Chris Sanders	.50	.20
❑ 85 Albert Connell	.50	.20
❑ 86 Robert Griffith	.50	.20
❑ 87 Germane Crowell	.50	.20
❑ 88 Tony Banks	.75	.30
❑ 89 Travis Taylor	.75	.30
❑ 90 Akili Smith	.50	.20
❑ 91 Michael Westbrook	.75	.30
❑ 92 Doug Flutie	1.25	.50
❑ 93 Ike Hilliard	.75	.30
❑ 94 Terry Glenn	.50	.20
❑ 95 Leslie Shepherd	.50	.20
❑ 96 Az-Zahir Hakim	.50	.20
❑ 97 La'Roi Glover	.50	.20
❑ 98 Peyton Manning	3.00	1.25
❑ 99 Jackie Harris	.50	.20
❑ 100 Edgerrin James	1.50	.60
❑ 101 Peerless Price	.75	.30
❑ 102 Jamal Anderson	1.25	.50
❑ 103 Keyshawn Johnson	1.25	.50
❑ 104 Derrick Mason	.75	.30
❑ 105 J.J. Stokes	.75	.30
❑ 106 Kevin Faulk	.75	.30
❑ 107 Tony Richardson	.50	.20
❑ 108 James Stewart	.75	.30
❑ 109 Tim Biakabutuka	.75	.30
❑ 110 Jon Kitna	1.25	.50
❑ 111 Thomas Jones	.75	.30
❑ 112 Steve McNair	1.25	.50
❑ 113 Sean Dawkins	.50	.20
❑ 114 Jerome Bettis	1.25	.50
❑ 115 Donovan McNabb	1.50	.60
❑ 116 Bill Schroeder	.75	.30
❑ 117 Rod Woodson	.75	.30
❑ 118 James McKnight	.75	.30
❑ 119 Daunte Culpepper	1.25	.50
❑ 120 Todd Husak	.50	.20
❑ 121 Shaun King	.50	.20
❑ 122 Tyrone Wheatley	.75	.30
❑ 123 Curtis Martin	1.25	.50
❑ 124 Terrell Davis	1.25	.50
❑ 125 Steve Beuerlein	.75	.30
❑ 126 Brad Johnson	1.25	.50
❑ 127 Joe Horn	.75	.30
❑ 128 Fred Taylor	1.25	.50
❑ 129 Brian Urlacher	2.00	.75
❑ 130 Ray Lewis	1.25	.50
❑ 131 Marshall Faulk	1.50	.60
❑ 132 Curtis Conway	.75	.30
❑ 133 Jason Sehorn	.50	.20
❑ 134 Jerome Pathon	.75	.30
❑ 135 Derrick Alexander	.75	.30

❑	136	Jerry Rice	2.50	1.00
❑	137	Jeff George	.75	.30
❑	138	Johnnie Morton	.75	.30
❑	139	Eric Moulds	.75	.30
❑	140	Duce Staley	1.25	.50
❑	141	Vinny Testaverde	.75	.30
❑	142	Eddie George	1.25	.50
❑	143	Shaun Alexander	1.50	.60
❑	144	Drew Bledsoe	1.50	.60
❑	145	Emmitt Smith	2.50	1.00
❑	146	Marvin Harrison	1.25	.50
❑	147	Frank Sanders	.50	.20
❑	148	Aaron Shea	.50	.20
❑	[illegible]	[illegible]	[illegible]	[illegible]
❑	150	Tony Gonzalez	.75	.30
❑	151	Marcus Robinson	1.25	.50
❑	152	Danny Farmer	.50	.20
❑	153	Warren Sapp	.75	.30
❑	154	Kurt Warner	2.50	1.00
❑	155	Jessie Armstead	.50	.20
❑	156	Lawyer Milloy	.75	.30
❑	157	Brian Griese	1.25	.50
❑	158	Jason Taylor	.50	.20
❑	159	Jeff Lewis	.50	.20
❑	160	Travis Prentice	.50	.20
❑	161	Tim Dwight	1.25	.50
❑	162	Kyle Brady	.50	.20
❑	163	Bubba Franks	.75	.30
❑	164	James Thrash	.75	.30
❑	165	Bobby Shaw	.50	.20
❑	166	Ron Dayne	1.25	.50
❑	167	Mike Alstott	1.25	.50
❑	168	Bruce Smith	.50	.20
❑	169	Jeff Graham	.50	.20
❑	170	Jeff Blake	.75	.30
❑	171	Laveranues Coles	1.25	.50
❑	172	Herman Moore	.75	.30
❑	173	Shannon Sharpe	.75	.30
❑	174	Corey Dillon	1.25	.50
❑	175	Ken Dilger	.50	.20
❑	176	Eddie Kennison	.50	.20
❑	177	Andre Rison	.75	.30
❑	178	Stephen Davis	1.25	.50
❑	179	Torry Holt	1.25	.50
❑	180	Samari Rollo	.50	.20
❑	181	Michael Strahan	.75	.30
❑	182	Plaxico Burress	1.25	.50
❑	183	Darnell Autry	.50	.20
❑	184	Wesley Walls	.50	.20
❑	185	Elvis Grbac	.75	.30
❑	186	Marcus Pollard	.50	.20
❑	187	Keith Poole	.50	.20
❑	188	Ryan Leaf	.75	.30
❑	189	Terrell Owens	1.25	.50
❑	190	Dedric Ward	.50	.20
❑	191	Donald Driver	.75	.30
❑	192	Larry Foster	.50	.20
❑	193	Priest Holmes	1.50	.60
❑	194	Sammy Morris	.50	.20
❑	195	Reggie Jones	.50	.20
❑	196	Kordell Stewart	.75	.30
❑	197	Sylvester Morris	.50	.20
❑	198	Aaron Brooks	1.25	.50
❑	199	Tai Streets	.50	.20
❑	200	Chad Pennington	2.00	.75
❑	201	Terrell Owens SH	1.25	.50
❑	202	Marshall Faulk SH	1.25	.50
❑	203	Mike Anderson SH	.75	.30
❑	204	Cris Carter SH	1.25	.50
❑	205	Corey Dillon SH	1.25	.50
❑	206	Daunte Culpepper SH	1.25	.50
❑	207	Peyton Manning SH	1.50	.60
❑	208	Torry Holt SH	1.25	.50
❑	209	Marvin Harrison SH	1.25	.50
❑	210	Edgerrin James SH	1.25	.50
❑	211	Sam Madison	.50	.20
❑	212	Jonathan Quinn	.50	.20
❑	213	Rob Morris	.50	.20
❑	214	E.G. Green	.50	.20
❑	215	David Sloan	.50	.20
❑	216	Jason Tucker	.50	.20
❑	217	Wali Rainer	.50	.20
❑	218	Jerry Azumah	.50	.20
❑	219	Dameyune Craig	.50	.20
❑	220	Jammi German	.50	.20
❑	221	LaDainian Tomlinson RC	300.00	150.00
❑	222	Quincy Morgan RC	20.00	7.50
❑	223	Steve Smith RC	40.00	20.00
❑	224	Santana Moss RC	30.00	12.50
❑	225	Koren Robinson RC	20.00	7.50
❑	226	Kevin Kasper RC	20.00	7.50
❑	227	Jamie Henderson RC	12.00	5.00
❑	228	Adam Archuleta RC	20.00	7.50
❑	229	Drew Brees RC	80.00	40.00
❑	230	Michael Stone RC	8.00	3.00
❑	231	Jamar Fletcher RC	12.00	5.00
❑	232	Eric Westmoreland RC	12.00	5.00
❑	233	[illegible] RC	12.00	5.00
❑	234	Gerard Warren RC	20.00	7.50
❑	235	Snoop Minnis RC	12.00	5.00
❑	236	Chris Chambers RC	25.00	12.50
❑	237	Damerien McCants RC	12.00	5.00
❑	238	Kevan Barlow RC	20.00	7.50
❑	239	Mike McMahon RC	20.00	7.50
❑	240	Jabari Holloway RC	12.00	5.00
❑	241	Travis Henry RC	30.00	15.00
❑	242	Derrick Blaylock RC	20.00	7.50
❑	243	Tim Hasselbeck RC	20.00	7.50
❑	244	Andre Carter RC	20.00	7.50
❑	245	Sage Rosenfels RC	20.00	7.50
❑	246	Cedrick Wilson RC	20.00	7.50
❑	247	Scotty Anderson RC	12.00	5.00
❑	248	Ken-Yon Rambo RC	12.00	5.00
❑	249	Marques Tuiasosopo RC	20.00	7.50
❑	250	Reggie Wayne RC	30.00	15.00
❑	251	Onomo Ojo RC	12.00	5.00
❑	252	James Jackson RC	20.00	7.50
❑	253	Moran Norris RC	8.00	3.00
❑	254	Rashard Casey RC	12.00	5.00
❑	255	Rudi Johnson RC	40.00	15.00
❑	256	Willie Middlebrooks RC	12.00	5.00
❑	257	Freddie Mitchell RC	20.00	7.50
❑	258	Deuce McAllister RC	40.00	20.00
❑	259	Chad Johnson RC	50.00	20.00
❑	260	David Terrell RC	20.00	7.50
❑	261	Jamal Reynolds RC	20.00	7.50
❑	262	Michael Vick RC	80.00	30.00
❑	263	Marcus Stroud RC	20.00	7.50
❑	264	Dan Alexander RC	20.00	7.50
❑	265	Jonathan Carter RC	12.00	5.00
❑	266	Bobby Newcombe RC	12.00	5.00
❑	267	Eddie Berlin RC	12.00	5.00
❑	268	LaMont Jordan RC	40.00	15.00
❑	269	Michael Bennett RC	20.00	7.50
❑	270	Shaun Rogers RC	20.00	7.50
❑	271	Travis Minor RC	12.00	5.00
❑	272	Jesse Palmer RC	[illegible]	7.50
❑	273	Derrick Gibson RC	12.00	5.00
❑	274	Chris Weinke RC	20.00	7.50
❑	275	Nate Clements RC	20.00	7.50
❑	276	Eric Kelly RC	8.00	3.00
❑	277	Justin Smith RC	20.00	7.50
❑	278	Ryan Pickett RC	8.00	3.00
❑	279	Anthony Thomas RC	20.00	7.50
❑	280	Will Allen RC	12.00	5.00
❑	281	Quincy Carter RC	20.00	7.50
❑	282	Richard Seymour RC	20.00	7.50
❑	283	Dan Morgan RC	20.00	7.50
❑	284	Tay Cody RC	8.00	3.00
❑	285	Alge Crumpler RC	25.00	10.00
❑	286	Robert Ferguson RC	20.00	7.50
❑	287	Will Peterson RC	12.00	5.00
❑	288	Tony Dixon RC	12.00	5.00
❑	289	Correll Buckhalter RC	20.00	7.50
❑	290	Rod Gardner RC	20.00	7.50
❑	291	Justin McCareins RC	20.00	7.50
❑	292	Josh Heupel RC	20.00	7.50
❑	293	Todd Heap RC	20.00	7.50
❑	294	Damione Lewis RC	12.00	5.00
❑	295	George Layne RC	12.00	5.00
❑	296	Jamie Winborn RC	12.00	5.00
❑	297	Billy Baber RC	8.00	3.00
❑	298	T.J. Houshmandzadeh RC	25.00	10.00
❑	299	Aaron Schobel RC	20.00	7.50
❑	300	Gary Baxter RC	12.00	5.00
❑	301	DeLawrence Grant RC	8.00	3.00
❑	302	Morlon Greenwood RC	12.00	5.00
❑	303	Shad Meier RC	12.00	5.00
❑	304	Torrance Marshall RC	20.00	7.50
❑	305	David Martin RC	12.00	5.00
❑	306	Anthony Henry RC	20.00	7.50
❑	307	Derrick Burgess RC	20.00	7.50
❑	308	Andre Dyson RC	8.00	3.00
❑	309	Ryan Helming RC	8.00	3.00
❑	310	Fred Smoot RC	20.00	7.50
❑	311	Arther Love RC	8.00	3.00
❑	312	John Capel RC	12.00	5.00
❑	313	Brandon Spoon RC	12.00	5.00
❑	314	Karon Riley RC	8.00	3.00
❑	315	Andre King RC	12.00	5.00
❑	316	Quentin McCord RC	12.00	5.00
❑	317	Zeke Moreno RC	20.00	7.50
❑	318	Francis St. Paul RC	12.00	5.00
❑	319	Richmond Flowers RC	12.00	5.00
❑	320	Derek Combs RC	12.00	5.00

2002 Topps Chrome

❑		COMP.SET w/o SP's (165)	50.00	20.00
❑	1	Anthony Thomas	.75	.30
❑	2	Jake Plummer	.75	.30
❑	3	Maurice Smith	.75	.30
❑	4	Jamal Lewis	1.25	.50
❑	5	Ray Lewis	1.25	.50
❑	6	Alex Van Pelt	.50	.20
❑	7	Chris Weinke	.75	.30
❑	8	Corey Dillon	.75	.30
❑	9	Quincy Morgan	.50	.20
❑	10	Rocket Ismail	.75	.30
❑	11	Brian Griese	1.25	.50
❑	12	Johnnie Morton	.75	.30
❑	13	Edgerrin James	1.50	.60
❑	14	Keenan McCardell	.50	.20
❑	15	Travis Minor	.75	.30
❑	16	Sylvester Morris	.50	.20
❑	17	Randy Moss	2.50	1.00
❑	18	Drew Bledsoe	1.50	.60
❑	19	Willie Jackson	.50	.20
❑	20	Michael Strahan	.75	.30
❑	21	Santana Moss	1.25	.50
❑	22	Duce Staley	1.25	.50
❑	23	Kendrell Bell	1.25	.50
❑	24	LaDainian Tomlinson	2.00	.75
❑	25	Terrell Owens	1.25	.50
❑	26	Shaun Alexander	1.50	.60
❑	27	Trung Canidate	.75	.30
❑	28	Mike Alstott	1.25	.50
❑	29	Kevin Dyson	.75	.30
❑	30	Rod Gardner	.75	.30
❑	31	David Boston	1.25	.50
❑	32	Michael Vick	2.50	1.00
❑	33	Qadry Ismail	.75	.30
❑	34	Peerless Price	.75	.30
❑	35	Rob Johnson	.75	.30
❑	36	Marcus Robinson	.75	.30
❑	37	Peter Warrick	.75	.30
❑	38	Kevin Johnson	.75	.30
❑	39	Ed McCaffrey	1.25	.50
❑	40	Shaun Rogers	.50	.20
❑	41	Marvin Harrison	1.25	.50
❑	42	Priest Holmes	1.50	.60
❑	43	Oronde Gadsden	.75	.30
❑	44	Terry Glenn	.75	.30
❑	45	Ike Hilliard	.75	.30
❑	46	Charles Woodson	.75	.30
❑	47	Freddie Mitchell	.75	.30

❑ 48 Drew Brees 1.25 .50
❑ 49 Jeff Garcia 1.25 .50
❑ 50 Kurt Warner 1.25 .50
❑ 51 Keyshawn Johnson 1.25 .50
❑ 52 Jevon Kearse .75 .30
❑ 53 Stephen Davis .75 .30
❑ 54 Shannon Sharpe .75 .30
❑ 55 Eric Moulds .75 .30
❑ 56 Muhsin Muhammad .75 .30
❑ 57 Brian Urlacher 2.00 .75
❑ 58 Chad Johnson 1.25 .50
❑ 59 Tim Couch .75 .30
❑ 60 Mike Anderson 1.25 .50
❑ 61 James Stewart .75 .30
❑ 62 Corey Bradford .50 .20
❑ 63 Reggie Wayne 1.25 .50
❑ 64 Mark Brunell 1.25 .50
❑ 65 Trent Green .75 .30
❑ 66 Zach Thomas 1.25 .50
❑ 67 Michael Bennett .75 .30
❑ 68 Troy Brown .75 .30
❑ 69 Amani Toomer .75 .30
❑ 70 Curtis Martin 1.25 .50
❑ 71 Tim Brown 1.25 .50
❑ 72 Correll Buckhalter .75 .30
❑ 73 Kordell Stewart .75 .30
❑ 74 Junior Seau 1.25 .50
❑ 75 Kevan Barlow .75 .30
❑ 76 Matt Hasselbeck .75 .30
❑ 77 Marshall Faulk 1.25 .50
❑ 78 Warren Sapp .75 .30
❑ 79 Frank Wycheck .50 .20
❑ 80 Michael Westbrook .50 .20
❑ 81 Travis Henry 1.25 .50
❑ 82 David Terrell 1.25 .50
❑ 83 Jon Kitna .75 .30
❑ 84 James Jackson .50 .20
❑ 85 Joey Galloway .75 .30
❑ 86 Rod Smith .75 .30
❑ 87 Germane Crowell .50 .20
❑ 88 Bill Schroeder .75 .30
❑ 89 Dominic Rhodes .75 .30
❑ 90 Fred Taylor 1.25 .50
❑ 91 Snoop Minnis .50 .20
❑ 92 Chris Chambers 1.25 .50
❑ 93 Daunte Culpepper 1.25 .50
❑ 94 Deuce McAllister 1.50 .60
❑ 95 Kerry Collins .75 .30
❑ 96 John Abraham .75 .30
❑ 97 Rich Gannon 1.25 .50
❑ 98 Tiki Barber 1.25 .50
❑ 99 Hines Ward 1.25 .50
❑ 100 Tom Brady 3.00 1.25
❑ 101 Tim Dwight .75 .30
❑ 102 Garrison Hearst .75 .30
❑ 103 Darrell Jackson .75 .30
❑ 104 Isaac Bruce 1.25 .50
❑ 105 Brad Johnson .75 .30
❑ 106 Steve McNair 1.25 .50
❑ 107 Champ Bailey .75 .30
❑ 108 Emmitt Smith 3.00 1.25
❑ 109 Mike McMahon 1.25 .50
❑ 110 Terrell Davis 1.25 .50
❑ 111 Antonio Freeman 1.25 .50
❑ 112 Jimmy Smith .75 .30
❑ 113 Tony Gonzalez .75 .30
❑ 114 Jay Fiedler .75 .30
❑ 115 Cris Carter 1.25 .50
❑ 116 David Patten .50 .20
❑ 117 Joe Horn .75 .30
❑ 118 Laveranues Coles .75 .30
❑ 119 Charlie Garner .75 .30
❑ 120 Donovan McNabb 1.50 .60
❑ 121 Jerome Bettis 1.25 .50
❑ 122 Curtis Conway .50 .20
❑ 123 Az-Zahir Hakim .50 .20
❑ 124 Warrick Dunn 1.25 .50
❑ 125 Eddie George 1.25 .50
❑ 126 Quincy Carter .75 .30
❑ 127 Ahman Green 1.25 .50
❑ 128 Peyton Manning 2.50 1.00
❑ 129 James McKnight .50 .20
❑ 130 Antowain Smith .75 .30
❑ 131 Ricky Williams 8.00 3.00
❑ 132 Chad Pennington 1.50 .60
❑ 133 Jerry Rice 2.50 1.00
❑ 134 Todd Pinkston .75 .30
❑ 135 Plaxico Burress .75 .30
❑ 136 Doug Flutie 1.25 .50
❑ 137 Koren Robinson .75 .30
❑ 138 Torry Holt 1.25 .50
❑ 139 Aaron Brooks 1.25 .50
❑ 140 Ron Dayne .75 .30
❑ 141 Vinny Testaverde .75 .30
❑ 142 Brett Favre 3.00 1.25
❑ 143 James Thrash .75 .30
❑ 144 Wayne Chrebet .75 .30
❑ 145 Derrick Mason .75 .30
❑ 146 Ahman Green WWU .75 .30
❑ 147 Peyton Manning WWU 1.25 .50
❑ 148 Kurt Warner WWU .75 .30
❑ 149 Daunte Culpepper WWU .75 .30
❑ 150 Tom Brady WWU 1.50 .60
❑ 151 Rod Gardner WWU .75 .30
❑ 152 Corey Dillon WWU .75 .30
❑ 153 Priest Holmes WWU 1.00 .40
❑ 154 Shaun Alexander WWU 1.00 .40
❑ 155 Randy Moss WWU 1.25 .50
❑ 156 Eric Moulds WWU .50 .20
❑ 157 Brett Favre WWU 1.50 .60
❑ 158 Todd Bouman WWU .50 .20
❑ 159 Dominic Rhodes WWU .50 .20
❑ 160 Marvin Harrison WWU .75 .30
❑ 161 Torry Holt WWU 1.25 .50
❑ 162 Derrick Mason WWU .50 .20
❑ 163 Jerry Rice WWU 1.25 .50
❑ 164 Donovan McNabb WWU 1.25 .50
❑ 165 Marshall Faulk WWU 1.25 .50
❑ 166 David Carr RC 20.00 7.50
❑ 167 Quentin Jammer RC 10.00 4.00
❑ 168 Mike Williams RC 8.00 3.00
❑ 169 Rocky Calmus RC 10.00 4.00
❑ 170 Travis Fisher RC 10.00 4.00
❑ 171 Dwight Freeney RC 15.00 6.00
❑ 172 Jeremy Shockey RC 40.00 15.00
❑ 173 Marquise Walker RC 8.00 3.00
❑ 174 Eric Crouch RC 10.00 4.00
❑ 175 DeShaun Foster RC 10.00 4.00
❑ 176 Roy Williams RC 20.00 7.50
❑ 177 Andre Davis RC 8.00 3.00
❑ 178 Alex Brown RC 10.00 4.00
❑ 179 Michael Lewis RC 10.00 4.00
❑ 180 Terry Charles RC 8.00 3.00
❑ 181 Clinton Portis RC 40.00 15.00
❑ 182 Dennis Johnson RC 5.00 2.00
❑ 183 Lito Sheppard RC 10.00 4.00
❑ 184 Ryan Sims RC 10.00 4.00
❑ 185 Raonall Smith RC 8.00 3.00
❑ 186 Albert Haynesworth RC 8.00 3.00
❑ 187 Eddie Freeman RC 5.00 2.00
❑ 188 Levi Jones RC 8.00 3.00
❑ 189 Josh McCown RC 12.00 5.00
❑ 190 Cliff Russell RC 8.00 3.00
❑ 191 Maurice Morris RC 10.00 4.00
❑ 192 Antwaan Randle El RC 12.00 5.00
❑ 193 Ladell Betts RC 10.00 4.00
❑ 194 Daniel Graham RC 10.00 4.00
❑ 195 David Garrard RC 20.00 7.50
❑ 196 Antonio Bryant RC 10.00 4.00
❑ 197 Patrick Ramsey RC 10.00 4.00
❑ 198 Kelly Campbell RC 8.00 3.00
❑ 199 Will Overstreet RC 5.00 2.00
❑ 200 Ryan Denney RC 8.00 3.00
❑ 201 John Henderson RC 10.00 4.00
❑ 202 Freddie Milons RC 8.00 3.00
❑ 203 Tim Carter RC 8.00 3.00
❑ 204 Kurt Kittner RC 8.00 3.00
❑ 205 Joey Harrington RC 12.00 5.00
❑ 206 Ricky Williams RC 8.00 3.00
❑ 207 Bryant McKinnie RC 8.00 3.00
❑ 208 Ed Reed RC 15.00 6.00
❑ 209 Josh Reed RC 10.00 4.00
❑ 210 Seth Burford RC 8.00 3.00
❑ 211 Javon Walker RC 15.00 6.00
❑ 212 Jamar Martin RC 8.00 3.00
❑ 213 Leonard Henry RC 8.00 3.00
❑ 214 Julius Peppers RC 20.00 7.50
❑ 215 Jabar Gaffney RC 10.00 4.00
❑ 216 Kalimba Edwards RC 10.00 4.00
❑ 217 Napoleon Harris RC 10.00 4.00
❑ 218 Ashley Lelie RC 20.00 7.50
❑ 219 Anthony Weaver RC 8.00 3.00
❑ 220 Bryan Thomas RC 8.00 3.00
❑ 221 Wendell Bryant RC 5.00 2.00
❑ 222 Damien Anderson RC 8.00 3.00
❑ 223 Travis Stephens RC 8.00 3.00
❑ 224 Rohan Davey RC 10.00 4.00
❑ 225 Mike Pearson RC 5.00 2.00
❑ 226 Marc Colombo RC 5.00 2.00
❑ 227 Phillip Buchanon RC 10.00 4.00
❑ 228 T.J. Duckett RC 10.00 4.00
❑ 229 Ron Johnson RC 8.00 3.00
❑ 230 Larry Tripplett RC 5.00 2.00
❑ 231 Randy Fasani RC 8.00 3.00
❑ 232 Keyuo Craver RC 8.00 3.00
❑ 233 Marquand Manuel RC 5.00 2.00
❑ 234 Jonathan Wells RC 10.00 4.00
❑ 235 Reche Caldwell RC 10.00 4.00
❑ 236 Luke Staley RC 8.00 3.00
❑ 237 Donte Stallworth RC 15.00 6.00
❑ 238 Levar Fisher RC 10.00 4.00
❑ 239 Lamar Gordon RC 10.00 4.00
❑ 240 William Green RC 10.00 4.00
❑ 241 Dusty Bonner RC 5.00 2.00
❑ 242 Craig Nall RC 10.00 4.00
❑ 243 Eric McCoo RC 5.00 2.00
❑ 244 David Thornton RC 5.00 2.00
❑ 245 Terry Jones RC 8.00 3.00
❑ 246 Lee Mays RC 10.00 4.00
❑ 247 Bryan Fletcher RC 5.00 2.00
❑ 248 Verron Haynes RC 10.00 4.00
❑ 249 Zak Kustok RC 10.00 4.00
❑ 250 Chad Hutchinson RC 8.00 3.00
❑ 251 Andra Davis RC 8.00 3.00
❑ 252 Wes Pate RC 5.00 2.00
❑ 253 Jon McGraw RC 5.00 2.00
❑ 254 Howard Green RC 5.00 2.00
❑ 255 Daryl Jones RC 8.00 3.00
❑ 256 David Priestley RC 8.00 3.00
❑ 257 Marques Anderson RC 10.00 4.00
❑ 258 Roosevelt Williams RC 5.00 2.00
❑ 259 Major Applewhite RC 10.00 4.00
❑ 260 Ronald Curry RC 10.00 4.00
❑ 261 Adrian Peterson RC 12.00 5.00
❑ 262 Tellis Redmon RC 8.00 3.00
❑ 263 Chester Taylor RC 20.00 7.50
❑ 264 Deion Branch RC 15.00 6.00
❑ 265 Tank Williams RC 5.00 2.00

2003 Topps Chrome

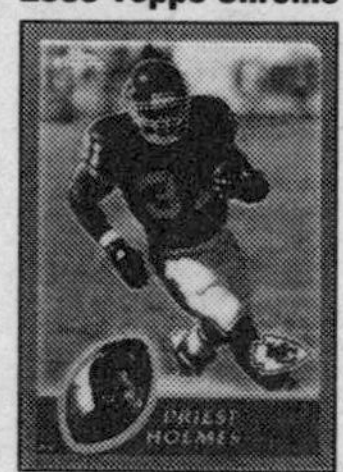

❑ COMP.SET w/o SP's (165) 40.00 15.00
❑ 1 Michael Vick 3.00 1.25
❑ 2 Josh Reed .75 .30
❑ 3 James Stewart .75 .30
❑ 4 Quincy Morgan .75 .30
❑ 5 Corey Bradford .50 .20
❑ 6 Fred Taylor 1.25 .50
❑ 7 David Patten .50 .20
❑ 8 Jerome Bettis 1.25 .50
❑ 9 Jerry Porter .75 .30
❑ 10 Steve McNair 1.25 .50
❑ 11 Stephen Davis .75 .30
❑ 12 Frank Wycheck .50 .20
❑ 13 Marcus Pollard .50 .20
❑ 14 David Terrell .75 .30

❑ 15	Bubba Franks	.75	.30
❑ 16	Trent Green	.75	.30
❑ 17	Mark Brunell	.75	.30
❑ 18	James Thrash	.50	.20
❑ 19	Mike Alstott	1.25	.50
❑ 20	Deuce McAllister	1.25	.50
❑ 21	Santana Moss	.75	.30
❑ 22	Jason Taylor	.50	.20
❑ 23	Corey Dillon	.75	.30
❑ 24	Jeff Blake	.50	.20
❑ 25	Ed McCaffrey	1.25	.50
❑ 26	Priest Holmes	1.50	.60
❑ 27	Tim D[illegible]	[illegible]	[illegible]
❑ 28	Curtis Martin	1.25	.50
❑ 29	Derrius Thompson	.50	.20
❑ 30	Jonathan Wells	.50	.20
❑ 31	William Green	.75	.30
❑ 32	Bill Schroeder	.75	.30
❑ 33	Amos Zereoue	.75	.30
❑ 34	Warren Sapp	.75	.30
❑ 35	Koren Robinson	.75	.30
❑ 36	Donovan McNabb	1.50	.60
❑ 37	Edgerrin James	1.25	.50
❑ 38	Kelly Holcomb	.75	.30
❑ 39	Daunte Culpepper	1.25	.50
❑ 40	Tommy Maddox	1.25	.50
❑ 41	Rod Gardner	.75	.30
❑ 42	T.J. Duckett	.75	.30
❑ 43	Drew Bledsoe	1.25	.50
❑ 44	Rod Smith	.75	.30
❑ 45	Peyton Manning	2.00	.75
❑ 46	Darrell Jackson	.75	.30
❑ 47	Brett Favre	3.00	1.25
❑ 48	Ashley Lelie	1.25	.50
❑ 49	Jeremy Shockey	2.00	.75
❑ 50	Hines Ward	1.25	.50
❑ 51	Jeff Garcia	1.25	.50
❑ 52	Eddie Kennison	.50	.20
❑ 53	Brian Urlacher	2.00	.75
❑ 54	Antwaan Randle El	1.25	.50
❑ 55	Eddie George	.75	.30
❑ 56	Derrick Brooks	.75	.30
❑ 57	Isaac Bruce	1.25	.50
❑ 58	Joe Horn	.75	.30
❑ 59	Jon Kitna	.75	.30
❑ 60	David Boston	.75	.30
❑ 61	Todd Heap	.75	.30
❑ 62	Lamar Smith	.50	.20
❑ 63	Germane Crowell	.50	.20
❑ 64	Kevin Johnson	.75	.30
❑ 65	Drew Brees	1.25	.50
❑ 66	Chad Lewis	.50	.20
❑ 67	Charlie Garner	.75	.30
❑ 68	Laveranues Coles	.75	.30
❑ 69	Shaun Alexander	1.25	.50
❑ 70	Kevan Barlow	.75	.30
❑ 71	Aaron Brooks	1.25	.50
❑ 72	Jake Plummer	.75	.30
❑ 73	Emmitt Smith	3.00	1.25
❑ 74	Terry Glenn	.50	.20
❑ 75	Michael Bennett	.75	.30
❑ 76	Deion Branch	1.25	.50
❑ 77	Keyshawn Johnson	1.25	.50
❑ 78	Marc Bulger	1.25	.50
❑ 79	Matt Hasselbeck	.75	.30
❑ 80	Garrison Hearst	.75	.30
❑ 81	Brian Griese	1.25	.50
❑ 82	Johnnie Morton	.75	.30
❑ 83	Patrick Ramsey	1.25	.50
❑ 84	Donald Driver	.75	.30
❑ 85	Joey Harrington	2.00	.75
❑ 86	Ricky Williams	1.25	.50
❑ 87	Jabar Gaffney	.75	.30
❑ 88	Duce Staley	.75	.30
❑ 89	Jimmy Smith	.75	.30
❑ 90	Reggie Wayne	.75	.30
❑ 91	Chad Johnson	1.25	.50
❑ 92	Steve Beuerlein	.50	.20
❑ 93	Joey Galloway	.75	.30
❑ 94	Curtis Conway	.50	.20
❑ 95	Brad Johnson	.75	.30
❑ 96	Jamal Lewis	1.25	.50
❑ 97	Terrell Owens	1.25	.50
❑ 98	Todd Pinkston	.75	.30
❑ 99	Keenan McCardell	.50	.20
❑ 100	Antonio Bryant	.75	.30
❑ 101	Eric Moulds	.75	.30
❑ 102	Jim Miller	.50	.20
❑ 103	Troy Brown	.75	.30
❑ 104	Rich Gannon	.75	.30
❑ 105	Chad Pennington	1.50	.60
❑ 106	Michael Strahan	.75	.30
❑ 107	Chris Chambers	1.25	.50
❑ 108	Antowain Smith	.75	.30
❑ 109	Derrick Mason	.75	.30
❑ 110	Michael Pittman	.50	.20
❑ 111	[illegible]	[illegible]	[illegible]
❑ 112	Tony Gonzalez	.75	.30
❑ 113	Marty Booker	.75	.30
❑ 114	Shannon Sharpe	.50	.20
❑ 115	Zach Thomas	1.25	.50
❑ 116	Plaxico Burress	.75	.30
❑ 117	Kurt Warner	1.25	.50
❑ 118	Warrick Dunn	.75	.30
❑ 119	Jay Fiedler	.75	.30
❑ 120	LaMont Jordan	1.25	.50
❑ 121	Kerry Collins	.75	.30
❑ 122	Jerry Rice	2.50	1.00
❑ 123	Randy Moss	2.00	.75
❑ 124	Tom Brady	3.00	1.25
❑ 125	Amani Toomer	.75	.30
❑ 126	Travis Henry	.75	.30
❑ 127	Chris Chandler	.50	.20
❑ 128	Ray Lewis	1.25	.50
❑ 129	Donte Stallworth	1.25	.50
❑ 130	David Carr	2.00	.75
❑ 131	Andre Davis	.50	.20
❑ 132	Travis Taylor	.75	.30
❑ 133	Steve Smith	1.25	.50
❑ 134	Tiki Barber	1.25	.50
❑ 135	Chad Hutchinson	.50	.20
❑ 136	Marshall Faulk	1.25	.50
❑ 137	Peerless Price	.75	.30
❑ 138	Ahman Green	1.25	.50
❑ 139	Julius Peppers	1.25	.50
❑ 140	LaDainian Tomlinson	1.25	.50
❑ 141	Muhsin Muhammad	.75	.30
❑ 142	Tim Couch	.50	.20
❑ 143	Clinton Portis	2.00	.75
❑ 144	Anthony Thomas	.75	.30
❑ 145	Marvin Harrison	1.25	.50
❑ 146	Priest Holmes WW	.75	.30
❑ 147	Drew Bledsoe WW	.75	.30
❑ 148	Tom Brady WW	1.25	.50
❑ 149	Shaun Alexander WW	.75	.30
❑ 150	Brett Favre WW	1.25	.50
❑ 151	Travis Henry WW	.50	.20
❑ 152	Marshall Faulk WW	.75	.30
❑ 153	Terrell Owens WW	.50	.20
❑ 154	Jeff Garcia WW	.50	.20
❑ 155	Plaxico Burress WW	.50	.20
❑ 156	Donovan McNabb WW	.75	.30
❑ 157	Ricky Williams WW	.75	.30
❑ 158	Michael Vick WW	1.50	.60
❑ 159	Steve Smith WW	.75	.30
❑ 160	Marvin Harrison WW	.50	.20
❑ 161	Chad Pennington WW	.75	.30
❑ 162	Jeremy Shockey WW	.75	.30
❑ 163	Tommy Maddox WW	.50	.20
❑ 164	Steve McNair WW	.50	.20
❑ 165	Rich Gannon WW	.50	.20
❑ 166	Carson Palmer RC	30.00	15.00
❑ 167	J.R. Tolver RC	6.00	2.50
❑ 168	Michael Haynes RC	8.00	3.00
❑ 169	Terrell Suggs RC	12.00	5.00
❑ 170	Rashean Mathis RC	6.00	2.50
❑ 171	Chris Kelsay RC	8.00	3.00
❑ 172	Brad Banks RC	6.00	2.50
❑ 173	Jordan Gross RC	6.00	2.50
❑ 174	Lee Suggs RC	8.00	3.00
❑ 175	Kliff Kingsbury RC	6.00	2.50
❑ 176	William Joseph RC	8.00	3.00
❑ 177	Kelley Washington RC	8.00	3.00
❑ 178	Jerome McDougle RC	8.00	3.00
❑ 179	Keenan Howry RC	8.00	3.00
❑ 180	Chris Simms RC	12.00	5.00
❑ 181	Alonzo Jackson RC	6.00	2.50
❑ 182	L.J. Smith RC	8.00	3.00
❑ 183	Mike Doss RC	8.00	3.00
❑ 184	Bobby Wade RC	8.00	3.00
❑ 185	Ken Hamlin RC	8.00	3.00
❑ 186	Brandon Lloyd RC	8.00	3.00
❑ 187	Justin Fargas RC	8.00	3.00
❑ 188	DeWayne Robertson RC	8.00	3.00
❑ 189	Bryant Johnson RC	8.00	3.00
❑ 190	Boss Bailey RC	8.00	3.00
❑ 191	Onterrio Smith RC	8.00	3.00
❑ 192	Doug Gabriel RC	8.00	3.00
❑ 193	Jimmy Kennedy RC	8.00	3.00
❑ 194	B.J. Askew RC	8.00	3.00
❑ 195	Taylor [illegible] RC	[illegible]	2.50
❑ 196	Dallas Clark RC	8.00	3.00
❑ 197	DeWayne White RC	6.00	2.50
❑ 198	Arnaz Battle RC	8.00	3.00
❑ 199	Kareem Kelly RC	6.00	2.50
❑ 200	Talman Gardner RC	8.00	3.00
❑ 201	Billy McMullen RC	6.00	2.50
❑ 202	Travis Anglin RC	4.00	1.50
❑ 203	Anquan Boldin RC	20.00	10.00
❑ 204	Osi Umenyiora RC	12.00	5.00
❑ 205	Byron Leftwich RC	25.00	10.00
❑ 206	Marcus Trufant RC	8.00	3.00
❑ 207	Sam Aiken RC	6.00	2.50
❑ 208	LaBrandon Toefield RC	8.00	3.00
❑ 209	Terry Pierce RC	6.00	2.50
❑ 210	Charles Rogers RC	8.00	3.00
❑ 211	Chaun Thompson RC	4.00	1.50
❑ 212	Chris Brown RC	8.00	3.00
❑ 213	Justin Gage RC	8.00	3.00
❑ 214	Kevin Williams RC	8.00	3.00
❑ 215	Willis McGahee RC	20.00	7.50
❑ 216	Victor Hobson RC	8.00	3.00
❑ 217	Brian St.Pierre RC	8.00	3.00
❑ 218	Nate Burleson RC	8.00	3.00
❑ 219	Calvin Pace RC	6.00	2.50
❑ 220	Larry Johnson RC	30.00	18.00
❑ 221	Andre Woolfolk RC	8.00	3.00
❑ 222	Tyrone Calico RC	8.00	3.00
❑ 223	Seneca Wallace RC	8.00	3.00
❑ 224	Domanick Davis RC	8.00	3.00
❑ 225	Rex Grossman RC	25.00	10.00
❑ 226	Artose Pinner RC	8.00	3.00
❑ 227	Jason Witten RC	15.00	6.00
❑ 228	Bennie Joppru RC	8.00	3.00
❑ 229	Bethel Johnson RC	8.00	3.00
❑ 230	Kyle Boller RC	8.00	3.00
❑ 231	Shaun McDonald RC	8.00	3.00
❑ 232	Musa Smith RC	8.00	3.00
❑ 233	Ken Dorsey RC	8.00	3.00
❑ 234	Johnathan Sullivan RC	6.00	2.50
❑ 235	Andre Johnson RC	15.00	6.00
❑ 236	Nick Barnett RC	8.00	3.00
❑ 237	Teyo Johnson RC	8.00	3.00
❑ 238	Terence Newman RC	15.00	6.00
❑ 239	Kevin Curtis RC	10.00	4.00
❑ 240	Dave Ragone RC	8.00	3.00
❑ 241	Ty Warren RC	8.00	3.00
❑ 242	Walter Young RC	4.00	1.50
❑ 243	Kevin Walter RC	6.00	2.50
❑ 244	Carl Ford RC	4.00	1.50
❑ 245	Cecil Sapp RC	6.00	2.50
❑ 246	Sultan McCullough RC	6.00	2.50
❑ 247	Eugene Wilson RC	8.00	3.00
❑ 248	Ricky Manning RC	8.00	3.00
❑ 249	Andrew Williams RC	6.00	2.50
❑ 250	Juston Wood RC	4.00	1.50
❑ 251	Cory Redding RC	6.00	2.50
❑ 252	Charles Tillman RC	10.00	4.00
❑ 253	Terrence Edwards RC	6.00	2.50
❑ 254	Adrian Madise RC	6.00	2.50
❑ 255	David Kircus RC	8.00	3.00
❑ 256	Zuriel Smith RC	4.00	1.50
❑ 257	Earnest Graham RC	8.00	3.00
❑ 258	Ronald Bellamy RC	6.00	2.50
❑ 259	John Anderson RC	4.00	1.50
❑ 260	David Tyree RC	6.00	2.50
❑ 261	Malaefou MacKenzie RC	4.00	1.50
❑ 262	Ahmaad Galloway RC	6.00	2.50
❑ 263	Brooks Bollinger RC	8.00	3.00
❑ 264	Gibran Hamdan RC	4.00	1.50
❑ 265	Taco Wallace RC	6.00	2.50
❑ 266	LaTarence Dunbar RC	6.00	2.50

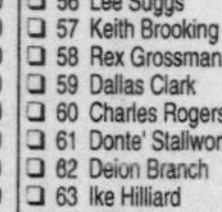
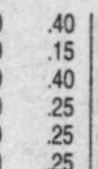
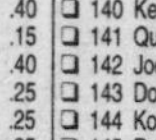
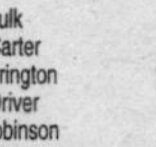

❑ 267 Justin Griffith RC 6.00 2.50
❑ 268 Bradie James RC 8.00 3.00
❑ 269 Danny Curley RC 4.00 1.50
❑ 270 Kenny Peterson RC 6.00 2.50
❑ 271 DeAndrew Rubin RC 4.00 1.50
❑ 272 Ryan Hoag RC 4.00 1.50
❑ 273 Rien Long RC 4.00 1.50
❑ 274 Troy Polamalu RC 30.00 15.00
❑ 275 Terrence Holt RC 6.00 2.50

2004 Topps Chrome

❑ COMP.SET w/o SP's (165) 30.00 12.50
❑ 1 Peyton Manning 1.50 .60
❑ 2 Patrick Ramsey .60 .25
❑ 3 Justin McCareins .40 .15
❑ 4 Matt Hasselbeck .60 .25
❑ 5 Chris Chambers .60 .25
❑ 6 Bubba Franks .60 .25
❑ 7 Eric Moulds .60 .25
❑ 8 Anquan Boldin 1.00 .40
❑ 9 Brian Urlacher 1.25 .50
❑ 10 Stephen Davis .60 .25
❑ 11 Michael Vick 2.00 .75
❑ 12 Dante Hall 1.00 .40
❑ 13 Chad Pennington 1.00 .40
❑ 14 Kevan Barlow .60 .25
❑ 15 Tommy Maddox .60 .25
❑ 16 Domanick Davis 1.00 .40
❑ 17 Dwight Freeney .60 .25
❑ 18 LaVar Arrington 2.00 .75
❑ 19 Troy Hambrick .40 .15
❑ 20 Jake Plummer .60 .25
❑ 21 Willis McGahee 1.00 .40
❑ 22 Steve McNair 1.00 .40
❑ 23 Kerry Collins .60 .25
❑ 24 Hines Ward 1.00 .40
❑ 25 Terrell Owens 1.00 .40
❑ 26 Jerome Pathon .40 .15
❑ 27 Andre Johnson 1.00 .40
❑ 28 DeShaun Foster .60 .25
❑ 29 Terrell Suggs .60 .25
❑ 30 Marcel Shipp .60 .25
❑ 31 Kyle Boller 1.00 .40
❑ 32 Javon Walker .60 .25
❑ 33 Ahman Green 1.00 .40
❑ 34 Travis Henry .60 .25
❑ 35 Randy McMichael .40 .15
❑ 36 Jerry Rice 2.00 .75
❑ 37 Travis Taylor .40 .15
❑ 38 Fred Taylor .60 .25
❑ 39 Zach Thomas 1.00 .40
❑ 40 Marques Tuiasosopo .60 .25
❑ 41 Laveranues Coles .60 .25
❑ 42 Thomas Jones .60 .25
❑ 43 Jamie Sharper .40 .15
❑ 44 Quincy Morgan .60 .25
❑ 45 Troy Brown .60 .25
❑ 46 Joey Galloway .60 .25
❑ 47 Justin Fargas .60 .25
❑ 48 Daunte Culpepper 1.00 .40
❑ 49 Keenan McCardell .40 .15
❑ 50 Priest Holmes 1.25 .50
❑ 51 Chad Johnson 1.00 .40
❑ 52 Marty Booker .60 .25
❑ 53 Tim Rattay .40 .15
❑ 54 Brian Westbrook .60 .25
❑ 55 Ricky Williams 1.00 .40
❑ 56 Lee Suggs 1.00 .40
❑ 57 Keith Brooking .40 .15
❑ 58 Rex Grossman 1.00 .40
❑ 59 Dallas Clark .60 .25
❑ 60 Charles Rogers .60 .25
❑ 61 Donte' Stallworth .60 .25
❑ 62 Deion Branch 1.00 .40
❑ 63 Ike Hilliard .40 .15
❑ 64 Michael Strahan .60 .25
❑ 65 Randy Moss 1.25 .50
❑ 66 Isaac Bruce .60 .25
❑ 67 Brad Johnson .60 .25
❑ 68 Warrick Dunn .60 .25
❑ 69 Josh McCown .60 .25
❑ 70 Donovan McNabb 1.25 .50
❑ 71 Shaun Alexander 1.00 .40
❑ 72 William Green .60 .25
❑ 73 Carson Palmer 1.25 .50
❑ 74 Quentin Griffin 1.00 .40
❑ 75 LaDainian Tomlinson 1.25 .50
❑ 76 Edgerrin James 1.00 .40
❑ 77 Santana Moss .60 .25
❑ 78 Marshall Faulk 1.00 .40
❑ 79 Tyrone Calico .60 .25
❑ 80 Marvin Harrison 1.00 .40
❑ 81 Tony Gonzalez .60 .25
❑ 82 Deuce McAllister 1.00 .40
❑ 83 Drew Brees 1.00 .40
❑ 84 Todd Pinkston .40 .15
❑ 85 Jeff Garcia 1.00 .40
❑ 86 Darrell Jackson .60 .25
❑ 87 Ray Lewis 1.00 .40
❑ 88 Billy Volek 1.00 .40
❑ 89 Rudi Johnson .60 .25
❑ 90 Julius Peppers 1.00 .40
❑ 91 Peter Warrick .60 .25
❑ 92 Trent Green .60 .25
❑ 93 Onterrio Smith .60 .25
❑ 94 Jerome Bettis 1.00 .40
❑ 95 Keyshawn Johnson .60 .25
❑ 96 Jamal Lewis 1.00 .40
❑ 97 Alge Crumpler .60 .25
❑ 98 Michael Bennett .60 .25
❑ 99 Jimmy Smith .60 .25
❑ 100 Brett Favre 2.50 1.00
❑ 101 Jerry Porter .60 .25
❑ 102 Marc Bulger 1.00 .40
❑ 103 David Carr 1.00 .40
❑ 104 Mark Brunell .60 .25
❑ 105 Aaron Brooks .60 .25
❑ 106 Plaxico Burress .60 .25
❑ 107 Correll Buckhalter .60 .25
❑ 108 Jevon Kearse .60 .25
❑ 109 Michael Pittman .40 .15
❑ 110 Clinton Portis 1.00 .40
❑ 111 Corey Dillon .60 .25
❑ 112 Steve Smith 1.00 .40
❑ 113 Eddie Kennison .40 .15
❑ 114 Amani Toomer .60 .25
❑ 115 Kelly Holcomb .60 .25
❑ 116 Torry Holt 1.00 .40
❑ 117 Eddie George .60 .25
❑ 118 Jeremy Shockey 1.00 .40
❑ 119 Jon Kitna .60 .25
❑ 120 Todd Heap .60 .25
❑ 121 Ashley Lelie .60 .25
❑ 122 Byron Leftwich 1.25 .50
❑ 123 Duce Staley .60 .25
❑ 124 Rod Gardner .60 .25
❑ 125 Tom Brady 2.50 1.00
❑ 126 Reggie Wayne .60 .25
❑ 127 Joe Horn .60 .25
❑ 128 Curtis Martin 1.00 .40
❑ 129 Charlie Garner .60 .25
❑ 130 Derrick Mason .60 .25
❑ 131 Marcus Robinson .60 .25
❑ 132 David Boston .60 .25
❑ 133 Drew Bledsoe 1.00 .40
❑ 134 Anthony Thomas .60 .25
❑ 135 Tiki Barber 1.00 .40
❑ 136 Terry Glenn .40 .15
❑ 137 A.J. Feeley 1.00 .40
❑ 138 Peerless Price .60 .25
❑ 139 Jake Delhomme 1.00 .40
❑ 140 Kevin Faulk .40 .15
❑ 141 Quincy Carter .60 .25
❑ 142 Joey Harrington 1.00 .40
❑ 143 Donald Driver .60 .25
❑ 144 Koren Robinson .60 .25
❑ 145 Rod Smith .60 .25
❑ 146 Anquan Boldin WW .40 .15
❑ 147 Jamal Lewis WW .60 .25
❑ 148 Priest Holmes WW 1.00 .40
❑ 149 Peyton Manning WW 1.00 .40
❑ 150 Marvin Harrison WW .60 .25
❑ 151 Steve McNair WW .60 .25
❑ 152 Travis Henry WW .40 .15
❑ 153 Torry Holt WW .60 .25
❑ 154 Tom Brady WW 1.00 .40
❑ 155 Ahman Green WW .60 .25
❑ 156 Donovan McNabb WW 1.00 .40
❑ 157 Deuce McAllister WW .60 .25
❑ 158 Domanick Davis WW .60 .25
❑ 159 Clinton Portis WW 1.00 .40
❑ 160 Rudi Johnson WW .40 .15
❑ 161 Brett Favre WW 1.00 .40
❑ 162 LaDainian Tomlinson WW .75 .30
❑ 163 Steve Smith WW .60 .25
❑ 164 Edgerrin James WW .60 .25
❑ 165 Ty Law WW .40 .15
❑ 166 Ben Roethlisberger RC 40.00 15.00
❑ 167 Ahmad Carroll RC 5.00 2.00
❑ 168 Johnnie Morant RC 5.00 2.00
❑ 169 Greg Jones RC 5.00 2.00
❑ 170 Michael Clayton RC 10.00 4.00
❑ 171 Josh Harris RC 5.00 2.00
❑ 172 Tatum Bell RC 10.00 4.00
❑ 173 Robert Gallery RC 5.00 2.00
❑ 174 B.J. Symons RC 5.00 2.00
❑ 175 Roy Williams RC 12.00 5.00
❑ 176 DeAngelo Hall RC 6.00 2.50
❑ 177 Jeff Smoker RC 5.00 2.00
❑ 178 Lee Evans RC 6.00 2.50
❑ 179 Michael Jenkins RC 5.00 2.00
❑ 180 Steven Jackson RC 15.00 6.00
❑ 181 Will Smith RC 5.00 2.00
❑ 182 Vince Wilfork RC 5.00 2.00
❑ 183 Ben Troupe RC 5.00 2.00
❑ 184 Chris Gamble RC 5.00 2.00
❑ 185 Kevin Jones RC 12.00 5.00
❑ 186 Jonathan Vilma RC 5.00 2.00
❑ 187 Dontarrious Thomas RC 5.00 2.00
❑ 188 Michael Boulware RC 5.00 2.00
❑ 189 Mewelde Moore RC 5.00 2.00
❑ 190 Drew Henson RC 5.00 2.00
❑ 191 D.J. Williams RC 5.00 2.00
❑ 192 Ernest Wilford RC 5.00 2.00
❑ 193 John Navarre RC 5.00 2.00
❑ 194 Jerricho Cotchery RC 5.00 2.00
❑ 195 Derrick Hamilton RC 4.00 1.50
❑ 196 Carlos Francis RC 4.00 1.50
❑ 197 Ben Watson RC 5.00 2.00
❑ 198 Reggie Williams RC 6.00 2.50
❑ 199 Devard Darling RC 5.00 2.00
❑ 200 Chris Perry RC 6.00 2.50
❑ 201 Derrick Strait RC 5.00 2.00
❑ 202 Sean Taylor RC 5.00 2.00
❑ 203 Michael Turner RC 6.00 2.50
❑ 204 Keary Colbert RC 5.00 2.00
❑ 205 Eli Manning RC 30.00 15.00
❑ 206 Julius Jones RC 15.00 6.00
❑ 207 Jason Babin RC 5.00 2.00
❑ 208 Cody Pickett RC 5.00 2.00
❑ 209 Kenechi Udeze RC 5.00 2.00
❑ 210 Rashaun Woods RC 5.00 2.00
❑ 211 Matt Schaub RC 15.00 6.00
❑ 212 Tommie Harris RC 5.00 2.00
❑ 213 Dwan Edwards RC 2.50 1.00
❑ 214 Shawn Andrews RC 5.00 2.00
❑ 215 Larry Fitzgerald RC 15.00 6.00
❑ 216 P.K. Sam RC 4.00 1.50
❑ 217 Teddy Lehman RC 5.00 2.00
❑ 218 Darius Watts RC 5.00 2.00
❑ 219 D.J. Hackett RC 4.00 1.50
❑ 220 Cedric Cobbs RC 5.00 2.00
❑ 221 Antwan Odom RC 5.00 2.00
❑ 222 Marquise Hill RC 4.00 1.50
❑ 223 Luke McCown RC 5.00 2.00

❑ 224 Triandos Luke RC 5.00 2.00
❑ 225 Kellen Winslow RC 10.00 4.00
❑ 226 Derek Abney RC 5.00 2.00
❑ 227 Chris Cooley RC 5.00 2.00
❑ 228 Dunta Robinson RC 5.00 2.00
❑ 229 Sean Jones RC 4.00 1.50
❑ 230 Philip Rivers RC 20.00 8.00
❑ 231 Craig Krenzel RC 5.00 2.00
❑ 232 Daryl Smith RC 5.00 2.00
❑ 233 Samie Parker RC 5.00 2.00
❑ 234 Ben Hartsock RC 5.00 2.00
❑ 235 J.P. Losman RC 10.00 4.00
❑ 236 Karlos Dansby RC 5.00 2.00
❑ 237 Ricardo Colclough RC 5.00 2.00
❑ 238 Bernard Berrian RC 6.00 2.50
❑ 239 Junior Siavii RC 5.00 2.00
❑ 240 Devery Henderson RC 5.00 2.00
❑ 241 Adimchinobe Echemandu RC 4.00 1.50
❑ 242 Patrick Crayton RC 5.00 2.00
❑ 243 Marcus Tubbs RC 5.00 2.00
❑ 244 Jamaar Taylor RC 5.00 2.00
❑ 245 Andy Hall RC 4.00 1.50
❑ 246 Darnell Dockett RC 4.00 1.50
❑ 247 Darrion Scott RC 5.00 2.00
❑ 248 Jim Sorgi RC 5.00 2.00
❑ 249 Jeff Dugan RC 2.50 1.00
❑ 250 Ryan Krause RC 4.00 1.50
❑ 251 Nate Lawrie RC 4.00 1.50
❑ 252 Casey Bramlet RC 4.00 1.50
❑ 253 Donnell Washington RC 5.00 2.00
❑ 254 Jonathan Smith RC 4.00 1.50
❑ 255 Tank Johnson RC 4.00 1.50
❑ 256 Keith Smith RC 4.00 1.50
❑ 257 Brandon Miree RC 4.00 1.50
❑ 258 Michael Gaines RC 4.00 1.50
❑ 259 Keiwan Ratliff RC 4.00 1.50
❑ 260 Stuart Schweigert RC 5.00 2.00
❑ 261 Derrick Ward RC 5.00 2.00
❑ 262 Matt Ware RC 5.00 2.00
❑ 263 Tim Anderson RC 5.00 2.00
❑ 264 Bradlee Van Pelt RC 5.00 2.00
❑ 265 Shawntae Spencer RC 5.00 2.00
❑ 266 Joey Thomas RC 5.00 2.00
❑ 267 Maurice Mann RC 4.00 1.50
❑ 268 Tim Euhus RC 5.00 2.00
❑ 269 Matt Mauck RC 5.00 2.00
❑ 270 Sloan Thomas RC 4.00 1.50
❑ 271 Jeris McIntyre RC 4.00 1.50
❑ 272 Randy Starks RC 4.00 1.50
❑ 273 Clarence Moore RC 5.00 2.00
❑ 274 Drew Carter RC 5.00 2.00
❑ 275 Sean Ryan RC 4.00 1.50
❑ RH00 Tom Brady RH 5.00 2.00

2005 Topps Chrome

❑ COMPLETE SET (275) 150.00 75.00
❑ COMP.SET w/o RC's (165) 30.00 12.50
❑ ROOKIE STATED ODDS 1:2 HOB/RET
❑ RH STATED ODDS 1:288 HOB/RET
❑ RH REFRACT.ODDS 1:17,884 H, 1:22,080 R
❑ 1 Deuce McAllister 1.00 .40
❑ 2 Sean Taylor .60 .25
❑ 3 Koren Robinson .60 .25
❑ 4 Tiki Barber 1.00 .40
❑ 5 LaDainian Tomlinson 1.25 .50
❑ 6 Lee Evans .60 .25
❑ 7 Aaron Brooks .60 .25
❑ 8 LaMont Jordan 1.00 .40
❑ 9 Dante Hall .60 .25
❑ 10 Daunte Culpepper 1.00 .40
❑ 11 Thomas Jones .60 .25
❑ 12 Warrick Dunn .60 .25
❑ 13 Willis McGahee 1.00 .40
❑ 14 Ed Reed .60 .25
❑ 15 Derrick Mason .60 .25
❑ 16 Jason Witten .60 .25
❑ 17 Chad Johnson 1.00 .40
❑ 18 Amani Toomer .60 .25
❑ 19 Joey Harrington 1.00 .40
❑ 20 [illegible] 1.00 .40
❑ 21 Brian Westbrook .60 .25
❑ 22 Matt Hasselbeck .60 .25
❑ 23 Michael Vick 1.50 .60
❑ 24 Kevin Jones 1.00 .40
❑ 25 Julius Peppers .60 .25
❑ 26 Michael Clayton 1.00 .40
❑ 27 Javon Walker .60 .25
❑ 28 Santana Moss .60 .25
❑ 29 Travis Henry .60 .25
❑ 30 Stephen Davis .60 .25
❑ 31 Larry Johnson 1.00 .40
❑ 32 Terrell Owens 1.00 .40
❑ 33 Ray Lewis 1.00 .40
❑ 34 Jake Plummer .60 .25
❑ 35 Philip Rivers 1.00 .40
❑ 36 Eli Manning 2.00 .75
❑ 37 Tedy Bruschi .60 .25
❑ 38 Adam Vinatieri 1.00 .40
❑ 39 J.P. Losman 1.00 .40
❑ 40 Zach Thomas 1.00 .40
❑ 41 Deion Branch .60 .25
❑ 42 Andre Johnson .60 .25
❑ 43 Marshall Faulk 1.00 .40
❑ 44 Bertrand Berry .50 .20
❑ 45 Terrell Suggs .60 .25
❑ 46 Tom Brady 2.50 1.00
❑ 47 Ashley Lelie .60 .25
❑ 48 Jonathan Wells .50 .20
❑ 49 Randy McMichael .50 .20
❑ 50 Charles Rogers .60 .25
❑ 51 Larry Fitzgerald 1.00 .40
❑ 52 Hines Ward 1.00 .40
❑ 53 Jason Taylor .50 .20
❑ 54 Ronde Barber .50 .20
❑ 55 T.J. Houshmandzadeh .50 .20
❑ 56 Keary Colbert .60 .25
❑ 57 DeAngelo Hall .60 .25
❑ 58 Chris Brown .60 .25
❑ 59 Chris Perry .60 .25
❑ 60 Steven Jackson 1.25 .50
❑ 61 Kyle Boller .60 .25
❑ 62 Rudi Johnson .60 .25
❑ 63 Roy Williams S .60 .25
❑ 64 Onterrio Smith .60 .25
❑ 65 Roy Williams WR 1.00 .40
❑ 66 Jerry Porter .60 .25
❑ 67 Edgerrin James 1.00 .40
❑ 68 Randy Moss 1.00 .40
❑ 69 Brian Griese .60 .25
❑ 70 Donovan McNabb 1.25 .50
❑ 71 Joe Horn .60 .25
❑ 72 Muhsin Muhammad .60 .25
❑ 73 Johnnie Morton .60 .25
❑ 74 Chad Pennington 1.00 .40
❑ 75 Torry Holt 1.00 .40
❑ 76 Marc Bulger 1.00 .40
❑ 77 Duce Staley .60 .25
❑ 78 Todd Heap .60 .25
❑ 79 Lee Suggs .60 .25
❑ 80 Patrick Ramsey .60 .25
❑ 81 Drew Bennett .60 .25
❑ 82 Michael Strahan .60 .25
❑ 83 Priest Holmes 1.00 .40
❑ 84 DeShaun Foster .60 .25
❑ 85 Corey Dillon .60 .25
❑ 86 Antonio Gates 1.00 .40
❑ 87 Trent Green .60 .25
❑ 88 Brandon Stokley .60 .25
❑ 89 Alge Crumpler .60 .25
❑ 90 Keyshawn Johnson .60 .25
❑ 91 Byron Leftwich 1.00 .40
❑ 92 Dunta Robinson .60 .25
❑ 93 Ben Roethlisberger 2.50 1.00
❑ 94 Rod Smith .60 .25
❑ 95 Robert Gallery .60 .25
❑ 96 Tony Gonzalez .60 .25
❑ 97 Steve McNair 1.00 .40
❑ 98 Jeremy Shockey 1.00 .40
❑ 99 Dominic Rhodes .50 .20
❑ 100 Michael Jenkins .60 .25
❑ 101 Jake Delhomme 1.00 .40
❑ 102 Jerome Bettis 1.00 .40
❑ 103 Jevon Kearse .60 .25
❑ 104 Plaxico Burress .60 .25
❑ 105 Dwight Freeney .60 .25
❑ 106 Marcus Robinson .60 .25
❑ 107 Rex Grossman .60 .25
❑ 108 Drew Henson .60 .25
❑ 109 Julius Jones 1.25 .50
❑ 110 Jamal Lewis 1.00 .40
❑ 111 Justin McCareins .50 .20
❑ 112 Billy Volek .60 .25
❑ 113 Curtis Martin 1.00 .40
❑ 114 Tatum Bell .60 .25
❑ 115 Domanick Davis .60 .25
❑ 116 Marvin Harrison 1.00 .40
❑ 117 Anquan Boldin .60 .25
❑ 118 Jimmy Smith .60 .25
❑ 119 Drew Brees 1.00 .40
❑ 120 Donte Stallworth .60 .25
❑ 121 Nate Burleson .60 .25
❑ 122 Fred Taylor .60 .25
❑ 123 Takeo Spikes .50 .20
❑ 124 Jonathan Ogden .50 .20
❑ 125 Michael Bennett .60 .25
❑ 126 Clinton Portis 1.00 .40
❑ 127 Ahman Green 1.00 .40
❑ 128 Drew Bledsoe 1.00 .40
❑ 129 Darrell Jackson .60 .25
❑ 130 Jonathan Vilma .60 .25
❑ 131 David Carr 1.00 .40
❑ 132 Champ Bailey .60 .25
❑ 133 Derrick Blaylock .50 .20
❑ 134 T.J. Duckett .60 .25
❑ 135 Shaun Alexander 1.25 .50
❑ 136 Peyton Manning 1.50 .60
❑ 137 Isaac Bruce .60 .25
❑ 138 LaVar Arrington 1.00 .40
❑ 139 Brett Favre 2.50 1.00
❑ 140 Allen Rossum .50 .20
❑ 141 Eric Moulds .60 .25
❑ 142 Carson Palmer 1.00 .40
❑ 143 Laveranues Coles .60 .25
❑ 144 Chester Taylor .60 .25
❑ 145 Reggie Wayne .60 .25
❑ 146 Curtis Martin LL .60 .25
❑ 147 Daunte Culpepper LL .60 .25
❑ 148 Muhsin Muhammad LL .50 .20
❑ 149 Shaun Alexander LL 1.00 .40
❑ 150 Trent Green LL .50 .20
❑ 151 Joe Horn LL .50 .20
❑ 152 Corey Dillon LL .50 .20
❑ 153 Peyton Manning LL 1.00 .40
❑ 154 Javon Walker LL .50 .20
❑ 155 Edgerrin James LL .60 .25
❑ 156 Jake Scott GM .50 .20
❑ 157 John Elway GM 2.00 .75
❑ 158 Dwight Clark GM .60 .25
❑ 159 Lawrence Taylor GM 1.00 .40
❑ 160 Joe Namath GM 1.25 .50
❑ 161 Richard Dent GM .60 .25
❑ 162 Peyton Manning GM 1.00 .40
❑ 163 Don Maynard GM .50 .20
❑ 164 Joe Greene GM 1.00 .40
❑ 165 Roger Staubach GM 1.25 .50
❑ 166 J.J. Arrington RC 5.00 2.00
❑ 167 Cedric Benson RC 12.00 5.00
❑ 168 Mark Bradley RC 5.00 2.00
❑ 169 Reggie Brown RC 5.00 2.00
❑ 170 Ronnie Brown RC 20.00 8.00
❑ 171 Jason Campbell RC 8.00 3.00
❑ 172 Maurice Clarett 5.00 2.00
❑ 173 Mark Clayton RC 5.00 2.00
❑ 174 Braylon Edwards RC 15.00 6.00
❑ 175 Ciatrick Fason RC 5.00 2.00

❑ 176 Charlie Frye RC 5.00 2.00
❑ 177 Frank Gore RC 12.00 5.00
❑ 178 David Greene RC 5.00 2.00
❑ 179 Vincent Jackson RC 5.00 2.00
❑ 180 Adam Jones RC 5.00 2.00
❑ 181 Matt Jones RC 8.00 3.00
❑ 182 Stefan LeFors RC 5.00 2.00
❑ 183 Heath Miller RC 10.00 4.00
❑ 184 Ryan Moats RC 5.00 2.00
❑ 185 Vernand Morency RC 5.00 2.00
❑ 186 Terrence Murphy RC 5.00 2.00
❑ 187 Kyle Orton RC 5.00 2.00
❑ 188 Roscoe Parrish RC 5.00 2.00
❑ 189 Courtney Roby RC 5.00 2.00
❑ 190 Aaron Rodgers RC 15.00 6.00
❑ 191 Carlos Rogers RC 6.00 2.50
❑ 192 Antrel Rolle RC 5.00 2.00
❑ 193 Eric Shelton RC 5.00 2.00
❑ 194 Alex Smith QB RC 20.00 8.00
❑ 195 Andrew Walter RC 5.00 2.00
❑ 196 Roddy White RC 5.00 2.00
❑ 197 Cadillac Williams RC 20.00 8.00
❑ 198 Mike Williams 5.00 2.00
❑ 199 Troy Williamson RC 5.00 2.00
❑ 200 Taylor Stubblefield RC 2.50 1.00
❑ 201 Dan Cody RC 5.00 2.00
❑ 202 David Pollack RC 5.00 2.00
❑ 203 Craig Bragg RC 4.00 1.50
❑ 204 Alvin Pearman RC 5.00 2.00
❑ 205 Marcus Maxwell RC 4.00 1.50
❑ 206 Brock Berlin RC 4.00 1.50
❑ 207 Khalif Barnes RC 4.00 1.50
❑ 208 Eric King RC 4.00 1.50
❑ 209 Alex Smith TE RC 5.00 2.00
❑ 210 Dante Ridgeway RC 4.00 1.50
❑ 211 Shaun Cody RC 5.00 2.00
❑ 212 Donte Nicholson RC 5.00 2.00
❑ 213 DeMarcus Ware RC 8.00 3.00
❑ 214 Lionel Gates RC 4.00 1.50
❑ 215 Fabian Washington RC 5.00 2.00
❑ 216 Brandon Jacobs RC 6.00 2.50
❑ 217 Noah Herron RC 5.00 2.00
❑ 218 Derrick Johnson RC 8.00 3.00
❑ 219 J.R. Russell RC 4.00 1.50
❑ 220 Adrian McPherson RC 5.00 2.00
❑ 221 Marcus Spears RC 5.00 2.00
❑ 222 Justin Miller RC 4.00 1.50
❑ 223 Marion Barber RC 8.00 3.00
❑ 224 Anthony Davis RC 4.00 1.50
❑ 225 Chad Owens RC 5.00 2.00
❑ 226 Craphonso Thorpe RC 4.00 1.50
❑ 227 Travis Johnson RC 4.00 1.50
❑ 228 Erasmus James RC 5.00 2.00
❑ 229 Mike Patterson RC 5.00 2.00
❑ 230 Airese Currie RC 5.00 2.00
❑ 231 Justin Tuck RC 5.00 2.00
❑ 232 Dan Orlovsky RC 5.00 2.00
❑ 233 Thomas Davis RC 5.00 2.00
❑ 234 Derek Anderson RC 8.00 3.00
❑ 235 Matt Roth RC 5.00 2.00
❑ 236 Chris Henry RC 5.00 2.00
❑ 237 Rasheed Marshall RC 5.00 2.00
❑ 238 Bryant McFadden RC 5.00 2.00
❑ 239 Darren Sproles RC 5.00 2.00
❑ 240 Fred Gibson RC 4.00 1.50
❑ 241 Barrett Ruud RC 5.00 2.00
❑ 242 Kelvin Hayden RC 4.00 1.50
❑ 243 Ryan Fitzpatrick RC 5.00 2.00
❑ 244 Patrick Estes RC 4.00 1.50
❑ 245 Zach Tuiasosopo RC 2.50 1.00
❑ 246 Luis Castillo RC 5.00 2.00
❑ 247 Lance Mitchell RC 4.00 1.50
❑ 248 Ronald Bartell RC 4.00 1.50
❑ 249 Jerome Mathis RC 5.00 2.00
❑ 250 Marlin Jackson RC 5.00 2.00
❑ 251 James Kilian RC 5.00 2.00
❑ 252 Roydell Williams RC 5.00 2.00
❑ 253 Joel Dreessen RC 4.00 1.50
❑ 254 Paris Warren RC 4.00 1.50
❑ 255 Dustin Fox RC 5.00 2.00
❑ 256 Ellis Hobbs RC 5.00 2.00
❑ 257 Mike Nugent RC 5.00 2.00
❑ 258 Channing Crowder RC 5.00 2.00
❑ 259 Kerry Rhodes RC 5.00 2.00
❑ 260 Jerome Collins RC 4.00 1.50
❑ 261 Stanford Routt RC 4.00 1.50
❑ 262 Madison Hedgecock RC 5.00 2.00
❑ 263 Rian Wallace RC 4.00 1.50
❑ 264 Larry Brackins RC 4.00 1.50
❑ 265 Manuel White RC 4.00 1.50
❑ 266 Corey Webster RC 5.00 2.00
❑ 267 Eric Moore RC 4.00 1.50
❑ 268 Kirk Morrison RC 5.00 2.00
❑ 269 Atiyyah Ellison RC 2.50 1.00
❑ 270 Travis Daniels RC 4.00 1.50
❑ 271 Boomer Grigsby RC 5.00 2.00
❑ 272 Alex Barron RC 2.50 1.00
❑ 273 Tab Perry RC 5.00 2.00
❑ 274 Cedric Houston RC 5.00 2.00
❑ 275 Kevin Burnett RC 5.00 2.00
❑ RH39 Deion Branch RH 5.00 2.00
❑ RH39R Deion Branch RHR/100 15.00 6.00

2006 Topps Chrome

❑ 1 Jonathan Vilma .60 .25
❑ 2 Chester Taylor .60 .25
❑ 3 Troy Polamalu 1.25 .50
❑ 4 Nathan Vasher .50 .20
❑ 5 Clinton Portis 1.00 .40
❑ 6 Willie Parker 1.25 .50
❑ 7 Lofa Tatupu .60 .25
❑ 8 Peyton Manning 1.50 .60
❑ 9 LaMont Jordan .60 .25
❑ 10 Jason Taylor .50 .20
❑ 11 Travis Taylor .50 .20
❑ 12 Derrick Johnson .60 .25
❑ 13 Jason Campbell .60 .25
❑ 14 Aaron Rodgers 1.00 .40
❑ 15 Deltha O'Neal .50 .20
❑ 16 LaDainian Tomlinson 1.25 .50
❑ 17 Keary Colbert .50 .20
❑ 18 Chris Chambers .60 .25
❑ 19 Chris Simms .60 .25
❑ 20 Troy Williamson .60 .25
❑ 21 Chad Johnson .60 .25
❑ 22 Jake Delhomme .60 .25
❑ 23 Willis McGahee 1.00 .40
❑ 24 Roddy White .60 .25
❑ 25 Rod Smith .60 .25
❑ 26 Zach Thomas 1.00 .40
❑ 27 Antonio Gates 1.00 .40
❑ 28 Michael Vick 1.00 .40
❑ 29 Antwaan Randle El .60 .25
❑ 30 Drew Bledsoe 1.00 .40
❑ 31 Randy McMichael .50 .20
❑ 32 Heath Miller .60 .25
❑ 33 Fred Taylor .60 .25
❑ 34 Alge Crumpler .60 .25
❑ 35 Roy Williams S .60 .25
❑ 36 Ryan Moats .50 .20
❑ 37 Dwight Freeney .60 .25
❑ 38 Jeremy Shockey 1.00 .40
❑ 39 Shawne Merriman .60 .25
❑ 40 Charlie Frye .60 .25
❑ 41 Reggie Wayne .60 .25
❑ 42 Alex Smith QB 1.00 .40
❑ 43 Jerome Bettis 1.00 .40
❑ 44 Chris Brown .60 .25
❑ 45 Michael Clayton .60 .25
❑ 46 Carlos Rogers .50 .20
❑ 47 DeAngelo Hall .60 .25
❑ 48 Drew Bennett .50 .20
❑ 49 Brandon Lloyd .60 .25
❑ 50 Corey Dillon .60 .25
❑ 51 Eli Manning 1.25 .50
❑ 52 Jerry Porter .60 .25
❑ 53 Carson Palmer 1.00 .40
❑ 54 Kevin Jones 1.00 .40
❑ 55 Andre Johnson .60 .25
❑ 56 Ray Lewis 1.00 .40
❑ 57 Kyle Orton .60 .25
❑ 58 Julius Jones 1.00 .40
❑ 59 Roy Williams WR 1.00 .40
❑ 60 Jonathan Ogden .50 .20
❑ 61 Antonio Pierce .50 .20
❑ 62 Larry Johnson 1.25 .50
❑ 63 Muhsin Muhammad .60 .25
❑ 64 Trent Green .60 .25
❑ 65 Tatum Bell .60 .25
❑ 66 Lee Evans .60 .25
❑ 67 Braylon Edwards 1.00 .40
❑ 68 Hines Ward 1.00 .40
❑ 69 Warrick Dunn .60 .25
❑ 70 Antonio Bryant .60 .25
❑ 71 Mewelde Moore .50 .20
❑ 72 Samkon Gado .60 .25
❑ 73 Mike Williams 1.00 .40
❑ 74 Marion Barber .60 .25
❑ 75 Samie Parker .50 .20
❑ 76 Julius Peppers .60 .25
❑ 77 Brian Westbrook .60 .25
❑ 78 Kevan Barlow .60 .25
❑ 79 Kyle Boller .50 .20
❑ 80 Donnie Edwards .50 .20
❑ 81 Courtney Roby .50 .20
❑ 82 Marc Bulger .60 .25
❑ 83 Steve Smith 1.00 .40
❑ 84 Ben Roethlisberger 1.50 .60
❑ 85 Byron Leftwich .60 .25
❑ 86 Isaac Bruce .60 .25
❑ 87 Kurt Warner .60 .25
❑ 88 Tiki Barber 1.00 .40
❑ 89 Derrick Mason .50 .20
❑ 90 Joe Horn .60 .25
❑ 91 Donovan McNabb 1.00 .40
❑ 92 DeShaun Foster .60 .25
❑ 93 Rex Grossman 1.00 .40
❑ 94 Randy Moss 1.00 .40
❑ 95 Tedy Bruschi 1.00 .40
❑ 96 Tony Gonzalez .60 .25
❑ 97 Cadillac Williams 1.00 .40
❑ 98 Torry Holt .60 .25
❑ 99 Philip Rivers 1.00 .40
❑ 100 Deuce McAllister .60 .25
❑ 101 Jason Witten .60 .25
❑ 102 Reggie Brown .75 .30
❑ 103 Ronnie Brown 1.00 .40
❑ 104 Deion Branch .60 .25
❑ 105 Terry Glenn .60 .25
❑ 106 Tom Brady 1.50 .60
❑ 107 Dallas Clark .50 .20
❑ 108 Mark Clayton 1.00 .40
❑ 109 D.J. Williams .50 .20
❑ 110 Matt Jones .60 .25
❑ 111 Ed Reed .60 .25
❑ 112 Reuben Droughns .60 .25
❑ 113 Matt Hasselbeck .60 .25
❑ 114 Anquan Boldin .60 .25
❑ 115 David Carr .60 .25
❑ 116 Domanick Davis .60 .25
❑ 117 Nate Burleson .60 .25
❑ 118 Shaun Alexander 1.00 .40
❑ 119 Dante Hall .60 .25
❑ 120 Santana Moss .60 .25
❑ 121 Brandon Stokley .60 .25
❑ 122 Larry Fitzgerald 1.00 .40
❑ 123 Marvin Harrison 1.00 .40
❑ 124 Steve McNair .60 .25
❑ 125 Osi Umenyiora .50 .20
❑ 126 Odell Thurman .50 .20
❑ 127 Josh McCown .60 .25
❑ 128 Curtis Martin 1.00 .40
❑ 129 Jake Plummer .60 .25
❑ 130 Cedric Benson 1.00 .40
❑ 131 J.P. Losman .60 .25

❑ 132	Joey Galloway	.60	.25
❑ 133	Brian Griese	.60	.25
❑ 134	Plaxico Burress	.60	.25
❑ 135	Brian Urlacher	1.00	.40
❑ 136	T.J. Houshmandzadeh	.60	.25
❑ 137	Todd Heap	.60	.25
❑ 138	Champ Bailey	.60	.25
❑ 139	Mark Brunell	.60	.25
❑ 140	Chris Cooley	.50	.20
❑ 141	Priest Holmes	.60	.25
❑ 142	Aaron Brooks	.60	.25
❑ 143	Steven Jackson	1.00	.40
❑ 144	Michael Strahan	.60	.25
❑ 145	Rudi Johnson	[illegible]	[illegible]
❑ 146	Terrell Owens	1.00	.40
❑ 147	John Abraham	.50	.20
❑ 148	Jon Kitna	.50	.20
❑ 149	LaVar Arrington	1.00	.40
❑ 150	Joe Jurevicius	.60	.25
❑ 151	Dominic Rhodes	.60	.25
❑ 152	Chad Pennington	.60	.25
❑ 153	Charles Woodson	.60	.25
❑ 154	Kerry Collins	.60	.25
❑ 155	Drew Brees	1.00	.40
❑ 156	Keyshawn Johnson	.60	.25
❑ 157	Mike Anderson	.60	.25
❑ 158	Jimmy Smith	.60	.25
❑ 159	Brett Favre	2.00	.75
❑ 160	Edgerrin James	1.00	.40
❑ 161	Jamal Lewis	.60	.25
❑ 162	Daunte Culpepper	1.00	.40
❑ 163	Eric Moulds	.60	.25
❑ 164	Patrick Ramsey	.60	.25
❑ 165	Ahman Green	.60	.25
❑ 166	Kamerion Wimbley RC	5.00	2.00
❑ 167	Bobby Carpenter RC	5.00	2.00
❑ 168	Abdul Hodge RC	5.00	2.00
❑ 169	P.J. Daniels RC	4.00	1.50
❑ 170	D'Qwell Jackson RC	4.00	1.50
❑ 171	Johnathan Joseph RC	4.00	1.50
❑ 172	Antonio Cromartie RC	5.00	2.00
❑ 173	Elvis Dumervil RC	2.50	1.00
❑ 174	Tamba Hali RC	5.00	2.00
❑ 175	Derek Hagan RC	5.00	2.00
❑ 176	Haloti Ngata RC	5.00	2.00
❑ 177	Manny Lawson RC	5.00	2.00
❑ 178	Kelly Jennings RC	5.00	2.00
❑ 179	Jason Allen RC	5.00	2.00
❑ 180	Mathias Kiwanuka RC	6.00	2.50
❑ 181	Marques Hagans RC	4.00	1.50
❑ 182	Devin Aromashodu RC	4.00	1.50
❑ 183	Brandon Johnson RC	4.00	1.50
❑ 184	Ingle Martin RC	5.00	2.00
❑ 185	Claude Wroten RC	2.50	1.00
❑ 186	Tye Hill RC	5.00	2.00
❑ 187	Ashton Youboty RC	5.00	2.00
❑ 188	DeMeco Ryans RC	6.00	2.50
❑ 189	Brodrick Bunkley RC	5.00	2.00
❑ 190	Thomas Howard RC	5.00	2.00
❑ 191	Ernie Sims RC	6.00	2.50
❑ 192	Rocky McIntosh RC	5.00	2.00
❑ 193	Donte Whitner RC	5.00	2.00
❑ 194	Anthony Schlegel RC	4.00	1.50
❑ 195	Jimmy Williams RC	5.00	2.00
❑ 196	Brett Basanez RC	5.00	2.00
❑ 197	Ben Obomanu RC	4.00	1.50
❑ 198	Jonathan Orr RC	4.00	1.50
❑ 199	Andre Hall RC	4.00	1.50
❑ 200	James Anderson RC	2.50	1.00
❑ 201	Darnell Bing RC	5.00	2.00
❑ 202	Jovon Bouknight RC	4.00	1.50
❑ 203	Gabe Watson RC	4.00	1.50
❑ 204	Garrett Mills RC	5.00	2.00
❑ 205	Jeff Webb RC	4.00	1.50
❑ 206	Kevin McMahan RC	4.00	1.50
❑ 207	D.J. Shockley RC	5.00	2.00
❑ 208	A.J. Nicholson RC	2.50	1.00
❑ 209	Cedric Humes RC	5.00	2.00
❑ 210	Winston Justice RC	5.00	2.00
❑ 211	Lawrence Vickers RC	4.00	1.50
❑ 212	Daniel Bullocks RC	5.00	2.00
❑ 213	Tim Day RC	4.00	1.50
❑ 214	Ko Simpson RC	4.00	1.50
❑ 215	Dusty Dvoracek RC	5.00	2.00
❑ 216	Davin Joseph RC	4.00	1.50
❑ 217	Dominique Byrd RC	4.00	1.50
❑ 218	Marcus Vick RC	4.00	1.50
❑ 219	John McCargo RC	4.00	1.50
❑ 220	Danieal Manning RC	5.00	2.00
❑ 221	Reggie Bush RC	20.00	8.00
❑ 222	A.J. Hawk RC	10.00	4.00
❑ 223	Vince Young RC	20.00	8.00
❑ 224	Matt Leinart RC	15.00	6.00
❑ 225	Kellen Clemens RC	8.00	3.00
❑ 226	Sinorice Moss RC	5.00	2.00
❑ 227	Laurence Maroney RC	12.00	5.00
❑ 228	DeAngelo Williams RC	12.00	5.00
❑ 229	[illegible]	[illegible]	[illegible]
❑ 230	LenDale White RC	10.00	4.00
❑ 231	Leonard Pope RC	5.00	2.00
❑ 232	Chad Greenway RC	5.00	2.00
❑ 233	Chad Jackson RC	5.00	2.00
❑ 234	Vernon Davis RC	10.00	4.00
❑ 235	Todd Watkins RC	4.00	1.50
❑ 236	David Thomas RC	5.00	2.00
❑ 237	Marcedes Lewis RC	5.00	2.00
❑ 238	Leon Washington RC	8.00	3.00
❑ 239	Will Blackmon RC	4.00	1.50
❑ 240	Michael Huff RC	6.00	2.50
❑ 241	Jerious Norwood RC	8.00	3.00
❑ 242	Reggie McNeal RC	4.00	1.50
❑ 243	Wali Lundy RC	5.00	2.00
❑ 244	Santonio Holmes RC	10.00	4.00
❑ 245	Jerome Harrison RC	5.00	2.00
❑ 246	Bruce Gradkowski RC	8.00	3.00
❑ 247	Maurice Drew RC	12.00	5.00
❑ 248	Brandon Williams RC	5.00	2.00
❑ 249	Anthony Fasano RC	5.00	2.00
❑ 250	Omar Jacobs RC	4.00	1.50
❑ 251	Domenik Hixon RC	4.00	1.50
❑ 252	Devin Hester RC	10.00	4.00
❑ 253	Maurice Stovall RC	5.00	2.00
❑ 254	Tarvaris Jackson RC	8.00	3.00
❑ 255	Michael Robinson RC	5.00	2.00
❑ 256	Mario Williams RC	8.00	3.00
❑ 257	Jason Avant RC	5.00	2.00
❑ 258	Brian Calhoun RC	5.00	2.00
❑ 259	Skyler Green RC	5.00	2.00
❑ 260	Greg Jennings RC	8.00	3.00
❑ 261	Charlie Whitehurst RC	5.00	2.00
❑ 262	Mike Hass RC	5.00	2.00
❑ 263	Brandon Marshall RC	5.00	2.00
❑ 264	Drew Olson RC	4.00	1.50
❑ 265	Demetrius Williams RC	5.00	2.00
❑ 266	Travis Wilson RC	5.00	2.00
❑ 267	Joe Klopfenstein RC	4.00	1.50
❑ 268	Joseph Addai RC	15.00	6.00
❑ 269	Brad Smith RC	5.00	2.00
❑ 270	Willie Reid RC	5.00	2.00
❑ RH40	Hines Ward RH	6.00	2.50

2007 Topps Chrome

❑ TC1	Matt Leinart	1.00	.40
❑ TC2	J.P. Losman	.75	.30
❑ TC3	Carson Palmer	1.00	.40
❑ TC4	Jay Cutler	1.00	.40
❑ TC5	Peyton Manning	1.50	.60
❑ TC6	Tom Brady	2.00	.75
❑ TC7	Chad Pennington	.75	.30
❑ TC8	Philip Rivers	1.00	.40
❑ TC9	Marc Bulger	.75	.30
❑ TC10	Edgerrin James	1.00	.40
❑ TC11	Willis McGahee	.75	.30
❑ TC12	Thomas Jones	.75	.30
❑ TC13	Marion Barber	.75	.30
❑ TC14	Fred Taylor	.75	.30
❑ TC15	Chester Taylor	.60	.25
❑ TC16	Reggie Bush	1.25	.50
❑ TC17	Willie Parker	1.00	.40
❑ TC18	Shaun Alexander	.75	.30
❑ TC19	LenDale White	.75	.30
❑ TC20	Larry Fitzgerald	.75	.30
❑ TC21	Lee Evans	.75	.30
❑ TC22	Muhsin Muhammad	[illegible]	[illegible]
❑ TC23	Rod Smith	.75	.30
❑ TC24	Andre Johnson	.75	.30
❑ TC25	Matt Jones	.75	.30
❑ TC26	Devery Henderson	.60	.25
❑ TC27	Plaxico Burress	.75	.30
❑ TC28	Randy Moss	1.00	.40
❑ TC29	Santonio Holmes	.75	.30
❑ TC30	Torry Holt	.75	.30
❑ TC31	Antwaan Randle El	.60	.25
❑ TC32	Todd Heap	.60	.25
❑ TC33	Tony Gonzalez	.75	.30
❑ TC34	Heath Miller	.60	.25
❑ TC35	Alex Smith TE	.60	.25
❑ TC36	Champ Bailey	.75	.30
❑ TC37	Roy Williams S	.75	.30
❑ TC38	Julius Peppers	.75	.30
❑ TC39	Jason Taylor	.60	.25
❑ TC40	Brian Urlacher	1.00	.40
❑ TC41	Marc Bulger LL	.60	.25
❑ TC42	Frank Gore LL	.75	.30
❑ TC43	Reggie Wayne LL	.60	.25
❑ TC44	Peyton Manning PB	1.25	.50
❑ TC45	Reggie Wayne PB	.60	.25
❑ TC46	Jason Taylor PB	.50	.20
❑ TC47	Troy Polamalu PB	.75	.30
❑ TC48	Tony Gonzalez PB	.60	.25
❑ TC49	Devin Hester PB	.75	.30
❑ TC50	LaDainian Tomlinson MVP	1.00	.40
❑ TC51	P.Manning/R.Wayne PSH	.60	.25
❑ TC52	New Orleans Saints PSH	.60	.25
❑ TC53	Peyton Manning PSH	1.25	.50
❑ TC54	T.Jones/C.Benson PSH	.60	.25
❑ TC55	Colts Defense PSH	.60	.25
❑ TC56	Steve McNair	.75	.30
❑ TC57	Rex Grossman	.75	.30
❑ TC58	Tony Romo	2.00	.75
❑ TC59	David Carr	.75	.30
❑ TC60	Tarvaris Jackson	1.00	.40
❑ TC61	Eli Manning	1.00	.40
❑ TC62	Ben Roethlisberger	1.25	.50
❑ TC63	Matt Hasselbeck	.75	.30
❑ TC64	Jason Campbell	.75	.30
❑ TC65	Warrick Dunn	.75	.30
❑ TC66	Jamal Lewis	.75	.30
❑ TC67	Cedric Benson	.75	.30
❑ TC68	Reuben Droughns	.75	.30
❑ TC69	Joseph Addai	1.25	.50
❑ TC70	Ronnie Brown	.75	.30
❑ TC71	Deuce McAllister	.75	.30
❑ TC72	Brian Westbrook	.75	.30
❑ TC73	Frank Gore	1.00	.40
❑ TC74	Cadillac Williams	.75	.30
❑ TC75	Anquan Boldin	.75	.30
❑ TC76	Mark Clayton	.75	.30
❑ TC77	Bernard Berrian	.60	.25
❑ TC78	Braylon Edwards	.75	.30
❑ TC79	Donald Driver	.75	.30
❑ TC80	Marvin Harrison	1.00	.40
❑ TC81	Troy Williamson	.60	.25
❑ TC82	Marques Colston	1.00	.40
❑ TC83	Laveranues Coles	.75	.30
❑ TC84	Hines Ward	1.00	.40
❑ TC85	Deion Branch	.75	.30
❑ TC86	Alge Crumpler	.75	.30
❑ TC87	Kellen Winslow	.75	.30
❑ TC88	Dallas Clark	.60	.25
❑ TC89	L.J. Smith	.60	.25
❑ TC90	Vernon Davis	.75	.30
❑ TC91	Sean Taylor	.60	.25
❑ TC92	Ronde Barber	.60	.25
❑ TC93	Brian Dawkins	.75	.30

Card	Player	Price 1	Price 2
❑ TC94	Dwight Freeney	.75	.30
❑ TC95	Ray Lewis	1.00	.40
❑ TC96	Peyton Manning LL	1.25	.50
❑ TC97	Larry Johnson LL	.75	.30
❑ TC98	Marvin Harrison LL	.75	.30
❑ TC99	LaDainian Tomlinson PB	1.00	.40
❑ TC100	Jeff Saturday PB	.50	.20
❑ TC101	Champ Bailey PB	.60	.25
❑ TC102	Frank Gore PB	.75	.30
❑ TC103	Walter Jones PB	.50	.20
❑ TC104	Tony Romo PB	1.50	.60
❑ TC105	Ronde Barber PB	.50	.20
❑ TC106	Larry Johnson PB	.75	.30
❑ TC107	Vince Young OROY	1.00	.40
❑ TC108	Asante Samuel PSH	.50	.20
❑ TC109	Tom Brady PSH	1.50	.60
❑ TC110	Devin Hester PSH	.75	.30
❑ TC111	Michael Vick SP	100.00	60.00
❑ TC112	Jake Delhomme	.75	.30
❑ TC113	Charlie Frye	.75	.30
❑ TC114	Brett Favre	2.00	.75
❑ TC115	Trent Green	.75	.30
❑ TC116	Drew Brees	.75	.30
❑ TC117	Donovan McNabb	1.00	.40
❑ TC118	Alex Smith QB	1.00	.40
❑ TC119	Vince Young	1.25	.50
❑ TC120	DeAngelo Williams	1.00	.40
❑ TC121	Rudi Johnson	.75	.30
❑ TC122	Julius Jones	.75	.30
❑ TC123	Larry Johnson	1.00	.40
❑ TC124	Laurence Maroney	1.00	.40
❑ TC125	Brandon Jacobs	.75	.30
❑ TC126	LaDainian Tomlinson	1.25	.50
❑ TC127	Steven Jackson	1.00	.40
❑ TC128	Clinton Portis	.75	.30
❑ TC129	Michael Jenkins	.75	.30
❑ TC130	Steve Smith	.75	.30
❑ TC131	Chad Johnson	.75	.30
❑ TC132	Roy Williams WR	.75	.30
❑ TC133	Reggie Wayne	.75	.30
❑ TC134	Reggie Williams	.75	.30
❑ TC135	Chris Chambers	.75	.30
❑ TC136	Sinorice Moss	.75	.30
❑ TC137	Reggie Brown	.75	.30
❑ TC138	Arnaz Battle	.60	.25
❑ TC139	Michael Clayton	.75	.30
❑ TC140	Santana Moss	.75	.30
❑ TC141	Desmond Clark	.60	.25
❑ TC142	Jeremy Shockey	.75	.30
❑ TC143	Antonio Gates	.75	.30
❑ TC144	Chris Cooley	.60	.25
❑ TC145	Devin Hester	1.00	.40
❑ TC146	Asante Samuel	.60	.25
❑ TC147	Troy Polamalu	1.00	.40
❑ TC148	DeMarcus Ware	.75	.30
❑ TC149	Michael Strahan	.75	.30
❑ TC150	A.J. Hawk	1.00	.40
❑ TC151	LaDainian Tomlinson LL	1.00	.40
❑ TC152	Chad Johnson LL	.60	.25
❑ TC153	LaDainian Tomlinson LL	1.00	.40
❑ TC154	Marvin Harrison PB	.75	.30
❑ TC155	Antonio Gates PB	.60	.25
❑ TC156	Shawne Merriman PB	.60	.25
❑ TC157	Drew Brees PB	.60	.25
❑ TC158	Steve Smith PB	.60	.25
❑ TC159	Julius Peppers PB	.60	.25
❑ TC160	DeMeco Ryans DROY	.60	.25
❑ TC161	Drew Brees PSH	.60	.25
❑ TC162	Reggie Bush PSH	1.00	.40
❑ TC163	Robbie Gould PSH	.50	.20
❑ TC164	Joseph Addai PSH	1.00	.40
❑ TC165	Adam Vinatieri PSH	.60	.25
❑ TC166	JaMarcus Russell RC	12.00	5.00
❑ TC167	Brady Quinn RC	15.00	6.00
❑ TC168	Drew Stanton RC	6.00	2.50
❑ TC169	Troy Smith RC	6.00	2.50
❑ TC170	Kevin Kolb RC	8.00	3.00
❑ TC171	Trent Edwards RC	10.00	4.00
❑ TC172	John Beck RC	10.00	4.00
❑ TC173	Jordan Palmer RC	5.00	2.00
❑ TC174	Chris Leak RC	4.00	1.50
❑ TC175	Isaiah Stanback RC	5.00	2.00
❑ TC176	Tyler Palko RC	5.00	2.00
❑ TC177	Jared Zabransky RC	5.00	2.00
❑ TC178	Jeff Rowe RC	4.00	1.50
❑ TC179	Zac Taylor RC	5.00	2.00
❑ TC180	Lester Ricard RC	4.00	1.50
❑ TC181	Adrian Peterson RC	40.00	15.00
❑ TC182	Marshawn Lynch RC	10.00	4.00
❑ TC183	Brandon Jackson RC	6.00	2.50
❑ TC184	Michael Bush RC	6.00	2.50
❑ TC185	Kenny Irons RC	5.00	2.00
❑ TC186	Antonio Pittman RC	4.00	1.50
❑ TC187	Tony Hunt RC	5.00	2.00
❑ TC188	Darius Walker RC	5.00	2.00
❑ TC189	Dwayne Wright RC	4.00	1.50
❑ TC190	Lorenzo Booker RC	5.00	2.00
❑ TC191	Kenneth Darby RC	5.00	2.00
❑ TC192	Chris Henry RB RC	5.00	2.00
❑ TC193	Selvin Young RC	6.00	2.50
❑ TC194	Brian Leonard RC	6.00	2.50
❑ TC195	Ahmad Bradshaw RC	6.00	2.50
❑ TC196	Gary Russell RC	5.00	2.00
❑ TC197	Kolby Smith RC	6.00	2.50
❑ TC198	Thomas Clayton RC	4.00	1.50
❑ TC199	Garrett Wolfe RC	6.00	2.50
❑ TC200	Calvin Johnson RC	15.00	6.00
❑ TC201	Ted Ginn Jr. RC	8.00	3.00
❑ TC202	Dwayne Jarrett RC	6.00	2.50
❑ TC203	Dwayne Bowe RC	10.00	4.00
❑ TC204	Sidney Rice RC	8.00	3.00
❑ TC205	Robert Meachem RC	5.00	2.00
❑ TC206	Anthony Gonzalez RC	8.00	3.00
❑ TC207	Craig Buster Davis RC	5.00	2.00
❑ TC208	Aundrae Allison RC	4.00	1.50
❑ TC209	Chansi Stuckey RC	4.00	1.50
❑ TC210	David Clowney RC	5.00	2.00
❑ TC211	Steve Smith USC RC	6.00	2.50
❑ TC212	Courtney Taylor RC	4.00	1.50
❑ TC213	Paul Williams RC	4.00	1.50
❑ TC214	Johnnie Lee Higgins RC	4.00	1.50
❑ TC215	Rhema McKnight RC	4.00	1.50
❑ TC216	Jason Hill RC	5.00	2.00
❑ TC217	Dallas Baker RC	4.00	1.50
❑ TC218	Greg Olsen RC	6.00	2.50
❑ TC219	Yamon Figurs RC	5.00	2.00
❑ TC220	Scott Chandler RC	4.00	1.50
❑ TC221	Matt Spaeth RC	5.00	2.00
❑ TC222	Ben Patrick RC	4.00	1.50
❑ TC223	Clark Harris RC	5.00	2.00
❑ TC224	Martrez Milner RC	4.00	1.50
❑ TC225	Alan Branch RC	4.00	1.50
❑ TC226	Amobi Okoye RC	5.00	2.00
❑ TC227	DeMarcus Tank Tyler RC	4.00	1.50
❑ TC228	Justin Harrell RC	5.00	2.00
❑ TC229	Gaines Adams RC	5.00	2.00
❑ TC230	Jamaal Anderson RC	4.00	1.50
❑ TC231	Adam Carriker RC	4.00	1.50
❑ TC232	Jarvis Moss RC	5.00	2.00
❑ TC233	Charles Johnson RC	3.00	1.25
❑ TC234	Anthony Spencer RC	5.00	2.00
❑ TC235	Quentin Moses RC	4.00	1.50
❑ TC236	LaMarr Woodley RC	5.00	2.00
❑ TC237	Victor Abiamiri RC	5.00	2.00
❑ TC238	Ray McDonald RC	4.00	1.50
❑ TC239	Tim Crowder RC	5.00	2.00
❑ TC240	Patrick Willis RC	10.00	4.00
❑ TC241	David Harris RC	4.00	1.50
❑ TC242	Buster Davis RC	4.00	1.50
❑ TC243	Lawrence Timmons RC	5.00	2.00
❑ TC244	Paul Posluszny RC	6.00	2.50
❑ TC245	Jon Beason RC	5.00	2.00
❑ TC246	Rufus Alexander RC	5.00	2.00
❑ TC247	Prescott Burgess RC	4.00	1.50
❑ TC248	Leon Hall RC	4.00	1.50
❑ TC249	Darrelle Revis RC	5.00	2.00
❑ TC250	Aaron Ross RC	5.00	2.00
❑ TC251	Daymeion Hughes RC	4.00	1.50
❑ TC252	Marcus McCauley RC	4.00	1.50
❑ TC253	Chris Houston RC	4.00	1.50
❑ TC254	Tanard Jackson RC	3.00	1.25
❑ TC255	Jonathan Wade RC	4.00	1.50
❑ TC256	Josh Wilson RC	4.00	1.50
❑ TC257	Eric Wright RC	5.00	2.00
❑ TC258	David Irons RC	3.00	1.25
❑ TC259	Laron Landry RC	6.00	2.50
❑ TC260	Reggie Nelson RC	4.00	1.50
❑ TC261	Michael Griffin RC	5.00	2.00
❑ TC262	Brandon Meriweather RC	5.00	2.00
❑ TC263	Eric Weddle RC	4.00	1.50
❑ TC264	Joe Thomas RC	5.00	2.00
❑ TC265	Levi Brown RC	5.00	2.00
❑ RH41	Peyton Manning RH	5.00	2.00

2003 Topps Draft Picks and Prospects

Card	Player	Price 1	Price 2
❑	COMPLETE SET (165)	50.00	25.00
❑ 1	Priest Holmes	1.25	.50
❑ 2	Tommy Maddox	1.00	.40
❑ 3	Donald Driver	.60	.25
❑ 4	Drew Bledsoe	1.00	.40
❑ 5	Tiki Barber	1.00	.40
❑ 6	Terrell Owens	1.00	.40
❑ 7	Rich Gannon	.60	.25
❑ 8	Isaac Bruce	1.00	.40
❑ 9	Stephen Davis	.60	.25
❑ 10	Peyton Manning	1.50	.60
❑ 11	Tony Gonzalez	.60	.25
❑ 12	Marty Booker	.60	.25
❑ 13	Warrick Dunn	.60	.25
❑ 14	Jimmy Smith	.60	.25
❑ 15	Troy Brown	.60	.25
❑ 16	Jerry Rice	2.00	.75
❑ 17	Curtis Conway	.40	.15
❑ 18	Kurt Warner	1.00	.40
❑ 19	Steve McNair	1.00	.40
❑ 20	Edgerrin James	1.00	.40
❑ 21	Aaron Brooks	1.00	.40
❑ 22	Joey Galloway	.60	.25
❑ 23	Peerless Price	.60	.25
❑ 24	Torry Holt	1.00	.40
❑ 25	Derrick Mason	.60	.25
❑ 26	Curtis Martin	1.00	.40
❑ 27	Daunte Culpepper	1.00	.40
❑ 28	Ahman Green	1.00	.40
❑ 29	Tim Couch	.40	.15
❑ 30	Ricky Williams	1.00	.40
❑ 31	Darrell Jackson	.60	.25
❑ 32	Keyshawn Johnson	1.00	.40
❑ 33	Jeff Garcia	1.00	.40
❑ 34	Charlie Garner	.60	.25
❑ 35	Randy Moss	1.50	.60
❑ 36	Rod Smith	.60	.25
❑ 37	Jamal Lewis	1.00	.40
❑ 38	Corey Dillon	.60	.25
❑ 39	Marvin Harrison	1.00	.40
❑ 40	Joe Horn	.60	.25
❑ 41	Laveranues Coles	.60	.25
❑ 42	Hines Ward	1.00	.40
❑ 43	Brad Johnson	.60	.25
❑ 44	Eddie George	.60	.25
❑ 45	Donovan McNabb	1.25	.50
❑ 46	Marshall Faulk	1.00	.40
❑ 47	Amani Toomer	.60	.25
❑ 48	Trent Green	.60	.25
❑ 49	Emmitt Smith	2.50	1.00
❑ 50	Brett Favre	2.50	1.00
❑ 51	Brian Griese	1.00	.40
❑ 52	Eric Moulds	.60	.25
❑ 53	Plaxico Burress	.60	.25
❑ 54	Fred Taylor	1.00	.40
❑ 55	Tom Brady	2.50	1.00
❑ 56	Michael Vick	2.50	1.00
❑ 57	Andre Davis	.40	.15

❑ 58	Chris Chambers	1.00	.40
❑ 59	Javon Walker	.60	.25
❑ 60	Marc Bulger	1.00	.40
❑ 61	LaDainian Tomlinson	1.00	.40
❑ 62	Chad Pennington	1.25	.50
❑ 63	Marc Boerigter	.60	.25
❑ 64	Rod Gardner	.60	.25
❑ 65	DeShaun Foster	.40	.15
❑ 66	Chris Redman	.40	.15
❑ 67	Chad Hutchinson	.40	.15
❑ 68	Deion Branch	1.00	.40
❑ 69	Jeremy Shockey	1.50	.60
❑ 70	Shaun Alexander	1.00	.40
❑ 71	Derrius Thompson	.40	.15
❑ [illegible]	[illegible]	[illegible]	[illegible]
❑ 73	Reggie Wayne	.60	.25
❑ 74	William Green	.60	.25
❑ 75	Julius Peppers	1.00	.40
❑ 76	Travis Henry	.60	.25
❑ 77	Marcel Shipp	.60	.25
❑ 78	Michael Bennett	.60	.25
❑ 79	Maurice Morris	.40	.15
❑ 80	Josh Reed	.60	.25
❑ 81	David Terrell	.60	.25
❑ 82	Drew Brees	1.00	.40
❑ 83	Jonathan Wells	.40	.15
❑ 84	Anthony Thomas	.60	.25
❑ 85	Quincy Morgan	.60	.25
❑ 86	Jerry Porter	.60	.25
❑ 87	Ron Johnson	.40	.15
❑ 88	Najeh Davenport	.40	.15
❑ 89	Lamar Gordon	.40	.15
❑ 90	Joey Harrington	1.50	.60
❑ 91	Donte Stallworth	1.00	.40
❑ 92	Kenny Watson	.40	.15
❑ 93	LaMont Jordan	1.00	.40
❑ 94	Antonio Bryant	.60	.25
❑ 95	Steve Smith	1.00	.40
❑ 96	T.J. Duckett	.60	.25
❑ 97	Patrick Ramsey	1.00	.40
❑ 98	Santana Moss	.60	.25
❑ 99	Chad Johnson	1.00	.40
❑ 100	Clinton Portis	1.50	.60
❑ 101	Reche Caldwell	.40	.15
❑ 102	Kevan Barlow	.60	.25
❑ 103	Deuce McAllister	1.00	.40
❑ 104	Koren Robinson	.40	.15
❑ 105	Todd Heap	.60	.25
❑ 106	Jabar Gaffney	.60	.25
❑ 107	Randy McMichael	.60	.25
❑ 108	Dwight Freeney	.60	.25
❑ 109	Antwaan Randle El	1.00	.40
❑ 110	David Carr	1.50	.60
❑ 111	Carson Palmer RC	6.00	2.50
❑ 112	Dahrran Diedrick RC	1.50	.60
❑ 113	Kyle Boller RC	1.50	.60
❑ 114	Terrell Suggs RC	2.50	1.00
❑ 115	Rien Long RC	.75	.30
❑ 116	Justin Gage RC	1.50	.60
❑ 117	William Joseph RC	1.50	.60
❑ 118	Chris Simms RC	2.50	1.00
❑ 119	Avon Cobourne RC	.75	.30
❑ 120	Victor Hobson RC	1.50	.60
❑ 121	Jason Gesser RC	1.50	.60
❑ 122	Ronald Bellamy RC	1.25	.50
❑ 123	Terence Newman RC	3.00	1.25
❑ 124	Terrence Edwards RC	1.25	.50
❑ 125	Sultan McCullough RC	1.25	.50
❑ 126	Kareem Kelly RC	1.25	.50
❑ 127	Jason Witten RC	2.50	1.00
❑ 128	Mike Doss RC	1.50	.60
❑ 129	Seneca Wallace RC	1.50	.60
❑ 130	Chris Brown RC	1.50	.60
❑ 131	Larry Johnson RC	6.00	3.00
❑ 132	Taylor Jacobs RC	1.25	.50
❑ 133	Jerome McDougle RC	1.50	.60
❑ 134	Kelley Washington RC	1.50	.60
❑ 135	Brad Banks RC	1.25	.50
❑ 136	DeWayne White RC	1.25	.50
❑ 137	LaBrandon Toefield RC	1.50	.60
❑ 138	Brian St.Pierre RC	1.50	.60
❑ 139	Kindal Moorehead RC	1.25	.50
❑ 140	Willis McGahee RC	4.00	1.50
❑ 141	Jimmy Kennedy RC	1.50	.60
❑ 142	Talman Gardner RC	1.50	.60
❑ 143	Chris Kelsay RC	1.50	.60
❑ 144	Cory Redding RC	1.25	.50
❑ 145	Dave Ragone RC	1.50	.60
❑ 146	Earnest Graham RC	1.50	.60
❑ 147	Andre Johnson RC	3.00	1.00
❑ 148	Boss Bailey RC	1.50	.60
❑ 149	Sam Aiken RC	1.25	.50
❑ 150	Byron Leftwich RC	5.00	2.00
❑ 151	Teyo Johnson RC	1.50	.60
❑ 152	Quentin Griffin RC	1.50	.60
❑ 153	Justin Fargas RC	1.50	.60
❑ 154	Bradie James RC	1.50	.60
❑ [illegible]	[illegible]	[illegible]	[illegible]
❑ 156	Marcus Trufant RC	1.50	.60
❑ 157	Ken Dorsey RC	1.50	.60
❑ 158	Onterrio Smith RC	1.50	.60
❑ 159	Bryant Johnson RC	1.50	.60
❑ 160	Charles Rogers RC	1.50	.60
❑ 161	Kliff Kingsbury RC	1.25	.50
❑ 162	Michael Haynes RC	1.50	.60
❑ 163	Bennie Joppru RC	1.50	.60
❑ 164	Brandon Lloyd RC	1.50	.60
❑ 165	Jarret Johnson RC	1.25	.50

2004 Topps Draft Picks and Prospects

❑	COMPLETE SET (165)	80.00	40.00
❑ 1	Steve McNair	1.00	.40
❑ 2	Stephen Davis	.60	.25
❑ 3	Chris Chambers	.60	.25
❑ 4	Curtis Martin	1.00	.40
❑ 5	Shaun Alexander	1.00	.40
❑ 6	Jon Kitna	.60	.25
❑ 7	Jimmy Smith	.60	.25
❑ 8	Travis Henry	.60	.25
❑ 9	Torry Holt	1.00	.40
❑ 10	Jamal Lewis	1.00	.40
❑ 11	Clinton Portis	1.00	.40
❑ 12	Aaron Brooks	.60	.25
❑ 13	Plaxico Burress	.60	.25
❑ 14	Trent Green	.60	.25
❑ 15	Chad Johnson	1.00	.40
❑ 16	Jake Delhomme	1.00	.40
❑ 17	David Boston	.60	.25
❑ 18	Joe Horn	.60	.25
❑ 19	Ahman Green	1.00	.40
❑ 20	Fred Taylor	.60	.25
❑ 21	Terrell Owens	1.00	.40
❑ 22	Brad Johnson	.60	.25
❑ 23	Laveranues Coles	.60	.25
❑ 24	Ricky Williams	1.00	.40
❑ 25	Peyton Manning	1.50	.60
❑ 26	Hines Ward	1.00	.40
❑ 27	Matt Hasselbeck	.60	.25
❑ 28	Marshall Faulk	1.00	.40
❑ 29	Tony Gonzalez	.60	.25
❑ 30	Marvin Harrison	1.00	.40
❑ 31	Eric Moulds	.60	.25
❑ 32	Chad Pennington	1.00	.40
❑ 33	Jerry Porter	.60	.25
❑ 34	Jeff Garcia	1.00	.40
❑ 35	Derrick Mason	.60	.25
❑ 36	Anthony Thomas	.60	.25
❑ 37	Drew Bledsoe	1.00	.40
❑ 38	Jake Plummer	.60	.25
❑ 39	Tiki Barber	1.00	.40
❑ 40	Brett Favre	2.50	1.00
❑ 41	Joey Harrington	1.00	.40
❑ 42	Daunte Culpepper	1.00	.40
❑ 43	LaVar Arrington	2.00	.75
❑ 44	Santana Moss	.60	.25
❑ 45	David Carr	1.00	.40
❑ 46	Randy Moss	1.25	.50
❑ 47	LaDainian Tomlinson	1.25	.50
❑ 48	Deuce McAllister	1.00	.40
❑ 49	Amani Toomer	.60	.25
❑ 50	Donovan McNabb	1.25	.50
❑ 51	Priest Holmes	1.25	.50
❑ [illegible]	[illegible]	[illegible]	[illegible]
❑ 53	Tom Brady	2.50	1.00
❑ 54	Edgerrin James	1.00	.40
❑ 55	Michael Vick	2.00	.75
❑ 56	Anquan Boldin	1.00	.40
❑ 57	Robert Ferguson	.40	.15
❑ 58	Onterrio Smith	.60	.25
❑ 59	Marques Tuiasosopo	.60	.25
❑ 60	Rudi Johnson	.60	.25
❑ 61	Alge Crumpler	.60	.25
❑ 62	Antonio Bryant	.60	.25
❑ 63	LaMont Jordan	1.00	.40
❑ 64	Lamar Gordon	.40	.15
❑ 65	Tim Rattay	.40	.15
❑ 66	Antwaan Randle El	1.00	.40
❑ 67	Ladell Betts	.40	.15
❑ 68	LaBrandon Toefield	.40	.15
❑ 69	Ashley Lelie	.60	.25
❑ 70	Marc Bulger	1.00	.40
❑ 71	Reggie Wayne	.60	.25
❑ 72	William Green	.60	.25
❑ 73	Josh Reed	.40	.15
❑ 74	T.J. Duckett	.60	.25
❑ 75	Andre Johnson	1.00	.40
❑ 76	Deion Branch	1.00	.40
❑ 77	Tyrone Calico	.60	.25
❑ 78	Jeremy Shockey	1.00	.40
❑ 79	Najeh Davenport	.40	.15
❑ 80	Byron Leftwich	1.25	.50
❑ 81	Correll Buckhalter	.60	.25
❑ 82	Justin McCareins	.40	.15
❑ 83	Carson Palmer	1.25	.50
❑ 84	Bryant Johnson	.40	.15
❑ 85	Patrick Ramsey	.60	.25
❑ 86	Justin Fargas	.60	.25
❑ 87	Dallas Clark	.60	.25
❑ 88	Kelly Campbell	.40	.15
❑ 89	DeShaun Foster	.60	.25
❑ 90	Charles Rogers	.60	.25
❑ 91	Donte' Stallworth	.60	.25
❑ 92	Dante Hall	1.00	.40
❑ 93	Randy McMichael	.40	.15
❑ 94	Marcel Shipp	.60	.25
❑ 95	Kyle Boller	1.00	.40
❑ 96	Steve Smith	1.00	.40
❑ 97	Brian Westbrook	.60	.25
❑ 98	Kevan Barlow	.60	.25
❑ 99	Darnerien McCants	.40	.15
❑ 100	Domanick Davis	1.00	.40
❑ 101	Andre' Davis	.40	.15
❑ 102	Nate Burleson	1.00	.40
❑ 103	Larry Johnson	1.25	.50
❑ 104	Drew Brees	1.00	.40
❑ 105	Koren Robinson	.60	.25
❑ 106	Quincy Carter	.60	.25
❑ 107	Javon Walker	.60	.25
❑ 108	Willis McGahee	1.00	.40
❑ 109	Chris Simms	.60	.25
❑ 110	Rex Grossman	1.00	.40
❑ 111	Steven Jackson RC	6.00	2.50
❑ 112	Greg Jones RC	2.00	.75
❑ 113	Brandon Everage RC	1.50	.60
❑ 114	DeAngelo Hall RC	2.50	1.00
❑ 115	Tatum Bell RC	4.00	1.50
❑ 116	B.J. Symons RC	2.00	.75
❑ 117	Michael Clayton RC	4.00	1.50
❑ 118	Jared Lorenzen RC	1.50	.60
❑ 119	Josh Harris RC	2.00	.75
❑ 120	Roy Williams RC	5.00	2.00
❑ 121	Mewelde Moore RC	2.00	.75
❑ 122	Jeff Smoker RC	2.00	.75

❑ 123 Lee Evans RC 2.50 1.00
❑ 124 Michael Jenkins RC 2.00 .75
❑ 125 Drew Henson RC 2.00 .75
❑ 126 Ben Watson RC 2.00 .75
❑ 127 Jerricho Cotchery RC 2.00 .75
❑ 128 Ben Troupe RC 2.00 .75
❑ 129 Chris Gamble RC 2.00 .75
❑ 130 Kevin Jones RC 5.00 2.00
❑ 131 Cody Pickett RC 2.00 .75
❑ 132 J.P. Losman RC 4.00 1.50
❑ 133 Michael Boulware RC 2.00 .75
❑ 134 Julius Jones RC 6.00 2.50
❑ 135 Keary Colbert RC 2.00 .75
❑ 136 Vince Wilfork RC 2.00 .75
❑ 137 Ernest Wilford RC 2.00 .75
❑ 138 John Navarre RC 2.00 .75
❑ 139 D.J. Williams RC 2.00 .75
❑ 140 Larry Fitzgerald RC 6.00 2.50
❑ 141 Quincy Wilson RC 1.50 .60
❑ 142 James Newson RC 1.50 .60
❑ 143 Reggie Williams RC 2.50 1.00
❑ 144 Devard Darling RC 2.00 .75
❑ 145 Chris Perry RC 2.50 1.00
❑ 146 Derrick Strait RC 2.00 .75
❑ 147 Teddy Lehman RC 2.00 .75
❑ 148 Michael Turner RC 2.50 1.00
❑ 149 Will Smith RC 2.00 .75
❑ 150 Eli Manning RC 15.00 6.00
❑ 151 Cedric Cobbs RC 2.00 .75
❑ 152 Ell Roberson UER RC 2.00 .75
❑ 153 Matt Schaub RC 6.00 2.50
❑ 154 Derrick Knight RC 1.50 .60
❑ 155 Rashaun Woods RC 2.00 .75
❑ 156 Jonathan Vilma RC 2.00 .75
❑ 157 Tommie Harris RC 2.00 .75
❑ 158 Dwan Edwards RC 1.50 .60
❑ 159 Will Poole RC 2.00 .75
❑ 160 Mike Williams RC 6.00 2.50
❑ 161 Philip Rivers RC 6.00 2.50
❑ 162 Sean Taylor RC 2.00 .75
❑ 163 Darius Watts RC 2.00 .75
❑ 164 Casey Clausen RC 2.00 .75
❑ 165 Ben Roethlisberger RC 20.00 10.00

2005 Topps Draft Picks and Prospects

❑ COMP.SET w/o AU's (165) 40.00 15.00
❑ COMP.SET w/o RC's (110) 25.00 10.00
❑ ONE ROOKIE PER PACK
❑ DRAFT PICK AUTO ODDS 1:1179H, 1:1182R
❑ UNPRICED GOLD SUPERFRACTORS #'d TO 1
❑ UNPRICED PRINTING PLATES #'d TO 1
❑ 1 Marvin Harrison 1.00 .40
❑ 2 Rudi Johnson .60 .25
❑ 3 Matt Hasselbeck .60 .25
❑ 4 Plaxico Burress .60 .25
❑ 5 Chad Pennington 1.00 .40
❑ 6 Jamal Lewis 1.00 .40
❑ 7 Terrell Owens 1.00 .40
❑ 8 LaDainian Tomlinson 1.25 .50
❑ 9 Tiki Barber 1.00 .40
❑ 10 Dante Hall .60 .25
❑ 11 Peyton Manning 1.50 .60
❑ 12 Marshall Faulk 1.00 .40
❑ 13 Donovan McNabb 1.25 .50
❑ 14 Randy Moss 1.00 .40
❑ 15 Muhsin Muhammad .60 .25
❑ 16 Deuce McAllister 1.00 .40
❑ 17 Fred Taylor .60 .25
❑ 18 Jake Plummer .60 .25
❑ 19 Javon Walker .60 .25
❑ 20 Tony Gonzalez .60 .25
❑ 21 Michael Vick 1.50 .60
❑ 22 Brett Favre 2.50 1.00
❑ 23 Joe Horn .60 .25
❑ 24 Jeremy Shockey 1.00 .40
❑ 25 Laveranues Coles .60 .25
❑ 26 Trent Green .60 .25
❑ 27 Alge Crumpler .60 .25
❑ 28 Curtis Martin 1.00 .40
❑ 29 Torry Holt 1.00 .40
❑ 30 Daunte Culpepper 1.00 .40
❑ 31 Aaron Brooks .60 .25
❑ 32 Priest Holmes 1.00 .40
❑ 33 Eric Moulds .60 .25
❑ 34 Jerome Bettis 1.00 .40
❑ 35 David Carr 1.00 .40
❑ 36 Chad Johnson 1.00 .40
❑ 37 Ahman Green 1.00 .40
❑ 38 Clinton Portis 1.00 .40
❑ 39 Drew Brees 1.00 .40
❑ 40 Darrell Jackson .60 .25
❑ 41 Corey Dillon .60 .25
❑ 42 Reggie Wayne .60 .25
❑ 43 Shaun Alexander 1.25 .50
❑ 44 Hines Ward 1.00 .40
❑ 45 Tom Brady 2.50 1.00
❑ 46 Isaac Bruce .60 .25
❑ 47 Byron Leftwich 1.00 .40
❑ 48 Chris Chambers .60 .25
❑ 49 Marc Bulger 1.00 .40
❑ 50 Edgerrin James 1.00 .40
❑ 51 Jake Delhomme 1.00 .40
❑ 52 Koren Robinson .60 .25
❑ 53 Brian Westbrook .60 .25
❑ 54 Reuben Droughns .60 .25
❑ 55 Joey Harrington 1.00 .40
❑ 56 Eli Manning 2.00 .75
❑ 57 Julius Jones 1.25 .50
❑ 58 Nick Goings .50 .20
❑ 59 T.J. Houshmandzadeh .50 .20
❑ 60 Ben Roethlisberger 2.50 1.00
❑ 61 Charles Rogers .60 .25
❑ 62 Billy Volek .60 .25
❑ 63 Drew Henson .60 .25
❑ 64 Andre Johnson .60 .25
❑ 65 Carson Palmer 1.00 .40
❑ 66 Anquan Boldin .60 .25
❑ 67 Lee Suggs .60 .25
❑ 68 Jerry Porter .60 .25
❑ 69 J.P. Losman 1.00 .40
❑ 70 Nate Burleson .60 .25
❑ 71 Lee Evans .60 .25
❑ 72 Tatum Bell .60 .25
❑ 73 Chester Taylor .60 .25
❑ 74 Philip Rivers 1.00 .40
❑ 75 Rex Grossman .60 .25
❑ 76 Willis McGahee 1.00 .40
❑ 77 Antonio Gates 1.00 .40
❑ 78 Steven Jackson 1.25 .50
❑ 79 Roy Williams WR 1.00 .40
❑ 80 Chris Simms .60 .25
❑ 81 Najeh Davenport .50 .20
❑ 82 Kevin Jones 1.00 .40
❑ 83 Jason Witten .60 .25
❑ 84 Brandon Lloyd .50 .20
❑ 85 Larry Johnson 1.00 .40
❑ 86 Ronald Curry .60 .25
❑ 87 Chris Brown .60 .25
❑ 88 Kyle Boller .60 .25
❑ 89 Chris Perry .60 .25
❑ 90 Keary Colbert .60 .25
❑ 91 Sean Taylor .60 .25
❑ 92 Greg Jones .50 .20
❑ 93 Larry Fitzgerald 1.00 .40
❑ 94 Michael Clayton 1.00 .40
❑ 95 Mewelde Moore .60 .25
❑ 96 Drew Bennett .60 .25
❑ 97 Reggie Williams .60 .25
❑ 98 Quentin Griffin .60 .25
❑ 99 Josh McCown .60 .25
❑ 100 Santana Moss .60 .25
❑ 101 Kellen Winslow 1.00 .40
❑ 102 Michael Jenkins .60 .25
❑ 103 Dunta Robinson .60 .25
❑ 104 Luke McCown .50 .20
❑ 105 Brandon Stokley .60 .25
❑ 106 Derrick Blaylock .50 .20
❑ 107 Ernest Wilford .50 .20
❑ 108 Domanick Davis .60 .25
❑ 109 Jonathan Vilma .60 .25
❑ 110 Dwight Freeney .60 .25
❑ 111 Alex Smith QB AU RC 120.00 60.00
❑ 112 Derrick Johnson AU RC 120.00 60.00
❑ 113 Charlie Frye AU RC 50.00 20.00
❑ 114 Ronnie Brown AU RC 120.00 60.00
❑ 115 Mike Williams AU 50.00 20.00
❑ 116 Erasmus James RC 2.00 .75
❑ 117 Alex Smith TE RC 2.00 .75
❑ 118 Dan Orlovsky RC 2.00 .75
❑ 119 Eric Shelton RC 2.00 .75
❑ 120 Reggie Brown RC 2.00 .75
❑ 121 Carlos Rogers RC 2.50 1.00
❑ 122 Dan Cody RC 2.00 .75
❑ 123 J.J. Arrington RC 2.00 .75
❑ 124 Travis Johnson RC 1.50 .60
❑ 125 Antrel Rolle RC 2.00 .75
❑ 126 Andrew Walter RC 2.00 .75
❑ 127 Craphonso Thorpe RC 1.50 .60
❑ 128 Bryan Randall RC 1.50 .60
❑ 129 Anttaj Hawthorne RC 1.50 .60
❑ 130 David Pollack RC 2.00 .75
❑ 131 Heath Miller RC 4.00 1.50
❑ 132 Charles Frederick RC 1.50 .60
❑ 133 Anthony Davis RC 1.50 .60
❑ 134 Chris Rix RC 1.50 .60
❑ 135 T.A. McLendon RC 1.50 .60
❑ 136 David Greene RC 2.00 .75
❑ 137 Timmy Chang RC 1.50 .60
❑ 138 Marcus Spears RC 2.00 .75
❑ 139 Airese Currie RC 2.00 .75
❑ 140 Chris Henry RC 2.00 .75
❑ 141 Josh Davis RC 1.50 .60
❑ 142 Jason Campbell RC 3.00 1.25
❑ 143 Barrett Ruud RC 2.00 .75
❑ 144 Courtney Roby RC 2.00 .75
❑ 145 Mike Patterson RC 2.00 .75
❑ 146 Jason White RC 2.00 .75
❑ 147 Fred Gibson RC 1.50 .60
❑ 148 Marion Barber RC 3.00 1.25
❑ 149 Braylon Edwards RC 6.00 2.50
❑ 150 Cadillac Williams RC 10.00 4.00
❑ 151 Kyle Orton RC 2.00 .75
❑ 152 Aaron Rodgers RC 6.00 2.50
❑ 153 Alvin Pearman RC 2.00 .75
❑ 154 Stefan LeFors RC 2.00 .75
❑ 155 Marlin Jackson RC 2.00 .75
❑ 156 Taylor Stubblefield RC 1.50 .60
❑ 157 Ciatrick Fason RC 2.00 .75
❑ 158 Kay-Jay Harris RC 1.50 .60
❑ 159 Frank Gore RC 4.00 1.50
❑ 160 Vernand Morency RC 2.00 .75
❑ 161 Adam Jones RC 2.00 .75
❑ 162 Troy Williamson RC 2.00 .75
❑ 163 Roddy White RC 2.00 .75
❑ 164 Thomas Davis RC 2.00 .75
❑ 165 Mark Clayton RC 2.00 .75
❑ 166 Craig Bragg RC 1.50 .60
❑ 167 Noah Herron RC 2.00 .75
❑ 168 Darren Sproles RC 2.00 .75
❑ 169 Terrence Murphy RC 2.00 .75
❑ 170 Walter Reyes RC 1.50 .60

2006 Topps Draft Picks and Prospects

❑ COMP.SET w/o SP's (165) 30.00 12.50
❑ COMP.SET w/o RC's (110) 15.00 6.00
❑ ONE ROOKIE CARD PER PACK
❑ 166-175 ROOKIE AU/100 ODDS 1:1282
❑ 1 Plaxico Burress .60 .25
❑ 2 Ahman Green .60 .25
❑ 3 Domanick Davis .60 .25
❑ 4 Andre Johnson .60 .25
❑ 5 Donovan McNabb 1.00 .40

❑ 6 Marvin Harrison 1.00 .40
❑ 7 Michael Vick 1.00 .40
❑ 8 Priest Holmes .60 .25
❑ 9 Torry Holt .60 .25
❑ 10 Marc Bulger .60 .25
❑ 11 Ben Roethlisberger 1.50 .60
❑ 12 Larry Fitzgerald 1.00 .40
❑ 13 Peyton Manning 1.50 .60
❑ 14 Chris Perry .60 .25
❑ 15 Antonio Gates 1.00 .40
❑ 16 Eli Manning 1.25 .50
❑ 17 Brett Favre 2.00 .75
❑ 18 Reggie Brown .75 .30
❑ 19 Curtis Martin 1.00 .40
❑ 20 Charlie Frye .60 .25
❑ 21 Tom Brady 1.50 .60
❑ 22 Cadillac Williams 1.00 .40
❑ 23 Trent Green .60 .25
❑ 24 Matt Jones .60 .25
❑ 25 Anquan Boldin .60 .25
❑ 26 Larry Johnson 1.25 .50
❑ 27 Rudi Johnson .60 .25
❑ 28 Marion Barber .60 .25
❑ 29 Jake Delhomme .60 .25
❑ 30 Philip Rivers 1.00 .40
❑ 31 Fred Taylor .60 .25
❑ 32 Frank Gore 1.00 .40
❑ 33 Shaun Alexander 1.00 .40
❑ 34 Chris Simms .60 .25
❑ 35 LaDainian Tomlinson 1.25 .50
❑ 36 Troy Williamson .60 .25
❑ 37 Clinton Portis 1.00 .40
❑ 38 Kyle Orton .60 .25
❑ 39 Tony Gonzalez .60 .25
❑ 40 Mark Clayton 1.00 .40
❑ 41 Steve Smith 1.00 .40
❑ 42 Heath Miller .60 .25
❑ 43 Warrick Dunn .60 .25
❑ 44 Alex Smith TE .50 .20
❑ 45 Chris Brown .60 .25
❑ 46 Billy Volek .60 .25
❑ 47 Tiki Barber 1.00 .40
❑ 48 Julius Jones 1.00 .40
❑ 49 Drew Bledsoe 1.00 .40
❑ 50 Charles Rogers .60 .25
❑ 51 Jake Plummer .60 .25
❑ 52 Greg Jones .50 .20
❑ 53 Chad Johnson .60 .25
❑ 54 Braylon Edwards 1.00 .40
❑ 55 Carson Palmer 1.00 .40
❑ 56 Scottie Vines .50 .20
❑ 57 Keary Colbert .50 .20
❑ 58 Alex Smith QB 1.00 .40
❑ 59 Roy Williams WR 1.00 .40
❑ 60 Roddy White .60 .25
❑ 61 Willis McGahee 1.00 .40
❑ 62 Michael Clayton .60 .25
❑ 63 Edgerrin James 1.00 .40
❑ 64 Aaron Rodgers 1.00 .40
❑ 65 Byron Leftwich .60 .25
❑ 66 Tatum Bell .60 .25
❑ 67 Daunte Culpepper 1.00 .40
❑ 68 Chris Henry .50 .20
❑ 69 Corey Dillon .60 .25
❑ 70 Ronnie Brown 1.00 .40
❑ 71 Kevin Jones 1.00 .40
❑ 72 J.P. Losman .60 .25
❑ 73 Steven Jackson 1.00 .40
❑ 74 Mike Williams 1.00 .40
❑ 75 Jeremy Shockey 1.00 .40
❑ 76 DeMarcus Ware .60 .25
❑ 77 LaMont Jordan .60 .25
❑ 78 Cedric Benson 1.00 .40
❑ 79 Ricky Williams .60 .25
❑ 80 Brandon Jones .50 .20
❑ 81 Brian Westbrook .60 .25
❑ 82 Willie Parker 1.25 .50
❑ 83 Hines Ward 1.00 .40
❑ 84 Ernest Wilford .50 .20
❑ 85 Matt Hasselbeck .60 .25
❑ [illegible]
❑ 87 Joey Galloway .60 .25
❑ 88 Odell Thurman .50 .20
❑ 89 Santana Moss .60 .25
❑ 90 Courtney Roby .50 .20
❑ 91 Deuce McAllister .60 .25
❑ 92 Derrick Johnson .60 .25
❑ 93 Drew Brees 1.00 .40
❑ 94 Michael Jenkins .60 .25
❑ 95 Jerome Bettis 1.00 .40
❑ 96 Osi Umenyiora .50 .20
❑ 97 Reggie Wayne .60 .25
❑ 98 Ryan Moats .50 .20
❑ 99 Randy Moss 1.00 .40
❑ 100 Samie Parker .50 .20
❑ 101 Mark Bradley .60 .25
❑ 102 Samkon Gado .60 .25
❑ 103 Matt Schaub .60 .25
❑ 104 Shaun McDonald .50 .20
❑ 105 D.J. Hackett .50 .20
❑ 106 Mewelde Moore .50 .20
❑ 107 Chester Taylor .60 .25
❑ 108 Greg Lewis .50 .20
❑ 109 Chris Cooley .50 .20
❑ 110 Todd DeVoe RC 1.00 .40
❑ 111 Joel Klopfenstein RC 2.00 .75
❑ 112 Devin Hester RC 5.00 2.00
❑ 113 Brad Smith RC 2.50 1.00
❑ 114 Jason Avant RC 2.50 1.00
❑ 115 Michael Robinson RC 2.50 1.00
❑ 116 Kellen Clemens RC 4.00 1.50
❑ 117 Anthony Fasano RC 2.50 1.00
❑ 118 Leon Washington RC 4.00 1.50
❑ 119 Laurence Maroney RC 6.00 2.50
❑ 120 Martin Nance RC 2.00 .75
❑ 121 Demetrius Williams RC 2.50 1.00
❑ 122 A.J. Nicholson RC 1.25 .50
❑ 123 Jimmy Williams RC 2.50 1.00
❑ 124 Michael Huff RC 3.00 1.25
❑ 125 Chad Jackson RC 2.50 1.00
❑ 126 Mike Hass RC 2.50 1.00
❑ 127 Brodie Croyle RC 6.00 2.50
❑ 128 Jerome Harrison RC 2.50 1.00
❑ 129 Hank Baskett RC 2.50 1.00
❑ 130 Santonio Holmes RC 5.00 2.00
❑ 131 Chad Greenway RC 2.50 1.00
❑ 132 Mario Williams RC 4.00 1.50
❑ 133 Charlie Whitehurst RC 2.50 1.00
❑ 134 Darrell Hackney RC 2.00 .75
❑ 135 DeMeco Ryans RC 3.00 1.25
❑ 136 Mathias Kiwanuka RC 3.00 1.25
❑ 137 Omar Jacobs RC 2.00 .75
❑ 138 Bruce Gradkowski RC 4.00 1.50
❑ 139 Drew Olson RC 2.00 .75
❑ 140 Maurice Stovall RC 2.50 1.00
❑ 141 Greg Jennings RC 4.00 1.50
❑ 142 D'Brickashaw Ferguson RC 2.50 1.00
❑ 143 Manny Lawson RC 2.50 1.00
❑ 144 Tamba Hali RC 2.50 1.00
❑ 145 Vernon Davis RC 5.00 2.00
❑ 146 Greg Lee RC 2.00 .75
❑ 147 Dominique Byrd RC 2.00 .75
❑ 148 Leonard Pope RC 2.50 1.00
❑ 149 Bobby Carpenter RC 2.50 1.00
❑ 150 Haloti Ngata RC 2.50 1.00
❑ 151 Marcedes Lewis RC 2.50 1.00
❑ 152 Ernie Sims RC 3.00 1.25
❑ 153 Ashton Youboty RC 2.50 1.00
❑ 154 D.J. Shockley RC 2.50 1.00
❑ 155 Paul Pinegar RC 2.00 .75
❑ 156 Maurice Drew RC 6.00 2.50
❑ 157 Jeremy Bloom RC 2.00 .75
❑ 158 Cory Rodgers RC 2.50 1.00
❑ 159 Abdul Hodge RC 2.50 1.00
❑ 160 Tye Hill RC 2.50 1.00
❑ 161 D'Qwell Jackson RC 2.00 .75
❑ 162 Jonathan Orr RC 2.00 .75
❑ 163 Antonio Cromartie RC 2.50 1.00
❑ 164 Todd Watkins RC 2.00 .75
❑ 165 Gerald Riggs RC 2.50 1.00
❑ 166 Matt Leinart AU RC 150.00 75.00
❑ 167 Reggie Bush AU RC 250.00 125.00
❑ 168 DeAngelo Williams AU RC 120.00 60.00
❑ 169 A.J. Hawk AU RC 125.00 75.00
❑ 170 Vince Young AU RC 200.00 100.00
❑ 171 Derek Hagan AU RC 50.00 25.00
❑ 172 Joseph Addai AU RC 135.00 75.00
❑ 173 Jay Cutler AU RC 150.00 75.00
❑ 174 Sinorice Moss AU RC 50.00 25.00
❑ 175 LenDale White AU RC 80.00 40.00
❑ RBML R.Bush/Leinart AU/25 300.00 150.00

2007 Topps Draft Picks and Prospects

❑ 1 Donovan McNabb 1.00 .40
❑ 2 Larry Johnson 1.00 .40
❑ 3 Willis McGahee .75 .30
❑ 4 Tom Brady 2.00 .75
❑ 5 Anquan Boldin .75 .30
❑ 6 Steve Smith .75 .30
❑ 7 Philip Rivers 1.00 .40
❑ 8 LaDainian Tomlinson 1.25 .50
❑ 9 Reuben Droughns .75 .30
❑ 10 Julius Jones .75 .30
❑ 11 Drew Brees .75 .30
❑ 12 Chad Johnson .75 .30
❑ 13 Ronnie Brown .75 .30
❑ 14 Brett Favre 2.00 .75
❑ 15 J.P. Losman .75 .30
❑ 16 Clinton Portis .75 .30
❑ 17 Edgerrin James 1.00 .40
❑ 18 Andre Johnson .75 .30
❑ 19 Fred Taylor .75 .30
❑ 20 Marc Bulger .75 .30
❑ 21 Peyton Manning 1.50 .60
❑ 22 Reggie Wayne .75 .30
❑ 23 Hines Ward 1.00 .40
❑ 24 Michael Vick 1.00 .40
❑ 25 Santana Moss .75 .30
❑ 26 Torry Holt .75 .30
❑ 27 Jake Delhomme .75 .30
❑ 28 Brian Westbrook .75 .30
❑ 29 Tony Gonzalez .75 .30
❑ 30 Larry Fitzgerald .75 .30
❑ 31 Matt Hasselbeck .75 .30
❑ 32 Kevin Jones .60 .25
❑ 33 Willie Parker 1.00 .40
❑ 34 Jeremy Shockey .75 .30
❑ 35 Marvin Harrison 1.00 .40
❑ 36 Warrick Dunn .75 .30
❑ 37 Ahman Green .75 .30
❑ 38 Ben Roethlisberger 1.25 .50
❑ 39 Randy Moss 1.00 .40
❑ 40 Rudi Johnson .75 .30
❑ 41 Carson Palmer 1.00 .40
❑ 42 Trent Green .75 .30
❑ 43 Plaxico Burress .75 .30

❑ 44 Steven Jackson 1.00 .40
❑ 45 Deuce McAllister .75 .30
❑ 46 Antonio Gates .75 .30
❑ 47 Cadillac Williams .75 .30
❑ 48 Eli Manning 1.00 .40
❑ 49 Rex Grossman .75 .30
❑ 50 Shaun Alexander .75 .30
❑ 51 DeAngelo Williams 1.00 .40
❑ 52 Joseph Addai 1.25 .50
❑ 53 Vince Young 1.25 .50
❑ 54 Matt Leinart 1.00 .40
❑ 55 Sinorice Moss .75 .30
❑ 56 Matt Jones .75 .30
❑ 57 Tony Romo 2.00 .75
❑ 58 Jay Cutler 1.00 .40
❑ 59 Marques Colston 1.00 .40
❑ 60 Vernon Davis .75 .30
❑ 61 Cedric Benson .75 .30
❑ 62 Mario Williams .75 .30
❑ 63 Hank Baskett .75 .30
❑ 64 Alex Smith QB 1.00 .40
❑ 65 Jason Campbell .75 .30
❑ 66 Mike Furrey .75 .30
❑ 67 Greg Jennings .75 .30
❑ 68 Laurence Maroney 1.00 .40
❑ 69 Charlie Frye .75 .30
❑ 70 Michael Robinson .75 .30
❑ 71 Michael Huff .75 .30
❑ 72 A.J. Hawk 1.00 .40
❑ 73 Marion Barber .75 .30
❑ 74 Santonio Holmes .75 .30
❑ 75 Kellen Winslow .75 .30
❑ 76 Reggie Bush 1.25 .50
❑ 77 Charlie Whitehurst .60 .25
❑ 78 Brad Smith .60 .25
❑ 79 Leon Washington .75 .30
❑ 80 Wali Lundy .60 .25
❑ 81 Owen Daniels .60 .25
❑ 82 Devin Hester 1.00 .40
❑ 83 Chad Jackson .60 .25
❑ 84 Braylon Edwards .75 .30
❑ 85 Bruce Gradkowski .75 .30
❑ 86 Tarvaris Jackson 1.00 .40
❑ 87 Derek Hagan .60 .25
❑ 88 Mike Bell .75 .30
❑ 89 Frank Gore 1.00 .40
❑ 90 LenDale White .75 .30
❑ 91 Chris Henry .60 .25
❑ 92 Kellen Clemens .75 .30
❑ 93 Nate Washington .60 .25
❑ 94 Jerious Norwood .75 .30
❑ 95 Maurice Jones-Drew 1.00 .40
❑ 96 Mark Clayton .75 .30
❑ 97 Jason Avant .60 .25
❑ 98 Mathias Kiwanuka .60 .25
❑ 99 Brandon Jacobs .75 .30
❑ 100 Chris Cooley .60 .25
❑ 101 Brady Quinn RC 8.00 3.00
❑ 102 Michael Bush RC 3.00 1.25
❑ 103 Leon Hall RC 2.00 .75
❑ 104 Jason Hill RC 2.50 1.00
❑ 105 Patrick Willis RC 5.00 2.00
❑ 106 Brian Leonard RC 3.00 1.25
❑ 107 Gaines Adams RC 2.50 1.00
❑ 108 Kenneth Darby RC 2.50 1.00
❑ 109 Marcus McCauley RC 2.00 .75
❑ 110 Paul Posluszny RC 3.00 1.25
❑ 111 Drew Stanton RC 3.00 1.25
❑ 112 Troy Smith RC 3.00 1.25
❑ 113 Garrett Wolfe RC 3.00 1.25
❑ 114 Chris Leak RC 2.00 .75
❑ 115 Joe Thomas RC 2.50 1.00
❑ 116 Paul Williams RC 2.00 .75
❑ 117 LaRon Landry RC 3.00 1.25
❑ 118 Aundrae Allison RC 2.00 .75
❑ 119 Kenny Irons RC 2.50 1.00
❑ 120 Kevin Kolb RC 4.00 1.50
❑ 121 Tyler Palko RC 2.50 1.00
❑ 122 Steve Smith USC RC 3.00 1.25
❑ 123 Steve Breaston RC 2.00 .75
❑ 124 Tyrone Moss RC 1.50 .60
❑ 125 LaMarr Woodley RC 2.50 1.00
❑ 126 Brandon Meriweather RC 2.50 1.00
❑ 127 Rhema McKnight RC 2.00 .75
❑ 128 Daymeion Hughes RC 2.00 .75
❑ 129 Jared Zabransky RC 2.50 1.00
❑ 130 Chansi Stuckey RC 2.00 .75
❑ 131 Amobi Okoye RC 2.50 1.00
❑ 132 Calvin Johnson RC 8.00 3.00
❑ 133 Marshawn Lynch RC 5.00 2.00
❑ 134 Ted Ginn Jr. RC 4.00 1.50
❑ 135 Adrian Peterson RC 20.00 8.00
❑ 136 Dwayne Jarrett RC 3.00 1.25
❑ 137 Greg Olsen RC 3.00 1.25
❑ 138 Adam Carriker RC 2.00 .75
❑ 139 Darius Walker RC 2.50 1.00
❑ 140 Robert Meachem RC 2.50 1.00
❑ 141 Jordan Palmer RC 2.50 1.00
❑ 142 JaMarcus Russell RC 6.00 2.50
❑ 143 DeShawn Wynn RC 2.50 1.00
❑ 144 Zach Miller RC 2.50 1.00
❑ 145 Lorenzo Booker RC 2.50 1.00
❑ 146 Selvin Young RC 3.00 1.25
❑ 147 Courtney Lewis RC 2.00 .75
❑ 148 Tony Hunt RC 2.50 1.00
❑ 149 Dwayne Bowe RC 5.00 2.00
❑ 150 Aaron Ross RC 2.50 1.00
❑ 151 Antonio Pittman RC 2.00 .75
❑ 152 Anthony Gonzalez RC 4.00 1.50
❑ 153 John Beck RC 5.00 2.00
❑ 154 Sidney Rice RC 4.00 1.50
❑ 155 Lawrence Timmons RC 2.50 1.00

2001 Topps Heritage

❑ COMPLETE SET (146) 300.00 150.00
❑ COMP.SET w/o SP's (110) 25.00 10.00
❑ 1 Ray Lewis 1.25 .50
❑ 2 Peter Warrick 1.25 .50
❑ 3 James Stewart .75 .30
❑ 4 Junior Seau 1.25 .50
❑ 5 Jeff George .75 .30
❑ 6 Amani Toomer .50 .20
❑ 7 Elvis Grbac .75 .30
❑ 8 David Boston 1.25 .50
❑ 9 Jimmy Smith .75 .30
❑ 10 Warrick Dunn 1.25 .50
❑ 11 Hines Ward 1.25 .50
❑ 12 Joe Horn .75 .30
❑ 13 Stephen Davis 1.25 .50
❑ 14 Tyrone Wheatley .75 .30
❑ 15 Brian Urlacher 2.00 .75
❑ 16 Fred Taylor 1.25 .50
❑ 17 Jerry Rice 2.50 1.00
❑ 18 Keyshawn Johnson 1.25 .50
❑ 19 Jay Fiedler 1.25 .50
❑ 20 Jamal Anderson 1.25 .50
❑ 21 Emmitt Smith 2.50 1.00
❑ 22 Tiki Barber 1.25 .50
❑ 23 Daunte Culpepper 1.25 .50
❑ 24 Torry Holt 1.25 .50
❑ 25 Peyton Manning 3.00 1.25
❑ 26 Eddie George 1.25 .50
❑ 27 Jamal Lewis 2.00 .75
❑ 28 Ricky Williams 1.25 .50
❑ 29 Ahman Green 1.25 .50
❑ 30 Ed McCaffrey 1.25 .50
❑ 31 Curtis Martin 1.25 .50
❑ 32 Isaac Bruce 1.25 .50
❑ 33 Doug Flutie 1.25 .50
❑ 34 Steve McNair 1.25 .50
❑ 35 Donovan McNabb 1.50 .60
❑ 36 Keenan McCardell .50 .20
❑ 37 Charlie Batch 1.25 .50
❑ 38 Cade McNown .50 .20
❑ 39 Terrell Owens 1.25 .50
❑ 40 Brad Johnson 1.25 .50
❑ 41 Robert Smith 1.25 .50
❑ 42 Muhsin Muhammad .75 .30
❑ 43 Kurt Warner 2.50 1.00
❑ 44 Lamar Smith .75 .30
❑ 45 Brian Griese 1.25 .50
❑ 46 Trent Dilfer .75 .30
❑ 47 Jeff Garcia 1.25 .50
❑ 48 Derrick Mason .75 .30
❑ 49 Drew Bledsoe 1.50 .60
❑ 50 Marshall Faulk 1.50 .60
❑ 51 Corey Dillon 1.25 .50
❑ 52 Tony Gonzalez .75 .30
❑ 53 Chad Lewis .50 .20
❑ 54 Shaun Alexander 1.50 .60
❑ 55 Edgerrin James 1.50 .60
❑ 56 Eric Moulds .75 .30
❑ 57 Aaron Brooks 1.25 .50
❑ 58 Zach Thomas 1.25 .50
❑ 59 Jerome Bettis 1.25 .50
❑ 60 Shannon Sharpe .75 .30
❑ 61 Kerry Collins .75 .30
❑ 62 Ricky Watters .75 .30
❑ 63 Tim Couch .75 .30
❑ 64 Marvin Harrison 1.25 .50
❑ 65 Tim Brown 1.25 .50
❑ 66 Mark Brunell 1.25 .50
❑ 67 Wayne Chrebet .75 .30
❑ 68 Terry Glenn .75 .30
❑ 69 Mike Anderson 1.25 .50
❑ 70 Randy Moss 2.50 1.00
❑ 71 Freddie Jones .50 .20
❑ 72 Ike Hilliard .75 .30
❑ 73 Derrick Alexander .75 .30
❑ 74 Travis Prentice .50 .20
❑ 75 Brett Favre 4.00 1.50
❑ 76 Rod Smith .75 .30
❑ 77 Troy Aikman 2.00 .75
❑ 78 Cris Carter 1.25 .50
❑ 79 Rich Gannon 1.25 .50
❑ 80 Charlie Garner .75 .30
❑ 81 Michael Pittman .50 .20
❑ 82 Jeff Graham .50 .20
❑ 83 Albert Connell .50 .20
❑ 84 Bill Schroeder .75 .30
❑ 85 Jeff Blake .75 .30
❑ 86 Jon Kitna 1.25 .50
❑ 87 Qadry Ismail .75 .30
❑ 88 Joey Galloway .75 .30
❑ 89 Charles Johnson .50 .20
❑ 90 Troy Brown .75 .30
❑ 91 Johnnie Morton .75 .30
❑ 92 Chris Chandler .75 .30
❑ 93 Donald Hayes .50 .20
❑ 94 Shaun King .50 .20
❑ 95 Vinny Testaverde .75 .30
❑ 96 James Allen .75 .30
❑ 97 Jake Plummer .75 .30
❑ 98 Antonio Freeman 1.25 .50
❑ 99 Sean Dawkins .50 .20
❑ 100 Ron Dayne 1.25 .50
❑ 101 Rob Johnson .75 .30
❑ 102 Kordell Stewart .75 .30
❑ 103 Akili Smith .50 .20
❑ 104 Shawn Jefferson .50 .20
❑ 105 Germane Crowell .50 .20
❑ 106 Kevin Johnson .75 .30
❑ 107 Steve Beuerlein .75 .30
❑ 108 Marcus Robinson 1.25 .50
❑ 109 Peerless Price .75 .30
❑ 110 Jerome Pathon .75 .30
❑ 111 Sage Rosenfels RC 8.00 3.00
❑ 112 Quincy Morgan RC 8.00 3.00
❑ 113 Chad Johnson RC 20.00 7.50
❑ 114 Josh Heupel RC 8.00 3.00
❑ 115 Anthony Thomas RC 8.00 3.00
❑ 116 Drew Brees RC 25.00 10.00
❑ 117 Kevan Barlow RC 8.00 3.00
❑ 118 Chris Chambers RC 12.00 5.00
❑ 119 Mike McMahon RC 8.00 3.00

❑ 120 Todd Heap RC	8.00	3.00
❑ 121 Leonard Davis RC	5.00	2.00
❑ 122 Richard Seymour RC	8.00	3.00
❑ 123 Robert Ferguson RC	8.00	3.00
❑ 124 Andre Carter RC	8.00	3.00
❑ 125 Jesse Palmer RC	8.00	3.00
❑ 126 Travis Minor RC	5.00	2.00
❑ 127 Rudi Johnson RC	15.00	6.00
❑ 128 Rod Gardner RC	8.00	3.00
❑ 129 Snoop Minnis RC	5.00	2.00
❑ 130 Koren Robinson RC	8.00	3.00
❑ 131 Chris Weinke RC	8.00	3.00
❑ 132 James Jackson RC	8.00	3.00
❑ 133 [illegible]	[illegible]	10.00
❑ 134 Marques Tuiasosopo RC	8.00	3.00
❑ 135 Michael Bennett RC	8.00	3.00
❑ 136 LaDainian Tomlinson RC	50.00	25.00
❑ 137 Freddie Mitchell RC	8.00	3.00
❑ 138 Deuce McAllister RC	15.00	6.00
❑ 139 Quincy Carter RC	8.00	3.00
❑ 140 Santana Moss RC	12.00	5.00
❑ 141 David Terrell RC	8.00	3.00
❑ 142 Reggie Wayne RC	15.00	6.00
❑ 143 Justin Smith RC	8.00	3.00
❑ 144 Gerard Warren RC	8.00	3.00
❑ 145 Travis Henry RC	15.00	6.00
❑ 146 Dan Morgan RC	8.00	3.00
❑ NNO Checklist CL	.50	.20

2005 Topps Heritage

❑ COMPLETE SET (400)	150.00	75.00
❑ COMP.SET w/o SPs (300)	40.00	15.00
❑ 58T SP PRINTED WITH 1958 TOPPS DESIGN		
❑ TBJ SP PRINTED W/THROWBACK JER.PHOTO		
❑ 1 Curtis Martin	1.00	.40
❑ 2 Javon Walker	.60	.25
❑ 3 Derrick Mason	.60	.25
❑ 4 Julius Jones	1.25	.50
❑ 5 Marc Bulger	1.00	.40
❑ 6 Reggie Wayne	.60	.25
❑ 7 Isaac Bruce	.60	.25
❑ 8 Ray Lewis	1.00	.40
❑ 9 Drew Bledsoe	1.00	.40
❑ 10 Michael Vick	1.50	.60
❑ 11 Charles Rogers	.60	.25
❑ 12 Lee Evans	.60	.25
❑ 13 Jake Plummer	.60	.25
❑ 14 Edgerrin James	1.00	.40
❑ 15 Hines Ward	1.00	.40
❑ 16 Peyton Manning	1.50	.60
❑ 17 Andre Johnson	.60	.25
❑ 18 Trent Green	.60	.25
❑ 19 Brian Westbrook	.60	.25
❑ 20 Kevin Jones	1.00	.40
❑ 21 Deuce McAllister	1.00	.40
❑ 22 Marvin Harrison	1.00	.40
❑ 23 Dwight Freeney	.60	.25
❑ 24 Ahman Green	1.00	.40
❑ 25 Plaxico Burress	.60	.25
❑ 26 Daunte Culpepper	1.00	.40
❑ 27 Corey Dillon	.60	.25
❑ 28 Joe Horn	.60	.25
❑ 29 Torry Holt	1.00	.40
❑ 30 Randy Moss	1.00	.40
❑ 31 Drew Brees	1.00	.40
❑ 32 Jonathan Vilma	.60	.25
❑ 33 Jerome Bettis	1.00	.40
❑ 34 Byron Leftwich	1.00	.40
❑ 35 Marshall Faulk	1.00	.40
❑ 36 Brett Favre	2.50	1.00
❑ 37 Steve McNair	1.00	.40
❑ 38 Rudi Johnson	.60	.25
❑ 39 Tiki Barber	1.00	.40
❑ 40 Muhsin Muhammad	.60	.25
❑ 41 Tony Gonzalez	.60	.25
❑ 42 Chad Pennington	1.00	.40
❑ 43 Shaun Alexander	1.25	.50
❑ 44 Jamal Lewis	1.00	.40
❑ 45 Antonio Gates	1.00	.40
❑ 46 LaDainian Tomlinson	1.25	.50
❑ 47 [illegible]	[illegible]	[illegible]
❑ 48 Jake Delhomme	1.00	.40
❑ 49 Chad Johnson	1.00	.40
❑ 50 Willis McGahee	1.00	.40
❑ 51 Jason Witten	.60	.25
❑ 52 J.P. Losman	1.00	.40
❑ 53 Donovan McNabb	1.25	.50
❑ 54A Eric Shelton RC	2.50	1.00
❑ 54B Eric Shelton 58T SP	3.00	1.25
❑ 55A Alex Smith QB RC	10.00	4.00
❑ 55B Alex Smith QB TBJ SP	12.00	5.00
❑ 56A Kyle Orton RC	2.50	1.00
❑ 56B Kyle Orton 58T SP	3.00	1.25
❑ 57A Andrew Walter RC	2.50	1.00
❑ 57B Andrew Walter TBJ SP	3.00	1.25
❑ 58A Ryan Moats RC	2.50	1.00
❑ 58B Ryan Moats 58T SP	3.00	1.25
❑ 59A Ciatrick Fason RC	2.50	1.00
❑ 59B Ciatrick Fason 58T SP	3.00	1.25
❑ 60A Vincent Jackson RC	2.50	1.00
❑ 60B Vincent Jackson 58T SP	3.00	1.25
❑ 61A Heath Miller RC	5.00	2.00
❑ 61B Heath Miller 58T SP	6.00	2.50
❑ 62A Carlos Rogers RC	3.00	1.25
❑ 62B Carlos Rogers TBJ SP	4.00	1.50
❑ 63A Terrence Murphy RC	2.50	1.00
❑ 63B Terrence Murphy 58T SP	3.00	1.25
❑ 64A Mike Williams	2.50	1.00
❑ 64B Mike Williams 58T SP	3.00	1.25
❑ 65A Vernand Morency RC	2.50	1.00
❑ 65B Vernand Morency 58T SP	3.00	1.25
❑ 66A Maurice Clarett	2.50	1.00
❑ 66B Maurice Clarett 58T SP	3.00	1.25
❑ 67A Roscoe Parrish RC	2.50	1.00
❑ 67B Roscoe Parrish 58T SP	3.00	1.25
❑ 68A Courtney Roby RC	2.50	1.00
❑ 68B Courtney Roby 58T SP	3.00	1.25
❑ 69 Tom Brady	2.50	1.00
❑ 70A David Greene RC	2.50	1.00
❑ 70B David Greene 58T SP	3.00	1.25
❑ 71A Antrel Rolle RC	2.50	1.00
❑ 71B Antrel Rolle 58T SP	3.00	1.25
❑ 72A Mark Bradley RC	2.50	1.00
❑ 72B Mark Bradley 58T SP	3.00	1.25
❑ 73A Frank Gore RC	5.00	2.00
❑ 73B Frank Gore 58T SP	6.00	2.50
❑ 74A Cedric Benson RC	6.00	2.50
❑ 74B Cedric Benson 58T SP	8.00	3.00
❑ 75A Derrick Johnson 62T RC	4.00	1.50
❑ 75B Derrick Johnson 58T SP	5.00	2.00
❑ 76A Reggie Brown RC	2.50	1.00
❑ 76B Reggie Brown 58T SP	3.00	1.25
❑ 77A Ronnie Brown RC	10.00	4.00
❑ 77B Ronnie Brown TBJ SP	12.00	5.00
❑ 78A Jason Campbell RC	4.00	1.50
❑ 78B Jason Campbell TBJ SP	5.00	2.00
❑ 79A Charlie Frye RC	2.50	1.00
❑ 79B Charlie Frye 58T SP	3.00	1.25
❑ 80 Jamie Sharper	.50	.20
❑ 81 Tony Romo	12.00	6.00
❑ 82 Rod Smith	.60	.25
❑ 83 Chester Taylor	.60	.25
❑ 84 Marcus Robinson	.60	.25
❑ 85 Terence Newman	.50	.20
❑ 86 Aaron Brooks	.60	.25
❑ 87 Kerry Collins	.60	.25
❑ 88 Brandon Lloyd	.50	.20
❑ 89 Michael Pittman	.50	.20
❑ 90 Sean Taylor	.60	.25
❑ 91 Michael Lewis	.50	.20
❑ 92 Jeremy Shockey	1.00	.40
❑ 93 Zach Thomas	1.00	.40
❑ 94 David Carr	1.00	.40
❑ 95 Champ Bailey	.60	.25
❑ 96 Julius Peppers	.60	.25
❑ 97 Brandon Stokley	.60	.25
❑ 98 Deion Branch	.60	.25
❑ 99 Charles Woodson	.60	.25
❑ 100 Darrell Jackson	.60	.25
❑ 101 Ronde Barber	.50	.20
❑ 102 Patrick Ramsey	.60	.25
❑ 103 Warrick Dunn	.60	.25
❑ 104 Takeo Spikes	.50	.20
❑ 105 Thomas Jones	.60	.25
❑ [illegible]	[illegible]	[illegible]
❑ 107 Najeh Davenport	.50	.20
❑ 108 Nate Burleson	.60	.25
❑ 109 Kelly Campbell	.50	.20
❑ 110 LaVar Arrington	1.00	.40
❑ 111 Joey Harrington	1.00	.40
❑ 112 DeAngelo Hall	.60	.25
❑ 113 Derrick Blaylock	.50	.20
❑ 114 Michael Clayton	1.00	.40
❑ 115 Adam Archuleta	.50	.20
❑ 116 Jason Taylor	.50	.20
❑ 117 Donald Driver	.60	.25
❑ 118 Dan Morgan	.50	.20
❑ 119 Michael Jenkins	.60	.25
❑ 120 Drew Henson	.60	.25
❑ 121 Jay Fiedler	.50	.20
❑ 122 Ladell Betts	.50	.20
❑ 123 Jonathan Ogden	.50	.20
❑ 124 Domanick Davis	.60	.25
❑ 125 Sebastian Janikowski	.50	.20
❑ 126 Cedrick Wilson	.50	.20
❑ 127 Marcus Trufant	.50	.20
❑ 128 Santana Moss	.60	.25
❑ 129 Tatum Bell	.60	.25
❑ 130 Jonathan Wells	.50	.20
❑ 131 Laveranues Coles	.60	.25
❑ 132 Josh McCown	.60	.25
❑ 133 Antonio Bryant	.50	.20
❑ 134 John Lynch	.60	.25
❑ 135 Roy Williams WR	1.00	.40
❑ 136 Adam Vinatieri	1.00	.40
❑ 137 Dominic Rhodes	.50	.20
❑ 138 Tyrone Calico	.60	.25
❑ 139 Keenan McCardell	.50	.20
❑ 140 Antonio Pierce	.50	.20
❑ 141 Chris Chambers	.60	.25
❑ 142 Bubba Franks	.60	.25
❑ 143 Mike Vanderjagt	.50	.20
❑ 144 Ernest Wilford	.50	.20
❑ 145 Bertrand Berry	.50	.20
❑ 146 David Garrard	.50	.20
❑ 147 DeShaun Foster	.60	.25
❑ 148 Rashaun Woods	.60	.25
❑ 149 Wes Welker	.50	.20
❑ 150 Allen Rossum	.50	.20
❑ 151 Mike Anderson	.60	.25
❑ 152 Keyshawn Johnson	.60	.25
❑ 153 Alge Crumpler	.60	.25
❑ 154 Dunta Robinson	.60	.25
❑ 155 Kyle Boller	.60	.25
❑ 156 William Green	.50	.20
❑ 157 Peter Warrick	.50	.20
❑ 158 Doug Gabriel	.50	.20
❑ 159 Ashley Lelie	.60	.25
❑ 160 Ronald Curry	.60	.25
❑ 161 Keary Colbert	.60	.25
❑ 162 Shawn Bryson	.50	.20
❑ 163 Tim Rattay	.50	.20
❑ 164 Jabar Gaffney	.50	.20
❑ 165 Doug Jolley	.50	.20
❑ 166 Keith Brooking	.50	.20
❑ 167 Brian Urlacher	1.00	.40
❑ 168 Chris Gamble	.60	.25
❑ 169 Kurt Warner	.60	.25
❑ 170 Duce Staley	.60	.25
❑ 171 Steve Smith	.60	.25
❑ 172 Anquan Boldin	.60	.25
❑ 173 Fred Taylor	.60	.25
❑ 174 Donnie Edwards	.50	.20
❑ 175 Clarence Moore	.50	.20
❑ 176 Corey Bradford	.50	.20

❑ 177	Dante Hall	.60	.25
❑ 178	Warren Sapp	.60	.25
❑ 179	Todd Heap	.60	.25
❑ 180	Mewelde Moore	.60	.25
❑ 181	John Abraham	.50	.20
❑ 182	Rex Grossman	.60	.25
❑ 183	Stephen Davis	.60	.25
❑ 184	Greg Jones	.50	.20
❑ 185	Jeremiah Trotter	.50	.20
❑ 186	Carson Palmer	1.00	.40
❑ 187	Simeon Rice	.60	.25
❑ 188	A.J. Feeley	.60	.25
❑ 189	Matt Schaub	.60	.25
❑ 190	Jamaar Taylor	.50	.20
❑ 191	Joey Galloway	.60	.25
❑ 192	Quentin Griffin	.60	.25
❑ 193	Amani Toomer	.60	.25
❑ 194	Michael Strahan	.60	.25
❑ 195	Travis Henry	.60	.25
❑ 196	Billy Volek	.60	.25
❑ 197	Robert Ferguson	.50	.20
❑ 198	Reggie Williams	.60	.25
❑ 199	Jeff Garcia	.60	.25
❑ 200	Mark Brunell	.60	.25
❑ 201	Derrick Brooks	.60	.25
❑ 202	Tommy Maddox	.50	.20
❑ 203	William Henderson	.50	.20
❑ 204	Bryant Johnson	.50	.20
❑ 205	Philip Rivers	1.00	.40
❑ 206	James Farrior	.50	.20
❑ 207	Terrence McGee	.50	.20
❑ 208	Bernard Berrian	.50	.20
❑ 209	Gus Frerotte	.50	.20
❑ 210	Mike Alstott	.60	.25
❑ 211	Luke McCown	.50	.20
❑ 212	Michael Bennett	.60	.25
❑ 213	Kenechi Udeze	.50	.20
❑ 214	Chris Perry	.60	.25
❑ 215	Robert Gallery	.60	.25
❑ 216	Lito Sheppard	.50	.20
❑ 217	Brian Finneran	.50	.20
❑ 218	Brian Griese	.60	.25
❑ 219	Kevin Curtis	.60	.25
❑ 220	LaMont Jordan	1.00	.40
❑ 221	Jerry Porter	.60	.25
❑ 222	Reuben Droughns	.60	.25
❑ 223	Dallas Clark	.50	.20
❑ 224	Kevan Barlow	.60	.25
❑ 225	Ken Lucas	.50	.20
❑ 226	Lee Suggs	.60	.25
❑ 227	Marcus Pollard	.50	.20
❑ 228	David Givens	.60	.25
❑ 229	T.J. Duckett	.60	.25
❑ 230	Chris Simms	.60	.25
❑ 231	Maurice Morris	.50	.20
❑ 232	Chris McAllister	.50	.20
❑ 233	Justin Fargas	.50	.20
❑ 234	Jimmy Smith	.60	.25
❑ 235	Aaron Stecker	.50	.20
❑ 236	Donte Stallworth	.60	.25
❑ 237	Darren Sproles RC	2.50	1.00
❑ 238	Justin McCareins	.50	.20
❑ 239	Adrian McPherson RC	2.50	1.00
❑ 240	Brian Dawkins	.50	.20
❑ 241	Travis Taylor	.50	.20
❑ 242	Fabian Washington RC	2.50	1.00
❑ 243	Jerramy Stevens	.50	.20
❑ 244	Anthony Davis RC	2.00	.75
❑ 245	Alex Smith TE RC	2.50	1.00
❑ 246	Ricky Williams	.60	.25
❑ 247	Marion Barber RC	4.00	1.50
❑ 248	Marcus Spears RC	2.50	1.00
❑ 249	Mike Nugent RC	2.50	1.00
❑ 250	Dat Nguyen	.50	.20
❑ 251	Derek Anderson RC	4.00	1.50
❑ 252	Terrence Holt	.50	.20
❑ 253	Dane Looker	.50	.20
❑ 254	Randy McMichael	.50	.20
❑ 255	Craig Bragg RC	2.00	.75
❑ 256	James Kilian RC	2.50	1.00
❑ 257	Airese Currie RC	2.50	1.00
❑ 258	Noah Herron RC	2.50	1.00
❑ 259	Dan Cody RC	2.50	1.00
❑ 260	Willie Parker	10.00	4.00
❑ 261	Travis Johnson RC	2.00	.75
❑ 262	Dan Orlovsky RC	2.50	1.00
❑ 263	Chris Baker	.50	.20
❑ 264	Luis Castillo RC	2.50	1.00
❑ 265	Travis Daniels RC	2.00	.75
❑ 266	Justin Miller RC	2.00	.75
❑ 267	J.R. Russell RC	2.00	.75
❑ 268	Lance Mitchell RC	2.00	.75
❑ 269	T.A. McLendon RC	1.25	.50
❑ 270	Jerricho Cotchery	.50	.20
❑ 271	Chad Owens RC	2.50	1.00
❑ 272	Tab Perry RC	2.50	1.00
❑ 273	Corey Webster RC	2.50	1.00
❑ 274	Fred Gibson RC	2.00	.75
❑ 275	Brandon Jones RC	2.50	1.00
❑ 276	DeWayne Robertson	.50	.20
❑ 277	Brock Berlin RC	2.00	.75
❑ 278	Nehemiah Broughton RC	2.00	.75
❑ 279	Shaun Cody RC	2.50	1.00
❑ 280	Anthony Wright	.50	.20
❑ 281	Damien Nash RC	2.00	.75
❑ 282	Ryan Fitzpatrick RC	2.50	1.00
❑ 283	Paris Warren RC	2.00	.75
❑ 284	Justin Tuck RC	2.50	1.00
❑ 285	Cedric Houston RC	2.50	1.00
❑ 286	Odell Thurman RC	2.50	1.00
❑ 287	Kirk Morrison RC	2.50	1.00
❑ 288	Josh Davis RC	2.00	.75
❑ 289	Craphonso Thorpe RC	2.00	.75
❑ 290	Sam Aiken	.50	.20
❑ 291	Stanley Wilson RC	2.00	.75
❑ 292	Jonathan Babineaux RC	2.00	.75
❑ 293	Darryl Blackstock RC	2.00	.75
❑ 294	Roydell Williams RC	2.50	1.00
❑ 295	Channing Crowder RC	2.50	1.00
❑ 296	Deandra Cobb RC	2.00	.75
❑ 297	Larry Brackins RC	1.25	.50
❑ 298	Bryant McFadden RC	2.50	1.00
❑ 299	Kevin Burnett RC	2.50	1.00
❑ 300	Barrett Ruud RC	2.50	1.00
❑ 301	Terrell Owens SP	5.00	2.00
❑ 302	Ben Roethlisberger SP	12.00	5.00
❑ 303	Eric Moulds SP	3.00	1.25
❑ 304	Eli Manning SP	10.00	4.00
❑ 305	Ed Reed SP	3.00	1.25
❑ 306	Larry Fitzgerald SP	5.00	2.00
❑ 307	Clinton Portis SP	5.00	2.00
❑ 308	Priest Holmes SP	5.00	2.00
❑ 309	Drew Bennett SP	3.00	1.25
❑ 310	Steven Jackson SP	6.00	2.50
❑ 311	Roy Williams S SP	3.00	1.25
❑ 312	Marcel Shipp SP	2.50	1.00
❑ 313	Peerless Price SP	2.50	1.00
❑ 314	Troy Vincent SP	2.50	1.00
❑ 315	Justin Gage SP	2.50	1.00
❑ 316	Nick Goings SP	2.50	1.00
❑ 317	Dennis Northcutt SP	2.50	1.00
❑ 318	Quincy Morgan SP	2.50	1.00
❑ 319	Darius Watts SP	3.00	1.25
❑ 320	Jason Elam SP	2.50	1.00
❑ 321	Nick Barnett SP	2.50	1.00
❑ 322	Tony Hollings SP	2.50	1.00
❑ 323	Samie Parker SP	2.50	1.00
❑ 324	Kelly Campbell SP	2.50	1.00
❑ 325	Kelly Holcomb SP	2.50	1.00
❑ 326	Darren Sharper SP	2.50	1.00
❑ 327	Tedy Bruschi SP	3.00	1.25
❑ 328	Ernie Conwell SP	2.50	1.00
❑ 329	Shaun Ellis SP	2.50	1.00
❑ 330	Teyo Johnson SP	2.50	1.00
❑ 331	Chris Brown SP	3.00	1.25
❑ 332	Quentin Jammer SP	2.50	1.00
❑ 333	Fred Smoot SP	2.50	1.00
❑ 334	Eric Parker SP	2.50	1.00
❑ 335	Steve Heiden SP	2.50	1.00
❑ 336	Troy Polamalu SP	8.00	3.00
❑ 337	Todd Pinkston SP	2.50	1.00
❑ 338	L.J. Smith SP	2.50	1.00
❑ 339	London Fletcher SP	2.50	1.00
❑ 340	Devery Henderson SP	2.50	1.00
❑ 341A	Troy Williamson SP RC	3.00	1.25
❑ 341B	Troy Williamson TBJ SP	3.00	1.25
❑ 342A	J.J. Arrington SP RC	3.00	1.25
❑ 342B	J.J. Arrington 58T SP	3.00	1.25
❑ 343A	Cadillac Williams SP SP	10.00	4.00
❑ 343B	Cadillac Williams TBJ SP	12.00	5.00
❑ 344A	Aaron Rodgers SP RC	10.00	4.00
❑ 344B	Aaron Rodgers 58T SP	12.00	5.00
❑ 345A	Matt Jones SP RC	5.00	2.00
❑ 345B	Matt Jones 58T SP	6.00	2.50
❑ 346A	Roddy White SP RC	3.00	1.25
❑ 346B	Roddy White 58T SP	4.00	1.50
❑ 347A	Braylon Edwards SP RC	10.00	4.00
❑ 347B	Braylon Edwards TBJ SP	12.00	5.00
❑ 348A	Adam Jones SP RC	3.00	1.25
❑ 348B	Adam Jones TBJ SP	4.00	1.50
❑ 349A	Mark Clayton SP RC	3.00	1.25
❑ 349B	Mark Clayton TBJ SP	3.00	1.25
❑ 350A	Stefan LeFors SP RC	3.00	1.25
❑ 350B	Stefan LeFors 58T SP	4.00	1.50
❑ 351	Alvin Pearman SP RC	3.00	1.25
❑ 352	Erasmus James SP RC	3.00	1.25
❑ 353	David Pollack SP RC	3.00	1.25
❑ 354	Brandon Jacobs SP RC	5.00	2.00
❑ 355	Chris Henry SP RC	3.00	1.25
❑ 356	Thomas Davis SP RC	3.00	1.25
❑ 357	Rasheed Marshall SP RC	3.00	1.25
❑ 358	Matt Roth SP RC	3.00	1.25
❑ 359	DeMarcus Ware SP RC	5.00	2.00
❑ 360	Matt Cassell SP RC	5.00	2.00
❑ 361	Stanford Routt SP RC	2.50	1.00
❑ 362	Marlin Jackson SP RC	3.00	1.25
❑ 363	Der.Johnson 59T SP ERR	5.00	2.00
❑ 364	Jerome Mathis SP RC	3.00	1.25
❑ 365	Lionel Gates SP RC	2.50	1.00

2006 Topps Heritage

❑	COMPLETE SET (497)	200.00	100.00
❑	COMP.SET w/o SP's (207)	40.00	15.00
❑ 1	LaVar Arrington	1.50	.60
❑ 2	Justin McCareins	.75	.30
❑ 3	Simeon Rice	.75	.30
❑ 4	Dennis Northcutt	.75	.30
❑ 5	Jason Campbell	1.00	.40
❑ 6	Ricardo Colclough	.75	.30
❑ 7	Marion Barber	1.00	.40
❑ 8	Samie Parker	.75	.30
❑ 9	Nick Barnett	.75	.30
❑ 10	David Garrard	.75	.30
❑ 11	Roy Williams S	1.00	.40
❑ 12	Adrian Peterson	.75	.30
❑ 13	Marcus Robinson	1.00	.40
❑ 14	Andrew Walter	1.00	.40
❑ 15	Cedric Houston	.75	.30
❑ 16	John Abraham	.75	.30
❑ 17	Alex Smith TE	.75	.30
❑ 18	Travis Henry	1.00	.40
❑ 19	Craig Krenzel	.75	.30
❑ 20	Brian Dawkins	1.00	.40
❑ 21	Bryant Young	.75	.30
❑ 22	Al Wilson	.75	.30
❑ 23	Nick Goings	.75	.30
❑ 24	Shaun Ellis	.75	.30
❑ 25	Marty Booker	.75	.30
❑ 26	Daniel Graham	.75	.30
❑ 27	Jim Sorgi	.75	.30
❑ 28	Sebastian Janikowski	.75	.30
❑ 29	Allen Rossum	.75	.30
❑ 30	Jim Kleinsasser	.75	.30
❑ 31	Lee Evans	1.00	.40
❑ 32	Alex Brown	.75	.30

❑ 33 Steve Hutchinson .75 .30
❑ 34 Sam Madison .75 .30
❑ 35 Aaron Rodgers 1.50 .60
❑ 36 Justin Griffith .75 .30
❑ 37 Terrence McGee .75 .30
❑ 38 Odell Thurman .75 .30
❑ 39 Marcus Trufant .75 .30
❑ 40 Courtney Roby .75 .30
❑ 41 Isaac Bruce 1.00 .40
❑ 42 Ben Watson .75 .30
❑ 43 Brandòn Stokley 1.00 .40
❑ 44 Koren Robinson 1.00 .40
❑ 45 Mark Clayton 1.50 .60
❑ 46 Darren Sproles .75 .30
❑ 47 Matt Leinart RC 10.00 4.00
❑ 48 Terrell Owens 1.50 .60
❑ 49 Antonio Pierce .75 .30
❑ 50 Mark Brunell 1.00 .40
❑ 51 T.J. Houshmandzadeh 1.00 .40
❑ 52 Chris Gamble .75 .30
❑ 53 Jason Witten 1.00 .40
❑ 54 Michael Huff RC 4.00 1.50
❑ 55 Joey Porter .75 .30
❑ 56 Eli Manning 2.00 .75
❑ 57 Ladell Betts .75 .30
❑ 58 Kevin Curtis .75 .30
❑ 59 Reggie Williams 1.00 .40
❑ 60 Alge Crumpler 1.00 .40
❑ 61 Joseph Addai RC 10.00 4.00
❑ 62 Todd Heap 1.00 .40
❑ 63 Trent Green 1.00 .40
❑ 64 Muhsin Muhammad 1.00 .40
❑ 65 Drew Bledsoe 1.50 .60
❑ 66 LenDale White RC 6.00 2.50
❑ 67 Kris Mangum .75 .30
❑ 68 Troy Vincent .75 .30
❑ 69 DeMarcus Ware 1.00 .40
❑ 70 Brian Westbrook 1.00 .40
❑ 71 Brandon Lloyd 1.00 .40
❑ 72 Corey Dillon 1.00 .40
❑ 73 Ernie Conwell .75 .30
❑ 74 Laveranues Coles 1.00 .40
❑ 75 Santana Moss 1.00 .40
❑ 76 Alvis Whitted .75 .30
❑ 77 Demorrio Williams 1.50 .60
❑ 78 Matt Hasselbeck 1.00 .40
❑ 79 Billy Volek 1.00 .40
❑ 80 Sean Taylor 1.00 .40
❑ 81 Plaxico Burress 1.00 .40
❑ 82 Frank Gore 1.50 .60
❑ 83 Chris McAlister .75 .30
❑ 84 Donnie Edwards .75 .30
❑ 85 Ed Reed 1.00 .40
❑ 86 Tarvaris Jackson RC 5.00 2.00
❑ 87 T.J. Duckett 1.00 .40
❑ 88 Rex Grossman 1.50 .60
❑ 89 Ronnie Brown 1.50 .60
❑ 90 James Farrior .75 .30
❑ 91 Mike Alstott .60 .25
❑ 92 Eddie Kennison .50 .20
❑ 93 Charlie Frye .60 .25
❑ 94 Deion Branch .60 .25
❑ 95 Brandon Jacobs SP 1.25 .50
❑ 96 Larry Fitzgerald 1.00 .40
❑ 97 Domanick Davis .60 .25
❑ 98 Terrence Holt .50 .20
❑ 99 Dan Morgan .50 .20
❑ 100 Shaun Alexander SP 2.00 .75
❑ 101 Shawne Merriman SP 1.25 .50
❑ 102 Roddy White .60 .25
❑ 103 Ashley Lelie .60 .25
❑ 104 Jevon Kearse .60 .25
❑ 105 Andre Johnson .60 .25
❑ 106 Matt Mauck .50 .20
❑ 107 Dwight Freeney SP 1.25 .50
❑ 108 Robert Gallery .50 .20
❑ 109 Chad Jackson SP RC 4.00 1.50
❑ 110 Marques Tuiasosopo .50 .20
❑ 111 LaMont Jordan SP 1.25 .50
❑ 112 Taylor Jacobs .50 .20
❑ 113 Byron Leftwich .60 .25
❑ 114 Fabian Washington .50 .20
❑ 115 Michael Jenkins .60 .25
❑ 116 Steven Jackson 1.00 .40
❑ 117 Ronald Curry .60 .25
❑ 118 J.P. Losman .60 .25
❑ 119 Patrick Crayton .50 .20
❑ 120 Javon Walker .60 .25
❑ 121 Daunte Culpepper SP 2.00 .75
❑ 122 Marc Bulger .60 .25
❑ 123 Kevin Jones SP 2.00 .75
❑ 124 Tom Brady 1.50 .60
❑ 125 Jay Cutler SP RC 12.00 5.00
❑ 126 Tony Gonzalez .60 .25
❑ 127 Warrick Dunn SP 1.25 .50
❑ 128 Michael Strahan .60 .25
❑ 129 Demetrius Williams SP RC 4.00 1.50
❑ 130 Charles Woodson .60 .25
❑ 131 Tiki Barber SP 2.00 .75
❑ 132 Hines Ward 1.00 .40
❑ 133 Brian Calhoun SP RC 4.00 1.50
❑ 134 Torry Holt .60 .25
❑ 135 Priest Holmes .60 .25
❑ 136 Philip Rivers 1.00 .40
❑ 137 Joey Harrington .60 .25
❑ 138 Donte Stallworth .60 .25
❑ 139 Ken Lucas .50 .20
❑ 140 Chad Morton .50 .20
❑ 141 Osi Umenyiora .50 .20
❑ 142 Jamal Lewis .60 .25
❑ 143 Derek Hagan RC 2.50 1.00
❑ 144 Deshaun Foster .60 .25
❑ 145 Michael Lewis .50 .20
❑ 146 Anquan Boldin .60 .25
❑ 147 Derrick Brooks .60 .25
❑ 148 Michael Turner .75 .30
❑ 149 Zach Thomas 1.00 .40
❑ 150 Carson Palmer 1.00 .40
❑ 151 Ryan Moats .50 .20
❑ 152 William Henderson .50 .20
❑ 153 Marcus Spears .50 .20
❑ 154 Travis Minor .50 .20
❑ 155 Scottie Vines .50 .20
❑ 156 Maurice Stovall RC 2.50 1.00
❑ 157 Dante Hall .60 .25
❑ 158 Chris Simms .60 .25
❑ 159 Zack Crockett .50 .20
❑ 160 Thomas Jones .60 .25
❑ 161 Marcus Pollard .50 .20
❑ 162 Troy Polamalu 1.25 .50
❑ 163 LeRon McCoy .50 .20
❑ 164 Najeh Davenport .50 .20
❑ 165 Keenan McCardell .50 .20
❑ 166 Chris Brown .60 .25
❑ 167 Derrick Johnson .60 .25
❑ 168 Chad Pennington .60 .25
❑ 169 Adam Jones .50 .20
❑ 170 Terry Glenn .60 .25
❑ 171 Antonio Bryant .60 .25
❑ 172 Jerramy Stevens .60 .25
❑ 173 Antrel Rolle .50 .20
❑ 174 Randy McMichael .50 .20
❑ 175 Orlando Pace .50 .20
❑ 176 Chris Perry .60 .25
❑ 177 Drew Bennett .50 .20
❑ 178 Cedric Benson 1.00 .40
❑ 179 Ernest Wilford .50 .20
❑ 180 Dunta Robinson .60 .25
❑ 181 Reggie Wayne .60 .25
❑ 182 Lito Sheppard .50 .20
❑ 183 Maurice Drew RC 6.00 2.50
❑ 184 Todd Bouman .50 .20
❑ 185 Marlin Jackson .50 .20
❑ 186 D.J. Williams .50 .20
❑ 187 DeAngelo Hall .60 .25
❑ 188 Bubba Franks .50 .20
❑ 189 Greg Jones .50 .20
❑ 190 Dominic Rhodes .60 .25
❑ 191 Dallas Clark .50 .20
❑ 192 Dre Bly .50 .20
❑ 193 Charlie Whitehurst 1.00 .40
❑ 194 Will Demps RC 1.00 .40
❑ 195 Champ Bailey .60 .25
❑ 196 Sinorice Moss RC 2.50 1.00
❑ 197 Jonathan Ogden .50 .20
❑ 198 Mike Peterson .50 .20
❑ 199 D.D. Lewis RC 1.25 .50
❑ 200 Vincent Jackson .50 .20
❑ 201 Stefan Lefors .50 .20
❑ 202 Willie Parker 1.25 .50
❑ 203 Antwaan Randle El .60 .25
❑ 204 Keary Colbert .50 .20
❑ 205 Tyrone Calico .50 .20
❑ 206 Mike Williams 1.00 .40
❑ 207 David Carr .60 .25
❑ 208 Braylon Edwards 1.00 .40
❑ 209 Michael Clayton .60 .25
❑ 210 Jerome Mathis .50 .20
❑ 211 Fred Taylor .60 .25
❑ 212 Jake Delhomme .60 .25
❑ 213 Roy Williams WR 1.00 .40
❑ 214 Curtis Martin 1.00 .40
❑ 215 Terrell Suggs .60 .25
❑ 216 Troy Williamson .60 .25
❑ 217 Marshall Faulk .60 .25
❑ 218 D'Brickashaw Ferguson RC 2.50 1.00
❑ 219 Kelly Holcomb .50 .20
❑ 220 Matt Jones .60 .25
❑ 221 Michael Vick 1.00 .40
❑ 222 Deuce McAllister .60 .25
❑ 223 Eric Moulds .60 .25
❑ 224 Ike Taylor .50 .20
❑ 225 D.J. Hackett .50 .20
❑ 226 Keyshawn Johnson .60 .25
❑ 227 Josh McCown .60 .25
❑ 228 Joe Horn .60 .25
❑ 229 Jonathan Vilma .60 .25
❑ 230 Warren Sapp .60 .25
❑ 231 Reggie Brown .75 .30
❑ 232 Clinton Portis 1.00 .40
❑ 233 Derrick Burgess .50 .20
❑ 234 Bob Sanders .60 .25
❑ 235 Lofa Tatupu .60 .25
❑ 236 Justin Fargas .50 .20
❑ 237 Kellen Clemens RC 4.00 1.50
❑ 238 Richard Seymour .50 .20
❑ 239 Jeff Garcia .60 .25
❑ 240 Shaun Cody .50 .20
❑ 241 Brad Johnson .60 .25
❑ 242 Edgerrin James 1.00 .40
❑ 243 Terence Newman .50 .20
❑ 244 Bernard Berrian .50 .20
❑ 245 Mike Anderson .60 .25
❑ 246 Ahman Green .60 .25
❑ 247 Erron Kinney .50 .20
❑ 248 David Pollack .50 .20
❑ 249 Kevin Faulk .50 .20
❑ 250 Laurence Maroney RC 6.00 2.50
❑ 251 Chad Johnson .60 .25
❑ 252 Antonio Gates 1.00 .40
❑ 253 Drew Brees 1.00 .40
❑ 254 Jake Plummer .60 .25
❑ 255 Mario Williams RC 4.00 1.50
❑ 256 Chester Taylor .60 .25
❑ 257 Shawn Bryson .50 .20
❑ 258 J.J. Arrington .60 .25
❑ 259 Robert Ferguson .50 .20
❑ 260 Reuben Droughns .60 .25
❑ 261 Tab Perry .50 .20
❑ 262 Troy Brown .60 .25
❑ 263 Luis Castillo .50 .20
❑ 264 Quincy Morgan .50 .20
❑ 265 Damon Huard .60 .25
❑ 266 Walter Jones .50 .20
❑ 267 Kyle Vanden Bosch .50 .20
❑ 268 Doug Gabriel .50 .20
❑ 269 Deltha O'Neal .50 .20
❑ 270 Randy Moss 1.00 .40
❑ 271 Omar Jacobs RC 2.00 .75
❑ 272 Kevan Barlow .60 .25
❑ 273 John Lynch .60 .25
❑ 274 Chris Cooley .50 .20
❑ 275 Zach Hilton .50 .20
❑ 276 Peter Warrick .50 .20
❑ 277 London Fletcher .50 .20
❑ 278 Nate Burleson .60 .25
❑ 279 Larry Foote .50 .20
❑ 280 Justin Miller .50 .20
❑ 281 Darius Watts .50 .20
❑ 282 Aaron Brooks .60 .25
❑ 283 Joey Galloway .60 .25
❑ 284 Darrell Jackson .60 .25

❑ 285 Alex Smith QB	1.00	.40
❑ 286 Vonnie Holliday	.50	.20
❑ 287 Nathan Vasher	.50	.20
❑ 288 Tatum Bell	.60	.25
❑ 289 Olin Kreutz	.50	.20
❑ 290 Duce Staley	.60	.25
❑ 291 Courtney Anderson	.50	.20
❑ 292 Tory James	.50	.20
❑ 293 Mike Vanderjagt	.50	.20
❑ 294 Mark Bradley	.60	.25
❑ 295 Kurt Warner	.60	.25
❑ 296 Ray Lewis	1.00	.40
❑ 297 Kassim Osgood	.50	.20
❑ 298 Trent Dilfer	.60	.25
❑ 299 Justin Gage	.50	.20
❑ 300 DeAngelo Williams RC	6.00	2.50
❑ 301 Luke McCown	.50	.20
❑ 302 Charles Rogers	.60	.25
❑ 303 Marcedes Lewis RC	2.50	1.00
❑ 304 Samari Rolle	.50	.20
❑ 305 Greg Lewis	.50	.20
❑ 306 Peter Boulware	.50	.20
❑ 307 Donald Driver	.60	.25
❑ 308 Travis Taylor	.50	.20
❑ 309 Quentin Jammer	.50	.20
❑ 310 Carlos Rogers	.50	.20
❑ 311 Peyton Manning	8.00	3.00
❑ 312 Reggie Bush RC	12.00	5.00
❑ 313 Vernon Davis RC	6.00	2.50
❑ 314 Brett Favre	10.00	4.00
❑ 315 Cadillac Williams	5.00	2.00
❑ 316 Donovan McNabb	5.00	2.00
❑ 317 Jason Avant RC	3.00	1.25
❑ 318 Ben Roethlisberger	8.00	3.00
❑ 319 Steve Smith	5.00	2.00
❑ 320 Vince Young RC	12.00	5.00
❑ 321 Willis McGahee	5.00	2.00
❑ 322 Jeremy Shockey	5.00	2.00
❑ 323 Rudi Johnson	3.00	1.25
❑ 324 Brian Urlacher	5.00	2.00
❑ 325 Rod Smith	3.00	1.25
❑ 326 Santonio Holmes RC	6.00	2.50
❑ 327 Larry Johnson	6.00	2.50
❑ 328 Julius Jones	5.00	2.00
❑ 329 Marvin Harrison	5.00	2.00
❑ 330 Chris Chambers	3.00	1.25
❑ 331 Takeo Spikes	2.50	1.00
❑ 332 Brian Griese	3.00	1.25
❑ 333 Steve McNair	3.00	1.25
❑ 334 Willie McGinest	2.50	1.00
❑ 335 Tedy Bruschi	5.00	2.00
❑ 336 Roydell Williams	2.50	1.00
❑ 337 Patrick Ramsey	3.00	1.25
❑ 338 Kyle Boller	2.50	1.00
❑ 339 Bethel Johnson	2.50	1.00
❑ 340 Jerry Porter	3.00	1.25
❑ 341 Shawntae Spencer	2.50	1.00
❑ 342 Drew Carter	2.50	1.00
❑ 343 Jason Elam	2.50	1.00
❑ 344 Michael Pittman	2.50	1.00
❑ 345 Edell Shepherd RC	1.50	.60
❑ 346 Maurice Hicks	2.50	1.00
❑ 347 Ron Dayne	3.00	1.25
❑ 348 Josh Reed	2.50	1.00
❑ 349 Lorenzo Neal	2.50	1.00
❑ 350 LaDainian Tomlinson	6.00	2.50
❑ 351 David Tyree	2.50	1.00
❑ 352 Keith Brooking	2.50	1.00
❑ 353 Devery Henderson	2.50	1.00
❑ 354 Daylon McCutcheon	2.50	1.00
❑ 355 Derrick Mason	2.50	1.00
❑ 356 Fred Smoot	2.50	1.00
❑ 357 Ronde Barber	2.50	1.00
❑ 358 Dan Kreider	3.00	1.25
❑ 359 Shayne Graham	2.50	1.00
❑ 360 Vernand Morency	3.00	1.25
❑ 361 Shawn Springs	2.50	1.00
❑ 362 Amani Toomer	3.00	1.25
❑ 363 Eric Parker	2.50	1.00
❑ 364 Jason Taylor	2.50	1.00
❑ 365 Keith Bulluck	2.50	1.00
❑ 366 Sam Gado	3.00	1.25
❑ 367 Cedrick Wilson	2.50	1.00
❑ 368 Mewelde Moore	2.50	1.00
❑ 369 Travis Daniels	2.50	1.00
❑ 370 Arnaz Battle	2.50	1.00
❑ 371 Kyle Orton	3.00	1.25
❑ 372 Dane Looker	2.50	1.00
❑ 373 Kellen Winslow	5.00	2.00
❑ 374 Julius Peppers	3.00	1.25
❑ 375 Jeremiah Trotter	2.50	1.00
❑ 376 L.J. Smith	2.50	1.00
❑ 377 Gibril Wilson	2.50	1.00
❑ 378 Adam Archuleta	2.50	1.00
❑ 379 Darren Sharper	2.50	1.00
❑ 380 Joe Jurevicius	3.00	1.25
❑ 381 Patrick Pass	2.50	1.00
❑ 382 A.J. Feeley	2.50	1.00
❑ 383 Leroy Hill	2.50	1.00
❑ 384 Corey Webster	2.50	1.00
❑ 385 Heath Miller	3.00	1.25
❑ 386 Cato June	3.00	1.25
❑ 387 Brad Hoover	2.50	1.00
❑ 388 Michael Boulware	2.50	1.00
❑ 389 Matt Schaub	3.00	1.25
❑ 390 Kirk Morrison	2.50	1.00
❑ 391 Kevin Carter	2.50	1.00
❑ 392 David Givens	3.00	1.25
❑ 393 Alvin Pearman	2.50	1.00
❑ 394 Brian Finneran	2.50	1.00
❑ 395 Ike Hilliard	2.50	1.00
❑ 396 Angelo Crowell	2.50	1.00
❑ 397 Charlie Adams	2.50	1.00
❑ 398 Neil Rackers	2.50	1.00
❑ 399 Brandon Jones	2.50	1.00
❑ 400 B.J. Sams	2.50	1.00
❑ 401 Kyle Johnson	2.50	1.00
❑ 402 Adam Vinatieri	3.00	1.25
❑ 403 Bryant Johnson	2.50	1.00
❑ 404 Bryan Fletcher	2.50	1.00
❑ 405 Channing Crowder	2.50	1.00
❑ 406 Jerricho Cotchery	2.50	1.00
❑ 407 A.J. Hawk RC	6.00	2.50

2003 Topps Total

❑ COMPLETE SET (550)	80.00	40.00
❑ 1 Rich Gannon	.50	.20
❑ 2 Travis Henry	.50	.20
❑ 3 Brian Finneran	.30	.10
❑ 4 Ed Hartwell	.30	.10
❑ 5 Az-Zahir Hakim	.30	.10
❑ 6 Rodney Peete	.30	.10
❑ 7 David Terrell	.50	.20
❑ 8 Matt Schobel	.30	.10
❑ 9 Andre Davis	.30	.10
❑ 10 Dexter Coakley	.30	.10
❑ 11 Rod Smith	.50	.20
❑ 12 Damerien McCants	.30	.10
❑ 13 Robert Ferguson	.30	.10
❑ 14 Kailee Wong	.30	.10
❑ 15 James Mungro	.30	.10
❑ 16 Fred Taylor	.75	.30
❑ 17 Tony Gonzalez	.50	.20
❑ 18 Randall Godfrey	.30	.10
❑ 19 Robert Thomas	.30	.10
❑ 20 Rohan Davey	.50	.20
❑ 21 Terrell Owens	.75	.30
❑ 22 Ron Dayne	.30	.10
❑ 23 Charlie Batch	.30	.10
❑ 24 Brian Westbrook	.50	.20
❑ 25 Plaxico Burress	.50	.20
❑ 26 Reche Caldwell	.30	.10
❑ 27 Fred Beasley	.30	.10
❑ 28 Anthony Simmons	.30	.10
❑ 29 Rod Woodson	.50	.20
❑ 30 Derrick Brooks	.50	.20
❑ 31 Shaun Ellis	.30	.10
❑ 32 Ladell Betts	.50	.20
❑ 33 Russell Davis	.30	.10
❑ 34 Warrick Dunn	.60	.20
❑ 35 Jeremy Shockey	1.25	.50
❑ 36 Alex Van Pelt	.30	.10
❑ 37 Todd Bouman	.30	.10
❑ 38 Kelly Campbell	.30	.10
❑ 39 Justin Smith	.30	.10
❑ 40 Jamel White	.30	.10
❑ 41 La'Roi Glover	.30	.10
❑ 42 Ian Gold	.30	.10
❑ 43 Robert Porcher	.30	.10
❑ 44 Jermaine Lewis	.30	.10
❑ 45 Marvin Harrison	.75	.30
❑ 46 Darren Sharper	.30	.10
❑ 47 Jamie Sharper	.30	.10
❑ 48 Tony Richardson	.30	.10
❑ 49 Moe Williams	.30	.10
❑ 50 Ricky Williams	.75	.30
❑ 51 Ty Law	.50	.20
❑ 52 Donte Stallworth	.75	.30
❑ 53 Shannon Sharpe	.50	.20
❑ 54 Santana Moss	.50	.20
❑ 55 Charlie Garner	.50	.20
❑ 56 Brian Dawkins	.50	.20
❑ 57 Dan Campbell	.30	.10
❑ 58 William Green	.50	.20
❑ 59 Ron Dugans	.30	.10
❑ 60 Darrell Jackson	.50	.20
❑ 61 Marc Bulger	.75	.30
❑ 62 Joe Jurevicius	.30	.10
❑ 63 Erron Kinney	.30	.10
❑ 64 Champ Bailey	.50	.20
❑ 65 Peerless Price	.50	.20
❑ 66 Gary Baxter	.30	.10
❑ 67 Chris Redman	.30	.10
❑ 68 London Fletcher	.30	.10
❑ 69 Dee Brown	.30	.10
❑ 70 Anthony Thomas	.50	.20
❑ 71 Jake Delhomme	.75	.30
❑ 72 Dorsey Levens	.30	.10
❑ 73 Roy Williams	.75	.30
❑ 74 Ashley Lelie	.75	.30
❑ 75 Joey Harrington	1.25	.50
❑ 76 William Henderson	.30	.10
❑ 77 Corey Bradford	.30	.10
❑ 78 Reggie Wayne	.50	.20
❑ 79 Kyle Brady	.30	.10
❑ 80 Trent Green	.50	.20
❑ 81 Bill Romanowski	.30	.10
❑ 82 Chike Okeafor RC	.75	.30
❑ 83 David Patten	.30	.10
❑ 84 Terrelle Smith	.30	.10
❑ 85 Kerry Collins	.50	.20
❑ 86 Derrick Mason	.50	.20
❑ 87 Trung Canidate	.50	.20
❑ 88 A.J. Feeley	.50	.20
❑ 89 Jason Gildon	.30	.10
❑ 90 Doug Flutie	.75	.30
❑ 91 Tai Streets	.30	.10
❑ 92 Keith Newman	.30	.10
❑ 93 Adam Archuleta	.30	.10
❑ 94 Simeon Rice	.50	.20
❑ 95 Eddie George	.50	.20
❑ 96 Frank Sanders	.30	.10
❑ 97 Freddie Jones	.30	.10
❑ 98 Charles Johnson	.30	.10
❑ 99 Keith Traylor	.30	.10
❑ 100 Drew Bledsoe	.75	.30
❑ 101 Muhsin Muhammad	.50	.20
❑ 102 Marques Anderson	.30	.10
❑ 103 Donald Hayes	.30	.10
❑ 104 Quincy Morgan	.50	.20
❑ 105 Chad Hutchinson	.30	.10
❑ 106 Mike Anderson	.50	.20
❑ 107 Randy McMichael	.50	.20
❑ 108 Vonnie Holliday	.30	.10
❑ 109 Marcus Coleman	.30	.10

110	Edgerrin James	.75	.30
111	Michael Lewis	.30	.10
112	Wayne Chrebet	.50	.20
113	Antwaan Randle El	.75	.30
114	Byron Chamberlain	.30	.10
115	Jeff Garcia	.75	.30
116	Kim Herring	.30	.10
117	Kenny Holmes	.30	.10
118	John Lynch	.50	.20
119	Doug Jolley	.30	.10
120	Duce Staley	.50	.20
121	Kordell Stewart	.50	.20
122	Stephen Alexander	.30	.10
123	Andre Carter	[illegible]	.10
124	Bobby Engram	.30	.10
125	Marshall Faulk	.75	.30
126	Peter Simon RC	.50	.20
127	Alge Crumpler	.50	.20
128	Kenny Watson	.30	.10
129	Duane Starks	.30	.10
130	Jeff Blake	.30	.10
131	Todd Heap	.50	.20
132	Bobby Shaw	.30	.10
133	Ricky Proehl	.30	.10
134	John Abraham	.30	.10
135	T.J. Houshmandzadeh	.30	.10
136	Brian Urlacher	1.25	.50
137	Darren Woodson	.30	.10
138	Steve Beuerlein	.30	.10
139	Cory Schlesinger	.30	.10
140	Ahman Green	.75	.30
141	Jabar Gaffney	.50	.20
142	Eddie Drummond	.30	.10
143	Stacey Mack	.30	.10
144	Johnnie Morton	.50	.20
145	Chris Chambers	.75	.30
146	Jim Kleinsasser	.30	.10
147	Tebucky Jones	.30	.10
148	Marcus Pollard	.30	.10
149	Tony Brackens	.30	.10
150	Chad Pennington	1.00	.40
151	Kevin Faulk	.30	.10
152	Michael Lewis	.30	.10
153	Mark Bruener	.30	.10
154	Tim Dwight	.50	.20
155	Jerry Rice	1.50	.60
156	Trent Dilfer	.50	.20
157	Jon Ritchie	.30	.10
158	Michael Pittman	.30	.10
159	Lamar Gordon	.30	.10
160	Rod Gardner	.50	.20
161	Ken Dilger	.30	.10
162	Doug Johnson	.30	.10
163	Peter Boulware	.30	.10
164	Jevon Kearse	.50	.20
165	Julius Peppers	.75	.30
166	Chris Chandler	.30	.10
167	Lorenzo Neal	.30	.10
168	Kevin Johnson	.50	.20
169	Kevin Hardy	.30	.10
170	KaRon Coleman	.30	.10
171	James Stewart	.50	.20
172	Tony Fisher	.30	.10
173	Billy Miller	.30	.10
174	Phillip Crosby	.30	.10
175	Priest Holmes	1.00	.40
176	Elvis Joseph	.30	.10
177	Bryan Gilmore	.30	.10
178	D'Wayne Bates	.30	.10
179	Quincy Carter	.50	.20
180	Joe Horn	.50	.20
181	Anthony Henry	.30	.10
182	Anthony Becht	.30	.10
183	Mike Peterson	.30	.10
184	James Thrash	.30	.10
185	Jerome Bettis	.75	.30
186	Marcellus Wiley	.30	.10
187	Tim Rattay	.50	.20
188	Maurice Morris	.30	.10
189	Jason Taylor	.30	.10
190	Keyshawn Johnson	.75	.30
191	John Simon	.30	.10
192	Fred Smoot	.30	.10
193	Wendell Bryant	.30	.10
194	Brandon Stokley	.50	.20
195	Kurt Warner	.75	.30
196	Steve Smith	.75	.30
197	Dez White	.30	.10
198	Jim Miller	.30	.10
199	Robert Griffith	.30	.10
200	Michael Vick	2.00	.75
201	Antonio Bryant	.50	.20
202	Laveranues Coles	.50	.20
203	Kalimba Edwards	.30	.10
204	Bubba Franks	.50	.20
205	David Carr	1.25	.50
206	Dwight Freeney	.50	.20
207	[illegible]	[illegible]	[illegible]
208	Reggie Tongue	.30	.10
209	Cam Cleeland	.30	.10
210	Michael Bennett	.50	.20
211	Antowain Smith	.50	.20
212	Warren Sapp	.50	.20
213	Ike Hilliard	.30	.10
214	Olandis Gary	.50	.20
215	Tim Brown	.75	.30
216	Kevin Dyson	.50	.20
217	Eddie Kennison	.30	.10
218	Junior Seau	.75	.30
219	Donnie Edwards	.30	.10
220	Shaun Alexander	.75	.30
221	Terrence Wilkins	.30	.10
222	Garrison Hearst	.50	.20
223	Keith Bulluck	.30	.10
224	Zeron Flemister	.30	.10
225	Jake Plummer	.50	.20
226	Chad Johnson	.75	.30
227	Travis Taylor	.50	.20
228	Josh Reed	.50	.20
229	James Farrior	.30	.10
230	Marty Booker	.50	.20
231	Todd Pinkston	.50	.20
232	Dennis Northcutt	.50	.20
233	Troy Hambrick	.30	.10
234	Roland Williams	.30	.10
235	Bill Schroeder	.50	.20
236	Javon Walker	.50	.20
237	Kevin Swayne	.30	.10
238	Dominic Rhodes	.50	.20
239	David Garrard	.30	.10
240	Mike Maslowski RC	.50	.20
241	Travis Minor	.30	.10
242	Terry Glenn	.30	.10
243	Deion Branch	.75	.30
244	Adrian Peterson	.30	.10
245	Tiki Barber	.75	.30
246	Ray Lewis	.75	.30
247	Marques Tuiasosopo	.50	.20
248	Chad Lewis	.30	.10
249	Takeo Spikes	[illegible]	.10
250	LaDainian Tomlinson	.75	.30
251	Stephen Davis	.50	.20
252	Koren Robinson	.50	.20
253	Daylon McCutcheon	.30	.10
254	Rob Johnson	.50	.20
255	Donovan McNabb	1.00	.40
256	Derrius Thompson	.30	.10
257	Marcel Shipp	.50	.20
258	Keith Brooking	.30	.10
259	Chris McAlister	.30	.10
260	Eric Moulds	.50	.20
261	Amos Zereoue	.50	.20
262	Drew Brees	.75	.30
263	Jon Kitna	.50	.20
264	Brad Johnson	.50	.20
265	Emmitt Smith	2.00	.75
266	Trevor Pryce	.30	.10
267	Mike McMahon	.50	.20
268	Patrick Ramsey	.75	.30
269	Jonathan Wells	.30	.10
270	Mark Brunell	.50	.20
271	Marc Boerigter	.50	.20
272	Rob Konrad	.30	.10
273	Derrick Alexander	.30	.10
274	Joey Galloway	.50	.20
275	Peyton Manning	1.25	.50
276	Najeh Davenport	.30	.10
277	Jesse Palmer	.30	.10
278	LaMont Jordan	.75	.30
279	Ernie Conwell	.30	.10
280	Hines Ward	.75	.30
281	Freddie Mitchell	.50	.20
282	Curtis Conway	.30	.10
283	Cedrick Wilson	.30	.10
284	Troy Brown	.50	.20
285	Torry Holt	.75	.30
286	Mike Alstott	.75	.30
287	Frank Wycheck	.30	.10
288	Jeremiah Trotter	.30	.10
289	Tyrone Wheatley	.30	.10
290	David Boston	.50	.20
[illegible]	[illegible]	[illegible]	[illegible]
292	Troy Walters	.30	.10
293	Warrick Holdman	.30	.10
294	Peter Warrick	.50	.20
295	Tim Couch	.30	.10
296	Aaron Glenn	.30	.10
297	Deuce McAllister	.75	.30
298	Michael Strahan	.50	.20
299	Tom Brady	2.00	.75
300	Brett Favre	2.00	.75
301	Isaac Bruce	.75	.30
302	Jimmy Smith	.50	.20
303	Dante Hall	.75	.30
304	James McKnight	.30	.10
305	Daunte Culpepper	.75	.30
306	Lawyer Milloy	.50	.20
307	Jerome Pathon	.30	.10
308	Steve McNair	.75	.30
309	Vinny Testaverde	.50	.20
310	Tommy Maddox	.75	.30
311	Amani Toomer	.50	.20
312	Aaron Brooks	.75	.30
313	Gus Frerotte	.30	.10
314	Kevan Barlow	.50	.20
315	Matt Hasselbeck	.50	.20
316	Clinton Portis	1.25	.50
317	Keenan McCardell	.30	.10
318	Zach Thomas	.75	.30
319	Curtis Martin	.75	.30
320	Jamal Lewis	.75	.30
321	T.J. Duckett	.50	.20
322	Jerry Porter	.50	.20
323	Randy Moss	1.25	.50
324	Rosevelt Colvin	.30	.10
325	Corey Dillon	.50	.20
326	Kelly Holcomb	.50	.20
327	Josh McCown	.50	.20
328	Ed McCaffrey	.75	.30
329	Mikhael Ricks	.30	.10
330	Donald Driver	.50	.20
331	Darling/Thompson/McKinnon	.30	.10
332	Hall/Carpenter/Buchanon	.30	.10
333	Thomas/Weaver/Gregg RC	1.00	.40
334	Winfield/Wire/Clements	.30	.10
335	Morgan/Fields/Witherspoon	.50	.20
336	Brown/Robinson RC/Daniels	.50	.20
337	Powell RC/Thornton/Williams RC	.50	.20
338	Taylor RC/Little/Bentley	.75	.30
339	Ekuban/Ellis/Myers	.30	.10
340	Gard/Dalton RC/Berry RC	.75	.30
341	Green/Curry RC/Holmes	.50	.20
342	Hunt RC/KGB/Walker RC	.75	.30
343	Walker/Deloach RC/Payne	.30	.10
344	Bratzke/Washington/Morris	.30	.10
345	Henderson/Coleman/Stroud	.50	.20
346	Hicks/Browning RC/Sims	.50	.20
347	A.Ogunleye RC/Chester RC	2.00	.75
348	Robbins/Mixon/Johnstone	.30	.10
349	Phifer/Johnson/Bruschi	.75	.30
350	Grant/Chase RC/Howard	.50	.20
351	Short/Jones RC/Barrow	.50	.20
352	Jones/Lewis/Cowart	.30	.10
353	Barton/Parrella/Harris	.30	.10
354	Whiting/Simon/Walker	.30	.10
355	Smith/Hamp/von Oel	1.00	.40
356	Williams RC/Fisk/Johnson	.50	.20
357	Smith/Ulbrich/Peterson	.30	.10
358	Cochran RC/Eaton/Randle	.50	.20
359	Lewis/Wistrom/Little	.30	.10
360	Rudd/Spires/Quarles RC	.75	.30
361	Haynesworth/Carter/Smith	.30	.10

❑ 362	Smith/Armstead/Upshaw	.30	.10
❑ 363	Ad.Wilson/Dex.Jackson RC	.75	.30
❑ 364	F.Wakefield/K.Vanden	.30	.10
❑ 365	K.Kasper/J.McAddley	.30	.10
❑ 366	B.Smith/P.Kerney	.30	.10
❑ 367	M.Jenkins/T.Gaylor	.30	.10
❑ 368	C.Draft/M.Stewart	.30	.10
❑ 369	J.Hunter/R.Johnson	.30	.10
❑ 370	C.Fuller/E.Reed	.50	.20
❑ 371	A.Schobel/J.Posey RC	.50	.20
❑ 372	P.Williams/S.Adams	.30	.10
❑ 373	D.Grant/M.Minter	.30	.10
❑ 374	B.Buckner/K.Jenkins	.30	.10
❑ 375	R.Howard RC/T.Cousin RC	.50	.20
❑ 376	M.Brown/M.Green	.50	.20
❑ 377	J.Azumah/R.W.McQuarters	.30	.10
❑ 378	B.Simmons/S.Foley	.30	.10
❑ 379	A.Hawkins/J.Burris	.30	.10
❑ 380	Jo.Armour RC/M.Manuel	.30	.10
❑ 381	G.Warren/O.Roye	.30	.10
❑ 382	C.Brown/K.Lang	.30	.10
❑ 383	D.Ross/M.Edwards	.30	.10
❑ 384	A.Singleton RC/D.Nguyen	.50	.20
❑ 385	A.Wilson/J.Mobley	.30	.10
❑ 386	D.O'Neal/K.Kennedy	.30	.10
❑ 387	L.Elliss/S.Rogers	.30	.10
❑ 388	C.Cash/D.Bly	.30	.10
❑ 389	B.Walker/C.Harris	.30	.10
❑ 390	H.Navies RC/N.Diggs	.30	.10
❑ 391	A.Harris/M.McKenzie	.30	.10
❑ 392	C.Clemons/J.Foreman	.30	.10
❑ 393	E.Brown/M.Stevens	.30	.10
❑ 394	B.Scioli/L.Tripplett	.30	.10
❑ 395	D.Macklin/W.Harris	.30	.10
❑ 396	A.Ayodele/H.Douglas	.30	.10
❑ 397	F.Bryant/J.Craft RC	.30	.10
❑ 398	D.Darius/M.McCree	.30	.10
❑ 399	S.Fujita/S.Barber	.50	.20
❑ 400	E.Warfield RC/W.Bartee	.75	.30
❑ 401	G.Wesley/J.Woods	.30	.10
❑ 402	P.Surtain/S.Madison	.30	.10
❑ 403	B.Marion/S.Knight	.30	.10
❑ 404	G.Biekert/H.Crockett	.30	.10
❑ 405	C.Claiborne/C.Hovan	.30	.10
❑ 406	C.Chavous/K.Irvin	.30	.10
❑ 407	C.Fauria/D.Graham	.30	.10
❑ 408	O.Smith/R.Harrison	.30	.10
❑ 409	A.Pleasant/R.Seymour	.30	.10
❑ 410	D.Smith/S.Hodge	.30	.10
❑ 411	A.Ambrose/D.Carter	.30	.10
❑ 412	M.Mitchell/D.Rodgers	.30	.10
❑ 413	W.Allen/W.Peterson	.30	.10
❑ 414	C.Griffin/K.Hamilton	.30	.10
❑ 415	O.Stoutmire/S.Williams	.30	.10
❑ 416	A.Beasley/D.Abraham	.30	.10
❑ 417	J.McGraw/S.Games	.30	.10
❑ 418	C.Woodson/P.Buchanon	.50	.20
❑ 419	T.Bryant/T.Armstrong	.30	.10
❑ 420	B.Taylor/T.Vincent	.30	.10
❑ 421	C.Emmons/N.Wayne	.30	.10
❑ 422	B.Alexander/C.Hope	.50	.20
❑ 423	J.Porter/K.Bell	.75	.30
❑ 424	C.Scott/D.Washington	.30	.10
❑ 425	B.Leber/R.McNeil	.30	.10
❑ 426	Q.Jammer/T.Cody	.30	.10
❑ 427	A.Plummer/J.Webster	.30	.10
❑ 428	T.Parrish/Z.Bronson	.30	.10
❑ 429	I.Mili/J.Stevens	.30	.10
❑ 430	K.Lucas/S.Springs	.30	.10
❑ 431	C.Brown/O.Huff	.30	.10
❑ 432	J.Duncan/T.Polley	.30	.10
❑ 433	A.Williams/T.Fisher	.30	.10
❑ 434	B.Kelly/R.Barber	.30	.10
❑ 435	A.Stecker/K.Williams	.30	.10
❑ 436	D.Bennett/J.McCareins	.50	.20
❑ 437	L.Schulters/T.Williams	.30	.10
❑ 438	A.Dyson/S.Rolle	.30	.10
❑ 439	I.Ohalete/M.Bowen	.30	.10
❑ 440	B.Noble/D.Wilkinson	.30	.10
❑ 441	Charles Rogers RC	1.25	.50
❑ 442	Jimmy Kennedy RC	1.25	.50
❑ 443	Kelley Washington RC	1.25	.50
❑ 444	Trent Smith RC	1.00	.40
❑ 445	Rashean Mathis RC	1.00	.40
❑ 446	Brian St.Pierre RC	1.25	.50
❑ 447	Bethel Johnson RC	1.25	.50
❑ 448	Alonzo Jackson RC	1.00	.40
❑ 449	Arnaz Battle RC	1.25	.50
❑ 450	Carson Palmer RC	6.00	2.50
❑ 451	Michael Haynes RC	1.25	.50
❑ 452	LaBrandon Toefield RC	1.25	.50
❑ 453	Earnest Graham RC	1.25	.50
❑ 454	Walter Young RC	.60	.25
❑ 455	Terry Pierce RC	1.00	.40
❑ 456	Talman Gardner RC	1.25	.50
❑ 457	J.T. Wall RC	.60	.25
❑ 458	DeWayne Robertson RC	1.25	.50
❑ 459	Bradie James RC	1.25	.50
❑ 460	Andre Johnson RC	2.50	1.00
❑ 461	Bobby Wade RC	1.25	.50
❑ 462	Chris Davis RC	1.00	.40
❑ 463	Kliff Kingsbury RC	1.00	.40
❑ 464	Osi Umenyiora RC	2.00	.75
❑ 465	Domanick Davis RC	1.25	.50
❑ 466	Sam Aiken RC	1.00	.40
❑ 467	Ty Warren RC	1.25	.50
❑ 468	Terence Newman RC	2.50	1.00
❑ 469	Zuriel Smith RC	.60	.25
❑ 470	Willis McGahee RC	3.00	1.25
❑ 471	David Kircus RC	1.25	.50
❑ 472	Billy McMullen RC	1.00	.40
❑ 473	Antwoine Sanders RC	.60	.25
❑ 474	Adrian Madise RC	1.00	.40
❑ 475	Byron Leftwich RC	4.00	1.50
❑ 476	Justin Gage RC	1.25	.50
❑ 477	Jason Witten RC	2.50	1.00
❑ 478	Lee Suggs RC	1.25	.50
❑ 479	Kareem Kelly RC	1.00	.40
❑ 480	Rex Grossman RC	4.00	1.50
❑ 481	Nate Burleson RC	1.25	.50
❑ 482	Chris Brown RC	1.25	.50
❑ 483	Julian Battle RC	1.00	.40
❑ 484	Carl Ford RC	.60	.25
❑ 485	Angelo Crowell RC	1.00	.40
❑ 486	Bennie Joppru RC	1.25	.50
❑ 487	Aaron Walker RC	1.00	.40
❑ 488	Brandon Green RC	1.00	.40
❑ 489	L.J. Smith RC	1.25	.50
❑ 490	Ken Dorsey RC	1.25	.50
❑ 491	Eugene Wilson RC	1.25	.50
❑ 492	Chaun Thompson RC	.60	.25
❑ 493	Kevin Curtis RC	1.50	.60
❑ 494	Marcus Trufant RC	1.25	.50
❑ 495	Andrew Williams RC	1.00	.40
❑ 496	Visanthe Shiancoe RC	1.00	.40
❑ 497	Terrence Edwards RC	1.00	.40
❑ 498	Rien Long RC	1.00	.40
❑ 499	Nick Barnett RC	1.25	.50
❑ 500	Larry Johnson RC	6.00	3.00
❑ 501	Ken Hamlin RC	1.25	.50
❑ 502	Johnathan Sullivan RC	1.00	.40
❑ 503	Jeremi Johnson RC	1.00	.40
❑ 504	William Joseph RC	1.25	.50
❑ 505	Boss Bailey RC	1.25	.50
❑ 506	Anquan Boldin RC	3.00	1.25
❑ 507	Dave Ragone RC	1.25	.50
❑ 508	DeJuan Groce RC	1.25	.50
❑ 509	Rashad Moore RC	1.00	.40
❑ 510	Mike Doss RC	1.25	.50
❑ 511	Kenny Peterson RC	1.00	.40
❑ 512	Justin Griffith RC	1.00	.40
❑ 513	Jordan Gross RC	1.00	.40
❑ 514	Terrence Holt RC	1.00	.40
❑ 515	Seneca Wallace RC	1.25	.50
❑ 516	Ovie Mughelli RC	.60	.25
❑ 517	Jerome McDougle RC	1.25	.50
❑ 518	Kevin Williams RC	1.25	.50
❑ 519	Musa Smith RC	1.25	.50
❑ 520	Teyo Johnson RC	1.25	.50
❑ 521	Victor Hobson RC	1.25	.50
❑ 522	Cory Redding RC	1.00	.40
❑ 523	Cecil Sapp RC	1.00	.40
❑ 524	Brandon Lloyd RC	1.25	.50
❑ 525	Chris Simms RC	2.00	.75
❑ 526	Artose Pinner RC	1.25	.50
❑ 527	DeWayne White RC	1.00	.40
❑ 528	Doug Gabriel RC	1.25	.50
❑ 529	Calvin Pace RC	1.00	.40
❑ 530	Onterrio Smith RC	1.25	.50
❑ 531	Terrell Suggs RC	2.00	.75
❑ 532	Ronald Bellamy RC	1.00	.40
❑ 533	Jimmy Wilkerson RC	1.00	.40
❑ 534	Travis Anglin RC	.60	.25
❑ 535	Tyrone Calico RC	1.25	.50
❑ 536	Keenan Howry RC	1.25	.50
❑ 537	Gibran Hamdan RC	.60	.25
❑ 538	Bryant Johnson RC	1.25	.50
❑ 539	Brad Banks RC	1.00	.40
❑ 540	Justin Fargas RC	1.25	.50
❑ 541	B.J. Askew RC	1.25	.50
❑ 542	J.R. Tolver RC	1.00	.40
❑ 543	Tully Banta-Cain RC	1.00	.40
❑ 544	Shaun McDonald RC	1.25	.50
❑ 545	Taylor Jacobs RC	1.00	.40
❑ 546	Ricky Manning RC	1.25	.50
❑ 547	Dallas Clark RC	1.25	.50
❑ 548	Juston Wood RC	.60	.25
❑ 549	Andre Woolfolk RC	1.25	.50
❑ 550	Kyle Boller RC	1.25	.50
❑ CL1	Checklist Card 1	.10	.02
❑ CL2	Checklist Card 2	.10	.02
❑ CL3	Checklist Card 3	.10	.02
❑ CL4	Checklist Card 4	.10	.02

2004 Topps Total

❑	COMPLETE SET (440)	80.00	40.00
❑ 1	Donovan McNabb	1.00	.40
❑ 2	Zach Thomas	.75	.30
❑ 3	Randy Moss	1.00	.40
❑ 4	Kerry Collins	.50	.20
❑ 5	Hines Ward	.75	.30
❑ 6	Tyrone Calico	.50	.20
❑ 7	Patrick Ramsey	.50	.20
❑ 8	Jeff Garcia	.75	.30
❑ 9	Aveion Cason	.30	.10
❑ 10	Stephen Davis	.50	.20
❑ 11	Marcel Shipp	.50	.20
❑ 12	T.J. Duckett	.50	.20
❑ 13	Chris McAlister	.30	.10
❑ 14	Peter Warrick	.50	.20
❑ 15	Ahman Green	.75	.30
❑ 16	Deion Branch	.75	.30
❑ 17	David Boston	.50	.20
❑ 18	Wayne Chrebet	.50	.20
❑ 19	Michael Strahan	.50	.20
❑ 20	Arnaz Battle	.50	.20
❑ 21	Darrell Jackson	.50	.20
❑ 22	Chris Chandler	.50	.20
❑ 23	Charlie Garner	.50	.20
❑ 24	James Thrash	.30	.10
❑ 25	LaDainian Tomlinson	1.00	.40
❑ 26	Jerry Porter	.50	.20
❑ 27	Jerome Pathon	.30	.10
❑ 28	Jerome Bettis	.75	.30
❑ 29	Eddie George	.50	.20
❑ 30	Jamal Lewis	.75	.30
❑ 31	Ricky Proehl	.30	.10
❑ 32	Josh Reed	.30	.10
❑ 33	David Terrell	.50	.20
❑ 34	Antonio Bryant	.50	.20
❑ 35	Domanick Davis	.75	.30
❑ 36	Artose Pinner	.30	.10
❑ 37	Jed Weaver	.30	.10
❑ 38	Johnnie Morton	.50	.20
❑ 39	Troy Edwards	.30	.10

❑ 40 Marvin Harrison .75 .30
❑ 41 Chris Hovan .30 .10
❑ 42 Boo Williams .30 .10
❑ 43 Ike Hilliard .30 .10
❑ 44 Sam Cowart .30 .10
❑ 45 Shaun Alexander .75 .30
❑ 46 Freddie Mitchell .50 .20
❑ 47 Garrison Hearst .50 .20
❑ 48 Joe Jurevicius .30 .10
❑ 49 Freddie Jones .30 .10
❑ 50 Michael Vick 1.50 .60
❑ 51 Mike Rucker .30 .10
❑ 52 Carson Palmer 1.00 .40
❑ 53 Az-Zahir Hakim .30 .10
❑ 54 Billy Miller .30 .10
❑ 55 Chad Pennington .75 .30
❑ 56 Charles Woodson .50 .20
❑ 57 Andre Carter .30 .10
❑ 58 Maurice Morris .30 .10
❑ 59 Leonard Little .30 .10
❑ 60 Travis Henry .50 .20
❑ 61 Thomas Jones .50 .20
❑ 62 Dennis Northcutt .30 .10
❑ 63 Quentin Griffin .75 .30
❑ 64 Joey Harrington .75 .30
❑ 65 Edgerrin James .75 .30
❑ 66 Cortez Hankton .30 .10
❑ 67 Jason Taylor .30 .10
❑ 68 Eddie Kennison .30 .10
❑ 69 Ty Law .50 .20
❑ 70 Aaron Brooks .50 .20
❑ 71 Antonio Gates .75 .30
❑ 72 Antwaan Randle El .75 .30
❑ 73 Kevan Barlow .50 .20
❑ 74 Chris Brown .75 .30
❑ 75 Clinton Portis .75 .30
❑ 76 Rod Gardner .50 .20
❑ 77 Isaac Bruce .50 .20
❑ 78 Mike Alstott .50 .20
❑ 79 Brian Westbrook .50 .20
❑ 80 Amani Toomer .50 .20
❑ 81 Justin Fargas .50 .20
❑ 82 Michael Bennett .50 .20
❑ 83 Dante Hall .75 .30
❑ 84 Marcus Pollard .30 .10
❑ 85 Fred Taylor .50 .20
❑ 86 Tai Streets .30 .10
❑ 87 Robert Ferguson .30 .10
❑ 88 Roy Williams S .50 .20
❑ 89 Lee Suggs .75 .30
❑ 90 Chad Johnson .75 .30
❑ 91 DeShaun Foster .50 .20
❑ 92 Alge Crumpler .50 .20
❑ 93 Travis Taylor .30 .10
❑ 94 London Fletcher .30 .10
❑ 95 Priest Holmes 1.00 .40
❑ 96 A.J. Feeley .75 .30
❑ 97 Kevin Faulk .30 .10
❑ 98 Shaun Ellis .30 .10
❑ 99 Tim Dwight .50 .20
❑ 100 Peyton Manning 1.25 .50
❑ 101 Dane Looker .50 .20
❑ 102 Mark Brunell .50 .20
❑ 103 Bryant Johnson .30 .10
❑ 104 Kelley Washington .30 .10
❑ 105 Rex Grossman .75 .30
❑ 106 William Green .50 .20
❑ 107 Keyshawn Johnson .50 .20
❑ 108 Trevor Pryce .30 .10
❑ 109 Donald Driver .50 .20
❑ 110 David Carr .75 .30
❑ 111 Marcus Robinson .50 .20
❑ 112 Justin McCareins .30 .10
❑ 113 Tim Brown .75 .30
❑ 114 James Farrior .30 .10
❑ 115 Deuce McAllister .75 .30
❑ 116 Simeon Rice .50 .20
❑ 117 Koren Robinson .50 .20
❑ 118 Kassim Osgood .30 .10
❑ 119 Tim Rattay .30 .10
❑ 120 Laveranues Coles .50 .20
❑ 121 Brian Finneran .30 .10
❑ 122 Todd Heap .50 .20
❑ 123 Bobby Shaw .30 .10
❑ 124 Anthony Thomas .50 .20
❑ 125 Brett Favre 2.00 .75
❑ 126 Dwight Freeney .50 .20
❑ 127 Randy McMichael .30 .10
❑ 128 David Givens .50 .20
❑ 129 Rich Gannon .50 .20
❑ 130 Tiki Barber .75 .30
❑ 131 Terrell Owens .75 .30
❑ 132 Drew Bennett .50 .20
❑ 133 Shawn Bryson .30 .10
❑ 134 Jabar Gaffney .50 .20
❑ 135 Jake Delhomme .75 .30
❑ 136 Warrick Dunn .50 .20
❑ 137 Brandon Lloyd .50 .20
❑ 138 Brad Johnson .50 .20
❑ 139 Jon Kitna .50 .20
❑ 140 Marshall Faulk .75 .30
❑ 141 Javon Walker .50 .20
❑ 142 Nate Burleson .75 .30
❑ 143 Jimmy Smith .50 .20
❑ 144 Adewale Ogunleye .50 .20
❑ 145 Trent Green .50 .20
❑ 146 Richard Seymour .30 .10
❑ 147 Donte' Stallworth .50 .20
❑ 148 Curtis Martin .75 .30
❑ 149 Todd Pinkston .30 .10
❑ 150 Steve McNair .75 .30
❑ 151 Josh McCown .50 .20
❑ 152 Ray Lewis .75 .30
❑ 153 Muhsin Muhammad .50 .20
❑ 154 Quincy Morgan .50 .20
❑ 155 Jake Plummer .50 .20
❑ 156 Jason Witten .50 .20
❑ 157 Dallas Clark .50 .20
❑ 158 Onterrio Smith .50 .20
❑ 159 Jeremy Shockey .75 .30
❑ 160 Ricky Williams .75 .30
❑ 161 Jevon Kearse .50 .20
❑ 162 Plaxico Burress .50 .20
❑ 163 Drew Brees .75 .30
❑ 164 Bobby Engram .30 .10
❑ 165 Torry Holt .75 .30
❑ 166 Ladell Betts .30 .10
❑ 167 Kelly Holcomb .50 .20
❑ 168 Vinny Testaverde .50 .20
❑ 169 Marty Booker .50 .20
❑ 170 Rudi Johnson .50 .20
❑ 171 Andra Davis .30 .10
❑ 172 Kurt Warner .75 .30
❑ 173 Troy Brown .50 .20
❑ 174 Jerry Rice 1.50 .60
❑ 175 Daunte Culpepper .75 .30
❑ 176 Darren Sharper .30 .10
❑ 177 Charles Rogers .50 .20
❑ 178 Ashley Lelie .50 .20
❑ 179 Correll Buckhalter .50 .20
❑ 180 Anquan Boldin .75 .30
❑ 181 Terrell Suggs .50 .20
❑ 182 Reggie Wayne .50 .20
❑ 183 Duce Staley .50 .20
❑ 184 Donnie Edwards .30 .10
❑ 185 Joe Horn .50 .20
❑ 186 LaVar Arrington 1.50 .60
❑ 187 Keenan McCardell .30 .10
❑ 188 Cedrick Wilson .30 .10
❑ 189 Bubba Franks .50 .20
❑ 190 Santana Moss .50 .20
❑ 191 Peerless Price .50 .20
❑ 192 Kyle Boller .75 .30
❑ 193 Julius Peppers .75 .30
❑ 194 Drew Bledsoe .75 .30
❑ 195 Marc Bulger .75 .30
❑ 196 Brian Urlacher 1.00 .40
❑ 197 Andre' Davis .30 .10
❑ 198 Terry Glenn .30 .10
❑ 199 Champ Bailey .50 .20
❑ 200 Tom Brady 2.00 .75
❑ 201 Chris Chambers .50 .20
❑ 202 Tommy Maddox .50 .20
❑ 203 Derrick Brooks .50 .20
❑ 204 Corey Dillon .50 .20
❑ 205 Matt Hasselbeck .50 .20
❑ 206 Keith Brooking .30 .10
❑ 207 Steve Smith .75 .30
❑ 208 Tony Gonzalez .50 .20
❑ 209 Joey Galloway .50 .20
❑ 210 Derrick Mason .50 .20
❑ 211 Quincy Carter .50 .20
❑ 212 Rod Smith .50 .20
❑ 213 Andre Johnson .75 .30
❑ 214 Rod Woodson .50 .20
❑ 215 Byron Leftwich 1.00 .40
❑ 216 Kevin Dyson .30 .10
❑ 217 Keith Bulluck .30 .10
❑ 218 Eric Moulds .50 .20
❑ 219 Jamie Sharper .30 .10
❑ 220 Takeo Spikes .30 .10
❑ 221 C.Pace/F.Wakefield .30 .10
❑ 222 B.Smith/P.Kerney .30 .10
❑ 223 E.Reed/G.Baxter .50 .20
❑ 224 A.Schobel/J.Posey .30 .10
❑ 225 K.Jenkins/B.Buckner .30 .10
❑ 226 J.Smith/D.Clemons .30 .10
❑ 227 M.Haynes/B.Robinson .30 .10
❑ 228 C.Brown/G.Warren .50 .20
❑ 229 T.Newman/D.Woodson .50 .20
❑ 230 R.Johnson/M.Fatafehi .30 .10
❑ 231 R.Porcher/J.Hall RC .75 .30
❑ 232 K.Gbaja-Biamila/C.Hunt .50 .20
❑ 233 A.Glenn/M.Coleman .30 .10
❑ 234 N.Harper RC/J.Jefferson .75 .30
❑ 235 H.Douglas/T.Brackens .30 .10
❑ 236 V.Holliday/E.Hicks .30 .10
❑ 237 S.Knight/A.Freeman .30 .10
❑ 238 S.Martin/N.Rogers .30 .10
❑ 239 R.Colvin/W.McGinest .30 .10
❑ 240 O.Stoutmire/S.Williams .30 .10
❑ 241 E.Barton/V.Hobson .30 .10
❑ 242 W.Sapp/T.Washington .50 .20
❑ 243 C.Simon/D.Walker .50 .20
❑ 244 T.Polamalu/M.Logan 2.00 .75
❑ 245 J.Williams/A.Dingle RC .30 .10
❑ 246 B.Young/B.Whiting .30 .10
❑ 247 K.Hamlin/D.Robinson RC .30 .10
❑ 248 D.Lewis/R.Pickett .30 .10
❑ 249 A.McFarland/G.Spires .30 .10
❑ 250 A.Haynesworth/R.Long .30 .10
❑ 251 I.Ohalete/M.Bowen .30 .10
❑ 252 B.Berry/K.King .30 .10
❑ 253 E.Johnson/E.Jasper .30 .10
❑ 254 C.Tillman/J.Azumah .50 .20
❑ 255 M.Wiley/L.Glover .30 .10
❑ 256 S.Rogers/D.Wilkinson .30 .10
❑ 257 G.Walker/R.Smith .30 .10
❑ 258 M.Doss/I.Bashir .30 .10
❑ 259 M.Stroud/J.Henderson .50 .20
❑ 260 R.Sims/C.Browning .30 .10
❑ 261 J.Seau/M.Greenwood .75 .30
❑ 262 K.Williams/K.Mixon .30 .10
❑ 263 T.Warren/K.Traylor .30 .10
❑ 264 W.Allen/W.Peterson .30 .10
❑ 265 D.Barrett/R.Tongue .30 .10
❑ 266 P.Buchanon/D.Gibson .30 .10
❑ 267 L.Sheppard/S.Brown .30 .10
❑ 268 B.Taylor/M.Trufant .50 .20
❑ 269 M.Washington/M.Barrow .30 .10
❑ 270 C.Draft/M.Stewart .30 .10
❑ 271 M.Brown/M.Green .50 .20
❑ 272 E.Brown/M.McCree .30 .10
❑ 273 P.Surtain/S.Madison .50 .20
❑ 274 B.Dawkins/M.Lewis .50 .20
❑ 275 S.Springs/F.Smoot .50 .20
❑ 276 McKinnon/Fisher/Thompson .30 .10
❑ 277 Webster/McBride RC/Scott .30 .10
❑ 278 Boulware/Hartwell/Thomas 1.00 .40
❑ 279 Vincent/Milloy/Clements .50 .20
❑ 280 Witherspoon/Morgan/Fields .50 .20
❑ 281 Simmons/Hardy/Webster .30 .10
❑ 282 Odom RC/Brown/Briggs 2.50 1.00
❑ 283 Holdman/Thompson/Lang .30 .10
❑ 284 Nguyen/Coakley/Singleton .30 .10
❑ 285 Wilson/Spragan RC/Holland .30 .10
❑ 286 Holmes/J.Davis RC/Bailey .75 .30
❑ 287 Barnett/Diggs/Navies .30 .10
❑ 288 Foreman/Peek/Wong .30 .10
❑ 289 Brock RC/Reagor/Tripplett .75 .30
❑ 290 Ayodele/Favors/Peterson .50 .20
❑ 291 Barber/Maslowsk/Fujita .50 .20

❑ 292 Claiborne/Henderson/Nattiel .50 .20
❑ 293 Bruschi/Phifer/Vrabel .75 .30
❑ 294 Grant/Howard/Sullivan .30 .10
❑ 295 Robbins/Joseph/Umenyiora .75 .30
❑ 296 Abra/Rober/Fergus.RC 1.25 .50
❑ 297 Harris/Rudd/Brayton .50 .20
❑ 298 Simoneau/Wayne/Jones .30 .10
❑ 299 Porter/Bell/Haggans RC 2.00 .75
❑ 300 Jammer/Davis/Florence .50 .20
❑ 301 Peterson/Ulbrich/Smith .30 .10
❑ 302 Simmons/Huff/Brown .30 .10
❑ 303 Tinoisamoa/Polley/Thomas .30 .10
❑ 304 Quarles/Wyms/Nece .30 .10
❑ 305 Carter/Hall/Sirmon .50 .20
❑ 306 Griffin/Daniels/Wynn .30 .10
❑ 307 Jackson/Wilson/Macklin .30 .10
❑ 308 Gregg/Douglas/Weaver .30 .10
❑ 309 Williams/Denney/Adams .30 .10
❑ 310 Hawkins/Minter/Manning .30 .10
❑ 311 James/Herring/Beckett .30 .10
❑ 312 Griffith/Little/Henry .30 .10
❑ 313 Lynch/Ferg.RC/Hern.RC .75 .30
❑ 314 Bly/Marion/Bryant .30 .10
❑ 315 Harris/Roman/McKenzie .30 .10
❑ 316 Thorn/Morris/Brackett RC 1.25 .50
❑ 317 Mathis/Darius/Bolden RC .50 .20
❑ 318 Warfield/Wesley/Woods .30 .10
❑ 319 Winfield/Russell RC/Chavous .50 .20
❑ 320 Harrison/Wilson/Poole .50 .20
❑ 321 Rodgers/Ruff/Hodge .30 .10
❑ 322 Green/Greisen/Emmons .30 .10
❑ 323 Von Oelhoffen/Smith/Hampton .75 .30
❑ 324 Godfrey/Foley/Leber .30 .10
❑ 325 Plummer/Parrish/Rumph .30 .10
❑ 326 Okeafor/Wistrom/Moore .30 .10
❑ 327 Archuleta/Williams/Butler .30 .10
❑ 328 Barber/Smith/Phillips .50 .20
❑ 329 Dyson/Schulters/Williams .30 .10
❑ 330 Thomas/Bellamy/Jones .30 .10
❑ 331 Philip Rivers RC 5.00 2.00
❑ 332 Dwan Edwards RC .75 .30
❑ 333 Ben Watson RC 1.50 .60
❑ 334 Karlos Dansby RC 1.50 .60
❑ 335 Cedric Cobbs RC 1.50 .60
❑ 336 Chris Perry RC 2.00 .75
❑ 337 Darius Watts RC 1.50 .60
❑ 338 Ricardo Colclough RC 1.50 .60
❑ 339 Derrick Hamilton RC 1.25 .50
❑ 340 Devard Darling RC 1.50 .60
❑ 341 Daryl Smith RC 1.50 .60
❑ 342 Luke McCown RC 1.50 .60
❑ 343 Dunta Robinson RC 1.50 .60
❑ 344 Keith Smith RC 1.25 .50
❑ 345 Ben Hartsock RC 1.50 .60
❑ 346 J.P. Losman RC 3.00 1.25
❑ 347 Chris Cooley RC 1.50 .60
❑ 348 Keary Colbert RC 1.50 .60
❑ 349 Tommie Harris RC 1.50 .60
❑ 350 Eli Manning RC 10.00 4.00
❑ 351 Kevin Jones RC 4.00 1.50
❑ 352 Lee Evans RC 2.00 .75
❑ 353 D.J. Williams RC 1.50 .60
❑ 354 Ben Troupe RC 1.50 .60
❑ 355 Mewelde Moore RC 1.50 .60
❑ 356 Michael Clayton RC 3.00 1.25
❑ 357 Michael Jenkins RC 1.50 .60
❑ 358 Adimchinobe Echemandu RC 1.25 .50
❑ 359 Rashaun Woods RC 1.50 .60
❑ 360 Bernard Berrian RC 2.00 .75
❑ 361 Carlos Francis RC 1.25 .50
❑ 362 Roy Williams RC 4.00 1.50
❑ 363 Sean Taylor RC 1.50 .60
❑ 364 Steven Jackson RC 5.00 2.00
❑ 365 Tatum Bell RC 3.00 1.25
❑ 366 Jonathan Vilma RC 1.50 .60
❑ 367 Derrick Strait RC 2.00 .75
❑ 368 Andy Hall RC 1.25 .50
❑ 369 Jason Babin RC 1.50 .60
❑ 370 Will Smith RC 1.50 .60
❑ 371 Kenechi Udeze RC 1.50 .60
❑ 372 Vince Wilfork RC 1.50 .60
❑ 373 Ahmad Carroll RC 1.50 .60
❑ 374 Marquise Hill RC 1.25 .50
❑ 375 Ben Roethlisberger RC 12.00 5.00
❑ 376 Chris Gamble RC 1.50 .60
❑ 377 Junior Siavii RC 1.50 .60
❑ 378 Teddy Lehman RC 1.50 .60
❑ 379 Antwan Odom RC 1.50 .60
❑ 380 DeAngelo Hall RC 2.00 .75
❑ 381 Nathan Vasher RC 2.00 .75
❑ 382 B.J. Symons RC 1.50 .60
❑ 383 Reggie Williams RC 2.00 .75
❑ 384 Michael Boulware RC 1.50 .60
❑ 385 Matt Schaub RC 5.00 2.00
❑ 386 Sean Jones RC 1.25 .50
❑ 387 Courtney Watson RC 1.50 .60
❑ 388 Nathaniel Adibi RC 1.50 .60
❑ 389 Devery Henderson RC 1.50 .60
❑ 390 Greg Jones RC 1.50 .60
❑ 391 Joey Thomas RC 1.50 .60
❑ 392 Drew Carter RC 1.50 .60
❑ 393 Julius Jones RC 5.00 2.00
❑ 394 Keyaron Fox RC 1.25 .50
❑ 395 Darrion Scott RC 1.50 .60
❑ 396 Rich Gardner RC 1.25 .50
❑ 397 Jeff Smoker RC 1.50 .60
❑ 398 Will Poole RC 1.50 .60
❑ 399 Samie Parker RC 1.50 .60
❑ 400 Larry Fitzgerald RC 5.00 2.00
❑ 401 Jerricho Cotchery RC 1.50 .60
❑ 402 Ernest Wilford RC 1.50 .60
❑ 403 Johnnie Morant RC 1.50 .60
❑ 404 Craig Krenzel RC 1.50 .60
❑ 405 Michael Turner RC 2.00 .75
❑ 406 D.J. Hackett RC 1.25 .50
❑ 407 P.K. Sam RC 1.25 .50
❑ 408 Triandos Luke RC 1.50 .60
❑ 409 Josh Harris RC 1.50 .60
❑ 410 Drew Henson RC 1.50 .60
❑ 411 John Navarre RC 1.50 .60
❑ 412 Cody Pickett RC 1.50 .60
❑ 413 Clarence Moore RC 1.50 .60
❑ 414 Michael Gaines RC 1.25 .50
❑ 415 Derek Abney RC 1.50 .60
❑ 416 Dontarrious Thomas RC 1.50 .60
❑ 417 Reggie Torbor RC 1.25 .50
❑ 418 Ryan Krause RC 1.25 .50
❑ 419 Travis LaBoy RC 1.50 .60
❑ 420 Kellen Winslow RC 3.00 1.25
❑ 421 Keiwan Ratliff RC 1.25 .50
❑ 422 Gilbert Gardner RC 1.25 .50
❑ 423 Jamaar Taylor RC 1.50 .60
❑ 424 Matt Ware RC 1.50 .60
❑ 425 Stuart Schweigert RC 1.50 .60
❑ 426 Marcus Tubbs RC 1.50 .60
❑ 427 Brandon Chillar RC 1.25 .50
❑ 428 Shawntae Spencer RC 1.50 .60
❑ 429 Marquis Cooper RC 1.25 .50
❑ 430 Derrick Ward RC 1.50 .60
❑ 431 Tim Euhus RC 1.50 .60
❑ 432 Patrick Crayton RC 1.50 .60
❑ 433 Caleb Miller RC 1.25 .50
❑ 434 Donnell Washington RC 1.50 .60
❑ 435 Thomas Tapeh RC 1.25 .50
❑ 436 Randy Starks RC 1.25 .50
❑ 437 Sloan Thomas RC 1.25 .50
❑ 438 Maurice Mann RC 1.25 .50
❑ 439 Jim Sorgi RC 1.50 .60
❑ 440 Nate Lawrie RC 1.25 .50

2005 Topps Total

❑ COMPLETE SET (550) 80.00 30.00
❑ COMP.PACKERS TIN (20) 20.00 10.00
❑ COMP.STEELERS TIN (20) 20.00 10.00
❑ 1 Michael Vick 1.00 .40
❑ 2 O.Kreutz/Q.Mitchell RC .40 .15
❑ 3 Re.Williams/Garrard/T.Edwards .50 .20
❑ 4 Terence Newman .40 .15
❑ 5 D.Jolley/C.Baker .40 .15
❑ 6 D.Clark/S.Will.RC/B.Hamilton .40 .15
❑ 7 Terrell Owens .75 .30
❑ 8 I.Ohalete/A.Wilson .40 .15
❑ 9 G.Walker/Payne/Rob.Smith .40 .15
❑ 10 Quentin Jammer .40 .15
❑ 11 Ke.Smith/D.Bly .40 .15
❑ 12 C.Taylor/Ogden/B.Sams .50 .20
❑ 13 Torry Holt .75 .30
❑ 14 W.Henderson/N.Davenport .40 .15
❑ 15 J.Siavii/Hicks/J.Allen .50 .20
❑ 16 Keith Bulluck .40 .15
❑ 17 K.Irvin/C.Chavous .40 .15
❑ 18 F.Jackson/A.Bryant/A.Davis .75 .30
❑ 19 Michael Pittman .40 .15
❑ 20 Vanderjagt/H.Smith RC .40 .15
❑ 21 J.Winborn/Ulbrich/D.Smith .40 .15
❑ 22 Reggie Wayne .50 .20
❑ 23 S.Lechler/Janikowski .40 .15
❑ 24 K.Mathis RC/J.Webster/B.Scott .40 .15
❑ 25 Daunte Culpepper .75 .30
❑ 26 W.Peterson/W.Allen .40 .15
❑ 27 T.Walter/F.Adams/L.Allen .40 .15
❑ 28 Tauscher/M.Flanagan/Clifton RC .40 .15
❑ 29 Jerome Bettis .75 .30
❑ 30 M.Brown/R.McQuarters .40 .15
❑ 31 Andre Johnson .50 .20
❑ 32 Toefield/G.Jones/Fuamatu-Ma'Afala .40 .15
❑ 33 G.Lewis/B.McMullen .75 .30
❑ 34 Kyle Boller .50 .20
❑ 35 Kacyvenski/T.White RC/Bates .40 .15
❑ 36 Chris Brown .50 .20
❑ 37 J.Phillips/B.Kelly .40 .15
❑ 38 Saturday RC/Diem RC/Ta.Glenn 1.25 .50
❑ 39 Clinton Portis .75 .30
❑ 40 M.Scifres/N.Kaeding .40 .15
❑ 41 Ke.Williams/Udeze/Johnstone .40 .15
❑ 42 Tony Parrish .40 .15
❑ 43 D.Armstrong/J.Gaffney .40 .15
❑ 44 F.Bryant/C.Cash/Te.Holt .40 .15
❑ 45 Kerry Collins .50 .20
❑ 46 M.Strong/M.Morris .50 .20
❑ 47 Robertson/J.Abraham/S.Ellis .40 .15
❑ 48 Darrell Jackson .50 .20
❑ 49 P.Price/A.Rossum .40 .15
❑ 50 A.Henry/N.Jones RC/Frazier RC .40 .15
❑ 51 Steven Jackson 1.00 .40
❑ 52 R.Sims/J.Browning .40 .15
❑ 53 Robbins/Umenyiora/W.Joseph .75 .30
❑ 54 Billy Volek .50 .20
❑ 55 A.Ayodele/Da.Smith .40 .15
❑ 56 I.Scott RC/Odom/T.Johnson .40 .15
❑ 57 Onterrio Smith .50 .20
❑ 58 M.Stover/D.Zastudil RC .40 .15
❑ 59 Hunt/Gbaja-Biamila/Kampman RC 2.00 .75
❑ 60 Dante Hall .50 .20
❑ 61 J.Peterson/B.Young .40 .15
❑ 62 Hardwick/Olivea RC/Oben .40 .15
❑ 63 Chad Pennington .75 .30
❑ 64 D.Clark/A.Moorehead .40 .15
❑ 65 B.Taylor/K.Richard RC .40 .15
❑ 66 K.Walker/J.Wade RC .40 .15
❑ 67 Jeremy Shockey .75 .30
❑ 68 Daylon McCutcheon .40 .15
❑ 69 Coakley/Claiborne/Tinoisamoa .40 .15
❑ 70 Roy Williams WR .75 .30
❑ 71 L.Schulters/Ta.Williams .40 .15
❑ 72 S.Brown/Hood RC/Wynn .40 .15
❑ 73 Sean Taylor .50 .20
❑ 74 L.Little/B.Chillar .40 .15
❑ 75 Boiman/R.Starks/Clauss RC .40 .15
❑ 76 Lee Suggs .50 .20
❑ 77 P.Crayton/T.Glenn .40 .15
❑ 78 Dansby/Darling/G.Hayes .40 .15
❑ 79 Nick Barnett .40 .15
❑ 80 R.Coleman/A.Lake RC .40 .15
❑ 81 Berrian/J.Gage/D.Clark .40 .15

❑ 82 Dominic Rhodes .40 .15
❑ 83 C.Moore/R.Hymes .40 .15
❑ 84 Fraley RC/Runyan/T.Thomas .40 .15
❑ 85 Philip Rivers .75 .30
❑ 86 A.Harris/A.Carroll .40 .15
❑ 87 B.Sanders/Doss/J.Jefferson 1.25 .50
❑ 88 Cesaire RC/Ja.Will/Dingle .40 .15
❑ 89 Eric Moulds .50 .20
❑ 90 P.Zellner RC/R.Davis .40 .15
❑ 91 K.Wong/Babin/A.Peek .40 .15
❑ 92 Tony Richardson .40 .15
❑ 93 G.Wesley/J.Woods .40 .15
❑ 94 Fabini/Goodwin RC/K.Mawae .40 .15
❑ 95 Tatum Bell .50 .20
❑ 96 K.Lewis RC/C.Emmons .40 .15
❑ 97 J.Galloway/W.Heller .50 .20
❑ 98 Tom Brady 2.00 .75
❑ 99 R.Babers/B.Walker .40 .15
❑ 100 Mickens/McGraw/Buckley .40 .15
❑ 101 Zach Thomas .75 .30
❑ 102 Co.Brown RC/A.Weaver .40 .15
❑ 103 A.Will/J.Butler/K.Garrett .40 .15
❑ 104 Troy Polamalu 1.25 .50
❑ 105 W.Sapp/T.Washington .50 .20
❑ 106 T.Johnson/Crockett/Morant .40 .15
❑ 107 Chris McAlister .40 .15
❑ 108 C.Stanley RC/K.Brown .40 .15
❑ 109 Drew Henson .50 .20
❑ 110 James Hall .40 .15
❑ 111 S.Player/N.Rackers .40 .15
❑ 112 D.Watts/A.Lelie .50 .20
❑ 113 J.David/N.Harper .40 .15
❑ 114 R.Curry/D.Gabriel .50 .20
❑ 115 R.Colclough/W.Williams .50 .20
❑ 116 C.Tillman/J.Azumah .40 .15
❑ 117 M.Kemoeatu RC/Ad.Thomas 1.00 .40
❑ 118 M.Roman/J.Thomas .40 .15
❑ 119 D.Henderson/M.Lewis .40 .15
❑ 120 M.Furrey/Manumaleuna 1.00 .40
❑ 121 R.Mahe/C.Buckhalter .50 .20
❑ 122 E.Kinney/T.Fleming .40 .15
❑ 123 W.Dunn/T.Duckett .50 .20
❑ 124 T.Euhus/M.Campbell .40 .15
❑ 125 P.Hunter/A.Glenn .40 .15
❑ 126 R.Tongue/D.Barrett .40 .15
❑ 127 S.Morris/L.Gordon .40 .15
❑ 128 R.Clark RC/S.Springs .40 .15
❑ 129 J.Miller/A.Vinatieri .75 .30
❑ 130 E.Warfield/W.Bartee .40 .15
❑ 131 Me.Moore/M.Bennett .50 .20
❑ 132 N.Goings/B.Hoover .40 .15
❑ 133 C.Harris/B.Macklin .40 .15
❑ 134 E.Drummond/R.Swinton .40 .15
❑ 135 J.Fargas/A.Whitted .40 .15
❑ 136 N.Clements/T.McGee RC .75 .30
❑ 137 T.Hollings/J.Wells .40 .15
❑ 138 D.Cooper RC/K.Thomas RC .40 .15
❑ 139 P.Dawson/D.Frost RC .40 .15
❑ 140 J.McCown/J.Navarre .50 .20
❑ 141 G.Ellis/K.Coleman .40 .15
❑ 142 G.Wilson/B.Alexander .40 .15
❑ 143 A.Woolfolk/L.Thompson .40 .15
❑ 144 E.Conwell/B.Williams .40 .15
❑ 145 D.Akers/Di.Johnson RC .40 .15
❑ 146 Hillenmeyer RC/L.Briggs 2.00 .75
❑ 147 R.Mathis RC/G.Brackett 1.50 .60
❑ 148 J.Rice/R.Alexander 1.25 .50
❑ 149 E.Coleman/D.Strait .40 .15
❑ 150 J.Hartwig RC/B.Troupe .40 .15
❑ 151 S.Davis/D.Florence .40 .15
❑ 152 P.Buchanon/M.Coleman .40 .15
❑ 153 S.Heiden/A.Shea .40 .15
❑ 154 T.Spikes/L.Fletcher .40 .15
❑ 155 T.Laboy/A.Odom .40 .15
❑ 156 A.Toomer/M.Cloud .50 .20
❑ 157 L.Tynes/C.Horn .50 .20
❑ 158 N.Diggs/P.Lenon RC .40 .15
❑ 159 R.Long/A.Haynesworth .40 .15
❑ 160 B.Askew/J.Sowell .40 .15
❑ 161 John Carney .40 .15
Mitch Berger
❑ 162 K.Campbell/J.Wiggins .40 .15
❑ 163 Jerramy Stevens .40 .15
❑ 164 Willis McGahee .75 .30

❑ 165 Ed Reed .50 .20
❑ 166 Muhsin Muhammad .50 .20
❑ 167 Donovin Darius .40 .15
❑ 168 E.J. Henderson .40 .15
❑ 169 Tony Banks .40 .15
❑ 170 Fred Taylor .50 .20
❑ 171 Jeremiah Trotter .40 .15
❑ 172 Adam Archuleta .40 .15
❑ 173 Marcus Trufant .40 .15
❑ 174 Steve McNair .75 .30
❑ 175 Ben Roethlisberger 2.00 .75
❑ 176 Derrick Blaylock .40 .15
❑ 177 Michael Strahan .50 .20
❑ 178 Robert Gallery .50 .20
❑ 179 Drew Brees .75 .30
❑ 180 David Kircus .60 .25
❑ 181 Robert Ferguson .40 .15
❑ 182 Jim Sorgi .40 .15
❑ 183 Alge Crumpler .50 .20
❑ 184 DeShaun Foster .50 .20
❑ 185 Reuben Droughns .50 .20
❑ 186 Charles Grant .40 .15
❑ 187 Jason Taylor .40 .15
❑ 188 James Thrash .50 .20
❑ 189 LaDainian Tomlinson 1.00 .40
❑ 190 Tim Rattay .40 .15
❑ 191 Jeff Garcia .50 .20
❑ 192 Jerricho Cotchery .40 .15
❑ 193 Chris Simms .50 .20
❑ 194 Jevon Kearse .50 .20
❑ 195 Kyle Brady .40 .15
❑ 196 Trent Green .50 .20
❑ 197 Antoine Winfield .40 .15
❑ 198 Deion Branch .50 .20
❑ 199 Rudi Johnson .50 .20
❑ 200 Lee Evans .50 .20
❑ 201 Stephen Davis .50 .20
❑ 202 Darnell Dockett .40 .15
❑ 203 Kurt Warner .50 .20
❑ 204 Quincy Morgan .40 .15
❑ 205 Daimon Shelton .40 .15
❑ 206 Champ Bailey .50 .20
❑ 207 Jamal Lewis .75 .30
❑ 208 Brett Favre 2.00 .75
❑ 209 Charles Woodson .50 .20
❑ 210 Koren Robinson .50 .20
❑ 211 Chris Chambers .50 .20
❑ 212 Dave Ragone .40 .15
❑ 213 Travis Minor .40 .15
❑ 214 Simeon Rice .50 .20
❑ 215 Tommy Maddox .40 .15
❑ 216 Aaron Stecker .40 .15
❑ 217 Dwight Freeney .50 .20
❑ 218 Thomas Jones .50 .20
❑ 219 Patrick Ramsey .50 .20
❑ 220 Travis Taylor .40 .15
❑ 221 Chris Weinke .40 .15
❑ 222 Marc Bulger .75 .30
❑ 223 James Farrior .40 .15
❑ 224 Billy Miller .40 .15
❑ 225 Mike Peterson .40 .15
❑ 226 Eddie Kennison .40 .15
❑ 227 Aaron Brooks .50 .20
❑ 228 Plaxico Burress .50 .20
❑ 229 Jerry Porter .50 .20
❑ 230 Joey Harrington .75 .30
❑ 231 Bubba Franks .50 .20
❑ 232 Michael Jenkins .50 .20
❑ 233 Larry Fitzgerald .75 .30
❑ 234 Troy Vincent .40 .15
❑ 235 Chad Johnson .75 .30
❑ 236 Roy Williams S .50 .20
❑ 237 Corey Dillon .50 .20
❑ 238 Donovan McNabb 1.00 .40
❑ 239 Marcus Robinson .50 .20
❑ 240 Derrick Brooks .50 .20
❑ 241 David Bowens RC .50 .20
❑ 242 Renaldo Wynn .40 .15
❑ 243 Kevan Barlow .50 .20
❑ 244 Antonio Gates .75 .30
❑ 245 Duce Staley .50 .20
❑ 246 Ernest Wilford .40 .15
❑ 247 Kevin Jones .75 .30
❑ 248 Julius Peppers .50 .20

❑ 249 Terrell Suggs .50 .20
❑ 250 Bertrand Berry .40 .15
❑ 251 Brian Simmons .40 .15
❑ 252 Jake Plummer .50 .20
❑ 253 Brian Urlacher .75 .30
❑ 254 Justin McCareins .40 .15
❑ 255 L.J. Smith .40 .15
❑ 256 Matt Hasselbeck .50 .20
❑ 257 Rashaun Woods .50 .20
❑ 258 Rodney Harrison .50 .20
❑ 259 Brandon Stokley .50 .20
❑ 260 [illegible]
❑ 261 J.P. Losman .75 .30
❑ 262 DeAngelo Hall .50 .20
❑ 263 Jake Delhomme .75 .30
❑ 264 Shaun Rogers .40 .15
❑ 265 Donald Driver .50 .20
❑ 266 Will Smith .40 .15
❑ 267 Brian Westbrook .50 .20
❑ 268 A.J. Feeley .50 .20
❑ 269 Marshall Faulk .75 .30
❑ 270 Marques Tuiasosopo .40 .15
❑ 271 Curtis Martin .75 .30
❑ 272 Jason Witten .50 .20
❑ 273 Kellen Winslow .75 .30
❑ 274 Corey Bradford .40 .15
❑ 275 Samari Rolle .40 .15
❑ 276 Anquan Boldin .50 .20
❑ 277 Adrian Peterson .40 .15
❑ 278 Javon Walker .50 .20
❑ 279 Fred Smoot .40 .15
❑ 280 Mike Alstott .50 .20
❑ 281 Randy McMichael .40 .15
❑ 282 Jay Fiedler .40 .15
❑ 283 Jamie Sharper .40 .15
❑ 284 Eli Manning 1.50 .60
❑ 285 Todd Pinkston .40 .15
❑ 286 La'Roi Glover .40 .15
❑ 287 Chris Perry .50 .20
❑ 288 David Carr .75 .30
❑ 289 Bryant Johnson .40 .15
❑ 290 Ray Lewis .75 .30
❑ 291 Tommie Harris .40 .15
❑ 292 Joe Horn .50 .20
❑ 293 Rod Smith .50 .20
❑ 294 Michael Clayton .75 .30
❑ 295 Tyrone Calico .50 .20
❑ 296 Santana Moss .50 .20
❑ 297 Hines Ward .75 .30
❑ 298 Jonathan Vilma .50 .20
❑ 299 Randy Moss .75 .30
❑ 300 Donte Stallworth .60 .20
❑ 301 Isaac Bruce .50 .20
❑ 302 Brian Griese .50 .20
❑ 303 Dennis Northcutt .40 .15
❑ 304 Michael Green .40 .15
❑ 305 Marvin Harrison .75 .30
❑ 306 Jimmy Smith .50 .20
❑ 307 Patrick Kerney .40 .15
❑ 308 Todd Heap .50 .20
❑ 309 Dan Morgan .40 .15
❑ 310 Charles Rogers .50 .20
❑ 311 Dunta Robinson .50 .20
❑ 312 Deuce McAllister .75 .30
❑ 313 Ronde Barber .40 .15
❑ 314 Brandon Lloyd .40 .15
❑ 315 Tiki Barber .75 .30
❑ 316 LaMont Jordan .75 .30
❑ 317 Lito Sheppard .40 .15
❑ 318 Laveranues Coles .50 .20
❑ 319 Drew Bennett .50 .20
❑ 320 Julius Jones 1.00 .40
❑ 321 Ahman Green .75 .30
❑ 322 Domanick Davis .50 .20
❑ 323 Byron Leftwich .75 .30
❑ 324 Nate Burleson .50 .20
❑ 325 David Givens .50 .20
❑ 326 Trent Dilfer .50 .20
❑ 327 T.J. Houshmandzadeh .40 .15
❑ 328 Keith Brooking .40 .15
❑ 329 Derrick Mason .50 .20
❑ 330 Ken Lucas .40 .15
❑ 331 Rex Grossman .50 .20
❑ 332 Edgerrin James .75 .30

❑ 333 Priest Holmes .75 .30
❑ 334 Donnie Edwards .40 .15
❑ 335 Pierson Prioleau RC .75 .30
❑ 336 Shaun Alexander 1.00 .40
❑ 337 D.J. Williams .40 .15
❑ 338 Peyton Manning 1.25 .50
❑ 339 Carson Palmer .75 .30
❑ 340 Keyshawn Johnson .50 .20
❑ 341 Tory James .40 .15
❑ 342 Drew Bledsoe .75 .30
❑ 343 Chris Gamble .50 .20
❑ 344 Mi.Lewis/B.Dawkins .50 .20
❑ 345 Forney/McClure RC/Weiner RC .40 .15
❑ 346 R.Smart/Kasay/J.Kyle .40 .15
❑ 347 J.Ferguson/Reeves/Nguyen .40 .15
❑ 348 Crocker/Lehan RC/M.Jameson .40 .15
❑ 349 Tyree/Ja.Taylor/T.Carter .40 .15
❑ 350 H.Thomas/D.Jones/Simoneau .40 .15
❑ 351 Royal/McCants/T.Jacobs .40 .15
❑ 352 Welker/D.Thompson/Gilmore .40 .15
❑ 353 D.Lewis/Pickett/Ty.Jackson .40 .15
❑ 354 F.Brown/F.Thomas/J.Bellamy .40 .15
❑ 355 Asomugha/M.Anderson/Schweigert .40 .15
❑ 356 M.Stroud/J.Hender/Favors .40 .15
❑ 357 W.Shields/Roaf/B.Waters RC .40 .15
❑ 358 Hamilton/Nalen/Lepsis .40 .15
❑ 359 J.Smith/Geathers/D.Clemons .40 .15
❑ 360 Wire/R.Baker/L.Milloy .40 .15
❑ 361 Ayanbadejo/J.Scobey/Hambrick .40 .15
❑ 362 St.Smith/Proehl/Colbert .50 .20
❑ 363 N.Harris/D.Thomas/Offord .40 .15
❑ 364 L.Neal/M.Turner/Pinnock .50 .20
❑ 365 Faneca/M.Smith RC/Hartings 1.25 .50
❑ 366 E.Moore/Pope/Ayanbadejo RC .75 .30
❑ 367 A.Plummer/Jo.Hanson RC/Spencer .40 .15
❑ 368 L.Betts/Brunell/C.Morton .50 .20
❑ 369 Pace/Timmerman/McCollum .40 .15
❑ 370 B.Thomas/Barton/Hobson .40 .15
❑ 371 S.Barber/K.Fox/K.Mitchell .40 .15
❑ 372 K.Edwards/Wilkinson/Redding .40 .15
❑ 373 Co.Jackson RC/Lang/McKinley .40 .15
❑ 374 Bannan/R.Edwards/S.Adams .40 .15
❑ 375 M.Schaub/D.White/Finneran .50 .20
❑ 376 Short/A.Wallace RC/K.Jenkins .40 .15
❑ 377 Leach/Carswell/Putzier .40 .15
❑ 378 Vrabel/T.Johnson/Bruschi .75 .30
❑ 379 Kiel/Je.Wilson RC/Fletcher .40 .15
❑ 380 Engelber/To.Brown RC/A.Adams .40 .15
❑ 381 Quarles/Gooch/D.White .40 .15
❑ 382 Madison/W.Poole/R.Howard .40 .15
❑ 383 Schneck RC/Gardocki/J.Reed .75 .30
❑ 384 J.Mitchell RC/Gross/Brzezinski RC .40 .15
❑ 385 Greisen/B.Green/A.Pierce .40 .15
❑ 386 C.Simon/D.Walker/McDougle .40 .15
❑ 387 D.Graham/Fauria/B.Watson .50 .20
❑ 388 E.Johnson/R.John/M.Coleman .40 .15
❑ 389 June/D.Thornton/Hutchins .50 .20
❑ 390 Teague/R.Tucker/M.Will.T .40 .15
❑ 391 M.Haynes/A.Brown/Ogunleye .75 .30
❑ 392 Ulmer RC/Br.Smith/De.Williams .40 .15
❑ 393 K.Faulk/Pass/Be.Johnson .50 .20
❑ 394 Tobeck RC/W.Jones/S.Hutchin .40 .15
❑ 395 V.Holliday/Y.Bell RC/K.Carter .40 .15
❑ 396 L.Foote/J.Porter/Al.Jackson .75 .30
❑ 397 Looker/K.Curtis/S.McDonald .50 .20
❑ 398 L.Marshall RC/C.Griffin/D.Evans .75 .30
❑ 399 D.Klecko/Izzo/R.Colvin .40 .15
❑ 400 M.Holland/Bentley/Gandy .40 .15
❑ 401 Petitgout/McKenzie RC
J.Whittle RC .40 .15
❑ 402 Sykes RC/Fatafehi/A.Wilson .40 .15
❑ 403 Meester RC/Ma.Will/Manuwai RC .40 .15
❑ 404 M.Schobel/K.Washing/Warrick .40 .15
❑ 405 M.Minter/R.Manning/C.Branch .40 .15
❑ 406 Jo.Reed/Jo.Smith/Aiken .40 .15
❑ 407 Birk/Liwienski/McKinnie .40 .15
❑ 408 Godfrey/Foley/Leber .40 .15
❑ 409 McFarland/Wyms/G.Spires .40 .15
❑ 410 E.Perry/Do.Lee/Booker .50 .20
❑ 411 Von Oelhoffen/Hoke RC/Aa.Smith .75 .30
❑ 412 B.Mitchell/Wistrom/Ra.Moore .40 .15
❑ 413 J.Green/Wilfork/T.Warren .50 .20
❑ 414 Middlebrooks/Lynch/N.Ferguson .40 .15
❑ 415 Reagor/R.Brock/Jo.Williams .40 .15
❑ 416 J.Dunn/S.Parker/La.Johnson .75 .30
❑ 417 La.Johnson/M.Wilkins RC/C.Miller .40 .15
❑ 418 Buckner/Moorehead/M.Rucker .40 .15
❑ 419 Denney/Kelsay/A.Schobel .40 .15
❑ 420 Singleton/B.James/K.O'Neil RC .40 .15
❑ 421 C.Thompson/Boyer/An.Davis .40 .15
❑ 422 D.Grant/Richardson RC/R.Mathis .40 .15
❑ 423 Schlesinger/Bryson/Pinner .40 .15
❑ 424 S.Johnson RC/R.Davis/Ru.Jones .40 .15
❑ 425 Phifer/Banta-Cain/McGinest .50 .20
❑ 426 McCardell/Osgood/E.Parker .40 .15
❑ 427 C.Woodard/Bernard/A.Cochran .40 .15
❑ 428 A.Battle/A.Walker/E.Johnson .40 .15
❑ 429 Salave'a RC/M.Wash/L.Arrington .75 .30
❑ 430 L.Mays/C.Wilson/Randle El .75 .30
❑ 431 D.Starks/E.Wilson/R.Gay .50 .20
❑ 432 Q.Griffin/M.Anderson/C.Sapp .50 .20
❑ 433 J.Thornton/L.Moore RC/Powell .40 .15
❑ 434 M.Gaines/Hankton/Seidman .40 .15
❑ 435 M.Haggan RC/Posey/A.Crowell .40 .15
❑ 436 O'Neal/M.Williams/K.Ratliff .40 .15
❑ 437 M.Light/Koppen RC/S.Neal RC .40 .15
❑ 438 C.Watson/D.Rodgers/J.Allen .50 .20
❑ 439 M.Boulware/Hamlin/Bierria RC .40 .15
❑ 440 T.Rogers RC/Unck RC/Roye .40 .15
❑ 441 Frank Gore RC 3.00 1.25
❑ 442 Mike Patterson RC 1.50 .60
❑ 443 DeMarcus Ware RC 2.50 1.00
❑ 444 Chris Henry RC 1.50 .60
❑ 445 Thomas Davis RC 1.50 .60
❑ 446 Justin Miller RC 1.25 .50
❑ 447 Shaun Cody RC 1.50 .60
❑ 448 Alex Barron RC .75 .30
❑ 449 Brock Berlin RC 1.25 .50
❑ 450 Travis Johnson RC 1.25 .50
❑ 451 Jerome Mathis RC 1.50 .60
❑ 452 Lance Mitchell RC 1.25 .50
❑ 453 Marlin Jackson RC 1.50 .60
❑ 454 Charlie Frye RC 1.50 .60
❑ 455 Luis Castillo RC 1.50 .60
❑ 456 Fred Gibson RC 1.25 .50
❑ 457 Dustin Fox RC 1.50 .60
❑ 458 Ryan Fitzpatrick RC 1.50 .60
❑ 459 Dan Orlovsky RC 1.50 .60
❑ 460 Justin Tuck RC 1.50 .60
❑ 461 Corey Webster RC 1.50 .60
❑ 462 Travis Daniels RC 1.25 .50
❑ 463 J.J. Arrington RC 1.50 .60
❑ 464 David Greene RC 1.50 .60
❑ 465 Alvin Pearman RC 1.50 .60
❑ 466 Manuel White RC 1.25 .50
❑ 467 Paris Warren RC 1.25 .50
❑ 468 Patrick Estes RC 1.25 .50
❑ 469 Cedric Houston RC 1.50 .60
❑ 470 David Pollack RC 1.50 .60
❑ 471 Craig Bragg RC 1.25 .50
❑ 472 Vincent Jackson RC 1.50 .60
❑ 473 Adam Jones RC 1.50 .60
❑ 474 Matt Jones RC 2.50 1.00
❑ 475 Stefan LeFors RC 1.50 .60
❑ 476 Heath Miller RC 3.00 1.25
❑ 477 Ryan Moats RC 1.50 .60
❑ 478 Vernand Morency RC 1.50 .60
❑ 479 Terrence Murphy RC 1.50 .60
❑ 480 Kyle Orton RC 1.50 .60
❑ 481 Roscoe Parrish RC 1.50 .60
❑ 482 Courtney Roby RC 1.50 .60
❑ 483 Aaron Rodgers RC 5.00 2.00
❑ 484 Carlos Rogers RC 2.00 .75
❑ 485 Antrel Rolle RC 1.50 .60
❑ 486 Eric Shelton RC 1.50 .60
❑ 487 Alex Smith QB RC 6.00 2.50
❑ 488 Andrew Walter RC 1.50 .60
❑ 489 Roddy White RC 1.50 .60
❑ 490 Cadillac Williams RC 6.00 2.50
❑ 491 Mike Williams 1.50 .60
❑ 492 Troy Williamson RC 1.50 .60
❑ 493 Kirk Morrison RC 1.50 .60
❑ 494 Tab Perry RC 1.50 .60
❑ 495 Chad Owens RC 1.50 .60
❑ 496 Lofa Tatupu RC 2.00 .75
❑ 497 Craphonso Thorpe RC 1.25 .50
❑ 498 Ryan Riddle RC .75 .30
❑ 499 Marcus Maxwell RC 1.25 .50
❑ 500 Barrett Ruud RC 1.50 .60
❑ 501 Stanley Wilson RC 1.25 .50
❑ 502 Mike Nugent RC 1.50 .60
❑ 503 Eric King RC 1.25 .50
❑ 504 Darryl Blackstock RC 1.25 .50
❑ 505 Attiyah Ellison RC .75 .30
❑ 506 Donte Nicholson RC 1.50 .60
❑ 507 Airese Currie RC 1.50 .60
❑ 508 Larry Brackins RC .75 .30
❑ 509 Joel Dreessen RC 1.25 .50
❑ 510 Cedric Benson RC 4.00 1.50
❑ 511 Mark Bradley RC 1.50 .60
❑ 512 Reggie Brown RC 1.50 .60
❑ 513 Ronnie Brown RC 6.00 2.50
❑ 514 Jason Campbell RC 2.50 1.00
❑ 515 Maurice Clarett 1.50 .60
❑ 516 Mark Clayton RC 1.50 .60
❑ 517 Braylon Edwards RC 5.00 2.00
❑ 518 Ciatrick Fason RC 1.50 .60
❑ 519 Dan Cody RC 1.50 .60
❑ 520 Taylor Stubblefield RC .75 .30
❑ 521 J.R. Russell RC 1.25 .50
❑ 522 Rian Wallace RC .40 .15
❑ 523 Anthony Davis RC 1.25 .50
❑ 524 Derek Anderson RC 2.50 1.00
❑ 525 Boomer Grigsby RC 1.50 .60
❑ 526 Rasheed Marshall RC 1.50 .60
❑ 527 Adrian McPherson RC 1.50 .60
❑ 528 Noah Herron RC 1.50 .60
❑ 529 Bryant McFadden RC 1.50 .60
❑ 530 Lionel Gates RC 1.25 .50
❑ 531 Matt Roth RC 1.50 .60
❑ 532 Derrick Johnson RC 2.50 1.00
❑ 533 Stanford Routt RC 1.25 .50
❑ 534 Brandon Jacobs RC 2.00 .75
❑ 535 Kevin Burnett RC 1.50 .60
❑ 536 Ryan Claridge RC 1.25 .50
❑ 537 James Kilian RC 1.50 .60
❑ 538 Oshiomogho Atogwe RC 1.25 .50
❑ 539 Fabian Washington RC 1.50 .60
❑ 540 Marion Barber RC 2.50 1.00
❑ 541 Anttaj Hawthorne RC 1.25 .50
❑ 542 Zach Tuiasosopo RC .75 .30
❑ 543 Ellis Hobbs RC 1.50 .60
❑ 544 Alex Smith TE RC 1.50 .60
❑ 545 Erasmus James RC 1.50 .60
❑ 546 Channing Crowder RC 1.50 .60
❑ 547 Kelvin Hayden RC 1.25 .50
❑ 548 Darren Sproles RC 1.50 .60
❑ 549 Marcus Spears RC 1.50 .60
❑ 550 Dante Ridgeway RC 1.25 .50
❑ CL1 Checklist 1 .10 .02
❑ CL2 Checklist 2 .10 .02
❑ CL3 Checklist 3 .10 .02
❑ CL4 Checklist 4 .10 .02
❑ BR1 Ben Roethlisberger Jumbo 6.00 3.00
❑ VL1 Vince Lombardi Jumbo 6.00 3.00

2006 Topps Total

❑ 1 C.Webster/S.Madison .40 .15
❑ 2 Randy Moss .75 .30
❑ 3 Garcia/Parry/Detmer .50 .20
❑ 4 Matt Jones .50 .20
❑ 5 C.Brown/G.Earl .40 .15
❑ 6 Anderson/Steinbach/Braham .40 .15
❑ 7 DeAngelo Hall .50 .20
❑ 8 J.P. Losman .50 .20

❑ 9 Kevin Jones .75 .30
❑ 10 K.Dorsey/F.Gore .75 .30
❑ 11 Nichol/Pearson RC/Allen .40 .15
❑ 12 Brandon Lloyd .50 .20
❑ 13 Jeremiah Trotter .40 .15
❑ 14 Stone/Grove/Sims .40 .15
❑ 15 Drew Brees .75 .30
❑ 16 Jason Taylor .40 .15
❑ 17 Tony Gonzalez .50 .20
❑ 18 Brandon Stokley .50 .20
❑ 19 Jake Plummer .50 .20
❑ 20 Braylon Edwards .75 .30
❑ 21 Berrian/Maynard/Gould RC .40 .15
❑ 22 B.Sams/M.Stover .40 .15
❑ 23 Darling/Huff/Dansby .40 .15
❑ 24 Julius Peppers .50 .20
❑ 25 Ferguson/Spears/Ellis .40 .15
❑ 26 D.Lee/D.Martin .40 .15
❑ 27 B.Johnson/B.Johnson .50 .20
❑ 28 Bethel Johnson .40 .15
❑ 29 Ellis/Robertson/Thomas .40 .15
❑ 30 Willie Parker 1.00 .40
❑ 31 E.Shepherd/I.Hilliard .40 .15
❑ 32 Troupe/Scaife/Mauck .40 .15
❑ 33 Marc Bulger .50 .20
❑ 34 M.Trufant/M.Boulware .40 .15
❑ 35 Hardwick/Oben/Olivea .40 .15
❑ 36 Ray Lewis .75 .30
❑ 37 S.Lefors/C.Weinke .40 .15
❑ 38 Kaesviharn/Pollack/Ohalete .40 .15
❑ 39 G.Jones/A.Pearman .40 .15
❑ 40 Allen/Hicks/Sims .40 .15
❑ 41 Tiki Barber .75 .30
❑ 42 N.Asomugha/F.Washington .40 .15
❑ 43 Lewis/Adams/Emanuel .40 .15
❑ 44 Rodney Harrison .40 .15
❑ 45 H.Smith/A.Vinatieri .50 .20
❑ 46 Orlovsky/Kitna/Bryson .50 .20
❑ 47 Bubba Franks .40 .15
❑ 48 A.Wilson/I.Gold .40 .15
❑ 49 Davis/Thompson/McGinest .40 .15
❑ 50 Nathan Vasher .40 .15
❑ 51 J.Greer/T.Vincent .40 .15
❑ 52 Rossum/Ptrsn/Koenen RC .40 .15
❑ 53 DeMarcus Ware .50 .20
❑ 54 L.Diamond RC/Booker .40 .15
❑ 55 McKinnie/Birk/Hutchinson .40 .15
❑ 56 Cole/Kearse/Patterson .50 .20
❑ 57 Tubbs/Wistrom/Fisher .40 .15
❑ 58 Curtis Martin .75 .30
❑ 59 D.Macklin/A.Rolle .40 .15
❑ 60 Lejeune/Howard/Bell .40 .15
❑ 61 Reggie Brown .60 .25
❑ 62 M.McKenzie/F.Thomas .40 .15
❑ 63 Fletcher/Hartsock/Sorgi .40 .15
❑ 64 Larry Fitzgerald .75 .30
❑ 65 E.Moulds/V.Morency .50 .20
❑ 66 Williams/Barnes/Naeole .40 .15
❑ 67 Trent Green .50 .20
❑ 68 D.Sproles/M.Turner .60 .25
❑ 69 Chillar/Glover/Tinoisamoa .50 .20
❑ 70 Chris Gamble .40 .15
❑ 71 A.Jones/M.Waddell .40 .15
❑ 72 Marshall/Washington/Daniels .40 .15
❑ 73 Hines Ward .75 .30
❑ 74 S.Knight/P.Surtain .40 .15
❑ 75 McKinney/Wade/Wiegert .40 .15
❑ 76 Rod Smith .50 .20
❑ 77 D.Henson/T.Romo 5.00 2.00
❑ 78 Franklin RC/Gregg/Pryce .40 .15
❑ 79 David Garrard .40 .15
❑ 80 D.Smith/M.Peterson .40 .15
❑ 81 Bowens/Traylor/Roth .40 .15
❑ 82 Simeon Rice .40 .15
❑ 83 M.Douglas/B.Young .40 .15
❑ 84 Thornton/Reynolds RC/Simon .40 .15
❑ 85 T.J. Houshmandzadeh .50 .20
❑ 86 L.Betts/J.Campbell .50 .20
❑ 87 Smith/Hartings/Faneca .50 .20
❑ 88 Antonio Pierce .40 .15
❑ 89 D.Bennett/R.Longwell .40 .15
❑ 90 Thomas/Manning/Poppinga .40 .15
❑ 91 Willis McGahee .75 .30
❑ 92 K.Smith/T.Holt .40 .15
❑ 93 Wilson/Samuel/Hobbs .50 .20
❑ 94 Pace/Timmerman/Barron .40 .15
❑ 95 Fred Taylor .50 .20
❑ 96 M.Doss/B.Sanders .50 .20
❑ 97 Joe/Briggs/Ayanbadejo .50 .20
❑ 98 Daunte Culpepper .75 .30
❑ 99 C.Perry/T.Perry .50 .20
❑ 100 Whitted/Janikowski/Lechler .40 .15
❑ 101 Julius Jones .75 .30
❑ 102 C.Lavalais/R.Coleman .40 .15
❑ 103 Rucker/Ciurciu RC/Wallace .40 .15
❑ 104 Rex Grossman .75 .30
❑ 105 Dunta Robinson .50 .20
❑ 106 Bockwoldt/Craft/Gleason .40 .15
❑ 107 Chad Pennington .50 .20
❑ 108 Heath Miller .50 .20
❑ 109 D.Hackett/N.Burleson .50 .20
❑ 110 Drew Bennett .40 .15
❑ 111 Williams/Godfrey/Castillo .40 .15
❑ 112 Doug Gabriel .40 .15
❑ 113 A.Toomer/B.Jacobs .50 .20
❑ 114 Travis Taylor .40 .15
❑ 115 Terrell Suggs .50 .20
❑ 116 Todd Heap .50 .20
❑ 117 Reese/Williams/Boley .40 .15
❑ 118 Odell Thurman .40 .15
❑ 119 D.Watts/S.Alexander .40 .15
❑ 120 Scobee/Hanson RC/Toefield .40 .15
❑ 121 Donovan McNabb .75 .30
❑ 122 A.Smith TE/A.Becht .40 .15
❑ 123 Adam Archuleta .40 .15
❑ 124 J.J. Arrington .50 .20
❑ 125 Johnson/Simmons/Miller .40 .15
❑ 126 Andruzzi/Bentley/Tucker .40 .15
❑ 127 Aaron Rodgers .75 .30
❑ 128 Brown/Gardner/Hobson .40 .15
❑ 129 Antonio Bryant .50 .20
❑ 130 Isaac Bruce .50 .20
❑ 131 Quarles/Nece/Ruud .40 .15
❑ 132 Williams/Elam/Sauerbrun .40 .15
❑ 133 B.Hoover/N.Goings .40 .15
❑ 134 Ward/Carter/Rolle .40 .15
❑ 135 Dante Hall .50 .20
❑ 136 Tom Brady 1.25 .50
❑ 137 R.Moats/C.Buckhalter .50 .20
❑ 138 Arnaz Battle .40 .15
❑ 139 Bernard/Hill/Lewis RC .40 .15
❑ 140 Kampman/Gbaja-Biamila/Jenkins .50 .20
❑ 141 Fowler RC/James/Burnett .40 .15
❑ 142 Warrick Dunn .50 .20
❑ 143 Eli Manning 1.00 .40
❑ 144 Clark/Brayton/Morrison .40 .15
❑ 145 Zach Thomas .75 .30
❑ 146 Anderson/Babin/Greenwood .40 .15
❑ 147 Ron Dayne .50 .20
❑ 148 D.Zastudil/P.Dawson .40 .15
❑ 149 Williams/Mosley/Johnson .40 .15
❑ 150 Donte Stallworth .50 .20
❑ 151 Shawne Merriman .50 .20
❑ 152 Thompson/Hentrich/Bironas .40 .15
❑ 153 Clinton Portis .75 .30
❑ 154 R.Curry/J.Morant .50 .20
❑ 155 Dwight Freeney .50 .20
❑ 156 B.Russell/D.McCutcheon .40 .15
❑ 157 Brown/Green/Tillman .50 .20
❑ 158 Takeo Spikes .40 .15
❑ 159 Kurt Warner .50 .20
❑ 160 Jonathan Vilma .50 .20
❑ 161 James Farrior .40 .15
❑ 162 D.Florence/Q.Jammer .40 .15
❑ 163 Kevan Barlow .50 .20
❑ 164 Haggans/Hampton/Smith .40 .15
❑ 165 Walter Jones .40 .15
❑ 166 Mayberry/Jacox RC/Holland .40 .15
❑ 167 Byron Leftwich .50 .20
❑ 168 Mike Williams WR .75 .30
❑ 169 Jason Witten .50 .20
❑ 170 Dennis Northcutt .40 .15
❑ 171 Baker/Clements/Wire .40 .15
❑ 172 Ronnie Cruz .40 .15
❑ 173 E.Henderson/E.James .40 .15
❑ 174 LaMont Jordan .50 .20
❑ 175 Tyrone Calico .40 .15
❑ 176 Nalen/Foster/Hamilton .40 .15
❑ 177 Sam Gado .50 .20
❑ 178 Randy McMichael .40 .15
❑ 179 Brown/Sheppard/Ware .40 .15
❑ 180 L.Little/A.Hargrove .40 .15
❑ 181 Cadillac Williams .75 .30
❑ 182 Feely/Morton/Tyree .40 .15
❑ 183 Dallas Clark .40 .15
❑ 184 Faggins/Sanders/Coleman .40 .15
❑ 185 V.Holliday/K.Carter .40 .15
❑ 186 Smith/Ulbrich/Winborn .40 .15
❑ 187 S.Player/N.Rackers .40 .15
❑ 188 Steve Smith .75 .30
❑ 189 Cassel/Graham/Watson .40 .15
❑ 190 J.Porter/L.Foote .40 .15
❑ 191 Jamal Lewis .50 .20
❑ 192 Michael Jenkins .50 .20
❑ 193 Michael Strahan .50 .20
❑ 194 Kyle Vanden Bosch .40 .15
❑ 195 Shields/Roaf/Waters .40 .15
❑ 196 Terry Glenn .50 .20
❑ 197 Griffith/Green/Wilson .40 .15
❑ 198 Philip Rivers .75 .30
❑ 199 Tuck/Joseph/Robbins .40 .15
❑ 200 LaDainian Tomlinson 1.00 .40
❑ 201 J.David/N.Harper .40 .15
❑ 202 Hall/Bailey/Rogers .40 .15
❑ 203 Donald Driver .50 .20
❑ 204 Reuben Droughns .50 .20
❑ 205 Wahle/Gross/Wharton .40 .15
❑ 206 Jonathan Ogden .40 .15
❑ 207 J.Bullocks/D.Smith .40 .15
❑ 208 Nugent/Miller/Graham RC .40 .15
❑ 209 Matt Hasselbeck .50 .20
❑ 210 Derrick Brooks .50 .20
❑ 211 Foxworth/Lynch/Ferguson .40 .15
❑ 212 Stewart/Unck/Fisk .40 .15
❑ 213 M.Will.T/Anderson RC/Villarrial .40 .15
❑ 214 Saturday/Glenn/Diem .40 .15
❑ 215 Larry Johnson 1.00 .40
❑ 216 Marcus Robinson .50 .20
❑ 217 Aaron Brooks .50 .20
❑ 218 Smith/Bartrum/Spach .40 .15
❑ 219 Steven Jackson .75 .30
❑ 220 Roy Williams WR .75 .30
❑ 221 L.Polite/P.Crayton .40 .15
❑ 222 Carson Palmer .75 .30
❑ 223 Brown/Kreutz/Tait .40 .15
❑ 224 Javon Walker .50 .20
❑ 225 J.Payton/T.Henry .50 .20
❑ 226 K.Rhodes/E.Coleman .40 .15
❑ 227 Ronnie Brown .75 .30
❑ 228 David Carr .50 .20
❑ 229 Terence Newman .40 .15
❑ 230 Grigsby/Bell/Mitchell .40 .15
❑ 231 M.Vrabel/R.Colvin .50 .20
❑ 232 Heitmann/Smiley/Harris .40 .15
❑ 233 Joey Galloway .50 .20
❑ 234 Keith Bulluck .40 .15
❑ 235 Hall/Frost/Brown .40 .15
❑ 236 Dockett/Smith/Okeafor .40 .15
❑ 237 Mike Anderson .50 .20
❑ 238 Kellen Winslow .75 .30
❑ 239 Tatum Bell .50 .20
❑ 240 A.Pinner/C.Schlesinger .40 .15
❑ 241 Roman/Underwood/Collins .40 .15
❑ 242 Reggie Wayne .50 .20
❑ 243 Reggie Williams .50 .20
❑ 244 Pope/Spragan/Crowder .40 .15
❑ 245 Courtney Watson .40 .15
❑ 246 G.Lewis/B.McMullen .40 .15
❑ 247 Troy Polamalu 1.00 .40
❑ 248 Smoker/Faulk/Looker .50 .20
❑ 249 Keyshawn Johnson .50 .20
❑ 250 J.Babineaux/C.Davis .40 .15
❑ 251 Marcel Shipp .40 .15
❑ 252 Brian Urlacher .75 .30
❑ 253 Haynesworth/LaBoy/Starks .40 .15
❑ 254 Derrick Burgess .40 .15
❑ 255 Harris/Thomas/Leber .40 .15
❑ 256 Henderson/Stroud/Hayward .40 .15
❑ 257 Travis Minor .40 .15
❑ 258 Rivera/Petitti/Johnson .40 .15
❑ 259 D.J. Williams .40 .15
❑ 260 Terrell Owens .75 .30

❑ 261 C.Wilson/D.Kreider .40 .15
❑ 262 Antonio Gates .75 .30
❑ 263 Ronde Barber .40 .15
❑ 264 Bryant Johnson .40 .15
❑ 265 Brett Favre 1.50 .60
❑ 266 C.Stanley/K.Brown .40 .15
❑ 267 McKenzie/Petitgout/O'Hara 1.00 .40
❑ 268 Chris Cooley .40 .15
❑ 269 Steve McNair .50 .20
❑ 270 Smith/Thornton/Geathers .40 .15
❑ 271 McClure/Forney/Lehr RC .40 .15
❑ 272 B.Sapp RC/McCleon/Warf .40 .15
❑ 273 Jeremy Shockey .75 .30
❑ 274 Chad Johnson .50 .20
❑ 275 Vincent RC/Flynn RC/Mulitalo .40 .15
❑ 276 Deuce McAllister .50 .20
❑ 277 Sapp/Kelly/Hamilton .50 .20
❑ 278 B.Manumaleuna/R.Fitzpatrick .50 .20
❑ 279 Spires/White/Wyms .40 .15
❑ 280 Josh McCown .50 .20
❑ 281 Derrick Johnson LB .50 .20
❑ 282 T.Bryant/C.Grant .40 .15
❑ 283 C.Houston/D.Blaylock .40 .15
❑ 284 David Givens .50 .20
❑ 285 Lindell/McGee/Moorman .40 .15
❑ 286 Charlie Frye .50 .20
❑ 287 Ahman Green .50 .20
❑ 288 Darren Sharper .40 .15
❑ 289 Justin McCareins .40 .15
❑ 290 Lofa Tatupu .50 .20
❑ 291 Brock/Reagor/Thomas .40 .15
❑ 292 Muhsin Muhammad .50 .20
❑ 293 Derrick Mason .40 .15
❑ 294 Jones/Mare/Welker .75 .30
❑ 295 Stecker/Henderson/Conwell .40 .15
❑ 296 Mawae/Roos/Olson .40 .15
❑ 297 M.Bradley/A.Peterson .50 .20
❑ 298 John Abraham .40 .15
❑ 299 Dockery/Rabach/Samuels .40 .15
❑ 300 Peyton Manning 1.25 .50
❑ 301 Alge Crumpler .50 .20
❑ 302 Mathis/Richardson/Grant .40 .15
❑ 303 Tedy Bruschi .75 .30
❑ 304 Snee/Diehl RC/Whittle 1.00 .40
❑ 305 J.Stevens/P.Warrick .50 .20
❑ 306 Trent Dilfer .50 .20
❑ 307 Marion Barber .50 .20
❑ 308 Robert Ferguson .40 .15
❑ 309 Chester Taylor .50 .20
❑ 310 Jerry Porter .50 .20
❑ 311 Buenning/Walker/Wade .40 .15
❑ 312 DeShaun Foster .50 .20
❑ 313 R.Parrish/K.Holcomb .40 .15
❑ 314 Chris Brown .50 .20
❑ 315 Woody/Backus/Raiola .40 .15
❑ 316 Andre Johnson .50 .20
❑ 317 S.Graham/K.Larson .40 .15
❑ 318 Mangum/Gaines/Shelton .40 .15
❑ 319 Ben Roethlisberger 1.25 .50
❑ 320 T.Devoe/C.Adams .75 .30
❑ 321 Jake Delhomme .50 .20
❑ 322 Chris Chambers .50 .20
❑ 323 Chris Simms .50 .20
❑ 324 Ed Reed .50 .20
❑ 325 Charles Rogers .50 .20
❑ 326 Eddie Kennison .40 .15
❑ 327 Seymour/Warren/Wilfork .40 .15
❑ 328 Lorenzo Neal .40 .15
❑ 329 Taylor Jacobs .40 .15
❑ 330 K.Mathis/L.Milloy .40 .15
❑ 331 Glenn/Henry/Reeves .40 .15
❑ 332 B.Dawkins/M.Lewis .50 .20
❑ 333 Edgerrin James .75 .30
❑ 334 Lee Evans .50 .20
❑ 335 Pat Williams .40 .15
❑ 336 Arrington/Torbor/Moore .75 .30
❑ 337 Roy Williams S .50 .20
❑ 338 Joe Horn .50 .20
❑ 339 Keenan McCardell .40 .15
❑ 340 Lee RC/Nedney/Hicks .40 .15
❑ 341 Mark Brunell .50 .20
❑ 342 Jimmy Smith .50 .20
❑ 343 Deltha O'Neal .40 .15
❑ 344 Chris McAlister .40 .15
❑ 345 T.Williamson/J.Kleinsasser .50 .20
❑ 346 N.Herron/A.Thurman .40 .15
❑ 347 A.Brown/A.Ogunleye .40 .15
❑ 348 Michael Vick .75 .30
❑ 349 Laveranues Coles .50 .20
❑ 350 Alex Smith QB .75 .30
❑ 351 Billy Volek .50 .20
❑ 352 Cato June .50 .20
❑ 353 J.Jurevicius/F.Jackson .50 .20
❑ 354 Keary Colbert .40 .15
❑ 355 Griffith/Schaub/White .50 .20
❑ 356 Smith/Payne/Walker .40 .15
❑ 357 Samie Parker .40 .15
❑ 358 Plaxico Burress .50 .20
❑ 359 R.Bartell/O.Atogwe .40 .15
❑ 360 C.Roby/R.Williams .40 .15
❑ 361 Springs/Harris/Prioleau .40 .15
❑ 362 A.Crowell/L.Fletcher .40 .15
❑ 363 Nick Barnett .40 .15
❑ 364 Antoine Winfield .40 .15
❑ 365 Will Smith .40 .15
❑ 366 J.Cotchery/B.Askew .40 .15
❑ 367 Brian Westbrook .50 .20
❑ 368 Jerome Mathis .40 .15
❑ 369 C.Moore/D.Darling .40 .15
❑ 370 Eric Parker .40 .15
❑ 371 Bly/Wilson/Kennedy .40 .15
❑ 372 Champ Bailey .50 .20
❑ 373 Cedric Benson .75 .30
❑ 374 Gray RC/Tobeck/Locklear .40 .15
❑ 375 L.Tynes/D.Colquitt .40 .15
❑ 376 Dan Morgan .40 .15
❑ 377 Posey/Schobel/Kelsay .40 .15
❑ 378 Ekuban/Brown/Myers .40 .15
❑ 379 Reed/Colclough/Gardocki .40 .15
❑ 380 M.Pollard/S.Vines .40 .15
❑ 381 McQuarters/Butler/Deloatch .40 .15
❑ 382 Fred Smoot .40 .15
❑ 383 Walter/Anderson/Crockett .50 .20
❑ 384 Dominic Rhodes .50 .20
❑ 385 T.Thompson/M.Vanderjagt .50 .20
❑ 386 Sullivan/Melton/Bryant .40 .15
❑ 387 M.Scifres/N.Kaeding .40 .15
❑ 388 Erron Kinney .40 .15
❑ 389 Bergen/Edwards/McCoy .40 .15
❑ 390 B.Jones/K.Brady .40 .15
❑ 391 McKinley/Pool/Baxter .40 .15
❑ 392 Jackson/Giordano/Hayden .40 .15
❑ 393 Keith Brooking .40 .15
❑ 394 Josh Reed .40 .15
❑ 395 Thomas Jones .50 .20
❑ 396 D.Johnson CB/S.Spencer .40 .15
❑ 397 Woolfolk/Clauss/Gardner .40 .15
❑ 398 Kyle Boller .40 .15
❑ 399 P.Pass/K.Faulk .40 .15
❑ 400 Routt/Schweigert/Riddle .40 .15
❑ 401 Donnie Edwards .40 .15
❑ 402 Michael Clayton .50 .20
❑ 403 Kasay/Kyle/Robertson .40 .15
❑ 404 A.Carroll/A.Harris .40 .15
❑ 405 Priest Holmes .50 .20
❑ 406 Jabar Gaffney .40 .15
❑ 407 Mewelde Moore .40 .15
❑ 408 Torry Holt .50 .20
❑ 409 Mark Clayton .75 .30
❑ 410 Shaun Alexander .75 .30
❑ 411 T.Tillman/T.Daniels .40 .15
❑ 412 Deion Branch .50 .20
❑ 413 Fraley/Andrews/Darilek RC .40 .15
❑ 414 Anquan Boldin .50 .20
❑ 415 T.James/K.Ratliff .40 .15
❑ 416 Ernest Wilford .40 .15
❑ 417 Moore/Jones/Kendall .40 .15
❑ 418 Brian Griese .50 .20
❑ 419 B.Kelly/J.Phillips .40 .15
❑ 420 Patrick Ramsey .50 .20
❑ 421 Corey Dillon .50 .20
❑ 422 Santana Moss .50 .20
❑ 423 Thomas/Edwards/Boulware .50 .20
❑ 424 Ashley Lelie .50 .20
❑ 425 G.Wilson/W.Demps .75 .30
❑ 426 Darrell Jackson .50 .20
❑ 427 Williams/Udeze/Scott .40 .15
❑ 428 K.Lucas/M.Minter .40 .15
❑ 429 Lee Suggs .40 .15
❑ 430 Kaczur/Mruczkowski/Gorin .40 .15
❑ 431 Robert Gallery .40 .15
❑ 432 Osgood/Feeley/Jackson .40 .15
❑ 433 Domanick Davis .50 .20
❑ 434 Osi Umenyiora .40 .15
❑ 435 Drew Bledsoe .75 .30
❑ 436 J.Gage/E.Berlin .40 .15
❑ 437 Rudi Johnson .50 .20
❑ 438 J.Fargas/M.Tuiasosopo .40 .15
❑ 439 Antwaan Randle El .50 .20
❑ 440 Marvin Harrison .75 .30
❑ 441 Brandon Marshall RC 1.50 .60
❑ 442 Wali Lundy RC 1.50 .60
❑ 443 Bruce Gradkowski RC 2.50 1.00
❑ 444 Leonard Pope RC 1.50 .60
❑ 445 Omar Jacobs RC 1.25 .50
❑ 446 Travis Wilson RC 1.50 .60
❑ 447 Derek Hagan RC 1.50 .60
❑ 448 Devin Hester RC 3.00 1.25
❑ 449 Willie Reid RC 1.50 .60
❑ 450 A.J. Hawk RC 3.00 1.25
❑ 451 DeAngelo Williams RC 4.00 1.50
❑ 452 Ashton Youboty RC 1.50 .60
❑ 453 Abdul Hodge RC 1.50 .60
❑ 454 Leon Washington RC 2.50 1.00
❑ 455 D'Qwell Jackson RC 1.25 .50
❑ 456 Johnathan Joseph RC 1.25 .50
❑ 457 Antonio Cromartie RC 1.50 .60
❑ 458 Michael Robinson RC 1.50 .60
❑ 459 Tye Hill RC 1.50 .60
❑ 460 Mathias Kiwanuka RC 2.00 .75
❑ 461 Vince Young RC 6.00 2.50
❑ 462 DeMeco Ryans RC 2.00 .75
❑ 463 Brodrick Bunkley RC 1.50 .60
❑ 464 Jay Cutler RC 5.00 2.00
❑ 465 Brad Smith RC 1.50 .60
❑ 466 Elvis Dumervil RC .75 .30
❑ 467 Cory Rodgers RC 1.50 .60
❑ 468 Davin Joseph RC 1.25 .50
❑ 469 Rocky McIntosh RC 1.50 .60
❑ 470 Jason Avant RC 1.50 .60
❑ 471 Anthony Schlegel RC 1.25 .50
❑ 472 Kamerion Wimbley RC 1.50 .60
❑ 473 Joseph Addai RC 5.00 2.00
❑ 474 Ernie Sims RC 2.00 .75
❑ 475 Jimmy Williams RC 1.50 .60
❑ 476 LenDale White RC 3.00 1.25
❑ 477 Brandon Williams RC 1.50 .60
❑ 478 Ko Simpson RC 1.25 .50
❑ 479 Jerious Norwood RC 2.50 1.00
❑ 480 P.J. Daniels RC 1.25 .50
❑ 481 Mario Williams RC 2.50 1.00
❑ 482 Santonio Holmes RC 3.00 1.25
❑ 483 Joe Klopfenstein RC 1.25 .50
❑ 484 Matt Leinart RC 5.00 2.00
❑ 485 Danieal Manning RC 1.50 .60
❑ 486 Andre Hall RC 1.25 .50
❑ 487 Chad Greenway RC 1.50 .60
❑ 488 Chad Jackson RC 1.50 .60
❑ 489 Skyler Green RC 1.50 .60
❑ 490 Donte Whitner RC 1.50 .60
❑ 491 Bobby Carpenter RC 1.50 .60
❑ 492 Jovon Bouknight RC 1.25 .50
❑ 493 Vernon Davis RC 3.00 1.25
❑ 494 Kevin McMahan RC 1.25 .50
❑ 495 D.J. Shockley RC 1.50 .60
❑ 496 A.J. Nicholson RC .75 .30
❑ 497 Brian Calhoun RC 1.50 .60
❑ 498 Tim Day RC 1.25 .50
❑ 499 Devin Aromashodu RC 1.25 .50
❑ 500 Charlie Whitehurst RC 1.50 .60
❑ 501 Sinorice Moss RC 1.50 .60
❑ 502 Maurice Stovall RC 1.50 .60
❑ 503 Laurence Maroney RC 4.00 1.50
❑ 504 James Anderson RC .75 .30
❑ 505 Darnell Bing RC 1.50 .60
❑ 506 Jerome Harrison RC 1.50 .60
❑ 507 Daniel Bullocks RC 1.50 .60
❑ 508 Will Blackmon RC 1.25 .50
❑ 509 Marcedes Lewis RC 1.50 .60
❑ 510 Lawrence Vickers RC 1.25 .50
❑ 511 Marques Hagans RC 1.25 .50
❑ 512 Jeremy Bloom RC 1.25 .50

❑ 513 Dominique Byrd RC	1.25	.50
❑ 514 Tarvaris Jackson RC	2.50	1.00
❑ 515 Dusty Dvoracek RC	1.50	.60
❑ 516 Brodie Croyle RC	4.00	1.50
❑ 517 Demetrius Williams RC	1.50	.60
❑ 518 Jason Allen RC	1.50	.60
❑ 519 Mike Hass RC	1.50	.60
❑ 520 Nick Mangold RC	1.25	.50
❑ 521 Brett Basanez RC	1.50	.60
❑ 522 Ben Obomanu RC	1.25	.50
❑ 523 Tamba Hali RC	1.50	.60
❑ 524 Gabe Watson RC	1.25	.50
❑ 525 Kelly Jennings RC	1.50	.60
❑ 526 Reggie Bush RC	[illegible]	[illegible]
❑ 527 Rod Wright RC	.75	.30
❑ 528 Reggie McNeal RC	1.25	.50
❑ 529 Jonathan Orr RC	1.25	.50
❑ 530 Haloti Ngata RC	1.50	.60
❑ 531 David Thomas RC	1.50	.60
❑ 532 Ingle Martin RC	1.50	.60
❑ 533 Anthony Fasano RC	1.50	.60
❑ 534 Winston Justice RC	1.50	.60
❑ 535 Manny Lawson RC	1.50	.60
❑ 536 Kellen Clemens RC	2.50	1.00
❑ 537 Adam Jennings RC	1.25	.50
❑ 538 Thomas Howard RC	1.50	.60
❑ 539 Cedric Humes RC	1.50	.60
❑ 540 Garrett Mills RC	1.50	.60
❑ 541 Jeff Webb RC	1.25	.50
❑ 542 Michael Huff RC	2.00	.75
❑ 543 Gerris Wilkinson RC	.75	.30
❑ 544 Maurice Drew RC	4.00	1.50
❑ 545 John McCargo RC	1.25	.50
❑ 546 Todd Watkins RC	1.25	.50
❑ 547 Marcus Vick RC	1.25	.50
❑ 548 Greg Jennings RC	2.50	1.00
❑ 549 P.J. Pope RC	1.25	.50
❑ 550 D'Brickashaw Ferguson RC	1.50	.60

2007 Topps Total

❑ 1 Cadillac Williams	.60	.25
❑ 2 Marcel Shipp/Troy Walters	.50	.20
❑ 3 Kerry Collins/Brandon Jones	.50	.20
❑ 4 J.J. Arrington	.60	.25
❑ 5 Albert Haynesworth	.50	.20
❑ 6 DeAngelo Hall	.60	.25
❑ 7 Kyle Vanden Bosch/Travis LaBoy Andre Woolfolk	.50	.20
❑ 8 Kyle Boller/Justin Green Demetrius Williams	.50	.20
❑ 9 Anquan Boldin	.60	.25
❑ 10 Anthony Thomas	.50	.20
❑ 11 Orlando Huff/Leonard Pope Darnell Dockett	.50	.20
❑ 12 Mike Rucker/Kris Jenkins	.50	.20
❑ 13 Musa Smith/Mike Anderson	.60	.25
❑ 14 DeShaun Foster	.60	.25
❑ 15 Mark Clayton	.60	.25
❑ 16 Mike Minter Ken Lucas Richard Marshall	.50	.20
❑ 17 Ed Reed	.60	.25
❑ 18 Devin Hester	.75	.30
❑ 19 Brian Moorman Craig Nall Rian Lindell	.50	.20
❑ 20 Jamal Lewis	.60	.25
❑ 21 Chris Gamble	.50	.20
❑ 22 Kenny Wright Leigh Bodden Tim Carter	.50	.20
❑ 23 Tommie Harris Tank Johnson	.50	.20
❑ 24 Ryan Tucker Kevin Shaffer RC Hank Fraley	.50	.20
❑ 25 Brad Maynard Robbie Gould Adrian Peterson Bears	.50	.20
❑ 26 Terence Newman Anthony Henry	.50	.20
❑ 27 T.J. Houshmandzadeh	.60	.25
❑ 28 Travis Henry	.60	.25
❑ 29 Julius Jones	.60	.25
❑ 30 Kyle Johnson Nick Ferguson Dre Bly	.50	.20
❑ 31 Leonard Davis Marco Rivera Andre Gurode	.50	.20
❑ 32 Aaron Kampman Kabeer Gbaja-Biamila	.60	.25
❑ 33 Demetrin Veal RC Gerard Warren	.50	.20
❑ 34 Brett Favre	1.50	.60
❑ 35 Mike Bell	.60	.25
❑ 36 Ron Dayne	.60	.25
❑ 37 Jon Kitna	.50	.20
❑ 38 Kris Brown Dexter Wynn Samkon Gado	.50	.20
❑ 39 Daniel Bullocks Fernando Bryant Kenoy Kennedy	.50	.20
❑ 40 Peyton Manning	1.25	.50
❑ 41 Matt Schaub	.60	.25
❑ 42 Matt Jones	.60	.25
❑ 43 Jim Sorgi Ben Utecht	.50	.20
❑ 44 Dennis Northcutt Josh Scobee Alvin Pearman	.50	.20
❑ 45 Dallas Clark	.50	.20
❑ 46 Kris Wilson Michael Bennett	.50	.20
❑ 47 Jeff Saturday Tarik Glenn Ryan Diem	.50	.20
❑ 48 Daunte Culpepper	.60	.25
❑ 49 Damon Huard	.50	.20
❑ 50 Bryant McKinnie Matt Birk Steve Hutchinson	.50	.20
❑ 51 Ty Law	.60	.25
❑ 52 Rosevelt Colvin Mike Vrabel	.50	.20
❑ 53 Brian Waters Casey Wiegmann Will Shields	.50	.20
❑ 54 Chad Jackson	.50	.20
❑ 55 Bobby Wade Tony Richardson	.50	.20
❑ 56 Tedy Bruschi	.75	.30
❑ 57 Antoine Winfield	.50	.20
❑ 58 Jammal Brown Jeff Faine Jon Stinchcomb	.50	.20
❑ 59 Matt Light Logan Mankins Dan Koppen	.50	.20
❑ 60 Michael Strahan	.60	.25
❑ 61 Marques Colston	.75	.30
❑ 62 Johnnie Morant Ronald Curry	.60	.25
❑ 63 Will Demps/Gibril Wilson	.50	.20
❑ 64 Warren Sapp	.60	.25
❑ 65 William Joseph Fred Robbins Barry Cofield	.50	.20
❑ 66 Chris Carr Sebastian Janikowski Shane Lechler	.50	.20
❑ 67 Cedric Houston	.50	.20
❑ 68 Nate Washington	.50	.20
❑ 69 Jonathan Vilma	.60	.25
❑ 70 Willie Parker	.75	.30
❑ 71 Sheldon Brown Lito Sheppard	.50	.20
❑ 72 Najeh Davenport Charlie Batch Dan Kreider	.50	.20
❑ 73 Jevon Kearse	.60	.25
❑ 74 Luis Castillo Jamal Williams	.50	.20
❑ 75 Darren Howard [illegible] Trent Cole	.50	.20
❑ 76 Vernon Davis	.60	.25
❑ 77 Antonio Gates	.60	.25
❑ 78 Chris Gray Chris Spencer Walter Jones	.50	.20
❑ 79 Terrence Kiel Drayton Florence Marlon McCree	.50	.20
❑ 80 Victor Adeyanju La'Roi Glover	.50	.20
❑ 81 Ashley Lelie	.60	.25
❑ 82 Torry Holt	.60	.25
❑ 83 Maurice Morris Mack Strong	.50	.20
❑ 84 Jermaine Phillips Will Allen Shelton Quarles	.50	.20
❑ 85 Shaun Alexander	.60	.25
❑ 86 Vince Young	1.00	.40
❑ 87 Orlando Pace Alex Barron Andy McCollum	.50	.20
❑ 88 Brandon Lloyd	.60	.25
❑ 89 Joey Galloway	.60	.25
❑ 90 Neil Rackers Scott Player	.50	.20
❑ 91 Peter Sirmon David Thornton	.50	.20
❑ 92 Bryant Johnson	.50	.20
❑ 93 Bo Scaife Cortland Finnegan Reynaldo Hill	.50	.20
❑ 94 John Abraham	.50	.20
❑ 95 Jason Campbell	.60	.25
❑ 96 Kelly Gregg Bart Scott Haloti Ngata	.60	.25
❑ 97 Adrian Wilson	.50	.20
❑ 98 Drew Carter Keary Colbert	.50	.20
❑ 99 Michael Jenkins D.J. Shockley Roddy White	.60	.25
❑ 100 Jake Delhomme	.60	.25
❑ 101 Terrell Suggs Trevor Pryce	.50	.20
❑ 102 Thomas Davis James Anderson Dan Morgan	.50	.20
❑ 103 Todd Heap	.50	.20
❑ 104 Bernard Berrian	.50	.20
❑ 105 Peerless Price	.50	.20
❑ 106 Chris Henry	.50	.20
❑ 107 Daimon Shelton Robert Royal Ryan Neufeld	.50	.20
❑ 108 Kellen Winslow	.60	.25
❑ 109 Rex Grossman	.60	.25
❑ 110 Kamerion Wimbley D'Qwell Jackson Andra Davis	.50	.20
❑ 111 Levi Jones Willie Anderson	.50	.20
❑ 112 Bradie James Akin Ayodele	.50	.20
❑ 113 Deltha O'Neal	.50	.20
❑ 114 Javon Walker	.60	.25
❑ 115 Jeremi Johnson Doug Johnson Reggie Kelly	.50	.20

❑ 116 Quincy Morgan Jason Elam Paul Ernster	.50	.20
❑ 117 Roy Williams S	.60	.25
❑ 118 Donald Driver	.60	.25
❑ 119 Miles Austin Mat McBriar Sam Hurd	.50	.20
❑ 120 Dunta Robinson Dexter McCleon	.50	.20
❑ 121 Devale Ellis RC Shaun McDonald	.50	.20
❑ 122 Wali Lundy	.50	.20
❑ 123 Tatum Bell	.60	.25
❑ 124 Owen Daniels Mark Bruener Jeb Putzier	.50	.20
❑ 125 Marquand Manuel Nick Collins Al Harris	.50	.20
❑ 126 Morlon Greenwood Shawn Barber Shantee Orr	.50	.20
❑ 127 Ahman Green	.60	.25
❑ 128 Marvin Harrison	.75	.30
❑ 129 Josh Thomas Corey Simon Raheem Brock	.50	.20
❑ 130 Chris Naeole Brad Meester Maurice Williams	.50	.20
❑ 131 Marcus Stroud John Henderson	.50	.20
❑ 132 Kendrell Bell Derrick Johnson	.50	.20
❑ 133 Byron Leftwich	.60	.25
❑ 134 Trent Green	.60	.25
❑ 135 Samie Parker	.50	.20
❑ 136 Mewelde Moore	.50	.20
❑ 137 Chris Chambers	.60	.25
❑ 138 Chris Kluwe/Artose Pinner Ryan Longwell	.50	.20
❑ 139 Travis Daniels/Michael Lehan Keith Adams	.50	.20
❑ 140 Richard Seymour	.50	.20
❑ 141 Jim Kleinsasser/Brooks Bollinger	.50	.20
❑ 142 Fred Thomas/Mike McKenzie	.50	.20
❑ 143 Darren Sharper	.50	.20
❑ 144 Will Smith	.50	.20
❑ 145 Ellis Hobbs/Asante Samuel Chad Scott	.50	.20
❑ 146 Brian Simmons/Scott Shanle Scott Fujita	.50	.20
❑ 147 Devery Henderson	.50	.20
❑ 148 Jeremy Shockey	.60	.25
❑ 149 Antonio Pierce/Reggie Torbor	.50	.20
❑ 150 Zack Crockett/Justin Fargas	.50	.20
❑ 151 Jerricho Cotchery	.50	.20
❑ 152 Dominic Rhodes	.60	.25
❑ 153 D'Brickashaw Ferguson Nick Mangold/Pete Kendall	.50	.20
❑ 154 Nnamdi Asomugha/Fabian Washington/Stuart Schweigert	.50	.20
❑ 155 Andrew Walter	.50	.20
❑ 156 Cedrick Wilson	.50	.20
❑ 157 Dirk Johnson/David Akers Reno Mahe	.50	.20
❑ 158 Troy Polamalu	.75	.30
❑ 159 Casey Hampton/Aaron Smith	.50	.20
❑ 160 Alan Faneca/Max Starks Marvel Smith	.50	.20
❑ 161 Shawne Merriman	.60	.25
❑ 162 Shaun Phillips/Randall Godfrey	.50	.20
❑ 163 Jonas Jennings/Larry Allen Kwame Harris	.50	.20
❑ 164 Nate Clements	.50	.20
❑ 165 Marcus Pollard/Seneca Wallace	.50	.20
❑ 166 Marcus Trufant/Jordan Babineaux Kelly Jennings	.50	.20
❑ 167 Nate Burleson	.50	.20
❑ 168 Isaac Bruce	.60	.25
❑ 169 Deion Branch	.60	.25
❑ 170 Alex Smith TE/Anthony Becht	.50	.20
❑ 171 Brandon Chillar/Pisa Tinoisamoa Will Witherspoon	.50	.20
❑ 172 Mark Jones/Matt Bryant Josh Bidwell	.50	.20
❑ 173 Michael Clayton	.60	.25
❑ 174 LenDale White	.60	.25
❑ 175 Lamont Thompson/Chris Hope	.50	.20
❑ 176 Chris Cooley	.50	.20
❑ 177 Santana Moss	.60	.25
❑ 178 Chike Okeafor/Bertrand Berry	.50	.20
❑ 179 Chris Samuels/Jon Jansen Randy Thomas	.50	.20
❑ 180 Matt Leinart	.75	.30
❑ 181 Michael Vick	.75	.30
❑ 182 Antrel Rolle/Roderick Hood Terrence Holt	.50	.20
❑ 183 Michael Koenen/Morten Andersen Allen Rossum	.50	.20
❑ 184 Joe Horn	.60	.25
❑ 185 Chris McAlister/Samari Rolle	.50	.20
❑ 186 Steve McNair	.60	.25
❑ 187 Roscoe Parrish	.50	.20
❑ 188 Sam Koch/Jonathan Ogden Matt Stover	.50	.20
❑ 189 J.P. Losman	.60	.25
❑ 190 John Kasay/Jason Baker	.50	.20
❑ 191 Kiwaukee Thomas/Ko Simpson Donte Whitner	.50	.20
❑ 192 Steve Smith	.60	.25
❑ 193 Cedric Benson	.60	.25
❑ 194 Rashied Davis	.50	.20
❑ 195 Bryan Robinson/Justin Smith	.50	.20
❑ 196 Mark Bradley/Brian Griese Desmond Clark	.60	.25
❑ 197 Dexter Jackson Keiwan Ratliff/Johnathan Joseph	.50	.20
❑ 198 Carson Palmer	.75	.30
❑ 199 Joe Jurevicius	.50	.20
❑ 200 Willie McGinest	.50	.20
❑ 201 Terry Glenn	.60	.25
❑ 202 Joshua Cribbs/Phil Dawson Dave Zastudil	.50	.20
❑ 203 DeMarcus Ware/Greg Ellis Marcus Spears	.60	.25
❑ 204 Bobby Carpenter/Aaron Glenn	.50	.20
❑ 205 Cory Redding/Shaun Rogers	.50	.20
❑ 206 Champ Bailey	.60	.25
❑ 207 T.J. Duckett	.50	.20
❑ 208 Damien Woody/Dominic Raiola Jeff Backus	.50	.20
❑ 209 Kevin Jones	.50	.20
❑ 210 Greg Jennings	.60	.25
❑ 211 Cullen Jenkins/Corey Williams Ryan Pickett	.50	.20
❑ 212 Anthony Weaver/Jason Babin	.50	.20
❑ 213 Andre Johnson	.60	.25
❑ 214 Kevin Walter/Jameel Cook Derrick Lewis	.50	.20
❑ 215 Hunter Smith/Terrence Wilkins Adam Vinatieri	.60	.25
❑ 216 Bob Sanders	.60	.25
❑ 217 Greg Jones/David Garrard	.60	.25
❑ 218 Reggie Wayne	.60	.25
❑ 219 Fred Taylor	.60	.25
❑ 220 Eddie Kennison	.50	.20
❑ 221 Marty Booker	.50	.20
❑ 222 Jeff Webb/Rod Gardner Dustin Colquitt	.50	.20
❑ 223 Ronnie Brown	.60	.25
❑ 224 Channing Crowder/Joey Porter	.50	.20
❑ 225 Jason Allen/Renaldo Hill Yeremiah Bell	.50	.20
❑ 226 Tarvaris Jackson	.75	.30
❑ 227 Kevin Williams/Pat Williams	.50	.20
❑ 228 Kenechi Udeze/Darrion Scott Dwight Smith	.50	.20
❑ 229 Tom Brady	1.50	.60
❑ 230 Roman Harper/Josh Bullocks	.50	.20
❑ 231 James Sanders/Rodney Harrison/Stephen Gostkowski	.50	.20
❑ 232 Terrance Copper	.50	.20
❑ 233 Brandon Jacobs	.60	.25
❑ 234 Drew Brees	.60	.25
❑ 235 Bryan Thomas/Shaun Ellis	.50	.20
❑ 236 Amani Toomer	.60	.25
❑ 237 Justin Miller	.50	.20
❑ 238 Jared Lorenzen/David Tyree Sinorice Moss	.60	.25
❑ 239 Brad Smith/Chris Baker	.50	.20
❑ 240 Derrick Burgess/Tyler Brayton	.50	.20
❑ 241 Jerry Porter	.60	.25
❑ 242 Michael Huff	.60	.25
❑ 243 Jeremiah Trotter	.50	.20
❑ 244 Kirk Morrison/Sam Williams Thomas Howard	.50	.20
❑ 245 Shawn Andrews/William Thomas Jon Runyan	.50	.20
❑ 246 Santonio Holmes	.60	.25
❑ 247 Jerame Tuman/Heath Miller	.50	.20
❑ 248 Eric Parker	.50	.20
❑ 249 Quentin Jammer	.50	.20
❑ 250 Marcus McNeill/Nick Hardwick Mike Goff	.50	.20
❑ 251 Mark Roman/Jeff Ulbrich Shawntae Spencer	.50	.20
❑ 252 Walt Harris/Michael Lewis	.50	.20
❑ 253 LeRoy Hill/Lofa Tatupu	.60	.25
❑ 254 Bryant Young	.50	.20
❑ 255 Darrell Jackson	.60	.25
❑ 256 Deon Grant/Brian Russell Michael Boulware	.50	.20
❑ 257 Drew Bennett	.50	.20
❑ 258 Steven Jackson	.75	.30
❑ 259 Dane Looker/Gus Frerotte Corey Chavous	.50	.20
❑ 260 Ike Hilliard/Michael Pittman	.50	.20
❑ 261 Simeon Rice	.50	.20
❑ 262 Roydell Williams	.50	.20
❑ 263 Mark Brunell/James Thrash	.60	.25
❑ 264 Ben Troupe/Kevin Mawae Erron Kinney	.50	.20
❑ 265 Clinton Portis	.60	.25
❑ 266 Larry Fitzgerald	.60	.25
❑ 267 Carlos Rogers/Fred Smoot Shawn Springs	.50	.20
❑ 268 Gerald Hayes/Calvin Pace Karlos Dansby	.50	.20
❑ 269 Warrick Dunn	.60	.25
❑ 270 Keith Brooking/Brian Finneran	.50	.20
❑ 271 Kynan Forney/Wayne Gandy Todd McClure	.50	.20
❑ 272 Jerious Norwood	.60	.25
❑ 273 Josh Reed/Shaud Williams	.50	.20
❑ 274 Willis McGahee	.60	.25
❑ 275 Terrence McGee	.50	.20
❑ 276 Ronnie Prude/Jarret Johnson Dawan Landry	.50	.20
❑ 277 Lee Evans	.60	.25
❑ 278 Keyshawn Johnson	.60	.25
❑ 279 Jordan Gross/Mike Wahle Will Montgomery	.50	.20
❑ 280 Alex Brown/Adewale Ogunleye	.50	.20
❑ 281 Muhsin Muhammad	.60	.25
❑ 282 Olin Kreutz/John Tait/Fred Miller	.50	.20
❑ 283 Glenn Holt RC/Kyle Larson Shayne Graham	.60	.25
❑ 284 Chris Perry	.50	.20
❑ 285 Derek Anderson/Ken Dorsey	.60	.25
❑ 286 Chad Johnson	.60	.25
❑ 287 Charlie Frye	.60	.25
❑ 288 Orpheus Roye/Ted Washington Robaire Smith	.50	.20
❑ 289 Jason Witten	.60	.25
❑ 290 Tony Romo	1.50	.60
❑ 291 D.J. Williams/Ian Gold Al Wilson	.50	.20
❑ 292 Ebenezer Ekuban/Kenard Lang	.50	.20
❑ 293 Paris Lenon/Boss Bailey	.50	.20
❑ 294 Rod Smith	.60	.25
❑ 295 Mike Furrey	.60	.25
❑ 296 Nick Harris/Jason Hanson Eddie Drummond	.50	.20
❑ 297 Robert Ferguson	.50	.20
❑ 298 Charles Woodson	.60	.25
❑ 299 Chad Clifton/Mark Tauscher Rob Davis	.50	.20
❑ 300 Travis Johnson/C.C. Brown Glenn Earl	.50	.20

- 301 Mario Williams .60 .25
- 302 Anthony McFarland/Robert Mathis .50 .20
- 303 George Wrighster/Marcedes Lewis .50 .20
- 304 Joseph Addai 1.00 .40
- 305 Maurice Jones-Drew .75 .30
- 306 Ernest Wilford .50 .20
- 307 Donovin Darius/Nick Greisen Mike Peterson .50 .20
- 308 Larry Johnson .75 .30
- 309 Derek Hagan .50 .20
- 310 Ron Edwards/James Reed Jimmy Wilkerson .50 .20
- 311 Zach Thomas .60 .25
- 312 Vonnie Holliday/Keith Traylor .50 .20
- 313 Jason Rader/L.J. Shelton Cleo Lemon .50 .20
- 314 Chester Taylor .50 .20
- 315 Jabar Gaffney/Reche Caldwell .50 .20
- 316 E.J. Henderson/Dontarrious Thomas/Ben Leber .50 .20
- 317 Donte Stallworth .60 .25
- 318 Jamie Martin/Mike Karney .50 .20
- 319 Hollis Thomas/Brian Young Charles Grant .50 .20
- 320 Reuben Droughns .60 .25
- 321 Eli Manning .75 .30
- 322 Corey Webster/R.W. McQuarters Sam Madison .50 .20
- 323 Erik Coleman/Kerry Rhodes .50 .20
- 324 Chad Pennington .60 .25
- 325 DeWayne Robertson Kimo Von Oelhoffen/Andre Dyson .50 .20
- 326 Courtney Anderson Robert Gallery/Randal Williams .50 .20
- 327 Randy Moss .75 .30
- 328 Brodrick Bunkley/Mike Patterson .50 .20
- 329 Correll Buckhalter .60 .25
- 330 Donovan McNabb .75 .30
- 331 Chris Gardocki/Jeff Reed .50 .20
- 332 Vincent Jackson .50 .20
- 333 Ben Roethlisberger 1.00 .40
- 334 Philip Rivers .75 .30
- 335 Larry Foote/Clark Haggans James Farrior .50 .20
- 336 Billy Volek/Brandon Manumaleuna Nate Kaeding .50 .20
- 337 Alex Smith QB .75 .30
- 338 Marques Douglas/Manny Lawson .50 .20
- 339 Maurice Hicks/Joe Nedney Andy Lee .50 .20
- 340 D.J. Hackett .50 .20
- 341 Julian Peterson .50 .20
- 342 Patrick Kerney/Bryce Fisher Rocky Bernard .50 .20
- 343 Randy McMichael Joe Klopfenstein .50 .20
- 344 Leonard Little .50 .20
- 345 Jeff Garcia .60 .25
- 346 Cato June/Derrick Brooks .60 .25
- 347 Mike Alstott .60 .25
- 348 Keith Bulluck .50 .20
- 349 Kevin Carter/Greg Spires Chris Hovan .50 .20
- 350 Courtney Roby/Craig Hentrich Rob Bironas .50 .20
- 351 London Fletcher Marcus Washington .50 .20
- 352 Edgerrin James .75 .30
- 353 Antwaan Randle El .50 .20
- 354 Obafemi Ayanbadejo Kurt Warner/Sean Morey .60 .25
- 355 Renaldo Wynn/Phillip Daniels Andre Carter .50 .20
- 356 Roy Williams WR .60 .25
- 357 Alge Crumpler .60 .25
- 358 Brian Dawkins .60 .25
- 359 Chris Crocker/Lawyer Milloy Jimmy Williams .50 .20
- 360 Reggie Bush 1.00 .40
- 361 Chris Kelsay/Angelo Crowell .50 .20
- 362 Sean Taylor .50 .20
- 363 Aaron Schobel .50 .20
- 364 Rock Cartwright/Ladell Betts Mike Sellers .50 .20
- 365 DeAngelo Williams .75 .30
- 366 Grady Jackson/Rod Coleman .50 .20
- 367 David Carr/Brad Hoover Michael Gaines .60 .25
- 368 Derrick Mason .50 .20
- 369 Brian Urlacher .75 .30
- 370 Ray Lewis .75 .30
- 371 Robert Geathers/Madieu Williams/Landon Johnson .50 .20
- 372 Langston Walker/Jason Peters Derrick Dockery .50 .20
- 373 Jason Wright/Jerome Harrison .50 .20
- 374 Julius Peppers .60 .25
- 375 Braylon Edwards .60 .25
- 376 Lance Briggs/Mark Anderson .60 .25
- 377 Jay Cutler .75 .30
- 378 Nathan Vasher/Charles Tillman Ricky Manning Jr .50 .20
- 379 Brandon Marshall/Daniel Graham/Patrick Ramsey .60 .25
- 380 Rudi Johnson .60 .25
- 381 Ernie Sims .50 .20
- 382 Marion Barber .60 .25
- 383 Bubba Franks/Aaron Hodgers .75 .30
- 384 Terrell Owens .75 .30
- 385 Vernand Morency .60 .25
- 386 Brad Johnson/Anthony Fasano Patrick Crayton .60 .25
- 387 Nick Barnett/Will Blackmon Abdul Hodge .50 .20
- 388 John Engelberger/Elvis Dumervil .50 .20
- 389 DeMeco Ryans .60 .25
- 390 John Lynch .60 .25
- 391 Rashean Mathis .50 .20
- 392 Shawn Bryson/Brian Calhoun Dan Campbell .50 .20
- 393 Brian Williams/Paul Spicer Reggie Hayward .50 .20
- 394 A.J. Hawk .75 .30
- 395 Tamba Hali/Jared Allen .50 .20
- 396 Gary Brackett/Rob Morris .50 .20
- 397 Jason Taylor .50 .20
- 398 Dwight Freeney .60 .25
- 399 Donnie Spragan/Matt Roth Travares Tillman .50 .20
- 400 Marlin Jackson/Matt Giordano Antoine Bethea .50 .20
- 401 Ty Warren/Vince Wilfork .50 .20
- 402 Reggie Williams .60 .25
- 403 Wes Welker .75 .30
- 404 Tony Gonzalez .60 .25
- 405 Laurence Maroney .75 .30
- 406 Patrick Surtain/Greg Wesley Sammy Knight .50 .20
- 407 Steve Weatherford/Michael Lewis John Carney .50 .20
- 408 Will Allen/Andre Goodman .50 .20
- 409 Plaxico Burress .60 .25
- 410 Troy Williamson .50 .20
- 411 Victor Hobson/Eric Barton .50 .20
- 412 Ben Watson/Matt Cassel Kevin Faulk .50 .20
- 413 Justin McCareins/Mike Nugent Ben Graham .60 .20
- 414 Deuce McAllister .60 .25
- 415 LaMont Jordan .60 .25
- 416 Osi Umenyiora/Mathias Kiwanuka .50 .20
- 417 Reggie Brown .60 .25
- 418 Shaun O'Hara/Kareem McKenzie Chris Snee .50 .20
- 419 Hines Ward .75 .30
- 420 Leon Washington .60 .25
- 421 Ike Taylor/Deshea Townsend Bryant McFadden .50 .20
- 422 Laveranues Coles .60 .25
- 423 Lorenzo Neal/Michael Turner .60 .25
- 424 Dhani Jones/Takeo Spikes .50 .20
- 425 Frank Gore .75 .30
- 426 Brian Westbrook .60 .25
- 427 Michael Robinson/Moran Norris Trent Dilfer .60 .25
- 428 Kevin Curtis/Hank Baskett Greg Lewis .60 .25
- 429 Fakhir Brown/Tye Hill .50 .20
- 430 LaDainian Tomlinson 1.00 .40
- 431 Marc Bulger .60 .25
- 432 Matt Wilhelm/Igor Olshansky Antonio Cromartie .50 .20
- 433 Chris Simms .50 .20
- 434 Derek Smith LB/Tully Banta-Cain .50 .20
- 435 Ronde Barber/Brian Kelly Phillip Buchanon .50 .20
- 436 Arnaz Battle .50 .20
- 437 David Givens .50 .20
- 438 Matt Hasselbeck .60 .25
- 439 Cornelius Griffin Rocky McIntosh .50 .20
- 440 Dominique Byrd/Jeff Wilkins Aaron Walker .50 .20
- 441 JaMarcus Russell RC 4.00 1.50
- 442 Brady Quinn RC 5.00 2.00
- 443 Drew Stanton RC 2.00 .75
- 444 Troy Smith RC 2.00 .75
- 445 Kevin Kolb RC 2.50 1.00
- 446 Trent Edwards RC 3.00 1.25
- 447 John Beck RC 3.00 1.25
- 448 Jordan Palmer RC 1.50 .60
- 449 Chris Leak RC 1.25 .50
- 450 Isiah Stanback RC 1.50 .60
- 451 Tyler Palko RC 1.50 .60
- 452 Jared Zabransky RC 1.50 .60
- 453 Jeff Rowe RC 1.25 .50
- 454 Zac Taylor RC 1.50 .60
- 455 Lester Ricard RC 1.25 .50
- 456 Adrian Peterson RC 12.00 5.00
- 457 Marshawn Lynch RC 3.00 1.25
- 458 Brandon Jackson RC 2.00 .75
- 459 Michael Bush RC 2.00 .75
- 460 Kenny Irons RC 1.50 .60
- 461 Antonio Pittman RC 1.25 .50
- 462 Tony Hunt RC 1.50 .60
- 463 Darius Walker RC 1.50 .60
- 464 Dwayne Wright RC 1.25 .50
- 465 Lorenzo Booker RC 1.50 .60
- 466 Kenneth Darby RC 1.50 .60
- 467 Chris Henry RC 1.50 .60
- 468 Selvin Young RC 2.00 .75
- 469 Brian Leonard RC 2.00 .75
- 470 Ahmad Bradshaw RC 2.00 .75
- 471 Gary Russell RC 1.50 .60
- 472 Kolby Smith RC 2.00 .75
- 473 Thomas Clayton RC 1.25 .50
- 474 Garrett Wolfe RC 2.00 .75
- 475 Calvin Johnson RC 5.00 2.00
- 476 Ted Ginn Jr. RC 2.50 1.00
- 477 Dwayne Jarrett RC 2.00 .75
- 478 Dwayne Bowe RC 3.00 1.25
- 479 Sidney Rice RC 2.50 1.00
- 480 Robert Meachem RC 1.50 .60
- 481 Anthony Gonzalez RC 2.50 1.00
- 482 Craig Buster Davis RC 1.50 .60
- 483 Aundrae Allison RC 1.25 .50
- 484 Chansi Stuckey RC 1.25 .50
- 485 David Clowney RC 1.50 .60
- 486 Steve Smith RC 2.00 .75
- 487 Courtney Taylor RC 1.25 .50
- 488 Paul Williams RC 1.25 .50
- 489 Johnnie Lee Higgins RC 1.25 .50
- 490 Rhema McKnight RC 1.25 .50
- 491 Jason Hill RC 1.50 .60
- 492 Dallas Baker RC 1.25 .50
- 493 Greg Olsen RC 2.00 .75
- 494 Yamon Figurs RC 1.50 .60
- 495 Scott Chandler RC 1.25 .50
- 496 Matt Spaeth RC 1.50 .60
- 497 Ben Patrick RC 1.25 .50
- 498 Clark Harris RC 1.50 .60
- 499 Martrez Milner RC 1.25 .50
- 500 Joe Newton RC 1.25 .50
- 501 Alan Branch RC 1.25 .50
- 502 Amobi Okoye RC 1.50 .60
- 503 DeMarcus Tank Tyler RC 1.25 .50
- 504 Justin Harrell RC 1.50 .60
- 505 Brandon Mebane RC 1.25 .50
- 506 Gaines Adams RC 1.50 .60
- 507 Jamaal Anderson RC 1.25 .50
- 508 Adam Carriker RC 1.25 .50

❑ 509 Jarvis Moss RC	1.50	.60
❑ 510 Charles Johnson RC	1.00	.40
❑ 511 Anthony Spencer RC	1.50	.60
❑ 512 Quentin Moses RC	1.25	.50
❑ 513 LaMarr Woodley RC	1.50	.60
❑ 514 Victor Abiamiri RC	1.50	.60
❑ 515 Ray McDonald RC	1.25	.50
❑ 516 Tim Crowder RC	1.50	.60
❑ 517 Patrick Willis RC	3.00	1.25
❑ 518 Brandon Siler RC	1.25	.50
❑ 519 David Harris RC	1.25	.50
❑ 520 Buster Davis RC	1.25	.50
❑ 521 Lawrence Timmons RC	1.50	.60
❑ 522 Paul Posluszny RC	2.00	.75
❑ 523 Jon Beason RC	1.50	.60
❑ 524 Rufus Alexander RC	1.50	.60
❑ 525 Earl Everett RC	1.25	.50
❑ 526 Stewart Bradley RC	1.50	.60
❑ 527 Prescott Burgess RC	1.25	.50
❑ 528 Leon Hall RC	1.25	.50
❑ 529 Darrelle Revis RC	1.50	.60
❑ 530 Aaron Ross RC	1.50	.60
❑ 531 Daymeion Hughes RC	1.25	.50
❑ 532 Marcus McCauley RC	1.25	.50
❑ 533 Chris Houston RC	1.25	.50
❑ 534 Tanard Jackson RC	1.00	.40
❑ 535 Jonathan Wade RC	1.25	.50
❑ 536 Josh Wilson RC	1.25	.50
❑ 537 Eric Wright RC	1.50	.60
❑ 538 A.J. Davis RC	1.00	.40
❑ 539 David Irons RC	1.00	.40
❑ 540 LaRon Landry RC	2.00	.75
❑ 541 Reggie Nelson RC	1.25	.50
❑ 542 Michael Griffin RC	1.50	.60
❑ 543 Brandon Meriweather RC	1.50	.60
❑ 544 Eric Weddle RC	1.25	.50
❑ 545 Aaron Rouse RC	1.50	.60
❑ 546 Josh Gattis RC	1.00	.40
❑ 547 Joe Thomas RC	1.50	.60
❑ 548 Levi Brown RC	1.50	.60
❑ 549 Tony Ugoh RC	1.25	.50
❑ 550 Ryan Kalil RC	1.25	.50

2005 Topps Turkey Red

❑ COMPLETE SET (299)	250.00	125.00
❑ COMP.SET w/o SP's (249)	60.00	25.00
❑ SP STATED ODDS 1:4		
❑ UNPRICED WOOD/1 ODDS 1:2072H, 1:2089R		
❑ 1A Eli Manning	2.00	.75
❑ 1B Eli Manning Ad Back	10.00	4.00
❑ 2 Clinton Portis	1.00	.40
❑ 3 Charles Woodson	.60	.25
❑ 4A Ray Lewis	1.00	.40
❑ 4B Ray Lewis Ad Back	5.00	2.00
❑ 5 Michael Clayton	1.00	.40
❑ 6 Eric Moulds	.60	.25
❑ 7 Derrick Blaylock	.50	.20
❑ 8 Carson Palmer	1.00	.40
❑ 9 Zach Thomas	1.00	.40
❑ 10 Dallas Clark	.50	.20
❑ 11 DeAngelo Hall	.60	.25
❑ 12 Terrell Owens	1.00	.40
❑ 13 Brian Griese	.60	.25
❑ 14 Dunta Robinson	.60	.25
❑ 15 Kevan Barlow	.60	.25
❑ 16 Jake Plummer	.60	.25
❑ 17 James Farrior	.50	.20
❑ 18A Peyton Manning	1.50	.60
❑ 18B Peyton Manning Ad Back	8.00	3.00
❑ 19 Michael Bennett	.60	.25
❑ 20 Brian Urlacher	1.00	.40
❑ 21 Dante Hall	.60	.25
❑ 22 Deion Branch	.60	.25
❑ 23 Billy Volek	.60	.25
❑ 24 Donald Driver	.60	.25
❑ 25 LaDainian Tomlinson CL	1.00	.40
❑ 26 Donte Stallworth CL	.50	.20
❑ 27 Joey Galloway	.60	.25
❑ 28 Joey Harrington	1.00	.40
❑ 29 T.J. Houshmandzadeh	.60	.25
❑ 30 LaDainian Tomlinson	1.25	.50
❑ 31 Darius Watts	.60	.25
❑ 32 Chris Gamble	.60	.25
❑ 33 Javon Walker	.60	.25
❑ 34 Kevin Curtis	.60	.25
❑ 35 Steven Jackson	1.25	.50
❑ 36 J.P. Losman	1.00	.40
❑ 37A Champ Bailey	.60	.25
❑ 37B Champ Bailey Ad Back	3.00	1.25
❑ 38 Tiki Barber	1.00	.40
❑ 39 LaVar Arrington	1.00	.40
❑ 40 Byron Leftwich	1.00	.40
❑ 41 Edgerrin James	1.00	.40
❑ 42 DeShaun Foster	.60	.25
❑ 43 Darrell Jackson	.60	.25
❑ 44 Julius Peppers	.60	.25
❑ 45 David Carr	1.00	.40
❑ 46 Drew Bennett	.50	.20
❑ 47 Antonio Gates	1.00	.40
❑ 48A Deuce McAllister	1.00	.40
❑ 48B Deuce McAllister Ad Back	5.00	2.00
❑ 49 Patrick Ramsey	.60	.25
❑ 50 Antonio Bryant	.60	.25
❑ 51 Quentin Jammer	.50	.20
❑ 52 Chris Brown	.60	.25
❑ 53 Eddie Kennison	.50	.20
❑ 54 Steve McNair	.60	.25
❑ 55 Corey Bradford	.50	.20
❑ 56 Chris Perry	.60	.25
❑ 57 Curtis Martin	1.00	.40
❑ 58 Mewelde Moore	.60	.25
❑ 59 Travis Taylor	.50	.20
❑ 60 Chad Pennington	1.00	.40
❑ 61 Chad Johnson	.60	.25
❑ 62 Kyle Boller	.60	.25
❑ 63 Tyrone Calico	.60	.25
❑ 64 Michael Pittman	.50	.20
❑ 65 Kerry Collins	.60	.25
❑ 66 Keary Colbert	.60	.25
❑ 67 LaMont Jordan CL	.50	.20
❑ 68 Robert Gallery	.60	.25
❑ 69 Derrick Mason	.60	.25
❑ 70 Brian Dawkins	.60	.25
❑ 71 Chris Simms	.60	.25
❑ 72 Marc Bulger	1.00	.40
❑ 73 Stephen Davis	.60	.25
❑ 74 Kurt Warner	.60	.25
❑ 75 Todd Heap	.60	.25
❑ 76 Domanick Davis CL	.50	.20
❑ 77 Shaun Alexander	1.00	.40
❑ 78 Jerry Porter	.60	.25
❑ 79 Chester Taylor	.60	.25
❑ 80A Michael Vick	1.00	.40
❑ 80B Michael Vick Ad Back	5.00	2.00
❑ 81 Justin McCareins	.50	.20
❑ 82 Fred Taylor	.60	.25
❑ 83 Laveranues Coles	.60	.25
❑ 84 Steve Smith	1.00	.40
❑ 85 Sean Taylor	.60	.25
❑ 86 Marvin Harrison	1.00	.40
❑ 87 Ashley Lelie	.60	.25
❑ 88 Willis McGahee	1.00	.40
❑ 89 Terence Newman	.50	.20
❑ 90 Joe Horn	.60	.25
❑ 91 Lee Suggs	.60	.25
❑ 92 Keyshawn Johnson	.60	.25
❑ 93 Desmond Clark	.50	.20
❑ 94 T.J. Duckett	.60	.25
❑ 95 Reggie Wayne	.60	.25
❑ 96 Donte Stallworth	.60	.25
❑ 97 Clarence Moore	.50	.20
❑ 98 Jason Witten	.60	.25
❑ 99 Jake Delhomme	1.00	.40
❑ 100 Julius Jones	1.25	.50
❑ 101 Ben Troupe	.50	.20
❑ 102 Hines Ward	1.00	.40
❑ 103 Domanick Davis	.60	.25
❑ 104 B.J. Sams	.50	.20
❑ 105 Marcus Robinson	.60	.25
❑ 106 Devery Henderson	.50	.20
❑ 107 Matt Hasselbeck	.60	.25
❑ 108 Antonio Pierce	.50	.20
❑ 109 Santana Moss	.60	.25
❑ 110 Adam Vinatieri	1.00	.40
❑ 111 Michael Strahan	.60	.25
❑ 112 Greg Jones	.50	.20
❑ 113 Drew Brees	1.00	.40
❑ 114 Marcus Robinson	.60	.25
❑ 115 Michael Jenkins	.60	.25
❑ 116 Randy McMichael	.50	.20
❑ 117 Jonathan Vilma	.60	.25
❑ 118 Greg Lewis	.50	.20
❑ 119 Ernest Wilford	.50	.20
❑ 120 Warrick Dunn	.60	.25
❑ 121 Shaun Alexander CL	.75	.30
❑ 122 Donnie Edwards	.50	.20
❑ 123 Antwaan Randle El	.60	.25
❑ 124 Rod Smith	.60	.25
❑ 125 Ed Reed	.60	.25
❑ 126 Muhsin Muhammad	.60	.25
❑ 127 L.J. Smith	.50	.20
❑ 128 Chris Chambers	.60	.25
❑ 129 Matt Schaub	.60	.25
❑ 130 Andre Johnson	.60	.25
❑ 131 Thomas Jones	.60	.25
❑ 132 Robert Ferguson	.50	.20
❑ 133 Jeremy Shockey	1.00	.40
❑ 134 William Green	.50	.20
❑ 135A Ben Roethlisberger	2.50	1.00
❑ 135B B. Roethlisberger Ad Back	12.00	5.00
❑ 136A Donovan McNabb	1.25	.50
❑ 136B Donovan McNabb Ad Back	6.00	2.50
❑ 137 Duce Staley	.60	.25
❑ 138 Larry Fitzgerald	1.00	.40
❑ 139 Charles Rogers	.60	.25
❑ 140 Mark Brunell	.60	.25
❑ 141 Kevin Jones	1.00	.40
❑ 142 LaMont Jordan	.60	.25
❑ 143 Aaron Brooks	.60	.25
❑ 144 Brian Westbrook	.60	.25
❑ 145 Larry Johnson	1.25	.50
❑ 146 Tommy Maddox	.50	.20
❑ 147 Corey Dillon	.60	.25
❑ 148 William Henderson	.50	.20
❑ 149 Tony Hollings	.50	.20
❑ 150 Lee Evans	.60	.25
❑ 151 Kelly Holcomb	.50	.20
❑ 152 Reuben Droughns	.60	.25
❑ 153 Keenan McCardell	.50	.20
❑ 154 Ricky Williams	.60	.25
❑ 155 Rashaun Woods	.60	.25
❑ 156 D.J. Williams	.50	.20
❑ 157 Tom Brady	2.00	.75
❑ 158 Eric Parker	.50	.20
❑ 159 Mike Anderson	.60	.25
❑ 160 Roy Williams WR	1.00	.40
❑ 161 Mike Vanderjagt	.50	.20
❑ 162 Ronald Curry	.60	.25
❑ 163 Priest Holmes	1.00	.40
❑ 164 Bernard Berrian	.50	.20
❑ 165 Brian Finneran	.50	.20
❑ 166 Tony Gonzalez	.60	.25
❑ 167 Chris McAlister	.50	.20
❑ 168 Gus Frerotte	.50	.20
❑ 169 Bryant Johnson	.50	.20
❑ 170 Jay Fiedler	.50	.20
❑ 171 Bubba Franks	.50	.20
❑ 172 Tony Romo	10.00	5.00
❑ 173 Jamal Lewis	.60	.25
❑ 174 Torry Holt	.60	.25
❑ 175 Ladell Betts	.50	.20
❑ 176 Bertrand Berry	.50	.20
❑ 177 Josh McCown	.60	.25
❑ 178 Jonathan Wells	.50	.20
❑ 179 Plaxico Burress	.60	.25

❑ 180	Rudi Johnson	.60	.25
❑ 181	Cedric Benson RC	5.00	2.00
❑ 182	Carlos Rogers RC	2.50	1.00
❑ 183	Terrence Murphy RC	2.00	.75
❑ 184	Frank Gore RC	5.00	2.00
❑ 185	Vincent Jackson RC	2.00	.75
❑ 186	Ciatrick Fason RC	2.00	.75
❑ 187	Alex Smith QB RC	8.00	3.00
❑ 188	Mike Williams	2.00	.75
❑ 189	Kyle Orton RC	2.00	.75
❑ 190A	Ronnie Brown RC	8.00	3.00
❑ 190B	Ronnie Brown	10.00	4.00
❑ 191	Charlie Frye RC	2.00	.75
❑ 192	Mark Bradley RC	2.00	.75
❑ 193	Antrel Rolle RC	2.00	.75
❑ 194	Roscoe Parrish RC	2.00	.75
❑ 195	Ryan Moats RC	2.00	.75
❑ 196	Andrew Walter RC	2.00	.75
❑ 197	Troy Williamson RC	2.00	.75
❑ 198	Cadillac Williams RC	8.00	3.00
❑ 199	Adam Jones RC	2.00	.75
❑ 200	Braylon Edwards RC	6.00	2.50
❑ 201	Vernand Morency RC	2.00	.75
❑ 202	Ryan Fitzpatrick RC	2.00	.75
❑ 203	Heath Miller RC	4.00	1.50
❑ 204	Eric Shelton RC	2.00	.75
❑ 205	Jason Campbell RC	2.50	1.00
❑ 206	David Pollack RC	2.00	.75
❑ 207	Stefan LeFors RC	2.00	.75
❑ 208	DeMarcus Ware RC	3.00	1.25
❑ 209	J.J. Arrington RC	2.00	.75
❑ 210	Marion Barber RC	3.00	1.25
❑ 211	Samkon Gado RC	2.00	.75
❑ 212	Roddy White RC	2.00	.75
❑ 213	Brandon Jacobs RC	2.50	1.00
❑ 214	Mark Clayton RC	2.00	.75
❑ 215	Alex Smith TE RC	2.00	.75
❑ 216	Darren Sproles RC	2.00	.75
❑ 217	Fabian Washington RC	2.00	.75
❑ 218	Brandon Jones RC	2.00	.75
❑ 219	Derrick Johnson RC	3.00	1.25
❑ 220	Dan Orlovsky RC	2.00	.75
❑ 221	Aaron Rodgers RC	6.00	2.50
❑ 222	Cedric Houston RC	2.00	.75
❑ 223	Reggie Brown RC	2.00	.75
❑ 224	Scottie Vines RC	2.00	.75
❑ 225	Willie Parker	8.00	3.00
❑ 226	Matt Jones RC	3.00	1.25
❑ 227	Odell Thurman RC	2.00	.75
❑ 228	Alvin Pearman RC	2.00	.75
❑ 229	Chris Henry RC	2.00	.75
❑ 230	Courtney Roby RC	2.00	.75
❑ 231	[illegible] Bruno	.60	.25
❑ 232	Warrick Dunn CL	.50	.20
❑ 233	Willis McGahee CL	.75	.30
❑ 234	Marcus Pollard	.50	.20
❑ 235	Jason Taylor	.50	.20
❑ 236	Joe Namath	5.00	2.00
❑ 237	Joe Montana	10.00	4.00
❑ 238	Barry Sanders	6.00	2.50
❑ 239	Jim Brown	5.00	2.00
❑ 240	Terry Bradshaw	6.00	2.50
❑ 241	Ahman Green	1.00	.40
❑ 242	Tiki Barber CL	.75	.30
❑ 243	Julius Jones CL	1.00	.40
❑ 244	Daunte Culpepper	1.00	.40
❑ 245	Edgerrin James CL	.75	.30
❑ 246	Trent Green	5.00	2.00
❑ 247	Dwight Freeney	5.00	2.00
❑ 248A	Brett Favre	12.00	5.00
❑ 248B	Brett Favre Ad Back	15.00	6.00
❑ 249	Marshall Faulk	8.00	3.00
❑ 250	Jerome Bettis	8.00	3.00
❑ 251	Nate Burleson	5.00	2.00
❑ 252	Brandon Lloyd	5.00	2.00
❑ 253	Randy Moss	8.00	3.00
❑ 254	Drew Bledsoe	8.00	3.00
❑ 255	Brandon Stokley	5.00	2.00
❑ 256	Takeo Spikes	4.00	1.50
❑ 257	Philip Rivers	8.00	3.00
❑ 258	Lito Sheppard	4.00	1.50
❑ 259	Jimmy Smith	5.00	2.00
❑ 260	Tatum Bell	5.00	2.00
❑ 261	Allen Rossum	4.00	1.50
❑ 262	Amani Toomer	5.00	2.00
❑ 263	Jabar Gaffney	4.00	1.50
❑ 264	Jonathan Ogden	4.00	1.50
❑ 265	John Abraham	4.00	1.50
❑ 266	Aaron Stecker	4.00	1.50
❑ 267	Jason Elam	4.00	1.50
❑ 268	Najeh Davenport	4.00	1.50
❑ 269	Alge Crumpler	5.00	2.00
❑ 270	Roy Williams S	5.00	2.00
❑ 271	Trent Dilfer	5.00	2.00
❑ 272	Anquan Boldin	5.00	2.00
❑ 273	Artose Pinner	4.00	1.50
❑ 274	David Garrard	4.00	1.50
❑ 275	[illegible]	[illegible]	[illegible]
❑ 276	Adam Archuleta	4.00	1.50
❑ 277	Jeremiah Trotter	4.00	1.50
❑ 278	Travis Henry	5.00	2.00
❑ 279	Rex Grossman	8.00	3.00
❑ 280	Maurice Morris	4.00	1.50
❑ 281	Mike Alstott	5.00	2.00
❑ 282	Justin Gage	4.00	1.50
❑ 283	Dennis Northcutt	4.00	1.50
❑ 284	David Givens	5.00	2.00
❑ 285	Dominic Rhodes	5.00	2.00
❑ 286	Gerald Ford	5.00	2.00
❑ 287	Ronald Reagan	5.00	2.00
❑ 288	John F. Kennedy	5.00	2.00
❑ 289	Ulysses S. Grant	5.00	2.00
❑ CL1	Jumbo Checklist 1	1.00	.40
❑ CL2	Jumbo Checklist 2	1.00	.40

2006 Topps Turkey Red

❑ 1	LaVar Arrington	1.00	.40
❑ 2	Heath Miller	.60	.25
❑ 3	Antwaan Randle El	.60	.25
❑ 4	Derrick Mason	.50	.20
❑ 5	Deshaun Foster	.60	.25
❑ 6	Andre Johnson	.60	.25
❑ 7	Jonathan Vilma	.60	.25
❑ 8	Trent Dilfer	.60	.25
❑ 9	Tatum Bell	.60	.25
❑ 10	Bubba Franks	.50	.20
❑ 11	T.J. Houshmandzadeh	.60	.25
❑ 12	Adam Vinatieri	.60	.25
❑ 13	Quentin Jammer	.50	.20
❑ 14	Jim Kleinsasser	.50	.20
❑ 15	Priest Holmes	.60	.25
❑ 16	Courtney Roby	.50	.20
❑ 17	Chris Simms	.60	.25
❑ 18	Terry Glenn	.60	.25
❑ 19	Jonathan Ogden	.50	.20
❑ 20	Andrew Walter	.60	.25
❑ 21	Lito Sheppard	.50	.20
❑ 22	Kevan Barlow	.60	.25
❑ 23	Santana Moss	.60	.25
❑ 24	Kelly Holcomb	.50	.20
❑ 25	Thomas Jones	.60	.25
❑ 26	Dennis Northcutt	.50	.20
❑ 27	Najeh Davenport	.50	.20
❑ 28	Edgerrin James	1.00	.40
❑ 29	Kevin Curtis	.50	.20
❑ 30	Brian Griese	.60	.25
❑ 31	Jason Taylor	.50	.20
❑ 32	T.J. Duckett	.60	.25
❑ 33	Antonio Bryant	.60	.25
❑ 34	Donald Driver	.60	.25
❑ 35	Brian Westbrook	.60	.25
❑ 36	Lofa Tatupu	.60	.25
❑ 37	Ben Troupe	.50	.20
❑ 38	Chris Cooley	.50	.20
❑ 39	Josh McCown	.60	.25
❑ 40	Chris Perry	.60	.25
❑ 41	Joe Horn	.60	.25
❑ 42	Kyle Boller	.50	.20
❑ 43	Keyshawn Johnson	.60	.25
❑ 44	Frank Gore	1.00	.40
❑ 45	Terence Newman	.50	.20
❑ 46	Devery Henderson	.50	.20
❑ 47	Michael Strahan	.60	.25
❑ 48	Ladell Betts	.50	.20
❑ 49	[illegible]	[illegible]	[illegible]
❑ 50	Anquan Boldin	.60	.25
❑ 51	Nathan Vasher	.50	.20
❑ 52	Dominic Rhodes	.60	.25
❑ 53	Travis Minor	.50	.20
❑ 54	Torry Holt	.60	.25
❑ 55	Sam Gado	.60	.25
❑ 56	Fred Taylor	.60	.25
❑ 57	Braylon Edwards	1.00	.40
❑ 58	Tyrone Calico	.60	.20
❑ 59	Derrick Burgess	.50	.20
❑ 60	Chester Taylor	.60	.25
❑ 61	Julius Peppers	.60	.25
❑ 62	L.J. Smith	.50	.20
❑ 63	Keenan McCardell	.50	.20
❑ 64	Lee Evans	.60	.25
❑ 65	Champ Bailey	.60	.25
❑ 66	Alex Smith QB	1.00	.40
❑ 67	Tedy Bruschi	1.00	.40
❑ 68	Roddy White	.60	.25
❑ 69	Marty Booker	.50	.20
❑ 70	Fred Smoot	.50	.20
❑ 71	A.J. Feeley	.50	.20
❑ 72	Kellen Winslow	1.00	.40
❑ 73	Curtis Martin	1.00	.40
❑ 74	Ronald Curry	.60	.25
❑ 75	Sam Madison	.50	.20
❑ 76	Keary Colbert	.50	.20
❑ 77	Marcus Pollard	.50	.20
❑ 78	James Farrior	.50	.20
❑ 79	Travis Henry	.60	.25
❑ 80	Samari Rolle	.50	.20
❑ 81	Rodney Harrison	.50	.20
❑ 82	Matt Schaub	.60	.25
❑ 83	Philip Rivers	1.00	.40
❑ 84	DeMarcus Ware	.60	.25
❑ 85	Reggie Wayne	.60	.25
❑ 86	Derrick Johnson	.60	.25
❑ 87	Travis Taylor	.50	.20
❑ 88	Antonio Pierce	.50	.20
❑ 89	Jamal Lewis	.60	.25
❑ 90	Aaron Brooks	.60	.25
❑ 91	Michael Pittman	.50	.20
❑ 92	Jerricho Cotchery	.50	.20
❑ 93	Shayne Graham	.50	.20
❑ 94	Dante Hall	.60	.25
❑ 95	Warrick Dunn	.60	.25
❑ 96	Mewelde Moore	.50	.20
❑ 97	Brandon Lloyd	.60	.25
❑ 98	Chris Gamble	.50	.20
❑ 99	Odell Thurman	.50	.20
❑ 100	Osi Umenyiora	.50	.20
❑ 101	Jerry Porter	.60	.25
❑ 102	Brandon Stokley	.60	.25
❑ 103	Clinton Portis	1.00	.40
❑ 104	Quentin Jammer	.50	.20
❑ 105	Reuben Droughns	.60	.25
❑ 106	Jason Campbell	.60	.25
❑ 107	LaBrandon Toefield	.50	.20
❑ 108	Nate Burleson	.60	.25
❑ 109	Antrel Rolle	.50	.20
❑ 110A	Steve McNair PS	.60	.25
❑ 110B	Steve McNair YS	.60	.25
❑ 111A	Chad Johnson PBB	.60	.25
❑ 111B	Chad Johnson No PBB	.60	.25
❑ 112	Steven Jackson	1.00	.40
❑ 113	Ron Dayne	.60	.25
❑ 114	Deion Branch	.60	.25
❑ 115	Ed Reed	.60	.25
❑ 116	Ty Law	.60	.25
❑ 117	Drew Bledsoe	1.00	.40

- ❑ 118 Chris McAlister .50 .20
- ❑ 119 Plaxico Burress .60 .25
- ❑ 120 Aaron Rodgers 1.00 .40
- ❑ 121 Tony Gonzalez .60 .25
- ❑ 122 David Givens .60 .25
- ❑ 123 Michael Vick 1.00 .40
- ❑ 124 Antonio Gates 1.00 .40
- ❑ 125 Darrell Jackson .60 .25
- ❑ 126 Adam Jones .50 .20
- ❑ 127 LaDainian Tomlinson CL 1.00 .40
- ❑ 128 Chad Pennington .60 .25
- ❑ 129 Kevin Faulk .50 .20
- ❑ 130 Isaac Bruce .60 .25
- ❑ 131 Tom Brady CL 1.25 .50
- ❑ 132 Deuce McAllister .60 .25
- ❑ 133 Laveranues Coles .60 .25
- ❑ 134 Donnie Edwards .50 .20
- ❑ 135 Brian Urlacher CL .75 .30
- ❑ 136 Dallas Clark .50 .20
- ❑ 137 Drew Bennett .50 .20
- ❑ 138 Domanick Davis .60 .25
- ❑ 139 Cadillac Williams CL .75 .30
- ❑ 140 David Garrard .50 .20
- ❑ 141 Shaun Alexander CL .75 .30
- ❑ 142 Troy Williamson .60 .25
- ❑ 143 Steve Smith CL .75 .30
- ❑ 144 Jake Plummer .60 .25
- ❑ 145 Carson Palmer CL .75 .30
- ❑ 146 DeAngelo Hall .60 .25
- ❑ 147 Michael Vick CL .75 .30
- ❑ 148 Kyle Vanden Bosch .50 .20
- ❑ 149 Larry Johnson CL 1.00 .40
- ❑ 150 LaDainian Tomlinson 1.25 .50
- ❑ 151 Dunta Robinson .60 .25
- ❑ 152 Muhsin Muhammad .60 .25
- ❑ 153 Steven Jackson CL .75 .30
- ❑ 154 David Pollack .50 .20
- ❑ 155 Mark Brunell .60 .25
- ❑ 156 Donovan McNabb 1.00 .40
- ❑ 157 Jeremy Shockey 1.00 .40
- ❑ 158 Corey Dillon .60 .25
- ❑ 159 Mark Clayton 1.00 .40
- ❑ 160 Vincent Jackson .50 .20
- ❑ 161 Kurt Warner .60 .25
- ❑ 162 Marcus Robinson .60 .25
- ❑ 163 Takeo Spikes .50 .20
- ❑ 164 Charles Rogers .60 .25
- ❑ 165 J.P. Losman .60 .25
- ❑ 166 Matt Jones .60 .25
- ❑ 167 Rod Smith .60 .25
- ❑ 168 Steve Smith 1.00 .40
- ❑ 169 Michael Vick 1.00 .40
- ❑ 170 Mike Vanderjagt .50 .20
- ❑ 171 Amani Toomer .60 .25
- ❑ 172 Deltha O'Neal .50 .20
- ❑ 173 Michael Jenkins .60 .25
- ❑ 174 David Carr .60 .25
- ❑ 175 Chris Brown .60 .25
- ❑ 176 Kevin Jones 1.00 .40
- ❑ 177 Roy Williams S .60 .25
- ❑ 178 Marvin Harrison 1.00 .40
- ❑ 179 Drew Brees 1.00 .40
- ❑ 180 John Abraham .50 .20
- ❑ 181 Joseph Addai RC SP 15.00 6.00
- ❑ 182 Sinorice Moss RC SP 5.00 2.00
- ❑ 183A Vince Young PS RC 8.00 3.00
- ❑ 183B Vince Young OS SP 20.00 8.00
- ❑ 184 Vernon Davis RC SP 10.00 4.00
- ❑ 185 Brandon Williams RC SP 5.00 2.00
- ❑ 186 Derek Hagan RC SP 5.00 2.00
- ❑ 187 Brian Calhoun RC SP 5.00 2.00
- ❑ 188 Mario Williams RC SP 8.00 3.00
- ❑ 189 DeAngelo Williams RC SP 12.00 5.00
- ❑ 190 Jay Cutler RC SP 15.00 6.00
- ❑ 191 A.J. Hawk RC SP 10.00 4.00
- ❑ 192 Reggie Bush RC 8.00 3.00
- ❑ 193 Laurence Maroney RC SP 12.00 5.00
- ❑ 194 D'Brickashaw Ferguson RC SP 5.00 2.00
- ❑ 195 Jason Avant RC SP 5.00 2.00
- ❑ 196 Brodie Croyle RC SP 12.00 5.00
- ❑ 197 Michael Huff RC SP 6.00 2.50
- ❑ 198 LenDale White RC SP 10.00 4.00
- ❑ 199 Marcedes Lewis RC SP 5.00 2.00
- ❑ 200 Travis Wilson RC SP 5.00 2.00
- ❑ 201 Haloti Ngata RC SP 5.00 2.00
- ❑ 202 Greg Jennings RC SP 8.00 3.00
- ❑ 203 Leon Washington RC SP 8.00 3.00
- ❑ 204 Tamba Hali RC SP 5.00 2.00
- ❑ 205 Santonio Holmes RC SP 10.00 4.00
- ❑ 206 Jerome Harrison RC SP 5.00 2.00
- ❑ 207 Tarvaris Jackson RC SP 8.00 3.00
- ❑ 208 Mathias Kiwanuka RC SP 6.00 2.50
- ❑ 209 Omar Jacobs RC SP 4.00 1.50
- ❑ 210 Alan Zemaitis RC SP 5.00 2.00
- ❑ 211 Demetrius Williams RC SP 5.00 2.00
- ❑ 212 Bobby Carpenter RC SP 5.00 2.00
- ❑ 213 Tye Hill RC SP 5.00 2.00
- ❑ 214 Chad Jackson RC SP 5.00 2.00
- ❑ 215 Joe Klopfenstein RC SP 4.00 1.50
- ❑ 216 Kamerion Wimbley RC SP 5.00 2.00
- ❑ 217 Michael Robinson RC SP 5.00 2.00
- ❑ 218 David Thomas RC SP 5.00 2.00
- ❑ 219 Charlie Whitehurst RC SP 5.00 2.00
- ❑ 220 Jerious Norwood RC SP 8.00 3.00
- ❑ 221 Bruce Gradkowski RC SP 8.00 3.00
- ❑ 222 Kellen Clemens RC SP 8.00 3.00
- ❑ 223 Thomas Howard RC SP 5.00 2.00
- ❑ 224 Anthony Fasano RC SP 5.00 2.00
- ❑ 225 Maurice Drew RC SP 12.00 5.00
- ❑ 226 Antonio Cromartie RC SP 5.00 2.00
- ❑ 227 Mike Bell RC SP 5.00 2.00
- ❑ 228 D'Qwell Jackson RC SP 4.00 1.50
- ❑ 229A Matt Leinart TIB RC 6.00 2.50
- ❑ 229B Matt Leinart SIB SP 20.00 8.00
- ❑ 230 Maurice Stovall RC SP 5.00 2.00
- ❑ 231A Carson Palmer BJ 1.00 .40
- ❑ 231A Carson Palmer WJ 1.00 .40
- ❑ 232 Courtney Anderson .50 .20
- ❑ 233 D.J. Williams .50 .20
- ❑ 234 Chris Chambers .60 .25
- ❑ 235 Zach Thomas 1.00 .40
- ❑ 236 Reggie Brown .75 .30
- ❑ 237 Cadillac Williams 1.00 .40
- ❑ 238 Randy McMichael .50 .20
- ❑ 239 Brian Urlacher 1.00 .40
- ❑ 240 Cedric Houston .50 .20
- ❑ 241 Marc Bulger .60 .25
- ❑ 242 Mike Anderson .60 .25
- ❑ 243 Allen Rossum .50 .20
- ❑ 244 William Henderson .50 .20
- ❑ 245 Eddie Kennison .50 .20
- ❑ 246 Adam Archuleta .50 .20
- ❑ 247 Ryan Moats .50 .20
- ❑ 248 D.J. Hackett .50 .20
- ❑ 249 Marion Barber .60 .25
- ❑ 250 Mike Alstott .60 .25
- ❑ 251 Shawne Merriman .60 .25
- ❑ 252 Byron Leftwich .60 .25
- ❑ 253 Dan Morgan .50 .20
- ❑ 254 Ronnie Brown 1.00 .40
- ❑ 255 Mark Bradley .60 .25
- ❑ 256 Mike Williams 1.00 .40
- ❑ 257 Ronde Barber .50 .20
- ❑ 258 Bernard Berrian .50 .20
- ❑ 259 Gibril Wilson .50 .20
- ❑ 260 Scottie Vines .50 .20
- ❑ 261 Rex Grossman 1.00 .40
- ❑ 262 Daniel Graham .50 .20
- ❑ 263 Ernest Wilford .50 .20
- ❑ 264 Javon Walker .60 .25
- ❑ 265 Corey Webster .50 .20
- ❑ 266 Jon Kitna .50 .20
- ❑ 267 Arnaz Battle .50 .20
- ❑ 268 Robert Ferguson SP 3.00 1.25
- ❑ 269 Cedric Benson 1.00 .40
- ❑ 270 Michael Clayton .60 .25
- ❑ 271 Brandon Jacobs .60 .25
- ❑ 272 Jason Witten SP 4.00 1.50
- ❑ 273A Randy Moss BS 1.00 .40
- ❑ 273B Randy Moss PS 1.00 .40
- ❑ 274 Daunte Culpepper SP 6.00 2.50
- ❑ 275 Ronnie Brown 1.00 .40
- ❑ 276 Dwight Freeney .60 .25
- ❑ 277 LaMont Jordan .60 .25
- ❑ 278 Jeremiah Trotter .50 .20
- ❑ 279A Hines Ward PO sky 1.00 .40
- ❑ 279B Hines Ward BY sky 1.00 .40
- ❑ 280A Tom Brady PBB 1.50 .60
- ❑ 280B Tom Brady No PBB 1.50 .60
- ❑ 281 Charles Woodson .60 .25
- ❑ 282A Shaun Alexander GJ 1.00 .40
- ❑ 282B Shaun Alexander WJ 1.00 .40
- ❑ 283 Eric Moulds .60 .25
- ❑ 284A Ben Roethlisberger BS 1.50 .60
- ❑ 284B Ben Roethlisberger PS 1.50 .60
- ❑ 285 Matt Hasselbeck .60 .25
- ❑ 286 Willis McGahee 1.00 .40
- ❑ 287 Carlos Rogers .50 .20
- ❑ 288 Brett Favre 2.00 .75
- ❑ 289 Larry Fitzgerald 1.00 .40
- ❑ 290 Billy Volek .60 .25
- ❑ 291 Julius Jones 1.00 .40
- ❑ 292 Trent Green .60 .25
- ❑ 293 Ashley Lelie .60 .25
- ❑ 294 Eli Manning 1.25 .50
- ❑ 295 Alge Crumpler .60 .25
- ❑ 296 Rudi Johnson .60 .25
- ❑ 297 Troy Polamalu 1.25 .50
- ❑ 298 Roy Williams WR 1.00 .40
- ❑ 299 Willie Parker 1.25 .50
- ❑ 300 Jake Delhomme .60 .25
- ❑ 301 Champ Bailey .60 .25
- ❑ 302 Ahman Green .60 .25
- ❑ 303 Robert Gallery .50 .20
- ❑ 304 Todd Heap .60 .25
- ❑ 305 Joey Harrington .60 .25
- ❑ 306 Terrell Owens 1.00 .40
- ❑ 307 Joey Galloway .60 .25
- ❑ 308A Larry Johnson OS 1.25 .50
- ❑ 308A Larry Johnson PS 1.25 .50
- ❑ 309 Brian Dawkins .60 .25
- ❑ 310 Ray Lewis 1.00 .40
- ❑ 311A Tiki Barber OS 1.00 .40
- ❑ 311B Tiki Barber BS SP 6.00 2.50
- ❑ 312 Donte Stallworth .60 .25
- ❑ 313 Eric Parker .50 .20
- ❑ 314 Charlie Frye .60 .25
- ❑ 315A Peyton Manning BYS 1.50 .60
- ❑ 315B Peyton Manning OS SP 40.00 15.00

2005 UD Mini Jersey Collection

- ❑ COMPLETE SET (100) 50.00 25.00
- ❑ 1 Kurt Warner .75 .30
- ❑ 2 Anquan Boldin .75 .30
- ❑ 3 Michael Vick 2.00 .75
- ❑ 4 Warrick Dunn .75 .30
- ❑ 5 Kyle Boller .75 .30
- ❑ 6 Ray Lewis 1.25 .50
- ❑ 7 Jake Delhomme 1.25 .50
- ❑ 8 DeShaun Foster .75 .30
- ❑ 9 Carson Palmer 1.25 .50
- ❑ 10 Chad Johnson 1.25 .50
- ❑ 11 Rudi Johnson .75 .30
- ❑ 12 Kellen Winslow 1.25 .50
- ❑ 13 Lee Suggs .75 .30
- ❑ 14 Julius Jones 1.50 .60
- ❑ 15 Drew Bledsoe 1.25 .50
- ❑ 16 Tatum Bell .75 .30
- ❑ 17 Jake Plummer .75 .30
- ❑ 18 Roy Williams WR 1.25 .50
- ❑ 19 Kevin Jones 1.25 .50
- ❑ 20 Brett Favre 3.00 1.25
- ❑ 21 Ahman Green 1.25 .50

❑ 22 David Carr 1.25 .50
❑ 23 Andre Johnson .75 .30
❑ 24 Peyton Manning 2.00 .75
❑ 25 Edgerrin James 1.25 .50
❑ 26 Marvin Harrison 1.25 .50
❑ 27 Byron Leftwich 1.25 .50
❑ 28 Fred Taylor .75 .30
❑ 29 Priest Holmes 1.25 .50
❑ 30 Trent Green .75 .30
❑ 31 Tony Gonzalez .75 .30
❑ 32 A.J. Feeley .75 .30
❑ 33 Randy McMichael .60 .25
❑ 34 Daunte Culpepper 1.25 .50
❑ 35 Nate Burleson .75 .30
❑ 36 Tom Brady 3.00 1.25
❑ 37 Corey Dillon .75 .30
❑ 38 Aaron Brooks .75 .30
❑ 39 Joe Horn .75 .30
❑ 40 Deuce McAllister 1.25 .50
❑ 41 Eli Manning 2.50 1.00
❑ 42 Tiki Barber 1.25 .50
❑ 43 Jeremy Shockey 1.25 .50
❑ 44 Chad Pennington 1.25 .50
❑ 45 Curtis Martin 1.25 .50
❑ 46 Santana Moss .75 .30
❑ 47 Randy Moss 1.25 .50
❑ 48 Kerry Collins .75 .30
❑ 49 Donovan McNabb 1.50 .60
❑ 50 Terrell Owens 1.25 .50
❑ 51 Brian Westbrook .75 .30
❑ 52 Ben Roethlisberger 3.00 1.25
❑ 53 Jerome Bettis 1.25 .50
❑ 54 Drew Brees 1.25 .50
❑ 55 LaDainian Tomlinson 1.50 .60
❑ 56 Kevan Barlow .75 .30
❑ 57 Tim Rattay .60 .25
❑ 58 Matt Hasselbeck .75 .30
❑ 59 Shaun Alexander 1.50 .60
❑ 60 Darrell Jackson .75 .30
❑ 61 Marc Bulger 1.25 .50
❑ 62 Steven Jackson 1.50 .60
❑ 63 Torry Holt 1.25 .50
❑ 64 Michael Pittman .60 .25
❑ 65 Brian Griese .75 .30
❑ 66 Michael Clayton 1.25 .50
❑ 67 Steve McNair 1.25 .50
❑ 68 Drew Bennett .75 .30
❑ 69 Clinton Portis 1.25 .50
❑ 70 Patrick Ramsey .75 .30
❑ 71 Alex Smith QB RC 8.00 3.00
❑ 72 Aaron Rodgers RC 6.00 2.50
❑ 73 Jason Campbell RC 3.00 1.25
❑ 74 Ronnie Brown RC 8.00 3.00
❑ 75 Cadillac Williams RC 8.00 3.00
❑ 76 Cedric Benson RC 5.00 2.00
❑ 77 J.J. Arrington RC 2.00 .75
❑ 78 Braylon Edwards RC 6.00 2.50
❑ 79 Troy Williamson RC 2.00 .75
❑ 80 Mike Williams 2.00 .75
❑ 81 Matt Jones RC 3.00 1.25
❑ 82 Mark Clayton RC 2.00 .75
❑ 83 Roddy White RC 2.00 .75
❑ 84 Reggie Brown RC 2.00 .75
❑ 85 Eric Shelton RC 2.00 .75
❑ 86 Peyton Manning SR 2.00 .75
❑ 87 Ben Roethlisberger SR 3.00 1.25
❑ 88 Julius Jones SR 1.50 .60
❑ 89 Michael Vick SR 2.00 .75
❑ 90 Tom Brady SR 3.00 1.25
❑ 91 Corey Dillon SR .75 .30
❑ 92 Terrell Owens SR 1.25 .50
❑ 93 Donovan McNabb SR 1.50 .60
❑ 94 Priest Holmes SR 1.25 .50
❑ 95 Kevin Jones SR 1.25 .50
❑ 96 Jerome Bettis SR 1.25 .50
❑ 97 Torry Holt SR 1.25 .50
❑ 98 Clinton Portis SR 1.25 .50
❑ 99 Drew Brees SR 1.25 .50
❑ 100 Tiki Barber SR 1.25 .50
❑ NNO Checklist Card .15 .05

2005 UD Portraits

❑ DRAFT PICK PRINT RUN 425 SER.#'d SETS
❑ 1 Larry Fitzgerald 3.00 1.25
❑ 2 Anquan Boldin 2.00 .75

❑ 3 Josh McCown 2.00 .75
❑ 4 Michael Vick 3.00 1.25
❑ 5 Alge Crumpler 2.00 .75
❑ 6 Peerless Price 1.50 .60
❑ 7 Ray Lewis 3.00 1.25
❑ 8 Jamal Lewis 2.00 .75
❑ 9 Todd Heap 2.00 .75
❑ 10 Derrick Mason 2.00 .75
❑ 11 J.P. Losman 3.00 1.25
❑ 12 Willis McGahee 3.00 1.25
❑ 13 Eric Moulds 2.00 .75
❑ 14 Jake Delhomme 3.00 1.25
❑ 15 DeShaun Foster 2.00 .75
❑ 16 Steve Smith 3.00 1.25
❑ 17 Brian Urlacher 3.00 1.25
❑ 18 Rex Grossman 3.00 1.25
❑ 19 Muhsin Muhammad 2.00 .75
❑ 20 Carson Palmer 3.00 1.25
❑ 21 Rudi Johnson 2.00 .75
❑ 22 Chad Johnson 2.00 .75
❑ 23 Julius Jones 4.00 1.50
❑ 24 Keyshawn Johnson 2.00 .75
❑ 25 Drew Bledsoe 3.00 1.25
❑ 26 Tatum Bell 2.00 .75
❑ 27 Jake Plummer 2.00 .75
❑ 28 Ashley Lelie 2.00 .75
❑ 29 Roy Williams WR 3.00 1.25
❑ 30 Kevin Jones 3.00 1.25
❑ 31 Joey Harrington 3.00 1.25
❑ 32 Brett Favre 8.00 3.00
❑ 33 Ahman Green 3.00 1.25
❑ 34 Javon Walker 2.00 .75
❑ 35 David Carr 3.00 1.25
❑ 36 Andre Johnson 2.00 .75
❑ 37 Domanick Davis 2.00 .75
❑ 38 Peyton Manning 5.00 2.00
❑ 39 Reggie Wayne 2.00 .75
❑ 40 Edgerrin James 3.00 1.25
❑ 41 Marvin Harrison 3.00 1.25
❑ 42 Byron Leftwich 3.00 1.25
❑ 43 Fred Taylor 2.00 .75
❑ 44 Jimmy Smith 2.00 .75
❑ 45 Priest Holmes 3.00 1.25
❑ 46 Larry Johnson 4.00 1.50
❑ 47 Trent Green 2.00 .75
❑ 48 A.J. Feeley 2.00 .75
❑ 49 Chris Chambers 2.00 .75
❑ 50 Randy McMichael 1.50 .60
❑ 51 Daunte Culpepper 3.00 1.25
❑ 52 Onterrio Smith 2.00 .75
❑ 53 Nate Burleson 2.00 .75
❑ 54 Tom Brady 6.00 2.50
❑ 55 Corey Dillon 2.00 .75
❑ 56 Deion Branch 2.00 .75
❑ 57 David Givens 2.00 .75
❑ 58 Aaron Brooks 2.00 .75
❑ 59 Deuce McAllister 3.00 1.25
❑ 60 Joe Horn 2.00 .75
❑ 61 Eli Manning 6.00 2.50
❑ 62 Jeremy Shockey 3.00 1.25
❑ 63 Tiki Barber 3.00 1.25
❑ 64 Chad Pennington 3.00 1.25
❑ 65 Curtis Martin 3.00 1.25
❑ 66 Jonathan Vilma 2.00 .75
❑ 67 Kerry Collins 2.00 .75
❑ 68 Jerry Porter 2.00 .75
❑ 69 Randy Moss 3.00 1.25
❑ 70 Donovan McNabb 4.00 1.50
❑ 71 Terrell Owens 3.00 1.25
❑ 72 Brian Dawkins 2.00 .75
❑ 73 Brian Westbrook 2.00 .75
❑ 74 Ben Roethlisberger 8.00 3.00
❑ 75 Jerome Bettis 3.00 1.25
❑ 76 Hines Ward 3.00 1.25
❑ 77 Duce Staley 2.00 .75
❑ 78 Drew Brees 3.00 1.25
❑ 79 LaDainian Tomlinson 4.00 1.50
❑ 80 Antonio Gates 3.00 1.25
❑ 81 Eric Parker 1.50 .60
❑ 82 Tim Rattay 1.50 .60
❑ 83 [illegible]
❑ 84 Eric Johnson 2.00 .75
❑ 85 Shaun Alexander 3.00 1.25
❑ 86 Darrell Jackson 2.00 .75
❑ 87 Matt Hasselbeck 2.00 .75
❑ 88 Marc Bulger 3.00 1.25
❑ 89 Steven Jackson 4.00 1.50
❑ 90 Marshall Faulk 3.00 1.25
❑ 91 Torry Holt 2.00 .75
❑ 92 Michael Pittman 1.50 .60
❑ 93 Brian Griese 2.00 .75
❑ 94 Michael Clayton 3.00 1.25
❑ 95 Steve McNair 2.00 .75
❑ 96 Billy Volek 2.00 .75
❑ 97 Chris Brown 2.00 .75
❑ 98 Clinton Portis 3.00 1.25
❑ 99 Patrick Ramsey 2.00 .75
❑ 100 Santana Moss 2.00 .75
❑ 101 Aaron Rodgers RC 15.00 6.00
❑ 102 Alex Smith QB RC 20.00 8.00
❑ 103 Charlie Frye RC 5.00 2.00
❑ 104 Andrew Walter RC 5.00 2.00
❑ 105 Jason Campbell RC 8.00 3.00
❑ 106 Dan Orlovsky RC 5.00 2.00
❑ 107 Derek Anderson RC 8.00 3.00
❑ 108 Kyle Orton RC 5.00 2.00
❑ 109 David Greene RC 5.00 2.00
❑ 110 James Kilian RC 4.00 1.50
❑ 111 Matt Jones RC 8.00 3.00
❑ 112 Cedric Benson RC 12.00 5.00
❑ 113 Ronnie Brown RC 20.00 8.00
❑ 114 Cadillac Williams RC 20.00 8.00
❑ 115 Ciatrick Fason RC 5.00 2.00
❑ 116 Vernand Morency RC 5.00 2.00
❑ 117 Eric Shelton RC 5.00 2.00
❑ 118 Maurice Clarett 5.00 2.00
❑ 119 Marion Barber RC 8.00 3.00
❑ 120 Anthony Davis RC 4.00 1.50
❑ 121 J.J. Arrington RC 5.00 2.00
❑ 122 Ryan Moats RC 5.00 2.00
❑ 123 Frank Gore RC 12.00 5.00
❑ 124 Alvin Pearman RC 5.00 2.00
❑ 125 Darren Sproles RC 5.00 2.00
❑ 126 Cedric Houston RC 5.00 2.00
❑ 127 Braylon Edwards RC 15.00 6.00
❑ 128 Troy Williamson RC 5.00 2.00
❑ 129 Mark Clayton RC 5.00 2.00
❑ 130 Chris Henry RC 5.00 2.00
❑ 131 Roddy White RC 5.00 2.00
❑ 132 Fred Gibson RC 4.00 1.50
❑ 133 Craphonso Thorpe RC 4.00 1.50
❑ 134 Terrence Murphy RC 5.00 2.00
❑ 135 Roydell Williams RC 4.00 1.50
❑ 136 Roscoe Parrish RC 5.00 2.00
❑ 137 Reggie Brown RC 5.00 2.00
❑ 138 Craig Bragg RC 4.00 1.50
❑ 139 Larry Brackins RC 4.00 1.50
❑ 140 Rasheed Marshall RC 5.00 2.00
❑ 141 J.R. Russell RC 4.00 1.50
❑ 142 Vincent Jackson RC 5.00 2.00
❑ 143 Dante Ridgeway RC 4.00 1.50
❑ 144 Chad Owens RC 5.00 2.00
❑ 145 Airese Currie RC 4.00 1.50
❑ 146 Marcus Maxwell RC 4.00 1.50
❑ 147 Paris Warren RC 4.00 1.50
❑ 148 Tab Perry RC 5.00 2.00
❑ 149 Jerome Mathis RC 5.00 2.00
❑ 150 Courtney Roby RC 5.00 2.00
❑ 151 Heath Miller RC 10.00 4.00
❑ 152 Alex Smith TE RC 5.00 2.00
❑ 153 Kevin Everett RC 5.00 2.00

❑ 154 Travis Johnson RC 2.50 1.00
❑ 155 Mike Patterson RC 4.00 1.50
❑ 156 DeMarcus Ware RC 8.00 3.00
❑ 157 Erasmus James RC 4.00 1.50
❑ 158 Dan Cody RC 5.00 2.00
❑ 159 David Pollack RC 5.00 2.00
❑ 160 Shaun Cody RC 5.00 2.00
❑ 161 Matt Roth RC 5.00 2.00
❑ 162 Marcus Spears RC 5.00 2.00
❑ 163 Jonathan Babineaux RC 4.00 1.50
❑ 164 Justin Tuck RC 5.00 2.00
❑ 165 Channing Crowder RC 5.00 2.00
❑ 166 Odell Thurman RC 5.00 2.00
❑ 167 Barrett Ruud RC 5.00 2.00
❑ 168 Lance Mitchell RC 4.00 1.50
❑ 169 Derrick Johnson RC 8.00 3.00
❑ 170 Shawne Merriman RC 8.00 3.00
❑ 171 Kevin Burnett RC 5.00 2.00
❑ 172 Darryl Blackstock RC 4.00 1.50
❑ 173 Antrel Rolle RC 5.00 2.00
❑ 174 Adam Jones RC 5.00 2.00
❑ 175 Fabian Washington RC 5.00 2.00
❑ 176 Carlos Rogers RC 6.00 2.50
❑ 177 Corey Webster RC 4.00 1.50
❑ 178 Justin Miller RC 4.00 1.50
❑ 179 Eric Green RC 2.50 1.00
❑ 180 Marlin Jackson RC 5.00 2.00
❑ 181 Luis Castillo RC 5.00 2.00
❑ 182 Thomas Davis RC 4.00 1.50
❑ 183 Kirk Morrison RC 5.00 2.00
❑ 184 Vincent Fuller RC 4.00 1.50
❑ 185 Donte Nicholson RC 5.00 2.00
❑ 186 Brodney Pool RC 4.00 1.50
❑ 187 Mike Nugent RC 5.00 2.00
❑ 188 Timmy Chang RC 4.00 1.50
❑ 189 Matt Cassel RC 8.00 3.00
❑ 190 Adrian McPherson RC 5.00 2.00
❑ 191 Gino Guidugli RC 2.50 1.00
❑ 192 Stefan LeFors RC 5.00 2.00
❑ 193 Marcus Randall RC 4.00 1.50
❑ 194 Brandon Jacobs RC 6.00 2.50
❑ 195 Walter Reyes RC 2.50 1.00
❑ 196 Mark Bradley RC 5.00 2.00
❑ 197 Josh Bullocks RC 5.00 2.00
❑ 198 Chase Lyman RC 2.50 1.00
❑ 199 Harry Williams RC 4.00 1.50
❑ 200 Mike Williams 5.00 2.00

2003 Ultimate Collection

❑ 1 Peyton Manning 8.00 3.00
❑ 2 Aaron Brooks 5.00 2.00
❑ 3 Joey Harrington 8.00 3.00
❑ 4 Brett Favre 12.00 5.00
❑ 5 Donovan McNabb 6.00 2.50
❑ 6 Jeff Garcia 5.00 2.00
❑ 7 Michael Vick 12.00 5.00
❑ 8 David Carr 8.00 3.00
❑ 9 Drew Brees 5.00 2.00
❑ 10 Chad Pennington 6.00 2.50
❑ 11 Drew Bledsoe 5.00 2.00
❑ 12 Tom Brady 12.00 5.00
❑ 13 Kurt Warner 5.00 2.00
❑ 14 Brad Johnson 3.00 1.25
❑ 15 Jay Fiedler 3.00 1.25
❑ 16 Tim Couch 2.00 .75
❑ 17 Trent Green 3.00 1.25
❑ 18 Daunte Culpepper 5.00 2.00
❑ 19 Keyshawn Johnson 5.00 2.00
❑ 20 Garrison Hearst 3.00 1.25
❑ 21 LaDainian Tomlinson 5.00 2.00
❑ 22 Emmitt Smith 12.00 5.00
❑ 23 Steve McNair 5.00 2.00
❑ 24 Chris Redman 2.00 .75
❑ 25 Chad Hutchinson 2.00 .75
❑ 26 Deuce McAllister 5.00 2.00
❑ 27 Eddie George 3.00 1.25
❑ 28 Marshall Faulk 5.00 2.00
❑ 29 Ahman Green 5.00 2.00
❑ 30 Julius Peppers 5.00 2.00
❑ 31 Priest Holmes 6.00 2.50
❑ 32 Edgerrin James 5.00 2.00
❑ 33 Jerry Rice 10.00 4.00
❑ 34 Ricky Williams 5.00 2.00
❑ 35 Anthony Thomas 3.00 1.25
❑ 36 Jerome Bettis 5.00 2.00
❑ 37 Shaun Alexander 5.00 2.00
❑ 38 Randy Moss 8.00 3.00
❑ 39 Jeremy Shockey 8.00 3.00
❑ 40 Patrick Ramsey 5.00 2.00
❑ 41 Clinton Portis 8.00 3.00
❑ 42 Terrell Owens 5.00 2.00
❑ 43 Corey Dillon 3.00 1.25
❑ 44 Mark Brunell 3.00 1.25
❑ 45 Rich Gannon 3.00 1.25
❑ 46 Curtis Martin 5.00 2.00
❑ 47 Josh McCown 3.00 1.25
❑ 48 Kerry Collins 3.00 1.25
❑ 49 Peerless Price 3.00 1.25
❑ 50 David Boston 3.00 1.25
❑ 51 Plaxico Burress 3.00 1.25
❑ 52 Marvin Harrison 5.00 2.00
❑ 53 Travis Henry 3.00 1.25
❑ 54 Brian Urlacher 8.00 3.00
❑ 55 Jake Plummer 3.00 1.25
❑ 56 Dave Ragone/750 RC 10.00 4.00
❑ 57 Brian St.Pierre AU/250 RC 20.00 8.00
❑ 58 Tony Romo/750 RC 100.00 50.00
❑ 59 Dallas Clark/750 RC 10.00 4.00
❑ 60 Kirk Farmer/750 RC 8.00 3.00
❑ 61 Juston Wood/750 RC 8.00 3.00
❑ 62 Justin Gage/750 RC 10.00 4.00
❑ 63 Sam Aiken/750 RC 8.00 3.00
❑ 64 LaBrandon Toefield/750 RC 10.00 4.00
❑ 65 L.J. Smith/750 RC 10.00 4.00
❑ 66 Domanick Davis/750 RC 10.00 4.00
❑ 67 Artose Pinner/750 RC 10.00 4.00
❑ 68 Dahrran Diedrick/750 RC 10.00 4.00
❑ 69 Lee Suggs/750 RC 10.00 4.00
❑ 70 Bethel Johnson/750 RC 10.00 4.00
❑ 71 Tyrone Calico/750 RC 10.00 4.00
❑ 72 Kevin Curtis/750 RC 12.00 5.00
❑ 73 Bobby Wade/750 RC 10.00 4.00
❑ 74 Brandon Lloyd/750 RC 10.00 4.00
❑ 75 Bryant Johnson/750 RC 10.00 4.00
❑ 76 J.R. Tolver/750 RC 8.00 3.00
❑ 77 Billy McMullen/750 RC 8.00 3.00
❑ 78 Nate Burleson/750 RC 10.00 4.00
❑ 79 Jason Johnson AU/250 RC 20.00 8.00
❑ 80 Talman Gardner/250 RC 15.00 6.00
❑ 81 Anquan Boldin/250 RC 50.00 20.00
❑ 82 Musa Smith/250 RC 15.00 6.00
❑ 83 Teyo Johnson/250 RC 20.00 8.00
❑ 84 Kyle Boller AU/250 RC 30.00 12.50
❑ 85 Carson Palmer AU/250 RC 350.00 175.00
❑ 86 Byron Leftwich AU/250 RC 100.00 50.00
❑ 87 Earnest Graham AU/250 RC 35.00 20.00
❑ 88 Chris Brown AU/250 RC 40.00 20.00
❑ 89 Chris Simms AU/250 RC 80.00 40.00
❑ 90 Kliff Kingsbury AU/250 RC 30.00 12.50
❑ 91 Jason Gesser/750 RC 10.00 4.00
❑ 92 Brad Banks AU/250 RC 25.00 10.00
❑ 93 Ken Dorsey AU/250 RC 30.00 12.50
❑ 94 Rex Grossman AU/250 RC 80.00 30.00
❑ 95 Willis McGahee AU/250 RC 120.00 60.00
❑ 96 Larry Johnson AU/250 RC [illegible] 150.00
❑ 97 Quentin Griffin AU/250 RC 30.00 12.50
❑ 98 Onterrio Smith AU/250 RC 30.00 12.50
❑ 99 Justin Fargas AU/250 RC 40.00 15.00
❑ 100 Kareem Kelly AU/250 RC 25.00 10.00
❑ 101 Arnaz Battle AU/250 RC 40.00 15.00
❑ 102 Kel Washington AU/250 RC 40.00 15.00
❑ 103 Seneca Wallace AU/250 RC 40.00 15.00
❑ 104 Taylor Jacobs AU/250 RC 25.00 10.00
❑ 105 Andre Johnson/750 RC 30.00 12.50
❑ 106 Charles Rogers/250 RC 15.00 6.00
❑ 107 Terrell Suggs AU/250 RC 40.00 15.00

2004 Ultimate Collection

❑ 1-65 PRINT RUN 750 SER.#'d SETS
❑ 66-91/99A/133-135 PRINT RUN 750 SETS
❑ 92-98 RC PRINT RUN 250 SER.#'d SETS
❑ 99B-124/131-132 AU RC PRINT RUN 250 SETS
❑ 125-130 AU RC PRINT RUN 150 SER.#'d SETS
❑ UNPRICED PLATINUM PRINT RUN 10 SETS
❑ 1 Emmitt Smith 10.00 4.00
❑ 2 Anquan Boldin 5.00 2.00
❑ 3 Michael Vick 10.00 4.00
❑ 4 Peerless Price 3.00 1.25
❑ 5 Kyle Boller 5.00 2.00
❑ 6 Jamal Lewis 5.00 2.00
❑ 7 Drew Bledsoe 5.00 2.00
❑ 8 Travis Henry 3.00 1.25
❑ 9 Stephen Davis 3.00 1.25
❑ 10 Jake Delhomme 5.00 2.00
❑ 11 Rex Grossman 5.00 2.00
❑ 12 Brian Urlacher 6.00 2.50
❑ 13 Carson Palmer 6.00 2.50
❑ 14 Chad Johnson 5.00 2.00
❑ 15 Jeff Garcia 5.00 2.00
❑ 16 Keyshawn Johnson 3.00 1.25
❑ 17 Roy Williams S 3.00 1.25
❑ 18 Jake Plummer 3.00 1.25
❑ 19 Joey Harrington 5.00 2.00
❑ 20 Charles Rogers 3.00 1.25
❑ 21 Ahman Green 5.00 2.00
❑ 22 Brett Favre 12.00 5.00
❑ 23 David Carr 5.00 2.00
❑ 24 Domanick Davis 5.00 2.00
❑ 25 Andre Johnson 5.00 2.00
❑ 26 Edgerrin James 5.00 2.00
❑ 27 Peyton Manning 8.00 3.00
❑ 28 Marvin Harrison 5.00 2.00
❑ 29 Byron Leftwich 6.00 2.50
❑ 30 Fred Taylor 3.00 1.25
❑ 31 Priest Holmes 6.00 2.50
❑ 32 Tony Gonzalez 3.00 1.25
❑ 33 Trent Green 3.00 1.25
❑ 34 Ricky Williams 5.00 2.00
❑ 35 Chris Chambers 3.00 1.25
❑ 36 Jay Fiedler 2.00 .75
❑ 37 Randy Moss 6.00 2.50
❑ 38 Daunte Culpepper 5.00 2.00
❑ 39 Tom Brady 12.00 5.00
❑ 40 Corey Dillon 3.00 1.25
❑ 41 Deuce McAllister 5.00 2.00
❑ 42 Aaron Brooks 3.00 1.25
❑ 43 Tiki Barber 5.00 2.00
❑ 44 Jeremy Shockey 5.00 2.00
❑ 45 Chad Pennington 5.00 2.00
❑ 46 Curtis Martin 5.00 2.00
❑ 47 Santana Moss 3.00 1.25
❑ 48 Jerry Rice 10.00 4.00
❑ 49 Rich Gannon 3.00 1.25
❑ 50 Donovan McNabb 6.00 2.50
❑ 51 Terrell Owens 5.00 2.00
❑ 52 Hines Ward 5.00 2.00
❑ 53 Plaxico Burress 3.00 1.25
❑ 54 LaDainian Tomlinson 6.00 2.50

❑ 55 Tim Rattay 2.00 .75
❑ 56 Matt Hasselbeck 3.00 1.25
❑ 57 Shaun Alexander 5.00 2.00
❑ 58 Marc Bulger 5.00 2.00
❑ 59 Marshall Faulk 5.00 2.00
❑ 60 Torry Holt 5.00 2.00
❑ 61 Brad Johnson 3.00 1.25
❑ 62 Steve McNair 5.00 2.00
❑ 63 Chris Brown 5.00 2.00
❑ 64 Mark Brunell 3.00 1.25
❑ 65 Clinton Portis 5.00 2.00
❑ 66 Michael Turner RC 15.00 6.00
❑ 67 Kris Wilson RC 10.00 4.00
❑ 68 [illegible]
❑ 69 Adimchinobe Echemandu RC 8.00 3.00
❑ 71 Thomas Tapeh RC 8.00 3.00
❑ 72 Chris Cooley RC 10.00 4.00
❑ 73 Cody Pickett RC 10.00 4.00
❑ 74 P.K. Sam RC 8.00 3.00
❑ 75 Ben Hartsock RC 10.00 4.00
❑ 76 Tim Euhus RC 10.00 4.00
❑ 77 Jammal Lord RC 10.00 4.00
❑ 78 Ricardo Colclough RC 10.00 4.00
❑ 79 D.J. Hackett RC 8.00 3.00
❑ 80 Ahmad Carroll RC 10.00 4.00
❑ 81 Troy Fleming RC 8.00 3.00
❑ 82 John Navarre RC 10.00 4.00
❑ 83 Craig Krenzel RC 10.00 4.00
❑ 84 Johnnie Morant RC 10.00 4.00
❑ 85 D.J. Williams RC 10.00 4.00
❑ 86 Jarrett Payton RC 10.00 4.00
❑ 87 Quincy Wilson RC 8.00 3.00
❑ 88 B.J. Symons RC 10.00 4.00
❑ 89 Tommie Harris RC 10.00 4.00
❑ 90 Jonathan Vilma RC 10.00 4.00
❑ 91 Karlos Dansby RC 10.00 4.00
❑ 92 Jerricho Cotchery RC 12.00 5.00
❑ 93 Samie Parker RC 12.00 5.00
❑ 94 Carlos Francis RC 10.00 4.00
❑ 95 Jim Sorgi RC 12.00 5.00
❑ 96 Derrick Hamilton RC 10.00 4.00
❑ 97 Dunta Robinson RC 12.00 5.00
❑ 98 Chris Gamble RC 12.00 5.00
❑ 99A Josh Harris RC 10.00 4.00
❑ 99B Devery Henderson AU RC 30.00 12.50
❑ 100 Julius Jones AU RC 100.00 40.00
❑ 101 Cedric Cobbs AU RC 25.00 10.00
❑ 102 Greg Jones AU RC 25.00 10.00
❑ 103 Tatum Bell AU RC 60.00 30.00
❑ 104 Michael Jenkins AU RC 25.00 10.00
❑ 105 Devard Darling AU RC 25.00 10.00
❑ 106 Lee Evans AU RC 40.00 20.00
❑ 107 Keary Colbert AU RC 30.00 12.50
❑ 108 Bernard Berrian AU RC 40.00 20.00
❑ 109 Ben Watson AU RC 30.00 12.50
❑ 110 Matt Schaub AU RC 150.00 75.00
❑ 111 Darius Watts AU RC 25.00 10.00
❑ 112 Kevin Jones AU RC 80.00 30.00
❑ 113 Luke McCown AU RC 25.00 10.00
❑ 114 DeAngelo Hall AU RC 40.00 20.00
❑ 115 Rashaun Woods AU RC 25.00 10.00
❑ 116 Michael Clayton AU RC 60.00 30.00
❑ 117 Ben Troupe AU RC 25.00 10.00
❑ 118 B.J. Sams AU RC 25.00 10.00
❑ 119 Reggie Williams AU RC 30.00 15.00
❑ 120 Chris Perry AU RC 40.00 15.00
❑ 121 Roy Williams AU RC 100.00 50.00
❑ 122 Robert Gallery AU RC 25.00 10.00
❑ 123 J.P. Losman AU RC 60.00 30.00
❑ 124 Steven Jackson AU RC 150.00 90.00
❑ 125 Drew Henson AU RC 25.00 10.00
❑ 126 Kellen Winslow AU RC 80.00 30.00
❑ 127 B.Roethlisberger AU RC 400.00 200.00
❑ 128 Philip Rivers AU RC 250.00 125.00
❑ 129 Larry Fitzgerald AU RC 120.00 60.00
❑ 130 Eli Manning AU RC 400.00 200.00
❑ 131 Ernest Wilford AU RC 25.00 10.00
❑ 132 Mewelde Moore AU RC 25.00 10.00
❑ 133 Will Smith RC 10.00 4.00
❑ 134 Kenechi Udeze RC 10.00 4.00
❑ 135 Matt Mauck RC 10.00 4.00

2005 Ultimate Collection

❑ 1-100/270-289 PRINT RUN 550 SER.#'d SETS
❑ 101-200/250-269 PRINT RUN 235 SETS
❑ AUTO PRINT RUN 225 UNLESS NOTED
❑ 1 Larry Fitzgerald 5.00 2.00
❑ 2 Anquan Boldin 3.00 1.25
❑ 3 Kurt Warner 3.00 1.25
❑ 4 Michael Vick 8.00 3.00
❑ 5 Warrick Dunn 3.00 1.25
❑ 6 Alge Crumpler 3.00 1.25
❑ 7 Ray Lewis 5.00 2.00
❑ 8 Deion Sanders 5.00 2.00
❑ 9 Kyle Boller 3.00 1.25
❑ 10 Derrick Mason 3.00 1.25
❑ 11 J.P. Losman 5.00 2.00
❑ 12 Willis McGahee 5.00 2.00
❑ 13 Lee Evans 3.00 1.25
❑ 14 Eric Moulds 3.00 1.25
❑ 15 Jake Delhomme 5.00 2.00
❑ 16 Keary Colbert 3.00 1.25
❑ 17 DeShaun Foster 3.00 1.25
❑ 18 Brian Urlacher 5.00 2.00
❑ 19 Rex Grossman 3.00 1.25
❑ 20 Muhsin Muhammad 3.00 1.25
❑ 21 Carson Palmer 5.00 2.00
❑ 22 Rudi Johnson 3.00 1.25
❑ 23 Chad Johnson 5.00 2.00
❑ 24 Julius Jones 6.00 2.50
❑ 25 Keyshawn Johnson 3.00 1.25
❑ 26 Drew Bledsoe 5.00 2.00
❑ 27 Tatum Bell 3.00 1.25
❑ 28 Jake Plummer 3.00 1.25
❑ 29 Ashley Lelie 3.00 1.25
❑ 30 Roy Williams WR 5.00 2.00
❑ 31 Kevin Jones 5.00 2.00
❑ 32 Jeff Garcia 3.00 1.25
❑ 33 Brett Favre 12.00 5.00
❑ 34 Ahman Green 5.00 2.00
❑ 35 Javon Walker 3.00 1.25
❑ 36 David Carr 5.00 2.00
❑ 37 Andre Johnson 3.00 1.25
❑ 38 Domanick Davis 3.00 1.25
❑ 39 Peyton Manning 8.00 3.00
❑ 40 Reggie Wayne 3.00 1.25
❑ 41 Edgerrin James 5.00 2.00
❑ 42 Marvin Harrison 5.00 2.00
❑ 43 Byron Leftwich 5.00 2.00
❑ 44 Fred Taylor 3.00 1.25
❑ 45 Jimmy Smith 3.00 1.25
❑ 46 Priest Holmes 5.00 2.00
❑ 47 Larry Johnson 5.00 2.00
❑ 48 Trent Green 3.00 1.25
❑ 49 A.J. Feeley 3.00 1.25
❑ 50 Chris Chambers 3.00 1.25
❑ 51 Randy McMichael 2.50 1.00
❑ 52 Daunte Culpepper 5.00 2.00
❑ 53 Michael Bennett 3.00 1.25
❑ 54 Nate Burleson 3.00 1.25
❑ 55 Tom Brady 12.00 5.00
❑ 56 Corey Dillon 3.00 1.25
❑ 57 Deion Branch 3.00 1.25
❑ 58 David Givens 3.00 1.25
❑ 59 Aaron Brooks 3.00 1.25
❑ 60 Deuce McAllister 5.00 2.00
❑ 61 Joe Horn 3.00 1.25
❑ 62 Eli Manning 10.00 4.00
❑ 63 Jeremy Shockey 5.00 2.00
❑ 64 Tiki Barber 5.00 2.00
❑ 65 Chad Pennington 5.00 2.00
❑ 66 Curtis Martin 5.00 2.00
❑ 67 Laveranues Coles 3.00 1.25
❑ 68 Kerry Collins 3.00 1.25
❑ 69 LaMont Jordan 5.00 2.00
❑ 70 Randy Moss 5.00 2.00
❑ 71 Donovan McNabb 6.00 2.50
❑ 72 Terrell Owens 5.00 2.00
❑ 73 Brian Dawkins 2.50 1.00
❑ 74 Brian Westbrook 3.00 1.25
❑ 75 Ben Roethlisberger 12.00 5.00
❑ 76 [illegible]
❑ 77 Hines Ward 5.00 2.00
❑ 78 Duce Staley 3.00 1.25
❑ 79 Drew Brees 5.00 2.00
❑ 80 LaDainian Tomlinson 6.00 2.50
❑ 81 Antonio Gates 5.00 2.00
❑ 82 Tim Rattay 2.50 1.00
❑ 83 Kevan Barlow 3.00 1.25
❑ 84 Eric Johnson 3.00 1.25
❑ 85 Shaun Alexander 6.00 2.50
❑ 86 Darrell Jackson 3.00 1.25
❑ 87 Matt Hasselbeck 3.00 1.25
❑ 88 Marc Bulger 5.00 2.00
❑ 89 Steven Jackson 6.00 2.50
❑ 90 Marshall Faulk 5.00 2.00
❑ 91 Torry Holt 5.00 2.00
❑ 92 Michael Pittman 2.50 1.00
❑ 93 Brian Griese 3.00 1.25
❑ 94 Michael Clayton 5.00 2.00
❑ 95 Steve McNair 5.00 2.00
❑ 96 Drew Bennett 3.00 1.25
❑ 97 Chris Brown 3.00 1.25
❑ 98 Clinton Portis 5.00 2.00
❑ 99 Patrick Ramsey 3.00 1.25
❑ 100 Santana Moss 3.00 1.25
❑ 101 James Kilian RC 10.00 4.00
❑ 102 Marlin Jackson RC 10.00 4.00
❑ 103 Corey Webster RC 10.00 4.00
❑ 104 Ryan Claridge RC 8.00 3.00
❑ 105 David Pollack RC 10.00 4.00
❑ 106 Deandra Cobb RC 8.00 3.00
❑ 107 Anttaj Hawthorne RC 8.00 3.00
❑ 108 Erasmus James RC 10.00 4.00
❑ 109 Dan Cody RC 10.00 4.00
❑ 110 Jerome Mathis RC 10.00 4.00
❑ 111 Barrett Ruud RC 10.00 4.00
❑ 112 Kevin Burnett RC 10.00 4.00
❑ 113 Jason White RC 10.00 4.00
❑ 114 Chase Lyman RC 8.00 3.00
❑ 115 Cedric Houston RC 10.00 4.00
❑ 116 Roydell Williams RC 10.00 4.00
❑ 117 Fred Gibson RC 8.00 3.00
❑ 118 Dustin Colquitt RC 8.00 3.00
❑ 119 Rasheed Marshall RC 10.00 4.00
❑ 120 Walter Reyes RC 8.00 3.00
❑ 121 Craig Bragg RC 8.00 3.00
❑ 122 Marcus Maxwell RC 8.00 3.00
❑ 123 LeRon McCoy RC 8.00 3.00
❑ 124 Harry Williams RC 8.00 3.00
❑ 125 Larry Brackins RC 8.00 3.00
❑ 126 J.R. Russell RC 8.00 3.00
❑ 127 Manuel White RC 8.00 3.00
❑ 128 Brandon Jones RC 10.00 4.00
❑ 129 Eric King RC 8.00 3.00
❑ 130 Travis Johnson RC 8.00 3.00
❑ 131 Mike Patterson RC 10.00 4.00
❑ 132 Marcus Spears RC 10.00 4.00
❑ 133 Darryl Blackstock RC 8.00 3.00
❑ 134 Michael Boley RC 8.00 3.00
❑ 135 Leroy Hill RC 10.00 4.00
❑ 136 Channing Crowder RC 10.00 4.00
❑ 137 Odell Thurman RC 10.00 4.00
❑ 138 Lance Mitchell RC 8.00 3.00
❑ 139 Jerome Collins RC 8.00 3.00
❑ 140 Stanford Routt RC 8.00 3.00
❑ 141 Justin Miller RC 8.00 3.00
❑ 142 Bryant McFadden RC 10.00 4.00
❑ 143 Eric Green RC 5.00 2.00
❑ 144 Fabian Washington RC 10.00 4.00
❑ 145 Antonio Perkins RC 8.00 3.00
❑ 146 Shaun Cody RC 10.00 4.00

❑ 147 Jonathan Babineaux RC 8.00 3.00
❑ 148 Ronald Bartell RC 8.00 3.00
❑ 149 Luis Castillo RC 10.00 4.00
❑ 150 Chris Carr RC 10.00 4.00
❑ 151 Justin Tuck RC 10.00 4.00
❑ 152 Brodney Pool RC 10.00 4.00
❑ 153 Matt Roth RC 10.00 4.00
❑ 154 DeMarcus Ware RC 15.00 6.00
❑ 155 Josh Bullocks RC 10.00 4.00
❑ 156 Vincent Fuller RC 8.00 3.00
❑ 157 Donte Nicholson RC 10.00 4.00
❑ 158 Rashied Davis RC 10.00 4.00
❑ 159 Nick Collins RC 10.00 4.00
❑ 160 Mike Nugent RC 10.00 4.00
❑ 161 Tyson Thompson RC 15.00 6.00
❑ 162 Darrent Williams RC 10.00 4.00
❑ 163 Kelvin Hayden RC 8.00 3.00
❑ 164 Oshiomogho Atogwe RC 8.00 3.00
❑ 165 Ryan Fitzpatrick RC 10.00 4.00
❑ 166 Stanley Wilson RC 8.00 3.00
❑ 167 Vonta Leach RC 10.00 4.00
❑ 168 Ellis Hobbs RC 10.00 4.00
❑ 169 Scott Starks RC 8.00 3.00
❑ 170 Lionel Gates RC 8.00 3.00
❑ 171 Alvin Pearman RC 10.00 4.00
❑ 172 Damien Nash RC 8.00 3.00
❑ 173 Noah Herron RC 10.00 4.00
❑ 174 Domonique Foxworth RC 10.00 4.00
❑ 175 Derrick Johnson CB RC 10.00 4.00
❑ 176 Lofa Tatupu RC 20.00 7.50
❑ 177 Daven Holly RC 10.00 4.00
❑ 178 Dante Ridgeway RC 8.00 3.00
❑ 179 Airese Currie RC 10.00 4.00
❑ 180 Adam Bergen RC 10.00 4.00
❑ 181 Kirk Morrison RC 10.00 4.00
❑ 182 Alfred Fincher RC 8.00 3.00
❑ 183 Jordan Beck RC 8.00 3.00
❑ 184 Sean Considine RC 10.00 4.00
❑ 185 Tab Perry RC 10.00 4.00
❑ 186 Travis Daniels RC 8.00 3.00
❑ 187 Paris Warren RC 8.00 3.00
❑ 188 Marviel Underwood RC 8.00 3.00
❑ 189 Jerome Carter RC 8.00 3.00
❑ 190 Kerry Rhodes RC 10.00 4.00
❑ 191 James Sanders RC 10.00 4.00
❑ 192 Stephen Spach RC 8.00 3.00
❑ 193 Bo Scaife RC 8.00 3.00
❑ 194 Andre Frazier RC 15.00 6.00
❑ 195 Alex Barron RC 5.00 2.00
❑ 196 Jammal Brown RC 10.00 4.00
❑ 197 Nehemiah Broughton RC 8.00 3.00
❑ 198 Elton Brown RC 5.00 2.00
❑ 199 David Baas RC 8.00 3.00
❑ 200 Joel Dreessen RC 8.00 3.00
❑ 201 Maurice Clarett AU/120 20.00 7.50
❑ 202 Craphonso Thorpe AU RC 15.00 6.00
❑ 203 Adam Jones AU RC 20.00 7.50
❑ 204 Mark Bradley AU RC 25.00 10.00
❑ 205 Vincent Jackson AU RC 30.00 15.00
❑ 206 Antrel Rolle AU RC 20.00 7.50
❑ 207 Heath Miller AU RC 50.00 25.00
❑ 208 Anthony Davis AU RC 15.00 6.00
❑ 209 Terrence Murphy AU RC 20.00 7.50
❑ 210 Chris Henry AU RC 25.00 12.50
❑ 211 Roscoe Parrish AU RC 20.00 7.50
❑ 212 Stefan LeFors AU RC 20.00 7.50
❑ 213 Derek Anderson AU RC 80.00 50.00
❑ 214 Darren Sproles AU RC 20.00 7.50
❑ 215 Adrian McPherson AU RC 20.00 7.50
❑ 216 Frank Gore AU RC 100.00 60.00
❑ 217 Marion Barber AU RC 100.00 60.00
❑ 218 Ryan Moats AU RC 25.00 12.50
❑ 219 Carlos Rogers AU RC 25.00 10.00
❑ 220 Vernand Morency AU RC 15.00 6.00
❑ 221 J.J. Arrington AU RC 20.00 7.50
❑ 222 Courtney Roby AU RC 20.00 7.50
❑ 223 Dan Orlovsky AU RC 20.00 7.50
❑ 224 Kyle Orton AU RC 25.00 10.00
❑ 225 David Greene AU RC 20.00 7.50
❑ 226 Roddy White AU/150 RC 30.00 12.50
❑ 227 Matt Jones AU/99 RC 60.00 30.00
❑ 228 Reggie Brown AU/150 RC 40.00 20.00
❑ 229 Mark Clayton AU/150 RC 40.00 20.00
❑ 230 Eric Shelton AU/150 RC 20.00 7.50
❑ 231 Ciatrick Fason AU/150 RC 20.00 7.50
❑ 232 Jason Campbell AU/150 RC 100.00 50.00
❑ 233 Charlie Frye AU/150 RC 50.00 20.00
❑ 234 Andrew Walter AU/150 RC 40.00 15.00
❑ 235 Troy Williamson AU/120 RC 40.00 20.00
❑ 236 Braylon Edwards AU/99 RC 120.00 60.00
❑ 237 Mike Williams AU/99 50.00 25.00
❑ 238 Cedric Benson AU/99 RC 120.00 60.00
❑ 239 Cadillac Williams AU/99 RC 120.00 60.00
❑ 240 Ronnie Brown AU/99 RC 120.00 60.00
❑ 241 Alex Smith QB AU/99 RC 120.00 60.00
❑ 242 Aaron Rodgers AU/99 RC 150.00 90.00
❑ 243 Matt Cassel AU RC 40.00 20.00
❑ 244 Brandon Jacobs AU RC 80.00 40.00
❑ 245 Alex Smith TE AU RC 20.00 7.50
❑ 246 Derrick Johnson AU RC 40.00 15.00
❑ 247 Chad Owens AU RC 30.00 15.00
❑ 248 Thomas Davis AU RC 20.00 7.50
❑ 249 Shawne Merriman AU RC 60.00 30.00
❑ 250 Gino Guidugli RC 5.00 2.00
❑ 251 Timmy Chang RC 8.00 3.00
❑ 252 Todd Mortensen RC 8.00 3.00
❑ 253 Bryan Randall RC 8.00 3.00
❑ 254 Brock Berlin RC 8.00 3.00
❑ 255 T.A. McLendon RC 5.00 2.00
❑ 256 Kay-Jay Harris RC 8.00 3.00
❑ 257 Bobby Purify RC 8.00 3.00
❑ 258 Steve Savoy RC 5.00 2.00
❑ 259 Keron Henry RC 5.00 2.00
❑ 260 Josh Davis RC 8.00 3.00
❑ 261 Chauncey Stovall RC 5.00 2.00
❑ 262 Efrem Hill RC 8.00 3.00
❑ 263 Sione Pouha RC 10.00 4.00
❑ 264 Jesse Lumsden RC 5.00 2.00
❑ 265 Vincent Burns RC 8.00 3.00
❑ 266 Brady Poppinga RC 10.00 4.00
❑ 267 Boomer Grigsby RC 10.00 4.00
❑ 268 Robert McCune RC 8.00 3.00
❑ 269 Fred Amey RC 8.00 3.00
❑ 270 T.J. Duckett 3.00 1.25
❑ 271 Jamal Lewis 5.00 2.00
❑ 272 Rod Gardner 3.00 1.25
❑ 273 Thomas Jones 3.00 1.25
❑ 274 Jason Witten 3.00 1.25
❑ 275 Roy Williams S 3.00 1.25
❑ 276 Mike Anderson 3.00 1.25
❑ 277 Joey Harrington 5.00 2.00
❑ 278 Charles Rogers 3.00 1.25
❑ 279 Donald Driver 3.00 1.25
❑ 280 Jabar Gaffney 2.50 1.00
❑ 281 Reggie Williams 3.00 1.25
❑ 282 Tony Gonzalez 3.00 1.25
❑ 283 Ricky Williams 3.00 1.25
❑ 284 Mewelde Moore 2.50 1.00
❑ 285 Plaxico Burress 3.00 1.25
❑ 286 Jerry Porter 3.00 1.25
❑ 287 Brandon Lloyd 2.50 1.00
❑ 288 Isaac Bruce 3.00 1.25
❑ 289 LaVar Arrington 5.00 2.00

2006 Ultimate Collection

❑ 1 Kurt Warner 3.00 1.25
❑ 2 Edgerrin James 5.00 2.00
❑ 3 Larry Fitzgerald 5.00 2.00
❑ 4 Anquan Boldin 3.00 1.25
❑ 5 Antrel Rolle 2.50 1.00
❑ 6 Karlos Dansby 2.50 1.00
❑ 7 Michael Vick 5.00 2.00
❑ 8 Warrick Dunn 3.00 1.25
❑ 9 DeAngelo Hall 3.00 1.25
❑ 10 Alge Crumpler 3.00 1.25
❑ 11 Roddy White 3.00 1.25
❑ 12 Michael Jenkins 3.00 1.25
❑ 13 Steve McNair 3.00 1.25
❑ 14 Jamal Lewis 3.00 1.25
❑ 15 Derrick Mason 2.50 1.00
❑ 16 Todd Heap 3.00 1.25
❑ 17 Mark Clayton 5.00 2.00
❑ 18 Ray Lewis 5.00 2.00
❑ 19 J.P. Losman 3.00 1.25
❑ 20 Willis McGahee 5.00 2.00
❑ 21 Lee Evans 3.00 1.25
❑ 22 Roscoe Parrish 2.50 1.00
❑ 23 Takeo Spikes 2.50 1.00
❑ 24 Nate Clements 2.50 1.00
❑ 25 Jake Delhomme 3.00 1.25
❑ 26 DeShaun Foster 3.00 1.25
❑ 27 Steve Smith 5.00 2.00
❑ 28 Keary Colbert 2.50 1.00
❑ 29 Julius Peppers 3.00 1.25
❑ 30 Chris Gamble 2.50 1.00
❑ 31 Rex Grossman 5.00 2.00
❑ 32 Thomas Jones 3.00 1.25
❑ 33 Cedric Benson 5.00 2.00
❑ 34 Muhsin Muhammad 3.00 1.25
❑ 35 Brian Urlacher 5.00 2.00
❑ 36 Nathan Vasher 2.50 1.00
❑ 37 Carson Palmer 5.00 2.00
❑ 38 Rudi Johnson 3.00 1.25
❑ 39 Chad Johnson 3.00 1.25
❑ 40 T.J. Houshmandzadeh 3.00 1.25
❑ 41 Odell Thurman 2.50 1.00
❑ 42 Deltha O'Neal 2.50 1.00
❑ 43 Charlie Frye 3.00 1.25
❑ 44 Reuben Droughns 3.00 1.25
❑ 45 Braylon Edwards 5.00 2.00
❑ 46 Joe Jurevicius 3.00 1.25
❑ 47 Kellen Winslow 5.00 2.00
❑ 48 Willie McGinest 2.50 1.00
❑ 49 Drew Bledsoe 5.00 2.00
❑ 50 Julius Jones 5.00 2.00
❑ 51 Terrell Owens 5.00 2.00
❑ 52 Terry Glenn 3.00 1.25
❑ 53 Jason Witten 3.00 1.25
❑ 54 DeMarcus Ware 3.00 1.25
❑ 55 Roy Williams S 3.00 1.25
❑ 56 Jake Plummer 3.00 1.25
❑ 57 Tatum Bell 3.00 1.25
❑ 58 Rod Smith 3.00 1.25
❑ 59 Javon Walker 3.00 1.25
❑ 60 Stephen Alexander 2.50 1.00
❑ 61 Champ Bailey 3.00 1.25
❑ 62 John Lynch 3.00 1.25
❑ 63 Jon Kitna 2.50 1.00
❑ 64 Kevin Jones 5.00 2.00
❑ 65 Roy Williams WR 5.00 2.00
❑ 66 Mike Williams 5.00 2.00
❑ 67 Marcus Pollard 2.50 1.00
❑ 68 Dre Bly 2.50 1.00
❑ 69 Brett Favre 10.00 4.00
❑ 70 Ahman Green 3.00 1.25
❑ 71 Donald Driver 3.00 1.25
❑ 72 Robert Ferguson 2.50 1.00
❑ 73 Charles Woodson 3.00 1.25
❑ 74 Kabeer Gbaja-Biamila 3.00 1.25
❑ 75 David Carr 3.00 1.25
❑ 76 Domanick Davis 3.00 1.25
❑ 77 Andre Johnson 3.00 1.25
❑ 78 Eric Moulds 3.00 1.25
❑ 79 Jeb Putzier 2.50 1.00
❑ 80 Dunta Robinson 3.00 1.25
❑ 81 Peyton Manning 8.00 3.00
❑ 82 Dominic Rhodes 3.00 1.25
❑ 83 Reggie Wayne 3.00 1.25
❑ 84 Marvin Harrison 6.00 2.00
❑ 85 Dallas Clark 2.50 1.00
❑ 86 Dwight Freeney 3.00 1.25
❑ 87 Bob Sanders 3.00 1.25
❑ 88 Byron Leftwich 3.00 1.25
❑ 89 Fred Taylor 3.00 1.25
❑ 90 Matt Jones 3.00 1.25

No.	Card	Price	Price
❑ 91	Ernest Wilford	2.50	1.00
❑ 92	Greg Jones	2.50	1.00
❑ 93	Mike Peterson	2.50	1.00
❑ 94	Trent Green	3.00	1.25
❑ 95	Larry Johnson	6.00	2.50
❑ 96	Samie Parker	2.50	1.00
❑ 97	Eddie Kennison	2.50	1.00
❑ 98	Tony Gonzalez	3.00	1.25
❑ 99	Patrick Surtain	2.50	1.00
❑ 100	Daunte Culpepper	5.00	2.00
❑ 101	Ronnie Brown	5.00	2.00
❑ 102	Chris Chambers	3.00	1.25
❑ 103	Marty Booker	2.50	1.00
❑ 104	Randy McMichael	2.50	1.00
❑ 105	Jason Taylor	2.50	1.00
❑ 106	Zach Thomas	5.00	2.00
❑ 107	Brad Johnson	3.00	1.25
❑ 108	Chester Taylor	3.00	1.25
❑ 109	Travis Taylor	2.50	1.00
❑ 110	Troy Williamson	3.00	1.25
❑ 111	Darren Sharper	2.50	1.00
❑ 112	Antoine Winfield	2.50	1.00
❑ 113	Tom Brady	8.00	3.00
❑ 114	Corey Dillon	3.00	1.25
❑ 115	Deion Branch	3.00	1.25
❑ 116	Ben Watson	2.50	1.00
❑ 117	Tedy Bruschi	5.00	2.00
❑ 118	Richard Seymour	2.50	1.00
❑ 119	Rodney Harrison	2.50	1.00
❑ 120	Drew Brees	5.00	2.00
❑ 121	Deuce McAllister	3.00	1.25
❑ 122	Joe Horn	3.00	1.25
❑ 123	Donte Stallworth	3.00	1.25
❑ 124	Will Smith	2.50	1.00
❑ 125	Fred Thomas	2.50	1.00
❑ 126	Eli Manning	6.00	2.50
❑ 127	Tiki Barber	5.00	2.00
❑ 128	Plaxico Burress	3.00	1.25
❑ 129	Jeremy Shockey	5.00	2.00
❑ 130	Osi Umenyiora	2.50	1.00
❑ 131	Michael Strahan	3.00	1.25
❑ 132	LaVar Arrington	5.00	2.00
❑ 133	Chad Pennington	3.00	1.25
❑ 134	Curtis Martin	5.00	2.00
❑ 135	Laveranues Coles	3.00	1.25
❑ 136	Justin McCareins	2.50	1.00
❑ 137	Jonathan Vilma	3.00	1.25
❑ 138	Shaun Ellis	2.50	1.00
❑ 139	Aaron Brooks	3.00	1.25
❑ 140	LaMont Jordan	3.00	1.25
❑ 141	Randy Moss	5.00	2.00
❑ 142	Doug Gabriel	2.50	1.00
❑ 143	Jerry Porter	3.00	1.25
❑ 144	Derrick Burgess	2.50	1.00
❑ 145	Donovan McNabb	5.00	2.00
❑ 146	Brian Westbrook	3.00	1.25
❑ 147	Reggie Brown	4.00	1.50
❑ 148	L.J. Smith	2.50	1.00
❑ 149	Jevon Kearse	3.00	1.25
❑ 150	Brian Dawkins	3.00	1.25
❑ 151	Ben Roethlisberger	8.00	3.00
❑ 152	Willie Parker	6.00	2.50
❑ 153	Hines Ward	5.00	2.00
❑ 154	Cedrick Wilson	2.50	1.00
❑ 155	Heath Miller	3.00	1.25
❑ 156	Joey Porter	2.50	1.00
❑ 157	Troy Polamalu	6.00	2.50
❑ 158	Philip Rivers	5.00	2.00
❑ 159	LaDainian Tomlinson	6.00	2.50
❑ 160	Keenan McCardell	2.50	1.00
❑ 161	Eric Parker	2.50	1.00
❑ 162	Antonio Gates	5.00	2.00
❑ 163	Shawne Merriman	3.00	1.25
❑ 164	Donnie Edwards	2.50	1.00
❑ 165	Alex Smith QB	5.00	2.00
❑ 166	Frank Gore	5.00	2.00
❑ 167	Antonio Bryant	3.00	1.25
❑ 168	Eric Johnson	3.00	1.25
❑ 169	Bryant Young	2.50	1.00
❑ 170	Shawntae Spencer	2.50	1.00
❑ 171	Matt Hasselbeck	3.00	1.25
❑ 172	Shaun Alexander	5.00	2.00
❑ 173	Darrell Jackson	3.00	1.25
❑ 174	Nate Burleson	3.00	1.25
❑ 175	Lofa Tatupu	3.00	1.25
❑ 176	Julian Peterson	2.50	1.00
❑ 177	Marc Bulger	3.00	1.25
❑ 178	Steven Jackson	5.00	2.00
❑ 179	Torry Holt	3.00	1.25
❑ 180	Kevin Curtis	2.50	1.00
❑ 181	Isaac Bruce	3.00	1.25
❑ 182	Leonard Little	2.50	1.00
❑ 183	Chris Simms	3.00	1.25
❑ 184	Cadillac Williams	5.00	2.00
❑ 185	Joey Galloway	3.00	1.25
❑ 186	Michael Clayton	3.00	1.25
❑ 187	Derrick Brooks	3.00	1.25
❑ 188	Ronde Barber	2.50	1.00
❑ 189	Billy Volek	3.00	1.25
❑ 190	Chris Brown	3.00	1.25
❑ 191	Drew Bennett	2.50	1.00
❑ 192	Travis Henry	3.00	1.25
❑ 193	Ben Troupe	2.50	1.00
❑ 194	Kyle Vanden Bosch	2.50	1.00
❑ 195	Sean Taylor	3.00	1.25
❑ 196	Mark Brunell	3.00	1.25
❑ 197	Clinton Portis	5.00	2.00
❑ 198	Santana Moss	3.00	1.25
❑ 199	Antwaan Randle El	3.00	1.25
❑ 200	Jason Campbell	3.00	1.25
❑ 201	Matt Leinart AU/99 RC	300.00	150.00
❑ 202	DeA.Williams AU/99 RC	150.00	75.00
❑ 203	Jay Cutler AU/99 RC	400.00	200.00
❑ 204	Joseph Addai AU/99 RC	250.00	125.00
❑ 205	L.Maroney AU/150 RC	150.00	75.00
❑ 206	Reggie Bush AU/99 RC	400.00	200.00
❑ 207	Santonio Holmes AU/99 RC	120.00	60.00
❑ 208	Vernon Davis AU/99 RC	80.00	40.00
❑ 209	Vince Young AU/99 RC	400.00	200.00
❑ 210	LenDale White AU/150 RC	80.00	40.00
❑ 211	Jerious Norwood AU/150 RC	80.00	40.00
❑ 212	Travis Wilson AU/150 RC	20.00	8.00
❑ 213	Brian Calhoun AU/150 RC	25.00	10.00
❑ 214	A.J. Hawk AU/99 RC	80.00	40.00
❑ 215	Greg Jennings AU/150 RC	60.00	30.00
❑ 216	Mario Williams AU/99 RC	50.00	25.00
❑ 217	Maurice Drew AU/150 RC	150.00	75.00
❑ 218	M.Lewis AU/150 RC EXCH	25.00	10.00
❑ 219	Skyler Green AU/275 RC	20.00	8.00
❑ 220	Derek Hagan AU/150 RC	20.00	8.00
❑ 221	Tarvaris Jackson AU/150 RC	100.00	50.00
❑ 222	Chad Jackson AU/150 RC	30.00	12.00
❑ 223	Sinorice Moss AU/99 RC	40.00	15.00
❑ 224	Kellen Clemens AU/150 RC	80.00	40.00
❑ 225	Leon Washington AU/150 RC	50.00	25.00
❑ 226	Michael Huff AU/150 RC	25.00	10.00
❑ 227	Omar Jacobs AU/150 RC EXCH	20.00	8.00
❑ 228	Charlie Whitehurst AU/150 RC	25.00	10.00
❑ 229	Michael Robinson AU/150 RC	30.00	12.00
❑ 230	Brandon Williams AU/150 RC	25.00	10.00
❑ 231	Leonard Pope AU/275 RC	15.00	6.00
❑ 232	Greg Lee AU/275 RC	12.00	5.00
❑ 233	D.J. Shockley AU/275 RC	20.00	8.00
❑ 234	Dem.Williams AU/275 RC	15.00	6.00
❑ 235	Reggie McNeal AU/275 RC	12.00	5.00
❑ 236	Jerome Harrison AU/275 RC	20.00	8.00
❑ 237	Anthony Fasano AU/275 RC	20.00	8.00
❑ 238	Brandon Marshall AU/275 RC	40.00	20.00
❑ 239	Ernie Sims AU/275 RC	25.00	10.00
❑ 240	Cory Rodgers AU/275 RC	12.00	5.00
❑ 241	Will Blackmon AU/275 RC	12.00	5.00
❑ 242	DeMeco Ryans AU/275 RC	30.00	15.00
❑ 243	Owen Daniels AU/275 RC	20.00	8.00
❑ 244	Josh Betts AU/275 RC	15.00	6.00
❑ 245	Chad Greenway AU/275 RC	20.00	8.00
❑ 246	Mike Hass AU/275 RC	15.00	6.00
❑ 247	Mathias Kiwanuka AU/275 RC	25.00	10.00
❑ 248	D.Ferguson AU/275 RC EXCH	20.00	8.00
❑ 249	Brad Smith AU/275 RC	20.00	8.00
❑ 250	Thomas Howard AU/275 RC	20.00	8.00
❑ 251	Jason Avant AU/275 RC	15.00	6.00
❑ 252	Brodrick Bunkley AU/275 RC	15.00	6.00
❑ 253	Willie Reid AU/275 RC	15.00	6.00
❑ 254	Kelly Jennings AU/275 RC	15.00	6.00
❑ 255	Jimmy Williams AU/275 RC	20.00	8.00
❑ 256	Joe Klopfenstein AU/275 RC	15.00	6.00
❑ 257	Tye Hill AU/275 RC	15.00	6.00
❑ 258	Dominique Byrd AU/275 RC	15.00	6.00
❑ 259	Maurice Stovall AU/150 RC	20.00	8.00
❑ 260	Bruce Gradkowski AU/275 RC	50.00	20.00
❑ 261	Abdul Hodge RC	10.00	4.00
❑ 262	Adam Jennings RC	8.00	3.00
❑ 263	Ahmad Brooks RC	8.00	3.00
❑ 264	Andrew Whitworth RC	5.00	2.00
❑ 265	Anthony Schlegel RC	8.00	3.00
❑ 266	Anthony Smith RC	12.00	5.00
❑ 267	Antonio Cromartie RC	10.00	4.00
❑ 268	Ashton Youboty RC	10.00	4.00
❑ 269	Ben Obomanu RC	8.00	3.00
❑ 270	Bennie Brazell RC	8.00	3.00
❑ 271	[illegible] RC	[illegible]	[illegible]
❑ 272	Bobby Carpenter RC	10.00	4.00
❑ 273	Brett Basanez RC	10.00	4.00
❑ 274	Brett Elliott RC	10.00	4.00
❑ 275	Brodie Croyle RC	30.00	15.00
❑ 276	Calvin Lowry RC	10.00	4.00
❑ 277	Cedric Griffin RC	8.00	3.00
❑ 278	Cedric Humes RC	10.00	4.00
❑ 279	Charles Davis RC	8.00	3.00
❑ 280	Charles Gordon RC	8.00	3.00
❑ 281	Chris Gocong RC	8.00	3.00
❑ 282	Claude Wroten RC	5.00	2.00
❑ 283	Clint Ingram RC	10.00	4.00
❑ 284	Cody Hodges RC	8.00	3.00
❑ 285	Corey Bramlet RC	8.00	3.00
❑ 286	Cory Ross RC	10.00	4.00
❑ 287	Damien Rhodes RC	8.00	3.00
❑ 288	Danieal Manning RC	10.00	4.00
❑ 289	Daniel Bullocks RC	10.00	4.00
❑ 290	Darnell Bing RC	10.00	4.00
❑ 291	Darrell Hackney RC	8.00	3.00
❑ 292	Darryl Tapp RC	8.00	3.00
❑ 293	Daryn Colledge RC	10.00	4.00
❑ 294	David Anderson RC	8.00	3.00
❑ 295	David Kirtman RC	8.00	3.00
❑ 296	David Pittman RC	8.00	3.00
❑ 297	David Thomas RC	10.00	4.00
❑ 298	Davin Joseph RC	8.00	3.00
❑ 299	Andre Hall RC	8.00	3.00
❑ 300	Delanie Walker RC	8.00	3.00
❑ 301	Demetrius Summers RC	5.00	2.00
❑ 302	Devin Aromashodu RC	8.00	3.00
❑ 303	Devin Hester RC	20.00	8.00
❑ 304	Donte Whitner RC	10.00	4.00
❑ 305	D'Qwell Jackson RC	8.00	3.00
❑ 306	Dusty Dvoracek RC	10.00	4.00
❑ 307	Elvis Dumervil RC	5.00	2.00
❑ 308	Eric Smith RC	8.00	3.00
❑ 309	Freddie Keiaho RC	8.00	3.00
❑ 310	Frostee Rucker RC	8.00	3.00
❑ 311	Garrett Mills RC	10.00	4.00
❑ 312	Gerris Wilkinson RC	5.00	2.00
❑ 313	Haloti Ngata RC	10.00	4.00
❑ 314	Ingle Martin RC	10.00	4.00
❑ 315	J.D. Runnels RC	8.00	3.00
❑ 316	James Anderson RC	5.00	2.00
❑ 317	Jason Allen RC	10.00	4.00
❑ 318	Jason Pociask RC	8.00	3.00
❑ 319	Hank Baskett RC	10.00	4.00
❑ 320	Jeff King RC	8.00	3.00
❑ 321	Jeff Webb RC	8.00	3.00
❑ 322	Jeremy Bloom RC	8.00	3.00
❑ 323	Jeremy Trueblood RC	8.00	3.00
❑ 324	Joel Klatt RC	8.00	3.00
❑ 325	John McCargo RC	8.00	3.00
❑ 326	Johnathan Joseph RC	8.00	3.00
❑ 327	Jon Alston RC	10.00	4.00
❑ 328	Jonathan Orr RC	8.00	3.00
❑ 329	Kamerion Wimbley RC	10.00	4.00
❑ 330	Kent Smith RC	10.00	4.00
❑ 331	Kevin McMahan RC	8.00	3.00
❑ 332	Ko Simpson RC	8.00	3.00
❑ 333	Lawrence Vickers RC	8.00	3.00
❑ 334	Manny Lawson RC	10.00	4.00
❑ 335	Marcus Demps RC	5.00	2.00
❑ 336	Marcus McNeill RC	8.00	3.00
❑ 337	Marcus Vick RC	8.00	3.00
❑ 338	Marques Colston RC	40.00	15.00
❑ 339	Marques Hagans RC	8.00	3.00
❑ 340	Matt Shelton RC	10.00	4.00
❑ 341	Nick Mangold RC	8.00	3.00
❑ 342	P.J. Daniels RC	8.00	3.00

❑ 343	P.J. Pope RC	8.00	3.00
❑ 344	Miles Austin RC	8.00	3.00
❑ 345	Quinn Sypniewski RC	8.00	3.00
❑ 346	Richard Marshall RC	8.00	3.00
❑ 347	Richie Ross RC	8.00	3.00
❑ 348	Rocky McIntosh RC	10.00	4.00
❑ 349	Roman Harper RC	8.00	3.00
❑ 350	Ryan Cook RC	8.00	3.00
❑ 351	Mike Bell RC	10.00	4.00
❑ 352	Deuce Lutui RC	8.00	3.00
❑ 353	Tamba Hali RC	10.00	4.00
❑ 354	Tim Massaquoi RC	8.00	3.00
❑ 355	Todd Watkins RC	8.00	3.00
❑ 356	Tony Scheffler RC	10.00	4.00
❑ 357	Drew Olson RC	8.00	3.00
❑ 358	Wali Lundy RC	10.00	4.00
❑ 359	Wendell Mathis RC	8.00	3.00
❑ 360	Winston Justice RC	10.00	4.00

2007 Ultimate Collection

❑ 1	Matt Leinart	6.00	2.50
❑ 2	Edgerrin James	6.00	2.50
❑ 3	Larry Fitzgerald	5.00	2.00
❑ 4	Anquan Boldin	5.00	2.00
❑ 5	Marion Barber	5.00	2.00
❑ 6	Jerious Norwood	5.00	2.00
❑ 7	Alge Crumpler	5.00	2.00
❑ 8	Steve McNair	5.00	2.00
❑ 9	Willis McGahee	5.00	2.00
❑ 10	Mark Clayton	5.00	2.00
❑ 11	J.P. Losman	5.00	2.00
❑ 12	Anthony Thomas	4.00	1.50
❑ 13	Lee Evans	5.00	2.00
❑ 14	Jake Delhomme	5.00	2.00
❑ 15	DeAngelo Williams	6.00	2.50
❑ 16	Steve Smith	5.00	2.00
❑ 17	Rex Grossman	5.00	2.00
❑ 18	Cedric Benson	5.00	2.00
❑ 19	Brian Urlacher	6.00	2.50
❑ 20	Carson Palmer	6.00	2.50
❑ 21	Rudi Johnson	5.00	2.00
❑ 22	Chad Johnson	5.00	2.00
❑ 23	T.J. Houshmandzadeh	5.00	2.00
❑ 24	Charlie Frye	5.00	2.00
❑ 25	Kellen Winslow	5.00	2.00
❑ 26	Braylon Edwards	5.00	2.00
❑ 27	Tony Romo	12.00	5.00
❑ 28	Julius Jones	5.00	2.00
❑ 29	Terrell Owens	6.00	2.50
❑ 30	Jay Cutler	6.00	2.50
❑ 31	Travis Henry	5.00	2.00
❑ 32	Javon Walker	5.00	2.00
❑ 33	Jon Kitna	4.00	1.50
❑ 34	Roy Williams WR	5.00	2.00
❑ 35	Tatum Bell	5.00	2.00
❑ 36	Brett Favre	20.00	8.00
❑ 37	Donald Driver	5.00	2.00
❑ 38	Greg Jennings	5.00	2.00
❑ 39	Matt Schaub	5.00	2.00
❑ 40	Ahman Green	5.00	2.00
❑ 41	Andre Johnson	5.00	2.00
❑ 42	Peyton Manning	10.00	4.00
❑ 43	Joseph Addai	8.00	3.00
❑ 44	Marvin Harrison	6.00	2.50
❑ 45	Reggie Wayne	5.00	2.00
❑ 46	Byron Leftwich	5.00	2.00
❑ 47	Maurice Jones-Drew	6.00	2.50
❑ 48	Fred Taylor	5.00	2.00
❑ 49	Brodie Croyle	6.00	2.50
❑ 50	Larry Johnson	6.00	2.50
❑ 51	Tony Gonzalez	5.00	2.00
❑ 52	Trent Green	5.00	2.00
❑ 53	Ronnie Brown	5.00	2.00
❑ 54	Chris Chambers	5.00	2.00
❑ 55	Tarvaris Jackson	6.00	2.50
❑ 56	Chester Taylor	4.00	1.50
❑ 57	Troy Williamson	4.00	1.50
❑ 58	Tom Brady	12.00	5.00
❑ 59	Laurence Maroney	6.00	2.50
❑ 60	Randy Moss	6.00	2.50
❑ 61	Drew Brees	5.00	2.00
❑ 62	Reggie Bush	8.00	3.00
❑ 63	Deuce McAllister	5.00	2.00
❑ 64	Marques Colston	6.00	2.50
❑ 65	Eli Manning	6.00	2.50
❑ 66	Brandon Jacobs	5.00	2.00
❑ 67	Plaxico Burress	5.00	2.00
❑ 68	Chad Pennington	5.00	2.00
❑ 69	Thomas Jones	5.00	2.00
❑ 70	Laveranues Coles	5.00	2.00
❑ 71	LaMont Jordan	5.00	2.00
❑ 72	Dominic Rhodes	5.00	2.00
❑ 73	Ronald Curry	5.00	2.00
❑ 74	Donovan McNabb	6.00	2.50
❑ 75	Brian Westbrook	5.00	2.00
❑ 76	Reggie Brown	5.00	2.00
❑ 77	Ben Roethlisberger	8.00	3.00
❑ 78	Willie Parker	6.00	2.50
❑ 79	Hines Ward	6.00	2.50
❑ 80	Philip Rivers	6.00	2.50
❑ 81	LaDainian Tomlinson	8.00	3.00
❑ 82	Antonio Gates	5.00	2.00
❑ 83	Alex Smith QB	6.00	2.50
❑ 84	Frank Gore	6.00	2.50
❑ 85	Darrell Jackson	5.00	2.00
❑ 86	Matt Hasselbeck	5.00	2.00
❑ 87	Shaun Alexander	5.00	2.00
❑ 88	Deion Branch	5.00	2.00
❑ 89	Marc Bulger	5.00	2.00
❑ 90	Steven Jackson	6.00	2.50
❑ 91	Torry Holt	5.00	2.00
❑ 92	Jeff Garcia	5.00	2.00
❑ 93	Cadillac Williams	5.00	2.00
❑ 94	Joey Galloway	5.00	2.00
❑ 95	Vince Young	8.00	3.00
❑ 96	LenDale White	5.00	2.00
❑ 97	David Givens	4.00	1.50
❑ 98	Jason Campbell	5.00	2.00
❑ 99	Clinton Portis	5.00	2.00
❑ 100	Santana Moss	5.00	2.00
❑ 101	Adrian Peterson AU/99 RC	700.00	400.00
❑ 102	Brady Quinn AU/99 RC	250.00	125.00
❑ 103	Calvin Johnson AU/99 RC	200.00	100.00
❑ 104	Dwayne Bowe AU/99 RC	100.00	50.00
❑ 105	JaMarcus Russell AU/99 RC	200.00	125.00
❑ 106	Kevin Kolb AU/99 RC	80.00	40.00
❑ 107	Marshawn Lynch AU/99 RC	200.00	100.00
❑ 108	Robert Meachem AU/99 RC	30.00	15.00
❑ 109	Sidney Rice AU/99 RC	50.00	20.00
❑ 110	Ted Ginn AU/99 RC	80.00	40.00
❑ 111	Anthony Gonzalez AU/150 RC	60.00	30.00
❑ 112	Brian Leonard AU/150 RC	25.00	10.00
❑ 113	Chris Henry AU/150 RC	25.00	10.00
❑ 114	Chris Leak AU/150 RC	20.00	8.00
❑ 115	Drew Stanton AU/150 RC	40.00	20.00
❑ 116	Dwayne Jarrett AU/150 RC	30.00	12.00
❑ 117	Gaines Adams AU/150 RC	25.00	10.00
❑ 118	Greg Olsen AU/150 RC	40.00	20.00
❑ 119	Jason Hill AU/150 RC	25.00	10.00
❑ 120	Joe Thomas AU/150 RC	25.00	10.00
❑ 121	Kenny Irons AU/150 RC	25.00	10.00
❑ 122	LaRon Landry AU/150 RC	30.00	12.00
❑ 123	Leon Hall AU/150 RC	20.00	8.00
❑ 124	Lorenzo Booker AU/150 RC	25.00	10.00
❑ 125	Michael Bush AU/150 RC	30.00	12.00
❑ 126	Steve Smith AU/150 RC	40.00	20.00
❑ 127	Trent Edwards AU/150 RC	60.00	30.00
❑ 128	Amobi Okoye AU/250 RC	20.00	8.00
❑ 129	Antonio Pittman AU/250 RC	15.00	6.00
❑ 130	Aundrae Allison AU/250 RC	15.00	6.00
❑ 131	Brandon Jackson AU/250 RC	30.00	15.00
❑ 132	Brandon Meriweather AU/250 RC	20.00	8.00
❑ 133	Chansi Stuckey AU/250 RC	15.00	6.00
❑ 134	Craig Buster Davis AU/250 RC	20.00	8.00
❑ 135	Dallas Baker AU/250 RC	15.00	6.00
❑ 136	Darrelle Revis AU/250 RC	20.00	8.00
❑ 137	David Ball AU/250 RC	12.00	5.00
❑ 138	David Clowney AU/250 RC	20.00	8.00
❑ 139	Daymeion Hughes AU/250 RC	15.00	6.00
❑ 140	Dwayne Wright AU/250 RC	15.00	6.00
❑ 141	Eric Wright AU/250 RC	20.00	8.00
❑ 142	Garrett Wolfe AU/250 RC	25.00	10.00
❑ 143	John Beck AU/250 RC	80.00	50.00
❑ 144	Johnnie Lee Higgins AU/250 RC	15.00	6.00
❑ 145	Jordan Palmer AU/250 RC	20.00	8.00
❑ 146	Kenneth Darby AU/250 RC	20.00	8.00
❑ 147	Kolby Smith AU/250 RC	40.00	20.00
❑ 148	LaMarr Woodley AU/250 RC	20.00	8.00
❑ 149	Lawrence Timmons AU/250 RC	20.00	8.00
❑ 150	Legedu Naanee AU/250 RC	15.00	6.00
❑ 151	Matt Moore AU/250 RC	40.00	20.00
❑ 152	Paul Williams AU/250 RC	15.00	6.00
❑ 153	Quentin Moses AU/250 RC	15.00	6.00
❑ 154	Reggie Nelson AU/250 RC	15.00	6.00
❑ 155	Rhema McKnight AU/250 RC	15.00	6.00
❑ 156	Selvin Young AU/250 RC	40.00	20.00
❑ 157	Sywelle Newton AU/250 RC	15.00	6.00
❑ 158	Tony Hunt AU/250 RC	20.00	8.00
❑ 159	Tyler Palko AU/250 RC	20.00	8.00
❑ 160	Zach Miller AU/250 RC	20.00	8.00

1991 Ultra

❑	COMPLETE SET (300)	20.00	7.50
❑ 1	Don Beebe	.05	.01
❑ 2	Shane Conlan	.05	.01
❑ 3	Pete Metzelaars	.05	.01
❑ 4	Jamie Mueller	.05	.01
❑ 5	Scott Norwood	.05	.01
❑ 6	Andre Reed	.10	.02
❑ 7	Leon Seals	.05	.01
❑ 8	Bruce Smith	.25	.08
❑ 9	Leonard Smith	.05	.01
❑ 10	Thurman Thomas	.25	.08
❑ 11	Lewis Billups	.05	.01
❑ 12	Jim Breech	.05	.01
❑ 13	James Brooks	.10	.02
❑ 14	Eddie Brown	.05	.01
❑ 15	Boomer Esiason	.10	.02
❑ 16	David Fulcher	.05	.01
❑ 17	Rodney Holman	.05	.01
❑ 18	Bruce Kozerski	.05	.01
❑ 19	Tim Krumrie	.05	.01
❑ 20	Tim McGee	.05	.01
❑ 21	Anthony Munoz	.10	.02
❑ 22	Leon White	.05	.01
❑ 23	Ickey Woods	.05	.01
❑ 24	Carl Zander	.05	.01
❑ 25	Brian Brennan	.05	.01
❑ 26	Thane Gash	.05	.01
❑ 27	Leroy Hoard	.10	.02
❑ 28	Mike Johnson	.05	.01
❑ 29	Reggie Langhorne	.05	.01
❑ 30	Kevin Mack	.05	.01
❑ 31	Clay Matthews	.10	.02
❑ 32	Eric Metcalf	.10	.02
❑ 33	Steve Atwater	.05	.01
❑ 34	Melvin Bratton	.05	.01
❑ 35	John Elway	1.25	.50

❑	36	Bobby Humphrey	.05	.01
❑	37	Mark Jackson	.05	.01
❑	38	Vance Johnson	.05	.01
❑	39	Ricky Nattiel	.05	.01
❑	40	Steve Sewell	.05	.01
❑	41	Dennis Smith	.05	.01
❑	42	David Treadwell	.05	.01
❑	43	Michael Young	.05	.01
❑	44	Ray Childress	.05	.01
❑	45	Cris Dishman RC	.05	.01
❑	46	William Fuller	.10	.02
❑	47	Ernest Givins	.10	.02
❑	48	John Grimsley UER	.05	.01
❑	49	Drew Hill	.05	.01
❑	50	Haywood Jeffires	.10	.02
❑	51	Sean Jones	.10	.02
❑	52	Johnny Meads	.05	.01
❑	53	Warren Moon	.25	.08
❑	54	Al Smith	.05	.01
❑	55	Lorenzo White	.05	.01
❑	56	Albert Bentley	.05	.01
❑	57	Duane Bickett	.05	.01
❑	58	Bill Brooks	.05	.01
❑	59	Jeff George	.25	.08
❑	60	Mike Prior	.05	.01
❑	61	Rohn Stark	.05	.01
❑	62	Jack Trudeau	.05	.01
❑	63	Clarence Verdin	.05	.01
❑	64	Steve DeBerg	.05	.01
❑	65	Emile Harry	.05	.01
❑	66	Albert Lewis	.05	.01
❑	67	Nick Lowery UER	.05	.01
❑	68	Todd McNair	.05	.01
❑	69	Christian Okoye	.05	.01
❑	70	Stephone Paige	.05	.01
❑	71	Kevin Porter UER	.05	.01
❑	72	Derrick Thomas	.25	.08
❑	73	Robb Thomas	.05	.01
❑	74	Barry Word	.05	.01
❑	75	Marcus Allen	.25	.08
❑	76	Eddie Anderson	.05	.01
❑	77	Tim Brown	.25	.08
❑	78	Mervyn Fernandez	.05	.01
❑	79	Willie Gault	.10	.02
❑	80	Ethan Horton	.05	.01
❑	81	Howie Long	.25	.08
❑	82	Vance Mueller	.05	.01
❑	83	Jay Schroeder	.05	.01
❑	84	Steve Smith	.05	.01
❑	85	Greg Townsend	.05	.01
❑	86	Mark Clayton	.10	.02
❑	87	Jim C. Jensen	.05	.01
❑	88	Dan Marino	1.25	.50
❑	89	Tim McKyer UER	.05	.01
❑	90	John Offerdahl	.05	.01
❑	91	Louis Oliver	.05	.01
❑	92	Reggie Roby	.05	.01
❑	93	Sammie Smith	.05	.01
❑	94	Hart Lee Dykes	.05	.01
❑	95	Irving Fryar	.10	.02
❑	96	Tommy Hodson	.05	.01
❑	97	Maurice Hurst	.05	.01
❑	98	John Stephens	.05	.01
❑	99	Andre Tippett	.05	.01
❑	100	Mark Boyer	.05	.01
❑	101	Kyle Clifton	.05	.01
❑	102	James Hasty	.05	.01
❑	103	Erik McMillan	.05	.01
❑	104	Rob Moore	.25	.08
❑	105	Joe Mott	.05	.01
❑	106	Ken O'Brien	.05	.01
❑	107	Ron Stallworth UER	.05	.01
❑	108	Al Toon	.10	.02
❑	109	Gary Anderson K	.05	.01
❑	110	Bubby Brister	.05	.01
❑	111	Thomas Everett	.05	.01
❑	112	Merril Hoge	.05	.01
❑	113	Louis Lipps	.05	.01
❑	114	Greg Lloyd	.25	.08
❑	115	Hardy Nickerson	.10	.02
❑	116	Dwight Stone	.05	.01
❑	117	Rod Woodson	.25	.08
❑	118	Tim Worley	.05	.01
❑	119	Rod Bernstine	.05	.01
❑	120	Marion Butts	.10	.02
❑	121	Gill Byrd	.05	.01
❑	122	Arthur Cox	.05	.01
❑	123	Burt Grossman	.05	.01
❑	124	Ronnie Harmon	.05	.01
❑	125	Anthony Miller	.10	.02
❑	126	Leslie O'Neal	.10	.02
❑	127	Gary Plummer	.05	.01
❑	128	Sam Seale	.05	.01
❑	129	Junior Seau	.25	.08
❑	130	Broderick Thompson	.05	.01
❑	131	Billy Joe Tolliver	.05	.01
❑	132	Brian Blades	.10	.02
❑	133	Jeff Bryant	.05	.01
❑	134	Derrick Fenner	.05	.01
❑	135	Jacob Green	.05	.01
❑	136	Andy Heck	.05	.01
❑	137	Patrick Hunter RC UER	.05	.01
❑	138	Norm Johnson	.05	.01
❑	139	Tommy Kane	.05	.01
❑	140	Dave Krieg	.10	.02
❑	141	John L. Williams	.05	.01
❑	142	Terry Wooden	.05	.01
❑	143	Steve Broussard	.05	.01
❑	144	Keith Jones	.05	.01
❑	145	Brian Jordan	.10	.02
❑	146	Chris Miller	.10	.02
❑	147	John Rade	.05	.01
❑	148	Andre Rison	.10	.02
❑	149	Mike Rozier	.05	.01
❑	150	Deion Sanders	.40	.15
❑	151	Neal Anderson	.10	.02
❑	152	Trace Armstrong	.05	.01
❑	153	Kevin Butler	.05	.01
❑	154	Mark Carrier DB	.10	.02
❑	155	Richard Dent	.10	.02
❑	156	Dennis Gentry	.05	.01
❑	157	Jim Harbaugh	.25	.08
❑	158	Brad Muster	.05	.01
❑	159	William Perry	.10	.02
❑	160	Mike Singletary	.10	.02
❑	161	Lemuel Stinson	.05	.01
❑	162	Troy Aikman	.75	.30
❑	163	Michael Irvin	.25	.08
❑	164	Mike Saxon	.05	.01
❑	165	Emmitt Smith	2.50	1.00
❑	166	Jerry Ball	.05	.01
❑	167	Michael Cofer	.05	.01
❑	168	Rodney Peete	.10	.02
❑	169	Barry Sanders	1.25	.50
❑	170	Robert Brown	.05	.01
❑	171	Anthony Dilweg	.05	.01
❑	172	Tim Harris	.05	.01
❑	173	Johnny Holland	.05	.01
❑	174	Perry Kemp	.05	.01
❑	175	Don Majkowski	.05	.01
❑	176	Brian Noble	.05	.01
❑	177	Jeff Query	.05	.01
❑	178	Sterling Sharpe	.25	.08
❑	179	Charles Wilson	.05	.01
❑	180	Keith Woodside	.05	.01
❑	181	Flipper Anderson UER	.05	.01
❑	182	Bern Brostek	.05	.01
❑	183	Pat Carter RC	.05	.01
❑	184	Aaron Cox	.05	.01
❑	185	Henry Ellard	.10	.02
❑	186	Jim Everett	.10	.02
❑	187	Cleveland Gary	.05	.01
❑	188	Jerry Gray	.05	.01
❑	189	Kevin Greene	.10	.02
❑	190	Mike Wilcher	.05	.01
❑	191	Alfred Anderson	.05	.01
❑	192	Joey Browner	.05	.01
❑	193	Anthony Carter	.10	.02
❑	194	Chris Doleman	.05	.01
❑	195	Rick Fenney	.05	.01
❑	196	Darrell Fullington	.05	.01
❑	197	Rich Gannon	.25	.08
❑	198	Hassan Jones	.05	.01
❑	199	Steve Jordan	.05	.01
❑	200	Mike Merriweather	.05	.01
❑	201	Al Noga	.05	.01
❑	202	Herschel Walker	.10	.02
❑	203	Wade Wilson	.10	.02
❑	204	Morten Andersen	.05	.01
❑	205	Gene Atkins	.05	.01
❑	206	Toi Cook RC	.05	.01
❑	207	Craig Heyward	.10	.02
❑	208	Dalton Hilliard	.05	.01
❑	209	Vaughan Johnson	.05	.01
❑	210	Eric Martin	.05	.01
❑	211	Brett Perriman	.25	.08
❑	212	Pat Swilling	.10	.02
❑	213	Steve Walsh	.05	.01
❑	214	Ottis Anderson	.10	.02
❑	215	Carl Banks	.05	.01
❑	216	Maurice Carthon	.05	.01
❑	217	Mark Collins	.05	.01
❑	218	Rodney Hampton	.25	.08
❑	219	Erik Howard	.05	.01
❑	220	Mark Ingram	.10	.02
❑	221	Pepper Johnson	.05	.01
❑	222	Dave Meggett	.10	.02
❑	223	Phil Simms	.10	.02
❑	224	Lawrence Taylor	.25	.08
❑	225	Lewis Tillman	.05	.01
❑	226	Everson Walls	.05	.01
❑	227	Fred Barnett	.25	.08
❑	228	Jerome Brown	.05	.01
❑	229	Keith Byars	.05	.01
❑	230	Randall Cunningham	.25	.08
❑	231	Byron Evans	.05	.01
❑	232	Wes Hopkins	.05	.01
❑	233	Keith Jackson	.10	.02
❑	234	Heath Sherman	.05	.01
❑	235	Anthony Toney	.05	.01
❑	236	Reggie White	.25	.08
❑	237	Rich Camarillo	.05	.01
❑	238	Ken Harvey	.10	.02
❑	239	Eric Hill	.05	.01
❑	240	Johnny Johnson	.05	.01
❑	241	Ernie Jones	.05	.01
❑	242	Tim McDonald	.05	.01
❑	243	Timm Rosenbach	.05	.01
❑	244	Jay Taylor	.05	.01
❑	245	Dexter Carter	.05	.01
❑	246	Mike Cofer	.05	.01
❑	247	Kevin Fagan	.05	.01
❑	248	Don Griffin	.05	.01
❑	249	Charles Haley	.10	.02
❑	250	Brent Jones	.25	.08
❑	251	Joe Montana UER	1.25	.50
❑	252	Darryl Pollard	.05	.01
❑	253	Tom Rathman	.05	.01
❑	254	Jerry Rice	.75	.30
❑	255	John Taylor	.10	.02
❑	256	Steve Young	.75	.30
❑	257	Gary Anderson RB	.05	.01
❑	258	Mark Carrier WR	.25	.08
❑	259	Chris Chandler	.25	.08
❑	260	Reggie Cobb	.05	.01
❑	261	Reuben Davis	.05	.01
❑	262	Willie Drewrey	.05	.01
❑	263	Ron Hall	.05	.01
❑	264	Eugene Marve	.05	.01
❑	265	Winston Moss UER	.05	.01
❑	266	Vinny Testaverde	.10	.02
❑	267	Broderick Thomas	.05	.01
❑	268	Jeff Bostic	.05	.01
❑	269	Earnest Byner	.05	.01
❑	270	Gary Clark	.25	.08
❑	271	Darrell Green	.05	.01
❑	272	Jim Lachey	.05	.01
❑	273	Wilber Marshall	.05	.01
❑	274	Art Monk	.10	.02
❑	275	Gerald Riggs	.05	.01
❑	276	Mark Rypien	.10	.02
❑	277	Ricky Sanders	.05	.01
❑	278	Alvin Walton	.05	.01
❑	279	Nick Bell RC	.05	.01
❑	280	Eric Bieniemy RC	.05	.01
❑	281	Jarrod Bunch RC	.05	.01
❑	282	Mike Croel RC	.05	.01
❑	283	Brett Favre RC	10.00	5.00
❑	284	Moe Gardner RC	.05	.01
❑	285	Pat Harlow RC	.05	.01
❑	286	Randal Hill RC	.10	.02
❑	287	Todd Marinovich RC	.05	.01

❑ 288	Russell Maryland RC	.25	.08
❑ 289	Dan McGwire RC	.05	.01
❑ 290	Ernie Mills RC UER	.10	.02
❑ 291	Herman Moore RC	.25	.08
❑ 292	Godfrey Myles RC	.05	.01
❑ 293	Browning Nagle RC	.05	.01
❑ 294	Mike Pritchard RC	.25	.08
❑ 295	Esera Tuaolo RC	.05	.01
❑ 296	Mark Vander Poel RC	.05	.01
❑ 297	Ricky Watters RC	1.50	.60
❑ 298	Chris Zorich RC	.25	.08
❑ 299	Checklist Card	.10	.02
❑ 300	Checklist Card	.10	.02

1991 Ultra Update

❑	COMP.FACT.SET (100)	30.00	12.50
❑ U1	Brett Favre	25.00	10.00
❑ U2	Moe Gardner	.10	.02
❑ U3	Tim McKyer	.10	.02
❑ U4	Bruce Pickens RC	.10	.02
❑ U5	Mike Pritchard	.40	.15
❑ U6	Cornelius Bennett	.20	.07
❑ U7	Phil Hansen RC	.10	.02
❑ U8	Henry Jones RC	.20	.07
❑ U9	Mark Kelso	.10	.02
❑ U10	James Lofton	.20	.07
❑ U11	Anthony Morgan RC	.10	.02
❑ U12	Stan Thomas	.10	.02
❑ U13	Chris Zorich	.20	.07
❑ U14	Reggie Rembert	.10	.02
❑ U15	Alfred Williams RC	.10	.02
❑ U16	Michael Jackson RC WR	.40	.15
❑ U17	Ed King RC	.10	.02
❑ U18	Joe Morris	.10	.02
❑ U19	Vince Newsome	.10	.02
❑ U20	Tony Casillas	.10	.02
❑ U21	Russell Maryland	.40	.15
❑ U22	Jay Novacek	.40	.15
❑ U23	Mike Croel	.10	.02
❑ U24	Gaston Green	.10	.02
❑ U25	Kenny Walker RC	.10	.02
❑ U26	Melvin Jenkins RC	.10	.02
❑ U27	Herman Moore	.40	.15
❑ U28	Kelvin Pritchett RC	.20	.07
❑ U29	Chris Spielman	.20	.07
❑ U30	Vinnie Clark RC	.10	.02
❑ U31	Allen Rice	.10	.02
❑ U32	Vai Sikahema	.10	.02
❑ U33	Esera Tuaolo	.10	.02
❑ U34	Mike Dumas RC	.10	.02
❑ U35	John Flannery RC	.10	.02
❑ U36	Allen Pinkett	.10	.02
❑ U37	Tim Barnett RC	.10	.02
❑ U38	Dan Saleaumua	.10	.02
❑ U39	Harvey Williams RC	.40	.15
❑ U40	Nick Bell	.10	.02
❑ U41	Roger Craig	.20	.07
❑ U42	Ronnie Lott	.20	.07
❑ U43	Todd Marinovich	.10	.02
❑ U44	Robert Delpino	.10	.02
❑ U45	Todd Lyght RC	.10	.02
❑ U46	Robert Young RC	.20	.07
❑ U47	Aaron Craver RC	.10	.02
❑ U48	Mark Higgs RC	.10	.02
❑ U49	Vestee Jackson	.10	.02
❑ U50	Carl Lee	.10	.02
❑ U51	Felix Wright	.10	.02
❑ U52	Darrell Fullington	.10	.02
❑ U53	Pat Harlow	.10	.02
❑ U54	Eugene Lockhart	.10	.02
❑ U55	Hugh Millen RC	.10	.02
❑ U56	Leonard Russell RC	.40	.15
❑ U57	Jon Vaughn RC	.10	.02
❑ U58	Quinn Early	.20	.07
❑ U59	Bobby Hebert	.10	.02
❑ U60	Rickey Jackson	.10	.02
❑ U61	Sam Mills	.20	.07
❑ U62	Jarrod Bunch	.10	.02
❑ U63	John Elliott	.10	.02
❑ U64	Jeff Hostetler	.20	.07
❑ U65	Ed McCaffrey RC	6.00	2.50
❑ U66	Kanavis McGhee RC	.10	.02
❑ U67	Mo Lewis RC	.20	.07
❑ U68	Browning Nagle	.10	.02
❑ U69	Blair Thomas	.10	.02
❑ U70	Antone Davis RC	.10	.02
❑ U71	Brad Goebel RC	.10	.02
❑ U72	Jim McMahon	.20	.07
❑ U73	Clyde Simmons	.10	.02
❑ U74	Randal Hill UER U71	.20	.07
❑ U75	Eric Swann RC	.40	.15
❑ U76	Tom Tupa	.10	.02
❑ U77	Jeff Graham RC WR	.40	.15
❑ U78	Eric Green	.10	.02
❑ U79	Neil O'Donnell RC	.40	.15
❑ U80	Huey Richardson RC	.10	.02
❑ U81	Eric Bieniemy	.10	.02
❑ U82	John Friesz	.40	.15
❑ U83	Eric Moten RC	.10	.02
❑ U84	Stanley Richard RC	.10	.02
❑ U85	Todd Bowles	.10	.02
❑ U86	Merton Hanks RC	.40	.15
❑ U87	Tim Harris	.10	.02
❑ U88	Pierce Holt	.10	.02
❑ U89	Ted Washington RC	.10	.02
❑ U90	John Kasay RC	.20	.07
❑ U91	Dan McGwire	.10	.02
❑ U92	Lawrence Dawsey RC	.20	.07
❑ U93	Charles McRae RC	.10	.02
❑ U94	Jesse Solomon	.10	.02
❑ U95	Robert Wilson RC	.10	.02
❑ U96	Ricky Ervins RC	.20	.07
❑ U97	Charles Mann	.10	.02
❑ U98	Bobby Wilson RC	.10	.02
❑ U99	Jerry Rice PV	1.50	.60
❑ U100	Nick Bell/J.McMahon CL	.10	.02

1992 Ultra

❑	COMPLETE SET (450)	15.00	6.00
❑ 1	Steve Broussard	.10	.02
❑ 2	Rick Bryan	.10	.02
❑ 3	Scott Case	.10	.02
❑ 4	Darion Conner	.10	.02
❑ 5	Bill Fralic	.10	.02
❑ 6	Moe Gardner	.10	.02
❑ 7	Tim Green	.10	.02
❑ 8	Michael Haynes	.20	.07
❑ 9	Chris Hinton	.10	.02
❑ 10	Mike Kenn	.10	.02
❑ 11	Tim McKyer	.10	.02
❑ 12	Chris Miller	.20	.07
❑ 13	Erric Pegram	.20	.07
❑ 14	Mike Pritchard	.20	.07
❑ 15	Andre Rison	.20	.07
❑ 16	Jessie Tuggle	.10	.02
❑ 17	Carlton Bailey RC	.10	.02
❑ 18	Howard Ballard	.10	.02
❑ 19	Cornelius Bennett	.20	.07
❑ 20	Shane Conlan	.10	.02
❑ 21	Kenneth Davis	.10	.02
❑ 22	Kent Hull	.10	.02
❑ 23	Mark Kelso	.10	.02
❑ 24	James Lofton	.20	.07
❑ 25	Keith McKeller	.10	.02
❑ 26	Nate Odomes	.10	.02
❑ 27	Jim Ritcher	.10	.02
❑ 28	Leon Seals	.10	.02
❑ 29	Darryl Talley	.10	.02
❑ 30	Steve Tasker	.20	.07
❑ 31	Thurman Thomas	.40	.15
❑ 32	Will Wolford	.10	.02
❑ 33	Jeff Wright	.10	.02
❑ 34	Neal Anderson	.10	.02
❑ 35	Trace Armstrong	.10	.02
❑ 36	Mark Carrier DB	.10	.02
❑ 37	Wendell Davis	.10	.02
❑ 38	Richard Dent	.20	.07
❑ 39	Shaun Gayle	.10	.02
❑ 40	Jim Harbaugh	.40	.15
❑ 41	Jay Hilgenberg	.10	.02
❑ 42	Darren Lewis	.10	.02
❑ 43	Steve McMichael	.20	.07
❑ 44	Anthony Morgan	.10	.02
❑ 45	Brad Muster	.10	.02
❑ 46	William Perry	.20	.07
❑ 47	John Roper	.10	.02
❑ 48	Lemuel Stinson	.10	.02
❑ 49	Tom Waddle	.10	.02
❑ 50	Donnell Woolford	.10	.02
❑ 51	Leo Barker RC	.10	.02
❑ 52	Eddie Brown	.10	.02
❑ 53	James Francis	.10	.02
❑ 54	David Fulcher UER	.10	.02
❑ 55	David Grant	.10	.02
❑ 56	Harold Green	.10	.02
❑ 57	Rodney Holman	.10	.02
❑ 58	Lee Johnson	.10	.02
❑ 59	Tim Krumrie	.10	.02
❑ 60	Tim McGee	.10	.02
❑ 61	Alonzo Mitz RC	.10	.02
❑ 62	Anthony Munoz	.20	.07
❑ 63	Alfred Williams	.10	.02
❑ 64	Stephen Braggs	.10	.02
❑ 65	Richard Brown RC	.10	.02
❑ 66	Randy Hilliard RC	.10	.02
❑ 67	Leroy Hoard	.20	.07
❑ 68	Michael Jackson	.20	.07
❑ 69	Mike Johnson	.10	.02
❑ 70	James Jones DT	.10	.02
❑ 71	Tony Jones T	.10	.02
❑ 72	Ed King	.10	.02
❑ 73	Kevin Mack	.10	.02
❑ 74	Clay Matthews	.20	.07
❑ 75	Eric Metcalf	.20	.07
❑ 76	Vince Newsome	.10	.02
❑ 77	Steve Beuerlein	.20	.07
❑ 78	Larry Brown DB	.10	.02
❑ 79	Tony Casillas	.10	.02
❑ 80	Alvin Harper	.20	.07
❑ 81	Issiac Holt	.10	.02
❑ 82	Ray Horton	.10	.02
❑ 83	Michael Irvin	.40	.15
❑ 84	Daryl Johnston	.40	.15
❑ 85	Kelvin Martin	.10	.02
❑ 86	Ken Norton	.20	.07
❑ 87	Jay Novacek	.20	.07
❑ 88	Emmitt Smith	3.00	1.50
❑ 89	Vinson Smith RC	.10	.02
❑ 90	Mark Stepnoski	.20	.07
❑ 91	Tony Tolbert	.10	.02
❑ 92	Alexander Wright	.10	.02
❑ 93	Steve Atwater	.10	.02
❑ 94	Tyrone Braxton	.10	.02
❑ 95	Michael Brooks	.10	.02
❑ 96	Mike Croel	.10	.02
❑ 97	John Elway	2.50	1.00
❑ 98	Simon Fletcher	.10	.02
❑ 99	Gaston Green	.10	.02

❑ 100 Mark Jackson .10 .02
❑ 101 Keith Kartz .10 .02
❑ 102 Greg Kragen .10 .02
❑ 103 Greg Lewis .10 .02
❑ 104 Karl Mecklenburg .10 .02
❑ 105 Derek Russell .10 .02
❑ 106 Steve Sewell .10 .02
❑ 107 Dennis Smith .10 .02
❑ 108 David Treadwell .10 .02
❑ 109 Kenny Walker .10 .02
❑ 110 Michael Young .10 .02
❑ 111 Jerry Ball .10 .02
❑ 112 Bennie Blades .10 .02
❑ 113 Lomas Brown .10 .02
❑ 114 Scott Conover RC .10 .02
❑ 115 Ray Crockett .10 .02
❑ 116 Mel Gray .20 .07
❑ 117 Willie Green .10 .02
❑ 118 Erik Kramer .20 .07
❑ 119 Dan Owens .10 .02
❑ 120 Rodney Peete .20 .07
❑ 121 Brett Perriman .40 .15
❑ 122 Barry Sanders 2.50 1.00
❑ 123 Chris Spielman .20 .07
❑ 124 Marc Spindler .10 .02
❑ 125 William White .10 .02
❑ 126 Tony Bennett .10 .02
❑ 127 Matt Brock .10 .02
❑ 128 LeRoy Butler .10 .02
❑ 129 Chuck Cecil .10 .02
❑ 130 Johnny Holland .10 .02
❑ 131 Perry Kemp .10 .02
❑ 132 Don Majkowski .10 .02
❑ 133 Tony Mandarich .10 .02
❑ 134 Brian Noble .10 .02
❑ 135 Bryce Paup .40 .15
❑ 136 Sterling Sharpe .40 .15
❑ 137 Darrell Thompson .10 .02
❑ 138 Mike Tomczak .10 .02
❑ 139 Vince Workman .10 .02
❑ 140 Ray Childress .10 .02
❑ 141 Cris Dishman .10 .02
❑ 142 Curtis Duncan .10 .02
❑ 143 William Fuller .10 .02
❑ 144 Ernest Givins .20 .07
❑ 145 Haywood Jeffires .20 .07
❑ 146 Sean Jones .10 .02
❑ 147 Lamar Lathon .10 .02
❑ 148 Bruce Matthews .10 .02
❑ 149 Bubba McDowell .10 .02
❑ 150 Johnny Meads .10 .02
❑ 151 Warren Moon .40 .15
❑ 152 Mike Munchak .20 .07
❑ 153 Bo Orlando RC .10 .02
❑ 154 Al Smith .10 .02
❑ 155 Doug Smith .10 .02
❑ 156 Lorenzo White .10 .02
❑ 157 Chip Banks .10 .02
❑ 158 Duane Bickett .10 .02
❑ 159 Bill Brooks .10 .02
❑ 160 Eugene Daniel .10 .02
❑ 161 Jon Hand .10 .02
❑ 162 Jeff Herrod .10 .02
❑ 163 Jessie Hester .10 .02
❑ 164 Scott Radecic .10 .02
❑ 165 Rohn Stark .10 .02
❑ 166 Clarence Verdin .10 .02
❑ 167 John Alt .10 .02
❑ 168 Tim Barnett .10 .02
❑ 169 Tim Grunhard .10 .02
❑ 170 Dino Hackett .10 .02
❑ 171 Jonathan Hayes .10 .02
❑ 172 Bill Maas .10 .02
❑ 173 Chris Martin .10 .02
❑ 174 Christian Okoye .10 .02
❑ 175 Stephone Paige .10 .02
❑ 176 Jayice Pearson RC .10 .02
❑ 177 Kevin Porter .10 .02
❑ 178 Kevin Ross .10 .02
❑ 179 Dan Saleaumua .10 .02
❑ 180 Tracy Simien RC .10 .02
❑ 181 Neil Smith .40 .15
❑ 182 Derrick Thomas .40 .15
❑ 183 Robb Thomas .10 .02
❑ 184 Barry Word .10 .02
❑ 185 Marcus Allen .40 .15
❑ 186 Eddie Anderson .10 .02
❑ 187 Nick Bell .10 .02
❑ 188 Tim Brown .40 .15
❑ 189 Mervyn Fernandez .10 .02
❑ 190 Willie Gault .20 .07
❑ 191 Jeff Gossett .10 .02
❑ 192 Ethan Horton .10 .02
❑ 193 Jeff Jaeger .10 .02
❑ 194 Howie Long .40 .15
❑ 195 Ronnie Lott .20 .07
❑ 196 Todd Marinovich .10 .02
❑ 197 Don Mosebar .10 .02
❑ 198 Jay Schroeder .10 .02
❑ 199 Anthony Smith .10 .02
❑ 200 Greg Townsend .10 .02
❑ 201 Lionel Washington .10 .02
❑ 202 Steve Wisniewski .10 .02
❑ 203 Flipper Anderson .10 .02
❑ 204 Robert Delpino .10 .02
❑ 205 Henry Ellard .20 .07
❑ 206 Jim Everett .20 .07
❑ 207 Kevin Greene .20 .07
❑ 208 Darryl Henley .10 .02
❑ 209 Damone Johnson .10 .02
❑ 210 Larry Kelm .10 .02
❑ 211 Todd Lyght .10 .02
❑ 212 Jackie Slater .10 .02
❑ 213 Michael Stewart .10 .02
❑ 214 Pat Terrell .10 .02
❑ 215 Robert Young .10 .02
❑ 216 Mark Clayton .20 .07
❑ 217 Bryan Cox .20 .07
❑ 218 Jeff Cross .10 .02
❑ 219 Mark Duper .10 .02
❑ 220 Harry Galbreath .10 .02
❑ 221 David Griggs .10 .02
❑ 222 Mark Higgs .10 .02
❑ 223 Vestee Jackson .10 .02
❑ 224 John Offerdahl .10 .02
❑ 225 Louis Oliver .10 .02
❑ 226 Tony Paige .10 .02
❑ 227 Reggie Roby .10 .02
❑ 228 Pete Stoyanovich .10 .02
❑ 229 Richmond Webb .10 .02
❑ 230 Terry Allen .40 .15
❑ 231 Ray Berry .10 .02
❑ 232 Anthony Carter .20 .07
❑ 233 Cris Carter .75 .30
❑ 234 Chris Doleman .10 .02
❑ 235 Rich Gannon .40 .15
❑ 236 Steve Jordan .10 .02
❑ 237 Carl Lee .10 .02
❑ 238 Randall McDaniel .10 .02
❑ 239 Mike Merriweather .10 .02
❑ 240 Harry Newsome .10 .02
❑ 241 John Randle .20 .07
❑ 242 Henry Thomas .10 .02
❑ 243 Bruce Armstrong .10 .02
❑ 244 Vincent Brown .10 .02
❑ 245 Marv Cook .10 .02
❑ 246 Irving Fryar .20 .07
❑ 247 Pat Harlow .10 .02
❑ 248 Maurice Hurst .10 .02
❑ 249 Eugene Lockhart .10 .02
❑ 250 Greg McMurtry .10 .02
❑ 251 Hugh Millen .10 .02
❑ 252 Leonard Russell .20 .07
❑ 253 Chris Singleton .10 .02
❑ 254 Andre Tippett .10 .02
❑ 255 Jon Vaughn .10 .02
❑ 256 Morten Andersen .10 .02
❑ 257 Gene Atkins .10 .02
❑ 258 Wesley Carroll .10 .02
❑ 259 Jim Dombrowski .10 .02
❑ 260 Quinn Early .20 .07
❑ 261 Bobby Hebert .10 .02
❑ 262 Joel Hilgenberg .10 .02
❑ 263 Rickey Jackson .10 .02
❑ 264 Vaughan Johnson .10 .02
❑ 265 Eric Martin .10 .02
❑ 266 Brett Maxie .10 .02
❑ 267 Fred McAfee RC .10 .02
❑ 268 Sam Mills .10 .02
❑ 269 Pat Swilling .10 .02
❑ 270 Floyd Turner .10 .02
❑ 271 Steve Walsh .10 .02
❑ 272 Stephen Baker .10 .02
❑ 273 Jarrod Bunch .10 .02
❑ 274 Mark Collins .10 .02
❑ 275 John Elliott .10 .02
❑ 276 Myron Guyton .10 .02
❑ 277 Rodney Hampton .20 .07
❑ 278 Jeff Hostetler .20 .07
❑ 279 Mark Ingram .10 .02
❑ 280 Pepper Johnson .10 .02
❑ 281 [illegible] [illegible] [illegible]
❑ 282 Leonard Marshall .10 .02
❑ 283 Kanavis McGhee .10 .02
❑ 284 Dave Meggett .20 .07
❑ 285 Bart Oates .10 .02
❑ 286 Phil Simms .20 .07
❑ 287 Reyna Thompson .10 .02
❑ 288 Lewis Tillman .10 .02
❑ 289 Brad Baxter .10 .02
❑ 290 Mike Brim RC .10 .02
❑ 291 Chris Burkett .10 .02
❑ 292 Kyle Clifton .10 .02
❑ 293 James Hasty .10 .02
❑ 294 Joe Kelly .10 .02
❑ 295 Jeff Lageman .10 .02
❑ 296 Mo Lewis .10 .02
❑ 297 Erik McMillan .10 .02
❑ 298 Scott Mersereau .10 .02
❑ 299 Rob Moore .20 .07
❑ 300 Tony Stargell .10 .02
❑ 301 Jim Sweeney .10 .02
❑ 302 Marvin Washington .10 .02
❑ 303 Lonnie Young .10 .02
❑ 304 Eric Allen .10 .02
❑ 305 Fred Barnett .40 .15
❑ 306 Keith Byars .10 .02
❑ 307 Byron Evans .10 .02
❑ 308 Wes Hopkins .10 .02
❑ 309 Keith Jackson .20 .07
❑ 310 James Joseph .10 .02
❑ 311 Seth Joyner .10 .02
❑ 312 Roger Ruzek .10 .02
❑ 313 Clyde Simmons .10 .02
❑ 314 William Thomas .10 .02
❑ 315 Reggie White .40 .15
❑ 316 Calvin Williams .20 .07
❑ 317 Rich Camarillo .10 .02
❑ 318 Jeff Faulkner .10 .02
❑ 319 Ken Harvey .10 .02
❑ 320 Eric Hill .10 .02
❑ 321 Johnny Johnson .10 .02
❑ 322 Ernie Jones .10 .02
❑ 323 Tim McDonald .10 .02
❑ 324 Freddie Joe Nunn .10 .02
❑ 325 Luis Sharpe .10 .02
❑ 326 Eric Swann .20 .07
❑ 327 Aeneas Williams .20 .07
❑ 328 Michael Zordich RC .10 .02
❑ 329 Gary Anderson K .10 .02
❑ 330 Bubby Brister .10 .02
❑ 331 Barry Foster .20 .07
❑ 332 Eric Green .10 .02
❑ 333 Bryan Hinkle .10 .02
❑ 334 Tunch Ilkin .10 .02
❑ 335 Carnell Lake .10 .02
❑ 336 Louis Lipps .10 .02
❑ 337 David Little .10 .02
❑ 338 Greg Lloyd .20 .07
❑ 339 Neil O'Donnell .20 .07
❑ 340 Rod Woodson .40 .15
❑ 341 Rod Bernstine .10 .02
❑ 342 Marion Butts .10 .02
❑ 343 Gill Byrd .10 .02
❑ 344 John Friesz .20 .07
❑ 345 Burt Grossman .10 .02
❑ 346 Courtney Hall .10 .02
❑ 347 Ronnie Harmon .10 .02
❑ 348 Shawn Jefferson .10 .02
❑ 349 Nate Lewis .10 .02
❑ 350 Craig McEwen RC .10 .02
❑ 351 Eric Moten .10 .02

❑ 352 Gary Plummer .10 .02
❑ 353 Henry Rolling .10 .02
❑ 354 Broderick Thompson .10 .02
❑ 355 Derrick Walker .10 .02
❑ 356 Harris Barton .10 .02
❑ 357 Steve Bono RC .40 .15
❑ 358 Todd Bowles .10 .02
❑ 359 Dexter Carter .10 .02
❑ 360 Michael Carter .10 .02
❑ 361 Keith DeLong .10 .02
❑ 362 Charles Haley .20 .07
❑ 363 Merton Hanks .20 .07
❑ 364 Tim Harris .10 .02
❑ 365 Brent Jones .20 .07
❑ 366 Guy McIntyre .10 .02
❑ 367 Tom Rathman .10 .02
❑ 368 Bill Romanowski .10 .02
❑ 369 Jesse Sapolu .10 .02
❑ 370 John Taylor .20 .07
❑ 371 Steve Young 1.50 .60
❑ 372 Robert Blackmon .10 .02
❑ 373 Brian Blades .20 .07
❑ 374 Jacob Green .10 .02
❑ 375 Dwayne Harper .10 .02
❑ 376 Andy Heck .10 .02
❑ 377 Tommy Kane .10 .02
❑ 378 John Kasay .10 .02
❑ 379 Cortez Kennedy .20 .07
❑ 380 Bryan Millard .10 .02
❑ 381 Rufus Porter .10 .02
❑ 382 Eugene Robinson .10 .02
❑ 383 John L. Williams .10 .02
❑ 384 Terry Wooden .10 .02
❑ 385 Gary Anderson RB .10 .02
❑ 386 Ian Beckles .10 .02
❑ 387 Mark Carrier WR .20 .07
❑ 388 Reggie Cobb .10 .02
❑ 389 Tony Covington .10 .02
❑ 390 Lawrence Dawsey .20 .07
❑ 391 Ron Hall .10 .02
❑ 392 Keith McCants .10 .02
❑ 393 Charles McRae .10 .02
❑ 394 Tim Newton .10 .02
❑ 395 Jesse Solomon .10 .02
❑ 396 Vinny Testaverde .20 .07
❑ 397 Broderick Thomas .10 .02
❑ 398 Robert Wilson .10 .02
❑ 399 Earnest Byner .10 .02
❑ 400 Gary Clark .40 .15
❑ 401 Andre Collins .10 .02
❑ 402 Brad Edwards .10 .02
❑ 403 Kurt Gouveia .10 .02
❑ 404 Darrell Green .10 .02
❑ 405 Joe Jacoby .10 .02
❑ 406 Jim Lachey .10 .02
❑ 407 Chip Lohmiller .10 .02
❑ 408 Charles Mann .10 .02
❑ 409 Wilber Marshall .10 .02
❑ 410 Brian Mitchell .20 .07
❑ 411 Art Monk .20 .07
❑ 412 Mark Rypien .10 .02
❑ 413 Ricky Sanders .10 .02
❑ 414 Mark Schlereth RC .10 .02
❑ 415 Fred Stokes .10 .02
❑ 416 Bobby Wilson .10 .02
❑ 417 Corey Barlow RC .10 .02
❑ 418 Edgar Bennett RC .40 .15
❑ 419 Eddie Blake RC .10 .02
❑ 420 Terrell Buckley RC .10 .02
❑ 421 Willie Clay RC .10 .02
❑ 422 Rodney Culver RC .10 .02
❑ 423 Ed Cunningham RC .10 .02
❑ 424 Mark D'Onofrio RC .10 .02
❑ 425 Matt Darby RC .10 .02
❑ 426 Charles Davenport RC .10 .02
❑ 427 Will Furrer RC .10 .02
❑ 428 Keith Goganious RC .10 .02
❑ 429 Mario Bailey RC .10 .02
❑ 430 Chris Hakel RC .10 .02
❑ 431 Keith Hamilton RC .20 .07
❑ 432 Aaron Pierce RC .10 .02
❑ 433 Amp Lee RC .10 .02
❑ 434 Scott Lockwood RC .10 .02
❑ 435 Ricardo McDonald RC .10 .02
❑ 436 Dexter McNabb RC .10 .02
❑ 437 Chris Mims RC .10 .02
❑ 438 Mike Mooney RC .10 .02
❑ 439 Ray Roberts RC .10 .02
❑ 440 Patrick Rowe RC .10 .02
❑ 441 Leon Searcy RC .10 .02
❑ 442 Siran Stacy RC .10 .02
❑ 443 Kevin Turner RC .10 .02
❑ 444 Tommy Vardell RC .10 .02
❑ 445 Bob Whitfield RC .10 .02
❑ 446 Darryl Williams RC .10 .02
❑ 447 Checklist 1-110 .10 .02
❑ 448 Checklist 111-224 .10 .02
❑ 449 Checklist 230-340 UER .10 .02
❑ 450 Checklist 341-450 .10 .02
❑ AD Super Bowl XXVII Strip 2.00 .75

1993 Ultra

❑ COMPLETE SET (500) 20.00 7.50
❑ 1 Vinnie Clark .10 .02
❑ 2 Darion Conner .10 .02
❑ 3 Eric Dickerson .20 .07
❑ 4 Moe Gardner .10 .02
❑ 5 Tim Green .10 .02
❑ 6 Roger Harper RC .10 .02
❑ 7 Michael Haynes .20 .07
❑ 8 Bobby Hebert .10 .02
❑ 9 Chris Hinton .10 .02
❑ 10 Pierce Holt .10 .02
❑ 11 Mike Kenn .10 .02
❑ 12 Lincoln Kennedy RC .10 .02
❑ 13 Chris Miller .20 .07
❑ 14 Mike Pritchard .20 .07
❑ 15 Andre Rison .20 .07
❑ 16 Deion Sanders .75 .30
❑ 17 Tony Smith RB .10 .02
❑ 18 Jessie Tuggle .10 .02
❑ 19 Howard Ballard .10 .02
❑ 20 Don Beebe .10 .02
❑ 21 Cornelius Bennett .20 .07
❑ 22 Bill Brooks .10 .02
❑ 23 Kenneth Davis .10 .02
❑ 24 Phil Hansen .10 .02
❑ 25 Henry Jones .10 .02
❑ 26 Jim Kelly .40 .15
❑ 27 Nate Odomes .10 .02
❑ 28 John Parrella RC .10 .02
❑ 29 Andre Reed .20 .07
❑ 30 Frank Reich .20 .07
❑ 31 Jim Ritcher .10 .02
❑ 32 Bruce Smith .40 .15
❑ 33 Thomas Smith RC .20 .07
❑ 34 Darryl Talley .10 .02
❑ 35 Steve Tasker .20 .07
❑ 36 Thurman Thomas .40 .15
❑ 37 Jeff Wright .10 .02
❑ 38 Neal Anderson .10 .02
❑ 39 Trace Armstrong .10 .02
❑ 40 Mark Carrier DB .10 .02
❑ 41 Curtis Conway RC .75 .30
❑ 42 Wendell Davis .10 .02
❑ 43 Richard Dent .20 .07
❑ 44 Shaun Gayle .10 .02
❑ 45 Jim Harbaugh .40 .15
❑ 46 Craig Heyward .20 .07
❑ 47 Darren Lewis .10 .02
❑ 48 Steve McMichael .20 .07
❑ 49 William Perry .20 .07
❑ 50 Carl Simpson RC .10 .02
❑ 51 Alonzo Spellman .10 .02
❑ 52 Keith Van Horne .10 .02
❑ 53 Tom Waddle .10 .02
❑ 54 Donnell Woolford .10 .02
❑ 55 John Copeland RC .20 .07
❑ 56 Derrick Fenner .10 .02
❑ 57 James Francis .10 .02
❑ 58 Harold Green .10 .02
❑ 59 David Klingler .10 .02
❑ 60 Tim Krumrie .10 .02
❑ 61 Ricardo McDonald .10 .02
❑ 62 Tony McGee RC .20 .07
❑ 63 Carl Pickens .20 .07
❑ 64 Lamar Rogers .10 .02
❑ 65 Jay Schroeder .10 .02
❑ 66 Daniel Stubbs .10 .02
❑ 67 Steve Tovar RC .10 .02
❑ 68 Alfred Williams .10 .02
❑ 69 Darryl Williams .10 .02
❑ 70 Jerry Ball .10 .02
❑ 71 David Brandon .10 .02
❑ 72 Rob Burnett .10 .02
❑ 73 Mark Carrier WR .20 .07
❑ 74 Steve Everitt RC .10 .02
❑ 75 Dan Footman RC .10 .02
❑ 76 Leroy Hoard .20 .07
❑ 77 Michael Jackson .20 .07
❑ 78 Mike Johnson .10 .02
❑ 79 Bernie Kosar .20 .07
❑ 80 Clay Matthews .20 .07
❑ 81 Eric Metcalf .20 .07
❑ 82 Michael Dean Perry .20 .07
❑ 83 Vinny Testaverde .20 .07
❑ 84 Tommy Vardell .10 .02
❑ 85 Troy Aikman 1.50 .60
❑ 86 Larry Brown DB .10 .02
❑ 87 Tony Casillas .10 .02
❑ 88 Thomas Everett .10 .02
❑ 89 Charles Haley .20 .07
❑ 90 Alvin Harper .20 .07
❑ 91 Michael Irvin .40 .15
❑ 92 Jim Jeffcoat .10 .02
❑ 93 Daryl Johnston .40 .15
❑ 94 Robert Jones .10 .02
❑ 95 Leon Lett RC .20 .07
❑ 96 Russell Maryland .10 .02
❑ 97 Nate Newton .20 .07
❑ 98 Ken Norton .20 .07
❑ 99 Jay Novacek .20 .07
❑ 100 Darrin Smith RC .20 .07
❑ 101 Emmitt Smith 3.00 1.25
❑ 102 Kevin Smith .20 .07
❑ 103 Mark Stepnoski .10 .02
❑ 104 Tony Tolbert .10 .02
❑ 105 Kevin Williams RC WR .40 .15
❑ 106 Steve Atwater .10 .02
❑ 107 Rod Bernstine .10 .02
❑ 108 Mike Croel .10 .02
❑ 109 Robert Delpino .10 .02
❑ 110 Shane Dronett .10 .02
❑ 111 John Elway 3.00 1.25
❑ 112 Simon Fletcher .10 .02
❑ 113 Greg Kragen .10 .02
❑ 114 Tommy Maddox .40 .15
❑ 115 Arthur Marshall RC .10 .02
❑ 116 Karl Mecklenburg .10 .02
❑ 117 Glyn Milburn RC .40 .15
❑ 118 Reggie Rivers RC .10 .02
❑ 119 Shannon Sharpe .40 .15
❑ 120 Dennis Smith .10 .02
❑ 121 Kenny Walker .10 .02
❑ 122 Dan Williams RC .10 .02
❑ 123 Bennie Blades .10 .02
❑ 124 Lomas Brown .10 .02
❑ 125 Bill Fralic .10 .02
❑ 126 Mel Gray .20 .07
❑ 127 Willie Green .10 .02
❑ 128 Jason Hanson .10 .02
❑ 129 Antonio London RC .10 .02
❑ 130 Ryan McNeil RC .40 .15
❑ 131 Herman Moore .40 .15
❑ 132 Rodney Peete .10 .02

❑ 133 Brett Perriman .40 .15
❑ 134 Kelvin Pritchett .10 .02
❑ 135 Barry Sanders 2.50 1.00
❑ 136 Tracy Scroggins .10 .02
❑ 137 Chris Spielman .20 .07
❑ 138 Pat Swilling .10 .02
❑ 139 Andre Ware .10 .02
❑ 140 Edgar Bennett .40 .15
❑ 141 Tony Bennett .10 .02
❑ 142 Matt Brock .10 .02
❑ 143 Terrell Buckley .10 .02
❑ 144 LeRoy Butler .10 .02
❑ 145 Mark Clayton .10 .02
❑ 146 Brett Favre 4.00 1.50
❑ 147 [illegible] .10 .02
❑ 148 Johnny Holland .10 .02
❑ 149 Bill Maas .10 .02
❑ 150 Brian Noble .10 .02
❑ 151 Bryce Paup .20 .07
❑ 152 Ken Ruettgers .10 .02
❑ 153 Sterling Sharpe .40 .15
❑ 154 Wayne Simmons RC .10 .02
❑ 155 John Stephens .10 .02
❑ 156 George Teague RC .20 .07
❑ 157 Reggie White .40 .15
❑ 158 Micheal Barrow RC .40 .15
❑ 159 Cody Carlson .10 .02
❑ 160 Ray Childress .10 .02
❑ 161 Cris Dishman .10 .02
❑ 162 Curtis Duncan .10 .02
❑ 163 William Fuller .10 .02
❑ 164 Ernest Givins .20 .07
❑ 165 Brad Hopkins RC .10 .02
❑ 166 Haywood Jeffires .20 .07
❑ 167 Lamar Lathon .10 .02
❑ 168 Wilber Marshall .10 .02
❑ 169 Bruce Matthews .10 .02
❑ 170 Bubba McDowell .10 .02
❑ 171 Warren Moon .40 .15
❑ 172 Mike Munchak .20 .07
❑ 173 Eddie Robinson .10 .02
❑ 174 Al Smith .10 .02
❑ 175 Lorenzo White .10 .02
❑ 176 Lee Williams .10 .02
❑ 177 Chip Banks .10 .02
❑ 178 John Baylor .10 .02
❑ 179 Duane Bickett .10 .02
❑ 180 Kerry Cash .10 .02
❑ 181 Quentin Coryatt .20 .07
❑ 182 Rodney Culver .10 .02
❑ 183 Steve Emtman .10 .02
❑ 184 Jeff George .40 .15
❑ 185 Jeff Herrod .10 .02
❑ 186 Jessie Hester .10 .02
❑ 187 Anthony Johnson .20 .07
❑ 188 Reggie Langhorne .10 .02
❑ 189 Roosevelt Potts RC .10 .02
❑ 190 Rohn Stark .10 .02
❑ 191 Clarence Verdin .10 .02
❑ 192 Will Wolford .10 .02
❑ 193 Marcus Allen .40 .15
❑ 194 John Alt .10 .02
❑ 195 Tim Barnett .10 .02
❑ 196 J.J.Birden .10 .02
❑ 197 Dale Carter .10 .02
❑ 198 Willie Davis .40 .15
❑ 199 Jaime Fields RC .10 .02
❑ 200 Dave Krieg .20 .07
❑ 201 Nick Lowery .10 .02
❑ 202 Charles Mincy RC .10 .02
❑ 203 Joe Montana 3.00 1.25
❑ 204 Christian Okoye .10 .02
❑ 205 Dan Saleaumua .10 .02
❑ 206 Will Shields RC .40 .15
❑ 207 Tracy Simien .10 .02
❑ 208 Neil Smith .40 .15
❑ 209 Derrick Thomas .40 .15
❑ 210 Harvey Williams .20 .07
❑ 211 Barry Word .10 .02
❑ 212 Eddie Anderson .10 .02
❑ 213 Patrick Bates RC .10 .02
❑ 214 Nick Bell .10 .02
❑ 215 Tim Brown .40 .15
❑ 216 Willie Gault .10 .02
❑ 217 Gaston Green .10 .02
❑ 218 Billy Joe Hobert RC .40 .15
❑ 219 Ethan Horton .10 .02
❑ 220 Jeff Hostetler .20 .07
❑ 221 James Lofton .20 .07
❑ 222 Howie Long .40 .15
❑ 223 Todd Marinovich .10 .02
❑ 224 Terry McDaniel .10 .02
❑ 225 Winston Moss .10 .02
❑ 226 Anthony Smith .10 .02
❑ 227 Greg Townsend .10 .02
❑ 228 Aaron Wallace .10 .02
❑ 229 Lionel Washington .10 .02
❑ 230 Steve Wisniewski .10 .02
❑ 231 Flipper Anderson .10 .02
❑ 232 Jerome Bettis RC 8.00 4.00
❑ 233 Marc Boutte .10 .02
❑ 234 Shane Conlan .10 .02
❑ 235 Troy Drayton RC .20 .07
❑ 236 Henry Ellard .20 .07
❑ 237 Jim Everett .20 .07
❑ 238 Cleveland Gary .10 .02
❑ 239 Sean Gilbert .20 .07
❑ 240 Darryl Henley .10 .02
❑ 241 David Lang .10 .02
❑ 242 Todd Lyght .10 .02
❑ 243 Anthony Newman .10 .02
❑ 244 Roman Phifer .10 .02
❑ 245 Gerald Robinson .10 .02
❑ 246 Henry Rolling .10 .02
❑ 247 Jackie Slater .10 .02
❑ 248 Keith Byars .10 .02
❑ 249 Marco Coleman .10 .02
❑ 250 Bryan Cox .10 .02
❑ 251 Jeff Cross .10 .02
❑ 252 Irving Fryar .20 .07
❑ 253 Mark Higgs .10 .02
❑ 254 Dwight Hollier RC .10 .02
❑ 255 Mark Ingram .10 .02
❑ 256 Keith Jackson .20 .07
❑ 257 Terry Kirby RC .40 .15
❑ 258 Dan Marino 3.00 1.25
❑ 259 O.J. McDuffie RC .40 .15
❑ 260 John Offerdahl .10 .02
❑ 261 Louis Oliver .10 .02
❑ 262 Pete Stoyanovich .10 .02
❑ 263 Troy Vincent .10 .02
❑ 264 Richmond Webb .10 .02
❑ 265 Jarvis Williams .10 .02
❑ 266 Terry Allen .40 .15
❑ 267 Anthony Carter .20 .07
❑ 268 Cris Carter .40 .15
❑ 269 Roger Craig .20 .07
❑ 270 Jack Del Rio .10 .02
❑ 271 Chris Doleman .10 .02
❑ 272 Qadry Ismail RC .40 .15
❑ 273 Steve Jordan .10 .02
❑ 274 Randall McDaniel .10 .02
❑ 275 Audray McMillian .10 .02
❑ 276 John Randle .20 .07
❑ 277 Sean Salisbury .10 .02
❑ 278 Todd Scott .10 .02
❑ 279 Robert Smith RC 2.50 1.00
❑ 280 Henry Thomas .10 .02
❑ 281 Ray Agnew .10 .02
❑ 282 Bruce Armstrong .10 .02
❑ 283 Drew Bledsoe RC 5.00 2.00
❑ 284 Vincent Brisby RC .40 .15
❑ 285 Vincent Brown .10 .02
❑ 286 Eugene Chung .10 .02
❑ 287 Marv Cook .10 .02
❑ 288 Pat Harlow .10 .02
❑ 289 Jerome Henderson .10 .02
❑ 290 Greg McMurtry .10 .02
❑ 291 Leonard Russell .20 .07
❑ 292 Chris Singleton .10 .02
❑ 293 Chris Slade RC .20 .07
❑ 294 Andre Tippett .10 .02
❑ 295 Brent Williams .10 .02
❑ 296 Scott Zolak .10 .02
❑ 297 Morten Andersen .10 .02
❑ 298 Gene Atkins .10 .02
❑ 299 Mike Buck .10 .02
❑ 300 Toi Cook .10 .02
❑ 301 Jim Dombrowski .10 .02
❑ 302 Vaughn Dunbar .10 .02
❑ 303 Quinn Early .20 .07
❑ 304 Joel Hilgenberg .10 .02
❑ 305 Dalton Hilliard .10 .02
❑ 306 Rickey Jackson .10 .02
❑ 307 Vaughan Johnson .10 .02
❑ 308 Reginald Jones .10 .02
❑ 309 Eric Martin .10 .02
❑ 310 Wayne Martin .10 .02
❑ 311 Sam Mills .10 .02
❑ 312 Brad Muster .10 .02
❑ 313 Willie Roaf RC .20 .07
❑ 314 Irv Smith RC [illegible] [illegible]
❑ 315 Wade Wilson .10 .02
❑ 316 Carlton Bailey .10 .02
❑ 317 Michael Brooks .10 .02
❑ 318 Derek Brown TE .10 .02
❑ 319 Marcus Buckley RC .10 .02
❑ 320 Jarrod Bunch .10 .02
❑ 321 Mark Collins .10 .02
❑ 322 Eric Dorsey .10 .02
❑ 323 Rodney Hampton .20 .07
❑ 324 Mark Jackson .10 .02
❑ 325 Pepper Johnson .10 .02
❑ 326 Ed McCaffrey .40 .15
❑ 327 Dave Meggett .10 .02
❑ 328 Bart Oates .10 .02
❑ 329 Mike Sherrard .10 .02
❑ 330 Phil Simms .20 .07
❑ 331 Michael Strahan RC 3.00 1.25
❑ 332 Lawrence Taylor .40 .15
❑ 333 Brad Baxter .10 .02
❑ 334 Chris Burkett .10 .02
❑ 335 Kyle Clifton .10 .02
❑ 336 Boomer Esiason .20 .07
❑ 337 James Hasty .10 .02
❑ 338 Johnny Johnson .10 .02
❑ 339 Marvin Jones RC .10 .02
❑ 340 Jeff Lageman .10 .02
❑ 341 Mo Lewis .10 .02
❑ 342 Ronnie Lott .20 .07
❑ 343 Leonard Marshall .10 .02
❑ 344 Johnny Mitchell .10 .02
❑ 345 Rob Moore .20 .07
❑ 346 Browning Nagle .10 .02
❑ 347 Coleman Rudolph RC .10 .02
❑ 348 Blair Thomas .10 .02
❑ 349 Eric Thomas .10 .02
❑ 350 Brian Washington .10 .02
❑ 351 Marvin Washington .10 .02
❑ 352 Eric Allen .10 .02
❑ 353 Victor Bailey RC .10 .02
❑ 354 Fred Barnett .20 .07
❑ 355 Mark Bavaro .10 .02
❑ 356 Randall Cunningham .40 .15
❑ 357 Byron Evans .10 .02
❑ 358 Andy Harmon RC .20 .07
❑ 359 Tim Harris .10 .02
❑ 360 Lester Holmes .10 .02
❑ 361 Seth Joyner .10 .02
❑ 362 Keith Millard .10 .02
❑ 363 Leonard Renfro RC .10 .02
❑ 364 Heath Sherman .10 .02
❑ 365 Vai Sikahema .10 .02
❑ 366 Clyde Simmons .10 .02
❑ 367 William Thomas .10 .02
❑ 368 Herschel Walker .20 .07
❑ 369 Andre Waters .10 .02
❑ 370 Calvin Williams .20 .07
❑ 371 Johnny Bailey .10 .02
❑ 372 Steve Beuerlein .20 .07
❑ 373 Rich Camarillo .10 .02
❑ 374 Chuck Cecil .10 .02
❑ 375 Chris Chandler .20 .07
❑ 376 Gary Clark .20 .07
❑ 377 Ben Coleman RC .10 .02
❑ 378 Ernest Dye RC .10 .02
❑ 379 Ken Harvey .10 .02
❑ 380 Garrison Hearst RC 1.50 .60
❑ 381 Randal Hill .10 .02
❑ 382 Robert Massey .10 .02
❑ 383 Freddie Joe Nunn .10 .02
❑ 384 Ricky Proehl .10 .02

❑ 385 Luis Sharpe .10 .02
❑ 386 Tyronne Stowe .10 .02
❑ 387 Eric Swann .20 .07
❑ 388 Aeneas Williams .10 .02
❑ 389 Chad Brown RC LB .20 .07
❑ 390 Dermontti Dawson .10 .02
❑ 391 Donald Evans .10 .02
❑ 392 Deon Figures RC .10 .02
❑ 393 Barry Foster .20 .07
❑ 394 Jeff Graham .20 .07
❑ 395 Eric Green .10 .02
❑ 396 Kevin Greene .20 .07
❑ 397 Carlton Haselrig .10 .02
❑ 398 Andre Hastings RC .20 .07
❑ 399 D.J. Johnson .10 .02
❑ 400 Carnell Lake .10 .02
❑ 401 Greg Lloyd .20 .07
❑ 402 Neil O'Donnell .40 .15
❑ 403 Darren Perry .10 .02
❑ 404 Mike Tomczak .10 .02
❑ 405 Rod Woodson .40 .15
❑ 406 Eric Bieniemy .10 .02
❑ 407 Marion Butts .10 .02
❑ 408 Gill Byrd .10 .02
❑ 409 Darren Carrington RC .10 .02
❑ 410 Darrien Gordon RC .10 .02
❑ 411 Burt Grossman .10 .02
❑ 412 Courtney Hall .10 .02
❑ 413 Ronnie Harmon .10 .02
❑ 414 Stan Humphries .20 .07
❑ 415 Nate Lewis .10 .02
❑ 416 Natrone Means RC .40 .15
❑ 417 Anthony Miller .20 .07
❑ 418 Chris Mims .10 .02
❑ 419 Leslie O'Neal .20 .07
❑ 420 Gary Plummer .10 .02
❑ 421 Stanley Richard .10 .02
❑ 422 Junior Seau .40 .15
❑ 423 Harry Swayne .10 .02
❑ 424 Jerrol Williams .10 .02
❑ 425 Harris Barton .10 .02
❑ 426 Steve Bono .20 .07
❑ 427 Kevin Fagan .10 .02
❑ 428 Don Griffin .10 .02
❑ 429 Dana Hall .10 .02
❑ 430 Adrian Hardy .10 .02
❑ 431 Brent Jones .20 .07
❑ 432 Todd Kelly RC .10 .02
❑ 433 Amp Lee .10 .02
❑ 434 Tim McDonald .10 .02
❑ 435 Guy McIntyre .10 .02
❑ 436 Tom Rathman .10 .02
❑ 437 Jerry Rice 2.00 .75
❑ 438 Bill Romanowski .10 .02
❑ 439 Dana Stubblefield RC .40 .15
❑ 440 John Taylor .20 .07
❑ 441 Steve Wallace .10 .02
❑ 442 Michael Walter .10 .02
❑ 443 Ricky Watters .40 .15
❑ 444 Steve Young 1.50 .60
❑ 445 Robert Blackmon .10 .02
❑ 446 Brian Blades .20 .07
❑ 447 Jeff Bryant .10 .02
❑ 448 Ferrell Edmunds .10 .02
❑ 449 Carlton Gray RC .10 .02
❑ 450 Dwayne Harper .10 .02
❑ 451 Andy Heck .10 .02
❑ 452 Tommy Kane .10 .02
❑ 453 Cortez Kennedy .20 .07
❑ 454 Kelvin Martin .10 .02
❑ 455 Dan McGwire .10 .02
❑ 456 Rick Mirer RC .40 .15
❑ 457 Rufus Porter .10 .02
❑ 458 Ray Roberts .10 .02
❑ 459 Eugene Robinson .10 .02
❑ 460 Chris Warren .20 .07
❑ 461 John L. Williams .10 .02
❑ 462 Gary Anderson RB .10 .02
❑ 463 Tyji Armstrong .10 .02
❑ 464 Reggie Cobb .10 .02
❑ 465 Eric Curry RC .10 .02
❑ 466 Lawrence Dawsey .10 .02
❑ 467 Steve DeBerg .10 .02
❑ 468 Santana Dotson .20 .07
❑ 469 Demetrius DuBose RC .10 .02
❑ 470 Paul Gruber .10 .02
❑ 471 Ron Hall .10 .02
❑ 472 Courtney Hawkins .10 .02
❑ 473 Hardy Nickerson .20 .07
❑ 474 Ricky Reynolds .10 .02
❑ 475 Broderick Thomas .10 .02
❑ 476 Mark Wheeler .10 .02
❑ 477 Jimmy Williams .10 .02
❑ 478 Carl Banks .10 .02
❑ 479 Reggie Brooks RC .20 .07
❑ 480 Earnest Byner .10 .02
❑ 481 Tom Carter RC .20 .07
❑ 482 Andre Collins .10 .02
❑ 483 Brad Edwards .10 .02
❑ 484 Ricky Ervins .10 .02
❑ 485 Kurt Gouveia .10 .02
❑ 486 Darrell Green .10 .02
❑ 487 Desmond Howard .20 .07
❑ 488 Jim Lachey .10 .02
❑ 489 Chip Lohmiller .10 .02
❑ 490 Charles Mann .10 .02
❑ 491 Tim McGee .10 .02
❑ 492 Brian Mitchell .20 .07
❑ 493 Art Monk .20 .07
❑ 494 Mark Rypien .10 .02
❑ 495 Ricky Sanders .10 .02
❑ 496 Checklist 1-126 .10 .02
❑ 497 Checklist 127-254 .10 .02
❑ 498 Checklist 255-382 .10 .02
❑ 499 Checklist 383-500 .10 .02
❑ 500 Inserts Checklist .10 .02

1994 Ultra

❑ COMPLETE SET (525) 25.00 10.00
❑ COMP.SERIES 1 (325) 12.00 5.00
❑ COMP.SERIES 2 (200) 12.00 5.00
❑ 1 Steve Beuerlein .20 .07
❑ 2 Gary Clark .20 .07
❑ 3 Randal Hill .10 .02
❑ 4 Seth Joyner .10 .02
❑ 5 Jamir Miller RC .20 .07
❑ 6 Ronald Moore .10 .02
❑ 7 Luis Sharpe .10 .02
❑ 8 Clyde Simmons .10 .02
❑ 9 Eric Swann .20 .07
❑ 10 Aeneas Williams .10 .02
❑ 11 Chris Doleman .10 .02
❑ 12 Bert Emanuel RC .40 .15
❑ 13 Moe Gardner .10 .02
❑ 14 Jeff George .40 .15
❑ 15 Roger Harper .10 .02
❑ 16 Pierce Holt .10 .02
❑ 17 Lincoln Kennedy .10 .02
❑ 18 Erric Pegram .10 .02
❑ 19 Andre Rison .20 .07
❑ 20 Deion Sanders .75 .30
❑ 21 Jessie Tuggle .10 .02
❑ 22 Cornelius Bennett .20 .07
❑ 23 Bill Brooks .10 .02
❑ 24 Jeff Burris RC .20 .07
❑ 25 Kent Hull .10 .02
❑ 26 Henry Jones .10 .02
❑ 27 Jim Kelly .40 .15
❑ 28 Marvcus Patton .10 .02
❑ 29 Andre Reed .20 .07
❑ 30 Bruce Smith .40 .15
❑ 31 Thomas Smith .10 .02
❑ 32 Thurman Thomas .40 .15
❑ 33 Jeff Wright .10 .02
❑ 34 Trace Armstrong .10 .02
❑ 35 Mark Carrier DB .10 .02
❑ 36 Dante Jones .10 .02
❑ 37 Erik Kramer .20 .07
❑ 38 Terry Obee .10 .02
❑ 39 Alonzo Spellman .10 .02
❑ 40 John Thierry RC .10 .02
❑ 41 Tom Waddle .10 .02
❑ 42 Donnell Woolford .10 .02
❑ 43 Tim Worley .10 .02
❑ 44 Chris Zorich .10 .02
❑ 45 John Copeland .10 .02
❑ 46 Harold Green .10 .02
❑ 47 David Klingler .10 .02
❑ 48 Ricardo McDonald .10 .02
❑ 49 Tony McGee .10 .02
❑ 50 Louis Oliver .10 .02
❑ 51 Carl Pickens .20 .07
❑ 52 Darnay Scott RC .75 .30
❑ 53 Steve Tovar .10 .02
❑ 54 Dan Wilkinson RC .20 .07
❑ 55 Darryl Williams .10 .02
❑ 56 Derrick Alexander WR RC .40 .15
❑ 57 Michael Jackson .20 .07
❑ 58 Tony Jones T .10 .02
❑ 59 Antonio Langham RC .20 .07
❑ 60 Eric Metcalf .20 .07
❑ 61 Stevon Moore .10 .02
❑ 62 Michael Dean Perry .20 .07
❑ 63 Anthony Pleasant .10 .02
❑ 64 Vinny Testaverde .20 .07
❑ 65 Eric Turner .10 .02
❑ 66 Tommy Vardell .10 .02
❑ 67 Troy Aikman 1.50 .60
❑ 68 Larry Brown DB .10 .02
❑ 69 Shante Carver RC .10 .02
❑ 70 Charles Haley .20 .07
❑ 71 Michael Irvin .40 .15
❑ 72 Leon Lett .10 .02
❑ 73 Nate Newton .10 .02
❑ 74 Jay Novacek .20 .07
❑ 75 Darrin Smith .10 .02
❑ 76 Emmitt Smith 2.50 1.00
❑ 77 Tony Tolbert .10 .02
❑ 78 Erik Williams .10 .02
❑ 79 Kevin Williams WR .20 .07
❑ 80 Steve Atwater .10 .02
❑ 81 Rod Bernstine .10 .02
❑ 82 Ray Crockett .10 .02
❑ 83 Mike Croel .10 .02
❑ 84 Shane Dronett .10 .02
❑ 85 Jason Elam .20 .07
❑ 86 John Elway 3.00 1.25
❑ 87 Simon Fletcher .10 .02
❑ 88 Glyn Milburn .20 .07
❑ 89 Anthony Miller .20 .07
❑ 90 Shannon Sharpe .20 .07
❑ 91 Gary Zimmerman .10 .02
❑ 92 Bennie Blades .10 .02
❑ 93 Lomas Brown .10 .02
❑ 94 Mel Gray .10 .02
❑ 95 Jason Hanson .10 .02
❑ 96 Ryan McNeil .10 .02
❑ 97 Scott Mitchell .20 .07
❑ 98 Herman Moore .40 .15
❑ 99 Johnnie Morton RC 1.50 .60
❑ 100 Robert Porcher .10 .02
❑ 101 Barry Sanders 2.50 1.00
❑ 102 Chris Spielman .20 .07
❑ 103 Pat Swilling .10 .02
❑ 104 Edgar Bennett .40 .15
❑ 105 Terrell Buckley .10 .02
❑ 106 Reggie Cobb .10 .02
❑ 107 Brett Favre 3.00 1.25
❑ 108 Sean Jones .10 .02
❑ 109 Ken Ruettgers .10 .02
❑ 110 Sterling Sharpe .20 .07
❑ 111 Wayne Simmons .10 .02
❑ 112 Aaron Taylor RC .10 .02
❑ 113 George Teague .10 .02
❑ 114 Reggie White .40 .15

❑ 115 Micheal Barrow .10 .02
❑ 116 Gary Brown .10 .02
❑ 117 Cody Carlson .10 .02
❑ 118 Ray Childress .10 .02
❑ 119 Cris Dishman .10 .02
❑ 120 Henry Ford RC .10 .02
❑ 121 Haywood Jeffires .20 .07
❑ 122 Bruce Matthews .10 .02
❑ 123 Bubba McDowell .10 .02
❑ 124 Marcus Robertson .10 .02
❑ 125 Eddie Robinson .10 .02
❑ 126 Webster Slaughter .10 .02
❑ 127 Trev Alberts RC .20 .07
❑ 128 Tony Bennett .10 .02
❑ 129 Ray Buchanan .10 .02
❑ 130 Quentin Coryatt .10 .02
❑ 131 Eugene Daniel .10 .02
❑ 132 Steve Emtman .10 .02
❑ 133 Marshall Faulk RC 6.00 2.50
❑ 134 Jim Harbaugh .40 .15
❑ 135 Roosevelt Potts .10 .02
❑ 136 John Stark .10 .02
❑ 137 Marcus Allen .40 .15
❑ 138 Donnell Bennett RC .40 .15
❑ 139 Dale Carter .10 .02
❑ 140 Tony Casillas .10 .02
❑ 141 Mark Collins .10 .02
❑ 142 Willie Davis .20 .07
❑ 143 Tim Grunhard .10 .02
❑ 144 Greg Hill RC .40 .15
❑ 145 Joe Montana 3.00 1.25
❑ 146 Tracy Simien .10 .02
❑ 147 Neil Smith .20 .07
❑ 148 Derrick Thomas .40 .15
❑ 149 Tim Brown .40 .15
❑ 150 James Folston RC .10 .02
❑ 151 Rob Fredrickson RC .20 .07
❑ 152 Jeff Hostetler .20 .07
❑ 153 Rocket Ismail .20 .07
❑ 154 James Jett .10 .02
❑ 155 Terry McDaniel .10 .02
❑ 156 Winston Moss .10 .02
❑ 157 Greg Robinson .10 .02
❑ 158 Anthony Smith .10 .02
❑ 159 Steve Wisniewski .10 .02
❑ 160 Flipper Anderson .10 .02
❑ 161 Jerome Bettis .60 .25
❑ 162 Isaac Bruce RC 4.00 2.00
❑ 163 Shane Conlan .10 .02
❑ 164 Wayne Gandy RC .10 .02
❑ 165 Sean Gilbert .10 .02
❑ 166 Todd Lyght .10 .02
❑ 167 Chris Miller .10 .02
❑ 168 Anthony Newman .10 .02
❑ 169 Roman Phifer .10 .02
❑ 170 Jackie Slater .10 .02
❑ 171 Gene Atkins .10 .02
❑ 172 Aubrey Beavers RC .10 .02
❑ 173 Tim Bowens RC .20 .07
❑ 174 J.B. Brown .10 .02
❑ 175 Marco Coleman .10 .02
❑ 176 Bryan Cox .10 .02
❑ 177 Irving Fryar .20 .07
❑ 178 Terry Kirby .40 .15
❑ 179 Dan Marino 3.00 1.25
❑ 180 Troy Vincent .10 .02
❑ 181 Richmond Webb .10 .02
❑ 182 Terry Allen .20 .07
❑ 183 Cris Carter .75 .30
❑ 184 Jack Del Rio .10 .02
❑ 185 Vencie Glenn .10 .02
❑ 186 Randall McDaniel .10 .02
❑ 187 Warren Moon .40 .15
❑ 188 David Palmer RC .40 .15
❑ 189 John Randle .20 .07
❑ 190 Todd Scott .10 .02
❑ 191 Todd Steussie RC .20 .07
❑ 192 Henry Thomas .10 .02
❑ 193 Dewayne Washington RC .20 .07
❑ 194 Bruce Armstrong .10 .02
❑ 195 Harlon Barnett .10 .02
❑ 196 Drew Bledsoe 1.00 .40
❑ 197 Vincent Brisby .20 .07
❑ 198 Vincent Brown .10 .02
❑ 199 Marion Butts .10 .02
❑ 200 Ben Coates .20 .07
❑ 201 Todd Collins .10 .02
❑ 202 Maurice Hurst .10 .02
❑ 203 Willie McGinest RC .40 .15
❑ 204 Ricky Reynolds .10 .02
❑ 205 Chris Slade .10 .02
❑ 206 Mario Bates RC .40 .15
❑ 207 Derek Brown RBK .10 .02
❑ 208 Vince Buck .10 .02
❑ 209 Quinn Early .20 .07
❑ 210 Jim Everett .20 .07
❑ 211 Michael Haynes .20 .07
❑ 212 Tyrone Hughes .20 .07
❑ 213 Joe Johnson RC .10 .02
❑ 214 Vaughan Johnson .10 .02
❑ 215 Willie Roaf .10 .02
❑ 216 Renaldo Turnbull .10 .02
❑ 217 Michael Brooks .10 .02
❑ 218 Dave Brown .20 .07
❑ 219 Howard Cross .10 .02
❑ 220 Stacey Dillard .10 .02
❑ 221 Jumbo Elliott .10 .02
❑ 222 Keith Hamilton .10 .02
❑ 223 Rodney Hampton .20 .07
❑ 224 Thomas Lewis RC .20 .07
❑ 225 Dave Meggett .10 .02
❑ 226 Corey Miller .10 .02
❑ 227 Thomas Randolph RC .10 .02
❑ 228 Mike Sherrard .10 .02
❑ 229 Kyle Clifton .10 .02
❑ 230 Boomer Esiason .20 .07
❑ 231 Aaron Glenn RC .40 .15
❑ 232 James Hasty .10 .02
❑ 233 Bobby Houston .10 .02
❑ 234 Johnny Johnson .10 .02
❑ 235 Mo Lewis .10 .02
❑ 236 Ronnie Lott .20 .07
❑ 237 Rob Moore .20 .07
❑ 238 Marvin Washington .10 .02
❑ 239 Ryan Yarborough RC .10 .02
❑ 240 Eric Allen .10 .02
❑ 241 Victor Bailey .10 .02
❑ 242 Fred Barnett .20 .07
❑ 243 Mark Bavaro .10 .02
❑ 244 Randall Cunningham .40 .15
❑ 245 Byron Evans .10 .02
❑ 246 William Fuller .10 .02
❑ 247 Andy Harmon .10 .02
❑ 248 William Perry .20 .07
❑ 249 Herschel Walker .20 .07
❑ 250 Bernard Williams RC .10 .02
❑ 251 Dermontti Dawson .10 .02
❑ 252 Deon Figures .10 .02
❑ 253 Barry Foster .10 .02
❑ 254 Kevin Greene .20 .07
❑ 255 Charles Johnson RC .40 .15
❑ 256 Levon Kirkland .10 .02
❑ 257 Greg Lloyd .20 .07
❑ 258 Neil O'Donnell .40 .15
❑ 259 Darren Perry .10 .02
❑ 260 Dwight Stone .10 .02
❑ 261 Rod Woodson .20 .07
❑ 262 John Carney .10 .02
❑ 263 Isaac Davis RC .10 .02
❑ 264 Courtney Hall .10 .02
❑ 265 Ronnie Harmon .10 .02
❑ 266 Stan Humphries .20 .07
❑ 267 Vance Johnson .10 .02
❑ 268 Natrone Means .40 .15
❑ 269 Chris Mims .10 .02
❑ 270 Leslie O'Neal .10 .02
❑ 271 Stanley Richard .10 .02
❑ 272 Junior Seau .40 .15
❑ 273 Harris Barton .10 .02
❑ 274 Dennis Brown .10 .02
❑ 275 Eric Davis .10 .02
❑ 276 William Floyd RC .40 .15
❑ 277 John Johnson .10 .02
❑ 278 Tim McDonald .10 .02
❑ 279 Ken Norton Jr. .20 .07
❑ 280 Jerry Rice 1.50 .60
❑ 281 Jesse Sapolu .10 .02
❑ 282 Dana Stubblefield .20 .07
❑ 283 Ricky Watters .20 .07
❑ 284 Bryant Young RC .60 .25
❑ 285 Steve Young 1.00 .40
❑ 286 Sam Adams RC .20 .07
❑ 287 Brian Blades .20 .07
❑ 288 Ferrell Edmunds .10 .02
❑ 289 Patrick Hunter .10 .02
❑ 290 Cortez Kennedy .20 .07
❑ 291 Rick Mirer .40 .15
❑ 292 Nate Odomes .10 .02
❑ 293 Ray Roberts .10 .02
❑ 294 Eugene Robinson .10 .02
❑ 295 Rod Stephens .10 .02
❑ 296 Chris Warren .20 .07
❑ 297 Marty Carter .10 .02
❑ 298 Horace Copeland .10 .02
❑ 299 Eric Curry .10 .02
❑ 300 Santana Dotson .20 .07
❑ 301 Craig Erickson .10 .02
❑ 302 Paul Gruber .10 .02
❑ 303 Courtney Hawkins .10 .02
❑ 304 Martin Mayhew .10 .02
❑ 305 Hardy Nickerson .20 .07
❑ 306 Errict Rhett RC .40 .15
❑ 307 Vince Workman .10 .02
❑ 308 Reggie Brooks .20 .07
❑ 309 Tom Carter .10 .02
❑ 310 Andre Collins .10 .02
❑ 311 Brad Edwards .10 .02
❑ 312 Kurt Gouveia .10 .02
❑ 313 Darrell Green .10 .02
❑ 314 Ethan Horton .10 .02
❑ 315 Desmond Howard .20 .07
❑ 316 Tre Johnson RC .10 .02
❑ 317 Sterling Palmer RC .10 .02
❑ 318 Heath Shuler RC .40 .15
❑ 319 Tyronne Stowe .10 .02
❑ 320 NFL 75th Anniversary .10 .02
❑ 321 Checklist .10 .02
❑ 322 Checklist .10 .02
❑ 323 Checklist .10 .02
❑ 324 Checklist .10 .02
❑ 325 Checklist .10 .02
❑ 326 Garrison Hearst .40 .15
❑ 327 Eric Hill .10 .02
❑ 328 Seth Joyner .10 .02
❑ 329 Jim McMahon .20 .07
❑ 330 Jamir Miller .10 .02
❑ 331 Ricky Proehl .10 .02
❑ 332 Clyde Simmons .10 .02
❑ 333 Chris Doleman .10 .02
❑ 334 Bert Emanuel .40 .15
❑ 335 Jeff George .40 .15
❑ 336 D.J. Johnson .10 .02
❑ 337 Terance Mathis .20 .07
❑ 338 Clay Matthews .10 .02
❑ 339 Tony Smith RB .10 .02
❑ 340 Don Beebe .10 .02
❑ 341 Bucky Brooks RC .10 .02
❑ 342 Jeff Burris .20 .07
❑ 343 Kenneth Davis .10 .02
❑ 344 Phil Hansen .10 .02
❑ 345 Pete Metzelaars .10 .02
❑ 346 Darryl Talley .10 .02
❑ 347 Joe Cain .10 .02
❑ 348 Curtis Conway .40 .15
❑ 349 Shaun Gayle .10 .02
❑ 350 Chris Gedney .10 .02
❑ 351 Erik Kramer .20 .07
❑ 352 Vinson Smith .10 .02
❑ 353 John Thierry .10 .02
❑ 354 Lewis Tillman .10 .02
❑ 355 Mike Brim .10 .02
❑ 356 Derrick Fenner .10 .02
❑ 357 James Francis .10 .02
❑ 358 Louis Oliver .10 .02
❑ 359 Darnay Scott .40 .15
❑ 360 Dan Wilkinson .20 .07
❑ 361 Alfred Williams .10 .02
❑ 362 Derrick Alexander WR .40 .15
❑ 363 Rob Burnett .10 .02
❑ 364 Mark Carrier WR .20 .07
❑ 365 Steve Everitt .10 .02
❑ 366 Leroy Hoard .10 .02

❑	367 Pepper Johnson	.10	.02
❑	368 Antonio Langham	.20	.07
❑	369 Shante Carver	.10	.02
❑	370 Alvin Harper	.20	.07
❑	371 Daryl Johnston	.20	.07
❑	372 Russell Maryland	.10	.02
❑	373 Kevin Smith	.10	.02
❑	374 Mark Stepnoski	.10	.02
❑	375 Darren Woodson	.20	.07
❑	376 Allen Aldridge RC	.10	.02
❑	377 Ray Crockett	.10	.02
❑	378 Karl Mecklenburg	.10	.02
❑	379 Anthony Miller	.20	.07
❑	380 Mike Pritchard	.10	.02
❑	381 Leonard Russell	.10	.02
❑	382 Dennis Smith	.10	.02
❑	383 Anthony Carter	.20	.07
❑	384 Van Malone RC	.10	.02
❑	385 Robert Massey	.10	.02
❑	386 Scott Mitchell	.20	.07
❑	387 Johnnie Morton	.60	.25
❑	388 Brett Perriman	.20	.07
❑	389 Tracy Scroggins	.10	.02
❑	390 Robert Brooks	.40	.15
❑	391 LeRoy Butler	.10	.02
❑	392 Reggie Cobb	.10	.02
❑	393 Sean Jones	.10	.02
❑	394 George Koonce	.10	.02
❑	395 Steve McMichael	.20	.07
❑	396 Bryce Paup	.20	.07
❑	397 Aaron Taylor	.10	.02
❑	398 Henry Ford	.10	.02
❑	399 Ernest Givins	.20	.07
❑	400 Jeremy Nunley RC	.10	.02
❑	401 Bo Orlando	.10	.02
❑	402 Al Smith	.10	.02
❑	403 Barron Wortham RC	.10	.02
❑	404 Trev Alberts	.20	.07
❑	405 Tony Bennett	.10	.02
❑	406 Kerry Cash	.10	.02
❑	407 Sean Dawkins RC	.40	.15
❑	408 Marshall Faulk	2.00	.75
❑	409 Jim Harbaugh	.40	.15
❑	410 Jeff Herrod	.10	.02
❑	411 Kimble Anders	.20	.07
❑	412 Donnell Bennett	.20	.07
❑	413 J.J. Birden	.10	.02
❑	414 Mark Collins	.10	.02
❑	415 Lake Dawson RC	.20	.07
❑	416 Greg Hill	.40	.15
❑	417 Charles Mincy	.10	.02
❑	418 Greg Biekert	.10	.02
❑	419 Rob Fredrickson	.20	.07
❑	420 Nolan Harrison	.10	.02
❑	421 Jeff Jaeger	.10	.02
❑	422 Albert Lewis	.10	.02
❑	423 Chester McGlockton	.10	.02
❑	424 Tom Rathman	.10	.02
❑	425 Harvey Williams	.20	.07
❑	426 Isaac Bruce	1.50	.60
❑	427 Troy Drayton	.10	.02
❑	428 Wayne Gandy	.10	.02
❑	429 Fred Stokes	.10	.02
❑	430 Robert Young	.10	.02
❑	431 Gene Atkins	.10	.02
❑	432 Aubrey Beavers	.10	.02
❑	433 Tim Bowens	.20	.07
❑	434 Keith Byars	.10	.02
❑	435 Jeff Cross	.10	.02
❑	436 Mark Ingram	.10	.02
❑	437 Keith Jackson	.10	.02
❑	438 Michael Stewart	.10	.02
❑	439 Chris Hinton	.10	.02
❑	440 Qadry Ismail	.40	.15
❑	441 Carlos Jenkins	.10	.02
❑	442 Warren Moon	.40	.15
❑	443 David Palmer	.20	.07
❑	444 Jake Reed	.20	.07
❑	445 Robert Smith	.40	.15
❑	446 Todd Steussie	.20	.07
❑	447 Dewayne Washington	.20	.07
❑	448 Marion Butts	.10	.02
❑	449 Tim Goad	.10	.02
❑	450 Myron Guyton	.10	.02
❑	451 Kevin Lee RC	.10	.02
❑	452 Willie McGinest	.40	.15
❑	453 Ricky Reynolds	.10	.02
❑	454 Michael Timpson	.10	.02
❑	455 Morten Andersen	.10	.02
❑	456 Jim Everett	.20	.07
❑	457 Michael Haynes	.20	.07
❑	458 Joe Johnson	.10	.02
❑	459 Wayne Martin	.10	.02
❑	460 Sam Mills	.10	.02
❑	461 Irv Smith	.10	.02
❑	462 Carlton Bailey	.10	.02
❑	463 Chris Calloway	.10	.02
❑	464 Mark Jackson	.10	.02
❑	465 Thomas Lewis	.20	.07
❑	466 Thomas Randolph	.10	.02
❑	467 Stevie Anderson RC	.10	.02
❑	468 Brad Baxter	.10	.02
❑	469 Aaron Glenn	.20	.07
❑	470 Jeff Lageman	.10	.02
❑	471 Johnny Mitchell	.10	.02
❑	472 Art Monk	.20	.07
❑	473 William Fuller	.10	.02
❑	474 Charlie Garner RC	1.25	.50
❑	475 Vaughn Hebron	.10	.02
❑	476 Bill Romanowski	.10	.02
❑	477 William Thomas	.10	.02
❑	478 Greg Townsend	.10	.02
❑	479 Bernard Williams	.10	.02
❑	480 Calvin Williams	.20	.07
❑	481 Eric Green	.10	.02
❑	482 Charles Johnson	.40	.15
❑	483 Carnell Lake	.10	.02
❑	484 Byron Bam Morris RC	.20	.07
❑	485 John L. Williams	.10	.02
❑	486 Darren Carrington	.10	.02
❑	487 Andre Coleman RC	.10	.02
❑	488 Isaac Davis	.10	.02
❑	489 Dwayne Harper	.10	.02
❑	490 Tony Martin	.40	.15
❑	491 Mark Seay RC	.40	.15
❑	492 Richard Dent	.20	.07
❑	493 William Floyd	.40	.15
❑	494 Rickey Jackson	.10	.02
❑	495 Brent Jones	.20	.07
❑	496 Ken Norton Jr.	.20	.07
❑	497 Gary Plummer	.10	.02
❑	498 Deion Sanders	.75	.30
❑	499 John Taylor	.20	.07
❑	500 Lee Woodall RC	.10	.02
❑	501 Bryant Young	.60	.25
❑	502 Sam Adams	.20	.07
❑	503 Howard Ballard	.10	.02
❑	504 Michael Bates	.10	.02
❑	505 Robert Blackmon	.10	.02
❑	506 John Kasay	.10	.02
❑	507 Kelvin Martin	.10	.02
❑	508 Kevin Mawae RC	.40	.15
❑	509 Rufus Porter	.10	.02
❑	510 Lawrence Dawsey	.10	.02
❑	511 Trent Dilfer RC	1.25	.50
❑	512 Thomas Everett	.10	.02
❑	513 Jackie Harris	.10	.02
❑	514 Errict Rhett	.20	.07
❑	515 Henry Ellard	.20	.07
❑	516 John Friesz	.20	.07
❑	517 Ken Harvey	.10	.02
❑	518 Ethan Horton	.10	.02
❑	519 Tre Johnson	.10	.02
❑	520 Jim Lachey	.10	.02
❑	521 Heath Shuler	.40	.15
❑	522 Tony Woods	.10	.02
❑	523 Checklist	.10	.02
❑	524 Checklist	.10	.02
❑	525 Checklist	.10	.02

1995 Ultra

❑	COMPLETE SET (550)	50.00	20.00
❑	COMP.SERIES 1 (350)	25.00	10.00
❑	COMP.SERIES 2 (200)	25.00	10.00
❑	1 Michael Bankston	.10	.02
❑	2 Larry Centers	.20	.07
❑	3 Garrison Hearst	.40	.15
❑	4 Eric Hill	.10	.02
❑	5 Seth Joyner	.10	.02
❑	6 Lorenzo Lynch	.10	.02
❑	7 Jamir Miller	.10	.02
❑	8 Clyde Simmons	.10	.02
❑	9 Eric Swann	.20	.07
❑	10 Aeneas Williams	.10	.02
❑	11 Devin Bush RC	.10	.02
❑	12 Ron Davis RC	.10	.02
❑	13 Chris Doleman	.10	.02
❑	14 Bert Emanuel	.40	.15
❑	15 Jeff George	.20	.07
❑	16 Roger Harper	.10	.02
❑	17 Craig Heyward	.20	.07
❑	18 Pierce Holt	.10	.02
❑	19 D.J. Johnson	.10	.02
❑	20 Terance Mathis	.20	.07
❑	21 Chuck Smith	.10	.02
❑	22 Jessie Tuggle	.10	.02
❑	23 Cornelius Bennett	.20	.07
❑	24 Ruben Brown RC	.40	.15
❑	25 Jeff Burris	.10	.02
❑	26 Matt Darby	.10	.02
❑	27 Phil Hansen	.10	.02
❑	28 Henry Jones	.10	.02
❑	29 Jim Kelly	.40	.15
❑	30 Mark Maddox RC	.10	.02
❑	31 Andre Reed	.20	.07
❑	32 Bruce Smith	.40	.15
❑	33 Don Beebe	.10	.02
❑	34 Kerry Collins RC	1.50	.60
❑	35 Darion Conner	.10	.02
❑	36 Pete Metzelaars	.10	.02
❑	37 Sam Mills	.20	.07
❑	38 Tyrone Poole RC	.40	.15
❑	39 Joe Cain	.10	.02
❑	40 Mark Carrier DB	.10	.02
❑	41 Curtis Conway	.40	.15
❑	42 Jeff Graham	.10	.02
❑	43 Raymont Harris	.10	.02
❑	44 Erik Kramer	.10	.02
❑	45 Rashaan Salaam RC	.20	.07
❑	46 Lewis Tillman	.10	.02
❑	47 Donnell Woolford	.10	.02
❑	48 Chris Zorich	.10	.02
❑	49 Jeff Blake RC	.75	.30
❑	50 Mike Brim	.10	.02
❑	51 Ki-Jana Carter RC	.40	.15
❑	52 James Francis	.10	.02
❑	53 Carl Pickens	.20	.07
❑	54 Darnay Scott	.20	.07
❑	55 Steve Tovar	.10	.02
❑	56 Dan Wilkinson	.20	.07
❑	57 Alfred Williams	.10	.02
❑	58 Darryl Williams	.10	.02
❑	59 Derrick Alexander WR	.40	.15
❑	60 Rob Burnett	.10	.02
❑	61 Steve Everitt	.10	.02
❑	62 Leroy Hoard	.10	.02
❑	63 Michael Jackson	.20	.07
❑	64 Pepper Johnson	.10	.02
❑	65 Tony Jones T	.10	.02
❑	66 Antonio Langham	.10	.02
❑	67 Anthony Pleasant	.10	.02
❑	68 Craig Powell RC	.10	.02
❑	69 Vinny Testaverde	.20	.07
❑	70 Eric Turner	.10	.02
❑	71 Troy Aikman	1.50	.60

❑ 72 Charles Haley .20 .07
❑ 73 Michael Irvin .40 .15
❑ 74 Daryl Johnston .20 .07
❑ 75 Robert Jones .10 .02
❑ 76 Leon Lett .10 .02
❑ 77 Russell Maryland .10 .02
❑ 78 Jay Novacek .20 .07
❑ 79 Darrin Smith .10 .02
❑ 80 Emmitt Smith 2.50 1.25
❑ 81 Kevin Smith .10 .02
❑ 82 Erik Williams .10 .02
❑ 83 Kevin Williams WR .20 .07
❑ 84 Sherman Williams RC .10 .02
❑ 85 Darren Woodson .20 .07
❑ 86 Elijah Alexander RC .10 .02
❑ 87 Steve Atwater .10 .02
❑ 88 Ray Crockett .10 .02
❑ 89 Shane Dronett .10 .02
❑ 90 Jason Elam .20 .07
❑ 91 John Elway 3.00 1.25
❑ 92 Simon Fletcher .10 .02
❑ 93 Glyn Milburn .10 .02
❑ 94 Anthony Miller .20 .07
❑ 95 Leonard Russell .10 .02
❑ 96 Shannon Sharpe .20 .07
❑ 97 Bennie Blades .10 .02
❑ 98 Lomas Brown .10 .02
❑ 99 Willie Clay .10 .02
❑ 100 Luther Elliss RC .10 .02
❑ 101 Mike Johnson .10 .02
❑ 102 Robert Massey .10 .02
❑ 103 Scott Mitchell .20 .07
❑ 104 Herman Moore .40 .15
❑ 105 Brett Perriman .20 .07
❑ 106 Robert Porcher .10 .02
❑ 107 Barry Sanders 2.50 1.00
❑ 108 Chris Spielman .20 .07
❑ 109 Edgar Bennett .20 .07
❑ 110 Robert Brooks .40 .15
❑ 111 LeRoy Butler .10 .02
❑ 112 Brett Favre 3.00 1.50
❑ 113 Sean Jones .10 .02
❑ 114 John Jurkovic .10 .02
❑ 115 George Koonce .10 .02
❑ 116 Wayne Simmons .10 .02
❑ 117 George Teague .10 .02
❑ 118 Reggie White .40 .15
❑ 119 Micheal Barrow .10 .02
❑ 120 Gary Brown .10 .02
❑ 121 Cody Carlson .10 .02
❑ 122 Ray Childress .10 .02
❑ 123 Cris Dishman .10 .02
❑ 124 Bruce Matthews .10 .02
❑ 125 Steve McNair RC 3.00 1.25
❑ 126 Marcus Robertson .10 .02
❑ 127 Webster Slaughter .10 .02
❑ 128 Al Smith .10 .02
❑ 129 Tony Bennett .10 .02
❑ 130 Ray Buchanan .10 .02
❑ 131 Quentin Coryatt .20 .07
❑ 132 Sean Dawkins .20 .07
❑ 133 Marshall Faulk 2.00 .75
❑ 134 Stephen Grant RC .10 .02
❑ 135 Jim Harbaugh .20 .07
❑ 136 Jeff Herrod .10 .02
❑ 137 Ellis Johnson RC .10 .02
❑ 138 Tony Siragusa .10 .02
❑ 139 Steve Beuerlein .20 .07
❑ 140 Tony Boselli RC .40 .15
❑ 141 Darren Carrington .10 .02
❑ 142 Reggie Cobb .10 .02
❑ 143 Kelvin Martin .10 .02
❑ 144 Kelvin Pritchett .10 .02
❑ 145 Joel Smeenge .10 .02
❑ 146 James O. Stewart RC 1.25 .50
❑ 147 Marcus Allen .40 .15
❑ 148 Kimble Anders .20 .07
❑ 149 Dale Carter .20 .07
❑ 150 Mark Collins .10 .02
❑ 151 Willie Davis .20 .07
❑ 152 Lake Dawson .20 .07
❑ 153 Greg Hill .20 .07
❑ 154 Trezelle Jenkins RC .10 .02
❑ 155 Darren Mickell .10 .02
❑ 156 Tracy Simien .10 .02
❑ 157 Neil Smith .20 .07
❑ 158 William White .10 .02
❑ 159 Joe Aska RC .10 .02
❑ 160 Greg Biekert .10 .02
❑ 161 Tim Brown .40 .15
❑ 162 Rob Fredrickson .10 .02
❑ 163 Andrew Glover RC .10 .02
❑ 164 Jeff Hostetler .20 .07
❑ 165 Rocket Ismail .20 .07
❑ 166 Napoleon Kaufman RC 1.25 .50
❑ 167 Terry McDaniel .10 .02
❑ 168 Chester McGlockton .20 .07
❑ 169 Anthony Smith .10 .02
❑ 170 Harvey Williams .10 .02
❑ 171 Steve Wisniewski .10 .02
❑ 172 Gene Atkins .10 .02
❑ 173 Aubrey Beavers .10 .02
❑ 174 Tim Bowens .10 .02
❑ 175 Bryan Cox .10 .02
❑ 176 Jeff Cross .10 .02
❑ 177 Irving Fryar .20 .07
❑ 178 Dan Marino 3.00 1.25
❑ 179 O.J. McDuffie .40 .15
❑ 180 Billy Milner RC .10 .02
❑ 181 Bernie Parmalee .20 .07
❑ 182 Troy Vincent .10 .02
❑ 183 Richmond Webb .10 .02
❑ 184 Derrick Alexander DE RC .10 .02
❑ 185 Cris Carter .40 .15
❑ 186 Jack Del Rio .10 .02
❑ 187 Qadry Ismail .20 .07
❑ 188 Ed McDaniel .10 .02
❑ 189 Randall McDaniel .10 .02
❑ 190 Warren Moon .20 .07
❑ 191 John Randle .20 .07
❑ 192 Jake Reed .20 .07
❑ 193 Fuad Reveiz .10 .02
❑ 194 Korey Stringer RC .20 .07
❑ 195 Dewayne Washington .20 .07
❑ 196 Bruce Armstrong .10 .02
❑ 197 Drew Bledsoe 1.00 .40
❑ 198 Vincent Brisby .10 .02
❑ 199 Vincent Brown .10 .02
❑ 200 Marion Butts .10 .02
❑ 201 Ben Coates .20 .07
❑ 202 Myron Guyton .10 .02
❑ 203 Maurice Hurst .10 .02
❑ 204 Mike Jones .10 .02
❑ 205 Ty Law RC 1.50 .60
❑ 206 Willie McGinest .20 .07
❑ 207 Chris Slade .10 .02
❑ 208 Mario Bates .20 .07
❑ 209 Quinn Early .20 .07
❑ 210 Jim Everett .10 .02
❑ 211 Mark Fields RC .40 .15
❑ 212 Michael Haynes .20 .07
❑ 213 Tyrone Hughes .20 .07
❑ 214 Joe Johnson .10 .02
❑ 215 Wayne Martin .10 .02
❑ 216 Willie Roaf .10 .02
❑ 217 Irv Smith .10 .02
❑ 218 Jimmy Spencer .10 .02
❑ 219 Winfred Tubbs .10 .02
❑ 220 Renaldo Turnbull .10 .02
❑ 221 Michael Brooks .10 .02
❑ 222 Dave Brown .20 .07
❑ 223 Chris Calloway .10 .02
❑ 224 Howard Cross .10 .02
❑ 225 John Elliott .10 .02
❑ 226 Keith Hamilton .10 .02
❑ 227 Rodney Hampton .20 .07
❑ 228 Thomas Lewis .20 .07
❑ 229 Thomas Randolph .10 .02
❑ 230 Mike Sherrard .10 .02
❑ 231 Michael Strahan .40 .15
❑ 232 Tyrone Wheatley RC 1.25 .50
❑ 233 Brad Baxter .10 .02
❑ 234 Kyle Brady RC .40 .15
❑ 235 Kyle Clifton .10 .02
❑ 236 Hugh Douglas RC .40 .15
❑ 237 Boomer Esiason .20 .07
❑ 238 Aaron Glenn .10 .02
❑ 239 Bobby Houston .10 .02
❑ 240 Johnny Johnson .10 .02
❑ 241 Mo Lewis .10 .02
❑ 242 Johnny Mitchell .10 .02
❑ 243 Marvin Washington .10 .02
❑ 244 Fred Barnett .20 .07
❑ 245 Randall Cunningham .40 .15
❑ 246 William Fuller .10 .02
❑ 247 Charlie Garner .40 .15
❑ 248 Andy Harmon .10 .02
❑ 249 Greg Jackson .10 .02
❑ 250 Mike Mamula RC .10 .02
❑ 251 Bill Romanowski .10 .02
❑ 252 Bobby Taylor RC .40 .15
❑ 253 William Thomas .10 .02
❑ 254 Calvin Williams .20 .07
❑ 255 Michael Zordich .10 .02
❑ 256 Chad Brown .20 .07
❑ 257 Mark Bruener RC .20 .07
❑ 258 Dermontti Dawson .20 .07
❑ 259 Barry Foster .20 .07
❑ 260 Kevin Greene .20 .07
❑ 261 Charles Johnson .20 .07
❑ 262 Carnell Lake .10 .02
❑ 263 Greg Lloyd .20 .07
❑ 264 Byron Bam Morris .10 .02
❑ 265 Neil O'Donnell .20 .07
❑ 266 Darren Perry .10 .02
❑ 267 Ray Seals .10 .02
❑ 268 Kordell Stewart RC 1.50 .60
❑ 269 John L. Williams .10 .02
❑ 270 Rod Woodson .20 .07
❑ 271 Jerome Bettis .40 .15
❑ 272 Isaac Bruce .75 .30
❑ 273 Kevin Carter RC .40 .15
❑ 274 Shane Conlan .10 .02
❑ 275 Troy Drayton .10 .02
❑ 276 Sean Gilbert .20 .07
❑ 277 Todd Lyght .10 .02
❑ 278 Chris Miller .10 .02
❑ 279 Anthony Newman .10 .02
❑ 280 Roman Phifer .10 .02
❑ 281 Robert Young .10 .02
❑ 282 John Carney .10 .02
❑ 283 Andre Coleman .10 .02
❑ 284 Courtney Hall .10 .02
❑ 285 Ronnie Harmon .10 .02
❑ 286 Dwayne Harper .10 .02
❑ 287 Stan Humphries .20 .07
❑ 288 Shawn Jefferson .10 .02
❑ 289 Tony Martin .20 .07
❑ 290 Natrone Means .20 .07
❑ 291 Chris Mims .10 .02
❑ 292 Leslie O'Neal .20 .07
❑ 293 Junior Seau .40 .15
❑ 294 Mark Seay .20 .07
❑ 295 Eric Davis .10 .02
❑ 296 William Floyd .20 .07
❑ 297 Merton Hanks .10 .02
❑ 298 Brent Jones .10 .02
❑ 299 Ken Norton Jr. .20 .07
❑ 300 Gary Plummer .10 .02
❑ 301 Jerry Rice 1.50 .60
❑ 302 Deion Sanders 1.00 .40
❑ 303 Jesse Sapolu .10 .02
❑ 304 J.J. Stokes RC .40 .15
❑ 305 Dana Stubblefield .20 .07
❑ 306 John Taylor .10 .02
❑ 307 Steve Wallace .10 .02
❑ 308 Lee Woodall .10 .02
❑ 309 Bryant Young .20 .07
❑ 310 Steve Young 1.25 .50
❑ 311 Sam Adams .10 .02
❑ 312 Howard Ballard .10 .02
❑ 313 Robert Blackmon .10 .02
❑ 314 Brian Blades .20 .07
❑ 315 Joey Galloway RC 1.50 .60
❑ 316 Carlton Gray .10 .02
❑ 317 Cortez Kennedy .20 .07
❑ 318 Rick Mirer .20 .07
❑ 319 Eugene Robinson .10 .02
❑ 320 Chris Warren .20 .07
❑ 321 Terry Wooden .10 .02
❑ 322 Derrick Brooks RC 1.50 .60
❑ 323 Lawrence Dawsey .10 .02

❑ 324	Trent Dilfer	.40	.15
❑ 325	Santana Dotson	.10	.02
❑ 326	Thomas Everett	.10	.02
❑ 327	Paul Gruber	.10	.02
❑ 328	Jackie Harris	.10	.02
❑ 329	Courtney Hawkins	.10	.02
❑ 330	Martin Mayhew	.10	.02
❑ 331	Hardy Nickerson	.10	.02
❑ 332	Errict Rhett	.20	.07
❑ 333	Warren Sapp RC	1.50	.60
❑ 334	Charles Wilson	.10	.02
❑ 335	Reggie Brooks	.20	.07
❑ 336	Tom Carter	.10	.02
❑ 337	Henry Ellard	.20	.07
❑ 338	Ricky Ervins	.10	.02
❑ 339	Darrell Green	.10	.02
❑ 340	Ken Harvey	.10	.02
❑ 341	Brian Mitchell	.10	.02
❑ 342	Cory Raymer RC	.10	.02
❑ 343	Heath Shuler	.20	.07
❑ 344	Michael Westbrook RC	.40	.15
❑ 345	Tony Woods	.10	.02
❑ 346	Checklist	.10	.02
❑ 347	Checklist	.10	.02
❑ 348	Checklist	.10	.02
❑ 349	Checklist	.10	.02
❑ 350	Checklist	.10	.02
❑ 351	Checklist	.10	.02
❑ 352	Checklist	.10	.02
❑ 353	Dave Krieg	.10	.02
❑ 354	Rob Moore	.20	.07
❑ 355	J.J. Birden	.10	.02
❑ 356	Eric Metcalf	.20	.07
❑ 357	Bryce Paup	.20	.07
❑ 358	Willie Green	.20	.07
❑ 359	Derrick Moore	.10	.02
❑ 360	Michael Timpson	.10	.02
❑ 361	Eric Bieniemy	.10	.02
❑ 362	Keenan McCardell	.40	.15
❑ 363	Andre Rison	.20	.07
❑ 364	Lorenzo White	.10	.02
❑ 365	Deion Sanders	1.00	.40
❑ 366	Wade Wilson	.10	.02
❑ 367	Aaron Craver	.10	.02
❑ 368	Michael Dean Perry	.10	.02
❑ 369	Rod Smith WR RC	12.00	5.00
❑ 370	Henry Thomas	.10	.02
❑ 371	Mark Ingram	.10	.02
❑ 372	Chris Chandler	.20	.07
❑ 373	Mel Gray	.10	.02
❑ 374	Flipper Anderson	.10	.02
❑ 375	Craig Erickson	.10	.02
❑ 376	Mark Brunell	1.00	.40
❑ 377	Ernest Givins	.10	.02
❑ 378	Randy Jordan	.10	.02
❑ 379	Webster Slaughter	.10	.02
❑ 380	Tamarick Vanover RC	.40	.15
❑ 381	Gary Clark	.10	.02
❑ 382	Steve Emtman	.10	.02
❑ 383	Eric Green	.10	.02
❑ 384	Louis Oliver	.10	.02
❑ 385	Robert Smith	.40	.15
❑ 386	Dave Meggett	.10	.02
❑ 387	Eric Allen	.10	.02
❑ 388	Wesley Walls	.20	.07
❑ 389	Herschel Walker	.20	.07
❑ 390	Ronald Moore	.10	.02
❑ 391	Adrian Murrell	.20	.07
❑ 392	Charles Wilson	.10	.02
❑ 393	Derrick Fenner	.10	.02
❑ 394	Pat Swilling	.10	.02
❑ 395	Kelvin Martin	.10	.02
❑ 396	Rodney Peete	.10	.02
❑ 397	Ricky Watters	.20	.07
❑ 398	Erric Pegram	.20	.07
❑ 399	Leonard Russell	.10	.02
❑ 400	Alexander Wright	.10	.02
❑ 401	Darrien Gordon	.10	.02
❑ 402	Alfred Pupunu	.10	.02
❑ 403	Elvis Grbac	.40	.15
❑ 404	Derek Loville	.10	.02
❑ 405	Steve Broussard	.10	.02
❑ 406	Ricky Proehl	.10	.02
❑ 407	Bobby Joe Edmonds	.10	.02
❑ 408	Alvin Harper	.10	.02
❑ 409	Dave Moore RC	.10	.02
❑ 410	Terry Allen	.20	.07
❑ 411	Gus Frerotte	.20	.07
❑ 412	Leslie Shepherd RC	.20	.07
❑ 413	Stoney Case RC	.10	.02
❑ 414	Frank Sanders RC	.40	.15
❑ 415	Roell Preston RC	.20	.07
❑ 416	Lorenzo Styles RC	.10	.02
❑ 417	Justin Armour RC	.10	.02
❑ 418	Todd Collins RC	1.25	.50
❑ 419	Darick Holmes RC	.20	.07
❑ 420	Kerry Collins	.60	.25
❑ 421	Tyrone Poole	.20	.07
❑ 422	Rashaan Salaam	.20	.07
❑ 423	Todd Sauerbrun RC	.10	.02
❑ 424	Ki-Jana Carter	.40	.15
❑ 425	David Dunn RC	.10	.02
❑ 426	Ernest Hunter RC	.10	.02
❑ 427	Eric Zeier RC	.40	.15
❑ 428	Eric Bjornson RC	.10	.02
❑ 429	Sherman Williams	.10	.02
❑ 430	Terrell Davis RC	2.50	1.00
❑ 431	Luther Elliss	.10	.02
❑ 432	Kez McCorvey RC	.10	.02
❑ 433	Antonio Freeman RC	1.25	.50
❑ 434	Craig Newsome RC	.10	.02
❑ 435	Steve McNair	1.50	.60
❑ 436	Chris Sanders RC	.20	.07
❑ 437	Zack Crockett RC	.20	.07
❑ 438	Ellis Johnson	.10	.02
❑ 439	Tony Boselli	.40	.15
❑ 440	James O. Stewart	.40	.15
❑ 441	Trezelle Jenkins	.10	.02
❑ 442	Tamarick Vanover	.40	.15
❑ 443	Derrick Alexander DE	.10	.02
❑ 444	Chad May RC	.10	.02
❑ 445	James A.Stewart RC	.10	.02
❑ 446	Ty Law	.40	.15
❑ 447	Curtis Martin RC	3.00	1.25
❑ 448	Will Moore RC	.10	.02
❑ 449	Mark Fields	.20	.07
❑ 450	Ray Zellars RC	.20	.07
❑ 451	Charles Way RC	.10	.02
❑ 452	Tyrone Wheatley	.40	.15
❑ 453	Kyle Brady	.40	.15
❑ 454	Wayne Chrebet RC	2.50	1.00
❑ 455	Hugh Douglas	.20	.07
❑ 456	Chris T.Jones RC	.10	.02
❑ 457	Mike Mamula	.10	.02
❑ 458	Fred McCrary RC	.10	.02
❑ 459	Bobby Taylor	.40	.15
❑ 460	Mark Bruener	.20	.07
❑ 461	Kordell Stewart	.60	.25
❑ 462	Kevin Carter	.20	.07
❑ 463	Lovell Pinkney RC	.10	.02
❑ 464	Johnny Thomas WR RC	.10	.02
❑ 465	Terrell Fletcher RC	.10	.02
❑ 466	Jimmy Oliver RC	.10	.02
❑ 467	J.J. Stokes	.40	.15
❑ 468	Christian Fauria RC	.20	.07
❑ 469	Joey Galloway	.60	.25
❑ 470	Derrick Brooks	.60	.25
❑ 471	Warren Sapp	.40	.15
❑ 472	Michael Westbrook	.40	.15
❑ 473	Garrison Hearst ES	.40	.15
❑ 474	Jeff George ES	.20	.07
❑ 475	Terance Mathis ES	.20	.07
❑ 476	Andre Reed ES	.20	.07
❑ 477	Bruce Smith ES	.40	.15
❑ 478	Lamar Lathon ES	.10	.02
❑ 479	Curtis Conway ES	.40	.15
❑ 480	Jeff Blake ES	.40	.15
❑ 481	Carl Pickens ES	.20	.07
❑ 482	Eric Turner ES	.10	.02
❑ 483	Troy Aikman ES	.75	.30
❑ 484	Michael Irvin ES	.40	.15
❑ 485	Emmitt Smith ES	1.25	.50
❑ 486	John Elway ES	1.50	.60
❑ 487	Shannon Sharpe ES	.20	.07
❑ 488	Herman Moore ES	.40	.15
❑ 489	Barry Sanders ES	1.25	.50
❑ 490	Brett Favre ES	1.50	.60
❑ 491	Reggie White ES	.40	.15
❑ 492	Haywood Jeffires ES	.10	.02
❑ 493	Sean Dawkins ES	.10	.02
❑ 494	Marshall Faulk ES	1.00	.40
❑ 495	Desmond Howard ES	.20	.07
❑ 496	Steve Bono ES	.20	.07
❑ 497	Derrick Thomas ES	.40	.15
❑ 498	Irving Fryar ES	.20	.07
❑ 499	Terry Kirby ES	.20	.07
❑ 500	Dan Marino ES	1.50	.60
❑ 501	O.J. McDuffie ES	.40	.15
❑ 502	Cris Carter ES	.40	.15
❑ 503	Warren Moon ES	.20	.07
❑ 504	Jake Reed ES	.20	.07
❑ 505	Drew Bledsoe ES	.40	.15
❑ 506	Ben Coates ES	.20	.07
❑ 507	Jim Everett ES	.10	.02
❑ 508	Rodney Hampton ES	.20	.07
❑ 509	Mo Lewis ES	.10	.02
❑ 510	Tim Brown ES	.40	.15
❑ 511	Jeff Hostetler ES	.20	.07
❑ 512	Rocket Ismail ES	.20	.07
❑ 513	Chester McGlockton ES	.20	.07
❑ 514	Fred Barnett ES	.20	.07
❑ 515	Greg Lloyd ES	.20	.07
❑ 516	Byron Bam Morris ES	.10	.02
❑ 517	Rod Woodson ES	.20	.07
❑ 518	Jerome Bettis ES	.40	.15
❑ 519	Isaac Bruce ES	.40	.15
❑ 520	Stan Humphries ES	.20	.07
❑ 521	Natrone Means ES	.20	.07
❑ 522	Junior Seau ES	.40	.15
❑ 523	William Floyd ES	.20	.07
❑ 524	Jerry Rice ES	.75	.30
❑ 525	Steve Young ES	.60	.25
❑ 526	Cortez Kennedy ES	.20	.07
❑ 527	Rick Mirer ES	.20	.07
❑ 528	Chris Warren ES	.20	.07
❑ 529	Trent Dilfer ES	.40	.15
❑ 530	Errict Rhett ES	.20	.07
❑ 531	Darrell Green ES	.10	.02
❑ 532	Heath Shuler ES	.20	.07
❑ 533	Stoney Case RO	.10	.02
❑ 534	Eric Zeier RO	.20	.07
❑ 535	Kerry Collins RO	.20	.07
❑ 536	Steve McNair RO	1.25	.50
❑ 537	Kordell Stewart RO	.60	.25
❑ 538	Rob Johnson RO RC	1.00	.40
❑ 539	Eric Ball EE	.10	.02
❑ 540	Darrick Brownlow EE	.10	.02
❑ 541	Paul Butcher EE	.10	.02
❑ 542	Carlester Crumpler EE	.10	.02
❑ 543	Maurice Douglas EE	.10	.02
❑ 544	Keith Elias EE RC	.10	.02
❑ 545	Kenneth Gant EE	.10	.02
❑ 546	Corey Harris EE	.10	.02
❑ 547	Andre Hastings EE	.20	.07
❑ 548	Thomas Homco EE	.10	.02
❑ 549	Lenny McGill EE	.10	.02
❑ 550	Mark Pike EE	.10	.02
❑ P1	Promo Sheet	2.00	.75
❑ P264	Byron Bam Morris Prototype	1.00	.40

1996 Ultra

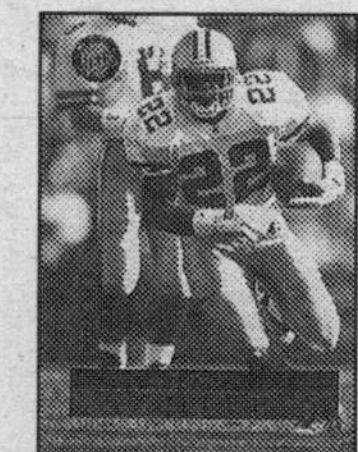

❑	COMPLETE SET (200)	25.00	10.00
❑ 1	Larry Centers	.25	.08
❑ 2	Garrison Hearst	.25	.08
❑ 3	Rob Moore	.25	.08

❑ 4 Eric Swann	.10	.02
❑ 5 Aeneas Williams	.10	.02
❑ 6 Bert Emanuel	.25	.08
❑ 7 Jeff George	.25	.08
❑ 8 Craig Heyward	.10	.02
❑ 9 Terance Mathis	.10	.02
❑ 10 Eric Metcalf	.10	.02
❑ 11 Cornelius Bennett	.10	.02
❑ 12 Darick Holmes	.10	.02
❑ 13 Jim Kelly	.50	.20
❑ 14 Bryce Paup	.10	.02
❑ 15 Bruce Smith	.25	.08
❑ 16 Mark Carrier WR	.10	.02
❑ 17 Kerry Collins	.50	.20
❑ 18 Lamar Lathon	.10	.02
❑ 19 Derrick Moore	.10	.02
❑ 20 Tyrone Poole	.10	.02
❑ 21 Curtis Conway	.50	.20
❑ 22 Jeff Graham	.10	.02
❑ 23 Raymont Harris	.25	.08
❑ 24 Erik Kramer	.10	.02
❑ 25 Rashaan Salaam	.25	.08
❑ 26 Jeff Blake	.50	.20
❑ 27 Ki-Jana Carter	.25	.08
❑ 28 Carl Pickens	.25	.08
❑ 29 Darnay Scott	.25	.08
❑ 30 Dan Wilkinson	.10	.02
❑ 31 Leroy Hoard	.10	.02
❑ 32 Michael Jackson	.25	.08
❑ 33 Andre Rison	.25	.08
❑ 34 Vinny Testaverde	.25	.08
❑ 35 Eric Turner	.10	.02
❑ 36 Troy Aikman	1.25	.50
❑ 37 Charles Haley	.25	.08
❑ 38 Michael Irvin	.50	.20
❑ 39 Daryl Johnston	.25	.08
❑ 40 Jay Novacek	.10	.02
❑ 41 Deion Sanders	.75	.30
❑ 42 Emmitt Smith	2.00	.75
❑ 43 Steve Atwater	.10	.02
❑ 44 Terrell Davis	1.00	.40
❑ 45 John Elway	2.50	1.00
❑ 46 Anthony Miller	.25	.08
❑ 47 Shannon Sharpe	.25	.08
❑ 48 Scott Mitchell	.25	.08
❑ 49 Herman Moore	.25	.08
❑ 50 Johnnie Morton	.25	.08
❑ 51 Brett Perriman	.10	.02
❑ 52 Barry Sanders	2.00	.75
❑ 53 Chris Spielman	.10	.02
❑ 54 Edgar Bennett	.25	.08
❑ 55 Robert Brooks	.50	.20
❑ 56 Mark Chmura	.25	.08
❑ 57 Brett Favre	2.50	1.00
❑ 58 Reggie White	.50	.20
❑ 59 Mel Gray	.10	.02
❑ 60 Haywood Jeffires	.10	.02
❑ 61 Steve McNair	1.00	.40
❑ 62 Chris Sanders	.25	.08
❑ 63 Rodney Thomas	.10	.02
❑ 64 Quentin Coryatt	.10	.02
❑ 65 Sean Dawkins	.10	.02
❑ 66 Ken Dilger	.25	.08
❑ 67 Marshall Faulk	.60	.25
❑ 68 Jim Harbaugh	.25	.08
❑ 69 Tony Boselli	.10	.02
❑ 70 Mark Brunell	.75	.30
❑ 71 Desmond Howard	.25	.08
❑ 72 Jimmy Smith	.50	.20
❑ 73 James O. Stewart	.25	.08
❑ 74 Marcus Allen	.50	.20
❑ 75 Steve Bono	.10	.02
❑ 76 Lake Dawson	.10	.02
❑ 77 Neil Smith	.25	.08
❑ 78 Derrick Thomas	.50	.20
❑ 79 Tamarick Vanover	.25	.08
❑ 80 Bryan Cox	.10	.02
❑ 81 Irving Fryar	.25	.08
❑ 82 Eric Green	.10	.02
❑ 83 Dan Marino	2.50	1.00
❑ 84 O.J. McDuffie	.25	.08
❑ 85 Bernie Parmalee	.10	.02
❑ 86 Cris Carter	.50	.20
❑ 87 Qadry Ismail	.25	.08

❑ 88 Warren Moon	.25	.08
❑ 89 Jake Reed	.25	.08
❑ 90 Robert Smith	.25	.08
❑ 91 Drew Bledsoe	.75	.30
❑ 92 Vincent Brisby	.10	.02
❑ 93 Ben Coates	.25	.08
❑ 94 Curtis Martin	1.00	.40
❑ 95 Willie McGinest	.10	.02
❑ 96 Dave Meggett	.10	.02
❑ 97 Mario Bates	.25	.08
❑ 98 Quinn Early	.10	.02
❑ 99 Jim Everett	.10	.02
❑ 100 Michael Haynes	.10	.02
❑ 101 Renaldo Turnbull	.10	.02
❑ 102 Dave Brown	.10	.02
❑ 103 Rodney Hampton	.25	.08
❑ 104 Mike Sherrard	.10	.02
❑ 105 Phillippi Sparks	.10	.02
❑ 106 Tyrone Wheatley	.25	.08
❑ 107 Hugh Douglas	.25	.08
❑ 108 Boomer Esiason	.25	.08
❑ 109 Aaron Glenn	.10	.02
❑ 110 Mo Lewis	.10	.02
❑ 111 Johnny Mitchell	.10	.02
❑ 112 Tim Brown	.50	.20
❑ 113 Jeff Hostetler	.10	.02
❑ 114 Rocket Ismail	.10	.02
❑ 115 Chester McGlockton	.10	.02
❑ 116 Harvey Williams	.10	.02
❑ 117 Fred Barnett	.10	.02
❑ 118 William Fuller	.10	.02
❑ 119 Charlie Garner	.25	.08
❑ 120 Ricky Watters	.25	.08
❑ 121 Calvin Williams	.10	.02
❑ 122 Kevin Greene	.25	.08
❑ 123 Greg Lloyd	.25	.08
❑ 124 Byron Bam Morris	.10	.02
❑ 125 Neil O'Donnell	.25	.08
❑ 126 Erric Pegram	.10	.02
❑ 127 Kordell Stewart	.50	.20
❑ 128 Yancey Thigpen	.25	.08
❑ 129 Rod Woodson	.25	.08
❑ 130 Jerome Bettis	.50	.20
❑ 131 Isaac Bruce	.50	.20
❑ 132 Troy Drayton	.10	.02
❑ 133 Sean Gilbert	.10	.02
❑ 134 Chris Miller	.10	.02
❑ 135 Andre Coleman	.10	.02
❑ 136 Ronnie Harmon	.10	.02
❑ 137 Aaron Hayden RC	.10	.02
❑ 138 Stan Humphries	.25	.08
❑ 139 Natrone Means	.25	.08
❑ 140 Junior Seau	.50	.20
❑ 141 William Floyd	.25	.08
❑ 142 Merton Hanks	.10	.02
❑ 143 Brent Jones	.10	.02
❑ 144 Derek Loville	.10	.02
❑ 145 Jerry Rice	1.25	.50
❑ 146 J.J. Stokes	.50	.20
❑ 147 Steve Young	1.00	.40
❑ 148 Brian Blades	.10	.02
❑ 149 Joey Galloway	.50	.20
❑ 150 Cortez Kennedy	.10	.02
❑ 151 Rick Mirer	.25	.08
❑ 152 Chris Warren	.25	.08
❑ 153 Derrick Brooks	.50	.20
❑ 154 Trent Dilfer	.50	.20
❑ 155 Alvin Harper	.10	.02
❑ 156 Jackie Harris	.10	.02
❑ 157 Hardy Nickerson	.10	.02
❑ 158 Errict Rhett	.25	.08
❑ 159 Terry Allen	.25	.08
❑ 160 Henry Ellard	.10	.02
❑ 161 Brian Mitchell	.10	.02
❑ 162 Heath Shuler	.25	.08
❑ 163 Michael Westbrook	.50	.20
❑ 164 Tim Biakabutuka RC	.50	.20
❑ 165 Tony Brackens RC	.50	.20
❑ 166 Rickey Dudley RC	.50	.20
❑ 167 Bobby Engram RC	.50	.20
❑ 168 Daryl Gardener RC	.10	.02
❑ 169 Eddie George RC	1.50	.60
❑ 170 Terry Glenn RC	1.25	.50
❑ 171 Kevin Hardy RC	.50	.20

❑ 172 Keyshawn Johnson RC	1.25	.50
❑ 173 Cedric Jones RC	.10	.02
❑ 174 Leeland McElroy RC	.25	.08
❑ 175 Jonathan Ogden RC	.50	.20
❑ 176 Lawrence Phillips RC	.50	.20
❑ 177 Simeon Rice RC	1.25	.50
❑ 178 Regan Upshaw RC	.10	.02
❑ 179 Justin Armour FI	.10	.02
❑ 180 Kyle Brady FI	.10	.02
❑ 181 Devin Bush FI	.10	.02
❑ 182 Kevin Carter FI	.10	.02
❑ 183 Wayne Chrebet FI	.75	.30
❑ 184 Napoleon Kaufman FI	.50	.20
❑ 185 Frank Sanders FI	.25	.08
❑ 186 Warren Sapp FI	.10	.02
❑ 187 Eric Zeier FI	.10	.02
❑ 188 Ray Zellars FI	.10	.02
❑ 189 Bill Brooks SW	.10	.02
❑ 190 Chris Calloway SW	.10	.02
❑ 191 Zack Crockett SW	.10	.02
❑ 192 Antonio Freeman SW	.50	.20
❑ 193 Tyrone Hughes SW	.10	.02
❑ 194 Daryl Johnston SW	.25	.08
❑ 195 Tony Martin SW	.10	.02
❑ 196 Keenan McCardell SW	.50	.20
❑ 197 Glyn Milburn SW	.10	.02
❑ 198 David Palmer SW	.10	.02
❑ 199 Checklist	.10	.02
❑ 200 Checklist	.10	.02
❑ P1 Promo Sheet	2.00	.75

1997 Ultra

❑ COMPLETE SET (350)	80.00	40.00
❑ COMP.SERIES 1 (200)	30.00	15.00
❑ COMP.SERIES 2 (150)	50.00	25.00
❑ 1 Brett Favre	2.50	1.25
❑ 2 Ricky Watters	.40	.15
❑ 3 Dan Marino	2.50	1.00
❑ 4 Bryan Still	.25	.08
❑ 5 Chester McGlockton	.25	.08
❑ 6 Tim Biakabutuka	.40	.15
❑ 7 Dave Brown	.25	.08
❑ 8 Mike Alstott	.60	.25
❑ 9 O.J. McDuffie	.40	.15
❑ 10 Mark Brunell	.75	.30
❑ 11 Michael Bates	.25	.08
❑ 12 Tyrone Wheatley	.40	.15
❑ 13 Eddie George	.60	.25
❑ 14 Kevin Greene	.40	.15
❑ 15 Jerris McPhail	.25	.08
❑ 16 Harvey Williams	.25	.08
❑ 17 Eric Swann	.25	.08
❑ 18 Carl Pickens	.40	.15
❑ 19 Terrell Davis	.75	.30
❑ 20 Charles Way	.25	.08
❑ 21 Jamie Asher	.25	.08
❑ 22 Qadry Ismail	.40	.15
❑ 23 Lawrence Phillips	.25	.08
❑ 24 John Friesz	.25	.08
❑ 25 Dorsey Levens	.60	.25
❑ 26 Willie McGinest	.25	.08
❑ 27 Chris T. Jones	.25	.08
❑ 28 Cortez Kennedy	.25	.08
❑ 29 Raymont Harris	.25	.08
❑ 30 William Roaf	.25	.08
❑ 31 Ted Johnson	.25	.08
❑ 32 Tony Martin	.40	.15

❑ 33	Jim Everett	.25	.08
❑ 34	Ray Zellars	.25	.08
❑ 35	Derrick Alexander WR	.40	.15
❑ 36	Leonard Russell	.25	.08
❑ 37	William Thomas	.25	.08
❑ 38	Karim Abdul-Jabbar	.40	.15
❑ 39	Kevin Turner	.25	.08
❑ 40	Robert Brooks	.40	.15
❑ 41	Kent Graham	.25	.08
❑ 42	Tony Brackens	.25	.08
❑ 43	Rodney Hampton	.40	.15
❑ 44	Drew Bledsoe	.75	.30
❑ 45	Barry Sanders	2.00	.75
❑ 46	Tim Brown	.60	.25
❑ 47	Reggie White	.60	.25
❑ 48	Terry Allen	.60	.25
❑ 49	Jim Harbaugh	.40	.15
❑ 50	John Elway	2.50	1.00
❑ 51	William Floyd	.40	.15
❑ 52	Michael Jackson	.40	.15
❑ 53	Larry Centers	.40	.15
❑ 54	Emmitt Smith	2.00	.75
❑ 55	Bruce Smith	.40	.15
❑ 56	Terrell Owens	.75	.30
❑ 57	Deion Sanders	.60	.25
❑ 58	Neil O'Donnell	.40	.15
❑ 59	Kordell Stewart	.60	.25
❑ 60	Bobby Engram	.40	.15
❑ 61	Keenan McCardell	.40	.15
❑ 62	Ben Coates	.40	.15
❑ 63	Curtis Martin	.75	.30
❑ 64	Hugh Douglas	.25	.08
❑ 65	Eric Moulds	.60	.25
❑ 66	Derrick Thomas	.60	.25
❑ 67	Byron Bam Morris	.25	.08
❑ 68	Bryan Cox	.25	.08
❑ 69	Rob Moore	.40	.15
❑ 70	Michael Haynes	.25	.08
❑ 71	Brian Mitchell	.25	.08
❑ 72	Alex Molden	.25	.08
❑ 73	Steve Young	.75	.30
❑ 74	Andre Reed	.40	.15
❑ 75	Michael Westbrook	.40	.15
❑ 76	Eric Metcalf	.40	.15
❑ 77	Tony Banks	.40	.15
❑ 78	Ken Dilger	.25	.08
❑ 79	John Henry Mills RC	.25	.08
❑ 80	Ashley Ambrose	.25	.08
❑ 81	Jason Dunn	.25	.08
❑ 82	Trent Dilfer	.60	.25
❑ 83	Wayne Chrebet	.60	.25
❑ 84	Ty Detmer	.40	.15
❑ 85	Aeneas Williams	.25	.08
❑ 86	Frank Wycheck	.25	.08
❑ 87	Jessie Tuggle	.25	.08
❑ 88	Steve McNair	.75	.30
❑ 89	Chris Slade	.25	.08
❑ 90	Anthony Johnson	.25	.08
❑ 91	Simeon Rice	.40	.15
❑ 92	Mike Tomczak	.25	.08
❑ 93	Sean Jones	.25	.08
❑ 94	Wesley Walls	.40	.15
❑ 95	Thurman Thomas	.60	.25
❑ 96	Scott Mitchell	.40	.15
❑ 97	Desmond Howard	.40	.15
❑ 98	Chris Warren	.40	.15
❑ 99	Glyn Milburn	.25	.08
❑ 100	Vinny Testaverde	.40	.15
❑ 101	James O.Stewart	.40	.15
❑ 102	Iheanyi Uwaezuoke	.25	.08
❑ 103	Stan Humphries	.40	.15
❑ 104	Terance Mathis	.40	.15
❑ 105	Thomas Lewis	.25	.08
❑ 106	Eddie Kennison	.40	.15
❑ 107	Rashaan Salaam	.25	.08
❑ 108	Curtis Conway	.40	.15
❑ 109	Chris Sanders	.25	.08
❑ 110	Marcus Allen	.60	.25
❑ 111	Gilbert Brown	.40	.15
❑ 112	Jason Sehorn	.40	.15
❑ 113	Zach Thomas	.60	.25
❑ 114	Bobby Hebert	.25	.08
❑ 115	Herman Moore	.40	.15
❑ 116	Ray Lewis	1.00	.40
❑ 117	Darnay Scott	.40	.15
❑ 118	Jamal Anderson	.60	.25
❑ 119	Keyshawn Johnson	.60	.25
❑ 120	Adrian Murrell	.40	.15
❑ 121	Sam Mills	.25	.08
❑ 122	Irving Fryar	.40	.15
❑ 123	Ki-Jana Carter	.25	.08
❑ 124	Gus Frerotte	.25	.08
❑ 125	Terry Glenn	.60	.25
❑ 126	Quentin Coryatt	.25	.08
❑ 127	Robert Smith	.40	.15
❑ 128	Jeff Blake	.40	.15
❑ 129	Natrone Means	.40	.15
❑ 130	Isaac Bruce	.60	.25
❑ 131	Lamar Lathon	.25	.08
❑ 132	Johnnie Morton	.40	.15
❑ 133	Jerry Rice	1.25	.50
❑ 134	Errict Rhett	.25	.08
❑ 135	Junior Seau	.60	.25
❑ 136	Joey Galloway	.40	.15
❑ 137	Napoleon Kaufman	.60	.25
❑ 138	Troy Aikman	1.25	.50
❑ 139	Kevin Hardy	.25	.08
❑ 140	Jimmy Smith	.40	.15
❑ 141	Edgar Bennett	.40	.15
❑ 142	Hardy Nickerson	.25	.08
❑ 143	Greg Lloyd	.25	.08
❑ 144	Dale Carter	.25	.08
❑ 145	Jake Reed	.40	.15
❑ 146	Cris Carter	.60	.25
❑ 147	Todd Collins	.25	.08
❑ 148	Mel Gray	.25	.08
❑ 149	Lawyer Milloy	.40	.15
❑ 150	Kimble Anders	.40	.15
❑ 151	Darick Holmes	.25	.08
❑ 152	Bert Emanuel	.40	.15
❑ 153	Marshall Faulk	.75	.30
❑ 154	Frank Sanders	.40	.15
❑ 155	Leeland McElroy	.25	.08
❑ 156	Rickey Dudley	.40	.15
❑ 157	Tamarick Vanover	.40	.15
❑ 158	Kerry Collins	.60	.25
❑ 159	Jeff Graham	.25	.08
❑ 160	Jerome Bettis	.60	.25
❑ 161	Greg Hill	.25	.08
❑ 162	John Mobley	.25	.08
❑ 163	Michael Irvin	.60	.25
❑ 164	Marvin Harrison	.60	.25
❑ 165	Jim Schwantz RC	.25	.08
❑ 166	Jermaine Lewis	.60	.25
❑ 167	Levon Kirkland	.25	.08
❑ 168	Nilo Silvan	.25	.08
❑ 169	Ken Norton	.25	.08
❑ 170	Yancey Thigpen	.40	.15
❑ 171	Antonio Freeman	.60	.25
❑ 172	Terry Kirby	.40	.15
❑ 173	Brad Johnson	.60	.25
❑ 174	Reidel Anthony RC	.60	.25
❑ 175	Tiki Barber RC	5.00	2.00
❑ 176	Pat Barnes RC	.60	.25
❑ 177	Michael Booker RC	.25	.08
❑ 178	Peter Boulware RC	.60	.25
❑ 179	Rae Carruth RC	.25	.08
❑ 180	Troy Davis RC	.40	.15
❑ 181	Corey Dillon RC	5.00	2.00
❑ 182	Jim Druckenmiller RC	.40	.15
❑ 183	Warrick Dunn RC	2.50	1.00
❑ 184	James Farrior RC	.60	.25
❑ 185	Yatil Green RC	.40	.15
❑ 186	Walter Jones RC	.60	.25
❑ 187	Tom Knight RC	.25	.08
❑ 188	Sam Madison RC	.60	.25
❑ 189	Tyrus McCloud RC	.25	.08
❑ 190	Orlando Pace RC	.60	.25
❑ 191	Jake Plummer RC	4.00	1.50
❑ 192	Dwayne Rudd RC	.60	.25
❑ 193	Darrell Russell RC	.25	.08
❑ 194	Sedrick Shaw RC	.40	.15
❑ 195	Shawn Springs RC	.40	.15
❑ 196	Bryant Westbrook RC	.25	.08
❑ 197	Danny Wuerffel RC	.60	.25
❑ 198	Reinard Wilson RC	.40	.15
❑ 199	Checklist	.25	.08
❑ 200	Checklist	.60	.25
❑ 201	Rick Mirer	.25	.08
❑ 202	Torrance Small	.25	.08
❑ 203	Ricky Proehl	.25	.08
❑ 204	Will Blackwell RC	.40	.15
❑ 205	Warrick Dunn	1.25	.50
❑ 206	Rob Johnson	.60	.25
❑ 207	Jim Schwantz	.25	.08
❑ 208	Ike Hilliard RC	1.25	.50
❑ 209	Chris Canty RC	.25	.08
❑ 210	Chris Boniol	.25	.08
❑ 211	Jim Druckenmiller	.25	.08
❑ 212	Tony Gonzalez RC	2.50	1.00
❑ 213	Scottie Graham	.25	.08
❑ 214	Byron Hanspard RC	.40	.15
❑ 215	Gary Brown	.25	.08
❑ 216	Darrell Russell	.25	.08
❑ 217	Sedrick Shaw	.40	.15
❑ 218	Boomer Esiason	.40	.15
❑ 219	Peter Boulware	.40	.15
❑ 220	Willie Green	.25	.08
❑ 221	Dietrich Jells	.25	.08
❑ 222	Freddie Jones RC	.40	.15
❑ 223	Eric Metcalf	.40	.15
❑ 224	John Henry Mills	.25	.08
❑ 225	Michael Timpson	.25	.08
❑ 226	Danny Wuerffel	.60	.25
❑ 227	Daimon Shelton RC	.25	.08
❑ 228	Henry Ellard	.25	.08
❑ 229	Flipper Anderson	.25	.08
❑ 230	Hunter Goodwin RC	.25	.08
❑ 231	Jay Graham RC	.40	.15
❑ 232	Duce Staley RC	6.00	2.50
❑ 233	Lamar Thomas	.25	.08
❑ 234	Rod Woodson	.40	.15
❑ 235	Zack Crockett	.25	.08
❑ 236	Ernie Mills	.25	.08
❑ 237	Kyle Brady	.25	.08
❑ 238	Jesse Campbell	.25	.08
❑ 239	Anthony Miller	.25	.08
❑ 240	Michael Haynes	.25	.08
❑ 241	Qadry Ismail	.40	.15
❑ 242	Tom Knight	.25	.08
❑ 243	Brian Manning RC	.25	.08
❑ 244	Derrick Mayes	.40	.15
❑ 245	Jamie Sharper RC	.40	.15
❑ 246	Sherman Williams	.25	.08
❑ 247	Yatil Green	.40	.15
❑ 248	Howard Griffith	.25	.08
❑ 249	Brian Blades	.25	.08
❑ 250	Mark Chmura	.40	.15
❑ 251	Chris Darkins	.25	.08
❑ 252	Willie Davis	.25	.08
❑ 253	Quinn Early	.25	.08
❑ 254	Marc Edwards RC	.25	.08
❑ 255	Charlie Jones	.25	.08
❑ 256	Jake Plummer	1.50	.60
❑ 257	Heath Shuler	.25	.08
❑ 258	Fred Barnett	.25	.08
❑ 259	William Henderson	.40	.15
❑ 260	Michael Booker	.25	.08
❑ 261	Chad Brown	.25	.08
❑ 262	Garrison Hearst	.40	.15
❑ 263	Leon Johnson RC	.40	.15
❑ 264	Antowain Smith RC	2.00	.75
❑ 265	Darnell Autry RC	.40	.15
❑ 266	Craig Heyward	.25	.08
❑ 267	Walter Jones	.25	.08
❑ 268	Dexter Coakley RC	.60	.25
❑ 269	Mercury Hayes	.25	.08
❑ 270	Brett Perriman	.25	.08
❑ 271	Chris Spielman	.25	.08
❑ 272	Kevin Greene	.40	.15
❑ 273	Kevin Lockett RC	.40	.15
❑ 274	Troy Davis	.40	.15
❑ 275	Brent Jones	.25	.08
❑ 276	Chris Chandler	.40	.15
❑ 277	Bryant Westbrook	.25	.08
❑ 278	Desmond Howard	.40	.15
❑ 279	Tyrone Hughes	.25	.08
❑ 280	Kez McCorvey	.25	.08
❑ 281	Stephen Davis	.60	.25
❑ 282	Steve Everitt	.25	.08
❑ 283	Andre Hastings	.25	.08
❑ 284	Marcus Robinson RC	5.00	2.00

❑ 285 Donnell Woolford .25 .08
❑ 286 Mario Bates .25 .08
❑ 287 Corey Dillon 2.00 .75
❑ 288 Jackie Harris .25 .08
❑ 289 Lorenzo Neal .25 .08
❑ 290 Anthony Pleasant .25 .08
❑ 291 Andre Rison .40 .15
❑ 292 Amani Toomer .40 .15
❑ 293 Eric Turner .25 .08
❑ 294 Elvis Grbac .40 .15
❑ 295 Cris Dishman .25 .08
❑ 296 Tom Carter .25 .08
❑ 297 Mark Carrier DB .25 .08
❑ 298 Orlando Pace .40 .15
❑ 299 Jay Riemersma RC .25 .08
❑ 300 Daryl Johnston .40 .15
❑ 301 Joey Kent RC .60 .25
❑ 302 Ronnie Harmon .25 .08
❑ 303 Rocket Ismail .40 .15
❑ 304 Terrell Davis .75 .30
❑ 305 Sean Dawkins .25 .08
❑ 306 Jeff George .40 .15
❑ 307 David Palmer .25 .08
❑ 308 Dwayne Rudd .25 .08
❑ 309 J.J. Stokes .40 .15
❑ 310 James Farrior .40 .15
❑ 311 William Fuller .25 .08
❑ 312 George Jones RC .40 .15
❑ 313 John Allred RC .25 .08
❑ 314 Tony Graziani RC .60 .25
❑ 315 Jeff Hostetler .25 .08
❑ 316 Keith Poole RC .60 .25
❑ 317 Neil Smith .40 .15
❑ 318 Steve Tasker .25 .08
❑ 319 Mike Vrabel RC 15.00 6.00
❑ 320 Pat Barnes .60 .25
❑ 321 James Hundon RC .60 .25
❑ 322 O.J. Santiago RC .40 .15
❑ 323 Billy Davis RC .25 .08
❑ 324 Shawn Springs .40 .15
❑ 325 Reinard Wilson .25 .08
❑ 326 Charles Johnson .40 .15
❑ 327 Micheal Barrow .25 .08
❑ 328 Derrick Mason RC 3.00 1.25
❑ 329 Muhsin Muhammad .40 .15
❑ 330 David LaFleur RC .25 .08
❑ 331 Reidel Anthony .40 .15
❑ 332 Tiki Barber 2.00 .75
❑ 333 Ray Buchanan .25 .08
❑ 334 John Elway 2.50 1.00
❑ 335 Alvin Harper .25 .08
❑ 336 Damon Jones RC .25 .08
❑ 337 Dedric Ward RC .40 .15
❑ 338 Jim Everett .25 .08
❑ 339 Jon Harris .25 .08
❑ 340 Warren Moon .60 .25
❑ 341 Rae Carruth .25 .08
❑ 342 John Mobley .25 .08
❑ 343 Tyrone Poole .25 .08
❑ 344 Mike Cherry RC .25 .08
❑ 345 Horace Copeland .25 .08
❑ 346 Deon Figures .25 .08
❑ 347 Antwuan Wyatt RC .25 .08
❑ 348 Tommy Vardell .25 .08
❑ 349 Checklist (201-324) .25 .08
❑ 350 Checklist (325-350/inserts) .25 .08
❑ S1A T.Davis Sample AU 80.00 40.00
❑ AU3 Dan Marino AU 100.00 40.00
❑ S1 Terrell Davis Sample 3.00 1.25

1998 Ultra

❑ COMPLETE SET (425) 120.00 50.00
❑ COMP.SERIES 1 (225) 80.00 30.00
❑ COMP.SERIES 2 (200) 50.00 25.00
❑ 1 Barry Sanders 2.50 1.00
❑ 2 Brett Favre 3.00 1.50
❑ 3 Napoleon Kaufman .75 .30
❑ 4 Robert Smith .75 .30
❑ 5 Terry Allen .75 .30
❑ 6 Vinny Testaverde .50 .20
❑ 7 William Floyd .30 .10
❑ 8 Carl Pickens .50 .20
❑ 9 Antonio Freeman .75 .30
❑ 10 Ben Coates .50 .20
❑ 11 Elvis Grbac .50 .20
❑ 12 Kerry Collins .50 .20
❑ 13 Orlando Pace .30 .10
❑ 14 Steve Broussard .30 .10
❑ 15 Terance Mathis .50 .20
❑ 16 Tiki Barber .75 .30
❑ 17 Cris Carter .75 .30
❑ 18 Eric Green .30 .10
❑ 19 Eric Metcalf .30 .10
❑ 20 Jeff George .50 .20
❑ 21 Leslie Shepherd .30 .10
❑ 22 Natrone Means .50 .20
❑ 23 Scott Mitchell .50 .20
❑ 24 Adrian Murrell .50 .20
❑ 25 Gilbert Brown .30 .10
❑ 26 Jimmy Smith .50 .20
❑ 27 Mark Bruener .30 .10
❑ 28 Troy Aikman 1.50 .60
❑ 29 Warrick Dunn .75 .30
❑ 30 Jay Graham .30 .10
❑ 31 Craig Whelihan RC .30 .10
❑ 32 Ed McCaffrey .50 .20
❑ 33 Jamie Asher .30 .10
❑ 34 John Randle .50 .20
❑ 35 Michael Jackson .30 .10
❑ 36 Rickey Dudley .30 .10
❑ 37 Sean Dawkins .30 .10
❑ 38 Andre Rison .50 .20
❑ 39 Bert Emanuel .50 .20
❑ 40 Jeff Blake .50 .20
❑ 41 Curtis Conway .50 .20
❑ 42 Eddie Kennison .50 .20
❑ 43 James McKnight .75 .30
❑ 44 Rae Carruth .30 .10
❑ 45 Tito Wooten RC .30 .10
❑ 46 Cris Dishman .30 .10
❑ 47 Ernie Conwell .30 .10
❑ 48 Fred Lane .30 .10
❑ 49 Jamal Anderson .75 .30
❑ 50 Lake Dawson .30 .10
❑ 51 Michael Strahan .50 .20
❑ 52 Reggie White .75 .30
❑ 53 Trent Dilfer .75 .30
❑ 54 Troy Brown .50 .20
❑ 55 Wesley Walls .50 .20
❑ 56 Chidi Ahanotu .30 .10
❑ 57 Dwayne Rudd .30 .10
❑ 58 Jerry Rice 1.50 .60
❑ 59 Johnnie Morton .50 .20
❑ 60 Sherman Williams .30 .10
❑ 61 Steve McNair .75 .30
❑ 62 Will Blackwell .30 .10
❑ 63 Chris Chandler .50 .20
❑ 64 Dexter Coakley .30 .10
❑ 65 Horace Copeland .30 .10
❑ 66 Jerald Moore .30 .10
❑ 67 Leon Johnson .30 .10
❑ 68 Mark Chmura .50 .20
❑ 69 Micheal Barrow .30 .10
❑ 70 Muhsin Muhammad .50 .20
❑ 71 Terry Glenn .75 .30
❑ 72 Tony Brackens .30 .10
❑ 73 Chad Scott .30 .10
❑ 74 Glenn Foley .50 .20
❑ 75 Keenan McCardell .50 .20
❑ 76 Peter Boulware .30 .10
❑ 77 Reidel Anthony .50 .20
❑ 78 William Henderson .50 .20
❑ 79 Tony Martin .50 .20
❑ 80 Tony Gonzalez .75 .30
❑ 81 Charlie Jones .30 .10
❑ 82 Chris Gedney .30 .10
❑ 83 Chris Calloway .30 .10
❑ 84 Dale Carter .30 .10
❑ 85 Ki-Jana Carter .30 .10
❑ 86 Shawn Springs .30 .10
❑ 87 Antowain Smith .75 .30
❑ 88 Eric Turner .30 .10
❑ 89 John Mobley .30 .10
❑ 90 Ken Dilger .30 .10
❑ 91 Bobby Hoying .50 .20
❑ 92 Curtis Martin .75 .30
❑ 93 Drew Bledsoe 1.25 .50
❑ 94 Gary Brown .30 .10
❑ 95 Marvin Harrison .75 .30
❑ 96 Todd Collins .30 .10
❑ 97 Chris Warren .50 .20
❑ 98 Danny Kanell .50 .20
❑ 99 Tony McGee .30 .10
❑ 100 Rod Smith .50 .20
❑ 101 Frank Sanders .50 .20
❑ 102 Irving Fryar .50 .20
❑ 103 Marcus Allen .75 .30
❑ 104 Marshall Faulk 1.00 .40
❑ 105 Bruce Smith .50 .20
❑ 106 Charlie Garner .50 .20
❑ 107 Paul Justin .30 .10
❑ 108 Randal Hill .30 .10
❑ 109 Erik Kramer .30 .10
❑ 110 Rob Moore .50 .20
❑ 111 Shannon Sharpe .50 .20
❑ 112 Warren Moon .75 .30
❑ 113 Zach Thomas .75 .30
❑ 114 Dan Marino 3.00 1.50
❑ 115 Duce Staley 1.00 .40
❑ 116 Eric Swann .30 .10
❑ 117 Kenny Holmes .30 .10
❑ 118 Merton Hanks .30 .10
❑ 119 Raymont Harris .30 .10
❑ 120 Terrell Davis .75 .30
❑ 121 Thurman Thomas .75 .30
❑ 122 Wayne Martin .30 .10
❑ 123 Charles Way .30 .10
❑ 124 Chuck Smith .30 .10
❑ 125 Corey Dillon .75 .30
❑ 126 Darnell Autry .30 .10
❑ 127 Isaac Bruce .75 .30
❑ 128 Joey Galloway .50 .20
❑ 129 Kimble Anders .50 .20
❑ 130 Aeneas Williams .30 .10
❑ 131 Andre Hastings .30 .10
❑ 132 Chad Lewis .50 .20
❑ 133 J.J. Stokes .50 .20
❑ 134 John Elway 3.00 1.25
❑ 135 Karim Abdul-Jabbar .75 .30
❑ 136 Ken Harvey .30 .10
❑ 137 Robert Brooks .50 .20
❑ 138 Rodney Thomas .30 .10
❑ 139 James Stewart .50 .20
❑ 140 Billy Joe Hobert .30 .10
❑ 141 Frank Wycheck .30 .10
❑ 142 Jake Plummer .75 .30
❑ 143 Jerris McPhail .30 .10
❑ 144 Kordell Stewart .75 .30
❑ 145 Terrell Owens .75 .30
❑ 146 Willie Green .30 .10
❑ 147 Anthony Miller .30 .10
❑ 148 Courtney Hawkins .30 .10
❑ 149 Larry Centers .30 .10
❑ 150 Gus Frerotte .30 .10
❑ 151 O.J. McDuffie .50 .20
❑ 152 Ray Zellars .30 .10
❑ 153 Terry Kirby .30 .10
❑ 154 Tommy Vardell .30 .10
❑ 155 Willie Davis .30 .10
❑ 156 Chris Canty .30 .10
❑ 157 Byron Hanspard .30 .10
❑ 158 Chris Penn .30 .10
❑ 159 Damon Jones .30 .10
❑ 160 Derrick Mayes .50 .20
❑ 161 Emmitt Smith 2.50 1.25

❑	162	Keyshawn Johnson	.75	.30
❑	163	Mike Alstott	.75	.30
❑	164	Tom Carter	.30	.10
❑	165	Tony Banks	.50	.20
❑	166	Bryant Westbrook	.30	.10
❑	167	Chris Sanders	.30	.10
❑	168	Deion Sanders	.75	.30
❑	169	Garrison Hearst	.75	.30
❑	170	Jason Taylor	.50	.20
❑	171	Jerome Bettis	.75	.30
❑	172	John Lynch	.50	.20
❑	173	Troy Davis	.30	.10
❑	174	Freddie Jones	.30	.10
❑	175	Herman Moore	.50	.20
❑	176	Jake Reed	.50	.20
❑	177	Mark Brunell	.75	.30
❑	178	Ray Lewis	.75	.30
❑	179	Stephen Davis	.30	.10
❑	180	Tim Brown	.75	.30
❑	181	Willie McGinest	.30	.10
❑	182	Andre Reed	.50	.20
❑	183	Darrien Gordon	.30	.10
❑	184	David Palmer	.30	.10
❑	185	James Jett	.50	.20
❑	186	Junior Seau	.75	.30
❑	187	Zack Crockett	.30	.10
❑	188	Brad Johnson	.75	.30
❑	189	Charles Johnson	.30	.10
❑	190	Eddie George	.75	.30
❑	191	Jermaine Lewis	.50	.20
❑	192	Michael Irvin	.75	.30
❑	193	Reggie Brown LB	.30	.10
❑	194	Steve Young	1.00	.40
❑	195	Warren Sapp	.50	.20
❑	196	Wayne Chrebet	.75	.30
❑	197	David Dunn	.30	.10
❑	198	Dorsey Levens CL	.50	.20
❑	199	Troy Aikman CL	.75	.30
❑	200	John Elway CL	.75	.30
❑	201	Peyton Manning RC	30.00	15.00
❑	202	Ryan Leaf RC	3.00	1.25
❑	203	Charles Woodson RC	4.00	1.50
❑	204	Andre Wadsworth RC	2.50	1.00
❑	205	Brian Simmons RC	2.50	1.00
❑	206	Curtis Enis RC	1.50	.60
❑	207	Randy Moss RC	20.00	10.00
❑	208	Germane Crowell RC	2.50	1.00
❑	209	Greg Ellis RC	1.50	.60
❑	210	Kevin Dyson RC	3.00	1.25
❑	211	Skip Hicks RC	2.50	1.00
❑	212	Alonzo Mayes RC	1.50	.60
❑	213	Robert Edwards RC	2.50	1.00
❑	214	Fred Taylor RC	5.00	2.00
❑	215	Robert Holcombe RC	2.50	1.00
❑	216	John Dutton RC	1.50	.60
❑	217	Vonnie Holliday RC	2.50	1.00
❑	218	Tim Dwight RC	3.00	1.25
❑	219	Tavian Banks RC	2.50	1.00
❑	220	Marcus Nash RC	1.50	.60
❑	221	Jason Peter RC	1.50	.60
❑	222	Michael Myers RC	1.50	.60
❑	223	Takeo Spikes RC	3.00	1.25
❑	224	Kivuusama Mays RC	1.50	.60
❑	225	Jacquez Green RC	2.50	1.00
❑	226	Doug Flutie	.75	.30
❑	227	Ike Hilliard	.50	.20
❑	228	Craig Heyward	.30	.10
❑	229	Kevin Hardy	.30	.10
❑	230	Jason Dunn	.30	.10
❑	231	Billy Davis	.30	.10
❑	232	Chester McGlockton	.30	.10
❑	233	Sean Gilbert	.30	.10
❑	234	Bert Emanuel	.50	.20
❑	235	Keith Byars	.30	.10
❑	236	Tyrone Wheatley	.50	.20
❑	237	Ricky Proehl	.30	.10
❑	238	Michael Bates	.30	.10
❑	239	Derrick Alexander	.50	.20
❑	240	Harvey Williams	.30	.10
❑	241	Mike Pritchard	.30	.10
❑	242	Paul Justin	.30	.10
❑	243	Jeff Hostetler	.30	.10
❑	244	Eric Moulds	.75	.30
❑	245	Jeff Burris	.30	.10
❑	246	Gary Brown	.30	.10
❑	247	Anthony Johnson	.30	.10
❑	248	Dan Wilkinson	.30	.10
❑	249	Chris Warren	.50	.20
❑	250	Chris Darkins	.30	.10
❑	251	Eric Metcalf	.30	.10
❑	252	Pat Swilling	.30	.10
❑	253	Lamar Smith	.50	.20
❑	254	Quinn Early	.30	.10
❑	255	Carlester Crumpler	.30	.10
❑	256	Eric Bieniemy	.30	.10
❑	257	Aaron Bailey	.30	.10
❑	258	Neil O'Donnell	.50	.20
❑	259	Rod Woodson	.50	.20
❑	260	Ricky Whittle	.30	.10
❑	261	Iheanyi Uwaezuoke	.30	.10
❑	262	Heath Shuler	.30	.10
❑	263	Darren Sharper	.50	.20
❑	264	John Henry Mills	.30	.10
❑	265	Marco Battaglia	.30	.10
❑	266	Yancey Thigpen	.30	.10
❑	267	Irv Smith	.30	.10
❑	268	Jamie Sharper	.30	.10
❑	269	Marcus Robinson	5.00	2.00
❑	270	Dorsey Levens	.75	.30
❑	271	Qadry Ismail	.50	.20
❑	272	Desmond Howard	.50	.20
❑	273	Webster Slaughter	.30	.10
❑	274	Eugene Robinson	.30	.10
❑	275	Bill Romanowski	.30	.10
❑	276	Vincent Brisby	.30	.10
❑	277	Errict Rhett	.50	.20
❑	278	Albert Connell	.30	.10
❑	279	Thomas Lewis	.30	.10
❑	280	John Farquhar RC	.30	.10
❑	281	Marc Edwards	.30	.10
❑	282	Tyrone Davis	.30	.10
❑	283	Eric Allen	.30	.10
❑	284	Aaron Glenn	.30	.10
❑	285	Roosevelt Potts	.30	.10
❑	286	Kez McCorvey	.30	.10
❑	287	Joey Kent	.50	.20
❑	288	Jim Druckenmiller	.30	.10
❑	289	Sean Dawkins	.30	.10
❑	290	Edgar Bennett	.30	.10
❑	291	Vinny Testaverde	.50	.20
❑	292	Chris Slade	.30	.10
❑	293	Lamar Lathon	.30	.10
❑	294	Jackie Harris	.30	.10
❑	295	Jim Harbaugh	.50	.20
❑	296	Rob Fredrickson	.30	.10
❑	297	Ty Detmer	.50	.20
❑	298	Karl Williams	.30	.10
❑	299	Troy Drayton	.30	.10
❑	300	Curtis Martin	.75	.30
❑	301	Tamarick Vanover	.30	.10
❑	302	Lorenzo Neal	.30	.10
❑	303	John Hall	.30	.10
❑	304	Kevin Greene	.50	.20
❑	305	Bryan Still	.30	.10
❑	306	Neil Smith	.50	.20
❑	307	Greg Lloyd	.30	.10
❑	308	Shawn Jefferson	.30	.10
❑	309	Aaron Taylor	.30	.10
❑	310	Sedrick Shaw	.30	.10
❑	311	O.J. Santiago	.30	.10
❑	312	Kevin Abrams	.30	.10
❑	313	Dana Stubblefield	.30	.10
❑	314	Daryl Johnston	.50	.20
❑	315	Bryan Cox	.30	.10
❑	316	Jeff Graham	.30	.10
❑	317	Mario Bates	.50	.20
❑	318	Adrian Murrell	.50	.20
❑	319	Greg Hill	.30	.10
❑	320	Jahine Arnold	.30	.10
❑	321	Justin Armour	.30	.10
❑	322	Ricky Watters	.50	.20
❑	323	Lamont Warren	.30	.10
❑	324	Mack Strong	.75	.30
❑	325	Darnay Scott	.50	.20
❑	326	Brian Mitchell	.30	.10
❑	327	Rob Johnson	.50	.20
❑	328	Kent Graham	.30	.10
❑	329	Hugh Douglas	.30	.10
❑	330	Simeon Rice	.50	.20
❑	331	Rick Mirer	.30	.10
❑	332	Randall Cunningham	.75	.30
❑	333	Steve Atwater	.30	.10
❑	334	Latario Rachal	.30	.10
❑	335	Tony Martin	.50	.20
❑	336	Leroy Hoard	.30	.10
❑	337	Howard Griffith	.30	.10
❑	338	Kevin Lockett	.30	.10
❑	339	William Floyd	.30	.10
❑	340	Jerry Ellison	.30	.10
❑	341	Kyle Brady	.30	.10
❑	342	Michael Westbrook	.50	.20
❑	343	Kevin Turner	.30	.10
❑	344	David LaFleur	.30	.10
❑	345	Robert Jones	.30	.10
❑	346	Dave Brown	.30	.10
❑	347	Kevin Williams	.30	.10
❑	348	Amani Toomer	.50	.20
❑	349	Amp Lee	.30	.10
❑	350	Bryce Paup	.30	.10
❑	351	Dewayne Washington	.30	.10
❑	352	Mercury Hayes	.30	.10
❑	353	Tim Biakabutuka	.50	.20
❑	354	Ray Crockett	.30	.10
❑	355	Ted Washington	.30	.10
❑	356	Pete Mitchell	.30	.10
❑	357	Billy Jenkins RC	.30	.10
❑	358	Troy Aikman CL	.75	.30
❑	359	Drew Bledsoe CL	.75	.30
❑	360	Steve Young CL	.75	.30
❑	361	Antonio Freeman NG	.50	.20
❑	362	Antowain Smith NG	.50	.20
❑	363	Barry Sanders NG	1.50	.60
❑	364	Bobby Hoying NG	.30	.10
❑	365	Brett Favre NG	2.00	.75
❑	366	Corey Dillon NG	.50	.20
❑	367	Dan Marino NG	2.00	.75
❑	368	Drew Bledsoe NG	.75	.30
❑	369	Eddie George NG	.50	.20
❑	370	Emmitt Smith NG	1.50	.60
❑	371	Herman Moore NG	.50	.20
❑	372	Jake Plummer NG	.50	.20
❑	373	Jerome Bettis NG	.50	.20
❑	374	Jerry Rice NG	1.00	.40
❑	375	Joey Galloway NG	.50	.20
❑	376	John Elway NG	2.00	.75
❑	377	Kordell Stewart NG	.50	.20
❑	378	Mark Brunell NG	.75	.30
❑	379	Keyshawn Johnson NG	.50	.20
❑	380	Steve Young NG	.75	.30
❑	381	Steve McNair NG	.50	.20
❑	382	Terrell Davis NG	.75	.30
❑	383	Tim Brown NG	.50	.20
❑	384	Troy Aikman NG	1.00	.40
❑	385	Warrick Dunn NG	.75	.30
❑	386	Ryan Leaf	3.00	1.25
❑	387	Tony Simmons RC	2.00	.75
❑	388	Rodney Williams RC	1.25	.50
❑	389	John Avery RC	2.00	.75
❑	390	Shaun Williams RC	2.00	.75
❑	391	Anthony Simmons RC	2.00	.75
❑	392	Rashaan Shehee RC	2.00	.75
❑	393	Robert Holcombe	2.00	.75
❑	394	Larry Shannon RC	1.25	.50
❑	395	Skip Hicks	2.00	.75
❑	396	Rod Rutledge RC	1.25	.50
❑	397	Donald Hayes RC	2.00	.75
❑	398	Curtis Enis	1.25	.50
❑	399	Mikhael Ricks RC	2.00	.75
❑	400	Brian Griese RC	6.00	2.50
❑	401	Michael Pittman RC	4.00	1.50
❑	402	Jacquez Green	2.00	.75
❑	403	Jerome Pathon RC	3.00	1.25
❑	404	Ahman Green RC	15.00	6.00
❑	405	Marcus Nash	1.25	.50
❑	406	Randy Moss	20.00	10.00
❑	407	Terry Fair RC	2.00	.75
❑	408	Jammi German RC	1.25	.50
❑	409	Stephen Alexander RC	2.00	.75
❑	410	Grant Wistrom RC	2.00	.75
❑	411	Charlie Batch RC	3.00	1.25
❑	412	Fred Taylor	4.00	1.50
❑	413	Pat Johnson RC	2.00	.75

❑ 414 Robert Edwards 2.00 .75
❑ 415 Keith Brooking RC 3.00 1.25
❑ 416 Peyton Manning 25.00 12.50
❑ 417 Duane Starks RC 1.25 .50
❑ 418 Andre Wadsworth 2.00 .75
❑ 419 Brian Alford RC 1.25 .50
❑ 420 Brian Kelly RC 2.00 .75
❑ 421 Joe Jurevicius RC 3.00 1.25
❑ 422 Tebucky Jones RC 1.25 .50
❑ 423 R.W. McQuarters RC 2.00 .75
❑ 424 Kevin Dyson 2.50 1.00
❑ 425 Charles Woodson 3.00 1.25
❑ R1 Reggie White COMM .60 .25
❑ P20 Jeff George Promo .75 .30

1999 Ultra

❑ COMPLETE SET (300) 100.00 40.00
❑ COMP.SET w/o SP's (250) 20.00 10.00
❑ 1 Terrell Davis .75 .30
❑ 2 Courtney Hawkins .30 .10
❑ 3 Cris Carter .75 .30
❑ 4 Darnay Scott .30 .10
❑ 5 Darrell Green .50 .20
❑ 6 Jimmy Smith .50 .20
❑ 7 Doug Flutie .75 .30
❑ 8 Michael Jackson .30 .10
❑ 9 Warren Sapp .50 .20
❑ 10 Greg Hill .30 .10
❑ 11 Karim Abdul-Jabbar .50 .20
❑ 12 Greg Ellis .30 .10
❑ 13 Dan Marino 2.50 1.00
❑ 14 Napoleon Kaufman .75 .30
❑ 15 Peyton Manning 2.50 1.00
❑ 16 Simeon Rice .50 .20
❑ 17 Tony Simmons .30 .10
❑ 18 [illegible] [illegible] .10
❑ 19 Charles Johnson .30 .10
❑ 20 Derrick Alexander .30 .10
❑ 21 Kent Graham .30 .10
❑ 22 Randall Cunningham .75 .30
❑ 23 Trent Green .75 .30
❑ 24 Chris Spielman .30 .10
❑ 25 Carl Pickens .50 .20
❑ 26 Bill Romanowski .30 .10
❑ 27 Jermaine Lewis .50 .20
❑ 28 Ahman Green .75 .30
❑ 29 Bryan Still .30 .10
❑ 30 Dorsey Levens .75 .30
❑ 31 Frank Wycheck .30 .10
❑ 32 Jerome Bettis .75 .30
❑ 33 Reidel Anthony .50 .20
❑ 34 Robert Jones .30 .10
❑ 35 Terry Glenn .75 .30
❑ 36 Tim Brown .75 .30
❑ 37 Eric Metcalf .30 .10
❑ 38 Kevin Greene .50 .20
❑ 39 Takeo Spikes .30 .10
❑ 40 Brian Mitchell .30 .10
❑ 41 Duane Starks .30 .10
❑ 42 Eddie George .75 .30
❑ 43 Joe Jurevicius .50 .20
❑ 44 Kimble Anders .50 .20
❑ 45 Kordell Stewart .50 .20
❑ 46 Leroy Hoard .30 .10
❑ 47 Rod Smith .50 .20
❑ 48 Terrell Owens .75 .30
❑ 49 Ty Detmer .50 .20
❑ 50 Charles Woodson .75 .30
❑ 51 Andre Rison .50 .20
❑ 52 Chris Slade .30 .10
❑ 53 Frank Sanders .50 .20
❑ 54 Michael Irvin .50 .20
❑ 55 Jerome Pathon .30 .10
❑ 56 Desmond Howard .50 .20
❑ 57 Billy Davis .30 .10
❑ 58 Anthony Simmons .30 .10
❑ 59 James Jett .50 .20
❑ 60 Jake Plummer .50 .20
❑ 61 John Avery .30 .10
❑ 62 Marvin Harrison .75 .30
❑ 63 Merton Hanks .30 .10
❑ 64 Ricky Proehl .30 .10
❑ 65 Steve Beuerlein .30 .10
❑ 66 Willie McGinest .30 .10
❑ 67 Bryce Paup .30 .10
❑ 68 Brett Favre 2.50 1.00
❑ 69 Brian Griese .75 .30
❑ 70 Curtis Martin .75 .30
❑ 71 Drew Bledsoe 1.00 .40
❑ 72 Jim Harbaugh .50 .20
❑ 73 Joey Galloway .50 .20
❑ 74 Natrone Means .50 .20
❑ 75 O.J. McDuffie .50 .20
❑ 76 Tiki Barber .75 .30
❑ 77 Wesley Walls .50 .20
❑ 78 Will Blackwell .30 .10
❑ 79 Bert Emanuel .50 .20
❑ 80 J.J. Stokes .50 .20
❑ 81 Steve McNair .75 .30
❑ 82 Adrian Murrell .50 .20
❑ 83 Dexter Coakley .30 .10
❑ 84 Jeff George .50 .20
❑ 85 Marshall Faulk 1.00 .40
❑ 86 Tim Biakabutuka .50 .20
❑ 87 Troy Drayton .30 .10
❑ 88 Ty Law .50 .20
❑ 89 Brian Simmons .30 .10
❑ 90 Eric Allen .30 .10
❑ 91 Jon Kitna .75 .30
❑ 92 Junior Seau .75 .30
❑ 93 Kevin Turner .30 .10
❑ 94 Larry Centers .30 .10
❑ 95 Robert Edwards .30 .10
❑ 96 Rocket Ismail .50 .20
❑ 97 Sam Madison .30 .10
❑ 98 Stephen Alexander .30 .10
❑ 99 Trent Dilfer .50 .20
❑ 100 Vonnie Holliday .30 .10
❑ 101 Charlie Garner .50 .20
❑ 102 [illegible] [illegible] [illegible]
❑ 103 Jamal Anderson .75 .30
❑ 104 Mike Vanderjagt .30 .10
❑ 105 Aeneas Williams .30 .10
❑ 106 Daryl Johnston .50 .20
❑ 107 Hugh Douglas .30 .10
❑ 108 Torrance Small .30 .10
❑ 109 Amani Toomer .30 .10
❑ 110 Amp Lee .30 .10
❑ 111 Germane Crowell .30 .10
❑ 112 Marco Battaglia .30 .10
❑ 113 Michael Westbrook .50 .20
❑ 114 Randy Moss 2.00 .75
❑ 115 Ricky Watters .50 .20
❑ 116 Rob Johnson .50 .20
❑ 117 Tony Gonzalez .75 .30
❑ 118 Charles Way .30 .10
❑ 119 Chris Penn .30 .10
❑ 120 Eddie Kennison .50 .20
❑ 121 Elvis Grbac .50 .20
❑ 122 Eric Moulds .75 .30
❑ 123 Terry Fair .30 .10
❑ 124 Tony Banks .50 .20
❑ 125 Chris Chandler .50 .20
❑ 126 Emmitt Smith 1.50 .60
❑ 127 Herman Moore .50 .20
❑ 128 Irv Smith .30 .10
❑ 129 Kyle Brady .30 .10
❑ 130 Lamont Warren .30 .10
❑ 131 Troy Davis .30 .10
❑ 132 Andre Reed .50 .20
❑ 133 Justin Armour .30 .10
❑ 134 James Hasty .30 .10
❑ 135 Johnnie Morton .50 .20
❑ 136 Reggie Barlow .30 .10
❑ 137 Robert Holcombe .30 .10
❑ 138 Sean Dawkins .30 .10
❑ 139 Steve Atwater .30 .10
❑ 140 Tim Dwight .75 .30
❑ 141 Wayne Chrebet .50 .20
❑ 142 Alonzo Mayes .30 .10
❑ 143 Mark Brunell .75 .30
❑ 144 Antowain Smith .75 .30
❑ 145 Byron Bam Morris .30 .10
❑ 146 Isaac Bruce .75 .30
❑ 147 Bryan Cox .30 .10
❑ 148 Bryant Westbrook .30 .10
❑ 149 Duce Staley .75 .30
❑ 150 Barry Sanders 2.50 1.00
❑ 151 La'Roi Glover RC .75 .30
❑ 152 Ray Crockett .30 .10
❑ 153 Tony Brackens .30 .10
❑ 154 Roy Barker .30 .10
❑ 155 Kerry Collins .50 .20
❑ 156 Andre Wadsworth .30 .10
❑ 157 Cameron Cleeland .30 .10
❑ 158 Koy Detmer .30 .10
❑ 159 Marcus Pollard .30 .10
❑ 160 Patrick Jeffers RC 6.00 2.50
❑ 161 Aaron Glenn .30 .10
❑ 162 Andre Hastings .30 .10
❑ 163 Bruce Smith .50 .20
❑ 164 David Palmer .30 .10
❑ 165 Erik Kramer .50 .20
❑ 166 Orlando Pace .30 .10
❑ 167 Robert Brooks .50 .20
❑ 168 Shawn Springs .30 .10
❑ 169 Terance Mathis .50 .20
❑ 170 Chris Calloway .30 .10
❑ 171 Gilbert Brown .30 .10
❑ 172 Charlie Jones .30 .10
❑ 173 Curtis Enis .30 .10
❑ 174 Eugene Robinson .30 .10
❑ 175 Garrison Hearst .50 .20
❑ 176 Jason Elam .30 .10
❑ 177 John Randle .50 .20
❑ 178 Keith Poole .30 .10
❑ 179 Kevin Hardy .30 .10
❑ 180 Keyshawn Johnson .75 .30
❑ 181 O.J. Santiago .30 .10
❑ 182 Jacquez Green .30 .10
❑ 183 Bobby Engram .50 .20
❑ 184 Damon Jones .30 .10
❑ 185 Freddie Jones .30 .10
❑ 186 [illegible] [illegible] [illegible]
❑ 187 Jerry Rice 1.50 .60
❑ 188 Joey Kent .30 .10
❑ 189 Lamar Smith .50 .20
❑ 190 John Elway 2.50 1.00
❑ 191 Leon Johnson .30 .10
❑ 192 Mark Chmura .50 .20
❑ 193 Peter Boulware .30 .10
❑ 194 Zach Thomas .75 .30
❑ 195 Marc Edwards .30 .10
❑ 196 Mike Alstott .75 .30
❑ 197 Yancey Thigpen .30 .10
❑ 198 Oronde Gadsden .50 .20
❑ 199 Rae Carruth .30 .10
❑ 200 Troy Aikman 1.50 .60
❑ 201 Shawn Jefferson .30 .10
❑ 202 Rob Moore .50 .20
❑ 203 Rickey Dudley .30 .10
❑ 204 Jason Taylor .30 .10
❑ 205 Curtis Conway .50 .20
❑ 206 Darrien Gordon .30 .10
❑ 207 Eric Green .30 .10
❑ 208 Jessie Armstead .30 .10
❑ 209 Keenan McCardell .50 .20
❑ 210 Robert Smith .75 .30
❑ 211 Mo Lewis .30 .10
❑ 212 Ryan Leaf .75 .30
❑ 213 Steve Young 1.00 .40
❑ 214 Tyrone Davis .30 .10
❑ 215 Chad Brown .30 .10
❑ 216 Ike Hilliard .30 .10
❑ 217 Jimmy Hitchcock .30 .10

❑ 218 Kevin Dyson	.50	.20
❑ 219 Levon Kirkland	.30	.10
❑ 220 Neil O'Donnell	.50	.20
❑ 221 Ray Lewis	.75	.30
❑ 222 Shannon Sharpe	.50	.20
❑ 223 Skip Hicks	.30	.10
❑ 224 Brad Johnson	.75	.30
❑ 225 Charlie Batch	.75	.30
❑ 226 Corey Dillon	.75	.30
❑ 227 Dale Carter	.30	.10
❑ 228 John Mobley	.30	.10
❑ 229 Hines Ward	.75	.30
❑ 230 Leslie Shepherd	.30	.10
❑ 231 Michael Strahan	.50	.20
❑ 232 R.W. McQuarters	.30	.10
❑ 233 Mike Pritchard	.30	.10
❑ 234 Antonio Freeman	.75	.30
❑ 235 Ben Coates	.50	.20
❑ 236 Michael Bates	.30	.10
❑ 237 Ed McCaffrey	.50	.20
❑ 238 Gary Brown	.30	.10
❑ 239 Mark Bruener	.30	.10
❑ 240 Mikhael Ricks	.30	.10
❑ 241 Muhsin Muhammad	.50	.20
❑ 242 Priest Holmes	1.25	.50
❑ 243 Stephen Davis	.75	.30
❑ 244 Vinny Testaverde	.50	.20
❑ 245 Warrick Dunn	.75	.30
❑ 246 Derrick Mayes	.30	.10
❑ 247 Fred Taylor	.75	.30
❑ 248 Drew Bledsoe CL	.50	.20
❑ 249 Eddie George CL	.50	.20
❑ 250 Steve Young CL	.50	.20
❑ 251 Jamal Anderson BB	.60	.25
❑ 252 D.Gordon/Romanowski BB	.30	.10
❑ 253 Shannon Sharpe BB	.30	.10
❑ 254 Terrell Davis BB	1.00	.40
❑ 255 Rod Smith BB	.30	.10
❑ 256 Rod Smith BB	.30	.10
❑ 257 John Elway BB	5.00	2.00
❑ 258 Tim Dwight BB	.60	.25
❑ 259 Elway/McC/Griff/Dav.BB	3.00	1.25
❑ 260 John Elway BB	5.00	2.00
❑ 261 Ricky Williams RC	6.00	2.50
❑ 262 Tim Couch RC	3.00	1.25
❑ 263 Chris Claiborne RC	1.50	.60
❑ 264 Champ Bailey RC	5.00	2.00
❑ 265 Torry Holt RC	8.00	3.00
❑ 266 Donovan McNabb RC	15.00	6.00
❑ 267 David Boston RC	3.00	1.25
❑ 268 Chris McAlister RC	2.50	1.00
❑ 269 Brock Huard RC	3.00	1.25
❑ 270 Daunte Culpepper RC	12.00	5.00
❑ 271 Matt Stinchcomb RC	1.50	.60
❑ 272 Edgerrin James RC	12.00	5.00
❑ 273 Jevon Kearse RC	6.00	2.50
❑ 274 Ebenezer Ekuban RC	2.50	1.00
❑ 275 Kris Farris RC	1.50	.60
❑ 276 Chris Terry RC	1.50	.60
❑ 277 Jerame Tuman RC	3.00	1.25
❑ 278 Akili Smith RC	2.50	1.00
❑ 279 Aaron Gibson RC	1.50	.60
❑ 280 Rahim Abdullah RC	2.50	1.00
❑ 281 Peerless Price RC	3.00	1.25
❑ 282 Antoine Winfield RC	2.50	1.00
❑ 283 Antuan Edwards RC	1.50	.60
❑ 284 Rob Konrad RC	3.00	1.25
❑ 285 Troy Edwards RC	2.50	1.00
❑ 286 John Thornton RC	1.50	.60
❑ 287 James Johnson RC	2.50	1.00
❑ 288 Gary Stills RC	1.50	.60
❑ 289 Mike Peterson RC	2.50	1.00
❑ 290 Kevin Faulk RC	3.00	1.25
❑ 291 Jared DeVries RC	1.50	.60
❑ 292 Martin Gramatica RC	1.50	.60
❑ 293 Montae Reagor RC	1.50	.60
❑ 294 Andy Katzenmoyer RC	2.50	1.00
❑ 295 Sedrick Irvin RC	1.50	.60
❑ 296 D'Wayne Bates RC	2.50	1.00
❑ 297 Amos Zereoue RC	3.00	1.25
❑ 298 Dre' Bly RC	3.00	1.25
❑ 299 Kevin Johnson RC	3.00	1.25
❑ 300 Cade McNown RC	2.50	1.00
❑ P247 Fred Taylor Promo	2.00	.75

2000 Ultra

❑ COMPLETE SET (249)	100.00	40.00
❑ COMP.SET w/o SP's (220)	20.00	7.50
❑ 1 Kurt Warner	1.50	.60
❑ 2 Derrick Alexander	.50	.20
❑ 3 Aaron Craver	.30	.10
❑ 4 Kevin Faulk	.50	.20
❑ 5 Marcus Robinson	.75	.30
❑ 6 Tony Banks	.50	.20
❑ 7 Jon Ritchie	.30	.10
❑ 8 Torry Holt	.75	.30
❑ 9 Joe Horn	.50	.20
❑ 10 Eddie George	.75	.30
❑ 11 Michael Westbrook	.50	.20
❑ 12 Gus Frerotte	.30	.10
❑ 13 Tim Brown	.75	.30
❑ 14 Tamarick Vanover	.30	.10
❑ 15 David Sloan	.30	.10
❑ 16 Darnay Scott	.30	.10
❑ 17 Junior Seau	.75	.30
❑ 18 Warren Sapp	.50	.20
❑ 19 Priest Holmes	1.00	.40
❑ 20 Jerry Rice	1.50	.60
❑ 21 Cade McNown	.30	.10
❑ 22 Johnnie Morton	.50	.20
❑ 23 Vinny Testaverde	.50	.20
❑ 24 James Jett	.30	.10
❑ 25 Tony Gonzalez	.50	.20
❑ 26 Charlie Batch	.75	.30
❑ 27 Tony Simmons	.30	.10
❑ 28 James Stewart	.50	.20
❑ 29 Corey Dillon	.75	.30
❑ 30 Ricky Williams	.75	.30
❑ 31 Ryan Leaf	.50	.20
❑ 32 Terry Allen	.50	.20
❑ 33 Freddie Jones	.30	.10
❑ 34 Terry Kirby	.30	.10
❑ 35 Charles Johnson	.50	.20
❑ 36 William Henderson	.50	.20
❑ 37 Stephen Alexander	.30	.10
❑ 38 Moe Williams	.50	.20
❑ 39 David Boston	.75	.30
❑ 40 Emmitt Smith	1.50	.60
❑ 41 Ken Oxendine	.30	.10
❑ 42 Byron Hanspard	.30	.10
❑ 43 Dwight Stone	.30	.10
❑ 44 Jim Harbaugh	.50	.20
❑ 45 Curtis Enis	.30	.10
❑ 46 Peerless Price	.50	.20
❑ 47 Terance Mathis	.50	.20
❑ 48 Mike Alstott	.75	.30
❑ 49 Rod Smith	.50	.20
❑ 50 Marshall Faulk	1.00	.40
❑ 51 Derrick Mayes	.50	.20
❑ 52 Keenan McCardell	.50	.20
❑ 53 Curtis Martin	.75	.30
❑ 54 Bobby Engram	.30	.10
❑ 55 Carl Pickens	.50	.20
❑ 56 Robert Smith	.75	.30
❑ 57 Ike Hilliard	.50	.20
❑ 58 Reidel Anthony	.50	.20
❑ 59 Jeff Graham	.30	.10
❑ 60 Mark Brunell	.75	.30
❑ 61 Joe Montgomery	.30	.10
❑ 62 Ed McCaffrey	.75	.30
❑ 63 Kenny Bynum	.30	.10
❑ 64 Curtis Conway	.50	.20
❑ 65 Trent Dilfer	.50	.20
❑ 66 Jake Reed	.50	.20
❑ 67 Jake Plummer	.50	.20
❑ 68 Tony Martin	.50	.20
❑ 69 Yatil Green	.30	.10
❑ 70 Keyshawn Johnson	.75	.30
❑ 71 Leroy Hoard	.30	.10
❑ 72 Skip Hicks	.30	.10
❑ 73 Marvin Harrison	.75	.30
❑ 74 Steve Beuerlein	.50	.20
❑ 75 Will Blackwell	.30	.10
❑ 76 Derek Loville	.30	.10
❑ 77 Warrick Dunn	.75	.30
❑ 78 Amos Zereoue	.75	.30
❑ 79 Ray Lucas	.50	.20
❑ 80 Randy Moss	1.50	.60
❑ 81 Wesley Walls	.30	.10
❑ 82 Jimmy Smith	.50	.20
❑ 83 Kordell Stewart	.50	.20
❑ 84 Brian Griese	.75	.30
❑ 85 Martin Gramatica	.30	.10
❑ 86 Chris Chandler	.50	.20
❑ 87 Reggie Barlow	.30	.10
❑ 88 Jeff George	.50	.20
❑ 89 Tavian Banks	.30	.10
❑ 90 Mushin Muhammad	.50	.20
❑ 91 Steve McNair	.75	.30
❑ 92 Hines Ward	.75	.30
❑ 93 Brian Mitchell	.30	.10
❑ 94 Daunte Culpepper	1.00	.40
❑ 95 Tim Dwight	.75	.30
❑ 96 Terrence Wilkins	.30	.10
❑ 97 Fred Lane	.30	.10
❑ 98 Brett Favre	2.50	1.00
❑ 99 Richie Anderson	.50	.20
❑ 100 Jamal Anderson	.75	.30
❑ 101 Doug Flutie	.75	.30
❑ 102 Charles Woodson	.50	.20
❑ 103 Jacquez Green	.30	.10
❑ 104 Olandis Gary	.75	.30
❑ 105 Steve Young	1.00	.40
❑ 106 Wayne Chrebet	.50	.20
❑ 107 Karim Abdul-Jabbar	.50	.20
❑ 108 Andre Rison	.50	.20
❑ 109 Eddie Kennison	.30	.10
❑ 110 Jevon Kearse	.75	.30
❑ 111 Tony Richardson RC	.50	.20
❑ 112 Jake Delhomme RC	3.00	1.25
❑ 113 Errict Rhett	.50	.20
❑ 114 Akili Smith	.30	.10
❑ 115 Tyrone Wheatley	.50	.20
❑ 116 Corey Bradford	.50	.20
❑ 117 J.J. Stokes	.50	.20
❑ 118 Simeon Rice	.50	.20
❑ 119 Brad Johnson	.75	.30
❑ 120 Edgerrin James	1.25	.50
❑ 121 Amani Toomer	.30	.10
❑ 122 O.J. McDuffie	.50	.20
❑ 123 Az-Zahir Hakim	.50	.20
❑ 124 Troy Edwards	.30	.10
❑ 125 Tim Biakabutuka	.50	.20
❑ 126 Jason Tucker	.30	.10
❑ 127 Charles Way	.30	.10
❑ 128 Terrell Davis	.75	.30
❑ 129 Garrison Hearst	.50	.20
❑ 130 Fred Taylor	.75	.30
❑ 131 Robert Holcombe	.30	.10
❑ 132 Frank Sanders	.50	.20
❑ 133 Morten Andersen	.30	.10
❑ 134 Cris Carter	.75	.30
❑ 135 Patrick Jeffers	.75	.30
❑ 136 Antonio Freeman	.75	.30
❑ 137 Jonathan Linton	.30	.10
❑ 138 Rashaan Shehee	.30	.10
❑ 139 Luther Broughton RC	.50	.20
❑ 140 Tim Couch	.50	.20
❑ 141 Keith Poole	.30	.10
❑ 142 Champ Bailey	.50	.20
❑ 143 Yancey Thigpen	.30	.10
❑ 144 Joey Galloway	.50	.20
❑ 145 Mac Cody	.30	.10
❑ 146 Damon Huard	.75	.30
❑ 147 Dorsey Levens	.50	.20
❑ 148 Donovan McNabb	1.25	.50
❑ 149 Jamie Asher	.30	.10
❑ 150 Peyton Manning	2.00	.75

❑ 151 Leslie Shepherd .30 .10
❑ 152 Charlie Rogers .30 .10
❑ 153 Tony Horne .30 .10
❑ 154 Jim Miller .30 .10
❑ 155 Richard Huntley .30 .10
❑ 156 Germane Crowell .30 .10
❑ 157 Natrone Means .30 .10
❑ 158 Justin Armour .30 .10
❑ 159 Drew Bledsoe 1.00 .40
❑ 160 Dedric Ward .30 .10
❑ 161 Allen Rossum .30 .10
❑ 162 Ricky Watters .50 .20
❑ 163 Kerry Collins .50 .20
❑ 164 James Johnson .30 .10
❑ 165 Elvis Grbac .50 .20
❑ 166 Larry Centers .30 .10
❑ 167 Rob Moore .50 .20
❑ 168 Jay Riemersma .30 .10
❑ 169 Bill Schroeder .50 .20
❑ 170 Deion Sanders .75 .30
❑ 171 Jerome Bettis .75 .30
❑ 172 Dan Marino 2.50 1.00
❑ 173 Terrell Owens .75 .30
❑ 174 Kevin Carter .30 .10
❑ 175 Lamar Smith .50 .20
❑ 176 Ken Dilger .30 .10
❑ 177 Napoleon Kaufman .50 .20
❑ 178 Kevin Williams .30 .10
❑ 179 Tremain Mack .30 .10
❑ 180 Troy Aikman 1.50 .60
❑ 181 Glyn Milburn .30 .10
❑ 182 Pete Mitchell .30 .10
❑ 183 Cameron Cleeland .30 .10
❑ 184 Qadry Ismail .50 .20
❑ 185 Michael Pittman .30 .10
❑ 186 Kevin Dyson .50 .20
❑ 187 Matt Hasselbeck .50 .20
❑ 188 Kevin Johnson .75 .30
❑ 189 Rich Gannon .75 .30
❑ 190 Stephen Davis .75 .30
❑ 191 Frank Wycheck .30 .10
❑ 192 Eric Moulds .75 .30
❑ 193 Jon Kitna .75 .30
❑ 194 Mario Bates .30 .10
❑ 195 Na Brown .30 .10
❑ 196 Jeff Blake .50 .20
❑ 197 Charles Evans .30 .10
❑ 198 Oronde Gadsden .50 .20
❑ 199 Donnell Bennett .30 .10
❑ 200 Isaac Bruce .75 .30
❑ 201 Olindo Mare .30 .10
❑ 202 Darnell McDonald .30 .10
❑ 203 Charlie Garner .50 .20
❑ 204 Shawn Jefferson .30 .10
❑ 205 Adrian Murrell .50 .20
❑ 206 Peter Boulware .30 .10
❑ 207 LeShon Johnson .30 .10
❑ 208 Herman Moore .50 .20
❑ 209 Duce Staley .75 .30
❑ 210 Sean Dawkins .30 .10
❑ 211 Antowain Smith .50 .20
❑ 212 Albert Connell .30 .10
❑ 213 Jeff Garcia .75 .30
❑ 214 Kimble Anders .30 .10
❑ 215 Shaun King .30 .10
❑ 216 Rocket Ismail .50 .20
❑ 217 Andrew Glover .30 .10
❑ 218 Rickey Dudley .30 .10
❑ 219 Michael Basnight .30 .10
❑ 220 Terry Glenn .50 .20
❑ 221 Peter Warrick RC 3.00 1.25
❑ 222 Ron Dayne RC 3.00 1.25
❑ 223 Thomas Jones RC 5.00 2.00
❑ 224 Joe Hamilton RC 2.50 1.00
❑ 225 Tim Rattay RC 3.00 1.25
❑ 226 Chad Pennington RC 8.00 3.00
❑ 227 Dennis Northcutt RC 3.00 1.25
❑ 228 Troy Walters RC 3.00 1.25
❑ 229 Travis Prentice RC 2.50 1.00
❑ 230 Shaun Alexander RC 15.00 6.00
❑ 231 J.R. Redmond RC 2.50 1.00
❑ 232 Chris Redman RC 2.50 1.00
❑ 233 Tee Martin RC 3.00 1.25
❑ 234 Tom Brady RC 60.00 30.00
❑ 235 Travis Taylor RC 3.00 1.25
❑ 236 R.Jay Soward RC 2.50 1.00
❑ 237 Jamal Lewis RC 8.00 3.00
❑ 238 Giovanni Carmazzi RC 2.00 .75
❑ 239 Dez White RC 3.00 1.25
❑ 240 LaVar Arrington RC SP 100.00 40.00
❑ 241 Laveranues Coles RC 4.00 1.50
❑ 242 Sherrod Gideon RC 2.00 .75
❑ 243 Trung Canidate RC 2.50 1.00
❑ 244 Michael Wiley RC 2.50 1.00
❑ 245 Anthony Lucas RC 2.00 .75
❑ 246 Darrell Jackson RC 6.00 2.50
❑ 247 Plaxico Burress RC 6.00 2.50
❑ 248 Reuben Droughns RC 4.00 1.50
❑ 249 Marc Bulger RC 6.00 2.50
❑ 250 Danny Farmer RC 2.50 1.00

2001 Ultra

❑ COMP.SET w/o SP's (250) 25.00 10.00
❑ 1 Daunte Culpepper .75 .30
❑ 2 Kurt Warner 1.50 .60
❑ 3 Emmitt Smith 1.50 .60
❑ 4 Eddie George .75 .30
❑ 5 Ron Dayne .75 .30
❑ 6 Zach Thomas .75 .30
❑ 7 Itula Mili .30 .10
❑ 8 Jake Reed .50 .20
❑ 9 James Stewart .50 .20
❑ 10 Terrence Wilkins .30 .10
❑ 11 Jeff Blake .50 .20
❑ 12 Kerry Collins .50 .20
❑ 13 Christian Fauria .30 .10
❑ 14 Jackie Harris .30 .10
❑ 15 Kevin Johnson .50 .20
❑ 16 Tony Martin .30 .10
❑ 17 Joey Galloway .50 .20
❑ 18 Junior Seau .75 .30
❑ 19 Jason Tucker .30 .10
❑ 20 Steve Beuerlein .30 .10
❑ 21 Mike Cloud .30 .10
❑ 22 Kevin Faulk .50 .20
❑ 23 Az-Zahir Hakim .30 .10
❑ 24 Charles Johnson .30 .10
❑ 25 Curtis Martin .75 .30
❑ 26 Eric Moulds .50 .20
❑ 27 Bill Schroeder .50 .20
❑ 28 Amani Toomer .30 .10
❑ 29 Obafemi Ayanbadejo .30 .10
❑ 30 Aaron Shea .30 .10
❑ 31 Ken Dilger .30 .10
❑ 32 Terry Glenn .30 .10
❑ 33 Rocket Ismail .50 .20
❑ 34 Dorsey Levens .30 .10
❑ 35 Brian Mitchell .30 .10
❑ 36 Tony Richardson .30 .10
❑ 37 Sam Madison .30 .10
❑ 38 Darren Sharper .30 .10
❑ 39 Derrick Alexander .50 .20
❑ 40 Aaron Brooks .75 .30
❑ 41 Casey Crawford .30 .10
❑ 42 Terrell Fletcher .30 .10
❑ 43 William Henderson .30 .10
❑ 44 Thomas Jones .50 .20
❑ 45 Keenan McCardell .30 .10
❑ 46 Chad Pennington 1.25 .50
❑ 47 Akili Smith .30 .10
❑ 48 Hines Ward .75 .30
❑ 49 Champ Bailey .50 .20
❑ 50 Cris Carter .75 .30
❑ 51 Corey Dillon .75 .30
❑ 52 Tony Gonzalez .50 .20
❑ 53 Darrell Jackson .75 .30
❑ 54 Chad Lewis .30 .10
❑ 55 Dave Moore .30 .10
❑ 56 Jay Riemersma .30 .10
❑ 57 J.J. Stokes .50 .20
❑ 58 Frank Wycheck .30 .10
❑ 59 Tiki Barber .75 .30
❑ 60 Tony Carter .30 .10
❑ 61 Rickey Dudley .30 .10
❑ 62 John Lynch .50 .20
❑ 63 Larry Foster .30 .10
❑ 64 Willie Jackson .30 .10
❑ 65 Jamal Lewis 1.25 .50
❑ 66 Herman Moore .50 .20
❑ 67 Andre Rison .50 .20
❑ 68 Michael Strahan .50 .20
❑ 69 Charlie Batch .75 .30
❑ 70 Larry Centers .30 .10
❑ 71 Ron Dugans .30 .10
❑ 72 Jeff Graham .30 .10
❑ 73 Edgerrin James 1.00 .40
❑ 74 Jermaine Lewis .30 .10
❑ 75 Charles Woodson .50 .20
❑ 76 Chris Redman .30 .10
❑ 77 Jon Ritchie .30 .10
❑ 78 Fred Taylor .75 .30
❑ 79 Jamal Anderson .75 .30
❑ 80 Isaac Bruce .75 .30
❑ 81 Terrell Davis .75 .30
❑ 82 Rich Gannon .75 .30
❑ 83 Joe Horn .50 .20
❑ 84 Eddie Kennison .50 .20
❑ 85 Steve McNair .75 .30
❑ 86 Travis Prentice .30 .10
❑ 87 Rod Smith .50 .20
❑ 88 Ricky Watters .50 .20
❑ 89 Michael Bates .30 .10
❑ 90 Byron Chamberlain .30 .10
❑ 91 Warrick Dunn .75 .30
❑ 92 Elvis Grbac .50 .20
❑ 93 Patrick Jeffers .50 .20
❑ 94 Ray Lewis .75 .30
❑ 95 Sammy Morris .30 .10
❑ 96 Marcus Robinson .75 .30
❑ 97 Travis Taylor .50 .20
❑ 98 Fred Beasley .30 .10
❑ 99 Chris Chandler .50 .20
❑ 100 Tim Dwight .75 .30
❑ 101 Ahman Green .75 .30
❑ 102 Shawn Jefferson .30 .10
❑ 103 Jeremy McDaniel .30 .10
❑ 104 Sylvester Morris .30 .10
❑ 105 John Randle .30 .10
❑ 106 Vinny Testaverde .50 .20
❑ 107 Anthony Becht .30 .10
❑ 108 Wayne Chrebet .50 .20
❑ 109 Stephen Boyd .30 .10
❑ 110 Jacquez Green .30 .10
❑ 111 MarTay Jenkins .30 .10
❑ 112 Jason Gildon .30 .10
❑ 113 Chad Morton .30 .10
❑ 114 Deion Sanders .75 .30
❑ 115 Yancey Thigpen .30 .10
❑ 116 Marty Booker .30 .10
❑ 117 Curtis Conway .50 .20
❑ 118 Jermaine Fazande .30 .10
❑ 119 Matthew Hatchette .30 .10
❑ 120 Pat Johnson .30 .10
❑ 121 Terance Mathis .50 .20
❑ 122 Terrell Owens .75 .30
❑ 123 Corey Simon .50 .20
❑ 124 Darrick Vaughn .30 .10
❑ 125 Drew Bledsoe 1.00 .40
❑ 126 Albert Connell .30 .10
❑ 127 Brett Favre 2.50 1.00
❑ 128 Marvin Harrison .75 .30
❑ 129 Keyshawn Johnson .75 .30
❑ 130 Derrick Mason .50 .20
❑ 131 Dennis Northcutt .50 .20
❑ 132 Shannon Sharpe .50 .20
❑ 133 Brian Urlacher 1.25 .50
❑ 134 Mike Anderson .75 .30
❑ 135 Mark Bruener .30 .10

❑ 136 Sean Dawkins .30 .10
❑ 137 Jeff Garcia .75 .30
❑ 138 Tony Horne .30 .10
❑ 139 Shaun King .30 .10
❑ 140 Cade McNown .30 .10
❑ 141 Peerless Price .50 .20
❑ 142 R.Jay Soward .30 .10
❑ 143 Tyrone Wheatley .50 .20
❑ 144 Richie Anderson .30 .10
❑ 145 Mark Brunell .75 .30
❑ 146 JaJuan Dawson .30 .10
❑ 147 Charlie Garner .50 .20
❑ 148 Desmond Howard .30 .10
❑ 149 Jon Kitna .50 .20
❑ 150 Duane Starks .30 .10
❑ 151 J.R. Redmond .30 .10
❑ 152 Duce Staley .75 .30
❑ 153 Dez White .30 .10
❑ 154 David Boston .75 .30
❑ 155 Tim Couch .50 .20
❑ 156 Jay Fiedler .75 .30
❑ 157 Jessie Armstead .30 .10
❑ 158 Rob Johnson .50 .20
❑ 159 Brad Johnson .75 .30
❑ 160 Derrick Mayes .30 .10
❑ 161 Jerome Pathon .50 .20
❑ 162 David Sloan .30 .10
❑ 163 Wesley Walls .30 .10
❑ 164 Shaun Alexander 1.00 .40
❑ 165 Derrick Brooks .75 .30
❑ 166 Germane Crowell .30 .10
❑ 167 Doug Flutie .75 .30
❑ 168 Ike Hilliard .50 .20
❑ 169 Hugh Douglas .30 .10
❑ 170 Wane McGarity .30 .10
❑ 171 Michael Pittman .30 .10
❑ 172 Shawn Bryson .30 .10
❑ 173 Richard Huntley .30 .10
❑ 174 Darnell Autry .30 .10
❑ 175 Plaxico Burress .75 .30
❑ 176 Trent Dilfer .50 .20
❑ 177 Jeff George .50 .20
❑ 178 Qadry Ismail .50 .20
❑ 179 Ryan Leaf .50 .20
❑ 180 Jim Miller .30 .10
❑ 181 Jerry Rice 1.50 .60
❑ 182 Kordell Stewart .50 .20
❑ 183 Ricky Williams .75 .30
❑ 184 James Allen .50 .20
❑ 185 Courtney Brown .50 .20
❑ 186 Reidel Anthony .30 .10
❑ 187 Bubba Franks .50 .20
❑ 188 Priest Holmes 1.00 .40
❑ 189 Napoleon Kaufman .30 .10
❑ 190 Trevor Pryce .30 .10
❑ 191 Jake Plummer .50 .20
❑ 192 Jimmy Smith .50 .20
❑ 193 Michael Wiley .30 .10
❑ 194 Brock Huard .30 .10
❑ 195 Troy Brown .50 .20
❑ 196 Stephen Davis .75 .30
❑ 197 Oronde Gadsden .50 .20
❑ 198 Brad Hoover .30 .10
❑ 199 La'Roi Glover .30 .10
❑ 200 Donovan McNabb 1.00 .40
❑ 201 Jerry Porter .50 .20
❑ 202 Robert Smith .50 .20
❑ 203 Justin Watson .30 .10
❑ 204 Tim Biakabutuka .50 .20
❑ 205 Laveranues Coles .75 .30
❑ 206 Marshall Faulk 1.00 .40
❑ 207 Jim Harbaugh .50 .20
❑ 208 Doug Johnson .30 .10
❑ 209 Tee Martin .50 .20
❑ 210 Muhsin Muhammad .50 .20
❑ 211 Darnay Scott .30 .10
❑ 212 Jeremiah Trotter .50 .20
❑ 213 Troy Aikman 1.25 .50
❑ 214 Kyle Brady .30 .10
❑ 215 Sam Cowart .30 .10
❑ 216 Darren Howard .30 .10
❑ 217 Donald Hayes .30 .10
❑ 218 Freddie Jones .30 .10
❑ 219 Ed McCaffrey .75 .30
❑ 220 David Patten .30 .10
❑ 221 Brian Griese .75 .30
❑ 222 Dedric Ward .30 .10
❑ 223 Jerome Bettis .75 .30
❑ 224 Greg Clark .30 .10
❑ 225 Bobby Engram .30 .10
❑ 226 Matt Hasselbeck .50 .20
❑ 227 James Jett .30 .10
❑ 228 Peyton Manning 2.00 .75
❑ 229 Randy Moss 1.50 .60
❑ 230 Warren Sapp .50 .20
❑ 231 James Thrash .50 .20
❑ 232 Mike Alstott .75 .30
❑ 233 Tim Brown .75 .30
❑ 234 Randall Cunningham .75 .30
❑ 235 Antonio Freeman .75 .30
❑ 236 Torry Holt .75 .30
❑ 237 Jevon Kearse .50 .20
❑ 238 James McKnight .50 .20
❑ 239 Marcus Pollard .30 .10
❑ 240 Lamar Smith .50 .20
❑ 241 Peter Warrick .75 .30
❑ 242 Donnell Bennett .30 .10
❑ 243 Joe Johnson .30 .10
❑ 244 Troy Edwards .30 .10
❑ 245 Trent Green .75 .30
❑ 246 Jason Taylor .30 .10
❑ 247 Aeneas Williams .30 .10
❑ 248 Johnnie Morton .50 .20
❑ 249 Frank Sanders .30 .10
❑ 250 Jason Sehorn .30 .10
❑ 251 Chris Weinke RC 6.00 2.50
❑ 252 Bobby Newcombe RC 4.00 1.50
❑ 253 LaDainian Tomlinson RC 40.00 20.00
❑ 254 Chad Johnson RC 15.00 6.00
❑ 255 Derrick Gibson RC 4.00 1.50
❑ 256 Sage Rosenfels RC 6.00 2.50
❑ 257 LaMont Jordan RC 12.00 5.00
❑ 258 Mike McMahon RC 6.00 2.50
❑ 259 Vinny Sutherland RC 4.00 1.50
❑ 260 Drew Brees RC 20.00 10.00
❑ 261 Deuce McAllister RC 12.00 5.00
❑ 262 Kevan Barlow RC 6.00 2.50
❑ 263 Jamar Fletcher RC 4.00 1.50
❑ 264 Gerard Warren RC 6.00 2.50
❑ 265 Todd Heap RC 6.00 2.50
❑ 266 Travis Henry RC 12.00 5.00
❑ 267 Quincy Morgan RC 6.00 2.50
❑ 268 Anthony Thomas RC 6.00 2.50
❑ 269 Andre Carter RC 6.00 2.50
❑ 270 Freddie Mitchell RC 6.00 2.50
❑ 271 Richard Seymour RC 6.00 2.50
❑ 272 Josh Booty RC 6.00 2.50
❑ 273 Robert Ferguson RC 6.00 2.50
❑ 274 Marques Tuiasosopo RC 6.00 2.50
❑ 275 Reggie Wayne RC 12.00 5.00
❑ 276 Jabari Holloway RC 4.00 1.50
❑ 277 Rudi Johnson RC 12.00 5.00
❑ 278 Michael Bennett RC 6.00 2.50
❑ 279 Snoop Minnis RC 4.00 1.50
❑ 280 Dan Morgan RC 6.00 2.50
❑ 281 Rod Gardner RC 6.00 2.50
❑ 282 Jesse Palmer RC 6.00 2.50
❑ 283 Michael Vick RC 20.00 8.00
❑ 284 Chris Chambers RC 10.00 4.00
❑ 285 James Jackson RC 6.00 2.50
❑ 286 David Terrell RC 6.00 2.50
❑ 287 Koren Robinson RC 6.00 2.50
❑ 288 Travis Minor RC 4.00 1.50
❑ 289 Santana Moss RC 10.00 4.00
❑ 290 Josh Heupel RC 6.00 2.50
❑ 291 Jamal Reynolds RC 6.00 2.50
❑ 292 Ken-Yon Rambo RC 4.00 1.50
❑ 293 Cedrick Wilson RC 6.00 2.50
❑ 294 Alge Crumpler RC 8.00 3.00
❑ 295 Fred Smoot RC 6.00 2.50
❑ 296 Dan Alexander RC 6.00 2.50
❑ 297 Tim Hasselbeck RC 6.00 2.50
❑ 298 Will Allen RC 4.00 1.50
❑ 299 Keith Adams RC 4.00 1.50
❑ 300 Heath Evans RC 4.00 1.50
❑ U301 Quincy Carter RC 6.00 2.50
❑ U302 Derrick Blaylock RC 6.00 2.50
❑ U303 Correll Buckhalter RC 6.00 2.50
❑ U304 A.J. Feeley RC 6.00 2.50
❑ U305 Milton Wynn RC 4.00 1.50
❑ U306 Kevin Kasper RC 6.00 2.50
❑ U307 Justin McCareins RC 6.00 2.50
❑ U308 Dave Dickenson RC 4.00 1.50
❑ U309 Steve Smith RC 15.00 7.50
❑ U310 Moran Norris RC 2.50 1.00

2002 Ultra

❑ COMP.SET w/o SP's (200) 25.00 10.00
❑ 1 Donovan McNabb 1.00 .40
❑ 2 Chad Pennington 1.00 .40
❑ 3 Shaun Alexander 1.00 .40
❑ 4 Corey Dillon .50 .20
❑ 5 Kurt Warner .75 .30
❑ 6 Ed McCaffrey .75 .30
❑ 7 Hugh Douglas .30 .10
❑ 8 Tony Gonzalez .50 .20
❑ 9 Travis Taylor .50 .20
❑ 10 Tony Boselli .30 .10
❑ 11 Chad Scott .30 .10
❑ 12 Ernie Conwell .30 .10
❑ 13 Brad Johnson .50 .20
❑ 14 Donald Hayes .30 .10
❑ 15 Emmitt Smith 2.00 .75
❑ 16 Jimmy Smith .50 .20
❑ 17 Anthony Becht .30 .10
❑ 18 Rod Gardner .50 .20
❑ 19 Muhsin Muhammad .50 .20
❑ 20 Troy Hambrick .30 .10
❑ 21 Keenan McCardell .30 .10
❑ 22 Laveranues Coles .50 .20
❑ 23 Kevin Dyson .50 .20
❑ 24 Grant Wistrom .30 .10
❑ 25 Eric Moulds .50 .20
❑ 26 Nate Clements .30 .10
❑ 27 Terrell Davis .75 .30
❑ 28 Aaron Glenn .30 .10
❑ 29 Eric Hicks .30 .10
❑ 30 Tiki Barber .75 .30
❑ 31 Jake Plummer .50 .20
❑ 32 Junior Seau .75 .30
❑ 33 Marshall Faulk .75 .30
❑ 34 Warrick Dunn .75 .30
❑ 35 Bill Gramatica .30 .10
❑ 36 Tim Couch .50 .20
❑ 37 Kabeer Gbaja-Biamila .50 .20
❑ 38 Kailee Wong .30 .10
❑ 39 David Patten .30 .10
❑ 40 Correll Buckhalter .50 .20
❑ 41 Troy Brown .50 .20
❑ 42 Drew Bledsoe 1.00 .40
❑ 43 Travis Henry .75 .30
❑ 44 Jim Miller .30 .10
❑ 45 Rod Smith .50 .20
❑ 46 Tai Streets .30 .10
❑ 47 Snoop Minnis .30 .10
❑ 48 Ron Dayne .50 .20
❑ 49 Tyrone Wheatley .50 .20
❑ 50 LaDainian Tomlinson 1.25 .50
❑ 51 Akili Smith .30 .10
❑ 52 Warren Sapp .50 .20
❑ 53 Adam Archuleta .30 .10
❑ 54 Chris Fuamatu-Ma'afala .30 .10
❑ 55 Marty Booker .30 .10
❑ 56 Trevor Pryce .30 .10
❑ 57 Peyton Manning 1.50 .60
❑ 58 Lamar Smith .50 .20
❑ 59 Amani Toomer .50 .20
❑ 60 Greg Biekert .30 .10

❑ 61	Marcellus Wiley	.30	.10
❑ 62	Ahmed Plummer	.30	.10
❑ 63	Mike Alstott	.75	.30
❑ 64	Gary Walker	.30	.10
❑ 65	Champ Bailey	.50	.20
❑ 66	Chris Redman	.30	.10
❑ 67	David Terrell	.75	.30
❑ 68	Mike McMahon	.75	.30
❑ 69	Marvin Harrison	.75	.30
❑ 70	Jay Fiedler	.50	.20
❑ 71	JaJuan Dawson	.30	.10
❑ 72	Charlie Garner	.50	.20
❑ 73	Curtis Conway	.30	.10
❑ 74	J.J. Stokes	.50	.20
❑ 75	Ronde Barber	.30	.10
❑ 76	Alge Crumpler	.50	.20
❑ 77	Jamir Miller	.30	.10
❑ 78	Brett Favre	2.00	.75
❑ 79	Randy Moss	1.50	.60
❑ 80	Joe Horn	.50	.20
❑ 81	Hines Ward	.75	.30
❑ 82	Lawyer Milloy	.50	.20
❑ 83	Aeneas Williams	.30	.10
❑ 84	Chris McAlister	.30	.10
❑ 85	Anthony Thomas	.50	.20
❑ 86	Johnnie Morton	.50	.20
❑ 87	Edgerrin James	1.00	.40
❑ 88	Chris Chambers	.75	.30
❑ 89	Michael Strahan	.50	.20
❑ 90	Charles Woodson	.50	.20
❑ 91	Tim Dwight	.50	.20
❑ 92	Kevan Barlow	.50	.20
❑ 93	Donnie Abraham	.30	.10
❑ 94	Peter Boulware	.30	.10
❑ 95	Marcus Robinson	.50	.20
❑ 96	Shaun Rogers	.30	.10
❑ 97	Dominic Rhodes	.50	.20
❑ 98	Zach Thomas	.75	.30
❑ 99	Kerry Collins	.50	.20
❑ 100	Tim Brown	.75	.30
❑ 101	Garrison Hearst	.50	.20
❑ 102	Steve McNair	.75	.30
❑ 103	Fred Smoot	.30	.10
❑ 104	Isaac Bruce	.75	.30
❑ 105	Jamal Lewis	.75	.30
❑ 106	Brian Urlacher	1.25	.50
❑ 107	Takeo Spikes	.30	.10
❑ 108	Marcus Pollard	.30	.10
❑ 109	Jason Taylor	.30	.10
❑ 110	Deuce McAllister	1.00	.40
❑ 111	Jerry Rice	1.50	.60
❑ 112	Terrell Owens	.75	.30
❑ 113	Eddie George	.75	.30
❑ 114	Rob Morris	.30	.10
❑ 115	Mike Brown	.75	.30
❑ 116	Joey Galloway	.50	.20
❑ 117	Fred Taylor	.75	.30
❑ 118	Rich Gannon	.75	.30
❑ 119	Chris Chandler	.50	.20
❑ 120	Koren Robinson	.50	.20
❑ 121	Dan Morgan	.30	.10
❑ 122	Rocket Ismail	.50	.20
❑ 123	Mark Brunell	.75	.30
❑ 124	John Abraham	.50	.20
❑ 125	Stephen Davis	.50	.20
❑ 126	Patrick Kerney	.30	.10
❑ 127	Anthony Henry	.30	.10
❑ 128	Scotty Anderson	.30	.10
❑ 129	Oronde Gadsden	.30	.10
❑ 130	Willie Jackson	.30	.10
❑ 131	Kendrell Bell	.75	.30
❑ 132	Ray Lewis	.75	.30
❑ 133	Quincy Carter	.50	.20
❑ 134	James Stewart	.50	.20
❑ 135	Travis Minor	.30	.10
❑ 136	Kyle Turley	.30	.10
❑ 137	Jason Gildon	.30	.10
❑ 138	David Boston	.75	.30
❑ 139	Justin Smith	.30	.10
❑ 140	Jamie Sharper	.30	.10
❑ 141	Antowain Smith	.50	.20
❑ 142	Freddie Mitchell	.50	.20
❑ 143	Frank Sanders	.30	.10
❑ 144	Kevin Johnson	.50	.20
❑ 145	Darren Sharper	.30	.10
❑ 146	Eric Johnson	.30	.10
❑ 147	Ty Law	.50	.20
❑ 148	James Thrash	.50	.20
❑ 149	Matt Hasselbeck	.50	.20
❑ 150	Peerless Price	.50	.20
❑ 151	T.J. Houshmandzadeh	.50	.20
❑ 152	Mike Anderson	.75	.30
❑ 153	Jermaine Lewis	.30	.10
❑ 154	Trent Green	.50	.20
❑ 155	Ron Dixon	.30	.10
❑ 156	Duce Staley	.75	.30
❑ 157	Drew Brees	.75	.30
❑ 158	Torry Holt	.75	.30
❑ 159	Keyshawn Johnson	.75	.30
❑ 160	Michael Vick	1.50	.60
❑ 161	Benjamin Gay	.30	.10
❑ 162	Bill Schroeder	.50	.20
❑ 163	Byron Chamberlain	.30	.10
❑ 164	Tedy Bruschi	.75	.30
❑ 165	Kordell Stewart	.50	.20
❑ 166	Deltha O'Neal	.30	.10
❑ 167	Quincy Morgan	.30	.10
❑ 168	Bubba Franks	.50	.20
❑ 169	Daunte Culpepper	.75	.30
❑ 170	Ricky Williams	4.00	1.50
❑ 171	Plaxico Burress	.50	.20
❑ 172	Trent Dilfer	.50	.20
❑ 173	Steve Smith	.75	.30
❑ 174	Greg Ellis	.30	.10
❑ 175	Tony Brackens	.30	.10
❑ 176	Santana Moss	.75	.30
❑ 177	Frank Wycheck	.30	.10
❑ 178	Michael Pittman	.30	.10
❑ 179	Peter Warrick	.50	.20
❑ 180	Antonio Freeman	.75	.30
❑ 181	Tom Brady	2.00	.75
❑ 182	Bobby Taylor	.30	.10
❑ 183	Jeff Garcia	.75	.30
❑ 184	Darrell Jackson	.50	.20
❑ 185	Chris Weinke	.50	.20
❑ 186	Darren Woodson	.30	.10
❑ 187	Hardy Nickerson	.30	.10
❑ 188	Wayne Chrebet	.50	.20
❑ 189	Samari Rolle	.30	.10
❑ 190	Jamal Anderson	.50	.20
❑ 191	James Jackson	.30	.10
❑ 192	Ahman Green	.75	.30
❑ 193	Michael Bennett	.50	.20
❑ 194	Aaron Brooks	.75	.30
❑ 195	Jerome Bettis	.75	.30
❑ 196	Jay Riemersma	.30	.10
❑ 197	Brian Griese	.75	.30
❑ 198	Priest Holmes	1.00	.40
❑ 199	Curtis Martin	.75	.30
❑ 200	Derrick Mason	.50	.20
❑ 201	Antonio Bryant RC	5.00	2.00
❑ 202	David Carr RC	10.00	4.00
❑ 203	Eric Crouch RC	5.00	2.00
❑ 204	Freddie Milons RC	4.00	1.50
❑ 205	Najeh Davenport RC	5.00	2.00
❑ 206	Rohan Davey RC	5.00	2.00
❑ 207	T.J. Duckett RC	5.00	2.00
❑ 208	DeShaun Foster RC	5.00	2.00
❑ 209	Jabar Gaffney RC	5.00	2.00
❑ 210	William Green RC	5.00	2.00
❑ 211	Joey Harrington RC	6.00	2.50
❑ 212	Travis Stephens RC	4.00	1.50
❑ 213	Julius Peppers RC	10.00	4.00
❑ 214	Adrian Peterson RC	6.00	2.50
❑ 215	Josh Reed RC	5.00	2.00
❑ 216	Mike Williams RC	5.00	2.00
❑ 217	Javon Walker RC	8.00	3.00
❑ 218	Marquise Walker RC	4.00	1.50
❑ 219	Patrick Ramsey RC	5.00	2.00
❑ 220	Lamar Gordon RC	5.00	2.00
❑ 221	David Garrard RC	10.00	4.00
❑ 222	Major Applewhite RC	5.00	2.00
❑ 223	Andre Davis RC	4.00	1.50
❑ 224	Roy Williams RC	10.00	4.00
❑ 225	Tim Carter RC	4.00	1.50
❑ 226	Ron Johnson RC	4.00	1.50
❑ 227	Randy Fasani RC	4.00	1.50
❑ 228	Ashley Lelie RC	10.00	4.00
❑ 229	Ladell Betts RC	5.00	2.00
❑ 230	Antwaan Randle El RC	6.00	2.50
❑ 231	Jonathan Wells RC	5.00	2.00
❑ 232	Brian Westbrook RC	10.00	4.00
❑ 233	Clinton Portis RC	15.00	6.00
❑ 234	Luke Staley RC	4.00	1.50
❑ 235	Cliff Russell RC	4.00	1.50
❑ 236	Jeremy Shockey RC	15.00	6.00
❑ 237	Donte Stallworth RC	8.00	3.00
❑ 238	Daniel Graham RC	5.00	2.00
❑ 239	Reche Caldwell RC	5.00	2.00
❑ 240	Ryan Sims RC	5.00	2.00

2003 Ultra

❑	COMP.SET w/o SP's (160)	30.00	12.50
❑ 1	Rich Gannon	.50	.20
❑ 2	Warren Sapp	.50	.20
❑ 3	Steve McNair	.75	.30
❑ 4	Donovan McNabb	1.00	.40
❑ 5	Chad Pennington	1.00	.40
❑ 6	Michael Vick	2.00	.75
❑ 7	Hines Ward	.75	.30
❑ 8	Terrell Owens	.75	.30
❑ 9	Brett Favre	2.00	.75
❑ 10	Jeremy Shockey	1.25	.50
❑ 11	William Green	.50	.20
❑ 12	Marvin Harrison	.75	.30
❑ 13	Mark Brunell	.50	.20
❑ 14	Todd Heap	.50	.20
❑ 15	Tim Couch	.30	.10
❑ 16	Javon Walker	.50	.20
❑ 17	Zach Thomas	.50	.20
❑ 18	Brian Westbrook	.50	.20
❑ 19	Matt Hasselbeck	.50	.20
❑ 20	Jevon Kearse	.50	.20
❑ 21	David Boston	.50	.20
❑ 22	Michael Bennett	.50	.20
❑ 23	James Mungro	.30	.10
❑ 24	Antowain Smith	.50	.20
❑ 25	Laveranues Coles	.50	.20
❑ 26	Curtis Conway	.30	.10
❑ 27	Peerless Price	.50	.20
❑ 28	Michael Strahan	.50	.20
❑ 29	Tommy Maddox	.75	.30
❑ 30	Dennis Northcutt	.50	.20
❑ 31	Rod Gardner	.50	.20
❑ 32	Marcel Shipp	.50	.20
❑ 33	Quincy Morgan	.50	.20
❑ 34	Reggie Wayne	.50	.20
❑ 35	Troy Brown	.50	.20
❑ 36	John Abraham	.30	.10
❑ 37	Tim Dwight	.50	.20
❑ 38	Jamal Lewis	.75	.30
❑ 39	Chad Hutchinson	.30	.10
❑ 40	Jerramy Stevens	.30	.10
❑ 41	Deion Branch	.75	.30
❑ 42	Jake Plummer	.50	.20
❑ 43	Junior Seau	.75	.30
❑ 44	T.J. Duckett	.50	.20
❑ 45	Emmitt Smith	2.00	.75
❑ 46	Edgerrin James	.75	.30
❑ 47	David Patten	.30	.10
❑ 48	Charlie Garner	.50	.20
❑ 49	Quentin Jammer	.30	.10
❑ 50	Corey Dillon	.50	.20
❑ 51	Rod Smith	.50	.20
❑ 52	Marc Boerigter	.50	.20
❑ 53	Michael Lewis	.30	.10
❑ 54	Kendrell Bell	.50	.20
❑ 55	Isaac Bruce	.75	.30

❑ 56 Warrick Dunn .50 .20
❑ 57 Antonio Bryant .50 .20
❑ 58 Peyton Manning 1.25 .50
❑ 59 Ty Law .50 .20
❑ 60 Jerry Rice 1.50 .60
❑ 61 Jeff Garcia .75 .30
❑ 62 Joey Galloway .50 .20
❑ 63 Aaron Glenn .30 .10
❑ 64 Aaron Brooks .75 .30
❑ 65 Tim Brown .75 .30
❑ 66 David Terrell .50 .20
❑ 67 Fred Smoot .30 .10
❑ 68 Brian Finneran .30 .10
❑ 69 Roy Williams .75 .30
❑ 70 Corey Bradford .30 .10
❑ 71 Deuce McAllister .75 .30
❑ 72 Jerry Porter .50 .20
❑ 73 Kevan Barlow .50 .20
❑ 74 Keith Brooking .30 .10
❑ 75 Brian Urlacher 1.25 .50
❑ 76 Jabar Gaffney .50 .20
❑ 77 Randy Moss 1.25 .50
❑ 78 Charles Woodson .50 .20
❑ 79 Darrell Jackson .50 .20
❑ 80 John Lynch .50 .20
❑ 81 Chester Taylor .30 .10
❑ 82 Anthony Thomas .50 .20
❑ 83 Jonathan Wells .30 .10
❑ 84 Daunte Culpepper .75 .30
❑ 85 Phillip Buchanon .30 .10
❑ 86 Koren Robinson .30 .10
❑ 87 Ronde Barber .30 .10
❑ 88 Julius Peppers .75 .30
❑ 89 Clinton Portis 1.25 .50
❑ 90 Jay Fiedler .50 .20
❑ 91 Donte Stallworth .75 .30
❑ 92 Marc Bulger .75 .30
❑ 93 Joe Jurevicius .30 .10
❑ 94 Jon Kitna .50 .20
❑ 95 Ricky Williams .75 .30
❑ 96 Joe Horn .50 .20
❑ 97 Jerome Bettis .75 .30
❑ 98 Kurt Warner .75 .30
❑ 99 Travis Henry .50 .20
❑ 100 Ahman Green .75 .30
❑ 101 Jimmy Smith .50 .20
❑ 102 Curtis Martin .75 .30
❑ 103 Simeon Rice .50 .20
❑ 104 Patrick Ramsey .75 .30
❑ 105 Josh Reed .50 .20
❑ 106 James Stewart .50 .20
❑ 107 Trent Green .50 .20
❑ 108 Randy McMichael .50 .20
❑ 109 Amos Zereoue .50 .20
❑ 110 Keyshawn Johnson .75 .30
❑ 111 DeShaun Foster .30 .10
❑ 112 Kevin Johnson .50 .20
❑ 113 Dwight Freeney .50 .20
❑ 114 Tom Brady 2.00 .75
❑ 115 Santana Moss .50 .20
❑ 116 LaDainian Tomlinson .75 .30
❑ 117 Joey Harrington 1.25 .50
❑ 118 Priest Holmes 1.00 .40
❑ 119 Amani Toomer .50 .20
❑ 120 Plaxico Burress .50 .20
❑ 121 Brad Johnson .50 .20
❑ 122 Champ Bailey .50 .20
❑ 123 Muhsin Muhammad .50 .20
❑ 124 Ashley Lelie .75 .30
❑ 125 Tony Gonzalez .50 .20
❑ 126 Kerry Collins .50 .20
❑ 127 Antwaan Randle El .75 .30
❑ 128 Torry Holt .75 .30
❑ 129 Ladell Betts .50 .20
❑ 130 Travis Taylor .30 .10
❑ 131 Marty Booker .50 .20
❑ 132 Patrick Surtain .30 .10
❑ 133 Duce Staley .50 .20
❑ 134 Shaun Alexander .75 .30
❑ 135 Eddie George .50 .20
❑ 136 Eric Moulds .50 .20
❑ 137 David Carr 1.25 .50
❑ 138 Fred Taylor .75 .30
❑ 139 Wayne Chrebet .50 .20
❑ 140 Bobby Taylor .30 .10
❑ 141 Derrick Brooks .50 .20
❑ 142 Stephen Davis .50 .20
❑ 143 Ray Lewis .75 .30
❑ 144 Kelly Holcomb .50 .20
❑ 145 Terry Glenn .30 .10
❑ 146 Jason Taylor .30 .10
❑ 147 Todd Pinkston .50 .20
❑ 148 Derrick Mason .50 .20
❑ 149 Chad Johnson .75 .30
❑ 150 Ed McCaffrey .50 .20
❑ 151 Tiki Barber .75 .30
❑ 152 Drew Brees .75 .30
❑ 153 Marshall Faulk .75 .30
❑ 154 Drew Bledsoe .75 .30
❑ 155 Andre Davis .30 .10
❑ 156 Donald Driver .50 .20
❑ 157 Chris Chambers .75 .30
❑ 158 Brian Dawkins .50 .20
❑ 159 Garrison Hearst .50 .20
❑ 160 Frank Wycheck .30 .10
❑ 161 Carson Palmer RC 15.00 6.00
❑ 162 Byron Leftwich RC 12.00 5.00
❑ 163 Charles Rogers RC 4.00 1.50
❑ 164 Andre Johnson RC 8.00 3.00
❑ 165 Chris Simms RC 6.00 2.50
❑ 166 Rex Grossman RC 12.00 5.00
❑ 167 Brandon Lloyd RC 4.00 1.50
❑ 168 Lee Suggs RC 4.00 1.50
❑ 169 Larry Johnson RC 15.00 7.50
❑ 170 Onterrio Smith RC 4.00 1.50
❑ 171 Dave Ragone RC 4.00 1.50
❑ 172 Taylor Jacobs RC 3.00 1.25
❑ 173 Kelley Washington RC 4.00 1.50
❑ 174 Bryant Johnson RC 4.00 1.50
❑ 175 Kyle Boller RC 4.00 1.50
❑ 176 Ken Dorsey RC 4.00 1.50
❑ 177 Kliff Kingsbury RC 3.00 1.25
❑ 178 Jason Gesser RC 4.00 1.50
❑ 179 Brian St.Pierre RC 4.00 1.50
❑ 180 Brad Banks RC 3.00 1.25
❑ 181 Seneca Wallace RC 4.00 1.50
❑ 182 Tony Romo RC 30.00 15.00
❑ 183 Terrell Suggs RC 6.00 2.50
❑ 184 Terence Newman RC 8.00 3.00
❑ 185 Willis McGahee RC 10.00 4.00
❑ 186 Justin Fargas RC 4.00 1.50
❑ 187 Musa Smith RC 4.00 1.50
❑ 188 Earnest Graham RC 4.00 1.50
❑ 189 Chris Brown RC 4.00 1.50
❑ 190 LaBrandon Toefield RC 4.00 1.50
❑ 191 Bennie Joppru RC 4.00 1.50
❑ 192 Jason Witten RC 8.00 3.00
❑ 193 Anquan Boldin RC 10.00 4.00
❑ 194 Talman Gardner RC 4.00 1.50
❑ 195 Justin Gage RC 4.00 1.50
❑ 196 Sam Aiken RC 3.00 1.25
❑ 197 Kevin Curtis RC 5.00 2.00
❑ 198 Terrence Edwards RC 3.00 1.25
❑ U199 DeWayne Robertson RC 4.00 1.50
❑ U200 Kevin Williams RC 4.00 1.50
❑ U201 Marcus Trufant RC 4.00 1.50
❑ U202 Jimmy Kennedy RC 4.00 1.50
❑ U203 Ty Warren RC 4.00 1.50
❑ U204 Michael Haynes RC 4.00 1.50
❑ U205 Jerome McDougle RC 4.00 1.50
❑ U206 Dallas Clark RC 4.00 1.50
❑ U207 William Joseph RC 4.00 1.50
❑ U208 Andre Woolfolk RC 4.00 1.50
❑ U209 Bethel Johnson RC 4.00 1.50
❑ U210 Teyo Johnson RC 4.00 1.50
❑ U211 Tyrone Calico RC 4.00 1.50
❑ U212 L.J. Smith RC 4.00 1.50
❑ U213 Nate Burleson RC 4.00 1.50
❑ U214 B.J. Askew RC 4.00 1.50
❑ U215 Billy McMullen RC 4.00 1.50
❑ U216 Domanick Davis RC 4.00 1.50
❑ U217 Doug Gabriel RC 4.00 1.50
❑ U218 Quentin Griffin RC 4.00 1.50

2004 Ultra

❑ COMP.SET w/o L13's (218) 60.00 25.00
❑ COMP.SET w/o SP's (200) 30.00 12.50
❑ COMP.UPDATE SET (21) 40.00 15.00
❑ L13 201-213 ROOKIE ODDS 1:100H,1:530R
❑ L13 ROOKIE PRINT RUN 500 SER.#'d SETS
❑ 214-232 ROOKIE STATED ODDS 1:4H,1:6R

❑ U234-U254 ODDS 2:1 TRADITION HOT PACK
❑ 1 Michael Vick 1.50 .60
❑ 2 Kelley Washington .30 .10
❑ 3 Rex Grossman .75 .30
❑ 4 Boss Bailey .50 .20
❑ 5 Johnnie Morton .50 .20
❑ 6 Michael Strahan .50 .20
❑ 7 Joey Porter .50 .20
❑ 8 Keenan McCardell .30 .10
❑ 9 Quincy Carter .50 .20
❑ 10 Travis Henry .50 .20
❑ 11 Bertrand Berry .30 .10
❑ 12 Marvin Harrison .75 .30
❑ 13 Ty Law .50 .20
❑ 14 Phillip Buchanon .30 .10
❑ 15 Kevan Barlow .50 .20
❑ 16 Eddie George .50 .20
❑ 17 Drew Bledsoe .75 .30
❑ 18 Antonio Bryant .50 .20
❑ 19 Marcus Pollard .30 .10
❑ 20 Brian Russell RC .75 .30
❑ 21 Santana Moss .50 .20
❑ 22 Julian Peterson .30 .10
❑ 23 Justin McCareins .30 .10
❑ 24 Ed Reed .50 .20
❑ 25 Charles Tillman .50 .20
❑ 26 Dat Nguyen .30 .10
❑ 27 Ricky Manning .30 .10
❑ 28 Dwight Freeney .50 .20
❑ 29 Zach Thomas .75 .30
❑ 30 Tiki Barber .75 .30
❑ 31 Jay Riemersma .30 .10
❑ 32 Joe Jurevicius .30 .10
❑ 33 Marcel Shipp .50 .20
❑ 34 Justin Gage .50 .20
❑ 35 Charles Rogers .50 .20
❑ 36 Eddie Kennison .30 .10
❑ 37 Deion Branch .75 .30
❑ 38 Matt Hasselbeck .50 .20
❑ 39 L.J. Smith .50 .20
❑ 40 Jamal Lewis .75 .30
❑ 41 Muhsin Muhammad .50 .20
❑ 42 Terence Newman .50 .20
❑ 43 Jabar Gaffney .50 .20
❑ 44 Junior Seau .75 .30
❑ 45 Jeremy Shockey .75 .30
❑ 46 Hines Ward .75 .30
❑ 47 Brad Johnson .50 .20
❑ 48 Kyle Boller .75 .30
❑ 49 Steve Smith .75 .30
❑ 50 Quincy Morgan .50 .20
❑ 51 Corey Bradford .30 .10
❑ 52 Ricky Williams .75 .30
❑ 53 Amani Toomer .50 .20
❑ 54 Plaxico Burress .50 .20
❑ 55 Derrick Brooks .50 .20
❑ 56 Dre Bly .30 .10
❑ 57 Terrell Suggs .50 .20
❑ 58 DeShaun Foster .50 .20
❑ 59 Andre Davis .30 .10
❑ 60 Rod Smith .50 .20
❑ 61 Andre Johnson .75 .30
❑ 62 Randy McMichael .30 .10
❑ 63 Ike Hilliard .30 .10
❑ 64 Antwaan Randle El .75 .30
❑ 65 Warren Sapp .50 .20
❑ 66 LaBrandon Toefield .30 .10
❑ 67 Chad Johnson .75 .30

No.	Player	Hi	Lo
❑ 68	Javon Walker	.50	.20
❑ 69	Jimmy Smith	.50	.20
❑ 70	Donte Stallworth	.50	.20
❑ 71	Brian Dawkins	.50	.20
❑ 72	Leonard Little	.30	.10
❑ 73	Ladell Betts	.30	.10
❑ 74	Ray Lewis	.75	.30
❑ 75	Stephen Davis	.50	.20
❑ 76	Dennis Northcutt	.30	.10
❑ 77	Ashley Lelie	.50	.20
❑ 78	Billy Miller	.30	.10
❑ 79	Chris Chambers	.50	.20
❑ 80	John Abraham	.30	.10
❑ 81	Quentin Jammer	.30	.10
❑ 82	Isaac Bruce	.50	.20
❑ 83	Peerless Price	.50	.20
❑ 84	Jake Delhomme	.75	.30
❑ 85	Lee Suggs	.75	.30
❑ 86	Shannon Sharpe	.50	.20
❑ 87	Domanick Davis	.75	.30
❑ 88	Daunte Culpepper	.75	.30
❑ 89	Shaun Ellis	.30	.10
❑ 90	Drew Brees	.75	.30
❑ 91	Torry Holt	.75	.30
❑ 92	Alge Crumpler	.50	.20
❑ 93	Mike Rucker	.50	.20
❑ 94	Tim Couch	.30	.10
❑ 95	Quentin Griffin	.75	.30
❑ 96	David Carr	.75	.30
❑ 97	Moe Williams	.30	.10
❑ 98	Chad Pennington	.75	.30
❑ 99	LaDainian Tomlinson	1.00	.40
❑ 100	Adam Archuleta	.30	.10
❑ 101	Julius Peppers	.75	.30
❑ 102	Clinton Portis	.75	.30
❑ 103	Marcus Stroud	.30	.10
❑ 104	Tom Brady	2.00	.75
❑ 105	Teyo Johnson	.30	.10
❑ 106	Terrell Owens	.75	.30
❑ 107	Keith Bulluck	.30	.10
❑ 108	Eric Moulds	.50	.20
❑ 109	Jake Plummer	.50	.20
❑ 110	Reggie Wayne	.50	.20
❑ 111	Tedy Bruschi	.50	.20
❑ 112	Rich Gannon	.50	.20
❑ 113	Tony Parrish	.30	.10
❑ 114	Steve McNair	.75	.30
❑ 115	T.J. Duckett	.50	.20
❑ 116	Peter Warrick	.50	.20
❑ 117	Donald Driver	.50	.20
❑ 118	Fred Taylor	.50	.20
❑ 119	Joe Horn	.50	.20
❑ 120	Jerry Porter	.50	.20
❑ 121	Marc Bulger	.75	.30
❑ 122	Trung Canidate	.30	.10
❑ 123	Warrick Dunn	.50	.20
❑ 124	Kelly Holcomb	.50	.20
❑ 125	Robert Ferguson	.30	.10
❑ 126	Byron Leftwich	1.00	.40
❑ 127	Michael Lewis	.30	.10
❑ 128	Jerry Rice	1.50	.60
❑ 129	Marshall Faulk	.75	.30
❑ 130	Patrick Ramsey	.50	.20
❑ 131	Josh McCown	.50	.20
❑ 132	Anthony Thomas	.50	.20
❑ 133	Joey Harrington	.75	.30
❑ 134	Dante Hall	.75	.30
❑ 135	Daniel Graham	.30	.10
❑ 136	Richard Seymour	.30	.10
❑ 137	Brandon Lloyd	.50	.20
❑ 138	Anquan Boldin	.75	.30
❑ 139	Jon Kitna	.50	.20
❑ 140	Nick Barnett	.50	.20
❑ 141	Priest Holmes	1.00	.40
❑ 142	Bethel Johnson	.50	.20
❑ 143	Shaun Alexander	.75	.30
❑ 144	Todd Heap	.50	.20
❑ 145	Brian Urlacher	1.00	.40
❑ 146	Peyton Manning	1.25	.50
❑ 147	Jason Taylor	.30	.10
❑ 148	Kerry Collins	.50	.20
❑ 149	Tommy Maddox	.50	.20
❑ 150	Charles Lee	.30	.10
❑ 151	Tim Rattay	.30	.10
❑ 152	Carson Palmer	1.00	.40
❑ 153	Brett Favre	2.00	.75
❑ 154	Trent Green	.50	.20
❑ 155	Aaron Brooks	.50	.20
❑ 156	Brian Westbrook	.50	.20
❑ 157	Itula Mili	.30	.10
❑ 158	Keith Brooking	.30	.10
❑ 159	Rudi Johnson	.50	.20
❑ 160	Najeh Davenport	.30	.10
❑ 161	Kevin Johnson	.30	.10
❑ 162	Boo Williams	.30	.10
❑ 163	Corey Simon	.50	.20
❑ 164	Darrell Jackson	.50	.20
❑ 165	Darnerien McCants	.30	.10
❑ 166	Willis McGahee	.75	.30
❑ 167	Terry Glenn	.30	.10
❑ 168	Dallas Clark	.50	.20
❑ 169	Randy Moss	1.00	.40
❑ 170	Charles Woodson	.50	.20
❑ 171	Jeff Garcia	.75	.30
❑ 172	Chris Brown	.75	.30
❑ 173	Emmitt Smith	1.50	.60
❑ 174	Marty Booker	.50	.20
❑ 175	Artose Pinner	.30	.10
❑ 176	Tony Gonzalez	.50	.20
❑ 177	Troy Brown	.50	.20
❑ 178	Freddie Mitchell	.50	.20
❑ 179	Marcus Trufant	.30	.10
❑ 180	London Fletcher	.30	.10
❑ 181	Roy Williams S	.50	.20
❑ 182	Edgerrin James	.75	.30
❑ 183	Michael Bennett	.50	.20
❑ 184	Jerald Sowell	.30	.10
❑ 185	David Boston	.50	.20
❑ 186	Derrick Mason	.50	.20
❑ 187	Bryant Johnson	.30	.10
❑ 188	Corey Dillon	.60	.20
❑ 189	Ahman Green	.75	.30
❑ 190	Vonnie Holliday	.30	.10
❑ 191	Deuce McAllister	.75	.30
❑ 192	Donovan McNabb	1.00	.40
❑ 193	Koren Robinson	.50	.20
❑ 194	Laveranues Coles	.50	.20
❑ 195	Takeo Spikes	.30	.10
❑ 196	Richie Anderson	.30	.10
❑ 197	Onterrio Smith	.50	.20
❑ 198	Curtis Martin	.75	.30
❑ 199	Antonio Gates	.75	.30
❑ 200	Champ Bailey	.50	.20
❑ 201	Eli Manning L13 RC	80.00	30.00
❑ 202	Philip Rivers L13 RC	50.00	25.00
❑ 203	Roy Williams L13 RC	50.00	20.00
❑ 204	Drew Henson L13 RC	20.00	7.50
❑ 205	Chris Perry L13 RC	25.00	10.00
❑ 206	Larry Fitzgerald L13 RC	50.00	20.00
❑ 207	Rashaun Woods L13 RC	20.00	7.50
❑ 208	Reggie Williams L13 RC	30.00	12.50
❑ 209	Mike Williams L13 RC	20.00	7.50
❑ 210	Kellen Winslow L13 RC	30.00	12.50
❑ 211	Steven Jackson L13 RC	50.00	20.00
❑ 212	Kevin Jones L13 RC	40.00	15.00
❑ 213	Ben Roethlisberger L13 RC	100.00	40.00
❑ 214	Michael Turner RC	6.00	2.50
❑ 215	Tatum Bell RC	8.00	3.00
❑ 216	Quincy Wilson RC	2.50	1.00
❑ 217	Devery Henderson RC	3.00	1.25
❑ 218	Ernest Wilford RC	4.00	1.60
❑ 219	Cody Pickett RC	4.00	1.50
❑ 220	Ryan Dinwiddie RC	2.50	1.00
❑ 221	J.P. Losman RC	8.00	3.00
❑ 222	Derrick Knight RC	2.50	1.00
❑ 223	Michael Jenkins RC	4.00	1.50
❑ 224	Greg Jones RC	4.00	1.50
❑ 225	Cedric Cobbs RC	4.00	1.50
❑ 226	Will Poole RC	4.00	1.50
❑ 227	Michael Clayton RC	8.00	3.00
❑ 228	Sean Taylor RC	4.00	1.50
❑ 229	Will Smith RC	4.00	1.50
❑ 230	Jonathan Vilma RC	4.00	1.50
❑ 231	Lee Evans RC	5.00	2.00
❑ 232	Julius Jones RC	12.00	5.00
❑ U234	D.J. Williams RC	5.00	2.00
❑ U235	Mewelde Moore RC	5.00	2.00
❑ U236	Ben Watson RC	5.00	2.00
❑ U237	Robert Gallery RC	5.00	2.00
❑ U238	DeAngelo Hall RC	6.00	2.50
❑ U239	Luke McCown RC	5.00	2.00
❑ U240	Ben Troupe RC	5.00	2.00
❑ U241	Keary Colbert RC	5.00	2.00
❑ U242	Matt Schaub RC	12.00	5.00
❑ U243	Kenechi Udeze RC	5.00	2.00
❑ U244	Jeff Smoker RC	5.00	2.00
❑ U245	Derrick Hamilton RC	4.00	1.50
❑ U246	Bernard Berrian RC	6.00	2.50
❑ U247	Devard Darling RC	5.00	2.00
❑ U248	Johnnie Morant RC	5.00	2.00
❑ U249	Vince Wilfork RC	5.00	2.00
❑ U250	Jerricho Cotchery RC	5.00	2.00
❑ U251	Darius Watts RC	5.00	2.00
❑ U252	Carlos Francis RC	4.00	1.50
❑ U253	P.K. Sam RC	4.00	1.50

2005 Ultra

No.	Player	Hi	Lo
❑	COMP.SET w/o RC's (200)	30.00	12.50
❑	201-213 L13 PRINT RUN 599 SER.#'d SETS		
❑	OVERALL ROOKIE ODDS 1:4 HOB, 1:5 RET		
❑ 1	Peyton Manning	1.25	.50
❑ 2	Brian Westbrook	.50	.20
❑ 3	Daunte Culpepper	.75	.30
❑ 4	Marvin Harrison	.75	.30
❑ 5	Edgerrin James	.75	.30
❑ 6	Reggie Wayne	.50	.20
❑ 7	Michael Vick	1.25	.50
❑ 8	Donte Stallworth	.50	.20
❑ 9	Brian Urlacher	.75	.30
❑ 10	Hines Ward	.75	.30
❑ 11	Charles Rogers	.50	.20
❑ 12	Roy Williams WR	.75	.30
❑ 13	Julius Peppers	.50	.20
❑ 14	Eric Moulds	.50	.20
❑ 15	Ray Lewis	.75	.30
❑ 16	Byron Leftwich	.75	.30
❑ 17	Fred Taylor	.50	.20
❑ 18	Andre Johnson	.50	.20
❑ 19	Travis Henry	.50	.20
❑ 20	Tom Brady	2.00	.75
❑ 21	Drew Bledsoe	.75	.30
❑ 22	Tiki Barber	.75	.30
❑ 23	Larry Fitzgerald	.75	.30
❑ 24	Jeff Garcia	.50	.20
❑ 25	Rex Grossman	.50	.20
❑ 26	Larry Johnson	.75	.30
❑ 27	Curtis Martin	.75	.30
❑ 28	Chad Pennington	.75	.30
❑ 29	Dwight Freeney	.50	.20
❑ 30	Peerless Price	.40	.15
❑ 31	Rich Gannon	.50	.20
❑ 32	Matt Hasselbeck	.50	.20
❑ 33	Clinton Portis	.75	.30
❑ 34	Jerry Rice	1.25	.50
❑ 35	Jeremy Shockey	.75	.30
❑ 36	Tony Gonzalez	.50	.20
❑ 37	Deuce McAllister	.75	.30
❑ 38	Shaun Alexander	1.00	.40
❑ 39	Peter Warrick	.50	.20
❑ 40	Isaac Bruce	.50	.20
❑ 41	Antonio Bryant	.40	.15
❑ 42	Mike Alstott	.50	.20
❑ 43	Domanick Davis	.50	.20
❑ 44	Jake Delhomme	.75	.30
❑ 45	Santana Moss	.50	.20
❑ 46	Ahman Green	.75	.30
❑ 47	David Carr	.75	.30
❑ 48	Kyle Boller	.50	.20

❑ 49 Chris Chambers .50 .20
❑ 50 Quentin Griffin .40 .15
❑ 51 Donovan McNabb 1.00 .40
❑ 52 Eli Manning 1.50 .60
❑ 53 Julius Jones 1.00 .40
❑ 54 Sean Taylor .50 .20
❑ 55 Javon Walker .50 .20
❑ 56 Randy Moss .75 .30
❑ 57 Thomas Jones .50 .20
❑ 58 Joey Harrington .75 .30
❑ 59 Michael Boulware .40 .15
❑ 60 Marshall Faulk .75 .30
❑ 61 Tony Parrish .40 .15
❑ 62 Bertrand Berry .40 .15
❑ 63 Alge Crumpler .50 .20
❑ 64 Aaron Brooks .50 .20
❑ 65 Muhsin Muhammad .50 .20
❑ 66 Simeon Rice .50 .20
❑ 67 Corey Dillon .50 .20
❑ 68 Willis McGahee .75 .30
❑ 69 Ben Roethlisberger 2.00 .75
❑ 70 Chad Johnson .75 .30
❑ 71 Jamal Lewis .75 .30
❑ 72 Drew Brees .75 .30
❑ 73 LaDainian Tomlinson 1.00 .40
❑ 74 Reuben Droughns .50 .20
❑ 75 Priest Holmes .75 .30
❑ 76 Jerry Porter .50 .20
❑ 77 Chris Brown .50 .20
❑ 78 Steve McNair .75 .30
❑ 79 Troy Brown .50 .20
❑ 80 Jerome Bettis .75 .30
❑ 81 Patrick Kerney .40 .15
❑ 82 Terrell Owens .75 .30
❑ 83 Brett Favre 2.00 .75
❑ 84 Carson Palmer .75 .30
❑ 85 Jake Plummer .50 .20
❑ 86 Tedy Bruschi .50 .20
❑ 87 Plaxico Burress .50 .20
❑ 88 Jonathan Vilma .50 .20
❑ 89 Ed Reed .50 .20
❑ 90 Brian Dawkins .40 .15
❑ 91 Anquan Boldin .50 .20
❑ 92 Vinny Testaverde .50 .20
❑ 93 David Givens .50 .20
❑ 94 Rudi Johnson .50 .20
❑ 95 Philip Rivers .75 .30
❑ 96 Jimmy Smith .50 .20
❑ 97 Emmitt Smith 3.00 1.25
❑ 98 Eric Johnson .50 .20
❑ 99 Jeremiah Trotter .40 .15
❑ 100 Duce Staley .50 .20
❑ 101 Warrick Dunn .50 .20
❑ 102 Nate Burleson .50 .20
❑ 103 Marc Bulger .75 .30
❑ 104 Joe Horn .50 .20
❑ 105 Rodney Harrison .40 .15
❑ 106 Zach Thomas .50 .20
❑ 107 Michael Clayton .75 .30
❑ 108 Derrick Brooks .50 .20
❑ 109 Michael Lewis .40 .15
❑ 110 Kurt Warner .50 .20
❑ 111 Jason Witten .50 .20
❑ 112 Roy Williams S .50 .20
❑ 113 Kabeer Gbaja-Biamila .50 .20
❑ 114 Torry Holt .75 .30
❑ 115 Tim Rattay .40 .15
❑ 116 Josh McCown .50 .20
❑ 117 Brian Griese .50 .20
❑ 118 Patrick Ramsey .50 .20
❑ 119 A.J. Feeley .50 .20
❑ 120 Kerry Collins .50 .20
❑ 121 Trent Green .50 .20
❑ 122 Billy Volek .50 .20
❑ 123 Travis Taylor .40 .15
❑ 124 T.J. Houshmandzadeh .40 .15
❑ 125 James Farrior .40 .15
❑ 126 Bryan Scott .40 .15
❑ 127 Lito Sheppard .40 .15
❑ 128 David Patten .40 .15
❑ 129 Antwaan Randle El .50 .20
❑ 130 Antonio Gates .75 .30
❑ 131 Brandon Stokley .40 .15
❑ 132 Keyshawn Johnson .50 .20
❑ 133 Amani Toomer .50 .20
❑ 134 Shawn Springs .40 .15
❑ 135 Eddie George .50 .20
❑ 136 Kevin Jones .75 .30
❑ 137 Darrell Jackson .50 .20
❑ 138 Ricky Manning .40 .15
❑ 139 Laveranues Coles .50 .20
❑ 140 Champ Bailey .50 .20
❑ 141 Rod Smith .50 .20
❑ 142 Ashley Lelie .50 .20
❑ 143 Charles Woodson .50 .20
❑ 144 Drew Bennett .50 .20
❑ 145 Derrick Mason .50 .20
❑ 146 Donovin Darius .40 .15
❑ 147 Dennis Northcutt .40 .15
❑ 148 Jamie Sharper .40 .15
❑ 149 Steven Jackson 1.00 .40
❑ 150 David Terrell .40 .15
❑ 151 Onterrio Smith .40 .15
❑ 152 Donald Driver .50 .20
❑ 153 Antoine Winfield .40 .15
❑ 154 Michael Pittman .40 .15
❑ 155 Dan Morgan .40 .15
❑ 156 Troy Polamalu 1.25 .50
❑ 157 Willie McGinest .40 .15
❑ 158 Justin McCareins .40 .15
❑ 159 Allen Rossum .40 .15
❑ 160 Deion Branch .50 .20
❑ 161 Deion Sanders .75 .30
❑ 162 Josh Reed .40 .15
❑ 163 Lee Evans .50 .20
❑ 164 Lee Suggs .50 .20
❑ 165 Dante Hall .50 .20
❑ 166 Eddie Kennison .40 .15
❑ 167 Ken Dorsey .40 .15
❑ 168 Andre Dyson .40 .15
❑ 169 Keith Bulluck .40 .15
❑ 170 Todd Pinkston .40 .15
❑ 171 Jevon Kearse .50 .20
❑ 172 Dunta Robinson .40 .15
❑ 173 Steve Smith .50 .20
❑ 174 Koren Robinson .40 .15
❑ 175 Freddie Mitchell .40 .15
❑ 176 L.J. Smith .40 .15
❑ 177 Kevin Curtis .40 .15
❑ 178 Marcus Robinson .40 .15
❑ 179 Kellen Winslow .75 .30
❑ 180 Reggie Williams .50 .20
❑ 181 Bubba Franks .50 .20
❑ 182 J.P. Losman .75 .30
❑ 183 Chris Perry .50 .20
❑ 184 Michael Jenkins .50 .20
❑ 185 T.J. Duckett .50 .20
❑ 186 Rashaun Woods .40 .15
❑ 187 Ben Watson .50 .20
❑ 188 Bryant Johnson .40 .15
❑ 189 Dallas Clark .40 .15
❑ 190 William Green .40 .15
❑ 191 Daniel Graham .40 .15
❑ 192 Jerramy Stevens .40 .15
❑ 193 DeShaun Foster .50 .20
❑ 194 Nick Goings .40 .15
❑ 195 Ronald Curry .40 .15
❑ 196 Kevan Barlow .50 .20
❑ 197 Kevin Faulk .40 .15
❑ 198 Eric Parker .40 .15
❑ 199 Keenan McCardell .40 .15
❑ 200 LaMont Jordan .75 .30
❑ 201 Alex Smith QB L13 RC 60.00 30.00
❑ 202 Aaron Rodgers L13 RC 60.00 25.00
❑ 203 Cedric Benson L13 RC 40.00 15.00
❑ 204 Braylon Edwards L13 RC 40.00 20.00
❑ 205 Ronnie Brown L13 RC 60.00 30.00
❑ 206 Cadillac Williams L13 RC 60.00 30.00
❑ 207 Troy Williamson L13 RC 20.00 7.50
❑ 208 Mark Clayton L13 RC 20.00 7.50
❑ 209 Charlie Frye L13 RC 20.00 7.50
❑ 210 Mike Williams L13 20.00 7.50
❑ 211 Marion Barber L13 RC 30.00 15.00
❑ 212 Eric Shelton L13 RC 20.00 7.50
❑ 213 Antrel Rolle L13 RC 20.00 7.50
❑ 214 Heath Miller RC 10.00 4.00
❑ 215 Dan Cody RC 5.00 2.00
❑ 216 Adam Jones RC 5.00 2.00
❑ 217 Derrick Johnson RC 8.00 3.00
❑ 218 Alex Smith TE RC 5.00 2.00
❑ 219 Kyle Orton RC 5.00 2.00
❑ 220 David Pollack RC 5.00 2.00
❑ 221 Erasmus James RC 5.00 2.00
❑ 222 Justin Tuck RC 5.00 2.00
❑ 223 Jason Campbell RC 8.00 3.00
❑ 224 Dan Orlovsky RC 5.00 2.00
❑ 225 Thomas Davis RC 5.00 2.00
❑ 226 J.J. Arrington RC 5.00 2.00
❑ 227 Roddy White RC 5.00 2.00
❑ 228 David Greene RC 5.00 2.00
❑ 229 Ciatrick Fason RC 5.00 2.00
❑ 230 Chris Henry RC 5.00 2.00
❑ 231 Reggie Brown RC 5.00 2.00
❑ 232 Vernand Morency RC 5.00 2.00
❑ 233 Carlos Rogers RC 6.00 2.50
❑ 234 Ryan Moats RC 5.00 2.00
❑ 235 Roscoe Parrish RC 5.00 2.00
❑ 236 Terrence Murphy RC 5.00 2.00
❑ 237 Shawne Merriman RC 8.00 3.00
❑ 238 Courtney Roby RC 5.00 2.00
❑ 239 Mark Bradley RC 5.00 2.00
❑ 240 Marcus Spears RC 5.00 2.00
❑ 241 Justin Miller RC 4.00 1.50
❑ 242 Matt Jones RC 8.00 3.00
❑ 243 DeMarcus Ware RC 8.00 3.00
❑ 244 Fabian Washington RC 5.00 2.00
❑ 245 Marlin Jackson RC 5.00 2.00
❑ 246 Corey Webster RC 5.00 2.00
❑ 247 Brandon Jacobs RC 6.00 2.50
❑ 248 Frank Gore RC 10.00 4.00

2006 Ultra

❑ 1 Larry Fitzgerald .75 .30
❑ 2 Anquan Boldin .50 .20
❑ 3 Kurt Warner .50 .20
❑ 4 Bryant Johnson .40 .15
❑ 5 Marcel Shipp .40 .15
❑ 6 J.J. Arrington .50 .20
❑ 7 Michael Vick .75 .30
❑ 8 Warrick Dunn .50 .20
❑ 9 T.J. Duckett .50 .20
❑ 10 Alge Crumpler .50 .20
❑ 11 Michael Jenkins .50 .20
❑ 12 DeAngelo Hall .50 .20
❑ 13 Kyle Boller .40 .15
❑ 14 Jamal Lewis .50 .20
❑ 15 Todd Heap .50 .20
❑ 16 Derrick Mason .40 .15
❑ 17 Ray Lewis .75 .30
❑ 18 Terrell Suggs .50 .20
❑ 19 J.P. Losman .50 .20
❑ 20 Willis McGahee .75 .30
❑ 21 Eric Moulds .50 .20
❑ 22 Lee Evans .50 .20
❑ 23 Roscoe Parrish .40 .15
❑ 24 Kelly Holcomb .40 .15
❑ 25 Jake Delhomme .50 .20
❑ 26 Steve Smith .75 .30
❑ 27 Stephen Davis .50 .20
❑ 28 Julius Peppers .50 .20
❑ 29 DeShaun Foster .50 .20
❑ 30 Keary Colbert .40 .15
❑ 31 Chris Gamble .40 .15
❑ 32 Kyle Orton .50 .20
❑ 33 Thomas Jones .50 .20
❑ 34 Rex Grossman .75 .30
❑ 35 Muhsin Muhammad .50 .20
❑ 36 Brian Urlacher .75 .30

❑ 37	Adrian Peterson	.40	.15
❑ 38	Carson Palmer	.75	.30
❑ 39	Chad Johnson	.50	.20
❑ 40	Rudi Johnson	.50	.20
❑ 41	Chris Perry	.50	.20
❑ 42	T.J. Houshmandzadeh	.50	.20
❑ 43	Chris Henry	.40	.15
❑ 44	Deltha O'Neal	.40	.15
❑ 45	Trent Dilfer	.50	.20
❑ 46	Reuben Droughns	.50	.20
❑ 47	Antonio Bryant	.75	.30
❑ 48	Braylon Edwards	.75	.30
❑ 49	Charlie Frye	.50	.20
[illegible]	[illegible]	[illegible]	[illegible]
❑ 51	Drew Bledsoe	.75	.30
❑ 52	Julius Jones	.75	.30
❑ 53	Keyshawn Johnson	.50	.20
❑ 54	Jason Witten	.50	.20
❑ 55	Roy Williams S	.50	.20
❑ 56	Marion Barber	.50	.20
❑ 57	Terry Glenn	.50	.20
❑ 58	Jake Plummer	.50	.20
❑ 59	Mike Anderson	.50	.20
❑ 60	Champ Bailey	.50	.20
❑ 61	Tatum Bell	.50	.20
❑ 62	Rod Smith	.50	.20
❑ 63	Ashley Lelie	.50	.20
❑ 64	Joey Harrington	.50	.20
❑ 65	Kevin Jones	.75	.30
❑ 66	Roy Williams WR	.75	.30
❑ 67	Mike Williams	.75	.30
❑ 68	Marcus Pollard	.40	.15
❑ 69	Jeff Garcia	.50	.20
❑ 70	Brett Favre	1.50	.60
❑ 71	Javon Walker	.50	.20
❑ 72	Donald Driver	.50	.20
❑ 73	Samkon Gado	.50	.20
❑ 74	Najeh Davenport	.40	.15
❑ 75	Robert Ferguson	.40	.15
❑ 76	David Carr	.50	.20
❑ 77	Domanick Davis	.50	.20
❑ 78	Andre Johnson	.50	.20
❑ 79	Jabar Gaffney	.40	.15
❑ 80	Corey Bradford	.40	.15
❑ 81	Dunta Robinson	.50	.20
❑ 82	Peyton Manning	1.25	.50
❑ 83	Edgerrin James	.75	.30
❑ 84	Marvin Harrison	.75	.30
❑ 85	Reggie Wayne	.50	.20
❑ 86	Dallas Clark	.40	.15
❑ 87	Dwight Freeney	.50	.20
❑ 88	Cato June	.50	.20
❑ 89	Byron Leftwich	.50	.20
❑ 90	Fred Taylor	.50	.20
❑ 91	Jimmy Smith	.50	.20
❑ 92	Matt Jones	.50	.20
❑ 93	Ernest Wilford	.40	.15
❑ 94	Greg Jones	.40	.15
❑ 95	Trent Green	.50	.20
❑ 96	Priest Holmes	.50	.20
❑ 97	Larry Johnson	1.00	.40
❑ 98	Tony Gonzalez	.50	.20
❑ 99	Dante Hall	.50	.20
❑ 100	Eddie Kennison	.40	.15
❑ 101	Gus Frerotte	.40	.15
❑ 102	Chris Chambers	.50	.20
❑ 103	Ronnie Brown	.75	.30
❑ 104	Ricky Williams	.50	.20
❑ 105	Randy McMichael	.40	.15
❑ 106	Zach Thomas	.75	.30
❑ 107	Daunte Culpepper	.75	.30
❑ 108	Nate Burleson	.50	.20
❑ 109	Michael Bennett	.40	.15
❑ 110	Mewelde Moore	.40	.15
❑ 111	Troy Williamson	.50	.20
❑ 112	Travis Taylor	.40	.15
❑ 113	Jermaine Wiggins	.40	.15
❑ 114	Tom Brady	1.25	.50
❑ 115	Corey Dillon	.50	.20
❑ 116	Deion Branch	.50	.20
❑ 117	Tedy Bruschi	.75	.30
❑ 118	David Givens	.50	.20
❑ 119	Patrick Pass	.40	.15
❑ 120	Aaron Brooks	.50	.20
❑ 121	Deuce McAllister	.50	.20

❑ 122	Joe Horn	.50	.20
❑ 123	Donte Stallworth	.50	.20
❑ 124	Antowain Smith	.40	.15
❑ 125	Devery Henderson	.40	.15
❑ 126	Eli Manning	1.00	.40
❑ 127	Tiki Barber	.75	.30
❑ 128	Jeremy Shockey	.75	.30
❑ 129	Plaxico Burress	.50	.20
❑ 130	Amani Toomer	.50	.20
❑ 131	Michael Strahan	.50	.20
❑ 132	Chad Pennington	.50	.20
❑ 133	Curtis Martin	.75	.30
❑ 134	Jonathan Vilma	.50	.20
[illegible]	[illegible]	[illegible]	[illegible]
❑ 136	Justin McCareins	.50	.20
❑ 137	Ty Law	.50	.20
❑ 138	Kerry Collins	.50	.20
❑ 139	LaMont Jordan	.50	.20
❑ 140	Randy Moss	.75	.30
❑ 141	Jerry Porter	.50	.20
❑ 142	Doug Gabriel	.40	.15
❑ 143	Zack Crockett	.40	.15
❑ 144	Donovan McNabb	.75	.30
❑ 145	Brian Westbrook	.50	.20
❑ 146	Terrell Owens	.75	.30
❑ 147	Jevon Kearse	.50	.20
❑ 148	L.J. Smith	.40	.15
❑ 149	Greg Lewis	.40	.15
❑ 150	Ben Roethlisberger	1.25	.50
❑ 151	Willie Parker	1.00	.40
❑ 152	Hines Ward	.75	.30
❑ 153	Jerome Bettis	.75	.30
❑ 154	Antwaan Randle El	.50	.20
❑ 155	Heath Miller	.50	.20
❑ 156	Joey Porter	.40	.15
❑ 157	Drew Brees	.75	.30
❑ 158	LaDainian Tomlinson	1.00	.40
❑ 159	Antonio Gates	.75	.30
❑ 160	Keenan McCardell	.40	.15
❑ 161	Donnie Edwards	.40	.15
❑ 162	Shawne Merriman	.50	.20
❑ 163	Eric Parker	.40	.15
❑ 164	Alex Smith	.75	.30
❑ 165	Kevan Barlow	.50	.20
❑ 166	Frank Gore	.75	.30
❑ 167	Brandon Lloyd	.50	.20
❑ 168	Eric Johnson	.50	.20
❑ 169	Julian Peterson	.40	.15
❑ 170	Matt Hasselbeck	.50	.20
❑ 171	Shaun Alexander	.75	.30
❑ 172	Darrell Jackson	.50	.20
❑ 173	Joe Jurevicius	.50	.20
❑ 174	Jerramy Stevens	.50	.20
❑ 175	D.J. Hackett	.40	.15
❑ 176	Marc Bulger	.50	.20
❑ 177	Steven Jackson	.75	.30
❑ 178	Torry Holt	.50	.20
❑ 179	Isaac Bruce	.50	.20
❑ 180	Kevin Curtis	.40	.15
❑ 181	Marshall Faulk	.50	.20
❑ 182	Chris Simms	.50	.20
❑ 183	Cadillac Williams	.75	.30
❑ 184	Michael Pittman	.40	.15
❑ 185	Michael Clayton	.40	.15
❑ 186	Joey Galloway	.50	.20
❑ 187	Brian Griese	.50	.20
❑ 188	Steve McNair	.50	.20
❑ 189	Chris Brown	.50	.20
❑ 190	Drew Bennett	.40	.15
❑ 191	Travis Henry	.50	.20
❑ 192	Ben Troupe	.40	.15
❑ 193	Billy Volek	.50	.20
❑ 194	Erron Kinney	.40	.15
❑ 195	Mark Brunell	.40	.15
❑ 196	Santana Moss	.40	.15
❑ 197	Clinton Portis	.75	.30
❑ 198	Chris Cooley	.40	.15
❑ 199	Ladell Betts	.40	.15
❑ 200	Sean Taylor	.50	.20
❑ 201	Matt Leinart L13 RC	100.00	50.00
❑ 202	Vince Young L13 RC	120.00	60.00
❑ 203	Reggie Bush L13 RC	150.00	75.00
❑ 204	D'Brick Ferguson L13 RC	25.00	10.00
❑ 205	DeAngelo Williams L13 RC	80.00	30.00
❑ 206	Jay Cutler L13 RC	80.00	40.00

❑ 207	A.J. Hawk L13 RC	80.00	30.00
❑ 208	Mario Williams L13 RC	40.00	15.00
❑ 209	Santonio Holmes L13 RC	60.00	25.00
❑ 210	Chad Greenway L13 RC	40.00	20.00
❑ 211	Laurence Maroney L13 RC	80.00	40.00
❑ 212	LenDale White L13 RC	50.00	20.00
❑ 213	Sinorice Moss L13 RC	40.00	20.00
❑ 214	A.J. Nicholson RC	2.50	1.00
❑ 215	Abdul Hodge RC	5.00	2.00
❑ 216	Jeremy Bloom RC	4.00	1.50
❑ 217	Anthony Fasano RC	5.00	2.00
❑ 218	Bobby Carpenter RC	5.00	2.00
❑ 219	Brian Calhoun RC	5.00	2.00
[illegible]	[illegible]	[illegible]	[illegible]
❑ 221	Chad Jackson RC	5.00	2.00
❑ 222	Charlie Whitehurst RC	5.00	2.00
❑ 223	Claude Wroten RC	2.50	1.00
❑ 224	Darnell Bing RC	5.00	2.00
❑ 225	Darrell Hackney RC	4.00	1.50
❑ 226	David Thomas RC	5.00	2.00
❑ 227	Demetrius Williams RC	5.00	2.00
❑ 228	Derek Hagan RC	5.00	2.00
❑ 229	Devin Hester RC	10.00	4.00
❑ 230	Dominique Byrd RC	4.00	1.50
❑ 231	D'Qwell Jackson RC	4.00	1.50
❑ 232	Elvis Dumervil RC	2.50	1.00
❑ 233	Haloti Ngata RC	5.00	2.00
❑ 234	Hank Baskett RC	5.00	2.00
❑ 235	Jason Avant RC	5.00	2.00
❑ 236	Jerome Harrison RC	5.00	2.00
❑ 237	Jimmy Williams RC	5.00	2.00
❑ 238	Joe Klopfenstein RC	4.00	1.50
❑ 239	Joseph Addai RC	15.00	6.00
❑ 240	Kellen Clemens RC	8.00	3.00
❑ 241	Cory Rodgers RC	5.00	2.00
❑ 242	Leon Washington RC	8.00	3.00
❑ 243	Leonard Pope RC	5.00	2.00
❑ 244	Marcedes Lewis RC	5.00	2.00
❑ 245	Martin Nance RC	4.00	1.50
❑ 246	Mathias Kiwanuka RC	6.00	2.50
❑ 247	Maurice Drew RC	12.00	5.00
❑ 248	Maurice Stovall RC	5.00	2.00
❑ 249	Michael Huff RC	6.00	2.50
❑ 250	Mike Hass RC	5.00	2.00
❑ 251	Omar Jacobs RC	4.00	1.50
❑ 252	Orien Harris RC	4.00	1.50
❑ 253	Owen Daniels RC	5.00	2.00
❑ 254	Reggie McNeal RC	4.00	1.50
❑ 255	DeMeco Ryans RC	6.00	2.50
❑ 256	Tamba Hali RC	5.00	2.00
❑ 257	Ernie Sims RC	6.00	2.50
❑ 258	Thomas Howard RC	5.00	2.00
❑ 259	Todd Watkins RC	4.00	1.50
❑ 260	Travis Wilson RC	5.00	2.00
❑ 261	Greg Lee RC	4.00	1.50
❑ 262	Tye Hill RC	5.00	2.00
❑ 263	Vernon Davis RC	10.00	4.00

2007 Ultra

❑	COMP.SET w/o RCs (200)	40.00	15.00
❑	HOBBY PRODUCED WITH SILVER HOLOFOIL		
❑ 1	Bryant Johnson	.75	.30
❑ 2	Matt Leinart	1.25	.50
❑ 3	Edgerrin James	1.25	.50
❑ 4	Larry Fitzgerald	1.00	.40
❑ 5	Anquan Boldin	1.00	.40
❑ 6	Jerious Norwood	1.00	.40
❑ 7	Roddy White	1.00	.40

❑ 8 Keith Brooking .75 .30
❑ 9 DeAngelo Hall 1.00 .40
❑ 10 Michael Vick 1.25 .50
❑ 11 Warrick Dunn 1.00 .40
❑ 12 Alge Crumpler 1.00 .40
❑ 13 Terrell Suggs .75 .30
❑ 14 Derrick Mason .75 .30
❑ 15 Todd Heap .75 .30
❑ 16 Ray Lewis 1.25 .50
❑ 17 Steve McNair 1.00 .40
❑ 18 Willis McGahee 1.00 .40
❑ 19 Mark Clayton 1.00 .40
❑ 20 Aaron Schobel .75 .30
❑ 21 Terrence McGee .75 .30
❑ 22 J.P. Losman 1.00 .40
❑ 23 Anthony Thomas .75 .30
❑ 24 Lee Evans 1.00 .40
❑ 25 Keyshawn Johnson 1.00 .40
❑ 26 DeAngelo Williams 1.25 .50
❑ 27 Julius Peppers 1.00 .40
❑ 28 Jake Delhomme 1.00 .40
❑ 29 DeShaun Foster 1.00 .40
❑ 30 Steve Smith 1.00 .40
❑ 31 Mark Anderson 1.00 .40
❑ 32 Devin Hester 1.25 .50
❑ 33 Bernard Berrian .75 .30
❑ 34 Muhsin Muhammad 1.00 .40
❑ 35 Rex Grossman 1.00 .40
❑ 36 Cedric Benson 1.00 .40
❑ 37 Brian Urlacher 1.25 .50
❑ 38 Reggie Kelly .75 .30
❑ 39 Carson Palmer 1.25 .50
❑ 40 Rudi Johnson 1.00 .40
❑ 41 Chad Johnson 1.00 .40
❑ 42 T.J. Houshmandzadeh 1.00 .40
❑ 43 Jamal Lewis 1.00 .40
❑ 44 Charlie Frye 1.00 .40
❑ 45 Braylon Edwards 1.00 .40
❑ 46 Kellen Winslow 1.00 .40
❑ 47 DeMarcus Ware 1.00 .40
❑ 48 Roy Williams S 1.00 .40
❑ 49 Jason Witten 1.00 .40
❑ 50 Marion Barber 1.00 .40
❑ 51 Tony Romo 2.50 1.00
❑ 52 Julius Jones 1.00 .40
❑ 53 Terrell Owens 1.25 .50
❑ 54 Terry Glenn 1.00 .40
❑ 55 Rod Smith 1.00 .40
❑ 56 Mike Bell 1.00 .40
❑ 57 Jason Elam .75 .30
❑ 58 Jay Cutler 1.25 .50
❑ 59 Champ Bailey 1.00 .40
❑ 60 Javon Walker 1.00 .40
❑ 61 Tatum Bell 1.00 .40
❑ 62 Jason Hanson .75 .30
❑ 63 Jon Kitna .75 .30
❑ 64 Kevin Jones .75 .30
❑ 65 Roy Williams WR 1.00 .40
❑ 66 Mike Furrey 1.00 .40
❑ 67 Charles Woodson 1.00 .40
❑ 68 Aaron Kampman 1.00 .40
❑ 69 Bubba Franks .75 .30
❑ 70 Brett Favre 2.50 1.00
❑ 71 Greg Jennings 1.00 .40
❑ 72 Donald Driver 1.00 .40
❑ 73 Ron Dayne 1.00 .40
❑ 74 DeMeco Ryans 1.00 .40
❑ 75 Jeb Putzier .75 .30
❑ 76 Matt Schaub 1.00 .40
❑ 77 Ahman Green 1.00 .40
❑ 78 Andre Johnson 1.00 .40
❑ 79 Terrence Wilkins .75 .30
❑ 80 Bob Sanders 1.00 .40
❑ 81 Dwight Freeney 1.00 .40
❑ 82 Dallas Clark .75 .30
❑ 83 Adam Vinatieri 1.00 .40
❑ 84 Peyton Manning 2.00 .75
❑ 85 Joseph Addai 1.50 .60
❑ 86 Marvin Harrison 1.25 .50
❑ 87 Reggie Wayne 1.00 .40
❑ 88 Rashean Mathis .75 .30
❑ 89 Matt Jones 1.00 .40
❑ 90 Fred Taylor 1.00 .40
❑ 91 Byron Leftwich 1.00 .40
❑ 92 David Garrard 1.00 .40
❑ 93 Reggie Williams 1.00 .40
❑ 94 Maurice Jones-Drew 1.25 .50
❑ 95 Damon Huard .75 .30
❑ 96 Dante Hall 1.00 .40
❑ 97 Eddie Kennison .75 .30
❑ 98 Trent Green 1.00 .40
❑ 99 Larry Johnson 1.25 .50
❑ 100 Tony Gonzalez 1.00 .40
❑ 101 Jason Taylor .75 .30
❑ 102 Randy McMichael .75 .30
❑ 103 Zach Thomas 1.00 .40
❑ 104 Daunte Culpepper 1.00 .40
❑ 105 Ronnie Brown 1.00 .40
❑ 106 Chris Chambers 1.00 .40
❑ 107 Troy Williamson .75 .30
❑ 108 Tony Richardson .75 .30
❑ 109 Tarvaris Jackson 1.25 .50
❑ 110 Chester Taylor .75 .30
❑ 111 Travis Taylor .75 .30
❑ 112 Richard Seymour .75 .30
❑ 113 Reche Caldwell .75 .30
❑ 114 Tedy Bruschi 1.25 .50
❑ 115 Ben Watson .75 .30
❑ 116 Tom Brady 2.50 1.00
❑ 117 Laurence Maroney 1.25 .50
❑ 118 Asante Samuel .75 .30
❑ 119 Michael Lewis .75 .30
❑ 120 Devery Henderson .75 .30
❑ 121 Mike Karney .75 .30
❑ 122 Will Smith .75 .30
❑ 123 Drew Brees 1.00 .40
❑ 124 Deuce McAllister 1.00 .40
❑ 125 Reggie Bush 1.50 .60
❑ 126 Marques Colston 1.25 .50
❑ 127 Michael Strahan 1.00 .40
❑ 128 Reuben Droughns 1.00 .40
❑ 129 Jeremy Shockey 1.00 .40
❑ 130 Eli Manning 1.25 .50
❑ 131 Brandon Jacobs 1.00 .40
❑ 132 Plaxico Burress 1.00 .40
❑ 133 Jonathan Vilma 1.00 .40
❑ 134 Jerricho Cotchery .75 .30
❑ 135 Thomas Jones 1.00 .40
❑ 136 Chad Pennington 1.00 .40
❑ 137 Leon Washington 1.00 .40
❑ 138 Laveranues Coles 1.00 .40
❑ 139 Dominic Rhodes 1.00 .40
❑ 140 Andrew Walter .75 .30
❑ 141 Randy Moss 1.25 .50
❑ 142 Ronald Curry 1.00 .40
❑ 143 LaMont Jordan 1.00 .40
❑ 144 Justin Fargas .75 .30
❑ 145 David Akers .75 .30
❑ 146 Correll Buckhalter 1.00 .40
❑ 147 Brian Dawkins 1.00 .40
❑ 148 L.J. Smith .75 .30
❑ 149 Donovan McNabb 1.25 .50
❑ 150 Brian Westbrook 1.00 .40
❑ 151 Reggie Brown 1.00 .40
❑ 152 Cedrick Wilson .75 .30
❑ 153 Aaron Smith .75 .30
❑ 154 Troy Polamalu 1.25 .50
❑ 155 Ben Roethlisberger 1.50 .60
❑ 156 Willie Parker 1.25 .50
❑ 157 Hines Ward 1.25 .50
❑ 158 Santonio Holmes 1.00 .40
❑ 159 Eric Parker .75 .30
❑ 160 Leslie O'Neal .75 .30
❑ 161 Shawne Merriman 1.00 .40
❑ 162 Philip Rivers 1.25 .50
❑ 163 LaDainian Tomlinson 1.50 .60
❑ 164 Antonio Gates 1.00 .40
❑ 165 Walt Harris .75 .30
❑ 166 Vernon Davis 1.00 .40
❑ 167 Alex Smith QB 1.25 .50
❑ 168 Frank Gore 1.25 .50
❑ 169 Arnaz Battle .75 .30
❑ 170 Maurice Morris .75 .30
❑ 171 Julian Peterson .75 .30
❑ 172 D.J. Hackett .75 .30
❑ 173 Lofa Tatupu 1.00 .40
❑ 174 Darrell Jackson 1.00 .40
❑ 175 Matt Hasselbeck 1.00 .40
❑ 176 Shaun Alexander 1.00 .40
❑ 177 Deion Branch 1.00 .40
❑ 178 Tye Hill .75 .30
❑ 179 Isaac Bruce 1.00 .40
❑ 180 Marc Bulger 1.00 .40
❑ 181 Steven Jackson 1.25 .50
❑ 182 Torry Holt 1.00 .40
❑ 183 Drew Bennett .75 .30
❑ 184 Jeff Garcia 1.00 .40
❑ 185 Michael Clayton 1.00 .40
❑ 186 Derrick Brooks 1.00 .40
❑ 187 Cadillac Williams 1.00 .40
❑ 188 Joey Galloway 1.00 .40
❑ 189 Ronde Barber .75 .30
❑ 190 Chris Simms .75 .30
❑ 191 Keith Bulluck .75 .30
❑ 192 LenDale White 1.00 .40
❑ 193 David Givens .75 .30
❑ 194 Vince Young 1.50 .60
❑ 195 Ladell Betts .75 .30
❑ 196 Chris Cooley .75 .30
❑ 197 Antwaan Randle El .75 .30
❑ 198 Jason Campbell 1.00 .40
❑ 199 Clinton Portis 1.00 .40
❑ 200 Santana Moss 1.00 .40
❑ 201 JaMarcus Russell L13 RC 25.00 10.00
❑ 202 Brady Quinn L13 RC 30.00 12.00
❑ 203 Calvin Johnson L13 RC 30.00 12.00
❑ 204 Joe Thomas L13 RC 10.00 4.00
❑ 205 Adrian Peterson L13 RC 80.00 30.00
❑ 206 Marshawn Lynch L13 RC 20.00 8.00
❑ 207 Ted Ginn Jr. L13 RC 15.00 6.00
❑ 208 Leon Hall L13 RC 8.00 3.00
❑ 209 Dwayne Bowe L13 RC 20.00 8.00
❑ 210 Steve Smith USC L13 RC 12.00 5.00
❑ 211 Robert Meachem L13 RC 10.00 4.00
❑ 212 LaRon Landry L13 RC 12.00 5.00
❑ 213 Dwayne Jarrett L13 RC 12.00 5.00
❑ 214 Darius Walker RC 6.00 2.50
❑ 215 Chris Leak RC 5.00 2.00
❑ 216 Darrelle Revis RC 6.00 2.50
❑ 217 Paul Posluszny RC 8.00 3.00
❑ 218 Daymeion Hughes RC 5.00 2.00
❑ 219 LaMarr Woodley RC 6.00 2.50
❑ 220 Garrett Wolfe RC 8.00 3.00
❑ 221 DeShawn Wynn RC 6.00 2.50
❑ 222 Alan Branch RC 5.00 2.00
❑ 223 Greg Olsen RC 8.00 3.00
❑ 224 Tyler Palko RC 6.00 2.50
❑ 225 Jordan Palmer RC 6.00 2.50
❑ 226 Drew Stanton RC 8.00 3.00
❑ 227 Jamaal Anderson RC 5.00 2.00
❑ 228 Eric Wright RC 6.00 2.50
❑ 229 Quentin Moses RC 5.00 2.00
❑ 230 Patrick Willis RC 12.00 5.00
❑ 231 Troy Smith RC 8.00 3.00
❑ 232 Amobi Okoye RC 6.00 2.50
❑ 233 Lawrence Timmons RC 6.00 2.50
❑ 234 H.B. Blades RC 5.00 2.00
❑ 235 Jared Zabransky RC 6.00 2.50
❑ 236 John Beck RC 12.00 5.00
❑ 237 Kevin Kolb RC 10.00 4.00
❑ 238 Matt Moore RC 10.00 4.00
❑ 239 Trent Edwards RC 12.00 5.00
❑ 240 Antonio Pittman RC 5.00 2.00
❑ 241 Brandon Jackson RC 8.00 3.00
❑ 242 Chris Henry RC 6.00 2.50
❑ 243 Dwayne Wright RC 5.00 2.00
❑ 244 Brian Leonard RC 8.00 3.00
❑ 245 Kenneth Darby RC 6.00 2.50
❑ 246 Kenny Irons RC 6.00 2.50
❑ 247 Kolby Smith RC 8.00 3.00
❑ 248 Lorenzo Booker RC 6.00 2.50
❑ 249 Drew Tate RC 5.00 2.00
❑ 250 Tanard Jackson RC 4.00 1.50
❑ 251 Michael Bush RC 8.00 3.00
❑ 252 Selvin Young RC 8.00 3.00
❑ 253 Tony Hunt RC 6.00 2.50
❑ 254 Tyrone Moss RC 4.00 1.50
❑ 255 Reggie Nelson RC 5.00 2.00
❑ 256 Zach Miller RC 6.00 2.50
❑ 257 Anthony Gonzalez RC 10.00 4.00
❑ 258 Adam Carriker RC 5.00 2.00
❑ 259 Sidney Rice RC 10.00 4.00
❑ 260 Aundrae Allison RC 5.00 2.00
❑ 261 Chansi Stuckey RC 5.00 2.00
❑ 262 Courtney Taylor RC 5.00 2.00

❑ 263 Craig Buster Davis RC 6.00 2.50
❑ 264 Dallas Baker RC 5.00 2.00
❑ 265 David Clowney RC 6.00 2.50
❑ 266 David Ball RC 4.00 1.50
❑ 267 Jason Hill RC 6.00 2.50
❑ 268 Johnnie Lee Higgins RC 5.00 2.00
❑ 269 Rhema McKnight RC 5.00 2.00
❑ 270 Gaines Adams RC 6.00 2.50
❑ 271 Mike Walker RC 5.00 2.00
❑ 272 Steve Breaston RC 5.00 2.00
❑ 273 Gary Russell RC 6.00 2.50
❑ 274 Marcus McCauley RC 5.00 2.00
❑ 275 Jarvis Moss RC 6.00 2.50
❑ 276 Syvelle Newton RC 5.00 2.00
❑ 277 DeMarcus Tank Tyler RC 5.00 2.00
❑ 278 Alvin Banks RC 5.00 2.00
❑ 279 Joel Filani RC 5.00 2.00
❑ 280 Chris Davis RC 5.00 2.00
❑ 281 Matt Trannon RC 5.00 2.00
❑ 282 Ryan Kalil RC 5.00 2.00
❑ 283 Levi Brown RC 6.00 2.50
❑ 284 Anthony Spencer RC 6.00 2.50
❑ 285 Brandon Meriweather RC 6.00 2.50
❑ 286 Chris Houston RC 5.00 2.00
❑ 287 Michael Griffin RC 6.00 2.50
❑ 288 Jon Beason RC 6.00 2.50
❑ 289 Legedu Naanee RC 5.00 2.00
❑ 290 Eric Weddle RC 5.00 2.00
❑ 291 Isaiah Stanback RC 6.00 2.50
❑ 292 Aaron Ross RC 6.00 2.50
❑ 293 Sabby Piscitelli RC 6.00 2.50
❑ 294 Charles Johnson RC 4.00 1.50
❑ 295 Buster Davis RC 5.00 2.00
❑ 296 Justin Harrell RC 6.00 2.50
❑ 297 Stewart Bradley RC 6.00 2.50
❑ 298 A.J. Davis RC 4.00 1.50
❑ 299 David Irons RC 4.00 1.50
❑ 300 Scott Chandler RC 5.00 2.00

1991 Upper Deck

❑ COMPLETE SET (700) 15.00 6.00
❑ COMP.FACT.SET (700) 25.00 10.00
❑ COMP.SERIES 1 SET (500) 10.00 4.00
❑ COMP.SERIES 2 SET (200) 5.00 2.00
❑ COMP.FACT.SERIES 2 (200) 6.00 2.50
❑ 1 Dan McGwire CL .05 .01
❑ 2 Eric Bieniemy RC .05 .01
❑ 3 Mike Dumas RC .05 .01
❑ 4 Mike Croel RC .05 .01
❑ 5 Russell Maryland RC .25 .08
❑ 6 Charles McRae RC .05 .01
❑ 7 Dan McGwire RC .05 .01
❑ 8 Mike Pritchard RC .25 .08
❑ 9 Ricky Watters RC 1.50 .60
❑ 10 Chris Zorich RC .25 .08
❑ 11 Browning Nagle RC .05 .01
❑ 12 Wesley Carroll RC .05 .01
❑ 13 Brett Favre RC 10.00 5.00
❑ 14 Rob Carpenter RC WR .05 .01
❑ 15 Eric Swann RC .25 .08
❑ 16 Stanley Richard RC .05 .01
❑ 17 Herman Moore RC .25 .08
❑ 18 Todd Marinovich RC .05 .01
❑ 19 Aaron Craver RC .05 .01
❑ 20 Chuck Webb RC .05 .01
❑ 21 Todd Lyght RC .05 .01
❑ 22 Greg Lewis RC .05 .01
❑ 23 Eric Turner RC .10 .02
❑ 24 Alvin Harper RC .25 .08
❑ 25 Jarrod Bunch RC .05 .01
❑ 26 Bruce Pickens RC .05 .01
❑ 27 Harvey Williams RC .25 .08
❑ 28 Randal Hill RC .10 .02
❑ 29 Nick Bell RC .05 .01
❑ 30 Jim Everett AT .10 .02
❑ 31 R.Cunningham/Jackson AT .05 .01
❑ 32 Steve DeBerg AT .05 .01
❑ 33 Warren Moon/D.Hill AT .10 .02
❑ 34 D.Marino/M.Clayton AT .50 .20
❑ 35 J.Montana/J.Rice AT .50 .20
❑ 36 Percy Snow .05 .01
❑ 37 Kelvin Martin .05 .01
❑ 38 Scott Case .05 .01
❑ 39 John Gesek RC .05 .01
❑ 40 Barry Word .05 .01
❑ 41 Cornelius Bennett .10 .02
❑ 42 Mike Kenn .05 .01
❑ 43 Andre Reed .10 .02
❑ 44 Bobby Hebert .05 .01
❑ 45 William Perry .10 .02
❑ 46 Dennis Byrd .05 .01
❑ 47 Martin Mayhew .05 .01
❑ 48 Issiac Holt .05 .01
❑ 49 William White .05 .01
❑ 50 JoJo Townsell .05 .01
❑ 51 Jarvis Williams .05 .01
❑ 52 Joey Browner .05 .01
❑ 53 Pat Terrell .05 .01
❑ 54 Joe Montana 3X UER 1.25 .50
❑ 55 Jeff Herrod .05 .01
❑ 56 Cris Carter .50 .20
❑ 57 Jerry Rice .75 .30
❑ 58 Brett Perriman .25 .08
❑ 59 Kevin Fagan .05 .01
❑ 60 Wayne Haddix .05 .01
❑ 61 Tommy Kane .05 .01
❑ 62 Pat Beach .05 .01
❑ 63 Jeff Lageman .05 .01
❑ 64 Hassan Jones .05 .01
❑ 65 Bennie Blades .05 .01
❑ 66 Tim McGee .05 .01
❑ 67 Robert Blackmon .05 .01
❑ 68 Fred Stokes RC .05 .01
❑ 69 Barney Bussey RC .05 .01
❑ 70 Eric Metcalf .10 .02
❑ 71 Mark Kelso .05 .01
❑ 72 Neal Anderson TC .05 .01
❑ 73 Boomer Esiason TC .05 .01
❑ 74 Thurman Thomas TC .25 .08
❑ 75 John Elway TC .50 .20
❑ 76 Eric Metcalf TC .10 .02
❑ 77 Vinny Testaverde TC .10 .02
❑ 78 Johnny Johnson TC .05 .01
❑ 79 Anthony Miller TC .10 .02
❑ 80 Derrick Thomas TC .10 .02
❑ 81 Jeff George TC .10 .02
❑ 82 Troy Aikman TC .40 .15
❑ 83 Dan Marino TC .50 .20
❑ 84 Randall Cunningham TC .10 .02
❑ 85 Deion Sanders TC .05 .01
❑ 86 Jerry Rice TC .40 .15
❑ 87 Lawrence Taylor TC .10 .02
❑ 88 Al Toon TC .05 .01
❑ 89 Barry Sanders TC .50 .20
❑ 90 Warren Moon TC .10 .02
❑ 91 Don Majkowski TC .05 .01
❑ 92 Andre Tippett TC .05 .01
❑ 93 Bo Jackson TC .30 .10
❑ 94 Jim Everett TC .10 .02
❑ 95 Art Monk TC .10 .02
❑ 96 Morten Andersen TC .05 .01
❑ 97 John L. Williams TC .05 .01
❑ 98 Rod Woodson TC .10 .02
❑ 99 Herschel Walker TC .10 .02
❑ 100 Checklist 1-100 .05 .01
❑ 101 Steve Young .75 .30
❑ 102 Jim Lachey .05 .01
❑ 103 Tom Rathman .05 .01
❑ 104 Earnest Byner .05 .01
❑ 105 Karl Mecklenburg .05 .01
❑ 106 Wes Hopkins .05 .01
❑ 107 Michael Irvin .25 .08
❑ 108 Burt Grossman .05 .01
❑ 109 Jay Novacek UER .25 .08
❑ 110 Ben Smith .05 .01
❑ 111 Rod Woodson .25 .08
❑ 112 Ernie Jones .05 .01
❑ 113 Bryan Hinkle .05 .01
❑ 114 Vai Sikahema .05 .01
❑ 115 Bubby Brister .05 .01
❑ 116 Brian Blades .10 .02
❑ 117 Don Majkowski .05 .01
❑ 118 Rod Bernstine .05 .01
❑ 119 Brian Noble .05 .01
❑ 120 Eugene Robinson .05 .01
❑ 121 John Taylor .10 .02
❑ 122 Vance Johnson .05 .01
❑ 123 Art Monk [illegible] [illegible]
❑ 124 John Elway 1.25 .50
❑ 125 Dexter Carter .05 .01
❑ 126 Anthony Miller .10 .02
❑ 127 Keith Jackson .10 .02
❑ 128 Albert Lewis .05 .01
❑ 129 Billy Ray Smith .05 .01
❑ 130 Clyde Simmons .05 .01
❑ 131 Merril Hoge .05 .01
❑ 132 Ricky Proehl .05 .01
❑ 133 Tim McDonald .05 .01
❑ 134 Louis Lipps .05 .01
❑ 135 Ken Harvey .10 .02
❑ 136 Sterling Sharpe .10 .02
❑ 137 Gill Byrd .05 .01
❑ 138 Tim Harris .05 .01
❑ 139 Derrick Fenner .05 .01
❑ 140 Johnny Holland .05 .01
❑ 141 Ricky Sanders .05 .01
❑ 142 Bobby Humphrey .05 .01
❑ 143 Roger Craig .10 .02
❑ 144 Steve Atwater .05 .01
❑ 145 Ickey Woods .05 .01
❑ 146 Randall Cunningham .25 .08
❑ 147 Marion Butts .10 .02
❑ 148 Reggie White .25 .08
❑ 149 Ronnie Harmon .05 .01
❑ 150 Mike Saxon .05 .01
❑ 151 Greg Townsend .05 .01
❑ 152 Troy Aikman .75 .30
❑ 153 Shane Conlan .05 .01
❑ 154 Deion Sanders .40 .15
❑ 155 Bo Jackson .30 .10
❑ 156 Jeff Hostetler .10 .02
❑ 157 Albert Bentley .05 .01
❑ 158 James Williams .05 .01
❑ 159 Bill Brooks .05 .01
❑ 160 Nick Lowery .05 .01
❑ 161 Ottis Anderson .10 .02
❑ 162 Kevin Greene .10 .02
❑ 163 Neil Smith .05 [illegible]
❑ 164 Jim Everett .10 .02
❑ 165 Derrick Thomas .25 .08
❑ 166 John L. Williams .05 .01
❑ 167 Timm Rosenbach .05 .01
❑ 168 Leslie O'Neal .10 .02
❑ 169 Clarence Verdin .05 .01
❑ 170 Dave Krieg .10 .02
❑ 171 Steve Broussard .05 .01
❑ 172 Emmitt Smith 2.50 1.00
❑ 173 Andre Rison .10 .02
❑ 174 Bruce Smith .25 .08
❑ 175 Mark Clayton .10 .02
❑ 176 Christian Okoye .05 .01
❑ 177 Duane Bickett .05 .01
❑ 178 Stephone Paige .05 .01
❑ 179 Fredd Young .05 .01
❑ 180 Mervyn Fernandez .05 .01
❑ 181 Phil Simms .10 .02
❑ 182 Pete Holohan .05 .01
❑ 183 Pepper Johnson .05 .01
❑ 184 Jackie Slater .05 .01
❑ 185 Stephen Baker .05 .01
❑ 186 Frank Cornish .05 .01
❑ 187 Dave Waymer .05 .01
❑ 188 Terance Mathis .10 .02
❑ 189 Darryl Talley .05 .01
❑ 190 James Hasty .05 .01
❑ 191 Jay Schroeder .05 .01
❑ 192 Kenneth Davis .05 .01
❑ 193 Chris Miller .10 .02

❑	194	Scott Davis	.05	.01
❑	195	Tim Green	.05	.01
❑	196	Dan Saleaumua	.05	.01
❑	197	Rohn Stark	.05	.01
❑	198	John Alt	.05	.01
❑	199	Steve Tasker	.10	.02
❑	200	Checklist 101-200	.05	.01
❑	201	Freddie Joe Nunn	.05	.01
❑	202	Jim Breech	.05	.01
❑	203	Roy Green	.05	.01
❑	204	Gary Anderson RB	.05	.01
❑	205	Rich Camarillo	.05	.01
❑	206	Mark Bortz	.05	.01
❑	207	Eddie Brown	.05	.01
❑	208	Brad Muster	.05	.01
❑	209	Anthony Munoz	.10	.02
❑	210	Dalton Hilliard	.05	.01
❑	211	Erik McMillan	.05	.01
❑	212	Perry Kemp	.05	.01
❑	213	Jim Thornton	.05	.01
❑	214	Anthony Dilweg	.05	.01
❑	215	Cleveland Gary	.05	.01
❑	216	Leo Goeas	.05	.01
❑	217	Mike Merriweather	.05	.01
❑	218	Courtney Hall	.05	.01
❑	219	Wade Wilson	.10	.02
❑	220	Billy Joe Tolliver	.05	.01
❑	221	Harold Green	.10	.02
❑	222	Al(Bubba) Baker	.10	.02
❑	223	Carl Zander	.05	.01
❑	224	Thane Gash	.05	.01
❑	225	Kevin Mack	.05	.01
❑	226	Morten Andersen	.05	.01
❑	227	Dennis Gentry	.05	.01
❑	228	Vince Buck	.05	.01
❑	229	Mike Singletary	.10	.02
❑	230	Rueben Mayes	.05	.01
❑	231	Mark Carrier WR	.25	.08
❑	232	Tony Mandarich	.05	.01
❑	233	Al Toon	.10	.02
❑	234	Renaldo Turnbull	.05	.01
❑	235	Broderick Thomas	.05	.01
❑	236	Anthony Carter	.10	.02
❑	237	Flipper Anderson	.05	.01
❑	238	Jerry Robinson	.05	.01
❑	239	Vince Newsome	.05	.01
❑	240	Keith Millard	.05	.01
❑	241	Reggie Langhorne	.05	.01
❑	242	James Francis	.05	.01
❑	243	Felix Wright	.05	.01
❑	244	Neal Anderson	.10	.02
❑	245	Boomer Esiason	.10	.02
❑	246	Pat Swilling	.10	.02
❑	247	Richard Dent	.10	.02
❑	248	Craig Heyward	.10	.02
❑	249	Ron Morris	.05	.01
❑	250	Eric Martin	.05	.01
❑	251	Jim C. Jensen	.05	.01
❑	252	Anthony Toney	.05	.01
❑	253	Sammie Smith	.05	.01
❑	254	Calvin Williams	.10	.02
❑	255	Dan Marino	1.25	.50
❑	256	Warren Moon	.25	.08
❑	257	Tommie Agee	.05	.01
❑	258	Haywood Jeffires	.10	.02
❑	259	Eugene Lockhart	.05	.01
❑	260	Drew Hill	.05	.01
❑	261	Vinny Testaverde	.10	.02
❑	262	Jim Arnold	.05	.01
❑	263	Steve Christie	.05	.01
❑	264	Chris Spielman	.10	.02
❑	265	Reggie Cobb	.05	.01
❑	266	John Stephens	.05	.01
❑	267	Jay Hilgenberg	.05	.01
❑	268	Brent Williams	.05	.01
❑	269	Rodney Hampton	.25	.08
❑	270	Irving Fryar	.10	.02
❑	271	Terry McDaniel	.05	.01
❑	272	Reggie Roby	.05	.01
❑	273	Allen Pinkett	.05	.01
❑	274	Tim McKyer	.05	.01
❑	275	Bob Golic	.05	.01
❑	276	Wilber Marshall	.05	.01
❑	277	Ray Childress	.05	.01
❑	278	Charles Mann	.05	.01
❑	279	Cris Dishman RC	.05	.01
❑	280	Mark Rypien	.10	.02
❑	281	Michael Cofer	.05	.01
❑	282	Keith Byars	.05	.01
❑	283	Mike Rozier	.05	.01
❑	284	Seth Joyner	.10	.02
❑	285	Jessie Tuggle	.05	.01
❑	286	Mark Bavaro	.05	.01
❑	287	Eddie Anderson	.05	.01
❑	288	Sean Landeta	.05	.01
❑	289	Howie Long/George Brett	.25	.08
❑	290	Reyna Thompson	.05	.01
❑	291	Ferrell Edmunds	.05	.01
❑	292	Willie Gault	.10	.02
❑	293	John Offerdahl	.05	.01
❑	294	Tim Brown	.25	.08
❑	295	Bruce Matthews	.10	.02
❑	296	Kevin Ross	.05	.01
❑	297	Lorenzo White	.05	.01
❑	298	Dino Hackett	.05	.01
❑	299	Curtis Duncan	.05	.01
❑	300	Checklist 201-300	.05	.01
❑	301	Andre Ware	.10	.02
❑	302	David Little	.05	.01
❑	303	Jerry Ball	.05	.01
❑	304	Dwight Stone UER	.05	.01
❑	305	Rodney Peete	.10	.02
❑	306	Mike Baab	.05	.01
❑	307	Tim Worley	.05	.01
❑	308	Paul Farren	.05	.01
❑	309	Carnell Lake	.05	.01
❑	310	Clay Matthews	.10	.02
❑	311	Alton Montgomery	.05	.01
❑	312	Ernest Givins	.10	.02
❑	313	Mike Horan	.05	.01
❑	314	Sean Jones	.10	.02
❑	315	Leonard Smith	.05	.01
❑	316	Carl Banks	.05	.01
❑	317	Jerome Brown	.05	.01
❑	318	Everson Walls	.05	.01
❑	319	Ron Heller	.05	.01
❑	320	Mark Collins	.05	.01
❑	321	Eddie Murray	.05	.01
❑	322	Jim Harbaugh	.25	.08
❑	323	Mel Gray	.10	.02
❑	324	Keith Van Horne	.05	.01
❑	325	Lomas Brown	.05	.01
❑	326	Carl Lee	.05	.01
❑	327	Ken O'Brien	.05	.01
❑	328	Dermontti Dawson	.05	.01
❑	329	Brad Baxter	.05	.01
❑	330	Chris Doleman	.05	.01
❑	331	Louis Oliver	.05	.01
❑	332	Frank Stams	.05	.01
❑	333	Mike Munchak	.10	.02
❑	334	Fred Strickland	.05	.01
❑	335	Mark Duper	.10	.02
❑	336	Jacob Green	.05	.01
❑	337	Tony Paige	.05	.01
❑	338	Jeff Bryant	.05	.01
❑	339	Lemuel Stinson	.05	.01
❑	340	David Wyman	.05	.01
❑	341	Lee Williams	.05	.01
❑	342	Trace Armstrong	.05	.01
❑	343	Junior Seau	.25	.08
❑	344	John Roper	.05	.01
❑	345	Jeff George	.25	.08
❑	346	Herschel Walker	.10	.02
❑	347	Sam Clancy	.05	.01
❑	348	Steve Jordan	.05	.01
❑	349	Nate Odomes	.05	.01
❑	350	Martin Bayless	.05	.01
❑	351	Brent Jones	.25	.08
❑	352	Ray Agnew	.05	.01
❑	353	Charles Haley	.10	.02
❑	354	Andre Tippett	.05	.01
❑	355	Ronnie Lott	.10	.02
❑	356	Thurman Thomas	.25	.08
❑	357	Fred Barnett	.25	.08
❑	358	James Lofton	.10	.02
❑	359	William Frizzell RC	.05	.01
❑	360	Keith McKeller	.05	.01
❑	361	Rodney Holman	.05	.01
❑	362	Henry Ellard	.10	.02
❑	363	David Fulcher	.05	.01
❑	364	Jerry Gray	.05	.01
❑	365	James Brooks	.10	.02
❑	366	Tony Stargell	.05	.01
❑	367	Keith McCants	.05	.01
❑	368	Lewis Billups	.05	.01
❑	369	Ervin Randle	.05	.01
❑	370	Pat Leahy	.05	.01
❑	371	Bruce Armstrong	.05	.01
❑	372	Steve DeBerg	.05	.01
❑	373	Guy McIntyre	.05	.01
❑	374	Deron Cherry	.05	.01
❑	375	Fred Marion	.05	.01
❑	376	Michael Haddix	.05	.01
❑	377	Kent Hull	.05	.01
❑	378	Jerry Holmes	.05	.01
❑	379	Jim Ritcher	.05	.01
❑	380	Ed West	.05	.01
❑	381	Richmond Webb	.05	.01
❑	382	Mark Jackson	.05	.01
❑	383	Tom Newberry	.05	.01
❑	384	Ricky Nattiel	.05	.01
❑	385	Keith Sims	.05	.01
❑	386	Ron Hall	.05	.01
❑	387	Ken Norton	.10	.02
❑	388	Paul Gruber	.05	.01
❑	389	Daniel Stubbs	.05	.01
❑	390	Ian Beckles	.05	.01
❑	391	Hoby Brenner	.05	.01
❑	392	Tory Epps	.05	.01
❑	393	Sam Mills	.05	.01
❑	394	Chris Hinton	.05	.01
❑	395	Steve Walsh	.05	.01
❑	396	Simon Fletcher	.05	.01
❑	397	Tony Bennett	.10	.02
❑	398	Aundray Bruce	.05	.01
❑	399	Mark Murphy	.05	.01
❑	400	Checklist 301-400	.05	.01
❑	401	Barry Sanders SL	.50	.20
❑	402	Jerry Rice SL	.40	.15
❑	403	Warren Moon SL	.10	.02
❑	404	Derrick Thomas SL	.10	.02
❑	405	Nick Lowery LL	.05	.01
❑	406	Mark Carrier DB LL	.10	.02
❑	407	Michael Carter	.05	.01
❑	408	Chris Singleton	.05	.01
❑	409	Matt Millen	.10	.02
❑	410	Ronnie Lippett	.05	.01
❑	411	E.J. Junior	.05	.01
❑	412	Ray Donaldson	.05	.01
❑	413	Keith Willis	.05	.01
❑	414	Jessie Hester	.05	.01
❑	415	Jeff Cross	.05	.01
❑	416	Greg Jackson RC	.05	.01
❑	417	Alvin Walton	.05	.01
❑	418	Bart Oates	.05	.01
❑	419	Chip Lohmiller	.05	.01
❑	420	John Elliott	.05	.01
❑	421	Randall McDaniel	.05	.01
❑	422	Richard Johnson CB RC	.05	.01
❑	423	Al Noga	.05	.01
❑	424	Lamar Lathon	.05	.01
❑	425	Rick Fenney	.05	.01
❑	426	Jack Del Rio	.10	.02
❑	427	Don Mosebar	.05	.01
❑	428	Luis Sharpe	.05	.01
❑	429	Steve Wisniewski	.05	.01
❑	430	Jimmie Jones	.05	.01
❑	431	Freeman McNeil	.05	.01
❑	432	Ron Rivera	.05	.01
❑	433	Hart Lee Dykes	.05	.01
❑	434	Mark Carrier DB	.10	.02
❑	435	Rob Moore	.25	.08
❑	436	Gary Clark	.25	.08
❑	437	Heath Sherman	.05	.01
❑	438	Darrell Green	.05	.01
❑	439	Jessie Small	.05	.01
❑	440	Monte Coleman	.05	.01
❑	441	Leonard Marshall	.05	.01
❑	442	Richard Johnson	.05	.01
❑	443	Dave Meggett	.10	.02
❑	444	Barry Sanders	1.25	.50
❑	445	Lawrence Taylor	.25	.08
❑	446	Marcus Allen	.25	.08
❑	447	Johnny Johnson	.05	.01
❑	448	Aaron Wallace	.05	.01

❑	449	Anthony Thompson	.05	.01
❑	450	D.Marino/S.DeBerg CL	.40	.15
❑	451	Andre Rison TM	.10	.02
❑	452	Thurman Thomas TM	.10	.02
❑	453	Neal Anderson MVP	.05	.01
❑	454	Boomer Esiason MVP	.05	.01
❑	455	Eric Metcalf MVP	.10	.02
❑	456	Emmitt Smith TM	1.25	.50
❑	457	Bobby Humphrey MVP	.05	.01
❑	458	Barry Sanders TM	.50	.20
❑	459	Sterling Sharpe TM	.10	.02
❑	460	Warren Moon TM	.10	.02
❑	461	Albert Bentley MVP	.05	.01
❑	462	Steve DeBerg MVP	.05	.01
❑	463	[illegible]	[illegible]	.01
❑	464	Henry Ellard MVP	.10	.02
❑	465	Dan Marino TM	.50	.20
❑	466	Anthony Carter MVP	.10	.02
❑	467	John Stephens MVP	.05	.01
❑	468	Pat Swilling MVP	.05	.01
❑	469	Ottis Anderson MVP	.10	.02
❑	470	Dennis Byrd MVP	.05	.01
❑	471	Randall Cunningham TM	.10	.02
❑	472	Johnny Johnson TM	.05	.01
❑	473	Rod Woodson TM	.10	.02
❑	474	Anthony Miller MVP	.10	.02
❑	475	Jerry Rice TM	.40	.15
❑	476	John L.Williams MVP	.05	.01
❑	477	Wayne Haddix MVP	.05	.01
❑	478	Earnest Byner MVP	.05	.01
❑	479	Doug Widell	.05	.01
❑	480	Tommy Hodson	.05	.01
❑	481	Shawn Collins	.05	.01
❑	482	Rickey Jackson	.05	.01
❑	483	Tony Casillas	.05	.01
❑	484	Vaughan Johnson	.05	.01
❑	485	Floyd Dixon	.05	.01
❑	486	Eric Green	.05	.01
❑	487	Harry Hamilton	.05	.01
❑	488	Gary Anderson K	.05	.01
❑	489	Bruce Hill	.05	.01
❑	490	Gerald Williams	.05	.01
❑	491	Cortez Kennedy	.25	.08
❑	492	Chet Brooks	.05	.01
❑	493	Dwayne Harper RC	.05	.01
❑	494	Don Griffin	.05	.01
❑	495	Andy Heck	.05	.01
❑	496	David Treadwell	.05	.01
❑	497	Irv Pankey	.05	.01
❑	498	Dennis Smith	.05	.01
❑	499	Marcus Dupree	.05	.01
❑	500	Checklist 401-500	.05	.01
❑	501	Wendell Davis	.05	.01
❑	502	Matt Bahr	.05	.01
❑	503	Bob Burnett RC	.10	.02
❑	504	Maurice Carthon	.05	.01
❑	505	Donnell Woolford	.05	.01
❑	506	Howard Ballard	.05	.01
❑	507	Mark Boyer	.05	.01
❑	508	Eugene Marve	.05	.01
❑	509	Joe Kelly	.05	.01
❑	510	Will Wolford	.05	.01
❑	511	Robert Clark	.05	.01
❑	512	Matt Brock RC	.05	.01
❑	513	Chris Warren	.25	.08
❑	514	Ken Willis	.05	.01
❑	515	George Jamison RC	.05	.01
❑	516	Rufus Porter	.05	.01
❑	517	Mark Higgs RC	.05	.01
❑	518	Thomas Everett	.05	.01
❑	519	Robert Brown	.05	.01
❑	520	Gene Atkins	.05	.01
❑	521	Hardy Nickerson	.10	.02
❑	522	Johnny Bailey	.05	.01
❑	523	William Frizzell	.05	.01
❑	524	Steve McMichael	.10	.02
❑	525	Kevin Porter	.05	.01
❑	526	Carwell Gardner	.05	.01
❑	527	Eugene Daniel	.05	.01
❑	528	Vestee Jackson	.05	.01
❑	529	Chris Goode	.05	.01
❑	530	Leon Seals	.05	.01
❑	531	Darion Conner	.05	.01
❑	532	Stan Brock	.05	.01
❑	533	Kirby Jackson RC	.05	.01
❑	534	Marv Cook	.05	.01
❑	535	Bill Fralic	.05	.01
❑	536	Keith Woodside	.05	.01
❑	537	Hugh Green	.05	.01
❑	538	Grant Feasel	.05	.01
❑	539	Bubba McDowell	.05	.01
❑	540	Vai Sikahema	.05	.01
❑	541	Aaron Cox	.05	.01
❑	542	Roger Craig	.10	.02
❑	543	Robb Thomas	.05	.01
❑	544	Ronnie Lott	.10	.02
❑	545	Robert Delpino	.05	.01
❑	546	Greg McMurtry	.05	.01
❑	547	Jim Morrissey RC	.05	.01
❑	548	Johnny Rembert	.05	.01
❑	549	Markus Paul RC	.05	.01
❑	550	Karl Wilson RC	.05	.01
❑	551	Gaston Green	.05	.01
❑	552	Willie Drewrey	.05	.01
❑	553	Michael Young	.05	.01
❑	554	Tom Tupa	.05	.01
❑	555	John Friesz	.25	.08
❑	556	Cody Carlson RC	.05	.01
❑	557	Eric Allen	.05	.01
❑	558	Thomas Benson	.05	.01
❑	559	Scott Mersereau RC	.05	.01
❑	560	Lionel Washington	.05	.01
❑	561	Brian Brennan	.05	.01
❑	562	Jim Jeffcoat	.05	.01
❑	563	Jeff Jaeger	.05	.01
❑	564	D.J. Johnson	.05	.01
❑	565	Danny Villa	.05	.01
❑	566	Don Beebe	.05	.01
❑	567	Michael Haynes	.25	.08
❑	568	Brett Faryniarz RC	.05	.01
❑	569	Mike Prior	.05	.01
❑	570	John Davis RC	.05	.01
❑	571	Vernon Turner RC	.05	.01
❑	572	Michael Brooks	.05	.01
❑	573	Mike Gann	.05	.01
❑	574	Ron Holmes	.05	.01
❑	575	Gary Plummer	.05	.01
❑	576	Bill Romanowski	.05	.01
❑	577	Chris Jacke	.05	.01
❑	578	Gary Reasons	.05	.01
❑	579	Tim Jorden RC	.05	.01
❑	580	Tim McKyer	.05	.01
❑	581	Johnnie Jackson RC	.05	.01
❑	582	Ethan Horton	.05	.01
❑	583	Pete Stoyanovich	.05	.01
❑	584	Jeff Query	.05	.01
❑	585	Frank Reich	.10	.02
❑	586	Riki Ellison	.05	.01
❑	587	Eric Hill	.05	.01
❑	588	Anthony Shelton RC	.05	.01
❑	589	Steve Smith	.05	.01
❑	590	Garth Jax RC	.05	.01
❑	591	Greg Davis RC	.05	.01
❑	592	Bill Maas	.05	.01
❑	593	Henry Rolling RC	.05	.01
❑	594	Keith Jones	.05	.01
❑	595	Tootie Robbins	.05	.01
❑	596	Brian Jordan	.10	.02
❑	597	Derrick Walker RC	.05	.01
❑	598	Jonathan Hayes	.05	.01
❑	599	Nate Lewis RC	.05	.01
❑	600	Checklist 501-600	.05	.01
❑	601	Croel/Lewis/Tray/Walk CL	.05	.01
❑	602	James Jones RC DT	.05	.01
❑	603	Tim Barnett RC	.05	.01
❑	604	Ed King RC	.05	.01
❑	605	Shane Curry RF	.05	.01
❑	606	Mike Croel	.05	.01
❑	607	Bryan Cox RC	.25	.08
❑	608	Shawn Jefferson RC	.10	.02
❑	609	Kenny Walker RC	.05	.01
❑	610	Michael Jackson RC WR	.25	.08
❑	611	Jon Vaughn RC	.05	.01
❑	612	Greg Lewis	.05	.01
❑	613	Joe Valerio RF	.05	.01
❑	614	Pat Harlow RC	.05	.01
❑	615	Henry Jones RC	.10	.02
❑	616	Jeff Graham RC WR	.25	.08
❑	617	Darryll Lewis RC	.10	.02
❑	618	Keith Traylor RC	.05	.01
❑	619	Scott Miller RF	.05	.01
❑	620	Nick Bell	.05	.01
❑	621	John Flannery RC	.05	.01
❑	622	Leonard Russell RC	.10	.02
❑	623	Alfred Williams RC	.05	.01
❑	624	Browning Nagle	.05	.01
❑	625	Harvey Williams	.10	.02
❑	626	Dan McGwire	.05	.01
❑	627	Favre/Pritchard/Pegram CL	.50	.20
❑	628	William Thomas RC	.05	.01
❑	629	Lawrence Dawsey RC	.10	.02
❑	630	Aeneas Williams RC	.25	.08
❑	631	Stan Thomas RF	.05	.01
❑	632	Randal Hill	.05	.01
❑	633	[illegible] RC	.05	.01
❑	634	Alvin Harper	.10	.02
❑	635	Esera Tuaolo RC	.05	.01
❑	636	Russell Maryland	.10	.02
❑	637	Anthony Morgan RC	.05	.01
❑	638	Erric Pegram RC	.25	.08
❑	639	Herman Moore	.25	.08
❑	640	Ricky Ervins RC	.10	.02
❑	641	Kelvin Pritchett RC	.10	.02
❑	642	Roman Phifer RC	.05	.01
❑	643	Antone Davis RC	.05	.01
❑	644	Mike Pritchard	.10	.02
❑	645	Vinnie Clark RC	.05	.01
❑	646	Jake Reed RC	.50	.20
❑	647	Brett Favre	4.00	1.50
❑	648	Todd Lyght	.05	.01
❑	649	Bruce Pickens	.05	.01
❑	650	Darren Lewis RC	.05	.01
❑	651	Wesley Carroll	.05	.01
❑	652	James Joseph RC	.10	.02
❑	653	Robert Delpino AR	.05	.01
❑	654	Deion Sanders/V.Glenn AR	.05	.01
❑	655	J.Rice/T.McDaniels AR	.30	.10
❑	656	B.Sanders/D.Thomas AR	.50	.20
❑	657	Ken Tippins AR	.05	.01
❑	658	Christian Okoye AR	.05	.01
❑	659	Rich Gannon	.25	.08
❑	660	Johnny Meads	.05	.01
❑	661	J.J.Birden RC	.10	.02
❑	662	Bruce Kozerski	.05	.01
❑	663	Felix Wright	.05	.01
❑	664	Al Smith	.05	.01
❑	665	Stan Humphries	.25	.08
❑	666	Alfred Anderson	.05	.01
❑	667	Nate Newton	.10	.02
❑	668	Vince Workman RC	.10	.02
❑	669	Ricky Reynolds	.05	.01
❑	670	Bryce Paup RC	.25	.08
❑	671	Gill Fenerty	.05	.01
❑	672	Darrell Thompson	.05	.01
❑	673	Anthony Smith	.05	.01
❑	674	Darryl Henley RC	.05	.01
❑	675	Brett Maxie	.05	.01
❑	676	Craig Taylor RC	.05	.01
❑	677	Steve Wallace	.10	.02
❑	678	Jeff Feagles RC	.05	.01
❑	679	James Washington RC	.05	.01
❑	680	Tim Harris	.05	.01
❑	681	Dennis Gibson	.05	.01
❑	682	Toi Cook RC	.05	.01
❑	683	Lorenzo Lynch	.05	.01
❑	684	Brad Edwards RC	.05	.01
❑	685	Ray Crockett RC	.05	.01
❑	686	Harris Barton	.05	.01
❑	687	Byron Evans	.05	.01
❑	688	Eric Thomas	.05	.01
❑	689	Jeff Criswell	.05	.01
❑	690	Eric Ball	.05	.01
❑	691	Brian Mitchell	.10	.02
❑	692	Quinn Early	.10	.02
❑	693	Aaron Jones	.05	.01
❑	694	Jim Dombrowski	.05	.01
❑	695	Jeff Bostic	.05	.01
❑	696	Tony Casillas	.05	.01
❑	697	Ken Lanier	.05	.01
❑	698	Henry Thomas	.05	.01
❑	699	Steve Beuerlein	.10	.02
❑	700	Checklist 601-700	.05	.01
❑	P1	Joe Montana Promo	2.50	1.00
❑	P2	Barry Sanders Promo	2.00	.75

❑ SP1 Darrell Green Fastest	.50	.20
❑ SP2 Don Shula 300th Win	2.00	.75

1992 Upper Deck

❑ COMPLETE SET (620)	15.00	6.00
❑ COMP.SERIES 1 (400)	10.00	4.00
❑ COMP.SERIES 2 (220)	5.00	2.50
❑ 1 Bennett/Buckley/McNabb C	.10	.02
❑ 2 Edgar Bennett RC	.25	.08
❑ 3 Eddie Blake RC	.05	.01
❑ 4 Brian Bollinger RC	.05	.01
❑ 5 Joe Bowden RC	.05	.01
❑ 6 Terrell Buckley RC	.05	.01
❑ 7 Willie Clay RC	.05	.01
❑ 8 Ed Cunningham RC	.05	.01
❑ 9 Matt Darby RC	.05	.01
❑ 10 Will Furrer RC	.05	.01
❑ 11 Chris Hakel RC	.05	.01
❑ 12 Carlos Huerta	.05	.01
❑ 13 Amp Lee RC	.05	.01
❑ 14 Ricardo McDonald RC	.05	.01
❑ 15 Dexter McNabb RC	.05	.01
❑ 16 Chris Mims RC	.05	.01
❑ 17 Derrick Moore RC	.10	.02
❑ 18 Mark D'Onofrio RC	.05	.01
❑ 19 Patrick Rowe RC	.05	.01
❑ 20 Leon Searcy RC	.05	.01
❑ 21 Torrance Small RC	.10	.02
❑ 22 Jimmy Smith RC	3.00	1.25
❑ 23 Tony Smith RC WR	.05	.01
❑ 24 Siran Stacy RC	.05	.01
❑ 25 Kevin Turner RC	.05	.01
❑ 26 Tommy Vardell RC	.05	.01
❑ 27 Bob Whitfield RC	.05	.01
❑ 28 Darryl Williams RC	.05	.01
❑ 29 Jeff Sydner RC	.05	.01
❑ 30 Mike Croel/L.Russell CL	.05	.01
❑ 31 Todd Marinovich ART	.05	.01
❑ 32 Leonard Russell ART	.05	.01
❑ 33 Nick Bell ART	.05	.01
❑ 34 Alvin Harper ART	.05	.01
❑ 35 Mike Pritchard ART	.05	.01
❑ 36 Lawrence Dawsey AR	.05	.01
❑ 37 Tim Barnett AR	.05	.01
❑ 38 John Flannery AR	.05	.01
❑ 39 Stan Thomas AR	.05	.01
❑ 40 Ed King AR	.05	.01
❑ 41 Charles McRae AR	.05	.01
❑ 42 Eric Moten AR	.05	.01
❑ 43 Moe Gardner AR	.05	.01
❑ 44 Kenny Walker AR	.05	.01
❑ 45 Esera Tuaolo AR	.05	.01
❑ 46 Alfred Williams AR	.05	.01
❑ 47 Bryan Cox AR	.05	.01
❑ 48 Mo Lewis AR	.05	.01
❑ 49 Mike Croel ART	.05	.01
❑ 50 Stanley Richard AR	.05	.01
❑ 51 Tony Covington AR	.05	.01
❑ 52 Larry Brown DB AR	.05	.01
❑ 53 Aeneas Williams AR	.05	.01
❑ 54 John Kasay AR	.05	.01
❑ 55 Jon Vaughn ART	.05	.01
❑ 56 David Fulcher	.05	.01
❑ 57 Barry Foster	.10	.02
❑ 58 Terry Wooden	.05	.01
❑ 59 Gary Anderson K	.05	.01
❑ 60 Alfred Williams	.05	.01
❑ 61 Robert Blackmon	.05	.01
❑ 62 Brian Noble	.05	.01
❑ 63 Terry Allen	.25	.08
❑ 64 Darrell Green	.05	.01
❑ 65 Darren Comeaux	.05	.01
❑ 66 Rob Burnett	.05	.01
❑ 67 Jarrod Bunch	.05	.01
❑ 68 Michael Jackson	.10	.02
❑ 69 Greg Lloyd	.10	.02
❑ 70 Richard Brown RC	.05	.01
❑ 71 Harold Green	.05	.01
❑ 72 William Fuller	.05	.01
❑ 73 Mark Carrier DB TC	.05	.01
❑ 74 David Fulcher TC	.05	.01
❑ 75 Cornelius Bennett TC	.05	.01
❑ 76 Steve Atwater TC	.05	.01
❑ 77 Kevin Mack TC	.05	.01
❑ 78 Mark Carrier WR TC	.05	.01
❑ 79 Tim McDonald TC	.05	.01
❑ 80 Marion Butts TC	.05	.01
❑ 81 Christian Okoye TC	.05	.01
❑ 82 Jeff Herrod TC	.05	.01
❑ 83 Emmitt Smith TC	.60	.25
❑ 84 Mark Duper TC	.05	.01
❑ 85 Keith Jackson TC	.05	.01
❑ 86 Andre Rison TC	.10	.02
❑ 87 John Taylor TC	.05	.01
❑ 88 Rodney Hampton TC	.10	.02
❑ 89 Rob Moore TC	.05	.01
❑ 90 Chris Spielman TC	.05	.01
❑ 91 Haywood Jeffires TC	.05	.01
❑ 92 Sterling Sharpe TC	.10	.02
❑ 93 Irving Fryar TC	.05	.01
❑ 94 Marcus Allen TC	.10	.02
❑ 95 Henry Ellard TC	.05	.01
❑ 96 Mark Rypien TC	.05	.01
❑ 97 Pat Swilling TC	.05	.01
❑ 98 Brian Blades TC	.05	.01
❑ 99 Eric Green TC	.05	.01
❑ 100 Anthony Carter TC	.05	.01
❑ 101 Burt Grossman	.05	.01
❑ 102 Gary Anderson RB	.05	.01
❑ 103 Neil Smith	.25	.08
❑ 104 Jeff Feagles	.05	.01
❑ 105 Shane Conlan	.05	.01
❑ 106 Jay Novacek	.10	.02
❑ 107 Bill Brooks	.05	.01
❑ 108 Mark Ingram	.05	.01
❑ 109 Anthony Munoz	.10	.02
❑ 110 Wendell Davis	.05	.01
❑ 111 Jim Everett	.10	.02
❑ 112 Bruce Matthews	.05	.01
❑ 113 Mark Higgs	.05	.01
❑ 114 Chris Warren	.10	.02
❑ 115 Brad Baxter	.05	.01
❑ 116 Greg Townsend	.05	.01
❑ 117 Al Smith	.05	.01
❑ 118 Jeff Cross	.05	.01
❑ 119 Terry McDaniel	.05	.01
❑ 120 Ernest Givins	.10	.02
❑ 121 Fred Barnett	.10	.02
❑ 122 Flipper Anderson	.05	.01
❑ 123 Floyd Turner	.05	.01
❑ 124 Stephen Baker	.05	.01
❑ 125 Tim Johnson	.05	.01
❑ 126 Brent Jones	.10	.02
❑ 127 Leonard Marshall	.05	.01
❑ 128 Jim Price	.05	.01
❑ 129 Jessie Hester	.05	.01
❑ 130 Mark Carrier WR	.10	.02
❑ 131 Bubba McDowell	.05	.01
❑ 132 Andre Tippett	.05	.01
❑ 133 James Hasty	.05	.01
❑ 134 Mel Gray	.10	.02
❑ 135 Christian Okoye	.05	.01
❑ 136 Earnest Byner	.05	.01
❑ 137 Ferrell Edmunds	.05	.01
❑ 138 Henry Ellard	.10	.02
❑ 139 Rob Moore	.10	.02
❑ 140 Brian Jordan	.10	.02
❑ 141 Clarence Verdin	.05	.01
❑ 142 Cornelius Bennett	.10	.02
❑ 143 John Taylor	.10	.02
❑ 144 Derrick Thomas	.25	.08
❑ 145 Thurman Thomas	.25	.08
❑ 146 Warren Moon	.25	.08
❑ 147 Vinny Testaverde	.10	.02
❑ 148 Steve Bono RC	.25	.08
❑ 149 Robb Thomas	.05	.01
❑ 150 John Friesz	.10	.02
❑ 151 Richard Dent	.10	.02
❑ 152 Eddie Anderson	.05	.01
❑ 153 Kevin Greene	.10	.02
❑ 154 Marion Butts	.05	.01
❑ 155 Barry Sanders	1.25	.50
❑ 156 Andre Rison	.10	.02
❑ 157 Ronnie Lott	.10	.02
❑ 158 Eric Allen	.05	.01
❑ 159 Mark Clayton	.10	.02
❑ 160 Terance Mathis	.10	.02
❑ 161 Darryl Talley	.05	.01
❑ 162 Eric Metcalf	.10	.02
❑ 163 Reggie Cobb	.05	.01
❑ 164 Ernie Jones	.05	.01
❑ 165 David Griggs	.05	.01
❑ 166 Tom Rathman	.05	.01
❑ 167 Bubby Brister	.10	.02
❑ 168 Broderick Thomas	.05	.01
❑ 169 Chris Doleman	.05	.01
❑ 170 Charles Haley	.10	.02
❑ 171 Michael Haynes	.10	.02
❑ 172 Rodney Hampton	.10	.02
❑ 173 Nick Bell	.05	.01
❑ 174 Gene Atkins	.05	.01
❑ 175 Mike Merriweather	.05	.01
❑ 176 Reggie Roby	.05	.01
❑ 177 Bennie Blades	.05	.01
❑ 178 John L. Williams	.05	.01
❑ 179 Rodney Peete	.10	.02
❑ 180 Greg Montgomery	.05	.01
❑ 181 Vince Newsome	.05	.01
❑ 182 Andre Collins	.05	.01
❑ 183 Erik Kramer	.10	.02
❑ 184 Bryan Hinkle	.05	.01
❑ 185 Reggie White	.25	.08
❑ 186 Bruce Armstrong	.05	.01
❑ 187 Anthony Carter	.10	.02
❑ 188 Pat Swilling	.05	.01
❑ 189 Robert Delpino	.05	.01
❑ 190 Brent Williams	.05	.01
❑ 191 Johnny Johnson	.05	.01
❑ 192 Aaron Craver	.05	.01
❑ 193 Vincent Brown	.05	.01
❑ 194 Herschel Walker	.10	.02
❑ 195 Tim McDonald	.05	.01
❑ 196 Gaston Green	.05	.01
❑ 197 Brian Blades	.10	.02
❑ 198 Rod Bernstine	.05	.01
❑ 199 Brett Perriman	.10	.02
❑ 200 John Elway	1.25	.50
❑ 201 Michael Carter	.05	.01
❑ 202 Mark Carrier DB	.05	.01
❑ 203 Cris Carter	.50	.20
❑ 204 Kyle Clifton	.05	.01
❑ 205 Alvin Wright	.05	.01
❑ 206 Andre Ware	.05	.01
❑ 207 Dave Waymer	.05	.01
❑ 208 Darren Lewis	.05	.01
❑ 209 Joey Browner	.05	.01
❑ 210 Rich Miano	.05	.01
❑ 211 Marcus Allen	.25	.08
❑ 212 Steve Broussard	.05	.01
❑ 213 Joel Hilgenberg	.05	.01
❑ 214 Bo Orlando RC	.05	.01
❑ 215 Clay Matthews	.10	.02
❑ 216 Chris Hinton	.05	.01
❑ 217 Al Edwards	.05	.01
❑ 218 Tim Brown	.25	.08
❑ 219 Sam Mills	.05	.01
❑ 220 Don Majkowski	.05	.01
❑ 221 James Francis	.05	.01
❑ 222 Steve Hendrickson RC	.05	.01
❑ 223 James Thornton	.05	.01
❑ 224 Byron Evans	.05	.01
❑ 225 Pepper Johnson	.05	.01
❑ 226 Darryl Henley	.05	.01
❑ 227 Simon Fletcher	.05	.01
❑ 228 Hugh Millen	.05	.01
❑ 229 Tim McGee	.05	.01
❑ 230 Richmond Webb	.05	.01
❑ 231 Tony Bennett	.05	.01

❑ 232 Nate Odomes .05 .01
❑ 233 Scott Case .05 .01
❑ 234 Dalton Hilliard .05 .01
❑ 235 Paul Gruber .05 .01
❑ 236 Jeff Lageman .05 .01
❑ 237 Tony Mandarich .05 .01
❑ 238 Cris Dishman .05 .01
❑ 239 Steve Walsh .05 .01
❑ 240 Moe Gardner .05 .01
❑ 241 Bill Romanowski .05 .01
❑ 242 Chris Zorich .10 .02
❑ 243 Stephone Paige .05 .01
❑ 244 Mike Croel .05 .01
❑ 245 Leonard Russell .10 .02
❑ 246 Mark Rypien .05 .01
❑ 247 Aeneas Williams .10 .02
❑ 248 Steve Atwater .05 .01
❑ 249 Michael Stewart .05 .01
❑ 250 Pierce Holt .05 .01
❑ 251 Kevin Mack .05 .01
❑ 252 Sterling Sharpe .25 .08
❑ 253 Lawrence Dawsey .10 .02
❑ 254 Emmitt Smith 1.50 .60
❑ 255 Todd Marinovich .05 .01
❑ 256 Neal Anderson .05 .01
❑ 257 Mo Lewis .05 .01
❑ 258 Vance Johnson .05 .01
❑ 259 Rickey Jackson .05 .01
❑ 260 Esera Tuaolo .05 .01
❑ 261 Wilber Marshall .05 .01
❑ 262 Keith Henderson .05 .01
❑ 263 William Thomas .05 .01
❑ 264 Rickey Dixon .05 .01
❑ 265 Dave Meggett .10 .02
❑ 266 Gerald Riggs .05 .01
❑ 267 Tim Harris .05 .01
❑ 268 Ken Harvey .05 .01
❑ 269 Clyde Simmons .05 .01
❑ 270 Irving Fryar .10 .02
❑ 271 Darion Conner .05 .01
❑ 272 Vince Workman .05 .01
❑ 273 Jim Harbaugh .25 .08
❑ 274 Lorenzo White .05 .01
❑ 275 Bobby Hebert .05 .01
❑ 276 Duane Bickett .05 .01
❑ 277 Jeff Bryant .05 .01
❑ 278 Scott Stephen .05 .01
❑ 279 Bob Golic .05 .01
❑ 280 Steve McMichael .10 .02
❑ 281 Jeff Graham .25 .08
❑ 282 Keith Jackson .10 .02
❑ 283 Howard Ballard .05 .01
❑ 284 Michael Brooks .05 .01
❑ 285 Freeman McNeil .10 .02
❑ 286 Rodney Holman .05 .01
❑ 287 Eric Bieniemy .05 .01
❑ 288 Seth Joyner .05 .01
❑ 289 Carwell Gardner .05 .01
❑ 290 Brian Mitchell .10 .02
❑ 291 Chris Miller .10 .02
❑ 292 Ray Berry .05 .01
❑ 293 Matt Brock .05 .01
❑ 294 Eric Thomas .05 .01
❑ 295 John Kasay .05 .01
❑ 296 Jay Hilgenberg .05 .01
❑ 297 Darrell Thompson .05 .01
❑ 298 Rich Gannon .25 .08
❑ 299 Steve Young .60 .25
❑ 300 Mike Kenn .05 .01
❑ 301 Emmitt Smith SL .60 .25
❑ 302 Haywood Jeffires SL .05 .01
❑ 303 Michael Irvin SL .25 .08
❑ 304 Warren Moon SL .10 .02
❑ 305 Chip Lohmiller SL .05 .01
❑ 306 Barry Sanders SL .50 .20
❑ 307 Ronnie Lott SL .10 .02
❑ 308 Pat Swilling SL .05 .01
❑ 309 Thurman Thomas SL .10 .02
❑ 310 Reggie Roby SL .05 .01
❑ 311 Moon/Irvin/T.Thomas CL .10 .02
❑ 312 Jacob Green .05 .01
❑ 313 Stephen Braggs .05 .01
❑ 314 Haywood Jeffires .10 .02
❑ 315 Freddie Joe Nunn .05 .01
❑ 316 Gary Clark .10 .02
❑ 317 Tim Barnett .05 .01
❑ 318 Mark Duper .05 .01
❑ 319 Eric Green .05 .01
❑ 320 Robert Wilson .05 .01
❑ 321 Michael Ball .05 .01
❑ 322 Eric Martin .05 .01
❑ 323 Alexander Wright .05 .01
❑ 324 Jessie Tuggle .05 .01
❑ 325 Ronnie Harmon .05 .01
❑ 326 Jeff Hostetler .10 .02
❑ 327 Eugene Daniel .05 .01
❑ 328 Ken Norton Jr. .10 .02
❑ 329 Reyna Thompson .05 .01
❑ 330 Jerry Ball .05 .01
❑ 331 Leroy Hoard .10 .02
❑ 332 Chris Martin .05 .01
❑ 333 Keith McKeller .05 .01
❑ 334 Brian Washington .05 .01
❑ 335 Eugene Robinson .05 .01
❑ 336 Maurice Hurst .05 .01
❑ 337 Dan Saleaumua .05 .01
❑ 338 Neil O'Donnell .10 .02
❑ 339 Dexter Davis .05 .01
❑ 340 Keith McCants .05 .01
❑ 341 Steve Beuerlein .10 .02
❑ 342 Roman Phifer .05 .01
❑ 343 Bryan Cox .10 .02
❑ 344 Art Monk .10 .02
❑ 345 Michael Irvin .25 .08
❑ 346 Vaughan Johnson .05 .01
❑ 347 Jeff Herrod .05 .01
❑ 348 Stanley Richard .05 .01
❑ 349 Michael Young .05 .01
❑ 350 Rod.Hampton/R.Cobb CL .10 .02
❑ 351 Jim Harbaugh MVP .10 .02
❑ 352 David Fulcher MVP .05 .01
❑ 353 Thurman Thomas MVP .10 .02
❑ 354 Gaston Green MVP .05 .01
❑ 355 Leroy Hoard MVP .05 .01
❑ 356 Reggie Cobb MVP .05 .01
❑ 357 Tim McDonald MVP .05 .01
❑ 358 Ronnie Harmon MVP UER .05 .01
❑ 359 Derrick Thomas MVP .10 .02
❑ 360 Jeff Herrod MVP .05 .01
❑ 361 Michael Irvin MVP .25 .08
❑ 362 Mark Higgs MVP .05 .01
❑ 363 Reggie White MVP .10 .02
❑ 364 Chris Miller MVP .05 .01
❑ 365 Steve Young MVP .30 .10
❑ 366 Rodney Hampton MVP .10 .02
❑ 367 Jeff Lageman MVP .05 .01
❑ 368 Barry Sanders MVP .50 .20
❑ 369 Haywood Jeffires MVP .05 .01
❑ 370 Tony Bennett MVP .05 .01
❑ 371 Leonard Russell MVP .05 .01
❑ 372 Jeff Jaeger MVP .05 .01
❑ 373 Robert Delpino MVP .05 .01
❑ 374 Mark Rypien MVP .05 .01
❑ 375 Pat Swilling MVP .05 .01
❑ 376 Cortez Kennedy MVP .10 .02
❑ 377 Eric Green MVP .05 .01
❑ 378 Cris Carter MVP .10 .02
❑ 379 John Roper .05 .01
❑ 380 Barry Word .05 .01
❑ 381 Shawn Jefferson .05 .01
❑ 382 Tony Casillas .05 .01
❑ 383 John Baylor RC .05 .01
❑ 384 Al Noga .05 .01
❑ 385 Charles Mann .05 .01
❑ 386 Gill Byrd .05 .01
❑ 387 Chris Singleton .05 .01
❑ 388 James Joseph .05 .01
❑ 389 Larry Brown DB .05 .01
❑ 390 Chris Spielman .10 .02
❑ 391 Anthony Thompson .05 .01
❑ 392 Karl Mecklenburg .05 .01
❑ 393 Joe Kelly .05 .01
❑ 394 Kanavis McGhee .05 .01
❑ 395 Bill Maas .05 .01
❑ 396 Marv Cook .05 .01
❑ 397 Louis Lipps .05 .01
❑ 398 Marty Carter RC .05 .01
❑ 399 Louis Oliver .05 .01
❑ 400 Eric Swann .10 .02
❑ 401 Troy Auzenne RC .05 .01
❑ 402 Kurt Barber .05 .01
❑ 403 Marc Boutte RC .05 .01
❑ 404 Dale Carter .10 .02
❑ 405 Marco Coleman .05 .01
❑ 406 Quentin Coryatt .05 .01
❑ 407 Shane Dronett RC .05 .01
❑ 408 Vaughn Dunbar .05 .01
❑ 409 Steve Emtman .05 .01
❑ 410 Dana Hall RC .05 .01
❑ 411 Jason Hanson RC .10 .02
❑ 412 Courtney Hawkins RC .10 .02
❑ 413 Terrell Buckley .05 .01
❑ 414 Robert Jones RC .05 .01
❑ 415 David Klingler .05 .01
❑ 416 Tommy Maddox 1.50 .60
❑ 417 Johnny Mitchell RC .05 .01
❑ 418 Carl Pickens .10 .02
❑ 419 Tracy Scroggins .05 .01
❑ 420 Tony Sacca RC .05 .01
❑ 421 Kevin Smith DB .05 .01
❑ 422 Alonzo Spellman .10 .02
❑ 423 Troy Vincent RC .05 .01
❑ 424 Sean Gilbert RC .10 .02
❑ 425 Larry Webster RC .05 .01
❑ 426 Carl Pickens/Klingler CL .10 .02
❑ 427 Bill Fralic .05 .01
❑ 428 Kevin Murphy .05 .01
❑ 429 Lemuel Stinson .05 .01
❑ 430 Harris Barton .05 .01
❑ 431 Dino Hackett .05 .01
❑ 432 John Stephens .05 .01
❑ 433 Keith Jennings RC .05 .01
❑ 434 Derrick Fenner .05 .01
❑ 435 Kenneth Gant RC .05 .01
❑ 436 Willie Gault .10 .02
❑ 437 Steve Jordan .05 .01
❑ 438 Charles Haley .10 .02
❑ 439 Keith Kartz .05 .01
❑ 440 Nate Lewis .05 .01
❑ 441 Doug Widell .05 .01
❑ 442 William White .05 .01
❑ 443 Eric Hill .05 .01
❑ 444 Melvin Jenkins .05 .01
❑ 445 David Wyman .05 .01
❑ 446 Ed West .05 .01
❑ 447 Brad Muster .05 .01
❑ 448 Ray Childress .05 .01
❑ 449 Kevin Ross .05 .01
❑ 450 Johnnie Jackson S .05 .01
❑ 451 Tracy Simien RC .05 .01
❑ 452 Don Mosebar .05 .01
❑ 453 Jay Hilgenberg .05 .01
❑ 454 Wes Hopkins .05 .01
❑ 455 Jay Schroeder .05 .01
❑ 456 Jeff Bostic .05 .01
❑ 457 Bryce Paup .25 .08
❑ 458 Dave Waymer .05 .01
❑ 459 Toi Cook .05 .01
❑ 460 Anthony Smith .05 .01
❑ 461 Don Griffin .05 .01
❑ 462 Bill Hawkins .05 .01
❑ 463 Courtney Hall .05 .01
❑ 464 Jeff Uhlenhake .05 .01
❑ 465 Mike Sherrard .05 .01
❑ 466 James Jones DT .05 .01
❑ 467 Jerrol Williams .05 .01
❑ 468 Eric Ball .05 .01
❑ 469 Randall McDaniel .05 .01
❑ 470 Alvin Harper .10 .02
❑ 471 Tom Waddle .05 .01
❑ 472 Tony Woods .05 .01
❑ 473 Kelvin Martin .05 .01
❑ 474 Jon Vaughn .05 .01
❑ 475 Gill Fenerty .05 .01
❑ 476 Aundray Bruce .05 .01
❑ 477 Morten Andersen .05 .01
❑ 478 Lamar Lathon .05 .01
❑ 479 Steve DeOssie .05 .01
❑ 480 Marvin Washington .05 .01
❑ 481 Herschel Walker .10 .02
❑ 482 Howie Long .25 .08
❑ 483 Calvin Williams .10 .02
❑ 484 Brett Favre 2.50 1.25

Card	Player	Mint	NrMt
❑ 485	Johnny Bailey	.05	.01
❑ 486	Jeff Gossett	.05	.01
❑ 487	Carnell Lake	.05	.01
❑ 488	Michael Zordich RC	.05	.01
❑ 489	Henry Rolling	.05	.01
❑ 490	Steve Smith	.05	.01
❑ 491	Vestee Jackson	.05	.01
❑ 492	Ray Crockett	.05	.01
❑ 403	Dexter Carter	.05	.01
❑ 494	Nick Lowery	.05	.01
❑ 495	Cortez Kennedy	.10	.02
❑ 496	Cleveland Gary	.05	.01
❑ 497	Kelly Stouffer	.05	.01
❑ 498	Carl Carter	.05	.01
❑ 499	Shannon Sharpe	.25	.08
❑ 500	Roger Craig	.10	.02
❑ 501	Willie Drewrey	.05	.01
❑ 502	Mark Schlereth RC	.05	.01
❑ 503	Tony Martin	.10	.02
❑ 504	Tom Newberry	.05	.01
❑ 505	Ron Hall	.05	.01
❑ 506	Scott Miller	.05	.01
❑ 507	Donnell Woolford	.05	.01
❑ 508	Dave Krieg	.10	.02
❑ 509	Eric Pegram	.10	.02
❑ 510	Checklist 401-510	.05	.01
❑ 511	Barry Sanders SBK	.60	.25
❑ 512	Thurman Thomas SBK	.10	.02
❑ 513	Warren Moon SBK	.10	.02
❑ 514	John Elway SBK	.50	.20
❑ 515	Ronnie Lott SBK	.10	.02
❑ 516	Emmitt Smith SBK	.60	.25
❑ 517	Andre Rison SBK	.10	.02
❑ 518	Steve Atwater SBK	.05	.01
❑ 519	Steve Young SBK	.30	.10
❑ 520	Mark Rypien SBK	.05	.01
❑ 521	Rich Camarillo	.05	.01
❑ 522	Mark Bavaro	.05	.01
❑ 523	Brad Edwards	.05	.01
❑ 524	Chad Hennings RC	.10	.02
❑ 525	Tony Paige	.05	.01
❑ 526	Shawn Moore	.05	.01
❑ 527	Sidney Johnson RC	.05	.01
❑ 528	Sanjay Beach RC	.05	.01
❑ 529	Kelvin Pritchett	.05	.01
❑ 530	Jerry Holmes	.05	.01
❑ 531	Al Del Greco	.05	.01
❑ 532	Bob Gagliano	.05	.01
❑ 533	Drew Hill	.05	.01
❑ 534	Donald Frank RC	.05	.01
❑ 535	Pio Sagapolutele RC	.05	.01
❑ 536	Jackie Slater	.05	.01
❑ 537	Vernon Turner	.05	.01
❑ 538	Bobby Humphrey	.05	.01
❑ 539	Audray McMillian	.05	.01
❑ 540	Gary Brown RC	.25	.08
❑ 541	Wesley Carroll	.05	.01
❑ 542	Nate Newton	.05	.01
❑ 543	Vai Sikahema	.05	.01
❑ 544	Chris Chandler	.25	.08
❑ 545	Nolan Harrison RC	.05	.01
❑ 546	Mark Green	.05	.01
❑ 547	Ricky Watters	.25	.08
❑ 548	J.J. Birden	.05	.01
❑ 549	Cody Carlson	.05	.01
❑ 550	Tim Green	.05	.01
❑ 551	Mark Jackson	.05	.01
❑ 552	Vince Buck	.05	.01
❑ 553	George Jamison	.05	.01
❑ 554	Anthony Pleasant	.05	.01
❑ 555	Reggie Johnson	.05	.01
❑ 556	John Jackson WR	.05	.01
❑ 557	Ian Beckles	.05	.01
❑ 558	Buford McGee	.05	.01
❑ 559	Fuad Reveiz UER	.05	.01
❑ 560	Joe Montana	1.25	.50
❑ 561	Phil Simms	.10	.02
❑ 562	Greg McMurtry	.05	.01
❑ 563	Gerald Williams	.05	.01
❑ 564	Dave Cadigan	.05	.01
❑ 565	Rufus Porter	.05	.01
❑ 566	Jim Kelly	.25	.08
❑ 567	Deion Sanders	.50	.20
❑ 568	Mike Singletary	.10	.02
❑ 569	Boomer Esiason	.10	.02
❑ 570	Andre Reed	.10	.02
❑ 571	James Washington	.05	.01
❑ 572	Jack Del Rio	.05	.01
❑ 573	Gerald Perry	.05	.01
❑ 574	Vinnie Clark	.05	.01
❑ 575	Mike Piel	.05	.01
❑ 576	Michael Dean Perry	.10	.02
❑ 577	Ricky Proehl	.05	.01
❑ 578	Leslie O'Neal	.10	.02
❑ 579	Russell Maryland	.05	.01
❑ 580	Eric Dickerson	.10	.02
❑ 581	Fred Strickland	.05	.01
❑ 582	Nick Lowery	.05	.01
❑ 583	Joe Milinichik RC	.05	.01
❑ 584	Mark Vlasic	.05	.01
❑ 585	James Lofton	.10	.02
❑ 586	Bruce Smith	.25	.08
❑ 587	Harvey Williams	.10	.02
❑ 588	Bernie Kosar	.10	.02
❑ 589	Carl Banks	.05	.01
❑ 590	Jeff George	.25	.08
❑ 591	Fred Jones RC	.05	.01
❑ 592	Todd Scott	.05	.01
❑ 593	Keith Jones	.05	.01
❑ 594A	Tootie Robbins ERR	.05	.01
❑ 594B	Tootie Robbins COR	.05	.01
❑ 595	Todd Philcox RC	.05	.01
❑ 596	Browning Nagle	.05	.01
❑ 597	Troy Aikman	.75	.30
❑ 598	Dan Marino	1.25	.50
❑ 599	Lawrence Taylor	.25	.08
❑ 600	Webster Slaughter	.05	.01
❑ 601	Aaron Cox	.05	.01
❑ 602	Matt Stover	.05	.01
❑ 603	Keith Sims	.05	.01
❑ 604	Dennis Smith	.05	.01
❑ 605	Kevin Porter	.05	.01
❑ 606	Anthony Miller	.10	.02
❑ 607	Ken O'Brien	.05	.01
❑ 608	Randall Cunningham	.25	.08
❑ 609	Timm Rosenbach	.05	.01
❑ 610	Junior Seau	.25	.08
❑ 611	Johnny Rembert	.05	.01
❑ 612	Rick Tuten	.05	.01
❑ 613	Willie Green	.05	.01
❑ 614	Sean Salisbury RC**/C	.05	.01
❑ 615	Martin Bayless	.05	.01
❑ 616	Jerry Rice	.75	.30
❑ 617	Randal Hill	.05	.01
❑ 618	Dan McGwire	.05	.01
❑ 619	Merril Hoge	.05	.01
❑ 620	Checklist 571-620	.05	.01
❑ A560	Joe Montana Blowup UDA	15.00	6.00
❑ A598	Dan Marino Blowup UDA	15.00	6.00
❑ SP3	James Lofton Yardage	.75	.30
❑ SP4	Art Monk Catches	.50	.20

1992 Upper Deck Gold

Card	Player	Mint	NrMt
❑	COMPLETE SET (50)	12.00	5.00
❑ G1	Steve Emtman RC	.10	.02
❑ G2	Carl Pickens RC	.30	.10
❑ G3	Dale Carter RC	.30	.10
❑ G4	Greg Skrepenak RC	.10	.02
❑ G5	Kevin Smith RC DB	.15	.05
❑ G6	Marco Coleman RC	.15	.05
❑ G7	David Klingler RC	.15	.05
❑ G8	Phillippi Sparks RC	.10	.02
❑ G9	Tommy Maddox RC	1.50	.60
❑ G10	Quentin Coryatt RC	.15	.05
❑ G11	Ty Detmer	.30	.10
❑ G12	Vaughn Dunbar RC	.10	.02
❑ G13	Ashley Ambrose RC	.30	.10
❑ G14	Kurt Barber RC	.10	.02
❑ G15	Chester McGlockton RC	.30	.10
❑ G16	Todd Collins RC	.10	.02
❑ G17	Steve Israel RC	.10	.02
❑ G18	Marquez Pope RC	.10	.02
❑ G19	Alonzo Spellman RC	.15	.05
❑ G20	Tracy Scroggins RC	.10	.02
❑ G21	Jim Kelly QC	.30	.10
❑ G22	Troy Aikman QC	.60	.25
❑ G23	Randall Cunningham QC	.30	.10
❑ G24	Bernie Kosar QC	.15	.05
❑ G25	Dan Marino QC	1.00	.40
❑ G26	Andre Reed	.15	.05
❑ G27	Deion Sanders	.50	.20
❑ G28	Randal Hill	.10	.02
❑ G29	Eric Dickerson	.15	.05
❑ G30	Jim Kelly	.30	.10
❑ G31	Bernie Kosar	.15	.05
❑ G32	Mike Singletary	.15	.05
❑ G33	Anthony Miller	.15	.05
❑ G34	Harvey Williams	.30	.10
❑ G35	Randall Cunningham	.30	.10
❑ G36	Joe Montana	1.25	.50
❑ G37	Dan McGwire	.10	.02
❑ G38	Al Toon	.15	.05
❑ G39	Carl Banks	.10	.02
❑ G40	Troy Aikman	.75	.30
❑ G41	Junior Seau	.30	.10
❑ G42	Jeff George	.30	.10
❑ G43	Michael Dean Perry	.15	.05
❑ G44	Lawrence Taylor	.30	.10
❑ G45	Dan Marino	1.25	.50
❑ G46	Jerry Rice	.75	.30
❑ G47	Boomer Esiason	.15	.05
❑ G48	Bruce Smith	.30	.10
❑ G49	Leslie O'Neal	.15	.05
❑ G50	Checklist Card	.10	.02

1993 Upper Deck

Card	Player	Mint	NrMt
❑	COMPLETE SET (530)	25.00	10.00
❑ 1	Mirer/Hearst/Con/Ken CL	.25	.08
❑ 2	Eric Curry RC	.05	.01
❑ 3	Rick Mirer RC	.25	.08
❑ 4	Dan Williams RC	.05	.01
❑ 5	Marvin Jones RC	.05	.01
❑ 6	Willie Roaf RC	.10	.02
❑ 7	Reggie Brooks RC	.10	.02
❑ 8	Horace Copeland RC	.10	.02
❑ 9	Lincoln Kennedy RC	.05	.01
❑ 10	Curtis Conway RC	.40	.15
❑ 11	Drew Bledsoe RC	2.50	1.00
❑ 12	Patrick Bates RC	.05	.01
❑ 13	Wayne Simmons RC	.05	.01
❑ 14	Irv Smith RC	.05	.01
❑ 15	Robert Smith RC	1.25	.50
❑ 16	O.J. McDuffie RC	.25	.08
❑ 17	Darrien Gordon RC	.05	.01
❑ 18	John Copeland RC	.10	.02
❑ 19	Derek Brown RC RBK	.05	.01
❑ 20	Jerome Bettis RC	5.00	2.50
❑ 21	Deon Figures RC	.05	.01

22	Glyn Milburn RC	.25	.08
23	Garrison Hearst RC	.75	.30
24	Qadry Ismail RC	.25	.08
25	Terry Kirby RC	.25	.08
26	Lamar Thomas RC	.05	.01
27	Tom Carter RC	.10	.02
28	Andre Hastings RC	.10	.02
29	George Teague RC	.10	.02
30	Tommy Maddox CL	.10	.02
31	David Klingler ART	.05	.01
32	Tommy Maddox ART	.10	.02
33	Vaughn Dunbar ART	.05	.01
34	Rodney Culver ART	.05	.01
35	Carl Pickens ART	.10	.02
36	Courtney Hawkins ART	.05	.01
37	Tyji Armstrong ART	.05	.01
38	Ray Roberts ART	.05	.01
39	Troy Auzenne ART	.05	.01
40	Shane Dronett ART	.05	.01
41	Chris Mims ART	.05	.01
42	Sean Gilbert ART	.05	.01
43	Steve Emtman ART	.05	.01
44	Robert Jones ART	.05	.01
45	Marco Coleman ART	.05	.01
46	Ricardo McDonald ART	.05	.01
47	Quentin Coryatt ART	.10	.02
48	Dana Hall ART	.05	.01
49	Darren Perry ART	.05	.01
50	Darryl Williams ART	.05	.01
51	Kevin Smith ART	.05	.01
52	Terrell Buckley ART	.05	.01
53	Troy Vincent ART	.05	.01
54	Lin Elliott ART	.05	.01
55	Dale Carter ART	.05	.01
56	Steve Atwater HIT	.05	.01
57	Junior Seau HIT	.10	.02
58	Ronnie Lott HIT	.05	.01
59	Louis Oliver HIT	.05	.01
60	Cortez Kennedy HIT	.05	.01
61	Pat Swilling HIT	.05	.01
62	Hitmen Checklist	.05	.01
63	Curtis Conway TC	.25	.08
64	Alfred Williams TC	.05	.01
65	Jim Kelly TC	.10	.02
66	Simon Fletcher TC	.05	.01
67	Eric Metcalf TC	.05	.01
68	Lawrence Dawsey TC	.05	.01
69	Garrison Hearst TC	.25	.08
70	Anthony Miller TC	.05	.01
71	Neil Smith TC	.05	.01
72	Jeff George TC	.10	.02
73	Emmitt Smith TC	.75	.30
74	Dan Marino TC	.75	.30
75	Clyde Simmons TC	.05	.01
76	Deion Sanders TC	.25	.08
77	Ricky Watters TC	.10	.02
78	Rodney Hampton TC	.10	.02
79	Brad Baxter TC	.05	.01
80	Barry Sanders TC	.60	.25
81	Warren Moon TC	.10	.02
82	Brett Favre TC	1.00	.40
83	Drew Bledsoe TC	1.25	.50
84	Eric Dickerson TC	.10	.02
85	Cleveland Gary TC	.05	.01
86	Earnest Byner TC	.05	.01
87	Wayne Martin TC	.05	.01
88	Rick Mirer TC	.25	.08
89	Barry Foster TC	.05	.01
90	Terry Allen TC	.10	.02
91	Vinnie Clark	.05	.01
92	Howard Ballard	.05	.01
93	Eric Ball	.05	.01
94	Marc Boutte	.05	.01
95	Larry Centers RC	.25	.08
96	Gary Brown	.05	.01
97	Hugh Millen	.05	.01
98	Anthony Newman RC	.05	.01
99	Darrell Thompson	.05	.01
100	George Jamison	.05	.01
101	James Francis	.05	.01
102	Leonard Harris	.05	.01
103	Lomas Brown	.05	.01
104	James Lofton	.10	.02
105	Jamie Dukes	.05	.01
106	Quinn Early	.10	.02
107	Ernie Jones	.05	.01
108	Torrance Small	.05	.01
109	Michael Carter	.05	.01
110	Aeneas Williams	.05	.01
111	Renaldo Turnbull	.05	.01
112	Al Smith	.05	.01
113	Troy Auzenne	.05	.01
114	Stephen Baker	.05	.01
115	Daniel Stubbs	.05	.01
116	Dana Hall	.05	.01
117	Lawrence Taylor	.25	.08
118	Ron Hall	.05	.01
119	Derrick Fenner	.05	.01
120	Martin Mayhew	.05	.01
121	Jay Schroeder	.05	.01
122	Michael Zordich	.05	.01
123	Ed McCaffrey	.25	.08
124	John Stephens	.05	.01
125	Brad Edwards	.05	.01
126	Don Griffin	.05	.01
127	Broderick Thomas	.05	.01
128	Ted Washington	.05	.01
129	Haywood Jeffires	.10	.02
130	Gary Plummer	.05	.01
131	Mark Wheeler	.05	.01
132	Ty Detmer	.25	.08
133	Derrick Walker	.05	.01
134	Henry Ellard	.10	.02
135	Neal Anderson	.05	.01
136	Bruce Smith	.25	.08
137	Cris Carter	.25	.08
138	Vaughn Dunbar	.05	.01
139	Dan Marino	1.50	.60
140	Troy Aikman	.75	.30
141	Randall Cunningham	.25	.08
142	Daryl Johnston	.25	.08
143	Mark Clayton	.05	.01
144	Rich Gannon	.25	.08
145	Nate Newton	.10	.02
146	Willie Gault	.05	.01
147	Brian Washington	.05	.01
148	Fred Barnett	.10	.02
149	Gill Byrd	.05	.01
150	Art Monk	.10	.02
151	Stan Humphries	.10	.02
152	Charles Mann	.05	.01
153	Greg Lloyd	.10	.02
154	Marvin Washington	.05	.01
155	Bernie Kosar	.10	.02
156	Pete Metzelaars	.05	.01
157	Chris Hinton	.05	.01
158	Jim Harbaugh	.05	[illegible]
159	Willie Davis	.25	.08
160	Leroy Thompson	.05	.01
161	Scott Miller	.05	.01
162	Eugene Robinson	.05	.01
163	David Little	.05	.01
164	Pierce Holt	.05	.01
165	James Hasty	.05	.01
166	Dave Krieg	.10	.02
167	Gerald Williams	.05	.01
168	Kyle Clifton	.05	.01
169	Bill Brooks	.05	.01
170	Vance Johnson	.05	.01
171	Greg Townsend	.05	.01
172	Jason Belser	.05	.01
173	Brett Perriman	.25	.08
174	Steve Jordan	.05	.01
175	Kelvin Martin	.05	.01
176	Greg Kragen	.05	.01
177	Kerry Cash	.05	.01
178	Chester McGlockton	.10	.02
179	Jim Kelly	.25	.08
180	Todd McNair	.05	.01
181	Leroy Hoard	.10	.02
182	Seth Joyner	.05	.01
183	Sam Gash RC	.25	.08
184	Joe Nash	.05	.01
185	Lin Elliott RC	.05	.01
186	Robert Porcher	.05	.01
187	Tommy Hodson	.05	.01
188	Greg Lewis	.05	.01
189	Dan Saleaumua	.05	.01
190	Chris Goode	.05	.01
191	Henry Thomas	.05	.01
192	Bobby Hebert	.05	.01
193	Clay Matthews	.10	.02
194	Mark Carrier WR	.10	.02
195	Anthony Pleasant	.05	.01
196	Eric Dorsey	.05	.01
197	Clarence Verdin	.05	.01
198	Marc Spindler	.05	.01
199	Tommy Maddox	.25	.08
200	Wendell Davis	.05	.01
201	John Fina	.05	.01
202	Alonzo Spellman	.05	.01
203	Darryl Williams	[illegible]	[illegible]
204	Mike Croel	.05	.01
205	Ken Norton Jr.	.10	.02
206	Mel Gray	.10	.02
207	Chuck Cecil	.05	.01
208	John Flannery	.05	.01
209	Chip Banks	.05	.01
210	Chris Martin	.05	.01
211	Donnie Brown	.05	.01
212	Vinny Testaverde	.10	.02
213	Nick Bell	.05	.01
214	Robert Delpino	.05	.01
215	Mark Higgs	.05	.01
216	Al Noga	.05	.01
217	Andre Tippett	.05	.01
218	Pat Swilling	.05	.01
219	Phil Simms	.10	.02
220	Ricky Proehl	.05	.01
221	William Thomas	.05	.01
222	Jeff Graham	.10	.02
223	Darion Conner	.05	.01
224	Mark Carrier DB	.05	.01
225	Willie Green	.05	.01
226	Reggie Rivers RC	.05	.01
227	Andre Reed	.10	.02
228	Deion Sanders	.50	.20
229	Chris Doleman	.05	.01
230	Jerry Ball	.05	.01
231	Eric Dickerson	.10	.02
232	Carlos Jenkins	.05	.01
233	Mike Johnson	.05	.01
234	Marco Coleman	.05	.01
235	Leslie O'Neal	.10	.02
236	Browning Nagle	.05	.01
237	Carl Pickens	.10	.02
238	Steve Emtman	.05	.01
239	Alvin Harper	.10	.02
240	Keith Jackson	.10	.02
241	Jerry Rice	1.00	.40
242	Cortez Kennedy	.10	.02
243	Tyji Armstrong	.05	.01
244	Troy Vincent	.05	.01
245	Randal Hill	.05	.01
246	Robert Blackmon	.05	.01
247	Junior Seau	.25	.08
248	Sterling Sharpe	.25	.08
249	Thurman Thomas	.25	.08
250	David Klingler	.05	.01
251	Jeff George	.25	.08
252	Anthony Miller	.10	.02
253	Earnest Byner	.05	.01
254	Eric Swann	.10	.02
255	Jeff Herrod	.05	.01
256	Eddie Robinson	.05	.01
257	Eric Allen	.05	.01
258	John Taylor	.10	.02
259	Sean Gilbert	.10	.02
260	Ray Childress	.05	.01
261	Michael Haynes	.10	.02
262	Greg McMurtry	.05	.01
263	Bill Romanowski	.05	.01
264	Todd Lyght	.05	.01
265	Clyde Simmons	.05	.01
266	Webster Slaughter	.05	.01
267	J.J. Birden	.05	.01
268	Aaron Wallace	.05	.01
269	Carl Banks	.05	.01
270	Ricardo McDonald	.05	.01
271	Michael Brooks	.05	.01
272	Dale Carter	.05	.01
273	Mike Pritchard	.10	.02

❑	274	Derek Brown TE	.05	.01
❑	275	Burt Grossman	.05	.01
❑	276	Mark Schlereth	.05	.01
❑	277	Karl Mecklenburg	.05	.01
❑	278	Rickey Jackson	.05	.01
❑	279	Ricky Ervins	.05	.01
❑	280	Jeff Bryant	.05	.01
❑	281	Eric Martin	.05	.01
❑	282	Carlton Haselrig	.05	.01
❑	283	Kevin Mack	.05	.01
❑	284	Brad Muster	.05	.01
❑	285	Kelvin Pritchett	.05	.01
❑	286	Courtney Hawkins	.05	.01
❑	287	Levon Kirkland	.05	.01
❑	288	Steve DeBerg	.05	.01
❑	289	Edgar Bennett	.25	.08
❑	290	Michael Dean Perry	.10	.02
❑	291	Richard Dent	.10	.02
❑	292	Howie Long	.25	.08
❑	293	Chris Mims	.05	.01
❑	294	Kurt Barber	.05	.01
❑	295	Wilber Marshall	.05	.01
❑	296	Ethan Horton	.05	.01
❑	297	Tony Bennett	.05	.01
❑	298	Johnny Johnson	.05	.01
❑	299	Craig Heyward	.10	.02
❑	300	Steve Israel	.05	.01
❑	301	Kenneth Gant	.05	.01
❑	302	Eugene Chung	.05	.01
❑	303	Harvey Williams	.10	.02
❑	304	Jarrod Bunch	.05	.01
❑	305	Darren Perry	.05	.01
❑	306	Steve Christie	.05	.01
❑	307	John Randle	.10	.02
❑	308	Warren Moon	.25	.08
❑	309	Charles Haley	.10	.02
❑	310	Tony Smith RB	.05	.01
❑	311	Steve Broussard	.05	.01
❑	312	Alfred Williams	.05	.01
❑	313	Terrell Buckley	.05	.01
❑	314	Trace Armstrong	.05	.01
❑	315	Brian Mitchell	.10	.02
❑	316	Steve Atwater	.05	.01
❑	317	Nate Lewis	.05	.01
❑	318	Richard Brown	.05	.01
❑	319	Rufus Porter	.05	.01
❑	320	Pat Harlow	.05	.01
❑	321	Anthony Smith	.05	.01
❑	322	Jack Del Rio	.05	.01
❑	323	Darryl Talley	.05	.01
❑	324	Sam Mills	.05	.01
❑	325	Chris Miller	.10	.02
❑	326	Ken Harvey	.05	.01
❑	327	Rod Woodson	.25	.08
❑	328	Tony Tolbert	.05	.01
❑	329	Todd Kinchen	.05	.01
❑	330	Brian Noble	.05	.01
❑	331	Dave Meggett	.05	.01
❑	332	Chris Spielman	.10	.02
❑	333	Barry Word	.05	.01
❑	334	Jessie Hester	.05	.01
❑	335	Michael Jackson	.10	.02
❑	336	Mitchell Price	.05	.01
❑	337	Michael Irvin	.25	.08
❑	338	Simon Fletcher	.05	.01
❑	339	Keith Jennings	.05	.01
❑	340	Vai Sikahema	.05	.01
❑	341	Roger Craig	.10	.02
❑	342	Ricky Watters	.25	.08
❑	343	Reggie Cobb	.05	.01
❑	344	Kanavis McGhee	.05	.01
❑	345	Barry Foster	.10	.02
❑	346	Marion Butts	.05	.01
❑	347	Bryan Cox	.05	.01
❑	348	Wayne Martin	.05	.01
❑	349	Jim Everett	.10	.02
❑	350	Nate Odomes	.05	.01
❑	351	Anthony Johnson	.10	.02
❑	352	Rodney Hampton	.10	.02
❑	353	Terry Allen	.25	.08
❑	354	Derrick Thomas	.25	.08
❑	355	Calvin Williams	.10	.02
❑	356	Pepper Johnson	.05	.01
❑	357	John Elway	1.50	.60
❑	358	Steve Young	.75	.30
❑	359	Emmitt Smith	1.50	.60
❑	360	Brett Favre	2.00	.75
❑	361	Cody Carlson	.05	.01
❑	362	Vincent Brown	.05	.01
❑	363	Gary Anderson RB	.05	.01
❑	364	Jon Vaughn	.05	.01
❑	365	Todd Marinovich	.05	.01
❑	366	Carnell Lake	.05	.01
❑	367	Kurt Gouveia	.05	.01
❑	368	Lawrence Dawsey	.05	.01
❑	369	Neil O'Donnell	.25	.08
❑	370	Duane Bickett	.05	.01
❑	371	Ronnie Harmon	.05	.01
❑	372	Rodney Peete	.05	.01
❑	373	Cornelius Bennett	.10	.02
❑	374	Brad Baxter	.05	.01
❑	375	Ernest Givins	.10	.02
❑	376	Keith Byars	.05	.01
❑	377	Eric Bieniemy	.05	.01
❑	378	Mike Brim	.05	.01
❑	379	Darren Lewis	.05	.01
❑	380	Heath Sherman	.05	.01
❑	381	Leonard Russell	.10	.02
❑	382	Brent Jones	.10	.02
❑	383	David Whitmore	.05	.01
❑	384	Ray Roberts	.05	.01
❑	385	John Offerdahl	.05	.01
❑	386	Keith McCants	.05	.01
❑	387	John Baylor	.05	.01
❑	388	Amp Lee	.05	.01
❑	389	Chris Warren	.10	.02
❑	390	Herman Moore	.25	.08
❑	391	Johnny Bailey	.05	.01
❑	392	Tim Johnson	.05	.01
❑	393	Eric Metcalf	.10	.02
❑	394	Chris Chandler	.10	.02
❑	395	Mark Rypien	.05	.01
❑	396	Christian Okoye	.05	.01
❑	397	Shannon Sharpe	.25	.08
❑	398	Eric Hill	.05	.01
❑	399	David Lang	.05	.01
❑	400	Bruce Matthews	.05	.01
❑	401	Harold Green	.05	.01
❑	402	Mo Lewis	.05	.01
❑	403	Terry McDaniel	.05	.01
❑	404	Wesley Carroll	.05	.01
❑	405	Richmond Webb	.05	.01
❑	406	Andre Rison	.10	.02
❑	407	Lonnie Young	.05	.01
❑	408	Tommy Vardell	.05	.01
❑	409	Gene Atkins	.05	.01
❑	410	Sean Salisbury	.05	.01
❑	411	Kenneth Davis	.05	.01
❑	412	John L. Williams	.05	.01
❑	413	Roman Phifer	.05	.01
❑	414	Bennie Blades	.05	.01
❑	415	Tim Brown	.25	.08
❑	416	Lorenzo White	.05	.01
❑	417	Tony Casillas	.05	.01
❑	418	Tom Waddle	.05	.01
❑	419	David Fulcher	.05	.01
❑	420	Jessie Tuggle	.05	.01
❑	421	Emmitt Smith SL	.75	.30
❑	422	Clyde Simmons SL	.05	.01
❑	423	Sterling Sharpe SL	.10	.02
❑	424	Sterling Sharpe SL	.10	.02
❑	425	Emmitt Smith SL	.75	.30
❑	426	Dan Marino SL	.75	.30
❑	427	Henry Jones SL	.05	.01
❑	428	Thurman Thomas SL	.10	.02
❑	429	Greg Montgomery SL	.05	.01
❑	430	Pete Stoyanovich SL	.05	.01
❑	431	Emmitt Smith CL	.40	.15
❑	432	Steve Young BB	.40	.15
❑	433	Jerry Rice BB	.50	.20
❑	434	Ricky Watters BB	.10	.02
❑	435	Barry Foster BB	.05	.01
❑	436	Cortez Kennedy BB	.05	.01
❑	437	Warren Moon BB	.10	.02
❑	438	Thurman Thomas BB	.10	.02
❑	439	Brett Favre BB	1.00	.40
❑	440	Andre Rison BB	.10	.02
❑	441	Barry Sanders BB	.60	.25
❑	442	Chris Berman CL	.05	.01
❑	443	Moe Gardner	.05	.01
❑	444	Robert Jones	.05	.01
❑	445	Reggie Langhorne	.05	.01
❑	446	Flipper Anderson	.05	.01
❑	447	James Washington	.05	.01
❑	448	Aaron Craver	.05	.01
❑	449	Jack Trudeau	.05	.01
❑	450	Neil Smith	.25	.08
❑	451	Chris Burkett	.05	.01
❑	452	Russell Maryland	.05	.01
❑	453	Drew Hill	.05	.01
❑	454	Barry Sanders	1.25	.50
❑	455	Jeff Cross	.05	.01
❑	456	Bennie Thompson	.05	.01
❑	457	Marcus Allen	.25	.08
❑	458	Tracy Scroggins	.05	.01
❑	459	LeRoy Butler	.05	.01
❑	460	Joe Montana	1.50	.60
❑	461	Eddie Anderson	.05	.01
❑	462	Tim McDonald	.05	.01
❑	463	Ronnie Lott	.10	.02
❑	464	Gaston Green	.05	.01
❑	465	Shane Conlan	.05	.01
❑	466	Leonard Marshall	.05	.01
❑	467	Melvin Jenkins	.05	.01
❑	468	Don Beebe	.05	.01
❑	469	Johnny Mitchell	.05	.01
❑	470	Darryl Henley	.05	.01
❑	471	Boomer Esiason	.10	.02
❑	472	Mark Kelso	.05	.01
❑	473	John Booty	.05	.01
❑	474	Pete Stoyanovich	.05	.01
❑	475	Thomas Smith RC	.10	.02
❑	476	Carlton Gray RC	.05	.01
❑	477	Dana Stubblefield RC	.25	.08
❑	478	Ryan McNeil RC	.25	.08
❑	479	Natrone Means RC	.25	.08
❑	480	Carl Simpson RC	.05	.01
❑	481	Robert O'Neal RC	.05	.01
❑	482	Demetrius DuBose RC	.05	.01
❑	483	Darrin Smith RC	.10	.02
❑	484	Micheal Barrow RC	.25	.08
❑	485	Chris Slade RC	.10	.02
❑	486	Steve Tovar RC	.05	.01
❑	487	Ron George RC	.05	.01
❑	488	Steve Tasker	.10	.02
❑	489	Will Furrer	.05	.01
❑	490	Reggie White	.25	.08
❑	491	Sean Jones	.05	.01
❑	492	Gary Clark	.10	.02
❑	493	Donnell Woolford	.05	.01
❑	494	Steve Beuerlein	.10	.02
❑	495	Anthony Carter	.10	.02
❑	496	Louis Oliver	.05	.01
❑	497	Chris Zorich	.05	.01
❑	498	David Brandon	.05	.01
❑	499	Bubba McDowell	.05	.01
❑	500	Adrian Cooper	.05	.01
❑	501	Bill Johnson	.05	.01
❑	502	Shawn Jefferson	.05	.01
❑	503	Siran Stacy	.05	.01
❑	504	James Jones DT	.05	.01
❑	505	Tom Rathman	.05	.01
❑	506	Vince Buck	.05	.01
❑	507	Kent Graham RC	.25	.08
❑	508	Darren Carrington RC	.05	.01
❑	509	Rickey Dixon	.05	.01
❑	510	Toi Cook	.05	.01
❑	511	Steve Smith	.05	.01
❑	512	Eric Green	.05	.01
❑	513	Phillippi Sparks	.05	.01
❑	514	Lee Williams	.05	.01
❑	515	Gary Reasons	.05	.01
❑	516	Shane Dronett	.05	.01
❑	517	Jay Novacek	.10	.02
❑	518	Kevin Greene	.10	.02
❑	519	Derek Russell	.05	.01
❑	520	Quentin Coryatt	.10	.02
❑	521	Santana Dotson	.10	.02
❑	522	Donald Frank	.05	.01
❑	523	Mike Prior	.05	.01
❑	524	Dwight Hollier RC	.05	.01
❑	525	Eric Davis	.05	.01

❑ 526 Dalton Hilliard .05 .01
❑ 527 Rodney Culver .05 .01
❑ 528 Jeff Hostetler .10 .02
❑ 529 Ernie Mills .05 .01
❑ 530 Craig Erickson .10 .02
❑ P231 Eric Dickerson Promo 1.25 .50

1994 Upper Deck

❑ COMPLETE SET (330) 25.00 12.50
❑ 1 Dan Wilkinson RC .20 .07
❑ 2 Antonio Langham RC .20 .07
❑ 3 Derrick Alexander WR RC .40 .15
❑ 4 Charles Johnson RC .40 .15
❑ 5 Bucky Brooks RC .10 .02
❑ 6 Trev Alberts RC .20 .07
❑ 7 Marshall Faulk RC 6.00 2.50
❑ 8 Willie McGinest RC .40 .15
❑ 9 Aaron Glenn RC .40 .15
❑ 10 Ryan Yarborough RC .10 .02
❑ 11 Greg Hill RC .40 .15
❑ 12 Sam Adams RC .20 .07
❑ 13 John Thierry RC .10 .02
❑ 14 Johnnie Morton RC .75 .30
❑ 15 LeShon Johnson RC .20 .07
❑ 16 David Palmer RC .40 .15
❑ 17 Trent Dilfer RC 1.25 .50
❑ 18 Jamir Miller RC .20 .07
❑ 19 Thomas Lewis RC .20 .07
❑ 20 Heath Shuler RC .40 .15
❑ 21 Wayne Gandy .10 .02
❑ 22 Isaac Bruce RC 4.00 2.00
❑ 23 Joe Johnson RC .10 .02
❑ 24 Mario Bates RC .40 .15
❑ 25 Bryant Young RC .60 .25
❑ 26 William Floyd RC .40 .15
❑ 27 Errict Rhett RC .40 .15
❑ 28 Chuck Levy RC .10 .02
❑ 29 Darnay Scott RC .75 .30
❑ 30 Rob Fredrickson RC .20 .07
❑ 31 Jamir Miller HW .10 .02
❑ 32 Thomas Lewis HW .10 .02
❑ 33 John Thierry HW .10 .02
❑ 34 Sam Adams HW .10 .02
❑ 35 Joe Johnson HW .10 .02
❑ 36 Bryant Young HW .30 .10
❑ 37 Wayne Gandy HW .10 .02
❑ 38 LeShon Johnson HW .10 .02
❑ 39 Mario Bates HW .20 .07
❑ 40 Greg Hill HW .20 .07
❑ 41 Andy Heck .10 .02
❑ 42 Warren Moon .40 .15
❑ 43 Jim Everett .20 .07
❑ 44 Bill Romanowski .10 .02
❑ 45 Michael Haynes .20 .07
❑ 46 Chris Doleman .10 .02
❑ 47 Merril Hoge .10 .02
❑ 48 Chris Miller .10 .02
❑ 49 Clyde Simmons .10 .02
❑ 50 Jeff George .40 .15
❑ 51 Jeff Burris RC .20 .07
❑ 52 Ethan Horton .10 .02
❑ 53 Scott Mitchell .20 .07
❑ 54 Howard Ballard .10 .02
❑ 55 Lewis Tillman .10 .02
❑ 56 Marion Butts .10 .02
❑ 57 Erik Kramer .20 .07
❑ 58 Ken Norton Jr. .20 .07
❑ 59 Anthony Miller .20 .07
❑ 60 Chris Hinton .10 .02
❑ 61 Ricky Proehl .10 .02
❑ 62 Craig Heyward .20 .07
❑ 63 Darryl Talley .10 .02
❑ 64 Tim Worley .10 .02
❑ 65 Derrick Fenner .10 .02
❑ 66 Jerry Ball .10 .02
❑ 67 Darrin Smith .10 .02
❑ 68 Mike Croel .10 .02
❑ 69 Ray Crockett .10 .02
❑ 70 Tony Bennett .10 .02
❑ 71 Webster Slaughter .10 .02
❑ 72 [illegible]
❑ 73 Charles Mincy .10 .02
❑ 74 Calvin Jones RC .10 .02
❑ 75 Henry Ellard .20 .07
❑ 76 Troy Vincent .10 .02
❑ 77 Sean Salisbury .10 .02
❑ 78 Pat Harlow .10 .02
❑ 79 James Williams RC LB .10 .02
❑ 80 Dave Brown .20 .07
❑ 81 Kent Graham .20 .07
❑ 82 Seth Joyner .10 .02
❑ 83 Deon Figures .10 .02
❑ 84 Stanley Richard .10 .02
❑ 85 Tom Rathman .10 .02
❑ 86 Rod Stephens .10 .02
❑ 87 Ray Seals .10 .02
❑ 88 Andre Collins .10 .02
❑ 89 Cornelius Bennett .20 .07
❑ 90 Richard Dent .20 .07
❑ 91 Louis Oliver .10 .02
❑ 92 Rodney Peete .10 .02
❑ 93 Jackie Harris .10 .02
❑ 94 Tracy Simien .10 .02
❑ 95 Greg Townsend .10 .02
❑ 96 Michael Stewart .10 .02
❑ 97 Irving Fryar .20 .07
❑ 98 Todd Collins .10 .02
❑ 99 Irv Smith .10 .02
❑ 100 Chris Calloway .10 .02
❑ 101 Kevin Greene .20 .07
❑ 102 John Friesz .20 .07
❑ 103 Steve Bono .20 .07
❑ 104 Brian Blades .20 .07
❑ 105 Reggie Cobb .10 .02
❑ 106 Eric Swann .20 .07
❑ 107 Mike Pritchard .10 .02
❑ 108 Bill Brooks .10 .02
❑ 109 Jim Harbaugh .40 .15
❑ 110 David Whitmore .10 .02
❑ 111 Eddie Anderson .10 .02
❑ 112 Ray Crittenden RC .10 .02
❑ 113 Mark Collins .10 .02
❑ 114 Brian Washington .10 .02
❑ 115 Barry Foster .10 .02
❑ 116 Gary Plummer .10 .02
❑ 117 Marc Logan .10 .02
❑ 118 John L. Williams .10 .02
❑ 119 Marty Carter .10 .02
❑ 120 Kurt Gouveia .10 .02
❑ 121 Ronald Moore .10 .02
❑ 122 Pierce Holt .10 .02
❑ 123 Henry Jones .10 .02
❑ 124 Donnell Woolford .10 .02
❑ 125 Steve Tovar .10 .02
❑ 126 Anthony Pleasant .10 .02
❑ 127 Jay Novacek .20 .07
❑ 128 Dan Williams .10 .02
❑ 129 Barry Sanders 2.50 1.00
❑ 130 Robert Brooks .40 .15
❑ 131 Lorenzo White .10 .02
❑ 132 Kerry Cash .10 .02
❑ 133 Joe Montana 3.00 1.25
❑ 134 Jeff Hostetler .20 .07
❑ 135 Jerome Bettis .60 .25
❑ 136 Dan Marino 3.00 1.25
❑ 137 Vencie Glenn .10 .02
❑ 138 Vincent Brown .10 .02
❑ 139 Rickey Jackson .10 .02
❑ 140 Carlton Bailey .10 .02
❑ 141 Jeff Lageman .10 .02
❑ 142 William Thomas .10 .02
❑ 143 Neil O'Donnell .40 .15
❑ 144 Shawn Jefferson .10 .02
❑ 145 Steve Young 1.00 .40
❑ 146 Chris Warren .20 .07
❑ 147 Courtney Hawkins .10 .02
❑ 148 Brad Edwards .10 .02
❑ 149 O.J.McDuffie .40 .15
❑ 150 David Lang .10 .02
❑ 151 Chuck Cecil .10 .02
❑ 152 Norm Johnson .10 .02
❑ 153 Pete Metzelaars .10 .02
❑ 154 Shaun Gayle .10 .02
❑ 155 Alfred Williams .10 .02
❑ [illegible]
❑ 157A Emmitt Smith ERR 1900 2.50 1.00
❑ 157B Emmitt Smith COR 2.50 1.00
❑ 158 Steve Atwater .10 .02
❑ 159 Robert Porcher .10 .02
❑ 160 Edgar Bennett .40 .15
❑ 161 Bubba McDowell .10 .02
❑ 162 Jeff Herrod .10 .02
❑ 163 Keith Cash .10 .02
❑ 164 Patrick Bates .10 .02
❑ 165 Todd Lyght .10 .02
❑ 166 Mark Higgs .10 .02
❑ 167 Carlos Jenkins .10 .02
❑ 168 Drew Bledsoe 1.00 .40
❑ 169 Wayne Martin .10 .02
❑ 170 Mike Sherrard .10 .02
❑ 171 Ronnie Lott .20 .07
❑ 172 Fred Barnett .20 .07
❑ 173 Eric Green .10 .02
❑ 174 Leslie O'Neal .10 .02
❑ 175 Brent Jones .20 .07
❑ 176 Jon Vaughn .10 .02
❑ 177 Vince Workman .10 .02
❑ 178 Ron Middleton .10 .02
❑ 179 Terry McDaniel .10 .02
❑ 180 Willie Davis .20 .07
❑ 181 Gary Clark .20 .07
❑ 182 Bobby Hebert .10 .02
❑ 183 Russell Copeland .10 .02
❑ 184 Chris Gedney .10 .02
❑ 185 Tony McGee .10 .02
❑ 186 Rob Burnett .10 .02
❑ 187 Charles Haley .20 .07
❑ 188 Shannon Sharpe .20 .07
❑ 189 Mel Gray .10 .02
❑ 190 George Teague .10 .02
❑ 191 Ernest Givins .20 .07
❑ 192 Ray Buchanan .10 .02
❑ 193 J.J. Birden .10 .02
❑ 194 Tim Brown .40 .15
❑ 195 Tim Lester .10 .02
❑ 196 Marco Coleman .10 .02
❑ 197 Randall McDaniel .10 .02
❑ 198 Bruce Armstrong .10 .02
❑ 199 Willie Roaf .10 .02
❑ 200 Greg Jackson .10 .02
❑ 201 Johnny Mitchell .10 .02
❑ 202 Calvin Williams .20 .07
❑ 203 Jeff Graham .10 .02
❑ 204 Darren Carrington .10 .02
❑ 205 Jerry Rice 1.50 .60
❑ 206 Cortez Kennedy .20 .07
❑ 207 Charles Wilson .10 .02
❑ 208 James Jenkins TE RC .10 .02
❑ 209 Ray Childress .10 .02
❑ 210 LeRoy Butler .10 .02
❑ 211 Randal Hill .10 .02
❑ 212 Lincoln Kennedy .10 .02
❑ 213 Kenneth Davis .10 .02
❑ 214 Terry Obee .10 .02
❑ 215 Ricardo McDonald .10 .02
❑ 216 Pepper Johnson .10 .02
❑ 217 Alvin Harper .20 .07
❑ 218 John Elway 3.00 1.25
❑ 219 Derrick Moore .10 .02
❑ 220 Terrell Buckley .10 .02
❑ 221 Haywood Jeffires .20 .07
❑ 222 Jessie Hester .10 .02
❑ 223 Kimble Anders .20 .07
❑ 224 Rocket Ismail .20 .07
❑ 225 Roman Phifer .10 .02

- ❑ 226 Bryan Cox .10 .02
- ❑ 227 Cris Carter .75 .30
- ❑ 228 Sam Gash .10 .02
- ❑ 229 Renaldo Turnbull .10 .02
- ❑ 230 Rodney Hampton .20 .07
- ❑ 231 Johnny Johnson .10 .02
- ❑ 232 Tim Harris .10 .02
- ❑ 233 Leroy Thompson .10 .02
- ❑ 234 Junior Seau .40 .15
- ❑ 235 Tim McDonald .10 .02
- ❑ 236 Eugene Robinson .10 .02
- ❑ 237 Lawrence Dawsey .10 .02
- ❑ 238 Tim Johnson .10 .02
- ❑ 239 Jason Elam .20 .07
- ❑ 240 Willie Green .10 .02
- ❑ 241 Larry Centers .40 .15
- ❑ 242 Erric Pegram .10 .02
- ❑ 243 Bruce Smith .40 .15
- ❑ 244 Alonzo Spellman .10 .02
- ❑ 245 Carl Pickens .20 .07
- ❑ 246 Michael Jackson .20 .07
- ❑ 247 Kevin Williams WR .20 .07
- ❑ 248 Glyn Milburn .20 .07
- ❑ 249 Herman Moore .40 .15
- ❑ 250 Brett Favre 3.00 1.25
- ❑ 251 Al Smith .10 .02
- ❑ 252 Roosevelt Potts .10 .02
- ❑ 253 Marcus Allen .40 .15
- ❑ 254 Anthony Smith .10 .02
- ❑ 255 Sean Gilbert .10 .02
- ❑ 256 Keith Byars .10 .02
- ❑ 257 Scottie Graham RC .20 .07
- ❑ 258 Leonard Russell .10 .02
- ❑ 259 Eric Martin .10 .02
- ❑ 260 Jarrod Bunch .10 .02
- ❑ 261 Rob Moore .20 .07
- ❑ 262 Herschel Walker .20 .07
- ❑ 263 Levon Kirkland .10 .02
- ❑ 264 Chris Mims .10 .02
- ❑ 265 Ricky Watters .20 .07
- ❑ 266 Rick Mirer .40 .15
- ❑ 267 Santana Dotson .20 .07
- ❑ 268 Reggie Brooks .20 .07
- ❑ 269 Garrison Hearst .40 .15
- ❑ 270 Thurman Thomas .40 .15
- ❑ 271 Johnny Bailey .10 .02
- ❑ 272 Andre Rison .20 .07
- ❑ 273 Jim Kelly .40 .15
- ❑ 274 Mark Carrier DB .10 .02
- ❑ 275 David Klingler .10 .02
- ❑ 276 Eric Metcalf .20 .07
- ❑ 277 Troy Aikman UER 1.50 .60
- ❑ 278 Simon Fletcher .10 .02
- ❑ 279 Pat Swilling .10 .02
- ❑ 280 Sterling Sharpe .20 .07
- ❑ 281 Cody Carlson .10 .02
- ❑ 282 Steve Emtman .10 .02
- ❑ 283 Neil Smith .20 .07
- ❑ 284 James Jett .10 .02
- ❑ 285 Shane Conlan .10 .02
- ❑ 286 Keith Jackson .10 .02
- ❑ 287 Qadry Ismail .40 .15
- ❑ 288 Chris Slade .10 .02
- ❑ 289 Derek Brown RBK .10 .02
- ❑ 290 Phil Simms .20 .07
- ❑ 291 Boomer Esiason .20 .07
- ❑ 292 Eric Allen .10 .02
- ❑ 293 Rod Woodson .20 .07
- ❑ 294 Ronnie Harmon .10 .02
- ❑ 295 John Taylor .20 .07
- ❑ 296 Ferrell Edmur .10 .02
- ❑ 297 Craig Erickson .10 .02
- ❑ 298 Brian Mitchell .10 .02
- ❑ 299 Dante Jones .10 .02
- ❑ 300 John Copeland .10 .02
- ❑ 301 Steve Beuerlein .20 .07
- ❑ 302 Deion Sanders .75 .30
- ❑ 303 Andre Reed .20 .07
- ❑ 304 Curtis Conway .40 .15
- ❑ 305 Harold Green .10 .02
- ❑ 306 Vinny Testaverde .20 .07
- ❑ 307 Michael Irvin .40 .15
- ❑ 308 Rod Bernstine .10 .02
- ❑ 309 Chris Spielman .20 .07
- ❑ 310 Reggie White .40 .15
- ❑ 311 Gary Brown .10 .02
- ❑ 312 Quentin Coryatt .10 .02
- ❑ 313 Derrick Thomas .40 .15
- ❑ 314 Greg Robinson .10 .02
- ❑ 315 Troy Drayton .10 .02
- ❑ 316 Terry Kirby .40 .15
- ❑ 317 John Randle .20 .07
- ❑ 318 Ben Coates .20 .07
- ❑ 319 Tyrone Hughes .20 .07
- ❑ 320 Corey Miller .10 .02
- ❑ 321 Brad Baxter .10 .02
- ❑ 322 Randall Cunningham .40 .15
- ❑ 323 Greg Lloyd .20 .07
- ❑ 324 Stan Humphries .20 .07
- ❑ 325 Dana Stubblefield .20 .07
- ❑ 326 Kelvin Martin .10 .02
- ❑ 327 Hardy Nickerson .20 .07
- ❑ 328 Desmond Howard .20 .07
- ❑ 329 Mark Carrier WR .20 .07
- ❑ 330 Daryl Johnston .20 .07
- ❑ P19 Joe Montana Promo 2.50 1.00

1995 Upper Deck

- ❑ COMPLETE SET (300) 30.00 12.50
- ❑ 1 Ki-Jana Carter RC .40 .15
- ❑ 2 Tony Boselli RC .40 .15
- ❑ 3 Steve McNair RC 4.00 1.50
- ❑ 4 Michael Westbrook RC .40 .15
- ❑ 5 Kerry Collins RC 2.00 .75
- ❑ 6 Kevin Carter RC .40 .15
- ❑ 7 James A.Stewart RC .10 .02
- ❑ 8 Joey Galloway RC 2.00 .75
- ❑ 9 Kyle Brady RC .40 .15
- ❑ 10 J.J. Stokes RC .40 .15
- ❑ 11 Derrick Alexander DE RC .10 .02
- ❑ 12 Warren Sapp RC 2.00 .75
- ❑ 13 Mark Fields RC .40 .15
- ❑ 14 Tyrone Wheatley RC 1.50 .60
- ❑ 15 Napoleon Kaufman RC 1.50 .60
- ❑ 16 James O. Stewart RC 1.50 .60
- ❑ 17 Luther Elliss RC .10 .02
- ❑ 18 Rashaan Salaam RC .20 .07
- ❑ 19 Jimmy Oliver RC .10 .02
- ❑ 20 Mark Bruener RC .20 .07
- ❑ 21 Derrick Brooks RC 2.00 .75
- ❑ 22 Christian Fauria RC .20 .07
- ❑ 23 Ray Zellars RC .20 .07
- ❑ 24 Todd Collins RC 1.25 .50
- ❑ 25 Sherman Williams RC .10 .02
- ❑ 26 Frank Sanders RC .40 .15
- ❑ 27 Rodney Thomas RC .20 .07
- ❑ 28 Rob Johnson RC 1.25 .50
- ❑ 29 Steve Stenstrom RC .10 .02
- ❑ 30 Curtis Martin RC 4.00 1.50
- ❑ 31 Gary Clark .10 .02
- ❑ 32 Troy Aikman 1.50 .60
- ❑ 33 Mike Sherrard .10 .02
- ❑ 34 Fred Barnett .20 .07
- ❑ 35 Henry Ellard .20 .07
- ❑ 36 Terry Allen .20 .07
- ❑ 37 Jeff Graham .10 .02
- ❑ 38 Herman Moore .40 .15
- ❑ 39 Brett Favre 3.00 1.25
- ❑ 40 Trent Dilfer .40 .15
- ❑ 41 Derek Brown RBK .10 .02
- ❑ 42 Andre Rison .20 .07
- ❑ 43 Flipper Anderson .10 .02
- ❑ 44 Jerry Rice 1.50 .60
- ❑ 45 Andre Reed .20 .07
- ❑ 46 Sean Dawkins .20 .07
- ❑ 47 Irving Fryar .20 .07
- ❑ 48 Vincent Brisby .10 .02
- ❑ 49 Rob Moore .20 .07
- ❑ 50 Carl Pickens .20 .07
- ❑ 51 Vinny Testaverde .20 .07
- ❑ 52 Ray Childress .10 .02
- ❑ 53 Eric Green .10 .02
- ❑ 54 Anthony Miller .20 .07
- ❑ 55 Lake Dawson .20 .07
- ❑ 56 Tim Brown .40 .15
- ❑ 57 Stan Humphries .20 .07
- ❑ 58 Rick Mirer .20 .07
- ❑ 59 Randal Hill .10 .02
- ❑ 60 Charles Haley .20 .07
- ❑ 61 Chris Calloway .10 .02
- ❑ 62 Calvin Williams .20 .07
- ❑ 63 Ethan Horton .10 .02
- ❑ 64 Cris Carter .40 .15
- ❑ 65 Curtis Conway .40 .15
- ❑ 66 Scott Mitchell .20 .07
- ❑ 67 Edgar Bennett .20 .07
- ❑ 68 Craig Erickson .10 .02
- ❑ 69 Jim Everett .10 .02
- ❑ 70 Terance Mathis .20 .07
- ❑ 71 Robert Young .10 .02
- ❑ 72 Brent Jones .10 .02
- ❑ 73 Bill Brooks .20 .07
- ❑ 74 Marshall Faulk 2.00 .75
- ❑ 75 O.J. McDuffie .40 .15
- ❑ 76 Ben Coates .20 .07
- ❑ 77 Johnny Mitchell .10 .02
- ❑ 78 Darnay Scott .20 .07
- ❑ 79 Derrick Alexander WR .40 .15
- ❑ 80 Lorenzo White .10 .02
- ❑ 81 Charles Johnson .20 .07
- ❑ 82 John Elway 3.00 1.25
- ❑ 83 Willie Davis .20 .07
- ❑ 84 James Jett .20 .07
- ❑ 85 Mark Seay .20 .07
- ❑ 86 Brian Blades .20 .07
- ❑ 87 Ronald Moore .10 .02
- ❑ 88 Alvin Harper .10 .02
- ❑ 89 Dave Brown .20 .07
- ❑ 90 Randall Cunningham .40 .15
- ❑ 91 Heath Shuler .20 .07
- ❑ 92 Jake Reed .20 .07
- ❑ 93 Donnell Woolford .10 .02
- ❑ 94 Barry Sanders 2.50 1.00
- ❑ 95 Reggie White .40 .15
- ❑ 96 Lawrence Dawsey .10 .02
- ❑ 97 Michael Haynes .20 .07
- ❑ 98 Bert Emanuel .40 .15
- ❑ 99 Troy Drayton .10 .02
- ❑ 100 Steve Young 1.25 .50
- ❑ 101 Bruce Smith .40 .15
- ❑ 102 Roosevelt Potts .10 .02
- ❑ 103 Dan Marino 3.00 1.25
- ❑ 104 Michael Timpson .10 .02
- ❑ 105 Boomer Esiason .20 .07
- ❑ 106 David Klingler .20 .07
- ❑ 107 Eric Metcalf .20 .07
- ❑ 108 Gary Brown .10 .02
- ❑ 109 Neil O'Donnell .20 .07
- ❑ 110 Shannon Sharpe .20 .07
- ❑ 111 Joe Montana 3.00 1.25
- ❑ 112 Jeff Hostetler .20 .07
- ❑ 113 Ronnie Harmon .10 .02
- ❑ 114 Chris Warren .20 .07
- ❑ 115 Larry Centers .20 .07
- ❑ 116 Michael Irvin .40 .15
- ❑ 117 Rodney Hampton .20 .07
- ❑ 118 Herschel Walker .20 .07
- ❑ 119 Reggie Brooks .20 .07
- ❑ 120 Qadry Ismail .20 .07
- ❑ 121 Chris Zorich .10 .02
- ❑ 122 Chris Spielman .20 .07
- ❑ 123 Sean Jones .10 .02
- ❑ 124 Errict Rhett .20 .07
- ❑ 125 Tyrone Hughes .20 .07
- ❑ 126 Jeff George .20 .07

❑ 127 Chris Miller .10 .02
❑ 128 Ricky Watters .20 .07
❑ 129 Jim Kelly .40 .15
❑ 130 Tony Bennett .10 .02
❑ 131 Terry Kirby .20 .07
❑ 132 Drew Bledsoe 1.00 .40
❑ 133 Johnny Johnson .10 .02
❑ 134 Dan Wilkinson .20 .07
❑ 135 Leroy Hoard .10 .02
❑ 136 Darryll Lewis .10 .02
❑ 137 Barry Foster .20 .07
❑ 138 Shane Dronett .10 .02
❑ 139 Marcus Allen .40 .15
❑ 140 Harvey Williams .10 .02
❑ 141 Tony Martin .20 .07
❑ 142 Rod Stephens .10 .02
❑ 143 Eric Swann .20 .07
❑ 144 Daryl Johnston .20 .07
❑ 145 Dave Meggett .10 .02
❑ 146 Charlie Garner .40 .15
❑ 147 Ken Harvey .10 .02
❑ 148 Warren Moon .20 .07
❑ 149 Steve Walsh .10 .02
❑ 150 Pat Swilling .10 .02
❑ 151 Terrell Buckley .10 .02
❑ 152 Courtney Hawkins .10 .02
❑ 153 Willie Roaf .10 .02
❑ 154 Chris Doleman .10 .02
❑ 155 Jerome Bettis .40 .15
❑ 156 Dana Stubblefield .20 .07
❑ 157 Cornelius Bennett .20 .07
❑ 158 Quentin Coryatt .20 .07
❑ 159 Bryan Cox .10 .02
❑ 160 Marion Butts .10 .02
❑ 161 Aaron Glenn .10 .02
❑ 162 Louis Oliver .10 .02
❑ 163 Eric Turner .10 .02
❑ 164 Cris Dishman .10 .02
❑ 165 John L. Williams .10 .02
❑ 166 Simon Fletcher .10 .02
❑ 167 Neil Smith .20 .07
❑ 168 Chester McGlockton .20 .07
❑ 169 Natrone Means .20 .07
❑ 170 Sam Adams .10 .02
❑ 171 Clyde Simmons .10 .02
❑ 172 Jay Novacek .20 .07
❑ 173 Keith Hamilton .10 .02
❑ 174 William Fuller .10 .02
❑ 175 Tom Carter .10 .02
❑ 176 John Randle .20 .07
❑ 177 Lewis Tillman .10 .02
❑ 178 Mel Gray .10 .02
❑ 179 George Teague .10 .02
❑ 180 Hardy Nickerson .10 .02
❑ 181 Mario Bates .20 .07
❑ 182 D.J. Johnson .10 .02
❑ 183 Sean Gilbert .20 .07
❑ 184 Bryant Young .20 .07
❑ 185 Jeff Burris .10 .02
❑ 186 Floyd Turner .10 .02
❑ 187 Troy Vincent .10 .02
❑ 188 Willie McGinest .20 .07
❑ 189 James Hasty .10 .02
❑ 190 Jeff Blake RC 1.00 .40
❑ 191 Stevon Moore .10 .02
❑ 192 Ernest Givins .10 .02
❑ 193 Byron Bam Morris .10 .02
❑ 194 Ray Crockett .10 .02
❑ 195 Dale Carter .20 .07
❑ 196 Terry McDaniel .10 .02
❑ 197 Leslie O'Neal .20 .07
❑ 198 Cortez Kennedy .20 .07
❑ 199 Seth Joyner .10 .02
❑ 200 Emmitt Smith 2.50 1.00
❑ 201 Thomas Lewis .20 .07
❑ 202 Andy Harmon .10 .02
❑ 203 Ricky Ervins .10 .02
❑ 204 Fuad Reveiz .10 .02
❑ 205 John Thierry .10 .02
❑ 206 Bennie Blades .10 .02
❑ 207 LeShon Johnson .20 .07
❑ 208 Charles Wilson .10 .02
❑ 209 Joe Johnson .10 .02
❑ 210 Chuck Smith .10 .02
❑ 211 Roman Phifer .10 .02
❑ 212 Ken Norton Jr. .20 .07
❑ 213 Bucky Brooks .10 .02
❑ 214 Ray Buchanan .10 .02
❑ 215 Tim Bowens .10 .02
❑ 216 Vincent Brown .10 .02
❑ 217 Marcus Turner .10 .02
❑ 218 Derrick Fenner .10 .02
❑ 219 Antonio Langham .10 .02
❑ 220 Cody Carlson .10 .02
❑ 221 Greg Lloyd .20 .07
❑ 222 Steve Atwater .10 .02
❑ 223 Donnell Bennett .20 .07
❑ 224 Rocket Ismail .20 .07
❑ 225 John Carney .10 .02
❑ 226 Eugene Robinson .10 .02
❑ 227 Aeneas Williams .10 .02
❑ 228 Darrin Smith .10 .02
❑ 229 Phillippi Sparks .10 .02
❑ 230 Eric Allen .10 .02
❑ 231 Brian Mitchell .10 .02
❑ 232 David Palmer .20 .07
❑ 233 Mark Carrier DB .10 .02
❑ 234 Dave Krieg .10 .02
❑ 235 Robert Brooks .40 .15
❑ 236 Eric Curry .10 .02
❑ 237 Wayne Martin .10 .02
❑ 238 Craig Heyward .20 .07
❑ 239 Isaac Bruce .75 .30
❑ 240 Deion Sanders 1.00 .40
❑ 241 Steve Tasker .20 .07
❑ 242 Jim Harbaugh .20 .07
❑ 243 Aubrey Beavers .10 .02
❑ 244 Chris Slade .10 .02
❑ 245 Mo Lewis .10 .02
❑ 246 Alfred Williams .10 .02
❑ 247 Michael Dean Perry .10 .02
❑ 248 Marcus Robertson .10 .02
❑ 249 Kevin Greene .20 .07
❑ 250 Leonard Russell .10 .02
❑ 251 Greg Hill .20 .07
❑ 252 Rob Fredrickson .10 .02
❑ 253 Junior Seau .40 .15
❑ 254 Rick Tuten .10 .02
❑ 255 Garrison Hearst .40 .15
❑ 256 Russell Maryland .10 .02
❑ 257 Michael Brooks .10 .02
❑ 258 Bernard Williams .10 .02
❑ 259 Reggie Roby .10 .02
❑ 260 Dewayne Washington .20 .07
❑ 261 Raymont Harris .10 .02
❑ 262 Brett Perriman .20 .07
❑ 263 LeRoy Butler .10 .02
❑ 264 Santana Dotson .10 .02
❑ 265 Irv Smith .10 .02
❑ 266 Ron George .10 .02
❑ 267 Marquez Pope .10 .02
❑ 268 William Floyd .20 .07
❑ 269 Matt Darby .10 .02
❑ 270 Jeff Herrod .10 .02
❑ 271 Bernie Parmalee .20 .07
❑ 272 Leroy Thompson .10 .02
❑ 273 Ronnie Lott .20 .07
❑ 274 Steve Tovar .10 .02
❑ 275 Michael Jackson .20 .07
❑ 276 Al Smith .10 .02
❑ 277 Rod Woodson .20 .07
❑ 278 Glyn Milburn .10 .02
❑ 279 Kimble Anders .20 .07
❑ 280 Anthony Smith .10 .02
❑ 281 Andre Coleman .10 .02
❑ 282 Terry Wooden .10 .02
❑ 283 Mickey Washington .10 .02
❑ 284 Steve Beuerlein .20 .07
❑ 285 Mark Brunell 1.00 .40
❑ 286 Keith Goganious .10 .02
❑ 287 Desmond Howard .20 .07
❑ 288 Darren Carrington .10 .02
❑ 289 Derek Brown TE .10 .02
❑ 290 Reggie Cobb .10 .02
❑ 291 Jeff Lageman .10 .02
❑ 292 Lamar Lathon .10 .02
❑ 293 Sam Mills .20 .07
❑ 294 Carlton Bailey .10 .02
❑ 295 Mark Carrier WR .20 .07
❑ 296 Willie Green .20 .07
❑ 297 Frank Reich .10 .02
❑ 298 Don Beebe .10 .02
❑ 299 Tim McKyer .10 .02
❑ 300 Pete Metzelaars .10 .02
❑ A19 Joe Montana 15.00 6.00
❑ A103 Dan Marino 15.00 6.00
❑ P1 Joe Montana Promo 2.00 .75
❑ P2 Joe Montana Promo 2.00 .75
Numbered 19
❑ P3 Marshall Faulk Promo 1.00 .40

1996 Upper Deck

❑ COMPLETE SET (300) 30.00 12.50
❑ 1 Keyshawn Johnson RC 1.25 .60
❑ 2 Kevin Hardy RC .50 .20
❑ 3 Simeon Rice RC 1.25 .50
❑ 4 Jonathan Ogden RC .50 .20
❑ 5 Cedric Jones RC .10 .02
❑ 6 Lawrence Phillips RC .50 .20
❑ 7 Tim Biakabutuka RC .50 .20
❑ 8 Terry Glenn RC 1.25 .50
❑ 9 Rickey Dudley RC .50 .20
❑ 10 Willie Anderson RC .10 .02
❑ 11 Alex Molden RC .10 .02
❑ 12 Regan Upshaw RC .10 .02
❑ 13 Walt Harris RC .10 .02
❑ 14 Eddie George RC 1.50 .60
❑ 15 John Mobley RC .10 .02
❑ 16 Duane Clemons RC .10 .02
❑ 17 Eddie Kennison RC .50 .20
❑ 18 Marvin Harrison RC 3.00 1.25
❑ 19 Daryl Gardener RC .10 .02
❑ 20 Leeland McElroy RC .25 .08
❑ 21 Eric Moulds RC 1.50 .60
❑ 22 Alex Van Dyke RC .25 .08
❑ 23 Mike Alstott RC 1.25 .50
❑ 24 Jeff Lewis RC .25 .08
❑ 25 Bobby Engram RC .50 .20
❑ 26 Derrick Mayes RC .50 .20
❑ 27 Karim Abdul-Jabbar RC .50 .20
❑ 28 Bobby Hoying RC .50 .20
❑ 29 Stepfret Williams RC .25 .08
❑ 30 Chris Darkins RC .10 .02
❑ 31 Stephen Davis RC 2.00 .75
❑ 32 Danny Kanell RC .50 .20
❑ 33 Tony Brackens RC .50 .20
❑ 34 Leslie O'Neal .10 .02
❑ 35 Chris Doleman .10 .02
❑ 36 Larry Brown .10 .02
❑ 37 Ronnie Harmon .10 .02
❑ 38 Chris Spielman .10 .02
❑ 39 John Jurkovic .10 .02
❑ 40 Shawn Jefferson .10 .02
❑ 41 William Floyd .25 .08
❑ 42 Eric Davis .10 .02
❑ 43 Willie Clay .10 .02
❑ 44 Marco Coleman .10 .02
❑ 45 Lorenzo White .10 .02
❑ 46 Neil O'Donnell .25 .08
❑ 47 Natrone Means .25 .08
❑ 48 Cornelius Bennett .10 .02
❑ 49 Steve Walsh .10 .02
❑ 50 Jerome Bettis .50 .20
❑ 51 Boomer Esiason .25 .08
❑ 52 Glyn Milburn .10 .02

❑ 53 Kevin Greene .25 .08
❑ 54 Seth Joyner .10 .02
❑ 55 Jeff Graham .10 .02
❑ 56 Darren Woodson .25 .08
❑ 57 Dale Carter .10 .02
❑ 58 Lorenzo Lynch .10 .02
❑ 59 Tim Brown .50 .20
❑ 60 Jerry Rice 1.25 .50
❑ 61 Garrison Hearst .25 .08
❑ 62 Eric Metcalf .10 .02
❑ 63 Leroy Hoard .10 .02
❑ 64 Thurman Thomas .50 .20
❑ 65 Sam Mills .10 .02
❑ 66 Curtis Conway .50 .20
❑ 67 Carl Pickens .25 .08
❑ 68 Deion Sanders .75 .30
❑ 69 Shannon Sharpe .25 .08
❑ 70 Herman Moore .25 .08
❑ 71 Robert Brooks .50 .20
❑ 72 Rodney Thomas .10 .02
❑ 73 Ken Dilger .25 .08
❑ 74 Mark Brunell .75 .30
❑ 75 Marcus Allen .50 .20
❑ 76 Dan Marino 2.50 1.00
❑ 77 Robert Smith .25 .08
❑ 78 Drew Bledsoe .75 .30
❑ 79 Jim Everett .10 .02
❑ 80 Rodney Hampton .25 .08
❑ 81 Adrian Murrell .25 .08
❑ 82 Daryl Hobbs RC .10 .02
❑ 83 Ricky Watters .25 .08
❑ 84 Yancey Thigpen .25 .08
❑ 85 Roman Phifer .10 .02
❑ 86 Tony Martin .25 .08
❑ 87 Dana Stubblefield .25 .08
❑ 88 Joey Galloway .50 .20
❑ 89 Errict Rhett .25 .08
❑ 90 Terry Allen .25 .08
❑ 91 Aeneas Williams .10 .02
❑ 92 Craig Heyward .10 .02
❑ 93 Vinny Testaverde .25 .08
❑ 94 Bryce Paup .10 .02
❑ 95 Kerry Collins .50 .20
❑ 96 Rashaan Salaam .25 .08
❑ 97 Dan Wilkinson .10 .02
❑ 98 Jay Novacek .10 .02
❑ 99 John Elway 2.50 1.00
❑ 100 Bennie Blades .10 .02
❑ 101 Edgar Bennett .25 .08
❑ 102 Darryll Lewis .10 .02
❑ 103 Marshall Faulk .60 .25
❑ 104 Bryan Schwartz .10 .02
❑ 105 Tamarick Vanover .25 .08
❑ 106 Terry Kirby .25 .08
❑ 107 John Randle .25 .08
❑ 108 Ted Johnson RC .50 .20
❑ 109 Mario Bates .25 .08
❑ 110 Phillippi Sparks .10 .02
❑ 111 Marvin Washington .10 .02
❑ 112 Terry McDaniel .10 .02
❑ 113 Bobby Taylor .10 .02
❑ 114 Carnell Lake .10 .02
❑ 115 Troy Drayton .10 .02
❑ 116 Darren Bennett .10 .02
❑ 117 J.J. Stokes .50 .20
❑ 118 Rick Mirer .25 .08
❑ 119 Jackie Harris .10 .02
❑ 120 Ken Harvey .10 .02
❑ 121 Rob Moore .25 .08
❑ 122 Jeff George .25 .08
❑ 123 Andre Rison .25 .08
❑ 124 Darick Holmes .10 .02
❑ 125 Tim McKyer .10 .02
❑ 126 Alonzo Spellman .10 .02
❑ 127 Jeff Blake .50 .20
❑ 128 Kevin Williams .10 .02
❑ 129 Anthony Miller .25 .08
❑ 130 Barry Sanders 2.00 .75
❑ 131 Brett Favre 2.50 1.25
❑ 132 Steve McNair 1.00 .40
❑ 133 Jim Harbaugh .25 .08
❑ 134 Desmond Howard .25 .08
❑ 135 Steve Bono .10 .02
❑ 136 Bernie Parmalee .10 .02
❑ 137 Warren Moon .25 .08
❑ 138 Curtis Martin 1.00 .40
❑ 139 Irv Smith .10 .02
❑ 140 Thomas Lewis .10 .02
❑ 141 Kyle Brady .10 .02
❑ 142 Napoleon Kaufman .50 .20
❑ 143 Mike Mamula .10 .02
❑ 144 Erric Pegram .10 .02
❑ 145 Isaac Bruce .50 .20
❑ 146 Andre Coleman .10 .02
❑ 147 Merton Hanks .10 .02
❑ 148 Brian Blades .10 .02
❑ 149 Hardy Nickerson .10 .02
❑ 150 Michael Westbrook .50 .20
❑ 151 Larry Centers .25 .08
❑ 152 Morten Andersen .10 .02
❑ 153 Michael Jackson .25 .08
❑ 154 Bruce Smith .25 .08
❑ 155 Derrick Moore .10 .02
❑ 156 Mark Carrier DB .10 .02
❑ 157 John Copeland .10 .02
❑ 158 Emmitt Smith 2.00 .75
❑ 159 Jason Elam .25 .08
❑ 160 Scott Mitchell .25 .08
❑ 161 Mark Chmura .25 .08
❑ 162 Blaine Bishop .10 .02
❑ 163 Tony Bennett .10 .02
❑ 164 Pete Mitchell .25 .08
❑ 165 Dan Saleaumua .10 .02
❑ 166 Pete Stoyanovich .10 .02
❑ 167 Cris Carter .50 .20
❑ 168 Vince Brisby .10 .02
❑ 169 Wayne Martin .10 .02
❑ 170 Tyrone Wheatley .25 .08
❑ 171 Mo Lewis .10 .02
❑ 172 Harvey Williams .10 .02
❑ 173 Calvin Williams .10 .02
❑ 174 Norm Johnson .10 .02
❑ 175 Mark Rypien .10 .02
❑ 176 Stan Humphries .25 .08
❑ 177 Derek Loville .10 .02
❑ 178 Christian Fauria .10 .02
❑ 179 Warren Sapp .10 .02
❑ 180 Henry Ellard .10 .02
❑ 181 Jamir Miller .10 .02
❑ 182 Jessie Tuggle .10 .02
❑ 183 Stevon Moore .10 .02
❑ 184 Jim Kelly .50 .20
❑ 185 Mark Carrier .10 .02
❑ 186 Chris Zorich .10 .02
❑ 187 Harold Green .10 .02
❑ 188 Chris Boniol .10 .02
❑ 189 Allen Aldridge .10 .02
❑ 190 Brett Perriman .10 .02
❑ 191 Chris Jacke .10 .02
❑ 192 Todd McNair .10 .02
❑ 193 Floyd Turner .10 .02
❑ 194 Jeff Lageman .10 .02
❑ 195 Derrick Thomas .50 .20
❑ 196 Eric Green .10 .02
❑ 197 Orlando Thomas .10 .02
❑ 198 Ben Coates .25 .08
❑ 199 Tyrone Hughes .10 .02
❑ 200 Dave Brown .10 .02
❑ 201 Brad Baxter .10 .02
❑ 202 Chester McGlockton .10 .02
❑ 203 Rodney Peete .10 .02
❑ 204 Willie Williams .10 .02
❑ 205 Kevin Carter .10 .02
❑ 206 Aaron Hayden RC .10 .02
❑ 207 Steve Young 1.00 .40
❑ 208 Chris Warren .25 .08
❑ 209 Eric Curry .10 .02
❑ 210 Brian Mitchell .10 .02
❑ 211 Frank Sanders .25 .08
❑ 212 Terance Mathis UER .10 .02
❑ 213 Eric Turner .10 .02
❑ 214 Bill Brooks .10 .02
❑ 215 John Kasay .10 .02
❑ 216 Erik Kramer .10 .02
❑ 217 Darnay Scott .25 .08
❑ 218 Charles Haley .25 .08
❑ 219 Steve Atwater .10 .02
❑ 220 Jason Hanson .10 .02
❑ 221 LeRoy Butler .10 .02
❑ 222 Cris Dishman .10 .02
❑ 223 Sean Dawkins .10 .02
❑ 224 James O. Stewart .25 .08
❑ 225 Greg Hill .25 .08
❑ 226 Jeff Cross .10 .02
❑ 227 Qadry Ismail .25 .08
❑ 228 Dave Meggett .10 .02
❑ 229 Eric Allen .10 .02
❑ 230 Chris Calloway .10 .02
❑ 231 Wayne Chrebet .75 .30
❑ 232 Jeff Hostetler .10 .02
❑ 233 Andy Harmon .10 .02
❑ 234 Greg Lloyd .25 .08
❑ 235 Toby Wright .10 .02
❑ 236 Junior Seau .50 .20
❑ 237 Bryant Young .25 .08
❑ 238 Robert Blackmon .10 .02
❑ 239 Trent Dilfer .50 .20
❑ 240 Leslie Shepherd .10 .02
❑ 241 Eric Swann .10 .02
❑ 242 Bert Emanuel .25 .08
❑ 243 Antonio Langham .10 .02
❑ 244 Steve Christie .10 .02
❑ 245 Tyrone Poole .10 .02
❑ 246 Jim Flanigan .10 .02
❑ 247 Tony McGee .10 .02
❑ 248 Michael Irvin .50 .20
❑ 249 Byron Bam Morris .10 .02
❑ 250 Terrell Davis 1.00 .40
❑ 251 Johnnie Morton .25 .08
❑ 252 Sean Jones .10 .02
❑ 253 Chris Sanders .25 .08
❑ 254 Quentin Coryatt .10 .02
❑ 255 Willie Jackson .25 .08
❑ 256 Mark Collins .10 .02
❑ 257 Randal Hill .10 .02
❑ 258 David Palmer .10 .02
❑ 259 Will Moore .10 .02
❑ 260 Michael Haynes .10 .02
❑ 261 Mike Sherrard .10 .02
❑ 262 William Thomas .10 .02
❑ 263 Kordell Stewart .50 .20
❑ 264 D'Marco Farr .10 .02
❑ 265 Terrell Fletcher .10 .02
❑ 266 Lee Woodall .10 .02
❑ 267 Eugene Robinson .10 .02
❑ 268 Alvin Harper .10 .02
❑ 269 Gus Frerotte .25 .08
❑ 270 Antonio Freeman .50 .20
❑ 271 Clyde Simmons .10 .02
❑ 272 Chuck Smith .10 .02
❑ 273 Steve Tasker .10 .02
❑ 274 Kevin Butler .10 .02
❑ 275 Steve Tovar .10 .02
❑ 276 Troy Aikman 1.25 .50
❑ 277 Aaron Craver .10 .02
❑ 278 Henry Thomas .10 .02
❑ 279 Craig Newsome .10 .02
❑ 280 Brent Jones .10 .02
❑ 281 Micheal Barrow .10 .02
❑ 282 Ray Buchanan .10 .02
❑ 283 Jimmy Smith .50 .20
❑ 284 Neil Smith .25 .08
❑ 285 O.J. McDuffie .25 .08
❑ 286 Jake Reed .25 .08
❑ 287 Ty Law .50 .20
❑ 288 Torrance Small .10 .02
❑ 289 Hugh Douglas .25 .08
❑ 290 Pat Swilling .10 .02
❑ 291 Charlie Garner .25 .08
❑ 292 Ernie Mills .10 .02
❑ 293 John Carney .10 .02
❑ 294 Ken Norton .10 .02
❑ 295 Cortez Kennedy .10 .02
❑ 296 Derrick Brooks .50 .20
❑ 297 Heath Shuler .25 .08
❑ 298 Reggie White .50 .20
❑ 299 Kimble Anders .25 .08
❑ 300 Willie McGinest .10 .02
❑ P96 Dan Marino Promo 2.00 .75
❑ MS1 Dan Marino 5.00 2.00
❑ MS2 Dan Marino 5.00 2.00
❑ P13 Dan Marino Promo 2.50 1.00

1997 Upper Deck

❑ COMPLETE SET (300) 40.00 20.00
❑ 1 Orlando Pace RC .60 .25
❑ 2 Darrell Russell RC .25 .08
❑ 3 Shawn Springs RC .40 .15
❑ 4 Bryant Westbrook RC .25 .08
❑ 5 Ike Hilliard RC 1.25 .50
❑ 6 Peter Boulware RC .60 .25
❑ 7 Tom Knight RC .25 .08
❑ 8 Yatil Green RC .40 .15
❑ 9 Tony Gonzalez RC 2.50 1.00
❑ 10 Reidel Anthony RC .60 .25
❑ 11 Warrick Dunn RC 2.50 1.00
❑ 12 Kenny Holmes RC .60 .25
❑ 13 Jim Druckenmiller RC .40 .15
❑ 14 James Farrior RC .60 .25
❑ 15 David LaFleur RC .25 .08
❑ 16 Antowain Smith RC 2.00 .75
❑ 17 Rae Carruth RC .25 .08
❑ 18 Dwayne Rudd RC .60 .25
❑ 19 Jake Plummer RC 4.00 1.50
❑ 20 Reinard Wilson RC .40 .15
❑ 21 Byron Hanspard RC .40 .15
❑ 22 Will Blackwell RC .40 .15
❑ 23 Troy Davis RC .40 .15
❑ 24 Corey Dillon RC 5.00 2.00
❑ 25 Joey Kent RC .60 .25
❑ 26 Renaldo Wynn RC .25 .08
❑ 27 Pat Barnes RC .60 .25
❑ 28 Kevin Lockett RC .40 .15
❑ 29 Darnell Autry RC .40 .15
❑ 30 Walter Jones RC .60 .25
❑ 31 Trevor Pryce RC .60 .25
❑ 32 Dan Marino SRF 1.25 .50
❑ 33 Steve Young SRF .25 .08
❑ 34 John Elway SRF 1.25 .50
❑ 35 Jerry Rice SRF .60 .25
❑ 36 Tim Brown SRF .60 .25
❑ 37 Deion Sanders SRF .60 .25
❑ 38 Troy Aikman SRF .60 .25
❑ 39 Barry Sanders SRF 1.00 .40
❑ 40 Emmitt Smith SRF 1.00 .40
❑ 41 Junior Seau SRF .60 .25
❑ 42 Neil Smith .40 .15
❑ 43 Brett Perriman .25 .08
❑ 44 Jim Everett .25 .08
❑ 45 Qadry Ismail .40 .15
❑ 46 Dana Stubblefield .25 .08
❑ 47 Bryant Young .25 .08
❑ 48 Ken Norton Jr. .25 .08
❑ 49 Terrell Owens .75 .30
❑ 50 Jerry Rice 1.25 .50
❑ 51 Steve Young .75 .30
❑ 52 Terry Kirby .40 .15
❑ 53 Chris Doleman .25 .08
❑ 54 Lee Woodall .25 .08
❑ 55 Merton Hanks .25 .08
❑ 56 Garrison Hearst .40 .15
❑ 57 Rashaan Salaam .25 .08
❑ 58 Raymont Harris .25 .08
❑ 59 Curtis Conway .40 .15
❑ 60 Bobby Engram .40 .15
❑ 61 Bryan Cox .25 .08
❑ 62 Walt Harris .25 .08
❑ 63 Tyrone Hughes .25 .08
❑ 64 Rick Mirer .25 .08
❑ 65 Jeff Blake .40 .15
❑ 66 Carl Pickens .40 .15
❑ 67 Darnay Scott .40 .15
❑ 68 Tony McGee .25 .08
❑ 69 Ki-Jana Carter .25 .08
❑ 70 Ashley Ambrose .25 .08
❑ 71 Dan Wilkinson .25 .08
❑ 72 Chris Spielman .25 .08
❑ 73 Todd Collins .25 .08
❑ 74 Andre Reed .40 .15
❑ 75 Quinn Early .25 .08
❑ 76 Eric Moulds .60 .25
❑ 77 Darick Holmes .25 .08
❑ 78 Thurman Thomas .60 .25
❑ 79 [illegible]
❑ 80 Bryce Paup .25 .08
❑ 81 John Elway 2.50 1.00
❑ 82 Terrell Davis .75 .30
❑ 83 Anthony Miller .25 .08
❑ 84 Shannon Sharpe .40 .15
❑ 85 Alfred Williams .25 .08
❑ 86 John Mobley .25 .08
❑ 87 Tory James .25 .08
❑ 88 Steve Atwater .25 .08
❑ 89 Darrien Gordon .25 .08
❑ 90 Mike Alstott .60 .25
❑ 91 Errict Rhett .25 .08
❑ 92 Trent Dilfer .60 .25
❑ 93 Courtney Hawkins .25 .08
❑ 94 Warren Sapp .40 .15
❑ 95 Regan Upshaw .25 .08
❑ 96 Hardy Nickerson .25 .08
❑ 97 Donnie Abraham RC .60 .25
❑ 98 Larry Centers .40 .15
❑ 99 Aeneas Williams .25 .08
❑ 100 Kent Graham UER .25 .08
❑ 101 Rob Moore .40 .15
❑ 102 Frank Sanders .40 .15
❑ 103 Leeland McElroy .25 .08
❑ 104 Eric Swann .25 .08
❑ 105 Simeon Rice .40 .15
❑ 106 Seth Joyner .25 .08
❑ 107 Stan Humphries .40 .15
❑ 108 Tony Martin .40 .15
❑ 109 Charlie Jones .25 .08
❑ 110 Andre Coleman UER 103 .25 .08
❑ 111 Terrell Fletcher .25 .08
❑ 112 Junior Seau .60 .25
❑ 113 Eric Metcalf .40 .15
❑ 114 Chris Penn .25 .08
❑ 115 Marcus Allen .60 .25
❑ 116 Greg Hill .25 .08
❑ 117 Tamarick Vanover .40 .15
❑ 118 Lake Dawson .25 .08
❑ 119 Derrick Thomas .60 .25
❑ 120 Dale Carter .25 .08
❑ 121 Elvis Grbac .40 .15
❑ 122 Aaron Bailey .25 .08
❑ 123 Jim Harbaugh .40 .15
❑ 124 Marshall Faulk .75 .30
❑ 125 Sean Dawkins .25 .08
❑ 126 Marvin Harrison .60 .25
❑ 127 Ken Dilger .25 .08
❑ 128 Tony Bennett .25 .08
❑ 129 Jeff Herrod .25 .08
❑ 130 Chris Gardocki .25 .08
❑ 131 Cary Blanchard .25 .08
❑ 132 Troy Aikman 1.25 .50
❑ 133 Emmitt Smith 2.00 .75
❑ 134 Sherman Williams .25 .08
❑ 135 Michael Irvin .60 .25
❑ 136 Eric Bjornson .25 .08
❑ 137 Herschel Walker .40 .15
❑ 138 Tony Tolbert .25 .08
❑ 139 Deion Sanders .60 .25
❑ 140 Daryl Johnston .40 .15
❑ 141 Dan Marino 2.50 1.00
❑ 142 O.J. McDuffie .40 .15
❑ 143 Troy Drayton .25 .08
❑ 144 Karim Abdul-Jabbar .40 .15
❑ 145 Stanley Pritchett .25 .08
❑ 146 Fred Barnett .25 .08
❑ 147 Zach Thomas .60 .25
❑ 148 Shawn Wooden RC .25 .08
❑ 149 Ty Detmer .40 .15
❑ 150 Derrick Witherspoon .25 .08
❑ 151 Ricky Watters .40 .15
❑ 152 Charlie Garner .40 .15
❑ 153 Chris T. Jones .25 .08
❑ 154 Irving Fryar .40 .15
❑ 155 Mike Mamula .25 .08
❑ 156 Troy Vincent .25 .08
❑ 157 Bobby Taylor .25 .08
❑ 158 Chris Boniol .25 .08
❑ 159 Devin Bush .25 .08
❑ 160 Bert Emanuel .40 .15
❑ 161 Jamal Anderson .60 .25
❑ 162 Terance Mathis .40 .15
❑ [illegible]
❑ 164 Ray Buchanan .25 .08
❑ 165 Chris Chandler .40 .15
❑ 166 Dave Brown .25 .08
❑ 167 Danny Kanell .25 .08
❑ 168 Rodney Hampton .40 .15
❑ 169 Tyrone Wheatley .40 .15
❑ 170 Amani Toomer .40 .15
❑ 171 Chris Calloway .25 .08
❑ 172 Thomas Lewis .25 .08
❑ 173 Phillippi Sparks .25 .08
❑ 174 Mark Brunell .75 .30
❑ 175 Keenan McCardell .40 .15
❑ 176 Willie Jackson .25 .08
❑ 177 Jimmy Smith .40 .15
❑ 178 Pete Mitchell .25 .08
❑ 179 Natrone Means .40 .15
❑ 180 Kevin Hardy .25 .08
❑ 181 Tony Brackens .25 .08
❑ 182 James O. Stewart .40 .15
❑ 183 Wayne Chrebet .60 .25
❑ 184 Keyshawn Johnson .60 .25
❑ 185 Adrian Murrell .40 .15
❑ 186 Neil O'Donnell .40 .15
❑ 187 Hugh Douglas .25 .08
❑ 188 Mo Lewis .25 .08
❑ 189 Marvin Washington .25 .08
❑ 190 Aaron Glenn .25 .08
❑ 191 Barry Sanders 2.00 .75
❑ 192 Scott Mitchell .40 .15
❑ 193 Herman Moore .40 .15
❑ 194 Johnnie Morton .40 .15
❑ 195 Glyn Milburn .25 .08
❑ 196 Reggie Brown LB .40 .15
❑ 197 Jason Hanson .25 .08
❑ 198 Steve McNair .75 .30
❑ 199 Eddie George .60 .25
❑ 200 Ronnie Harmon .25 .08
❑ 201 Chris Sanders .25 .08
❑ 202 Willie Davis .25 .08
❑ 203 Frank Wycheck .25 .08
❑ 204 Darryll Lewis .25 .08
❑ 205 Blaine Bishop .25 .08
❑ 206 Robert Brooks .40 .15
❑ 207 Brett Favre 2.50 1.25
❑ 208 Edgar Bennett .40 .15
❑ 209 Dorsey Levens .60 .25
❑ 210 Derrick Mayes .40 .15
❑ 211 Antonio Freeman .60 .25
❑ 212 Mark Chmura .40 .15
❑ 213 Reggie White .60 .25
❑ 214 Gilbert Brown .40 .15
❑ 215 LeRoy Butler .25 .08
❑ 216 Craig Newsome .25 .08
❑ 217 Kerry Collins .60 .25
❑ 218 Wesley Walls .40 .15
❑ 219 Muhsin Muhammad .40 .15
❑ 220 Anthony Johnson .25 .08
❑ 221 Tim Biakabutuka .40 .15
❑ 222 Kevin Greene .40 .15
❑ 223 Sam Mills .25 .08
❑ 224 John Kasay .25 .08
❑ 225 Micheal Barrow .25 .08
❑ 226 Drew Bledsoe .75 .30
❑ 227 Curtis Martin .75 .30
❑ 228 Terry Glenn .60 .25
❑ 229 Ben Coates .40 .15
❑ 230 Shawn Jefferson .25 .08
❑ 231 Willie McGinest .25 .08
❑ 232 Ted Johnson .25 .08

❑ 233	Lawyer Milloy	.40	.15
❑ 234	Ty Law	.40	.15
❑ 235	Willie Clay	.25	.08
❑ 236	Tim Brown	.60	.25
❑ 237	Rickey Dudley	.40	.15
❑ 238	Napoleon Kaufman	.60	.25
❑ 239	Chester McGlockton	.25	.08
❑ 240	Rob Fredrickson	.25	.08
❑ 241	Terry McDaniel	.25	.08
❑ 242	Desmond Howard	.40	.15
❑ 243	Jeff George	.40	.15
❑ 244	Isaac Bruce	.60	.25
❑ 245	Tony Banks	.40	.15
❑ 246	Lawrence Phillips UER 247	.25	.08
❑ 247	Kevin Carter	.25	.08
❑ 248	Roman Phifer	.25	.08
❑ 249	Keith Lyle	.25	.08
❑ 250	Eddie Kennison	.40	.15
❑ 251	Craig Heyward	.25	.08
❑ 252	Vinny Testaverde	.40	.15
❑ 253	Derrick Alexander WR	.40	.15
❑ 254	Michael Jackson	.40	.15
❑ 255	Byron Bam Morris	.25	.08
❑ 256	Eric Green	.25	.08
❑ 257	Ray Lewis	1.00	.40
❑ 258	Antonio Langham	.25	.08
❑ 259	Michael McCrary	.25	.08
❑ 260	Gus Frerotte	.25	.08
❑ 261	Terry Allen	.60	.25
❑ 262	Brian Mitchell	.25	.08
❑ 263	Michael Westbrook	.40	.15
❑ 264	Sean Gilbert	.25	.08
❑ 265	Rich Owens	.25	.08
❑ 266	Ken Harvey	.25	.08
❑ 267	Jeff Hostetler	.25	.08
❑ 268	Michael Haynes	.25	.08
❑ 269	Mario Bates	.25	.08
❑ 270	Renaldo Turnbull UER 273	.25	.08
❑ 271	Ray Zellars	.25	.08
❑ 272	Joe Johnson	.25	.08
❑ 273	Eric Allen	.25	.08
❑ 274	Heath Shuler	.25	.08
❑ 275	Daryl Hobbs	.25	.08
❑ 276	John Friesz	.25	.08
❑ 277	Brian Blades	.25	.08
❑ 278	Joey Galloway	.40	.15
❑ 279	Chris Warren	.40	.15
❑ 280	Lamar Smith	.60	.25
❑ 281	Cortez Kennedy	.25	.08
❑ 282	Chad Brown	.25	.08
❑ 283	Warren Moon	.60	.25
❑ 284	Jerome Bettis	.60	.25
❑ 285	Charles Johnson	.40	.15
❑ 286	Kordell Stewart	.60	.25
❑ 287	Erric Pegram	.25	.08
❑ 288	Norm Johnson	.25	.08
❑ 289	Levon Kirkland	.25	.08
❑ 290	Greg Lloyd	.25	.08
❑ 291	Carnell Lake	.25	.08
❑ 292	Brad Johnson	.60	.25
❑ 293	Cris Carter	.60	.25
❑ 294	Jake Reed	.40	.15
❑ 295	Robert Smith	.40	.15
❑ 296	Derrick Alexander DE	.25	.08
❑ 297	John Randle	.40	.15
❑ 298	Dixon Edwards	.25	.08
❑ 299	Orlanda Thomas	.25	.08
❑ 300	Dewayne Washington	.25	.08

1998 Upper Deck

❑	COMPLETE SET (255)	200.00	75.00
❑	COMP.SET w/o SP's (213)	25.00	12.50
❑ 1	Peyton Manning RC	50.00	25.00
❑ 2	Ryan Leaf RC	5.00	2.00
❑ 3	Andre Wadsworth RC	3.00	1.25
❑ 4	Charles Woodson RC	6.00	2.50
❑ 5	Curtis Enis RC	2.50	1.00
❑ 6	Grant Wistrom RC	3.00	1.25
❑ 7	Greg Ellis RC	2.50	1.00
❑ 8	Fred Taylor RC	8.00	3.00
❑ 9	Duane Starks RC	2.50	1.00
❑ 10	Keith Brooking RC	5.00	2.00
❑ 11	Takeo Spikes RC	5.00	2.00
❑ 12	Jason Peter RC	2.50	1.00

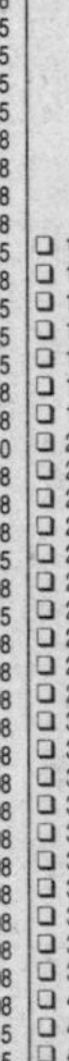

❑ 13	Anthony Simmons RC	3.00	1.25
❑ 14	Kevin Dyson RC	5.00	2.00
❑ 15	Brian Simmons RC	3.00	1.25
❑ 16	Robert Edwards RC	3.00	1.25
❑ 17	Randy Moss RC	30.00	15.00
❑ 18	John Avery RC	3.00	1.25
❑ 19	Marcus Nash RC	2.50	1.00
❑ 20	Jerome Pathon RC	5.00	2.00
❑ 21	Jacquez Green RC	3.00	1.25
❑ 22	Robert Holcombe RC	3.00	1.25
❑ 23	Pat Johnson RC	3.00	1.25
❑ 24	Germane Crowell RC	3.00	1.25
❑ 25	Joe Jurevicius RC	5.00	2.00
❑ 26	Skip Hicks RC	3.00	1.25
❑ 27	Ahman Green RC	25.00	10.00
❑ 28	Brian Griese RC	10.00	4.00
❑ 29	Hines Ward RC	20.00	10.00
❑ 30	Tavian Banks RC	3.00	1.25
❑ 31	Tony Simmons RC	3.00	1.25
❑ 32	Victor Riley RC	2.50	1.00
❑ 33	Rashaan Shehee RC	3.00	1.25
❑ 34	R.W. McQuarters RC	3.00	1.25
❑ 35	Flozell Adams RC	2.50	1.00
❑ 36	Tra Thomas RC	2.50	1.00
❑ 37	Greg Favors RC	3.00	1.25
❑ 38	Jon Ritchie RC	3.00	1.25
❑ 39	Jesse Haynes RC	2.50	1.00
❑ 40	Ryan Sutter RC	2.50	1.00
❑ 41	Mo Collins RC	2.50	1.00
❑ 42	Tim Dwight RC	5.00	2.00
❑ 43	Chris Chandler	.40	.15
❑ 44	Byron Hanspard	.25	.08
❑ 45	Jessie Tuggle	.25	.08
❑ 46	Jamal Anderson	.60	.25
❑ 47	Terance Mathis	.40	.15
❑ 48	Morten Andersen	.25	.08
❑ 49	Jake Plummer	.60	.25
❑ 50	Mario Bates	.40	.15
❑ 51	Frank Sanders	.40	.15
❑ 52	Adrian Murrell	.40	.15
❑ 53	Simeon Rice	.40	.15
❑ 54	Aeneas Williams	.25	.08
❑ 55	Eric Swann UER	.25	.08
❑ 56	Jim Harbaugh	.40	.15
❑ 57	Michael Jackson	.25	.08
❑ 58	Peter Boulware	.25	.08
❑ 59	Errict Rhett	.40	.15
❑ 60	Jermaine Lewis	.40	.15
❑ 61	Eric Zeier	.40	.15
❑ 62	Rod Woodson	.40	.15
❑ 63	Rob Johnson	.60	.25
❑ 64	Antowain Smith	.60	.25
❑ 65	Bruce Smith	.40	.15
❑ 66	Eric Moulds	.60	.25
❑ 67	Andre Reed	.40	.15
❑ 68	Thurman Thomas	.60	.25
❑ 69	Lonnie Johnson	.25	.08
❑ 70	Kerry Collins	.40	.15
❑ 71	Kevin Greene	.40	.15
❑ 72	Fred Lane	.25	.08
❑ 73	Rae Carruth	.25	.08
❑ 74	Michael Bates	.25	.08
❑ 75	William Floyd	.25	.08
❑ 76	Sean Gilbert	.25	.08
❑ 77	Erik Kramer	.25	.08
❑ 78	Edgar Bennett	.25	.08
❑ 79	Curtis Conway	.40	.15
❑ 80	Darnell Autry	.25	.08
❑ 81	Ryan Wetnight RC	.25	.08
❑ 82	Walt Harris	.25	.08
❑ 83	Bobby Engram	.40	.15
❑ 84	Jeff Blake	.40	.15
❑ 85	Carl Pickens	.40	.15
❑ 86	Darnay Scott	.40	.15
❑ 87	Corey Dillon	.60	.25
❑ 88	Reinard Wilson	.25	.08
❑ 89	Ashley Ambrose	.25	.08
❑ 90	Troy Aikman	1.25	.50
❑ 91	Michael Irvin	.60	.25
❑ 92	Emmitt Smith	2.00	.75
❑ 93	Deion Sanders	.60	.25
❑ 94	David LaFleur	.25	.08
❑ 95	Chris Warren	.40	.15
❑ 96	Darren Woodson	.25	.08
❑ 97	John Elway	2.50	1.00
❑ 98	Terrell Davis	.60	.25
❑ 99	Rod Smith	.40	.15
❑ 100	Shannon Sharpe	.40	.15
❑ 101	Ed McCaffrey	.40	.15
❑ 102	Steve Atwater	.25	.08
❑ 103	John Mobley	.25	.08
❑ 104	Darrien Gordon	.25	.08
❑ 105	Barry Sanders	2.00	.75
❑ 106	Scott Mitchell	.40	.15
❑ 107	Herman Moore	.40	.15
❑ 108	Johnnie Morton	.40	.15
❑ 109	Robert Porcher	.25	.08
❑ 110	Bryant Westbrook	.25	.08
❑ 111	Tommy Vardell	.25	.08
❑ 112	Brett Favre	2.50	1.00
❑ 113	Dorsey Levens	.60	.25
❑ 114	Reggie White	.60	.25
❑ 115	Antonio Freeman	.60	.25
❑ 116	Robert Brooks	.40	.15
❑ 117	Mark Chmura	.40	.15
❑ 118	Derrick Mayes	.40	.15
❑ 119	Gilbert Brown	.25	.08
❑ 120	Marshall Faulk	.75	.30
❑ 121	Jeff Burris	.25	.08
❑ 122	Marvin Harrison	.60	.25
❑ 123	Quentin Coryatt	.25	.08
❑ 124	Ken Dilger	.25	.08
❑ 125	Zack Crockett	.25	.08
❑ 126	Mark Brunell	.60	.25
❑ 127	Bryce Paup	.25	.08
❑ 128	Tony Brackens	.25	.08
❑ 129	Renaldo Wynn	.25	.08
❑ 130	Keenan McCardell	.40	.15
❑ 131	Jimmy Smith	.40	.15
❑ 132	Kevin Hardy	.25	.08
❑ 133	Elvis Grbac	.40	.15
❑ 134	Tamarick Vanover	.25	.08
❑ 135	Chester McGlockton	.25	.08
❑ 136	Andre Rison	.40	.15
❑ 137	Derrick Alexander	.40	.15
❑ 138	Tony Gonzalez	.60	.25
❑ 139	Derrick Thomas	.60	.25
❑ 140	Dan Marino	2.50	1.00
❑ 141	Karim Abdul-Jabbar	.60	.25
❑ 142	O.J. McDuffie	.40	.15
❑ 143	Yatil Green	.25	.08
❑ 144	Charles Jordan	.25	.08
❑ 145	Brock Marion	.25	.08
❑ 146	Zach Thomas	.60	.25
❑ 147	Brad Johnson	.60	.25
❑ 148	Cris Carter	.60	.25
❑ 149	Jake Reed	.40	.15
❑ 150	Robert Smith	.60	.25
❑ 151	John Randle	.40	.15
❑ 152	Dwayne Rudd	.25	.08
❑ 153	Randall Cunningham	.60	.25
❑ 154	Drew Bledsoe	1.00	.40
❑ 155	Terry Glenn	.60	.25
❑ 156	Ben Coates	.40	.15
❑ 157	Willie Clay	.25	.08
❑ 158	Chris Slade	.25	.08
❑ 159	Derrick Cullors RC	.25	.08
❑ 160	Ty Law	.40	.15
❑ 161	Danny Wuerffel	.40	.15
❑ 162	Andre Hastings	.25	.08
❑ 163	Troy Davis	.25	.08

❑ 164	Billy Joe Hobert	.25	.08
❑ 165	Eric Guliford	.25	.08
❑ 166	Mark Fields	.25	.08
❑ 167	Alex Molden	.25	.08
❑ 168	Danny Kanell	.40	.15
❑ 169	Tiki Barber	.60	.25
❑ 170	Charles Way	.25	.08
❑ 171	Amani Toomer	.40	.15
❑ 172	Michael Strahan	.40	.15
❑ 173	Jessie Armstead	.25	.08
❑ 174	Jason Sehorn	.40	.15
❑ 175	Glenn Foley	.40	.15
❑ 176	Curtis Martin	.60	.25
❑ 177	Aaron Glenn	.25	.08
❑ 178	Keyshawn Johnson	.60	.25
❑ 179	James Farrior	.25	.08
❑ 180	Wayne Chrebet	.60	.25
❑ 181	Keith Byars	.25	.08
❑ 182	Jeff George	.40	.15
❑ 183	Napoleon Kaufman	.60	.25
❑ 184	Tim Brown	.60	.25
❑ 185	Darrell Russell	.25	.08
❑ 186	Rickey Dudley	.25	.08
❑ 187	James Jett	.40	.15
❑ 188	Desmond Howard	.40	.15
❑ 189	Bobby Hoying	.40	.15
❑ 190	Charlie Garner	.40	.15
❑ 191	Irving Fryar	.40	.15
❑ 192	Chris T. Jones	.25	.08
❑ 193	Mike Mamula	.25	.08
❑ 194	Troy Vincent	.25	.08
❑ 195	Kordell Stewart	.60	.25
❑ 196	Jerome Bettis	.60	.25
❑ 197	Will Blackwell	.25	.08
❑ 198	Levon Kirkland	.25	.08
❑ 199	Carnell Lake	.25	.08
❑ 200	Charles Johnson	.25	.08
❑ 201	Greg Lloyd	.25	.08
❑ 202	Donnell Woolford	.25	.08
❑ 203	Tony Banks	.40	.15
❑ 204	Amp Lee	.25	.08
❑ 205	Isaac Bruce	.60	.25
❑ 206	Eddie Kennison	.40	.15
❑ 207	Ryan McNeil	.25	.08
❑ 208	Mike Jones	.25	.08
❑ 209	Ernie Conwell	.25	.08
❑ 210	Natrone Means	.40	.15
❑ 211	Junior Seau	.60	.25
❑ 212	Tony Martin	.40	.15
❑ 213	Freddie Jones	.25	.08
❑ 214	Bryan Still	.25	.08
❑ 215	Rodney Harrison	.40	.15
❑ 216	Steve Young	.75	.30
❑ 217	Jerry Rice	1.25	.50
❑ 218	Garrison Hearst	.60	.25
❑ 219	J.J. Stokes	.40	.15
❑ 220	Ken Norton	.25	.08
❑ 221	Greg Clark	.25	.08
❑ 222	Terrell Owens	.60	.25
❑ 223	Bryant Young	.25	.08
❑ 224	Warren Moon	.60	.25
❑ 225	Jon Kitna	.60	.25
❑ 226	Ricky Watters	.40	.15
❑ 227	Chad Brown	.25	.08
❑ 228	Joey Galloway	.40	.15
❑ 229	Shawn Springs	.25	.08
❑ 230	Cortez Kennedy	.25	.08
❑ 231	Trent Dilfer	.60	.25
❑ 232	Warrick Dunn	.60	.25
❑ 233	Mike Alstott	.60	.25
❑ 234	Warren Sapp	.40	.15
❑ 235	Bert Emanuel	.40	.15
❑ 236	Reidel Anthony	.40	.15
❑ 237	Hardy Nickerson	.25	.08
❑ 238	Derrick Brooks	.60	.25
❑ 239	Steve McNair	.60	.25
❑ 240	Yancey Thigpen	.25	.08
❑ 241	Anthony Dorsett	.25	.08
❑ 242	Blaine Bishop	.25	.08
❑ 243	Kenny Holmes	.25	.08
❑ 244	Eddie George	.60	.25
❑ 245	Chris Sanders	.25	.08
❑ 246	Gus Frerotte	.25	.08
❑ 247	Terry Allen	.60	.25
❑ 248	Dana Stubblefield	.25	.08
❑ 249	Michael Westbrook	.40	.15
❑ 250	Darrell Green	.40	.15
❑ 251	Brian Mitchell	.25	.08
❑ 252	Ken Harvey	.25	.08
❑ CL1	Troy Aikman CL	.60	.25
❑ CL2	Dan Marino CL	.75	.30
❑ CL3	Herman Moore CL	.40	.15

1999 Upper Deck

❑	COMPLETE SET (270)	100.00	50.00
❑	COMP.SET w/o SP's (225)	25.00	12.50
❑ 1	Jake Plummer	.50	.20
❑ 2	Adrian Murrell	.50	.20
❑ 3	Rob Moore	.50	.20
❑ 4	Larry Centers	.30	.10
❑ 5	Simeon Rice	.50	.20
❑ 6	Andre Wadsworth	.30	.10
❑ 7	Frank Sanders	.50	.20
❑ 8	Tim Dwight	.75	.30
❑ 9	Ray Buchanan	.30	.10
❑ 10	Chris Chandler	.50	.20
❑ 11	Jamal Anderson	.75	.30
❑ 12	O.J. Santiago	.30	.10
❑ 13	Danny Kanell	.30	.10
❑ 14	Terance Mathis	.50	.20
❑ 15	Priest Holmes	1.25	.50
❑ 16	Tony Banks	.50	.20
❑ 17	Ray Lewis	.75	.30
❑ 18	Patrick Johnson	.30	.10
❑ 19	Michael Jackson	.30	.10
❑ 20	Michael McCrary	.30	.10
❑ 21	Jermaine Lewis	.50	.20
❑ 22	Eric Moulds	.75	.30
❑ 23	Doug Flutie	.75	.30
❑ 24	Antowain Smith	.75	.30
❑ 25	Rob Johnson	.50	.20
❑ 26	Bruce Smith	.50	.20
❑ 27	Andre Reed	.50	.20
❑ 28	Thurman Thomas	.50	.20
❑ 29	Fred Lane	.30	.10
❑ 30	Wesley Walls	.50	.20
❑ 31	Tim Biakabutuka	.50	.20
❑ 32	Kevin Greene	.30	.10
❑ 33	Steve Beuerlein	.30	.10
❑ 34	Muhsin Muhammad	.50	.20
❑ 35	Rae Carruth	.30	.10
❑ 36	Bobby Engram	.50	.20
❑ 37	Curtis Enis	.30	.10
❑ 38	Edgar Bennett	.30	.10
❑ 39	Erik Kramer	.30	.10
❑ 40	Steve Stenstrom	.30	.10
❑ 41	Alonzo Mayes	.30	.10
❑ 42	Curtis Conway	.50	.20
❑ 43	Tony McGee	.30	.10
❑ 44	Darnay Scott	.30	.10
❑ 45	Jeff Blake	.50	.20
❑ 46	Corey Dillon	.75	.30
❑ 47	Ki-Jana Carter	.30	.10
❑ 48	Takeo Spikes	.30	.10
❑ 49	Carl Pickens	.50	.20
❑ 50	Ty Detmer	.50	.20
❑ 51	Leslie Shepherd	.30	.10
❑ 52	Terry Kirby	.30	.10
❑ 53	Marquez Pope	.30	.10
❑ 54	Antonio Langham	.30	.10
❑ 55	Jamir Miller	.30	.10
❑ 56	Derrick Alexander DT	.30	.10
❑ 57	Troy Aikman	1.50	.60
❑ 58	Rocket Ismail	.50	.20
❑ 59	Emmitt Smith	1.50	.60
❑ 60	Michael Irvin	.50	.20
❑ 61	David LaFleur	.30	.10
❑ 62	Chris Warren	.30	.10
❑ 63	Deion Sanders	.75	.30
❑ 64	Greg Ellis	.30	.10
❑ 65	John Elway	2.50	1.00
❑ 66	Bubby Brister	.30	.10
❑ 67	Terrell Davis	.75	.30
❑ 68	Ed McCaffrey	.50	.20
❑ 69	John Mobley	.30	.10
❑ 70	Bill Romanowski	.30	.10
❑ 71	Rod Smith	.50	.20
❑ 72	Shannon Sharpe	.50	.20
❑ 73	Charlie Batch	.75	.30
❑ 74	Germane Crowell	.30	.10
❑ 75	Johnnie Morton	.30	.10
❑ 76	Barry Sanders	2.50	1.00
❑ 77	Robert Porcher	.30	.10
❑ 78	Stephen Boyd	.30	.10
❑ 79	Herman Moore	.50	.20
❑ 80	Brett Favre	2.50	1.00
❑ 81	Mark Chmura	.30	.10
❑ 82	Antonio Freeman	.75	.30
❑ 83	Robert Brooks	.50	.20
❑ 84	Vonnie Holliday	.30	.10
❑ 85	Bill Schroeder	.75	.30
❑ 86	Dorsey Levens	.75	.30
❑ 87	Santana Dotson	.30	.10
❑ 88	Peyton Manning	2.50	1.00
❑ 89	Jerome Pathon	.30	.10
❑ 90	Marvin Harrison	.75	.30
❑ 91	Ellis Johnson	.30	.10
❑ 92	Ken Dilger	.30	.10
❑ 93	E.G. Green	.30	.10
❑ 94	Jeff Burris	.30	.10
❑ 95	Mark Brunell	.75	.30
❑ 96	Fred Taylor	.75	.30
❑ 97	Jimmy Smith	.50	.20
❑ 98	James Stewart	.50	.20
❑ 99	Kyle Brady	.30	.10
❑ 100	Dave Thomas RC	.30	.10
❑ 101	Keenan McCardell	.50	.20
❑ 102	Elvis Grbac	.50	.20
❑ 103	Tony Gonzalez	.75	.30
❑ 104	Andre Rison	.50	.20
❑ 105	Donnell Bennett	.30	.10
❑ 106	Derrick Thomas	.75	.30
❑ 107	Warren Moon	.75	.30
❑ 108	Derrick Alexander WR	.50	.20
❑ 109	Dan Marino	2.00	1.00
❑ 110	O.J. McDuffie	.50	.20
❑ 111	Karim Abdul-Jabbar	.50	.20
❑ 112	John Avery	.30	.10
❑ 113	Sam Madison	.30	.10
❑ 114	Jason Taylor	.30	.10
❑ 115	Zach Thomas	.75	.30
❑ 116	Randall Cunningham	.75	.30
❑ 117	Randy Moss	2.00	.75
❑ 118	Cris Carter	.75	.30
❑ 119	Jake Reed	.50	.20
❑ 120	Matthew Hatchette	.30	.10
❑ 121	John Randle	.50	.20
❑ 122	Robert Smith	.75	.30
❑ 123	Drew Bledsoe	1.00	.40
❑ 124	Ben Coates	.50	.20
❑ 125	Terry Glenn	.75	.30
❑ 126	Ty Law	.50	.20
❑ 127	Tony Simmons	.30	.10
❑ 128	Ted Johnson	.30	.10
❑ 129	Tony Carter	.30	.10
❑ 130	Willie McGinest	.30	.10
❑ 131	Danny Wuerffel	.30	.10
❑ 132	Cameron Cleeland	.30	.10
❑ 133	Eddie Kennison	.50	.20
❑ 134	Joe Johnson	.30	.10
❑ 135	Andre Hastings	.30	.10
❑ 136	La'Roi Glover RC	.75	.30
❑ 137	Kent Graham	.30	.10
❑ 138	Tiki Barber	.75	.30
❑ 139	Gary Brown	.30	.10

	Card	High	Low
❑	140 Ike Hilliard	.30	.10
❑	141 Jason Sehorn	.30	.10
❑	142 Michael Strahan	.50	.20
❑	143 Amani Toomer	.30	.10
❑	144 Kerry Collins	.50	.20
❑	145 Vinny Testaverde	.50	.20
❑	146 Wayne Chrebet	.50	.20
❑	147 Curtis Martin	.75	.30
❑	148 Mo Lewis	.30	.10
❑	149 Aaron Glenn	.30	.10
❑	150 Steve Atwater	.30	.10
❑	151 Keyshawn Johnson	.75	.30
❑	152 James Farrior	.30	.10
❑	153 Rich Gannon	.75	.30
❑	154 Tim Brown	.75	.30
❑	155 Darrell Russell	.30	.10
❑	156 Rickey Dudley	.30	.10
❑	157 Charles Woodson	.75	.30
❑	158 James Jett	.50	.20
❑	159 Napoleon Kaufman	.75	.30
❑	160 Duce Staley	.75	.30
❑	161 Doug Pederson	.30	.10
❑	162 Bobby Hoying	.50	.20
❑	163 Koy Detmer	.30	.10
❑	164 Kevin Turner	.30	.10
❑	165 Charles Johnson	.30	.10
❑	166 Mike Mamula	.30	.10
❑	167 Jerome Bettis	.75	.30
❑	168 Courtney Hawkins	.30	.10
❑	169 Will Blackwell	.30	.10
❑	170 Kordell Stewart	.50	.20
❑	171 Richard Huntley	.50	.20
❑	172 Levon Kirkland	.30	.10
❑	173 Hines Ward	.75	.30
❑	174 Trent Green	.75	.30
❑	175 Marshall Faulk	1.00	.40
❑	176 Az-Zahir Hakim	.30	.10
❑	177 Amp Lee	.30	.10
❑	178 Robert Holcombe	.30	.10
❑	179 Isaac Bruce	.75	.30
❑	180 Kevin Carter	.30	.10
❑	181 Jim Harbaugh	.50	.20
❑	182 Junior Seau	.75	.30
❑	183 Natrone Means	.50	.20
❑	184 Ryan Leaf	.75	.30
❑	185 Charlie Jones	.30	.10
❑	186 Rodney Harrison	.30	.10
❑	187 Mikhael Ricks	.30	.10
❑	188 Steve Young	1.00	.40
❑	189 Terrell Owens	.75	.30
❑	190 Jerry Rice	1.50	.60
❑	191 J.J. Stokes	.50	.20
❑	192 Irv Smith	.30	.10
❑	193 Bryant Young	.30	.10
❑	194 Garrison Hearst	.50	.20
❑	195 Jon Kitna	.75	.30
❑	196 Ahman Green	.75	.30
❑	197 Joey Galloway	.50	.20
❑	198 Ricky Watters	.50	.20
❑	199 Chad Brown	.30	.10
❑	200 Shawn Springs	.30	.10
❑	201 Mike Pritchard	.30	.10
❑	202 Trent Dilfer	.50	.20
❑	203 Reidel Anthony	.50	.20
❑	204 Bert Emanuel	.50	.20
❑	205 Warrick Dunn	.75	.30
❑	206 Jacquez Green	.30	.10
❑	207 Hardy Nickerson	.30	.10
❑	208 Mike Alstott	.75	.30
❑	209 Eddie George	.75	.30
❑	210 Steve McNair	.75	.30
❑	211 Kevin Dyson	.50	.20
❑	212 Frank Wycheck	.30	.10
❑	213 Jackie Harris	.30	.10
❑	214 Blaine Bishop	.30	.10
❑	215 Yancey Thigpen	.30	.10
❑	216 Brad Johnson	.75	.30
❑	217 Rodney Peete	.30	.10
❑	218 Michael Westbrook	.50	.20
❑	219 Skip Hicks	.30	.10
❑	220 Brian Mitchell	.30	.10
❑	221 Dan Wilkinson	.30	.10
❑	222 Dana Stubblefield	.30	.10
❑	223 Kordell Stewart CL	.50	.20
❑	224 Fred Taylor CL	.75	.30
❑	225 Warrick Dunn CL	.50	.20
❑	226 Champ Bailey RC	3.00	1.25
❑	227 Chris McAlister RC	1.50	.60
❑	228 Jevon Kearse RC	4.00	1.50
❑	229 Ebenezer Ekuban RC	1.50	.60
❑	230 Chris Claiborne RC	1.00	.40
❑	231 Andy Katzenmoyer RC	1.50	.60
❑	232 Tim Couch RC	2.00	.75
❑	233 Daunte Culpepper RC	10.00	4.00
❑	234 Akili Smith RC	1.50	.60
❑	235 Donovan McNabb RC	12.00	5.00
❑	236 Sean Bennett RC	1.00	.40
❑	237 Brock Huard RC	2.00	.75
❑	238 Cade McNown RC	1.50	.60
❑	239 Shaun King RC	1.50	.60
❑	240 Joe Germaine RC	1.50	.60
❑	241 Ricky Williams RC	5.00	2.00
❑	242 Edgerrin James RC	10.00	4.00
❑	243 Sedrick Irvin RC	1.00	.40
❑	244 Kevin Faulk RC	2.00	.75
❑	245 Rob Konrad RC	2.00	.75
❑	246 James Johnson RC	1.50	.60
❑	247 Amos Zereoue RC	2.00	.75
❑	248 Torry Holt RC	6.00	2.50
❑	249 D'Wayne Bates RC	1.50	.60
❑	250 David Boston RC	2.00	.75
❑	251 Dameane Douglas RC	2.00	.75
❑	252 Troy Edwards RC	1.50	.60
❑	253 Kevin Johnson RC	2.00	.75
❑	254 Peerless Price RC	2.00	.75
❑	255 Antoine Winfield RC	1.50	.60
❑	256 Mike Cloud RC	1.50	.60
❑	257 Joe Montgomery RC	1.50	.60
❑	258 Jermaine Fazande RC	1.50	.60
❑	259 Scott Covington RC	2.00	.75
❑	260 Aaron Brooks RC	5.00	2.00
❑	261 Patrick Kerney RC	2.00	.75
❑	262 Cecil Collins RC	1.00	.40
❑	263 Chris Greisen RC	1.50	.60
❑	264 Craig Yeast RC	1.50	.60
❑	265 Karsten Bailey RC	1.50	.60
❑	266 Reginald Kelly RC	1.00	.40
❑	267 Al Wilson RC	1.50	.60
❑	268 Jeff Paulk RC	1.00	.40
❑	269 Jim Kleinsasser RC	2.00	.75
❑	270 Darrin Chiaverini RC	1.50	.60

2000 Upper Deck

	Card	High	Low
❑	COMPLETE SET (1-270)	120.00	60.00
❑	COMP.SET w/o SPs (222)	30.00	12.50
❑	1 Jake Plummer	.50	.20
❑	2 Michael Pittman	.30	.10
❑	3 Rob Moore	.50	.20
❑	4 David Boston	.75	.30
❑	5 Frank Sanders	.50	.20
❑	6 Aeneas Williams	.30	.10
❑	7 Kwamie Lassiter	.30	.10
❑	8 Rob Fredrickson	.30	.10
❑	9 Tim Dwight	.75	.30
❑	10 Chris Chandler	.50	.20
❑	11 Jamal Anderson	.75	.30
❑	12 Shawn Jefferson	.30	.10
❑	13 Ken Oxendine	.30	.10
❑	14 Terance Mathis	.50	.20
❑	15 Bob Christian	.30	.10
❑	16 Qadry Ismail	.50	.20
❑	17 Jermaine Lewis	.50	.20
❑	18 Rod Woodson	.50	.20
❑	19 Michael McCrary	.30	.10
❑	20 Tony Banks	.50	.20
❑	21 Peter Boulware	.30	.10
❑	22 Shannon Sharpe	.50	.20
❑	23 Peerless Price	.50	.20
❑	24 Rob Johnson	.50	.20
❑	25 Eric Moulds	.75	.30
❑	26 Doug Flutie	.75	.30
❑	27 Jay Riemersma	.30	.10
❑	28 Antowain Smith	.50	.20
❑	29 Jonathan Linton	.30	.10
❑	30 Muhsin Muhammad	.50	.20
❑	31 Patrick Jeffers	.75	.30
❑	32 Steve Beuerlein	.50	.20
❑	33 Natrone Means	.30	.10
❑	34 Tim Biakabutuka	.50	.20
❑	35 Michael Bates	.30	.10
❑	36 Chuck Smith	.30	.10
❑	37 Wesley Walls	.30	.10
❑	38 Cade McNown	.30	.10
❑	39 Curtis Enis	.30	.10
❑	40 Marcus Robinson	.75	.30
❑	41 Eddie Kennison	.50	.20
❑	42 Bobby Engram	.50	.20
❑	43 Glyn Milburn	.30	.10
❑	44 Marty Booker	.50	.20
❑	45 Akili Smith	.30	.10
❑	46 Corey Dillon	.75	.30
❑	47 Darnay Scott	.50	.20
❑	48 Tremain Mack	.30	.10
❑	49 Dámon Griffin	.30	.10
❑	50 Takeo Spikes	.30	.10
❑	51 Tony McGee	.30	.10
❑	52 Tim Couch	.50	.20
❑	53 Kevin Johnson	.75	.30
❑	54 Darrin Chiaverini	.30	.10
❑	55 Jamir Miller	.30	.10
❑	56 Errict Rhett	.50	.20
❑	57 Terry Kirby	.30	.10
❑	58 Marc Edwards	.30	.10
❑	59 Troy Aikman	1.50	.60
❑	60 Emmitt Smith	1.50	.60
❑	61 Rocket Ismail	.50	.20
❑	62 Jason Tucker	.30	.10
❑	63 Dexter Coakley	.30	.10
❑	64 Joey Galloway	.50	.20
❑	65 Wane McGarity	.30	.10
❑	66 Terrell Davis	.75	.30
❑	67 Olandis Gary	.75	.30
❑	68 Brian Griese	.75	.30
❑	69 Gus Frerotte	.30	.10
❑	70 Byron Chamberlain	.30	.10
❑	71 Ed McCaffrey	.75	.30
❑	72 Rod Smith	.50	.20
❑	73 Al Wilson	.30	.10
❑	74 Charlie Batch	.75	.30
❑	75 Germane Crowell	.30	.10
❑	76 Sedrick Irvin	.30	.10
❑	77 Johnnie Morton	.50	.20
❑	78 Robert Porcher	.30	.10
❑	79 Herman Moore	.50	.20
❑	80 James Stewart	.50	.20
❑	81 Brett Favre	2.50	1.00
❑	82 Antonio Freeman	.75	.30
❑	83 Bill Schroeder	.50	.20
❑	84 Dorsey Levens	.50	.20
❑	85 Corey Bradford	.50	.20
❑	86 De'Mond Parker	.30	.10
❑	87 Vonnie Holliday	.30	.10
❑	88 Peyton Manning	2.00	.75
❑	89 Edgerrin James	1.25	.50
❑	90 Marvin Harrison	.75	.30
❑	91 Ken Dilger	.30	.10
❑	92 Terrence Wilkins	.30	.10
❑	93 Marcus Pollard	.30	.10
❑	94 Fred Lane	.30	.10
❑	95 Mark Brunell	.75	.30
❑	96 Fred Taylor	.75	.30
❑	97 Jimmy Smith	.50	.20
❑	98 Keenan McCardell	.50	.20
❑	99 Carnell Lake	.30	.10
❑	100 Tavian Banks	.30	.10

❑ 101 Kyle Brady	.30	.10
❑ 102 Hardy Nickerson	.30	.10
❑ 103 Elvis Grbac	.50	.20
❑ 104 Tony Gonzalez	.50	.20
❑ 105 Derrick Alexander WR	.50	.20
❑ 106 Donnell Bennett	.30	.10
❑ 107 Mike Cloud	.30	.10
❑ 108 Donnie Edwards	.30	.10
❑ 109 Jay Fiedler	.75	.30
❑ 110 James Johnson	.30	.10
❑ 111 Tony Martin	.50	.20
❑ 112 Damon Huard	.75	.30
❑ 113 O.J. McDuffie	.50	.20
❑ 114 Thurman Thomas	.50	.20
❑ 115 Zach Thomas	.75	.30
❑ 116 Oronde Gadsden	.50	.20
❑ 117 Randy Moss	1.50	.60
❑ 118 Robert Smith	.75	.30
❑ 119 Cris Carter	.75	.30
❑ 120 Matthew Hatchette	.30	.10
❑ 121 Daunte Culpepper	1.00	.40
❑ 122 Leroy Hoard	.30	.10
❑ 123 Drew Bledsoe	1.00	.40
❑ 124 Terry Glenn	.50	.20
❑ 125 Troy Brown	.50	.20
❑ 126 Kevin Faulk	.30	.10
❑ 127 Lawyer Milloy	.50	.20
❑ 128 Ricky Williams	.75	.30
❑ 129 Keith Poole	.30	.10
❑ 130 Jake Reed	.50	.20
❑ 131 Cam Cleeland	.30	.10
❑ 132 Jeff Blake	.50	.20
❑ 133 Andrew Glover	.30	.10
❑ 134 Kerry Collins	.50	.20
❑ 135 Amani Toomer	.50	.20
❑ 136 Joe Montgomery	.30	.10
❑ 137 Ike Hilliard	.50	.20
❑ 138 Tiki Barber	.75	.30
❑ 139 Pete Mitchell	.30	.10
❑ 140 Ray Lucas	.50	.20
❑ 141 Mo Lewis	.30	.10
❑ 142 Curtis Martin	.75	.30
❑ 143 Vinny Testaverde	.50	.20
❑ 144 Wayne Chrebet	.50	.20
❑ 145 Dedric Ward	.30	.10
❑ 146 Tim Brown	.75	.30
❑ 147 Rich Gannon	.75	.30
❑ 148 Tyrone Wheatley	.50	.20
❑ 149 Napoleon Kaufman	.50	.20
❑ 150 Charles Woodson	.50	.20
❑ 151 Darrell Russell	.30	.10
❑ 152 James Jett	.30	.10
❑ 153 Rickey Dudley	.30	.10
❑ 154 Jon Ritchie	.30	.10
❑ 155 Duce Staley	.75	.30
❑ 156 Donovan McNabb	1.25	.50
❑ 157 Torrance Small	.30	.10
❑ 158 Allen Rossum	.30	.10
❑ 159 Mike Mamula	.30	.10
❑ 160 Na Brown	.30	.10
❑ 161 Charles Johnson	.50	.20
❑ 162 Kent Graham	.30	.10
❑ 163 Troy Edwards	.30	.10
❑ 164 Jerome Bettis	.75	.30
❑ 165 Hines Ward	.75	.30
❑ 166 Kordell Stewart	.50	.20
❑ 167 Levon Kirkland	.30	.10
❑ 168 Richard Huntley	.30	.10
❑ 169 Marshall Faulk	1.00	.40
❑ 170 Kurt Warner	1.50	.60
❑ 171 Torry Holt	.75	.30
❑ 172 Isaac Bruce	.75	.30
❑ 173 Kevin Carter	.30	.10
❑ 174 Az-Zahir Hakim	.50	.20
❑ 175 Ricky Proehl	.30	.10
❑ 176 Jermaine Fazande	.30	.10
❑ 177 Curtis Conway	.50	.20
❑ 178 Freddie Jones	.30	.10
❑ 179 Junior Seau	.75	.30
❑ 180 Jeff Graham	.30	.10
❑ 181 Jim Harbaugh	.50	.20
❑ 182 Rodney Harrison	.30	.10
❑ 183 Steve Young	1.00	.40
❑ 184 Jerry Rice	1.50	.60
❑ 185 Charlie Garner	.50	.20
❑ 186 Terrell Owens	.75	.30
❑ 187 Jeff Garcia	.75	.30
❑ 188 Fred Beasley	.30	.10
❑ 189 J.J. Stokes	.50	.20
❑ 190 Ricky Watters	.50	.20
❑ 191 Jon Kitna	.75	.30
❑ 192 Derrick Mayes	.50	.20
❑ 193 Sean Dawkins	.30	.10
❑ 194 Charlie Rogers	.30	.10
❑ 195 Mike Pritchard	.30	.10
❑ 196 Cortez Kennedy	.30	.10
❑ 197 Christian Fauria	.30	.10
❑ 198 Warrick Dunn	.75	.30
❑ 199 Shaun King	.30	.10
❑ 200 Mike Alstott	.75	.30
❑ 201 Warren Sapp	.50	.20
❑ 202 Jacquez Green	.30	.10
❑ 203 Reidel Anthony	.30	.10
❑ 204 Dave Moore	.30	.10
❑ 205 Keyshawn Johnson	.75	.30
❑ 206 Eddie George	.75	.30
❑ 207 Steve McNair	.75	.30
❑ 208 Kevin Dyson	.50	.20
❑ 209 Jevon Kearse	.75	.30
❑ 210 Yancey Thigpen	.30	.10
❑ 211 Frank Wycheck	.30	.10
❑ 212 Isaac Byrd	.30	.10
❑ 213 Neil O'Donnell	.30	.10
❑ 214 Brad Johnson	.75	.30
❑ 215 Stephen Davis	.75	.30
❑ 216 Michael Westbrook	.50	.20
❑ 217 Albert Connell	.30	.10
❑ 218 Brian Mitchell	.30	.10
❑ 219 Bruce Smith	.50	.20
❑ 220 Stephen Alexander	.30	.10
❑ 221 Jeff George	.50	.20
❑ 222 Adrian Murrell	.30	.10
❑ 223 Courtney Brown RC	4.00	1.50
❑ 224 John Engelberger RC	2.50	1.00
❑ 225 Deltha O'Neal RC	4.00	1.50
❑ 226 Corey Simon RC	4.00	1.50
❑ 227 R.Jay Soward RC	2.50	1.00
❑ 228 Marc Bulger RC	8.00	3.00
❑ 229 Raynoch Thompson RC	2.50	1.00
❑ 230 Deon Grant RC	2.50	1.00
❑ 231 Darrell Jackson RC	8.00	3.00
❑ 232 Chris Cole RC	2.50	1.00
❑ 233 Trevor Gaylor RC	2.50	1.00
❑ 234 John Abraham RC	4.00	1.50
❑ 235 Chris Redman RC	2.50	1.00
❑ 236 Joe Hamilton RC	2.50	1.00
❑ 237 Chad Pennington RC	10.00	4.00
❑ 238 Tee Martin RC	4.00	1.50
❑ 239 Giovanni Carmazzi RC	2.00	.75
❑ 240 Tim Rattay RC	4.00	1.50
❑ 241 Ron Dayne RC	4.00	1.50
❑ 242 Shaun Alexander RC	20.00	7.50
❑ 243 Thomas Jones RC	6.00	2.50
❑ 244 Reuben Droughns RC	4.00	1.50
❑ 245 Jamal Lewis RC	10.00	4.00
❑ 246 Michael Wiley RC	2.50	1.00
❑ 247 J.R. Redmond RC	2.50	1.00
❑ 248 Travis Prentice RC	2.50	1.00
❑ 249 Todd Husak RC	4.00	1.50
❑ 250 Trung Canidate RC	2.50	1.00
❑ 251 Brian Urlacher RC	15.00	6.00
❑ 252 Anthony Becht RC	4.00	1.50
❑ 253 Bubba Franks RC	4.00	1.50
❑ 254 Tom Brady RC	60.00	35.00
❑ 255 Peter Warrick RC	4.00	1.50
❑ 256 Plaxico Burress RC	8.00	3.00
❑ 257 Sylvester Morris RC	2.50	1.00
❑ 258 Dez White RC	4.00	1.50
❑ 259 Travis Taylor RC	4.00	1.50
❑ 260 Todd Pinkston RC	4.00	1.50
❑ 261 Dennis Northcutt RC	4.00	1.50
❑ 262 Jerry Porter RC	5.00	2.00
❑ 263 Laveranues Coles RC	5.00	2.00
❑ 264 Danny Farmer RC	2.50	1.00
❑ 265 Curtis Keaton RC	2.50	1.00
❑ 266 Sherrod Gideon RC	2.00	.75
❑ 267 Ron Dugans RC	2.00	.75
❑ 268 Steve McNair CL	.50	.20
❑ 269 Jake Plummer CL	.50	.20
❑ 270 Antonio Freeman CL	.50	.20

2001 Upper Deck

❑ COMPLETE SET (280)	300.00	150.00
❑ COMP.SET w/o SP's (180)	25.00	10.00
❑ 1 Jake Plummer	.50	.20
❑ 2 David Boston	.75	.30
❑ 3 Thomas Jones	.50	.20
❑ 4 Frank Sanders	.30	.10
❑ 5 Eric Zeier	.30	.10
❑ 6 Jamal Anderson	.75	.30
❑ 7 Chris Chandler	.50	.20
❑ 8 Shawn Jefferson	.30	.10
❑ 9 Darrick Vaughn	.30	.10
❑ 10 Terance Mathis	.50	.20
❑ 11 Jamal Lewis	1.25	.50
❑ 12 Shannon Sharpe	.50	.20
❑ 13 Elvis Grbac	.50	.20
❑ 14 Ray Lewis	.75	.30
❑ 15 Qadry Ismail	.50	.20
❑ 16 Chris Redman	.30	.10
❑ 17 Rob Johnson	.75	.30
❑ 18 Eric Moulds	.50	.20
❑ 19 Sammy Morris	.30	.10
❑ 20 Shawn Bryson	.30	.10
❑ 21 Jeremy McDaniel	.30	.10
❑ 22 Muhsin Muhammad	.50	.20
❑ 23 Brad Hoover	.30	.10
❑ 24 Tim Biakabutuka	.50	.20
❑ 25 Steve Beuerlein	.30	.10
❑ 26 Jeff Lewis	.30	.10
❑ 27 Wesley Walls	.30	.10
❑ 28 Cade McNown	.30	.10
❑ 29 James Allen	.50	.20
❑ 30 Marcus Robinson	.75	.30
❑ 31 Brian Urlacher	1.25	.50
❑ 32 Bobby Engram	.30	.10
❑ 33 Peter Warrick	.75	.30
❑ 34 Corey Dillon	.75	.30
❑ 35 Akili Smith	.30	.10
❑ 36 Danny Farmer	.30	.10
❑ 37 Ron Dugans	.30	.10
❑ 38 Jon Kitna	.75	.30
❑ 39 Tim Couch	.50	.20
❑ 40 Kevin Johnson	.50	.20
❑ 41 Travis Prentice	.30	.10
❑ 42 Spergon Wynn	.30	.10
❑ 43 Errict Rhett	.30	.10
❑ 44 Dennis Northcutt	.50	.20
❑ 45 Courtney Brown	.50	.20
❑ 46 Tony Banks	.30	.10
❑ 47 Emmitt Smith	1.50	.60
❑ 48 Joey Galloway	.50	.20
❑ 49 Rocket Ismail	.50	.20
❑ 50 Randall Cunningham	.75	.30
❑ 51 James McKnight	.50	.20
❑ 52 Terrell Davis	.75	.30
❑ 53 Mike Anderson	.75	.30
❑ 54 Brian Griese	.75	.30
❑ 55 Rod Smith	.50	.20
❑ 56 Ed McCaffrey	.75	.30
❑ 57 Eddie Kennison	.50	.20
❑ 58 Olandis Gary	.50	.20
❑ 59 Charlie Batch	.75	.30
❑ 60 Germane Crowell	.30	.10
❑ 61 James O. Stewart	.50	.20

Card	Low	High
❑ 62 Johnnie Morton	.50	.20
❑ 63 Brett Favre	2.50	1.00
❑ 64 Antonio Freeman	.75	.30
❑ 65 Dorsey Levens	.50	.20
❑ 66 Ahman Green	.75	.30
❑ 67 Bill Schroeder	.50	.20
❑ 68 Peyton Manning	2.00	.75
❑ 69 Edgerrin James	1.00	.40
❑ 70 Marvin Harrison	.75	.30
❑ 71 Jerome Pathon	.50	.20
❑ 72 Ken Dilger	.30	.10
❑ 73 Mark Brunell	.75	.30
❑ 74 Fred Taylor	.75	.30
❑ 75 Jimmy Smith	.50	.20
❑ 76 Keenan McCardell	.30	.10
❑ 77 R.Jay Soward	.30	.10
❑ 78 Todd Collins	.30	.10
❑ 79 Tony Gonzalez	.50	.20
❑ 80 Derrick Alexander	.50	.20
❑ 81 Tony Richardson	.30	.10
❑ 82 Sylvester Morris	.30	.10
❑ 83 Oronde Gadsden	.50	.20
❑ 84 Lamar Smith	.50	.20
❑ 85 Jay Fiedler	.75	.30
❑ 86 Jason Taylor	.30	.10
❑ 87 Ray Lucas	.30	.10
❑ 88 O.J. McDuffie	.30	.10
❑ 89 Randy Moss	1.50	.60
❑ 90 Cris Carter	.75	.30
❑ 91 Daunte Culpepper	.75	.30
❑ 92 Moe Williams	.50	.20
❑ 93 Troy Walters	.30	.10
❑ 94 Drew Bledsoe	1.00	.40
❑ 95 Terry Glenn	.50	.20
❑ 96 Kevin Faulk	.50	.20
❑ 97 J.R. Redmond	.30	.10
❑ 98 Troy Brown	.50	.20
❑ 99 Ricky Williams	.75	.30
❑ 100 Jeff Blake	.50	.20
❑ 101 Joe Horn	.50	.20
❑ 102 Albert Connell	.30	.10
❑ 103 Aaron Brooks	.75	.30
❑ 104 Chad Morton	.30	.10
❑ 105 Kerry Collins	.50	.20
❑ 106 Amani Toomer	.50	.20
❑ 107 Ron Dayne	.75	.30
❑ 108 Tiki Barber	.75	.30
❑ 109 Ike Hilliard	.50	.20
❑ 110 Ron Dixon	.30	.10
❑ 111 Jason Sehorn	.30	.10
❑ 112 Vinny Testaverde	.50	.20
❑ 113 Wayne Chrebet	.50	.20
❑ 114 Curtis Martin	.75	.30
❑ 115 Dedric Ward	.30	.10
❑ 116 Laveranues Coles	.75	.30
❑ 117 Windrell Hayes	.30	.10
❑ 118 Tim Brown	.75	.30
❑ 119 Rich Gannon	.75	.30
❑ 120 Tyrone Wheatley	.50	.20
❑ 121 Charlie Garner	.50	.20
❑ 122 Andre Rison	.50	.20
❑ 123 Charles Woodson	.50	.20
❑ 124 Trace Armstrong	.30	.10
❑ 125 Duce Staley	.75	.30
❑ 126 Donovan McNabb	1.00	.40
❑ 127 Darnell Autry	.30	.10
❑ 128 Charles Johnson	.30	.10
❑ 129 Torrance Small	.30	.10
❑ 130 Kordell Stewart	.50	.20
❑ 131 Jerome Bettis	.75	.30
❑ 132 Plaxico Burress	.75	.30
❑ 133 Bobby Shaw	.30	.10
❑ 134 Troy Edwards	.30	.10
❑ 135 Marshall Faulk	1.00	.40
❑ 136 Kurt Warner	1.50	.60
❑ 137 Isaac Bruce	.75	.30
❑ 138 Torry Holt	.75	.30
❑ 139 Trent Green	.75	.30
❑ 140 Az-Zahir Hakim	.30	.10
❑ 141 Junior Seau	.75	.30
❑ 142 Curtis Conway	.50	.20
❑ 143 Doug Flutie	.75	.30
❑ 144 Jeff Graham	.30	.10
❑ 145 Freddie Jones	.30	.10
❑ 146 Marcellus Wiley	.30	.10
❑ 147 Jeff Garcia	.75	.30
❑ 148 Jerry Rice	1.50	.60
❑ 149 Fred Beasley	.30	.10
❑ 150 Terrell Owens	.75	.30
❑ 151 J.J. Stokes	.50	.20
❑ 152 Garrison Hearst	.50	.20
❑ 153 Ricky Watters	.30	.10
❑ 154 Shaun Alexander	1.00	.40
❑ 155 Matt Hasselbeck	.50	.20
❑ 156 Brock Huard	.30	.10
❑ 157 Darrell Jackson	.75	.30
❑ 158 John Randle	.30	.10
❑ 159 Warrick Dunn	.75	.30
❑ 160 Shaun King	.30	.10
❑ 161 Ryan Leaf	.50	.20
❑ 162 Mike Alstott	.75	.30
❑ 163 Jacquez Green	.30	.10
❑ 164 Brad Johnson	.75	.30
❑ 165 Keyshawn Johnson	.75	.30
❑ 166 Eddie George	.75	.30
❑ 167 Steve McNair	.75	.30
❑ 168 Neil O'Donnell	.30	.10
❑ 169 Derrick Mason	.50	.20
❑ 170 Frank Wycheck	.30	.10
❑ 171 Kevin Dyson	.50	.20
❑ 172 Jevon Kearse	.50	.20
❑ 173 Jeff George	.50	.20
❑ 174 Stephen Davis	.75	.30
❑ 175 Larry Centers	.30	.10
❑ 176 Michael Westbrook	.50	.20
❑ 177 Stephen Alexander	.50	.20
❑ 178 Ron Dayne	.75	.30
❑ 179 Donovan McNabb	1.00	.40
❑ 180 Jimmy Smith	.50	.20
❑ 181 Adam Archuleta RC	5.00	2.00
❑ 182 A.J. Feeley RC	5.00	2.00
❑ 183 Alex Bannister RC	3.00	1.25
❑ 184 Alge Crumpler RC	6.00	2.50
❑ 185 Andre Carter RC	5.00	2.00
❑ 186 Andre Dyson RC	2.00	.75
❑ 187 Anthony Thomas RC	5.00	2.00
❑ 188 Arther Love RC	2.00	.75
❑ 189 Bobby Newcombe RC	3.00	1.25
❑ 190 Brandon Spoon RC	5.00	2.00
❑ 191 Carlos Polk RC	2.00	.75
❑ 192 Casey Hampton RC	5.00	2.00
❑ 193 Cedrick Wilson RC	5.00	2.00
❑ 194 Chad Johnson RC	12.00	5.00
❑ 195 Chris Chambers RC	8.00	3.00
❑ 196 Chris Taylor RC	3.00	1.25
❑ 197 Chris Weinke RC	5.00	2.00
❑ 198 Correll Buckhalter RC	6.00	2.50
❑ 199 Damione Lewis RC	3.00	1.25
❑ 200 Dan Alexander RC	5.00	2.00
❑ 201 Dan Morgan RC	5.00	2.00
❑ 202 Willie Middlebrooks RC	3.00	1.25
❑ 203 David Terrell RC	5.00	2.00
❑ 204 Derrick Gibson RC	3.00	1.25
❑ 205 Deuce McAllister RC	10.00	4.00
❑ 206 Drew Brees RC	20.00	10.00
❑ 207 Edgerton Hartwell RC	2.00	.75
❑ 208 Fred Smoot RC	5.00	2.00
❑ 209 Freddie Mitchell RC	5.00	2.00
❑ 210 Gary Baxter RC	3.00	1.25
❑ 211 Gerard Warren RC	5.00	2.00
❑ 212 Hakim Akbar RC	2.00	.75
❑ 213 Heath Evans RC	3.00	1.25
❑ 214 Jabari Holloway RC	3.00	1.25
❑ 215 Jamal Reynolds RC	5.00	2.00
❑ 216 Jamar Fletcher RC	3.00	1.25
❑ 217 James Jackson RC	5.00	2.00
❑ 218 Jamie Winborn RC	3.00	1.25
❑ 219 Jesse Palmer RC	5.00	2.00
❑ 220 Josh Booty RC	5.00	2.00
❑ 221 Josh Heupel RC	5.00	2.00
❑ 222 Justin Smith RC	5.00	2.00
❑ 223 Karon Riley RC	2.00	.75
❑ 224 Ken Lucas RC	3.00	1.25
❑ 225 Kenyatta Walker RC	2.00	.75
❑ 226 Ken-Yon Rambo RC	3.00	1.25
❑ 227 Kevan Barlow RC	5.00	2.00
❑ 228 Kevin Kasper RC	5.00	2.00
❑ 229 Koren Robinson RC	5.00	2.00
❑ 230 LaDainian Tomlinson RC	60.00	30.00
❑ 231 LaMont Jordan RC	10.00	4.00
❑ 232 Leonard Davis RC	3.00	1.25
❑ 233 Marcus Stroud RC	5.00	2.00
❑ 234 Marques Tuiasosopo RC	5.00	2.00
❑ 235 Snoop Minnis RC	3.00	1.25
❑ 236 Michael Bennett RC	5.00	2.00
❑ 237 Michael Stone RC	2.00	.75
❑ 238 Mike McMahon RC	5.00	2.00
❑ 239 Michael Vick RC	20.00	8.00
❑ 240 Moran Norris RC	2.00	.75
❑ 241 Morlon Greenwood RC	3.00	1.25
❑ 242 Nate Clements RC	5.00	2.00
❑ 243 Orlando Huff RC	2.00	.75
❑ 244 Quincy Morgan RC	5.00	2.00
❑ 245 Reggie Wayne RC	10.00	4.00
❑ 246 Richard Seymour RC	5.00	2.00
❑ 247 Robert Ferguson RC	5.00	2.00
❑ 248 Rod Gardner RC	5.00	2.00
❑ 249 Rudi Johnson RC	10.00	4.00
❑ 250 Sage Rosenfels RC	5.00	2.00
❑ 251 Santana Moss RC	8.00	3.00
❑ 252 Scotty Anderson RC	3.00	1.25
❑ 253 Sedrick Hodge RC	2.00	.75
❑ 254 Shaun Rogers RC	5.00	2.00
❑ 255 Steve Hutchinson RC	3.00	1.25
❑ 256 T.J. Houshmandzadeh RC	6.00	2.50
❑ 257 Tay Cody RC	2.00	.75
❑ 258 George Layne RC	3.00	1.25
❑ 259 Todd Heap RC	5.00	2.00
❑ 260 Tommy Polley RC	5.00	2.00
❑ 261 Tony Dixon RC	3.00	1.25
❑ 262 Brian Allen RC	2.00	.75
❑ 263 Torrance Marshall RC	5.00	2.00
❑ 264 Travis Henry RC	10.00	4.00
❑ 265 Travis Minor RC	3.00	1.25
❑ 266 Vinny Sutherland RC	3.00	1.25
❑ 267 Will Allen RC	3.00	1.25
❑ 268 Derrick Blaylock RC	5.00	2.00
❑ 269 Zeke Moreno RC	5.00	2.00
❑ 270 Chris Barnes RC	3.00	1.25
❑ 271 Dee Brown RC	5.00	2.00
❑ 272 Reggie White RC	3.00	1.25
❑ 273 Derek Combs RC	3.00	1.25
❑ 274 Steve Smith RC	12.00	6.00
❑ 275 John Capel RC	3.00	1.25
❑ 276 Justin McCareins RC	5.00	2.00
❑ 277 Darnerien McCants RC	3.00	1.25
❑ 278 Eddie Berlin RC	3.00	1.25
❑ 279 Francis St. Paul RC	3.00	1.25
❑ 280 Quincy Carter RC	5.00	2.00

2002 Upper Deck

Card	Low	High
❑ COMP.SET w/o SP's (180)	25.00	10.00
❑ 1 Jake Plummer	.50	.20
❑ 2 Marcel Shipp	.75	.30
❑ 3 David Boston	.75	.30
❑ 4 Arnold Jackson	.30	.10
❑ 5 Frank Sanders	.30	.10
❑ 6 Freddie Jones	.30	.10
❑ 7 Michael Vick	1.50	.60
❑ 8 Jamal Anderson	.50	.20
❑ 9 Warrick Dunn	.75	.30
❑ 10 Maurice Smith	.30	.10
❑ 11 Shawn Jefferson	.30	.10
❑ 12 Chris Redman	.30	.10
❑ 13 Jeff Blake	.30	.10

❑ 14 Jamal Lewis .75 .30
❑ 15 Travis Taylor .50 .20
❑ 16 Ray Lewis .75 .30
❑ 17 Chris McAlister .30 .10
❑ 18 Drew Bledsoe 1.00 .40
❑ 19 Travis Henry .75 .30
❑ 20 Larry Centers .30 .10
❑ 21 Eric Moulds .50 .20
❑ 22 Reggie Germany .30 .10
❑ 23 Peerless Price .50 .20
❑ 24 Chris Weinke .50 .20
❑ 25 Lamar Smith .50 .20
❑ 26 Nick Goings .30 .10
❑ 27 Muhsin Muhammad .50 .20
❑ 28 Isaac Byrd [illegible] .10
❑ 29 Wesley Walls .30 .10
❑ 30 Jim Miller .30 .10
❑ 31 Anthony Thomas .50 .20
❑ 32 Dez White .30 .10
❑ 33 David Terrell .75 .30
❑ 34 Marty Booker .50 .20
❑ 35 Brian Urlacher 1.25 .50
❑ 36 Jon Kitna .50 .20
❑ 37 Corey Dillon .50 .20
❑ 38 Peter Warrick .50 .20
❑ 39 Darnay Scott .30 .10
❑ 40 Chad Johnson .75 .30
❑ 41 Tim Couch .50 .20
❑ 42 James Jackson .30 .10
❑ 43 JaJuan Dawson .30 .10
❑ 44 Kevin Johnson .50 .20
❑ 45 Quincy Morgan .30 .10
❑ 46 Courtney Brown .50 .20
❑ 47 Quincy Carter .50 .20
❑ 48 Emmitt Smith 2.00 .75
❑ 49 Joey Galloway .50 .20
❑ 50 Rocket Ismail .50 .20
❑ 51 Ken-Yon Rambo .30 .10
❑ 52 Brian Griese .75 .30
❑ 53 Terrell Davis .75 .30
❑ 54 Mike Anderson .75 .30
❑ 55 Shannon Sharpe .50 .20
❑ 56 Ed McCaffrey .75 .30
❑ 57 Rod Smith .50 .20
❑ 58 Mike McMahon .75 .30
❑ 59 James Stewart .50 .20
❑ 60 Az-Zahir Hakim .30 .10
❑ 61 Desmond Howard .30 .10
❑ 62 Germane Crowell .30 .10
❑ 63 Brett Favre 2.00 .75
❑ 64 Ahman Green .75 .30
❑ 65 Antonio Freeman .75 .30
❑ 66 Terry Glenn .50 .20
❑ 67 Kabeer Gbaja-Biamila .50 .20
❑ 68 Kent Graham .30 .10
❑ 69 James Allen .50 .20
❑ 70 Corey Bradford .30 .10
❑ 71 Jermaine Lewis .30 .10
❑ 72 Jamie Sharper .30 .10
❑ 73 Peyton Manning 1.50 .60
❑ 74 Edgerrin James 1.00 .40
❑ 75 Dominic Rhodes .50 .20
❑ 76 Marvin Harrison .75 .30
❑ 77 Qadry Ismail .50 .20
❑ 78 Mark Brunell .75 .30
❑ 79 Fred Taylor .75 .30
❑ 80 Stacey Mack .30 .10
❑ 81 Jimmy Smith .50 .20
❑ 82 Keenan McCardell .30 .10
❑ 83 Trent Green .50 .20
❑ 84 Priest Holmes 1.00 .40
❑ 85 Derrick Alexander .50 .20
❑ 86 Johnnie Morton .50 .20
❑ 87 Snoop Minnis .30 .10
❑ 88 Tony Gonzalez .50 .20
❑ 89 Jay Fiedler .50 .20
❑ 90 Ricky Williams 2.50 1.00
❑ 91 Chris Chambers .75 .30
❑ 92 Oronde Gadsden .30 .10
❑ 93 Zach Thomas .75 .30
❑ 94 Daunte Culpepper .75 .30
❑ 95 Michael Bennett .50 .20
❑ 96 Randy Moss 1.50 .60
❑ 97 Sean Dawkins .30 .10
❑ 98 Tom Brady 2.00 .75
❑ 99 Antowain Smith .50 .20
❑ 100 David Patten .30 .10
❑ 101 Troy Brown .50 .20
❑ 102 Adam Vinatieri .75 .30
❑ 103 Aaron Brooks .75 .30
❑ 104 Deuce McAllister 1.00 .40
❑ 105 Jake Reed .50 .20
❑ 106 Jerome Pathon .50 .20
❑ 107 Joe Horn .50 .20
❑ 108 Kyle Turley .30 .10
❑ 109 Kerry Collins .50 .20
❑ 110 Ron Dayne .50 .20
❑ 111 Tiki Barber .75 .30
❑ 112 [illegible] [illegible] [illegible]
❑ 113 Ike Hilliard .50 .20
❑ 114 Michael Strahan .50 .20
❑ 115 Vinny Testaverde .50 .20
❑ 116 Chad Pennington 1.00 .40
❑ 117 Curtis Martin .75 .30
❑ 118 Santana Moss .75 .30
❑ 119 Laveranues Coles .50 .20
❑ 120 Wayne Chrebet .50 .20
❑ 121 Rich Gannon .75 .30
❑ 122 Charlie Garner .50 .20
❑ 123 Jerry Rice 1.50 .60
❑ 124 Tim Brown .75 .30
❑ 125 Charles Woodson .50 .20
❑ 126 Donovan McNabb 1.00 .40
❑ 127 Duce Staley .75 .30
❑ 128 Correll Buckhalter .50 .20
❑ 129 Freddie Mitchell .50 .20
❑ 130 James Thrash .50 .20
❑ 131 Todd Pinkston .50 .20
❑ 132 Kordell Stewart .50 .20
❑ 133 Jerome Bettis .75 .30
❑ 134 Chris Fuamatu-Ma'afala .30 .10
❑ 135 Hines Ward .75 .30
❑ 136 Plaxico Burress .50 .20
❑ 137 Kendrell Bell .75 .30
❑ 138 Doug Flutie .75 .30
❑ 139 Drew Brees .75 .30
❑ 140 LaDainian Tomlinson 1.25 .50
❑ 141 Curtis Conway .30 .10
❑ 142 Tim Dwight .50 .20
❑ 143 Junior Seau .75 .30
❑ 144 Jeff Garcia .75 .30
❑ 145 Garrison Hearst .50 .20
❑ 146 Kevan Barlow .50 .20
❑ 147 Terrell Owens .75 .30
❑ 148 J.J. Stokes .50 .20
❑ 149 Trent Dilfer .50 .20
❑ 150 Shaun Alexander 1.00 .40
❑ 151 Ricky Watters .50 .20
❑ 152 Bobby Engram .30 .10
❑ 153 Koren Robinson .50 .20
❑ 154 Kurt Warner .75 .30
❑ 155 Marshall Faulk .75 .30
❑ 156 Isaac Bruce .75 .30
❑ 157 Ricky Proehl .30 .10
❑ 158 Terrence Wilkins .30 .10
❑ 159 Torry Holt .75 .30
❑ 160 Brad Johnson .50 .20
❑ 161 Shaun King .30 .10
❑ 162 Rob Johnson .50 .20
❑ 163 Mike Alstott .75 .30
❑ 164 Michael Pittman .30 .10
❑ 165 Keyshawn Johnson .75 .30
❑ 166 Steve McNair .75 .30
❑ 167 Eddie George .75 .30
❑ 168 Derrick Mason .50 .20
❑ 169 Kevin Dyson .50 .20
❑ 170 Frank Wycheck .30 .10
❑ 171 Jevon Kearse .50 .20
❑ 172 Danny Wuerffel .50 .20
❑ 173 Stephen Davis .50 .20
❑ 174 Michael Westbrook .30 .10
❑ 175 Rod Gardner .50 .20
❑ 176 Champ Bailey .50 .20
❑ 177 Darrell Green .30 .10
❑ 178 Kurt Warner CL .50 .20
❑ 179 Brett Favre CL 1.00 .40
❑ 180 Randy Moss CL .75 .30
❑ 181 David Boston SS 4.00 1.50
❑ 182 Jake Plummer SS 2.50 1.00
❑ 183 Michael Vick SS 8.00 3.00
❑ 184 Drew Bledsoe SS 5.00 2.00
❑ 185 Anthony Thomas SS 2.50 1.00
❑ 186 Tim Couch SS 2.50 1.00
❑ 187 Emmitt Smith SS 10.00 4.00
❑ 188 Ahman Green SS 4.00 1.50
❑ 189 Brett Favre SS 10.00 4.00
❑ 190 Edgerrin James SS 5.00 2.00
❑ 191 Peyton Manning SS 8.00 3.00
❑ 192 Mark Brunell SS 4.00 1.50
❑ 193 Daunte Culpepper SS 4.00 1.50
❑ 194 Randy Moss SS 8.00 3.00
❑ 195 Tom Brady SS 10.00 4.00
❑ 196 [illegible] SS 4.00 1.50
❑ 197 Ricky Williams SS 4.00 1.50
❑ 198 Curtis Martin SS 4.00 1.50
❑ 199 Jerry Rice SS 8.00 3.00
❑ 200 Donovan McNabb SS 5.00 2.00
❑ 201 Jerome Bettis SS 4.00 1.50
❑ 202 Kordell Stewart SS 2.50 1.00
❑ 203 LaDainian Tomlinson SS 6.00 2.50
❑ 204 Jeff Garcia SS 4.00 1.50
❑ 205 Terrell Owens SS 4.00 1.50
❑ 206 Shaun Alexander SS 5.00 2.00
❑ 207 Kurt Warner SS 4.00 1.50
❑ 208 Marshall Faulk SS 4.00 1.50
❑ 209 Keyshawn Johnson SS 4.00 1.50
❑ 210 Steve McNair SS 4.00 1.50
❑ 211 Damien Anderson RC 5.00 2.00
❑ 212 Jason McAddley RC 5.00 2.00
❑ 213 Josh McCown RC 8.00 3.00
❑ 214 Josh Scobey RC 4.00 1.50
❑ 215 Preston Parsons RC 3.00 1.25
❑ 216 Dusty Bonner RC 3.00 1.25
❑ 217 Kahlil Hill RC 5.00 2.00
❑ 218 Kurt Kittner RC 5.00 2.00
❑ 219 T.J. Duckett RC 6.00 2.50
❑ 220 Chester Taylor RC 6.00 2.50
❑ 221 Kalimba Edwards RC 6.00 2.50
❑ 223 Ron Johnson RC 5.00 2.00
❑ 224 Tellis Redmon RC 5.00 2.00
❑ 225 Wes Pate RC 3.00 1.25
❑ 226 David Priestley RC 5.00 2.00
❑ 227 Josh Reed RC 6.00 2.50
❑ 228 Mike Williams RC 5.00 2.00
❑ 229 Ryan Denney RC 5.00 2.00
❑ 230 DeShaun Foster RC 6.00 2.50
❑ 231 Julius Peppers RC 12.00 5.00
❑ 232 Randy Fasani RC 5.00 2.00
❑ 233 Adrian Peterson RC 8.00 3.00
❑ 234 Alex Brown RC 6.00 2.50
❑ 235 Gavin Hoffman RC 3.00 1.25
❑ 236 Levi Jones RC 5.00 2.00
❑ 237 Andra Davis RC 5.00 2.00
❑ 238 Andre Davis RC 5.00 2.00
❑ 239 William Green RC 6.00 2.50
❑ 240 Antonio Bryant RC 6.00 2.50
❑ 241 Chad Hutchinson RC 5.00 2.00
❑ 242 Roy Williams RC 12.00 5.00
❑ 243 Woody Dantzler RC 5.00 2.00
❑ 244 Ashley Lelie RC 12.00 5.00
❑ 245 Clinton Portis RC 20.00 7.50
❑ 246 Lamont Thompson RC 5.00 2.00
❑ 247 James Mungro RC 6.00 2.50
❑ 248 Joey Harrington RC 8.00 3.00
❑ 249 Luke Staley RC 5.00 2.00
❑ 250 Craig Nall RC 6.00 2.50
❑ 251 Javon Walker RC 10.00 4.00
❑ 252 Najeh Davenport RC 6.00 2.50
❑ 253 David Carr RC 12.00 5.00
❑ 254 Saleem Rasheed RC 6.00 2.50
❑ 255 Mike Rumph RC 6.00 2.50
❑ 256 Jabar Gaffney RC 6.00 2.50
❑ 257 Jonathan Wells RC 6.00 2.50
❑ 258 Dwight Freeney RC 10.00 4.00
❑ 259 Larry Tripplett RC 3.00 1.25
❑ 260 David Garrard RC 12.00 5.00
❑ 261 John Henderson RC 6.00 2.50
❑ 262 Ryan Sims RC 6.00 2.50
❑ 263 Leonard Henry RC 5.00 2.00
❑ 264 Brian Allen RC 5.00 2.00
❑ 265 Atrews Bell RC 3.00 1.25
❑ 266 Bryant McKinnie RC 5.00 2.00

❑ 267 Kelly Campbell RC 5.00 2.00
❑ 268 Raonall Smith RC 5.00 2.00
❑ 269 Antwoine Womack RC 5.00 2.00
❑ 270 Daniel Graham RC 6.00 2.50
❑ 271 Deion Branch RC 10.00 4.00
❑ 272 Sam Simmons RC 3.00 1.25
❑ 273 Rohan Davey RC 6.00 2.50
❑ 274 Charles Grant RC 6.00 2.50
❑ 275 Derrick Lewis RC 3.00 1.25
❑ 276 Donte Stallworth RC 10.00 4.00
❑ 277 J.T. O'Sullivan RC 5.00 2.00
❑ 278 Keyuo Craver RC 5.00 2.00
❑ 279 Ricky Williams RC 5.00 2.00
❑ 280 Bryan Thomas RC 5.00 2.00
❑ 281 Jeremy Shockey RC 20.00 7.50
❑ 282 Tim Carter RC 5.00 2.00
❑ 283 Larry Ned RC 2.50 1.00
❑ 284 Napoleon Harris RC 4.00 1.50
❑ 285 Phillip Buchanon RC 6.00 2.50
❑ 286 Ronald Curry RC 6.00 2.50
❑ 287 Brian Westbrook RC 12.00 5.00
❑ 288 Freddie Milons RC 5.00 2.00
❑ 289 Lito Sheppard RC 6.00 2.50
❑ 290 Antwaan Randle El RC 8.00 3.00
❑ 291 Lee Mays RC 2.50 1.00
❑ 292 Daryl Jones RC 5.00 2.00
❑ 293 Justin Peelle RC 3.00 1.25
❑ 294 Quentin Jammer RC 4.00 1.50
❑ 295 Reche Caldwell RC 6.00 2.50
❑ 296 Seth Burford RC 5.00 2.00
❑ 297 Terry Charles RC 5.00 2.00
❑ 298 Brandon Doman RC 5.00 2.00
❑ 299 Maurice Morris RC 6.00 2.50
❑ 300 Eric Crouch RC 6.00 2.50
❑ 301 Lamar Gordon RC 6.00 2.50
❑ 302 Marquise Walker RC 5.00 2.00
❑ 303 Tracey Wistrom RC 5.00 2.00
❑ 304 Travis Stephens RC 5.00 2.00
❑ 305 Herb Haygood RC 3.00 1.25
❑ 306 Albert Haynesworth RC 5.00 2.00
❑ 307 Rocky Calmus RC 6.00 2.50
❑ 308 Cliff Russell RC 5.00 2.00
❑ 309 Ladell Betts RC 6.00 2.50
❑ 310A Patrick Ramsey RC 6.00 2.50
❑ 310B Ed Reed RC 10.00 4.00

2003 Upper Deck

❑ COMP.SET w/o SP's (180) 25.00 10.00
❑ 1 Brad Johnson .50 .20
❑ 2 Derrick Brooks .50 .20
❑ 3 Simeon Rice .50 .20
❑ 4 Warren Sapp .50 .20
❑ 5 Thomas Jones .50 .20
❑ 6 Mike Alstott .75 .30
❑ 7 Michael Pittman .30 .10
❑ 8 Tim Brown .75 .30
❑ 9 Rich Gannon .50 .20
❑ 10 Charlie Garner .50 .20
❑ 11 Jerry Porter .50 .20
❑ 12 Phillip Buchanon .30 .10
❑ 13 Charles Woodson .50 .20
❑ 14 James Thrash .30 .10
❑ 15 Duce Staley .50 .20
❑ 16 Brian Westbrook .50 .20
❑ 17 Correll Buckhalter .50 .20
❑ 18 Koy Detmer .30 .10
❑ 19 Brian Dawkins .50 .20
❑ 20 Jon Ritchie .30 .10
❑ 21 Ahman Green .75 .30
❑ 22 Donald Driver .50 .20
❑ 23 Bubba Franks .50 .20
❑ 24 Javon Walker .50 .20
❑ 25 Kabeer Gbaja-Biamila .50 .20
❑ 26 Robert Ferguson .30 .10
❑ 27 Eddie George .50 .20
❑ 28 Jevon Kearse .50 .20
❑ 29 Billy Volek .75 .30
❑ 30 Frank Wycheck .30 .10
❑ 31 Derrick Mason .50 .20
❑ 32 Tommy Maddox .75 .30
❑ 33 Jerome Bettis .75 .30
❑ 34 Antwaan Randle El .75 .30
❑ 35 Amos Zereoue .50 .20
❑ 36 Hines Ward .75 .30
❑ 37 Jeff Garcia .75 .30
❑ 38 Terrell Owens .75 .30
❑ 39 Tim Rattay .50 .20
❑ 40 Brandon Doman .30 .10
❑ 41 Tai Streets .30 .10
❑ 42 Garrison Hearst .50 .20
❑ 43 Kerry Collins .50 .20
❑ 44 Tiki Barber .75 .30
❑ 45 Amani Toomer .50 .20
❑ 46 Jesse Palmer .30 .10
❑ 47 Tim Carter .30 .10
❑ 48 Michael Strahan .50 .20
❑ 49 Ike Hilliard .30 .10
❑ 50 Marvin Harrison .75 .30
❑ 51 Peyton Manning 1.25 .50
❑ 52 Marcus Pollard .30 .10
❑ 53 James Mungro .30 .10
❑ 54 Reggie Wayne .50 .20
❑ 55 Peerless Price .50 .20
❑ 56 Warrick Dunn .50 .20
❑ 57 T.J. Duckett .50 .20
❑ 58 Keith Brooking .30 .10
❑ 59 Doug Johnson .30 .10
❑ 60 Brian Finneran .30 .10
❑ 61 Chad Pennington 1.00 .40
❑ 62 Curtis Martin .75 .30
❑ 63 Marvin Jones .30 .10
❑ 64 Wayne Chrebet .50 .20
❑ 65 LaMont Jordan .75 .30
❑ 66 Curtis Conway .30 .10
❑ 67 Vinny Testaverde .50 .20
❑ 68 Tim Couch .30 .10
❑ 69 William Green .50 .20
❑ 70 Andre Davis .30 .10
❑ 71 Quincy Morgan .50 .20
❑ 72 Dennis Northcutt .50 .20
❑ 73 Kelly Holcomb .50 .20
❑ 74 Jake Plummer .50 .20
❑ 75 Mike Anderson .75 .30
❑ 76 Ashley Lelie .75 .30
❑ 77 Ed McCaffrey .75 .30
❑ 78 Shannon Sharpe .30 .10
❑ 79 Rod Smith .50 .20
❑ 80 Terrell Davis .75 .30
❑ 81 Antowain Smith .50 .20
❑ 82 Kevin Faulk .30 .10
❑ 83 David Patten .30 .10
❑ 84 Deion Branch .75 .30
❑ 85 Troy Brown .50 .20
❑ 86 Rohan Davey .50 .20
❑ 87 Jay Fiedler .50 .20
❑ 88 Randy McMichael .50 .20
❑ 89 Derrius Thompson .30 .10
❑ 90 Jason Taylor .30 .10
❑ 91 Zach Thomas .75 .30
❑ 92 Ricky Williams .75 .30
❑ 93 Deuce McAllister .75 .30
❑ 94 Donte Stallworth .75 .30
❑ 95 Jerome Pathon .30 .10
❑ 96 Michael Lewis .30 .10
❑ 97 Joe Horn .50 .20
❑ 98 Priest Holmes 1.00 .40
❑ 99 Johnnie Morton .50 .20
❑ 100 Eddie Kennison .30 .10
❑ 101 Dante Hall .75 .30
❑ 102 Tony Gonzalez .50 .20
❑ 103 Marc Boerigter .50 .20
❑ 104 Drew Brees .75 .30
❑ 105 David Boston .50 .20
❑ 106 Reche Caldwell .30 .10
❑ 107 Tim Dwight .50 .20
❑ 108 Doug Flutie .75 .30
❑ 109 Drew Bledsoe .75 .30
❑ 110 Eric Moulds .50 .20
❑ 111 Alex Van Pelt .30 .10
❑ 112 Charles Johnson .30 .10
❑ 113 Takeo Spikes .30 .10
❑ 114 Josh Reed .50 .20
❑ 115 Ladell Betts .50 .20
❑ 116 Laveranues Coles .50 .20
❑ 117 Champ Bailey .50 .20
❑ 118 Trung Canidate .50 .20
❑ 119 Kenny Watson .30 .10
❑ 120 Rod Gardner .50 .20
❑ 121 Kurt Warner .75 .30
❑ 122 Lamar Gordon .30 .10
❑ 123 Shaun McDonald RC .75 .30
❑ 124 Marc Bulger .75 .30
❑ 125 Isaac Bruce .75 .30
❑ 126 Torry Holt .75 .30
❑ 127 Matt Hasselbeck .50 .20
❑ 128 Maurice Morris .30 .10
❑ 129 Bobby Engram .30 .10
❑ 130 Darrell Jackson .50 .20
❑ 131 Koren Robinson .50 .20
❑ 132 Chris Redman .30 .10
❑ 133 Todd Heap .50 .20
❑ 134 Travis Taylor .50 .20
❑ 135 Ron Johnson .30 .10
❑ 136 Ray Lewis .75 .30
❑ 137 Jake Delhomme .75 .30
❑ 138 Muhsin Muhammad .50 .20
❑ 139 Stephen Davis .50 .20
❑ 140 Julius Peppers .75 .30
❑ 141 Rodney Peete .30 .10
❑ 142 Mark Brunell .50 .20
❑ 143 Jimmy Smith .50 .20
❑ 144 Kyle Brady .30 .10
❑ 145 Kevin Lockett .30 .10
❑ 146 David Garrard .30 .10
❑ 147 Fred Taylor .75 .30
❑ 148 Michael Bennett .50 .20
❑ 149 Ronald Bellamy RC 1.00 .40
❑ 150 Randy Moss 1.25 .50
❑ 151 D'Wayne Bates .30 .10
❑ 152 Josh McCown .50 .20
❑ 153 Marquise Walker .30 .10
❑ 154 Jeff Blake .30 .10
❑ 155 Freddie Jones .30 .10
❑ 156 Marcel Shipp .50 .20
❑ 157 Troy Hambrick .30 .10
❑ 158 Joey Galloway .50 .20
❑ 159 Terry Glenn .30 .10
❑ 160 Roy Williams .75 .30
❑ 161 Antonio Bryant .50 .20
❑ 162 Quincy Carter .50 .20
❑ 163 Anthony Thomas .50 .20
❑ 164 Marty Booker .50 .20
❑ 165 Dez White .30 .10
❑ 166 Adrian Peterson .30 .10
❑ 167 Kordell Stewart .50 .20
❑ 168 David Terrell .50 .20
❑ 169 Jabar Gaffney .50 .20
❑ 170 Bennie Joppru RC 1.00 .40
❑ 171 Corey Bradford .30 .10
❑ 172 David Carr 1.25 .50
❑ 173 James Stewart .50 .20
❑ 174 Ty Detmer .30 .10
❑ 175 Az-Zahir Hakim .30 .10
❑ 176 Bill Schroeder .50 .20
❑ 177 Jon Kitna .50 .20
❑ 178 Chad Johnson .75 .30
❑ 179 Ron Dugans .30 .10
❑ 180 Peter Warrick .50 .20
❑ 181 Brett Favre SS 10.00 4.00
❑ 182 Emmitt Smith SS 12.00 5.00
❑ 183 LaDainian Tomlinson SS 5.00 2.00
❑ 184 Joey Harrington SS 8.00 3.00
❑ 185 Brian Urlacher SS 8.00 3.00
❑ 186 Daunte Culpepper SS 5.00 2.00
❑ 187 Jamal Lewis SS 5.00 2.00

❑ 188 Shaun Alexander SS 5.00 2.00
❑ 189 Marshall Faulk SS 5.00 2.00
❑ 190 Travis Henry SS 4.00 1.50
❑ 191 Trent Green SS 4.00 1.50
❑ 192 Aaron Brooks SS 5.00 2.00
❑ 193 Chris Chambers SS 5.00 2.00
❑ 194 Tom Brady SS 10.00 4.00
❑ 195 Clinton Portis SS 8.00 3.00
❑ 196 Kevin Johnson SS 4.00 1.50
❑ 197 Santana Moss SS 4.00 1.50
❑ 198 Michael Vick SS 12.00 5.00
❑ 199 Edgerrin James SS .75 .30
❑ 200 Jeremy Shockey SS 8.00 3.00
❑ 201 Kevan Barlow SS 4.00 1.50
❑ 202 Plaxico Burress SS 4.00 1.50
❑ 203 Steve McNair SS 5.00 2.00
❑ 204 Donovan McNabb SS 6.00 2.50
❑ 205 Jerry Rice SS 10.00 4.00
❑ 206 Keyshawn Johnson SS 5.00 2.00
❑ 207 Patrick Ramsey SS 5.00 2.00
❑ 208 Stephen Davis SS 4.00 1.50
❑ 209 Corey Dillon SS 4.00 1.50
❑ 210 Chad Hutchinson SS 4.00 1.50
❑ 211 Brad Banks RC 4.00 1.50
❑ 212 Kliff Kingsbury RC 4.00 1.50
❑ 213 Jason Gesser RC 5.00 2.00
❑ 214 Jason Johnson RC 3.00 1.25
❑ 215 Brian St.Pierre RC 5.00 2.00
❑ 216 Ken Dorsey RC 5.00 2.00
❑ 217 Seneca Wallace RC 5.00 2.00
❑ 218 Brooks Bollinger RC 5.00 2.00
❑ 219 Chris Brown RC 6.00 2.00
❑ 220 B.J Askew RC 5.00 2.00
❑ 221 Earnest Graham RC 5.00 2.00
❑ 222 Quentin Griffin RC 5.00 2.00
❑ 223 Musa Smith RC 5.00 2.00
❑ 224 Artose Pinner RC 5.00 2.00
❑ 225 Domanick Davis RC 5.00 2.00
❑ 226 Anquan Boldin RC 12.00 5.00
❑ 227 Talman Gardner RC 5.00 2.00
❑ 228 Brandon Lloyd RC 6.00 2.00
❑ 229 Bryant Johnson RC 5.00 2.00
❑ 230 Kareem Kelly RC 4.00 1.50
❑ 231 Arnaz Battle RC 5.00 2.00
❑ 232 Keenan Howry RC 5.00 2.00
❑ 233 Justin Gage RC 5.00 2.00
❑ 234 Tyrone Calico RC 5.00 2.00
❑ 235 Teyo Johnson RC 5.00 2.00
❑ 236 Malaefou MacKenzie RC 3.00 1.25
❑ 237 Terence Newman RC 10.00 5.00
❑ 238 Marcus Trufant RC 5.00 2.00
❑ 239 Mike Doss RC 5.00 2.00
❑ 240 Terrell Suggs RC 8.00 3.00
❑ 241 Carson Palmer RC 30.00 15.00
❑ 242 Byron Leftwich RC 25.00 10.00
❑ 243 Rex Grossman RC 25.00 10.00
❑ 244 Kyle Boller RC 8.00 3.00
❑ 245 Dave Ragone RC 8.00 3.00
❑ 246 Chris Simms RC 12.00 5.00
❑ 247 Larry Johnson RC 30.00 15.00
❑ 248 Lee Suggs RC 6.00 2.00
❑ 249 Justin Fargas RC 8.00 3.00
❑ 250 Onterrio Smith RC 8.00 3.00
❑ 251 Willis McGahee RC 20.00 7.50
❑ 252 Charles Rogers RC 5.00 2.00
❑ 253 Andre Johnson RC 15.00 6.00
❑ 254 Taylor Jacobs RC 8.00 3.00
❑ 255 Kelley Washington RC 8.00 3.00
❑ 256 Tony Romo RC 40.00 20.00
❑ 257 Jerel Myers RC 4.00 1.50
❑ 258 Kirk Farmer RC 4.00 1.50
❑ 259 Kevin Walter RC 5.00 2.00
❑ 260 Gibran Hamdan RC 4.00 1.50
❑ 261 Juston Wood RC 4.00 1.50
❑ 262 Travis Anglin RC 4.00 1.50
❑ 263 Marquel Blackwell RC 4.00 1.50
❑ 264 Jason Thomas RC 5.00 2.00
❑ 265 Carl Ford RC 4.00 1.50
❑ 266 Walter Young RC 4.00 1.50
❑ 267 Sultan McCullough RC 5.00 2.00
❑ 268 Dahrran Diedrick RC 6.00 2.50
❑ 269 Cecil Sapp RC 5.00 2.00
❑ 270 Doug Gabriel RC 6.00 2.50
❑ 271 LaBrandon Toefield RC 6.00 2.50
❑ 272 Adrian Madise RC 5.00 2.00
❑ 273 J.R. Tolver RC 5.00 2.00
❑ 274 Kevin Curtis RC 8.00 3.00
❑ 275 Bobby Wade RC 6.00 2.50
❑ 276 Sam Aiken RC 5.00 2.00
❑ 277 Mike Bush RC 4.00 1.50
❑ 278 Billy McMullen RC 5.00 2.00
❑ 279 Bethel Johnson RC 5.00 2.00
❑ 280 David Kircus RC 5.00 2.00
❑ 281 Zuriel Smith RC 4.00 1.50
❑ 282 LaTarence Dunbar RC 5.00 2.00
❑ 283 Nate Burleson RC 6.00 2.00
❑ 284 Antwone Savage RC 4.00 1.50
❑ 285 Terrence Edwards RC 5.00 2.00

2004 Upper Deck

❑ COMPLETE SET (275) 135.00 75.00
❑ COMP.SET w/o SP's (250) 60.00 30.00
❑ COMP.SET w/o RC's (200) 25.00 10.00
❑ 201-225 ROOKIE STATED ODDS 1:8
❑ 226-275 ROOKIE STATED ODDS 1:1
❑ UNPRICED PRINT PLATE PRINT RUN 1 SET
❑ 1 Anquan Boldin .75 .30
❑ 2 Josh McCown .50 .20
❑ 3 Emmitt Smith 1.50 .60
❑ 4 Freddie Jones .30 .10
❑ 5 Marcel Shipp .50 .20
❑ 6 Shaun King .30 .10
❑ 7 Michael Vick 1.50 .60
❑ 8 T.J. Duckett .50 .20
❑ 9 Peerless Price .50 .20
❑ 10 Warrick Dunn .50 .20
❑ 11 Keith Brooking .30 .10
❑ 12 Brian Finneran .30 .10
❑ 13 Anthony Wright .30 .10
❑ 14 Kyle Boller .75 .30
❑ 15 Jamal Lewis .75 .30
❑ 16 Todd Heap .50 .20
❑ 17 Ray Lewis .75 .30
❑ 18 Terrell Suggs .50 .20
❑ 19 Travis Taylor .30 .10
❑ 20 Drew Bledsoe .75 .30
❑ 21 Willis McGahee .75 .30
❑ 22 Eric Moulds .50 .20
❑ 23 Travis Henry .50 .20
❑ 24 Takeo Spikes .30 .10
❑ 25 Josh Reed .30 .10
❑ 26 Lawyer Milloy .50 .20
❑ 27 Stephen Davis .50 .20
❑ 28 Jake Delhomme .75 .30
❑ 29 Steve Smith .75 .30
❑ 30 DeShaun Foster .50 .20
❑ 31 Dan Morgan .30 .10
❑ 32 Julius Peppers .75 .30
❑ 33 Rod Smart .30 .10
❑ 34 Rex Grossman .75 .30
❑ 35 Thomas Jones .50 .20
❑ 36 Marty Booker .50 .20
❑ 37 Anthony Thomas .50 .20
❑ 38 Brian Urlacher 1.00 .40
❑ 39 Justin Gage .50 .20
❑ 40 Chad Johnson .75 .30
❑ 41 Carson Palmer 1.00 .40
❑ 42 Peter Warrick .50 .20
❑ 43 Jon Kitna .50 .20
❑ 44 Kelley Washington .30 .10
❑ 45 Rudi Johnson .50 .20
❑ 46 Jeff Garcia .75 .30
❑ 47 Dennis Northcutt .30 .10
❑ 48 Lee Suggs .75 .30
❑ 49 Andre Davis .30 .10
❑ 50 Quincy Morgan .50 .20
❑ 51 Kelly Holcomb .50 .20
❑ 52 Keyshawn Johnson .50 .20
❑ 53 Quincy Carter .50 .20
❑ 54 Antonio Bryant .50 .20
❑ 55 Terry Glenn .30 .10
❑ 56 Terence Newman .50 .20
❑ 57 Roy Williams S .50 .20
❑ 58 Champ Bailey .50 .20
❑ 59 Jake Plummer .50 .20
❑ 60 Quentin Griffin .75 .30
❑ 61 John Lynch .50 .20
❑ 62 Rod Smith .50 .20
❑ 63 Ashley Lelie .50 .20
❑ 64 Joey Harrington .75 .30
❑ 65 Az-Zahir Hakim .30 .10
❑ 66 Charles Rogers .50 .20
❑ 67 Tai Streets .30 .10
❑ 68 Shawn Bryson .30 .10
❑ 69 Artose Pinner .30 .10
❑ 70 Brett Favre 2.00 .75
❑ 71 Nick Barnett .50 .20
❑ 72 Ahman Green .75 .30
❑ 73 Kabeer Gbaja-Biamila .50 .20
❑ 74 Javon Walker .50 .20
❑ 75 Donald Driver .50 .20
❑ 76 Tim Couch .30 .10
❑ 77 David Carr .75 .30
❑ 78 Corey Bradford .30 .10
❑ 79 J.J. Moses .30 .10
❑ 80 Domanick Davis .75 .30
❑ 81 Jabar Gaffney .50 .20
❑ 82 Andre Johnson .75 .30
❑ 83 Marvin Harrison .75 .30
❑ 84 Peyton Manning 1.25 .50
❑ 85 Dallas Clark .50 .20
❑ 86 Edgerrin James .75 .30
❑ 87 Reggie Wayne .50 .20
❑ 88 Dwight Freeney .50 .20
❑ 89 Byron Leftwich 1.00 .40
❑ 90 LaBrandon Toefield .30 .10
❑ 91 Fred Taylor .50 .20
❑ 92 Troy Edwards .30 .10
❑ 93 Jimmy Smith .50 .20
❑ 94 Kyle Brady .30 .10
❑ 95 Trent Green .50 .20
❑ 96 Tony Gonzalez .50 .20
❑ 97 Dante Hall .75 .30
❑ 98 Priest Holmes 1.00 .40
❑ 99 Eddie Kennison .30 .10
❑ 100 Johnnie Morton .50 .20
❑ 101 Jay Fiedler .30 .10
❑ 102 Junior Seau .75 .30
❑ 103 Ricky Williams .75 .30
❑ 104 Chris Chambers .50 .20
❑ 105 Zach Thomas .75 .30
❑ 106 David Boston .50 .20
❑ 107 A.J. Feeley .75 .30
❑ 108 Daunte Culpepper .75 .30
❑ 109 Onterrio Smith .50 .20
❑ 110 Randy Moss 1.00 .40
❑ 111 Moe Williams .30 .10
❑ 112 Michael Bennett .50 .20
❑ 113 Jim Kleinsasser .30 .10
❑ 114 Tom Brady 2.00 .75
❑ 115 Kevin Faulk .30 .10
❑ 116 Deion Branch .75 .30
❑ 117 Corey Dillon .50 .20
❑ 118 Troy Brown .50 .20
❑ 119 Adam Vinatieri .75 .30
❑ 120 Tedy Bruschi .50 .20
❑ 121 Aaron Brooks .50 .20
❑ 122 Deuce McAllister .75 .30
❑ 123 Donte' Stallworth .50 .20
❑ 124 Joe Horn .50 .20
❑ 125 Jerome Pathon .30 .10
❑ 126 Boo Williams .30 .10
❑ 127 Jeremy Shockey .75 .30
❑ 128 Kurt Warner .75 .30
❑ 129 Amani Toomer .50 .20

❑ 130 Tiki Barber .75 .30
❑ 131 Ike Hilliard .30 .10
❑ 132 Michael Strahan .50 .20
❑ 133 Chad Pennington .75 .30
❑ 134 Santana Moss .50 .20
❑ 135 Wayne Chrebet .50 .20
❑ 136 Curtis Martin .75 .30
❑ 137 LaMont Jordan .75 .30
❑ 138 Justin McCareins .30 .10
❑ 139 Jerry Rice 1.50 .60
❑ 140 Rich Gannon .50 .20
❑ 141 Tim Brown .75 .30
❑ 142 Jerry Porter .50 .20
❑ 143 Warren Sapp .50 .20
❑ 144 Charles Woodson .50 .20
❑ 145 Donovan McNabb 1.00 .40
❑ 146 Brian Westbrook .50 .20
❑ 147 Todd Pinkston .30 .10
❑ 148 Jevon Kearse .50 .20
❑ 149 Freddie Mitchell .50 .20
❑ 150 Correll Buckhalter .50 .20
❑ 151 Terrell Owens .75 .30
❑ 152 Tommy Maddox .50 .20
❑ 153 Duce Staley .50 .20
❑ 154 Plaxico Burress .50 .20
❑ 155 Hines Ward .75 .30
❑ 156 Antwaan Randle El .75 .30
❑ 157 Jerome Bettis .75 .30
❑ 158 Kendrell Bell .50 .20
❑ 159 LaDainian Tomlinson 1.00 .40
❑ 160 Doug Flutie .75 .30
❑ 161 Quentin Jammer .30 .10
❑ 162 Drew Brees .75 .30
❑ 163 Reche Caldwell .30 .10
❑ 164 Tim Dwight .50 .20
❑ 165 Tim Rattay .30 .10
❑ 166 Kevan Barlow .50 .20
❑ 167 Brandon Lloyd .50 .20
❑ 168 Cedrick Wilson .30 .10
❑ 169 Julian Peterson .30 .10
❑ 170 Ahmed Plummer .30 .10
❑ 171 Matt Hasselbeck .50 .20
❑ 172 Koren Robinson .50 .20
❑ 173 Shaun Alexander .75 .30
❑ 174 Darrell Jackson .50 .20
❑ 175 Marcus Trufant .30 .10
❑ 176 Bobby Engram .30 .10
❑ 177 Marc Bulger .75 .30
❑ 178 Torry Holt .75 .30
❑ 179 Marshall Faulk .75 .30
❑ 180 Orlando Pace .30 .10
❑ 181 Isaac Bruce .50 .20
❑ 182 Kyle Turley .30 .10
❑ 183 Brad Johnson .50 .20
❑ 184 Charlie Garner .50 .20
❑ 185 Keenan McCardell .30 .10
❑ 186 Mike Alstott .50 .20
❑ 187 Derrick Brooks .50 .20
❑ 188 Brian Griese .50 .20
❑ 189 Steve McNair .75 .30
❑ 190 Chris Brown .75 .30
❑ 191 Eddie George .50 .20
❑ 192 Tyrone Calico .50 .20
❑ 193 Derrick Mason .50 .20
❑ 194 Drew Bennett .50 .20
❑ 195 Mark Brunell .50 .20
❑ 196 LaVar Arrington 1.50 .60
❑ 197 Clinton Portis .75 .30
❑ 198 Laveranues Coles .50 .20
❑ 199 Patrick Ramsey .50 .20
❑ 200 Rod Gardner .50 .20
❑ 201 Eli Manning RC 30.00 15.00
❑ 202 Larry Fitzgerald RC 15.00 6.00
❑ 203 Michael Jenkins RC 5.00 2.00
❑ 204 Ben Roethlisberger RC 40.00 15.00
❑ 205 Philip Rivers RC 15.00 7.50
❑ 206 Kellen Winslow RC 10.00 4.00
❑ 207 Kevin Jones RC 12.00 5.00
❑ 208 Steven Jackson RC 15.00 6.00
❑ 209 Reggie Williams RC 6.00 2.50
❑ 210 Chris Perry RC 6.00 2.50
❑ 211 Roy Williams RC 12.00 5.00
❑ 212 Rashaun Woods RC 5.00 2.00
❑ 213 Chris Gamble RC 5.00 2.00
❑ 214 Sean Taylor RC 5.00 2.00
❑ 215 Robert Gallery RC 5.00 2.00
❑ 216 Ben Troupe RC 5.00 2.00
❑ 217 Lee Evans RC 6.00 2.50
❑ 218 Michael Clayton RC 10.00 4.00
❑ 219 J.P. Losman RC 10.00 4.00
❑ 220 Devery Henderson RC 5.00 2.00
❑ 221 Drew Henson RC 5.00 2.00
❑ 222 DeAngelo Hall RC 6.00 2.50
❑ 223 Julius Jones RC 15.00 6.00
❑ 224 Ben Watson RC 5.00 2.00
❑ 225 Greg Jones RC 5.00 2.00
❑ 226 D.J. Williams RC 1.50 .60
❑ 227 Tommie Harris RC 1.50 .60
❑ 228 Shawn Andrews RC 1.50 .60
❑ 229 Vince Wilfork RC 2.00 .75
❑ 230 Dunta Robinson RC 1.50 .60
❑ 231 Will Smith RC 1.50 .60
❑ 232 Jonathan Vilma RC 1.50 .60
❑ 233 Ricardo Colclough RC 1.50 .60
❑ 234 Ahmad Carroll RC 1.50 .60
❑ 235 Karlos Dansby RC 1.50 .60
❑ 236 Matt Ware RC 1.50 .60
❑ 237 Jim Sorgi RC 1.50 .60
❑ 238 Will Poole RC 1.50 .60
❑ 239 Derrick Strait RC 1.50 .60
❑ 240 Andy Hall RC 1.25 .50
❑ 241 Nathan Vasher RC 2.00 .75
❑ 242 D.J. Hackett RC 1.25 .50
❑ 243 Jason Babin RC 1.50 .60
❑ 244 Derrick Hamilton RC 1.25 .50
❑ 245 Michael Boulware RC 1.50 .60
❑ 246 Michael Turner RC 2.00 .75
❑ 247 Sean Jones RC 1.25 .50
❑ 248 Ernest Wilford RC 1.50 .60
❑ 249 Cedric Cobbs RC 1.50 .60
❑ 250 Tatum Bell RC 4.00 1.50
❑ 251 Bernard Berrian RC 2.00 .75
❑ 252 Vernon Carey RC 1.25 .50
❑ 253 Kenechi Udeze RC 1.50 .60
❑ 254 P.K. Sam RC 1.25 .50
❑ 255 Ben Hartsock RC 1.50 .60
❑ 256 Chris Cooley RC 1.50 .60
❑ 257 Josh Harris RC 1.50 .60
❑ 258 Cody Pickett RC 1.50 .60
❑ 259 Carlos Francis RC 1.25 .50
❑ 260 Devard Darling RC 1.50 .60
❑ 261 Johnnie Morant RC 1.50 .60
❑ 262 John Navarre RC 1.50 .60
❑ 263 Kris Wilson RC 1.50 .60
❑ 264 Jerricho Cotchery RC 1.50 .60
❑ 265 Darius Watts RC 1.50 .60
❑ 266 Quincy Wilson RC 1.25 .50
❑ 267 Maurice Mann RC 1.25 .50
❑ 268 Samie Parker RC 1.50 .60
❑ 269 B.J. Symons RC 1.50 .60
❑ 270 Matt Schaub RC 6.00 2.50
❑ 271 Jeff Smoker RC 1.50 .60
❑ 272 Craig Krenzel RC 1.50 .60
❑ 273 Luke McCown RC 1.50 .60
❑ 274 Mewelde Moore RC 1.50 .60
❑ 275 Keary Colbert RC 2.00 .75

2005 Upper Deck

❑ COMPLETE SET (275) 250.00 125.00
❑ COMP.SET w/o SP's (250) 60.00 30.00
❑ COMP.SET w/o RC's (200) 30.00 12.50
❑ 201-225 ROOKIE STATED ODDS 1:8
❑ 226-275 ROOKIE STATED ODDS 1:1
❑ 1 Larry Fitzgerald .75 .30
❑ 2 Anquan Boldin .50 .20
❑ 3 Kurt Warner .50 .20
❑ 4 Josh McCown .50 .20
❑ 5 Bryant Johnson .40 .15
❑ 6 Duane Starks .40 .15
❑ 7 Michael Vick 1.25 .50
❑ 8 Warrick Dunn .50 .20
❑ 9 T.J. Duckett .50 .20
❑ 10 Peerless Price .40 .15
❑ 11 Alge Crumpler .50 .20
❑ 12 Patrick Kerney .40 .15
❑ 13 Ed Reed .50 .20
❑ 14 Ray Lewis .75 .30
❑ 15 Kyle Boller .50 .20
❑ 16 Ma'Ake Kemoeatu RC .75 .30
❑ 17 Jamal Lewis .75 .30
❑ 18 Derrick Mason .50 .20
❑ 19 J.P. Losman .75 .30
❑ 20 Willis McGahee .75 .30
❑ 21 Lawyer Milloy .40 .15
❑ 22 Lee Evans .50 .20
❑ 23 Eric Moulds .50 .20
❑ 24 Takeo Spikes .40 .15
❑ 25 Jake Delhomme .75 .30
❑ 26 DeShaun Foster .50 .20
❑ 27 Keary Colbert .50 .20
❑ 28 Stephen Davis .50 .20
❑ 29 Nick Goings .40 .15
❑ 30 Julius Peppers .50 .20
❑ 31 Rex Grossman .50 .20
❑ 32 Brian Urlacher .75 .30
❑ 33 Thomas Jones .50 .20
❑ 34 Muhsin Muhammad .50 .20
❑ 35 Anthony Thomas .50 .20
❑ 36 Bernard Berrian .40 .15
❑ 37 Carson Palmer .75 .30
❑ 38 Chad Johnson .75 .30
❑ 39 Peter Warrick .40 .15
❑ 40 T.J. Houshmandzadeh .40 .15
❑ 41 Rudi Johnson .50 .20
❑ 42 Justin Smith .40 .15
❑ 43 Jeff Garcia .50 .20
❑ 44 Lee Suggs .50 .20
❑ 45 William Green .40 .15
❑ 46 Kellen Winslow .75 .30
❑ 47 Dennis Northcutt .40 .15
❑ 48 Antonio Bryant .40 .15
❑ 49 Julius Jones 1.00 .40
❑ 50 Drew Bledsoe .75 .30
❑ 51 Keyshawn Johnson .50 .20
❑ 52 Al Johnson .40 .15
❑ 53 Jason Witten .50 .20
❑ 54 Roy Williams S .50 .20
❑ 55 Jake Plummer .50 .20
❑ 56 Champ Bailey .50 .20
❑ 57 Tatum Bell .50 .20
❑ 58 Reuben Droughns .50 .20
❑ 59 Ashley Lelie .50 .20
❑ 60 Rod Smith .50 .20
❑ 61 Kevin Jones .75 .30
❑ 62 Roy Williams WR .75 .30
❑ 63 Charles Rogers .50 .20
❑ 64 Joey Harrington .75 .30
❑ 65 Az-Zahir Hakim .40 .15
❑ 66 Dre Bly .40 .15
❑ 67 Brett Favre 2.00 .75
❑ 68 Javon Walker .50 .20
❑ 69 Ahman Green .75 .30
❑ 70 Donald Driver .50 .20
❑ 71 Robert Ferguson .40 .15
❑ 72 Nick Barnett .40 .15
❑ 73 David Carr .75 .30
❑ 74 Domanick Davis .50 .20
❑ 75 Andre Johnson .50 .20
❑ 76 Jabar Gaffney .40 .15
❑ 77 Dunta Robinson .50 .20
❑ 78 Jamie Sharper .40 .15
❑ 79 Peyton Manning 1.25 .50
❑ 80 Edgerrin James .75 .30
❑ 81 Marvin Harrison .75 .30
❑ 82 Reggie Wayne .50 .20

❑ 83 Brandon Stokley	.50	.20
❑ 84 Dwight Freeney	.50	.20
❑ 85 Byron Leftwich	.75	.30
❑ 86 Fred Taylor	.50	.20
❑ 87 Jimmy Smith	.50	.20
❑ 88 Greg Jones	.40	.15
❑ 89 Donovin Darius	.40	.15
❑ 90 Reggie Williams	.50	.20
❑ 91 Priest Holmes	.75	.30
❑ 92 Larry Johnson	.75	.30
❑ 93 Tony Gonzalez	.50	.20
❑ 94 Trent Green	.50	.20
❑ 95 Eddie Kennison	.40	.15
❑ 96 Johnnie Morton	[illegible]	[illegible]
❑ 97 Jason Taylor	.40	.15
❑ 98 A.J. Feeley	.50	.20
❑ 99 Sammy Morris	.40	.15
❑ 100 Chris Chambers	.50	.20
❑ 101 Randy McMichael	.40	.15
❑ 102 Zach Thomas	.75	.30
❑ 103 Antoine Winfield	.40	.15
❑ 104 Daunte Culpepper	.75	.30
❑ 105 Michael Bennett	.50	.20
❑ 106 Nate Burleson	.50	.20
❑ 107 Onterrio Smith	.50	.20
❑ 108 Marcus Robinson	.50	.20
❑ 109 Tom Brady	2.00	.75
❑ 110 Corey Dillon	.50	.20
❑ 111 David Givens	.50	.20
❑ 112 David Patten	.40	.15
❑ 113 Adam Vinatieri	.75	.30
❑ 114 Troy Brown	.50	.20
❑ 115 Aaron Brooks	.50	.20
❑ 116 Deuce McAllister	.75	.30
❑ 117 Joe Horn	.50	.20
❑ 118 Donte Stallworth	.50	.20
❑ 119 Charles Grant	.40	.15
❑ 120 Jerome Pathon	.40	.15
❑ 121 Eli Manning	1.50	.60
❑ 122 Tiki Barber	.75	.30
❑ 123 Amani Toomer	.50	.20
❑ 124 Jeremy Shockey	.75	.30
❑ 125 Michael Strahan	.50	.20
❑ 126 Plaxico Burress	.50	.20
❑ 127 Chad Pennington	.75	.30
❑ 128 Curtis Martin	.75	.30
❑ 129 Laveranues Coles	.50	.20
❑ 130 Wayne Chrebet	.50	.20
❑ 131 Jonathan Vilma	.50	.20
❑ 132 Justin McCareins	.40	.15
❑ 133 Kerry Collins	.50	.20
❑ 134 Jerry Porter	.50	.20
❑ 135 LaMont Jordan	.75	.30
❑ 136 Randy Moss	.75	.30
❑ 137 Barry Sims	.40	.15
❑ 138 Warren Sapp	.50	.20
❑ 139 Donovan McNabb	1.00	.40
❑ 140 Brian Westbrook	.50	.20
❑ 141 Terrell Owens	.75	.30
❑ 142 Jevon Kearse	.50	.20
❑ 143 Brian Dawkins	.50	.20
❑ 144 Ben Roethlisberger	2.00	.75
❑ 145 Jerome Bettis	.75	.30
❑ 146 Duce Staley	.50	.20
❑ 147 Cedrick Wilson	.40	.15
❑ 148 Hines Ward	.75	.30
❑ 149 Antwaan Randle El	.50	.20
❑ 150 Troy Polamalu	1.25	.50
❑ 151 Philip Rivers	.75	.30
❑ 152 Drew Brees	.75	.30
❑ 153 LaDainian Tomlinson	1.00	.40
❑ 154 Antonio Gates	.75	.30
❑ 155 Reche Caldwell	.40	.15
❑ 156 Eric Parker	.40	.15
❑ 157 Kevan Barlow	.50	.20
❑ 158 Tim Rattay	.40	.15
❑ 159 Eric Johnson	.50	.20
❑ 160 Rashaun Woods	.50	.20
❑ 161 Brandon Lloyd	.40	.15
❑ 162 Julian Peterson	.40	.15
❑ 163 Matt Hasselbeck	.50	.20
❑ 164 Shaun Alexander	1.00	.40
❑ 165 Michael Boulware	.40	.15
❑ 166 Darrell Jackson	.50	.20

❑ 167 Koren Robinson	.50	.20
❑ 168 Marcus Trufant	.40	.15
❑ 169 Marc Bulger	.75	.30
❑ 170 Steven Jackson	1.00	.40
❑ 171 Marshall Faulk	.75	.30
❑ 172 Issac Bruce	.50	.20
❑ 173 Torry Holt	.75	.30
❑ 174 Michael Clayton	.75	.30
❑ 175 Michael Pittman	.40	.15
❑ 176 Brian Griese	.50	.20
❑ 177 Joey Galloway	.50	.20
❑ 178 Derrick Brooks	.50	.20
❑ 179 Josh Savage RC	.50	.20
❑ 180 [illegible]	[illegible]	[illegible]
❑ 181 Chris Brown	.50	.20
❑ 182 Billy Volek	.50	.20
❑ 183 Ben Troupe	.40	.15
❑ 184 Drew Bennett	.50	.20
❑ 185 Clinton Portis	.75	.30
❑ 186 Mark Brunell	.50	.20
❑ 187 Patrick Ramsey	.50	.20
❑ 188 Sean Taylor	.50	.20
❑ 189 LaVar Arrington	.75	.30
❑ 190 Santana Moss	.50	.20
❑ 191 David Terrell	.50	.20
❑ 192 Deion Branch	.50	.20
❑ 193 Chester Taylor	.50	.20
❑ 194 Derrick Blaylock	.40	.15
❑ 195 Shaun Ellis	.40	.15
❑ 196 Terrell Suggs	.50	.20
❑ 197 Charles Woodson	.50	.20
❑ 198 Jason Elam	.40	.15
❑ 199 Lawrence Tynes RC	.50	.20
❑ 200 David Akers	.40	.15
❑ 201 Alex Smith QB RC	25.00	10.00
❑ 202 Aaron Rodgers RC	20.00	7.50
❑ 203 Ronnie Brown RC	25.00	10.00
❑ 204 Cadillac Williams RC	25.00	10.00
❑ 205 Braylon Edwards RC	20.00	7.50
❑ 206 Antrel Rolle RC	6.00	2.50
❑ 207 Cedric Benson RC	15.00	6.00
❑ 208 Troy Williamson RC	6.00	2.50
❑ 209 Mark Clayton RC	6.00	2.50
❑ 210 Matt Jones RC	10.00	4.00
❑ 211 Reggie Brown RC	6.00	2.50
❑ 212 Charlie Frye RC	6.00	2.50
❑ 213 Heath Miller RC	12.00	5.00
❑ 214 Vincent Jackson RC	6.00	2.50
❑ 215 Andrew Walter RC	6.00	2.50
❑ 216 Roddy White RC	6.00	2.50
❑ 217 Adam Jones RC	6.00	2.50
❑ 218 J.J. Arrington RC	6.00	2.50
❑ 219 Eric Shelton RC	6.00	2.50
❑ 220 Terrence Murphy RC	6.00	2.50
❑ 221 Frank Gore RC	12.00	5.00
❑ 222 Roscoe Parrish RC	6.00	2.50
❑ 223 Jason Campbell RC	10.00	4.00
❑ 224 Carlos Rogers RC	8.00	3.00
❑ 225 Mike Williams	6.00	2.50
❑ 226 Erasmus James RC	6.00	2.50
❑ 227 Travis Johnson RC	1.50	.60
❑ 228 Dan Cody RC	2.00	.75
❑ 229 Thomas Davis RC	2.00	.75
❑ 230 David Pollack RC	2.00	.75
❑ 231 David Greene RC	2.00	.75
❑ 232 Alex Smith TE RC	2.00	.75
❑ 233 Ryan Moats RC	2.00	.75
❑ 234 Ciatrick Fason RC	2.00	.75
❑ 235 Vernand Morency RC	2.00	.75
❑ 236 Fred Gibson RC	6.00	2.50
❑ 237 Craphonso Thorpe RC	1.50	.60
❑ 238 Kevin Everett RC	2.00	.75
❑ 239 Kyle Orton RC	2.00	.75
❑ 240 Derek Anderson RC	3.00	1.25
❑ 241 Derrick Johnson RC	3.00	1.25
❑ 242 Mark Bradley RC	2.00	.75
❑ 243 Chris Henry RC	2.00	.75
❑ 244 DeMarcus Ware RC	3.00	1.25
❑ 245 Luis Castillo RC	2.00	.75
❑ 246 Mike Patterson RC	2.00	.75
❑ 247 Brodney Pool RC	2.00	.75
❑ 248 Barrett Ruud RC	2.00	.75
❑ 249 Darren Sproles RC	2.00	.75
❑ 250 Stefan LeFors RC	2.00	.75

❑ 251 Josh Bullocks RC	2.00	.75
❑ 252 Kevin Burnett RC	2.00	.75
❑ 253 Lofa Tatupu RC	2.50	1.00
❑ 254 Matt Roth RC	2.00	.75
❑ 255 Shaun Cody RC	2.00	.75
❑ 256 Shawne Merriman RC	3.00	1.25
❑ 257 Corey Webster RC	2.00	.75
❑ 258 Channing Crowder RC	2.00	.75
❑ 259 Justin Miller RC	1.50	.60
❑ 260 Eric Green RC	1.00	.40
❑ 261 Marcus Spears RC	2.00	.75
❑ 262 Marlin Jackson RC	2.00	.75
❑ 263 Odell Thurman RC	2.00	.75
❑ 264 Mike Nugent RC	2.00	.75
❑ 265 Marion Barber RC	3.00	1.25
❑ 266 Anttaj Hawthorne RC	1.50	.60
❑ 267 Dan Orlovsky RC	2.00	.75
❑ 268 Fabian Washington RC	2.00	.75
❑ 269 Justin Tuck RC	2.00	.75
❑ 270 Jerome Mathis RC	2.00	.75
❑ 271 Ronald Bartell RC	1.50	.60
❑ 272 Kirk Morrison RC	2.00	.75
❑ 273 Adrian McPherson RC	2.00	.75
❑ 274 Matt Cassel RC	6.00	2.50
❑ 275 Maurice Clarett	2.00	.75

2006 Upper Deck

❑ COMP.SET w/o RC's (200)	30.00	12.00
❑ 1 Larry Fitzgerald	.75	.30
❑ 2 Anquan Boldin	.50	.20
❑ 3 J.J. Arrington	.50	.20
❑ 4 Kurt Warner	.50	.20
❑ 5 Neil Rackers	.40	.15
❑ 6 Edgerrin James	.75	.30
❑ 7 Michael Vick	.75	.30
❑ 8 Alge Crumpler	.50	.20
❑ 9 Warrick Dunn	.50	.20
❑ 10 Michael Jenkins	.50	.20
❑ 11 Roddy White	.50	.20
❑ 12 DeAngelo Hall	.50	.20
❑ 13 Jamal Lewis	.50	.20
❑ 14 Derrick Mason	.40	.15
❑ 15 Todd Heap	.50	.20
❑ 16 Kyle Boller	.40	.15
❑ 17 Ray Lewis	.75	.30
❑ 18 Ed Reed	.50	.20
❑ 19 Willis McGahee	.75	.30
❑ 20 Lee Evans	.50	.20
❑ 21 J.P. Losman	.50	.20
❑ 22 Rashad Baker	.40	.15
❑ 23 Takeo Spikes	.40	.15
❑ 24 Aaron Schobel	.40	.15
❑ 25 Steve Smith	.75	.30
❑ 26 Jake Delhomme	.50	.20
❑ 27 DeShaun Foster	.50	.20
❑ 28 Keary Colbert	.40	.15
❑ 29 Julius Peppers	.50	.20
❑ 30 Ma'Ake Kemoeatu	.40	.15
❑ 31 Rex Grossman	.75	.30
❑ 32 Muhsin Muhammad	.50	.20
❑ 33 Brian Urlacher	.75	.30
❑ 34 Thomas Jones	.50	.20
❑ 35 Cedric Benson	.75	.30
❑ 36 Nathan Vasher	.40	.15
❑ 37 Rudi Johnson	.50	.20
❑ 38 Chad Johnson	.50	.20
❑ 39 T.J. Houshmandzadeh	.50	.20

❑ 40 Chris Henry .40 .15
❑ 41 Deltha O'Neal .40 .15
❑ 42 Odell Thurman .40 .15
❑ 43 Carson Palmer .75 .30
❑ 44 Charlie Frye .50 .20
❑ 45 Reuben Droughns .50 .20
❑ 46 Braylon Edwards .75 .30
❑ 47 Kellen Winslow Jr. .75 .30
❑ 48 Steve Heiden .40 .15
❑ 49 Joe Jurevicius .50 .20
❑ 50 Drew Bledsoe .75 .30
❑ 51 Julius Jones .75 .30
❑ 52 Terrell Owens .75 .30
❑ 53 Terry Glenn .50 .20
❑ 54 Jason Witten .50 .20
❑ 55 DeMarcus Ware .50 .20
❑ 56 Roy Williams S .50 .20
❑ 57 Jake Plummer .50 .20
❑ 58 Tatum Bell .50 .20
❑ 59 Al Wilson .40 .15
❑ 60 Rod Smith .50 .20
❑ 61 Ashley Lelie .50 .20
❑ 62 Champ Bailey .50 .20
❑ 63 Javon Walker .50 .20
❑ 64 Jon Kitna .40 .15
❑ 65 Kevin Jones .75 .30
❑ 66 Roy Williams WR .75 .30
❑ 67 Mike Williams .75 .30
❑ 68 Marcus Pollard .40 .15
❑ 69 Dre Bly .40 .15
❑ 70 Brett Favre 1.50 .60
❑ 71 Ahman Green .50 .20
❑ 72 Donald Driver .50 .20
❑ 73 Robert Ferguson .40 .15
❑ 74 Bubba Franks .40 .15
❑ 75 Kabeer Gbaja-Biamila .50 .20
❑ 76 David Carr .50 .20
❑ 77 Domanick Davis .50 .20
❑ 78 Andre Johnson .50 .20
❑ 79 Eric Moulds .50 .20
❑ 80 Jeb Putzier .40 .15
❑ 81 Dunta Robinson .50 .20
❑ 82 Peyton Manning 1.25 .50
❑ 83 Dominic Rhodes .50 .20
❑ 84 Reggie Wayne .50 .20
❑ 85 Marvin Harrison .75 .30
❑ 86 Dallas Clark .40 .15
❑ 87 Dwight Freeney .50 .20
❑ 88 Bob Sanders .50 .20
❑ 89 Byron Leftwich .50 .20
❑ 90 Fred Taylor .50 .20
❑ 91 Greg Jones .40 .15
❑ 92 Ernest Wilford .40 .15
❑ 93 John Henderson .40 .15
❑ 94 Matt Jones .50 .20
❑ 95 Trent Green .50 .20
❑ 96 Larry Johnson 1.00 .40
❑ 97 Priest Holmes .50 .20
❑ 98 Eddie Kennison .40 .15
❑ 99 Tony Gonzalez .50 .20
❑ 100 Dante Hall .50 .20
❑ 101 Daunte Culpepper .75 .30
❑ 102 Ronnie Brown .75 .30
❑ 103 Marty Booker .40 .15
❑ 104 Chris Chambers .50 .20
❑ 105 Randy McMichael .40 .15
❑ 106 Zach Thomas .75 .30
❑ 107 Brad Johnson .50 .20
❑ 108 Chester Taylor .50 .20
❑ 109 Antoine Winfield .40 .15
❑ 110 Koren Robinson .50 .20
❑ 111 Travis Taylor .40 .15
❑ 112 Darren Sharper .40 .15
❑ 113 Tom Brady 1.25 .50
❑ 114 Corey Dillon .50 .20
❑ 115 Deion Branch .50 .20
❑ 116 Reche Caldwell .40 .15
❑ 117 Ben Watson .40 .15
❑ 118 Tedy Bruschi .75 .30
❑ 119 Rodney Harrison .40 .15
❑ 120 Drew Brees .75 .30
❑ 121 Deuce McAllister .50 .20
❑ 122 Joe Horn .50 .20
❑ 123 Donte Stallworth .50 .20
❑ 124 Devery Henderson .40 .15
❑ 125 Will Smith .40 .15
❑ 126 Eli Manning 1.00 .40
❑ 127 Tiki Barber .75 .30
❑ 128 Plaxico Burress .50 .20
❑ 129 Amani Toomer .50 .20
❑ 130 Jeremy Shockey .75 .30
❑ 131 Michael Strahan .50 .20
❑ 132 Osi Umenyiora .40 .15
❑ 133 Chad Pennington .50 .20
❑ 134 Curtis Martin .75 .30
❑ 135 Justin McCareins .40 .15
❑ 136 Laveranues Coles .50 .20
❑ 137 Jonathan Vilma .50 .20
❑ 138 Shaun Ellis .40 .15
❑ 139 Aaron Brooks .50 .20
❑ 140 LaMont Jordan .50 .20
❑ 141 Randy Moss .75 .30
❑ 142 Jerry Porter .50 .20
❑ 143 Doug Gabriel .40 .15
❑ 144 Derrick Burgess .40 .15
❑ 145 Donovan McNabb .75 .30
❑ 146 Brian Westbrook .50 .20
❑ 147 Jevon Kearse .50 .20
❑ 148 Reggie Brown .60 .25
❑ 149 L.J. Smith .40 .15
❑ 150 Brian Dawkins .50 .20
❑ 151 Ben Roethlisberger 1.25 .50
❑ 152 Willie Parker 1.00 .40
❑ 153 Hines Ward .75 .30
❑ 154 Cedrick Wilson .40 .15
❑ 155 Heath Miller .50 .20
❑ 156 Joey Porter .40 .15
❑ 157 Troy Polamalu 1.00 .40
❑ 158 Philip Rivers .75 .30
❑ 159 LaDainian Tomlinson 1.00 .40
❑ 160 Keenan McCardell .40 .15
❑ 161 Eric Parker .40 .15
❑ 162 Antonio Gates .75 .30
❑ 163 Shawne Merriman .50 .20
❑ 164 Donnie Edwards .40 .15
❑ 165 Alex Smith QB .75 .30
❑ 166 Frank Gore .75 .30
❑ 167 Antonio Bryant .50 .20
❑ 168 Eric Johnson .50 .20
❑ 169 Arnaz Battle .40 .15
❑ 170 Bryant Young .40 .15
❑ 171 Matt Hasselbeck .50 .20
❑ 172 Shaun Alexander .75 .30
❑ 173 Darrell Jackson .50 .20
❑ 174 Etric Pruitt .50 .20
❑ 175 Julian Peterson .40 .15
❑ 176 Lofa Tatupu .50 .20
❑ 177 Marc Bulger .50 .20
❑ 178 Steven Jackson .75 .30
❑ 179 Torry Holt .50 .20
❑ 180 Kevin Curtis .40 .15
❑ 181 Isaac Bruce .50 .20
❑ 182 Leonard Little .40 .15
❑ 183 Chris Simms .50 .20
❑ 184 Cadillac Williams .75 .30
❑ 185 Joey Galloway .50 .20
❑ 186 Michael Clayton .50 .20
❑ 187 Derrick Brooks .50 .20
❑ 188 Ronde Barber .40 .15
❑ 189 Billy Volek .50 .20
❑ 190 Chris Brown .50 .20
❑ 191 Drew Bennett .40 .15
❑ 192 Ben Troupe .40 .15
❑ 193 David Givens .50 .20
❑ 194 Adam Jones .40 .15
❑ 195 Mark Brunell .50 .20
❑ 196 Clinton Portis .75 .30
❑ 197 Santana Moss .50 .20
❑ 198 Chris Cooley .40 .15
❑ 199 Antwaan Randle El .50 .20
❑ 200 Sean Taylor .50 .20
❑ 201 A.J. Hawk RC 12.00 5.00
❑ 202 Anthony Fasano RC 6.00 2.50
❑ 203 Brian Calhoun RC 6.00 2.50
❑ 204 Chad Greenway RC 6.00 2.50
❑ 205 Chad Jackson RC 6.00 2.50
❑ 206 DeAngelo Williams RC 15.00 6.00
❑ 207 D'Brickashaw Ferguson RC 6.00 2.50
❑ 208 Brodie Croyle RC 15.00 6.00
❑ 209 Haloti Ngata RC 6.00 2.50
❑ 210 Jay Cutler RC 20.00 8.00
❑ 211 Joseph Addai RC 20.00 8.00
❑ 212 Laurence Maroney RC 15.00 6.00
❑ 213 LenDale White RC 12.00 5.00
❑ 214 Maurice Drew RC 15.00 6.00
❑ 215 Mario Williams RC 10.00 4.00
❑ 216 Matt Leinart RC 20.00 8.00
❑ 217 Maurice Stovall RC 6.00 2.50
❑ 218 Michael Huff RC 8.00 3.00
❑ 219 Reggie Bush RC 25.00 10.00
❑ 220 Santonio Holmes RC 12.00 5.00
❑ 221 Sinorice Moss RC 6.00 2.50
❑ 222 Kellen Clemens RC 10.00 4.00
❑ 223 Tarvaris Jackson RC 10.00 4.00
❑ 224 Vernon Davis RC 12.00 5.00
❑ 225 Vince Young RC 25.00 10.00
❑ 226 Donte Whitner RC 2.50 1.00
❑ 227 Antonio Cromartie RC 2.50 1.00
❑ 228 Ashton Youboty RC 2.50 1.00
❑ 229 Bobby Carpenter RC 2.50 1.00
❑ 230 Brad Smith RC 2.50 1.00
❑ 231 Brandon Williams RC 2.50 1.00
❑ 232 Dominique Byrd RC 2.00 .75
❑ 233 Brodrick Bunkley RC 2.50 1.00
❑ 234 Charlie Whitehurst RC 2.50 1.00
❑ 235 Demetrius Williams RC 2.50 1.00
❑ 236 Cory Rodgers RC 2.50 1.00
❑ 237 Daniel Bullocks RC 2.50 1.00
❑ 238 Manny Lawson RC 2.50 1.00
❑ 239 Darrell Hackney RC 2.00 .75
❑ 240 Darryl Tapp RC 2.00 .75
❑ 241 David Thomas RC 2.50 1.00
❑ 242 DeMeco Ryans RC 3.00 1.25
❑ 243 Derek Hagan RC 2.50 1.00
❑ 244 Devin Hester RC 5.00 2.00
❑ 245 D'Qwell Jackson RC 2.00 .75
❑ 246 Brandon Marshall RC 2.50 1.00
❑ 247 Ernie Sims RC 3.00 1.25
❑ 248 Gabe Watson RC 2.00 .75
❑ 249 Jason Allen RC 2.50 1.00
❑ 250 Greg Jennings RC 4.00 1.50
❑ 251 Marcus Vick RC 2.00 .75
❑ 252 Jason Avant RC 2.50 1.00
❑ 253 Jeremy Bloom RC 2.00 .75
❑ 254 Jerome Harrison RC 2.50 1.00
❑ 255 Joe Klopfenstein RC 2.00 .75
❑ 256 Johnathan Joseph RC 2.00 .75
❑ 257 Jimmy Williams RC 2.50 1.00
❑ 258 Kamerion Wimbley RC 2.50 1.00
❑ 259 Leon Washington RC 4.00 1.50
❑ 260 Marcedes Lewis RC 2.50 1.00
❑ 261 Marcus McNeill RC 2.00 .75
❑ 262 Mathias Kiwanuka RC 3.00 1.25
❑ 263 Leonard Pope RC 2.50 1.00
❑ 264 Tamba Hali RC 2.50 1.00
❑ 265 Mike Hass RC 2.50 1.00
❑ 266 Omar Jacobs RC 2.00 .75
❑ 267 Jerious Norwood RC 4.00 1.50
❑ 268 Owen Daniels RC 2.50 1.00
❑ 269 P.J. Daniels RC 2.00 .75
❑ 270 Ray Edwards RC 2.00 .75
❑ 271 Michael Robinson RC 2.50 1.00
❑ 272 Rocky McIntosh RC 2.50 1.00
❑ 273 Travis Wilson RC 2.50 1.00
❑ 274 Tye Hill RC 2.50 1.00
❑ 275 Thomas Howard RC 2.50 1.00

2007 Upper Deck

❑ 1 Karlos Dansby .50 .20
❑ 2 Edgerrin James .75 .30
❑ 3 Matt Leinart .75 .30
❑ 4 Larry Fitzgerald .60 .25
❑ 5 Anquan Boldin .60 .25
❑ 6 Joe Horn .60 .25
❑ 7 Michael Jenkins .60 .25
❑ 8 Michael Vick .75 .30
❑ 9 Warrick Dunn .60 .25
❑ 10 Alge Crumpler .60 .25
❑ 11 Derrick Mason .50 .20
❑ 12 Ed Reed .60 .25
❑ 13 Willis McGahee .60 .25
❑ 14 Steve McNair .60 .25

❑	15	Mark Clayton	.60	.25
❑	16	Todd Heap	.50	.20
❑	17	Ray Lewis	.75	.30
❑	18	J.P. Losman	.60	.25
❑	19	Peerless Price	.50	.20
❑	20	Lee Evans	.60	.25
❑	21	Anthony Thomas	.50	.20
❑	22	David Carr	.60	.25
❑	23	DeAngelo Williams	.75	.30
❑	24	Julius Peppers	.60	.25
❑	25	Jake Delhomme	.60	.25
❑	26	DeShaun Foster	.60	.25
❑	27	Steve Smith	.60	.25
❑	28	Muhsin Muhammad	.60	.25
❑	29	Rex Grossman	.60	.25
❑	30	Desmond Clark	.50	.20
❑	31	Devin Hester	.75	.30
❑	32	Cedric Benson	.60	.25
❑	33	Bernard Berrian	.50	.20
❑	34	Brian Urlacher	.75	.30
❑	35	Justin Smith	.50	.20
❑	36	T.J. Houshmandzadeh	.60	.25
❑	37	Carson Palmer	.75	.30
❑	38	Rudi Johnson	.60	.25
❑	39	Chad Johnson	.60	.25
❑	40	Kamerion Wimbley	.50	.20
❑	41	Charlie Frye	.60	.25
❑	42	Tim Carter	.50	.20
❑	43	Jamal Lewis	.60	.25
❑	44	Kellen Winslow	.60	.25
❑	45	Braylon Edwards	.60	.25
❑	46	Roy Williams S	.60	.25
❑	47	Marion Barber	.60	.25
❑	48	Jason Witten	.60	.25
❑	49	Terry Glenn	.60	.25
❑	50	DeMarcus Ware	.60	.25
❑	51	Tony Romo	1.50	.60
❑	52	Julius Jones	.60	.25
❑	53	Terrell Owens	.75	.30
❑	54	Mike Bell	.60	.25
❑	55	John Lynch	.60	.25
❑	56	Rod Smith	.60	.25
❑	57	Travis Henry	.60	.25
❑	58	Jay Cutler	.75	.30
❑	59	Javon Walker	.60	.25
❑	60	Champ Bailey	.60	.25
❑	61	Tatum Bell	.60	.25
❑	62	Mike Furrey	.60	.25
❑	63	Jon Kitna	.50	.20
❑	64	Kevin Jones	.50	.20
❑	65	Roy Williams WR	.60	.25
❑	66	Bubba Franks	.50	.20
❑	67	Charles Woodson	.60	.25
❑	68	Brett Favre	1.50	.60
❑	69	Donald Driver	.60	.25
❑	70	A.J. Hawk	.75	.30
❑	71	Ahman Green	.60	.25
❑	72	DeMeco Ryans	.60	.25
❑	73	Matt Schaub	.60	.25
❑	74	Andre Johnson	.60	.25
❑	75	Mario Williams	.60	.25
❑	76	Ron Dayne	.60	.25
❑	77	Dwight Freeney	.60	.25
❑	78	Dallas Clark	.50	.20
❑	79	Peyton Manning	1.25	.50
❑	80	Marvin Harrison	.75	.30
❑	81	Reggie Wayne	.60	.25
❑	82	Joseph Addai	1.00	.40
❑	83	Matt Jones	.60	.25
❑	84	David Garrard	.60	.25
❑	85	Ernest Wilford	.50	.20
❑	86	Reggie Williams	.60	.25
❑	87	Maurice Jones-Drew	.75	.30
❑	88	Fred Taylor	.60	.25
❑	89	Byron Leftwich	.60	.25
❑	90	Eddie Kennison	.50	.20
❑	91	Samie Parker	.50	.20
❑	92	Derrick Johnson	.50	.20
❑	93	Trent Green	.60	.25
❑	94	Larry Johnson	.75	.30
❑	95	Tony Gonzalez	.60	.25
❑	96	Damon Huard	.50	.20
❑	97	Zach Thomas	.60	.25
❑	98	Daunte Culpepper	.60	.25
❑	99	Ronnie Brown	.60	.25
❑	100	Jason Taylor	.50	.20
❑	101	Chris Chambers	.60	.25
❑	102	Antoine Winfield	.50	.20
❑	103	Ryan Longwell	.50	.20
❑	104	Chester Taylor	.50	.20
❑	105	Tarvaris Jackson	.75	.30
❑	106	Troy Williamson	.50	.20
❑	107	Rodney Harrison	.50	.20
❑	108	Randy Moss	.75	.30
❑	109	Stephen Gostkowski	.50	.20
❑	110	Donte Stallworth	.60	.25
❑	111	Tom Brady	1.50	.60
❑	112	Laurence Maroney	.75	.30
❑	113	Ben Watson	.50	.20
❑	114	Tedy Bruschi	.75	.30
❑	115	Charles Grant	.50	.20
❑	116	Michael Lewis	.50	.20
❑	117	Drew Brees	.60	.25
❑	118	Marques Colston	.75	.30
❑	119	Reggie Bush	1.00	.40
❑	120	Deuce McAllister	.60	.25
❑	121	Amani Toomer	.60	.25
❑	122	Reuben Droughns	.60	.25
❑	123	Michael Strahan	.60	.25
❑	124	Plaxico Burress	.60	.25
❑	125	Osi Umenyiora	.50	.20
❑	126	Eli Manning	.75	.30
❑	127	Jeremy Shockey	.60	.25
❑	128	Brandon Jacobs	.60	.25
❑	129	Jonathan Vilma	.60	.25
❑	130	Jerricho Cotchery	.50	.20
❑	131	Chris Baker	.50	.20
❑	132	Chad Pennington	.60	.25
❑	133	Leon Washington	.60	.25
❑	134	Laveranues Coles	.60	.25
❑	135	Nnamdi Asomugha	.50	.20
❑	136	Dominic Rhodes	.60	.25
❑	137	Warren Sapp	.60	.25
❑	138	Justin Fargas	.50	.20
❑	139	Ronald Curry	.60	.25
❑	140	Brian Dawkins	.60	.25
❑	141	L.J. Smith	.50	.20
❑	142	Mike Patterson	.50	.20
❑	143	Brian Westbrook	.60	.25
❑	144	Reggie Brown	.60	.25
❑	145	Donovan McNabb	.75	.30
❑	146	Hines Ward	.75	.30
❑	147	James Farrior	.50	.20
❑	148	Ike Taylor	.50	.20
❑	149	Santonio Holmes	.60	.25
❑	150	Ben Roethlisberger	1.00	.40
❑	151	Willie Parker	.75	.30
❑	152	Troy Polamalu	.75	.30
❑	153	Michael Turner	.60	.25
❑	154	Vincent Jackson	.50	.20
❑	155	Nate Kaeding	.50	.20
❑	156	Philip Rivers	.75	.30
❑	157	Antonio Gates	.60	.25
❑	158	Shawne Merriman	.60	.25
❑	159	LaDainian Tomlinson	1.00	.40
❑	160	Arnaz Battle	.50	.20
❑	161	Nate Clements	.50	.20
❑	162	Ashley Lelie	.60	.25
❑	163	Alex Smith QB	.75	.30
❑	164	Frank Gore	.75	.30
❑	165	Vernon Davis	.60	.25
❑	166	Mack Strong	.50	.20
❑	167	Lofa Tatupu	.60	.25
❑	168	Maurice Morris	.50	.20
❑	169	Bobby Engram	.50	.20
❑	170	Matt Hasselbeck	.60	.25
❑	171	Shaun Alexander	.60	.25
❑	172	Deion Branch	.60	.25
❑	173	Leonard Little	.50	.20
❑	174	Pisa Tinoisamoa	.50	.20
❑	175	Drew Bennett	.50	.20
❑	176	Steven Jackson	.75	.30
❑	177	Marc Bulger	.60	.25
❑	178	Torry Holt	.60	.25
❑	179	Isaac Bruce	.60	.25
❑	180	Ronde Barber	.50	.20
❑	181	Chris Simms	.50	.20
❑	182	Mike Alstott	.60	.25
❑	183	Derrick Brooks	.60	.25
❑	184	Cadillac Williams	.60	.25
❑	185	Michael Clayton	.60	.25
❑	186	Joey Galloway	.60	.25
❑	187	Brandon Jones	.50	.20
❑	188	Keith Bulluck	.50	.20
❑	189	Nick Harper	.50	.20
❑	190	David Givens	.50	.20
❑	191	Vince Young	1.00	.40
❑	192	LenDale White	.60	.25
❑	193	Mark Brunell	.60	.25
❑	194	Sean Taylor	.50	.20
❑	195	Chris Cooley	.50	.20
❑	196	Brandon Lloyd	.60	.25
❑	197	Jason Campbell	.60	.25
❑	198	Clinton Portis	.60	.25
❑	199	Santana Moss	.60	.25
❑	200	Antwaan Randle El	.50	.20
❑	201	Levi Brown RC	4.00	1.50
❑	202	Alan Branch RC	3.00	1.25
❑	203	Buster Davis RC	3.00	1.25
❑	204	Steve Breaston RC	3.00	1.25
❑	205	Justin Blalock RC	2.50	1.00
❑	206	Chris Houston RC	3.00	1.25
❑	207	Laurent Robinson RC	3.00	1.25
❑	208	Ben Grubbs RC	3.00	1.25
❑	209	Troy Smith RC	5.00	2.00
❑	210	Yamon Figurs RC	4.00	1.50
❑	211	Le'Ron McClain RC	3.00	1.25
❑	212	Trent Edwards RC	8.00	3.00
❑	213	Dwayne Wright RC	3.00	1.25
❑	214	Jon Beason RC	4.00	1.50
❑	215	Ryan Kalil RC	3.00	1.25
❑	216	Dan Bazuin RC	3.00	1.25
❑	217	Garrett Wolfe RC	5.00	2.00
❑	218	Michael Okwo RC	3.00	1.25
❑	219	Chris Leak RC	3.00	1.25
❑	220	Leon Hall RC	3.00	1.25
❑	221	Jeff Rowe RC	3.00	1.25
❑	222	Eric Wright RC	4.00	1.50
❑	223	Isaiah Stanback RC	4.00	1.50
❑	224	Anthony Spencer RC	4.00	1.50
❑	225	Jarvis Moss RC	4.00	1.50
❑	226	Tim Crowder RC	4.00	1.50
❑	227	Ikaika Alama-Francis RC	4.00	1.50
❑	228	Justin Harrell RC	4.00	1.50
❑	229	Brandon Jackson RC	5.00	2.00
❑	230	James Jones RC	6.00	2.50
❑	231	Jacoby Jones RC	4.00	1.50
❑	232	Tony Ugoh RC	3.00	1.25
❑	233	Daymeion Hughes RC	3.00	1.25
❑	234	Reggie Nelson RC	3.00	1.25
❑	235	Justin Durant RC	3.00	1.25
❑	236	Turk McBride RC	3.00	1.25
❑	237	DeMarcus Tank Tyler RC	3.00	1.25
❑	238	Kolby Smith RC	5.00	2.00
❑	239	Lorenzo Booker RC	4.00	1.50
❑	240	Marcus McCauley RC	3.00	1.25
❑	241	Brandon Meriweather RC	4.00	1.50
❑	242	Antonio Pittman RC	3.00	1.25
❑	243	Usama Young RC	3.00	1.25
❑	244	Aaron Ross RC	4.00	1.50
❑	245	Zak DeOssie RC	3.00	1.25
❑	246	Darrelle Revis RC	4.00	1.50
❑	247	David Harris RC	3.00	1.25
❑	248	Zach Miller RC	4.00	1.50
❑	249	Johnnie Lee Higgins RC	3.00	1.25

❑ 250 Michael Bush RC 5.00 2.00
❑ 251 Quentin Moses RC 3.00 1.25
❑ 252 Victor Abiamiri RC 4.00 1.50
❑ 253 Tony Hunt RC 4.00 1.50
❑ 254 Stewart Bradley RC 4.00 1.50
❑ 255 Lawrence Timmons RC 4.00 1.50
❑ 256 LaMarr Woodley RC 4.00 1.50
❑ 257 Matt Spaeth RC 4.00 1.50
❑ 258 Eric Weddle RC 3.00 1.25
❑ 259 Scott Chandler RC 3.00 1.25
❑ 260 Anthony Waters RC 3.00 1.25
❑ 261 Joe Staley RC 3.00 1.25
❑ 262 Jason Hill RC 4.00 1.50
❑ 263 Josh Wilson RC 3.00 1.25
❑ 264 Brandon Mebane RC 3.00 1.25
❑ 265 Adam Carriker RC 3.00 1.25
❑ 266 Jonathan Wade RC 3.00 1.25
❑ 267 Arron Sears RC 3.00 1.25
❑ 268 Sabby Piscitelli RC 4.00 1.50
❑ 269 Quincy Black RC 3.00 1.25
❑ 270 Michael Griffin RC 4.00 1.50
❑ 271 Chris Henry RB RC 4.00 1.50
❑ 272 Paul Williams RC 3.00 1.25
❑ 273 Chris Davis RC 3.00 1.25
❑ 274 H.B. Blades RC 3.00 1.25
❑ 275 Jordan Palmer RC 4.00 1.50
❑ 276 JaMarcus Russell RC 10.00 4.00
❑ 277 Calvin Johnson RC 12.00 5.00
❑ 278 Brady Quinn RC 12.00 5.00
❑ 279 Adrian Peterson RC 30.00 12.00
❑ 280 Marshawn Lynch RC 8.00 3.00
❑ 281 Ted Ginn Jr. RC 6.00 2.50
❑ 282 LaRon Landry RC 5.00 2.00
❑ 283 Jamaal Anderson RC 3.00 1.25
❑ 284 Amobi Okoye RC 4.00 1.50
❑ 285 Dwayne Bowe RC 8.00 3.00
❑ 286 Greg Olsen RC 5.00 2.00
❑ 287 Gaines Adams RC 4.00 1.50
❑ 288 Patrick Willis RC 8.00 3.00
❑ 289 Drew Stanton RC 5.00 2.00
❑ 290 Kevin Kolb RC 6.00 2.50
❑ 291 John Beck RC 8.00 3.00
❑ 292 Anthony Gonzalez RC 6.00 2.50
❑ 293 Sidney Rice RC 6.00 2.50
❑ 294 Robert Meachem RC 4.00 1.50
❑ 295 Joe Thomas RC 4.00 1.50
❑ 296 Dwayne Jarrett RC 5.00 2.00
❑ 297 Kenny Irons RC 4.00 1.50
❑ 298 Brian Leonard RC 5.00 2.00
❑ 299 Craig Buster Davis RC 4.00 1.50
❑ 300 Steve Smith USC RC 5.00 2.00

2005 Upper Deck ESPN

❑ COMP.SET w/o RC's (100) 25.00 10.00
❑ DRAFT PICK STATED ODDS 1:4
❑ 1 Larry Fitzgerald .75 .30
❑ 2 Josh McCown .50 .20
❑ 3 Anquan Boldin .50 .20
❑ 4 Michael Vick 1.25 .50
❑ 5 Warrick Dunn .50 .20
❑ 6 Peerless Price .40 .15
❑ 7 Alge Crumpler .50 .20
❑ 8 Jamal Lewis .75 .30
❑ 9 Kyle Boller .50 .20
❑ 10 Derrick Mason .50 .20
❑ 11 Willis McGahee .75 .30
❑ 12 J.P. Losman .75 .30
❑ 13 Eric Moulds .50 .20
❑ 14 Jake Delhomme .75 .30
❑ 15 Steve Smith .50 .20
❑ 16 DeShaun Foster .50 .20
❑ 17 Muhsin Muhammad .50 .20
❑ 18 Thomas Jones .50 .20
❑ 19 Rex Grossman .50 .20
❑ 20 Chad Johnson .75 .30
❑ 21 Carson Palmer .75 .30
❑ 22 Rudi Johnson .50 .20
❑ 23 Lee Suggs .50 .20
❑ 24 Kellen Winslow .75 .30
❑ 25 Luke McCown .40 .15
❑ 26 Julius Jones 1.00 .40
❑ 27 Keyshawn Johnson .50 .20
❑ 28 Drew Bledsoe .75 .30
❑ 29 Tatum Bell .50 .20
❑ 30 Jake Plummer .50 .20
❑ 31 Rod Smith .50 .20
❑ 32 Roy Williams WR .75 .30
❑ 33 Kevin Jones .75 .30
❑ 34 Joey Harrington .75 .30
❑ 35 Jeff Garcia .50 .20
❑ 36 Brett Favre 2.00 .75
❑ 37 Javon Walker .50 .20
❑ 38 Ahman Green .75 .30
❑ 39 David Carr .75 .30
❑ 40 Andre Johnson .50 .20
❑ 41 Domanick Davis .50 .20
❑ 42 Peyton Manning 1.25 .50
❑ 43 Edgerrin James .75 .30
❑ 44 Marvin Harrison .75 .30
❑ 45 Byron Leftwich .75 .30
❑ 46 Fred Taylor .50 .20
❑ 47 Jimmy Smith .50 .20
❑ 48 Priest Holmes .75 .30
❑ 49 Trent Green .50 .20
❑ 50 Tony Gonzalez .50 .20
❑ 51 Larry Johnson .75 .30
❑ 52 Chris Chambers .50 .20
❑ 53 A.J. Feeley .50 .20
❑ 54 Randy McMichael .40 .15
❑ 55 Daunte Culpepper .75 .30
❑ 56 Nate Burleson .50 .20
❑ 57 Michael Bennett .50 .20
❑ 58 Tom Brady 2.00 .75
❑ 59 Deion Branch .50 .20
❑ 60 Corey Dillon .50 .20
❑ 61 Aaron Brooks .50 .20
❑ 62 Deuce McAllister .75 .30
❑ 63 Joe Horn .50 .20
❑ 64 Eli Manning 1.50 .60
❑ 65 Jeremy Shockey .75 .30
❑ 66 Tiki Barber .75 .30
❑ 67 Plaxico Burress .50 .20
❑ 68 Chad Pennington .75 .30
❑ 69 Curtis Martin .75 .30
❑ 70 Laveranues Coles .50 .20
❑ 71 Jerry Porter .50 .20
❑ 72 Randy Moss .75 .30
❑ 73 Kerry Collins .50 .20
❑ 74 Donovan McNabb 1.00 .40
❑ 75 Brian Westbrook .50 .20
❑ 76 Terrell Owens .75 .30
❑ 77 Ben Roethlisberger 2.00 .75
❑ 78 Jerome Bettis .75 .30
❑ 79 Hines Ward .75 .30
❑ 80 Drew Brees .75 .30
❑ 81 LaDainian Tomlinson 1.00 .40
❑ 82 Antonio Gates .75 .30
❑ 83 Tim Rattay .40 .15
❑ 84 Eric Johnson .50 .20
❑ 85 Rashaun Woods .50 .20
❑ 86 Matt Hasselbeck .50 .20
❑ 87 Shaun Alexander 1.00 .40
❑ 88 Darrell Jackson .50 .20
❑ 89 Marc Bulger .75 .30
❑ 90 Marshall Faulk .75 .30
❑ 91 Torry Holt .75 .30
❑ 92 Brian Griese .50 .20
❑ 93 Michael Pittman .40 .15
❑ 94 Michael Clayton .75 .30
❑ 95 Steve McNair .75 .30
❑ 96 Chris Brown .50 .20
❑ 97 Drew Bennett .50 .20
❑ 98 Clinton Portis .75 .30
❑ 99 Patrick Ramsey .50 .20
❑ 100 Santana Moss .50 .20
❑ 101 Aaron Rodgers RC 8.00 3.00
❑ 102 Alex Smith QB RC 10.00 4.00
❑ 103 Charlie Frye RC 2.50 1.00
❑ 104 Andrew Walter RC 2.50 1.00
❑ 105 David Greene RC 2.50 1.00
❑ 106 Dan Orlovsky RC 2.50 1.00
❑ 107 Derek Anderson RC 4.00 1.50
❑ 108 Cadillac Williams RC 10.00 4.00
❑ 109 Ronnie Brown RC 10.00 4.00
❑ 110 Ciatrick Fason RC 2.50 1.00
❑ 111 Cedric Benson RC 6.00 2.50
❑ 112 Vincent Jackson RC 2.50 1.00
❑ 113 Eric Shelton RC 2.50 1.00
❑ 114 Frank Gore RC 5.00 2.00
❑ 115 Braylon Edwards RC 8.00 3.00
❑ 116 Roddy White RC 2.50 1.00
❑ 117 Troy Williamson RC 2.50 1.00
❑ 118 Craphonso Thorpe RC 2.00 .75
❑ 119 Mark Clayton RC 2.50 1.00
❑ 120 Fred Gibson RC 2.00 .75
❑ 121 Reggie Brown RC 2.50 1.00
❑ 122 Matt Jones RC 4.00 1.50
❑ 123 David Pollack RC 2.50 1.00
❑ 124 Derrick Johnson RC 4.00 1.50
❑ 125 Erasmus James RC 2.50 1.00
❑ 126 Antrel Rolle RC 2.50 1.00
❑ 127 Thomas Davis RC 2.50 1.00
❑ 128 Adam Jones RC 2.50 1.00
❑ 129 Corey Webster RC 2.50 1.00
❑ 130 Marlin Jackson RC 2.50 1.00
❑ 131 Brodney Pool RC 2.50 1.00
❑ 132 Mark Bradley RC 2.50 1.00
❑ 133 Stefan LeFors RC 2.50 1.00
❑ 134 Alex Smith TE RC 2.50 1.00
❑ 135 Heath Miller RC 5.00 2.00
❑ 136 Jason Campbell RC 4.00 1.50
❑ 137 Kyle Orton RC 2.50 1.00
❑ 138 Vernand Morency RC 2.50 1.00
❑ 139 Carlos Rogers RC 3.00 1.25
❑ 140 J.J. Arrington RC 2.50 1.00
❑ 141 Ryan Moats RC 2.50 1.00
❑ 142 Chris Henry RC 2.50 1.00
❑ 143 Terrence Murphy RC 2.50 1.00
❑ 144 Fabian Washington RC 2.50 1.00
❑ 145 Roscoe Parrish RC 2.50 1.00
❑ 146 Kevin Everett RC 2.50 1.00
❑ 147 Travis Johnson RC 2.00 .75
❑ 148 Mike Williams 2.50 1.00
❑ 149 Maurice Clarett 2.50 1.00
❑ 150 Channing Crowder RC 2.50 1.00
❑ 151 Odell Thurman RC 2.00 .75
❑ 152 DeMarcus Ware RC 4.00 1.50
❑ 153 Shawne Merriman RC 4.00 1.50
❑ 154 Jerome Mathis RC 2.50 1.00
❑ 155 Marcus Spears RC 2.50 1.00
❑ 156 Luis Castillo RC 2.50 1.00
❑ 157 Darren Sproles RC 2.50 1.00
❑ 158 Marion Barber RC 4.00 1.50
❑ 159 Justin Tuck RC 2.50 1.00
❑ 160 Courtney Roby RC 2.50 1.00

2007 Upper Deck First Edition

❑ 1 Matt Leinart	.40	.15
❑ 2 Larry Fitzgerald	.30	.12
❑ 3 Anquan Boldin	.30	.12
❑ 4 Michael Vick	.40	.15
❑ 5 Warrick Dunn	.30	.12
❑ 6 Alge Crumpler	.30	.12
❑ 7 Steve McNair	.30	.12
❑ 8 Mark Clayton	.30	.12
❑ 9 Todd Heap	.25	.10
❑ 10 Ray Lewis	.40	.15
❑ 11 J.P. Losman	.30	.12
❑ 12 Lee Evans	.30	.12
❑ 13 Anthony Thomas	.25	.10
❑ 14 Jake Delhomme	.30	.12
❑ 15 DeShaun Foster	.30	.12
❑ 16 Steve Smith	.30	.12
❑ 17 Cedric Benson	.30	.12
❑ 18 Bernard Berrian	.25	.10
❑ 19 Brian Urlacher	.40	.15
❑ 20 Carson Palmer	.40	.15
❑ 21 Rudi Johnson	.30	.12
❑ 22 Chad Johnson	.30	.12
❑ 23 Kellen Winslow	.30	.12
❑ 24 Braylon Edwards	.30	.12
❑ 25 Tony Romo	.75	.30
❑ 26 Julius Jones	.30	.12
❑ 27 Terrell Owens	.40	.15
❑ 28 Jay Cutler	.40	.15
❑ 29 Javon Walker	.30	.12
❑ 30 Champ Bailey	.30	.12
❑ 31 Jon Kitna	.25	.10
❑ 32 Kevin Jones	.25	.10
❑ 33 Roy Williams WR	.30	.12
❑ 34 Brett Favre	.75	.30
❑ 35 Donald Driver	.30	.12
❑ 36 A.J. Hawk	.40	.15
❑ 37 Andre Johnson	.30	.12
❑ 38 Mario Williams	.30	.12
❑ 39 Ron Dayne	.30	.12
❑ 40 Peyton Manning	.60	.25
❑ 41 Marvin Harrison	.40	.15
❑ 42 Reggie Wayne	.30	.12
❑ 43 Joseph Addai	.50	.20
❑ 44 Maurice Jones-Drew	.40	.15
❑ 45 Fred Taylor	.30	.12
❑ 46 Byron Leftwich	.30	.12
❑ 47 Larry Johnson	.40	.15
❑ 48 Tony Gonzalez	.30	.12
❑ 49 Damon Huard	.25	.10
❑ 50 Ronnie Brown	.30	.12
❑ 51 Jason Taylor	.25	.10
❑ 52 Chris Chambers	.30	.12
❑ 53 Chester Taylor	.25	.10
❑ 54 Tarvaris Jackson	.40	.15
❑ 55 Troy Williamson	.25	.10
❑ 56 Tom Brady	.75	.30
❑ 57 Laurence Maroney	.40	.15
❑ 58 Ben Watson	.25	.10
❑ 59 Asante Samuel	.25	.10
❑ 60 Chad Pennington	.30	.12
❑ 61 Leon Washington	.30	.12
❑ 62 Laveranues Coles	.30	.12
❑ 63 Eli Manning	.40	.15
❑ 64 Jeremy Shockey	.30	.12
❑ 65 Brandon Jacobs	.30	.12
❑ 66 Drew Brees	.30	.12
❑ 67 Marques Colston	.40	.15
❑ 68 Reggie Bush	.50	.20
❑ 69 Deuce McAllister	.30	.12
❑ 70 Jerry Porter	.30	.12
❑ 71 Justin Fargas	.25	.10
❑ 72 Randy Moss	.40	.15
❑ 73 Brian Westbrook	.30	.12
❑ 74 Reggie Brown	.30	.12
❑ 75 Donovan McNabb	.40	.15
❑ 76 Ben Roethlisberger	.50	.20
❑ 77 Willie Parker	.40	.15
❑ 78 Troy Polamalu	.40	.15
❑ 79 Antonio Gates	.30	.12
❑ 80 Shawne Merriman	.30	.12
❑ 81 LaDainian Tomlinson	.50	.20
❑ 82 Alex Smith QB	.40	.15
❑ 83 Frank Gore	.40	.15
❑ 84 Vernon Davis	.30	.12
❑ 85 Steven Jackson	.40	.15
❑ 86 Marc Bulger	.30	.12
❑ 87 Torry Holt	.30	.12
❑ 88 Isaac Bruce	.30	.12
❑ 89 Matt Hasselbeck	.30	.12
❑ 90 Shaun Alexander	.30	.12
❑ 91 Deion Branch	.30	.12
❑ 92 Cadillac Williams	.30	.12
❑ 93 Michael Clayton	.30	.12
❑ 94 Joey Galloway	.30	.12
❑ 95 Vince Young	.50	.20
❑ 96 LenDale White	.30	.12
❑ 97 Jason Campbell	.30	.12
❑ 98 Clinton Portis	.30	.12
❑ 99 Santana Moss	.30	.12
❑ 100 Antwaan Randle El	.25	.10
❑ 101 JaMarcus Russell RC	4.00	1.50
❑ 102 Brady Quinn RC	5.00	2.00
❑ 103 Calvin Johnson RC	5.00	2.00
❑ 104 Adrian Peterson RC	12.00	5.00
❑ 105 Joe Thomas RC	1.50	.60
❑ 106 Levi Brown RC	1.50	.60
❑ 107 Gaines Adams RC	1.50	.60
❑ 108 Adam Carriker RC	1.25	.50
❑ 109 Ted Ginn Jr. RC	2.50	1.00
❑ 110 Anthony Gonzalez RC	2.50	1.00
❑ 111 Troy Smith RC	2.00	.75
❑ 112 Leon Hall RC	1.25	.50
❑ 113 LaMarr Woodley RC	1.50	.60
❑ 114 Alan Branch RC	1.25	.50
❑ 115 Patrick Willis RC	3.00	1.25
❑ 116 Reggie Nelson RC	1.25	.50
❑ 117 Paul Posluszny RC	2.00	.75
❑ 118 Dwayne Bowe RC	3.00	1.25
❑ 119 Steve Smith RC	2.00	.75
❑ 120 Dwayne Jarrett RC	2.00	.75
❑ 121 Marshawn Lynch RC	3.00	1.25
❑ 122 Darius Walker RC	1.50	.60
❑ 123 Daymeion Hughes RC	1.25	.50
❑ 124 LaRon Landry RC	2.00	.75
❑ 125 Jon Beason RC	1.50	.60
❑ 126 Lawrence Timmons RC	1.50	.60
❑ 127 Drew Stanton RC	2.00	.75
❑ 128 Trent Edwards RC	3.00	1.25
❑ 129 John Beck RC	3.00	1.25
❑ 130 Kevin Kolb RC	2.50	1.00
❑ 131 Amobi Okoye RC	1.50	.60
❑ 132 Michael Bush RC	2.00	.75
❑ 133 Darrelle Revis RC	1.50	.60
❑ 134 H.B. Blades RC	1.25	.50
❑ 135 Jamaal Anderson RC	1.25	.50
❑ 136 Robert Meachem RC	1.50	.60
❑ 137 Sidney Rice RC	2.50	1.00
❑ 138 Craig Davis RC	1.50	.60
❑ 139 Paul Williams RC	1.25	.50
❑ 140 Greg Olsen RC	2.00	.75
❑ 141 Jarvis Moss RC	1.50	.60
❑ 142 Justin Harrell RC	1.50	.60
❑ 143 DeMarcus Tank Tyler RC	1.25	.50
❑ 144 Aaron Ross RC	1.50	.60
❑ 145 Chris Houston RC	1.25	.50
❑ 146 Brandon Meriweather RC	1.50	.60
❑ 147 Eric Weddle RC	1.25	.50
❑ 148 Lorenzo Booker RC	1.50	.60
❑ 149 Buster Davis RC	1.25	.50
❑ 150 Antonio Pittman RC	1.25	.50
❑ 151 Chris Henry RC	1.50	.60
❑ 152 Kenny Irons RC	1.50	.60
❑ 153 Brandon Jackson RC	2.00	.75
❑ 154 Tony Hunt RC	1.50	.60
❑ 155 Brian Leonard RC	2.00	.75
❑ 156 Garrett Wolfe RC	2.00	.75
❑ 157 Yamon Figurs RC	1.50	.60
❑ 158 Johnnie Lee Higgins RC	1.25	.50
❑ 159 Jordan Palmer RC	1.50	.60
❑ 160 Chris Leak RC	1.25	.50
❑ 161 Rhema McKnight RC	1.25	.50
❑ 162 Dwayne Wright RC	1.25	.50
❑ 163 Matt Moore RC	2.50	1.00
❑ 164 Jeff Rowe RC	1.25	.50
❑ 165 Zach Miller RC	1.50	.60
❑ 166 Ben Patrick RC	1.25	.50
❑ 167 Joe Staley RC	1.25	.50
❑ 168 Eric Wright RC	1.50	.60
❑ 169 Aundrae Allison RC	1.25	.50
❑ 170 Steve Breaston RC	1.25	.50
❑ 171 David Harris RC	1.25	.50
❑ 172 Brandon Siler RC	1.25	.50
❑ 173 Tim Shaw RC	1.25	.50
❑ 174 Selvin Young RC	2.00	.75
❑ 175 Michael Griffin RC	1.50	.60
❑ 176 Kenneth Darby RC	1.50	.60
❑ 177 Anthony Spencer RC	1.50	.60
❑ 178 Charles Johnson RC	1.00	.40
❑ 179 Quentin Moses RC	1.25	.50
❑ 180 DeShawn Wynn RC	1.50	.60
❑ 181 Scott Chandler RC	1.25	.50
❑ 182 Stewart Bradley RC	1.50	.60
❑ 183 Ahmad Bradshaw RC	2.00	.75
❑ 184 Matt Spaeth RC	1.50	.60
❑ 185 Ray McDonald RC	1.25	.50
❑ 186 Ben Grubbs RC	1.25	.50
❑ 187 Jon Abbate RC	1.00	.40
❑ 188 Victor Abiamiri RC	1.50	.60
❑ 189 Courtney Taylor RC	1.25	.50
❑ 190 A.J. Davis RC	1.00	.40
❑ 191 Nate Harris RC	1.25	.50
❑ 192 Jonathan Wade RC	1.25	.50
❑ 193 Tim Crowder RC	1.50	.60
❑ 194 Legedu Naanee RC	1.25	.50
❑ 195 Quinn Pitcock RC	1.25	.50
❑ 196 Marcus McCauley RC	1.25	.50
❑ 197 Sabby Piscitelli RC	1.50	.60
❑ 198 Tanard Jackson RC	1.00	.40
❑ 199 Josh Gattis RC	1.00	.40
❑ 200 Rufus Alexander RC	1.50	.60

1997 Upper Deck Legends

❑ COMPLETE SET (208)	80.00	30.00
❑ 1 Bart Starr	2.50	1.00
❑ 2 Jim Brown	2.50	1.00
❑ 3 Joe Namath	3.00	1.25
❑ 4 Walter Payton	5.00	2.00
❑ 5 Terry Bradshaw	3.00	1.25
❑ 6 Franco Harris	.60	.25
❑ 7 Dan Fouts	.60	.25
❑ 8 Steve Largent	.60	.25
❑ 9 Johnny Unitas	2.50	1.00
❑ 10 Gale Sayers	1.50	.60
❑ 11 Roger Staubach	3.00	1.25
❑ 12 Tony Dorsett	.60	.25
❑ 13 Fran Tarkenton	1.50	.60
❑ 14 Charley Taylor	.40	.15
❑ 15 Ray Nitschke	.60	.25
❑ 16 Jim Ringo	.40	.15
❑ 17 Dick Butkus	1.50	.60
❑ 18 Fred Biletnikoff	.60	.25
❑ 19 Lenny Moore	.40	.15
❑ 20 Len Dawson	.60	.25
❑ 21 Lance Alworth	.40	.15
❑ 22 Chuck Bednarik	.40	.15
❑ 23 Raymond Berry	.40	.15
❑ 24 Donnie Shell	.30	.10
❑ 25 Mel Blount	.40	.15
❑ 26 Willie Brown	.40	.15
❑ 27 Ken Houston	.30	.10
❑ 28 Larry Csonka	.60	.25
❑ 29 Mike Ditka	1.25	.50
❑ 30 Art Donovan	.40	.15
❑ 31 Sam Huff	.40	.15
❑ 32 Lem Barney	.30	.10

❑ 33 Hugh McElhenny .40 .15
❑ 34 Otto Graham .75 .30
❑ 35 Joe Greene .60 .25
❑ 36 Mike Rozier .30 .10
❑ 37 Lou Groza .40 .15
❑ 38 Ted Hendricks .30 .10
❑ 39 Elroy Hirsch .40 .15
❑ 40 Paul Hornung .75 .30
❑ 41 Charlie Joiner .40 .15
❑ 42 Deacon Jones .40 .15
❑ 43 Bill Bradley .30 .10
❑ 44 Floyd Little .30 .10
❑ 45 Willie Lanier .30 .10
❑ 46 Bob Lilly .40 .15
❑ 47 Sid Luckman .40 .15
❑ 48 John Mackey .30 .10
❑ 49 Don Maynard .40 .15
❑ 50 Mike McCormack .30 .10
❑ 51 Bobby Mitchell .40 .15
❑ 52 Ron Mix .40 .15
❑ 53 Marion Motley .30 .10
❑ 54 Leo Nomellini .40 .15
❑ 55 Mark Duper .30 .10
❑ 56 Mel Renfro .30 .10
❑ 57 Jim Otto .40 .15
❑ 58 Alan Page .40 .15
❑ 59 Joe Perry .40 .15
❑ 60 Andy Robustelli .30 .10
❑ 61 Lee Roy Selmon .40 .15
❑ 62 Jackie Smith .40 .15
❑ 63 Art Shell .40 .15
❑ 64 Jan Stenerud .30 .10
❑ 65 Gene Upshaw .40 .15
❑ 66 Y.A. Tittle .60 .25
❑ 67 Paul Warfield .60 .25
❑ 68 Kellen Winslow .40 .15
❑ 69 Randy White .40 .15
❑ 70 Larry Wilson .30 .10
❑ 71 Willie Wood .40 .15
❑ 72 Jack Ham .40 .15
❑ 73 Jack Youngblood .30 .10
❑ 74 Dan Abramowicz .30 .10
❑ 75 Dick Anderson .30 .10
❑ 76 Ken Anderson .40 .15
❑ 77 Steve Bartkowski .30 .10
❑ 78 Bill Bergey .30 .10
❑ 79 Rocky Bleier .40 .15
❑ 80 Cliff Branch .40 .15
❑ 81 John Brodie .30 .10
❑ 82 Bobby Bell .30 .10
❑ 83 Billy Cannon .30 .10
❑ 84 Gino Cappelletti .30 .10
❑ 85 Harold Carmichael .30 .10
❑ 86 Dave Casper .30 .10
❑ 87 Wes Chandler .30 .10
❑ 88 Todd Christensen .30 .10
❑ 89 Dwight Clark .40 .15
❑ 90 Mark Clayton .30 .10
❑ 91 Cris Collinsworth .30 .10
❑ 92 Roger Craig .40 .15
❑ 93 Randy Cross .30 .10
❑ 94 Isaac Curtis .30 .10
❑ 95 Mike Curtis .30 .10
❑ 96 Ben Davidson .30 .10
❑ 97 Fred Dean .30 .10
❑ 98 Tom Dempsey .30 .10
❑ 99 Eric Dickerson .40 .15
❑ 100 Lynn Dickey .30 .10
❑ 101 John McKay LL .30 .10
❑ 102 Carl Eller .30 .10
❑ 103 Chuck Foreman .30 .10
❑ 104 Russ Francis .30 .10
❑ 105 Joe Gibbs LL .40 .15
❑ 106 Gary Garrison .30 .10
❑ 107 Randy Gradishar .30 .10
❑ 108 L.C. Greenwood .40 .15
❑ 109 Rosey Grier .30 .10
❑ 110 Steve Grogan .30 .10
❑ 111 Ray Guy .30 .10
❑ 112 John Hadl .30 .10
❑ 113 Jim Hart .30 .10
❑ 114 George Halas LL .40 .15
❑ 115 Mike Haynes .30 .10
❑ 116 Charlie Hennigan .30 .10
❑ 117 Chuck Howley .30 .10
❑ 118 Harold Jackson .30 .10
❑ 119 Tom Jackson .30 .10
❑ 120 Ron Jaworski .30 .10
❑ 121 John Jefferson .30 .10
❑ 122 Billy Johnson .30 .10
❑ 123 Ed Too Tall Jones .40 .15
❑ 124 Jack Kemp 1.50 .60
❑ 125 Jim Kiick .30 .10
❑ 126 Billy Kilmer .40 .15
❑ 127 Jerry Kramer .40 .15
❑ 128 Paul Krause .30 .10
❑ 129 Daryle Lamonica .30 .10
❑ 130 Bill Walsh LL .40 .15
❑ 131 James Lofton .30 .10
❑ 132 Hank Stram LL .30 .10
❑ 133 Archie Manning .40 .15
❑ 134 Jim Marshall .30 .10
❑ 135 Harvey Martin .30 .10
❑ 136 Tommy McDonald .30 .10
❑ 137 Max McGee .40 .15
❑ 138 Reggie McKenzie .30 .10
❑ 139 Karl Mecklenburg .30 .10
❑ 140 Tom Landry LL .60 .25
❑ 141 Terry Metcalf .30 .10
❑ 142 Matt Millen .30 .10
❑ 143 Earl Morrall .30 .10
❑ 144 Mercury Morris .30 .10
❑ 145 Chuck Noll LL .40 .15
❑ 146 Joe Morris .30 .10
❑ 147 Mark Moseley .30 .10
❑ 148 Haven Moses .30 .10
❑ 149 Chuck Muncie .30 .10
❑ 150 Anthony Munoz .40 .15
❑ 151 Tommy Nobis .30 .10
❑ 152 Babe Parilli .30 .10
❑ 153 Drew Pearson .40 .15
❑ 154 Ozzie Newsome .30 .10
❑ 155 Jim Plunkett .40 .15
❑ 156 William Perry .30 .10
❑ 157 Johnny Robinson .30 .10
❑ 158 Ahmad Rashad .40 .15
❑ 159 George Rogers .30 .10
❑ 160 Sterling Sharpe .40 .15
❑ 161 Billy Sims .40 .15
❑ 162 Sid Gillman LL .30 .10
❑ 163 Mike Singletary .60 .25
❑ 164 Charlie Sanders .30 .10
❑ 165 Bubba Smith .30 .10
❑ 166 Ken Stabler 2.00 .75
❑ 167 Freddie Solomon .30 .10
❑ 168 John Stallworth .40 .15
❑ 169 Dwight Stephenson .40 .15
❑ 170 Vince Lombardi LL 1.00 .40
❑ 171 Weeb Ewbank LL .30 .10
❑ 172 Lionel Taylor .30 .10
❑ 173 Otis Taylor .30 .10
❑ 174 Joe Theismann .60 .25
❑ 175 Bob Trumpy .30 .10
❑ 176 Mike Webster .30 .10
❑ 177 Jim Zorn .30 .10
❑ 178 Joe Montana 5.00 2.00
❑ 179 Packers Superbowl SM .40 .15
❑ 180 Bart Starr SM 1.25 .50
❑ 181 Max McGee SM .40 .15
❑ 182 Joe Namath SM 1.50 .60
❑ 183 Johnny Unitas SM 1.25 .50
❑ 184 Len Dawson SM .40 .15
❑ 185 Chuck Howley SM .30 .10
❑ 186 Roger Staubach SM 1.50 .60
❑ 187 Paul Warfield SM .40 .15
❑ 188 Larry Csonka SM .40 .15
❑ 189 Fran Tarkenton SM .60 .25
❑ 190 Terry Bradshaw SM 1.50 .60
❑ 191 Ken Stabler SM .75 .30
❑ 192 Fred Biletnikoff SM .40 .15
❑ 193 Chuck Foreman SM .30 .10
❑ 194 Harvey Martin SM .30 .10
❑ 195 Tony Dorsett SM .40 .15
❑ 196 Terry Bradshaw SM 1.50 .60
❑ 197 John Stallworth SM .30 .10
❑ 198 Franco Harris SM .40 .15
❑ 199 Ken Anderson SM .30 .10
❑ 200 Joe Theismann SM .40 .15
❑ 201 Jim Plunkett SM .30 .10
❑ 202 Roger Craig SM .30 .10
❑ 203 William Perry SM .30 .10
❑ 204 Steve Grogan SM .30 .10
❑ 205 Joe Montana SM 2.50 1.00
❑ 206 Russ Francis SM .30 .10
❑ 207 Joe Montana SM 2.50 1.00
❑ 208 Joe Montana SM 2.50 1.00

2000 Upper Deck Legends

❑ COMPLETE SET (132) 400.00 200.00
❑ COMP.SET w/o SP's (90) 20.00 7.50
❑ 1 Jake Plummer .30 .10
❑ 2 Jamal Anderson .50 .20
❑ 3 Doug Flutie .50 .20
❑ 4 Jim Kelly .60 .25
❑ 5 Dick Butkus 1.00 .40
❑ 6 Mike Singletary .50 .20
❑ 7 Gale Sayers 1.00 .40
❑ 8 Boomer Esiason .30 .10
❑ 9 Anthony Munoz .30 .10
❑ 10 Otto Graham .30 .10
❑ 11 Jim Brown 1.25 .50
❑ 12 Ozzie Newsome .20 .07
❑ 13 Bob Lilly .30 .10
❑ 14 Troy Aikman 1.25 .50
❑ 15 Emmitt Smith 1.25 .50
❑ 16 Roger Staubach 1.25 .50
❑ 17 Deion Sanders .50 .20
❑ 18 Tony Dorsett .50 .20
❑ 19 Terrell Davis .50 .20
❑ 20 John Elway 2.00 .75
❑ 21 Charlie Batch .50 .20
❑ 22 Brett Favre 2.00 .75
❑ 23 Bart Starr 1.50 .60
❑ 24 Reggie White .50 .20
❑ 25 Earl Campbell .50 .20
❑ 26 Peyton Manning 1.50 .60
❑ 27 Edgerrin James 1.00 .40
❑ 28 Johnny Unitas 1.25 .50
❑ 29 Marvin Harrison .50 .20
❑ 30 Mark Brunell .50 .20
❑ 31 Fred Taylor .50 .20
❑ 32 Len Dawson .50 .20
❑ 33 Dan Marino 2.00 .75
❑ 34 Bob Griese .50 .20
❑ 35 Mark Duper .20 .07
❑ 36 Thurman Thomas .30 .10
❑ 37 Fran Tarkenton 1.00 .40
❑ 38 Randy Moss 1.25 .50
❑ 39 Cris Carter .50 .20
❑ 40 Gary Anderson .20 .07
❑ 41 John Randle .30 .10
❑ 42 Drew Bledsoe .75 .30
❑ 43 Archie Manning .30 .10
❑ 44 Ricky Williams .50 .20
❑ 45 Frank Gifford .50 .20
❑ 46 Kerry Collins .30 .10
❑ 47 Phil Simms .30 .10
❑ 48 Vinny Testaverde .30 .10
❑ 49 Curtis Martin .50 .20
❑ 50 Keyshawn Johnson .50 .20
❑ 51 Joe Namath 1.25 .50
❑ 52 Marcus Allen .60 .25
❑ 53 Bruce Smith .30 .10
❑ 54 Ken Stabler 1.25 .50
❑ 55 Fred Biletnikoff .50 .20

❑ 56 Howie Long .60 .25
❑ 57 Ron Jaworski .20 .07
❑ 58 Harold Carmichael .20 .07
❑ 59 Kordell Stewart .30 .10
❑ 60 Levon Kirkland .20 .07
❑ 61 Mel Blount .30 .10
❑ 62 Jerome Bettis .50 .20
❑ 63 John Stallworth .30 .10
❑ 64 Franco Harris .60 .25
❑ 65 Jim Harbaugh .30 .10
❑ 66 Kellen Winslow .30 .10
❑ 67 Charlie Joiner .20 .07
❑ 68 Junior Seau .50 .20
❑ 69 Jerry Rice 1.25 .50
❑ 70 Steve Young 1.00 .40
❑ 71 Joe Montana 2.50 1.00
❑ 72 Roger Craig .30 .10
❑ 73 Ronnie Lott .30 .10
❑ 74 Jon Kitna .50 .20
❑ 75 Steve Largent .50 .20
❑ 76 Ricky Watters .30 .10
❑ 77 Kurt Warner 1.25 .50
❑ 78 Marshall Faulk .75 .30
❑ 79 Isaac Bruce .50 .20
❑ 80 Merlin Olsen .30 .10
❑ 81 Lee Roy Selmon .20 .07
❑ 82 Tim Brown .50 .20
❑ 83 Tim Couch .30 .10
❑ 84 Mike Alstott .50 .20
❑ 85 Eddie George .50 .20
❑ 86 Steve McNair .50 .20
❑ 87 Brad Johnson .50 .20
❑ 88 Sonny Jurgensen .50 .20
❑ 89 Art Monk .30 .10
❑ 90 Joe Theismann .50 .20
❑ 91 Ray Nitschke TCL 10.00 4.00
❑ 92 Doak Walker TCL 10.00 4.00
❑ 93 Thurman Thomas TCL 10.00 4.00
❑ 94 Jim Brown TCL 12.00 5.00
❑ 95 Sammy Baugh TCL 15.00 6.00
❑ 96 Reggie White TCL 10.00 4.00
❑ 97 Eric Dickerson TCL 10.00 4.00
❑ 98 Paul Hornung TCL 10.00 4.00
❑ 99 Deion Sanders TCL 12.00 5.00
❑ 100 Bronko Nagurski TCL 10.00 4.00
❑ 101 Walter Payton TCL 25.00 12.50
❑ 102 Jim Thorpe TCL 12.00 5.00
❑ 103 Ron Dayne RC 6.00 2.50
❑ 104 Tim Rattay RC 6.00 2.50
❑ 105 Brian Urlacher RC 25.00 10.00
❑ 106 Bubba Franks RC 6.00 2.50
❑ 107 Chad Pennington RC 15.00 6.00
❑ 108 Chris Cole RC 5.00 2.00
❑ 109 Chris Redman RC 5.00 2.00
❑ 110 Courtney Brown RC 6.00 2.50
❑ 111 Curtis Keaton RC 5.00 2.00
❑ 112 Dennis Northcutt RC 10.00 4.00
❑ 113 Dez White RC 6.00 2.50
❑ 114 Giovanni Carmazzi RC 10.00 4.00
❑ 115 J.R. Redmond RC 5.00 2.00
❑ 116 JaJuan Dawson RC 10.00 4.00
❑ 117 Jamal Lewis RC 15.00 6.00
❑ 118 Jerry Porter RC 8.00 3.00
❑ 119 Laveranues Coles RC 8.00 3.00
❑ 120 Peter Warrick RC 6.00 2.50
❑ 121 Plaxico Burress RC 12.00 5.00
❑ 122 R.Jay Soward RC 5.00 2.00
❑ 123 Reuben Droughns RC 8.00 3.00
❑ 124 Ron Dixon RC 5.00 2.00
❑ 125 Ron Dugans RC 10.00 4.00
❑ 126 Shaun Alexander RC 30.00 12.50
❑ 127 Sylvester Morris RC 5.00 2.00
❑ 128 Thomas Jones RC 10.00 4.00
❑ 129 Todd Pinkston RC 6.00 2.50
❑ 130 Travis Prentice RC 5.00 2.00
❑ 131 Travis Taylor RC 10.00 4.00
❑ 132 Trung Canidate RC 5.00 2.00

2001 Upper Deck Legends

❑ COMP.SET w/o SP's (90) 30.00 12.50
❑ 1 Jake Plummer .50 .20
❑ 2 Jamal Anderson .75 .30
❑ 3 Ray Lewis .75 .30
❑ 4 Johnny Unitas 1.50 .60
❑ 5 Jamal Lewis 1.50 .60
❑ 6 Andre Reed .50 .20
❑ 7 Jim Kelly 1.25 .50
❑ 8 Thurman Thomas .50 .20
❑ 9 Rob Johnson .50 .20
❑ 10 Brian Urlacher 1.50 .60
❑ 11 Dick Butkus 1.50 .60
❑ 12 Gale Sayers 1.50 .60
❑ 13 James Allen .50 .20
❑ 14 Corey Dillon .75 .30
❑ 15 Jim Brown 1.50 .60
❑ 16 Tim Couch .50 .20
❑ 17 Joey Galloway .50 .20
❑ 18 Emmitt Smith 2.00 .75
❑ 19 Randy White .50 .20
❑ 20 Roger Staubach 1.50 .60
❑ 21 Troy Aikman 1.50 .60
❑ 22 Tony Dorsett .75 .30
❑ 23 Brian Griese .75 .30
❑ 24 Floyd Little .30 .10
❑ 25 John Elway 3.00 1.25
❑ 26 Mike Anderson .75 .30
❑ 27 Terrell Davis .75 .30
❑ 28 Barry Sanders 2.00 .75
❑ 29 Charlie Batch .75 .30
❑ 30 Bart Starr 2.00 .75
❑ 31 Paul Hornung .75 .30
❑ 32 Reggie White .75 .30
❑ 33 Warren Moon .75 .30
❑ 34 Edgerrin James 1.25 .50
❑ 35 Peyton Manning 2.50 1.00
❑ 36 Mark Brunell .75 .30
❑ 37 Tony Gonzalez .50 .20
❑ 38 Eric Dickerson .50 .20
❑ 39 Jack Youngblood .30 .10
❑ 40 Jay Fiedler .75 .30
❑ 41 Lamar Smith .50 .20
❑ 42 Dan Marino 3.00 1.25
❑ 43 Oronde Gadsden .50 .20
❑ 44 Cris Carter .75 .30
❑ 45 Fran Tarkenton 1.25 .50
❑ 46 Daunte Culpepper .75 .30
❑ 47 Randy Moss 2.00 .75
❑ 48 Robert Smith .30 .10
❑ 49 Drew Bledsoe 1.25 .50
❑ 50 Archie Manning .50 .20
❑ 51 Jeff Blake .50 .20
❑ 52 Ricky Williams .75 .30
❑ 53 Kerry Collins .50 .20
❑ 54 Ron Dayne .75 .30
❑ 55 Lawrence Taylor .75 .30
❑ 56 Wayne Chrebet .50 .20
❑ 57 Vinny Testaverde .50 .20
❑ 58 Joe Namath 1.50 .60
❑ 59 Jim Plunkett .50 .20
❑ 60 George Blanda .75 .30
❑ 61 Tim Brown .75 .30
❑ 62 Jerry Rice 2.00 .75
❑ 63 Ken Stabler 1.50 .60
❑ 64 Marcus Allen 1.25 .50
❑ 65 Donovan McNabb 1.25 .50
❑ 66 Harold Carmichael .30 .10
❑ 67 Franco Harris 1.25 .50
❑ 68 Jerome Bettis .75 .30
❑ 69 Terry Bradshaw 1.50 .60
❑ 70 Doug Flutie .75 .30
❑ 71 Lance Alworth .50 .20
❑ 72 Junior Seau .75 .30
❑ 73 Kellen Winslow .50 .20
❑ 74 Dan Fouts .75 .30
❑ 75 Joe Montana 5.00 2.00
❑ 76 Terrell Owens .75 .30
❑ 77 Jeff Garcia .75 .30
❑ 78 Steve Young 1.25 .50
❑ 79 Matt Hasselbeck .50 .20
❑ 80 Kurt Warner 2.00 .75
❑ 81 Marshall Faulk 1.25 .50
❑ 82 Brad Johnson .75 .30
❑ 83 Eddie George .75 .30
❑ 84 Charley Taylor .50 .20
❑ 85 Stephen Davis .75 .30
❑ 86 Jeff George .50 .20
❑ 87 John Riggins 1.25 .50
❑ 88 Joe Theismann .75 .30
❑ 89 Michael Westbrook .50 .20
❑ 90 Sonny Jurgensen .75 .30
❑ 91 Andre Carter RC 8.00 3.00
❑ 92 Cedrick Wilson RC 8.00 3.00
❑ 93 Kevan Barlow RC 8.00 3.00
❑ 94 Anthony Thomas RC 8.00 3.00
❑ 95 David Terrell RC [illegible] [illegible]
❑ 96 Chad Johnson RC 20.00 7.50
❑ 97 Justin Smith RC 8.00 3.00
❑ 98 Rudi Johnson RC 15.00 6.00
❑ 99 T.J. Houshmandzadeh RC 10.00 4.00
❑ 100 Brandon Spoon RC 8.00 3.00
❑ 101 Nate Clements RC 8.00 3.00
❑ 102 Travis Henry RC 15.00 6.00
❑ 103 Kevin Kasper RC 8.00 3.00
❑ 104 Willie Middlebrooks RC 5.00 2.00
❑ 105 Gerard Warren RC 8.00 3.00
❑ 106 James Jackson RC 8.00 3.00
❑ 107 Quincy Morgan RC 8.00 3.00
❑ 108 Bobby Newcombe RC 5.00 2.00
❑ 109 Arnold Jackson RC 5.00 2.00
❑ 110 Carlos Polk RC 3.00 1.25
❑ 111 Drew Brees RC 25.00 10.00
❑ 112 LaDainian Tomlinson RC 60.00 30.00
❑ 113 Tay Cody RC 3.00 1.25
❑ 114 Zeke Moreno RC 8.00 3.00
❑ 115 Snoop Minnis RC 5.00 2.00
❑ 116 George Layne RC 5.00 2.00
❑ 117 Derrick Blaylock RC 8.00 3.00
❑ 118 Reggie Wayne RC 15.00 6.00
❑ 119 Tony Dixon RC 5.00 2.00
❑ 120 Quincy Carter RC 8.00 3.00
❑ 121 Chris Chambers RC 12.00 5.00
❑ 122 Jamar Fletcher RC 5.00 2.00
❑ 123 Josh Heupel RC 8.00 3.00
❑ 124 Travis Minor RC 5.00 2.00
❑ 125 A.J. Feeley RC [illegible] [illegible]
❑ 126 Correll Buckhalter RC 10.00 4.00
❑ 127 Freddie Mitchell RC 8.00 3.00
❑ 128 Alge Crumpler RC 10.00 4.00
❑ 129 Michael Vick RC 25.00 10.00
❑ 130 Vinny Sutherland RC 5.00 2.00
❑ 131 Marcus Stroud RC 8.00 3.00
❑ 132 Mike McMahon RC 8.00 3.00
❑ 133 Scotty Anderson RC 5.00 2.00
❑ 134 Shaun Rogers RC 8.00 3.00
❑ 135 Jesse Palmer RC 8.00 3.00
❑ 136 Will Allen RC 5.00 2.00
❑ 137 LaMont Jordan RC 15.00 6.00
❑ 138 Santana Moss RC 12.00 5.00
❑ 139 Reggie White RC 5.00 2.00
❑ 140 Jamal Reynolds RC 8.00 3.00
❑ 141 Robert Ferguson RC 8.00 3.00
❑ 142 Torrance Marshall RC 8.00 3.00
❑ 143 Chris Weinke RC 8.00 3.00
❑ 144 Dan Morgan RC 8.00 3.00
❑ 145 Steve Smith RC 20.00 7.50
❑ 146 Dee Brown RC 8.00 3.00
❑ 147 Arther Love RC 3.00 1.25
❑ 148 Hakim Akbar RC 3.00 1.25
❑ 149 Jabari Holloway RC 5.00 2.00
❑ 150 Derek Combs RC 5.00 2.00
❑ 151 Derrick Gibson RC 5.00 2.00
❑ 152 Ken-Yon Rambo RC 5.00 2.00
❑ 153 Marques Tuiasosopo RC 8.00 3.00
❑ 154 Adam Archuleta RC 8.00 3.00
❑ 155 Tommy Polley RC 8.00 3.00

❑ 156 Brian Allen RC	3.00	1.25
❑ 157 Milton Wynn RC	5.00	2.00
❑ 158 Francis St.Paul RC	5.00	2.00
❑ 159 Edgerton Hartwell RC	3.00	1.25
❑ 160 Gary Baxter RC	5.00	2.00
❑ 161 Todd Heap RC	8.00	3.00
❑ 162 Chris Barnes RC	5.00	2.00
❑ 163 Fred Smoot RC	8.00	3.00
❑ 164 Rod Gardner RC	8.00	3.00
❑ 165 Sage Rosenfels RC	8.00	3.00
❑ 166 Damerien McCants RC	5.00	2.00
❑ 167 Deuce McAllister RC	15.00	6.00
❑ 168 Moran Norris RC	3.00	1.25
❑ 169 Sedrick Hodge RC	3.00	1.25
❑ 170 Alex Bannister RC	5.00	2.00
❑ 171 Heath Evans RC	5.00	2.00
❑ 172 Josh Booty RC	8.00	3.00
❑ 173 Ken Lucas RC	5.00	2.00
❑ 174 Koren Robinson RC	8.00	3.00
❑ 175 Chris Taylor RC	5.00	2.00
❑ 176 Andre Dyson RC	3.00	1.25
❑ 177 Dan Alexander RC	8.00	3.00
❑ 178 Justin McCareins RC	8.00	3.00
❑ 179 Eddie Berlin RC	5.00	2.00
❑ 180 Michael Bennett RC	8.00	3.00

2004 Upper Deck Legends

❑ COMP.SET w/o SP's (90)	20.00	7.50
❑ 91-110 LEGENDS/1250 ODDS 1:24		
❑ 111-190 ROOKIE/650 ODDS 1:12		
❑ 1 Josh McCown	.50	.20
❑ 2 Emmitt Smith	1.50	.60
❑ 3 Michael Vick	1.50	.60
❑ 4 Peerless Price	.50	.20
❑ 5 Ray Lewis	.75	.30
❑ 6 Kyle Boller	.75	.30
❑ 7 Deion Sanders	.75	.30
❑ 8 Drew Bledsoe	.75	.30
❑ 9 Travis Henry	.50	.20
❑ 10 Eric Moulds	.50	.20
❑ 11 Steve Smith	.75	.30
❑ 12 Stephen Davis	.50	.20
❑ 13 Jake Delhomme	.75	.30
❑ 14 Rex Grossman	.75	.30
❑ 15 Brian Urlacher	1.00	.40
❑ 16 Thomas Jones	.50	.20
❑ 17 Chad Johnson	.75	.30
❑ 18 Rudi Johnson	.50	.20
❑ 19 Carson Palmer	1.00	.40
❑ 20 William Green	.50	.20
❑ 21 Andre Davis	.30	.10
❑ 22 Jeff Garcia	.75	.30
❑ 23 Roy Williams S	.50	.20
❑ 24 Eddie George	.50	.20
❑ 25 Keyshawn Johnson	.50	.20
❑ 26 Reuben Droughns	.50	.20
❑ 27 Jake Plummer	.50	.20
❑ 28 Champ Bailey	.50	.20
❑ 29 Charles Rogers	.50	.20
❑ 30 Joey Harrington	.75	.30
❑ 31 Ahman Green	.75	.30
❑ 32 Brett Favre	2.00	.75
❑ 33 Javon Walker	.50	.20
❑ 34 David Carr	.75	.30
❑ 35 Domanick Davis	.75	.30
❑ 36 Andre Johnson	.75	.30
❑ 37 Marvin Harrison	.75	.30
❑ 38 Edgerrin James	.75	.30
❑ 39 Peyton Manning	1.25	.50
❑ 40 Byron Leftwich	1.00	.40
❑ 41 Fred Taylor	.50	.20
❑ 42 Trent Green	.50	.20
❑ 43 Tony Gonzalez	.50	.20
❑ 44 Priest Holmes	1.00	.40
❑ 45 Zach Thomas	.75	.30
❑ 46 Chris Chambers	.50	.20
❑ 47 Jay Fiedler	.30	.10
❑ 48 Daunte Culpepper	.75	.30
❑ 49 Randy Moss	1.00	.40
❑ 50 Onterrio Smith	.50	.20
❑ 51 Tom Brady	2.00	.75
❑ 52 Deion Branch	.75	.30
❑ 53 Corey Dillon	.50	.20
❑ 54 Deuce McAllister	.75	.30
❑ 55 Aaron Brooks	.50	.20
❑ 56 Joe Horn	.50	.20
❑ 57 Tiki Barber	.75	.30
❑ 58 Kurt Warner	.75	.30
❑ 59 Jeremy Shockey	.75	.30
❑ 60 Chad Pennington	.75	.30
❑ 61 Santana Moss	.50	.20
❑ 62 Curtis Martin	.75	.30
❑ 63 Kerry Collins	.50	.20
❑ 64 Jerry Rice	1.50	.60
❑ 65 Jerry Porter	.50	.20
❑ 66 Terrell Owens	.75	.30
❑ 67 Jevon Kearse	.50	.20
❑ 68 Donovan McNabb	1.00	.40
❑ 69 Hines Ward	.75	.30
❑ 70 Plaxico Burress	.50	.20
❑ 71 Duce Staley	.50	.20
❑ 72 Drew Brees	.75	.30
❑ 73 LaDainian Tomlinson	1.00	.40
❑ 74 Tim Rattay	.30	.10
❑ 75 Brandon Lloyd	.50	.20
❑ 76 Kevan Barlow	.50	.20
❑ 77 Shaun Alexander	.75	.30
❑ 78 Koren Robinson	.50	.20
❑ 79 Matt Hasselbeck	.50	.20
❑ 80 Marshall Faulk	.75	.30
❑ 81 Torry Holt	.75	.30
❑ 82 Marc Bulger	.75	.30
❑ 83 Brian Griese	.50	.20
❑ 84 Derrick Brooks	.50	.20
❑ 85 Steve McNair	.75	.30
❑ 86 Derrick Mason	.50	.20
❑ 87 Chris Brown	.75	.30
❑ 88 Mark Brunell	.50	.20
❑ 89 Laveranues Coles	.50	.20
❑ 90 Clinton Portis	.75	.30
❑ 91 Dick Butkus	8.00	3.00
❑ 92 Gale Sayers	6.00	2.50
❑ 93 Mike Ditka	5.00	2.00
❑ 94 Jim Brown	8.00	3.00
❑ 95 Roger Staubach	8.00	3.00
❑ 96 Troy Aikman	6.00	2.50
❑ 97 John Elway	8.00	3.00
❑ 98 Barry Sanders	8.00	3.00
❑ 99 Bart Starr	10.00	4.00
❑ 100 Paul Hornung	5.00	2.00
❑ 101 Len Dawson	5.00	2.00
❑ 102 Dan Marino	10.00	4.00
❑ 103 Fran Tarkenton	6.00	2.50
❑ 104 Archie Manning	5.00	2.00
❑ 105 Joe Namath	8.00	3.00
❑ 106 Ken Stabler	6.00	2.50
❑ 107 Lynn Swann	6.00	2.50
❑ 108 Terry Bradshaw	8.00	3.00
❑ 109 Joe Montana	12.00	5.00
❑ 110 Joe Theismann	5.00	2.00
❑ 111 Bernard Berrian RC	6.00	2.50
❑ 112 Ben Hartsock RC	5.00	2.00
❑ 113 Karlos Dansby RC	5.00	2.00
❑ 114 Thomas Tapeh RC	4.00	1.50
❑ 115 Keary Colbert RC	5.00	2.00
❑ 116 Ben Troupe RC	5.00	2.00
❑ 117 Jonathan Vilma RC	5.00	2.00
❑ 118 Jamaar Taylor RC	5.00	2.00
❑ 119 Ben Roethlisberger RC	40.00	15.00
❑ 120 Samie Parker RC	5.00	2.00
❑ 121 Dunta Robinson RC	5.00	2.00
❑ 122 Dontarrious Thomas RC	5.00	2.00
❑ 123 Adimchinobe Echemandu RC	4.00	1.50
❑ 124 Darius Watts RC	5.00	2.00
❑ 125 Ben Watson RC	5.00	2.00
❑ 126 Terry Johnson RC	4.00	1.50
❑ 127 D.J. Hackett RC	4.00	1.50
❑ 128 Devery Henderson RC	5.00	2.00
❑ 129 Kellen Winslow Jr. RC	10.00	4.00
❑ 130 Travis LaBoy RC	5.00	2.00
❑ 131 Maurice Mann RC	4.00	1.50
❑ 132 Rashaun Woods RC	5.00	2.00
❑ 133 Michael Turner RC	6.00	2.50
❑ 134 Junior Siavii RC	5.00	2.00
❑ 135 Johnnie Morant RC	5.00	2.00
❑ 136 Larry Fitzgerald RC	15.00	6.00
❑ 137 Kevin Jones RC	12.00	5.00
❑ 138 Will Smith RC	5.00	2.00
❑ 139 Robert Gallery RC	5.00	2.00
❑ 140 Michael Jenkins RC	5.00	2.00
❑ 141 Cedric Cobbs RC	5.00	2.00
❑ 142 Igor Olshansky RC	5.00	2.00
❑ 143 Josh Harris RC	5.00	2.00
❑ 144 Michael Clayton RC	10.00	4.00
❑ 145 Mewelde Moore RC	5.00	2.00
❑ 146 Jason Babin RC	5.00	2.00
❑ 147 Cody Pickett RC	5.00	2.00
❑ 148 Lee Evans RC	6.00	2.50
❑ 149 Greg Jones RC	5.00	2.00
❑ 150 Marcus Tubbs RC	5.00	2.00
❑ 151 Craig Krenzel RC	5.00	2.00
❑ 152 Roy Williams RC	12.00	5.00
❑ 153 Tatum Bell RC	10.00	4.00
❑ 154 Kenechi Udeze RC	5.00	2.00
❑ 155 Shawn Andrews RC	5.00	2.00
❑ 156 Reggie Williams RC	6.00	2.50
❑ 157 Julius Jones RC	15.00	6.00
❑ 158 Vince Wilfork RC	5.00	2.00
❑ 159 Vernon Carey RC	4.00	1.50
❑ 160 Eli Manning RC	30.00	12.50
❑ 161 Devard Darling RC	5.00	2.00
❑ 162 Sean Taylor RC	5.00	2.00
❑ 163 Teddy Lehman RC	5.00	2.00
❑ 164 Jammal Lord RC	5.00	2.00
❑ 165 J.P. Losman RC	10.00	4.00
❑ 166 Jerricho Cotchery RC	5.00	2.00
❑ 167 Ahmad Carroll RC	5.00	2.00
❑ 168 Michael Boulware RC	5.00	2.00
❑ 169 Quincy Wilson RC	4.00	1.50
❑ 170 Derrick Hamilton RC	4.00	1.50
❑ 171 Kris Wilson RC	5.00	2.00
❑ 172 D.J. Williams RC	5.00	2.00
❑ 173 P.K. Sam RC	4.00	1.50
❑ 174 Matt Schaub RC	15.00	6.00
❑ 175 Ernest Wilford RC	5.00	2.00
❑ 176 Chris Gamble RC	5.00	2.00
❑ 177 Courtney Watson RC	5.00	2.00
❑ 178 Drew Henson RC	5.00	2.00
❑ 179 Chris Perry RC	6.00	2.50
❑ 180 Tommie Harris RC	5.00	2.00
❑ 181 Marquis Cooper RC	4.00	1.50
❑ 182 Philip Rivers RC	15.00	6.00
❑ 183 Carlos Francis RC	4.00	1.50
❑ 184 DeAngelo Hall RC	6.00	2.50
❑ 185 Daryl Smith RC	5.00	2.00
❑ 186 Troy Fleming RC	4.00	1.50
❑ 187 Luke McCown RC	5.00	2.00
❑ 188 Steven Jackson RC	15.00	6.00
❑ 189 Ricardo Colclough RC	5.00	2.00
❑ 190 Gilbert Gardner RC	4.00	1.50

2005 Upper Deck Legends

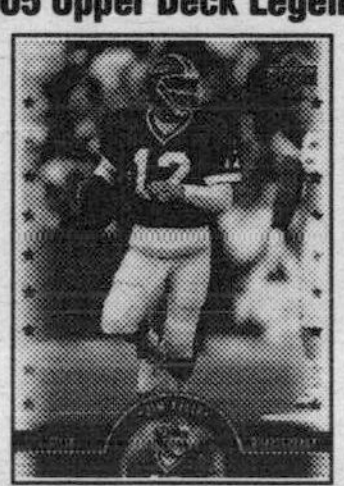

❑ COMP.SET w/o SP's (100)	20.00	7.50
❑ ROOKIE PRINT RUN 725 SER.#'d SETS		
❑ 100-195 LEG.PRINT RUN 1025 SER.#'d SETS		
❑ 1 Charley Taylor	.50	.20
❑ 2 Roger Craig	.50	.20
❑ 3 Ozzie Newsome	.50	.20
❑ 4 Rocky Bleier	.75	.30
❑ 5 Russ Francis	.40	.15
❑ 6 Jerry Rice	1.50	.60
❑ 7 Pat Haden	.40	.15
❑ 8 Brett Favre	2.00	.75
❑ 9 Joe Ferguson	.40	.15
❑ 10 Ed Jones	.50	.20
❑ 11 Joe Washington	.40	.15
❑ 12 John Brodie	.40	.15
❑ 13 Peyton Manning	1.25	.50
❑ 14 Mark Van Eeghen	.40	.15
❑ 15 William Perry	.50	.20
❑ 16 Bob Brown	.40	.15
❑ 17 Herb Adderley	.40	.15
❑ 18 Deion Sanders	1.00	.40
❑ 19 Lenny Moore	.50	.20
❑ 20 Tom Mack	.40	.15
❑ 21 Jim McMahon	.75	.30
❑ 22 Bobby Mitchell	.50	.20
❑ 23 John Mackey	.40	.15
❑ 24 Curtis Martin	.75	.30
❑ 25 Junior Seau	.50	.20
❑ 26 Harold Jackson	.40	.15
❑ 27 Jim Zorn	.40	.15
❑ 28 Chuck Foreman	.40	.15
❑ 29 Willie Brown	.40	.15
❑ 30 Cliff Branch	.50	.20
❑ 31 Jerry Kramer	.50	.20
❑ 32 Harry Carson	.40	.15
❑ 33 Chuck Noll	.50	.20
❑ 34 Len Hauss	.40	.15
❑ 35 Jim Plunkett	.50	.20
❑ 36 Ollie Matson	.50	.20
❑ 37 Billy Kilmer	.50	.20
❑ 38 Jim Marshall	.40	.15
❑ 39 Dan Dierdorf	.40	.15
❑ 40 Jim Kelly	1.00	.40
❑ 41 Vince Ferragamo	.40	.15
❑ 42 Ottis Anderson	.40	.15
❑ 43 Charlie Joiner	.40	.15
❑ 44 George Blanda	.75	.30
❑ 45 Drew Pearson	.50	.20
❑ 46 Andre Reed	.50	.20
❑ 47 Merlin Olsen	.50	.20
❑ 48 Paul Warfield	.50	.20
❑ 49 James Lofton	.40	.15
❑ 50 Art Donovan	.50	.20
❑ 51 Dwight Clark	.50	.20
❑ 52 Raymond Berry	.50	.20
❑ 53 L.C. Greenwood	.50	.20
❑ 54 Dave Casper	.40	.15
❑ 55 Don Maynard	.50	.20
❑ 56 Bud Grant	.40	.15
❑ 57 Roman Gabriel	.50	.20
❑ 58 Cris Collinsworth	.50	.20
❑ 59 Joe Theismann	.75	.30
❑ 60 Paul Hornung	.75	.30
❑ 61 Alan Page	.50	.20
❑ 62 Deacon Jones	.50	.20
❑ 63 Steve Largent	.75	.30
❑ 64 Phil Simms	.50	.20
❑ 65 Floyd Little	.40	.15
❑ 66 Archie Manning	.75	.30
❑ 67 Ken Stabler	1.00	.40
❑ 68 Fran Tarkenton	1.00	.40
❑ 69 Len Dawson	.75	.30
❑ 70 Mike Ditka	.75	.30
❑ 71 Conrad Dobler	.40	.15
❑ 72 Jack Lambert	.75	.30
❑ 73 Marcus Allen	.75	.30
❑ 74 Bo Jackson	1.00	.40
❑ 75 Jerome Bettis	.75	.30
❑ 76 Jack Ham	.50	.20
❑ 77 Marshall Faulk	.75	.30
❑ 78 Mike Singletary	.75	.30
❑ 79 Bob Griese	.75	.30
❑ 80 Dick Butkus	1.25	.50
❑ 81 Gale Sayers	1.00	.40
❑ 82 Earl Campbell	.75	.30
❑ 83 Dan Fouts	.75	.30
❑ 84 Franco Harris	1.00	.40
❑ 85 Steve Young	1.00	.40
❑ 86 Tony Dorsett	.75	.30
❑ 87 Jim Brown	1.25	.50
❑ 88 Roger Staubach	1.25	.50
❑ 89 Troy Aikman	1.00	.40
❑ 90 Barry Sanders	1.25	.50
❑ 91 Bernie Kosar	.50	.20
❑ 92 Dan Marino	2.00	.75
❑ 93 John Elway	1.25	.50
❑ 94 Randy Moss	.75	.30
❑ 95 Joe Montana	2.50	1.00
❑ 96 Joe Montana CL	1.25	.50
❑ 97 Dan Marino CL	1.00	.40
❑ 98 John Elway CL	.75	.30
❑ 99 Gale Sayers CL	.50	.20
❑ 100 Paul Hornung CL	.50	.20
❑ 101 Aaron Rodgers RC	15.00	6.00
❑ 102 Alex Smith QB RC	20.00	8.00
❑ 103 Cadillac Williams RC	20.00	8.00
❑ 104 Ronnie Brown RC	20.00	8.00
❑ 105 Ciatrick Fason RC	5.00	2.00
❑ 106 Charlie Frye RC	5.00	2.00
❑ 107 Derek Anderson RC	8.00	3.00
❑ 108 Braylon Edwards RC	15.00	6.00
❑ 109 Roddy White RC	6.00	2.00
❑ 110 Thomas Davis RC	5.00	2.00
❑ 111 Jason Campbell RC	8.00	3.00
❑ 112 Andrew Walter RC	5.00	2.00
❑ 113 Kyle Orton RC	5.00	2.00
❑ 114 David Greene RC	5.00	2.00
❑ 115 Cedric Benson RC	12.00	5.00
❑ 116 Vernand Morency RC	5.00	2.00
❑ 117 Eric Shelton RC	5.00	2.00
❑ 118 Maurice Clarett	5.00	2.00
❑ 119 Brandon Jacobs RC	6.00	2.50
❑ 120 Anthony Davis RC	4.00	1.50
❑ 121 Marion Barber RC	8.00	3.00
❑ 122 J.J. Arrington RC	5.00	2.00
❑ 123 Ryan Moats RC	5.00	2.00
❑ 124 Frank Gore RC	10.00	4.00
❑ 125 Stefan LeFors RC	5.00	2.00
❑ 126 Darren Sproles RC	5.00	2.00
❑ 127 Cedric Houston RC	5.00	2.00
❑ 128 Troy Williamson RC	5.00	2.00
❑ 129 Mark Clayton RC	5.00	2.00
❑ 130 Chris Henry RC	5.00	2.00
❑ 131 Fred Gibson RC	4.00	1.50
❑ 132 Craphonso Thorpe RC	4.00	1.50
❑ 133 Terrence Murphy RC	5.00	2.00
❑ 134 Dan Orlovsky RC	5.00	2.00
❑ 135 Roscoe Parrish RC	5.00	2.00
❑ 136 Reggie Brown RC	5.00	2.00
❑ 137 Craig Bragg RC	4.00	1.50
❑ 138 Larry Brackins RC	2.50	1.00
❑ 139 Adrian McPherson RC	5.00	2.00
❑ 140 Matt Jones RC	8.00	3.00
❑ 141 Heath Miller RC	10.00	4.00
❑ 142 Alex Smith TE RC	5.00	2.00
❑ 143 Kevin Everett RC	5.00	2.00
❑ 144 Jerome Mathis RC	5.00	2.00
❑ 145 Travis Johnson RC	4.00	1.50
❑ 146 Channing Crowder RC	5.00	2.00
❑ 147 Mike Williams	5.00	2.00
❑ 148 Barrett Ruud RC	5.00	2.00
❑ 149 Marcus Spears RC	5.00	2.00
❑ 150 Derrick Johnson RC	8.00	3.00
❑ 151 Shawne Merriman RC	8.00	3.00
❑ 152 Kevin Burnett RC	5.00	2.00
❑ 153 Erasmus James RC	5.00	2.00
❑ 154 Dan Cody RC	5.00	2.00
❑ 155 David Pollack RC	5.00	2.00
❑ 156 Antrel Rolle RC	5.00	2.00
❑ 157 Adam Jones RC	5.00	2.00
❑ 158 Mark Bradley RC	5.00	2.00
❑ 159 Carlos Rogers RC	6.00	2.50
❑ 160 Vincent Jackson RC	5.00	2.00
❑ 161 DeMarcus Ware RC	8.00	3.00
❑ 162 Corey Webster RC	5.00	2.00
❑ 163 Justin Miller RC	4.00	1.50
❑ 164 Eric Green RC	2.50	1.00
❑ 165 Marlin Jackson RC	5.00	2.00
❑ 166 Herb Adderley LH	3.00	1.25
❑ 167 Fran Tarkenton LH	6.00	2.50
❑ 168 Troy Aikman LH	6.00	2.50
❑ 169 Charlie Joiner LH	3.00	1.25
❑ 170 George Blanda LH	5.00	2.00
❑ 171 Jim Kelly LH	6.00	2.50
❑ 172 Joe Montana LH	12.00	5.00
❑ 173 Jack Ham LH	4.00	1.50
❑ 174 Marcus Allen LH	5.00	2.00
❑ 175 Tony Dorsett LH	5.00	2.00
❑ 176 Barry Sanders LH	8.00	3.00
❑ 177 Paul Warfield LH	4.00	1.50
❑ 178 Dan Marino LH	10.00	4.00
❑ 179 John Elway LH	8.00	3.00
❑ 180 Franco Harris LH	6.00	2.50
❑ 181 Mike Singletary LH	5.00	2.00
❑ 182 Gale Sayers LH	6.00	2.50
❑ 183 Bob Griese LH	5.00	2.00
❑ 184 Dan Fouts LH	5.00	2.00
❑ 185 Earl Campbell LH	5.00	2.00
❑ 186 Jim Brown LH	8.00	3.00
❑ 187 Dick Butkus LH	8.00	3.00
❑ 188 Paul Hornung LH	5.00	2.00
❑ 189 Roger Staubach LH	8.00	3.00
❑ 190 Steve Largent LH	5.00	2.00
❑ 191 Ryan Fitzpatrick RC	5.00	2.00
❑ 192 Alvin Pearman RC	5.00	2.00
❑ 193 Courtney Roby RC	5.00	2.00
❑ 194 Chase Lyman RC	4.00	1.50
❑ 195 Roydell Williams RC	5.00	2.00

2006 Upper Deck Legends

❑ COMP.SET w/o RC's (100)	20.00	8.00
❑ RC PRINT RUN 750 SER.#'d SETS		
❑ 1 Marshall Faulk	.50	.20
❑ 2 John Elway	1.25	.50
❑ 3 Barry Sanders	1.25	.50
❑ 4 Dan Marino	1.50	.60
❑ 5 Troy Aikman	1.00	.40
❑ 6 Roger Staubach	1.25	.50
❑ 7 Curtis Martin	.75	.30
❑ 8 O.J. McDuffie	.50	.20
❑ 9 Steve Young	1.00	.40
❑ 10 Jim Kelly	1.00	.40
❑ 11 Dan Fouts	.75	.30
❑ 12 Franco Harris	.75	.30
❑ 13 Christian Okoye	.50	.20
❑ 14 Craig Morton	.50	.20

❑ 15 Doug Flutie .50 .20
❑ 16 Gale Sayers 1.00 .40
❑ 17 Bob Griese .75 .30
❑ 18 Jim Plunkett .75 .30
❑ 19 Marvin Harrison .75 .30
❑ 20 L.C. Greenwood .50 .20
❑ 21 Len Dawson .75 .30
❑ 22 Ken Stabler 1.00 .40
❑ 23 Fran Tarkenton 1.00 .40
❑ 24 Herman Moore .40 .15
❑ 25 Joe Theismann .75 .30
❑ 26 Paul Hornung .75 .30
❑ 27 Herschel Walker .50 .20
❑ 28 Randy Moss .75 .30
❑ 29 Drew Pearson .50 .20
❑ 30 Don Maynard .50 .20
❑ 31 Dwight Clark .50 .20
❑ 32 Golden Richards .40 .15
❑ 33 Wesley Walker .50 .20
❑ 34 Greg Landry .40 .15
❑ 35 Mick Tingelhoff .40 .15
❑ 36 Ken O'Brien .40 .15
❑ 37 Emerson Boozer .40 .15
❑ 38 Reggie McKenzie .40 .15
❑ 39 Wally Hilgenberg .40 .15
❑ 40 Jan Stenerud .40 .15
❑ 41 Roger Craig .75 .30
❑ 42 Joe Cribbs .50 .20
❑ 43 Reggie Rucker .40 .15
❑ 44 Louis Lipps .40 .15
❑ 45 Rick Upchurch .40 .15
❑ 46 Ben Roethlisberger 1.50 .60
❑ 47 Rocket Ismail .50 .20
❑ 48 Gary Clark .50 .20
❑ 50 Dwight Stephenson .40 .15
❑ 51 Joe Klecko .40 .15
❑ 52 John Hannah .50 .20
❑ 53 John Cappelletti .50 .20
❑ 54 Tiki Barber .75 .30
❑ 55 Coy Bacon .40 .15
❑ 56 A.J. Duhe .40 .15
❑ 57 Brett Favre 2.00 .75
❑ 58 Jon Kolb .40 .15
❑ 59 Rich Saul .40 .15
❑ 60A Antonio Freeman .50 .20
❑ 60B Diron Talbert .40 .15
❑ 61 John Taylor .50 .20
❑ 62 Ron McDole .40 .15
❑ 63 Jethro Pugh .40 .15
❑ 64 Joe Jacoby .50 .20
❑ 65 Steve Smith .75 .30
❑ 66 Terrell Owens .75 .30
❑ 67 Charle Young .40 .15
❑ 68 Roy Jefferson .50 .20
❑ 69 Gary Fencik .40 .15
❑ 70 Terry Metcalf .50 .20
❑ 71 Johnny Rodgers .50 .20
❑ 72 Charles White .50 .20
❑ 73 Billy Sims .75 .30
❑ 74 Neal Anderson .50 .20
❑ 75 Marlin Briscoe .40 .15
❑ 76 Edgerrin James .75 .30
❑ 77 LaDainian Tomlinson 1.00 .40
❑ 78 Steve DeBerg .50 .20
❑ 79 Randy Grossman .50 .20
❑ 80 Ickey Woods .50 .20
❑ 81 Donovan McNabb .75 .30
❑ 82 Ron Mix .50 .20
❑ 83 Gerald Riggs Sr. .40 .15
❑ 84 Curt Warner .50 .20
❑ 85 Everson Walls .40 .15
❑ 86 Mike Quick .50 .20
❑ 87 Shaun Alexander .75 .30
❑ 88 Al Toon .50 .20
❑ 89 Nat Moore .50 .20
❑ 90 Michael Vick .75 .30
❑ 91 Carson Palmer .75 .30
❑ 92 Tom Brady 1.25 .50
❑ 93 Gary Garrison .40 .15
❑ 94 Fred Dean .40 .15
❑ 95 Bob Trumpy .50 .20
❑ 96 Doug Cosbie .50 .20
❑ 97 Tommy Kramer .50 .20
❑ 98 Peyton Manning 1.25 .50
❑ 99 John Brockington .50 .20
❑ 100 Stanley Morgan .50 .20
❑ 101 A.J. Hawk RC 12.00 5.00
❑ 102 Abdul Hodge RC 6.00 2.50
❑ 103 Antonio Cromartie RC 6.00 2.50
❑ 104 Anthony Fasano RC 6.00 2.50
❑ 105 Brandon Marshall RC 6.00 2.50
❑ 106 Ben Obomanu RC 5.00 2.00
❑ 107 Bobby Carpenter RC 6.00 2.50
❑ 108 Brad Smith RC 6.00 2.50
❑ 109 Erik Meyer RC 5.00 2.00
❑ 110 Brandon Williams RC 6.00 2.50
❑ 111 Brian Calhoun RC 6.00 2.50
❑ 112 Brodie Croyle RC 15.00 6.00
❑ 113 Frostee Rucker RC 5.00 2.00
❑ 114 Bruce Eugene RC 5.00 2.00
❑ 115 Bruce Gradkowski RC 10.00 4.00
❑ 116 Cedric Humes RC 6.00 2.50
❑ 117 Chad Greenway RC 6.00 2.50
❑ 118 Chad Jackson RC 6.00 2.50
❑ 119 Charles Davis RC 5.00 2.00
❑ 120 Charlie Whitehurst RC 6.00 2.50
❑ 121 Jason Allen RC 6.00 2.50
❑ 122 Cory Rodgers RC 6.00 2.50
❑ 123 Cory Ross RC 6.00 2.50
❑ 124 D.J. Shockley RC 6.00 2.50
❑ 125 Darnell Bing RC 6.00 2.50
❑ 126 Darrell Hackney RC 5.00 2.00
❑ 127 D'Brickashaw Ferguson RC 6.00 2.50
❑ 128 DeAngelo Williams RC 15.00 6.00
❑ 129 DeMeco Ryans RC 8.00 3.00
❑ 130 Demetrius Williams RC 6.00 2.50
❑ 131 Derek Hagan RC 6.00 2.50
❑ 132 Devin Aromashodu RC 5.00 2.00
❑ 133 Devin Hester RC 12.00 5.00
❑ 134 Dominique Byrd RC 5.00 2.00
❑ 135 Donte Whitner RC 6.00 2.50
❑ 136 DonTrell Moore RC 5.00 2.00
❑ 137 D'Qwell Jackson RC 5.00 2.00
❑ 138 Ernie Sims RC 8.00 3.00
❑ 139 John McCargo RC 5.00 2.00
❑ 140 Gerald Riggs Jr. RC 6.00 2.50
❑ 141 Greg Jennings RC 12.00 5.00
❑ 142 Greg Lee RC 5.00 2.00
❑ 143 Haloti Ngata RC 6.00 2.50
❑ 144 Johnathan Joseph RC 5.00 2.00
❑ 145 Jason Avant RC 6.00 2.50
❑ 146 Jay Cutler RC 20.00 8.00
❑ 147 Jeff King RC 5.00 2.00
❑ 148 Jeff Webb RC 5.00 2.00
❑ 149 Jeremy Bloom RC 5.00 2.00
❑ 150 Jerious Norwood RC 10.00 4.00
❑ 151 Jerome Harrison RC 6.00 2.50
❑ 152 Jimmy Williams RC 6.00 2.50
❑ 153 Joe Klopfenstein RC 5.00 2.00
❑ 154 Jonathan Orr RC 5.00 2.00
❑ 155 Joseph Addai RC 20.00 8.00
❑ 156 Josh Betts RC 5.00 2.00
❑ 157 Matt Baker RC 6.00 2.50
❑ 158 Kamerion Wimbley RC 6.00 2.50
❑ 159 Kellen Clemens RC 10.00 4.00
❑ 160 Ko Simpson RC 5.00 2.00
❑ 161 Laurence Maroney RC 15.00 6.00
❑ 162 Lawrence Vickers RC 5.00 2.00
❑ 163 LenDale White RC 12.00 5.00
❑ 164 Leon Washington RC 10.00 4.00
❑ 165 Leonard Pope RC 6.00 2.50
❑ 166 Marcedes Lewis RC 6.00 2.50
❑ 167 Marcus Vick RC 5.00 2.00
❑ 168 Mario Williams RC 10.00 4.00
❑ 169 Marques Hagans RC 5.00 2.00
❑ 170 Martin Nance RC 5.00 2.00
❑ 171 Mathias Kiwanuka RC 8.00 3.00
❑ 172 Matt Bernstein RC 3.00 1.25
❑ 173 Matt Leinart RC 20.00 8.00
❑ 174 Maurice Drew RC 15.00 6.00
❑ 175 Maurice Stovall RC 6.00 2.50
❑ 176 Michael Huff RC 8.00 3.00
❑ 177 Michael Robinson RC 6.00 2.50
❑ 178 Mike Hass RC 6.00 2.50
❑ 179 Miles Austin RC 5.00 2.00
❑ 180 Omar Jacobs RC 5.00 2.00
❑ 181 Owen Daniels RC 6.00 2.50
❑ 182 P.J. Daniels RC 5.00 2.00
❑ 183 Quinton Ganther RC 5.00 2.00
❑ 184 Reggie Bush RC 40.00 15.00
❑ 185 Reggie McNeal RC 5.00 2.00
❑ 186 Santonio Holmes RC 12.00 5.00
❑ 187 Sinorice Moss RC 6.00 2.50
❑ 188 Skyler Green RC 6.00 2.50
❑ 189 T.J. Williams RC 6.00 2.50
❑ 190 Tamba Hali RC 6.00 2.50
❑ 191 Manny Lawson RC 6.00 2.50
❑ 192 Tarvaris Jackson RC 10.00 4.00
❑ 193 Travis Wilson RC 6.00 2.50
❑ 194 Tye Hill RC 6.00 2.50
❑ 195 Vernon Davis RC 12.00 5.00
❑ 196 Vince Young RC 25.00 10.00
❑ 197 Wali Lundy RC 6.00 2.50
❑ 198 Wendell Mathis RC 5.00 2.00
❑ 199 Will Blackmon RC 5.00 2.00
❑ 200 Willie Reid RC 6.00 2.50

1999 Upper Deck MVP

❑ COMPLETE SET (220) 25.00 10.00
❑ 1 Jake Plummer .30 .10
❑ 2 Adrian Murrell .30 .10
❑ 3 Larry Centers .20 .07
❑ 4 Frank Sanders .30 .10
❑ 5 Andre Wadsworth .20 .07
❑ 6 Rob Moore .30 .10
❑ 7 Simeon Rice .30 .10
❑ 8 Jamal Anderson .50 .20
❑ 9 Chris Chandler .30 .10
❑ 10 Chuck Smith .20 .07
❑ 11 Terance Mathis .30 .10
❑ 12 Tim Dwight .50 .20
❑ 13 Ray Buchanan .20 .07
❑ 14 O.J. Santiago .20 .07
❑ 15 Eric Zeier .30 .10
❑ 16 Priest Holmes .75 .30
❑ 17 Michael Jackson .20 .07
❑ 18 Jermaine Lewis .30 .10
❑ 19 Michael McCrary .20 .07
❑ 20 Rob Johnson .30 .10
❑ 21 Antowain Smith .50 .20
❑ 22 Thurman Thomas .30 .10
❑ 23 Doug Flutie .50 .20
❑ 24 Eric Moulds .50 .20
❑ 25 Bruce Smith .30 .10
❑ 26 Andre Reed .30 .10
❑ 27 Fred Lane .20 .07
❑ 28 Tim Biakabutuka .30 .10
❑ 29 Rae Carruth .20 .07
❑ 30 Wesley Walls .30 .10
❑ 31 Steve Beuerlein .20 .07
❑ 32 Muhsin Muhammad .30 .10
❑ 33 Erik Kramer .20 .07
❑ 34 Edgar Bennett .20 .07
❑ 35 Curtis Conway .30 .10
❑ 36 Curtis Enis .20 .07
❑ 37 Bobby Engram .30 .10
❑ 38 Alonzo Mayes .20 .07
❑ 39 Corey Dillon .50 .20
❑ 40 Jeff Blake .30 .10
❑ 41 Carl Pickens .30 .10
❑ 42 Darnay Scott .20 .07
❑ 43 Tony McGee .20 .07
❑ 44 Ki-Jana Carter .20 .07
❑ 45 Ty Detmer .30 .10
❑ 46 Terry Kirby .20 .07

❑ 47 Justin Armour	.20	.07
❑ 48 Freddie Solomon	.20	.07
❑ 49 Marquez Pope	.20	.07
❑ 50 Antonio Langham	.20	.07
❑ 51 Troy Aikman	1.00	.40
❑ 52 Emmitt Smith	1.00	.40
❑ 53 Deion Sanders	.50	.20
❑ 54 Rocket Ismail	.30	.10
❑ 55 Michael Irvin	.30	.10
❑ 56 Chris Warren	.20	.07
❑ 57 Greg Ellis	.20	.07
❑ 58 John Elway	1.50	.60
❑ 59 Terrell Davis	.50	.20
❑ 60 Rod Smith	.30	.10
❑ 61 Shannon Sharpe	.30	.10
❑ 62 Ed McCaffrey	.30	.10
❑ 63 John Mobley	.20	.07
❑ 64 Bill Romanowski	.20	.07
❑ 65 Barry Sanders	1.50	.60
❑ 66 Johnnie Morton	.30	.10
❑ 67 Herman Moore	.30	.10
❑ 68 Charlie Batch	.50	.20
❑ 69 Germane Crowell	.20	.07
❑ 70 Robert Porcher	.20	.07
❑ 71 Brett Favre	1.50	.60
❑ 72 Antonio Freeman	.50	.20
❑ 73 Dorsey Levens	.50	.20
❑ 74 Mark Chmura	.30	.10
❑ 75 Vonnie Holliday	.20	.07
❑ 76 Bill Schroeder	.50	.20
❑ 77 Marshall Faulk	.60	.25
❑ 78 Marvin Harrison	.50	.20
❑ 79 Peyton Manning	1.50	.60
❑ 80 Jerome Pathon	.20	.07
❑ 81 E.G. Green	.20	.07
❑ 82 Ellis Johnson	.20	.07
❑ 83 Mark Brunell	.50	.20
❑ 84 Jimmy Smith	.30	.10
❑ 85 Keenan McCardell	.30	.10
❑ 86 Fred Taylor	.50	.20
❑ 87 James Stewart	.30	.10
❑ 88 Kevin Hardy	.20	.07
❑ 89 Elvis Grbac	.30	.10
❑ 90 Andre Rison	.30	.10
❑ 91 Derrick Alexander WR	.30	.10
❑ 92 Tony Gonzalez	.50	.20
❑ 93 Donnell Bennett	.20	.07
❑ 94 Derrick Thomas	.50	.20
❑ 95 Tamarick Vanover	.20	.07
❑ 96 Dan Marino	1.50	.60
❑ 97 Karim Abdul-Jabbar	.30	.10
❑ 98 Zach Thomas	.50	.20
❑ 99 O.J. McDuffie	.30	.10
❑ 100 John Avery	.20	.07
❑ 101 Sam Madison	.20	.07
❑ 102 Randall Cunningham	.50	.20
❑ 103 Cris Carter	.50	.20
❑ 104 Robert Smith	.50	.20
❑ 105 Randy Moss	1.25	.50
❑ 106 Jake Reed	.30	.10
❑ 107 Matthew Hatchette	.20	.07
❑ 108 John Randle	.30	.10
❑ 109 Drew Bledsoe	.60	.25
❑ 110 Terry Glenn	.50	.20
❑ 111 Ben Coates	.30	.10
❑ 112 Ty Law	.30	.10
❑ 113 Tony Simmons	.20	.07
❑ 114 Ted Johnson	.20	.07
❑ 115 Danny Wuerffel	.20	.07
❑ 116 Lamar Smith	.30	.10
❑ 117 Sean Dawkins	.20	.07
❑ 118 Cameron Cleeland	.20	.07
❑ 119 Joe Johnson	.20	.07
❑ 120 Andre Hastings	.20	.07
❑ 121 Kent Graham	.20	.07
❑ 122 Gary Brown	.20	.07
❑ 123 Amani Toomer	.20	.07
❑ 124 Tiki Barber	.50	.20
❑ 125 Ike Hilliard	.20	.07
❑ 126 Jason Sehorn	.20	.07
❑ 127 Vinny Testaverde	.30	.10
❑ 128 Curtis Martin	.50	.20
❑ 129 Keyshawn Johnson	.50	.20
❑ 130 Wayne Chrebet	.30	.10
❑ 131 Mo Lewis	.20	.07
❑ 132 Steve Atwater	.20	.07
❑ 133 Donald Hollas	.20	.07
❑ 134 Napoleon Kaufman	.50	.20
❑ 135 Tim Brown	.50	.20
❑ 136 Darrell Russell	.20	.07
❑ 137 Rickey Dudley	.20	.07
❑ 138 Charles Woodson	.50	.20
❑ 139 Koy Detmer	.20	.07
❑ 140 Duce Staley	.50	.20
❑ 141 Charlie Garner	.30	.10
❑ 142 Doug Pederson	.20	.07
❑ 143 Jeff Graham	.20	.07
❑ 144 Charles Johnson	.20	.07
❑ 145 Kordell Stewart	.30	.10
❑ 146 Jerome Bettis	.50	.20
❑ 147 Hines Ward	.50	.20
❑ 148 Courtney Hawkins	.20	.07
❑ 149 Will Blackwell	.20	.07
❑ 150 Richard Huntley	.30	.10
❑ 151 Levon Kirkland	.20	.07
❑ 152 Trent Green	.50	.20
❑ 153 Tony Banks	.30	.10
❑ 154 Isaac Bruce	.50	.20
❑ 155 Eddie Kennison	.30	.10
❑ 156 Az-Zahir Hakim	.20	.07
❑ 157 Amp Lee	.20	.07
❑ 158 Robert Holcombe	.20	.07
❑ 159 Ryan Leaf	.50	.20
❑ 160 Natrone Means	.30	.10
❑ 161 Jim Harbaugh	.30	.10
❑ 162 Junior Seau	.50	.20
❑ 163 Charlie Jones	.20	.07
❑ 164 Rodney Harrison	.20	.07
❑ 165 Steve Young	.60	.25
❑ 166 Jerry Rice	1.00	.40
❑ 167 Garrison Hearst	.30	.10
❑ 168 Terrell Owens	.50	.20
❑ 169 J.J. Stokes	.30	.10
❑ 170 Bryant Young	.20	.07
❑ 171 Ricky Watters	.30	.10
❑ 172 Joey Galloway	.30	.10
❑ 173 Jon Kitna	.50	.20
❑ 174 Ahman Green	.50	.20
❑ 175 Mike Pritchard	.20	.07
❑ 176 Chad Brown	.20	.07
❑ 177 Warrick Dunn	.50	.20
❑ 178 Trent Dilfer	.30	.10
❑ 179 Mike Alstott	.50	.20
❑ 180 Reidel Anthony	.30	.10
❑ 181 Bert Emanuel	.30	.10
❑ 182 Jacquez Green	.20	.07
❑ 183 Hardy Nickerson	.20	.07
❑ 184 Steve McNair	.50	.20
❑ 185 Eddie George	.50	.20
❑ 186 Yancey Thigpen	.20	.07
❑ 187 Frank Wycheck	.20	.07
❑ 188 Kevin Dyson	.30	.10
❑ 189 Jackie Harris	.20	.07
❑ 190 Blaine Bishop	.20	.07
❑ 191 Skip Hicks	.20	.07
❑ 192 Michael Westbrook	.30	.10
❑ 193 Stephen Alexander	.20	.07
❑ 194 Leslie Shepherd	.20	.07
❑ 195 Jeff Hostetler	.20	.07
❑ 196 Brian Mitchell	.20	.07
❑ 197 Dan Wilkinson	.20	.07
❑ 198 Terrell Davis CL	.50	.20
❑ 199 Troy Aikman CL	.50	.20
❑ 200 Tim Couch CL	.50	.20
❑ 201 Ricky Williams RC	2.50	1.00
❑ 202 Tim Couch RC	1.00	.40
❑ 203 Akili Smith RC	.75	.30
❑ 204 Daunte Culpepper RC	5.00	2.00
❑ 205 Torry Holt RC	3.00	1.25
❑ 206 Edgerrin James RC	5.00	2.00
❑ 207 David Boston RC	1.00	.40
❑ 208 Peerless Price RC	1.00	.40
❑ 209 Chris Claiborne RC	.50	.20
❑ 210 Champ Bailey RC	1.25	.50
❑ 211 Cade McNown RC	.75	.30
❑ 212 Jevon Kearse RC	1.50	.60
❑ 213 Joe Germaine RC	.75	.30
❑ 214 D'Wayne Bates RC	.75	.30
❑ 215 Dameane Douglas RC	.50	.20
❑ 216 Troy Edwards RC	.75	.30
❑ 217 Sedrick Irvin RC	.50	.20
❑ 218 Brock Huard RC	1.00	.40
❑ 219 Amos Zereoue RC	1.00	.40
❑ 220 Donovan McNabb RC	6.00	2.50

2000 Upper Deck MVP

❑ COMPLETE SET (218)	25.00	10.00
❑ 1 Jake Plummer	.30	.10
❑ 2 Michael Pittman	.20	.07
❑ 3 Rob Moore	.30	.10
❑ 4 David Boston	.50	.20
❑ 5 Frank Sanders	.30	.10
❑ 6 Aeneas Williams	.20	.07
❑ 7 Kwamie Lassiter	.20	.07
❑ 8 Tim Dwight	.50	.20
❑ 9 Chris Chandler	.30	.10
❑ 10 Jamal Anderson	.50	.20
❑ 11 Shawn Jefferson	.20	.07
❑ 12 Qadry Ismail	.30	.10
❑ 13 Jermaine Lewis	.20	.07
❑ 14 Rod Woodson	.30	.10
❑ 15 Michael McCrary	.20	.07
❑ 16 Tony Banks	.30	.10
❑ 17 Peter Boulware	.20	.07
❑ 18 Shannon Sharpe	.30	.10
❑ 19 Peerless Price	.30	.10
❑ 20 Rob Johnson	.30	.10
❑ 21 Eric Moulds	.50	.20
❑ 22 Doug Flutie	.50	.20
❑ 23 Muhsin Muhammad	.30	.10
❑ 24 Patrick Jeffers	.50	.20
❑ 25 Steve Beuerlein	.30	.10
❑ 26 Tim Biakabutuka	.30	.10
❑ 27 Michael Bates	.20	.07
❑ 28 Cade McNown	.20	.07
❑ 29 Curtis Enis	.20	.07
❑ 30 Marcus Robinson	.50	.20
❑ 31 Shane Matthews	.30	.10
❑ 32 Bobby Engram	.30	.10
❑ 33 Glyn Milburn	.20	.07
❑ 34 Akili Smith	.20	.07
❑ 35 Corey Dillon	.50	.20
❑ 36 Darnay Scott	.30	.10
❑ 37 Tremain Mack	.20	.07
❑ 38 Tim Couch	.30	.10
❑ 39 Kevin Johnson	.50	.20
❑ 40 Darrin Chiaverini	.20	.07
❑ 41 Jamir Miller	.20	.07
❑ 42 Errict Rhett	.30	.10
❑ 43 Troy Aikman	1.00	.40
❑ 44 Emmitt Smith	1.00	.40
❑ 45 Rocket Ismail	.30	.10
❑ 46 Jason Tucker	.20	.07
❑ 47 Dexter Coakley	.20	.07
❑ 48 Joey Galloway	.30	.10
❑ 49 Greg Ellis	.20	.07
❑ 50 Terrell Davis	.50	.20
❑ 51 Olandis Gary	.50	.20
❑ 52 Brian Griese	.50	.20
❑ 53 Ed McCaffrey	.50	.20
❑ 54 Rod Smith	.30	.10
❑ 55 Trevor Pryce	.20	.07
❑ 56 Charlie Batch	.50	.20
❑ 57 Germane Crowell	.20	.07
❑ 58 Johnnie Morton	.30	.10

❑ 59 Robert Porcher	.20	.07
❑ 60 Luther Elliss	.20	.07
❑ 61 James Stewart	.30	.10
❑ 62 Brett Favre	1.50	.60
❑ 63 Antonio Freeman	.50	.20
❑ 64 Bill Schroeder	.30	.10
❑ 65 Dorsey Levens	.30	.10
❑ 66 Peyton Manning	1.25	.50
❑ 67 Edgerrin James	.75	.30
❑ 68 Marvin Harrison	.50	.20
❑ 69 Ken Dilger	.20	.07
❑ 70 Terrence Wilkins	.20	.07
❑ 71 Mark Brunell	.50	.20
❑ 72 Fred Taylor	.50	.20
❑ 73 Jimmy Smith	.30	.10
❑ 74 Keenan McCardell	.30	.10
❑ 75 Carnell Lake	.20	.07
❑ 76 Tony Brackens	.20	.07
❑ 77 Kevin Hardy	.20	.07
❑ 78 Hardy Nickerson	.20	.07
❑ 79 Elvis Grbac	.30	.10
❑ 80 Tony Gonzalez	.30	.10
❑ 81 Derrick Alexander	.30	.10
❑ 82 Donnell Bennett	.20	.07
❑ 83 James Hasty	.20	.07
❑ 84 Jay Fiedler	.50	.20
❑ 85 James Johnson	.20	.07
❑ 86 Tony Martin	.30	.10
❑ 87 Damon Huard	.50	.20
❑ 88 O.J. McDuffie	.30	.10
❑ 89 Oronde Gadsden	.30	.10
❑ 90 Zach Thomas	.50	.20
❑ 91 Sam Madison	.20	.07
❑ 92 Jeff George	.30	.10
❑ 93 Randy Moss	1.00	.40
❑ 94 Robert Smith	.50	.20
❑ 95 Cris Carter	.50	.20
❑ 96 Matthew Hatchette	.20	.07
❑ 97 Drew Bledsoe	.60	.25
❑ 98 Terry Glenn	.30	.10
❑ 99 Troy Brown	.30	.10
❑ 100 Kevin Faulk	.30	.10
❑ 101 Lawyer Milloy	.30	.10
❑ 102 Ricky Williams	.50	.20
❑ 103 Keith Poole	.20	.07
❑ 104 Jake Reed	.30	.10
❑ 105 Cam Cleeland	.20	.07
❑ 106 Jeff Blake	.30	.10
❑ 107 Andrew Glover	.20	.07
❑ 108 Kerry Collins	.30	.10
❑ 109 Amani Toomer	.20	.07
❑ 110 Joe Montgomery	.20	.07
❑ 111 Ike Hilliard	.30	.10
❑ 112 Michael Strahan	.30	.10
❑ 113 Jessie Armstead	.20	.07
❑ 114 Ray Lucas	.30	.10
❑ 115 Keyshawn Johnson	.50	.20
❑ 116 Curtis Martin	.50	.20
❑ 117 Vinny Testaverde	.30	.10
❑ 118 Wayne Chrebet	.30	.10
❑ 119 Dedric Ward	.20	.07
❑ 120 Tim Brown	.50	.20
❑ 121 Rich Gannon	.50	.20
❑ 122 Tyrone Wheatley	.30	.10
❑ 123 Napoleon Kaufman	.30	.10
❑ 124 Charles Woodson	.30	.10
❑ 125 Darrell Russell	.20	.07
❑ 126 Duce Staley	.50	.20
❑ 127 Donovan McNabb	.75	.30
❑ 128 Torrance Small	.20	.07
❑ 129 Allen Rossum	.20	.07
❑ 130 Brian Dawkins	.50	.20
❑ 131 Troy Vincent	.20	.07
❑ 132 Troy Edwards	.20	.07
❑ 133 Jerome Bettis	.50	.20
❑ 134 Hines Ward	.50	.20
❑ 135 Kordell Stewart	.30	.10
❑ 136 Levon Kirkland	.20	.07
❑ 137 Kent Graham	.20	.07
❑ 138 Marshall Faulk	.60	.25
❑ 139 Kurt Warner	1.00	.40
❑ 140 Torry Holt	.50	.20
❑ 141 Isaac Bruce	.50	.20
❑ 142 Kevin Carter	.20	.07
❑ 143 Az-Zahir Hakim	.30	.10
❑ 144 Todd Lyght	.20	.07
❑ 145 Jermaine Fazande	.20	.07
❑ 146 Curtis Conway	.30	.10
❑ 147 Freddie Jones	.20	.07
❑ 148 Junior Seau	.50	.20
❑ 149 Jeff Graham	.20	.07
❑ 150 Ryan Leaf	.30	.10
❑ 151 Rodney Harrison	.20	.07
❑ 152 Steve Young	.60	.25
❑ 153 Jerry Rice	1.00	.40
❑ 154 Charlie Garner	.30	.10
❑ 155 Terrell Owens	.50	.20
❑ 156 Jeff Garcia	.50	.20
❑ 157 Bryant Young	.20	.07
❑ 158 Lance Schulters	.20	.07
❑ 159 Ricky Watters	.30	.10
❑ 160 Jon Kitna	.50	.20
❑ 161 Derrick Mayes	.30	.10
❑ 162 Sean Dawkins	.20	.07
❑ 163 Cortez Kennedy	.20	.07
❑ 164 Chad Brown	.20	.07
❑ 165 Warrick Dunn	.50	.20
❑ 166 Shaun King	.20	.07
❑ 167 Mike Alstott	.50	.20
❑ 168 Warren Sapp	.30	.10
❑ 169 Jacquez Green	.20	.07
❑ 170 Derrick Brooks	.50	.20
❑ 171 John Lynch	.30	.10
❑ 172 Donnie Abraham	.20	.07
❑ 173 Eddie George	.50	.20
❑ 174 Steve McNair	.50	.20
❑ 175 Kevin Dyson	.30	.10
❑ 176 Jevon Kearse	.50	.20
❑ 177 Yancey Thigpen	.20	.07
❑ 178 Frank Wycheck	.20	.07
❑ 179 Eddie Robinson	.20	.07
❑ 180 Samari Rolle	.20	.07
❑ 181 Brad Johnson	.50	.20
❑ 182 Stephen Davis	.50	.20
❑ 183 Michael Westbrook	.30	.10
❑ 184 Albert Connell	.20	.07
❑ 185 Brian Mitchell	.20	.07
❑ 186 Bruce Smith	.30	.10
❑ 187 Stephen Alexander	.20	.07
❑ 188 Peter Warrick RC	.60	.25
❑ 189C Cutout Card/Arrington	10.00	4.00
❑ 190 Chris Redman RC	.50	.20
❑ 191 Courtney Brown RC	.60	.25
❑ 192 Brian Urlacher RC	2.50	1.00
❑ 193 Plaxico Burress RC	1.25	.50
❑ 194 Corey Simon RC	.60	.25
❑ 195 Bubba Franks RC	.60	.25
❑ 196 Deon Grant RC	.50	.20
❑ 197 Michael Wiley RC	.50	.20
❑ 198 Tim Rattay RC	.60	.25
❑ 199 Ron Dayne RC	.60	.25
❑ 200 Sylvester Morris RC	.50	.20
❑ 201 Shaun Alexander RC	3.00	1.25
❑ 202 Dez White RC	.60	.25
❑ 203 Thomas Jones RC	1.00	.40
❑ 204 Reuben Droughns RC	.75	.30
❑ 205 Travis Taylor RC	.60	.25
❑ 206 Trevor Gaylor RC	.40	.15
❑ 207 Jamal Lewis RC	1.50	.60
❑ 208 Chad Pennington RC	1.50	.60
❑ 209 J.R. Redmond RC	.50	.20
❑ 210 Laveranues Coles RC	.75	.30
❑ 211 Travis Prentice RC	.50	.20
❑ 212 R.Jay Soward RC	.50	.20
❑ 213 Todd Pinkston RC	.60	.25
❑ 214 Dennis Northcutt RC	.60	.25
❑ 215 Shyrone Stith RC	.40	.15
❑ 216 Tee Martin RC	.60	.25
❑ 217 Giovanni Carmazzi RC	.40	.15
❑ 218 Drew Bledsoe CL	.30	.10
❑ 219 Steve Young CL	.30	.10
❑ 220A Donovan McNabb CL SP	30.00	15.00
❑ 220B D.McNabb CL SP Emb.	30.00	15.00

2001 Upper Deck MVP

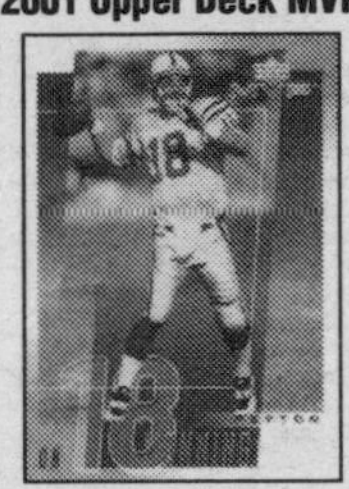

❑ COMPLETE SET (330)	50.00	20.00
❑ 1 Jake Plummer	.30	.10
❑ 2 David Boston	.50	.20
❑ 3 Thomas Jones	.30	.10
❑ 4 Michael Pittman	.20	.07
❑ 5 Frank Sanders	.20	.07
❑ 6 MarTay Jenkins	.20	.07
❑ 7 Pat Tillman RC	20.00	10.00
❑ 8 Tywan Mitchell	.20	.07
❑ 9 Jamal Anderson	.50	.20
❑ 10 Doug Johnson	.20	.07
❑ 11 Ephraim Salaam RC	.50	.20
❑ 12 Chris Chandler	.30	.10
❑ 13 Shawn Jefferson	.20	.07
❑ 14 Tim Dwight	.50	.20
❑ 15 Terance Mathis	.30	.10
❑ 16 Jamal Lewis	.75	.30
❑ 17 Shannon Sharpe	.30	.10
❑ 18 Trent Dilfer	.30	.10
❑ 19 Ray Lewis	.50	.20
❑ 20 Qadry Ismail	.30	.10
❑ 21 Travis Taylor	.30	.10
❑ 22 Chris Redman	.20	.07
❑ 23 Priest Holmes	.60	.25
❑ 24 Rod Woodson	.30	.10
❑ 25 Jamie Sharper	.20	.07
❑ 26 Doug Flutie	.50	.20
❑ 27 Rob Johnson	.30	.10
❑ 28 Eric Moulds	.30	.10
❑ 29 Sammy Morris	.20	.07
❑ 30 Shawn Bryson	.20	.07
❑ 31 Antowain Smith	.30	.10
❑ 32 Jeremy McDaniel	.20	.07
❑ 33 Sam Cowart	.20	.07
❑ 34 Muhsin Muhammad	.30	.10
❑ 35 Brad Hoover	.20	.07
❑ 36 Tim Biakabutuka	.30	.10
❑ 37 Steve Beuerlein	.20	.07
❑ 38 Donald Hayes	.20	.07
❑ 39 Jeff Lewis	.20	.07
❑ 40 Dameyune Craig	.20	.07
❑ 41 Wesley Walls	.20	.07
❑ 42 Isaac Byrd	.20	.07
❑ 43 Cade McNown	.20	.07
❑ 44 James Allen	.30	.10
❑ 45 Marcus Robinson	.50	.20
❑ 46 Brian Urlacher	.75	.30
❑ 47 Jim Miller	.20	.07
❑ 48 Curtis Enis	.20	.07
❑ 49 Eddie Kennison	.30	.10
❑ 50 Marty Booker	.20	.07
❑ 51 Bobby Engram	.20	.07
❑ 52 Peter Warrick	.50	.20
❑ 53 Corey Dillon	.50	.20
❑ 54 Akili Smith	.20	.07
❑ 55 Danny Farmer	.20	.07
❑ 56 Brandon Bennett	.20	.07
❑ 57 Curtis Keaton	.20	.07
❑ 58 Ron Dugans	.20	.07
❑ 59 Takeo Spikes	.20	.07
❑ 60 Scott Mitchell	.20	.07
❑ 61 Tim Couch	.30	.10
❑ 62 Kevin Johnson	.30	.10
❑ 63 Travis Prentice	.20	.07
❑ 64 Spergon Wynn	.20	.07

❑ 65 Errict Rhett .20 .07
❑ 66 David Patten .20 .07
❑ 67 Dennis Northcutt .30 .10
❑ 68 Aaron Shea .20 .07
❑ 69 Courtney Brown .30 .10
❑ 70 Troy Aikman .75 .30
❑ 71 Emmitt Smith 1.00 .40
❑ 72 Joey Galloway .30 .10
❑ 73 Rocket Ismail .30 .10
❑ 74 Randall Cunningham .50 .20
❑ 75 Anthony Wright .20 .07
❑ 76 James McKnight .30 .10
❑ 77 Dexter Coakley .20 .07
❑ 78 Terrell Davis .50 .20
❑ 79 Mike Anderson .50 .20
❑ 80 Brian Griese .50 .20
❑ 81 Rod Smith .30 .10
❑ 82 Ed McCaffrey .50 .20
❑ 83 Olandis Gary .30 .10
❑ 84 Trevor Pryce .20 .07
❑ 85 John Mobley .20 .07
❑ 86 Charlie Batch .50 .20
❑ 87 Germane Crowell .20 .07
❑ 88 James O. Stewart .30 .10
❑ 89 Johnnie Morton .30 .10
❑ 90 Herman Moore .30 .10
❑ 91 Mario Bates .20 .07
❑ 92 Desmond Howard .20 .07
❑ 93 Stephen Boyd .20 .07
❑ 94 Chris Claiborne .30 .10
❑ 95 Kurt Schulz .20 .07
❑ 96 Brett Favre 1.50 .60
❑ 97 Antonio Freeman .50 .20
❑ 98 Dorsey Levens .20 .07
❑ 99 Ahman Green .50 .20
❑ 100 Matt Hasselbeck .30 .10
❑ 101 De'Mond Parker .20 .07
❑ 102 Bill Schroeder .30 .10
❑ 103 Bubba Franks .30 .10
❑ 104 Donald Driver .30 .10
❑ 105 Darren Sharper .20 .07
❑ 106 Peyton Manning 1.25 .50
❑ 107 Edgerrin James .60 .25
❑ 108 Marvin Harrison .50 .20
❑ 109 Jerome Pathon .30 .10
❑ 110 Terrence Wilkins .20 .07
❑ 111 Ken Dilger .20 .07
❑ 112 Marcus Pollard .20 .07
❑ 113 Brad Scioli RC .50 .20
❑ 114 Mark Brunell .50 .20
❑ 115 Fred Taylor .50 .20
❑ 116 Jimmy Smith .30 .10
❑ 117 Jamie Martin .30 .10
❑ 118 Keenan McCardell .20 .07
❑ 119 Kyle Brady .20 .07
❑ 120 R.Jay Soward .20 .07
❑ 121 Alvis Whitted .20 .07
❑ 122 Brant Boyer RC .20 .07
❑ 123 Elvis Grbac .30 .10
❑ 124 Tony Gonzalez .30 .10
❑ 125 Derrick Alexander .30 .10
❑ 126 Tony Richardson .20 .07
❑ 127 Frank Moreau .20 .07
❑ 128 Sylvester Morris .20 .07
❑ 129 Kevin Lockett .20 .07
❑ 130 Donnie Edwards .20 .07
❑ 131 Oronde Gadsden .30 .10
❑ 132 Lamar Smith .30 .10
❑ 133 Jay Fiedler .50 .20
❑ 134 James Johnson .20 .07
❑ 135 Thurman Thomas .20 .07
❑ 136 Leslie Shepherd .20 .07
❑ 137 Tony Martin .20 .07
❑ 138 O.J. McDuffie .20 .07
❑ 139 Zach Thomas .50 .20
❑ 140 Randy Moss 1.00 .40
❑ 141 Bubby Brister .20 .07
❑ 142 Cris Carter .50 .20
❑ 143 Daunte Culpepper .50 .20
❑ 144 Moe Williams .30 .10
❑ 145 Troy Walters .20 .07
❑ 146 Chris Walsh RC .20 .07
❑ 147 Matthew Hatchette .20 .07
❑ 148 Kailee Wong .20 .07
❑ 149 Robert Griffith .20 .07
❑ 150 Drew Bledsoe .60 .25
❑ 151 Terry Glenn .20 .07
❑ 152 Kevin Faulk .30 .10
❑ 153 J.R. Redmond .20 .07
❑ 154 Tony Carter .20 .07
❑ 155 Patrick Pass .20 .07
❑ 156 Troy Brown .30 .10
❑ 157 Tony Simmons .20 .07
❑ 158 Michael Bishop .20 .07
❑ 159 Lawyer Milloy .30 .10
❑ 160 Ricky Williams .50 .20
❑ 161 Jeff Blake .30 .10
❑ 162 Joe Horn .30 .10
❑ 163 Aaron Brooks .50 .20
❑ 164 La'Roi Glover .20 .07
❑ 165 Chad Morton .20 .07
❑ 166 Keith Mitchell RC .30 .10
❑ 167 Willie Jackson .20 .07
❑ 168 Robert Wilson .20 .07
❑ 169 Jake Reed .30 .10
❑ 170 Kerry Collins .30 .10
❑ 171 Amani Toomer .20 .07
❑ 172 Ron Dayne .50 .20
❑ 173 Tiki Barber .50 .20
❑ 174 Greg Comella .20 .07
❑ 175 Ike Hilliard .30 .10
❑ 176 Joe Jurevicius .20 .07
❑ 177 Ron Dixon .20 .07
❑ 178 Jason Sehorn .20 .07
❑ 179 Michael Strahan .30 .10
❑ 180 Vinny Testaverde .30 .10
❑ 181 Wayne Chrebet .30 .10
❑ 182 Curtis Martin .50 .20
❑ 183 Richie Anderson .20 .07
❑ 184 Dedric Ward .20 .07
❑ 185 Laveranues Coles .50 .20
❑ 186 Windrell Hayes .20 .07
❑ 187 Chad Pennington .75 .30
❑ 188 Tim Brown .50 .20
❑ 189 Rich Gannon .50 .20
❑ 190 Tyrone Wheatley .30 .10
❑ 191 Napoleon Kaufman .20 .07
❑ 192 Jon Ritchie .20 .07
❑ 193 James Jett .20 .07
❑ 194 Rickey Dudley .20 .07
❑ 195 Andre Rison .30 .10
❑ 196 Eric Allen .20 .07
❑ 197 Charles Woodson .30 .10
❑ 198 Duce Staley .50 .20
❑ 199 Donovan McNabb .60 .25
❑ 200 Darnell Autry .20 .07
❑ 201 Chad Lewis .20 .07
❑ 202 Charles Johnson .20 .07
❑ 203 Torrance Small .20 .07
❑ 204 Todd Pinkston .20 .07
❑ 205 Brian Mitchell .20 .07
❑ 206 Hugh Douglas .20 .07
❑ 207 David Akers RC .30 .10
❑ 208 Kordell Stewart .30 .10
❑ 209 Jerome Bettis .50 .20
❑ 210 Bobby Shaw .20 .07
❑ 211 Hines Ward .50 .20
❑ 212 Plaxico Burress .50 .20
❑ 213 Courtney Hawkins .20 .07
❑ 214 Troy Edwards .20 .07
❑ 215 Earl Holmes .20 .07
❑ 216 Richard Huntley .20 .07
❑ 217 Marshall Faulk .60 .25
❑ 218 Kurt Warner 1.00 .40
❑ 219 Isaac Bruce .50 .20
❑ 220 Torry Holt .50 .20
❑ 221 Trent Green .50 .20
❑ 222 Justin Watson .20 .07
❑ 223 Trung Canidate .30 .10
❑ 224 Az-Zahir Hakim .20 .07
❑ 225 Ricky Proehl .20 .07
❑ 226 Dexter McCleon .20 .07
❑ 227 London Fletcher .20 .07
❑ 228 Junior Seau .50 .20
❑ 229 Curtis Conway .30 .10
❑ 230 Rodney Harrison .20 .07
❑ 231 Jeff Graham .20 .07
❑ 232 Freddie Jones .20 .07
❑ 233 Reggie Jones .20 .07
❑ 234 Ronney Jenkins .20 .07
❑ 235 Trevor Gaylor .20 .07
❑ 236 Jeff Garcia .50 .20
❑ 237 Jerry Rice 1.00 .40
❑ 238 Charlie Garner .30 .10
❑ 239 Terrell Owens .50 .20
❑ 240 J.J. Stokes .30 .10
❑ 241 Fred Beasley .20 .07
❑ 242 Tim Rattay .30 .10
❑ 243 Garrison Hearst .20 .07
❑ 244 Ricky Watters .30 .10
❑ 245 Shaun Alexander .60 .25
❑ 246 Jon Kitna .30 .10
❑ 247 Brock Huard .20 .07
❑ 248 Darrell Jackson .50 .20
❑ 249 James Williams WR .20 .07
❑ 250 Sean Dawkins .20 .07
❑ 251 John Hilliard RC .20 .07
❑ 252 Warrick Dunn .50 .20
❑ 253 Shaun King .20 .07
❑ 254 Ryan Leaf .30 .10
❑ 255 Mike Alstott .50 .20
❑ 256 Jacquez Green .20 .07
❑ 257 Reidel Anthony .20 .07
❑ 258 Derrick Brooks .50 .20
❑ 259 John Lynch .30 .10
❑ 260 Warren Sapp .30 .10
❑ 261 Eddie George .50 .20
❑ 262 Steve McNair .50 .20
❑ 263 Rodney Thomas .20 .07
❑ 264 Derrick Mason .30 .10
❑ 265 Yancey Thigpen .20 .07
❑ 266 Frank Wycheck .20 .07
❑ 267 Chris Sanders .20 .07
❑ 268 Carl Pickens .20 .07
❑ 269 Kevin Dyson .20 .07
❑ 270 Jevon Kearse .30 .10
❑ 271 Jeff George .30 .10
❑ 272 Stephen Davis .50 .20
❑ 273 Brad Johnson .50 .20
❑ 274 Albert Connell .20 .07
❑ 275 James Thrash .30 .10
❑ 276 Michael Westbrook .30 .10
❑ 277 Stephen Alexander .20 .07
❑ 278 Deion Sanders .50 .20
❑ 279 Champ Bailey .30 .10
❑ 280 Todd Husak .20 .07
❑ 281 Dan Morgan RC 1.00 .40
❑ 282 Josh Booty RC 1.00 .40
❑ 283 Michael Vick RC 4.00 1.50
❑ 284 Mike McMahon RC 1.00 .40
❑ 285 Reggie White RC .60 .25
❑ 286 Chris Weinke RC 1.00 .40
❑ 287 Drew Brees RC 4.00 1.50
❑ 288 Sage Rosenfels RC 1.00 .40
❑ 289 Marques Tuiasosopo RC 1.00 .40
❑ 290 Josh Heupel RC 1.00 .40
❑ 291 David Rivers RC .60 .25
❑ 292 Kevin Kasper RC 1.00 .40
❑ 293 Jesse Palmer RC 1.00 .40
❑ 294 LaDainian Tomlinson RC 15.00 6.00
❑ 295 Deuce McAllister RC 2.00 .75
❑ 296 Kevan Barlow RC 1.00 .40
❑ 297 LaMont Jordan RC 2.00 .75
❑ 298 James Jackson RC 1.00 .40
❑ 299 Anthony Thomas RC 1.00 .40
❑ 300 Correll Buckhalter RC 1.25 .50
❑ 301 Travis Henry RC 2.00 .75
❑ 302 Dan Alexander RC 1.00 .40
❑ 303 Travis Minor RC .60 .25
❑ 304 Derrick Gibson RC .60 .25
❑ 305 Rudi Johnson RC 2.00 .75
❑ 306 Michael Bennett RC 1.00 .40
❑ 307 Alge Crumpler RC 1.25 .50
❑ 308 Todd Heap RC 1.00 .40
❑ 309 Snoop Minnis RC .60 .25
❑ 310 Santana Moss RC 1.50 .60
❑ 311 Reggie Wayne RC 2.00 .75
❑ 312 Koren Robinson RC 1.00 .40
❑ 313 Chris Chambers RC 1.50 .60
❑ 314 David Terrell RC 1.00 .40
❑ 315 Rod Gardner RC 1.00 .40
❑ 316 Quincy Morgan RC 1.00 .40

❑ 317 Ken-Yon Rambo RC	.60	.25
❑ 318 Vinny Sutherland RC	.60	.25
❑ 319 David Allen RC	.60	.25
❑ 320 Bobby Newcombe RC	.60	.25
❑ 321 Ronney Daniels RC	.40	.15
❑ 322 T.J. Houshmandzadeh RC	1.25	.50
❑ 323 Chad Johnson RC	2.50	1.00
❑ 324 Freddie Mitchell RC	1.00	.40
❑ 325 Moran Norris RC	.40	.15
❑ 326 Ron Dayne CL	.30	.10
❑ 327 Mike Anderson CL	.20	.07
❑ 328 Jamal Lewis CL	.40	.15
❑ 329 Brian Urlacher CL	.40	.15
❑ 330 Darren Howard CL	.20	.07

2002 Upper Deck MVP

❑ COMPLETE SET (300)	50.00	20.00
❑ 1 Arnold Jackson	.20	.07
❑ 2 Dave Brown	.20	.07
❑ 3 David Boston	.50	.20
❑ 4 Frank Sanders	.20	.07
❑ 5 Jake Plummer	.30	.10
❑ 6 MarTay Jenkins	.20	.07
❑ 7 Freddie Jones	.20	.07
❑ 8 Jamal Anderson	.30	.10
❑ 9 Keith Brooking	.20	.07
❑ 10 Michael Vick	1.00	.40
❑ 11 Rodney Thomas	.20	.07
❑ 12 Shawn Jefferson	.20	.07
❑ 13 Tony Martin	.20	.07
❑ 14 Warrick Dunn	.50	.20
❑ 15 Brandon Stokley	.30	.10
❑ 16 Chris McAlister	.20	.07
❑ 17 Chris Redman	.20	.07
❑ 18 Ray Lewis	.50	.20
❑ 19 Sam Gash	.20	.07
❑ 20 Travis Taylor	.30	.10
❑ 21 Terry Allen	.20	.07
❑ 22 Drew Bledsoe	.60	.25
❑ 23 Alex Van Pelt	.20	.07
❑ 24 Eric Moulds	.30	.10
❑ 25 Kenyatta Wright	.20	.07
❑ 26 Larry Centers	.20	.07
❑ 27 Peerless Price	.30	.10
❑ 28 Shawn Bryson	.20	.07
❑ 29 Travis Henry	.50	.20
❑ 30 Chris Weinke	.30	.10
❑ 31 Lamar Smith	.30	.10
❑ 32 Isaac Byrd	.50	.20
❑ 33 Muhsin Muhammad	.30	.10
❑ 34 Nick Goings	.20	.07
❑ 35 Richard Huntley	.20	.07
❑ 36 Tim Biakabutuka	.20	.07
❑ 37 Wesley Walls	.20	.07
❑ 38 Anthony Thomas	.30	.10
❑ 39 Brian Urlacher	.75	.30
❑ 40 David Terrell	.50	.20
❑ 41 Dez White	.20	.07
❑ 42 Jim Miller	.20	.07
❑ 43 Larry Whigham	.20	.07
❑ 44 Marty Booker	.20	.07
❑ 45 Chris Chandler	.30	.10
❑ 46 Corey Dillon	.30	.10
❑ 47 Darnay Scott	.20	.07
❑ 48 Jon Kitna	.30	.10
❑ 49 Peter Warrick	.30	.10
❑ 50 Ron Dugans	.20	.07
❑ 51 Scott Mitchell	.20	.07
❑ 52 Chad Johnson	.50	.20
❑ 53 Courtney Brown	.30	.10
❑ 54 JaJuan Dawson	.20	.07
❑ 55 James Jackson	.20	.07
❑ 56 Kevin Johnson	.30	.10
❑ 57 Quincy Morgan	.20	.07
❑ 58 Rickey Dudley	.20	.07
❑ 59 Tim Couch	.30	.10
❑ 60 Chris Sanders	.20	.07
❑ 61 Emmitt Smith	1.25	.50
❑ 62 Joey Galloway	.30	.10
❑ 63 Ken-Yon Rambo	.20	.07
❑ 64 La'Roi Glover	.20	.07
❑ 65 Quincy Carter	.30	.10
❑ 66 Rocket Ismail	.30	.10
❑ 67 Darren Woodson	.20	.07
❑ 68 Ryan Leaf	.30	.10
❑ 69 Chester McGlockton	.20	.07
❑ 70 Brian Griese	.50	.20
❑ 71 Shannon Sharpe	.30	.10
❑ 72 Kevin Kasper	.20	.07
❑ 73 Mike Anderson	.50	.20
❑ 74 Olandis Gary	.30	.10
❑ 75 Rod Smith	.30	.10
❑ 76 Terrell Davis	.50	.20
❑ 77 Anthony Carter	.20	.07
❑ 78 Az-Zahir Hakim	.20	.07
❑ 79 Charlie Batch	.30	.10
❑ 80 Chris Claiborne	.20	.07
❑ 81 Cory Schlesinger	.20	.07
❑ 82 Desmond Howard	.20	.07
❑ 83 Germane Crowell	.20	.07
❑ 84 James Stewart	.30	.10
❑ 85 Mike McMahon	.50	.20
❑ 86 Bill Schroeder	.30	.10
❑ 87 Ahman Green	.50	.20
❑ 88 Brett Favre	1.25	.50
❑ 89 Bubba Franks	.30	.10
❑ 90 Antonio Freeman	.50	.20
❑ 91 Donald Driver	.30	.10
❑ 92 Kabeer Gbaja-Biamila	.30	.10
❑ 93 William Henderson	.20	.07
❑ 94 Corey Bradford	.20	.07
❑ 95 Jamie Sharper	.20	.07
❑ 96 Jermaine Lewis	.20	.07
❑ 97 Kailee Wong	.20	.07
❑ 98 Matt Stevens	.20	.07
❑ 99 Tony Boselli	.20	.07
❑ 100 James Allen	.30	.10
❑ 101 Aaron Glenn	.20	.07
❑ 102 Edgerrin James	.60	.25
❑ 103 Dominic Rhodes	.30	.10
❑ 104 Marcus Pollard	.20	.07
❑ 105 Marvin Harrison	.50	.20
❑ 106 Peyton Manning	1.00	.40
❑ 107 Qadry Ismail	.30	.10
❑ 108 Reggie Wayne	.50	.20
❑ 109 Stacey Mack	.20	.07
❑ 110 Elvis Joseph	.20	.07
❑ 111 Fred Taylor	.50	.20
❑ 112 Jimmy Smith	.30	.10
❑ 113 Jonathan Quinn	.20	.07
❑ 114 Keenan McCardell	.20	.07
❑ 115 Mark Brunell	.50	.20
❑ 116 Trent Green	.30	.10
❑ 117 Derrick Alexander	.30	.10
❑ 118 Johnnie Morton	.30	.10
❑ 119 Snoop Minnis	.20	.07
❑ 120 Mike Cloud	.20	.07
❑ 121 Priest Holmes	.60	.25
❑ 122 Tony Gonzalez	.30	.10
❑ 123 Tony Richardson	.20	.07
❑ 124 Ricky Williams	1.00	.40
❑ 125 Chris Chambers	.50	.20
❑ 126 James McKnight	.20	.07
❑ 127 Jay Fiedler	.30	.10
❑ 128 Zach Thomas	.50	.20
❑ 129 Oronde Gadsden	.30	.10
❑ 130 Ray Lucas	.20	.07
❑ 131 Randy Moss	1.00	.40
❑ 132 Spergon Wynn	.20	.07
❑ 133 Cris Carter	.50	.20
❑ 134 Daunte Culpepper	.50	.20
❑ 135 Doug Chapman	.20	.07
❑ 136 Michael Bennett	.30	.10
❑ 137 Tom Brady	1.25	.50
❑ 138 Troy Brown	.30	.10
❑ 139 Adam Vinatieri	.50	.20
❑ 140 Antowain Smith	.30	.10
❑ 141 David Patten	.20	.07
❑ 142 Donald Hayes	.20	.07
❑ 143 J.R. Redmond	.20	.07
❑ 144 Willie Jackson	.20	.07
❑ 145 Jerome Pathon	.30	.10
❑ 146 Jake Reed	.30	.10
❑ 147 Aaron Brooks	.50	.20
❑ 148 John Carney	.20	.07
❑ 149 Deuce McAllister	.60	.25
❑ 150 Joe Horn	.30	.10
❑ 151 Kyle Turley	.20	.07
❑ 152 Robert Wilson	.20	.07
❑ 153 Tiki Barber	.50	.20
❑ 154 Amani Toomer	.30	.10
❑ 155 Ike Hilliard	.30	.10
❑ 156 Jason Sehorn	.20	.07
❑ 157 Joe Jurevicius	.20	.07
❑ 158 Kerry Collins	.30	.10
❑ 159 Michael Strahan	.30	.10
❑ 160 Ron Dayne	.30	.10
❑ 161 Wayne Chrebet	.30	.10
❑ 162 Chad Pennington	.60	.25
❑ 163 Curtis Martin	.50	.20
❑ 164 LaMont Jordan	.50	.20
❑ 165 Laveranues Coles	.30	.10
❑ 166 Marvin Jones	.20	.07
❑ 167 Santana Moss	.50	.20
❑ 168 Vinny Testaverde	.30	.10
❑ 169 Tyrone Wheatley	.30	.10
❑ 170 Charles Woodson	.30	.10
❑ 171 Charlie Garner	.30	.10
❑ 172 Jerry Rice	1.00	.40
❑ 173 John Parrella	.20	.07
❑ 174 Jon Ritchie	.20	.07
❑ 175 Rich Gannon	.50	.20
❑ 176 Tim Brown	.50	.20
❑ 177 Todd Pinkston	.30	.10
❑ 178 Correll Buckhalter	.30	.10
❑ 179 Donovan McNabb	.60	.25
❑ 180 Duce Staley	.50	.20
❑ 181 Freddie Mitchell	.30	.10
❑ 182 Hugh Douglas	.20	.07
❑ 183 James Thrash	.30	.10
❑ 184 Koy Detmer	.20	.07
❑ 185 Troy Edwards	.20	.07
❑ 186 Chris Fuamatu-Ma'afala	.20	.07
❑ 187 Hines Ward	.50	.20
❑ 188 Jerome Bettis	.50	.20
❑ 189 Kendrell Bell	.50	.20
❑ 190 Kordell Stewart	.30	.10
❑ 191 Mark Bruener	.20	.07
❑ 192 Plaxico Burress	.30	.10
❑ 193 Tim Dwight	.30	.10
❑ 194 Curtis Conway	.20	.07
❑ 195 Doug Flutie	.50	.20
❑ 196 Drew Brees	.50	.20
❑ 197 Junior Seau	.50	.20
❑ 198 LaDainian Tomlinson	.75	.30
❑ 199 Marcellus Wiley	.20	.07
❑ 200 Rodney Harrison	.20	.07
❑ 201 Stephen Alexander	.20	.07
❑ 202 Terrell Owens	.50	.20
❑ 203 Andre Carter	.20	.07
❑ 204 Cedrick Wilson	.20	.07
❑ 205 Fred Beasley	.20	.07
❑ 206 Garrison Hearst	.30	.10
❑ 207 J.J. Stokes	.30	.10
❑ 208 Jeff Garcia	.50	.20
❑ 209 Kevan Barlow	.30	.10
❑ 210 Tai Streets	.20	.07
❑ 211 Doug Evans	.20	.07
❑ 212 Bobby Engram	.20	.07
❑ 213 Darrell Jackson	.30	.10
❑ 214 James Williams	.20	.07
❑ 215 John Randle	.20	.07
❑ 216 Koren Robinson	.30	.10
❑ 217 Matt Hasselbeck	.30	.10
❑ 218 Shaun Alexander	.60	.25

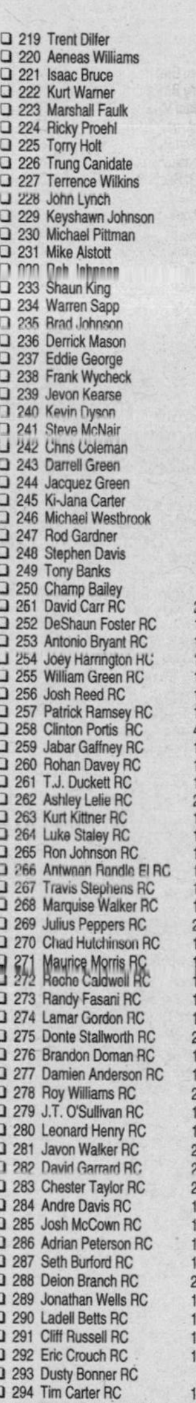

❑ 219	Trent Dilfer	.30	.10
❑ 220	Aeneas Williams	.20	.07
❑ 221	Isaac Bruce	.50	.20
❑ 222	Kurt Warner	.50	.20
❑ 223	Marshall Faulk	.50	.20
❑ 224	Ricky Proehl	.20	.07
❑ 225	Torry Holt	.50	.20
❑ 226	Trung Canidate	.30	.10
❑ 227	Terrence Wilkins	.20	.07
❑ 228	John Lynch	.30	.10
❑ 229	Keyshawn Johnson	.50	.20
❑ 230	Michael Pittman	.20	.07
❑ 231	Mike Alstott	.50	.20
❑ 232	Rob Johnson	.20	.10
❑ 233	Shaun King	.20	.07
❑ 234	Warren Sapp	.30	.10
❑ 235	Brad Johnson	.30	.10
❑ 236	Derrick Mason	.30	.10
❑ 237	Eddie George	.50	.20
❑ 238	Frank Wycheck	.20	.07
❑ 239	Jevon Kearse	.30	.10
❑ 240	Kevin Dyson	.30	.10
❑ 241	Steve McNair	.50	.20
❑ 242	Chris Coleman	.20	.07
❑ 243	Darrell Green	.20	.07
❑ 244	Jacquez Green	.20	.07
❑ 245	Ki-Jana Carter	.20	.07
❑ 246	Michael Westbrook	.20	.07
❑ 247	Rod Gardner	.30	.10
❑ 248	Stephen Davis	.30	.10
❑ 249	Tony Banks	.20	.07
❑ 250	Champ Bailey	.30	.10
❑ 251	David Carr RC	2.50	1.00
❑ 252	DeShaun Foster RC	1.25	.50
❑ 253	Antonio Bryant RC	1.25	.50
❑ 254	Joey Harrington RC	1.50	.60
❑ 255	William Green RC	1.25	.50
❑ 256	Josh Reed RC	1.25	.50
❑ 257	Patrick Ramsey RC	1.25	.50
❑ 258	Clinton Portis RC	4.00	1.50
❑ 259	Jabar Gaffney RC	1.25	.50
❑ 260	Rohan Davey RC	1.25	.50
❑ 261	T.J. Duckett RC	1.25	.50
❑ 262	Ashley Lelie RC	2.50	1.00
❑ 263	Kurt Kittner RC	1.00	.40
❑ 264	Luke Staley RC	1.00	.40
❑ 265	Ron Johnson RC	1.00	.40
❑ 266	Antwaan Randle El RC	1.50	.60
❑ 267	Travis Stephens RC	1.00	.40
❑ 268	Marquise Walker RC	1.00	.40
❑ 269	Julius Peppers RC	2.50	1.00
❑ 270	Chad Hutchinson RC	1.00	.40
❑ 271	Maurice Morris RC	1.25	.50
❑ 272	Reche Caldwell RC	1.25	.50
❑ 273	Randy Fasani RC	1.00	.40
❑ 274	Lamar Gordon RC	1.25	.50
❑ 275	Donte Stallworth RC	2.00	.75
❑ 276	Brandon Doman RC	1.00	.40
❑ 277	Damien Anderson RC	1.00	.40
❑ 278	Roy Williams RC	2.50	1.00
❑ 279	J.T. O'Sullivan RC	1.00	.40
❑ 280	Leonard Henry RC	1.00	.40
❑ 281	Javon Walker RC	2.00	.75
❑ 282	David Garrard RC	2.50	1.00
❑ 283	Chester Taylor RC	2.50	1.00
❑ 284	Andre Davis RC	1.00	.40
❑ 285	Josh McCown RC	1.50	.60
❑ 286	Adrian Peterson RC	1.50	.60
❑ 287	Seth Burford RC	1.00	.40
❑ 288	Deion Branch RC	2.00	.75
❑ 289	Jonathan Wells RC	1.25	.50
❑ 290	Ladell Betts RC	1.25	.50
❑ 291	Cliff Russell RC	1.00	.40
❑ 292	Eric Crouch RC	1.25	.50
❑ 293	Dusty Bonner RC	.60	.25
❑ 294	Tim Carter RC	1.00	.40
❑ 295	Brian Westbrook RC	2.50	1.00
❑ 296	Quentin Jammer RC	1.25	.50
❑ 297	Brian Poli-Dixon RC	1.00	.40
❑ 298	Donovan McNabb CL	.30	.10
❑ 299	Curtis Martin CL	.20	.07
❑ 300	Tom Brady CL	.60	.25

2003 Upper Deck MVP

❑	COMPLETE SET (440)	60.00	30.00
❑ 1	Brad Johnson	.30	.10
❑ 2	Dexter Jackson RC	.50	.20
❑ 3	Derrick Brooks	.30	.10
❑ 4	Simeon Rice	.30	.10
❑ 5	Warren Sapp	.30	.10
❑ 6	John Lynch	.30	.10
❑ 7	Joe Jurevicius	.20	.07
❑ 8	Ronde Barber	.20	.07
❑ 9	Mike Alstott	.50	.20
❑ 10	Michael Pittman	.20	.07
❑ 11	Keyshawn Johnson	.50	.20
❑ 12	Jerry Rice	1.00	.40
❑ 13	Tim Brown	.50	.20
❑ 14	Rich Gannon	.30	.10
❑ 15	Charlie Garner	.30	.10
❑ 16	Jerry Porter	.30	.10
❑ 17	Sebastian Janikowski	.20	.07
❑ 18	Zack Crockett	.20	.07
❑ 19	Tyrone Wheatley	.20	.07
❑ 20	Bill Romanowski	.20	.07
❑ 21	Charles Woodson	.30	.10
❑ 22	Rod Woodson	.30	.10
❑ 23	Donovan McNabb	.60	.25
❑ 24	James Thrash	.20	.07
❑ 25	Duce Staley	.30	.10
❑ 26	Brian Westbrook	.30	.10
❑ 27	A.J. Feeley	.30	.10
❑ 28	Koy Detmer	.20	.07
❑ 29	Brian Dawkins	.30	.10
❑ 30	Dorsey Levens	.20	.07
❑ 31	Jon Ritchie	.20	.07
❑ 32	Todd Pinkston	.30	.10
❑ 33	Chad Lewis	.20	.07
❑ 34	Brett Favre	1.25	.50
❑ 35	Ahman Green	.50	.20
❑ 36	Donald Driver	.30	.10
❑ 37	Bubba Franks	.30	.10
❑ 38	Javon Walker	.20	.07
❑ 39	Kabeer Gbaja-Biamila	.30	.10
❑ 40	Robert Ferguson	.20	.07
❑ 41	Tony Fisher	.20	.07
❑ 42	Marques Anderson	.20	.07
❑ 43	Ryan Longwell	.20	.07
❑ 44	Craig Nall	.20	.07
❑ 45	Steve McNair	.50	.20
❑ 46	Eddie George	.30	.10
❑ 47	Jevon Kearse	.30	.10
❑ 48	Kevin Carter	.20	.07
❑ 49	Samari Rolle	.20	.07
❑ 50	Keith Bulluck	.20	.07
❑ 51	Joe Nedney	.20	.07
❑ 52	Robert Holcombe	.20	.07
❑ 53	Drew Bennett	.30	.10
❑ 54	Frank Wycheck	.20	.07
❑ 55	Derrick Mason	.30	.10
❑ 56	Tommy Maddox	.50	.20
❑ 57	Jerome Bettis	.50	.20
❑ 58	Plaxico Burress	.30	.10
❑ 59	Antwaan Randle El	.50	.20
❑ 60	Amos Zereoue	.30	.10
❑ 61	Chris Fuamatu-Ma'afala	.20	.07
❑ 62	Jason Gildon	.20	.07
❑ 63	Kendrell Bell	.30	.10
❑ 64	Dewayne Washington	.20	.07

❑ 65	Jeff Reed RC	2.50	1.00
❑ 66	Hines Ward	.50	.20
❑ 67	Jeff Garcia	.50	.20
❑ 68	Terrell Owens	.50	.20
❑ 69	Andre Carter	.20	.07
❑ 70	Tai Streets	.20	.07
❑ 71	Tim Rattay	.30	.10
❑ 72	Eric Johnson	.30	.10
❑ 73	Cedrick Wilson	.20	.07
❑ 74	Brandon Doman	.20	.07
❑ 75	Kevan Barlow	.30	.10
❑ 76	Bryant Young	.20	.07
❑ 77	Garrison Hearst	.30	.10
❑ 78	Kerry Collins	.30	.10
❑ 79	Daryl Jones	.20	.07
❑ 80	Tiki Barber	.50	.20
❑ 81	Amani Toomer	.30	.10
❑ 82	Tim Carter	.20	.07
❑ 83	Michael Strahan	.30	.10
❑ 84	Ike Hilliard	.20	.07
❑ 85	Brian Mitchell	.20	.07
❑ 86	Ron Dixon	.20	.07
❑ 87	Jeremy Shockey	.75	.30
❑ 88	Marvin Harrison	.50	.20
❑ 89	Peyton Manning	.75	.30
❑ 90	Edgerrin James	.50	.20
❑ 91	Dominic Rhodes	.30	.10
❑ 92	Brock Huard	.20	.07
❑ 93	Marcus Pollard	.20	.07
❑ 94	James Mungro	.20	.07
❑ 95	Dwight Freeney	.30	.10
❑ 96	Reggie Wayne	.30	.10
❑ 97	Rob Morris	.20	.07
❑ 98	Michael Vick	1.25	.50
❑ 99	Warrick Dunn	.30	.10
❑ 100	T.J. Duckett	.30	.10
❑ 101	Keith Brooking	.20	.07
❑ 102	Ray Buchanan	.20	.07
❑ 103	Alge Crumpler	.30	.10
❑ 104	Quentin McCord	.20	.07
❑ 105	Doug Johnson	.20	.07
❑ 106	Brian Finneran	.20	.07
❑ 107	Peerless Price	.30	.10
❑ 108	Chad Pennington	.60	.25
❑ 109	Curtis Martin	.50	.20
❑ 110	Laveranues Coles	.30	.10
❑ 111	Wayne Chrebet	.30	.10
❑ 112	LaMont Jordan	.50	.20
❑ 113	Anthony Becht	.20	.07
❑ 114	Marvin Jones	.20	.07
❑ 115	Mo Lewis	.20	.07
❑ 116	Sam Cowart	.20	.07
❑ 117	Vinnie Testaverde	.30	.10
❑ 118	Santana Moss	.30	.10
❑ 119	Tim Couch	.20	.07
❑ 120	William Green	.30	.10
❑ 121	Andre Davis	.20	.07
❑ 122	Quincy Morgan	.30	.10
❑ 123	Kevin Johnson	.30	.10
❑ 124	James Jackson	.20	.07
❑ 125	Jamel White	.20	.07
❑ 126	Robert Griffith	.20	.07
❑ 127	Dennis Northcutt	.30	.10
❑ 128	Josh Booty	.20	.07
❑ 129	Kelly Holcomb	.30	.10
❑ 130	Jake Plummer	.30	.10
❑ 131	Olandis Gary	.30	.10
❑ 132	Clinton Portis	.75	.30
❑ 133	Mike Anderson	.50	.20
❑ 134	Ashley Lelie	.50	.20
❑ 135	Ed McCaffrey	.50	.20
❑ 136	Shannon Sharpe	.30	.10
❑ 137	Rod Smith	.30	.10
❑ 138	John Mobley	.20	.07
❑ 139	Jason Elam	.20	.07
❑ 140	Terrell Davis	.50	.20
❑ 141	Tom Brady	1.25	.50
❑ 142	Christian Fauria	.20	.07
❑ 143	Antowain Smith	.30	.10
❑ 144	Kevin Faulk	.20	.07
❑ 145	Ty Law	.30	.10
❑ 146	Lawyer Milloy	.30	.10
❑ 147	David Patten	.20	.07
❑ 148	Deion Branch	.50	.20

❑ 149 Troy Brown	.30	.10
❑ 150 Rohan Davey	.30	.10
❑ 151 Adam Vinatieri	.50	.20
❑ 152 Jay Fiedler	.30	.10
❑ 153 Chris Chambers	.50	.20
❑ 154 Randy McMichael	.30	.10
❑ 155 Rob Konrad	.20	.07
❑ 156 Morlon Greenwood	.20	.07
❑ 157 Derrius Thompson	.20	.07
❑ 158 Travis Minor	.20	.07
❑ 159 Olindo Mare	.20	.07
❑ 160 Jason Taylor	.20	.07
❑ 161 Zach Thomas	.50	.20
❑ 162 Ricky Williams	.50	.20
❑ 163 Aaron Brooks	.50	.20
❑ 164 Deuce McAllister	.50	.20
❑ 165 Donte Stallworth	.50	.20
❑ 166 Jerome Pathon	.20	.07
❑ 167 J.T. O'Sullivan	.20	.07
❑ 168 Darrin Smith	.20	.07
❑ 169 Michael Lewis	.20	.07
❑ 170 John Carney	.20	.07
❑ 171 Kyle Turley	.20	.07
❑ 172 Joe Horn	.30	.10
❑ 173 Trent Green	.30	.10
❑ 174 Priest Holmes	.60	.25
❑ 175 Johnnie Morton	.30	.10
❑ 176 Eddie Kennison	.20	.07
❑ 177 Marvcus Patton	.20	.07
❑ 178 Omar Easy	.20	.07
❑ 179 Derrick Blaylock	.30	.10
❑ 180 Snoop Minnis	.20	.07
❑ 181 Dante Hall	.50	.20
❑ 182 Tony Gonzalez	.30	.10
❑ 183 Marc Boerigter	.30	.10
❑ 184 Drew Brees	.50	.20
❑ 185 David Boston	.30	.10
❑ 186 Stephen Alexander	.20	.07
❑ 187 Quentin Jammer	.20	.07
❑ 188 Donnie Edwards	.20	.07
❑ 189 LaDainian Tomlinson	.50	.20
❑ 190 Junior Seau	.50	.20
❑ 191 Reche Caldwell	.20	.07
❑ 192 Lorenzo Neal	.20	.07
❑ 193 Tim Dwight	.30	.10
❑ 194 Doug Flutie	.30	.10
❑ 195 Drew Bledsoe	.50	.20
❑ 196 Travis Henry	.30	.10
❑ 197 Eric Moulds	.30	.10
❑ 198 Alex Van Pelt	.20	.07
❑ 199 Charles Johnson	.20	.07
❑ 200 Nate Clements	.20	.07
❑ 201 Takeo Spikes	.20	.07
❑ 202 Bobby Shaw	.20	.07
❑ 203 London Fletcher	.20	.07
❑ 204 Sammy Morris	.20	.07
❑ 205 Josh Reed	.30	.10
❑ 206 Patrick Ramsey	.50	.20
❑ 207 Ladell Betts	.30	.10
❑ 208 Chad Morton	.20	.07
❑ 209 Trung Canidate	.30	.10
❑ 210 Kenny Watson	.20	.07
❑ 211 Jessie Armstead	.20	.07
❑ 212 Fred Smoot	.20	.07
❑ 213 Champ Bailey	.30	.10
❑ 214 Bruce Smith	.20	.07
❑ 215 Rod Gardner	.30	.10
❑ 216 Kurt Warner	.50	.20
❑ 217 Troy Edwards	.20	.07
❑ 218 Adam Archuleta	.20	.07
❑ 219 Grant Wistrom	.20	.07
❑ 220 Marshall Faulk	.50	.20
❑ 221 Jeff Wilkins	.20	.07
❑ 222 Aeneas Williams	.20	.07
❑ 223 Lamar Gordon	.20	.07
❑ 224 Marc Bulger	.50	.20
❑ 225 Isaac Bruce	.50	.20
❑ 226 Torry Holt	.50	.20
❑ 227 Matt Hasselbeck	.30	.10
❑ 228 Maurice Morris	.20	.07
❑ 229 Bobby Engram	.20	.07
❑ 230 Darrell Jackson	.30	.10
❑ 231 James Williams	.20	.07
❑ 232 Chad Brown	.20	.07
❑ 233 Anthony Simmons	.20	.07
❑ 234 Shaun Alexander	.50	.20
❑ 235 Koren Robinson	.30	.10
❑ 236 Chris Redman	.20	.07
❑ 237 Jamal Lewis	.50	.20
❑ 238 Brandon Stokley	.30	.10
❑ 239 Peter Boulware	.20	.07
❑ 240 Randy Hymes RC	.30	.10
❑ 241 Todd Heap	.30	.10
❑ 242 Travis Taylor	.30	.10
❑ 243 Ron Johnson	.20	.07
❑ 244 Ray Lewis	.50	.20
❑ 245 Jake Delhomme	.50	.20
❑ 246 DeShaun Foster	.20	.07
❑ 247 Dee Brown	.20	.07
❑ 248 Steve Smith	.50	.20
❑ 249 Kevin Dyson	.30	.10
❑ 250 Muhsin Muhammad	.30	.10
❑ 251 Stephen Davis	.30	.10
❑ 252 Julius Peppers	.50	.20
❑ 253 Rodney Peete	.20	.07
❑ 254 Mark Brunell	.30	.10
❑ 255 Jimmy Smith	.30	.10
❑ 256 Kyle Brady	.20	.07
❑ 257 Kevin Lockett	.20	.07
❑ 258 Quinn Gray	.20	.07
❑ 259 Tony Brackens	.20	.07
❑ 260 Marco Coleman	.20	.07
❑ 261 David Garrard	.20	.07
❑ 262 Fred Taylor	.50	.20
❑ 263 Daunte Culpepper	.50	.20
❑ 264 Michael Bennett	.30	.10
❑ 265 D'Wayne Bates	.20	.07
❑ 266 Cedric James	.20	.07
❑ 267 Kelly Campbell	.20	.07
❑ 268 Derrick Alexander	.20	.07
❑ 269 Byron Chamberlain	.20	.07
❑ 270 Shaun Hill	.20	.07
❑ 271 Randy Moss	.75	.30
❑ 272 Josh McCown	.30	.10
❑ 273 Thomas Jones	.30	.10
❑ 274 Wendell Bryant	.20	.07
❑ 275 Kevin Kasper	.20	.07
❑ 276 Jason McAddley	.20	.07
❑ 277 Emmitt Smith	1.25	.50
❑ 278 Preston Parsons	.20	.07
❑ 279 Freddie Jones	.20	.07
❑ 280 Marcel Shipp	.30	.10
❑ 281 Chad Hutchinson	.20	.07
❑ 282 Troy Hambrick	.20	.07
❑ 283 Dat Nguyen	.20	.07
❑ 284 Michael Wiley	.20	.07
❑ 285 Joey Galloway	.30	.10
❑ 286 Terry Glenn	.20	.07
❑ 287 La'Roi Glover	.20	.07
❑ 288 Roy Williams	.50	.20
❑ 289 Antonio Bryant	.50	.20
❑ 290 Quincy Carter	.30	.10
❑ 291 Anthony Thomas	.30	.10
❑ 292 Marty Booker	.30	.10
❑ 293 Dez White	.20	.07
❑ 294 Marcus Robinson	.30	.10
❑ 295 Kordell Stewart	.30	.10
❑ 296 David Terrell	.30	.10
❑ 297 John Davis	.20	.07
❑ 298 Mike Brown	.30	.10
❑ 299 Brian Urlacher	.75	.30
❑ 300 Jabar Gaffney	.30	.10
❑ 301 Jonathan Wells	.20	.07
❑ 302 JaJuan Dawson	.20	.07
❑ 303 Corey Bradford	.20	.07
❑ 304 Frank Murphy	.20	.07
❑ 305 Billy Miller	.20	.07
❑ 306 Aaron Glenn	.20	.07
❑ 307 Avion Black	.20	.07
❑ 308 David Carr	.75	.30
❑ 309 Joey Harrington	.75	.30
❑ 310 James Stewart	.30	.10
❑ 311 Ty Detmer	.20	.07
❑ 312 Jason Hanson	.20	.07
❑ 313 Bill Schroeder	.30	.10
❑ 314 Mikhael Ricks	.20	.07
❑ 315 Scotty Anderson	.20	.07
❑ 316 Robert Porcher	.20	.07
❑ 317 Az-Zahir Hakim	.20	.07
❑ 318 Jon Kitna	.30	.10
❑ 319 Ron Dugans	.20	.07
❑ 320 Chad Johnson	.50	.20
❑ 321 Brandon Bennett	.20	.07
❑ 322 T.J. Houshmandzadeh	.20	.07
❑ 323 Rudi Johnson	.50	.20
❑ 324 Kevin Hardy	.20	.07
❑ 325 Corey Dillon	.30	.10
❑ 326 Peter Warrick	.30	.10
❑ 327 Carson Palmer RC	5.00	2.00
❑ 328 Byron Leftwich RC	4.00	1.50
❑ 329 Rex Grossman RC	4.00	1.50
❑ 330 Kyle Boller RC	1.25	.50
❑ 331 Dave Ragone RC	1.25	.50
❑ 332 Chris Simms RC	2.00	.75
❑ 333 Brad Banks RC	1.00	.40
❑ 334 Kliff Kingsbury RC	1.00	.40
❑ 335 Jason Gesser RC	1.25	.50
❑ 336 Jason Johnson RC	.60	.25
❑ 337 Brian St.Pierre RC	1.25	.50
❑ 338 Ken Dorsey RC	1.25	.50
❑ 339 Seneca Wallace RC	1.25	.50
❑ 340 Seth Marler RC	1.00	.40
❑ 341 Tony Romo RC	30.00	15.00
❑ 342 J.T. Wall RC	.60	.25
❑ 343 Kirk Farmer RC	.60	.25
❑ 344 Ricky Manning RC	1.25	.50
❑ 345 B.J. Askew RC	1.25	.50
❑ 346 Juston Wood RC	.60	.25
❑ 347 Jeremi Johnson RC	1.00	.40
❑ 348 Tom Lopienski RC	1.00	.40
❑ 349 Justin Griffith RC	1.00	.40
❑ 350 Ovie Mughelli RC	.60	.25
❑ 351 Bradie James RC	1.25	.50
❑ 352 Larry Johnson RC	5.00	2.50
❑ 353 Lee Suggs RC	1.25	.50
❑ 354 Justin Fargas RC	1.25	.50
❑ 355 Chris Brown RC	1.25	.50
❑ 356 Onterrio Smith RC	1.25	.50
❑ 357 Willis McGahee RC	3.00	1.25
❑ 358 Claude Diggs RC	.60	.25
❑ 359 Lance Briggs RC	4.00	1.50
❑ 360 Earnest Graham RC	1.25	.50
❑ 361 Quentin Griffin RC	1.25	.50
❑ 362 Michael Haynes RC	1.25	.50
❑ 363 Musa Smith RC	1.25	.50
❑ 364 Artose Pinner RC	1.25	.50
❑ 365 Domanick Davis RC	1.25	.50
❑ 366 LaBrandon Toefield RC	1.25	.50
❑ 367 Bethel Johnson RC	1.25	.50
❑ 368 Sultan McCullough RC	1.00	.40
❑ 369 Dahrran Diedrick RC	1.25	.50
❑ 370 Soloman Bates RC	.60	.25
❑ 371 Andrew Pinnock RC	1.00	.40
❑ 372 Charles Rogers RC	1.25	.50
❑ 373 Andre Johnson RC	2.50	1.00
❑ 374 Taylor Jacobs RC	1.00	.40
❑ 375 Anquan Boldin RC	3.00	1.25
❑ 376 Talman Gardner RC	1.25	.50
❑ 377 Brandon Lloyd RC	1.25	.50
❑ 378 Bryant Johnson RC	1.25	.50
❑ 379 Kelley Washington RC	1.25	.50
❑ 380 Kareem Kelly RC	1.00	.40
❑ 381 Arnaz Battle RC	1.25	.50
❑ 382 Billy McMullen RC	1.00	.40
❑ 383 Kennan Howry RC	1.25	.50
❑ 384 Nate Burleson RC	1.25	.50
❑ 385 Doug Gabriel RC	1.25	.50
❑ 386 J.R. Tolver RC	1.00	.40
❑ 387 Wayne Hunter RC	.60	.25
❑ 388 Teyo Johnson RC	1.25	.50
❑ 389 Eric Steinbach RC	1.00	.40
❑ 390 Kevin Curtis RC	1.50	.60
❑ 391 Bobby Wade RC	1.25	.50
❑ 392 Sam Aiken RC	1.00	.40
❑ 393 Willie Pile RC	1.25	.50
❑ 394 Jerel Myers RC	.60	.25
❑ 395 Tyrone Calico RC	1.25	.50
❑ 396 Terrence Edwards RC	1.00	.40
❑ 397 Travis Anglin RC	.60	.25
❑ 398 Antwone Savage RC	.60	.25
❑ 399 Cato June RC	1.50	.60
❑ 400 Charles Drake RC	.60	.25

❑ 401 Ronald Bellamy RC	1.00	.40
❑ 402 Justin Gage RC	1.25	.50
❑ 403 Mat McBriar RC	.60	.25
❑ 404 Kevin Garrett RC	.60	.25
❑ 405 Kenny Peterson RC	1.00	.40
❑ 406 L.J. Smith RC	1.25	.50
❑ 407 Jason Witten RC	2.50	1.00
❑ 408 Dallas Clark RC	1.25	.50
❑ 409 DeWayne White RC	1.00	.40
❑ 410 Mike Seidman RC	.60	.25
❑ 411 Aaron Walker RC	1.00	.40
❑ 412 Bennie Joppru RC	1.25	.50
❑ 413 Mike Pinkard RC	.60	.25
❑ 414 [illegible]	[illegible]	.25
❑ 415 Trent Smith RC	1.00	.40
❑ 416 George Wrighster RC	1.00	.40
❑ 417 Terrell Suggs RC	2.00	.75
❑ 418 Tully Banta-Cain RC	1.00	.40
❑ 419 Jerome McDougle RC	1.25	.50
❑ 420 William Joseph RC	1.25	.50
❑ 421 DeWayne Robertson RC	1.25	.50
❑ 422 Jimmy Kennedy RC	1.25	.50
❑ 423 Chris Kelsay RC	1.25	.50
❑ 424 Kevin Williams RC	1.25	.50
❑ 425 Boss Bailey RC	1.25	.50
❑ 426 Terry Pierce RC	1.00	.40
❑ 427 Terence Newman RC	2.50	1.00
❑ 428 Marcus Trufant RC	1.25	.50
❑ 429 Mike Doss RC	1.25	.50
❑ 430 Dennis Weathersby RC	.60	.25
❑ 431 Matt Wilhelm RC	1.25	.50
❑ 432 Andre Woolfolk RC	1.25	.50
❑ 433 Shane Walton RC	.60	.25
❑ 434 DeJuan Groce RC	1.25	.50
❑ 435 Antwoine Sanders RC	.60	.25
❑ 436 Julian Battle RC	1.00	.40
❑ 437 Brett Favre CL	.60	.25
❑ 438 Chad Pennington CL	.30	.10
❑ 439 David Carr CL	.50	.20
❑ 440 Drew Brees CL	.30	.10

2000 Upper Deck Pros and Prospects

❑ COMPLETE SET (126)	600.00	300.00
❑ COMP.SET w/o SP's (84)	20.00	7.50
❑ 1 Jake Plummer	.30	.10
❑ 2 Michael Pittman	.20	.07
❑ 3 Tim Dwight	.50	.20
❑ 4 Chris Chandler	.30	.10
❑ 5 Qadry Ismail	.30	.10
❑ 6 Shannon Sharpe	.30	.10
❑ 7 Peerless Price	.30	.10
❑ 8 Rob Johnson	.30	.10
❑ 9 Eric Moulds	.50	.20
❑ 10 Muhsin Muhammad	.30	.10
❑ 11 Patrick Jeffers	.50	.20
❑ 12 Steve Beuerlein	.30	.10
❑ 13 Cade McNown	.20	.07
❑ 14 Curtis Enis	.20	.07
❑ 15 Marcus Robinson	.50	.20
❑ 16 Akili Smith	.20	.07
❑ 17 Corey Dillon	.50	.20
❑ 18 Tim Couch	.30	.10
❑ 19 Kevin Johnson	.50	.20
❑ 20 Errict Rhett	.30	.10
❑ 21 Troy Aikman	1.00	.40
❑ 22 Emmitt Smith	1.00	.40
❑ 23 Rocket Ismail	.30	.10
❑ 24 Terrell Davis	.50	.20
❑ 25 Olandis Gary	.50	.20
❑ 26 Brian Griese	.50	.20
❑ 27 Ed McCaffrey	.50	.20
❑ 28 Charlie Batch	.50	.20
❑ 29 Germane Crowell	.20	.07
❑ 30 James O. Stewart	.30	.10
❑ 31 Brett Favre	1.50	.60
❑ 32 Antonio Freeman	.50	.20
❑ 33 Dorsey Levens	.30	.10
❑ 34 Peyton Manning	1.25	.50
❑ 35 Edgerrin James	.75	.30
❑ 36 Marvin Harrison	.50	.20
❑ 37 Mark Brunell	.50	.20
❑ 38 Fred Taylor	.50	.20
❑ 39 Jimmy Smith	.30	.10
❑ 40 Elvis Grbac	.30	.10
❑ 41 Tony Gonzalez	.30	.10
❑ 42 Damon Huard	.50	.20
❑ 43 James Johnson	.20	.07
❑ 44 Jay Fiedler	.50	.20
❑ 45 Randy Moss	1.00	.40
❑ 46 Robert Smith	.50	.20
❑ 47 Cris Carter	.50	.20
❑ 48 Drew Bledsoe	.60	.25
❑ 49 Terry Glenn	.30	.10
❑ 50 Ricky Williams	.50	.20
❑ 51 Jeff Blake	.30	.10
❑ 52 Keith Poole	.20	.07
❑ 53 Kerry Collins	.30	.10
❑ 54 Amani Toomer	.20	.07
❑ 55 Vinny Testaverde	.30	.10
❑ 56 Keyshawn Johnson	.50	.20
❑ 57 Curtis Martin	.50	.20
❑ 58 Tim Brown	.50	.20
❑ 59 Rich Gannon	.50	.20
❑ 60 Tyrone Wheatley	.30	.10
❑ 61 Duce Staley	.50	.20
❑ 62 Donovan McNabb	.75	.30
❑ 63 Troy Edwards	.20	.07
❑ 64 Jerome Bettis	.60	.20
❑ 65 Marshall Faulk	.60	.25
❑ 66 Kurt Warner	1.00	.40
❑ 67 Torry Holt	.50	.20
❑ 68 Isaac Bruce	.50	.20
❑ 69 Junior Seau	.50	.20
❑ 70 Jeff Graham	.20	.07
❑ 71 Steve Young	.60	.25
❑ 72 Jerry Rice	1.00	.40
❑ 73 Charlie Garner	.30	.10
❑ 74 [illegible]	[illegible]	[illegible]
❑ 75 Jon Kitna	.50	.20
❑ 76 Warrick Dunn	.50	.20
❑ 77 Shaun King	.20	.07
❑ 78 Mike Alstott	.50	.20
❑ 79 Eddie George	.50	.20
❑ 80 Steve McNair	.50	.20
❑ 81 Kevin Dyson	.30	.10
❑ 82 Brad Johnson	.50	.20
❑ 83 Stephen Davis	.50	.20
❑ 84 Michael Westbrook	.30	.10
❑ 85 Peter Warrick RC	12.00	5.00
❑ 86 LaVar Arrington RC	40.00	15.00
❑ 87 Chris Redman RC	10.00	4.00
❑ 88 Courtney Brown RC	12.00	5.00
❑ 89 Plaxico Burress RC	25.00	10.00
❑ 90 Corey Simon RC	12.00	5.00
❑ 91 Bubba Franks RC	12.00	5.00
❑ 92 Deon Grant RC	10.00	4.00
❑ 93 Brian Urlacher RC	40.00	15.00
❑ 94 Ron Dayne RC	12.00	5.00
❑ 95 Sylvester Morris RC	10.00	4.00
❑ 96 Shaun Alexander RC	50.00	25.00
❑ 97 Dez White RC	12.00	5.00
❑ 98 Thomas Jones RC	20.00	7.50
❑ 99 Travis Taylor RC	12.00	5.00
❑ 100 Kwame Cavil RC	6.00	2.50
❑ 101 Jamal Lewis RC	25.00	10.00
❑ 102 Chad Pennington RC	25.00	10.00
❑ 103 J.R. Redmond RC	10.00	4.00
❑ 104 Sebastian Janikowski RC	12.00	5.00
❑ 105 Anthony Lucas RC	6.00	2.50
❑ 106 Travis Prentice RC	10.00	4.00
❑ 107 Danny Farmer RC	10.00	4.00
❑ 108 Sherrod Gideon RC	6.00	2.50
❑ 109 Todd Pinkston RC	12.00	5.00
❑ 110 Dennis Northcutt RC	12.00	5.00
❑ 111 Tim Rattay RC	12.00	5.00
❑ 112 Troy Walters RC	12.00	5.00
❑ 113 Michael Wiley RC	10.00	4.00
❑ 114 R.Jay Soward RC	10.00	4.00
❑ 115 Trung Canidate RC	10.00	4.00
❑ 116 Reuben Droughns RC	15.00	6.00
❑ 117 Rondell Mealey RC	6.00	2.50
❑ 118 Chris Coleman RC	12.00	5.00
❑ 119 Giovanni Carmazzi RC	10.00	4.00
❑ 120 Trevor Insley RC	10.00	4.00
❑ 121 Shyrone Stith RC	10.00	4.00
❑ 122 Gari Scott RC	6.00	2.50
❑ 123 Tee Martin RC	12.00	5.00
❑ 124 Tom Brady RC	350.00	200.00
❑ 125 Marcus Knight RC	10.00	4.00
❑ 126 Jerry Porter RC	25.00	10.00
❑ 127 Brad Hoover RC	5.00	2.00
❑ 128 Chad Morton RC	8.00	3.00
❑ 129 Charles Lee RC	5.00	2.00
❑ 130 Damon Hodge RC	5.00	2.00
❑ 131 Darrell Jackson RC	15.00	6.00
❑ 132 Doug Johnson RC	8.00	3.00
❑ 133 Frank Moreau RC	5.00	2.00
❑ 134 JaJuan Dawson RC	5.00	2.00
❑ 135 Jake Delhomme RC	30.00	15.00
❑ 136 Jarious Jackson RC	5.00	2.00
❑ 137 Joe Hamilton RC	5.00	2.00
❑ 138 Larry Foster RC	5.00	2.00
❑ 139 Laveranues Coles RC	10.00	4.00
❑ 140 Aaron Shea RC	8.00	3.00
❑ 141 Matt Lytle RC	5.00	2.00
❑ 142 Mike Anderson RC	15.00	6.00
❑ 143 Ron Dixon RC	5.00	2.00
❑ 144 Ronney Jenkins RC	5.00	2.00
❑ 145 Sammy Morris RC	6.00	2.50
❑ 146 Shockmain Davis RC	5.00	2.00
❑ 147 Spergon Wynn RC	5.00	2.00
❑ 148 Todd Husak RC	8.00	3.00
❑ 149 Trevor Gaylor RC	5.00	2.00
❑ 150 Tywan Mitchell RC	5.00	2.00
❑ 151 Windrell Hayes RC	5.00	2.00
❑ 152 Bobby Shaw RC	5.00	2.00

2001 Upper Deck Pros and Prospects

❑ COMP.SET w/o SP's (90)	15.00	6.00
❑ 1 Jake Plummer	.30	.10
❑ 2 David Boston	.50	.20
❑ 3 Jamal Anderson	.50	.20
❑ 4 Doug Johnson	.20	.07
❑ 5 Maurice Smith	.30	.10
❑ 6 Jamal Lewis	.75	.30
❑ 7 Shannon Sharpe	.30	.10
❑ 8 Trent Dilfer	.30	.10
❑ 9 Doug Flutie	.50	.20
❑ 10 Rob Johnson	.30	.10
❑ 11 Eric Moulds	.50	.20
❑ 12 Muhsin Muhammad	.30	.10
❑ 13 Brad Hoover	.20	.07
❑ 14 Tim Biakabutuka	.30	.10
❑ 15 Cade McNown	.20	.07

❑ 16 James Allen	.30	.10
❑ 17 Marcus Robinson	.50	.20
❑ 18 Brian Urlacher	.75	.30
❑ 19 Peter Warrick	.50	.20
❑ 20 Corey Dillon	.50	.20
❑ 21 Tim Couch	.30	.10
❑ 22 Kevin Johnson	.30	.10
❑ 23 Travis Prentice	.20	.07
❑ 24 Troy Aikman	.75	.30
❑ 25 Emmitt Smith	1.00	.40
❑ 26 Terrell Davis	.50	.20
❑ 27 Mike Anderson	.50	.20
❑ 28 Brian Griese	.50	.20
❑ 29 Charlie Batch	.50	.20
❑ 30 Germane Crowell	.20	.07
❑ 31 James Stewart	.30	.10
❑ 32 Brett Favre	1.50	.60
❑ 33 Antonio Freeman	.50	.20
❑ 34 Dorsey Levens	.30	.10
❑ 35 Ahman Green	.50	.20
❑ 36 Peyton Manning	1.25	.50
❑ 37 Edgerrin James	.60	.25
❑ 38 Marvin Harrison	.50	.20
❑ 39 Mark Brunell	.50	.20
❑ 40 Fred Taylor	.50	.20
❑ 41 Jimmy Smith	.30	.10
❑ 42 Elvis Grbac	.30	.10
❑ 43 Tony Gonzalez	.30	.10
❑ 44 Derrick Alexander	.30	.10
❑ 45 Oronde Gadsden	.30	.10
❑ 46 Lamar Smith	.30	.10
❑ 47 Jay Fiedler	.50	.20
❑ 48 Randy Moss	1.00	.40
❑ 49 Moe Williams	.30	.10
❑ 50 Cris Carter	.50	.20
❑ 51 Daunte Culpepper	.50	.20
❑ 52 Drew Bledsoe	.60	.25
❑ 53 Terry Glenn	.30	.10
❑ 54 Ricky Williams	.50	.20
❑ 55 Jeff Blake	.30	.10
❑ 56 Joe Horn	.30	.10
❑ 57 Aaron Brooks	.50	.20
❑ 58 La'Roi Glover	.20	.07
❑ 59 Kerry Collins	.30	.10
❑ 60 Amani Toomer	.30	.10
❑ 61 Ron Dayne	.50	.20
❑ 62 Vinny Testaverde	.30	.10
❑ 63 Wayne Chrebet	.30	.10
❑ 64 Curtis Martin	.50	.20
❑ 65 Tim Brown	.50	.20
❑ 66 Rich Gannon	.50	.20
❑ 67 Tyrone Wheatley	.30	.10
❑ 68 Duce Staley	.50	.20
❑ 69 Donovan McNabb	.60	.25
❑ 70 Kordell Stewart	.30	.10
❑ 71 Jerome Bettis	.50	.20
❑ 72 Marshall Faulk	.60	.25
❑ 73 Kurt Warner	1.00	.40
❑ 74 Isaac Bruce	.50	.20
❑ 75 Junior Seau	.50	.20
❑ 76 Curtis Conway	.30	.10
❑ 77 Jeff Garcia	.50	.20
❑ 78 Jerry Rice	1.00	.40
❑ 79 Charlie Garner	.30	.10
❑ 80 Terrell Owens	.50	.20
❑ 81 Ricky Watters	.20	.07
❑ 82 Shaun Alexander	.60	.25
❑ 83 Warrick Dunn	.50	.20
❑ 84 Shaun King	.20	.07
❑ 85 Derrick Brooks	.50	.20
❑ 86 Eddie George	.50	.20
❑ 87 Steve McNair	.50	.20
❑ 88 Brad Johnson	.50	.20
❑ 89 Jeff George	.30	.10
❑ 90 Stephen Davis	.50	.20
❑ 91 Jamal Reynolds RC	12.00	5.00
❑ 92 Justin Smith RC	12.00	5.00
❑ 93 Dan Morgan RC	12.00	5.00
❑ 94 Deuce McAllister RC	25.00	10.00
❑ 95 Drew Brees RC	50.00	20.00
❑ 96 Josh Booty RC	12.00	5.00
❑ 97 Mike McMahon RC	12.00	5.00
❑ 98 Sage Rosenfels RC	12.00	5.00
❑ 99 Marques Tuiasosopo RC	12.00	5.00
❑ 100 Josh Heupel RC	12.00	5.00
❑ 101 Heath Evans RC	8.00	3.00
❑ 102 Reggie White RC	8.00	3.00
❑ 103 Tim Hasselbeck RC	12.00	5.00
❑ 104 LaDainian Tomlinson RC	80.00	40.00
❑ 105 Kevan Barlow RC	12.00	5.00
❑ 106 LaMont Jordan RC	25.00	10.00
❑ 107 James Jackson RC	12.00	5.00
❑ 108 Anthony Thomas RC	12.00	5.00
❑ 109 Correll Buckhalter RC	15.00	6.00
❑ 110 Travis Henry RC	25.00	10.00
❑ 111 Dan Alexander RC	12.00	5.00
❑ 112 Travis Minor RC	8.00	3.00
❑ 113 Rudi Johnson RC	30.00	12.50
❑ 114 Michael Bennett RC	12.00	5.00
❑ 115 Todd Heap RC	12.00	5.00
❑ 116 Snoop Minnis RC	8.00	3.00
❑ 117 Santana Moss RC	20.00	7.50
❑ 118 Reggie Wayne RC	25.00	10.00
❑ 119 Koren Robinson RC	12.00	5.00
❑ 120 Chris Chambers RC	20.00	7.50
❑ 121 David Terrell RC	12.00	5.00
❑ 122 Rod Gardner RC	12.00	5.00
❑ 123 Quincy Morgan RC	12.00	5.00
❑ 124 Ken-Yon Rambo RC	8.00	3.00
❑ 125 Ronney Daniels RC	5.00	2.00
❑ 126 Ja'Mar Toombs RC	8.00	3.00
❑ 127 Bobby Newcombe RC	8.00	3.00
❑ 128 Cedrick Wilson RC	12.00	5.00
❑ 129 Chad Johnson RC	40.00	15.00
❑ 130 Shaun Rogers RC	12.00	5.00
❑ 131 Robert Ferguson RC	12.00	5.00
❑ 132 Kevin Kasper RC	12.00	5.00
❑ 133 Chris Weinke JSY RC	20.00	7.50
❑ 134 Freddie Mitchell JSY RC	15.00	6.00
❑ 135 Michael Vick JSY RC	50.00	20.00
❑ 136 Chris Taylor RC	8.00	3.00
❑ 137 Vinny Sutherland RC	8.00	3.00
❑ 138 Gerard Warren RC	12.00	5.00
❑ 139 Torrance Marshall RC	12.00	5.00
❑ 140 Jesse Palmer RC	12.00	5.00

2003 Upper Deck Pros and Prospects

❑ COMP.SET w/o SP's (90)	20.00	7.50
❑ 1 Jake Plummer	.60	.25
❑ 2 David Boston	.60	.25
❑ 3 Warrick Dunn	.60	.25
❑ 4 T.J. Duckett	.60	.25
❑ 5 Chris Redman	.40	.15
❑ 6 Jamal Lewis	1.00	.40
❑ 7 Drew Bledsoe	1.00	.40
❑ 8 Travis Henry	.60	.25
❑ 9 Eric Moulds	.60	.25
❑ 10 Peerless Price	.60	.25
❑ 11 Rodney Peete	.60	.25
❑ 12 Julius Peppers	1.00	.40
❑ 13 Anthony Thomas	.60	.25
❑ 14 Brian Urlacher	1.50	.60
❑ 15 Marty Booker	.60	.25
❑ 16 David Terrell	.60	.25
❑ 17 Corey Dillon	.60	.25
❑ 18 Peter Warrick	.60	.25
❑ 19 Jon Kitna	.60	.25
❑ 20 Tim Couch	.40	.15
❑ 21 Andre Davis	.40	.15
❑ 22 Quincy Morgan	.60	.25
❑ 23 Dennis Northcutt	.60	.25
❑ 24 Roy Williams	1.00	.40
❑ 25 Emmitt Smith	2.50	1.00
❑ 26 Joey Galloway	.60	.25
❑ 27 Antonio Bryant	.60	.25
❑ 28 Brian Griese	1.00	.40
❑ 29 Clinton Portis	1.50	.60
❑ 30 Shannon Sharpe	.60	.25
❑ 31 Joey Harrington	1.50	.60
❑ 32 Az-Zahir Hakim	.40	.15
❑ 33 Brett Favre	2.50	1.00
❑ 34 Robert Ferguson	.40	.15
❑ 35 Donald Driver	.60	.25
❑ 36 David Carr	1.50	.60
❑ 37 Jabar Gaffney	.60	.25
❑ 38 Edgerrin James	1.00	.40
❑ 39 Marvin Harrison	1.00	.40
❑ 40 Reggie Wayne	.60	.25
❑ 41 Mark Brunell	.60	.25
❑ 42 Fred Taylor	1.00	.40
❑ 43 Priest Holmes	1.25	.50
❑ 44 Trent Green	.60	.25
❑ 45 Marc Boerigter	.60	.25
❑ 46 Jay Fiedler	.60	.25
❑ 47 Chris Chambers	1.00	.40
❑ 48 Randy McMichael	.60	.25
❑ 49 Randy Moss	1.50	.60
❑ 50 Daunte Culpepper	1.00	.40
❑ 51 Michael Bennett	.60	.25
❑ 52 Antowain Smith	.60	.25
❑ 53 David Patten	.40	.15
❑ 54 Troy Brown	.60	.25
❑ 55 Aaron Brooks	1.00	.40
❑ 56 Joe Horn	.60	.25
❑ 57 Donte Stallworth	1.00	.40
❑ 58 Amani Toomer	.60	.25
❑ 59 Kerry Collins	.60	.25
❑ 60 Tiki Barber	1.00	.40
❑ 61 Santana Moss	.60	.25
❑ 62 Curtis Martin	1.00	.40
❑ 63 Wayne Chrebet	.60	.25
❑ 64 Rich Gannon	.60	.25
❑ 65 Charlie Garner	.60	.25
❑ 66 Tim Brown	1.00	.40
❑ 67 Donovan McNabb	1.25	.50
❑ 68 Duce Staley	.60	.25
❑ 69 Hines Ward	1.00	.40
❑ 70 Antwaan Randle El	1.00	.40
❑ 71 Plaxico Burress	.60	.25
❑ 72 Jerome Bettis	1.00	.40
❑ 73 Junior Seau	1.00	.40
❑ 74 LaDainian Tomlinson	1.00	.40
❑ 75 Tai Streets	.40	.15
❑ 76 Kevan Barlow	.60	.25
❑ 77 Garrison Hearst	.60	.25
❑ 78 Jeff Garcia	1.00	.40
❑ 79 Shaun Alexander	1.00	.40
❑ 80 Matt Hasselbeck	.60	.25
❑ 81 Marshall Faulk	1.00	.40
❑ 82 Marc Bulger	1.00	.40
❑ 83 Torry Holt	1.00	.40
❑ 84 Isaac Bruce	1.00	.40
❑ 85 Brad Johnson	.60	.25
❑ 86 Keyshawn Johnson	1.00	.40
❑ 87 Steve McNair	1.00	.40
❑ 88 Kevin Dyson	.60	.25
❑ 89 Patrick Ramsey	1.00	.40
❑ 90 Ladell Betts	.60	.25
❑ 91 Marcel Shipp SP	2.50	1.00
❑ 92 Michael Vick SP	8.00	3.00
❑ 93 Ray Lewis SP	3.00	1.25
❑ 94 Josh Reed SP	2.50	1.00
❑ 95 Josh McCown SP	2.50	1.00
❑ 96 Kelly Holcomb SP	2.50	1.00
❑ 97 William Green SP	2.50	1.00
❑ 98 Chad Hutchinson SP	1.50	.60
❑ 99 Rod Smith SP	2.50	1.00
❑ 100 James Stewart SP	2.50	1.00
❑ 101 Ahman Green SP	3.00	1.25
❑ 102 Peyton Manning SP	5.00	2.00
❑ 103 Jimmy Smith SP	2.50	1.00
❑ 104 Tony Gonzalez SP	2.50	1.00
❑ 105 Ricky Williams SP	3.00	1.25

❑ 106 Jason Taylor SP 1.50 .60
❑ 107 Tom Brady SP 6.00 2.50
❑ 108 Deuce McAllister SP 3.00 1.25
❑ 109 Jeremy Shockey SP 5.00 2.00
❑ 110 Chad Pennington SP 4.00 1.50
❑ 111 Jerry Rice SP 6.00 2.50
❑ 112 A.J. Feeley SP 2.50 1.00
❑ 113 Tommy Maddox SP 3.00 1.25
❑ 114 Drew Brees SP 3.00 1.25
❑ 115 Terrell Owens SP 3.00 1.25
❑ 116 Maurice Morris SP 1.50 .60
❑ 117 Kurt Warner SP 3.00 1.25
❑ 118 Derrick Brooks SP 2.50 1.00
❑ 119 Eddie George SP 2.50 1.00
❑ 120 Rod Gardner SP 2.50 1.00
❑ 121 Leftwich AU RC/Pnn.AU/250 60.00 30.00
❑ 122 Dorsey AU RC/Test/2000 20.00 7.50
❑ 123 Palmer AU RC/Mnn.AU/250 250.00 150.00
❑ 124 Simms AU RC/Bru.AU/250 50.00 30.00
❑ 125 A.Johnson RC/S.Moss 20.00 7.50
❑ 126 Banks AU RC/Brks.AU/250 30.00 12.50
❑ 127 J.R. Tolver RC/Hakim 4.00 1.50
❑ 128 J.Myers RC/J.Reed 2.50 1.00
❑ 129 R.Bellamy RC/A.Toomer 4.00 1.50
❑ 130 J.Gesser RC/D.Bledsoe 5.00 2.00
❑ 131 Kingsbury AU RC/S.Baugh 20.00 7.50
❑ 132 K.Boller RC/Brees AU/500 50.00 20.00
❑ 133 L.Johnson RC/Thomas AU 40.00 20.00
❑ 134 K.Kelly AU RC/Morton/2000 20.00 7.50
❑ 135 B.Johnson RC/Gard.AU/500 20.00 7.50
❑ 136 Johnson RC/Couch AU/500 25.00 10.00
❑ 137 T.Suggs AU RC/Nmll/2000 20.00 7.50
❑ 138 Ragone RC/Brnll AU/500 30.00 15.00
❑ 139 M.Smith RC/C.Trippi 5.00 2.00
❑ 140 J.Wood RC/J.Harrington 4.00 1.50
❑ 141 J.Thomas RC/Michael Vick 5.00 2.00
❑ 142 Graham AU RC/E.Smt/2000 30.00 15.00
❑ 143 McGahee AU RC/Jms/2000 50.00 20.00
❑ 144 R.Lee RC/Alexander AU/500 30.00 15.00
❑ 145 A.Boldin RC/J.Walker 12.00 5.00
❑ 146 Jacobs AU RC/Cald AU/250 30.00 12.50
❑ 147 T.Gardner RC/L.Coles 5.00 2.00
❑ 148 B.Wade RC/D.Northcutt 5.00 2.00
❑ 149 McMullen RC/Bruce AU/500 20.00 7.50
❑ 150 A.Cobourne RC/A.Zereoue 2.50 1.00
❑ 151 B.James RC/F.Kinard 5.00 2.00
❑ 152 Washing AU RC/Prc/2000 25.00 10.00
❑ 153 E.Steinbach RC/J.Parker 4.00 1.50
❑ 154 J.Kennedy RC/E.Stautner 5.00 2.00
❑ 155 R.Long RC/A.Weinmeister 2.50 1.00
❑ 156 C.Brown AU RC/Andr/2000 25.00 10.00
❑ 157 T.Johnson RC/T.Gonzalez 5.00 2.00
❑ 158 S.Smith RC/M.Morris 8.00 3.00
❑ 159 Fargas AU RC/Portis/2000 20.00 7.50
❑ 160 S.Wallace RC/A.Randle El 5.00 2.00
❑ 161 St.Pierre RC/Mann AU/500 80.00 40.00
❑ 162 Toefield RC/Tmln AU/500 80.00 40.00
❑ 163 M.Blackwell RC/Culpepper 2.50 1.00
❑ 164 K.Howry RC/A.J.Feeley 5.00 2.00
❑ 165 J.Gage RC/K.Farmer RC 5.00 2.00
❑ 166 S.Witten RC/A.Davis 2.50 1.00
❑ 167 Weathersby RC/A.Williams 2.50 1.00
❑ 168 B.Bailey RC/C.Bailey 6.00 2.50
❑ 169 B.Lloyd RC/K.Kittner 5.00 2.00
❑ 170 D.Gabriel RC/C.Chambers 5.00 2.00
❑ 171 A.Gbaja-Biamila RC/KGB 5.00 2.00
❑ 172 D.Diedrick RC/A.Green 5.00 2.00
❑ 173 K.Curtis RC/K.Dyson 6.00 2.50
❑ 174 McCull RC/McAll.AU/500 25.00 12.50
❑ 175 M.Bush RC/M.Trufant RC 5.00 2.00
❑ 176 Z.Hilton RC/S.Aiken RC 4.00 1.50
❑ 177 Newman RC/Woolfolk RC 12.00 6.00
❑ 178 T.Calico RC/K.Holcomb 6.00 2.50
❑ 179 J.T. Wall RC/T.Edwards RC 8.00 3.00
❑ 180 C.Paus RC/M.Seidman RC 8.00 3.00
❑ 181 L.J. Smith RC/M.Battaglia 5.00 2.00
❑ 182 Griffin AU RC/Sav.RC/2000 20.00 7.50
❑ 183 L.Suggs RC/M.Vick 15.00 6.00
❑ 184 B.Askew RC/B.Joppru RC 5.00 2.00
❑ 185 M.Pinkard RC/Todd Heap 2.50 1.00
❑ 186 A.Battle RC/Tim Brown 5.00 2.00
❑ 187 C.Rogers RC/P.Burress 5.00 2.00
❑ 188 A.Pinnock RC/D.Staley 4.00 1.50
❑ 189 Grossman RC/Mnn.AU/500 100.00 50.00
❑ 190 G.Wrighster RC/J.Peelle 4.00 1.50
❑ KBBF K.Boller/B.Favre AU/25 200.00 125.00
❑ RGBF Grossman/Favre AU/25 200.00 100.00

2005 Upper Deck Rookie Debut

❑ COMP.SET w/o SP's (100) 20.00 10.00
❑ ROOKIE STATED ODDS 1:3
❑ UNPRICED BLUE PRINT RUN 15 SETS
❑ 1 Larry Fitzgerald .75 .30
❑ 2 Kurt Warner .50 .20
❑ 3 Anquan Boldin .50 .20
❑ 4 Michael Vick 1.25 .50
❑ 5 Warrick Dunn .50 .20
❑ 6 Peerless Price .40 .15
❑ 7 Jamal Lewis .75 .30
❑ 8 Derrick Mason .50 .20
❑ 9 Kyle Boller .50 .20
❑ 10 Willis McGahee .75 .30
❑ 11 J.P. Losman .75 .30
❑ 12 Eric Moulds .50 .20
❑ 13 Stephen Davis .50 .20
❑ 14 Jake Delhomme .75 .30
❑ 15 Steve Smith .50 .20
❑ 16 Thomas Jones .50 .20
❑ 17 Brian Urlacher .75 .30
❑ 18 Rex Grossman .50 .20
❑ 19 Carson Palmer .75 .30
❑ 20 Rudi Johnson .50 .20
❑ 21 Chad Johnson .75 .30
❑ 22 Kellen Winslow .75 .30
❑ 23 Luke McCown .40 .15
❑ 24 Lee Suggs .50 .20
❑ 25 Drew Bledsoe .75 .30
❑ 26 Keyshawn Johnson .50 .20
❑ 27 Julius Jones 1.00 .40
❑ 28 Roy Williams S .50 .20
❑ 29 Jake Plummer .50 .20
❑ 30 Tatum Bell .50 .20
❑ 31 Rod Smith .50 .20
❑ 32 Roy Williams WR .75 .30
❑ 33 Joey Harrington .75 .30
❑ 34 Kevin Jones .75 .30
❑ 35 Brett Favre 2.00 .75
❑ 36 Javon Walker .50 .20
❑ 37 Ahman Green .75 .30
❑ 38 David Carr .75 .30
❑ 39 Andre Johnson .50 .20
❑ 40 Domanick Davis .50 .20
❑ 41 Peyton Manning 1.25 .50
❑ 42 Marvin Harrison .75 .30
❑ 43 Edgerrin James .75 .30
❑ 44 Reggie Wayne .50 .20
❑ 45 Byron Leftwich .75 .30
❑ 46 Jimmy Smith .50 .20
❑ 47 Fred Taylor .50 .20
❑ 48 Priest Holmes .75 .30
❑ 49 Trent Green .50 .20
❑ 50 Tony Gonzalez .50 .20
❑ 51 Chris Chambers .50 .20
❑ 52 Sammy Morris .40 .15
❑ 53 A.J. Feeley .50 .20
❑ 54 Daunte Culpepper .75 .30
❑ 55 Nate Burleson .50 .20
❑ 56 Michael Bennett .50 .20
❑ 57 Tom Brady 2.00 .75
❑ 58 David Givens .50 .20
❑ 59 Corey Dillon .50 .20
❑ 60 Ty Law .50 .20
❑ 61 Aaron Brooks .50 .20
❑ 62 Joe Horn .50 .20
❑ 63 Deuce McAllister .75 .30
❑ 64 Eli Manning 1.50 .60
❑ 65 Tiki Barber .75 .30
❑ 66 Amani Toomer .50 .20
❑ 67 Chad Pennington .75 .30
❑ 68 Curtis Martin .75 .30
❑ 69 Santana Moss .50 .20
❑ 70 Jerry Porter .50 .20
❑ 71 Randy Moss .75 .30
❑ 72 Kerry Collins .50 .20
❑ 73 Donovan McNabb 1.00 .40
❑ 74 Terrell Owens .75 .30
❑ 75 Brian Westbrook .50 .20
❑ 76 Ben Roethlisberger 2.00 .75
❑ 77 Hines Ward .75 .30
❑ 78 Jerome Bettis .75 .30
❑ 79 Duce Staley .50 .20
❑ 80 Drew Brees .75 .30
❑ 81 LaDainian Tomlinson 1.00 .40
❑ 82 Antonio Gates .75 .30
❑ 83 Tim Rattay .40 .15
❑ 84 Kevan Barlow .50 .20
❑ 85 Eric Johnson .50 .20
❑ 86 Matt Hasselbeck .50 .20
❑ 87 Shaun Alexander 1.00 .40
❑ 88 Darrell Jackson .50 .20
❑ 89 Marc Bulger .75 .30
❑ 90 Marshall Faulk .75 .30
❑ 91 Torry Holt .75 .30
❑ 92 Chris Simms .50 .20
❑ 93 Michael Clayton .75 .30
❑ 94 Michael Pittman .40 .15
❑ 95 Steve McNair .75 .30
❑ 96 Drew Bennett .50 .20
❑ 97 Chris Brown .50 .20
❑ 98 Clinton Portis .75 .30
❑ 99 Patrick Ramsey .50 .20
❑ 100 Laveranues Coles .50 .20
❑ 101 Gino Guidugli RC 1.50 .60
❑ 102 Kyle Orton RC 3.00 1.25
❑ 103 David Greene RC 3.00 1.25
❑ 104 Charlie Frye RC 3.00 1.25
❑ 105 Andrew Walter RC 3.00 1.25
❑ 106 Dan Orlovsky RC 3.00 1.25
❑ 107 Jason White RC 3.00 1.25
❑ 108 Sonny Cumbie RC 2.50 1.00
❑ 109 Ronnie Brown RC 12.00 5.00
❑ 110 Cadillac Williams RC 12.00 5.00
❑ 111 Anthony Davis RC 2.50 1.00
❑ 112 Kay-Jay Harris RC 2.50 1.00
❑ 113 Walter Reyes RC 2.50 1.00
❑ 114 Darren Sproles RC 3.00 1.25
❑ 115 Mark Clayton RC 3.00 1.25
❑ 116 Braylon Edwards RC 10.00 4.00
❑ 117 Charles Frederick RC 2.50 1.00
❑ 118 Fred Gibson RC 2.50 1.00
❑ 119 Craphonso Thorpe RC 2.50 1.00
❑ 120 Terrence Murphy RC 3.00 1.25
❑ 121 Antrel Rolle RC 3.00 1.25
❑ 122 Marlin Jackson RC 3.00 1.25
❑ 123 Corey Webster RC 3.00 1.25
❑ 124 Travis Johnson RC 2.50 1.00
❑ 125 Shawne Merriman RC 5.00 2.00
❑ 126 Aaron Rodgers RC 10.00 4.00
❑ 127 Alex Smith QB RC 12.00 5.00
❑ 128 T.A. McLendon RC 1.50 .60
❑ 129 Troy Williamson RC 3.00 1.25
❑ 130 Ryan Moats RC 3.00 1.25
❑ 131 Vernand Morency RC 3.00 1.25
❑ 132 Brock Berlin RC 2.50 1.00
❑ 133 J.J. Arrington RC 3.00 1.25
❑ 134 Frank Gore RC 6.00 2.50
❑ 135 Chris Henry RC 3.00 1.25
❑ 136 Roscoe Parrish RC 3.00 1.25
❑ 137 Alex Smith TE RC 3.00 1.25
❑ 138 Ciatrick Fason RC 3.00 1.25
❑ 139 Marion Barber RC 5.00 2.00
❑ 140 J.R. Russell RC 2.50 1.00
❑ 141 Heath Miller RC 6.00 2.50

❑ 142 Marcus Spears RC 3.00 1.25
❑ 143 Alvin Pearman RC 3.00 1.25
❑ 144 David Pollack RC 3.00 1.25
❑ 145 Erasmus James RC 3.00 1.25
❑ 146 Noah Herron RC 3.00 1.25
❑ 147 Dan Cody RC 3.00 1.25
❑ 148 Eric Shelton RC 3.00 1.25
❑ 149 Anttaj Hawthorne RC 2.50 1.00
❑ 150 Steve Savoy RC 1.50 .60
❑ 151 Mike Patterson RC 3.00 1.25
❑ 152 Kirk Morrison RC 3.00 1.25
❑ 153 Airese Currie RC 3.00 1.25
❑ 154 Derrick Johnson RC 5.00 2.00
❑ 155 Darryl Blackstock RC 2.50 1.00
❑ 156 Mike Williams 3.00 1.25
❑ 157 Ernest Shazor RC 3.00 1.25
❑ 158 James Butler RC 2.50 1.00
❑ 159 Thomas Davis RC 3.00 1.25
❑ 160 Carlos Rogers RC 4.00 1.50
❑ 161 Mark Bradley RC 3.00 1.25
❑ 162 Jerome Mathis RC 3.00 1.25
❑ 163 Justin Miller RC 2.50 1.00
❑ 164 Donte Nicholson RC 3.00 1.25
❑ 165 Derek Anderson RC 5.00 2.00
❑ 166 Brandon Browner RC 2.50 1.00
❑ 167 Domonique Foxworth RC 3.00 1.25
❑ 168 Kevin Burnett RC 3.00 1.25
❑ 169 Lorenzo Alexander RC 2.50 1.00
❑ 170 Oshiomogho Atogwe RC 2.50 1.00
❑ 171 Dustin Fox RC 3.00 1.25
❑ 172 Jamaal Brimmer RC 1.50 .60
❑ 173 Ryan Fitzpatrick RC 3.00 1.25
❑ 174 Bill Swancutt RC 2.50 1.00
❑ 175 Barrett Ruud RC 3.00 1.25
❑ 176 Channing Crowder RC 3.00 1.25
❑ 177 Timmy Chang RC 2.50 1.00
❑ 178 Chris Rix RC 2.50 1.00
❑ 179 Justin Tuck RC 3.00 1.25
❑ 180 Adam Jones RC 3.00 1.25
❑ 181 Bryant McFadden RC 3.00 1.25
❑ 182 Taylor Stubblefield RC 1.50 .60
❑ 183 Vincent Jackson RC 3.00 1.25
❑ 184 Craig Bragg RC 2.50 1.00
❑ 185 Reggie Brown RC 3.00 1.25
❑ 186 Roddy White RC 3.00 1.25
❑ 187 Jason Campbell RC 5.00 2.00
❑ 188 Derek Wake RC 3.00 1.25
❑ 189 Josh Davis RC 2.50 1.00
❑ 190 Mike Nugent RC 3.00 1.25
❑ 191 Maurice Clarett 3.00 1.25
❑ 192 Brandon Jacobs RC 4.00 1.50
❑ 193 Matt Jones RC 5.00 2.00
❑ 194 Chad Owens RC 3.00 1.25
❑ 195 Paris Warren RC 2.50 1.00
❑ 196 Tab Perry RC 3.00 1.25
❑ 197 Jovan Haye RC 2.50 1.00
❑ 198 Cedric Benson RC 8.00 3.00
❑ 199 Bobby Purify RC 2.50 1.00
❑ 200 Stefan LeFors RC 3.00 1.25

2006 Upper Deck Rookie Debut

❑ COMP.SET w/o RC's (100) 25.00 10.00
❑ 101-200 ROOKIES ONE PER PACK
❑ 201-260 AU ROOKIE ODDS 1:28
❑ 1 Anquan Boldin .50 .20
❑ 2 Larry Fitzgerald .75 .30
❑ 3 Edgerrin James .75 .30
❑ 4 Warrick Dunn .50 .20
❑ 5 Alge Crumpler .50 .20
❑ 6 Michael Vick .75 .30
❑ 7 Jamal Lewis .50 .20
❑ 8 Derrick Mason .40 .15
❑ 9 Steve McNair .50 .20
❑ 10 Willis McGahee .75 .30
❑ 11 Lee Evans .50 .20
❑ 12 J.P. Losman .50 .20
❑ 13 Steve Smith .75 .30
❑ 14 Jake Delhomme .50 .20
❑ 15 DeShaun Foster .50 .20
❑ 16 Rex Grossman .75 .30
❑ 17 Brian Urlacher .75 .30
❑ 18 Thomas Jones .50 .20
❑ 19 Carson Palmer .75 .30
❑ 20 Chad Johnson .50 .20
❑ 21 T.J. Houshmandzadeh .50 .20
❑ 22 Rudi Johnson .50 .20
❑ 23 Charlie Frye .50 .20
❑ 24 Reuben Droughns .50 .20
❑ 25 Braylon Edwards .75 .30
❑ 26 Terrell Owens .75 .30
❑ 27 Julius Jones .75 .30
❑ 28 Drew Bledsoe .75 .30
❑ 29 Terry Glenn .50 .20
❑ 30 Jake Plummer .50 .20
❑ 31 Tatum Bell .50 .20
❑ 32 Javon Walker .50 .20
❑ 33 Kevin Jones .75 .30
❑ 34 Roy Williams WR .75 .30
❑ 35 Jon Kitna .40 .15
❑ 36 Brett Favre 1.50 .60
❑ 37 Donald Driver .50 .20
❑ 38 Ahman Green .50 .20
❑ 39 David Carr .50 .20
❑ 40 Domanick Davis .50 .20
❑ 41 Andre Johnson .50 .20
❑ 42 Peyton Manning 1.25 .50
❑ 43 Reggie Wayne .50 .20
❑ 44 Marvin Harrison .75 .30
❑ 45 Byron Leftwich .50 .20
❑ 46 Greg Jones .40 .15
❑ 47 Ernest Wilford .40 .15
❑ 48 Trent Green .50 .20
❑ 49 Larry Johnson 1.00 .40
❑ 50 Tony Gonzalez .50 .20
❑ 51 Daunte Culpepper .75 .30
❑ 52 Ronnie Brown .75 .30
❑ 53 Chris Chambers .50 .20
❑ 54 Brad Johnson .50 .20
❑ 55 Chester Taylor .50 .20
❑ 56 Troy Williamson .50 .20
❑ 57 Tom Brady 1.25 .50
❑ 58 Deion Branch .50 .20
❑ 59 Corey Dillon .50 .20
❑ 60 Drew Brees .75 .30
❑ 61 Deuce McAllister .50 .20
❑ 62 Joe Horn .50 .20
❑ 63 Eli Manning 1.00 .40
❑ 64 Tiki Barber .75 .30
❑ 65 Plaxico Burress .50 .20
❑ 66 Michael Strahan .50 .20
❑ 67 Chad Pennington .50 .20
❑ 68 Curtis Martin .75 .30
❑ 69 Jonathan Vilma .50 .20
❑ 70 Aaron Brooks .50 .20
❑ 71 Randy Moss .75 .30
❑ 72 LaMont Jordan .50 .20
❑ 73 Donovan McNabb .75 .30
❑ 74 Brian Westbrook .50 .20
❑ 75 L.J. Smith .40 .15
❑ 76 Ben Roethlisberger 1.25 .50
❑ 77 Hines Ward .75 .30
❑ 78 Willie Parker 1.00 .40
❑ 79 LaDainian Tomlinson 1.00 .40
❑ 80 Philip Rivers .75 .30
❑ 81 Antonio Gates .75 .30
❑ 82 Alex Smith QB .75 .30
❑ 83 Antonio Bryant .50 .20
❑ 84 Frank Gore .75 .30
❑ 85 Matt Hasselbeck .50 .20
❑ 86 Shaun Alexander .75 .30
❑ 87 Nate Burleson .50 .20
❑ 88 Julian Peterson .40 .15
❑ 89 Torry Holt .50 .20
❑ 90 Marc Bulger .50 .20
❑ 91 Steven Jackson .75 .30
❑ 92 Cadillac Williams .75 .30
❑ 93 Chris Simms .50 .20
❑ 94 Joey Galloway .50 .20
❑ 95 Drew Bennett .40 .15
❑ 96 David Givens .50 .20
❑ 97 Chris Brown .50 .20
❑ 98 Clinton Portis .75 .30
❑ 99 Santana Moss .50 .20
❑ 100 Antwaan Randle El .50 .20
❑ 101 Todd Watkins RC 3.00 1.25
❑ 102 Damarius Bilbo RC 3.00 1.25
❑ 103 Troy Bergeron RC 3.00 1.25
❑ 104 Jerious Norwood RC 6.00 2.50
❑ 105 Adam Jennings RC 3.00 1.25
❑ 106 Haloti Ngata RC 4.00 1.50
❑ 107 Ed Hinkel RC 4.00 1.50
❑ 108 P.J. Daniels RC 3.00 1.25
❑ 109 Quinn Sypniewski RC 3.00 1.25
❑ 110 Donte Whitner RC 4.00 1.50
❑ 111 John McCargo RC 3.00 1.25
❑ 112 Chris Denney RC 2.00 .75
❑ 113 Richard Marshall RC 3.00 1.25
❑ 114 Brett Basanez RC 4.00 1.50
❑ 115 Nate Salley RC 3.00 1.25
❑ 116 Jeff King RC 3.00 1.25
❑ 117 Danieal Manning RC 4.00 1.50
❑ 118 Devin Hester RC 8.00 3.00
❑ 119 P.J. Pope RC 3.00 1.25
❑ 120 Johnathan Joseph RC 3.00 1.25
❑ 121 Andrew Whitworth RC 2.00 .75
❑ 122 Ethan Kilmer RC 4.00 1.50
❑ 123 Bennie Brazell RC 3.00 1.25
❑ 124 Erik Meyer RC 3.00 1.25
❑ 125 J.D. Runnels RC 3.00 1.25
❑ 126 Kamerion Wimbley RC 4.00 1.50
❑ 127 D'Qwell Jackson RC 3.00 1.25
❑ 128 Lawrence Vickers RC 3.00 1.25
❑ 129 Bobby Carpenter RC 4.00 1.50
❑ 130 Demetrius Summers RC 2.00 .75
❑ 131 Tony Scheffler RC 4.00 1.50
❑ 132 Domenik Hixon RC 3.00 1.25
❑ 133 Daniel Bullocks RC 4.00 1.50
❑ 134 Joe Klopfenstein RC 3.00 1.25
❑ 135 Joel Klatt RC 3.00 1.25
❑ 136 Daryn Colledge RC 4.00 1.50
❑ 137 Brandon Marshall RC 4.00 1.50
❑ 138 Brandon Williams RC 4.00 1.50
❑ 139 Ingle Martin RC 4.00 1.50
❑ 140 Matt Baker RC 4.00 1.50
❑ 141 David Anderson RC 3.00 1.25
❑ 142 Charles Spencer RC 2.00 .75
❑ 143 Wali Lundy RC 4.00 1.50
❑ 144 Mario Williams RC 6.00 2.50
❑ 145 David Kirtman RC 3.00 1.25
❑ 146 Tamba Hali RC 4.00 1.50
❑ 147 Bernard Pollard RC 3.00 1.25
❑ 148 Derrick Ross RC 3.00 1.25
❑ 149 Jeff Webb RC 3.00 1.25
❑ 150 De'Arrius Howard RC 4.00 1.50
❑ 151 Chris Hannon RC 3.00 1.25
❑ 152 Jason Allen RC 4.00 1.50
❑ 153 Devin Aromashodu RC 3.00 1.25
❑ 154 Cedric Griffin RC 3.00 1.25
❑ 155 Ryan Cook RC 3.00 1.25
❑ 156 Jason Carter RC 3.00 1.25
❑ 157 Barrick Nealy RC 3.00 1.25
❑ 158 Wendell Mathis RC 3.00 1.25
❑ 159 David Thomas RC 4.00 1.50
❑ 160 Garrett Mills RC 4.00 1.50
❑ 161 Roman Harper RC 3.00 1.25
❑ 162 Marques Colston RC 15.00 6.00
❑ 163 Travis Wilson RC 4.00 1.50
❑ 164 Anthony Mix RC 3.00 1.25
❑ 165 Nick Mangold RC 3.00 1.25
❑ 166 Brett Elliott RC 4.00 1.50
❑ 167 Antonio Cromartie RC 4.00 1.50
❑ 168 Kevin McMahan RC 3.00 1.25
❑ 169 Derek Hagan RC 3.00 1.25

❑	170 Marcedes Lewis RC	4.00	1.50
❑	171 Kent Smith RC	4.00	1.50
❑	172 John Madsen RC	4.00	1.50
❑	173 Charlie Whitehurst RC	4.00	1.50
❑	174 Deuce Lutui RC	3.00	1.25
❑	175 Jeremy Bloom RC	3.00	1.25
❑	176 Cedric Humes RC	4.00	1.50
❑	177 Jason Avant RC	4.00	1.50
❑	178 Brodie Croyle RC	10.00	4.00
❑	179 Marcus McNeill RC	3.00	1.25
❑	180 Manny Lawson RC	4.00	1.50
❑	181 Delanie Walker RC	3.00	1.25
❑	182 Kelly Jennings RC	4.00	1.50
❑	183 Darryl Tapp RC	[illegible]	[illegible]
❑	184 Ben Obomanu RC	3.00	1.25
❑	185 Travis Lulay RC	3.00	1.25
❑	186 Matt Henshaw RC	3.00	1.25
❑	187 Clinton Solomon RC	3.00	1.25
❑	188 Marques Hagans RC	3.00	1.25
❑	189 Davin Joseph RC	3.00	1.25
❑	190 Jeremy Trueblood RC	3.00	1.25
❑	191 T.J. Williams RC	4.00	1.50
❑	192 Alan Zemaitis RC	4.00	1.50
❑	193 Quinton Ganther RC	3.00	1.25
❑	194 Cody Hodges RC	3.00	1.25
❑	195 Jesse Mahelona RC	3.00	1.25
❑	196 Rocky McIntosh RC	4.00	1.50
❑	197 Mike Espy RC	4.00	1.50
❑	198 Willie Reid RC	4.00	1.50
❑	199 Jonathan Orr RC	3.00	1.25
❑	200 Joe Rubin RC	3.00	1.25
❑	201 A.J. Hawk AU/200* RC	60.00	30.00
❑	202 Anthony Fasano AU RC	15.00	6.00
❑	203 Ashton Youboty AU RC	10.00	4.00
❑	204 Brad Smith AU RC	12.00	5.00
❑	205 Thomas Howard AU RC	10.00	4.00
❑	206 Will Blackmon AU RC	10.00	4.00
❑	207 Brian Calhoun AU/200* RC	20.00	8.00
❑	208 Terrence Whitehead AU RC	10.00	4.00
❑	209 Brodrick Bunkley AU RC	10.00	4.00
❑	210 Bruce Gradkowski AU RC	30.00	12.00
❑	211 Chad Greenway AU RC	15.00	6.00
❑	212 Chad Jackson AU/200* RC	25.00	10.00
❑	213 Mike Bell AU RC	20.00	8.00
❑	214 Clint Ingram AU RC	15.00	6.00
❑	215 Josh Betts AU RC	10.00	4.00
❑	216 D.J. Shockley AU RC	15.00	6.00
❑	217 D.Ferguson AU RC	12.00	5.00
❑	218 DeA.Williams AU/25* RC	250.00	125.00
❑	219 DeMeco Ryans AU RC	12.00	5.00
❑	220 Demetrius Williams AU RC	10.00	4.00
❑	221 Martin Nance AU RC	10.00	4.00
❑	222 Dominique Byrd AU RC	12.00	5.00
❑	223 Drew Olson AU RC	10.00	4.00
❑	224 Ernie Sims AU RC	12.00	5.00
❑	225 Gerald Riggs AU RC	12.00	5.00
❑	226 Greg Jennings AU RC	40.00	20.00
❑	227 Greg Lee AU RC	10.00	4.00
❑	228 Hank Baskett AU RC	12.00	5.00
❑	229 Jay Cutler AU/50* RC	400.00	200.00
❑	230 DonTrell Moore AU RC	10.00	4.00
❑	231 Jerome Harrison AU RC	15.00	6.00
❑	232 Jimmy Williams AU RC	12.00	5.00
❑	233 Darnell Bing AU RC	10.00	4.00
❑	234 Joseph Addai AU RC	100.00	50.00
❑	235 Kellen Clemens AU/200* RC	25.00	15.00
❑	236 Maroney AU/50* RC	200.00	100.00
❑	237 LenDale White AU/200* RC	40.00	20.00
❑	238 Leon Washington AU RC	25.00	10.00
❑	239 Leonard Pope AU RC	12.00	5.00
❑	240 Cory Rodgers AU RC	10.00	4.00
❑	241 Darrell Hackney AU RC	10.00	4.00
❑	242 Mathias Kiwanuka AU RC	15.00	6.00
❑	243 Matt Leinart AU/50* RC	400.00	200.00
❑	244 Maurice Drew AU/300* RC	60.00	30.00
❑	245 Maurice Stovall AU/300* RC	20.00	8.00
❑	246 Michael Huff AU/300* RC	20.00	8.00
❑	247 Michael Robinson AU RC	10.00	4.00
❑	248 Mike Hass AU RC	10.00	4.00
❑	249 Omar Jacobs AU RC	10.00	4.00
❑	250 Owen Daniels AU RC	20.00	8.00
❑	251 Reggie Bush AU/25* RC	500.00	250.00
❑	252 Reggie McNeal AU RC	10.00	4.00
❑	253 S.Holmes AU/120* RC	50.00	25.00
❑	254 Sinorice Moss AU/240* RC	25.00	10.00
❑	255 Tarvaris Jackson AU/300* RC	50.00	25.00
❑	256 Andre Hall AU RC	10.00	4.00
❑	257 Tye Hill AU RC	12.00	5.00
❑	258 V.Davis AU/100* RC EXCH	50.00	25.00
❑	259 Vince Young AU/25* RC	500.00	250.00
❑	260 Winston Justice AU RC	12.00	5.00

2005 Upper Deck Rookie Premiere

❑	COMPLETE SET (30)	20.00	10.00
❑	1 Ciatrick Fason	.75	.30
❑	2 Alex Smith QB	3.00	1.25
❑	3 Antrel Rolle	.75	.30
❑	4 Cadillac Williams	3.00	1.25
❑	5 Ronnie Brown	3.00	1.25
❑	6 Charlie Frye	.75	.30
❑	7 Roddy White	.75	.30
❑	8 Braylon Edwards	2.50	1.00
❑	9 Mark Bradley	.75	.30
❑	10 Vincent Jackson	.75	.30
❑	11 Matt Jones	1.25	.50
❑	12 Stefan LeFors	.75	.30
❑	13 Kyle Orton	.75	.30
❑	14 Troy Williamson	.75	.30
❑	15 Mark Clayton	.75	.30
❑	16 Aaron Rodgers	2.50	1.00
❑	17 Cedric Benson	2.00	.75
❑	18 Mike Williams	.75	.30
❑	19 Adam Jones	.75	.30
❑	20 Reggie Brown	.75	.30
❑	21 J.J. Arrington	.75	.30
❑	22 Andrew Walter	.75	.30
❑	23 David Greene	.75	.30
❑	24 Roscoe Parrish	.75	.30
❑	25 Terrence Murphy	.75	.30
❑	26 Jason Campbell	1.25	.50
❑	27 Maurice Clarett	.75	.30
❑	28 Frank Gore	2.00	.75
❑	29 Ryan Moats	.75	.30
❑	30 Checklist Card	.75	.30

2006 Aspire

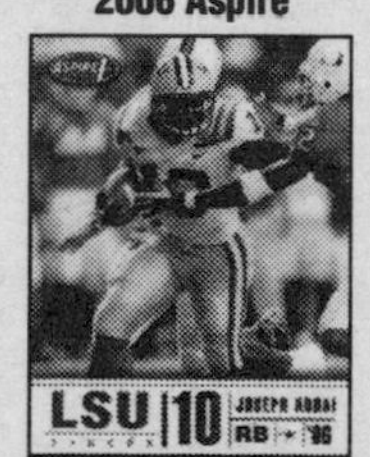

❑	COMPLETE SET (36)	25.00	10.00
❑	1 Reggie Bush	4.00	1.50
❑	2 Matt Leinart	3.00	1.25
❑	3 Vince Young	4.00	1.50
❑	4 Mario Williams	1.50	.60
❑	5 Michael Huff	1.25	.50
❑	6 Vernon Davis	2.00	.75
❑	7 LenDale White	2.00	.75
❑	8 Brodie Croyle	2.50	1.00
❑	9 Drew Olson	.75	.30
❑	10 Maurice Drew	2.50	1.00
❑	11 Tye Hill	1.00	.40
❑	12 Michael Robinson	1.00	.40
❑	13 Joseph Addai	3.00	1.25
❑	14 Paul Pinegar	.75	.30
❑	15 Jimmy Williams	1.00	.40
❑	16 D.J. Shockley	1.00	.40
❑	17 Mike Hass	1.00	.40
❑	18 Demetrius Williams	1.00	.40
❑	19 Reggie McNeal	.75	.30
❑	20 Charlie Whitehurst	1.00	.40
❑	21 Maurice Stovall	1.00	.40
❑	22 Sinorice Moss	1.00	.40
❑	23 Jason Avant	1.00	.40
❑	24 Omar Jacobs	.75	.30
❑	25 Laurence Maroney	2.50	1.00
❑	26 Martin Nance	.75	.30
❑	27 Leonard Pope	1.00	.40
❑	28 Rodrique Wright	.50	.20
❑	29 David Thomas	1.00	.40
❑	30 Will Blackmon	.75	.30
❑	31 Dominique Byrd	.75	.30
❑	32 D'Brickashaw Ferguson	1.00	.40
❑	33 Reggie Bush	4.00	1.50
❑	34 Matt Leinart	3.00	1.25
❑	35 Vince Young	4.00	1.50
❑	36 Jay Cutler	3.00	1.25

2007 Aspire

❑	1 JaMarcus Russell	2.50	1.00
❑	2 Brady Quinn	3.00	1.25
❑	3 Drew Stanton	1.25	.50
❑	4 John Beck	2.00	.75
❑	5 Trent Edwards	2.00	.75
❑	6 Troy Smith	1.50	.60
❑	7 Kevin Kolb	1.50	.60
❑	8 Jared Zabransky	1.00	.40
❑	9 Jordan Palmer	1.00	.40
❑	10 Chris Leak	.75	.30
❑	11 Adrian Peterson	8.00	3.00
❑	12 Marshawn Lynch	2.00	.75
❑	13 Brian Leonard	1.00	.40
❑	14 Antonio Pittman	.75	.30
❑	15 Kenny Irons	1.00	.40
❑	16 Michael Bush	1.25	.50
❑	17 Darius Walker	1.00	.40
❑	18 Calvin Johnson	3.00	1.25
❑	19 Robert Meachem	1.00	.40
❑	20 Dwayne Bowe	2.00	.75
❑	21 Sidney Rice	1.50	.60
❑	22 Craig Buster Davis	1.00	.40
❑	23 Steve Smith USC	1.25	.50
❑	24 Anthony Gonzalez	1.50	.60
❑	25 Greg Olsen	1.25	.50

❑ 26 Zach Miller	.75	.30
❑ 27 Levi Brown	1.00	.40
❑ 28 Gaines Adams	1.00	.40
❑ 29 Leon Hall	.75	.30
❑ 30 Ted Ginn Jr.	1.50	.60
❑ 31 Patrick Willis	1.50	.60
❑ 32 Adam Carriker	.75	.30
❑ 33 Aaron Ross	1.00	.40

1996 Press Pass

❑ COMPLETE SET (55)	20.00	7.50
❑ 1 Keyshawn Johnson	1.50	.60
❑ 2 Jonathan Ogden	.60	.25
❑ 3 Duane Clemons	.20	.07
❑ 4 Kevin Hardy	.20	.07
❑ 5 Eddie George	2.50	1.00
❑ 6 Karim Abdul-Jabbar	.60	.25
❑ 7 Terry Glenn	.60	.25
❑ 8 Leeland McElroy	.40	.15
❑ 9 Simeon Rice	.75	.30
❑ 10 Roman Oben	.20	.07
❑ 11 Daryl Gardener	.20	.07
❑ 12 Marcus Coleman	.20	.07
❑ 13 Christian Peter	.20	.07
❑ 14 Tim Biakabutuka	.60	.25
❑ 15 Eric Moulds	1.50	.60
❑ 16 Chris Darkins	.20	.07
❑ 17 Andre Johnson	.20	.07
❑ 18 Lawyer Milloy	.60	.25
❑ 19 Jon Runyan	.20	.07
❑ 20 Mike Alstott	1.50	.60
❑ 21 Jeff Hartings	.60	.25
❑ 22 Amani Toomer	1.25	.50
❑ 23 Danny Kanell	.60	.25
❑ 24 Marco Battaglia	.20	.07
❑ 25 Stephen Davis	1.50	.60
❑ 26 Johnny McWilliams	.20	.07
❑ 27 Israel Ifeanyi	.20	.07
❑ 28 Scott Slutzker	.20	.07
❑ 29 Bryant Mix	.20	.07
❑ 30 Brian Roche	.20	.07
❑ 31 Stanley Pritchett	.20	.07
❑ 32 Jerome Woods	.20	.07
❑ 33 Tommie Frazier	.40	.15
❑ 34 Stepfret Williams	.20	.07
❑ 35 Ray Mickens	.20	.07
❑ 36 Alex Van Dyke	.20	.07
❑ 37 Bobby Hoying	.60	.25
❑ 38 Tony Brackens	.60	.25
❑ 39 Dietrich Jells	.20	.07
❑ 40 Jason Odom	.20	.07
❑ 41 Randall Godfrey	.20	.07
❑ 42 Willie Anderson	.20	.07
❑ 43 Tony Banks	.60	.25
❑ 44 Michael Cheever	.20	.07
❑ 45 Je'Rod Cherry	.20	.07
❑ 46 Chris Doering	.20	.07
❑ 47 Steve Taneyhill	.20	.07
❑ 48 Kyle Wachholtz	.20	.07
❑ 49 Dusty Zeigler	.20	.07
❑ 50 Derrick Mayes	.40	.15
❑ 51 Orpheus Roye	.20	.07
❑ 52 Sedric Clark	.20	.07
❑ 53 Richard Huntley	.40	.15
❑ 54 Donnie Edwards	.60	.25
❑ 55 Zach Thomas CL	.60	.25
❑ RED Lawrence Phillips	6.00	2.50
❑ P1 Tim Biakabutuka Promo	1.00	.40

1997 Press Pass

❑ COMPLETE SET (49)	20.00	7.50
❑ 1 Orlando Pace	.50	.20
❑ 2 Warrick Dunn	1.25	.50
❑ 3 Danny Wuerffel	.50	.20
❑ 4 Darnell Autry	.20	.07
❑ 5 Troy Davis	.20	.07
❑ 6 Jake Plummer	2.00	.75
❑ 7 Corey Dillon	2.50	1.00
❑ 8 Reidel Anthony	.50	.20
❑ 9 Byron Hanspard	.30	.10
❑ 10 Tiki Barber	2.50	1.00
❑ 11 Ike Hilliard	.50	.20
❑ 12 Rae Carruth	.20	.07
❑ 13 Yatil Green	.30	.10
❑ 14 Peter Boulware	.50	.20
❑ 15 Jim Druckenmiller	.30	.10
❑ 16 Pat Barnes	.20	.07
❑ 17 Trevor Pryce	.50	.20
❑ 18 Kevin Lockett	.20	.07
❑ 19 Koy Detmer	.50	.20
❑ 20 Bryant Westbrook	.20	.07
❑ 21 Darrell Russell	.20	.07
❑ 22 Tony Gonzalez	1.25	.50
❑ 23 Shawn Springs	.30	.10
❑ 24 Chris Canty	.20	.07
❑ 25 David LaFleur	.20	.07
❑ 26 Dwayne Rudd	.20	.07
❑ 27 Bob Sapp	.50	.20
❑ 28 Mike Vrabel	2.00	.75
❑ 29 Antowain Smith	1.00	.40
❑ 30 Keith Poole	.20	.07
❑ 31 Sedrick Shaw	.30	.10
❑ 32 Tremain Mack	.20	.07
❑ 33 Matt Russell	.20	.07
❑ 34 Reinard Wilson	.30	.10
❑ 35 Marc Edwards	.30	.10
❑ 36 Greg Jones	.20	.07
❑ 37 Michael Booker	.20	.07
❑ 38 James Farrior	.50	.20
❑ 39 Danny Wuerffel HL	.30	.10
❑ 40 Troy Davis HL	.20	.07
❑ 41 Corey Dillon HL	1.00	.40
❑ 42 Jake Plummer HL	.75	.30
❑ 43 Peter Boulware HL	.30	.10
❑ 44 Eddie Robinson CO	.50	.20
❑ 45 Bobby Bowden CO	.75	.30
❑ 46 Steve Spurrier CO	1.25	.50
❑ 47 Gary Barnett CO	.20	.07
❑ 48 Joe Paterno CO SP	50.00	20.00
❑ 49 Tom Osborne CO	1.25	.50
❑ 50 Jarrett Irons CL	.20	.07

1998 Press Pass

❑ COMPLETE SET (50)	20.00	7.50
❑ 1 Peyton Manning	8.00	4.00
❑ 2 Ryan Leaf	.50	.20
❑ 3 Charles Woodson	.75	.30
❑ 4 Andre Wadsworth	.30	.10
❑ 5 Randy Moss	5.00	2.00
❑ 6 Curtis Enis	.25	.08
❑ 7 Tra Thomas	.25	.08
❑ 8 Flozell Adams	.25	.08
❑ 9 Jason Peter	.25	.08
❑ 10 Brian Simmons	.30	.10
❑ 11 Takeo Spikes	.50	.20
❑ 12 Michael Myers	.25	.08
❑ 13 Kevin Dyson	.50	.20
❑ 14 Grant Wistrom	.30	.10
❑ 15 Fred Taylor	1.25	.50
❑ 16 Germane Crowell	.30	.10
❑ 17 Sam Cowart	.30	.10
❑ 18 Anthony Simmons LB	.30	.10
❑ 19 Robert Edwards	.30	.10
❑ 20 Shaun Williams	.30	.10
❑ 21 Phil Savoy	.25	.08
❑ 22 Leonard Little	.50	.20
❑ 23 Saladin McCullough	.25	.08
❑ 24 Duane Starks	.25	.08
❑ 25 John Avery	.30	.10
❑ 26 Vonnie Holliday	.50	.20
❑ 27 Tim Dwight	.50	.20
❑ 28 Donovin Darius	.30	.10
❑ 29 Alonzo Mayes	.25	.08
❑ 30 Jerome Pathon	.50	.20
❑ 31 Brian Kelly	.30	.10
❑ 32 Hines Ward	2.50	1.25
❑ 33 Jacquez Green	.30	.10
❑ 34 Marcus Nash	.25	.08
❑ 35 Ahman Green	2.50	1.00
❑ 36 Joe Jurevicius	.50	.20
❑ 37 Tavian Banks	.30	.10
❑ 38 Donald Hayes	.30	.10
❑ 39 Robert Holcombe	.30	.10
❑ 40 E.G. Green	.30	.10
❑ 41 John Dutton	.25	.08
❑ 42 Skip Hicks	.30	.10
❑ 43 Pat Johnson	.30	.10
❑ 44 Keith Brooking	.50	.20
❑ 45 Alan Faneca	1.00	.40
❑ 46 Steve Spurrier CO	1.00	.40
❑ 47 Mike Price CO	.25	.08
❑ 48 Bobby Bowden CO	.30	.10
❑ 49 Tom Osborne CO	1.00	.40
❑ 50 Peyton Manning CL	1.50	.60
❑ P1 Randy Moss Promo	4.00	1.50

1999 Press Pass

❑ COMPLETE SET (45)	20.00	7.50
❑ 1 Ricky Williams	1.25	.50
❑ 2 Tim Couch	.60	.25
❑ 3 Champ Bailey	1.00	.40
❑ 4 Chris Claiborne	.30	.10

❑ 5 Donovan McNabb 3.00 1.25
❑ 6 Edgerrin James 2.50 1.00
❑ 7 Akili Smith 1.00 .40
❑ 8 John Tait .30 .10
❑ 9 Jevon Kearse 1.50 .60
❑ 10 Torry Holt 1.50 .60
❑ 11 Troy Edwards .40 .15
❑ 12 Chris McAlister .40 .15
❑ 13 Daunte Culpepper 2.50 1.00
❑ 14 Andy Katzenmoyer .40 .15
❑ 15 David Boston .60 .25
❑ 16 Ebenezer Ekuban .40 .15
❑ 17 Peerless Price .60 .25
❑ 18 Shaun King .40 .15
❑ 19 Joe Germaine .40 .15
❑ 20 Brock Huard .60 .25
❑ 21 Michael Bishop .60 .25
❑ 22 Amos Zereoue .60 .25
❑ 23 Sedrick Irvin .30 .10
❑ 24 Autry Denson .40 .15
❑ 25 Kevin Faulk .60 .25
❑ 26 James Johnson .40 .15
❑ 27 D'Wayne Bates .40 .15
❑ 28 Kevin Johnson 1.00 .40
❑ 29 Tai Streets .60 .25
❑ 30 Craig Yeast .40 .15
❑ 31 Dre' Bly .60 .25
❑ 32 Anthony Poindexter .30 .10
❑ 33 Jared DeVries .30 .10
❑ 34 Rob Konrad .60 .25
❑ 35 Dat Nguyen .60 .25
❑ 36 Cade McNown .40 .15
❑ 37 Scott Covington .60 .25
❑ 38 Jon Jansen .30 .10
❑ 39 Rufus French .30 .10
❑ 40 [illegible]
❑ 41 Aaron Gibson .30 .10
❑ 42 Kris Farris .30 .10
❑ 43 Anthony McFarland .30 .10
❑ 44 Matt Stinchcomb .40 .15
❑ 45 Dee Miller CL .30 .10

2000 Press Pass

❑ COMPLETE SET (45) 25.00 10.00
❑ 1 Peter Warrick .50 .20
❑ 2 Travis Claridge .25 .08
❑ 3 Courtney Brown .60 .25
❑ 4 Plaxico Burress 1.00 .40
❑ 5 Chad Pennington 1.00 .40
❑ 6 Thomas Jones .75 .30
❑ 7 Ron Dayne .50 .20
❑ 8 Brian Urlacher 2.00 .75
❑ 9 Corey Simon .60 .25
❑ 10 Chris Samuels .40 .15
❑ 11 Stockar McDougle .25 .08
❑ 12 Deon Grant .40 .15
❑ 13 Cosey Coleman .25 .08
❑ 14 Sylvester Morris .40 .15
❑ 15 Shyrone Stith .40 .15
❑ 16 Shaun Alexander 2.50 1.00
❑ 17 Dez White .50 .20
❑ 18 [illegible]
❑ 19 Tim Rattay .50 .20
❑ 20 Todd Pinkston .50 .20
❑ 21 John Abraham .50 .20
❑ 22 R.Jay Soward .40 .15
❑ 23 Shaun Ellis .50 .20
❑ 24 Keith Bulluck .50 .20
❑ 25 Jerry Porter .60 .25
❑ 26 Darren Howard .40 .15
❑ 27 Joe Hamilton .40 .15
❑ 28 Deltha O'Neal .50 .20
❑ 29 Chris Redman .40 .15
❑ 30 Deon Dyer .40 .15
❑ 31 Jamal Lewis 1.00 .40
❑ 32 Chris Hovan .40 .15
❑ 33 Raynoch Thompson .40 .15
❑ 34 Travis Taylor .50 .20
❑ 35 Sebastian Janikowski .50 .20
❑ 36 Travis Prentice .40 .15
❑ 37 Tom Brady 20.00 10.00
❑ 38 Tee Martin .50 .20
❑ 39 J.R. Redmond .40 .15
❑ 40 Dennis Northcutt .50 .20
❑ 41 Laveranues Coles .60 .25
❑ 42 Danny Farmer .40 .15
❑ 43 Darrell Jackson 1.00 .40
❑ 44 Chris McIntosh .25 .08
❑ 45 Peter Warrick CL .40 .15
❑ P1 Peter Warrick Promo 2.00 .75

2001 Press Pass

❑ COMPLETE SET (50) 25.00 10.00
❑ COMP.FACTORY SET (46) 25.00 10.00
❑ COMP.SET w/o SP's (45) 20.00 7.50
❑ 1 Michael Vick CL 1.50 .60
❑ 2 Drew Brees 3.00 1.25
❑ 3 Michael Vick 3.00 1.25
❑ 4 Chris Weinke .75 .30
❑ 5 Marques Tuiasosopo .75 .30
❑ 6 Josh Booty .75 .30
❑ 7 Josh Heupel .75 .30
❑ 8 Sage Rosenfels .75 .30
❑ 9 Mike McMahon .75 .30
❑ 10 Deuce McAllister 2.00 .75
❑ 11 LaDainian Tomlinson 12.00 5.00
❑ 12 LaMont Jordan 1.50 .60
❑ 13 James Jackson .75 .30
❑ 14 Travis Henry 2.00 .75
❑ 15 Anthony Thomas .75 .30
❑ 16 Travis Minor .60 .25
❑ 17 Michael Bennett .75 .30
❑ 18 Kevan Barlow .75 .30
❑ 19 Rudi Johnson 1.50 .60
❑ 20 Santana Moss 1.50 .60
❑ 21 Quincy Morgan .75 .30
❑ 22 Rod Gardner .75 .30
❑ 23 David Terrell .75 .30
❑ 24 Chris Chambers 1.50 .60
❑ 25 Reggie Wayne 2.00 .75
❑ 26 Ken-Yon Rambo .60 .25
❑ 27 Chad Johnson 2.00 .75
❑ 28 Snoop Minnis .60 .25
❑ 29 Freddie Mitchell .75 .30
❑ 30 Koren Robinson .75 .30
❑ 31 [illegible]
❑ 32 Robert Ferguson .75 .30
❑ 33 Todd Heap .75 .30
❑ 34 Steve Hutchinson .60 .25
❑ 35 Leonard Davis .60 .25
❑ 36 Kenyatta Walker .40 .15
❑ 37 Justin Smith .75 .30
❑ 38 Jamal Reynolds .75 .30
❑ 39 Richard Seymour .75 .30
❑ 40 Shaun Rogers .75 .30
❑ 41 Gerard Warren .75 .30
❑ 42 Jamar Fletcher .60 .25
❑ 43 Gary Baxter .60 .25
❑ 44 Nate Clements .75 .30
❑ 45 Derrick Gibson .60 .25
❑ 46 Drew Brees PP 6.00 2.50
❑ 47 Michael Vick PP 6.00 2.50
❑ 48 Deuce McAllister PP 4.00 1.50
❑ 49 LaDainian Tomlinson PP 15.00 6.00
❑ 50 David Terrell PP 1.00 .40

2002 Press Pass

❑ COMPLETE SET (50) 40.00 15.00
❑ COMP.SET w/o SP's (45) 25.00 10.00
❑ 1 David Carr 2.00 .75
❑ 2 Eric Crouch 1.00 .40
❑ 3 Rohan Davey 1.00 .40
❑ 4 David Garrard 2.00 .75
❑ 5 Joey Harrington 1.25 .50
❑ 6 Kurt Kittner .75 .30
❑ 7 David Neill .75 .30
❑ 8 Patrick Ramsey 1.00 .40
❑ 9 Antwaan Randle El 1.25 .50
❑ 10 Damien Anderson .75 .30
❑ 11 T.J. Duckett 1.00 .40
❑ 12 DeShaun Foster 1.00 .40
❑ 13 Lamar Gordon 1.00 .40
❑ 14 William Green 1.00 .40
❑ 15 Leonard Henry .75 .30
❑ 16 Adrian Peterson 1.25 .50
❑ 17 Clinton Portis 4.00 1.50
❑ 18 Jonathan Wells 1.00 .40
❑ 19 Brian Westbrook 2.00 .75
❑ 20 Antonio Bryant 1.00 .40
❑ 21 Reche Caldwell 1.00 .40
❑ 22 Kelly Campbell .75 .30
❑ 23 Andre Davis .75 .30
❑ 24 Jabar Gaffney 1.00 .40
❑ 25 Ron Johnson .75 .30
❑ 26 Ashley Lelie 2.00 .75
❑ 27 Josh Reed 1.00 .40

- ❑ 28 Cliff Russell .75 .30
- ❑ 29 Donte Stallworth 1.50 .60
- ❑ 30 Javon Walker 1.50 .60
- ❑ 31 Marquise Walker .75 .30
- ❑ 32 Daniel Graham 1.00 .40
- ❑ 33 Jeremy Shockey 4.00 1.50
- ❑ 34 Bryant McKinnie .75 .30
- ❑ 35 Mike Pearson .50 .20
- ❑ 36 Mike Williams .75 .30
- ❑ 37 Phillip Buchanon 1.00 .40
- ❑ 38 Quentin Jammer 1.00 .40
- ❑ 39 Kalimba Edwards 1.00 .40
- ❑ 40 Julius Peppers 2.00 .75
- ❑ 41 Wendell Bryant .50 .20
- ❑ 42 John Henderson 1.00 .40
- ❑ 43 Ryan Sims 1.00 .40
- ❑ 44 Roy Williams 2.00 .75
- ❑ 45 David Carr CL 1.00 .40
- ❑ 46 David Carr PP 4.00 1.50
- ❑ 47 Joey Harrington PP 3.00 1.25
- ❑ 48 T.J. Duckett PP 2.00 .75
- ❑ 49 Donte Stallworth PP 4.00 1.50
- ❑ 50 William Green PP 2.50 1.00

2003 Press Pass

- ❑ COMPLETE SET (50) 50.00 20.00
- ❑ COMP.SET w/o SP's (45) 25.00 10.00
- ❑ 1 Brad Banks .75 .30
- ❑ 2 Kyle Boller 1.00 .40
- ❑ 3 Ken Dorsey 1.00 .40
- ❑ 4 Jason Gesser 1.00 .40
- ❑ 5 Rex Grossman 3.00 1.25
- ❑ 6 Kliff Kingsbury .75 .30
- ❑ 7 Byron Leftwich 3.00 1.25
- ❑ 8 Carson Palmer 4.00 1.50
- ❑ 9 Dave Ragone 1.00 .40
- ❑ 10 Chris Simms 1.50 .60
- ❑ 11 Brian St.Pierre 1.00 .40
- ❑ 12 Chris Brown 1.00 .40
- ❑ 13 Avon Cobourne .50 .20
- ❑ 14 Dahrran Diedrick 1.00 .40
- ❑ 15 Justin Fargas 1.00 .40
- ❑ 16 Earnest Graham 1.00 .40
- ❑ 17 Larry Johnson 4.00 2.00
- ❑ 18 Willis McGahee 2.50 1.00
- ❑ 19 Musa Smith 1.00 .40
- ❑ 20 Onterrio Smith 1.00 .40
- ❑ 21 Lee Suggs 1.00 .40
- ❑ 22 Anquan Boldin 2.50 1.00
- ❑ 23 Talman Gardner 1.00 .40
- ❑ 24 Taylor Jacobs .75 .30
- ❑ 25 Andre Johnson 2.00 .75
- ❑ 26 Bryant Johnson 1.00 .40
- ❑ 27 Brandon Lloyd 1.00 .40
- ❑ 28 Charles Rogers 1.00 .40
- ❑ 29 Kelley Washington 1.00 .40
- ❑ 30 Teyo Johnson 1.00 .40
- ❑ 31 Bennie Joppru 1.00 .40
- ❑ 32 Jason Witten 2.00 .75
- ❑ 33 Andrew Pinnock .75 .30
- ❑ 34 Jordan Gross .75 .30
- ❑ 35 Kwame Harris .75 .30
- ❑ 36 Eric Steinbach .75 .30
- ❑ 37 Brett Williams .50 .20
- ❑ 38 Terence Newman 2.00 .75
- ❑ 39 Marcus Trufant 1.00 .40
- ❑ 40 Andre Woolfolk 1.00 .40
- ❑ 41 Terrell Suggs 1.50 .60
- ❑ 42 Jimmy Kennedy 1.00 .40
- ❑ 43 Boss Bailey 1.00 .40
- ❑ 44 Mike Doss 1.00 .40
- ❑ 45 Carson Palmer CL 1.50 .60
- ❑ 46 Carson Palmer PP 8.00 3.00
- ❑ 47 Byron Leftwich PP 6.00 2.50
- ❑ 48 Charles Rogers PP 2.00 .75
- ❑ 49 Kyle Boller PP 2.00 .75
- ❑ 50 Andre Johnson PP 4.00 1.50

2004 Press Pass

- ❑ COMPLETE SET (50) 50.00 20.00
- ❑ COMP.SET w/o SP's (45) 30.00 12.50
- ❑ 1 Casey Clausen 1.00 .40
- ❑ 2 Craig Krenzel 1.00 .40
- ❑ 3 J.P. Losman 2.00 .75
- ❑ 4 Eli Manning 5.00 2.50
- ❑ 5 Luke McCown 1.00 .40
- ❑ 6 John Navarre 1.00 .40
- ❑ 7 Cody Pickett 1.00 .40
- ❑ 8 Philip Rivers 3.00 1.25
- ❑ 9 Ben Roethlisberger 6.00 2.50
- ❑ 10 Matt Schaub 3.00 1.25
- ❑ 11 Cedric Cobbs 1.00 .40
- ❑ 12 Steven Jackson 3.00 1.25
- ❑ 13 Kevin Jones 2.50 1.00
- ❑ 14 Greg Jones 1.00 .40
- ❑ 15 Julius Jones 3.00 1.25
- ❑ 16 Jarrett Payton 1.00 .40
- ❑ 17 Chris Perry 1.25 .50
- ❑ 18 Michael Turner 1.25 .50
- ❑ 19 Quincy Wilson .75 .30
- ❑ 20 Jason Wright .50 .20
- ❑ 21 Bernard Berrian 1.25 .50
- ❑ 22 Michael Clayton 2.00 .75
- ❑ 23 Devard Darling 1.00 .40
- ❑ 24 Lee Evans 1.25 .50
- ❑ 25 Larry Fitzgerald 3.00 1.25
- ❑ 26 Devery Henderson 1.00 .40
- ❑ 27 Michael Jenkins 1.00 .40
- ❑ 28 Darius Watts 1.00 .40
- ❑ 29 Mike Williams 1.00 .40
- ❑ 30 Roy Williams WR 2.50 1.00
- ❑ 31 Rashaun Woods 1.00 .40
- ❑ 32 Ben Troupe 1.00 .40
- ❑ 33 Shawn Andrews 1.00 .40
- ❑ 34 Robert Gallery 1.00 .40
- ❑ 35 Tommie Harris 1.00 .40
- ❑ 36 Vince Wilfork 1.00 .40
- ❑ 37 Will Smith 1.00 .40
- ❑ 38 Teddy Lehman 1.00 .40
- ❑ 39 Jonathan Vilma 1.00 .40
- ❑ 40 D.J. Williams 1.00 .40
- ❑ 41 DeAngelo Hall 1.25 .50
- ❑ 42 Dunta Robinson 1.00 .40
- ❑ 43 Derrick Strait 1.00 .40
- ❑ 44 Keith Smith .75 .30
- ❑ 45 Eli Manning CL 3.00 1.25
- ❑ 46 Eli Manning PP 10.00 4.00
- ❑ 47 Ben Roethlisberger PP 12.00 5.00
- ❑ 48 Larry Fitzgerald PP 6.00 2.50
- ❑ 49 Roy Williams PP 5.00 2.00
- ❑ 50 Philip Rivers PP 6.00 2.50

2005 Press Pass

- ❑ COMPLETE SET (50) 50.00 25.00
- ❑ COMP.SET w/o PP'S (45) 30.00 12.50
- ❑ POWER PICK STATED ODDS 1:14 H/R
- ❑ UNPRICED HOBBY SOLO PRINT RUN 1 SET
- ❑ 1 Derek Anderson 1.50 .60
- ❑ 2 Brock Berlin .75 .30
- ❑ 3 Charlie Frye 1.00 .40
- ❑ 4 Gino Guidugli .50 .20
- ❑ 5 David Greene 1.00 .40
- ❑ 6 Stefan LeFors 1.00 .40
- ❑ 7 Dan Orlovsky 1.00 .40
- ❑ 8 Kyle Orton 1.00 .40
- ❑ 9 Aaron Rodgers 3.00 1.25
- ❑ 10 Alex Smith QB 4.00 1.50
- ❑ 11 Andrew Walter 1.00 .40
- ❑ 12 Jason White 1.00 .40
- ❑ 13 J.J. Arrington 1.00 .40
- ❑ 14 Ronnie Brown 4.00 1.50
- ❑ 15 Anthony Davis .75 .30
- ❑ 16 Kay-Jay Harris .75 .30
- ❑ 17 T.A. McLendon .50 .20
- ❑ 18 Ryan Moats 1.00 .40
- ❑ 19 Vernand Morency 1.00 .40
- ❑ 20 Cadillac Williams 4.00 1.50
- ❑ 21 Mark Bradley 1.00 .40
- ❑ 22 Reggie Brown 1.00 .40
- ❑ 23 Mark Clayton 1.00 .40
- ❑ 24 Braylon Edwards 3.00 1.25
- ❑ 25 Fred Gibson .75 .30
- ❑ 26 Terrence Murphy 1.00 .40
- ❑ 27 J.R. Russell .75 .30
- ❑ 28 Craphonso Thorpe .75 .30
- ❑ 29 Roddy White 1.00 .40
- ❑ 30 Mike Williams 1.00 .40
- ❑ 31 Troy Williamson 1.00 .40
- ❑ 32 Heath Miller 2.00 .75
- ❑ 33 Alex Smith TE 1.00 .40
- ❑ 34 Khalif Barnes .75 .30
- ❑ 35 Jammal Brown 1.00 .40
- ❑ 36 Brandon Browner .75 .30
- ❑ 37 Marlin Jackson 1.00 .40
- ❑ 38 Carlos Rogers 1.25 .50
- ❑ 39 Antrel Rolle 1.00 .40
- ❑ 40 Dan Cody 1.00 .40
- ❑ 41 Erasmus James 1.00 .40
- ❑ 42 David Pollack 1.00 .40
- ❑ 43 Anttaj Hawthorne .75 .30
- ❑ 44 Derrick Johnson 1.50 .60
- ❑ 45 Ronnie Brown CL 2.00 .75
- ❑ 46 Cadillac Williams PP 8.00 3.00
- ❑ 47 Aaron Rodgers PP 6.00 2.50
- ❑ 48 Alex Smith QB PP 8.00 3.00
- ❑ 49 Braylon Edwards PP 6.00 3.00
- ❑ 50 Mike Williams PP 2.00 .75

2006 Press Pass

❑ COMPLETE SET (50)	50.00	20.00
❑ COMP.SET w/o SP's (45)	25.00	10.00
❑ POWER PICK ODDS 1:14		
❑ UNPRICED SOLO SER.#'d TO 1		
❑ 1 Brodie Croyle	2.50	1.00
❑ 2 Jay Cutler	3.00	1.25
❑ 3 Omar Jacobs	.75	.30
❑ 4 Matt Leinart	3.00	1.25
❑ 5 Drew Olson	.75	.30
❑ 6 Michael Robinson	1.00	.40
❑ 7 D.J. Shockley	1.00	.40
❑ 8 Brad Smith	1.00	.40
❑ 9 Marcus Vick	.75	.30
❑ 10 Charlie Whitehurst	1.00	.40
❑ 11 Vince Young	4.00	1.50
❑ 12 Joseph Addai	3.00	1.25
❑ 13 Reggie Bush	4.00	1.50
❑ 14 Jerome Harrison	1.00	.40
❑ 15 Laurence Maroney	2.50	1.00
❑ 16 Leon Washington	1.50	.60
❑ 17 LenDale White	2.00	.75
❑ 18 DeAngelo Williams	2.50	1.00
❑ 19 Jason Avant	1.00	.40
❑ 20 Derek Hagan	1.00	.40
❑ 21 Chris Hannon	.75	.30
❑ 22 Santonio Holmes	2.00	.75
❑ 23 Chad Jackson	1.00	.40
❑ 24 Greg Lee	.75	.30
❑ 25 Sinorice Moss	1.00	.40
❑ 26 Martin Nance	.75	.30
❑ 27 Maurice Stovall	1.00	.40
❑ 28 Travis Wilson	1.00	.40
❑ 29 Dominique Byrd	.75	.30
❑ 30 Vernon Davis	2.00	.75
❑ 31 Marcedes Lewis	1.00	.40
❑ 32 Leonard Pope	1.00	.40
❑ 33 Jimmy Williams	1.00	.40
❑ 34 Darnell Bing	1.00	.40
❑ 35 Michael Huff	1.25	.50
❑ 36 Mathias Kiwanuka	1.25	.50
❑ 37 Mario Williams	1.50	.60
❑ 38 Haloti Ngata	1.00	.40
❑ 39 Gabe Watson	.75	.30
❑ 40 Rodrique Wright	.50	.20
❑ 41 D'Brickashaw Ferguson	1.00	.40
❑ 42 Chad Greenway	1.00	.40
❑ 43 A.J. Hawk	2.50	1.00
❑ 44 DeMeco Ryans	1.25	.50
❑ 45 Reggie Bush CL	2.00	.75
❑ 46 Reggie Bush PP	8.00	3.00
❑ 47 Matt Leinart PP	6.00	2.50
❑ 48 Vince Young PP	8.00	3.00
❑ 49 A.J. Hawk PP	5.00	2.00
❑ 50 DeAngelo Williams PP	5.00	2.00

2007 Press Pass

❑ COMPLETE SET (105)	60.00	25.00
❑ COMP.SET w/o SP's (100)	40.00	15.00
❑ 101-105 POWER PICK ODDS 1:14		
❑ UNPRICED SOLO SER.#'d TO 1		
❑ 1 Chris Leak	.60	.25
❑ 2 Brady Quinn	2.50	1.00
❑ 3 JaMarcus Russell	2.00	.75
❑ 4 Troy Smith	1.25	.50
❑ 5 Drew Stanton	1.00	.40
❑ 6 Michael Bush	1.00	.40
❑ 7 Tony Hunt	.75	.30
❑ 8 Kenny Irons	.75	.30
❑ 9 Brandon Jackson	1.00	.40
❑ 10 Marshawn Lynch	1.50	.60
❑ 11 Adrian Peterson	6.00	2.50
❑ 12 Antonio Pittman	.60	.25
❑ 13 Brian Leonard	.75	.30
❑ 14 Dwayne Bowe	1.50	.60
❑ 15 Ted Ginn Jr.	1.25	.50
❑ 16 Anthony Gonzalez	1.25	.50
❑ 17 Dwayne Jarrett	1.00	.40
❑ 18 Calvin Johnson	2.50	1.00
❑ 19 Robert Meachem	.75	.30
❑ 20 Sidney Rice	1.25	.50
❑ 21 Garrett Wolfe	1.00	.40
❑ 22 Leon Hall	.60	.25
❑ 23 Gaines Adams	.75	.30
❑ 24 Jamaal Anderson	.60	.25
❑ 25 Alan Branch	.60	.25
❑ 26 Amobi Okoye	.75	.30
❑ 27 Paul Posluszny	1.00	.40
❑ 28 Lawrence Timmons	.75	.30
❑ 29 LaRon Landry	1.00	.40
❑ 30 Reggie Nelson	.60	.25
❑ 31 John Beck	1.50	.60
❑ 32 Trent Edwards	1.50	.60
❑ 33 Kevin Kolb	1.25	.50
❑ 34 Jordan Palmer	.75	.30
❑ 35 Lorenzo Booker	.75	.30
❑ 36 Darius Walker	.75	.30
❑ 37 Dwayne Wright	[illegible]	[illegible]
❑ 38 DeShawn Wynn	1.00	.40
❑ 39 Zach Miller	.60	.25
❑ 40 Greg Olsen	1.00	.40
❑ 41 Aundrae Allison	.60	.25
❑ 42 Dallas Baker	.60	.25
❑ 43 Jason Hill	.60	.25
❑ 44 Steve Smith USC	1.00	.40
❑ 45 Darrelle Revis	.75	.30
❑ 46 Aaron Ross	.75	.30
❑ 47 Adam Carriker	.60	.25
❑ 48 Charles Johnson	.50	.20
❑ 49 Jarvis Moss	.75	.30
❑ 50 Patrick Willis	1.25	.50
❑ 51 John Beck LDR	1.50	.60
❑ 52 JaMarcus Russell LDR	2.00	.75
❑ 53 Troy Smith LDR	1.25	.50
❑ 54 Jordan Palmer LDR	.75	.30
❑ 55 Kevin Kolb LDR	1.25	.50
❑ 56 Brady Quinn LDR	2.50	1.00
❑ 57 Garrett Wolfe LDR	1.00	.40
❑ 58 Dwayne Wright LDR	.60	.25
❑ 59 Ahmad Bradshaw LDR	1.00	.40
❑ 60 Johnnie Lee Higgins LDR	.60	.25
❑ 61 Robert Meachem LDR	.75	.30
❑ 62 Rhema McKnight LDR	.60	.25
❑ 63 Calvin Johnson LDR	2.50	1.00
❑ 64 Joel Filani LDR	.60	.25
❑ 65 Dwayne Bowe LDR	1.50	.60
❑ 66 Daymeion Hughes LDR	.60	.25
❑ 67 Reggie Nelson LDR	.60	.25
❑ 68 LaMarr Woodley TC	.75	.30
❑ 69 Troy Smith TC	1.25	.50
❑ 70 Brady Quinn TC	2.50	1.00
❑ 71 Calvin Johnson TC	2.50	1.00
❑ 72 Paul Posluszny TC	1.00	.40
❑ 73 Aaron Ross TC	.75	.30
❑ 74 Patrick Willis TC	1.25	.50
❑ 75 Troy Smith AA	1.25	.50
❑ 76 Marshawn Lynch AA	1.50	.60
❑ 77 Johnnie Lee Higgins AA	.60	.25
❑ 78 Dwayne Jarrett AA	1.00	.40
❑ 79 Calvin Johnson AA	2.50	1.00
❑ 80 Robert Meachem AA	.75	.30
❑ 81 Zach Miller AA	.60	.25
❑ 82 Gaines Adams AA	.75	.30
❑ 83 Paul Posluszny AA	1.00	.40
❑ 84 Leon Hall AA	.60	.25
❑ 85 LaRon Landry AA	1.00	.40
❑ 86 Reggie Nelson AA	.60	.25
❑ 87 Aaron Ross AA	.75	.30
❑ 88 M.Lynch/D.Hughes TM	.60	.25
❑ 89 C.Leak/R.Nelson TM	.60	.25
❑ 90 L.Booker/L.Thomas TM	.75	.30
❑ 91 J.Russell/D.Bowe TM	2.00	.75
❑ 92 B.Jackson/A.Carriker TM	.60	.25
❑ 93 B.Quinn/D.Walker TM	2.50	1.00
❑ 94 T.Smith/A.Pittman TM	.60	.25
❑ 95 T.Ginn Jr./A.Gonzalez TM	1.25	.50
❑ 96 T.Hunt/P.Posluszny TM	1.00	.40
❑ 97 D.Jarrett/S.Smith TM	1.00	.40
❑ 98 Joseph Addai SS	2.00	.75
❑ 99 Reggie Bush SS	2.00	.75
❑ 100 Vince Young SS	2.00	.75
❑ 101 Brady Quinn PP	6.00	2.50
❑ 102 JaMarcus Russell PP	5.00	2.00
❑ 103 Adrian Peterson PP	15.00	6.00
❑ 104 Calvin Johnson PP	6.00	2.50
❑ 105 Ted Ginn Jr. PP	3.00	1.25

2002 Press Pass JE

❑ COMPLETE SET (45)	25.00	10.00
❑ 1 David Carr	2.00	.75
❑ 2 Julius Peppers	2.00	.75
❑ 3 Joey Harrington	1.25	.50
❑ 4 Mike Williams	.75	.30
❑ 5 Quentin Jammer	1.00	.40
❑ 6 Ryan Sims	1.00	.40
❑ 7 Bryant McKinnie	.75	.30
❑ 8 Roy Williams	2.00	.75
❑ 9 John Henderson	1.00	.40
❑ 10 Wendell Bryant	.50	.20
❑ 11 Donte Stallworth	1.50	.60
❑ 12 Jeremy Shockey	4.00	1.50
❑ 13 William Green	1.00	.40
❑ 14 Phillip Buchanon	1.00	.40
❑ 15 T.J. Duckett	1.00	.40
❑ 16 Ashley Lelie	2.00	.75
❑ 17 Javon Walker	1.50	.60
❑ 18 Daniel Graham	1.00	.40
❑ 19 Jerramy Stevens	1.00	.40
❑ 20 Patrick Ramsey	1.00	.40
❑ 21 Jabar Gaffney	1.00	.40
❑ 22 DeShaun Foster	1.00	.40
❑ 23 Kalimba Edwards	1.00	.40
❑ 24 Josh Reed	1.00	.40
❑ 25 Mike Pearson	.50	.20
❑ 26 Andre Davis	.75	.30

❑ 27 Reche Caldwell 1.00 .40
❑ 28 Clinton Portis 4.00 1.50
❑ 29 Maurice Morris 1.00 .40
❑ 30 Ladell Betts 1.00 .40
❑ 31 Antwaan Randle El 1.25 .50
❑ 32 Antonio Bryant 1.00 .40
❑ 33 Josh McCown 1.25 .50
❑ 34 Lamar Gordon 1.00 .40
❑ 35 Marquise Walker .75 .30
❑ 36 Cliff Russell .75 .30
❑ 37 Brian Westbrook 2.00 .75
❑ 38 Eric Crouch 1.00 .40
❑ 39 Jonathan Wells 1.00 .40
❑ 40 David Garrard 2.00 .75
❑ 41 Rohan Davey 1.00 .40
❑ 42 Ron Johnson .75 .30
❑ 43 Kurt Kittner .75 .30
❑ 44 Adrian Peterson 1.25 .50
❑ 45 David Carr CL 1.00 .40

2003 Press Pass JE

❑ COMPLETE SET (45) 25.00 10.00
❑ 1 Boss Bailey 1.00 .40
❑ 2 Brad Banks .75 .30
❑ 3 Anquan Boldin 2.50 1.00
❑ 4 Kyle Boller 1.00 .40
❑ 5 Chris Brown 1.00 .40
❑ 6 Avon Cobourne .50 .20
❑ 7 Ken Dorsey 1.00 .40
❑ 8 Justin Fargas 1.00 .40
❑ 9 Talman Gardner 1.00 .40
❑ 10 Jason Gesser 1.00 .40
❑ 11 Earnest Graham 1.00 .40
❑ 12 Jordon Gross .75 .30
❑ 13 Rex Grossman 3.00 1.25
❑ 14 Kwame Harris .75 .30
❑ 15 Taylor Jacobs .75 .30
❑ 16 Larry Johnson 4.00 2.00
❑ 17 Bryant Johnson 1.00 .40
❑ 18 Andre Johnson 2.00 .75
❑ 19 Teyo Johnson 1.00 .40
❑ 20 William Joseph 1.00 .40
❑ 21 Bennie Joppru 1.00 .40
❑ 22 Jimmy Kennedy 1.00 .40
❑ 23 Kliff Kingsbury .75 .30
❑ 24 Byron Leftwich 3.00 1.25
❑ 25 Brandon Lloyd 1.25 .40
❑ 26 Jerome McDougle 1.00 .40
❑ 27 Willis McGahee 2.50 1.00
❑ 28 Terence Newman 2.00 .75
❑ 29 Carson Palmer 4.00 1.50
❑ 30 Terry Pierce .75 .30
❑ 31 Dave Ragone 1.00 .40
❑ 32 DeWayne Robertson 1.00 .40
❑ 33 Charles Rogers 1.00 .40
❑ 34 Chris Simms 1.50 .60
❑ 35 Musa Smith 1.00 .40
❑ 36 Onterrio Smith 1.00 .40
❑ 37 Brian St.Pierre 1.00 .40
❑ 38 Lee Suggs 1.00 .40
❑ 39 Terrell Suggs 1.50 .60
❑ 40 Marcus Trufant 1.00 .40
❑ 41 Seneca Wallace 1.00 .40
❑ 42 Kelley Washington 1.00 .40
❑ 43 Jason Witten 2.00 .75
❑ 44 Andre Woolfolk 1.00 .40
❑ 45 Byron Leftwich CL 2.00 .75

2006 Press Pass Legends

❑ COMP.SET w/o SP's (90) 40.00 20.00
❑ UNPRICED PLATINUM PRINT RUN 1
❑ UNPRICED PRINT PLATES SER.#'d TO 1
❑ UNPRICED RED PRINT RUN 5
❑ 1 Brodie Croyle 3.00 1.25
❑ 2 Tarvaris Jackson 2.00 .75
❑ 3 Derek Hagan 1.25 .50
❑ 4 Devin Aromashodu 1.00 .40
❑ 5 Mathias Kiwanuka 1.50 .60
❑ 6 Omar Jacobs 1.00 .40
❑ 7 Tye Hill 1.25 .50
❑ 8 Charlie Whitehurst 1.25 .50
❑ 9 Joe Klopfenstein 1.00 .40
❑ 10 Chad Jackson 1.25 .50
❑ 11 Leon Washington 2.00 .75
❑ 12 Ernie Sims 1.50 .60
❑ 13 Leonard Pope 1.25 .50
❑ 14 D.J. Shockley 1.25 .50
❑ 15 Joseph Addai 4.00 1.50
❑ 16 Vernon Davis 2.50 1.00
❑ 17 DeAngelo Williams 3.00 1.25
❑ 18 Sinorice Moss 1.25 .50
❑ 19 Martin Nance 1.00 .40
❑ 20 Jason Avant 1.25 .50
❑ 21 Laurence Maroney 3.00 1.25
❑ 22 Brad Smith 1.25 .50
❑ 23 Mario Williams 2.00 .75
❑ 24 Brett Basanez 1.25 .50
❑ 25 Anthony Fasano 1.25 .50
❑ 26 Maurice Stovall 1.25 .50
❑ 27 Bobby Carpenter 1.25 .50
❑ 28 A.J. Hawk 3.00 1.25
❑ 29 Santonio Holmes 2.50 1.00
❑ 30 Ashton Youboty 1.25 .50
❑ 31 Travis Wilson 1.25 .50
❑ 32 Haloti Ngata 1.25 .50
❑ 33 Demetrius Williams 1.25 .50
❑ 34 Mike Hass 1.25 .50
❑ 35 Michael Robinson 1.25 .50
❑ 36 Greg Lee 1.00 .40
❑ 37 Cory Rodgers 1.25 .50
❑ 38 Michael Huff 1.50 .60
❑ 39A Vince Young Clr 5.00 2.00
❑ 39B Vince Young B&W 8.00 3.00
❑ 40 Reggie McNeal 1.00 .40
❑ 41 Bruce Gradkowski 2.00 .75
❑ 42 Darrell Hackney 1.00 .40
❑ 43 Maurice Drew 3.00 1.25
❑ 44 Marcedes Lewis 1.25 .50
❑ 45 Drew Olson 1.00 .40
❑ 46 Darnell Bing 1.25 .50
❑ 47A Reggie Bush Clr 5.00 2.00
❑ 47B Reggie Bush B&W 8.00 3.00
❑ 48 Dominique Byrd 1.00 .40
❑ 49A Matt Leinart Clr 4.00 1.50
❑ 49B Matt Leinart B&W 6.00 2.50
❑ 50 LenDale White 2.50 1.00
❑ 51A Jay Cutler Clr 4.00 1.50
❑ 51B Jay Cutler B&W 6.00 2.50
❑ 52 D'Brickashaw Ferguson 1.25 .50
❑ 53 Marcus Vick 1.00 .40
❑ 54 Jimmy Williams 1.25 .50
❑ 55 Jerome Harrison 1.25 .50
❑ 56 Ozzie Newsome 1.25 .50
❑ 57 Ken Stabler 2.00 .75
❑ 58A Bo Jackson B&W 2.00 .75
❑ 58B Bo Jackson Clr 3.00 1.25
❑ 59 Steve Spurrier 2.00 .75
❑ 60 Charlie Ward 1.25 .50
❑ 61 Fran Tarkenton 2.00 .75
❑ 62 Herschel Walker 1.25 .50
❑ 63 Billy Cannon 1.25 .50
❑ 64 Y.A. Tittle 1.50 .60
❑ 65 Roger Craig 1.50 .60
❑ 66 Tommie Frazier 1.25 .50
❑ 67 Rocky Bleier 1.50 .60
❑ 68A Tim Brown B&W 1.50 .60
❑ 68B Tim Brown Clr 2.50 1.00
❑ 69 Paul Hornung 1.50 .60
❑ 70 Joe Theismann 1.50 .60
❑ 71 Howard Cassady 1.25 .50
❑ 72 Archie Griffin 1.00 .40
❑ 73 Jack Tatum 1.00 .40
❑ 74 Paul Warfield 1.25 .50
❑ 75 Brian Bosworth 1.50 .60
❑ 76 Billy Sims 1.25 .50
❑ 77A Barry Sanders B&W 2.50 1.00
❑ 77B Barry Sanders Clr 4.00 1.50
❑ 78 Thurman Thomas 1.25 .50
❑ 79 Jack Ham 1.25 .50
❑ 80 Franco Harris 1.50 .60
❑ 81A Dan Marino B&W 3.00 1.25
❑ 81B Dan Marino Clr 5.00 2.00
❑ 82 Len Dawson 1.50 .60
❑ 83 Jim Plunkett 1.25 .50
❑ 84 Bob Lilly 1.25 .50
❑ 85 Steve Largent 1.50 .60
❑ 86 Ronnie Lott 1.25 .50
❑ 87 Bobby Bowden 1.50 .60
❑ 88 Bo Schembechler 1.00 .40
❑ 89 Darrell Royal 1.25 .50
❑ 90 Ara Parseghian 1.25 .50
❑ 91 Johnny Lattner SP 5.00 2.00
❑ 92 Desmond Howard SP 6.00 2.50

2007 Press Pass Legends

❑ 1 Kenneth Darby 1.25 .50
❑ 2 Chris Henry 1.25 .50
❑ 3 Zach Miller 1.00 .40
❑ 4 Jamaal Anderson 1.00 .40
❑ 5 Kenny Irons 1.25 .50
❑ 6 Courtney Taylor 1.00 .40
❑ 7 John Beck 2.50 1.00
❑ 8 Daymeion Hughes 1.00 .40
❑ 9 Marshawn Lynch 2.50 1.00
❑ 10 Gaines Adams 1.25 .50
❑ 11 Chansi Stuckey 1.00 .40
❑ 12 Aundrae Allison 1.00 .40
❑ 13 Dallas Baker 1.00 .40
❑ 14 Chris Leak 1.00 .40
❑ 15 Jarvis Moss 1.25 .50
❑ 16 Reggie Nelson 1.00 .40
❑ 17 DeShawn Wynn 1.50 .60
❑ 18 Paul Williams 1.00 .40
❑ 19 Dwayne Wright 1.00 .40
❑ 20 Lorenzo Booker 1.25 .50
❑ 21 Buster Davis 1.00 .40
❑ 22 Lawrence Timmons 1.25 .50

❑	23 Quentin Moses	1.00	.40
❑	24 Calvin Johnson	4.00	1.50
❑	25 Kevin Kolb	2.00	.75
❑	26 Michael Bush	1.50	.60
❑	27 Amobi Okoye	1.25	.50
❑	28 Kolby Smith	1.50	.60
❑	29 Joseph Addai	1.50	.60
❑	30 Dwayne Bowe	2.50	1.00
❑	31 Craig Buster Davis	1.25	.50
❑	32 LaRon Landry	1.50	.60
❑	33 JaMarcus Russell	3.00	1.25
❑	34 Greg Olsen	1.50	.60
❑	35 Alan Branch	1.00	.40
❑	36 Leon Hall	1.00	.40
❑	37 Drew Stanton	1.50	.60
❑	38 Adam Carriker	1.00	.40
❑	39 Brandon Jackson	1.50	.60
❑	40 Jeff Rowe	1.00	.40
❑	41 Garrett Wolfe	1.50	.60
❑	42 Brady Quinn	4.00	1.50
❑	43 Ted Ginn Jr.	2.00	.75
❑	44 Anthony Gonzalez	2.00	.75
❑	45 Antonio Pittman	1.00	.40
❑	46 Troy Smith	2.00	.75
❑	47 Adrian Peterson	10.00	4.00
❑	48 Patrick Willis	2.50	1.00
❑	49 Tony Hunt	1.25	.50
❑	50 Paul Posluszny	1.50	.60
❑	51 Darrelle Revis	1.25	.50
❑	52 Brian Leonard	1.25	.50
❑	53 Sidney Rice	2.00	.75
❑	54 Trent Edwards	2.50	1.00
❑	55 Robert Meachem	1.25	.50
❑	56 Michael Griffin	1.25	.50
❑	57 Aaron Ross	1.25	.50
❑	58 Vince Young	1.50	.60
❑	59 Joel Filani	1.00	.40
❑	60 Dwayne Jarrett	1.50	.60
❑	61 Steve Smith USC	1.50	.60
❑	62 Johnnie Lee Higgins	1.00	.40
❑	63 Jordan Palmer	1.25	.50
❑	64 David Clowney	1.25	.50
❑	65 Jason Hill	1.25	.50
❑	66 Ozzie Newsome	1.25	.50
❑	67 Ken Stabler	2.00	.75
❑	68 Bart Starr	2.50	1.00
❑	69 Pat Sullivan	1.00	.40
❑	70 Doug Flutie	1.50	.60
❑	71 Ty Detmer	1.00	.40
❑	72 Danny Wuerffel	1.00	.40
❑	73 Jack Youngblood	1.50	.60
❑	74 Fred Biletnikoff	1.50	.60
❑	75 Herschel Walker	1.25	.50
❑	76 Dick Butkus	2.00	.75
❑	77 Y.A. Tittle	1.50	.60
❑	78 Randy White	1.25	.50
❑	79 Jerry Rice	2.50	1.00
❑	80 Joe Bellino	1.00	.40
❑	81 Tommie Frazier	1.25	.50
❑	82 Tom Osborne	1.25	.50
❑	83 Tom Rathman	1.00	.40
❑	84 Johnny Rodgers	1.00	.40
❑	85 Mike Rozier	1.00	.40
❑	86 Jerome Bettis	1.50	.60
❑	87 Paul Hornung	1.50	.60
❑	88 Alan Page	1.00	.40
❑	89 Rudy Ruettiger	1.50	.60
❑	90 Joe Theismann	1.50	.60
❑	91 Archie Griffin	1.00	.40
❑	92 Brian Bosworth	1.50	.60
❑	93 Steve Owens	1.00	.40
❑	94 Billy Sims	1.25	.50
❑	95 Archie Manning	1.50	.60
❑	96 Raymond Berry	1.25	.50
❑	97 James Lofton	1.00	.40
❑	98 Marcus Allen	1.50	.60
❑	99 John Hannah	1.00	.40
❑	100 Dick Butkus CL	1.25	.50

2001 Press Pass SE

❑	COMPLETE SET (45)	40.00	20.00
❑	1 Michael Vick	3.00	1.25
❑	2 Drew Brees	3.00	1.25
❑	3 Quincy Carter	.75	.30
❑	4 Marques Tuiasosopo	.75	.30
❑	5 Chris Weinke	.75	.30
❑	6 Sage Rosenfels	.75	.30
❑	7 Jesse Palmer	.75	.30
❑	8 Mike McMahon	.75	.30
❑	9 Josh Booty	.75	.30
❑	10 Josh Heupel	.75	.30
❑	11 LaDainian Tomlinson	10.00	4.00
❑	12 Deuce McAllister	2.00	.75
❑	13 Michael Bennett	.75	.30
❑	14 Anthony Thomas	.75	.30
❑	15 LaMont Jordan	1.50	.60
❑	16 Travis Henry	2.00	.75
❑	17 James Jackson	.75	.30
❑	18 Kevan Barlow	.75	.30
❑	19 Travis Minor	.60	.25
❑	20 Rudi Johnson	1.50	.60
❑	21 David Terrell	.75	.30
❑	22 Koren Robinson	.75	.30
❑	23 Rod Gardner	.75	.30
❑	24 Santana Moss	1.50	.60
❑	25 Freddie Mitchell	.75	.30
❑	26 Reggie Wayne	2.00	.75
❑	27 Quincy Morgan	.75	.30
❑	28 Chris Chambers	1.50	.60
❑	29 Robert Ferguson	.75	.30
❑	30 Chad Johnson	2.00	.75
❑	31 Snoop Minnis	.60	.25
❑	32 Todd Heap	.75	.30
❑	33 Steve Hutchinson	.60	.25
❑	34 Leonard Davis	[illegible]	[illegible]
❑	35 Kenyatta Walker	.40	.15
❑	36 Justin Smith	.75	.30
❑	37 Andre Carter	.75	.30
❑	38 Jamal Reynolds	.75	.30
❑	39 Gerard Warren	.75	.30
❑	40 Richard Seymour	.75	.30
❑	41 Damione Lewis	.60	.25
❑	42 Jamar Fletcher	.60	.25
❑	43 Nate Clements	.75	.30
❑	44 Derrick Gibson	.60	.25
❑	45 David Terrell CL	.60	.25

2004 Press Pass SE

❑	COMPLETE SET (40)	30.00	15.00
❑	1 Shawn Andrews	1.00	.40
❑	2 Casey Clausen	1.00	.40
❑	3 Michael Clayton	2.00	.75
❑	4 Cedric Cobbs	1.00	.40
❑	5 Devard Darling	1.00	.40
❑	6 Lee Evans	1.25	.50
❑	7 Larry Fitzgerald	3.00	1.25
❑	8 Robert Gallery	1.00	.40
❑	9 DeAngelo Hall	1.25	.50
❑	10 Tommie Harris	1.00	.40
❑	11 Ben Hartsock	1.00	.40
❑	12 Devery Henderson	1.00	.40
❑	13 Steven Jackson	3.00	1.25
❑	14 Michael Jenkins	1.00	.40
❑	15 Greg Jones	1.00	.40
❑	16 Kevin Jones	2.50	1.00
❑	17 Teddy Lehman	1.00	.40
❑	18 J.P. Losman	2.00	.75
❑	19 Eli Manning	5.00	2.00
❑	20 Mewelde Moore	1.00	.40
❑	21 John Navarre	1.00	.40
❑	22 Jarrett Payton	1.00	.40
❑	23 Chris Perry	1.25	.50
❑	24 Cody Pickett	1.00	.40
❑	25 Philip Rivers	3.00	1.25
❑	26 Ben Roethlisberger	6.00	2.50
❑	27 Matt Schaub	3.00	1.25
❑	28 Will Smith	1.00	.40
❑	29 Ben Troupe	1.00	.40
❑	30 Michael Turner	1.25	.50
❑	31 Ben Watson	1.00	.40
❑	32 Darius Watts	1.00	.40
❑	33 Vince Wilfork	1.00	.40
❑	34 Mike Williams	1.00	.40
❑	35 Reggie Williams	1.25	.50
❑	36 Roy Williams WR	2.50	1.00
❑	37 Quincy Wilson	.75	.30
❑	38 Rashaun Woods	1.00	.40
❑	39 Jason Wright	.75	.30
❑	40 Eli Manning CL	3.00	1.25
❑	NNO Eli Manning Mini Helmet	120.00	60.00

2005 Press Pass SE

❑	COMPLETE SET (40)	25.00	10.00
❑	1 Charlie Frye	1.00	.40
❑	2 David Greene	1.00	.40
❑	3 Gino Guidugli	.50	.20
❑	4 Stefan LeFors	1.00	.40
❑	5 Dan Orlovsky	1.00	.40
❑	6 Kyle Orton	1.00	.40
❑	7 Aaron Rodgers	3.00	1.25
❑	8 Alex Smith QB	4.00	1.50
❑	9 Andrew Walter	1.00	.40
❑	10 Jason White	1.00	.40
❑	11 J.J. Arrington	1.00	.40
❑	12 Marion Barber	1.50	.60
❑	13 Ronnie Brown	4.00	1.50
❑	14 Anthony Davis	.75	.30
❑	15 Ciatrick Fason	1.00	.40
❑	16 T.A. McLendon	.50	.20
❑	17 Vernand Morency	1.00	.40

❑ 18 Walter Reyes	.75	.30
❑ 19 Cadillac Williams	4.00	1.50
❑ 20 Mark Bradley	1.00	.40
❑ 21 Reggie Brown	1.00	.40
❑ 22 Mark Clayton	1.00	.40
❑ 23 Braylon Edwards	3.00	1.25
❑ 24 Fred Gibson	.75	.30
❑ 25 Chris Henry	1.00	.40
❑ 26 Terrence Murphy	1.00	.40
❑ 27 J.R. Russell	.75	.30
❑ 28 Craphonso Thorpe	.75	.30
❑ 29 Roddy White	1.00	.40
❑ 30 Mike Williams	1.00	.40
❑ 31 Troy Williamson	1.00	.40
❑ 32 Heath Miller	2.00	.75
❑ 33 Alex Smith TE	1.00	.40
❑ 34 Jammal Brown	1.00	.40
❑ 35 Marlin Jackson	1.00	.40
❑ 36 Antrel Rolle	1.00	.40
❑ 37 Dan Cody	1.00	.40
❑ 38 Derrick Johnson	1.50	.60
❑ 39 Thomas Davis	1.00	.40
❑ 40 Aaron Rodgers CL	2.00	.75

2006 Press Pass SE

❑ COMPLETE SET (40)	30.00	12.50
❑ 1 Joseph Addai	3.00	1.25
❑ 2 Jason Avant	1.00	.40
❑ 3 Reggie Bush	4.00	1.50
❑ 4 Dominique Byrd	.75	.30
❑ 5 Brodie Croyle	2.50	1.00
❑ 6 Jay Cutler	3.00	1.25
❑ 7 Vernon Davis	2.00	.75
❑ 8 Maurice Drew	2.50	1.00
❑ 9 Anthony Fasano	1.00	.40
❑ 10 D'Brickashaw Ferguson	1.00	.40
❑ 11 Bruce Gradkowski	1.50	.60
❑ 12 Darrell Hackney	.75	.30
❑ 13 Derek Hagan	1.00	.40
❑ 14 Jerome Harrison	1.00	.40
❑ 15 A.J. Hawk	2.50	1.00
❑ 16 Santonio Holmes	2.00	.75
❑ 17 Michael Huff	1.25	.50
❑ 18 Chad Jackson	1.00	.40
❑ 19 Omar Jacobs	.75	.30
❑ 20 Matt Leinart	3.00	1.25
❑ 21 Marcedes Lewis	1.00	.40
❑ 22 Laurence Maroney	2.50	1.00
❑ 23 Reggie McNeal	.75	.30
❑ 24 Sinorice Moss	1.00	.40
❑ 25 Martin Nance	.75	.30
❑ 26 Haloti Ngata	1.00	.40
❑ 27 Leonard Pope	1.00	.40
❑ 28 Michael Robinson	1.00	.40
❑ 29 D.J. Shockley	1.00	.40
❑ 30 Maurice Stovall	1.00	.40
❑ 31 Marcus Vick	.75	.30
❑ 32 Leon Washington	1.50	.60
❑ 33 LenDale White	2.00	.75
❑ 34 Charlie Whitehurst	1.00	.40
❑ 35 Jimmy Williams	1.00	.40
❑ 36 Mario Williams	1.50	.60
❑ 37 DeAngelo Williams	2.50	1.00
❑ 38 Demetrius Williams	1.00	.40
❑ 39 Vince Young	4.00	1.50
❑ 40 Vince Young CL	2.00	.75

2007 Press Pass SE

❑ 1 Reggie Nelson	.75	.30
❑ 2 Patrick Willis	1.50	.60
❑ 3 Brian Leonard	1.00	.40
❑ 4 Sidney Rice	1.50	.60
❑ 5 Robert Meachem	1.00	.40
❑ 6 Chris Leak	.75	.30
❑ 7 Calvin Johnson	3.00	1.25
❑ 8 Charles Johnson	.60	.25
❑ 9 Kevin Kolb	1.50	.60
❑ 10 Drew Stanton	1.25	.50
❑ 11 Antonio Pittman	.75	.30
❑ 12 Troy Smith	1.50	.60
❑ 13 Steve Smith USC	1.25	.50
❑ 14 Leon Hall	.75	.30
❑ 15 Brandon Jackson	1.25	.50
❑ 16 Ted Ginn Jr.	1.50	.60
❑ 17 Aundrae Allison	.75	.30
❑ 18 DeShawn Wynn	1.25	.50
❑ 19 Dwayne Wright	.75	.30
❑ 20 Michael Bush	1.25	.50
❑ 21 Dwayne Bowe	2.00	.75
❑ 22 Adam Carriker	.75	.30
❑ 23 Paul Posluszny	1.25	.50
❑ 24 Aaron Ross	1.00	.40
❑ 25 Lorenzo Booker	1.00	.40
❑ 26 Jamaal Anderson	.75	.30
❑ 27 Zach Miller	.75	.30
❑ 28 Dallas Baker	.75	.30
❑ 29 Adrian Peterson	8.00	3.00
❑ 30 Dwayne Jarrett	1.25	.50
❑ 31 Greg Olsen	1.25	.50
❑ 32 Darius Walker	1.00	.40
❑ 33 Alan Branch	.75	.30
❑ 34 Marshawn Lynch	2.00	.75
❑ 35 JaMarcus Russell	2.50	1.00
❑ 36 Anthony Gonzalez	1.50	.60
❑ 37 Gaines Adams	1.00	.40
❑ 38 Craig Buster Davis	1.00	.40
❑ 39 Jason Hill	.75	.30
❑ 40 Kenny Irons	1.00	.40
❑ 41 John Beck	2.00	.75
❑ 42 Lawrence Timmons	1.00	.40
❑ 43 Trent Edwards	2.00	.75
❑ 44 Tony Hunt	1.00	.40
❑ 45 Darrelle Revis	1.00	.40
❑ 46 Jarvis Moss	1.00	.40
❑ 47 LaRon Landry	1.25	.50
❑ 48 Brady Quinn	3.00	1.25
❑ 49 Jordan Palmer	1.00	.40
❑ 50 Rhema McKnight	.75	.30

1999 SAGE

❑ COMPLETE SET (50)	30.00	15.00
❑ 1 Rahim Abdullah	.60	.25
❑ 2 Jerry Azumah	.60	.25
❑ 3 Champ Bailey	1.25	.50
❑ 4 D'Wayne Bates	.60	.25
❑ 5 Michael Bishop	1.00	.40
❑ 6 David Boston	1.00	.40
❑ 7 Fernando Bryant	.60	.25
❑ 8 Tony Bryant	.60	.25
❑ 9 Chris Claiborne	.40	.15
❑ 10 Mike Cloud	.60	.25
❑ 11 Cecil Collins	.40	.15
❑ 12 Tim Couch	1.00	.40
❑ 13 Daunte Culpepper	4.00	1.50
❑ 14 Jared DeVries	.60	.25
❑ 15 Adrian Dingle	.60	.25
❑ 16 Antuan Edwards	.60	.25
❑ 17 Troy Edwards	.60	.25
❑ 18 Kevin Faulk	1.00	.40
❑ 19 Rufus French	.40	.15
❑ 20 Martin Gramatica	.40	.15
❑ 21 Torry Holt	2.50	1.00
❑ 22 Sedrick Irvin	.40	.15
❑ 23 Edgerrin James	4.00	1.50
❑ 24 Jon Jansen	.40	.15
❑ 25 Andy Katzenmoyer	.60	.25
❑ 26 Jevon Kearse	2.50	1.00
❑ 27 Patrick Kerney	1.00	.40
❑ 28 Lamar King	.60	.25
❑ 29 Shaun King	.60	.25
❑ 30 Jim Kleinsasser	1.00	.40
❑ 31 Rob Konrad	1.00	.40
❑ 32 Brian Kuklick	.60	.25
❑ 33 Chris McAlister	.60	.25
❑ 34 Darnell McDonald	.60	.25
❑ 35 Reggie McGrew	.60	.25
❑ 36 Donovan McNabb	5.00	2.00
❑ 37 Cade McNown	.60	.25
❑ 38 Dat Nguyen	1.00	.40
❑ 39 Solomon Page	.40	.15
❑ 40 Mike Peterson	1.00	.40
❑ 41 Anthony Poindexter	.60	.25
❑ 42 Peerless Price	1.00	.40
❑ 43 Mike Rucker	1.00	.40
❑ 44 L.J. Shelton	.40	.15
❑ 45 Akili Smith	1.50	.60
❑ 46 John Tait	.40	.15
❑ 47 Fred Vinson	.60	.25
❑ 48 Al Wilson	1.00	.40
❑ 49 Antoine Winfield	.60	.25
❑ 50 Damien Woody	.60	.25

2000 SAGE

- ❑ COMPLETE SET (50) 15.00 6.00
- ❑ 1 John Abraham .75 .30
- ❑ 2 Shaun Alexander 4.00 1.50
- ❑ 3 LaVar Arrington 3.00 1.25
- ❑ 4 Courtney Brown 1.00 .40
- ❑ 5 Keith Bulluck .75 .30
- ❑ 6 Plaxico Burress 1.50 .60
- ❑ 7 Giovanni Carmazzi .40 .15
- ❑ 8 Kwame Cavil .40 .15
- ❑ 9 Cosey Coleman .40 .15
- ❑ 10 Laveranues Coles 1.00 .40
- ❑ 11 Tim Couch .75 .30
- ❑ 12 Ron Dayne .75 .30
- ❑ 13 Reuben Droughns 1.00 .40
- ❑ 14 Shaun Ellis .75 .30
- ❑ 15 John Engelberger .60 .25
- ❑ 16 Danny Farmer .60 .25
- ❑ 17 Dwayne Goodrich .75 .30
- ❑ 18 Deon Grant .60 .25
- ❑ 19 Chris Hovan .60 .25
- ❑ 20 Darren Howard .60 .25
- ❑ 21 Todd Husak .75 .30
- ❑ 22 Thomas Jones 1.25 .50
- ❑ 23 Curtis Keaton .60 .25
- ❑ 24 Jamal Lewis 1.50 .60
- ❑ 25 Anthony Lucas .40 .15
- ❑ 26 Tee Martin .75 .30
- ❑ 27 Stockar McDougle .40 .15
- ❑ 28 Corey Moore .40 .15
- ❑ 29 Rob Morris .60 .25
- ❑ 30 Sammy Morris .75 .30
- ❑ 31 Sylvester Morris .60 .25
- ❑ 32 Chad Pennington 2.00 .75
- ❑ 33 Todd Pinkston .75 .30
- ❑ 34 Ahmed Plummer .75 .30
- ❑ 35 Jerry Porter 1.00 .40
- ❑ 36 Travis Prentice .60 .25
- ❑ 37 Tim Rattay .75 .30
- ❑ 38 Chris Redman .60 .25
- ❑ 39 J.R. Redmond .60 .25
- ❑ 40 Chris Samuels .60 .25
- ❑ 41 Brandon Short .60 .25
- ❑ 42 Corey Simon 1.00 .40
- ❑ 43 R.Jay Soward .60 .25
- ❑ 44 Shyrone Stith .60 .25
- ❑ 45 Raynoch Thompson .60 .25
- ❑ 46 Brian Urlacher 3.00 1.25
- ❑ 47 Todd Wade .40 .15
- ❑ 48 Troy Walters .75 .30
- ❑ 49 Dez White .75 .30
- ❑ 50 Michael Wiley .60 .25

2001 SAGE

- ❑ COMPLETE SET (50) 20.00 7.50
- ❑ 1 Will Allen .60 .25
- ❑ 2 Adam Archuleta .75 .30
- ❑ 3 Jeff Backus .60 .25
- ❑ 4 Alex Bannister .60 .25
- ❑ 5 Gary Baxter .60 .25
- ❑ 6 Michael Bennett .60 .25
- ❑ 7 Josh Booty .75 .30
- ❑ 8 Drew Brees 3.00 1.25
- ❑ 9 Correll Buckhalter 1.00 .40
- ❑ 10 Quincy Carter .75 .30
- ❑ 11 Chris Chambers 1.50 .60
- ❑ 12 Alge Crumpler 1.00 .40
- ❑ 13 Andre Dyson .40 .15
- ❑ 14 Robert Ferguson .75 .30
- ❑ 15 Jamar Fletcher .60 .25
- ❑ 16 Rod Gardner .75 .30
- ❑ 17 Reggie Germany .60 .25
- ❑ 18 Derrick Gibson .60 .25
- ❑ 19 Casey Hampton .75 .30
- ❑ 20 Tim Hasselbeck .75 .30
- ❑ 21 Todd Heap .75 .30
- ❑ 22 Travis Henry 1.00 .40
- ❑ 23 Josh Heupel .75 .30
- ❑ 24 Willie Howard .60 .25
- ❑ 25 Steve Hutchinson .60 .25
- ❑ 26 James Jackson .75 .30
- ❑ 27 Rudi Johnson 1.50 .60
- ❑ 28 LaMont Jordan 1.50 .60
- ❑ 29 Torrance Marshall .75 .30
- ❑ 30 Deuce McAllister 2.00 .75
- ❑ 31 Willie Middlebrooks .60 .25
- ❑ 32 Quincy Morgan .75 .30
- ❑ 33 Santana Moss 1.50 .60
- ❑ 34 Jesse Palmer .75 .30
- ❑ 35 Carlos Polk .40 .15
- ❑ 36 Ken-Yon Rambo .60 .25
- ❑ 37 Jamal Reynolds .75 .30
- ❑ 38 Koren Robinson .75 .30
- ❑ 39 Richard Seymour .75 .30
- ❑ 40 Justin Smith .75 .30
- ❑ 41 Fred Smoot .75 .30
- ❑ 42 Marcus Stroud .75 .30
- ❑ 43 David Terrell .75 .30
- ❑ 44 LaDainian Tomlinson 10.00 4.00
- ❑ 45 Ja'Mar Toombs .60 .25
- ❑ 46 Michael Vick 3.00 1.25
- ❑ 47 Kenyatta Walker .40 .15
- ❑ 48 Gerard Warren .75 .30
- ❑ 49 Reggie Wayne 2.00 .75
- ❑ 50 Jamie Winborn .60 .25

2002 SAGE

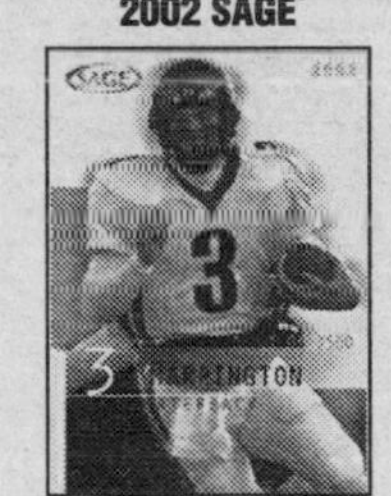

- ❑ COMPLETE SET (45) 40.00 15.00
- ❑ 1 Ladell Betts 1.50 .60
- ❑ 2 Antonio Bryant 1.50 .60
- ❑ 3 Reche Caldwell 1.50 .60
- ❑ 4 Kelly Campbell 1.25 .50
- ❑ 5 David Carr 4.00 1.50
- ❑ 6 Tim Carter 1.25 .50
- ❑ 7 Eric Crouch 1.50 .60
- ❑ 8 Ronald Curr 1.50 .60
- ❑ 9 Rohan Davey 1.50 .60
- ❑ 10 Andre Davis 1.25 .50
- ❑ 11 T.J. Duckett 1.50 .60
- ❑ 12 Randy Fasani 1.25 .50
- ❑ 13 DeShaun Foster 1.50 .60
- ❑ 14 Dwight Freeney 2.50 1.00
- ❑ 15 Jabar Gaffney 1.50 .60
- ❑ 16 Lamar Gordon 1.50 .60
- ❑ 17 Daniel Graham 1.50 .60
- ❑ 18 Joey Harrington 2.00 .75
- ❑ 19 Napoleon Harri 1.50 .60
- ❑ 20 Albert Haynesworth 1.25 .50
- ❑ 21 John Henderson 5.00 2.00
- ❑ 22 Chad Hutchinson 1.25 .50
- ❑ 23 Quentin Jammer 1.50 .60
- ❑ 24 Ron Johnson 1.25 .50
- ❑ 25 Kurt Kittner 1.25 .50
- ❑ 26 Ashley Lelie 3.00 1.25
- ❑ 27 Bryant McKinnie 1.25 .50
- ❑ 28 Maurice Morris 1.50 .60
- ❑ 29 David Neill 1.25 .50
- ❑ 30 J.T. O'Sullivan 1.25 .50
- ❑ 31 [illegible]
- ❑ 32 Clinton Portis 6.00 2.50
- ❑ 33 Patrick Ramsey 1.50 .60
- ❑ 34 Josh Reed 1.50 .60
- ❑ 35 Cliff Russell 1.25 .50
- ❑ 36 Lito Sheppard 1.50 .60
- ❑ 37 Jeremy Shockey 6.00 2.50
- ❑ 38 Luke Staley 1.25 .50
- ❑ 39 Donte Stallworth 2.50 1.00
- ❑ 40 Travis Stephens 1.25 .50
- ❑ 41 Chester Taylor 2.50 1.00
- ❑ 42 Larry Tripplett .75 .30
- ❑ 43 Javon Walker 2.50 1.00
- ❑ 44 Marquise Walker 1.25 .50
- ❑ 45 Jonathan Wells 1.50 .60

2003 SAGE

- ❑ COMPLETE SET (45) 25.00 10.00
- ❑ 1 Sam Aiken 1.25 .50
- ❑ 2 Boss Bailey 1.50 .60
- ❑ 3 Brad Banks 2.00 .75
- ❑ 4 Tully Banta-Cain 1.25 .50
- ❑ 5 Arnaz Battle 1.50 .60
- ❑ 6 Ronald Bellamy 1.25 .50
- ❑ 7 Kyle Boller 1.50 .60
- ❑ 8 Chris Brown 1.50 .60
- ❑ 9 Tyrone Calico 1.50 .60
- ❑ 10 Dallas Clark 1.50 .60
- ❑ 11 Kevin Curtis 2.00 .75
- ❑ 12 Sammy Davis 1.50 .60
- ❑ 13 Dahrran Diedrick 1.50 .60
- ❑ 14 Ken Dorsey 1.50 .60
- ❑ 15 Justin Fargas 1.50 .60
- ❑ 16 Justin Gage 1.50 .60
- ❑ 17 Jason Gesser 1.50 .60
- ❑ 18 Cie Grant 1.50 .60
- ❑ 19 Rex Grossman 5.00 2.00
- ❑ 20 E.J. Henderson 1.50 .60
- ❑ 21 Taylor Jacobs 1.25 .50
- ❑ 22 Bryant Johnson 1.50 .60
- ❑ 23 Larry Johnson 6.00 3.00
- ❑ 24 Teyo Johnson 1.50 .60
- ❑ 25 Kliff Kingsbury 1.25 .50
- ❑ 26 Brandon Lloyd 1.50 .60
- ❑ 27 Rashean Mathis 1.25 .50
- ❑ 28 Jerome McDougle 1.50 .60
- ❑ 29 Willis McGahee 4.00 1.50
- ❑ 30 Billy McMullen 1.25 .50
- ❑ 31 Terence Newman 3.00 1.25

❑ 32 Donnie Nickey	1.25	.50
❑ 33 Terry Pierce	1.25	.50
❑ 34 Dave Ragone	1.50	.60
❑ 35 Charles Rogers	1.50	.60
❑ 36 Chris Simms	2.50	1.00
❑ 37 Musa Smith	1.50	.60
❑ 38 Lee Suggs	1.50	.60
❑ 39 Terrell Suggs	2.50	1.00
❑ 40 Marcus Trufant	1.50	.60
❑ 41 Seneca Wallace	1.50	.60
❑ 42 Kelley Washington	1.50	.60
❑ 43 Matt Wilhelm	1.50	.60
❑ 44 Jason Witten	3.00	1.25
❑ 45 George Wrighster	1.25	.50

2004 SAGE

❑ COMPLETE SET (46)	30.00	12.50
❑ STATED PRINT RUN 3200 SETS		
❑ 1 Tatum Bell	2.50	1.00
❑ 2 Bernard Berrian	1.50	.60
❑ 3 Michael Boulware	1.25	.50
❑ 4 Drew Carter	1.25	.50
❑ 5 Maurice Clarett	1.50	.60
❑ 6 Casey Clausen	1.25	.50
❑ 7 Michael Clayton	2.50	1.00
❑ 8 Chris Collins	1.00	.40
❑ 9 Karlos Dansby	1.25	.50
❑ 10 Devard Darling	1.25	.50
❑ 11 Lee Evans	1.50	.60
❑ 12 Clarence Farmer	1.00	.40
❑ 13 Chris Gamble	1.25	.50
❑ 14 Jake Grove	1.00	.40
❑ 15 DeAngelo Hall	1.50	.60
❑ 16 Josh Harris	1.25	.50
❑ 17 Tommie Harris	1.25	.50
❑ 18 Devery Henderson	1.25	.50
❑ 19 Steven Jackson	4.00	1.50
❑ 20 Michael Jenkins	1.25	.50
❑ 21 Greg Jones	1.25	.50
❑ 22 Kevin Jones	3.00	1.25
❑ 23 Sean Jones	1.00	.40
❑ 24 Derrick Knight	1.00	.40
❑ 25 Craig Krenzel	1.25	.50
❑ 26 Jared Lorenzen	1.00	.40
❑ 27 Eli Manning	6.00	3.00
❑ 28 John Navarre	1.25	.50
❑ 29 Chris Perry	1.50	.60
❑ 30 Cody Pickett	1.25	.50
❑ 31 Will Poole	1.25	.50
❑ 32 Philip Rivers	4.00	1.50
❑ 33 Ell Roberson	1.25	.50
❑ 34 Dunta Robinson	1.25	.50
❑ 35 Ben Roethlisberger	8.00	3.00
❑ 36 Rod Rutherford	1.00	.40
❑ 37 P.K. Sam	1.00	.40
❑ 38 Matt Schaub	4.00	1.50
❑ 39 Will Smith	1.25	.50
❑ 40 Jeff Smoker	1.25	.50
❑ 41 Ben Troupe	1.25	.50
❑ 42 Ernest Wilford	1.25	.50
❑ 43 Reggie Williams	1.25	.50
❑ 44 Roy Williams WR	3.00	1.25
❑ 45 Quincy Wilson	1.00	.40
❑ 46 Rashaun Woods	1.25	.50

2005 SAGE

❑ COMPLETE SET (54)	30.00	12.50
❑ 1 Derek Anderson	2.00	.75
❑ 2 J.J. Arrington	1.25	.50
❑ 3 Marion Barber	2.00	.75
❑ 4 Brock Berlin	1.00	.40
❑ 5 Jammal Brown	1.25	.50
❑ 6 Reggie Brown	1.25	.50
❑ 7 Ronnie Brown	5.00	2.00
❑ 8 Jason Campbell	2.00	.75
❑ 9 Mark Clayton	1.25	.50
❑ 10 Channing Crowder	1.25	.50
❑ 11 Anthony Davis	1.00	.40
❑ 12 Josh Davis	1.00	.40
❑ 13 Thomas Davis	1.25	.50
❑ 14 Ciatrick Fason	1.25	.50
❑ 15 Ryan Fitzpatrick	1.25	.50
❑ 16 Charlie Frye	1.25	.50
❑ 17 Fred Gibson	1.00	.40
❑ 18 Johnathan Goddard	1.00	.40
❑ 19 Frank Gore	2.50	1.00
❑ 20 David Greene	1.25	.50
❑ 21 Kay-Jay Harris	1.00	.40
❑ 22 Marlin Jackson	1.25	.50
❑ 23 Brandon Jacobs	1.50	.60
❑ 24 Derrick Johnson	1.50	.60
❑ 25 Matt Jones	2.00	.75
❑ 26 T.A. McLendon	1.00	.40
❑ 27 Adrian McPherson	1.25	.50
❑ 28 Justin Miller	1.00	.40
❑ 29 Vernand Morency	1.25	.50
❑ 30 Terrence Murphy	1.25	.50
❑ 31 Dan Orlovsky	1.25	.50
❑ 32 Kyle Orton	1.25	.50
❑ 33 Roscoe Parrish	1.25	.50
❑ 34 Brodney Pool	1.25	.50
❑ 35 Dante Ridgeway	1.00	.40
❑ 36 Chris Rix	1.00	.40
❑ 37 Aaron Rodgers	4.00	1.50
❑ 38 Carlos Rogers	1.50	.60
❑ 39 J.R. Russell	1.00	.40
❑ 40 Alex Smith TE	1.25	.50
❑ 41 Alex Smith QB	5.00	2.00
❑ 42 Taylor Stubblefield	1.00	.40
❑ 43 Craphonso Thorpe	1.00	.40
❑ 44 Andrew Walter	1.25	.50
❑ 45 DeMarcus Ware	2.00	.75
❑ 46 Fabian Washington	1.25	.50
❑ 47 Corey Webster	1.25	.50
❑ 48 Jason White	1.25	.50
❑ 49 Roddy White	1.25	.50
❑ 50 Cadillac Williams	5.00	2.00
❑ 51 Troy Williamson	1.25	.50
❑ 52 Maurice Clarett	1.25	.50
❑ 53 Ben Roethlisberger	4.00	1.50
❑ 54 Antrel Rolle	1.25	.50

2006 SAGE

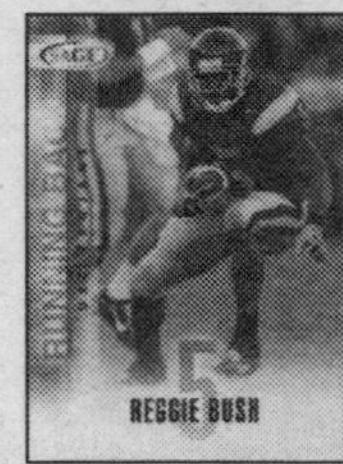

❑ 1 Joseph Addai	4.00	1.50
❑ 2 Devin Aromashodu	1.00	.40
❑ 3 Jason Avant	1.25	.50
❑ 4 Hank Baskett	1.25	.50
❑ 5 Mike Bell	1.25	.50
❑ 6 Will Blackmon	1.00	.40
❑ 7 Daniel Bullocks	1.25	.50
❑ 8 Reggie Bush	5.00	2.00
❑ 9 Dominique Byrd	1.00	.40
❑ 10 Brian Calhoun	1.25	.50
❑ 11 Bobby Carpenter	1.25	.50
❑ 12 Antonio Cromartie	1.25	.50
❑ 13 Brodie Croyle	3.00	1.25
❑ 14 Jay Cutler	4.00	1.50
❑ 15 Vernon Davis	2.50	1.00
❑ 16 Anthony Fasano	1.25	.50
❑ 17 D'Brickashaw Ferguson	1.25	.50
❑ 18 Charles Gordon	1.00	.40
❑ 19 Bruce Gradkowski	2.00	.75
❑ 20 Skyler Green	1.25	.50
❑ 21 Jerome Harrison	1.25	.50
❑ 22 Mike Hass	1.25	.50
❑ 23 Taurean Henderson	1.25	.50
❑ 24 Devin Hester	2.50	1.00
❑ 25 Tye Hill	1.25	.50
❑ 26 Michael Huff	1.50	.60
❑ 27 Tarvaris Jackson	2.00	.75
❑ 28 Omar Jacobs	1.00	.40
❑ 29 Maurice Drew	3.00	1.25
❑ 30 Winston Justice	1.25	.50
❑ 31 Matt Leinart	4.00	1.50
❑ 32 Laurence Maroney	3.00	1.25
❑ 33 Reggie McNeal	1.00	.40
❑ 34 Marcus McNeill	.60	.25
❑ 35 Erik Meyer	1.00	.40
❑ 36 Sinorice Moss	1.25	.50
❑ 37 Martin Nance	1.00	.40
❑ 38 Drew Olson	1.00	.40
❑ 39 Jonathan Orr	1.00	.40
❑ 40 Paul Pinegar	1.00	.40
❑ 41 Leonard Pope	1.25	.50
❑ 42 Gerald Riggs Jr.	1.25	.50
❑ 43 Michael Robinson	1.25	.50
❑ 44 DeMeco Ryans	1.50	.60
❑ 45 D.J. Shockley	1.25	.50
❑ 46 Ernie Sims	1.50	.60
❑ 47 Dwayne Slay	1.00	.40
❑ 48 Maurice Stovall	1.25	.50
❑ 49 David Thomas	1.25	.50
❑ 50 Leon Washington	2.00	.75
❑ 51 Pat Watkins	1.25	.50
❑ 52 LenDale White	2.50	1.00
❑ 53 Charlie Whitehurst	1.25	.50
❑ 54 Demetrius Williams	1.25	.50
❑ 55 Jimmy Williams	1.25	.50
❑ 56 Mario Williams	2.00	.75
❑ 57 Rodrique Wright	.60	.25
❑ 58 Ashton Youboty	1.25	.50
❑ 59 Vince Young	5.00	2.00
❑ 60 Alan Zemaitis	1.25	.50

2007 SAGE

❑ 1 Gaines Adams 1.25 .50
❑ 2 Aundrae Allison 1.00 .40
❑ 3 Dallas Baker 1.00 .40
❑ 4 David Ball 1.00 .40
❑ 5 John Beck 2.50 1.00
❑ 6 Dwayne Bowe 2.50 1.00
❑ 7 Alan Branch 1.00 .40
❑ 8 Steve Breaston 1.00 .40
❑ 9 Levi Brown 1.25 .50
❑ 10 Michael Bush 1.50 .60
❑ 11 Adam Carriker 1.00 .40
❑ 12 David Clowney 1.25 .50
❑ 13 Ken Darby 1.25 .50
❑ 14 Craig Buster Davis 1.25 .50
❑ 15 Trent Edwards 2.50 1.00
❑ 16 Earl Everett 1.00 .40
❑ 17 Yamon Figurs 1.25 .50
❑ 18 Joel Filani 1.00 .40
❑ 19 Ted Ginn Jr. 2.00 .75
❑ 20 Anthony Gonzalez 2.00 .75
❑ 21 Michael Griffin 1.25 .50
❑ 22 Leon Hall 1.00 .40
❑ 23 Chris Henry 1.25 .50
❑ 24 Johnnie Lee Higgins 1.00 .40
❑ 25 Jason Hill 1.25 .50
❑ 26 David Irons .75 .30
❑ 27 Kenny Irons 1.25 .50
❑ 28 Calvin Johnson 4.00 1.50
❑ 29 Ryan Kalil 1.00 .40
❑ 30 Kevin Kolb 2.00 .75
❑ 31 Chris Leak 1.00 .40
❑ 32 Brian Leonard 1.25 .50
❑ 33 Marshawn Lynch 2.50 1.00
❑ 34 Robert Meachem 1.25 .50
❑ 35 Brandon Meriweather 1.25 .50
❑ 36 Zach Miller 1.00 .40
❑ 37 Jarvis Moss 1.25 .50
❑ 38 Greg Olsen 1.50 .60
❑ 39 Tyler Palko 1.00 .40
❑ 40 Jordan Palmer 1.25 .50
❑ 41 Adrian Peterson 10.00 4.00
❑ 42 Antonio Pittman 1.00 .40
❑ 43 Brady Quinn 4.00 1.50
❑ 44 Sidney Rice 2.00 .75
❑ 45 Aaron Ross 1.25 .50
❑ 46 Jeff Rowe 1.00 .40
❑ 47 JaMarcusÂ Russell 3.00 1.25
❑ 48 Kolby Smith 1.50 .60
❑ 49 Steve Smith USC 1.50 .60
❑ 50 Troy Smith 2.00 .75
❑ 51 Jason Snelling 1.00 .40
❑ 52 Isaiah Stanback 1.25 .50
❑ 53 Drew Stanton 1.50 .60
❑ 54 Courtney Taylor 1.00 .40
❑ 55 Lawrence Timmons 1.25 .50
❑ 56 DeMarcus Tank Tyler 1.00 .40
❑ 57 Darius Walker 1.25 .50
❑ 58 Paul Williams 1.00 .40
❑ 59 Patrick Willis 2.00 .75
❑ 60 Garrett Wolfe 1.50 .60
❑ 61 LaMarr Woodley 1.25 .50
❑ 62 Jared Zabransky 1.25 .50

2000 SAGE HIT

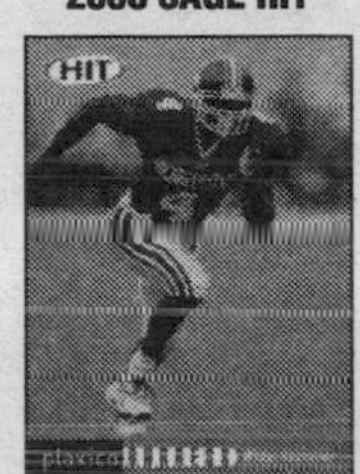

❑ COMPLETE SET (50) 25.00 10.00
❑ 1 Jerry Porter 1.00 .40
❑ 2 Tim Couch .75 .30
❑ 3 Chris Samuels .60 .25
❑ 4 Plaxico Burress 1.50 .60
❑ 5 Michael Wiley .60 .25
❑ 6 Thomas Jones 1.25 .50
❑ 7 Chris Redman .60 .25
❑ 8 Anthony Lucas .40 .15
❑ 9 Kwame Cavil .40 .15
❑ 10 Chad Pennington 2.00 .75
❑ 11 LaVar Arrington 4.00 1.50
❑ 12 Giovanni Carmazzi .40 .15
❑ 13 Tim Rattay .75 .30
❑ 14 Laveranues Coles 1.00 .40
❑ 15 Mario Edwards .60 .25
❑ 16 John Engelberger .60 .25
❑ 17 Tee Martin .75 .30
❑ 18 R.Jay Soward .60 .25
❑ 19 Ahmed Plummer .75 .30
❑ 20 Na'il Diggs .60 .25
❑ 21 J.R. Redmond .60 .25
❑ 22 Dez White .75 .30
❑ 23 Reuben Droughns 1.00 .40
❑ 24 Sylvester Morris .60 .25
❑ 25 Cosey Coleman .40 .15
❑ 26 Corey Moore .40 .15
❑ 27 Curtis Keaton .60 .25
❑ 28 Danny Farmer .60 .25
❑ 29 Travis Claridge .40 .15
❑ 30 Troy Walters .75 .30
❑ 31 Jamal Lewis 1.50 .60
❑ 32 Shaun King .40 .15
❑ 33 Ron Dayne .75 .30
❑ 34 Keith Bulluck .75 .30
❑ 35 Corey Simon 1.00 .40
❑ 36 Deon Dyer .60 .25
❑ 37 Shaun Alexander 4.00 1.50
❑ 38 Shyrone Stith .60 .25
❑ 39 Shaun Ellis .75 .30
❑ 40 Todd Pinkston .75 .30
❑ 41 Travis Prentice .60 .25
❑ 42 Chris Hovan .60 .25
❑ 43 Brandon Short .60 .25
❑ 44 Brian Urlacher 3.00 1.25
❑ 45 Rob Morris .75 .30
❑ 46 Raynoch Thompson .60 .25
❑ 47 Deon Grant .60 .25
❑ 48 Stockar McDougle .40 .15
❑ 49 Darren Howard .60 .25
❑ 50 Courtney Brown 1.00 .40

2001 SAGE HIT

❑ COMPLETE SET (50) 25.00 10.00
❑ 1 David Terrell .75 .30
❑ 2 Jamar Fletcher .60 .25
❑ 3 Koren Robinson .75 .30

❑ 4 Ken-Yon Rambo .60 .25
❑ 5 LaDainian Tomlinson 8.00 4.00
❑ 6 Santana Moss 1.50 .60
❑ 7 Michael Vick 3.00 1.25
❑ 8 Steve Hutchinson .60 .25
❑ 9 Robert Ferguson .75 .30
❑ 10 Torrance Marshall .75 .30
❑ 11 Scotty Anderson .75 .30
❑ 12 Derrick Gibson .60 .25
❑ 13 Marcus Stroud .75 .30
❑ 14 Josh Heupel .75 .30
❑ 15 Drew Brees 3.00 1.25
❑ 16 Gerard Warren .75 .30
❑ 17 Quincy Carter .75 .30
❑ 18 Gary Baxter .60 .25
❑ 19 Alex Bannister .60 .25
❑ 20 Travis Henry 2.00 .75
❑ 21 Andre Dyson .40 .15
❑ 22 Deuce McAllister 2.00 .75
❑ 23 Rod Gardner .75 .30
❑ 24 Jamie Winborn .60 .25
❑ 25 Will Allen .60 .25
❑ 26 Kenyatta Walker .40 .15
❑ 27 Tim Hasselbeck .75 .30
❑ 28 Alge Crumpler 1.00 .40
❑ 30 LaMont Jordan 1.50 .60
❑ 31 Jeff Backus .60 .25
❑ 32 Rudi Johnson 1.50 .60
❑ 33 Willie Howard .60 .25
❑ 34 Josh Booty .75 .30
❑ 35 Todd Heap .75 .30
❑ 36 Correll Buckhalter 1.00 .40
❑ 37 Jesse Palmer .75 .30
❑ 38 Carlos Polk .40 .15
❑ 39 Richard Seymour .75 .30
❑ 40 Adam Archuleta .75 .30
❑ 41 James Jackson .75 .30
❑ 42 Willie Middlebrooks .60 .25
❑ 43 Ja'Mar Toombs .60 .25
❑ 44 Chris Chambers 1.50 .60
❑ 45 Reggie Germany .60 .25
❑ 46 Casey Hampton .75 .30
❑ 47 Reggie Wayne 2.00 .75
❑ 48 Jamal Reynolds .75 .30
❑ 49 Justin Smith .75 .30
❑ 50 Quincy Morgan .75 .30

2002 SAGE HIT

❑ COMPLETE SET (48) 30.00 12.50
❑ 1 John Henderson 1.25 .50

❑ 2 Tim Carter	1.00	.40
❑ 3 Joey Harrington	1.50	.60
❑ 4 Marquise Walker	1.00	.40
❑ 5 Quentin Jammer	1.25	.50
❑ 6 Rohan Davey	1.25	.50
❑ 7A Eric Crouch QB	1.25	.50
❑ 7B Eric Crouch RB	1.25	.50
❑ 8 David Carr	3.00	1.25
❑ 9 Maurice Morris	1.25	.50
❑ 10 Jabar Gaffney	1.25	.50
❑ 11 David Neill	1.00	.40
❑ 12 Randy Fasani	1.00	.40
❑ 13 Alex Brown	1.25	.50
❑ 14 J.T. O'Sullivan	1.00	.40
❑ 15 Kurt Kittner	1.00	.40
❑ 16 Ashley Lelie	2.50	1.00
❑ 17 Reche Caldwell	1.25	.50
❑ 18 T.J. Duckett	1.25	.50
❑ 19 Chester Taylor	2.50	1.00
❑ 20 Jonathan Wells	1.25	.50
❑ 21 Kelly Campbell	1.00	.40
❑ 22 Bryant McKinnie	1.00	.40
❑ 23 Lito Sheppard	1.25	.50
❑ 24 Donte Stallworth	2.00	.75
❑ 25 Josh Reed	1.25	.50
❑ 26 DeShaun Foster	1.25	.50
❑ 27 Patrick Ramsey	1.25	.50
❑ 28 Clinton Portis	5.00	2.00
❑ 29 Albert Haynesworth	1.00	.40
❑ 31 Cliff Russell	1.00	.40
❑ 32 Luke Staley	1.00	.40
❑ 33 Ron Johnson	1.00	.40
❑ 34 Travis Stephens	1.00	.40
❑ 35 Chad Hutchinson	1.00	.40
❑ 36 Lamar Gordon	1.25	.50
❑ 37 Larry Tripplett	.60	.25
❑ 38 Napoleon Harris	1.25	.50
❑ 39 Daniel Graham	1.25	.50
❑ 40 Antonio Bryant	1.25	.50
❑ 41 Javon Walker	2.00	.75
❑ 42 Brian Poli-Dixon	1.00	.40
❑ 43 Jeremy Shockey	5.00	2.00
❑ 44 Andre Davis	1.00	.40
❑ 45 Ladell Betts	1.25	.50
❑ 46 Michael Vick	1.25	.50
❑ NNO David Carr CL	1.25	.50

2003 SAGE HIT

❑ COMPLETE SET (48)	25.00	10.00
❑ 1 Charles Rogers	1.00	.40
❑ 2 Willis McGahee	2.50	1.00
❑ 3 Amaz Battle	1.00	.40
❑ 4 Terence Newman	2.00	.75
❑ 5 Larry Johnson	4.00	2.00
❑ 6 Taylor Jacobs	.75	.30
❑ 7 Kyle Boller	1.00	.40
❑ 8 Rex Grossman	3.00	1.25
❑ 9 Jerome McDougle	1.00	.40
❑ 10 Jason Witten	2.00	.75
❑ 11 Ken Dorsey	1.00	.40
❑ 12 Justin Gage	1.00	.40
❑ 13 Andy Groom	.75	.30
❑ 14 Seneca Wallace	1.00	.40
❑ 15 Dave Ragone	1.00	.40
❑ 16 Kliff Kingsbury	.75	.30
❑ 17 Jason Gesser	1.00	.40
❑ 18 George Wrighster	.75	.30
❑ 19 Ronald Bellamy	.75	.30
❑ 20 Donnie Nickey	.75	.30
❑ 21 Billy McMullen	.75	.30
❑ 22 Lee Suggs	1.00	.40
❑ 23 Chris Brown	1.00	.40
❑ 24 Bryant Johnson	1.00	.40
❑ 25 Justin Fargas	1.00	.40
❑ 26 Brandon Lloyd	1.00	.40
❑ 27 Tyrone Calico	1.00	.40
❑ 28 Sam Aiken	.75	.30
❑ 29 Cie Grant	1.00	.40
❑ 30 Dahrran Diedrick	1.00	.40
❑ 31 Kelley Washington	1.00	.40
❑ 32 Musa Smith	1.00	.40
❑ 33 Kevin Curtis	1.25	.50
❑ 34 Terry Pierce	.75	.30
❑ 35 Matt Wilhelm	1.00	.40
❑ 36 Rashean Mathis	.75	.30
❑ 37 Brad Banks	.75	.30
❑ 38 Tully Banta-Cain	.75	.30
❑ 39 Sammy Davis	1.00	.40
❑ 40 Teyo Johnson	1.00	.40
❑ 41 Chris Simms	1.50	.60
❑ 42 E.J. Henderson	1.00	.40
❑ 43 Terrell Suggs	1.50	.60
❑ 44 Dallas Clark	1.00	.40
❑ 45 Marcus Trufant	1.00	.40
❑ 46 Boss Bailey	1.00	.40
❑ 47 David Carr	1.50	.60
❑ NNO Charles Rogers CL	1.00	.40

2004 SAGE HIT

❑ COMPLETE SET (46)	30.00	12.50
❑ 1 Reggie Williams	1.25	.50
❑ 2 Bernard Berrian	1.25	.50
❑ 3 Lee Evans	1.25	.50
❑ 4 Roy Williams WR	2.50	1.00
❑ 5 Josh Harris	1.00	.40
❑ 6 Greg Jones	1.00	.40
❑ 7 Ben Roethlisberger	6.00	2.50
❑ 8 Drew Carter	1.00	.40
❑ 9 Devery Henderson	1.00	.40
❑ 10 Eli Manning	5.00	2.00
❑ 11 Karlos Dansby	1.00	.40
❑ 12 Michael Jenkins	1.00	.40
❑ 13 Maurice Clarett	1.25	.50
❑ 14 Michael Clayton	2.00	.75
❑ 15 Casey Clausen	1.00	.40
❑ 16 John Navarre	1.00	.40
❑ 17 Philip Rivers	3.00	1.25
❑ 18 Jeff Smoker	1.00	.40
❑ 19 Ernest Wilford	1.00	.40
❑ 20 Derrick Knight	.75	.30
❑ 21 Chris Gamble	1.00	.40
❑ 22 Jared Lorenzen	.75	.30
❑ 23 Chris Perry	1.25	.50
❑ 24 Rod Rutherford	.75	.30
❑ 25 Kevin Jones	2.50	1.00
❑ 26 Michael Boulware	1.00	.40
❑ 27 Tatum Bell	2.00	.75
❑ 28 Will Poole	1.00	.40
❑ 29 Jake Grove	.75	.30
❑ 30 Eli Roberson	1.00	.40
❑ 31 Devard Darling	1.00	.40
❑ 32 Dunta Robinson	1.00	.40
❑ 33 Cody Pickett	1.00	.40
❑ 34 Steven Jackson	3.00	1.25
❑ 35 Matt Schaub	3.00	1.25
❑ 36 Sean Jones	.75	.30
❑ 37 Tommie Harris	1.00	.40
❑ 38 Chris Collins	.75	.30
❑ 39 Will Smith	1.00	.40
❑ 40 DeAngelo Hall	1.25	.50
❑ 41 Rashaun Woods	1.00	.40
❑ 42 Ben Troupe	1.00	.40
❑ 43 Quincy Wilson	.75	.30
❑ 44 P.K. Sam	.75	.30
❑ 45 Clarence Farmer	.75	.30
❑ NNO Eli Manning CL	3.00	1.25
❑ EM Eli Manning SEC/30	50.00	20.00

2005 SAGE HIT

❑ COMPLETE SET (50)	25.00	10.00
❑ 1 Craphonso Thorpe	.75	.30
❑ 2 Derrick Johnson	1.50	.60
❑ 3 Frank Gore SP	2.50	1.00
❑ 4 Ciatrick Fason	1.00	.40
❑ 5 Charlie Frye	1.00	.40
❑ 6 Antrel Rolle	1.00	.40
❑ 7 Dan Orlovsky	1.00	.40
❑ 8 Aaron Rodgers	3.00	1.25
❑ 9 Mark Clayton	1.00	.40
❑ 10 Thomas Davis	1.00	.40
❑ 11 Alex Smith QB	4.00	1.50
❑ 12 Fred Gibson SP	1.00	.40
❑ 13 Maurice Clarett SP	1.25	.50
❑ 14 David Greene	1.00	.40
❑ 15 Carlos Rogers	1.25	.50
❑ 16 Andrew Walter	1.00	.40
❑ 17 Jason Campbell	1.50	.60
❑ 18 Jason White	1.00	.40
❑ 19 Matt Jones	1.50	.60
❑ 20 Marion Barber SP	2.00	.75
❑ 21 Taylor Stubblefield	.75	.30
❑ 22 Jammal Brown SP	1.25	.50
❑ 23 Ronnie Brown	4.00	1.50
❑ 24 Cadillac Williams	4.00	1.50
❑ 25 Kay-Jay Harris	.75	.30
❑ 26 Reggie Brown	1.00	.40
❑ 27 Troy Williamson	1.00	.40
❑ 28 Anthony Davis	.75	.30
❑ 29 Josh Davis SP	1.00	.40
❑ 30 J.J. Arrington	1.00	.40
❑ 31 Alex Smith TE	1.00	.40
❑ 32 Corey Webster SP	1.25	.50
❑ 33 Vernand Morency	1.00	.40
❑ 34 Derek Anderson	1.50	.60
❑ 35 DeMarcus Ware SP	2.00	.75
❑ 36 Kyle Orton	1.00	.40
❑ 37 Brock Berlin	.75	.30
❑ 38 Marlin Jackson	1.00	.40
❑ 39 Channing Crowder	1.00	.40
❑ 40 Roddy White	1.00	.40
❑ 41 Roscoe Parrish	1.00	.40
❑ 42 Adrian McPherson	1.00	.40

❑ 43 Brodney Pool	1.00	.40
❑ 44 T.A. McLendon	.75	.30
❑ 45 Terrence Murphy	1.00	.40
❑ 46 Chris Rix	.75	.30
❑ 47 Ben Roethlisberger SP	4.00	1.50
❑ 48 Dante Ridgeway SP	1.00	.40
❑ 49 Justin Miller	.75	.30
❑ 50 Johnathan Goddard SP	1.00	.40
❑ ROY Roethlisberger ROY/100	20.00	7.50

2006 SAGE HIT

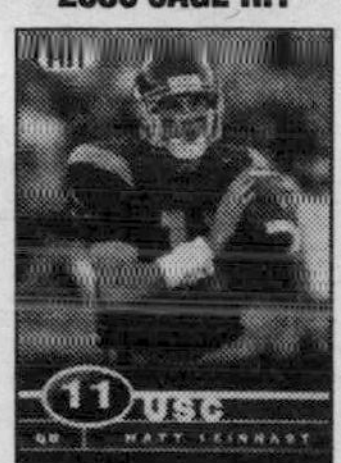

❑ COMPLETE SET (55)	25.00	10.00
❑ #56 ISSUED AT 2006 ANAHEIM NATIONAL		
❑ 1 Reggie McNeal	.75	.30
❑ 2 Jimmy Williams SP	1.00	.40
❑ 3 D.J. Shockley SP	1.00	.40
❑ 4 Omar Jacobs	.75	.30
❑ 5 Reggie Bush	4.00	1.50
❑ 6 Charlie Whitehurst	1.00	.40
❑ 7 Michael Huff	1.25	.50
❑ 8 Tye Hill	1.00	.40
❑ 9 Mario Williams	1.50	.60
❑ 10 Vince Young	4.00	1.50
❑ 11 Matt Leinart UER	3.00	1.25
❑ 12 Brodie Croyle	2.50	1.00
❑ 13 Paul Pinegar	.75	.30
❑ 14 Drew Olson	.75	.30
❑ 15 Martin Nance	.75	.30
❑ 16 David Thomas	1.00	.40
❑ 17 Dwayne Slay SP	.75	.30
❑ 18 Vernon Davis	2.00	.75
❑ 19 Taurean Henderson SP	1.00	.40
❑ 20 Maurice Drew	2.50	1.00
❑ 21 LenDale White	2.00	.75
❑ 22 Laurence Maroney	2.50	1.00
❑ 23 Leon Washington	1.50	.60
❑ 24 Erik Meyer SP	.75	.30
❑ 25 Maurice Stovall	1.00	.40
❑ 26 Ashton Youboty	1.00	.40
❑ 27 Devin Aromashodu	.75	.30
❑ 28 Mike Hass	1.00	.40
❑ 29 Jonathan Orr	.75	.30
❑ 30 Joseph Addai	3.00	1.25
❑ 31 Leonard Pope	1.00	.40
❑ 32 Michael Robinson	1.00	.40
❑ 33 Mike Bell	1.00	.40
❑ 34 Ernie Sims SP	1.25	.50
❑ 35 Skyler Green	1.00	.40
❑ 36 Demetrius Williams	1.00	.40
❑ 37 Winston Justice	1.00	.40
❑ 38 Sinorice Moss	1.00	.40
❑ 39 Charles Gordon SP	.75	.30
❑ 40 Gerald Riggs	1.00	.40
❑ 41 Jerome Harrison	1.00	.40
❑ 42 Bobby Carpenter	1.00	.40
❑ 43 Dominique Byrd	.75	.30
❑ 44 Bruce Gradkowski	1.50	.60
❑ 45 Rodrique Wright	.50	.20
❑ 46 D'Brickashaw Ferguson	1.00	.40
❑ 47 Daniel Bullocks SP	1.00	.40
❑ 48 Jason Avant	1.00	.40
❑ 49 Will Blackmon	.75	.30
❑ 50 Devin Hester SP	2.00	.75
❑ 51 Alan Zemaitis SP	1.00	.40
❑ 52 Hank Baskett	1.00	.40
❑ 53 Cadillac Williams ROY SP	3.00	1.25
❑ 54 Bush/Leinart CL SP	3.00	1.25
❑ 55 Vince Young CL SP	2.00	.75
❑ 56 Jay Cutler	3.00	1.25

2007 SAGE HIT

❑ COMPLETE SET (64)	25.00	10.00
❑ 1 Paul Williams	.75	.30
❑ 2 JaMarcus Russell	2.50	1.00
❑ 3 Robert Meachem	1.00	.40
❑ 4 Sidney Rice	1.50	.60
❑ 5 Drew Stanton	1.25	.50
❑ 6 Jeff Rowe	.60	.25
❑ 7 Zach Miller	.75	.30
❑ 8 Joel Filani	.75	.30
❑ 9 Chris Henry	1.00	.40
❑ 10 Brady Quinn	3.00	1.25
❑ 11 Anthony Gonzalez	1.50	.60
❑ 12 Chris Leak	.75	.30
❑ 13 David Clowney	1.00	.40
❑ 14 Isaiah Stanback	1.00	.40
❑ 15 Steve Breaston	.75	.30
❑ 16 Yamon Figurs	1.00	.40
❑ 17 Lawrence Timmons	1.00	.40
❑ 18 Greg Olsen	1.25	.50
❑ 19 Michael Bush	1.25	.50
❑ 20 Alan Branch	.75	.30
❑ 21 Johnnie Lee Higgins	.75	.30
❑ 22 Aundrae Allison	.75	.30
❑ 23 Kenny Irons	1.00	.40
❑ 24 Marshawn Lynch	2.00	.75
❑ 25 Earl Everett	.75	.30
❑ 26 Courtney Taylor	.75	.30
❑ 27 Michael Griffin	1.00	.40
❑ 28 Adrian Peterson	8.00	3.00
❑ 29 Leon Hall	.75	.30
❑ 30 David Ball	.75	.30
❑ 31 Aaron Ross	1.00	.40
❑ 32 John Beck	2.00	.75
❑ 33 Kolby Smith	1.25	.50
❑ 34 Ken Darby	1.00	.40
❑ 35 Trent Edwards	2.00	.75
❑ 36 Craig Buster Davis	1.00	.40
❑ 37 Ryan Kalil	.75	.30
❑ 38 Jason Snelling	.75	.30
❑ 39 Tyler Palko	.75	.30
❑ 40 Dwayne Bowe	2.00	.75
❑ 41 Dallas Baker	.75	.30
❑ 42 Steve Smith USC	1.25	.50
❑ 43 Jason Hill	.75	.30
❑ 44 Kevin Kolb	1.50	.60
❑ 45 Jared Zabransky	1.00	.40
❑ 46 Brian Leonard	1.00	.40
❑ 47 Darius Walker	1.00	.40
❑ 48 Adam Carriker	.75	.30
❑ 49 Patrick Willis	1.50	.60
❑ 50 Troy Smith	1.50	.60
❑ 51 Brandon Meriweather	1.00	.40
❑ 52 Jarvis Moss	1.00	.40
❑ 53 Levi Brown	1.00	.40
❑ 54 David Irons	.60	.25
❑ 55 Garrett Wolfe	1.25	.50
❑ 56 LaMarr Woodley	1.00	.40
❑ 57 DeMarcus Tank Tyler	.75	.30
❑ 58 Jordan Palmer	1.00	.40
❑ 59 Antonio Pittman	.75	.30
❑ 60 Gaines Adams	1.00	.40
❑ 61 Calvin Johnson	3.00	1.25
❑ ML Matt Leinart	1.50	.60
❑ RB Reggie Bush	2.00	.75
❑ VY Vince Young	2.00	.75

2008 SAGE HIT

❑ COMPLETE SET (50)	7.50	20.00
❑ 1 John David Booty	.75	2.00
❑ 2 Will Franklin	.30	.75
❑ 3 Danny Woodhead	.75	2.00
❑ 4 Limas Sweed	.75	2.00
❑ 5 Joe Flacco	.75	2.00
❑ 6 Brian Brohm	1.25	3.00
❑ 7 Chad Henne	1.25	3.00
❑ 8 Marcus Thomas	.30	.75
❑ 9 Early Doucet	.50	1.25
❑ 10 Dennis Dixon	.60	1.50
❑ 11 Xavier Adibi	.40	1.00
❑ 12 Matt Ryan	1.50	4.00
❑ 13 T.C. Ostrander	.30	.75
❑ 14 Bernard Morris	.30	.75
❑ 15 Sam Baker	.25	.60
❑ 16 Adrian Arrington	.40	1.00
❑ 17 Kevin O'Connell	.30	.75
❑ 18 Jacob Hester	.60	1.50
❑ 19 Keenan Burton	.30	.75
❑ 20 Darius Reynaud	.40	1.00
❑ 21 Keon Lattimore	.30	.75
❑ 22 Tashard Choice	.40	1.00
❑ 23 Jake Long	1.00	2.50
❑ 24 Paul Smith	.40	1.00
❑ 25 Jamaal Charles	.50	1.25
❑ 26 Yvenson Bernard	.40	1.00
❑ 27 Alex Brink	.50	1.25
❑ 28 James Hardy	.40	1.00
❑ 29 Martin Rucker	.30	.75
❑ 30 Steve Slaton	.75	2.00
❑ 31 Derrick Harvey	.30	.75
❑ 32 Andre Callender	.40	1.00
❑ 33 Jabari Arthur	.30	.75
❑ 34 Bruce Hocker	.40	1.00
❑ 35 Kalvin McRae	.30	.75
❑ 36 Lawrence Jackson	.30	.75
❑ 37 Tyrell Johnson	.40	1.00
❑ 38 Marcus Howard	.40	1.00
❑ 39 Sam Keller	.50	1.25
❑ 40 Keith Rivers	.40	1.00
❑ 41 Brandon Flowers	.30	.75
❑ 42 Adarius Bowman	.30	.75
❑ 43 Ricky Santos	.40	1.00
❑ 44 Jordon Dizon	.30	.75
❑ 45 Robert Jordan	.30	.75
❑ 46 Maurice Purify	.60	1.50
❑ 47 Lavelle Hawkins	.30	.75
❑ 48 Jason Rivers	.40	1.00
❑ 49 John Carlson	.40	1.00
❑ 50 Vernon Gholston	.60	1.50

Acknowledgments

Every year we make active solicitations for expert input. We are particularly appreciative of the help (however extensive or cursory) provided for this volume. We receive many inquiries, comments, and questions regarding material within this book. In fact, each and every one is read and digested. Time constraints, however, prevent us from personally replying. But keep sharing your knowledge. Even though we cannot respond to each letter, you are making significant contributions to the hobby through your interest and comments.

The effort to continually refine and improve our books also involves a growing number of people and types of expertise on our home team. Our company boasts a substantial Sports Data Publishing team, which strengthens our ability to provide comprehensive analysis of the marketplace.

Our football analysts played a major part in compiling this year's book, traveling thousands of miles during the past year to attend sportscard shows and visit card shops around the United States and Canada. The Beckett Football specialists are Brian Fleischer and Dan Hitt (Senior Manager of SDP).

Dave Lee's input as Beckett Football editor this past year helped immeasurably; Rich Klein as research analyst and primary proofer also added many hours of painstaking work.

The effort was ably assisted by the rest of the SDP Team: Matt Brumley, Keith Hower, Grant Sandground (Senior Price Guide Editor), and Tim Trout.

The price-gathering and analytical talents of this fine group of hobbyists have helped make our Beckett team stronger, while making this guide and its companion monthly Price Guide more widely recognized as the hobby's most reliable and relied-upon source of pricing information.

In addition, Bill Sutherland and Soma Madhdhipitla contributed many programming improvements to make this process smoother. Also, this book could not be produced without the fine work of our prepress team. Under the leadership of Pete Adauto, Gean Paul Figari was responsible for the layout and general presentation of this book.